Seventh Edition

MANAGERS
and the LEGAL
ENVIRONMENT

STRATEGIES FOR THE 21ST CENTURY

CONSTANCE E. BAGLEY

Yale School of Management

SOUTH-WESTERN
CENGAGE Learning·

Australia • Brazil • Japan • Korea • Mexico • Singapore • Spain • United Kingdom • United States

SOUTH-WESTERN
CENGAGE Learning·

**Managers and the Legal Environment:
Strategies for the 21st Century, 7e**
Constance E. Bagley

Editor-in-Chief: Rob Dewey

Sr. Acquisitions Editor: Vicky True-Baker

Sr. Developmental Editor: Jan Lamar

Editorial Assistant: Tammy Grega

Sr. Content Project Manager: Tamborah Moore

Sr. Media Editor: Kristen Meere

Manufacturing Planner: Kevin Kluck

Sr. Marketing Communications Manager:
Libby Shipp

Production Service: MPS Limited

Sr. Art Director: Michelle Kunkler

Internal Designer: Lisa Albonetti

Cover Images: © Olaru Radian-Alexandru/
Shutterstock; © jovannig/Veer

Rights Acquisitions Specialist: Amber Hosea

Image Permissions Researcher: Sarah Golden,
Vignesh Sadhasivam/PMG

Text Permissions Researcher: Kristine Janssens/
PMG

For product information and technology assistance, contact us at
Cengage Learning Customer & Sales Support, 1-800-354-9706
**For permission to use material form this text or product,
submit all requests online at www.cengage.com/permissions**
Further permissions questions can be emailed to
permissionrequest@cengege.com

ExamView® is a registered trademark of eInstruction Corp. Windows is a registered trademark of the Microsoft Corporation used herein under license. Macintosh and Power Macintosh are registered trademarks of Apple Computer, Inc. used herein under license.

Library of Congress Control Number: 2012938896

ISBN-13: 978-1-111-53063-1

ISBN-10: 1-111-53063-7

South-Western
5191 Natorp Boulevard
Mason, OH 45040
USA

Cengage Learning products are represented in Canada by Nelson Education, Ltd.

For your course and learning solutions, visit **www.cengage.com**

Purchase any of out products at your local college store or at our preferred online store **www.cengagebrain.com**

Printed in the United States of America
1 2 3 4 5 6 7 16 15 14 13 12

DEDICATION

Contents in Brief

TABLE OF CONTENTS

ABOUT THE AUTHOR

CONSTANCE E. BAGLEY

Constance E. Bagley is Professor in the Practice of Law and Management at the Yale School of Management, where she teaches Law for Executives, Legal Aspects of Entrepreneurship, and State and Society. She joined the Yale faculty in 2007 and received the Excellence in Teaching Award in 2009. Previously, she was an Associate Professor of Business Administration at the Harvard Business School and Senior Lecturer in Law and Management at the Stanford University Graduate School of Business. Before joining the Stanford faculty in 2000, she was a corporate securities partner in the San Francisco office of Bingham McCutchen. She was a member of the faculty of the Young Presidents' Organization (YPO) International University for Presidents in Hong Kong and the Czech Republic and is the author of *Winning Legally: How Managers Can Use the Law to Create Value, Marshal Resources, and Manage Risk* (2005) and the coauthor (with Craig E. Dauchy) of *The Entrepreneur's Guide to Business Law* (4th ed. 2011).

Professor Bagley is President of the Academy of Legal Studies in Business (the Academy), received the Academy's Senior Faculty Award of Excellence in 2006, and serves as a staff editor of the *American Business Law Journal*. She is also a member of the Advisory Board of the Wharton School's Zicklin Center for Ethics Research at the University of Pennsylvania and served on the Financial Industry Regulatory Authority's National Adjudicatory Council from 2005 to 2008.

She received her J.D., *magna cum laude*, from the Harvard Law School, where she was invited to join the *Harvard Law Review*. She received her A.B., with Honors and Distinction, from Stanford University, where she was elected to Phi Beta Kappa her junior year. In recognition of her pioneering work on the intersection of law and management, she received an honorary doctorate in economics from Lund University in 2011. Professor Bagley is a member of the State Bar of California (inactive) and the State Bar of New York.

PREFACE

It is hard to imagine a time when understanding the interplay of law, business, and society was more important to successful and responsible management. Law both reflects societal expectations and changes in response to them. The subprime mortgage crisis of 2008 led predictably to the Dodd–Frank Wall Street Reform and Consumer Protection Act of 2010 and the creation of the Consumer Financial Protection Bureau. Concerns about persistently high unemployment rates led to the Jumpstart Our Business Startups Act of 2012, which relaxed the securities law requirements applicable to certain emerging growth companies.

After the Supreme Court opened the floodgates for direct corporate electioneering in *Citizens United v. Federal Election Commission*,[1] shareholders began demanding that firms be more transparent about their political activities. Proposed legislation to stop Internet piracy led to the shutdown of Wikipedia and a shroud on Google in protest. Meanwhile, Google's announcement in 2012 of new privacy policies that permit it to aggregate data from Internet searches, YouTube viewings, and Android smartphone GPS tracking raised heightened concerns about consumer privacy in the electronic age.

The seventh edition of *Managers and the Legal Environment: Strategies for the 21st Century* includes not only traditional business law topics, such as agency, contracts, torts, criminal law, antitrust, and employment law, but also other topics of vital concern to business managers, such as privacy protections, constitutional law, intellectual property, corporate governance, securities regulation, bankruptcy, and environmental law. As its title implies, the text is designed as a "hands-on," transactional guide for future and current business managers and leaders, including entrepreneurs.[2] It provides a broad and detailed understanding of how law affects daily management decisions and business strategies and offers tools that managers can use to manage more effectively. The text also highlights traps for the unwary so managers can both spot legal issues before they become legal problems and effectively handle the inevitable legal disputes that will arise in the course of doing business. No manager operating in the complex and ever-changing global business environment of the twenty-first century can compete successfully without such knowledge.

At a minimum, it is critical for managers to know where the lines are on the field—what is legal and what is not.

The conviction in 2011 of high-profile hedge fund managers, including billionaire Raj Rajaratnam, for insider trading is just the latest reminder of the perils of not complying with the law.

Yet staying out of trouble is only part of the picture. Law does not just regulate; it also enables and facilitates.[3]

A key objective of *Managers and the Legal Environment: Strategies for the 21st Century* is to reframe students' understanding of the relationship of law to business. Rather than focusing just on regulation and viewing law and ethics purely as constraints to be complied with and reacted to, this text teaches future managers the value of legal astuteness—the ability to practice strategic compliance management and to pursue opportunities to use the law and legal tools to increase both the total value created and the share of that value captured by the firm.[4]

To achieve legal astuteness, managers must learn to bridge the communications gaps that can occur when they work with attorneys. They need to develop a common language. This book helps future managers develop legal literacy and an appreciation of the role of law in the effective and ethical management of their businesses.

The text tightly integrates the treatment of law and management and helps students develop the ability to exercise informed judgment when managing the legal dimensions of business. Law is not presented in a vacuum. Instead, its relevance to management is made explicit at the beginning of every chapter. Court cases are chosen for their managerial relevance. Each chapter ends not with a summary of black-letter law but with a discussion of ways managers can use the laws and legal tools discussed in the chapter to create value, marshal resources, and manage risk.

The text provides practical examples of how managers can use the law strategically and tactically to craft solutions that make it possible to attain the core business objectives without incurring undue legal or business risk. For example, the chapter on intellectual property explains how firms can use copyrights, patents, and trade secret protection to capture the value of the intellectual capital they create. It also discusses the use of trademarks to protect brand equity.

---

1. 130 S. Ct. 876 (2010).

2. Additional readings on the legal aspects of entrepreneurship can be found in CONSTANCE E. BAGLEY & CRAIG E. DAUCHY, THE ENTREPRENEUR'S GUIDE TO BUSINESS LAW (4th ed. 2011).

3. M.C. Suchman, D.J. Steward & C.A. Westfall, *The Legal Environment of Entrepreneurship: Observations on the Legitimization of Venture Finance in Silicon Valley,* in THE ENTREPRENEURSHIP DYNAMIC: ORIGINS OF ENTREPRENEURSHIP AND THE EVOLUTION OF INDUSTRIES (C.B. Schoonhoven & E. Romanell eds., 2001).

4. Constance E. Bagley, *Winning Legally: The Value of Legal Astuteness,* 33 ACAD. MGMT. REV. 378 (2008).

The topics covered in *Managers and the Legal Environment: Strategies for the 21st Century* demonstrate its focus on meeting the needs of business managers and leaders. The chapter on international business transactions illustrates the overall approach of the text. It includes not only a discussion of the Foreign Corrupt Practices Act and such key legal concepts as sovereign immunity, but also a detailed discussion of the blend of legal, financial, operational, and logistical issues that often will determine the success or failure of an international investment transaction or joint venture. The discussion of the case against Shell under the Alien Tort Statute for alleged human rights violations in Nigeria[5] requires students to think critically about the legal and social responsibilities of business and to consider whether a corporation can be a person entitled to engage in political speech under the First Amendment, but not a person for purposes of liability for violations of international law.

The legal topics discussed in the main body of the text are on the leading edge of business regulation. They include the Dodd–Frank Wall Street Reform and Consumer Protection Act of 2010, the most sweeping financial reform since the Great Depression; the constitutionality of the Patient Protection and Affordable Care Act; the application of the National Labor Relations Act to social media postings by employees; the 2011 U.S. Supreme Court decision limiting the power of bankruptcy courts to decide certain core counterclaims[6]; federal preemption of state-law product liability claims; shareholder activism and the invalidation of the Securities and Exchange Commission's proxy access rule, which would have given significant shareholders the right to include their nominees in management's proxy materials; the patentability of business processes, genes, and medical correlations; copyright law in cyberspace; mandatory arbitration of employment and consumer disputes; employer liability for sexual harassment; and selective disclosure of inside information to hedge funds and securities analysts.

This text is suitable for a class in the legal environment of business and a business law course at the undergraduate, M.B.A., executive M.B.A., or executive education levels. The objective is a comprehensive and challenging, yet approachable and understandable, text that will work both for those with substantial work experience and for those who are studying business at the undergraduate level for the first time.

PEDAGOGICAL FEATURES

Each chapter of *Managers and the Legal Environment: Strategies for the 21st Century* employs a wide array of effective teaching devices that reinforce the goals of the text.

Conceptual Frameworks

The seventh edition presents several conceptual frameworks to help students better understand the intersection of law, management, and ethics. Exhibit 1.1 presents the systems approach to business and society. The model explains how public law and societal expectations affect a firm's competitive environment and the value and uniqueness of its resources and capabilities. It also shows how a firm's action prompts changes in the public rules and how managers can use the law and the tools it offers to pursue opportunity and capture value while managing the attendant risks. Exhibit 1.2 shows how managers can use the law to affect the competitive environment, and Exhibit 1.3 shows how legal considerations affect each activity in the value chain. Based on the author's analysis of literally thousands of cases, statutes, and regulations, Exhibits 1.4 through 1.8 present a typology of the underlying rationales of the U.S. public law governing businesses. As Chapter 1 points out, other countries tend to have laws that further many of these same objectives, albeit with varying degrees of emphasis on the different objectives and varying ways of furthering them.

Exhibit 1.9 summarizes a variety of legal tools available during various stages of business development (ranging from evaluating the opportunity and defining the value proposition to harvest) to further the managerial objectives of creating realizable value and managing risk. By mapping legal tools against these key managerial objectives, Exhibit 1.9 seeks to frame the legal aspects of management in terms more readily accessible to students of business. Exhibit 2.1 presents the Ethical Business Leader's Decision Tree,[7] which is a tool that managers and their counsel can use to evaluate the legal and ethical aspects of their strategy and its implementation. The *In Brief* in Chapter 20 presents a decision tree for understanding how the business judgment rule is applied to board decisions. Finally, the insider trading decision tree shows when trades based on material nonpublic information violate the securities and mail and wire fraud laws.

A Case in Point

Each chapter presents two to six cases, set off from the body of the text, as examples of business law in action. These cases represent crucial court decisions that have shaped important business law concepts or present key legal conflicts that managers will address in their careers. Included are many modern cases that represent the most current statement of the law. These include *Pliva v. Mensing*,[8] in which the U.S. Supreme Court held that federal law preempts state-law failure-to-warn claims in

---

5. Kiobel v. Royal Dutch Petroleum Co., 621 F.3d 111 (2d Cir. 2010), *cert. granted*, 132 S. Ct. 472 (2011) (Case 24.3).

6. Stern v. Marshall, 131 S. Ct. 2594 (2011) (Case 23.2).

7. This first appeared in Constance E. Bagley, *The Ethical Leader's Decision Tree*, 81 HARV. BUS. REV. 18 (Feb. 2003).

8. 131 S. Ct. 2567 (2011) (Case 10.4).

the case of generic drug labels approved by the Food and Drug Administration; the Supreme Court's invalidation of California's ban on the sale of violent video games to minors in *Brown v. Entertainment Merchants Association*;[9] and the split in the circuits as to whether a breach of the duty of loyalty automatically terminates an agent's authority to access the employer's computers in violation of the Computer Fraud and Abuse Act.[10] Other traditional cases, such as *Meinhard v. Salmon* (Case 5.1) and *MacPherson v. Buick Motor Co.* (Case 10.1), are used to show early developments in the law that remain applicable today. The selection and approach to cases are guided by the author's goals of teaching students how to use the law strategically and how to identify legal issues before they become legal problems.

The format of each *A Case in Point* is designed to convey a detailed understanding of the case while simultaneously covering a large range of material. The case citation and facts are followed by a statement of the issue presented, which reinforces the legal principle being illustrated by the case. Each case discussion then proceeds with a presentation of the court's decision and then a description of the result.

The opinions in at least one case in each chapter are presented in the language of the court, edited for clarity and brevity. Excerpts from dissenting opinions are used occasionally to demonstrate how reasonable people can come to different conclusions about the same facts. This is important for two reasons. First, today's dissent may be tomorrow's majority opinion. Second, comparing the arguments raised in the opinion with those of the dissent requires, and strengthens the student's ability to engage in, critical analysis. Each edited case is followed by two thought-provoking critical thinking questions that challenge the student's understanding of the court's language and reasoning and encourage the student to consider the ramifications of the decision for future cases and managerial decisions.

The opinions in the remaining cases in each chapter are summarized, thereby permitting the coverage of more cases and concepts than would be feasible if all cases were in the language of the court. The author believes that students benefit from reading a more rigorous treatment of cases than is provided by the short briefs found in many texts. Thus, students are provided with a detailed recitation of the facts, the issues, the court's reasoning, and the result.

Many cases also include comments that place the case in its proper legal and managerial context. A comment might explain why the case is important, why the court decided it a certain way, or what the ramifications are for business actors. This helps students understand how an individual case helps shape the legal environment as a whole. In addition, the comments encourage students to think critically about court decisions and the conduct of the managers involved.

International Coverage, *Global View,* and *International Snapshots*

The seventh edition includes one of the most expansive integrated treatments of international business regulation available in a general legal environment or business law textbook. The text addresses the international aspects of the legal environment in three ways. First, the chapter on international business (Chapter 24) provides a transactional, integrated discussion of international business transactions, including the use of letters of credit, sovereign immunity, and compliance with local labor laws. Second, many chapters includes a boxed section entitled *Global View*, which discusses key differences between U.S. law and the laws applied in the European Union, Japan, Canada, and other countries. For example, the product liability and consumer protection chapters (Chapters 10 and 17) describe the relevant European Union Directives. The chapter on civil rights and employment discrimination (Chapter 13) discusses European, Japanese, and Indian discrimination law. The chapter on directors, officers, and controlling shareholders (Chapter 20) discusses corporate takeovers in Germany. Finally, a number of chapters also highlight international considerations in short boxed features called *International Snapshots*. For example, the Chinese approach to capital punishment for economic crimes is discussed in an *International Snapshot* in the criminal law chapter (Chapter 14).

Focus on Ethics

This text places great emphasis on ethical concerns, stimulating students to consider how their actions as managers and business leaders must incorporate considerations of ethics and social responsibility. Ethical considerations are emphasized in four ways. First, Chapter 2, "Ethics and the Law," includes topics such as rampant accounting fraud by companies intent on managing their earnings to meet analyst expectations, exploitation of foreign workers, the marketing of tobacco and beer to children, and conflicts of interest in the securities, insurance brokerage, and mutual fund industries. Second, ethical considerations are highlighted throughout the text in separate boxed sections entitled *Ethical Consideration*. Third, each chapter includes a section entitled *A Manager's Dilemma: Putting It into Practice*, which requires students to consider how ethics factor into managerial decisions. Finally, ethical considerations are raised in many of the end-of-chapter *Questions and Case Problems*.

These ethical considerations are commentaries on how standards of ethics and social responsibility do (and

---

9. 131 S. Ct. 2929 (2011) (Case 4.3).

10. United States v. Nosal, 642 F.3d 781 (9th Cir. 2011), *reh'g en banc granted*, 661 F.3d 1180 (9th Cir. 2011).

sometimes do not) inform the process of lawmaking. The text discusses the ethical implications of business decisions made in response to legal rules, as well as the moral boundaries of the legal regime.

Economic, Historical, and Political Perspectives

Many chapters have a separate boxed section that puts the law in that chapter into economic, historical, or political perspective. For example, the environmental law chapter (Chapter 15) explains the economic concept of externalities, and the chapter on public and private offerings of securities (Chapter 21) shows the progression from the Securities Act of 1933 to the JOBS Act of 2012. The employment agreement chapter (Chapter 12) discusses the politics of immigration reform at both the state and the federal levels.

These *Perspectives* add a real-world dimension to the material. Too often law is presented in a vacuum, divorced from the larger political and economic context in which the law is created. The goal of these sections is to heighten students' awareness of these larger forces. In addition, business managers should be made aware of the complicated interplay between economics and the law. That interplay is crucial to the operation of a business, but it is often less than predictable.

In Brief

To provide a visual aid for the student, each chapter contains at least one boxed summary, an *In Brief,* which breaks down into digestible pieces the key elements of material presented in that chapter. In some cases, this may be represented in the form of a flow chart; in others, it may appear in the form of a decision tree or matrix.

The Responsible Manager

Each chapter includes a section entitled *The Responsible Manager.* This section is an in-depth discussion of the crucial legal considerations that the successful manager must take into account. *The Responsible Manager* sections summarize key takeaways from each chapter, but they are far more than a mere summary of legal rules. In a concise yet sophisticated manner, they alert managers to the legal issues they must spot in order to avoid violating the law or plunging the company into expensive, time-consuming litigation. In addition, these sections highlight the ethical concerns managers need to confront to adequately serve their company and community.

These sections play a vital role in establishing this text as a "must-have" for upcoming and practicing business managers. In *The Responsible Manager* section for a particular area of the law, managers will find a wealth of practical information that will bring them up to speed on the key legal issues in that area. These sections are not mere checklists—they

contain a depth of analysis that is demanded by the complex, real-life nature of the problems at hand.

As examples, *The Responsible Manager* section for the chapter on courts and dispute resolution (Chapter 3) provides a step-by-step guide to setting up an effective alternative dispute resolution procedure. The torts chapter (Chapter 9) provides a manager's guide to reducing risks of exposure for tort liability. The international business transactions chapter (Chapter 24) highlights the issues likely to arise in transactions involving more than one country and suggests strategies for managing successfully in a global setting.

A Manager's Dilemma: Putting It into Practice

Each chapter includes a section entitled *A Manager's Dilemma: Putting It into Practice,* which requires students to analyze the legal, business, and ethical aspects of a managerial decision and to make a recommendation for action. Many of these sections are based on recent cases or news accounts. For example, the agency chapter asks whether an investment bank creating a zero-sum derivative contract has a legal or ethical obligation to disclose to the buyer of the long position that the buyer of the short position selected the assets whose value will determine which client loses the money invested.

Inside Story

Each chapter concludes with a section called *Inside Story,* which contains mini-cases that present fascinating and detailed descriptions of real-world business situations. A strong effort has been made to include up-to-the-minute, cutting-edge business situations. The *Inside Stories* include the regulatory regime created by the Dodd–Frank Act (Chapter 6); the Toyota unintended acceleration cases (Chapter 10); the effects of the subprime mortgage crisis on foreclosure and lending practices (Chapters 18 and 23); and the Foreign Corrupt Practices Act cases against Siemens and Halliburton (Chapter 24). The *Inside Stories* bring the legal conflicts and developments to life and reinforce the students' appreciation for how such conflicts are played out in the real world.

Classic battles are also included. For example, the *Pennzoil v. Texaco* case study is the *Inside Story* for the contracts chapter (Chapter 7). It includes excerpts from the court's opinion and the legal documents so that students can have the experience of seeing such material firsthand.

Defined Terms, Key Words and Phrases, and Glossary

Throughout the text, all crucial legal terms are placed in italics and defined immediately. A list of key terms used in a chapter appears immediately before the end-of-chapter

Questions and Case Problems, with a page reference to the place where that term is defined.

In addition to the references to defined terms contained in *Key Words and Phrases,* there is also a comprehensive glossary at the end of the text. The *Glossary* defines each term that has been set in italics anywhere in the text. The definitions of terms in the *Glossary* and the *Key Words and Phrases* help convey the concepts and improve the students' legal and business vocabulary.

End-of-Chapter *Questions and Case Problems*

Each chapter is followed by eight thought-provoking questions and case problems that require students to synthesize, review, and apply the material. The questions are diverse. Some are mini-cases that require students to figure out the legal and business issues and make a managerial decision. Others are based directly on specific cases, presenting real-world legal conflicts or decisions as opportunities for students to apply the appropriate law and engage in critical thinking. For example, the intellectual property chapter includes a question addressing the scope of Myriad Genetics' patent on the BRCA1 and BRCA2 genes.[11] In most chapters, more than half the questions are based on actual cases, with the citation provided for enterprising students who want to look up the case in preparation for class.

✪ CHANGES IN THE SEVENTH EDITION

The seventh edition represents the most significant revision of the text since the publication of the first edition in 1991. In recognition that less is more, the seventh edition is substantially shorter than the sixth. Many chapters have been streamlined, making them more readily accessible to students. The separate chapter on executive compensation (former Chapter 14) has been deleted because aspects were too specialized for many users.[12] Topics of broad application, such as the discussion of ERISA, were moved to the chapter on the employment agreement (Chapter 12). Other aspects of executive compensation are now addressed in the chapter on officers, directors, and controlling shareholders (Chapter 20). The deletion of the more specialized material on executive compensation made it possible to add new material on labor relations, including state limits on the right of public employees to bargain collectively.

As the line between the real and virtual worlds has blurred, it became necessary to integrate the discussion of transactions using the Internet with the treatment of brick-and-mortar business. This includes the use of electronic agents to form contracts, the enforceability of browse-wrap agreements, and the labor laws applicable to employees, regardless of whether they are chatting near the water cooler or on Facebook.

The seventh edition provides a cutting-edge analysis of key developments that have dramatically altered the legal landscape since the publication of the sixth edition and draws more explicit links between chapters. Many of the cases presented as *A Case in Point* are new. They include the U.S. Supreme Court's rulings on mandatory arbitration of consumer complaints, the constitutionality of a state law banning the sale of physician-identifying pharmaceutical prescribing information to drug companies without the consent of the physicians, the validity of an Arizona statute permitting the revocation of the charter of Arizona corporations that repeatedly hire undocumented workers, the ability of female employees at Wal-Mart and other companies to bring a class action for employment discrimination, affirmative action to avoid claims of disparate impact race discrimination, retaliation claims brought under Title VII by the fiancé of an employee who complained of gender discrimination, and the criminal liability of Jeffery Skilling and other executives for honest-services fraud. The real property chapter (Chapter 18) includes a key foreclosure decision rendered by the Massachusetts Supreme Judicial Court in 2011 and the agreement reached in 2012 with state attorneys general, the U.S. Department of Justice, and major banks, whereby the banks agreed to pay $26 billion to settle allegations of robo-signing and other improper mortgage foreclosure and servicing practices. The international transactions chapter includes a U.S. court of appeals decision invalidating an Oklahoma constitutional amendment prohibiting state courts from considering Sharia and other international law when deciding cases.[13] When an earlier case remains the best pedagogical tool to illustrate a principle, it has been retained.

The seventh edition embeds the provisions of new federal legislation, such as the Dodd–Frank Act and the Patient Protection and Affordable Care Act, in the relevant chapters. The text includes new regulations and administrative guidance, including the Equal Employment Opportunity Commission's 2011 regulations implementing the Americans with Disabilities Act Amendments Act of 2008 and guidance from the National Labor Relations Board on when employees' use of social media to criticize their employer constitutes protected concerted action under the National Labor Relations Act. The text also discusses recent international developments, including a massive judgment awarded by a court in Ecuador against Chevron for environmental damage to the rain forests and Chevron's attempt to use a New York court to enjoin its

---

11. Ass'n for Molecular Pathology v. U.S. Patent & Trademark Office, 2011 WL 3211513 (Fed. Cir. 2011).

12. For those interested in equity compensation, see BAGLEY &. DAUCHY, *supra* note 2, at 91–112.

13. Awad v. Ziriax, 2012 WL 50636 (10th Cir. Jan. 10, 2012) (Case 24.1).

enforcement outside Equador,[14] as well as the agreement reached in the November 2011 round of climate-change talks to work toward a post-Kyoto international agreement that would require not only the developed countries but also China, India, and other developing countries to reduce the emission of greenhouse gases.

Many of the end-of-chapter *Questions and Case Problems* are new. For example, the criminal law chapter (Chapter 14) includes an end-of-chapter question based on the 2012 U.S. Supreme Court decision requiring a warrant before the police can put a GPS tracking device on a suspect's vehicle.[15] The constitutional law chapter (Chapter 4) includes a question on the validity of state limits on campaign contributions.

Most of the *Inside Stories* and the *Economic, Historical,* and *Political Perspectives* are also new or have been substantially revised to reflect the latest developments. For example, the *Inside Story* in the environmental law chapter discusses BP's massive oil spill in the Gulf of Mexico.

ANCILLARY COMPONENTS

Instructor's Resource CD-ROM (IRCD)

The IRCD includes the following supplements: *Answer Manual, Instructor's Manual, Test Bank, ExamView*™, PowerPoint slides, and transparency masters of the exhibits in the text.

Answer Manual for End-of-Chapter *Questions and Case Problems* and *A Manager's Dilemma*

A complete and separate *Answer Manual,* prepared by the author, identifies the issues presented in each *A Manager's Dilemma* and in the end-of-chapter *Questions and Case Problems.* It provides thorough, cogent model answers to facilitate teaching by the Socratic and case methods. It is available on the IRCD and the *Companion Website* (login.cengage.com).

Instructor's Manual

The *Instructor's Manual* was developed by Joseph A. Zavaletta, Jr., J.D. This manual includes chapter outlines, case summaries, and teaching suggestions. It is available on the IRCD and the *Companion Website* (login.cengage.com).

Test Bank

The *Test Bank* was developed by Vonda Laughlin of Carson-Newman College. It contains true/false test

questions, multiple-choice test questions, and essay test questions. The Test Bank also includes multi-subject final exam essay questions prepared by the author. It is available on the IRCD and the *Companion Website* (login.cengage.com).

ExamView™

ExamView™ is a computerized testing software program containing all of the questions in the printed test bank. This program is an easy-to-use test creation software package compatible with Microsoft Windows. Instructors can add or edit questions and provide customized instructions. It is available on the IRCD.

PowerPoint Slides

A set of PowerPoint slides prepared by Joseph A. Zavaletta, Jr., provides outlines of topics covered in each chapter, which can be used for lecture or review.

Textbook *Companion Website* and *Internet Sources*

Available at login.cengage.com, the *Companion Website* offers an array of teaching and learning resources. They include interactive quizzes to help students study the material covered in the text as well as instructor supplements (for instructors only). It also includes *Internet Sources,* a list of websites (including their electronic addresses or URLs) relevant to the text, which gives instructors and students a starting point for online legal research.

OTHER TEACHING AIDS

Student Guide to the Sarbanes–Oxley Act

A brief overview of the Sarbanes–Oxley Act for business students, which explains the Sarbanes–Oxley Act, what is required of whom, and how it might affect students in their business life, is available as an optional bundle item with a new text.

Business Law Digital Video Library

Featuring more than eighty segments on the most important topics in business law, the Business Law Digital Video Library helps students make the connection between their textbook and the business world. Five types of clips are represented: (1) *Legal Conflicts in Business* clips feature modern business scenarios; (2) *Ask the Instructor* clips offer concept review; (3) *Drama of the Law* clips present classic legal situations; (4) *LawFlix* clips feature segments from well-known and recent motion pictures; and (5) *Real World Legal* clips explore conflicts that arise in a variety

---

14. Chevron Corp. v. Naranjo, 667 F.3d 232 (2d Cir. 2012) (Case 24.5).
15. United States v. Jones, 132 S. Ct. 945 (2012).

of business environments. Together, these clips bring the legal environment and business law to life. Access to the Business Law Digital Video Library is free when bundled with a new text. If access to the Business Law Digital Video Library did not come packaged with the text, students can purchase it online at www.cengagebrain.com. At the cengagebrain.com home page, students should search for the ISBN of the textbook title (which is set forth on the back cover of the book), using the search box at the top of the page. This will take the student to the product page where companion resources can be found.

BUSINESS SCHOOL CASES PREPARED BY THE AUTHOR

Professor Bagley has coauthored a variety of business school cases that can be purchased separately and used together with *Managers and the Legal Environment* in both business law and legal environment of business classes. Her Harvard Business School cases include *BitTorrent* and *Warner Bros. and BitTorrent* (copyrights and licensing agreements), *Priceline versus Microsoft* (patents), *X-IT and Kidde* (ethics, trade secrets, and patents), and *USG Corporation (A), (B),* and *(C)* (litigation, lobbying, product liability, and bankruptcy). For a complete list, please go to hbsp.harvard.edu and search the author field for "Bagley." Her Yale School of Management cases include *BP in Russia* (ethics and international business transactions), *From Politics to Law: U.S. Healthcare Reform 2011* (sources of law, constitutional law, and healthcare reform), *Jim Flores, ControlTrix* (employment discrimination and wrongful termination), *Kirkwood* (contracts), *Morgan Life Sciences* (securities regulation and insider trading), *Research in Motion's BlackBerry: Balancing Privacy Rights and National Security* (privacy), and *South Africa's Energy Crisis: Reconciling Economic Growth with Environmental Protection* (environmental protection). For a complete list, please go to winninglegally.com.

ACKNOWLEDGMENTS

The author gratefully acknowledges Diane W. Savage, coauthor of both the fifth and sixth editions, for her contributions to *Managers and the Legal Environment* and wishes her all the best with the free time she has now that she has retired as a coauthor. A number of academics and practitioners reviewed portions of this manuscript and the first six editions, and provided valuable guidance, correction, and helpful commentary. The author thanks each of them.

Reviewers and others who provided insight for this edition include:

Lee Ann E. Butler, *Rice University*

Timothy J. Fogarty, *Case Western Reserve University*

Kapp L. Johnson, *California Lutheran College*

Ida M. Jones, *California State University, Fresno*

Rachel Kowal, *NYU Stern School of Business*

Daniel Louviere, *Florida State College-Jacksonville*

Doug McCloskey, *Fontbonne University (St. Louis)*

Robert J. Rhead, *Central Michigan University*

Joan Schmit, *University of Wisconsin–Madison*

Ira C. Selkowitz, *University of Colorado Denver Business School*

Alan B. Talarczyk, *Edgewood College*

Reviewers and others who provided insight for the sixth edition include:

A. David Austill, *Union University*

Michael Bixby, *Boise State University*

Linda Christiansen, *Indiana University Southeast*

John W. Collis, *St. Ambrose University*

Steven J. Green, *University of California at Berkeley and Davis*

John Hale, partner, *Cooley LLP*

Susan L. Martin, *Hofstra University*

Virginia G. Maurer, *University of Florida*

Christopher H. Meakin, *University of Texas at Austin*

Buff Miller, partner, *Cooley LLP*

Susan A. O'Sullivan, *Seton Hall University*

Nancy Wojitas, partner, *Cooley LLP*

Reviewers and others who provided insight for the fifth edition include:

Lynda M. Applegate, *Harvard Business School*

Steven Arsenault, *College of Charleston*

Carliss Y. Baldwin, *Harvard Business School*

Frederick Baron, partner, *Cooley LLP*

Todd Bontemps, special counsel, *Cooley LLP*

Susan Boyd, *University of Tulsa*

Tom Cary, *City University*

Thomas Cavenagh, *North Central College*

Patrick Costello, partner, *Bialson, Bergen & Schwab*

Larry Alan Di Matteo, *University of Florida*

Steve Fackler, partner, *Gibson, Dunn & Crutcher LLP*

Ian Feinberg, partner, *Mayer Brown Rowe & Maw*

Stephen Friedlander, partner, *Cooley LLP*

William E. Fruhan, Jr., *Harvard Business School*

Bill Galliani, partner, *Cooley LLP*

Robert Gebhard, partner, *Sedgwick Detert, Moran & Arnold*

Ernest W. King, *University of Southern Mississippi*

Virginia G. Maurer, *University of Florida*

Ellwood F. Oakley III, *Georgia State University*

David A. Redle, *The University of Akron*

Cindy Schipani, *University of Michigan*

Lillian Stenfeld, partner, *Sedgwick Detert, Moran & Arnold*

Anita Stork, partner, *Covington & Burling LLP*

Lois Voelz, partner, *Cooley LLP*

Mark Webber, associate, *Osborne Clarke*

Reviewers and others who provided insight for the fourth edition include:

Robert W. Emerson, *University of Florida*

Joan T. A. Gabel, *University of Missouri*

Steven J. Green, *University of California at Berkeley and Davis*

Laurie A. Lucas, *Arkansas Technical University*

Claude Mosseri-Marlio, *Schiller University and American Business School in Paris*

Lynn Sharp Paine, *Harvard Business School*

Arthur Segel, *Harvard Business School*

John A. Wrieden, *Florida International University*

Reviewers for the third edition include:

Royce de R. Barondes, *Louisiana State University*

Susan M. Denbo, *Rider College*

Joan T. A. Gabel, *Georgia State University*

Ernest W. King, *University of Southern Mississippi*

Eugene P. O'Connor, *Canisius College*

Lou Ann Simpson, *Drake University*

Reviewers for the second edition include:

Barbara Ahna, *Pacific Lutheran University*

Rodolfo Camacho, *Oregon State University*

Kenneth D. Crews, *Indiana University*

James G. Frierson, *East Tennessee State University*

John P. Geary, *Appalachian State University*

David G. Jaeger, *Case Western Reserve University*

Arthur Levine, *California State University–Long Beach*

Susan L. Martin, *Hofstra University*

William F. Miller, *Stanford University*

Alan R. Thiele, *University of Houston*

Reviewers for the first edition include:

Thomas M. Apke, *California State University, Fullerton*

Dawn Bennett-Alexander, *University of Georgia*

Robert L. Cherry, *Appalachian State University*

Frank B. Cross, *University of Texas at Austin*

Charles J. Cunningham, *University of Tampa*

Michael Engber, *Ball State University*

Andrea Giampetro Meyer, *Loyola College, Maryland*

James P. Hill, *Central Michigan University*

Tom Jackson, *University of Vermont*

Roger J. Johns, Jr., *Eastern New Mexico University*

Jack E. Karns, *East Carolina University*

Mary C. Keifer, *Ohio University*

Nancy Kubasek, *Bowling Green University*

Paul Lansing, *University of Iowa*

Nancy R. Mansfield, *Georgia State University*

Arthur J. Marinelli, *Ohio University*

John McMahon, *Stanford University*

Gregory C. Mosier, *Oklahoma State University*

Patricia H. Nunley, *Baylor University*

Mark M. Phelps, *University of Oregon*

Michael W. Pustay, *Texas A&M University*

Roger Richman, *University of Hartford*

John C. Ruhnka, *University of Colorado at Denver*

Linda B. Samuels, *George Mason University*

Susan Samuelson, *Boston University*

Rudy Sandoval, *University of Texas at San Antonio*

John E. H. Sherry, *Cornell University*

S. Jay Sklar, *Temple University*

Larry D. Strate, *University of Nevada at Las Vegas*

Gary L. Tidwell, *College of Charleston*

William V. Vetter, *Wayne State University*

William H. Walker, *Indiana Purdue University at Ft. Wayne*

Darryl Webb, *University of Alabama*

Any mistakes or inadequacies are the author's responsibility.

The author thanks Quinnipiac Law School students Thomas R. Hollowell, Ivette Konopka, Brittany Paz, and Michael A. Hespeler as well as Columbia Law School student Sandra Hudak for their research and cite-checking assistance. She would also like to acknowledge the word processing and editing support, productivity, hard work, and grace under pressure of faculty assistants Paula Blanchette, Lauren Hudak, and Melissa Studer. Thank you for your invaluable assistance in converting my illegible scribbles and multiple riders into a finished manuscript.

Thanks to Publisher Rob Dewey, Senior Acquisitions Editor Vicky True-Baker, Senior Developmental Editor Jan Lamar, Executive Marketing Director Lisa Lysne, Senior Art Director Michelle Kunkler, and Senior Media Editor Kristen Meere for their insightful and creative suggestions for this seventh edition. Thanks also to Senior Production Editor Tammy Moore and copyeditor extraordinaire Pat Lewis for their excellent work, even temper while meeting a seemingly impossible production schedule, and their tolerance of multiple missed author deadlines. Thanks also to Liah Rose, Edward Dionne, and the other members of the MPS Limited team for getting the book into type in record time. Finally, thanks to the Dean's Office at the Yale School of Management for the generous support of this edition.

Constance E. Bagley
Yale School of Management

The principal cases are in bold type. Cases cited or discussed are in light type. Cases in notes are indicated by "n" after the page number,

C

X

Y

Z

UNIT

I

FOUNDATIONS
OF THE
LEGAL AND REGULATORY
ENVIRONMENT

CHAPTER 1

LAW, VALUE CREATION, AND RISK MANAGEMENT

INTRODUCTION

WINNING LEGALLY[1]

Governments immerse modern organizations "in a sea of law."[2] Public law provides the rules of the game[3] within which firms compete to create and capture value. Law does more than regulate and constrain, however. It also enables and facilitates.[4] Indeed, multiple-country studies reveal that the efficiency of a country's capital markets is directly related to the country's legal environment.[5] Researchers found a statistically significant relationship between a country's economic prosperity, as measured by the per capita gross domestic product, and each of the following:

- Judicial independence.
- Adequacy of legal recourse.
- Police protection of business.
- Demanding product standards.
- Stringent environmental regulations.
- Quality laws relating to information technology.
- Extent of intellectual property protection.
- Effectiveness of antitrust laws.[6]

For example, adequate protection of minority shareholder rights increases investment in new ventures.[7] Conversely, excessive regulation, including burdensome licensing requirements and filing fees, can hamper new venture formation.[8]

"Legally astute" managers who understand and proactively manage the legal aspects of business can use the law and the legal system to increase both the total value created and the share of that value captured by the firm.[9] As Tom Hinthorne remarked, "[L]awyers and corporate leaders who understand the law and the structures of power in the U.S.A. have a unique capacity to protect and enhance share-owner wealth."[10] For example, companies can use patents, copyrights, trademarks, and trade secrets to differentiate their products, command premium prices, erect barriers to entry, sustain first-mover advantage, and reduce costs. Managers can also make their own "private law" by entering into contracts and crafting certain governance structures. A variety of legal tools, ranging from insurance policies to contractual indemnification provisions and limitations on liability, can help firms allocate and manage risk. Finally, managers can lobby and work with regulators to change the rules of the game.

> ## CHAPTER OVERVIEW
> The purpose of this chapter is to provide a framework for analyzing the intersection of law and management. It introduces the *systems approach to*
>
> *CONTINUED*

1. *See generally* CONSTANCE E. BAGLEY, WINNING LEGALLY: HOW TO USE THE LAW TO CREATE VALUE, MARSHAL RESOURCES, AND MANAGE RISK (2005).
2. Lauren B. Edelman & Mark C. Suchman, *The Legal Environments of Organizations*, 23 ANN. REV. SOC. 479 (1997).
3. DOUGLASS C. NORTH, INSTITUTIONS, INSTITUTIONAL CHANGE AND ECONOMIC PERFORMANCE 3–4 (1990).
4. Mark C. Suchman, D.J. Steward & C.A. Westfall, *The Legal Environment of Entrepreneurship: Observations on the Legitimization of Venture Finance in Silicon Valley, in* THE ENTREPRENEURSHIP DYNAMIC: ORIGINS OF ENTREPRENEURSHIP AND THE EVOLUTION OF INDUSTRIES (C.B. Schoonhoven & E. Romanell, eds., 2001).
5. R. La Porta, F. Lopez-de-Silanes, A. Shleifer & R.W. Vishny, *Legal Determinants of External Finance*, 52 J. FIN. 1131 (1997).
6. Michael E. Porter, *Enhancing the Microeconomic Foundations of Prosperity: The Current Competitiveness Index, in* WORLD ECONOMIC FORUM, THE GLOBAL COMPETITIVENESS REPORT 2001–2002 (2002).
7. S. Johnson, R. La Porta, F. Lopez-de-Silanes & A. Shleifer, *Tunneling*, 90 AM. ECON. REV. 22 (2000).
8. S. Djankov, R. La Porta, F. Lopez-de-Silanes & A. Shleifer, *The Regulation of Entry*, 117 Q.J. ECON. 1 (2002).
9. *See* Constance E. Bagley, *Winning Legally: The Value of Legal Astuteness*, 33 ACAD. MGMT. REV. 378 (2008).
10. Tom Hinthorne, *Predatory Capitalism, Pragmatism, and Legal Positivism in the Airlines Industry*, 18 STRATEGIC MGMT. J. 509 (1996). *See also* George J. Siedel, *Six Forces and the Legal Environment of Business: The Relative Value of Business Law Among Business School Core Courses*, 37 AM. BUS. L.J. 37 (2000).

business and society, a descriptive framework that integrates legal and societal considerations with mainstream theories of competitive advantage and social responsibility. We then outline the four primary public policies furthered by business regulation in the United States. The chapter concludes with a discussion of how legally astute managers can enhance realizable firm value.

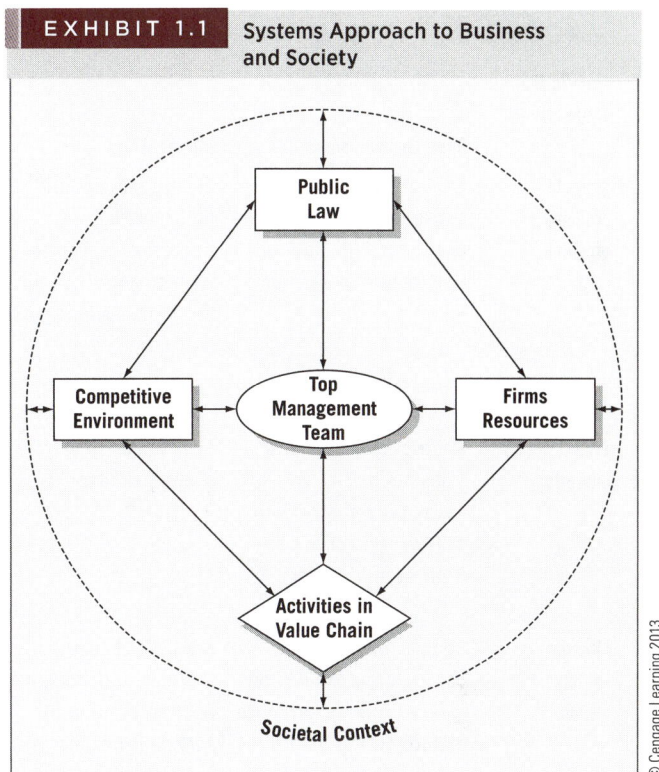

EXHIBIT 1.1 Systems Approach to Business and Society

© Cengage Learning 2013

THE SYSTEMS APPROACH TO BUSINESS AND SOCIETY

Society grants rights and powers to business, but society can revoke those rights and powers if firms do not act responsibly.[11] As Tom Stephens, CEO of Manville Corporation, put it when he decided to add labels to Manville's fiberglass products, warning of possible carcinogenic risks, "The laws of society are more powerful than any law that Congress can put on the books. Woe to any businessman who doesn't read the laws of society and understand them."[12] As a result, "the task of anticipating, understanding, evaluating, and responding to public policy developments within the host environment is itself a critical managerial task."[13]

As seen in Exhibit 1.1, firms operate within a broader societal context, which directly affects the competitive environment and the value of firm resources.[14] At the center is the top management team (TMT), which evaluates and pursues opportunities for value creation and capture while managing the attendant risks. Given the characteristics of the members of the TMT and their values, the parameters set by the public law, the firm's position within the competitive environment, and the nature and uniqueness of the firm's resources, the TMT defines the value proposition and selects and performs the activities in the value chain.

Meeting Societal Expectations

The systems approach recognizes that "business decisions consist of continuous, interrelated economic and moral components."[15] It also builds on stakeholder theory's insight that firms have relationships with many constituent groups, which both affect and are affected by the actions of the firm.[16]

Effect of Law on the Competitive Environment and the Firm's Resources

Law helps shape the competitive environment and affects each of the *five forces*, identified by Michael Porter, that determine the attractiveness of an industry: buyer power, supplier power, the competitive threat posed by current rivals, the availability of substitutes, and the threat of new entrants.[17] Exhibit 1.2 shows how managers can use law to affect these forces and also indicates the public policies behind the relevant laws.

Law also affects the allocation, marshaling, value, and distinctiveness of the firm's resources. Under the *resource-based view (RBV)* of the firm, a firm's resources can be a source of sustained competitive advantage if they are valuable, rare, and imperfectly imitable by competitors and have no strategically equivalent substitutes.[18] Legal

11. D.J. Wood, *Corporate Social Performance Revisited,* 16 ACAD. MGMT. REV. 691 (1991).

12. William Glaberson, *Of Manville, Morals and Mortality,* N.Y. TIMES, Oct. 9, 1988.

13. LEE E. PRESTON & JAMES E. POST, PRIVATE MANAGEMENT AND PUBLIC POLICY: THE PRINCIPLE OF PUBLIC RESPONSIBILITY 4 (1975).

14. *See generally* Constance E. Bagley, *What's Law Got to Do with It?: Integrating Law and Strategy,* 47 AM. BUS. L.J. 587 (2010).

15. D.L. Swanson, *Addressing a Theoretical Problem by Reorienting the Corporate Social Performance Model,* 20 ACAD. MGMT. REV. 43 (1995).

16. Thomas Donaldson & Lee E. Preston, *The Stakeholder Theory of the Corporation: Concepts, Evidence, and Implications,* 20 ACAD. MGMT. REV. 65 (1995).

17. Michael E. Porter, *How Competitive Forces Shape Strategy, in* ON COMPETITION 21–22 (1996). *See also* RICHARD G. SHELL, MAKE THE RULES OR YOUR RIVALS WILL (2004).

18. Margaret A. Peteraf & Jay B. Barney, *Unraveling the Resource-Based Tangle,* 24 MANAGERIAL & DECISION ECON. 309 (2003). *See also* GEORGE J. SIEDEL, USING LAW FOR COMPETITIVE ADVANTAGE (2002).

EXHIBIT 1.2	Using Law to Affect the Competitive Environment

Public Policy Objectives	Porter's Five Forces				
	Direct Competition	Threat of Entry	Substitution	Supplier Power	Buyer Power
Promote economic growth	Obtain development subsidies, tax breaks for domestic firm; litigate application of antitrust laws	Secure patents and other intellectual property (IP) rights; lobby for protectionist tariffs to advantage domestic firms	Secure trademarks; bundle products	Enter into long-term supply contracts	Secure cost-plus government contracts and no-bid contracts from Department of Defense; enter into exclusive dealing contracts; use contracts or IP to bundle products
Protect worker interests	Restrict availability of visas needed by rivals; lobby for tighter OSHA or FDA regulations to detriment of lesser rivals	Seek limits on overseas outsourcing	Enter into employment agreements with covenants not to compete; subject stock to vesting	Litigate definition of "employee"	Lobby for ban on products made with child or slave labor
Promote consumer welfare	Seek to outlaw competing products on safety grounds; promote expedited regulatory approval of generic drugs; disclose product ingredients and place of manufacture	Impose licensing regime; demand posting of bond by service providers	Seek to outlaw substitute products on safety grounds	Require labeling of "foreign" parts	Require purchasers to buy services from state-licensed providers
Promote public welfare	Obtain ethanol-style subsidies for firm's product; lobby for tougher environmental standards	Resist reforms designed to reduce the costs of incorporating, obtaining licenses, and issuing securities	Seek to grandfather existing products and facilities from new taxes and regulatory requirements	Lobby for reduced import duties on foreign suppliers	Lobby for domestic content requirements and higher transportation taxes; promote bans on the payment of bribes

SOURCE: Bagley, *supra* note 14, at 599.

astuteness is a valuable managerial capability that may be a source of sustained competitive advantage.[19] Conversely, failure to integrate law into the development of strategy and of action plans can place a firm at a competitive disadvantage and imperil its economic viability.[20]

Consider the fall of Enron and its once venerable accounting firm Arthur Andersen (described in the "Inside Story" in Chapter 2) and the collapse of WorldCom in the wake of massive accounting fraud; the implosion of Barings, England's oldest merchant bank, after illegal trades by Nick Leeson; and the collapse of mortgage brokerage firms implicated in predatory lending (described further in the "Inside Story" in Chapter 18). Violation of the criminal laws can also land an executive in prison, as happened to Jeffrey Skilling, former CEO of Enron,

who was convicted of fraud and sentenced to more than twenty-four years in prison.

Even if the firm survives, noncompliance destroys value. Illegal conduct can put a firm at a competitive disadvantage by diverting funds from strategic investments, tarnishing the firm's image with customers and other stakeholders, raising capital costs, and reducing sales volume.[21] Researchers found that Fortune 500 firms convicted of illegal conduct earned significantly lower returns on assets than unconvicted firms. In the case of WorldCom, $200 billion of shareholder value was lost in less than a year, making it the largest corporate fraud in history.[22]

---

19. Bagley, *supra* note 14.
20. Bagley, *supra* note 9.

21. Melissa S. Baucus & David A. Baucus, *Paying the Piper: An Empirical Examination of Long-Term Financial Consequences of Illegal Corporate Behavior*, 40 ACAD. MGMT. J. 129 (1997).
22. *See* Richard Breeden, *Restoring Trust*, filed with the WorldCom bankruptcy court on August 26, 2003.

In contrast, at least under certain circumstances, the ability to proactively go beyond the letter of the law can result in competitive advantage.[23] Legally astute management teams practice *strategic compliance management*.[24] They view the cost of complying with government regulations as an investment, not an expense. Instead of just complying with the letter of the law, they seek out and embrace operational changes that will enable them to convert regulatory constraints into innovation opportunities.[25]

Proactive strategies for dealing with the interface between a firm's business and the natural environment that go beyond environmental regulatory compliance have been associated with improved financial performance.[26] Yet firms' ability to reduce pollution became a source of competitive advantage only after managers replaced the mindset of reducing pollution to meet government end-pipe restrictions with a search for ways to use environment-friendly processes to create value.[27]

Law and the Value Chain

As seen in Exhibit 1.3, each activity in the value chain has legal aspects. From a firm's choice of business entity to the warranties it offers and the contracts it negotiates, law pervades the activities of the firm, affecting both its internal organization and its external relationships with customers, suppliers, and competitors.

Law Is Dynamic

The systems approach recognizes the dynamic nature of law. Law affects the market and market players, but market players also affect the law and the way it is interpreted, applied, and changed over time. Thus, law is not just a static external force acting upon managers and their firms. Instead, law and organizations are "endogenously coevolutionary."[28] By lobbying legislators and members of the executive branch, forming coalitions, and working directly with regulatory bodies, managers can help shape the environment in which they do business.[29] As with any other activity, managers engaged in lobbying and other political activities must be mindful of the ethical aspects of their actions.

Unfortunately, enlightened self-interest is not always a substitute for government regulation. Paul Krugman criticized former Federal Reserve Board Chair Alan Greenspan and other banking regulators for ignoring warnings about the predatory lending practices that contributed to the subprime mortgage crisis in 2007–2008.[30] Krugman quoted a 1963 essay in which Greenspan dismissed as a "collectivist myth" the idea that business leaders, left to their own devices, would "attempt to sell unsafe food and drugs, fraudulent securities and shoddy buildings"; instead, Greenspan asserted that "it is in the self-interest of every businessman to have a reputation for honest dealings and a quality product." Krugman faulted Greenspan for putting "ideology above public protection."[31] Greenspan himself subsequently remarked: "Those of us who look to the self-interest of lending institutions to protect shareholder equity have to be in a state of shocked disbelief."[32]

Laws enacted in response to corporate misdeeds often impose greater restrictions and costs on business than would have been imposed had firms acted more responsibly at the outset. A prime example is the Dodd–Frank Wall Street Reform and Consumer Protection Act of 2010 (discussed in Chapters 6, 17, 18, 21, and 23), which was enacted after widespread abuses in the subprime mortgage market led to near-global financial collapse.

LAW AND PUBLIC POLICY

Public law—the formal rules embodied in constitutions, statutes enacted by legislatures, judicial decisions rendered by courts, and regulations promulgated by administrative agencies—both reflects and helps shape social expectations. The laws and regulations applicable to U.S. business further four primary public policy objectives: promoting economic growth, protecting workers, promoting consumer welfare, and promoting public welfare. This typology is depicted in Exhibit 1.4.

Other major economic powers tend to have laws that further these same objectives, albeit with varying degrees of emphasis on the different objectives and varying ways of furthering them.[33] Indeed, much of the current debate on what constitutes good corporate governance turns on

---

23. Bagley, *supra* note 9.

24. Bagley, *supra* note 1.

25. Regulation may prompt firms to innovate, making them more competitive. Barry M. Mitnick, *The Strategic Uses of Regulation—and Deregulation*, in Corporate Political Agency: The Construction of Competition in Public Affairs (Barry M. Mitnick ed., 1993); Michael E. Porter & C. van der Linde, *Green and Competitive*, Harv. Bus. Rev., May 1995, at 120.

26. *See* William Q. Judge & Thomas J. Douglas, *Performance Implications of Incorporating Natural Environmental Issues into the Strategic Planning Process: An Empirical Assessment*, 35 J. Mgmt. Stud. 241 (1998); Robert D. Klassen & D. Clay Whybark, *The Impact of Environmental Technologies in Manufacturing Performance*, 42 Acad. Mgmt. J. 599 (1999).

27. Chad Nehrt, *Maintainability of First Mover Advantages When Environmental Regulations Differ Between Countries*, 23 Acad. Mgmt. Rev. 77 (1998).

28. Edelman & Suchman, *supra* note 2, at 501.

29. *See* L.G. Weber, *Citizenship and Democracy: The Ethics of Corporate Lobbying*, 6 Bus. Ethics Q. 253 (1996).

30. *Id.*

31. Paul Krugman, *Disastrous De-Regulation: For Greenspan and Bush, Ideology Trumps Oversight*, Pittsburgh Post-Gazette, Dec. 22, 2007, at B7.

32. Alan Greenspan, *We Will Never Have a Perfect Model of Risk*, Fin. Times, Mar. 17, 2008, at 13.

33. For example, Germany seeks to promote economic growth by facilitating the capital markets, but its goal of protecting workers has led to the system of codetermination whereby half of the members of the supervisory boards of large German corporations are elected by the workers and unions, and half are elected by the shareholders.

EXHIBIT 1.3	Law and the Value Chain

Support Activities	Firm infrastructure	Limited liability, corporate governance, choice of business entity, tax planning & securities regulation				
	Human resource management	Employment contracts, at-will employment, wrongful termination, bans on discrimination, equity compensation, Fair Labor Practices Act, National Labor Relations Act, workers' compensation & Employment Retirement Income Security Act				
	Technology development	Intellectual property protection, nondisclosure agreements, assignments of inventions, covenants not to compete, licensing agreements & product liability				
	Procurement	Contracts, Uniform Commercial Code, Convention on the International Sale of Goods, bankruptcy laws, securities regulation & Foreign Corrupt Practices Act				
		Inbound logistics	**Operations**	**Outbound logistics**	**Marketing and sales**	**Service**
		Contracts Antitrust limits on exclusive dealing contracts Environmental compliance	Workplace safety & labor relations Environmental compliance Process patents and trade secrets	Contracts Environmental compliance	Contracts Uniform Commercial Code Convention on the International Sale of Goods Consumer protection laws, including privacy protection Bans on deceptive or misleading advertising or sales practices Antitrust limits on vertical and horizontal market division, tying & predatory pricing Import/export controls World Trade Organization	Strict product liability Warranties Waivers & limitations of liability Doctrine of unconscionability Customer privacy
		Primary Activities				**Margin**

SOURCES: Diagram and text in roman type from MICHAEL E. PORTER, COMPETITIVE ADVANTAGE: CREATING AND SUSTAINING SUPERIOR PERFORMANCE (1985); text in italic type adapted from BAGLEY, *supra* note 1, and M.E. Porter & M.R. Kramer, *Strategy and Society: The Link Between Competitive Advantage and Corporate Social Responsibility,* HARV. BUS. REV., Dec. 2006, at 78.

EXHIBIT 1.4   Underlying Public Policy Rationales of U.S. Laws

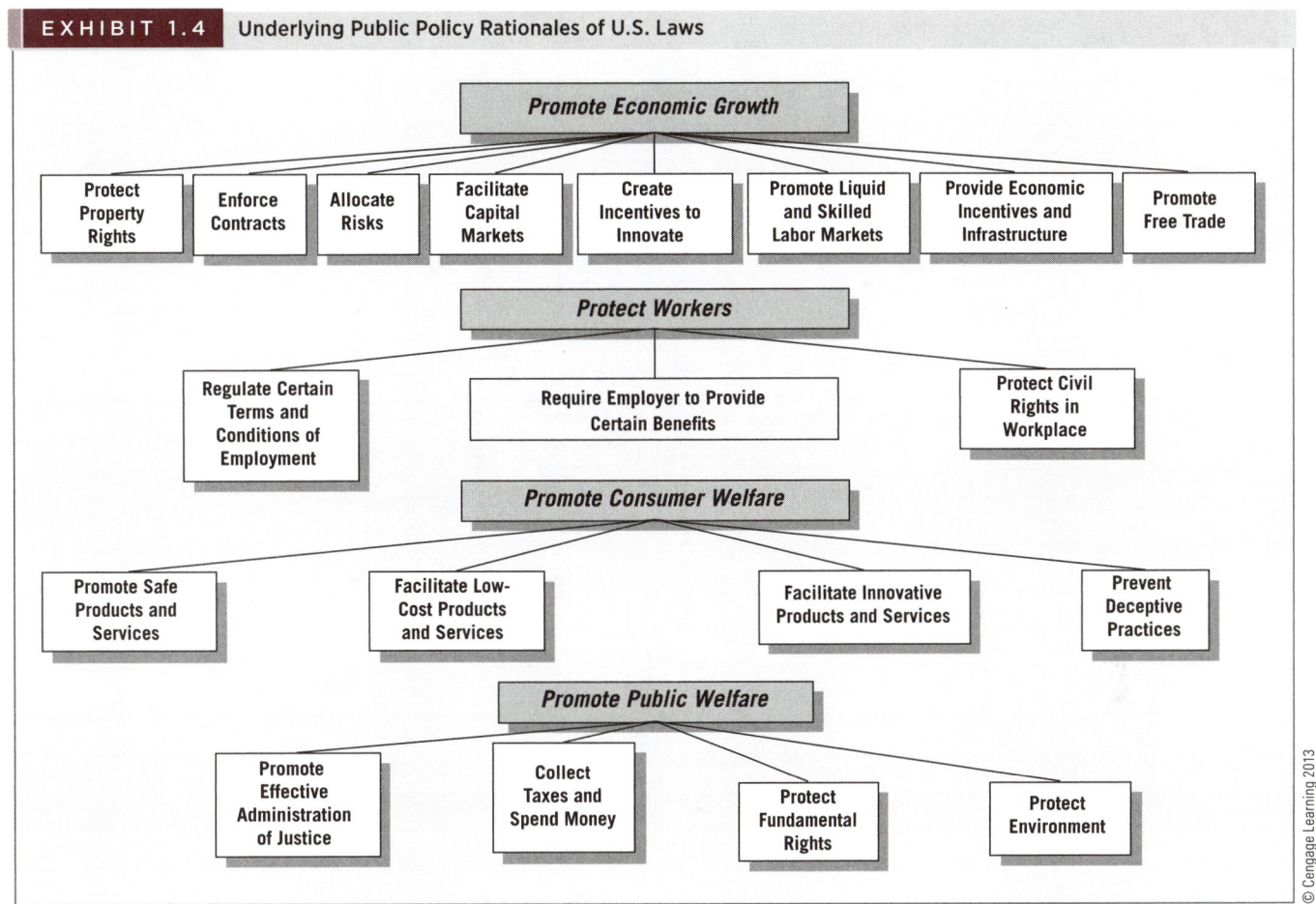

how much weight each country gives to the interests of shareholders, debtholders, employees, customers, and suppliers and to the protection of the environment.

Promoting Economic Growth

Various laws and regulations promote economic growth. As Exhibit 1.5 shows, this is done by protecting private property rights; enforcing private agreements; allocating risks;[34] facilitating the raising of capital; creating incentives to innovate; promoting liquid and skilled labor markets; providing subsidies, tax incentives, and infrastructure; and promoting free trade in the global markets.

Protecting Workers

Worker protection constitutes a second major public policy underlying U.S. business law. As depicted in Exhibit 1.6, this is accomplished by regulating certain

terms and conditions of employment, requiring the employer to provide certain benefits, and protecting workers' civil rights. Complying with these requirements imposes costs on employers that society, acting through the legislature and the courts, has deemed it appropriate for employers to bear.

Promoting Consumer Welfare

As shown in Exhibit 1.7, business regulation is designed to promote consumer welfare by encouraging the sale of safe and innovative products and services at a fair price, preventing deceptive practices, and protecting consumer privacy.

Promoting Public Welfare

As depicted in Exhibit 1.8, business regulation promotes public welfare by ensuring the effective administration of justice, collecting taxes and spending money, protecting fundamental rights, and protecting the environment.

---

34. For an excellent discussion of government's role in allocating risk, see DAVID A. MOSS, WHEN ALL ELSE FAILS: GOVERNMENT AS THE ULTIMATE RISK MANAGER (2001).

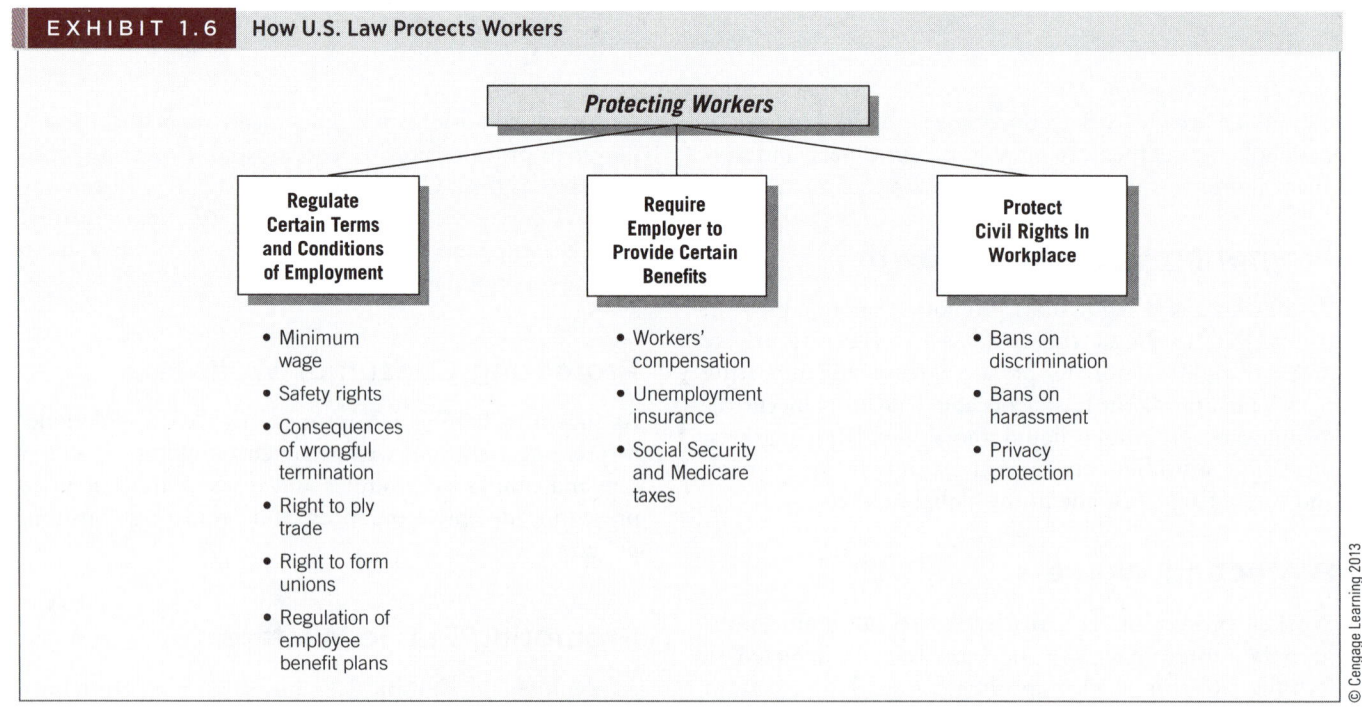

EXHIBIT 1.5   How U.S. Law Promotes Economic Growth

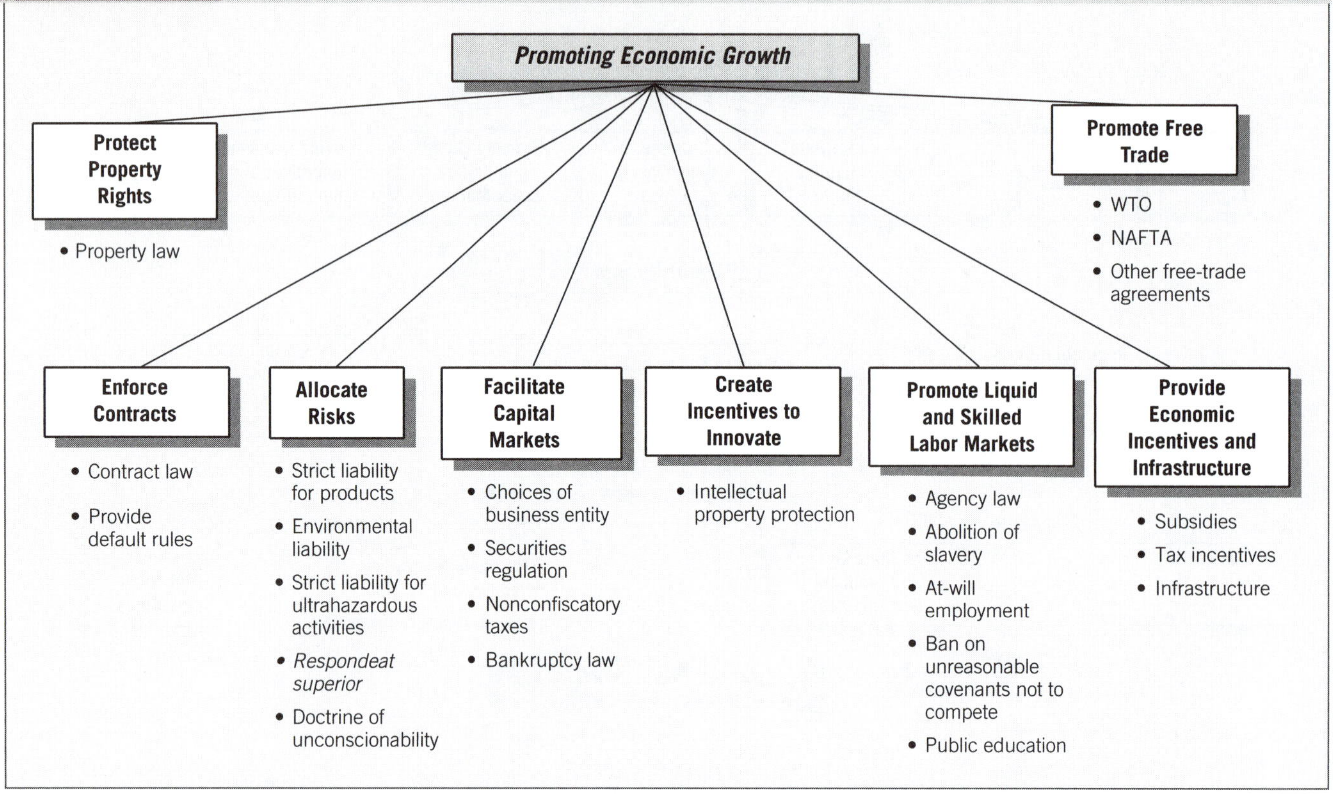

Promoting Economic Growth

Protect Property Rights
- Property law

Promote Free Trade
- WTO
- NAFTA
- Other free-trade agreements

Enforce Contracts
- Contract law
- Provide default rules

Allocate Risks
- Strict liability for products
- Environmental liability
- Strict liability for ultrahazardous activities
- *Respondeat superior*
- Doctrine of unconscionability

Facilitate Capital Markets
- Choices of business entity
- Securities regulation
- Nonconfiscatory taxes
- Bankruptcy law

Create Incentives to Innovate
- Intellectual property protection

Promote Liquid and Skilled Labor Markets
- Agency law
- Abolition of slavery
- At-will employment
- Ban on unreasonable covenants not to compete
- Public education

Provide Economic Incentives and Infrastructure
- Subsidies
- Tax incentives
- Infrastructure

© Cengage Learning 2013

EXHIBIT 1.6   How U.S. Law Protects Workers

Protecting Workers

Regulate Certain Terms and Conditions of Employment
- Minimum wage
- Safety rights
- Consequences of wrongful termination
- Right to ply trade
- Right to form unions
- Regulation of employee benefit plans

Require Employer to Provide Certain Benefits
- Workers' compensation
- Unemployment insurance
- Social Security and Medicare taxes

Protect Civil Rights In Workplace
- Bans on discrimination
- Bans on harassment
- Privacy protection

© Cengage Learning 2013

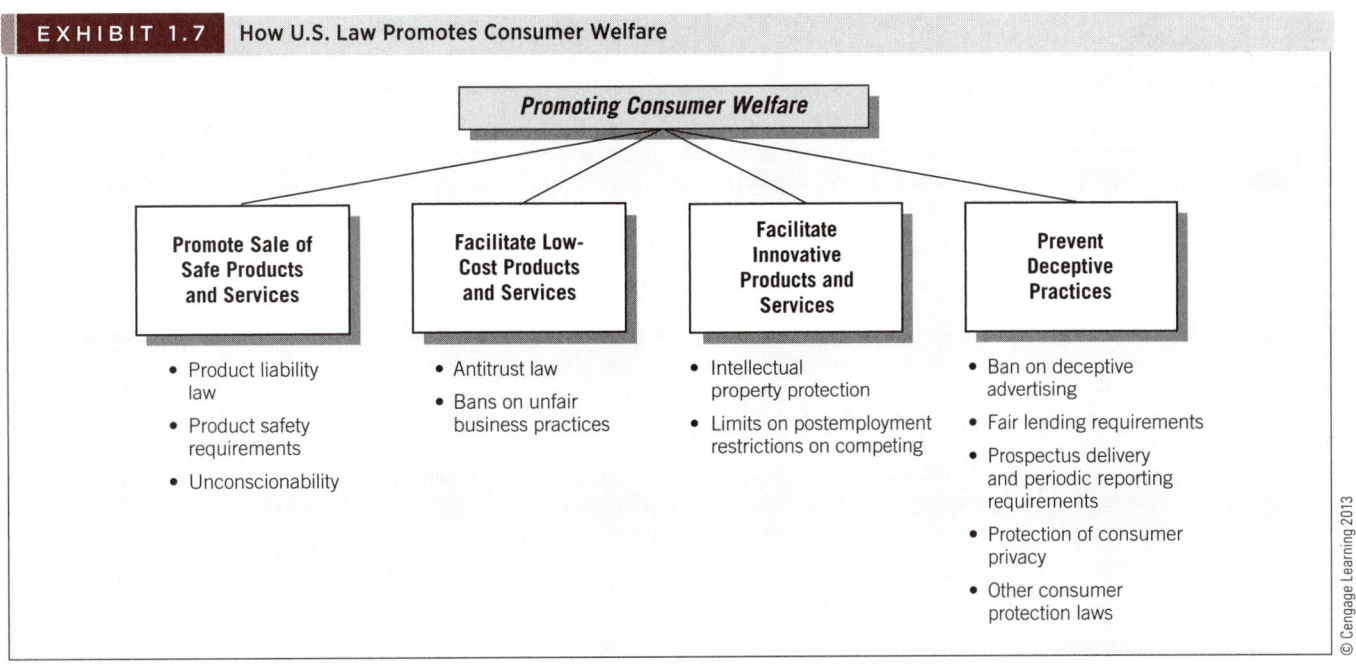

EXHIBIT 1.7   How U.S. Law Promotes Consumer Welfare

EXHIBIT 1.8   How U.S. Law Promotes Public Welfare

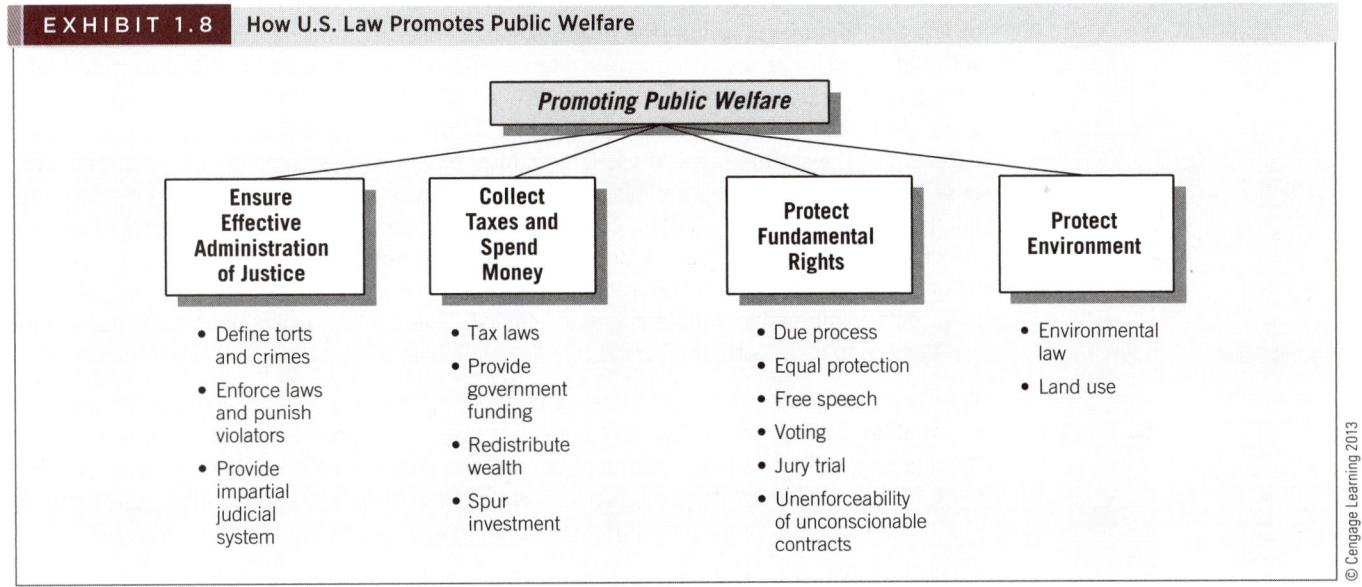

Policy Conflicts

Sometimes, these public policies conflict. In the following case, the Supreme Court considered whether the public policy of ensuring freedom of expression outweighed the interest of physicians in keeping their prescribing practices private and the interest of the state in reducing health-care expenses.

| A CASE IN POINT | *Summary* | Case 1.1 |

Sorrell v. IMS Health Inc.

Supreme Court of the United States
131 S. Ct. 2653 (2011).

FACTS   A Vermont statute prohibited pharmacies from selling prescriber-identifying information for marketing prescription drugs without the prescriber's consent. Data miners analyze such information and sell it to pharmaceutical manufacturers, which use the information to refine their sales pitches to physicians and thereby increase sales of brand-name drugs. Vermont data miners and an association of brand-name drug manufacturers challenged the statute as a violation of their free-speech rights under the First Amendment of the U.S. Constitution (as applied to the states by the Fourteenth Amendment).

ISSUE PRESENTED   Is a state law banning the sale of prescriber-identifying information to pharmaceutical firms without the prescriber's consent constitutional?

SUMMARY OF OPINION   The U.S. Supreme Court began by noting that speech in aid of drug manufacturing is protected by the Free Speech Clause of the First Amendment. The Vermont statute precluded detailers—drug reps who meet with physicians to provide additional details about brand-name drugs and often free samples—from obtaining prescriber-identifying information but permitted its purchase by others. Because it disfavored speech with a particular content—marketing—and disfavored specific speakers, namely, detailers, the statute was subject to "heightened judicial scrutiny." For the statute to pass muster, Vermont had to show that it directly advanced a substantial government interest and that it was drawn to achieve that interest.

Vermont argued that the law was necessary to protect the privacy of prescribing physicians and to reduce the likelihood that physicians will prescribe expensive brand-name drugs that are not in the best interests of patients or the State. The legislature found that detailing "increases the cost of health care and health insurance; encourages hasty and excessive reliance on brand-name drugs, before the profession has observed their effectiveness as compared with older and less expensive generic alternatives; and fosters disruptive and repeated marketing visits tantamount to harassment." While conceding that these interests were "significant," the Court concluded that they did not justify the burden the statute placed on protected expression. The statute made prescribing information available to an almost unlimited audience (including researchers and health departments promoting the use of generic drugs) but banned its sale to "a narrow class of disfavored speakers." Even if pharmaceutical marketing efforts influence prescribing practices, "the State may not seek to remove a popular but disfavored product from the marketplace by prohibiting truthful, nonmisleading advertisements that contain impressive endorsements or catchy jingles." As for disruptive visits, physicians are free not to meet with detailers.

The Court acknowledged that "[t]he capacity of technology to find and publish personal information . . . presents serious and unresolved issues with respect to personal privacy and the dignity it seeks to save." If Vermont banned the sale of prescriber-identifying information except in narrow circumstances, "then the State might have a strong position." But Vermont "cannot engage in content-based discrimination to advance its own side of a debate."

COMMENTS   In a dissent in which Justices Ginsburg and Kagan joined, Justice Breyer argued that this regulation of commercial speech should be evaluated under a less strict "intermediate" standard, which upholds laws and regulations that significantly restrict speech "as long as they also 'directly advance' a 'substantial' government interest that could not 'be served as well by a more limited restriction.'" He cautioned: "If the Court means to create constitutional barriers to regulatory rules that might affect the *content* of a commercial message, it has embarked upon an unprecedented task—a task that threatens significant judicial interference with widely accepted regulatory activity." The dissent charged that the majority approach "threatens to return us to a happily bygone era when judges scrutinized legislation for its interference with economic liberty. History shows that the power was much abused and resulted in the constitutionalization of economic theories preferred by individual jurists. See *Lochner* v. *New York*, 198 U.S. 45, 75–76 (1905) (Holmes, J., dissenting)."

⟨A⟩ THE LEGALLY ASTUTE MANAGER

At its core, *legal astuteness* is the ability of a manager to communicate effectively with counsel and to work together to solve complex problems.[35] For example, legally astute managers can (1) negotiate contracts as complements to trust building and other relational governance techniques to define and strengthen relationships and reduce transaction costs, (2) protect and enhance the realizable value of the firm's resources, (3) create options through contracts and other legal tools, and (4) convert regulatory constraints into opportunities.[36]

As discussed further in "The Responsible Manager," legal astuteness has four components:

- A set of value-laden attitudes about the importance of law to the firm's success.

- A proactive approach to legal issues and regulation.

- The ability to exercise informed judgment when managing the legal aspects of business.

- Context-specific knowledge of the law and the appropriate use of legal tools.[37]

Exhibit 1.9 shows how legally astute managers can use law to create and capture value and to manage risk during the five stages of business development:

- Evaluating the opportunity and defining the value proposition, which includes developing the business concept for exploiting the opportunity.

- Assembling the team.

- Raising capital.

- Developing, producing, and marketing the product or service.

- Harvesting the opportunity, through sale of the venture, an initial public offering (IPO) of stock, or reinvestment and renewal.[38]

Exhibit 1.9 does not purport to be an all-inclusive list of techniques for using the law to increase realizable value while managing risk. Rather, it is intended to suggest both the variety and the pervasive nature of the tools available.

---

35. Bagley, *supra* note 9.

36. *Id.*

37. *Id.*

38. Professors Stevenson, Roberts, and Grousbeck break down the entrepreneurial process into five steps: (1) evaluating the opportunity, (2) developing the business concept, (3) assessing required resources both human and capital, (4) acquiring needed resources, and (5) managing and harvesting the venture. HOWARD H. STEVENSON, MICHAEL J. ROBERTS & H. IRVING GROUSBECK, NEW BUSINESS VENTURES AND THE ENTREPRENEUR 17–21 (2d ed. 1985). The five steps in Exhibit 1.9 are based on this model with modifications to reflect the fact that very different but significant legal issues arise in the course of marshaling human resources and raising money and in the course of managing the development, production, marketing, and sale of the product or service and in harvesting the venture.

EXHIBIT 1.9 Legal Tools for Increasing Realizable Value While Managing Risk

Evaluating Opportunity and Defining Value Proposition	Assembling Team	Raising Capital	Developing, Producing, Marketing, and Selling Product or Service	Harvesting
• Ask whether idea is patentable or otherwise protectable. • Examine branding possibilities.	• Choose appropriate form of business entity and issue equity to founders early. • Structure appropriate equity incentives for employees. • Enter into nondisclosure agreements and assignments of inventions.	• Be prepared to negotiate downside and sideways protection and upside rights for preferred stock. • Be prepared to subject at least some founders' stock to vesting. • Sell stock in exempt transaction.	• Implement trade secret policy. • Consider patent protection for new business processes and other inventions. Select a strong trademark and protect it. Register copyrights. • Enter into licensing agreements. • Create options to buy and sell. • Secure distribution rights. • Decide whether to buy or build, then enter into contracts.	• If investor, exercise demand registration rights or board control to force IPO or sale of company. Rely on exemptions for sale of restricted stock. Ask whether employee vesting accelerates on an IPO or sale. • Negotiate and document arrangements with underwriter or investment banker.

CONTINUED

EXHIBIT 1.9	Legal Tools for Increasing Realizable Value While Managing Risk (Continued)			
Evaluating Opportunity and Defining Value Proposition	Assembling Team	Raising Capital	Developing, Producing, Marketing, and Selling Product or Service	Harvesting
• Ask whether anyone else has rights to opportunity.	• Document founders' arrangements and subject founders' shares to vesting. • Analyze any covenants not to compete or trade secret issues. • Require arbitration or mediation of disputes. • Comply with antidiscrimination laws in hiring and firing. Institute harassment policy. • Avoid wrongful termination by documenting performance issues. • Caution employees on discoverability of e-mail. • Provide whistleblower protection.	• Be prepared to make representations and warranties in stock-purchase agreement with or without knowledge qualifiers. • Choose business entity with limited liability. • Respect corporate form to avoid piercing of corporate veil.	• Enter into purchase and sale contracts. • Impose limitations on liability and use releases. • Buy insurance for product liabilities. Recall unsafe products. • Create safe workplace. • Institute compliance system. • Do due diligence before buying or leasing property to avoid environmental problems. No horizontal price-fixing or tying, but product integration is generally OK. • Be active in finding business solutions to legal disputes. • Avoid misleading advertising. • File tax returns on time and pay taxes when due. Do tax planning.	• Be mindful of difference between letter of intent and contract of sale. • Consider entering into no-shop agreements if buyer. Negotiate fiduciary out if seller. • Disclose fully in prospectus or acquisition agreement. Secure indemnity rights. • Perform due diligence. • Allocate risk of unknown. • Make sure board of directors is informed and disinterested. • Ban insider trading and police trades.

© Cengage Learning 2013

GLOBAL VIEW

Lobbying in the European Union

"This shows you are never too old to get surprised,"[39] remarked sixty-six-year-old Jack Welch, CEO of General Electric, after the European Commission rejected GE's proposed $40 billion merger with Honeywell International on the grounds that the vertical combination would have anticompetitive effects in the European Union (EU).[40] The deal would have vertically integrated two aerospace industry leaders. GE builds engines and leases aircraft, while Honeywell makes avionics components. The decision marked the first time a merger of two U.S.-based corporations was derailed by EU officials.[41] Welch remarked, "In this case, the European regulators' demands exceeded anything I or our European advisers imagined, and differed sharply from antitrust counterparts in the U.S. and Canada."[42]

GE's experience is illustrative of the new reality facing U.S.-based corporations wishing to gain access to the 500 million consumers in the EU's twenty-seven members: finalizing a deal will require spending significant time in Brussels, Belgium, the EU's center of operations.[43] "Every company of a certain size has a Washington representative. Increasingly the same is true of Brussels," commented Hogan & Hartson LLP partner Raymond S. Calamaro.[44] An estimated 15,000 lobbyists are now pursuing their clients' interests before the EU.[45]

CONTINUED

Norebbo/Shutterstock

39. *GE Pessimistic on Merger*, CNNMoney.com, June 14, 2001, http://money.cnn.com/2001/06/14/europe/ge/.

40. Edmund Andrews & Paul Meller, *Europe Ends Bid by G.E. for Honeywell*, N.Y. Times, July 4, 2001, at 1.

41. *Id.*

42. *GE Pessimistic on Merger*, *supra* note 39.

43. *European Imperialism*, Wall St. J., Oct. 31, 2007, at A20.

44. Nicholas Kulish, *Euro Brash*, Wash. Monthly, Apr. 1, 2004, at 24.

45. Carol Matlack, *Why Brussels Is Abuzz with Lobbyists*, Bus. Wk., Oct. 29, 2007, at 81.

GE hired Finsbury International Political and Regulatory Advisers to present its position to regulators in individual nations,[46] but the company apparently underestimated the level of resistance it faced. GE did not make concerted efforts to influence the outcome until after the competition commission, a branch of the European Commission, released a preliminary draft opinion opposing the combination.[47] The competition commission makes recommendations to the EU regarding issues that affect economic competition within the member states.[48] After the adverse preliminary opinion was released, GE representatives met with competition regulators and official members of the European Commission,[49] but by then the die had been cast.

GE's U.S. competitors, including United Technologies and Rockwell International,[50] and foreign rivals, such as Rolls Royce, lobbied aggressively against the deal.[51] European antitrust regulators are often more sympathetic to competitors than U.S. authorities are. "The European Union's process offers a lot more credence to competitors," commented a Washington-based management consultant.[52] He added, "In the U.S., they listen to competitors but don't give them as much weight."[53]

According to Mario Monti, the EU Commissioner in charge of competition from 1999 to 2004, objectivity was not an issue. Three months before the GE–Honeywell merger was rejected, he commented: "We are sufficiently non-naive as to be able to discount the elements provided by competitors for their vested interests."[54] Although GE appealed the European Commission's decision, the appeal ultimately was unsuccessful, and the company was ordered to pay the legal costs of the EU and its allies, including Rolls Royce.[55]

GE and Honeywell are not the only companies to run afoul of European competition officials. EU regulators blocked WorldCom's proposed $130 billion purchase of Sprint in 2000. In 2007 alone, the EU levied more than $3.6 billion in antitrust fines, including a $689 million fine against Microsoft for abusing its dominant position.[56]

European companies have also seen their merger plans scuttled by the European Commission. In 2000, Volvo and Scania, the two Swedish truck manufacturers, abandoned a proposed $7 billion merger due to antitrust concerns.[57]

As Europe continues to consolidate its economic power, its impact on corporate planning and strategy will become even more evident. Consumer privacy, emissions standards, chemical usage, and accounting standards are just a few areas where EU and U.S. law differ.[58] Companies doing business globally may find themselves having to conform to EU regulations when they impose higher standards than the United States. As discussed further in Chapter 2, General Electric CEO Jeff Immelt (Welch's successor) seized this as an opportunity for economic growth when GE launched its ecomagination campaign in 2005 and touted its energy-efficient and lower-emission hybrid locomotives, aircraft engines, and compact fluorescent light bulbs. Managers hoping to participate in creating the rules governing their business would be wise to start booking flights to Brussels.

46. Boris Grondahl & James Ledbetter, *Cutting Europe's Red Tape*, Industry Standard, July 9, 2001, *available at* http://findarticles.com/p/articles/mi_m0HWW/is_27_4/ai_76964767.

47. Andrew Ross Sorkin, *G.E.-Honeywell: If at First . . .* , N.Y. Times, June 27, 2001, at 1.

48. Andrew Ross Sorkin, *U.S. Businesses Turn to Europe to Bar Mergers*, N.Y. Times, June 19, 2001, at 1.

49. *Id.*

50. *Id.*

51. Paul Meller, *Another Step in Killing Deal for Honeywell*, N.Y. Times, June 26, 2001, at 1.

52. Andrews & Meller, *supra* note 40.

53. *Id.*

54. *Id.*

55. Paul Meller, *GE and Honeywell Lose Merger Appeal*, Int'l Herald Trib., Dec. 14, 2005.

56. Matlack, *supra* note 45.

57. Sorkin, *supra* note 48.

58. Kulish, *supra* note 44; *European Imperialism*, *supra* note 43.

THE RESPONSIBLE MANAGER

DEVELOPING A LEGALLY ASTUTE TOP MANAGEMENT TEAM

Legal astuteness begins with respect for both the letter and the spirit of the law. Legally astute management teams appreciate the importance of meeting society's expectations of appropriate behavior and recognize that "the moral aspects of choice" are the "final component of strategy."[59]

Legally astute managers include legal considerations at each stage of strategy development and implementation. They bring counsel in early and do not wait to seek legal advice until after a deal has been struck or a problem has arisen. They demand legal advice that is business oriented and expect their lawyers to help them address business opportunities and threats in ways that are legally permissible, effective, and efficient.

Legally astute managers accept responsibility for managing the legal dimensions of business and recognize that it is the job of the general manager, not the lawyer, to decide which allocation of resources and rewards makes the most

59. E.P. Learned, C.R. Christensen, K.R. Andrews & W.D. Guth, Business Policy: Text and Cases 578 (1969).

CONTINUED

business sense. They understand that legal analysis is often ambiguous and that managing the legal aspects of business requires the exercise of informed judgment. Even the most skilled and experienced advisers, including lawyers, sometimes get it wrong. A lawyer's judgment can be clouded by personal interests, such as increasing billable hours or angling for more power within the firm, or by oversensitivity to risk or overconfidence bias.[60] Legally astute managers take this into account when factoring in legal advice. At the end of the day, as long as counsel has not advised that a particular course of action is illegal, it is up to the management team to determine whether a particular risk is worth taking or a particular opportunity is worth pursuing.

As discussed further in Chapter 3, every legal dispute is a business problem requiring a business solution.[61] Legally

astute managers take responsibility for managing their disputes and do not hand them off to their lawyers with a "you-take-care-of-it" approach.

Legally astute managers have context-specific knowledge of the law and the application of legal tools. Managers who can harness the creative power of legal language are more adept at seeing and shaping the legal structure of their world. They are also better equipped to communicate effectively with their lawyers.

The law offers a variety of tools that legally astute management teams can use to increase realizable value and to manage risks. For example, the choice of business entity (e.g., corporation, partnership, or limited liability company) will determine the investors' liability for the debts of the business, the rights and responsibilities of the managers and equity holders, and the level at which tax is levied. The legal tools of greatest relevance to managers will vary with the firm's overall strategy, its external environment, and the stage of development of the business. Certain tools, such as contracts, have broad application.

---

60. D.C. Langevoort & R.K. Rasmussen, *Skewing the Results: The Role of Lawyers in Transmitting Legal Rules*, 5 S. Cal. L. Rev. 375 (1997).

61. Constance E. Bagley, *Legal Problems Showing a Way to Do Business*, Fin. Times, Nov. 27, 2000, at 2.

A Manager's Dilemma

Putting It into Practice

Guanxi: Networking or Bribery?

Johanna Lu is the new head of international business development for Dexter Motors, a leading manufacturer of heavy truck engines. Dexter has recently entered into a joint venture with the Chinese state automotive company to produce fuel-efficient, low-emission engines. From conversations with business school classmates working in China, Lu knows that companies in China engage in a variety of political activities. These range from providing gifts or money, inviting government officials to banquets, hiring the children of government officials, and electing executives as national or local congresspersons, to engaging in *guanxi* (relationship-based) lobbying,[62] making charitable contributions, and reporting important issues to the government.

Only two laws apply to corporate political activities in China.[63] The Election Act of China gives businesspeople the right to be elected as congresspersons. The Criminal Law of

China prohibits businesses from paying bribes to government officials, but a payment of money is not considered a bribe unless the amount is significant.

A survey of 195 executives attending the Huazhong University of Science and Technology (HUST) revealed a consensus that it is unethical to give money or gifts to government officials or to provide paid travel.[64] Even though paying honoraria for speaking, inviting government officials to banquets, and hiring the offspring of officials are ethically questionable in the West, most of the HUST respondents considered such activities ethically acceptable.[65]

Lu knows that her success will depend in part on her ability to work cooperatively with a variety of Chinese government officials. A friend has suggested that she encourage Dexter's local manager to seek election as a congressperson as part of a broader political action initiative. Should Lu encourage the manager to run for office? Engage in *guanxi* lobbying to encourage the district leaders to impose stiffer emissions and mileage requirements for heavy trucks? Hire the son of a prominent local official?

---

62. For a discussion of *guanxi*, see Xiao-Ping Chen & Chao C. Chen, *On the Intricacies of the Chinese* Guanxi *Development*, 21 Asia Pac. J. Mgmt. 305, 306 (2004) (defining *guanxi* as "an informal, particularist personal connection between two individuals who are bounded by an implicit psychological contract to follow the social norm of *guanxi*, such as maintaining a long-term relationship, mutual commitment, loyalty, and obligation").

63. Yongqiang Gao & Wenchuan Wei, *Are Corporate Political Actions Ethical? An Investigation of Executives in Chinese Enterprises*, 1 Int'l J. Bus. Innovation & Res. 464 (2007).

64. *Id.*

65. *Id.*

INSIDE STORY

Ronald McDonald, Mickey Mouse, and Childhood Obesity

The food and beverage industry spends about $2 billion a year marketing products directly to children.[66] As childhood obesity has increased, advocacy groups, such as Action for Children's Television (ACT), and government actors, from Congress to the Federal Trade Commission (FTC) to state legislatures, have pressured "family-oriented" companies to consider the impact of their advertising on children's diets.[67] While certain industry leaders have responded to this pressure by voluntarily restricting their advertising to preempt calls for tougher government restrictions on ads aimed at children, others oppose not only stricter government regulation but even voluntary restrictions.

The Childhood Obesity Problem and the Advertising Link

An alarming 17% of children and adolescents between the ages of two and nineteen are obese.[68] Since 1980, the number of overweight children has doubled, and the number of obese adolescents has almost tripled.[69] During the twenty-nine year period from 1977 to 2006, meals eaten or prepared outside the home increased by 31%.[70] Commercially prepared food often has more fats and sugars than home-cooked meals.

An Institute of Medicine review of 123 empirical studies concluded that "television advertising 'influences children to prefer and request high-calorie and low-nutrient foods and beverages,' and 'influences the short term consumption of children ages 2–12.'"[71] As many as 23% of the food-related ads kids see on TV are for fast food, so children are being exposed to tens of thousands of fast-food commercials each year.[72] Consequently,

researchers suggest that a ban on fast-food commercials could reduce the number of obese young children by 18%.[73] Nevertheless, proposals to limit advertising to children face stiff political opposition and heightened judicial scrutiny, given the U.S. Supreme Court's invalidation of a California statute banning the sale of violent video games to children[74] and its invalidation of a Vermont statute restricting the sale of physician-identifying prescribing information to pharmaceutical companies.[75]

Efforts to Reduce Childhood Obesity Through Industry Self-Regulation

Historically, food advertisers have successfully fought off enhanced government oversight of advertising to children. In 1974, the industry created the Children's Advertising Review Unit (CARU), a voluntary association, to forestall proposed government regulations that would have curbed marketing targeted at children.[76] Following a protracted battle, during which members of Congress were lobbied hard by advertising representatives, Congress rescinded the FTC's jurisdiction over advertising to children in 1980 and left oversight of children's advertising to the CARU.[77]

Self-regulation has proved largely ineffective, however. A study reported in the *Archives of Pediatrics & Adolescent Medicine* found that children were seeing more fast-food commercials in 2009 than they were six years earlier.[78]

As the public has become more concerned about childhood obesity, some members of Congress have begun to reconsider the decision to take away the FTC's jurisdiction over the fairness of children's advertising.[79] In addition, the Federal Communications Commission is considering a ban on certain types of children's advertising, including interactive commercials.[80] State legislatures in more than thirty states have proposed requiring labels on fast food or limiting the availability of junk food in schools, or both.[81] After the Obama

CONTINUED

---

66. Dan Eggen & Lyndsey Layton, *Industries Lobby Against Voluntary Nutrition Guidelines for Food Marketed to Kids*, Wash. Post, July 9, 2011.

67. Jess Alderman, Jason Smith, Ellen Fried & Richard Daynard, *Prevention and Treatment: Solutions Beyond the Individual: Application of Law to the Childhood Obesity Epidemic*, 35 J.L. Med. & Ethics 90, 94 (Spring 2007).

68. Cynthia Ogden & Margaret Carroll, *Prevalence of Obesity Among Children and Adolescents: United States, Trends 1963–1965 Through 2007–2008*, June 4, 2010, *available at* http://www.cdc.gov/nchs/data/hestat/obesity_child_07_08/obesity_child_07_08.pdf.

69. Alderman *et al.*, *supra* note 67.

70. Meredith Melnick, *Is Commercially Prepared Food Responsible for Childhood Weight Gain?* Time Healthland, July 25, 2011, *available at* http://healthland.time.com/2011/07/25/is-commercially-prepared-food-responsible-for-childhood-weight-gain/ (reporting on a study published in the *Journal of the American Dietetic Association*, which looked at the eating habits of 35,000 children).

71. Juliet B. Schor & Margaret Ford, *Perspectives on the Problem: From Tastes Great to Cool: Children's Food Marketing and the Rise of the Symbolic*, 35 J.L. Med. & Ethics 10, 12 (Spring 2007).

72. *Fast Food TV Ads Linked to Child Obesity, Study Finds*, FOXNews.com, Nov. 20, 2008, http://www.foxnews.com/story/0,2933,455028,00.html.

73. *Id.*

74. Brown v. Entm't Merch. Ass'n, 131 S. Ct. 2729 (2011) (Case 4.3).

75. Sorrell v. IMS Health Inc., 131 S. Ct. 2653 (2011) (holding that "the State may not seek to remove a popular but disfavored product from the marketplace by prohibiting truthful, nonmisleading advertisements that contain . . . catchy jingles.") (Case 1.1).

76. Alderman et al., *supra* note 67.

77. *Id.*

78. Amy Norton, *Junk Food Still Stars in TV Ads Seen by Kids*, Reuters Health, Aug. 9, 2011, *available at* http://www.reuters.com/article/2011/08/09/us-junk-food-idUSTRE7783XS20110809.

79. *Id.*

80. *Id.* at 99.

81. Schor & Ford, *supra* note 71.

administration proposed voluntary guidelines for the types of food advertised to children, giants in the food industry created two groups to respond to the proposed new guidelines: the Children's Food and Beverage Advertising Initiative and the Sensible Food Policy Coalition.

The Children's Food and Beverage Advertising Initiative began in 2006 as a response to calls for greater self-regulation of food advertising to children. The initiative now comprises seventeen companies, including Coca-Cola, Kraft Foods, and General Mills, which have pledged to improve the nutritional content of the food featured in ads geared toward children. In July 2011, the initiative announced that it had developed uniform nutrition criteria for food advertisements to children, which will go into effect in 2014. The criteria, which are based on U.S. dietary guidelines, include, for example, a limit on ads aimed at children for cereals containing more than 10 grams of sugar per serving.

Some of the nation's largest food makers, fast-food chains, and media companies (including Viacom and Time Warner) have taken a different tack and are opposing even voluntary advertising restrictions.[82] Their advocacy group—the Sensible Food Policy Coalition—is leading a campaign to derail even voluntary nutritional guidelines, arguing that parents, not lawmakers, should be responsible for deciding what their children will eat and whether they can have toys with their meals.[83] Those arguments have thwarted a number of proposed bans across the country.[84]

McDonald's Role in the Controversy

McDonald's mascot clown—Ronald McDonald—is prominently featured in so many advertisements that "[he] is as recognizable as Santa Claus."[85] McDonald's fast-food-plus-toy children's meal is "arguably the most successful marketing strategy in human history . . . turning a visit to a fast food restaurant into a favored activity for children."[86] A Happy Meal consisting of a cheeseburger, small fries, and 1% milk contains 640 calories and almost as many total grams of fat—26—as a Big Mac.[87]

Corporate Accountability International and others advocacy groups have called for an end to Ronald's role in marketing unhealthy food to children.[88] One advocate dubbed

Ronald "a deep-fried Joe Camel for the 21st century."[89] Camel Cigarettes had used the "cool" Joe Camel cartoon character in its cigarette ads in the 1990s, but it was forced to retire the character after a study published in *The Journal of the American Medical Association* found that Joe Camel was more recognizable to preschoolers than Mickey Mouse.[90] In response to Ronald's critics, McDonald's CEO James Skinner announced that the clown mascot was not nearing retirement; he also criticized the calls to retire Ronald to the exclusion of other fast-food mascots.[91]

Disney Takes a Stand

Even though the ability to market films ranging from *Toy Story 2* to *Aladdin* directly to parents and children grabbing a quick bite to eat at McDonald's had been an advantage, Disney announced in 2006 that it was not renewing its co-marketing agreement with McDonald's.[92] Although spokespeople for both companies denied that health concerns played any role in the decision to terminate one of the fast-food chain's most successful marketing strategies,[93] Disney announced new advertising guidelines five months later. Disney CEO Robert Iger remarked, "A company such as ours, with the reach we have, has a responsibility because of how much we can influence people's opinions and behavior." He also noted the strategic implications of the new guidelines: "There's also a business opportunity here."[94]

If opportunities are gauged by what consumers think, then Iger was correct. A *Wall Street Journal*/Harris Interactive poll conducted just one month after his statement found that 65% of American adults believed that food advertising was a major factor contributing to the increase in obesity among children.[95] As part of the initiative announced by Iger, Disney will permit its characters to pitch children's foods only if they meet these guidelines:

- Appropriate kid-sized portions do not exceed a cap on calories.

- Total fat does not exceed 30% of calories for main and side dishes and 35% of calories for snacks.

CONTINUED

---

82. Sharon Bernstein, *Fast-Food Industry Quietly Fights Ban*, PITTSBURGH TRIB. REV., May 22, 2011, *available at* http://www.pittsburghlive.com/x/pittsburghtrib/business/s_738333.html.

83. *Id.*

84. *Id.*

85. Andrea Simakis, *Ronald McDonald: Evil Genius? The Kid-Friendly Clown Is Under Fire for Leading Our Children Astray*, PLAIN DEALER (Cleveland), May 21, 2011, at E1.

86. Schor & Ford, *supra* note 71.

87. Nutritional information as disclosed on McDonald's website (last visited Aug. 12, 2011). Nutritional data for popular food items are available at http://nutrition.mcdonalds.com/nutritionexchange/nutritionfacts.pdf. Happy Meals nutritional data are available at http://nutrition.mcdonalds.com/nutrionexchange/Happy_Meals_Nutrition.List.pdf.

88. *Id.*

89. *Id.*

90. Mary B. Meaden, Comment, *Joe Camel and the Targeting of Minors in Tobacco Advertising: Before and After* 44 Liquormart v. Rhode Island, 31 NEW ENG. L. REV. 1011 (1997).

91. Simakis, *supra* note 85.

92. Rachel Abramowitz, *Disney Loses Its Appetite for Happy Meal Tie-Ins*, L.A. TIMES, May 8, 2006, at A1.

93. Eric Noe, *Did Childhood-Obesity Worries Kill Disney-McDonald's Pact?* ABCNEWS.GO.COM, May 8, 2006, http://abcnews.go.com/Business/story?id=1937651 &page=1.

94. Merissa Marr & Janet Adamy, *Disney Pulls Its Characters from Junk Food*, WALL ST. J., Oct. 17, 2006, at D1.

95. Beckey Bright, *More Americans See Childhood Obesity as Major Problem in U.S., Poll Finds*, WALL ST. J. ONLINE, http://online.wsj.com/article/SB115190208989196887.html.

- Saturated fat does not exceed 10% of calories for main dishes, side dishes, and snacks.

- Added sugar does not exceed 10% of calories for main dishes and side dishes and 25% of calories for snacks.

- Disney will continue to license special-occasion sweets such as birthday cakes and seasonal candy as part of its product range but will limit the number of indulgence items in its licensed portfolio to 15%. In addition, most special-occasion sweets will be available in single-serving packets.[96]

In addition, Disney altered the default makeup of the kids' meals in its theme parks.[97] Milk, juice, or water replaced soft drinks, and a healthier side dish (such as applesauce or carrots) replaced french fries. In the fall of 2007, Disney also began marketing an agricultural line branded as Disney Garden. The line includes teriyaki sugar snap peas, honey orange carrot coins, and an assortment of miniature fruits.[98]

The Center for Science in the Public Interest, an advocacy group that has lobbied against marketing to children, commended Disney's dietary and character use guidelines, saying the move put Disney "head, shoulders, and ears" above other children's entertainment companies, such as Nickelodeon's parent company Viacom, Inc. whose "programming is filled with junk-food ads and whose characters grace all kinds of junk-food packaging."[99] Critics, however, questioned the sincerity of Disney's efforts to link itself to healthier food choices. They pointed to continued junk food ads on the company's websites and on its ABC television network, as well as the continued presence of McDonald's vending carts in Disney theme parks.[100]

McDonald's Reconsiders

In 2011, McDonald's announced its own initiative to make Happy Meals healthier. McDonald's plans to reduce the calorie count of Happy Meals by 20% by cutting the size of a serving of french fries in half and including a serving of fruits or vegetables. McDonald's also announced that it would eliminate the caramel dipping sauces served with apple slices.[101] The new Happy Meals were to be available in limited areas in the fall of 2011 before expanding nationwide.[102] McDonald's already prominently displays the nutritional content of its food on the packaging of each item, making it easier for parents to know what their children are eating.

Even modest steps like these could protect the fast-food chain from onerous future regulations as the laws governing food and advertising and consumer sentiment continue to evolve. They might also contribute to enhanced market share. PepsiCo's healthy food brands, including Quaker Oats and Tropicana, are among the firm's fastest-growing products. Long before other major food companies took steps against trans fats, PepsiCo removed the artery-clogging fats from its Frito Lay potato chips and other snacks and then touted their absence in its packaging and marketing.

---

96. Press Release, Walt Disney Company, The Walt Disney Company Introduces New Food Guidelines to Promote Healthier Kids' Diets (Oct. 16, 2006), *available at* http://corporate.disney.go.com/news/corporate/2006/2006_1016_food_guidelines.html.

97. *Id.*

98. *Disney Characters to Push Produce*, CNNMONEY.COM, Oct. 12, 2007, http://money.cnn.com/2007/10/12/news/companies/disney_characters.ap/index.htm?postversion=2007101212.

99. Marr & Adamy, *supra* note 94.

100. Drew McLellan, *Does Disney Really Care If Your Kids Are Fat?* THE MARKETING MINUTE BLOG, Oct. 30, 2007, http://www.drewsmarketingminute.com/2007/10/does-disney-rea.html?referer=sphere_related_content.

101. Kristeen Moore, *Nutrition Changes Underway for McDonald's Happy Meals*, THIRDAGE, Aug. 7, 2011, *available at* http://www.thirdage.com/news/nutrition-changes-underway-for-mcdonald-s-happy-meals_08-07-2011.

102. Vanessa Evans, *Childhood Obesity Rates Force Fast Food Chains to Revamp Their Menus*, YAHOO! NEWS, Aug. 2, 2011, http://news.yahoo.com/childhood-obesity-rates-force-fast-food-chains-revamp-175100616.html.

KEY WORDS AND PHRASES

legal astuteness 11

strategic compliance management 5

systems approach to business and society 2

QUESTIONS AND CASE PROBLEMS

This chapter introduced important conceptual frameworks to be used while reading the cases and text and analyzing the Questions and Case Problems in each of the chapters that follow. Questions to consider include:

1. What public policies are furthered by this law? To what extent are there conflicts among the policies served, and how will they affect the way the law in this area is interpreted, applied, and changed?

2. What effect does this body of law or legal tool have on the competitive environment and the firm's resources?

3. Where does this body of law or legal tool fit in the value chain?

4. How can managers responsibly help shape this aspect of the legal environment?

5. How could the managers in this case have avoided the litigation that ensued?

6. What are the "moral aspects of choice" implicated by the conduct at issue?

7. Does this conduct meet societal expectations? If not, what new laws would be likely to result if a substantial number of firms acted this way?

8. Did the manager in this situation exemplify the four components of legal astuteness? If not, what could the manager have done differently?

CHAPTER 2

ETHICS AND THE LAW

INTRODUCTION

ETHICS MATTER

When asked which qualities were most important for successful leaders, legendary investor Warren Buffett responded, "Integrity, intelligence and energy. Without the first, the other two will kill you."[1]

Compliance with the law is just the baseline for effective and responsible managerial action. Legally astute managers consider not only what the firm *can* do but also what it *should* do.[2] Greatness in the global marketplace requires attention to ethics and social responsibility as well as to the financial return to shareholders.[3] Conversely, failure to meet the firm's responsibilities to employees, customers, the community, and the environment "puts at risk the company's ability to operate, grow, and deliver future value to shareholders."[4]

Good ethics are simply good business. As the Business Roundtable, the leading association of CEOs in the United States, proclaimed, "[Long-term] shareholder value is enhanced when a corporation treats its employees well, serves its customers well, fosters good relationships with suppliers, maintains an effective compliance program and strong corporate governance practices, and has a reputation for civic responsibility."[5]

Maintaining a reputation for integrity and honesty is more important than ever as customers vote with their feet and boycott clothing made in sweatshops in Mauritius or gasoline made from oil transported in pipelines built with slave labor in Burma (Myanmar). As General Electric learned after its protracted and ultimately unsuccessful battle with the Environmental Protection Agency about cleaning up the PCBs it had (at the time, lawfully) dumped into the Hudson River, "governments are customers too."[6] They not only purchase goods and services but also directly affect the firm's regulatory environment. For example, in 2011 Rupert Murdoch's News Corporation was forced to abandon its $12 billion bid to acquire full control of British Sky Broadcasting, Britain's largest pay-television broadcaster, after word leaked that News Corporation reporters had illegally hacked into phones in the United Kingdom and elsewhere.[7]

Current and prospective employees also care. When evaluating a potential employer, job hunters use postings on social network sites, questions in job interviews, and contacts with present and past employees to search for clues to a firm's ethical values. The mere existence of a code of conduct or a toothless ethics program is not enough to attract individuals who are not just looking for employment, but also want to protect their personal integrity, retirement savings, and future employability by working only for upstanding organizations. For many of the same reasons, the ethical reputation of an employer makes a difference to its current employees as well.

Finally, as demonstrated graphically by the passage of the Dodd–Frank Wall Street Reform and Consumer Protection Act of 2010,[8] corporate conduct that violates society's expectations can also result in "[n]ew forms of regulation or effective enforcement . . . without regard for feasibility

1. Ibolya Balog, *Ethics on Their Shoulders: Boards Bear the Burden*, ACCT. TODAY, Nov. 27, 2006, *available at* http://www.accountingtoday.com/ato_issues/2006_21/22603-1.html (last visited Aug. 21, 2011).

2. C. ROLAND CHRISTENSEN ET AL., BUSINESS POLICY: TEXT AND CASES 121 (6th ed. 1987). On legal astuteness, *see* Constance E. Bagley, *Winning Legally: The Value of Legal Astuteness*, 33 ACAD. MGMT. REV. 378 (2008).

3. LYNN SHARP PAINE, VALUE SHIFT: WHY COMPANIES MUST MERGE SOCIAL AND FINANCIAL IMPERATIVES TO ACHIEVE SUPERIOR PERFORMANCE (2003). *See also* Constance E. Bagley & Karen L. Page, *The Devil Made Me Do It: Replacing Corporate Director's Veil of Secrecy with the Mantle of Stewardship*, 36 SAN DIEGO L. REV. 897 (1999).

4. ROBERT S. KAPLAN & DAVID P. NORTON, STRATEGY MAPS: CONVERTING INTANGIBLE ASSETS INTO TANGIBLE OUTCOMES 165 (2004).

5. *Principles of Corporate Governance*, BUS. ROUNDTABLE, Mar. 31, 2010, *available at* http://businessroundtable.org/studies-and-reports/2010-principles-of-corporate-governance/(last visted Aug. 21, 2011).

6. Constance E. Bagley et al., *General Electric Ecomagination: An Examination of GE's Corporate Environmental Strategy* (Yale Sch. of Mgmt. Case No. 08-041, 2008).

7. Jeremy W. Peters & John F. Burns, *Father and Son Split on Tactics in Murdoch Family Drama*, N.Y. TIMES, July 13, 2011.

8. Pub. L. No. 111-203, 124 Stat. 1376 (2010).

or cost."[9] Accordingly, "government regulation is not a good substitute for knowledgeable self-restraint."[10]

CHAPTER OVERVIEW

The purpose of this chapter is to provide a framework for analyzing how ethics, business, and law interact. It explains the business leader's role in setting the ethical tone of the firm and provides an example of an executive who failed to fill that role. The chapter then presents the Ethical Business Leader's Decision Tree, a tool managers can use to evaluate the legal and ethical aspects of their strategy and its implementation.[11] After examining several incidents in which companies failed to meet societal expectations for ethical behavior, the chapter concludes by providing several positive examples of responsible behavior and suggesting steps managers can take to promote ethical behavior.

---

9. CHRISTENSEN ET AL., *supra* note 2, at 461.

10. *Id.*

11. Adapted from Constance E. Bagley, *The Ethical Leader's Decision Tree*, HARV. BUS. REV., Feb. 1, 2003, at 18.

THE RELATIONSHIP BETWEEN LAW AND ETHICS

The law does not prohibit all "bad" behavior. An action that is unethical may nonetheless be legal. In finding that former executives of General Development Corporation had not violated a criminal law even though they had "behaved badly," the U.S. Court of Appeals for the Eleventh Circuit explained:

> [I]t is true that these men behaved badly. We live in a fallen world. But "bad men, like good men, are entitled to be tried and sentenced in accordance with law." And, the fraud statutes do not cover all behavior which strays from the ideal; Congress has not yet criminalized all sharp conduct, manipulative acts, or unethical transactions. We might prefer that [the defendants] would have told these customers to shop around before buying. But, "there are . . . things . . . which we wish that people should do, which we like or admire them for doing, perhaps dislike or despise them for not doing, but yet admit that they are not bound to do."[12]

The following case exemplifies the failure of the law to address all unethical conduct.

---

12. United States v. Brown, 79 F.3d 1550, 1562 (11th Cir. 1996).

| A CASE IN POINT | *Summary* | Case 2.1 |

Bammert v. Don's Super Valu, Inc.

Supreme Court of Wisconsin
646 N.W.2d 365 (Wis. 2002).

FACTS   For some twenty-six years, Karen Bammert worked at Don's Super Valu, Inc. in Menomonie, Wisconsin. Her husband was a sergeant in the Menomonie police department. On one occasion, Bammert's husband administered a breathalyzer test to Nona Williams, the wife of Don Williams, owner of Don's Super Valu. Nona failed the test and was arrested for drunk driving. Don's Super Valu then fired Karen Bammert, allegedly in retaliation for her husband's participation in the arrest.

Karen Bammert was an at-will employee. Although at-will employees can generally be fired for any reason or for no reason at all without risk of judicial action, there is a public policy exception to this rule in Wisconsin, which allows an at-will employee to recover for wrongful termination "when the discharge is contrary to a fundamental and well-defined public policy as evidenced by existing law." Bammert sued Don's Super Valu for wrongful discharge, claiming that her firing was contrary to both the public policy against drunk driving and the public policy promoting marriage, both of which were reflected in existing Wisconsin law.

The trial court rejected Bammert's argument and dismissed the complaint for failure to state a claim. The court of appeals affirmed, and the Supreme Court of Wisconsin accepted review.

ISSUE PRESENTED   Does the public policy exception to the employment-at-will doctrine apply when an at-will employee is fired in retaliation for the lawful actions of her nonemployee spouse?

SUMMARY OF OPINION   The Supreme Court of Wisconsin began by pointing out that the public policy exception was intended to be a narrow one. For purposes of this exception, a public policy must be clearly articulated, fundamental, and well defined. The court went on to stress the value and importance of the employment-at-will doctrine and advised that employment contracts are the best way to protect against unjust firings.

CONTINUED

After acknowledging that the policies implicated in this case were clearly articulated, fundamental, and well defined, the court noted that previous cases had not addressed the vindication of a public policy by a third party: "Bammert was not fired for her participation in the enforcement of the laws against drunk driving; she was fired for her husband's participation." Previous cases had dealt with behavior only within the context of employment.

The Wisconsin Supreme Court concluded that "[e]xtending [the public policy exception] to discharges for fulfillment of an affirmative obligation which the law places on a relative would go too far, and have no logical stopping point." The court feared that the exception, once expanded to include "police officers' spouses fired in retaliation for the officers' conduct in the line of duty," might expand to "spouses of prosecutors, judges, . . . or IRS agents." The court questioned whether "discharges in retaliation for the conduct of nonemployee parents, children, and siblings" would be included in such an exception. The court concluded that the public policy exception to the employment-at-will doctrine should not be expanded to protect an at-will employee from firing in retaliation for the actions of his or her nonemployee spouse.

RESULT The Supreme Court of Wisconsin declined to expand the public policy exception to the employment-at-will doctrine and affirmed the dismissal of Bammert's complaint, leaving her with no legal recourse.

COMMENTS The Wisconsin Supreme Court acknowledged that Bammert's firing was retaliatory and "reprehensible." The dissenting judge lamented that "society owes its police officers a duty not to put them in the no-win position that Bammert's husband was placed in." Some would argue that courts and lawmakers should expand the law to punish all unethical behavior. But even though courts can and do retroactively expand or contract the law when they elect to interpret it broadly or narrowly, such judicial alteration of the law can lead to inconsistent outcomes when today's case becomes tomorrow's precedent.

© Cengage Learning 2013

Ethics and law are related, however. First, a judge or jury's assessment of the ethical character of an action may determine how the law is interpreted and applied in a given case.[13] Second, law often reflects society's consensus about what constitutes appropriate behavior. Third, law can help define the roles managers play, how they play those roles, and whether they have played them well.[14] Fourth, patterns of unethical behavior tend to result in illegal behavior over time. As Martin L. Grass put it prior to being sentenced to eight years in prison for accounting fraud while CEO of Rite Aid: "In early 1999, when things started to go wrong financially, I did some things to try to hide that fact. Those things were wrong. They were illegal."[15] Therefore, creating an organization that encompasses exemplary conduct may be the best way to prevent damaging misconduct.[16] Finally, as noted earlier,

unethical conduct tends, over time, to lead to more onerous business regulation. Passage of the Sarbanes–Oxley Act of 2002[17] in the wake of widespread accounting fraud and of the Foreign Corrupt Practices Act of 1977[18] in response to the payment of government bribes by Gulf Oil, Lockheed Aircraft, and other major U.S. corporations are but two examples of this phenomenon.[19]

THE ETHICAL TONE IS SET AT THE TOP

The chief executive officer plays the most significant role in instilling a sense of ethics throughout the organization. As William F. May, chair of the Trinity Center for Ethics and Corporate Policy, explained: "The CEO has a unique responsibility; he's a role model. What he does, how he lives, and the principles under which he operates become pretty much those the rest of the corporation

13. MODEL RULES OF PROF'L CONDUCT R. 2.1 cmt. 2 (2002) ("moral and ethical considerations impinge upon most legal questions and may decisively influence how the law will be applied").

14. J. Nesteruk, *A New Role for Legal Scholarship in Business Ethics*, 36 AM. BUS. L.J. 515 (1999).

15. Mark Maremont, *Rite Aid's Ex-CEO Sentenced to 8 Years for Accounting Fraud*, WALL ST. J., May 28, 2004, at A3.

16. Lynn Sharp Paine, *Managing for Organizational Integrity*, HARV. BUS. REV., Mar.–Apr. 1994, at 106, 117.

17. Pub. L. No. 107-204, 116 Stat. 745 (2002).

18. 15 U.S.C. § 78dd-1.

19. *See* Gisela Bolte, Jonathan Beaty & Christopher Byrons, *Big Profits in Big Bribery*, TIME, Mar. 16, 1981, *available at* http://www.time.com/time/magazine/article/0,9171,922462,00.html (last visited Aug. 21, 2011).

emulate."[20] Ben Heineman, Jr., former general counsel at General Electric, expanded this leadership responsibility to include all corporate executives and noted how even small quips or gestures can hinder company ethics objectives:

> Companies are preternaturally attuned to leadership hypocrisy. The stirring call for performance with integrity at the large company meeting can be eroded by the cynical comment an executive makes at a smaller meeting, by the winks and nods that implicitly sanction improprieties, by personal actions (dishonesty, lack of candor) that contradict company values. It is fundamental: A culture of high standards for employees requires high standards from the CEO and the senior operating and staff officers.[21]

This is not to downplay the role of middle management. An employee's immediate supervisor often has the most direct effect on the employee's choices. Nevertheless, direction from the top signals to middle management that the CEO has a serious commitment to ethics.

A corporation cannot establish an ethical culture overnight but can achieve it through strong leadership and support from the CEO and the board of directors. Conversely, failure to create an ethical culture that enables employees to do what is right can have catastrophic effects.

The Imperial CEO

In 2010, the average CEO of a company in the Standard and Poor's 500 Index took home $11.4 million in pay, or more than 300 times as much as the average worker.[22] The multiple was less than 150 in 1990.[23] Critics of overly generous executive compensation packages argue that putting CEOs on a compensatory pedestal often leads to greedy and unethical behavior and reinforces narcissistic tendencies. Indeed, some even argue that narcissistic personality disorder (recognized and classified by the American Psychiatric Association) is prevalent within the corporate world for exactly this reason.[24] Sam Vaknin, former director of an Israeli investment firm, who was himself diagnosed with narcissistic personality disorder

while imprisoned for engaging in stock manipulation, described the disorder: "The narcissist lacks empathy—the ability to put himself in other people's shoes. . . . He does not recognize boundaries—personal, corporate or legal."[25] Perhaps the "poster child" of the imperial CEO is Dennis Kozlowski of Tyco International.

Tyco's Dennis Kozlowski

Leo Dennis Kozlowski took over as CEO of Tyco in 1992 and became chair in 1993. In May 2001, at the pinnacle of his career, Kozlowski appeared on the cover of *BusinessWeek*. Less than two years later, Kozlowski was forced to resign when he was charged with tax evasion after allegedly having art he had bought in New York shipped out of state to avoid paying $1 million in New York sales tax. Soon thereafter, Kozlowski and Mark H. Swartz, Tyco's former chief financial officer (CFO), were charged with stealing $600 million from the company. During Kozlowski's reign, Tyco's stock price dropped from a high of $63.21 in 2001 to a low of $6.98 in 2002.[26]

At trial, uncontested testimony revealed that Kozlowski had had sexual affairs with at least two Tyco employees and spent tens of millions of Tyco's money to purchase and outfit apartments in New York.[27] Kozlowski allegedly spent $2 million on his wife's birthday party and billed half of the cost to Tyco. Among other items paid for as corporate expenses were a $6,000 shower curtain, a $15,000 poodle-shaped umbrella stand, a $6,300 sewing basket, two sets of sheets for $5,960, a $2,200 wastebasket, coat hangers totaling $2,900, and a $445 pincushion.[28]

Ironically, about a month before prosecutors announced the tax evasion charges, Kozlowski had cautioned graduating students at St. Anselm's College:

> As you go forward in life, you will become leaders of families, communities and even companies. . . . You will be confronted with questions every day that test your morals. The questions will get tougher and the consequences will become more severe. Think carefully, and for your sake, do the right thing, not the easy thing.[29]

In 2005, a jury convicted Kozlowski of grand larceny, conspiracy, and fraud. He was sentenced to eight and a third to twenty-five years in prison.[30] He will not be

20. Alden Lank, *The Ethical Criterion in Business Decision Making: Operational or Imperative?* in Touche Ross & Co., Ethics in American Business: A Special Report 28 (1998) (hereinafter Touche Report).

21. Ben W. Heineman, Jr., *Avoiding Integrity Land Mines*, Harv. Bus. Rev., Apr. 2007, at 100.

22. *2011 Executive Paywatch*, American Federation of Labor–Congress of Industrial Organizations, http://www.aflcio.org/corporatewatch/paywatch (last visited Aug. 25, 2011). Section 953(b) of the Dodd–Frank Act requires public companies to disclose the ratio of CEO pay to that of the median worker.

23. Phred Dvorak, *Theory and Practice: Limits on Executive Pay: Easy to Set, Hard to Keep*, Wall St. J., Apr. 9, 2007, at B1.

24. Tim Race, *New Economy; Like Narcissus, Executives Are Smitten, and Undone, by Their Own Images*, N.Y. Times, July 29, 2002, at C4.

25. *Id.*

26. Floyd Norris, *Tyco to Pay $3 Billion to Settle Investor Lawsuits*, N.Y. Times, May 16, 2007, at 1.

27. Alex Berenson, *The Tyco Mistrial: The Chief; Tyco Chief and His Deputy Avoid Convictions, but Not Tattered Reputations*, N.Y. Times, Apr. 3, 2004, at C5.

28. Linda Hales, *The Curtain That Just Won't Wash*, Wash. Post, Apr. 3, 2004, at C1.

29. Berenson, *supra* note 27.

30. Mark Maremont, *Tyco Figures Will Be Jailed at Least Seven Years*, Wall St. J., Sept. 20, 2005, at C1.

eligible for parole until January 17, 2014.[31] In addition, Kozlowski must repay $97 million to Tyco and is responsible for another $70 million in fines.[32]

THE ETHICAL BUSINESS LEADER'S DECISION TREE

The *Ethical Business Leader's Decision Tree* in Exhibit 2.1 provides a tool business leaders and their counsel can use to evaluate the legal and ethical aspects of their strategy and its implementation.

Is the Action Legal?

Managers should first ask themselves whether the proposed action is legal. Legality is addressed at the outset to reinforce the notion that legal compliance is the baseline standard. If an action is not in accordance with the letter and the spirit of the law, then, regardless of the likely effect on shareholder

value, the action should not be taken. Although the spirit of a law is more vague than its letter, managers must attend to both components because "[w]hen you try to keep to the letter of the law while undermining the spirit, you are likely to violate the letter in the end."[33]

Would It Maximize Shareholder Value?

The filter for shareholder value is intended to require managers to consider early on whether the interests of the shareholders—the group given the ultimate legal authority to change management—are being served by the proposed action. Yet the inquiry need not stop there.

Contrary to popular belief, maximization of shareholder value, so-called *shareholder primacy*, is not legally mandated, except in very narrow circumstances.[34] The courts and many state legislatures have made it abundantly clear that the directors' obligation is to manage the corporation "for the best interest of the corporation." In deciding what is in the best interest of the corporation, the

31. *Inmate Population Information Search*, N.Y. State Dep't of Corrections and Community Supervision, http://nysdocslookup.docs. state.ny.us/GCA00P00/WIQ3/WINQ130 (last visited Aug. 25, 2011).

32. Maremont, *supra* note 30.

33. Mark Gimein, *The Skilling Trap*, Bus. Wk., June 12, 2006, at 31.

34. *See* Bagley & Page, *supra* note 3.

EXHIBIT 2.1   The Ethical Business Leader's Decision Tree

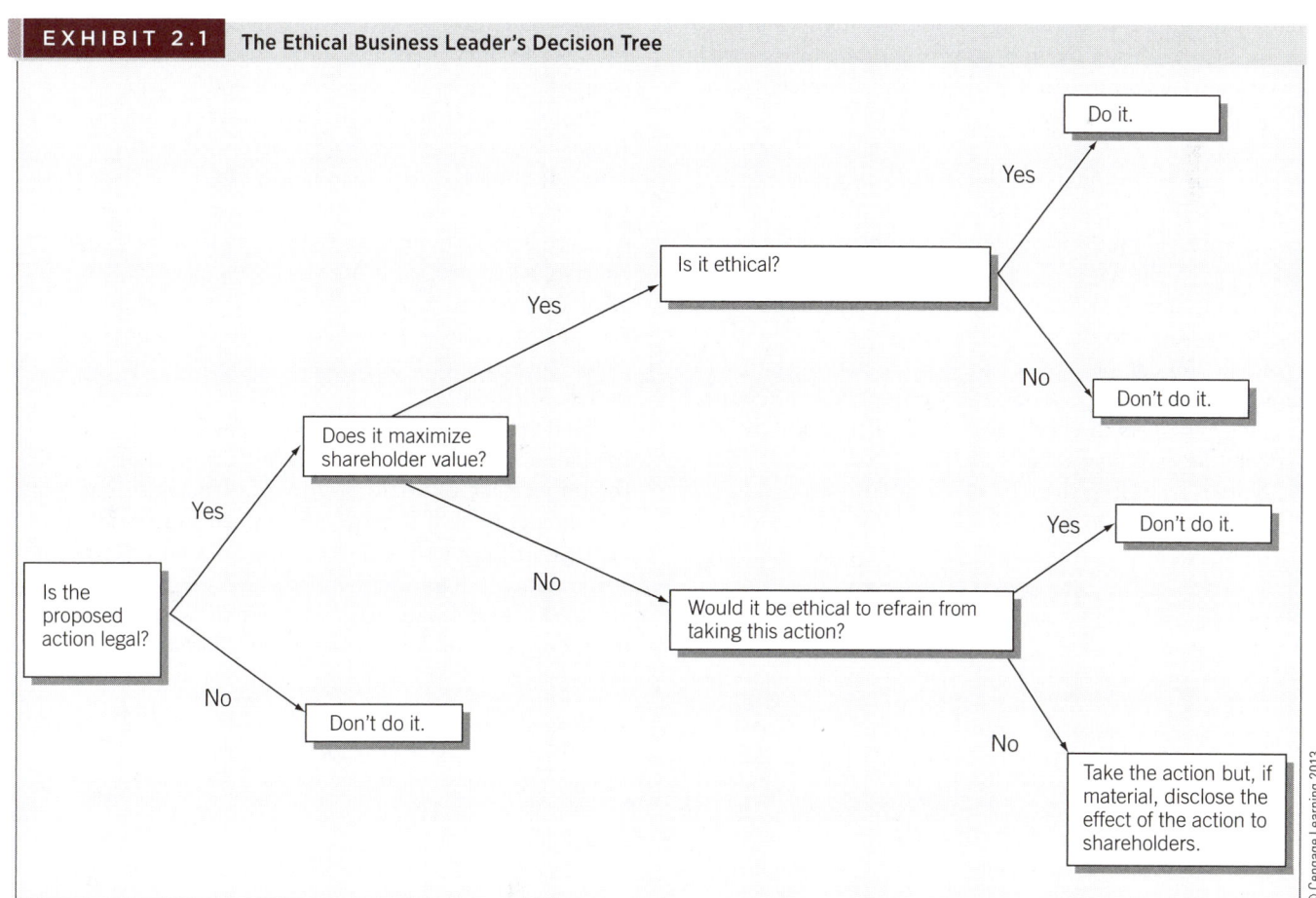

© Cengage Learning 2013

board may legitimately consider not only how a decision might affect the shareholders but also how it might affect employees, customers, suppliers, and the community where the corporation does business.[35] Legislatures in a majority of the states have enacted so-called constituency statutes, which expressly authorize the boards of corporations incorporated there to take into account all stakeholders and constituencies even when a change in control or breakup of the corporation has become inevitable.[36]

Although Delaware, where a majority of the *Fortune 500* companies are incorporated, does not have a constituency statute, the Delaware Supreme Court has made it clear that the role of the director shifts from "being a protector of the corporate bastion" to being an "auctioneer" charged with obtaining the highest realizable short-term value for the shareholders only when the breakup of the corporation or a change of control has become inevitable.[37] As explained more fully in Chapter 20, the Delaware Supreme Court defines change of control narrowly. For example, it ruled that there was no change of control when two publicly traded companies combined because control was vested in a large disaggregated group of public shareholders before and after the transaction.[38] As a result, the Time, Inc. board could legally rebuff an any-or-all cash bid by Paramount favored by Time's shareholders and pursue a merger with Warner Communications even though a majority of the Time shareholders, if asked, would have voted against the merger with Warner. The Time board justified its decision by asserting that a merger with Paramount would impair Time's journalistic integrity and imperil the Time culture.

Thus, the CEO who asserted, "I have a duty to maximize value for my shareholders. I can't let my own sense of right and wrong get in the way," was just plain wrong as a matter of law. CEOs or board members may *choose* to do things in the name of the corporation that they would feel wrong doing in their personal lives, but they are not legally *required* to do so. In the same way that medical ethics do not compel a physician to do something that violates his or her own personal ethics, corporate law does not require managers to check their sense of right and wrong outside the executive suite.

Notwithstanding the lack of a legal duty to maximize shareholder value, Milton Friedman, a Nobel Prize winner in economics, and his followers would have the inquiry stop here. In his seminal article *The Social Responsibility of Business Is to Increase Its Profits*,[39] he asserted that the only guiding criterion for the corporation should be profitability within the confines of the law. He argued that it is not the role of business to promote social ends in and of themselves. Friedman asserted that a corporation is an "artificial person" with no true responsibilities to any constituencies other than its owners, the shareholders. When a company makes a decision to spend money for a social cause, it is in essence making the decision for someone else and spending someone else's money for a general social interest.

Friedman argued that spending money in ways that are not consistent with shareholder wishes is tantamount to imposing a tax and unilaterally deciding where the money will be spent. Because taxation is a governmental function and only the government has sufficient legislative and judicial protections to ensure that taxation and expenditures fairly reflect the desires of the public, a corporation making taxation decisions on its own would render the executive "simultaneously legislator, executive and jurist."

Friedman concluded his landmark article by asserting that "social responsibility" is an inherently collectivist attitude and a "fundamentally subversive doctrine." In a free society, "there is one and only one social responsibility of business—to use its resources and engage in activities designed to increase its profits so long as it stays within the rules of the game, which is to say, engages in open and free competition without deception or fraud."

Professors Henry Mintzberg, Robert Simons, and Kunal Basu characterized the assertion that corporations exist solely to maximize shareholder value as a "half-truth" that contributed significantly to the "syndrome of selfishness" that took hold of corporations and society in the late twentieth and early twenty-first century.[40] They argued that focusing on shareholder value without taking account of other stakeholders' interests "reflects a fallacious separation of the economic and social consequences of decisionmaking."[41]

Even economist Michael C. Jensen, a staunch believer in shareholder primacy, acknowledged in a 2001 article the importance of focusing on long-term, not short-term, shareholder value: "Short-term profit maximization at the expense of long-term value creation is a sure way to destroy value."[42] Jensen explained, "In order to maximize value, corporate managers must not only satisfy, but enlist the support of, all corporate stakeholders—customers,

---

35. Unocal Corp. v. Mesa Petroleum Co., 493 A.2d 946 (Del. 1985).

36. *See, e.g.,* Steven M.H. Wallman, *The Proper Interpretation of Corporate Constituency Statutes and Formulations of Director Duties*, 21 STETSON L. REV. 163 (1991). *See also* Steven J. Haymore, *Public(ly Oriented) Companies: B Corporations and the Delaware Stakeholder Provision Dilemma*, 64 VAND. L. REV. 1311, 1340 (2011) (thirty-one states have some version of constituency statute).

37. Revlon, Inc. v. MacAndrews & Forbes Holdings, Inc., 506 A.2d 173 (Del. 1986).

38. Paramount Commc'ns, Inc. v. QVC Network, Inc., 637 A.2d 34 (Del. 1994).

39. MILTON FRIEDMAN, AN ECONOMIST'S PROTEST: COLUMNS IN POLITICAL ECONOMY 177–84 (1972).

40. Henry Mintzberg et al., *Beyond Selfishness*, MIT SLOAN MGMT. REV., Fall 2002, at 67.

41. *Id.* at 69.

42. Michael C. Jensen, *Value Maximization, Stakeholder Theory, and the Corporate Objective Function*, 14(1) J. APPLIED CORP. FIN. 8, 16 (2001).

employees, managers, suppliers, local communities."[43] He cautioned that "we cannot maximize the long-term market value of an organization if we ignore or mistreat any important constituency."[44]

Thus, a myopic focus on shareholder value can result not only in unfair treatment of nonshareholder constituencies but also in harm to the shareholders.[45] In the age of the Internet and 24/7 cable news networks, misdeeds in faraway places are often featured on the evening news at home the same day. Nongovernment organizations (NGOs) and other interest groups track and report on the working conditions in overseas factories, the dumping of hazardous waste and spoliation of forests and rivers, the exploitation of indigenous peoples, and the sale of shoddy and dangerous products. As former General Electric general counsel Heineman noted, "The changes in laws, regulations, stakeholder expectations, and media scrutiny that have taken place over the past decade can now make a major lapse in integrity catastrophic."[46]

Edward Simon, president of Herman Miller, went even further and encouraged managers to focus not just on avoiding harm but on doing good: "Why can't we do good works at work? . . . Business is the only institution that has a chance, as far as I can see, to fundamentally improve the injustice that exists in the world."[47]

Is the Action Ethical?
What Is Ethical?

The next question to consider is whether the proposed action would be ethical. But how does one define what constitutes good ethical behavior? This is sometimes difficult, in part because there are numerous and diverse ethical theories. Ultimately, each manager has a personal responsibility to decide what is right.

Teleological and Deontological Schools

The two main schools of ethical thought are teleological and deontological. *Teleological theory* is concerned with consequences. The ethical good of an action is to be judged by the effect of the action on others. *Deontological theory* focuses more on the motivation and principle behind an action than on the consequences.

For example, suppose that a construction company donates materials to build shelters for the homeless. In judging this action within the teleological framework, the fact that some homeless people are given housing is the important issue. Within a deontological framework, one would want

to know why the company was motivated to supply the materials for the shelters. As another example, suppose that an employer promises to throw a party if the firm reaches profitability and then breaks the promise. Under teleological theory, as long as the consequences of breaking the promise are insignificant, the action of breaking the promise is not in and of itself bad. Deontological theory, however, would suggest that there is something intrinsically wrong with breaking a promise, no matter what the consequences. Thus, a particular action can be evaluated differently, depending on the system under which it is examined.

A brief examination of several theories within these two schools further illustrates their differences. *Utilitarianism* is a major teleological system that operates under the proposition that the ideal is to maximize the total benefit for everyone involved. Under a utilitarian theory, no one person's particular interest is given more weight than another's, but rather the utility of everyone as a group is maximized.

For example, suppose that a $10,000 bonus pool is to be divided among three project managers and that their marginal benefits from receiving a portion of the money can be quantified. Imagine that the money can be allocated in either of two ways: Under Distribution 1, the three persons benefit 6, 12, and 24 units, respectively. Under Distribution 2, the three persons benefit 8, 12, and 16 units, respectively. A utilitarian would want Distribution 1 because the total benefit (6 + 12 + 24 = 42) is greater than under Distribution 2 (8 + 12 + 16 = 36). The utilitarian would not be concerned that the other distribution seems more equal and fair or that under the benefit-maximizing utility distribution, the worst-off person has considerably less than the worst-off person in Distribution 2.

In contrast, *Rawlsian moral theory*, a deontological theory, aims to maximize the plight of the worst-off person in society by developing principles behind a "veil of ignorance." Each person in society is to imagine that he or she does not know what his or her allotment of society's resources will be and then to decide which principles should govern society's interactions. John Rawls believed that behind the veil of ignorance individuals would create a system that benefited the least-well-off people most. According to this theory, Distribution 2 should be favored because it is the one that would be preferred by the person who faced the possibility of getting the worst share.

Kantian theory is another important deontological line of thought. In examining the ethical worth of an action, Immanuel Kant's categorical imperative looks to the form of the action rather than the intended result. The form of an action can be delineated into universalizability and reversibility. *Universalizability* asks whether one would want everyone to act in this manner; *reversibility* looks to whether one would want such a rule applied to oneself.

For example, suppose that a manager is deciding how long a break to give the workers on an assembly line. In choosing between a system allowing a ten-minute break every three hours with bathroom breaks whenever

43. *Id.* at 8, 9.

44. *Id.*

45. Bagley & Page, *supra* note 3.

46. Heineman, *supra* note 21.

47. Quoted in PETER M. SENGE, THE FIFTH DISCIPLINE: THE ART AND PRACTICE OF THE LEARNING ORGANIZATION 5 (1990).

necessary versus a longer lunch break, the manager might ask—under universalizability—whether he or she would like a world in which all companies applied a similar system. Under reversibility, the manager would decide whether he or she would want to be subjected to a particular break system as an employee.

Some proponents of the deontological school would argue that courses of action that confer incidental benefits on stakeholders are not truly ethical if they were motivated primarily by the desire to maximize shareholder value. This appears to elevate form over function. An action that confers a benefit (incidentally or otherwise) on stakeholders in addition to maximizing shareholder value is clearly more ethical than two alternatives: maximizing shareholder value without conferring any benefit on other stakeholders or maximizing shareholder value while harming other stakeholders.

Comparative Justice

The consequences of an action motivated by a certain ethical system can also be evaluated within a comparative justice framework. This framework allows the rights-based moral theories of Kant or Rawls to be compared to, for example, a utilitarian framework. Distributive, compensatory, and retributive theories of justice are the three main categories within this framework.

Distributive justice focuses on how the burden and benefits of a particular system are distributed. An ideal system maximizes the overall pie by dividing it in a way that provides enough incentives to entice persons to produce more. The system also concerns itself with a fair distribution of these goods—compensating those who contributed while still upholding a certain minimum standard. For example, the use of progressively higher income tax rates for those with more income and earned income tax credits for those earning the least can be understood within a distributive justice framework.

Behavioral economists George A. Akerlof and Robert J. Shiller explain that notions of fairness are central to how individuals determine what is an acceptable distribution.[48] Faced with a choice of receiving nothing at all or accepting far less than the other party, most people would prefer to deny the other party the satisfaction of receiving more than his or her fair share even if that means failing to agree on a distribution and receiving nothing.

Compensatory justice aims at compensating people for the harm done by others. For example, if someone is found to be responsible for making another person miss five days of work, a compensatory system of justice would demand that the victim be somehow compensated for the lost wages.

Retributive justice is also concerned with the harm people do to others, but here the focus is more on how to deter them

from inflicting further harm. For example, suppose that X steals an idea from Y and makes $10,000. If the idea had not been stolen, Y would have made $5,000. Under a compensatory framework, X would compensate Y for the thievery by paying Y $5,000. Under a retributive framework, X should be taught that stealing an idea is wrong. Thus, X would be required to give up any benefit and pay Y $10,000.

How Do Business Leaders Define Ethics?

Many business leaders associate ethics with such concepts as integrity, fairness, and honesty. For more than seventy-five years, the J.C. Penney Company has considered ethical business behavior to be behavior that conforms to the Golden Rule: Do unto others as you would have them do unto you. Carly Fiorina, former CEO of Hewlett-Packard, remarked, "Good leadership means doing the right thing when no one's watching."[49]

The CEO of a highly successful Scandinavian multinational tells his managers to conjure up the following scenario: Assume that the decision you are about to make in Timbuktu becomes public knowledge in our home country, the host country, and significant developing countries where our company is operating. Assume further that you, as the decision maker, are called upon to defend the decision on television both at home and abroad. If you think you can defend it successfully in these public forums, the probability is high that your decision is ethical.[50]

Actions That Might Maximize Shareholder Value but Would Be Unethical

Some actions may be legal and maximize at least short-term shareholder value but are nonetheless unethical. Evidence suggests that, if asked, most shareholders would not want managers to act unethically even if doing so would boost the financial return. Seventy-five percent of investors polled in a 2007 Pepperdine University survey indicated that they would likely withdraw their investment—even if that meant sacrificing a high return—if they learned that a company was engaged in unethical but legal behavior.[51]

Ethical business leaders will not sacrifice their ethics to secure a short-term gain. Joseph Neubauer, CEO of Aramark Worldwide Corporation, walked away from two well-priced and fully negotiated overseas acquisitions that

---

48. GEORGE A. AKERLOF & ROBERT J. SHILLER, ANIMAL SPIRITS: HOW HUMAN PSYCHOLOGY DRIVES THE ECONOMY, AND WHY IT MATTERS FOR GLOBAL CAPITALISM 22–24 (2009).

49. Stephen Overell, *Blowing Your Own Credibility*, PERSONNEL TODAY, May 27, 2003, at 13.

50. TOUCHE REPORT, *supra* note 20, at 48.

51. Press Release, Pepperdine University, Study: Investors Likely to Move Investments if Board Engages in Legal but Unethical Behavior (June 26, 2007), *available at* http://bschool.pepperdine.edu/newsroom/index.php/2007/06/study-investors-likely-to-move-investments-if-board-engages-in-legal-but-unethical-behavior-2/ (last visited Aug. 25, 2011).

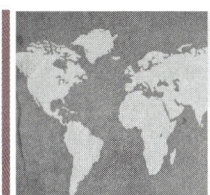

HISTORICAL PERSPECTIVE

Aquinas on Law and Ethics

Saint Thomas Aquinas (1225?–1274), a theologian and philosopher, believed that an unjust law could not properly be considered a law at all. The only true laws were those that followed eternal law—as far as eternal law could be discovered by the use of human reason and revelation. Eternal law is the orderly governance of the acts and movements of all creatures by God as the divine governor of the universe. Because not every individual follows a natural inclination to do good—that is, to act virtuously in order to achieve happiness and avoid evil—human laws are framed to train, and sometimes compel, a person to do what is right, as well as to restrain the person from doing harm to others. According to Aquinas, for human law to be considered law, that is, binding on human conscience, it must be just. To be just, a human law must be (1) consonant with a reasoned determination of the universal good; (2) within the power of individuals to fulfill; (3) clearly expressed by legitimate authority; (4) approved by custom, that is, the declaration of right reason by a community; and (5) widely promulgated. To the extent that human law is just, it is in concert with eternal law, as discerned through human reason, and it is binding on individuals. Human laws that promote private benefit over the common good are unjust, and individuals are bound not to obey them. Instead, individuals should "disregard them, oppose them, and do what [they] can to revoke them."[a]

Most modern legal theorists separate the question of a law's status as law from the question of its inherent morality. They argue that a law may help to resolve moral issues, punish immoral action, and serve a moral purpose (as, for example, when laws permit participation in government); yet a law need not be inherently moral to be a real law. In this so-called positive-law view, any law counts as a real law if it has been created according to recognized procedures by someone with the recognized authority to do so—for instance, a king in a monarchy or, in the U.S. system, a legislature, judge, or administrative agency. A properly created law may, of course, be criticized as immoral. Some people may even wish to disobey it. But they do so in the full knowledge that they are disobeying a valid law.

In the United States, the split between legal and moral debate has always been less clear than positive-law theorists might wish. Americans have always given their moral debates a peculiarly legal flavor, mainly because certain important but ambiguous phrases in the U.S. and state constitutions invite a person to "constitutionalize" moral questions. Moral questions are readily translatable into questions about the meaning and scope of the constitutional doctrines of due process of law, liberty, equal protection under the laws, or cruel and unusual punishment. For example, in upholding a woman's right to have an abortion, the U.S. Supreme Court stated: "At the heart of liberty is the right to define one's own concept of existence, of meaning, of the universe, and of the mystery of human life."[b]

It has become a national trait of Americans to expect their constitutions to support their moral convictions. Just as Aquinas believed that unjust laws could not accord with eternal law, many Americans believe that unjust laws cannot be constitutional. Perhaps it is for this reason that many of the most controversial American moral debates, such as those on slavery, segregation, affirmative action, same-sex marriage, abortion, student-led prayer in public school, capital punishment, and the right to die, have focused on the interpretation of constitutions or have been framed in terms of possible constitutional amendments. In some ways, the tendency in the United States to look to constitutions for substantiation of the just quality of law is akin to the use by theologians of the Judeo–Christian scriptures as supernatural revelation of knowledge of the universal good that is eternal law.

As this comparison of present-day constitutional analysis to thirteenth-century theology indicates, the past is often a valuable pointer to the future. At the same time, one must be able to distinguish differences between doctrines that prevailed in the past and those that should prevail in the future. In this regard, it is important to recall the positivists' distinction between law and morals. If people confuse what's "allowed" with what's "right," they risk cutting their ethical discussions short and missing opportunities both for the encouragement of morality by law and for the reform of law in the light of society's morals.

---

a. P. GLENN, A TOUR OF THE SUMMA 170 (1978).
b. Planned Parenthood of Se. Pa. v. Casey, 505 U.S. 833 (1992).

were perfectly suited to Aramark's goal of international expansion after a closer look at their operations and books revealed unsavory business practices. He justified the loss of time and money, stating, "It takes a lifetime to build a reputation, and only a short time to lose it all."[52]

Actions That Neither Maximize Shareholder Value nor Are Ethically Mandated

If an action does not maximize shareholder value and the firm has no ethical reason to act, the action should not be taken. Indeed, taking actions that will not maximize shareholder value without any other justification might result in liability for waste of corporate assets.

Actions That Do Not Maximize Shareholder Value but Are Nonetheless Ethically Required

Sometimes, firms will have an ethical reason to act, even though acting will not maximize shareholder value (at least not in the short term). These situations can present the most difficult issues for ethical business decision making. When shareholder value and ethics appear to be at odds, managers should follow the ethical high road. Failure to meet societal expectations of ethical behavior can tarnish a firm's reputation, erode employee morale, and result in more onerous business regulation.

When managers take actions that could have a material adverse effect on today's shareholders, they should disclose the actions and the reasons for taking them to the shareholders.[53] Otherwise, managers might be tempted to use social responsibility as a fig leaf to cover up mediocre performance or self-dealing.

Consider a company establishing a manufacturing facility overseas in a country that has much less stringent environmental laws than the United States. The managers legally may and should consider not only the possibility that those laws might later be tightened and applied retroactively to require costly cleanups that will adversely affect shareholder value, but also the cost of installing pollution-control equipment and the potential harm that would result if the equipment were not installed. Thus, top management might feel ethically compelled to install $5 million worth of pollution-control equipment in a country that does not require such equipment if a failure to do so would cause $100 million worth of damage or certain loss of life or serious physical injury. Spending that money may even provide a source of competitive advantage over firms that wait until more costly "tail-pipe" regulations are put into effect. If the company elects to spend a material amount

of the shareholders' money to install such equipment, the board should disclose the decision and the reasons for it in the company's periodic reports to shareholders.

Finding the "Sweet Spot"

Ethical behavior need not be a drag on corporate performance, nor merely incidental. Ideal courses of action are ethically sound and maximize shareholder value. Great managers reframe issues and work hard to create such solutions. When asked whether he would rather be a good corporate citizen or maximize profits, Ralph Larsen, CEO of Johnson & Johnson, responded, "Yes."[54] He rejected what he termed the "tyranny of the 'or'" and refused to treat social responsibility and profit maximization as mutually exclusive.

Similarly, in 2005 General Electric launched a major "green" initiative, dubbed "ecomagination," both to restore its image after it initially refused to clean up the PCBs it had dumped in the Hudson River and to capitalize on the demand for more energy-efficient products. CEO Jeff Immelt announced that GE would double its annual spending on research and development of "clean technology," including lower-emission turbines, aircraft engines, locomotives, and other products designed to produce fewer greenhouse gases (GHGs), to $1.5 billion a year by 2010.[55] GE met that goal in 2009 and then committed to invest an additional $10 billion in ecomagination products by 2015.[56] GE also committed to reducing its own GHG emissions and water usage. By 2010, GE had reduced its GHG emissions by 22%, compared with 2004, and its water usage by 30%, compared with 2006. Employing the motto "green is green," Immelt remarked, "My environmental agenda is not about being trendy or moral. It's about accelerating economic growth."[57]

Strategy guru Michael E. Porter and corporate social responsibility specialist Mark Kramer express similar sentiments. While asserting that "[t]he most important thing a corporation can do for society . . . is to contribute to a prosperous economy," Porter and Kramer recognize that successful corporations need a healthy society.[58] They contend that social responsibility "can be much more than a cost, a constraint, or a charitable deed—it can be a source of opportunity, innovation, and competitive advantage."[59]

---

52. Nanette Byrnes et al., *The Good CEO*, BUS. WK., Sept. 23, 2002, at 80.

53. Bagley & Page, *supra* note 3.

54. Quoted in Ira M. Millstein, *The Responsible Board*, 52 BUS. LAW. 407, 408–09 (1997).

55. Amanda Griscom Little, *G.E.'s Green Gamble*, VANITY FAIR, July 2006, *available at* http://www.vanityfair.com/politics/features/2006/07/generalelectric200607 (last visited Aug. 25, 2011).

56. General Electric, *Ecomagination 2010 Annual Report*, *available at* http://files.gecompany.com/ecomagination/progress/GE_ecomagination_2010AnnualReport.pdf (last visited Aug. 25, 2011).

57. Little, *supra* note 55.

58. Michael E. Porter & Mark R. Kramer, *Strategy and Society: The Link Between Competitive Advantage and Corporate Social Responsibility*, HARV. BUS. REV., Dec. 2006, at 78.

59. *Id.*

Rather than trying to take on all the ills of the world, companies should, according to Porter and Kramer, focus on social issues that intersect with their particular business and value proposition. Managers should first eliminate as many negative value-chain impacts, such as emissions and waste and depletion of scarce natural resources, as possible. Then, they should identify areas of the social context where they can create "shared value" for the firm and society through a small number of initiatives that both generate competitive advantage for the firm and benefit society.[60] Examples include Toyota's Prius, a hybrid gasoline–electric vehicle that both reduced emissions and gave Toyota a distinct position with customers, and Whole Foods Market's ability to charge premium prices for healthful food products that are (1) sourced from local farmers, (2) sold in stores that are constructed with a minimum of virgin raw materials and utilize electricity offset by renewable wind energy credits, and (3) increasingly delivered in trucks powered by biofuels.[61]

Third-generation former Timberland CEO Jeffrey Swartz explained that "corporate responsibility isn't an option—it's part of our company's DNA, as well as a competitive advantage." He continued:

> Today, we embrace corporate responsibility consciously and deliberately. We believe in our ability and responsibility to make socially and environmentally responsible decisions that benefit our business, the outdoors and our communities. These are not commitments we make altruistically. On the contrary, our strategic sustainability programs help build a stronger company—improving our bottom line as well as our ability to improve our physical and social environment. We call this our Earthkeepers philosophy, and it drives everything we do.[62]

This is not to suggest that ethics always pay. Sometimes, good guys do come in last and crime pays.

Approaches to Resolving the Tension Between Short-Term Results and Long-Term Value

Managers can take affirmative steps to help resolve the tension between short-term economic results and long-term value creation and capture.

Soften the Edges

To avoid or reduce layoffs, many companies soften the edges of difficult economic times by cutting personnel costs through other means. Less draconian measures include hiring freezes, shortening the workweek, reducing pay and bonuses, eliminating bonuses altogether, reducing salary increases, reassigning employees, and offering buyout packages to employees who might be considering leaving anyway.[63]

When declining demand for its goods caused Levi Strauss & Co. to close eleven U.S. plants, lay off 5,900 employees, and move more of its manufacturing offshore, the company committed to providing a $245 million employee package. Levi gave employees eight months' notice, as much as three weeks of severance pay for every year of service, up to eighteen months of medical coverage, an enhanced early retirement program, and a flexible allowance of up to $6,000 for training and start-up expenses.[64]

Lobby for Changes in the Law or the Enactment of Codes of Conduct

In many instances, corporations or coalitions of corporations have the economic and political power to lobby for changes in applicable law. By encouraging the passage and enforcement of laws prohibiting unethical conduct, such as the dumping of hazardous waste or the use of child labor, managers can ensure that they compete on a level playing field.

After the United States enacted the Foreign Corrupt Practices Act of 1977, which prohibits U.S. companies from paying bribes to government officials, General Electric and other U.S. firms successfully lobbied for tougher international standards. (This act is discussed in detail in Chapter 24.) In 1999, the Organization of Economic Co-operation and Development (OECD) adopted a convention criminalizing bribes to government officials and recommended a prohibition on the tax deductibility of bribes.[65] The OECD comprises thirty-four nations from North and South America, Europe, Asia–Pacific, and the Middle East, representing more than half of the goods and services produced worldwide.

Transparency International's 2008 Bribe Payers Index ranks the top leading export countries by their companies' inclination to bribe abroad. Companies based in China, India, Mexico, and Russia were among the most likely to pay bribes[66] even though China, Mexico, and Russia had previously ratified the United Nations Convention Against Corruption,[67] which requires its sovereign parties to

---

60. *Id.* at 88.

61. *Id.* at 88–91.

62. Timberland Company, *Timberland Responsibility: Executive Commitment,* *available at* http://responsibility.timberland.com/executive-commitment/ (last visited Jan. 23, 2012).

63. Karen F. Lehr, *Smart Companies Use Alternatives Instead of Layoffs,* WASH. BUS. J., Nov. 12. 2001.

64. Miles Socha, *Bad Day at Levi's: 11 Plants to Close, Costing 5,900 Jobs,* WOMEN'S WEAR DAILY, Feb. 23, 1999, at 1.

65. G. Pascal Zachary, *Industrialized Countries Agree to Adopt Rules to Curb Bribery,* WALL ST. J., Feb. 16, 1999, at A18.

66. *2008 Transparency International Bribe Payers Index,* TRANSPARENCY INT'L, *available at* http://www.transparency.org/news_room/in_focus/2008/bpi_2008 (last visited Aug. 25, 2011).

67. For a list of the 140 signatories as of May 1, 2011, see United Nations Convention Against Corruption, U.N. Office on Drugs & Crime, *available at* http://www.unodc.org/unodc/en/treaties/CAC/signatories. html (last visited Aug. 25, 2011).

legislate against bribing and influence peddling. India ratified the U.N. Convention on May 1, 2011, and it remains to be seen how that will affect India's future performance. Transparency International cautioned: "Corruption in and by business hollows out the very basis on which its own existence and success depends: the functioning and sound governance of markets. Corrupt practices invalidate the social licence to operate, breaking the legitimacy and trust that business depends upon in society."[68]

Adopt an Ethics Program

Managers can help make ethics a priority within the firm by enacting a code of conduct, establishing an ethics training program, arranging a formal system for reporting misconduct, and setting up an ethics advice line or office. When Christine Lagarde replaced Dominique Strauss-Kahn as managing director of the International Monetary Fund (IMF), her contract required her "to observe the highest standards of ethical conduct, consistent with the values of integrity, impartiality and discretion."[69] IMF spokesperson William Murray explained, "The fund has made a conscious decision to elaborate on what the highest ethical standards are via this contract."[70] Lagarde's predecessor had resigned in 2011 after being indicted for sexually assaulting a hotel maid.[71] Some had questioned the IMF board's decision to leave Strauss-Kahn in place in 2008 after he had an undisclosed affair with an IMF staffer. In May 2011, before Strauss-Kahn's arrest, the IMF (1) added a requirement that IMF employees disclose sexual relationships with other IMF employees so that any conflicts of interest could be addressed and (2) instituted mandatory ethics training concerning harassment, bullying, and other forms of intimidation.

Employees are more likely to report misconduct when they know that management will take appropriate corrective action and protect those who report unethical conduct.[72] In fact, the more elements an organization's ethics program has, the more likely employees are to report misconduct.[73] The reasons employees most often cite for not reporting misconduct are a lack of confidence that

corrective action will be taken and a lack of trust that the report will be kept confidential.[74] Perhaps most important, employees who work for organizations with more comprehensive ethics programs are more satisfied with their organizations than those with less comprehensive programs.[75]

Walk the Walk

Managers should resist the temptation to settle for "the appearance of a compliant reputation."[76] As Richard S. Gruner warned, "Compliance programs that are treated by management as a sham tend to encourage cynicism by employees. Such cynicism, in turn, tends to cause employees to pay less attention to legal requirements and to be more willing to commit offenses."[77] It takes discipline for managers to maintain this kind of commitment to ethical standards, but many firms are already exemplifying that discipline.

Employees pay attention to what managers do, not just to what they say. As a result, failure to sanction or even terminate employees who act unethically signals a lack of commitment to ethics and integrity at the top. When a firm dismisses an employee who personally acted unethically, the business consequences may be painful, especially when the employee has been a high performer. Even so, the connection between the individual's behavior and the dismissal is clear. On at least two occasions, General Electric faced a more difficult scenario: whether to hold business unit leaders responsible for ethical lapses by their subordinates.[78] One case involved procurement fraud and the other falsification of regulatory documents. Even though neither unit leader had participated in or known of the transgressions, both had failed to create an ethical culture within their respective units. At GE, this shortcoming was deemed equivalent to commercial failure, and both individuals were asked to leave the company.

Individual Responsibility

Individual employees, particularly those without substantial authority, are faced with a daunting task when they see their company acting in an unethical manner or are asked to engage in unethical behavior themselves. The individual should first determine whether the activity is illegal. Supervisors and managers cannot legally require subordinates to engage in illegal behavior. As discussed further in Chapter 12, even at-will employees are generally

68. *Global Corruption Report 2009*, TRANSPARENCY INT'L, *available at* http://www.transparency.org/publications/gcr/gcr_2009#sum (last visited Aug. 25, 2011).

69. Howard Schneider, *First Up for New IMF Chief Christine Lagarde: Ethics Training*, WASH. POST, July 5, 2011.

70. *Id.*

71. The indictment against Strauss-Kahn was subsequently dismissed. *See* Chris Dolmetsch & David McLaughlin, *Strauss-Kahn Faces Lawsuit, French Probe After Charges Dismissed*, BLOOMBERG, Aug. 24, 2011, *available at* http://www.bloomberg.com/news/2011-08-23/strauss-kahn-sexual-assault-charges-are-dismissed-by-new-york-city-judge.html (last visited Aug. 25, 2011).

72. ETHICS RESOURCE CENTER, NATIONAL BUSINESS ETHICS SURVEY 42 (2003).

73. *Id.*

74. *Id.* at 43.

75. *Id.* at 58.

76. Quoted in William S. Laufer, *Corporate Liability, Risk Shifting, and the Paradox of Compliance*, 52 VAND. L. REV. 1343, 1372 (1999).

77. *Id.* at 1372 n.127.

78. Heineman, *supra* note 21.

protected from discharge in retaliation for refusing to commit an illegal act. Furthermore, if an employee chooses to follow orders (and breaks the law), the fact that the employee was ordered to do so by a superior is no defense in a criminal trial. Thus, if asked to engage in illegal behavior, an employee is fully justified in "just saying 'no'" and is well advised to do so.

If an employee is asked to engage in legal, but unethical, behavior, the course of action is often less clear. First, the employee should review the company's code of conduct for guidance. Often consulting an ombudsperson or calling an ethics hotline, if available, is a good idea. Sometimes, it may be worthwhile to make others (coworkers, managers, supervisors, or even the board of directors) aware of the ethical implications of the situation because those implications may not be apparent to persons who are not intimately involved in the specific case. Higher-ups in the organization can sometimes provide "air cover" to protect a subordinate from retaliation. If no one else takes interest, a careful appraisal of one's own personal beliefs; an assessment of the social, environmental, or other ethical consequences of the action; and a realistic understanding of the consequences of refusing to take the action are all essential to deciding how to proceed.

Sometimes, managers have conflicting responsibilities and must decide "[w]hat to do when one clear right thing must be left undone in order to do another or when doing the right thing requires doing something wrong."[79] When trying to resolve problems that raise questions of personal integrity and moral identity, Professor Joe Badaracco calls on managers to ask, "Who am I?" and "What is my moral center?"[80] When managers with power over others are faced with organizational challenges, they should ask, "Who are we? What do we stand for? What norms and values guide how we work together and treat each other? How do we define ourselves as a human institution?"[81]

Jim Metcalf, the president and chief operating officer of USG Corporation, the largest manufacturer of building materials in the United States (including Sheetrock brand wallboard), remarked when describing USG's approach to the multitude of asbestos cases it faced in 2001:

> We were committed to doing what was best for the shareholders and all stakeholders. Before joining USG as a trainee, I worked in a steel mill during the summer while attending college at The Ohio State University. It's important to remember who you are and where you're from. Then you fight like hell to be good stewards.[82]

FAILING TO MEET SOCIETAL EXPECTATIONS

Companies have suffered severe financial setbacks as a result of decisions that, in hindsight, were perceived by the public as unethical. Given their reliance on individual retail sales, consumer products companies are particularly sensitive to public perception. As William D. Smithburg, then chair and CEO of the Quaker Oats Company, wrote: "[I] know ethical behavior is sound business practice because every day at the Quaker Oats Company I am reminded that we succeed or fail according to the trust consumers have in us."[83] Senior executives must negotiate with stakeholders to define the firm's role in society and its relationship with its customers, employees, and investors.[84]

Customers and Clients

Socially responsible businesses place a heavy emphasis on the safety of their products. Huge costs have been associated with failure to meet the public's perception of what is safe. Mattel's massive recall of lead-tainted toys made in China, the subject of the "Inside Story" in Chapter 17, is just one example of the perils of failing to ensure the safety of consumer products. Similarly, shoddy service or conflicts of interest can tarnish brands and cost hundreds of millions in fines.

General Motors and the Chevrolet Malibu's Exploding Fuel Tank

In 1999, General Motors Corporation was ordered to pay $4.8 billion in punitive damages and $107.89 million in compensatory damages to six people who were burned when their 1979 Chevrolet Malibu exploded after its fuel tank was ruptured in a crash.[85] Internal GM memos introduced during the trial suggested that GM executives had decided that redesigning the fuel system to reduce fire risk at a cost of $8.59 per car would impose a greater cost than paying claims for fuel-fire deaths. A key memo written by a GM engineer estimated that each death from burns from a fuel-related fire would cost the company $200,000. Based on that amount, the memo calculated that such deaths would cost $2.40 for every one of the potentially dangerous vehicles that had been sold. The memo cautioned, however, that "a human fatality is really beyond value, subjectively."[86] After the case, the GM lawyer stated

79. Joseph Badaracco, Jr., Defining Moments: When Managers Must Choose Between Right and Right 6 (1997).

80. *Id.* at 13.

81. *Id.*

82. Interview with the author. *See* Constance E. Bagley & Eliot Sherman, *USG Corporation (C)* (Harvard Bus. Sch. Case No. 807-121, 2007).

83. Touche Report, *supra* note 20, at 45.

84. *Id.* at 22–23.

85. Subsequent to the decision in this case, the U.S. Supreme Court ruled that "few awards exceeding a single-digit ratio between punitive damages and compensatory damages, to a significant degree, will satisfy due process." State Farm Mut. Auto. Ins. Co. v. Campbell, 538 U.S. 408, 425 (2003).

86. Jeffrey Ball & Milo Geyelin, *GM Ordered by Jury to Pay $4.9 Billion— Auto Maker Plans to Appeal Huge California Verdict in Fuel-Tank-Fire Case*, Wall St. J., July 12, 1999, at A3.

that the company had no plans to notify owners of cars with the same fuel system as the Malibu that the system was dangerous.

The GM case is reminiscent of Ford Motor Company's ultimately very costly decision to produce the Ford Pinto without safety modifications to keep the gas tank from rupturing when rear-ended at low speeds. Ford managers relied on a classic cost–benefit analysis, which compared the $4 to $8 cost of the alterations with the cost of defending the lawsuits stemming from injuries or deaths caused by the exploding gas tanks.[87]

Conflicts of Interest: Goldman Sachs

Undisclosed conflicts of interest erode client confidence. Venerable investment bank Goldman Sachs paid a $550 million fine to settle allegations by the Securities and Exchange Commission (SEC) that it had violated the securities laws when it sold derivatives contracts based on the performance of a portfolio of subprime mortgage-backed securities without disclosing that it had permitted another Goldman client, who was effectively shorting the same portfolio, to select many of the mortgage-backed securities on which the derivatives were based. Critics also accused Goldman of spreading negative rumors about the Greek sovereign debt market while serving as an adviser to the Greek government. Goldman CEO Lloyd Blankfein attracted further negative attention when he responded to criticism about high executive compensation at Goldman by asserting that Goldman was doing "God's work."[88] Nobel economics laureate Joseph Stiglitz commented, "That Goldman's chief executive saw himself as doing 'God's work' as his firm sold short products that it created, or disseminated scurrilous rumours about a country for which it was serving as an 'adviser,' suggests a parallel universe, with different mores and values."[89] Although Goldman Sachs did not admit liability, Blankfein conceded that Goldman had made an error of judgment.[90] Conduct by Goldman and other banks during the subprime mortgage bubble contributed to the passage of the Dodd–Frank Wall Street Reform and Consumer Protection Act, the most sweeping financial reform since the Great Depression.[91]

"Sorry—I live in a parallel universe."

Employees

A number of firms have lost business in the wake of allegations of questionable workplace practices, including using child labor, contracting work to sweatshops, and engaging in employment discrimination. For example, Texaco lost $1 billion in market capitalization in one day in 1996 after a group of its African American employees filed a Title VII class-action suit alleging racial discrimination in hiring and promotion. The complaint included racist comments made by a member of top management who had been secretly recorded by a disgruntled employee. After the Reverend Jesse Jackson organized a consumer boycott, Texaco agreed to pay more than $100 million to settle the charges of racial discrimination and to implement a comprehensive diversity program.

Discrimination costs more than money. It also saps employee morale. After the lawsuit, employee morale hit lows not seen since the $10.5 billion verdict rendered against Texaco when it was sued by Pennzoil over the acquisition of Getty Oil (discussed in the "Inside Story" in Chapter 7). One executive, who had suffered through the Pennzoil ordeal, said that friends called and asked how she could work at a "place like that." She commented, "It's one thing to be called stupid; it's another to be called a bigot."[92]

Texaco's newly elected CEO, Peter Bijur, responded to the lawsuit by summoning his top management team and instructing them to get the word out to all managers that there would be zero tolerance of racial epithets, taunts, and joking on the job. When one officer asked whether Bijur thought this was realistic, given the somewhat rowdy atmosphere on oil rigs and the like, Bijur responded, "Tell the local managers that if they can't enforce this policy, then you will replace them." He went on to say, "And if

87. *See* Grimshaw v. Ford Motor Co., 119 Cal. App. 3d 757, 777 (1981).

88. Joseph Stiglitz, *The Fraught Road to World Financial Reform*, 6/10/10 INDEP. FIN. REV. (NZ) 17, 2010 WLNR 11759320 (June 10, 2010).

89. *Id.*

90. James Quinn, *Goldman Boss Admits Handling of Conflicts "Can Be a Little Off,"* TELEGRAPH, May 5, 2010, *available at* http://www.telegraph.co.uk/finance/newsbysector/banksandfinance/7683202/Goldman-boss-admits-handling-of-conflicts-can-be-a-little-off.html (last visited Aug. 27, 2011).

91. Brady Dennis, *Obama Signs Financial Overhaul into Law*, WASH. POST, July 22, 2010, at A13.

92. CONSTANCE E. BAGLEY, WINNING LEGALLY: HOW MANAGERS CAN USE THE LAW TO CREATE VALUE, MARSHAL RESOURCES, AND MANAGE RISK (2005).

you can't find managers who can enforce this policy, I'll replace you."[93] Although Bijur's predecessor, Al deCrane, had circulated memos about Texaco's policies against discrimination, Bijur went a step further and instituted a policy requiring an African American and a woman to be present at each human resources meeting to ensure that there would be no repeat of the odious comments that had triggered the lawsuit.[94]

Investors: Managed Earnings

In an effort to meet securities analysts' earnings expectations and thereby avoid the punishing drop in stock price that usually follows a company's announcement that its earnings were below Wall Street's estimates, a number of public companies have managed earnings.[95] They used what Arthur Levitt, former chair of the SEC, called "accounting hocus-pocus" to recognize revenue improperly, take unjustified restructuring charges, and create "cookie-jar reserves" that could be used to smooth out earnings by making up earnings shortfalls in later periods.[96] When the truth is finally revealed, the resultant drop in market capitalization can be dramatic. For example, the disclosure of improper inflation of operating income and other accounting irregularities at Cendant caused the company's stock to drop by more than $14 billion in a single day.

Enron

As described more fully in the "Inside Story" for this chapter, Enron Corporation's increasingly aggressive accounting, which began as clever tricks and grew into complex and illegal schemes, led to the energy giant's demise in 2001.[97] Enron was a dog-eat-dog world where short-term shareholder value was paramount, and the "deal" was everything.

The Environment

Failure to meet societal expectations concerning the protection of the environment can tarnish a firm's reputation, wreak ecological havoc, and hurt innocent people.

BP's Deepwater Horizon *Oil Spill*

As discussed more fully in the "Inside Story" in Chapter 15, in 2010 BP, p.l.c. was involved in the worst environmental disaster since the *Exxon Valdez* ran aground in 1989 and spilled 10.9 million barrels of crude oil onto the pristine beaches of Prince William Sound in Alaska. The *Deepwater Horizon* rig above a BP well in mile-deep water in the Gulf of Mexico exploded, killing eleven workers and spilling 4.1 million barrels of crude oil into the gulf. Although BP blamed the owner of the rig, Transocean, Ltd., for the spill, BP's mishandling of the entire episode led to the replacement of CEO Tony Hayward and the establishment of a $20 billion escrow fund to cover claims and cleanup. By 2011, BP had taken total charges against earnings of more than $40 billion for costs associated with the spill.

The *Deepwater Horizon* disaster followed the 2005 explosion at a BP oil refinery in Texas City, Texas, which killed fifteen workers, and the 2006 leak in BP's pipeline in Alaska's North Shore, which spilled more than 5,000 barrels of crude oil. The Occupational Safety and Health Administration found more than 300 health and safety violations at the Texas City refinery, and the Environmental Protection Agency concluded that the Alaska spill was caused by BP's failure to properly inspect and maintain the pipeline to prevent corrosion. Although BP America's chair and president Bob Malone had announced in 2007 that "we have made real progress in the areas of process safety performance and risk management,"[98] another BP employee was killed in the same Texas City refinery in early 2008.

Robert Dudley, Hayward's replacement as CEO of BP, embarrassed the firm in 2011 when he negotiated a $7.8 billion strategic alliance with the state-owned Russian oil company Rosneft in violation of the TNK–BP shareholder agreement with a group of Russian oil oligarchs.[99] BP and Rosneft agreed to a deal whereby (1) BP would swap 5% of its stock for 10% of the stock of Rosneft, and (2) BP and Rosneft would spend $2 billion to explore an area in the South Kara Sea in the Russian Arctic estimated to have as much potential as the North Sea. The High Court in London ruled that the shareholder agreement made TNK–BP BP's exclusive partner for oil exploration in Russia. The *New York Times* reported that "BP's lawyers had understood that the agreement with Rosneft was 'on the edge' of violating the TNK–BP shareholder agreement," but BP still proceeded without first obtaining the consent of its TNK–BP Russian partner.[100] Apparently, BP had assumed that Russian Premier Vladimir Putin would keep the oligarchs from blocking the deal, but that "turned out to be a bad bet on BP's part."[101] Instead of siding with BP, Putin rebuked the company for failing to

93. *Id.*

94. *Id.*

95. *See* Carol J. Loomis, *Lies, Damned Lies, and Managed Earnings*, FORTUNE, Aug. 2, 1999, at 74.

96. ARTHUR LEVITT, TAKING ON THE STREET (2003).

97. *See* BETHANY MCLEAN & PETER ELKIND, THE SMARTEST GUYS IN THE ROOM: THE AMAZING RISE AND SCANDALOUS FALL OF ENRON (2003).

98. Press Release, BP, p.l.c., BP America Announces Resolution of Texas City, Texas, Alaska, Propane Trading, Law Enforcement Investigations (Oct. 25, 2007), *available at* http://www.bp.com/genericarticle.do?categoryId=2012968&contentId=7037819 (last visited Aug. 27, 2011).

99. Constance E. Bagley et al., *BP in Russia* (Yale Sch. of Mgmt. CASE No. 11-014, 2011).

100. Julia Werdigier & Andrew E. Kramer, *Setback in Rosneft Deal Suggests BP Misread Russia*, N.Y. TIMES, Apr. 8, 2011.

101. *Id.*

meet its contractual obligations. Thus, rather than achieving Dudley's espoused goal of showcasing the "new BP," the incident renewed concerns about the top management team's judgment.

Some had questioned BP's willingness to deal with Rosneft at all, given that Rosneft had acquired its vast Russian oil assets from the firm Yukos, at a fraction of their fair value, by effectively nationalizing Yukos after its owner Mikhail Khodorkovsky was imprisoned on trumped-up charges of tax evasion. A former Putin aide had called the purchase of the Yukos assets "the theft of the century."[102] The *Financial Times* characterized BP's willingness to do a deal with Rosneft as a recognition of the "realpolitik" of dealing with the regimes controlling much of the world's oil reserves.[103] In August 2011, ExxonMobil announced a multibillion-dollar deal with Rosneft, which was apparently brokered by Putin.

Disposal of Electronics

According to environmental groups, high-tech garbage is causing substantial health and safety risks in China, India, Nigeria, Pakistan, and other developing countries. Businesses in the United States that offer to recycle retired electronics are often not recycling them responsibly, perhaps because dismantling and reusing the waste in America is substantially more expensive than the alternatives. For instance, it costs ten times more to dismantle and reuse the materials in a computer monitor in the United States than to ship it to China for recycling.[104] Up to 80% of electronics waste collected in America for recycling ends up in developing countries where laborers tear the waste apart, often by hand, to extract traces of copper, small amounts of gold, and other valuable minerals.[105]

The health and environmental risks are substantial because the waste contains many toxic materials. An average fourteen-inch monitor contains five to eight pounds of lead, which can seep into groundwater or disperse into the air if the monitor is crushed and burned. Semiconductor chips contain cadmium; computer exteriors contain chromium; batteries and switches contain mercury; and circuit boards contain brominated flame retardants.[106] As workers pick apart the waste and its toxic ingredients disperse into the soil, water, and air, people in China are suffering high incidences of birth defects, infant mortality, tuberculosis, blood diseases, and severe respiratory problems.[107] Recently, several

U.S. computer companies, including Dell, started offering more responsible recycling services.[108]

Communities

A number of firms have wrestled with issues related to their responsibilities to the communities in which they do business. For example, the public has put pressure on corporations and institutional investors to invest responsibly, that is, in a way that does not lend support to unjust, oppressive regimes. For instance, many companies with direct or indirect economic ties to South Africa were the subject of consumer boycotts and shareholder resolutions prohibiting investment in South Africa. South Africa's policy of racial segregation (called *apartheid*) relegated its black citizens to second-class status in employment, housing, and opportunity. The boycotts and shareholder resolutions were critical in helping end apartheid in South Africa, a result for which Nelson Mandela and F.W. de Klerk won the Nobel Peace Prize in 1993.

Energy giant Chevron Corporation, which purchased rival Unocal in 2005, has been sharply criticized for its continuous involvement with the $1.2 billion Yadana pipeline in the country of Burma.[109] Rather than ceding power after a free election won by an opposing party, Burma's military leaders took control in 1990 and renamed the country Myanmar. The government has since established a reputation as one of the most oppressive in the world.

Chevron is the largest U.S. investor remaining in Burma. Burma's state-owned oil company, Unocal's partner on the pipeline, has allegedly been involved in rapes, murders, and slavery.[110] President Clinton banned any new American investments in Burma in April 1997,[111] but Unocal's existing investment was grandfathered.[112] In May 2004, President George W. Bush labeled the military government an "extraordinary threat" to U.S. interests and renewed an import ban against the country.[113] In 2007, the U.S. government imposed additional sanctions prohibiting American banks and companies from doing business with fourteen Burmese officials, including the country's military ruler, General Than Shwe, and froze any assets held in the United States by those individuals.[114]

102. Steven Lee Myers, *From Ashes of Yukos, New Russian Oil Giant Emerges*, N.Y. TIMES, Mar. 27, 2007.

103. Editorial, *BP's Realpolitik in the Russian Arctic*, FIN. TIMES, Jan. 17, 2011.

104. Peter S. Goodman, *China Serves as Dump Site for Computers*, WASH. POST, Feb. 24, 2003, at A1.

105. *Id.*

106. *Id.*; P.J. Huffstutter, *Recycled Electronics Pose a Health Hazard in Asia*, L.A. TIMES, Feb. 26, 2002, pt. 3, at 1.

107. Goodman, *supra* note 104.

108. Tom Zeller, Jr., *Few Rules for Recycling Electronics*, N.Y. TIMES, May 31, 2009.

109. David R. Baker, *Chevron's Links to Burma Stir Critics to Demand It to Pull Out*, S.F. CHRON., Oct. 4, 2007, at A1.

110. Lisa Girion, *Unocal in Burma Lawsuit Talks*, L.A. TIMES, Dec. 14, 2004.

111. The U.S. Supreme Court struck down a Massachusetts statute barring state entities from buying goods or services from companies doing business with Myanmar in *Crosby v. National Foreign Trade Council*, 530 U.S. 363 (2000).

112. Jay Solomon & James Hookway, *U.S. Slaps Financial Sanctions on Mynamar*, WALL ST. J., Sept. 28, 2007, at A3.

113. *Unocal's Shareholders Reject Bid for Dissidents' Access to Board*, L.A. TIMES, May 25, 2004, at C2.

114. Solomon & Hookway, *supra* note 112.

In 2004, Charles Williamson, Unocal's chair and CEO, defended the company's involvement in Burma, calling it "good for stockholders . . . and the country."[115] Several years later, Chevron vice chair Peter Robertson pointed out that Chevron has paid for teachers and doctors in affected communities and stated: "I'm convinced that hundreds of thousands of people in Burma have benefited. . . . They benefit from us being there."[116]

In 2011, EarthRights International charged that Norway's sovereign wealth fund had violated its own guidelines for responsible investment by investing $4.8 billion in fifteen oil and gas companies doing business in Burma, including Chevron and France's Total. EarthRights asserted that Norway had invested "despite evidence that those companies are currently complicit in human rights abuses or pose an unreasonable risk of contributing to abuses in the future."[117]

POSITIVE ACTION

Although examples of corporate misdeeds abound, there are also encouraging instances of responsible corporate behavior.

Customers and Product Safety: Johnson & Johnson and Tylenol

Johnson & Johnson's Tylenol success story is a classic illustration of socially responsible behavior. In September 1982, several Tylenol capsules were tampered with and laced with cyanide poison. As soon as the first deaths were reported, the company recalled 31 million bottles of Tylenol at a cost of approximately $100 million.

James Burke, chair of Johnson & Johnson during the Tylenol scare, credited Johnson & Johnson's code of ethics with helping the company deal with the crisis.[118] Johnson & Johnson's code begins: "We believe that our first responsibility is to the doctors, nurses and patients, to mothers and fathers, and all others who use our products and services. In meeting their need, everything we do must be of high quality."[119] Burke recalled, "Dozens of people had to make hundreds of decisions on the fly. There was no doubt in their minds that the public was

going to come first in this issue because we had spelled it out [in our credo] as their responsibility."[120]

Although the short-term economic costs of the Tylenol recall were enormous, within a matter of months Johnson & Johnson was able to regain the market share it had lost. By living up to its reputation for integrity and social responsibility, Johnson & Johnson enhanced both its public image and its long-term profitability. That image was later tarnished, however, by claims that Johnson & Johnson had been slow to warn consumers that Tylenol can cause liver damage[121] and by the company's agreement in 2011 to pay more than $70 million in fines to settle SEC charges that it paid kickbacks and bribed physicians to garner more business—both incidents are vivid reminders of the importance of being ever vigilant to protect a firm's reputation.[122]

Employees: Auditing of Supplier Work Conditions

For many years, American companies claimed that their foreign factories were not stereotypical sweatshops, but they stubbornly refused to release the reports detailing the audits they used to substantiate those claims. A number of companies now go public with the audit reports. Adidas, Hanesbrand, Nike,[123] and other firms post the results of their factory audits on the Fair Labor Association (FLA) website (http://www.fairlabor.org). This has put pressure on other companies, particularly those with less than stellar human rights reputations, to publicize their audits as well. Although certain critics claim that the inspection regime is "watered down,"[124] some accountability is better than none at all.

Environment: Socially Responsible Investment

Individual and institutional investors continue to promote more environmentally responsible behavior. In 1989, the Coalition for Environmentally Responsible Economies (CERES) promulgated investor guidelines that focus on environmental awareness and corporate activities, such as

---

115. *Unocal's Shareholders Reject Bid, supra* note 113.

116. Baker, *supra* note 109.

117. Press Release, EarthRights International, Recent Killings Near Gas Pipelines in Burma as Norwegian Government Announces Updated Investments in Companies in Burma's Energy Sector (Mar. 23, 2011), *available at* http://www.earthrights.org/sites/default/files/documents/EarthRights_Press_Release_23_Mar_2011_5.pdf (last visited Aug. 27, 2011).

118. Richard S. Tedlow & Wendy K. Smith, *James Burke: A Career in American Business (A)* (Harvard Bus. Sch. Case No. 389-177, 2005).

119. Quoted in PATRICK E. MURPHY, EIGHTY EXEMPLARY ETHICS STATEMENTS 123 (1998).

120. Stanley J. Modic, *Corporate Ethics: From Commandments to Commitment*, INDUSTRY WK., Dec. 14, 1987, at 33.

121. *See* Thomas Easton, *Medicine, J&J's Dirty Little Secret*, FORBES, Jan. 12, 1998, at 42.

122. Joshua Gallu & Alex Nussbaum, *Johnson & Johnson Will Pay $70 Million over Bribery Claims*, BLOOMBERG, Apr. 8, 2011, *available at* http://www.bloomberg.com/news/2011-04-08/johnson-johnson-will-pay-70-million-to-resolve-bribery-claims.html (last visited Aug. 27, 2011).

123. Nike had an in-house staff of ninety-seven that inspected 600 factories in the two-year period ending in 2004 and graded them. Maria S. Eitel, the Nike vice president for corporate responsibility, commented: "You haven't heard about us recently because we have had our head down doing it the hard way. Now we have a system to deal with the labor issue, not a crisis mentality." Quoted in Stanley Holmes, *The New Nike*, BUS. WK., Sept. 20, 2004, at 78, 84.

124. Aaron Bernstein, *Sweatshops: Finally, Airing the Dirty Linen*, BUS. WK., June 23, 2003, at 100.

using and preserving natural resources, safely disposing of pollutants, marketing safe products, and reducing environmental risks. CERES is a diverse network of 130 investors, environmentalists, labor unions, and community advocates. By 2011, more than eighty companies (including Consolidated Edison, General Motors, and Sunoco) had endorsed the CERES principles.[125]

CERES launched the Investor Network on Climate Risk (INCR) in 2003 with ten institutional investors controlling $600 billion in assets. By 2011, the group included almost a hundred investors managing $9.5 trillion.

Many large mutual fund companies, 401(k) retirement plans, and college saving plans offer socially responsible options,[126] and American investors are investing in responsible funds and companies in increasing numbers.[127] The Social Investment Forum reported that $3 trillion was invested in U.S. socially responsible funds in 2010, up 34% since 2005. For example, Vanguard's Social Index fund grew from $77 million in 2001 to $553.1 million in 2011.

Europe has seen a similar growth in socially responsible funds.[128] The European Social Investment Forum reported that in 2009 the managers of five trillion euros of invested European capital took environmental, social, and governance factors into account when investing, up 87% from 2007. Pursuant to regulations that went into effect in 2000 and 2010, pension-fund trustees and other investment managers in the United Kingdom must disclose in their statement of investment principles the extent, if any, to which they consider social, environmental, or ethical factors when deciding in which companies to invest.[129] Certain other European countries have similar laws. Experts have called for the SEC to adopt comparable disclosure requirements in the United States.[130]

PROMOTING ETHICAL BEHAVIOR

In addition to leading by example, CEOs and other managers use a variety of techniques to promote ethical behavior.

---

125. The list of companies, investors, and other affiliates is available at www.ceres.org (last visited July 18, 2011).

126. Jilian Mincer, *Socially Responsible Funds Grow*, WALL ST. J., May 29, 2007, at D2.

127. This is not to suggest, however, that capital does not continue to flow to companies engaged in more venal pursuits. The Vice Fund, which invests solely in companies involved in alcoholic beverages, tobacco, casinos, gaming machines and facilities, and aerospace and defense, had $86 million under management in 2011. The Vice Fund (Vicex) prospectus is available at www.vicefund.com (last visited July 17, 2011).

128. Sara Calian & Tamzin Booth, *Ethical-Investment Practices Expand in U.K. in Response to New Legislation*, WALL ST. J., June 19, 2000, at A15B.

129. As of December 6, 2010, all U.K. investment managers must disclose whether they adhere to the U.K. Stewardship Code. *See* European Fund and Asset Management Association, *available at* www.efama.org (last visited July 17, 2011).

130. Bagley & Page, *supra* note 3.

Craft a Mission Statement

Corporations sometimes include ethical language in their corporate mission statements. Even if there is no express reference to ethics, companies may stress their responsibilities to employees, customers, and society at large. For example, Toyo Glass Company, a Japanese supplier of glass products, includes the following statement:

1. Our objective is to contribute our share of work towards the happiness of the public at large.

2. Profit is not our first aim to attain, it is a natural outgrowth of successful business activities.

3. Everybody is expected to do his duty as a service to the public, individually and collectively, and thus to benefit the property of his own as well as others.[131]

Adopt a Code of Ethics

Business leaders consider a code of ethics to be one of the most effective measures for encouraging ethical business behavior. A code of ethics is a written set of rules or standards that states the company's principles and clarifies its expectations of employee conduct in various situations. Although these codes vary from company to company, they govern such areas as selling and marketing practices, conflicts of interest, political activities, and product safety and quality.

Having a code of conduct in place before a crisis strikes is essential. Bowen H. "Buzz" McCoy, one of *National Real Estate Investor Magazine*'s 100 real estate "icons" of the twentieth century, observed that "if a common sense of values has not been discussed and articulated before an ethical issue intrudes unexpectedly, it is too late."[132]

A company code of ethics is ineffective without proper implementation, however. Enron had a great policy on paper. It is not enough simply to state general rules; the code must show employees how the principles apply to particular decisions. The code should be a living document that is reviewed periodically to meet new circumstances. Managers should go over the code with personnel to ensure that they understand the company's values. The company should also pay increased attention to ethical standards in recruiting, hiring, and setting compensation.

Provide Ethics Training

Employers should supplement the written code with ethics education programs. Companies cite two primary goals of ethics training: (1) developing a general awareness of ethics in business and (2) drawing attention to practical

---

131. ROBERT E. ALLINSON, GLOBAL DISASTERS: INQUIRIES INTO MANAGEMENT ETHICS (1994).

132. Bowen H. McCoy, *Real Estate Ethics*, 4 REAL EST. REV. 27, 31 (2000).

ethical issues. Sixty percent of the companies that provide ethics training do so during the orientation process for new employees.

Several companies have developed innovative methods for educating their employees in ethics. Aircraft manufacturer Boeing offers an online quiz (with answers) to try to guide its staff through the whole gamut of moral quandaries from how to deal with employees who fiddle with their expenses to suppliers who ask for kickbacks.[133] In the wake of repeated scandals, Citigroup instituted mandatory online ethics training for all Citigroup employees worldwide.[134]

Ethics training may be particularly important for business managers. Research indicates that students planning a career in business are more likely to cheat than students planning to pursue other disciplines (87% of undergraduate business students and 56% of graduate business students admitted that they had cheated on at least one test).[135] Other research supports the assertion that business students are more tolerant of unethical behavior than other students.[136] Moreover, courses in classic economics may enhance students' tendencies to act in a selfish manner.[137] Nonetheless, business schools are trying to increase the scope and quality of their ethics coverage.

To preserve the reputation of tomorrow's business leaders and to prevent unethical behavior in the future, there must be a renewed focus on trustworthiness and personal responsibility in business schools.[138] Many business schools offer stand-alone courses in ethics or corporate responsibility and business law, and most try to integrate such topics into strategy and accounting courses, among others. The Yale School of Management has developed an integrated core curriculum that trains students to analyze business decisions from a variety of perspectives, including investors, employees, customers, competitors, and state and society.[139]

Provide Oversight

In an effort to enforce ethical standards, some companies have set up oversight committees, and many large firms employ at least one full-time ethics officer. The Ethics and Compliance Officer Association has grown from a dozen members in 1992 to more than 1,200 members in 2011.[140] The association's member companies include more than half of the *Fortune* 100. Defense and engineering giant United Technologies has an international network of more than 450 "business practice officers," who are responsible for distributing and reinforcing a code of ethics in thirty-three languages to its employees around the world.[141]

In general, ethics committees are responsible for setting standards and policy and for handling employee complaints or infractions. Executive officers or directors of the company are often members. Ombudspersons investigate employee complaints. Judiciary boards usually decide cases of ethics code violations.

Another method of oversight is the social audit. Increasingly, companies have been performing social audits of their activities in sensitive or controversial areas. For example, a semiconductor company might conduct an internal audit of its disposal of chemical waste, or a bank might audit the reporting practices of its securities trading division.

A 2000 study of social auditing revealed that corporate financial performance typically improves with increased social responsibility. The companies studied increased their efficiency and productivity, lowered legal exposure and risk to the company's reputation, and reduced direct and overhead costs as a result of adopting socially responsible practices.[142] The financial payback to the company was between six and twenty times the audit cost over periods of six months to three years.[143]

Make It Easier to Blow the Whistle

Many employees are reluctant to "blow the whistle"—to report illegal or unethical conduct that they observe at work—for fear of being considered a troublemaker or of being fired. As discussed in Chapter 12, a number of federal, state, and local laws prohibit reprisals against employees who report activities that they believe violate a law, rule, or regulation.

Even with legislative and judicial protections, whistleblowers still suffer. Edna Ottney, a quality assurance

133. Boeing Frontiers Online, *Ethics Training Module Online*, Sept. 2003, http://www.boeing.com/news/frontiers/archive/2003/september/i_nan2.html; Boeing Education and Awareness, *available at* http://www.boeing.com/companyoffices/aboutus/ethics/education.htm.

134. Hamilton Nolan, *Citigroup Kicks Off Internal Efforts to Clarify Standards*, PR Wk., Apr. 4, 2005, at 3. On more than one occasion, CEO and lawyer Charles O. Prince commented, "My goal for Citi is to be the most respected global financial services company." Prince resigned in late 2007 as the company faced upwards of $4 billion in losses related to the collapse of the subprime mortgage market.

135. Donald L. McCabe & Linda Klebe Trevino, *Cheating Among Business Students: A Challenge for Business Leaders and Educators*, 19 J. Mgmt. Educ. 205, 209–10 (1995).

136. M. Lynette Smyth & James R. Davis, *An Examination of Student Cheating in the Two-Year College*, 31 Community C. Rev. 17 (2003).

137. F. Ferraro, J. Pfeffer & R.I. Sutton, *Economics Language and Assumptions: How Theories Can Become Self-Fulfilling*, 30 Acad. Mgmt. Rev. 8 (2005).

138. Carolyn Y. Woo, *Personally Responsible*, BizEd, May–June 2003, at 22, *available at* http://www.aacsb.edu/publications/archives/mayjune03/p22-27.pdf (last visited Aug. 27, 2011).

139. A description is available at http://www.mba.yale.edu.

140. Ethics and Compliance Officer Association, *ECOA Global Network*, *available at* http://www.theecoa.org.

141. This information was gleaned from the United Technologies website, http://utc.com/Governance/Ethics (last visited Aug. 27, 2011).

142. Sandra Waddock & Neil Smith, *Corporate Responsibility Audits: Doing Well by Doing Good*, MIT Sloan Mgmt. Rev., Winter 2000, at 75, 76.

143. *Id.* at 82.

engineer who has investigated employee concerns in the nuclear power industry since 1985, reported that 90% of the 1,700 whistleblowers she interviewed had experienced negative reactions. A person who reported violations at the Comanche Peak nuclear plant in Glen Rose, Texas, warned: "Be prepared for old friends to suddenly become distant. Be prepared to change your type of job and lifestyle. Be prepared to wait years for blind justice to prevail."[144]

A manager can make it easier for employees to blow the whistle by protecting them from retaliation by their immediate supervisor and coworkers. A manager provides moral and psychological support by emphasizing to coworkers the courage shown by the whistleblower and by providing free counseling to deal with any victimization by coworkers.

---

144. Quoted in Joel Chineson, *Bureaucrats with Conscience*, LEGAL TIMES, Apr. 17, 1989, at 50.

HONOR OR THE MORALS OF THE MARKETPLACE?

In the case of partners and certain other relationships of confidence and trust, the law imposes a *fiduciary duty* to act in the best interest of the other party. In the oft-quoted words of Chief Judge Cardozo:

> Many forms of conduct permissible in a workaday world for those acting at arm's length are forbidden to those bound by fiduciary ties. A trustee is held to something stricter than the morals of the market place. Not honesty alone, but the punctilio of an honor the most sensitive, is then the standard of behavior.[145]

In the following case, the judges on the New York Court of Appeals (the highest court in New York) wrestled with the extent of the duties a finder owes its client.

---

145. Meinhard v. Salmon, 164 N.E. 545 (N.Y. 1928) (Case 5.1).

| A CASE IN POINT | *In the Language of the Court* | Case 2.2 |

Northeast General Corp. v. Wellington Advertising, Inc.

Court of Appeals of New York
624 N.E.2d 129 (N.Y. 1993).

FACTS   In 1988, Northeast General Corporation entered into an agreement with Wellington Advertising, Inc. whereby Northeast agreed to act "as a non-exclusive independent investment banker and business consultant for the purposes of finding and presenting candidates for purchase, sale, merger or other business combination." The agreement further provided that Northeast General would be entitled to a finder's fee, based on the size of the transaction, if a transaction was completed within three years of Wellington's introduction to the "found" buying party. In the course of his discussion with Northeast's new president, Dunton, Wellington's president, Arpadi, had confided that he was "terrified" he "would lose everything" in a bad merger.

Margolis, one of Northeast General's agents, consulted with Dunton and then introduced Sternau to Arpadi as a potential purchaser of Wellington. Ultimately, Sternau and Wellington entered into an acquisition agreement. Before introducing Sternau to Wellington, Dunton was informed by an unidentified investment banker that Sternau had a reputation for buying companies, removing assets, rendering the companies borderline insolvent, and leaving minority investors unprotected. Dunton did not disclose this information to Wellington prior to the closing of the Wellington–Sternau deal.

After Northeast introduced Sternau to Wellington, but prior to the signing of the acquisition agreement, Dunton called Arpadi and offered further help with the transaction. Arpadi declined that help and discouraged Dunton from any further involvement. After the acquisition agreement was signed, companies controlled by Sternau purchased the controlling stock of Wellington, leaving Wellington's principals, including Arpadi, as minority investors. Ultimately, Wellington was rendered insolvent, and Arpadi and other minority investors suffered financial losses. Wellington delivered a check to Northeast for its finder services but stopped payment before the check could be negotiated.

Northeast sued Wellington to recover its finder's fee. After a trial, the jury found in favor of Northeast and awarded it the agreed finder's fee. The trial court judge set aside the jury's verdict. The judge's decision, which rested on arguments of public policy, imposed a fiduciary-like duty on finders to disclose adverse information to their clients. The appellate division court upheld the trial court judge's action, and Northeast appealed.

CONTINUED

ISSUE PRESENTED   Does a finder–seller agreement create a relationship of trust with a "fiduciary-like" obligation on the finder to share information with the seller regarding the potential buyer's bad reputation?

OPINION   BELLACOSA, J., writing on behalf of the New York Court of Appeals:

Before courts can infer and superimpose a duty of the finest loyalty, the contract and relationship of the parties must be plumbed. We recognize that "[m]any forms of conduct, permissible in a workaday world for those acting at arm's length, are forbidden to those bound by fiduciary ties" (*Meinhard v. Salmon*, 249 N.Y. 458, 464 (1928).) Chief Judge Cardozo's oft-quoted maxim is a timeless reminder that "[a] trustee is held to something stricter than the morals of the market place. Not honesty alone, but the punctilio of an honor the most sensitive" (*Id.*). If the parties find themselves or place themselves in the milieu of the "workaday" mundane market place, and if they do not create their own relationship of higher trust, courts should not ordinarily transport them to the higher realm of relationship and fashion the stricter duty for them.

The Northeast–Wellington agreement contains no cognizable fiduciary terms or relationship. The dissent ascribes inordinate weight to the titles non-exclusive "independent investment banker and business consultant." These terms in the context of this agreement are not controlling, since Dunton did not perform the services of an investment banker or consultant. Instead, Dunton's sole function was "for purposes of finding and presenting candidates." That drives the analysis of this case because he was a traditional finder functioning under a finder's agreement, and his role ceased when he found and presented someone. The finder was not described or given the function of an agent, partner or co-venturer.

Probing our precedents and equitable principles unearths no supportable justification for such a judicial interposition, however highly motivated and idealistic. Indeed, responding to this fine instinct would inappropriately propel the courts into reformation of service agreements between commercially knowledgeable parties in this and perhaps countless other situations and transactions as well.

This Court may sense a sympathetic impulse to balance what it may view as the equities of a situation such as this. The hard judicial obligation, however, is to be intellectually disciplined against that tug. Instead, courts must focus on the precise law function reposed in them in such circumstances, which is to construe and enforce the meaning and thrust of the contract of the parties, not to purify their efforts.

The character of the Northeast–Wellington agreement was not one of trust importing duties beyond finding a prospect. The fact that Wellington did not employ its own independent, traditional methods to check out the reputation of the prospect and accepted what turned out to be a bad prospect does not warrant this Court rescuing it from its soured deal by any post-agreement fiduciary lifeline.

The commonplace mores of the market place suffice and are appropriate to govern relationships established by a contract of the type involved here, which contemplates and asks nothing more of the parties than performance of a simple service. In sum, defendants' financial losses from their market mishap with Sternau is not reason enough to propel a sweeping new fiduciary-like doctrine into finders' agreements.

DISSENT   HANCOCK, J., dissenting from the majority opinion:

The established rule is that "[a] fiduciary relationship is one founded on trust or confidence reposed by one person in the integrity and fidelity of another. The term is a very broad one. It is said that the relation exists, and that relief is granted, in all cases in which influence has been acquired and abused, in which confidence has been reposed and betrayed. The origin of the confidence and the source of the influence are immaterial. The rule embraces both technical fiduciary relations and those informal relations which exist whenever one man trusts in and relies upon another. Out of such a relation, the law raises the rules that neither party may exert influence or pressure upon the other."

CONTINUED

The narrow question applying the above rules is whether Arpadi's and Dunton's relationship exhibits sufficient trust and de facto control upon which to ground Dunton's duty to disclose negative information regarding the very deal he was promoting. The record reveals more than enough evidence to demonstrate both elements. By imparting confidential business details as well as his personal plans and intentions, Arpadi reposed trust in Dunton as a business counselor to find candidates likely to conform to Arpadi's investment goals. Arpadi expected Dunton to perform as a finder with Arpadi's interests at heart, i.e., not to remain silent as Wellington was being circled by a corporate predator. Dunton exerted de facto control and influence over Arpadi by fostering Arpadi's false belief that there was no reason not to accept Sternau as a suitable candidate. Dunton's review of the intimate details of Arpadi's business marked Dunton's acceptance of that trust. There is no doubt that as regards the proposed merger with [Sternau's company], Dunton and Arpadi stood in a fiduciary relation to each other.

There is a final point. Even if only the agreement between Northeast and Arpadi were to be considered, the law would, I submit, imply a duty on the part of Dunton to disclose critical adverse information in these circumstances. Indeed, I believe that many would agree that even the "morals of the market place" would require it. Surely [Dunton] should not be rewarded for his failure.

RESULT   The judgment for Wellington was reversed by the New York Court of Appeals, and Wellington was ordered to pay the finder's fee to Northeast General.

CRITICAL THINKING QUESTIONS

1. What language could Wellington have added to its contract with Northeast to ensure that it was apprised of the reputation of any proposed buyer?

2. The court stated that a broker, who helps negotiate a deal and thereby brings the parties to an agreement, has a fiduciary duty to act in the best interests of the person who hired him or her. Should a finder, who merely introduces the parties, be governed by a lesser ethical standard?

© Cengage Learning 2013

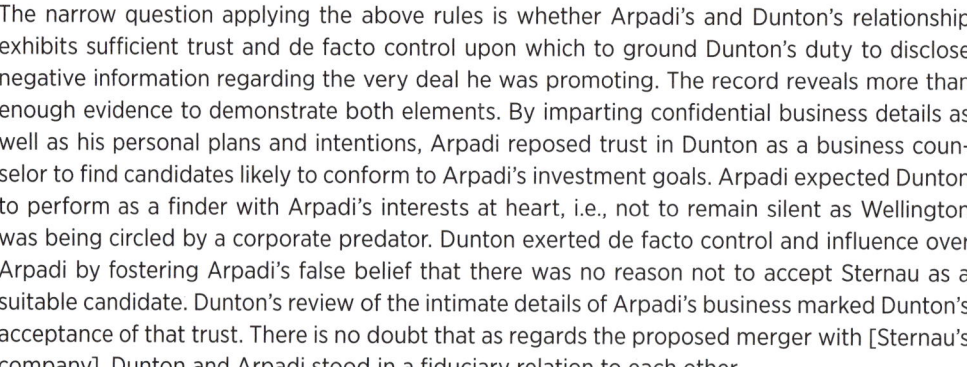

GLOBAL VIEW

"When Ethics Travel"[146]

With the rapid globalization of the marketplace, many corporations face complex ethical challenges abroad. Sometimes, actions regarded as ethically unacceptable in the United States are common practice in foreign countries. How should managers deal with such differences? Corporations take diverse approaches. One method is simply to conform to host-country customs; another is to apply home-country customs uniformly and ignore host-country customs. Both of these extreme approaches present problems. Universally conforming to host-country customs places no limits on the potential abuses that take place in developing countries. The opposite approach, however, amounts to ethical imperialism and leaves no room for legitimate local norms.

Professors Dunfee and Donaldson, of the Wharton School at the University of Pennsylvania, argued that the better option is to balance the opportunity for local identity with the acknowledgment that certain values transcend individual communities.

They called these transcendent values "hypernorms." One such hypernorm, known as the efficiency hypernorm, requires that economic agents efficiently utilize resources when their society has a stake. Another hypernorm, at least in democratic or quasi-democratic states, values citizen participation in political affairs. Both of these hypernorms relate to the controversial international business ethics issue of bribery.

Although bribery is prevalent in many countries, it is overwhelmingly regarded as ethically (and legally) wrong, even in those countries where it is widespread. Thus, for that reason alone, bribery should not be viewed as an acceptable norm, even where it is common. But bribery often also interferes with the two hypernorms described above. The efficiency hypernorm frequently proscribes bribery in business dealings because bribe recipients make decisions based on bribes rather than price and quality. Business decisions based on bribery, therefore, undermine the market mechanism. Bribery of high-level government

CONTINUED

146. This discussion is based on Thomas Donaldson & Thomas W. Dunfee, *When Ethics Travel: The Promise and Peril of Global Business Ethics*, 41 CAL. MGMT. REV. 45 (1999).

officials in democratic and quasi-democratic states violates the hypernorm that values citizen participation in political affairs. This is because such bribery undercuts accountability to the citizenry in favor of an official's personal gain.

Managers must make other, far more subtle, ethical judgments in international management. Although many legitimate cultural norms that are not proscribed by hypernorms are consistent from culture to culture, others fall into an area known as moral free space. Consider the following value matrix shown to 567 managers in twelve nations:

1. Clean, obedient, polite, responsible, and self-controlled.
2. Forgiving, helpful, loving, and cheerful.
3. Broad-minded, capable, and courageous.
4. Imaginative, independent, and intellectual.

© Cengage Learning 2013

Japanese managers assigned a significantly high priority to the first value dimension (i.e., clean, obedient, polite, responsible, and self-controlled). In contrast, Swedish and Brazilian managers assigned a significantly high priority to the third (i.e., broad-minded, capable, and courageous). Thus, managers in different countries value different characteristics. Many managers in Hong Kong, for instance, view taking credit for the work of another as more unethical than bribery or gaining competitor information.

A global manager would be well advised to understand and respect such cultural differences, rather than trample them with moral imperialism. In the end, a manager unprepared to balance moral tensions is unprepared for the international business realm where subtle, and not so subtle, cultural differences abound.

Mike Price/Shutterstock

THE RESPONSIBLE MANAGER

ENSURING ETHICAL CONDUCT

Ethical behavior is reinforced when (1) top management exemplifies the company's values and takes a leadership role in programs to promote ethics, (2) managers work to create "shared value" for both the corporation and society, (3) the company creates an atmosphere of openness and trust in which employees feel comfortable reporting violations, and (4) managers engage in activities to enhance and reward ethical behavior at every operational level of the company.

High ethical standards and business success go hand in hand. Although ethics alone may not ensure long-term success, unethical behavior often leads to illegal activity and can result in business failure. Members of top management cannot just pay lip service to this notion. Rather, they should show a dedication and commitment to ethics.

The manager should recognize the critical importance of self-esteem at both the individual and the organizational levels. In the same way that a woman cannot be a little bit pregnant, a manager cannot be a little bit unethical. Once a person starts breaking the little rules, he or she is destined to fall into bigger ethical lapses, often culminating in illegal behavior. If a manager will cheat on the little stuff, imagine what he or she will do when the stakes really matter.

Sometimes, even the best managers fail to be true to their ethical resolutions. But it is critical not to let such lapses go unnoticed. Instead, ethical managers pick themselves up from the ground and reorient their sights to the high ground. Managers who set their sights on the stars are far more likely to reach the top of the mountain than those who aim for the foothills.

Managers should strive to strike a proper balance between economic performance and ethics and look for opportunities to create shared value for the firm and society. A strong ethical culture is a prerequisite to long-term profitability, and social responsibility may be a source of competitive advantage. Managers should look at the firm honestly and objectively, then ask themselves what factors, including industry pressure or internal corporate structure, inhibit employees from being ethical.

A corporation needs a clearly written policy, such as a code of ethics. This policy must be legitimized and reinforced through formal and informal interaction with the entire management, beginning with the board of directors and the CEO. It should include procedural steps for reporting violations of the code of ethics and enforcing the code. The company should include a reference to the code of ethics in its employment agreements.

A company should institute ethics training, including setting up a forum to discuss ethical dilemmas. In deciding whether a course of action is ethically right, managers should ask whether it is fair or unfair to the firm's personnel, customers, and suppliers and to the communities where it does business. Managers should consider the direct and indirect results of a particular decision, including the impact on public image. They should ask themselves how much short-term benefit they are willing to forgo for long-term gain.

Ethics are related to laws, but they are not identical. The legal thing to do is usually the right thing to do—but

CONTINUED

managers often have to go beyond their legal obligations to act ethically.

The law acknowledges that in a business deal, misunderstandings may arise, unforeseen events may occur, expected gains may disappear, or dislikes may develop that tempt one party to act in bad faith. By requiring each party to act in good faith, the law significantly reduces the risk of a party breaking faith.[147] When reading the chapters that follow, consider whether the courts, in applying the law, are doing anything more than requiring businesspersons to do what they knew or suspected they really should have been doing all along.

147. *See* Robert S. Summers, *"Good Faith," in General Contract Law and the Sales Provisions of the Uniform Commercial Code*, 54 VA. L. REV. 195 (1968).

A MANAGER'S DILEMMA

Putting It into Practice

Quantifying the Value of Life

André Gastaux is the CEO of Euro Air, a large international airline with an excellent safety record, having had only two fatal crashes in its fifty years of operations. Unfortunately, a flight from New York to Paris with 350 passengers crashed off the coast of Canada, killing everyone on board.

Gastaux has tentatively decided to compensate all of the victims' families immediately by giving each of them a $150,000 check. Euro Air's insurers have complained that these payments would be overly generous and premature, and they have advised Euro Air not to make any payments until the claims are litigated in court, a process that could take several years. Euro Air's lawyers and its insurers have also advised Gastaux to offer the families of non-American passengers a smaller sum than he offers American families because the non-American passengers earned substantially less than the American passengers and only U.S. courts award large damages to the families of airplane crash victims. Should Gastaux delay making payments to the families of the victims? Should he offer every family the same amount of money even though he knows that the courts in many of the countries with citizens on the doomed plane would award far less if the cases were litigated? What factors should Gastaux consider in making these decisions?

INSIDE STORY

Enron Implodes

Largely due to the brilliance and foresight of its CEO Harvard MBA Jeffrey K. Skilling and wunderkind CFO Andrew S. Fastow, Enron Corporation evolved in the 1990s from a modest gas pipeline company into an energy giant and a Wall Street favorite. At its pinnacle, the corporation was the nation's seventh-largest public company by revenue, with 32,000 employees worldwide.

The firm filed for bankruptcy in 2001 after it became apparent that its executives had improperly employed a number of structured finance tools, such as special-purpose entities, and fraudulent devices to hide debt, manufacture profits, and fabricate capital.[148] Enron's employees lost not only their jobs but also more than $3 billion in Enron stock held in the company's 401(k) retirement and employee stock ownership plans.[149]

According to the felony charges filed against Richard A. Causey, the company's former chief accounting officer, the reported value of one Enron asset known as Mariner Energy was arbitrarily increased by $100 million in 2000 so that Enron could meet its projected earnings for the quarter—the same quarter in which Enron had collected, but not reported, profits from the California energy crisis. Enron reported profits from sham sales of assets to an investment partnership called LJM2, which Fastow controlled. The profits were not legitimate because Enron had agreed to bear any losses after the sales. To make matters worse, Enron had used its own stock to hedge and secure its obligations.

LJM2 also acted as a nominally independent investor in Enron's off-the-books partnerships. The law required such partnerships to obtain at least 3% of their capital from an independent investor. This requirement was intended to ensure the legitimacy of off-the-books deals. At least one set of off-the-books partnerships, called the Raptors, received the 3% from LJM2. Fastow went so far as to arrange for LJM2 to retrieve its

148. The discussion that follows is based on MCLEAN & ELKIND, *supra* note 97, and other public sources.

149. Jo Thomas, *Enron's Collapse: Fading Nest Eggs; Labor Dept. Reviews Ban on Stock Sale*, N.Y. TIMES, Jan. 24, 2002, at C6.

CONTINUED

3% (plus a substantial profit) before the Raptors engaged in any hedging. This guaranteed Enron compensation if one of its assets lost value. Thus, LJM2, the "independent" investor, did not have any true interest in the Raptors or the legitimacy of their dealings.

Because Enron had used its own stock to hedge its obligations, the scheme depended on the maintenance of Enron's high stock price to achieve its purpose. After the stock price began to fall, Enron's faults began to surface, causing the stock to drop farther, exposing more problems. The pressure to meet earnings projections and hide volatile results increased as time went on. At some point, executives at Enron began taking illegal actions to avoid exposing the corporation's frail state. Burdened by $67 billion of debt, the company collapsed.

In 2004, Fastow pleaded guilty to two counts of wire and securities fraud and was sentenced to six years in prison.[150] In 2006, former chair Kenneth L. Lay and former CEO Skilling were found guilty of fraud and conspiracy. Lay's conviction was vacated after he died of a heart attack two months before his appeal could be heard. Skilling was sentenced to twenty-four years in prison and began serving his sentence on December 13, 2006. The U.S. Supreme Court reversed his conviction for three counts of violating the "right of honest services"[151] but remanded to the appeals court the question of whether his conviction for more than twenty-five counts of substantive securities fraud, wire fraud, making false representations to Enron's auditors, and insider trading should stand.[152] Arthur Andersen, LLP, the accounting firm responsible for auditing Enron's financial statements, saw its criminal conviction for obstruction of justice overturned by the Supreme Court,[153] but not before the company had collapsed.[154]

Enron's collapse also spawned a host of civil litigation. A lawsuit filed on behalf of former Enron employees who lost their investments in Enron's retirement accounts ultimately netted $265 million.[155] Former Enron shareholders recovered $7.2 billion in settlements through a lawsuit that named former Enron executives and directors as well as Enron's investment banking partners as defendants.[156] Citigroup alone agreed to pay $1.66 billion to settle claims that it had misrepresented Enron's financial condition to secure the company's investment banking business.[157]

---

150. Fastow was originally expected to serve a ten-year sentence per his plea agreement; however, the trial judge reduced the sentence to six years.

151. 18 U.S.C. § 1346.

152. Skilling v. United States, 130 S. Ct. 2896 (2010) (Case 14.5). The Supreme Court limited section 1346 to schemes to defraud involving bribes and kickbacks.

153. Arthur Andersen, LLP v. United States, 544 U.S. 696 (2005) (jury instructions erroneously stated that Arthur Andersen could be found guilty even if the jury did not find that Andersen employees acted with knowledge and intent to commit a crime).

154. Linda Greenhouse, *Justices Reject Auditor Verdict in Enron Scandal*, N.Y. TIMES, June 1, 2005, at 1.

155. Kristen Hays, *Data Error Stalls Enron Payouts to Employees*, HOUS. CHRON., July 3, 2007, at 1.

156. Kristen Hays, *Possible $7.2 Billion Enron Settlement Emerges*, HOUS. CHRON., July 28, 2007, at 1.

157. Eric Dash, *Citigroup Resolves Claims That It Helped Enron Deceive Investors*, N.Y. TIMES, Mar, 27, 2008.

KEY WORDS AND PHRASES

apartheid 34	fiduciary duty 38	shareholder primacy 23
compensatory justice 26	Kantian theory 25	teleological theory of ethics 25
deontological theory of ethics 25	Rawlsian moral theory 25	universalizability 25
distributive justice 26	retributive justice 26	utilitarianism 25
Ethical Business Leader's Decision Tree 23	reversibility 25	

QUESTIONS AND CASE PROBLEMS

1. Christine Bancroft is a twenty-five-year-old blonde with a face and a figure that some of her male colleagues thought seemed better suited to the cover of the *Sports Illustrated* swimsuit issue than *Advertising Age*. After spending her first three months as an analyst at the privately held advertising boutique Scot Wayne More, sitting in her cubicle doing research on the Hispanic market, she looked forward to the day she would have a chance to wow clients with the finely honed marketing skills she had acquired while pursuing her MBA at Northwestern University.

Christine knew that Allen Scot and Bart Wayne had a reputation for entertaining clients from out of town at San Francisco's all-male Pacific Union Club, so she was pleasantly surprised when Allen asked her to join him and Bart for lunch with Andrew Wise at the World Trade Club. Wise was an account executive from the Cincinnati headquarters of Quinn & Inder, the second-largest consumer products firm in the United States. At first, Christine thought that she'd been invited to discuss their plans to extend Quinn & Inder's reach into the Hispanic youth market. But when she asked Bart how she might best prepare for the meeting, he smiled and said, "Just wear that little black dress you wore at the firm's holiday party and leave the talking to Allen and me. Andrew asked for California, so we're giving him California."

What should Christine do? What would you do if you were head of human resources for Scot Wayne More and overheard the conversation between Bart and Christine while waiting in Allen's office to go over an offer letter for a new hire? [Inspired in part by Joseph L. Badaracco, Jr., Defining Moments: When Managers Must Choose Between Right and Right (1997).]

2. During Hurricane Irene in 2011, many people anticipated flooding and widespread power outages. Hotel Le Bleu in Brooklyn, New York, which typically offers rooms for $250 per night, raised its prices to $999 per night during the storm, knowing that people would pay the price rather than go to a shelter. Those who planned on staying in their homes even if they lost power rushed to hardware stores to buy batteries and generators. As a hotel operator or hardware store owner, you know that you can expect a significant increase in business during times of impending natural disasters. Do you raise prices? Even if you raise prices, you expect that you will still run out of merchandise as people stockpile goods in preparation for the disaster. As a result, those who may need the merchandise the most may not be able to purchase it. Should you monitor the needs of your customers and sell to only those customers most in need? Would raising your prices serve the same purpose (i.e., at higher prices, people are more likely to buy an item only if they really need it)? Would your answer vary depending on the socioeconomic composition of your customer base? [Based on Chris MacDonald, *Post-Hurricane-Irene Business Ethics Roundup*, Canadian Bus., Aug. 29, 2011, *available at* http://www.canadianbusiness.com/blog/business_ethics/42445--post-hurricane-irene-business-ethics-roundup (last visited Aug. 29, 2011).]

3. Zandra Quartney is a manager/buyer in charge of purchasing children's shoes for a large retail store chain. She is also a die-hard football fan. This year, the Super Bowl will be played in the Superdome in New Orleans, her hometown. Quartney's favorite team, the Steelers, is expected to reach the Super Bowl.

Currently, the store chain carries four brands of children's rain boots. In an effort to streamline its product line, the CEO has decided to cut back to three brands of rain boots, leaving to Quartney the decision of which brand to cut. Assume that all four brands are equally profitable. If the makers of Brand One send Quartney a pair of Super Bowl tickets, should she accept them? Does it matter whether the maker of Brand One is also a close friend of hers?

4. Assume the same facts as in Question 3, except that Brand One underperforms the other three brands. How, if at all, should that affect Quartney's decision? What if it is mid-January and the Steelers are definitely in the Super Bowl? Quartney has waited her entire life to watch the Steelers play in the Super Bowl. Even if she would not accept the tickets before, should she accept them now? Can she get out of her dilemma by offering to pay the face value of the tickets? Should she accept the tickets if she has already decided to discontinue Brand One?

5. Ginny Portoff, a recent graduate of New York University, is a first-year associate with the McBain Consulting Group. The partner in charge of a major strategy study for an important new client in the shipping business has asked Portoff to call low-level employees in competing shipping companies to gather competitive data to be used to devise a winning strategy for the client. The partner instructed her not to identify the client but to introduce herself as a consultant doing an analysis of the shipping industry.

Assume that Portoff knows that senior managers in the competing firms would consider the data she is collecting proprietary and would not talk with her at all if they knew that she worked for a direct competitor. Is it ethical for Portoff to question the lower-level employees without revealing that she is working for a direct competitor? What should she do if after telling the partner that she considers it unethical to make the calls, the partner tells her that consultants do this all the time and that refusal to make the calls would be a career-limiting move?

6. Indra Wu, a sales rep at Rite Engineering, attended a trade show and conference at company expense. Many exhibitors donated prizes, which were awarded to attendees based on a drawing of free tickets given to all attendees upon registration. Wu won a $12,000 plasma television in one of the drawings. The winner's certificate included the winner's name with no mention of the company.

What should Wu do? What should Wu's supervisor do if she learns of the prize from someone other than Wu?

7. Social networking sites such as MySpace, Facebook, and Twitter have become increasingly popular. Most people are members of at least one social networking site. By reading an individual's page, one can see his or her pictures, the people he or she is communicating with, what is written on the page, and even what the individual writes on others' pages. Many people, however, have restricted access to their personal information by adjusting their privacy settings to better protect their privacy. The only way to see such a person's entire page is to become his or her "friend." You are a manager of an investment banking firm. Members of the managerial staff have an interest in discovering background information about potential employees and also have concerns about how employees are using their time while at work. You would like to find out more about your employees, so you, as a manager, are considering sending a "friend" or "follow" request to a subordinate employee for the sole purpose of getting access to that person's "private" page. Is this ethical? Should it be legal? Would it be ethical (or legal) to ask applicants to open their pages during a job interview? If a manager finds information

on a social networking site that may warrant disciplinary action, such as abusive comments about fellow employees or threats against the safety of the workplace, should the manager act on it in his or her managerial capacity? Is it ethical (or legal) for an employee to use a smart phone to secretly record an end-of-year performance evaluation?[Based on Marie-Andrée Weiss, *The Use of Social Media Sites Data by Business Organizations in Their Relationship with Employees*, 15(2) J. Internet L. 16 (2011).]

8. In April 2009, Andrea Teofilo left the Stanford Graduate School of Business to become the founder and CEO of gopublicnow.com, a securities brokerage firm specializing in helping young companies use the Internet to raise money from the public. Her company went public on March 2, 2011. On September 7, 2011, Teofilo personally sold one million shares of stock for $75 million. She used $10 million of the proceeds to buy a large house in Atherton, California, an easy commute to the company's Silicon Valley offices. Teofilo still owns another four million shares.

Gopublicnow.com employs thirty senior computer programmers who are paid a starting salary of $125,000 and given stock options potentially worth millions. The company also employs five janitors who empty the trash, clean the latrines, and vacuum the senior programmers' work areas. These janitors are paid approximately $15,000 a year. Due to the astronomical cost of living in Silicon Valley, several janitors with children have second jobs and rent out space in their one-bedroom apartments to make additional money to support their families. Four of the company's janitors are non-English-speaking immigrants from Mexico who are desperate for employment and, as a result, are willing to work for the low salary.

Although there is a large pool of unskilled workers willing to work as janitors for $15,000 a year, the market for skilled programmers is so tight that gopublicnow.com has had to institute special incentives to keep the programmers happy. Most recently, the senior programmer was given a Tesla sports car to celebrate the completion of an important piece of code.

What ethical and business considerations should a corporation and its CEO consider when setting the salaries for the different types of workers it employs?

CHAPTER 3

SOURCES OF LAW, COURTS, AND DISPUTE RESOLUTION

INTRODUCTION

EQUAL JUSTICE UNDER THE LAW

"Equal justice under the law," the inscription on the front of the U.S. Supreme Court building in Washington, D.C., is a reminder that the judicial system is intended to protect the legal rights of those who come before a court. In 1790, President George Washington underscored the importance of the judiciary when he told the U.S. Supreme Court: "I have always been persuaded that the stability and success of the National Government, and consequently the happiness of the American people, would depend in a considerable degree on the interpretation and execution of its laws."

Commercial litigation is big business. In addition to the parties themselves, hedge funds and other investors, such as Juridica Investments Ltd. and Burford Capital Management, have started bankrolling multimillion-dollar patent infringement, antitrust, and other types of cases.[1]

In a litigation-prone society, it is important for managers to understand the judicial system and be prepared to use it, when appropriate, to protect their rights and the rights of their companies. By the same token, managers should recognize when pursuing litigation is not in the company's best interest. Appreciating the pros and cons of the common alternatives to litigation permits managers to find the right resolution mechanism for the particular problem at hand.

CHAPTER OVERVIEW

This chapter first explains how to read a case citation and outlines the sources of law, including constitutions, statutes, regulations, and common law. It then introduces the federal and state court systems, including standing to sue and jurisdiction.

The chapter discusses factors managers should consider when selecting a dispute resolution mechanism and when deciding whether to settle. Next it outlines the litigation process and describes various alternative dispute resolution techniques, such as mediation and arbitration. The chapter concludes with a discussion of discovery, document retention and deletion policies, and attorney–client privilege.

HOW TO READ A CASE CITATION

When an appellate court decides a case, the court writes an opinion, which is usually published in one or more *reporters*—collections of court opinions. Some trial courts also publish opinions. The citation of a case (the *cite*) includes the following information:

1. The plaintiff's name.
2. The defendant's name.
3. The volume number and title of the reporter in which the case is reported.
4. The page number at which the case report begins.
5. The court that decided the case (if the court is not indicated, it is understood to be the state supreme court or the U.S. Supreme Court, depending on the reporter in which the case appears).
6. The year in which the case was decided.

When a lawsuit is originally filed, the case name appears as *plaintiff v. defendant*. If the case is appealed, the case name usually appears as *appellant* or *petitioner* (the person who is appealing the case or seeking a writ of certiorari) *v. appellee* or *respondent* (the other party). So, if the defendant loses at the trial level and appeals the decision to a higher court, the name of the defendant (now the appellant) will appear first in the case citation.

---

1. *Third-Party Investors Funding Major Commercial Lawsuits*, CORP. COUNS. WKLY. (BNA), Mar. 17, 2010, at 88.

For example, *Nafta Traders, Inc. v. Quinn*, 339 S.W.3d 84 (Tex. 2011), indicates that in 2011 the Texas Supreme Court issued an opinion in a case involving Nafta Traders as the petitioner and Quinn as the respondent. The case is reported in volume 339 of the third series of the South Western Reporter, beginning on page 84. *In re Freeway Foods of Greensboro, Inc.*, 449 B.R. 254 (Bankr. M.D.N.C. 2011), refers to the bankruptcy proceedings of Freeway Foods. The case is reported in volume 449 of the Bankruptcy Reporter, beginning on page 254.[2] The parenthetical information indicates that this is a U.S. Bankruptcy Court sitting in the Middle District of North Carolina and that the case was decided in 2011.

Some cases are reported in more than one reporter. For example, the famous New York taxicab case discussed in Chapter 19, *Walkovszky v. Carlton*, is cited as 18 N.Y.2d 414, 223 N.E.2d 6, 276 N.Y.S.2d 585 (1966). One may locate this case in volume 18 of the second series of New York Reports, in volume 223 of the second series of the North Eastern Reporter, or in volume 276 of the second series of the New York Supplement.

Opinions are also available online from Westlaw at Westlaw.com and from LexisNexis. An opinion that has not yet been published in a printed reporter receives an alphanumeric designation until it is given a published cite of the type described above. For example, *In re Bernard L. Madoff Investment Securities LLC* is available online at Westlaw.com; WL 3568936 is its temporary number until it is published in the third series of the Federal Reporter. The same case in the LexisNexis database has the cite 2011 U.S. App. LEXIS 16884 (2d Cir. Aug. 16, 2011). Once the case is in print, the citation will change from WL 3568936 or 2011 U.S. App. LEXIS 16884 to a citation with the volume and page number in "F.3d."

SOURCES OF LAW

Federal and state courts look to the U.S. and state constitutions, statutes, regulations, and common (or case) law to ascertain the applicable law.

Constitutions

Courts may be called on to interpret the U.S. or state constitutions. For example, lawsuits concerning random drug testing of employees have centered on whether this testing violates the Fourth Amendment ban on unreasonable searches and other constitutional provisions guaranteeing the right to privacy.

Statutes

Congress enacts statutes in such areas as antitrust, food and drugs, patents and copyrights, labor relations, and civil rights. For example, Title 42 of the United States Code, Section 2000(a), provides that "all persons shall be entitled to the full and equal enjoyment of the goods, services, facilities, privileges, advantages, and accommodations of any place of public accommodation . . . without discrimination or segregation on the grounds of race, color, religion or national origin." State legislatures also adopt statutes covering a broad range of topics, from requirements for a will to the formation and governance of corporations to rights of employers. For example, section 16600[3] of the California Business and Professions Code generally invalidates employee covenants not to compete except in connection with the sale of an employee's stock in a transaction involving the sale of the corporation as a going concern.

Regulations

Courts sometimes hear cases arising under federal and state regulations. *Regulations* are provisions issued by federal and state administrative agencies and executive departments to interpret and implement statutes enacted by the legislature. For example, the Securities and Exchange Commission issues regulations governing the sale of securities, and the Bureau of Citizenship and Immigration Services in the Department of Homeland Security issues regulations governing immigration and naturalization as a U.S. citizen. Federal regulations and rules are printed in the multivolume *Code of Federal Regulations (CFR)*, which is revised and updated every year. Administrative rules and regulations are discussed in Chapter 6.

Common Law

Common law is case law—the legal rules made by judges when they decide a case where no constitution, statute, or regulation exists to resolve the dispute. Common law originated in England. U.S. common law includes all of the case law of England and the American colonies before the American Revolution, as well as American case law decided since the colonial period.

Stare Decisis

Common law is developed through the doctrine of *stare decisis*, which means "to abide by decided cases." Once a court resolves a particular issue, other courts in the same jurisdiction addressing a similar legal problem will generally follow that court's decision.

A legal rule established by a court's decision may be either persuasive or authoritative. A decision is persuasive if it reasonably and fairly resolves the dispute. Another

---

2. When quoting a particular passage from an opinion, one should include the page number on which the quotation is found after the first page number of the case in the reporter. A comma should separate the two numbers.

3. CAL. BUS. & PROF. CODE § 16600.

court confronting a similar dispute will probably choose to apply the same reasoning. An authoritative decision, by contrast, is one that must be followed, regardless of its persuasive power. As the U.S. Court of Appeals for the Seventh Circuit explained:

> Whether a decision is authoritative depends on a variety of factors, of which the most important is the relationship between the court that decided it and the court to which it is cited later as a precedent. The simplest relationship is hierarchical: the decisions of a superior court in a unitary system bind the inferior courts. The most complex relationship is between a court and its own previous decisions.
>
> A court must give considerable weight to its own decisions unless and until they have been overruled or undermined by the decisions of a higher court, or other supervening developments, such as a statutory overruling. But [a court] is not absolutely bound by [its previous rulings], and must give fair consideration to any substantial argument that a litigant makes for overruling a previous decision.[4]

Every court must follow a decision of the U.S. Supreme Court, unless powerfully convinced that the Supreme Court itself would change its decision at the first possible opportunity.

Reversing U.S. Supreme Court Precedent The U.S. Supreme Court rarely overrules its previous decisions, but it does do so on occasion. In *Planned Parenthood of Southeastern Pennsylvania v. Casey*,[5] the Court articulated four primary questions to be considered when deciding whether an earlier decision should be overruled:

1. Has the prior decision's central rule proved unworkable?

2. Can the rule be changed without serious inequity to those who have relied on it, or would such a change significantly damage the stability of the society governed by the rule in question?

3. Has the law's growth in the intervening years left the prior decision's central rule a doctrinal anachronism discounted by society?

4. Have the prior decision's premises of fact so greatly changed since the decision was issued as to render its central holding somehow irrelevant or unjustifiable in dealing with the issue it addressed?

Courts apply *stare decisis* more "rigidly" in statutory cases than in constitutional cases.[6] In addition, the fact that a case involves property or contract rights giving rise to reliance interests argues against overruling precedent.[7]

Consider the Supreme Court's explanation in *Casey* of why the "separate but equal" rule for applying the Fourteenth Amendment's equal protection guarantee test, first adopted in *Plessy v. Ferguson*,[8] was appropriately overruled in *Brown v. Board of Education*,[9] the 1954 school-desegregation case:

> In *Plessy v. Ferguson* the Court held that legislatively mandated racial segregation in public transportation was no denial of equal protection and rejected the argument that racial separation enforced by the legal machinery of American society treats the black race as inferior. The *Plessy* Court considered "the underlying fallacy of the plaintiff's argument to consist in the assumption that the enforced separation of the two races stamps the colored race with a badge of inferiority. If this be so, it is not by reason of anything found in the act, but solely because the colored race chooses to put that construction upon it." Whether, as a matter of historical fact, the Justices in the *Plessy* majority believed this or not, this understanding of the implication of segregation was the stated justification for the Court's opinion. But this understanding of the facts and the rule it was stated to justify were repudiated in *Brown v. Board of Education.* . . .
>
> The Court in *Brown* addressed these facts of life by observing that whatever may have been the understanding in *Plessy's* time of the power of segregation to stigmatize those who were segregated with a "badge of inferiority," it was clear by 1954 that legally sanctioned segregation had just such an effect, to the point that racially separate public educational facilities were deemed inherently unequal. Society's understanding of the facts upon which a constitutional ruling was sought in 1954 was thus fundamentally different from the basis claimed for the decision in 1896. While we think *Plessy* was wrong the day it was decided, . . . we must also recognize that the *Plessy* Court's explanation for its decision was so clearly at odds with the facts apparent to the Court in 1954 that the decision to reexamine *Plessy* was on this ground alone not only justified but required.

In *Casey*, the Supreme Court declined the invitation by right-to-life groups to overrule its decision in *Roe v. Wade*[10] upholding the right of a woman to have an abortion before the fetus becomes viable. Subsequent decisions, especially the decision in Gonzales v. Carhart,[11] which upheld a federal statute criminalizing certain late-term abortions not necessary to save the life of the mother, have curtailed that right.

In the majority opinion in *Leegin Creative Leather Products, Inc. v. PSKS, Inc.*,[12] written by Chief Justice Roberts, the Supreme Court overruled the *per se* ban on

---

4. Colby v. J.C. Penney Co., 811 F.2d 1119, 1123 (7th Cir. 1987).

5. 505 U.S. 833 (1992).

6. Fed. Election Comm'n v. Wis. Right to Life, 551 U.S. 449 (2007).

7. Payne v. Tennessee, 501 U.S. 808 (1991).

8. 163 U.S. 537 (1896).

9. 347 U.S. 483 (1954).

10. 410 U.S. 113 (1973).

11. 550 U.S. 124 (2007).

12. 551 U.S. 877 (2007).

minimum resale price maintenance established in 1911 in *Dr. Miles Medical Co. v. John D. Park & Sons Co.*[13] and reaffirmed in 1997 in *State Oil Co. v. Khan*[14] just ten years earlier. Even though *Casey* is widely recognized as the Supreme Court's most definitive statement on *stare decisis*, Chief Justice Roberts did not even cite *Casey* when explaining why the Court was overruling almost a hundred years of precedent.[15] In a dissent joined by Justices Ginsburg, Souter, and Stevens, Justice Breyer asserted that "every stare decisis concern this Court has ever mentioned counsels against overruling" the *per se* ban on minimum prices established in *Dr. Miles Medical.*[16] Similarly, the dissenting minority in *Citizens United*[17] sharply criticized the majority for failing to follow precedent.

Splits in the Circuits   Just as one trial court does not have to follow another trial court, the court of appeals above the trial court need not follow other appellate courts. A court of appeals in one circuit does not have to follow a decision by a court of appeals in another circuit. When different courts of appeals disagree on a legal issue, there is said to be a *split in the circuits.* Thus, if the U.S. Court of Appeals for the Tenth Circuit (based in Denver) interprets a federal air pollution regulation in a certain way, the U.S. Court of Appeals for the Sixth Circuit (based in Cincinnati) may follow that interpretation, but it is not compelled to do so. The authority of the Tenth Circuit does not reach beyond its own geographic boundaries. However, a federal district court in Tulsa, which is within the Tenth Circuit, would be compelled to interpret the regulation in accordance with the decision of the Court of Appeals for the Tenth Circuit.

Restatements

Today, many rules that originated as common law have been collected into *restatements* compiled after careful study by the American Law Institute, a prestigious group of legal scholars, practicing attorneys, and judges. There are restatements of various areas of the law, such as torts, contracts, property, and trusts. The restatements are persuasive rather than authoritative. They do not compel a judge to make a particular decision unless the rule has been adopted by the state's legislature or its highest court.

---

13. 220 U.S. 373 (1911).

14. 522 U.S. 3 (1997).

15. Leegin Creative Leather Prods., Inc. v. PSKS, Inc., 551 U.S. 877 (2007). It would be easier for the Roberts Court to overturn *Roe v. Wade* using the lax standard applied in *Leegin Products* than the stricter standard articulated in *Casey.*

16. *Id.*

17. Citizens United v. Fed. Election Comm'n, 130 S. Ct. 876, 938 (2010).

THE U.S. AND STATE COURT SYSTEMS

The United States has two judicial systems: federal and state. Federal and state courts have different *subject matter jurisdiction*, meaning that they have the power to hear different kinds of cases. In general, federal courts are courts of limited subject matter jurisdiction, meaning that they can adjudicate only certain types of cases. As discussed further in Chapter 4, the jurisdiction of the federal courts arises from the U.S. Constitution and statutes enacted by Congress. By contrast, state constitutions and statutes give state courts general subject matter jurisdiction, so they can hear any type of dispute. The two coexisting judicial systems are a result of the federalism created by the U.S. Constitution, which gives certain powers to the federal government while reserving other powers to the states.

The diagram in Exhibit 3.1 shows the basic structure of the federal and state court systems. In practice, this structure is more complex than the diagram indicates. For example, an applicant may appeal an adverse decision from the U.S. Patent and Trademark Office to the Board of Patent Appeals and Interferences. The person may then appeal an unfavorable ruling from this court to the Court of Appeals for the Federal Circuit. Alternatively, the applicant may appeal the unfavorable ruling of the Board of Patent Appeals and Interferences by filing a civil action, in the U.S. District Court for the District of Columbia, against the Commissioner of the U.S. Patent and Trademark Office.

FEDERAL JURISDICTION

Federal courts derive their legal power to hear civil cases from three sources: federal question jurisdiction, diversity jurisdiction, and jurisdiction when the United States is a party. The Eleventh Amendment to the U.S. Constitution generally protects a state (or an agency thereof) from being sued without its consent in a federal court. Congress can abrogate this immunity only if it unequivocally expresses its intention to do so and acts pursuant to a constitutional grant of authority, such as Section 5 of the Fourteenth Amendment. Chapter 4 addresses this shield in more detail.

Federal Question Jurisdiction

Federal courts have nonexclusive jurisdiction over cases involving a federal question. A *federal question* exists when the dispute concerns federal law, that is, a legal right arising under the U.S. Constitution, a federal statute, federal common law, a treaty of the United States, or an administrative regulation issued by a federal government agency. Cases involving a federal question may also be brought in state court, but the defendant has the right to remove such a case to federal court if the defendant so chooses. There is no minimum monetary requirement for lawsuits involving a federal question.

EXHIBIT 3.1   Structure of the Federal and State Court Systems in the United States

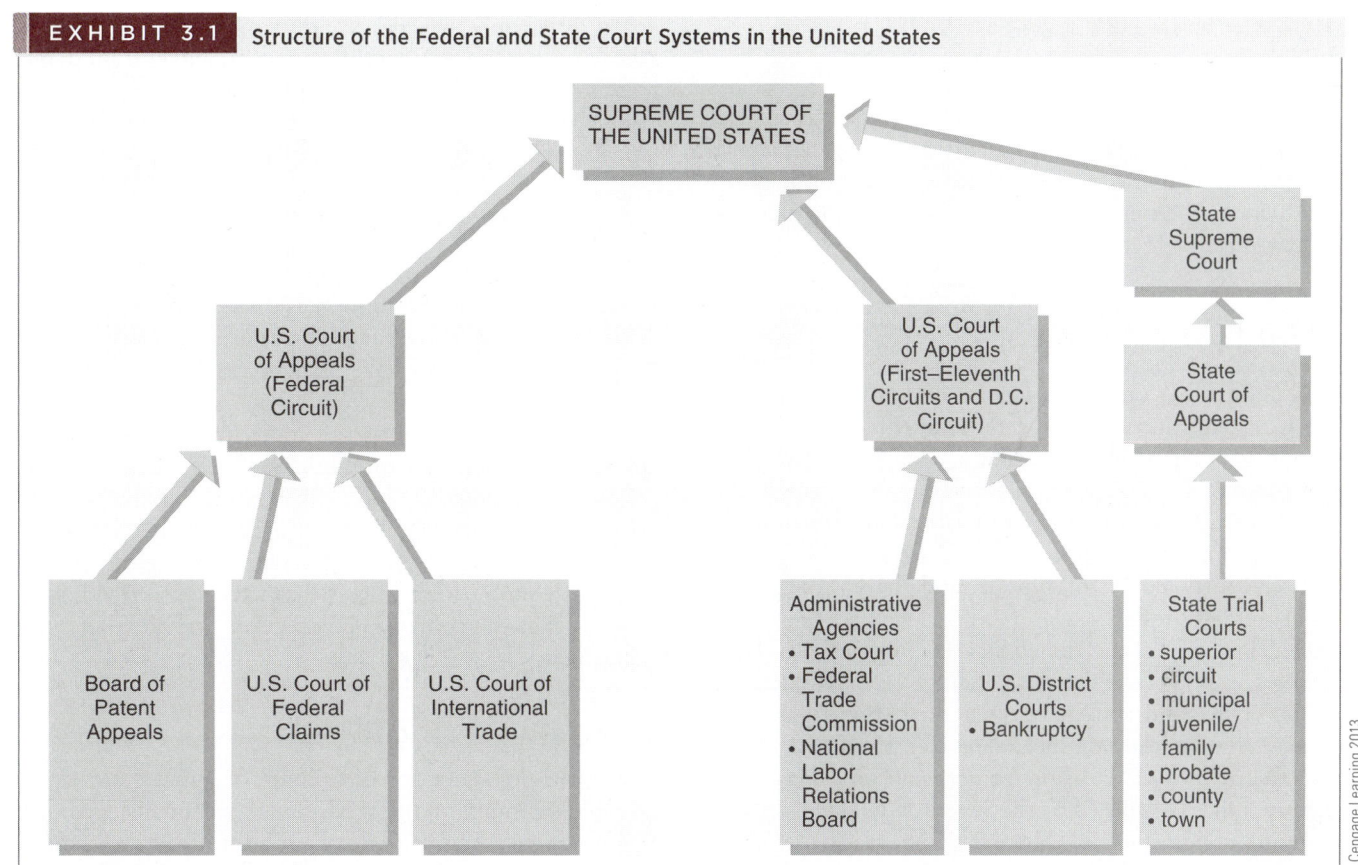

© Cengage Learning 2013

Diversity Jurisdiction

Diversity jurisdiction exists when a lawsuit is between citizens of two different states, or between a citizen of a state and a citizen of a foreign country, and the amount in controversy, exclusive of interest and all costs, exceeds $75,000. The purpose of the monetary requirement is to prevent trivial cases from overwhelming the federal judicial system. Diversity cases may also be brought in state court. The defendant may remove the case to federal court as long as the amount in controversy exceeds $75,000.

Diversity jurisdiction was traditionally justified by the fear that state courts might be biased against the out-of-state party. In federal district court, all litigants are in a neutral forum, and there should be no local prejudice for the home team.

Most diversity cases do not involve federal statutes or the U.S. Constitution and thus could also be resolved pursuant to state law in state court. In a landmark case, *Erie Railroad Co. v. Tompkins,*[18] the U.S. Supreme Court held that a federal court exercising its diversity jurisdiction must apply state law to the dispute unless the lawsuit concerns the U.S. Constitution or a federal statute. The *Erie doctrine*, as the holding of this case is known, ensures that the outcome of a diversity case in federal court will be similar to the outcome in a state court because the same state law will govern either adjudication. This prevents

litigants (the parties to a lawsuit) from *forum shopping* between federal and state courts in an attempt to have the more favorable law govern their dispute.

A federal court hearing a diversity case will apply the *conflict-of-law rules* promulgated by the state in which it is sitting to determine which state's law should govern the dispute. For example, if a New York state court would apply the law of the state where an accident occurred to a lawsuit alleging negligent operation of a motor vehicle, then a federal court sitting in New York City hearing a case involving an automobile accident in Connecticut would apply Connecticut law to determine whether the driver was negligent.

Determining Citizenship

An individual is a citizen of the state where that person has his or her legal residence or domicile. An individual may have a house in more than one state but is a citizen only of the state he or she considers home.

A corporation, in contrast, may have dual citizenship. A corporation is deemed a citizen of both (1) the state in which it has been incorporated and (2) the state where it has its principal place of business. For this purpose, the corporation's principal place of business is the state "where its officers direct, control, and coordinate the corporation's activities," the corporation's so-called nerve center.[19]

---

18. 304 U.S. 64 (1938).

19. Hertz Corp. v. Friend, 130 S. Ct. 1181 (2010).

Jurisdiction in Cases in Which the United States Is a Party

Federal courts have exclusive jurisdiction over all lawsuits in which the U.S. government, or an officer or agency thereof, is the plaintiff or the defendant. As with federal question jurisdiction, there is no minimum monetary requirement for lawsuits in which the United States is a party.

FEDERAL COURTS

The main function of the federal courts is to interpret the U.S. Constitution and the laws of the United States. Congress's first piece of legislation, "An Act to Establish the Judicial Courts of the United States," created the federal district courts. Two years later, Congress created the federal courts of appeals. The three-tiered system of district courts, courts of appeals, and the U.S. Supreme Court remains today.

The President of the United States nominates each judge who serves on a federal court. The U.S. Senate, pursuant to its "advice and consent" power, then votes to approve or reject the judicial nominees. The Constitution does not impose any age or citizenship requirements on judicial candidates. Once confirmed by the Senate, federal judges have a lifetime appointment to the bench. They may be removed

from office only by legislative impeachment if they violate the law. Lifetime tenure protects federal judges from public reprisal for making unpopular or difficult decisions. As a result, the federal judiciary is more independent than either the executive or the legislative branch.

U.S. District Courts

The U.S. district courts are the trial courts of the federal system. Currently, the country is divided into ninety-four judicial districts. Each state has at least one district; the more populous states have as many as four. Exhibit 3.2 shows the various districts.

Many districts have two or more divisions. For example, the main location for the U.S. District Court for the Southern District of Florida is Miami, but that district also has courts in Key West, Fort Lauderdale, West Palm Beach, and Fort Pierce. Thus, a plaintiff may file its lawsuit with the nearest federal district court, provided, of course, that the court has jurisdiction over the particular controversy.

U.S. Courts of Appeals

The primary functions of a court of appeals are (1) to review decisions of the trial courts within its territory; (2) to review decisions of certain administrative agencies

EXHIBIT 3.2   Map of Federal Judicial Districts and Circuits

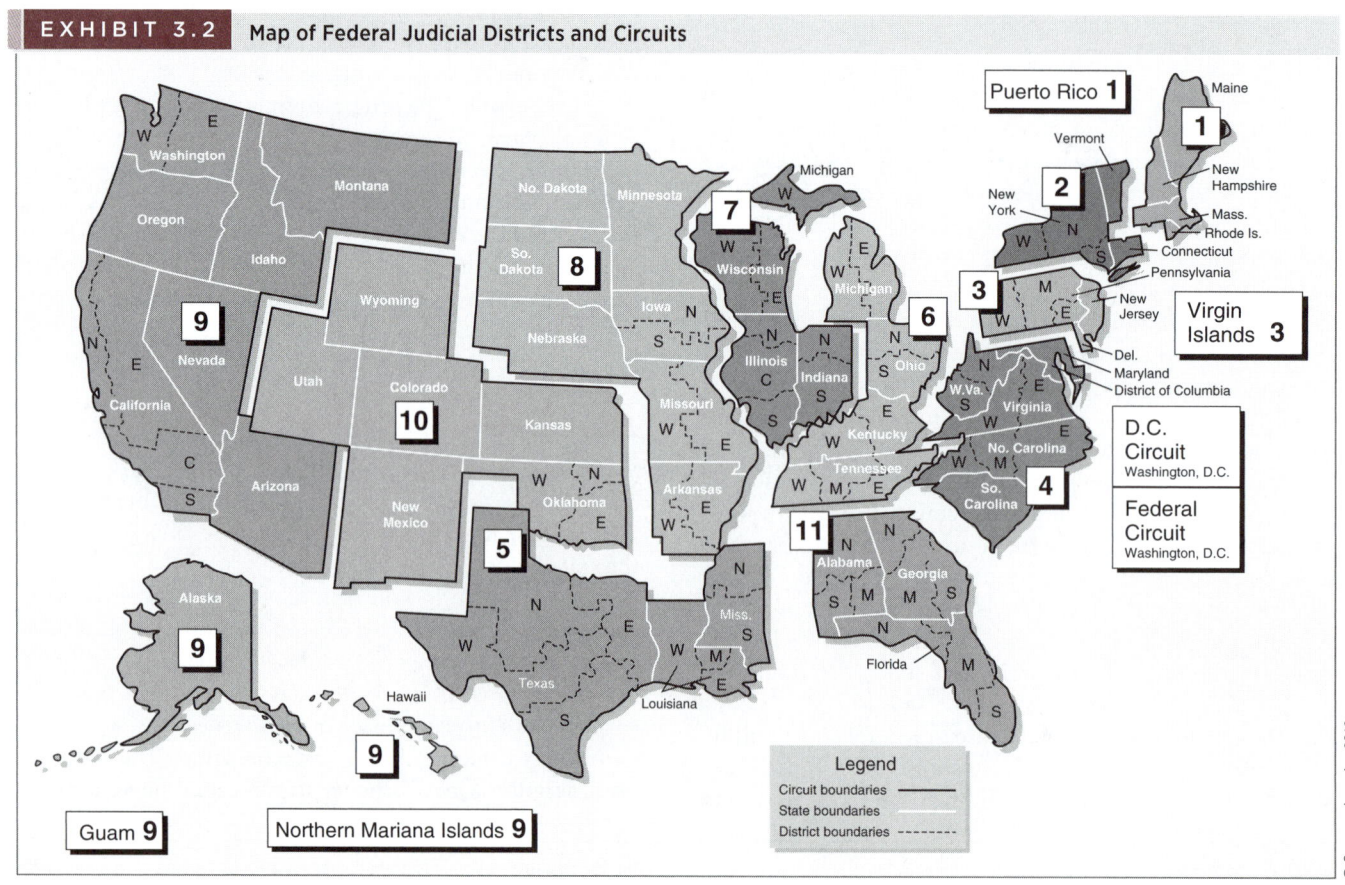

© Cengage Learning 2013

and commissions; and (3) to issue *writs*, or orders, to lower courts or to litigants. Only final decisions of lower courts are appealable. A decision is final if it conclusively resolves a discrete issue in a dispute or the entire controversy. The court of appeals can affirm or reverse the decision of the lower court. It may also *vacate*, or nullify, the previous court's ruling and *remand* the case—send it back to the lower court for reconsideration in light of the appellate court's opinion.

Cases before the courts of appeals are usually presented to a panel of three judges. Occasionally, all the judges of a court of appeals will sit together to hear and decide a particularly important or close case. This is called an *en banc* (or *in banc*) *hearing*. Frequently, the panel of judges will decide an appeal based on the legal briefs, or written memoranda, submitted to the court, rather than hearing oral arguments presented by the lawyers.

There are thirteen courts of appeals, one for each of the twelve regional circuits in the United States and one for the Federal Circuit. The Ninth Circuit, encompassing nine states and Guam, is the largest circuit, with twenty-six active judges and three vacancies. The Court of Appeals for the First Circuit has only six active judges. Exhibit 3.3 lists the states and territories included within each circuit.

The Court of Appeals for the Federal Circuit, created in 1982, does not have jurisdiction over a specific geographic region but rather hears appeals from various specialized federal courts, including the Court of Federal Claims, the Court of International Trade, and the International Trade Commission, which handles disputes involving unfair practices in import trade. The Federal Circuit also hears all cases involving patents.

Specialized Federal Courts

The federal system has several specialized courts that resolve legal disputes within particular subject areas.

The bankruptcy courts are units of the federal district courts that hear proceedings involving the bankruptcy laws and regulations of the United States. When General Motors (automotive manufacturer), United Airlines, and Lehman Brothers (investment bank) filed for protection from their creditors under Chapter 11 of the bankruptcy laws, they did so in federal bankruptcy court. (The law of bankruptcy is discussed in Chapter 23.)

The tax courts hear taxpayer petitions or appeals regarding federal income, estate, and gift taxes. The Court of International Trade has jurisdiction over disputes involving tariffs, or import taxes, and trade laws. This court also hears cases on appeal from the U.S. International Trade Commission. The U.S. Court of Appeals for the Armed Forces hears cases from the lower courts and tribunals within the armed services. Military veterans and their families may petition the U.S. Court of Appeals for Veterans Claims to review administrative decisions regarding their entitlement to veterans' benefits.

U.S. Supreme Court

The U.S. Supreme Court comprises one chief justice and eight associate justices. At least six justices must be present to hear a case. A majority of the cases heard by the Supreme Court are on appeal from the U.S. courts of appeals. A decision by a state supreme court is also appealable to the U.S. Supreme Court, but only when the case concerns the U.S. Constitution or some other federal law. The Supreme Court may also hear direct appeals from a federal district court decision declaring an act of the U.S. Congress unconstitutional.

The Supreme Court has *discretionary review*, meaning that it decides which cases within its jurisdiction it will adjudicate. When it agrees to hear a case, the Supreme Court issues a *writ of certiorari*, ordering the lower court

EXHIBIT 3.3	Geographic Regions of the U.S. Courts of Appeals
Circuit	**Region**
District of Columbia	District of Columbia
First	Maine, Massachusetts, New Hampshire, Puerto Rico, and Rhode Island
Second	Connecticut, New York, and Vermont
Third	Delaware, New Jersey, Pennsylvania, and Virgin Islands
Fourth	Maryland, North Carolina, South Carolina, Virginia, and West Virginia
Fifth	Canal Zone, Louisiana, Mississippi, and Texas
Sixth	Kentucky, Michigan, Ohio, and Tennessee
Seventh	Illinois, Indiana, and Wisconsin
Eighth	Arkansas, Iowa, Minnesota, Missouri, Nebraska, North Dakota, and South Dakota
Ninth	Alaska, Arizona, California, Guam, Hawaii, Idaho, Montana, Nevada, Oregon, and Washington
Tenth	Colorado, Kansas, New Mexico, Oklahoma, Utah, and Wyoming
Eleventh	Alabama, Florida, and Georgia
Federal	Based in Washington, D.C., but hears cases dealing with patents and certain other matters from all regions

to certify the record of proceedings below and send it up to the Supreme Court. Four justices must vote to hear a case before a writ can be issued. If a writ was sought but denied by the Supreme Court, the citation for the case will indicate *"cert. denied."*

The Supreme Court will not decide cases that involve a political question. A *political question* is a dispute that is more appropriately decided by democratically elected officials in the executive or the legislative branch of government. Nonetheless, the Court effectively determined the outcome of the 2000 U.S. presidential election in *Bush v. Gore*[20] when it prohibited Florida from doing a manual recount of the ballots.

STATE COURTS

State courts handle the bulk of litigated disputes in the United States. Each state's constitution creates the judicial branch of government for that state. For example, the Constitution of Texas provides:

> [T]he judicial power of this State shall be vested in one Supreme Court, in one Court of Criminal Appeals, in Courts of Appeals, in District Courts, in County Courts, in Commissioners Courts, in Courts of Justices of the Peace, and in such other courts as may be provided by law.[21]

The state constitution then provides the details of the state judicial system. These include the number of justices sitting on the state's supreme court, the jurisdiction of the state courts, the geographic districts of the various appellate courts, the way in which justices and judges are selected or appointed, and the tenure of justices and judges.

State Trial Courts

At the lowest level of the state trial court system are several courts of limited jurisdiction. These courts decide minor criminal matters, small civil suits, and other specialized legal disputes. Examples include traffic courts, small claims courts, juvenile courts, and family courts. In these courts, the procedures are often informal. Parties may appear without lawyers, the court may not keep a complete transcript or recording of the proceedings, and the technical rules of evidence and formal courtroom procedures may not apply. The jurisdiction of a small claims court is usually limited to disputes involving less than, for example, $5,000. Any dispute involving more than this amount must be heard by a higher-level trial court.

The second level of state trial courts consists of courts of general or unlimited jurisdiction. These courts have formal courtroom procedures, apply the standard rules of evidence, and record all proceedings.

In 2002, the State of Michigan created the first "cybercourt" to hear business-related litigation. Circuit court judges preside over the court, which uses videoconferencing, digital record keeping, and other online tools. All filings and briefs are filed online. The court's goal is to expedite business litigation involving more than $25,000 and significantly lower its cost.

State Appellate Courts

A state appellate court is similar to its counterpart in the federal system. It usually consists of a panel of three judges who review lower court rulings for errors in the application of the law or the procedures followed. An appellate court may affirm, reverse, or vacate and remand any final decision of a lower court. The appellate court usually accepts the trial judge's or jury's findings of fact, unless a particular finding is clearly unsupported by the evidence presented at trial. The appellate court is not required to accept the lower court's conclusions of law, however; it may consider legal issues *de novo*, or anew, as if the trial court had not resolved any questions of law.

State Supreme Court

Each state has one court that acts as the highest judicial authority in that state. Most states call that court the supreme court. (In New York, the highest state court is called the New York Court of Appeals; the intermediate appellate court is called the Supreme Court, Appellate Division; and the state trial courts are called Supreme Courts.) The number of justices on a state supreme court varies from three to nine.

A state supreme court usually has discretionary jurisdiction over all decisions of a court of appeals. A state supreme court may also have jurisdiction over cases where a statute of the state or the United States has been ruled unconstitutional in whole or in part. In addition, the state supreme court will decide all appeals in criminal cases in which a sentence of death has been imposed.

STANDING

Courts will not hear a case unless it involves a real and substantial controversy and resolving the lawsuit will provide actual relief to one party.[22] Further, the party pursuing the litigation must have standing to sue. *Standing* means that the party seeking relief (1) is the proper party to advance the litigation, (2) has a personal interest in the outcome of the suit, and (3) will benefit from a favorable

---

20. 531 U.S. 98 (2000).
21. Tex. Const. art. V, § 1.

22. United States v. Hays, 515 U.S. 737 (1995).

INTERNATIONAL SNAPSHOT

In 2002, the European Union (EU) adopted the Brussels Conventions to standardize the rules for determining where suits involving e-commerce may be brought. A person may bring suit (1) in the EU state where he or she is domiciled; (2) in the EU state where the defendant is domiciled; (3) in the place of performance when the case involves a contract dispute; or (4) in the place the harmful act occurred in the event of a tortious (that is, wrongful) act. The Brussels Conventions are designed to ensure that courts in the EU use the same jurisdiction standards for e-commerce as for commerce not involving the Internet.

ruling.[23] A party challenging an administrative agency's interpretation of a statute must be arguably "within the zone of interests" to be regulated or protected under the statute in question.[24]

PERSONAL JURISDICTION

For a court to hear a case, the court must have personal jurisdiction over the defendant. *Personal jurisdiction* means that the court has legal authority over the parties to the lawsuit. Personal jurisdiction may be based on the residence or activities of the person being sued (called *in personam jurisdiction*) or on the location of the property at issue in the lawsuit (called *in rem jurisdiction*). For example, if an individual does any business in a state, then he or she is properly within the jurisdiction of that state's courts. Owning property in a state, causing a personal injury or property damage within the state, or even paying alimony or child support to someone living within the state might justify the exercise of personal jurisdiction by that state's courts.[25]

Most states have *long-arm statutes*, which can subject an out-of-state defendant to jurisdiction in the state, as long as constitutional due process requirements are satisfied. The Due Process Clause exists, in part, to give "a degree of predictability to the legal system that allows potential defendants to structure their primary conduct with some minimum assurance as to where that conduct will and will not render them liable to suit."[26] The critical test is whether the defendant has certain *minimum contacts* with the state "such that the maintenance of the suit does not offend 'traditional notions of fair play and substantial justice.'"[27]

The courts generally require that the nonresident defendant (1) have done some act or consummated some transaction in the jurisdiction in which it is being sued or (2) have purposefully availed itself of the privilege of conducting activities in that state, thereby invoking the benefits and protections of the forum. Courts have held that negotiating business contracts by means of telephone calls, the mail, or even a fax machine is sufficient to give a court personal jurisdiction over an individual or corporation. Personal jurisdiction may also be proper over a nonresident defendant who committed an intentional tort outside the forum when the tortious conduct was aimed at the forum and the brunt of the harm was felt by the plaintiff in the forum.[28]

Service of process, which notifies the defendant of the filing of a lawsuit, has traditionally been accomplished either by mail or by personally handing a prospective defendant a copy of the complaint. If a party is physically present in the forum, personal service will always be considered proper regardless of the party's contact with the forum. The Supreme Court has gone as far as to allow someone merely vacationing in a state to be served and then forced to answer to charges in that state.[29] Service via alternative means, such as fax or e-mail, may also be acceptable if the plaintiff obtains prior approval from the court.[30]

Personal Jurisdiction and the Internet

The global reach of the Internet has raised complicated issues about the permissible scope of personal jurisdiction based on use of the Internet. In general, "the likelihood that personal jurisdiction can be constitutionally exercised is directly proportionate to the nature and quality of commercial activity that an entity conducts

---

23. Stated more technically by the U.S. Supreme Court, to establish standing, "First, the plaintiff must have suffered an 'injury in fact'—an invasion of a legally protected interest which is (a) concrete and particularized and (b) 'actual or imminent, not conjectural' or 'hypothetical.' Second, there must be a causal connection between the injury and the conduct complained of—the injury has to be 'fairly . . . trace[able] to the challenged action of the defendant, and not . . . the result [of] the independent action of some third party not before the court.' Third, it must be 'likely,' as opposed to merely 'speculative,' that the injury will be 'redressed by a favorable decision.'" Lujan v. Defenders of Wildlife, 504 U.S. 555, 560–61 (1992).

24. Nat'l Credit Union Admin. v. First Nat'l Bank & Trust Co., 522 U.S. 479 (1998) (commercial banks had standing to challenge the National Credit Union Administration's determination that the Federal Credit Union Act permitted federal credit unions comprising unrelated employer groups). Congress responded to this litigation by passing legislation that expressly adopted the NCUA's interpretation.

25. The Anticybersquatting Consumer Protection Act gave trademark owners the ability to bring an *in rem* suit to invalidate an Internet domain name registration by a cybersquatter, a person who wrongfully registers a domain name to extract money from the trademark owner. 15 U.S.C. § 1125(d) (2006). *In rem* jurisdiction is available only in situations where the plaintiff has "disproved" the existence of personal jurisdiction. Heathmount A.E. v. Technodome.com, 106 F. Supp. 2d 860 (E.D. Va. 2000). Cybersquatting is discussed further in Chapter 11.

26. World-Wide Volkswagen Corp. v. Woodson, 444 U.S. 286, 297 (1980).

27. Int'l Shoe Co. v. Washington, 326 U.S. 310, 316 (1945) (quoting Milliken v. Meyer, 311 U.S. 457, 463 (1940)).

28. Price v. Socialist People's Libyan Arab Jamahiriya, 294 F.3d 82 (D.C. Cir. 2002).

29. Burnham v. Superior Court of Cal., 495 U.S. 604 (1990).

30. *See* Brockmeyer v. May, 383 F.3d 798, 805–806 (9th Cir. 2004).

over the Internet."[31] The U.S. District Court for the Western District of Pennsylvania adopted a sliding scale, stating:

> At one end of the spectrum are situations where a defendant clearly does business over the Internet. If the defendant enters into contracts with residents of a foreign jurisdiction that involved the knowing and repeated transmission of computer files over the Internet, personal jurisdiction is proper. At the opposite end are situations where a defendant has simply posted information on an Internet Web site that is accessible to users in foreign jurisdictions. A passive Web site that does little more than make information available to those who are interested in it is not grounds for the exercise of personal jurisdiction. The middle ground is occupied by interactive Web sites where a user can exchange information with the host computer. In these cases, the exercise of jurisdiction is determined by examining the level of interactivity and commercial nature of the exchange of information that occurs on the Web site.[32]

On one end of that spectrum lies *Pavlovich v. Superior Court*,[33] the first case involving jurisdiction based on Internet postings to reach the California Supreme Court. In this case, Pavlovich, a Texas resident, was sued in California for posting on the Internet decryption codes that could be used to decode and copy DVDs. The plaintiff, DVD Copy Control Association, Inc., claimed that Pavlovich, the president of Media Driver, LLC, facilitated the illegal copying of DVDs and thereby reduced sales of authorized DVDs by motion picture companies based in California. The California Supreme Court ruled that posting the codes merely provided information that was accessible to users in foreign jurisdictions. It did not subject the defendants to personal jurisdiction in California because the website did not, in itself, have any particular contact with California.[34]

At the other end of the spectrum lies *Aitken v. Communications Workers of America*.[35] Two agents of the Communications Workers of America labor union, posing as Verizon managers, sent spam e-mails to Verizon employees touting the benefits of union membership and disparaging Verizon's employment practices. Verizon and the managers whose identities had been stolen asserted a variety of claims in a Virginia federal court, including violations of federal and state anti-spam laws, defamation, invasion of privacy, and conspiracy. The district court ruled that the agents' spamming activities subjected them to personal jurisdiction in Virginia because they had

"intentionally [sent] scores of emails to '@verizonbusiness.com' email addresses, the servers for which are located in Virginia, and transmitt[ed] the emails to the targeted Verizon employees, including some employees located in Virginia."[36]

CHOICE OF FORUM, WAIVER OF RIGHT TO TRIAL BY JURY, AND CHOICE OF LAW

Parties to a contract may specify in advance where any disputes will be litigated. This is done by including a *choice-of-forum clause*. A contract may also include a waiver of the right to a jury trial or, as discussed more fully later in this chapter, provide that disputes will be decided by a method other than litigation, such as arbitration. The parties may also agree in advance which law will govern any future dispute. This section is often entitled "Governing Law" or "Choice of Law." A court will usually uphold the contracting parties' choice of forum and law.

Choice of Forum

Courts in the United States will honor clauses in a valid contract requiring disputes to be resolved in another forum under its laws unless (1) the clause was fraudulently included in the contract, (2) enforcement would deprive a party "of his day in court," or (3) enforcement would contravene a strong public policy of the forum in which suit is brought.[37] Parties should take care in how they word such provisions, however. Even when a clause appears at first blush to require all disputes to be litigated in a particular forum, a court may read the clause narrowly and apply it to only those disputes clearly specified in the clause.

For example, a U.S. citizen filed suit in New York against the English companies involved in recording and producing his albums.[38] The parties' agreement stipulated that any dispute "that may arise out of the [contract]" would be resolved by English law in an English court. The Second Circuit ruled that the artist could not bring his breach-of-contract claim for unpaid royalties in a U.S. court because the contract clearly laid out the defendant's payment obligations.

The court also ruled, however, that the artist could assert his causes of action for federal copyright infringement, as well as unfair competition and unjust enrichment under state law, in a U.S. court because they did not "arise out of" the contract. The court reasoned that the term "arise out of" did not encompass all claims that "have some possible relationship with the contract, including claims that may only 'relate to,' be 'associated with,'

---

31. Zippo Mfg. Co. v. Zippo Dot Com, 952 F. Supp. 1119, 1124 (W.D. Pa. 1997).

32. *Id.* at 1124.

33. 58 P.3d 2 (Cal. 2002).

34. *Id.*

35. 496 F. Supp. 2d 653 (E.D. Va. 2007).

36. *Id.* at 659.

37. The Bremen v. Zapata Off Shore Co., 407 U.S. 1 (1972).

38. Phillips v. Audio Active, Ltd., 494 F.3d 378 (2d Cir. 2007).

or 'arise in connection with' the contract." To be covered by the choice-of-forum clause, the claim had to originate from the recording contract. Because the plaintiff's ownership of the music was based on authorship, not on the contract, the clause did not apply to those claims. As a result, the U.S. courts were free to assert jurisdiction over the copyright infringement, unfair competition, and unjust enrichment claims.

Doctrine of Forum Non Conveniens

If there is no applicable choice-of-forum clause and the plaintiff has sued in a place that is inconvenient for the defendant, then the defendant may file a motion for a change of *venue*, that is, location, under the doctrine of *forum non conveniens*.[39] Although a federal district court in one state may transfer the case to a federal district court in another state, a state court can only transfer the case to another location within that state. The following case identifies the factors courts take into account when deciding whether to grant a motion for change of venue.

---

39. Abbott Labs. v. Takeda Pharm. Co., 476 F.3d 421, 426 (7th Cir. 2007) (holding that a forum selection clause is a "substitute" for the doctrine of *forum non conveniens*, not another name for it).

A CASE IN POINT	*Summary*	Case 3.1

Radeljak v. Daimler-Chrysler Corp.

Supreme Court of Michigan
719 N.W.2d 40 (Mich. 2006).

FACTS An automobile accident in Croatia involving a Jeep Grand Cherokee manufactured by DaimlerChrysler resulted in the death of one passenger and injuries to the driver and other passengers. The families of the victims, all Croatian residents and citizens, sued in Wayne County, Michigan, where DaimlerChrysler had automotive plants. They alleged that the transmission of the Jeep Grand Cherokee had slipped from park into reverse, causing the vehicle to roll into a ravine.

The trial court in Michigan granted DaimlerChrysler's motion to dismiss on the basis of *forum non conveniens*. The court concluded that Croatia would be a more convenient forum because the accident occurred in Croatia, the victims were Croatian, Croatian law would most likely apply, and the transmission—the allegedly defective product—had been designed and manufactured outside the United States. On appeal, the Michigan appellate court held that the lower court had abused its discretion because Wayne County was not a "seriously inconvenient" forum. DaimlerChrysler appealed.

ISSUE PRESENTED May a Michigan court dismiss a case under the *forum non conveniens* doctrine in favor of another more appropriate forum even though litigation in Michigan would not be "seriously inconvenient" for the defendant?

SUMMARY OF OPINION The Michigan Supreme Court acknowledged that trial court judges are generally within the bounds of their discretionary powers in applying the *forum non conveniens* doctrine. The court explained, however, that the dispositive issue in deciding whether to apply the doctrine is not the residency of either party, but the determination of which forum best serves the convenience of the parties and the interests of justice. The Michigan Supreme Court ruled that there was no requirement that a forum be "seriously inconvenient" for a *forum non conveniens* dismissal.

The court then reviewed the factors the trial court had used in analyzing the motion to dismiss based on *forum non conveniens* to determine whether it had abused its discretion in granting the defendant's motion. Four of the seven private factors considered by the trial court favored neither forum over the other, but three favored Croatia: (1) "ease of access to sources of proof," because it would be easier for the plaintiffs in Croatia to obtain documents related to the choice of transmissions from Michigan than it would be for the defendant in Michigan to obtain documents from Croatia related to the accident; (2) "other practical problems which contribute to the ease, expense, and expedition of the trial," because a Michigan trial would not allow the defendant to include third-party Croatians who could be responsible for the plaintiffs' injuries; and (3) "possibility of viewing the premises," because it would be almost impossible for a Michigan jury to visit the crash site. The three public factors considered by the trial court also weighed in favor of trying the case in Croatia: (1) the goal of avoiding court congestion, (2) the fact that many of the people concerned about the proceeding lived in Croatia, and (3) the burden of jury duty on a community with little relationship to the incident.

CONTINUED

RESULT The Michigan Supreme Court ruled that the trial court had not abused its discretion when it granted the defendant's motion to dismiss. The plaintiffs could not force DaimlerChrysler to defend the case in Michigan even though the automobile manufacturer had extensive operations there.

COMMENTS In her dissent, Justice Kelly argued that the plaintiffs' choice of forum should be given deference unless the balance of *forum non conveniens* factors strongly favored the defendant. Because the plaintiffs in this case had not filed suit in Michigan merely to "vex," "harass," or "oppress" the defendant, she argued, their choice of forum should have been respected.

Waiver of Right to Jury Trial

As discussed more fully in Chapter 4, the U.S. and state constitutions guarantee the right to trial by jury in all criminal cases and most civil cases. Increasingly, though, employers, residential lessors, banks, lenders, and other firms are requiring employees and customers to agree in advance to waive their right to a jury trial.[40] The dispute is still litigated, but it is decided by a judge, not a jury. Studies suggest that judges find in favor of employees in roughly the same proportion of cases as juries, but judges tend to award substantially lower damages than juries. Although courts in New York, Massachusetts, and Florida have generally upheld these prelitigation waivers, courts in California and Georgia have refused to enforce them.

Choice of Law

Even if a court sitting in a particular jurisdiction agrees to hear a case, it still may not apply the law of that state to the dispute. The question of which jurisdiction's law to apply comes up not only in the context of diversity cases heard in federal court but also in state court actions involving the citizens of more than one state. This question is governed by a complicated set of conflict-of-laws rules. In general, the jurisdiction that has the greatest governmental interest in the dispute will provide the governing law. Put another way, the selection of the governing law is guided by a grouping of contacts: the state with the strongest contacts with the litigants and the subject matter of the litigation has the greatest interest in the application of its law.[41]

Sometimes a state will use formalistic rules, however. For example, some states look only to where a contract was entered into to decide which state's contract law

should govern a dispute. For example, because Pennzoil and Getty Oil Company entered into their acquisition agreement in New York, the trial court in Texas applied New York's contract law to determine whether the preliminary negotiations had ripened into a binding contract.[42]

LAWS FAVORING SETTLEMENT OR ALTERNATIVE DISPUTE RESOLUTION OVER LITIGATION

Like other business decisions, choosing a dispute resolution mechanism involves many trade-offs. Litigation is expensive and takes a toll on management and employees. In addition to generating legal fees, lawsuits distract management from the company's business, risk damaging the firm's public image, and jeopardize relationships with the opposing party. Instead of automatically taking legal conflicts to the courthouse, more firms than ever are using *alternative dispute resolution (ADR)* techniques, such as negotiation, mediation, arbitration, med-arb, arb-med, minitrials, and summary jury trials, to resolve disputes. They are discussed in detail later in this chapter. The use of ADR techniques in international disputes is discussed in Chapter 24.

The government promotes settlement and other alternatives to litigation in a variety of ways, including requiring courts to refer appropriate cases to ADR programs,[43] mandating pretrial settlement conferences, penalizing plaintiffs who reject favorable settlement offers, limiting the ability of a party to introduce willingness to negotiate as evidence of fault, providing liberal discovery, and generally enforcing agreements to arbitrate. In addition, federal legislation requires federal agencies to use ADR to resolve administrative cases.[44] The states have also supported efforts to use ADR rather than the courts to resolve disputes.

40. Jane Spencer, *Waiving Your Right to a Jury Trial*, WALL ST. J., Aug. 17, 2003, at D1.

41. When more than one state or country has an interest in the outcome of a case, the court is permitted to apply the laws of different places to different issues, under the doctrine of *depeçage. See, e.g.,* Berg Chilling Sys., Inc. v. Hull Corp. 435 F.3d 455 (3d Cir. 2006) (court applied Pennsylvania law to determine whether the purchase of a Pennsylvania corporation had successor liability for defective products sold by the acquired firm and New Jersey law to determine whether the purchaser's disclaimer of successor liability in the purchase contract violated New Jersey public policy).

42. This case is the subject of the "Inside Story" in Chapter 7.

43. *See, e.g.,* Alternative Dispute Resolution Act of 1998, 28 U.S.C. § 652.

44. For example, the Administrative Dispute Resolution Act of 1996 requires federal agencies to look at their mission to see where ADR might be effective. 5 U.S.C. §§ 571–585.

These efforts appear to be working. Although Americans are filing cases in court at a record pace, partly due to the growing U.S. population, the percentage of cases that actually go to trial before a jury or the bench (in a *bench trial*, a judge, not a jury, decides all issues) has steadily decreased over the last thirty years.

In a classic example of the active role judges can play in promoting settlement, the judge assigned to ten of the breach-of-contract suits brought in 1975 by twenty-seven utility companies against Westinghouse Corporation forced the chief executives concerned to meet in his office to try to settle the case. Westinghouse, then the thirty-sixth largest corporation in the United States, with a net worth of roughly $2.3 billion, had breached its contracts to deliver about 70 million pounds of uranium after the price of uranium had more than doubled. The plaintiffs sought damages of up to $2.6 billion. If the court had forced Westinghouse to pay damages, Westinghouse would have been crippled financially and might not have been able to complete the construction of certain nuclear power plants that it was building for the same utility companies. The judge concluded that a business solution to the lawsuits, rather than a strictly legal one, was needed:

> I am tired of pussyfooting and, more than that, I am tired of talking to lawyers when other, more powerful men, who have the ultimate power of decision, have not been here. . . . Any decision I hand down will hurt someone and, because of the potential damage, I want to make it clear that it will happen only because certain captains of industry could not together work out their problems so that the hurt might have been held to a minimum.[45]

Inventive and mutually beneficial settlements were reached in many of the cases.[46]

TORTIOUS DISPUTE RESOLUTION

Although the law supports settlements and alternative dispute resolution, managers are not immune from the law simply because they pursue alternative mechanisms to resolve their disputes. The applicability of tort and criminal law is a good example.

As discussed in Chapter 9, a *tort* is a civil wrong causing injury to a person, his or her property, or certain economic relationships. A party who intentionally misleads another by making a material misrepresentation of fact on which the plaintiff reasonably relied to his or her detriment may be liable for fraudulent misrepresentation. Although mere "puffing"—general statements that exaggerate a party's negotiation goals or downplay its willingness to settle—is generally permissible, affirmative misstatements are not. Thus, if the board of directors of a defendant company has authorized the settlement of a case for $100,000, corporate counsel may say that the company does not want to settle for more than $100,000, but counsel may not state that the board has formally disapproved any settlement for an amount greater than $100,000.[47] Material misrepresentations not only may result in the obligation to pay damages for the harm caused by the misrepresentation but may also invalidate any agreement to settle the dispute.

Furthermore, an overly aggressive attempt to "resolve" a dispute by force or threats—"making an offer he can't refuse," as Don Corleone put it in *The Godfather*—may constitute criminal extortion or assault and expose the manager to liability for damages for civil assault, intentional infliction of emotional distress, defamation, invasion of privacy, disparagement, injurious falsehood, interference with contractual obligations, or interference with prospective business advantage. Attempting to settle a conflict outside of court does not exempt managers from the law.

CLASS ACTIONS

If the conduct of the defendant affected numerous persons in a common way, the case may be brought as a *class action* by a representative of the class of persons affected. This was done in the silicone-breast-implant cases involving Dow Corning and others, as well as the smoking cases brought against the tobacco companies. Class actions are the norm in actions alleging securities fraud. The Class Action Fairness Act[48] permits defendants to remove certain civil class actions to federal court.

Written notice of the formation of the class must be mailed to all potential class members. Until recently, it was difficult to do this effectively. Now the Internet and websites, such as Findlaw.com and numerous small sites, have made finding and joining these suits much easier.[49]

Anyone who wants to litigate separately can opt out of the class. If a person does not opt out, he or she is a member of the class and will be bound by any decision or settlement reached in the class action. The court hearing the case must certify the class and approve any settlement.

In the following case, the U.S. Supreme Court considered whether more than a million female Wal-Mart employees could sue as a class for employment discrimination under Title VII of the Civil Rights Act of 1964.

---

45. William Eagan, *The Westinghouse Uranium Contracts: Commercial Impracticality and Related Matters*, 18 Am. Bus. L.J. 281 (1980).

46. *Id.*

47. ABA Standing Comm. on Ethics & Prof'l Responsibility, Formal Op. 06-439 (Apr. 12, 2006).

48. 28 U.S.C. § 1453.

49. Dina Temple-Raston, *Class-Action Lawsuits Gain Strength on the Web*, N.Y. Times, July 28, 2002, at 10.

Wal-Mart Stores, Inc. v. Dukes

Supreme Court of the United States
131 S. Ct. 2541 (2011).

FACTS   Three current or former female Wal-Mart employees sued Wal-Mart in a nationwide class action on behalf of 1.5 million female Wal-Mart employees who alleged that Wal-Mart had discriminated against them on the basis of their sex in both pay and promotions in violation of Title VII of the Civil Rights Act of 1964. In addition to injunctive and declaratory relief, the plaintiffs sought an award of back pay and punitive damages.

Pay and promotion decisions at Wal-Mart are generally left to local managers' broad discretion, which is exercised "in a largely subjective manner." Higher corporate authorities have discretion to set the pay of salaried store managers and their deputies within preestablished ranges.

Candidates for Wal-Mart's management training program must meet certain objective criteria, including an above-average performance rating, at least one year's tenure in the applicant's current position, and a willingness to relocate. Except for those requirements, regional and district managers have discretion to use their own judgment when selecting candidates for management training. Promotion to a higher position—such as assistant manager, co-manager, or store manager—is similarly at the discretion of the employee's superiors after prescribed objective factors are satisfied.

The plaintiffs did not allege that Wal-Mart has any express corporate policy against the advancement of women. Rather, they claimed that the local managers exercise their discretion over pay and promotions disproportionately in favor of men, leading to an unlawful disparate impact on female employees. The plaintiffs argued that because Wal-Mart is aware of this effect, Wal-Mart's refusal to "cabin," or limit, its managers' authority amounts to disparate treatment. The trial and appeals courts certified the class, and Wal-Mart appealed.

ISSUE PRESENTED   Does this class meet the requirements for class certification under Federal Rules of Civil Procedure 23(a) and (b)(2)? In particular, is there sufficient commonality among the class members?

Opinion SCALIA, J., writing on behalf of the U.S. Supreme Court:

We are presented with one of the most expansive class actions ever. . . .

I

. . . .

Importantly for our purposes, respondents [the plaintiffs] claim that the discrimination to which they have been subjected is common to all Wal-Mart's female employees. The basic theory of their case is that a strong and uniform "corporate culture" permits bias against women to infect, perhaps subconsciously, the discretionary decision making of each one of Wal-Mart's thousands of managers—thereby making every woman at the company the victim of one common discriminatory practice. Respondents therefore wish to litigate the Title VII claims of all female employees at Wal-Mart's stores in a nationwide class action.

Class certification is governed by Federal Rule of Civil Procedure 23. . . .

II

. . . The crux of this case is commonality—the rule requiring a plaintiff to show that "there are questions of law or fact common to the class." . . . Commonality requires the plaintiff to demonstrate that the class members "have suffered the same injury." This does not mean merely that they have all suffered a violation of the same provision of law. . . . Their claims must depend upon a common contention—for example, the assertion of discriminatory bias on the part of the same supervisor. That common contention, moreover, must be of such a nature that it is capable of class wide resolution—which means that determination of its truth or falsity will resolve an issue that is central to the validity of each one of the claims in one stroke.

. . . .

CONTINUED

In this case, proof of commonality necessarily overlaps with respondents' merits contention that Wal-Mart engages in a *pattern or practice* of discrimination. That is so because, in resolving an individual's Title VII claim, the crux of the inquiry is "the reason for a particular employment decision." Here respondents wish to sue about literally millions of employment decisions at once. Without some glue holding the alleged *reasons* for all those decisions together, it will be impossible to say that examination of all the class members' claims for relief will produce a common answer to the crucial question *why was I disfavored.*

. . . .

Wal-Mart's announced policy forbids sex discrimination, and . . . the company imposes penalties for denials of equal employment opportunity. The only evidence of a "general policy of discrimination" respondents produced was the testimony of Dr. William Bielby, their sociological expert. Relying on "social framework" analysis, Bielby testified that Wal-Mart has a "strong corporate culture," that makes it vulnerable to "gender bias.". . . "At his deposition . . . Dr. Bielby conceded that he could not calculate whether 0.5 percent or 95 percent of the decisions at Wal-Mart might be determined by stereotyped thinking.". . . [T]his is the essential question on which [the plaintiffs'] theory of commonality depends. If Bielby admittedly has no answer to that question, we can safely disregard what he has to say. . . .

The only corporate policy that the plaintiffs' evidence convincingly establishes is Wal-Mart's "policy" of *allowing discretion* by local supervisors over employment matters. On its face, of course, that is just the opposite of a uniform employment practice that would provide the commonality needed for a class action; it is a policy *against having* uniform employment practices. . . .

To be sure we have recognized that "in appropriate cases," giving discretion to lower-level supervisors can be the basis of Title VII liability under a disparate-impact theory—since "an employer's undisciplined system of subjective decisionmaking [can have] precisely the same effects as a system pervaded by impermissible intentional discrimination." But the recognition that this type of Title VII claim "can" exist does not lead to the conclusion that every employee in a company using a system of discretion has such a claim in common. To the contrary, left to their own devices most managers in any corporation—and surely most managers in a corporation that forbids sex discrimination—would select sex-neutral, performance-based criteria for hiring and promotion that produce no actionable disparity at all. Others may choose to reward various attributes that produce disparate impact—such as scores on general aptitude tests or educational achievements. And still other managers may be guilty of intentional discrimination that produces a sex-based disparity. In such a company, demonstrating the invalidity of one manager's use of discretion will do nothing to demonstrate the invalidity of another's. A party seeking to certify a nationwide class will be unable to show that all the employees' Title VII claims will in fact depend on the answers to common questions.

Respondents have not identified a common mode of exercising discretion that pervades the entire company—aside from their reliance on Dr. Bielby's social framework analysis that we have rejected. . . . Respondents attempt to make that showing by means of statistical and anecdotal evidence, but their evidence falls well short.

The statistical evidence consists primarily of regression analyses performed by Dr. Richard Drogin, a statistician, and Dr. Marc Bendick, a labor economist. Drogin conducted his analysis region-by-region, comparing the number of women promoted into management positions with the percentage of women in the available pool of hourly workers. After considering regional and national data, Drogin concluded that "there are statistically significant disparities between men and women at Wal-Mart . . . [and] these disparities . . . can be explained only by gender discrimination." Bendick compared work-force data from Wal-Mart and competitive retailers and concluded that Wal-Mart "promotes a lower percentage of women than its competitors."

CONTINUED

Even if they are taken at face value, these studies are insufficient to establish that respondents' theory can be proved on a classwide basis. . . . [I]nformation about disparities at the regional and national level does not establish the existence of disparities at individual stores, let alone raise the inference that a company-wide policy of discrimination is implemented by discretionary decisions at the store and district level.

There is another, more fundamental, respect in which respondents' statistical proof fails. Even if it established (as it does not) a pay or promotion pattern that differs from the nationwide figures or the regional figures in *all* of Wal-Mart's 3,400 stores, that would still not demonstrate that commonality of issue exists. Some managers will claim that the availability of women, or quailified women, or interested women, in their stores' area does not mirror the national or regional statistics. And almost all of them will claim to have been applying some sex-neutral, performance-based criteria—whose nature and effects will differ from store to store. . . .

Respondents' anecdotal evidence suffers from the same defects, and in addition is too weak to raise any inference that all the individual, discretionary personnel decisions are discriminatory. . . . Even if every single one of these accounts is true, that would not demonstrate that the entire company "operate[s] under a general policy of discrimination," which is what respondents must show to certify a company-wide class.

III

We also conclude that respondents' claims for backpay were improperly certified under Federal Rule of Civil Procedure 23(b)(2) [which applies when "the party opposing the class has acted or refused to act on grounds that apply generally to the class, so that final injunctive relief or corresponding declaratory relief is appropriate respecting the class as a whole."] We now hold that claims for monetary relief may not be certified under that provision at least where (as here) the monetary relief is not incidental to the injunctive or declaratory relief.

RESULT   The judgment of the court of appeals was reversed. The plaintiffs could not sue as a class.

COMMENTS   In an opinion by Justice Ginsburg, in which Justices Breyer, Sotomayor, and Kagan joined, these four justices concurred in the majority opinion's conclusion that the class should not have been certified under Federal Rule of Civil Procedure 23(b)(2), but they dissented from the holding that the plaintiffs did not satisfy Rule 23(a)(2)'s commonality requirement. Citing the following evidence, the dissent argued that the common question of whether Wal-Mart's discretionary pay and promotion policies gave rise to unlawful sex discrimination satisfied Rule 23(a)(2):

> Women fill 70 percent of the hourly jobs in the retailer's stores but make up only "33 percent of management employees." "[T]he higher one looks in the organization the lower the percentage of women." The plaintiffs' "largely uncontested descriptive statistics" also show that women working in the company's stores "are paid less than men in every region" and "that the salary gaps widens over time even for men and women hired into the same jobs at the same time."

> The District Court identified "systems for . . . promoting in-store employees" that were "sufficiently similar across regions and stores" to conclude that "the manner in which these systems affect the class raises issue that are common to all class members." The selection of employees for promotion to in-store management "is fairly characterized as a 'tap on the shoulder' process," in which managers have discretion about whose shoulder to tap. Vacancies are not regularly posted; from among those employees satisfying minimum qualifications, managers choose whom to promote on the basis of their own subjective impressions.

> Wal-Mart's compensation policies also operate uniformly across stores, the District Court found. The retailer leaves open a $2 band for every position's hourly pay rate. Wal-Mart provides no standards or criteria for setting wages within that band, and thus does nothing to counter unconscious bias on the part of supervisors.

CONTINUED

Wal-Mart's supervisors do not make their discretionary decisions in a vacuum. The District Court reviewed means Wal-Mart used to maintain a "carefully constructed . . . corporate culture," such as frequent meetings to reinforce the common way of thinking, regular transfers of managers between stores to ensure uniformity throughout the company, monitoring of stores "on a close and constant basis," and "Wal-Mart TV," "broadcas[t] . . . into all stores."

The plaintiffs' evidence, including class members' tales of their own experiences, suggests that gender bias suffused Wal-Mart's company culture. Among illustrations, senior management often refer to female associates as "little Janie Qs." One manager told an employee that "[m]en are here to make a career and women aren't." A committee of female Wal-Mart executives concluded that "[s]tereotypes limit the opportunities offered to women."

Finally, the plaintiffs presented an expert's appraisal to show that the pay and promotions disparities at Wal-Mart "can be explained only by gender discrimination and not by . . . neutral variables."

Justice Ginsburg explained: "Managers, like all humankind, may be prey to biases of which they are unaware. The risk of discrimination is heightened when those managers are predominantly of one sex, and are steeped in a corporate culture that perpetuates gender stereotypes." She cited a study finding that "[o]rchestras that permitted reviewers to see the [musicians auditioning] hired far fewer female musicians than orchestras that conducted blind auditions, in which candidates played behind opaque screens."[50]

The dissent cited the case of *Watson v. Fort Worth Bank & Trust*[51] for the proposition that "'discretionary employment practices' can give rise to Title VII claims, not only when such practices are motivated by discriminatory intent but also when they produce discriminatory results." Accordingly:

A finding that Wal-Mart's pay and promotions practices in fact violate the law would be the first step in the usual order of proof for plaintiffs seeking individual remedies for company-wide discrimination. That each individual employee's unique circumstances will ultimately determine whether she is entitled to backpay or damages should not factor into the Rule 23(a)(2) determination.

CRITICAL THINKING QUESTIONS

1. On the issue of commonality, which opinion do you find more persuasive, the majority or the dissent?

2. Supervisors at New York Telephone Company were told, when deciding on promotions, to start with objective criteria, then to look at the candidate "as a total individual," and finally to consider whether "this person [is] going to be successful in our business."[52] Evaluate this policy from a legal and business perspective.

---

50. Claudia Goldin & Cecelia Rouse, *Orchestrating Impartiality: The Impact of "Blind" Auditions on Female Musicians*, 90 AM. ECON. REV. 715, 738 (2000).

51. 487 U.S. 977 (1988). *See also* Wards Cove Packing Co. v. Atonio, 490 U.S. 642, 657 (1989), in which the Court recognized that subjective decision making in the employment context can give rise to a disparate impact violation under Title VII.

52. Leisner v. N.Y. Tel. Co., 358 F. Supp. 359, 364–65 (S.D.N.Y. 1973).

Although corporate defendants have historically condemned class actions as an easy way for an eager plaintiff and his or her lawyer to get to court, some companies now view class actions as a "strategic management tool" that can end litigation nightmares and work to their advantage by avoiding potentially devastating jury awards, reducing litigation costs, and limiting long-term liability.[53]

---

53. Richard B. Schmitt, *The Deal Makers: Some Firms Embrace the Widely Dreaded Class-Action Lawsuit*, WALL ST. J., July 18, 1996, at A1.

A product liability class action can have the following advantages: (1) the settlement can bind not only present class members but also future claimants; (2) standardized payment schedules can avoid the risk of widely divergent jury awards; (3) some claimants who suffered less harm than others can be excluded from the settlement; and (4) the filing of suits and the settlement can occur on the same day.[54]

CIVIL PROCEDURE: LITIGATION STEPS

Civil procedure refers to the methods, procedures, and practices that govern the processing of a civil lawsuit from start to finish. Each court system has its own rules or guidelines to ensure the orderly processing of litigation. The *Federal Rules of Civil Procedure (FRCP)* control the trial practices in all of the U.S. district courts. Each federal district court may also adopt its own local rules, which apply only within that district, to supplement the federal rules. Individual judges may even have their own particular rules for certain procedures in their courts.

Each state has a set of rules governing the procedures in the state trial court system. Often, the state rules are similar to the federal rules. Separate sets of rules govern practice

before the various appellate courts and supreme courts. These rules address every requirement, from the time deadline for filing an appeal to the contents of the notice of appeal and the paper size, line spacing, and type style for briefs filed with the court.

Filing, Prosecuting, and Defending Against a Claim

The plaintiff's complaint, the defendant's answer (including any counterclaim), and any reply to the answer filed by the plaintiff are referred to as the *pleadings*. Exhibit 3.4 provides a typical timeline for a suit filed in federal court.

Complaint

The *complaint* briefly states a grievance and alleges (1) the particular facts giving rise to the dispute; (2) the legal reason why the plaintiff is entitled to a remedy; and (3) the *prayer*, or request for relief. The complaint should also explain why this particular court has jurisdiction over the alleged dispute and indicate whether the plaintiff requests a jury trial. If the plaintiff does not request a jury trial within the time limit, that right is deemed to be waived.

Summons

After the plaintiff files the complaint, the clerk of the court prepares a summons. The *summons* officially notifies the defendant that a lawsuit is pending against it in a particular court and that it must file a response to

---

54. Catherine Yan, *Look Who's Talking Settlement*, Bus. Wk., July 18, 1994, at 72.

| EXHIBIT 3.4 | Typical Timeline for a Suit Filed in Federal Court |

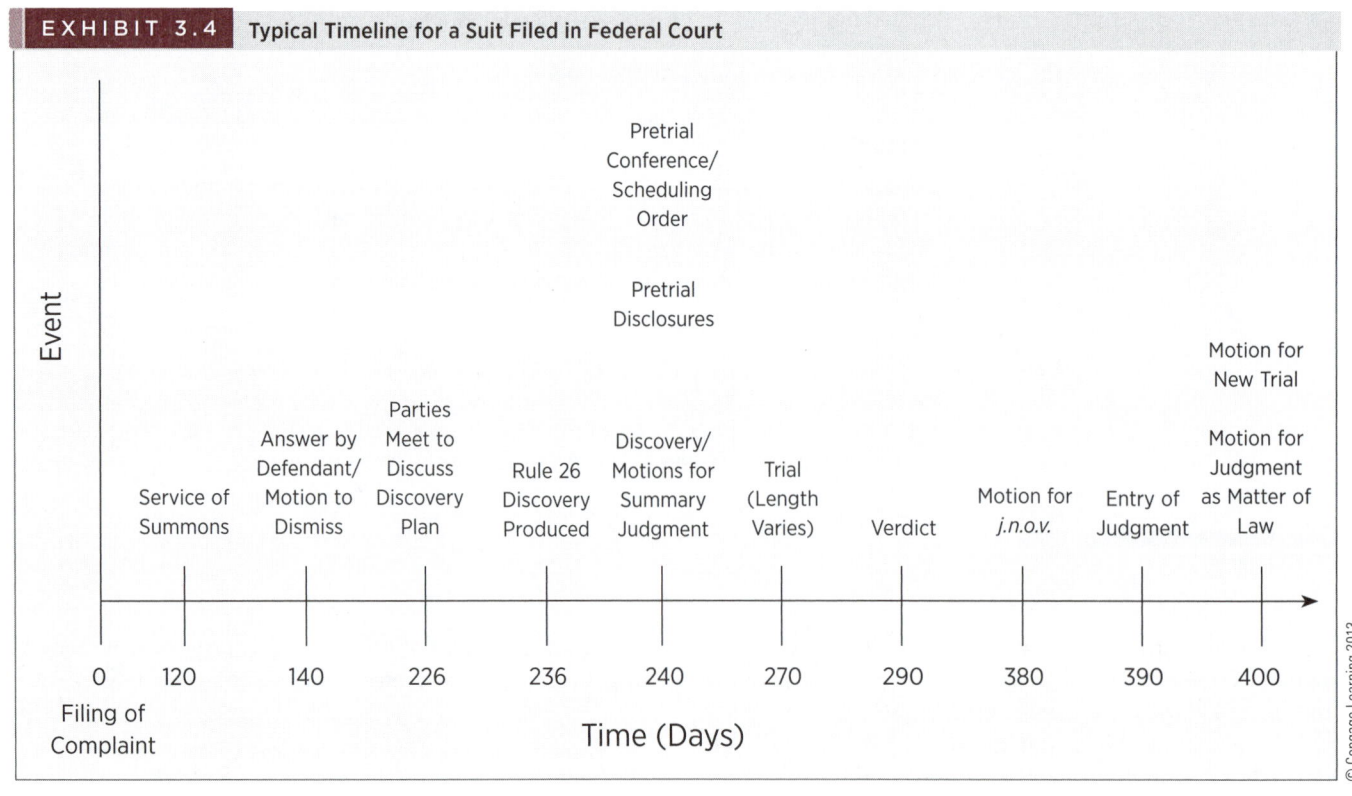

© Cengage Learning 2013

the complaint within a certain number of days. The clerk then stamps the official seal of the court on the summons. Next, the plaintiff or the clerk serves the official summons and complaint on the defendant. Service is usually completed by sending the documents to the defendant by mail.

Answer and Counterclaim

The defendant's *answer* may admit or deny the various allegations in the complaint. If the defendant believes that it lacks sufficient information to assess the truth of an allegation, it should state this. Such a statement has the effect of a denial. The answer may also deny that the law provides relief for the plaintiff's claim regardless of whether the plaintiff's factual allegations are true.

The answer may put forth affirmative defenses to the allegations in the complaint. An *affirmative defense* admits that the defendant has acted in a certain way but claims either (1) that the defendant's conduct was not the real or legal cause of harm to the plaintiff or (2) that the defendant's conduct is excused for some reason. An example of an affirmative defense in a contract case is the requirement under the statute of frauds (discussed in Chapter 7) that certain agreements must be in writing to be enforceable.

An answer may also include a *counterclaim*, a legal claim by the defendant against the plaintiff. The counterclaim need not be related to the plaintiff's claim.

Default Judgment

If the defendant does not file an answer within the time required, a *default judgment* may be entered in favor of the plaintiff. The defendant may, however, ask the court to set aside the default judgment if there were extenuating circumstances for not filing an answer to the complaint on time.

Pretrial Activity

Before the trial begins, the parties conduct discovery (discussed later in this chapter) and the attorneys for each party and the judge usually meet to discuss certain issues.

Pretrial Motions

A lawsuit may be resolved by the judge before trial pursuant to either a motion to dismiss or a motion for summary judgment. A *motion* formally requests the court to take some action.

Motion to Dismiss   A *motion to dismiss* seeks to terminate the lawsuit on the ground that the plaintiff's claim is technically inadequate. A judge will grant a motion to dismiss if (1) the court lacks jurisdiction over the subject matter or the parties involved, (2) the plaintiff failed to properly serve the complaint on the defendant, or (3) the

plaintiff has failed to state a claim on which relief can be granted. If a case is *dismissed with prejudice*, the plaintiff is precluded from asserting the same claims in another case. If a case is *dismissed without prejudice*, however, the plaintiff is permitted to refile the complaint (or an amended version thereof) and recommence litigation of the same claims.

A party may file a motion to dismiss immediately after the complaint and answer have been filed. This is known as a *motion for judgment on the pleadings*. One party, usually the defendant, argues that the complaint alone demonstrates that the action is futile.

The moving party may file *affidavits*, that is, sworn statements, or other written evidence in an attempt to show that the cause of action is without merit. When information or documents other than the pleadings are involved, the motion becomes a *motion for summary judgment*.

Summary Judgment   Judges normally decide all questions of law, and juries resolve all disputes over factual matters. A judge will grant *summary judgment* when (1) all of the written evidence before the court clearly establishes that there are no disputed issues of material fact and (2) a party is entitled to judgment in its favor as a matter of law. If there is even a scintilla, that is, even the slightest bit, of evidence that casts doubt on an important fact in the lawsuit, the judge will not grant summary judgment. A judge may, however, grant summary judgment on some issues of the case and let the other issues proceed to trial. This is called a *partial summary judgment*.

Pretrial and Status Conferences

During pretrial and status conferences, the attorneys for the litigants meet with the judge to discuss the progress of their case. Such conferences may be held either in open court or in the judge's chambers. Topics addressed typically include:

- Prospects for settlement of the dispute.
- Issues raised by the pleadings.
- Any amendments to the pleadings.
- Scheduling of future discovery and a plan for the timely completion of discovery.
- The status of pending motions or prospective motions that a party may file.
- The schedule for the disclosure of production of exhibits.

As noted earlier, the judge will often hold a *settlement conference* to give each side a candid assessment of the strengths and weaknesses of its case and the likely outcome if the case goes to trial. If a settlement clearly is not feasible, then the pretrial conference will focus on formulating an efficient plan for the trial.

Under FRCP Rule 16, parties are required to alert the court early on about potential issues related to the discovery of electronically stored information, such as e-mails. Electronic document retention policies are discussed in more depth later in this chapter.

Trial

A trial usually goes through the following stages:

1. Selection of the jury (if the trial is before a jury). The judge or attorneys may question the potential jurors.

2. Opening statements, first by the plaintiff's attorney and then by the defendant's attorney.

3. Presentation of evidence and witnesses by the plaintiff's attorney. This consists of:

   a. Direct examination of witnesses by the plaintiff's attorney.

   b. Cross-examination of witnesses by the defendant's attorney.

   c. Redirect examination by the plaintiff's attorney.

   d. Recross-examination by the defendant's attorney.

   e. Redirect and recross-examination until both sides have no further questions to ask.

4. Presentation of evidence and witnesses by the defendant's attorney. This consists of:

   a. Direct examination of witnesses by the defendant's attorney.

   b. Cross-examination of witnesses by the plaintiff's attorney.

   c. Redirect and recross-examination until both sides have no further questions to ask.

5. Motion for a directed verdict by either attorney.

6. Closing arguments, first by the plaintiff's attorney, then by the defendant's attorney, and then rebuttal by the plaintiff's attorney.

7. The judge's instructions to the jury.

8. Jury deliberations.

9. Announcement of the jury verdict.

Selection of Jury

Each side may challenge any number of jurors for cause during the questioning of potential jurors, which is called *voir dire.* Cause includes any relationship between the potential juror and any of the parties or their counsel. Most jurisdictions also permit a limited number of preemptory challenges. These can be used by counsel to remove potential jurors who counsel thinks might be inclined to decide for the other side. It is unconstitutional to use a preemptory challenge to remove a potential juror due to race or gender, however.[55]

---

55. *See* Batson v. Kentucky, 476 U.S. 79 (1986) and Rice v. Collins, 546 U.S. 333 (2006) (race); J.E.B. v. Alabama, 511 U.S. 127 (1994) (gender).

ethical consideration

You are a manager of Dow Chemical Company, overseeing the silicone-breast-implant litigation across the United States. Your market research tells you that most individuals distrust Big Business and that most consumers cannot identify many products of your company, except those involved in the litigation. With an upcoming trial in Louisiana, you are considering conducting a full-scale advertising campaign to boost Dow Chemical's public image. The goal is to influence public opinion in the jurisdiction of the suit, thereby creating a positive image in the minds of potential jurors. You have several options for the campaign:

1. Emphasize Dow Chemical's citizenship: employee volunteers, donations to charities, and the improvement of society as a result of Dow's products.

2. Describe the benefits of silicone products. Without mentioning the breast-implant issue, tell numerous heart-wrenching tales about how silicone products have saved the lives of children.

3. Begin the final campaign the week before jury selection. Highlight the greed of attorneys who represent plaintiffs in such cases, and lament the growing litigiousness of our society. The final slogan: "You can stop the greedy lawyers!"

4. Same as option 3, but also argue that silicone breast implants do no harm.

What should you do? If you were the plaintiff, how would you respond to these tactics?

SOURCE: *See* Richard B. Schmitt, *Can Corporate Advertising Sway Juries?*, WALL ST. J., Mar. 3, 1997, at B1.

Motion for a Directed Verdict

After all the evidence has been presented, either attorney may ask the judge to grant a motion for a *directed verdict.* The moving party asserts that the other side has not produced enough evidence to support the legal claim or defense alleged. The motion requests that the judge take the case away from the jury and direct that a verdict be entered in favor of the party making the motion. If the judge agrees that there is not even an iota of evidence to support one party's claim or defense, then he or she will issue a directed verdict in favor of the other party. This does not happen very frequently.

Jury Verdict

After both sides have presented their closing arguments, the judge instructs the jury on applicable rules of law. After deliberating in private, the jury delivers its verdict, specifying both the prevailing party and the relief to which that party is entitled. In federal court, the six-person jury verdict must be unanimous. In state courts, a unanimous jury verdict is not always required. Frequently, nine out of twelve votes is sufficient.

Posttrial Motions

The announcement of the jury verdict does not necessarily conclude the case. Either party may make a motion to set aside the verdict or to have the case retried.

Judgment Notwithstanding the Verdict

Immediately after the jury has rendered its verdict and the jury has been excused from the courtroom, the attorney for the losing party may make a motion for a *judgment notwithstanding the verdict*. Such a judgment, also known as a *judgment n.o.v.*, from the Latin *non obstante veredicto*, or *j.n.o.v.*, reverses the jury verdict on the ground that the evidence of the prevailing party was so weak that no reasonable jury could have resolved the dispute in that party's favor. The judge will deny the motion if there is any reasonable possibility that the evidence could support the jury verdict.

New Trial

The judge may order a new trial if there were serious errors in the trial process. Examples include misconduct on the part of the attorneys or the jurors and the improper admission of evidence that severely prejudiced one party's chances for a fair trial.

Appeals

If the trial judge does not grant the motion for a *j.n.o.v.* or a new trial, the losing party can appeal the decision. The appellate court will review the manner in which the trial judge applied the law to the case and conducted the trial. The appeals court can review the presentation of evidence at trial, the denial of a motion for a directed verdict, the jury instructions, and even the jury award of damages. The appellate court will not review the facts *de novo* and will reverse a judge's findings of fact only if they are clearly erroneous.

If the appellant loses before the court of appeals, it may want to have the supreme court consider the decision. Appeals are expensive, however, so the losing party should seriously consider the likelihood of success at the higher court before pursuing an appeal.

ALTERNATIVE DISPUTE RESOLUTION

In many cases, negotiation, mediation, and other alternative dispute resolution (ADR) procedures can help the company maintain a relationship with the opposing party, reduce legal expenses, dispose of issues relatively quickly, and allow for flexible business-oriented solutions. Certain

forms of ADR, such as mediation, are usually accepted readily by the opposing party—the proceeding is informal and can be terminated at any time, and a mediator can also protect the confidentiality of sensitive data that might be made public during litigation. Others, such as arbitration, usually have to be agreed to in advance.

There are three basic varieties of ADR: negotiation, mediation, and arbitration. By mixing these with each other and the formal judicial system, a manager has four more options: minitrials, med-arb, arb-med, and summary jury trials. Some companies negotiate ADR clauses into all of their standard business contracts. Other companies leave it to their attorneys to decide which disputes are better resolved by ADR than by litigation.

Negotiation

Negotiation is the give-and-take people engage in when coming to terms with each other. One can view negotiation along several different dimensions. First, negotiation can be either forward looking with concern for desired relationships—*transactional negotiation*—or backward looking to address past events that have caused disagreement—*dispute negotiation*. For example, two firms involved in a joint venture might engage in a transactional negotiation, whereas a steel manufacturer that failed to deliver I-beams and the construction company that has already paid for them would engage in a dispute negotiation. In the former, both parties are looking to the future with positive expectations; in the latter, the parties are looking to the past and apportioning blame. Conflicts need not be simply one or the other. Labor negotiations often have elements of both transactions and disputes. The parties must work together in the future but may also feel the need to apportion blame for the event that precipitated the crisis.

Second, negotiation can be viewed as involving a fixed or a growing pie. In *distributive* or *zero-sum negotiations*, the only issue is the distribution of a fixed pie. In contrast, in *integrative* or *variable-sum negotiations*, mutual gains are possible as parties trade lower-valued resources for higher-valued ones.

Distributive negotiations can easily become adversarial and strain even the closest relationships. With nothing to do but fight over the same pie, the parties inevitably do fight. Integrating other issues into the discussion creates the possibility of trade-offs that allow both parties to gain relative to their distributive starting point.

For example, consider a dispute between the manufacturer of a telecommunications device and the supplier of one of the device's critical components. The supplier delivered the component as scheduled, but the component failed to work properly in the device, causing significant friction between the manufacturer and the supplier. It is unclear which party caused the problem. In distributive negotiations, the parties would merely battle over who should absorb the resulting loss, a process that could irreversibly injure the manufacturer–supplier relationship and lead to litigation. By looking beyond the boundaries of the original transaction and dispute, however, the parties may be able to create value between them. For instance, the supplier may have the capacity to expedite delivery of a modified component at very little cost in a short period of time. The manufacturer, in turn, might highly value the ability to secure this modified component. Thus, the parties could strike a deal whereby the manufacturer agrees to pay the original amount owed plus a small premium for replacement in exchange for the supplier's agreement to expedite a modified component. Both parties receive more than was originally due and preserve their relationship.

Texaco CEO James Kinnear successfully employed this strategy to resolve a $300 million dispute with a major customer that had sued Texaco for a variety of business torts. Texaco had agreed to supply oil at a fixed price to an aging plant that the customer had kept open only to preserve the value of the nontransferable fixed-price contract. The two CEOs first met to hear evidence from lawyers from both sides. After it became clear that a speedy resolution of the legal claims was unlikely, Kinnear negotiated a deal whereby Texaco agreed to let the customer transfer the fixed-price contract to a more efficient plant in exchange for the customer's agreement to drop the lawsuit.[56]

---

56. Constance E. Bagley, Winning Legally: Using the Law to Create Value, Marshal Resources, and Manage Risk 203–204 (2005).

INTERNATIONAL SNAPSHOT

In negotiating across cultures or in international settings, cultural myopia is a serious barrier to success. For instance, eye contact implies dramatically different attitudes in Japan and the United States. In the United States, a negotiator who avoids eye contact will be perceived as being intimidated or shifty. In Japan, that same behavior is taken as a sign of respect. When signals are misinterpreted, complex negotiations become even more difficult. Consider the Tokyo conference room where respectful officials of Mitsubishi avoid eye contact as they begin discussions with the aggressive owners of a Texas car dealership who rarely avert their eyes. What of teetotalling in Moscow? Bare heads in Jerusalem? Shoed feet in Beijing?[a]

The following excerpt from an essay written by an anonymous Japanese negotiator provides insight into how the Japanese view the American style of negotiation:

Often they [the Americans] argue among themselves in public, so it is safe to assume that they argue even more in private. This is part of their idea of adversary proceedings and they seem to feel no shame about such embarrassing behavior....

Americans like to concentrate on one problem at a time. They seem not to understand that the whole picture is more important, and they spend little time on developing a general understanding of the views and interests of both sides. Since

their habit of focusing on one issue often forces a direct disagreement, they often propose setting the issue aside, but they come back to it later with the same attitude and concentration. A negotiation with them may therefore become a series of small conflicts and we must always make a special effort to give proper attention to the large areas of agreement and common interest.[b]

---

a. For discussions of issues in cross-cultural negotiation, see Frank E. A. Sader & Jeffrey Z. Rubin, *Culture, Negotiation, and Eye of the Beholder*, 7 Negotiation J. 249 (1991); Stephen E. Weiss, *Negotiating with "Romans"—Part 1*, MIT Sloan Mgmt. Rev. 51 (Winter 1994); John L. Graham, *The Japanese Negotiation Style: Characteristics of a Distinct Approach*, 9 Negotiation J. 123 (1993).

b. Yuko Yanagida et al., Law and Investment in Japan 219–20 (1994).

Liability for Failed Negotiations

In the United States, it is difficult to establish legal liability on the grounds that a party did not finalize a contract after a series of negotiations. As explained more fully in Chapter 7, a party negotiating in the United States is generally free to terminate negotiations for any or no reason at any time prior to contract formation. For example, in *Apothekernes Laboratorium for Special Praeparater v. IMC Chemical Group, Inc.*,[57] IMC's board of directors rejected a negotiated deal with Apothekernes after a letter of intent had been signed and IMC's negotiator had assured Apothekernes that the board would approve the deal. Even though the negotiators had a meeting of the minds, the U.S. appeals court held that there was no contract because the letter of intent expressly stated that the terms were "subject to our concluding an Agreement of Sale which shall be acceptable to the Boards of Directors of our respective corporations, whose discretion shall in no way be limited by this letter."[58] In some jurisdictions, however, a covenant of good faith and trust applies to negotiations even if they do not ripen into a contract.[59]

Mediation

Mediation is another less hostile and less costly alternative to a lawsuit. In *mediation*, the parties agree to try to reach a solution with the assistance of a neutral third party who helps them find a mutually satisfactory resolution. This third party is the *mediator*. Unlike a

---

57. 873 F.2d 155 (7th Cir. 1989).

58. *Id.* at 156.

59. *See, e.g.*, the Tokyo High Court's decision in *D. James Wan Kim Min v. Mitsui Bussan K.K.* (1987), excerpted in Yuko Yanagida et al., Law and Investment in Japan 223–29 (1994) ("In the event that preparation between two parties progresses towards conclusion of an agreement and the first party comes to expect that the agreement will surely be concluded, the second party becomes obligated under the principles of good faith and trust to try to conclude the agreement, in order not to injure the expectation of the first party.").

judge, a mediator cannot dictate a solution; the parties must come to a resolution themselves and then agree to abide by it.

Mediation can offer resolutions that are speedy, inexpensive, and logistically simple when compared to litigation. Like negotiation, mediation can lead to joint gains and help preserve relationships that might otherwise break under the strain of conflict. In a survey of 1,000 large U.S. corporations, 81% of the respondents indicated that they used mediation because it provides "a more satisfactory process" than litigation; 66% said it provides more "satisfactory settlements"; and 59% asserted that it "preserves good relationships."[60]

Companies in a variety of industries have saved money, time, and other resources by mediating. Chubb & Son, Inc. has resolved nearly a dozen disputes under mediation pacts with other insurance companies and saved between $150,000 and $200,000 per case. The Travelers Insurance Company found that more than 85% of the cases it submitted to mediation were settled. Even when a settlement could not be reached, the mediation process helped the litigants focus on the most important issues, which allowed for a quicker resolution at trial.[61]

The Mediation Process

By definition, mediation is a flexible process that allows for many different structures, rules, and procedures. Because parties are less likely to agree to anything once a dispute has arisen, mediation organizations have evolved sets of default rules to which disputants can subscribe in advance of a specific conflict or to which they can defer once a conflict has arisen. Disputants are also free to establish alternative ground rules that are specifically tailored to their particular conflict and needs.

In many ways, mediation is an extension of the negotiation process. A mediator's role is to guide the parties through a structured set of discussions about the issues and alternatives and to suggest ways to resolve the dispute fairly. He or she confers with both parties, together and in private, and points out the elements in dispute and the areas of agreement. Because mediators can allow parties to vent their feelings and encourage them to at least acknowledge each other's perspectives, mediation can diffuse difficult interpersonal tensions. If the parties can reach an agreement, they often formalize the arrangement with contracts, public statements, or letters of understanding.

Although not pronouncing final judgment, a mediator can powerfully affect the outcome of the dispute. Unlike the parties, a mediator can offer compromises without fear of appearing weak or too eager to settle. By asking some questions but not others, the mediator can move the discussion toward or away from an issue. By suggesting solutions and reacting to proposals, the mediator can influence both parties' attitudes toward fairness, risk aversion, and trust. A skilled mediator knows how to bring disputing parties to genuine settlement; an unskilled mediator can push parties into agreements they later regret or, worse, can inflame the situation.

When to Use Mediation

Mediation is an appropriate option only when the parties sincerely desire to settle their dispute. If they are unwilling to compromise or seek to harm their opponents, mediation will be a frustrating waste of time. Conversely, parties who wish to preserve their relationship may find that mediation is their best option. Litigation and arbitration frequently leave the parties feeling negative about each other.

The more uncertain a party's legal claims are, the more attractive mediation often is. If the law is clear and one party's rights are clearly being violated, compromise may appear unnecessary. When the law is uncertain, mediation allows parties to resolve their differences without being subjected to undeveloped, ill-formed, or uncertain legal doctrine.

The need for privacy may also make some disputes more appropriate for mediation. Lawsuits require the filing of public documents and can alert the media to sensitive areas of business. A company may wish to keep trade secrets, controversial research, organizational structures, and internal training documents from the front pages of newspapers. Suppliers and customers may also become nervous if problems that could have been kept confidential are reported in the press. "Keeping it between ourselves" is much more realistic if few outsiders are involved.

Dangers   Critics of mediation point to the lack of procedural protections. Some parties may be surprised to find that legal rights that would be protected in litigation are not protected in mediation. Parties with equal bargaining power may wisely agree to trade such rights for expediency. When one party has superior bargaining power, however, it may unfairly take advantage of the other side. For example, in a mediation of a conflict between a landlord and rent-controlled tenants over a rat infestation, the tenants might accept the placing of rat traps instead of the full-scale extermination that the housing code and a court would mandate.

Mediation may also effect changes in the distribution of power in a relationship. For example, introducing mediation into a nonunion plant may effectively defuse tensions and hinder efforts to unionize the plant.[62] Before agreeing to mediation, parties should consider the possibility

---

60. DAVID LIPSKY & RONALD SEEBER, THE APPROPRIATE RESOLUTION OF CORPORATE DISPUTES: A REPORT ON THE GROWING USE OF ADR BY U.S. CORPORATIONS (1998).

61. Margaret A. Jacobs, *Industry Giants Join Movement to Mediate*, WALL ST. J., July 21, 1997, at B1.

62. WILLIAM L. URY ET AL., GETTING DISPUTES RESOLVED 52 (1988).

of such consequences, including possible effects on continued adjudication of the dispute, future dealings with the opponent, and the firm's reputation with internal and external constituencies.

Preserving Confidentiality

Ensuring confidentiality is central to negotiation and mediation. If parties do not feel comfortable revealing important, sensitive information, they are less likely to identify opportunities for mutual gain. Unlike negotiation, mediation allows disputants to confide in a third party without fear of being exploited. Whether the mediation process involves caucusing or shuttle diplomacy, confiding in a mediator can allow the mediator to identify potential gains and point them out to the parties. If that confidentiality is doubted, the parties will withhold useful but potentially damaging information. Even worse, if the promise of confidentiality is not honored, the parties will come to regret their decision to mediate.

To protect such confidences, many states extend legal privileges to mediators; others do so only if the parties have agreed to keep communications with the mediator confidential. Although federal law does not directly address the question, federal courts have shown a willingness to recognize a mediation privilege, even if doing so deprives a party of truthful probative evidence.[63]

Selecting a Mediator

Mediation agreements may or may not specify how a mediator will be selected. According to the Society of Professionals in Dispute Resolution (SPDR), qualified mediators (1) understand the negotiating process and the role of advocacy, (2) earn trust and maintain acceptability, (3) convert the parties' positions into needs and interests, (4) screen out nonmediable issues, (5) help the parties invent creative options, (6) help the parties identify principles and criteria that will guide their decision making, (7) help the parties assess their nonsettlement alternatives, (8) help the parties make their own informed choices, and (9) help the parties assess whether their agreement can be implemented.[64]

The CPR International Institute for Conflict Prevention and Resolution (CPR), a nonprofit alliance of 500 major corporations and law firms, offers a standard mediation clause for parties to incorporate into their contracts: "The parties shall endeavor to resolve any dispute arising out of or relating to this Agreement by mediation under the CPR Mediation Procedure. Unless otherwise agreed, the parties will select a mediator from the CPR Panels of Distinguished Neutrals." The Panels of Distinguished Neutrals are the CPR's rosters of 700

attorneys, former judges, legally trained executives, and academics who can mediate disputes. The CPR is a strong proponent of self-administered ADR, in which the parties and the mediator manage the process themselves. Self-administered ADR provides the parties with optimum control over the dispute resolution process and is cheaper and more efficient.

Arbitration

Arbitration is the resolution of a dispute by a neutral third party, called an *arbitrator*. The process is consensual and created by a contract.

Although *nonbinding arbitration* is certainly an option, most parties enter *binding arbitration* whereby they agree to be bound by the arbitrator's decision. In *final-offer arbitration*, used most notably in baseball salary disputes, each side submits its "best and final" offer to the arbitrator, who then chooses one of the two proposals. Such a structure strongly encourages the parties to submit fair and reasonable offers. Otherwise, the less reasonable party is likely to lose with no chance for further concessions. Without its binding nature, such an exercise would be pointless. Nonetheless, the result of nonbinding arbitration can serve as a guide to what is fair. If a neutral third party has heard the strongest evidence and best arguments of both sides in a dispute, his or her opinion can serve as a baseline for what a court might decide.

Arbitration Process

Arbitration is the most formal of the ADR methods. It differs from both negotiation, in which there is no structure unless the parties first negotiate one, and mediation, in which the mediator focuses more on creating dialogue than on enforcing a technical format. Arbitration is more like a trial.

Because appointing arbitrators takes time, arbitration may not be suitable in certain disputes, such as violations of noncompete agreements or intellectual property infringement, when immediate injunction relief is necessary to avoid irreparable harm. As a result, parties often include carve-outs in their arbitration agreement for such claims or provide that courts can order interim relief pending arbitration.

The first stage of arbitration is usually a *prehearing*, in which the parties may submit trial-like briefs, supporting documents, and other written statements making their case. Because neither federal nor state statutes grant arbitrators the authority to use discovery devices at this stage, prehearing discovery is usually limited to what the parties voluntarily disclose unless the parties agreed to greater discovery when they agreed to arbitrate the dispute.

The *hearing* is more structured than the prehearing and is often adversarial. The precise structure varies from arbitration to arbitration, but Rule 32 of the Commercial

---

63. *See, e.g.*, NLRB v. Macaluso, 618 F.2d 51 (9th Cir. 1980).

64. NAT'L INST. OF DISPUTE RESOLUTION, DISPUTE RESOLUTION FORUM (May 9, 1989).

Arbitration Rules, Conduct of Proceedings, promulgated by the American Arbitration Association (AAA), provides an illustration:

> The claimant shall present evidence to support its claim. The respondent shall then present evidence to support its defense. Witnesses for each party shall also submit to questions from the arbitrator and the adverse party. The arbitrator has the discretion to vary this procedure, provided that the parties are treated with equality and that each party has the right to be heard and is given a fair opportunity to present its case.

Although arbitrators, unlike judges, are not required to apply detailed rules of evidence or procedure, many arbitrators believe that compliance with some of these rules is useful and necessary. Arbitrators may also subpoena documents and third-party witnesses for the hearing but generally cannot require a third party to appear for depositions or produce documents prior to the hearing.[65]

After considering all the evidence presented in the prehearing and the hearing, the arbitrator makes his or her award in the final, *posthearing* phase. Often the award is not accompanied by any discussion or explanation of the decision. "Written opinions can be dangerous because they identify targets for the losing party to attack," warns one arbitration scholar.[66] In a profession neither subject to appeal nor constrained by precedent, arbitrators may be reluctant to give extra grist to the loser's mill. The U.S. Supreme Court, however, has noted that "a well-reasoned opinion tends to engender confidence in the integrity of the process and aids in clarifying the underlying agreement."[67] In some settings, such as federal labor arbitrations under the auspices of the National Labor Relations Board (NLRB), arbitrators are required to write an opinion. Also, parties can insist on an opinion as part of their contract with the arbitrator.

Choice of Arbitrator

The choice of an arbitrator is crucial. Unlike a judge's decision, which can be set aside if erroneous, an arbitrator's ruling is generally binding and not subject to appeal. In addition, arbitration offers the opportunity to select a decision maker familiar with the industry or form of dispute.

An arbitration clause may list the names of potential arbitrators. If so, the parties should check the availability of these candidates before enlisting them. Like judges and their courts, particular arbitrators may be too busy to provide speedy resolution. Alternatively, the arbitration clause may defer the selection of an arbitrator to the

American Arbitration Association (AAA), which represents 18,000 arbitrators, or another dispute resolution organization. Arbitrators from the AAA are skilled, and the association makes special efforts to identify arbitrators experienced in handling particular types of disputes. The AAA decides how many arbitrators to appoint (usually from one to three) and may include arbitrators from different professions, unless the arbitration clause specifies the number and kind of arbitrators desired. Arbitration clauses often provide that each party will choose its own arbitrator and that these two will pick a third. In some states, the government itself is willing to intervene. In New York, for instance, a court may name the arbitrator upon application by either party.[68] The Federal Arbitration Act has a similar provision.[69]

The Delaware Court of Chancery adopted rules effective on February 1, 2010, that permit business entities to submit certain business disputes to arbitration by judges or masters sitting permanently on the Court of Chancery.[70] To be eligible, (1) the parties must consent to arbitration by the Court of Chancery, and (2) at least one party must be a business entity organized under Delaware law or have its principal place of business in Delaware. Disputes involving consumers are not eligible. Claims solely for monetary damages (as compared with claims for injunctive or declaratory relief) must have amounts in controversy in excess of $1 million. Arbitration decisions can be appealed to the Delaware Supreme Court.

Arbitration Clauses

Parties typically agree to arbitrate their disputes by including an *arbitration clause* in their contract. Most arbitration clauses simply state that the parties will arbitrate all disputes relating to or arising out of their contract—leaving the parties to fight over the specifics of arbitration after a dispute arises. Instead, parties should specify in the agreement the types of issues and disputes to be resolved through arbitration as well as the procedure and rules to be used at the arbitration. It is far easier for parties to negotiate these terms at the beginning of their relationship than later after a dispute has arisen. The agreement should expressly state whether the arbitration will be binding or nonbinding. Parties should also stipulate the scope of discovery available, the types of permissible damages awards (including whether punitive damages will be available),[71] the location of the hearings, a reasonable timetable for resolving the dispute, and any other procedural matters on which they can agree.

---

65. *See* Life Receivables Trust v. Syndicate 102 at Lloyd's of London, 549 F.3d 210 (2d Cir. 2008).

66. R. COULSON, BUSINESS ARBITRATION—WHAT YOU NEED TO KNOW 29 (3d ed. 1986).

67. United Steelworkers of Am. v. Enter. Wheel & Car Corp., 363 U.S. 593, 598 (1960).

68. N.Y. C.P.L.R. 7504 (CONSOL. 2011).

69. 9 U.S.C. § 5.

70. Interview, *Delaware Court of Chancery Adopts New Arbitration Rules*, CORP. COUNS. WKLY. (BNA), Apr. 7, 2010, at 112.

71. In some states, such as Illinois, an arbitrator cannot award punitive damages unless the parties expressly authorize such an award.

HISTORICAL PERSPECTIVE

Early Binding Arbitration

In one of the earliest examples of ADR, two women brought their dispute over the maternity of an infant boy to a leading official:

> Then the king [Solomon] said, "The one says, 'This is my son, who is living, and your son is the dead one'; and the other says, 'No! For your son is the dead one, and my son is the living one.' "
>
> And the king said, "Get me a sword." So they brought a sword before the king. And the king said, "Divide the living child in two, and give half to the one and half to the other."
>
> Then the woman whose child was the living one spoke to the king for she was deeply stirred over her son and said, "Oh my lord, give her the living child and by no means kill him."
>
> But the other said, "He shall be neither mine nor yours; divide him!"
>
> Then the king answered and said, "Give the first woman the living child and by no means kill him. She is his mother."
>
> When all Israel heard of the judgment which the king had handed down, they feared the king; for they saw that the wisdom of God was in him to administer justice.[a]

_____

a. 1 *Kings* 3:23–28.

© Cengage Learning 2013

To minimize conflict over such specifics, parties often designate that arbitrations will be conducted according to the rules of a third-party organization, such as the American Arbitration Association. Such organizations have evolved certain rules and procedures that may serve as defaults for disputing parties. Unfortunately, these rules rarely include provisions concerning the scope of discovery and limits on punitive damages. Parties are better served by including specific provisions concerning these matters.

When drafting a contract, managers should consider the scope of any arbitration clause. In *mandatory arbitration*, one party will not do business with the other unless he or she agrees to arbitrate any future claims. Usually, the parties to the contract are the parties to the arbitration. Sometimes, however, a dispute may arise between parties to several different contracts. For example, there may be a dispute between a construction subcontractor and an architect. The parties should ensure that each contract contains an arbitration clause and that each party agrees to a consolidated arbitration with other parties on related issues.

The more standard and reasonable an arbitration clause, the less likely it is to spawn derivative litigation questioning the obligation to arbitrate. When there is a challenge to the entire contract, however, a claimant may be able to bring suit in a court of law.[72]

Judicial Enforcement of Arbitration Clauses: Federal Arbitration Act

In 1920, New York enacted the first arbitration statute in the United States, giving parties the right to settle current disputes and resolve future ones through private arbitration. The New York act served as a model for the Uniform Arbitration Act enacted thirty-five years later. Today, most states have amended their laws to conform to the Uniform Arbitration Act, making agreements to arbitrate and arbitration awards judicially enforceable.

Congress passed what is now known as the *Federal Arbitration Act (FAA) in 1925*. Many years later, the Supreme Court proclaimed that in enacting the law, "Congress declared a national policy favoring arbitration and withdrew the power of the states to require a judicial forum for the resolution of claims which the contracting parties agreed to resolve by arbitration."[73]

Section 2 of the FAA provides that arbitration agreements in contracts concerning interstate commerce are "valid, irrevocable, and enforceable, save upon such grounds as exist at law or in equity for the revocation of any contract." By placing arbitration agreements on the same footing as other contracts, Congress precluded the states from "singling out arbitration agreements for suspect status."[74] For example, the Supreme Court struck down a Montana law that rendered an arbitration clause unenforceable unless "[n]otice that [the] contract is subject to arbitration" was "typed in underlined capital letters on the first page of the contract."[75] Montana's first-page notice requirement conflicted with the FAA because it applied only to arbitration agreements and not to all contracts.

In the following case, the Supreme Court considered whether an arbitration clause prohibiting class actions could be invalidated as unconscionable under state law.

_____

72. Spahr v. Secco, 330 F.3d 1266 (10th Cir. 2003).

73. Southland Corp. v. Keating, 465 U.S. 1, 2 (1984).

74. Doctor's Assocs., Inc. v. Casarotto, 517 U.S. 681, 687 (1996).

75. *Id.* at 683.

winnond/Shutterstock

| A CASE IN POINT | *Summary* | Case 3.3 |

AT&T Mobility LLC v. Concepcion

Supreme Court of the United States
131 S. Ct. 1740 (2011).

FACTS   In 2002, Vincent and Liza Concepcion purchased AT&T Mobility cellular telephone service, which was advertised as including the provision of free phones. AT&T did not charge them for the phones, but they were charged $30.22 in sales tax based on the phones' retail value. The contract provided for arbitration of all disputes between the parties, but required that claims be brought in the parties' "individual capacity, and not as a plaintiff or class member in any purported class or representative proceeding."

The Concepcions subsequently filed a complaint against AT&T alleging, among other things, that AT&T had engaged in false advertising and fraud by charging sales tax on phones it advertised as free. The complaint was later consolidated with a putative class action.

AT&T moved to compel arbitration under the terms of its contract with the Concepcions. The Concepcions opposed the motion, contending that the arbitration agreement was unconscionable and unlawfully exculpatory under California law because it disallowed classwide procedures. In particular, the plaintiffs cited the California Supreme Court's decision in *Discover Bank v. Supreme Court,*[76] in which the court ruled that a ban on class proceedings is an unconscionable waiver of liability when it occurs:

> in a consumer contract of adhesion in a setting in which disputes between the contracting parties predictably involve small amounts of damages, and when it is alleged that the party with the superior bargaining power has carried out a scheme to deliberately cheat large numbers of consumers out of individually small sums of money.

California courts have applied this doctrine to invalidate contractual provisions prohibiting class litigation or class arbitration. The U.S. Court of Appeals for the Ninth Circuit invalidated the arbitration clause, and AT&T appealed.

ISSUE PRESENTED   Does section 2 of the FAA preempt a California rule (the so-called *Discover Bank* rule) classifying most collective-arbitration waivers in consumer contracts as unconscionable?

SUMMARY OF OPINION   The U.S. Supreme Court rejected the Concepcions' argument that the *Discover Bank* rule is a ground that "exist[s] at law or in equity for the revocation of any contract" under section 2 of the FAA. The fact that California law also prohibits waivers of class litigation did not save the *Discover Bank* rule as applied to arbitration agreements.

Like the state-law rule requiring exhaustion of administrative remedies before arbitration, which the Supreme Court struck down in *Preston* v. *Ferrer,*[77] California's *Discover Bank* rule impermissibly interferes with arbitration:

> Although the rule does not *require* classwide arbitration, it allows any party to a consumer contract to demand it *ex post.* The rule is limited to adhesion contracts, but the times in which consumer contracts were anything other than adhesive are long past. The rule also requires that damages be predictably small, and that the consumer allege a scheme to cheat consumers. The former requirement, however, is toothless and malleable (the Ninth Circuit has held that damages of $4,000 are sufficiently small), and the latter has no limiting effect, as all that is required is an allegation. . . . Consumers remain free to bring and resolve their disputes on a bilateral basis under *Discover Bank,* and some may well do so; but there is little incentive for lawyers to arbitrate on behalf of individuals when they may do so for a class and reap far higher fees in the process. And faced with inevitable class arbitration, companies would have less incentive to continue resolving potentially duplicative claims on an individual basis.

CONTINUED

76. 113 P.3d. 1100 (Cal. 2005).
77. 552 U.S 346, 357–58 (2008).

In *Stolt-Nielsen*,[78] the Supreme Court held that an arbitration panel exceeded its power under the FAA when it ordered class-action arbitration in the absence of an express provision in the arbitration agreement permitting class arbitration. Switching from bilateral to class arbitration "sacrifices the principal advantage of arbitration—its informality—and makes the process slower, more costly, and more likely to generate procedural morass than final judgment." Because classwide arbitration affects absent parties, additional procedural protections are required. In addition, class proceedings make it far more difficult to maintain confidentiality. Finally, classwide arbitration greatly increases the risks of uncorrectable errors for defendants:

> Defendants are willing to accept the costs of these errors in arbitration, since their impact is limited to the size of individual disputes, and presumably outweighed by savings from avoiding the courts. But when damages allegedly owed to tens of thousands of potential claimants are aggregated and decided at once, the risk of an error will often become unacceptable. Faced with even a small chance of a devastating loss, defendants will be pressured into settling questionable claims.

The majority rejected the dissent's assertion that class arbitration was "necessary to prosecute small-dollar claims that might otherwise slip through the legal system," reasoning that even if that were true, the states still could not require a procedure that is inconsistent with the FAA. Accordingly, the FAA preempted California's *Discover Bank* rule.

RESULT The judgment of the Ninth Circuit was reversed. The plaintiffs could not bring their claims in a class litigation or class arbitration. Instead, they had to litigate their claims in their individual capacity.

COMMENTS In a dissent by Justice Breyer, in which Justices Ginsburg, Sotomayor, and Kagan joined, Justice Breyer faulted the majority for making the "wrong comparison." Instead of comparing the complexity of class arbitration with that of bilateral arbitration, the "*relevant* comparison is . . . between class arbitration and judicial class actions. After all, in respect to the relevant set of contracts, the *Discover Bank* rule similarly and equally sets aside clauses that forbid class procedures—whether arbitration procedures or ordinary judicial procedures are at issue."

Contrary to the majority's assertion that arbitration is poorly suited to high-stake disputes, the dissent cited a $500 million settlement in 2011 of a drug dispute submitted to arbitration, the initiation of an arbitration proceeding in 2010 involving Kraft and Starbucks that could result in an award in excess of $1.5 billion, and an $833 million award to IBM in 1988 in its licensing dispute with Fujitsu.

The dissent argued that agreements prohibiting the consolidation of claims can prompt large numbers of consumers cheated out of individually small amounts of money to abandon their claims. Not only does the consumer face the hassle of filling out forms and waiting on hold for phone calls to be answered, but "[w]hat rational lawyer would have signed on to represent the Concepcions in litigation for the possibility of fees stemming from a $30.22 claim?"

---

78. Stolt-Nielsen S.A. v. Animal Feeds Int'l Corp., 130 S. Ct. 1758 (2010) (holding that "a party may not be compelled under the FAA to submit to class arbitration unless there is a contractual basis for concluding that the party *agreed* to do so").

Arbitration of Statutory Rights The U.S. Supreme Court has enforced arbitration clauses, even when the rights at issue were protected by federal law. The Court has upheld agreements to arbitrate claims under the Securities Act of 1933,[79] the Securities Exchange Act of 1934,[80] the Racketeer Influenced and Corrupt Organizations Act (RICO),[81] and the antitrust laws.[82] By agreeing to arbitrate a statutory claim, the Court reasoned, a party does not forgo the substantive rights afforded by the statute. The agreement means only that the resolution of the dispute will be in an arbitral, rather than a judicial, forum.

---

79. Rodriguez de Quijas v. Shearson/Am. Express, Inc., 490 U.S. 477 (1989).

80. Shearson/Am. Express v. McMahon, 482 U.S. 220 (1987), *reh'g denied*, 483 U.S. 1056 (1987).

81. *Id.*

82. Mitsubishi Motors Corp. v. Soler Chrysler-Plymouth, Inc., 473 U.S. 614 (1985).

Employment Disputes Employees are increasingly being required to sign applications or employment agreements that require mandatory arbitration of all future claims, including discrimination claims arising out of Title VII of the Civil Rights Act of 1964.

An employee's agreement to arbitrate is clear when the employee signs an application form or agreement requiring arbitration, receives something of value from the employer, and is given a copy of the relevant arbitration rules. Some jurisdictions will infer an employee's agreement to arbitrate if the employee continues to work for the firm after receiving notice of the company's policy requiring all employees to arbitrate their claims. In *Howard v. Oakwood Homes Corp.*,[83] a North Carolina court found that an employee's continued employment with the company after she received a written notice of the employer's required program of dispute resolution reflected her assent to the terms of the agreement. As a result, she was compelled to arbitrate her claims of wrongful termination pursuant to the terms of the dispute resolution program.

In contrast, in *Rosenberg v. Merrill Lynch, Pierce, Fenner & Smith, Inc.*,[84] the First Circuit ruled that Merrill Lynch could not compel Rosenberg, a financial consultant who filed a suit against the company alleging age and gender discrimination, to arbitrate these claims because the company had not provided her with proper notice of its policy regarding arbitration. Although Rosenberg had signed a standard securities industry form agreeing to arbitrate certain claims, Merrill Lynch never provided her with a copy of the relevant arbitration rules. To ensure that an agreement to arbitrate will be enforceable, employers should make sure both that the agreement is supported by consideration (something of value from the employer) and that conspicuous notice of the obligation to arbitrate, including relevant arbitration rules, is given to the employee or applicant.

Even though the FAA by its terms does not apply to "contracts of employment of seamen, railroad engineers, or any other class of workers engaged in foreign or interstate commerce,"[85] the U.S. Supreme Court in *Circuit City Stores v. Adams*[86] read that exclusion narrowly to apply only to contracts involving employees in the transportation industries. All other employment contracts are subject to the FAA, meaning that courts must enforce agreements to arbitrate even where the employee is asserting Title VII claims. Employees who have signed individual or collective bargaining agreements to arbitrate can also be required to arbitrate age discrimination claims under the Age Discrimination in Employment Act[87] and statutory claims under the Employment Retirement Income Security Act (ERISA), which governs pensions and other benefits.[88]

In the Department of Defense Appropriations Act for Fiscal Year 2010,[89] Congress limited the ability of defense contractors and subcontractors with defense contracts in excess of $1 million to require arbitration of Title VII claims and claims by employees arising out of "sexual harassment, including assault and battery; intentional infliction of emotional distress, false imprisonment, or negligent hiring, supervision, or retention."[90] This provision applies only to funds appropriated under the Act, but the Dodd–Frank Wall Street Reform and Consumer Protection Act gave the Securities and Exchange Commission the power to ban predispute arbitration clauses in certain brokerage contracts.

The employee's agreement to arbitrate in no way limits the relief, including damages, that the Equal Employment Opportunity Commission (EEOC) is entitled to recover on the employee's behalf in a court of law, however.[91] The EEOC may file a claim in court on its own behalf against an employer, even if the employee involved had entered into an enforceable arbitration agreement, if the EEOC is either (1) seeking a permanent injunction enjoining an employer from engaging in discriminatory practices or (2) enforcing the individual rights of the employee.

Judicial Review of Awards

The FAA lists only four circumstances in which an arbitration award may be set aside by a court: (1) the award was procured by corruption, fraud, or undue means; (2) the arbitrator was demonstrably impartial or corrupt; (3) the arbitrator engaged in misconduct by refusing to postpone the hearing when given sufficient reason or by refusing to hear pertinent evidence; and (4) the arbitrator exceeded his or her powers or executed them so badly that a final award on the issue put to arbitration was not made. These are the only grounds on which a court may modify or vacate an arbitration award under the FAA.[92] As New York's highest court stated more than three decades ago, "[a]n arbitrator's paramount responsibility is to reach an equitable result, and the courts will not assume the role of overseers to mold the award to conform

83. 516 S.E.2d 879 (N.C. App. 1999).

84. 170 F.3d 1 (1st Cir. 1999).

85. 9 U.S.C. § 1.

86. 532 U.S. 105 (2001). In a dissenting opinion, in which Justices Ginsburg and Breyer joined, Justice Stevens asserted that the legislative history of section 1 of the FAA made it clear that the act "was not intended to apply to employment contracts at all."

87. Gilmer v. Interstate/Johnson Lane Corp., 500 U.S. 20 (1991) (individual agreements); 14 Penn Plaza LLC v. Pyett, 556 U.S. 247 (2009) (collective bargaining agreement).

88. Shearson Lehman/Am. Express v. Bird, 493 U.S. 884 (1989).

89. Department of Defense Appropriations Act of 2010, Pub. L. No. 111-118, 123 Stat. 3409 (2010).

90. *Id. See also* Peter S. Pantaleo, Claudia T. Salomon & Tara M. Lee, *Contractors Note: Legislation Bans Mandatory Arbitration Clauses for Certain Employment Disputes*, DLA PIPER LAB. & EMP. ALERT, Jan. 13, 2010.

91. EEOC v. Waffle House, Inc., 534 U.S. 279 (2002).

92. Hall St. Assocs., L.L.C. v. Mattel, Inc., 128 S. Ct. 1396 (2008).

to their sense of justice. Thus, an arbitrator's award will not be vacated for errors of law and fact committed by the arbitrator."[93] Because arbitrators' rulings are final even if the arbitrators lack professional training or are actually incompetent,[94] it is very much in the interest of the parties to learn as much as they can about potential arbitrators.

Although parties to arbitration generally have the right to tailor their own procedural rules, the Ninth Circuit held that the parties could not by contract give a court broader review power than is granted by the FAA.[95] The parties in that case had agreed to permit a judge to overturn an arbitration award if he concluded that it was not supported by substantial evidence. The Ninth Circuit ruled that the parties had no authority to supplant congressional determinations of judicial limits.

Hybrids

Various hybrid forms of ADR are available, including med-arb, arb-med, minitrials, summary jury trials, and collaborative law.

Med-Arb

In *med-arb*, the parties to a dispute enter mediation with the commitment to submit to binding arbitration if mediation fails to resolve the conflict. A danger of med-arb is that honesty in mediation could become damaging revelation in arbitration, especially if the mediator then acts as arbitrator. Looking ahead to such a possibility, parties in the "med" stage of med-arb may be reluctant to participate openly and in good faith, thus ensuring the final "arb" stage from the beginning. To avoid this, it is usually preferable to specify that a different person will act as arbitrator if mediation fails to resolve the conflict.

Arb-Med

Parties using arbitration/mediation *(arb-med)* present their case to an arbitrator who makes an award but keeps it secret while the parties try to resolve the dispute through mediation. If the mediation fails, then the arbitrator's award is unsealed and becomes binding on the parties.

Minitrial

In a *minitrial*, lawyers conduct discovery for a limited period, usually a few weeks. They then exchange legal briefs or memoranda of law. At this point, the top managers of the two businesses hear the lawyers from each side present their case in a trial format. The presentations are moderated by a neutral third party, often an attorney or a judge.

After the minitrial, the managers of the two businesses meet to settle the case. If they are unable to reach a settlement, the presiding third party can issue a nonbinding opinion. The managers can then meet again to try to settle on the basis of the third-party opinion.

Minitrials have several advantages. Like litigation, they allow a thorough investigation and presentation of the parties' claims. But, unlike litigation, they give the managers the opportunity to work out their differences directly rather than through their attorneys. By shortening the time for discovery and presentation of the case, minitrials can reduce the possibility of the two sides becoming locked into opposing positions. The presence of a neutral third party gives the process an added element of discipline. Should the managers come to an impasse in their discussions, the third party can offer suggestions about a settlement. Finally, minitrials can be relatively private.

Because minitrials involve discovery, the production of briefs, oral argument, and the hiring of a third party, they can still be fairly expensive. Only when disputes are expected to involve large damages awards or protracted litigation do minitrials make economic sense.

Summary Jury Trial

In a *summary jury trial (SJT)*, parties to a dispute put their cases before a real jury, which renders a nonbinding decision. Like nonbinding arbitration, this allows the parties to assess how a decision maker might decide the case in a real trial. The result is often the basis for a negotiated settlement. Like minitrials, SJTs offer disputants the opportunity to present their best case in a trial-like setting. Because the SJT makes use of abbreviated procedures, the result is achieved more quickly and with less expense.

A unique feature of SJTs is that they can be used like focus groups. Disputants often debrief jurors after the trial to find out how and why they reached their decision. Like discovery, this helps align the parties' information and expectations, so there is less reason to go through the expense of a formal trial. For example, a car accident victim suing for $5 million may balk at the insurance company's offer of $50,000 to settle the claim. If the jury in an SJT renders an award of only $75,000, the plaintiff will be more willing to consider settlement. If the jury awards $3 million, however, the defendant insurance company will be forced to reconsider its settlement offer. Either way, the parties' expectations will be brought closer together, making settlement more likely.

---

93. Sprinzen v. Nomberg, 389 N.E.2d 456, 458 (N.Y. 1979).

94. IDS Ins. Co. v. Royal Alliance Assocs., 266 F.3d 645 (7th Cir. 2001). American Express accused the arbitrators of incompetence and not addressing the issues, but the court found that to be immaterial because all parties had agreed to be bound by the arbitrator's decision.

95. Kyocera Corp. v. Prudential-Bache T Servs., 341 F.3d 987 (9th Cir. 2003), *cert. dismissed*, 540 U.S. 1098 (2004).

Collaborative Law and Other Techniques

Collaborative law attempts to combine mediation and negotiation into a more efficient, cheaper, more satisfying, and ultimately more successful form of dispute resolution. Attorneys who practice collaborative law attempt to work out both business and family disputes without going to court. Competent collaborative professionals can now be found in virtually every state in the United States and throughout the world,[96] and tens of thousands of cases have been resolved using the collaborative law model.[97]

Usually, collaborative law negotiations are four-way meetings with attorneys and clients present. The lawyers enter into contracts with their clients, requiring them to seek other attorneys to represent them if the negotiations break down and the dispute goes to court. This removes any incentive the attorneys might otherwise have to go to trial.[98]

Ombudspersons can also help parties resolve conflict. Such a person hears complaints, engages in fact-finding, and generally promotes dispute resolution through information methods such as counseling or mediation. An ombudsperson allows aggrieved parties to vent their concerns and alert *related* parties to problems before they become *opposing* parties.

The "In Brief" summarizes the most common ADR techniques in use today.

96. Stu Webb & Ron Ousky, *History and Development of Collaborative Practice*, 49 Fam. Ct. Rev. 213 (2011).

97. Christopher M. Fairman, *Growing Pains: Changes in Colaborative Law and the Challenge of Legal Ethics*, 30 Campbell L. Rev. 237, 239 (2008). The American Bar Association ethics committee concluded that collaborative law practice does not violate the Model Rules of Professional Conduct as long as the lawyer engaging in the practice first obtains informed consent from the client. ABA Standing Comm. on Ethics & Prof'l Responsibility, Formal Op. 07–447 (Aug. 9, 2007).

98. Steven Keeva, *Working It Out Amicably*, 89 A.B.A. J. 66–67 (June 2003).

IN BRIEF

Models of Alternative Dispute Resolution

	Negotiation	Mediation	Arbitration	Med-Arb/Arb-Med	Minitrial	Summary Jury Trial
How are the disputants represented?	Disputants represent themselves, or legal counsel negotiates on their behalf.	By themselves	By legal counsel	By legal counsel	By legal counsel	By legal counsel
Who makes the final decision?	Disputants mutually decide.	Disputants mutually decide.	If binding arbitration, arbitrator decides.	Arbitrator if parties cannot agree	Disputants mutually decide.	Jury
How are the facts found and standards of judgment set?	Parties decide ad hoc.	Parties decide ad hoc.	Arbitrator decides based on preset rules, e.g., those of the AAA.	Parties and arbitrator decide.	Parties decide ad hoc.	Rules of court
What is the source for the standard of resolution?	Mutual agreement	Mutual agreement	Arbitrator's sense of fairness	Arbitrator's sense of fairness	Mutual agreement	Jury's sense of fairness
How will the resolution by enforced?	Agreement is usually turned into a contract that is enforceable by the courts.	Agreement is usually turned into a contract that is enforceable by the courts.	By the courts, according to the agreement to arbitrate the dispute	By the courts, according to the agreement to arbitrate the dispute	Agreement is usually turned into a contract that is enforceable by the courts.	By the courts
Who will pay the dispute resolution fees?	Parties decide ad hoc.	Parties decide ad hoc.	Parties decide before entering arbitration, often in arbitration clause.	Parties decide in advance.	Parties decide ad hoc.	Parties decide ad hoc.

DISCOVERY

Before a trial is held and sometimes before an arbitration hearing or minitrial is conducted, the parties collect evidence to support their claims through a process called *discovery*. Discovery includes *depositions*, which are written or oral questions asked of any person who may have helpful information about the facts of the case; *interrogatories*, which are written questions to the parties in the case and their attorneys; and *requests for production of documents*, such as medical records and personnel files. In addition, personal notes and computer files, including e-mail correspondence and instant messages, are also subject to discovery. Discovery also extends to wireless devices, such as the Subscriber Identity Module (SIM) card in cellular phones, BlackBerry or iPhone devices, USB portable drives, and digital cards.[99]

Discovery is designed to promote settlement and more efficient trials by reducing the *asymmetric information* problem, which arises because each party has information not possessed by the other party. If both the plaintiff and the defendant have similar information, there is less uncertainty to resolve through a lengthy and expensive trial. Discovery also preserves evidence. For example, depositions preserve the testimony of important witnesses who may otherwise be unavailable at trial. Finally, discovery reduces the number of legal issues to be presented at trial because the parties can see beforehand which claims they have evidence to support and which ones are not worth pursuing.

In general, parties may obtain discovery regarding any matter relevant to the dispute. Exceptions include certain information protected by the attorney–client privilege, the attorney–client work-product doctrine, and other privileges discussed later in this chapter. Failing to produce all discoverable documents can result in penalties and damage a company's case.

Corporate executives who would never write damaging statements in official company correspondence are often indiscreet or impolitic in e-mails and other electronic messages, forgetting that they are subject to discovery in a lawsuit. As one commentator remarked, "E-mail is a truth serum."[100] Managers should never put anything in an e-mail, instant message, or text that they would not put in a written memo to the file. Parties are frequently able to recover "deleted" e-mail messages from backup tapes and hard drives. In fact, computer specialists can restore e-mail messages from magnetic tapes even if they have been overwritten several times.[101] In addition, almost all instant messaging (IM) programs automatically save all communications in log files, making these files discoverable.[102] Stanford Law School professor Joseph Grundfest, a former member of the Securities and Exchange Commission, commented: "It's remarkable how many corporate executives don't understand that the 'e' in email stands for both evidence and eternal."[103]

Discovery is labor-intensive and therefore very expensive. Frequently, it involves hours and days of depositions and hundreds of interrogatories. The strategy behind such a plan can be twofold: to wear down the opposing party by making the lawsuit more expensive than a victory would be worth, or to keep the papers flowing at such a rate that the other side cannot discern what all the documents really state. Such tactics often lead to discovery disputes that end up before the court. Taken too far, these strategies can lead to discovery abuse, which reduces the already slow pace of litigation, significantly increases costs, and can anger judges. Congress has responded by limiting discovery in some circumstances, such as securities fraud cases subject to the Private Securities Litigation Reform Act, which is discussed further in Chapter 22.

DOCUMENT RETENTION AND DELETION

Federal and state regulations require companies to retain certain records. The *Code of Federal Regulations* contains more than 2,400 regulations requiring that certain types of business records be maintained for specific periods of time. Many regulatory agencies have increased their retention requirements, forcing some companies to increase their file capacities by more than 15% a year. With the proliferation of electronic documents, e-mails, text messaging, and IM, electronic communications are quickly becoming the most voluminous files that a document-management system must handle. Many companies do not have effective policies regarding document retention and deletion. Failure to implement an effective policy can have disastrous effects. For example, if a document retention policy calls for destruction of e-mail without regard to content or the existence of a threatened lawsuit or government investigation, the company risks violating federal obstruction of justice statutes and discovery rules and incurring judicial sanctions.[104] In addition, a court may instruct the jury that it can assume that documents not properly produced were damaging to the nonproducing party's case.[105] This is known as a *spoliation inference*. For example, a jury rendered a $1.45 billion verdict against investment bank Morgan Stanley after the firm failed to preserve and produce e-mails and then concealed its failure to do so.[106]

99. Derek Hill, *Wireless Technology: A Minefield for Litigation*, L.A. Times, May 14, 2007, at 11.

100. David S. Bennahum, *Old E-mail Never Dies*, Wired, May 1999, at 102.

101. *Id.* at 109.

102. Deborah H. Juhnke & David P. Stenhouse, *Instant Messaging: What You Can't See Can Hurt You (in Court)*, DiscoveryResources, *available at* http://www.discoveryresources.org/pdfFiles/TL_InstantMessaging.pdf.

103. Scott Thurm, *Whole Foods CEO Serves Up Heated Words for FTC*, Wall St. J., June 27, 2007, at A2.

104. Jima Anne Kato, *The Brave New World of Electronic Discovery and Document Management*, 49 Orange County Law. 6, 13 (2007).

105. *See, e.g.*, Scott v. IBM Corp., 196 F.R.D. 233 (D.N.J. 2000).

106. Coleman (Parent) Holdings Inc. v. Morgan Stanley & Co., Fla. Cir. Ct., No. 2003-CA-005045 A1, *jury verdict*, May 18, 2005. This litigation is discussed in Corp. Couns. Wkly. (BNA), May 25, 2005, at 162.

As former "Big Five" accounting firm Arthur Andersen learned the hard way when it was convicted of obstruction of justice after shredding a "significant" amount of correspondence and papers relating to its audit of Enron Corporation, it is illegal to destroy potentially relevant documents in the face of a threatened or pending lawsuit or government investigation. The "smoking gun" was an e-mail in which Nancy Temple, one of Andersen's top attorneys, encouraged auditors in the Houston office to abide by Andersen's document retention policy. The prosecution contended that the e-mail directed employees to destroy evidence in the face of a pending government investigation. Even though Andersen's conviction for obstructing justice was eventually overturned by the U.S. Supreme Court,[107] the firm never recovered from the ensuing government investigation and criminal indictment.[108]

Largely in response to Andersen's behavior, the Sarbanes–Oxley Act made it a felony punishable by up to twenty years in prison to alter or destroy documents with intent to impair their use in an official proceeding.[109] Moreover, accountants who knowingly and willfully fail to keep audit documents and work papers for at least five years are subject to up to ten years of imprisonment.[110]

In general, documents that a company is not required to retain for any business or legal purpose should be eliminated from company files pursuant to a comprehensive record retention plan.[111] If the documents to be destroyed contain sensitive personal information, such as Social Security numbers, financial data, and medical records, then they should be shredded, erased, or otherwise modified to make the personal information undecipherable.[112] Consumer privacy is discussed further in Chapter 9.

A well-designed and well-executed document-management program can (1) reduce corporate liability; (2) protect trade secrets and other confidential firm information; (3) protect employee privacy, especially as it relates to medical information; (4) reduce storage costs; and (5) save on litigation costs.[113] Time and money are wasted when corporate staff and lawyers are forced to search for documents during discovery. With an organized document-management program, a company knows exactly what documents are in its possession and where these documents are located. It is critical to remember, however, that the duty to preserve any document, including electronic files, either by law or court order will always override a document-management program, no matter how well planned. As a result, every plan should include a litigation hold procedure that suspends the usual disposal procedures (including the erasing of backup tapes) when there is reason to believe the documents are relevant to pending or even potential litigation.[114]

Even if a company has been careful to destroy unnecessary records, duplicates may exist in an employee's personal files, diaries, calendars, notebooks, laptops, and wireless devices, where they are still subject to discovery. For example, the Weyerhaeuser Company paid $200 million in a case after company documents were found in personal files in the home of a retired company administrative assistant. Companies should therefore include this type of record in their document-management programs.

Necessary Elements of a Document Retention Program

To stand up in court, a document retention program must satisfy several requirements.

- *Well planned and systematic.* The program must be well planned and systematic. Companies should appoint a single person (perhaps the compliance officer) or department to be responsible for supervising, auditing, and enforcing the document-management program.[115] Policies should be established as to the types of documents to be destroyed, including documents stored on computer servers, desktop and laptop computers, and portable digital devices. As long as no lawsuit or government investigation is threatened or pending, documents not otherwise required to be retained for a business purpose should be systematically destroyed according to an established time frame (for example, when they reach a certain age).

- *No destruction in the face of a potential lawsuit or government investigation.* It is illegal to destroy documents when the company has notice of a potential lawsuit or government investigation. A company cannot wait until a suit is formally filed against it to stop destroying relevant documents. It must halt destruction as soon as it has good reason to believe that a suit is likely to be filed or an investigation started. Companies that did not halt destruction of documents have been forced to pay damages even when they acted accidentally. For example, in *Carlucci v. Piper Aircraft Corp.,*[116] flight data essential to the case were missing.

---

107. Arthur Andersen LLP v. United States, 544 U.S. 696 (2005).

108. *Managing E-mail Risk: An Executive Leadership Guide*, TG GROUP AMERICAS, Apr. 28, 2003, at 4 ("Arthur Andersen's deleting of e-mail was a cornerstone in the investigation that later damaged the firm's reputation and led many clients to take their business elsewhere").

109. 18 U.S.C. §§ 1501–1520.

110. 18 U.S.C. § 1520.

111. Dan P. Sedor, *Problem: Information Explosion Meets Electronic Discovery; Solution: Practical Pre-Litigation Records Retention Planning*, CORP. COUNS. WKLY. (BNA), Mar. 8, 2006, at 80.

112. Section 1798.81 of the California Civil Code requires businesses having custody of personal information about California residents to take all reasonable steps to destroy personal customer data in this fashion.

113. Much of the discussion of document retention that follows is based on the work of John Ruhnka, Bard Family Term Professor of Entrepreneurship at the University of Colorado at Denver Business School, and Robert B. Austin, CRM, CSP, of Austin Associates, Denver. *See* John Ruhnka & Robert Austin, *Design Considerations for Document Retention/Destruction Programs*, 1 CORP. CONFIDENTIALITY & DISCLOSURE LETTER 2 (1988).

114. Sedor, *supra* note 111, at 79.

115. *Id.*

116. 102 F.R.D. 472 (S.D. Fla. 1984).

The judge did not believe Piper Aircraft's claim that it had not deliberately destroyed the relevant document. The judge issued a directed verdict for the plaintiff and rendered a $10 million judgment against Piper.

- *No selective destruction.* The importance of a systematic document-management program cannot be emphasized enough. The court will scrutinize whether document destruction was done in the ordinary course of business. Any hint of selective destruction jeopardizes the defensibility of a document-management program and enhances the likelihood that a judge will instruct the jury to assume that the missing evidence would have been damaging to the party that destroyed it. As several practitioners warned, "The adverse inference instruction can be and often is case-determinative."[117]

ATTORNEY–CLIENT PRIVILEGE, ATTORNEY WORK-PRODUCT DOCTRINE, AND OTHER PRIVILEGES

Although generally any person with knowledge of facts relevant to a case can be required to testify in depositions or at trial, the attorney–client privilege and other privileges designed to protect certain relationships limit the introduction of certain types of evidence.

Attorney–Client Privilege

Perhaps the most important limitation on discovery and testimony at trial is the *attorney–client privilege.* It dates back to the sixteenth century and provides that a court cannot force the disclosure of confidential communications between a client and his or her attorney. The privilege survives after the client is no longer represented by the attorney and even after the client's death.

The attorney–client privilege is intended to promote the administration of justice. An attorney is better able to advise and represent a client if the client discloses the complete facts. Clients are more likely to make a full and frank disclosure of the facts if they know that the attorney cannot be compelled to pass the information on to adverse parties. The privilege may also help to prevent unnecessary litigation because an attorney who knows all the facts should be better able to assess whether litigation is justified.

To be protected by the privilege, a communication must occur between the attorney and the client. The communication must also be made in confidence. If the client knows that the communication will be relayed to others or makes the communication in the presence of third parties, there is no confidentiality and therefore no privilege. Thus, statements that William J. Ruehle, chief financial officer at

Broadcom Corporation, had made to Broadcom's outside counsel were admissible in his criminal trial for illegally backdating stock options because he knew that Broadcom planned to disclose his statements to the outside auditors.[118] The court characterized Ruehle's "subjective shock and surprise" about the government's use of these statements in the criminal case as "frankly of no consequence here."

The attorney–client privilege belongs to the client alone and can be waived by the client. The attorney, however, has an obligation to alert the client to the existence of the privilege and, if necessary, to invoke it on the client's behalf. The client can waive the privilege over the attorney's objection if the client so desires.

To assert a personal claim of privilege for communications with corporate counsel, individual employees must prove that (1) they sought legal advice from corporate counsel; (2) they made it clear that they were seeking advice in their individual, not representative, capacities; (3) counsel communicated with them in their individual capacities, knowing that a possible conflict could arise; (4) their communications were confidential; and (5) the substance of their communications concerned personal legal affairs not the company's business or general affairs.[119] Satisfying this five-part test can be very difficult, so employees should generally assume that the privilege for conversations with corporate counsel belongs to the corporation and therefore can be waived by the corporation.

Corporate Clients

A corporation can communicate with its attorney only through its officers, directors, employees, and agents. Although communications between a corporate client and an attorney can be protected by attorney–client privilege, it can be difficult to determine which element of the corporation is the client. In *Upjohn Co. v. United States,*[120] the Supreme Court ruled that, in cases brought in federal court, the privilege protects the communications or discussions of any company employee with counsel as long as the subject matter of the communication relates to that employee's duties and the communication is made at the direction of a corporate superior (the *subject matter test*). Thus, communications between a corporation's attorneys and any of the corporation's employees, not just a small, upper-level group, are protected under the federal attorney–client privilege as long as those communications pass the subject matter test. The Court also ruled that the attorney–client privilege extends to communications made to both in-house and outside counsel as long as the attorneys are acting in a legal capacity. In contrast, most European countries do not extend the privilege to in-house attorneys.[121]

---

117. Interview, *Records Retention Policies: Why They Are Necessary for Corporations and Who Is Responsible for Them,* CORP. COUNS. WKLY. (BNA), Dec. 6, 2006, at 376, 374.

118. United States v. Ruehle, 583 F.3d 600 (9th Cir. 2009).

119. United States v. Graf, 610 F.3d 1148 (9th Cir. 2010) (adopting test articulated in *In re* Bevil, Bresler, & Schulman Asset Mgmt. Corp., 805 F.2d 120 (3d Cir. 1986)).

120. 449 U.S. 383 (1981).

121. Case C-550/07P, Akzo Nobel Chems. Ltd. v. European Comm'n (E.C.J. 2010).

A number of state courts and the British House of Lords do not apply *Upjohn*'s subject matter test. Instead, they apply the control group test and extend the privilege only to communications between counsel and upper-echelon employees who are in a position to control, or at least take a substantial role in making, the decision about the action the corporation might take based on the corporate attorney's advice.[122]

The decision in *Upjohn* did not resolve all of the uncertainties regarding the application of attorney–client privilege to corporations. The Supreme Court did not decide whether the attorney–client privilege applies to communications with former employees. Nor did it specify what constitutes a voluntary waiver of the attorney–client privilege by a corporation. Finally, there is still uncertainty about the protection the privilege gives corporations in suits brought against them by shareholders.

Guidelines   Following the Supreme Court's decision in *Upjohn*, experts have suggested several techniques to keep communications within the scope of the federal attorney–client privilege.[123] They include the following:

1. Because communication between an attorney and a corporation is protected only when a client is seeking or receiving legal advice, not business advice, corporations should request legal advice in writing and assign communication with the attorney to a specific employee who has responsibility over the subject matter at issue. How the interactions of an attorney and client are characterized can determine whether a court will find them to be protected. In *Satcom International Group PLC v. Orbcomm International Partners LP*,[124] the district court held that Virginia's attorney–client privilege protected discussions between corporate executives and the company's lawyer at a meeting called for the purpose of making a legal decision, even though this decision had commercial ramifications, as long as the corporation's counsel was present to provide legal advice and all discussion concerned the legal decision. Even documents that appear to be business in nature may fall under the privilege if they are created in connection with threatened or pending litigation.

2. Corporations should make sure that all communication between employees and corporate counsel is directed by senior management and that the employees know they must keep all communications confidential. Sharing communications too widely within the corporation—beyond the employees with a need-to-know—can waive the privilege.[125] Forwarding an e-mail from counsel to a third party, such as the corporation's

public relations firm, will also destroy the privilege. For example, a large bank forfeited its privilege when it shared the attorney's communication with its investment advisers.[126]

3. Employees should deal directly with counsel (not through intermediaries) and maintain confidential files and documentation.

4. When a corporation gives a government agency access to its communications or files, the corporation should negotiate a written agreement of confidentiality with the agency. Even with such an agreement, however, documents disclosed to the government lose the protection of the attorney–client privilege and therefore are discoverable in civil and class-action suits brought by private parties.[127]

Limitations

The attorney to whom the communication is made must be a practicing attorney at the time of the communication, and the person making the communication must be a current or prospective client seeking legal advice. A conversation between the client and the attorney about nonlegal matters is not protected. In *United States v. Frederick*,[128] the U.S. Court of Appeals for the Seventh Circuit held that neither the attorney–client privilege nor the work-product doctrine (discussed below) protected documents created by or communications with a lawyer who was acting as both an attorney and a tax preparer in preparing a client's tax returns. The court reasoned that a taxpayer "must not be allowed, by hiring a lawyer to do the work that an accountant, or other tax preparer, or the taxpayer himself, normally would do, to obtain greater protection from government investigations than a taxpayer who did not use a lawyer as his tax preparer." Similarly, in *Cavallaro v. United States*,[129] the U.S. Court of Appeals for the First Circuit ruled that the attorney–client privilege did not protect documents produced by an accounting firm helping the lawyers for two companies arrange a merger. The accounting company had not been retained to facilitate legal representation; it was merely providing accounting advice.

The attorney–client privilege does not protect client communications that are made to further a crime or other illegal act. The party seeking to vitiate attorney-client privilege under this *crime-fraud exception* must show by a preponderance of the evidence that (1) "the client was engaged in or planning a criminal or fraudulent scheme when it sought the advice of counsel to further the scheme" and (2) "the attorney–client communications for which production is sought are sufficiently related to and were made in furtherance of the intended, or present, continuing illegality."[130] Thus, if an executive asks his or her attorney the best way to embezzle money without being caught, that conversation is not privileged.

122. *Id.*

123. This discussion is based in large part on Dennis J. Block & Sanford F. Remz, *After "Upjohn": The Uncertain Confidentiality of Corporate Internal Investigative Files*, A.B.A. Sec. Litig.: Recent Developments in Attorney–Client Privilege, Work-Product Doctrine and Confidentiality of Communications Between Counsel and Client (1983).

124. 1999 WL 76847 (S.D.N.Y. Feb. 16, 1999).

125. Verschoth v. Time Warner, Inc., 2001 U.S. Dist. LEXIS 3174 (S.D.N.Y. Mar. 22, 2001).

126. Stenovich v. Wachtell, Lipton, Rosen & Katz, 756 N.Y.S.2d 367 (N.Y. App. Div. 2003).

127. *See, e.g.*, *In re* Qwest Commc'ns Int'l Inc., 450 F.3d 1179 (10th 2006).

128. 182 F.3d 496 (7th Cir. 1999), *cert. denied*, 528 U.S. 1154 (2000).

129. 284 F.3d 236 (1st Cir. 2002).

130. *In re* Napster, Inc. Copyright Litig., 479 F.3d 1078 (9th Cir. 2007).

Similarly, the Florida Court of Appeal rejected the tobacco companies' claim of attorney–client privilege for eight confidential documents, including attorneys' notes from in-house meetings on legal strategy.[131] Because the documents contained evidence that the tobacco attorneys had participated in an industry-wide conspiracy to defraud the public about the dangers of smoking, the documents came within the exception for communications to further commission of fraud or a crime. This ruling was instrumental in the tobacco industry's decision to enter into a multibillion-dollar settlement of claims related to the dangers of smoking.

Reporting Up the Ladder and Reporting Out

Section 307 of the Sarbanes–Oxley Act of 2002 greatly expanded the responsibility of corporate attorneys representing public companies to report "up the ladder" to a higher corporate authority evidence of material violations of securities laws, breaches of fiduciary duty, and "similar" violations of Securities and Exchange Commission (SEC) rules.[132] The goal is to promote greater corporate responsibility by requiring lower-level lawyers to report wrongdoing to the supervising attorney. If nothing is done to remedy the situation, then the supervising attorney must report to the CEO. If the situation remains unresolved, then the supervising attorney must report the violation to the board of directors. The SEC rules permit (but do not require) counsel for publicly traded companies to "report out" confidential information to the SEC (1) to prevent the company from committing a material violation of the securities laws likely to cause substantial financial injury to the company or its investors, (2) to prevent the company from committing fraud or perjury in an SEC proceeding, or (3) to ameliorate the financial consequences of a material violation in which the lawyer's services were used.[133] At least in certain states, disclosure is permitted even if state professional ethics rules would otherwise preclude it.[134]

Amendments to Rule 1.13 of the American Bar Association's (ABA's) Model Rules of Professional Conduct enacted in 2003 in response "to the corporate scandals of the Enron era"[135] generally require an attorney representing a corporation to "report up the ladder" any violation by an employee of a legal obligation to the corporation and any violation of law by an employee that is likely to result in substantial injury to the corporation.[136] A number of states pattern their rules of professional conduct on the ABA's model rules. Rule 1.13 gives attorneys the right (but not the obligation) to reveal client confidences to third parties (that is, to "report out") if the highest authority fails to address a clear violation of law that is reasonably certain to result in substantial injury to the corporation.[137]

Attorney Work Product

The attorney *work-product doctrine* protects certain information that an attorney prepares in the course of his or her work. This information includes the private memoranda created by the attorney and his or her personal thoughts while preparing a case for trial. The rationale behind the work-product rule is that lawyers, while performing their duties, must "work with a certain degree of privacy, free from unnecessary intrusion by opposing parties and their counsel."[138] Work-product materials may be obtained only with a showing of extreme necessity, such that the failure to obtain the materials would unduly prejudice an attorney's case or create hardship and injustice.

The work-product doctrine is broader than the attorney–client privilege and thus may protect materials that are not protected by the privilege. For example, even though a court concluded that a corporation had waived the attorney–client privilege regarding notes summarizing its counsel's legal advice at board meetings by permitting an assistant to one of the directors to attend the meetings, the assistant's notes were still protected by the work-product doctrine because they summarized the lawyer's advice regarding litigation against the corporation.[139]

The U.S. Court of Appeals for the First Circuit refused to extend work-product protection to tax accrual work papers prepared by lawyers and others in Textron, Inc.'s tax department to support the tax reserve calculations used in its financial statements, reasoning that "the work product privilege is aimed at protecting work done for litigation, not in preparing financial statements."[140] In contrast, the U.S. Court of Appeals for the District of Columbia Circuit held that a corporation did not waive work-product protection when it disclosed tax-related documents to its independent auditor,[141] making it likely that the U.S. Supreme Court will ultimately have to resolve this split in the circuits.

Other Privileges

A party may also assert several other privileges to protect information the opposing party seeks to discover. Discussions between a physician and patient are privileged unless the patient has made his or her medical condition

---

131. 66 U.S.L.W. 1111 (Aug. 19, 1997).

132. Thomas G. Bost, *Corporate Lawyers After the Big Quake: The Conceptual Fault Line in the Professional Duty of Confidentiality*, 19 GEO. J. LEGAL ETHICS 1089 (2006).

133. 17 C.F.R. pt. 205, § 205.3(d)(2).

134. North Carolina State Bar Ethics Comm., Formal Op. 2005-9 (Jan. 20, 2006).

135. MODEL RULES OF PROF'L CONDUCT R. 1.13 cmt. (2007).

136. MODEL RULES OF PROF'L CONDUCT R. 1.13 (2007).

137. *Id.*

138. Hickman v. Taylor, 329 U.S. 495, 510 (1947).

139. Nat'l Educ. Training Group, Inc. v. SkillSoft Corp., 1999 WL 378337 (S.D.N.Y. June 10, 1999).

140. United States v. Textron Inc., 577 F.3d 21, 31–32 (1st Cir. 2009) (en banc).

141. United States v. Deloitte LLP, 610 F.3d 129 (D.C. Cir. 2010).

an issue at trial. For example, a person claiming damages for a back injury resulting from a workplace accident will be deemed to have waived the privilege at least as to any medical history relating to his or her back. The U.S. Supreme Court has recognized a privilege protecting discussions between a psychologist or licensed social worker and a patient as well.[142] The priest–penitent privilege protects disclosures made to a priest or other minister during confession. The Fifth Amendment to the U.S. Constitution gives any person the right to refuse to testify if it would tend to incriminate him or her.

Several courts have recognized a privilege for corporate "self-critical analysis," on the grounds that the forced

disclosure of such potentially negative information could deter socially beneficial investigation and evaluation. For instance, in *Tice v. American Airlines, Inc.*,[143] the plaintiffs sought to obtain American Airlines' "top-to-bottom" safety reports in connection with their claim that the forced retirement of airline pilots over the age of sixty constituted age discrimination. The court upheld American Airlines' claim of privilege, emphasizing that "the public has a strong interest in preserving the free flow of airline safety [monitoring- and improvement-] related information."[144]

---

142. Jaffee v. Redmond, 518 U.S. 1 (1996).

143. 192 F.R.D. 270 (N.D. Ill. 2000).
144. *Id.* at 273.

Mike Price/Shutterstock

THE RESPONSIBLE MANAGER

ACCEPTING RESPONSIBILITY FOR MANAGING DISPUTES

Legal disputes often arise in business, and an amicable solution to them is not always possible. Some form of dispute resolution then becomes the next step. Legally astute managers treat legal disputes like any other business problem that requires a business solution.[145] Businesspeople usually need legal advice to make an informed decision but should resist the temptation to just "leave it to the lawyers." Law firms often wrongly assume that they call the shots and may spend more time and money on a case than the client intended.[146] Companies can reduce litigation costs by maintaining frequent contact with counsel.

To Sue or Not to Sue

Members of upper management and, in some cases, the full board of directors should be involved in deciding when to sue or use ADR, when to settle or dismiss, and how vigorously to defend. Sometimes the managers and employees intimately involved in a dispute lack the perspective and objectivity to evaluate the merits of a particular dispute resolution decision.

Frequently, parties file a lawsuit without giving sufficient thought to the various consequences. Before filing a lawsuit, managers should consider the following:

- Are the likelihood of recovery and the amount of recovery enough to justify the cost and disruption of litigation?

- Will the defendant be able to satisfy a judgment against it?

- Is the defendant likely to raise a counterclaim?

- Does the company need to preserve its relationship with the other party, or is this conflict the last interaction with that party?

- Will mutual resolution of the conflict make the company a desirable business partner, or will potential disputants be encouraged to seek conflict because the company appears weak and unwilling to defend itself vigorously?

- Will suing cause any ill will among customers, suppliers, or sources of corporate financing?

- Is the right decision more important than a quick resolution, or is time of the essence?

- Will public attention help in resolving the conflict, or does the matter require confidentiality?

The win–lose nature of lawsuits usually makes it impossible for both parties to claim satisfaction, save face, or forgive-and-forget. After a lawsuit, at best one party feels vindicated and the other feels wronged. Even the ostensible winner often feels angry about the time and money spent getting what it felt was its due to begin with. Or, as Jay Walker, founder of Priceline.com, put it, "It's not a matter of who wins. It's a matter of who loses less."[147]

Sometimes a lawsuit is worth pursuing simply to establish a company's credibility as one that will fight to support a legitimate business position. Notwithstanding Walker's distaste for litigation, he concluded that Priceline had to sue Microsoft Corporation and Expedia after Expedia began using reverse auctions to sell hotel rooms in violation of Priceline's patent: "[W]e concluded that the IP [intellectual property] was at the core of our ability to differentiate

CONTINUED

---

145. BAGLEY, *supra* note 56.

146. Ann Davis, *Businesses' Poor Communications with Law Firms Is Found Costly*, WALL ST. J., July 17, 1997, at B5.

147. Michael J. Roberts & Constance E. Bagley, *Priceline.com and Microsoft* (B) 1–3 (Harvard Bus. Sch. Case No. 802-082, 2001).

ourselves in an environment of low barriers to entry and the ease of imitation."[148]

If applied too rigidly, however, a philosophy favoring litigation can be expensive and may do more harm than good. Often communication, or the lack thereof, can make the difference between a minor disagreement and protracted litigation. Sometimes what the other party really wants is just an apology, a strategy Mike France of *BusinessWeek* dubbed the "mea culpa defense."[149] He called on executives to acknowledge their mistakes and apologize instead of stonewalling. As Andrew Meyer, a prominent Boston plaintiffs' lawyer who represents victims of malpractice, further explained: "The hardest case for me to bring is the case where the defense has admitted error [and apologized to the injured patient]. If you have no conflict, you have no story, no debate. And it doesn't play well."[150]

Deciding Whether to Settle

Parties should always consider settling the suit. Recent figures show that more than 90% of cases settle out of court, saving all parties the time, cost, and ill will of a trial. Filing a lawsuit can be a tactic to encourage settlement of a dispute that neither party really wishes to bring to trial.

Settlement is more likely when pursuing the lawsuit all the way to trial is not cost-efficient. For example, if a plaintiff alleges that a product is defective and caused her a loss of $4,500, the legal expenses will far exceed the original loss. Discovery alone is likely to cost more than $4,500. In such a case, it is usually in both parties' interest to settle the dispute if at all possible. If the plaintiff's claim is similar to many other identical claims that may be brought against the company, however, settling the

first claim could appear to commit the defendant to paying all the other claims, too. Other lawsuits unlikely to settle include (1) cases presenting legal questions—such as the meaning of an ambiguous term in a contract—that the court should clarify to avoid future disputes between the same parties, (2) cases that could bring a large recovery if the plaintiff wins and no great harm if it loses, and (3) cases where one side has acted so unreasonably that settlement is impossible.

Establishing an ADR Program

To promote more efficient methods of resolving disputes, companies often institute an ADR program. To be successful, ADR programs require support from the managers, not just the lawyers.[151] The program should involve (1) in-house counsel; (2) the executives and corporate managers; (3) outside counsel; (4) the company's adversaries; and (5) certain field personnel, such as insurance industry claims personnel. Training of these various players is also essential.

The general counsel or another appropriate person should explain the benefits of an ADR program to company officers and executives. High-level management should demonstrate a commitment to the program. The company also needs to make clear that management's early and personal involvement in addressing disputes entering the ADR program is crucial to effectively resolving the matter.

Continuous feedback from all participants is essential to monitor, refine, and improve the program. Frequently, corporate managers are in a position to discover a weakness in a particular ADR procedure that could harm the company. The company may wish to designate one employee as the ADR "point person" who monitors the program to ensure that flaws are corrected and strengths are further enhanced.

---

148. *Id.*

149. Mike France, *Mea Culpa Defense*, Bus. Wk., Aug. 26, 2002, at 77.

150. Quoted in Rachel Zimmerman, *Doctors' New Tool to Fight Lawsuits: Saying "I'm Sorry,"* Wall St. J., May 18, 2004.

151. This discussion is based in part on Center for Public Resources, Mainstreaming: Corporate Strategies for Systematic ADR Use (1989).

A MANAGER'S DILEMMA

Putting It into Practice

The Propriety of Confidential Settlements

One way to avoid future claims is to settle a case pursuant to a *confidentiality agreement*, whereby the parties agree not to disclose the terms of the settlement. Such settlements may delay future lawsuits or even save the company from liability because the public may never hear about the settled claim. Also, in the event that future claims are filed, the plaintiffs will not know the economic particulars associated with the settlement, so they may settle for less than the original claim. Such settlements are a mainstay in conflict resolution and

litigation in America, but in 2002, ten federal judges in South Carolina voted to ban all secret settlements on the ground that they often hide information that could be valuable to the public.[152] The judges cited the Ford–Firestone tire tread separation cases in which secret settlements deprived the public of the knowledge that

CONTINUED

---

152. *See* Adam Liptak, *South Carolina Judges Seek to Ban Secret Settlements*, N.Y. Times, Sept. 2, 2002, at A1.

some Firestone tires were dangerously defective when installed on Ford Explorer SUVs. Had they been aware, lives might have been saved. Change seems to be in the wind, and that wind is blowing against confidential settlements. Nevertheless, for now they remain an indispensable tool in minimizing exposure for companies. If you were a manager responsible for major litigation, what factors would you take into account in deciding whether to insist on a confidentiality clause in an agreement? What factors might lead you to *not* insist on confidentiality?

© Cengage Learning 2013

INSIDE STORY

Crafting a Litigation Strategy

Once a company has concluded that a dispute cannot be resolved without litigation, the managers and counsel need to work together to develop a strategy for the litigation. Experts recommend that companies construct a prelitigation "decision tree," which determines at each step of the proceeding the chances of prevailing or losing, the costs of going forward, and the potential amount of recovery.[153] Developing a decision tree forces a company to conduct a substantial factual and legal analysis of its claim.

Litigation Strategies for Plaintiffs

When planning to file a lawsuit, the plaintiff must decide which legal claim is most likely to succeed. Courts can impose monetary penalties or "sanctions" on companies, individuals, and attorneys who file lawsuits without sufficient facts or the legal basis to support their claims.

The attorney and client should then select a court in which to file the lawsuit. State courts are usually skilled in handling a variety of business disputes ranging from contract matters to personal-injury cases. Federal courts are often more accustomed to handling complex business litigation, such as cases involving federal securities law or employment-discrimination laws. Other considerations about where to file include (1) the convenience and location of necessary witnesses and documents, (2) the location of trial counsel, (3) the reputation and size of the company and its opponent in a particular area, and (4) the possibility of favorable or unfavorable publicity.

Texas plaintiffs' lawyer Anthony Buzbee came under fire after he told a small gathering of maritime defense lawyers that filing lawsuits in Starr County on the western edge of the Rio Grande Valley in Texas on behalf of workers hurt at sea "probably adds about seventy-five percent to the value of the case."[154] He claimed that when he has an injured Hispanic client before a completely Hispanic jury and a Hispanic judge in Starr County, "you need to just show that the guy was working, and that he was hurt."[155] According to the American Tort Reform Association, the five venues most hostile to defendants are, in order:

1. West Virginia.
2. South Florida.
3. Rio Grande Valley and Gulf Coast, Texas.
4. Cook County, Illinois.
5. Madison County, Illinois.[156]

Pretrial Preparation

Having decided to file a lawsuit, the company should carefully select the personnel who will act as contacts with the attorneys. These individuals should have substantial authority in the company and ensure that the necessary information and documents are gathered for the attorneys.

Executives or senior management who will be involved in the lawsuit or with the corporate attorneys should not handle public relations. This could lead to disputes regarding waiver of the attorney–client privilege.

The company should also tell all employees not to destroy any documents that may be relevant to the lawsuit. Destruction of these documents, particularly after the claim is filed, can be harmful and even illegal.

Top management should tell employees not to discuss the lawsuit with anyone, including family or close friends. Casual comments about bankrupting the opposing party or teaching an opponent a lesson may turn up as testimony at trial, with undesirable consequences.

The company and its attorney should develop a budget for the lawsuit. Then, at each step of the case, strategic options can be discussed on the basis of cost–benefit analysis. The budget should include not only the attorneys' fees but also

CONTINUED

153. See Roger Fisher, *He Who Pays the Piper*, HARV. BUS. REV., Mar.–Apr. 1985, at 150. *See also* Joseph A. Grundfest & Peter H. Huang, *The Unexpected Value of Litigation: A Real Options Perspective*, 58 STAN. L. REV. 1267 (2005).

154. Nathan Koppel, *A Lawyer's Speech Opens a New Venue in Ongoing Battle*, WALL ST. J., Feb. 27, 2007, at B1.

155. *Id.*

156. *Id.* at B2.

(1) the cost of employee time, (2) damage to company morale, (3) disruption of business, and (4) other hidden expenses. A budget will help the company manager and lawyer decide whether to pursue the lawsuit or attempt to settle.

All courts urge the parties to confer and settle the case if possible. The judge will act as a settlement mediator and objectively assist counsel in recognizing the strengths and weaknesses of their cases. Many state courts require a settlement conference before a specially designated settlement judge. The parties may also hire retired judges, professional mediators, law school professors, or mediators who are part of a bar association settlement program to facilitate settlement.

Litigation Strategies for Defendants

A defendant receiving a complaint and summons notifying it that a lawsuit has been filed should never let the lawsuit go unattended. The defendant should plan a defense strategy and follow it step by step. Factual and legal preparation should be done promptly so that important evidence—such as the memory of key witnesses—is not lost.

When a company is served with a complaint, it should try to determine why the plaintiff felt it necessary to sue. Some of the factors may include (1) whether prior bargaining or negotiations with the plaintiff broke down, and why; (2) whether

the company's negotiator was pursuing the wrong tactics or following an agenda inconsistent with the company's best interests; and (3) whether the lawsuit resulted from bad personnel practices that the company still needs to correct.

The defendant should always promptly consider the possibility of a settlement and review the ways in which amicable negotiations could be commenced or resumed. Senior executives should get together and decide whether it would be beneficial to discuss the lawsuit with the plaintiff. Referring to Texaco's failure to negotiate a settlement with Pennzoil (subject of the "Inside Story" in Chapter 7), then Texaco Deputy Chair James Kinnear remarked, "The case should have and could have been settled."[157] The defendant may also want to consider mediation or arbitration as alternatives to an expensive trial. Sometimes an apology can be more important than a vigorous defense in a case where the plaintiff feels unjustly wronged.

If the lawsuit cannot be settled, then the defendant should proceed with the same steps required of the plaintiff—plan a strategy, prepare a budget for the action, and so on. If the suit was filed in a state court, the defendant must decide whether it is possible and desirable to move the action to federal court.

---

157. BAGLEY, *supra* note 56, at 205.

KEY WORDS AND PHRASES

affidavit   65

affirmative defense   65

alternative dispute resolution (ADR)   58

answer   65

appellant   47

appellee   47

arbitration   70

arbitrator   70

attorney–client privilege   80

bench trial   59

binding arbitration   70

cert. denied   54

choice-of-forum clause   56

cite   47

civil procedure   64

class action   59

Code of Federal Regulations (CFR)   78

common law   48

complaint   64

confidentiality agreement   84

conflict-of-law rules   51

counterclaim   65

de novo   54

default judgment   65

defendant   47

deposition   78

directed verdict   66

discovery   78

dismissed with prejudice   65

dismissed without prejudice   65

diversity jurisdiction   51

en banc hearing   53

Erie doctrine   51

Federal Arbitration Act (FAA)   72

federal question   50

Federal Rules of Civil Procedure (FRCP)   64

final-offer arbitration   70

forum non conveniens   57

forum shopping   51

hearing   70

in personam jurisdiction   55

in rem jurisdiction   55

interrogatory   78

judgment n.o.v (*j.n.o.v.*)   67

judgment notwithstanding the verdict   67

long-arm statute   55

mandatory arbitration   72

med-arb   76

mediation   68

minitrial   76

motion   65

motion for judgment on the pleadings   65

motion for summary judgment   65

QUESTIONS AND CASE PROBLEMS

1. Answer the following questions with regard to the case *Bush v. Gore*, 531 U.S. 98 (2000):
   a. In what year was the case decided?
   b. Which court decided the case?
   c. Can you tell from the cite which party originally brought the lawsuit or which party brought the appeal?
   d. Suppose that you want to cite the following passage that appeared on page 111:

   > None are more conscious of the vital limits on judicial authority than are the members of this Court, and none stand more in admiration of the Constitution's design to leave the selection of the President to the people, through their legislatures, and to the political sphere. When contending parties invoke the process of the courts, however, it becomes our unsought responsibility to resolve the federal and constitutional issues the judicial system has been forced to confront.

   Where would the page designation go?

2. Nine individuals who had been exposed to asbestos filed a class-action complaint against multiple asbestos manufacturers on behalf of the class of individuals who had not previously sued asbestos manufacturers and either (1) had been exposed to asbestos attributable to the defendants through their occupations or the occupation of a household member or (2) had a spouse or family member who had been exposed to asbestos. The size of the class was indeterminate but was estimated at hundreds of thousands, perhaps millions, of individuals. Only half of the named plaintiffs currently manifested medical conditions as a result of exposure; others had allegedly been exposed to asbestos but had not yet developed any asbestos-related medical condition. The lead plaintiffs and defendants reached a proposed settlement agreement and sought class certification and court approval of the settlement. Why might the defendant manufacturers want the court to certify this class? Should the class be certified? [*Amchem Products, Inc. v. Windsor*, 521 U.S. 591 (1997).]

3. FC Schaffer & Associates, Inc. is an engineering firm based in Louisiana that did business with ODA Trading Agency, an Ethiopian entity that represents businesses wanting to do business in Ethiopia. Endrias, the founder and owner of ODA, employs Mesfin Gebreyes and an independent contractor, Kifle Gebre. Endrias left Ethiopia to live in the United States for five years. Shortly after Endrias's departure, Kifle learned that the Ethiopian Sugar Corporation was going to build a sugar mill and ethanol plant in Ethiopia. Kifle then contacted Schaffer about bidding for the project. Schaffer was interested and entered into a contract with ODA that provided that Schaffer would pay a commission to ODA if it was the successful bidder on the project. Schaffer was the low bidder and was chosen to build the mill and plant.

   Two months after Schaffer was awarded the contract, Endrias returned to Ethiopia and contacted Schaffer to introduce himself as the owner of ODA. Schaffer had never worked with or heard of Endrias and decided to enter into a new agreement with Mesfin and Kifle. This agreement purported to supersede the prior agreement between Schaffer and ODA. Schaffer refused to pay any commission to ODA under the first agreement, and Endrias sued Schaffer for breach of contract in the U.S. District Court for the Middle District of Louisiana. Can Endrias sue Schaffer in federal court? What law will apply to the breach-of-contract claim—federal law, the state law of Louisiana, or the law of Ethiopia? [*ODA v. FC Schaffer & Associates, Inc.*, 204 F.3d 639 (5th Cir. 2000).]

4. John W. Ferron, an Ohio resident, sued 411 Web Directory and National Programming Service in Ohio in connection with the transmittal by 411 Web Directory of 168 e-mail messages advertising the availability of "Dish Network" satellite television products and services to consumers. 411 Web Directory has no contacts with the state of Ohio beyond transmitting the e-mails. Does an Ohio court have personal jurisdiction over this defendant? [*Ferron v. 411 Web Directory*, 2009 U.S. Dist. LEXIS 109898 (July 6, 2009).]

5. In a securities case, the plaintiff sought to compel documents regarding a merger between EdgeMark Financial Corporation and Old Kent Financial Corporation. EdgeMark retained David Olson of Donaldson, Lufkin & Jenrette (DLJ) to act as its investment banker in connection

with the merger. EdgeMark sent a number of documents to Olson that it claims are protected by the attorney–client privilege. The plaintiff argues that these documents are no longer protected by the privilege because disclosure to Olson resulted in waiver of the privilege. EdgeMark argues that after the plaintiff's counsel threatened to sue, EdgeMark's and DLJ's interests became "inextricably linked" because the litigation jeopardized the merger. As a result, EdgeMark argues, the documents are protected under the "common interest" rule, which is an exception to the general rule under the attorney–client privilege that the privilege is waived when a document is disclosed to a third party. The common interest rule protects from disclosure communications between one party and an attorney for another party when the parties are engaged in a joint defense effort. DLJ is not a party to the lawsuit and has not been asked to assist in the defense. Has the attorney–client privilege been waived, or does the common interest rule preserve the privilege? [*Blanchard v. EdgeMark Financial Corp.*, 192 F.R.D. 233 (N.D. Ill. 2000).]

6. A group of plaintiffs, including the American Civil Liberties Union, journalists, scholars, and lawyers, filed a lawsuit challenging the U.S. government's warrantless international Terrorist Surveillance Program (TSP) as a violation of their constitutional rights and the Foreign Intelligence Surveillance Act of 1978 (FISA). In the wake of the September 11, 2001 terrorist attacks, President George W. Bush instituted the TSP and instructed the National Security Agency (NSA) to intercept without a warrant telephone and e-mail communications involving at least one party located outside the United States who the NSA has "a reasonable basis to conclude . . . is a member of al Qaeda, affiliated with al Qaeda, or a member of an organization affiliated with al Qaeda, or working in support of al Qaeda." The plaintiffs asserted that they communicated with persons living overseas who were the types of people targeted by the TSP and were therefore likely to have been subjected to the NSA's eavesdropping. The district court granted summary judgment in the plaintiffs' favor and enjoined the NSA from utilizing the TSP. The court concluded that "three publicly acknowledged facts about the TSP—(1) it eavesdrops, (2) without warrants, (3) on international telephone and e-mail communications in which at least one of the parties is a suspected al Qaeda affiliate—were sufficient to establish standing" and constituted a violation of the Fourth Amendment to the U.S. Constitution. The NSA appealed on the grounds that the plaintiffs lacked standing because they could not prove that they personally had been injured by the program. The NSA invoked the state secrets doctrine (which bans the discovery or admission of evidence that would "expose [confidential] matters which, in the interest of national security, should not be

divulged")[158] to deny the plaintiffs access to the records of which conversations had been recorded in warrantless wiretaps. Do individuals have standing to challenge a warrantless international wiretapping program when they cannot prove that their conversations were intercepted? Should it matter that the defendant invoked privilege to make such information unavailable? [*American Civil Liberties Union v. National Security Agency*, 493 F.3d 644 (6th Cir. 2007).]

7. Margaret Quinn sued her employer Nafta Traders, Inc. for sex discrimination in violation of Texas law after Nafta terminated her employment. Nafta's employee handbook provides that "a dispute arising out of [the] employment relationship . . . or its termination" must be submitted to binding arbitration. The arbitration agreement further provides that the "arbitrator does not have authority (i) to render a decision which contains a reversible error of state or federal law, or (ii) to apply a cause of action or remedy not expressly provided for under existing state or federal law." The arbitrator awarded Quinn $30,000 in back pay, $30,000 in mental anguish damages, $29,031 in "special damages," $104,828 in attorney's fees, and costs. Nafta moved to vacate this award, arguing that the arbitrator had inappropriately applied federal law to a state-law claim and awarded double recovery to Quinn. Is a provision in an arbitration agreement limiting the arbitrator's authority to render a decision containing reversible error of state or federal law enforceable? [*Nafta Traders, Inc. v. Quinn*, 339 S.W.3d 84 (Tex. 2011).]

8. A group of music companies and others sued various parties that financed Napster's illegal peer-to-peer music sharing service, including media conglomerate Bertelsmann, for copyright infringement. The plaintiffs sought discovery of privileged attorney–client communications between Bertelsmann and its lawyer concerning the $50 million loan, convertible into equity, that Bertelsmann made to Napster in 2000. The plaintiffs claimed that "Bertelsmann used its lawyers to create sham loan documents that were designed to disguise what was, in fact, a purchase of control of Napster" and that "Bertelsmann, acting through its lawyers, attempted to defraud the courts by omitting from the loan documents a side agreement that allowed Napster to channel some of the $50 million into Napster's litigation expenses." Bertelsmann denied the existence of a secret side agreement and "argued that evidence that it structured a corporate transaction to limit its liability did not prove either that the loan documents were a sham or that they were intended to defraud the courts." Are the communications discoverable? [*In re Napster, Inc. Copyright Litigation*, 479 F.3d 1078 (9th Cir. 2007).]

---

158. United States v. Reynolds, 345 U.S. 1, 10 (1953); *see also* United States v. Richardson, 418 U.S. 166, 179 (1974).

CHAPTER 4

CONSTITUTIONAL BASES FOR BUSINESS REGULATION

INTRODUCTION

EFFECT OF THE U.S. CONSTITUTION ON BUSINESS

The U.S. Constitution gives the federal and state governments the power to regulate many business activities. It also provides that certain rights cannot be taken away from individuals and organizations. Responsibility for regulating business at the federal level is allocated to the three branches of government: the legislative (the Congress, which consists of the House of Representatives and the Senate), the executive (which includes the President), and the judicial (which includes the U.S. Supreme Court).

The Constitution became effective in 1789. The first ten amendments, called the Bill of Rights, were added in 1791. Since then seventeen other amendments have been added.

Although this chapter focuses on the U.S. Constitution, many of the legal and policy issues discussed have analogues in the constitutions of states and other countries. For example, many jurisdictions afford a certain degree of protection for commercial speech and prescribe the procedures that must be followed before a person can be deprived of life, liberty, or property.

Constitution's Commerce Clause to this doctrine is explored. Finally, the chapter outlines the individual rights established by the Constitution and the various methods of protecting those rights. Among the various constitutional issues addressed in this chapter are the rights to free speech, freedom of association and religion, and due process guaranteed under the Bill of Rights, and the concepts of substantive due process and equal protection. Eminent domain is discussed briefly in this chapter and more fully in Chapter 18.

CHAPTER OVERVIEW

This chapter first discusses the structure of the U.S. government and the allocation of different responsibilities to its three branches. The scope of the powers of the federal courts and the concept of judicial review are outlined, as is the Supremacy Clause. The chapter also describes the scope of executive and legislative power. This is followed by an analysis of conflicts that can arise among the three branches.

The chapter then discusses the doctrine of *federalism*, which serves to allocate power between the federal government and the various state governments. The central importance of the

STRUCTURE OF GOVERNMENT

The Constitution divides governmental power between the federal government and the state governments, giving the federal government only the powers specified therein. Without a constitutional grant of power, the federal government cannot act. All powers not expressly given to the federal government in the Constitution rest with either the states or the people.

Both the states and the federal government often regulate the same business activity. For example, there are both federal and state laws governing environmental protection, antitrust, and retail banking. If a state law conflicts with a federal law, however, the federal law takes precedence over, or *preempts*, the state law.

SEPARATION OF POWERS

Within the federal government, power is divided among the judicial branch (the courts), the executive branch (the President and cabinet departments), and the legislative branch (the Congress). This division of power among the three branches is typically referred to as the *separation of powers*.

The Judicial Power

The power of the judiciary is established in the Constitution: Article I gives Congress the authority to establish federal courts, and Article III provides the basis for the federal courts' judicial power.

Article III

Article III of the Constitution vests judicial power in the Supreme Court of the United States and such other lower courts as Congress may establish. Federal judicial power extends to all cases or controversies:

- Arising under the Constitution, laws, or treaties of the United States.
- Of admiralty and maritime jurisdiction.
- In which the United States is a party.
- Between two or more states.
- Between a state and citizens of another state.
- Between citizens of different states.
- Between citizens of the same state claiming lands under grants of different states.
- Between a state or citizens thereof and foreign states, citizens, or subjects.

In other words, the federal courts have *subject matter jurisdiction* to decide such cases.

Article III gives the Supreme Court *appellate jurisdiction* in all such cases, that is, the power to hear appeals from a lower court's decision. The Supreme Court also has *original jurisdiction* over cases affecting ambassadors and cases in which a state is a party. These cases are actually tried in the Supreme Court, not in a lower court. Today, the Supreme Court's original jurisdiction is used mainly to decide controversies between states.

Congress has used its authority under Article III to establish federal district courts and courts of appeals. (The structure of the federal court system was discussed in Chapter 3.) All cases that fall under one of the categories listed above, except those in which the Supreme Court has original jurisdiction, are tried in federal district courts or, in some instances, in state courts with a right to remove them to federal court.

Article I

Article I allows Congress to establish special courts other than the federal district courts and courts of appeals established under Article III. These specialized courts are often granted administrative as well as judicial powers. Examples include the U.S. Tax Court, the U.S. Bankruptcy Court, and the courts of the District of Columbia.

Judicial Review

Federal courts also have the power to review acts of the other two branches of the federal government to determine whether they violate the Constitution. This power of *judicial review* makes the federal judiciary a watchdog over the government.

Even though the Constitution did not explicitly grant the federal courts this power, the U.S. Supreme Court established its power of judicial review in 1803 in the landmark decision *Marbury v. Madison*.[1] The Supreme Court reasoned that one of its functions is to determine what the law is. Because the written Constitution is the fundamental and paramount law of the land, any law enacted by Congress that conflicts with the Constitution must be void.

The Executive Power

The executive power of the President is defined in Article II, Section 1, of the Constitution. Various executive functions may be delegated within the executive branch by the President or by Congress.

Article II, Section 2, enables the President, with the advice and consent of the Senate, to appoint the Justices of the U.S. Supreme Court. (The politics involved in such appointments are discussed in the "Inside Story" in this chapter.) It also gives the President the authority to appoint all ambassadors and consuls and all other officers of the United States whose appointments are not provided for elsewhere in the Constitution.

Article II, Section 2, also empowers the President to grant reprieves and pardons for offenses against the United States, except in cases of impeachment. President George W. Bush used this power to commute the thirty-month prison sentence that Lewis Libby received for leaking the names of undercover Central Intelligence Agency operatives; only the portion of his sentence involving probation and a fine was left intact.[2]

Article I, Section 7, grants the President the power either to approve or to disapprove acts of Congress before they take effect. The President thus has *veto power* over laws that do not meet his or her approval. Congress can *override* a President's veto by a two-thirds vote of both the House of Representatives and the Senate.

The President has extensive power over foreign affairs. Although only Congress can formally declare war, the President may take other military action through the President's power as commander in chief of the armed forces under Article II, Section 2. President George W. Bush used this power in 2003 to invade Iraq.

The President also has the power to make treaties with the advice and consent of the Senate—that is, with two-thirds of the senators voting to ratify the treaty. The President may also make executive agreements, which do not require the advice and consent of the Senate. These agreements are superior to state law, but not to federal law.

1. 5 U.S. (1 Cranch) 137 (1803).
2. Sheryl Gay Stolberg, *Bush Spares Libby 30-Month Jail Term*, N.Y. TIMES, July 2, 2007.

(Treaties and executive agreements are discussed further in Chapter 24.)

The Legislative Power

Article I, Section 8, of the Constitution enumerates the powers of the Congress, which consists of the House of Representatives and the Senate. Among other things, Congress has the power to:

- Regulate commerce with foreign nations and among the states.
- Spend to provide for the common defense and general welfare.
- Coin money.
- Establish post offices.
- Levy and collect taxes.
- Issue patents and copyrights.
- Declare war.
- Raise and support armies.

Congress also has the power to make such laws as are "necessary and proper" to carry out any power vested in the U.S. government.

Conflicts Between the Branches

Inherent in this system of checks and balances is the potential for conflict between the branches of government. At times, the power of one branch of the government must be curbed to ensure the integrity of another branch.

For example, the President has a type of immunity known as *executive privilege*, which protects against the forced disclosure of presidential communications made in the exercise of executive power. Vice President Dick Cheney and other senior officials in the executive branch successfully invoked executive privilege to avoid having to produce information about the National Energy Task Policy Development Group that Cheney chaired.[3]

Executive privilege also provides the President "absolute immunity from damages liability predicated on his official acts."[4] Such immunity does not, however, protect the President during his or her term of office from civil litigation over events that occurred before he or she took office.[5]

The principle of separation of powers has been successfully invoked to invalidate certain legislation. In *Clinton v. City of New York*,[6] the Supreme Court struck down the *line item veto* given to the President by Congress in the Line Item Veto Act of 1996.[7] The line item veto allowed the President to sign a bill into law, then cancel any dollar amounts that he or she believed to be fiscally irresponsible. Because the veto gave the President the power to strike specific provisions from tax and spending bills, which usually include thousands of separate, discrete provisions, the President could shape budgetary policy without having to make the stark choice to accept or to reject an entire package of provisions. Congress could effectively override any particular line item veto by adopting a disapproval bill by a two-thirds vote of both houses.

The U.S. Supreme Court ruled that the Act impermissibly altered the "single, finely wrought and exhaustively considered, procedure" in Article I, Section 7, of the U.S. Constitution, which requires that laws be approved by both houses of Congress (*bicameralism*) and then be presented to the President.[8] The Court stated that the President must approve all parts of a bill or reject it *in toto*. The amendment and repeal of statutes must meet these same requirements. If the Act were valid, it would authorize the President to create a different law—one whose text was not voted on by either house of Congress or presented to the President for signature. The Court concluded that if there is to be a new procedure in which the President will play a different role in determining the final text of what may become a law, "such change must come not by legislation but through the amendment procedures set forth in Article V of the Constitution."

SUPREMACY CLAUSE AND PREEMPTION

The Supremacy Clause of Article VI states that the Constitution, laws, and treaties of the United States take precedence over state laws and that the judges of the state courts must follow federal law. Any federal or state laws enacted in violation of the Constitution or ratified treaties are void. State law is preempted when it directly conflicts with federal law (*express preemption*) or when Congress has manifested an intent to regulate the entire area without state participation (*field preemption*). Ultimately, preemption depends on the specificity of federal regulation, any statutory language addressing preemption, and the nature of the conflict between the federal and state approaches.

In *Geier v. American Honda Motor Co.*,[9] the U.S. Supreme Court held that the National Traffic and Motor Vehicle Safety Act of 1996 (the Safety Act) preempted state product liability claims based on a manufacturer's failure to equip a vehicle with air bags. Whereas the Safety Act deliberately provided the manufacturers of cars with a range of choices among different passive restraint devices and sought a gradual phase-in of passive restraints to allow more time for manufacturers to develop better systems,

---

3. Cheney v. U.S. Dist. Court for D.C., 542 U.S. 367 (2004).
4. Nixon v. Fitzgerald, 457 U.S. 731 (1982).
5. Clinton v. Jones, 520 U.S. 681 (1997).
6. 524 U.S. 417 (1998).
7. 2 U.S.C. § 691 *et seq.*

8. Clinton v. City of New York, 524 U.S. 417, 419 (1998).
9. 529 U.S. 861 (2000).

the state law imposed a duty to install an air bag. This presented an obstacle to the variety and mix of devices contemplated by the federal statute. As discussed further in Chapter 10, subsequent Supreme Court cases have been mixed in their deference to state product liability laws.

In 2011, the Supreme Court ruled that the Federal Immigration Reform and Control Act (IRCA) did not preempt provisions in the Legal Arizona Workers Act of 2007 that require employers to use E-Verify to confirm applicants' eligibility to work in the United States and authorize the suspension or revocation of business licenses for firms that knowingly or intentionally employ ineligible workers.[10] E-Verify is a voluntary Internet-based system that Congress created for verifying an individual's work-authorization status. Although the IRCA expressly preempts state laws imposing civil or criminal penalties for employing unauthorized workers, the statute's "saving clause" excludes from preemption "licensing and similar laws." The Court concluded that the Arizona statute came within the savings clause and that it was permissible for Arizona to require use of E-Verify.

FEDERALISM

The Constitution limits the federal government's powers to those expressly granted in the Constitution. State governments, on the other hand, have general powers not specified in the Constitution. These general powers, sometimes termed the *police power*, include the power to protect the health, safety, welfare, and morals of state residents.

Some powers are exclusively federal because the Constitution expressly limits the states' exercise of those powers. Exclusive federal powers include the power to make treaties, to coin money, and to impose duties on imports. Other powers are inherently in the states' domain, such as the power to structure state and local governments.

The Eleventh Amendment

The Eleventh Amendment was added to the Constitution in 1798 to further protect the division of power between the federal and state governments. It immunizes states from lawsuits in federal court brought by citizens of another state or nation. It has been interpreted broadly to also bar (1) suits against a state in federal court by citizens of that same state[11] and (2) suits against a state by any party in state court.[12] A state may waive its sovereign immunity, but it must do so voluntarily, explicitly, and in accordance with its own law.

Congress has enacted numerous laws that purport to *abrogate*, or annul, the states' Eleventh Amendment immunity. In reviewing the constitutionality of such legislation, the Supreme Court has held that a state cannot be required to litigate in federal court unless Congress both unequivocally (1) expressed its intent to abrogate that immunity and (2) acted pursuant to a valid grant of constitutional authority.

Section 5 of the Fourteenth Amendment gives Congress the power to bar states from depriving any person of life, liberty, or property without due process of law. To invoke Section 5, Congress must identify conduct that violates the Fourteenth Amendment and tailor its legislation to remedy or prevent that conduct. Although Congress may enact "prophylactic legislation" that "prohibit[s] a somewhat broader swath of conduct, including that which is not itself forbidden by the [Fourteenth] Amendment's text,"[13] Congress may not use Section 5 to "substantively redefine" the meaning of the states' legal obligations under the Fourteenth Amendment.

The Supreme Court surprised many in 1999 when it ruled that states could not be sued in federal court for patent infringement under the Patent Remedy Act.[14] The Court ruled that Congress could not abrogate state sovereign immunity pursuant to its powers under Article I to issue patents or to regulate interstate commerce. The Court also rejected the argument that Congress could rely on Section 5 of the Fourteenth Amendment, because Congress had not identified either a pattern of unremedied patent infringement by the states or a pattern of constitutional violations. Absent evidence that states were depriving patenters of property and leaving them without a remedy under state law, Congress could not sustain the Patent Remedy Act as a valid exercise of its Section 5 power.

In contrast, the Supreme Court held that the State of Tennessee could be sued in federal court for failure to provide handicap access to its courthouses in violation of Title II of the Americans with Disabilities Act of 1990.[15] Title II provides that "no qualified individual with a disability shall, by reason of such disability, be excluded from participation in or be denied the benefits of services, programs or activities of a public entity, or be subjected to discrimination by any such entity."[16] The plaintiffs, who both had paraplegia and used wheelchairs for mobility, sought damages because they were denied access to, and denied the services of, state courthouses due to their disabilities. In particular, one plaintiff alleged that he was compelled to crawl up two flights of stairs to answer criminal charges on the second floor of a courthouse because there was no elevator. When he refused to crawl again on his second appearance, he was arrested and jailed for failure to appear.

The Court ruled that Congress's exercise of its Section 5 prophylactic power was supported by a history and pattern

---

10. Chamber of Commerce v. Whiting, 131 S. Ct. 1968 (2011).

11. Hans v. Louisiana, 134 U.S. 1 (1890).

12. Alden v. Maine, 527 U.S. 706 (1999).

13. Nev. Dep't of Human Res. v. Hibbs, 538 U.S. 721, 756 (2003).

14. Fla. Prepaid Postsecondary Educ. Expense Bd. v. Coll. Sav. Bank & United States, 527 U.S. 627 (1999).

15. Tennessee v. Lane, 541 U.S. 509 (2004).

16. 42 U.S.C. §§ 12131–12165.

of violations of the fundamental rights of disabled persons. A 1983 U.S. Civil Rights Commission report revealed that 76% of public programs and services housed in state-owned buildings were not handicap accessible. Disabled persons had been unequally deprived of fundamental rights in a number of contexts, including voting, marriage, service on juries, unjustified commitment, abuse and neglect, zoning decisions, the penal system, and public education. The Court concluded that Title II was an appropriate response to this history and pattern of unequal treatment and that the remedy that Congress adopted in Title II—to "take reasonable measures to remove architectural and other barriers to accessibility"—was "reasonably targeted to a legitimate end."

Dual Sovereignty

The Supreme Court reaffirmed the system of dual federal and state sovereignty when it struck down provisions of the Brady Handgun Violence Prevention Act that required state law enforcement officers to receive reports from gun dealers regarding prospective handgun sales and to conduct background checks on prospective handgun purchasers.[17] The Court stated that "[t]he Federal Government's power would be augmented immeasurably and impermissibly if it were able to impress into its service—and at no cost to itself—the police officers of the 50 States."

In *Reno v. Condon*,[18] however, the Supreme Court upheld the Driver's Privacy Protection Act of 1994, which restricts a state's ability to disclose personal information contained in the records of the state department of motor vehicles without the driver's consent. The Court rejected the contention that the Act violated the Tenth Amendment's federalism principles, holding that the Act was a proper exercise of Congress's authority to regulate interstate commerce under the Commerce Clause:

> The motor vehicle information, which the States have historically sold, is used by insurers, manufacturers, direct marketers, and others engaged in interstate commerce to contact drivers with customized solicitations. The information is also used in the stream of interstate commerce by various public and private entities for matters related to interstate motoring. Because drivers' personal, identifying information is, in this context, an article of commerce, its sale or release into the interstate stream of business is sufficient to support congressional regulation.

THE COMMERCE CLAUSE

Another boundary between federal and state powers is the Constitution's *Commerce Clause*, contained in Article I, Section 8. The Commerce Clause, which gives Congress the power to regulate commerce with other nations, with Indian tribes, and between states, is a source of federal authority and a restraint on state action. The commerce power has been interpreted to allow federal regulation of such areas as interstate travel, labor relations, and discrimination in accommodations. As explained below, over time the U.S. Supreme Court has changed its view of the scope of the Commerce Clause.

1824 to 1887

Chief Justice John Marshall wrote the first Supreme Court decision involving the Commerce Clause in the 1824 case *Gibbons v. Ogden*.[19] A state-granted steamboat monopoly affecting navigation between New York and New Jersey violated a federal statute regulating interstate commerce. The Court held that under the Supremacy Clause, the federal statute prevailed. In the decision, Justice Marshall expressed his view that interstate commerce—which he defined as "commerce which concerns more states than one"—included every activity having any interstate impact. The Commerce Clause gave Congress the power to regulate all such activities.

1887 to 1937

From 1887 to 1937, the Supreme Court viewed the Commerce Clause quite differently from Chief Justice Marshall. During this period, the Court interpreted "commerce" narrowly, holding that activities such as mining and manufacturing were not commerce and could not be regulated by Congress under the Commerce Clause.[20] The Supreme Court was not persuaded by the fact that the products of these activities would later enter interstate commerce. Toward the end of this period, the Court struck down various pieces of New Deal legislation, arguing that the Commerce Clause did not grant Congress the power to regulate such activities.

1937 to 1995

A turning point in the Supreme Court's attitude came in 1937 in *NLRB v. Jones & Laughlin Steel Corp.*[21] The Court held that Congress could regulate labor relations in a manufacturing plant that manufactured steel subsequently shipped across state lines. From 1937 until 1995, virtually all federal regulation of commerce was upheld under the Commerce Clause. As long as the legislation had a "substantial economic effect" on interstate commerce, it was upheld as a valid exercise of the commerce power.

For example, in *Heart of Atlanta Motel, Inc. v. United States*,[22] the Supreme Court upheld Title II of the

---

17. Printz v. United States, 521 U.S. 898 (1997).
18. 528 U.S. 141 (2000).
19. 22 U.S. (1 Wheat.) 1 (1824).
20. *See* Carter v. Carter Coal, 298 U.S. 238 (1936); A.L.A. Schechter Poultry Corp. v. United States, 295 U.S. 495 (1935).
21. 301 U.S. 1 (1937).
22. 379 U.S. 241 (1964).

Civil Rights Act of 1964, which prohibits discrimination or segregation on the grounds of race, color, religion, or national origin in any inn, hotel, motel, or other establishment of more than five rooms that provides lodging to transient guests. The party challenging the Act—the Heart of Atlanta Motel—had followed a practice of refusing to rent rooms to African Americans, and it stated its intention to continue to do so. The operator of the motel solicited patronage from both inside and outside the state of Georgia through billboards, signs, and various national advertising media, including magazines of national circulation. Approximately 75% of its registered guests were from out of state.

The Court noted that the population had become increasingly mobile, with millions of people of all races traveling from state to state. Because African Americans in particular were subjected to discrimination in transient accommodations, they were forced to travel great distances to secure lodging, which impaired their ability to travel to other states.

In *Katzenbach v. McClung*,[23] the Supreme Court upheld the application of the Civil Rights Act to a restaurant because a substantial portion of the food that it served had previously moved in interstate commerce. The Court reasoned that the restaurant's discrimination against African Americans, who were potential customers, resulted in its selling less food that had traveled in interstate commerce. Thus, the discrimination had a substantial effect on interstate commerce.

1995 to the Present

In 1995, in *United States v. Lopez*,[24] the Supreme Court again changed course when it struck down the Federal Gun-Free School Zone Act provision banning guns near schools as being beyond Congress's power under the Commerce Clause. The Court found that the statute was not a regulation of the use of the channels of interstate commerce, an attempt to prohibit the interstate transportation of a commodity through the channels of interstate commerce, or an attempt to protect an instrumentality of interstate commerce or a thing in interstate commerce. The Court ruled that the law was not sustainable as a regulation of an activity that substantially affects interstate commerce because its terms had nothing to do with commerce or any sort of economic enterprise.

The Court rejected the government's argument that the statute was constitutional because possession of a firearm at school might result in violent crime, which in turn would (1) affect the functioning of the national economy by increasing costs and reducing people's willingness to travel to parts of the country deemed unsafe and (2) reduce national productivity by threatening the

learning environment. The Court reasoned that the "cost of crime" argument would give Congress the power to regulate not only all violent crime, but also all activities that might lead to violent crime. Similarly, the "national productivity" argument would empower Congress to regulate any activity related to the economic productivity of individual citizens, including family laws governing marriage, child support, and divorce. As a result, there would be virtually no limitation on federal power, even in areas such as criminal law and education where the states historically have been sovereign. The Court also noted that Congress had failed to state any factual findings justifying the adoption of the Gun-Free School Zone Act.

In *United States v. Morrison*,[25] the Court struck down the Violent Crimes Against Women Act, even though the Act was supported by numerous congressional findings regarding the serious impact that gender-motivated violence has on victims and their families. Christy Brzonkala, a student at Virginia Polytechnic Institute, had sued Virginia Tech and two fellow students who allegedly assaulted and repeatedly raped her, under section 13981 of the Act, which states that "persons within the United States have the right to be free from crimes of violence motivated by gender."[26] Chief Justice Rehnquist, writing for the majority, found that the existence of congressional findings is not sufficient, by itself, to sustain the constitutionality of Commerce Clause legislation. The Court also rejected the argument that Congress may regulate noneconomic violent criminal conduct based solely on that conduct's aggregate effect in interstate commerce, noting that

the concern that we expressed in *Lopez* that Congress might use the Commerce Clause to completely obliterate the Constitution's distribution between national and local authority seems well founded. . . . If accepted, [petitioners'] reasoning would allow Congress to regulate any crime as long as the nationwide, aggregated impact of that crime has substantial effects on employment, production, transit, or consumption.[27]

In 2000, the Supreme Court also ruled that Congress could not apply the federal arson statute to the burning of a private home.[28] The statute made it a crime for any person to damage or destroy "by means of fire or an explosive, any . . . property used in interstate or foreign commerce or in any activity affecting interstate or foreign commerce." The government argued that the burned Indiana home was used in at least three activities affecting commerce: (1) the homeowner used the house as collateral to obtain a mortgage from an Oklahoma lender, (2) the house was used to obtain an insurance policy from a Wisconsin

---

23. 379 U.S. 294 (1964).
24. 514 U.S. 549 (1995).

25. 529 U.S. 598 (2000).
26. 42 U.S.C. § 13981 (1994).
27. Morrison v. United States, 529 U.S. 598 (2000).
28. Jones v. United States, 529 U.S. 848 (2000).

insurer, and (3) the house received natural gas from out-side Indiana. The Court rejected these arguments, noting that under this reasoning

> hardly a building in the land would fall outside the federal statute's domain. Practically every building in our cities, towns, and rural areas is constructed with supplies that have moved in interstate commerce, served by utilities that have an interstate connection, financed or insured by enterprises that do business across state lines, or bears some other trace of interstate commerce.[29]

Because the private residence was used for everyday family living, not commerce or any activity affecting commerce, the federal arson law did not apply. Unlike *Morrison*, where the Court struck down the Violent Crimes Against Women Act in its entirety, the Court in *Jones* did not strike down the arson statute as unconstitutional on its face. Congress could legitimately regulate damage or destruction to property that was in fact used in interstate or foreign commerce or in activities affecting such commerce, so the statute was valid as applied to such conduct.

The Patient Protection and Affordable Care Act of 2010[30] required all individuals to purchase health insurance by 2014 or pay a monetary penalty. Opponents of the massive federal health-care reform law, which some critics derisively called "Obamacare," challenged the law as an unconstitutional assertion of federal power. The following case addressed this issue.

---

29. *Id.* at 857.

30. Pub. L. No. 111-148, 124 Stat. 119 (2010).

A CASE IN POINT	*Summary*	Case 4.1

Florida v. U.S. Department of Health and Human Services

United States Court of Appeals for the Eleventh Circuit
648 F.3d 1235 (11th Cir. 2011), *cert. granted*, 2011 U.S. LEXIS 8094 (U.S. Nov. 14, 2011).

FACTS   On March 23, 2010, Congress passed the Patient Protection and Affordable Care Act,[31] a massive health-care reform law designed to improve access to the health-care and health insurance markets and to reduce the cost of health care. The Act (1) created tax incentives for small businesses to buy health insurance for their employees and required many large employers to do so; (2) provided for the creation of state-operated "health benefit exchanges," which allow individuals and small businesses to use collective buying power to obtain price-competitive insurance; (3) expanded Medicaid eligibility to help lower-income families obtain health insurance; (4) barred insurance companies from denying coverage to or increasing rates for people with preexisting conditions; and (5) imposed the "Requirement to Maintain Minimum Essential Coverage."[32]

The minimum essential coverage provision (also known as "the insurance mandate") requires Americans or their employers to buy essential health-care insurance by January 1, 2014. Individuals who fail to maintain coverage at the beginning of each month are required to pay either a flat rate penalty or a penalty based on household income (not to exceed the dollar amount per year of the "Bronze" package, the lowest-level health-care package offered by Health Care Exchanges), with exceptions for those individuals who cannot afford coverage or face particular hardship with respect to their capability to obtain coverage.[33]

Soon after Congress passed the Act, twenty-six states, two private individuals (Mary Brown and Kaj Ahlburg), and the National Federation of Independent Business brought suit against the Secretaries of the U.S. Health and Human Services Department (HHS), the U.S. Treasury, and the U.S. Department of Labor (collectively, the "Government"). The plaintiffs challenged the constitutionality of the Act in its entirety, claiming that Congress lacked the power to impose the individual mandate under the Commerce Clause.

In January 2011, Florida district court Judge Roger Vinson ruled that the entire law was unconstitutional, because it rested on what he held was the unconstitutional and nonseverable mandate.[34] Congress did not include a *severability clause*, which would have made the balance of the Act enforceable even if the mandate was struck down. The court cited evidence that the

CONTINUED

---

31. *Id.*

32. 26 U.S.C. § 5000A (2010).

33. *Id.*

34. Florida *ex rel.* Bondi v. U.S. Dep't of Health & Human Servs., 780 F. Supp. 2d 1256 (N.D. Fla. 2011).

mandate was an indispensable part of Congress's overall plan to reform health care and that Congress would not have passed the Act without the ability to impose the mandate. Judge Vinson stayed his decision, pending expedited appeal to the U.S. Court of Appeals for the Eleventh Circuit or the U.S. Supreme Court,[35] and the plaintiffs appealed.

ISSUES PRESENTED   Is an act that requires individuals to purchase health insurance or pay a penalty a valid exercise of Congress's power under the Commerce Clause? If not, is it a valid exercise of Congress's power under the Taxing Clause? If the mandate is unconstitutional, may it be severed from the entirety of the Act?

SUMMARY OF OPINION   The U.S. Court of Appeals for the Eleventh Circuit began its analysis by noting that the minimum coverage provision, like all congressional enactments, is presumed to be constitutional unless it can be shown that Congress exceeded its constitutional power. Congress has "broad and sweeping" power in this field, but this power must be exerted with caution so as not to "effectively obliterate the distinction between what is national and what is local and create a completely centralized government."

The court began its Commerce Clause analysis with *Wickard v. Filburn*,[36] in which the U.S. Supreme Court upheld the Agricultural Adjustment Act. That Act sought to control the volume of wheat in interstate commerce by placing acreage limits on farms, even where the overage was due to the farmers' personal use of the wheat. The Supreme Court upheld this line of reasoning in *Gonzales v. Raich*,[37] when it rejected an as-applied challenge to the Controlled Substances Act by plaintiffs in California who legally used marijuana for medicinal purposes. The court also reviewed the Supreme Court's decisions in various other cases, including *Heart of Atlanta Motel v. United States*,[38] *United States v. Lopez*,[39] and *United States v. Morrison*.[40]

The court also analyzed precedent under the Necessary and Proper Clause,[41] which gives Congress authority to enact laws "necessary and proper" for executing its power under the Commerce Clause. For example, in *United States v. Comstock*,[42] the Supreme Court held that Congress acted within its Article I powers in enacting a federal civil-commitment statute that authorized the U.S. Department of Justice to detain mentally ill, sexually dangerous prisoners beyond the duration of their sentences.

The Eleventh Circuit noted that the U.S. Court of Appeals for the Sixth Circuit had upheld the mandate in *Thomas More Law Center v. Obama*.[43] The Sixth Circuit concluded that the mandate was a valid regulation of participation in the national market for health care, not just the market for health insurance.[44] That court reasoned that (1) individuals' decisions not to buy insurance had a substantial effect on the interstate market for health care, and (2) Congress could have rationally concluded that the individual mandate was necessary for the success of its larger economic plan to stabilize health-care costs. The Sixth Circuit noted that virtually every individual consumes health care at some point in his or her life and that people receive those services regardless of their ability to pay due to the Emergency Medical Treatment and Active Labor Act,[45] thereby shifting the cost of health care to third parties. The Sixth Circuit distinguished the mandate from the statutes struck down in *Lopez* and *Morrison*, reasoning that the relationship between the decision not to buy insurance and interstate commerce was far less attenuated.

CONTINUED

---

35. Florida *ex rel.* Bondi v. U.S. Dep't of Health & Human Servs., 2011 WL 723117 (N.D. Fla. Mar. 3, 2011).

36. 317 U.S. 111 (1942).

37. 545 U.S. 1 (2005).

38. 379 U.S. 241 (1964). *See supra* text accompanying note 22.

39. 514 U.S. 549 (1995). *See supra* text accompanying note 24.

40. 529 U.S. 598 (2000). *See supra* text accompanying note 25.

41. U.S. CONST. art. I, § 8, cl. 18.

42. 130 S. Ct. 1949 (2010).

43. 651 F.3d 529 (6th Cir. 2011).

44. *Id.*

45. 42 U.S.C. § 1395dd (2003).

The Eleventh Circuit rejected this analysis, reasoning that, historically, Congress has regulated *activity* in the stream of commerce. In contrast, this Act attempts to regulate *inactivity* by imposing a penalty on individuals who have chosen not to purchase health insurance. Because the Supreme Court has never spoken on this issue, however, the Eleventh Circuit found itself unable to base its decision on this dichotomy.

Instead, the Eleventh Circuit based its analysis on (1) the unprecedented nature of the individual mandate, which, for the first time, "override[s]" ordinary decisions by Americans in their everyday lives in determining "what products to buy, where to invest or save, and how to pay for future contingencies such as their retirement, their children's educations, and their health care"; (2) the absence of sufficient and meaningful limiting principles; and (3) the far-reaching implications for the U.S. federalist structure.

The court suggested that the unprecedented nature of this Act can indicate an *absence* of congressional power. There are only a few instances in which citizens have been required to take action: they have a duty to serve on juries, register for the draft, file tax returns, and respond to the census. All of these require an individual to interact with the government. In contrast, the mandate requires an individual to enter into a compulsory contract with a private company. The court distinguished the mandate from the military draft, which the Supreme Court characterized as "a duty owed to the government as a condition of citizenship" with deep history both in the United States and in other countries around the world.

The Eleventh Circuit also distinguished the Supreme Court's decision in *Wickard*. Even though the wheat production restrictions potentially forced farmers to purchase wheat on the open market, this was not a mandate: farmers could have decided to make due with the wheat they had available, they could have ceased part of their farming operations, or they could have redirected their endeavors so that they required less wheat. At no point did Congress require farmers to purchase more wheat; they were left with a choice. Thus, the Act's economic mandate to purchase insurance is even more far reaching than *Wickard*, which is considered "perhaps the most far reaching example of Commerce Clause authority over intrastate activity."[46]

The Eleventh Circuit noted that the Supreme Court had declined to expand the substantial effects and aggregation doctrines in *Lopez*. Because those who currently do not have insurance are not *in* the stream of commerce, allowing the federal government to regulate this previously unregulated area would "expand the substantial effects doctrine to one of unlimited scope." If an individual's decision not to purchase insurance were subject to the aggregation principle, the Eleventh Circuit found itself "unable to conceive of any product whose purchase Congress could not mandate under this line of argument."

The court then looked at the broad scope of the regulation and concluded that the individual mandate was "woefully" overinclusive. The Act is not directed at those who pay for none or for only a portion of their health care, that is, those responsible for cost-shifting. Nor is it even tied to those who consume health care. The individual mandate is applied across the board, without regard to whether the regulated individuals receive, or have ever received, uncompensated care—or, indeed, seek any care at all, either now or in the future. The Act contains no language "which might limit its reach to a discrete set of [activities] that additionally have an explicit connection with or effect on interstate commerce."

The Eleventh Circuit found that the regulation intrudes on insurance, which is an industry traditionally governed by the states pursuant to their police power.[47] As a result, it has a potentially "far-reaching" impact on the U.S. federalist structure. A state may, if it chooses,

CONTINUED

---

46. United States v. Lopez, 514 U.S. 549, 560 (1995).

47. Prior to the Supreme Court's decision in *United States v. South-Eastern Underwriters*, 322 U.S. 533 (1944), the regulation of the insurance industry was reserved exclusively to the states. A year later, in response to the Court's decision, Congress passed the McCarran–Ferguson Act, 15 U.S.C. §§ 1011–1015 (1945), which preserved state control over the insurance industry because Congress considered it a "local matter."

require individuals to purchase health insurance. When the federal government issues an individual mandate, however, it is telling states how to employ their police power. This federalism concern, together with the other "indicia of constitutional infirmity," led the court to conclude that the mandate is not a valid exercise of Congress's power to regulate interstate commerce.

The Eleventh Circuit also rejected the government's assertion that the individual mandate is a constitutional exercise of Congress's power under the Taxing Clause. Even though the mandate is housed in the Internal Revenue Code and produces revenue, it cannot be fairly characterized as a tax. As the Supreme Court has repeatedly recognized, "there is a firm distinction between a tax and a penalty." A tax is "'an enforced contribution to provide for the support of government,'" whereas a penalty "'is an exaction imposed by statute as punishment for an unlawful act.'"

The court looked to the plain language of the statute, principles of statutory construction, and the legislative history, all of which "overwhelmingly establish that the individual mandate is not a tax, but rather a penalty." The statute "over and over again" explicitly describes the mandate as a penalty without ever describing it as a tax. Additionally, the court noted, "Congress knows full well how to enact a tax when it chooses to do so." Indeed, the Act contains many other provisions that Congress explicitly described as a "tax." Presumably, Congress "did not indiscriminately use the word 'tax' in some provisions but not in others." Further, the purpose of the mandate is not to raise revenue for the government, "but rather to . . . reduce the number of uninsured and to create . . . effective health insurance markets that make health insurance more widely available."

Although the court concluded that the individual mandate was an unconstitutional exercise of Congress's commerce and taxing powers, it concluded that the mandate could be severed from the rest of the Act. The district court had invalidated the entire Act, in part, because the final version did not contain a severability clause, whereas an early version of the bill did. The lower court had also viewed the mandate as essential to Congress's objective of controlling health-care costs. The Eleventh Circuit disagreed. The Supreme Court has made it clear that "[u]nless it is *evident* that the Legislature would not have enacted those provisions which are within its power, independently of that which is not, the invalid part may be dropped if what is left is *fully operative as a law*." Senate and House drafting manuals state that "in light of Supreme Court precedent in favor of severability, severability clauses are unnecessary unless they specifically state that all or some portions of the statute *should not* be severed."

The Eleventh Circuit found provisions in the Act that were "wholly unrelated" to the individual mandate or to private insurance. It acknowledged, however, that Congress had explicitly provided in the Act that the individual mandate was essential to two of the insurance reforms—guaranteed issuance of health insurance and the prohibition on exclusions for preexisting conditions. Nonetheless, the court concluded that these two reforms would reduce both the number of uninsured and underwriting costs, so they would accomplish the main goals of the Act even without the individual mandate. Also, the Act does not contain a nonseverability clause and makes no cross-reference to these two reforms that makes their existence dependent on the enforceability of the individual mandate. Moreover, the mandate is limited in its operation: it includes a number of exceptions and exemptions and does no more than require that individuals obtain coverage that satisfies the mandate. It does not require health insurance with any particular minimum level of benefits. Because it was not *evident* that Congress would not have enacted those two provisions or the rest of the Act if not for the individual mandate, the remaining sections of the Act were severable from the invalid individual mandate.

RESULT The appeals court upheld the district court's finding that the minimum essential coverage provision was unconstitutional, but it reversed the holding that this made the entire Act invalid. The mandate was severable, so the balance of the Act remained in force.

CONTINUED

COMMENTS   Judge Vinson (the Florida trial judge whose decision invalidating the entire Act was appealed to the Eleventh Circuit) acknowledged that the "individual mandate has raised some novel issues regarding the Constitutional role of the federal government about which reasonable and intelligent people (and reasonable and intelligent jurists) can disagree."[48] The Supreme Court agreed to hear the case during its 2011–2012 term to resolve the split in the Circuits.

Like the Eleventh Circuit (and unlike the Sixth Circuit), a district court judge in Virginia (which is in the Fourth Circuit) struck down the mandate as unconstitutional in 2010, but left the rest of the law's provisions intact.[49] Judge Henry E. Hudson found no precedent for Congress using the Commerce Clause to impose a federal penalty for an individual's decision "*not* to participate in interstate commerce," in this case, by refusing to purchase health insurance. The court rejected the argument that "uninsured people [cannot] sit passively on the market sidelines," because, by their inaction, they substantially increase overall health-care costs through emergency room care and other measures. The court also rejected the assertion that the penalty is essentially a tax, which the federal government has wide latitude to levy. Judge Hudson cited several instances when the Obama administration asserted that the penalty was not a tax, in part, to prevent opponents from claiming that the Act would lead to higher taxes during a recession.

48. Florida *ex rel.* Bondi v. U.S. Dep't of Health & Human Servs., 2011 WL 723117 at *8 (N.D. Fla. Mar. 3, 2011).
49. Virginia *ex rel.* Cuccinelli v. Sebelius, 728 F. Supp. 2d 768 (E.D. Va. 2010).

© Cengage Learning 2013

Limits on State Powers

Federal powers enumerated in the Constitution impose many limits on state action. This chapter discusses only the limits on state power resulting from the commerce power, but the principles apply to other federal powers as well.

As mentioned earlier, when Congress has indicated a policy by acting, its action preempts state action because the Supremacy Clause makes federal laws supreme over state laws. Even when Congress has not taken action, the *"dormant"* or *"negative"* Commerce Clause may impose restrictions on state action.

Dormant or Negative Commerce Clause

The idea behind the dormant Commerce Clause is that the grant of power to Congress under the Commerce Clause implies a negative converse that restricts states from passing laws that improperly discriminate against interstate commerce. Since the mid-1930s, the U.S. Supreme Court has tried to clarify when state regulation affecting interstate commerce is valid in the absence of preempting federal regulation. When evaluating a dormant Commerce Clause challenge, the Court first looks at whether the statute is discriminatory or neutral on its face. If the statute is facially discriminatory, it is presumed to be unconstitutional. For example, in *City of Philadelphia v. New Jersey,*[50] the Court held that a New Jersey statute prohibiting the importation of most "solid or liquid waste which originated or was collected outside the territorial limits of the State" violated the Commerce Clause because it imposed

on out-of-state commercial interests "the full burden of conserving the State's remaining landfill."

Even if a state statute is facially neutral, it is presumed to be unconstitutional if it has a discriminatory purpose or effect. For example, the Supreme Court invalidated a North Carolina statute that prohibited the sale of apples that bore a grade other than the applicable U.S. grade.[51] Although neutral on its face, the statute's effect was to discriminate against Washington apples, which bore their own state's grade on the container, a grade that was equal to or more stringent than the U.S. grade.

The presumption of unconstitutionality can be rebutted if the state can demonstrate under a strict scrutiny standard that the law is necessary (i.e., that no other nondiscriminatory means were available) to serve a compelling state objective or a legitimate local interest.[52] For example, the Court upheld a Minnesota statute banning plastic, nonreturnable milk containers in the face of claims that it discriminated against interstate commerce.[53] The statute was not "simple protectionism"—it regulated evenhandedly by prohibiting all milk retailers from selling their products in plastic containers, and it applied regardless of whether the milk, the containers, or the sellers were from inside or outside the state.

If the Court finds that the purpose and effect of the state statute are not discriminatory, but that it has some

50. 437 U.S. 617 (1978).
51. Hunt v. Wash. State Apple Adver. Comm'n, 432 U.S. 333 (1977).
52. This presumption is particularly hard to rebut when the state statute is discriminatory on its face. The Supreme Court has upheld only one facially discriminatory state law. *See* Maine v. Taylor, 477 U.S. 131 (1986).
53. Minnesota v. Clover Leaf Creamery Co., 449 U.S. 456 (1981).

impact on interstate commerce, the Court will then balance the burden on interstate commerce against the local state interest and its putative benefit. If the interstate impacts are infrequent or insubstantial in relation to the benefits to the state, then the Court will uphold the state law.[54]

FEDERAL FISCAL POWERS

Two other federal powers, the taxing and spending powers, have been invoked to regulate traditionally local "police problems" as well as purely economic problems.

The Constitution grants the federal government a broad taxing power. The only specific limitations are that (1) direct taxes on anything but income and capitation (per head) taxes must be allocated among the states in proportion to population, and (2) all custom duties and excise taxes must be uniform throughout the United States. In addition, no duty may be levied on exports from any state. The Fifth Amendment's Due Process Clause is also a general limitation on Congress's taxing power.

Taxes have an economic impact on business.[55] The federal government has imposed taxes in order to affect the behavior of businesses as well as to raise revenues. The Supreme Court has upheld both types of taxes under the government's power to tax without regard to the purpose behind the tax. As noted earlier, a key issue in the litigation surrounding the insurance mandate imposed by the Patient Protection and Affordable Care Act of 2010 is whether the penalty for noncompliance can be justified as a federal tax.[56]

Congress has the power to spend in order to provide for the common defense and general welfare. An exercise of the spending power will be upheld as long as it does not violate a specific check on the federal power.

PROTECTION OF INDIVIDUAL LIBERTIES

The Constitution and the Bill of Rights guarantee certain individual rights, including freedom of speech, association, and religion; due process; compensation for takings; equal protection; and the right to a jury trial.

The Constitution

Although most explicit guarantees of individual liberty are found in the amendments to the Constitution, the original Constitution contains three specific guarantees of individual rights: (1) the Contracts Clause, (2) a ban on ex post facto laws, and (3) a prohibition against bills of attainder. In addition, the Constitution guarantees the privileges and immunities associated with being a U.S. citizen.

The Contracts Clause

Article I, Section 10, of the Constitution specifically prohibits a state legislature from impairing the obligation of existing contracts. The Fifth Amendment imposes a similar bar on federal legislation that would retroactively impair the obligations of a contract. In *Calfarm Insurance Co. v. Deukmejian*,[57] insurance companies raised issues under the federal and state Contracts Clauses in connection with insurance law changes mandated by California Proposition 103, a voter initiative that made fundamental changes to the regulation of automobile and other types of insurance and imposed new restrictions on an insurance company's ability to refuse to renew an automobile insurance policy entered into prior to enactment of the initiative. Seven insurers and the Association of California Insurance Companies sued to invalidate the initiative as an unconstitutional law impairing the obligations of contracts because the restrictions on renewal applied to policies issued before enactment of Proposition 103.

The California Supreme Court upheld the nonrenewal restrictions. The decision rested, in part, on the fact that insurance is a highly regulated industry in which further regulation can reasonably be anticipated. In addition, the court found that the public interest in making insurance available to all Californians and the fear that insurance companies would refuse to renew in California, leaving drivers without the car insurance required by law, was sufficient, when measured against the relatively low degree of impairment of contract rights involved, to justify the nonrenewal restrictions. The court explained:

> Although the language of the Contracts Clause is facially absolute, its prohibition must be accommodated to the inherent police power of the State "to safeguard the vital interests of its people." This Court has long recognized that a statute does not violate the Contracts Clause simply because it has the effect of restricting, or even barring altogether, the performance of duties created by contracts entered into prior to its enactment. Thus, a state prohibition law may be applied to contracts for the sale of beer that were valid when entered into, a law barring lotteries may be applied to lottery tickets that were valid when issued, and a workmen's compensation law may be applied to employers and employees operating under pre-existing contracts of employment that made no provision for work-related injuries.[58]

---

54. *See* Pike v. Bruce Church, Inc., 397 U.S. 137 (1970).

55. For a discussion of how to integrate tax considerations into business strategy, *see* Mark A. Wolfson et al., Taxes and Business Strategy: A Planning Approach (4th ed. 2009).

56. *Compare* Thomas More Law Ctr. v. Obama, 651 F.3d 529 (6th Cir. 2011) (Sutton, J., concurring in part and delivering the opinion of the court in part) (the majority opinion did not need to address the Taxing Clause issue because it found the individual mandate constitutional under the Commerce Clause, but the concurring opinion would have upheld the mandate as a valid tax) *with* Florida v. U.S. Dep't of Health & Human Servs., 648 F.3d 1235 (11th Cir. 2011), *cert. granted*, 2011 U.S. LEXIS 8094 (U.S. Nov. 14, 2011) (Case 4.1) (holding that the mandate was a penalty, not a tax).

57. 771 P.2d 1247 (Cal. 1989).

58. *Id.* at 1261.

Ex Post Facto Laws

Article I, Section 9, and Article I, Section 10, prohibit laws that punish actions that were not illegal when performed, also known as *ex post facto laws*. Ex post facto laws are discussed in greater detail in Chapter 14.

Bills of Attainder

Article I, Section 9, prohibits the federal government from enacting laws to punish specific individuals. Such laws are termed *bills of attainder*.

Privileges and Immunities

Article IV, Section 2, of the Constitution guarantees the privileges and immunities of citizens of the United States, that is, the rights that go with being a citizen of the federal government, such as the right to vote in a federal election and the right to travel. Article IV provides that citizens of each state shall receive all the privileges and immunities of citizens of other states. These provisions prohibit any unreasonable discrimination between the citizens of different states. Any such discrimination must reasonably relate to legitimate state or local purposes.

The Bill of Rights

The first ten amendments of the Constitution constitute the *Bill of Rights*. The first eight amendments contain specific guarantees of individual liberties that limit the power of the federal government. Importantly, the last two make clear that the federal government's powers are limited and enumerated, whereas the rights of the people go beyond those listed in the Constitution.

The First Amendment guarantees freedom of religion, speech, press, and assembly and prohibits laws establishing religion. The Second Amendment grants persons the right to bear arms. In *District of Columbia v. Heller*,[59] the U.S. Supreme Court invalidated the District of Columbia's total ban on handguns and its requirement that licensed firearms kept in the home be disassembled or bound by a trigger lock. The Court ruled: "Under any of the standards of scrutiny that we have applied to enumerated constitutional rights, banning from the home 'the most preferred firearm in the nation to keep and use for protection of one's home and family,' would fail constitutional muster" under the Second Amendment.[60] Although the Court upheld an individual's right to possess a firearm unconnected with service in a militia and to use it for traditionally lawful purposes, such as self-defense within the home, the Court left undisturbed cases upholding laws barring felons and mentally ill persons from bearing arms and laws prohibiting the carrying of "dangerous and unusual weapons," such as M-16 rifles and sawed-off shotguns.[61] The Third Amendment provides that no soldier shall be quartered in any house.

The Fourth Amendment prohibits unreasonable searches and seizures and provides that warrants shall be issued only upon probable cause. The following case considered whether it is constitutional for schools to require random drug testing of student athletes.

---

59. 554 U.S. 570 (2008).

60. *Id.* at 628.

61. *See* United States v. Emerson, 270 F.3d 203 (5th Cir. 2001); United States v. Marzzarella, 614 F.3d 85 (3d Cir. 2010).

| A CASE IN POINT | *In the Language of the Court* | Case 4.2 |

Board of Education of Independent School District No. 92 of Pottawatomie County v. Earls

Supreme Court of the United States
536 U.S. 822 (2002).

FACTS The Tecumseh, Oklahoma school district adopted a policy requiring all student-athletes to consent to urinalysis drug testing as a condition of participating in extracurricular activities. In effect, this gave schools the right to test athletes without any suspicion of drug use. Earls, along with another student and their parents, claimed that this policy violated the Fourth Amendment to the U.S. Constitution's ban on unreasonable searches.

ISSUE PRESENTED Does requiring student-athletes to take a drug test without any suspicion of drug use violate the Fourth Amendment?

OPINION THOMAS, J., writing for the U.S. Supreme Court:

The Fourth Amendment to the United States Constitution protects "[t]he right of the people to be secure in their persons, houses, papers, and effects, against unreasonable searches and seizures." Searches by public school officials, such as the collection of urine samples, implicate Fourth Amendment interests. We must therefore review the School District's Policy for "reasonableness," which is the touchstone of the constitutionality of a governmental search.

Respondents argue that drug testing must be based at least on some level of individualized suspicion. It is true that we generally determine the reasonableness of a search by balancing

CONTINUED

the nature of the intrusion on the individual's privacy against the promotion of legitimate governmental interests. But we have long held that "the Fourth Amendment imposes no irreducible requirement of [individualized] suspicion.". . . "[I]n certain limited circumstances, the Government's need to discover such latent or hidden conditions, or to prevent their development, is sufficiently compelling to justify the intrusion on privacy entailed by conducting such searches without any measure of individualized suspicion." Therefore, in the context of safety and administrative regulations, a search unsupported by probable cause may be reasonable "when 'special needs, beyond the normal need for law enforcement, make the warrant and probable-cause requirement impracticable.'"

In *Vernonia*,[62] this Court held that the suspicionless drug testing of athletes was constitutional. The Court, however, did not simply authorize all school drug testing, but rather conducted a fact-specific balancing of the intrusion on the children's Fourth Amendment rights against the promotion of legitimate governmental interests. Applying the principles of *Vernonia* to the somewhat different facts of this case, we conclude that Tecumseh's Policy is also constitutional.

[*Editor's note:* Justice Thomas went on to identify and examine several factors influencing the Court's decision, including the nature of the students' privacy being compromised by the drug testing, the degree to which a urinalysis is intrusive to the students, and the urgency of a school's need to obtain results quickly. After discussing and weighing these factors, the Court ruled that the policy was appropriately tailored to further the school district's goal of lower drug use among its student-athletes.]

RESULT   Random drug testing of student-athletes was constitutional.

DISSENT   GINSBURG, J., joined by O'CONNOR, STEVENS, and SOUTER, JJ., dissenting:

"[T]he legality of a search of a student," this Court has instructed, "should depend simply on the reasonableness, under all the circumstances, of the search.". . . The particular testing program upheld today is not reasonable; it is capricious, even perverse: [Tecumseh's] policy targets for testing a student population least likely to be at risk from illicit drugs and their damaging effects. I therefore dissent. . . .

Concern for student health and safety is basic to the school's caretaking, and it is undeniable that "drug use carries a variety of health risks for children, including death from overdose."

Those risks, however, are present for all schoolchildren. *Vernonia* cannot be read to endorse invasive and suspicionless drug testing of all students upon any evidence of drug use, solely on the ground that drugs jeopardize the life and health of those who use them.

CRITICAL THINKING QUESTIONS

1. Do you find the argument of the majority or the dissent more persuasive?
2. How would you reconcile the Court's reasoning in this case with its invalidation of California's ban on the sale of violent video games to minors in *Brown v. Entertainment Merchants Association*?[63]

62. Vernonia Sch. Dist. 47J v. Acton, 515 U.S. 646 (1995).
63. 131 S. Ct. 2729 (2011) (Case 4.3).

The Fifth Amendment (1) contains the grand jury requirements; (2) forbids *double jeopardy* (that is, being tried twice for the same crime); (3) prohibits forcing a person to be a witness against himself or herself; (4) prohibits the deprivation of life, liberty, or property without due process of law; and (5) requires just compensation when private property is taken for public use. The Sixth Amendment guarantees a speedy and public jury trial in all criminal prosecutions. The Seventh Amendment gives the right to a jury trial in almost all civil (that is, noncriminal) cases when the value in dispute is greater than $20. The Eighth Amendment prohibits excessive bails and fines as well as cruel and unusual punishment. Aspects of the Fourth, Fifth, and Sixth Amendments relevant to criminal cases are discussed in Chapter 14.

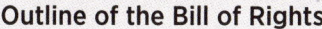

IN BRIEF

Outline of the Bill of Rights

Amendment I

No law establishing religion

Freedom of religion

Freedom of speech

Freedom of press

Right to assembly and petition

Amendment II

Well-regulated militia and right to keep and bear arms

Amendment III

Restrictions on quartering soldiers in homes

Amendment IV

No unreasonable search and seizure

Requirements for warrants

Amendment V

Presentment or indictment of a grand jury required for
    capital or otherwise infamous crime

Prohibition on double jeopardy

Prohibition on compulsory self-incrimination

Due process required before taking life, liberty, or property

Just compensation for taking private property

Amendment VI

In criminal prosecutions:

Right to a speedy and public trial

Right to a jury trial

Right to confront witnesses

Right to counsel

Amendment VII

Right to a jury trial in most civil cases

Amendment VIII

No excessive bail

No excessive fines

No cruel and unusual punishment

Amendment IX

Rights of the people not limited to those listed in the
    Constitution

Amendment X

Powers not delegated to the United States in the
    Constitution are reserved to the states or the people,
    except for those powers prohibited to the states by the
    Constitution, which are reserved to the people

© Cengage Learning 2013

Christoph Weihs/Shutterstock

Applicability to the States

The Fourteenth Amendment provides that no state shall "deprive any person of life, liberty, or property, without due process of law" (the *Due Process Clause*) and that "[n]o State shall make or enforce any law which shall abridge the privileges or immunities of citizens of the United States" (the *Privileges and Immunities Clause*).

After the Fourteenth Amendment was passed, some argued that the Due Process Clause and the Privileges and Immunities Clause made the entire Bill of Rights applicable to state governments. The Supreme Court rejected this theory, holding that the provisions in the Bill of Rights are incorporated into the Fourteenth Amendment, and therefore binding on the states, only if they are fundamental to the American system of law or are safeguards "essential to liberty in the American scheme of justice."[64] These include freedom of speech and religion.[65] As a result, if a state government were to abridge the freedom of speech, for example, it would violate the First Amendment as applied to state governments through the Fourteenth Amendment. Similarly, the Supreme Court ruled that a state ban on handguns violated the fundamental right to bear arms under the Second Amendment.[66]

Provisions held not to apply to the states via the Fourteenth Amendment's Due Process Clause include the Fifth Amendment's requirement of a grand jury indictment before any criminal prosecution and the Seventh Amendment's guarantee of a jury trial in civil cases.[67] Although the Eighth Amendment's prohibition against the imposition of excessive bail has not been explicitly applied to the states, the Supreme Court has assumed that it applied in a number of state cases.[68] The Fifth Amendment's prohibition against the taking of property without just compensation has not been incorporated into the Fourteenth Amendment, but the due process guarantee in the Fourteenth Amendment has been interpreted to provide the same protection.[69] The Supreme Court has not yet determined whether the Third Amendment, which prohibits the quartering of soldiers in private houses, and the Eighth Amendment's provision banning excessive fines are applicable to state governments.[70]

64. Duncan v. Louisiana, 391 U.S. 145 (1968).

65. *See* Lovell v. City of Griffin, Ga., 303 U.S. 444 (1938).

66. McDonald v. City of Chicago, 130 S. Ct. 3020 (2010).

67. Hurtado v. California, 110 U.S. 516 (1884); Minneapolis & St. Louis R.R. Co. v. Bombolis, 241 U.S. 211 (1916).

68. *See* Schilb v. Kuebel, 404 U.S. 357, 365 (1971).

69. *See* Chicago, B. & Q. R.R. Co. v. City of Chicago, 166 U.S. 226 (1897).

70. The U.S. Court of Appeals for the Second Circuit found incorporation of the Third Amendment in *Engblom v. Carey*, 677 F.2d 957 (2d Cir. 1982).

FREEDOM OF SPEECH AND PRESS

Although the First Amendment states that "Congress shall make no law . . . abridging the freedom of speech, or of the press," the U.S. Supreme Court has not applied the First Amendment to protect all speech to the same degree. The type of speech most clearly protected is political speech, including speech critical of governmental policies and officials. Some types of expression—bribery, perjury, and obscenity—are not protected at all by the First Amendment.

A government may violate the right to free speech not only by forbidding speech, but by commanding it as well. For example, the U.S. Supreme Court ruled that Massachusetts had violated the First Amendment when it ordered organizers of South Boston's St. Patrick's Day Parade to include a group of gay and lesbian Bostonians of Irish ancestry.[71] This compulsory inclusion of a group imparting a message the organizers did not wish to convey was unconstitutional.

Determining whether a type of speech is protected by the First Amendment is only the first step of the analysis. Even if a certain expression is protected, under certain circumstances the expression may still be regulated without violating the First Amendment.

For example, public school students have First Amendment rights, but the Supreme Court has upheld certain limits on such rights. In *Morse v. Frederick*,[72] the Supreme Court ruled that the principal of a high school in Juneau, Alaska, could discipline a student who displayed a fourteen-foot banner bearing the phrase "Bong Hits 4 Jesus" as the Olympic Torch Relay passed in front of the school. School policy prohibited messages promoting illegal drug use. Noting that "school boards know that peer pressure is perhaps 'the single most important factor leading school-children to take drugs,' and that students are more likely to use drugs when the norms in school appear to tolerate such behavior," the Court held that the "First Amendment does not require schools to tolerate at school events student expression that contributes to those dangers."

"Clear and Present Danger" Test

Throughout most of the nineteenth and early twentieth centuries, Congress followed the mandate of the First Amendment literally and made "no law" restricting freedom of speech, assembly, or the press. In response to vocal resistance to World War I, Congress passed the Espionage Act of 1917 and the Sedition Act of 1918. Charles Schenck, a dissident, was convicted under the Espionage Act for circulating to men who had been called and accepted for military service a document that stated that the draft violated the Thirteenth Amendment, which prohibits slavery or involuntary servitude. In 1919, the Supreme Court, in an opinion by Justice Oliver Wendell Holmes, first articulated the *"clear and present danger" test* and affirmed Schenck's conviction.[73]

The Supreme Court explained that many things that might be said in peacetime are not allowed in time of war:

> [T]he character of every act depends upon the circumstances in which it is done. The most stringent protection of free speech would not protect a man in falsely shouting fire in a theatre and causing a panic. . . . [The] question in every case is whether the words used are used in such circumstances and are of such a nature as to create a *clear and present danger* that they will bring about the substantive evils that Congress has a right to prevent. (Emphasis added.)[74]

During the height of the Cold War, the clear and present danger test was applied in an expansive manner to restrict First Amendment freedoms even more severely, but the test became stricter and more protective of free speech in the 1960s. In *Brandenburg v. Ohio*, the Supreme Court held that "the constitutional guarantees of free speech and free press do not permit a State to forbid or proscribe advocacy of the use of force or of law violation except where such advocacy is directed to inciting or producing imminent lawless action and is likely to incite or produce such action."[75]

In 1997, the U.S. Court of Appeals for the Fourth Circuit ruled that the First Amendment did not bar a wrongful-death suit against the publisher of *Hit Man: A Technical Manual for Independent Contractors*, a 130-page manual of detailed factual instructions on how to become a professional killer.[76] A convicted murderer had used the book to commit a triple homicide. The publisher stipulated that it had targeted the market of murderers, would-be murderers, and other criminals and that it knew and intended that criminals would immediately use the book to solicit, plan, and commit murder. The court rejected the publisher's claim that this was abstract advocacy protected under *Brandenburg v. Ohio*, reasoning that "this book constitutes the archetypal example of speech which, because it methodically and comprehensively prepares and steels its audience to specific criminal conduct through exhaustively detailed instructions on the planning, commission, and concealment of criminal conduct, finds no preserve in the First Amendment."

Defamation of Public Figures by Media

Defamatory words—words that harm a person's reputation—are protected by the First Amendment, even

---

71. Hurley v. Irish-American Gay, Lesbian & Bisexual Group of Boston, 515 U.S. 557 (1995).

72. 551 U.S. 393 (2007).

73. Schenck v. United States, 249 U.S. 47 (1919).

74. *Id.* at 52.

75. 395 U.S. 444, 447 (1969).

76. Rice v. Paladin Enter., Inc., 128 F.3d 233 (4th Cir. 1997).

when they are false, if they are made by a media defendant (such as a newspaper or television network) about a public figure without knowledge they were false, that is, without actual malice. Defamation is discussed further in Chapter 9.

Obscenity

Obscene material does not enjoy any protection under the First Amendment. Material is obscene if it (1) appeals to a prurient or sordid and perverted interest in sex; (2) has no serious literary, artistic, political, or scientific merit; and (3) is on the whole offensive to the average person in the community.[77] Applying this test, the U.S. Court of Appeals for the Second Circuit held that the label for Bad Frog Beer, which depicts a frog with its middle finger raised, was perhaps in bad taste, but not obscene.[78]

Pornography on the Internet

Since 1995, Congress has struggled with how to protect children from pornography on the Internet. Most attempts to ban indecent but not obscene materials have not withstood judicial scrutiny.[79] For example, the Supreme Court struck down provisions of the Communications Decency Act (CDA)[80] that banned "indecent transmissions" and "patently offensive displays" in public forums accessible by children, including the Internet.[81] The Court rejected the government's analogy to broadcast media, which have traditionally enjoyed less First Amendment protection. Unlike other media, the Internet does not have an extensive history of government regulation, it is not a scarce resource in need of monitored allocation, and it is not intrusive into individuals' homes. Instead, the Court analogized the Internet to a public square, where speech is given heightened protection. Although it struck down much of the CDA, the Court left in place its prohibition of online transmission of obscene speech. The Supreme Court also upheld the Children's Internet Protection Act of 2000 (CIPA),[82] which requires public schools and libraries to install Internet filters on their computers so that children cannot view depictions that are harmful, obscene, or child pornography.[83]

Commercial Speech

Unlike political speech, commercial speech, especially advertising, has always been subject to reasonable regulations regarding the time, place, and manner of such speech. In addition, the state may prohibit false commercial speech, as well as explicitly or inherently misleading commercial speech. To determine whether content-based regulation of commercial speech violates the First Amendment, the Supreme Court has formulated the following test. First, the speech must concern lawful activity and not be misleading. Even if the speech satisfies this requirement, the First Amendment still allows the government to restrict it as long as (1) the asserted governmental interest in regulating the speech is substantial, (2) the regulation directly advances the governmental interest asserted, and (3) the restriction is no more extensive than necessary to serve that interest.[84] Determining whether the regulation is no more extensive than necessary does not require the least restrictive means;[85] it requires only a "reasonable fit" between the government's purpose and the means chosen to achieve it.

Advertising, Data Mining, and Video Games

The Supreme Court has struck down a variety of federal and state laws restricting liquor and tobacco advertisements, including a federal provision prohibiting statements of alcohol content on malt beverage labels unless state law required disclosure[86] and a Rhode Island statute prohibiting the advertisement of liquor prices except at the point of sale.[87] The Court also struck down Massachusetts regulations that banned certain point-of-sale advertising in retail stores that was visible from the outside and also prohibited

> outdoor advertising of cigarettes, smokeless tobacco, and cigars, including advertising in enclosed stadiums and advertising from within a retail establishment that is directed toward or visible from the outside of the establishment, in any location that is within [a] 1,000 foot radius of any public playground, playground area in a public park, elementary school or secondary school.[88]

While acknowledging the state's valid interest in preventing smoking by minors, the Court explained in the Massachusetts case that "a speech regulation cannot unduly impinge on the speaker's ability to propose a

---

77. Miller v. California, 413 U.S. 15, 24 (1973).

78. Bad Frog Brewery v. N.Y. State Liquor Auth., 134 F.3d 87 (2d Cir. 1998). The Bad Frog label can be seen at http://www.badfrog.com/ (last visited Aug. 5, 2011).

79. *See, e.g.,* Ashcroft v. Free Speech Coal., 535 U.S. 234 (2002) (striking down a ban on nonobscene "virtual" child pornography except as applied to images involving real children or images that are the product of sexual abuse); Am. Civil Liberties Union v. Ashcroft, 542 U.S. 656 (2004) (striking down Child Online Protection Act of 1998).

80. Pub. L. No. 104-104, 110 Stat. 133 (1996).

81. Reno v. Am. Civil Liberties Union, 521 U.S. 844 (1997).

82. Pub. L. No. 106-554, 114 Stat. 2763 (2000).

83. United States. v. Am. Library Ass'n, Inc., 539 U.S. 194 (2003).

84. Cent. Hudson Gas & Elec. Corp. v. Pub. Serv. Comm'n of N.Y., 447 U.S. 557, 566 (1980).

85. Bd. of Trustees, State Univ. of N.Y. v. Fox, 492 U.S. 469, 477 (1989).

86. Rubin v. Coors Brewing Co., 514 U.S. 476 (1995).

87. 44 Liquormart, Inc. v. Rhode Island, 517 U.S. 484 (1996).

88. Lorillard Tobacco Co. v. Reilly, 533 U.S. 525 (2001).

commercial transaction and the adult listener's opportunity to obtain information about products."[89]

As discussed in Chapter 1, the Supreme Court struck down a Vermont statute banning pharmacies from selling prescriber-identifying information to data miners and pharmaceutical companies.[90] In the following case, the Supreme Court considered whether a state could prohibit the sale of graphically violent video games to minors.

---

89. *Id.* at 565.

90. Sorrell v. IMS Health Inc., 131 S. Ct. 2653 (2011) (Case 1.1).

| A CASE IN POINT | *In the Language of the Court* | Case 4.3 |

Brown v. Entertainment Merchants Association

Supreme Court of the United States
131 S. Ct. 2729 (2011).

FACTS California Assembly Bill 1179 (2005)[91] prohibits the sale or rental of "violent video games" to minors and requires their packaging to be labeled "18." The Act covers games "in which the range of options available to a player includes killing, maiming, dismembering, or sexually assaulting an image of a human being, if those acts are depicted" in a manner that "[a] reasonable person, considering the game as a whole, would find appeals to a deviant or morbid interest of minors"; that is "patently offensive to prevailing standards in the community as to what is suitable for minors"; and that "causes the game, as a whole, to lack serious literary, artistic, political, or scientific value for minors." Violation of the Act is punishable by a civil fine of up to $1,000.

Entertainment Merchants Association, which represents the video game and software industries, brought a preenforcement constitutional challenge. The U.S. Court of Appeals for the Ninth Circuit concluded that the Act violated the First Amendment and permanently enjoined its enforcement. The State of California appealed.

ISSUE PRESENTED May a state prohibit the sale or rental of graphically violent video games to minors?

OPINION SCALIA, J., writing on behalf of the U.S. Supreme Court:

II

California correctly acknowledges that video games qualify for First Amendment protection. . . . Like the protected books, plays, and movies that preceded them, video games communicate ideas—and even social messages—through many familiar literary devices (such as characters, dialogue, plot, and music) and through features distinctive to the medium (such as the player's interaction with the virtual world). That suffices to confer First Amendment protection. . . .

Last Term, in *Stevens,*[92] we held that new categories of unprotected speech may not be added to the list by a legislature that concludes certain speech is too harmful to be tolerated. *Stevens* concerned a federal statute purporting to criminalize the creation, sale, or possession of certain depictions of animal cruelty. . . . We held that statute to be an impermissible content-based restriction on speech. There was no American tradition of forbidding the *depiction of* animal cruelty—though States have long had laws against *committing* it.

. . . .

As in *Stevens,* California has tried to make violent-speech regulation look like obscenity regulation by appending a saving clause required for the latter. That does not suffice. Our cases have been clear that the obscenity exception to the First Amendment does not cover whatever a legislature finds shocking, but only depictions of "sexual conduct."

. . . .

. . . "[M]inors are entitled to a significant measure of First Amendment protection, and only in relatively narrow and well-defined circumstances may government bar public dissemination of protected materials to them." No doubt a State possesses legitimate power to protect children from harm, but that does not include a free-floating power to restrict the ideas to which children may be exposed. . . .

CONTINUED

---

91. Cal. Civ. Code Ann. §§ 1746–1746.5.

92. United States v. Stevens, 130 S. Ct. 1577 (2010).

California's argument would fare better if there were a longstanding tradition in this country of specially restricting children's access to depictions of violence, but there is none. Certainly the *books* we give children to read—or read to them when they are younger—contain no shortage of gore. *Grimm's Fairy Tales*, for example, are grim indeed. As her just deserts for trying to poison Snow White, the wicked queen is made to dance in red hot slippers "till she fell dead on the floor, a sad example of envy and jealousy." Cinderella's evil stepsisters have their eyes pecked out by doves. And Hansel and Gretel (children!) kill their captor by baking her in an oven.

High-school reading lists are full of similar fare. Homer's Odysseus blinds Polyphemus the Cyclops by grinding out his eye with a heated stake. In the *Inferno*, Dante and Virgil watch corrupt politicians struggle to stay submerged beneath a lake of boiling pitch, lest they be skewered by devils above the surface. And Golding's *Lord of the Flies* recounts how a school-boy called Piggy is savagely murdered by other children while marooned on an island. . . .

California claims that video games present special problems because they are "interactive," in that the player participates in the violent action on screen and determines its outcome. The latter feature is nothing new: Since at least the publication of *The Adventures of You: Sugarcane Island* in 1969, young readers of choose-your-own-adventure stories have been able to make decisions that determine the plot by following instructions about which page to turn to. As for the argument that video games enable participation in the violent action, that seems to us more a matter of degree than of kind. As Judge Posner has observed, all literature is interactive.

. . . .

III

Because the Act imposes a restriction on the content of protected speech, it is invalid unless California can demonstrate that it passes strict scrutiny—that is, unless it is justified by a compelling government interest and is narrowly drawn to serve that interest. . . .

California cannot meet that standard. At the outset, it acknowledges that it cannot show a direct causal link between violent video games and harm to minors. . . .

. . . California relies primarily on the research of Dr. Craig Anderson and a few other research psychologists whose studies purport to show a connection between exposure to violent video games and harmful effects on children. These studies have been rejected by every court to consider them, and with good reason: They do not prove that violent video games *cause* minors to *act* aggressively (which would at least be a beginning). Instead, "[n]early all of the research is based on correlation, not evidence of causation, and most of the studies suffer from significant, admitted flaws in methodology." They show at best some correlation between exposure to violent entertainment and minuscule real-world effects, such as children's feeling more aggressive or making louder noises in the few minutes after playing a violent game than after playing a nonviolent game.

Even taking for granted Dr. Anderson's conclusions that violent video games produce some effect on children's feelings of aggression, those effects are both small and indistinguishable from effects produced by other media. In his testimony in a similar lawsuit, Dr. Anderson admitted that the "effect sizes" of children's exposure to violent video games are "about the same" as that produced by their exposure to violence on television. And he admits that the same effects have been found when children watch cartoons starring Bugs Bunny or the Road Runner, or when they play video games like Sonic the Hedgehog that are rated "E" (appropriate for all ages), or even when they "vie[w] a picture of a gun."

Of course, California has (wisely) declined to restrict Saturday morning cartoons, the sale of games rated for young children, or the distribution of pictures of guns. The consequence is that its regulation is wildly underinclusive when judged against its asserted justification, which in our view is alone enough to defeat it. . . .

The Act is also seriously underinclusive in another respect . . . . The California Legislature is perfectly willing to leave this dangerous, mind-altering material in the hands of children so

CONTINUED

long as one parent (or even an aunt or uncle) says it's OK. And there are not even any requirements as to how this parental or avuncular relationship is to be verified; apparently the child's or putative parent's, aunt's, or uncle's say-so suffices. That is not how one addresses a serious social problem.

California claims that the Act is justified in aid of parental authority: By requiring that the purchase of violent video games can be made only by adults, the Act ensures that parents can decide what games are appropriate. At the outset, we note our doubts that punishing third parties for conveying protected speech to children *just in case* their parents disapprove of that speech is a proper governmental means of aiding parental authority. . . .

But leaving that aside, California cannot show that the Act's restrictions meet a substantial need of parents who wish to restrict their children's access to violent video games but cannot do so. The video-game industry has in place a voluntary rating system designed to inform consumers about the content of games. . . . This system does much to ensure that minors cannot purchase seriously violent games on their own, and that parents who care about the matter can readily evaluate the games their children bring home. Filling the remaining modest gap in concerned-parents' control can hardly be a compelling state interest.

And finally, the Act's purported aid to parental authority is vastly overinclusive. Not all of the children who are forbidden to purchase violent video games on their own have parents who *care* whether they purchase violent video games. While some of the legislation's effect may indeed be in support of what some parents of the restricted children actually want, its entire effect is only in support of what the State thinks parents *ought* to want. This is not the narrow tailoring to "assisting parents" that restriction of First Amendment rights requires.

RESULT   The California ban on sales of violent video games to minors was struck down as an unconstitutional infringement of minors' free speech.

CRITICAL THINKING QUESTIONS

1. In his dissent, Justice Thomas asserted that the "historical evidence shows that the founding generation believed parents had absolute authority over their minor children," making it "absurd to suggest that such a society understood 'the freedom of speech' to include a right to speak to minors (or a corresponding right of minors to access speech) without going through the minors' parents." If he is right about the historical evidence, how, if at all, should that affect the resolution of this case?

2. In *Ginsberg v. New York*,[93] the Court upheld a statute prohibiting the sale of nude pictures to minors. In his dissent in *Entertainment Merchants*, Justice Breyer raised the following question: "But what sense does it make to forbid selling to a 13-year-old boy a magazine with an image of a nude woman, while protecting a sale to that 13-year-old of an interactive video game in which he actively, but virtually, binds and gags the woman, then tortures and kills her?" How would you respond to his query?

93. 390 U.S. 629 (1968).

Political Speech

Since the passage of the Tillman Act in 1907,[94] federal law has prohibited corporations from using general treasury funds to make direct contributions to candidates for federal office. The Taft-Hartley Act of 1947 extended the ban to independent expenditures that expressly advocated the election or defeat of a candidate. The Bipartisan Campaign Reform Act of 2002 (also known as the BCRA or the McCain–Feingold Act) prohibits corporations and unions from using their general treasury funds for publicly distributed "electioneering communications" or for speech expressly advocating the election or defeat of a candidate within thirty days of a primary election or sixty days of a general election.[95] In 2003, the Supreme Court upheld

94. "Tillman Act," ch. 420, 34 Stat. 864 (1907) (an Act to prohibit corporations from making money contributions in connection with political elections).

95. 2 U.S.C. § 441b.

the BCRA's limits on electioneering communications in *McConnell v. Federal Election Commission*.[96] The holding of *McConnell* rested to a large extent on the Court's decision in *Austin v. Michigan Chamber of Commerce*,[97] which upheld a Michigan law that banned corporate independent expenditures that supported or opposed any candidate for state office. An independent expenditure is political speech not coordinated with the candidate. In 2010, the Supreme Court overruled both decisions in *Citizens United v. Federal Election Commission*,[98] which invalidated both section 203's limit on corporate independent expenditures and section 441b's prohibition on the use of corporate treasury funds for electioneering communications or express advocacy.

Citizens United, a nonprofit organization, had released a film entitled *Hillary: The Movie* in theaters and on DVD and then wanted to make the film available through video-on-demand within thirty days of the 2008 presidential primary elections. This 90-minute documentary was highly critical of Hillary Clinton, then a senator from New York and a candidate for the Democratic Party's presidential nomination. Although Citizens United received most of its funds from donations by individuals, a small portion of its funds came from for-profit corporations.

Fearing that both the film and the ads would be covered by section 441b's ban on corporate-funded expenditures, thereby subjecting the organization to civil and criminal penalties, Citizens United sought a ruling that the statute was unconstitutional as applied to the video-on-demand distribution of *Hillary*. After the appeals court struck down the statute as applied to Citizens United, the Supreme Court took the unusual step of asking the parties to rebrief the case on the issue of whether the statute—on its face—violated the First Amendment.

In a five-to-four opinion written by Justice Kennedy, the Supreme Court held that both sections 203 and 441b of the BCRA were unconstitutional on their face because they suppressed political speech based on the speaker's identity as a corporation. The Court first concluded that it could not resolve the case on other, narrower grounds. It rejected Citizens United's contention that section 441b did not cover *Hillary* because a single video-on-demand transmission is sent only to a requesting cable converter box and therefore is not publicly distributed. It also rejected the assertion that *Hillary* was not "express advocacy or its functional equivalent," characterizing it as "a feature-length negative advertisement that urges viewers to vote against Senator Clinton for President." The Court also rejected Citizens United's assertion that

section 441b should be invalidated as applied to movies shown through video-on-demand.

The Court then characterized section 441b's prohibition on corporate independent expenditures as an impermissible ban on speech that was designed "to silence entities whose voices the Government deems to be suspect," namely, corporations. The Court explained that First Amendment protection extends to corporations, rejecting "the argument that political speech of corporations or other associations should be treated differently under the First Amendment simply because such associations are not 'natural persons.'" Even though corporations can create political action committees (PACs), a PAC is a separate association and is expensive to operate. Accordingly, "[e]ven if a PAC could somehow allow a corporation to speak—and it does not—the option to form PACs does not alleviate the First Amendment problems with § 441b." Section 441b was, therefore, subject to strict scrutiny.

The Government asserted three compelling interests to sustain section 441b's ban: the antidistortion interest, the anticorruption interest, and the shareholder-protection interest. The Court rejected all three.

In *Austin*, the Court had ruled that the government's interest in preventing "the corrosive and distorting effects of immense aggregations of wealth that are accumulated with the help of the corporate form and that have little or no correlation to the public's support for the corporation's political ideas" (the so-called antidistortion interest) was sufficiently compelling to validate the ban on independent expenditures. But the *Citizens United* Court based its decision on earlier cases in which the Supreme Court had rejected the proposition that the government has an interest "in equalizing the relative ability of individuals and groups to influence the outcome of elections."[99] The Court explained that the "rule that political speech cannot be limited based on a speaker's wealth is a necessary consequence of the premise that the First Amendment generally prohibits the suppression of political speech based on the speaker's identity."

Although media corporations are exempt from section 441b's ban on corporate expenditures, the Court reasoned that *Austin*'s antidistortion rationale would produce the "dangerous, and unacceptable, consequence" that Congress could diminish the voice of wealthy media corporations "to put them on par with other media entities." The Court explained:

> *Austin* interferes with the "open marketplace" of ideas protected by the First Amendment. It permits the Government to ban the political speech of millions of associations of

---

96. 540 U.S. 93 (2003). In *Federal Election Commission v. Wisconsin Right to Life*, 551 U.S. 449 (2007), the Court limited section 441b's ban to advertisements that contained "the functional equivalent of express advocacy."

97. 494 U.S. 652 (1990).

98. 130 S. Ct. 876 (2010).

99. In *Buckley v. Valeo*, 424 U. S. 1 (1976) (per curiam), the U.S. Supreme Court upheld limits on campaign contributions by individuals but struck down limits on campaign expenditures. In *Davis v. Federal Election Commission*, 554 U.S. 724 (2008), the Court also invalidated the BCRA provision that increased the cap on contributions to one candidate if the opponent made certain expenditures from personal funds.

citizens. Most of these are small corporations without large amounts of wealth. This fact belies the Government's argument that the statute is justified on the ground that it prevents the "distorting effects of immense aggregations of wealth." It is not even aimed at amassed wealth.

The censorship we now confront is vast in its reach. The Government has "muffle[d] the voices that best represent the most significant segments of the economy." And "the electorate [has been] deprived of information, knowledge and opinion vital to its function."

The Court rejected the Government's argument that corporate political speech could be banned in order to prevent corruption or its appearance:

[I]ndependent expenditures do not lead to, or create the appearance of, *quid pro quo* corruption. In fact, there is only scant evidence that independent expenditures even ingratiate. Ingratiation and access, in any event, are not corruption. . . . If elected officials succumb to improper influences from independent expenditures; if they surrender their best judgment; and if they put expediency before principle, then surely there is cause for concern. We must give weight to attempts by Congress to seek to dispel either the appearance or the reality of these influences. The remedies enacted by law, however, must comply with the First Amendment; and, it is our law and our tradition that more speech, not less, is the governing rule.

The Court also rejected the assertion that the ban was necessary to ensure that dissenting shareholders are not compelled to fund corporate political speech. The First Amendment does not give Congress that power. In any event, the Court found "little evidence of abuse that cannot be corrected by shareholders 'through the procedures of corporate democracy.'"

The Court acknowledged that under the doctrine of *stare decisis*, "our precedent is to be respected unless the most convincing of reasons demonstrates that adherence to it puts us on a course that is sure error." Factors to consider include "workability, the antiquity of the precedent, the reliance interests at stake, and of course whether the decision was well reasoned," as well as whether "experience has pointed up the precedent's shortcomings."

The Court argued that *Austin* was not well reasoned and contravened earlier cases striking down limits on campaign contributions by individuals. The Court found no "serious reliance interests" at stake. Even though state and federal legislatures may have enacted bans on corporate expenditures believing that those bans were constitutional, "This is not a compelling interest for *stare decisis*. If it were, legislative acts could prevent us from overruling our own precedents, thereby interfering with our duty 'to say what the law is.' *Marbury v. Madison*, 5 U.S. 137 (1803)."

The majority opinion left open the question of whether the Government has a compelling interest in preventing foreign individuals or associations from influencing U.S. elections, stating that "Section 441b . . . would be overbroad even if we assumed, *arguendo*, that the Government has a compelling interest in limiting foreign influence over our political process."

Eight of the Court's nine Justices rejected Citizens United's challenge to the disclaimer and disclosure requirements in section 311 of the BCRA, which provide that televised electioneering communications funded by anyone other than a candidate must include a disclaimer that "' _____ is responsible for the content of this advertising.'"[100] Although disclaimer and disclosure requirements burden the ability to speak, they "impose no ceiling on campaign-related activities" and "do not prevent anyone from speaking." As a result, section 311 was valid as applied to *Hillary*.

Justice Kennedy concluded his majority opinion with the following remarks:

When word concerning the plot of the movie *Mr. Smith Goes to Washington* reached the circles of Government, some officials sought, by persuasion, to discourage its distribution. Under *Austin*, though, officials could have done more than discourage its distribution—they could have banned the film. After all, it, like *Hillary*, was speech funded by a corporation that was critical of Members of Congress. *Mr. Smith Goes to Washington* may be fiction and caricature; but fiction and caricature can be a powerful force.

Modern day movies, television comedies, or skits on Youtube.com might portray public officials or public policies in unflattering ways. . . . Governments are often hostile to speech, but under our law and our tradition it seems stranger than fiction for our Government to make this political speech a crime. Yet this is the statute's purpose and design.

Some members of the public might consider *Hillary* to be insightful and instructive; some might find it to be neither high art nor a fair discussion on how to set the Nation's course; still others simply might suspend judgment on these points but decide to think more about issues and candidates. Those choices and assessments, however, are not for the Government to make. "The First Amendment underwrites the freedom to experiment and to create in the realm of thought and speech. Citizens must be free to use new forms, and new forums, for the expression of ideas. The civic discourse belongs to the people, and the Government may not prescribe the means used to conduct it."

---

100. Justice Thomas joined in the parts of the majority opinion striking down the independent expenditure provisions of the Act but dissented in the part in which the Court upheld the Act's disclaimer and disclosure provisions. In his dissent, Justice Thomas cited reports by amici that donors have been "blacklisted, threatened, or otherwise targeted for retaliation." Citizens United v. Fed. Election Comm'n, 130 S. Ct. 876, 980 (2010) (Thomas, J., concurring in part, dissenting in part).

In a dissent joined by Justices Ginsburg, Breyer, and Sotomayor, Justice Stevens characterized the conceit that corporations must be treated identically to natural persons in the political sphere as "not only inaccurate but also inadequate to justify the Court's disposition of this case," stating:

> In the context of election to public office, the distinction between corporate and human speakers is significant. Although they make enormous contributions to our society, corporations are not actually members of it. They cannot vote or run for office. Because they may be managed and controlled by nonresidents, their interests may conflict in fundamental respects with the interests of eligible voters. The financial resources, legal structure, and instrumental orientation of corporations raise legitimate concerns about their role in the electoral process. Our lawmakers have a compelling constitutional basis, if not also a democratic duty, to take measures designed to guard against the potentially deleterious effects of corporate spending in local and national races.

Although business corporations have been "effectively delegated responsibility for ensuring society's economic welfare," they "have no consciences, no beliefs, no feelings, no thoughts, no desires." "Corporations help structure and facilitate the activities of human beings," but they "are not themselves members of 'We the People' by whom and for whom our Constitution was established."

The dissent faulted the majority for deciding the case "on a basis relinquished below, not included in the questions presented to us by the litigants, and argued here only in response to the Court's invitation. This procedure is unusual and inadvisable for a court." Moreover, the dissent argued, the majority violated the doctrine of *stare decisis* when it overturned the decision in *Austin*. If the doctrine of *stare decisis* "is to do any meaningful work in supporting the rule of law, it must at least demand a significant justification, beyond the preferences of five Justices, for overturning settled doctrine." Justice Stevens asserted:

> The only relevant thing that has changed since *Austin* and *McConnell* is the composition of this Court. Today's ruling thus strikes at the vitals of *stare decisis*, "the means by which we ensure that the law will not merely change erratically, but will develop in a principled and intelligible fashion" that "permits society to presume that bedrock principles are founded in the law rather than in the proclivities of individuals."

The dissent characterized as "nonsense" the majority's assertion that corporate political speech has been suppressed altogether or that a piece of fiction such as *Mr. Smith Goes to Washington* might be covered. The statute leaves "open many additional avenues for corporations' political speech."

As for the Court's claim that the First Amendment bans identity-based distinctions, the dissent argued that Congress is permitted to take "the special characteristics of the corporate structure" into account in an electoral context, in part because of "the distinctive potential of corporations to corrupt the electoral process," and in part because "'corporations' First Amendment speech and association interests are derived largely from those of their members and of the public in receiving information.'" When corporations, as a class, are distinguished from noncorporations, "there is a lesser risk that regulatory distinctions will reflect invidious discrimination or political favoritism." The majority's "assumption that the identity of a speaker has no relevance to the Government's ability to regulate political speech would lead to some remarkable conclusions," including the possibility that it "may be a First Amendment problem that corporations are not permitted to vote, given that voting is, among other things, a form of speech."[101]

As for the original intent of the Framers of the Constitution:

> The Framers . . . took it as a given that corporations could be comprehensively regulated in the service of the public welfare. Unlike our colleagues, they had little trouble distinguishing corporations from human beings, and when they constitutionalized the right to free speech in the First Amendment, it was the free speech of individual Americans that they had in mind.[102]

The dissent argued that the Government has a strong interest not only in preventing *quid pro quo* relationships but also in preventing corporations from exerting undue influence on an elected official's judgment or creating the appearance of undue influence:

> Corruption can take many forms. Bribery may be the paradigm case. But the difference between selling a vote and selling access is a matter of degree, not kind. And selling access is not qualitatively different from giving special preference to those who spent money on one's behalf. Corruption operates along a spectrum, and the majority's apparent belief that *quid pro quo* arrangements can be neatly demarcated from other improper influences does not accord with the theory or reality of politics. It certainly does not accord with the [100,000-page] record Congress developed in passing BCRA, a record that stands as a remarkable testament to the energy and ingenuity with which corporations, unions, lobbyists, and politicians may go about scratching each other's backs—and which amply supported Congress' determination to target a limited set of especially destructive practices.

---

101. According to the dissent, "The Court all but confesses that a categorical approach to speaker identity is untenable when it acknowledges that Congress might be allowed to take measures aimed at 'preventing foreign individuals or associations from influencing our Nation's political process.'" *Id.* at 948 n.51 (Stevens, J., concurring in part, dissenting in part).

102. Indeed, Justice Stevens noted, "Thomas Jefferson famously fretted that corporations would subvert the Republic." *Id.* at 949.

. . . A democracy cannot function effectively when its constituent members believe laws are being bought and sold. . . .

As a class, corporations tend to be more attuned to the complexities of the legislative process and more directly affected by tax and appropriations measures that receive little public scrutiny; they also have vastly more money with which to try to buy access and votes. Business corporations must engage the political process in instrumental terms if they are to maximize shareholder value. The unparalleled resources, professional lobbyists, and single-minded focus they bring to this effort . . . make *quid pro quo* corruption and its appearance inherently more likely when they (or their conduits or trade groups) spend unrestricted sums on elections.

Congress, the dissent argued, also had a legitimate interest in protecting shareholders:

When corporations use general treasury funds to praise or attack a particular candidate for office, it is the shareholders, as the residual claimants, who are effectively footing the bill. Those shareholders who disagree with the corporation's electoral message may find their financial investments being used to undermine their political convictions.

The dissent rejected the Court's assertion that shareholder abuses could be corrected "through the procedures of corporate democracy," stating: "In practice, however, many corporate lawyers will tell you that 'these rights are so limited as to be almost nonexistent,' given the internal authority wielded by boards and managers and the expansive protections afforded by the business judgment rule."[103] Nor does the option of divestiture solve the problem. By the time shareholders learn that a corporation has funded objectionable electioneering, "[t]he injury to the shareholders' expressive rights has already occurred; they might have preferred to keep that corporation's stock in their portfolio for any number of economic reasons; and they may incur a capital gains tax or other penalty from selling their shares, changing their pension plan, or the like."

The decision in *Citizens United* left standing provisions in the Bipartisan Campaign Reform Act prohibiting direct or in-kind contributions to federal candidates.[104] It remains to be seen how the Supreme Court will address this issue.[105]

---

103. Chapter 20 discusses this rule, which insulates directors from most shareholder suits.

104. *Citizens United*, 130 S. Ct. at 909 ("Citizens United has not made direct contributions to candidates, and it has not suggested that the Court should reconsider whether contribution limits should by subjected to rigorous First Amendment scrutiny.").

105. In *Iowa Right to Life Committee, Inc. v. Smithson*, 750 F. Supp. 2d 1020 (S.D. Iowa 2010), the U.S. District Court for the Southern District of Iowa found it unlikely that the plaintiff would succeed in its claim that a ban on corporate campaign contributions was unconstitutional. In contrast, the Colorado Supreme Court invalidated a Colorado constitutional amendment that banned campaign contributions by companies, labor unions, hospitals, and other with sole-source government contracts, that is, contracts not secured by soliciting at least three bids. Dallman v. Ritter, 225 P.3d 610 (Colo. 2010) (en banc).

"If you prick a corporation, does it not bleed? If you tickle it, does it not laugh? If you poison it, does it not die?"

Encryption

In *Junger v. Daley*,[106] a professor challenged the Export Administration Regulations insofar as they attempted to restrict him from posting on his website the human readable source code of an encryption software program that he had written to demonstrate how computers work. The professor claimed that the regulations were vague, overly broad, and an impermissible prior restraint in violation of the First and Fifth Amendments to the Constitution. The U.S. Court of Appeals for the Sixth Circuit agreed: "Because computer source code is an expressive means for the exchange of information and ideas about computer programming, we hold that it is protected by the First Amendment." As such, the court determined that the regulations should be subjected to intermediate scrutiny, or the *substantially related test*, which requires the government to prove that the regulations further a governmental interest that is "important" or "substantial" and that they prevent real, not conjectural, harm "in a direct and material way." Having concluded that the First Amendment protects computer source code, the Sixth Circuit remanded the case to the district court for further consideration of the professor's constitutional claims under the substantially related test.

Academic Research

The First Amendment also protects academic research. During the U.S. government's antitrust suit against Microsoft Corporation for illegal monopolization, Microsoft sought to compel two university professors to produce notes and tape recordings of the interviews they

---

106. 209 F.3d 481 (6th Cir. 2000).

conducted with Netscape's employees while researching their book *Competing on Internet Time: Lessons from Netscape and Its Battle with Microsoft.* The U.S. Court of Appeals for the First Circuit denied access, reasoning that the academics, in gathering and disseminating information, were acting almost as journalists. Compelling disclosure of their research materials would impede "the free flow of information to the public, thus denigrating a fundamental First Amendment value."[107]

English-Only Laws

Freedom of speech issues also arise in connection with "English-only" laws, which require government employees to conduct all government business in English. This topic is discussed in Chapter 13.

Prior Restraints

Prior restraints of speech, such as prohibiting in advance a demonstration in a public area, are considered a more drastic infringement on free speech than permitting the speech to occur but then punishing it afterwards. Restrictions concerning the time, place, and manner of speech are usually acceptable under the First Amendment, but regulations that restrict speech in traditional public forums are scrutinized closely.

For example, the City of Dallas adopted an ordinance regulating "sexually oriented businesses," defined as any "adult arcade, adult bookstore or adult video store, adult cabaret, adult motel, adult motion picture theater, adult theater, escort agency, nude model studio, or sexual encounter center." The ordinance regulated such businesses through zoning, licensing, and inspections. It also banned motels that rented rooms for fewer than ten hours; such rooms are often used for prostitution. The Supreme Court struck down all of the ordinance, except the ban on ten-hour motels, as a prior restraint on speech that did not comply with the procedural safeguards for that type of regulation. In upholding the provision prohibiting motels from renting rooms for fewer than ten hours, the Court rejected the argument that the ordinance unconstitutionally interfered with the right of association. On behalf of the majority, Justice Sandra Day O'Connor stated, "Any 'personal bonds' that are formed from the use of a motel room for fewer than 10 hours are not those that have 'played a critical role in the culture and traditions of the Nation by cultivating and transmitting shared ideals and beliefs.'"[108] Similarly, the Supreme Court upheld a ban on nude dancing in 2000.[109]

Prior restraints can be particularly problematic for members of the media, who may need to publish immediately or not at all. For example, during a suit by Procter & Gamble against Bankers Trust for negligent sale of financial derivative products, *BusinessWeek* obtained confidential documents about both parties that had emerged from their court-approved secret discovery process. The trial court granted the litigants' request for a temporary restraining order (TRO) to keep *BusinessWeek* from immediately publishing the information and later enjoined the magazine from ever publishing it. The U.S. Court of Appeals for the Sixth Circuit struck down the injunction as a violation of the First Amendment.[110] Noting that "[a] prior restraint comes to a court 'with a heavy presumption against its constitutional validity,'" the Sixth Circuit concluded that the trial court's grounds for granting the TRO were insufficient to meet the high standard required for prior restraint.

Nonspeech Business

The First Amendment also protects seemingly nonspeech business. The U.S. Court of Appeals for the Ninth Circuit affirmed a lower court's decision enjoining California's Santa Clara County from enforcing its ban on gun sales at the county's fairgrounds.[111] The county had argued that rather than regulating speech, the ban regulated the unprotected conduct of selling guns. The trial court disagreed and found that "some type of speech is necessarily involved in the sale of any gun."[112] The appeals court agreed and ruled that the offer to buy constituted protected commercial speech. Although the county asserted an interest in curtailing gun possession, the court ruled that the ban did not directly advance that interest.

RIGHT OF ASSOCIATION

Closely related to the right to free speech and press is the constitutional right of association. In 2000, the U.S. Supreme Court struck down California's law requiring political parties to hold open primaries in which any registered voter could vote to select a party's candidate for elected office.[113] The Court reasoned:

> Proposition 198 forces petitioners to adulterate their candidate-selection process—the "basic function of a political party"—by opening it up to persons wholly unaffiliated with the party. Such forced association has the likely outcome—indeed, in this case the intended outcome—of changing the parties' message. We can think of no heavier burden on a political party's associational freedom.

107. Cusamano v. Microsoft Corp., 162 F.3d 708, 717 (1st Cir. 1998).

108. FW/PBS, Inc. v. City of Dallas, 493 U.S. 215 (1990).

109. City of Erie v. Pap's A.M., 529 U.S. 277 (2000).

110. Procter & Gamble v. Bankers Trust, 78 F.3d 219 (6th Cir. 1996).

111. Nordyke v. Santa Clara County, Cal., 110 F.3d 707 (9th Cir. 1997).

112. Nordyke v. Santa Clara County, Cal., 933 F. Supp. 903, 906 (N.D. Cal. 1996).

113. Cal. Democratic Party v. Jones, 530 U.S. 567 (2000).

Similar issues arise when city or state governments enact laws banning discriminatory clubs. The courts will balance the First Amendment rights of association and free speech against the government's social policy against discrimination. To increase the likelihood that such laws will be upheld, most antidiscrimination statutes apply only to clubs of a certain size where business is conducted.

In *Warfield v. Peninsula Golf & Country Club*,[114] the California Supreme Court held that a private country club that allowed nonmembers, for a fee, to use its golf course, tennis courts, or dining areas was a "business establishment" and therefore subject to the state law prohibiting discrimination against women and minorities. It will generally be assumed that business is conducted in a private club if the member's employer pays for club dues, meals, or drinks or if it is the site of company-sponsored events.

In *Boy Scouts of America v. Dale*,[115] the U.S. Supreme Court held that applying a New Jersey law that prohibits discrimination based on sexual orientation in places of public accommodation to the Boy Scouts of America (BSA) was an unconstitutional violation of the BSA's First Amendment right of association. The Supreme Court stated that the forced inclusion of an unwanted person in a group infringes the group's freedom of expressive association if the person's presence significantly affects the group's ability to advocate public or private viewpoints. But freedom of association is not absolute. It can be overridden "by regulations adopted to serve compelling state interests, unrelated to the suppression of ideas, that cannot be achieved through means significantly less restrictive of associational freedom."

The Court noted that the BSA is an expressive association that teaches, among other values, that "homosexual conduct is not morally straight" and does "not want to promote homosexual conduct as a legitimate form of behavior." The Court concluded that the forced inclusion of a gay man as an assistant scoutmaster would significantly affect the organization's expression and significantly burden its right to oppose homosexual conduct. The Court held that the state interests embodied in the law did not justify such a severe intrusion on the BSA's right to freedom of expressive association.

FREEDOM OF RELIGION

Two clauses of the First Amendment deal with religion. The *Establishment Clause* prohibits the establishment of a religion by the federal government. The same ban applies to state governments through the Due Process Clause of the Fourteenth Amendment. The *Free Exercise Clause* prohibits certain, but not all, restrictions on the practice of religion.

Religion in government offices is a difficult issue that may bring the Establishment and Free Exercise Clauses into conflict. In 1996, the U.S. Court of Appeals for the Ninth Circuit ruled unconstitutional a near total ban on religious activity in the workplace imposed by the California Department of Education's Child Nutrition and Food Distribution Division.[116] Tensions arose in the division between computer analyst Monte Tucker and his supervisor after Tucker refused to stop signing office memos with his name and the acronym "SOTLJC," which stood for "Servant of the Lord Jesus Christ." After several warnings, the supervisor suspended Tucker and prohibited all employees from displaying religious materials outside their cubicles, engaging in any religious advocacy, and putting any acronym or other symbol on office communications. Although the state asserted its interest in avoiding workplace disruption and the appearance of religious endorsement (which would constitute a violation of the Establishment Clause), the appeals court concluded that these interests were outweighed by Tucker's constitutional right to talk about religion. Such issues also come up in the private sector, which is regulated by various statutes barring discrimination based on religion (discussed in Chapter 13).

Establishment Clause

The Establishment Clause requires the government to remain neutral in matters of religion. Although federal taxpayers have standing to challenge congressional action alleged to be in violation of the Establishment Clause,[117] they have no standing to challenge spending paid for out of general executive branch appropriations.[118]

The U.S. Supreme Court has ruled that the Establishment Clause prohibits teacher- or student-led prayer (including benedictions at football games or graduations) in public schools.[119] It does not, however, preclude the federal government from providing secular books and other teaching materials and supplies to parochial schools on the same basis that they are given to public schools.[120] The Supreme Court also ruled that an Ohio school voucher program that allowed parents to use public money to pay for tuition at private schools, including religious schools, did not violate the Establishment Clause.[121]

A pair of five-to-four U.S. Supreme Court decisions in 2005 highlights the divisions among the members of the Court concerning the government's obligation to exhibit neutrality toward religion. *Van Orden v. Perry*[122] involved a six-foot by three-and-one-half-foot stone monument engraved with the Ten Commandments that was erected by the Fraternal Order of Eagles in 1941 and displayed on the grounds of the Texas State Capitol, along with sixteen

---

114. 896 P.2d 776 (Cal. 1995).
115. 530 U.S. 640 (2000).

116. Tucker v. Cal. Dep't of Educ., 97 F.3d 1204 (9th Cir. 1996).
117. Flast v. Cohen, 392 U.S. 83 (1968).
118. Hein v. Freedom From Religion Found., 551 U.S. 587 (2007).
119. Santa Fe Indep. Sch. Dist. v. Doe, 530 U.S. 290 (2000).
120. Mitchell v. Helms, 530 U.S. 793 (2000).
121. Zelman v. Simmons-Harris, 536 U.S. 639 (2002).
122. 545 U.S. 677 (2005).

other monuments and twenty-one historical markers, which purported to commemorate the "people, ideals, and events that compose Texan identity." *McCreary County, Kentucky v. ACLU*[123] involved a large, gold-framed copy of the Ten Commandments that was prominently displayed in the courthouse in McCreary County, Kentucky. When the display was challenged by the American Civil Liberties Union (ACLU), the county authorized a second, expanded display that added eight more documents that either had a religious theme or highlighted a religious element of the document. After a district court enjoined that display, the county created a third display consisting of nine equal-sized documents—the Ten Commandments and eight American "foundational documents," including the Declaration of Independence, the Bill of Rights, and Magna Carta.

The Supreme Court upheld the Texas display in *Van Orden* but struck down the Kentucky display in *McCreary*. Justices Scalia, Thomas, Kennedy, and Rehnquist would have upheld the displays in both cases, on the basis that displays incorporating the Ten Commandments are common in many government buildings and have "an undeniable historical meaning." Justice Breyer joined with them only in *Van Orden* and for a completely different reason. He reasoned that the Establishment Clause was designed to accomplish a separation between church and state but did not require the government to purge all mention of the religious from the public sphere. He pointed out that there was no exact test that could dictate a resolution of such fact-specific cases but concluded that the Texas display was permissible. In *McCreary*, however, Justice Breyer voted to strike down the display, reasoning that the government violates the Establishment Clause when it acts with "the ostensible and predominant purpose of advancing religion." He found the evidence of religious purpose in the Kentucky display overwhelming.

Free Exercise Clause

In *Jimmy Swaggart Ministries v. Board of Equalization*,[124] the U.S. Supreme Court held that the imposition of general taxes on the sale of religious materials does not contravene the Free Exercise Clause of the First Amendment. The tax was only a small fraction of any sale, and it applied neutrally to all relevant sales regardless of the nature of the seller or purchaser. The Court also held that the tax did not violate the Establishment Clause. There was little evidence of administrative entanglement between religion and the government. The government was not involved in the organization's day-to-day activities, and the imposition of the tax did not require the state to inquire into the religious content of the items sold or the religious motivation behind selling or purchasing them.

THE FOURTH AMENDMENT

As discussed earlier in this chapter and in Chapter 14, the Fourth Amendment protects against unreasonable search and seizure.

DUE PROCESS

The Due Process Clauses of the Fifth Amendment (which applies to the federal government) and the Fourteenth Amendment (which applies to the states) prohibit depriving any person of life, liberty, or property without due process of law. *Procedural due process* focuses on the fairness of the legal proceeding. *Substantive due process* focuses on the fundamental rights protected by the Due Process Clauses.

Procedural Due Process

When a governmental action affects a person's life, liberty, or property, the due process requirement applies, and some form of notice and hearing is required. Explaining the notice requirement, the Supreme Court stated:

> [A] . . . fundamental requirement of due process in any proceeding which is to be accorded finality is notice, reasonably calculated, under all the circumstances, to apprise interested parties of the pendency of the action and afford them an opportunity to present their objections. . . . The notice must be of such nature as reasonably to convey the required information, and it must afford a reasonable time for those interested to make their appearance.[125]

The type of hearing required varies depending on the nature of the action, but some opportunity to be heard must be provided. In general, greater procedural protections are afforded to criminal defendants because the possibility of imprisonment and even death in capital cases is at stake.

The Due Process Clause of the Fourteenth Amendment has been interpreted to make virtually all of the procedural requirements in the Bill of Rights applicable to state criminal proceedings. These rights are discussed in Chapter 14.

Substantive Due Process

Disputes have raged over the years as to what are the fundamental rights—the rights with which the government may not interfere—possessed by people in our society. It has been argued that such rights and liberty interests, including the right to privacy, are guaranteed by the Due Process Clauses of the Fifth and Fourteenth Amendments. This protection of fundamental rights is known as substantive due process. The notion of substantive due process was not wholeheartedly accepted by the Supreme Court until the end of the nineteenth century, mainly because substantive due process rights are not specifically listed in the Constitution.

---

123. 545 U.S. 844 (2005).
124. 493 U.S. 378 (1990).

125. Mullane v. Cent. Hanover Bank & Trust Co., 339 U.S. 306, 314 (1950).

Limit on Economic Regulation

The Supreme Court first invalidated a state law on substantive due process grounds in 1897.[126] The Court held that a Louisiana law prohibiting anyone from obtaining insurance on Louisiana property from any marine insurance company that had not complied in all respects with Louisiana law violated the fundamental right to make contracts.

Early in the twentieth century, the concept was applied to more controversial areas, such as state statutes limiting working hours. In *Lochner v. New York*,[127] the Supreme Court struck down a New York statute that prohibited the employment of bakery employees for more than ten hours a day or sixty hours a week on the basis that it interfered with the employers' and employees' fundamental right to contract with each other. From 1905 to 1937, the Supreme Court invoked the doctrine of substantive due process to invalidate a number of laws relating to regulation of prices, labor relations, and conditions for entry into business.[128]

In 1937, the Supreme Court reversed direction. After President Franklin Delano Roosevelt threatened to "pack" the Court (discussed further in the "Inside Story"), the Justices upheld a minimum-wage law for women in Washington,[129] thereby overruling an earlier decision striking down a similar statute. In 1938, the Court upheld a statute that prohibited the interstate shipment of "filled" milk (milk to which any fat or oil other than milk fat has been added).[130] The Court made it clear that if any set of facts, either known or imaginable, provided a rational basis for *economic* legislation, then the legislation would not be held to violate substantive due process. Under this test, economic regulation is rarely constrained by substantive due process.

Protection of Fundamental Rights

Substantive due process challenges are given more weight when fundamental rights other than the right to make contracts are at issue. Laws that limit fundamental rights violate substantive due process unless they can be shown to promote a compelling or overriding governmental interest.

Fundamental rights and liberty interests protected by the Due Process Clause include the guarantees of the Bill of Rights, the right to marry and to have children, the right to raise children, the right to travel, the right to vote, and the right to associate with other people. The fundamental rights protected by substantive due process are not limited to those specifically enumerated in the Constitution or the Bill of Rights.

Right to Privacy   Substantive due process was extended to the right to privacy in *Griswold v. Connecticut*.[131] The executive director of the Planned Parenthood League of Connecticut and a physician who served as medical director for the league's New Haven center were charged with giving birth control advice in violation of a Connecticut statute that prohibited the use of any drug, medicinal article, or instrument to prevent conception.

Finding that the Connecticut statute was an unconstitutional invasion of individuals' right to privacy, the Supreme Court discussed the penumbra of rights surrounding each guarantee in the Bill of Rights. The Court defined *penumbra* as the peripheral rights that are implied by the specifically enumerated rights. For example, the Court noted that the First Amendment's guarantee of freedom of the press necessarily includes the right to distribute, the right to receive, the right to read, freedom of inquiry, freedom of thought, freedom to teach, and freedom of association. The Fourth Amendment, which prohibits unreasonable searches and seizures, similarly includes a "right to privacy, no less important than any other right carefully and particularly reserved to the people." The Supreme Court found that the Connecticut statute encroached on the right to privacy in marriage.

The Supreme Court first held that a woman's right to have an abortion is protected by the right to privacy in *Roe v. Wade*.[132] The Court restated and reaffirmed *Roe*'s essential holding in *Planned Parenthood of Southeastern Pennsylvania v. Casey*,[133] reiterating that state regulation of access to abortion procedures must protect "the health of the woman," even after the fetus has become viable. In *Gonzales v. Carhart*,[134] the Court upheld by a five-to-four vote the Partial-Birth Abortion Ban Act of 2003, which prohibited knowingly performing late-term abortions not necessary to save the life of a mother.[135] The Court concluded that "the legitimate interest of the Government in protecting the life of the fetus that may become a child" was sufficient to justify encroachment on a woman's right to privacy.

126. Allegeyer v. Louisiana, 165 U.S. 578 (1897).

127. 198 U.S. 45 (1905).

128. In his dissent in *Sorrell v. IMS Health Inc.*, 131 S. Ct. 2653 (2011) (Case 1.1), Justice Breyer cautioned that invalidation of Vermont's ban on selling prescriber-identifying information could presage a "retur[n] to the bygone era" of *Lochner* "in which it was common practice for this Court to strike down economic regulations adopted by a State based on the Court's own notions of the most appropriate means for the State to implement its considered policies" (quoting Justice Rehnquist's dissent in Cent. Hudson Gas & Elec. Corp. v. Pub. Serv. Comm'n of N.Y., 447 U.S. 557, 589 (1980)).

129. W. Coast Hotel Co. v. Parrish, 300 U.S. 379 (1937).

130. United States v. Carolene Prods. Co., 304 U.S. 144 (1938).

131. 381 U.S. 479 (1965).

132. 410 U.S. 113 (1973).

133. 505 U.S. 833, 846 (1992).

134. 550 U.S. 124 (2007).

135. 18 U.S.C. § 1531(a) (2003). The Act defines "partial-birth abortion" as a procedure in which the doctor "(A) deliberately and intentionally vaginally delivers a living fetus until, in the case of a head-first presentation, the entire fetal head is outside the [mother's] body . . . , or, in the case of breech presentation, any part of the fetal trunk past the navel is outside the [mother's] body . . . , for the purpose of performing an overt act that the person knows will kill the partially delivered living fetus;" and "(B) performs the overt act, other than completion of delivery, that kills the fetus."

Dissenting Justices Ginsburg, Souter, Stevens, and Breyer called the majority opinion "alarming" and stated:

> In candor, the Act, and the Court's defense of it, cannot be understood as anything other than an effort to chip away at a right declared again and again by this Court—and with increasing comprehension of its centrality to women's lives. A decision so at odds with our jurisprudence should not have staying power.

The right to privacy is relevant in other areas as well. For example, the Supreme Court upheld a person's right to refuse life-sustaining treatment (such as lifesaving hydration and nutrition)[136] and upheld an Oregon voter proposition permitting physician-assisted suicide.[137] In another case,[138] a schoolteacher successfully sued a board of education, alleging that her teaching contract was not renewed because she was an unwed mother and her pregnancy had been by means of artificial insemination. In 2003, the Supreme Court, overruling an earlier decision, held that a Texas statute criminalizing the act of sodomy performed by consenting adults in private impermissibly infringed on their constitutionally protected right of privacy.[139] Mandatory drug testing also presents privacy issues. As will be discussed further in Chapter 13, the Supreme Court has upheld certain regulations concerning drug testing for public employees.

Limits on Punitive Damages

In certain cases involving torts, or civil wrongs, the jury is entitled to award the plaintiff not only compensatory damages equal to the plaintiff's actual loss but also *punitive* or *exemplary damages*, designed to punish and make an example of the defendant. In *BMW of North America v. Gore*,[140] the Supreme Court held that courts reviewing punitive damages awards should consider three guideposts to determine whether the award is so excessive that it violates the Fourteenth Amendment's Due Process Clause: (1) the degree of reprehensibility of the defendant's misconduct, (2) the disparity between the actual or potential harm suffered and the punitive damages award, and (3) the difference between the punitive damages awarded by the jury and the civil penalties authorized or imposed in similar cases.

Subsequent to the *BMW* decision, a Utah jury awarded Curtis Campbell $2.6 million in compensatory damages and $145 million in punitive damages (reduced to $1 million and $25 million, respectively, by the trial court) in his action against State Farm Insurance for its bad-faith refusal to pay an insurance claim within the policy limits. Although investigators and witnesses had concluded

that Campbell caused an automobile accident that killed one person and permanently disabled another, State Farm rejected offers by the injured parties to settle their claims within Campbell's policy limits ($25,000 per claimant) and took the case to trial. State Farm had assured the Campbells that their assets were safe, that State Farm would represent their interests, and that they did not need separate counsel. When the jury found Campbell liable for $185,849, State Farm refused to cover the excess liability over the policy limit of $50,000. Campbell then sued State Farm for bad faith, fraud, and intentional infliction of emotional distress. Applying the *BMW* guidelines, the Utah Supreme Court upheld the $145 million punitive damages award, noting State Farm's massive wealth and the clandestine nature of its actions.

On appeal, however, the U.S. Supreme Court reversed, holding that "in practice, few awards exceeding a single-digit ratio between punitive and compensatory damages, to a significant degree, will satisfy due process."[141] The Court found that the $145 million award was neither reasonable nor proportionate to the wrong committed and was therefore an irrational and arbitrary deprivation of State Farm's property. During the damages portion of the trial, the Campbells had introduced evidence that showed that State Farm had a national policy of meeting fiscal goals by capping payouts on claims and described fraudulent practices by State Farm outside Utah that bore no relationship to third-party automobile claims. The Court held that a jury must be instructed that it may not use "evidence of out-of-state conduct to punish a defendant for action that was lawful in the jurisdiction where it occurred." It also found that a jury could not use evidence of "[a] defendant's dissimilar acts, independent from the acts upon which liability was premised," as the basis for a punitive damages award.

In *Philip Morris USA v. Williams*,[142] the U.S. Supreme Court held that evidence of harm caused to third parties by similar conduct could be used to show that the conduct that harmed the plaintiff also posed a substantial risk to others and therefore was particularly reprehensible. But the Court ruled that such evidence could not be used to punish the defendant directly for harm to those nonparties.

In *Exxon Shipping Co. v. Baker*,[143] the U.S. Supreme Court cited data showing that the median ratio of punitive to compensatory awards across the board is less than one-to-one and held that a one-to-one ratio was a fair upper limit in maritime cases. The *Exxon Shipping* Court made it clear that it was articulating a federal common law rule applicable only to maritime cases and was not setting a constitutional limit. Nonetheless, the Court noted the unpredictability of high punitive awards and suggested that

---

136. Cruzan v. Dir., Mo. Dep't of Health, 497 U.S. 261 (1990).

137. Gonzales v. Oregon, 546 U.S. 243 (2006).

138. Cameron v. Bd. of Educ. of the Hillsboro, Ohio, City Sch. Dist., 795 F. Supp. 228 (S.D. Ohio 1991).

139. Lawrence v. Texas, 539 U.S. 558 (2003).

140. 517 U.S. 559 (1996).

141. State Farm Mut. Auto. Ins. Co. v. Campbell, 538 U.S. 408, 425 (2003).

142. 549 U.S. 346 (2007).

143. 554 U.S. 471 (2008).

the law should threaten violators with "a fair probability of suffering in a like degree when they wreak like damage."

Along with the substantive due process requirements illustrated in cases such as *State Farm*, there is a procedural due process requirement that punitive damage awards must be subject to appellate review. In *Honda Motor Co. v. Oberg*,[144] an Oregon jury had awarded $5 million in punitive damages to a plaintiff injured in a three-wheel all-terrain vehicle accident. Honda wanted to appeal the penalty, but Oregon's constitution barred review of punitive awards unless there was no evidence to support the jury's decision. The U.S. Supreme Court concluded that the Oregon rule violated due process and was insufficient to protect Honda's constitutional rights.

COMPENSATION FOR TAKINGS

One of the first provisions of the Bill of Rights incorporated into the Fourteenth Amendment was the Fifth Amendment provision that private property may not be taken for public use without just compensation. State and federal governments have the power of *eminent domain*, which is the power to take property for public uses, such as building a school, park, or airport. If property is taken from a private owner for such a purpose, the owner is entitled to just compensation. As discussed further in Chapter 18, a more complex situation arises when the government does not physically take the property but imposes regulations that restrict its use.

In a sense, all regulations take some aspect of property away from the owner. The question is when does a regulation constitute a taking that requires compensation.

For example, the Federal Communications Commission regulated the rates a utility company could charge for the attachment of television cables to the company's poles. The Supreme Court held that the regulation was not a taking as long as the rates were not set so low as to be unjust and confiscatory.[145]

In *Eastern Enterprises v. Apfel*,[146] the Supreme Court invalidated the Coal Industry Retiree Health Benefits Act of 1992 under which Eastern Enterprises, a former coal mine operator that had ceased its mine operations in 1987, was required to contribute an annual premium of $5 million to a health fund for coal workers. The Act was enacted to remedy the shortfalls in the preexisting multi-employer benefits plans the coal industry had negotiated with the United Mine Workers union. It required all companies that had signed on to the union plans to contribute to a new health fund and to pay for their former employees even if the amount exceeded a company's obligation under the negotiated plan. The Supreme Court struck down

the Act as an unconstitutional "taking" of private property without compensation, holding that a law violates the Fifth Amendment if "[1] it imposes severe retroactive liability [2] on a limited class of parties that could not have anticipated the liability, and [3] the extent of that liability is substantially disproportionate to the parties' experience."

EQUAL PROTECTION

The Equal Protection Clause of the Fourteenth Amendment provides that no state shall "deny to any person within its jurisdiction the equal protection of the laws." A comparable limitation is imposed on the federal government by the Due Process Clause of the Fifth Amendment.

Establishing Discrimination

To challenge a statute on equal protection grounds, it is first necessary to establish that the statute discriminates against a class of persons. Discrimination may be found on the face of the statute, in its application, or in its purpose. The statute may (1) explicitly (on its face) treat different classes of persons differently; (2) contain no classification, but government officials may apply it differently to different classes of people; or (3) be neutral on its face and in its application but have the purpose of creating different burdens for different classes of persons.

In determining whether a facially neutral law is a device to discriminate against certain classes of people, the Supreme Court looks at three things: (1) the practical or statistical impact of the statute on different classes of persons, (2) the history of the problems that the statute seeks to solve, and (3) the legislative history of the statute. Even if a government action has a disproportionate effect on a racial minority group, it will be upheld if there was no racially discriminatory purpose or intent.[147]

Tests for Judging the Validity of Discrimination

The Supreme Court uses three different tests to determine the constitutionality of various types of discrimination, depending on how the statute classifies the persons concerned.

Rational Basis Test

The *rational basis test* applies to all classifications that relate to matters of economics or social welfare. Under this test, a classification will be upheld if there is any conceivable basis on which the classification might relate to a legitimate governmental interest. For example, a system of

---

144. 512 U.S. 415 (1994).

145. FCC v. Fla. Power Corp., 480 U.S. 245, 253 (1987).

146. 524 U.S. 498 (1998).

147. *See* Arlington Heights v. Metro. Hous. Dev. Corp., 429 U.S. 252 (1977) (upholding a largely white suburb's refusal to rezone to permit multifamily dwellings for low- and moderate-income tenants, including members of racial minorities).

progressive taxation, in which persons with higher income are required to pay taxes at a higher marginal rate, passes muster under this test. It is a rare regulation that cannot meet this minimal standard.

Strict Scrutiny Test

A classification that determines who may exercise a fundamental right or a classification based on certain suspect traits, such as race or color, is subject to strict scrutiny. Under the *strict scrutiny test*, a classification will be held valid only if it is necessary to promote a compelling state interest and is narrowly tailored to achieve that interest. The right to privacy, the right to vote, the right to travel, and certain other guarantees in the Bill of Rights are fundamental rights subject to strict scrutiny. Rights such as welfare payments, housing, education, and government employment are not fundamental rights.

Substantially Related Test

The Supreme Court occasionally applies a third test, which is stricter than the rational basis test but less strict than strict scrutiny. This intermediate-level test, known as the substantially related test, applies to classifications such as gender and legitimacy of birth. Under this test, a classification will be upheld if it is substantially related to an important governmental interest.

Racial Discrimination

Racial discrimination was the major target of the Fourteenth Amendment, so it is clear that racial classifications are suspect. Nonetheless, from 1896 to 1954, the "separate but equal" doctrine allowed governments to provide separate services for minorities as long as they were equal to the services provided for whites. For example, in *Plessy v. Ferguson*,[148] the U.S. Supreme Court upheld a law requiring all railway companies to provide separate but equal accommodations for African American and white passengers. Fifty-eight years later, the Supreme Court ruled in *Brown v. Board of Education*[149] that the separate but equal doctrine had no place in education. The Justices unanimously held that "segregation of children in public schools solely on the basis of race, even though the physical facilities and other 'tangible' factors may be equal, deprives the children of the minority group of equal educational opportunities." Supreme Court rulings following *Brown* made it clear that no governmental entity may segregate people because of their race or national origin.

Complications concerning racial classifications continue to arise in the area of affirmative action programs intended to benefit racial or ethnic minorities. A debate raged over whether strict scrutiny should be applied only to legislation that discriminates against a minority or to any legislation that generally discriminates based on race. The Supreme Court resolved that issue in *Adarand Constructors, Inc. v. Peña*,[150] when it held that all racial classifications—whether imposed by federal, state, or local government—are subject to strict scrutiny. In *Adarand*, the white owner of a construction company successfully challenged regulations adopted by the U.S. Department of Transportation that used race-based presumptions in awarding lucrative federal highway project contracts to economically disadvantaged businesses.

In 2009, the Supreme Court ruled that the City of New Haven violated Title VII of the Civil Rights Act of 1964 when it disregarded job-related examinations that resulted in no nonwhite firefighters being eligible for promotion.[151] The Court found that the City intentionally discriminated against the nonblacks who would have been promoted had the scores been used. Because the plaintiffs alleged only a violation of Title VII, the Court did not reach the question of whether race-based employment action not necessary to remedy past discrimination can withstand strict scrutiny under the Fourteenth Amendment.

A number of cases have raised the question of whether universities and schools can consider an applicant's race when deciding whether to admit the student. In *Grutter v. Bollinger*,[152] the U.S. Supreme Court considered the constitutionality of the University of Michigan Law School's admissions policy, which required admissions officials to consider diversity as one of a list of factors in evaluating potential students. Although the admissions policy did not define diversity solely in terms of race and ethnicity, and did not restrict the types of diversity eligible for consideration, the policy affirmed the school's commitment to diversity, with specific references to African American, Hispanic, and Native American students. After the law school denied admission to Ms. Grutter, a white Michigan resident with a 3.8 GPA and a high LSAT score, she filed suit alleging, among other things, that the school had discriminated against her on the basis of race in violation of the Fourteenth Amendment.

The Supreme Court ruled that the Equal Protection Clause did not prohibit the law school's narrowly tailored use of race in admissions decisions to further a compelling interest in obtaining the educational benefits that flow from a diverse student body. Applying the strict scrutiny test, the Court found that the law school's use of race was justified by a compelling state interest. The Court noted that "[a] core purpose of the Fourteenth Amendment was to do away with all governmentally imposed discrimination based on race" and stated that race-conscious admissions policies should therefore be limited in time. Observing that it had been twenty-five years since Justice Powell first

148. 163 U.S. 537 (1896).
149. 347 U.S. 483 (1954).

150. 515 U.S. 200 (1995).
151. Ricci v. DeStefano, 129 S. Ct. 2658 (2009) (Case 13.1).
152. 539 U.S. 306 (2003).

approved the use of race to further an interest in student body diversity, the Court stated that "[w]e expect that 25 years from now, the use of racial preferences will no longer be necessary to further the interest approved today."

Although the Supreme Court voted five-to-four to uphold the use of race by the University of Michigan Law School in *Grutter*, in *Gratz v. Bollinger* it struck down the University of Michigan's undergraduate admissions policy, which awarded points to African Americans, Hispanics, and Native Americans on an admissions rating scale.[153] The Court concluded that this use of race was not "narrowly tailored" to achieve the university's diversity goals.

Similarly, in *Parents Involved in Community Schools v. Seattle School District No. 1*,[154] the Court held that a Seattle public school district that had not operated legally segregated schools could not voluntarily adopt a student assignment plan that relied on race to determine which public high schools children attended. Nor could a school district in Jefferson County, Kentucky, whose court-ordered desegregation decree had been dissolved, use racial guidelines to assign elementary school students to particular schools.[155] The Court distinguished the compelling state intent in higher education upheld in *Grutter*, which "was not focused on race alone but encompassed 'all factors that may contribute to student body diversity,' " "as part of a broader effort to achieve 'exposure to widely diverse people, cultures, ideas, and viewpoints'. . . ." In contrast, for certain students in Seattle and Jefferson County, race alone was determinative. Noting that before *Brown v. Board of Education*, "schoolchildren were told where they could and could not go to school based on the color of their skin," the Court concluded that the two school districts had "not carried the heavy burden of demonstrating that we should allow this once again—even for very different reasons." In short, "the way to stop discrimination on the basis of race is to stop discriminating on the basis of race."

In his dissent, Justice Stevens found "a cruel irony in the Chief Justice's reliance on our decision in *Brown v. Board of Education*," which he said reminded him of Anatole France's observation that "'the majestic equality of the la[w], forbid[s] rich and poor alike to sleep under bridges, to beg in the streets, and to steal their bread.'" Justice Stevens faulted Chief Justice John Roberts's majority opinion for failing to note that it was only black schoolchildren who were so ordered: "[H]istory books do not tell stories of white children struggling to attend black schools. In this and other ways, the Chief Justice rewrites the history of one of this Court's most important decisions."

Private employers are not limited by the Equal Protection Clause, which applies only to governmental actors, such as state and local governments, schools, and police departments. However, as explained in Chapter 13, private entities are subject to Title VII of the Civil Rights Act and other regulations imposed by federal and state antidiscrimination statutes.

Other Forms of Discrimination

The U.S. Supreme Court has applied the substantially related test to laws that classify on the basis of gender, illegitimacy, and alienage.

Gender

In *United States v. Virginia*,[156] the Supreme Court ruled that the Virginia Military Institute, an all-male, state-supported military college, violated the Equal Protection Clause by excluding women. The Court held that classifications based on gender must (1) serve important governmental objectives, (2) be substantially related to achieving those objectives, and (3) rest on an "exceedingly persuasive justification." This decision can be read to require gender classifications to meet a standard somewhere between intermediate and strict scrutiny. In prior cases, the Court invalidated statutory provisions that gave female workers fewer benefits for their families than male workers;[157] upheld differential treatment for women when it was compensatory for past discrimination, but not when it unreasonably denied benefits to men;[158] upheld a statutory rape law that applied only to male offenders;[159] upheld exempting women from the draft;[160] and upheld disability insurance policies that excluded insurance benefits for costs relating to pregnancy, but not other disabilities.[161] Gender discrimination is discussed further in Chapter 13.

Illegitimacy

Classifications based on the legitimacy of children will be held invalid unless substantially related to a proper state interest. The Supreme Court will usually look at the purpose behind the classification and will not uphold any law intended to punish children born out of wedlock.

Alienage

Aliens, that is, persons who are not citizens of the United States, do not receive the protection of all constitutional guarantees, many of which apply only to citizens. For example, in 1990, the Supreme Court held that the Fourth Amendment prohibition of search and seizure without a

---

153. 539 U.S. 244 (2003).

154. 551 U.S. 701 (2007).

155. Meredith v. Jefferson County Bd. of Ed., 551 U.S. 701 (2007). This case was consolidated with the Seattle school district case.

156. 518 U.S. 515 (1996).

157. *See* Ariz. Governing Comm. for Tax Deferred Annuity & Deferred Comp. Plans v. Norris, 463 U.S. 1073 (1983).

158. *See* Johnson v. Transp. Agency, Santa Clara County, Cal., 480 U.S. 616 (1987).

159. *See* Michael M. v. Super. Ct. of Sonoma County, 450 U.S. 464 (1981).

160. *See* Rostker v. Goldberg, 453 U.S. 57 (1981).

161. *See* Geduldig v. Aiello, 417 U.S. 484 (1974).

warrant did not apply to a drug raid of an alien's premises in Mexico.[162] Because of Congress's *plenary* (or absolute) power to regulate aliens and immigration, classifications imposed by the federal government based on alienage are valid as long as they are not arbitrary and unreasonable. State and local laws that classify on the basis of alienage are subject to strict scrutiny, however, except for state laws discriminating against alien participation in certain state government positions, which are evaluated under the rational basis test. Foreign organizations without property or presence in the United States also have no constitutional rights.[163]

RIGHT TO JURY TRIAL

The Seventh Amendment provides that "[i]n Suits at common law, where the value in controversy shall exceed twenty dollars, the right of trial by jury shall be preserved." The phrase "suits at common law" refers to suits in which legal rights are to be ascertained and monetary damages awarded, in contrast to suits where only equitable rights and remedies (such as injunctions) are recognized. To determine whether a particular action will resolve legal rights, a court must analyze both the nature of the issues involved and the remedy sought. In particular, a court will compare the suits to eighteenth-century actions brought before the American Revolution in the courts of England prior to the merger of the courts of law and equity and examine the remedy sought to determine whether it is legal or equitable in nature.[164] In this two-part analysis, the second inquiry is more important than the first.

As previously discussed, the Seventh Amendment has not been interpreted to apply to the states. As a result, there is no federal constitutional requirement that jury trials be held in state court civil cases. When a federal court is hearing a case involving state law, the matter becomes more complicated. In *GTFM, LLC v. TKN Sales, Inc.*,[165] the U.S. Court of Appeals for the Second Circuit ruled that when a federal court has jurisdiction in a case based solely on diversity of citizenship (that is, when no federal question is involved), the federal court should require a jury trial only if a state court in that state would require a jury trial.

---

162. United States v. Verdugo-Urquidez, 494 U.S. 259 (1990).

163. People's Mojahedin Org. of Iran v. Dep't of State, 182 F.3d 17 (D.C. Cir. 1999).

164. *See* Chauffers, Teamsters & Helpers Local No. 391 v. Terry, 494 U.S. 558 (1990).

165. 257 F.3d 235 (2d Cir. 2001).

GLOBAL VIEW

Free Speech Rights in the European Union

Freedom of speech, or expression, is the concept that individuals should be able to express themselves freely, without governmental intervention. The right to freedom of speech is guaranteed under international law through a number of human rights instruments, including Article 19 of the Universal Declaration of Human Rights, which was adopted by the General Assembly of the United Nations in 1948. Article 19 provides that "[e]veryone has the right to freedom of opinion and expression; this right includes freedom to hold opinions without interference and to seek, receive and impart information and ideas through any media and regardless of frontiers." In practice, however, there is a "free speech" spectrum along which countries may be placed, with the United States providing the most freedom, totalitarian countries providing the least, and most European Union countries falling somewhere in the middle.

The First Amendment to the U.S. Constitution provides that "Congress shall make no law . . . abridging the freedom of speech, or of the press . . . ." The U.S. concept of free speech requires the government to refrain from interfering in individual expression, subject to narrow exceptions. The European approach, set forth in Article 10 of the Convention for the Protection of Human Rights and Fundamental Freedoms, affirms that everyone has the right to freedom of expression; however, it also states that the exercise of free speech "carries with it duties and responsibilities" and "may be subject to such formalities, conditions, restrictions and penalties as are prescribed by law and are necessary in a democratic society."[166] In Europe, the concept of free speech includes the idea that the government should prevent certain types of prohibited speech through active intervention. This approach is followed in most other democratic countries, including Australia, Canada, and Japan.[167]

Racist speech provides an example of the differences between the U.S. and the European approach to regulation of expression. Racist speech in the United States is protected political speech, no matter how disgusting, dangerous, or extreme it may be. As Supreme Court Justice Oliver Wendell Holmes stated: "The principle of free thought is not free

CONTINUED

---

166. 213 U.N.T.S. 222, *entered into force* Sept. 3, 1953, *as amended by* Protocols Nos. 3, 5, 8, and 11, *which entered into force* Sept. 21, 1970, Dec. 20, 1971, Jan. 1, 1990, and Nov. 1, 1998, *respectively.*

167. Benoît Frydman & Isabelle Rorive, *Regulating Internet Content Through Intermediaries in Europe and the USA*, 23 ZEITSCHRIFT FUR RECHTSSOZIOLOGIE 41 (2002), *available at* http://www.isys.ucl.ac.be/etudes/cours/linf2202/Frydman_&_Rorive_2002.pdf (last visited Aug. 6, 2011).

thought for those who agree with us but freedom for the thought we hate."[168]

Many European countries, however, including France, the Netherlands, Germany, and Denmark, have laws against inciting hatred and violence.[169] Such laws have led to criminal convictions and, in the case of foreigners, expulsion. In recent European speech cases:

- An Austrian court sentenced British historian David Irving to three years in prison for denying the Holocaust.[170]

- A German court convicted a sixty-one-year-old businessman of insulting Islam by selling toilet paper printed with the word "Quran," the Muslim holy book.[171]

- A French court ordered three French intellectuals and the publisher of the nation's premier newspaper, *Le Monde,* to pay 1 euro each to Attorneys Without Borders for defaming Jews in an op-ed article.[172]

- An Italian judge ordered journalist Oriana Fallaci to stand trial on charges that she defamed Islam in her book, *The Force of Reason,* when she wrote that Islam "sows hatred in the place of love and slavery in the place of freedom."[173] Fallaci died in 2006, while on trial.

- London Mayor Ken Livingston received a four-week suspension for comparing a Jewish journalist to a Nazi concentration camp guard.[174]

The growth of the Internet has highlighted these differences, as countries have attempted to apply their own free speech standards to Internet communications. An early example of this occurred in the late 1990s, when La Ligue Contre Racisme et L'Antisemitisme (LICRA) and L'Union Des Etudiants Juifs de France (UEJF) filed a complaint in France against Yahoo!, asserting that the sale of Nazi memorabilia on Yahoo!'s auction site violated a French law that prohibits the sale or display of symbols that incite racism. In May 2000,

a French court ruled that there were sufficient links with France to give it jurisdiction to hear the complaint. Specifically, the court found that the auctions of Nazi memorabilia were open to bidders worldwide (including France), that the viewing and display of these objects in France caused a public nuisance and violated French criminal law, and that Yahoo! was aware that French residents used its site. The court issued a preliminary injunction against Yahoo! pending further review.[175]

In response to Yahoo!'s argument that it was technologically impossible to block French users from the auction sites, the judge ordered three technology experts—one American, one French, and one other European—to study the issue and present their findings to the court. Based on their conclusion that Yahoo! could achieve a significant filtering success rate, the French court issued an order for Yahoo! to prevent French Internet users from accessing auction sites with Nazi paraphernalia within three months or face a fine of 15,244.90 euros per day.

Under pressure from U.S. organizations, Yahoo! banned hate-related goods from its auction site and removed numerous pro-Nazi Web pages from Geocities, although it claimed that these actions had nothing to do with the French judge's decision. At the same time, Yahoo! filed suit in a federal district court in California against LICRA and UEJF seeking a declaratory judgment that the French decision was unenforceable in the United States because it violated the First Amendment. In November 2001, the district court voided the French court's decision,[176] but the U.S. Court of Appeals for the Ninth Circuit reversed this decision in 2004 on the basis that it had no personal jurisdiction over the French plaintiffs.[177]

The case sparked a controversy in the United States, where many saw it as the censoring of a U.S. publication by a foreign country. The U.S. Court of Appeals for the Ninth Circuit agreed to hear the case en banc, and on January 1, 2006, the panel issued an opinion that, like the earlier three-judge panel, reversed the judgment of the district court and remanded the case with directions to dismiss the action. The court noted that "Yahoo! is necessarily arguing that it has a First Amendment right to violate French criminal law and to facilitate the violation of French criminal law by others . . . . the extent—indeed the very existence—of such an extraterritorial right under the First Amendment is uncertain."[178]

CONTINUED

---

168. *United States v. Schwimmer,* 279 U.S. 644, 654–55 (1929). The U.S. Supreme Court did, however, rule that state and local governments could permissibly draft carefully tailored statutes banning cross burning conducted with an intent to intimidate. The Court noted that the Ku Klux Klan had historically used burning crosses as "a tool of intimidation and a threat of impending violence" to African Americans. Nonetheless, the Court ruled that the government could not prohibit ritualistic cross burning conducted not to intimidate but to symbolize "shared group identity and ideology," because such ritualistic practices constituted political speech. *Virginia v. Black,* 538 U.S. 343 (2003).

169. *European Hate Speech Laws,* Legal Project, 2011, http://www.legal-project.org/issues/european-hate-speech-laws (last visited Aug. 5, 2011).

170. *Austrian Court Jails British Historian for Holocaust Denial,* European Jewish Press, Feb. 21, 2006, *available at* http://www.ejpress.org/article/news/uk/6105 (last visited Aug. 5, 2011).

171. César G. Soriano, *Europe Struggles to Balance Free Speech, Limits on Expression,* USA Today, Feb. 26, 2006.

172. Craig S. Smith, *Free Speech and Hate Speech: French Ruling Roils the Water,* N.Y. Times, June 27, 2005.

173. *Id.*

174. *Mayor Is Suspended over Nazi Jibe,* BBC News, Feb. 24, 2006, *available at* http://news.bbc.co.uk/2/hi/uk_news/england/london/4746016.stm (last visited Aug. 5, 2011).

175. Peter D. Trooboff, *Recent "Yahoo!" Ruling,* Nat'l L.J., Mar. 6, 2006, *available at* http://www.cov.com/files/Publication/a4f2de20-f384-49fe-8957-973c20895265/Presentation/PublicationAttachment/e777c041-431f-43ec-9d35-9e0ca1c06d65/oid6796.pdf (last visited Aug. 5, 2011).

176. *Yahoo! Inc. v. La Ligue Contre Le Racisme et L'Antisemitisme,* 145 F. Supp. 2d 1168 (N.D. Cal. 2001). Under the principle of comity, courts will respect and enforce judgments of foreign tribunals. However, Judge Jeremy Fogel noted that the principle of comity is not without exceptions. Generally, U.S. courts will not enforce foreign judgments that are inconsistent with fundamental U.S. public policies. Here, the French court decision ran counter to the First Amendment's free speech protections.

177. *Yahoo! Inc. v. La Ligue Contre Le Racisme et L'Antisemitisme,* 379 F.3d 1120 (9th Cir. 2004).

178. *Yahoo! Inc. v. LICRA,* 433 F.3d 1199, 1221 (9th Cir. 2006).

Attempts to establish international standards for racist speech on the Internet have made some progress. In November 2002, the Council of Europe (CoE)[179] approved an Additional Protocol to the Cybercrime Convention on the Criminalization of Acts of a Racist or Xenophobic Nature Committed Through Computer Systems that would make it illegal to distribute or publish anything online that "advocates, promotes or incites hatred [or]

discrimination." Although the United States is a signatory to the Cybercrime Convention,[180] which is designed to encourage other countries to enact computer crime and intellectual property laws, and participated in the drafting and negotiation of the Protocol, it has informed the CoE that it will not become a party to the Protocol because it believes that the final version of the Protocol is not consistent with the First Amendment.[181]

179. The Council of Europe consists of forty-seven member states, including all of the members of the European Union, and was established in 1949 primarily as a forum to uphold and strengthen human rights and to promote democracy and the rule of law in Europe. The CoE has been the negotiating forum for a number of conventions on criminal matters in which the United States has participated.

180. Forty-seven countries have signed the Convention on Cybercrime; of these, thirty-one (including Germany, Italy, the United Kingdom, and the United States) have ratified it.

181. Declan McCullagh, *U.S. Won't Support Net "Hate Speech" Ban*, CNET News.com, Nov. 15, 2002, http://news.com.com/2100-1023-965983.html (last visited Aug. 5, 2011).

© Cengage Learning 2013

THE RESPONSIBLE MANAGER

PRESERVING CONSTITUTIONAL RIGHTS

Although the Constitution is directed primarily at establishing and limiting the powers of the federal and state governments, its provisions have a profound effect on private actors in society. The costs are usually high, but at times a company may find it worthwhile to challenge a regulation on constitutional grounds. This was true for the pharmaceutical companies that successfully challenged Vermont's ban on the sale of prescriber-identifying information[182] and for State Farm, the insurance company that successfully challenged the $145 million punitive damages award against it.[183]

182. Sorrell v. IMS Health Inc., 131 S. Ct. 2653 (2011) (Case 1.1).
183. State Farm Mut. Auto. Ins. Co. v. Campbell, 538 U.S. 408 (2003).

Managers often have an interest in influencing legislation or other government action through direct lobbying or political action committees. When pursuing change, it is important to know the constitutional limitations placed on different government segments. In addition, the ability of corporations and labor unions to fund advertisements for specific candidates raises a host of ethical issues.

Although many provisions in the Constitution apply only to government actions, managers of private organizations should be aware of the societal values reflected in the Constitution. These include the right to fair and equal treatment and respect for the individual.

© Cengage Learning 2013

A MANAGER'S DILEMMA

Putting It into Practice

Personal Privacy in Text Messages on Employer-Provided Mobile Phones

In 2001, the City of Ontario, California, issued twenty alphanumeric pagers capable of sending and receiving text messages to members of its SWAT team in an effort to help the team mobilize and respond more efficiently in emergency situations. The City made it clear that these pagers were subject to auditing per its "Computer Usage, Internet, and E-Mail Policy." Within the first month, certain employees began going over their monthly allowances for text messages. For the first year, the employees were informed of the overages and given the opportunity to reimburse the City for the cost; in exchange, the City agreed not to audit the messages to determine whether they were, in

fact, work related. The City subsequently determined that this arrangement was not workable, so it audited the bills of employees who went over their monthly allowances for a two-month period. After reviewing the transcripts, the City discovered that one employee had sent and received 457 text messages in one month, 399 of which were not work related. In addition, many were sexually explicit. Can the City discipline this employee without violating his First and Fourth Amendment rights? What about the rights of the recipients of the employee's text messages?[184]

184. City of Ontario, California v. Quon, 130 S. Ct. 2619 (2010).

© Cengage Learning 2013

INSIDE STORY

Effect of Politics on Supreme Court Appointments

The nomination process for the U.S. Supreme Court has grown increasingly politicized and controversial over time. Nomination to the Supreme Court now brings along with it a process of public scrutiny akin to running for national political office. Politics, however, is not new to the process of selecting Justices.

Franklin Delano Roosevelt was probably the first President to attempt explicitly and publicly to use the power of judicial appointment to change the Court's position on key political issues. Frustrated because the Supreme Court was invalidating much of his New Deal legislation, Roosevelt introduced a Court-packing bill that would have added one Justice to the Court for every sitting Justice who had reached the age of seventy, thereby increasing the Court's membership to fifteen. By appointing additional Justices, Roosevelt hoped to gain a majority sympathetic to his programs. Although the bill was never passed by the Senate, the Court quickly capitulated and abandoned its commitment to limited government, especially regarding economic liberty.

Other presidents have made considerations of diversity and representation key to their selection of nominees. President Lyndon Johnson's appointment of Thurgood Marshall took into consideration for the first time the need for African Americans to be represented on the Court. The appointments of Sandra Day O'Connor (the first female member of the Court) by President Ronald Reagan in 1981, Clarence Thomas (the second African American) by the elder George Bush in 1991, and Sonia Sotomayor (the first Hispanic) by President Barack Obama in 2009 served to expand and maintain the Court's gender and racial diversity.

In 1987, President Ronald Reagan nominated Robert Bork, a well-known conservative constitutional scholar with an extensive "paper trail" of opinions and writings on constitutional matters. Lengthy Senate hearings in which Bork was forced to attempt to explain the reasoning behind some of his more radical statements over the years, and the resultant political uproar across the nation, led the Senate to deny his confirmation to the Court.

The 1991 nomination of Clarence Thomas to the "black seat" on the Supreme Court, vacated by Justice Thurgood Marshall's resignation, was supposed to be straightforward and noncontroversial but resulted in another Bork-like public spectacle. Thomas seemed to be a safe bet: his writings and opinions were sparse and generally without controversy. After completing an initial hearing, however, Thomas was called back before the Judiciary Committee to face allegations of sexual harassment by Anita Hill, an African American law professor and former colleague. The ensuing melee became a circus in which actors on both sides paraded before the committee, asserting their versions of the truth. Thomas, undaunted by the allegations, charged the committee with conducting a "high-tech lynching of uppity-blacks." This aggressive challenge to the senators dulled the edge of their remaining questions, and the Senate subsequently approved Thomas by a vote of fifty-two to forty-eight.

When President Bill Clinton nominated Ruth Bader Ginsburg to the Court, the politics swirled around the question of whether the Senate should apply an abortion "litmus test" to her appointment in light of the changing Supreme Court position on the pivotal issue of whether a woman has a constitutional right to an abortion. In an effort to preempt potential litmus test–type questions, Judge Ginsburg began her hearing with opening remarks that hinted at the inappropriateness of deciding a case in advance and promised to impartially hear each case before the Court "without reaching out to cover cases not yet seen." She was easily confirmed by a vote of ninety-six to three, and her hearing served as an opportunity to reduce hostility in the nomination process.

Since the confirmation of President George W. Bush's appointees Chief Justice John Roberts, Jr., and Justice Samuel Alito, the Supreme Court has taken an undeniable turn to the right, which could become one of the enduring legacies of President Bush's tenure.[185] At the conclusion of the first full Term on which Justices Roberts and Alito served, one Court watcher commented that "at the end of a course-changing, gut-wrenching Supreme Court term littered with heated 5–4 decisions, one bit of clarity is shining through: The Roberts Court, and especially its newest member, Samuel Alito, are both very conservative and very pro-business—more so than any Supreme Court in decades."[186]

Indeed, when control of one or both of the other branches of government is in the hands of another party, there can be occasional head-butting. During the State of the Union address in January 2010, President Obama "called out" the Supreme Court on what he believed was a poor decision in the *Citizens United*[187] case, stating, "Well I don't think American elections should be bankrolled by America's most powerful interests, or worse, by foreign entities. They should be decided by the American people, and that's why I'm urging Democrats and Republicans to pass a bill that helps to right

CONTINUED

---

185. Linda Greenhouse, *In Steps Big and Small, Supreme Court Moved Right*, N.Y. Times, July 1, 2007, at A1.

186. Tony Mauro, *A Mind for Business*, Legal Times, July 2, 2007, *available at* http://www.law.com/jsp/article.jsp?id=1183107990440.

187. Citizens United v. Fed. Election Comm'n, 130 S. Ct. 876 (2010).

this wrong."[188] Justice Alito, sitting in the front row at the time with the other members of the Court, reportedly mouthed "not true" in response.[189] Later, Chief Justice Roberts indicated that he was "troubled" by President Obama's remarks. Although the Chief Justice said that he had no problem with politicians criticizing a decision of the Court, because it is part of their job, he took issue with the "setting, circumstance and decorum" of the President's remarks, implying that the State of the Union address was not the appropriate place to voice such disapproval. The Chief Justice characterized the State of the Union address as a "political pep rally" where the Justices are expected to sit expressionless while "Congress literally surrounds them," jeering and hollering.[190] Justices Alito, Scalia,

and Thomas did not attend the State of the Union address in January 2011.[191]

President Obama's nominees Sonia Sotomayor and Elena Kagan were both appointed with bipartisan support. Although Sotomayor had been a sitting judge of the U.S. Court of Appeals for the Second Circuit prior to her appointment to the Supreme Court, Kagan (former dean of Harvard Law School) had no prior judicial experience. Some commentators suggested that her absence of a record that could be used by conservatives in the Senate to oppose her confirmation was a net plus.

---

188. Kasie Hunt, *Justice Alito Mouths "Not True,"* POLITICO, Jan. 27, 2010, *available at* http://www.politico.com/blogs/politicolive/0110/Justice_Alitos_You_lie_moment.html (last visited Aug. 8, 2011).

189. *Id.*

190. Ariane de Vogue, *Chief Justice Roberts "Troubled" by Scene at State of the Union Address*, ABC NEWS, Mar. 10, 2010, *available at* http://abcnews.go.com/Politics/chief-justice-roberts-troubled-scene-state-union/story?id=10063937 (last visited Aug. 8, 2011).

191. *See* Jess Bravin, *Six on Supreme Court to Attend State of the Union*, WALL ST. J., Jan. 25, 2011. Justice Thomas indicated that he no longer attends the speeches because they have become "so partisan and it's very uncomfortable for a judge to sit there." *See Supreme Court Justice Alito Plans to Skip Next State of the Union Address*, FOX NEWS, Oct. 16, 2010, *available at* http://www.foxnews.com/politics/2010/10/16/supreme-court-justice-alito-plans-skip-state-union-address/ (last visited Aug. 8, 2011).

KEY WORDS AND PHRASES

QUESTIONS AND CASE PROBLEMS

1. What factors should managers and labor union leaders take into account when deciding whether to support specific candidates for office?

2. Most of the athletic shoes sold by Nike, Inc. are manufactured by female workers under the age of twenty-four employed by subcontractors in China, Vietnam, and Indonesia. Beginning in March 1993, Nike assumed responsibility for its subcontractors' compliance with applicable local laws and regulations regarding minimum wages, overtime, safety, health, and environmental protection. In 1996, the television program *48 Hours* reported that Nike products were made in factories where workers were paid less than the applicable minimum wage; were required to work overtime and encouraged to work more

than the legal overtime limits; were subjected to physical, verbal, and sexual abuse; and were exposed to toxic chemicals, noise, heat, and dirt, in violation of applicable occupational health and safety laws. These allegations were repeated in articles published in a variety of media.

In response, Nike issued press releases, letters to newspapers, letters to university presidents and athletic directors, and other documents (including full-page advertisements in leading newspapers) stating that the allegations were false and misleading, that its workers were paid in accordance with applicable local laws, and received free meals and medical care, and that their working conditions complied with safety and health rules. Marc Kasky sued Nike on behalf of the general public under California Business and Professions Code sections 17204 and 17535, claiming that Nike's statements were false and misleading and were made with knowledge or reckless disregard of California laws prohibiting false and misleading statements. Nike moved to dismiss the complaint on the grounds, among others, that its statements were protected by the First Amendment to the U.S. Constitution. Can a corporation participating in a public debate be subjected to liability for factual inaccuracies? [*Kasky v. Nike, Inc.*, 45 P.3d 243 (Cal. 2002), *cert. granted*, 537 U.S. 1099 (2003), *cert. dismissed as improvidently granted*, 539 U.S. 654 (2003).]

3. Most wine in the United States is distributed through a three-tier network that developed after the repeal of Prohibition. First, the winery obtains a permit to sell wine. Next, the winery sells its wine to a licensed wholesaler, who pays excise taxes and delivers the wine to a retailer. The retailer then sells the wine to consumers. As demand for wine has increased over the last two decades, the number of wineries has grown to more than 2,000, including many small wineries. Meanwhile, the number of wholesalers has declined from several thousand to a few hundred. As a result, many small wineries are unable to find wholesalers to carry their wine and are trying to market their wine directly to consumers.

Juanita Swedenburg runs the Swedenburg Estate Vineyard in Middleburg, Virginia. People from all over the United States visit her winery and purchase wine to take home with them. Once they get home, many call the winery or use its website to order more bottles. However, the laws in twenty-six states prohibit the direct shipment of wine to consumers across state lines. The states claim that the Twenty-first Amendment, which repealed Prohibition, gives them the authority to regulate the importation of alcohol. Their claim is based on Section 2 of the amendment, which states that "[t]he transportation or importation into any state, territory, or possession of the United States for delivery or use therein of intoxicating liquors, in violation of the laws thereof, is hereby prohibited." Swedenburg, other winery owners, and wine lovers challenged the direct-shipment laws. Are these direct-shipment laws constitutional? Explain why or why not. [*Granholm v. Heald*, 544 U.S. 460 (2005).]

4. John and Judith Rapanos were accused of destroying wetlands, without a permit, on three central Michigan sites that they hoped to develop. Regulators sought as much as

$1.4 million in fines and restoration of the site. Rapanos argued that his land is far away from the nearest river tributary—twenty miles in the case of one site. The U.S. Court of Appeals for the Sixth Circuit concluded, however, that the Clean Water Act covered the property because the land had a hydrological connection to navigable waterways because it ultimately drained into either the Tittabawassee River or Lake Huron. Rapanos argued that extending the Clean Water Act's jurisdiction to every intrastate wetland with any sort of hydrological connection to navigable waters, no matter how tenuous or remote, exceeds Congress's constitutional power to regulate commerce among the states. Is the Clean Water Act, which gives permitting authority to the U.S. Army Corps of Engineers, for wetlands that are not adjacent to a river or other navigable waterway, but are hydrologically connected to these waterways because they drain into a tributary of a river or navigable waterway, a constitutional exercise of Congress's power under the Commerce Clause? Explain why or why not. [*Rapanos v. United States*, 547 U.S. 715 (2006).]

5. The State of Washington created a new college scholarship program, pursuant to which it awarded Promise Scholarships to low- and middle-income students who had achieved an excellent academic record in high school. Joshua Davey was awarded one of the Promise Scholarships. The director of financial aid at Northwest College, however, determined that Davey did not meet the enrollment requirements for the Promise Scholarship because he was pursuing a degree in pastoral ministries. Davey filed a lawsuit in which he alleged that the provision of the Washington law that denied Promise Scholarships to students pursuing a degree in theology is unconstitutional. What arguments can Davey make? What arguments can the state make in its defense? Who will win the lawsuit? [*Locke v. Davey*, 540 U.S. 712 (2004).]

6. Section 1464 of Title 18 of the U.S. Code provides that "[w]hoever utters any obscene, indecent, or profane language by means of radio communication shall be fined under this title or imprisoned not more than two years, or both." The Federal Communications Commission (FCC) defined "indecent" speech as "language that describes, in terms patently offensive as measured by contemporary community standards for the broadcast medium, sexual or excretory activities and organs, at times of the day when there is a reasonable risk that children may be in the audience." In the years prior to 2004, the FCC held that a single, nonliteral use of an expletive was not actionably indecent. However, after the 2003 Golden Globes, where U2 Band member Bono stated "this is really, really, fucking brilliant," the FCC changed its position and held that a single, nonliteral use of an expletive (called a "fleeting expletive") could be actionably "indecent" under the statute (this new standard was called the "Golden Globes standard"). The FCC then found that four programs were in violation of the statute under the new policy, including the 2002 Billboard Music Awards, the 2003 Billboard Music Awards, certain episodes of *NYPD Blue*, and CBS's *The Early Show*. All four programs involved "fleeting expletives," and the FCC proclaimed that any use of "fuck" or "shit" was indecent and profane, regardless of how the

word was used in a sentence or how many times it was used. A number of networks, including NBC Universal, Fox Television Stations, Inc., CBS Broadcasting, Inc., and ABC, Inc., filed petitions for reconsideration of this policy, as well as constitutional challenges on First Amendment grounds. The networks' administrative argument, that the FCC's interpretation of the statute was arbitrary and capricious, failed in the Supreme Court, where the Court found that "[t]he Commission could reasonably conclude that the pervasiveness of foul language, and the coarsening of public entertainment in other media such as cable, justify more stringent regulation of broadcast programs so as to give conscientious parents a relatively safe haven for their children." Is the FCC's "Golden Globes standard" constitutional? What arguments can be made by the FCC? By the networks? What public policies are implicated? [*Fox Television Stations, Inc. v. FCC*, 613 F.3d 317 (2d Cir. 2010), *cert. granted*, 131 S. Ct. 3065 (2011).]

7. In an effort to protect the community from salmonella-infected eggs, the U.S. Department of Agriculture (USDA) issued interim regulations that restricted the interstate sale and transportation of eggs and poultry from flocks determined under the regulations to be contaminated. If a federal or state representative traced an outbreak to a flock, then the flock would be designated a "study flock." The USDA would collect samples from the study flock to determine whether the birds were infected. If any of these tests came out positive, the flock would then be designated a "test flock," and its movement in interstate commerce would be restricted. In addition, a number of birds from the test flock would be killed so that their blood and internal organs could be tested. If those tests came back positive in even a single bird, the flock would be deemed an "infected flock" until either the flock was retested with no positive results, or the flock's housing was depopulated, cleaned, disinfected, and repopulated with new birds.

In 1990, salmonella outbreaks were traced to three houses belonging to Rose Acre Farms, and flocks from those houses subsequently tested positive. As a result, the USDA labeled them "test flocks" and restricted their interstate movement. For organ testing, USDA officials removed and killed sixty hens from each of the three houses. At least one hen tested positive, so the houses were designated as "infected houses." Initially, Rose Acre attempted retesting to see whether the flocks would pass inspection; when that proved fruitless, Rose Acre began to depopulate and sanitize the houses. The houses were empty for long periods of time while awaiting USDA inspection. The restrictions on the three houses were not lifted until 1992. In the meantime, Rose Acre was able to sell the eggs from those houses (which comprised 43% of its total egg production) only to breaker plants where eggs are pasteurized for use in products such as cake mixes; the value of eggs sold to these plants is reduced by 10%. Rose Acre filed suit pursuant to the Fifth Amendment, alleging an uncompensated taking of its eggs and hens. Was this a "taking" for Fifth Amendment purposes? What result? [*Rose Acre Farms, Inc. v. United States*, 559 F.3d 1260 (2009), *cert. denied, Rose Acre Farms, Inc. v. United States*, 130 S.Ct. 1501 (2010).]

8. The Arizona Citizens Clean Election Act provides that after a privately financed candidate has raised or spent a specified amount, each dollar spent by that candidate will be matched, almost dollar-for-dollar, by a direct payment of public money to publicly funded opponents. Is the Arizona statute constitutional? [*Arizona Free Enterprise Club's Freedom Club PAC v. Bennett*, 131 S. Ct. 2806 (2011).]

A Minnesota statute bans direct corporate contributions to political candidates and requires corporations wishing to make independent expenditures advocating the election or defeat of a candidate to either (1) form and register an independent expenditure political fund or (2) contribute to an existing fund. The treasurer of such a fund must segregate its funds, keep certain records, and make the records available for audit. Is the Minnesota statute constitutional? [*Minnesota Citizens Concerned for Life, Inc. v. Swanson*, 640 F.3d 304 (8th Cir. 2011); *see also* Ognibene v. Parkes, 2011 U.S. App. LEXIS 25301 (2d Cir. Dec. 21, 2011).]

CHAPTER 5

AGENCY

INTRODUCTION

AGENCY AND THE CONDUCT OF BUSINESS

Agency is perhaps the most pervasive legal relationship in the business world. In an *agency* relationship, one person—the *agent*—acts for or represents another person—the *principal*. The principal delegates a portion of his or her power to the agent. The agent then manages the assigned task and exercises the discretion given by the principal. The agency relationship can be created by an express or implied agreement or by law.

Businesses of all kinds require the assistance of agents in order to conduct multiple operations in various locations. Indeed, without the law of agency, corporations could not function at all. Only through its human agents can a corporation enter into any kind of binding agreement.

CHAPTER OVERVIEW

This chapter defines and discusses the central principles of agency law. First, it describes the different methods by which an agency relationship can be formed. The chapter identifies the different types of agency relationships (employer–employee and principal–independent contractor) and the consequences that flow from each. It examines the duties an agent owes to the principal and an agent's authority to enter into agreements that bind the principal. Finally, the chapter discusses the extent to which a principal may be liable for the tortious or illegal conduct of an agent.

---

enters into an agreement of a type that must be in writing to be enforceable (such as an agreement for the sale of real property), then the agent's signature on the agreement will not bind the principal unless the agency relationship itself is evidenced by some signed writing. This is called the *equal dignities rule.*

An agency agreement can also be implied from conduct. For example, suppose that Techno Phones, Inc. agrees that its sales representative, Computers International (CI), will sell Techno's smartphones to retailers and end users. CI solicits sales for Techno, and Techno pays CI a commission for each sale. An agency relationship exists between Techno and CI, even if they have not entered into a formal agreement.

Agency relationships can be formed without agreement based on apparent authority. *Apparent authority,* also referred to as *agency by estoppel,* occurs when a person leads another to believe that someone else is his or her agent and is thereafter estopped (prevented) from denying it. For example, suppose that Jack causes Kendra to believe that Lori is his agent, and Kendra, relying on this, proceeds to deal with Lori. Even if Lori is not in fact Jack's agent, Kendra's reliance creates an agency by estoppel. As a result, Lori's dealings with Kendra will bind Jack.

An agency relationship can also be formed without agreement by ratification. If a principal approves or accepts the benefits of the actions of an otherwise unauthorized agent, he or she has formed an *agency by ratification.*

FORMATION OF AN AGENCY RELATIONSHIP

The agency relationship is consensual in nature and is typically created by agreement of the parties, which can usually be either written or oral. If, however, the agent

TYPES OF AGENCY RELATIONSHIPS

An agent may be either an employee of the principal or an independent contractor.

Employer–Employee

The most common form of agency relationship is the employer-employee relationship, sometimes still referred to as the master-servant relationship. The basic characteristic of this relationship is that the employer has the right to control the conduct of the employee. The employee may have the authority to bind the employer to a contract under theories of actual or apparent authority.

Principal (Client)–Independent Contractor

An *independent contractor*, such as a lawyer working for a client or a plumber working for a house builder, is not an employee of the person paying for his or her services because the independent contractor's conduct is not fully subject to that person's control. The person hiring an independent contractor bargains only for results.

An independent contractor may or may not be an agent. Generally, an agency relationship exists when the hiring person gives the independent contractor authority to enter into contracts on his or her behalf. For example, suppose that a builder contracts to build a house for Ken for $200,000. Ken has no control over the builder's manner of doing the work because the house is one of a large group of houses that the builder is constructing in a housing subdivision. The builder is not Ken's agent. In contrast, if Ken expressly authorized the builder to buy redwood siding from a lumber company on his behalf, the independent contractor would be Ken's agent for purposes of buying the siding.

Distinguishing Between Employees and Independent Contractors

The determination of whether a worker is an employee or an independent contractor is a legal issue with several important consequences. These include the liability of the principal for the worker's wrongful misconduct, as well as the principal's duty to deduct and pay certain taxes on behalf of the worker and to permit the worker to participate in employee benefit plans.

Under the doctrine of *respondeat superior* ("let the master answer"), employers are liable for the torts (and many crimes) of their employees, as long as the employee was acting within the scope of employment. In contrast, persons hiring independent contractors are generally not liable for torts committed by the independent contractor.

Employers are required to deduct or pay income, Social Security, and unemployment taxes for employees but not for independent contractors. Independent contractors are responsible for paying their own self-employment taxes. Moreover, independent contractors are generally not eligible for the same fringe benefits provided to employees, such as medical insurance, stock options, and 401(k) retirement plans. Although the distinction between employees and independent contractors is an important one, there is no bright-line test to distinguish one from the other.

Whether a person is an independent contractor or an employee depends on what he or she does, not on how the relationship is characterized by the parties. Thus, the label used in a contract does not determine the status of a worker. Courts and regulatory agencies frequently look at a variety of factors, including the following:

1. How much control can the employer exercise over the details of the work?
2. Is the employed person engaged in an occupation distinct from that of the employer?
3. Is the kind of work being done usually performed under the direction of an employer or by a specialist without supervision?
4. What degree of skill does the work require?
5. Does the employer provide the worker with tools and a place of work?
6. For how long is the worker employed?
7. Is the worker paid on the basis of time or by the job?
8. Does the worker offer his or her services to the public at large?

Employee status is more likely to be found for workers who are lower paid and less skilled, lack bargaining power, and have a high degree of economic dependence on their employers.

Because an employer does not pay employment taxes and may not provide fringe benefits for independent contractors, employers may be tempted to hire temporary workers and independent contractors as a less costly alternative to hiring employees, but this decision could turn out to be an expensive mistake. During the 1980s, Microsoft employed a number of freelance workers as independent contractors to perform services as software testers, production editors, proofreaders, formatters, and indexers. The freelancers often worked on teams with regular employees, sharing the same supervisors, performing identical tasks, and working the same hours. Unlike employees, however, they were not permitted to assign their work to others, were not invited to official company functions, and were not paid overtime wages. In addition, the freelancers were required to submit invoices for their services, documenting their hours and the projects on which they worked, and they were paid through the accounts receivable department rather than Microsoft's payroll department.

Although the freelancers had acknowledged in their Independent Contractor Agreements that they were independent contractors and had agreed to be responsible for all federal and state taxes, tax withholding, and Social Security taxes, the Internal Revenue Service (IRS) concluded that Microsoft had misclassified these workers and that they should have been classified as employees for withholding and employment tax purposes. Microsoft therefore was required to (1) pay overdue employer withholding taxes, (2) issue retroactive W-2 forms to allow the freelancers to recover Microsoft's share of Social Security taxes (which they had been required to pay), and (3) pay the freelancers retroactively for any overtime they had worked.

After learning of the IRS rulings, eight freelancers, on behalf of themselves and as representatives of the class of freelance workers, filed a lawsuit against Microsoft, seeking various employee benefits, including benefits under an employee stock purchase plan (ESPP), which allowed employees to purchase company stock at 85% of the fair market value on either the first or the last day of each six-month offering period, whichever was lower. Microsoft denied liability because each of these workers had signed an Independent Contractor Agreement that expressly provided that the worker was personally responsible for all of his or her own benefits. The U.S. Court of Appeals for the Ninth Circuit ruled that the approximately 10,000 current and former independent contractors and longtime "temporary" employees at Microsoft who worked at least half-time, or five months a year, had become "common law" employees of the company and thus were entitled to compensation for their exclusion from the ESPP.[1] At the time of the decision, analysts estimated that Microsoft would have to pay approximately $100 million to the workers.

1. Vizcaino v. Microsoft, 173 F.3d 713, 723 (9th Cir. 1999).

Many companies responded to the *Microsoft* decision by leasing workers from temporary employment agencies instead of hiring them directly. This arrangement may not be fail-safe, however. The fact that leased workers are on the payroll of an employment agency does not preclude them from being considered employees of the company—the agency and company could be considered joint employers.

To determine whether a company is a joint employer of leased workers, a manager should consider such factors as whether the company (1) supervises the workers, (2) has the ability to hire and fire, (3) is involved in day-to-day labor relations, (4) establishes wage rates, or (5) has the power to promote or discipline the worker. As with questions surrounding the independent contractor label, the bottom line is that if leased employees are treated the same as regular employees, they may be treated as common law employees of the company.

FIDUCIARY DUTY

In agreeing to act on behalf of the principal, the agent becomes a *fiduciary*. Loyalty, obedience, and care are the hallmarks of the fiduciary relationship. An agent has a duty to act solely for the benefit of his or her principal in all matters directly connected with the agency undertaking. This is the *duty of loyalty*. For example, if Adrienne is entrusted with the power to buy a piece of land for Pierre, she cannot buy the best piece of land for herself instead. An agent is also obligated to obey all reasonable orders of his or her principal. For example, if Adrienne refuses to follow Pierre's order to purchase a particular parcel of property, her insubordination would violate the *duty of obedience*.

The following classic case examines the contours of the duty of loyalty.

A CASE IN POINT	*In the Language of the Court*	Case 5.1

Meinhard v. Salmon

Court of Appeals of New York
164 N.E. 545 (N.Y. 1928).

FACTS In 1902, Louisa Gerry leased the Bristol Hotel in New York City to the defendant, Walter Salmon, for a term of twenty years, beginning in 1902 and ending in 1922. Salmon was to renovate the hotel building for use as shops and offices at a cost of $200,000. Salmon needed funds to complete his proposed renovations, so he persuaded Morton Meinhard to act as a financial backer. Salmon and Meinhard entered into a joint venture agreement with the following terms: Meinhard agreed to pay to Salmon one-half of the money necessary to reconstruct, alter, manage, and operate the property, and Salmon agreed to pay to Meinhard 40% of the net profits for the first five years of the lease and 50% for the years thereafter. If there were losses, each party was to bear them equally. Salmon, however, was to have sole power to "manage, lease, underlet and operate" the building.

In January 1922, with less than four months of the lease to run, Elbridge Gerry, who had become the owner of the property, approached Salmon, and they agreed to enter into a new twenty-year lease for the Bristol Hotel and an entire tract of property surrounding it. The new lessee (the entity leasing the property) was the Midpoint Realty Company, which was owned and controlled by Salmon. Under the new lease, the Bristol Hotel would eventually be torn down, and new buildings would be built on the old Bristol site and adjacent lots at a cost of

CONTINUED

$3 million. Salmon did not tell Meinhard about the new lease between Gerry and the Midpoint Realty Company, which was signed and delivered on January 25, 1922, and Meinhard did not learn of the existence of the new project until February, after the new lease had been signed.

Meinhard demanded to be included in the new lease, but Salmon and Gerry refused, and Meinhard sued. A referee found in favor of Meinhard but limited his interest in (and corresponding obligations under) the lease to 25%. Both the plaintiff and the defendant cross-appealed to the Appellate Division of the New York Supreme Court. On appeal, Meinhard was awarded one-half of the interest in (and corresponding obligations under) the lease. Salmon appealed to the New York Court of Appeals, the highest state court in New York.

ISSUE PRESENTED   Did Salmon, as Meinhard's joint venturer, have a relationship of trust (or *fiduciary duty*) to Meinhard that obligated him to give Meinhard the opportunity to be included in a new lease covering property that was originally leased by Salmon on behalf of the joint venture?

OPINION   CARDOZO, C.J. (later a Justice of the U.S. Supreme Court), writing for the New York Court of Appeals:

Joint adventurers, like copartners, owe to one another, while the enterprise continues, the duty of the finest loyalty. Many forms of conduct permissible in a workaday world for those acting at arm's length, are forbidden to those bound by fiduciary ties. A trustee is held to something stricter than the morals of the market place. Not honesty alone, but the punctilio of an honor the most sensitive, is then the standard of behavior. As to this there has developed a tradition that is unbending and inveterate. Uncompromising rigidity has been the attitude of courts of equity when petitioned to undermine the rule of undivided loyalty by the "disintegrating erosion" of particular exceptions. Only thus has the level of conduct for fiduciaries been kept at a level higher than that trodden by the crowd. It will not consciously be lowered by any judgment of this court.

The owner of the [property], Mr. Gerry, had vainly striven to find a tenant who would favor his ambitious scheme of demolition and construction. Baffled in the search, he turned to the defendant Salmon [who was] in possession of the Bristol, the keystone of the project. . . . To the eye of an observer, Salmon held the lease as owner in his own right, for himself and no one else. In fact he held it as a fiduciary, for himself and another, sharers in a common venture. If this fact had been proclaimed, if the lease by its terms had run in favor of a partnership, Mr. Gerry, we may fairly assume, would have laid before the partners, and not merely before one of them, his plan for reconstruction. . . . The trouble about [Salmon's] conduct is that he excluded his coadventurer from any chance to compete, from any chance to enjoy the opportunity for benefit that had come to him alone by virtue of his agency. This chance, if nothing more, he was under a duty to concede.

. . . .

We have no thought to hold that Salmon was guilty of a conscious purpose to defraud. Very likely he assumed in all good faith that with the approaching end of the venture he might ignore his coadventurer and take the extension for himself. He had given to the enterprise time and labor as well as money. He had made it a success. Meinhard, who had given money, but neither time nor labor, had already been richly paid. There might seem to be something grasping in his insistence upon more. Such recriminations are not unusual when coadventurers fall out. They are not without their force if conduct is to be judged by the common standards of competitors. That is not to say that they have pertinency here. Salmon had put himself in a position in which thought of self was to be renounced, however hard the abnegation. He was much more than a coadventurer. He was a managing coadventurer. For him and for those like him the rule of undivided loyalty is relentless and supreme.

RESULT   The judgment for the plaintiff, Meinhard, was affirmed. He was granted one-half of the interest in (and corresponding obligations under) the new lease between Salmon and Gerry.

CONTINUED

COMMENTS   In *Meinhard v. Salmon*, the court seemed to assume without explanation that joint venturers had a fiduciary duty to one another. Judges can disagree on what types of business relations give rise to a standard that is "stricter than the morals of the market place," thereby creating a fiduciary duty. Furthermore, there is even disagreement as to what constitutes the proper morals of the marketplace. In *Northeast General Corp. v. Wellington Advertising*, decided by the New York Court of Appeals, the same court that decided *Meinhard v. Salmon*, a majority of the judges concluded that a finder hired by the seller of a business to find a buyer of a majority interest in the business did not have a fiduciary duty to disclose to the seller the unsavory reputation of the potential buyer.[2] The dissenting judge disagreed. He argued that there was a fiduciary relationship between the parties and that, even if there were not, the morals of the marketplace would require disclosure.

---

2.   624 N.E.2d 129 (N.Y. 1993) (Case 2.2).

© Cengage Learning 2013

An agent also has a duty to act with due care. This *duty of care* includes a duty to avoid mistakes, whether through negligence, recklessness, or intentional misconduct. Some states require an agent to use the same level of care a person would use in the conduct of his or her own affairs. Others use a comparative approach: an agent must exercise the same level of care that a reasonable person in a like situation would use. Application of these duties to officers, directors, and controlling shareholders is discussed in Chapter 20.

Sometimes, it is not clear whether an agency relationship has been established between an independent contractor and its employer, thereby imposing a fiduciary obligation on the contractor. This was the issue in the following case dealing with the lead managing underwriter of an initial public offering.

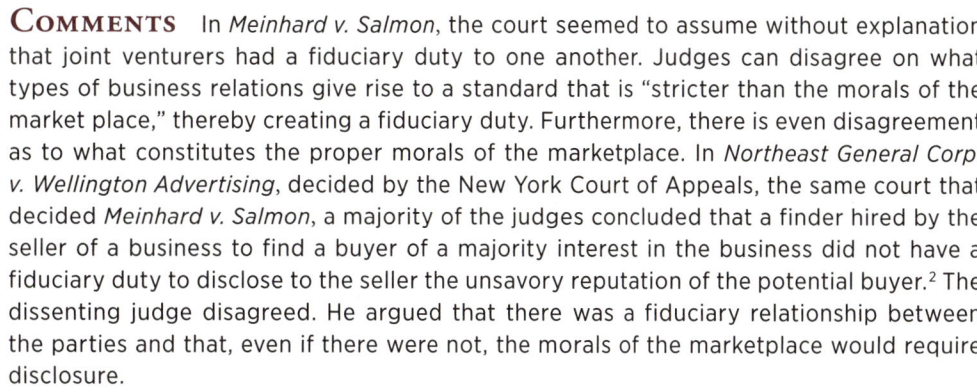

| A CASE IN POINT | *Summary* | Case 5.2 |

EBC I, Inc. v. Goldman, Sachs & Co.

Court of Appeals of New York
832 N.E.2d 26 (N.Y. 2005).

FACTS   In the 1990s, eToys, Inc., an Internet retailer specializing in the sale of products for children, retained Goldman Sachs as lead managing underwriter for the initial public offering (IPO) of its stock. On April 19, 1999, eToys and Goldman entered into an underwriting agreement pursuant to which eToys agreed to sell 8,320,000 shares of its stock to Goldman and the other underwriters for $18.65 per share. eToys also granted Goldman an option to buy an additional 1,248,000 shares at the same price to cover overallotments. The agreement obligated Goldman to offer the shares for public sale on the terms set forth in the prospectus, which fixed the initial offering price at $20 per share, capping Goldman's maximum return from the sale of eToys' stock at $12,916,800, which represented 6.75% of the offering proceeds.

On the first day of trading, eToys' stock opened at $79 per share, rose as high as $85 per share, then closed at $76.56. Six months later, however, the stock fell below $20 and never rose above the IPO price again. In March 2001, eToys filed a voluntary petition for reorganization under Chapter 11 of the U.S. Bankruptcy Code. The bankruptcy court appointed the Official Committee of Unsecured Creditors and authorized it to bring an action alleging breach of fiduciary duty, among other things, on behalf of eToys, now known as EBC I, Inc.

The complaint alleged that eToys had relied on Goldman for its expertise in pricing the IPO and that Goldman gave advice to eToys without disclosing that it had entered into arrangements whereby its customers "were obligated to kick back to Goldman a portion of any profits that they made" from the sale of eToys securities subsequent to the IPO. Because a lower IPO price would result in higher profits to these clients on resale and a higher payment to Goldman for the allotment, the plaintiff alleged that Goldman had an incentive to advise eToys to underprice its stock. As a result of this undisclosed conflict, Goldman was allegedly paid 20% to 40% of its clients' profits from trading the eToys securities.

CONTINUED

The New York trial court denied Goldman's motion to dismiss the cause of action for breach of fiduciary duty, finding that the complaint sufficiently raised an issue as to the existence of an informal fiduciary relationship. The New York Appellate Division affirmed, and Goldman appealed to the New York Court of Appeals (New York's highest court).

ISSUE PRESENTED Does advice provided to a client by underwriters on "market conditions" give rise to a fiduciary duty?

SUMMARY OF OPINION   Although the New York Court of Appeals conceded that the underwriting contract itself might not have created any fiduciary duty, it noted that the plaintiff had alleged eToys "was induced to and did repose confidence in Goldman's knowledge and expertise to advise it as to a fair IPO price and engage in honest dealings with eToys' best interest in mind." The court rejected Goldman's contention that requiring disclosure of Goldman's compensation arrangements with its customers would conflict with an underwriter's general duty to investors under the Securities Act of 1933. It also rejected Goldman's argument that there could be no fiduciary duty in this case because eToys and Goldman functioned as a typical seller and buyer. Unlike a typical buyer, who purchases a seller's goods at wholesale and resells at the highest possible profit, Goldman and eToys allegedly agreed that Goldman would receive a fixed profit from the sale of the securities. As a result, eToys had a further reason to trust that Goldman would act in eToys' interest. Finally, the court rejected Goldman's warning that finding a fiduciary duty in this case would have a significant impact on the underwriting industry and concluded:

> To the extent that underwriters function, among other things, as expert advisors to their clients on market conditions, a fiduciary duty may exist. We stress, however, that the fiduciary duty we recognize is limited to the underwriter's role as advisor. We do not suggest that underwriters are fiduciaries when they are engaged in activities other than rendering expert advice.

RESULT   The court affirmed the denial of Goldman's motion to dismiss the plaintiff's cause of action for breach of fiduciary duty. Due to their relationship of higher trust, Goldman's failure to disclose a material conflict of interest, namely, the alleged profit-sharing arrangement with prospective IPO investors, established a valid claim for breach of fiduciary duty.

AGENT'S ABILITY TO BIND THE PRINCIPAL TO CONTRACTS ENTERED INTO BY THE AGENT

An agent has the ability to bind the principal in legal relations with third parties if the agent has actual or apparent authority to do so. Even in the absence of such authority, the principal may be bound by the unauthorized acts of the agent if the principal subsequently ratifies those acts. A principal can be bound even if his or her identity is undisclosed to the third party.

Actual Authority

The principal may give the agent *actual authority* to enter into agreements on his or her behalf; that is, the principal may give consent for the agent to act for and bind the principal. This consent (or authority) may be express or implied.

One reason to keep minutes of meetings of the board of directors of a corporation is to answer agency questions that may arise from corporate transactions. Board minutes, when read in conjunction with corporate bylaws, can be used to determine whether an officer had actual authority to execute an agreement or to take other actions on behalf of the corporation.

Failure to document an employee's authority can lead to unintended consequences. For example, Billy Mauldin sued WorldCom, which had acquired his employer, seeking to enforce stock option agreements that provided for accelerated vesting if he suffered diminished responsibility or pay within two years of a change of control event. The option agreements gave the compensation committee broad discretion to determine all issues arising under the plan. The agreements also provided that the committee could designate company employees to assist in the administration of the plan. WorldCom's senior vice president Dennis Sickle, who was not a member of the compensation committee, had denied Maudlin's request for accelerated vesting. Because the committee had neither delegated its authority to Sickle before he denied Mauldin's request nor thereafter expressly ratified Sickle's action in duly recorded minutes, Sickle had no authority to act on behalf of the committee.[3]

---

3.   Mauldin v. WorldCom, Inc., 263 F.3d 1205 (10th Cir. 2001).

Express Authority

Express authority may be given by the principal's actual words, for example, a request that the agent hire an architect to design a new office. Express authority may also be given by an action that indicates the principal's consent, for example, by sending the agent a check for the architect's retainer. An agent has express authority if the agent has a justifiable belief that the principal has authorized the agent to do what he or she is doing.

Implied Authority

Once an agent is given express authority, he or she also has *implied authority* to do whatever is reasonable to complete the task at hand. To determine an agent's implied authority, courts look to the usual and customary authority of the agent. *Usual authority* is the authority that the agent has been allowed to exercise in the past. For example, if a principal has allowed its purchasing agent to enter into contracts with a dollar value of up to $50,000, the agent has implied authority to continue to enter into such transactions. *Customary authority* consists of the authority that agents of that type normally would have. For example, the vice president of purchasing for a trucking business, because of his or her position, has the implied authority to purchase trucks. There are limits to such implied authority, however. For example, the vice president of purchasing for a trucking division does not have the implied authority to buy an office building. Similarly, an officer of a corporation does not have the authority to bind the corporation to sell or grant rights to purchase shares of its stock; stock issuances must be approved by the corporation's board of directors.

Authority of Electronic Agents

Electronic agents are autonomous computer programs that can be dispatched by the user to execute certain tasks. For example, an electronic agent can search the Internet and retrieve relevant information or serve as a "personal shopping agent" (sometimes called a "shopping bot") that makes purchases on behalf of its user.[4]

A prominent feature of electronic commerce is the *click-wrap agreement* whereby users assent by clicking on an acceptance box.[5] As discussed in Chapter 8, click-wrap agreements are generally enforceable as long as the user affirmatively gives assent and the terms are prominently displayed.[6] The use of electronic agents raises an interesting legal question: What happens when an electronic agent comes across a click-wrap agreement?[7] Traditional agency law does not offer clear guidance as to whether an electronic device can bind an individual to a contract.

The Uniform Computer Information Transactions Act (UCITA), a proposed uniform commercial code for software licenses and other computer information transactions, provides that the user of an electronic agent will be bound by its operations. Section 107 states that a person who uses an electronic agent is bound by its operations "even if no individual was aware of or reviewed the agent's operations or the results of the operations."[8] However, UCITA has been enacted into law in only two states (Virginia and Maryland), and it appears unlikely that it will be enacted into law by any other states.

The Electronic Signatures in Global and National Commerce Act of 2000 (E-Sign) and the Uniform Electronic Transactions Act[9] provide that a contract in or affecting interstate or foreign commerce may not be denied legal effect, validity, or enforceability solely because it involved the action of an electronic agent, as long as the action is "legally attributable to the person to be bound." At a minimum, E-Sign requires that a consumer will not be bound unless the consumer "consents electronically, or confirms his or her consent electronically, in a manner that reasonably demonstrates that the consumer can access information in the electronic form that will be used to provide the information that is the subject of the consent."[10] Unfortunately, however, E-Sign contains no further discussion of when the actions of an electronic agent will be attributed to the person to be bound. E-Sign recognizes that the operations of electronic agents may result in agreements that are binding on the user of the electronic agent; however, it provides little guidance regarding the circumstances under which a court will find such

---

4. The Uniform Electronic Transactions Act defines "electronic agent" as "a computer program or an electronic or other automated means used independently to initiate an action or respond to electronic records or performances in whole or in part, without review or action by an individual." Unif. Elec. Transactions Act § 2(6), 7A U.L.A. 21 (1999).

5. The term "click-wrap agreement" is derived from the term "shrink-wrap agreement." Under a "shrink-wrap license," users are deemed to have assented to a licensing agreement with a software manufacturer by their act of tearing open the shrink-wrap covering the software package. The U.S. Court of Appeals for the Seventh Circuit held that shrink-wrap licenses are generally enforceable in *ProCD, Inc. v. Zeidenberg,* 86 F.3d 1447 (7th Cir. 1996).

6. *See, e.g.*, Feldman v. Google, Inc., 513 F. Supp. 2d 229 (E.D. Pa. 2007).

7. Electronic agents may someday have the natural language abilities to parse through contract provisions and accept only those terms their users have preprogrammed. But at least for the near term, these agents will likely be able only to accept or to reject online contracts in full.

8. *The Uniform Computer Information Transactions Act (UCITA): A Firestorm of Controversy,* Online Libr. & Microcomputers, May 1, 2000.

9. The Uniform Electronic Transactions Act (UETA) is a model law that has been adopted by forty-seven states, the District of Columbia, and the U.S. Virgin Islands. Section 14 of UETA provides that a contract may be formed between (1) electronic agents, even if no individual was aware of or reviewed the electronic agents' actions or the resulting terms and agreements, and (2) an electronic agent and an individual, acting on the individual's own behalf or for another person, including interactions where the individual performs actions that the individual is free to refuse to perform and which the individual knows or has reason to know will cause the electronic agent to complete the transaction or performance. Section 5(b) of UETA, however, limits the application of UETA to transactions where the parties have agreed to conduct that transaction by electronic means.

10. 15 U.S.C. § 7001.

agreements to be binding. Courts have concluded that the operations of electronic agents can bind their users to the terms of online agreements based on the contract doctrine that a user's taking of a benefit that is offered subject to stated conditions constitutes the user's assent if the benefit is taken with knowledge of the terms of the offer.

In the first U.S. case involving an automated system of communication, a federal district court held that the response of the seller's computer and issuance of a tracking number for a purchase order did not amount to an acceptance of the buyer's offer because the telephone computer ordering system performed automated, ministerial acts that could not constitute an acceptance.[11]

The U.S. Court of Appeals for the Second Circuit reached a different result in *Register.com, Inc. v. Verio, Inc.*[12] Verio had used an electronic agent known as a search robot to perform multiple successive queries on Register.com's website to obtain contact information for Internet domain registrants for solicitation purposes. The terms of use published on Register.com's website home page conditioned use of its database on the user's assent to such terms and expressly prohibited solicitation. This type of agreement is known as a *browse-wrap agreement.* Unlike a click-wrap agreement, which requires the user to expressly assent to its terms, a browse-wrap agreement states that the user is deemed to assent to its terms by its continued use of the website. The court rejected Verio's assertion that it was never contractually bound by Register.com's terms of use, reasoning that Verio had assented to such terms by repeatedly using Register.com's website. The court also rejected Verio's argument that it did not form a contract with Register.com when its search robot collected information from the database. Chapter 8 discusses other cases dealing with click-wrap and browse-wrap agreements not involving use of an electronic agent.

Apparent Authority

Apparent authority is created when a third party reasonably believes that an agent has authority to act for and bind the principal. This belief may be based on the principal's words or acts or on knowledge that the principal has allowed its agent to engage in certain activities on its behalf over an extended period of time.

In *CSX Transportation, Inc. v. Recovery Express, Inc.,*[13] Albert Arillotta, a partner of Interstate Demolition and Environmental Corporation (IDEC), contacted Len Whitehead of CSX, a seller of out-of-service railcars, by e-mail. Arillotta used albert@recoveryexpress.com as his e-mail address and represented that he was from "interstate demolition and recovery express." After several e-mail and telephone exchanges, CSX delivered railcars to a location specified by

Arillotta and sent invoices totaling $115,000 to IDEC at its Boston office. When Arillotta's check bounced, CSX sued IDEC and Recovery Express, a company that shared office space with IDEC, for breach of contract. Whitehead testified that, based on Arillotta's e-mail address and representations, he believed Arillotta was representing Recovery and IDEC and was authorized to act on their behalf. Recovery denied that Arillotta had ever worked for it, indicating that Arillotta had acquired his Recovery e-mail address as the result of another venture between Recovery and IDEC. The court characterized the case as an attempt by CSX "to shift the consequences of its own gullibility to someone else" through use of the doctrine of apparent authority. Observing that apparent authority is established not by the agent's words or conduct, but by those of the principal, the court concluded that the e-mail domain name, by itself, was not sufficient as a matter of law to cloak Arillotta with authority to act on behalf of Recovery.

Ratification

The principal can bind himself or herself to an agent's unauthorized acts through *ratification,* that is, affirmation, of the prior acts. When an act has been ratified, it is then treated as if the principal had originally authorized it.

Ratification, like authorization, can be either express or implied. *Express ratification* occurs when the principal, through words or behavior, manifests an intent to be bound by the agent's act. For example, a principal could ratify an agent's unauthorized purchase of a truck by

IN BRIEF

Agent's Authority to Bind the Principal

Actual Authority (express and implied)	P → A	Principal communicates authority directly to Agent either by expressly authorizing certain acts (express) or by expressly authorizing certain acts that naturally suggest the power to do related collateral acts (implied).
Apparent Authority/ Estoppel	P → TP	Principal, by words, actions, or the position it puts the Agent in, leads Third Party to reasonably believe that the Agent has authority.
Ratification	P → TP	Principal agrees, by words or by acccepting the benefits of the Agent's act, to be bound by the act even though it was not authorized at the time the Agent acted.

Christoph Weihs/Shutterstock

© Cengage Learning 2013

11. Corinthian Pharm. Sys., Inc. v. Lederle Labs., 724 F. Supp. 605 (S.D. Ind. 1989).

12. 356 F.3d 393 (2d Cir. 2004).

13. 415 F. Supp. 2d 6 (D. Mass. 2006).

saying "OK" or simply by paying the bill for the vehicle. *Implied ratification* occurs when the principal, by silence or failure to repudiate the agent's act, acquiesces in it.

Use of Undisclosed Principal

An agent may lawfully conceal the principal's identity or even his or her existence. This may be desirable when, for instance, the principal is trying to buy up adjacent properties in an area before news of a business venture is made public, or if the principal's wealth would cause the seller to demand a higher price. If the third party does not know that the agent is acting for the principal (*an undisclosed principal*), the principal will nonetheless be bound by any contract the agent enters into with actual authority. In some states, an agent who negotiates a contract with a third party can be sued for breach of the contract, unless the agent discloses both that he or she is acting on behalf of a principal and the identity of the principal. If the agent acts without authority, the principal will not be bound; however, the agent may be personally liable on such a contract.

---

ethicalconsideration

Is it ethical to use an agent to enter into a contract with a third party who has made it clear that he or she is unwilling to enter into a deal with the undisclosed principal? How might a manager protect against that possibility?

 LIABILITY FOR TORTS OF AGENTS

A principal may be liable for not only the contracts but also the torts of its agents. According to the doctrine of *respondeat superior*, an agent's employer will be liable for any injuries or damage to the property of another that the agent causes while acting within the scope of his or her employment. If the principal is required to pay damages to a third party because of an agent's negligence, the principal has the right to demand reimbursement from the agent.

Liability for Torts of Employees Acting Within the Scope of Employment

Many cases in this area turn on whether the employee was acting within the scope of employment. (Torts of independent contractors are discussed in a later section.) What constitutes scope of employment? Some of the relevant factors include (1) whether the employee's act was authorized by the employer, (2) the extent to which the employer's interests were advanced by the act, (3) whether the employer furnished the instrumentality (for example, the truck or machine) that caused the injury, and (4) whether the employer had reason to know the employee would perform the act. Even an action that violates the law may be within the scope of employment if the employee performed the act to serve the employer. For example, when a salesperson lies to a customer to make a sale, the tortious conduct is within the scope of employment because it benefits the employer by increasing sales, even though it may violate the employer's policy as well as the law.

It is often not clear whether an agent is acting within the scope of employment. Courts tend to use the term "detour" to refer to a slight deviation from the employer's business and "frolic" to refer to conduct that in no way serves the interests of the employer. Detours are deemed to be within the scope of employment, but frolics are not. The following case illustrates how difficult it can be to determine whether a deviation is a detour or a frolic.

A CASE IN POINT	*Summary*	Case 5.3

O'Shea v. Welch

United States Court of Appeals for the Tenth Circuit 350 F.3d 1101 (10th Cir. 2003).

FACTS   Anthony Welch, an Osco store manager, was driving from his store to the Osco District Office to deliver football tickets from a vendor for distribution among Osco managers. Welch frequently made trips for Osco using his own car. During his drive, Welch remembered that he needed some routine maintenance on his car and made a spur of the moment decision to turn left into a service station for an estimate. Welch allegedly failed to yield in making the turn and struck John O'Shea's car. O'Shea, who was injured, filed a suit against Welch and Osco, claiming that Welch was negligent and that Osco was liable for damages under a theory of *respondeat superior*. The trial court dismissed Osco from the case, reasoning that even if the trip had been within the scope of Welch's employment, the attempted stop at the service station was not. O'Shea appealed.

ISSUE PRESENTED   Is an employee acting within the scope of his employment when he turns into a service station for nonemergency maintenance on his car while driving to deliver a vendor's gift to his employer's office?

SUMMARY OF OPINION   The U.S. Court of Appeals for the Tenth Circuit observed that there were no Kansas cases directly on point but concluded that Kansas would apply the "slight

CONTINUED

deviation" rule, which has been adopted by approximately half of the states. Pursuant to this rule, a court determines "whether the employee was on a frolic or a detour; the latter is a deviation that is sufficiently related to the employment to fall within its scope, while the former is the pursuit of the employee's personal business as a substantial deviation from . . . the employment."

Courts have considered the following factors in determining whether the employee embarked on a detour or on a frolic: (1) the employee's intent; (2) the nature, time, and place of the deviation; (3) the time consumed in the deviation; (4) the work for which the employee was hired; (5) the incidental acts reasonably expected by the employer; and (6) the freedom allowed the employee in performing his or her job responsibilities. Applying these factors to this case, the court found:

> [Welch's] stop for routine maintenance on a car used for business purposes could be considered enough of a mixed purpose by a jury to keep him within the scope of his employment with Osco.
>
> . . . At the time of the accident, he had not entered the service station. He was technically still on the road en route to the District Office. Because the accident occurred on this road, not at the service station, a jury could decide that Mr. Welch had not yet abandoned his employment for a personal errand at the time of the accident. It was unclear how long the estimate would have taken. However, we do know that if he had deviated at the time of the accident, the length of the deviation was only a few minutes or less.

RESULT   The court remanded the issue of whether Welch was acting within the scope of his employment to the district court for determination by a jury at trial.

CRITICAL THINKING QUESTIONS

1. In the classic case of *Riley v. Standard Oil Co. of New York*,[14] a child was hit and severely injured by Million, a truck driver employed by Standard Oil of New York. The driver had been instructed to drive a company truck from the Standard Oil mill to a nearby freight yard. Before leaving the mill, however, he drove to his sister's house, which was about four blocks in the opposite direction from the freight yard. Million unloaded some scrap wood at her house, and then, while driving to the freight yard, he hit the child. Should Standard Oil of New York be liable for Million's accident? Would your answer be different if the accident had occurred on the way to Million's sister's house? What other factors might affect your answer?

2. What public policy considerations are involved in cases like this? Is it relevant that the employer is often in a better position to pay victims or insure against liability?

14. 132 N.E. 97 (N.Y. 1921).

© Cengage Learning 2013

Liability for Torts of Employees Acting Outside the Scope of Employment

Even if an employee was acting outside the scope of employment, the employer may be liable for the employee's action if (1) the employer intended the employee's conduct or its consequences, (2) the employee's high rank in the company makes him or her the employer's alter ego, (3) the employee's action can be attributed to the employer's own negligence or recklessness, (4) the employee uses apparent authority to act or to speak on behalf of the employer and there was reliance upon apparent authority, or (5) the employee was aided in accomplishing the tort by the existence of the agency relationship (the *aided-in-the-agency-relation theory*). The California Supreme Court used the aided-in-the-agency-relation theory to hold a city liable for a uniformed police officer who used his badge of authority to persuade a woman to get into his car and then raped her.[15] In contrast, the U.S. Court of Appeals for the First Circuit, applying Maine law, found that a trucking company was not liable for the actions of a driver who attacked and stabbed a motorist in an incident of "road rage" that occurred while the driver was driving a tractor-trailer for the company, because his attack was not actuated by a purpose to serve the trucking company.[16] As discussed in Chapter 13, the aided-in-the-agency-relation theory can

15. Mary M. v. City of Los Angeles, 814 P.2d 1341 (Cal. 1991).
16. Nichols v. Land Transp. Corp., 223 F.3d 21 (1st Cir. 2000).

also be used in certain cases to impose liability on employers for sexual or racial harassment by supervisors.

Liability for Torts of Independent Contractors

The *respondeat superior* doctrine typically applies only to the actions of employees. Principals may be held liable for the torts of independent contractors only in extraordinary circumstances, usually involving highly dangerous acts or nondelegable duties. For instance, if a principal hires an independent contractor to blast boulders off its land, the principal will be liable for any injuries or damages resulting from the blast. In other words, a principal cannot avoid liability for damages resulting from ultrahazardous activities simply by contracting out the work. Similarly, the South Carolina Supreme Court ruled that a hospital could not escape liability for the medical care provided by hiring physicians as independent contractors.[17]

LIABILITY OF THE PRINCIPAL FOR VIOLATIONS OF LAW BY THE AGENT

Under the theory of *vicarious liability*, a company can be held liable for violations of civil law by its employee even if a manager told the employee not to violate the law. As discussed further in Chapter 14, employers and sometimes supervisors may even face criminal prosecution for crimes committed by employees.

---

17. Simmons v. Tuomey Reg'l Med. Ctr., 533 S.E.2d 312 (S.C. 2000).

Mike Price/Shutterstock

THE RESPONSIBLE MANAGER

WORKING WITH AGENTS

The relationship between a manager and his or her employer is one of trust. As an agent, a manager owes the employer fiduciary duties, which are most often summarized as the duty of care, the duty of obedience, and the duty of loyalty. The duty of care requires a manager to avoid grossly negligent, reckless, or intentional behavior that would harm the company. Rarely will an act of simple negligence be treated as a breach of fiduciary duty. The duty of obedience requires the manager to follow his or her employer's reasonable orders. The duty of loyalty imposes more complex obligations. It requires a manager to avoid self-dealing or for-profit activity that competes with the employer's business. In other words, a manager has a duty to act solely for the benefit of his or her employer in all matters related to its business. This duty includes an obligation to notify the employer of all relevant facts—all that the agent knows, the principal should know.

A manager should review the scope of authority granted to the company's workers and consider the company's potential liability for the actions of those workers. Perhaps the most determinable aspect of this relationship is whether the worker is deemed an employee or an independent contractor. A manager may prefer to label workers as independent contractors rather than employees for several reasons—for instance, to lower tax and benefits costs or to reduce exposure to liability. As noted earlier, however, the legal status of workers will be determined by the manner in which they are used, not by the label written into employment agreements.

Once a manager has hired an agent, he or she should carefully define the scope of the agent's authority. If the manager does not do this, the company may find itself bound by unanticipated contracts. For example, a manager might inadvertently give a purchasing agent the apparent authority to bind the business to a large purchase of supplies, above the actual needs of the business. A manager can help avoid scope-of-authority problems by making explicit, unambiguous statements to third parties that specify the limits on an employee's ability to enter into a binding contract. When using an employee or other agent to deal with third parties, a manager should also monitor transactions and business records, such as credit card bills, to avoid conduct that might legally ratify an otherwise unauthorized agreement entered into by the agent.

The manager should ensure that the work environment and the machines and other equipment used in the business are safe. He or she should also stress to the employees the importance not only of complying with the law, but also of being concerned about safety and ethical behavior. These concerns pertain mostly to the duties owed by employers to their employees. But employers may owe similar duties even to workers properly termed independent contractors, depending on where the independent contractor works and how much control the employer exerts over that work.

Finally, an employer should seek to minimize its potential liability for the wrongdoing of its workers. Because the employer will be liable for employee torts committed within the scope of employment, a manager should attempt to decrease the risk of such vicarious liability by training employees to be careful and by defining the employees' scope of employment as narrowly as possible. It is also important not to set overly ambitious production targets or delivery deadlines that cause workers to rush unduly to complete the job. For example, after Domino's Pizza drivers caused several

CONTINUED

traffic accidents, the firm dropped its guarantee of pizza delivery within thirty minutes.[18]

In light of an employer's potential liability under the aided-in-the-agency-relation theory for acts outside the scope of employment, managers should exercise particular care when giving an employee authority or an instrumentality (such as a company truck) that could be misused. Managers should ensure both that the employee is trustworthy and that any persons under the employee's control have the ability to complain to someone other than the supervisor. Because a company cannot avoid liability for injuries caused while it is engaged in an ultrahazardous activity, even if it

is working through an independent contractor, managers should ensure that the company has adequate liability insurance. Finally, as discussed in Chapter 14, employers may be responsible for the criminal acts of employees. For example, if an employee violates an industry-related regulation during the normal course of employment, the employer could be held vicariously liable. In some situations, the supervising manager may be liable as well.

Although having a policy against illegal practices and conducting in-house training may not insulate the employer and its owner from civil liability for criminal acts of its lower-level employees, these steps reduce the chance an employee will break the law in the first place. They also reduce the likelihood that punitive damages will be assessed against the employer and its owner.

---

18. GEORGE J. SIEDEL, USING THE LAW FOR COMPETITIVE ADVANTAGE 54–55 (2002).

A MANAGER'S DILEMMA

Putting It into Practice

To Disclose or Not Disclose?

Danimark Investment Bank has decided to structure and market to its clients a new securities product comprising collateralized debt obligations (CDOs) directly tied to a reference portfolio of credit-card-backed securities (CCBS). CDOs are zero-sum investments, so one party's gain is always the other party's loss.

Anthony Karol is the managing partner at Danimark responsible for the launch of the new securities. He knows that Danimark's client Nelipern & Co., a large hedge fund, will play a significant role in selecting the securities in the reference portfolio. Karol also knows that the investors' interests in the portfolio will be adverse to Nelipern's interests. While Nelipern has shorted the equity of the CDOs (so Nelipern will make money if their value falls), the counterparties will be long the portfolio, so they will lose money if it performs badly. Does Danimark have a legal duty or an ethical obligation to

disclose Nelipern's role in the selection process to potential investors? Is it enough if Danimark's marketing materials to potential investors disclose that Nelipern helped select the portfolio, or should Danimark also disclose Nelipern's adverse interests in the performance of the portfolio? Is this situation any different from a transaction in which an investment bank sells stock belonging to one client to another client?

Now suppose that the largest long-term investor in the portfolio, I-Analytics International, has the privilege and responsibility of independently approving the selection of the CCBS in the portfolio. If I-Analytics uses its own methods and approves the CCBS in the portfolio, how, if at all, should that affect Karol's analysis? Should it matter whether the offering circular states that I-Analytics selected the portfolio? Should it matter that Danimark plans to buy the securities for its own firm account?

INSIDE STORY

HP Discovers Corporate Spying Is an Ultrahazardous Activity

Corporate demand for private investigative services has grown steadily since the 1980s. For example, in 2000 Oracle acknowledged that it had hired detectives who attempted to obtain the trash of a think tank that had defended the aggressive

business practices of Oracle's archrival, Microsoft Corporation. Companies that hire private investigators (PIs) generally share three characteristics: (1) they are desperate to obtain sensitive information, (2) they have been unable to obtain the information

CONTINUED

through ordinary means, and (3) they often feel that the targets of their investigation have been fighting dirty.[19] Companies typically subcontract their investigative work to independent PI firms. One of the benefits of subcontracting the work is that it should shield the company from liability because employers are not liable for torts committed by an independent contractor, unless the contractor engages in an ultrahazardous activity. The experience of Hewlett-Packard (HP) has made it clear, however, that both the company and its management may be held liable, legally and in the court of public opinion, for the acts of independent PIs.

In 2005, HP was a $90 billion publicly held company that prided itself on "commitment to uncompromising integrity."[20] For several years, however, HP had suffered from leaks of confidential information. The leaks became a subject of increased concern for Patricia Dunn, chair of the board of directors, when an unidentified person leaked the board's selection of Mark Hurd as CEO to replace Carly Fiorina. The leak caused Hurd to reconsider whether he would take the job, and last-minute negotiations were required to allay his concerns. Frustrated by these and other leaks that suggested that a top-level insider was the source, Dunn hired a Boston-based PI, Ron DeLia, to find the source of the leaks. Dunn named the investigation Project Kona because she was vacationing in Hawaii at the time.

Two months later, Dunn mailed a seven-page report from DeLia to HP's general counsel Ann Baskins. The report discussed phone record searches and an investigative technique known as "pretexting" whereby a person pretends to be someone else, typically over the phone, in order to obtain information. DeLia later recalled that Baskins was curious about pretexting and concerned about its legality. When Baskins asked DeLia whether pretexting was lawful, DeLia replied that he was aware of no laws that made it illegal or of any criminal prosecutions for pretexting. E-mails showed that pretexting continued through August 2005 when Anthony Gentilucci, the manager of HP Global Security investigations, reported that the investigators still had not discovered the source of the leaks.

When confidential information about a potential HP acquisition was leaked to CNET Networks in January 2006, HP initiated a new investigation, dubbed Kona II. Kevin Hunsaker, the senior HP counsel assigned to the investigations, reported regularly to both Baskins and Dunn. On several occasions, Baskins asked Hunsaker to explore the legality of pretexting further. In response, Hunsaker had several e-mail and phone conversations with DeLia, who continued to assure him that pretexting was legal. Hunsaker also engaged in approximately one hour of online legal research himself. At separate times, DeLia and Gentilucci consulted DeLia's outside attorney, John Kiernan (with whom DeLia shared office space), who confirmed that pretexting was not a crime.

On March 10, 2006, Hunsaker sent a draft report to Dunn, Baskins, and Hurd. It identified board member and renowned physicist George Keyworth II as the source of the leaks. On March 15, Baskins and Dunn told Hurd that the investigators had concluded that Keyworth was the leaker. After consulting with Larry Sonsini, HP's outside attorney, they told the directors at the May 18 board meeting that Keyworth was the leaker. Despite strong protests about how the investigation was conducted from HP director and prominent venture capitalist Tom Perkins, the board voted six to three to ask Keyworth to resign. Keyworth refused to resign, but Perkins quit in protest. On May 22, HP filed a Form 8-K with the Securities and Exchange Commission (SEC) that announced Perkins's resignation but gave no reason for his departure.

During the summer, Perkins sent a series of e-mails and letters to the HP board in which he challenged the legality of the investigation and informed the board that he considered the Form 8-K filed on May 22 to be defective.[21] Unsatisfied with HP's responses, Perkins told the California Attorney General's Office, the SEC, and others about the investigation, including the pretexting. He also notified the SEC that he objected to how HP had portrayed his resignation in its Form 8-K filing. Facing a storm of media criticism about its actions, HP asked its outside counsel to conduct an internal investigation of the propriety of the leak investigation. The law firm's report concluded that while the use of pretexting may not have been illegal at the time, subcontractors may have used Social Security numbers while pretexting, "which more likely than not violates federal law."[22]

After the scandal continued to build steam during September, HP hired a second outside law firm to conduct another internal investigation. The company also filed a new document with the SEC that outlined the investigation and admitted that HP had spied on at least two HP employees, seven members of the HP board, and nine reporters and their relatives.

On September 8, federal prosecutors from the U.S. Attorney's Office in San Francisco contacted the company to talk about the pretexting. Staff from the House Energy and Commerce Committee called the same day to say they were interested in talking to management about the investigation. On September 12, HP announced that Dunn would step down as chair in January 2007 but would remain on the board and that Keyworth would resign from the board. Keyworth and Perkins agreed not to sue HP over what happened, and the company agreed not to sue them.

CONTINUED

---

19. Michael Orey, *Corporate Snoops*, BusinessWeek.com, Oct. 9, 2006, http://www.businessweek.com/magazine/content/06_41/b4004008.htm.

20. HP Global Citizenship Report: Ethics and Compliance, *available at* http://www.hp.com/hpinfo/globalcitizenship/07gcreport/ethics.html.

21. If a director sends a letter to the board detailing his or her reasons for resigning, the company must file the letter within two business days of filing the Form 8-K announcing the resignation. HP did not file Perkins's letter or otherwise amend its 8-K. Instead, Baskins wrote back that it would be "inappropriate" to change the 8-K because it was accurate when it was filed.

22. Susan Beck, *Where Will the Troubles End for Sonsini and HP?*, Am. Law., Dec. 6, 2006, *available at* http://www.law.com/jsp/ihc/PubArticleIHC.jsp?id=1165320502955.

Unfortunately for HP and its executives, however, the story did not end there. As more damaging details about the investigation continued to dribble out, Dunn was forced to resign from the board. HP executives and others associated with the investigation were required to appear before congressional committees investigating the incident. During one congressional hearing, Baskins announced her resignation and refused to answer questions, citing her Fifth Amendment rights against self-incrimination.

In October 2006, California Attorney General Bill Lockyer brought felony criminal charges against three of the employees of the PIs (DeLia, Matthew DePante, and Bryan Wagner),[23] as well as HP board member Dunn and HP employee Hunsaker. All five defendants were charged with fraudulent wire communications, wrongful use of computer data, identity theft, and conspiracy. The first three charges carried a maximum penalty of three years in prison and a fine of $10,000. The conspiracy charge carried a maximum of one year in prison and a $25,000 fine. Attorney General Lockyer had no trouble holding the HP executives responsible for illegal activities conducted by HP's subcontractors. At the time the criminal charges were announced, he stated, "The person who orchestrated these illegal practices should be held accountable, not just those who carried them out."

On May 14, 2007, Hunsaker, DeLia, and DePante pleaded no contest to misdemeanor counts in the boardroom spying case, and the court offered to dismiss the case against them if they each completed ninety-six hours of community service and paid restitution to the victims. The court dismissed the criminal case against Dunn. It also dismissed the criminal case against Wagner because he had previously pleaded guilty to two federal felony charges. Wagner faced up to five years in prison and a fine of up to $250,000.

In exchange for the California Attorney General's agreement not to file a civil action, HP agreed to pay $14.5 million to settle civil charges related to the company's investigation. Without admitting any liability, HP agreed that for five years it would (1) employ a chief ethics and compliance officer, (2) expand the role of its chief privacy officer to review HP's investigation practices, (3) expand its employee and vendor codes

to ensure they address ethical standards regarding investigations, and (4) retain an expert in the field of investigations to assist the company's chief ethics officer with regard to investigations. Of the total settlement, $13.5 million funded a new state law enforcement fund to fight violations of privacy and intellectual property rights, $650,000 represented statutory damages, and $350,000 was paid to reimburse the Attorney General's Office for the costs of its investigation.

In May 2007, HP entered into a settlement agreement with the SEC concerning its federal investigation of HP's handling of Tom Perkins's resignation from the board of directors. Under the agreement, HP agreed to a cease and desist order issued by the SEC, which stated that HP should not have limited its disclosure to the fact that Perkins had resigned. Instead, HP should also have reported that Perkins had resigned because of a disagreement with its practices, and the company should have "provided a brief description of the circumstances around the disagreement."

Even then, the story was not over. In May 2007, three journalists from CNET Networks, whose private records had been scrutinized by investigators hired by HP, announced that they intended to sue HP for invasion of privacy. Counsel for the journalists indicated that the suit would seek punitive damages against HP for its actions in connection with the spy investigation. Several other reporters who were investigated also commenced settlement negotiations with HP. HP settled cases with the New York Times Company and three *BusinessWeek* journalists in 2008 for undisclosed amounts.[24]

The HP incident also hastened passage of a federal law, the Telephone Records and Privacy Protection Act of 2006, which made it illegal for a person to use fraud to obtain individual customer billing records and other customer information from telephone companies. The Act also prohibited the selling of such illegally obtained records. Violators of the Act face fines and up to ten years in prison. Although some argued that passage of the Act meant that pretexting was not already a violation of federal law, that was cold comfort to HP, Dunn, and the others implicated in the spying scandal.

---

23. DePante was the manager of the information broker in Melbourne, Florida, that DeLia hired to conduct the pretexting activities, and Wagner was the employee who actually engaged in the pretexting.

24. Nancy Gohring, *HP Settles Pretexting Cases*, PCWORLD, Feb. 14, 2008, *available at* http://www.pcworld.com/article/142524/hp_settles_pretexting_cases.html.

KEY WORDS AND PHRASES

actual authority 134	aided-in-the-agency-relation theory 138	electronic agents 135
agency 129	apparent authority 129	equal dignities rule 129
agency by estoppel 129	duty of care 133	express authority 135
agency by ratification 129	duty of loyalty 131	fiduciary duty 132
agent 129	duty of obedience 131	implied authority 135

QUESTIONS AND CASE PROBLEMS

1. Singer was employed by General Automotive Manufacturing Company (GAMC) as its general manager from 1953 until 1959. He had worked in the machine-shop field for more than thirty years and enjoyed a fine reputation in machine-shop circles.

   GAMC was a small company with only five employees and a low credit rating. Singer attracted a large volume of business to GAMC and was invaluable in bolstering the company's credit rating. At times, when collections were slow, Singer paid the customer's bill to GAMC and waited for his own reimbursement until the customer remitted. Also, when work was slack, Singer would finance the manufacture of unordered parts and wait for recoupment until the stockpiled parts were sold. Some parts were never sold, and Singer personally absorbed the loss on them.

   While working for GAMC, Singer set up his own sideline operation, in which he acted as a machinist–consultant. As orders came in to GAMC through him, Singer would decide that some of them required equipment GAMC lacked or that GAMC could not do the job at a competitive price. For such orders, Singer would give the customer a price, then deal with another machine shop to do the work at a lower price, and pocket the difference. Singer conducted his operation without notifying GAMC of the orders that it (through Singer) did not accept.

   Contending that Singer's sideline business was in direct competition with its business, GAMC sued Singer for breach of fiduciary duty. What result? What were Singer's duties to GAMC as its agent? Was Singer's operation of a sideline business ethical? Would it have been ethical if he had disclosed it to his GAMC superiors? [*General Automotive Manufacturing Co. v. Singer,* 120 N.W.2d 659 (Wis. 1963).]

2. NTG Telecommunications, which was interested in purchasing a computer network for its office, received a promotional letter from IBM regarding IBM's PC Server 310, Small Business Solution, a computer network server designed for and marketed to small businesses. The letter stated: "When you're ready to get down to business, give us a call. . . . We'll give you the name of the IBM business partner nearest you, as well as answer any questions you might have." The Small Business Solution was available only through an IBM business partner, which is an entity authorized to resell IBM products.

   Jud Berkowitz, president of NTG, contacted Frank Cubbage of Sun Data Services, an IBM business partner, regarding the Small Business Solution. Berkowitz decided to purchase the Small Business Solution after being informed by Cubbage that it was compatible with Windows 95, the operating system installed on each of the networked computers. After he installed the server, NTG started having serious computer problems, which were not resolved until NTG replaced PerfectOffice (which was sold as part of the Small Business Solution) with Lotus Smart

   Suite. Berkowitz sued IBM for fraud based in part on Cubbage's representation that the Small Business Solution was compatible with Windows 95. IBM argued that Cubbage's statement could not be attributed to it because a formal licensing or dealership agreement does not create an agency relationship. How should the court rule? [*NTG Telecommunications, Inc. v. IBM, Inc.,* 2000 U.S. Dist. LEXIS 6279 (E.D. Pa. May 8, 2000).]

3. Rodney and Ydonna Smith divorced in 1998 after having one child. In 1999, Ydonna went to work for Sears in its retail-debt collections department, where she collected debts from existing Sears account holders who were behind on their payments. In that capacity, and for that purpose, Ydonna had access to a computer and password that allowed her to use a Sears information system to obtain certain information on customers from their credit reports. At the same time, Ydonna was also trying to obtain child support payments from Rodney, but neither she nor the State of Mississippi could locate him. Ydonna used the Sears credit information system fourteen times to access Rodney's credit report in an effort to find his current address, in violation of the Fair Credit Reporting Act (FCRA). When Rodney discovered these inquiries, he complained to Sears, which fired Ydonna for violating its policy by accessing Rodney's credit report. Rodney subsequently sued Sears to recover damages for alleged violation of the FCRA, based on Ydonna's inquiries. Is Sears vicariously liable for Ydonna's violations of the FCRA? [*Smith v. Sears, Roebuck & Co.,* 276 F. Supp. 2d 603 (S.D. Miss. 2003).]

4. Shortly after hiring Corte Adams, Goodyear Tires transferred him from his home near Houston to Bryan, Texas, to work on commercial trucks. After the transfer, Adams continued to live in Houston and commuted two hours each way to work. Although Adams owned his own car, Goodyear allowed him to use a company-owned pickup truck to commute to and from work. Once or twice a week, Adams either picked up tires at the Houston shop on his way to work and delivered them to Bryan, or he dropped off tires from Bryan at the Houston shop on the way home. With his boss's knowledge, Adams also used the Goodyear truck during working hours to run some personal errands.

   After Adams left work in the company truck on a Friday, he delivered tires to the Houston shop at 7 P.M.; stopped for Chinese takeout; and then drove to his father's house, which was about ten miles from his home, where he ate dinner, drank a few beers, and fell asleep. At 1 A.M., he woke up and drove the truck to a store to buy cigarettes for his father. On the way back to his father's house, Adams fell asleep at the wheel and hit another car, severely injuring himself and the other driver. After the driver sued Adams and Goodyear, Goodyear's insurance company Travelers Indemnity Company refused to cover Adams or to defend or indemnify him in the lawsuit. Adams then sued Travelers and Goodyear. Travelers argued that Adams was not an "insured" under its policy with Goodyear because he did not have permission to use the truck when the accident occurred. Did Adams have implied permission to use the truck? Is Goodyear (and therefore Travelers) liable for damages arising out of the accident? If so, on what basis? [*Adams v. Travelers Indemnity of Connecticut,* 465 F.3d 156 (5th Cir. 2006).]

5. Frederick Richmond agreed to sell UForma Shelby Business Forms, Inc., a business forms printing business, to Samuel Peters pursuant to a stock-purchase agreement at a price of $3.6 million to be paid in annual installments. The amount of each installment was one-half the amount by which the profits of UForma and Miami Systems, Inc., another company owned by Peters, exceeded the 1988 and 1989 average annual profits of Miami Systems alone. The agreement stated that this formula might result in no payment being made in some years. At the time of the sale, UForma was operating at a loss. The sales agreement also stated that Peters should operate UForma according to "sound business practices." Peters paid Richmond $496,057 for 1990 and $147,368 for 1991. Because the earnings of UForma and Miami Systems were insufficient to trigger a payment under the formula in the agreement, Peters paid Richmond nothing for the years 1992 through 1995. Richmond sued Peters for breach of contract and breach of fiduciary duty, alleging that he was entitled to additional payments and that Peters had not operated UForma in accordance with sound business practices. How should the court rule? [*Richmond v. Peters,* 1998 U.S. App. LEXIS 30114 (6th Cir. 1998), *reh'g denied,* 173 F.3d 429 (6th Cir. 1999).]

6. H&R Block's tax filing service allows customers to obtain faster tax refunds in two ways: (1) the customer can pay $25 for H&R Block to file the return with the Internal Revenue Service electronically, in which case the customer will receive the refund in two weeks; or (2) if the customer wants the funds even faster, H&R Block can arrange a loan from a third-party bank in the amount of the customer's refund through its Rapid Anticipation Loan (RAL) program. H&R Block benefited financially from each RAL in at least one way, and potentially in as many as three ways. First, H&R Block received a "license fee" of $3 to $9 for every RAL referred to a lending bank. Second, its affiliate, H&R Block Financial, purchased about one-half of the RALs from lender banks. Third, under an arrangement with Sears, Roebuck & Co., H&R Block encouraged RAL customers to cash their checks at Sears and received a fee equal to 15% of the check-cashing fee that Sears charged for cashing the loan checks. H&R Block did not disclose its financial participation in the RAL program to its customers.

Joyce Green filed a class-action suit on behalf of all Maryland customers who obtained RAL bank loans, claiming, among other things, that H&R Block had breached its fiduciary duty by failing to disclose the benefits it received from the lending institutions to which it referred its customers. What arguments will Green make? What arguments will H&R Block make in its defense? Could H&R Block have added language to its customer contracts to ensure that it would not owe any fiduciary obligations to its customers? Even if H&R Block is found not to have a fiduciary obligation to its customers, was it ethical for H&R Block to receive fees for the RAL program and not disclose them to its customers? [*Green v. H&R Block, Inc.,* 735 A.2d 1039 (Md. Ct. App. 1999).]

7. The plaintiffs were models in a "fitness fashion show," featured as part of the Working Women's Survival Show exhibition at a convention center in St. Louis, Missouri. B.P.S., doing business as Wells Fargo Guard Service, had contracted with the city to provide guards at the center. Security arrangements at the convention center included a number of television surveillance cameras scattered around the center, which were monitored on small screens in a central control room. The direction in which each camera was pointing could be adjusted manually or automatically in the control room. The control room also had a large screen that the guards could use to view the images from the cameras or to monitor what was being taped on the VCR. The purpose of having the VCR was to enable the guards to videotape suspicious activities. The Wells Fargo guards were told to practice taping on the VCR.

Promoters for the Working Women's Survival Show had a makeshift curtained dressing area set up near the stage for the models in the fashion show. Unbeknownst to the models, the dressing area was in a location that could be monitored by one of the surveillance cameras. That fortuity was discovered by two Wells Fargo guards, Rook and Smith. Rook had the rank of captain at Wells Fargo, denoting supervisory capacity, though there was testimony that when he worked in the control room, he had no supervisory authority. Another supervisor with disputed supervisory authority, Ramey, walked by the control room and saw the guards using the large screen to view women in a state of undress. Ramey said that he thought the guards were watching pornographic tapes that they had brought to work. (There was testimony that the guards watched their own pornographic tapes in the control room.) Either Smith or Rook (each accused the other) focused the camera on the plaintiffs and taped them as they were changing clothes for the fashion show. Is Wells Fargo Guard Service liable for the unauthorized actions of its agents, even if those actions were done for reasons of personal pleasure rather than for work? [*Doe v. B.P.S. Guard Service, Inc., d/b/a Wells Fargo Guard Service,* 945 F.2d 1422 (8th Cir. 1991).]

8. The Southern Pacific Transportation Company was transporting eighteen boxcars loaded with bombs belonging to the U.S. government from Hawthorne, Nevada, to Port Chicago, California, pursuant to a contract with the Navy. While in Southern Pacific's yard in Roseville, California, the boxcars exploded, causing personal injuries and property damage and resulting in a lawsuit.

Assume that Southern Pacific used due care in transporting the bombs. Is it nonetheless liable for the damage caused by the explosion? Should the government be liable? How could Southern Pacific have protected itself from this lawsuit? Who would be liable if, instead of bombs exploding, deadly chemicals were spilled while being transported? [*Chavez v. Southern Pacific Transportation Co.,* 413 F. Supp. 1203 (E.D. Cal. 1976); *Indiana Harbor Belt Railroad v. American Cyanamid Co.,* 916 F.2d 1174 (7th Cir. 1990).]

CHAPTER 6

ADMINISTRATIVE LAW

INTRODUCTION

IMPORTANCE OF ADMINISTRATIVE AGENCIES

Administrative law concerns the powers and procedures of administrative agencies, such as the Internal Revenue Service (IRS), which collects taxes, and the Securities and Exchange Commission (SEC), which regulates the securities markets. The activities of administrative agencies affect nearly everyone, frequently on a daily basis. Administrative agencies set limits on pollution and emissions and regulate disposal of hazardous waste. They regulate the Internet, radio and television, food and drugs, and health and safety. By working with administrative agencies, managers can help shape the regulatory environment in which they do business. For example, Vonage Holdings and other Internet companies offering phone service helped their fledgling industry get off the ground when they persuaded the Federal Communications Commission not to impose the same burdensome universal access requirements applicable to landlines.[1]

Federal and state administrative agencies solve practical problems that cannot be handled effectively by the legislatures or the courts. Agencies make rules to effectuate legislative enactments; they resolve conflicts by formal adjudication, a courtlike proceeding; they carry out informal discretionary actions; and they conduct investigations regarding compliance with specific laws and regulations. Although usually part of the executive branch, administrative agencies can rightly be called a fourth branch of government.

Failure to comply with applicable regulations can result in the revocation of licenses and permits and in the imposition of stiff fines. In 2007, BP Products North America agreed to pay a total of $287 million in fines to the U.S. Environmental Protection

Agency, the U.S. Commodity Futures Trading Commission, and the U.S. Department of Justice for violating regulations under the Clean Air Act, the Clean Water Act, and the Commodity Exchange Act.[2] The company was also forced to pay more than $80 million in restitution to affected parties and to make more than $400 million worth of safety improvements.

CHAPTER OVERVIEW

This chapter discusses the various ways in which administrative agencies operate and addresses the key principles of administrative law. Constitutional issues include separation of powers, delegation of authority, and the protections afforded by the Bill of Rights. Issues arising from the judicial review of agency actions include the doctrines of ripeness and exhaustion of administrative remedies. Doctrines that limit the decision-making power of agencies include the principles that agencies are bound by their own rules and that they must explain the basis for their decisions. We also explain how to find the rules of a particular agency and how to obtain documents from the government.

HOW ADMINISTRATIVE AGENCIES ACT

An administrative agency functions in four primary ways: making rules, conducting formal adjudications, taking informal discretionary actions, and conducting investigations.

---

1. Yuki Noguchi, *FCC Asserts Role as Internet Phone Regulators*, WASH. POST, Nov. 10, 2004, at E1. FCC Chair Michael K. Powell declared, "This landmark order recognizes that a revolution has occurred. Internet voice services have cracked the 19-century mold to the great benefit of consumers." *Id. See also* Vonage Holdings Corp. v. Minn. PUC, 394 F.3d 568 (8th Cir. 2004) (upholding an injunction prohibiting Minnesota from imposing common carrier telecommunications regulation upon Vonage).

2. Press Release, U.S. Commodity Futures Trading Comm'n, BP Agrees to Pay a Total of $303 Million in Sanctions to Settle Charges of Manipulation and Attempted Manipulation in the Propane Market (Oct. 25, 2007), *available at* http://www.cftc.gov (last visited Aug. 18, 2011); Press Release, U.S. Envtl. Prot. Agency, BP to Pay Largest Criminal Fine Ever for Air Violations (Oct. 25, 2007), *available at* http://www.epa.gov.

Making Rules

Congress and the state legislatures frequently lack the time, human resources, and expertise to enact detailed regulations. Sometimes issues are so politically sensitive that elected officials lack the will to make the tough decisions. In such cases, the legislature will often pass a law setting forth general principles and guidelines and will delegate authority to an administrative agency to carry out this legislative intent. The agency will then follow a three-step procedure to promulgate appropriate rules or regulations.

Notice to the Public

First, the administrative agency gives notice to the public of its intent to propose a rule. Generally, the agency publishes the proposed rule and gives the public an opportunity to submit written comments. Comment letters are helpful to an agency and can influence the final rule. A comment letter usually (1) identifies the person that is concerned, (2) explains why that person is concerned, (3) suggests a specific change in the language of the proposed rule, and (4) provides factual information to support its position.

The Mercatus Center, an independent think tank associated with George Mason University that receives funding from many sources, has been particularly successful in promoting less rigorous business regulation. Mercatus provides formal comment letters that analyze whether the costs of a proposed rule exceed the benefits, whether the rule disadvantages consumers or small businesses, and whether there are less burdensome alternatives.[3]

Agencies may, but are not always required to, hold a formal public hearing. They always allow people to comment on proposed rules by meeting informally with or telephoning the agency personnel. If a company is particularly concerned about a proposed rule, it should both call and meet with the proposing agency about its concerns.

Evaluation

Second, the administrative agency evaluates the comments, responds to them, and decides on the scope and extent of the final rule. If the comments prompt the agency to make substantial changes in the proposed rule, the agency may publish a revised proposed rule for public comment.

Adoption

Third, the agency will formally adopt the rule by publishing it in the *Federal Register* along with an explanation of the changes. The *Federal Register* is published daily by the U.S. Government Printing Office. Rules that are not properly published there are void. The final rule will also be *codified,* that is, added to the *Code of Federal Regulations*

(CFR). The CFR contains fifty titles and includes the regulations of approximately 400 federal agencies and bureaus.

The Administrative Procedure Act (APA) requires notice to the public and an opportunity to comment before a federal agency can promulgate a rule. Rules of agency procedure and general statements of policy are exempted from this requirement. Courts have the power to review final agency actions and binding legal rules but not mere guidelines.

The federal government has attempted to make the regulatory process less cumbersome and time-consuming, more informal, and less vulnerable to judicial review by applying the Japanese style of negotiating with the major affected groups in an effort to obtain a consensus on the substance of new regulations. Congress facilitated this process by adopting amendments to the APA entitled the Negotiated Rulemaking Act.[4] In this process, known as *regulatory negotiations,* or *reg. neg.,* an agency convenes a committee representing all of the interests that will be significantly affected by the regulation to develop a proposed rule.[5] Such committees have considered a broad range of regulatory issues, from construction safety standards for cranes and derricks to the management of dogs within the Golden Gate National Recreation Area.

Conducting Formal Adjudications

Courts do not have the time, money, or personnel to hear all cases that might arise in the course of regulating individual and corporate behavior. Consequently, legislatures frequently give administrative agencies the responsibility for solving specific types of legal disputes, such as who is entitled to government benefits or whether civil penalties should be imposed on regulated industries.

Formal agency adjudications are courtlike proceedings that can be presided over by one or more members of the agency or by an *administrative law judge (ALJ).* The presiding official is entitled to administer oaths, issue subpoenas, rule on offers of proof and relevant evidence, authorize depositions, and decide the case at hand.

These formal adjudications typically include a prehearing discovery phase. The hearing itself is conducted like a trial. Each side presents its evidence under oath, and testimony is subject to cross-examination. The main difference between administrative adjudications and courtroom trials is that there is never a jury at the administrative level.

An administrative agency's decision in a formal adjudication can be appealed to a court. Agency actions setting rates for natural gas or providing licenses for dams are examples of the types of cases that regularly go to court. In most instances, judicial review of an agency action is based on the *record,* that is, the oral and written evidence

---

3. Bob Davis, *In Washington, Tiny Think Tank Wields Big Stick on Regulation,* WALL ST. J., July 16, 2004, at A1.

4. 5 U.S.C. § 561 *et seq.*

5. Notice of Intent to Negotiate Proposed Rule on All Appropriate Inquiry, 68 Fed. Reg. 10,675, 10,677 (Mar. 6, 2003).

HISTORICALPERSPECTIVE

From Revolutionary War Vets to Homeland Security

Administrative agencies date back to the country's earliest days. The first Congress established three administrative agencies, including one for the payment of benefits to Revolutionary War veterans. The Patent Office was created in 1790, and ten other federal administrative agencies were established before the Civil War.

At three critical junctures in U.S. history, Congress has made extensive use of administrative agencies. During the Progressive Era, from 1885 until 1914, Congress turned to agencies such as the Interstate Commerce Commission, the Federal Reserve Board, the Federal Trade Commission, and the Food and Drug Administration to solve problems involving railroads and shipping,

banks, trade, and food and drugs. In response to the stock market crash in 1929 and the Great Depression that followed, Congress created many agencies to deal with the crisis and delegated broad authority to them. The Securities and Exchange Commission was given broad powers to regulate the offer and sale of securities, the brokerage industry, and the securities exchanges. Finally, during the dawn of the environmental era in the 1970s, Congress turned extensively to federal administrative agencies, especially the Environmental Protection Agency, to regulate hazardous waste disposal and restrict pollution.

Following the terrorist attacks of September 11, 2001, Congress created

the Department of Homeland Security to be responsible for civilian aspects of national security. In creating the department, Congress undertook a massive reorganization of the government structure. Several long-standing agencies, including the U.S. Customs Service and the Immigration and Naturalization Service, as well as newer bodies, such as the Transportation Security Administration, were transferred to Homeland Security's oversight.[a]

---

[a] Section 402 of the Homeland Security Act (HSA) of 2002, Pub. L. No. 107-296, 116 Stat. 2135 (Nov. 25, 2002). *See also* Department of Homeland Security Organizational Chart, *available at* http://www.dhs.gov/xlibrary/assets/DHS_OrgChart.pdf.

© Cengage Learning 2013

---

presented at the administrative hearing. The court's review is limited to determining whether the administrative agency acted properly based on the evidence reflected in the record. In some cases, the laws governing the administrative adjudication provide for a *de novo* (i.e., new) proceeding in court, where the entire matter is litigated from the beginning.

Taking Informal Discretionary Actions

The basic role of administrative agencies is to provide a practical decision-making process for repetitive, frequent actions that are inappropriate to litigate in the courts. These *informal discretionary actions* have been called the lifeblood of administrative agencies. Common examples are the awarding of governmental grants and loans, the resolution of workers' compensation claims, the administration of welfare benefits, the informal resolution of tax disputes, and the determination of Social Security claims. Informal discretionary action also governs most applications to governmental agencies for licenses, leases, and permits, such as leases of federal lands and the registration of securities offerings.

Informal discretionary actions also include contracting, planning, and negotiation. Thus, the process of negotiating a contract with a governmental agency to supply parts for military equipment or to build bridges or highways is

within the realm of administrative law. In fact, most of what governmental agencies do falls within the category of informal discretionary action.

The most noteworthy aspect of these informal actions is their lack of clear procedural rules. In court, there is a strict set of rules and procedures to be followed, and a specific person (the judge) is assigned to hear the case. In informal discretionary actions, the agency frequently has no formal procedures, such as notice to the public, opportunity to file briefs, or opportunity to submit oral testimony. Informal agency actions can lead to quick and practical problem resolution, but they can also lead to seemingly endless administrative paper shuffling.

Conducting Investigations

Many administrative agencies have the responsibility to determine whether a regulated company or person is complying with the applicable laws and regulations. They can use their subpoena power to make mandatory requests for information, conduct interviews, and perform searches. Based on these investigations, the agencies may file administrative suits seeking civil penalty assessments, or they may go to court and seek civil and criminal penalties.

Since 1970, governmental agencies have increasingly relied on their investigatory and prosecutorial powers. ChoicePoint, Inc., which collects, analyzes, and sells consumer data, faced probes by the Federal Trade Commission (FTC) and the Securities and Exchange Commission (SEC) after it sold personal information, including names and Social Security numbers, to criminals.[6] The company paid a $15 million fine to the FTC, one of the largest ever levied by that body, for failing to verify the identity of more than 100 dummy corporations that purchased sensitive personal information about 163,000 individuals. The SEC investigated alleged insider trading activity in the months following the company's discovery of the error and its disclosure of that issue to the public.

The investigatory powers possessed by administrative agencies can lead to fines ranging from thousands of dollars to hundreds of millions of dollars, as well as other penalties. For example, an SEC investigation led to former Qwest Communications CEO Joseph Nacchio being ordered to pay a $19 million fine, give back another $52 million in ill-gotten investment profits, and serve six years in prison for insider trading.[7]

ADMINISTRATIVE AGENCIES AND THE CONSTITUTION

Constitutional issues raised by the creation of administrative agencies concern separation of powers, proper delegation of authority, and the limits imposed on agency actions by the Bill of Rights.

Separation of Powers

The U.S. Constitution provides for a legislature, an executive, and a judiciary. This division of power creates a system of checks and balances to preserve liberty. It does not specifically provide for administrative agencies, thus raising the question of whether the delegation of legislative and judicial powers to an administrative agency is constitutional.

The few cases addressing this issue have upheld the constitutionality of this "fourth branch" of government. In 1856, the U.S. Supreme Court upheld the authority of the Department of the Treasury to audit accounts for money owed to the United States by customs collectors and to issue a warrant for the money owed. The Court rejected the argument that only the courts of the United States were empowered to perform such activities.[8]

In 1935, in a case involving the Federal Trade Commission, the Supreme Court explained with approval that the FTC was an administrative body created by Congress to carry out legislative policies in accordance with a prescribed legislative standard and to act as a legislative or judicial aide by performing rulemaking and adjudicatory functions. It found no constitutional violation in allowing an administrative agency to perform judicial and legislative functions. The Court did not, however, provide much explanation as to why this was permissible.[9] Justice Jackson subsequently stated:

> [Administrative bodies] have become a veritable fourth branch of the Government which has deranged our three-branch legal theories as much as the concept of a fourth dimension unsettles our three dimensional thinking. . . . Administrative agencies have been called quasi-legislative, quasi-executive or quasi-judicial, as the occasion required. . . . The mere retreat to the qualifying "quasi". . . is a smooth cover which we draw over our confusion as we might use a counterpane to conceal a disordered bed.[10]

The Supreme Court upheld the cross-branch nature of administrative agencies when it validated a Federal Communications Commission (FCC) interpretation of a statutory term that conflicted with the Ninth Circuit's prior interpretation of the same term.[11] The Court held that the FCC's interpretation was authoritative because Congress had delegated to administrative agencies the power to interpret ambiguous language in statutes within their jurisdiction. That delegation was not discarded merely because a court had interpreted the language before the proper agency had adopted its rule interpreting the term.[12] In his dissent, Justice Scalia scorned the decision as "inventing yet another breathtaking novelty: judicial decisions subject to reversal by Executive officers."[13] He raised a host of problematic consequences that could stem from permitting agencies to simultaneously ignore prior court interpretations and construct regulations.[14]

In the following case, the Supreme Court considered the constitutionality of the Public Company Accounting Oversight Board, a nonprofit corporation given the authority by Congress to regulate the auditors of public companies.

---

6. Christopher Conkey & Ann Carrns, *ChoicePoint to Pay $15 Million to Settle Consumer-Privacy Case*, WALL ST. J., Jan. 27, 2006, at A2.

7. Carrie Johnson, *Former Qwest Chief Gets 6-Year Prison Term; Nacchio to Pay $71 Million in Insider-Trading Case*, WASH. POST, July 28, 2007, at D1.

8. Den *ex dem.* Murray v. Hoboken Land & Improvement Co., 59 U.S. 272 (1856). *See also* Noriega-Perez v. United States, 179 F.3d 1166 (9th Cir. 1999) (upholding the authority of an administrative law judge to impose a civil fine for violations of the Immigration and Nationality Act).

9. Humphrey's Ex'r v. United States, 295 U.S. 602 (1935).

10. FTC v. Ruberoid Co., 343 U.S. 470, 487–88 (1952).

11. Nat'l Cable & Telecomms. Ass'n v. Brand X Internet Servs., 545 U.S. 967 (2005). In contrast, in *INS v. Chadha*, 462 U.S. 919 (1983), the Supreme Court struck down a statute that gave either house of Congress the right to pass a resolution overturning a decision by the Immigration and Naturalization Service (INS) suspending the deportation of a deportable alien. The Supreme Court reasoned that the resolution passed by the House of Representatives revising the INS decision was essentially legislative. As such, it required passage by both houses of Congress and presentment to the President for signature or veto.

12. Nat'l Cable, 545 U.S. at 980, 982–83.

13. *Id.* at 1016 (Scalia, J., dissenting).

14. *Id.* at 1017.

| A CASE IN POINT | *In the Language of the Court* | Case 6.1 |

Free Enterprise Fund v. Public Company Accounting Oversight Board

Supreme Court of the United States
130 S. Ct. 3138 (2010).

FACTS   The Free Enterprise Fund and a Nevada accounting firm filed a constitutional challenge to the creation of the Public Company Accounting Oversight Board (PCAOB), an entity created by the Sarbanes–Oxley Act (SOX) to oversee and regulate the auditors of public companies. The five members of the PCAOB are appointed by the Securities and Exchange Commission (SEC or Commission) after consultation with the Chair of the Board of Governors of the Federal Reserve and the Secretary of the Treasury. No PCAOB rule becomes effective unless and until the SEC approves it after the SEC's notice-and-comment proceedings. Before approving a rule, the SEC must find that it is "consistent with the requirements of [SOX] and the securities law, or is necessary or appropriate in the public interest or for the protection of investors."

The plaintiffs made several constitutional challenges. They claimed that the appointment of the PCAOB members violated the separation of powers because the members were not removable at will by the President. The President can remove SEC commissioners only for cause, and the SEC can remove the PCAOB members only for cause. The plaintiffs also claimed that the appointment of the PCAOB members by the SEC violated the Appointments Clause of the U.S. Constitution (Article II, Section 2), which empowers the President to appoint "Officers of the United States" while giving Congress the power to vest the appointment of "inferior officers" in the President, courts of law, or heads of departments. The plaintiffs argued that because PCAOB members are neither appointed nor supervised on a day-to-day basis by principal officers directly accountable to the President, they are not inferior officers and therefore must be appointed by the President. Despite the provisions specifying that Board members are not Government officials for statutory purposes, the parties agreed that the Board is "part of the Government" for constitutional purposes and that its members are "Officers of the United States" who "exercis[e] significant authority pursuant to the laws of the United States."

ISSUE PRESENTED   Did the provisions protecting members of the Board from removal only by the SEC for good cause violate the doctrine of separation of powers?

OPINION   ROBERTS, C.J., writing for the U.S. Supreme Court:

We are asked . . . to consider a new situation not yet encountered by the Court. . . . May the President be restricted in his ability to remove a principal officer, who is in turn restricted in his ability to remove an inferior officer, even though that inferior officer determines the policy and enforces the laws of the United States?

We hold that such multilevel protection from removal is contrary to Article II's vesting of the executive power in the President. The President cannot "take Care that the Laws be faithfully executed" if he cannot oversee the faithfulness of the officers who execute them. Here the President cannot remove an officer who enjoys more than one level of good-cause protection, even if the President determines that the officer is neglecting his duties or discharging them improperly. That judgment is instead committed to another officer, who may or may not agree with the President's determination, and whom the President cannot remove simply because that officer disagrees with him. This contravenes the President's "constitutional obligation to ensure the faithful execution of the laws."

The willful violation of any Board rule is treated as a willful violation of the Securities Exchange Act of 1934—a federal crime punishable by up to 20 years' imprisonment or $25 million in fines. And the Board itself can issue severe sanctions in its disciplinary proceedings, up to and including the permanent revocation of a firm's registration, a permanent ban on a person's associating with any registered firm, and money penalties of $15 million ($750,000 for a natural person).

The Act places the Board under the SEC's oversight, particularly with respect to the issuance of rules or the imposition of sanctions (both of which are subject to Commission approval and alteration). But the individual members of the Board are substantially insulated from the

CONTINUED

Commission's control. The Commission cannot remove Board members at will, but only "for good cause shown," "in accordance with" certain procedures. Those procedures require a Commission finding, "on the record" and "after notice and opportunity for a hearing," that the Board member

> "(A) has willfully violated any provision of th[e] Act, the rules of the Board, or the securities laws;
>
> "(B) has willfully abused the authority of that member; or
>
> "(C) without reasonable justification or excuse, has failed to enforce compliance with any such provision or rule, or any professional standard by any registered public accounting firm or any associated person thereof."

Removal of a Board member requires a formal Commission order and is subject to judicial review. Similar procedures govern the Commission's removal of officers and directors of the private self-regulatory organizations [such as the New York Stock Exchange]. The parties agree that the Commissioners cannot themselves be removed by the President except under the standard of "inefficiency, neglect of duty, or malfeasance in office."

III

We hold that the dual for-cause limitations on the removal of Board members contravene the Constitution's separation of powers.

A

The Constitution provides that "[t]he executive Power shall be vested in a President of the United States of America." . . .

. . . .

. . . Congress [may, however, confer] good-cause tenure on the principal officers of certain independent agencies [such as the Federal Trade Commission]. . . . Because "one who holds his office only during the pleasure of another, cannot be depended upon to maintain an attitude of independence against the latter's will," the Court held that Congress had power to "fix the period during which [the Commissioners] shall continue in office, and to forbid their removal except for cause in the meantime."

The Act before us does something quite different. It not only protects Board members from removal except for good cause, but withdraws from the President any decision on whether that good cause exists. That decision is vested instead in other tenured officers—the Commissioners—none of whom is subject to the President's direct control. The result is a Board that is not accountable to the President, and a President who is not responsible for the Board.

. . . .

A second level of tenure protection changes the nature of the President's review. Now the Commission cannot remove a Board member at will. The President therefore cannot hold the Commission fully accountable for the Board's conduct, to the same extent that he may hold the Commission accountable for everything else that it does. The Commissioners are not responsible for the Board's actions. They are only responsible for their own determination of whether the Act's rigorous good-cause standard is met. And even if the President disagrees with their determination, he is powerless to intervene—unless that determination is so unreasonable as to constitute "inefficiency, neglect of duty, or malfeasance in office."

This novel structure does not merely add to the Board's independence, but transforms it. Neither the President, nor anyone directly responsible to him, nor even an officer whose conduct he may review only for good cause, has full control over the Board. The President is stripped of the power our precedents have preserved, and his ability to execute the laws—by holding his subordinates accountable for their conduct—is impaired.

CONTINUED

That arrangement is contrary to Article II's vesting of the executive power in the President. Without the ability to oversee the Board, or to attribute the Board's failings to those whom he *can* oversee, the President is no longer the judge of the Board's conduct. He is not the one who decides whether Board members are abusing their offices or neglecting their duties. He can neither ensure that the laws are faithfully executed, nor be held responsible for a Board member's breach of faith. This violates the basic principle that the President "cannot delegate ultimate responsibility or the active obligation to supervise that goes with it," because Article II "makes a single President responsible for the actions of the Executive Branch."

The diffusion of power carries with it a diffusion of accountability. The people do not vote for the "Officers of the United States." They instead look to the President to guide the "assistants or deputies . . . subject to his superintendence." Without a clear and effective chain of command, the public cannot "determine on whom the blame or the punishment of a pernicious measure, or series of pernicious measures ought really to fall." . . .

. . . .

Indeed, this case presents an even more serious threat to executive control than an "ordinary" dual for-cause standard. Congress enacted an unusually high standard that must be met before Board members may be removed. A Board member cannot be removed except for willful violations of the Act, Board rules, or the securities laws; willful abuse of authority; or unreasonable failure to enforce compliance—as determined in a formal Commission order, rendered on the record and after notice and an opportunity for a hearing. The Act does not even give the Commission power to fire Board members for violations of *other* laws that do not relate to the Act, the securities laws, or the Board's authority. The President might have less than full confidence in, say, a Board member who cheats on his taxes; but that discovery is not listed among the grounds for removal under § 7217(d)(3).

. . . .

IV

Petitioners' complaint argued that the Board's "freedom from Presidential oversight and control" rendered it "and all power and authority exercised by it" in violation of the Constitution. We reject such a broad holding. Instead, we agree with the Government that the unconstitutional tenure provisions are severable from the remainder of the statute.

 . . . Concluding that the removal restrictions are invalid leaves the Board removable by the Commission at will, and leaves the President separated from Board members by only a single level of good-cause tenure. The Commission is then fully responsible for the Board's actions, which are no less subject than the Commission's own functions to Presidential oversight.

[*Editor's note:* The Court rejected claims that the Board members were principal officers who could only be appointed by the President with advice and consent from the Senate. Instead, they are inferior officers whose appointment Congress permissibly vested in the full Securities and Exchange Commission.]

RESULT   The petitioners were not entitled to broad injunctive relief against the Board's continued operations. The Board can regulate public accounting firms, but its members can be removed at will by the SEC.

CRITICAL THINKING QUESTIONS

1. Why is it constitutional to have one, but not two, layers of for-cause termination protection?

2. The dissent argued that "the justification for insulating the 'technical experts' on the Board from fear of losing their jobs due to political influence is particularly strong." Do you agree? How, if it all, should that factor into the constitutional analysis?

Delegation of Authority

The delegation-of-authority issue concerns the nature and degree of direction the legislature must give to administrative agencies. Because Article I of the Constitution vests all legislative powers in the Congress, "when Congress confers decision-making authority upon agencies, *Congress* must 'lay down by legislative act an intelligible principle to which the person or body authorized to [act] is directed to conform.'"[15]

The Supreme Court has refused to uphold the delegation of power to administrative agencies in only two cases. One case concerned the delegation of power regarding shipments of oil between states in excess of government-set quotas.[16] The second case concerned the delegation of authority to the president to determine codes of fair competition for various trades and industries.[17] In both cases, the Supreme Court held that although Congress was free to allow agencies to make rules within prescribed limits, Congress itself must lay down the policies and establish the standards. Both before and after these two cases, however, the Supreme Court has upheld vague standards, such as those requiring rules to be set "in the public interest," "for the public convenience, interest or necessity," or "to prevent unfair methods of competition."

Limits Imposed by the Bill of Rights

There is very little limit to the investigatory powers of administrative agencies. Although agencies must comply with constitutional principles protecting freedom from self-incrimination and from unreasonable search and seizure, over time these protections have been severely eroded.

Self-Incrimination

The Fifth Amendment's protection against self-incrimination does not apply to records that the government requires to be kept. Specifically, the Fifth Amendment protections do not apply to records that are regulatory in nature, are of a kind that the party has customarily kept, and have at least some public aspect to them. It does, however, protect individuals from having to testify concerning the content of the records. In addition, the Fifth Amendment's protection against self-incrimination does not apply to corporations.

Probable Cause

In carrying out their investigatory powers, administrative agencies are not required to have probable cause—that is, reason to suspect a violation—before beginning an investigation. An agency may inquire into regulated behavior merely to satisfy itself that the law is being upheld. For example, the IRS needs no specific cause to audit a company's tax returns.

Search and Seizure

In the administrative arena, the courts have largely obliterated the Fourth Amendment's protection against unreasonable searches and seizures. Particularly for highly regulated industries, such as liquor and firearms, government regulators can conduct full inspections of property and records almost without restriction.

Right to Jury Trial

The Seventh Amendment right to a jury trial extends only to cases for which a right to trial by jury existed in common law before the enactment of the Seventh Amendment. Because administrative agencies adjudicate statutory rights that were unknown at the time the Seventh Amendment was enacted, there is no constitutional right to a jury in a formal adjudication before an administrative agency.[18]

PRINCIPLES OF ADMINISTRATIVE LAW

General principles of administrative law include choice of approach and the need for actual authority to act.

Choice of Approach

In some cases, Congress will require the agency to enact a regulatory program and will provide a deadline for the issuance of final regulations (for an example, see the "Inside Story" in this chapter). In the absence of congressional direction, administrative agencies have a fundamental right to decide whether to promulgate regulations or to proceed on a case-by-case basis.[19] The right to proceed on a case-by-case basis is necessary because an administrative agency cannot anticipate every problem it might encounter. Problems could arise that are so specialized and varying in nature as to be impossible to capture within the boundaries of a general rule.

Authority to Act

Administrative agencies can be compared to large corporations in size, structure, and, to some extent, function. Agencies provide benefits, sign contracts, and produce products. In the private arena, a person acting on behalf of an organization may bind the organization in accordance with not only the person's actual authority but also his or her apparent authority (concepts discussed in Chapter 5). Under the rules for governmental agencies, there is only actual authority.

The Supreme Court has repeatedly upheld the fundamental principle that government employees acting

---

15. Whitman v. Am. Trucking Ass'ns, 531 U.S. 457 (2001) (emphasis in original).

16. Panama Ref. Co. v. Ryan, 293 U.S. 388 (1935).

17. A.L.A. Schechter Poultry Corp. v. United States, 295 U.S. 495 (1935).

18. *See* Wickwire v. Reinecke, 275 U.S. 101 (1927); NLRB v. Jones & Laughlin Steel Corp., 301 U.S. 1 (1937).

19. SEC v. Chenery Corp., 332 U.S. 194 (1947).

"H.U.D. called the F.A.A. The F.A.A. called the S.E.C. The S.E.C. called G.S.A. G.S.A. called O.M.B. O.M.B. called Y-O-U."

Dean Vietor / The New Yorker Collection/www.cartoonbank.com

beyond their authority cannot bind the government. For example, in 1917, the Supreme Court held that the United States was not bound by acts of its officials who, on behalf of the government, entered into an agreement that was not permitted by law.[20] The Court rejected the argument that the neglect of duty by officers of the government was a defense to the suit by the United States to enforce a public right to protect a public interest.

The uninitiated naturally rely on the word of a government employee as to the scope of his or her authority. This is a mistake. In fact, it is incumbent upon anyone dealing with governmental agencies to make sure that the person he or she is dealing with is authorized to act and that the proposed actions are permitted by law.

20. Utah Power & Light Co. v. United States, 243 U.S. 389 (1947).

This rule is intended to prevent personal actions from circumventing congressional intent and the formal process of law. Unfortunately, the rule also takes away the incentive for the government to make sure that its officials know the law and administer it properly.

JUDICIAL REVIEW OF AGENCY ACTIONS

Congress, or the appropriate state legislature, sets the standards for judicial review of agency actions. If the courts control agency action with too heavy a hand, an agency can grind to a halt. If too little oversight is exercised, agencies can run roughshod over individual rights. Some agency actions are not reviewable because they are within the discretion of the agency; others are mere guidelines without the force of law.[21] Most agency actions, however, are reviewable by the courts, but the basic standard of review is highly deferential to the agency. Once it has been determined that an agency has the authority to act, its actions will be given the "highest deference possible."[22]

Review of Rulemaking and Informal Discretionary Actions

Courts will generally uphold an agency's action unless it is arbitrary and capricious. Under the *arbitrary and capricious standard*, if the agency chooses from among several courses of action, the court will presume the validity of the chosen course unless it is shown to lack any rational basis.

21. *See, e.g.,* Ctr. for Auto Safety v. Nat'l Highway Traffic Safety Admin., 452 F.3d 798 (D.C. Cir. 2006).

22. United States v. Mead Corp., 533 U.S. 218 (2001).

Christoph Weihs/Shutterstock

IN BRIEF

Seven Basic Steps for Working Successfully with an Administrative Agency

STEP 1
Investigate the applicable standards that will govern the agency's actions.

STEP 2
Identify and evaluate the agency's formal structure.

STEP 3
Determine what facts are before the agency.

STEP 4
Identify the interests of others who may be involved in the decision-making process.

STEP 5
Adopt a strategy to achieve the desired goal.

STEP 6
Eliminate any adverse impact on other interested parties.

STEP 7
Get involved in the administrative process early and stay involved.

Nonetheless, courts will invalidate any regulation that is inconsistent with the statute pursuant to which the agency was acting. In *Ragsdale v. Wolverine World Wide, Inc.*,[23] the U.S. Supreme Court invalidated a regulation promulgated by the Department of Labor (DOL) that gave an employee the right to an additional twelve weeks of family or medical leave if the employer failed to notify the employee that the twelve weeks of leave provided by the Family and Medical Leave Act ran concurrently with the thirty weeks of paid disability leave provided by the employer. The Court ruled that DOL regulations could not grant entitlements that extended beyond those set forth in the statute and were inconsistent with the statute's purpose. In this case, the statute's purpose was to encourage more generous employer policies, which was exactly what this employer provided.

Courts also will not defer to an agency action when Congress has not expressly delegated rulemaking authority

to the agency. In *Gonzales v. Oregon*,[24] the Supreme Court ruled that the U.S. Attorney General did not have the power to determine whether physician-assisted suicide qualified as a legitimate medical practice under the Controlled Substances Act (CSA). Analyzing the language of the CSA, the Court determined that the law was intended to fight recreational drug use, not to impose federal limitations on the way controlled substances could be utilized in the course of medical care. "[W]hen Congress wants to regulate medical practice in the given scheme," wrote the Court, "it does so by explicit language in the statute," not through an "implicit" or "oblique form." As a result, the Attorney General's Interpretive Ruling prohibiting physicians from prescribing drugs to help a patient commit suicide was invalid.

In the following case, the court considered whether the Federal Communications Commission could regulate Internet service providers' network management policies.

---

23. 535 U.S. 81 (2002).

24. 546 U.S. 243 (2006).

A CASE IN POINT

Comcast Corp. v. FCC

United States Court of Appeals for the District of Columbia Circuit
600 F.3d 642 (D.C. Cir. 2010).

Summary   Case 6.2

FACTS In 2007, subscribers to Comcast's high-speed Internet service discovered that the company was interfering with their use of peer-to-peer networking applications (such as BitTorrent), which allow users to share large files directly with one another without the use of a central server. Nonprofit advocacy organizations filed a complaint with the Federal Communications Commission and, together with public interest groups, a petition for a declaratory ruling. They argued that Comcast's actions violated the FCC's policy statement that consumers are entitled to run applications and use servers of their liking. Comcast defended its actions as necessary to manage scarce network capacity because the peer-to-peer programs use significant amounts of bandwidth.

The Commission issued an order ruling that Comcast had improperly interfered with consumers' use of applications and their ability to access the content of their choice. The FCC found that Comcast had other methods that it could use to manage network traffic. Comcast agreed to change its system, so the Commission simply ordered it to make a disclosure of the new approach. Nonetheless, Comcast petitioned for review, objecting on three grounds: (1) the Commission failed to justify its jurisdiction over network management practices, (2) the Commission's adjudicatory action was procedurally flawed, and (3) parts of the Order were arbitrary and capricious.

ISSUE PRESENTED Does the FCC have the authority to regulate an Internet service provider's network management practices?

SUMMARY OF OPINION The U.S. Court of Appeals for the District of Columbia Circuit began by noting that the FCC agreed that it has no express statutory authority to regulate network management practices. Therefore, the practice must be validated by the Communications Act of 1934, which gives the Commission power to "perform any and all acts, make such rules and regulations, and issue such orders, not inconsistent with this chapter, as may be necessary in the execution of its functions."[25] The Commission could exercise this power "only when two conditions are satisfied: (1) the Commission's general jurisdictional grant under Title I [of the Communications Act] covers the regulated subject and (2) the

CONTINUED

---

25. 47 U.S.C. § 154(i).

regulations are reasonably ancillary to the Commission's effective performance of its statutorily mandated responsibilities."[26] Comcast conceded that the Commission's action satisfied the first requirement under the Communications Act because Internet service qualifies as "interstate and foreign communication by wire" under Title I.[27]

The court then considered whether the Order was reasonably ancillary to the Commission's effective performance of provisions of the Communications Act that either set forth congressional policy or delegate regulatory authority. The Commission argued that the congressional policy set forth in the reasons the Commission was created[28] and in a provision entitled "Protection for private blocking and screening of offensive material"[29] justified its actions. However, the court found that neither of those sections delegated regulatory authority. They are only statements of policy; they cannot provide the basis for the Commission's use of ancillary power absent a link to specifically delegated powers under the Act. To allow the Commission to act without that link would be inconsistent with prior case law and would render the Commission's ancillary jurisdiction limitless. The court further determined that none of the statutory provisions that the Commission relied on to support its exercise of ancillary authority granted regulatory authority over this matter.

RESULT   The court struck down the FCC's antidiscrimination order because it was not reasonably ancillary to the Commission's statutorily mandated duties.

COMMENTS   On December 21, 2010, the Federal Communications Commission adopted an Order titled, "In the Matter of Preserving Open Internet Broadband Industry Practices,"[30] which attempts to preserve the Internet as an open forum through three basic rules: (1) transparency, (2) no blocking, and (3) no unreasonable discrimination.[31] The FCC relied on section 70 of the Telecommunications Act of 1996[32] as a source of direct authority to adopt the Order. Section 70 gives the Commission the power to take actions that encourage the deployment of advanced communications capability.[33] The FCC also asserted ancillary authority based on various provisions of Titles II, III, and VI of the 1996 Act.

Commissioner Robert M. McDowell voted against the new rules and predicted that they would not withstand judicial scrutiny.[34] He accused the Commission of improperly trying to circumvent the *Comcast* decision and argued that the 1996 Act did not give the FCC authority to regulate Internet management policies. McDowell further argued that the rules, contrary to their intended purpose, will cause irreparable harm to broadband investment and consumers at a time when the existing law provides ample consumer protection.

---

26. Am. Library Ass'n v. FCC, 406 F.3d 689, 691–92 (D.C. Cir. 2005).

27. 47 U.S.C. § 152(a).

28. 47 U.S.C. § 151.

29. 47 U.S.C. § 230.

30. 25 FCC Rcd. 17905.

31. *Id.* at 17906.

32. Pub. L. No. 104-104, 110 Stat. 56 (1996).

33. *Supra* note 30, at 17966–17989.

34. *Statement of Commissioner Robert M. McDowell, Before the Subcommittee on Intellectual Property, Competition and the Internet*, 2011 WL 1691824 (FCC May 5, 2011).

Although positive actions by agencies often grab headlines, sometimes not acting at all can have just as lasting and powerful an effect. An appeals court invalidated an FCC rule requiring regional telephone companies—such as Verizon Communications, BellSouth Corporation, and Qwest Communications International—to lease their local networks to national telephone companies and long-distance carriers, such as MCI and AT&T, at a discounted rate.[35] Rather than appealing that ruling to the Supreme Court, the FCC, Justice Department, and Commerce Department supported it, thereby abandoning the existing FCC rule.[36] Increased competition

---

35. U.S. Telecom Ass'n v. FCC, 359 F.3d 554 (D.C. Cir. 2004).

36. Anne Marie Squeo & Almar Latour, *U.S. Sides with Bells in Battle over Local Calling*, WALL ST. J., June 10, 2004, at A1.

in the phone industry spurred by nontraditional challengers, such as wireless, cable, and voice-over-Internet companies, had diminished the FCC's concern over the domination of local phone service by a small number of players.[37]

Review of Factual Findings

An agency's factual findings are determinations that can be made without reference to the relevant law or regulation. The arbitrary and capricious standard of judicial review is not applied to the agency's factual findings. Instead, courts use a *substantial evidence standard* to review factual findings in formal adjudications. Under this standard, courts determine whether the evidence in the record could reasonably support the agency's conclusion.[38] Courts will defer to an agency's reasonable factual determinations, even if the record would support other factual conclusions. This standard of review is similar to an appellate court's review of jury verdicts. Courts acknowledge that the agency's fact finder is generally in a better position to judge the credibility of witnesses and to evaluate evidence, especially if the evidence is highly technical or scientific.

---

37. *Id.*
38. Consol. Edison Co. of NY v. NLRB, 305 U.S. 197 (1938).

Review of Statutory Interpretations

Courts will generally defer to an agency's *construction* (i.e., interpretation) of a statute within its area of expertise. This permits those with relevant practical experience to have the greatest influence in deciding how to implement a particular law. Although the Supreme Court's position on this issue has varied somewhat, its most recent cases have reinforced the rule of deference to any "reasonable" administrative interpretation of law.[39] As noted above, the Supreme Court even granted deference to agency interpretations that conflicted with prior judicial interpretations of the statutory language at issue.[40] However, if "the agency's interpretation goes beyond the limits of what is ambiguous and contradicts [language that in the Court's] view is quite clear," then the Court will invalidate the agency's policy.[41]

In the following case, the U.S. Supreme Court considered whether the Environmental Protection Agency had properly interpreted statutory language in the Clean Air Act when it concluded that it did not have the authority to enact auto emissions regulations to combat global warming by reducing the amount of greenhouse gases in the atmosphere.

---

39. *See, e.g.,* Chevron U.S.A. Inc. v. Natural Res. Def. Council, Inc., 467 U.S. 837 (1984).
40. Nat'l Cable & Telecomms. Ass'n v. Brand X Internet Servs., 545 U.S. 967 (2005).
41. Whitman v. Am. Trucking Ass'ns, 531 U.S. 457 (2001) ("The EPA may not construe the statute in a way that completely nullifies textually applicable provisions meant to limit its discretion.").

| A CASE IN POINT | *Summary* | Case 6.3 |

Massachusetts v. Environmental Protection Agency

Supreme Court of the United States
549 U.S. 497 (2007).

FACTS   In 1999, a collection of nineteen private energy and environmental groups filed a rulemaking petition with the Environmental Protection Agency (EPA). Noting that the former general counsel of the EPA had confirmed that the agency had the power to regulate carbon dioxide, the groups petitioned the EPA to combat global warming by limiting "greenhouse gas emissions from new motor vehicles," including carbon dioxide, pursuant to section 202 of the Clear Air Act (the Act).

The EPA denied the petition for two reasons. First, despite previous contrary rulings by its own attorneys, the EPA claimed that the Act did not authorize the agency to regulate carbon dioxide. Although Congress had promulgated legislation to combat climate change, it had not specifically directed the EPA to address the issue. In particular, the agency reasoned that greenhouse gases, including carbon dioxide, could not be considered "air pollutants" as the term was used in the Act. Furthermore, the EPA argued that because the Department of Transportation (DOT) already oversaw detailed fuel economy standards, crafting the EPA's own set of emissions standards would be superfluous at best and create a statutory conflict at worst. Second, even if the Act did grant the necessary authority, the EPA reasoned that the timing was not right to enact such regulations. The agency asserted that doing so would conflict with other congressional actions aimed at remediating climate change. Moreover, the EPA claimed that the link between greenhouse gases and climate change was scientifically uncertain.

CONTINUED

A coalition of states (including Massachusetts), local governments, and private organizations sought judicial review of the agency's decision, alleging that the EPA had "abdicated its responsibility under the [Act] to regulate [auto] emissions." After the U.S. Court of Appeals for the District of Columbia Circuit ruled in the EPA's favor, the Supreme Court granted the writ of certiorari due to "the unusual importance of the underlying issue."

ISSUES PRESENTED   Does the EPA have statutory authority to regulate greenhouse gas emissions from new motor vehicles? If so, are its stated reasons for refusing to do so consistent with the Clean Air Act?

SUMMARY OF OPINION   As a preliminary matter, the U.S. Supreme Court ruled that the petitioners had standing to challenge the EPA's actions in court, in part because Massachusetts owned coastal land that would be lost to rising seas caused by global warming. Although EPA action to restrict greenhouse emissions would not completely solve the climate change problem, it would be an incremental step offering the state some protection. (Standing is discussed further later in this chapter.)

The Court then examined the statutory language related to the EPA's emissions regulation powers. Section 202 of the Act calls for the EPA to regulate auto emissions if the agency judges them an "air pollutant . . . which may reasonably be anticipated to endanger public health or welfare." The Act goes on to define "air pollutant" as "any physical, chemical . . . substance or matter which . . . enters the ambient air" and to define "welfare" to include effects on weather and climate. The Court determined that this statutory language was unambiguous and therefore precluded the EPA's restrictive reading of the term "air pollutant" to exclude greenhouse gases. The Court reasoned that Congress's other efforts to fight global warming gave no guidance for interpreting the Act and, in any event, did nothing to diminish the EPA's power to regulate greenhouse gas emissions under the Act. Additionally, the Court concluded that the fact that the DOT had established fuel efficiency standards in no way absolved the EPA of its statutory regulatory responsibility. Two agencies with overlapping obligations can coordinate their efforts to avoid inconsistency.

Having determined that the EPA had the authority to regulate greenhouse gas emissions, the Court then analyzed whether the agency had properly refused to do so. Under the Act, the EPA may refuse to act only if it either (1) determines that an air pollutant poses no danger to public health and welfare or (2) provides a reasonable explanation for why it is unable or unwilling to engage in making a determination on that issue. The EPA had noted the potential policy impediments to formulating a regime for limiting the emission of greenhouse gases, but it had made no statement about whether sufficient scientific information existed to determine whether carbon dioxide and other greenhouse gases posed a danger to public health and welfare. Given the EPA's failure to articulate a rationale for not reaching a determination, the EPA's actions were "arbitrary, capricious, . . . or otherwise not in accordance with law."

RESULT   The Court reversed the lower court's decision and remanded the case for further proceedings. The EPA had the power to regulate greenhouse gases, and its reasons for inaction were not consistent with its responsibilities under the Clean Air Act.

COMMENTS   The dissent acknowledged that global warming may be the most pressing environmental problem of our time but argued that the Court cannot use that concern to usurp the discretion Congress gave the EPA to decide whether to promulgate rules governing matters within its jurisdiction. According to the dissent, the EPA was within its congressionally granted rights when it refused to regulate greenhouse gas emissions.

In 2011, members of Congress introduced multiple bills to prevent or delay the EPA's regulation of greenhouse gas emissions.[42] For example, the House of Representatives added House Bill 153 to the Full-Year Continuing Appropriations Act (House Bill 1) during floor debate, but House Bill 1 subsequently failed in the Senate.

---

42. Gabriel Nelson & Phil Taylor, *Appropriations: House Eyes Steep Cuts and Policy Riders for EPA, Interior,* GREENWIRE, July 6, 2011.

Limited Review of Procedures

Absent extremely compelling circumstances, administrative agencies are free to fashion their own rules of procedure and to pursue their own methods of inquiry when discharging their broad and varied duties. A court is not free to impose on an agency its view as to what procedures the agency must follow; the court may only require the agency to comply with its own procedural rules and to conform to the requirements of the Due Process Clause.[43]

The reason for these highly deferential review standards is evident: the role of administrative agencies is to relieve the burden on the courts by having the agencies make their own adjudications. If the courts engaged in a searching inquiry of all factual questions and exercised their own judgment on policy or procedural issues, then the effectiveness of administrative agencies would be greatly diminished.

No Right to Probe the Mental Processes of the Agency

One of the most critical points of administrative law concerns the extent to which a court can inquire into the process by which an administrative agency makes its decision. This issue was one of the first decided in the administrative law arena. It was resolved in a case involving a decision of the Secretary of Agriculture that made news headlines at the end of the New Deal era.[44]

The Packers and Stockyards Act authorized the Secretary of Agriculture to determine reasonable rates for services rendered by cattle-marketing agencies. The marketing agencies of the Kansas Stockyards challenged the ultimate price set as too low. The federal district court had allowed the marketing agents to require the Secretary to appear in person at the trial. He was questioned at length regarding the process by which he had reached his decision about the rates. The interrogation included questions as to what documents he had studied and the nature of his consultations with subordinates. The Supreme Court held that this questioning into the mental processes of the Secretary was improper.

Today, formal federal review procedures limit judicial review of agency actions to the record compiled before the agency. Thus, once an administrative process is complete, there is generally no judicial opportunity to inquire into the whys and wherefores of the decision-making process. Without this shield from judicial review, agency actions would be tied up in court.

Although a court may not inquire into the decision-making process, the legislature may probe agency officials to determine why they acted as they did. In fact, Congress regularly holds oversight hearings on how agencies are administering the law. Criticism from a key member of Congress or a congressional committee can lead to newspaper headlines and prompt changes in agency policies. Congress can also use the appropriation process to withhold funds from disfavored programs and to fund favored ones.

Timing of Review

Two judicial doctrines are designed to prevent cases from being prematurely transferred from the administrative arena to the courts: the doctrines of exhaustion of administrative remedies and of ripeness.

Exhaustion

Exhaustion of administrative remedies concerns the timing and substance of the administrative review process. The general rule is that a court will not entertain an appeal to review the administrative process until the agency has had the chance to act and the party challenging the agency's actions has pursued all possible avenues of relief before the agency. This requirement conserves judicial resources. A party is not required to exhaust all administrative avenues when that would be futile, however.

In *Harline v. Drug Enforcement Administration*,[45] the U.S. Court of Appeals for the Tenth Circuit considered when the exhaustion of remedies requirement may properly be waived due to futility. Harline brought suit in federal district court before exhausting all remedies available before the Drug Enforcement Administration (DEA). He claimed that the DEA's use of an administrative law judge employed by the DEA violated his procedural due process rights to a fair and impartial tribunal and argued that the court should waive the exhaustion requirement. The court stated that exhaustion is waivable either by the agency or at the court's discretion when the plaintiff's interest in prompt resolution is so great that it renders the doctrine of exhaustion inappropriate. As a result, courts have discretion to waive the exhaustion requirement only when (1) the plaintiff asserts a colorable (i.e., plausible) constitutional claim collateral to the substantive issues of the administrative law proceeding, (2) exhaustion would result in irreparable harm, and (3) exhaustion would be futile. Applying this test, the court concluded that Harline's general claims of due process violations were insufficient to justify waiver of the exhaustion requirement in this case.

---

43. Vt. Yankee Nuclear Power Corp. v. Natural Res. Def. Council, Inc., 435 U.S. 519 (1978).

44. United States v. Morgan, 313 U.S. 409 (1941).

45. 148 F.3d 1199 (10th Cir. 1998).

Statutes and agency rules often provide that courts reviewing an administrative agency's action may not rule on issues that a party failed to raise with the agency.[46] In cases where the regulatory language is silent on issue exhaustion, the court will determine whether issues not previously raised should be permitted to be brought before the court by assessing whether the administrative proceedings were sufficiently adversarial in nature to draw out all of a party's arguments.[47] For example, the Supreme Court held that an individual pursuing judicial review of denial of benefits by the Social Security Administration had not waived issues she had failed to raise in administrative proceedings.[48] An administrative law judge (ALJ) had denied Juatassa Sims's claim for disability and supplemental security income benefits under the Social Security Act, and the Social Security Appeals Council denied her request for a review of that decision. Sims filed suit in district court, contending that the ALJ (1) made selective use of the record, (2) posed defective questions to a vocational expert, and (3) should have ordered a consultative examination. After the appeals court held that it could not consider the second and third contentions because Sims had not raised them in her request for review by the Appeals Council, Sims appealed to the U.S. Supreme Court

The Court reversed on the grounds that the reasons for requiring issue exhaustion were not present in Social Security proceedings. Although many administrative proceedings are adversarial, Social Security proceedings are primarily inquisitorial. The ALJ has the duty to investigate the facts and develop the arguments both for and against granting benefits. As a result, the Court ruled, the adversarial development of issues by the parties was not essential. Therefore, a party who exhausted administrative remedies available from the Social Security Appeals Council need not also exhaust issues in order to preserve judicial review of them.

Ripeness

The *ripeness* doctrine helps ensure that courts are not forced to decide hypothetical questions. Courts will not hear cases until they are "ripe" for decision. The issue of ripeness most frequently arises in pre-enforcement review of statutes and ordinances; this occurs when review is sought after a rule is adopted but before the agency seeks to apply the rule in a particular case. The general rule is that agency action is ripe for judicial review when the impact of the action is sufficiently direct and immediate as to make review appropriate.[49]

Standing to Sue

To obtain judicial review of a federal agency's action, the plaintiff must have *standing* to sue. Standing involves three elements. First, the plaintiff must have suffered an injury in fact, that is, an invasion of a legally protectable interest that is (a) concrete and particularized and (b) actual or imminent, not conjectural or hypothetical. Second, the injury must be fairly traceable to the challenged action. Third, it must be "likely," as opposed to merely "speculative," that the injury will be redressed, at least in part, by a favorable decision.[50]

In the following case, the court considered whether an "average" U.S. citizen had standing to sue the Secretary of Agriculture for policies he felt might be exposing him and the rest of the country to added health risks.

---

46. Sims v. Apfel, 530 U.S. 103, 107–08 (2000).

47. *See e.g.*, Delta Found., Inc. v. Thompson, 303 F.3d 551 (5th Cir. 2002) (holding issue exhaustion not required by any statute, or regulation governing Health and Human Services proceedings).

48. *Sims*, 530 U.S. 103.

49. *See* Abbott Labs. v. Gardner, 387 U.S. 136 (1967) (pre-enforcement review of FDA generic drug-labeling rule was appropriate because the issue was purely legal, the regulations represented final agency action and the impact of the rules was direct and immediate).

50. Lujan v. Defenders of Wildlife, 504 U.S. 555 (1992). *See also* Larson v. Valente, 456 U.S. 228, 244 n.15 (1982) (holding that it is not required that the decision remedy all of the plaintiff's injuries).

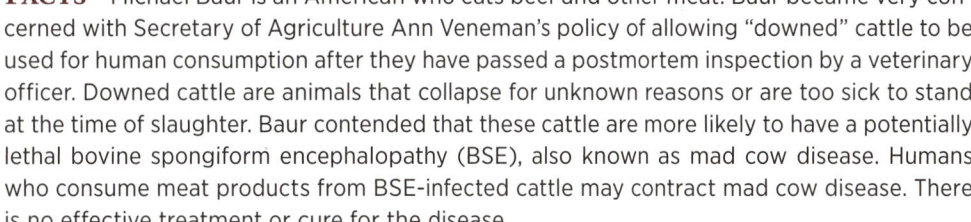

| A CASE IN POINT | *In the Language of the Court* | Case 6.4 |

Baur v. Veneman

United States Court of Appeals for the Second Circuit
352 F. 3d 625 (2d Cir. 2003).

FACTS Michael Baur is an American who eats beef and other meat. Baur became very concerned with Secretary of Agriculture Ann Veneman's policy of allowing "downed" cattle to be used for human consumption after they have passed a postmortem inspection by a veterinary officer. Downed cattle are animals that collapse for unknown reasons or are too sick to stand at the time of slaughter. Baur contended that these cattle are more likely to have a potentially lethal bovine spongiform encephalopathy (BSE), also known as mad cow disease. Humans who consume meat products from BSE-infected cattle may contract mad cow disease. There is no effective treatment or cure for the disease.

CONTINUED

Baur sued Veneman in her capacity as Secretary of the Department of Agriculture (USDA) in an attempt to ban the use of downed livestock. Baur claimed that the British outbreak of mad cow disease had already demonstrated the very real threat of human disease through exposure to BSE—a threat made all the more serious by scientific research suggesting that downed cattle in the United States might already be infected with an unidentified variant of BSE. He also argued that preventing the human consumption of downed cattle was necessary because "current [BSE] surveillance efforts, including slaughterhouse inspection procedures," could provide only limited screening.

ISSUE PRESENTED   Does mere exposure to BSE give a private citizen standing to challenge the USDA's policy on the human consumption of downed cows?

OPINION   STRAUB, J., writing for the U.S. Court of Appeals for the Second Circuit:

On appeal, the parties frame a narrow question for us to consider: whether Baur's allegation that he faces an increased risk of contracting a food-borne illness from the consumption of downed livestock constitutes a cognizable injury-in-fact for Article III standing purposes. . . . To establish Article III standing, a plaintiff must . . . allege, and ultimately prove, that he has suffered an injury-in-fact that is fairly traceable to the challenged action of the defendant, and which is likely to be redressed by the requested relief.

The government does not contest causation and redressibility, and it seems clear that if the alleged risk of disease transmission from downed livestock qualifies as a cognizable injury-in-fact then Baur's injury is fairly traceable to the USDA's decision to permit the use of such livestock for human consumption and could be redressed if the court granted Baur's request for equitable relief.

In this case, only the injury-in-fact requirement of Article III standing is at issue. To qualify as a constitutionally sufficient injury-in-fact, the asserted injury must be "concrete and particularized" as well as "actual or imminent, not 'conjectural' or 'hypothetical,' [and] in evaluating whether the alleged injury is concrete and particularized, we assess whether the injury 'affect[s] the plaintiff in a personal and individual way.'. . . "

Here, the government largely concedes, at least for the purposes of this type of administrative action, that relevant injury-in-fact may be the increased risk of disease transmission caused by exposure to a potentially dangerous food product. . . . In the specific context of food and drug safety suits, however, we conclude that such injuries are cognizable for standing purposes, where the plaintiff alleges exposure to potentially harmful products.

. . . Like threatened environmental harm, the potential harm from exposure to dangerous food products or drugs "is by nature probabilistic," yet an unreasonable exposure to risk may itself cause cognizable injury. Significantly, the very purpose of the Federal Meat Inspection Act and the Federal Food, Drug and Cosmetic Act, the statutes which Baur alleges the USDA has violated, is to ensure the safety of the nation's food supply and to minimize the risk to public health from potentially dangerous food and drug products.

Baur must allege that he faces a direct risk of harm which rises above mere conjecture. While the standard for reviewing standing at the pleading stage is lenient, a plaintiff cannot rely solely on conclusory allegations of injury or ask the court to draw unwarranted inferences in order to find standing. Given the potentially expansive and nebulous nature of enhanced risk claims, we agree that plaintiffs like Baur must allege a "credible threat of harm" to establish injury-in-fact based on exposure to enhanced risk. In evaluating the degree of risk sufficient to support standing, however, we are mindful that "Supreme Court precedent teaches us that the injury in fact requirement . . . is qualitative, not quantitative, in nature.". . .

There are two critical factors that weigh in favor of concluding that standing exists in this case: (1) the fact that government studies and statements confirm several of Baur's key

CONTINUED

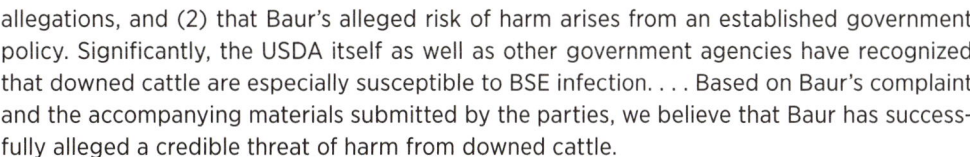

allegations, and (2) that Baur's alleged risk of harm arises from an established government policy. Significantly, the USDA itself as well as other government agencies have recognized that downed cattle are especially susceptible to BSE infection. . . . Based on Baur's complaint and the accompanying materials submitted by the parties, we believe that Baur has successfully alleged a credible threat of harm from downed cattle.

RESULT   The court vacated the earlier judgment against Baur and remanded the case back to the lower court to be heard. Baur had standing to challenge the USDA's policy on downed cows.

COMMENTS   The dissent argued that Baur did not have standing because he had asserted only a generalized grievance and could not distinguish himself from the millions of other Americans who regularly consume beef.

CRITICAL THINKING QUESTIONS

1. Should it matter that Baur could not distinguish himself from any other American who eats beef?

2. Ordinarily, a harm must have already occurred or be imminent for a court to hear a case. Baur could not demonstrate such an injury or the immediacy of an injury to him. Nonetheless, the court permitted his case to proceed. Why did the court not require Baur to demonstrate that he had contracted BSE or had almost eaten a product infected with it?

© Cengage Learning 2013

DECISION-MAKING POWER OF AGENCIES

There are a number of doctrines that limit administrative agencies' decision-making powers.

Only Delegated Powers

The general rule is that an administrative agency may do only what Congress or the state legislature has authorized it to do. Agency action contrary to or in excess of its delegated authority is void.

Obligation to Follow Own Rules

Not only are agencies required to act within the authority delegated to them, but they are also required to follow their own rules and regulations. When an administrative agency adopts a regulation, it becomes binding on the public. It also binds the agency. For example, in *Service v. Dulles*,[51] the Supreme Court held that a State Department employee could not be discharged without being provided reasons because that would be contrary to the State Department's own regulations regarding discharges under its Loyalty Security Program.

At the federal level, one of the most prominent procedural obligations is the requirement to prepare an environmental impact statement before approving major federal actions. The National Environmental Policy Act (NEPA),

passed in 1969, dramatically changed the way all federal agencies conduct their business.

Before 1969, an agency could focus exclusively on its substantive legal obligations (the legal rules that define the rights and duties of the agency and of persons dealing with it) and on its own duly adopted procedural obligations (the rules that define the manner in which these rights and duties are enforced). With NEPA's passage, each federal agency assumed a new procedural obligation to consider the environmental impacts of its proposed actions and the alternatives to those impacts. Each of the hundreds of thousands of federal actions must comply with NEPA. As a result, each agency attempts to document its compliance as a routine part of its procedures. The agencies have not found it easy to meet these procedural requirements. Hundreds of cases have invalidated agency actions as a result of the failure to meet this obligation.

Explanation of Decisions

As discussed earlier in this chapter, courts will not inquire into the mental processes of the decision maker. The corollary to this principle is that an agency must explain the basis for its decisions and show that it has taken into account all relevant considerations as required by the statute. If an agency makes a decision and fails to provide an adequate explanation of why it acted, then the courts will invalidate the agency's action.[52] In some instances,

---

51. 354 U.S. 363 (1957).

52. *See, e.g.,* Motor Vehicle Mfrs. Ass'n of United States v. State Farm Mut. Auto. Ins. Co., 463 U.S. 29 (1983).

however, the court may permit the agency to explain deficiencies in the record and to add supplementary explanations of why it acted. The judiciary's insistence that an agency make a reasoned decision, supported by an explanation of why it acted, is a major restraint on improper agency action.

FINDING AN AGENCY'S RULES AND PROCEDURES

In addition to rules and regulations set forth in officially published documents such as the *Federal Register* and the *Code of Federal Regulations*, federal agencies maintain internal guidance documents. For example, the U.S. Forest Service controls millions of acres of timberland. Although the Service's formal rules are few, it publishes a manual and a handbook containing thousands of pages of guidance on such topics as how to conduct timber sales. Such manuals and handbooks are an important source of law, agency practice, and policy. The Internet has made many of these materials more readily accessible. Reports of court cases provide equivalent information, but cases decided by agency adjudication usually are not reported.

Finding the rules is just a small part of the difficult task of complying with administrative rules and regulations. A small business typically must comply with more than two dozen regulatory procedures at the local, state, and federal levels in order to open.[53] This task is made even more difficult by the fact that relatively few places provide help to a small business trying to figure out the many regulations with which it must comply. Although the Small Business Administration, neighborhood economic development organizations, and banks may offer some guidance, few private small-business consultants specialize in the regulatory aspect of opening a business.

OBTAINING DOCUMENTS FROM AN AGENCY

In court proceedings and in formal agency adjudications, documents may be obtained by discovery. In other situations, individuals are entitled to obtain copies of government records pursuant to federal and state statutes. The federal statute authorizing this procedure is the Freedom of Information Act (FOIA).[54] Under the FOIA, any citizen may request records of the government on any subject of

interest. Unlike discovery, a FOIA request need not show the relevance of the documents to any particular legal proceeding or that the requester has any specific interest in the documents. It is sufficient that the requester seeks the documents.

In theory, the FOIA provides an easy way to obtain documents from a government agency. The agency is required to respond to a document request within ten days. In practice, months, weeks, or even years may pass before the government responds to a FOIA request. Moreover, requesters are required to pay the cost of locating and copying the records. However, these costs are waived for public interest groups, newspaper reporters, and certain other requesters.

Not all documents in the government's possession are available for public inspection. The FOIA exempts:

1. Records required by an executive order to be kept secret in the interest of national defense or foreign policy.

2. Records related solely to the internal personnel rules and practice of an agency.

3. Records exempted from disclosure by another statute.

4. Trade secrets or confidential commercial and financial information.

5. Interagency memorandums or decisions that reflect the deliberative process.

6. Personnel files and other files that, if disclosed, would constitute a clearly unwarranted invasion of personal privacy.

7. Information compiled for law enforcement purposes.

8. Reports prepared on behalf of an agency responsible for the regulation of financial institutions.

9. Geological information concerning wells.

The government is not required to withhold information under any of these exemptions. It may do so or not at its discretion.

From the perspective of those doing business with the government, the FOIA provides an excellent opportunity to learn who is communicating with the agency and what the agency is thinking about a particular matter. The FOIA can also be useful in obtaining government studies and learning generally about government activities.

Frequently, regulated companies are required to submit confidential information to the government. From the perspective of a company submitting such information, the FOIA presents a danger of disclosure to competitors. To protect information from disclosure, the company should mark each document as privileged and confidential so that government officials reviewing FOIA requests will not inadvertently disclose it.

Each federal agency has its own set of regulations relating to FOIA requests. These regulations must be complied with strictly, or consideration of the request may be greatly delayed.

---

53. Kenneth Howe, *Maze of Regulations*, S.F. CHRON., Oct. 29, 1997, at D1.
54. 5 U.S.C. § 552.

THE RESPONSIBLE MANAGER

WORKING WITH ADMINISTRATIVE AGENCIES

It is important for managers to be active, rather than re-active or passive, participants in administrative decision making and processes. Indeed, the ability to help shape the regulatory environment can be a source of competitive advantage. American Express and MCI both adopted corporate political strategies that allowed them to help shape the rules for financial services firms and telecommunications.[55] In contrast, the major U.S. automakers missed opportunities to work with the Environmental Protection Agency to create livable rules on fleet gasoline mileage requirements.[56]

Seven basic recommendations for working successfully with an administrative agency were offered in the "In Brief" on page 153. As recommended in Step 1, a manager working with an agency should first investigate the basic legal standards that will govern the agency's actions in the matter at hand. These include the agency's laws, its regulations, and its internal manuals and procedures. It is also important to discover how the agency's past history and the current political environment are affecting the way the agency administers its laws and regulations. Agencies, like any other bureaucracy, tend to have biases in how they carry out the applicable laws and regulations.

These investigations are important for three reasons. First, a manager needs to know what facts must be presented in order to prevail on a claim. Second, it is possible that the agency personnel may not know the applicable legal standard. Many administrative agencies have little access to legal advice and find it helpful to have a clear presentation of the law under which a person is proceeding. Third, it is important to know the law at the outset of an administrative proceeding because, under the doctrine of exhaustion of administrative remedies, issues not raised before the agency are generally deemed to be waived if the matter is later brought before a court.

The second step is for the manager to learn how the agency operates by identifying and evaluating its formal structure. Administrative agencies can have complicated structures. Because the power to make decisions may be vested in more than one official, it is important to know all of the decision maker's options before proceeding. A person can start at the top, the middle, or the bottom. The important point is to start at the right place. Finding out where that is takes some effort.

Next, the manager needs to determine what facts the agency already has (Step 3). In a judicial proceeding, the parties create the record by filing documents with the court. All parties have access to those documents and share the same factual record. The same is not true in an administrative agency proceeding. The factual record may be scattered about the agency in different files and offices. To function effectively before the agency, a manager must identify and locate this record.

Step 4 recommends that the manager identify the interests of other agencies or parties who may be involved in the decision-making process. In a court proceeding, all the parties to a case are known; in an administrative matter, the parties may not be designated formally. It helps to identify the people concerned at the outset and to determine how the proposed action will affect them.

Upon completing this background information, the manager should adopt a strategy to achieve the desired goal (Step 5). Investigation of an administrative matter could show that the agency lacks the authority to do what is proposed. In that case, the manager must persuade the agency to adopt new rules or go to the legislature to have new laws adopted. The most significant task, however, is to decide whether additional factual information should be gathered and presented to the agency. The record before the agency will normally be the record in court. The use of experts during the administrative process and the submission of key documents are important.

In reviewing a proposed action, the manager may find that the action would have undesirable impacts on other interested parties (Step 6). Elimination of those impacts is an effective way to avoid costly disputes.

Finally, as recommended in Step 7, the manager needs to participate in the administrative process at the earliest possible time and to continue participating throughout the proceedings. Once set in motion, agencies tend to stay in motion unless they are deflected by an outside force. The greater the momentum that has gathered, the harder it is to move the agency off the path it is pursuing. Therefore, it is important to participate early in the process in an effort to influence the agency before it makes up its mind rather than after.

55. David B. Yoffie & Sigrid Bergenstein, *Creating Political Advantage: The Rise of the Corporate Political Entrepreneur*, 28 Cal. Mgmt. Rev. 124 (1985). *See also* David B. Yoffie, *Corporate Strategy for Political Action: A Rational Model, in* Business Strategy and Public Policy 92–111 (A. Marcus et al. eds., 1987).

56. Paul R. Lawrence & Nitin Nohria, Driven: How Human Nature Shapes Our Choices 234–39 (2001).

Mike Price/Shutterstock

A MANAGER'S DILEMMA

Putting It into Practice

Getting into Bed with the Regulators

Dora Reilly is the executive vice president of DNA in Combat, Inc., a genetic-engineering company based in Cambridge, Massachusetts. Eighteen months ago she filed an application with the Food and Drug Administration (FDA) for approval of a promising anticancer drug, DBL. Two months ago she met Gene Splice at an après-ski party and invited him to her room at the ski lodge to listen to her MP3 collection. After that night, Splice returned to his job as a senior specialist in the division of the FDA responsible for approving new drugs based on recombinant DNA, and Reilly returned to Cambridge. Two weeks after her return,

Splice wrote Reilly a letter on FDA letterhead, saying, "It was nice to see your name cross my desk on your company's petition for approval of DBL. I'd really like to see you again—why don't you fly down this weekend?"

Reilly considered requesting that the petition be referred to another specialist at the FDA. However, she is concerned that that would delay the approval process by at least eighteen months. Her chief scientist has advised her that a key competitor is expected to have a similar drug on the market in four months. What should she do? What would you advise her to do if you were head of human resources for Combat, Inc.?

INSIDE STORY

The Devil Is in the Details: Dodd–Frank's Massive Delegation of Authority to Administrative Agencies

The Dodd–Frank Wall Street Reform and Consumer Protection Act[57] was signed into law on July 21, 2010.[58] Its objective is "to promote the financial stability of the United States by improving accountability and transparency of the nation's financial system" and "to ensure American consumers get the clear, accurate information they need to shop for mortgages, credit cards, and other financial products, and protect them from hidden fees, abusive terms, and deceptive practices."[59] Dodd–Frank's ultimate success or failure will depend in large part on the authority Congress delegated to a combination of new and existing administrative agencies, including the newly created Consumer Financial Protection Bureau (CFPB).

The Consumer Financial Protection Bureau

The CFPB is a new independent regulatory agency within the Federal Reserve System,[60] designed to be a "watchdog"[61] over the financial sector. In addition to having authority to

adjudicate in all matters involving home mortgages and student lenders, the agency has the authority to make rules governing any "financial institution" and other "non-financial institutions" having assets of more than $10 billion, such as debt collectors and consumer reporting agencies.[62] Banks and credit unions with assets of $10 billion or less are regulated by another agency.[63] Authority to regulate consumer credit was previously spread among a number of administrative agencies, including the Office of the Comptroller of the Currency, Office of Thrift Supervision, Federal Deposit Insurance Corporation, Federal Reserve Board, National Credit Union Administration, Department of Housing and Urban Development, and Federal Trade Commission.[64] This fragmentation of power left loopholes and allowed issues to fall through the cracks, unnoticed by agencies and lawmakers who were tasked with safeguarding the financial system.

When promulgating rules and regulations, the CFPB will consult with experts in the field as well as with regulators from other agencies, including the Federal Reserve Board, to arrive at the best possible solutions to the problems. Following the publication of the CFPB's rules, there is a process through which regulators may appeal rules that they think could put the safety of the banking system or the stability of the financial system at risk.[65]

CONTINUED

57. Pub. L. No. 111-203, 124 Stat. 1376 (2010).

58. *Summary of the Dodd–Frank Wall Street Reform and Consumer Protection Act*, DAVIS POLK, July 21, 2010, *available at* http://www.davispolk.com/files/Publication/7084f9fe-6580-413b-b870-b7c025ed2ecf/Presentation/PublicationAttachment/1d4495c7-0be0-4e9a-ba77-f786fb90464a/070910_Financial_Reform_Summary.pdf.

59. Brief Summary of the Dodd–Frank Wall Street Reform and Consumer Protection Act, S. COMM. ON BANKING, HOUSING & URBAN AFFAIRS, at 1, *available at* http://banking.senate.gov/public/_files/070110_Dodd_Frank_Wall_Street_Reform_comprehensive_summary_Final.pdf (last visited Aug. 24, 2011) [hereinafter Dodd–Frank Summary].

60. *Id.* at 2.

61. *Id.*

62. *Id.*

63. *Id.*

64. *Id.* at 2–3.

65. *Id.* at 3.

Within the CFPB, Dodd–Frank mandates the creation of a subagency, the Office of Financial Literacy, which is primarily tasked with educating members of the public on financial matters so that they can avoid entering into risky loans.[66] The Office is also required to set up a Consumer Complaint Hotline so that consumers can alert the agency to unfair business practices that might have previously gone unnoticed.[67]

The CFPB has already proved politically controversial. Although Harvard Law School professor Elizabeth Warren was key to the creation of the new agency and many regarded her as the logical first chair, opposition by conservative Republicans in Congress prompted President Obama to instead nominate Richard Cordray, the former Ohio Attorney General and the CFPB's director of enforcement.[68] Although experts expected Cordray to be confirmed in September 2011,[69] his confirmation was delayed by political wrangling in the Senate.

A Multitier System of Banks

Dodd–Frank will bring about a "multi-tier system of banks"[70] in which the larger banks are highly regulated but the smaller community banks are not. The new regime is designed to constrain the growth of large financial institutions (those deemed "too big to fail"). Their cost of capital will rise not only because of the cost of complying with the additional regulations, but also because suppliers of capital to these banks will face an increased risk that the government may take over the institution.[71]

Financial Stability Oversight Council

Dodd–Frank also created the Financial Stability Oversight Council, an independent investigatory council whose members are drawn from the CFPB and the other government agencies charged with monitoring the financial sector, including the Federal Reserve, SEC, Commodity Futures Trading Commission, Office of the Comptroller of the Currency, Federal Deposit Insurance Corporation, Federal Housing Finance Agency, and National Credit Union Administration. The Secretary of the Treasury chairs the Council.[72] Its members may evaluate market conditions and make recommendations to the Federal Reserve for increasingly strict rules regarding capital, leverage, risk

management, liquidity, and other requirements as companies grow in size and complexity.[73] The goal of these rules is to provide a disincentive for companies to grow "too big to fail" and to impose stringent requirements on those companies that, in the Council's view, pose a "significant risk" to the financial system.[74] The newly created Office of Financial Research within the Department of the Treasury will analyze data and monitor any emerging risks to the economy and publish this information periodically for the public and Congress.[75]

The Council may also require, by a two-thirds vote, that a nonbank financial entity not currently under the supervision of the Federal Reserve be regulated by the Fed if the Council members determine that the failure of such entity would have negative effects on the financial system or if its activities pose a threat to the financial stability of the United States.[76] In perhaps its most extreme power, the Council may require a "large, complex" company to divest some of its assets if two-thirds of the Council members find that the company poses a "grave" threat to the financial stability of the United States.[77] The Act specifies that such an action should be used only "as a last resort."[78]

The Federal Reserve Board

The Federal Reserve Board is responsible for defining the terms "significant bank holding company" and "significant nonbank holding company." The Board also determines which nonbanks are deemed to be "predominantly engaged" in financial activities and therefore subject to regulation. It set the maximum permissible interchange fee that debit card issuers may charge for an electronic debt transaction as the sum of 21 cents per transaction and 5 basis points multiplied by the value of the transaction, or approximately 23 cents for the average $38 debit card transaction.[79]

Dodd–Frank significantly curtailed certain powers of the Federal Reserve. In addition to giving other administrative agencies the right to "make suggestions" regarding proposed regulations, Dodd–Frank expressly prohibits the Fed from using its emergency lending authority under section 13(3) of the Federal Reserve Act[80] to bail out an individual company[81] without first obtaining approval from the Secretary of the Treasury. The Fed had used that authority to bail out

CONTINUED

66. *Id.*

67. *Id.*

68. *Richard Cordray to Lead Consumer Financial Protection Bureau*, Huffington Post, July 17, 2011, http://www.huffingtonpost.com/2011/07/17/richard-cordray-cfpb-elizabeth-warren_n_900967.html.

69. Alan S. Kaplinsky, *Cordray Nomination as Director on Hold*, CFPB Monitor, Aug. 3, 2011, *available at* http://www.cfpbmonitor.com/2011/08/03/cordray-nomination-as-director-on-hold/.

70. Tom Brown, *The Dodd–Frank Bill: What People Are Saying and Why Most Are Wrong*, SeekingAlpha.com, July 21, 2010, http://seekingalpha.com/article/215510-the-dodd-frank-bill-what-people-are-saying-and-why-most-are-wrong.

71. *Id.*

72. Dodd–Frank Summary, *supra* note 59.

73. *Id.* at 4.

74. *Id.*

75. *Id.*

76. *Id.*

77. *Id.*

78. *Id.*

79. Regulation II (Debit Card Interchange Fees and Routing), 76 Fed. Reg. 43,394 (July 20, 2011).

80. Section 13(3) of the Federal Reserve Act, 12 U.S.C. § 343, authorizes loans to parties that meet certain eligibility requirements.

81. Dodd–Frank Summary, *supra* note 59, at 6.

investment bank Bear Stearns. For the Treasury to approve such a loan, the firm must not be insolvent and must demonstrate its ability to repay the loan.[82] If the Fed makes such loans in the future, it must disclose information concerning them to the public.[83] All loans under the Fed's section 13(3) emergency lending power must also be reviewed by the General Accountability Office (GAO),[84] an independent agency that works for Congress and investigates how the federal government spends taxpayer dollars.[85] The President selects the head of the GAO—the Comptroller General of the United States—from a list of candidates proposed by Congress, and he or she serves for a fifteen-year term.[86]

The Dodd–Frank Act also calls for a study of the entire Federal Reserve System to ascertain whether "the current system effectively represents the public or whether there are actual or potential conflicts of interest."[87] This opens the door to a potential future reshaping of the Federal Reserve System.

The Relationship Between the CFTC and the SEC: The Regulation of Swaps

In addition to transferring responsibilities from existing regulatory agencies to the CFPB, Dodd–Frank also clarified the authority of the SEC and the Commodity Futures Trading Commission (CFTC) to regulate a category of derivatives known as over-the-counter (OTC) swaps.[88] Section 721(b) of the Act defines "swap" to include the following:

> a put, call, cap, floor, collar, or similar option of any kind that is for the purchase or sale, or based on the value, of 1 or more interest or other rates, currencies, commodities, securities, instruments of indebtedness, indices, quantitative measures, or other financial or economic interests or property of any kind.

Credit default swaps were central to the near collapse of insurance giant AIG and several other firms during the financial crisis of 2008.

It was originally recommended that the SEC and CFTC be consolidated into one agency,[89] but this proved to be politically infeasible, in part because the different congressional committees responsible for overseeing the SEC and CFTC did not want to relinquish their power. Instead, Dodd–Frank gave the SEC the authority to regulate security-based swap products, markets, and participants; non-security-based swaps are subject to CFTC regulation.[90] Accordingly, the CFTC is prohibited from issuing any rule or regulation with respect to or otherwise providing oversight or regulation of "security-based swaps," "security-based swap dealers," "major security-based participants," "security-based swap data repositories," "persons associated with a security-based swap dealer or major security-based swap participant," "eligible contract participants with respect to security-based swaps," or "swap execution facilities" with respect to security-based swaps.[91] The SEC is similarly prohibited from issuing any rule or regulation or otherwise regulating or providing oversight for non-security-based swaps.[92] Any swaps that do not fit neatly into either of these two spheres (so-called mixed swaps) are to be regulated by the SEC and the CFTC jointly.[93] Dodd–Frank also requires the SEC and the CFTC to treat all products or entities that are "economically or functionally similar" in a "similar fashion."[94]

Dodd–Frank requires the two agencies to consult "to the extent possible" prior to engaging in any rulemaking or adjudications in the swaps area.[95] This "consultation" provision was a compromise designed to ameliorate problems arising from having two agencies responsible for regulating a single area.

Timetable for New Rules

Dodd–Frank called for the promulgation of 400 new rules.[96] One year after the Act's passage, the various agencies had finalized 38 rules, missed the deadlines for finalizing 26 rules, proposed 121 rules, and awaited future deadlines for 215 rules.[97] Industry groups are lobbying intensely to tailor the new rules to their best interests. For example, General Electric and other firms are seeking to exempt certain financial and energy swaps from further regulation. The CFTC and the SEC missed Congress's deadline of July 16, 2011, for the new swaps regulations in part because of the difficulty of distinguishing between firms using swaps as part of speculative investment strategies, such as a hedge fund betting on changes in interest

CONTINUED

---

82. *Id.* at 7.

83. *Id.*

84. Pauline Smale, Cong. Research Serv., RS20826, Structures and Functions of the Federal Reserve System, 7 (Nov. 10, 2010), *available at* http://www.fas.org/sgp/crs/misc/RS20826.pdf.

85. *About GAO*, U.S. Gov't Accountability Office, http://www.gao.gov/about/index.html (last visited Aug. 25, 2011).

86. *Id.*

87. *Id.*

88. Harold Bloomenthal & Samuel Wolff, *International Capital Markets and Securities Regulation, Section 31A:2: Division of Regulatory Authority*, 10A Int'l Cap. Markets & Sec. Reg. § 31A:2 (updated May 2011).

89. *Department of the Treasury Blueprint for a Modernized Financial Regulatory Structure*, DechertOnPoint, June 2008, at 3, *available at* http://www.dechert.com/library/FRE-FS-WCSL-SA-06-08-Department_of_The_Treasury_Blueprint.pdf.

90. Bloomenthal & Wolff, *supra* note 88.

91. Dodd–Frank Act, § 712(b)(1).

92. Dodd–Frank Act, at § 712(b)(2).

93. *Id.*

94. *Id.*

95. *Id.*, at § 712(a)(7).

96. *Dodd–Frank Progress Report*, Davis Polk, July 2011, at 8, *available at* http://www.davispolk.com/files/uploads/FIG//July2011_Dodd.Frank.Progress.Report.pdf.

97. *Id.* at 10.

rates or commodity prices, and other companies using swaps to stabilize operating expenses, such as a beer company trying to protect itself from sharp fluctuations in the price of ingredients such as hops.[98]

Litigation may be an even more potent way to shape the contours of the new rules and ultimately the reform (or not) of the financial sector. In July 2011, the U.S. Court of Appeals for the District of Columbia Circuit struck down the SEC's newly enacted proxy rules designed to make it easier for shareholders to nominate company directors.[99] This decision suggests that "while lobbying might yield the occasional loophole, judicial rulings can halt new rules altogether."[100]

---

98. David S. Hilzenrath, *Overwhelmed Regulators Give Wall Street a Reprieve*, WASH. POST, June 10, 2011.

99. Bus. Roundtable v. SEC, 647 F.3d 1144 (D.C. Cir. 2011) (Case 19.5).

100. Ben Protess, *Court Ruling Offers Path to Challenge Dodd–Frank*, N.Y. TIMES, Aug. 17, 2011.

KEY WORDS AND PHRASES

QUESTIONS AND CASE PROBLEMS

1. A statute gives the Department of the Interior the power to allow or to curtail mining within the national forests "as the best interests of all users of the national forest shall dictate." Is this a valid delegation of legislative power to the agency, or is it too broad a delegation of power?

2. After Congress decided to set stricter limits on harmful car emissions, the Environmental Protection Agency (EPA) was directed to devise a test for all automobiles to determine if they were in compliance with the stringent new emissions standard. The EPA, already stretched thin by many preexisting projects, issued the CAP 2000 regulation, which requires all automobile manufacturers to devise their own tests for their automobiles. The EPA hopes this measure will do three things: cut down on the cost of producing its own test, force automobile manufacturers to share in the cost of producing cleaner cars, and result in an even more effective test for emissions.

    Ethyl Corporation produces gasoline additives. Because the automobile companies will now devise their tests behind closed doors, Ethyl will have a more difficult time producing additives that will pass emission standards. Ethyl sued the EPA, challenging the CAP regulation. What arguments should Ethyl advance to persuade the court to strike down the EPA regulation? How else might Ethyl affect the EPA's rulemaking? [*Ethyl Corp. v.* EPA, 306 F.3d 1144 (D.C. Cir. 2002).]

3. The Food and Drug Administration (FDA), which is charged with implementation of the Federal Food, Drug and Cosmetic Act, refused to approve the cancer-treatment drug Laetrile on the ground that it failed to meet the statute's safety and effectiveness standards. Terminally ill cancer patients sued, claiming that the safety and effectiveness standards implemented by the FDA could have no reasonable application to drugs used by the terminally ill. The statute contained no explicit exemption for drugs used by the terminally ill. The U.S. court of appeals reviewing the case agreed with the plaintiffs and approved intravenous injections of Laetrile for terminally ill cancer patients. The U.S. Government appealed to the Supreme Court. Under what standard should the Supreme Court review the FDA's determination that an exemption from the Federal Food, Drug and Cosmetic Act should not be implied for drugs used by the terminally ill? [*United States v. Rutherford,* 442 U.S. 544 (1979).]

4. In 1985, President Ronald Reagan signed into law the Gramm-Rudman-Hollings Act. The purpose of the Act was to reduce the federal deficit by setting a maximum deficit amount for fiscal years 1986 to 1991, progressively reducing the budget deficit to zero by 1991.

    If the federal budget deficit failed to be reduced as the Act required, an automatic budget process was to take effect. The Comptroller would calculate, on a program-by-program basis, the amount of reductions needed to meet the target. He or she would then report that amount to the President, who was required to issue a sequestration order mandating these reductions. (A *sequestration order* directs spending levels to be reduced below the levels authorized in the original budget.) Unless Congress then acted to modify the budget to reduce the deficit to the required level, the sequestrations would go into effect.

The Comptroller, unlike the employees of the executive branch and agency officials, does not serve at the pleasure of the President. He or she can be removed from office only by Congress.

Opponents of the Gramm-Rudman-Hollings Act argued that the Comptroller's role in the automatic budget process was an exercise of executive functions. Because the Comptroller was controlled by Congress, they argued that this role violated the constitutional requirement of separation of powers. Were they right? [*Bowsher v. Synar*, 478 U.S. 714 (1986).]

5. The Supreme Court has recognized that administrative inspections may be conducted without warrants in some situations when a company's business concerns an industry that has a history of government oversight and, as a result, has a reduced expectation of privacy. The Court has held that a warrantless search will be found reasonable in the context of a pervasively regulated business if (1) there is a "substantial" government interest underlying the regulatory scheme pursuant to which the search is made; (2) the warrantless inspection is necessary to further the regulatory scheme; and (3) the inspection program, in terms of the certainty and regularity of its application, provides a constitutionally adequate substitute for a warrant. Based on this standard, would the Court allow warrantless administrative inspections to occur in the following industries: (a) firearms, (b) mining, (c) pharmaceutical, and (d) computer software design? [*In re Subpoenas Duces Tecum*, 51 F. Supp. 2d 726 (W.D. Va. 1999).]

6. James O'Hagan was a partner in the law firm of Dorsey & Whitney in Minneapolis, Minnesota. In July 1988, the London-based company Grand Metropolitan PLC (Grand Met) retained Dorsey & Whitney as local counsel for a potential tender offer for the common stock of the Pillsbury Company, headquartered in Minneapolis. Both Grand Met and Dorsey & Whitney took precautions to protect the confidentiality of Grand Met's tender offer plans. O'Hagan, who was not working on the deal, began purchasing Pillsbury stock and call options for Pillsbury stock. When Grand Met announced its tender offer in October, the price of Pillsbury stock rose to $60 per share. O'Hagan sold his Pillsbury call options and stock, making a profit of more than $4.3 million.

The Securities and Exchange Commission (SEC) initiated an investigation into O'Hagan's transactions that culminated in a fifty-seven-count indictment, charging O'Hagan with, among other counts, violation of Rule 14e-3(a). Rule 14e-3(a) was adopted by the SEC pursuant to section 14(e) of the Securities Exchange Act of 1934. Section 14(e) reads in relevant part:

It shall be unlawful for any person . . . to engage in fraudulent, deceptive, or manipulative acts or practices, in connection with any tender offer. . . . The [SEC] shall, for the purposes of this subsection, by rules and regulations define, and prescribe means reasonably designed to prevent, such acts and practices as are fraudulent, deceptive, or manipulative.

Relying on section 14(e)'s rulemaking authorization, the SEC promulgated Rule 14e-3(a) in 1980. Traders violate Rule 14e-3(a) if they trade on the basis of material nonpublic information concerning a pending tender offer that they know or have reason to know has been acquired "directly or indirectly" from an insider of the offeror or the target, or someone working on their behalf. Rule 14e-3(a) requires traders who fall within its ambit to abstain from trading or to disclose the nonpublic information, without regard to whether the trader owes a preexisting fiduciary duty to respect the confidentiality of the information. In contrast, courts have interpreted section 14(e) to apply only to situations in which the person trading violated a fiduciary duty by trading. Did the SEC exceed its rulemaking authority by adopting Rule 14e-3(a) without requiring a showing that the trading at issue entailed a breach of fiduciary duty? [*United States v. O'Hagan*, 521 U.S. 642 (1997).]

7. Section 7(a)(2) of the Endangered Species Act of 1973 (ESA) is intended to protect species of animals against threats to their continuing existence caused by humans. The ESA instructs the Secretary of the Interior to promulgate a list of those endangered or threatened species and requires each federal agency, in consultation with the Secretary of the Interior, to ensure that any action authorized, funded, or carried out by such agency is not likely to jeopardize the continued existence of any endangered or threatened species.

In 1978, the Department of the Interior and the Department of Commerce promulgated a joint regulation stating that the obligations imposed by section 7(a)(2) extended to actions taken in foreign nations. Thus, any actions taken by the United States would require consultation with the Department of the Interior. The Secretary of the Interior, however, reinterpreted the section to require consultation only for actions taken in the United States or on the high seas.

Almost immediately, organizations dedicated to wildlife conservation and other environmental causes sued Manuel Lujan, the Secretary of the Interior, and sought an injunction requiring the Secretary to promulgate a new regulation restoring the initial interpretation of the geographic scope. They claimed that U.S.-funded projects in Egypt and Sri Lanka would significantly reduce endangered and threatened species in those areas. Two members of Defenders of Wildlife, Joyce Kelly and Amy Skilbred, submitted affidavits indicating that they had traveled to foreign countries to observe endangered species (the Nile crocodile in Egypt, the Asian elephant and leopard in Sri Lanka) and that they planned to do so in the future. The U.S. Supreme Court ruled that Kelly and Skilbred did not have standing to challenge the new interpretation.

In *Bennett v. Spear*, however, the Court held that ranchers in irrigation districts that would be directly affected economically by a Fish and Wildlife Service finding regarding two endangered species of fish had standing to challenge it. Why did they have standing when Kelly and Skilbred did not? [*Lujan v. Defenders of Wildlife*, 504 U.S. 555 (1992); *Bennett v. Spear*, 520 U.S. 154 (1997).]

8. Section 3(a)(8) of the Securities Act of 1933, which governs the sale of any security through interstate commerce, exempts "annuity contracts" subject to state insurance laws from the federal registration, disclosure, and antifraud requirements of the Act. Rule 151A, which the SEC adopted in 2007, provides that fixed indexed annuities (FIAs) are not annuity contracts within the meaning of the Act and are therefore not exempt from SEC regulation. FIAs are hybrid financial products that combine aspects of fixed annuities with aspects of securities. Like a traditional fixed annuity, which yields a guaranteed interest rate, an FIA has a guaranteed minimum return. But like the return on a security, the expected return on an FIA depends on the performance of a securities index, such as the Nasdaq 100 Index. As a result, the actual yield is more variable than that of a traditional annuity, resulting in greater investment risk for the purchaser. Under Rule 151A, even if an annuity is issued by a state-licensed insurance company, it is still not deemed an "annuity" within the meaning of section 3(a)(8) if (1) its yield is calculated after the crediting period and (2) the amounts payable "are more likely than not to exceed the amounts guaranteed under the contract."

Section 2(b) of the Act specifies that the SEC has a responsibility to consider the effect that a new rule of this sort will have on efficiency, competition, and capital formation. In its attempt to meet this requirement, the SEC provided general statements, including the claim that Rule 151A would enhance competition by providing greater clarity to an area of law that was unclear and would improve efficiency by requiring fuller disclosure to investors. The SEC made no finding to determine whether the proposed rule would provide better results than those obtained under the existing state-law regime.

If you were the manager of an insurance company seeking to challenge Rule 151A, what arguments would you make? What arguments would you expect the SEC to make in its defense? What standard will a court apply when evaluating the rule and the SEC's findings? Is Rule 151A valid? [*American Equity Investment Life Insurance Co. v. SEC*, 613 F.3d 166 (D.C. Cir. 2010).]

UNIT
II

THE LEGAL ENVIRONMENT

CHAPTER 7

CONTRACTS

INTRODUCTION

WHY CONTRACT LAW IS IMPORTANT

Contracts are critical to the conduct of business in the United States and internationally. The principles of contract law determine which agreements will be enforced by the courts. Contract law allows a company to make plans to move its offices into a new building, knowing that the lease gives it an enforceable right to exclusive use of the space for the term of the lease at the specified rent. Similarly, an owner can rent space, knowing that the tenant will be required to pay rent and to comply with the other terms of the lease. An employee can leave his or her current employer and begin work for a start-up company, knowing that the new firm will grant the stock options it promised when it recruited the employee. All of the parties to these transactions expect that their agreements will be enforceable.

Contract law is based on case law, statutes, and tradition, subject to slight variations from state to state. Many states follow the Restatement (Second) of Contracts, which is the basis for much of the discussion in this chapter. Common law contracts include employment agreements and other contracts involving services, leases and sales of real property, loan agreements, stock-purchase agreements, settlement agreements, and joint venture agreements. Commercial transactions involving the sale of goods, that is, movable personal property, are governed by Article 2 of the Uniform Commercial Code (UCC). Article 2, as well as the laws governing the sale of goods internationally and contracts for the sale and licensing of software, is discussed in Chapter 8. The "In Brief" in Chapter 8 (page 225) summarizes key differences among common law contracts, the UCC, the Convention on Contracts for the International Sale of Goods, and the Uniform Computer Information Transactions Act.

CHAPTER OVERVIEW

This chapter discusses the elements necessary for a valid contract: agreement (formed by an offer and acceptance), consideration, contractual capacity, and legality. It explains the equitable doctrine of promissory estoppel and the enforcement of an agreement to negotiate. Promissory estoppel can, in certain circumstances, result in limited relief for a party who has relied on a promise even though it lacks one or more of the elements required for a contract. The equitable doctrine of unconscionability, on the other hand, allows a court to elect not to enforce all or a portion of an otherwise enforceable contract. The chapter discusses the need for genuine assent and the effects of fraud and duress, as well as issues concerning a misunderstanding or mistake about the meaning of a contract or the facts underlying the contract. The chapter explains the requirement that certain contracts be in writing and the rules for looking beyond the written terms of an agreement to discern the parties' intentions. It discusses damages for breach of contract and court orders for specific performance. The chapter concludes with a brief look at acquisition agreements.

BASIC REQUIREMENTS OF A CONTRACT

A *contract* is a legally enforceable promise or set of promises. If the promise is broken, the person to whom the promise was made—the *promisee*—has certain legal rights against the person who made the promise—the *promisor*. If the promisor fails to carry out its promise, the promisee may be able to recover money damages, or it may be able to get an injunction, that is, a court order forcing the promisor to perform the promise.

Formation of a valid contract requires four basic elements: (1) there must be an agreement between the parties, formed by an offer and acceptance; (2) the parties' promises must be supported by something of value, known as consideration; (3) both parties must have the capacity to enter into a contract; and (4) the contract must have a legal purpose.

In addition, courts may invalidate contracts that do not reflect a true "meeting of the minds." For instance, if one party is induced to enter into a contract by fraud, duress, or misrepresentation, courts may refuse to enforce the contract because both parties did not genuinely assent to its terms.

AGREEMENT

A valid contract requires an offer and acceptance resulting in agreement between the two parties. Contract law has traditionally treated offer and acceptance as a rather sterile, step-by-step process. Despite its incongruity with the fluid nature of business deal making today, this narrow view continues to give the rules governing contract formation a formalistic flavor.

Offer

An *offer* is a manifestation of willingness to enter into a bargain that justifies another person in understanding that his or her assent will conclude the bargain. An offer is effective if (1) the *offeror* (the person making the offer) has an intention to be bound by the offer, (2) the terms of the offer are reasonably definite, and (3) the offer is communicated to the *offeree* (the intended recipient).

Intention

Courts will evaluate the offeror's outward expression of intent, not his or her secret intention. Thus, if a reasonable person would consider an offeror's statement to be a serious offer, an offer has been made. Offers made in obvious jest or in the heat of anger do not meet the intention requirement because a reasonable person would know the offer was not serious. This objective standard of contract interpretation makes it possible to plan one's business based on reasonable expectations of what the other party's words mean.

Most advertisements are treated not as offers but as invitations to negotiate. Sellers do not have an unlimited ability to provide services or an unlimited supply of goods. If advertisements were offers, then everyone who "accepted" could sue the seller for breach of contract if the seller's supply ran out. An advertisement will be treated as an offer only in the rare case where a seller makes a promise so definite that it is clearly binding itself to the conditions stated. This can arise, for example, when the advertisement calls for some performance by the offeree, such as providing information that leads to the recovery of a lost or stolen article.

Definiteness

An offer will form the basis for a contract only when the essential terms of the agreement are set forth. If essential terms (such as price, subject matter, duration of the contract, and manner of payment) are left open, then there is no contract.

Communication

The offeror must communicate the offer to the offeree. For instance, a Good Samaritan who returns a lost briefcase cannot claim a reward offered by the owner if he or she did not know about the reward beforehand.

Termination of Offer

An offer can be terminated either by operation of law or by action of the parties.

Termination by Operation of Law   An offer terminates when the time for acceptance specified by the offeror has elapsed or after a reasonable period has elapsed if the offeror did not specify a time. Death or incapacitation of either party terminates an offer, as does destruction of the subject matter.

Termination by Action of the Parties   The offeror can *revoke* the offer—that is, cancel it—at any time before the offeree accepts. An offer is also terminated if the offeree rejects it or makes a new offer, which is referred to as a *counteroffer*. A counteroffer constitutes a rejection of the original offer and reverses the roles of the original offeror and offeree. If Misha responds to a job offer with a salary of $100,000 a year by saying, "That salary is too low, but I'll take the job at $120,000 per year," he is making a counteroffer, which terminates the original offer. Inquiring into the terms of an offer is not a rejection, however. Had Misha responded, "Does that include a five-week vacation?" it would have constituted an inquiry into terms, which would not terminate the original offer.

Irrevocable Offers

An *irrevocable offer* cannot be terminated by the offeror. Irrevocable offers arise (1) when an option contract has been created and (2) when an offeree has relied on an offer to his or her detriment.

Option Contracts   An *option contract* is created when an offeror agrees to hold an offer open for a certain amount of time in exchange for some consideration from the other party. Under such an agreement, the offeror cannot revoke the offer until the time for acceptance has expired. For example, in exchange for a $200 payment by the offeree, a company might agree to keep the position of general manager open for ten days while the offeree decides whether to take the job.

Detrimental Reliance   An irrevocable offer may also occur when an offeree has changed his or her position because of justifiable reliance on the offer. Sometimes courts will hold that such detrimental reliance makes the offer irrevocable.

Suppose Aunt Leila offers the use of her Maui condo to her niece Christina during spring break in exchange for Christina's promise to fix a hole in the condo roof during her stay. Under traditional contract law, Aunt Leila could revoke this offer at any time before Christina accepts. But suppose Christina relies on this offer, purchases a nonrefundable plane ticket to Maui, and passes up the opportunity to rent other condos for her stay. The modern view of this situation is quite different from traditional contract law. If Aunt Leila should reasonably have known that Christina would act to her detriment in reliance on the offer, then the doctrine of promissory estoppel would make the offer irrevocable. In other words, Aunt Leila would be estopped—or barred—from revoking her offer. The doctrine of promissory estoppel is described in more detail below.

Acceptance

Acceptance is a response by the person receiving the offer that indicates willingness to enter into the agreement proposed in the offer. For example, if Indra says to Dayle, "I'll give you $100 to install my new computer software package," and Dayle says, "OK," a contract has been formed. Indra is now legally obliged to give Dayle the money, and Dayle is obliged to install the software.

Both offer and acceptance can be oral, written, or implied by conduct. If, for example, a manager offers a consultant $5,000 to develop a business plan for her company, the consultant can accept orally or in writing, or the consultant can accept the offer by starting work on the business plan. The acceptance is implied by the consultant's action, even though he did not actually say, "I accept your offer."

Mode of Acceptance

The offeror is the "master of his offer" in that he or she can specify the means and manner of acceptance. For example, the offeror could specify that the offer can be accepted only by a facsimile (fax) sent to a stated fax number and that the acceptance is not effective until it is actually received. Absent such a provision, acceptance is effective

upon dispatch of the acceptance. Thus, if a person mails a properly addressed envelope with adequate postage containing a letter accepting an offer, a contract is formed when the letter is put in the mailbox; the offeror cannot thereafter revoke the offer.

Many online service providers modify their terms of service by simply posting the updated terms of service on their websites. Joe Douglas challenged this practice on behalf of all users of Talk America after he learned that the service provider had modified its service contract to add service charges and an arbitration clause. Talk America had posted the revised contract on its website, but it did not otherwise notify users that the contract had been changed. (Although the court hearing the case did not mention it, Talk America's original service contract included language that purported to give it the right to change the terms at any time.) Talk America moved to compel arbitration based on the modified service contract, claiming that Douglas's continued use of the service after the revised terms were posted had constituted his acceptance of them. The U.S. Court of Appeals for the Ninth Circuit disagreed, stating:

> Parties to a contract have no obligation to check the terms on a periodic basis in order to learn whether they have been changed by the other side. Indeed, a party can't unilaterally change the terms of a contract; it must obtain the other party's consent before so doing. This is because a revised contract is merely an offer and does not bind the parties until it is accepted. . . . Even if Douglas' continued use of Talk America's service could be considered assent, such assent can only be inferred after he received proper notice of the proposed changes.[1]

Mirror Image Rule

The traditional concept of contract formation requires that what the offeree accepts must be exactly the same as what the offeror has offered. If it is not, the *mirror image rule* dictates that no contract has been formed.

Suppose Alyssa offers to rent to Roberto 6,000 square feet of office space in Houston for $60 per square foot per year. Roberto accepts the offer of 6,000 square feet of office space but says he wants ten free underground parking spaces as well. The requirements of the mirror image rule have not been met because Roberto's acceptance is not unequivocal. Accordingly, there is no contract; Roberto's request for the parking spaces is considered a counteroffer, not an acceptance.

Intent to Be Bound

Formalistic rules of contract formation often do not reflect the realities of how businesses enter into agreements. A joint venture agreement between contractors to build

---

1. Douglas v. U.S. Dist. Court, 495 F.3d 1062,1066 (9th Cir. 2007).

a hydroelectric dam, for example, can involve months of negotiations and a series of letters, memoranda, and draft contracts. As a result, it is sometimes difficult to determine precisely when the parties have entered into a legally binding contract.

At some point in the negotiations, the parties will usually manifest an intention, either orally or in writing, to enter into a contract. Such *intent to be bound* can create an enforceable contract even if nonessential terms must still be hammered out or a more definitive agreement is contemplated. Courts will look at the specific facts of each case when determining whether the parties regarded themselves as having completed a bargain.

In general, to determine the enforceability of preliminary agreements, courts examine (1) the intent of the parties to be bound and (2) the definiteness of the terms of the agreement. Most litigation concerning the enforceability of preliminary agreements with open terms has involved the issue of intent, as in the landmark case of *Pennzoil v. Texaco*, discussed in the "Inside Story" for this chapter. In that case, the court ruled that Getty Oil, the Getty Trust, and the Getty Museum intended to be bound by a four-page "memorandum of agreement" calling for the sale of Getty Oil to Pennzoil, even though the memorandum was not expressly made binding and the consummation of the multibillion-dollar deal was subject to execution of a definitive agreement.

In deciding whether the parties intended to be bound, courts look to a variety of factors, including (1) the degree to which the terms of the agreement are spelled out; (2) the circumstances of the parties (e.g., the importance of the deal to them); (3) the parties' prior course of dealing with each other, if any; and (4) the parties' behavior after execution of the agreement (for example, issuing a press release announcing a deal may demonstrate intent).

The parties can make a preliminary agreement nonbinding by stating their intention not to be bound. However, courts will honor such a statement only if it is expressed in the clearest language. Titling an agreement a "letter of intent" or using the phrase "formal agreement to follow" might not be enough to prove that the parties did not intend to be bound if their other conduct suggests otherwise.

CONSIDERATION

In addition to offer and acceptance, formation of a valid contract requires that each side provide something of value, known as *consideration,* which can be money, an object, a service, a promise, or a giving up of the right to do something the promisor has the legal right to do. For instance, an adult's promise to quit smoking for five years constitutes consideration because the promisor is giving up something he or she is legally entitled to do. A promise to take property off the market for thirty days constitutes consideration, as does a promise to conduct a midyear audit.

A promise to do something illegal, such as to pay an illegal bribe to a government official, does not constitute valid consideration, however. Likewise, a promise to fulfill a preexisting legal obligation, that is, to do something the promisor is already obligated to do—either by law or by contract—is not consideration.

Suppose Brett's Builders Corporation (BBC) has a contract to build a production facility for Hardware, Inc. for $15 million. Halfway through the project, BBC demands an additional $3 million to finish the project. Because it wants the project completed as quickly as possible, Hardware promises to pay the additional $3 million. Hardware's promise is not enforceable by BBC because BBC's promise to "finish the project" did not constitute consideration. BBC was already contractually obligated to build the facility in its entirety for $15 million. This type of situation is explored further in the discussion of contract modification below.

Adequacy of Consideration

Generally, courts will not scrutinize the value of the consideration or the fairness of a contract. A court will deem consideration adequate—and hold the parties to their bargain—unless it concludes that the purported consideration is a sham. Hence, the adage that even a peppercorn can be adequate consideration. The rare exception to this rule is the unconscionability doctrine discussed below.

Bilateral and Unilateral Contracts

Consideration can be either a promise to do a certain act or the performance of the act itself.

A *bilateral contract* is a promise given in exchange for another promise. One party agrees to do one thing, and the other party agrees to do something in return. For example, Ibrahim promises to give Mercedes $10 if she promises to drive him to business school. The exchange of promises represents consideration and makes the promises binding.

A *unilateral contract* is a promise given in exchange for an act. For example, Ibrahim promises to give Mercedes $10 if she drives him to business school. Mercedes can accept the contract only by driving Ibrahim to business school, and no contract is formed until she does so.

Mutuality of Obligation in Bilateral Contracts

The corollary of consideration in the case of bilateral contracts is the concept of *mutuality of obligation.* To be enforceable, a bilateral contract must limit the behavior of both parties in some fashion. If one party has full freedom of action, there is no contract.

Mutuality of obligation applies only to bilateral contracts. In the case of a unilateral contract, the promisor becomes bound only after the promisee has performed the required act. Thus, in the example above, Ibrahim has no obligation to pay Mercedes $10 until she drives him to school.

Illusory Promise   A promise that neither confers any benefit on the promisee nor subjects the promisor to any detriment is an *illusory promise.* Because there is no mutuality of obligation in such a case, the resulting agreement is unenforceable. A classic case[2] involved a coal company, Wickham, which had agreed to sell at a certain price all the coal that Farmers' Lumber, a lumber company, wanted to purchase from Wickham. The Iowa Supreme Court held that Farmers' Lumber's promise to purchase only what it wanted to purchase, which could be nothing at all, was illusory. Because there was no consideration flowing from Farmers' Lumber to Wickham, there was no contract. Farmers' Lumber could have avoided the finding of an illusory contract by agreeing to purchase all the coal it needed from Wickham. Such an agreement is called a requirements contract.

Requirements and Output Contracts   In a *requirements contract,* the buyer agrees to buy all its requirements of a specified commodity, such as steel, from the seller, and the seller agrees to meet those requirements. The parties do not know how much steel the buyer will actually need, but, whatever that amount is, the buyer will buy it all from that seller. Because the buyer is precluded from buying steel from another supplier, there is a binding contract even if the buyer did not originally expect to need any steel.

In an *output contract,* the buyer promises to buy all the output that the seller produces. Again, the parties do not how know many units that will be, but the seller must sell all its output to that buyer. The seller cannot sell any of its product to another buyer.

These types of contracts are not enforceable if the requirement or output is unreasonable or out of proportion to prior requirements or outputs. The buyer cannot take advantage of the seller by increasing its requirement to triple the usual amount. The seller will not be required to sell anything over the reasonable or usual amount required by the buyer.

Conditional Promises

Promises conditioned on the occurrence or nonoccurrence of an event often look illusory, but they are enforceable as long as the promisor is bound by conditions beyond his or her control. If satisfaction of the condition is within the control of one party, however, conditional clauses will be treated as illusory promises. For example, courts usually disallow clauses that condition an agreement on the approval of a party's own lawyer.

There are three types of *conditions:* (1) conditions precedent, (2) conditions concurrent, and (3) conditions subsequent. A *condition precedent* is an event that must occur before performance under a contract is due. For example, Lockheed Martin agreed to sell one of its operations to BTN pursuant to a contract that required BTN to demonstrate that it had "resources and assets necessary and sufficient to conduct the [transferred business] and to perform its obligations and contracts." When Lockheed demanded evidence that BTN was in compliance with this condition, BTN was unable to satisfy Lockheed. After Lockheed terminated the contract, BTN sued for breach of contract. The U.S. Court of Appeals for the Fourth Circuit concluded that Lockheed had not breached the contract because BTN had not satisfied the condition precedent.[3]

A *condition concurrent* occurs when the mutual duties of performance are to take place simultaneously. For example, a buyer's obligation to pay for stock often does not become absolute until the seller tenders or delivers the stock certificates. Similarly, the seller's obligation to deliver the stock certificates does not become absolute until the buyer tenders or makes payment.

A *condition subsequent* operates to terminate an existing contractual obligation if the condition occurs. For example, a partner agrees to sell his share of the partnership for ten times the partnership's earnings, unless an audit of the partnership's books shows earnings of less than $5 million. The partner will not be obligated to sell if the audit reveals earnings of less than $5 million (that is, if the condition subsequent occurs).

CAPACITY

A valid contract also requires that both parties possess the capacity to enter into an agreement. *Capacity* is a legal term that refers to a person's ability to understand the nature and effect of an agreement. The widely accepted rule is that minors and mentally incompetent persons lack capacity because they are unable to protect their own interests.

As a result, the law generally gives minors and incompetent persons the power to repudiate their contractual obligations. In other words, such contracts are *voidable* at the option of the person lacking capacity: that person can enforce the contract if it is advantageous for him or her to do so, or disavow the contract if it is not. In some states, minors also have the right to retain any property they acquired under the voidable contract even though they have

---

2. Wickham & Burton Coal Co. v. Farmers' Lumber Co., 179 N.W. 417 (Iowa 1920).

3. Bi-Tech North, Inc. v. Lockheed Martin Corp., 2005 U.S. App. LEXIS 4026 (4th Cir. Mar. 10, 2005).

avoided their own contract obligations. In many states, though, minors cannot repudiate their contractual obligations if they misrepresented their age to the other party.

Contracts entered into by incompetent persons have the potential to be void, voidable (at the option of the incompetent person), or valid. If the party has been legally found incompetent and a guardian has been appointed for him or her, the contract is void. If the party simply lacked the mental capacity to comprehend the subject matter, the contract is voidable. If the incompetent person was able to understand the nature and effect of the agreement, however, then the contract is valid, even if he or she lacked capacity to engage in other activities.

These voidability rules are subject to certain limitations. Both minors and mentally incompetent persons are held to contracts for necessaries, such as food, clothing, and shelter. Otherwise, no one would be willing to provide the necessaries a minor or mentally incompetent person needs to survive. Both minors and mentally incompetent persons can *ratify* (agree to be bound by) contracts after they reach majority or gain competency.

LEGALITY

Contracts must have a legal purpose. Contracts that are contrary to a statute or to public policy are illegal and are generally considered void—that is, they are not valid contracts.

Licensing Statutes

Many states require licenses to conduct particular kinds of business, ranging from real estate and securities broker licenses to chauffeur and contractor licenses. Licensing statutes often provide that if a party fails to have a required license, the other party to the contract does not have to fulfill its side of the bargain, usually payment. This is true even if the unlicensed party performed the work perfectly and the other party knew beforehand that the person doing the work was unlicensed.

Other Contracts Contrary to Statute

Sometimes a statute will expressly make certain types of contracts illegal. For example, *usury statutes* limit the interest rate on loans and usually provide that any loan agreement in violation of the statute is unenforceable. In some jurisdictions, this means that no interest can be collected; in some states, the principal amount of the loan is also not collectible. Loans that violate the usury statutes also violate criminal law.

Other examples of *illegal contracts* include price-fixing agreements in violation of the antitrust laws; bribes; wagering contracts or bets in violation of applicable gambling laws; and unreasonable covenants not to compete. To be reasonable, a *covenant not to compete* entered into in connection with the sale of a business must be reasonable as to scope of activities, length of time, and geographic area, and must be necessary to protect trade secrets or goodwill. The enforceability of covenants not to compete in the employment context is discussed in Chapter 12.

PROMISSORY ESTOPPEL

The primary exception to the rule that only promises supported by consideration will be enforced is the doctrine of promissory estoppel. *Promissory estoppel* (sometimes referred to as *detrimental reliance* or *unjust enrichment*) applies only if the injured party can prove there was (1) a promise and (2) justifiable reliance on the promise (3) that was foreseeable and (4) resulted in injustice.

Promise

In a classic case,[4] Red Owl Stores promised Hoffman that he could acquire a Red Owl grocery store franchise for $10,000. While the parties were negotiating the terms of a deal, the franchisor encouraged Hoffman to sell his bakery, to get more experience, and to move to another area. The franchisor subsequently increased the capital amount required, and the deal fell through. Even though the negotiation had not yet ripened into a contract, Hoffman sued for the losses he suffered by relying on Red Owl's promise about the capital required.

Justifiable Reliance

The promise must cause the promisee to take an action that he or she would not otherwise have taken. In the *Red Owl* case, Hoffman relied on Red Owl's promise when he sold his bakery and moved to the area of the new store. If he had not sold his business or moved, there would have been no reliance, and Red Owl's breach of promise would not entitle him to recover damages.

Foreseeability

The action taken in reliance on the promise must be reasonably foreseeable by the promisor. It was foreseeable that Hoffman would sell his business and move as a result of Red Owl's promise.

Injustice

A promise that has been reasonably relied on will give rise to relief only if the failure to provide relief would cause injustice. Legal scholars have debated the exact meaning of "injustice," but a good rule of thumb is to ask whether the promisee has been harmed by his or her reliance on the promise.

---

4. Hoffman v. Red Owl Stores, 133 N.W.2d 267 (Wis. 1965).

PRECONTRACTUAL LIABILITY FOR FAILURE TO NEGOTIATE IN GOOD FAITH

Under traditional contract law, the offeror is free to revoke an offer at any time before it is accepted without risk of *precontractual liability*. A party entering negotiations does so at the risk that the negotiations will break off. Courts typically will impose a duty to negotiate in good faith only if a letter of intent between the two parties specifically imposes that duty. For example, Venture Associates had sent Zenith Data a letter of intent that stated, "this letter is intended to evidence the preliminary understanding which

we have reached . . . and our mutual intent to negotiate in good faith to enter into a definitive Purchase Agreement." Based on the wording in the letter of intent, the U.S. district court held that the two parties had entered into an enforceable preliminary agreement to negotiate in good faith.[5]

In the following case, the court considered whether Baskin Robbins had a good faith duty to negotiate even though there was no written agreement that required the parties to negotiate in good faith.

---

5. Venture Assocs. Corp. v. Zenith Data Sys. Corp., 887 F. Supp. 1014 (N.D. Ill. 1995).

| A CASE IN POINT | *In the Language of the Court* | Case 7.1 |

Copeland v. Baskin Robbins

Court of Appeal of California
117 Cal. Rptr. 2d 875 (Cal. Ct. App. 2002).

FACTS   When Baskin Robbins announced its intention to close its ice cream manufacturing plant in Vernon, California, Copeland expressed an interest in acquiring it. Copeland's offer was contingent on the execution of a co-packing agreement whereby Baskin Robbins would agree to purchase the ice cream that Copeland manufactured in the plant. In May 1999, Baskin Robbins sent Copeland a letter that stated:

> This letter details the terms which our . . . executives have approved for subletting and sale of our Vernon manufacturing facility/equipment and a product supply agreement. . . . (1) Baskin Robbins will sell [Copeland] Vernon's ice cream manufacturing equipment . . . for $1,300,000 cash. . . . (2) Baskin Robbins would agree, subject to a separate co-packaging agreement and negotiated pricing, to provide [Copeland] a three year co-packing agreement for 3,000,000 gallons in year 1, 2,000,000 gallons in year 2 and 2,000,000 in year 3. . . . If the above is acceptable please acknowledge by returning a copy of this letter with a non-refundable check for three thousand dollars. . . . We should be able to coordinate a closing [within] thirty days thereafter.

Copeland signed a statement at the bottom of the letter agreeing that "[t]he above terms are acceptable" and returned the letter to Baskin Robbins along with the $3,000 deposit.

Thereafter, the negotiations of the co-packing agreement broke down with regard to several items. In July 1999, Baskin Robbins terminated the co-packing negotiations entirely and returned Copeland's $3,000 deposit. Copeland then declined Baskin Robbins's offer to proceed with the agreement for the sale and lease of the Vernon plant assets.

Copeland filed a lawsuit for breach of contract, alleging that Baskin Robbins had breached its May 1999 letter agreement to negotiate the terms of a co-packing agreement by "unreasonably and wrongfully refusing to enter into any co-packing agreement with [him]." The trial court granted Baskin Robbins's motion for summary judgment on the ground that the letter failed as a contract because the essential terms of the co-packing deal were never agreed to and there was no reasonable basis on which to determine them.

ISSUE PRESENTED   Can a party to failed contract negotiations successfully sue for breach of a contract to negotiate an agreement, or is such a "contract" merely an unenforceable "agreement to agree"?

OPINION   JOHNSON, Acting P.J., writing for the California Court of Appeal:

When Baskin Robbins refused to continue negotiating the terms of the co-packing agreement, Copeland faced a dilemma. "Many millions of dollars" in anticipated profits had melted away

CONTINUED

like so much banana ripple ice cream on a hot summer day. . . . [H]e could proceed with the contract for the purchase and lease of the Vernon plant's assets and use those assets to produce ice cream for other retailers. But . . . without the Baskin Robbins co-packing agreement he could not afford to purchase the assets and pay the on-going costs of operating the plant while he searched for other business. Alternatively, he could attempt to sue Baskin Robbins for breach of the co-packing agreement on the theory the terms of the agreement set out in the May 1999 letter plus additional terms supplied by the court constituted an enforceable contract. Such a suit, however, had a slim prospect of success. . . . It is still the general rule that where any of the essential elements of a promise are reserved for the future agreement of both parties, no legal obligation arises until such "future agreement is made."

Copeland chose a third course. Rather than insist the parties had formed a co-packing contract and Baskin Robbins had breached it, he claimed the May 1999 letter constituted a contract to negotiate the remaining terms of the co-packing agreement and Baskin Robbins breached this contract by refusing without excuse to continue negotiations or, alternatively, by failing to negotiate in good faith. This path too has its difficulties. No reported California case has held breach of a contract to negotiate an agreement gives rise to a cause of action for damages. . . . We believe, however, these difficulties could be overcome in an appropriate case.

Initially, we see no reason why in principle the parties could not enter into a valid, enforceable contract to negotiate the terms of the co-packing agreement. A contract, after all, is "an agreement to do or not to do a certain thing." Persons are free to contract to do just about anything that is not illegal or immoral. Conducting negotiations to buy and sell ice cream is neither.

A contract to negotiate the terms of an agreement is not, in form or substance, an "agreement to agree." If, despite their good faith efforts, the parties fail to reach ultimate agreement on the terms in issue the contract to negotiate is deemed performed and the parties are discharged from their obligations. Failure to agree is not, itself, a breach of the contract to negotiate. A party will be liable only if a failure to reach ultimate agreement results from a breach of the party's obligation to negotiate or to negotiate in good faith. . . .

. . . Baskin Robbins maintains that there are sound public policy reasons for not enforcing a contract to negotiate an agreement. In doing so, we would be injecting a covenant of good faith and fair dealing into the negotiation process whether or not the parties specifically agreed to such a term. . . . Most parties, Baskin Robbins suggests, would prefer to risk losing their out-of-pocket costs if the negotiation fails rather than risk losing perhaps millions of dollars in expectation damages if their disappointed negotiating partner can prove bad faith. Finally, Baskin Robbins argues, any precontractual wrong-doing can be adequately remedied by existing causes of action for unjust enrichment, promissory fraud and promissory estoppel. . . .

. . . [W]e believe there are sound public policy reasons for protecting parties to a business negotiation from bad faith practices by their negotiating partners. Gone are the days when our ancestors sat around a fire and bargained for the exchange of stones axes for bear hides. Today the stakes are much higher and negotiations are much more complex. Deals are rarely made in a single negotiating session. Rather, they are the product of a gradual process in which agreements are reached piecemeal on a variety of issues in a series of face-to-face meetings, telephone calls, e-mails and letters involving corporate officers, lawyers, bankers, accountants, architects, engineers and others. . . . [C]ontracts today are not formed by discrete offers, counter-offers and acceptances. Instead they result from a gradual flow of information between the parties followed by a series of compromises and tentative agreements on major points which are finally refined into contract terms. These slow contracts are not only time consuming but costly. For these reasons, the parties should have some assurance "their investments in time and money and effort will not be wiped out by the other party's footdragging or change of heart or taking advantage of a vulnerable position created by the negotiation.". . .

CONTINUED

For obvious reasons, damages for breach of a contract to negotiate an agreement are measured by the injury the plaintiff suffered in relying on the defendant to negotiate in good faith. This measure encompasses the plaintiff's out-of-pocket costs in conducting the negotiations and may or may not include lost opportunity costs. The plaintiff cannot recover for lost expectations (profits) because there is no way of knowing what the ultimate terms of the agreement would have been or even if there would have been an ultimate agreement.

RESULT Because Copeland failed to establish any reliance damages, Baskin Robbins was entitled to summary judgment. Baskin Robbins had breached its duty to negotiate in good faith, but Copeland was unable to prove that it had suffered losses in reliance on Baskin Robbins's promise.

CRITICAL THINKING QUESTIONS

1. What other causes of action might Copeland have been able to allege against Baskin Robbins?

2. How could Baskin Robbins have structured the negotiations to avoid any potential liability when it elected to break off the negotiations related to the co-packing agreement?

© Cengage Learning 2013

In addition to imposing liability for a breach of the duty to negotiate in narrow circumstances, American courts will impose precontractual liability on theories of misrepresentation or promissory estoppel.[6] For example, the Supreme Court of Washington found misrepresentation when the owner of a warehouse told the lessee that he intended to renew the lease for three years, but in fact was negotiating the sale of the facility to someone else.[7]

⊕ UNCONSCIONABILITY

A contract term is *unconscionable* if it is so oppressive or fundamentally unfair as to "shock the conscience of the court."[8] A 1750 English case defined an unconscionable contract as one that "no honest man in his senses and not under delusion would make on one hand, and as no honest and fair man would accept on the other."[9] This concept is applied most often to consumer contracts where the consumer may have little or no bargaining power. The seller dictates the terms of the contract, and the buyer can take it or leave it.

One state's settlement with the tobacco industry provides a vivid illustration. In August 1997, the State of Florida settled a suit against the tobacco industry for more than $11 billion. The State had hired a group of outside attorneys to represent it in the case, in exchange for a 25%

contingency fee. The settlement agreement with the tobacco industry called for attorneys' fees to be determined by an independent arbitrator. Several of the State's outside attorneys then went to court in an effort to enforce their 25% contingency-fee contract.

A Florida state judge denied their claim on unconscionability grounds. The court stated that a fee of tens of millions of dollars or perhaps even hundreds of millions could be reasonable, "but a fee of 2.8 *billion* dollars simply shocks the conscience of the court." The court calculated that if the twelve principal lawyers had worked around the clock from the outset of negotiations in mid-1994 through the end of 1997, they would be paid the equivalent of $7,716 per hour if the contingency-fee agreement were upheld. The court found these figures to be "patently ridiculous" and "per se unreasonable."[10]

Courts usually refuse to enforce contract terms that they find unconscionable. Unconscionability has both a procedural and a substantive element. When the term is central to the contract, the court can either rewrite the term (for example, by substituting a fair market price) or void the entire contract.

Procedural Element

The procedural element of unconscionability focuses on two factors: oppression and surprise. *Oppression* arises from an inequality of bargaining power that results in no real negotiation and an absence of meaningful choice for one party to the contract. *Surprise* arises when the terms of

6. For a classic summary of the law in this area, see E. Allen Farnsworth, *Precontractual Liability and Preliminary Agreements: Fair Dealing and Failed Negotiations*, 87 COLUM. L. REV. 217 (1987).

7. Markov v. ABC Transfer & Storage Co., 457 P.2d 535 (Wash. 1969).

8. Eyre v. Potter, 56 U.S. 42, 60 (1853).

9. Earl of Chesterfield v. Janssen, (1750) 28 Eng. Rep. 82 (Ch.); 2 Ves. Sen. 125.

10. John McKinnon, *Florida Judge Blocks Lawyers' Bid to Collect Tobacco-Accord Fee*, WALL ST. J., Nov. 13, 1997, at B3.

HISTORICALPERSPECTIVE

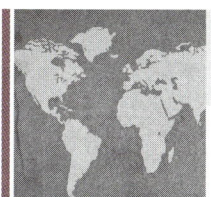

Origins of the Equitable Doctrines of Promissory Estoppel and Unconscionability

Until the 1870s, the English legal system had both courts of law and courts of equity. The courts of law enforced the laws, but the range of claims that could be heard was narrow and the procedures that governed them were complicated and technical. As a result, many meritorious claimants were denied relief by the courts of law.

In such cases, a claimant could still seek relief by filing a petition with the king (or queen). Over time, the royal secretarial department, referred to as the Chancery, began to resemble a judicial body and became known as the "Court of Chancery." The Chancery courts, also referred to as equity courts, were more concerned than the courts of law with reaching a fair result, even if it did not fit within the strict letter of the law.

Although the state and federal court systems of the United States initially replicated England's dual court system, the northern states had eliminated equity courts by the late 1700s. A dual system of U.S. federal courts of law and equity continued until 1937. As equity courts were eliminated, equity powers were merged into the courts of law so that a plaintiff could seek both

legal and equitable relief in the same action. Today, only four U.S. states—Arkansas, Delaware, Mississippi, and Tennessee—have completely separate Courts of Chancery. The most notable of these is the Court of Chancery in Delaware, which is renowned throughout the world as the preeminent forum for corporate matters.

There are two important equitable contract doctrines—promissory estoppel and unconscionability. The doctrine of promissory estoppel enforces some promises even though the injured party cannot establish all of the elements for a binding contract. Conversely, the doctrine of unconscionability allows a court to refuse to enforce an otherwise valid and enforceable contract or contract provision. An early antecedent—the Code of Justinian's doctrine of *laesio enormis* barred the enforcement of contracts for the sale of land or goods for less than one half of the "just price."[a]

The coming of the Industrial Revolution and the emergence of large corporations in the mid-1800s brought about fundamental changes in the mode of analysis of contract law.

As goods became more complex, the seller typically knew more about them than the buyer did, and the bargaining power of large corporations often greatly exceeded that of the individuals with whom they contracted. Thus, a greater number of contracts failed to satisfy the "equal footing" condition necessary to make freedom of contract efficiency enhancing. Courts became less hesitant to intervene to protect a party to a contract who was perceived to be weaker, and the doctrine of unconscionability was expanded to cover situations where the parties were not on an equal footing. Nevertheless, courts remain reluctant to find unconscionability in negotiated contracts between two business parties because of a desire to encourage predictability in commercial transactions. As a result, most successful unconscionability defenses in breach of contract cases involve form contracts between a business and an individual. Form contracts are usually drafted by the party with the superior bargaining position.

a. James Gordley, *Equality in Exchange*, 69 CALIF. L. REV. 1587 (1981).

© Cengage Learning 2013

the contract are hidden in a densely printed form drafted by the party seeking to enforce these terms.

Substantive Element

Substantive unconscionability cannot be defined precisely. Courts have talked in terms of "overly harsh" or "one-sided" results. One commentator has pointed out that unconscionability turns not only on a "one-sided" result, but also on an absence of justification for it. The most detailed and specific commentaries observe that a contract is largely an allocation of risk between the parties; therefore, a contractual term is substantively suspect if it reallocates the risk of the bargain in an objectively unreasonable or unexpected manner. But not all unreasonable risk allocations

are unconscionable. The greater the unfair surprise or the inequality of bargaining power, the less likely the courts will tolerate an unreasonable risk allocation.

Liability Releases

The user of a facility is sometimes asked to sign a general release, especially before embarking on a dangerous activity such as skydiving or race car driving. A *general release* purports to relieve the owner of the facility of any liability, including liability for negligence that results in injuries to a person using the facility. A number of earlier cases held that the exculpatory language in a general release agreement was invalid because the agreement was unconscionable. More recently, however, releases have been enforced when (1) the language of the release evidences a clear and unambiguous intent to exonerate the would-be defendant from liability; (2) there was no vast difference in the parties' bargaining power at the time the release was executed; and (3) enforcement of the clause is not injurious to the public health, morals, or confidence in administration of the laws and does not violate public policy.[11] Courts generally will not enforce releases that purport to relieve a party from liability for an "intentional, willful or fraudulent act or gross, wanton negligence."[12]

The court in the following case considered whether a release required before using a dirt bike park was enforceable.

---

12. *Id. See also* Atkins v. Swimwest Family Fitness Ctr., 691 N.W.2d 334 (Wis. 2005) (refusing to enforce a combined swimming-pool guest registration and release form that did not require a separate signature for the exculpatory clause and purported to release the pool operator from all liability "without regard to fault").

11. *See, e.g.*, Schmidt v. United States, 912 P.2d 871 (Okla. 1996).

| A CASE IN POINT | *In the Language of the Court* | Case 7.2 |

Kurashige v. Indian Dunes, Inc.

California Court of Appeal
246 Cal. Rptr. 310 (Cal. Ct. App. 1988).

FACTS   Members of the general public used Indian Dunes Park for motorcycle dirt bike riding. On December 21, 1982, Kurashige was injured while riding his motorcycle on the park's trails. Before using the park, Kurashige had signed a general release agreement, which was printed in red ink with 10-point bold type and capital letters saying: "SINCE ALL MOTORBIKE RIDING IS DANGEROUS WE REQUIRE ALL RIDERS AND VISITORS TO ASSUME ALL RISK BY SIGNING THIS GENERAL RELEASE." At the bottom of the agreement, the words "MOTORCYCLING IS DANGEROUS" were printed in red in 17-point bold type. Below the agreement were three columns of 28 lines each for the riders to sign. Printed on each of the 84 lines were the words "THIS IS A RELEASE" in capital letters.

The agreement provided in pertinent part that each of the undersigned:

> Hereby Releases, Waives, Discharges and Covenants not to sue [defendants], all for purposes herein referred to as Releasees, from all liability to the Undersigned . . . for all loss or damage and any claim or demands therefor, on account of injury to the person or property or resulting in death of the Undersigned, whether caused by the negligence of Releasees or otherwise while the Undersigned is upon the Park premises.

Kurashige suffered injury and sued the owner of Indian Dunes. The trial court granted summary judgment in favor of Indian Dunes. By granting the motion for summary judgment, the court took the issue of liability away from the jury and decided as a matter of law that the defendant should prevail. Kurashige appealed.

ISSUE PRESENTED   Is the exculpatory language in a general release agreement enforceable as a general matter and, more specifically, as against a claim of unconscionability?

OPINION   SPENCER, J., writing for the California Court of Appeal:

[*Editor's note:* The court began by considering whether any general release, regardless of terms, was valid. Relying on *Tunkl v. Regents of the University of California*,[13] the court held that an exculpatory provision may stand only if it does not involve "the public interest."]

. . . [T]he "General Release" agreement used here was printed legibly, contained adequate, clear and explicit exculpatory language and indicated defendants were to be absolved from the consequences of their own negligence. Furthermore, it did not involve the public interest: defendants' business was not generally thought to be suitable for public regulation; defendants did not perform a service of great importance to the public, and the business was not a matter of practical necessity for members of the public; and defendants' customers did not place their persons under defendants' control.

. . . .

[The court then addressed the plaintiff's contention that the general release was unconscionable.] Turning to the procedural element of unconscionability, the first question is whether the

CONTINUED

---

13. 383 P.2d 441 (Cal. 1963).

"General Release" agreement was oppressive, whether there was "an inequality in bargaining power which result[ed] in no real negotiation and 'an absence of meaningful choice.'"[14] The record shows there was no real negotiation; the "General Release agreement was preprinted and all users of Indian Dunes Park were required to sign it before using the park. However, the record does not show plaintiff had no meaningful choice in deciding to sign the agreement.... There is no evidence plaintiff could not have ridden his motorcycle elsewhere without the constraints imposed upon him by defendant.

The next question is whether plaintiff was surprised by supposedly agreed-upon terms hidden within a printed form drafted by defendants. The entire release agreement was printed at the top of the form signed by plaintiff. Warnings as to the dangers of motorcycling, the rider's assumption of the risk and the release and waiver of all liability stood out and the exculpatory provisions of the agreement were clearly set forth. Thus, the agreement was not procedurally unconscionable.

In examining the issue of substantive unconscionability, one question to be asked is whether the agreement was one-sided and, if so, whether the one-sidedness was justified. A further question is whether the agreement reallocated the risks of the bargain in an objectively unreasonable or unexpected manner. Risk reallocation which will be subjected to special scrutiny is that in which the risk shifted to a party is one that only the other party can avoid. Clearly, the agreement here was one-sided; all of the risk was reallocated to the Park's user, plaintiff. As previously discussed, the risk reallocation was not unexpected; the agreement clearly indicated the user assumed all risk of his use of the Park's facilities.

Was the risk reallocation objectively unreasonable? One signing the agreements warrants he knows "the present condition [of the Park and] that said condition may become more hazardous and dangerous during the time [he is] upon said premises." The agreement warned the user motorcycling is dangerous; implicit in the knowledge of the danger of motorcycling "is the knowledge that riding over rough, uneven terrain in an outdoor park poses a risk of injury from a fall" or other accident.[15] Moreover, to a certain extent, the risk of injury is conditioned upon the user's skill and experience as a motorcycle rider, factors over which the Park's owners and operators have no control. In view of the foregoing, the risk reallocation was not unreasonable and the "General Release" agreement was not substantively unconscionable.

RESULT The appeals court upheld the general release and affirmed the trial court's grant of summary judgment for the defendant, Indian Dunes.

COMMENTS It would appear that the court would limit the use of a general release in a county hospital. Would it matter if the hospital was private?

CRITICAL THINKING QUESTIONS

1. Would the result in this case have been different if the plaintiff had been thrown from his bike after riding into a barbed-wire fence not visible from the hill he had just crested? What if there had been a big hole on the other side of the hill?

2. What would the court consider a practical necessity for members of the public? A bus? A cosmetic surgery clinic? A public park for camping that charges a small fee?

14. A & M Produce Co. v. FMC Corp., 186 Cal. Rptr. 114 (Cal. Ct. App. 1982).
15. Coates v. Newhall Land & Farming, Inc., 236 Cal. Rptr. 181 (Cal. Ct. App. 1987).

© Cengage Learning 2013

GENUINENESS OF ASSENT

Even a contract that meets all the requirements of validity (agreement, consideration, capacity, and legality) may not be enforceable if there was no true "meeting of the minds" between the two parties. In other words, a court will refuse to enforce a contract if it feels one or both of the parties did not genuinely assent to its terms. The discussion below examines a variety of problems that could prevent a true meeting of the minds, including fraud, duress, ambiguity, and mistake.

Fraud

A contract is voidable if it is tainted with fraud. There are two types of fraud: fraud in the factum and fraud in the inducement. *Fraud in the factum* occurs when, because of a *misrepresentation,* or untrue statement of material fact, one party does not understand that he or she is entering into a contract or does not understand one or more essential terms of the contract. For example, if a person were given a deed to sign for the transfer of real property, after being told that the document was an employment agreement, the deed could be voided by the defrauded party.

The second type of fraud, *fraud in the inducement,* occurs when a party makes a false statement to persuade the other party to enter into an agreement. If a jeweler tells a customer that the stone in a ring is a diamond when the jeweler knows it is zirconium, the purchaser would have the right to rescind, or cancel, the agreement to purchase the ring based on fraud in the inducement. A contract is not voidable due to fraudulent misrepresentation, unless the misrepresentation was material to the bargain and was reasonably relied on by the party seeking to void the contract.

Fraud in the inducement also occurs when a party has a duty to disclose information to the other party but fails to do so. The duty to disclose often arises out of a special relationship between the parties (that is, a fiduciary relationship), such as between an officer and a corporation or between a trustee and a beneficiary. For example, a partner who knows the true value of a piece of property cannot sell it to a fellow partner without disclosing the true value. Parties engaged in arm's-length transactions cannot affirmatively misrepresent a fact, but as a general rule, they do not have a duty to disclose every fact that might be material to the other party.

Promissory fraud occurs when one party makes a promise without any intention of carrying it out. This is a misrepresentation of intent, rather than a misrepresentation of fact. Because a promise to do something necessarily implies the intention to perform, when a promise is made without such an intention, there is an implied misrepresentation of fact that can give the other party the right to rescind the contract. Promissory fraud is a tort as well as a defense to a contract action, and punitive damages may be available if the injured party can prove that the other party acted with malice.

Duress

A contract is voidable if one party was forced to enter into it through fear created by threats. Thus, inducing someone to sign a contract by physical threat, blackmail, or extortion is *duress*. Duress is present only if the threatened act is wrongful or illegal. Therefore, more subtle forms of pressure, such as an implied threat that at-will employees will lose their jobs unless they sign agreements waiving certain rights to employee benefits, do not constitute duress.

Historically, economic duress was usually not enough to invalidate a contract. Early common law provided that a contract could be voided only if the party claiming duress could show that the agreement was entered into for fear of loss of life or limb, mayhem, or imprisonment. Today, however, courts are willing to set aside contracts on the basis of economic duress when (1) the party alleging economic duress involuntarily accepted the terms of another, (2) the circumstances permitted no other alternative, and (3) the circumstances resulted from the other party's wrongful and oppressive conduct. For example, a court found economic duress when a company deliberately withheld payment of an acknowledged debt of $260,000, knowing that the other party had no choice but to accept its offer of $97,500 in settlement of the debt because of that party's own pressing debts.[16]

Under the related doctrine of *undue influence,* a court may invalidate an agreement if one party exercised improper persuasion on the other that made genuine assent impossible. Improper persuasion may result from such factors as constant pressure, a need for the victim to act quickly, unavailability of independent advice, or the weakness or infirmity of the victim. For example, if an invalid living alone, with few contacts with the outside world and dependent on a caregiver, agreed to sell her house to the caregiver at a bargain price, a court might set aside that agreement based on undue influence.

Ambiguity

Misunderstandings may arise from ambiguous language in a contract or from a mistake as to the facts. If the terms of a contract are subject to differing interpretations, some courts will construe the ambiguity against the party who drafted the agreement. More often, courts will apply the following rule: The party who would be adversely affected by a particular interpretation can void the contract when (1) both interpretations are reasonable and (2) the parties either both knew or both did not know of the different interpretations. If only one party knew or had reason to know of the other's interpretation, the court will find for the party who did not know or did not have reason to know of the difference.

In a case involving Mark Suwyn, an executive vice president of International Paper Company (the world's largest paper company), a federal court refused to enforce a noncompete agreement to prevent Suwyn from joining Louisiana-Pacific, a producer of wood products.[17] Suwyn had signed a broad covenant not to compete with International Paper after allegedly being assured by International Paper's chairman and CEO that the

---

16. Totem Marine Tug & Barge, Inc. v. Alyeska Pipeline Serv. Co., 584 P.2d 15 (Alaska 1978).

17. William M. Carley, *CEO Gets Hard Lesson in How Not to Keep His Top Lieutenants,* WALL ST. J., Feb. 11, 1998, at A1.

covenant was aimed at preventing Suwyn from going to one of the big paper companies. Suwyn had attached to the signed agreement a note indicating that it was meant to prevent him from joining a major paper company, such as Georgia-Pacific, Champion, or Weyerhaeuser. Because Louisiana-Pacific did not make paper and was not on the list, Suwyn argued that he was free to join the company. International Paper countered that the noncompete agreement included wood products, such as plywood and lumber, that both companies produced. The judge found there was no contract: Suwyn and International Paper had such different meanings in mind that there had been no real agreement on the scope of the noncompete.

Mistake of Fact

Like a misunderstanding due to ambiguity, a *mistake of fact* by both parties can make a contract voidable. As a general rule, a unilateral mistake of fact by one party does not make a contract voidable. This rule has two narrow exceptions, however. A mistaken party may void a contract when either (1) the mistaken party has made an unintentional mistake in preparing its offer that makes the offer too good to be true or (2) the nonmistaken party is guilty of blameworthy conduct, such as fraud or misrepresentation.

A court's willingness to undo a contract based on a mistaken assumption of fact depends heavily on the particular circumstances. The court will look at three factors to determine if a mistake has been made: (1) the substantiality of the mistake, (2) whether the risks were allocated, and (3) timing.

Substantiality of the Mistake

A court is more likely to void the contract when the mistake has a material effect on one of the parties. For example, in the classic case *Raffles v. Wichelhaus*,[18] two parties had signed a contract in which Wichelhaus agreed to buy 125 bales of cotton to be brought by Raffles from India on a ship named *Peerless*. Unbeknown to both parties, there were two ships named *Peerless*, both sailing out of Bombay during the same year. Raffles meant the *Peerless* that was sailing in December, and Wichelhaus meant the *Peerless* that was sailing in October. When the cotton arrived on the later ship, Wichelhaus refused to complete the purchase. Raffles then sued for breach of contract. The English court held that the contract was voidable due to the mutual mistake of fact. The court described the situation as one of "latent ambiguity" and declared that there was no meeting of the minds and therefore no contract.

The three-month delay had made the cotton worthless to the buyer, and thus the mistake was substantial. If the delay had been only a few days, the court would probably have enforced the contract. On the other hand, even if the delay had been only a few days, if the buyer had planned to resell the cotton on the open market and the price of cotton had dropped sharply during that period, the mistake would probably have been substantial enough to make the contract voidable.

Allocation of the Risks

If one party accepts a risk, then that party must bear the consequences even if it is doubtful that the risk will materialize. If the parties have not expressly allocated a risk, a court will sometimes place the risk on the party who had access to the most information. In other cases, the court might impose the risk on the party better able to bear it.

Timing

The party alleging a mistake of fact must give prompt notice when the mistake is discovered. If too much time passes before the other party is notified, undoing the contract might create more problems than letting it stand.

Mistake of Judgment

A *mistake of judgment* occurs when the parties make an erroneous assessment about some aspect of what is bargained for. For example, in a futures contract a seller agrees to sell a buyer a crop of sugar in three months at a price of fifty cents per pound. The seller is betting that the market price in three months will be less than fifty cents. The buyer is betting that the market price will be higher. One of them will be mistaken, but the futures contract will still be valid. This is a mistake of judgment. Such a mistake is not a valid defense to enforcement of the contract.

The line between judgment and fact can sometimes be unclear. In *CTA, Inc. v. United States*,[19] a company that entered into a contract to provide technical support services to the government included labor rates for its workers that were substantially lower than the market rates. After realizing this discrepancy, the company argued that it had made a mistake in the numbers contained in the labor rates set forth in its bid. The court rejected this argument and found that the company had made an error in business judgment, not a mistake of fact. Had the labor rates been obviously in error, the court would probably have found a mistake of fact justifying withdrawal of the bid.

Another example is the classic case of *Sherwood v. Walker*.[20] A seller agreed to sell a barren cow for a low price, but before the sale closed, the seller discovered the cow was pregnant and therefore was worth about ten times the agreed-on price. As a result, the seller refused to proceed with the sale, and the buyer sued for breach of contract. The Michigan Supreme Court held that the contract was based on a mutual mistake of fact that made the contract unenforceable. The court reasoned:

---

18. (1864) 159 Eng. Rep. 375 (Exch.).

19. 44 Fed. Cl. 684 (Fed. 1999).
20. 33 N.W. 919 (Mich. 1887).

If there is a difference or misapprehension as to the substance of the thing bargained for; if the thing actually delivered or received is different in substance from the thing bargained for, and intended to be sold, then there is no contract . . . A barren cow is substantially a different creature than a breeding one.

A dissenting judge argued that the case involved a mistake in judgment. The buyer had believed the cow could be made to breed, in spite of the seller's statements to the contrary, and the seller disagreed. As the majority and dissenting opinions in this case demonstrate, different judges may reach different conclusions as to whether a mistake is one of fact or judgment.

Much of contract law comes down to the expectations of the parties involved. In the cow case, the seller did not believe the cow was fertile. The buyer did not make known his secret belief that the cow could be made to breed. From the seller's point of view, the transaction was for a barren cow with no chance of breeding, but the buyer did not see the transaction that way. The case might have come out differently if the buyer had explicitly said to the seller, "I know you believe the cow is barren, but I believe she can be made to breed, and I'm willing to take the chance in buying her."

Although disclosing all expectations may make for firm contracts, it may not be the most effective negotiating technique. For example, had the buyer convinced the seller that the cow might be fertile, the seller would probably have demanded a higher price. One of the challenges of business is balancing the slim (but expensive) chances of litigation against the desire to capture value not apparent to the other party.

STATUTE OF FRAUDS

Although most oral contracts are enforceable, many states have a statute, called the *statute of frauds*, which requires certain types of contracts to be evidenced by some form of written communication. If a contract covered by the statute of frauds is oral, it is still valid, but the courts will not enforce the contract if the statute of frauds is raised as a defense. Therefore, if neither party raises the issue, the contract will be enforced. Similarly, even if the party seeking to enforce the contract has not signed anything, it can still enforce the contract against a party who has signed a writing embodying the essential terms of the deal.

There are four traditional justifications for requiring certain contracts to be evidenced by writing. First, requiring a written document avoids fraudulent claims that an oral contract was made. Second, the existence of a written document avoids false claims as to the terms of the contract. Third, the statute of frauds encourages persons to put their agreements in writing, thereby reducing the risk of future misunderstandings. Fourth, the writing required

by the statute has the psychological effect of reinforcing the importance of the parties' decision to enter into a contract.

Transactions Subject to the Statute of Frauds

Contracts that must be evidenced by some writing include (1) a contract for the transfer of any interest in real property (such as a deed, lease, or option to buy), (2) a promise to pay the debt of another person, (3) an agreement that by its terms cannot be performed within a year, and (4) a *prenuptial agreement* (that is, an agreement entered into before marriage that sets forth the manner in which the parties' assets will be distributed and the support to which each party will be entitled in the event of divorce).

The statute of frauds issue that arises most often in litigation is whether a contract can by its terms be performed within one year. If it cannot—that is, if the contract is longer than one year in duration—then it must be put in writing to be enforceable.

A typical "performed within one year" case involves an oral promise of "lifetime employment." For example, in *McInerney v. Charter Golf, Inc.*,[21] a golf-apparel sales representative received an offer to join a rival company, which promised to pay him an 8% commission. When notified of this offer, his current employer orally promised to guarantee the sales rep a 10% commission "for the remainder of his life," subject to discharge only for dishonesty or disability. The sales rep accepted this offer and passed up the rival's offer. When he was fired three years later, he sued for breach of contract.

The Illinois Supreme Court ruled that a lifetime employment contract is intended to be permanent. It inherently anticipates a relationship of long duration—certainly longer than one year. Thus, the court found that the contract was subject to the statute of frauds and accordingly unenforceable because it was not in writing.

Other courts have taken a contrasting approach and construe the words "cannot be performed" to mean "not capable of being performed within one year." Because, theoretically, an employee can die at any time, these courts reason that lifetime employment contracts are *capable* of being performed within one year. As a result, they deem such contracts to be outside the scope of the statute of frauds and valid even if not in writing.

The statute of frauds does not require the agreement to be embodied in a formal, legal-looking document. An agreement can be represented by an exchange of letters that refer to each other, even if no single letter is sufficient to reflect all essential terms. Details or particulars can be omitted; only the essential terms must be stated. A writing may satisfy the statute of frauds even if the party never delivers or communicates it to the other party. What

---

21. 680 N.E.2d 1347 (Ill. 1997).

is essential depends on the agreement, its context, and the subsequent conduct of the parties. Under the *equal dignities rule,* if an agent acts on behalf of another (the principal) in signing an agreement of the type that must, under the statute of frauds, be in writing, the authority of the agent to act on behalf of the principal must also be in writing. Thus, an individual signs a written *power of attorney* to authorize a person, called an attorney-in-fact (who need not be a lawyer), to sign documents on the individual's behalf. Corporations authorize officers to sign through a combination of written authority specified in the bylaws of the corporation and the minutes of the governing body, the board of directors.

If there is clear evidence that a person made an oral promise, a court will often strain to recharacterize the nature of the agreement so that it does not come within the statute of frauds.[22] One cannot count on such leniency, however, so the prudent manager will put any agreements that might fall within the statute of frauds in writing. As the U.S. Court of Appeals for the Seventh Circuit stated:

> It is astounding in this day and age to find it necessary to repeat [the] admonition [to "get it in writing"], but no less so than to find a sophisticated party willing to leverage an agreement involving multiple years and millions of dollars solely on the enforceability of a simple handshake.[23]

THE PAROL EVIDENCE RULE

Under the *parol evidence rule,* when there is an unambiguous written contract that the parties intended would encompass their entire agreement, parol (that is, oral) evidence of prior or contemporaneous statements is inadmissible in court and cannot be used to interpret, vary, or add to the terms of the written contract. A court usually will not look beyond the "four corners" of the document to discern the intentions of the parties.

For example, in *White v. Security Pacific Financial Services, Inc.,*[24] the borrower plaintiffs tried to introduce evidence that the lender defendant had fraudulently induced them to execute a promissory note by assuring them that its sole recourse upon default would be under a deed of trust that collateralized the loan. The court found that this evidence could not be admitted because it contradicted the parties' written agreement.

Clarifying Ambiguous Language

The parol evidence rule does not prohibit the parties from presenting evidence to show what the contract means. Thus, courts are willing to look beyond the written agreement if its language is ambiguous. For example, if the contract stated that a party was to purchase a carload of tomatoes, the parol evidence rule would not be violated if the party presented evidence showing that "carload" in the relevant commercial setting means a train carload, not a Chevy truckload. This evidence merely explains the ambiguous term "carload"; it does not vary the term. Parol evidence is also admissible to show mistake, fraud, or duress.

CHANGED CIRCUMSTANCES

Contracts often contain provisions for a variety of future events so that the parties involved can allocate the risks of different outcomes. It is not always possible to anticipate every occurrence, however. Three theories are used to address this situation: impossibility, impracticability, and frustration of purpose.

Impossibility

Suppose that Antonio signs a contract to sell Trevor computer chips of a special type manufactured only in Antonio's factory. Before he can manufacture the computer chips, however, the factory burns down through no fault of Antonio's, making it impossible for him to perform the contract. Assume that the destruction of Antonio's factory is a changed circumstance that neither party contemplated when they made the contract.

Trevor is not entitled to money damages for Antonio's nonperformance because Antonio is discharged from his obligations due to *impossibility.* If, however, the computer chips could be manufactured in another factory, Antonio would have an obligation to have them manufactured there after his factory burned down. This would be the case even if having the chips manufactured at the other facility would cost Antonio more money.

Impracticability

Closely related to impossibility is the concept of *impracticability,* where performance is possible but commercially impractical. As a rule, impracticability is difficult to prove.

Impracticability was invoked by several shipping companies in 1967 when political turmoil in the Middle East gave rise to the temporary closing of the Suez Canal. A number of merchant ships had to detour around the Cape of Good Hope at the southern tip of Africa. The detour increased shipping costs so much that the shipping companies suffered substantial losses. Several of these companies sued to nullify the contracts they had entered into before

---

22. *See, e.g.,* Wilson Floors Co. v. Sciota Park, Ltd., 377 N.E.2d 514 (Ohio 1978) (oral promise by construction lender to pay subcontractor if he returned to work served lender's own pecuniary interest, so the agreement did not have to be in writing to be enforceable).

23. Trustmark Ins. Co. v. Gen. & Cologne Life Re of Am., 424 F.3d 542, 544 (7th Cir. 2005).

24. No. 5079754 (Cal. July 21, 1999), *cert. denied,* 528 U.S. 1160 (2000).

the Suez Canal was closed. They claimed performance was impractical and sought to recover the full costs of sailing the longer route around the Cape of Good Hope. In only one case did the court grant relief. The other courts found that the added costs were not so great as to make performance impracticable. (Chapter 8 addresses impracticability in contracts for the sale of goods.)

Frustration of Purpose

Frustration of purpose occurs when performance is possible, but changed circumstances have made the contract useless to one or both of the parties. A famous example is the King Edward VII coronation case[25] in which Henry contracted to rent a room in London from Krell for the acknowledged purpose of viewing King Edward VII's coronation procession. Krell had advertised the room as one that would be good for viewing the procession. When the King became ill with appendicitis and the coronation was postponed, Henry refused to pay for the apartment. Krell then sued. The English court ruled that Henry did not have to pay because the entire reason for the contract had been "frustrated."

Note that performance of the contract was not impossible: Henry could still have rented the room. The outcome of the case would have been different if the room had not been rented for the express purpose of viewing the procession. In that case, Krell would have won because the purpose of the contract would have been for just the rental of the room, not for the viewing of the procession.

The contract defense of frustration requires that (1) the expressed purpose in making the contract is frustrated, (2) without the defendant's fault, (3) by the occurrence of an event, the nonoccurrence of which was a basic assumption on which the contract was made. The frustration defense is unavailable if the defendant helped cause the frustrating event or if the parties were aware of the possibility of the frustrating event when they entered into the contract.

Contracts with the Government and the Sovereign Acts Doctrine

When a party's performance is made illegal or impossible because of a new law, performance of the contract is usually discharged, and damages are not awarded. But what happens when a party contracts with the government, and the government then promulgates a new law that makes its own performance impossible? If it no longer wishes to be bound by a contract, can the government discharge its obligations by changing the law to make performance illegal?

According to the *sovereign acts doctrine*, the government generally cannot be held liable for breach of contract due to legislative or executive acts. Because one Congress

cannot bind a later Congress, the general rule is that subsequent acts of the government can discharge the government's preexisting contractual obligations.

This doctrine has limits, however. If Congress passes legislation deliberately targeting its existing contractual obligation, the defense otherwise provided by the sovereign acts doctrine is unavailable.[26] The government is not prevented from changing the law, but it must pay damages for its legislatively chosen breach. On the other hand, if a new law of general application indirectly affects a government contract, making the government's performance impossible, the sovereign acts doctrine will protect the government in a subsequent suit for breach of contract.

CONTRACT MODIFICATION

Traditional contract law does not allow a contract modification that changes the obligations of only one party, because no consideration has been given by the other party. Over time, lawyers have developed a variety of techniques to meet the formal requirements of consideration. One technique is *novation*, by which a new party is substituted for one of the old parties, and a new contract is written (with the consent of all old and new parties) to effect the desired change. Another technique is formal change, where the consideration for the desired modification is a formal but meaningless change, such as making the payment in cash rather than with a bank check. Similarly, if both parties agree to terminate the contract and enter into a new one, the new contract will be valid.

DISCHARGE OF CONTRACT

Once a manager has entered into a legally enforceable contract, his or her next concern is determining when the contractual obligations have been satisfied or terminated, that is, *discharged*. Most commonly, discharge of contracts occurs when both parties have fully performed their obligations to one another. But what happens when one party performs and the other does not? Or when one party performs only some of its obligations under the contract? These questions are answered under the rules on discharging contracts.

If one party fails to perform a contract according to its essential terms, such as by not performing a service after receiving payment, that party has *materially breached* the contract. Any material breach of a contract discharges the nonbreaching party from its obligations and provides grounds to sue for damages. A breach is minor if the essential terms and purpose of the contract have been fulfilled. In the case of a minor breach, the nonbreaching party must still perform its contractual obligations, but it may

25. Krell v. Henry, [1903] 2 K.B. 740 (C.A.).

26. United States v. Winstar Corp., 518 U.S. 839 (1996).

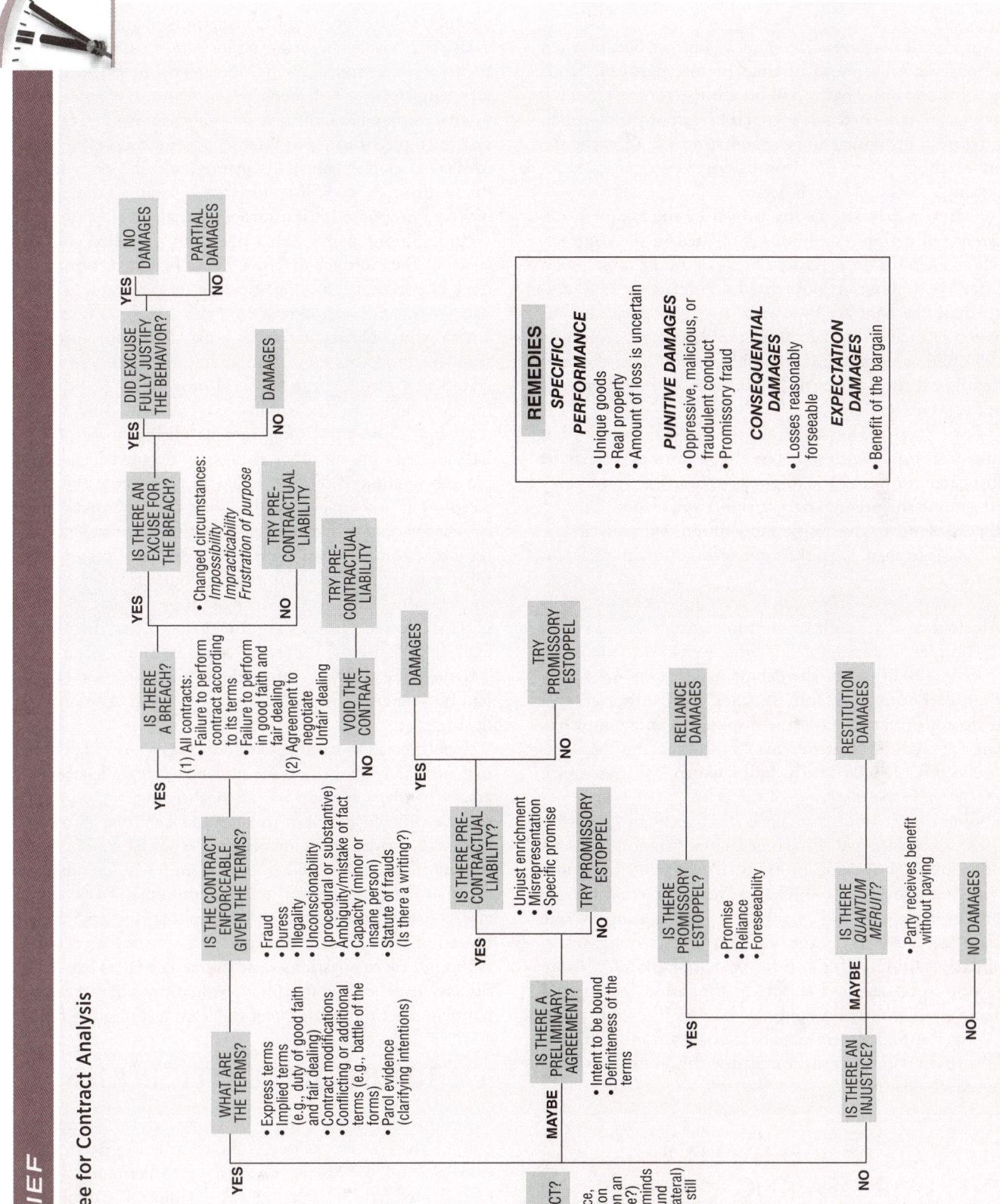

IN BRIEF

Decision Tree for Contract Analysis

SOURCE: This decision tree was prepared by Sheila Bonini with information and input from Constance E. Bagley. Used by permission.

suspend performance until the breach is cured or sue for damages.

An *anticipatory repudiation* of a contract occurs when one party knows ahead of time (before performance is due) that the other party will breach the contract. Such a repudiation is treated as a material breach of the contract. By treating an anticipatory repudiation as a breach, the nonbreaching party can avoid having to wait to take action until an actual breach occurs.

Contracts may also be discharged by the failure or occurrence of certain conditions stipulated in the contract, such as a condition precedent or a condition subsequent, as discussed above. If both parties agree, they may also terminate the contract by *mutual rescission*. A mutual rescission is itself a type of contract and, as such, requires a valid offer, acceptance, and consideration. Often the consideration is the agreement by both parties not to enforce their legal obligations.

If one party prefers to retain the original contract but wants to contract with someone else, a third party may be substituted for one of the original parties. The third party will assume the original party's rights and responsibilities. All parties must agree to the substitution. Formally, a new contract is formed, with the same terms but with different parties.

An *accord and satisfaction* is any agreement to accept performance that is different from what is called for in the contract. For example, assume a creditor believes he is owed $100,000, but the debtor believes she owes only $75,000. An *accord* is formed when the creditor accepts the debtor's offer to settle the dispute for an amount less than the creditor claims is due (say, by cashing the debtor's check for $80,000 with "Full Payment" written on it). *Satisfaction* is the discharge of the debt.

Sometimes a valid contract is discharged by operation of law. Certain types of changed circumstances, such as impossibility, impracticability, or frustration of purpose (described above), may discharge the contractual obligations of both parties. A bankruptcy proceeding by one party can also discharge its contractual obligations. Similarly, failing to file suit for breach of contract before the time specified in a statute of limitations has passed effectively discharges a contract, because the courts will no longer enforce it. In many states, an action for breach of a written contract must be filed within four years after the breach occurs.

DUTY OF GOOD FAITH AND FAIR DEALING

Every contract contains an implied covenant of good faith and fair dealing in its performance that imposes on each party a duty not to do anything that will deprive the other party of the benefits of the agreement. One court defined a lack of good faith as "some type of affirmative action

consisting of at least . . . a design to mislead or to deceive another."[27] The covenant has been implied and enforced in a variety of contexts, including insurance contracts, agreements to make mutual wills, agreements to sell real property, employment agreements, and leases. (Its application in the employment context is discussed in Chapter 12.) For example, if an insurance company refuses an offer to settle a claim against the insured within policy limits, many jurisdictions will require the insurance company to pay whatever amount is awarded at trial.

In addition, claims that a party has complied with the letter of the contract may not be sufficient to satisfy the duty of good faith and fair dealing. For example, Disney had entered into an agreement with Marsu B.V., pursuant to which Disney agreed to create half-hour animated films for broadcast on television and to coordinate a merchandising campaign that would provide broad exposure for "Marsupilami," a cartoon character owned by Marsu. Although Disney did some merchandising, its effort was halfhearted; among other things, it assigned junior employees to the project and failed to coordinate the campaign with the television broadcast. A memo written by Disney stated that "we have neither the time nor the resources to do Marsu right" and "we have lots of other Disney priorities, more important both financially and strategically." The U.S. Court of Appeals for the Ninth Circuit rejected Disney's argument that it had fulfilled its express obligations under the terms of the contract and affirmed the district court's determination that Disney had breached the implied covenant of good faith and fair dealing.[28]

The precise meanings of "good faith" and "fair dealing" are the subject of extended debate among legal scholars. What was considered fair dealing twenty years ago may be considered unfair today, and vice versa. Two commonly used rules of thumb offer some guidance. Managers should ask themselves whether an action would embarrass them or their company if it became public. They should also consider whether they would follow the same course of action if they were dealing with a friend or relative. Although these questions raise moral as well as legal considerations, they are useful in evaluating whether a contemplated action would meet the legal test of good faith.

THIRD-PARTY BENEFICIARIES

A person who is not a party to a contract can sometimes enforce the contract between the contracting parties. For example, suppose Sheila agrees to sell to Fernando a piece of real property in exchange for a $100,000 payment by Fernando to Jack. Fernando is the promisor, Sheila is the promisee, and Jack is the *third-party beneficiary*, or

---

27. Bunge Corp. v. Recker, 519 F.2d 449, 452 (8th Cir. 1975).
28. Marsu B.V. v. Walt Disney Co., 185 F.3d 932 (9th Cir. 1999).

intended beneficiary. A person is not a third-party beneficiary with legal rights to enforce the contract unless the contracting parties intended to benefit that party.

Creditor Beneficiary

If the promisee entered into the contract to discharge a duty he or she owed to the third party, then the third party is a *creditor beneficiary* and has the right to enforce the contract between the promisor and promisee. The third party must prove, however, that the promisee intended the contract to satisfy his or her obligation to the third party. For example, if Sheila owes Jack $100,000 and she and Fernando agree that she will sell land to Fernando to pay off that debt, Jack has enforceable rights under the contract as a creditor beneficiary. If the contract is not carried out, Jack can sue Fernando directly to compel performance. Jack also has the option of suing Sheila for the $100,000 she owes him.

Donee Beneficiary

A *donee beneficiary* is created when the promisee does not owe an obligation to the third party, but rather wishes to confer a gift. For example, if Sheila agreed to sell her property to Fernando for $100,000 in order to make a $100,000 gift to Jack, Jack would be a donee beneficiary and could enforce the contract in most jurisdictions, but only against Fernando. Some jurisdictions, such as New York, require a family relationship between the donee beneficiary and the promisee before allowing the beneficiary to sue under the contract.

REMEDIES

If one party breaches a contract, the other is entitled to monetary damages or, in some instances, a court order requiring performance. The purpose of damages is to put the plaintiff in the position it would have been in had the contract been performed. A secondary purpose is to discourage breaches of contract. Because the U.S. legal system recognizes that sometimes it is economically efficient to breach a contract, courts generally will not allow punitive damages, traditionally a tort remedy, in contract cases. However, courts have developed several exceptions that allow for the award of punitive damages in cases involving (1) a breach of a promise to marry; (2) a breach of a fiduciary duty; or (3) a breach of a contract, the performance of which involves a public duty or is regulated by public authorities, such as contracts involving public utilities, common carriers, or insurance companies.

Over the years the courts have developed a variety of methods to measure appropriate monetary damages in contract cases. The three standard measures are (1) expectation, (2) reliance, and (3) restitution. The interest to be compensated determines which of these measures

is most appropriate in a particular case. These measures may seem similar, but the resulting damages awards can be very different, as discussed below. In certain situations, a court may also order the equitable remedies of specific performance or injunctive relief.

Expectation Damages

Expectation damages give the plaintiff the benefit of its bargain, putting the plaintiff in the cash position it would have been in if the contract had been fulfilled. The general formula for expectation damages is Expectation Damages = Compensatory Damages + Consequential Damages + Incidental Damages − Avoidable Losses.

Compensatory Damages

Compensatory damages are the amount necessary to make up for the economic loss caused by the breach of contract. For example, suppose an independent contractor agrees to work for Peabody Manufacturing Company for $15 per hour for one week. When the time comes to start work, the contractor reneges. Peabody can find another independent contractor elsewhere, but the market price is now $20 per hour. Instead of spending $600 for a forty-hour workweek, Peabody must now pay $800. Peabody's compensatory damages are the difference between the two expenditures, or $200.

Consequential Damages

In addition to damages that compensate for the breach itself, the plaintiff is entitled to *consequential damages*, that is, compensation for losses that occur as a foreseeable result of the breach. For example, suppose Peabody contracts with another person at $20 per hour, but the new contractor cannot start working immediately. If the two-week delay causes Peabody to be late in delivering its product to one of its customers, any late fees that Peabody must pay will also be included in the consequential damages.

Two principles operate to limit consequential damages: (1) the damages must be reasonably foreseeable and (2) they must be reasonably certain.

Foreseeability Consequential damages will be awarded only if the breaching party knew, or should have known, that the loss would result from a breach of the contract.

For example, in the classic case *Hadley v. Baxendale*,[29] the plaintiff was a mill owner who sent a broken crankshaft by carrier to be repaired. Because this was the only crankshaft the mill owned, the mill was completely shut down until the carrier returned with the repaired crankshaft. When the carrier did not deliver the shaft as quickly as promised, the mill owner sued the carrier for profits lost during the time the mill was closed. The English appellate court observed that most mills had more than one

---

29. (1854) 156 Eng. Rep. 145.

crankshaft, so the carrier had no way of knowing that nondelivery of the crankshaft would result in the closure of the mill. As a result, the court did not award damages for lost profits: they were neither reasonably foreseeable nor a natural consequence of the carrier's breach.

Uncertainty of Damages   Sometimes it is not possible to know what the benefit of the bargain would have been. For example, Publisher & Sons signs a contract to publish Rachel Author's first book. Publisher later decides not to publish the book. To what damages is Rachel entitled? The benefit of her bargain would be the royalties from a published book, but the parties have no way to measure how much those royalties would have been. Because Rachel has the burden of proving the amount of her loss, she may collect very little in damages.

Similarly, new businesses have no record of past profits by which to estimate the loss caused by a breach. Traditionally, this prevented start-ups from collecting anything for lost profits. Today, however, with more sophisticated methods for projecting future profits, new businesses are having more success recovering damages.

Incidental Damages

Incidental damages are the lesser and relatively minor damages that a nonbreaching party incurs. Examples of incidental damages include the charges, expenses, and commissions incurred in stopping delivery; the cost of the transportation, care, and custody of goods after a buyer's default; and the expenses incurred in connection with the return or subsequent disposition of goods that are the subject of a contract.

Mitigation of Damages

The nonbreaching party has a duty to use reasonable efforts to *mitigate,* or lessen, the amount of damages that flow from the breach. As a general rule, the nonbreaching party cannot recover damages that it could have reasonably avoided. This gives the nonbreaching party an incentive to make the best of a bad situation.

For example, suppose Arjay Automotive and Hazmat, a hazardous-waste collection company, enter into a contract whereby Hazmat agrees to pick up Arjay's hazardous waste for a fee of $500 per pickup. If Hazmat fails to pick up the hazardous waste, Arjay should *cover*—find another hazardous-waste collection company at the current market price, say, $625 per pickup, at the time of the breach. Arjay will still be entitled to compensatory damages, measured by the difference between the market price at the time it learned of the breach ($625 per pickup) and the contract price ($500 per pickup), plus any consequential damages, such as extra storage fees, late fees, and incidental damages incurred in finding a substitute hazardous-waste collection company.

If Arjay elects not to cover, it is limited to compensatory damages (as measured above) and cannot recover any

consequential damages that could have been prevented by covering, such as storage fees from the date a substitute firm could have picked up the waste. If no cover is available, Arjay is entitled to foreseeable consequential damages resulting from the breach.

Additionally, Arjay must avoid compounding damages from the breach. If hazardous-waste collection services are available at both $625 and $650 per pickup and the quality is the same, then Arjay is required to purchase at the lower price. Thus, its expectation damages are limited to $125 per pickup. Any expenses incurred by Arjay in reasonably attempting to mitigate damages, such as the costs of finding another collection company, are also recoverable consequential damages, regardless of whether the efforts were successful.

From the seller's perspective, the duty to mitigate damages works similarly. For example, suppose Beta Software Company contracts to develop a customized program for Arturo Architects, LLC, a small architecture firm. Beta learns midway through the development process that Arturo plans to breach the contract. Beta should cover by finding another buyer for the software and then charge Arturo for the difference between the contract price and the resale price (compensatory damages), plus any consequential damages. If no other buyer is available, perhaps because the program is too customized, Beta should immediately stop its work and charge Arturo for expenses incurred plus the expected net profit.

Reliance Damages

Reliance damages compensate the nonbreaching party for any expenditures it made in reliance on the contract. Reliance damages are an alternative to expectation damages when it is not possible to determine the expectation damages. Reliance damages are also awarded in promissory estoppel cases, where expectation damages are generally not allowed. Instead of giving the plaintiff the benefit of the bargain, reliance damages return it to the position it was in before the contract was formed.

For example, a seller agrees to sell a buyer a heavy drill press. The buyer tells the seller that it has invested in renovation work to strengthen the floor where the drill press will be installed. The seller then sells the drill press to someone else. Reliance damages require the seller to reimburse the buyer for the renovation expenses.

Restitution and *Quantum Meruit*

Whereas reliance damages look at what the plaintiff has lost, *restitution* looks at what the other party has gained from the transaction. The usual measure of restitution is the amount it would cost the recipient of the benefit to buy that benefit elsewhere.

A court will order restitution under the doctrine of *quantum meruit* if one party has received a benefit for which it has not paid even though there was no contract between the parties. The obligation to give restitution is implied as a matter of law. For example, suppose that an entrepreneur asks an advertising agency to place an advertisement. The advertising agency contracts with an industry publication to place the advertisement but fails to pay for it. Under the doctrine of *quantum meruit*, the agency's default on payment renders the entrepreneur liable to the publication for the value of the benefit the entrepreneur received (the advertisement). The entrepreneur must pay the publication even though there was no contract between the entrepreneur and the publication.

A court may also order restitution in cases where (1) a plaintiff seeks to rescind, or cancel, a contract that it entered into based on fraud or mutual mistake, or (2) the defendant has breached an executory contract (i.e., a contract under which the parties have continuing obligations to perform). Rescission terminates the parties' rights under the contract, and restitution restores the parties to the position they were in prior to entering the contract by requiring them to return any benefits they received under the contract.

Liquidated Damages

The parties to a contract may include a clause that specifies the amount of money to be paid if one of them should later breach the agreement. Such *liquidated damages* clauses are frequently used in real estate and construction contracts. Because courts will not enforce penalties in contract cases, clauses that provide for damages that are substantially higher than the losses will not be enforced. The amount of the liquidated damages should be the parties' best estimate of what the expectation damages would be.

Specific Performance and Injunctive Relief

Instead of awarding monetary damages, a court may order the breaching party to complete the contract as promised. *Specific performance* is ordered only when (1) the goods are unique (for example, an antique car or a painting), (2) the subject of the contract is real property, or (3) the amount of the loss is so uncertain that there is no fair way to calculate damages.

Courts never force an employee to provide services under an employment contract because that would constitute involuntary servitude in violation of the Thirteenth Amendment to the U.S. Constitution. For example, if a CEO who has agreed to work for a corporation for five years walks out after three years, the court will not force her to continue her employment. The court may, however, issue an injunction barring her from working for someone else.

CONTRACTS RELATING TO MERGERS AND ACQUISITIONS

A corporation can acquire control of another corporation (the *target*) by merger, a sale of stock by the target's shareholders, or a sale of substantially all the assets of the target.[30] A *merger agreement* is an agreement between two companies to combine into a single entity. Mergers and sales of substantially all the assets generally cannot be completed until the transaction is approved by the shareholders of both the acquiring and the target company.

Mergers and acquisitions are usually highly negotiated transactions that are governed by detailed acquisition agreements containing *representations and warranties* (statements about the entity being sold and the buyer), *covenants* (promises to do or refrain from doing something), and conditions (events that must occur before either party has a duty to *close*, or consummate, the transaction, as well as events that will terminate a party's obligation to close). The seller's representations and warranties typically cover such matters as the proper organization of the entity as a corporation, the accuracy of its financial statements, title to its assets, the absence of undisclosed liabilities, the absence of undisclosed legal proceedings, and its compliance with all laws and contractual obligations by which it is bound. Seller covenants typically include promises (1) to conduct the business in the ordinary course until the closing date, (2) to refrain from entering into any new major contracts, and (3) to permit access to the business to enable the buyer to conduct due diligence.

Acquisition agreements in transactions involving private companies typically provide for indemnification by the seller for breaches of its representations, warranties, and covenants. The seller may also require the buyer to include indemnification provisions if the buyer is purchasing the target with shares of the buyer's stock. Public company acquisition agreements typically do not include indemnification clauses because collecting indemnification from numerous public shareholders would be virtually impossible. If, however, one or several shareholders own a controlling block, then they may be required to provide indemnification, at least up to the value of the consideration they receive in the sale.

The indemnification provisions often limit the seller's or the buyer's exposure to some percentage of the total purchase price. In some agreements, different ceilings apply to different types of liabilities. In addition, the provisions may stipulate that breaches of representations, warranties, or covenants must be material before indemnification will be available. For example, the parties might agree that a

---

30. Acquisitions are discussed in detail in Constance E. Bagley & Craig E. Dauchy, Entrepreneur's Guide to Business Law, 628–704 (4th ed. 2011).

claim must be worth at least $100,000 before the seller has an obligation to pay any damages to the buyer. If the parties decide to establish a dollar threshold, they must also decide whether the threshold should be a deductible amount or whether the indemnifying party should provide "dollar one" coverage. For example, under an agreement that uses the deductible approach, if the claim is $150,000 and the threshold is $100,000, the indemnifying party would be liable for only $50,000, the excess over $100,000. In contrast, if the agreement uses the dollar one coverage approach, the party would be liable for the full amount of $150,000.

The issue of time limits on indemnification obligations is frequently one of the most controversial negotiating points in an acquisition agreement. The indemnifying party usually wants a shorter period than the applicable statute of limitations, and many acquisition agreements will place some time limit on indemnification obligations. The seller typically argues that the buyer, as the owner and operator of the business, should discover any misstatements within a certain period of time. The buyer, however, often argues for longer time limits for tax claims, environmental claims, intellectual property claims, and capitalization matters, as these problems may not surface for years.

GLOBAL VIEW

Contracting with Foreign Entities

When entering into contracts with companies in other nations, it is important to remember that most non-English-speaking countries follow the civil law tradition—a system of jurisprudence that was originally used in the Roman Empire. Civil law countries rely primarily on civil codes, or statutes, rather than case-by-case common law to develop rules for behavior. In contrast, the law in the United States and England stems from a common law tradition.

Most civil law countries do not recognize certain common law contract principles. For example, many civil law countries do not require consideration to make a contract binding. In addition, although common law countries generally treat contracts with the government in the same way as contracts with private entities, civil law countries have different rules for private and public entities.

Remedies for nonperformance also differ. A U.S. court will enter an order for specific performance or injunctive relief only if it finds that damages would not be an adequate remedy. In contrast, civil law courts award specific performance in most contract cases.

In general, common law countries, such as the United Kingdom, do not recognize a common law duty to negotiate in good faith and thus do not impose liability for its breach. In contrast, civil law countries, including France, Germany, the Netherlands, and Japan, have been more willing to impose a good faith obligation during the negotiation of a contract.[31] In 1994, the International Institute for the Unification of Private Law (Unidroit) published its Principles of International Commercial Contracts (Unidroit Principles), which set forth general rules for international commercial contracts for services. The Unidroit Principles are used primarily in international arbitration. Unidroit Article 2.1.15(2) provides that one who

"breaks off negotiations in bad faith is liable for the losses caused to the other party." Like the American Law Institute's Restatements of the Law, the Unidroit Principles are not designed to be codified into statutes. As a result, in many international agreements, there may be an expectation that parties have a duty to negotiate in good faith, and they can be held liable if they fail to do so.

The Commission on European Contract law, better known as the Lando-Commission, has produced a draft version of a complete code of European Contract Law. Even though the Code has not yet been enacted, the parties to an international contract may adopt the Principles. If a dispute arises, a court or arbitrator will then apply the Principles instead of national rules of law. Although the parties are free to exclude or vary most of the Principles, certain provisions are considered to be of such importance as to be mandatory. These include the provisions (1) requiring each party to act from the outset of contract negotiations in accordance with good faith and fair dealing and (2) dealing with invalidity caused by mistake, fraud, threat, undue influence, and unfair contract terms.

Because of the differences in each country's laws regarding contract interpretation, performance, and remedies, it is generally appropriate for parties to a multinational contract to include a provision that specifies which country's laws will govern the contract (a *choice-of-law provision*). It may also be appropriate to include a provision that specifies which country's courts will have exclusive jurisdiction over any dispute involving the contract (a *choice-of-forum provision*). As explained in Chapter 3, courts will generally honor such provisions. Finally, many contracts involving parties located in different countries will include an agreement that any disputes will be arbitrated, rather than tried in court. Arbitration awards are enforceable in the more than 130 countries that have signed the United Nations Convention on Recognition and Enforcement of Foreign Arbitral Awards. These provisions are discussed in more detail in Chapter 24.

---

31. *See* D. James Wan Kim Min v. Mitsui Bussan K.K. (Tokyo High Ct. 1987), cited in YUKO YANAGIDA ET AL., LAW AND INVESTMENT IN JAPAN 223–29 (1994).

THE RESPONSIBLE MANAGER

ACTING IN GOOD FAITH AND DEALING FAIRLY

Legally astute managers appreciate the importance of dealing fairly in negotiations.[32] The standard of fair dealing ordinarily requires that (1) each party must actually negotiate and refrain from imposing improper conditions on the negotiation, (2) each party must disclose enough about parallel negotiations to allow the other party to make a counterproposal, and (3) each party must continue to negotiate until an impasse or an agreement has been reached.

In general, managers who are parties to a negotiation should describe as specifically as possible the duty of fair dealing to which they have agreed. Instead of simply pledging to use their "best efforts" to negotiate fairly, the parties should specify whether the negotiations are to be exclusive, how long they must continue, and what must be held in confidence. Given the uncertain state of the law on these matters, no drafter should leave these items to be filled in by a court.

Managers should avoid signing a letter of intent unless they intend to be bound by its proposed terms. Many courts will let a jury decide whether there was intent to be bound even if the letter states that it is not meant to be binding. If a letter of intent is necessary to obtain financing or to begin due diligence, then a manager who does not intend to be bound if negotiations of the definitive agreement break down should consider inserting clear language into the letter stating that it is not binding, that there is no contract unless and until the parties execute a definitive written contract, and that the letter creates no obligation to negotiate in good faith and cannot be reasonably relied upon. The manager should also label the document as a "tentative proposal" or "status letter," and he or she should not sign it.[33]

It is almost always preferable to put the terms of an agreement in writing. A manager should always read a contract before signing it. If the terms are unfamiliar or unclear, the manager should consult with an attorney. A manager should never sign a contract he or she does not understand.

It is rarely to a manager's advantage to try to slip a provision by the other party that the manager knows would be unacceptable if it were pointed out. It is far preferable to hash out any ambiguities at the negotiation stage, while the parties are on good terms and in the mood to make a deal. Positions tend to polarize once the agreement is signed and a dispute arises.

Similarly, it is inappropriate and often unethical to bury offensive terms in a preprinted form contract in the hope that the other party will not spot them. Courts sometimes refuse to enforce such terms, especially when they conflict with the position taken in the negotiations or are contrary to the spirit of the deal. Not only does it make both legal and ethical sense to abide by the covenant of good faith and fair dealing in negotiating a contract, but it is also good business. Contract litigation is expensive and time-consuming and can destroy relationships.

Managers should also ensure that they are not tortiously interfering with the contract of another. As *Pennzoil v. Texaco,* discussed in the "Inside Story" in this chapter demonstrates, even a very large company can be driven into bankruptcy if its executives guess wrong on whether there is a contract or whether their deal tortiously interferes with it.

It is sometimes tempting to view the drafting and review of contracts as a necessary evil. Legally astute managers realize, however, that contract drafting and negotiation can provide opportunities to strengthen business relationships and to protect key assets, such as trade secrets and patentable ideas that give a firm a competitive edge.

---

32. Constance E. Bagley, *Winning Legally: The Value of Legal Astuteness,* 33 ACAD. MGMT. REV. 385 (2008).

33. *See* William G. Schopf et al., *When a Letter of Intent Goes Wrong,* 5 BUS. L. TODAY 31 (Jan.–Feb. 1996).

© Cengage Learning 2013

A MANAGER'S DILEMMA

Putting It into Practice

Trials and Tribulations

HEM Pharmaceuticals Corporation designed a new drug, Ampligen, to fight chronic fatigue syndrome. Typically, new medicines go through several phases of clinical evaluation before approval by the Food and Drug Administration (FDA) and general release onto the market. As a part of the process, HEM began a clinical trial with ninety-two patients to evaluate the effectiveness, side effects, and risks of Ampligen. The patients signed consent forms that warned them of the experimental nature of Ampligen and the possible side effects. The

CONTINUED

patients were free to withdraw from the trial at any time, but if they remained in the study, they were required to accept the risks of treatment, forgo other drugs, not become pregnant, and submit to intensive and uncomfortable testing for one year. In return, after the trial ended, they would be entitled to receive Ampligen for a full year at no charge. At the end of the trial, a manager at HEM considered refusing to provide the year's supply of the drug to the patients free of charge on the grounds that there was no binding contract. If you were that manager, what would you do? Why? [*Dahl v. HEM Pharmaceuticals Corp.*, 7 F.3d 1399 (9th Cir. 1993).]

INSIDE STORY

Pennzoil v. Texaco

Texaco's ill-fated acquisition of Getty Oil remains a leading case both on when negotiations ripen into a contract and on what constitutes tortious interference with a contract.

The Facts[34]

On December 28, 1983, Pennzoil Company announced an unsolicited, public tender offer for 16 million shares of Getty Oil Company at a price of $100 per share. Soon thereafter, Pennzoil contacted both Gordon Getty and a representative of the J. Paul Getty Museum to discuss the tender offer and the possible purchase of Getty Oil by Pennzoil. Gordon Getty was a director of Getty Oil and also the trustee of the Sara Getty Trust, which owned approximately 40% of the outstanding shares of Getty Oil. The Getty Museum held approximately 12% of the shares of Getty Oil. In the first two days of January 1984, representatives of Pennzoil, Gordon Getty, and the Museum negotiated a "Memorandum of Agreement" whereby Pennzoil would buy 3/7ths of Getty for $110 a share. Gordon Getty was to become chair of the board, and Hugh Liedtke, the chief executive officer of Pennzoil, was to become chief executive officer of the new company. The plan also provided that Pennzoil and the Trust were to try in good faith to agree upon a plan to restructure Getty Oil within a year, but if they could not reach an agreement, the assets of Getty Oil were to be divided between them, 3/7ths to Pennzoil and 4/7ths to the Trust.

The Memorandum of Agreement stated that it was subject to the approval of the board of Getty Oil and would expire by its own terms if not approved at the board meeting scheduled to begin on January 2. Liedtke signed the Memorandum of Agreement on behalf of Pennzoil; Gordon Getty signed a counterpart on behalf of the Trust before the Getty Oil board meeting on January 2; and Harold Williams, the president of the Museum, signed it shortly after the board meeting began.

The Getty Oil board voted to reject the Memorandum of Agreement price of $110 per share as too low. On the morning of January 3, Getty Oil's investment banker, Geoffrey Boisi, began calling other companies, seeking a higher bid than Pennzoil's for Getty Oil.

When the board reconvened at 3 p.m. on January 3, a revised Pennzoil proposal was presented, offering $110 per share plus a $3 "stub" to be paid from the proceeds of the sale of ERC, a Getty oil subsidiary. Each shareholder was to receive a pro rata share of the proceeds in excess of $1 billion, but in any case, a minimum of $3 per share at the end of five years. During the meeting, Boisi briefly informed the board of the status of his inquiries of other companies that might be interested in bidding for the company. He reported some preliminary indications of interest, but no definite bid yet.

After a recess, the Museum's president (who was also a director of Getty Oil) moved that the Getty board accept Pennzoil's proposal provided that the guaranteed minimum for the stub be raised to $5. The board voted fifteen to one to approve this counterproposal to Pennzoil. The board then voted themselves and Getty's officers and advisers indemnity for any liability arising from the events of the past few months. There was evidence that during another brief recess of the board meeting, the counteroffer of $110 plus a $5 stub was presented to and accepted by Pennzoil. After Pennzoil's acceptance was conveyed to the Getty board, the meeting was adjourned, congratulations were exchanged, and many of the individuals present, including several Pennzoil representatives, shook hands. Most board members then left town for their respective homes.

As soon as the board meeting adjourned on the evening of January 3, some thirty lawyers began working around the clock to draw up the definitive merger documents and the press release to announce the deal. Both were supposed to be completed by the next morning, but only the press release was ready. Typed on Getty Oil letterhead, the January 4, 1984 press release announced that Getty Oil and Pennzoil had "agreed in

---

34. This statement of facts is based on the opinion of the Texas Court of Appeals in *Texaco, Inc. v. Pennzoil Co.*, 729 S.W.2d 768 (Tex. Ct. App. 1987), *cert. dismissed*, 485 U.S. 994 (1988).

CONTINUED

principle" on the terms of the Memorandum of Agreement, but with a price of $110 plus a $5 stub. It further stated: "The transaction is subject to execution of a definitive merger agreement, approval by the stockholders of Getty Oil and completion of various governmental filing and waiting period requirements." Later that day, Pennzoil issued an identical press release.

The Memorandum of Agreement is set forth in Exhibit 7.1, which Liedtke signed separately as a counterpart.[35] Getty and Pennzoil had an agreement in principle, but did they have a contract?

35. James Shannon, Texaco and the $10 Billion Jury 172 (1988).

EXHIBIT 7.1   The Pennzoil–Getty Memorandum of Agreement

Memorandum of Agreement

January 2, 1984

The following plan (the "Plan") has been developed and approved by (i) Gordon P. Getty, as Trustee (the "Trustee") of the Sarah C. Getty Trust dated December 31, 1934 (the "Trust"), which Trustee owns 31,805,800 shares (40.2% of the total outstanding shares) of Common Stock, without par value, of Getty Oil Company (the "Company"), which shares as well as all other outstanding shares of such Common Stock are hereinafter referred to as the "Shares", (ii) The J. Paul Getty Museum (the "Museum"), which Museum owns 9,320,340 Shares (11.8% of the total outstanding Shares), and (iii) Pennzoil Company ("Pennzoil"), which owns 593,900 Shares through a subsidiary, Holdings Incorporated, a Delaware corporation (the "Purchaser"). The Plan is intended to assure that the public shareholders of the Company and the Museum will receive $110 per Share for all their Shares, a price which is approximately 40% above the price at which the Company's Shares were trading before Pennzoil's subsidiary announced its Offer (hereinafter described) and 10% more than the price which Pennzoil's subsidiary offered in its Offer for 20% of the Shares. The Trustee recommends that the Board of Directors of the Company approve the Plan. The Museum desires that the Plan be considered by the Board of Directors and has executed the Plan for that purpose.

1. **Pennzoil agreement.** Subject to the approval of the Plan by the Board of Directors of the Company as provided in paragraph 6 hereof, Pennzoil agrees to cause the Purchaser promptly to amend its Offer to Purchase dated December 28, 1983 (the "Offer") for up to 16,000,000 Shares so as:

   (a) to increase the Offer price to $110 per Share, net to the Seller in cash and

   (b) to increase the number of Shares subject to the Offer to 23,406,100 (being 24,000,000 Shares less 593,900 now owned by the Purchaser).

2. **Company agreement.** Subject to approval of the Plan by the Board of Directors of the Company as provided in paragraph 6 hereof, the Company agrees:

   (a) to purchase forthwith all 9,320,340 Shares owned by the Museum at a purchase price of $110 per Share (subject to adjustment before or after closing in the event of any increase in the Offer price or in the event any higher price is paid by any person who hereafter acquires 10 percent or more of the outstanding Shares) payable either (at the election of the Company) in cash or by means of a promissory note of the Company, dated as of the closing date, payable to the order of the Museum, due on or before thirty days from the date of issuance, bearing interest at a rate equivalent to the prime rate as in effect at Citibank, N.A. and backed by an irrevocable letter of credit (the "Company Note").

   (b) to proceed promptly upon completion of the Offer by the Purchaser with a cash merger transaction whereby all remaining holders of Shares (other than the Trustee and Pennzoil and its subsidiaries) will receive $110 per Share in cash, and

   (c) in consideration of Pennzoil's agreement provided for in paragraph 1 hereof and in order to provide additional assurance that the Plan will be consummated in accordance with its terms, to grant to Pennzoil hereby the option, exercisable at Pennzoil's election at any time on or before the later of consummation of the Offer referred to in paragraph 1 and the purchase referred to in (a) of this paragraph 2, to purchase from the Company up to 8,000,000 Shares of Common Stock of the Company held in the treasury of the Company at a purchase price of $110 per share in cash.

3. **Museum agreement.** Subject to approval of the Plan by the Board of Directors of the Company as provided in paragraph 6 hereof, the Museum agrees to sell to the Company forthwith all 9,320,340 Shares owned by the Museum at a purchase price of $110 per Share (subject to adjustment before or after closing as provided in paragraph 2(a)) payable either (at the election of the Company) in cash or by means of the Company Note referred to in paragraph 2(c).

4. **Trustee and Pennzoil agreement.** The Trustee and Pennzoil hereby agree with each other as follows:

   (a) **Ratio of Ownership of Shares.** The Trustee may increase its holdings to up to 32,000,000 Shares and Pennzoil may increase its holdings to up to 24,000,000 Shares of the approximately 79,132,000 outstanding Shares. Neither the Trustee nor Pennzoil

CONTINUED

will acquire in excess of such respective amounts without the prior written agreement of the other, it being the agreement between the Trustee and Pennzoil to maintain a relative Share ratio of 4 (for the Trustee) to 3 (for Pennzoil). In connection with the Offer in the event that more than 23,406,100 Shares are duly tendered to the Purchaser, the Purchaser may (if it chooses) purchase any excess over 23,406,000; provided, however, (i) the Purchaser agrees to sell any such excess Shares to the Company (and the company shall agree to purchase) forthwith at $110 per Share and (ii) pending consummation of such sale to the Company the Purchaser shall grant to the Trustee the irrevocable proxy to vote such excess Shares.

(b) **Restructuring plan.** Upon completion of the transactions provided for in paragraphs 1, 2 and 3 hereof, the Trustee and Pennzoil shall endeavor in good faith to agree upon a plan for the restructuring of the Company. In the event that for any reason the Trustee and Pennzoil are unable to agree upon a mutually acceptable plan on or before December 31, 1984, then the Trustee and Pennzoil hereby agree to cause the Company to adopt a plan of complete liquidation of the Company pursuant to which (i) any assets which are mutually agreed to be sold shall be sold and the net proceeds therefrom shall be used to reduce liabilities of the Company and (ii) individual interests in all remaining assets and liabilities shall be distributed to the shareholders pro rata in accordance with their actual ownership interest in the Company. In connection with the plan of distribution, Pennzoil agrees (if requested by the Trustee) that it will enter into customary joint operating agreements to operate any properties so distributed and otherwise to agree to provide operating management for any business and operations requested by the Trustee on customary terms and conditions.

(c) **Board of Directors and Management.** Upon completion of the transactions provided for in paragraphs 1, 2 and 3 hereof, the Trustee and Pennzoil agree that the Board of Directors of the Company shall be composed of approximately fourteen Directors who shall be mutually agreeable to the Trustee and Pennzoil (which Directors may include certain present Directors) and who shall be nominated by the Trustee and Pennzoil, respectively, in the ratio of 4 to 3. The Trustee and Pennzoil agree that the senior management of the Company shall include Gordon P. Getty as Chairman of the Board, J. Hugh Liedtke as President and Chief Executive Officer and Blaine P. Kerr as Chairman of the Executive Committee.

(d) **Access to Information.** Pennzoil, the Trustee and their representatives will have access to all information concerning the Company necessary or pertinent to accomplish the transactions contemplated by the Plan.

(e) **Press releases.** The Trustee and Pennzoil (and the Company upon approval of the Plan) will coordinate any press releases or public announcements concerning the Plan and any transactions contemplated hereby.

5. **Compliance with regulatory requirements.** The Plan shall be implemented in compliance with applicable regulatory requirements.

6. **Approval by the Board of Directors.** This Plan is subject to approval by the Board of Directors of the Company at the meeting of the Board being held on January 2, 1984, and will expire if not approved by the Board. Upon such approval the Company shall execute three or more counterparts of the "Joinder by the Company" attached to the Plan and deliver one such counterpart to each of the Trustee, the Museum and Pennzoil.

IN WITNESS WHEREOF, this Plan, or a counterpart hereof, has been signed by the following officials thereunto duly authorized this January 2, 1984.

/s/ Gordon P. Getty
_____
Gordon P. Getty as Trustee of the Sarah C. Getty Trust

The J. Paul Getty Museum

By /s/ Harold Williams
_____
Harold Williams, President

Pennzoil Company
By J. Hugh Liedtke,
_____
J. Hugh Liedtke, Chairman of the Board and Chief Executive Officer

Joinder by the Company

The foregoing Plan has been approved by the Board of Directors.

GETTY OIL COMPANY
By _____

January 2, 1984

CONTINUED

On January 4, Boisi continued to contact other companies throughout the day, looking for a higher price than Pennzoil had offered. After talking briefly with Boisi, Texaco management called several meetings with its in-house financial planning group.

On January 5, the *Wall Street Journal* reported that an agreement had been reached between Pennzoil and the Getty entities, describing essentially the terms contained in the Memorandum of Agreement. The Pennzoil board met to ratify the actions of its officers in negotiating an agreement with the Getty entities, and Pennzoil's attorneys periodically attempted to contact the other parties' advisers and attorneys to continue work on the transaction agreement. While the Pennzoil lawyers were negotiating the final documents, Texaco, Inc. offered to buy all of Getty oil for $125 a share in cash.

The Texaco deal was much simpler than the Pennzoil deal. Texaco simply bought out everyone for $125 a share in cash. At 9 A.M. on January 6, the Getty board of directors held another board meeting at which it withdrew its previous counterproposal to Pennzoil and unanimously voted to accept Texaco's offer. Texaco immediately issued a press release announcing that Getty Oil and Texaco would merge.

Soon after the Texaco press release appeared, Pennzoil telexed the Getty entities, demanding that they honor their agreement with Pennzoil. Later that day, prompted by the telex, Getty Oil filed a suit in Delaware for declaratory judgment that it was not bound to any contract with Pennzoil. The merger agreement between Texaco and Getty Oil was signed on January 6; the stock purchase agreement with the Museum was signed on January 6; and the stock exchange agreement with the Trust was signed on January 8, 1984.

On January 10, 1984, Pennzoil filed suit in Delaware against Getty Oil, Gordon Getty, the Getty Museum, and Texaco. Pennzoil wanted specific performance—that is, a court order that would give it back its deal with Getty. A few days later, after discovering that Texaco had agreed to indemnify Getty Oil from any claims arising out of its sale to Texaco, Pennzoil added tortious interference with a contract to its claims against Texaco.

The Delaware case was to be tried before a judge, not a jury. Through some legal maneuvering on Pennzoil's part and Texaco's failure to file an answer in the Delaware case right away, the case against Texaco ended up in a Texas state court before a jury. (The suits against Getty, the Trust, and the Museum continued in Delaware.)

To win its suit against Texaco for tortuous interference, Getty had to prove (1) the existence of a contract, (2) Texaco's knowledge of the contract, (3) Texaco's intentional inducement of a breach of the contract, and (4) damages.[36] Texaco asserted that Pennzoil never had a contract because the parties had not yet agreed on the essential terms of the deal and that, even if a contract did exist, Texaco did not tortiously interfere with it.

At trial, Pennzoil made this an issue of honor and the value of a man's word, asserting that a handshake could and often did seal a bargain. At the 1984 Pennzoil stockholder meeting, Hugh Liedtke described the decision to sue Texaco:

> It's one thing to play hardball. It's quite another thing to play foul ball. Conduct such as Texaco's is not made legal simply by protestations that the acts involved were, in fact, legal. All too often such assertions go unchallenged, and so slip into some sort of legal limbo, and become accepted as the norm by default. In this way, actions previously considered amoral somehow become clothed in respectability.[37]

Texaco countered that, handshakes notwithstanding, the Getty board of directors left the January 3 meeting without signing the memorandum of agreement. Texaco also pointed out that it had not made an offer until it was invited to do so by Getty. John McKinley, chairman of Texaco, had repeatedly asked whether Getty Oil was free to deal and was assured by Gordon Getty and by the Getty Museum that there was no contract with Pennzoil. In addition, under the law of New York, where all the deals were made, a contract does not exist until the parties have agreed on all the essential terms of the deal. Texaco argued that a five-page memorandum could not possibly cover all the essential terms in a $5 billion deal involving four parties (Pennzoil, Getty Oil Company, the Sarah Getty Trust, and the Getty Museum).

Texas Justice

For four and a half months, the two sides presented their evidence. Before the jury retired to the jury room, the judge instructed the jurors on how to apply the law to the facts they had heard. The word "contract" never appeared in the jury instructions. Instead, the judge used the word "agreement."

The Calculation of Damages

On the issue of damages, Pennzoil presented a single witness, who testified that the jury should award "replacement" damages, rather than expectation damages. He asserted that if Getty Oil had honored its deal with Pennzoil, it would have cost Pennzoil $3.4 billion, or $3.40 per barrel, to acquire the one billion barrels that it would have owned as a result of its 3/7ths ownership of Getty Oil's reserves. With the deal destroyed, Pennzoil's expert testified, Pennzoil would have to drill from scratch at a cost of $10.87 per barrel: $10.87 per barrel minus $3.40 per barrel times one billion barrels equaled $7.47 billion in replacement costs—three times the price that Pennzoil had agreed to pay to purchase its 3/7ths

CONTINUED

---

36. *See, e.g.,* Kronos, Inc. v. AVX Corp., 612 N.E.2d 289 (N.Y. 1993).

37. Adapted from Thomas Petzinger, Jr., Oil and Honor: The Texaco–Pennzoil Wars 275–76 (1987).

interest in Getty Oil. Under a benefit of the bargain analysis, Pennzoil had lost the opportunity to buy 32 million shares of Getty Oil at $112.50 each—shares that Texaco subsequently purchased for $126 each—or a total of $496 million ($15.50 per share times 32 million shares). Even though Texaco's counsel argued to the jury that the replacement damages claimed by Pennzoil were inappropriate, Texaco elected not to call an expert witness or to introduce other evidence on the issue of damages.[38]

The jury returned a verdict in favor of Pennzoil against Texaco for tortious interference with a contract and awarded Pennzoil $7.53 billion in compensatory damages. The jury also awarded $3 billion in punitive damages, or $1 billion for each indemnity given—$1 billion for the indemnity to Gordon Getty, $1 billion for the indemnity to Getty Oil, and $1 billion for the indemnity to the Getty Museum—after concluding that the indemnitees had acted outrageously. The punitive damages were eventually reduced to $1 billion. The compensatory damages were not changed.

What did the judges for the Court of Appeals for the First Supreme Judicial District of Texas think of all this? In a lengthy opinion, excerpted below, they upheld the jury's verdict.

Excerpts from the Opinion of the Texas Court of Appeals: Legal Analysis

Under New York law, if parties do not intend to be bound to an agreement until it is reduced to writing and signed by both parties, then there is no contract until that event occurs. If there is no understanding that a signed writing is necessary before the parties will be bound, and the parties have agreed upon all substantial terms, then an informal agreement can be binding, even though the parties contemplate evidencing their agreement in a formal document later.

Thus, under New York law, the parties are given the power to obligate themselves informally or only by a formal signed writing, as they wish. The emphasis in deciding when a binding contract exists is on intent rather than on form.

To determine intent, a court must examine the words and deeds of the parties, because these constitute the objective signs of such intent. Only the outward expressions of intent are considered—secret or subjective intent is immaterial to the question of whether the parties were bound.

Although the magnitude of the transaction here was such that normally a signed writing would be expected, there was sufficient evidence to support an inference by the jury that the expectation was satisfied here initially by the Memorandum of Agreement, signed by a majority of shareholders of Getty Oil and approved by the board with a higher price, and by the transaction agreement in progress that had been intended to memorialize the agreement previously reached.

Texaco claims that even if the parties intended to bind themselves before a definitive document was signed, no binding contract could result because the terms that they intended to include in their agreement were too vague and incomplete to be enforceable as a matter of law. . . . The question of whether the agreement is sufficiently definite to be enforceable is a difficult one. The facts of the individual case are decisively important. . . .

Texaco's attempts to create additional "essential" terms from the mechanics of implementing the agreement's existing provisions are unpersuasive. The terms of the agreement found by the jury are supported by the evidence, and the promises of the parties are clear enough for a court to recognize a breach and to determine the damages resulting from that breach.

The Fallout

Burdened by the largest damages award in U.S. history, Texaco filed for bankruptcy in 1987 after its appeals in the Texas courts failed. As part of its reorganization plan, Texaco agreed to settle the case with Pennzoil for $3 billion.

This case had a tremendous impact on Wall Street, which the *Wall Street Journal* dubbed "the Texaco chill." Investment banker Alan Rothenberg summarized the new attitude: "No longer can we say, 'We stole a deal fair and square.'"[39] In legal circles, the arguments still continue as to whether the Texas judges properly understood New York contract law and the jury reached the correct verdict.[40]

---

38. Apparently, Texaco's lawyers did not want to dignify Pennzoil's claims by introducing evidence of the damages to which Pennzoil would be entitled if the jury concluded that Texaco had tortiously interfered with its contract to buy 3/7ths of Getty Oil. Bagley, *supra* note 32.

39. PETZINGER, *supra* note 37, at 459–60.

40. A subsequent Texas Supreme Court decision, *Wal-Mart Stores, Inc. v. Sturges*, 52 S.W.3d 711 (Tex. 2001), made it more difficult to recover damages in an action claiming interference with a prospective contractual relationship. In this case, Sturges had sued Wal-Mart, claiming that it had tortiously interfered with its prospective lease. A trial court found Wal-Mart liable and awarded Sturges $1 million in actual damages and $500,000 in punitive damages. The Texas Supreme Court reversed, holding that when a case involves a prospective business relationship, as opposed to a signed contract, "aggressive but legal interference" cannot be attacked as tortious interference.

KEY WORDS AND PHRASES

QUESTIONS AND CASE PROBLEMS

1. Brian Olson, a hedge fund operator, sued his investing partners Andreas Halvorsen and David Ott for breach of contract, claiming that they had orally amended the compensation provisions in their limited liability company (LLC) operating agreements. The written agreements provided that if a founder left, he would receive only his capital account and earned compensation for that year. Over a year-and-a-half period, Olson's lawyers prepared and circulated nine drafts of a new operating agreement that would have given each founder a declining percentage of his interest for six years upon retirement or death. None of the three founders ever signed this new operating agreement. Although Olson was paid more than $100 million after he left the LLCs in 2005 (which represented his 2005 earned compensation and capital accounts), he claimed that Halvorsen and Ott had orally agreed to pay him the six-year declining interest contemplated by the draft operating agreement.

The LLCs were formed under Delaware law, which for more than a century has provided that contracts that cannot be performed within a year must be in writing. A Delaware statute enacted decades later provides that an LLC is not required to sign its "limited liability agreement." The Delaware LLC Act defines this to include "any agreement (whether referred to as a limited liability company agreement, operating agreement or otherwise) written, oral or implied, of the member or members as to the affairs of a limited liability company and the conduct of its business." (6 Del. C. § 18-101(7).) Is Olson entitled to receive more than his 2005 earned compensation and capital account? [*Olson v. Halvorsen*, 986 A.2d 1150 (Del. 2009).]

2. In 1999, the plaintiff sold his New York–based public relations firm, Lobsenz Stevens, to the defendants, Publicis S.A., a French global communications company, and its American subsidiary. The sale involved two contracts: a stock-purchase agreement pursuant to which the plaintiff sold all of his stock in the firm to the defendants, and an employment agreement pursuant to which the plaintiff was to continue as chairman and CEO of the new company, named Publicis-Dialog (PD), for three years. Under the stock-purchase agreement, the plaintiff received an initial payment of $3,044,000 and stood to earn "earn-out" payments of up to $4 million contingent upon PD achieving certain levels of earnings before interest and taxes during the three calendar years after the closing. The employment agreement described the plaintiff's duties as the "customary duties of a Chief Executive Officer." Within six months of the closing, signs of financial problems appeared, including the loss of PD's largest pre-acquisition client. In March 2001, the plaintiff was removed as CEO of the business and given several options, including leaving the firm, staying and working on new business, and a third option of coming up with another alternative. Thereafter, Bob Bloom, former chair and CEO of Publicis USA, and the plaintiff exchanged a series of e-mails, which culminated in a March 28 message from Bloom that set forth his understanding of the parties' terms regarding the plaintiff's new role at PD as follows:

    > Thus I suggested an allocation of your time that would permit the majority of your effort to go against new business development (70%). I also suggested that the remaining time be allocated to maintaining/growing the former Lobsenz Stevens clients (20%) and involvement in management/operations of the unit (10%). This option, it would seem, is in your best interest because it offers the best opportunity for you to achieve your stated goal of a full earn-out. When I suggested this option, you seemed to have considerable enthusiasm for it and expressed your satisfaction with it so I, of course, assumed that it was an option you preferred.

    The plaintiff responded with an e-mail that stated, among other things, "I accept your proposal with total enthusiasm and excitement. . . . I'm psyched again and will do everything in my power to generate business, maintain profits, work well with others and move forward." Bloom responded that he was "thrilled with [the plaintiff's] decision." Each of the e-mail transmissions bore the typed name of the sender at the foot of the message. The plaintiff subsequently filed a lawsuit based on the terms of the original employment agreement and filed a motion for summary judgment claiming that the e-mail exchanges did not constitute "signed writings" within the meaning of the statute of frauds. What arguments would you make on behalf of the defendants? Which party do you think will prevail? [*Stevens v. Publicis, S.A.,* 854 N.Y.S.2d 690 (2008).]

3. Factors, a company in the business of purchasing accounts receivable and lending money to other businesses, asked Unisearch to conduct a Uniform Commercial Code (UCC) search on its behalf for liens against The Benefit Group, Inc. Unisearch completed the search and sent Factors an invoice along with a search report showing no security interests. The invoice was identical to forty-seven others that Unisearch had previously sent to Factors. On receiving the report, Factors lent $100,000 to The Benefit Group, secured by its existing and future accounts receivable and other business assets. A year later, The Benefit Group defaulted, and when Factors tried to foreclose on the collateral, it discovered a prior UCC filing under the name of "The Benefits Group, Inc." Factors sued Unisearch, alleging breach of contract and negligence. Prior to trial, Unisearch brought a motion for summary judgment on damages, claiming that its liability was limited to $25 because a clause in its invoice limited liability for any action arising out of or related to the contract to that amount. The limitation of liability was printed on the front of the one-page invoice in the upper right-hand corner in a shaded box. Factors argued that the limitation of liability was unenforceable. Is the limitation of liability unenforceable? On what basis? [*Puget Sound Financial, L.L.C. v. Unisearch, Inc.,* 47 P.3d 940 (Wash. 2002).]

4. Lanci was involved in an automobile accident with an uninsured motorist. Lanci and Metropolitan Insurance Company entered settlement negotiations and ultimately agreed to settle all claims for $15,000. Lanci's correspondence accepting the settlement offer clearly indicated his belief that his policy limit was $15,000. However, Lanci did not have a copy of his policy, and, in fact, his policy limit was $250,000. When Lanci learned the correct policy limit, he refused to accept the settlement proceeds of $15,000. Should Lanci be able to void the contract? On what basis? [*Lanci v. Metropolitan Insurance Co.,* 564 A.2d 972 (Pa. Super. Ct. 1989).]

5. Hydrotech Systems, Ltd., a New York corporation, agreed to sell wave-pool equipment to Oasis Waterpark, an amusement park in Palm Springs, California. Although Hydrotech was not licensed to install such equipment in California, it agreed to install the wave-pool equipment after Oasis promised to arrange for a California-licensed contractor to "work with" Hydrotech on any construction.

    The contract between Hydrotech and Oasis called for Oasis to withhold a specific portion of the contract price pending satisfactory operation of the wave pool. Although the pool functioned properly after installation, Oasis continued to withhold payment for both the equipment and the installation services.

    Section 7031 of the California Business and Professions Code states that a suit may not be brought in a California court to recover compensation for any act or contract that requires a California contractor's license, unless the plaintiff alleges and proves that he or she was duly licensed at all times during the performance.

    Can Hydrotech recover its compensation due under the contract? Does Hydrotech have a valid action against Oasis for fraud? Is it ethical for Oasis to use the California law to defend itself? [*Hydrotech Systems, Ltd. v. Oasis Waterpark,* 803 P.2d 370 (Cal. 1991).]

6. Tractebel Energy Marketing, a power plant designer and builder, wanted to build a power plant. Environmental

Protection Agency regulations required new power plants to offset the anticipated increase in overall emissions by purchasing emission reduction credits. Companies acquired these credits by installing better technology in existing plants or shutting down existing operations. Through a broker, DuPont entered into a contract to sell 1,000 tons of nitrogen oxide emission credits to Tractebel. Shortly thereafter, however, the New Jersey Department of Environmental Protection revoked DuPont's credits, citing new regulations. When DuPont refused to perform the contract, Tractebel sued for breach. What arguments will DuPont claim in its defense? Who will prevail in this action? [*Tractebel Energy Marketing, Inc. v. E.I. DuPont DeNemours & Co.*, 118 S.W.3d 60 (Tex. App.–Houston 2003).]

7. As lawyers assembled closing documents for a refinancing of part of the outstanding debt of United States Lines (USL), a secretary working on "Amendment No. 1 to the First Preferred Ship Mortgage" omitted three zeros from the number representing USL's outstanding indebtedness to Prudential Insurance. As a result, the document showed the amount of Prudential's first mortgage as "$92,855.00" instead of "$92,885,000.00." No one noticed the error until eight months later when USL defaulted on the notes secured by the amended mortgage and went bankrupt.

When Prudential tried to foreclose its $92,885,000 first mortgage, USL's bankruptcy trustee objected, arguing that the mortgage should be limited to $92,885. In addition, General Electric Capital Corporation (GECC), which had lent money to USL secured by a second mortgage, brought suit for a declaration that Prudential's first mortgage was valid only to the extent of $92,855. Because GECC had lent money to USL secured by a mortgage junior to that to Prudential, GECC stood to gain by reducing the value of Prudential's first mortgage.

GECC had been intimately involved in USL's financing for some years and knew that Prudential had a $92,885,000 first mortgage. Neither GECC nor any other creditor of USL asserted that it had relied on erroneous information about the amount of USL's outstanding debt.

If you had been the manager of GECC in charge of the USL account, what would you have done once the typo was discovered? Is Prudential legally entitled to a $92,885,000 first mortgage? What would be the ethical thing to do? [*See* Andrew Kull, *Zero-Based Morality: The Case of the $31 Million Typo*, 1 Bus. L. Today 11 (July–Aug. 1992).]

8. On September 29, 2008, at a time when Wachovia bank teetered on the edge of insolvency, the Federal Deposit Insurance Corporation (FDIC) voted to authorize financial assistance to facilitate the acquisition of Wachovia by Citigroup pursuant to section 13 of the Federal Deposit Insurance Act. The FDIC also recommended that the Secretary of the Treasury invoke the "systemic risk" provision in section 13, which authorizes the FDIC to take action to avoid or mitigate serious adverse effects on economic conditions or financial stability. That same day, Wachovia and Citigroup entered into a nonbinding agreement in principle whereby Citigroup would acquire Wachovia's operations for $1 per share. They also entered into an exclusivity agreement in which Wachovia agreed that it would not solicit acquisition proposals from any third party or enter into negotiations with any third party for the purpose of securing an acquisition proposal. On October 2, 2008, while Wachovia and Citigroup were still negotiating, Wells Fargo made an unsolicited offer to acquire Wachovia for $7 per share. Unlike the Citigroup deal, the Wells Fargo offer did not require any FDIC assistance. Wachovia and Wells Fargo signed a definitive merger agreement on October 3, 2008, and announced the merger that same day.

Also on October 3, 2008, President Bush signed the Emergency Economic Stabilization Act.[41] Section 126(c) of the Act provided:

> [No provision in any existing or future agreement that] affects, restricts, or limits the ability of any person to offer or acquire . . . all or part of any insured depository institution . . . in connection with any transaction in which the [FDIC] exercises its authority under Section 11 or 13 [of the Federal Deposit Insurance Act], shall be enforceable against or impose any liability on such person, as such enforcement or liability shall be contrary to public policy.

Does section 126(c) violate the Contracts Clause of the U.S. Constitution? Is the Wachovia–Citigroup exclusivity agreement enforceable? If not, what effect is that holding likely to have on the willingness of future acquirers to acquire a bank in distress? [*Wachovia Corp. v. Citigroup, Inc.*, 634 F. Supp. 2d 445 (S.D.N.Y. 2009).]

---

41. Pub. L. No. 110-343, 122 Stat. 3765 (2008).

CHAPTER 8

SALES, LICENSING, AND E-COMMERCE

INTRODUCTION

SALES OF GOODS, LICENSING OF SOFTWARE, AND ELECTRONIC COMMERCE

Virtually all commercial enterprises engage in the purchase or sale of goods and the licensing of software. Sales of goods within the United States are governed by Article 2 of the Uniform Commercial Code (UCC); most international sales are governed by the Convention on Contracts for the International Sale of Goods. The UCC does not govern the rendering of services or the sale of land. Contracts for selling services or land are governed by common law contract principles, which are discussed in Chapter 7.

There is no comparable uniform law for software licenses. Although the National Conference of Commissioners on Uniform State Laws adopted the Uniform Computer Information Transactions Act (UCITA) as a model law in 2003, only Virginia and Maryland have enacted it into law, and it appears unlikely to be enacted by other states. Perhaps because of this lack of a uniform law, many courts have applied Article 2 of the UCC to such transactions, either directly or by analogy.

The Internet has transformed the way businesses and individuals conduct business in the United States and throughout the world. According to the Census Bureau, e-commerce transactions by manufacturers, wholesalers, service providers, and retailers amounted to $3.371 trillion in 2009 and are expected to continue to grow in coming years.[1] Due to the speed at which technology is developing and the range of novel issues it presents, state and national governments are scrambling to enact laws that protect consumers and businesses, while facilitating electronic sales transactions using the Internet. In addition, the international reach of the Internet is forcing countries throughout the world to engage in legal cooperation and collaboration.

---

1. Census numbers are from U.S. Census Bureau, *E-Stats*, May 26, 2011, *available at* http://www.census.gov/econ/estats/2009/2009reportfinal.pdf.

CHAPTER OVERVIEW

This chapter begins by addressing when Article 2 applies. It then discusses the application of Article 2 to software licenses, the Uniform Computer Information Transactions Act, and an issue unique to software licenses: whether parties to a software license are free to broaden the protection, or to narrow the defenses, afforded by federal intellectual property law. The chapter then deals with contract formation, including issues arising from the process of formation in the software environment and on the Internet. Major questions involve the enforcement of contract terms that become available only after assent and/or are presented in a take-it-or-leave-it standard form. The chapter also discusses the UCC approach to the battle of the forms, which occurs when the form accepting an offer contains terms different from those on the form that constitutes the offer. Next, it discusses the Uniform Electronic Transactions Act and the Electronic Signatures in Global and National Commerce Act.

The chapter also addresses the special warranty provisions of the UCC, including express warranties and implied warranties of merchantability and fitness for a particular purpose. It explains how the risk of loss is allocated and a buyer's right to reject nonconforming goods. The chapter then reviews excuses for nonperformance, including unconscionability and commercial impracticability, and remedies for unexcused nonperformance. Finally, the chapter discusses the rules applicable to the international sale of goods and compares them with the rules applicable to domestic sales transactions governed by the UCC.

ARTICLE 2 OF THE UCC

The Uniform Commercial Code deals with a broad range of commercial transactions, from the use of negotiable instruments to secured transactions. It was promulgated in the early 1940s under the joint authority of the American Law Institute (ALI) and the National Conference of Commissioners on Uniform State Laws (NCCUSL) to bring greater certainty and predictability to an increasingly national commercial system.

The UCC is a model law, which means that it must be enacted into law by a state legislature to become effective in that state. Because the UCC is approved by both the ALI and the NCCUSL, however, it has generally been accepted by the states more readily than model laws promulgated by only the NCCUSL.

What Types of Contracts Are Covered by Article 2?

Article 2 of the UCC deals with contracts for the sale of goods, and it has been adopted in every state except Louisiana. Section 2-105 of the UCC defines *goods* as "all things (including specially manufactured goods) which are movable at the time of identification to the contract for sale." *Identification to the contract* means the designation—by marking, setting aside, or other means—of the particular goods that are to be supplied under the contract.

Sometimes it is not clear whether an activity should be characterized as a sale of goods or a sale of services. For example, when a hospital performs a blood transfusion, is it selling blood or rendering medical services? This distinction can be critical for purposes of both the UCC warranties and product liability in tort (discussed in Chapter 10). Many states have addressed precisely this issue by passing special amendments to their versions of the UCC. These so-called blood shield statutes define blood transfusions as the provision of services, rather than the sale of goods, in order to limit hospital and blood bank liability for reasons of public policy.[2] In other states, the common law has led to the conclusion that such sales are incidental to the provision of medical services and are therefore outside the scope of the UCC.[3]

Similarly, there can be an issue as to whether something attached to land is considered goods or land. This gray area includes *fixtures*, which are items of personal property that are attached to real property and cannot be removed without substantial damage. Fixtures are not considered goods under Article 2 and, like real property, are generally subject to the common law contract principles described in Chapter 7. As discussed further below, courts have also struggled with whether software falls within the definition of "goods" and whether software licenses are "contracts for the sale of goods."

The UCC regulates sales of goods by both merchants and nonmerchants, but different rules may apply to them. Section 2-104 of the UCC defines a *merchant* as "a person who deals in goods of the kind or otherwise by his occupation holds himself out as having knowledge or skill peculiar to the practices or goods involved in the transaction."

SOFTWARE LICENSES

Software is a series of instructions to a computer that can be expressed in written form or as a series of electronic impulses. Software can be embodied on a disk, a CD-ROM, or another tangible medium like other hard goods subject to Article 2. Unlike hard goods, however, the value of the software is not the medium, but the instructions themselves. As the U.S. District Court for the Northern District of California pointed out in *Adobe Systems, Inc. v. Stargate Software, Inc.*:

> The CD-ROM itself [on which the Adobe software was embedded] is worth not much more than a nominal amount, and it is the [software] code that justifies the purchase price of the [Adobe software] product. That being the case, the economic reality of [the] transaction is that a consumer is ultimately paying for the software contained on the CD-ROM, rather than the CD-ROM itself.[4]

In addition, unlike most other goods, software can be "readily and easily copied on a mass scale in an extraordinarily short amount of time" or distributed on the Internet for little or no cost.[5]

Vendors initially chose to license, rather than sell, their software because it was unclear at that time whether copyright law protected computer programs. Even though amendments to the Copyright Act in 1976 made it clear that computer programs are copyrightable, vendors have continued to distribute their software products through licensing agreements because licenses offer certain advantages to the licensor. A sales agreement generally imposes no continuing obligations on the purchaser other than an obligation to pay the purchase price. A software license, however, generally includes a number of continuing obligations, such as limitations on the right to make copies of the software, limitations on the number of computers on which the program may be installed, prohibitions against sublicensing, restrictions on the use of the software to provide services to third parties, prohibitions against modifying the software, and prohibitions against reverse engineering. By licensing, rather than selling the software, the vendor can avoid the *doctrine of first sale*, embodied in

---

2. *See, e.g.*, Zichichi v. Middlesex Mem'l Hosp., 528 A.2d 805 (Conn. 1987); Pleasant v. Dow Corning Corp., 1993 WL 1156110 (D.D.C. Jan. 7, 1993).

3. *See, e.g.*, Lovett v. Emory Univ., Inc., 156 S.E.2d 923 (Ga. Ct. App. 1967).

4. 216 F. Supp. 2d 1051, 1055 (N.D. Cal. 2002).

5. *Id.* at 1059.

section 109(a) of the Copyright Act, which provides that "the owner of a particular copy . . . lawfully made under this title, or any person authorized by such owner, is entitled, without the authority of the copyright owner, to sell or otherwise dispose of the possession of that copy . . . ."

Law Applicable to Software Licenses

Most cases addressing the subject have held, either directly or by analogy, that Article 2 of the UCC applies to most transactions involving software.[6] Although Article 2 does not answer all of the legal issues that arise in regard to software licenses, especially terms that strike at the balance between promoting public welfare by granting exclusive rights and promoting public welfare through competition fueled in part by the broad distribution of information, it has worked reasonably well for the issues that it covers, such as contract formation, the battle of the forms, quality warranties, disclaimers of warranty, and remedies. The remainder of this chapter includes references to a number of cases involving computer software that have applied Article 2 when addressing these issues.

Efforts to create a comprehensive uniform state law for software licensing have been largely unsuccessful. Although the NCCUSL adopted the Uniform Computer Information Transactions Act (UCITA) as a model law, only two states (Maryland and Virginia) have adopted it.

Many sectors of the software industry strongly supported UCITA, but consumer advocates, technology trade associations, law professors, the American Library Association, the Consumers Union, the Institute of Electrical and Electronics Engineers, and a long list of state attorneys general opposed it. Critics complained that UCITA provided too much protection to software companies and not enough to consumers. The critics not only strongly opposed giving software vendors the right to monitor the use of their products by accessing computers remotely, but also argued that UCITA would weaken the warranty protection consumers receive under software licenses and make it more difficult to sue software vendors that sell faulty programs. Five states have adopted anti-UCITA laws that limit the power of their courts to apply UCITA by virtue of a choice-of-law determination.

In 2003, the NCCUSL and ALI approved amendments to Article 2 that expressly included embedded software within Article 2 but excluded "information" from the definition of "goods." This exclusion would appear to exclude electronic transfers of computer software from the scope of Article 2. Although Oklahoma adopted the "information" exclusion, other states have not followed suit. Because prospects for the widespread adoption of the 2003

amendments by the states are not good,[7] this chapter does not address these amendments in detail.

In 2005, the ALI decided that the statutory path for regulation of software licenses was not promising and that courts were likely to continue to develop software licensing law as a matter of case law for at least the near future. As a result, the ALI generated *Principles of the Law of Software Contracts*, which reviews the existing case law and recommends best practices for use by judges and lawyers. The first volume, which was published in 2010, covers basic definitions, their scope, and general terms; the formation and enforcement of software contracts; performance; and available remedies.[8]

Interplay Between License Provisions and Intellectual Property Law

The imposition of continuing license restrictions on software has raised a number of issues regarding enforceability. License restrictions have been challenged and, in some cases, invalidated, on the basis that they conflict with applicable intellectual property law, violate public policy, or are unconscionable.

Two types of provisions are particularly susceptible to attack: (1) provisions that purport to expand the exclusive rights conferred by copyright or other intellectual property laws, and (2) provisions that narrow statutory or common law limits on the owner's exclusive rights. For example, Lasercomb America, Inc. licensed its computer-aided design/manufacturing die-making software program—Interact—to Holiday Steel pursuant to Lasercomb's standard ninety-nine-year software license agreement. The agreement prohibited the person to whom the license was granted from developing or selling during the term of the license or for one year thereafter any computer-assisted die-making software without Lasercomb's prior written consent. When Lasercomb discovered that several Holiday Steel executives had made unauthorized copies of Interact, it sued Holiday Steel and two executives for breach of contract and copyright infringement. Although the defendants did not dispute that they had made unauthorized copies of Interact, they argued that Lasercomb

---

6. RESTATEMENT (THIRD) OF TORTS § 19 cmt. d (1997) (stating "[u]nder the [UCC] software that is mass-marketed is considered a good" and citing numerous cases); *UCITA Update*, COM. L. REP., Oct. 2003, at 146–48.

7. In 2004, Oklahoma enacted the exclusion of "information" from the definition of goods under Article 2, although it did not enact any other portion of the 2003 amendments. Oklahoma also excluded a "license of information" from the definition of "contract for sale." Jean Braucher, *Contracting Out of Article 2 Using a "License" Label: A Strategy That Should Not Work for Software Products*, 46 LOY. L.A. L. REV. 261, 270 (2007). In February 2010, Oklahoma proposed amendments to forty-nine sections of Article 2 and four sections of Article 2A. Cynthia Lee Starnes, *UCC Forms with Practice Comments*, MICH. COMP. LAWS ANN., current through July 2011, 1 MICH. UCC FORMS ANN. art. 2 (3d ed. 2011).

8. *See* AM. LAW INST., PRINCIPLES OF THE LAW OF SOFTWARE CONTRACTS (2010), http://www.ali.org/index.cfm?fuseaction=publications.ppage&node_id=121.

was barred from recovering for infringement because of copyright misuse.

Even though the defendants had not signed an agreement with Lasercomb, they proved at trial that at least one Interact licensee had entered into a Lasercomb agreement that included the restrictive provision. The U.S. Court of Appeals for the Fourth Circuit found that this provision constituted a misuse of copyright that barred Lasercomb from suing any party, including the defendants, for infringement of its copyright in the Interact program:

> Lasercomb undoubtedly has the right to protect against copying of the Interact code. Its standard licensing agreement, however, goes much further and essentially attempts to suppress any attempt by the licensee to independently implement the idea which Interact expresses. The agreement forbids the licensee to develop or assist in developing *any* kind of computer-assisted die-making software. . . . Although one or another licensee might succeed in negotiating out the noncompete provisions, this does not negate the fact that Lasercomb is attempting to use its copyright in a manner adverse to the public policy embodied in copyright law, and that it has succeeded in doing so with at least one licensee.[9]

Users have also successfully challenged license provisions that narrow or exclude statutory or common law limits on exclusive rights, including terms restricting distribution of noncopyrightable factual information, prohibiting assignment, mandating grant-back licenses, and prohibiting reverse engineering. For example, in *Alcatel USA, Inc. v. DGI Technologies, Inc.*, the U.S. Court of Appeals for the Fifth Circuit found a copyright misuse when a license agreement prohibited the reverse engineering necessary to test compatibility between a microprocessor card and an operating system. The court stressed that the copyright owner could not "indirectly seek[] to obtain patent-like protection of its hardware—its microprocessor card—through the enforcement of its software copyright."[10]

Although federal intellectual property law does not expressly preempt state-law enforcement of private agreements, the policies underlying federal intellectual property laws may preempt certain provisions. Preemption issues are heightened when software is distributed under a "take-it-or-leave-it" standard form agreement. For example, although the Court of Appeals for the Federal Circuit enforced a contractual prohibition against reverse engineering in *Bowers v. Baystate Technologies, Inc.*,[11] the dissent would have invalidated the prohibition on the basis that a state cannot eliminate the fair use defense by enforcing such a provision in a nonnegotiable shrink-wrap license agreement (shrink-wraps are discussed later in the chapter). As with certain other contract provisions, sometimes less is more.

---

9. Lasercomb Am., Inc. v. Reynolds, 911 F.2d 970, 978 (4th Cir. 1990).
10. 166 F.3d 772, 793 (5th Cir. 1999).
11. 320 F.3d 1317 (Fed. Cir. 2003).

CONTRACT FORMATION

The UCC permits a contract to be enforced if the parties intended a binding contract, even though important terms may have been left open for later agreement. If a dispute later arises over a missing term, the court may simply use a "gap-filler" as provided by the UCC. The court will fill in missing terms, however, only if the party attempting to enforce the contract can prove that there was a genuine agreement, not a mere proposal or intention to continue negotiations. As with common law contracts, a mutual mistake of fact concerning an essential term of sale, but not a mistake of judgment, will preclude the formation of a sales contract.

Offer

The UCC does not define the term *offer*, although it is used in several important sections. Therefore, traditional common law principles (discussed in Chapter 7) determine whether an offer has been made. Under the UCC, neither an invitation for bids nor a price quotation is an offer. Similarly, a proposal by a sales representative that is subject to approval by the home office is not an offer.

Acceptance

The UCC does not define *acceptance* either, except to state that an acceptance may contain terms additional to or different from those in the offer. This is different from the common law *mirror image rule*, which requires the acceptance to contain the exact same terms as the offer. Unless the offeror indicates unambiguously that his or her offer can be accepted only in a particular way, an offer may be accepted in any manner and by any medium that is reasonable in the circumstances.

ethical consideration

Devon Cartagena, a dealer in antiques, sees a desk for sale for $50 at a garage sale and recognizes it as a Louis XV desk worth $15,000. Does he have a legal or ethical obligation to disclose the true value to the person holding the garage sale? Should it matter that difficult financial circumstances made it necessary for the homeowner to sell the desk? Should Cartagena get some reward for the effort he has spent in becoming an expert in antiques and for the time he has spent pawing through junk at countless garage sales?

A person recently sold a map for $3 that later turned out to be worth more than $19 million. Does the buyer have a moral duty to share the windfall with the seller? Would the seller have a moral duty to share the loss if the buyer paid $19 million for a map worth only $3?

What if a framed picture sold for $25 turns out to have an original copy of the U.S. Constitution behind the picture? Is this a mistake of judgment or of fact? What, if anything, is the buyer's ethical responsibility to the seller in such a case?

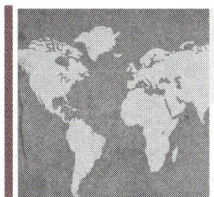

HISTORICALPERSPECTIVE

From Medieval Guilds to Online Arbitration

The increased use of the Internet by businesses and individuals, combined with the lack of established legal rules, has resulted in the development of private legal institutions.[a] For example, individuals doing business on the Internet have devised ways to ensure that the information they transmit to each other will remain confidential and be used only in an authorized manner. In addition, Internet companies have established online mediation and dispute resolution sites that allow consumers to resolve their disputes without filing claims in courts. Although these private legal regimes may be revolutionary in that they are being used in connection with a new technology, private legal regimes have emerged at other times in history when individuals needed to protect their rights and the existing legal regime was inadequate to do so.

In medieval Europe, the nation-state had not yet developed, so merchants and traders could not rely on a central government to enforce laws or contracts to protect their trading activities. As long-distance trade became more common, traders and merchants began to venture beyond the protection of a local ruler or entrusted agents to carry and deliver their goods to fairs and markets in other countries. Because the merchants needed a mechanism to protect their interests, they developed private organizations, or guilds, and courts enforced by groups of

merchants. To determine whether an unknown trader or agent was trustworthy, merchants turned to each other for information about the stranger's reputation. Merchants refused to trade with parties who breached commitments to pay or to perform services, and they organized guildwide embargoes to freeze out members of the guild who violated its rules.

Similarly, in modern society, members of private organizations often agree to be governed by a legal regime created and enforced by the organization. For example, a number of trade associations have rules that govern relationships among their members and establish procedures for resolving disputes arising from breaches of these rules. Although these associations base their rules on public law, such as contract law, their legal regimes typically rely on simple rules, which they interpret and apply literally.

Stock exchanges, such as the New York Stock Exchange and Nasdaq, also operate under quasi-private legal regimes. Members of an exchange must comply with its rules and are subject to its monitoring, investigation, and enforcement mechanisms. These exchanges are not subject just to a set of private rules, however. Their private rules are subject to review by the Securities and Exchange Commission and the courts, and they also incorporate public laws.

The rapid development of e-commerce is also driving the development of a private legal regime. The Internet is decentralized by design, and its ever-changing technology and ability to reach billions of consumers in countries all over the world present enormous challenges for local and international legal regulation. In addition to using the World International Property Organization (WIPO) and the Internet Corporation for Assigned Names and Numbers (ICANN) to resolve domain name disputes, companies are using private law regimes to deal with consumer concerns about privacy on the Internet and secure transmissions of sensitive data (such as credit card numbers) by establishing "Seal" programs. For example, TRUSTe, a nonprofit corporation founded by the Online Privacy Alliance (a group of leading Internet firms), the Electronic Frontier Foundation (a public interest group), and the Boston Consulting Group (a management consulting firm), has established a set of practices regarding user privacy to which a company wishing to display the TRUSTe seal must adhere. TRUSTe enforces its policies by several methods including a dispute resolution process.

a. This discussion is based on Gillian K. Hadfield, *Privatizing Commercial Law: Lessons from the Middle and Digital Ages*, 7 N.Z. Bus. L.Q. 287 (2001).

Battle of the Forms

In a *battle of the forms*, the parties negotiate the essential terms of the contract (for example, quantity, quality, and delivery date) but neglect to bargain over items that are less immediately important (for example, whether disputes will be subject to arbitration, for how long a period after delivery the buyer may assert complaints of defects, or on whom the risk of loss during shipment falls). The parties then exchange standard printed forms, each of which is

filled with fine print listing all kinds of terms advantageous to the party that drew up the form. Often goods are shipped, received, and paid for before both parties have expressly accepted the same document as their contract. As a result of these exchanges, two questions arise: (1) Is there a contract? (2) If so, what are its terms?

The UCC calls a truce in the battle of the forms by effectively abolishing the mirror image rule. It is not necessary for an offer and acceptance to match exactly in order for a contract for the sale of goods to exist. Unlike the rule under common law, adding to or modifying terms in the offer does not make the acceptance a counteroffer.

Definite Response   A definite and timely assent to an offer constitutes an acceptance. The presence of additional or different terms is not a bar to contract formation. The crucial inquiry is whether the parties intended to close a deal. Under section 2-207, a contract exists whenever the parties act as if there is a contract between them. It is not necessary to determine which document constitutes the offer and which the acceptance. If the offeree's response manifests the intent to enter into a deal, the offer has been accepted. For example, if additional or different terms merely appear in the standard printed language of a form contract, it is likely that the offeree intended to close a deal. Once the contract is formed, the only issue to be decided is what are its terms.

If, however, the response indicates only a willingness to continue negotiations, it is not an acceptance but a counteroffer. For example, an additional or different term that directly pertains to one of the negotiated terms, such as price or quantity, is evidence that the parties are still negotiating and have not reached an agreement.

Conditional Response   If the offeree wants to make a counteroffer rather than an acceptance, he or she should state clearly that acceptance is conditioned on the offeror's agreement to the additional or different terms. The safest course is to use the language of the UCC: "This acceptance is expressly made conditional on offeror's assent to all additional or different terms contained herein. Should offeror not give assent to said terms, there is no contract between the parties." Less direct language (such as "The acceptance of your order is subject to the conditions set forth herein" or "Acceptance of this order is expressly limited to the conditions of purchase printed on the reverse side") has been held to be an acceptance rather than a counteroffer.

Acceptance with Missing Terms   What happens when the parties ship, receive, and pay for goods without first agreeing on all material terms? In that case, section 2-207(3) provides that the terms of the contract will be those on which the writings exchanged by the parties agree, supplemented by the UCC's gap-fillers where needed.

Acceptance with Additional Terms   What is the effect of an acceptance that includes additional terms without expressly making the contract subject to the offeror's agreeing to those terms? The answer depends on whether the parties are merchants. Under section 2-207(2), if either of the parties is not a merchant, additional terms are construed as proposals for additions to the contract that the acceptance has created. Unless the offeror expressly agrees to the added provisions, they do not become part of the contract. In contrast, if all parties are merchants, the additional provisions in the acceptance automatically become part of the contract, unless (1) the offer expressly limits acceptance to the terms of the offer, (2) the new terms materially alter the original offer, or (3) the party making the original offer notifies the other party within a reasonable time that it objects to the new terms. If any one of these exceptions applies, the additional terms serve as proposals requiring the express consent of the offeror to become part of the contract.

Acceptance with Different Terms   What is the effect of different—as opposed to additional—terms in an acceptance when the acceptance is not expressly made subject to the offeror's agreeing to those terms? As in the case of additional terms in a response to an offer, different terms neither defeat the acceptance nor impede the formation of the contract. But do the different terms become part of the contract? Surprisingly, the language of section 2-207 does not address this situation. Under common law, the courts usually found that an offeree's response to an offer that contained different terms was a counteroffer that the offeror accepted by continuing its performance. The following case illustrates how most courts applying the UCC deal with this situation.

A CASE IN POINT	*Summary*	Case 8.1

Richardson v. Union Carbide Industrial Gases, Inc.

Superior Court of New Jersey, Appellate Division
790 A.2d 962 (N.J. Super. 2002).

FACTS   Prior to 1988, Hoeganaes Corporation used furnace 2S for annealing iron powders. In 1988, Hoeganaes undertook to convert furnace 2S to a distalloy furnace. As part of the conversion, Hoeganaes bought a powder transporter system from Rage Engineering, Inc. to transport iron to the input end of the furnace.

The Rage proposal included the following language, in all capital letters, at the bottom of each page:

> ANY PURCHASE ORDER ISSUED AS A RESULT OF THIS QUOTE IS MADE EXPRESSLY SUBJECT TO THE TERMS AND CONDITIONS ATTACHED HERETO IN LIEU OF ANY CONFLICTING TERMS PROPOSED BY PURCHASER.

CONTINUED

The terms and conditions attached to the proposal were standard, boilerplate terms that were never discussed by Rage and Hoeganaes. They included the following provisions:

> LIMITATION OF ACCEPTANCE. This sale (including all services) is limited to and expressly made conditional on Purchaser's assent to these Terms and Conditions as well as all other provisions contained in any other document to which these terms or conditions are attached. . . .
>
> . . . .
>
> INDEMNITY. Purchaser shall indemnify and hold Seller harmless against and in respect of any loss, claim or damage (including costs of suit and attorneys' fees) or other expense incident to or in connection with: the goods/equipment; . . . unless such loss, claim or damage is due solely and directly to the negligence or willful misconduct of Seller.

Hoeganaes included the following language in boldface type at the bottom of its purchase order:

> THIS ORDER IS ALSO SUBJECT TO THE TERMS AND CONDITIONS ON THE REVERSE SIDE OF THIS PAGE[.]

The reverse side of the Hoeganaes purchase order included the following terms and conditions:

> 1. Compliance with Terms and Conditions of Order—The terms and conditions set forth below, along with the provisions set forth on the front page hereof, constitute the entire contract of purchase and sale between Buyer and Seller. Any provisions in the Seller's acceptance, acknowledgment or other response to this Order which are different from or in addition to any of the terms and conditions and other provisions of this Order . . . shall not become a part of Buyer's contract of purchase and sale. . . .
>
> . . . .
>
> 14. Indemnification—Seller agrees to indemnify and hold harmless Buyer, . . . from and against all losses, damages, liabilities, claims, demands (including attorneys' fees), and suits at law or equity that arise out of . . . any act of omission or commission, negligent or otherwise, of Seller, . . . or otherwise out of the performance or attempted performance by Seller of this purchase order.

Except as expressed in the boilerplate forms they exchanged, neither side objected to the language in the documents, and the contract was performed. The furnace exploded, however, and Jeffrey Richardson, a Hoeganaes employee who was injured in the explosion, filed suit against a number of defendants, including Hoeganaes and Rage. In its answer, Rage cross-complained against Hoeganaes for contractual indemnification. Rage filed a motion for summary judgment seeking contractual indemnification from Hoeganaes, and Hoeganaes cross-moved for summary judgment seeking dismissal of Rage's indemnification claim. The trial court granted Hoeganaes's motion and dismissed Rage's claim for indemnification. Rage appealed.

ISSUES PRESENTED   If the parties have performed, but the buyer's and seller's pre-printed forms contain contradictory terms, is there a contract? If so, what are its terms?

SUMMARY OF OPINION   The Appellate Division of the New Jersey Superior Court observed that when faced with conflicting terms in contracts in similar circumstances, courts have used three approaches:

> The majority view [the so-called knockout rule] is that the conflicting terms fall out and, if necessary, are replaced by suitable UCC gap-filler provisions.
>
> The minority view is that the offeror's terms control because the offeree's different terms cannot be saved by . . . 2-207(2), because that section applies only to additional terms.

CONTINUED

The third view assimilates "different" to "additional" so that the terms of the offer prevail over the different terms in the acceptance only if the latter are materially different. This is the least adopted approach.

The court then concluded that the "knockout" rule is preferable and should be adopted. The court reasoned that the other approaches were "inequitable and unjust" and were contrary to the policy behind section 2-207, which was to jettison the common law "mirror image" rule by recognizing the existence of a contract even when certain terms conflicted or were unresolved. The court quoted the motion judge who had stated:

> The truth is, and this really is the truth, what's happening is some little person some place writing these little—trying to plan it out, trying to conflict these things out, but the business people are out there delivering and taking money. And if the people really want to really get into all of this, then they should have taken their stuff away and they should have said, ooh, you know, we—you know, this is real here and, sorry, I'm not going to be able to take your check and, sorry, you're not going to be able to keep the stuff, but they're not doing that. They're just playing a little game with forms.

As a result, even though Rage's offer had specifically limited acceptance to its terms, Rage's indemnity clause did not become part of the contract because the terms of the parties' writings had conflicting indemnification provisions.

RESULT   The appeals court affirmed the trial court's decision to strike the contradictory indemnity provisions.

COMMENTS   By formally adopting the knockout rule instead of the common law approach, the appeals court made it much harder to game the system by exchanging preprinted forms with boilerplate rejection of the other party's terms. Because conflicting terms may simply be thrown out and replaced by UCC gap-fillers, managers using such forms should be aware of which UCC provisions might replace their standard terms.

Software Licenses and Online Purchase Agreements

The sale of software licenses in stores, by mail, and over the Internet and the sale of other goods online have resulted in several specialized forms of licenses and other purchase agreements that have raised new issues about what constitutes acceptance. In *ProCD, Inc. v. Zeidenberg*,[12] the U.S. Court of Appeals for the Seventh Circuit upheld the enforceability of a software license agreement that was "encoded on the CD-ROM disks, as well as printed on the manual, and which appear[ed] on a user's screen every time the software [ran]." The court acknowledged that use of a *shrink-wrap license*, which places the license terms on the outside of the box containing the software, was not practical in this instance. It was sufficient for the vendor to include a notice on the box stating that the software was purchased subject to an enclosed license, because the software could not be used unless and until the purchaser was shown the license and manifested his or her acceptance by using the software after having an opportunity to read the license.

A second type of license, a click-wrap, is frequently used for software that is distributed over the Internet. A *click-wrap license* presents the user with a notice on his or her computer screen that requires the user to agree to the terms of the license by clicking on an icon. The software cannot be obtained or used until the icon is clicked. The few cases that have considered click-wrap licenses have generally found them to be enforceable.[13]

Some websites use a third type of software license, a browse-wrap. A *browse-wrap agreement* is an online agreement that appears on a website but does not require the user to take any action to express his or her consent to the agreement. To be enforceable, a browse-wrap agreement must, at a minimum, be conspicuous.

For example, Netscape offered its SmartDownload program free of charge on its website to all those who visited the site and indicated, by clicking their mouse on a designated box, that they wished to obtain the software. The sole reference on the page to the license agreement appeared in text that was visible only if the visitor scrolled down through the page to the next screen, which

---

12. 86 F.3d 1447 (7th Cir. 1996).

13. *See, e.g.*, Adsit Co. v. Gustin, 874 N.E.2d 1018 (Ind. App. 2007); Feldman v. Google, Inc., 513 F. Supp. 2d 229 (E.D. Pa. 2007).

included the following invitation to review the license agreement: "Please review and agree to the terms of the Netscape SmartDownload software license agreement before downloading and using the software." Visitors were not required to indicate their assent to the license agreement, or even to view it, before proceeding to download the software. When users sued Netscape, claiming that the SmartDownload software transmitted information to Netscape about their online activity, the U.S. Court of Appeals for the Second Circuit held that the plaintiffs were not bound by the arbitration clause in the license agreement, because "a reference to the existence of license terms on a submerged screen is not sufficient to place consumers on inquiry or constructive notice of those terms."[14]

In a subsequent case, the Appellate Court of Illinois enforced a prominently displayed browse-wrap agreement.[15] The plaintiffs had purchased computers on Dell's website. To make their purchases, the plaintiffs had completed online forms on five separate web pages, each of which included a hyperlink entitled "Terms and Conditions of Sale." A hyperlink to these conditions was also provided on Dell's marketing page. In addition, the last three of the five forms the plaintiffs filled out to submit the order stated: "All sales are subject to Dell's Term[s] and Conditions of Sale." The court found that this statement, in conjunction with the conspicuously located hyperlinks on multiple forms completed by the plaintiffs, would "put a reasonable person on notice that there are terms and conditions attached to the purchase and that it would be wise to find out what the terms and conditions were before making a purchase." To avoid any uncertainty about the enforceability of a browse-wrap agreement, vendors should require purchasers or licensees to click "I accept" before completing the sale.

Consideration

Contracts for the sale of goods ordinarily must have consideration to be enforceable. However, a *firm offer*, that is, a signed offer by a merchant that indicates that the offer will be kept open, is not revocable for lack of consideration. The offer must be kept open during the time stated or, if none is stated, for a reasonable period of time, up to a maximum of three months. This rule is just one example of how the UCC provides more stringent standards for merchants than for nonmerchants.

Under the UCC, an agreement to modify a contract is binding even if there is no consideration for the modification as long as the modification was made in good faith. If the original contract was required to be in writing to satisfy the statute of frauds, however, then the agreement to modify the contract must be in writing also.

14. Specht v. Netscape, 306 F.3d 17 (2d Cir. 2002).
15. Hubbert v. Dell Corp., 359 Ill. App. 3d 976 (2005).

STATUTE OF FRAUDS

Section 2-201 of the UCC is a *statute of frauds*. It provides that a contract for the sale of goods for $500 or more is unenforceable unless it is at least partly in writing. The provision states:

1. There must be some writing evidencing the sale of goods.
2. The writing must be signed by the party against whom enforcement is sought.
3. The writing must specify the quantity of the goods sold.

"Some Writing"

Statutes of fraud generally require all the essential terms of the contract to be in writing, so the UCC's requirement for "some writing" is relatively lenient. The official comments to section 2-201 state: "All that is required is that the writing afford a basis for believing that the offered oral evidence rests on a real transaction. It may be written in lead pencil on a scratch pad." The comments go on to provide: "The price, time and place of payment or delivery, the general quality of the goods, or any particular warranties may all be omitted."

The only term that must appear in the writing is the quantity of goods to be sold because it is necessary to provide a basis for awarding money damages in the event of a breach. The contract is not enforceable beyond the quantity of goods shown in the writing. If no quantity is specified, the contract is unenforceable unless (1) the goods were specially manufactured for the buyer and are not suitable for sale to others in the ordinary course of the seller's business, (2) the defendant admits in a judicial proceeding that there was an agreement, or (3) payment for the goods was made and accepted or the goods were received and accepted.

Signature

The writing must be signed by the party against whom enforcement is sought, unless the sale is between merchants and (1) a confirmation of the contract has been received, (2) the party receiving it has reason to know its contents, and (3) that party has not made a written objection within ten days after the confirmation was received. For example, an invoice that a seller sent to a buyer would be a contract enforceable against the buyer if the buyer did not respond within ten days after receiving the invoice.

ELECTRONIC CONTRACTS: THE UNIFORM ELECTRONIC TRANSACTIONS ACT AND THE E-SIGN ACT

With the rise of e-commerce, more and more transactions are taking place electronically. Most states now give most types of contracts executed electronically the same legal effect as physical paper contracts, and federal law requires the recognition of many electronic agreements.

Uniform Electronic Transactions Act

As of 2011, forty-seven states, the District of Columbia, the Virgin Islands, and Puerto Rico had enacted the Uniform Electronic Transactions Act (UETA), which sets forth four basic rules regarding contracts entered into by parties that agree to conduct business electronically:

1. A record or signature may not be denied legal effect or enforceability solely because it is in electronic form.

2. A contract may not be denied legal effect or enforceability solely because an electronic record was used in its formation.

3. An electronic record satisfies a law that requires a record to be in writing.

4. An electronic signature satisfies a law that requires a signature.[16]

Under UETA, almost any mark or process intended to sign an electronic record will constitute an electronic signature, including a typed name at the bottom of an e-mail message, a faxed signature, and a "click-through" process on a computer screen whereby a person clicks "I agree" on a web page. The essential element necessary to determine the validity of an electronic signature is whether the person intended the process or mark provided to act as a signature and whether it can be attributed to that person.

E-Sign Act

In an effort to ensure more uniform treatment of electronic transactions across the United States, Congress enacted the Electronic Signatures in Global and National Commerce Act, more commonly known as the E-Sign Act, effective October 1, 2000. Consistent with UETA, the E-Sign Act provides that a signature, contract, or other record "may not be denied legal effect, validity, or enforceability solely because it is in electronic form."[17] The provisions of the E-Sign Act are very similar to those of UETA, except that UETA, where enacted, applies to intrastate transactions, whereas the E-Sign Act governs only transactions in interstate and foreign commerce. Moreover, the provisions of the E-Sign Act are mandatory.

The E-Sign Act expressly preempts all state laws inconsistent with its provisions. The E-Sign Act does, however, demonstrate some flexibility toward those states that have adopted UETA by allowing state law "to modify, limit, or supersede" the provisions of the E-Sign Act to the extent that such variations are not inconsistent with the Act.

What variations will ultimately be considered "inconsistent" is not entirely clear and may have to be determined by the courts.

Exclusions

To protect those individuals or companies that choose not to conduct business electronically or do not have access to computers, the E-Sign Act and UETA require that the use or acceptance of electronic records or electronic signatures be voluntary. Moreover, under the E-Sign Act, if a business is legally bound to produce information to a consumer in writing, electronic records may be used only if the business first secures the consumer's informed consent.

Notwithstanding the broad scope of the E-Sign Act and UETA, several classes of documents are not covered by their provisions and thus may not be considered fully enforceable if transacted electronically. Both UETA and the E-Sign Act exclude:

- Wills, codicils, and trusts.
- Contracts or records relating to adoption, divorce, or other matters of family law.
- Contracts governed by certain provisions of the UCC in effect in each state.

Unlike UETA, the E-Sign Act also excludes:

- Court orders and notices and other official court documents.
- Notices of cancellation or termination of utility services.
- Notices regarding credit agreements secured by, or rental agreements for, a primary residence (for example, eviction notices).

INTERNATIONAL SNAPSHOT

By 2011, most countries had enacted basic legislation addressing the issue of electronic signatures.[a] Some countries, including the United Kingdom, Canada, and Australia, take a minimalist approach akin to that of the E-Sign Act. They provide that electronic signatures and records fulfill most existing requirements but do not advocate protocols or technology to speed up implementation of electronic transactions. Other countries, such as Germany and Italy, are more prescriptive; they restrict the types of technology and techniques that can be used and sometimes require an authentication process to validate electronic signatures. Others use a blended approach that outlines standards for certificate authorities and cryptographic digital signatures and establishes a wide basis for acceptance of electronic signatures for legal purposes. This blended approach is currently gaining popularity in a number of countries.

© Cengage Learning 2013

---

16. UNIFORM ELECTRONIC TRANSACTIONS ACT (1999), *available at* http://www.law.upenn.edu/bll/archives/ulc/ecom/ueta_final.pdf (last visited Aug. 30, 2011); David Schumacher, *U.S. Addresses Legal Issues Raised by Electronic Trading*, 4/1/00 INT'L FIN. L. REV. 19 (2000).

17. Electronic Signatures in Global and National Commerce Act, 15 U.S.C. § 7001(a)(1).

a. *International Law*, SIGNNOW, 2011, https://signnow.com/resources/international-digital-and-electronic-signature-law (last visited July 27, 2011).

- Notices of cancellation or termination of health or life insurance benefits.
- Notices of recall.
- Documents required to accompany the transport of hazardous materials, pesticides, or other toxic materials.

DUTY OF GOOD FAITH UNDER THE UCC

Section 1-304 of the UCC states that "[e]very contract or duty within this Act imposes an obligation of good faith in its performance and enforcement." "Good faith" is defined in section 1-201(b)(20) as "honesty in fact and observance of reasonable commercial standards of fair dealing." Section 1-304 imposes on each party a duty not to do anything that will deprive the other party of the benefits of the agreement. One court defined "good faith" as "a compact reference to an implied undertaking not to take opportunistic advantage in a way that could not have been contemplated at the time of drafting, and which therefore was not resolved explicitly by the parties."[18] Good faith in the case of a merchant has been interpreted as the observance of reasonable commercial standards of fair dealing in the trade.

The UCC applies to the enforcement, performance, or modification of a contract for the sale of goods, but not to the formation or procurement of a contract. For example, the Texas Supreme Court refused to invalidate a mutual release of liabilities for violation of good faith after characterizing the mutual release as the formation, not the modification, of a contract.[19]

WARRANTIES

Goods delivered pursuant to a contract may not live up to the buyer's expectations. In many such cases, the buyer can sue the seller for breaching an express or implied warranty that the goods sold would have certain qualities or would perform in a certain way.

The UCC's warranty provisions attempt to determine which attributes of the goods the parties have agreed on. The UCC allows a great deal of flexibility in determining which warranties apply, permitting consideration of the description of the goods, the seller's words, common uses in the trade, the price paid, and the extent to which the buyer communicated particular needs to the seller. As a result, the seller of goods may find itself bound, perhaps unintentionally, by one of the three warranties provided by the UCC: express warranty, implied warranty of merchantability, and implied warranty of fitness for a particular purpose.

Express Warranty

An *express warranty* is an explicit guarantee by the seller that the goods will have certain qualities. Section 2-313 of the UCC has two requirements for the creation of an express warranty. First, the seller must (a) make a statement or promise relating to the goods, (b) provide a description of the goods, or (c) furnish a sample or model of the goods. Second, this statement, promise, description, sample, or model must become a "part of the basis of the bargain" between the seller and the buyer. This second requirement is intended to ensure that the buyer actually relied on the seller's statement when making a purchasing decision. Although the UCC does not define "part of the basis of the bargain," most courts have interpreted it as requiring the buyer to prove reliance. For example, if a car dealer asserts that a car can go 130 mph and the buyer responds that she will never take it above 55, in most jurisdictions the buyer would be unable to recover for breach of warranty if the car failed to go over 75 mph because the buyer could not prove reliance on the statement.

Puffing

Section 2-313(2) provides that a warranty may be found even though the seller never used the word "warranty" or "guarantee" and had no intention of making a warranty. However, if a seller is merely *puffing*—that is, expressing an opinion about the quality of the goods—he or she has not made a warranty. For example, a car salesperson's statement that "this is a top-notch car" is puffing, whereas a factual statement such as "it will get twenty-five miles to the gallon" is an express warranty. Unfortunately, the line between opinion and fact is not always easy to draw. Much turns on the circumstances surrounding the representation, including the identities and relative knowledge of the parties involved.

A number of courts employ a two-prong test to distinguish warranty language from opinion. The first prong is whether the seller asserted a fact of which the buyer was ignorant. If so, the assertion may be a warranty. The second prong is whether the seller merely stated a view on something about which the buyer could be expected to have formed his or her own opinion and whether the buyer could judge the validity of the seller's statement. In this second instance, the seller's statement is an opinion, not an express warranty. The following case illustrates the distinction between sales talk and a warranty.

18. Brooklyn Bagel Boys, Inc. v. Earthgrains Refrigerated Dough Prods., Inc., 212 F.3d 373, 382 (7th Cir. 2000).

19. El Paso Natural Gas Co. v. Minco Oil & Gas, Inc., 8 S.W.3d 309 (Tex. 1999).

| A CASE IN POINT | *In the Language of the Court* | Case 8.2 |

MacNeil Automotive Products, Ltd. v. Cannon Automotive, Ltd.

United States District Court for the Northern District of Illinois
715 F. Supp. 2d 786 (N.D. Ill. 2010).

FACTS   MacNeil Automotive was under contract to provide floor mats to Hyundai and BMW for use in their automobiles. MacNeil in turn contracted with Cannon Automotive for the manufacture of these floor mats. After MacNeil learned that the carpet and rubber portions of the floor mats provided to it by Cannon did not properly adhere, MacNeil sued Cannon for breach of express warranty. Cannon had assured MacNeil that it could "manufacture a quality mat" with "carpet that properly adhered to the mat," that Cannon's mats would "meet MacNeil's and Hyundai's expectations of quality," and that Cannon's mats "would be suitable for their purposes." Cannon asserted that the statements alleged did not amount to an express warranty.

ISSUE PRESENTED   What types of statements by a seller about the quality of goods constitute an express warranty?

OPINION   GOTTSCHALL, J., writing for the U.S. District Court for the Northern District of Illinois:

In order to be actionable for a claim of express warranty, the statement made must be (1) regarding a fact (something that can be proven false, rather than an opinion); (2) of which the buyer is ignorant; and (3) becomes the basis of the parties' bargain. Statements walk a fine line between opinion and fact. Statements made by sellers that a product is "of good quality" and that the buyer would be pleased with the quality of the product are merely "sales talk" and do not constitute express warranties. However, statements that the product would "work for a reasonable period of time" and are "free of defects" are more specific factual representations that would be considered express warranties. In contrast, the statements in the case at bar that the floor mats would be "quality mats" and would "meet . . . expectations of quality," and "would be suitable for their purposes" do not constitute express warranties because they are vague representations that do not assert specific facts of which MacNeil was ignorant. Additionally, these guarantees do not appear to be bargained for between the parties so as to form the basis of their agreement.

The representation by Cannon that they would provide "carpet that properly adhered to the mat" is more specific and does constitute an express warranty. MacNeil was ignorant of the manner in which the carpet would adhere to the mat in Hyundais whereas Cannon possessed this knowledge. Also, the record indicates that MacNeil was concerned about the mats' ability to adhere properly to the carpet, given prior issues with Cannon, and it appears that these representations on the part of Cannon were made in response to these concerns. Therefore, the representations by Cannon that it would provide "carpet that properly adhered to the mat" appear to be a basis of the bargain between the two parties.

RESULT   The district court granted Cannon's motion to dismiss MacNeil's claims of breach of express warranty in part, but denied the motion as to Cannon's specific alleged representation regarding the carpet-mat adhesion.

CRITICAL THINKING QUESTIONS

1. Assume that Cannon's representations that it would produce a mat that would adhere to the carpet were made during oral negotiations between the parties. Further assume that the written contract that the parties entered into after the negotiations contained no representations about the mats but did contain a clause that stated "this written contract represents the entire agreement of the parties." Would the case have turned out differently?

2. Suppose that instead of making personal assurances to MacNeil as to the quality of its product, Cannon maintained a website on which it stated that its product was "of better quality" than a number of specific named competitors because it used superior materials. Would this statement of good quality then constitute an express warranty?

Implied Warranty of Merchantability

The *implied warranty of merchantability* guarantees that the goods are reasonably fit for the general purpose for which they are sold and that they are properly packaged and labeled. The warranty applies to all goods sold by merchants in the normal course of business. It does not depend on the seller's statements or use of a sample or model. Rather, it depends on the identity of the seller as a merchant who deals in goods of a certain kind.

To be merchantable under section 2-314(2) of the UCC, goods must (1) pass without objection in the trade under the contract description; (2) be fit for the ordinary purposes for which such goods are used; (3) be within the variations permitted by the agreement and be of even kind, quality, and quantity within each unit and among all units involved; (4) be adequately contained, packaged, and labeled as the agreement may require; and (5) conform to the promises or affirmations of fact made on the container or label, if any. Fungible goods, such as grain, must be of average quality within the contract description.

Reasonable Expectations

The key issue in determining merchantability is whether the goods do what a reasonable person would expect them to do. The contract description is crucial. Goods considered merchantable under one contract may be considered not merchantable under another. A bicycle with a cracked frame and bent wheels is not fit for the ordinary purpose for which bicycles are used, but it will pass under a contract for the sale of scrap metal.

When no contract description exists, breach is most frequently based on the claim that the goods are not fit "for the ordinary purposes for which such goods are used." Proof that the goods are imperfect or flawed is often insufficient to succeed on this claim. Even imperfect goods can be fit for their ordinary purposes.

In *Lescs v. William R. Hughes, Inc.*,[20] a homeowner filed a claim against Dow Chemical Company when she became ill after moving into a house that had been sprayed with insecticide manufactured by Dow. The homeowner argued that Dow had breached the implied warranty of merchantability by marketing an unreasonably dangerous product. The U.S. Court of Appeals for the Fourth Circuit rejected her claim that the insecticide failed to meet consumer expectations because the warning label on the pesticide had been approved by the Environmental Protection Agency. The court reasoned that "it would be anomalous to hold 'that a consumer is entitled to expect a product to perform more safely than its government mandated warnings indicate.'" (In contrast, as discussed further in Chapter 9, courts have held defendants liable for the tort of negligence even when their conduct satisfied the government standards.)

Implied Warranty of Fitness for a Particular Purpose

The *implied warranty of fitness for a particular purpose,* set forth in section 2-315 of the UCC, guarantees that the goods are fit for a particular purpose beyond the scope of ordinary purposes for which the seller recommended them. Broad in scope, this warranty may apply to merchants and nonmerchants alike.

Unlike the implied warranty of merchantability, the implied warranty of fitness for a particular purpose does not arise in connection with every sale of goods. It will be implied only if four elements are present: (1) the buyer had a particular purpose for the goods, (2) the seller knew or had reason to know of that purpose, (3) the buyer relied on the seller's expertise, and (4) the seller knew or had reason to know of the buyer's reliance. Although the warranty usually arises when the seller is a merchant with some level of skill or judgment, it is not restricted to such circumstances.

A "particular purpose" differs from the ordinary purpose for which a good is used in that a particular purpose contemplates a specific use by the buyer that is peculiar to that buyer or that buyer's business. For example, a seller may know that a particular customer will be using a pair of shoes to climb mountains, not just walking. By contrast, the ordinary purpose is that contemplated by the concept of merchantability. For example, an apartment community successfully sued its pool service company for breach of the implied warranty of fitness after the company sandblasted and repainted the apartment community's pool using a primer that the company had recommended. The court found:

> Plaintiff [the pool service company] knew, or should have known, that Defendant was reasonably relying upon Plaintiff to specify the correct preparation method (sandblasting) and the paint and primer for the indoor and outdoor pools in light of such preparation. Plaintiff breached this warranty when it recommended an incompatible primer for pools that were sandblasted and rough, like the pools at [Defendant].[21]

Disproving Reliance

To prove that the buyer did not rely on the seller's expertise, the seller may try to show that (1) the buyer's expertise was equal to or superior to the seller's, (2) the buyer relied on the skill and judgment of persons hired by the buyer, or (3) the buyer supplied the seller with detailed specifications or designs that the seller was to follow.

Identifiable patents and trademarks can play an interesting role in this area of the law. If the buyer insists on a particular brand and style, he or she cannot be relying on

---

20. 168 F.3d 482 (4th Cir. 1999).

21. Horizon Chem. Co. v. OPR L.P., 2004 WL 3030054 (Minn. D. Ct. Sept. 2, 2004).

the seller's skill or judgment; hence, no implied warranty results. The mere fact that a good has an identifiable patent or trademark, however, does not prove nonreliance, especially if the seller recommended the product to the buyer.

Disclaiming Warranties and Limiting Liability

The seller can avoid responsibility for the quality of the goods under any of these warranties. First, the seller need not make any express warranties. This may be difficult to do, however, because even a simple description of the goods may constitute a warranty. Second, a seller may disclaim any warranties of quality if it follows specifically delineated rules in the UCC designed to ensure that the buyer is aware of, and assents to, the disclaimers. To be effective, (1) a disclaimer of the implied warranty of merchantability must mention merchantability and, if in writing, must be conspicuous; and (2) a disclaimer of the implied warranty of fitness must be in writing and conspicuous.[22] Language to exclude all implied warranties (for example, "AS IS" or "WITH ALL FAULTS") is also sufficient if it makes plain that there is no implied warranty. Third, the seller can refrain from professing expertise with respect to the goods and leave the selection to the buyer.

More commonly, the seller limits its responsibility for the quality of the goods by limiting the remedies available to the buyer in the event of a breach of warranty. A typical method is to include a provision limiting the seller's responsibility for defective goods to repair or replacement. Unless this remedy is clearly identified as exclusive, however, it will be interpreted as additional to all other remedies set forth in the UCC. In addition, a limited or exclusive remedy will not be enforced if the remedy fails in its purpose or operates to deprive either party of the substantial value of the bargain. In that case, the remedies in the UCC will govern as if the parties had not agreed on any remedies of their own.[23] Sellers may also limit their liability by including disclaimers of liability for special or consequential damages and by capping their liability for direct damages to the amounts received under the contract. Some states limit a seller's right to limit liability, especially for personal injury.

Finally, under the UCC, a seller is not an absolute insurer of the quality of goods sold. To recover for breach of warranty, a buyer must prove that (1) the seller made an express or implied warranty under the UCC; (2) the goods were defective at the time of the sale; (3) the loss or injury was caused by the defect rather than the buyer's negligent or inappropriate use of the goods; and (4) the

seller has no affirmative defenses, such as a disclaimer of warranty.

Strict Product Liability versus Breach of Warranty

As an alternative (or, in some cases, in addition) to suing for breach of warranty, the plaintiff may sue in tort for strict product liability (discussed in Chapter 10). A product liability claim may succeed where a breach-of-warranty claim would not. This may happen when there is no contractual relationship between the buyer and the seller. But the remedies available may differ. Product liability actions generally permit recovery only for bodily injury or property damage caused by a defective product. In contrast, warranty actions permit recovery of economic damage suffered by the purchaser who has purchased an inferior or defective product.

MAGNUSON–MOSS WARRANTY ACT

The Magnuson–Moss Warranty Act[24] is a federal law that protects consumers against deception in warranties. It gives a consumer purchaser of a product the right to sue a manufacturer or retailer for failing to comply with the Act or the terms of a written or implied warranty arising from the Act. The Act was adopted "to improve the adequacy of information available to consumers, to prevent deception, and to improve competition in the marketing of consumer products."[25]

Nothing in the Act requires a supplier of consumer products to give a written warranty; the Act applies only when a seller chooses to do so. If the seller does make a written promise or affirmation of fact, however, then it must also state whether the warranty is full or limited to inform the average consumer about the level of protection provided. A *full warranty* gives the consumer the right to free repair or replacement of a defective product. To earn the designation of "full warranty," a warranty must meet minimum standards provided in the Act. A *limited warranty* might restrict the availability of free repair or replacement.

RIGHT TO REJECT NONCONFORMING GOODS

Generally, a buyer that has contracted to purchase goods from a seller must fulfill its obligation and pay for those goods. A buyer has the right to reject nonconforming goods, however. Under section 2-601 of the UCC, if the

22. *See* U.C.C. § 2-316(2).
23. U.C.C. § 2-719(2) cmt. 1 (1962).

24. 15 U.S.C. §§ 2301–12.
25. 15 U.S.C. § 2302(a).

goods or the tender of delivery fails to conform to the contract in any respect, the buyer may reject any or all of the goods. Section 2-602 requires that any rejection be made within a reasonable time after the goods are delivered. After such a rejection, the buyer may not treat the goods as if it owned them. If the buyer has taken possession of the goods before rejecting them, then it must hold the goods with reasonable care for a time sufficient to allow the seller to remove them. As the following case illustrates, the right to reject can be waived by a buyer who continues to use the goods after notifying the seller of its dissatisfaction.

| A CASE IN POINT | *Summary* | Case 8.3 |

Midwest Hatchery & Poultry Farms, Inc. v. Doorenbos Poultry, Inc.

Court of Appeals of Iowa
783 N.W.2d 56 (Iowa App. 2010).

Facts   Doorenbos Poultry produces and sells chicken eggs. Hens begin to lay eggs at approximately seventeen or eighteen weeks old and are most productive in laying eggs when they are between twenty and eighty weeks old. Doorenbos slaughters its older hens at the end of their productive life and replaces them with young hens—called pullets—that are seventeen or eighteen weeks old. Doorenbos contracted with Midwest Hatchery to purchase 112,000 pullets at eighteen weeks of age, to be delivered on December 28, 2006, at a cost of $1.27 per pullet, plus the cost to feed them from the time of hatching to the date of delivery. The contract provided, "Deliveries are subject to availability of the Products, availability of transportation, and availability due to demand from Seller's other customers." The contract also provided, "If Seller breaches this Contract, at Seller's option, customer is entitled to either replacement or refund of the price paid by Customer."

Prior to the agreed-on delivery date, Midwest notified Doorenbos that it would be unable to deliver the pullets on December 28. Doorenbos agreed to the delay and canceled plans to dispose of the 110,000 chickens at its facility that had reached the end of their productive life. Between January 16 and 18, 2007, Midwest delivered 115,581 pullets to Doorenbos, and Doorenbos slaughtered the older hens. However, the pullets delivered by Midwest were between thirteen and fourteen weeks old rather than eighteen weeks old as contracted. Doorenbos could not return the pullets because it had already slaughtered its old hens. Additionally, the building that housed the hens did not have heat, as Doorenbos relied on the body heat of the birds to keep the pipes from freezing in the January cold. The pullets provided by Midwest did not begin laying eggs until February 18, 2007. In the meantime, Doorenbos incurred costs to feed and house the pullets without generating any revenue from egg production.

In August 2007, Midwest sent Doorenbos an invoice for $267,916.76, but Doorenbos paid only $184,135.18, the amount that it believed should have been the cost for the younger pullets, and kept all of the pullets. Midwest sued Doorenbos to recover the balance, and Doorenbos filed a counterclaim for breach of contract. The trial court entered summary judgment in favor of Midwest following a bench trial, and Doorenbos appealed from that judgment.

Issue Presented   Under what circumstances will the buyer of nonconforming goods be deemed to have accepted them?

Summary of Opinion   The Court of Appeals of Iowa explained that when a buyer is not satisfied with the goods it receives, it has three options: (1) reject the nonconforming goods, (2) accept the goods and later revoke acceptance, or (3) accept the goods and sue for damages resulting from the nonconformity. If the buyer accepts the goods, then it must pay at the contract rate for any goods accepted. A buyer is deemed to have accepted goods if the buyer "take[s] or retain[s] them in spite of their nonconformity" or "does any act inconsistent with the seller's ownership."

The court found substantial evidence to conclude that Doorenbos had accepted the pullets within the meaning of these definitions. Doorenbos still had the pullets that Midwest had delivered and was selling their eggs. It had refused Midwest's request for return of the birds in August 2007. Although the owner of Doorenbos testified that he did not know that he could cancel the order, this did not alter the result. Doorenbos could, however, sue

CONTINUED

for breach of contract to recover the damages it suffered as a result of the nonconforming hens.

RESULT Doorenbos was ordered to pay the remaining $83,781.58 balance due under the contract. The court also affirmed Doorenbos's award of $31,732.79 on its counterclaim for breach of contract against Midwest, which left a net amount of $52,048.79 to be paid by Doorenbos.

ALLOCATION OF RISK OF LOSS

Goods can be lost in transit due to events such as fire, earthquake, flood, and theft. In the absence of an agreement to the contrary, UCC section 2-509 places the risk of loss on the party controlling the goods at the time loss occurs, because that party is better able to insure against loss and to take precautions to protect the goods. Section 2-319 expressly authorizes the buyer and seller to allocate risk of loss between them as they see fit and provides shorthand symbols, such as "FOB" (free on board), with defined meanings, to facilitate the expression of such an agreement between the parties.

It is important to note that Article 2's definitions of FOB, FAS, CIF, C&F, and Delivery Ex Ship are inconsistent with INCOTERMS, a set of thirteen primary trade terms, including FAS, FOB, CPT, and CIF, as well as several secondary terms, created by the international mercantile community acting through the International Chamber of Commerce. Traders throughout the world incorporate INCOTERMS into their international sales contracts. The terms are revised every ten years; the latest revision is INCOTERMS, eighth edition, 2010.

For example, the INCOTERMS version of FOB is used only when goods are transported by sea or inland waterway. It requires that the seller load the goods on board the vessel nominated by the buyer. Cost and risk are divided when the goods are actually on board the vessel. The seller must clear the goods for export. The buyer must instruct the seller about the details of the vessel and the port where the goods are to be loaded, and there is no reference to, or provision for, the use of a carrier or forwarder. The seller also has an express obligation to provide any information that the buyer needs to obtain insurance.

Goods Shipped by Carrier

If a sales contract requires or authorizes the seller to ship the goods by carrier, the risk of loss passes to the buyer (1) at the time the goods are properly delivered to the carrier, if the contract does not require delivery at a particular destination; or (2) at the time the carrier tenders the goods to the buyer at the specified destination, if the contract specifies one. If nothing is said about delivery, the contract is not a delivery contract and does not require delivery to the destination.

If the parties indicate that shipment is to be made "FOB seller's place of business" (or "FCA seller's place of business" if INCOTERMS are used), delivery at a particular place is not required, so the risk of loss shifts to the buyer once the goods are properly placed in the possession of the carrier. An indication in the contract that shipment is to be made "FOB buyer's place of business" (or "FCA buyer's place of business" if INCOTERMS are used) means that delivery at a particular place is required, so the risk of loss will not shift to the buyer until the goods are tendered to the buyer at its place of business. The parties' selection of an FOB (or FCA) term in a sales contract controls the allocation of the risk of loss even if contrary language exists elsewhere in the contract.

Goods Held by Independent Warehouse

When the goods are in the possession of an independent warehouse and the seller provides the buyer with a document enabling it to pick up the goods at the warehouse, the risk of loss passes to the buyer when the buyer receives the document entitling it to pick up the goods.

All Other Cases

When the goods are neither to be shipped by carrier nor held by an independent warehouse, the allocation of the risk of loss in transit depends on whether the seller is a merchant. (As mentioned earlier, a seller is a merchant if he or she possesses experience and special knowledge relating to the goods in question.) If the seller is a merchant, the risk of loss passes to the buyer only when the buyer receives physical possession of the goods. If the seller is not a merchant, the risk passes to the buyer upon *tender of delivery*, which occurs when the seller notifies the buyer that it has the goods ready for delivery.

UNCONSCIONABILITY

A party is normally bound by the terms of a contract into which he or she enters. If, however, the contract is so unfair as to shock the conscience of the court, the judge may decline to enforce the offending terms or the entire contract.

Section 2-302(1) of the UCC provides procedural guidelines for judicial review of unconscionable clauses in contracts for the sale of goods, but it does not define "unconscionable." The official comments, however, do provide some guidance. For example, comment 1 to section 2-302 states:

> The basic test is whether, in the light of the general background and the commercial needs of the particular trade or case, the clauses involved are so one-sided as to be unconscionable under the circumstances existing at the time of the making of the contract. . . . The principle is one of the prevention of oppression and unfair surprise . . . and not of disturbance of allocation of risks because of superior bargaining power.

In deciding whether a contract is unconscionable, the court considers evidence in addition to the contractual language, particularly whether (1) the contractual obligation was bargained for and (2) the parties understood and accepted the obligation. As under common law (discussed in Chapter 7), *unconscionability* can be either procedural (relating to the bargaining process) or substantive (relating to the provisions of the contract).

Procedural Unconscionability

A contract is procedurally unconscionable when one party is induced to enter the contract without having any meaningful choice. For example, in highly concentrated industries with few competitors, all the sellers may offer the same unfair contracts on a "take-it-or-leave-it" basis. Such contracts are known as *adhesion contracts*. They are most prevalent in consumer transactions where bargaining power is unequal.

It is also procedurally unconscionable for a seller to tuck oppressive clauses into the fine print or for high-pressure salespersons to mislead illiterate consumers. In commercial transactions, however, it is presumed that the parties have the sophistication to bargain knowledgeably. Hence, procedural unconscionability is more difficult to prove in a commercial setting.

---

ethicalconsideration

Merchants that sell goods on credit to low-income customers often charge a very high rate of interest. Some businesspeople suggest that because low-income persons are statistically more likely to default on loans, creditors must charge a higher interest rate to protect themselves against the increased risk of default. They argue that if sellers are not allowed to charge higher interest rates or prices, low-income buyers will not be able to buy goods on credit. How should a manager balance the need for low-income persons to have credit to buy goods with the need for businesses to make a profit? Are such higher rates and prices ethical? Should there be any limit to what a seller can charge for credit?

Substantive Unconscionability

A contract is substantively unconscionable if its terms are unduly harsh or oppressive or unreasonably favorable to one side, such as when the price is excessive or one party's rights and remedies are unreasonably limited. The courts have not agreed on any well-defined test for determining when a price is so excessive as to be unconscionable. However, prices that were two to three times the price of similar goods sold in the same area have been held unconscionable.

COMMERCIAL IMPRACTICABILITY

The UCC has adopted the doctrine of *commercial impracticability* rather than the common law doctrine of strict impossibility discussed in Chapter 7. Section 2-615 states that unless the contract provides otherwise, a failure to perform is not a breach if performance is made impractical by an event unforeseen by the contract. Section 2-615, the associated official comments, and the cases that have arisen under section 2-615 establish certain criteria that a party seeking discharge from performance must show.

Failure of Underlying Condition

First, a party must show that there was a failure of an underlying condition of the contract, that is, a condition that was not included in the parties' bargain. Contracts provide fully for certain occurrences, and the seller is assumed to have included an appropriate "insurance premium" when setting the contract price. Other risks are deemed too remote and uncertain to be included in the contract price. The function of the court in applying the doctrine of commercial impracticability is to determine which risks were, or properly should have been, allocated to the buyer and which to the seller.

Unforeseen Contingency

In addition to showing that a condition was not reflected in the contract price, a seller seeking discharge must prove that the contingency that prevents performance was both unforeseen and unforeseeable. To some extent every occurrence is foreseeable—there is always some probability that a fire will destroy the anticipated source of supply, that a key person will die, or that various acts of God will occur. Legally, however, a foreseeable contingency is one that the parties should have contemplated in the circumstances surrounding the contracting. If there is a standard trade custom for allocating the risk, it is assumed that a particular contract follows that custom unless it specifies differently.

Official Comment 4 provides an illustrative, but not exhaustive, list of contingencies that are considered unforeseeable. Wars and embargoes are considered unforeseeable; market fluctuations are not.

Impracticable Performance

Even if a party is able to show that there was a failure of an underlying condition of the contract and that it did not implicitly assume the risk of this occurrence, the party must still prove that performance was impracticable. Increased cost alone is not sufficient reason to excuse performance unless it is a marked increase. In one case, a ten- to twelve-fold increase was considered sufficient. In another case, the court observed, "We are not aware of any cases where something less than a 100% cost increase has been held to make a seller's performance impracticable."[26] Transactions that have merely become unprofitable will not be excused. Sellers cannot rely on section 2-615 to get them out of a bad bargain.

Some of the most famous cases dealing with the issue of impracticability involved Westinghouse Electric Corporation and its unsuccessful attempts in the mid-1970s to avoid its obligation to supply 70 million pounds of uranium pursuant to fixed-price contracts with twenty-seven utilities after a sharp increase in uranium prices.[27] Westinghouse claimed that the potential loss of $2 billion made it commercially impractical to meet its obligations. In 1976, Westinghouse brought suit against its uranium suppliers, claiming that an international cartel had caused an unforeseen and precipitous increase in the price of uranium.

As discussed in Chapter 3, the judges involved in the ensuing litigation between Westinghouse and the utilities saw the conflict as primarily a business issue and pushed for settlement. On October 27, 1978, the U.S. District Court for the Eastern District of Virginia concluded that Westinghouse had not met its burden of establishing that it was entitled to be excused from its contractual obligations under section 2-615 of the UCC. The court did not issue its supporting findings of facts and conclusions of law at the time, however; instead, the court urged the parties to settle as it was reluctant for the case to serve as legal precedent. As noted in Chapter 3, most of the cases did, in fact, settle.

REMEDIES

The UCC generally tries to put the nonbreaching party in the same position it would have been in if the contract had been performed. This is usually done through the award of money damages.

Seller's Remedies

If a buyer wrongfully cancels a contract or refuses to accept delivery of the goods covered by the contract, the seller is entitled to damages under section 2-708 of the UCC. The measure of direct damages is the difference between the market price at the time and place for delivery and the unpaid contract price, less expenses saved because of the buyer's breach. If this measure of damages is inadequate to put the seller in as good a position as performance would have, then the seller is entitled to recover the profit (including reasonable overhead) that it would have made from full performance by the buyer. Such a seller is called a *lost volume seller*. The courts split on whether to allow sellers to recover consequential damages under Article 2.

Buyer's Remedies

If a seller wrongfully fails to deliver the goods or repudiates the contract, or if the buyer justifiably rejects the tendered goods, then under section 2-711 of the UCC the buyer has several choices. The buyer may cancel the contract and recover as much of the price as has been paid and then either (1) *cover*, that is, buy the goods elsewhere and be reimbursed for the extra cost of the substitute goods, or (2) recover damages for nondelivery.

If the buyer elects to cover under section 2-712, it must make, in good faith and without unreasonable delay, a reasonable purchase of substitute goods. The buyer may then recover from the seller the difference between the cost of cover and the contract price. If the buyer elects not to cover, then under section 2-713 the buyer is entitled to direct damages. The measure of *direct damages* is the difference between the market price at the time the buyer learned of the breach and the contract price. Section 2-715 of the UCC also permits the buyer to recover *consequential damages* for (1) any loss resulting from general or particular requirements and needs of the buyer that the seller at the time of contracting had reason to know and that could not reasonably be prevented by cover or otherwise, and (2) injury to person or property proximately resulting from any breach of warranty.

Specific Performance

If the promised goods are unique, then under section 2-716 of the UCC a court may order the seller to deliver them to the buyer, that is, order *specific performance*. For example, if there is only one antique Mercedes-Benz of a certain vintage, then damages alone will not be adequate to remedy the loss suffered by the disappointed buyer. Only delivery of the promised car will suffice. If the car is one of thousands, however, monetary damages will suffice because an equivalent car can be purchased elsewhere.

---

26. Publicker Indus., Inc. v. Union Carbide Corp., 17 U.C.C. Rep. Serv. 989 (E.D. Pa. 1975).

27. This discussion is based on William Eagan, *The Westinghouse Uranium Contracts: Commercial Impracticability and Related Matters*, 18 Am. Bus. L.J. 281 (1980).

GLOBAL VIEW

The Convention on Contracts for the International Sale of Goods

Article 2 of the UCC largely unified the laws of the separate states in the United States governing the domestic sale of goods. International sales of goods, however, remain outside the scope of the UCC. As international trade and the global economy grew throughout the twentieth century, the need for more uniform laws throughout the world became apparent. The Convention on Contracts for the International Sale of Goods (CISG), promulgated under the auspices of the United Nations, became effective in 1988. As of August 2011, the Convention had been ratified by seventy-seven countries, including many of the world's largest economies; among the signatories are Canada, China, France, Germany, Japan, Russia, Singapore, and the United States.[28] Today, the signatories to CISG account for nearly three-quarters of the world's imports and exports.[29]

Scope of the Convention

CISG sets out substantive provisions of law to govern the formation of international sales contracts between merchants and the rights and obligations of buyers and sellers engaged in such transactions.[30] Unless both parties expressly opt out of the Convention, CISG automatically applies to (1) sales contracts between merchants with places of business in different countries, if those countries are bound by the Convention ("contracting states"), and (2) sales contracts between merchants with places of business in different countries, if the application of choice-of-law rules of either of these countries would apply the law of a contracting state to the transaction. In other words, sales contracts meeting these requirements will be governed by CISG even if they make no reference to it. Although parties located in contracting states may expressly elect not to have CISG govern their sales contracts, a provision that only calls for the application of the laws of a contracting state does not constitute such an opt-out.

CISG does not apply to sales (1) of goods bought for personal, family, or household use, unless the seller, at any time before or at the conclusion of the contract, neither knew nor ought to have known that the goods were bought for any such use; (2) by auction; (3) on execution [of a judgment] or otherwise by authority of law; (4) of stocks, shares, investment securities, negotiable instruments, or money; (5) of ships, vessels, hovercraft, or aircraft; and (6) of electricity. As for the distinction between goods and services, CISG does not apply to contracts in which goods are sold in conjunction with services unless the preponderance of the obligations of the seller consists of the supply of goods. It also does not govern the liability of the seller for death or personal injury to any person caused by the seller's goods.

CISG applies to oral as well as written contracts of sale. CISG contains no statute of frauds requiring certain contracts to be in writing, unless one party has its place of business in a country that has made a reservation to CISG in this regard. The United States did not make this reservation.

Legal scholars are split over the question of whether CISG is applicable to e-commerce transactions. Although the formation of contracts for the international sale of physical goods by electronic means is generally regarded as covered by CISG,[31] the question of whether the international sale of "digital (intangible) goods" would be covered by CISG is controversial.[32]

Offer and Acceptance

Under CISG, an offer becomes effective when it reaches the offeree, and it may be withdrawn if the withdrawal reaches the offeree before or at the same time as the offer. Until a contract is concluded, an offeror may revoke its offer if the revocation reaches the offeree before the offeree has dispatched its acceptance. An offer cannot be revoked, however, if the offer indicates that it is irrevocable or if the offeree reasonably relied on its irrevocability. Even if irrevocable, an offer is terminated when the offeree's rejection reaches the offeror.

A contract is concluded at the moment acceptance of an offer becomes effective; a statement made by the offeree indicating its assent constitutes such an acceptance. Conduct indicating assent is also acceptance, but silence or inactivity

CONTINUED

---

28. For parties to the convention, see United Nations Treaty Collection, *United Nations Convention on Contracts for the International Sale of Goods*, http://treaties.un.org/Pages/ViewDetails.aspx?src=TREATY&mtdsg_no=X-10&chapter=10&lang=en (last visited Aug. 30, 2011). Several of the world's largest economies, including Brazil, South Korea, and the United Kingdom, have not yet ratified the Convention.

29. Lachmi Singh, *China's Implementation of the UN Sales Convention Through Arbitral Tribunals*, 48 COLUM. J. TRANSNAT'L L. 242, 271 (2010).

30. Article 4 of CISG sets forth the basic principle: "This Convention governs only the formation of the contract of sale and the rights and obligations of the seller and the buyer arising from such a contract. In particular, except as otherwise provided in this Convention, it is not concerned with: (1) the validity of the contract or of any of its provisions or of any usage; [or] (b) the effect which the contract may have on the property in the goods sold." For extensive materials relating to CISG, including international cases and commentary, see the Pace University School of Law's website on the Convention, http:www.cisg.law.pace.edu/cisg/guide.html.

31. Siegfried Eiselen, *Electronic Commerce and the UN Convention on Contracts for the International Sale of Goods (CISG) 1980*, 6 EDI L. REV. 21–46 (1999).

32. *See* Hiroo Sono, *The Applicability and Non-Applicability of the CISG to Software Transactions, in* SHARING INTERNATIONAL COMMERCIAL LAW ACROSS NATIONAL BOUNDARIES: FESTSCHRIFT FOR ALBERT H. KRITZER ON THE OCCASION OF HIS EIGHTIETH BIRTHDAY 512–26 (Camilla B. Andersen & Ulrich G. Schroeter, eds., 2008); Jacqueline Mowbray, *The Application of the United Nations Convention on Contracts for the International Sale of Goods to E-Commerce Transactions: The Implications for Asia*, 7 VINDOBONA J. INT'L COM. L. & ARB. 121–50 (2003).

does not in itself amount to acceptance under CISG. An acceptance becomes effective when it reaches the offeror, although an acceptance is not effective if it fails to reach the offeror within the time the offeror has specified for such acceptance. If the offeror has not specified a time, then the acceptance must reach the offeror within a reasonable time. If the offer is oral, however, it must be accepted by the offeree immediately unless circumstances indicate otherwise.

Recognizing the importance of custom and practice, CISG also provides that if the parties have established practices between themselves, the offeree may accept the offer by performing an appropriate act, such as sending the goods or paying the price, without notifying the offeror. In such a case, acceptance is effective as soon as such act is performed. Such acceptance by performance without notification differs from the UCC, which allows for acceptance by performance but requires notification.

Battle of the Forms

An important difference between the UCC and CISG is the approach to the battle of the forms. Under CISG, a reply to an offer that purports to be an acceptance but contains additional terms or other modifications that *materially* alter the terms of the offer is a rejection of the offer and constitutes a counteroffer. Thus, under CISG, there is no contract in this situation. If, however, the modifications in the reply to an offer do *not materially* alter the terms of the offer and the offeror fails to object in a timely fashion, then there is a contract under CISG. In that situation, the contract will include the terms of the offer with the modifications stated in the acceptance. CISG lists categories of differences that are presumed to alter the terms of the offer in a material respect: price, payment, quality and quantity of the goods, place and time of delivery, extent of one party's liability to the other, and settlement of disputes. The list leaves little for the sphere of "immateriality" and largely effects the old mirror image rule. As explained earlier, under the UCC, an acceptance with additional or conflicting terms may still result in a contract unless the offeree clearly specifies that there will not be a contract unless the offeror accepts the additions or modifications.

Good Faith

CISG provides that it is to be interpreted with regard for promoting "the observance of good faith in international trade." As noted earlier, section 1-304 of the UCC provides that "[e]very contract or duty within this Act imposes an obligation of good faith in its performance and enforcement." The UCC provision at first appears to be broader than the CISG principle, which literally applies only to the interpretation of CISG rather than the conduct of merchants under it. Throughout CISG, however, there are numerous requirements of "reasonableness," such as those for giving notice, making substitutions, relying, measuring inconvenience and expense, delaying performance, examining goods, incurring expenses, and making excuses.

Certain commentators have suggested that the combination of CISG's requirements of good faith in interpretation and of reasonableness in so many areas of merchant behavior creates a broad, albeit uncertain, duty for merchants to conduct themselves with good faith.[33] If that interpretation is correct, then, for example, if a seller requests additional time to deliver goods, a buyer would be required to act in good faith when deciding whether to grant that request. The buyer could not simply decide to enforce the letter of the contract to the seller's detriment if the delay would not, in fact, adversely affect the buyer. This would contrast with the UCC's *perfect tender rule*, which gives the buyer an absolute right to reject any goods not meeting all the contract requirements, including time of delivery.

Implied Warranties

Under CISG, the seller must deliver goods that are of the quantity, quality, and description required by the contract, and such goods must be packaged as specified by the contract. Like the UCC, the Convention holds sellers liable for implied warranties of merchantability and fitness for particular use and for any express warranties they make.[34] CISG makes clear, however, that the implied warranty of merchantability does not attach if the buyer knew that the goods were not fit for ordinary use.

Obligations of the Parties

CISG sets forth the main obligations of both the seller (in Chapter II: Delivery of goods and handing over of documents) and the buyer (in Chapter III: Payment of the price and taking delivery). CISG also deals with breach of contract of the parties and their failure to perform.

Exclusion of CISG from Agreements

U.S. lawyers tend to opt out of CISG in written agreements because of uncertainty regarding the legal consequences of its application. Because CISG differs from the UCC (and for that matter from the laws that govern the sales of goods in other jurisdictions) in several aspects, in some instances it might offer an attractive legal alternative (often only to one of the parties, depending on the role of such party and the otherwise applicable law). The parties should try to understand what their rights and obligations under CISG would be so that they can make an informed decision about its use; if the parties decide that they want to exclude CISG from an agreement, they will need to ensure that it is excluded correctly and completely.

33. *See, e.g.*, Phanesh Koneru, *The International Interpretation of the UN Convention on Contracts for the International Sale of Goods: An Approach Based on General Principles*, 6 MINN. J. GLOBAL TRADE 105 (1997).

34. 15 U.S.C. app. (1987). Convention on Contracts for the International Sale of Goods, art. 35: "Except where the parties have agreed otherwise, the goods do not conform with the contract unless they: (a) are fit for the purposes for which goods of the same description would ordinarily be used; (b) are fit for any particular purpose expressly or impliedly made known to the seller at the time of the conclusion of the contract, except where the circumstances show that the buyer did not rely, or that it was unreasonable for him to rely, on the seller's skill and judgment; (c) possess the qualities of goods which the seller has held out to the buyer as a sample or model; (d) are contained or packaged in the manner usual for such goods or, where there is no such manner, in a manner adequate to preserve and protect the goods."

IN BRIEF

Comparison of Article 2 of the UCC, Common Law, UCITA, and CISG

	Scope	Battle of the Forms	Warranties	Statute of Frauds
Article 2 of UCC	Sale of goods	If both parties are merchants, additional terms are generally incorporated; if not, mirror image rule applies. For different terms, "knockout" rule applies.	1. Implied warranties of merchantability and fitness for a particular purpose 2. Any express warranties made	Sale of $500 or more
Common Law	1. Provision of services 2. Contracts for sale of land or securities 3. Loan agreements	Mirror image rule	Any express warranties made	1. Transfer of real estate 2. Contract cannot be performed within one year 3. Prenuptial agreement 4. Agreement to pay debt of another
UCITA	Computer information (including software, computer games, and online access)	Contract even if acceptance has additional or different terms, unless acceptance materially alters the offer	1. Warranty of noninterference and noninfringement 2. Implied warranties of merchantability of computer program, informational content, fitness for licensee's particular purpose, and fitness for system integration 3. Any express warranties made	Contract for $5,000 or more
CISG	Sale of goods by merchants in different countries unless parties opt out	In practice, mirror image rule	1. Implied warranties of merchantability and fitness for a particular use 2. Any express warranties made	None

THE RESPONSIBLE MANAGER

OPERATING UNDER VARIOUS LEGAL REGIMES

Any manager who enters into contracts on behalf of a business should know which body of contract law will govern the transaction. In particular, the manager should determine whether the transaction is governed by Article 2 of the UCC, the common law rules concerning contracts, CISG, or UCITA. Article 2 applies only to the sale of goods, not services or real property.

Although some things are clearly goods, others may be more difficult to categorize. CISG will apply to most international sales of goods unless the parties affirmatively opt out of its provisions. In Maryland and Virginia, the Uniform Computer Information Transactions Act governs contracts to license or buy software, computer programs, multimedia products,

computer games, and online access. In the forty-eight states that have not enacted UCITA, courts will likely apply Article 2 to software licenses, either directly or by analogy. A manager should obtain legal advice if there is any doubt as to which body of law controls in a particular situation.

Managers should be aware of the requirements that must be met for the valid formation of a contract under the different regimes. In particular, managers should focus on one of the key elements in creating a valid contract: the process of offer and acceptance. This knowledge is crucial to ensuring that the company can enforce the contracts it has entered into and wishes to uphold. In addition, a manager may have

CONTINUED

a valid reason to attempt to avoid an agreement that was not formed in the correct manner. Only if the manager knows the rules of contract formation can he or she assess whether a contract was validly created.

The manner of making an appropriate offer is the same under the UCC and common law. A manager should note, however, that Article 2 allows an offeree to accept an offer, even if the offeree's acceptance contains terms additional to or different from those in the offer. In contrast, CISG in practice generally imposes the mirror image rule applied by the common law. The rules in this area and the corresponding case law are both complex and fact specific. Nonetheless, it is crucial that managers understand these rules before they engage in negotiations. Failure to develop this understanding can lead to unexpected results. A manager or company may be legally bound to a contract even when there was no intention to be bound. Or a manager may inadvertently extinguish an offer by proposing modifications that ultimately the offeree might have been willing to forgo.

Article 2 of the UCC, CISG, and UCITA establish three types of warranties that buyers may rely on when purchasing goods or computer information. Managers should be aware of how each warranty is created, how the warranties are applied, and how liability for products can be limited. These warranties also provide guidelines for managers as to what is expected from a product in terms of quality and suitability for its intended use. It is essential that managers

obtain legal advice in this area because lawsuits for breach of warranty can lead to large awards of damages that are far in excess of the purchase price. Managers must provide adequate instruction and training to salespersons and agents about express and implied warranties. Aggressive salespersons willing to say whatever it takes to close a deal may unwittingly cause their company to be held liable under an implied warranty of fitness for a particular purpose when the seller never intended to make such a warranty.

Managers should also be familiar with the legal doctrines that allow parties legally to back out of contracts. The doctrine of impracticability can protect a party when unexpected changes in circumstances make performance commercially ruinous, though not literally impossible. The doctrine of unconscionability provides guidelines on the legal limits to one-sided contracts. Managers should keep in mind that sometimes more is less; extracting onerous concessions from a weaker party may backfire and cause a judge to declare a set of provisions invalid *in toto*, when less onerous provisions might have passed judicial muster.

Both the UCC and CISG require the parties to act in good faith and in a commercially reasonable manner. Managers should avoid acting in an arbitrary manner and try to accommodate the reasonable requests of the other side (e.g., a seller's request to delay delivery when the delay would not have an adverse effect on the buyer's business).

A MANAGER'S DILEMMA

Putting It into Practice

When Is a Seller Responsible for a Known Software Defect?

Mortenson, a nationwide construction contractor, had used Timberline's Bid Analysis software to assist with its preparation of bids for several years. In 1993, Mortenson issued a purchase order to Softworks, an authorized Timberline dealer, for eight copies of a new version of Bid Analysis. The purchase order did not include a clause stating that the order constituted the entire agreement of the parties. Softworks signed the purchase order and ordered the software from Timberline. The full text of the Timberline license agreement was set forth on the outside of each diskette pouch and in the inside cover of the instruction manuals delivered to Mortenson. The license agreement included the following warning:

> CAREFULLY READ THE FOLLOWING TERMS AND CONDITIONS BEFORE USING THE PROGRAMS. USE OF THE PROGRAMS INDICATES YOUR ACKNOWLEDGEMENT THAT YOU HAVE READ THIS LICENSE, UNDERSTAND IT, AND AGREE TO BE BOUND

> BY ITS TERMS AND CONDITIONS. IF YOU DO NOT AGREE TO THESE TERMS AND CONDITIONS, PROMPTLY RETURN THE PROGRAMS AND USER MANUALS TO THE PLACE OF PURCHASE AND YOUR PURCHASE PRICE WILL BE REFUNDED. YOU AGREE THAT YOUR USE OF THE PROGRAM ACKNOWLEDGES THAT YOU HAVE READ THIS LICENSE, UNDERSTAND IT, AND AGREE TO BE BOUND BY ITS TERMS AND CONDITIONS.

Mortenson's chief estimator claimed that Mortenson never saw any of the licensing information or any of the manuals because the software was installed by Softworks.

Mortenson subsequently used the Precision Bid Analysis software to prepare a bid for a project. On the day of the bid, the software allegedly malfunctioned many times and gave the following message: "Abort: Cannot find alternate." Nevertheless, Mortenson submitted a bid generated by the software. After Mortenson was awarded

CONTINUED

the project, it learned that the bid was approximately $1.95 million lower than it had intended. Mortenson sued Timberline and Softworks for breach of express and implied warranties. After the suit was filed, a Timberline internal memorandum surfaced stating that "[a] bug has been found . . . that results in two rather obscure problems." The memo explained that "[t]hese problems only happen if the following [four] conditions are met." Apparently, other Timberline customers had encountered the same problem, and a new version of the software had been sent to some of these customers. After extensive investigation, Timberline's lead programmer acknowledged that Mortenson's error message appeared when the four conditions were met.[35]

Did Timberline have an ethical obligation to notify all of its customers when it became aware of the defect in its software that could result in significant errors in the calculation of bids? Is Timberline's disclaimer of consequential damages enforceable? Is it unconscionable to allow Timberline to use the disclaimer of consequential damages to avoid liability to its customers for a known product defect?

---

35. M.A. Mortenson Co. v. Timberline Software Corp., 998 P.2d 305 (Wash. 2000).

INSIDE STORY

The Top Five Most Unfair Software License Terms

An IT manager purchases new software for the firm. She opens the box and inserts the CD-ROM for download onto the company server. A screen immediately appears and informs the IT manager that before she can continue to download the software, she must agree to each and every term set forth in a very lengthy, complex legal contract. With no opportunity to bargain or negotiate the terms, she faces a choice: (1) agree to each term contained in the license agreement or (2) immediately close the program and return the software.

Managers often associate the term *contract of adhesion* with a form agreement that a consumer with little bargaining power must accept as a condition to purchasing a freezer or other household product. Yet a 2011 study by Forrester Analysts reveals that software companies impose harsh and unfair licensing terms as a condition to businesses' receiving the most up-to-date software for their firms. According to Forrester, the five most unfair software license terms do the following:

1. Provide for maintenance repricing whereby the software company reserves the right to alter the price of maintenance at its discretion.

2. Insist that all licenses are considered to be purchased for live use even when the licensee is merely evaluating the software.

3. Impose maintenance fees on shelfware, that is, software not currently used by the licensee.

4. Limit functionality enhancements to new products instead of including them in the maintenance contract.

5. Retain the right of the licensor to change licensing policies at any time.[36]

Other common unfair software license terms include charging to fix software bugs, requiring that pricing and contract terms be kept confidential, charging for the use of modules that customers cannot control or track, insisting that the licensee purchase all licenses before implementation commences, packaging product enhancements as new products, and requiring that licenses be purchased up front instead of being phased in over time in accordance with project milestones.[37]

Maintenance charges are among the most contested terms. Maintenance fees give the licensee the right to receive both software updates that increase the speed and efficiency of the software and access to experts at the software company to address software issues when they arise.[38] Oracle and other companies typically charge an annual rate for maintenance equal to 22% of the license list price.[39] Licenses are often sold at a discounted

CONTINUED

---

36. Cliff Saran, *The Five Software Licensing Tricks CIOs Hate*, COMPUTERWEEKLY.COM, July 20, 2011, http://www.computerweekly.com/Articles/2011/07/20/247340/The-five-software-licensing-tricks-CIOs-hate.htm (last visited July 21, 2011).

37. Forrester Analysts, *Please Vote in Our Unfair Licensing Policies Survey*, COMPUTER WORLD UK, Mar. 24, 2011, http://blogs.computerworlduk.com/sourcing-and-vendor-management/2011/03/please-vote-in-our-unfair-licensing-policies-survey/index.htm (last visited July 23, 2011).

38. *See* Mary Hayes Weier, *Software Maintenance Fees: Time for This Model to Change?*, INFORMATIONWEEK, Jan. 24, 2009, at 1, http://www.informationweek.com/news/software/enterprise_apps/212902014 (last visited July 21, 2011).

39. *Id.* at 1.

price, but instead of basing the maintenance fee on the discounted price, software companies use the list price to calculate the fee.[40] The licensing term deemed most unfair by Forrester is the maintenance repricing provision, which gives the software company the right to increase the maintenance rate at will.

Software companies earn considerable money from maintenance charges. For example, Oracle generates 51% of its revenues from maintenance fees.[41] Often, these maintenance charges are not open to negotiation,[42] so the user must either pay the 22% fee or do without the upgrades that only the software company can provide. Although software companies justify these fees as necessary to pay for product improvements and updates,[43] Forrester's Ray Wang estimates that between 70% and 80% of the maintenance fees demanded are not used for this purpose.[44]

Software companies generally do not offer a personalized maintenance package. As a result, businesses cannot purchase only the services they require.[45] For example, if a company wants to purchase only upgrades while outsourcing its day-to-day maintenance for fixing bugs and the like to another firm at a lower price, there is no opportunity to negotiate a discount on the flat 22% rate.

Duncan Jones of Forrester Analysts recommends that businesses reject unfair license terms.[46] Some companies have taken this advice and turned to third-party maintenance firms that will service the software at a significantly lower price.[47] Although this move is risky because the business will no longer have the right to innovative updates that only the licensing software company can provide, widespread rejection of unfair terms may enable the market to regulate software companies' use of such terms, or, at the very least, result in the reduction of maintenance costs.

---

40. Saran, *supra* note 36.
41. *Id.* at 2.
42. *Id.* at 1.
43. *Id.* at 3.
44. *Id.*

45. *Id.* at 4.
46. *Id.* at 1.
47. Weier, *supra* note 38, at 1.

KEY WORDS AND PHRASES

acceptance   208

adhesion contracts   221

battle of the forms   209

browse-wrap agreement   212

click-wrap license   212

commercial impracticability   221

consequential damages   222

cover   222

direct damages   222

doctrine of first sale   206

express warranty   215

firm offer   213

fixtures   206

full warranty   218

goods   206

implied warranty of fitness for a particular purpose   217

implied warranty of merchantability   217

limited warranty   218

merchant   206

mirror image rule   208

offer   208

perfect tender rule   224

puffing   215

shrink-wrap license   212

specific performance   222

statute of frauds   213

unconscionability   221

QUESTIONS AND CASE PROBLEMS

1. Before deciding what remedies are available under Article 2 of the UCC, one must first determine whether the transaction involved the sale of goods. Consider the following cases.

   a. Wachter, a construction company, entered into a contract to purchase an accounting and project management software package from DCI, a company that develops, markets, and supports software for construction companies. The package included "installation of the software, a full year of maintenance, and a training and consulting package." Was the contract for a sale of goods or services? [*Wachter Management Co. v. Dexter & Chaney, Inc.*, 144 P.3d 747 (Kan. 2006).]

   b. A customer sued a New York restaurant for breach of warranty after a glass of water allegedly exploded in his hand during the course of a meal. Does the claim involve the sale of goods? [*Gunning ex rel. Gunning v. Small Feast Caterers, Inc.*, 777 N.Y.S.2d 268 (Sup. 2004).]

   c. Brenda Brandt underwent an operation at the Sarah Bush Lincoln Health Center to implant a ProtoGen Sling to resolve her urinary incontinence. Instead of solving the problem, the sling resulted in serious complications and was subsequently removed. After the device was recalled by its manufacturer, Brandt sued the Health Center for breach of warranty. Does the claim involve the sale of goods or services? [*Brandt v. Boston Scientific Corp.*, 792 N.E.2d 296 (Ill. 2003).]

2. Joseph Boud visited Wasatch Marine, a Salt Lake City retailer run by SDNCO, Inc., that sells yachts manufactured by Cruisers. During the visit, Wasatch gave Boud a copy of Cruisers' sales brochure, which included a photograph of Cruisers' 3375 Esprit model apparently moving at a high rate of speed. The photograph had the following caption:

> Offering the best performance and cruising accommodations in its class, the 3375 Esprit offers a choice of either stern drive or inboard power, superb handling and sleeping accommodations for six.

Based in part on the photo and caption, Boud took a test-drive and signed a contract to purchase a 3375 Esprit model yacht for more than $150,000. During the test-drive and a subsequent test-drive a week later, the yacht manifested several electrical and mechanical problems. Pursuant to a limited warranty in its sales contract, Wasatch serviced the yacht and attempted to fix the problems. After the problems persisted during a third test-drive, Boud sought to cancel the sales contract. Cruisers responded by offering to repair or replace the defective parts in accordance with its limited warranty. Boud filed a lawsuit seeking rescission on the basis that the photograph and caption were themselves an express warranty and that Cruisers and Wasatch had breached this warranty. How will Wasatch respond? Will the court find in favor of Boud or the defendant? On what basis? [*Boud v. SDNCO, Inc.*, 54 P.3d 1131 (Utah 2002).]

3. Hardie-Tynes Manufacturing Company subcontracted with Hunger United States Special Hydraulic Cylinders Corporation to manufacture two hydraulic cylinders to be used in construction of the Jordanelle Dam in Utah. After Hardie-Tynes sent a request for quotations for Hunger's best price for the two cylinders, Hunger responded with a letter providing specific quantity, price, delivery, and payment terms. Both parties agreed that this constituted an offer to contract. A copy of Hunger's standard terms and conditions, which included a provision attempting to specify a mode of acceptance and limiting acceptance to Hunger's terms, accompanied the offer. None of the terms related to payment of attorneys' fees in the event of a contract dispute.

Hardie-Tynes accepted Hunger's offer by sending a purchase order, which required payment of attorneys' fees in the event that Hardie-Tynes commenced litigation upon Hunger's default. Like Hunger, Hardie-Tynes limited the agreement to its own terms.

The cylinders manufactured by Hunger did not comply with government standards. Hardie-Tynes sued Hunger for breach of contract and claimed that it was entitled to recover attorneys' fees. Did Hunger and Hardie-Tynes enter into a contract? If so, what were its terms? Would your answer differ if the transaction were governed by CISG? [*Hunger United States Special Hydraulic Cylinders Corp. v. Hardie-Tynes Manufacturing Co.*, 41 U.C.C. Rep. Serv. 2d 165 (10th Cir. 2000).]

4. Aquila, a public utility that produces electrical power, contracted with C.W. Mining for C.W. to provide Aquila with 1,550,000 tons of coal during the years 2004–2006. The contract contained a force majeure clause, which provided:

> THE TERM "FORCE MAJEURE" AS USED HEREIN SHALL MEAN ANY AND ALL CAUSES BEYOND THE REASONABLE CONTROL OF THE PARTY FAILING TO PERFORM, INCLUDING BUT NOT LIMITED TO ACTS OF GOD; . . . LABOR DISPUTES; BOYCOTTS; LOCKOUTS; LABOR AND MATERIAL SHORTAGES; . . . ; BREAKDOWNS OF OR DAMAGE TO PLANTS, EQUIPMENT, OR FACILITIES; . . . OR OTHER CAUSES OF A SIMILAR NATURE WHICH WHOLLY OR PARTLY PREVENT OR MAKE UNREASONABLY COSTLY (I) THE MINING, DELIVERING, OR LOADING OF THE COAL BY SELLER; OR (II) THE RECEIVING, TRANSPORTING, ACCEPTING, OR UTILIZING OF THE COAL BY BUYER AT THE STATION. TO BE CONSIDERED UNREASONABLE SUCH INCREASED COSTS MUST BE SUBSTANTIAL AND SUSTAINED SO THAT MINING IS NO LONGER POSSIBLE. THIS SECTION SHALL NOT BE CONSTRUED TO REQUIRE EITHER PARTY TO PREVENT, SETTLE OR OTHERWISE AVOID OR TERMINATE A STRIKE, WORK SLOWDOWN, OR OTHER SIMILAR LABOR ACTION.

The provision also required that written notice of the force majeure be given.

Less than a week after signing the contract, C.W. was hit by a labor strike that continued for two years. In addition, C.W. suffered several roof collapses, necessitating the closure of two of its mines. C.W. notified Aquila that it considered the strike a force majeure event and that its coal shipments would be reduced as a result; however, C.W. never notified Aquila that it considered the geological issues that led to the collapse of the roofs in the mines to be a force majeure event. Aquila accepted the coal that C.W. was able to deliver and purchased the remainder of the coal it required on the spot market, but it sent C.W. a letter stating that it did not excuse C.W. from its obligations under the contract. Almost a year later, C.W. informed Aquila of its intent to cancel the contract entirely, citing the force majeure provision. After the cancellation, Aquila entered into another long-term contract with Consolidated Coal under terms that were less favorable to Aquila, including higher prices for coal with higher sulfur content. Aquila sued C.W. for damages incurred as a result of C.W.'s nonperformance under the contract. How should C.W. respond? What result? [*Aquila, Inc. v. C.W. Mining*, 545 F.3d 1258 (10th Cir. 2008).]

5. In 1991, Brian Yarusso catapulted over the handlebars of his off-road motorcycle while traveling over a series of dirt moguls at a dirt motocross track in Newark, Delaware. He landed on his head, flipped over, and came to rest face down in the dirt. As a result of the accident, Yarusso suffered quadriplegia. Yarusso was wearing a full complement of safety equipment, including a Bell Moto-5 helmet, a full-face motocross helmet that was designed for off-road use. The Bell Moto-5 helmet complied with the U.S. Department of Transportation standards and was also certified by the Snell Foundation, a leading worldwide helmet research and testing laboratory. The owner's manual for the helmet included the following:

> **Five Year Limited Warranty:** Any Bell helmet found by the factory to be defective in materials or workmanship within five years from the date of purchase will be repaired or replaced at the option of the manufacturer. . . . This warranty is expressly in lieu of all other warranties, and any implied warranties of merchantability or fitness for a particular purpose created hereby, are limited in duration to the same duration of the express warranty herein. Bell shall not be liable for any incidental or consequential damages. . . .

> **Introduction:** Your new Moto-5 helmet is another in the long line of innovative off-road helmets from Bell. . . . [T]he primary function of a helmet is to reduce the harmful effects of a blow to the head. However, it is important to recognize that the wearing of a helmet is not an assurance of absolute protection. NO HELMET CAN PROTECT THE WEARER AGAINST ALL FORESEEABLE IMPACTS.

Yarusso filed suit against Bell. He testified at trial that he had purchased the helmet based on Bell's assertion that the helmet's primary function was to reduce the harmful effects of a blow to the head. On what grounds could Yarusso sue Bell? What will Bell argue in its defense? Who will prevail? Could Bell have done anything that would have avoided this lawsuit? [*Bell Sports, Inc. v. Yarusso*, 759 A.2d 582 (Del. 2000).]

6. Carole Van Tassell made online purchases of products from ChefsCatalog.com, a website owned by Pikes Peak. After the purchase, Pikes Peak transmitted her credit and debit card information to United Marketing without her knowledge or consent. United Marketing used her information to enroll her in a negative-option membership program, resulting in charges of $14.95 per month until she finally discovered the charges and called to cancel membership

in the program. When Van Tassell sued for consumer fraud, Pikes Peak sought to compel arbitration, claiming that Van Tassell had agreed to the arbitration clause in the Conditions of Use on the ChefsCatalog.com website when she made her purchase. Van Tassell argued that she was not bound by the Conditions of Use because they were not sufficiently conspicuous to provide the notice necessary for formation of an enforceable browse-wrap agreement. Although the Conditions of Use were hyperlinked on the ChefsCatalog.com website under the "Consumer Service" link, they were not hyperlinked on the checkout page. Is Van Tassell required to arbitrate her claims? [*Van Tassell v. United Marketing Group, LLC*, 2011 U.S. Dist. LEXIS 72088 (N.D. Ill. July 5, 2011.]

7. American Brass manufactured and sold brass and copper products, primarily in coil form. This manufacturing process generated a considerable amount of waste in the form of dust that American Brass sold to Westmin Corporation for use in a trace mineral premix that Westmin in turn sold to Nufeeds, Inc. for use in its cattle feed products. When it found dioxin in the dust, Nufeeds was forced to recall its cattle feed products. Nufeeds then sued American Brass for breach of the warranty of merchantability. What arguments can American Brass make in its defense? Who should win? [*Nufeeds v. Westmin Corp.*, 59 U.C.C. Rep. Serv. 2d 422 (Md. 2006).]

8. Cablescope, a cable supply and installation firm, entered into a contract pursuant to which ASK Technologies agreed to sell, deliver, and install new computer hardware and software. An ASK technician began to install the ASK system at Cablescope's offices, but numerous bugs in the system were discovered during the installation. Cablescope found that the technician was either unwilling or unable to perform the work required to integrate the system with Cablescope's existing system. As a result, Cablescope informed ASK that it was dissatisfied with the technician's work and did not want him to return. In the following weeks, Cablescope informed ASK twice by letter that the installation had not been adequately performed. On the basis of ASK's nonperformance, Cablescope refused to pay for the equipment and services supplied by ASK, although it continued to use the system for the next nine months.

ASK sued to recover payments plus interest for the computer system and services provided to Cablescope, alleging breach of contract. What is Cablescope's defense? How will the court decide? Why? [*ASK Technologies, Inc. v. Cablescope, Inc.*, 2003 WL 22400201 (S.D.N.Y. Oct. 20, 2003).]

CHAPTER 9

TORTS AND PRIVACY PROTECTION

INTRODUCTION

WHAT IS A TORT?

A *tort* is a civil wrong resulting in injury to a person or property. A tort case is brought by the injured party to obtain compensation for the wrong done. A crime, by contrast, is a wrong to society that is prosecuted by the state. (Criminal law is discussed in Chapter 14.) Even though a crime may be committed against an individual, the victim is not a party to a criminal action. Criminal law is generally concerned with protecting society and punishing the criminal, not with compensating the victim.

The distinctions between tort and criminal law are not always as clear as they first appear, however. A criminal statute might call for the criminal to compensate the victim. The victim might sue the perpetrator of the crime in tort, using the violation of a criminal statute as a basis for the tort claim. In some instances, tort law, like criminal law, purports to protect society through the award of punitive damages.

CHAPTER OVERVIEW

This chapter first discusses intentional torts, which fall into three general categories: (1) torts that protect individuals from physical and mental harm, (2) torts that protect interests in property, and (3) torts that protect certain economic interests and business relationships. The chapter then addresses negligence (including an accountant's liability to third parties) and strict liability. Tortious activity by more than one individual or entity raises the issues of vicarious liability and apportioned responsibility. Finally, the chapter discusses laws dealing with the privacy and security of personal information.

ELEMENTS OF AN INTENTIONAL TORT AND DEFENSES

Intentional torts require the plaintiff to prove (1) actual or implied intent, (2) a voluntary act by the defendant, (3) causation, and (4) injury or harm. The act must be the actual and legal cause of the injury. The act required depends on the specific intentional tort. A single set of facts may give rise to claims under more than one tort.

Intent

Intent is the subjective desire to cause the consequences of an act. *Actual intent* can be shown by evidence that the defendant intended a specific consequence to a particular individual. Intent is implied if the defendant knew that the consequences of the act were certain or substantially certain, even if he or she did not actually intend any consequence at all.

As the degree of certainty of the result decreases, the defendant's conduct loses the character of intent and becomes recklessness. As the result becomes even less certain, the act becomes negligence, which is discussed later in this chapter. For example, if Metro Corporation's custodian, Ted, dumped garbage out of Metro's third-floor office window onto a busy sidewalk and hit Alexa, the law would likely imply intent to hit Alexa. Even though Ted may have had no subjective intention of hitting Alexa with the garbage, throwing it onto a busy sidewalk was substantially certain to result in at least one pedestrian being hit. However, if late one night Ted put garbage in the middle of the sidewalk in front of the office building for morning pickup and Alexa tripped over it, the intent to cause harm is not so clear. If intent is not established, Ted will not be liable for the intentional tort of battery, which requires intent to bring about a harmful or offensive contact. Alexa might still be able to establish negligence, however, if she can show that a reasonable person would not have left the garbage on the sidewalk.

Intent may be transferred. If the defendant intended to hit one person, but instead hit the plaintiff, the intent requirement is met as to the plaintiff.

Defenses

Even if a plaintiff has proved all the elements of an intentional tort, the defendant may raise a legal defense to absolve himself or herself of liability. The most frequently raised defense is consent. If the plaintiff consented to the defendant's act, there is no tort. Even if the plaintiff did not explicitly consent, the law may imply consent. For example, a professional athlete injured during practice is deemed to have consented to the physical contact attendant to practice. The defendant may also be absolved of liability by a claim of self-defense or defense of others.

INTENTIONAL TORTS TO PROTECT PERSONS

The intentional torts of battery, assault, false imprisonment, intentional infliction of emotional distress, defamation, and invasion of privacy are designed to protect individuals from physical and mental harm.

Battery

Tort law recognizes a right to have one's body be free from harmful or offensive contact. Battery is the violation of that right.

Battery is intentional, nonconsensual, harmful, or offensive contact with the plaintiff's body or with something in contact with it. Offensive contact, such as dousing a person with water or spitting in his or her face, may be a battery, even if the plaintiff has suffered no physical harm. The contact may be by the defendant directly or by something the defendant has set in motion. For example, putting poison in someone's food is a battery.

A company president committed battery when he spanked an employee with a carpenter's level in a hazing ritual while other employees watched.[1] The jury awarded $6,000 for pain and suffering and loss of consortium, and $1 million in punitive damages. The trial court found the punitive damages award excessive and reduced it to $130,000.

Assault

The tort of assault also protects the right to have one's body left alone. Unlike battery, however, it does not require contact. *Assault* is an intentional, nonconsensual act that gives rise to the apprehension (though not necessarily the fear) that a harmful or offensive contact is imminent.

Generally, assault requires some act, such as a threatening gesture, plus the ability to follow through immediately with a battery. A punch thrown from close range that misses its target may be an assault, but a threat to punch someone out of punching range is not. For example, if someone makes a threatening gesture and says, "I would hit you if I weren't behind this desk," and is in fact behind a desk, there is no assault because the immediacy requirement has not been met. Similarly, the threat "I'll beat you up if you come to class next week" is not immediate enough to be an assault.

False Imprisonment

The tort of false imprisonment protects the right to be free from restraint of movement. *False imprisonment* is intentional, nonconsensual confinement by physical barriers, by physical force, or by threats of force. It requires that the plaintiff either knew he or she was confined or suffered harm as a result of the confinement.

False imprisonment has been found when the plaintiff's freedom of movement was restricted because of force applied to the plaintiff's valuable property. For example, it is false imprisonment if a store clerk grabs a package from a customer walking out the door, because the customer cannot be expected to abandon the package to leave the store.

Shopkeepers who detain and later release a person mistakenly suspected of shoplifting are sometimes sued for false imprisonment. Most states have legislation exempting shopkeepers from such claims if the shopkeeper acted in good faith and the detention was made in a reasonable manner, for a reasonable time, and was based on reasonable cause.

Intentional Infliction of Emotional Distress

The tort of intentional infliction of emotional distress protects the right to peace of mind. The law has been slow to provide redress for purely mental injuries and is still evolving in this area. Jurisdictions differ sharply in their acceptance of this tort. In most jurisdictions, to prove *intentional infliction of emotional distress*, a plaintiff must show (1) outrageous conduct by the defendant; (2) intent to cause, or reckless disregard of the probability of causing, emotional distress; (3) severe emotional suffering; and (4) actual and proximate (or legal) causation of the emotional distress. The mental distress must be *foreseeable*, in other words, a condition that a reasonable person could have anticipated as a result of his or her actions. The defendant is liable only to the extent that the plaintiff's response is reasonably within the range of normal human emotions. The reluctance of courts to accept intentional infliction of emotional distress as an independent tort most likely stems from fear that plaintiffs will file false claims. Therefore, some jurisdictions also require a physical manifestation of the emotional distress.

---

1. Smith v. Phillips Getschow Co., 616 N.W.2d 526 (Wis. 2000).

The defendant's acts must be outrageous or intolerable. Insulting, abusive, threatening, profane, or annoying conduct is not in itself a tort. Everyone is expected to be hardened to a certain amount of abuse. In determining outrageousness, courts consider both the context of the conduct and the relationship of the parties. For example, an employee can expect to be subjected to evaluation and criticism in the workplace, and neither criticism nor discharge is in itself outrageous. On the other hand, sexual harassment by a supervisor in the workplace is less tolerated than it might be if, for example, a patron in a nightclub engaged in the same conduct.

In *Ford v. Revlon, Inc.*,[2] the Supreme Court of Arizona found Revlon liable for intentional infliction of emotional distress after its employee, Leta Fay Ford, was harassed by her supervisor, the manager for the purchasing department. In addition to making vulgar and threatening remarks to Ford, the manager held her in a chokehold and fondled her at a company picnic. Ford repeatedly complained to management, but Revlon did not confront the supervisor for nine months. Indeed, one manager to whom Ford complained told her that her complaint was too hot to handle and encouraged her to try not to think about her predicament. Ford not only suffered emotional distress but also developed physical complications, including high blood pressure and chest pains, as a result of her stressful work environment. Revlon had a specific policy and several guidelines for handling sexual harassment claims but recklessly disregarded them.

Defamation

Defamation is the communication (often termed *publication*) to a third party of an untrue statement, asserted as fact, that injures the plaintiff's reputation by exposing him or her to "hatred, ridicule or contempt." *Libel* is written defamation, and *slander* is spoken defamation. The distinction between libel and slander is sometimes blurred with respect to modern communications.

Different rules apply to the requirement of injury to reputation depending on whether the defamation is spoken or written. In an action for slander, the plaintiff must prove that he or she has suffered actual harm, such as the loss of credit, a job, or customers, unless the statement is so obviously damaging that it falls into the category of slander *per se*. *Slander per se* means that the words are slanderous in and of themselves. For example, a statement that a person has committed a serious crime, is guilty of sexual misconduct, or is not fit to conduct business is slander *per se*. In an action for libel, the law presumes injury; that

is, no actual harm need be shown unless the statement on its face is not damaging.

An opinion is defamation only if it implies a statement of objective fact. In *Sagan v. Apple Computer, Inc.*,[3] noted astronomer Carl Sagan sued for libel when Apple changed its code name for a new personal computer from "Carl Sagan" to "Butt-Head Astronomer" after Sagan demanded that the company cease using his name. The court ruled that the dispositive question in determining whether a statement of opinion can form the basis of a libel action is whether a reasonable fact finder could conclude that the statement implies an assertion of fact. The court found that a reasonable fact finder would conclude that Apple was not making a statement of fact about Sagan's competency as an astronomer in using the figurative term "Butt-Head" and would understand that the company was using the figurative term to retaliate in a humorous and satirical way for Sagan's reaction to Apple's use of his name. In addition, the court found that the statement that Sagan was a "Butt-Head Astronomer" could not rest on a core of objective evidence, so it could not be proved true or false.

In contrast, the U.S. Court of Appeals for the Second Circuit found that a lawyer's libel claim against the American Association of University Women's Legal Advocacy Fund (AAUW) was based on a statement of fact, not opinion.[4] In its directory of attorneys willing to consult with women considering bringing gender discrimination claims, the AAUW published an entry that stated: "At least one plaintiff has described Flamm as an 'ambulance chaser' with interest only in 'slam dunk cases.'" The appeals court found that this statement contained in a "fact-laden" directory did not simply express an opinion, but could reasonably be interpreted to imply a factual statement that Flamm engaged in the unethical solicitation of clients and took only easy cases.

The requirement of publication generally means that the statement must be made in the presence of a third person. Thus, the statement "You are a thief" made in a one-on-one conversation is not defamation. However, some courts have adopted the doctrine of *self-publication* to give an employee a claim for defamation when an employer, in firing an employee, makes a false assertion that the employer could reasonably expect that the employee would be required to repeat to a prospective employer.

Defenses and Privileges

Truth is an absolute defense to a defamation claim in most jurisdictions. The law presumes that the plaintiff has a pristine reputation, but it will not protect a reputation the plaintiff does not deserve. The burden is on the defendant to prove that the derogatory statements are true.

2. 734 P.2d 580 (Ariz. 1987). *But see* Hoffman-La Roche, Inc. v. Zeltwinger, 144 S.W.3d 438 (Tex. 2004) (dismissing a claim for infliction of emotional distress based on sexual harassment because it was based on the same facts as the plaintiff's causes of action for violation of the Texas statute prohibiting sexual harassment).

3. 874 F. Supp. 1072 (C.D. Cal. 1994).
4. Flamm v. Am. Ass'n of Univ. Women, 201 F.3d 144 (2d Cir. 2000).

Other defenses to defamation actions are framed in terms of privilege and may be asserted in a number of circumstances. An *absolute privilege* cannot be lost. A *qualified privilege* can be lost under certain conditions. If the defendant has an absolute privilege, he or she can publish with impunity a statement he or she knows to be false. The defendant can even do so with the most evil intention. Absolute privilege is limited to situations in which (1) the plaintiff has consented to the publication, (2) the statement is made by a government official in the performance of governmental duties, (3) the statement is made by participants in judicial proceedings, or (4) the statement is made between spouses.

There is a qualified privilege (1) to make statements to protect one's own personal interests, including statements to a peer review committee; (2) to make statements to protect legitimate business interests, such as statements to a prospective employer; and (3) to provide information for the public interest, such as credit reports. A qualified privilege can be lost if the person making the statement abuses the privilege.

Public Figures and Media Defendants   The media, such as newspapers, television, online news sources, and radio, have a qualified privilege that is almost absolute when they are commenting on a public official or a public figure. The U.S. Supreme Court, in applying the First Amendment right of freedom of the press, has held that a public official or public figure cannot recover damages for defamation by a media defendant absent a showing of *actual malice.* That means the plaintiff must prove that the statement was made with the knowledge that it was false or with a reckless disregard as to whether it was false. (Other aspects of the First Amendment are discussed in Chapter 4.)

Public officials include legislators, judges, and police officers. *Public figures* are those who are injected into the public eye by reason of the notoriety of their achievements or the vigor and success with which they seek the public's attention. A private individual does not automatically become a public figure simply because he or she is involved in a public event, however.[5]

A publicly traded corporation is generally considered a public figure, however, and thus must prove actual malice to prevail in a defamation suit. Because proving actual malice can be difficult, a corporation that anticipates that the press may publish an unfavorable story about its business may take proactive steps to counteract the negative publicity, rather than try to initiate a defamation action after the fact in court. In October 1999, the diet product company Metabolife International, Inc. became concerned that ABC would broadcast an unfair report on the medical risks of a dietary supplement sold by Metabolife. The company therefore posted on the Internet

a complete, unedited, videotaped interview between an ABC News correspondent and the company's chief executive. Although ABC said that Metabolife's decision to post the interview on the Internet would not affect the interview that it broadcast, television executives indicated that in the future networks might ask interviewees to agree not to make material from the interview public until after it is broadcast on television.[6]

A plaintiff who is not a public figure does not need to prove malice to prevail in a defamation action. A private plaintiff can recover if the defendant acted with knowledge, acted in reckless disregard of the facts, or was negligent in failing to ascertain the facts. If the plaintiff proceeds on a negligence theory, he or she must prove actual damages, such as loss of business or out-of-pocket costs. If the plaintiff proves malice, however, then damages are presumed, so no proof of damages is required.

Statutory Defenses   In addition to common law privileges, statutory defenses may protect speakers. For instance, the Communications Decency Act of 1996 (CDA) provides that no provider or user of an interactive computer service will be held liable for defamatory content provided by a third party.[7] Applying this statute, the U.S. Court of Appeals for the Fourth Circuit refused to hold America Online (AOL) liable for defamation when an unidentified user posted offensive (and false) messages related to the bombing of the Oklahoma City federal building and attributed these messages to the plaintiff.[8]

Invasion of Privacy

Invasion of privacy is a violation of the right to keep personal matters to oneself. As the Minnesota Supreme Court explained: "The right to privacy is an integral part of our humanity; one has a public persona, exposed and active, and a private persona, guarded and reserved. The heart of our liberty is choosing which parts of our lives shall become public and which parts we shall hold close."[9] Invasion of privacy can take several forms.

Intrusion is objectionable prying, such as eavesdropping or unauthorized rifling through files. Injunctions or court orders are usually available to prevent further intrusion. There must be a reasonable expectation of privacy in the thing into which there is intrusion. For example, there is no legitimate expectation of privacy in conversations in a public restaurant. The tort of intrusion does not require publication of the information obtained.

Public disclosure of private facts requires publication of non-newsworthy private facts, for example, by stating in

---

5. Wells v. Liddy, 186 F.3d 505 (4th Cir. 1999).

6. Bill Carter, *Anxious Pill Maker Puts ABC Interview of Its Chief on the Web*, N.Y. TIMES, Oct. 7, 1999.

7. 47 U.S.C. § 230.

8. Zeran v. Am. Online, Inc., 129 F.3d 327 (4th Cir. 1997).

9. Bodah v. Lakeville Motor Express, Inc., 663 N.W.2d 550, 553 (Minn. 2003).

a newspaper that the plaintiff does not pay debts or posting such a notice in a public place. The matter must be private, such that a reasonable person would find publication offensive. Unlike in a defamation case, truth is not a defense. In *Benz v. Washington Newspaper Publishing Co., LLC*,[10] a plaintiff sued for public disclosure of private facts when a former acquaintance posted her home and work e-mail addresses and phone numbers on a website in response to advertisements seeking sexual relations. The

U.S. District Court for the District of Columbia denied the defendant's motion to dismiss the action, concluding that the plaintiff's contact information constituted private facts, even though it was already available on the Internet, because "[i]ndividuals have a privacy interest in their home addresses and phone numbers."

In the following case, the Minnesota Supreme Court considered whether employees could recover for invasion of privacy when their employer distributed their names and Social Security numbers in a manner that could allow a third party to steal and misuse the numbers.

---

10. 2006 WL 2844896 (D.D.C. Sept. 29, 2006).

| **A CASE IN POINT** | ***Summary*** | **Case 9.1** |

Bodah v. Lakeville Motor Express, Inc.

Minnesota Supreme Court
663 N.W.2d 550 (Minn. 2003).

FACTS   Lakeville Motor Express, Inc. (LME) is a trucking company operating primarily in Minnesota. LME sent a facsimile containing the names and Social Security numbers of 204 LME employees to its sixteen terminals across six states with a coversheet that was addressed simply to "Terminal Managers." The purpose of the fax was to allow LME to keep better records of accidents and injuries throughout its trucking network. Four months later, after being advised of the potential for identity theft, Peter Martin, president of LME, sent a letter of apology to all employees informing them of the mistake. The letter also notified them that the information was not shared with anyone other than the terminal managers and that Martin had instructed all terminal managers to destroy or return the list. Despite the president's apology and assurances, several employees filed a class-action suit on behalf of all 204 employees alleging invasion of privacy. The trial court dismissed the case in favor of LME, but the court of appeals reversed and found for the plaintiffs. The defendants appealed this judgment.

ISSUE PRESENTED   Does a company violate its employees' right to privacy by transmitting their names and Social Security numbers in an unsecured manner that could lead to identity theft?

SUMMARY OF OPINION   After concluding that it had the authority to review the earlier findings of the lower courts, the Minnesota Supreme Court explained the rationale behind recognizing the tort of invasion of privacy.

In order to find invasion of privacy, (1) the defendant must have publicized some aspect of the plaintiff's life, (2) that information must not be a legitimate concern of the public, and (3) disclosure must be offensive to a reasonable person. The employees' Social Security numbers qualified under the second and third prongs of the test because the public would have no reason to know the numbers, and many found their distribution offensive and potentially dangerous. Therefore, the case turned on the meaning of publication in the first prong.

LME maintained that faxing the numbers to its terminal managers did not constitute publication because the general public never saw the numbers. The employees argued that it constituted publication because (1) the names and corresponding Social Security numbers were sent to sixteen terminals in six states with no warning of the confidential nature of the information; (2) no corrective action was taken for at least four months; and (3) most importantly, there was no guarantee that the numbers were ever destroyed. As a result, they could still be used maliciously. The court ruled that "publicity" means that "the matter is made public, by communicating it to the public at large, or to so many persons that the matter must be regarded as substantially certain to become one of public knowledge."

RESULT   Distribution of the facsimile did not constitute publication, so there was no invasion of privacy. The lawsuit was dismissed.

Even if a person does not intend to make private facts, such as Social Security numbers public, that person may still be liable for negligence if he or she failed to take reasonable steps to keep the information confidential:

> [I]f an unauthorized transmission of private data actually resulted in pecuniary loss due to identity theft, a plaintiff may be able to bring a negligence action. Likewise, a plaintiff may have a cause of action for negligent infliction of emotional distress if, because private information was shared, the plaintiff suffered severe emotional distress with accompanying physical manifestations.[11]

Technological developments, especially the Internet, have made it possible to amass large amounts of detailed personal information. Concerned that traditional tort law causes of action, such as invasion of privacy, were not sufficient to protect against identity theft and other violations of privacy, state and federal governments have enacted a plethora of laws dealing with the security and unauthorized use and disclosure of private data. Privacy legislation is addressed later in this chapter, and identity theft is the subject of the "Inside Story."

Appropriation of a person's name or likeness may be an invasion of privacy. For example, using a fictitious testimonial in an advertisement would be a tort, as would using a person's picture in an advertisement or article with which he or she has no connection. In *Brown v. Ames*,[12] a group of blues musicians, songwriters, and music producers successfully sued a music producer and record label for distributing cassettes, CDs, posters, and other products using the names and likenesses of the performers. The U.S. Court of Appeals for the Fifth Circuit ruled in the plaintiffs' favor by applying Texas state law, which allows recovery for unauthorized appropriation of names or likenesses if the plaintiff can prove that (1) the defendant misappropriated the plaintiff's name or likeness for the value associated with it and not in an incidental manner or for a newsworthy purpose, (2) the plaintiff can be identified from the publication, and (3) the defendant derived some advantage or benefit.

Public figures from President John F. Kennedy to Britney Spears have required employees to sign confidentiality agreements, which prohibit them from talking about their famous employers, even after their employment has been terminated. Oprah Winfrey, who also requires employees to sign nondisclosure agreements, won her case against a former employee who had planned on writing a book about her time with Oprah. Courts enforce these agreements to protect celebrities' privacy.[13]

INTENTIONAL TORTS THAT PROTECT PROPERTY

The torts of trespass to land, nuisance, conversion, and trespass to personal property protect interests in property.

Trespass to Land

The previously described torts involved interference with personal rights. *Trespass to land* is an interference with a property right. It is an invasion of real property (that is, land) without the consent of the owner. The land need not be injured by the trespass. The intent required is the intent to enter the property, not the intent to trespass. Thus, a mistake as to ownership is irrelevant.

Trespass may also occur below the surface and in the airspace above the land. Throwing something, such as trash, on the land and shooting bullets over it may be a trespass, even though the perpetrator was not standing on the plaintiff's land.

Refusing to move something that at one time the plaintiff permitted the defendant to place on the land may also be a trespass. For example, if the plaintiff gave the defendant permission to leave a forklift on the plaintiff's land for one month, and it was left for two, the defendant may be liable for trespass.

Trespass may also occur if an individual permitted access to property does a wrongful act in excess of and in abuse of the authorized entry. In *Food Lion, Inc. v. Capital Cities/ABC, Inc.*,[14] two ABC reporters used false résumés to obtain jobs at Food Lion supermarkets in order to videotape unsanitary meat-handling practices at the markets. Food Lion sued, alleging that the reporters had committed trespass by secretly videotaping while working at the supermarkets. The U.S. Court of Appeals for the Fourth Circuit ruled that the two reporters had breached their duty of loyalty to the company as employees by videotaping in nonpublic areas, thereby nullifying Food Lion's consent for them to enter the property. Accordingly, the reporters had committed trespass. However, the court rejected Food Lion's argument that misrepresentation on a job application nullifies the consent given to an employee to enter the employer's property and thereby turns the employee into a trespasser.

Nuisance

Nuisance is a nontrespassory interference with the use and enjoyment of real property, for example, by an annoying odor or noise. The focus of nuisance claims is on the plaintiff's harm, not on the degree of the defendant's fault. Therefore, even innocent behavior by the

---

11. *Bodah*, 663 N.W.2d at 556 n.5.

12. 201 F.3d 654 (5th Cir. 2000).

13. Coady v. Harpo, Inc., 719 N.E.2d 244 (N.Y. 1999); Margaret Graham Tebo, *Zipped Lips*, A.B.A. J., Sept. 2000, at 16.

14. 194 F.3d 505 (4th Cir. 1999).

defendant is actionable—that is, may be the basis for a claim—if that behavior resulted in unreasonable and substantial interference with the use and enjoyment of the plaintiff's property. To determine whether the defendant's conduct resulted in unreasonable interference, the court will balance the utility of the activity creating the harm, and the burden of preventing it, against the nature and the gravity of the harm. For example, hammering noise during the remodeling of a house may be less likely to constitute a nuisance than playing loud music late at night purely for recreation. Nuisance can be public or private.

Public Nuisance

Public nuisance is unreasonable and substantial interference with the public health, safety, peace, comfort, convenience, or use of land. An action for public nuisance is usually brought by the government. However, a private citizen who experiences special harm different from that experienced by the general public may also bring a suit for public nuisance.

Guns   After a number of states and cities sued gun dealers and gun makers under a theory of public nuisance for distributing firearms in a way that would make them more accessible to juveniles and criminals,[15] Congress passed the Protection of Lawful Commerce in Arms Act of 2005 (PLCAA).[16] The Act bans suits seeking to hold gun manufacturers and dealers liable in civil actions for damages when their weapons are used in crimes; an exception allows certain suits involving defective weapons or criminal behavior by a gun maker or dealer, such as knowingly selling a gun to a person who failed a criminal background check. In addition, thirty-six states have passed legislation granting gun makers immunity.[17]

In the following case, the court considered whether the PLCAA precludes lawsuits under the California civil codes.

---

15. In *City of Cincinnati v. Beretta USA Corp.*, 768 N.E.2d 1136 (Ohio 2002), the Ohio Supreme Court ruled that prosecutors could proceed with public nuisance claims against gun makers, but in *Grunow v. Valor Corp. of Florida*, 2003 WL 22020032 (Fla. Cir. Ct. 2003), a Florida appellate court set aside a trial court verdict in favor of the plaintiff.

16. Pub. L. No. 109-92, 119 Stat. 2095 (2005) (codified at 15 U.S.C. §§ 7901–7903).

17. *Immunity Statutes/Manufacturer Liability*, Legal Community Against Violence (Aug. 12, 2009), http://www.lcav.org/content/immunity_statutes.pdf. One notable exception is California, which repealed a law that had protected gun manufacturers in the state. Fox Butterfield, *Gun Industry Is Gaining Immunity from Suits*, N.Y. Times, Sept. 1, 2002, at 19.

A CASE IN POINT	*Summary*	Case 9.2

Ileto v. Glock, Inc.

United States Court of Appeals for the Ninth Circuit
565 F.3d 1126 (9th Cir. 2009).

Facts   In 1999, Bufford Furrow shot and injured five people, including three young children, at a Jewish Community Center in Granada Hills, California. Later he shot and killed a postal worker. At the time, Furrow illegally possessed at least seven firearms. The shooting victims and their family members brought suit solely under the California civil statutes for negligence, emotional distress, and wrongful death against the manufacturers, importers, distributors, and dealers of the firearms used by the assailant during the attack. The district court dismissed the case against the two licensed firearm manufacturers but permitted the suit against the unlicensed foreign firearm seller to proceed. The plaintiffs and the foreign manufacturer appealed.

Issue Presented   Does the PLCAA give gun violence victims the ability to bring a suit under California tort statutes against licensed manufacturers of firearms? Against an unlicensed foreign manufacturer?

Summary of Opinion   The U.S. Court of Appeals for the Ninth Circuit began by noting that the PLCAA requires federal courts, subject to certain exceptions, to dismiss every qualified civil liability action against a licensed firearm manufacturer or seller. Both Glock and RSR were licensed manufacturers and sellers. Thus, the actions against those two defendants had to be dismissed unless they came within a specified exception. The plaintiffs argued that the so-called predicate exception—section 7903(5)(A)(iii)—applied. That section provides that the PLCAA does not preempt an action where "a manufacturer or seller of a qualified product knowingly violated a state or federal statute applicable to the sale or marketing of the product, and the violation was a proximate cause of the harm for which relief is sought." The plaintiffs did not allege a knowing violation of any California statute other than

CONTINUED

California's general tort statute, but they argued that the California tort statute nonetheless qualified as a predicate statute.

The court rejected this argument. It explained that Congress intended for the PLCAA to pre-empt general tort law claims, such as the plaintiffs', even when the causes of action were codified into a civil code, as is the case in California. Thus, the district court properly held that the plaintiffs' California claims against the two licensed manufacturers were preempted by the PLCAA.

The court then rejected the plaintiffs' various constitutional challenges to the PLCAA, including the assertion that the PLCAA violated the doctrine of separation of powers by impinging on the role of the judiciary. Congress amended the applicable law for pending and future cases, not for decided cases, so it did not upset final judicial judgments. The court also rejected the plaintiffs' argument that the PLCAA violated their equal protection and due process rights. There was nothing arbitrary or irrational about Congress's decision to protect licensed gun manufacturers, and the plaintiffs had a full hearing before the trial court.

Finally, the court addressed defendant China North's appeal from the district court's order finding that the PLCAA did not preempt the plaintiffs' claims against it. Although China North claimed to be a "manufacturer or seller of a qualified product," it was not a federally licensed manufacturer or seller of firearms. As a result, state-law claims against it were not preempted.

RESULT   The trial court's decision was affirmed. Under the PLCAA, claims under California's general tort law brought against the unlicensed foreign manufacturer of firearms could proceed, but the claims against the two licensed gun manufacturers were dismissed.

COMMENTS   The U.S. Court of Appeals for the Second Circuit reached a similar result when it found that a state criminal nuisance statute did not come within the predicate exception to the PLCAA.[18] In contrast, the Indiana Court of Appeals ruled in 2007 that the federal law did not bar a public nuisance suit by the City of Gary against several gun manufacturers.[19] The court reasoned that the federal law seeks to prevent lawsuits that try to use the judicial system to circumvent the legislative branch, but noted that Gary's claim rested on a state law passed by the Indiana legislature. The court also cited an exception to the immunity provisions of the federal law that allows certain cases to go forward if plaintiffs can show that the manufacturers knowingly violated a statute applicable to the sale and marketing of firearms.

---

18. City of New York v. Beretta U.S.A. Corp., 524 F.3d 384, 404 (2d Cir. 2008). The Act was also upheld in *District of Columbia v. Beretta U.S.A. Corp.*, 940 A.2d 163 (D.C. 2008).

19. Smith & Wesson Corp. v. City of Gary, 875 N.E.2d 422 (Ind. Ct. App. 2007).

Greenhouse Gases   As discussed in Chapter 15, both individual states and private parties have sued power companies alleging that their production of greenhouse gases constitutes a public nuisance under federal and state law.[20]

Private Nuisance

Private nuisance is interference with an individual's use and enjoyment of his or her land. Flooding that destroys crops, polluting a stream, or playing loud music late at night in a residential neighborhood can constitute a private nuisance.

For example, the Wisconsin Supreme Court held that stray voltage that reduced a dairy herd's milk production was actionable on a private nuisance theory.[21] The court noted that the common law doctrine of private nuisance is broad enough to meet a wide variety of possible invasions and flexible enough to adapt to changing social values and conditions.

Conversion

Conversion is the exercise of dominion and control over the personal property, rather than the real property, of another. This tort protects the right to have personal

---

20. *See, e.g.,* Am. Elec. Power Co., Inc. v. Connecticut, 131 S. Ct. 2527 (2011).

21. Vogel v. Grant-Lafayette Elec. Co-op., 548 N.W.2d 829 (Wis. 1996).

property left alone. It is the tort claim a plaintiff asserts to recover the value of property that was stolen, destroyed, or substantially altered by a defendant.

The intent element for conversion does not include a wrongful motive. It merely requires the intent to exercise dominion or control over goods, inconsistent with the plaintiff's rights. The defendant does not have to know that the goods belonged to the plaintiff.

Trespass to Personal Property

When personal property is interfered with but not converted—that is, taken, destroyed, or substantially altered—there is a *trespass to personal property* (sometimes referred to as *trespass to chattels*). No wrongful motive must be shown. The intent required is the intent to exercise control over the plaintiff's personal property. For example, an employer who took an employee's car on a short errand without the employee's permission committed a trespass to personal property. If instead the employer damaged the car or drove it for several thousand miles, thereby lowering its value, the employer would be liable for conversion.

Trespass to chattels can include demonstrations that involve private property on private land. For example, a logging company successfully sued six members of an environmental group who climbed on and chained themselves to the company's logging equipment.[22] The members of the environmental group were required to pay punitive damages for demonstrating against government policies while on private property. The court ruled that the assessment of punitive damages did not violate the protesters' First Amendment rights.

Internet auction powerhouse eBay, Inc. successfully sued Bidder's Edge, Inc. when it discovered that Bidder's Edge had used an automated system to pull information off eBay's website. All eBay users are required to agree to the eBay User Agreement, which specifically forbids such data mining. Bidder's Edge argued that eBay's website is public and that it had a right to use that public information. The court disagreed and ruled that Bidder's Edge's actions constituted a trespass to chattels. Even though eBay's website is public, eBay's servers are private property, and the unauthorized use of even a small portion of a server's capacity deprived eBay of its ability to use its personal property in the way it saw fit.[23]

In *Intel Corp. v. Hamidi*,[24] the California Supreme Court considered whether Intel could use the theory of trespass to chattels to prevent Hamidi, a former employee, from sending e-mails to Intel employees. Hamidi gained access to Intel e-mail addresses through a floppy disk that was sent to him anonymously. He then sent six e-mail messages to about 35,000 Intel e-mail addresses over a twenty-one-month span. Although the trial court granted Intel's motion for summary judgment and enjoined Hamidi from sending further e-mails, the California Supreme Court reversed and dismissed the lawsuit. The court distinguished this case from cases in which Internet service providers (ISPs) had successfully relied on trespass to chattels to sue spammers, noting:

> In those cases . . . the underlying complaint was that the extraordinary quantity of [unsolicited commercial e-mail] impaired the computer system's functioning. In the present case, the claimed injury is located in the disruption or distraction caused to recipients by the contents of the e-mail messages, an injury entirely separate from, and not directly affecting, the possession or value of personal property.[25]

INTENTIONAL TORTS THAT PROTECT CERTAIN ECONOMIC INTERESTS AND BUSINESS RELATIONSHIPS

Certain economic interests and business relationships are protected by the torts of fraudulent misrepresentation, disparagement, injurious falsehood, malicious prosecution, interference with contractual relations, participation in a breach of fiduciary duty, interference with prospective business advantage, and bad faith.

Fraudulent Misrepresentation

The tort of *fraudulent misrepresentation*, also called *fraud* or *deceit*, protects economic interests and the right to be treated fairly and honestly. Fraud requires proof that the defendant either (1) intentionally misled the plaintiff by making a material misrepresentation of fact on which the plaintiff relied or (2) omitted to state a material fact when the defendant had a duty to speak because of a special relationship with the plaintiff. Intent can be constructive—in other words, a court will sometimes impute a fraudulent intent if the defendant showed reckless disregard for the truth. For example, a shareholder who relied to his or her detriment on an intentionally misleading accountant's opinion regarding the company's financial statements might sue the accountant for fraud.

Everyone has a duty to refrain from affirmatively misrepresenting the facts, that is, from lying. But, as explained in Chapter 5, as a general rule, parties dealing

22. Huffman & Wright Logging Co. v. Wade, 857 P.2d 101 (Or. 1993).
23. eBay, Inc. v. Bidder's Edge, Inc., 100 F. Supp. 2d 1058 (N.D. Cal. 2000).
24. 71 P.3d 296 (Cal. 2003).
25. *Id.* at 300–301.

at arm's length are not required to disclose all facts that might be relevant to the other party's decision. If, however, one party is a fiduciary (a person entrusted to protect the interests of another), then he or she has a *fiduciary duty* to act with integrity and in the best interests of the other party. This means that the fiduciary must disclose all relevant facts to the other party even if that party has not asked any questions. For example, if an executive is negotiating to buy a piece of property from his or her corporation, the executive must volunteer all information known to him or her that might affect the terms (such as the price) on which the corporation would be willing to sell the property.

Occasionally, a court will impose an affirmative duty to disclose even if the party required to disclose is not a fiduciary. For example, in *Brass v. American Film Technologies, Inc.*,[26] the defendant American Film Technologies (AFT) convinced Brass and other plaintiffs to buy warrants that could be used to acquire common stock, but AFT failed to reveal that the underlying stock was restricted and could not be freely traded for a period of two years. On discovering the omission, the plaintiffs sued for fraud. The court held that because AFT had superior knowledge about the restrictions on its securities, it had a duty to reveal those restrictions and its failure to do so was fraudulent concealment.

In contrast, the Supreme Court of Georgia held that physicians do not have a common law or statutory duty to disclose to a patient personal factors that might adversely affect their professional performance.[27] Cleveland sued his urologist for negligently performing unnecessary surgery on him and for fraudulently concealing the urologist's illegal use and abuse of cocaine. The court held that although a doctor has a common law duty to answer a patient's questions regarding medical or procedural risks, the doctor does not have the duty to disclose personal factors such as illicit drug use. The court ruled that the patient could sue the doctor for professional negligence, but could not base a claim of fraud on the physician's failure to disclose his drug use.

A mere expression of opinion generally is not a valid basis for a fraud claim. Although statements as to future actions are generally deemed opinions and therefore not actionable, they can constitute fraud when (1) the defendant held itself out to be specially qualified and the plaintiff acted reasonably in relying on the defendant's superior knowledge, (2) the opinion is that of a fiduciary or other trusted person, or (3) the defendant stated its opinion as an existing fact or as implying facts that justify a belief in its truth.

To state a claim of fraud, a plaintiff must establish that he or she suffered damages as a result of the fraud. In *Maio v. Aetna, Inc.*,[28] a class of persons enrolled in Aetna's health maintenance organization (HMO) plan filed a claim alleging that the company had engaged in a fraudulent scheme to induce individuals to enroll in the HMO plan by representing that Aetna's primary commitment was to maintain and improve the quality of health care given to its members. The class alleged that, in fact, Aetna was driven primarily by financial and administrative considerations. The U.S. District Court for the Eastern District of Pennsylvania ruled that the plaintiffs' vague allegation that "quality of care" might suffer in the future was too hypothetical an injury to confer standing. The court also found that Aetna's general assertions about its commitment to "quality of care" were "mere puffery" and could not serve as the basis for a fraud claim.

Disparagement

Disparagement is the publication of statements derogatory to the quality of the plaintiff's business, to the business in general, or even to the plaintiff's personal affairs, in order to discourage others from dealing with the plaintiff. To prove disparagement, the plaintiff must show that the defendant made false statements about the quality or ownership of the plaintiff's goods or services, knowing that the statements were false or with conscious indifference as to their truth, and that the statements caused actual harm.

Injurious Falsehood

Knowingly making false statements may give rise to a claim for *injurious falsehood*. For example, a false statement that the plaintiff has gone out of business or does not carry certain goods is a tort if it results in economic loss to the plaintiff.

The range of damages available for injurious falsehood is more restricted than for defamation. Injurious falsehood permits recovery of only pecuniary (that is, monetary) losses related to business operations, whereas defamation permits recovery for loss of reputation, including emotional damages, as well.

Defenses

The defenses available to the defendant in a defamation action also apply to injurious falsehood. When the statement involves a comparison of goods, the privilege in an injurious falsehood case is even broader than the privilege available in defamation. For example, a defendant who favorably compares his or her own goods to those of a competitor is privileged, even though the defendant may not honestly believe that his or her own goods are superior.

---

26. 987 F.2d 142 (2d Cir. 1993).
27. Albany Urology Clinic PC v. Cleveland, 528 S.E.2d 777 (Ga. 2000).

28. 1999 WL 800315 (E.D. Pa. Sept. 29, 1999), *aff'd*, 221 F.3d 472 (3d Cir. 2000).

Malicious Prosecution and Defense

A plaintiff can successfully sue for *malicious prosecution* by showing that a prior proceeding was instituted against him or her maliciously and without probable cause or factual basis. In addition, the earlier case must have been resolved in the plaintiff's favor. This tort originated from the tort of misuse of the criminal process but has been adapted to redress malicious civil prosecution as well. A victorious plaintiff can recover damages for attorneys' fees paid in connection with the prior action, injury to reputation, and psychological distress.

Courts frequently state that the malicious prosecution action is disfavored under the law. Because the action has the potential to produce a chilling effect that discourages legitimate claims, courts have been reluctant to expand its reach.

Nevertheless, one state expanded the doctrine to recognize an action for *malicious defense.* In *Aronson v. Schroeder*,[29] the defendant allegedly created false material evidence while serving as defense counsel in a prior case and then gave false testimony concerning the evidence. In a ruling for the plaintiff, the New Hampshire Supreme Court stated:

> [W]hen a defense is commenced maliciously or is based upon false evidence and perjury or is raised for an improper purpose, the litigant is not made whole if the only remedy is reimbursement of counsel fees. It follows that upon proving malicious defense, the aggrieved party is entitled to the same damages as are recoverable in a malicious prosecution claim.[30]

Massachusetts,[31] Hawaii,[32] and Kansas[33] have rejected this expansion of the doctrine.

Interference with Contractual Relations and Participation in a Breach of Fiduciary Duty

The tort of *interference with contractual relations* protects the right to enjoy the benefits of legally binding agreements. It provides a remedy when the defendant intentionally induces another person to breach a contract with the plaintiff. The defendant must know of the existence of the contract between the plaintiff and the other person, or there must be sufficient facts that a reasonable person would be led to believe that such a contract existed. Interference with contractual relations requires intent to interfere. Thus, courts usually require that the defendant induce the contracting party to breach, rather than merely create the opportunity for the breach. Similarly, a defendant who knowingly participates in, or induces, a breach of fiduciary duty by another commits the tort of *participation in a breach of fiduciary duty.*

In some jurisdictions, interference with contractual relations also requires an unacceptable purpose. If good grounds exist for the interference, the defendant is not liable. For example, if a manager of a corporation is incompetent, then a stockholder of the corporation may be entitled to induce a breach of the employment agreement between the manager and the corporation. The stockholder's motive would be to protect his or her investment. On the other hand, a defendant may not interfere with another person's contract in order to attract customers or employees away from that person.

Perhaps the most famous case involving tortious interference with a contract was *Pennzoil v. Texaco*,[34] discussed in the "Inside Story" in Chapter 7. In 1983, Pennzoil and Getty Oil Company negotiated an agreement for a merger. During the process of drafting the final merger documents, Texaco offered a better price for Getty and agreed to indemnify Getty for any claims that might be asserted by Pennzoil. After Getty accepted Texaco's offer, Pennzoil sued Texaco for tortious interference with a contract. Under New York law, Pennzoil had to prove (1) the existence of a valid contract, (2) Texaco's knowledge of the existence of the contract, (3) Texaco's intentional inducement of a breach of that contract, and (4) damages incurred by Pennzoil as a result of the breach of contract. A jury decided against Texaco and awarded $10.5 billion to Pennzoil. The case was ultimately settled for $3 billion.

Defense

As in defamation, truth is a defense to a claim for interference with contractual relations. There is no liability if a true statement was made to induce another to break off relations with the plaintiff.

Interference with Prospective Business Advantage

Courts are less willing to award damages for interference with prospective contracts than they are to protect existing contracts. To prove *interference with prospective business advantage*, the plaintiff must prove that the defendant intentionally interfered with a relationship the plaintiff sought to develop and that the interference caused the plaintiff's loss. In rare cases, however, courts have permitted recovery when the defendant was merely negligent.

---

29. 671 A.2d 1023 (N.H. 1995).

30. *Id.* at 1028.

31. *See* Iantosca v. Merrill Lynch Pierce Fenner & Smith, Inc., 2009 WL 981389 (Mass. Super. 2008).

32. *See* Young v. Allstate Ins. Co., 119 Haw. 403, 198 P.3d 66 (2008).

33. *See* Wilkinson v. Shoney's Inc., 4 P.3d 1149 (Kan. 2000).

34. *See* Texaco, Inc. v. Pennzoil Co., 729 S.W.2d 768 (Tex. Ct. App. 1987).

In one case,[35] Baum Research and Development Company, a manufacturer of wooden baseball bats, filed a claim of tortious interference with prospective economic advantage against several manufacturers of aluminum baseball bats, a trade association of bat manufacturers, and the National Collegiate Athletic Association. Baum claimed that the defendants had prevented it from establishing relationships with amateur baseball teams and had disrupted its sale of bats to these teams by, among other things, disseminating false information about the Baum Hitting Machine manufactured by Baum, thereby inducing baseball teams to terminate arrangements with Baum for the use of its wooden bats, and to remove and destroy Baum bats and replace them with aluminum bats. The court stated that the necessary elements of tortious interference with economic relations are (1) the existence of a valid business relationship or expectancy, (2) knowledge of the relationship or expectancy on the part of the interferor, (3) intentional interference inducing or causing a breach or termination of a relationship or expectancy, and (4) damages. Concluding that the company "had more than a mere hope for business opportunities or the innate optimism of a salesman,"[36] the court ruled that Baum had a valid claim of tortious interference with economic relations.

Defenses

Interference with prospective business advantage is usually done by a competitor or at least by one who stands to benefit from the interference. Most jurisdictions recognize a privilege to act for one's own financial gain. Competing fairly is not a tort. For the purposes of competition, a defendant may attempt to increase its business by cutting prices, offering rebates, refusing to deal with the plaintiff, secretly negotiating with the plaintiff's customers, or refusing to deal with third parties unless they agree not to deal with the plaintiff.

In some jurisdictions, the plaintiff has the burden of showing that the defendant acted from a motive other than financial gain, such as revenge. In others, the defendant has the burden of proving that he or she acted only for financial gain. Any purpose sufficient to create a privilege to disturb existing contractual relations will also justify interference with prospective business advantage. As in defamation and interference with contractual relations, truth is a defense. Some jurisdictions have also applied the First Amendment defenses available in defamation cases.

Bad Faith

Bad faith conduct by one party to a contract to the other party may serve as the basis for a tort claim of *bad faith*. This claim is separate and independent from a breach-of-contract claim. Typically, a claim of bad faith is brought by an insured against an insurance company for breaching its duty to act in good faith in handling and paying claims. The plaintiff must show that the insurer failed to exercise good faith in processing a claim and that there was no reasonable justification for the insurer's refusal to pay it.

NEGLIGENCE

Intent is an essential element of every intentional tort. Negligence does not include the element of intent. Rather, the focus is on the reasonableness of the defendant's conduct. Negligence requires that all people take appropriate care in any given situation. It does not require that the defendant intended, or even knew, that his or her actions would harm the plaintiff. In fact, a defendant's conduct might still be negligent even if the defendant was full of concern for the plaintiff's safety. It is enough that the defendant acted carelessly or, in other words, that his or her conduct created an unreasonable risk of harm.

Negligence is defined as conduct that involves an unreasonably great risk of causing injury to another person or damage to property. To establish liability for negligence, the plaintiff must show that (1) the defendant owed a duty to the plaintiff to act in conformity with a certain standard of conduct, that is, to act reasonably under the circumstances; (2) the defendant breached that duty by failing to conform to the standard; (3) a reasonably close causal connection exists between the plaintiff's injury and the defendant's breach; and (4) the plaintiff suffered an actual loss or injury.

Duty

A person with a *legal duty* to another is required to act reasonably under the circumstances to avoid harming the other person. The required standard of care is what a reasonable person of ordinary prudence would do in the circumstances. It is not graduated to include the reasonably slow person, the reasonably forgetful person, or the reasonable person of low intelligence. In determining duty, the law allows reasonable mistakes of judgment in some circumstances. In emergency situations, the duty is to act as a reasonable person would act in the circumstances. The defendant is expected to anticipate emergencies. Drivers must drive defensively. Innkeepers must anticipate fires and install smoke alarms and, in some cases, sprinkler systems, and must provide fire escapes and other fire-safety features. Owners of swimming pools in subdivisions with children must fence their property.

As explained further below, most states take a formalistic approach to duty and alter the scope of the defendant's liability depending on the court's characterization of the

---

35. *In re* Baseball Bat Antitrust Litig., 75 F. Supp. 2d 1189 (D. Kan. 1999).
36. *Id.* at 1203.

injured party (e.g., trespasser versus business guest). In 1993, the New Jersey Supreme Court articulated a more general framework: "Whether a person owes a duty of reasonable care toward another turns on whether the imposition of such a duty satisfies an abiding sense of basic fairness under all of the circumstances in light of considerations of public policy."[37] For that court, the analysis involves balancing many factors, including the relationship between the parties, the nature of the attendant risk, the opportunity and ability to exercise care, and the public interest in the proposed solution. As discussed further below, courts are split on whether an employer has a duty to take reasonable precautions to protect third parties from injury by employees ordered home because they are intoxicated.[38]

Duty to Rescue

In the United States, there is no general duty to rescue. (In contrast, certain countries, such as France and Brazil, require bystanders to try to help those in danger, if trying to help will not put the bystanders at risk.) However, once one undertakes a rescue, the law imposes a duty to act as a reasonable person and not to abandon the rescue effort unreasonably. Thus, if Ciril Wyatt sat on a riverbank and watched Edward Donnelly drown, she would not be liable in negligence for Donnelly's death. But if Wyatt saw Donnelly drowning, jumped in her boat, sped to him, tried to pull him into the boat, and then changed her mind and let him drown, she would be liable.

A special relationship between two people may create a duty to rescue. If Donnelly were Wyatt's husband or child or parent, Wyatt would have a duty to rescue him. Other relationships that create a duty to rescue are employer and employee; innkeeper and guest; teacher and student; employee of a bus, train, or other common carrier and passenger; and possibly team members, hunting partners, and hiking partners.

There is also a duty to rescue those whom one has placed in peril. For example, if Wyatt had been driving her boat in a negligent manner, thereby causing Donnelly to fall overboard, she would have a duty to rescue him.

Duty of Landlord to Tenant

In general, a landlord has a duty to provide adequate security to protect tenants from foreseeable criminal acts of a third party. Relevant issues are whether (1) the property was in a high-crime area, (2) there had been earlier criminal acts, (3) there was a failure to maintain locks, and (4) the landlord had knowledge of prior criminal acts.

In *Sharon P. v. Arman, Ltd.*,[39] the plaintiff was sexually assaulted in an underground commercial parking garage below her office building. She sued the garage owner for failing to take measures to prevent criminal acts in the garage. The California Supreme Court ruled that a commercial landlord owes a duty to take reasonable steps to secure common areas against foreseeable criminal acts of third parties that are likely to occur in the absence of such precautionary measures. Under this standard, a court must balance the foreseeability of the harm against the burden imposed on the landlord if required to take precautionary measures. The court found that the garage had a ten-year history with no assaults and stated that "absent any prior similar incidents or other indications of a reasonably foreseeable risk of violent criminal assaults in that location, we cannot conclude defendants were required to secure the area against such crime."[40]

Duty of Landowner or Tenant to Third Parties

A landowner or possessor of land (such as a tenant) has a legal duty to keep the property reasonably safe. Such a person may be liable for injury that occurs outside the premises as well as on them. For example, a landowner may be liable for harm caused when water from a cooling tower spills onto the highway; when sparks from a locomotive engine, which is not properly maintained, start a fire on adjacent property; or when snow falls from a roof onto the highway.

A landowner must exercise care in demolishing or constructing buildings on his or her property and in excavating his or her land. Landowners have been held liable when, after being hit by a car, a pole on a landowner's property collapsed and injured a pedestrian, and when a landowner erected a sign that obstructed the view and caused an accident.

A landowner has a general duty to inspect his or her property and keep it in repair, and he or she may be liable if a showroom window, a downspout, a screen, or a loose sign falls and injures someone. In a few jurisdictions, landowners have a duty to maintain sidewalks that abut (are right next to) their property.

Traditional Approach to Premises Liability Traditionally, the liability associated with injury on the premises of another has hinged on the distinctions among trespassers, licensees, and invitees. The possessor owes the least duty to a trespasser and the greatest duty to an invitee.

Duty to Trespassers In general, a possessor of property owes no duty to an undiscovered trespasser. If a substantial number of trespassers are in the habit of entering at a particular place, however, then the possessor of the property has a duty to take reasonable care to discover and to protect the trespassers from activities he or she carries on.

---

37. Hopkins v. Fox & Lazo Realtors, 625 A.2d 1110, 1116 (N.J. 1993).
38. *See* Lett v. Collis Foods, Inc., 605 S.W.3d 95 (Tenn. Ct. App. 2001) and the authorities cited therein.
39. 989 P.2d 121 (Cal. 1999).
40. *Id.* at 133.

Some courts have also established a duty to protect such trespassers from dangerous conditions, such as concealed high-tension wires, that do not result from the possessor's activities. Some jurisdictions require the possessor to exercise reasonable care once he or she knows of the trespasser's presence.

Trespassing children are owed a higher level of duty. The *attractive nuisance* doctrine imposes liability for physical injury to child trespassers caused by artificial conditions on the land if (1) the possessor knew or should have known that children were likely to trespass; (2) the condition is one the possessor would reasonably know involved an unreasonable risk of injury to such children; (3) because of their youth, the children did not discover the condition or realize the risk involved; (4) the utility to the possessor of maintaining the condition is not great; (5) the burden of eliminating the risk is slight compared with the magnitude of the risk to the children; and (6) the possessor fails to exercise reasonable care to protect the children.

Duty to Licensees   A *licensee* is anyone who is on the land of another person with the possessor's express or implied consent. The licensee enters for his or her own purposes, not for those of the possessor. Social guests and uninvited sales representatives are licensees.

The possessor must exercise reasonable care for the protection of a licensee. This duty differs from that owed to a trespasser because the possessor is required to look out for licensees before they enter the land. The possessor is not required to inspect for unknown dangers, however. The duty arises only when the possessor has actual knowledge of a risk.

Duty to Invitees   An *invitee*, or business visitor, is someone who enters the premises for purposes of the possessor's business. The possessor owes a higher duty to an invitee than to a licensee. The possessor must protect invitees against known dangers and also against those dangers that the possessor might discover with reasonable care.

A customer is clearly an invitee and is accordingly owed a higher duty of care than a licensee such as a social guest. Managers thus have particular reason to be concerned about invitees. Every year businesses must deal with thousands of "slip and fall" cases brought by customers who have fallen due to wet floors, icy sidewalks, or broken steps.

In the following case, the court addressed the duty of an employer to protect an employee from a guard dog on the premises.

A CASE IN POINT	*Summary*	Case 9.3

Labaj v. VanHouten

Court of Appeals of Texas
322 S.W.3d 416 (Tex. Ct. App. 2010).

FACTS   DeeAnnVanHouten was an employee of Third Coast Auto Group, LP (TCAG), working in a TCAG used-car lot as a title clerk. On May 30, 2007, VanHouten left the front office to check a car for licensing papers. When she reached the garage, she was told by a coworker that the car was located in the back lot. VanHouten was unaware that there was a guard dog in the back lot; while she was looking at a Ford Mustang, the dog attacked her, pulled her to the ground, and detached part of her leg muscle. VanHouten filed suit alleging three theories of liability against her employer: (1) strict liability, (2) negligent handling, and (3) negligence. The jury found in favor of VanHouten and awarded her $50,000 in damages. The defendant appealed, arguing that the trial court had erred in failing to grant its motions for summary judgment, a directed verdict, and a new trial because there was no evidence that the dog had dangerous propensities abnormal to its class.

ISSUE PRESENTED   In order to find an employer negligent for failing to protect an employee from being attacked by a dog, does the dog have to possess abnormally dangerous propensities?

SUMMARY OF OPINION   The Court of Appeals of Texas began by noting that if an animal has aggressive tendencies and the owner has knowledge of that propensity, then the owner can be subject to strict liability. If the animal is not vicious, the owner can still be subject to liability for negligent handling of the animal if the owner intentionally causes the animal to do harm or is negligent in failing to prevent harm. Thus, to prevail on a negligence claim, the plaintiff must prove that (1) the defendant was the owner or possessor of the animal, (2) the defendant owed a duty to exercise reasonable care to prevent the animal from injuring others, (3) the defendant breached that duty, and (4) the defendant's breach proximately caused the plaintiff's injury.

When a person is injured on the property of another, the duty owed by the landlord depends on the status of the person injured on the premises. When the plaintiff is an invitee, the defendant must exercise ordinary care to keep the premises reasonably safe, but if the

CONTINUED

plaintiff is merely a licensee, the only duty owed by the defendant is to refrain from gross negligence. Because VanHouten was an invitee, the defendant owed her a duty to exercise reasonable care in keeping the property safe. In dog bite cases, whether a duty exists depends, in part, on whether risk of injury is foreseeable.

Liability may attach even though the injured person does not establish that the dog had dangerous propensities. A plaintiff satisfies his or her burden of proof by establishing that the owner had constructive notice of facts that would put an ordinary person on notice that the animal could cause harm. Whether the owner had that notice is a question of fact for the jury.

Here, the dog, a pitbull, had been on the lot for several weeks as a guard dog intended to deter anyone from vandalizing or stealing parts. TCAG's manager Steven Quiroz testified that he thought the dog should be restrained during the day so that it could not hurt clientele and employees going through the area. He also testified that the dog was recently injured and a new mother, which generally makes a dog especially protective. Quiroz further admitted that he did not take any precautions to protect employees or customers from the dog and that no warning signs were posted. The court reasoned that under these circumstances, the evidence was sufficient to find that TCAG owed a duty to ensure that invitees were adequately warned of the dog's presence. The facts also showed that there was more than a scintilla of evidence to support the jury verdict that TCAG breached its duty and caused VanHouten's injuries.

RESULT   The jury award in favor of the plaintiff was affirmed. An employer can be negligent for failing to protect an employee from getting attacked by a dog, even if the dog is not known to possess abnormally dangerous propensities.

© Cengage Learning 2013

Invitees of a possessor of property, such as contractors, may also have a duty to other persons admitted onto the property by the owner. Contractors that create a dangerous condition while working at a construction site may be held liable for an injury caused by the dangerous condition after the contractor leaves the site and turns its work over to the property owner. In *Brent v. Unocal, Inc.,*[41] ARCO Alaska, Inc. hired Unocal, Inc., as an independent contractor, to perform excavation and install sheet piling as part of a bridge construction project. After Unocal had finished its work and turned the property over to ARCO, construction worker William Brent was injured while working on the site, when he fell into a hole created by Unocal. The Supreme Court of Alaska held Unocal was liable under section 385 of the Restatement (Second) of Torts, which states that "a contractor is held to the standard of reasonable care for the protection of third parties who may foreseeably be endangered by his negligence, even after acceptance of the work by the contractor." Section 385 reflects the majority rule adopted by courts that have considered this issue.

A business's duty to invitees may even include an obligation to protect invitees from criminal conduct by third parties. States have been mixed in their application of this standard. In *Delgado v. Trax Bar & Grill,*[42] the California Supreme Court held that a bar did not have a duty to employ burdensome measures to protect patrons in its parking lot in the absence of prior similar incidents, but that did not absolve it of liability. The court adopted a "sliding scale balancing test" formulation: where there is evidence of prior similar incidents, burdensome measures like hiring guards or using security cameras are mandated, and where there is evidence of something less than prior similar acts, "minimally burdensome measures" are required. For example, in a lawsuit filed by the victim of a vicious assault against an all-night restaurant, the court noted that there was evidence of fistfights and robberies but no evidence of similar assaults. Although there was no duty for the restaurant to take burdensome measures in this case, the court concluded that it was up to a jury to decide whether the failure of the restaurant employees to take any action violated the obligation to take "minimally burdensome" measures such as calling 911.[43]

The Washington Supreme Court, on the other hand, denied a claim by an assaulted convenience store patron based on the store's failure to provide security personnel.[44] The court reasoned that imposing a requirement that businesses provide guards in all cases would unfairly shift responsibility for policing from the government to the private sector. In *dicta*, the court said that a duty to

41. 969 P.2d 627 (Alaska 1998).
42. 113 P.3d 1159 (Cal. 2005).

43. Morris IV v. De La Tore, 113 P.3d 1182 (Cal. 2005).
44. Nivens v. 7-11 Hoagy's Corner, 943 P.2d 286 (Wash. 1997).

provide security guards may arise if "[the] construction or maintenance of the premises brings about a . . . peculiar temptation . . . for criminal misconduct"[45] by third parties, but such facts were not present in that case.

Reasonable Care Approach to Liability to Third Parties for Injuries on Premises   The traditional approach of classifying one who enters a tenant's or landowner's property as a trespasser, licensee, or invitee has fallen into disfavor in certain jurisdictions. Determining the proper classification of an injured plaintiff is often difficult and may require courts and juries to sift through hundreds of pages of testimony. Moreover, a person's status could change over the course of a day or a transaction. For example, an intruder would be deemed a trespasser, but if the landowner spotted the intruder and permitted him or her to remain, then the trespasser's status could shift to licensee. The New York Court of Appeals put it this way: "[I]t remains a curiosity of the law that the duty owed to a plaintiff on exit may have been many times greater than that owed him on his entrance, though he and the premises all the while remained the same."[46]

To eliminate this potential for confusion, a number of jurisdictions have abandoned the traditional "trichotomy." According to the West Virginia Supreme Court, "[A]t least 25 jurisdictions have abolished or largely abandoned the licensee/invitee distinction. Among these 25 jurisdictions that have broken with past tradition, at least 17 have eliminated or fundamentally altered the distinction. Another eight of the 25 have eliminated even the trespasser distinction."[47]

Some jurisdictions have adopted a standard of *reasonable care under the circumstances* in lieu of the traditional trichotomy. Under this standard, courts require all landowners to act in a reasonable manner with respect to entrants on their land, with liability hinging on the foreseeability of harm. For example, the New York Court of Appeals collapsed all three of the old standards into a single reasonable care standard, which it explained "should be no different than that applied in the usual negligence action."[48] Other jurisdictions, such as North Carolina, have eliminated the distinction between licensees and invitees, but continue to treat trespassers differently because they had no right to enter the land. In determining whether the landowner has exercised reasonable care, courts will consider the identity of the person entering the property and the reasons why that person entered.[49] Illinois eliminated the distinction between invitees and licensees by statute.[50]

Breach of Duty

Once it is determined that the defendant owed the plaintiff a duty, the next issue in a negligence case is whether the defendant breached that duty. In many cases, the required standard of conduct will be that of a reasonable person. A person who is specially trained to practice a profession or trade, however, will be held to the higher standard of care of a reasonably skilled member of that profession or trade. For example, the professional conduct of a doctor, architect, pilot, attorney, or accountant will be measured against the standard of the profession. A specialist within a profession will be held to the standard of specialists.

The court will also look to statutes and regulations to determine whether the defendant's conduct amounted to a breach of duty. Some jurisdictions merely allow the statute to be introduced into evidence to establish the standard of care. In other jurisdictions, however, once the plaintiff shows that the defendant violated a statute and the violation caused the injury, the burden shifts to the defendant to prove that he or she was not negligent. This is often an impossible burden to satisfy. This rule, sometimes referred to as *negligence per se*, applies only when the statute or regulation was designed to protect a class of persons from the type of harm suffered by the plaintiff and the plaintiff is a member of the class to be protected.

Courts will also look to the custom or practice of others under similar circumstances to determine the standard of care. Although the custom in the industry may be given great weight, it is ordinarily not dispositive or conclusive.

Res Ipsa Loquitur

The doctrine of *res ipsa loquitur*—"the thing speaks for itself"—allows the plaintiff to prove breach of duty and causation (discussed below) indirectly. *Res ipsa loquitur* applies when an accident has occurred, and it is obvious, although there is no direct proof, that the accident would not have happened without someone's negligence. For example, if a postoperative X-ray shows a surgical clamp in the plaintiff's abdomen, one can reasonably infer that the surgeon negligently left it, even if no one testifies as to how the clamp got there.

Res ipsa loquitur has three requirements. First, the plaintiff's injury must have been caused by a condition or instrumentality that was within the defendant's exclusive control. This requirement eliminates the possibility that persons not named as defendants were responsible for the condition that gave rise to the injury. Second, the accident must be of such a nature that it ordinarily would not occur in the absence of negligence by the defendant. Third, the accident must not be due to the plaintiff's own negligence.

Once *res ipsa loquitur* is established, jurisdictions vary as to its effect. In some jurisdictions, it creates a presumption of negligence, and the plaintiff is entitled to a directed verdict (whereby the judge directs the jury to find in favor

---

45. *Id.* at 290.

46. Basso v. Miller, 352 N.E.2d 868 (N.Y. 1976).

47. Mallet v. Pickens, 522 S.E.2d 436 (W. Va. 1999).

48. *Basso*, 352 N.E.2d at 868.

49. Nelson v. Freeland, 507 S.E.2d 882 (N.C. 1998).

50. 740 Ill. Comp. Stat. Ann. § 130/2.

of the plaintiff), unless the defendant can prove he or she was not responsible. This rule has the effect of shifting the burden of proof, normally with the plaintiff, to the defendant. Other jurisdictions leave the burden of proof with the plaintiff, requiring the jury to weigh the inference of negligence and to find the defendant negligent only if the preponderance of the evidence (including the *res ipsa* inference) favors such a finding.

Causal Connection

In addition to establishing duty and breach, a plaintiff claiming negligence must prove that the defendant's breach of duty caused the injury. The causation requirement has two parts: actual cause and proximate (or legal) cause.

Actual Cause

To establish *actual cause*, the plaintiff must prove that he or she would not have been harmed but for the defendant's negligence. The defendant is not liable if the plaintiff's injury would have occurred in the absence of the defendant's conduct. For example, if George Broussard put a garbage can on the sidewalk for morning pickup and Anna Chang came along and broke her ankle, Broussard's conduct would not be the actual cause of Chang's injury if it was established that Chang had caught her heel in the sidewalk, turned her ankle, and then bumped into Broussard's garbage can.

When the plaintiff names more than one defendant, the actual-cause test may become a *substantial-factor test*: Was the defendant's conduct a substantial factor in bringing about the plaintiff's injury?

A further problem may arise if more than one individual could possibly have been the negligent party. A classic case involved two hunters shooting quail on an open range.[51] Both shot at exactly the same time, using identical shotguns. A shot from one of the guns accidentally hit another hunter. Clearly, only one of the two defendants caused the injury, but there was no way to determine which one it was. The court imposed the burden on each defendant to prove that he had not caused the injury. Because neither could do so, both were held liable for the whole injury.

Proximate Cause

Once the plaintiff has proved that the defendant's conduct is an actual cause of the plaintiff's injury, he or she must also prove that it is the *proximate cause*, that is, that the defendant had a duty to protect the particular plaintiff against the particular conduct that injured him or her. Through the requirement of proximate cause, the law places limits on the defendant's liability.

The defendant is not required to compensate the plaintiff for injuries that were unforeseeable, even if the defendant's conduct was careless. Courts apply the foreseeability requirement in two different ways. Some courts limit the defendant's liability to those consequences that were foreseeable. Others look to whether the plaintiff was a foreseeable plaintiff, that is, whether the plaintiff was within the *zone of danger* caused by the defendant's careless conduct.

A classic case involved Mrs. Palsgraf, who was injured when scales on a railroad platform fell on her.[52] Two railroad employees were helping a man carrying a bulky package climb onto a moving train. Unbeknownst to the employees, the package contained fireworks. The man dropped the package and the fireworks exploded, causing the scales, which were located many feet away, to fall on the unfortunate Mrs. Palsgraf. She sued the railroad for negligence. The New York Court of Appeals ruled that even if the employees had failed to use due care, Mrs. Palsgraf's injury was not foreseeable. Because the railroad's employees' actions were not the proximate cause of her injury, the railroad was not liable for negligence.

As a general rule, a company is not liable for the criminal acts of third parties, unless the company knew or should have known that its negligence might allow the crime to occur.[53] Following the attack on the federal building in Oklahoma City in 1995, plaintiffs alleged negligence on the part of the manufacturer of the fertilizer that Terry Nichols and Timothy McVeigh used to concoct their bomb. The court dismissed the claim, finding as a matter of law that the terrorist activity was not reasonably foreseeable to the company.[54] In short, the company had no duty to protect against consumers using its product to blow up buildings because the company could not have anticipated such a use.

In a subsequent suit following the first World Trade Center attack in 1993, the court again dismissed claims against a fertilizer manufacturer on foreseeability grounds.[55] The concurrence did, however, signal to corporate America that society would expect companies to be more wary of the potential for terrorists to misuse products and services in the future, stating that the opinion "rest[ed] largely on a slender and temporal reed."[56]

Courts revisited the issue of the foreseeability of terrorists' acts in the wake of the September 11, 2001 attacks. The plaintiffs claimed that the airlines' negligence led to the injuries and damage suffered that day.[57] While noting the novelty of the type of attack,

51. Summers v. Tice, 199 P.2d 1 (Cal. 1948).

52. Palsgraf v. Long Island R.R. Co., 162 N.E. 99 (N.Y. 1928).

53. Gaines-Tabb v. ICI Explosives, USA, Inc., 160 F.3d 613 (10th Cir. 1998).

54. *Id.* at 621.

55. Port Auth. of New York & New Jersey v. Arcadian Corp., 189 F.3d 305, 315 (3d Cir. 1999).

56. *Id.* at 321.

57. *In re* Sept. 11 Litig., 280 F. Supp. 2d 279 (S.D.N.Y. 2003).

the court rejected the position of the judges deciding the Oklahoma City and 1993 World Trade Center cases and refused to rule as a matter of law that terrorist acts were unforeseeable. The court explained: "While it may be true that terrorists had not before deliberately flown airplanes into buildings, the airlines reasonably could foresee that crashes causing death and destruction on the ground [were] a hazard that would arise should hijackers take control of a plane."[58]

Injury

Finally, even if a defendant is negligent, the plaintiff cannot recover, unless he or she can show that he or she, or his or her property, was injured as a result of the defendant's conduct.

This injury requirement is often the controlling factor in actions for *negligent infliction of emotional distress*. The traditional rule is that a plaintiff cannot recover for negligent infliction of emotional distress, unless he or she can show some form of physical injury. In cases involving exposure to the human immunodeficiency virus (HIV), however, courts have permitted plaintiffs to recover for emotional distress (over the fear of contracting HIV) without requiring that they actually have contracted the virus. Courts have set forth objective standards that prevent someone from basing an action on an irrational fear that he or she contracted HIV. In *Williamson v. Waldman*,[59] the New Jersey Supreme Court held that a plaintiff can recover if a reasonable person would have experienced emotional distress over the prospect of contracting HIV under the circumstances. This hypothetical reasonable person would, however, be presumed to have "then-current, accurate, and generally available" knowledge concerning the transmission of HIV. Again, an irrational fear of catching the virus would not be a valid basis for an emotional distress suit.

Defenses to Negligence

In some jurisdictions, the defendant may absolve itself of part or all of the liability for negligence by proving that the plaintiff was also negligent. There may also be statutory defenses and common law limits on damages.

Contributory Negligence

Under the doctrine of *contributory negligence*, if the plaintiff was also negligent in any manner, he or she cannot recover any damages from the defendant. Thus, if a plaintiff was 5% negligent and the defendant was 95% negligent, the plaintiff's injury would go unredressed. To address this inequity, most courts have replaced the

doctrine of contributory negligence with that of comparative negligence.

Comparative Negligence

Under the doctrine of *comparative negligence*, the plaintiff may recover the proportion of his or her loss attributable to the defendant's negligence. For example, in *Lara v. Nevitt*,[60] plaintiff Ramon Lara was asleep in the sleeper berth of his son's big rig truck when the defendant lost control of his car and hit the truck. The jury found that Lara was 50% at fault because he was not wearing the seat belt or safety restraints that went across the bed in the sleeper berth. As a result, he could recover only 50% of his loss.

Comparative negligence may take two forms: ordinary and pure. In an *ordinary comparative negligence* jurisdiction, the plaintiff may recover only if he or she is less culpable than the defendant. Thus, if the plaintiff is found 51% negligent and the defendant 49% negligent, the plaintiff cannot recover. In a *pure comparative negligence* state, the plaintiff may recover for any amount of the defendant's negligence, even if the plaintiff was the more negligent party. For example, if the plaintiff was 80% negligent and the defendant was 20% negligent, the plaintiff may recover 20% of his or her loss.

Assumption of Risk

The *assumption of risk* defense requires that the plaintiff (1) knew the risk was present and understood its nature and (2) voluntarily chose to incur the risk. This defense applies when the plaintiff, in advance of the defendant's wrongdoing, expressly or impliedly consented to take the chance of injury from the defendant's actions. Such consent, like consent to an intentional tort, relieves the defendant of any liability. For example, the plaintiff assumes the risk if he or she, knowing that a car has faulty brakes, consents to take the chance of injury by riding in the car, or if he or she voluntarily chooses to walk where the defendant has negligently scattered broken glass.

Sometimes courts use duty to determine the viability of the assumption of risk defense. In *Mosca v. Lichtenwalter*,[61] a man who went ocean fishing and was accidentally struck in the eye by the sinker of another man's fishing pole unsuccessfully sued the other fisherman for negligence. The California Court of Appeal found that the injury arose from a risk inherent in the activity of sport fishing and that imposing a duty on the other fisherman would alter the fundamental nature of the sport.

Similarly, a Boston court dismissed a lawsuit brought by a Red Sox baseball fan who was hit by a fly ball. There are limits, however, on the risk that plaintiffs assume. The New Jersey Supreme Court held that the general rule that

58. *Id.* at 296.
59. 696 A.2d 14 (N.J. 1997).

60. 19 Cal. Rptr. 3d 865 (Cal. Ct. App. 2004).
61. 68 Cal. Rptr. 2d 58 (Cal. Ct. App. 1997).

baseball fans agree to assume a risk of injury from a foul ball or thrown bat applies when the injury occurs in the stands, but does not extend to other areas, including concourses or mezzanine areas. As a result, the court found that a ballpark patron hit by a foul ball while buying a beer from a vending cart on the mezzanine could sue the park owner for negligence.[62] Similarly, a New York court held that a college baseball player could sue her coach and university for injuries she incurred when her coach struck her in the face with a bat while demonstrating batting techniques. The court held it was not foreseeable that a coach with years of experience would swing a bat without ensuring that the player was out of range.[63]

Economic Loss Rule

In many states, the *economic loss rule* bars a plaintiff who is in privity of contract with the defendant or who has entered into a commercial transaction involving the defendant from bringing a lawsuit for negligence based solely on economic losses (as distinct from damages resulting from personal injury or property damage).[64] The theory is that parties who could have bargained for contractual protections, such as an express warranty, should be relegated to the remedies available under commercial law and not afforded tort remedies designed for accidents that cause property damage or personal injury.[65]

Statutory Defenses

In addition to common law privileges, there may also be statutory defenses. For example, the U.S. District Court for the Western District of Texas held that the immunity provision of the Communications Decency Act of 1996[66] barred a suit for negligence, gross negligence, fraud, and negligent misrepresentation brought against MySpace by the mother of a fourteen-year-old girl who was sexually assaulted by a man she met through the website.[67]

---

62. Maisonave v. Newark Bears Prof'l Baseball Club, Inc., 881 A.2d 700 (N.J. 2005).

63. Mark Fass, *Court Finds Exception to Assumed Risk Doctrine in Case of Student Hit by Bat-Swinging Coach*, N.Y. L.J., Jan. 11, 2008, *available at* http://www.law.com/jsp/article.jsp?id=1199786731062.

64. *See, e.g.*, Banknorth N.A. v. BJ's Wholesale Club, Inc., 442 F. Supp. 2d 206 (M.D. Pa. 2006) (holding that a retailer is not liable to a bank that issued Visa cards for losses the bank suffered because the retailer negligently failed to adequately secure cardholder information).

65. Miller v. U.S. Steel, 902 F.2d 573 (7th Cir. 1990) (holding that a purchaser of steel that could have obtained an express warranty from U.S. Steel or the general contractors could not sue U.S. Steel for negligence).

66. The Communications Decency Act of 1996, 47 U.S.C. § 230, states that "[n]o provider or user of an interactive computer service shall be treated as the publisher or speaker of any information provided by another content provider."

67. Doe v. MySpace, Inc., 474 F. Supp. 2d 843 (W.D. Tex. 2007).

LIABILITY OF ACCOUNTANTS AND OTHER PROFESSIONALS TO THIRD PARTIES

The liability of professionals to third parties varies depending on the professional's degree of fault and on the jurisdiction.

Intentional Misrepresentation

If an accountant, attorney, or other professional commits fraud, he or she is liable not only to the client, but also to any other person whom the accountant (or other professional) reasonably should have foreseen would rely on the intentional misrepresentation. For example, suppose that an auditor issued an audit opinion to a company's board of directors stating that its financial statements were prepared in accordance with generally accepted accounting principles, even though the auditor knew that they contained material misstatements. In this case, the auditor could be sued for fraud by not only the company but also its shareholders. If the auditor knew that the company would be giving the audited financial statements to a bank, then the auditor could also be liable to the bank, if it relied on the audit letter when extending credit.

Negligent Misrepresentation

If the claim is for professional negligence, or *malpractice*, however, rather than for fraud, the class of parties eligible to sue is more limited. Clearly, a professional owes a duty of due care to the client, and the client can sue for malpractice if the professional fails to satisfy that duty. But a professional may not have a duty to a third party with whom he or she does not have a contractual relationship.

Accountants

Courts have developed three main approaches to the duty of care owed by a public accountant to third parties who rely on the accountant's reports. New York's "near privity" approach, which several states have followed, is the most restrictive. In New York, a plaintiff claiming negligent misrepresentation against an accountant with whom the plaintiff had no contractual relationship must establish three elements: (1) the accountant must have been aware that the reports would be used for a particular purpose, (2) a known party must have been intended to rely on the reports to further that purpose, and (3) there must be some conduct by the accountant "linking" him or her to that known party. This strict limitation on the class of potential plaintiffs represents a policy determination by the New York courts that accountants will not, merely by contracting with a particular client, expose themselves to liability to an indeterminate class in an indeterminate amount for an indeterminate time.[68]

The most liberal approach, which few jurisdictions have adopted, extends an accountant's liability to all persons whom the accountant should reasonably foresee might obtain and rely on the accountant's report. States adopting the foreseeability approach compare defective audits to defective products and refuse to insulate auditors with a privity requirement, when manufacturers of defective products are strictly liable regardless of their relationship with the end user.[69]

The majority view is set forth in section 552 of the Restatement (Second) of Torts (1977):

> [A]n accountant's duty is limited to the client and third parties whom the accountant or client intends the information to benefit. The Restatement approach recognizes that an accountant's duty should extend beyond those in privity or near-privity with the accountant, but is not so expansive as to impose liability where the accountant knows only the possibility of distribution to anyone, and their subsequent reliance.

Attorneys

Courts have also taken a variety of approaches when considering whether lawyers are liable to nonclients. In 1995, the New Jersey Supreme Court held a property seller's attorney liable to the buyer for providing incomplete inspection reports in the course of a sale of land.[70] Although the attorney claimed that he had no duty to the purchaser

and therefore could not be liable, the court disagreed. The court ruled that when an attorney knows or should know that a nonclient buyer will rely on his or her professional capacity, then the attorney owes a duty to the third party and may be liable for breaching that duty.

In litigation surrounding the massive fraud at Enron (subject of the "Inside Story" in Chapter 2), the U.S. District Court for the Southern District of Texas noted that Texas law requires privity of contract for malpractice liability but held that claims for fraudulent or negligent misrepresentation may be brought by persons whom the attorney had reason to know would rely on the information and who justifiably relied on it.[71] Thus:

> [P]rofessionals, including lawyers and accountants, when they take the affirmative step of speaking out, whether individually or as essentially an author or co-author in a statement or report, whether identified or not, about their client's financial condition, do have a duty to third parties not in privity not to knowingly or with severe recklessness issue materially misleading statements on which they intend or have reason to expect that those third parties will rely.

Accordingly, Enron's law firm Vinson & Elkins could be held liable for Securities and Exchange Commission reports it created even though it was not named in the documents.

In the following case, the South Dakota Supreme Court took a less expansive approach when considering whether a corporate lawyer was liable for malpractice when sued by the investors and directors of a corporation he represented.

---

68. *See, e.g.*, White v. Guarente, 372 N.E.2d 315 (N.Y. 1977).

69. ML–Lee Acquisition Fund, L.P. v. Deloitte & Touche, 463 S.E.2d 618 (S.C. Ct. App. 1995).

70. Petrillo v. Bachenberg, 655 A.2d 1354 (N.J. 1995).

71. *In re* Enron Corp. Secs., Derivative and ERISA Litig., 235 F. Supp. 2d 549 (S.D. Tex. 2002).

A CASE IN POINT	*In the Language of the Court*	Case 9.4

Chem-Age Industries, Inc. v. Glover

Supreme Court of South Dakota
652 N.W.2d 756 (S.D. 2002).

FACTS   Alan Glover represented Byron Dahl, an entrepreneur, in a number of business transactions. At some point, Glover, acting on behalf of Dahl, approached Roger Pederson and Garry Shepard about investing in a start-up company called Chem-Age Industries. Pederson and Shepard agreed to invest in the company in exchange for stock and became members of the board of directors. Soon thereafter, both investors became suspicious when the credit cards in the company's name began to accrue large balances due to charges by Dahl for what appeared to be personal items. Pederson and Shepard asked Dahl and Glover about the charges and were informed that Chem-Age Industries was in negotiations with another company to be bought out and that the charges would be paid with the proceeds from that sale. During this meeting, Glover stated that he "represented Chem-Age Industries" and that Chem-Age was owned by Dahl. Shortly after this meeting, Chem-Age failed to pay its taxes and was dissolved entirely. Pederson and Shepard sued both Dahl and Glover for negligent misrepresentation and Glover for legal malpractice.

ISSUE PRESENTED   Does a company's corporate counsel have a duty to the company's investors and directors such that the counsel can be held liable to them for legal malpractice?

CONTINUED

OPINION KONENKAMP, J., writing for the Supreme Court of South Dakota:

To prevail in a legal malpractice claim, a plaintiff must prove: (1) the existence of an attorney–client relationship giving rise to a duty; (2) the attorney, either by an act or a failure to act, breached that duty; (3) the attorney's breach of duty proximately caused injury to the client; and (4) the client sustained actual damage. Whether an attorney–client relationship existed is ordinarily a question of fact. Here, we will examine the elements for an attorney–client relationship regarding, first, the corporation and, next, the individual plaintiffs.

. . . .

Dahl hired Glover to organize the business as a corporation. By his own admission, Glover's involvement with Dahl was directly related to that incorporation, notwithstanding Dahl's earlier engagement of Glover on personal matters before and independent of the events at issue here. . . . Glover contends nonetheless that he did not represent the corporation. This is clearly a question of material fact. In the absence of some indication otherwise, Glover can be deemed the attorney for the corporation, even if he was also representing Dahl personally. An attorney may represent both a corporation and individuals in the corporation. . . . If it is shown that he represented the corporation, then it follows that Glover had a duty to the client corporation.

. . . .

South Dakota recognizes that an attorney–client relationship may arise expressly or impliedly from the parties' conduct. Such a relationship is created when: (1) a person seeks advice or assistance from an attorney; (2) the advice or assistance sought pertains to matters within the attorney's professional competence; and (3) the attorney expressly or impliedly agrees to give or indeed gives the advice or assistance. . . . Here, the individual plaintiffs sought no advice from Glover. Correspondingly, Glover never agreed to advise or assist them. . . . Glover had no personal consultation with Pederson and Shepard in creating the corporation. [Therefore, although Glover did owe a duty to the corporation, and the corporation may in turn have owed the plaintiffs a duty, Glover did not directly owe them a duty as individual shareholders or directors of the corporation.]

. . . .

We earlier found that no attorney–client relationship existed between Glover and the two investor-directors, Pederson and Shepard. We now turn to the question whether Glover may have owed a fiduciary duty to them or to the corporation, even in the absence of an attorney–client relationship. To ascertain a fiduciary duty, we must find three things: (1) plaintiffs reposed "faith, confidence and trust" in Glover; (2) plaintiffs were in a position of "inequality, dependence, weakness, or lack of knowledge" and, (3) Glover exercised "dominion, control or influence" over plaintiffs' affairs.

. . . .

Plaintiffs Pederson and Shepard have submitted no evidence to show how they were in a confidential relationship with Glover, where they depended on him specifically to protect their investment interests and, where Glover exercised dominance and influence over their business affairs. On the contrary, they never consulted with Glover during the time he is alleged to have breached a fiduciary duty to them.

. . . .

Holding attorneys liable for aiding and abetting the breach of a fiduciary duty in rendering professional services poses both a hazard and a quandary for the legal profession. On the one hand, overbroad liability might diminish the quality of legal services, since it would impose "self protective reservations" in the attorney–client relationship. Attorneys acting in a professional capacity should be free to render advice without fear of personal liability

CONTINUED

to third persons if the advice later goes awry. On the other hand, the privilege of rendering professional services not being absolute, lawyers should not be free to substantially assist their clients in committing tortious acts. To protect lawyers from meritless claims, many courts strictly interpret the common law elements of aiding and abetting the breach of a fiduciary duty.

The substantial assistance requirement carries with it a condition that the lawyer must actively participate in the breach of a fiduciary duty. Merely acting as a scrivener for a client is insufficient. A plaintiff must show that the attorney defendant rendered "substantial assistance" to the breach of duty, not merely to the person committing the breach. In *Granewich*,[72] the lawyers facilitated the squeeze-out, not just by providing legal advice and drafting documents, but by sending letters containing misrepresentations and helping to amend by-laws eliminating voting requirements that protected the minority shareholder's interest.

Another condition to finding liability for assisting in the breach of a fiduciary duty is the requirement that the assistance be "knowing." Knowing participation in a fiduciary's breach of duty requires both knowledge of the fiduciary's status as a fiduciary and knowledge that the fiduciary's conduct contravenes a fiduciary duty.

Although Glover may not have taken any active role in defrauding the investor-directors and may not have owed any direct fiduciary duty to them, Dahl did owe such a duty, and a material question of fact exists on whether Glover substantially assisted Dahl in breaching that duty. It may be that Glover, as much as Pederson and Shepard, was duped by Dahl's conniving business dealings, but that is for a jury to decide.

Result   Although Pederson and Shepard could not sue Glover for legal malpractice or breach of fiduciary duty, they could sue him for aiding and abetting a breach of fiduciary duty by Dahl. To prevail, they had to show that Glover was aware of Dahl's breach and substantially assisted him in breaching his duty.

Comments   In the wake of the collapse of Enron Corporation, WorldCom, and other firms, experts disagreed over what should be the "gatekeeper" role of lawyers and auditors.[73] As explained in Chapter 3, the Sarbanes–Oxley Act requires corporate counsel to "report up-the-ladder" ongoing material violations of securities laws or breaches of fiduciary duty to the board of directors. The subprime mortgage crisis of 2007–2008 has brought the issue to the fore again.

Critical Thinking Questions

1. Should corporate lawyers be liable to the shareholders for malpractice? Why or why not?
2. Should a corporate attorney who discovers a breach of fiduciary duty by an officer and director be required to disclose that breach to all of the other directors?

72. Granewich v. Harding, 985 P.2d 788 (Or. 1999).
73. John C. Coffee, Jr., *The Attorney as Gatekeeper: An Agenda for the SEC*, 103 Colum. L. Rev. 1293 (2003).

Investment Bankers

The issues surrounding attorney and auditor liability to third parties closely parallel those surrounding the liability of investment bankers who issue fairness opinions in leveraged buyouts. Should shareholders be able to sue the investment bankers directly for negligent misrepresentation? Do investment bankers owe shareholders a duty? The actual client of the investment banker is the board of directors of the target company. Nevertheless, some courts have upheld negligent misrepresentation actions by shareholders against investment bankers on a foreseeability basis.[74]

74. For an excellent discussion of the potential liability of investment bankers to shareholders, see Bill Shaw & Edward J. Gac, *Fairness Opinions in Leveraged Buy Outs: Should Investment Bankers Be Directly Liable to Shareholders?*, 23 Sec. Reg. L.J. 293 (1995). *See, e.g.*, Dowling v. Narragansett Capital Corp., 735 F. Supp. 1105 (R.I. 1990).

NEGLIGENT HIRING AND LIABILITY FOR EMPLOYEE RECOMMENDATIONS

Employers face potential liability for negligently hiring incompetent employees and for harm caused by former employees for whom the prior employer wrote a favorable letter of recommendation.

Negligent Hiring

An employer may be held liable even for the negligent or tortious conduct of employees acting outside the scope of employment if the employer breached its duty to use care in hiring competent employees. (As explained in Chapter 5 and further below, employers are always liable for torts committed by employees acting within the scope of their employment.) Under the theory of *negligent hiring*, the proximate cause of the plaintiff's injury is the employer's negligence in hiring the employee, rather than the employee's wrongful act. A plaintiff must prove that (1) the employer was required to investigate the employee and failed to do so, (2) an investigation would have revealed the unsuitability of the employee for the job, and (3) it was unreasonable for the employer to hire the employee in light of the information the employer knew or should have known. In addition, the plaintiff must prove that (1) the employee was "unfit" for the employment position, (2) the employer knew or should have known that the employee was unfit for the position, and (3) the employee's particular unfitness proximately caused the plaintiff's injury.

Duty of Employers to Third Parties for Employee Recommendations

In recent years, many employers have backed away from providing letters of recommendation, primarily because of the fear of lawsuits.[75] Employers have chosen instead to issue "no comment" or "name, rank, and serial number" reference letters largely because writing a substantive reference may put them in a "damned if you do, damned if you don't" legal conundrum. Employers who disclose "too much" negative information may be subject to a defamation suit by the former employee. Employers who disclose "too little" negative information may be held liable to injured third parties for negligent misrepresentation.[76] In an

effort to respond to the problem, at least thirty-five states have enacted statutes offering some protection to employers who make recommendations in good faith.[77]

STRICT LIABILITY

Strict liability is liability without fault, that is, without either intent or negligence. Strict liability is imposed in two circumstances: (1) in product liability cases (the subject of Chapter 10) and (2) in cases involving abnormally dangerous, that is, ultrahazardous, activities.

Ultrahazardous Activities

If the defendant's activity is ultrahazardous, the defendant is strictly liable for any injuries that result. An activity is *ultrahazardous* if it (1) necessarily involves a risk of serious harm to persons or property that cannot be eliminated by the exercise of utmost care and (2) is not a matter of common usage. In most jurisdictions, liability does not attach until a court determines that the dangerous activity is inappropriate to the particular location.

Courts have found the following activities ultrahazardous: (1) storing flammable liquids in quantity in an urban area, (2) pile driving, (3) blasting, (4) crop dusting, (5) fumigating with cyanide gas, (6) constructing a roof that allows snow to fall off onto a highway, (7) emitting of noxious fumes by a manufacturing plant located in a settled area, (8) locating oil wells or refineries in populated communities, (9) test-firing solid-fuel rocket motors, and (10) keeping wild animals or a domestic animal known to be vicious.

In contrast, courts have considered parachuting, drunk driving, maintaining power lines, and letting water escape from an irrigation ditch not to be ultrahazardous. Similarly, discharging fireworks is not ultrahazardous because the risk of serious harm could be eliminated by proper manufacture.

Under strict liability, once the court determines that the activity is abnormally dangerous, it is irrelevant that the defendant observed a high standard of care. For example, if the defendant's blasting injured the plaintiff, it is irrelevant that the defendant took every precaution available. Although evidence of such precautions might prevent the plaintiff from recovering under a theory of negligence, it does not affect strict liability. Evidence of due care would, however, prevent an award of punitive damages. Adequate liability insurance is particularly important for companies engaged in ultrahazardous activities.

---

75. Note, *Addressing the Cloud over Employee References: A Survey of Recently Enacted State Legislation*, 39 Wm. & Mary L. Rev. 177 (1997).

76. *See, e.g.,* Randi W. v. Muroc Joint Unified Sch. Dist., 929 P.2d 582 (Cal. 1997) (finding liability). *But see* Richland Sch. Dist. v. Mabton Sch. Dist., 45 P.3d 580 (Wash. App. 2002) (finding that a former employer did not owe a school custodian's new employer a duty to disclose dismissal charges of child molestation, on the basis that it was not foreseeable that a person with the custodian's record of minor disciplinary problems and dismissal charges posed a foreseeable risk of physical harm).

77. For a clever way a prospective employer may be able to finesse this issue, see Pierre Mornell, Hiring Smart (1999). Dr. Mornell recommended that the prospective employer call the former employer at a time when the supervisor is unlikely to be in the office and leave a voice message asking the supervisor to return the call only if the supervisor considers the former employee to be an excellent candidate.

RESPONDEAT SUPERIOR AND VICARIOUS LIABILITY

Under certain circumstances, a person can be held vicariously liable for the negligent, or in some cases the intentional, conduct of another.

Respondeat Superior

As discussed in Chapter 5, under the doctrine of *respondeat superior*—"let the master answer"—a "master" or employer is vicariously liable for the torts of the "servant" or employee if the employee was acting within the scope of his or her employment. The doctrine of *respondeat superior* may also apply when the person is not paid, but acts on behalf of another out of friendship or loyalty, or as a volunteer.

Underlying the doctrine of *respondeat superior* is the policy of allocating the risk of doing business to those who stand to profit from the undertaking. Because the employer benefits from the business, it is deemed more appropriate for the employer to bear the risk of loss than for the innocent customer or bystander to do so. The employer is in a better position to absorb such losses or to shift them, through liability insurance or price increases, to insurers and customers and, thus, to the community in general.

Liability for Torts Committed Within the Scope of Employment

An employer is directly liable for its own negligence in hiring or supervising an employee. In addition, the employer may be vicariously liable for an employee's wrongful acts, even though the employer had no knowledge of them and in no way directed them, if the acts were committed while the employee was acting within the scope of employment. To be within the scope of employment, activities must be closely connected to what the employee is employed to do or reasonably incidental to it. Whether an act was in the scope of employment is an issue for the jury to decide. (Scope of employment is discussed in greater detail in Chapter 5.)

In the following case, the court considered whether an employer was liable for injury to a customer caused by a cashier who was just "joking around."

| **A CASE IN POINT** | *In the Language of the Court* | **Case 9.5** |

Burlarley v. Wal-Mart Stores, Inc.

New York Supreme Court, Appellate Division
75 A.D.3d 955 (N.Y. App. Div. 2010).

FACTS   The plaintiff and his wife were checking out at the Wal-Mart store in Kingston, New York, when the cashier, in an effort to make her work shift go by faster, jokingly pretended to ring up items for vastly more than they were worth and threw various items at the plaintiff. The plaintiff told her to stop, which the cashier initially did. When the plaintiff turned away, however, the cashier threw a bag containing a pair of shoes and shampoo at his face, injuring the plaintiff. He then sued Wal-Mart.

Wal-Mart moved for summary judgment, arguing that the doctrine of *respondeat superior* did not apply because the cashier was not acting within the scope of her employment when she hit the plaintiff with the bag. The trial court granted the motion, and the plaintiff appealed.

ISSUE PRESENTED   Is an employer vicariously liable for injury to a customer caused by an employee who was joking around during her shift?

OPINION   MERCURE, J., writing for the Supreme Court of New York, Appellate Division:

The doctrine of respondeat superior renders an employer "vicariously liable for the tortious acts of its employees only if those acts were committed in furtherance of the employer's business and within the scope of employment." Factors relevant to a determination of whether an employee's acts fall within the scope of employment include: "the connection between the time, place, and occasion for the act; the history of the relationship between the employer and employee as spelled out in actual practice; whether the act is one commonly done by such an employee; the extent of departure from normal methods of performance; and whether the specific act was one that the employer could reasonably have anticipated." While this inquiry generally presents questions of fact, summary judgment is appropriate if the undisputed facts demonstrate that the doctrine is inapplicable.

In our view, the Supreme Court properly concluded that throwing a full bag of heavy items at an unsuspecting customer's face as a "joke" is not commonly done by a cashier and, indeed, substantially departs from a cashier's normal methods of performance. Moreover, the

CONTINUED

cashier's actions arose not from any work-related motivation, but rather her desire to pass the time and relieve mounting frustration with her job. Nor did the employer have any reason to anticipate that the cashier would engage in the complained-of behavior, in light of the fact that she had worked as a cashier for several years without any significant disciplinary problems. Accordingly . . . the cashier acted for purely personal reasons and "not in the furtherance of any duty owed to" defendant.

RESULT   Summary judgment in favor of the defendant store was affirmed. Wal-Mart was not liable to the plaintiff.

CRITICAL THINKING QUESTIONS

1. Would Wal-Mart have been liable if the employee had a history of acting inappropriately with customers?

2. Based on the court's reasoning in this case, would the owner of an appliance store be liable if one of its repairmen raped a customer while in her house for a service call?

© Cengage Learning 2013

Courts have held the employer vicariously liable for an accident caused by the negligence of an employee who drove after drinking alcohol at a company function, on the grounds that the injury-producing event—the consumption of alcohol—occurred while the employee was acting within the scope of his employment by attending a company function.[78] For example, in *Dickinson v. Edwards*,[79] the Washington Supreme Court ruled that an employer hosting a banquet is liable under *respondeat superior* if the plaintiff establishes that (1) the employee consumed alcohol at a party hosted by the employer at which the employee's presence was requested or required by the employer, (2) the employee caused the accident while driving from the banquet, and (3) the proximate cause of the accident (the intoxication) occurred at the time the employee negligently consumed the alcohol. The Rhode Island Supreme Court went so far as to find an employer responsible for workers' compensation benefits, when an employee got drunk at a Christmas party and fell from a third-floor window.[80]

If intentional conduct caused the plaintiff's injury, courts will look to the nexus, or connection, between the conduct and the employment. In general, an employer is liable for his or her employee's intentional torts if the wrongful act in any way furthered the employer's purpose, however misguided the manner of furthering that purpose. Often intentional torts do not further the employer's business and are therefore outside the scope of employment. For example, one court found a security company not liable when one of its security guards raped a worker in a client's building, even though the guard used his position to create the circumstances for the rape.[81]

Employer Liability Based on the Aided-in-the-Agency Doctrine

Other courts will apply the *aided-in-the-agency doctrine* (discussed in Chapters 5 and 13) and look beyond the scope of employment to determine whether the employee exercised authority conferred by, or used assets provided by, the employer. Thus, one court held a county vicariously liable for battery, among other things, when one of its law enforcement officers stopped a woman, placed her in his patrol car, drove to an isolated place, and threatened to rape and murder her.[82] Other courts have refused to impose liability in such cases.

Other Types of Vicarious Liability

Under certain circumstances, an employer may be vicariously, or indirectly, liable for harm caused by an employee even when the employee was not acting within the scope of employment and did not exercise authority conferred by, or use assets provided by, the employer. Courts are most likely to impose vicarious liability when the employer took an action (or failed to act) and thereby increased the likelihood that an employee would commit a tort.

For example, the employer may be responsible for the safe passage home of an employee who was not intoxicated, but was tired from working too many consecutive hours. In *Robertson v. LeMaster*,[83] LeMaster was an employee of the Norfolk and Western Railway Company. He was doing heavy manual labor, including lifting railroad ties and shoveling coal. After thirteen hours at work, he told his supervisor that he was tired and wanted to go home. The supervisor told him to continue working. This happened several times, until finally LeMaster said that he could no longer work because he was too tired. His supervisor told him that if he would not work, he should get his

78. *See, e.g.,* Chastain v. Litton Sys., Inc., 694 F.2d 957 (4th Cir. 1982); Wong-Leong v. Hawaiian Indep. Refinery, Inc., 879 P.2d 538 (Haw. 1994).

79. 716 P.2d 814 (Wash. 1986).

80. Beauchesne v. David London & Co., 375 A.2d 920 (R.I. 1977).

81. Rabon v. Guardsmark, Inc., 571 F.2d 1277 (4th Cir. 1978).

82. White v. County of Orange, 212 Cal. Rptr. 493 (Cal. Ct. App. 1985).

83. 301 S.E.2d 563 (W. Va. 1983).

bucket and go home. LeMaster had been at work a total of twenty-seven consecutive hours. On his way home, he fell asleep at the wheel and was involved in an accident, causing injuries to Robertson. Robertson sued the railroad.

The Supreme Court of Appeals of West Virginia concluded that requiring LeMaster to work such long hours and then setting him loose on the highway in an obviously exhausted condition was sufficient to sustain a claim against the railroad. The court found that the issue in this case was not whether the railway failed to control LeMaster while he was driving on the highway, but rather whether the railroad's conduct prior to the accident created a foreseeable risk of harm. The court concluded that the railway's actions created such a foreseeable risk.

Courts are split on whether to impose liability on an employer who sends home an intoxicated employee who injures a third party en route. In *Otis Engineering Corp. v. Clark*,[84] a supervisor at Otis Engineering sent an employee home because he was drunk. The employee had a history of drinking at work and was intoxicated on the evening in question. Unfortunately, the employee was involved in a fatal automobile accident on his way home from work—the employee was killed as were two women traveling in another automobile. The husbands of the two women brought a wrongful death action against Otis. Historically, employers were not responsible for accidents caused by employees traveling to and from work. The Texas Supreme Court broke new ground and held that the corporation had a duty to prevent the intoxicated employee from causing an unreasonable risk of harm to others. The court explained that "changing social conditions [have] led constantly to the recognition of new duties. . . . [T]he courts will find a duty where, in general reasonable men would recognize it and agree that it exists."[85]

Prior to *Otis*, no case in Texas had established a duty for employers in such a situation. This case is an example of how the law can be changed, in a sense retroactively, to hold parties to a higher standard than they might have previously expected. Because courts and lawmakers generally push the law toward higher standards, rather than lower ones, managers should make sure that they constantly reach for higher, more ethical standards.

The Arizona Court of Appeals reached a different conclusion on similar facts in *Riddle v. Arizona Oncology Services, Inc.*[86] An Arizona Oncology Services (AOS) supervisor sent an employee home because she was high on cocaine. The employee had a history of drug abuse and had consumed cocaine while at work on the date in question. On her way home, the employee drove her vehicle across the centerline and collided with Steven Riddle's vehicle, seriously injuring Riddle. Riddle brought a personal-injury action against AOS. The Arizona Court of Appeals expressly declined to follow the Texas Supreme Court's decision in *Otis* and held that AOS had no duty to protect a third party from injury allegedly caused by the employee.

The Tennessee Court of Appeals also refused to impose liability on the employer of a woman who arrived at work intoxicated and then caused an accident off-premises after insisting on driving her own car home.[87] Tennessee has adopted the Restatement (Second) of Torts (1965), which provides:

> There is no duty so to control the conduct of a third person as to prevent him from causing physical harm to another unless
>
> (a) a special relation exists between the actor and the third person which imposes a duty upon the actor to control the third person's conduct, or
>
> (b) a special relation exists between the actor and the other which gives to the other a right to protection.

The court noted:

> [The employer] did not contribute to, condone, or seek to accommodate, her intoxication. It did not require her to drive home; in fact, it attempted to find her safe passage home, but she refused. In sum, the employer did not provide her mobility she otherwise did not have; it did not encourage her to drive home; and it did not contribute to the condition that made it unsafe for her to drive. In effect, the employer "did no more than acquiesce in [her] determination to drive [her] own car."

The Supreme Judicial Court of Massachusetts addressed a more complicated situation in the following case.

---

84. 668 S.W.2d 307 (Tex. 1983).
85. *Id.* at 310.

86. 924 P.2d 468 (Ariz. Ct. App. 1996).
87. Lett v. Collis Foods, Inc., 605 S.W.3d 95 (Tenn. Ct. App. 2001).

A CASE IN POINT	*Summary*	Case 9.6

Lev v. Beverly Enterprises-Massachusetts, Inc.

Supreme Judicial Court of Massachusetts
929 N.E.2d 303 (Mass. 2010).

Facts   Charles Lev sued Beverly Enterprises for injuries he sustained as a result of an automobile accident caused by Beverly employee John Ahern. Ahern left his shift at approximately 5:30 p.m. He then drove to a restaurant where he was joined by his supervisor (who was also a close friend). The two discussed an upcoming Department of Public Health survey, and Ahern purchased two drinks. At 7 p.m., Ahern was driving home when he struck the plaintiff with his car as the plaintiff was crossing the street, causing severe injuries.

CONTINUED

The plaintiff alleged that Ahern was working within the scope of his employment when he became intoxicated and then negligently operated his vehicle. Lev also alleged that Beverly, acting through the supervisor, should have known Ahern was intoxicated and prevented him from driving. The trial judge granted Beverly's motion for summary judgment, and the plaintiff appealed.

Issue Presented   Is an employer liable for negligence if an intoxicated employee causes an automobile accident after leaving a restaurant where he discussed work with his supervisor over drinks?

Summary of Opinion   The Supreme Judicial Court of Massachusetts ruled that Beverly was not vicariously liable for the torts of its employee Ahern. The court explained that the conduct of an agent is within the scope of employment if it is of the kind he is employed to perform. The scope of employment generally does not include travel to and from home to a place of employment. Here, the scope of Ahern's employment ended when he left the restaurant to travel home. He was no longer acting on behalf of or under the direction or control of Beverly when he struck and injured the plaintiff. As a result, his actions could not be imputed to Beverly under the doctrine of *respondeat superior.*

The court then considered the plaintiff's argument that Beverly should be liable under employer-host liability. The court began by noting that the existence of a duty of care is a question of law, making summary judgment appropriate. The duty of care owed by a social host to a guest is limited to those occasions when the host controls the alcohol that is provided to guests. This same standard of care test is applicable to the employer-host relationship. Here, the supervisor did not provide the alcohol to Ahern, so Beverly owed no duty to the plaintiff under an employer-host theory of liability.

The plaintiff further argued that Beverly owed a duty of care to the plaintiff under traditional theories of negligence because of the employer's "special relationship" with employees. The court rejected this argument, reasoning that the existence of a duty of care is predicated on a plaintiff's reasonable expectations and reliance that a defendant will anticipate harmful acts of third persons and take measures to protect the plaintiff from harm. When two employees meet at a restaurant to socialize and talk about work, an employer cannot be expected to be foresee that it should act to protect all potential plaintiffs from an employee's misbehavior. Ahern's employment with the defendant did not facilitate his ability to harm the plaintiff, so there was no special relationship giving rise to a duty of care.

The court also concluded that Beverly's alcohol abuse policy did not impose a duty of care on the supervisor and, hence, Beverly to prohibit Ahern from consuming alcohol. As a general rule, there is no duty to control another person's conduct to prevent that person from harming a third party. The court refused to impose a duty on employers to monitor the off-premises conduct of their employees to ensure that harm does not come to third parties.

© Cengage Learning 2013

⟨⟩ SUCCESSOR LIABILITY

As explained further in Chapter 10, under the doctrine of *successor liability*, individuals or entities that purchase a business may be held liable for product defects and certain other tortious acts of the previous owner. For example, if a company buys the assets of a ladder manufacturer and continues in the same line of business, the acquiring company may be liable for defective ladders manufactured and sold before the acquisition.

⟨⟩ DAMAGES

Tort damages generally attempt to restore the plaintiff to the same position he or she was in before the tort occurred. (In contrast, contract damages try to place the plaintiff in the position he or she would have been in had the contract been performed, as explained in Chapter 7.) Tort damages may include punitive as well as compensatory damages.

Actual (or Compensatory) Damages

Actual damages, also known as *compensatory damages*, measure the cost to repair or replace an item or the decrease in market value caused by the tortious conduct. Actual damages may also include compensation for medical expenses, lost wages, and pain and suffering.

Punitive Damages

Punitive damages, also known as *exemplary damages*, may be awarded to punish the defendant and deter others from engaging in similar conduct. Punitive damages are awarded only in cases of outrageous misconduct.

The amount of punitive damages may properly be based on the defendant's degree of culpability and wealth. But, as discussed in Chapter 4, the U.S. Supreme Court has indicated that, except in egregious cases, the ratio of punitive damages to actual damages should be in the single digits.[88]

Several states have limited punitive damages awards to situations in which the plaintiff can prove by clear and convincing evidence that the defendant was guilty of oppression, fraud, or malice. Nevertheless, as discussed in the "Political Perspective," business leaders continue to call for legislative reform to cap or eliminate punitive damages as part of more general tort reform. Indeed, the head of the American Manufacturers Association declared, "[Trial lawyers are] the pariahs of the business community, which is more frightened by them than terrorists, China, or high energy prices."[89]

The desire to curb punitive damages seems to be largely limited to product liability cases, however, where businesses are defendants but rarely plaintiffs. In areas where businesses tend to be plaintiffs as well as defendants (such as contracts, unfair competition, and misleading advertising), reform of punitive damages appears to be less of a priority.[90]

88. *See* State Farm Mut. Auto. Ins. Co. v. Campbell, 538 U.S. 408 (2003).

89. Richard A. Oppel Jr. & Glen Justice, *The 2004 Election: The Response: Kerry Gains Campaign Ace, Risking Anti-Lawyer Anger*, N.Y. TIMES, July 7, 2004.

90. Richard B. Schmitt, *Why Businesses Sometimes Like Punitive Awards*, WALL ST. J., Dec. 11, 1995, at B1.

POLITICAL | PERSPECTIVE

The Attack on Tort Law

For years, critics and supporters of the U.S. tort system have advanced largely unchanged arguments about the perceived need for tort reform.[a] The topic became an election-year issue in 2004, when Vice President Dick Cheney called on challenger, Senator John Edwards, to defend his record as a trial lawyer and his approach to tort reform during the vice presidential debate.

Critics assert that the tort system has a random, Russian roulette flavor to it. To buttress this claim, they point to several cases where juries granted multimillion-dollar punitive damages awards to injured plaintiffs. These well-publicized horror stories include a $2.9 million award to an elderly woman, Stella Liebeck, who

received third-degree burns after spilling McDonald's coffee on her lap;[b] a $4 million award against BMW for selling as new a car that had been damaged by acid rain and repainted;[c] and a $150 million award against General Motors in a case where the plaintiff who was injured in a single-car accident had admittedly consumed at least one beer and was not wearing a seat belt.[d]

The critics argue that large and unpredictable jury awards have resulted in sharply higher liability insurance rates, which in turn may (1) increase the cost of vital products and services, (2) stifle innovation in valuable but potentially dangerous products, and (3) render U.S. firms less equipped to compete with rivals abroad. Moreover,

they claim that attorneys' fees and administrative costs are so extensive that less than half of the amount awarded by verdict or settlement is paid to the injured plaintiffs.

Supporters of the present tort system respond that it is the one place where the average citizen can battle the powerful on nearly equal terms. They claim that without the threat of lawsuits and their accompanying discovery process, large corporations would have every incentive to conceal harmful information about the effects of their products. The supporters believe that if any reform of the system is necessary, judicial review and self-policing would be more effective tools than legislation at either the state or the federal level.[e]

CONTINUED

Statistical studies claim to show a connection between so-called frivolous lawsuits and the impediment of economic growth in the area. For example, in 2002, the U.S. Chamber of Commerce singled out Mississippi as the "jackpot justice" state where tort lawyers were running amok and businesses were leaving in droves.[f] The basic premise, as it has played out in Mississippi, is that jurors assume they can force big business to be more responsible by awarding large settlements against businesses in favor of the ordinary person. In 2004, Mississippi enacted comprehensive tort reform that, among other things, capped noneconomic actual damages in medical malpractice actions at $500,000; capped noneconomic actual damages in nonmedical malpractice cases at $1 million; capped punitive damages based on the defendant's net worth; abolished joint and several liability; immunized innocent sellers from strict liability for defective products; and changed premises liability to provide immunity to premises owners for death or injury to contractors or their employees if the contractor knew or should have known of the danger.[g] Although the American Tort Reform Association claimed that these reforms were responsible for new investments in the state,[h] a 2010 study by the U.S. Chamber Institute for Legal Reform found that U.S. businesses still ranked Mississippi's tort liability system forty-eighth in terms of its reasonableness and balance.[i]

Other studies contradict claims of a "litigation explosion." A report issued by the U.S. Department of Justice's Bureau of Justice Statistics shows that the number of tort cases resolved in U.S. district courts fell 79% between 1985 and 2003. In fiscal years 2002 and 2003, 98% of personal-injury cases were resolved by mediation, settled out of court, or handled in some nontrial disposition. Only 2% of the actions filed required trials to be resolved.[j] In addition, according to the U.S. Department of Justice, the amount of damages awarded in tort cases is declining. The median inflation-adjusted payout in all tort (personal-injury) cases dropped more than 50% between 1992 and 2001, to $28,000.[k]

Furthermore, punitive damages awards are both extremely rare and usually closely related to the amount of compensatory damages. In 2001, juries awarded punitive damages in only 5.3% of the tort cases won by plaintiffs, and the median inflation-adjusted award in these cases was only $25,000.[l] Of course, fear of large punitive damages awards may cause businesses to settle cases for larger amounts than they would otherwise have agreed to pay. Large awards make headlines, but when they are reduced on appeal, as often happens, the reduction receives much less attention. Even the $2.9 million award in the notorious McDonald's coffee case, for example, was reduced to $400,000.[m] The 2003 U.S. Supreme Court decision in *State Farm Mutual Automobile Insurance Co. v. Campbell*,[n] which held that "few awards exceeding a single-digit ratio between punitive and compensatory damages . . . will satisfy due process," has also resulted in reductions in the size of punitive damages awards on appeal.

Although efforts to enact broad federal legislation to limit tort damages have been unsuccessful, the Class Action Fairness Act of 2005 moved many class actions from state courts into federal courts, thereby limiting the scope of such actions and the ability of plaintiffs to forum shop for the friendliest jurisdiction. In 2004, California voters approved Proposition 64, a ballot initiative that required plaintiffs to prove they were injured by an alleged violation of the state's unfair competition law in order to participate in class-action litigation. This victory triggered a movement by tort reform groups and lawyers representing some of the nation's largest corporations to enact similar legislation in other states. As part of these efforts, tort reformers have drafted model legislation that would require consumers to have suffered economic losses or injury from a company's misstatements in order to file a class action. Plaintiffs' lawyers argue that requiring reliance and actual injury will present major roadblocks to future consumer litigation. "The idea that a reliance requirement be injected into consumer protection statutes is a horrible idea," according to Todd Heyman, a partner at Shapiro Haber & Urmy who sued Philip Morris over "light" cigarettes in Massachusetts. He argues that such a requirement will, in effect, constitute a "free pass" for companies to make false statements about their products without being held accountable.[o]

The American Justice Partnership (AJP), launched in January 2005 by the National Association of Manufacturers, has been encouraging businesses to push for tort reform through the courts by targeting rules of law the AJP believes keep useful information from juries. The issues list may expand, but the AJP has targeted collateral source rules, which bar the jury from learning that the plaintiff received compensation from sources other than the defendant and from reducing damages awards based on that information; rules barring jurors from learning the impact of joint and several liability; rules preventing jurors from considering a plaintiff's failure to wear a seat belt in automobile accident cases and lowering damages or finding contributory negligence as a result; bans on allowing jurors to consider that a plaintiff was under the influence of drugs or alcohol, speeding, or asleep at the wheel in product defect cases; and bars on disclosing to jurors hearing toxic tort cases that the plaintiff was exposed to the hazardous materials from sources other than the defendant (including other defendants with whom the plaintiff has previously settled). As one critic of the tort reform movement, Richard W. Wright, a professor at the Chicago-Kent College

CONTINUED

of Law, noted: "[Proponents of tort reform are] frustrated that their arguments are not seen as valid by legislatures and courts. So now they're going after juries. They're asking courts to 'let juries hear this,' but they're really saying, 'Let's let juries change common law.'"[p]

In 2011, thirty-two new tort reform measures were enacted in states across the country, including Arizona, North Carolina, and Texas. The American Tort Reform Association called 2011 the "most productive year for enactment of meaningful state civil justice reforms in recent memory."[q]

---

a. *See, e.g.*, George Melloan, *Rule of Law or Rule of Lawyers?*, WALL ST. J., Nov. 21, 2000, at A27.
b. Andrea Gerlin, *A Matter of Degree: How a Jury Decided That a Coffee Spill Is Worth $2.9 Million*, WALL ST. J., Sept. 1, 1994, at A1.
c. The Alabama Supreme Court subsequently reduced this award to $2 million. BMW of North Am., Inc. v. Gore, 646 So. 2d 619 (Ala. 1994). The U.S. Supreme Court then declared the $2 million award void as "grossly excessive" and unconstitutional. BMW of North Am., Inc. v. Gore, 517 U.S. 559 (1996). On remand, the Alabama Supreme Court further reduced the award to $50,000. BMW of North Am., Inc. v. Gore, 701 So. 2d 507 (Ala. 1997).
d. Eric Peters, *Captious Spin on the Wheel of Misfortune*, WASH. POST, June 10, 1996, at A17.
e. Philip Shuchman, *It Isn't That the Tort Lawyers Are So Right, It's Just That the Tort Reformers Are So Wrong*, 49 RUTGERS L. REV. 485 (1997).
f. Todd Buchholz, *The High Cost of "Jackpot Justice,"* WALL ST. J., July 8, 2002, at A23.
g. Wells Marble & Hurst, PLLC, *Tort Reform* (2004), *available at* http://library.findlaw.com/2004/Aug/24/133556.html.
h. *How Tort Reform Works*, AM. TORT REFORM ASS'N, *available at* http://www.atra.org/wrap/files.cgi/7964_howworks.html.
i. Lawsuit Climate 2010: Rating the States, 2010 U.S. Chamber of Commerce State Liability Systems Ranking Study, *available at* http://www.instituteforlegalreform.org/sites/default/files/images2/stories/documents/pdf/lawsuitclimate2010/2010LawsuitClimateReport.pdf.
j. U.S. Dep't of Justice, *Federal Tort Filings Down*, *available at* http://www.atla.org/pressroom/research/bjs2005.aspx.
k. Thomas H. Cohen & Steven K. Smith, *Civil Trial Cases and Verdicts in Large Counties, 2001*, Bureau of Justice Statistics, U.S. Dep't of Justice, Apr. 2004, *available at* http://www.bjs.gov/content/pub/pdf/ctcvlc01.pdf.
l. Ctr. for Justice and& Democracy, *Mythbuster! Punitive Damages: Rare, Reasonable, and Effective*, *available at* http://www.centerjd.org/archives/illinois/facts/MB_2007punitives.pdf.
m. Gerlin, *supra* note b. See Liebeck v. McDonald's Restaurants, 1994 WL 16777706 (N.M. Dist. 1994).
n. 538 U.S. 408, 410 (2003).
o. Amanda Bronstad, *Tort Reform's Next Big Push*, NAT'L L.J., Sept. 7, 2006, *available at* http://www.law.com/jsp/law/LawArticleFriendly.jsp?id=1157462044386.
p. Terry Carter, *Case-by-Case Tort Reform*, 92 A.B.A. J., June 2006, at 46.
q. Darren McKinney, *States Enact More Than 30 New Tort Reform Laws as 2011 Legislative Sessions Wind Down: State Competition for Economic Growth and Jobs Seen as Driving Factor*, AM. TORT REFORM ASS'N, June 17, 2011, *available at* http://www.atra.org/newsroom/releases.php?id=8601.

EQUITABLE RELIEF

If a monetary award cannot adequately compensate for the plaintiff's loss, courts may give *equitable relief*. For example, the court may issue an *injunction*, that is, a court order, to prohibit the defendant from continuing a certain course of activity. This remedy is particularly appropriate for torts such as trespass or nuisance, when the plaintiff wants the defendant to stop violating the plaintiff's rights. The court may also issue an injunction ordering the defendant to take certain action. For example, a newspaper could be ordered to publish a retraction. In determining whether to grant injunctive relief, the courts will balance the hardship to the defendant against the benefit to the plaintiff.

LIABILITY OF MULTIPLE DEFENDANTS

A plaintiff may name numerous defendants. In some cases, the defendants may ask the court to join, or add, other defendants. As a result, when a court determines liability and damages, it must grapple with the problem of allocating the damages among multiple defendants.

Joint and Several Liability

Under the doctrine of *joint and several liability*, multiple defendants are jointly (that is, collectively) liable and also severally (that is, individually) liable. This means that once the court determines that multiple defendants are at fault, the plaintiff may collect the entire judgment from any one of them, regardless of the degree of that defendant's fault. Thus, it is possible that a defendant who played a minor role in causing the plaintiff's injury might have to pay all the damages. This is particularly likely when only one defendant is solvent and has money to pay the damages.

Many states have adopted statutes that limit the doctrine of joint and several liability for tort defendants. Most states that have abolished joint and several liability have moved to a contributory regime. For example, if a defendant was only 1% responsible for causing the plaintiff's injuries, then that defendant will not be liable for more than 1% of the total damages award even if the defendants responsible for 99% of the harm lack the funds to pay the judgment against them.

Contribution and Indemnification

The doctrines of contribution and indemnification can mitigate the harsh effects of joint and several liability.

Contribution distributes the loss among several defendants by requiring each to pay its proportionate share. For example, if the owner of a landfill had to pay $1 million to clean up hazardous waste deposited in the landfill by two manufacturers, then the landfill owner can sue the manufacturers to recover all or part of the cleanup costs. *Indemnification* allows a defendant to shift its individual loss to other defendants whose relative blame is greater. The other defendants can be ordered to reimburse the one that has discharged a joint liability. For example, a truck manufacturer might require a seat manufacturer to indemnify it if a defective seat caused an accident for which the truck manufacturer was held liable. It is important to keep in mind, however, that the rights to contribution and indemnification are worthless to a defendant if all the other defendants are insolvent or lack sufficient assets to contribute their share.

PRIVACY PROTECTION

In part because private tort actions alone have not been able to stop the avalanche of privacy violations that have occurred in recent years, state and federal governments have enacted a plethora of laws regulating the collection, transmission, storage, use, and disclosure of private data. In addition, as discussed in detail in the "Global View" in this chapter, strict privacy protections in the European Union and elsewhere apply to U.S. firms doing business with residents of these other countries.

State Legislation

The states have taken the lead in formulating consumer privacy policy in the United States. State statutes fall into three general categories: (1) bills to prohibit or limit the financial industry's use of account-related information, (2) bills to regulate the use of information collected by online service providers and websites, and (3) bills to prevent state agencies from selling information about people who do business with the state, including obtaining driver's licenses.[91] As noted in Chapter 4, Congress passed federal legislation banning the sale of driver's license information.

California has been particularly active. In 1999, California took the lead when it passed a law that limits the information that supermarkets can demand from customers as a condition of signing up for grocery club discount cards. Supermarkets had been selling data about their customers' purchases of items such as liquor and tobacco to insurance companies.[92] In 2000, California

created the first statewide Office of Privacy Protection in the nation, with the mission of promoting the privacy rights of California consumers.[93]

In 2004, California established an information security standard requiring businesses that own or license personal information about a California resident to implement and maintain "reasonable security measures" to protect that information; health-care providers, which are already regulated under the Health Insurance Portability and Accountability Act (HIPAA), discussed below, and other entities governed by the HIPAA privacy rules issued by the federal Department of Health and Human Services were excluded.[94] The statute defines "reasonable security measures" as "procedures and practices appropriate to the nature of the information to protect the personal information from unauthorized access, destruction, use, modification, or disclosure."[95] The law applies to any business, regardless of where it is located, that owns or licenses personal information about a California resident. For example, if a company based in Maine outsources warranties to a third party in New York, then the Maine company will have to determine how that third party uses information about its California customers and ensure that it has adequate security measures in place.[96] California also requires firms to notify customers if their personal identifying information is improperly disclosed to third parties.[97]

Opponents of states' efforts to protect consumers' privacy argue that the different states are creating a patchwork of conflicting rules, undermining efforts to enact federal legislation on privacy. But some consumer privacy advocates hope that enacting strong state privacy laws will put pressure on Congress to enact stronger federal privacy legislation.

Federal Trade Commission Actions

For a number of years, the Federal Trade Commission (FTC) has taken the position that it is an unfair or deceptive trade practice under section 5(a) of the Federal Trade Commission Act[98] for firms to fail to honor their own privacy policies. In 2006, consumer data broker ChoicePoint, Inc. agreed to pay $10 million in civil

---

91. Rachel Zimmerman & Glenn R. Simpson, *Lobbyists Swarm to Stop Tough Privacy Bills in States*, WALL ST. J., Apr. 21, 2000, at A16.

92. Super Market Club Card Act, CAL. CIV. CODE § 1749.60 *et seq.*

93. CAL. CIV. CODE § 1798.81.5, *available at* http://www.leginfo.ca.gov/cgi-bin/displaycode?section=civ&group=01001-02000&file=1798.80-1798.84.

94. California Assembly Bill 1950 (2004), *available at* http://info.sen.ca.gov/pub/03-04/bill/asm/ab_1901-1950/ab_1950_bill_20040929_chaptered.pdf.

95. *Id.*

96. In 2004, *California Again Leads States in Passage of Privacy-Related Legislation*, 9 ELECTRONIC COM. & L. REP. 843 (Oct. 13, 2004).

97. CAL. CIV. CODE §§ 1798.29, 1798.82, 1798.4.

98. See Appendix F, Federal Trade Commission Act of 1914 [Excerpts].

penalties (the largest civil penalty in FTC history) and $5 million in consumer redress to settle FTC charges that its security and record-handling procedures violated consumers' privacy rights and federal laws. Among other things, the agency charged that ChoicePoint had violated the FTC Act by making false and misleading statements about its privacy policies, including statements in its published privacy principles, such as "ChoicePoint does not distribute information to the general public and monitors the use of its public record information to ensure appropriate use." The settlement also required ChoicePoint to implement an information security program and to obtain third-party security audits every other year for ten years.[99]

The FTC had warned firms in 2004 that a company's failure to protect sensitive consumer information could itself be an "unfair" practice, even if the company did not promise to keep its data secure.[100] The FTC stressed that security is an ongoing process, not a static checklist. Therefore, companies must remain proactive in data protection.

The FTC subsequently brought an action against BJ's Wholesale Club, claiming that the company's failure to protect its customers' information was an unfair practice, because it caused substantial injury that was not avoidable by the customers and that was not outweighed by offsetting benefits to customers or consumers. The FTC alleged that fraudulent purchases were made using counterfeit copies of credit and debit cards used at BJ's stores. In 2005, BJ's settled the FTC charges by agreeing to implement a comprehensive security program and to obtain third-party security audits every other year for twenty years.[101]

The FTC Disposal Rule, promulgated pursuant to the Fair and Accurate Credit Transaction Act of 2003,[102] requires recipients of consumer information to take "reasonable measures to protect against unauthorized access to or use of [sensitive consumer] information in connection with its disposal."[103] It calls for data destruction policies commensurate with the sensitivity of the data, the size of the business, the costs and benefits of different disposal methods, and relevant technological changes. The rule applies to individuals and organizations of any size that obtain information from consumer reporting agencies, including resellers of consumer reports, lenders,

insurers, employers, landlords, government agencies, mortgage brokers, car dealers, and individuals who obtain consumer reports on prospective domestic or home employees.

In 2010, Google created a scandal when it revealed that it had captured large quantities of private e-mail and other Internet traffic from unencrypted routers via its Street View photography cars. The company admitted that it had been "mistakenly collecting samples of payload data from open WiFi Networks' in direct contravention of its previously stated privacy claims."[104] Google subsequently removed the cars from service to purge the code.

In 2011, Facebook settled charges by the FTC that the social networking giant had engaged in unfair or deceptive practices in violation of the FTC Act when it promised to keep users' personal information private, then unilaterally changed its privacy policy in 2009 and repeatedly made the information public.[105] Although Facebook did not have to pay a fine as part of the settlement, it agreed to twenty years of privacy audits and promised to obtain users' express approval before making their personal information public in a manner that materially exceeds the restrictions imposed by a user's privacy settings.[106] Facebook appointed a chief privacy officer and a chief privacy counsel as part of what founder and CEO Mark Zuckerberg described as Facebook's' commitment "to making Facebook the leader in transparency and control around privacy."[107] Representative Edward Markey (D-Mass.) remarked, "When it comes to its users' privacy Facebook's policy should be: 'Ask for permission, don't assume it.'"[108]

Financial Information: Gramm-Leach-Bliley Act

The Gramm-Leach-Bliley Financial Modernization Act of 1999[109] requires financial institutions to provide privacy protections to consumers. The law applies to banks, debt collectors, credit counselors, retailers, and travel agencies. Financial institutions must give notice to their customers before sharing personal information with other entities and give customers the right to opt out of disclosures

99. *See* Press Release, Fed. Trade Comm'n, ChoicePoint Settles Data Security Breach Charges (Jan. 26, 2006), *available at* http://www.ftc.gov/opa/2006/01/choicepoint.shtm.

100. *Lax Security Could Bring FTC Enforcement Under "Unfair" Practices Section of FTC Act*, 72 U.S.L.W. 2744 (June 8, 2004).

101. Press Release, Fed. Trade Comm'n, BJ's Wholesale Club Settles FTC Charges (June 16, 2005), *available at* http://www.ftc.gov/opa/2005/06/bjswholesale.shtm.

102. 16 C.F.R. pt. 682.

103. *Id.*

104. Gareth Halfacree, *Google Admits Street View WiFi Sniffing*, Bit-Tech, May 17, 2010, *available at* http://www.bit-tech.net/news/bits/2010/05/17/google-admits-street-view-wifi-sniffing/1.

105. Jessica Guynn, *Facebook Settles Privacy Complaint with Federal Trade Commission*, L.A. Times, Nov. 29, 2011; Cecilia Kang, *Facebook Settles Privacy Complaint, Agrees to Ask Permission for Privacy Changes*, Wash. Post, Nov. 29, 2011.

106. In the Matter of Facebook, Inc., 2011 WL 6092532 (F.T.C. Nov. 29, 2011).

107. Guynn, *supra* note 105.

108. *Id.*

109. 15 U.S.C. §§ 6801–6809.

to third parties. The Gramm-Leach-Bliley Act does not preempt states from implementing stricter privacy regulations, and a number of states have enacted or introduced their own financial privacy legislation.[110]

The FTC and seven other financial regulatory agencies (including the Federal Deposit Insurance Corporation, the Federal Reserve Board, and the Securities and Exchange Commission) have issued regulations that implement the privacy protections provided by the statute. The government has attempted to force businesses to better safeguard consumers' information through the Safeguard Rule contained in the Gramm-Leach-Bliley Act.

The *Safeguard Rule* requires financial services firms to (1) promulgate a written information security plan, (2) designate at least one employee to coordinate the plan, (3) identify and assess the risks to customer financial information, and (4) evaluate the safeguards for controlling these risks. To come within the Safeguard Rule, the firm must also (1) regularly monitor and test the plan, (2) select appropriate service providers and contract with them to implement the safeguards, and (3) evaluate and adjust the plan as material circumstances change. According to the FTC, its ultimate goal is to promote awareness among companies about the importance of protecting sensitive information, while allowing the companies to tailor a plan based on their size, scope, and level of sensitive information.[111] Although some companies have called for stricter guidelines for determining whether a particular plan satisfies the rule,[112] the FTC claims that its requirements are simple and straightforward.

Medical Information: HIPAA

The U.S. Department of Health and Human Services has issued regulations, under the Health Insurance Portability and Accountability Act of 1996 (HIPAA), on maintaining the privacy of personal medical information.[113] At first blush, the regulations appear to apply only to health-care providers (such as doctors, hospitals, and nurses), group health plans (such as HMOs and self-insured plans that have fifty or more participants or are administered by an entity other than the employer that established and maintained the plan), and health-care clearinghouses that process claims. Upon a closer reading, it becomes clear that, in fact, almost all employers that provide health-care coverage to their employees are affected by the privacy regulations and required to

develop privacy policies and procedures to safeguard protected health information.[114]

Protected health information includes any information relating to a person's health that (1) was created by a health-care provider, health plan, employer, or health-care clearinghouse; and (2) identifies the person to whom the health information relates. For example, if, as is usually the case, the employer acts as the plan sponsor, then the employer must establish "firewalls" to ensure that private health information is used only for purposes of plan administration and not for any other employment-related decisions, such as termination of employment.

Any person who knowingly discloses individually identifiable health information to an unauthorized person can be fined up to $50,000 or imprisoned for up to one year or both.[115] If the defendant acted under false pretenses, the maximum penalty increases to not more than $100,000 and five years in prison; if the defendant acted with intent to "sell, transfer, or use individually identifiable health information for commercial advantage, personal gain, or malicious harm," the maximum penalty rises to not more than $250,000 and ten years in prison.

Although courts have consistently held that there is no private right of action under HIPAA, plaintiffs have been allowed to use HIPAA standards to establish that defendants failed to adequately protect their sensitive medical information. For example, an appellate court allowed an invasion of privacy lawsuit to proceed, citing HIPAA standards in its determination that a doctor owed a duty of confidentiality to his patients.[116] In another case, an appellate court held that HIPAA could be used to establish the standard of care in a negligence action.[117]

Children's Online Privacy Protection Act

The Children's Online Privacy Protection Act of 1998 (COPPA)[118] prevents websites from collecting personal information from children under age thirteen without parental consent. Parental consent can be in the form of a note, credit card number, or e-mail with a password. Websites must disclose what personal information they collect from children and how they use it, including whether they share it with third parties.

In 2001, the FTC approved the self-regulatory program of the Children's Advertising Review Unit of the Council

---

110. Eileen Canning, *States Legislating Financial Privacy Before Federal Regulators Even Issue Draft*, 68 U.S.L.W. 2453 (2000).

111. *Id.*

112. Michael Bologna, *Attorneys Claim That FTC Safeguards Rule Has Been Greeted with Confusion, Uncertainty*, 8 U.S.L.W. 746 (2003).

113. 42 U.S.C. §§ 1320d–1320d-8; *see also* 45 C.F.R. pts. 160, 164 (Final Rules for Administrative Data Standards and for Security and Privacy of Individually Identifiable Health Information) (2000).

114. *See generally* Linda Abdel-Malek, *HIPAA Privacy Rules Impact Employers*, N.Y. L.J., May 14, 2001, at 5.

115. 42 U.S.C. § 1320d-6.

116. Sorensen v. Barbuto, 143 P.3d 295 (Utah Ct. App. 2006).

117. Acosta v. Byrum, 638 S.E.2d 246 (N.C. Ct. App. 2006).

118. 5 U.S.C. §§ 6501–6506. *See also* 16 C.F.R. pt. 312 (implementing FTC regulations).

of Better Business Bureaus as the first "safe-harbor" program under COPPA. Companies that establish and comply with approved self-regulatory programs are deemed to have complied with COPPA.

In 2011, the operators of twenty online "virtual worlds" agreed to pay a $3 million civil penalty to settle FTC charges that they had illegally collected and disclosed children's personal information in violation of COPPA.[119] Playdom, Inc., a prominent developer of online games, operated twenty websites where users could access games and other activities, some of which were specifically directed to children. According to the FTC, between 2006 and 2010, more than 400,000 children registered on Playdom's general audience sites, and more than 800,000 additional users registered on the children's site. The FTC alleged that Playdom collected children's ages and e-mail addresses and then allowed children to publicly post personal information, including their names, e-mail addresses, and location, without providing proper notice and obtaining parental consent. The complaint also charged that Playdom had misrepresented its privacy policy by claiming that it would prohibit children under thirteen from posting personal information. In addition to imposing the $3 million

penalty, the settlement order barred Playdom from violating COPPA's rule that parental consent must be obtained before personal information is collected and from misrepresenting its information practices regarding children.

Proposed Legislation

In 2011, Senators John Kerry (D-Mass.) and John McCain (R-Ariz.) introduced the Commercial Privacy Bill of Rights Act of 2011,[120] which would impose certain limits on the commercial data collecting industry.[121] The bill would create the nation's first comprehensive privacy law. It would require companies that gather personal information to obtain permission before collecting and sharing sensitive religious, medical, and financial information with outside entities. Although the Interactive Advertising Bureau, the trade association for most online tracking firms, criticized the bill for giving too much discretion to the FTC, the bill received support from a variety of groups and firms, including the Center for Democracy and Technology, the Consumers Union, Microsoft, eBay, Intel, Hewlett-Packard, and Facebook.[122]

---

119. *See* Press Release, Fed. Trade Comm'n, Operators of Online "Virtual Worlds" to Pay $3 Million to Settle FTC Charges That They Illegally Collected and Disclosed Children's Personal Information (May 12, 2011), *available at* http://www.ftc.gov/opa/2011/05/playdom.shtm.

120. Commercial Privacy Bill of Rights Act of 2011, S. 799, 112th Cong. (2011).

121. Julia Angwin, *Senators Offer Privacy Bill to Protect Personal Data*, WALL ST. J., Apr. 13, 2011, at B1.

122 *Id.*

GLOBAL VIEW

International Privacy Laws

Today's online world and the increasing use of "the cloud" to store data offer unprecedented possibilities for the global exchange of information and data, including the exchange and transfer of personal information. The risks and problems that come with the unregulated exchange of personal information have led many jurisdictions around the world to enact privacy laws, regulations, and rules that deal with its collection, processing, storage, disclosure, and use.

Although definitions and understanding of the term "privacy" vary from jurisdiction to jurisdiction, common elements include the freedom or protection of individuals and sometimes groups (including selective freedom or protection of individuals and groups) from unauthorized or unwanted intrusion into or observation of their personal information and the violation of its integrity. Often, data protection is seen as being part of privacy or being closely connected to it.[123]

The type of protection, as well as the speed, level of completeness, and depth of regulation and implementation, varies from country to country. Increasingly, countries have addressed the cross-border transfer of personal information and taken steps to prevent the circumvention of existing national laws governing the storage, processing, and disclosure of information through "off-shoring" of these activities. Accordingly, when multinational companies doing business outside their home country, including offering products or services on the Internet, collect personal information from residents of a foreign country, they are likely to fall under the privacy laws and regulations in that country.

The following provides a brief overview of the privacy laws and regulations in several key jurisdictions.

European Union

In 1995, the European Union (EU) implemented the EU Data Protection Directive (Directive 95/46/EC), which deals with

---

123. Privacy International, a nonprofit organization based in the United Kingdom, provides more information about the different understandings and definitions of privacy at its website, http://www.privacyinternational.org/article.shtml?cmd[347]=x-347-559062.

CONTINUED

the processing of personal information and its free movement. As with other EU directives, the provisions of the Data Protection Directive had to be incorporated into national law by each of the EU's members to become binding in those states. Consequently, there is some variation in the privacy laws among the EU's member states.

The Data Protection Directive requires a company that processes personal information (or "personal data," the term used by the Directive) to register with the respective data protection supervisory authority before it starts collecting personal information. An important principle of the Directive is that personal information generally should not be collected, unless the collection is (1) proportional (meaning adequate and not excessive relative to its purpose), (2) transparent (meaning that the affected individual must be informed as to the circumstances of the collection and consent to it), and (3) for a legitimate purpose. The Directive allows personal information to be transferred into third countries (countries outside the EU) only if the third country provides an adequate level of protection for the information.

Although the United States is not regarded as providing adequate protection,[124] the EU and the U.S. Department of Commerce negotiated a safe-harbor arrangement to allow the transfer of personal information from any EU member state to the United States under certain circumstances.[125] Under this arrangement, U.S. companies must adhere to seven principles set forth in the Directive: notice, choice, onward transfer, security, data integrity, access, and enforcement, as determined by self-assessment or assessment of a third party, with re-certification required each year.[126]

Several members of the EU have expressed concerns about Google's Street View mapping feature and regard it as an invasion of privacy. In 2010, the Czech Republic refused to give Google permission to expand the feature there. Similarly, the German government gave its citizens the right to opt out of Street View.[127]

Canada

Canada is generally regarded as having relatively strict privacy laws, and the EU considers Canada to be a third country that provides adequate protection of personal information under the EU Data Protection Directive. Major privacy legislation includes the Canadian Privacy Act of 1983, which regulates the collection, processing, and use of personal information by government authorities; the (Federal) Personal Information Protection and Electronic Documents Act (PIPEDA) of 1999, which governs the collection of personal information by private organizations and companies; and the (Provincial) Personal Information Protection Act (PIPA) of 2004. The Privacy Commissioner of Canada, a special authority that can audit collecting authorities and entities and investigate complaints, also performs privacy-related research and publishes privacy-related information to increase the awareness of the general public.[128]

Canada has expressed particular concern about privacy issues posed by the social networking site Facebook. In 2010, the Privacy Commissioner launched an investigation into changes that Facebook had unilaterally made in its privacy settings, which prompted Facebook to be more transparent about sharing its members' data.[129]

Asia-Pacific Economic Cooperation

The twenty-one countries of the Asia-Pacific Economic Cooperation (APEC) have created the APEC Privacy Framework, which was endorsed by the APEC ministers in 2005. The Framework addresses the cross-border transfer of personal information and is aimed at providing guidance to businesses in APEC member countries on common privacy issues by setting up nine principles: prevention of harm, integrity of personal information, notice, security safeguards, collection limitations, access and correction, use of personal information, accountability, and choice.[130] As of 2011, no APEC country had ratified the Framework, however, and it is not clear that the Framework will be sufficient for APEC members to be considered third countries with adequate protection of personal information under the EU Data Protection Directive.

---

124. More information about EU privacy rules and regulations and data protection initiatives can be found at http://ec.europa.eu/justice_home/fsj/privacy/index_en.htm.

125. For an overview of Commission decisions on the adequacy of personal data protections in third countries, see http://ec.europa.eu/justice_home/fsj/privacy/thridcountries/index_en.htm.

126. See the *Commission Decision of 26 July 2000 Pursuant to Directive 95/46/EC of the European Parliament and of the Council on the Adequacy of the Protection Provided by the Safe Harbour Privacy Principles and Related Frequently Asked Questions Issued by the US Department of Commerce,* available at http://eur-lex.europa.eu/LexUriServ/LexUriServ.do?uri=CELEX:32000D0520:EN:HTML.

127. *Czech Republic Bans Google "Street View": Watchdog Says Mapping Feature Invades People's Privacy,* MSNBC.com, Sept. 22, 2010, http://www.msnbc.msn.com/id/39302384/ns/technology_and_science/t/czech-republic-bans-google-street-view/#.TqMFNc1jNGo.

128. More information about Canadian privacy laws can be found at http://www.privacylawyer.ca/index.html.

129. Troy McMullen, *Canada's Privacy Commission Probes Facebook over Users Private Information,* ABC News, Jan. 29, 2010, *available at* http://abcnews.go.com/Technology/canada-investigates-facebook-privacy-settings/story?id=9691133.

130. The text of the APEC Privacy Framework can be found at http://www.ag.gov.au/www/agd/rwpattach.nsf/VAP/(03995EABC73F94816C2AF4AA2645824B)-APEC+Privacy+Framework.pdf/$file/APEC+Privacy+Framework.pdf.

THE RESPONSIBLE MANAGER

REDUCING TORT RISKS

Managers should implement ongoing programs of education and monitoring to reduce the risks of tort liability. Because torts can be committed in numerous ways, the programs should cover all possible sources of liability. For example, the management of a company that does not respond satisfactorily to an allegation of sexual harassment may be liable for intentional infliction of emotional distress. Statements made by company representatives about an individual or product can constitute defamation.

In addition to preventing intentional torts, managers should work to prevent their employees from committing acts of negligence, which can lead to large damages awards against the company. Any tort-prevention program must recognize that under the principle of *respondeat superior*, employers will be held liable for any torts their employees commit in the scope of their employment. It is crucial, therefore, to define the scope of employment clearly.

Managers should use care to avoid committing torts that are related to contractual relations and competition with other firms. For example, a company may be held liable for interference with contractual relations if a court finds that the company intentionally tried to induce a party to breach a contract. Also, although competition itself is permissible, intentionally seeking to sabotage the efforts of another firm is not. Managers may need to consult counsel when they are unsure whether their activity has crossed the line from permissible competition to tortious interference with a prospective business advantage.

Managers need to pay attention to any personal information that they are collecting. Although U.S. law does not require all businesses to establish privacy policies, certain industries, including the health-care industry and financial institutions, are regulated under federal privacy laws. In addition, the Federal Trade Commission has taken action against companies that have failed to take reasonable steps to protect the personal information of their users. Failure to comply with the various state, federal, and international laws regulating the collection, use, and storage of personal information may not only give rise to substantial liability and criminal prosecution, but may also lead to unhappy customers. International privacy laws are discussed in this chapter's "Global View."

A program of overall risk management and reduction is essential to limit the potential of tort liability. It is often desirable to designate one person to be in charge of risk management. That person should keep track of all claims and determine which areas of the business merit special attention. The head of risk management should be free to report incidents and problems to the chief executive officer and the board of directors, in much the same way as an internal auditor reports directly to the independent directors on the audit committee. This enhances independence and reduces the fear of reprisals if the risk manager blows the whistle on high-ranking managers.

A MANAGER'S DILEMMA

Putting It into Practice

Negotiating Customer Privacy with Big Brother

In 2010, Research in Motion's BlackBerry smartphone offered its corporate clients the ultimate in smartphone security. All messages were encrypted before leaving the device and then routed through a series of Network Operating Centers in Canada. This security made it difficult for anyone to eavesdrop on BlackBerry calls, texts, or e-mails. As a result, the BlackBerry became the device of choice for many government and corporate clients.

Several countries, however, including India and the United Arab Emirates , however, became concerned that the security features would make it difficult for them to protect their citizens from criminals and terrorists. Their concern was not unfounded: the 2008 Mumbai attacks had been orchestrated using BlackBerrys.

In 2010, the UAE demanded that RIM either provide a way for the UAE to monitor the communications of BlackBerry users or have BlackBerry service cut off. How should RIM respond? Would it make a difference if RIM suspected that a country wanted its encryption codes primarily in order to crack down on political dissidents? Would RIM customers have a cause of action against RIM if information they expected to remain secure was secretly compromised?[131]

---

131. *See* Constance E. Bagley, Sally Gunz & Andrea Nagy Smith, *Research in Motion: Compromise BlackBerry Security, or Give Up Emerging Markets?* (Yale Sch. of Mgmt. Case No. 11-011, Apr. 7, 2011).

INSIDE STORY

What's in a Name? Fighting Identity Theft

Identity theft is the illegal practice of gaining access to other people's identifying information (such as Social Security and credit card numbers) and then using it to the thief's advantage. In the past, getting the personal information necessary to make identity theft profitable meant going through the garbage or stealing mail, both of which could easily be combated by potential victims. Now, however, with more and more business being done online, individuals often have to disclose sensitive information on the Internet, which is far less private than the U.S. mail or even the kitchen garbage can.

In 2010, identity theft was the number one complaint at the Consumer Sentinel Network (CSN), a secure online database of consumer complaints available exclusively to law enforcement.[132] More than 8 million adults were victims of identity fraud in 2010, with a mean fraud amount per victim of $4,607.[133] The mean consumer out-of-pocket cost for identity theft was $631 per incident in 2010. New account fraud was responsible for the greatest fraud amount, accounting for $17 billion.

The financial services companies that are the keepers of a significant amount of individual personal data have already lost billions of dollars and stand to lose billions more as identity theft victims sue the companies for allowing the theft of their information.[134] The Financial Services Technology Consortium, a coalition of leading financial services firms and technology companies, has been trying to develop technology to combat *phishing* scams, in which fraudulent websites or e-mails ask for credit card and bank account numbers and other personal information.[135] Spyware makes it possible for outsiders to see everything in a computer's memory.

The growing threat has spawned new legislation. Texas and California have enacted laws prohibiting businesses from printing Social Security numbers on health plan and employer ID cards and prohibiting banks from including Social Security numbers on bank statements and other documents sent by mail. Senate Bill 1457 gave Californians a private right of action to sue persons who send commercial e-mail that is false or misleading.

The Fair and Accurate Credit Transactions Act of 2003 (FACT Act)[136] made identity theft a federal offense and provides specific remedies for victims. It also made it a crime to post Social Security numbers on a website with the intent to aid and abet a crime.[137] In early 2004, a computer technician became the first person to be convicted under the federal statute.

The FACT Act makes it possible for victims to work with creditors to block negative information from appearing on their credit reports if the problems occurred as a result of identity theft. In conjunction with the FACT Act, the Federal Trade Commission has instituted a number of measures that enable theft victims to place "fraud alerts" on their credit reports that tell the credit reporting agencies to contact the consumer directly because he or she may be an identity theft victim.[138] Consumers seeking to bring suit against credit bureaus that made mistakes leading to identity theft must file these claims within two years of the actual mistake, regardless of whether the victim learned about the mistake in that time.[139]

Those who suspect they are victims of identity theft should quickly place a fraud alert on all credit accounts with a credit bureau. The United States has three main credit agencies—Experian, Equifax, and TransUnion. Alerting one will effectively alert all three. Next, victims must fill out an FTC "ID Theft Affidavit," which is similar to a police report. A copy should be sent to any company that might have had unauthorized activity with a victimized account. Finally, an actual police report should be filled out, as the credit bureaus will often take action only pursuant to an official police report.[140] Finally, victims should consult the ID Theft Data Clearinghouse, the government's database on all ID theft, which can help them repair the damage to their credit and their lives.[141]

The best way to protect against identity theft is to be proactive. Adam Cohen of *Time* recommends the following:[142]

1. Install a firewall and virus protection. A firewall acts like a gatekeeper to a network of computers so that a single place can deny any unauthorized access into the network (by hackers, for example) and out of the network (by employees surfing the Web, for example).

CONTINUED

---

132. *Consumer Sentinel Network Databook for January–December 2010*, Fed. Trade Comm'n, March 2010, *available at* http://www.ftc.gov/sentinel/reports/sentinel-annual-reports/sentinel-cy2010.pdf.

133. Javelin Strategy & Research, *2011 Identity Fraud Survey Report*, IDsafety.net, *available at* http://www.idsafety.net/report.php.

134. *See, e.g.,* TRW v. Andrews, 534 U.S. 19 (2001).

135. *Financial Consortium, Technology Firms Gird for Battle Against Phishing Scams*, 9 Electronic Com. & L. Rep. 842 (Oct. 13, 2004).

136. 18 U.S.C. § 10-28(A)(7).

137. Press Release, U.S. Attorney's Office, Central District of California, No. 03-052 (Apr. 16, 2004).

138. *FACT Act Regulatory Plan Defines ID Theft, Requirements for Credit Report Fraud Alerts*, 72 U.S.L.W. 2652–53 (2004).

139. Amy Borrus, *To Catch an Identity Thief*, Bus. Wk., Mar. 31, 2003, at 91.

140. Andrea Chipman, *Stealing You*, Wall St. J., April 26, 2004, at R8.

141. For more information, see http://www.consumer.gov/idtheft.

142. Much of the following list is derived from Adam Cohen, *Internet Insecurity*, Time, July 2, 2001, at 47–51.

2. Do not download files from people you do not know or trust. Almost all viruses are spread by innocuous looking files, including MP3 music files.

3. Many popular Web browsers store the user's name and address in their system. Security holes can allow other websites to obtain this information and make a permanent record of it. Users should make sure the preferences for their Web browser are secure and that the browser does not disclose this information.

4. Some websites reserve the right to share whatever information they obtain with third parties. Usually, however, they must offer the option of "opting out" of this practice at the website. Users should exercise their opt-out rights.

5. Users should not accept cookies unless they are aware of their origin. *Cookies* are bits of code sent by websites that identity the user to the site at a future visit. Cookies are how websites, such as eBay and Amazon, know a particular user has returned. Usually, cookies are harmless, but they can interact with other computer processes. Most browsers permit users to decide whether or not to accept cookies. Users should accept cookies only from websites they trust.

6. All secure, reputable websites encrypt data. The browser will tell the user when data are being encrypted. Users should not send sensitive data unless the website indicates that they are encrypted. Otherwise, anyone online can obtain this information.

7. Periodically clear the browser of cached data. A cache is a record the computer keeps of websites to allow faster access to them later. Unfortunately, this acts like a roadmap to the websites the user has visited. Even if the websites visited are safe, virus software can transmit these data back to unauthorized users who can use the information.

8. To avoid exposing sensitive company or personal information to potential Internet thieves, promulgate a thorough and well-thought-out Internet policy that limits employees to job-related Internet use.

KEY WORDS AND PHRASES

QUESTIONS AND CASE PROBLEMS

1. Christian and Britt Ewens, owners and residents of a luxury condominium in New York City, sued the owner of the adjacent unit, Federico Maccherone, for negligence and private nuisance. The Ewens claimed that Maccherone's "excessive smoking" caused secondhand smoke to seep through the walls into their unit. They also alleged that because there was a building-wide ventilation system, there was "odor migration." The condominium declaration and bylaws did not prohibit smoking. Who should prevail? [*Ewen v. Maccherone*, 927 N.Y.S. 2d 274 (N.Y. App. Div. 2011).]

2. A school bus driver's attention was diverted momentarily from the road when a bee flew in the window of the bus and stung him on the neck. While the driver ducked his head and tried with his left hand to extricate the bee from under his collar, the bus veered to the left and onto the shoulder of the road, a distance of about seventy-five feet. At this point, the driver raised his head and saw what had happened. He tried to turn the bus back onto the road, but was unable to do so because of the soft condition of the shoulder. The bus went down into a shallow ditch, tilting first to the left and then to the right before it could be stopped. This motion of the bus caused one of the students to be thrown from her seat and injured. The student sued for negligence. What must the student argue in order to prevail? Will the student win her case? [*Schultz v. Cheney School District No. 360*, 371 P.2d 59 (Wash. 1962).]

3. A recent college graduate created the website http://www.harassthem.com, where the visitor is encouraged to provide private or defamatory content for a fee. In addition, the website encourages posters to provide dirt on the victims. Is the website operator liable for any defamatory information posted? Would it be liable if a stalker used the site to track down a former boss's address and then attacked her at her home? [*Fair Housing Counsel of San Fernando Valley v. Roommates.com*, 521 F.3d 1157 (9th Cir. 2008).]

4. CRST Van Expedited, Inc., a trucking company, sponsors a driver training program to help its new hires become certified truck drivers. At a certain point in the training program, the driver trainer must sign a one-year employment contract with CRST if he or she wants to continue employment with the company. The employment contract provides that CRST will pay the costs associated with the training and certification but it requires the employee to reimburse a portion of these costs if he or she is terminated for cause or voluntarily quits. After obtaining their truck driver certifications at CRST's expense, two CRST employees were solicited for employment by Werner, a competitor. CRST claimed that Werner had a pattern of waiting for CRST to train drivers and then luring them away. Does CRST have any legal basis for suing Werner or the employees? If so, on what basis? What damages would be available? Did Werner act ethically? [*CRST Van Expedited, Inc. v. Werner Enterprises, Inc.*, 479 F.3d 1099 (9th Cir. 2007).]

5. After two years of negotiations, the four shareholders and founders of Access, Inc. sold their health-care start-up to a subsidiary of Res-Care, Inc. and agreed to stay on as employees, based on assurances from the buyer that Res-Care would not merge with VOCA of North Carolina. The Access shareholders had explained to Res-Care that they were all former employees of VOCA and had left to form Access because of differences over the way VOCA was run. They made it clear to Res-Care that they would not sell their shares without assurances that they would never be affiliated with VOCA or their former supervisor.

   Res-Care's chief development officer told the shareholders that his company was not interested in buying VOCA because it had poor profits and was poorly managed. Res-Care's vice president of the central region made similar assurances in a later meeting.

   A week after the Access shareholders signed the deal, Res-Care announced that it had signed a letter of intent to buy VOCA. The Access shareholders' former boss at VOCA was given the job of statewide director, thereby becoming the Access shareholders' new supervisor.

   Do the former Access shareholders have any legal basis for suing Res-Care? Assume that the acquisition agreement between the Access shareholders and Res-Care contained no representation or warranty by Res-Care regarding a possible merger with VOCA, and that it contained a standard merger clause stating that the written acquisition agreement superseded any and all prior negotiations and oral statements. What could the Access shareholders have done to avoid this dispute? [*Godfrey v. Res-Care, Inc.*, 598 S.E.2d 396 (N.C. App. 2004).]

6. A class-action lawsuit is filed against a number of alcoholic beverage producers, asserting that the defendants target underage consumers in a manner that is "deliberate, reckless, and illegal," and that such actions constitute unfair,

deceptive, and unconscionable practices in violation of state consumer protection statutes and are negligent. The plaintiffs claim that the defendants use advertisements and marketing campaigns that are likely to appeal to minors, because the ads employ video games and animation, attractive models, and social situations and humor with which minors can identify. Could the companies be found liable for targeting a youthful audience? Should they be? What moral responsibility, if any, do the companies have? [*Hakki v. Zima Co.*, 2006 WL 852126 (D.C. Super. 2006), *aff'd*, 926 A.2d 722 (D.C. App. 2007).]

7. Bruce Marecki, an employee of Crystal Rock Spring Water Company, attended a seminar sponsored by the company at a Ramada Inn. At the seminar, he drank several beers. After the seminar ended, he was planning to go to happy hour at the hotel, but at a separate location from the seminar room. Instead, he left the hotel to purchase cigarettes after discovering that the cigarette machine in the hotel was broken. While he was driving to a store to buy cigarettes, he rear-ended another car and caused injuries to the driver. The driver sued Crystal Rock Spring Water Company under the doctrine of *respondeat superior*. Should the company be liable for the injuries the driver suffered? What if Crystal Rock Spring Water Company had not supplied the liquor at the seminar, but had allowed it to be served? What if Marecki had had nothing to drink at the seminar, but then drank at the happy hour with his coworkers and had an accident when he was driving home after socializing with them? What if the seminar was optional and Marecki had no obligation to attend? [*Sheftic v. Marecki*, 1999 Conn. Super. LEXIS 2953 (Conn. Oct. 22, 1999).]

8. Harold Tod Parrot was employed as vice president of sales by Capital Corporation, a privately held investment adviser. Parrot purchased 40,500 shares of Capital stock, pursuant to a stock-purchase agreement that provided that upon termination of Parrot's employment, the company would repurchase his shares at fair market value. The fair market value was to be determined by the accounting firm Coopers & Lybrand, which had been retained by Capital Corporation for that purpose. Several years after the stock purchase, Parrot was terminated. He then sought to sell his shares back to Capital Corporation at fair market value. Parrot objected to the price of the shares established by Coopers & Lybrand in the company's most recent biannual report and sued both Capital Corporation and Coopers & Lybrand. His complaint against Coopers & Lybrand alleged professional negligence and negligent misrepresentation. He argued that the accountants had changed the valuation methodology, at Capital's request, in order to reduce the price of the shares and, as a result, Parrot was induced to accept a lesser value for his stock. Does Parrot's suit against Coopers & Lybrand have merit? [*Parrot v. Coopers & Lybrand, LLP*, 702 N.Y.S.2d 40 (2000), *aff'd*, 95 N.Y.2d 479 (2000).]

CHAPTER 10

PRODUCT LIABILITY

INTRODUCTION

DEFINITION OF PRODUCT LIABILITY

Product liability is the legal liability manufacturers and sellers have for defective products that cause injury to the purchaser, a user, or a bystander, or their property. Liability extends to anyone in the chain of distribution: manufacturers, distributors, wholesalers, and retailers.

Today, more than forty states in the United States have adopted strict product liability, whereby an injured person may recover damages without having to show that the defendant was negligent or otherwise at fault. No contractual relationship between the defendant and the injured person is necessary. The injured person merely needs to show that the defendant sold the product in a defective or dangerous condition and that the defect caused his or her injury.

CHAPTER OVERVIEW

This chapter discusses the evolution of the strict liability doctrine, beginning with its origin in warranty and negligence theories. It then focuses on the bases for strict liability, including manufacturing defect, design defect, and failure to warn. The chapter examines who may be held liable for defective products and the allocation of liability among multiple defendants. It discusses defenses to product liability claims, including the courts' increasing acceptance of the preemption defense to preclude state-law product liability claims and legislative reforms designed to correct perceived abuses in the system. The chapter concludes with a description of the law of product liability in the European Union.

THEORIES OF RECOVERY

The primary theories on which a product liability claim can be brought are breach of warranty, negligence, and strict liability.

Breach of Warranty

In a warranty action, the reasonableness of the manufacturer's actions is not at issue. Rather, the question is whether the quality, characteristics, and safety of the product were consistent with the implied or express representations made by the seller. A buyer may bring a warranty action whenever the product fails to meet the standards that the seller represented to the buyer at the time of purchase.

Common Law Warranties and Privity of Contract

A common law breach-of-warranty action is based on principles of contract law. To recover, an injured person must be in a contractual relationship with the seller, a requirement known as *privity of contract*. It necessarily precludes recovery by those persons, such as bystanders, who have no contractual relationship with the seller.

UCC Warranties

As explained in Chapter 8, a warranty under the Uniform Commercial Code (UCC) may be either express or implied. An express warranty is an affirmation made by the seller relating to the quality of the goods sold. An implied warranty is created by law and guarantees the merchantability of the goods sold and, in some circumstances, their fitness for a particular purpose. The UCC includes alternate provisions regarding the need for privity, from which adopting states may choose. These range from (1) provisions limiting liability to those in privity with the seller (and members of their household and guests who (a) may reasonably be expected to use, consume, or be affected by the goods and (b) are personally injured by breach of the warranty) to (2) provisions extending liability not only to those in privity but also to "any person who may reasonably be expected to use, consume or be affected by the goods and who is injured by breach of the warranty."[1]

---

1. U.C.C. § 2-318.

Negligence

In the following landmark case, the New York Court of Appeals found the defendant manufacturer liable for negligence even though there was no contractual relationship between the manufacturer and the plaintiff. Although

liability in *MacPherson* was still based on the negligence principles of reasonableness and due care, the New York Court of Appeals abandoned the privity requirement in this case, making it an important forerunner to the doctrine of strict product liability.

| **A CASE IN POINT** | *Summary* | **Case 10.1** |

MacPherson v. Buick Motor Co.

Court of Appeals of New York
111 N.E. 1050 (N.Y. 1916).

FACTS   MacPherson purchased a new Buick car with wooden wheels from a Buick Motor Company dealer who had previously purchased the car from its manufacturer, Buick Motor Company. MacPherson was injured when the car ran into a ditch after one of the car's wheels collapsed due to defective wood used for the spokes. The wheel had been made by a manufacturer other than Buick.

MacPherson sued Buick Motor Company directly. He proved that Buick could have discovered the defect by reasonable inspection and that such an inspection had not been conducted. No claim was made that the manufacturer knew of the defect and willfully concealed it. After the trial court found in favor of MacPherson, Buick appealed.

ISSUE PRESENTED   May a consumer who purchases a product from a retailer sue the manufacturer directly for negligent manufacture of the product even though there is no contract between the consumer and the manufacturer?

SUMMARY OF OPINION   The New York Court of Appeals held that Buick could be held liable for negligence. As a manufacturer, it owed a duty to any person who could foreseeably be injured as a result of a defect in an automobile it manufactured. The court stated that a manufacturer's duty to inspect varies with the nature of the thing to be inspected. The more probable the danger, the greater the need for caution. Because the action was one in tort for negligence, no contract between the plaintiff and the defendant was required.

RESULT   New York's highest court affirmed the lower court's finding that the manufacturer Buick Motor Company was liable for the injuries sustained by the plaintiff. Buick was found negligent for not inspecting the wheels and was responsible for the finished product sold by its dealer.

COMMENTS   This case established the rule, still applicable today, that a manufacturer can be liable for failure to exercise reasonable care in the manufacture of a product when such failure involves an unreasonable risk of bodily harm to users of the product. This rule is embodied in sections 1 and 2(a) of the Restatement (Third) of Torts: Products Liability (1998).[2]

---

2.   This rule also appeared in the RESTATEMENT (SECOND) OF TORTS § 395 (1977).

To prove negligence in a products case, the injured party must show that the defendant did not use reasonable care in designing or manufacturing its product or in providing adequate warnings. A manufacturer can be found negligent even if the product met all regulatory requirements because, under some circumstances, a reasonably prudent manufacturer would have taken additional precautions.[3] As discussed later in this chapter, the only exception is when a federally mandated standard is deemed to have preempted state product liability law.[4]

It can be difficult to prove negligence. Moreover, injured persons have often been negligent themselves in their use or misuse of the product. This precludes recovery in a contributory negligence state and reduces recovery in a comparative negligence state.

Courts will not permit a plaintiff to prove negligence by introducing evidence of *subsequent remedial measures* taken by a defendant after an injury to improve a product. This rule is designed to encourage companies to continually strive to improve the safety of their products. If subsequent safety measures could be used to establish negligence, companies would be deterred from improving their products.

---

3.   *See, e.g.,* Brooks v. Beech Aircraft Corp., 902 P.2d 54 (N.M. 1995).
4.   *See, e.g.,* Horn v. Thoratec Corp., 376 F.3d 163 (3d Cir. 2004).

Strict Liability in Tort

Strict liability in tort allows a person injured by an unreasonably dangerous product to recover damages from the manufacturer or seller of the product even in the absence of a contract or negligent conduct on the part of the manufacturer or seller. Because the defect in the product is the basis for liability, the injured person may recover damages even if the seller exercised all possible care in the manufacture and sale of the product.

In 1963, in *Greenman v. Yuba Power Products, Inc.*,[5] the California Supreme Court became the first state supreme court in the United States to adopt strict product liability. The case involved a consumer who was injured while using a Shopsmith combination power tool that could be used as a saw, drill, and wood lathe. Claiming that the tool was defective and not suitable to perform the work for which it was intended, Greenman sued the manufacturer and the retailer who had sold the power tool to his wife for breach of express and implied warranties and for negligent construction of the tool. The California Supreme Court ruled that a manufacturer is strictly liable in tort when it places an article on the market, knowing that the product is to be used without inspection for defects, and it proves to have a defect that causes injury to a human being.

Rationale

The legal principle of strict product liability is grounded in considerations of public policy. The rationale has four basic parts:

1. The law should protect consumers against unsafe products. Consumers are often unable to insure against all risks. In addition, consumers should be able to rely on the marketing of manufacturers.

2. The cost of injury should be borne by the parties best able to prevent, detect, eliminate, and insure against product defects: manufacturers and others in the chain of distribution. Because the manufacturers and sellers of products can insure against the losses caused by their products and pass these costs on to all consumers in the form of higher prices, they are in the best position to bear and spread the costs of product liability.

3. Imposing strict liability encourages manufacturers to go the extra mile to produce safer products and to improve existing products by investing in careful product design, manufacture, testing, and quality control. Manufacturers should not escape liability simply because they typically do not sign a formal contract with the end user of their product (or with nonusers who might be injured by their product). Negligence liability alone does not provide sufficient incentives to induce manufacturers to make safe products.

4. The law should give sellers an incentive to deal with reputable manufacturers.

In short, the goal of strict product liability is to force companies to internalize the costs of the injuries caused by their products.

Elements of a Strict Liability Claim

For a defendant to be held strictly liable, the plaintiff must prove that (1) the plaintiff, or the plaintiff's property, was harmed by the product; (2) the injury was caused by a defect in the product; and (3) the defect existed at the time the product left the defendant and did not substantially change along the way. Most states have followed the formulation of section 402A of the Restatement (Second) of Torts, which states:

1. One who sells any product in a defective condition unreasonably dangerous to the user or consumer or to his property is subject to liability for physical harm thereby caused to the ultimate user or consumer, or to his property, if

   a. the seller is engaged in the business of selling such a product, and

   b. it is expected to and does reach the user or consumer without substantial change in the condition in which it is sold.

2. The rule stated in Subsection (1) applies although

   a. the seller has exercised all possible care in the preparation and sale of his product, and

   b. the user or consumer has not bought the product from or entered into any contractual relation with the seller.

In some cases, the plaintiffs may base their suit on the anticipation of becoming ill or suffering physical injury as a result of being exposed to a toxic product, such as asbestos. In 2003, the U.S. Supreme Court ruled that asymptomatic plaintiffs exposed to asbestos could sue if they had a reasonable fear of developing cancer and at least some physical injury.[6] In *Petito v. A.H. Robins Co.*,[7] the Florida Court of Appeal recognized a cause of action for "medical monitoring" for plaintiffs who had been prescribed the weight-loss drugs Fenfluramine and Phentermine. Although they had no physical injuries, the class members argued that taking the drugs had placed them at a substantially increased risk of developing serious cardiac and circulatory damage, including heart valve damage. The court required manufacturers and sellers to pay for a court-supervised program of medical testing, monitoring, and study of the class, reasoning, "[O]ne can hardly dispute that an individual has just as great an interest in avoiding expensive diagnostic examinations as in avoiding physical injury."[8]

The American Law Institute (ALI) promulgated the Restatement (Third) of Torts: Products Liability in 1998. Restatements provide judges and lawyers with a

5. 377 P.2d 897 (Cal. 1963).

6. Norfolk & Western Ry. Co. v. Ayers, 538 U.S. 135 (2003).

7. 750 So. 2d 103 (Fla. Dist. Ct. App. 1999).

8. *Id.* at 105.

comprehensive view of the status of American case law (drawn from a survey of courts throughout the country) and the rationale behind it. They also reflect the drafters' vision of the way that a particular area of the law should evolve. As explained in Chapter 3, courts are free to follow or ignore the restatement's formulation.

Like the Restatement (Second) of Torts, the Restatement (Third) imposes strict liability for manufacturing defects. In the case of design defects and defects based on inadequate instructions or warnings, however, it imposes a standard predicated on negligence. Because a majority of states still follow the Restatement (Second), the discussion that follows is, except as otherwise noted, based on that restatement. We will return to the Restatement (Third) standard for defects in design, instructions, and warnings later in this chapter.

LITIGATION STRATEGY AND THE AVAILABILITY OF PUNITIVE DAMAGES

Although negligence and breach of warranty are alleged in most product liability cases, they play a secondary role compared with strict liability. Under strict liability, the injured person does not have the burden of proving negligence and does not have to be in privity with the seller. Thus, strict liability is easier to prove than either negligence or breach of warranty.

Nonetheless, plaintiffs' attorneys usually try to prove negligence as well as strict liability. Proof of negligence will often stir the jury's emotions, leading to higher damages awards and, in some cases, to punitive damages.[9] For example, in 2006, a jury awarded $9 million in punitive damages on top of $4.5 million in compensatory damages to a plaintiff who had taken Vioxx pain medication, after finding that Merck had withheld information about the drug's health risks from the Food and Drug Administration.[10] Jury foreperson Timothy Kile explained the jury's thought process: "[Merck is] responsible for people taking the medication and putting it in their bodies. To not put information out there about public safety that I feel you have a responsibility to put out there, that's willful and wanton."[11] (Chapter 4 discusses court-imposed limitations on punitive damages.)

Once the plaintiff has raised the issue of negligence, the defendant is permitted to introduce evidence that its products were "state of the art" and manufactured with due care. Such evidence would otherwise be inadmissible in strict liability cases governed by the Restatement (Second) and manufacturing defect cases governed by the Restatement (Third).

---

9. Punitive damages are discussed further in Chapters 4 and 9.

10. Alex Berenson, *Merck Jury Adds $9 Million in Damages*, N.Y. Times, Apr. 12, 2006, at C1.

11. *Id.*

IN BRIEF

Theories of Product Liability*

	Contract—Breach of Warranty	Tort—Negligence	Tort—Strict Liability
What needs to be shown?	Express (stated in the contract) or implied (by law) warranty. Implied warranties are merchantability and sometimes fitness for a particular purpose.	1. The injured party (or property) was injured (damaged) by the product, resulting in an actual loss. 2. The defendant owed a duty to the injured party. 3. The defendant did not use reasonable care in designing the product, manufacturing the product, or providing adequate warnings. 4. The defect caused the injury or damage. 5. The injury was reasonably foreseeable.	1. The injured party (or property) was harmed by a defective product (i.e., has a design defect, a manufacturing defect, or a failure to adequately warn) that is unreasonably dangerous (i.e., the danger extends beyond that contemplated by the ordinary consumer who purchases with ordinary knowledge in the community). 2. The product reached the consumer without substantial change in the condition in which it was sold. 3. The seller is engaged in the business of selling the product.

CONTINUED

	Contract—Breach of Warranty	*Tort—Negligence*	*Tort—Strict Liability*
Is privity of contract required?	Yes, for common law warranties; varies by state for UCC warranties	No	No
Who is covered?	Only the parties in privity of contract under common law; under the UCC, parties in privity, members of their household and guests personally injured by the breach, and, in certain states, any reasonably foreseeable user or bystander	Purchasers, users, and bystanders (Note: Purchasers of used property generally are not covered.)	Same as Tort—Negligence
Who is liable?	Only the parties in privity of contract under common law; seller who made the warranty under the UCC	The person(s) who acted negligently	Anyone in the commercial chain of distribution: component manufacturers, manufacturers, distributors, wholesalers, and retailers (but not casual sellers and, in some jurisdictions, there are limitations on the liability of component manufacturers, wholesalers, and retailers)
Is "fault" required?	No	Yes—failure to use reasonable care in designing, manufacturing (including inspecting for defects in components), or providing adequate warnings	No
What if the injured person negligently used or misused the product?	For express warranties, the terms of the warranty generally bar or severely limit recovery. For implied warranties, especially fitness for a particular purpose, the result will be fact specific.	In contributory negligence states—no recovery. In comparative negligence states—reduced recovery. Unforeseeable misuse will generally bar recovery.	Contributory negligence does not apply. In some jurisdictions, comparative fault can reduce awards. Unforeseeable misuse will generally bar recovery.
What if the product was "state of the art"? (Note: States differ as to the standard used to establish "state of the art.")	Generally no recovery	Generally precludes claims for negligent design. Manufacturing defects and failure-to-warn claims are still available.	Generally irrelevant
What if the product met all federal and state regulatory standards?	Generally irrelevant as to express warranties but may eliminate any claim under implied warranties	If the standards do not preempt state product liability law—no effect. If the standards do preempt state product liability law—recovery is limited to the preemption limitations.	Same as Tort—Negligence
What damages are recoverable?	Economic only	Economic damages, bodily injury, property damage, and pain and suffering	Same as Tort—Negligence
Are punitive damages available?	No	Yes if the defendant's conduct was grossly negligent or reckless	No

*Key assumptions:

1. The defendant sold a product, not a service.

2. The defendant was not engaged in an ultrahazardous activity.

3. The product was not unavoidably unsafe.

4. The court will apply something similar to the Restatement (Second).

5. Variations among jurisdictions have not been noted in all possible circumstances.

WHAT IS A PRODUCT?

Strict liability in tort applies only to products, not services and other intangibles. What qualifies as a *product* is sometimes not clear.

Products versus Services or Information

In some cases, it is unclear whether an injury was caused by a defective product or a negligently performed service. For example, a person may be injured by a needle used by a dentist or the hair solution used by a beautician. Some courts apply strict liability in these situations. Other courts will treat the product as incidental to the service and not apply strict liability.

Courts that have addressed the definition-of-product question have required that the item giving rise to liability be tangible. But what happens when harm results from defective information contained in a book or other tangible item? Is the "product" the information or the physical characteristics of the item in which the information is embedded?

In the case of books, courts have generally taken the position that "the tangible portion of the book, the binding and printing . . . is a good[;] the thought and ideas contained therein are not."[12] For example, mushroom enthusiasts who had relied on descriptions in a book entitled *The Encyclopedia of Mushrooms* to determine which wild mushrooms were safe to eat, but become critically ill after eating a poisonous variety, could not bring a strict product liability claim based on the erroneous information.[13] The court reasoned that the allegedly defective "product" was a collection of ideas and expressions, not a tangible item. The First Amendment to the U.S. Constitution evidences the high value placed on the unfettered exchange of ideas; this could be seriously inhibited by the threat of strict liability for the contents of books. Courts have used similar reasoning to dismiss product claims based on a dieting guide,[14] an instruction guide for a floor hockey game,[15] video games,[16] and scuba diving lessons.[17]

In contrast, courts have allowed product liability claims to proceed against publishers of written materials that are akin to specialized instruments. For example, a court ruled that aeronautical charts are sufficiently tangible to qualify as products because they provide visual representations of technical information, such as headings, distances, and minimum altitudes required by pilots.[18] The charts were not merely thoughts and expressions. Similarly, if the information at issue is characterized as "an integral part of a product in a 'smart good,' such as a computerized braking system in a car," then strict product liability will apply.[19]

Software

With the evolution of the digital age, courts have also considered whether software is sufficiently tangible to be considered a product. Certain scholars argue that "the reasons for treating software differently from all other products no longer withstand close scrutiny, if they ever did," and they have called for "the extension of strict liability to defective software at the earliest opportunity."[20] But courts have reached varying results.

A federal court applying Louisiana law ruled that the software State Farm Insurance used to calculate home damage estimates was a product under the state's product liability law.[21] The homeowners had alleged that State Farm had intentionally programmed the software to underestimate the costs of repairing or replacing property damage suffered during Hurricane Katrina in 2005. In reaching its decision, the court relied on a Louisiana Supreme Court ruling on a tax code issue. In that case, Louisiana's highest court, reaching back to Roman law, had held that software is a "corporeal movable," or physical thing capable of being moved, not an "incorporeal movable," or abstract concept such as a legal right.[22] (Note that Louisiana is not a common law jurisdiction.)

In another case, which examined the issue outside of the product liability context, the U.S. Court of Appeals for the Fourth Circuit came to the opposite conclusion. It characterized computer files and operating systems as "abstract ideas, logic, instructions, and information," not tangible products.[23] Accordingly, America Online's insurance policy, which covered only physical harm to tangible items, did not cover liability for claims brought by customers who alleged that AOL's update software had corrupted their electronic data and altered the operating systems in their computers. The Eighth Circuit, however, held that software that caused a subscriber to lose use of his computer did cause damage to a tangible product within the meaning of a general liability insurance policy.[24]

12. Smith v. Linn, 563 A.2d 123, 126 (Pa. Super. Ct. 1989).

13. Winter v. G.P. Putnam's Sons, 938 F.2d 1033 (9th Cir. 1991).

14. Gorran v. Atkins Nutritionals, Inc., 464 F. Supp. 2d 315 (S.D.N.Y. 2006).

15. Garcia v. Kusan, Inc., 655 N.E.2d 1290 (Mass. App. Ct. 1995).

16. Wilson v. Midway Games, 198 F. Supp. 2d 167 (D. Conn. 2002).

17. Isham v. Padi Worldwide Corp., 2007 WL 2460776 (D. Haw. Aug. 23, 2007).

18. Aetna Cas. & Sur. Co. v. Jeppesen & Co., 642 F.2d 339 (9th Cir. 1981).

19. Michael Traynor, *Information Liability and the Challenges for Law Reform: An Introductory Note, in* CONSUMER PROTECTION IN THE AGE OF THE INFORMATION ECONOMY 81, 82 (Jane K. Winn ed., 2006).

20. Frances E. Zollers, Andrew McMullin, Sandra N. Hurd & Peter Shears, *No More Soft Landings for Software: Liability for Defects in an Industry That Has Come of Age*, 21 SANTA CLARA COMPUTER & HIGH TECH. L.J. 745, 782 (2005).

21. Schafer v. State Farm Fire & Cas. Co., 507 F. Supp. 2d 587 (E.D. La. 2007).

22. South Cent. Bell Tel. Co. v. Barthelemy, 643 So. 2d 1240, 1244 (La. 1994).

23. Am. Online, Inc. v. St. Paul Mercury Ins. Co., 347 F.3d 89, 96 (4th Cir. 2003).

24. Eyeblaster, Inc. v. Fed. Ins. Co., 613 F.3d 797 (8th Cir. 2009).

Fixtures and Structural Improvements

A similar issue arises when a telephone pole or other product installed in the ground is defective. Some courts take the position that fixtures of this type are structural improvements of real property and, as such, are not products for purposes of product liability actions. For example, the Florida Court of Appeal held that a conveyor was a structural improvement as a matter of law and not subject to strict liability.[25]

Other courts, such as the Alabama Supreme Court, have ruled that telephone poles maintain their product characteristics even after being attached to real property.[26] Alabama's top court has also treated the following structural improvements as products: (1) a conveyor belt installed in a grain-storage facility,[27] (2) a gas water heater in a home,[28] (3) a cylindrical rotary soybean conditioner located in a soybean extraction facility,[29] and (4) a diving board that had been installed with an in-ground, vinyl-lined swimming pool.[30] The court reasoned that the policies underlying strict product liability have little relation to the policies underlying the fixtures doctrine even though the two do intersect in some instances.[31] As a result, the application of product liability law should not be totally dependent upon the intricacies of real property law. Similarly, the U.S. District Court for the District of South Carolina treated a conveyor belt as a product under South Carolina law.[32] A New Jersey Superior Court recognized that a pool was an improvement to real property but ruled that it was still subject to strict liability under state law.[33]

In contrast, the Alabama Supreme Court ruled that certain items, such as fireplaces[34] and multilayered exterior wall systems,[35] that become part of the structure once installed are not products because they "will have the same useful life as the house or building itself and will not need to be replaced over the life of the building."[36]

WHAT MAKES A PRODUCT DEFECTIVE?

An essential element for recovery in strict liability is proof of a defect in the product. The injured party must show that (1) the product was defective when it left the hands of the manufacturer or seller, and (2) the defect made the product unreasonably dangerous. Typically, a product is dangerous if its characteristics do not meet the consumer's expectations. For example, a consumer expects that a step-ladder will not break when someone stands on the bottom step. Not all situations are so clear-cut, however.

John Wade, a noted American jurist whose articles are frequently cited by courts,[37] set forth the following factors for determining whether a product is defective:

1. The usefulness and desirability of the product—its utility to the user and to the public as a whole.

2. The safety aspects of the product—the likelihood that it will cause injury and the probable seriousness of the injury.

3. The availability of a substitute product that would meet the same need and not be as unsafe.

4. The manufacturer's ability to eliminate the unsafe character of the product without impairing its usefulness or making it too expensive to maintain its utility.

5. The user's ability to avoid danger by the exercise of care in the use of the product.

6. The user's anticipated awareness of the dangers inherent in the product and their avoidability, because of general public knowledge of the obvious condition of the product or of the existence of suitable warnings or instructions.

7. The feasibility, on the part of the manufacturer, of spreading the loss by setting the price of the product or carrying liability insurance.[38]

Manufacturing Defect

A *manufacturing defect* is a flaw in a product that occurs during production, such as a failure to meet the design specifications. A product with a manufacturing defect is not like the others rolling off the production line. For example, suppose the driver's seat in a truck is designed to be bolted to the frame. If a worker forgets to tighten the bolts, the loose seat will be a manufacturing defect.

Design Defect

A *design defect* occurs when a product manufactured according to specifications is, nonetheless, due to its inadequate design or a poor choice of materials, unreasonably dangerous to users. Typically, a design is defective when the product is not safe for its intended or reasonably foreseeable use. A highly publicized example was the Ford Pinto, which a jury found to be defectively designed because the car's fuel tank was too close to the rear axle, causing the tank to rupture when the car was struck from behind.

25. Plaza v. Fisher Dev., Inc., 971 So. 2d 918 (Fla. Dist. Ct. App. 2008).

26. Bell v. T.R. Miller Mill Co., 768 So. 2d 953 (Ala. 2000).

27. Beam v. Tramco, Inc., 655 So. 2d. 979 (Ala. 1995).

28. Sears, Roebuck & Co. v. Harris, 630 So. 2d. 1018 (Ala. 1993).

29. McDaniel v. French Oil Mill Mach. Co., 623 So. 2d 1146 (Ala. 1993).

30. King v. S.R. Smith, Inc., 578 So. 2d 1285 (Ala. 1991).

31. *Bell*, 768 So. 2d at 957.

32. Ervin v. Cont'l Conveyor & Equip. Co., 674 F. Supp. 2d 709 (D.S.C. 2009).

33. Dziewiecki v. Bakula, 824 A.2d 241 (N.J. Super. Ct. App. Div. 2003).

34. Wells v. Clowers Constr. Co., 476 So. 2d 105 (Ala. 1985).

35. Keck v. Dryvit Sys., 830 So. 2d 1 (Ala. 2002).

36. *Id.* at 6.

37. *See, e.g.*, Nunnally v. R.J. Reynolds Tobacco Co., 869 So. 2d 373 (Miss. 2004).

38. *Id.* at 379–80.

Inadequate Warnings, Labeling, or Instructions

To avoid charges of *failure to warn*, a product must carry adequate warnings of the risks involved in its foreseeable use. To prevail in a failure-to-warn case, most states require the plaintiff to prove that "the defendant did not adequately warn of a particular risk that was known or knowable in light of the generally recognized and prevailing best scientific and medical knowledge available at the time of manufacture and distribution."[39] For example, the manufacturer of a ladder must warn the user not to stand on the top step. A product must also be accompanied by instructions for its safe use. For example, sellers have been found liable for failing to provide adequate instructions about the proper use and capacity of a hook and the assembly and use of a telescope and sun filter.

Although a warning can shield a manufacturer from liability for a *properly* manufactured and designed product, it cannot shield the manufacturer from liability for a *defectively* manufactured or designed product. For example, an automobile manufacturer cannot escape liability for defectively designed brakes merely by warning that "under certain conditions this car's brakes may fail." As will be explained later, in cases involving certain

---

39. Anderson v. Owens-Corning Fiberglass Corp., 810 P.2d 549, 558 (Cal. 1991).

---

ethical consideration

You are a manager of a major manufacturing corporation. An interview with a low-level engineer leads you to believe that the design specifications for your model PaZazz-4 are, in fact, the cause of numerous deaths. You are facing a wrongful death and product liability suit for defective design. The plaintiffs have not deposed this engineer, even though his name was provided as one of the hundreds who worked on this project. Thus, although you believe the design for PaZazz-4 was defective, it will be extremely difficult—if not impossible—for the plaintiffs to prove this. What should you do?

© Cengage Learning 2013

products, such as certain types of vaccines, that are unavoidably unsafe, the adequacy of the warning determines whether a product known to be dangerous is also "defective."

Bilingual Warnings

The United States is a heterogeneous country, and diversity is one of its great strengths. With diversity can come challenges, however. Misunderstandings may arise due to differences in culture or language. Legislatures in states with substantial non-English-speaking populations have recognized the need for bilingual or multilingual documents in such areas as voting and public services. The following case addresses the need for bilingual warnings on nonprescription drugs.

| A CASE IN POINT | *Summary* | Case 10.2 |

Ramirez v. Plough, Inc.

Supreme Court of California
863 P.2d 167 (Cal. 1993).

FACTS   In March 1986, when he was less than four months old, plaintiff Jorge Ramirez exhibited symptoms of a cold or similar upper respiratory infection. To relieve these symptoms, Ramirez's mother gave him St. Joseph's Aspirin for Children (SJAC), a nonprescription drug manufactured and distributed by Plough, Inc. The product label stated that the dosage for a child under two years old was "as directed by doctor." Moreover, the package displayed this warning:

> Warning: Reye Syndrome is a rare but serious disease which can follow flu or chicken pox in children and teenagers. While the cause of Reye Syndrome is unknown, some reports claim aspirin may increase the risk of developing this disease. Consult doctor before use in children or teenagers with flu or chicken pox.

The warnings were provided only in English, although Plough was aware that non-English-speaking Hispanics purchased the product. Ramirez's mother, who could read only Spanish, did not consult a doctor before using SJAC to treat Ramirez's condition. After two days, Ramirez's mother took him to a hospital, where the doctor advised her to administer Dimetapp or Pedialyte (nonprescription medications that do not contain aspirin); she disregarded the advice and continued to treat Ramirez with SJAC. Ramirez thereafter developed the potentially fatal Reye syndrome, resulting in severe neurological damage, including cortical blindness, spastic quadriplegia, and mental retardation.

CONTINUED

Ramirez sued Plough, alleging that he contracted Reye syndrome as a result of ingesting SJAC. He sought compensatory and punitive damages on, among other things, a theory of product liability. The complaint alleged that SJAC was defective when it left the defendant's control and that the product's reasonably foreseeable use involved a substantial and not readily apparent danger of which the defendant failed to warn adequately.

Finding no duty to warn and no causal relation between the defendant's actions and the plaintiff's illness, the trial court granted summary judgment for the defendant. On appeal, the appellate court reversed after concluding that a jury should decide whether the English warnings were adequate. The defendant appealed.

ISSUE PRESENTED May a manufacturer of nonprescription drugs that can lead to a deadly illness when taken as normally expected incur tort liability for distributing its products with warnings only in English when the manufacturer knows that there are non-English-reading users?

SUMMARY OF OPINION The California Supreme Court began by noting that a manufacturer of nonprescription drugs has a duty to warn purchasers about dangers of its products. The issue under consideration was whether the defendant's duty to warn required it to provide label or package warnings in Spanish.

The court acknowledged that although the Food and Drug Administration (FDA) encourages labeling that meets the needs of non-English speakers, it only requires manufacturers to provide full labeling in English for all nonprescription drugs except those distributed solely in Puerto Rico or another territory where the predominant language is not English.

Although the California legislature had enacted laws to protect non-English speakers in certain circumstances, California did not have a law requiring labeling in a foreign language. Because the state and federal statutes expressly required only English labeling, the court decided not to intrude on a matter it deemed best handled by the legislature.

RESULT Because both state and federal law require warnings in English but not in any other language, the drug manufacturer was not liable in tort for failing to label the aspirin with warnings in a language other than English. Ramirez's case was dismissed.

COMMENTS The California Supreme Court was influenced by the FDA's experience with Spanish inserts for prescription drugs. Recognizing that "the United States is too heterogeneous to enable manufacturers, at reasonable cost and with reasonable simplicity, to determine exactly where to provide alternative language inserts," the FDA for a time required manufacturers, as an alternative to multilingual or bilingual inserts, to provide Spanish-language translations of their patient package inserts on request to doctors and pharmacists. The FDA later concluded that manufacturers were having difficulty obtaining accurate translations, and eventually it abandoned the patient package insert requirement for prescription drugs altogether.

CRITICAL THINKING QUESTIONS

1. Would the result have been different if the nonprescription medicine had been for an illness particular to a certain non-English-speaking group residing in the United States?

2. Should it matter whether a drug company advertises a particular medicine in a language other than English?

© Cengage Learning 2013

Causation Requirement

To prevail on a failure-to-warn claim, the plaintiff must show that (1) the defendant breached a duty to warn and (2) the defendant's failure to warn was the *proximate cause* (or legal cause) of the plaintiff's injuries. The question of proximate cause is one for the jury to determine. As a result, the vast majority of courts will not disturb a jury's finding that a failure to warn was the proximate cause of an injury. However, in an extreme case—one in which the court believes no reasonable person could have deemed the failure to warn a proximate cause of the plaintiff's injury—the court may set aside a verdict on causation grounds.

Unavoidably Unsafe Products

If the societal value of using an *unavoidably unsafe product* outweighs the risk of harm from its use, the manufacturer may be exonerated from liability as long as it provided proper warnings. For example, certain drugs are generally beneficial, but are known to have harmful side effects in some situations. The authors of both the Restatement (Second) and the Restatement (Third) recognized that there should be a separate concept of product liability for manufacturers of prescription drugs and medical devices.

Comment b to section 6 of the Restatement (Third) articulated the rationale behind this special treatment:

> The traditional refusal by courts to impose tort liability for defective designs of prescription drugs and medical devices is based on the fact that a prescription drug or medical device entails a unique set of risks and benefits. What may be harmful to one patient may be beneficial to another. Under Subsection (c) [of section 6] a drug is defectively designed only when it provides no net benefit to any class of patients. . . . [M]anufacturers must have ample discretion to develop useful drugs and devices without subjecting their design decisions to the ordinary test applicable to products generally.[40]

Nearly every jurisdiction in the United States has followed this reasoning in some form or another.[41] For example, the manufacturer of the Sabin oral polio vaccine was held not strictly liable to an individual who contracted polio from the vaccine.[42] The odds of contracting polio from the vaccine were one in a million. The drug's benefits outweighed its dangers, and the manufacturer's warning about the remote risk of harm was reasonably adequate.[43]

WHO MAY BE STRICTLY LIABLE FOR PRODUCT DEFECTS?

In theory, each party in the chain of distribution may be strictly liable for product defects: manufacturers, distributors, wholesalers, and retailers. Although disclaimers of liability are generally ineffective, parties in the chain of distribution may (and should) enter into contracts giving them a right to *indemnity* (that is, reimbursement) if they are found liable for defects caused by other members of the distribution chain.

Manufacturers of Products and Component Parts

A manufacturer will be held strictly liable for its defective products regardless of how remote the manufacturer is from the final user of the product. The only requirement for strict liability is that the manufacturer be in the business of selling the injury-causing product. The manufacturer may be held liable even when the distributor makes final inspections, corrections, and adjustments of the product.

Manufacturers of component parts are frequently sued as well and are generally liable for any defects in the components they produce. But the maker of a component part is not liable for defective design specifications for the entire product as long as (1) the component is not itself defective, and (2) the component manufacturer did not participate in the design of the finished product.[44] For example, the maker of a nondefective seat installed in a garbage truck was not liable to either the driver of the truck or the truck manufacturer when the driver was hurt after the truck rolled over.[45] The truck manufacturer designed the garbage truck and chose which seat to install, and its own attorney had "admitted that 'there isn't anything wrong with the seat.'"[46]

Wholesalers

Wholesalers are usually held strictly liable for defects in the products they sell. In some jurisdictions, however, a wholesaler is not liable for latent or hidden defects if the wholesaler sells the products in exactly the same condition it received them.

Retailers

A retailer may also be held strictly liable. For example, in the automobile industry, retailers have a duty to inspect and care for the products. In several jurisdictions, however, a retailer will not be liable if it did not contribute to the defect and played no part in the manufacturing process.

Sellers of Used Goods and Occasional Sellers

Sellers of used goods are usually not held strictly liable because they are not within the original chain of distribution of the product.[47] In addition, the custom in the used-goods market is that there are no warranties or expectations relating to the quality of the products (although some jurisdictions have adopted rules requiring warranties for used cars). A seller of used goods is, however, strictly liable for any defective repairs or replacements he or she makes. Occasional sellers, such as people who host garage sales, are not strictly liable.

---

40. RESTATEMENT (THIRD) OF TORTS: PRODUCTS LIABILITY § 6 cmt. b (1998).

41. *See* RESTATEMENT (SECOND) OF TORTS § 402A cmt. k (1977).

42. Johnson v. Am. Cyanamid Co., 718 P.2d 1318 (Kan. 1986).

43. *Id.* at 1324–25.

44. See RESTATEMENT (THIRD) OF TORTS: PRODUCTS LIABILITY § 5 (1998).

45. Bostrom Seating, Inc. v. Crane Carrier Co., 140 S.W.3d 681 (Tex. 2004).

46. *Id.* at 684.

47. Allenberg v. Bentley Hedges Travel Serv., Inc., 22 P.3d 223 (Okla. 2001).

SUCCESSOR, MARKET-SHARE, AND PREMISES LIABILITY

Companies may also face product liability because they acquired the firm that sold the defective product, they sold an undifferentiated product, or they operated premises tainted by defective products.

Successor Liability

Most states employ the traditional *successor liability* rule: a corporation purchasing or acquiring the assets of another is liable for the acquired company's product liability and other debts only when (1) there is a consolidation or merger of the two corporations,[48] (2) the acquirer expressly or impliedly agrees to assume such obligations, or (3) the transaction was wrongfully entered into to escape liability.[49] A minority of jurisdictions have adopted one of two additional bases for successor liability: the product-line theory and the continuity-of-enterprise approach.

Under the *product-line theory,* espoused by the California Supreme Court,[50] a successor that continues to manufacture the same product line as its predecessor, under the same name and with no outward indication of any change of ownership, may be held liable for product liability claims resulting from that product line, even if the particular item was manufactured and sold by the acquired firm prior to the acquisition. Courts applying the *continuity-of-enterprise approach* look for constancy between the buyer and seller organizations to determine whether the successor company is essentially "a mere continuation or reincarnation of the predecessor entity."[51] Among the factors a court will analyze are similarity of management, personnel, assets, facilities, operations, and shareholders, and whether the successor holds itself out to the public as a continuing enterprise.[52] For example, several people injured in a boating accident caused by defects in the craft successfully used the continuity-of-enterprise approach to sue the company that succeeded the boat manufacturer.[53] Although the name of the company changed, the owners, officers, employees, address, phone number, and line of business remained the same.

Market-Share Liability

When there are multiple manufacturers of identical products, the injured party may not be able to prove which of the defendant manufacturers sold the product that caused the injury. In certain unusual cases, particularly those involving prescription drugs, the court may allocate liability on the basis of each defendant's share of the market. This doctrine of *market-share liability* was developed by the California Supreme Court in *Sindell v. Abbott Laboratories*[54] to address the specific problem of DES litigation.

Women whose mothers took the drug diethylstilbestrol (DES) during pregnancy alleged that they were injured by the DES, which, among other things, increased the daughters' likelihood of developing cancer. Many of the plaintiffs could not pinpoint which manufacturer was directly responsible for their injuries, so they sought damages from a number of DES manufacturers.

Several factors made it difficult to identify particular DES manufacturers. All manufacturers made DES from an identical chemical formula. Druggists typically filled prescriptions from whatever stock they had on hand. During the twenty-four years that DES was sold for use during pregnancy, more than three hundred companies entered and left the market. The harmful effects of DES were not discovered until many years after the plaintiffs' mothers had used the drug.

By the time the lawsuit was filed, memories had faded, records had been lost, and witnesses had died. Given the difficulty of identifying the defendant responsible for each plaintiff, the court held that the fairest approach was to apportion liability based on each manufacturer's national market share. The court reasoned that it was more appropriate that the loss be borne by those who produced the drug than by those who suffered injury.

Although the New York Court of Appeals applied market-share liability in DES cases,[55] it characterized the DES situation as "a singular case." The Appellate Division of the Supreme Court of New York (New York's intermediate appeals court) refused to extend the doctrine to lead-based paints because (1) 20% of the lead pigments could have been manufactured by defendants not named in the litigation; (2) the plaintiffs were unable to identify the years in which the house was painted, making it impossible to determine which defendants manufactured paint during the relevant period; (3) lead-based paints were not uniform, fungible products; and (4) there was no signature injury in lead poisoning cases.[56] In contrast, the Wisconsin Supreme Court extended the doctrine to lead-based paint,[57] and a federal court in New York imposed

48. The de facto merger doctrine is discussed in Chapter 19.
49. *See, e.g.,* Nissen Corp. v. Miller, 594 A.2d 564, 565–66 (Md. 1991) (adopting the traditional successor liability exceptions).
50. Ray v. Alad Corp., 560 P.2d 3 (Cal. 1977). *But see, e.g.,* Semenetz v. Sherling & Walden, Inc., 851 N.E.2d 1170 (N.Y. 2006) (declining to adopt the "product-line" exception).
51. *Nissen Corp.,* 594 A.2d at 565–66.
52. Turner v. Bituminous Cas. Co., 244 N.W.2d 873 (Mich. 1976).
53. Patin v. Thoroughbred Power Boats, 294 F.3d 640 (5th Cir. 2002) (applying Florida law).

54. 607 P.2d 924 (Cal. 1980).
55. Hymowitz v. Eli Lilly & Co., 539 N.E.2d 1069 (N.Y. 1989).
56. Brenner v. Am. Cyanamid Co., 699 N.Y.S.2d 848 (N.Y. App. Div. 1999).
57. Thomas v. Mallett, 701 N.W.2d 523 (Wis. 2005).

market-share liability in a case involving well-water contamination by oil companies.[58]

Many jurisdictions have rejected market-share liability outright.[59] It has been criticized for being a simplistic response to a complex problem and for implying that manufacturers must be the insurers of all their industry's products. Market-share liability has also been challenged on the constitutional ground that it violates a defendant's right to due process of law because it denies a defendant the opportunity to prove that its individual products did not cause the plaintiff's injury.

Premises Liability

Courts have imposed liability on building owners for asbestos-related diseases on a *premises liability* theory. Under this theory, a building owner may be found liable under a theory of negligence for violating its general duty to manage the premises and warn of asbestos dangers.[60] This is in addition to the liability imposed on the manufacturers of the asbestos-laden insulation, roofing, or other materials. The same theory has been applied to buildings with mold.

PRODUCT LIABILITY CLASS ACTIONS

Product liability cases are frequently resolved through class actions, a procedural device that allows a large number of plaintiffs to recover against a defendant in a single case. Lawsuits involving the tobacco industry, silicone breast implants, and harmful diet drugs were all resolved through class actions. The U.S. Supreme Court's decisions in both *Amchem Products, Inc. v. Windsor*[61] and *Wal-Mart v. Dukes*[62] have made class certification more difficult.

The Ohio Supreme Court refused to certify a class of more than 4,000 workers exposed to beryllium at an Ohio job site who were seeking the creation of a medical monitoring program.[63] The members of the proposed class spanned forty-six years, multiple contractors, and multiple locations within the plant. The court concluded that "lack of cohesiveness is fatal."[64] As a result, the individual questions outweighed the questions common to the class.

Rule 23(b)(1)(B) of the Federal Rules of Civil Procedure provides a mechanism to resolve class actions in which the total of the aggregated liquidated claims exceeds the fund available to satisfy them (*limited fund class actions*). In the *Fibreboard* asbestos class action, the U.S. Supreme Court made it clear that the trial court itself must determine whether the fund is limited.[65] Thus, it was improper for the trial court to simply accept an agreement among the lead plaintiffs, the insurance companies, and the manufacturer as to the maximum amount the insurance companies could be required to pay tort victims.

COMMON LAW DEFENSES

The defendant in a product liability case may raise the traditional common law tort defenses of assumption of risk and, in some jurisdictions, a variation of comparative negligence known as comparative fault. Other defenses, such as obvious risk, sophisticated user, unforeseeable misuse of the product, the government-contractor defense, and the state-of-the-art defense, may be available only in product liability cases. These defenses are sometimes codified into state statutes, and their acceptance varies from state to state. Finally, under certain circumstances, state product liability law is preempted by federal law.

Assumption of Risk

Under the doctrine of *assumption of risk,* when a person voluntarily and unreasonably assumes the risk of a known danger, the manufacturer is not liable for any resulting injury. For example, under Michigan law, if the claimant voluntarily exposed himself or herself to a risk, and that risk was the proximate cause of the injury, then recovery is completely barred.[66] Thus, if a ladder bears a conspicuous warning not to stand on the top step, but a person steps on it anyway and falls, the ladder manufacturer will not be liable for any injuries caused by the fall.

On the other hand, a Washington appellate court found no assumption of risk when a grinding disc exploded and hit a person in the eye.[67] The court reasoned that although the injured person should have been wearing goggles, he could not have anticipated that a hidden defect in the disc would cause it to explode. By not wearing goggles, the injured person assumed only the risk that dust or small particles of wood or metal would lodge in his eyes.

Comparative Fault

Contributory negligence by the plaintiff is not a defense in a strict liability action. Nevertheless, in some states, the plaintiff's damages may be reduced by the degree to which

---

58. *In re* Methyl Tertiary Butyl Ether Prods. Liab. Litig., 175 F. Supp. 2d 593 (S.D.N.Y. 2001).

59. *See, e.g.,* Doe v. Baxter Healthcare Corp., 380 F.3d 399 (8th Cir. 2004) (rejected theory on "broad policy grounds," in case involving hemophiliac who allegedly acquired HIV after taking the drug Factor VIII).

60. *CA App. Ct. Reverses Exxon Nonsuit Ruling*, Asbestos Litig. Rep., July 16, 1999. *See, e.g.,* John Crane, Inc. v. Jones, 604 S.E.2d 822 (Ga. 2004).

61. 521 U.S. 591 (1997) (refusing to certify class containing both symptomatic and asymptomatic asbestos plaintiffs because the class members had different interests).

62. 131 S. Ct. 2541 (2011) (Case 3.2).

63. Wilson v. Brush Wellman, Inc., 817 N.E.2d 59 (Ohio 2004).

64. *Id.* at 65.

65. Ortiz v. Fibreboard Corp., 527 U.S. 815 (1999).

66. Mich. Comp. Laws § 600.2947(3) (2011).

67. Haugen v. Minn. Mining & Mfg. Co., 550 P.2d 71 (Wash. App. 1976).

his or her own negligence contributed to the injury. This doctrine is known as *comparative fault.*

For example, Michigan law provides that the negligence of the plaintiff does not bar recovery, but damages are reduced by his or her degree of fault—that is, the negligence attributed to the plaintiff.[68] Under Illinois law, if the jury finds that the degree of the plaintiff's fault exceeds 50%, then the plaintiff cannot recover damages. If the jury finds that the degree of the plaintiff's fault is less than 50%, the plaintiff can recover damages, but the damages will be reduced in proportion to the plaintiff's fault.[69]

Obvious Risk

If the use of a product carries an *obvious risk*, the manufacturer will not be held liable for injuries that result from ignoring the risk. Although a plaintiff will argue that the manufacturer had a duty to warn of the dangers of a foreseeable use of the product, courts often apply the standard that a manufacturer need not warn of a danger that is generally known and recognized.

For example, in *Maneely v. General Motors Corp.,*[70] two men who rode in the cargo bed of a pickup truck sued GM after sustaining serious injuries in a collision. The men argued that GM failed to warn of the dangers of riding in a cargo bed. The court rejected their claims, noting that a manufacturer should not bear the paternalistic responsibility of warning users of every possible risk that could arise from use of its product. As the public generally recognizes the dangers of riding unrestrained in the cargo bed of a moving pickup truck, GM had no duty to warn of those dangers.

Sophisticated User

The California Supreme Court articulated a *sophisticated user defense* in product liability and toxic tort actions in 2008, holding that a "manufacturer is not liable to a sophisticated user of its product for failure to warn of a risk,

harm or danger if the sophisticated user knew or *should have known* of that risk, harm, or danger."[71] The court ruled that the sophisticated user's actual knowledge was irrelevant, reasoning that "it would be nearly impossible for a manufacturer to predict or determine whether a given user or member of the sophisticated group actually has knowledge of the dangers because of the infinite number of idiosyncrasies." Rather, the duty to warn is measured by what is generally known or should have been known by the class of sophisticated users and not by the individual plaintiff's subjective knowledge. The court also made clear that the relevant time for determining user sophistication is at the time of the plaintiff's injury, rather than the date that the product was manufactured or distributed.

Unforeseeable Misuse of the Product

A manufacturer or seller is entitled to assume that its product will be used in a normal manner. The manufacturer or seller will not be held liable for injuries resulting from abnormal use of its product. For example, unforeseeable misuse of a product is a defense under Indiana law if it is the proximate cause of the harm and the misuse is not reasonably expected by the seller at the time the seller conveyed the product to another party.[72] On the other hand, unusual use that is reasonably foreseeable may be deemed a normal use. For example, operating a lawn mower with the grass bag removed was held to be a foreseeable use, and the manufacturer was liable to a bystander injured by an object that shot out of the unguarded mower.[73]

As a general rule, a company is not liable for the criminal acts of third parties using its products unless the company knew or should have known that its negligence might allow the crime to occur.[74] In the following case, the court considered whether a video game manufacturer was strictly liable for a teenager's shooting spree.

---

68. MICH. COMP. LAWS § 600.2959 (2011).
69. 735 ILL. COMP. STAT. ANN. § 5/2-1116 (2011).
70. 108 F.3d 1176 (9th Cir. 1997).
71. Johnson v. Am. Standard, Inc., 179 P.3d 905 (Cal. 2008).
72. IND. CODE ANN. § 34-20-6-4.
73. LaPaglia v. Sears Roebuck & Co., 531 N.Y.S.2d 623 (N.Y. App. Div. 1988).
74. Gaines-Tabb v. ICI Explosives, USA, Inc., 160 F.3d 613, 621 (10th Cir. 1998).

A CASE IN POINT	*Summary*	Case 10.3

James v. Meow Media Inc.

United States Court of Appeals for the Sixth Circuit
300 F.3d 683 (6th Cir. 2002).

FACTS   In 2002, a teenager in Kentucky went on a shooting spree, killing a number of his classmates at the high school he attended. The families of the victims brought a suit against Meow Media, Inc., which makes and sells video games. The families claimed that the defendant's games desensitized the shooter to violence, thereby leading to the tragedy.

ISSUE PRESENTED   Is the creator of a video game, movie, or Internet site that contains violent images and themes liable under either a theory of negligence or strict product liability when children who view these images act violently?

CONTINUED

SUMMARY OF OPINION   The U.S. Court of Appeals for the Sixth Circuit first addressed the negligence claim. In order to prove negligence, the plaintiffs needed to prove three separate elements: (1) the defendant owed a duty of care to the victims, (2) it breached that duty of care, and (3) the breach was the proximate cause of the injury.

To find a duty of care, the plaintiffs had to show that the shooter's actions were reasonably foreseeable by the defendant. After a lengthy discussion, the court concluded that the shooting was so aberrant as to be unforeseeable by the video game producer. Furthermore, there is a general rule, with few exceptions, that no one is responsible for the "intentional criminal acts of a third party." In this case, the shooter's intentional act of murder, regardless of the situation, made his act unforeseeable to the defendant. Since there was no duty of care, the defendant could not have breached a duty of care to the victims.

The court then considered whether the plaintiffs had proved proximate cause by establishing a direct connection between the action (in this case, the shooting) and the defendant's conduct (distributing video games). The court reiterated that the shooter's actions were intentional criminal acts and found, in keeping with a century of precedent, that a third party's criminal act functions as an intervening act, rendering all actions before that act not the proximate cause of the injury.

The court also addressed the defendant's actions in light of the First Amendment guarantees of free speech and expression. Like virtually all U.S. courts, the Sixth Circuit was "loathe to attach tort liability to the dissemination of ideas."

Finally, the court characterized the plaintiffs' theory that the defendant's works were defective products as "deeply flawed." In a prior case decided more than a decade before, the court had ruled that the "words and pictures" contained in the board game *Dungeons and Dragons* were not products. In light of the changing times and rash of school shootings, the court revisited the issue rather than flatly rejecting the claim based on its earlier ruling. Nonetheless, it concluded that the same logic should apply in this case.

RESULT   The plaintiffs had no valid product liability claim. Their suit was dismissed.

COMMENTS   The unforeseeability of intentional criminal acts is generally a defense to liability, but if the product is intended to be used in furtherance of a criminal act, the defendant cannot avail itself of that protection. Thus, the publisher of a book entitled *Hit Man*, billed as an instruction manual for murder and actually used by a convicted killer to carry out his crime, was held liable for wrongful death.[75]

75. Rice v. Paladin Enter., 128 F.3d 233 (4th Cir. 1997).

© Cengage Learning 2013

As discussed in Chapter 9, courts will impose new duties to reflect changing societal expectations. For example, certain courts have permitted plaintiffs to pursue claims against gun manufacturers[76] and drug makers[77] for contributing to a "gray market" in their respective products through faulty distribution designs. The courts ruled that the companies' sales practices made it reasonably foreseeable that their products would reach consumers who were prohibited from owning the items, in the case of gun manufacturers, or that the products would be dangerously altered, in the case of drug manufacturers.

Other courts have dismissed such claims. As discussed in Chapter 9, courts in future cases may be willing to hold manufacturers liable for the misuse of their products by terrorists.

Government-Contractor Defense

Under the *government-contractor defense*, a manufacturer of products under contract to the government can avoid product liability if (1) the product was produced according to government specifications, (2) the manufacturer possessed less knowledge about the specifications than did the government agency, (3) the manufacturer exercised proper skill and care in production, and (4) the manufacturer did not deviate from the specifications.

76. Ileto v. Glock, 349 F.3d 1191 (9th Cir. 2003).

77. Fagan v. Amerisourcebergen Corp., 356 F. Supp. 2d 198 (E.D.N.Y. 2004).

The rationale for this immunity is that the manufacturer is acting merely as an agent of the government; to hold the manufacturer liable would unfairly shift the insurance burden from the government to the manufacturer. As discussed below, the Homeland Security Act extended this defense to certain products designed to thwart terrorists.

State-of-the-Art Defense

In some states, the *state-of-the-art defense* shields a manufacturer from liability for a defective design if no safer product design is generally recognized as being possible. As discussed further below, the Restatement (Third) would require all plaintiffs asserting defective design to prove the existence of an alternative design.

The contours of the state-of-the-art defense are often first laid down by judges, then codified by state legislatures. For example, an Arizona statute provides a defense "if the plans or designs for the product or the methods and techniques of manufacturing, inspecting, testing and labeling the product conformed with the state of the art at the time the product was first sold by defendant."[78]

State courts have split over two aspects of this defense. First, even states that recognize the state-of-the art defense have defined "state of the art" differently. A majority of the states that accept the defense deem "state of the art" to refer to what is technologically feasible at the time of design. Accordingly, a manufacturer may have a duty to use a safer design even if the custom of the industry is to use a less safe alternative.[79] Certain states define "state of the art" either in terms of industry custom (e.g., New Jersey[80]) or in terms of compliance with existing governmental regulations (e.g., Illinois[81]).

Second, in states that do not recognize the state-of-the-art defense, there is a split on whether to even allow the introduction of evidence of alternative designs in defective design cases. Certain courts have ruled that state-of-the-art evidence is irrelevant, and therefore inadmissible, in strict product liability cases because it improperly focuses the jury's attention on the reasonableness of the manufacturer's conduct. The overwhelming majority of states, however, hold that state-of-the-art evidence is relevant simply to determining the adequacy of the product's design.

The state-of-the art defense has also been applied in certain failure-to-warn cases. For example, a Missouri statute provides that if the defendant can prove that the dangerous nature of the product was not known and could not reasonably have been discovered at the time the product was placed in the stream of commerce, then the defendant will not be held liable for failure to warn.[82]

Preemption Defense

Perhaps the most significant and controversial of the defenses to product liability is the *preemption defense*, whereby certain federal laws and regulations that set minimum safety standards are held to preempt state-law product liability claims. For example, the National Traffic and Motor Vehicle Safety Act sets standards for automobiles, and the Safe Medical Devices Act sets standards for medical devices. Manufacturers that meet those standards will sometimes be granted immunity from product liability claims on the grounds of federal preemption. The rationale for deferring to the federal regulatory scheme is that allowing states to impose fifty different sets of requirements would frustrate the purpose of a uniform federal scheme. As a representative of the medical device industry put it, "What it boils down to is whether we want to have the experts at the FDA tell us what is a safe pacemaker, or do we want each jury designing its own pacemaker—one doing it one way in Brooklyn and one doing it another way in Missouri?"[83]

Manufacturing groups want preemption to serve as a "silver bullet" defense, effectively eliminating the possibility of state-law product liability claims in any sphere governed by federal safety law and regulation. In practice, compliance with a regulatory scheme is not always a valid defense. Instead, the availability of the preemption defense depends largely on the language and context of the federal statute at issue. In recent years, courts have struggled to determine whether federal safety statutes preempt state product liability claims involving tobacco, outboard motors, and faulty medical devices.

Tobacco

In *Cipollone v. Liggett Group*,[84] the U.S. Supreme Court concluded that broad language in the Public Health Cigarette Smoking Act of 1969 preempted claims based on a failure to warn and the neutralization of federally mandated warnings to the extent that those claims relied on omissions or inclusions in a tobacco company's advertising or promotions. The Court ruled that the Act did not preempt claims based on express warranty, intentional fraud and misrepresentation, or conspiracy, however, which left room for lawsuits that ultimately cost the tobacco industry more than $300 billion.

---

78. Ariz. Rev. Stat. § 12-683(1).

79. *See* Potter v. Chicago Pneumatic Tool Co., 694 A.2d, 1319, 1347 (Conn. 1997).

80. N.J. Stat. Ann. § 2A:58C-3.

81. 735 Ill. Comp. Stat. Ann. § 5/2-2107.

82. Mo. Rev. Stat. § 537.764.

83. Paul M. Barrett, *Lora Lohr's Pacemaker May Alter Liability Law*, Wall St. J., Apr. 9, 1996, at B1 (quoting Victor Schwartz).

84. 505 U.S. 504 (1992).

Outboard Motors

Sprietsma v. Mercury Marine[85] involved state common law tort claims arising out of the death of a woman who fell off a boat and was struck by a propeller manufactured by the defendant. The U.S. Supreme Court concluded that these claims were not preempted by the Federal Boat Safety Act of 1971 (FBSA) or by the U.S. Coast Guard's decision not to issue a regulation requiring propeller guards on boat motors. The FBSA's preemption clause prohibits states from enforcing "a law or regulation establishing a recreational vessel or associated equipment performance or other safety standard or imposing a requirement for associated equipment" that is not identical to a federal regulation. The Court scrutinized the wording of this clause to discern whether it preempted common law claims:

> First, the article "a" before "law or regulation" implies a discreteness—which is embodied in statutes and regulations—that is not present in the common law. Second, because "a word is known by the company it keeps," the terms "law" and "regulation" used together in the pre-emption clause indicate that Congress pre-empted only positive enactments. If "law" were read broadly so as to include the common law, it might also be interpreted to include regulations, which would render the express reference to "regulation" in the pre-emption clause superfluous.[86]

Nor did the scope of the statute indicate that Congress intended federal law to occupy the field exclusively. There was no implied conflict preemption because a private party could comply with both state and federal requirements.

Finally, the Coast Guard's decision not to adopt a regulation requiring propeller guards on motorboats was deemed not to be "the functional equivalent of a regulation prohibiting all States and their political subdivisions from adopting such a regulation." Even though the Coast Guard's decision "was undoubtedly intentional and carefully considered, it does not convey an 'authoritative' message of a federal policy against propeller guards."

Medical Devices and Drugs

In general, the more rigorous the federal regulatory process, the more likely that product liability claims will be preempted. *Medtronic, Inc. v. Lohr*[87] involved a pacemaker that the Food and Drug Administration (FDA) had cleared pursuant to an exemption from thorough review for medical devices "substantially equivalent" to devices already on the market.[88] Because the Medtronic pacemaker had not undergone rigorous premarket regulatory examination, the plaintiff's state-law product liability claims were not preempted.[89]

In a case involving a Medtronic catheter that *had* undergone the more thorough premarket approval process,[90] the U.S. Supreme Court ruled that state tort liability claims of strict liability, breach of warranty, and negligent design were preempted by the Medical Device Amendments of 1976 (MDA).[91] The MDA provides:

> Except as provided in subsection (b) of this section, no State or political subdivision of a State may establish or continue in effect with respect to a device intended for human use any requirement—
>
> (1) which is different from, or in addition to, any requirement applicable under this chapter to the device, and
>
> (2) which relates to the safety or effectiveness of the device or to any other matter included in a requirement applicable to the device under this chapter.[92]

The Court observed that premarket approval is an "arduous" process. The FDA spends an average of 1,200 hours reviewing each application and grants approval only if it finds there is a "reasonable assurance" of a device's "safety and effectiveness." Because the benefits are weighed against the risk of injury, the FDA may approve a device that poses substantial risks if it offers great benefit in light of the available alternatives.

The MDA expressly preempts only state requirements "different from or in addition to, any requirement applicable . . . to the device" under federal law. Hence, once the FDA grants premarket approval of a device, the manufacturer cannot deviate from the specifications in its approval application.

The Court ruled that common law causes of action for negligence and strict liability imposed "requirements" that were different from those that the FDA required and were therefore preempted. The Court reasoned:

> State tort law that requires a manufacturer's catheters to be safer, but hence less effective, than the model the FDA has approved disrupts the federal scheme no less than state regulatory law to the same effect. Indeed, one would think that tort law, applied by juries under a negligence or strict-liability standard, is less deserving of preservation. A state statute, or a regulation adopted by a state agency, could at least be expected to apply cost-benefit analysis similar to that applied by the experts at the FDA: How many more lives will be saved by a device which, along with its greater effectiveness, brings a greater risk of harm? A jury, on the

---

85. 537 U.S. 51 (2002).

86. *Id.* at 63.

87. 518 U.S. 470 (1996).

88. 21 U.S.C. § 510(k).

89. This interpretation was supported by the FDA's proposal of regulations to clarify its position.

90. Riegel v. Medtronic, Inc., 552 U.S. 312 (2008).

91. Federal Food, Drug, and Cosmetic Act, 21 U.S.C. § 360k (1976).

92. *Id.*

other hand, sees only the cost of a more dangerous design, and is not concerned with its benefits; the patients who reaped those benefits are not represented in court.[93]

The Court also ruled, however, that federal law did not preempt state laws providing for damages for claims premised on a violation of FDA regulations, reasoning that such state laws "parallel," but do not add to, federal requirements.

The dissent in *Riegel* quoted a statement by the former general counsel of the FDA acknowledging that "FDA regulation of a device cannot anticipate and protect against all safety risks to individual consumers." Until the FDA filed an amicus brief arguing for total preemption in the *Riegel* case, the agency's position had been that FDA approval and state tort liability each provided "a significant, yet distinct, layer of consumer protection." As a result, preempting state-law claims "would result in the loss of a significant layer of consumer protection."[94]

In 2008, an evenly split U.S. Supreme Court affirmed a New York court ruling that federal law does not preempt claims against a drug company that fraudulently gained FDA approval of the drug in question.[95] One year later, in *Wyeth v. Levine*,[96] the Supreme Court held that FDA approval of a brand-name drug label does not preempt an inadequate warning claim under state law. The plaintiff had developed gangrene and had to have her forearm amputated after receiving an injection of Wyeth's antinausea drug Phenergan by the "IV-push" method, whereby a drug is injected directly into a patient's vein. She sued Wyeth for failing to warn of the risks associated with the "IV-push" method and failing to instruct clinicians to administer the drug through the safer "IV-drip" method. The Court found substantial evidence that Congress did not intend for FDA oversight to be the exclusive means of ensuring drug safety and effectiveness. The Court noted that "the FDA has limited resources to conduct postapproval monitoring of drug safety," and manufacturers "have superior access to information about their drugs." This was not a case where it was impossible for a private party to comply with both the federal and state requirements: Wyeth could have satisfied both its state-law duty to provide a stronger warning and its federal labeling duties by seeking FDA approval of a strengthened label. In fact, the FDA's changes-being-effected (CBE) procedures authorize drug manufacturers to alter labels to reflect new safety information pending FDA review of the new label.

In the following case, the Court considered whether the same rule should apply to labels on generic drugs.

---

93. *Riegel*, 552 U.S. at 325. The Court noted: "The Riegels [the plaintiffs] . . . invoke §360h(d), which provides that compliance with certain FDA orders 'shall not relieve any person from liability under Federal or State law.' This indicates that some state-law claims are not pre-empted, as we held in *Lohr*. But it could not possibly mean that *all* state-law claims are not pre-empted, since that would deprive the MDA pre-emption clause of all content. And it provides no guidance as to which state-law claims are pre-empted and which are not." *Id.* at 325 n.4.

94. *Id.* at 337–38 (Ginsburg, J., dissenting).

95. Warner-Lambert Co. v. Kent, 552 U.S. 440 (2008). The Court was evenly split, with Chief Justice Roberts recusing himself. By rule, an evenly divided Court affirms the lower court ruling, but carries no precedential weight. Linda Greenhouse, *Court Allows Suit Against Drug Maker*, N.Y. Times, Mar., 4, 2008, at 21.

96. 555 U.S. 555 (2009).

| A CASE IN POINT | *In the Language of the Court* | Case 10.4 |

Pliva, Inc. v. Mensing

Supreme Court of the United States
131 S. Ct. 2567 (2011).

FACTS Consumers brought separate actions in state courts against a generic drug manufacturer alleging that the manufacturer was liable under state tort law for failing to provide adequate warning labels for metoclopramide, the generic version of Reglan. The consumers alleged that due to the inadequate warning labels, they used the drug over a number of years, which caused them to develop tardive dyskinesia, a severe neurological disorder. The manufacturers in both suits argued that federal statutes and FDA regulations preempted state tort claims. The U.S. Courts of Appeals for the Fifth and Eighth Circuits disagreed and held that the consumers' claims were not preempted. The U.S. Supreme Court granted certiorari.

ISSUE PRESENTED Does the federal law requirement that generic drugs must bear the same FDA-approved labels as their brand-name counterparts preempt state-law claims for failure to warn?

OPINION THOMAS, J., writing on behalf of the U.S. Supreme Court:

Pre-emption analysis requires us to compare federal and state law. We therefore begin by identifying the state tort duties and federal labeling requirements applicable to the Manufacturers. It is undisputed that Minnesota and Louisiana tort law require a drug manufacturer that is or should be aware of its product's danger to label that product in a way that renders it reasonably safe.

. . . .

CONTINUED

Federal law imposes far more complex drug labeling requirements. . . .

. . . Under [the Drug Price Competition and Patent Term Restoration Act, 98 Stat. 1585, commonly called the Hatch–Waxman Amendments], "generic drugs" can gain FDA approval simply by showing equivalence to a reference listed drug that has already been approved by the FDA. This allows manufacturers to develop generic drugs inexpensively, without duplicating the clinical trials already performed on the equivalent brand-name drug. A generic drug application must also "show that the [safety and efficacy] labeling proposed . . . is the same as the labeling approved for the [brand-name] drug."

As a result, brand-name and generic drug manufacturers have different federal drug labeling duties. A brand-name manufacturer seeking new drug approval is responsible for the accuracy and adequacy of its label. A manufacturer seeking generic drug approval, on the other hand, is responsible for ensuring that its warning label is the same as the brand name's.

[*Editor's note:* Deferring to the FDA's interpretation of its changes-being-effected and generic labeling regulations, the Court rejected the plaintiffs' claims that the manufacturers could have strengthened their labels either by using the FDA's CBE process, which allows manufacturers to change labels when needed, or by sending "Dear Doctor" letters providing additional warnings. Nonetheless, the Court assumed, for purposes of deciding this case, that federal law requires generic drug manufacturers to ask the FDA for assistance in convincing the brand-name manufacturer to adopt a stronger label if necessary.]

The Supremacy Clause establishes that federal law "shall be the supreme Law of the Land . . . any Thing in the Constitution or Laws of any State to the Contrary notwithstanding." U.S. Const., Art. VI, cl. 2. Where state and federal law "directly conflict," state law must give way. We have held that state and federal law conflict where it is "impossible for a private party to comply with both state and federal requirements."

We find impossibility here. . . . If the Manufacturers had independently changed their labels to satisfy their state-law duty, they would have violated federal law. . . . Federal law, however, demanded that generic drug labels be the same at all times as the corresponding brand-name drug labels.

The federal duty to ask the FDA for help in strengthening the corresponding brand-name label, assuming such a duty exists, does not change this analysis. Although requesting FDA assistance would have satisfied the Manufacturers' federal duty, it would not have satisfied their state tort-law duty to provide adequate labeling. State law demanded a safer label; it did not instruct the Manufacturers to communicate with the FDA about the possibility of a safer label.

. . . Thus, federal law would permit the Manufacturers to comply with the state labeling requirements if, and only if, the FDA and the brand-name manufacturer changed the brand-name label to do so.

[The plaintiffs] assert that when a private party's ability to comply with state law depends on approval and assistance from the FDA, proving pre-emption requires that party to demonstrate that the FDA would not have allowed compliance with state law. Here, they argue, the Manufacturers cannot bear their burden of proving impossibility because they did not even *try* to start the process that might ultimately have allowed them to use a safer label. This is a fair argument, but we reject it.

The question for "impossibility" is whether the private party could independently do under federal law what state law requires of it. . . . Accepting [the plaintiffs"] argument would render conflict pre-emption largely meaningless because it would make most conflicts between state and federal law illusory. We can often imagine that a third party or the Federal Government *might* do something that makes it lawful for a private party to accomplish under federal law what state law requires of it. . . .

CONTINUED

If these conjectures suffice to prevent federal and state law from conflicting for Supremacy Clause purposes, it is unclear when, outside of express pre-emption, the Supremacy Clause would have any force. We do not read the Supremacy Clause to permit an approach to pre-emption that renders conflict pre-emption all but meaningless. The Supremacy Clause, on its face, makes federal law "the supreme Law of the Land" even absent an express statement by Congress.

. . . To decide these cases, it is enough to hold that when a party cannot satisfy its state duties without the Federal Government's special permission and assistance, which is dependent on the exercise of judgment by a federal agency, that party cannot independently satisfy those state duties for pre-emption purposes.

We recognize that from the perspective of [the plaintiffs], finding pre-emption here but not in *Wyeth* makes little sense. Had [they] taken Reglan, the brand-name drug prescribed by their doctors, *Wyeth* would control and their lawsuits would not be pre-empted. But because pharmacists, acting in full accord with state law, substituted generic metoclopramide instead, federal law pre-empts these lawsuits. We acknowledge the unfortunate hand that federal drug regulation has dealt [the plaintiffs] and others similarly situate

But "it is not this Court's task to decide whether the statutory scheme established by Congress is unusual or even bizarre." . . . As always, Congress and the FDA retain the authority to change the law and regulations if they so desire.

RESULT   The decisions of both courts of appeals were reversed. The state-law failure-to-warn claims were preempted by federal law.

DISSENT   SOTOMAYOR, J., dissenting (joined by BREYER, GINSBURG, and KAGAN, JJ.):

The Court gets one thing right: This outcome "makes little sense."

. . . .

The Court today invokes the doctrine of impossibility pre-emption to hold that federal law immunizes generic-drug manufacturers from all state-law failure-to-warn claims because they cannot unilaterally change their labels. I cannot agree. We have traditionally held defendants claiming impossibility to a demanding standard: Until today, the mere possibility of impossibility had not been enough to establish pre-emption.

The Food and Drug Administration (FDA) permits—and, the Court assumes, requires—generic-drug manufacturers to propose a label change to the FDA when they believe that their labels are inadequate. If it agrees that the labels are inadequate, the FDA can initiate a change to the brand-name label, triggering a corresponding change to the generic labels. Once that occurs, a generic manufacturer is in full compliance with both federal law and a state-law duty to warn. Although generic manufacturers may be able to show impossibility in some cases, petitioners, generic manufacturers of metoclopramide (Manufacturers), have shown only that they *might* have been unable to comply with both federal law and their state-law duties to warn [the plaintiffs]. This, I would hold, is insufficient to sustain their burden.

The Court strains to reach the opposite conclusion. It invents new principles of pre-emption law out of thin air to justify its dilution of the impossibility standard. It effectively rewrites our decision in *Wyeth v. Levine*. . . . And a plurality of the Court tosses aside our repeated admonition that courts should hesitate to conclude that Congress intended to pre-empt state laws governing health and safety.

CRITICAL THINKING QUESTIONS

1. The FDA took the position that there was no federal preemption in this case. Why did the Court not give deference to that position?

2. What will be the likely effects of this decision on prescibing physicians, patients, and insurance companies? Has the Court promoted economic efficiency?

OTHER LEGISLATIVE LIMITS ON LIABILITY

Legislative reforms have changed many of the common law rules discussed earlier in this chapter. For example, a number of states have enacted legislation to limit non-manufacturers' liability and joint liability, cap punitive damages, deter frivolous suits, and limit the time within which a product liability suit may be brought.

Limitations on Nonmanufacturers' Liability

Rather than holding all companies in the chain of distribution liable, many state legislatures have limited the liability of nonmanufacturers. For example, a Minnesota statute provides that once an injured person files a claim against the manufacturer of the product, the court must, in most cases, dismiss the strict liability claims against any other defendants. A nonmanufacturer can still be held strictly liable, however, if it was involved in the design or manufacture of the product or provided instructions or warnings about the defect, or if it knew of or created the defect. The nonmanufacturer may also be held strictly liable if the manufacturer is no longer in business or cannot satisfy a judgment against it.[97]

An Illinois statute provides that an action against a defendant other than the manufacturer will be dismissed unless the plaintiff can show that (1) the defendant had some control over the design or manufacture of the product, or instructed or warned the manufacturer about the alleged defect; (2) the defendant actually knew of the defect; or (3) the defendant created the defect.[98]

---

97. MINN. STAT. § 544.41 (2010).
98. 735 ILL. COMP. STAT. ANN. § 5/2-621.

Limitations on Joint Liability

Traditionally, all defendants in a strict liability action were held jointly and severally liable. Each defendant was held liable not only for the injuries it severally—that is, individually—caused, but also for all of the injuries caused by the other defendants jointly. Thus, a firm such as USG Corporation, which had used asbestos in only a small subset of its products, was held jointly and severally liable for personal-injury claims asserted by workers who had been exposed to asbestos in products manufactured by other firms, such as Johns Manville and GAF, that were in bankruptcy and unable to pay their share of the liability.[99]

At least thirty-eight states have placed limits on joint and several liability, and many have abolished joint liability altogether.[100] For example, an Oregon statute limits joint and several liability as follows:

> Liability of each defendant for non-economic damages is several, not joint. Liability of a defendant who is less than 25 percent at fault for economic damages is several only. Liability of a defendant who is 25 percent or more at fault for the economic damages is joint and several, except that a defendant whose fault is less than the plaintiff's is liable only for that percentage of the recoverable economic damages.[101]

As noted earlier, "innocent" parties in the chain of distribution may, by contract, require indemnification from the co-defendants at fault for the product defect at issue. But, absent a limitation on joint liability, an indemnification provision will not relieve a member of the chain of distribution from its obligation to pay the share of any insolvent co-defendant.

---

99. *See* Constance E. Bagley & Eliot Sherman, *USG Corporation (A), (B), & (C)* (Harv. Bus. Sch.. Case Nos. 807-090, 807-120 & 807-121, 2007).
100. David Olsen, *Minnesota: Key Reform Bills Head for State Senate*, METROPOLITAN CORP. COUNS., Feb. 2000.
101. OR. REV. STAT. § 31.610.

POLITICAL | PERSPECTIVE

Lobbying for Limitations on Product Liability

Over the last several decades, U.S. businesses have taken steps to influence both the creation and the interpretation of product liability laws.

Companies can obtain legislative insulation by persuading lawmakers to include protection in the core of the bill or to attach a "rider" to another piece of legislation. For example, the SAFETY Act,[a] which promotes the development of anti-terrorism tools, (1) grants exclusive federal

CONTINUED

jurisdiction over sellers of "qualified anti-terrorism technology"; (2) limits the liability of sellers of qualified anti-terrorism technologies to an amount of liability insurance coverage specified for each individual technology; (3) prohibits joint and several liability for noneconomic damages, so sellers are liable only for the percentage of noneconomic damages that is proportionate to their responsibility for the harm; (4) bars punitive damages and prejudgment interest; and (5) creates a rebuttable presumption that the seller is entitled to the "government-contractor defense," provided that its "qualified anti-terrorism technology" is certified by the Department of Homeland Security as an "Approved Product for Homeland Security."

Riders are essentially add-ons and do not have to be related to the primary thrust of the bill. For example, under pressure from the White House, Congress added a rider to the Homeland Security Act of 2002[b] to protect drug companies from certain liability suits.[c]

Although firms in some industries (including light aircraft) have successfully lobbied for certain congressional limits on product liability, DaimlerChrysler assistant general counsel Stephen B. Hantler claimed that "the greatest return on investment is at the state level." By 2011, business groups had procured the following victories at the state level:

- Limits on punitive damages (32 states).

- Limits on pain and suffering damages (23 states).

- Restrictions on class-action lawsuits (10 states).

- Reduction in size of bonds needed to appeal a verdict (38 states).

- Bar on ability of out-of-state plaintiffs to file suit in a jurisdiction with which they have no connection (8 states).[d]

In addition, Michigan now severely restricts consumers' ability to initiate litigation against pharmaceutical companies in that state, and six states allow only a few select types of asbestos suits.[e] Statehouse lobbyists have also pushed to make it harder for affluent individuals to avoid jury duty.[f]

Business representatives have also sought to extend their influence to the state courtrooms where most product liability cases are heard. More than half of the states elect their judges, and corporate interest groups have actively supported the campaigns of those candidates seen as sympathetic to business interests.[g] For example, in 2006 candidates for the position of chief justice of the Alabama Supreme Court received more than $8 million in contributions from business and nonbusiness interests.[h] Overall, contributions to state supreme court candidates rose from $83 million in the 1990s to more than $206 million in the period from 2000 to 2009.[i]

In the 1990s, while George W. Bush was governor of Texas, his aide (and subsequent White House deputy chief of staff) Karl Rove was instrumental in shifting the makeup of the Texas Supreme Court from 100% Democratic to 100% Republican.[j] In 2004, business groups outspent plaintiffs' lawyers in the Texas State Supreme Court elections for the first time ($21.5 million in campaign contributions from the business groups versus $13.3 million from the plaintiffs' bar).[k] The Texas courts have made it increasingly difficult for plaintiffs to bring mass-injury class actions, and big jury verdicts have become more vulnerable on appeal. During its 2005-2006 term, the Texas Supreme Court ruled against consumers in 83% of the cases.[l] Frederick M. Baron, a Dallas plaintiffs' attorney specializing in asbestos and industrial toxin cases, remarked, "When you have a large verdict that you receive from a jury,

you can't settle the case anymore because the defendants will walk in and say: 'We know we're going to win in the Supreme Court.'"[m]

Federal judges are appointed, but that does not eliminate the possibility of corporate influence. The U.S. Chamber of Commerce, which has spent an estimated $21 million lobbying influential federal policymakers—from White House staffers to members of Congress to regulating agency officials—endorses U.S. Supreme Court candidates and lobbies for their nomination.[n] For example, the Chamber ardently supported President George W. Bush's Court appointees Chief Justice John Roberts and Justice Samuel Alito.[o]

a. Support Antiterrorism by Fostering Effective Technologies Act, Pub. L. No. 107-296, §§ 861–865, 116 Stat. 2238 (2002). *See also* 6 C.F.R. pt. 25.3.

b. Pub. L. No. 107-296, 116 Stat. 2229 (2002).

c. Dan Morgan, *Homeland Bill Rider Aids Drugmakers; Measure Would Block Suits over Vaccines, FBI Powers Would Also Grow*, Wash. Post, Nov. 15, 2002, at A7.

d. Harvey L. Kaplan & Jon A. Strongman, *Developments in U.S. Product Liability and Issues Related to Foreign Manufacturers*, Practical Law Co., Aug. 1, 2011, http://us.practicallaw.com/6-501-9379#a733973.

e. Michael Orey, *How Business Trounced the Trial Lawyers*, Bus. Wk., Jan. 8, 2007, at 44.

f. Lorraine Woellert, *Tort Reform: A Little Here, a Little There*, Bus. Wk., Jan. 8, 2003, at 60.

g. Mike France & Lorraine Woellert, *The Battle over the U.S. Courts*, Bus. Wk., Sept. 27, 2004, at 36.

h. Robert Barnes, *Judicial Races Now Rife with Politics*, Wash. Post, Oct. 28, 2007, at A1.

i. Bryant Furlow, *Campaign Contributions to Judges Skyrocket Across U.S.*, N.M. Indep., Aug. 16, 2010, *available at* http://newmexicoindependent.com/61710/campaign-contributions-to-judges-skyrocket-across-u-s.

j. Orey, *supra* note d.

k. *Id.*

l. *Id.*

m. Quoted in *id.*, at 49–50.

n. Jeffrey Rosen, *Supreme Court, Inc.*, N.Y. Times, Mar. 16, 2008, at MM38.

o. *Id.*

Caps on Punitive Damages

Large awards of punitive damages by U.S. juries have been criticized for providing windfalls to injured parties far in excess of their actual losses and for motivating plaintiffs and their lawyers to engage in expensive and wasteful litigation rather than settling cases. Both legislatures and courts have sought to solve this problem by capping punitive damages.

More than thirty states have enacted legislation limiting punitive damages awards. These reforms have typically taken three basic forms. Certain states have either limited the availability of punitive damages or require a higher standard of proof (such as clear and convincing evidence rather than a mere preponderance of evidence) before punitives will be awarded; a few states have done both. For example, North Dakota requires plaintiffs to prove oppression, fraud, or actual malice before claiming punitive damages.[102] Other states have placed outright caps on punitive damages (Georgia, for instance, caps punitives at $250,000)[103] or have tied punitive damages to compensatory damages (in Florida, for example, punitives cannot exceed three times compensatory damages).[104] Finally, a few states (such as New Hampshire) have banned punitive awards altogether.[105]

As discussed in Chapter 4, the Supreme Court has also limited punitive damage awards.

Penalties for Frivolous Suits

Some states have enacted penalties to deter frivolous lawsuits. For example, a Wisconsin statute provides that if a claim or defense is found to be frivolous, the prevailing party can be awarded its legal costs and attorneys' fees.[106] Minnesota and North Dakota have similar statutes.[107]

Statutes of Limitations

A *statute of limitations* is a time limit, set by statute, within which a lawsuit must be brought. Ordinarily, the statute of limitations starts to run at the time a person is injured. There are exceptions, however.

Discovery-of-Injury and Revival Statutes

In many cases involving exposure to certain products, such as asbestos, the plaintiff did not become aware of the injury until after the statute of limitations had run out. This situation led to the adoption of *discovery-of-injury statutes*, which generally provide that the statute of limitations for asbestos and certain other claims does not begin to run until the person discovers the injury from exposure to asbestos.

When information about the prenatal injuries caused by the drug DES emerged, state legislatures passed *revival statutes* permitting plaintiffs to file lawsuits that had previously been barred by the running of the statute of limitations. DES manufacturers unsuccessfully argued that the revival statutes violated their rights to due process of law and to equal protection of the laws because the statutes typically apply to only a few substances, such as DES or asbestos, and not to other dangerous chemical substances. Most courts rejected these arguments and held that state revival statutes have a rational basis and that legislatures enacting such statutes are acting within their broad discretion.[108] More recently, revival statutes were enacted to extend the time in which women may sue for injuries caused by silicone breast implants.

As injuries are increasingly being discovered long after exposure, many states have amended their statutes of limitations to define more precisely when a cause of action arises. For example, the Ohio statute provides that:

- An asbestos cause of action arises when the claimant learns or should have realized that he or she was injured by exposure to asbestos, whichever is earlier.

- An Agent Orange cause of action involving exposure of a veteran to chemical defoliants or herbicides arises when the claimant learns that he or she was injured by the exposure.

- A DES drug cause of action arises when the claimant learns from a physician that her injury might be related to her prenatal DES exposure or when she should have realized that she had such an injury, whichever is earlier.[109]

Statutes of Repose

A *statute of repose* cuts off the right to assert a cause of action after a specified period of time from the delivery of the product. A statute of repose is different from a statute of limitations, which measures the time period from the time when the injury occurred. Thus, under a ten-year statute of repose, a person injured eleven years after the product was delivered would be time-barred from suing by the statute of repose, though not by the statute of limitations.

For example, Cessna and other light airplane manufacturers lobbied Congress hard for the General Aviation Revitalization Act, which was enacted in 1994. The Act created an eighteen-year statute of repose, which limited an aircraft manufacturer's liability for performance of an aircraft after the first eighteen years of the aircraft's life. Because the average aircraft was thirty years old in 1994, the Act significantly limited the product liability exposure of aircraft manufacturers.[110] A fifteen-year statute of

102. N.D. Cent. Code § 32-03.2-11.

103. Ga. Code Ann. § 51-12-5.1(g).

104. Fla. Stat. § 768.73(1).

105. *E.g.,* N.H. Rev. Stat. Ann. § 507:16.

106. Wis. Stat. § 802.05.

107. Minn. Stat. § 11.03; N.D. Civ. P. R. 11.

108. *See, e.g.,* Hymowitz v. Eli Lilly & Co., 539 N.E.2d 1069 (N.Y. 1989).

109. Ohio Rev. Code Ann. § 2305.10.

110. Allen Michel et al., *Protecting Future Product Liability Claimants,* Am. Bankr. Inst. J., Dec. 1999, at 3–4.

repose in Texas barred a lawsuit against the manufacturer of a Houston hospital elevator that had decapitated a physician because the elevator was more than fifteen years old at the time of the accident.[111]

Statutes of repose have usually been upheld on the ground that they serve a legitimate state purpose, such as encouraging manufacturers to upgrade their products. Absent a statute of repose, a manufacturer might not upgrade, out of fear that upgrading might be seen as an admission that the earlier version was inadequate.

Useful Life Statutes

Some states have enacted useful life statutes. *Useful life statutes* are similar to statutes of limitation and repose in that they provide manufacturers and sellers some protection from liability after a particular period of time has expired, but they differ in that they define that period as the length of time a product is expected to safely provide utility to the user. Furthermore, these laws do not absolutely eliminate liability. Instead, useful life statutes establish a rebuttable presumption about how long consumers can continue safely using a product.

---

111. Michael Orey, *How Business Trounced the Trial Lawyers*, Bus. Wk., Jan. 8, 2007, at 44.

EXHIBIT 10.1 **Summary of Defenses**

Theory of Liability	Defenses
Breach of warranty	No privity of contract
	Statute of limitations
Negligence	Defendant used reasonable care
	Contributory or comparative negligence
	Preemption
	Statute of limitations
	Assumption of risk
Strict liability in tort	Unavoidably unsafe product
	Comparative fault (only reduces damages)
	Assumption of risk
	Obvious risk
	Sophisticated user
	Abnormal misuse
	Government contractor
	State of the art
	Preemption
	Statute of repose
	Useful life statute

© Cengage Learning 2013

The details of the statutes vary significantly. For example, Idaho statutorily defines the same presumptive ten-year lifetime for all products,[112] but Minnesota requires a multifactor analysis to determine the useful life of the product at issue.[113] Other states combine useful life and statute of repose concepts in legislation limiting product liability.

Exhibit 10.1 summarizes the defenses available for product cases based on breach of warranty, negligence, and strict liability.

TOBACCO, GUNS, AND BIG FOOD

Plaintiffs' lawyers have targeted tobacco, guns, and, more recently, fatty and high-calorie foods for high stakes product liability litigation.

Tobacco

One of the most dramatic applications of product liability law has been the lawsuits against tobacco companies for illness, death, and medical expenses resulting from the use of tobacco or from secondhand smoke. In 1998, forty-six of the fifty states that had filed claims to recover billions they had spent on health-care costs related to smoking settled with the tobacco industry for $206 billion—the largest civil settlement in U.S. history.[114] The remaining four states had previously entered into settlements with tobacco companies totaling $40 billion. In 2000, the U.S. government softened its stance against tobacco. Instead of trying to recover $280 billion in profits from the tobacco companies for their alleged wrongful acts, the government sought $14 billion to pay for antismoking campaigns and programs to help current smokers quit. In 2006, the U.S. District Court for the District of Columbia ruled that Philip Morris, its parent Altria, and other cigarette companies had violated the civil provisions of the Racketeer Influenced and Corrupt Organization Act (RICO) but refused to order the companies to pay the $14 billion requested by the federal government. The U.S. Court of Appeals for the District of Columbia upheld that ruling in 2009, and the U.S. Supreme Court denied Philip Morris's petition for certiorari in 2010.[115]

Individual plaintiffs have successfully pursued their cases as well. In early 2008, the Oregon Supreme Court reinstated for a third time an award of nearly $80 million in punitive damages to an Oregon widow whose husband died of lung cancer brought on by smoking.[116] The

---

112. Idaho Code Ann. § 6-1403.

113. Minn. Stat. § 604.03.

114. Milo Geyelin, *States Agree to $206 Billion Tobacco Deal*, Wall St. J., Nov. 23, 1998, at B13.

115. United States v. Philip Morris USA, Inc., 449 F. Supp. 2d 1 (D.D.C. 2006), *aff'd in part & vacated in part*, 566 F.3d 1095 (D.C. Cir. 2009), *cert. denied*, 130 S. Ct. 3501 (2010).

116. *Oregon High Court Upholds $80M Award in Philip Morris Case*, Dow Jones Newswires, Jan. 31, 2008.

U.S. Supreme Court had twice sent the case back to the Oregon court for reconsideration of the punitive damages award.[117]

But in 2008 an intermediate appellate court in New York reversed a judgment awarding $3.4 million in compensatory damages and $17.1 million in punitive damages to a seventy-three-year-old lung cancer victim.[118] The court ruled that the plaintiff had failed to prove that Brown & Williamson Holdings and Philip Morris negligently designed cigarettes by continuing to market regular cigarettes with higher levels of tar and nicotine than so-called light cigarettes. The court rejected the plaintiff's assertion that a cigarette's function is merely "to be lit, burned, and inhaled," finding instead that individuals smoke for the taste and psychological effects of nicotine and tar. Under New York law, a manufacturer cannot be held liable for declining to "adopt an alternative product design that has not been shown to retain the 'inherent usefulness' the product offers when manufactured according to the more risky (but otherwise lawful) design that was actually used." The court concluded that the plaintiff had failed to prove that lower-tar, low-nicotine cigarettes would "have been acceptable to consumers that constitute the market for the allegedly defective product [regular cigarettes]." The dissenting judges argued that the test of consumer acceptability amounted to "nothing more than a cynical effort by the [tobacco companies] to maintain the commercial advantages of continuing to sell unreasonably dangerous addictive products to addicts."

In a set of class-action suits, plaintiff smokers claimed that tobacco companies had deceptively promoted low-tar "light" cigarettes as healthier alternatives to regular cigarettes while knowing that this was not true.[119] They were seeking more than $100 billion in compensation. The U.S. Second Circuit held that the plaintiffs could not establish loss causation—that is, proximate causation—on a classwide basis, so they could not bring the case as a class action.[120] In 2009, Congress passed the Federal Family Smoking Prevention and Tobacco Control Act, giving the FDA the power to regulate tobacco products by stopping youth-focused marketing, banning candy-flavored cigarettes, prohibiting misleading marketing, requiring full disclosure of ingredients, and strengthening warning label requirements. It also requires the nicotine levels in cigarettes to be reduced.[121]

The United States is not the only country where the tobacco industry faces legal problems. Litigation in India and Uganda has led to smoking bans and limits on cigarette advertising.[122] The governments of Guatemala, Nicaragua, and Venezuela unsuccessfully filed claims in the federal district court in Washington, D.C., in an effort to recover health-care expenses related to smoking.[123] Similar suits have been filed in the courts of other countries. In addition, individual suits have been brought against the tobacco industry in a number of countries, including Argentina, Canada, Germany, Ireland, Israel, Japan, Sri Lanka, Thailand, and Turkey. In addition to civil proceedings, government officials in Canada and Colombia have alleged that tobacco companies committed crimes by participating in smuggling and money laundering activities.[124]

Guns

After the enormous success of the litigation against the tobacco industry, cities and counties launched a similar attack against the gun industry. Unlike the tobacco industry, however, which has companies with deep pockets and vast assets to satisfy claims for damages, the gun industry comprises generally small, mostly privately held companies with annual sales of only $2.5 billion.[125] Nuisance suits against gun manufacturers are discussed in Chapter 9.

In early 2000, two Clinton administration lawyers—the deputy general counsel of Housing and Urban Development and the general counsel at the Treasury Department, which helped oversee the Bureau of Alcohol, Tobacco and Firearms—presented a list of gun-control demands to Ed Schultz, the CEO of Smith & Wesson Corporation. Smith & Wesson, a unit of Britain's Tomkins PLC, is America's largest maker of handguns. Schultz initially responded by asking one of the lawyers how old he was. When the lawyer answered that he was thirty-four years old, Schultz said, "If you live a good long life, you will not live to see this proposal happen." Two months later, however, Smith & Wesson agreed to a settlement based on that initial proposal. In particular, Smith & Wesson agreed to make a number of changes, including the following:

- All guns would be shipped with external child safety locks.

---

117. Philip Morris v. Williams, 549 U.S. 346 (2007).

118. Rose v. Brown & Williamson Tobacco Corp., 855 N.Y.S.2d 119 (N.Y. App. Div. 2008).

119. Lorraine Woellert, Jane Sasseen & Nanette Byrnes, *Tobacco May Be Partying Too Soon*, Bus. Wk., July 24, 2006, at 26.

120. Schwab v. Phillip Morris USA, Inc., 449 F. Supp. 2d 92 (E.D.N.Y. 2006), *rev'd*, McLaughlin v. Am. Tobacco Co., 522 F.3d 215 (2d Cir. 2008).

121. Press Release, The White House, Fact Sheet: The Family Smoking Prevention and Tobacco Control Act of 2009 (June 22, 2009), *available at* http://whitehouse.gov/the_press_office/Fact-sheet-and-expected-attendees-for-todays-Rose-Garden-bill-signing.

122. *Oregon High Court, supra* note 116.

123. In 1999, the U.S. District Court for the District of Columbia dismissed Guatemala's claim, finding that the harms were "too remote." *In re* Tobacco/Governmental Health Care Costs Litig., 83 F. Supp. 2d 125 (D.C.C. 1999). In 2002, the remainder of these cases were dismissed by a Florida state court for failure to state a claim. Republic of Venezuela v. Philip Morris Co., 827 So. 2d 332 (Fla. App. 3 Dist. 2002).

124. Richard A. Daynard et al., *Litigants Worldwide Blaming Then Branding Big Tobacco in Court*, WORLDPAPER, June 1, 2000.

125. Paul Barrett, *As Lawsuits Loom, Gun Industry Presents a Fragmented Front*, WALL ST. J., Dec. 9, 1998, at A1.

- Within two years, all pistols would be manufactured with internal safety locks.

- Within one year, all firearms would be made child-proof.

- Handguns would have to pass a stringent performance test.

- The company would devote 2% of its gross revenues to developing a "smart" gun that can be fired only by its owner.

The company also agreed to develop a code of conduct for its dealers and distributors that would require background checks on purchases and would forbid sales to anyone who had not passed a safety exam or taken a training class.

Commentators compared Smith & Wesson's settlement with Liggett Group's decision to break ranks with the other tobacco companies and settle its tobacco cases. But whereas Liggett was a small tobacco company, Smith & Wesson was one of the most powerful companies in the gun industry. Eliot Spitzer, the New York attorney general involved in designing the Smith & Wesson settlement, commented, "The idea all along was that one responsible company would break away from the rest of the industry and that would be leverage to use against the rest."[126]

More recently, however, gun-control advocates have experienced setbacks. As discussed in Chapter 9, the Protection of Lawful Commerce in Arms Act,[127] state statutes, and judicial setbacks have made it even harder for plaintiffs' lawyers to hold gun manufacturers liable for deaths and injuries caused by gun fire. As discussed in Chapter 4, the U.S. Supreme Court invalidated the D.C. law prohibiting handguns and requiring trigger locks or similar devices on firearms in the home[128] and then struck down the Chicago law banning the possession of handguns.[129]

Food

As discussed in the "Inside Story" in Chapter 1, "Big Food" has come under fire for selling fatty and high-calorie foods, ranging from Big Macs and fries at McDonald's to sugar-laden sodas in schools. New York City became the first major U.S. city to ban trans fats in restaurants and to require restaurants to provide written nutritional information for each item on the menu. Although the plaintiffs lost most of the early cases alleging

that fast foods caused them to gain weight and to develop diabetes and related conditions, cases based on failure to warn and misleading advertising targeted at children might ultimately have a greater likelihood of success.

PROBLEMS WITH THE PRODUCT LIABILITY SYSTEM AND THE RESTATEMENT (THIRD) APPROACH TO DESIGN DEFECTS AND FAILURES TO WARN

Although strict product liability is predicated on the assumption that manufacturers are in the best position to insure against loss or to spread the risk of loss among their customers, in practice, insurance policies often are available only with a substantial deductible, if at all. This leads to increased manufacturing costs and higher prices.

The strict product liability scheme also takes its toll on industry efficiency and competitiveness. Companies have become unwilling to invest in product creation or modification because this may be seen as an admission of fault. In most jurisdictions, product modification is admissible as evidence of the product's prior defective condition. Companies find themselves in a no-win situation: failing to remedy a defect may expose the company to punitive damages in a negligence case, but remedying the defect may expose the company to compensatory damages in subsequent suits.

Informed by these concerns, the American Law Institute (ALI) approved the Restatement (Third) of Torts: Products Liability in 1997. The new restatement proposed bold changes in the doctrine of product liability. As noted earlier, however, no court is bound by the restatement's formulation of product liability law. As of 2011, only a minority of states had adopted the Restatement (Third) approach, either in whole or in part.[130]

Design Defects and the Reasonable-Alternative-Design Requirement

Instead of imposing strict liability for defectively designed products, the Restatement (Third) requires that any claim of design defect be supported by a showing of a reasonable alternative design.

In the following case, the South Carolina Supreme Court considered whether to accept the Restatement (Third)'s *reasonable-alternative-design requirement* or permit a plaintiff to recover for a design defect based on the consumer expectations test.

126. Paul M. Barrett, Vanessa O'Connell & Joe Mathews, *Glock May Accept Handgun Restrictions—Austrian Firm May Follow Lead of Smith & Wesson to Avoid U.S. Sanctions*, WALL ST. J., Mar. 20, 2000, at A3.

127. The U.S. Court of Appeals for the Second Circuit upheld the constitutionality of the Act in *New York City v. Beretta U.S.A. Corp.*, 524 F.3d 384 (2d Cir. 2008).

128. District of Columbia v. Heller, 554 U.S. 570 (2008).

129. McDonald v. City of Chicago, 130 S. Ct. 3020 (2010) (extended *Heller* to the states).

130. George W. Conk, *Punctuated Equilibrium: Why Section 402A Flourished and the Third Restatement Languished*, 26 REV. LITIG. 799, 840–43 (2007).

| A CASE IN POINT | *In the Language of the Court* | Case 10.5 |

Branham v. Ford Motor Co.

Supreme Court of South Carolina
701 S.E.2d 5 (S.C. 2010).

FACTS   Jesse Branham III, a passenger in a Bronco 4×2 truck driven by Cheryl Hale, was injured when the truck rolled over, throwing him out of the vehicle. No one was wearing a seat belt. Hale had taken her eyes off the road to turn toward the backseat to quiet the children sitting there. When the right rear wheel left the road, Hale overcorrected to the left, causing the truck to roll over. Branham sued Hale for negligence and Ford Motor Company for negligence and strict liability. He alleged that Ford's failure to install a different suspension system constituted a design defect. Ford engineers had criticized the Bronco's Twin I-Beam design and suggested more stable (but also more expensive) alternatives. The jury returned a verdict against Hale and Ford for $16 million in actual damages and $15 million in punitive damages. Ford appealed.

ISSUE PRESENTED   Should South Carolina adopt the Restatement (Third) approach to design defects, which requires the plaintiff to show the existence of a reasonable alternative design before a product will be deemed unreasonably dangerous, or permit recovery based on the consumer expectations test?

OPINION   KITTRIDGE, J., writing on behalf of the South Carolina Supreme Court:

We next address Ford's two-fold argument that: (1) Branham failed to prove a reasonable alternative design pursuant to the risk-utility test; and (2) South Carolina law requires a risk-utility test in design defect cases to the exclusion of the consumer expectations test.

For a plaintiff to successfully advance a design defect claim, he must show that the design of the product caused it to be "unreasonably dangerous." In South Carolina, we have traditionally employed two tests to determine whether a product was unreasonably dangerous as a result of a design defect: (1) the consumer expectations test and (2) the risk-utility test.

In *Claytor v. General Motors Corp.*,[131] this Court phrased the consumer expectations test as follows: "The test of whether a product is or is not defective is whether the product is unreasonably dangerous to the consumer or user given the conditions and circumstances that foreseeably attend use of the product."

The *Claytor* Court articulated the risk-utility test in the following manner: "[N]umerous factors must be considered [when determining whether a product is unreasonably dangerous], including the usefulness and desirability of the product, the cost involved for added safety, the likelihood and potential seriousness of injury, and the obviousness of danger."

Ford contends Branham failed to present evidence of a feasible alternative design. Implicit in Ford's argument is the contention that a product may only be shown to be defective and unreasonably dangerous by way of a risk-utility test, for by its very nature, the risk-utility test requires a showing of a reasonable alternative design. Branham counters, arguing that under *Claytor* he may prove a design defect by resort to the consumer expectations test or the risk-utility test. Branham also argues that regardless of which test is required, he has met both, including evidence of a feasible alternative design. We agree with Branham's contention that he produced evidence of a feasible alternative design. Branham additionally points out that the jury was charged on the consumer expectations test *and* the risk-utility test.

As discussed above, Branham challenged the design of the Ford Bronco II by pointing to the MacPherson suspension as a reasonable alternative design. A former Ford vice president, Thomas Feaheny, testified that the MacPherson suspension system would have significantly increased the handling and stability of the Bronco II, making it less prone to rollovers. Branham's expert, Dr. Richardson, also noted that the MacPherson suspension system would have enhanced vehicle stability by lowering the vehicle center of gravity. There was further evidence that the desired sport utility features of the Bronco II would not have been compromised by

CONTINUED

131. 286 S.E.2d 129, 131 (S.C. 1982).

using the MacPherson suspension. Moreover, there is evidence that use of the MacPherson suspension would not have increased costs. Whether this evidence satisfies the risk-utility test is ultimately a jury question. But it is evidence of a feasible alternative design, sufficient to survive a directed verdict motion.

While the consumer expectations test fits well in manufacturing defect cases, we do agree with Ford that the test is ill-suited in design defect cases. We hold today that the exclusive test in a products liability design case is the risk-utility test with its requirement of showing a feasible alternative design. In doing so, we recognize our Legislature's presence in the area of strict liability for products liability.

In 1974, our Legislature adopted the *Restatement (Second) of Torts* § 402A (1965), and identified its comments as legislative intent.[132]. . . Since the adoption of section 402A, the American Law Institute published the *Restatement (Third) of Torts: Products Liability* (1998). The third edition effectively moved away from the consumer expectations test for design defects, and towards a risk-utility test. We believe the Legislature's foresight in looking to the American Law Institute for guidance in this area is instructive.

The Legislature has expressed no intention to foreclose court consideration of developments in products liability law. For example, this Court's approval of the risk-utility test in *Claytor* yielded no legislative response. We thus believe the adoption of the risk-utility test in design defect cases in no manner infringes on the Legislature's presence in this area. Some form of a risk-utility test is employed by an overwhelming majority of the jurisdictions in this country. Some of these jurisdictions exclusively employ a risk-utility test, while others do so with a hybrid of the risk-utility and the consumer expectations test, or an explicit either-or option. States that exclusively employ the consumer expectations test are a decided minority.

We believe that in design defect cases the risk-utility test provides the best means for analyzing whether a product is designed defectively. Unlike the consumer expectations test, the focus of a risk-utility test centers upon the alleged defectively designed product. The risk-utility test provides objective factors for a trier of fact to analyze when presented with a challenge to a manufacturer's design. Conversely, we find the consumer expectations test and its focus on the consumer ill-suited to determine whether a product's design is unreasonably dangerous.

. . . .

. . . The very nature of feasible alternative design evidence entails the manufacturer's decision to employ one design over another. This weighing of costs and benefits attendant to that decision is the essence of the risk-utility test.

This approach is in accord with the current edition of the Restatement of Torts:

> A product . . . is defective in design when the foreseeable risks of harm posed by the product could have been reduced or avoided by the adoption of a reasonable alternative design by the seller or other distributor, or a predecessor in the commercial chain of distribution, and the omission of the alternative design renders the product not reasonably safe.[133]

In every design defect case the central recurring fact will be a product that failed causing damage to a person or his property. Consequently, the focus will be whether the product was made safe enough. This inquiry is the core of the risk-utility balancing test in design defect cases, yet we do not suggest a jury question is created merely because a product can be made safer. We adhere to our longstanding approval of the principle that a product is not in a

CONTINUED

---

132. S.C. Code Ann. §§ 15-73-10–30 (2005).

133. Restatement (Third) of Torts: Products Liability § 2(b) (1998).

defective condition unreasonably dangerous merely because it "can be made more safe." As we observed in *Marchant v. Mitchell Distributing Co.*

> Most any product can be made more safe. Automobiles would be more safe with disc brakes and steel-belted radial tires than with ordinary brakes and ordinary tires, but this does not mean that an automobile dealer would be held to have sold a defective product merely because the most safe equipment is not installed. By a like token, a bicycle is more safe if equipped with lights and a bell, but the fact that one is not so equipped does not create the inference that the bicycle is defective and unreasonably dangerous.[134]

. . . .

In sum, in a product liability design defect action, the plaintiff must present evidence of a reasonable alternative design. The plaintiff will be required to point to a design flaw in the product and show how his alternative design would have prevented the product from being unreasonably dangerous. This presentation of an alternative design must include consideration of the costs, safety and functionality associated with the alternative design. On retrial, Branham's design defect claim will proceed pursuant to the risk-utility test and not the consumer expectations test.

III

Notwithstanding the existence of ample evidence to withstand a directed verdict motion on the handling and stability design defect claim, we reverse and remand for a new trial. There are three reasons we reverse and remand the finding of liability and award of actual damages. First, this case implicates two evidentiary rules related to products liability cases. The first rule provides that whether a product is defective must be measured against information known at the time the product was placed into the stream of commerce. When a claim is asserted against a manufacturer, post-manufacture evidence is generally not admissible. The second rule provides that evidence of similar incidents is admissible where there is a substantial similarity between the other incidents and the accident in dispute tending to prove or disprove some fact in controversy. Evidence was introduced that violated both of these rules. Third, Branham's closing argument was a direct appeal to the passion and prejudice of the jury. And although not a standalone ground for reversal, we find that because Ford and Hale were joint tortfeasors, it was error to require the jury to apportion responsibility between the defendants.

RESULT   The state supreme court overturned the jury verdict and ordered a new trial. To prevail in the new trial, the plaintiff would have to show a reasonable alternative design.

CRITICAL THINKING QUESTIONS

1. How do the approaches of the Restatement (Second) and the Restatement (Third) differ?
2. Should the plaintiff or the defendant have the burden of proving the existence of a reasonable alternative design?

134. 240 S.E.2d 511 (S.C. 1977).

© Cengage Learning 2013

Failure to Warn of Foreseeable Risks or to Provide Reasonable Instructions

In failure-to-warn cases, the Restatement (Third) embodied the majority view that defendants are liable only if they failed to warn of risks that were foreseeable at the time of sale.[135] It further interjected a negligence standard by providing that a product "is defective because of inadequate instructions or warnings when the foreseeable risks of harm posed by the product could have been reduced or avoided by the provision of *reasonable* instructions or warnings by the [defendant], . . . and the omission of the instructions or warnings renders the product not reasonably safe."[136]

135. *See, e.g.*, Powers v. Taser Int'l, Inc., 174 P.3d 777 (Ariz. Ct. App. 2007) (defendant is not liable for failure to warn against risks that were unforeseeable at the time of sale).

136. RESTATEMENT (THIRD) OF TORTS: PRODUCTS LIABILITY § 2(c) (1998) (emphasis added).

GLOBAL VIEW

Product Liability in the European Union

In 1985, after nearly a decade of debate, the Council of Ministers of the European Union (EU) adopted a product liability directive designed to provide increased consumer protection and to harmonize competitive conditions within the EU.[137] The directive's basic purpose is to hold manufacturers strictly liable for injuries caused by defects in their products. This represented a fundamental change for manufacturers of products marketed in Europe. Traditionally, injured consumers in most of the member states had to prove both negligence and privity of contract in order to recover damages from the producer of a defective product. Only France had previously imposed strict product liability.

The directive does not apply to services, which continue to be governed solely by national law. In June 1999, following separate outbreaks of mad cow disease, *E. coli*, and salmonella, the European Commission adopted an amendment to the 1985 directive that extended product liability to cover agricultural products.[138] The European Commission decided to leave the directive unchanged in 2006, after finding that its goals were being accomplished.[139] The European Commission revisited the directive in 2011 and again left it unchanged, but indicated that it would follow any developments closely to determine whether any changes were needed in its next report.[140]

Comparison with U.S. Strict Liability

The liability of manufacturers under the EU product liability directive is very similar to the strict liability doctrine applied in most of the United States. To recover damages, an injured party has to prove the existence of a defect, an injury, and a causal relationship between the defect and the injury. (Plaintiffs may also sue under the traditional negligence and contract laws of the EU member states.) In determining whether a product is defective, courts in the EU countries, like those in the United States, consider such factors as the product's foreseeable uses and the instructions and warnings provided by the manufacturer.

Unlike in the United States, however, a supplier or wholesaler is not strictly liable unless the injured party is unable to identify the manufacturer. In this instance, the supplier can escape liability by informing the injured person of the manufacturer's identity. Like the Restatement (Third), the directive provides for a "development risks" or state-of-the-art defense. A producer can escape liability by proving that the state of scientific knowledge when the product went into circulation was insufficient to allow it to discover the defect.

Other available defenses are similar to those available in most jurisdictions in the United States. For example, a manufacturer will not be liable if (1) the manufacturer did not put the product into circulation, (2) the defect did not exist when the product went into circulation, (3) the product was a component that was neither manufactured nor distributed by the manufacturer of the overall product, or (4) the defect was due to compliance of the product with mandatory regulations. The manufacturer of a component part will not be liable if the defect was attributable to the overall design of the product into which the component was fitted.

The directive includes both a statute of limitations and a statute of repose. An injured person must sue within three years of when he or she knew, or should have known, of the injury, the defect, and the manufacturer's identity. A manufacturer's liability will be extinguished ten years after the product was put into circulation, unless the injured party has commenced proceedings in the meantime. Thus, as in certain states in the United States, a defect that does not become manifest until eleven years after the product went into circulation may leave the injured person without a remedy. Most EU member states previously had thirty-year statutes of repose.

Importers of products into the EU are strictly liable under the directive. Thus, U.S. exporters may be required to indemnify overseas importers. It is important for U.S. exporters to carry product liability insurance that covers lawsuits in the EU and to adhere to EU safety standards.

137. 1985 O.J. (L 210) 29.

138. John R. Schmertz, Jr. & Mike Meier, *EU Amends Product Liability Directive to Include Agricultural Products*, INT'L L. UPDATE, June 1999.

139. Report from the Commission to the Council, the European Parliament and the European Economic and Social Committee: Third report on the application of Council Directive on the approximation of laws, regulations and administrative provisions of the Member States concerning liability for defective products (85/374/EEC of 25 July 1985, amended by Directive 1999/34/EC of the European Parliament and of the Council of 10 May 1999), COM(2006) 496 final, *available at* http://ec.europa.eu/prelex/detail_dossier_real.cfm?CL=en&DosId=194649.

140. Report from the Commission to the European Parliament, the Council and the European Economic and Social Committee: Fourth report on the application of Council Directive 85/374/EEC of 25 July 1985 on the approximation of the laws, regulations and administrative provisions of the Member States concerning liability for defective products amended by Directive 1999/34/EC of the European Parliament and of the Council of 10 May 1999, *available at* http://eur-lex.europa.eu/LexUriServ/LexUriServ.do?uri=COM:2011:0547:FIN:EN:PDF.

THE RESPONSIBLE MANAGER

REDUCING PRODUCT LIABILITY RISK

Managers have a responsibility to their customers and investors to minimize their company's exposure to liability in the design, manufacture, assembly, and use of its products. Legally astute managers will implement a product safety program to ensure that products are sold in a legally safe condition and will take appropriate steps to discover and correct any defects that may come to light after the product is sold. The goal should be to prevent injuries. If an accident does occur, evidence of a product safety program is crucial for limiting the manufacturer's liability for punitive damages and containing damage to the brand.

Managers should ensure that their products are performing as intended over the lives of the products and that the products have as little adverse effect on the environment as possible under current technology. It is helpful to establish a product safety committee and to conduct regular safety audits to identify and correct problems. The advice of experienced counsel can be helpful in this area.

Managers should have a thorough understanding of all statutes, regulations, and administrative rulings to which a product must conform. Failure of the product to comply with any of these rules will typically be deemed a product defect. Mere conformance with these rules is considered a minimum requirement, however, and does not automatically release a manufacturer from liability.

To protect against potential liabilities, managers should implement internal loss-control procedures, obtain adequate insurance protection, and seek the advice of product liability counsel from the earliest stages of product development. If a product carries risks even with normal use, warnings must be provided to consumers. Managers should make sure that contracts properly disclaim and limit product liability and, to the extent possible, include indemnification provisions, particularly if the product will be used as a component part by another manufacturer. If the firm is acquiring another company, managers should examine potential product liability exposure created by the purchase. With the variety of jurisdictional approaches to successor liability, managers should seek legal advice to help them assess and structure the acquisition.

Nonetheless, accidents and product defects will occur. One of the most difficult, and ethically challenging, decisions a manager must make is whether to undertake subsequent remedial measures. When a product is found to be inherently defective, it is in society's best interest for the manufacturer to fix the dangerous condition or to improve the design; nevertheless, manufacturers may fear that such remedies will be used as evidence against them in subsequent proceedings. For this reason, some courts refuse to allow plaintiffs to submit evidence of subsequent remedial measures as proof that the original design was defective.

Legally astute managers recall defective products and constantly strive to improve designs and processes to ensure the safety of the firm's products. Even when there is no legal obligation to recall a product, a recall can mitigate potential liability, exemplify the company's commitment to protecting consumers, and protect the brand. But once undertaken, recalls must be performed properly. Careless recalls expose the company to negligence claims.

© Cengage Learning 2013

A MANAGER'S DILEMMA

Putting It into Practice

Should a Medical Device Manufacturer Pay for Precautionary Hip Implant Replacements?

In 2010, the DePuy Orthopaedics unit of Johnson & Johnson recalled two kinds of hip implants that had deteriorated after being placed in the patient. About 12% to 13% of patients needed a second hip replacement within five years of receiving the recalled DePuy implant. Problems with the implants had been reported for several years before the recall, and orthopedic experts have expressed dismay that DePuy did not stop selling the devices earlier.

CONTINUED

Johnson & Johnson has stated that it will cover the cost of monitoring and treating patients with hip implants, including the cost of replacement surgery, if necessary. But this offer does not necessarily extend to paying for new implants that patients who received the DePuy devices but have not experienced problems might request immediately as a precaution. Johnson & Johnson's credo states that health-care professionals and patients are most important to the company, followed by its employees, then the community, and finally its shareholders and the attempt to maintain a profitable company. How should Johnson & Johnson handle this situation?[141]

141. Natasha Singer, *Johnson & Johnson Recalls Hip Implants*, N.Y. Times, Aug. 26, 2010; Robert Lowes, *Johnson & Johnson Unit Recalls 2 Hip Replacement Systems*, Medscape News, Aug. 30, 2010, *available at*, http://www.medscape.com/viewarticle/727699; Johnson & Johnson Credo, *available at*, http://www.jnj.com/wps/wcm/connect/c7933f004f5563df9e22be1bb31559c7/jnj_ourcredo_english_us_8.5x11_cmyk.pdf?MOD=AJPERES.

© Cengage Learning 2013

INSIDE STORY

Toyota Recalls Millions of Vehicles due to "Unintended Acceleration"

In February 2011, Toyota Motor Corporation announced that it was recalling 2.17 million vehicles due to problems resulting from stuck accelerator pedals.[142] These recalls were only the most recent in a series that has seen Toyota recall more than 14 million vehicles globally since 2009. Most of the recalls were connected with "sudden" or "unintended" acceleration. Toyota attributed the recalls to "floor mat entrapment," which can cause gas pedals to become stuck. Others claimed, however, that there were defects in the design of the gas pedal or in the vehicles' software. Although Toyota initially tried to blame a U.S. component manufacturer for any defects in the pedal, the manufacturer showed that it had manufactured the component in the pedal to Toyota's specifications.

After investigating incidents of unintended acceleration, the National Highway Traffic Safety Administration (NHTSA) found no evidence of a defect in the gas pedal itself or in the software. Instead, the NHTSA concluded that the floor mats were to blame. The NHTSA ordered Toyota to recall the affected vehicles and pay $48.8 million in fines—the maximum allowed under the law—for delaying the sudden-acceleration recalls and an unrelated 2005 recall.[143] Due largely to these defects, Toyota's sales declined by 0.4% in 2010 while the rest of the auto industry reported an increase in sales of 13.4%.

The vehicle malfunctions and recalls opened the gates to a flood of litigation by persons injured in accidents caused by the stuck gas pedals and car owners alleging that the defects reduced the market value of their vehicles.[144] Insurance companies seeking to recoup the money paid to settle claims arising out of such accidents have also sued.[145]

In 2011, Toyota won the first unintended-acceleration case brought to trial when the jury concluded that the accident was caused by driver error, not the floor mats.[146] Toyota had settled a California case out of court in 2010 for an undisclosed amount.[147]

The unfavorable publicity and the recalls "dealt a devastating blow"[148] to a brand previously known for its high quality. Federal regulators and others sharply criticized Toyota for the way it had handled the complaints of unintended acceleration. An embarrassed Akio Toyoda, Toyota's president and the grandson of the founder, apologized before Congress in 2010.

CONTINUED

142. Nick Bunkley, *Toyota to Recall Over 2 Million Vehicles for Gas Pedal Flaws*, N.Y. Times, Feb. 25, 2011, at B4.

143. Nick Bunkley, *In Detroit, Toyota Vows to Earn Trust*, N.Y. Times, Jan. 11, 2011, Late Ed., at B1.

144. *In re* Toyota Motor Corp., 2011 U.S. Dist. LEXIS 52529 (D.C. Cal. May 13, 2011).

145. *See, e.g., In re* Toyota Motor Corp. Unintended Acceleration Mktg., Sales Practices, and Prods. Liab. Litig., 754 F. Supp. 2d 1145 (C.D. Cal. 2010); Chad Hemney, *Seven Insurers File Subrogation Lawsuits Against Toyota*, Prop. & Casualty, Jan. 5, 2011, at sec. 1; Brent M. Rosenthal, *Toxic Torts and Mass Torts*, 64 S.M.U. L. Rev. 583 (2011).

146. *Toyota Wins First Trial over Alleged Unintended Acceleration*, PracticeView Database, Apr. 5, 2011; Katie LaBarre, *Court Clears Toyota in First Unintended Acceleration Lawsuit*, U.S. News, Apr. 4, 2011, *available at* http://usnews.rankingsandreviews.com/cars-trucks/daily-news/110404-Court-Clears-Toyota-in-First-Unintended-Acceleration-Lawsuit/.

147. Nick Bunkley, *Toyota Settles Suit over Death of Family in California Crash*, N.Y. Times, Sept. 19, 2010, Late Ed., at A28 (Toyota reached an undisclosed settlement amount with a family whose members were the victims of a crash near San Diego in 2009).

148. *Toyota Panel: Centralized Control Hurt Response to Acceleration Crisis*, 30(25) Westlaw J. Automotive 3 (June 7, 2011).

hxdbzxy/Shutterstock

In May 2011, a seven-member panel appointed by Toyota to investigate the matter issued a report entitled "A Road Forward."[149] The report stated that "Toyota initially reacted to consumer complaints such as [unintended acceleration], 'sticky pedals' and other issues with a degree of skepticism and defensiveness."[150] The panel faulted managers for not adequately applying the key principles of the "Toyota Way," which is based on the twin pillars of "continuous improvement and respect for people." Toyota tended to treat feedback from external sources such as regulators, customers, and independent rating agencies differently from feedback from employees within the company.[151] Because decision making on vehicle design, recalls, and communications had always been tightly controlled by Toyota in Japan, the company tended to ignore local complaints.

Although Toyota did not accept all of the panel's recommendations, it did appoint a global chief safety officer.

Unlike most companies, which assign the responsibility for ensuring safety to specific employees and executives, Toyota had previously lumped safety into the larger issue of "quality," thereby making it everyone's responsibility. One panel member, a former president of the Insurance Institute for Highway Safety, asserted that Toyota's "safety philosophy might suffer from the old adage, 'When everyone is responsible, no one is accountable.'" Toyota also gave its American executives more authority to make decisions rather than just reporting information back to the company's headquarters in Japan.[152]

The panel stated, "Although Toyota is in the car manufacturing business, it—like most modern corporations—is also a decision factory." As a result, "Toyota's reputation in North America increasingly will be based as much on the quality of its decision-making as on the quality of its vehicles."[153]

---

149. "A Road Forward: The Report of the Toyota North American Quality Advisory Panel" is available at http://www.insideline.com/toyota/toyota-safety-panel-uncovers-automakers-inadequacies-in-recall-crisis.html.

150. *Toyota Panel, supra* note 148.

151. *Id.*

152. *Id.*

153. *Id.*

KEY WORDS AND PHRASES

QUESTIONS AND CASE PROBLEMS

1. Stephanie Good smoked "light" Marlboro and Cambridge cigarettes for more than fifteen years. Light cigarettes have lower levels of nicotine and tar than regular cigarettes but can be even more harmful. Good sued the cigarette manufacturer Philip Morris under the Maine Unfair Trade Practices Act (MUTPA), claiming that by labeling the cigarettes "light" and "lower tar and nicotine," Philip Morris intentionally deceived consumers into believing that the health risks were not as great as with regular cigarettes. The MUTPA bans unfair methods of competition and unfair or deceptive acts or practices in the conduct of any trade or commerce. The cigarette manufacturer had labeled the packages in accordance with the Federal Cigarette Labeling and Advertising Act and Federal Trade Commission regulations. Is Good's claim for intentional deception under the MUTPA preempted by federal law? [*Altria Group, Inc. v. Good*, 555 U.S. 70 (2008).]

2. Johnson was a trained and certified heating, ventilation, and air-conditioning (HVAC) technician with a "universal" certification, the highest obtainable from the Environmental Protection Agency. He purchased R-22 refrigerant manufactured by American Standard and used it in maintaining and repairing air-conditioning units. Johnson sued American Standard for negligence, failure to warn, and design defect, alleging that the R-22 refrigerant exposed him to phosgene gas, causing him to develop pulmonary fibrosis. He admitted receiving and reading the Material Safety Data Sheets (MSDS) with each of his purchases of R-22 refrigerant, but claimed that he did not understand that heating the R-22 refrigerant could produce allegedly harmful phosgene exposures. Who should prevail? Should the result be the same if Johnson did not purchase the R-22 refrigerant himself but was an employee of a company that would qualify as a sophisticated user? What public policies are implicated in cases such as this? [*Johnson v. American Standard, Inc.*, 179 P.3d 904 (Cal. 2008).]

3. Roy Mercurio drove his Nissan Altima into a tree in the middle of the night at a speed of approximately thirty-five miles per hour. When the car struck the tree, the passenger compartment collapsed, and Mercurio was seriously injured. He was driving while intoxicated with a blood alcohol content of at least 0.18%. Mercurio brought a product liability action against Nissan on the grounds that the car was not crashworthy. Nissan argued that the claim should be dismissed, asserting as defenses assumption of risk and unforeseeable misuse of the car in that Mercurio was driving while intoxicated. Mercurio argued that evidence of his blood alcohol level at the time of the accident was irrelevant and should be excluded. How should the court rule? What public policies are at issue here? [*Mercurio v. Nissan Motor Corp.*, 81 F. Supp. 2d 859 (N.D. Ohio 2000).]

4. Terrell Redman, a senior vice president of Alligator Corporation, is evaluating a potential acquisition for the company. The entity he wishes to acquire has several divisions, two of which manufacture chemicals and industrial tools.

   a. What risks does the acquisition present to Alligator Corporation under product liability law?

   b. Are there ways to limit the company's exposure?

   c. To the extent that product liability law will expose Alligator to liability for the acquired company's prior conduct, what steps must be taken at the time of the acquisition to ensure Alligator's ability to defend potential claims? [*See, e.g., Tolo v. Wexco*, 993 F.2d 884 (9th Cir. 1993).]

5. Rochelle Black's husband worked as an auto mechanic in the Air Force from 1971 to 1986. When he died of lung cancer in 1991, Mrs. Black sued forty-eight asbestos manufacturers, alleging that her husband's death had been caused by his exposure to asbestos-containing products while working as an auto mechanic. She based her claims on market-share liability. Although she conceded that market-share liability would be inappropriate if she were alleging injury from exposure to many different types of asbestos products, she argued that she should be allowed to proceed in her market-share claims against four manufacturers of asbestos-containing "friction products," including brake and clutch products. These four companies produced friction products, that contained between 7% and 7.5% asbestos fibers. How should the court rule? What if the range of asbestos fibers in the products produced by the four companies was 40% to 60%? [*Black v. Abex Corp.*, 603 N.W.2d 182 (N.D. 1999).]

6. Laura Hollister was a business student at Northwestern University. She attended a business school party and then returned to her apartment with a friend. When Hollister left the party, she was intoxicated. She woke the next morning with no memory of subsequent events after she had returned to her apartment, but she had third-degree burns over 55% of her body. From the evidence, police determined that she had been cooking; when she reached for the cupboard over the stove, her shirt brushed against the hot burner and caught fire. Hollister brought an action against the department store where her mother purchased the shirt on the grounds that the shirt was defective because it lacked a warning regarding its extreme flammability. The department store argued that the danger inherent in having clothing come into contact with a hot stove is "open and obvious." How should the court rule? [*Hollister v. Dayton Hudson Corp.*, 201 F.3d 731 (6th Cir. 2000).]

7. Richard Welge loved to sprinkle peanuts on his ice cream sundaes. One day Karen Godfrey, with whom Welge boarded, bought a 24-ounce vacuum-sealed plastic-capped glass jar of peanuts at a convenience store in Chicago. To obtain a $2 rebate that the manufacturer was offering to anyone who bought a "party" item, such as peanuts, Godfrey needed proof of her purchase from the jar of peanuts. Using an Exacto knife, she removed the part of the label that contained the bar code. She then placed the jar on top of the refrigerator. About a week later, Welge removed the plastic seal from the jar, uncapped it, took some peanuts, replaced the cap, and returned the jar to the top of the refrigerator, all without incident.

   A week later, Welge took down the jar, removed the plastic cap, spilled some peanuts into his left hand to put on his sundae, and replaced the cap with his right hand. But as he pushed the cap down on the open jar, the jar shattered. His hand was severely cut and is now, he claims, permanently impaired.

   Welge brought suit and named three defendants: the convenience store, the manufacturer of the peanuts, and the manufacturer of the jar itself. From whom will Welge be able to recover? On what theories? What defenses, if any, are available to the defendants? [*Welge v. Planters Lifesavers Co.*, 17 F.3d 209 (7th Cir. 1994).]

8. Darleen Johnson was driving her Ford car under rainy conditions on a two-lane highway through Missouri. The car's front tires had a reasonable amount of tread remaining on them, but the back tires were nearly bald.

For an undetermined reason, Johnson lost control of the car, spun into the other lane, and collided with a pickup truck driven by Kathyleen Sammons. Johnson was killed instantly.

Johnson's father claimed that the inboard C.V. joint boot on the front axle was torn, which allowed debris to contaminate the joint. (The boot is a covering that contains the grease that lubricates the joint.) This contamination allegedly made the joint act like a brake on the left front wheel and caused Johnson's car to pivot around that wheel and into the path of the oncoming pickup truck. Ford admits that the joint boot can become torn, which will allow contamination of the joint. In its manuals, Ford recommends periodic inspection of the boots. However, Ford contends that the joint on Johnson's car was contaminated during or after the accident. Ford also contends that contamination of the joint could not result in the joint seizing and creating a loss of steering control, and that the worst that could result from contamination would be some vibration and noise. According to Ford, Johnson's accident was caused by road conditions and driving error. The case is submitted to the jury on theories of strict liability and negligent design and manufacture. Is Ford liable for Johnson's death? Are there any additional arguments that Ford can raise in its defense? [*Johnson v. Ford Motor Co.*, 988 F.2d 573 (9th Cir. 1993).

CHAPTER 11

INTELLECTUAL PROPERTY

INTRODUCTION

STRATEGIC IMPORTANCE OF INTELLECTUAL PROPERTY

Legally astute managers recognize that intellectual property (IP) is an essential part of their business. As Horatio Gutierrez, vice president and deputy general counsel in Microsoft's intellectual property and licensing group, observed, "We're moving toward a global economy where the true strategic asset is IP."[1] Google's agreement to pay more than $12 billion to acquire Motorola Mobility's 17,000 cellphone patents and other assets in 2011 is just the latest example of this phenomenon.[2]

Intellectual property is any product or result of a mental process that is given legal protection against unauthorized use. There are four basic types: patents, copyrights, trademarks, and trade secrets. The Semiconductor Chip Protection Act of 1984 created a fifth, highly specialized form of intellectual property, the registered mask work. Different types of intellectual property are protected in different ways, and the protections apply to different aspects of a product.

International piracy, or the unauthorized reproduction and distribution of patented, copyrighted, or trademarked goods, is a major issue today. In support of the Stop Online Piracy Act (SOPA), introduced in the U.S. House of Representatives in October 2011, several members of Congress claimed that intellectual property theft costs America's economy more than $100 billion per year and has caused the loss of thousands of jobs.[3] According to industry executives, piracy not only depletes the profits of American companies but can also, in the case of fake drugs, threaten people's lives. Both SOPA and the companion Senate bill, the Protect IP Act (PIPA), would restrict access to websites hosting pirated content. The bills faced strong opposition from Google, Internet service providers, and others.[4]

CHAPTER OVERVIEW

This chapter describes the law of patents, copyrights, mask work rights, trademarks, and trade secrets in detail. The chapter concludes with a discussion of international intellectual property protection and the growing trend toward harmonization of national laws.

PATENTS

A *patent* is a government-granted right to exclude others from making, using, or selling an invention. Article I of the U.S. Constitution specifically grants Congress the power "to promote the Progress of Science and useful Arts, by securing for limited times to . . . Inventors the exclusive Right to their . . . Discoveries." There are three types of patents in the United States: utility, design, and plant patents. The patent holder is not required to personally make use of the invention. After

---

1. PricewaterhouseCoopers, Exploiting Intellectual Property in a Complex World 9 (2007), *available at* http://www.pwc.com/extweb/pwcpublications.nsf/docid/F5DBAFA7B3F4501D852570830007AD84/$File/tecv4ip.pdf.

2. Scott Martin, Jon Swartz & Byron Acolido, *Google Buys Motorola Mobility to "Supercharge" Android OS,* USA Today, Aug. 15, 2011. *See also* Alexander Krasnikov, Saurabh Mishra & David Orozco, *Evaluating the Financial Impact of Branding Using Trademarks: A Framework and Empirical Evidence,* 73(6) J. Marketing 154 (2009).

3. Press Release, H. Comm. on the Judiciary, Bipartisan Bill Combats Online Piracy (Oct. 26, 2011), *available at* http://judiciary.house.gov/news/HR%203261%20Introduced.html.

4. Richard Verrier, *Hollywood Regroups after Losing Battle over Anti-Piracy Bills,* L.A. Times, Jan. 21, 2012.

EXHIBIT 11.1	Top Ten Private-Sector Patent Recipients for the 2010 Calendar Year

Organization	Number of Patents in 2010
International Business Machines	5,866
Samsung Electronics	4,518
Microsoft	3,086
Canon Kabushiki Kaisha	2,551
Panasonic	2,443
Toshiba	2,212
Sony	2,130
Intel	1,652
LG Electronics	1,488
Hewlett-Packard Development Co.	1,480

SOURCE: U.S. Patent & Trademark Office, *Patenting by Organizations 2010* (2011), *available at* http://www.uspto.gov/web/offices/ac/ido/oeip/taf/topo_10.htm#PartB.

a period of time, the patent expires and the invention is dedicated to the public. Patents are one of the oldest recognized forms of intellectual property but, as discussed in the "Inside Story" in this chapter, the U.S. patent laws were revised substantially in 2011 by the Leahy–Smith America Invents Act (AIA).[5] Certain provisions went into effect when the bill was signed into law on September 16, 2011; others take effect on September 16, 2012; and still others, including some of the most important, are not effective until September 16, 2013. Except as otherwise noted, the text that follows reflects all the changes effected by the AIA.

The most significant change brought about by the AIA is a shift to a first-to-file system. Under the law in effect until March 2013, an inventor must file the patent application within one year after the invention is either described in a printed publication in the United States or a foreign country, or publicly used or sold in the United States. This rule is referred to as the *statutory bar*. In other countries, the patent application must be filed *before* the invention is described in a publication, publicly used, or sold. Under the AIA, U.S. patent law is now closer to the system used in other countries. Effective March 2013, patent protection is unavailable in the United States if the invention is disclosed by anyone other than the inventor before the patent application is filed (unless the person who disclosed the invention derived it from the original inventor's work). If the inventor discloses the invention, then he or she must file the patent application within one year after disclosure.

If two individuals independently create the same invention, then the U.S. patent goes to the first to invent until September 16, 2013, at which point the patent will go to the first to file the patent application (assuming in both cases that there is no statutory bar). This change brings the United States into line with the rest of the world, which grants the patent to the first to file.

The Patent and Trademark Office (PTO), an agency of the U.S. Department of Commerce, is responsible for issuing patents. The PTO issued its first patent in 1790. Since that time, the PTO has issued more than 8 million patents. It granted 244,341 patents in 2010 alone, almost a 40% increase from the number issued in 2000.[6] The types of patents issued by the PTO have varied dramatically over the years, particularly in the last century. The top ten private-sector patent recipients for the 2010 calendar year are identified in Exhibit 11.1.

Utility Patents

To be eligible for a *utility patent*, the most frequently issued type of patent, an invention must be (1) novel, (2) useful, (3) nonobvious, and (4) patentable subject matter. To be patentable subject matter, it must be (1) a process, machine, manufacture, or composition of matter, or (2) a novel, useful, and nonobvious improvement thereof.

Novel

An invention is *novel* if it was not anticipated, that is, not previously known or used by others in the United States and not previously patented or described in a printed publication in any country. Even if the invention is novel, it will be denied patent protection if its novelty merely represents an obvious development over existing technology, also referred to as *prior art*.

5. Leahy–Smith America Invents Act, Pub. L. No. 112-29, 125 Stat. 284–381 (2011).

6. U.S. Patent & Trademark Office, *U.S. Patent Statistics Chart: Calendar Years 1963–2010* (2011), *available at* http://www.uspto.gov/web/offices/ac/ido/oeip/taf/us_stat.htm.

Nonobvious

When deciding whether an invention is nonobvious, the courts consider the scope and content of the prior art, differences between the claimed invention and the prior art, the level of ordinary skill in the art, and secondary indicia of nonobviousness.[7] A combination of two inventions can be nonobvious even if there is no prior art suggesting that they be combined.[8]

Useful

To be approved, an application for a utility patent must satisfy the *utility requirement*; that is, the invention must have a practical or real-world benefit. If the PTO issues a utility patent, the patent owner has the exclusive right to make, use, sell, and import for use the invention for a nonrenewable period of twenty years from the date on which the patent application was filed.

Patentable Subject Matter

There is no protection for nonstatutory subject matter, such as abstract ideas (rather than specific applications of ideas), mental processes, naturally occurring substances, arrangements of printed matter, scientific principles, or laws of nature.

Biotechnology In *Diamond v. Chakrabarty*,[9] a microbiologist sought patent protection for his invention of a live, human-made, genetically engineered bacterium capable of breaking down crude oil. Although the patent examiner rejected the application, the U.S. Supreme Court held on appeal that living organisms can be patented if they are human-made. Stating that the patent statute should include "anything under the sun that is *made* by man," the Supreme Court extended patent protection to the new organism.

The Supreme Court recognized that its decision in *Chakrabarty* would determine whether research efforts would be accelerated by the hope of reward or slowed by the want of incentives. The availability of patents made it possible for small biotechnology firms to attract venture capitalists and other investors, thereby spawning a whole new industry.

In 1987, the PTO confirmed that nonnaturally occurring, nonhuman, multicellular living organisms (including animals) are patentable subject matter. The PTO issued a patent in 1988 on a transgenic mouse that was engineered to be susceptible to cancer.

According to the PTO, human gene sequences are also patentable subject matter. Specifically, a gene patent covers "the genetic composition isolated from its natural state and processed through purifying steps that separate the gene from other molecules naturally associated with it."[10] More than 4,000 genes, or 20% of the almost 24,000 human genes, have been claimed in U.S. patents.[11] More than twenty human pathogens are privately owned, including haemophilus influenza and hepatitis C. Many gene patents have been associated with research leading to the treatment of the related disease.

Gene patenting (which has always been controversial) sparked new controversy when the PTO issued a patent to Human Genome Sciences, Inc. for a gene found to serve as a platform from which the AIDS virus can infect cells of the body. Concerns arose over the effect of giving one company the ability to control medical research related to a life-threatening disease, especially when that company may not appreciate or be able to realize the medical value of the gene.[12] In response to concerns that patents were being issued on genes before the inventors had ascertained the gene's function, in 2001 the PTO issued guidelines for examination of gene applications to ensure compliance with the utility requirement.[13]

ethical consideration

Children with Canavan disease, an inherited disorder, begin to display symptoms at three months of age. They never crawl or walk, suffer seizures, eventually become paralyzed, and die by adolescence. Canavan families around the world donated tissue and money to identify the gene that causes the disease so that a test could be developed to tell parents if they were at risk of producing a child with the disorder. When the gene was identified by a researcher at Miami Children's Hospital Research Institute, a New York hospital promised that it would offer the test, free of charge, to all who wanted it, but Miami Children's, which had patented the gene, refused to allow any health-care provider to offer the test without paying a royalty. Is it ethical to require families at risk for Canavan disease (including those who had contributed money and tissue to Miami Children's research) to pay for the test? Is it ethical to require researchers to pay royalties if they wish to study this disease further?

© Cengage Learning 2013

7. Graham v. John Deere, 383 U.S. 1, 17–18 (1966).

8. In *KSR International Co. v. Teleflex, Inc.*, 550 U.S. 398 (2007), the Supreme Court made it easier for a person that is seeking to invalidate a patent on an invention that is an obvious innovation given preexisting patents and inventions. While not overruling the Federal Circuit's TSM ("teaching, suggestion, or motivation") test, which required some "motivation or suggestion to combine the prior art teachings" for an obviousness invalidation, the Supreme Court declared that the TSM test provides a "helpful insight" but should not be used as a "rigid rule."

9. 447 U.S. 303 (1980).

10. Notice, 66 Fed. Reg. 1092 (Jan. 5, 2001).

11. Ass'n for Molecular Pathology v. USPTO, 653 F.3d 1329 (Fed. Cir. 2011); Stefan Lovgren, *One-Fifth of Human Genes Have Been Patented, Study Reveals*, NAT'L GEOGRAPHIC NEWS, Oct. 13, 2005, *available at* http://news.nationalgeographic.com/news/2005/10/1013_051013_gene_patent.html; *see also* DNA Patent Database, *available at* http://dnapatents.georgetown.edu/ (last visited Oct. 1, 2011).

12. For an excellent collection of articles on the pros and cons of gene patents, see MIT TECH. REV. (Sept.–Oct. 2000). *See also* Michael Crichton, *Patenting Life*, N.Y. TIMES, Feb. 13, 2007, at A23.

13. 66 Fed.Reg. 1092.

Computer Software   The law's embrace of software patents began in 1981, when the Supreme Court held that if a "claim containing a mathematical formula implements or applies that formula in a structure or process, which when considered as a whole, is performing a function which the patent laws were designed to protect (e.g., transforming or reducing an article to a different state or thing), then the claim [may be patentable]."[14] After this decision, developers successfully acquired software patents at a quickening pace.

Most software code is not published, so much of the relevant prior art is not accessible to the PTO examiners. In 2007, the PTO began a pilot program called the Peer to Patent project, which opened up the patent examination process to the public. On a website interface, and with the consent of the inventor, the public can view the applications, submit prior art references, and evaluate the prior art references submitted by others. The PTO examiner is provided with the top-ten references, as well as commentary. The PTO began its third run of the pilot in October 2010 and expanded the subject matter included from the original focus on computer software to life sciences, telecommunications, and business methods.[15]

Business Method Patents   In recent years, some of the most criticized patents have been patents on "business method" inventions, particularly in connection with the Internet and electronic commerce. Some of the most "notorious" e-commerce business method patents include Amazon.com's patent for the "one-click" shopping system, Priceline.com's patent for the online reverse auction, and Microsoft's patent on "e-commerce." Notwithstanding heightened PTO review of applications seeking protection for e-commerce-based business methods, 17,231 business method applications were filed in 2010, and 3,649 patents were issued.[16]

In the following case, the U.S. Supreme Court was encouraged to revisit the issue of whether business processes should be patentable at all.

---

14. Diamond v. Diehr, 450 U.S. 175, 192 (1981).

15. U.S. Patent & Trademark Office, *Peer Review Pilot FY 2011*, http://www.uspto.gov/patents/init_events/peerpriorartpilotindex.jsp (last visited Nov. 16, 2011).

16. *Id.*

| **A CASE IN POINT** | ***Summary*** | **Case 11.1** |

Bilski v. Kappos

Supreme Court of the United States
130 S. Ct. 3218 (2010).

FACTS   Bilski and Warsaw filed an application for patent protection for an alleged invention of a business process that explained how buyers and sellers of commodities in the energy market could protect against the risk of price changes by hedging. The patent examiner rejected the application. The Board of Patent Appeals and Interferences and the U.S. Court of Appeals for the Federal Circuit affirmed the rejection.

Claim 1 in the patent application described a series of steps instructing how to hedge risk, claim 4 placed claim 1's concept into a mathematical formula, and the remaining claims explained how claims 1 and 4 could be applied to minimize risks resulting from fluctuations in market demand for energy suppliers and consumers.

ISSUE PRESENTED   Is a business process that explains how buyers and sellers of commodities in the energy market can use hedging to protect against price fluctuations patentable?

SUMMARY OF OPINION   The U.S. Supreme Court began by noting that four categories of inventions are eligible for patent protection under the Patent Act: processes, machines, manufactures, and compositions of matter.[17] An invention or discovery is not patent eligible if it is a law of nature, a physical phenomenon, or an abstract idea.

The Court then considered two proposed categorical limitations on the availability of "process" patents: (1) the machine-or-transformation test and (2) a categorical exclusion for business method patents. The U.S. Court of Appeals for the Federal Circuit had ruled that a process had to meet the *machine-or-transformation* test to be patent eligible. To satisfy that test, a process must either (1) be tied to a particular machine or apparatus or (2) transform a particular article into a different state or thing. While finding the test "useful" when determining the patent eligibility of a process, the Court concluded that making it the exclusive test for

CONTINUED

---

17. 35 U.S.C. § 101.

determining whether processes are patentable would incorporate limitations not implicated by the Patent Act's text, purpose, or design.

The Court then rejected a categorical exclusion of business methods' patentability. The term "method" is within the statute's definition of "process," and it may include at least some methods of doing business.

Although federal law contemplates the existence of some business patent methods, the Court still found this particular process to be patent ineligible. The inventors sought to patent both the concept of hedging risk and the application of that concept to energy markets, but the Court concluded that these were patent-ineligible abstract ideas. The Court noted, "Hedging is a fundamental economic practice long prevalent in our system of commerce and taught in any introductory finance class." The remaining claims were simply examples of how hedging can be used in energy markets.

RESULT The judgment of the court of appeals was affirmed. The claimed invention was not a patent-eligible process because it was an abstract idea.

COMMENTS Justice Stevens concurred in the judgment but argued that business methods should be categorically excluded from patentability because they have traditionally been excluded from patentability in the United States.[18] Justice Breyer agreed with Justice Stevens's opinion that business methods are not patent eligible.

18. Prior to the decision by the U.S. Court of Appeals for the Federal Circuit in *State Street Bank & Trust Co. v. Signature Financial Group, Inc.*, 149 F.3d 1368 (Fed. Cir. 1998) (upholding a patent on a method for calculating the daily net asset value of a "fund of funds" investment company), courts had held that business processes are not patentable.

Design Patents

A *design patent* protects any novel, original (rather than nonobvious), and ornamental (rather than useful) design for an article of manufacture. Design patents protect against copying the appearance or shape of an article, such as a computer tablet, a perfume bottle, a typeface, or the icons and screen displays used in computer programs. A design dictated by function rather than aesthetic concerns cannot be protected by a design patent, but it may be protectable by a utility patent. A design patent has a duration of fourteen years from the date on which the patent application is filed.

Traditionally, design patents have rarely been used in the United States; other forms of protection, such as unfair competition law, have been relied on instead. Recently, however, the use of design patents has been increasing, in part because the application process is simpler and less expensive than for utility patents.

Plant Patents

Plant patents protect any distinct and new variety of plant that is asexually reproduced (that is, not reproduced by means of seeds). The variety must not exist naturally. Thus, a plant patent will not be issued to someone who merely discovers a wild plant not previously known to exist. Once a plant patent is granted, the patent owner has the exclusive right to exclude others from asexually reproducing, using, or selling the plant. In 2001, the U.S. Supreme Court affirmed that plant patents do not foreclose utility patent protection for the same plants.[19] Like utility patents, plant patents have a duration of twenty years from the date the application is filed.

Obtaining Patent Protection

To obtain patent protection in the United States, the inventor must file a patent application with the PTO. Each patent application contains four parts: the specifications, the claims, the drawings (except in chemical cases), and a declaration by the inventor.

Specifications

The *specifications* must describe the invention (as defined by the claims) in its best mode and the manner and process of making and using the invention, in such a way that a person skilled in the relevant field could make and use it. The description of the *best mode* must be the best way the inventor knows to make the invention at the time of filing the application. All descriptions must be clear, concise, and exact.

19. J.E.M. AG Supply, Inc. v. Pioneer Hi-Bred Int'l, Inc., 534 U.S. 124 (2001).

Claims

The *claims* (the numbered paragraphs at the end of the patent) describe the elements of the invention that the patent will protect. Any element not specifically set forth in the claims is unprotected by the patent. Thus, drafting the claims is crucial to obtaining adequate protection.

Drawings and Declaration by the Inventor

The *drawings* must show the claimed invention. The *declaration by the inventor* must state that the inventor has reviewed the application and believes that he or she is the first inventor of the invention. The inventor must also make full disclosure of any known relevant prior art. Knowing the prior developments assists the patent attorney in drafting the claims to avoid the prior art; it also permits the patent examiner to determine whether the patent is novel or would have been obvious to those familiar with the relevant field.

Review by Patent Examiner

In the vast majority of cases, the patent examiner will initially reject the application, as being precluded by prior inventions or otherwise failing to meet the statutory requirements. The inventor may then either present arguments (and in extreme cases, evidence) to contest the rejection or seek to amend the application to overcome the examiner's objections. If the application is finally rejected, the inventor can either refile the application as a *continuation application* or appeal to the PTO's Board of Appeals and subsequently to the U.S. Court of Appeals for the Federal Circuit. The inventor alternatively has the option to sue the Director of the PTO in the U.S. District Court for the District of Columbia. Once the examiner agrees that a patent should be issued, and the examiner and applicant agree on the precise language of the claims, a patent will be issued.

Postissuance Challenges

Competitors and others can challenge a patent after it is issued. For example, under the America Invents Act, a competitor can bring a derivation proceeding in which it claims that the applicant derived or stole the invention.

In *Medimmune, Inc. v. Genentech, Inc.*,[20] the Supreme Court held that a patent licensing agreement is not equivalent to a settlement between the parties. As a result, to avoid later claims of willful infringement, a company can accept a license from a party whose claim to the patent the licensee considers invalid but still preserve the right to subsequently challenge the validity of the underlying patent.

Provisional Patent Applications

Since 1995, inventors have been able to file provisional patent applications, which can be filed without formal patent claims. The provisional application provides a low-cost way to establish an early filing date for the later, nonprovisional patent application. A provisional application must be followed by a nonprovisional application within twelve months.

Types of Infringement

A U.S. patent may be infringed in three ways: directly, indirectly, or contributorily.

Direct Patent Infringement

Direct patent infringement is the making, use, or sale of any patented invention within the United States during the term of the U.S. patent. Direct infringement can be committed innocently and unintentionally. When an accused device or process does not have precisely each element of a particular claim of a patent (that is, the patent is not literally infringed), but the patented invention is replicated in a product or process that works in substantially the same way and accomplishes substantially the same result, a direct infringement can be found under the *doctrine of equivalents*. In 2002, the U.S. Supreme Court narrowed the reach of this doctrine so that it is now effectively available only to inventors who did not amend their patent applications in order to satisfy patentability requirements.[21] Because the patent examiner asks the majority of patent applicants to amend their applications to satisfy these requirements, the doctrine of equivalents now provides patent owners with considerably less recourse against competitors who design around their patents.

Indirect Patent Infringement

Indirect patent infringement, also referred to as *inducement to infringe*, is a party's active inducement of another party to infringe a patent. For example, if a film company encouraged consumers to play its DVDs on a brand of player that it knows violated Philips's data compression patents, that would constitute active inducement to infringe. Indirect and contributory infringement require some knowledge or intent that a patent will be infringed.

Contributory Patent Infringement

Contributory patent infringement occurs when one party knowingly sells an item with one specific use that will result in the infringement of another's patent. For example, if a company sells a computer add-on card for a specific use that will infringe another's patent, the sale is a contributory infringement even though the add-on card itself does not infringe any patent.

---

20. 549 U.S. 118 (2007).

21. Festo Corp. v. Shoketsu Kinzoku Kogyo Kabushiki Co., 535 U.S. 722 (2002).

Defenses

A defendant to a patent-infringement action may claim a variety of defenses, including (1) noninfringement of the patent, (2) invalidity of the patent, (3) misuse of the patent, or (4) innocent infringement.

Noninfringement

The defense of *noninfringement* asserts that the allegedly infringing matter does not fall within the claims of the issued patent. Under this defense, the specific language of the patent claims is compared with the allegedly infringing matter. If the allegedly infringing matter is not described by the patent claims, the defense of noninfringement is successful. The doctrine of *file-wrapper estoppel* prevents a patent owner from asserting any claim interpretation at odds with the application on file with the PTO. Because the patent holder has previously negotiated the scope of his or her invention with the PTO, the patent holder may not renegotiate that scope in a subsequent court proceeding.

The proper construction of the words in patent claims is a matter of law for the court, not the jury, to decide.[22] The Supreme Court reasoned that "[t]he construction of written instruments is one of those things that judges often do and are likely to do better than jurors unburdened by training in exegesis."[23]

Invalidity

A patent is presumed to be valid, but a court may find it invalid if (1) the invention was not novel, useful, or nonobvious when the patent was issued; (2) the patent covers nonstatutory subject matter, such as an abstract idea, a scientific principle, or a mental process; (3) a statutory bar was created by a publication or sale of the invention prior to the filing of the patent application; or (4) any other requirement of the patent law was not met. Thus, for example, if a third party discloses an invention before an applicant discloses it or files a patent application, then the applicant is barred from getting a patent on the disclosed invention.

Patent Misuse

A *patent misuse* defense asserts that although the defendant has infringed a valid patent, the patent holder has abused its patent rights and therefore has lost, at least temporarily, its right to enforce them. Improperly expanding the physical or temporal scope of a patent constitutes patent misuse. For example, forcing a party to sign a license agreement that calls for royalty payments beyond the expiration of the patent would be a patent misuse. Seeking to enforce a patent obtained through inequitable conduct might also be a patent misuse. Requiring a licensee to purchase nonpatentable products as a condition

to obtaining a license for patented products is no longer treated as patent misuse, but, as discussed in Chapter 16, it may, under certain circumstances, be an illegal tie under the antitrust laws.

The patent holder is barred from recovering for any infringement of its patent during the period of misuse. If the patent holder later "purges" itself of the misuse, it may recover for any subsequent infringement. For example, if a provision in a patent license caused the patent misuse, eliminating the provision from all of the patent holder's patent licenses would enable the holder to once again enforce the patent, but the holder would not be entitled to judicial relief for conduct prior to the effective date of the purge.

Innocent Infringement

A defendant may claim innocent infringement if the patented item did not carry adequate notice of its patent status. Although this is not a complete defense to patent infringement, a patent owner cannot sue for damages arising out of infringement occurring before the defendant received actual notice of infringement. In the case of physical products, notice is normally given by putting the patent number on the product or its packaging. In the case of intangible patented items, such as business processes, the patent owner generally does not need to provide any patent marking to recover damages for the full period of infringement, although at least two cases have held that marking is required for a method or system patent if the patent owner sold the patented system over the Internet.[24]

First Sale Doctrine

Under the *first sale doctrine*, an authorized sale of a patented article exhausts the patent holder's exclusive rights as to that article, to the extent that the article embodies the invention. As a result, the patent holder is precluded from obtaining any further royalties or imposing any further restrictions on the article or its subsequent sale or transfer. For example, the owner of a patent on eyeglass frames cannot use the patent law to prevent a distributor from selling the frames to a discounter. As discussed in Chapter 16, the manufacturer may, however, be able to terminate its agreement with the distributor because it sold the product for less than the suggested sale price.

Remedies

If a valid patent has been infringed, the patent holder may seek preliminary and permanent injunctive relief and damages, as well as court costs and attorneys' fees.

---

22. Markman v. Westview Instruments, Inc., 517 U.S. 370 (1996).

23. *Id.* at 388.

24. Northbrook Digital Corp. v. Browster, Inc., 2008 WL 4104695, at *4 (D. Minn. Aug. 26, 2008); IMX, Inc. v. Lendingtree, LLC, 2005 WL 3465555, at *4 (D. Del. Dec. 14, 2005).

Injunctive Relief

A patent holder may seek a preliminary injunction to prevent any further infringement of the patent pending the court's ultimate decision. Most courts, however, are reluctant to grant injunctive relief before they have determined that a valid patent has actually been infringed. For many years, U.S. courts granted permanent injunctive relief almost as a matter of right after a finding of infringement. This gave so-called patent trolls tremendous leverage "to charge exorbitant fees to companies that seek to buy licenses to practice the patent."[25] The term *patent troll* is generally understood to refer to a nonpracticing entity that purchases one or more patents with the intent to enforce the patents against infringers, rather than to manufacture a patented product or supply a patented service. It has also been used to refer to a company that files patent applications covering new technologies, waits for others to develop and create markets for these technologies, and then sues these newcomers for patent infringement after they are locked into using the patented technologies.

A patent trolls operates much like any other firm that seeks to exploit its patent portfolio except that the troll focuses on extracting money from existing users of the patent rather than practicing or seeking out new applications for the patented technology. The patent troll often starts by sending demand letters to smaller companies, hoping that early settlements with these companies will encourage others to agree to take licenses as well.

In 2006, for example, Research in Motion, maker of the BlackBerry smartphone, paid $612.5 million in royalties to patent troll NTP to avoid an injunction that would have shut down BlackBerry service.[26] NTP was a one-person firm that had no employees and made no products. In the early 1990s, NTP filed for, and ultimately obtained, a series of patents premised on wireless e-mail. Then NTP sat back and waited for others to develop the wireless e-mail market. During the litigation, the PTO reexamined all seven of NTP's patents and had issued notices rejecting all of them by the end of 2005. After the court refused to delay the litigation pending the final outcome of the reexamination process, and with the threat of another injunction looming over its head, RIM agreed to settle the case.[27] RIM had no right to a refund of the $612 million it paid NTP even if the PTO eventually overturned NTP's patents.

In 2006, the U.S. Supreme Court ruled in *eBay Inc. v. MercExchange, L.L.C.*[28] that the "right to exclude others

from making, using, offering for sale, or selling the invention"[29] granted by the Patent Act did not justify a general rule in favor of permanent injunctive relief when patent infringement is found. Because the Patent Act provides that injunctive relief may issue only "in accordance with the principles of equity,"[30] a plaintiff must satisfy the traditional four-factor test to obtain a permanent injunction. These factors include demonstrating that (1) an irreparable injury exists; (2) the remedies available at law, such as monetary damages, are inadequate; (3) an injunction is appropriate given the balance of hardships between the plaintiff and the defendant; and (4) the public interest would not be disserved by a permanent injunction. In short, the decision to grant or deny injunctive relief in patent cases lies within the equitable discretion of the district court, which must be exercised consistent with the traditional four-factor injunctive relief test.

The Supreme Court's decision in *eBay Inc. v. MercExchange* was rendered several months after RIM settled its case with NTP. Had NTP been required to meet the traditional four-factor test for equitable relief, RIM would almost certainly have paid far less than $612.5 million, whether in a negotiated settlement or in a judicial award of damages.

Damages

Damages may be awarded based on (1) the patent holder's lost profits (in the case of a patent holder practicing its invention), (2) the infringer's profits, or (3) a reasonable royalty for the infringer's use of the invention. To this, court costs, as fixed by the court, may be added. The court also has discretion (1) to increase the damages award by up to three times for intentional or willful infringement and (2) to award attorneys' fees in exceptional cases.

The instant-camera litigation between Polaroid Corporation and Eastman Kodak Company illustrates the potential for large damages awards for patent infringement. In the 1970s, Kodak sought a license from Polaroid to produce instant cameras and film, but the parties never reached an agreement. When Kodak nonetheless introduced an instant camera and film in 1976, Polaroid sued for patent infringement. A federal district court held that Kodak had infringed twenty claims of seven Polaroid patents and enjoined Kodak from any further infringements. The injunction terminated Kodak's instant-camera business, leaving it with $200 million worth of useless manufacturing equipment and $600 million in losses.[31] Kodak was later ordered to pay Polaroid $910 million for infringing its patents, including $454.2 million in lost profits and royalties and $455.3 million in interest.[32] In 2009,

25. eBay Inc. v. MercExchange, L.L.C., 547 U.S. 388, 396 (2006) (Kennedy, J. concurring).

26. Press Release, Research in Motion, Research in Motion and NTP Sign Definitive Settlement Agreement to End Lititgation (Mar. 3, 2006), *available at* http://press.rim.com/release.jsp?id=981).

27. Rob Kelley, *BlackBerry Maker, NTP Ink $612 Million Settlement*, CNNMoney.com, Mar. 2, 2006, http://money.cnn.com/2006/03/03/ technology/rimm_ntp/index.htm.

28. 547 U.S. 388 (2006).

29. 35 U.S.C. § 154(a)(1).

30. 35 U.S.C. § 283.

31. Polaroid Corp. v. Eastman Kodak Co., 789 F.2d 1556 (Fed. Cir. 1986).

32. Lawrence Ingrassia & James S. Hirsch, *Polaroid's Patent-Case Award, Smaller Than Anticipated, Is a Relief for Kodak*, Wall St. J., Oct. 15, 1990, at A3.

Centocor was awarded $1.67 billion for lost profits and reasonable royalties on its arthritis drug Remicade after Abbott was found to have infringed with its Humira product.[33]

Patent litigation is a high stakes game for both established market participants and small companies, but the prohibitive cost of patent litigation can make it much more difficult for small companies to recover damages from larger firms. Some corporations purposely lengthen and complicate the discovery process in order to strain the resources of their smaller challengers. Nevertheless, patent rights can provide a David with an effective means to strike down a Goliath. For example, a jury awarded i4i $290 million after finding that Microsoft had infringed i4i's patent on a method for editing computer documents.[34]

COPYRIGHTS

A *copyright* is the legal right to prevent others from copying an original expression embodied in any original work of authorship fixed in a tangible medium. Copyright protects the expression, not the underlying ideas in the work. The owner has exclusive rights to reproduce, distribute, display, and perform the work. The owner also has the exclusive right to create *derivative works*, that is, works based on the copyrighted work. The Semiconductor Chip Protection Act of 1984 provides copyright-like protection for the layout or topography of an integrated circuit, but the duration of protection is limited to ten years.

The United States Copyright Act of 1976 requires that the material for which copyright protection is sought be original (not copied) and fall within one of the following categories: (1) literary works; (2) musical works; (3) dramatic works; (4) pantomimes and choreographic works; (5) pictorial, graphic, and sculptural works; (6) motion pictures and other audiovisual works; and (7) sound recordings. Best-selling novels, award-winning films, off-the-shelf software packages, and compact discs are all copyrightable works. So are restaurant menus, digital videodiscs, designer linens, plush toy animals, and cereal boxes as well as original blogs or photographs posted on YouTube.

The Act requires that the works be fixed in a tangible medium from which they can be perceived, reproduced, or communicated. For example, stories may be fixed in written manuscripts, computer software on computer memory chips, recordings of songs on digital recorders, and the staging of a play recorded on videotape. Copyright does not extend to names, familiar phrases, government publications, standardized information, or facts.

In addition to being fixed, the works must be sufficiently original—have some degree of creativity—to qualify for protection. As mentioned, facts are not copyrightable. A compilation of facts may be eligible for copyright protection, but only to the extent that the selection, coordination, or arrangement of the facts is original. As the U.S. Supreme Court explained in *Feist Publications v. Rural Telephone Co.*, "[t]he sine qua non of copyright is originality."[35] In that case, Feist, a publisher of a rural telephone directory, sued Rural Telephone for copying its listings in its rival telephone directory. Feist argued that because it had invested substantial time and effort in compiling and arranging the factual listings, the data were copyrightable. The Supreme Court rejected this "sweat of the brow" argument, holding that originality is the critical element of copyright protection and that the alphabetical arrangement of the phone listings was not sufficiently original to entitle Feist to copyright protection.

If an author can establish the fixity and originality of a work, copyright protection is automatic and entitles the author to the exclusive economic rights to (1) reproduce the copyrighted work, (2) prepare derivative works based on the copyrighted work, (3) distribute copies or phonorecords of the copyrighted work to the public, (4) perform the copyrighted work publicly, and (5) display the copyrighted work publicly.

Ownership and Scope of Protection

The creator of the work or, in the case of a work made for hire, the party for whom the work was prepared, is the author of the copyrighted work. A work is deemed a *work made for hire* when either (1) an employee created the work within the scope of his or her employment or (2) the work is in one of nine listed categories that is specially commissioned through a signed writing that states that the work is a "work made for hire."

The author of a copyrighted work can transfer ownership by an assignment of copyright. Parties that commission independent contractors to produce works that fall outside the nine listed categories, such as computer programs, often seek copyright assignments.

The advent of nonprint media and electronic databases led to disputes between freelance writers and photographers on one side, and the newspapers and magazines that buy their work on the other, about who owns the electronic or digital rights. The Supreme Court ruled that the owner of a copyright for a collective work (in this case, the publisher of the newspaper or magazine) has the right to revise the individual works, but it does not automatically have the right to republish them in an electronic database. This ruling underscores the importance of negotiating an assignment of rights that clearly applies to any known or future media.[36]

33. Centocor Ortho Biotech v. Abbott Labs., 2009 WL 5248493 (E.D. Tex. June 29, 2009).

34. Microsoft Corp. v. i4i Ltd. P'ship, 131 S. Ct. 2238 (2011).

35. 499 U.S. 340, 345 (1991).

36. Tasini v. New York Times Co., 533 U.S. 483 (2001).

Expression Versus Idea

The Copyright Act prohibits unauthorized copying of the *protected expression* of a work, but the underlying ideas embodied in the work remain freely usable by others. As the Supreme Court stated in *Feist*, "copyright assures authors the right to their original expression, but encourages others to build freely upon the ideas and information conveyed by a work."[37] In particular, section 102 of the Act excludes from copyright protection any "idea, procedure, process, system, method of operation, concept, principle or discovery, regardless of the form in which it is described, explained, illustrated, or embodied." For example, the use of buttons on a video camera labeled "Play" and "Fast Forward" would be an unprotectable method of operation.[38]

When an idea and its expression are inseparable, the *merger doctrine* dictates that the expression is not copyrightable. If it were, the copyright would confer a monopoly over the idea. Thus, a manufacturer of a karate video game cannot keep a competitor from producing another video game based on standard karate moves and rules. The idea of a karate game (including game procedures, karate moves, background scenes, a referee, and the use of computer graphics) is not protected expression. The manufacturer can, however, keep a competitor from copying any original graphics it has used in the game, as long as they are separable from the idea of karate or of a karate video game.

Useful Article Doctrine

The *useful article doctrine* provides that copyright protection does not extend to the useful application of an idea. The Copyright Act defines pictorial, graphic, and sculptural works to include "works of artistic craftsmanship insofar as their form but not their mechanical or utilitarian aspects are concerned." For example, blank forms used to record, rather than convey, information are considered noncopyrightable useful articles.

If the expression of a pictorial, graphic, or sculptural work cannot be identified separately from and exist independently of such utilitarian aspects, courts will deny copyright protection to the whole work. An example of an article whose expression is separable from its utilitarian aspects would be a lamp that incorporates a statue of a woman in its base. An example of an article whose expression is not separable from its utilitarian aspects is the layout of an integrated circuit. Although a drawing of the circuit is copyrightable, the actual circuitry is not copyrightable, because it is impossible to separate the utilitarian aspect of the circuit from its expression or layout. It is the layout of the circuit that enables the circuit to operate correctly. The circuit may be patentable, however. In addition, the layout or topography of the circuit may be protectable as a registered mask work under the Semiconductor Chip Protection Act of 1984.[39]

Preemption of State Law

Because the Copyright Act is a federal statute, it preempts any state law that enforces rights "equivalent" to one of the exclusive rights in federal copyright. Nonetheless, copyright law does not preempt a state law if the state-protected rights are qualitatively different from those protected under federal copyright.

The U.S. Court of Appeals for the Fifth Circuit ruled that state tort claims for misappropriation of the names and likenesses of music artists were not preempted by federal copyright law.[40] The defendants had allegedly marketed CDs and cassettes of musical performances by the plaintiff artists without obtaining copyright permission and had used the artists' names and likenesses to assist in the illegal marketing effort. The artists sued for copyright infringement and for misappropriation. In deciding that the misappropriation claim was not preempted, the court emphasized that names and likenesses are not copyrightable and therefore could not be the subject of a federal copyright claim.

Term of Protection

The Sonny Bono Copyright Term Extension Act of 1998[41] extended the duration of U.S. copyrights by twenty years. If the author is a known individual, the term is now the life of the author plus 70 years. For a work made for hire or for an anonymous or pseudonymous work, the term is the lesser of 95 years after first publication or 120 years after creation of the work. Publishers and librarians unsuccessfully challenged the constitutionality of the Act on the basis that it was not "necessary and proper" to achieve the purpose of "promoting the progress of science and useful arts." The Supreme Court upheld the extension, citing congressional authority to determine the scope and duration of copyright protection.[42]

Copyright Formalities: Registration and Notice

U.S. copyright law does not require authors to either register their works with the Copyright Office or affix a notice to the work itself, but it confers substantial benefits on those who do.

---

37. 499 U.S. 340, 349–50 (1991).

38. *See, e.g.*, Lotus Dev. Corp. v. Borland Int'l, Inc., 49 F.3d 807 (1st Cir. 1995), *aff'd*, 516 U.S. 233 (1996) (holding that Lotus 1-2-3's choice of spreadsheet menu command terms, such as "Exit" or "Save," was part of the method of operation and therefore not copyrightable).

39. 17 U.S.C.A. §§ 901–914.

40. Brown v. Ames, 201 F.3d 654 (5th Cir. 2000).

41. 17 U.S.C.A. § 304 (2002).

42. Eldred v. Ashcroft, 537 U.S. 186 (2003).

Copyright Notice

Although copyright notices are not mandatory for works first published after March 1, 1989, use of a notice precludes an infringer from claiming innocent infringement in mitigation of actual or statutory damages.[43] Proper U.S. copyright notice for works distributed within the United States includes these elements: "Copyright" or "Copr." or "©," the year of first publication, and the name of the copyright owner.

Copyright Registration

U.S. copyright owners cannot sue for infringement until they register with the Copyright Office. Statutory damages and attorneys' fees are available only if either (1) the work was registered prior to the infringement at issue, or (2) the owner registered the work within ninety days after first publication. Availability of statutory damages (up to $30,000 per infringement or up to $150,000 per willful infringement) can be particularly important for a start-up—or a more established company selling a new product—because the absence of historical sales can make it very difficult to prove actual damages (discussed later under "Remedies"). Registration also creates a legal presumption of ownership and copyright validity, which can be extremely helpful to a plaintiff in a copyright-infringement suit.

Copyright Infringement

Copyright infringement occurs when a party copies, modifies, displays, performs, or distributes a copyrighted work without the owner's permission. The plaintiff in a copyright-infringement suit must show (1) substantial similarity of the protected expression, not merely substantial similarity of the ideas contained in the work, and (2) that the alleged infringer had access to the plaintiff's work.

Types of Infringement

Copyright infringement may take three forms: direct, contributory, or vicarious.

Direct Infringement   *Direct copyright infringement* occurs when the copyright owner alleges that the defendant violated at least one of the five exclusive rights of the copyright holder. For example, the Princeton University Press and other publishers successfully sued a Michigan copy shop for direct infringement when the copy shop reproduced and sold excerpts of a variety of copyrighted works selected by professors without obtaining the publishers' permission to do so.[44]

Contributory Infringement   A party may also be liable for *contributory copyright infringement*—inducing, causing, or materially contributing to the infringing conduct of another with knowledge of the infringing activity. Recent case law on contributory infringement is based on the seminal Supreme Court decision in *Sony Corp. of America v. Universal City Studios, Inc.*[45] In 1984, Universal City Studios alleged that Sony, by manufacturing and selling the Betamax videocassette recorder, contributed to the infringement, of Universal's copyrights on programs broadcast over the public airwaves, which viewers could copy using their VCRs. The Court held that the sale of copying equipment does not constitute contributory infringement if the product has substantial noninfringing uses. In Sony's case, the trial court had found that time-shifting of television programs by private, noncommercial viewers, so they could view the programs later, was such a substantial noninfringing use. As a result, Sony's manufacture and sale of VCRs did not contributorily infringe on Universal's copyrights.[46]

Vicarious Infringement   A defendant may face *vicarious copyright liability* for a direct infringer's actions if the defendant (1) has the right and ability to control the infringer's acts and (2) receives a direct financial benefit from the infringement. Unlike contributory infringement, vicarious infringement does not require that the defendant know of the primary infringement. Although "direct financial benefit" certainly includes receiving a percentage of the value of each illegal sale, it is not limited to such per-unit arrangements.

The *Napster* case illustrates how the Sony-Betamax principle of "substantial noninfringing use" and vicarious liability principles apply to peer-to-peer networks. In Napster's original system, users downloaded free file-sharing software from the Napster website that enabled them to (1) make MP3 files stored on their hard drives available to other Napster users, (2) search for MP3 files stored on other users' computers, and (3) transfer exact copies of those files from one computer to another. By uploading MP3 file names to Napster network servers, users added to the collective library of files available for transfer to any user logged into Napster. The music industry brought suit, claiming that Napster had engaged in contributory and vicarious copyright infringement.

Because there can be no contributory or vicarious liability without direct infringement by a third party, the U.S. Court of Appeals for the Ninth Circuit first considered whether Napster's users engaged in direct infringement.[47] Napster argued that its users did not directly infringe because they were engaged in a fair use of the

---

43. For works published before March 1, 1989, most copyright authorities agree that owners should continue to use a copyright notice to avoid the risk of releasing the work into the public domain.

44. Princeton Univ. Press v. Mich. Document Serv., Inc., 99 F.3d 1381 (6th Cir. 1996).

45. 464 U.S. 417 (1984).

46. Courts have also applied the concept of contributory infringement to trademark law. *See* Hard Rock Cafe Licensing Corp. v. Concession Serv., Inc., 955 F.2d 1143 (7th Cir. 1992).

47. A & M Records, Inc. v. Napster, Inc., 239 F.3d 1004 (9th Cir. 2001).

material ("fair use" is discussed in the next section). The Ninth Circuit disagreed, holding that the users were engaged in wholesale, commercial copying of copyright-protected works. The court then found Napster liable for both contributory and vicarious infringement. Napster contributorily infringed because it knowingly encouraged and assisted its users' direct infringement. Napster met the two-prong vicarious liability test as well: (1) the availability of the infringing material attracted customers, thereby increasing the user base on which Napster's future revenues depended; and (2) Napster's ability to control access to its servers and its software was sufficient to give it the requisite right and ability to supervise the infringing activity.

This and subsequent court decisions contributed to Napster's demise and its resurrection as a paid subscription service, but the file-sharing seed had been planted. Grokster, StreamCast, and other systems arose to take Napster's place. Unlike Napster, these companies provided free software that allowed users to connect to a decentralized file-sharing network of computers. There was no centralized server, and any computer on the network could function as a server if it met the technical requirements. Neither Grokster nor StreamCast maintained control over entry to the network. In their continuing battle against

peer-to-peer file-sharing software, a number of music publishers and motion picture studios (the copyright owners) sued Grokster and StreamCast (the software distributors) for contributory and vicarious liability. The copyright owners claimed that the software distributors enabled users of their software to illegally copy and transmit copyrighted materials.

The U.S. Court of Appeals for the Ninth Circuit distinguished the *Napster* decision and found Grokster not liable for contributing or vicarious infringement.[48] The Ninth Circuit held that the software distributors were not contributorily infringing because, unlike Napster, they did not provide the "site and facilities" for infringement or otherwise materially contribute to the users' direct infringement. Similarly, the software distributors were not vicariously liable because, unlike Napster, they did not operate an integrated service and therefore had no ability to block access to infringing users.

The U.S. Supreme Court granted certiorari and invoked the theory of inducement to infringe from patent law to hold Grokster liable for inducing copyright infringement by its users in the following case.

---

48. Metro-Goldwyn-Mayer Studios, Inc. v. Grokster Ltd., 380 F.3d 1154 (9th Cir. 2004).

A CASE IN POINT	*Summary*	Case 11.2

MGM Studios, Inc. v. Grokster, Ltd.

Supreme Court of the United States 545 U.S. 913 (2005).

FACTS Grokster, Ltd. and StreamCast Networks both distributed electronic file-sharing software that implemented a peer-to-peer network sharing system, which allowed users' computers to directly communicate and share files, including music and video. This differed from the earlier Napster model, which had not only distributed file-sharing software, but had also operated network servers that maintained a centralized index of users and files. After Napster was sued for facilitating copyright infringement, the defendants marketed themselves as legal Napster alternatives. The defendants asserted that they were not liable for secondary infringement, because there were no centralized servers and they maintained no control over entry to the decentralized file-sharing network of computers operated solely by the users of their software.

MGM and a group of copyright owners, including motion picture studios, recording companies, songwriters, and music publishers (MGM), sued the defendants for copyright infringement based on either contributory or vicarious theories of secondary liability. After the district court granted summary judgment for the defendants and the U.S. Court of Appeals for the Ninth Circuit affirmed, the plaintiffs appealed.

ISSUE PRESENTED When a product is capable of both lawful and unlawful use, under what circumstances is a distributor of that product liable for acts of copyright infringement by third parties who use the product?

SUMMARY OF OPINION In a unanimous decision, the U.S. Supreme Court observed that it had dealt with secondary copyright infringement in only one recent case, *Sony Corp. v. Universal City Studios*. The Court noted that there was no evidence in that case that Sony had expressed any intent to promote infringing uses of its VCRs. The Court had held Sony not liable for contributory infringement because the VCR was "capable of commercially significant noninfringing uses." The Court agreed with MGM that the Ninth Circuit had misapplied *Sony*,

CONTINUED

which the Ninth Circuit had read to mean that a producer can never be contributorily liable if its product is capable of substantial lawful use. The Court concluded that *Sony* was never meant to preclude other theories of secondary liability.

The Court then discussed the history of the active inducement theory of liability in patent cases and concluded that it should apply equally to copyright cases. The theory requires intent to promote infringement as shown by "clear expression or other affirmative steps taken to foster infringement," the distribution of a device suitable for infringing use, and evidence of actual direct infringement by a third party.

The Court then considered the evidence to determine whether the intent element of the inducement test was satisfied. First, internal documents and advertisements aiming the software at former Napster users showed that each defendant was actively aiming its product toward a known source of demand for copyright infringement. Second, the lack of development of any filtering tools or other mechanisms to prevent users from engaging in infringing activity, "underscore[d] Grokster's and StreamCast's intentional facilitation of their users' infringement."[49] Third, the Court emphasized the defendants' business model, which relied on selling advertising space and turned on high-volume use, which the record showed was infringing. The Court concluded that the defendants were not passive recipients of information regarding the infringing use of their software; instead, each defendant had as its objective that its software be used for infringing uses and clearly and actively encouraged such infringement.[50] With "evidence of infringement on a gigantic scale," the Court easily found that the other two elements of the inducement test were satisfied to the extent needed to survive summary judgment.

RESULT   The Court reversed the summary judgment in favor of the defendants and remanded the case for further proceedings, including reconsideration of MGM's motion for summary judgment.

COMMENTS   The *Grokster* decision offered little guidance on whether a company can be liable for distributing file-sharing software if it is not actively inducing, encouraging, or promoting its use. Three Justices (Ginsburg, Rehnquist, and Kennedy) said yes, if the product is primarily used for infringement. Three other Justices (Breyer, Stevens, and O'Connor), however, said no, as long as there is evidence that the product is capable of being used in a noninfringing way.

CRITICAL THINKING QUESTIONS

1. What does this decision mean for companies that distribute Internet browsers, CD burners, MP3 players, and other technologies that are frequently used by their customers to infringe? What does this decision mean for companies like YouTube?

2. Would you expect this decision to have a chilling effect on the development of new copying and sharing technologies?

---

49. The Court made clear, however, that in the absence of other evidence of intent, the failure to take affirmative steps to prevent infringement is not in and by itself enough to find infringement under the inducement theory, if the product is capable of substantial noninfringing uses, as in *Sony*.

50. The Court noted that evidence supported the conclusion that the defendants' unlawful objective was "unmistakable."

Defenses to Copyright Infringement

Defenses to copyright-infringement claims include the doctrines of fair use, first sale, and copyright misuse.

Fair Use Doctrine

The *fair use doctrine*, embodied in section 107 of the Copyright Act, provides that a person may infringe the copyright owner's exclusive rights without liability, if he or she engages in such activities as literary criticism, social comment, news reporting, education, scholarship, or research. To decide what constitutes fair use, courts balance the public benefit of the defendant's use against any detrimental effect on the copyright owner's interests. In doing so, they consider (1) the purpose and character of the use (including whether it was for profit), (2) the economic effect of the use on the copyright owner, (3) the nature of the work used, and (4) the amount of the work used.

Courts often find that all four factors in the fair use test tilt in favor of one party or of the other. In some cases, however, the court must weigh the various factors. For example, in *Perfect 10, Inc. v. Amazon.com, Inc.*, the plaintiff operated an Internet website that marketed and sold copyrighted images of nude models. Some website publishers republished Perfect 10's images on the Internet without authorization. Google's search engine automatically indexed some of the webpages containing Perfect 10's images and provided reduced-size, "thumbnail" versions of them in response to user inquiries. From 2001 through 2004, Perfect 10 repeatedly notified Google that these thumbnail images infringed its copyright, and in 2004 it filed a lawsuit against Google. The trial court granted a preliminary injunction against Google's use of the images, but the U.S. Court of Appeals for the Ninth Circuit reversed the decision and held that Google was protected by the fair use doctrine.[51] The court acknowledged that the nature of the copyrighted work weighed slightly in favor of Perfect 10; the economic effect of the use and the amount of the work used, however, weighed in neither party's favor because there was no proven adverse effect of Google's use on Perfect 10's market and Google's use was reasonable in relation to the purpose of the copying. Finally, citing the Supreme Court's decision in *Campbell v. Acuff* (discussed below), the court considered the purpose and character of the use. The court found that this factor weighed heavily in Google's favor because its use was transformative, in that Google used the work in a different context by transforming it into a new creation, and this was more significant than any other incidental superseding use or the minor commercial aspects of Google's search engine.

Fair use arguments are common in the academic environment. As mentioned earlier, a publisher successfully sued a Michigan copy shop that was in the business of preparing course readers for university professors.[52] The professors excerpted a variety of copyrighted works, which the copy shop then compiled and sold to students without the permission of the copyright owners. The U.S. Court of Appeals for the Sixth Circuit noted that the copy shop's motivation was commercial profit, not education; the "transformative value" was slight, at best; the excerpts were substantial; and the market value of the original works was indeed harmed. As a result, the court found that the copy shop was liable for copyright infringement and enjoined it from further infringement.

In *Campbell v. Acuff-Rose Music, Inc.*,[53] the U.S. Supreme Court held that a parody that uses only as much of the lyrics and music of the original work as is necessary

to make it recognizable constitutes a fair use, even if the copied part is the heart of the original work. The group 2 Live Crew had parodied Roy Orbison's song "Pretty Woman."[54]

First Sale Doctrine

Under the *first sale doctrine*, codified in section 109(a) of the Copyright Act, a copyright owner has exhausted its statutory right to control distribution of a copyrighted item once the owner sells the item and thereby puts it in the stream of commerce. As a result, once the copyright owner sells a copyrighted product, it cannot prevent its resale or transfer to others. The U.S. Supreme Court has held that the first sale doctrine applies even when the product is sold outside the United States with the expectation that it will not be resold in the United States.[55] This decision dealt a blow to U.S. companies trying to combat the *gray market*, in which products are sold outside the normal channel of distribution, often at a discounted price.[56]

Copyright Misuse

Modeled after the patent misuse doctrine, copyright misuse exists when a copyright owner leverages his or her statutory copyright to gain control over areas outside the copyright's intended scope. For example, if a copyright owner licenses its software on the condition that the licensee may not use its competitors' products or develop complementary products, that action will constitute copyright misuse. If a court finds misuse, the copyright owner cannot enforce its copyright against infringers until the misuse has been purged.

Piracy

Piracy is a problem for many companies, but especially for software companies, which lose billions of dollars each year because of illegal copying or pirating of their software. The Business Software Alliance estimated that worldwide losses from all software piracy in 2010 amounted to nearly $59 billion.[57]

As discussed earlier, music publishers and film studios are being challenged by the file-sharing technologies that help evaders become ever more elusive. To identify illegal copying, the Recording Industry Association of America (RIAA)

51. 487 F.3d 701 (9th Cir. 2007).

52. Princeton Univ. Press v. Mich. Document Serv., Inc., 99 F.3d 1381 (6th Cir. 1996).

53. 510 U.S. 569 (1994).

54. *See also* Suntrust Bank v. Houghton Mifflin Co., 268 F.3d 1257 (11th Cir. 2001) (holding that a parody of *Gone with the Wind* was transformative and unlikely to serve as a market substitute for the original work).

55. Quality King Distrib., Inc. v. L'anza Research Int'l, Inc., 523 U.S. 135 (1998).

56. *See* Edward Felsenthal, *Copyright Scope Limited for Some Firms*, WALL ST. J., Mar. 10, 1998, at B5.

57. Business Software Alliance, *Eighth Annual BSA Global Software 2010 Piracy Study*, May 2011, *available at* http://portal.bsa.org/globalpiracy2010/.

ECONOMIC PERSPECTIVE

Intellectual Property Rights and Incentives to Innovate

A basic tenet of neoclassical economic theory is that productive efficiency and allocative efficiency will be achieved through free competition by private parties interested in maximizing their own welfare. Productive efficiency exists when competition among individual producers drives all but the lowest-cost producers of goods or services out of the market. Allocative efficiency exists when scarce societal resources are allocated to the production of various goods and services up to the point at which the cost of producing each good or service equals the benefit society reaps from its use.

In general, U.S. economic policy is to foster the functioning of free markets in which individuals may compete. For example, the antitrust laws, discussed in Chapter 16, are designed to protect competition by prohibiting any individual entity or group of entities from monopolizing an industry.

The area of intellectual property is a seeming exception to the general free-market orientation of the U.S. economy. Patent laws provide inventors with the opportunity to gain a legally enforceable monopoly to prevent the manufacture, use, and sale of their inventions for a limited time.

The economic rationale for granting monopolies to inventors is based on the high value of innovation to society and the need to provide incentives to inventors. Without legal rules protecting the ownership of inventions, once a valuable new product or cost-saving technique is introduced, others could immediately copy and profit from it, even though they bore none of the cost of its creation. Technological advances are crucial to a growing economy. Development of new techniques increases productive efficiency, thereby expanding the quantity of goods and services that can be produced with a given level of societal resources. Development of new products meeting previously unfulfilled needs increases the welfare of society as a whole. Such innovation has taken on increasing importance for the United States in the international context. Although countries with lower-cost labor have a competitive advantage in the manufacture of goods with established production techniques, the United States' competitive advantage lies in its ability to develop new technologies.

Individuals will produce innovations only up to the point at which the rewards they reap equal their costs. To ensure that innovations are produced fully up to the point at which the social cost equals the social benefit (that is, to ensure allocative efficiency), the law must guarantee to innovators a significant part of the benefit from their innovations. The U.S. solution to this problem is to provide inventors whose inventions meet the requirements for a patent with a limited monopoly to exclude others from the manufacture, use, and sale of those inventions. This system ensures that inventors will be able to capture the full benefit of their inventions during the period of their monopoly and that the innovation will be freely available to others thereafter. The stringent requirements for patents are designed to prevent unnecessary restrictions on free competition. In fact, overly broad patents can actually hamper innovation.

An important secondary objective is to give the scientific community access to state-of-the-art technology. Without a legal monopoly, innovators would keep their advances secret to prevent others from copying them. Such secrecy would result in waste of scarce societal resources, as other researchers would struggle to discover what is already known.

The World Bank has identified property rights, including intellectual property rights, as one of the keys to energizing countries in transition to market-based economies. Many developing and transitioning economies have already adopted intellectual property laws similar to those of the developed nations, but, as the World Bank acknowledges, these laws are difficult to enforce. Nevertheless, enforcement of these laws will encourage development of intellectual property and the foreign investment needed to spur growth.

---

uses *web robots*, which search and index the Internet for specific content by visiting websites, requesting documents based on certain criteria, and following up with potential infringers. Companies are also using encryption, watermarking, and mandatory online activation. The RIAA has brought a number of high-profile lawsuits against college students, elementary and high school students, and many other casual music downloaders since 2003. It has also put pressure on universities to discourage illegal file sharing by students and faculty. The Motion Pictures Association of America has also aggressively targeted pirates.

Remedies

Under the Copyright Act, a plaintiff can recover both its actual damages and the defendant's profits attributable to the infringements, to the extent that these are not duplicative. Alternatively, if the copyright is registered within three months of first publication or prior to the alleged infringement, a plaintiff may elect to recover statutory damages (which can be up to $30,000 for infringement and up to $150,000 for willful infringement), as well as attorneys' fees under certain circumstances. Injunctive relief, the seizure of infringing copies, and exclusion of infringing copies from import into the United States may also be available.

Although the Copyright Act does not provide a statutory right to a jury trial, a defendant in a copyright-infringement suit in which the copyright owner seeks statutory damages is entitled to a jury trial under the Seventh Amendment to the U.S. Constitution.[58] The defendant also has the right to have the jury determine the amount of statutory damages.

The Digital Millennium Copyright Act (DMCA) may apply to copyright violations as well. In a civil action, a court may impose injunctions and award damages, costs, and attorneys' fees. It may also order impounding, modification, or destruction of any devices or products involved in the violation. The court may punish repeat offenders by awarding treble damages.

Criminal Liability

Willful infringers may face criminal penalties as well as civil remedies. The No Electronic Theft Act punishes with fines and prison time those who copy compact discs, videocassettes, or software worth more than $1,000 without permission of the copyright holder. The law requires no proof that the defendant commercially gained from the infringement.[59] It is also a crime to fraudulently use or remove a copyright notice or to make false representations in connection with a copyright application.

The DMCA also imposes criminal sanctions of up to $500,000 in fines and up to five years' imprisonment for violators a court finds to be willful or motivated by financial gain. Repeat offenders face increased fines (up to $1 million) and up to ten years in prison.

REGISTERED MASK WORK

The Semiconductor Chip Protection Act of 1984 created a highly specialized form of intellectual property, the *registered mask work*. Semiconductor masks are detailed transparencies representing the topological layout of semiconductor chips. The mask work was the first significant new intellectual property right introduced in the United States in nearly one hundred years. The Act gives the owner copyright-like exclusive rights in the registered mask work for a period of ten years and prohibits its copying or use by others, although reverse engineering is specifically allowed. The law was aimed primarily at counterfeiters who replicate semiconductor masks for a chip already on the

market and produce the chips without having to expend their own resources on development. Remedies include injunctive relief, damages, and impoundment of the infringing mask and chips.

TRADEMARKS

Trademarks—words or symbols (such as brand names) that identify the source of goods or services—are also legally protected. Because trademarks tend to embody or represent the goodwill of the business, they are not legally transferable without that goodwill. Trademarks are protected for an indefinite time and can be valuable marketing and business assets. The packaging or dressing of a product may also be protected under the trademark laws as *trade dress*.

Most people associate a particular trademark with the product to which it is applied, without considering how this association has been generated. For example, when consumers purchase Apple computers or smartphones, they usually do not think about how the word for a type of fruit has become representative of that particular brand of personal computer or smartphone. Trademark law concerns itself with just such questions: how trademarks are created, how trademark rights arise, how such rights are preserved, and why certain marks are given greater protection than others.[60] The PTO registered 221,090 trademarks in 2010 alone.[61]

Ownership and Scope of Protection

The federal trademark act, known as the Lanham Act, and the 1988 Trademark Law Revision Act[62] define a trademark as "any word, name, symbol, or device or any combination thereof adopted and used by a manufacturer or merchant to identify and distinguish his goods, including a unique product, from those manufactured or sold by others, and to indicate the source of the goods, even if that source is unknown."

This definition has been interpreted as recognizing four different purposes of a trademark: (1) to provide an identification symbol for a particular merchant's goods, (2) to indicate that the goods to which the trademark has been applied are from a single source, (3) to guarantee that all goods to which the trademark has been applied are of a constant quality, and (4) to advertise the goods.

A trademark tells a consumer where a product comes from and who is responsible for its creation. A trademark also implies that all goods sold under the mark are of a consistent level of quality. A consumer purchasing french fries at a McDonald's restaurant, for instance, can

58. *See* Feltner v. Columbia Pictures Television, Inc., 523 U.S. 340 (1998).

59. No Electronic Theft Act of 1997, Pub. L. No. 105-147, 111 Stat. 2678 (1997).

60. Ron Zapata, *Patent Infringement Actions Declining: Study*, IP L. BULL., Feb. 27, 2007, *available at* http://www.law360.com/texas/articles/19358/patent-infringement-actions-declining-study.

61. U.S. Patent & Trademark Office, *Performance and Accountability Report Fiscal Year 2010*, at 56, *available at* http://www.uspto.gov/about/stratplan/ar/2010/USPTOFY2010PAR.pdf.

62. 15 U.S.C. §§ 1051–1072.

reasonably expect them to taste as good as those sold at any other McDonald's. The trademark does not necessarily reveal the product's manufacturer. For example, the trademark Bose identifies a brand of speaker. We may not know whether the manufacturer is a company called Bose, but we know that all speakers bearing the Bose mark are sponsored by a single company (or its licensees).

For producers, a trademark represents the goodwill of a business, that is, an accumulation of satisfied customers who will continue buying from that business. Trademark rights are largely determined by the perceptions and associations in the minds of the buying public, so maintaining a strong trademark is essential to preserving the success of a business. The top brand names for 2010 are listed in Exhibit 11.2.

In a phenomenon known as "trademark bullying," large corporations have sued start-ups to prevent them from using potentially confusing trademarks. For example, even though the PTO granted Christy Prunier a trademark on her line of skin care products, which she named after her daughter Willa, Procter and Gamble sued her, claiming that her trademark "Willa" was too similar to its "Wella" hair care brand. The parties settled on the eve of trial pursuant to a confidential agreement that permitted Prunier to continue to use the Willa name for her skin care line.[63]

Although most trademarks are verbal or graphic, trademark law also protects distinctive shapes, odors, packaging, and sounds. Apple, Inc. trademarked the three-dimensional shape of its iPod.[64] Both the unique shape of the Coca-Cola bottle and the sound of NBC's three chimes have trademark protection. Color may also qualify as a trademark. In *Qualitex Co. v. Jacobson Products Co.*,[65] the U.S.

Supreme Court articulated two principal criteria for determining whether trademark protection is available for a color: (1) the color must have attained secondary meaning so that it identifies and distinguishes a particular brand, and (2) the color must not serve a useful function, because granting trademark protection in this circumstance would amount to the grant of monopoly control.

Other Marks

Trademarks should not be confused with other forms of legally protected identifying marks, such as service marks, trade names, and certification marks.

Service Marks

A trademark is used in connection with a tangible product; a *service mark* is used in connection with services. The law concerning service marks is almost identical to that of trademarks.

Trade Names

Whereas a trademark is used to identify and distinguish products, a *trade name* identifies a company, partnership, or business. Trade names cannot be registered under federal law, unless they are also used as trademarks or service marks. The use of a trade name—evidenced by the filing of articles of incorporation or a fictitious business name statement—gives the company using the name certain common law rights, however.

Certification Marks

A *certification mark* placed on a product indicates that the product has met the certifier's standards of safety or quality. An example is the "Good Housekeeping" seal of approval placed on certain consumer goods.

---

63. Andrew Martin & Peter Lattman, *P.&G. Settles Trademark Suit Against Start-Up Business*, N.Y. TIMES, OCT. 15, 2011, at B4.

64. David Orozco & James Conley, *Innovation, Shape of Things to Come*, WALL ST. J., May 12, 2008, at R6.

65. 514 U.S. 159 (1995).

EXHIBIT 11.2	Most Valuable Brand Names in 2010	
2010 Rank	**2010 Brand Value (in millions)**	**Percentage Change (from prior year)**
1. Coca-Cola	$70,452	+2%
2. IBM	64,727	+7
3. Microsoft	60,895	+7
4. Google	43,557	+36
5. General Electric	42,808	−10
6. McDonald's	33,578	+4
7. Intel	32,015	+4
8. Nokia	29,495	−15
9. Disney	28,731	+1
10. Hewlett-Packard (HP)	26,192	+12

SOURCE: *Best Global Brands 2010*, INTERBRAND, *available at* http://interbrand.com/en/best-global-brands/best-global-brands-2008/best-global-brands-2010.aspx.

The Varying Distinctiveness of Trademarks

As shown on Exhibit 11.3, different types of marks fall on a distinctiveness continuum. The same word can be fanciful or arbitrary, suggestive, descriptive, or generic, depending on the product on which it is used.

Fanciful and Arbitrary Marks

Fanciful or arbitrary marks are often called strong marks because they are immediately protectable.

A *fanciful mark* is a coined term that has no prior meaning, until used as a trademark in connection with a particular product. Fanciful marks are usually made-up words, such as Kodak for camera products and Exxon for gasoline.

Arbitrary marks are real words whose ordinary meaning has nothing to do with the trademarked product, for example, Camel for cigarettes and Shell for gasoline.

Suggestive Marks

A *suggestive mark* suggests something about the product without directly describing it. After seeing the mark, a consumer must use his or her imagination to determine the nature of the goods. For instance, Chicken of the Sea does not immediately create an association with tuna fish; it merely suggests some type of seafood.

Descriptive Marks

Descriptive marks specify certain characteristics of the goods, such as size or color, proposed uses, the intended consumers of the goods, or the effect of using the goods. Laudatory terms, such as First Rate or Gold Medal, are also considered descriptive marks. Geographic terms and personal names are also descriptive marks.

Descriptive marks are initially unprotectable, but they can become protectable if they acquire *secondary meaning*, that is, a mental association by the buyer that links the mark with a single source of the product. Through secondary meaning, a mark obtains distinctiveness. Once this occurs, the mark is granted trademark protection.

Establishment of secondary meaning depends on a number of factors, such as the amount of advertising, the type of market, the number of sales, and consumer recognition and response. The testimony of random buyers or of product dealers may be required to prove that a mark has acquired secondary meaning. For example, the term "Holiday Inn" has acquired secondary meaning because the public associates that term with a particular provider of hotel services, and not with hotel services in general.

Geographic Terms Geographic descriptive terms are usually considered nondistinctive unless a secondary meaning has been established. Geographic terms used in an arbitrary manner are distinctive, however, for example, Salem for cigarettes and North Pole for bananas.

Personal Names Personal first names and surnames are not distinctive. But an arbitrary use of a historical name, such as Lincoln for a savings bank, does not require secondary meaning to be protectable.

Generic Terms

Trademark law grants no protection to generic terms, such as "spoon" or "software," because doing so would permit a producer to monopolize a term that all producers should be able to use equally. It would not make any sense to permit one manufacturer to obtain the exclusive right to use the word "computer," for example, and thereby force all competitors to come up with a new word, rather than a brand name, for the same type of product. Generic terms are not protected even when they acquire secondary meaning.

Many terms that were once enforceable trademarks have become generic. For example, "escalator" was once the brand name of a moving staircase, and "cellophane" was a plastic wrap developed by DuPont. Due to misuse or

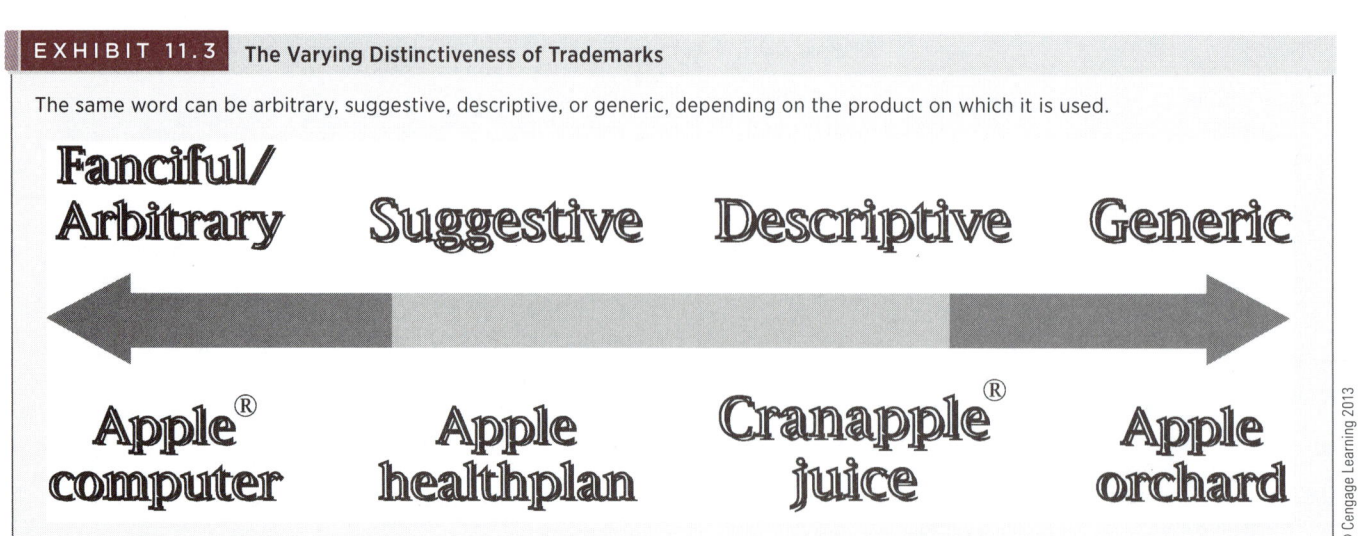

EXHIBIT 11.3 The Varying Distinctiveness of Trademarks

The same word can be arbitrary, suggestive, descriptive, or generic, depending on the product on which it is used.

Fanciful/Arbitrary — Suggestive — Descriptive — Generic

Apple® computer — Apple healthplan — Cranapple® juice — Apple orchard

© Cengage Learning 2013

negligence by the owners, these marks lost their connection with particular brands and became ordinary words. That is why Xerox Corporation engages in substantial advertising to explain that you don't "Xerox" a document, you "copy" it on a Xerox copier.

For terms that describe products made by only one company, the problem of *genericism*—the use of the product name as a generic name—is acute. Without competitive products, buyers may begin to think of the trademark as indicative of what the product is rather than where the product comes from. Manufacturers can try to avoid this problem by always using the trademark as an adjective in conjunction with a generic noun. It is all right to say "Kleenex tissue" or "I'm going to use the Google search engine for research," but not "a Kleenex" or "I'm going to Google that research topic." Once the buying public starts using the mark as a synonym for the product, rather than as a means of distinguishing its source, loss of the trademark is imminent.

Creating Rights in a Trademark

U.S. trademark owners initially obtain rights by using the mark in commerce or filing an "intent to use" application with the PTO. Following use in interstate commerce, owners may obtain additional rights by federal registration. State registration requires only intrastate use.

Trademark Searches

A company about to use a new trademark should first conduct a trademark search to determine whether use of the proposed mark will constitute an infringement. The time, money, and effort spent on promotion and advertising will be wasted if use of the mark is ultimately prohibited.

There are various ways to search a mark. The PTO's records provide information on federally registered marks; the office of the secretary of state can usually provide relevant data for that state's registered marks. Both state and federal registrations describe the mark and the goods it identifies, the owners of the mark, the date of registration, and the date on which the mark was first used. Most of this registration material has been computerized and can be accessed online.

"I'm not wasting my life online—I'm building my brand."

Barbara Smaller/The New Yorker Collection/www.cartoonbank.com

Searching for unregistered common law marks is more difficult. Trade and telephone directories are often a good source of common law marks. Some searches can be done by anyone using the Internet. There are also professional trademark search firms that search databases for customers. Although there is always the risk that a new mark or a common law user may be untraceable, any search is better than no search. Searching is evidence of a good faith effort to determine whether any other entity has preexisting rights in a mark.

Common Law Rights in a Trademark

A trademark is used in commerce if it is physically attached to goods that are then sold or distributed. Each subsequent use of a trademark creates greater rights, because increased sales and advertising generate greater customer awareness of the mark as representing the product. Use is also necessary to establish secondary meaning for descriptive marks.

In the United States, the first person to sell the goods under a mark becomes the owner and senior user of the mark. The mark is protected immediately, provided that it was adopted and used in good faith and without actual or constructive knowledge of any superior rights in the mark.

There is an exception to the rule of first use. If a subsequent, or junior, user establishes a strong consumer identification with its mark in a separate geographic area, the junior user may be granted superior rights for that area. By failing to expand its business to other parts of the country, the senior user takes the risk that a junior user may be permitted to use the same or a confusingly similar mark in a distant area. The junior user's use must be in good faith; that is, the junior user must take reasonable steps to determine whether any preexisting mark is confusingly similar to the one it plans to use.

This geographic rule is inapplicable, however, if the senior user has applied for or obtained federal registration (discussed in the next section). Once the senior user has filed an application or has obtained federal registration, it is permitted to claim nationwide constructive notice of the mark. This precludes any use of the mark—even a good faith use—by a junior user. Even with an application pending or registration, however, the senior user may not take any action against the junior user in a geographically removed area until the senior user is likely to expand into that area.

Federal Registration

Although not a requirement for obtaining U.S. rights in a mark, registration on the federal Principal Register provides (1) constructive notice of a claim of ownership in all fifty states, which makes it easier to enjoin subsequent users; (2) prima facie evidence of ownership; (3) the "incontestable" right (subject to certain defenses) to use the mark, obtainable after five years of continuous use following registration; and (4) the right to prevent importation into the United States of articles bearing an infringing mark.

Trademarks are grouped into different classes, covering more than forty different industries and goods. When a trademark is registered, the holder of the mark must specify the particular class to which the mark belongs. Although a single trademark may be registered in more than one classification, it is also possible for the same mark to be registered by different holders for different types of products.

Certain marks that do not qualify for registration on the Principal Register may be registered on the Supplemental Register. Such registration does not afford the owner any of the above benefits, however, and should be pursued only on the advice of counsel.

The PTO conducts federal registration of trademarks. An applicant may file either an "actual use" application or an "intent to use" application. For the latter, the applicant must state a bona fide intent to use the mark and must then commence use and provide the PTO with a statement of use within six months of receiving notice that its application is entitled to registration. The six-month period can be extended for up to thirty months, giving applicants a total of three years from the date of the notice of allowance in which to file the statement of use. Registration is postponed until the applicant actually uses the mark. The applicant has priority rights, however, against any party who did not use the same mark or file an application for it before the filing date of the intent to use application.

State Registration

Although state registration does not provide as much protection as federal registration, it does offer certain benefits. In most states, registration can be obtained within a few weeks of filing and is proof of ownership of the mark. For marks that are not eligible for federal registration, state registration usually provides at least some protection as long as there has been sufficient use of the mark.

State registration cannot preempt or narrow the rights granted by federal registration. For example, a junior user with a state registration predating a senior user's federal registration gains exclusive rights in the mark only in the geographic area of continuous usage preceding the federal registration, and not the entire state. A state trademark law that purported to reserve the entire state for the junior user would be preempted by the Lanham Act.

Loss of Trademark Rights

Failure to use one's mark—known as *abandonment*—may result in the loss of rights. A federally registered mark that has been abandoned can be used by a junior user. Trademark searches can reveal whether a previously registered trademark has lost its enforceability. There are two types of abandonment: actual and constructive.

Actual Abandonment

Actual abandonment occurs when an owner discontinues use of the mark with the intent not to resume use. Mere nonuse for a limited period does not result in loss of protection. After two years of nonuse, however, there is a presumption of abandonment. Because protection for federally registered marks is nationwide, the abandonment must be nationwide for loss of rights to result.

Constructive Abandonment

Constructive abandonment results when the owner does something, or fails to do something, that causes the mark to lose its distinctiveness. Constructive abandonment can result from a mark lapsing into genericism through improper use. It can also result from an owner's failure to adequately control companies licensed to use its mark. Thus, a licensor should carefully exercise quality controls and approval procedures for its licensees' products in order to ensure a consistent quality level.

Trademark Infringement

To establish direct trademark infringement, a trademark owner must prove (1) the validity of the mark (note that a federally registered mark is prima facie valid), (2) priority of usage of the mark, and (3) a likelihood of confusion in the minds of the purchasers of the products in question. A trademark owner may also allege vicarious and/or contributory infringement of his or her marks.

Proving validity and priority of usage is fairly straightforward if the mark is registered. If the mark is not registered, such proof is a factual matter. Establishing likelihood of confusion, on the other hand, involves subjectively weighing a variety of factors. These may include (1) the similarity of the two marks with respect to appearance, sound, connotation, and commercial impression; (2) the similarity of the goods; (3) the similarity of the channels of trade in which the goods are sold; (4) the strength of the marks, as evidenced by the amount of sales and advertising, and the length of use; (5) the use of similar marks by third parties with respect to related goods and services; (6) the length of time of concurrent use without actual confusion; and (7) the extent and nature of any actual confusion of the two marks in the marketplace.[66]

Taking advantage of trademark confusion does not necessarily amount to infringement. In 1996, the U.S. Court of Appeals for the Sixth Circuit ruled that a travel agency had not infringed Holiday Inns' trademark in its vanity toll-free telephone number by using a similar number.[67] To promote itself, Holiday Inns had widely publicized its toll-free reservation line as 1-800-HOLIDAY, which translates to 1-800-465-4329 on a numeric keypad. Perhaps anticipating

---

66. *See, e.g.,* Interstellar Starship Servs., Ltd. v. Epix, Inc., 304 F.3d 936 (9th Cir. 2002).

67. Holiday Inns, Inc. v. 800 Reservation, Inc., 86 F.3d 619 (6th Cir. 1996).

that dialers would mistake Holiday Inns' letter "O" for the number zero, the travel agency reserved the toll-free number 1-800-405-4329 for its own use. Though acknowledging the potential for confusion, the court rejected Holiday Inns' claim of trademark infringement. The travel agency did not create the confusion; it merely took advantage of it.

The following case involved a lawsuit brought by 1-800 Contacts against WhenU.com because WhenU had delivered advertisements of 1-800's competitors to computer users who accessed 1-800's website. Before the court could consider infringement, it had to decide whether WhenU. com had "used" 1-800's trademarks.

| A CASE IN POINT | *In the Language of the Court* | Case 11.3 |

1-800 Contacts, Inc. v. WhenU. com, Inc.

United States Court of Appeals for the Second Circuit
414 F.3d 400 (2d Cir. 2005).

FACTS WhenU.com is an Internet marketing company that provides its proprietary "SaveNow" software without charge to computer users, usually as part of a software bundle that the user voluntarily downloads from the Internet. Once installed, the SaveNow software requires no action by the user to activate its operations. Instead, the software responds to a user's Internet activities by generating pop-up advertisement windows that are relevant to the activities. To deliver this contextually relevant advertising, the SaveNow software employs an internal directory with about 32,000 website addresses and address fragments, 29,000 search terms, and 1,200 keyword algorithms that correlate with particular consumer interests. It screens the words that a user types into a web browser or search engine, or that appear within the Internet sites that a user visits. When the software recognizes a term, it randomly selects an advertisement from the corresponding product or service category to deliver to the user's computer screen at roughly the same time the website or search results sought by the user appear.

The plaintiff, 1-800 Contacts, filed a complaint alleging, among other things, that WhenU was infringing its trademarks by causing pop-up ads of 1-800's competitors to appear on a user's screen when the user accessed 1-800's website. If a SaveNow user who has accessed the 1-800 website and has received a WhenU.com pop-up advertisement does not want to view the ad or the advertiser's website, the user can click on the visible part of the 1-800 window, which moves the 1-800 site to the front of the screen display, with the pop-up ad moving behind the website window. Alternatively, the user can close the pop-up website by clicking on its close button. If the user clicks on the pop-up ad, the main browser window containing the 1-800 website will be navigated to the website of the advertiser that was featured inside the pop-up ad.

ISSUE PRESENTED Does WhenU "use" 1-800's trademarks within the meaning of the Lanham Act by delivering advertisements of 1-800's competitors to computer users who have intentionally accessed 1-800's website?

OPINION WALKER, C.J., writing for the U.S. Court of Appeals for the Second Circuit:

The Lanham Act defines "use in commerce," in relevant part, as follows:

. . . For purposes of this Chapter, a mark shall be deemed to be in use in commerce—

(1) on goods when—(A) it is placed in any manner on the goods or their containers or the displays associated therewith or on the tags or labels affixed thereto, or if the nature of the goods makes such placement impracticable, then on documents associated with the goods or the sale, and (B) the goods are sold or transported in commerce, and

(2) on services when it is used or displayed in the sale or advertising of services and the services are rendered in commerce. . . .

. . . [W]e note that WhenU does not "use" 1-800's trademark in the manner ordinarily at issue in an infringement claim: it does not "place" 1-800 trademarks on any goods or services in order to pass them off as emanating from or authorized by 1-800. The fact is that WhenU does not reproduce or display 1-800's trademarks at all, nor does it cause the trademarks to be displayed to a . . . user. Rather, WhenU reproduces 1-800's website address, www.1800contacts. com, which is similar, but not identical to, 1-800's 1-800CONTACTS trademark.

CONTINUED

... [I]t is plain that WhenU is using 1-800's website address precisely because it is a website address, rather than because it bears any resemblance to 1-800's trademark, because the only place WhenU reproduces the address is in the SaveNow directory. Although the directory resides in the ... user's computer, it is inaccessible to both the ... user and the general public. Thus, the appearance of 1-800's website address in the directory does not create a possibility of visual confusion with 1-800's mark. More important, a WhenU pop-up ad cannot be triggered by a ... user's input of the 1-800 trademark or the appearance of that trademark on a webpage accessed by the ... user.

A company's internal utilization of a trademark in a way that does not communicate it to the public is analogous to an individual's private thoughts about a trademark. Such conduct simply does not violate the Lanham Act, which is concerned with the use of trademarks in connection with the sale of goods or services in a manner likely to lead to consumer confusion as to the source of such goods or services. ...

... Absent improper use of 1-800's trademark, ... such conduct does not violate the Lanham Act. ... Indeed it is routine for vendors to seek specific "product placement" in retail stores precisely to capitalize on their competitors' name recognition. For example, a drug store typically places its own store-brand generic products next to the trademarked products they emulate in order to induce a customer who has specifically sought out the trademarked product to consider the store's less-expensive alternative. WhenU employs this same marketing strategy by informing ... users who have sought out a specific trademarked product about available coupons, discounts, or alternative products that may be of interest to them.

... Not only are "use," "in commerce," and "likelihood of confusion" three distinct elements of a trademark infringement claim, but "use" must be decided as a threshold matter because, while any number of activities may be "in commerce" or create a likelihood of confusion, no such activity is actionable under the Lanham Act absent the "use" of a trademark. Because 1-800 has failed to establish such "use," its trademark infringement claims fail.

RESULT   The appellate court reversed the district court's entry of a preliminary injunction and remanded the case with instructions to dismiss with prejudice 1-800's trademark-infringement claims against WhenU.

CRITICAL THINKING QUESTIONS

1. Would the court have reached the same conclusion if WhenU's pop-up ads displayed the 1-800 trademark? If WhenU's activities altered or affected 1-800's website? If WhenU diverted or misdirected users away from 1-800's website, or altered the results a user obtained when searching with the 1-800 trademark or website address?

2. Through programs like Google's AdWare, advertisers can choose to have their ads triggered when an Internet user searches a keyword (which may include a third party's trademark) that the advertiser has "purchased" from Google. Is this a "use in interstate commerce"?

The Federal Trademark Dilution Act[68] allows the owner of a famous mark to sue for injunctive relief from a party whose commercial use of a mark "begins after the mark has become famous and causes dilution of the distinctive quality of the mark." Dilution can result from "blurring" or "tarnishment." *Blurring* occurs when the nonfamous mark reduces the strong association between the owner of the famous mark and its products. *Tarnishment* occurs when use of the famous mark in connection with a particular category of goods or goods of an inferior quality reduces the positive image associated with the products bearing the famous mark. For example, use of candyland. com for a child pornography website tarnished the value of Hasbro's popular trademarked "Candy Land" children's game.[69]

68. 15 U.S.C. §§ 1125, 1127.

69. Hasbro, Inc. v. Internet Entm't Grp., Ltd., 1996 WL 84853 (W.D. Wash. Feb. 9, 1996).

In 2003, the U.S. Supreme Court held that a trademark owner must prove actual dilution, not just the potential for dilution, to prevail in an action under the Federal Trademark Dilution Act.[70] Congress responded by amending the statute to require only a showing of a likelihood of dilution.[71]

Damages are available only if the defendant willfully intended to trade on the reputation of the famous mark's owner or to cause dilution of the famous mark; in this event, the trademark owner is entitled to recover its damages and costs, as well as the dilutor's profits. Unlike in an action for trademark infringement, relief is available even if the other mark does not cause consumer confusion as to the source of the product.

Defenses

Possible defenses in trademark-infringement cases include the first sale and fair use doctrines, nominative use, genericity, and the First Amendment.

First Sale Doctrine

The first sale doctrine provides that a trademark owner cannot act against resellers of products after the first sale of the product. The idea behind the first sale doctrine is that the trademark owner had the chance to control the quality of the product and to make money on the first sale of the trademarked product. The first sale doctrine attempts to strike a balance among (1) trademark law's goal of allowing producers to reap the benefits of their reputation, (2) consumers' desire to receive what they bargain for, and (3) the public interest in maintaining competitive markets by limiting a producer's control of resale.

The first sale doctrine applies only when the seller is legally selling genuine trademarked goods. In 2003, Taylor Made Golf, a manufacturer of trademarked golf clubs, successfully sued MJT Consulting for selling Taylor Made clubs without authorization.[72] MJT had taken defective club heads that had been rejected and discarded by Taylor Made, affixed alternative shafts and grips, and then sold the "new" clubs under the Taylor Made trademark. MJT's defense was that it had bought the club heads from a middleman (that represented that it had bought the club heads from another middleman) and that Taylor Made's infringement claim was therefore invalid under the first sale doctrine. Pointing to factual evidence that the club heads were originally manufactured by Taylor Made and that Taylor Made did not intend them to be sold to anyone, the court rejected MJT's first sale defense.

Fair Use

The defense of fair use is available when a trademark user truthfully uses a competitor's mark to identify the competitor's product for the user's own purposes. To establish fair use, a defendant must show that its use is (1) other than as a mark, (2) in a descriptive sense, and (3) in good faith (the user must not intend to capitalize on the mark's goodwill or reputation).

Nominative Use

A defendant is not liable for trademark infringement if its use is *nominative use*, that is, if it uses the mark to talk about the mark itself. For example, Century 21, Coldwell Banker, and ERA Franchise Systems sued Lending Tree, an Internet real estate referral service, for using their trademarks on its website. Lending Tree asserted a nominative use defense. The U.S. Court of Appeals for the Third Circuit took a bifurcated approach. It ruled that the plaintiff must first demonstrate that the defendant's use of the plaintiff's mark is likely to create confusion. If the plaintiff meets this burden, the defendant must then prove the nominative fair use defense by showing that (1) the use of the plaintiff's mark is necessary to describe both the plaintiff's product or service and the defendant's product and service, (2) the defendant has used only as much of the plaintiff's mark as is necessary to describe the plaintiff's product, and (3) the defendant's conduct or language reflects the true and accurate relationship between the plaintiff and the defendant's product.[73] The court remanded the case to the trial court to determine if the defendant's use of the plaintiffs' trademarks was likely to cause consumer confusion and, if so, whether such use of the marks amounted to nominative fair use.

Genericity

As discussed earlier, genericity can be a defense when a trademark owner brings suit over a trademark that is arguably a generic term. Trademark owners must take appropriate measures to ensure that their marks are not, and do not become, generic.

First Amendment

Defendants may claim a First Amendment defense when their use of another's trademark is part of their communicative or expressive message and thus is protected as free speech. For example, courts have upheld consumers' rights to criticize corporations or service providers through websites that use the corporation's trademarked name. Courts have protected these so-called gripe sites as protected speech, even though the corporations often allege that the

---

70. Moseley v. V Secret Catalogue, Inc., 537 U.S. 418 (2003).

71. 15 U.S.C. § 1127.

72. Taylor Made Golf Co. v. MJT Consulting Grp., LLC, 265 F. Supp. 2d 732 (N.D. Tex. 2003).

73. *See* Century 21 Real Estate Corp. v. Lending Tree, Inc., 425 F.3d 211 (3d Cir. 2005).

sites confuse other consumers, hurt their business, and dilute their trademarks.[74]

Remedies for Trademark Infringement

One of the most common remedies for trademark infringement is injunctive relief. Courts may also award damages, measured either by the owner's lost sales and profits due to the infringement, or by economic injury to the owner's goodwill and reputation. To the extent they are not duplicative, courts may award the trademark owner the profits that the infringer earned through its use of the mark. In cases of flagrant infringement, a court may take the unusual step of awarding attorneys' fees to the trademark owner. Finally, in the particular case of trafficking in goods or services that knowingly use a *counterfeit mark*, the Lanham Act imposes substantial fines and/or imprisonment.[75]

DOMAIN NAMES AND CYBERSQUATTING

The Internet Corporation for Assigned Names and Numbers (ICANN) is the regulatory body that oversees the Internet's address system. Internet addresses are called *domain names*. The top-level domain is the domain name's suffix, which characterizes the type of organization. For example, ".edu" is used by educational organizations, and ".com" is used by commercial organizations. Country codes, such as ".fr" for France, serve as top-level domain names. The secondary domain identifies the specific organization. For example, in the domain name "cnn.com," the "cnn" identifies Cable News Network. As the Internet increasingly is used to conduct business, companies seek domain names that easily identify their web locations. Disputes have arisen when entities have registered domain names that are confusingly similar to another business's trademark. Unlike the trademark system, where more than one company can register the same mark for non-competitive products or services, only one entity can own the right to each domain name.

Domain names are registered on a first-come, first-served basis. Because the registrar does not check whether use of the name by the person seeking registration would violate someone else's trademark, the practice of

cybersquatting developed: an individual would register famous trademarks as domain names and then offer to sell them to the trademark owner for a "ransom."[76]

To combat this practice, ICANN developed a worldwide, fast-track, online domain name dispute resolution policy (UDRP), which became effective in 1999. Under the UDRP, a trademark owner who proves cybersquatting can receive an order from an arbitration panel that the domain name be canceled or transferred to the trademark owner. To prove cybersquatting under the UDRP, the complainant must prove that (1) the disputed domain name is identical or misleadingly similar to a trademark to which the complainant has rights, (2) the respondent has no legitimate rights in the domain name, and (3) the domain name is being held and used in bad faith. A successful complainant is not entitled to money damages under the UDRP.

Even though the U.S. Department of Commerce had designated ICANN to set up a global system for Internet management, including trademark issues, Congress passed the Anticybersquatting Consumer Protection Act of 1999 (ACPA),[77] before it was clear whether ICANN's process would be able to solve the cybersquatting problem. The ACPA, which became effective on November 29, 1999, created a separate, federal remedy, applicable only to domestic name registrations. Under the ACPA, a complainant must prove that (1) the defendant has a bad faith intent to profit from a mark, including a name of the defendant that is protected as a mark; and (2) registers, traffics in, or uses a domain name that (a) in the case of a mark that is distinctive at the time of registration of the domain name, is identical or confusingly similar to that mark; or (b) in the case of a famous mark that is famous at the time of registration of the domain name, is identical or confusingly similar to or dilutive of that mark. The ACPA's definition of cybersquatting is broader than ICANN's definition in that it makes bad faith alone actionable, regardless of use. In addition to authorizing a court to order the forfeiture or cancellation of a domain name or the transfer of the domain name to the owner of the mark, the ACPA also authorizes the award of actual or statutory damages of not less than $1,000 and not more than $100,000 per domain name.

TRADE DRESS

In addition to protecting registered marks, the Lanham Act also protects *trade dress*, that is, the packaging or dressing of a product. Trade dress includes all elements making up the total visual image by which a product is presented to customers, as defined by its overall composition and design.

---

74. Tresa Baldas, *The Cost of Griping on the Web: Lawsuits*, Nat'l L.J., Dec. 2, 2004, *available at* http://www.law.com/jsp/nlj/PubArticleNLJ.jsp?id=900005419466.

75. The Lanham Act defines a "counterfeit mark" as "(a) a spurious mark (i) that is used in connection with trafficking in goods or services; (ii) that is identical with, or substantially indistinguishable from, a registered trademark; and (iii) the use of which is likely to cause confusion or mistake or to deceive; or (b) a spurious designation that is identical with, or substantially indistinguishable from, the holder of the right to use the designation." 18 U.S.C. § 2320(e).

76. *See, e.g.*, Panavision Int'l, L.P. v. Toeppen, 141 F.3d 1316 (9th Cir. 1998).

77. 15 U.S.C. § 1125(d).

The elements of trade dress infringement parallel those of trademark infringement, with the likelihood of consumer confusion as the core issue. In one case, Best Cellars successfully sued Grape Finds for copying the style and arrangement of its retail wine shops.[78] Best Cellars' business model was predicated on demystifying wine purchases for unsophisticated shoppers by using a "wall of wine" racking system and other distinctive visual displays. Grape Finds started using the same system. The court ruled that Best Cellars' store arrangements were arbitrary and therefore protectable, and granted a preliminary injunction to prevent Grape Finds from using the same system in its stores.

Trade dress protection may not be claimed for functional product features.[79] In general, a product feature is functional if it is essential to the use or purpose of the article, or if it affects the cost or quality of the article.

✦ TRADE SECRETS

In our free-market system, the demand for modern technologies and innovation may lead to unauthorized disclosure of sensitive information. Trade secret law is necessary to protect the owners of such information.

A *trade secret* is information that gives a business an advantage over its competitors that do not know the information. The classic example of a trade secret is the formula for Coca-Cola. Trade secrets are protected for an indefinite time.

Know-how—detailed information on how to make or do something—can be a trade secret, or it can be show-how. *Show-how* is nonsecret information used to teach someone how to make or do something; it is generally not protectable.

Scope of Protection

The growing value of trade secrets has been accompanied by increasingly high stakes litigation. In 2011, a jury found Kolon Industries, Inc. liable for willful and malicious misappropriation of trade secrets from DuPont related to aramid fibers used in Kevlar body armor. It awarded DuPont almost $920 million in compensatory damages,[80] one of the largest amounts ever awarded in defense of business processes and technologies.[81] As of 2011, the case was on appeal.

Trade secret law is primarily the province of the states. Until 1996, courts developed the law of trade secrets on a case-by-case basis, applying the laws of the relevant state.

Courts based their decisions on tort theories in cases involving theft or misappropriation of trade secrets and on contract theories when a special relationship or duty was present. Many trade secret cases involved a combination of the two theories. Now courts also consider the federal Economic Espionage Act, which intersects with these traditional state-law approaches.

Common Law

The most widely accepted common law definition of "trade secret" is contained in the Restatement (Second) of Torts. Section 757, comment b, provides:

> A trade secret may consist of any formula, pattern, device, or compilation of information which is used in one's business, and which gives him an opportunity to obtain an advantage over competitors who do not know or use it. It may be a formula for a chemical compound, a process of manufacturing, treating or preserving materials, a pattern for a machine or other device, or a list of customers.

Section 39 of the Restatement of Unfair Competition defines "trade secret" as "any information that can be used in the operation of a business or other enterprise and that is sufficiently valuable and secret to afford an actual or potential economic advantage over others."

The courts have developed a number of factors to determine whether specific information qualifies as a trade secret. These factors include (1) the extent to which the information is known outside the business, (2) the extent to which measures are taken to protect the information, (3) the value of the information, (4) the amount of money or time spent to develop the information, and (5) the ease of duplicating the information.

Unfortunately, even with this formal definition and set of factors, a certain amount of guesswork is still required to determine whether a particular type of information qualifies as a trade secret under the common law. Faced with only slightly different factual settings, the courts have classified identical types of information differently.

The Uniform Trade Secrets Act

In 1979, the National Conference of Commissioners on Uniform State Laws (NCCUSL) promulgated the Uniform Trade Secrets Act (UTSA) in an attempt to provide a coherent framework for trade secret protection. NCCUSL hoped to eliminate the unpredictability of the common law by providing a more comprehensive definition of trade secrets. In particular, NCCUSL expanded the common law definition by adding the terms "method," "program," and "technique" to the Restatement's list of types of protected information. The intention was to specifically include know-how (technical knowledge, methods, and experience). In addition, NCCUSL broadened the common law definition by deleting the requirement that the

---

78. Best Cellars, Inc. v. Grape Finds at Dupont, Inc., 90 F. Supp. 2d 431 (S.D.N.Y. 2000).

79. TraffixDevices, Inc. v. Mktg. Displays, Inc., 532 U.S. 23 (2001).

80. *Jury Returns $919 Million for DuPont in Trade Secrets Theft Case*, McGuireWoods LLP (Sept. 15, 2011), *available at* http://www.mcguirewoods.com/news-resources/item.asp?item=6125.

81. News Release, E.I. du Pont de Nemours & Co., DuPont Wins Trade Secret Case Against Kolon Industries (Sept. 16, 2011), *available at* http://www2.dupont.com/Media_Center/en_US/daily_news/september/article20110916.html.

secret be continuously used in a business. Accordingly, the UTSA defines a trade secret as:

Information, including a formula, pattern, compilation, program, device, method, technique, or process, that (1) derives independent economic value, actual or potential, from not being generally known to, and not being readily ascertainable by proper means by, other persons who can obtain economic value from its disclosure or use; and (2) is the subject of efforts that are reasonable under the circumstances to maintain its secrecy.

Although the common law does not protect information unless it is in use, the UTSA definition is broad enough to include (1) information that has potential value from being secret, (2) information regarding one-time events, and (3) negative information, such as test results showing what will not work for a particular process or product.

The most significant difference between the UTSA and the common law definitions is in the overall approach to determining whether information is protectable as a trade secret. As discussed above, at common law a fairly objective five- or six-part test was developed. Although many courts adopted a reasonableness standard when interpreting the individual factors of the test, the focus was on objectivity, as delineated in this test. The UTSA uses a more flexible test, indicating that the steps taken to preserve the information as a trade secret must be reasonable and that the owner must derive independent economic value from secrecy. Although the "independent economic value" factor is subjective, a number of courts now use it as part of their trade secret test.

Adopted, at least in part, in forty-five states, the UTSA has only partially fulfilled its goal of standardizing trade secret law. States have tended to enact only those parts of the UTSA that embody the existing common law of the particular state. Consequently, in states that have adopted the UTSA, the courts rely on a combination of the common law and the UTSA. Although the UTSA seems to have fallen short of its goal of establishing consistent protection for trade secrets, it may provide broader protection to owners of trade secrets in states that have adopted it. Its definition of the term "trade secret" is broader than the common law definition, so the burden of proof on the owner is reduced. In addition, the UTSA provides more effective remedies.

Criminal Liability Under the Economic Espionage Act

The Federal Economic Espionage Act of 1996[82] imposes criminal liability (including fines and prison sentences) on any person who intentionally or knowingly steals a trade secret or knowingly receives or purchases a wrongfully obtained trade secret. The Act's definition of trade secret is substantially similar to the definition in the Uniform Trade Secrets Act.

Although the Economic Espionage Act was prompted by a desire to remedy perceived problems created by foreign thefts of trade secrets from U.S. businesses, it applies to any trade secret related to or included in products placed in interstate commerce. Organizations (other than foreign instrumentalities) can be fined up to $5 million (or two times the greater of the defendant's gain or the trade secret owner's loss). Foreign instrumentalities, defined as entities substantially owned or controlled by a foreign government, can be fined up to $10 million; individuals knowingly benefiting a foreign instrumentality can be fined up to $500,000 and imprisoned up to fifteen years.

The Act has extraterritorial application: it applies to any violation outside the United States by a U.S. citizen, a resident alien or an organization organized in the United States. It also applies to violations outside the United States if any act in furtherance of the offense was committed in the United States.

The government has moved swiftly to add violations of the Economic Espionage Act to its arsenal of potential actions against white-collar criminals. A disgruntled former employee of Replacement Aircraft Parts who offered to sell secret manufacturing details to competitors was sentenced to thirty months in prison after pleading guilty to criminal violation of the Economic Espionage Act.[83]

Creating Rights in a Trade Secret

In contrast to the formal process required for patent and copyright protection, no lengthy application and filing procedures are needed for trade secret protection. No review or approval by a governmental agency is required. To create and protect a trade secret, one need only develop and maintain a trade secret protection program. When the information being protected has a short shelf life, trade secret protection may be a more practical solution than copyright or patent protection.

Trade secrets are immediately protectable and continue to be protectable as long as the information remains confidential and is not developed independently by someone else. Material that would not qualify for patent or copyright protection is often protectable as a trade secret. A trade secret need not be as unique as a patentable invention or as original as a copyrightable work. It only needs to provide a competitive advantage. It may be merely an idea that has been kept secret, such as a way to organize common machines in an efficient manner, a marketing plan, or a formula for mixing the ingredients of a product. Trade secrets can also consist of a compilation of information, even though each component part of the compilation is generally known.

In addition, obtaining patent and copyright protection usually requires the disclosure of valuable information.

---

82. 18 U.S.C. §§ 1831–1839.

83. United States v. Lange, 312 F.3d 263 (7th Cir. 2002).

IN BRIEF

Advantages and Disadvantages of Different Types of Intellectual Property Protection

	Patent	Copyright	Trade Secret	Trademark
Benefits	Very strong protection; provides exclusive right to make, use, and sell an invention	Prevents copying of a wide array of artistic and literary expressions, including software; very inexpensive	Very broad protection for sensitive, competitive information; very inexpensive	Protects corporate image and identity by protecting marks that customers use to identify a business; prevents others from using confusingly similar identifying marks
Duration	20 years from date of filing the patent application	Life of author plus 70 years; for works made for hire, 95 years from year of first publication or 120 years from year of creation, whichever is shorter	For as long as the information remains valuable and is kept confidential	Indefinitely as long as the mark is not abandoned and steps are taken to police its use
Weaknesses	High standards of patentability; often expensive and time-consuming to pursue (especially when overseas patents are needed); must disclose invention to the public	Protects only the particular way an idea is expressed, not the idea itself; apparent lessening of protection for software; hard to detect copying in digital age	No protection from accidental disclosure, independent creation by a competitor, or disclosure by someone without a duty to maintain confidentiality	Can be lost or weakened if not appropriately used and enforced; can be costly if multiple overseas registrations are needed
Required Steps	Detailed filing with U.S. Patent and Trademark Office, which performs a search for prior art and can impose hefty fees	None required, though notice and registration can strengthen rights	Take reasonable steps to protect—generally, a trade secret protection program	Only need to use mark in commerce, though filing with U.S. Patent and Trademark Office is usually desirable to gain stronger protections
U.S. Rights Valid Internationally?	No. Separate patent examinations and filings are required in each country; however, a single international patent application can be filed with the national patent office or the World International Property Organization, and a single filing in the European Patent Office can cover a number of European countries.	Generally, yes	No. Trade secret laws vary significantly by country, and some countries have no trade secret laws	No. Separate filings are required in foreign jurisdictions, and a mark available in the United States may not be available overseas. A single CTM filing can cover a number of European countries, however.

SOURCE: Adapted from CONSTANCE E. BAGLEY & CRAIG E. DAUCHY, THE ENTREPRENEUR'S GUIDE TO BUSINESS LAW 572–73 (4th ed. 2012).

There is always a risk that after the sensitive information has been revealed, the reviewing agency will not grant the protection. To avoid this risk, trade secret protection may be the safest course of action.

There are two disadvantages to using trade secret protection, however. First, maintaining a full-fledged protection program can be expensive because confidentiality procedures must be continuously and rigidly followed to preserve trade secret status. Second, trade secret protection provides no protection against reverse engineering or independent discovery, and the uncertainty of protection may limit the productive uses of the trade secret.

Protecting a Trade Secret

Misappropriation of trade secrets most commonly occurs as a result of inadvertent disclosures or employee disclosures. To properly protect trade secret information, the owner must develop a program to preserve its confidentiality. In almost every jurisdiction, the test of a trade secret program's adequacy may be reduced to the question of whether the owner has taken reasonable precautions to preserve the confidentiality of his or her trade secrets.

A trade secret program should cover four areas: (1) notification, (2) identification, (3) security, and (4) exit interviews.

Notification

The first critical element is a written notice, which should be posted, to confirm that all employees have been made aware of the trade secret program. Ideally, the company's trade secret policy should be explained to each new employee during orientation, and each new employee should sign a confidentiality agreement that specifies how long confidentiality will be required.[84]

Labeling, such as using a rubber stamp to denote confidential material and posting signs in areas containing sensitive materials, is another means of notification. Some authorities, however, believe that labeling may actually hurt the trade secret status of information because, in practice, it can be difficult to ensure consistent and continuous labeling procedures. These authorities claim that failure to label some documents may be seen as evidence that the information in those documents should not be afforded trade secret status.

The company should also provide written notice to any consultant, vendor, joint venturer, or other party to whom a trade secret must be revealed. This notice should take the form of a confidentiality agreement that describes the protected information and limits the receiving party's rights to use it. Without such notice, the receiving party may be unaware of the nature of the information and unwittingly release it into the public domain.

A nondisclosure agreement (NDA) can serve as the basis for recovery if a court later determines that the party who gained access to trade secrets used or disclosed them in violation of the agreement. For example, in *Celeritas Technologies, Ltd. v. Rockwell International Corp.*,[85] the parties entered into negotiations for licensing Celeritas's "de-emphasis technology," a method for reducing high-frequency noise in cellular communications. Prior to allowing access to the information, Celeritas asked Rockwell to sign an NDA. The licensing negotiations ultimately failed, and Rockwell subsequently developed its own modem chips that incorporated de-emphasis technology. The same engineers who had access to Celeritas's technology under the NDA worked on Rockwell's de-emphasis technology project. Celeritas brought suit claiming, among other things, breach of the NDA. Because the technology was not readily ascertainable in the public domain and was found to have come directly from Celeritas, the court concluded that Rockwell had breached the NDA and that Celeritas was entitled to damages.

Sometimes an NDA may contain a "residuals" provision, which permits either party to use and exploit any information that representatives of the nondisclosing party learned in the course of the subject negotiations or engagement and retained in their minds. This can create a very large loophole in the restrictions on nondisclosure.

Identification

There is some debate about the appropriate method of identifying trade secrets. One view is that everything in the workplace, or pertaining to the business, is a trade secret, but a court will most likely deem this umbrella approach to be overly restrictive of commerce and therefore against public policy. Such a finding could undermine the company's trade secret program, exposing all of its trade secrets to unrecoverable misappropriation.

At the other extreme is a program that attempts to specify every one of the company's trade secrets. This approach may be too narrow because any legitimate trade secrets that are not specified will not be protected. Also, it is often difficult to pinpoint all of a company's potential trade secrets. For example, although it may be easy to designate all research and development projects as trade secrets, gray areas such as sales data, customer lists, or marketing surveys may cause problems. The best solution may be a program that specifies as much information as possible, while also including a limited number of catchall categories.

Security

Measures must be taken to ensure that trade secret information remains secret, at least from the public. The disclosure of a trade secret, whether intentional (for example, as part of a sale) or by mistake, destroys any legal protection. Access to trade secret information should therefore be limited to those who truly have a need to know. Hard copies of trade secret information should be locked in secure filing cabinets or a secure room. Photocopying machines should be placed as far as possible from trade secret files. Digital confidential information should be encrypted and password protected.

A company should also guard against unintentional disclosure of a trade secret during a public tour of the facility. An offhand remark in the hall overheard by a visitor, or a formula left written on a chalkboard in plain view of a tour group, is all that is needed. The best way to avoid this situation is to keep all trade secrets in areas restricted from public access. If such physical barriers are not possible, visitors' access should be controlled through a system that logs in all visitors, identifies them with badges, and keeps track of them while they are on the premises.

Employees may inadvertently disclose trade secrets when participating in trade groups, conferences, and conventions, and through publication of articles in trade journals and other periodicals. To avoid this problem, an employer should consistently remind its employees and contractors of when and how to talk about the company's business activities.

---

84. Many confidentiality agreements do not include a fixed term. Instead, they require an employee to maintain confidentiality as long as the information remains confidential and is not otherwise publicly released by the employer.

85. 150 F.3d 1354 (Fed. Cir. 1998).

Exit Interviews

When an employee who has had access to trade secrets leaves the company, he or she should be given an exit interview. The exit interview provides an opportunity to reinforce the confidentiality agreement that the employee signed on joining the company. If no confidentiality agreement exists, the exit interview is even more important because it provides the notice and possibly the identification necessary to legally protect the employer's trade secrets. The exit interview also lets the departing employee know that the company is serious about protecting its trade secrets and that any breach of confidentiality could result in legal proceedings against him or her. After such a warning, any misappropriation would be deliberate and could therefore result in punitive damages.

Misappropriation of Trade Secrets

An individual misappropriates a trade secret when he or she (1) uses or discloses the trade secret of another or (2) learns of a trade secret through improper means. The UTSA defines "improper means" by a list of deceitful actions. They include theft, bribery, misrepresentation, breach or inducement of a breach of a duty to maintain secrecy, and espionage through electronic or other means. The list is not exclusive, however, and anything that strikes a court as improper would probably qualify as an improper means.

In one misappropriation case, Wyeth, a large pharmaceutical company, sued Natural Biologics for misappropriating its secret manufacturing process for Premarin, a highly profitable hormone replacement therapy drug.[86] Pretrial discovery uncovered a series of phone calls between Natural Biologics and a retired Wyeth scientist who had been instrumental in developing the Premarin manufacturing process. The court determined that these calls gave the fledgling company all the knowledge it needed to copy the process. Because Natural Biologics had improperly obtained this information, the court issued a permanent injunction forbidding it from using the information or in any way engaging in drug development processes.

Inevitable Disclosure Doctrine

Some courts have recognized a form of employee misappropriation under the *inevitable disclosure doctrine*, which recognizes that former employees who go to work for a competitor in a similar capacity will inevitably rely on and disclose the trade secrets gained in their former employment.

The inevitable disclosure doctrine was first recognized by a federal appeals court in *PepsiCo, Inc. v. Redmond*.[87]

William Redmond, Jr. worked as a senior marketing manager for PepsiCo in its Pepsi-Cola North America division. Redmond had just completed work on the strategic marketing plans for All Sport (a sports drink that competed against Gatorade) and PepsiCo's powdered teas (which competed against Snapple, among others). In November 1994, Redmond accepted an offer from Quaker Oats to work as the vice president of field operations in Quaker's combined Gatorade and Snapple drinks subsidiary. PepsiCo sued to enjoin Redmond from working at Quaker Oats on grounds of threatened misappropriation.

The U.S. Court of Appeals for the Seventh Circuit held that a company may prove trade secret misappropriation by demonstrating that the employee's new position will inevitably lead him to rely on his ex-employer's trade secrets. Because of the competition between All Sport and Gatorade, the court concluded that Redmond could not help but rely on PepsiCo's trade secrets as he planned Gatorade's future course. Specifically, Quaker Oats would have a substantial advantage by knowing how PepsiCo would price, distribute, and market its sports drinks. The court likened the situation to that faced by a football team whose key player leaves to play for another team and takes the playbook with him.

By recognizing the notion of inevitable disclosure as being within the UTSA's provision of "threatened disclosure," the *PepsiCo* case gives employers greater leverage over departing employees and a powerful weapon against competitors who lure away valuable employees. For example, after initiating a lawsuit, Campbell Soup Company entered into a settlement agreement with H.J. Heinz that allowed the former head of Campbell's U.S. soup business to join the Heinz tuna and pet-food businesses, but only on the condition that he stay out of the soup business for one year.

Although a number of courts have accepted the inevitable disclosure doctrine in some form, other courts have hesitated to apply the doctrine. For example, in *Earthweb, Inc. v. Schlack*,[88] the U.S. District Court for the Southern District of New York refused to apply the inevitable disclosure doctrine in circumstances where a noncompete agreement was considered overbroad and thus unenforceable. The court reasoned that "the inevitable disclosure doctrine treads an exceedingly narrow path through judicially disfavored territory. Absent evidence of actual misappropriation by an employee, the doctrine should be applied in only the rarest of cases."[89] In *FLIR Systems Inc. v. William Parrish*,[90] the California Court of Appeal went further, declaring: "The doctrine of inevitable disclosure is not the law in California."

86. Wyeth v. Natural Biologics, Inc., 2003 WL 22282371 (D. Minn. 2003), *aff'd*, 395 F.3d 897 (8th Cir. 2005).
87. 54 F.3d 1262 (7th Cir. 1995).
88. 71 F. Supp. 2d 299 (S.D.N.Y. 1999), *aff'd*, 205 F.3d 1322 (2d Cir. 2000).
89. *Id.* at 310.
90. 174 Cal. App. 4th 1270 (2009).

Remedies for Trade Secret Misappropriation

Once a trade secret has been misappropriated, the law provides a choice of remedies, which are not mutually exclusive.

Injunctions

A court may issue an injunction ordering the misappropriator to refrain from disclosing or using the stolen trade secret. An injunction is available only to prevent irreparable harm, however. If the trade secret has already been disclosed, an injunction may no longer be appropriate to protect the trade secret. The court may, however, still enjoin the misappropriator from using the information so that the misappropriator will not benefit from his or her wrongful act. In this situation, the injunction is often combined with an award of damages.

The owner may also be able to seek an injunction or damages from anyone receiving the misappropriated trade secret or anyone hiring the individual who misappropriated it. For example, as mentioned earlier, the court issued a permanent injunction against Natural Biologics forbidding it from any drug development, because its entire drug manufacturing business was based on information stolen from Wyeth.

Finally, an injunction may also be appropriate when an individual threatens to use or disclose a trade secret, although the real damage has not yet occurred. In the *PepsiCo* case, the former PepsiCo employee was not permitted to work for Quaker Oats, until the information he had in his head about PepsiCo's marketing strategy became stale and lacked competitive value.

Damages

When the owner of the trade secret has suffered financial harm, courts often award money damages, based on either a contract or a tort theory. Under the tort theory of trade secrets, the purpose of the damages is not only to make the owner whole, but also to disgorge any profits the misappropriator may have made due to his or her wrongful act. The key to the tort measure of damages is that there was either a harm or an unjust gain, or both. The contract theory of trade secrets, on the other hand, measures damages by the loss of value of the trade secret to the owner as a result of a breach of contract. Courts determine the loss of value by adding the general loss to any special losses resulting from the breach and subtracting any costs avoided by the owner as a result of the breach.

The technical differences between the two measures of damages make little practical difference. Most courts will attempt to fairly compensate the owner of a misappropriated trade secret regardless of how the case is characterized.

Punitive Damages

Punitive damages are available when the misappropriation was willful and wanton. Under the UTSA, the court may award double the ordinary damages if it finds willful and malicious misappropriation; in some states, courts may award attorneys' fees as well.

Criminal Liability

As described earlier, the Economic Espionage Act criminalizes the theft of trade secrets and imposes fines and imprisonment on those convicted under it. In addition, many state statutes also impose criminal liability for theft of trade secrets. Although criminal charges are less common than civil charges, in part due to the higher standard of proof for a criminal conviction, they still occur.

GLOBAL VIEW

The Move Toward Harmonization of Intellectual Property Regimes

Several multinational treaties are attempting to harmonize the application of intellectual property laws across jurisdictions. Although they do not alter the substantive criteria that each jurisdiction applies to determine whether patent, trademark, or copyright protection is available, the treaties seek to coordinate the registration and recognition process among signatory countries.[91]

In most countries, if two entities file for protection of the same invention or trademark, the entity that filed first receives protection. This can be a problem for an inventor or trademark owner who files for protection in one country and later discovers that someone else has subsequently filed for protection of the same invention or trademark in another country. The International Convention for the Protection of Industrial Property Rights (known as the Paris Convention) addresses this problem by encouraging reciprocal recognition of patents, trademarks, service marks, and similar forms of intellectual property rights among its eighty-plus signatory nations. Each signatory nation grants nationals of other signatory nations a grace period after filing in their home country, within which to

---

91. One academic cautioned: "Notwithstanding these harmonization efforts, countries—both developed and less developed—have become increasingly dissatisfied with the international intellectual property regime. . . . To protect themselves and to reclaim autonomy over their intellectual property policies, [they] have recently pushed for measures that frustrate the harmonization project." Peter K. Yu, *Five Disharmonizing Trends in the International Intellectual Property Regime* 2 (Michigan State Univ. Coll. of Law, Legal Studies Research Paper Series No. 03-28, 2006).

CONTINUED

file corresponding patent or trademark applications. Patent applicants have one year and trademark owners have six months.

The Paris Convention does not alter the substantive requirements of the laws of each nation, so patent or trademark protection in one country does not necessarily translate into protection in another country. Differing rules governing eligibility may mean that actions in one's home country that do not compromise protection there may forfeit protection abroad (for example, disclosure or sale of inventions prior to filing for a patent).

Patents

The Patent Cooperation Treaty (PCT) allows an inventor to file a single international patent application to preserve the right to seek patent protection in each contracting country, rather than having to initially apply for separate patents in many different countries. The inventor may file this application either with the national patent office (e.g., the PTO for U.S. inventors) or the International Bureau of the World Intellectual Property Organization (WIPO).

Every international patent application is subject to an "international search" by an International Searching Authority. The search results include a list of citations of prior art relevant to the international patent application claims and information regarding possible relevance of the citations to questions of novelty and inventiveness (nonobviousness). This information enables the applicant to evaluate its chances of obtaining patents in the countries designated. An applicant may also have an international preliminary examination of the patent, which provides even more information about the invention's patentability. This information helps an applicant decide whether to file applications in individually designated countries.

The patent practice of other countries is often different from that of the United States. For example, foreign laws regarding statutory bars are radically different from U.S. patent law. A rule of thumb is that any public disclosure of an invention prior to filing the patent application will prevent an inventor from obtaining foreign patent protection. Also, some jurisdictions are more receptive to certain types of patents than others. In Europe, there are significant obstacles to obtaining patents on certain types of software innovations, including business methods. Some countries do not permit composition patents for pharmaceuticals, although they may receive some protection under process patents. Given these differences, managers should discuss the rules that apply in foreign jurisdictions with an attorney prior to disclosure or sale of any patentable invention.

Copyrights

International copyright protection has also begun to harmonize. Under the Berne Convention and the Universal Copyright Convention, American works receive the same protection that is afforded to the works of a national in foreign countries that are signatories of the same treaty.

In May 2001, the European Union (EU) approved a Copyright Directive to update and harmonize member state copyright laws to bring them into conformity with the WIPO Treaty and the WIPO Performances and Phonograms Treaty. The Copyright Directive outlaws the manufacture of devices that facilitate the circumvention of technology used for copyright protection. The Directive also provides authors with the exclusive right to authorize or prohibit communication of their work to the public by wire or wireless means, including interactive Internet sites that offer such works without the author's permission. In contrast to the DMCA in the United States, however, the Directive contains several different, yet still compliant, implementation methods regarding exceptions, penalties, and remedies that allow each country to modify the rules as needed. As of 2011, all EU countries had enacted the legislation required for compliance with the Directive.

Trademarks

Every country has its own methods for determining what is a protectable trademark, how to obtain and maintain trademarks, and the scope of protection available for trademarks. In contrast to the United States, in most countries use of a mark confers no rights; the first person to register the mark owns the rights to use it. In addition, registration of a trademark in the United States confers no rights in foreign countries, although a U.S. registration can provide an easy basis for registration of corresponding trademarks in countries that participate in multilateral trademark conventions with the United States.

Currently, several overlapping international regimes govern trademark applications, reflecting the trend toward increased global harmonization. As noted earlier, under the Paris Convention, an owner has a six-month grace period from the date a trademark registration application is filed in his or her home country to file in other signatory countries. As long as the foreign filing is made within that grace period, it is treated as if it had been filed in the foreign jurisdiction on the date the home country filing occurred.

The Madrid Protocol allows for centralized international registration of trademarks. The United States joined the Madrid Protocol in 2003, and there were eighty-five signatory countries as of December 2011.[92] A U.S. trademark owner can register the trademark in all signatory countries by filing a single application at WIPO's International Bureau in Geneva or at the U.S. PTO. Many lawyers see this process as beneficial and believe that it will substantially reduce the time and expense associated with trademark application filings. Others, however, point to differences in protection between national trademark regimes that may prove disadvantageous to U.S. trademark holders who use the WIPO registration process. For example, the PTO application requires narrower

CONTINUED

92. Madrid System for the International Registration of Marks, Summary Report for the Year 2010, *available at* http://www.wipo.int/export/sites/www/madrid/en/statistics/pdf/summary2010.pdf.

descriptions of goods and services than are required in many countries. As a result, a U.S. trademark holder may be better off filing separate, broader applications in each relevant foreign country.

The Pan American Convention recognizes the right of a trademark owner in one signatory country to successfully challenge the registration or use of that same trademark in another country. The key issue is whether persons using or applying to register the mark had knowledge of the existence and continuous use of the mark in any of the member states on goods of the same category.

For EU members, the Community Trade Mark (CTM) can confer protection in the entire EU. The CTM does not replace national rights or Madrid Protocol rights but coexists with them. A CTM can only be registered, assigned, or canceled with respect to the entire EU.

In an effort to attract foreign investment and trade, several nations have enacted laws to harmonize their trademark procedures with the international community. For example, in 1997 Japan enacted a trademark law to address the accumulation of unused registered trademarks by allowing anyone to petition for the cancellation of a mark that has gone unused and by making it more difficult to defend against such petitions. The law also shortened the time required to approve trademark applications. This made it easier for non-Japanese businesses to register and protect their marks in Japan. Among its many provisions, the law allowed for the registration of three-dimensional marks for the first time.

Trade Secrets

International trade secret protection is perhaps the least codified and harmonized aspect of intellectual property; thus, this area is the riskiest for U.S. companies doing business abroad. A primary concern is that countries differ in their interpretation of what constitutes a trade secret. For example, in the EU, trade secrets must be fixed in a tangible medium to be legally recognized. Japan does not recognize trade secrets as protectable property in and of themselves; instead, Japanese law forbids unfair acts of acquiring, disclosing, or using information in a manner that harms the trade secret owner. Other countries, like the Philippines, provide no legal protection at all for trade secrets.

Some countries recognize the importance of trade secrets but have legislation that forces their disclosure. For example, at one time, India required foreign companies to create joint venture arrangements that result in compulsory technology transfers to Indian companies. In 1977, Coca-Cola abandoned its Indian operations rather than divulge the trade secret for its secret formula. In China, government approval is required for any licensing agreement involving trade secrets; if the parties fail to comply, the trade secret owner forfeits the trade secret after ten years.

Most foreign countries will enforce reasonable nondisclosure restrictions in contracts, at least against parties to the contract; however, most countries do not recognize the tort law aspect of trade secrets that is recognized in the United States. In some countries, the judicial process itself may destroy the confidential character of the misappropriated information.

THE RESPONSIBLE MANAGER

PROTECTING INTELLECTUAL PROPERTY RIGHTS

Some of a company's most important assets may be intangible forms of intellectual property. Consider the formula for Coke, never registered as a patent, but kept as a trade secret by generations of executives at the Coca-Cola Company. In addition to protecting his or her company's own intellectual property, a manager should also ensure that the company does not infringe the intellectual property rights of others, whether they be trade secrets, patents, copyrights, or trademarks.

Problems frequently arise when a manager leaves the employment of one company to assume a position at another. During the exit interview, employees should be reminded of their obligations, and materials and computers being removed from the employer's premises should be inspected. It is critical that the manager and the new

employer ensure that no confidential information, including trade secrets, is conveyed to the new employer, either in the form of documents or as information in the manager's head. At the time of hire, the employer should determine whether the potential employee is bound by a restrictive covenant. Moreover, a company should provide written notice to all employees that it has a policy against receiving, using, or purchasing any trade secrets belonging to third parties. Misappropriation of trade secrets is a civil and criminal offense.

If the manager cannot fulfill all the duties of his or her new job without using the prior employer's trade secrets, the new employer should scale back the manager's activities and responsibilities. This can be accomplished by having the former employer and the new employer agree

CONTINUED

that the manager will not assume responsibility for certain product lines that compete with his or her former employer's until a date when the strategic and other confidential information known by the manager is stale. If possible, the departing manager should negotiate this issue as part of his or her severance arrangement, rather than wait for a costly lawsuit to be brought by the former employer.

Because international trade secret protection is the least codified and least harmonized aspect of intellectual property, a manager should consult with local counsel before making trade secrets available, by license or otherwise, in a foreign country. Patents, copyrights, and trademarks also provide legal protection for different aspects of a company's intellectual property. Patents are extremely important to high-tech companies and some e-commerce firms. Royalties from patents can add tens or even hundreds of millions of dollars to a company's revenues. A manager should develop a global patent strategy as each jurisdiction gives the holder exclusive rights only in the granting jurisdiction. Although the United States is shifting from a "first-to-invent" to a "first-to-file" approach in issuing patents (as discussed in the "Inside Story" in this chapter), major differences between U.S. and non-U.S. patent regimes persist.

Patents also have an important strategic use as a defensive measure in the event that another company claims patent infringement. In such a case, it is very helpful for a manager to have patents that can be used as bargaining chips to negotiate a settlement, which often takes the form of a cross-license. When Google CEO Larry Page announced the company's $12.5 billion deal to acquire Motorola Mobility, he specifically referenced the need to counter what he called anticompetitive patent activities by Microsoft and Apple.[93] Apple cofounder Steve Jobs had reportedly threatened "thermonuclear war" over Google's release of the Android operating system for smartphones, which directly competed with Apple's iPhones.[94]

Copyrights prevent others from copying literary works, musical works, sound recordings, computer software, and other forms of expression fixed in a tangible medium. A manager should consult with an experienced copyright attorney to ensure that his or her company obtains copyright ownership when it commissions, or contracts with, a third party to prepare a copyrighted work. A manager should also discuss with an attorney what, if any, copyright protection is available for a work in any foreign jurisdiction in which the company wants to distribute the work, and what steps are necessary to obtain such protection. A manager should be aware that copyright registration with the U.S. Copyright Office is a prerequisite for filing an infringement suit for a work of U.S. origin. Statutory damages and attorneys' fees are available only to owners who have registered the work within ninety days of first publication or prior to the infringement that forms the basis of the suit. Because the timing of the registration is critical, a manager should consult with a copyright attorney before publication of an important copyrighted work.

Trademarks that identify brands of goods or services are protected for an indefinite time. Managers must work to preserve trademarks, however. Once the buying public starts using the trademark as a synonym for the product, rather than as a means of distinguishing its source, loss of the trademark is imminent. The trademark registration process can be complex and confusing. It can also take up to eighteen months after an application is filed for a federal registration to be issued. Early consultation with legal counsel is therefore strongly advised.

A company may benefit from technology licensing. The volume of such arrangements, which offer advantages and disadvantages for both the licensor and the licensee, has increased dramatically since World War II and continues to accelerate.

Finally, managers should evaluate the adequacy of the company's insurance coverage for losses and claims related to electronic commerce and intellectual property. In light of the importance of computers, it is crucial to ensure that policies for property damage and business interruption cover damage to hardware and software, loss of data, and business disruptions caused by a virus, hacker attack, or other electronic assault. Commercial general liability policies, which provide coverage for liability a company may face for harm to third parties, usually cover bodily injury, property damage, personal injury, and advertising injury. Emerging issues include whether data are tangible property, whether the insertion of a defective computer part or software into a larger system causes property damage, and whether any company with a website is in the business of advertising and therefore is not covered by the usual advertising injury provisions, which can cover intellectual property infringement and defamation claims.

Some insurance companies are attempting to eliminate coverage for cyberspace and e-commerce claims from traditional policies, often with the hope of selling specialty policies to cover cyber-risks. Although the new specialty policies are potentially valuable, policyholders must be careful to assess the gaps in coverage that can result if traditional "all-risk" liability coverage is replaced with a patchwork of specialty policies. Also, the language of the new policies can vary widely, so managers need to ensure that the coverage chosen matches the risks. Finally, managers should be aware that the new language used in these policies will inevitably result in disputes about its meaning.

93. Martin, Swartz & Acolido, *supra* note 2.

94. *Steve Jobs Vowed to "Destroy" Android*, BBC, Oct. 21, 2011, http://www.bbc.co.uk/news/technology-15400984.

A MANAGER'S DILEMMA

Putting It into Practice

A Patent for Your Thoughts

In the 1980s, three university doctors conducting research into vitamin deficiencies found a correlation between high levels of an amino acid called homocysteine in the blood and deficiencies of two essential vitamins—folate and cobalamin. The doctors also developed more accurate methods for testing body fluids for homocysteine by using gas chromatography and mass spectrometry. They obtained a patent that claims a process for helping to diagnose deficiencies of folate and cobalamin. The patent contained several claims that covered the researchers' new methods for testing homocysteine levels using gas chromatography and mass spectrometry. Competitive Technologies, Inc. (CTI) eventually acquired ownership of the patent, which it licensed to Metabolite Laboratories, Inc.

In 1991, Laboratory Corporation of America (LabCorp) entered into a license agreement with Metabolite pursuant to which Metabolite granted LabCorp the right to use the tests described in the patent in consideration of a royalty equal to 27.5% of LabCorp's related revenues. The agreement permitted LabCorp to terminate the arrangement if a more cost-effective commercial alternative became available that did not infringe a valid and enforceable claim of the CTI patent.

By 1998, growing recognition that elevated homocysteine levels might predict risk of heart disease led to increased testing demand, and other companies began to produce alternative testing procedures. LabCorp decided to use a test for elevated homocysteine levels that was developed by Abbott Laboratories. LabCorp continued to pay royalties to Metabolite when it used the patented Metabolite tests, but LabCorp did not pay Metabolite royalties when it used the Abbott test, which it had concluded did not fall within the patent's claims.

In response, CTI and Metabolite sued LabCorp for patent infringement and breach of the license agreement.[95] The plaintiffs did not claim that LabCorp's use of the

Abbott test infringed the CTI patent's claims for testing homocysteine. Instead, they accused LabCorp of indirect infringement, arguing that LabCorp induced its customers to infringe claim 13 of the patent, which reads in full as follows:

> A method for detecting a deficiency of cobalamin or folate in warm-blooded animals comprising the steps of: assaying a body fluid for an elevated level of total homocysteine; and correlating an elevated level of total homocysteine in said body fluid with a deficiency of cobalamin or folate.

The plaintiffs argued that claim 13 created a protected monopoly over the process of "correlating" test results and potential vitamin deficiencies. The parties agreed that the words "assaying a body fluid" refer to the use of any test, whether patented or unpatented, that determines whether a body fluid has an "elevated level of total homocysteine."

At trial, the inventors testified that claim 13's "correlating" step consists simply of a physician's recognition that a test showing an elevated homocysteine level—by that very fact—indicates that the patient is likely to have a cobalamin or folate deficiency. Because the natural relationship between homocysteine and vitamin deficiency was well known by then, the inventors acknowledged that the "correlating" step would automatically occur in the mind of any competent doctor. Therefore, the plaintiffs asserted, LabCorp was liable for inducing infringement of the patent when it conducted the Abbott test and reported homocysteine levels to its physician customers who, because of their training, would automatically reach a conclusion about whether the person tested was suffering from a vitamin deficiency.

Should claim 13 be invalidated on the basis that it improperly seeks to claim a basic scientific relationship between homocysteine and vitamin deficiency? What public policies are implicated? Was it legal, and was it ethical, for CTI and Metabolite to acquire the CTI patent and to seek to enforce it in this way? Was it legal, and was it ethical, for LabCorp to encourage doctors to order diagnostic tests for measuring homocysteine levels?

---

95. *Metabolite Labs., Inc. v. Lab. Corp. of Am. Holdings*, 370 F.3d 1354 (Fed. Cir. 2004), *cert. granted in part*, 546 U.S. 999 (2005), *and cert. dismissed in part*, 548 U.S. 124 (2006). *See also* Mayo Collaborative Serv. v. Prometheus Labs., 2012 WL 912952 (U.S., Mar. 20, 2012).

INSIDE STORY

Congress Passes Sweeping Patent Reform

On September 16, 2011, President Obama signed into law the American Invents Act of 2011 (AIA),[96] the most sweeping reform of the U.S. patent laws since the Patent Act of 1952. The Act passed the House of Representatives by a vote of 304–117 and the Senate by a vote of 89–9. The AIA made changes in several key areas, including a shift from a first-to-invent to a first-to-file system and the implementation of new post-grant review procedures within the PTO. The AIA also added special provisions for "financial products or services" business method patents.

With the passage of the AIA in 2011, the United States adopted a first-to-file system, effective September 16, 2013, making the U.S. patent system more similar to that used in the rest of the world. Nevertheless, the U.S. first-to-file system will be distinctly American, as it will allow the inventor to disclose his or her invention before applying for a U.S. patent, as long as that disclosure is made one year or less before the effective filing date of the application. Aside from this limited disclosure exception, the scope of prior art is expanded under the AIA. For example, public use and sale of the invention in a foreign country count as prior art under the AIA. Additionally, under the U.S. first-to-file system, there will no longer be interference proceedings to determine who was the first to invent; instead, there will be derivation proceedings to determine whether the first-to-file inventor derived his or her invention from a subsequent applicant's work. If so, then the patent will go to the person who actually invented the work, even though he or she filed a subsequent patent application.

The AIA also established a process whereby the PTO can review patents after they are granted ("post-grant" review) to determine whether they are valid. Post-grant review may be sought within nine months of the issuance of the patent by any third party that wishes to challenge the patent on any basis. After that nine-month period, a third party may seek *inter partes* review, which has a higher standard and is limited to challenging the patent based on prior art patents and printed publications. Post-grant review is designed to eradicate invalid patents more promptly than judicial review in litigation.

Several important provisions in earlier versions of the bill did not make it into the final act. They included a provision that would have limited damages in cases where the infringed patent constituted only a minor portion of the defendant's product to the proportionate value of the infringed patent within the larger product rather than the overall sales of the entire product. A clearer definition of willful infringement and further restrictions on forum shopping were also deleted from the final bill. A provision that would have eliminated fee diversion, a practice whereby the fees collected by the PTO in excess of its approved budget are used by the government as general revenues, was also dropped. The PTO has a large backlog of patent applications, and supporters of this provision argued that the PTO should be allowed to keep its fees so that it can hire more examiners to deal with that backlog and satisfy its new obligations under the AIA. Critics asserted that eliminating fee diversion would unduly interfere with Congress's ability to oversee the PTO as part of the appropriations process.

The shift to a first-to-file system proved even more contentious. Critics claimed that it unfairly advantaged larger corporations. Indeed, some argued that eliminating the first-to-invent system was inconsistent with the authority the Constitution gave Congress to promote inventions by issuing patents. While DuPont CEO Ellen Kullman praised the AIA for bringing "the U.S. patent system into the 21st century and [helping] speed and expand the innovation capacity of the American economy, creating new technologies, products and jobs,"[97] Silicon Valley entrepreneur Henry Nothhaft sharply criticized it: "[T]his change [to a first-to-file system] will cripple job creation in the United States and lead to even more economic advancement from our overseas competitors."[98]

---

96. Leahy–Smith America Invents Act, Pub. L. No. 112-29, 125 Stat. 284–381 (2011).

97. News Release, E.I. du Pont de Nemours & Co., DuPont Chair and CEO Ellen Kullman Attends U.S. Presidential Bill Signing, (Sept. 19, 2011), *available at* http://www2.dupont.com/Media_Center/en_US/daily_news/september/article20110919.html.

98. Henry R. Nothhaft, *"First to File" Is Threat to Job Creation*, THE HILL (Feb. 25, 2011), http://thehill.com/blogs/congress-blog/economy-a-budget/146149-first-to-file-is-threat-to-job-creation.

KEY WORDS AND PHRASES

QUESTIONS AND CASE PROBLEMS

1. Myriad Genetics, Inc. has patents for isolated DNA sequences associated with a predisposition to breast and ovarian cancers (the BRCA1 and BCRA2 genes) and for diagnostic methods of identifying mutations in those DNA sequences. A group of plaintiffs challenged the validity of the patents in court. The challenged patents include (1) a patent over the composition of isolated DNA sequences related to breast and ovarian cancers; (2) a patent for the method of comparing/analyzing isolated DNA sequences (which can be accomplished by mere inspection); and (3) a patent for the method of screening potential cancer therapeutics through changes in cell growth rates, which involves growing cells, determining cell growth rates, and comparing growth rates. Are the isolated DNA sequences a product of nature and thus patent ineligible? Are these methods of comparing DNA sequences too abstract to patent? Is the method for screening potential cancer therapeutics too abstract to be a patent-ineligible scientific principle, or does it include transformative steps that are patent eligible? Would making a correlation between the presence of the BRCA1 and BRCA2 genes and a heightened risk of breast and ovarian cancer be patentable? [*Ass'n for Molecular Pathology v. U.S. Patent & Trademark Office,* 2011 WL 3211513 (Fed. Cir. 2011).]

2. The Digital Millennium Copyright Act (DMCA) includes a "safe harbor" provision under which a service provider is granted immunity from copyright infringement "by reason of the storage [of infringing content] at the direction of a user." To be eligible for this safe harbor exception, the provider must (1) have no "actual knowledge" of infringement; (2) not be aware of "facts or circumstances from which infringing activity is apparent"; (3) on gaining knowledge of the infringing content, act "expeditiously to remove" the infringing material; and (4) "not receive a financial benefit directly attributable to the infringing activity" if the service provider has the ability to control such activity. The service provider must also have a designated agent to receive notifications of claimed infringement, but it is not obligated to monitor users' activity or "affirmatively [seek] facts indicating infringing activity." YouTube hosts a website on which users can upload video files and view videos posted by others. Viacom, along with several other content providers, sued YouTube for copyright-infringing content uploaded by users on its website. If YouTube has the ability to monitor users to identify infringement, should it be required to do so? If YouTube is notified of infringing video files, should it be required to seek out all other files infringing the same content? Should it matter that infringing content as a whole brings more traffic to YouTube than noninfringing content does? Is it ethical for YouTube to keep content on its site that it knows is infringing? If you were the head of the Motion Picture Association of America or a major television network, what legislative changes might you propose to protect your intellectual property? If you

were YouTube's CEO, how would you respond? [*Viacom Int'l Inc. v. YouTube, Inc.*, 2010 WL 2532404 (S.D.N.Y. June 23, 2010).]

3. Article I, Section 8, Clause 8, of the U.S. Constitution (the Copyright Clause) grants Congress the power to grant copyrights to authors, but only for "limited [t]imes" and to "promote the [p]rogress of the useful [a]rts." Section 514 of the Uruguay Round Agreements Act (URAA) granted copyright protection to various foreign works that were previously in the public domain in the United States. In effect, section 514 extended copyright protection to works that had previously not been eligible for copyright protection and were therefore in the public domain. Is this provision constitutional? What policy arguments would you make for and against the provision? [*Golan v. Holder*, 609 F.3d 1076 (10th Cir. 2010), *cert. granted*, 131 S. Ct. 160 (2011).]

4. A hypothetical new communications product is described below. After reading the product description, think up three trademarks for this product: one that is fanciful, arbitrary, or suggestive; one that is geographic, descriptive, or a personal name; and one that is nondistinctive.

New Product Description

This new product incorporates global positioning technology into a multifunctional device that is worn like a watch. Not only does the device provide the time, but it also allows others to determine the location of the device and thus the location of the person. Moreover, the device is equipped to send and receive simple e-mail messages. The device may be especially suited for parents hoping to track remotely the whereabouts of their children. The location of the device can be determined through an online site that requires input of an identifying password.

5. Toy company Mattel sued MGA Entertainment for misappropriation of trade secrets, including the concept for the popular Bratz fashion doll. MGA counterclaimed that Mattel had misappropriated its trade secrets in violation of California's Uniform Trade Secrets Act, which defines "trade secret" as information that (1) "derives independent economic value . . . from not being generally known" and (2) "is the subject of efforts that are reasonable under the circumstances to maintain its secrecy." One of the issues was whether Mattel, and later MGA, took "reasonable efforts" to protect the alleged "trade secrets." MGA permitted retailers and the press to access its toy showrooms and product information displayed in "planogram" rooms operated by retailers, but it disallowed other toy vendors. Should MGA have required members of the press to sign nondisclosure agreements before viewing its products? How else might MGA have protected its proprietary information? [*Mattel, Inc. v. MGA Entertainment, Inc.*, 782 F. Supp. 2d 911 (C.D. Cal. 2011).]

6. McNeil Nutritionals sells Splenda, a highly successful national brand of sucralose, in yellow boxes and bags with blue lettering; the name "Splenda" is on the front in italicized blue lettering, surrounded by a white, oval-shaped cloud. The boxes and bags display photographs of different physical props, such as a white cup of coffee with a saucer, a glass and pitcher of iced tea, and a bowl of cereal and a scoop of Splenda behind a piece of pie on a plate. Heartland Sweeteners (the defendant) also sells its private label and store brands in yellow boxes and bags, with blue or black lettering (some outlined in white) and photographs of various items that can use the sweetener. Applying the following ten-factor test to determine whether there is a likelihood of confusion, does Heartland's packaging infringe McNeil's packaging? What other facts would you need to know? What steps could Heartland take to avoid a finding of infringement?

The ten factors are (1) degree of similarity between the plaintiff's trade dress and the allegedly infringing trade dress; (2) strength of the plaintiff's trade dress; (3) price of the goods and other factors indicative of the care and attention expected of consumers when making a purchase; (4) length of time the defendant has used the trade dress without evidence of actual confusion arising; (5) intent of the defendant in adopting its trade dress; (6) evidence of actual confusion; (7) whether the goods, although not competing, are marketed through the same channels of trade and advertised through the same media; (8) extent to which the targets of the parties' sales efforts are the same; (9) relationship of the goods in the minds of consumers because of the similarity of function; and (10) other facts suggesting the consuming public might expect the plaintiff to manufacture a product in the defendant's market, or that the plaintiff is likely to expand into that market. [*McNeil Nutritionals, LLC v. Heartland Sweeteners, LLC*, 511 F.3d 350 (3d Cir. 2007).]

7. BitTorrent developed a peer-to-peer file sharing technology that facilitates the transfer of large files on the Internet. Although computer designers at Silicon Graphics and Red Hat Software have used the technology for the lawful transfer of computer files, other users have used it to make and transfer illegal copies of copyrighted movies. BitTorrent published the software as open source without restrictions on its use. Like Grokster but unlike Napster, BitTorrent maintains no list of files transferred by its users and has no ability to monitor its users' activities. Unlike at Grokster, no one at BitTorrent ever encouraged users to use the software to make illegal copies of content. To the contrary, Bram Cohen of BitTorrent exhorted users not to use the software for illegal purposes. You are David Chao, a partner at DCM Capital, and are considering making an equity investment in BitTorrent. What factors would you consider when making your decision? If you were the head of Warner Brothers' home video unit, would you give BitTorrent a license to sell your films? On what conditions, if at all? [Constance E. Bagley & Reed Martin, *BitTorrent* (Harvard Bus. Sch. Case No. 806-169, 2006); Constance E. Bagley & Reed Martin, *Warner Bros. and BitTorrent* (Harvard Bus. Sch. Case No. 807-012, 2007).]

8. FairTest, a nonprofit organization dedicated to improving standardization tests, posted data on its website that demonstrated that minorities and low-income students score lower on the SAT and ACT than white and upper-class students. The College Board, the nonprofit that administers the SAT, demanded that FairTest remove the data, claiming that it was using College Board copyrighted data without permission. The College Board has a formal process by which it grants permission to organizations wishing to use its data; FairTest did not use this process. In reply, FairTest alleged that the data were not owned by the College Board and that, even if they were, the data are widely available in the public domain, thus removing them from copyright protection. Does FairTest's defense have merit? [*See* http://www.chillingeffects.org/responses/notice.cgi?NoticeID=1519; http://www.susanohanian.org/show_atrocities.php?id=3323.]

UNIT
III

HUMAN RESOURCES

CHAPTER 12

THE EMPLOYMENT AGREEMENT

INTRODUCTION

EMPLOYEE RIGHTS, POWERS, AND PROTECTION

Over the past eighty years, there has been an explosion of laws regulating the employment relationship. In the 1930s, as a result of the union movement, employees acquired economic and political power in their dealings with employers. With the emergence of the civil rights movement and the antidiscrimination legislation of the 1960s, employers began to examine their hiring and other employment practices more closely with respect to the treatment of women, minorities, and other protected groups. (Antidiscrimination laws are discussed in Chapter 13.) Laws concerning worker safety challenged employers to make the workplace safer. Federal and state whistleblower statutes prohibited retaliation against employees who complained to a governmental agency about working conditions or accounting practices that they believed violated the law. The Employee Retirement Income Security Act (ERISA) and other statutes required employers to manage pension funds in a prudent manner to protect employees' retirement benefits and regulated health-care and other employee benefits. Concerns about illegal workers led to both federal and state legislation dealing with undocumented workers.

The courts have also developed new common law doctrines that limit a U.S. employer's traditional right to discharge an employee for any reason. These judicial decisions have moved U.S. employment law closer to the European model, which requires an employer to show just cause for a discharge. Under the current law, an employer may be bound by contracts with its employees without even knowing it. Managers must devote both attention and resources to complying with the sometimes bewildering array of statutes, regulations, and common law principles that bear on their relations with their employees.

CHAPTER OVERVIEW

This chapter discusses the traditional U.S. rule that employees can be terminated at will and the exceptions to this rule. It examines the tort of fraudulent inducement and the enforceability of covenants not to compete. The laws relating to drug testing, genetic testing, lie detector tests, and certain hiring practices are also addressed. The chapter explains the employer's responsibility for worker safety; laws related to workers' pay, including minimum-wage and overtime payments; and several other federal laws that affect the employment relationship. In addition, the chapter explores pensions and other employee benefits. It also discusses the coverage and application of the National Labor Relations Act (NLRA), which governs union and other concerted action activities in the United States. Finally, the chapter examines how U.S. immigration law affects domestic employment of foreign workers and discusses the wrongful termination laws in the European Union and certain other jurisdictions.

AT-WILL EMPLOYMENT

For more than one hundred years, the American rule has been that an employment agreement of indefinite duration is an *at-will contract*; that is, the employee can quit at any time, and the employer can discharge the employee at any time, for any or no reason, with or without advance notice. All states originally followed this rule. Today, however, in many states, the at-will rule has been largely buried under its exceptions. Although some courts have declined to recognize these exceptions, the trend is toward some level of protection against discharge in certain circumstances.

Employees Not Subject to the At-Will Rule

Public employees, employees who have express employment contracts for a fixed term, and unionized workers are generally not subject to the at-will rule.

Public Employees

Most employees of federal, state, and local government agencies work under civil service or merit systems that provide for tenure, require just cause for discharge, and guarantee administrative procedures to determine whether there is just cause for discharge.

Employees with Individual Contracts

A private-sector employee can avoid at-will status by negotiating a contract that provides for a specific term of employment and defines how the contract can be terminated. Although employers almost always reserve the right to fire an employee, the employment contract may require some level of severance pay if the termination is without cause. Negotiated contracts requiring just cause for termination by the employer may also provide some level of payment and benefits if the employee quits "for good reason," which is often defined to include being required to move more than fifty miles from the original place of employment or having one's duties and responsibilities substantially changed or reduced.

Union Contracts

Other employees rely on union contracts, which almost universally require just cause for termination and establish grievance procedures whereby an employee can challenge his or her discharge.

Wrongful Discharge

Beginning in the early 1970s, courts in a number of states began to recognize exceptions to the at-will doctrine in new causes of action for *wrongful discharge*, that is, termination of employment without good cause. Wrongful discharge is a common law–based claim supported by three theories: public policy, implied contract, and implied covenant of good faith and fair dealing. These causes of action are based on both contract and tort law.

The Public Policy Exception

One of the earliest exceptions to the at-will rule was the *public policy exception*. Even if an individual is an at-will employee, in most states the employer is prohibited from discharging the employee for a reason that violates public policy.[1] The greatest protection is given to an employee discharged due to a refusal to commit an unlawful act, such as perjury or price-fixing, at the employer's request. Indeed, an employer's request that an employee violate a criminal statute—or even a noncriminal regulation—is almost always deemed to be a wrongful discharge in violation of public policy.

Sources of Public Policy

Different jurisdictions vary in what they recognize as a legitimate source of public policy. Some states, including West Virginia and Georgia, accept only statements of public policy that are expressly set forth in state or federal constitutions, statutes, or judicial decisions.

Most states, however, will consider a range of sources, including statutes, constitutional provisions, administrative regulations, professional codes of ethics, and, in some cases, common law. For example, an employee claimed that she was terminated by Central Indiana Gas Company for filing a workers' compensation claim. Although no state statute prohibited such a discharge, the Indiana Supreme Court held that "retaliatory discharge for filing a workmen's compensation claim is a wrongful, unconscionable act and should be actionable in a court of law."[2] The court further observed that an employee must be able to exercise his or her right under the Indiana workers' compensation statute without fear of reprisal in order for the public policy of the statute to be realized.

The California Supreme Court held that an attorney could base a claim of retaliatory discharge on allegations that he was terminated for refusing to violate a mandatory ethical duty embodied in the rules of attorney professional conduct.[3] Andrew Rose, former in-house counsel at General Dynamics, had filed a claim for retaliatory discharge, alleging that he had been fired because he had (1) spearheaded an investigation of drug use at the company that resulted in the termination of more than sixty employees; (2) protested the company's failure to investigate the bugging of the office of the chief of security, a criminal offense; and (3) advised company officials that General Dynamics' salary policy might be in violation of the minimum-wage and overtime provisions of the Fair Labor Standards Act, which could potentially expose the company to several hundred million dollars in backpay claims.

In contrast, in *Jacobson v. Knepper & Moga, P.C.*,[4] the Illinois Supreme Court held that an attorney who had been fired by his firm after complaining that it was violating the Fair Debt Collection Practices Act could not recover for retaliatory discharge. The court found that the public policy protected by the Act (protecting debtors' property and ensuring them due process) was already adequately safeguarded by the ethical obligations imposed by the rules of attorney professional conduct, making it unnecessary to expand the tort of retaliatory discharge to protect the discharged employee attorney.

---

1. The common law policy exception to the at-will doctrine has been adopted in forty-three states. Timothy J. Coley, *Getting Noticed: Direct and Indirect Power-Allocation in the Contemporary American Labor Market*, 59 Cath. U. L. Rev. 965, 986 (2010). New York and Florida, the third and fourth most populous states in the United States, do not recognize any form of the public policy exception. *Id.* at 986 n.116.

2. Frampton v. Cent. Ind. Gas Co., 297 N.E.2d 425 (Ind. 1973).

3. General Dynamics Corp. v. Superior Court, 876 P.2d 487 (Cal. 1994).

4. 706 N.E.2d 491 (Ill. 1998).

Whistleblowing Protection   In addition to protecting employees from discharge for exercising a right or duty, or for refusing to break the law, the public policy exception also protects employees from discharge for reporting an employer's unlawful or wrongful conduct (*whistleblowing*). In whistleblower cases, courts balance the public interest in the enforcement of laws, the whistleblower's interest in being protected from reprisal, and the employer's interest in managing its workforce. As discussed below, certain statutory and constitutional provisions may protect whistleblowers as well.

Remedies   In *Tameny v. Atlantic Richfield Co.*,[5] the California Supreme Court held that an employee might maintain both tort and contract actions if the employee's discharge violated fundamental principles of public policy. As a result, tort damages for pain and suffering, and possibly punitive damages, were available.

Implied Contracts

Most jurisdictions recognize the contract-based *implied contract* judicial exception to the at-will rule, in which the parties' conduct is found to imply a contract that limits the employer's right to discharge even when there is no written or express oral contract. Some factors that can give rise to an implied obligation to discharge the employee only for good cause are that the person (1) has been a long-term employee; (2) has never been formally criticized or warned about his or her conduct; (3) has received raises, bonuses, and promotions throughout his or her career; (4) has been assured that his or her employment would continue if he or she did a good job or that the company did not terminate employees at his or her level except for good cause; and (5) has been assured by management that he or she was doing a good job. Other relevant factors include the personnel policies or practices of the employer and the practices of the industry in which the employee is engaged.

In some states, a personnel manual stating that it is the employer's policy to release employees for just cause only, together with oral assurances that the employee will be with the company as long as he or she does his or her job properly, can create a binding contractual obligation on the company to terminate only for good cause. This obligation may arise in the absence of negotiations or any meeting of the minds, or even when the policy has not been communicated to the employee.[6]

For example, Woodstock Soapstone Company's personnel policy stated that an employee was entitled to two written warnings in a twelve-month period prior to termination for "willful or repeated violations, or exaggerated

[sic] behavior not in the best interest of the company or its employees." Prior to her termination, Havill continually clashed with a corporate reorganization consultant hired by Woodstock to redefine employment duties. After the consultant complained to Woodstock's management about Havill's "rude" and "insubordinate" behavior, Woodstock fired her, without providing the written warning required by its personnel policy. When Havill sued, the Vermont Supreme Court held Woodstock liable for damages arising out of its breach of the implied promise of "just cause" termination and progressive discipline.[7]

Other states, however, have been unwilling to treat written personnel policies as contracts. In one case, an employee of Citibank claimed that he could be discharged only for cause based on provisions of a personnel manual. A New York appellate court rejected this argument and held that the manual did not impose any legal obligation on the employer, because the employee was still free to terminate the relationship at will.[8] Similarly, in a case involving Westinghouse Electric Corporation, the North Carolina Court of Appeals held that unilaterally implemented employment policies are not part of the employment contract, unless expressly included in it.[9]

Even when an implied contract is found to exist, an employer may legally terminate an employee suspected of misconduct if, acting in good faith and following an investigation that is appropriate under the circumstances, the employer has reasonable grounds for believing that the employee engaged in misconduct. For example, a male manager was terminated following charges of sexual harassment by two female employees. The employer conducted a thorough investigation but was unable to determine with certainty whether harassment had taken place. Because the employer felt that the accusers were credible, and its investigator concluded that the harassment more likely than not had occurred, the company terminated the manager. He sued for wrongful termination, and the jury awarded him $1.78 million, after apparently finding that the charges against him were false. The California Supreme Court reversed and sent the case back for retrial so that the jury could determine whether, following a reasonable investigation, the company had a good faith belief that the manager had engaged in sexual harassment. If so, the company would not be liable for breach of the implied employment contract.[10]

Implied Covenant of Good Faith and Fair Dealing

Courts in a minority of states have also recognized an exception to the at-will employment relationship for the

5. 610 P.2d 1330 (Cal. 1980).

6. *See* Toussaint v. Blue Cross & Blue Shield of Mich., 292 N.W.2d 880 (Mich. 1980).

7. Havill v. Woodstock Soapstone Co., 865 A.2d 335 (Vt. 2004).

8. Edwards v. Citibank, N.A., 425 N.Y.S.2d 327 (1980).

9. Walker v. Westinghouse Elec. Corp., 335 S.E.2d 79 (N.C. App. 1985).

10. Cotran v. Rollins Hudig Hall Int'l, Inc., 69 Cal. Rptr. 2d 900 (1998).

breach of the *implied covenant of good faith and fair dealing*, that is, the *bad faith exception*.[11] For example, the Illinois Court of Appeals held that former at-will employees of Allstate Insurance could sue for breach of the implied covenant of good faith after Allstate pressured them to resign or retire, without disclosing that it was considering a sweetened severance package for employees who decided to stay.[12]

The bad faith exception to the at-will doctrine has been interpreted differently in the states that have recognized it. Most courts restrict the recovery in these actions to contract damages.[13] Courts in Texas, New Mexico, Florida, and Wisconsin have expressly declined to recognize an implied covenant of good faith and fair dealing in employment cases.

Treatment of Stock Options Stock options have become a key component of damages alleged in wrongful termination lawsuits, and their treatment can vary significantly depending on the jurisdiction. For example, in *Scully v. US WATS, Inc.*,[14] the U.S. Court of Appeals for the Third Circuit found that US WATS had wrongfully deprived Mark Scully of his employee stock options when it terminated him without warning on December 30, 1996, effective immediately. US WATS had hired Scully in May 1995 to serve as president and chief operations officer for a two-year period. As an inducement to remain the full two years, the company granted him an option to purchase 850,000 shares of stock that would vest over the same period. The plan provided that all options would expire on termination of employment. When Scully attempted to exercise his option to purchase the 600,000 shares that had vested, US WATS refused to honor the option, claiming that the option had automatically expired when he was fired. Noting that the district court had found that the "real reason for the defendants' actions, or at least a principal reason," was that US WATS had granted more stock options than it could fulfill and would have to report this to the Securities and Exchange Commission (SEC) unless it could eliminate some of the options before December 31, 1996, the Third Circuit upheld the district court's award of $626,442, which represented the value of Scully's stock options, lost wages, and interest.

In contrast, in *Benard v. Netegrity, Inc.*,[15] a U.S. district court in New York dismissed a claim that Netegrity had wrongfully discharged Benard to prevent his stock options from vesting. The court found that Netegrity had

not promised Benard any fixed term of employment and that there was no requirement of "good faith in an at-will employment relationship."

STATUTORY AND CONSTITUTIONAL PROTECTION FOR WHISTLEBLOWERS

As noted briefly earlier, courts may protect whistleblowers from retaliatory discharge under the public policy exception. In addition, both state and federal statutes provide some protection for whistleblowers.

State Statutory Protection

A number of states have statutes that provide whistleblower protection for terminated employees. They include New York, which does not have a common law public policy exception to at-will employment. The New York state statute protecting private-sector whistleblowers provides, among other things, that an employer may not take any retaliatory personnel action against an employee because such employee "discloses, or threatens to disclose to a supervisor or to a public body an activity, policy or practice of the employer that is in violation of law, rule or regulation which violation creates and presents a substantial and specific danger to the public health or safety . . . ."[16]

California's whistleblower statute is similar to New York's, but it does not limit protection to violations of law that create a danger to public health or safety.[17] The California attorney general also maintains a hotline that whistleblowers can use to report violations of laws by corporations.[18] (For further discussion of the protection available under a state whistleblower statute, see this chapter's "Inside Story.")

Federal Statutory Protection

There are also a number of federal whistleblower statutes. Many of these apply only to federal employees who report violations by governmental agencies or employees. The Sarbanes–Oxley Act of 2002 (SOX)[19] added several whistleblower provisions applicable to nongovernment employees. One provides criminal penalties for public and private company employers who retaliate against a person who provides truthful information relating to the commission of a federal offense to a law

11. *Id.*

12. Linker v. Allstate Ins. Co., 794 N.E.2d 945 (Ill.App. 2003).

13. *See* Foley v. Interactive Data Corp., 47 Cal. 3d 654 (1988).

14. 238 F.3d 497 (3d Cir. 2001).

15. No. 00 Civ. 3001 (LMM), 2000 WL 1760796 (S.D.N.Y. Nov. 30, 2000).

16. N.Y. Lab. Law § 740.

17. Cal. Lab. Code § 1102.5(b).

18. Cal. Lab. Code § 1102.7(a).

19. 18 U.S.C. § 1514A.

enforcement officer.[20] Another provision, which applies only to public companies, prohibits a company from discharging, demoting, suspending, threatening, harassing, or in any other manner discriminating against an employee in the terms and conditions of employment because of any lawful act done by the employee, including providing information to a federal regulatory or law enforcement agency, a member or committee of

Congress, or any person with supervisory authority over the employee or who has the authority to investigate misconduct.[21]

In the following case, the court considered whether an employee fired after reporting financial reporting irregularities suffered illegal retaliation under SOX.

---

20. *Id.*

---

21. *See generally* Beverley H. Earle & Gerald A. Madek, *The Mirage of Whistleblower Protection Under Sarbanes–Oxley: A Proposal for Change,* 44 Am. Bus. L. J. 1 (2007).

| A CASE IN POINT | *In the Language of the Court* | Case 12.1 |

Nance v. Time Warner Cable, Inc.

United States Court of Appeals for the Ninth Circuit
433 F. App'x 502 (9th Cir. 2011).

FACTS Arnold Nance told his superiors about an inconsistency in the way Comcast and Time Warner Cable (TWC) calculated their subscriber counts prior to the purchase of Comcast assets by TWC. Nance communicated these findings to his superiors and subsequently was terminated. He filed suit, alleging wrongful termination in violation of public policy under California tort law based on the whistleblower protections in the Sarbanes–Oxley Act. The trial court granted summary judgment for the employer, and Nance appealed.

ISSUE PRESENTED Is communicating immaterial inconsistencies in record keeping to supervisors considered protected activity under the Sarbanes–Oxley Act?

OPINION MEMORANDUM Nance's complaint alleges a violation of California tort law under *Tameny v. Atlantic Richfield Co.*,[22] which recognized the tort of wrongful termination in violation of public policy. Under California law, the first step in analyzing a *Tameny* claim is to determine whether the former employee was "engaged in a protected activity."

Nance contends he was engaged in protected activity because he brought to light accounting misstatements and SEC violations in TWC's financial reports. Therefore, he argues, his conduct is a protected activity under the whistleblower protection provision of the Sarbanes–Oxley Act (SOX).

Under § 1514A of SOX an employee cannot be terminated for providing information "regarding any conduct which the employee reasonably believes constitutes a violation of [a federal fraud statute], any rule or regulation of the Securities and Exchange Commission, or any provision of Federal law relating to fraud against shareholders." In order to be protected by the anti-retaliatory provision an "employee's communications must 'definitively and specifically' relate to one of the listed categories of fraud or securities violations" in § 1514A. Additionally, the employee must have "a subjective belief that the conduct being reported violated a listed law" and "this belief must be objectively reasonable." Nance has failed to meet any of these requirements.

The issue about which Nance communicated with his superiors, possible errors in Comcast's subscriber count, did not relate to one of the listed categories of fraud or securities violations, let alone definitively and specifically. . . . None of Nance's statements [about the inconsistency between the ways Comcast and TWC calculated their subscriber counts] linked the inconsistency to fraud or to a securities violation. Nance was not required to use the word "fraud" or to cite the code section he believed was violated, but his statements must still be related to fraudulent or otherwise illegal conduct in order to be protected.

Nor did he suggest that TWC was violating SEC regulations by not reporting the problem. In his e-mail informing his superior of the exceptions he intended to make, Nance identified one of the other exceptions as a possible SOX violation but made no similar statement about the

CONTINUED

---

22. 610 P.2d 1330 (Cal. 1980).

subscriber count issue. Even when Nance suggested to another TWC official that the information should be disclosed, his reason was that it "impacts other partners in the partnership," not that failure to disclose it would be a securities violation.

Nance's statements about the subscriber count inconsistency also demonstrate that, at the time, he did not have a subjective belief that TWC was engaging in fraudulent or illegal activities. [Even when he] finally did raise the issue, he also certified that he did not believe that there had been any fraudulent activity in regards to TWC's financial statements. While this provision was part of the boilerplate language of the letter, so were the other provisions to which Nance made his exceptions.

Finally, Nance's purported belief that TWC had engaged in fraudulent or illegal activities would not have been objectively reasonable. In order to have an objectively reasonable belief, "the complaining employee's theory of such fraud must at least approximate the basic elements of a claim of securities fraud." Nance's theory of fraud was deficient in several key ways. Notably, it was missing the element of materiality because the alleged problems, according to Nance, had a financial impact of an amount which Time Warner's outside auditor . . . concluded was immaterial to a corporation the size of Time Warner. . . .

As Nance was not engaged in a protected activity, a necessary element to his claim, summary judgment was appropriate.

RESULT The appellate court affirmed the trial court's summary judgment for the employer. Nance was not entitled to whistleblower protection under SOX or California tort law.

CRITICAL THINKING QUESTIONS

1. Should the employee bear the burden of deciding whether a misstatement is material?
2. Would the result in this case have been the same if Nance had crossed out the boilerplate language about the absence of fraudulent activity?

The Dodd–Frank Wall Street Reform and Consumer Protection Act[23] added further whistleblower protections. Sections 748 and 922 provide that no employer may discharge, demote, suspend, threaten, harass, or in any other manner discriminate against a whistleblower in the terms and conditions of employment because of any lawful act done by the whistleblower in (1) providing information to the SEC; (2) assisting in any investigation or judicial or administrative action of the SEC based on or related to such information; or (3) making disclosures that are required or protected under the Sarbanes–Oxley Act, the Securities Exchange Act of 1934, and any other law, rule, or regulation subject to the jurisdiction of the SEC.

Claims of Constitutional Protection by Public Employees

Some discharged government workers have attempted to claim whistleblower protection under the First Amendment to the U.S. Constitution. *Garcetti v. Ceballos*[24]

involved Richard Ceballos, a deputy district attorney for the Los Angeles County District Attorney's Office, who had written a memo to his supervisors recommending that they dismiss a case due to inaccuracies in an affidavit used to obtain a critical search warrant. Several discussions with his supervisors followed, but the supervisors ultimately decided to proceed with the case. When the trial court held a hearing on the motion challenging the warrant, Ceballos testified that he believed the affidavit was inaccurate, but the trial court rejected the challenge to the warrant.

After these events, Ceballos claimed that he suffered employment retaliation, including reassignment, transfer to another courthouse, and denial of a promotion. He filed suit, claiming that his employer's retaliation violated the First and Fourteenth Amendments because the memo was a protected form of speech.

The U.S. Supreme Court rejected his constitutional claims. Although "the First Amendment protects a public employee's right, in certain circumstances, to speak as a citizen addressing matters of public concern," Ceballos "spoke as a prosecutor fulfilling a responsibility to advise his supervisor about how best to proceed with a pending case," not as a citizen. As a result, the Constitution did not insulate his communications from employer discipline.

23. Pub. L. No. 111-203, 124 Stat. 1376 (2010).
24. 547 U.S. 410 (2006).

The Court reasoned: "Government employers, like private employers, need a significant degree of control over their employees' words and actions; without it, there would be little chance for the efficient provision of public services." But because "a citizen who works for the government is nonetheless a citizen," when public "employees are speaking as citizens about matters of public concern, they must face only those speech restrictions that are necessary for their employers to operate efficiently and effectively." The Court recognized that "[e]xposing governmental inefficiency and misconduct is a matter of considerable significance," but concluded that a "powerful network of legislative enactments," such as labor codes and whistleblower protection laws, protects employees and provides checks on supervisors who would order unlawful or otherwise inappropriate actions.

The dissent was far less sanguine about the ability of the "patchwork" of statutory whistleblower protections to protect government whistleblowers from vindictive bosses:

> To begin with, speech addressing official wrongdoing may well fall outside protected whistle-blowing. . . . Some state statutes protect all government workers . . . others stop at state employees. Some limit protection to employees who tell their bosses before they speak out; others forbid bosses from imposing any requirement to warn. . . . My point here is not to disparage particular statutes or speak here to the merits of interpretations by other federal courts, but merely to show the current understanding of statutory protection: individuals doing the same sorts of governmental jobs and

IN BRIEF

Limits on At-Will Employment

The employer's right to terminate an employee without cause may be subject to and restricted by:

- Express statutory abrogation of terminable at-will employment
- Statutory prohibition of discrimination on specified characteristic (e.g., race, gender, age)
- Statutory prohibition of discrimination for protected activity (e.g., collective bargaining, protected leaves of absence, off-duty lawful conduct)
- Civil service systems
- Union contracts
- Express employment contracts (oral or written)
- The public policy exception
- Implied contracts
- The implied covenant of good faith and fair dealing
- Fraudulent inducement
- Whistleblower statutes

---

ethical consideration

What role, if any, should the law play in penalizing an employer who lies to its employee about the reason for termination in order to persuade the employee to resign? What role do ethics play in this situation?

---

saying the same sorts of things addressed to civic concerns will get different protection depending on the local, state, or federal jurisdiction that happened to employ them.[25]

Hence, the dissent argued, "private and public interests in addressing official wrongdoing and threats to health and safety can outweigh the government's stake in the efficient implementation of policy, and when they do public employees who speak on these matters in the course of their duties should be eligible to claim First Amendment protection."[26]

FRAUDULENT INDUCEMENT

During difficult economic times, a business may engage in exaggeration to keep and attract highly qualified personnel. For example, in the course of recruiting Andrew Lazar to work as Rykoff's West Coast general manager for contract design, a vice president of Rykoff made a number of fraudulent statements, including that the current head of the department in which Lazar would work had plans to retire and that Lazar would be groomed for that position, that Rykoff was very strong financially, and that Lazar would receive annual reviews and raises. Lazar alleged that he resigned from his position as president of a family-owned company in New York, relocated his family to Los Angeles, and began employment at Rykoff based on these false statements. The trial court dismissed most of Lazar's claims, but the California Supreme Court held that Lazar had stated a cause of action for fraudulent inducement.[27]

In a more recent case, however, the New York Court of Appeals dismissed a fraudulent inducement action brought by five at-will investment managers who alleged that they had reasonably relied on fraudulent no-merger promises by Dreyfus Corporation in accepting and continuing employment with Dreyfus and in turning down other job opportunities. The court held:

> In that the length of employment is not a material term of at-will employment, a party cannot be injured merely by the termination of the contract—neither party can be said to have reasonably relied upon the other's promise not to terminate the contract. Absent injury independent of termination, plaintiffs cannot recover damages for what is at bottom an alleged breach of contract in the guise of a tort.[28]

---

25. *Id.* at 440–41 (Souter, J., dissenting).

26. *Id.* at 428.

27. Lazar v. Rykoff-Sexton, Inc., 909 P.2d 981 (Cal. 1996).

28. Smalley v. Dreyfus Corp., 882 N.E.2d 882 (N.Y. 2008).

NONCOMPETE AGREEMENTS

A *covenant not to compete* is a device, ancillary to another agreement (such as an employment contract), that is designed to protect a company's interests by limiting a former employee's ability to use trade secrets in working for a competitor or setting up a competing business. Enforcing a noncompete agreement can be difficult because rules vary by jurisdiction. For example, California and Georgia severely limit the enforceability of noncompete agreements.

Even in states that permit noncompetes, courts will enforce only reasonable restrictions on competition. Unreasonableness can be found on many grounds, including duration of limitation, geographic extent, scope of activities prohibited, and the employer's relation to the interests being protected. For example, the Nevada Supreme Court invalidated a noncompete agreement that restricted a lighting- retrofitting employee from competing with his former employer within a 100-mile radius of the former employer's site for five years.[29] The duration placed a great hardship on the employee and was not necessary to protect the former employer's interests.

The majority of states recognize an employer's investment of time and money to develop customer and client relationships as a legitimate employer interest that can justify a noncompete agreement. In the following case, the Texas Supreme Court considered whether an employer's promise to provide specialized training or confidential information in the course of at-will employment could support enforcement of a covenant not to compete.

---

29. Jones v. Deeter, 913 P.2d 1272 (Nev. 1996). *See also* Rollins Burdick Hunter of Wis., Inc. v. Hamilton, 304 N.W.2d 752 (Wis. 1981).

A CASE IN POINT	*In the Language of the Court*	Case 12.2

Alex Sheshunoff Management Services, L.P. v. Johnson

Supreme Court of Texas
209 S.W.3d 644 (Tex. 2006).

FACTS   Alex Sheshunoff Management Services (ASM) provides consulting services to banks and other financial institutions. ASM hired Kenneth Johnson as an at-will employee in 1993. In September 1997, ASM promoted Johnson to director of its "Affiliation Program," a program designed to maintain relationships with clients and prospective clients. A few months later, ASM presented Johnson with an employment agreement that provided that "[e]ither party may elect to terminate this Agreement at any time for any reason," subject to employer and employee notice provisions. The employer notice provision stated that ASM would give notice of termination to Johnson, unless the termination stemmed from employee misconduct, but also allowed ASM to terminate Johnson immediately as long as ASM paid him a specified fee.

The Agreement required ASM to provide Johnson with training as follows:

> To assist Employee in the performance of his/her duties, Employer agrees to provide to Employee, special training regarding Employer's business methods and access to certain confidential and proprietary information and materials belonging to Employer, its affiliates, and to third parties, including but not limited to, customers and prospects of the Employer who have furnished such information and materials to Employer under obligations of confidentiality.

The Agreement also provided that for one year after his termination, Johnson would not provide consulting services to any ASM clients for whom Johnson had "provided fee based services in excess of 40 hours within the last year of employment," and would not "solicit or aid any other party in soliciting any affiliation member or previously identified prospective client or affiliation member."

After Johnson signed the Agreement, ASM provided him with confidential information and paid for him to receive training. In early 2001, Johnson participated in confidential meetings regarding ASM's plans to introduce a bank overdraft protection product. The market leader for such products, Strunk & Associates, contacted Johnson in early 2002 about hiring him. In March 2002, Johnson told ASM he was leaving to work for Strunk.

ASM sued Johnson, alleging breach of the covenant not to compete in the Agreement and seeking injunctive relief and damages. Strunk intervened. The court granted a temporary injunction, and Strunk and Johnson moved for summary judgment, arguing that the covenant not to compete was unenforceable because ASM had provided no consideration in exchange for it. The district court granted the summary judgment motions, and the court of appeals affirmed.

CONTINUED

ISSUE PRESENTED   Can an employer's promise to an at-will employee to provide special training and access to confidential information support enforcement of a covenant not to compete under Texas law?

OPINION   WILLETT, J., writing for the Texas Supreme Court:

The Covenants Not to Compete Act (Act) states:

> [A] covenant not to compete is enforceable if it is ancillary to or part of an otherwise enforceable agreement at the time the agreement is made to the extent that it contains limitations as to time, geographical area, and scope of activity to be restrained that are reasonable and do not impose a greater restraint than is necessary to protect the goodwill or other business interest of the promisee.

. . . .

In the pending case, ASM promised to disclose confidential information and to provide specialized training under the Agreement, and Johnson promised not to disclose confidential information. The covenant was ancillary to or part of the agreement . . . .

. . . .

In the pending case, the court of appeals correctly held that . . . the agreement was illusory insofar as it required ASM to provide confidential information and specialized training. . . . There was no promise to provide such training and access after the employee had been terminated. . . . Under the notice provision applicable to the employer, ASM could terminate Johnson immediately and without notice so long as it paid a specified sum to Johnson. The promises to provide confidential information and training to Johnson were therefore illusory at the time the agreement was executed. . . .

. . . .

. . . [W]e hold that a covenant not to compete is not unenforceable under the Covenants Not to Compete Act solely because the employer's promise is executory when made. If the agreement becomes enforceable after the agreement is made because the employer performs his promise under the agreement and a unilateral contract is formed, the covenant is enforceable if all other requirements under the Act are met. In the pending case, these other requirements were met and, by the time Johnson left ASM, the agreement had become an enforceable unilateral contract because ASM had provided confidential information and specialized training as promised to Johnson, and Johnson had promised in return to preserve the confidences of his employer.

RESULT   The Texas Supreme Court reversed the judgment of the court of appeals that ASM should take nothing against Johnson and Strunk and remanded the case to the trial court for further proceedings. The covenant not to compete was ancillary to or part of an enforceable unilateral contract to provide confidential information and specialized training, so it was enforceable if all the other requirements in the statute were met.

CRITICAL THINKING QUESTIONS

1. How would this court have decided this case if ASM had not shared any confidential information or provided any training to Johnson until after he announced his departure and then had quickly shared such information in an attempt to ensure the enforceability of the noncompete?

2. The court held that ASM's agreement to either provide notice of termination or pay an agreed-on sum in lieu of notice was not adequate consideration for the noncompete, because a prior decision interpreted the Covenants Not to Compete Act as requiring that "the consideration given by the employer in the otherwise enforceable agreement must give rise to the employer's interest in restraining the employee from competing," and the noncompete "must be designed to enforce the employee's consideration or return promise." Do you agree with the court's interpretation of the Covenants Not to Compete Act? For example, should an employer be able to extract a binding noncompete in consideration for payment of a bonus? A promotion? A salary increase? If not, why not?

Due to differences in state laws, disputes can arise regarding which law to apply to noncompete agreements. For example, an employee working in Ohio signed a noncompete with his employer, Convergys, which included an Ohio choice-of-law provision. When the employee resigned to work for a competitor in Georgia, he filed a lawsuit in Georgia seeking a declaration that the noncompete was unenforceable. The district court concluded that it could not follow "a contractual selection of law of a foreign state where such chosen law would contravene the public policy of Georgia," declared the noncompete void, and granted an injunction against Convergys that prohibited the company from seeking to enforce the noncompete in any court nationwide. On appeal, the U.S. Court of Appeals for the Eleventh Circuit found that although Georgia was entitled to enforce its public policy interests within its borders, "Georgia cannot in effect apply its public policy decisions nationwide—the public policy of Georgia is not that everywhere [sic]. To permit a nationwide injunction would in effect interfere both with parties' ability to contract and their ability to enforce appropriately derived expectations." As a result, the court modified the injunction to preclude Convergys only from enforcing the noncompete in Georgia.[30]

Even if an employment agreement does not contain an express noncompete, provisions having a similar effect will be unenforceable in a jurisdiction that bans noncompetes. AfterImpaxx acquired Pac-West Labels, it asked a Pac-West employee to sign the following covenant: "For a period of one (1) year following the termination of employment, I will not (1) call on, solicit or take away any of Pac-West Label's customers or potential customers with whom I have had any dealings as a result of my employment by Pac-West Labels." When the employee refused, Impaxx fired him. The employee then sued for wrongful termination under the rule that termination of an employee for refusal to sign an unenforceable covenant not to compete violates public policy. The employee also alleged that the identity of Pac-West's customers was not a trade secret. Impaxx moved for judgment on the pleadings on the ground that the covenant was not a "true" covenant not to compete, but a mere limited restrictive covenant not to solicit. The California Court of Appeal disagreed, stating:

> This clause is less restrictive, and less anti-competitive, than the broad, traditional anti-competitive clauses . . . It is nevertheless anti-competitive—why else would they ask employees to sign it? More to the point, "Anti-solicitation covenants are void as unlawful business restraints except where their enforcement is necessary to protect trade secrets."[31]

Clawback provisions, which give an employer the right to recoup some or all of an employee's stock option gain if he or she goes to work for a competitor within a certain period of time following exercise of the option, have also led to litigation. The outcome varies depending on which state's law governs. Although such provisions are enforceable under New York law, they are not enforceable in California.[32]

Employers may attempt to prevent other companies from poaching employees in an overly aggressive fashion. In *Reeves v. Hanlon,*[33] the California Supreme Court held that although competition between companies for at-will employees is encouraged, inducing the termination of an at-will employment relationship may be tortious intentional interference with prospective economic advantage if the new employer engages in "independently wrongful acts" when inducing the employee to join its ranks. The court defined "independently wrongful acts" as acts "proscribed by constitutional, statutory, regulatory, common law, or other determinable legal standard." The defendants had left their former employer, an immigration law firm, then induced six other employees to leave to join their new law practice. The court found the defendants liable

30. Keener v. Convergys Corp., 342 F.3d 1264 (11th Cir. 2003).
31. Thompson v. Impaxx, Inc., 113 Cal. App. 4th 1425 (2003).
32. Richmond Tech., Inc. v. Aumtech Bus. Solutions, 2011 WL 2607158 (N.D. Cal. July 1, 2011) (rejecting the U.S. Court of Appeals for the Ninth Circuit's holding in an earlier case that a California court would have enforced a clawback provision against a California resident pursuant to a contract subject to New York law: "California courts have been clear in their expression that [there is] a strong public policy of the state which should not be diluted by judicial fiat.").
33. 33 Cal. 4th 1140 (2004).

for damages suffered by the prior firm because they had also mounted "a campaign to deliberately disrupt plaintiff's business" by having employees resign without notice, leaving no status reports of outstanding matters or deadlines, destroying the firm's computer files and forms, taking confidential information, and improperly soliciting the firm's clients.

RECOMMENDATIONS FOR FORMER EMPLOYEES

Employers are often asked to give references regarding former employees to prospective employers. As discussed in Chapter 9, if the employer's reference is not fair and the employer has impugned the individual's reputation, he or she can sue the employer for defamation.

Certain courts recognize a common law conditional privilege for references. For example, *Deutsch v. Chesapeake Center*,[34] involved a reverend who was hired as director of an overnight lodging and meeting facility for church groups but was terminated as a result of accusations of racism and sexual harassment. When he applied for a position as a church pastor in another community, his former employer told the prospective employer of the charges that had resulted in the termination. The reverend sued his former employer for defamation, but the U.S. District Court for the District of Maryland dismissed his claim, finding that the former employer's statements were protected by a conditional privilege to communicate information concerning a former employee to a prospective employer.

In contrast, the U.S. District Court for the Eastern District of Pennsylvania concluded that a principal's comments regarding a teacher's poor performance during a faculty meeting were not protected by the privilege.[35] The principal had abused the privilege by publishing the defamatory statements to the entire faculty and including allegedly defamatory matter not reasonably believed to be necessary for the purpose of informing the faculty that certain teachers' contracts would not be renewed.

There is a growing trend toward statutory protection for employers that disclose information about a former employee's performance. The most basic statutes provide that an employer is immune from suit if it provides information about an existing or former employee to a prospective employer, although some statutes limit immunity to the disclosure of "job performance information."[36]

Traditionally, defamation law requires publication, meaning that the communicator of the defamatory information must disclose the information to a third party, such as a prospective employer. Under the *doctrine of self-publication*, a defamatory communication by an employer to the employee may constitute publication if the employer could reasonably foresee that the employee would be required to repeat the communication, for instance, to a prospective employer. The doctrine is designed to provide a cause of action to the job-seeking employee who is forced to self-publicize a former employer's defamatory statement. Only four states continue to recognize a cause of action for self-publication, and only two states, Iowa and Kansas, have done so in an employment context.[37] The majority of the other states have rejected the doctrine for various reasons. First, a number of courts have found that the doctrine would "encourage employers to curtail communications with employees, and the employees' prospective employers, for fear of liability." Second, courts fear that by providing plaintiffs with so much control over the cause of action, the recognition of compelled self-publication defamation could discourage them from mitigating damages. Finally, courts have reasoned that the doctrine of compelled self-defamation conflicts with the employment-at-will doctrine.[38]

If the employee signs a waiver and release form releasing potential claims, then an employer may be protected against liability for defamation claims by a former employee. For example, after Bethany Bardin was laid off by Lockheed, she applied for a job as a police officer with the Los Angeles Police Department. As part of the application process, she signed a "Release and Waiver" form, which authorized a background investigation and provided that former employers were cleared "from any and all liability for damage of whatever kind." The police department notified Bardin that her application was suspended because she had failed to disclose employment problems at Lockheed, including a complaint related to her drinking. Bardin sued Lockheed, but the court found that the language in the waiver and release form protected Lockheed from liability.[39]

Nevertheless, employers should be cautious when giving recommendations for former employees. A growing number of job applicants are hiring third-party companies to investigate what their former employers are saying about them.[40] Companies should have a written policy outlining who may provide references and what information can be provided to companies seeking a reference. Some companies obtain a standard release, giving express permission to provide references, from all departing employees.

34. 27 F. Supp. 2d 642 (D. Md. 1998).

35. MacCord v. Christian Acad., 1998 WL 848067 (E.D. Pa. 1998).

36. Garen Dodge, *Work Place Trends: New Job Reference Immunity Law*, WILEY REIN LLP, July 25, 2005, *available at* http://www.wileyrein.com/publication_newsletters.cfm?sp=newsletter&year=2005&ID=13.

37. Emery v. Ne. Ill. Reg'l Commuter R.R. Corp., 880 N.E.2d 1002 (Ill. App. Ct. 2007).

38. *Id.* at 1028.

39. Bardin v. Lockheed Aeronautical Sys. Co., 82 Cal. Rptr. 2d 726 (Cal. Ct. App. (1999).

40. Marci Alboher Nusbaum, *Executive Life; When a Reference Is a Tool for Snooping*, N.Y. TIMES, Oct. 19, 2003, at BU12.

Although fear of a defamation claim may tempt an employer to give an overly positive recommendation, this is not prudent. As noted in Chapter 9, an employer giving an untrue assessment of a former employee may be liable to the new employer who relies on the recommendation and also to third parties physically harmed as a foreseeable result of the recommendation.[41]

EMPLOYER TESTING AND SURVEILLANCE

Employers often administer tests to employees in an effort to increase productivity, manage legal risks, and cut costs. Certain testing and surveillance activities may conflict with an employee's right to privacy, however.

Drug Testing

Many employers have adopted drug-screening programs for their employees and applicants to avoid the decreased productivity, quality control problems, absenteeism, on-the-job accidents, and employee theft that can result from drug and alcohol abuse. According to the Society for Human Resource Management, 57% of companies in the United States test their employees for drugs.[42] Some employers use drug testing in conjunction with a comprehensive drug program that provides education and assistance to an employee with a drug or an alcohol problem.

The issue of drug testing generally comes before the courts in the context of discipline or discharge of an employee for refusing to take a test. An employee may challenge a drug test in many ways. The employee may claim that (1) the test breached his or her employment contract; (2) there was no justification for the test; (3) it violated the public policy that protects privacy; (4) he or she was defamed by false accusations of drug use based on an erroneous test; (5) he or she suffered emotional distress, especially if the test result was in error; or (6) the testing disproportionately affected employees of one race or gender and therefore was discriminatory.

Whether testing will be deemed permissible in a particular situation depends on four factors: (1) the scope of the testing program, (2) whether the employer is a public or private employer, (3) any state constitutional guarantees of a right to privacy, and (4) any state statutes regulating drug testing.

Scope of Testing Program

The first major factor, scope, concerns who is being tested: all employees (random testing); only employees in a specific job where the employer believes there is a legitimate job-related need (for example, nuclear power plant employees); groups of employees (for example, all employees in one facility because there is a general suspicion of drug use within that group); or specific individuals who are believed to be using drugs. The smaller the group to be tested and the more specific the reason for testing, the more likely that a court will uphold the test. Random testing is the most difficult to defend.

Public Versus Private Employees

Because public employees are protected by the U.S. Constitution's Fourth Amendment prohibition against unreasonable searches and seizures and by the right to privacy, there are greater limits on testing public employees than on testing private-sector employees. It has long been recognized that urine tests and blood tests are a substantial intrusion on bodily privacy and are therefore searches subject to regulation when imposed on public employees. The right to privacy guaranteed by the U.S. Constitution protects against invasions of privacy by public actors (i.e., state and federal governments or agencies), but does not protect against invasions by private (i.e., nongovernmental) actors. Similarly, the Fourth Amendment ban on unreasonable searches and seizures applies only to governmental activity. As a result, there are greater limits on testing public employees than on testing private-sector employees. With some exceptions, there is no federal constitutional limitation on drug testing in the private sector.

In *Skinner v. Railway Labor Executives' Association*,[43] the U.S. Supreme Court held that railroads can be required to test public employees involved in a major train accident and have the authority to test employees who violate certain safety rules. The Court reasoned that any intrusion on individual privacy rights in the railroad context was outweighed by the government's compelling interest in public and employee safety. The Supreme Court also upheld mandatory drug testing of U.S. Customs Service employees in line for transfer or promotion to certain sensitive positions involving drug interdiction or the handling of firearms.[44] Although there was no perceived drug problem among Customs employees, the Court held that the need for national security and the extraordinary safety hazards attendant to the positions involved justified the program.

In *Knox County Education Association v. Knox County Board of Education*,[45] the U.S. Court of Appeals for the Sixth Circuit held that subjecting public school teachers to drug and alcohol testing did not violate their constitutional right to privacy. Of primary importance in the

41. *See, e.g.*, Randi W. v. Muroc Joint Unified Sch. Dist., 929 P.2d 582 (Cal. 1997).

42. *SHRM Poll: Drug Testing Efficacy*, Soc'y for Human Res. Mgmt., Sept. 7, 2011, *available at* http://www.shrm.org/Research/SurveyFindings/Articles/Pages/lDrugTestingEfficacy.aspx.

43. 489 U.S. 602 (1989).

44. Nat'l Treasury Emps. Union v. Von Raab, 489 U.S. 656 (1989).

45. 158 F.3d 361 (6th Cir. 1998).

court's decision was the unique role that teachers play by accepting *in loco parentis* (in place of the parents) obligations to ensure the safety of children and to serve as role models. The court commented that "teachers must expect with this extraordinary responsibility, they will be subject to scrutiny to which other civil servants or professionals might not be subjected, including drug testing."[46]

State Constitutional Protection

Many state constitutions also guarantee the right to privacy. Some states extend this right to private invasions of privacy; others limit it to governmental intrusions, not to alleged violations by private entities.

The California Court of Appeal held that a pupillary-reaction test given to all employees of Kerr–McGee Corporation at its chemical plant in Trono, California, might violate the California Constitution's right to privacy, depending on the intrusiveness of the test and the employer's safety needs.[47] The test consisted of shining a light in the person's eye and observing how much the pupil contracted. Although the court acknowledged that the pupillary test was less intrusive than urine, blood, or breath tests, it held that the trial court needed more facts to determine just how intrusive the test was. In contrast, the Alaska Supreme Court held that the right to privacy in the Alaska state constitution did not shield its citizens from drug tests by a private employer.[48]

State Statutory Regulation

Many states have enacted legislation regarding drug testing of private employees, which often sets forth the notice procedures an employer must follow before asking an employee to submit to a drug test. In Vermont, for example, before administering the test, the employer must give the employee a copy of a written policy describing the circumstances under which persons may be tested, the drugs that will be screened, the procedures involved, and the consequences of a positive result.

A number of states have comprehensive drug- and alcohol-testing laws that require reasonable suspicion or probable cause before an employer may test. The requirements for establishing reasonable suspicion or probable cause vary from state to state. For instance, Connecticut permits testing when "the employer has reasonable suspicion that the employee is under the influence of drugs or alcohol which adversely affects or could adversely affect such employee's job performance."[49] Other states take the opposite approach and encourage broad, fair, and consistent testing in order to promote drug-free workplaces. For

example, Alabama permits discounted workers' compensation insurance premiums for employers that follow fair testing procedures, including random testing.[50]

Although private employers, as well as public employers, may face some limits on implementing a drug-testing program, it should be noted that all employers have the right to make and enforce rules prohibiting drug use or possession on work premises, as well as rules prohibiting employees from being under the influence of drugs while at work. When an employee exhibits visible signs of intoxication or impairment, or inadequate performance, the employer may take disciplinary action. Because of the inadequacy of drug tests and the uncertainty about the scope of employees' rights, however, the employer may wish instead to develop programs that provide assistance and drug education, and to counsel employees about the performance problems that drug abuse can cause.

Genetic Testing and Health Monitoring

Genetic testing predicts whether a person has a genetic predisposition for developing a certain disease, although the accuracy of such tests is unproven.[51] Employers may be motivated to perform genetic tests to avoid hiring workers they believe are likely to take sick leave, resign, or retire early because of health reasons, or to reduce costs by lowering absenteeism rates and health insurance premiums kept high by unhealthy workers.[52]

As discussed more fully in Chapter 13, the Genetic Information Nondiscrimination Act of 2008[53] prohibits employers engaged in any industry affecting interstate commerce with fifteen or more employees from using genetic information to make decisions about hiring, firing, or compensation.[54] Although Nancy Wexler, president of the Hereditary Disease Foundation, praised the Act for giving people with hereditary diseases a weapon and a tool, she also noted, "It's very hard to prove why somebody is firing you."[55] Genetic testing may also violate Title VII when employees or applicants are singled out for testing based

46. *Id.* at 384.

47. Semore v. Pool, 217 Cal. App. 3d 1087 (Cal. Ct. App. 1990).

48. Luedtke v. Nabors Alaska Drilling, Inc., 768 P.2d 1123 (Alaska 1989).

49. CONN. GEN. STAT. ANN. § 31-51x.

50. Alabama seeks to maximize productivity, enhance competitive positions of its companies in the marketplace, and reach companies' "desired levels of success without experiencing the costs, delays, and tragedies associated with work related accidents resulting from substance abuse by employees." ALA. CODE § 25-5-330 *et seq.*

51. *Genetic Discrimination in the Workplace Fact Sheet*, AM. CIVIL LIBERTIES ASS'N, Dec. 31, 2000, *available at* http://www.aclu.org/technology-and-liberty/genetic-discrimination-workplace-factsheet.

52. Human Genome Project Information, *Genetics Privacy and Legislation*, OAK RIDGE NAT'L LAB., *available at* http://www.ornl.gov/sci/techresources/Human_Genome/elsi/lesislat.shtml (last visited Sept. 15, 2011).

53. 42 U.S.C.A. § 2000ff-1.

54. 42 U.S.C.A. § 2000e(b).

55. Amy Harmon, *Congress Passes Bill to Bar Bias Based on Genes*, N.Y. TIMES, May 2, 2008, at P1.

on race or gender.[56] The Americans with Disabilities Act (ADA) may also provide employees with a cause of action for genetic testing.

At least thirty-five states have enacted laws outlawing genetic discrimination in the workplace.[57] These laws generally fit within one of three types of legislation: (1) laws prohibiting discrimination in employment based on genetic characteristics, (2) laws prohibiting employers from requiring applicants or employees to undergo genetic testing, and (3) laws banning discrimination based on genetic test results or the refusal to take a genetic test.[58] Private employers may also have liability under state constitutions that protect employees from invasions of privacy.

When employees are exposed to dangerous chemicals or conditions as part of their jobs, regular health monitoring is encouraged, and in some instances, it is required by standards adopted by the Occupational Safety and Health Administration.[59] Presumably, even when regulations do not require monitoring, an employer may choose to require participation in the health monitoring program as a condition of employment in positions affected by hazardous exposure.

Polygraph Testing of Employees

Polygraph testing is another area where an employee's right to privacy may limit an employer's investigative rights. The Employee Polygraph Protection Act of 1988 (EPPA)[60] generally makes it unlawful for employers to (1) ask an applicant or employee to take a polygraph exam or other lie detector test, (2) rely on or inquire about the results of a lie detector test that an applicant or employee has taken, (3) take or threaten to take any adverse action against an applicant or employee because of a refusal to take a lie detector test or on the basis of the results of such a test, or (4) take or threaten to take any adverse action against an employee or applicant who has filed a complaint or participated in a proceeding relating to the polygraph law.

These rights cannot be waived by the employee in advance. For example, a federal district court held that a bartender could still sue for violation of the EPPA even though she had signed a release form stating that her employer had reasonable suspicion of theft before the employer requested that she take a polygraph test.[61] The court held that an employee can waive rights or procedures under the EPPA only pursuant to a written settlement of a pending lawsuit.

The EPPA does not completely ban the use of polygraph exams, however. Employers may test employees who are reasonably suspected of conduct injurious to the business, as well as applicants or employees in certain businesses involving security services or the handling of drugs. In addition, the EPPA does not restrict federal, state, or local government employers from administering polygraph exams.

A majority of states, however, have laws that restrict the use of polygraph examinations and require additional safeguards when these tests are administered. For example, a number of states and the District of Columbia prevent employers from requesting that an applicant or employee take a lie detector test as a condition of employment.[62] Even when lie detector tests are permitted, no question should be asked during the test that could not lawfully be asked on an application form or during an interview.

Employee Surveillance in an Electronic Age

Companies check up on their employees by using a variety of strategies, including listening in on cellphones, inspecting computer files, reading e-mails, and conducting video surveillance. Companies monitor their employees for several reasons. For example, regulated industries, such as telemarketing and securities trading, may conduct surveillance to show their compliance with regulations.

Employees' use of the Internet, e-mail, instant messaging (IM), and employee blogs raises a number of issues for employers. From a productivity standpoint, employers are concerned that employees waste company time by using the Internet for personal reasons during working hours. In addition, employees may subject their employers to liability, such as potential discrimination claims resulting from sexually explicit statements or ethnic slurs in e-mails and blogs, and copyright and trademark violations due to unauthorized downloading of third-party content. Employees' personal use of the employer's computers may also disrupt and endanger the employer's business by allowing for easy, instantaneous, and unauthorized transfer of trade secrets.[63]

As a result of these concerns, 84% of the companies surveyed by the American Management Association (AMA) have formal written policies regulating the use of

---

56. Samantha French, *Genetic Testing in the Workplace: The Employer's Coin Toss*, 2002 DUKE L. & TECH. REV. 15 (2002).

57. *Genetic Employment Laws*, NAT'L CONFERENCE ON STATE LEGISLATURES, *updated* Jan. 2008, *available at* http://www.ncsl.org/IssuesResearch/Health/GeneticEmploymentLaws/tabid/14280/Default.aspx (last visited Sept. 15, 2011).

58. French, *supra* note 56.

59. *See, e.g.*, 29 C.F.R. § 1910.1450 & apps. A & B.

60. 29 U.S.C. §§ 2001–2009 (1988).

61. Long v. Mango's Tropical Cafe, Inc., 958 F. Supp. 612 (S.D. Fla. 1997).

62. JOHN F. BUCKLEY IV & RONALD M. GREEN, 2010 STATE BY STATE GUIDE TO HUMAN RESOURCES LAW tbl.8-1 (2010).

63. *See* Robert Sprague, *From Taylorism to the Omnipticon: Expanding Employee Surveillance Beyond the Workplace*, 25 J. MARSHALL J. COMPUTER & INFO. L. 1, 4 (Winter 2007).

their e-mail systems by employees,[64] 66% monitor employee Internet use,[65] 43% monitor employee e-mails,[66] and 31% have fired an employee for improper use of the Internet or e-mail while at work.[67] For example, in 2009 PNC Bank in New Jersey fired two women for sending sexually explicit jokes by e-mail at work.[68]

Although the AMA survey found that less than 25% of participating companies had a written policy regarding corporate or personal blogs, a number of companies (including Delta Airlines, Google, Microsoft, Wells Fargo, and Starbucks) have fired employees for inappropriate blogging. In most of these cases, the employer was concerned about the widespread circulation of confidential company information, such as corporate trade secrets or the e-mail addresses of top executives. Because the employees were employed at will, posting statements that were critical of their company or coworkers in a personal blog was enough to get them fired.[69] As a result, some employees who blog about work-related items do so anonymously under a pseudonym. Even that may not prevent termination—Nintendo employee Jessica Zenner was terminated after her bosses linked her to an "anonymous" blog criticizing several of her coworkers.[70] As discussed below, employers must be mindful of the protections afforded by the National Labor Relations Act before disciplining an employee for comments about work-related matters.

Employer surveillance goes well beyond employee use of the Internet. Fully 45% of employers surveyed by the AMA monitor time spent on the telephone and track phone numbers called, while 16% actually record employees' phone conversations. Employers are also using global positioning system (GPS) technology to track company vehicles, cellphones, and employee identification cards. Surveillance of this sort is still in its infancy, but 8% of participating employers track the location of company vehicles and 3% monitor employees movements through their cellphones. Employer surveillance of Internet use and e-mail is more common in office settings, whereas GPS is used more frequently in service industries, such as delivery firms.

Because employers have a legitimate interest in monitoring their employees and most private employees at least do not have a reasonable expectation of privacy when using company-owned equipment, most courts have upheld a private employer's right to monitor and regulate employees' workplace movements, e-mail, and use of computers.[71] In most states, the employer is not even required to notify employees that they are being monitored.[72] In 2004, the U.S. Court of Appeals for the Third Circuit ruled that an employer may read and access employees' e-mails without violating the Electronic Communications Privacy Act, which bars the interception of any electronic communication or the unauthorized access of stored communications, as long as the employer reads only e-mail messages that were already sent and stored on the company's own e-mail system.[73] In 2005, a New Jersey appellate court went even further by holding that an employer was negligent when it failed to monitor the Internet sites an employee was visiting after supervisors became aware that the employee had a history of visiting pornographic websites on the job.[74]

Under certain circumstances, however, surveillance may transgress employees' privacy rights, particularly when government employees are involved. The watershed case in this area was *O'Connor v. Ortega*.[75] In that case, the U.S. Supreme Court ruled that a public employee may, in certain circumstances, enjoy a reasonable expectation of privacy in the workplace. The employee's privacy interest must be balanced, however, by the "operational realities" of the workplace. Since *Ortega*, lower courts have considered (1) whether the employee was provided an exclusive working space, (2) the nature of the employment, and (3) whether the employee was on notice that parts of the workplace were subject to employer intrusions. For example, in *Vega-Rodriguez v. Puerto Rico Telephone Co.*,[76] the U.S. Court of Appeals for the First Circuit held that governmental security operators, sitting in an open, undifferentiated work area, who monitored computer banks to detect alarm-system signals, had no reasonable expectation of privacy. As a result, the public employer's soundless video surveillance of the workplace did not violate the employees' Fourth Amendment rights.

In the following case, the U.S. Supreme Court considered whether a public employer may read transcripts of an employee's text messages without a warrant.

64. Kate M. Jackson, *Mixing Blogging with Work Can Lead to Unemployment*, Boston Globe, July 3, 2005, *available at* http://www.boston.com/jobs/globe/articles/070305_blogs.html.

65. *2007 Electronic Monitoring & Surveillance Survey*, Am. Mgmt. Ass'n, Feb. 28, 2008, *available at* http://press.amanet.org/press-releases/177/2007-electronic-monitoring-surveillance-survey.

66. *Id.*

67. Daniel B. Garrie & Rebecca Wong, *The Future of Consumer Web Data: A European/US Perspective*, 15 Int'l J.L. & Info. Tech. 129, 136 (2007).

68. Tatiana Morales, *Fired for Sending E-mail*, CBSNews.com, Feb. 11, 2009, http://www.cbsnews.com/stories/2004/08/17/earlyshow/living/caught/main636589.shtml.

69. *See* Jackson, *supra* note 64.

70. *See* Jonah Spangenthal-Lee, *Game Over: Nintendo Contractor Fired for Blog*, Simply Forums, Sept. 19, 2007, http://forum.simplyhired.com/showthread.php?t=11468.

71. *See* Sprague, *supra* note 63, at 22.

72. *See 2007 Electronic Monitoring*, *supra* note 65.

73. *See* Fraser v. Nationwide Mut. Ins. Co., 352 F.3d 107 (3d Cir. 2004).

74. *See* Doe v. XYC Corp., 887 A.2d 1156, 1158 (N.J. Super. Ct. App. Div. 2005).

75. 480 U.S. 709 (1987).

76. 110 F.3d 174 (1st Cir. 1997).

| A CASE IN POINT | *Summary* | Case 12.3 |

City of Ontario v. Quon

United States Supreme Court
130 S. Ct. 2619 (2010).

FACTS   In 2001, the City of Ontario, California, issued alphanumeric pagers capable of sending and receiving text messages to Quon and other SWAT team members in order to help the team mobilize and respond to emergency situations. Arch Wireless provided wireless service for the pagers. Its service contract with the City allotted each pager 25,000 characters sent or received each month.

Before acquiring the pagers, the City announced a "Computer Usage, Internet and E-Mail Policy" applicable to all employees. Among other provisions, it specified that the City "reserves the right to monitor and log all network activity including e-mail and Internet use, with or without notice. Users should have no expectation of privacy or confidentiality when using these resources." Quon signed a statement acknowledging that he had read and understood the policy.

On its face, the policy did not apply to text messaging. An e-mail sent on a City computer was transmitted through the City's own data servers, but a text message sent on one of the City's pagers was transmitted using wireless radio frequencies from an individual pager to a receiving station owned by Arch Wireless. Arch Wireless retained a copy of the text messages on its computer servers.

Although the policy did not cover text messages by its explicit terms, the City held a staff meeting on April 18, 2002, which Quon attended, and made clear to employees that messages sent on the pagers would be considered e-mail messages and that text messages would fall under the City's policy as public information and would be eligible for auditing. Chief Scharf distributed a memorandum summarizing comments from the meeting to Quon and other City personnel on April 29, 2002.

Within the first or second billing cycle after the pagers were distributed, Quon exceeded his monthly text message character allotment. Duke, the officer in charge of the account, told Quon about the overage and reminded him that messages sent on the pagers were "considered e-mail and could be audited." After Duke suggested that Quon reimburse the City for the overage fee rather than have Duke audit the messages, Quon wrote a check to the City for the overage. Duke offered the same arrangement to other employees who incurred overage fees.

Over the next few months, Quon exceeded his character limit three or four times. Each time he reimbursed the City. At a meeting in October, Duke told Chief Scharf that he had become "tired of being a bill collector." Scharf then decided to determine whether the existing character limit was too low—that is, whether officers such as Quon were having to pay fees for sending work-related messages—or if the overages were for personal messages. Scharf told Duke to request transcripts of text messages sent in August and September by Quon and the other employee who had exceeded the character allowance.

After reviewing the transcripts, Duke discovered that many of the messages sent and received on Quon's pager were not work related; some were sexually explicit. The internal affairs division of the Ontario Police Department (OPD) concluded that Quon had violated the department's rules by pursuing personal matters while on duty, and he was disciplined.

Quon filed suit, alleging that the City had violated his Fourth Amendment rights against unreasonable search and seizure because he had a reasonable expectation of privacy in the content of his text messages. Although a jury concluded that Quon had a reasonable expectation of privacy, it concluded that the search was reasonable because the purpose of the audit was to determine the efficacy of the character limit. The U.S. Court of Appeals for the Ninth Circuit reversed, and the City appealed.

ISSUES PRESENTED   Does an employee have a reasonable expectation of privacy in text messages sent and received on his employer-provided pager? If so, is a subsequent search of the content of those text messages reasonable if it is for a legitimate, work-related purpose?

CONTINUED

SUMMARY OF OPINION   The U.S. Supreme Court explained that "[i]ndividuals do not lose Fourth Amendment rights merely because they work for the government instead of a private employer." Nonetheless, "special needs, beyond the normal need for law enforcement" can make the warrant and probable cause requirement impracticable for government employers.

The Court cautioned that a "broad holding concerning employees' privacy expectations vis-à-vis employer-provided technological equipment might have implications for future cases that cannot be predicted." Instead, the Court decided the case on narrower grounds, reasoning that even if (1) Quon had a reasonable expectation of privacy in the text messages sent on the pager provided to him by the City, (2) the review of the transcript of his messages constituted a search within the meaning of the Fourth Amendment, and (3) the principles applicable to a government employer's search of an employee's physical office apply with at least the same force when the employer intrudes on the employee's privacy in the electronic sphere. Hence, the City did not necessarily violate the Fourth Amendment by obtaining and reviewing the transcripts. Although warrantless searches are generally *per se* unreasonable under the Fourth Amendment, there are exceptions, including the need to accommodate the "special needs" of the workplace. In particular, when a public employer conducts a search for a noninvestigatory, work-related purpose or investigates work-related misconduct, a warrantless search is reasonable if it is "justified at its inception" and is not excessively intrusive in light of the circumstances giving rise to the search.

In this case, the search was justified at its inception. The City and the OPD had a legitimate interest in ensuring that employees were not being forced to pay out of their own pockets for work-related expenses and that the City was not paying for extensive personal communications.

Reviewing the transcripts was an expedient and efficient way for the City to determine whether Quon's overages were the result of work-related messaging or personal use. The scope of the search was not excessively intrusive. Quon had exceeded his monthly allotment a number of times, but the OPD requested transcripts for only the months of August and September 2002. Even if Quon expected some level of privacy in the contents of his messages, it would not have been reasonable for a law enforcement officer like Quon to conclude that his on-the-job communications messages were immune from scrutiny, especially after the City told him that his messages were subject to auditing. Under the circumstances, a reasonable employee would be aware that sound management principles might require the audit of messages to determine whether the pager was being appropriately used.

The Supreme Court rejected the Ninth Circuit's reasoning that the search was unreasonable in part because the City had a "host of simple ways to verify the efficacy of the 25,000 character limit" without intruding on Quon's Fourth Amendment rights. The Court found that approach inconsistent with controlling precedents: "This Court has 'repeatedly refused to declare that only the "least intrusive" search practicable can be reasonable under the Fourth Amendment.'"

RESULT   The decision of the U.S. Court of Appeals for the Ninth Circuit was reversed. The search did not violate the Fourth Amendment.

COMMENTS   The Court noted that the "OPD's audit of messages on Quon's employer-provided pager was not nearly as intrusive as a search of his personal e-mail account or pager, or a wiretap on his home phone line, would have been," thereby leaving open the question of whether such a search would violate the Fourth Amendment.

To avoid problems and resolve conflicts with employees, companies should establish policies for employees' use of the Internet, e-mail, IM, and blogs and the employer's monitoring of employees' computers, cellphones, and other work equipment. Employees should also be trained in the proper use of this equipment. The policies should prohibit the sending of unlawful, offensive, or defamatory statements, and unauthorized disclosures of trade secrets, via the corporate e-mail system. Employees should also be informed that they have no expectations of privacy when using the employer's electronic resources, vehicles, and other equipment and that the company has the right to monitor use and content without notice. In addition, companies should establish security measures and educate their employees about the related policies and the manner in which the employer will enforce them.

RESPONSIBILITY FOR WORKER SAFETY

Both federal and state laws require employers to provide a reasonably safe workplace.

Occupational Safety and Health Act

The Occupational Safety and Health Act of 1970 (the OSH Act)[77] requires employers to establish safe and healthful working environments. The federal agency responsible for enforcing the provisions of the OSH Act is the Occupational Safety and Health Administration (OSHA). This agency is also authorized by Congress to regulate additional workplace issues, including exposure to hazardous chemicals, protective gear, fire protection, and workplace temperatures and ventilation. About half of the states have enacted similar legislation and established enforcement agencies at the state level. Typically, in states with approved employment health and safety programs, OSHA defers to the state agency for enforcement activities.

An employer governed by the OSH Act has a general duty to provide a safe workplace, which includes the obligation to abate workplace hazards that are causing or are likely to cause death or serious physical harm to employees.[78] Conditions that are obviously dangerous or are regarded by the employer or other employers in the industry as dangerous are considered to be *recognized hazards*. What constitutes a recognized hazard is not entirely clear. The term's reach is broad and includes anything from sharp objects to radiation to repetitive stress injuries.[79]

Dealing with the Threat of Terrorism

As a result of the terrorist attacks on the World Trade Center and elsewhere on September 11, 2001, OSHA has encouraged employers to implement emergency action plans to ensure employee safety in the event of another terrorist attack.[80] OSHA recommends that employers have plans for evacuation, anthrax risk management, and tightened security at building entrances and exits.

OSHA Inspections

In general, OSHA inspectors are allowed to enter and inspect a workplace at any reasonable time, without prior notice. During the inspection, the OSHA investigator may review company records, check for compliance with the relevant OSHA standards, inspect fire-protection and other safety equipment, examine the company's safety and health-management programs, interview employees, walk through the facility, and employ other reasonable investigative techniques. The inspection should not unreasonably disrupt the operations of the employer's establishment.

When the inspection has been completed, the inspector meets with the employer and the employee representative, if any, to review the results of the inspection. If appropriate, the inspector will issue a written citation for violations.

In March 2010, OSHA announced that it had sent letters to approximately 15,000 employers that needed to correct workplace safety and health hazards.[81] The letters directed the employers to various resources available through OSHA, including the agency's free on-site consultation program for employers with 250 or fewer employees. The employers that received the letters had severe workplace injury ratios higher than the national average in their respective industries. In most cases, the employers had DART rates (rates of injuries and illnesses resulting in days away from work, restricted work activities, or job transfers) that were twice the national average.[82]

Record-Keeping and Posting Requirements

OSHA requires employers to maintain certain records, including the OSHA Form 300, which lists and summarizes all work-related injuries and illnesses.[83] (Certain industries, such as retail, finance, and insurance, are exempt from this record-keeping requirement.) A summary of these records must be posted annually at the job site. In addition, employers must post in a conspicuous place (1) OSHA's official Job Safety Poster; (2) any OSHA citations for violations; and (3) notices of imminent danger to employees, including exposure to toxic substances.

77. Pub. L. No. 91-596, 84 Stat. 1590 (1970) (codified as amended at 29 U.S.C. §§ 651–678).

78. *See* 29 U.S.C. § 654(a)(1); Fabi Constr. Co. v. Sec'y of Labor, 508 F.3d 1077, 1081 (D.C. Cir. 2007).

79. Employers have an obligation under the General Duty Clause, 29 U.S.C. § 654 (Section 5(a)(1)), to keep a workplace free from recognized serious hazards, including ergonomic hazards; *see* Occupational Safety & Health Admin., *Ergonomics: Enforcement, available at* http://www.osha.gov/SLTC/ergonomics/faqs.html. OSHA also produces Safety and Health Information Bulletins (SHIBs) to help identify hazards associated with specific industries or practices; *see* http://www.osha.gov/dts/shib/index.html.

80. Occupational Safety & Health Admin., *My Company Has a Credible Risk of Anthrax Exposure; What Should I Do to Prepare?* (2001), *available at* http://www.osha.gov/SLTC/etools/anthrax/credible_risk.html.

81. Eric. J. Conn & James A. Lastowka, *OSHA to 15,000 U.S. Employers: "Ready or Not, Here We Come,"* RELIABLE PLANT, *available at* http://www.reliableplant.com/Read/23548/OSHA-here-we-come.

82. *Id.*

83. Occupational Safety & Health Adm., *OSHA Forms for Recording Work-Related Injuries and Illnesses, available at* http://www.osha.gov/recordkeeping/new-osha300form1-1-04.pdf.

Civil Violations

OSHA can cite employers for six types of civil violations: (1) willful violations, which are deliberate or intentional, for which a fine of at least $5,000 and up to $70,000 may be imposed for each violation; (2) repeated violations, involving another violation of a previously cited section, for which fines up to $70,000 may be imposed; (3) serious violations, which have a substantial likelihood of resulting in death or serious bodily harm, for which a penalty of up to $7,000 per violation must be imposed; (4) other than serious violations, which involve hazards that are not likely to cause death or serious bodily harm, for which a fine of up to $7,000 per violation may be imposed; (5) "failure to abate" violations, for which civil penalties of up to $7,000 may be assessed for each day a violation continues beyond the prescribed abatement date; and (6) *de minimis* (that is, unimportant) violations, for which no notice is posted and no penalty is imposed.[84]

For purposes of issuing violations, the U.S. Court of Appeals for the Fifth Circuit has held that the hazardous condition is the proper unit of prosecution, rather than the number of employees exposed to the hazardous condition.[85] Thus, if eighty-seven employees were threatened by a chemical explosion, one violation (the explosion), rather than eighty-seven (the number of individuals exposed to the risk of heat, burns, and flying debris as a result of the explosion), may be cited. An individual employee can be a unit of prosecution when the violation is unique to the employee, however, such as a failure to train the employee.[86]

If OSHA finds a violation, the employer is required to remedy the problem immediately. If remedial action is not taken, OSHA will seek a court order to ensure compliance. The employer may either settle the violation or seek review of the OSHA decision by the Occupational Safety and Health Review Commission. OSHA may penalize egregious violations by imposing a separate fine for each violation, rather than an overall fine for a group of violations. Additionally, evidence that shows a clear violation of OSHA standards can sometimes support punitive damages.[87]

The aggregation of multiple serious violations can result in significant fines. In 2009, OSHA levied a record fine of more than $87 million against BP Products North America, Inc. for continuing safety violations at its Texas City, Texas oil refinery.[88] After 15 BP workers were killed and another 180 injured in an explosion at the facility in 2005, OSHA had cited BP for 301 willful violations of worker safety laws, levied a $21 million fine, and secured BP's agreement to take corrective action to eliminate potential hazards at the facility.[89] The record 2009 fine included $56.7 million in fines for noncompliance with the terms of the 2005 agreement (including 270 notifications of failure to abate, which resulted in a penalty of $7,000 times 30 days, the period during which the conditions remained unabated). The 2009 fine also included $30.7 million in penalties for 439 new willful violations for failure to follow industry-accepted controls on the pressure relief safety systems and other process safety management violations.[90]

Federal Criminal Penalties

OSHA can refer a case to the Justice Department for criminal prosecution when a willful violation of safety laws causes the death of an employee or an employer provides false information to OSHA.[91] In this context, "willful" means that the employer demonstrated either "intentional disregard" of safety laws or "plain indifference" toward them. Willful violations resulting in the death of an employee are misdemeanors, punishable by $250,000 in fines for an individual or up to $500,000 for a corporation, imprisonment of up to six months, or both.[92] Providing OSHA with false information is also a misdemeanor and is punishable by a maximum of six months in jail and a $10,000 fine.[93] The OSH Act also makes it a crime for anyone to provide advance notice of a surprise OSHA inspection. This is punishable by a maximum of six months in jail and a $1,000 fine.[94]

Critics have faulted OSHA for rarely seeking federal criminal penalties even in cases of worker death due to willful safety violations.[95] In addition, some members of Congress have introduced legislation to substantially increase the penalties for OSHA violations.[96]

Voluntary Compliance Measures

Along with concerns about the small number of criminal prosecutions, some have criticized OSHA for policies that favor voluntary employer compliance over new mandatory

84. Occupational Safety & Health Admin., *OSH Act, OSHA Standards, Inspections, Citations and Penalties*, available at http://www.osha.gov/doc/outreachtraining/htmlfiles/introsha.html.

85. Reich v. Arcadian Corp., 110 F.3d 1192 (5th Cir. 1997).

86. Eric K. Ho, Ho Ho Ho Express., Houston Fruitland, Inc., 20 BNA OSHC 1361, at 78 (Nos. 98-1645 & 98-1646, 2003).

87. Schoenbaum Ltd., LLC v. Lenox Pines, LLC, 262 Ga. App. 457, 472 (2003).

88. Marlena Telvick, *The Penalty for Killing a Worker?* PBS, Feb. 5, 2008, available at http://www.pbs.org/wgbh/pages/frontline/mcwane/penalty/ (last visited July 3, 2008).

89. News Release, U.S. Dep't of Labor, Occupational Safety & Health Admin., U.S. Department of Labor OSHA Issues Record-Breaking Fines to BP (Oct. 30, 2009), *available at* http://www.osha.gov/pls/oshaweb/owadisp.show_document?p_table=NEWS_RELEASES&p_id=16674.

90. *Id.*

91. *See* 29 U.S.C. § 666(e).

92. *Id.*

93. *See* 29 U.S.C. § 666(g).

94. *See* 29 U.S.C. § 666(f).

95. David Barstow, *U.S. Rarely Seeks Charges for Deaths in Workplace*, N.Y. Times, Dec. 22, 2003, at A1.

96. Protecting America's Workers Act, S. 1166, 112th Cong. (2011)

regulations.[97] Some industries have applauded these efforts, but critics claim the voluntary focus and reduced regulatory guidance have made OSHA less effective.

State Analogues to OSHA

The OSH Act encourages states to create their own job safety and health programs. If a state program meets various OSHA benchmarks, the state can gain more control over its own health and safety regulation. When a state program has met all of OSHA's requirements, OSHA may give "final approval" and relinquish its authority to regulate occupational safety and health matters covered by that program. Only a state program that is "at least as effective" as comparable federal standards will gain this final approval from OSHA. The state program may also govern hazards not addressed by federal standards. As of 2011, OSHA had given final approval to plans covering both private-sector and public employees in twenty-two states and plans covering public employees in five other states.[98]

Where state regulatory programs exist, employees may file formal complaints regarding workplace safety with either the OSHA regional administrator or the appropriate state program. In addition, anyone finding deficiencies with the state program itself may file a complaint with the regional administrator. OSHA investigates all such complaints and requires the state to take corrective actions when necessary.

State Criminal Penalties

In addition to the federal criminal penalties that may be imposed under the OSH Act, state prosecutors may also charge employers with a broad range of crimes, including manslaughter or reckless homicide, when a violation results in an employee's death. For example, in May 2011, the owner of California C&R, Inc. pleaded guilty to, among other things, involuntary manslaughter and willfully violating a Cal/OSHA safety order in connection with the 2008 death of an employee who fell off a four-story apartment building after Cal/OSHA had issued the company a citation for failing to have a site safety plan. The owner was sentenced to one year in prison. The foreman pleaded guilty to leaving a worker unprotected, a misdemeanor, and was sentenced to six months in jail.[99]

Recently, some states have substantially increased the severity of penalties for workplace safety violations. In California for example, willful violations causing an employee's death or prolonged bodily impairment can be prosecuted either as misdemeanors, with maximum penalties of one year in prison and a fine of $100,000, or as felonies, with maximum penalties of a fine of $1.5 million for a corporation or $250,000 for an individual, and three years in prison.[100]

Tort Liability for Violence in the Workplace

Employers also face potential tort liability for violence in the workplace perpetrated by employees or their former lovers or spouses. Workplace violence is among the top four leading causes of fatal occupational injuries in the United States, resulting in more than 3,000 deaths and 15,000 injuries between 2006 and 2010, as well as costing employers $121 billion annually.[101]

A 2005 survey of workplace violence prevention found that less than 30% of businesses surveyed had a crisis program or policy to address workplace violence. To help prevent domestic violence from spilling over into the workplace, some companies hold seminars on domestic-violence issues on company time, provide a twenty-four-hour telephone counseling service for employees and their partners, and tap the phones of workers who fear an attack and provide them with escorts to and from parking lots. Sometimes, the employer seeks restraining orders in its name to keep alleged abusers from potential victims' work sites.[102]

Once an employer is informed about the risk of violence or takes an interest in the case, it exposes itself to liability for negligence if it fails to take reasonable steps to prevent injury. In 2010, a woman was killed while working in a restricted employee area at an Old Navy store by a former boyfriend who shot her and then himself. The family of the victim filed suit against Old Navy for at least $50,000, claiming that the incident could have been prevented and that the store's poor security contributed to the shooting because the shooter was able to enter via a private employee entrance.[103]

---

97. Kris Maher, *OSHA Drawing Democratic Fire over Regulations—Agency Criticized for Emphasizing Voluntary Action*, Wall St. J., Apr. 10, 2008, at A4.

98. Occupational Safety & Health Admin., *Frequently Asked Questions About State Occupational Safety and Health Plans*, available at http://www.osha.gov/dcsp/osp/faq.html.

99. Press Release, Dep't of Indus. Relations' Div., Cal/OSHA Referral to DA Leads to Conviction of Roofing Contractor and Foreman (May 23, 2011), available at http://www.dir.ca.gov/dirnews/2011/ir2011-12.html.

100. Occupational Safety & Health State Plan Ass'n, *2007 OSHSPA Report: Grassroots Workplace Protection* (2007), at 53, available at http://www.orosha.org/grassroots/pdf/2007-oshspa-report.pdf; Kevin Donahue, *State Increases Cal OSHA Penalties*, EHS Today, Nov. 10, 1999, http://ehstoday.com/news/ehs_imp_32581/.

101. Press Release, Occupational Safety & Health Admin., *OSHA Issues Compliance Directive to Address Workplace Violence* (Sept. 8, 2011), available at http://www.osha.gov/pls/oshaweb/owadisp.show_document?p_table=NEWS_RELEASES&p_id=20637; W. Barry Nixon, *Workplace Violence Prevention Fact Sheet*, Workplace Violence News, June 30, 2011.

102. U.S. Dep't of Justice, Federal Bureau of Investigation, Workplace Violence: Issues in Response 44–45 (Mar. 1, 2004), available at http://www.fbi.gov/stats-services/publications/workplace-violence.

103. Bj Lutz, *Family of Woman Shot at Loop Old Navy Sues Store*, NBC (Chicago), July 2, 2010, available at http://www.nbcchicago.com/news/local/old-navy-loop-shooting-lawsuit-97623189.html.

Workers' Compensation

State workers' compensation statutes provide income and coverage of medical expenses for employees[104] who suffer work-related accidents or illnesses.[105] The statutes are based on the principle that the risks of injury in the workplace should be borne by industry. The system is no-fault, and an employee is entitled to monetary benefits from the employer, regardless of the level of safety in the work environment and the degree to which the employee's carelessness contributed to the incident. Workers receive medical treatment and benefits sooner and with more certainty, as a trade-off for receiving smaller total compensation than civil litigation might bring.

The amount of workers' compensation received by an employee is determined by a set schedule, based on the employee's loss of earning power. Usually, the employee receives payments of a specified amount at regular intervals over a definite period of time. In most cases, benefits include medical, surgical, hospital, nursing, and burial services in addition to payment of compensation.[106] Workers' compensation can be provided through (1) self-insurance, (2) insurance purchased through a state fund, or (3) insurance purchased through a private company.

Generally, workers' compensation benefits paid by the employer are the employee's sole remedy for workplace injuries. Some courts have recognized exceptions to this general rule, however, and allow employees to sue employers in tort for their injuries, in addition to collecting workers' compensation, for the following: (1) nonphysical injuries resulting from the tort of intentional infliction of emotional distress; (2) mental distress, indignity, or loss of wages or promotion opportunities due to sexual harassment; (3) injury to reputation caused by an employer's defamatory statements; and (4) both physical and nonphysical injuries resulting from an employer's intentional tort or misconduct.[107]

For example, the New Jersey Supreme Court held that an employer's intentional removal of a safety device from a machine was an intentional wrong that would remove the employer's immunity from a tort suit.[108] In contrast, a New Jersey appellate court dismissed a suit brought on behalf of a security guard killed during a robbery, holding that the dangers faced by security guards did not amount to a "substantial certainty" that injury would occur and, therefore, did not satisfy the intentional tort exception to the workers' compensation exclusive remedy.[109]

MINIMUM WAGE, OVERTIME, AND CHILD LABOR

The Federal Fair Labor Standards Act (FLSA),[110] enacted in 1938 and amended many times thereafter, was established primarily to regulate the minimum wage, overtime pay, and the use of child labor. Many, if not all, states have established wage and hour regulations as well. In general, when federal and state laws vary, employers must abide by the stricter law. Because of the wide variance in state laws, this discussion focuses on federal law.

Who Is Covered?

The FLSA applies to employees who individually are engaged in interstate commerce, or in the production of goods for interstate commerce, or who are employed by employers of any size that participate in interstate commerce, or in the production of goods for interstate commerce.

The FLSA does not apply to independent contractors. As discussed in Chapter 5, proper characterization of workers as employees or independent contractors can be hotly contested.

Who Is Liable for Violations?

Individuals as well as corporations may be held liable for violations under the FLSA. In *Herman v. RSR Security Services Ltd.*,[111] the U.S. Court of Appeals for the Second Circuit ruled that Murray Portnoy, a principal in a labor relations firm, exercised sufficient control over a security company's employees to be held liable as an employer for violations of the FLSA's minimum-wage, overtime, and record-keeping requirements. Portnoy partially owned the security company, funded its start-up costs, and chaired its board of directors. The court affirmed a judgment of $160,000 against Portnoy.

The issue is more complicated when state employees are involved. In *Luder v. Endicott*,[112] the U.S. Court of Appeals for the Seventh Circuit held that the Eleventh Amendment barred a suit against the warden and other supervisors in a Wisconsin state penitentiary who allegedly violated the FLSA by altering hourly workers' time sheets and not compensating them for their work. The court ruled that the plaintiffs, who were suing the supervisors in their individual capacities because a suit against the State of Wisconsin was barred by the Eleventh Amendment, could not bring a suit against the supervisors because the effect of suing the supervisors was the same as suing the State. In 2008, however, the U.S. District Court in the Western District of Kentucky disagreed, arguing that although the decision in *Luder* might

---

104. Independent contractors are generally excluded from workers' compensation.

105. *See* Constance E. Bagley & Craig E. Dauchy, The Entrepreneur's Guide to Business Law 232–34 (4th ed. 2012).

106. 82 Am. Jur. 2d *Workers' Compensation* § 6 (2011).

107. *Id.* §§ 62, 58, 73, 74.

108. Laidlow v. Hariton Mach. Co., 790 A.2d 884 (N.J. 2002).

109. Fisher v. Sears, Roebuck & Co., 883 A.2d 650 (N.J. Super. 2003).

110. 29 U.S.C. §§ 201–219.

111. 172 F.3d 132 (2d Cir. 1999).

112. 253 F.3d 1020 (7th Cir. 2001).

be the best policy result, the "simplest and plain reading of the FLSA" permits a public officer to be sued in his individual capacity.[113] The Kentucky court reasoned that policy considerations are for the legislature, not the courts, to decide.

Hours Worked and Overtime

The FLSA does not limit the number of hours that an employee may work in a workweek or workday, as long as the employee is paid appropriate overtime. (But, as noted in Chapter 9, if an employer forces an employee to work too many hours, the employer may be liable under common law negligence for injury to a third party resulting from the employee's fatigue.) The FLSA requires that, with certain exceptions, every employee be paid one and one-half times the regular rate of pay for hours worked in excess of forty hours in a workweek. The "regular rate" is not necessarily the hourly wage, but includes all cash compensation for the workweek. In most cases, employers can exclude profits from certain employer-provided stock options, stock appreciation rights, and bona fide stock purchases from the calculation of regular pay rates when calculating overtime pay.[114]

The FLSA permits state and local governments to comply with the statute's overtime provisions by giving employees compensatory time (comp time) in lieu of overtime pay.[115] *Comp time* is extra paid vacation time granted instead of extra pay for overtime work.

Compensation

The FLSA requires that employees be compensated for all hours worked. This includes the time employees spend putting on required protective gear, donning and doffing the gear, and walking to and from the locker room to the production floor.[116] The time employees spend before donning protective gear or after doffing it is not compensable under the FLSA, however.

In general, the hours that an employer knows or has reason to know that an employee has worked are deemed hours worked even if the employer has not asked the employee to work those hours. If an employee is asked to be on standby—that is, available to return to work while off duty—the hours spent on standby will not be counted as hours worked if the employee is generally free to use the time for his or her own purposes.

Minimum Wage

In 1938, the FLSA established the first minimum wage at 25 cents per hour. The minimum wage in 2011 is $7.25 per hour.[117] States often impose higher minimum wages.

More than 140 localities (including Baltimore, Detroit, Milwaukee, Minneapolis, Portland (Oregon), and St. Louis) require certain employers to provide wages and employee benefits higher than either federal or state minimum wages.[118] Called *living wage ordinances*, these programs require employers to pay wages approximating the real cost of living in the locality, which is often significantly higher than the applicable state or federal minimum wage. Unlike state and federal minimum-wage laws, living wage ordinances often target only certain businesses, such as recipients of city contracts, lessees of city property, or larger businesses with more employees and higher earnings. RUI One Corporation, which owned and operated a restaurant located on an open space preserve held in public trust by the City of Berkeley, California, unsuccessfully challenged Berkeley's living wage ordinance under the Equal Protection and Due Process Clauses of the U.S. and California Constitutions.[119] The ordinance applied only to five employers that (1) were located on the open space preserve, (2) had a minimum number of employees, and (3) earned an annual revenue of more than $350,000.[120] The U.S. Court of Appeals for the Ninth Circuit held that RUI was not unfairly targeted by the ordinance. RUI operated its restaurant on the highly desirable open space preserve under a privilege granted by the City. Ultimately, the court reasoned, cities should be allowed leeway to approach the problem of their working poor by implementing their living wage ordinances incrementally.

Exempt Employees

Certain types of employees are exempt from the FLSA minimum-wage and overtime requirements, including many executive, administrative, professional, computer, and outside sales employees. In August 2004, the Wage and Hour Division of the Department of Labor updated the regulations that define the characteristics of these exempt employees in terms of salary and work duties to more accurately reflect the realities of the contemporary workplace.[121]

To qualify as an *exempt employee*, the employee must (1) be paid a minimum salary amount, (2) be paid on a "salary basis," and (3) meet the "duties test" for the particular exemption. All other employees are *nonexempt employees*

---

113. Fraternal Order of Police Barkley Lodge v. Fletcher, 618 F. Supp. 2d 712, 721 (W.D. Ky. 2008).

114. *See* U.S. Dep't of Labor, Office of the Assistant Sec'y for Policy/Office of Compliance Assistance Policy, *FLSA Overtime Calculator Advisor, Statutory Exclusions*, available at http://www.dol.gov/elaws/esa/flsa/otcalc/docstatexc.asp.

115. 1985 Amendment to the Fair Labor Standards Act, Pub. L. No. 99-150, 99 Stat. 787, § 2(a) (1985).

116. IBP, Inc. v. Alvarez, 546 U.S. 21 (2005).

117. U.S. Dep't of Labor, Wage & Hour Div., *Minimum Wage*, available at http://www.dol.gov/whd/minimumwage.htm.

118. Trisha B. Philips, *Living Wage for Research Subjects*, 39 J. L. MED. & ETHICS 243, 248 (2011).

119. RUI One Corp. v. City of Berkeley, 371 F.3d 1137 (9th Cir. 2004).

120. *Id.* at 1145.

121. *See generally* 29 C.F.R. § 541.0.

and must be paid both the minimum wage and the overtime required by the FLSA. The regulations also provide that certain types of jobs do not qualify for the exemptions from the FLSA minimum-wage and overtime requirements. Nonexempt workers include manual laborers and other blue-collar workers, as well as police officers, firefighters, paramedics, and other public safety "first responders."[122]

Minimum Salary

Employees who earn less than $455 per week ($23,660 annualized) are automatically considered nonexempt. The Labor Department has also adopted a "bright-line" test whereby highly paid employees—those earning an annual salary of at least $100,000 per year (including commissions and nondiscretionary bonuses)—are considered exempt as long as the employer can show that they regularly perform at least one of the exempt duties or responsibilities of an executive, administrative, or professional employee. For employees earning between $23,660 and $100,000, the FLSA provides a test based on the types of duties the employee performs to determine whether the employee is exempt.

Child Labor

The FLSA child-labor provisions were enacted to stop the early twentieth-century abuses of many employers who employed children at minimal wages. It is illegal to employ anyone under the age of fourteen, except in specified agricultural occupations. Children aged fourteen or fifteen may work in some occupations, but only if the employment occurs outside school hours and does not exceed daily and weekly hour limits. Individuals aged sixteen to eighteen may work in manufacturing occupations, but not in jobs that the Secretary of Labor has declared to be particularly hazardous, such as jobs entailing exposure to radioactive materials or operation of a power-driven woodworking machine, a hoisting apparatus, a metal-forming machine, or a circular or band saw.

Modern-Day Slavery

Human trafficking, which often involves the recruitment and smuggling of foreign nationals into the United States to force them to work in factories, fields, or homes, amounts to "modern-day slavery." Human Rights Watch estimates that every year 800,000 to 900,000 men, women, and children are trafficked across international borders into forced labor or slavery-like conditions.[123] The Victims of Trafficking and Violence Protection Act

of 2000 (TVPA)[124] made prosecution of human trafficking in the United States more effective and increased the statutory maximum sentences that traffickers face.

EMPLOYEE BENEFITS

A variety of federal and state statutes govern employee benefits.

Employee Retirement Income Security Act of 1974 (ERISA)

Prior to the enactment of the Employee Retirement Income Security Act of 1974 (ERISA),[125] many employees who had expected to receive pension payments on retirement received either no benefits or far lower benefits than they had anticipated. Plan officials made ill-advised pension investments, employees who quit or were discharged received few or no vested benefits, and employers terminated underfunded plans or left them within sufficient assets to cover their obligations. Congress enacted ERISA to help remedy these problems, but its scope goes far beyond pensions. As discussed further below, ERISA preempts many state laws governing pensions and employer-sponsored health maintenance organizations and other employee benefits.

Coverage

ERISA governs most retirement plans (referred to as *pension plans*) as well as many other types of employer-sponsored employee benefit plans (referred to as *welfare benefit plans*). With regard to pension plans, ERISA (1) establishes minimum funding requirements and participation and vesting standards; (2) imposes fiduciary obligations on pension plan administrators; (3) requires detailed disclosure and reporting of certain pension plan information; (4) imposes substantial restrictions on the investment of pension plan assets; and (5) requires pension plan administrators to provide annual, audited financial statements to the government and participants. An employer must also maintain records of each employee's years of service and vesting percentage.

Types of Pension Plans

In a *defined benefit pension plan*, the employer guarantees that the participant will receive an annual benefit for life following retirement (or the actuarial equivalent of such benefit), based on the formulas in the plan, regardless of the total contributions made to the plan or the plan's investment performance. Thus, the employer bears the economic risk of poor investment performance (and enjoys the benefits of superior financial performance). The employer

---

122. 29 C.F.R. § 541.3.

123. Martin Patt, *Human Trafficking & Modern-Day Slavery*, Oct. 15, 2010, *available at* http://gvnet.com/humantrafficking/00-HumanTrafficking.htm.

124. Pub. L. No. 106-386, 114 Stat 1464 (2000).

125. 29 U.S.C. §§ 1001–1461 (1974).

is required to fund the defined benefit pension plan on an annual basis based on reasonable actuarial assumptions.

In contrast, in a *defined contribution pension plan*, the employer makes no guarantee as to any particular benefit on retirement. Instead, the retirement benefit is whatever can be funded by the balance in the participant's account at retirement. Thus, the participant bears the economic risk of poor investment performance (and enjoys the benefits of superior investment performance). The employer's obligation to make contributions to a defined contribution pension plan depends on the terms of the plan. Some defined contribution pension plans provide for a fixed percentage of the participant's compensation. Other plans are totally discretionary with the employer on a year-by-year basis.

A *401(k) plan* is a defined contribution pension plan funded with contributions by the participants or a combination of participant and employer contributions. Both 401(k) plans and *SIMPLE plans* (plans for employers with fewer than 100 employees that are similar to 401(k) plans but have stricter rules and simpler administration) allow employees to defer a portion of their salaries on a pretax basis into an investment fund set up by the company. By law, participation in 401(k) plans cannot be too heavily weighted in favor of higher compensated employees, so companies generally offer a partial match to encourage broad participation in these voluntary plans. The match can be in cash or any investment vehicle the company chooses, including company stock. Over time, many employers have abandoned their traditional defined benefit plans in favor of 401(k) plans, thereby shifting more of the investment risk to employees.[126]

An *employee stock ownership plan (ESOP)* can provide numerous tax and other benefits for employees, the company, and shareholders. ESOPs are tax-qualified, however, so they must meet many coverage, nondiscrimination, distribution, and other Internal Revenue Code requirements. Among other things, ESOPs must not discriminate in favor of highly compensated employees, and the Internal Revenue Code's distribution rules require the employer to repurchase the stock after an employee terminates employment at the election of the employee (if a market does not otherwise exist). An ESOP's assets must be invested primarily in stock of the sponsoring employer, and an ESOP is the only plan that is allowed to borrow funds on the credit of the sponsoring company to acquire employer stock to hold as a plan asset in the ESOP trust.

Fiduciary Duties

ERISA provides that officers and trustees of both defined benefit pension plans and defined contribution pension plans are fiduciaries who are required to act solely in the interests of the plan's participants and beneficiaries in providing benefits and defraying expenses.[127] In particular, section 409 of ERISA imposes fiduciary duties on plan administrators relating to the proper management, administration, and investment of plan assets in order to ensure that the benefits authorized by the plan are ultimately paid to plan participants.

Trustees of private pension plans must use the "prudent person" investment standard when investing pension funds. This rule requires trustees to employ "the care, skill, prudence and diligence under the circumstances then prevailing that a prudent man acting in a like capacity and familiar with such matters would use in the conduct of an enterprise of a like character and with like aims."[128]

Participants in a defined benefit plan are not entitled to receive more than their accrued benefits, however: "Since a decline in the value of a plan's assets does not alter accrued benefits, members similarly have no entitlement to share in a plan's surplus—even if it is partially attributable to the investment growth of their contributions."[129] As a result, Hughes Aircraft Company did not violate its fiduciary duties when it stopped making contributions to a defined benefit plan with a $1 billion surplus, amended the plan to include an early retirement program with additional benefits to certain eligible employees, and then amended the plan again to provide that new participants could not contribute to the plan and would receive fewer benefits.

In *Massachusetts Mutual Life Insurance Co. v. Russell*,[130] the U.S. Supreme Court held that section 502(a)(2) of ERISA provides remedies only for the defined benefit pension plans themselves, not for individual participants in those plans. Misconduct by the administrator of a defined benefit pension plan will not affect an individual participant's entitlement to benefits unless it creates or enhances the risk of default by the entire plan. In contrast, the U.S. Supreme Court ruled in *LaRue v. DeWolff, Boberg & Associates, Inc.*,[131] that a participant in a defined contribution pension plan may sue a fiduciary whose alleged misconduct impaired the value of plan assets in the participant's individual 401(k) account.

The Pension Protection Act of 2006

In the first two years of the twenty-first century, thousands of Enron employees lost virtually all of their retirement savings while some Enron executives retained significant wealth by selling their Enron stock prior to its decline in value. The retirement security of employees at many other major corporations was similarly undermined.

126. Investment Company Institute, *401(k) Plans: A 25-Year Retrospective*, Res. Persp., Nov. 2006, at 1, *available at* http://www.ici.org/pdf/per12-02.pdf (last visited Sept. 2, 2008).

127. Richard H. Koppes & Maureen L. Reilly, *An Ounce of Prevention: Meeting the Fiduciary Duty to Monitor an Index Fund Through Relationship Investing*, 20 J. Corp. L. 413, 426 (1995).

128. *Id.* (citing 29 U.S.C. § 1104 (Supp. 1990)).

129. Hughes Aircraft Co. v. Jacobson, 525 U.S. 432, at 440–41 (1999).

130. 473 U.S. 134 (1985).

131. 552 U.S. 248 (2008).

The Pension Protection Act of 2006,[132] a 900-page omnibus law, was passed in part to prevent similar abuses in the future. It requires 401(k) plans and other defined contribution pension plans that hold publicly traded employer stock to allow participants and beneficiaries to divest the employer shares. Plans are required to offer at least three different types of investment options, in addition to employer stock, in order to satisfy a variety of risk tolerances among participants and beneficiaries. The Act also requires 401(k) quarterly statements to warn employees that holding more than 20% of their portfolio in any one company or industry could leave them inadequately diversified. To encourage employee participation, the Act allows companies to automatically enroll 401(k)-eligible employees in the plan and to automatically increase worker contributions every year. Participation in 401(k) plans is 85% where the employer automatically enrolls eligible employees, but only 67% where there is no automatic enrollment.[133] Plan participation for eligible employees had increased to 75.8% by 2010.[134] The Act also boosted the portability of 401(k) plans, making it easier for employees to roll over funds. Thus, for example, employees who work at a nonprofit organization can roll their 403(b) plans into a 401(k) if they go to work for a for-profit corporation. The Act also allows the plan provider chosen by the employer to offer investment advice to workers.

In an effort to address the deteriorating funding of many defined benefit pension plans and, in some cases, the termination of plans when a plan sponsor was unable to meet its funding obligations, many of the Act's provisions aimed at requiring defined benefit pension plans to meet more stringent funding rules. The Act requires contributions to underfunded plans that, in most cases, are sufficient to fully fund the plan within seven years. It requires that minimum contributions be made quarterly for certain underfunded plans. The Act requires larger contributions when a defined benefit plan is "at risk," and it limits benefit increases and acceleration of payments by underfunded plans. Finally, it increased the limit on deductible contributions to 150% of a defined pension plan's current liability.

401(k) Litigation   As the number of employees with 401(k) plans has grown, the number of lawsuits targeting 401(k) plan fiduciaries, including corporate executives, company directors, and investment committee members, has also grown. Litigation involving 401(k) plans increased significantly after a 2002 lawsuit against Enron, on behalf of 224,000 employees, led to a $220 million settlement, according to the law firm that was co-lead counsel.

In 2008, four former Wellpoint, Inc. employees filed a lawsuit against the health insurance giant over the losses that its 401(k) retirement plan suffered when the company announced a sharp drop in profits for the previous year.[135] The lawsuit alleged that Wellpoint's officers breached their fiduciary duties by failing to promptly inform 401(k) participants that the company's business was worsening.

Wal-Mart employees are suing the world's largest company for breach of its fiduciary duties with respect to the company's $9.5 billion 401(k) plan. The suit alleges that the company breached its duties as a fiduciary by allowing its 401(k) plan participants to be charged "unreasonably expensive" fees in violation of ERISA requirements that fees be reasonable. The plaintiffs claim the fees were too high because Wal-Mart's plan offers participants retail mutual funds rather than less expensive institutional funds "despite the ready availability of reasonably priced options, particularly for a massive plan like Wal-Mart's with tremendous potential to leverage economies of scale."[136] Although the district court dismissed the complaint, the U.S. Court of Appeals for the Eighth Circuit reversed and remanded the case to the district court for trial.[137]

Welfare Benefit Plans

Medical, dental, disability, and other welfare benefit plans are also subject to ERISA's rules on reporting, disclosure, and fiduciary responsibility. For example, employers must provide employees with a summary plan description, a summary annual report, and a summary of any material modifications to the plan. Further, the employer or plan administrator must maintain sufficient records, usually including the employee's age, hours worked, salary, and contributions, to calculate each employee's benefits.

Other employee benefits (which may not be part of a formal plan) are also covered by ERISA if a reasonable person could determine, from the surrounding circumstances, the existence of the intended benefits, the beneficiaries, the financing for the benefits, and the procedures for receiving the benefits. Many types of group severance pay plans are deemed to be either welfare plans or, less commonly, pension plans and are thus regulated by ERISA. Individually negotiated severance agreements, however, generally are not.

132. *See* U.S. Dep't of Labor, Emp. Benefits Sec. Admin., *Pension Protection Act*, *available at* http://www.dol.gov/EBSA/pensionreform.html (last visited Sept. 28, 2011).

133. Edward Jacobson, *Aon Hewitt: 401(k) Participation Rate Rises*, National Underwriter Life & Health, May 24, 2011, *available at* http://www.lifeandhealthinsurancenews.com/News/2011/5/Pages/Aon-Hewitt-401k-Participation-Rate-Rises.aspx.

134. *Id.*

135. J.K. Wall, *401(k) Losses Bite Wellpoint*, Newsnet.com, June 16, 2008, http://www.insurancenewsnet.com/article.asp?a=top_lh&id=96069.

136. Mark Bruno, *Wal-Mart Suit Hits 401(k) Fees*, Fin. Wk., Apr. 28, 2008, *available at* http://www.financialweek.com/apps/pbcs.dll/article?AID=/20080428/REG/156632963/1028.

137. Robert Steyer, *Execs Keeping An Eye on Major Court Cases*, Pensions & Investments, Jan. 24, 2011, *available at* http://www.pionline.com/article/20110124/PRINTSUB/301249985/.

Federal Preemption

ERISA was designed "to provide a uniform regulatory regime over employee benefit plans,"[138] and it expressly supersedes "any and all State laws insofar as they may now or hereafter relate to any employee benefit plan . . . ." Thus, a state law is preempted if it has a connection with or relates to an employee benefit plan.[139]

ERISA does not preempt all state laws, however, the U.S. Supreme Court held in *UNUM Life Insurance Co. of America v. Ward*.[140] The case involved a long-term group disability policy that UNUM had issued to Management Analysis Company (MAC) as a benefit plan governed by ERISA. The policy required that proof of claims be furnished to UNUM within a certain limited period of time. John Ward, a MAC employee, became disabled and qualified for state disability benefits. When Ward inquired, MAC informed him that its long-term disability plan covered his condition, and Ward submitted a benefits application. MAC processed the application and forwarded it to UNUM, which advised Ward that his claim was untimely. California's notice-prejudice rule provides that an insurer cannot avoid liability when proof of claim is untimely, unless the insurer can show that it suffered actual prejudice from the delay. Under California's agency rule, a California employer that administers an insured group health plan should be deemed to act as the agent of the insurance company. Ward argued that, under this rule, his notice to MAC sufficed to supply timely notice to the insurance company.

The U.S. Supreme Court concluded that ERISA did not preempt the notice-prejudice rule because it regulates insurance, an area traditionally governed by state law. By allowing a longer period to file than the minimum filing terms mandated by federal law, the state law complemented rather than contradicted ERISA. The Court also ruled, however, that the agency rule related to an employee benefit plan and was, therefore, preempted by ERISA. Preemption in connection with health maintenance organizations is discussed below.

Judicial Review of Benefit Determinations

Courts apply principles of trust law when reviewing benefit determinations by plan administrators or other fiduciaries under ERISA.[141] When a plan gives the administrator discretionary authority to determine eligibility for benefits or to interpret the plan, a court will not overturn an administrator's decision unless there has been an abuse of discretion. In contrast, if the plan is silent or does not give the administrator discretionary authority to determine eligibility, then a court will conduct a de novo review of the decision and not give deference to the administrator's decision.

If a benefit plan gives discretion to an administrator who is operating under a conflict of interest, however, then the courts will weigh the conflict as a factor in determining whether there has been an abuse of discretion. For example, an employer that both administers an ERISA plan and determines whether a participant is eligible for benefits is deemed to have a conflict of interest:

> In such a circumstance, "every dollar provided in benefits is a dollar spent by . . . the employer; and every dollar saved . . . is a dollar in [the employer's] pocket." The employer's fiduciary interest may counsel in favor of granting a borderline claim while its immediate financial interest counsels to the contrary. Thus, the employer has an "interest . . . conflicting with that of the beneficiaries," the type of conflict that judges must take into account when they review the discretionary acts of a trustee of a common-law trust.[142]

Similarly, an insurance company that both evaluates claims for benefits and pays benefits claims is deemed to have a conflict, which should "be weighed as a 'factor in determining whether there is an abuse of discretion.'"[143] Even though an insurance company administering a plan for an employer may have a greater incentive than a self-administering employer to process claims accurately, the employer's own conflict may extend to its selection of an insurance company to administer the plan. In addition, "ERISA imposes higher-than-marketplace standards on insurers."[144]

For example, Metropolitan Life Insurance (MetLife) was an administrator and the insurer of the insurance plan for Sears, Roebuck & Co. The plan gave MetLife the discretionary authority to determine the validity of employees' benefits claims and provided that MetLife, as insurer, would pay the claims.

After Wanda Glenn, a Sears employee, was diagnosed with severe dilated cardiomyopathy, a heart condition whose symptoms include fatigue and shortness of breath, she applied in June 2000 for short-term disability benefits under her disability insurance plan. MetLife concluded that she could not "perform the material duties of [her] own job" and therefore met the plan's standard for an initial twenty-four months of benefits. MetLife also referred Glenn to a law firm to assist her in applying for Social Security disability benefits, some of which MetLife would be entitled to receive as an offset to her plan benefits. In April 2002, an administrative law judge found that Glenn's illness prevented her "from performing any jobs [for which she could qualify] existing in significant numbers in the

138. Aetna Health Inc. v. Davila, 542 U.S. 200, 208 (2004).

139. Shaw v. Delta Air Lines, Inc., 463 U.S. 85, 96–97 (1983).

140. 526 U.S. 358 (1999).

141. Firestone Tire & Rubber Co. v. Bruch, 489 U.S. 101 (1989).

142. Metro. Life Ins. Co. v. Glenn, 554 U.S. 105, 112 (2008).

143. *Id.* at 115.

144. *Id.*

national economy" and granted her permanent disability payments retroactive to April 2000. Glenn kept none of these backdated benefits: three-quarters were paid to MetLife, and the remainder (plus some additional money) was paid to her lawyers.

The Sears plan provided that Glenn had to meet a stricter standard to continue receiving disability benefits after twenty-four months. This standard required that her medical condition render her incapable of performing not only her own job, but also "the material duties of any gainful occupation for which" she was "reasonably qualified." MetLife denied Glenn the extended benefits because it found that she was "capable of performing full time sedentary work." Glenn sought federal court review under ERISA, but the district court denied her relief. The U.S. Court of Appeals for the Sixth Circuit reversed, and MetLife appealed. The U.S. Supreme Court affirmed the Sixth Circuit's holding that MetLife had abused its discretion when it denied Glenn long-term disability benefits, reasoning:

> The Court of Appeals' opinion in the present case illustrates the combination-of-factors method of review. . . . The Court of Appeals gave the conflict weight to some degree; its opinion suggests that, in context, the court would not have found the conflict alone determinative. The court instead focused more heavily on other factors. In particular, the court found questionable the fact that MetLife had encouraged Glenn to argue to the Social Security Administration that she could do no work, received the bulk of the benefits of her success in doing so (the remainder going to the lawyers it recommended), and then ignored the agency's finding in concluding that Glenn could in fact do sedentary work. This course of events was not only an important factor in its own right (because it suggested procedural unreasonableness), but also would have justified the court in giving more weight to the conflict (because MetLife's seemingly inconsistent positions were both financially advantageous). And the court furthermore observed that MetLife had emphasized a certain medical report that favored a denial of benefits, had deemphasized certain other reports that suggested a contrary conclusion, and had failed to provide its independent vocational and medical experts with all of the relevant evidence. All these serious concerns, taken together with some degree of conflicting interests on MetLife's part, led the court to set aside MetLife's discretionary decision.[145]

Review of Decisions by HMOs   Health maintenance organizations (HMOs) that provide care pursuant to employer-sponsored health plans are subject to ERISA

and have spawned much litigation. One landmark case involved Cynthia Herdrich, who was covered by Carle Clinic Association P.C., Health Alliance Medical Plans, Inc., and Carle Health Insurance Management Company, Inc. (collectively Carle) through her husband's employer, State Farm Insurance Company.[146] During a physical exam, Dr. Lori Pegram, a Carle doctor, discovered an inflamed mass in Herdrich's abdomen. Instead of ordering an immediate ultrasound at the local hospital, Dr. Pegram decided that Herdrich could wait eight more days for an ultrasound at a facility staffed by Carle. Before the scheduled ultrasound, Herdrich's appendix ruptured, causing peritonitis.

Herdrich sued Pegram and Carle for medical malpractice and fraud. She also argued that the provision of medical services under the Carle HMO, which rewarded its physicians for limiting medical care to cut costs, was a breach of Carle's duty under ERISA because it created an incentive to make decisions in the physicians' self-interest rather than in the exclusive interests of their patients. The Supreme Court rejected her ERISA claims. It distinguished between pure "eligibility decisions," which turn on a plan's coverage of a particular condition or medical procedure for its treatment and are covered by ERISA, and "treatment decisions," which are choices about how to go about diagnosing and treating a patient's condition and are not covered by ERISA. Observing that the decisions that Herdrich claimed were fiduciary in character were mixed eligibility and treatment decisions, the Court held that such mixed decisions by HMO physicians were not fiduciary decisions under ERISA: "Traditional trustees administer a medical trust by paying out money to buy medical care, whereas physicians making mixed eligibility decisions consume the money as well. Private trustees do not make treatment judgments, whereas treatment judgments are what physicians reaching mixed decisions do make, by definition."

In contrast, in *Aetna Health Inc. v. Davila*,[147] the Supreme Court held that benefit determinations made by an HMO (even if "infused with medical judgment") are pure eligibility decisions—not mixed eligibility decisions like those made indirectly by a physician. As a result, state-law claims based on benefit determinations are preempted by ERISA.

The case consolidated two separate suits against HMOs. One suit involved Ruby Calad, who underwent a hysterectomy but was ordered by her HMO to leave the hospital one day later, despite her doctor's opposition. Calad suffered complications and was rushed to the emergency room several days later. The other suit involved Juan Davila, who nearly died of internal bleeding when his HMO refused to pay for a medication prescribed by his doctor and insisted he use a cheaper pain relief medication instead. Calad and Davila alleged that the HMOs' refusals to cover the requested services violated their duty of care when making

---

145. *Id.* at 118.

146. Pegram v. Herdrich, 530 U.S. 211 (2000).
147. 542 U.S. 200 (2004).

health-care treatment decisions and "proximately caused" the plaintiffs' injuries in violation of the Texas Health Care Liability Act, a patients' rights law giving patients the right to sue their managed care organizations for certain wrongful coverage decisions that resulted in injury or death.

The Supreme Court held that Calad's and Davila's state-law claims were completely preempted by ERISA. Writing for the majority, Justice Thomas distinguished the case from *Pegram*, in which the Court had held that Congress did not intend an HMO to be treated as a fiduciary under ERISA "to the extent it makes mixed eligibility decisions acting through its physicians."[148] In contrast, the coverage decisions of the HMOs in *Aetna* were not made by physicians or employers of the physicians. Because they were pure eligibility decisions, they were governed by ERISA. In their concurring opinion in *Aetna*, Justices Ginsburg and Breyer joined "the rising judicial chorus urging that Congress and [this] Court revisit what is an unjust and increasingly tangled ERISA regime."[149] They also referenced an amicus brief filed by the U.S. Solicitor General, which suggested that some form of "make whole" relief is available against a breaching fiduciary under ERISA.[150]

In an effort to avoid the HMOs' traditional defense that claims regarding quality of care should be filed under ERISA, a group of chronically ill and disabled patients sued two HMOs and a physicians' group under the Americans with Disabilities Act (ADA). They claimed that the defendants violated the ADA by limiting care for chronically ill patients. Although the case was ultimately settled, a Texas federal court judge had held earlier that the ADA prevents HMOs from discriminating against patients with disabilities.[151]

Penalties

ERISA imposes various penalties for failure to conform to its requirements. Plan participants or beneficiaries may sue for lost benefits and loss of the plan's tax benefits. Any plan fiduciary that breaches a duty is personally liable for the losses resulting from the breach. ERISA also provides civil penalties for breach of its prohibited transaction rules (which bar many transactions between an ERISA plan and a fiduciary of that plan) of up to 100% of the amount of the prohibited transaction.[152]

To minimize costs and maximize benefit levels, many employers with union employees under collective bargaining agreements belong to multiemployer pension plans. Under the Multiemployer Pension Plan Amendments Act of 1980, withdrawal from such a plan may result in stiff penalties.

Consolidated Omnibus Budget Reconciliation Act (COBRA)

The Consolidated Omnibus Budget Reconciliation Act of 1985 (COBRA)[153] was enacted in 1986 to allow group health, dental, and visual benefits to continue for employees who are terminated voluntarily or involuntarily (unless the discharge was for gross misconduct), and for employees whose hours are reduced to the point at which coverage would normally cease. COBRA applies to employers of twenty or more workers that sponsor a group health plan.[154] Employers must notify employees of their rights when they begin participation in a group health plan or when coverage has been threatened by an event such as termination or reduced hours. Employers who fail to comply with COBRA's requirements are subject to adverse tax consequences.[155]

Eligible employees must be given at least sixty days from the date their coverage ceases to elect to have their coverage continued for them and their covered spouse and dependents. If coverage continuation is elected, the employer is required to extend, for up to eighteen months, coverage identical to that provided under the plan for similarly situated employees. The eligible employee electing COBRA coverage must pay the entire premium, plus an administrative fee of up to an additional 2% of the cost of coverage. If the employee declines to continue coverage, the employer has no further coverage obligations.

An employer may discontinue coverage for any one of five reasons: (1) the employer ceases to provide group health coverage to any of its employees; (2) the premium for the coverage is not paid; (3) the employee, or former employee, becomes insured under another group plan; (4) the employee, or former employee, becomes eligible for Medicare; or (5) a spouse of the employee, or former employee, is divorced, remarries, and becomes covered under the new spouse's plan.

Health Insurance Portability and Accountability Act (HIPAA)

The Health Insurance Portability and Accountability Act of 1996 (HIPAA)[156] provides special protection for individuals with lifelong illnesses who change jobs and, as discussed in Chapter 9, imposes strict patient confidentiality requirements. Its principal provisions cover all companies with fifty or more employees.

HIPAA requires that new employees and their dependents be eligible for health insurance coverage by the new

---

148. *Id.* at 231.

149. *Id.* at 222.

150. *Id.* at 223.

151. Zamora-Quezada v. HealthTexas Med. Grp. of San Antonio, 34 F. Supp. 2d 433, 440 (W.D. Tex. 1998).

152. 29 U.S.C. §§ 1106, 1132 (1974).

153. Pub. L. No. 99-272, 100 Stat. 82 (1986) (codified as amended in scattered sections of 29 U.S.C.).

154. Churches and federal government agencies are exempt from COBRA.

155. Pub. L. No. 100-647, 102 Stat. 3342 (1988) (codified as amended in scattered sections of 26 U.S.C.).

156. Pub. L. No. 104-191, 110 Stat. 1936 (1996) (codified in scattered sections of 18, 26, 29, 42 U.S.C.).

employer without an exclusion (or higher premiums) for preexisting conditions if they had health insurance for at least eighteen months provided by the previous employer and joined the new company within sixty-three days of leaving the previous employer. The previous employer must provide a certificate to a leaving employee documenting the previous coverage. HIPAA also provides that the duration of an employee's previous coverage may be applied to fulfilling a new employer's waiting period.

The Act also extended COBRA for up to twenty-nine months for individuals who leave work as a result of illness or disability, provided that they apply within sixty days of leaving. In addition, HIPAA requires companies to offer the same health coverage whether the illness is physical or mental. It also provided greater health-related tax deductions for self-employed individuals.

Despite its multiple provisions, HIPAA did not resolve all issues related to health insurance reform. Among other things, HIPAA did not include insurance pools for small businesses, nor did it raise the lifetime caps on insurance benefits.

Patient Protection and Affordable Care Act of 2010

The Patient Protection and Affordable Care Act, a sweeping health-care reform act signed into law in 2010, prohibits insurers from denying health-care coverage (or charging higher premiums) due to preexisting conditions. It also requires employers with 200 or more full-time employees to automatically enroll new employees in health-care coverage. Firms with fifty or more employees that do not offer health insurance to employees must pay a shared responsibility payment of $750 per employee if the government has to subsidize the employees' health care.[157] In this regime, individuals, employers, insurers, and the government all share responsibility for helping to expand health-care coverage. The shared responsibility payment of the employer is another facet of the individual mandate that helps the government subsidize individuals' health insurance when the employer does not offer insurance. Very small businesses (twenty-five or fewer full-time employees) may get tax credits to participate in health-care exchanges.[158] As discussed in Chapter 4, the Supreme Court heard oral arguments in March 2012 in a case challenging the constitutionality of the insurance mandate in the Act.

WORKER ADJUSTMENT AND RETRAINING NOTIFICATION ACT

The Worker Adjustment and Retraining Notification Act of 1988 (WARN Act)[159] requires an employer to provide timely notice to its employees of a proposal to close a plant or to reduce its workforce permanently. The Act applies to employers with 100 or more employees, either all working full-time or working an aggregate of at least 4,000 hours per week.

The WARN Act[160] requires employers to give employees sixty days' advance notice of any plant closing that will result in a loss of employment during any thirty-day period for fifty or more employees. A shutdown of a product line or operation within a plant is included within the Act's definition of a plant closing. The Act also requires sixty days' notice for a layoff during any thirty-day period that affects at least 500 employees or, at least 50 employees if they comprise one-third of the workforce. Employers must give written notice of the plant closing or layoff to each representative of the affected employees or, if there is no representative, to each affected employee, as well as to the state and local governments where the layoff or plant closing will occur.

The Act permits an employer to order the shutdown of a plant before the conclusion of the sixty-day notice period if (1) at the time notice would have been required, the employer was actively seeking capital or business that would enable it to avoid or postpone the shutdown, and the employer reasonably and in good faith believed that giving the required notice would preclude it from obtaining the needed business or capital; or (2) the plant closing or mass layoff was caused by a natural disaster or by business circumstances that were not reasonably foreseeable at the time notice would have been required.

The WARN Act does not apply to (1) the closing of a temporary facility, (2) a closing or mass layoff that results from the completion of a particular project if the affected employees were hired with the understanding that their employment would not continue beyond the duration of the project, or (3) a closing or layoff that results from a strike or lockout that is not intended to evade the requirements of the Act.

Aggrieved employees are entitled to receive back wages and benefits for each day that the employer is in violation of the WARN Act. The court has discretion to award the prevailing party reasonable attorneys' fees. In addition, an employer who violates the Act may be subject to a civil penalty of up to $30,000, to be paid to the affected communities.

---

157. Henry J. Kaiser Family Found., *Explaining Health Care Reform: What Is an Employer "Pay-or-Play" Requirement?*, FOCUS ON HEALTH REFORM, May 2009, *available at* http://www.kff.org/healthreform/upload/7907. pdf; Senate Democrats, *Responsible Reform for the Middle Class, The Patient Protection and Affordable Care Act, Detailed Summary, available at* http://dpc.senate.gov/healthreformbill/healthbill04.pdf.

158. Internal Revenue Serv., *Small Business Health Care Tax Credit for Small Employees*, Sept. 7, 2011, *available at* http://www.irs.gov/ newsroom/article/0,,id=223666,00.html.

---

159. 29 U.S.C. §§ 2101–2109.

160. 29 U.S.C. § 2101.

IMMIGRATION LAW

There are more than 11.1 million illegal immigrants living in the United States[161] and about 7 million illegal workers.[162] Immigration law has thus become an increasingly important concern for employers.

Immigration Reform and Control Act of 1986

Under the Immigration Reform and Control Act of 1986,[163] employers may hire only persons eligible to legally work in the United States, that is, U.S. citizens and noncitizens (so-called aliens) authorized to work in the United States. An employer can be fined up to $16,000[164] and imprisoned for up to six months for each illegal alien knowingly hired.[165] During 2010, U.S. Immigration and Customs Enforcement (ICE), the investigation and enforcement branch of the Department of Homeland Security (DHS), secured immigration-related fines, judgments, judicial forfeitures, and restitutions against employers totaling approximately $36.6 million, coupled with 196 arrests.[166] In 2011, ICE announced its largest nationwide worksite raids to date, arresting more than 2,900 undocumented workers in a coordinated effort in all fifty states and four U.S. territories.[167]

Obtaining Authorization

The primary way that aliens gain authorization to work in the United States is by obtaining a work visa. The U.S. government offers a number of visas based on different classifications including, for example, as (1) a student, (2) an educational or cultural exchange visitor, (3) a professional worker from Canada or Mexico authorized to work in the United States under the North American Free Trade Agreement, or (4) a foreign employee of an overseas company who is temporarily transferred to the United States.

Many U.S. employers rely on the employment of foreign workers with an *H-1B visa*, which is available only for workers in professional and specialty occupations (generally those requiring a bachelor's degree or its equivalent), such as computer programmers, engineers, doctors, or fashion models,[168] where the employer can show an inability to recruit qualified workers in the United States. Employers generally apply for the visa on behalf of the foreign worker; it authorizes the worker to work in the United States for up to six years (with some exceptions). During a worker's tenure, he or she is entitled to the same wages, benefits, and working conditions as other similarly situated employees. The U.S. government caps the number of H1-B visas granted each year. For 2011, this cap was set at 65,000 workers, with an exemption from the cap for up to 20,000 master's and Ph.D. graduates from U.S. universities.

Verifying Authorization

The U.S. government requires that all employers verify the identity and employment eligibility of all persons they hire.[169] This includes completing the Employment Eligibility Verification Form, also called the *I-9*, which must be kept on file by the employer for at least three years for purposes of government audits. Employers may also ask a potential employee questions regarding his or her work status. The questions should not identify a candidate by his or her national origin or citizenship status, however, because doing so could expose the employer to an employment-discrimination claim.[170] Questions that may be asked include "Can you, if hired, show that you are legally authorized to work in the United States?"

In 2007, the DHS issued new regulations that would have required all U.S. employers to either fire employees who did not resolve Social Security discrepancies or face liability for employing unauthorized workers. The American Federation of Labor–Congress of Industrial Organizations (AFL-CIO), the American Civil Liberties Union, and other organizations filed a lawsuit challenging these regulations in August 2007, and the U.S. District Court for the Northern District of California issued a preliminary injunction against their implementation.[171] The judge subsequently granted the DHS's motion for additional time to revise the regulations to address the

161. Jeffrey S. Passel & D'Vera Cohn, *U.S. Unauthorized Immigration Flows Are Down Sharply Since Mid-Decade*, PEW HISPANIC CTR., Sept. 1, 2010, *available at* http://pewhispanic.org/files/reports/126.pdf.

162. *Id.* at 8–9.

163. 8 U.S.C. § 1101 (1952).

164. Rules and Regulations, 73 Fed. Reg. 10,130 (Feb. 26, 2007).

165. 8 U.S.C. § 1324a.

166. *Oversight Hearing on U.S. Immigration and Customs Enforcement: Priorities and the Rules of Law, H. Comm. on the Judiciary, Subcomm. on Immigration Policy & Enforcement*, 112th Cong. (Oct. 12, 2011) (statement of Joe Morton, Director, U.S. Immigration & Customs Enforcement), *available at* http://www.dhs.gov/ynews/testimony/20111012-morton-ice-oversight.shtm.

167. Michael Muskal, *Immigration Raids Net 2,900 Criminals in Largest National Crackdown*, L.A. TIMES, Sept. 28, 2011, *available at* http://latimesblogs.latimes.com/nationnow/2011/09/immigration-raids-net-2900-criminals.html.

168. U.S. Dep't of Labor, *Employment Law Guide: Workers in Professional and Specialty Occupations (H-1B Visas)*, *available at* http://www.dol.gov/compliance/guide/h1b.htm(last visited Sept. 20, 2011).

169. U.S. Dep't of Labor, *Employment Law Guide: Authorized Workers*, *available at* http://www.dol.gov/asp/programs/guide/aw.htm (last visited June 3, 2008).

170. Letter from Nguyen Van Hanh, Director of the Office of Refugee Resettlement, and Juan Carlos Benitez, Special Counsel to the Office of Special Counsel for Immigration-Related Unfair Employment Practices, Civil Rights Div., U.S. Dep't of Justice, to State Refugee Coordinators, National Voluntary Agencies & Other Interested Parties, *available at* http://www.acf.hhs.gov/programs/orr/policy/oscj_lt.htm (last visited Sept. 20, 2011).

171. Am. Fed'n of Labor v. Chertoff, 552 F. Supp. 2d 999 (N.D. Cal. 2007).

court's concerns, but the plaintiffs assured the court that they would seek a permanent injunction no matter what changes the DHS made to the regulations.[172] The DHS rescinded the rule, effective November 2009, but then republished the August 2007 final rule with no substantive changes.[173]

Legislative Reform: States Rush in Where Congress Fears to Tread

Efforts at comprehensive federal immigration reform have failed.[174] In 2007, for example, President George W. Bush proposed that illegal aliens who had entered the United States before 2007 should be allowed to stay in the country as long as they met certain rules and conditions. The

proposal also included a temporary worker program that would have created two-year work visas and a new system for applying for permanent non-U.S. citizen resident status (green cards). The Bush proposal failed due to lack of sufficient congressional support, however, as did subsequent proposals by the Obama administration.

With federal legislation stalled, the states have rushed to fill the void. According to the National Conference of State Legislatures, forty-seven states enacted 346 immigration resolutions in 2010 alone. Many of these laws sought to deter illegal immigration by targeting illegal immigrants, but many also sought to encourage integration into the community by providing additional support for English language education.

Arizona has passed several of the toughest laws. The Legal Arizona Workers Act of 2007[175] provides that any Arizona employer caught more than once knowingly or intentionally hiring unauthorized workers is subject to having its charter revoked, effectively shutting down the business. The U.S. Supreme Court considered the constitutionality of the Arizona statute in the following case.

---

172. *Id.* at 47.

173. Safe Harbor Procedures for Employers Who Receive a No-Match Letter: Clarification, Final Regulatory Flexibility Analysis, 8 C.F.R. pt. 274a (2009).

174. Hope Yen, *Number of Illegal Immigrants in U.S. Steady at 11.2M*, CBSNEWS.COM, Feb. 1, 2011, http://www.cnsnews.com/news/article/number-illegal-immigrants-us-steady-112m.

175. Ariz. Rev. Stat. Ann. §§ 23-211, 212, 212.01.

A CASE IN POINT	*Summary*	Case 12.4

Chamber of Commerce of the United States v. Whiting

Supreme Court of the United States
131 S. Ct. 1968 (2011).

FACTS   The Legal Arizona Workers Act of 2007 provides that if an individual files a complaint alleging that an employer has hired an unauthorized alien, the attorney general or the county attorney must first verify the employee's work authorization with the federal government pursuant to section 1373(c) of the Immigration Reform and Control Act.[176] The Arizona law expressly prohibits state, county, or local officials from attempting "to independently make a final determination on whether an alien is authorized to work in the United States." If the section 1373(c) inquiry reveals that a worker is an unauthorized alien, the attorney general or the county attorney must notify U.S. Immigration and Customs Enforcement (ICE) officials and local law enforcement, and bring an action against the employer.

For a first instance of *knowingly* employing an unauthorized alien, the law requires the court to order the employer to (1) terminate the employment of all unauthorized aliens and (2) file quarterly reports on all new hires for a probationary period of three years. The court may also "order the appropriate agencies to suspend all licenses . . . that are held by the employer for [a period] not to exceed ten business days." These include the corporate charter and other business licenses a firm needs to operate legally in Arizona. For a second knowing violation, the adjudicating court must "permanently revoke all licenses that are held by the employer specific to the business location where the unauthorized alien performed work."

For a first *intentional* violation, the court must order the employer to (1) terminate the employment of all unauthorized aliens and (2) file quarterly reports on all new hires for a probationary period of five years. The court must also suspend all the employer's licenses for a minimum of ten days. A second intentional violation requires the permanent revocation of all business licenses. With respect to both knowing and intentional violations, a violation qualifies as a "second violation" only if it occurs at the same business location as the first violation, during the time that the employer is already on probation for a violation at that location.

CONTINUED

---

176. 8 U.S.C. § 1373(c).

The Arizona law also requires that "every employer, after hiring an employee, shall verify the employment eligibility of the employee" by using the federal E-Verify service. Congress authorized this voluntary Internet-based system in the Illegal Immigration Reform and Immigrant Responsibility Act of 1996 (IIRIRA),[177] but generally prohibited the Secretary of Homeland Security from requiring any person outside the federal government to use the system. Under the Arizona law, proof of employment authorization through the E-Verify program creates a rebuttable presumption that an employer did not knowingly employ an unauthorized alien.

The Chamber of Commerce of the United States and others challenged the Arizona law, arguing that it was preempted by federal immigration law. After the U.S. Court of Appeals for the Ninth Circuit upheld the Arizona law, the Chamber appealed. The U.S. Government filed an amicus brief in support of the Chamber, arguing that the Arizona statute was unconstitutional.

ISSUE PRESENTED   Does federal immigration law preempt the provisions of the Legal Arizona Workers Act?

SUMMARY OF OPINION   The U.S. Supreme Court began by noting that the Immigration Reform and Control Act (IRCA) expressly preempts states from imposing "civil or criminal sanctions" on those who employ unauthorized aliens, "other than through licensing and similar laws." The Court concluded that the licensing provisions in the Arizona law "fall squarely" within this savings clause and that federal law did not impliedly preempt the requirement that Arizona employers use the E-Verify system.

The Arizona statute defined "license" as "any agency permit, certificate, approval, registration, charter or similar form of authorization that is required by law and that is issued by any agency for the purposes of operating a business in" Arizona. The Court noted that this definition "largely parrots" the definition of "license" in the Federal Administrative Procedures Act. The Arizona law further defined "licenses" to include articles of incorporation, certificates of partnership, and authorizations for foreign companies to do business in Arizona. The Court concluded that all three types of documents were licenses, or at least very "similar" to licenses, so they were "comfortably within the savings clause."

The Court rejected the argument advanced by the Chamber of Commerce and the United States as amicus that the Arizona law was not a "licensing" law because it operated only to suspend and revoke licenses rather than to grant them. The Court found such a construction of the term contrary to "the definition that Congress itself has codified."

In summary, although IRCA expressly preempted certain state powers dealing with the employment of unauthorized aliens, it expressly preserved others. Because Arizona's licensing law fell within the confines of the authority Congress chose to leave to the states, it was not expressly preempted.

A four-justice plurality of the Court then concluded that the Act was not impliedly preempted. (Because Justice Kagan did not participate in the decision, only eight justices voted on the case.) The plurality reasoned that Arizona's verification procedures permissibly implemented the sanctions that Congress expressly allowed the state to pursue through its licensing laws. Indeed, "Arizona went the extra mile in ensuring that its law closely tracks IRCA's provisions in all material respects." Because Arizona provides that a state court "shall consider *only* the federal government's determination" when deciding "whether an employee is an unauthorized alien," there could, by definition, be no conflict between state and federal law as to worker authorization, at either the investigatory or the adjudicatory stage.

The plurality acknowledged that "[l]icense suspension and revocation are significant sanctions," but characterized them as "typical attributes of a licensing regime." Both Arizona and federal law permit the suspension or revocation of licenses for failing to comply with applicable laws.

CONTINUED

---

177. 110 Stat. 3009-655.

The plurality rejected the Chamber of Commerce's assertion (which Justice Breyer echoed in his dissent) that "employers will err on the side of discrimination rather than risk the 'business death penalty' by 'hiring unauthorized workers.'" The Arizona law covers only knowing or intentional violations and requires permanent revocation of a license only after a second knowing or intentional violation at the same business location, and only if the second violation occurs while the employer is still on probation for the first. The plurality concluded: "These limits ensure that licensing sanctions are imposed only when an employer's conduct fully justifies them. An employer acting in good faith need have no fear of the sanctions."

A majority of the Court then found that the Act's required use of the federal E-Verify system to determine whether an employee is authorized to work was not impliedly preempted by IIRIRA. Although the federal law constrained federal action, it did not preclude the states from requiring use of the system.

The Court concluded that Arizona's use of E-Verify did not conflict with the federal scheme. Congress authorized the development of E-Verify "to ensure reliability in employment authorization verification, combat counterfeiting of identity documents, and protect employee privacy." Indeed, the federal government has consistently expanded and encouraged the use of E-Verify. Furthermore, "the consequences of not using E-Verify under the Arizona law are the same as the consequences of not using the system under federal law. In both instances, the only result is that the employer forfeits the otherwise available rebuttable presumption that it complied with the law."

Result   The judgment of the U.S. Court of Appeals for the Ninth Circuit was affirmed. Arizona's unauthorized alien employment law was not preempted by federal immigration law.

Comments   States have spent a significant amount of money defending the constitutionality of their immigration laws. By February 2011, Arizona had spent more than $1.5 million. Officials in Nebraska estimate that it will cost approximately $1 million per year to defend their ban on hiring or renting property to illegal immigrants, resulting in a potential 18% increase in property taxes.

© Cengage Learning 2013

Arizona's Support Our Law Enforcement and Safe Neighborhoods Act,[178] which was signed into law in 2010, requires law enforcement officials to inquire about a person's immigration status during a valid investigatory stop or arrest and permits officers to detain a person to make inquiries into his or her immigration status if the person cannot produce valid documentation. It also permits police officers to effect warrantless arrests based on probable cause that the person has committed an act that would justify a civil removal from the United States by federal authorities. The Act also makes it a misdemeanor under Arizona law for an unauthorized worker to work in Arizona. Private citizens can sue law enforcement officials if they are not properly enforcing the immigration law.[179]

The day before this law was scheduled to go into effect, a federal district court issued a preliminary injunction.[180] On April 11, 2011, the U.S. Court of Appeals for the Ninth Circuit upheld the injunction, finding that "Congress . . . created a comprehensive and carefully calibrated scheme . . . for adjudicating and enforcing civil removability" and therefore the state may not have the authority to "unilaterally transform state and local law enforcement officers into a state-controlled DHS [Department of Homeland Security] force to carry out its declared policy of attrition."[181] The Ninth Circuit noted that the Arizona statute had already had a "deleterious" effect on the United States' relations with Mexico and other countries.

In 2010, President Barack Obama signed into law a $600 billion bill focused on border security. The President

---

178. 2010 Ariz. Sess. Laws, ch. 113 (2010), as amended by 2010 Ariz. Sess. Laws, ch. 211 (2010) (commonly known as "S.B. 1070").

179. American Immigration Council, Immigration Policy Ctr., *Q&A Guide to State Immigration Laws, available at* http://www.immigrationpolicy.org/special-reports/qa-guide-state-immigration-laws.

180. United States v. Arizona, 703 F. Supp. 2d 980 (D. Ariz. 2011)

181. United States v. Arizona, 641 F.3d 339 (9th Cir. 2011), *cert. granted*, 132 S. Ct. 845 (2011). *But see* United States v. Alabama, 2011 WL 4469941 (N.D. Ala. Sept. 28, 2011) (enjoining some but not all provisions in the Beason-Hammon Alabama Taxpayer & Citizen Protection Act).

announced in 2011 that the federal government would be vigorously attacking unconstitutional state immigration laws, thereby ensuring that immigration reform would be an important issue in the 2012 presidential campaign. Many argue that the only solution is a comprehensive approach to immigration reform that (1) addresses the reasons people come to the United States (to work, to be with family, and to build a new life); (2) requires people who are here without authorization to register, pay taxes, and learn English; and (3) uses smart workplace, border, and interior-enforcement strategies to enforce U.S. immigration laws.[182]

LABOR–MANAGEMENT RELATIONS

Before the mid-1930s, attempts by employees to band together and demand better wages and working conditions were largely ineffective. Employers squelched attempts to organize by lawfully discharging union organizers. In addition, organized economic actions, such as strikes and picketing, were enjoined as unlawful conspiracies. Starting in the 1930s, Congress attempted to equitably balance the economic power of employers, individual employees, and unions by comprehensively regulating labor–management relations. The laws are aimed both at providing employees with greater economic bargaining power and at curbing union excess and corruption.[183]

The central statute governing labor relations in most private industries is the National Labor Relations Act (NLRA).[184] An earlier similar law, the Railway Labor Act,[185] was enacted to govern railroads and, later, airlines. Although public-sector employees have since been granted similar rights under both federal and state laws, as discussed in the "Political Perspective," such rights have come under siege. Union membership has also been declining. The percentage of organized workers in the private sector, which was 12% in 1929, was only 6.9% in 2010[186]—the lowest percentage in eighty years.

Applicability of National Labor Relations Act

Section 7 of the NLRA grants rights only to employees. It does not grant rights to independent contractors or to supervisors. The NLRA defines *supervisor* to mean:

> Any individual having authority, in the interest of the employer, to hire, transfer, suspend, lay off, recall, promote, discharge, assign, reward or discipline other employees, or responsibility to direct them, or to adjust their grievances, or effectively to recommend such action, if in connection with the foregoing the exercise of such authority is not of a merely routine or clerical nature, but requires the use of independent judgment.

Union Representation Elections

The five-member National Labor Relations Board (NLRB) oversees *representation elections*, that is, elections among employees to decide whether they want a union to represent them for collective bargaining. The procedure for conducting a representation election is initiated by filing a petition with a regional office of the NLRB. The NLRB will hold an election only in an *appropriate collective bargaining unit* of employees. To form such a unit, the group of employees must share a community of interest, meaning that they have similar compensation, working conditions, and supervision, and work under the same general employer policies.

Under current labor law, the NLRB will certify a union as the employees' exclusive representative if it is elected by either (1) a majority signature drive or (2) a secret NLRB election, which is held if more than 30% of employees in a bargaining unit sign statements asking for representation by a union. A company can demand a secret ballot election supervised by the NLRB after being presented with the requisite number of union cards. Many consider a secret ballot election to be the more effective method of determining whether employees desire union representation because it allows their voices to be heard without coercion, intimidation, or peer pressure. In a signature drive, union organizers solicit employees' signatures on union authorization cards in an unsupervised and public process that may encourage some employees to sign simply to "get the union off their backs."

The Employee Free Choice Act (H.R. 800), a top priority for organized labor, would amend the NLRA to authorize *card-check elections*, whereby an employer would be required to recognize a union after being presented with union authorization cards signed by a majority of eligible workers on its payroll if there is no evidence of illegal coercion. The proposed law would also provide for liquidated damages of three times back pay if employers were found to have unlawfully terminated pro-union employees. Although the House of Representatives passed the bill in 2007, it was filibustered by Republicans in the Senate. Subsequent efforts to pass the bill also failed.[187] In 2010, in response to the proposed legislation, four states passed constitutional amendments guaranteeing a secret ballot to determine union recognition.

---

182. American Immigration Council, *supra* note 179.

183. *See generally* Norris–La Guardia Act, 29 U.S.C. §§ 101–115; Wagner Act, 29 U.S.C. §§ 151–169; Taft–Hartley Act, 29 U.S.C. §§ 141–144.

184. 29 U.S.C. § 151 (1935).

185. 45 U.S.C. § 151 *et seq.* (1926).

186. Robert J. Samuelson, *Is Organized Labor Obsolete?*, Wash. Post, Feb. 28, 2011.

187. Employee Free Choice Act of 2009, H.R. 1409, 111th Cong. (2009); *see* GovTrack.us, http://www.govtrack.us/congress/bill.xpd?bill=h111-1409.

After an election is held, the losing party may file objections to it. If the objections are deemed to be without merit, the NLRB will certify the election. If the objections are meritorious, the NLRB will conduct a new election. Once a union is elected, it is the employees' exclusive bargaining representative and has a statutory duty under section 8(b)(1) of the NLRA to represent all employees fairly when engaging in collective bargaining (without regard to their union affiliation) and when enforcing the collective bargaining agreement.[188]

Duty to Bargain in Good Faith

Once a union election is certified, both the employer and the union have a duty to bargain collectively in good faith. Employers must approach negotiations with an honest and serious intent to engage in give-and-take bargaining in an attempt to reach an agreement. This obligation to bargain in good faith does not, however, compel either party to agree to a proposal or make concessions.

Unfair Labor Practices by Employers

Section 8(a) of the NLRA prohibits employers from engaging in specified activities against employees or their unions. Such activities, known as *unfair labor practices*, are investigated and prosecuted by the general counsel of the NLRB and his or her representatives. As of January 2012, the NLRB requires all employers to post a notice informing employees of their rights under the NLRA.[189] Failure to post such a notice may be treated as an unfair labor practice under the NLRA.

No Interference or Retaliation

It is illegal for an employer to interfere with, restrain, or coerce employees in the exercise of their section 7 rights to organize and bargain collectively and to engage in other protected concerted activities. This prohibition covers a wide range of employer conduct, including (1) threatening employees with any adverse action for organizing or supporting a union, (2) promising employees any benefits if they abandon support for a union, (3) interrogating employees about union sentiment or activity, and (4) engaging in surveillance of employees' union activities. For example, the U.S. Court of Appeals for the First Circuit held that an employer committed an unfair labor practice when it fired a truck driver after he was seen giving an unidentified person a half-block ride in a company truck. The employer argued that it had fired the truck driver for violating its "one strike and you're out" policy against letting nonemployees ride in company trucks, but the court found that the employer knew that the employee was actively organizing for a union and would not have fired him if he had not been involved in the union activities.[190]

Protection for Concerted Activities and Use of Social Media

The NLRA protects employees who engage in concerted activities for mutual aid and protection and also prohibits an employer from enforcing an overly broad rule against soliciting other employees (perhaps for union support) or distributing literature on company premises. For example, an employer may not retaliate against a group of employees who complain to management about some aspect of their working conditions, such as poor lighting in the workplace. For an activity to be a *concerted activity*, it must be "engaged in with or on the authority of other employees, and not solely by and on behalf of the employee himself"[191] and relate to the terms and conditions of employment. Note that an activity need not be related to the formation of a union to be a protected concerted activity. These rules apply to many employee communications using Facebook, Twitter, and other social media.

In August 2011, the NLRB announced decisions in fourteen social media cases to help employers predict how such issues will be handled in the future. The decisions addressed employees' postings on social media networks such as Facebook and Twitter, union postings on Facebook and YouTube, and the lawfulness of employers' social media policies and rules.

The NLRB found concerted action in a case where over several months, an employee (the advocate) was involved in conversations with other employees about why clients were not seeking services from the employer. Finally, one coworker suggested that the advocate meet with the Executive Director to discuss the issue. In preparation for this meeting, one coworker posted on Facebook that her coworkers did not help the employer's clients enough and asked her coworkers how they felt. After four coworkers responded to the Facebook post, they were discharged along with the advocate. The NLRB explained that such actions were protected concerted activity because the advocate was acting with or on the authority of other employees; the posts commented on staffing and job performance and, therefore, implicated the terms and conditions of employment; and the posting was initiated in preparation for a meeting with the employer.[192]

---

188. Vaca v. Sipes, 386 U.S. 171 (1967).

189. Dianne Rose LaRocca, *NLRB Postpones Implementation Date of Notice-Posting Rule: What Employers Should Know*, DLA PIPER, Oct. 6, 2011, *available at* http://www.dlapiper.com/nlrb-postpones-implementation-date-of-notice-posting-rule-what-employers-should-know/.

190. Holsum de Puerto Rico, Inc. v. NLRB, 456 F.3d 265 (1st Cir. 2006).

191. Meyers Indus., Inc., 268 N.L.R.B. 493, 497 (1984).

192. Memorandum from Lafe E. Soloman, Nat'l Labor Relations Bd., Office of the Gen. Counsel, Report of the Acting General Counsel Concerning Social Media Cases Within the Last Year 3 (Aug. 18, 2011), *available at* http://www.huntonlaborblog.com/uploads/file/NLRB_Provides_Guidance_For_Social_Media.pdf.

The NLRB also found protected concerted activity in a case where a salesperson employed at a luxury automobile dealership posted pictures on Facebook from a work event and criticized the employer for providing inexpensive food and beverages. Prior to the event, the advocate, along with other salespeople, had been complaining about the employer's handling of the event. The employees were concerned that the inexpensive food and beverages would send the wrong message to their clients and negatively affect their sales and commissions. The NLRB determined that these postings were a protected concerted activity because the advocate had been complaining with coworkers about the food for the event and had told his coworkers that he would be placing the pictures on Facebook. Thus, the salesperson was vocalizing the sentiment of his coworkers. The post was related to the terms and conditions of employment because the choice of refreshments could affect the employees' commissions.[193]

Conversely, the NLRB found no protected concerted activity where the employee of a newspaper posted a tweet critical of the paper's copyeditors, tweets about homicides in the city where the paper was published, and several tweets with sexual content on his work-related Twitter account. Because there was no evidence that he had discussed these issues with his coworkers, his termination did not violate the NLRA.[194]

The Board also determined that a bartender did not engage in protected concerted activity when he posted a complaint on Facebook about his employer's tipping policy in response to a query from a nonemployee. The employee had never raised the issue with management or his coworkers, and no other employees commented on or responded to his Facebook posts. The NLRB determined that the employee was acting solely on his own behalf, so there was no protected concerted activity.[195]

There was also no concerted activity when a store employee posted on Facebook a comment about the "tyranny" at the store after an interaction with a new assistant manager. He also noted that a lot of the employees were about to quit. Although other coworkers posted supportive comments, there was no concerted activity because the posting did not include any language indicating that the employee sought to initiate or induce coworkers to engage in collective action. It was merely an individual gripe.[196]

The NLRB also clarified what constitutes an acceptable social media policy. It struck down a policy that (1) prohibited employees from using any social media that might violate, compromise, or disregard the rights and reasonable expectations of privacy or confidentiality of any person or entity; (2) prohibited any communication or post that would embarrass, harass, or defame the employer, its

employees, officer board members, representatives, or staff members; and (3) prohibited statements that lacked truthfulness or might damage the reputation or goodwill of the employer, its staff, or employees. The prohibition on the use of social media to discuss confidential matters did not explain what was confidential and lacked appropriate limits. The policy was overbroad because it could reasonably be construed as prohibiting protected conduct.[197]

A social media policy that precluded employees from pressuring their coworkers to connect or communicate with them via social media was lawful, however, because it could not reasonably be read to restrict section 7 activity. Its prohibition against pressuring coworkers was sufficiently specific to apply only to harassing conduct.[198]

No Union Domination or Assistance

An employer may not dominate or assist a labor organization. The employer may not instigate, encourage, or directly participate in the formation of a labor organization, nor may it give financial support to a labor organization. These provisions were enacted to prevent employers from assisting compliant organizations in becoming representatives of their employees and then imposing "sweetheart" collective bargaining contracts—that is, contracts unduly favorable to the employer.

No Discrimination or Retaliation

The NLRA prohibits employers from discriminating against any employee to encourage or discourage membership in any labor organization. If an employee has been unlawfully discharged, the NLRB may order that the employee be reinstated and given full back pay. It is also an unfair labor practice for an employer to discharge or otherwise discriminate against an employee because he or she has filed charges with, or given testimony to, the NLRB, either in a representation proceeding or pursuant to an unfair labor practice charge.

Violation of Duty to Bargain in Good Faith

If an employer does not bargain in good faith, a union may seek redress through the NLRB. Remedies may include damages payable to employees or injunctive relief.

Lawful and Unlawful Strikes, Lockouts, and Other Economic Action

Labor law permits both employers and labor organizations to engage in certain tactics against each other, known as "economic action," to influence the other party to reach agreement in collective bargaining. Strikes and related publicity tactics such as picketing form an important part of the economic actions available to labor organizations.

---

193. *Id.* at 7–8.
194. *Id.* at 12–13.
195. *Id.* at 14–15.
196. *Id.* at 17–18.

197. *Id.* at 19–20.
198. *Id.* at 21.

POLITICAL | PERSPECTIVE

States Slash Collective Bargaining Rights of Government Workers

In March 2011, the Wisconsin legislature passed Wisconsin Act 10, also known as the Budget Repair Bill, which effectively eliminated collective bargaining rights for a majority of state employees.[a] The Act reduced public employee unions' ability to bargain for benefits for their members and undercut the unions' ability to collect dues, thereby making it more difficult for them to raise money for advertising and lobbying efforts. To blunt opposition from the powerful police and firefighters unions, the legislature excepted them from the bill.

Advocates of the Budget Repair Bill projected that it would produce savings of $30 million in the 2011 budget year, helping to close the state's $137 million budget gap. They argued that because state workers in effect had a monopoly on public service jobs, they should have fewer rights to force high wages and generous pensions from the state.

The meaure faced considerable opposition, however. While 80,000 people protested the bill at rallies at the state capitol, fourteen Wisconsin Senate Democrats fled to a neighboring state in an effort to delay the vote on the bill. In order to force a vote, Senate Republicans stripped the bill of its fiscal items, which would have required a quorum of twenty for a

vote, and then passed the bill by an eighteen-to-one margin.[b]

Within days after the bill was signed into law, county officials filed suit against the state, claiming that the law was passed illegally because the legislature failed to give the proper twenty-four-hours notice required by the state's open-meetings law. The Wisconsin Supreme Court, however, reinstated the collective bargaining law, ruling that committees of lawmakers were not subject to the open-meetings law.[c]

The Ohio legislature had enacted a similar measure aimed at curbing public employee unions in March 2011. Championed by the state's newly elected Republican governor, the law limited public workers' rights to bargain for health insurance, ended automatic pay increases, and infringed on teachers' rights to pick their classes and schools.[d] As in Wisconsin, the bill aroused substantial opposition, including some 5,000 protesters at the state capitol. In a referendum held in November 2011, Ohio voters rejected the measure by a vote of 62% to 28%.[e] Richard Trumka, president of the AFL-CIO labor federation, remarked, "Ohio sent a message to every politician out there: Go in and make war on your employees rather than make jobs with your employees, and you do so at your own peril."[f]

The legality of state laws limiting public employees' collective bargaining rights has also been questioned in federal court. In March 2011, a federal judge issued a temporary injunction against an Illinois anti-union bill, ruling that the Illinois state legislature could not limit or impede collective bargaining rights because such state action is preempted by the National Labor Relations Act.[g]

a. Gannett Analysis, *What's in Wisconsin's New Law?*, USA Today, Mar. 12, 2011, *available at* http://www.usatoday.com/news/nation/2011-03-12-wisconsin-law-analysis_N.htm.

b. Mary Spicuzza & Clay Barbour, *Budget Repair Bill Passes Senate, Thursday Vote Set in Assembly*, Wis. St. J., Mar. 10, 2011.

c. *Ex rel.* Ozanne v. Fitzgerald, 334 Wis. 2d 70 (2011).

d. Andy Kroll, *What's Happening in Wisconsin Explained*, Mother Jones, Mar. 17, 2011, *available at* http://motherjones.com/mojo/2011/02/whats-happening-wisconsin-explained.

e. Sabrina Tavernise, *Ohio Turns Back a Law Limiting Unions' Rights*, N.Y. Times, Nov. 8, 2011.

f. AP Worldstream, *Ohio Voters Reject Republican-Backed Union Limits*, HighBeam Res., Nov. 9, 2011, *available at* http://www.highbeam.com/doc/1A1-3ed310d6c00c4fbe-a6e994eacf8664e9.html.

g. *See* Local 727, Int'l Bhd. of Teamsters v. Metro. Pier & Exposition Auth., 784 F. Supp. 2d 1008 (N.D. Ill. 2011).

There are two kinds of lawful strikes: economic strikes and unfair labor practice strikes. An *economic strike* occurs when a union is unable to extract acceptable terms and conditions of employment through collective bargaining. An employer subjected to an economic strike may hire permanent replacements for the positions vacated by the striking employees. If it does so, the employer is not required to reinstate striking employees who offer to return to work unless the departure of replacements creates vacancies. An *unfair labor*

practice strike occurs when workers strike an employer wholly or partly to protest an unfair labor practice and the employer's conduct is in fact found to violate the NLRA. Workers who engage in an unfair labor practice strike have a right to be reinstated if they make an unconditional offer to return to work.

Striking employees may have no legal protection or reinstatement rights if they conduct a "wildcat" strike by violating a "no-strike" provision in their collective bargaining agreements. Slowdowns, intermittent strikes, and work stoppages are also unprotected activities. Otherwise lawful strikes may result in liability for striking employees if the workers' tactics violate local safety or public peace ordinances or the state penal code (e.g., assault and battery).

The NLRA prohibits unduly lengthy *recognitional picketing* (whose purpose is to force the employer to recognize the union as a collective bargaining agent for its employees). It also outlaws *secondary boycotts*, which are certain threats or tactics against an outside company to induce the third party to put pressure (usually by withholding business) on the employer with which the union has a dispute. The NLRB permits employers to lock out full-term strikers while allowing nonstrikers and crossovers to continue working. In July 2011, after the league, the team owners, and the players' union could not reach an agreement on salary caps, players' salaries and benefits, contracts, annual raises, and how to split revenue, the National Basketball Association imposed a lockout.[199]

Non-Strike-Related Unfair Labor Practices by Unions

Unions may not coerce employees to join the union or support its activities. A union is also prohibited from coercing employees to join, or refrain from abandoning, a strike. Unions are prohibited from discriminating against represented employees on the basis of race, gender, national origin, union membership, or internal union political affiliations. A union may not cause or attempt to cause an employer to discriminate against an employee on the basis of union affiliation or activities.

---

199. Mitch Lawrence, *A Summary of the Sticking Points of the NBA Lockout Between the Players and the Owners*, N.Y. DAILY NEWS, July 1, 2011.

GLOBAL VIEW

The Right to Continued Employment

Most foreign countries do not share the U.S. concept of "employment at will" and instead provide employees with greater rights to continued employment.

The European Union

Although the European Union (EU) has worked on harmonizing many employment laws of its member states, it has not attempted to bring uniformity to the laws related to termination of employment.[200] No member states recognize the U.S. concept of employment at will. Instead, each country has specific laws on unfair dismissal and/or general civil code provisions that apply to the termination of employment contracts. Although the specifics of these laws vary, they all give employees a basis for challenging a dismissal on the grounds that it is unfair and provide a mechanism for adjudicating such claims.

For example, employers in the United Kingdom are generally free to agree with their employees to whatever employment relationship suits them both, subject to certain statutory restrictions. Under English law, an employee has two sets of rights: contractual and statutory. Contractual rights are governed by the employee's employment contract, whether they are express or implied by custom or law, and they are enforced by a suit for wrongful dismissal. Wrongful dismissal occurs when an employer dismisses an employee in breach of its contractual obligations. An employee's normal remedy for breach of contract is to sue for damages, which are limited to the amount required to put the employee in the position he or she would have been in had the contract been performed.

Statutory restrictions are set forth in various statutes, the most important of which are the Employee Rights Agreement 1996 (ERA 1996) and the Employment Act 2002 (EA 2002). Statutory rights are enforced by a claim for unfair dismissal. To bring a claim for unfair dismissal, an employee must show that he or she was dismissed for a reason listed in section 95 of the ERA 1996, such as a union-related reason, the assertion of a statutory right, a reason involving health and safety, a reason related to working time or the assertion of rights under the national minimum-wage law, a reason connected with trade union recognition or bargaining arrangements, and, in certain circumstances, taking part in a protected industrial action. The three remedies for unfair dismissal are (1) reinstatement, which treats the employee as if he or she had never been dismissed; (2) reengagement, in which the employee returns to the same or a similar job; and (3) compensation, which consists of a basic award calculated on a strict formula and a compensatory award, based on what the tribunal considers just and equitable according to the loss sustained by the employee as a result of the dismissal.

French workers are entitled to significantly more benefits and legal protection than their counterparts in the United States or the United Kingdom. French law requires "just cause" for dismissal: an employer must justify an employee's

---

200. *See generally* INTERNATIONAL LABOR AND EMPLOYMENT LAWS 1-68 (Timothy J. Darby & William L. Keller eds., 2007).

CONTINUED

dismissal and will be subject to legal sanctions if it is unable to do so.[201] During any agreed-on trial period, a French employee can be dismissed without formalities or particular reasons. Once the trial period has elapsed, however, the employer must prove that any dismissal is for legitimate reasons (either for cause or as a result of a reduction in force due to economic factors).[202] Case law has accepted that "just cause" includes professional incompetence, insufficient results, professional shortcomings, loss of confidence in the employee, and sexual harassment.

Unless terminated for gross negligence or willful misconduct, the employee is entitled to (1) a payment or indemnity, set by statute, if he or she has at least two years of uninterrupted seniority; (2) any accrued but unused vacation pay; (3) and an indemnity equal to the salary he or she would have received during the notice period if the employer wants to pay the employee in lieu of providing the required notice. In addition, if the employee is dismissed without legitimate reason, he or she is entitled to receive compensation and damages for abusive breach of the employment contract. An employer's failure to comply with the statutory dismissal procedure also gives rise to damages even if the dismissal was justified.

Japan

Japanese employment laws are employee-friendly, especially when compared with U.S. law. There is no concept of "at-will"

---

201. *See generally id.* at 3-1 to 3-18.

202. Ordinance 2005-83 of August 2, 2005, created the "new hire contract," which provides that for private-sector employees during the first two years of employment, by an employer of up to twenty people, either the employer or the employee may terminate the new hire contract for personal reasons, without complying with standard dismissal procedures.

employment, and employers' rights to terminate employees are limited by statute, case law, and custom.

The Labor Contracts Law, which became effective March 1, 2008, provides that an employer can dismiss an employee only for just cause; the absence of just cause gives rise to a claim of abuse of the right of dismissal. In addition, a fixed-term employment contract cannot be terminated without a compelling reason. Finally, the law restricts an employer's right to continually renew short-term employment contracts. The Labor Tribunal Law established an industrial tribunal system to quickly and efficiently settle employment disputes, including those related to termination of employment.

India

India views the employment relationship as a contract that is subject to judicial intervention. Thus, the courts have implemented procedural safeguards shielding employees from indiscriminate termination by employers.[203] Although Indian law starts from the common law premise that an employee can be terminated by an employer without giving a reason, this position has been modified by legislative intervention and by case law. Some instances of misconduct may justify termination without notice or payment in lieu of notice, but employers are generally required to provide some form of compensation to a terminated employee. In addition, most employers with more than 100 employees must seek permission from the labor department of the government before dismissing or laying off a worker, or shutting down, irrespective of financial condition.

---

203. Jaivir Singh, *The Law, Labour and Development in India*, paper presented at the Annual World Bank Conference on Development Economics in Oslo, Norway (June 24–26, 2002).

Mike Price/Shutterstock

THE RESPONSIBLE MANAGER

AVOIDING WRONGFUL DISCHARGE SUITS AND OTHER EMPLOYEE PROBLEMS

If an employer wants to preserve the traditional legal right to discharge employees at will, it should take steps to ensure that it does not inadvertently limit this right. To illustrate, an employee seeking to establish at-will employment might include the following language above the employee signature line of an application form: "I understand that, if hired, my employment can be terminated at any time, with or without cause, at either my employer's or my option." Inclusion of such language reminds the employee that the employment is at will, verifies that he or she was so informed, and lessens the likelihood that the employee will be able to establish an implied contractual right to be discharged only for cause.

Additionally, employers hiring at-will employees should avoid making statements during interviews that could create an impression that the applicant will not be fired without good cause. "Employees are never fired from here without good reason," "Your job will be secure, as long as you do your work," and "We treat our employees like family" are examples of such statements.

If an employer chooses to have a policy of progressive discipline, the policy should state that it does not alter at-will employment and that all decisions on progressive discipline—whether to apply it, what steps to take or skip—are within the company's sole discretion. If specific rules

CONTINUED

of conduct are listed, the manual should describe them as examples, not an exhaustive list, and inform employees that violation of a stated rule is not required for termination, because employment remains terminable at will. Supervisors and managers, as well as the human resources staff, should be trained to administer the policy, to document performance problems, and to counsel employees about the need to improve, but not to portray the policy as an entitlement.

Conversely, if an employer wants its employees to make firm-specific investments of time, talent, and commitment, then at-will employment may not be suitable. Because an employer's human resource practices can affect its competitive position, the determination of what practices are most suitable for a given firm should be made by the top management team, not just the lawyers.[204]

If a company wants to impose a covenant not to compete on its employees, it should consider what state's law will apply to the covenant. Given that different states apply different standards for reviewing noncompetes, the company must structure each agreement in a way that courts will recognize and uphold. The company should also clarify the specific roles and responsibilities of a given employee so that the noncompete is not overly restrictive, thereby reducing the risk of judicial invalidation. Finally, the company should provide consideration, such as a bonus or a promotion, before imposing a noncompete covenant on existing employees.[205]

The FLSA imposes numerous obligations on employers.[206] Most importantly, an employer must carefully classify its employees, as exempt or nonexempt, to ensure that it pays overtime to all employees who are not exempt from the FLSA overtime pay obligations. For example, nonexempt employees required to work through lunch must be compensated. Employers cannot dock salary for late arrivals or partial-day absences of exempt employees. Employers should factor in bonus payments, prorated to a weekly rate of pay, when calculating overtime payments to nonexempt employees. Although commuting time to and from work is not compensable, employers must consider whether they should compensate for commuting time when a nonexempt employee travels from home directly to a client's site rather than to the employer's site. Although outside salespeople are exempt, salespeople who work at the employer's place of business are not exempt.

Most managers in the United States have a visceral negative reaction to attempts to unionize their workers, believing that unions interfere with management control in the workplace and hinder efforts to achieve competitive levels of costs, quality, and productivity. Nevertheless, some academics argue that there is systemic empirical evidence indicating that unions are positively associated with higher training expenditures, successful employee involvement, and successful quality-improvement programs and organizational innovation. Indeed, many of the best-known examples of high-performance production systems occur at unionized plants, such as those at Xerox, Corning, Levi-Strauss, and AT&T.[207] These and other benefits of a well-regulated workforce—and the assistance of a labor organization to achieve that objective—may become apparent to management faced with organizing desires in its workforce.

At a minimum, employers must ensure that they do not unlawfully interfere with lawful union organizing efforts or other concerted activity. Managers should review their social media and other policies to reflect the developing law in this area. Perhaps the best defense against a lawsuit and unwanted union activities is to create a corporate culture where employees feel appreciated, which includes (1) compensating them fairly, (2) providing honest feedback about job requirements and performance, and (3) offering multiple outlets where employees can voice complaints and suggest improvements.

204. Jeffrey Pfeffer, The Human Equation: Building Profits by Putting People First (1998).

205. Some jurisdictions state that a continued at-will employment relationship amounts to consideration for a noncompetition agreement. *See* Lake Land Emp't Grp. of Akron, LLC v. Columber, 101 Ohio St. 3d 242 (2004).

206. *See* Simon Nadel, *FLSA: The Law Employers Love to Hate Is Scrutinized in Light of the New Economy*, 68 U.S.L.W. 2771 (2000).

207. Pfeffer, *supra* note 204, at 226.

A Manager's Dilemma

Putting It into Practice

Making Employment Decisions in Difficult Times

Gita Bhandari joined your social-network start-up in 2009, immediately after graduating from Carnegie Mellon University. She turned down better-paying consulting and investment banking opportunities to get in on the ground floor of a young, fast-growing company. As compensation, Bhandari receives a nominal salary and stock options. Because the company's product will require three years to bring to market, the options do not vest for three years. This means that Bhandari forfeits all of the stock options if she leaves the company before 2012.

CONTINUED

In 2011, the company began having serious problems. Even though the project is on schedule and is anticipated to be a huge success, costs are skyrocketing, and your investors demand a significant reduction in operating expenses.

You are considering firing Bhandari. Although she has performed well, Bhandari was the most recent person hired. She is an at-will employee, but, considering that she has less than one year to go until she can exercise her stock options, you fear a lawsuit, especially given the company's close-knit character. At this critical stage, the legal fees alone from a wrongful termination lawsuit could bankrupt the company.

Should you fire Bhandari to reduce operating expenses? Can you threaten to fire her if she does not agree to surrender some of her options? If Bhandari is terminated, on what basis could she sue the company? Would she prevail? How could you have structured the relationship to avoid this potential lawsuit?

INSIDE STORY

The FCC's News Distortion Rules and Whistleblower Protection

In December 1996, WTVT-TV, a subsidiary of Fox Television, hired Jane Akre and her husband, Steve Wilson, as an investigative reporting team. Soon thereafter they began to work on a series about the use of Monsanto's recombinant bovine growth hormone (rBGH) in Florida dairy cattle. rBGH is a genetically engineered hormone sold to dairy farmers, who inject it into their cows to increase milk production. It is controversial because some evidence suggests that rBGH may promote cancer in humans who drink milk from rBGH-treated cows. The EU has banned rBGH due to human health concerns.

Three days before the series was scheduled to air, Fox TV executives received a letter from Monsanto's lawyers stating that Monsanto would suffer "enormous damage" if the series ran. Station management temporarily delayed broadcast of the series and re-reviewed it for accuracy. When the station decided to go forward with the broadcast a week later, it received a second letter from Monsanto that warned of "dire consequences" for Fox if the series aired. At this point, WTVT pulled the story. Over the next weeks, Akre and Wilson produced seventy-three station-mandated rewrites, all of which were rejected by WTVT management.

According to Akre and Wilson, they cooperated with every WTVT request to revise the series, until they were asked to misrepresent the facts as they knew them—specifically, they refused to include a statement that there was "no difference" between hormone-treated and untreated milk. Wilson claimed that the WTVT station manager told them, "We paid $3 billion for these television stations. We will decide what the news is. The news is what we tell you it is." He then told the reporters that he would fire them for insubordination and that another reporter would make the required changes. When Akre and Wilson threatened to file a complaint with the Federal Communications Commission (FCC) if that happened, WTVT offered them large cash settlements if they would keep quiet about the story. They refused the offer and ultimately were fired in December 1997.

The WTVT managers insisted that they had made a good faith effort to edit the series but that the reporters were uncooperative and the series remained too "biased and one-sided" to broadcast. The station contended that the reporters were fired for "unreasonable and intemperate behavior [which] did not advance [WTVT's] interests in providing quality news programming to its viewers."

Akre and Wilson sued WTVT alleging, among other things, that their terminations violated Florida's whistleblower statute, because they were fired in retaliation for resisting WTVT's attempts to distort or suppress the rBGH story and for threatening to report the alleged news distortion to the FCC. The Florida whistleblower statute prohibits retaliation against employees who have "[d]isclosed, or threatened to disclose" employer conduct that "is in violation of" a law, rule, or regulation. After listening to five weeks of evidence, a six-person jury found that WTVT had retaliated against Akre in response to her threat to disclose the alleged news distortion to the FCC and awarded her $425,000 in damages. The jury found against Wilson on the same claim. Both Wilson and WTVT appealed.

The Florida appellate court reversed the trial court's decision, finding that WTVT's termination of Akre for threatening to report WTVT's attempts to distort the news did not violate the Florida whistleblower statute. Reading the statute narrowly, the court found that the FCC's policy against the intentional falsification of the news, which the FCC refers to as its "news distortion policy," did not qualify as a "law, rule or regulation." The court stated that the FCC had never

CONTINUED

published its news distortion policy as a regulation. Even if the policy qualified as a rule, it was never "adopted," as defined by another Florida statute.

During the appeal, WTVT asserted that there were no written rules against distorting news in the media. The station argued that, under the First Amendment, broadcasters have the right to lie or deliberately distort news reports on public airwaves. WTVT did not dispute Akre's claim that it pressured her to broadcast a false story; it simply claimed that it had a right to do so.[208]

208. *See generally Jury Verdict Overturned on Legal Technicality*, BGH BULL., http://www.foxbghsuit.com; Sheldon Rampton & John Stauber, *Monsanto and Fox: Partners in Censorship*, PR WATCH (Ctr. for Media and Democracy), Second Quarter 1998, Vol. 5, No. 2, *available at* http://www.prwatch.org/prwissues/1998Q2/foxbgh.html; New World Commc'n of Tampa, Inc. v. Akre, 866 So. 2d 1231 (Fla. App. 2003).

KEY WORDS AND PHRASES

appropriate collective bargaining unit   377

at-will contract   344

bad faith exception   347

comp time   365

concerted activity   378

covenant not to compete   351

defined benefit pension plan   366

defined contribution pension plan   367

doctrine of self-publication   354

economic strike   380

exempt employee   365

401(k) plan   367

H-1B visa   373

I-9   373

implied contract   346

implied covenant of good faith and fair dealing   347

living wage ordinances   365

nonexempt employees   365

pension plans   366

public policy exception   345

recognitional picketing   381

recognized hazards   361

representation elections   377

secondary boycotts   381

supervisor   377

unfair labor practice strike   380

unfair labor practices   378

welfare benefit plans   366

whistleblowing   346

wrongful discharge   345

QUESTIONS AND CASE PROBLEMS

1. Jeff Hemphill was an internal audit manager at Celanese, a publicly traded chemicals company. In 2007, he began work on an internal audit of a Celanese construction project in Ocotlan, Mexico. The team of auditors he managed identified several potential violations of law and company policy at the Ocotlan project, which were described in an audit report. Hemphill also reported these issues to his superiors, including Donna Wegner, and requested that a forensic auditor be hired to determine if any fraud had been committed in connection with these accounting problems. Hemphill additionally raised the issues with Gary Rowan, a Celanese compliance officer.

Hemphill participated in the further investigation of the accounting problems at the Ocotlan project. The Celanese auditors eventually determined that several Celanese employees had violated company policy, but not any laws, and one employee was removed from the project.

In June 2007, after the Ocotlan audit, Wegner told Hemphill that in order to create a better working environment he should "not develop issues." Around this time,

Hemphill also worked on another project reviewing the travel and entertainment records for several Celanese employees. Hemphill and his staff discovered certain violations of the company's policies. Hemphill later testified that, in his view, these violations created the risk of a "books and records violation" of Securities and Exchange Commission (SEC) rules. Hemphill advised Wegner of the violations and asked to raise the issues with Celanese's audit committee. Wegner rebuffed this request.

In August 2007, while Hemphill's secretary was arranging to rent a boat for a corporate outing, Hemphill began yelling at her in an abusive manner about her handling of the matter. Two Celanese employees witnessed the incident. Hemphill's behavior was reported to the director of human resources, and an investigation was conducted by an investigator who had no prior knowledge of Hemphill. The head of human resources advised Wegner of the investigation. The secretary and employee witnesses said that Hemphill had acted in an aggressive and unprofessional manner and that he was "outrageously rude and completely unprofessional"; his behavior was "atrocious," and it was "a one-sided rant by Mr. Hemphill . . . she was spoken to like a dog." Hemphill denied yelling or otherwise engaging in unprofessional behavior.

After concluding the investigation, the investigator recommended that Hemphill be terminated due to his "lying during a formal investigation, harassment of an employee, and creating a negative work environment for the team and those around him." The head of human resources concurred, and Wegner fired Hemphill.

Hemphill filed suit, claiming violations of the whistle-blower protection provisions of the Sarbanes–Oxley Act. He alleged that he was terminated in retaliation for the reports he filed regarding the Ocotlan audit and the travel and expenses audit. The district court granted Celanese's motion for summary judgment, after concluding that Hemphill had failed to establish the last prima facie element of his claim: that his protected activity was a "contributing factor" to his termination. The district court also determined that, even assuming Hemphill had established his prima facie claim, Celanese had rebutted the claim with clear and convincing evidence that Celanese would have terminated Hemphill regardless of his protected activity. How should the appeals court rule? Should it matter whether the director of HR was aware of the audit discrepancies? What public policies are at stake here? What firm values? [*Hemphill v. Celanese Corp.*, 430 Fed. App'x 341 (5th Cir. 2011).]

2. Ernest Bins, who had worked for Exxon for fifteen years, heard rumors in the months before his retirement that the company was considering offering a lump-sum retirement incentive under the employee benefit plan covered by ERISA. In response to his inquiries, a benefits counselor and human resources adviser told Bins that they knew nothing about whether the rumor was true. Less than two weeks after Bins retired, Exxon publicly announced the very retirement incentive about which he had inquired. Bins sued, claiming that the company had breached its duties as an ERISA fiduciary in not disclosing the potential change in ERISA benefits to all employees who might be affected. Who should prevail? Did Exxon act ethically? [*Bins v. Exxon Co. U.S.A.*, 189 F.3d 929 (9th Cir. 1999), *reh'g en banc*, 220 F.3d 1042 (9th Cir. 2000).]

3. In early 2011, several former and current employees of the GoalPost Sports Bar and Grill discovered that they owed state income taxes for 2010 related to their GoalPost compensation. At least one employee brought the issue to GoalPost's attention and requested that the matter be placed on the agenda for discussion at an upcoming management meeting with employees. Thereafter, a former employee posted on her Facebook page a statement, which included a shorthand expletive, expressing dissatisfaction that she owed money. She also asserted that the GoalPost's owners could not even do paperwork correctly. One current employee, Jeffrey, responded to this posting by clicking "Like." Two other employees commented that they had never owed money before; one of them also referred to telling GoalPost, "We will discuss this at

the meeting." Two of GoalPost's customers joined in the conversation, as did another current employee, Brittany. She asserted that she also owed money and referred to one of GoalPost's owners as "[s]uch an asshole." Neither Jeffrey nor Brittany was working on the day the Facebook conversation occurred. When Brittany reported to work the next day, she was told that her employment was terminated due to her Facebook posting and because she was not "loyal enough" to work for GoalPost anymore. When Jeffrey reported to work, he was confronted by GoalPost about the Facebook conversation and was also terminated. Thereafter, Brittany received a letter from GoalPost's attorney stating that legal action would be initiated against her unless she retracted the "defamatory" statements regarding GoalPost and its principals that she had posted on Facebook. Was either Jeffrey or Brittany engaged in protected concerted action under the National Labor Relations Act when they made their Facebook postings? Can GoalPost terminate them? Should it? [Memorandum from Lafe E. Soloman, National Labor Relations Board, Office of the General Counsel, Report of the Acting General Counsel Concerning Social Media Cases Within the Last Year 3 (Aug. 18, 2011), *available at* http://www.huntonlaborblog.com/uploads/file/NLRB_Provides_Guidance_For_Social_Media.pdf.]

4. In March 2001, forty-three-year-old Peter Barnes read an ad in the *Chicago Tribune* stating that Pentrix, Inc. was seeking experienced word processors to work in its Chicago office. Pentrix is a national corporation specializing in the design and manufacture of handheld computers. The ad stated that Pentrix was looking for "experienced word processors seeking a career in a stable and growing company." On March 8, 2001, Barnes interviewed with Renee Thompson, the head of Pentrix's word processing department in Chicago. Thompson was impressed with Barnes's prior experience and assured him that although Pentrix was a national corporation, the employees in Pentrix were like a family and looked after one another. Thompson offered Barnes a job at the end of the interview, and Barnes began work on March 15, 2001.

Barnes received an updated policy manual from the personnel department every year that he worked for Pentrix. In addition to discussing such things as vacation, salary, and benefits, the policy manual described Pentrix's progressive discipline system.

Pentrix's progressive discipline system consisted of three basic steps. First, an employee's supervisor must discuss the employee's deficiencies with the employee and suggest ways for the employee to improve his or her work performance. Second, the employee must receive written notice of his or her poor performance with suggestions of how the performance can improve. Third, the employee must receive a written warning that if the employee's performance does not improve, he or she will be terminated.

The manual provided that in cases of "material misconduct" a supervisor had the discretion to decide whether to follow the progressive discipline procedures. The policy manual also provided that Pentrix had complete discretion to decide who would be discharged in the event of a company layoff.

In 2003, the following language was added to the policy manual:

> These policies are simply guidelines to management. Pentrix reserves the right to terminate or change them at any time or to elect not to follow them in any case. Nothing in these policies is intended or should be understood as creating a contract of employment or a guarantee of continued employment with Pentrix. Employment at Pentrix remains terminable at the will of either the employee or Pentrix at any time for any reason or for no reason.

Barnes signed an acknowledgment of receipt of the 2003 policy manual.

Barnes received several good performance reviews during the time he worked at Pentrix. On a few occasions, Thompson discussed with Barnes the importance of arriving at work on time, but no record was kept of the times that he was late. In Barnes's 2005 and 2006 performance evaluations, Thompson noted that he should proofread his work more carefully.

In October 2010, Barnes received an offer to work as a word processor for Lintog, another computer manufacturing corporation in Chicago. Barnes discussed this offer with Thompson. Thompson persuaded Barnes to remain at Pentrix by suggesting that he might be promoted to day-shift word processing supervisor when the current day-shift supervisor resigned. The day-shift supervisor has yet to resign from Pentrix.

Barnes was discharged from Pentrix on July 1, 2011. Thompson told Barnes that he was being fired because Pentrix was experiencing a slowdown and that two word processors were being let go in each of Pentrix's twenty offices across the country. Thompson wrote on the separation notice placed in Barnes's personnel file that Barnes was being discharged as a result of a workforce reduction. Before leaving on July 1, Barnes saw Olga Svetlana, Pentrix's vice president of computer design, getting into her car. Svetlana said to Barnes, "Too bad about your job, but maybe this will teach you to stop leaking our computer designs to other companies."

Barnes had trouble sleeping and felt depressed after being fired from Pentrix. He waited three weeks before he began looking for another job. He then submitted an application to Lintog, the company that had offered him a job in 2010. Rob Grey, the head of the word processing department at Lintog, called Renee Thompson at Pentrix to find out why Barnes had left. Thompson responded that Barnes had worked in Pentrix's word processing department for more than ten years and was discharged as a result of a slowdown. Barnes interviewed with Grey on July 26, 2011. During the interview, Grey asked Barnes why he had left his job at Pentrix. Barnes responded that although he was officially told that he was being discharged because of a reduction in force, he was fired because he was wrongly suspected of leaking

the corporation's computer designs. Barnes was not hired by Lintog.

a. What claims might Barnes bring against Pentrix?
b. If you were investigating whether Barnes could successfully sue Pentrix, what information would you want to know?
c. What damages might Barnes be entitled to recover?

5. Le Ann McAteer, a landscaper, suffered a job-related injury on July 11, 2005, when she tripped over a cement parking stop while using a weedeater in a parking lot. She did not report this injury to her employer, SilverleafResorts, until September 2005, which was after her employment with Silverleaf had ended.

   Silverleaf does not subscribe to Texas workers' compensation insurance. Instead, it provides benefits to its employees through the Silverleaf Club Employee Injury Benefit Plan (the Plan), which is governed by ERISA. The Plan gives no-fault benefits to employees in the event of a job-related injury and requires arbitration of any disputes regarding benefits. McAteer enrolled in the Plan and signed an agreement that the Plan would provide the exclusive avenue of relief for on-the-job injuries.

   After leaving Silverleaf, McAteer submitted an injury claim form to the Plan, where it was reviewed by the Plan's administrator, Providence Risk Services, Inc. Providence issued an initial determination denying McAteer's claim because she had not timely reported her injury, had not sought advance approval for her medical treatment, and had not used a Plan-approved physician. McAteer did not pursue an administrative appeal. McAteer then brought a state-law negligence action under Texas law against her former employer for allegedly failing to maintain a safe workplace environment. Silverleaf argued that her state-law claims were preempted by ERISA. Who should prevail? [*McAteer v. Silverleaf Resorts, Inc.*, 514 F.3d 411 (5th Cir. 2008).]

6. Lisa Mull was a line operator at Zeta Consumer Products' plastic-bag manufacturing facility in New Jersey. One of Mull's duties was to work with a machine known as a "winder," which winds plastic bags onto spools for packaging and delivery. The machine's frequent malfunctions required Mull to clear the jam and replace the nylon ropes that turned the machine's cylinders. On one occasion, after Mull had turned off the machine by pressing the stop button on the control panel, the winder suddenly began to operate, pulling Mull's left hand into the machine and causing serious injuries, including amputation of two fingers.

   Several months before the accident, OSHA had cited Zeta for failing to provide its employees with so-called lockout/tagout procedures, which are designed to control the release of hazardous energy when a worker is servicing or performing maintenance on equipment or machinery. Also prior to the date of Mull's injury, another line operator had sustained injuries similar to Mull's; Zeta was aware of the injuries. In addition, other line operators indicated that Zeta, motivated by a desire to enhance productivity, had altered the original design of the winder by removing safety interlock switches (which prevent the machine from operating when the access cover is open). Line operators had also complained to management that Zeta failed to post warnings on the winder to inform workers of its "sudden start-up" capabilities or that the safety interlock switches had been removed.

Mull sued the employer for damages, and Zeta moved for summary judgment on the basis that Mull's sole remedy was recovery under New Jersey's Workers' Compensation Act. What, if any, OSHA liability does Zeta face based on these facts? How should the court rule? Should Zeta be concerned about any other potential liability arising out of these facts? [*Mull v. Zeta Consumer Products*, 823 A.2d 782 N.J. (2003).]

7. Have any of the employers in the following cases terminated an employee in violation of public policy? Has each employer acted ethically?

   a. Elizabeth M. Stewart was a highly talented salesperson for Cendant Mobility Services Corporation. Stewart's husband was also employed by Cendant as an executive in the operations department. During a major corporate reorganization, Cendant terminated Stewart's husband. Shortly thereafter, Stewart spoke with James Simon, Cendant's executive vice president of sales, regarding her concerns about how her employment with Cendant might be affected if her husband ultimately found employment with a competitor. Simon told Stewart that her husband's employment would have no bearing on her employment with Cendant and that she had no reason to be concerned about her status at Cendant because she was a highly valued employee. On the basis of these assurances, Stewart continued in her position with Cendant and did not pursue other employment opportunities.

   Nearly one year after Cendant's reorganization, Cendant learned that Stewart's husband was working for a competitor and subsequently reduced her duties and limited her interaction with clients. Cendant also requested that Stewart verbally agree to a document that purported to delineate her obligations to Cendant in relation to her husband's work on behalf of any competitor of Cendant. When Stewart declined to agree to this document, Cendant terminated her employment. [*Stewart v. Cendant Mobility Services Corp.*, 836 A.2d 736 (Conn. 2003).]

   b. Dohme claimed that he was fired by Eurand America, Inc. because he had expressed concerns to outside parties about the safety of the Eurand workplace. In 2002, Dohme had discussed with his neighbor, who was a captain with the local fire department, the design of a pump that Dohme believed had started a fire at the plant. In 2003, he had communicated his workplace-safety concerns to an insurance adjuster who conducted an on-site evaluation of Eurand's facility to assess the building and its operations. Prior to the insurance adjuster's visit, Eurand had sent an interoffice e-mail to all its employees explaining that the facility would be inspected by the adjuster and that only the employees identified in that e-mail were to have contact with the adjuster. Even though Dohme was not on the list, he spoke with the adjuster anyway. In his suit against Eurand, he contended that he was terminated because of his "perceived role in an on-site insurance adjuster's discovery of certain violations relative to [Eurand America's] fire alarm system, which jeopardized workplace safety and placed employees in [an] unreasonable and dangerous setting." Eurand America claimed that Dohme was terminated for contributing to the violations the adjuster found in his inspection and for insubordination. [*Dohme v. Eurand America, Inc.*, 2011 WL 4108354 (Ohio Sept. 15, 2011).]

   c. A nonexempt employee alleged that she was discharged after thirty years of employment with the Cleveland Clinic Foundation because she complained about being underpaid and requested remediation. She also claimed that she was forced to falsify her timekeeping records during her employment at the clinic. [*DeMell v. Cleveland Clinic Foundation*, 2007 WL 1705094 (Ohio App. 8 Dist. June 14, 2007).]

   d. An employee hired as an "environmental/assistant safety manager" complained about La-Z-Boy's handling of injured employees on a number of occasions. Among other incidents, she submitted a memorandum in which she stated that employees' injury claims were being intentionally mismanaged and that the claim adjuster was hostile to employees who filed workers' compensation claims. She also informed the human resources director that the "alternate duty assignments" given to injured employees were demeaning. When she told La-Z-Boy's vice president that an employee had been injured and that his benefits were being improperly denied, she alleged that she was told "she would be fired if she ever talked to any employees about their Workers' Compensation issues or their injuries." Several months later while she was on maternity leave, she was informed that she had been terminated and her position had been filled. [*Touchard v. La-Z-Boy, Inc.*, 148 P.3d 945 (Utah 2006).]

   e. Collotype Labels suspended Luke after learning that he had lied about having his position covered when he took time off. While he was suspended, Luke sent an e-mail to a Collotype manager in another office, entitled "trouble brewing," that related to various complaints raised by a number of Collotype employees. The next day, Collotype terminated Luke's employment for insubordination and provided him with a termination memorandum stating that one of the reasons for his termination was that he had been soliciting signatures for a letter denouncing the company's management. [*Luke v. Collotype Labels USA, Inc.*, 159 Cal. App. 4th 1463 (2008).]

   f. Brent Voss is a partial owner of two companies, Liberty Holdings, Inc. and Premier Concrete Pumping, L.L.C. In 2004, Nathan Berry began working for Liberty Holdings. On June 5, 2006, a concrete pumper truck owned by Premier struck and injured

Berry, who was on his way home from work. Berry filed a personal-injury lawsuit against Premier for the injuries he sustained in the collision. Berry ultimately settled this claim within the policy limits of Premier's insurance coverage.

Approximately nine months after the settlement, Liberty Holdings terminated Berry's employment. Berry filed suit against Liberty Holdings, asserting an intentional tort claim for wrongful termination in violation of public policy. Berry alleged that Liberty Holdings terminated his employment "because he engaged in the protected activity of bringing a claim for personal injury" against Premier. [*Berry v. Liberty Holdings, Inc.*, 803 N.W.2d 106 (Iowa 2011).]

8. Frontline Processing's Internet service provider tipped off the FBI that a Frontline employee had accessed child pornography from a work computer, and the FBI immediately contacted Frontline's information technology (IT) department, which investigated further. The IT employees determined that Jeffrey Ziegler, Frontline's director of operations, had searched for and accessed child pornography from his work computer, and they started monitoring his Internet activity through his browser's cache files, where they found evidence of child pornography. Frontline routinely monitored workplace computers, and its employees were aware of its monitoring capabilities.

Members of the Frontline IT department obtained a key to Ziegler's office from the chief financial officer, entered the office, and made two copies of Ziegler's computer hard drive. Frontline's corporate counsel turned over all the materials to the FBI and indicated that the company would comply fully with the investigation.

Ziegler argued that the FBI obtained the materials without a warrant and, thus, conducted an illegal search that violated the Fourth Amendment. Even though the district court found that the FBI had directed the company to enter Ziegler's office and make the copies, it denied his motions, explaining that Ziegler had no expectation of privacy in "the files he accessed on the Internet." Does an employee have an expectation of privacy in his workplace computer sufficient to suppress images of child pornography sought to be admitted into evidence in a criminal prosecution? If so, could the employer provide valid consent to a search of the employee's computer? [*United States v. Ziegler*, 474 F.3d 1184 (9th Cir. 2007).]

CHAPTER 13

CIVIL RIGHTS AND EMPLOYMENT DISCRIMINATION

INTRODUCTION

LAWS DESIGNED TO ELIMINATE EMPLOYMENT DISCRIMINATION

The abolition of slavery after the Civil War and the civil rights movement of the 1960s were two great forces behind modern civil rights legislation. From the Civil Rights Act of 1866 to the Genetic Information Nondiscrimination Act of 2008, the law has moved in a direction to eliminate discrimination based on race, gender, color, religion, national origin, age, disability, or genetics information. Civil rights laws help ensure that every member of society has the opportunity to reach his or her full potential and promote economic growth by expanding the pool of qualified workers.

Managers who fail to adopt and enforce policies to ensure compliance with federal and state legislation prohibiting employment discrimination put their companies at risk of being penalized by large fines and judgments. The Equal Employment Opportunity Commission (EEOC) secured financial settlements of $364.6 million in 2010.[1] In 2011, the EEOC achieved the largest settlement in history under the Americans with Disabilities Act. Verizon Communications agreed to pay $20 million and to provide equitable relief to settle a nationwide class disability discrimination lawsuit in which the plaintiffs alleged that the company had denied reasonable accommodations to hundreds of employees and disciplined or fired them pursuant to Verizon's "no fault" attendance plans.[2] With the EEOC facing a backlog of more than 70,000 cases,[3] private litigation of employment-discrimination claims has become increasingly important. In 2010, Novartis Pharmaceuticals Corporation agreed to pay $175 million to settle a class-action lawsuit for sex and pregnancy discrimination. A federal jury had awarded the class

$250 million in punitive damages after concluding that Novartis had intentionally discriminated against more than 5,000 female sales representatives in the period from 2002 to 2007.[4] Employment discrimination is not just expensive to defend in court; it also tarnishes the employer's reputation and jeopardizes its relationship with employees, customers, and investors.

CHAPTER OVERVIEW

This chapter provides an overview of federal legislation barring employment discrimination, with special attention to Title VII of the Civil Rights Act, the Age Discrimination in Employment Act (ADEA), the Americans with Disabilities Act (ADA), the Family and Medical Leave Act, and the Uniformed Services Employment and Reemployment Rights Act. It illustrates the various legal theories pursued under each piece of legislation and shows how those theories relate to legal and appropriate behavior by managers in a business environment. The chapter also discusses how discrimination laws apply to affirmative action and the hiring of contingent or temporary workers. The chapter concludes with an overview of the ways that other countries approach workplace discrimination and diversity.

OVERVIEW OF CIVIL RIGHTS LEGISLATION

The federal statutes that forbid various kinds of discrimination in employment are summarized in Exhibit 13.1. Many states have passed their own fair employment acts, which in

---

1. Equal Emp't Opportunity Comm'n, *FY 2011 Performance and Accountability, available at* http://www.eeoc.gov/2011par_discussion.cfm.

2. Press Release, Equal Emp't Opportunity Comm'n, Verizon to Pay $20 Million to Settle Nationwide EEOC Disability Suit (July 6, 2011), *available at* http://www.eeoc.gov/eeoc/newsroom/release/7-6-11a.cfm.

3. Equal Emp't Opportunity Comm'n, *supra* note 1.

4. *Jury in Novartis Sex Bias Lawsuit Awards $250 Million in Punitive Damages*, CORP. COUNS. WKLY. (BNA), May 26, 2010, at 161.

EXHIBIT 13.1	Major Pieces of Federal Civil Rights Legislation		
Statute	**Major Provisions**	**Employers Subject to Statute**	**Comments**
Civil Rights Act of 1866[a] (Section 1981)	Prohibits racial discrimination by employers of any size in the making and enforcement of contracts, including employment contracts.	All public and private employers	The bar against racial discrimination applies not only to hiring, promotion, and termination, but also to working conditions, such as racial harassment, and to breaches of contract occurring during the term of the contract.
Equal Pay Act of 1963[b]	Mandates equal pay for equal work without regard to gender.	All public and private employers with 20 or more employees (including federal, state, and local governments)	
Title VII of the Civil Rights Act of 1964[c] (Title VII)	Prohibits discrimination in employment on the basis of race, color, religion, national origin, or sex. Later amended to provide that discrimination on the basis of sex includes discrimination on the basis of pregnancy, childbirth, or related medical conditions.	All public and private employers with 15 or more employees (including federal, state, and local governments)	
Age Discrimination in Employment Act of 1967[d] (ADEA), as amended by Older Workers' Benefit Protection Act of 1990[e]	Protects persons 40 years and older from discrimination on the basis of age. The Older Workers' Benefit Protection Act prohibits age discrimination in providing employee benefits and establishes minimum standards for waiver of one's rights under the ADEA.	All public and private employers with 20 or more employees (including federal, state, and local governments)	
Vietnam Era Veterans' Readjustment Assistance Acts of 1972 and 1974[f]	Require affirmative action to employ disabled Vietnam-era veterans.	Employers holding federal contracts of $10,000 or more	Enforced by U.S. Department of Labor.
Vocational Rehabilitation Act of 1973[g]	Prohibits discrimination against the physically and mentally disabled. Imposes affirmative-action obligations on employers having contracts with the federal government in excess of $2,500.	Employers receiving federal financial assistance of any amount	Enforced by U.S. Department of Labor. This legislation was the precursor to and guided the development of the Americans with Disabilities Act.
Uniformed Services Employment and Reemployment Rights Act of 1994[h]	Gives employees who served in the military at any time the right to be reinstated in employment without loss of benefits and the right not to be discharged without cause for one year following such reinstatement.	All public and private employers	
Immigration Reform and Control Act of 1986[i] (IRCA)	Prohibits discrimination against applicants or employees based on national origin or citizenship status.	All private employers with 4 or more employees	If employer has 15 or more employees, plaintiff must file national origin discrimination claims under Title VII.

CONTINUED

EXHIBIT 13.1	Major Pieces of Federal Civil Rights Legislation (Continued)		
Statute	Major Provisions	Employers Subject to Statute	Comments
Americans with Disabilities Act of 1990 (ADA), as amended by the ADA Amendments Act of 2008[j] (ADAAA)	Prohibits discrimination in employment on the basis of a person's disability. Also requires businesses to provide "reasonable accommodation" to the disabled unless such an accommodation would result in "undue hardship" on business operations.	All private employers with 15 or more employees	The ADA is the most sweeping civil rights measure since the Civil Rights Act of 1964.
Civil Rights Act of 1991[k]	Caps compensatory and punitive damages for discrimination on basis of sex or religion at $50,000 for employers of 100 or fewer employees, $100,000 for employers with 101 to 200 employees, $200,000 for employers with 201 to 500 employees, and $300,000 for employers with more than 500 employees, as well as limited the ability to challenge affirmative-action litigated judgments and consent decrees. Also extended coverage of the major civil rights statutes to the staffs of the President and the Senate.		
Family and Medical Leave Act of 1993,[l] as amended in 2009 by the National Defense Act for Fiscal Year 2010[m] (NDA)	Designed to allow employees to take time off from work to handle domestic responsibilities, such as the birth or adoption of a child or the care of an elderly parent. Employees are guaranteed job security despite familial responsibilities. NDA amendment expands coverage for "qualifying exigency" leave to eligible employees with covered family members in the Regular Armed Forces and coverage for "military caregiver leave" to eligible employees who are the spouse, son, daughter, parent, or next of kin of certain veterans with a "serious injury or illness."	Private employers with 50 or more employees at work sites within 75 miles of each other	Part-time employees are excluded from the Act's coverage and are not to be counted in calculating the 50 employees necessary for an employer to be covered by the Act.
Genetic Information Nondiscrimination Act of 2008[n] (GINA)	Prohibits employers, group health plans, and health insurers from discriminating based on genetic information.	All public and private employers with 15 or more employees (including federal, state, and local governments)	Employers are prohibited from hiring, firing, placing, or making promotional decisions based solely on an individual's genetic information, but there is no cause of action for disparate impact.

a. 42 U.S.C. § 1981.
b. 29 U.S.C. § 206(d).
c. 42 U.S.C. §§ 2000e–2000e-17.
d. 29 U.S.C. §§ 621–634.
e. 29 U.S.C. § 623 (1990).
f. 38 U.S.C. § 4100 *et seq.*
g. 29 U.S.C. §§ 701–797.
h. 38 U.S.C. §§ 4301–4335.
i. Pub. L. No. 99-603, 100 Stat. 3359 (1986) (codified as amended in scattered sections of the U.S.C.).
j. 42 U.S.C. §§ 12101–12213, as amended by Pub. L. No. 110-325, 122 Stat. 3553 (2008).
k. Pub. L. No. 102-106, 105 Stat. 1071 (1991) (codified in scattered sections of the U.S.C.) (1991).
l. 29 U.S.C. §§ 2601–2654.
m. Pub. L. No. 111-84, 123 Stat. 2190 (2009).
n. Pub. L. No. 110-233, 122 Stat. 881 (2008).

some instances provide greater protection than their federal counterparts.[5] The federal statutes apply only to employees, not independent contractors. (See Chapter 5 for a discussion of the difference between employees and contractors.)

Although the statutes described in Exhibit 13.1 have created a far more level playing field for all workers, progress can be slow. For example, the Equal Pay Act was enacted in 1963, but as of 2010, women still earned only 77.4% of what men earned annually.[6]

Enforcement

The Equal Employment Opportunity Commission (EEOC) is the primary enforcer of civil rights legislation in the United States. A part of the Department of Justice, the EEOC processes hundreds of complaints, investigating and evaluating their merit. An individual challenging an employment practice must file a complaint with the EEOC within the specified *charging period*. For example, Title VII claims must be filed within 180 days after the alleged unlawful employment practice occurred. If a claim is unfounded or not filed in a timely manner, it will be dismissed.

In *Ledbetter v. Goodyear Tire & Rubber Co.*,[7] Lily Ledbetter sued Goodyear Tire under Title VII and the Equal Pay Act, alleging that sexually discriminatory and negative performance evaluations earlier in her tenure resulted in lower pay than her male colleagues throughout the rest of her career. The U.S. Supreme Court rejected her claims for the pay periods before the 180-day charging period. The Lily Ledbetter Fair Pay Act of 2009[8] effectively overturned this decision. The aggrieved person may now recover back pay for up to two years preceding the filing of the EEOC claim.

If a timely claim withstands initial inquiry and the EEOC is unable to pursue the case due to staff and resource constraints, the agency will provide a right-to-sue letter to the private party. Without this administrative permission, private litigants cannot initiate suits under various statutes, including Title VII and the ADA. As explained in Chapter 3, employers can require individual employees to arbitrate civil rights' disputes, but this does not preclude the EEOC from suing the employer in a court of law for damages payable to the aggrieved employee.

Definition of Adverse Employment Action

In most discrimination cases, the employee must establish that his or her employer subjected him or her to an adverse employment action. For example, section 703(a) of Title VII forbids discrimination "with respect to . . . compensation, terms, conditions or privileges of employment, based on an individual's race, color, religion, national origin, or sex."[9] *Adverse employment action* includes demotions, reductions in pay, refusals to hire or promote, and other actions that adversely affect the individual's employment status or opportunities in a tangible manner. It also includes giving unwarranted negative job evaluations, subjecting an employee to disadvantageous transfers or assignments, depriving an employee of support services, cutting off challenging assignments, moving an employee from a spacious office to a dingy closet, forcing an employee to jump through hoops in order to obtain severance benefits, making and soliciting from coworkers negative comments about an employee, needlessly delaying authorization for medical treatment, requiring an employee to work without a lunch break, and changing an employee's schedule without notification. To prove an adverse employment action, "a plaintiff must show that a reasonable employee would have found the challenged action materially adverse."[10] (The showing of adverse action necessary to support a retaliation claim is discussed later in this chapter.)

Remedies

Available remedies in discrimination cases generally include compensation for lost salary and benefits (*back pay*); hiring, wage adjustments, promotion, reinstatement, and other injunctive relief to stop prohibited discriminatory actions; and *front pay* equal to what the employee would have received had he or she not been discharged. Front pay is generally awarded when reinstatement is inappropriate because the position is unavailable or hostility raises a practical barrier.

The plaintiff may also recover compensatory damages for future pecuniary losses, emotional pain and suffering, inconvenience, mental anguish, loss of enjoyment of life, and other nonpecuniary losses. While front pay is limited in duration because it compensates for the immediate effects of discrimination, lost future earnings compensate an employee for a lifetime of diminished earnings resulting from the reputational harm suffered as a result of discrimination. Therefore, an employee may be awarded both front pay and damages for lost future earnings.[11] As discussed more fully later in this chapter, punitive damages may be available under certain circumstances as well.

---

5. For example, fourteen states currently have passed laws barring employment discrimination based on gender identity. *See Non-Discrimination Laws: State by State Information—Map*, Am. Civil Liberties Union (Sept. 21, 2011), *available at* http://www.aclu.org/maps/non-discrimination-laws-state-state-information-map.

6. Ariane Hegewisch, Claudia Williams & Amber Henderson, *The Gender Wage Gap: 2010*, Inst. For Women's Policy Research (Sept. 2011), *available at* http://www.iwpr.org/initiatives/pay-equity-and-discrimination.

7. 550 U.S. 618 (2007).

8. Pub.L. No. 111-2, 123 Stat. 5 (2009).

9. 42 U.S.C. § 2000e-2(a).

10. Burlington N. & Santa Fe Ry. v. White, 548 U.S. 53 (2006).

11. Williams v. Pharmacia, Inc., 137 F.3d 944 (7th Cir. 1998).

For example, the U.S. Court of Appeals for the Sixth Circuit affirmed a jury's award of more than $1 million to a former employee of Tyson Foods who, during the five weeks she worked at the plant, was sexually harassed by male coworkers who made sexually explicit comments to her, engaged in behavior such as "wolf-whistling" and staring, touched her breasts and buttocks on one occasion, attempted to kiss her on one occasion, and repeatedly asked to have sex with her.[12] Such incidents occurred ten to fifteen times per day. When she reported the harassment to her direct supervisor in accordance with the company's sexual harassment policy, he moved her to another section of the line but did not investigate the allegations as required by company policy. As a result of the harassment, she did not return to work and was subsequently terminated for job abandonment. At her exit interview, she reported the harassment to the human resources manager, who also failed to follow the company's policy and investigate the allegations. The jury awarded the former employee $750,000 for past and future emotional distress, $65,818.29 in back pay, $64,545 in front pay, and $400,000 in punitive damages.

TITLE VII

Title VII bans discrimination based on an individual's race, color, religion, national origin, or sex. Title VII claims generally fall within one of four broad categories: traditional discrimination, harassment, failure to accommodate religious beliefs, and retaliation.

Traditional Discrimination Claims

Litigation in traditional Title VII actions has produced two distinct legal theories of discrimination: (1) disparate treatment and (2) disparate impact.

Disparate Treatment

A plaintiff claiming *disparate treatment* must prove that the employer intentionally discriminated against him or her by denying a benefit or privilege of employment (such as a promotion or pay raise) because of his or her race, color, religion, sex, or national origin. The U.S. Supreme Court has established a systematic approach for proving these claims.[13] First, the employee must prove a prima facie case, which entails proving that (1) he or she is a member of a class of persons protected by Title VII; and (2) he or she was denied a position or benefit that he or she sought, for which he or she was qualified, and that was available. If the employee proves the prima facie case, the employer

then must present evidence, but need not prove, that it had legitimate, nondiscriminatory grounds for its decision, such as the employee's lack of qualifications or poor job performance. Once the employer meets its burden of producing evidence, the employee then must prove that the grounds offered by the employer were merely a pretext for the employer's actions and that intentional discrimination was the true reason.

In *Frank v. United Airlines, Inc.*,[14] the U.S. Court of Appeals for the Ninth Circuit held that United Airlines' use of different weight policies for male and female flight attendants was illegal disparate treatment on the basis of sex. The airline required female flight attendants to meet weight limits based on suggested weights for medium body frames, but permitted male flight attendants to meet weight limits based on large body frames. The court held that United failed to show that having thinner female than male flight attendants affected the flight attendants' ability to greet passengers, move luggage, push carts, or provide physical assistance in emergencies. The court found that the plaintiffs had successfully established that United's reasons were a pretext and that the different weight limits for male and female flight attendants constituted illegal discrimination. In fact, the court concluded, the discriminatory weight requirement may have actually hindered female employees' job performance.

Disparate Impact

The *disparate impact* theory arose out of Title VII class actions brought in the 1970s against large employers. These suits challenged testing and other selection procedures, claiming that they systematically excluded women or particular ethnic groups from certain types of jobs. It is not necessary to prove intentional discrimination to prevail in a disparate impact case. Discrimination can be established by proving that an employment practice, although neutral on its face, disproportionately affects a protected group in a negative way.

For example, the owner of a sausage plant implemented a strength test for entry-level jobs that required repetitive lifting of up to thirty-five pounds to a height of sixty inches. The EEOC established its prima facie case by showing that 46% of the individuals hired for these jobs were women before the test was adopted, but the number of women hired dropped to 15% after implementation of the test. The employer attempted to show that the test "related to safe and efficient job performance and [was] consistent with business necessity" by presenting evidence that the test effectively gauged the skills needed for the job and that there was a consistent decline in the number of work-related injuries after the test was implemented. But there was also evidence that the downward trend in injuries had begun before the adoption of the strength test, when the employer had

---

12. West v. Tyson Foods, Inc., F. App'x 624 (6th Cir. 2010).

13. *See* McDonnell Douglas Corp. v. Green, 411 U.S. 792 (1973). *See also* Ash v. Tyson Foods, Inc., 546 U.S. 454 (2006).

14. 216 F.3d 845 (9th Cir. 2000).

instituted other measures to reduce injuries. The U.S. Court of Appeals for the Eighth Circuit found that the employer had not presented sufficient evidence of business necessity because it had not shown that these other safety measures could not have produced the same results. As a result, the court affirmed the jury's verdict that use of the strength test had an unlawful disparate impact on female applicants.[15]

The business justification offered by an employer to justify the disparate impact must relate to job performance. Inconvenience, annoyance, or expense to the employer will not suffice. For example, a Latina applicant who is denied employment because she failed an

English-language test might challenge the language requirement. If she has applied for a sales job, the employer might be able to justify the requirement on the ground that ability to communicate with customers is an indispensable qualification. On the other hand, if she has applied for a job on the production line, that justification would probably not suffice unless her duties would include communicating with others in English. As under disparate treatment analysis, the burden of persuasion ultimately rests with the plaintiff.

In the following case, the Supreme Court considered whether an employer could disregard job-related test results to the detriment of high-scoring white firefighters for fear that using them would subject the employer to a disparate impact lawsuit by African American firefighters.

---

15. EEOC v. Dial Corp., 469 F.3d 735 (8th Cir. 2006).

A CASE IN POINT

Ricci v. DeStefano

Supreme Court of the United States
129 S. Ct. 2658 (2009).

Summary   Case 13.1

Facts   In 2003, the City of New Haven administered an objective examination developed by Industrial/Organizational Solutions, Inc. (IOS) to identify which firefighters should be promoted. Based on the examination results, the only candidates eligible for promotion to lieutenant were ten whites, and the only candidates eligible for promotion to captain were seven whites and two Hispanics. The City decided not to certify or consider the test results based on its belief that doing so could subject the City to a lawsuit alleging that the test had a disparate impact on minority firefighters in violation of Title VII.

IOS had conducted a series of interviews, ride-alongs, and questionnaires to identify the tasks, knowledge, skills, and abilities essential to the positions. Throughout the analyses, IOS deliberately oversampled minority firefighters to ensure that the examinations would not unintentionally favor white candidates. The assessors of the examination were also deliberately chosen so that each three-member panel included two minority members.

Seventeen white firefighters and one Hispanic firefighter who likely would have been promoted based on their test results sued, alleging that the City had violated Title VII when it refused to certify the exam results. After the U.S. Court of Appeals for the Second Circuit found for the City, the plaintiffs appealed.

Issue Presented   Under Title VII, may an employer refuse to certify test results that would make a disproportionate number of white candidates eligible for promotion in comparison with minority candidates due to fear of disparate impact discrimination litigation?

Summary of Opinion   The U.S. Supreme Court began by noting that Title VII prohibits both intentional discrimination (disparate treatment) and certain facially neutral practices that are discriminatory in operation (disparate impact). An employer may defend against liability for disparate impact by demonstrating that the practice is "job related for the position in question and consistent with business necessity." Even if the employer meets that burden, however, a plaintiff may still prevail if he or she can show that the employer refused to adopt an available alternative employment practice that has less disparate impact and serves the employer's legitimate needs.

The City rejected the test results solely because the higher-scoring candidates were white. This race-conscious discriminatory conduct constituted illegal disparate treatment unless the City had a lawful justification.

The Court held that an employer may not engage in intentional discrimination for the asserted purpose of avoiding or remedying an unintentional disparate impact unless the employer has "a strong basis in evidence to believe it will be subject to disparate-impact liability if it fails to

CONTINUED

take the race-conscious, discriminatory action." Applying this standard, the Court concluded that the City violated Title VII when it discarded the test results. There was no evidence that the tests were flawed. They were job related, and there was no evidence of other, equally valid and less discriminatory tests available to the City. The Court explained, "Fear of litigation alone cannot justify an employer's reliance on race to the detriment of individuals who passed the examinations and qualified for promotions." If the City had certified the test results and then faced a suit based on disparate impact, "it should be clear that the City would [have avoided] disparate-impact liability based on the strong basis in evidence that, had it not certified the results, it would have been subject to disparate-treatment liability."

RESULT   The Supreme Court reversed the Second Circuit's decision. The City had engaged in illegal disparate treatment discrimination.

COMMENTS   In his concurrence, Justice Scalia noted that the majority opinion had failed to address an issue that it will eventually have to confront, namely, "Whether, or to what extent, are the disparate-impact provisions of Title VII of the Civil Rights Act of 1964 consistent with the Constitution's guarantee of equal protection [under the Fourteenth Amendment]?"

In her dissent, Justice Ginsburg (joined by Justices Stevens, Souter, and Breyer) argued that the majority had ignored substantial evidence of flaws in the tests and had failed to acknowledge alternative and better testing methods used in other cities. Moreover, the dissent argued, the City merely needed "good cause" to believe it would be subject to disparate impact litigation before deciding not to consider the test results.

Disparate impact analysis may be applied not only to objective selection criteria, such as tests and degree requirements, but also to subjective bases for decisions, such as interviews and supervisor evaluations.[16] Although the U.S. Supreme Court refused to certify a class comprising millions of female Wal-Mart employees suing for sex discrimination,[17] the individual women were permitted to sue Wal-Mart in an individual capacity for maintaining a highly discretionary promotion policy that resulted in a disproportionately small percentage of women being promoted. As the Court explained, "[G]iving discretion to lower-level supervisors can be the basis of Title VII liability under a disparate-impact theory—since 'an employer's undisciplined system of subjective decision-making [can have] precisely the same effects as a system pervaded by impermissible intentional discrimination'"[18] Thus, an employer violated Title VII when it instructed supervisors to start with objective measures, then to "look at the individual as a total individual," and finally to ask and answer the question, "Is this person going to be successful in our business?"[19] As Justice Ginsburg stated in her dissent in the *Wal-Mart* case, "It is hardly surprising that for many managers, the ideal candidate was someone with characteristics similar to their own."[20]

Harassment

Employees can bring claims for harassment in violation of Title VII on the basis of sex, race, color, religion, or national origin. The most prevalent type of harassment claim is sexual harassment, and thus the law regarding harassment has been largely developed in the context of sexual harassment claims.[21] Nevertheless, the analysis used in sexual harassment cases is applied to claims of harassment on the basis of race, color, religion, and national origin as well.

Sexual Harassment

Sexual harassment law is based on language in Title VII that prohibits discrimination "because of sex" and is one of the more complex and emotional issues in anti-discrimination law. Sexual harassment can be asserted by male or female employees. Sexual harassment charges brought by men accounted for 16.4% of all sexual harassment charges filed with the EEOC (including claims filed with state and local agencies that have a work sharing agreement with the EEOC) in 2010, up from 11.6% in 1997.[22] The vast majority of such charges involved harassment by other men.

16. *See* Allen v. City of Chicago, 351 F.3d 306 (7th Cir. 2003).

17. Wal-Mart Stores, Inc. v. Dukes, 131 S. Ct. 2541 (2011) (Case 3.2).

18. *Id*. at 2554 (quoting Watson v. Fort Worth Bank & Trust, 487 U.S. 977, 990–91 (1988)).

19. Leisner v. New York Tel. Co., 358 F. Supp. 359 (S.D.N.Y. 1973).

20. *Wal-Mart Stores*, 131 S. Ct. at 2564.

21. EMPLOYMENT DISCRIMINATION LAW 1384 (Barbara Lindemann & Paul Grossman eds., 2007).

22. Equal Emp't Opportunity Comm'n, *Sexual Harassment Charges: FY 1997–2010, available at* http://eeoc.gov/eeoc/statistics/enforcement/sexual_harassment.cfm.

***Quid Pro Quo* Harassment**   Early on, the courts recognized that a specific, job-related adverse action, such as denial of a promotion, in retaliation for a person's refusal to respond to his or her supervisor's sexual advances is a violation of Title VII. Such retaliation, which is referred to as *quid pro quo harassment*, is a theory unique to sexual harassment claims.

Hostile Environment Harassment   A threat of adverse job action in retaliation for rebuffing sexual advances does not constitute *quid pro quo* harassment if the threat is not carried out. Instead, it is a form of *hostile environment harassment.*[23] Employees can bring claims for hostile environment harassment on the basis of race, color, religion, and national origin as well.

In *Meritor Savings Bank, FSB v. Vinson,*[24] the U.S. Supreme Court first ruled that creation of a hostile environment by sexual harassment is a form of sex discrimination barred by Title VII, even if the employee cannot show a concrete economic effect on employment, such as discharge or denial of a raise or promotion, to establish a violation. Not every sexually offensive comment or act constitutes actionable sexual harassment, however; there must be sufficient offensive conduct to give rise to a pervasively hostile atmosphere. This determination should be based on the totality of the circumstances.

In *Harris v. Forklift Systems, Inc.,*[25] the U.S. Supreme Court held that a showing of a serious effect on an employee's psychological well-being, or other injury, is not necessary for a hostile work environment claim under Title VII, reasoning that "Title VII comes into play before the harassing conduct leads to a nervous breakdown." The Court ruled in favor of a female manager of an equipment-rental company who was harassed for two years by its president. In the presence of other employees, the president said such things as, "You're a woman, what do you know?" and "We need a man as the rental manager," and called her "a dumb-ass woman." The president also made sexual innuendos, suggesting that they "go to the Holiday Inn to negotiate her raise," and occasionally asked female employees to get coins from his front pants pocket. Despite the employee's complaints, the sexual comments continued.

Defining a Hostile Work Environment   To determine whether there is a hostile or abusive environment, courts look at all the circumstances, including (1) the frequency and severity of the discriminatory conduct; (2) whether it is physically threatening or humiliating, or merely an offensive utterance; and (3) whether it unreasonably interferes with the employee's work performance.

To be actionable under Title VII, sexual harassment must be so severe or pervasive as to alter the conditions of the victim's employment and create an abusive work environment. For example, the U.S. Court of Appeals for the Seventh Circuit ruled that a supervisor's multiple and direct propositions for sex during a business meeting were sufficiently severe to create a hostile work environment.[26] The U.S. Supreme Court has ruled that "'simple teasing,' offhand comments, and isolated incidents (unless extremely serious) will not amount to discriminatory changes in the terms and conditions of employment."[27] The conduct must be "extreme." These standards for judging hostility are sufficiently demanding to prevent plaintiffs from converting Title VII into a "general civility code"; they are intended to filter out "complaints attacking 'the ordinary tribulations of the workplace, such as the sporadic use of abusive language, gender-related jokes, and occasional teasing.'"

In *Duncan v. General Motors Corp.,*[28] for example, the U.S. Court of Appeals for the Eighth Circuit concluded that a male supervisor did not create a hostile work environment when he showed three-dimensional models of sexual organs and a picture of a naked woman to a female subordinate. The court stated that such action, while "boorish, chauvinistic, and decidedly immature," did not create an objectively hostile work environment where the plaintiff's employment had been altered.

Although some courts have held that a one-time incident is not enough to create a hostile environment, the trend in both sexual harassment suits and other claims of harassment appears to be to find a hostile environment if the incident is severe enough and involves a supervisor. In *Brooks v. San Mateo, California,*[29] the U.S. Court of Appeals for the Ninth Circuit held that a single incident in which a male coworker touched a female employee's breast and stomach while she was answering a 911 emergency call was not sufficient to establish a hostile work environment. The employee suffered no physical injury, and the employer took prompt steps to remove the male employee from the workplace. The court noted that a single incident involving a supervisor was more likely to result in employer liability for hostile environment than comparable conduct by a coworker.

Certain state courts have upheld claims for hostile environment in so-called paramour cases (where coworkers claim an employee has received preferential treatment as a result of having sexual relations with a supervisor),[30] but a majority of federal courts have struck down such claims.[31] For example, in *Ackel v. National Communications, Inc.,*[32] the plaintiff complained that she was replaced by her supervisor's paramour as a result of favoritism based on their sexual relationship. The U.S. Court of Appeals for the

---

23. Burlington Indus., Inc. v. Ellerth, 524 U.S. 742 (1998).
24. 477 U.S. 57 (1986).
25. 510 U.S. 17 (1993).

26. Quantock v. Shared Mktg. Servs., Inc., 312 F.3d 899 (7th Cir. 2002).
27. Faragher v. City of Boca Raton, 524 U.S. 775, 788 (1998).
28. 300 F.3d 928 (8th Cir. 2002), *aff'd*, 538 U.S. 994 (2003).
29. 229 F.3d 917 (9th Cir. 2000).
30. Miller v. Dep't of Corr., 36 Cal. 4th 446 (2005).
31. Riggs v. County of Banner, 159 F. Supp. 2d 1158 (D. Neb. 2001).
32. 339 F.3d 376 (5th Cir. 2003).

Fifth Circuit stated that "courts have held that when an employer discriminates in favor of a paramour, such an action is not sex-based discrimination, as the favoritism, while unfair, disadvantages both sexes alike for reasons other than gender."[33]

Same-Sex Sexual Harassment In *Oncale v. Sundowner Offshore Services, Inc.*, the U.S. Supreme Court held that Title VII prohibits same-sex harassment; in other words, it prohibits harassment where the harasser is the same sex as the employee being harassed.[34] Acknowledging that same-sex harassment was not the evil Congress sought to remedy when it passed Title VII, the Court nevertheless saw "no justification in the statutory language or our precedents for a categorical rule excluding same-sex harassment claims from the coverage of Title VII." However, the Court was careful to explain that to be actionable, the harassment must be tied to some type of gender discrimination: it must be "discrimination because of sex." Thus, the Court explained, "The critical issue is whether members of one sex are exposed to disadvantageous terms or conditions of employment to which members of the other sex are not exposed." The Supreme Court called on courts and juries to use "common sense" to differentiate sex discrimination from horseplay, noting that a pat on the bottom by a football coach to a player running onto the field may not constitute sex discrimination, but similar touching of a secretary might.[35]

Applying the standard set forth in *Oncale*, the U.S. Court of Appeals for the Fifth Circuit found that obnoxious comments by a male supervisor about a male employee's sexuality, inappropriate touching of the employee's private body parts, and spitting tobacco juice on him could constitute sex discrimination if the plaintiff could show that the same-sex harasser's actions were "explicit or implicit proposals of sexual activity" and that there was "credible evidence that the harasser was homosexual."[36] Such evidence would prove that the same-sex employee would not have been harassed if he had been a member of the opposite sex.

Sexual Orientation and Transgender Harassment The *Oncale* decision did not extend Title VII protection to harassment based on a person's sexual orientation. Although legislation to amend Title VII to include sexual orientation has been introduced in every term of Congress since 1975, it has not been enacted. The U.S. Supreme Court has suggested, however, that homosexual employees may state *sexual stereotyping* claims under Title VII against employers who discriminated against them because they were not "manly" enough men or "womanly" enough women.[37] There is also authority in many of the circuits for applying Title VII to cases in which an employee claims that he or she was subjected to harassment due to the discomfort or hostility of fellow employees because of the employee's gender nonconformity.[38]

For example, in *Rene v. MGM Grand Hotel, Inc.*, a gay male alleged that his harassers grabbed and poked at his genitals, but there was no evidence that any of his harassers had expressed any interest in engaging in sexual activity with Rene. The court found that harassment that included touching body parts was "inescapably [harassment] because of sex." The court held that an employee's sexual orientation is irrelevant for purposes of Title VII and neither provides nor precludes a cause of action for sexual harassment: "That the harasser is, or may be, motivated by hostility based on sexual orientation is . . . irrelevant. . . . It is enough that the harasser engaged in severe or pervasive unwelcome physical conduct of a sexual nature."[39]

Racial, National Origin, and Religious Harassment

Like claims of hostile environment harassment on the basis of sex, harassment claims based on race, color, national origin, or religion are evaluated according to the rule in

IN BRIEF

Elements of a Sexual Harassment Claim

Unwelcome sexual advances, requests for sexual favors, and other verbal or physical conduct of a sexual nature constitute sexual harassment when:

1. An individual's employment depends on submission to such conduct;
2. Submission to or rejection of such conduct is used as the basis of employment decisions; or
3. Such conduct unreasonably interferes with the individual's work performance or creates an intimidating, hostile, or offensive working environment.

To establish a claim of hostile environment sexual harassment under Title VII, the plaintiff must show that:

1. The harassment created an abusive working environment;
2. The harassment was based on sex; and
3. The harassment was so severe or pervasive as to alter the conditions of the victim's employment.

Christoph Weihs/Shutterstock

---

33. *Id.* at 382 (quoting Green v. Adm'rs of the Tulane Educ. Fund, 284 F.3d 642 (5th Cir. 2002)).

34. 523 U.S. 75 (1988).

35. *Id.*

36. La Day v. Catalyst Tech., Inc., 302 F.3d 474, 478 (5th Cir. 2002).

37. Price Waterhouse v. Hopkins, 490 U.S. 228 (1989) *superseded in part on other grounds by statute*, Civil Rights Act of 1991, Pub.L. No. 102-166, 105 Stat. 1074.

38. *See, e.g.*, Rene v. MGM Grand Hotel, Inc., 305 F.3d 1061 (9th Cir. 2002) (en banc), and cases cited therein.

39. *Id.*

Harris v. Forklift Systems, Inc.[40] Courts examine the total-ity of the circumstances to determine whether an employee was exposed to a hostile environment. In *Azimi v. Jordan's Meats, Inc.*,[41] a Muslim immigrant from Afghanistan sued his employer, claiming that he was subjected to racial or ethnic harassment. The U.S. Court of Appeals for the First Circuit affirmed the jury's finding of a hostile work envi-ronment, noting that the incidents of maltreatment were

"outrageous" and included numerous disparaging remarks about the employee's religion, physical intimidation (one coworker grabbed him by the neck and tried to shove pork in his mouth), and other offensive conduct, often done anonymously (for example, an unsigned note left in his locker with a swastika on one side and a hate message con-taining racial and religious epithets on the other, pieces of pork placed in the pockets of his work jacket, and a picture of Osama Bin Laden hung in his locker).

In the following case, the court considered whether re-peated offensive comments by a coworker created a racially hostile work environment.

40. 510 U.S. 17 (1993).
41. 456 F.3d 228 (1st Cir. 2006).

A CASE IN POINT

Green v. Franklin National Bank of Minneapolis

United States Court of Appeals for the Eighth Circuit
459 F.3d 903 (8th Cir. 2006).

In the Language of the Court   Case 13.2

FACTS Linda Green, an African American female, worked as a teller for Franklin National Bank from March 2002 until her termination on August 26, 2002. She was transferred to the Washington Avenue branch in April after she complained that a teller at the branch where she worked had called her "stupid." Beginning in May 2002, Green worked with Jared Howard, a Caucasian male teller at the Washington branch. According to Green, Howard began harass-ing her and using racial slurs to describe her. Specifically, he called her "monkey," "black mon-key," and "chimpanzee" on at least eight occasions during a three-month period. On August 7, Howard sent her an e-mail that said, "Just wanted to let you know . . . You got a funny shaped head." Although Green asked Howard to stop using racial slurs, he persisted and engaged in other conduct toward her that she found demeaning. Green reported Howard's racial harass-ment to Kim Reep, her supervisor, who told her that she could not do anything for Green and that Green should report the conduct to Wayne Erdman, a vice president of the bank. In July, Green complained about Howard's racial harassment to Erdman, who said he would speak to Howard about it. (According to Green, Erdman never spoke with Howard about Green's com-plaint.) On August 1, Reep gave Howard a warning about his racially insensitive comments; Reep gave him a second warning on August 6.

According to the bank president, the company's policy on sexual harassment also applied to racial harassment and specified that after an employee notified his or her direct super-visor of harassment, the supervisor was required to investigate the claim. The supervisor was also responsible for attempting to resolve the complaint. There was no requirement to report harassment to the bank president. On beginning her employment, Green had signed a form acknowledging that she understood the bank's harassment policy. When Green received the e-mail about her "funny shaped head," she forwarded it to Reep, who discussed it with Erdman. The bank terminated Howard later in August 2002.

The district court granted summary judgment for the bank on Green's hostile work environ-ment claim because it found that (1) the harassment was not severe or pervasive enough to be actionable, and (2) the bank's response was adequate to preclude liability.

ISSUE PRESENTED Does repeated use of the term "monkey" and other similar words make out a prima facie case of racial harassment?

OPINION MELLOY, J., writing for the U.S. Court of Appeals for the Eighth Circuit:

In the present matter, Green's allegations about Howard's statements to her are sufficient to be actionable. His comments were frequent and directed at Green. . . .

Green had told Howard that she thought the term "Monkey" was roughly equivalent to "Nigger." Other courts have agreed with Green's assessment of calling African-Americans "monkeys." "To suggest that a human being's physical appearance is essentially a caricature of a jungle beast goes far beyond the mere unflattering; it is degrading and humiliating in the

CONTINUED

extreme." The use of the term "monkey" and other similar words have been part of actionable racial harassment claims across the country. Primate rhetoric has been used to intimidate African-Americans and monkey imagery has been significant in racial harassment in other contexts as well.

In all, there are eight alleged instances of Howard using racially insensitive terms toward Green in a three-month time frame. We have found just a few incidents in a longer time span to be sufficient for a hostile work environment.

. . . .

Taking all inferences in the light most favorable to Green, we find sufficient severity and pervasiveness of harassment for Green's claim to be actionable.

. . . .

However, we affirm the grant of summary judgment on the hostile work environment claim because Green has failed to show that Franklin National Bank did not take the proper remedial action. Title VII does not necessarily require that an employer fire a harasser. Nonetheless, Franklin National Bank did fire Howard to end the harassment against Green.

RESULT The appeals court upheld the summary judgment for the bank. Even though Howard's statements were sufficient to establish a hostile work environment, the bank had a defense because it took prompt and appropriate remedial action once Green reported the harassment to her supervisor.

COMMENTS As is explained more fully in the next section, in cases involving harassment by a coworker, employers have a defense from liability if they can show that they took appropriate corrective measures once they knew or should have known of the harassment. In this case, the court concluded that warning and then ultimately firing Howard was an adequate response.

CRITICAL THINKING QUESTIONS

1. Red Mendoza filed a sexual harassment action in which she claimed that her supervisor constantly followed her and watched her. In two instances, he looked her up and down, stopped in her groin area, and made a sniffing motion. On another occasion, he passed by her and rubbed his right hip against her left hip and touched her shoulders. Has Mendoza met her burden of proving a hostile work environment?[42]

2. Hythem Al-Salem, an immigrant from Libya, asserted that over six months he overheard a coworker call him "camel jockey" and a "sand nigger." He also alleged that a coworker offered him pork, even though he knew Al-Salem's religion forbade it, and that he had heard of his supervisor's comments that he would not be promoted. Has he met his burden of proving a hostile work environment?[43]

42. *See* Mendoza v. Borden, 195 F.3d 1238, 1245 (11th Cir. 1999).
43. *See* Al-Salem v. Bucks Cnty. Water & Sewer Auth., 1999 WL 167729 (E.D. Pa. Mar. 25, 1999).

Employer and Supervisor Liability for Hostile Environment

As explained in Chapter 5, employers are vicariously liable under the doctrine of *respondeat superior* for all torts committed by employees acting within the scope of employment. As a result, if a supervisor fails to promote an employee because of his or her national origin, for example, the employer is liable for discrimination because the supervisor was acting within the scope of employment when deciding whom to promote. But when a supervisor harasses an employee (either by demanding sexual favors or by creating a hostile environment), the supervisor is rarely acting within the scope of his or her employment.

The U.S. Supreme Court has drawn on general principles of agency law to determine when an employer is liable for the creation of a hostile environment. Under section 219(2) of the Restatement (Second) of Agency, an employer is liable for torts of employees not acting in the scope of employment if (1) the employer intended the conduct, (2) the employee's high rank makes him or her the employer's alter ego, (3) the employer was negligent, or (4) the employee was aided in accomplishing the tort by the existence of the agency relation.[44]

Negligence An employer is negligent with respect to harassment if it knew or should have known of the harassment but failed to stop it by taking appropriate corrective measures. This negligence standard governs hostile environment by coworkers (and probably customers with whom the employee must deal as part of his or her job). For example, in *Ferris v. Delta Air Lines, Inc.,*[45] the U.S. Court of Appeals for the Second Circuit found that Delta was responsible for a sexually hostile work environment that allowed the plaintiff flight attendant to be raped by a male coworker. Delta was on notice that the male employee had previously raped three other flight attendants, yet it failed to take any action against him. The court stated that Delta had a "responsibility to warn or protect likely future victims."

Aided-in-the-Agency-Relation and Supervisor Harassment In *quid pro quo* sexual harassment cases and hostile environment cases, the employer is always vicariously liable under the aided-in-the-agency-relation standard when a supervisor takes a tangible employment action against a subordinate (such as firing, failing to promote, reassigning with significantly different responsibilities, or reducing benefits). Thus, in such cases, the employer is vicariously liable for the hostile environment created by a supervisor with immediate (or successively higher) authority over the victimized employee, regardless of whether the employer knew or should have known about the supervisor's conduct.

INTERNATIONAL SNAPSHOT

In 2004, Infosys Technologies, India's largest software exporter, settled its second sexual harassment lawsuit against one of its former officers and directors, Phaneesh Murthy. Murthy was accused of harassing two American women employed in Infosys's Fremont, California office. The suit sent shockwaves through Indian software companies with U.S. operations. In 2004, the two lawsuits were settled, one for $80,000 and the other for $3 million.[a]

---

a. *Infy, Phaneesh Murthy Settle Case*, Times of Inida, Nov. 24, 2004, *available at* http://timesofindia.indiatimes.com/Infy-Phaneesh-Murthy-settle-case/articleshow/935032.cms; SarithaRai, *Harassment Suit in U.S. Shifts India's Work Culture*, N.Y. Times, Sept. 5, 2002.

In *Faragher v. City of Boca Raton,*[46] the U.S. Supreme Court applied the aided-in-the-agency-relation standard to a case involving the creation of a hostile environment by a supervisor who threatened to take tangible adverse employment action but did not do so. The Court acknowledged that in a sense a harassing supervisor is always assisted in his or her conduct by the supervisory relationship: "When a fellow employee harasses, the victim can walk away or tell the offender where to go, but it may be difficult to offer such responses to a supervisor" with the power to hire, fire, and set work schedules and pay raises.

Even so, the Court felt constrained by its prior holding in *Meritor Savings Bank v. Vinson* that the employer is not automatically liable for harassment by a supervisor. It also noted that the primary objective of Title VII is to avoid harm. To implement that statutory policy, the Court considered it appropriate "to recognize the employer's affirmative obligation to prevent violations and give credit here to employers who make the reasonable efforts to discharge their duty." At the same time, the Court acknowledged an employee's duty to avoid or mitigate harm. If the employee unreasonably failed to avail himself or herself of the employer's preventive or remedial apparatus, the employee should not recover damages that could have been avoided if he or she had done so. Accordingly, the Court held that if the supervisor's harassment does not culminate in a tangible employment action, then the employer may raise an affirmative defense to liability or damages.

To establish the defense, the employer must prove two things: (1) it exercised reasonable care to prevent and promptly correct any harassing behavior, and (2) the employee unreasonably failed to take advantage of any preventive or corrective opportunities provided by the employer or to avoid harm otherwise. For example, in *Hill v. American General Finance, Inc.,*[47] Louise Hill, a lending/collection administrator, filed a racial and sexual harassment lawsuit against American General Finance (AGF). The U.S. Court of Appeals for the Seventh Circuit affirmed the district court's decision dismissing Hill's action on the basis that AGF's policies were adequate and Hill had failed to take reasonable steps to notify the company of her harassment. In determining whether the company took corrective action, the court noted that AGF had several policies and procedures in place to help employees deal with harassment, including an equal employment policy and a sexual harassment policy. In addition, the company had established a complaint procedure that allowed aggrieved employees to report to a number of different managers. The court found that after receiving Hill's notice of harassment, the company took immediate corrective action by launching an investigation regarding her allegations. As a result of this investigation, the company punished the supervisor who had harassed her.

---

44. *See* Burlington Indus., Inc. v. Ellerth, 524 U.S. 742 (1998).
45. 277 F.3d 128 (2d Cir. 2001).

46. 524 U.S. 775 (1998).
47. 218 F.3d 639 (7th Cir. 2000).

Personal Liability As a general rule, courts have not held supervisors personally liable for discrimination against a subordinate employee in violation of Title VII.[48] However, the U.S. Court of Appeals for the Second Circuit has held that supervisors may be held personally liable for harassment under other federal statutes.[49] In addition, supervisors may be held personally liable under some state anti-discrimination statutes.[50]

Duty to Accommodate Religious Beliefs

Religious discrimination charges filed with the EEOC rose from 1,709 in 1997 to 3,790 in 2010.[51] These claims include not only refusals to hire or promote based on religious prejudice, but also allegations that employers would not give employees flexible schedules so that they could attend religious ceremonies or adjust workplace dress codes to accommodate clothing mandated by the employee's religion. A growing number of religious discrimination cases involve Christian and Muslim employees who bring their religious views into the workplace.[52]

Retaliation

Title VII and other statutes prohibit both employment discrimination and retaliation against an employee for exercising his or her protected rights. To prove a case of retaliation, an employee must demonstrate that (1) the employee's activity was protected by Title VII; (2) the employer knew of the employee's exercise of protected rights; (3) the employer took some adverse employment action against the employee, or the employee was subjected to severe or pervasive retaliatory harassment by a supervisor; and (4) there was a causal connection between the protected activity and the adverse employment action or harassment. Generally, plaintiffs file a retaliation claim in conjunction with an underlying claim of discrimination. To succeed on a claim for retaliation, however, a plaintiff does not need to prevail on his or her Title VII discrimination claim.[53] Both current and former employees can sue for retaliation.[54]

Whereas the anti-discrimination provision in Title VII expressly limits its scope to actions that affect employment or alter workplace conditions, the anti-retaliation provision is broader. The employee need only show that a reasonable employee would have found the challenged action materially adverse, that is, that it might well "have 'dissuaded a reasonable worker from making or supporting a charge of discrimination.'"[55] For example, the Supreme Court upheld a finding of retaliation when the Burlington Northern and Santa Fe Railway transferred Sheila White from forklift duty to standard track laborer tasks after she filed a complaint with the EEOC alleging sexual harassment by her supervisor. She was also suspended for thirty-seven days without pay for insubordination. Burlington ultimately reinstated her with back pay after concluding that she had not been insubordinate.

Burlington did not question the jury's determination that the motivation for the company's actions was retaliation. Instead, it questioned the statutory significance of the harm caused, arguing that the reassignment of duties should not constitute retaliatory discrimination where, as here, the former and present duties fell within the same job category. Burlington also argued that the suspension was not significant because White was reinstated with back pay.

The Court rejected Burlington's assertions. First, it concluded that the jury was not required to find that the challenged actions were related to the terms or conditions of employment. Although reassignment of job duties is not automatically actionable, a particular reassignment may be materially adverse and "should be judged from the perspective of a reasonable person in the plaintiff's position, considering 'all the circumstances.'" In this case, the jury had considerable evidence that the track laborer duties were "more arduous and dirtier" than the forklift operator position. The Court also found that White's suspension was adverse, because many reasonable employees would find a month without a paycheck to be a serious hardship. Second, it ruled that the jury's finding that each of these actions was "materially adverse" was adequately supported by the evidence.

In *Fine v. Ryan International Airlines*,[56] the U.S. Court of Appeals for the Seventh Circuit found that Ryan illegally retaliated against Fine by firing her a day after she submitted a letter outlining her multiple experiences of sexual discrimination at the company. Although Ryan claimed that Fine was fired because she "routinely missed work and was always hard to get along with," there were no written complaints about either Fine's attendance or her interpersonal skills in her personnel file.

In contrast, in *Antonio v. Sygma Network, Inc.*,[57] Gladys Antonio was unable to prove that her employer terminated her in retaliation for reporting that her supervisor, Dena Johnson, had told her that she had offensive body odor, which the supervisor attributed to Antonio's culture. Johnson

---

48. *See, e.g.*, Udoinyion v. Guardian Sec., 440 Fed. App'x 731 (11th Cir. 2011).

49. Patterson v. County of Oneida, N.Y., 375 F.3d 206 (2d Cir. 2004).

50. Dantz v. Apple Ohio LLC, 277 F. Supp. 2d 794 (N.D. Ohio 2003).

51. Equal Emp't Opportunity Comm'n, *Religion-Based Charges: FY 1997–2010, available at* http://www.eeoc.gov/eeoc/statistics/enforcement/religion.cfm (last visited Oct. 23, 2011).

52. *See, e.g.*, Jason Hoppin, *Cubicle Postings Merited Firing*, RECORDER, Jan. 7, 2004, at 1.

53. Fine v. Ryan Int'l Airlines, 305 F.3d 746 (7th Cir. 2002).

54. Robinson v. Shell Oil Co., 519 U.S. 337 (1997).

---

55. Burlington N. & Santa Fe Ry. Co. v. White, 548 U.S. 53 (2006).

56. 305 F.3d 746 (7th Cir. 2002).

57. 458 F.3d 1177 (10th Cir. 2006). *Accord* Adewole v. PSI Servs., Inc., 2011 WL 2938137 (D.D.C. July 18, 2011).

had terminated Antonio nine months after she made the complaint when she failed to return to work as scheduled after returning to Zimbabwe for a vacation. Although the court assumed that Antonio's complaint regarding Johnson's "culture" remark constituted protected opposition to discrimination, it agreed with the district court that Johnson's termination of Antonio nine months later was too temporally remote to support an inference of causation.

Actions allegedly taken to prevent further harassment may be deemed retaliation under Title VII if they harm the employee's employment situation. For example, in *DiLenno v. Goodwill Industries of Mid-Eastern Pennsylvania*,[58] the U.S. Court of Appeals for the Third Circuit found that transferring an employee to a job that the employer knew she could not perform was retaliation for her complaint that her manager was sexually harassing her. The plaintiff was transferred from her job of tagging and pricing clothing to a job requiring her to sort through clothes contributed to Goodwill. The employee's phobia of "critters," such as mice, insects, and bugs found in these bags of clothing, prevented her from performing the job. The court explained that "[i]t is important to take a plaintiff's job-related attributes into account when determining whether a lateral transfer was an adverse employment action."

The U.S. Court of Appeals for the Second Circuit held that even involuntary participation in Title VII proceedings by an employee accused of sexual harassment qualifies as protected activity. As a result, it found that an employer violated Title VII when it retaliated against an employee who had successfully defended himself against harassment charges.[59]

In the following case, the Supreme Court considered whether a man could sue for retaliation under Title VII after he was fired because his fiancée had filed a complaint of discrimination against their mutual employer.

---

58. 162 F.3d 235 (3d Cir. 1998).

59. Deravin v. Kerik, 335 F.3d 195 (2d Cir. 2003).

| A CASE IN POINT | *In the Language of the Court* | Case 13.3 |

Thompson v. North American Stainless, LP

Supreme Court of the United States
131 S. Ct. 863 (2011).

FACTS   Until 2003, both the petitioner, Eric Thompson, and his fiancée, Miriam Regalado, were employees of North American Stainless (NAS). In February 2003, North American was notified by the EEOC that Regalado had filed sex discrimination charges against the company. Thompson was fired three weeks later. Thompson filed a charge with the EEOC and then sued under Title VII, alleging that North American had fired him to retaliate against Regalado for filing her charge with the EEOC.

The trial court granted summary judgment to North American, finding that Title VII "does not permit third party retaliation claims." After the U.S. Court of Appeals for the Sixth Circuit affirmed that decision, Thompson appealed.

ISSUE PRESENTED   Does Title VII create a cause of action for third-party victims of retaliation?

OPINION   SCALIA, J., writing on behalf of the U.S. Supreme Court:

II

. . . Title VII's antiretaliation provision prohibits any employer action that "well might have dissuaded a reasonable worker from making or supporting a charge of discrimination."

We think it obvious that a reasonable worker might be dissuaded from engaging in protected activity if she knew that her fiancé would be fired. . . . NAS raises the concern, however, that prohibiting reprisals against third parties will lead to difficult line-drawing problems concerning the types of relationships entitled to protection. Perhaps retaliating against an employee by firing his fiancée would dissuade the employee from engaging in protected activity, but what about firing an employee's girlfriend, close friend, or trusted co-worker?

Although we acknowledge the force of this point, we do not think it justifies a categorical rule that third-party reprisals do not violate Title VII. . . .

We must also decline to identify a fixed class of relationships for which third-party reprisals are unlawful. We expect that firing a close family member will almost always meet the *Burlington*[60]

CONTINUED

---

60. Burlington N. & Santa Fe Ry. Co. v. White, 548 U.S. 53 (2006).

standard, and inflicting a milder reprisal on a mere acquaintance will almost never do so, but beyond that we are reluctant to generalize. As we explained in *Burlington*, "the significance of any given act of retaliation will often depend upon the particular circumstances." Given the broad statutory text and the variety of workplace contexts in which retaliation may occur, Title VII's antiretaliation provision is simply not reducible to a comprehensive set of clear rules. We emphasize, however, that "the provision's standard for judging harm must be objective," so as to "avoi[d] the uncertainties and unfair discrepancies that can plague a judicial effort to determine a plaintiff's unusual subjective feelings."

III

The more difficult question in this case is whether Thompson may sue NAS for its alleged violation of Title VII. The statute provides that "a civil action may be brought . . . by the person claiming to be aggrieved." . . . It is arguable that the aggrievement referred to is nothing more than the minimal Article III standing, which consists of injury in fact caused by the defendant and remediable by the court. . . .

. . . If any person injured in the Article III sense by a Title VII violation could sue, absurd consequences would follow. For example, a shareholder would be able to sue a company for firing a valuable employee for racially discriminatory reasons, so long as he could show that the value of his stock decreased as a consequence. . . . [T]herefore [we] conclude that the term "aggrieved" must be construed more narrowly than the outer boundaries of Article III.

At the other extreme from the position that "person aggrieved" means anyone with Article III standing, NAS argues that it is a term of art that refers only to the employee who engaged in the protected activity. We know of no other context in which the words carry this artificially narrow meaning, and if that is what Congress intended it would more naturally have said "person claiming to have been discriminated against" rather than "person claiming to be aggrieved." We see no basis in text or prior practice for limiting the latter phrase to the person who was the subject of unlawful retaliation. . . .

In our view there is a common usage of the term "person aggrieved" that avoids the extremity of equating it with Article III. . . . The Administrative Procedure Act . . . authorizes suit to challenge a federal agency by any "person . . . adversely affected or aggrieved . . . within the meaning of a relevant statute." We have held that this language establishes a regime under which a plaintiff may not sue unless he "falls within the 'zone of interests' sought to be protected by the statutory provision whose violation forms the legal basis for his complaint." . . . We hold that the term "aggrieved" in Title VII incorporates this test, enabling suit by any plaintiff with an interest "arguably [sought] to be protected by the statutes," while excluding plaintiffs who might technically be injured in an Article III sense but whose interests are unrelated to the statutory prohibitions in Title VII.

Applying that test here, we conclude that Thompson falls within the zone of interests protected by Title VII. Thompson was an employee of NAS, and the purpose of Title VII is to protect employees from their employers' unlawful actions. Moreover, accepting the facts as alleged, Thompson is not an accidental victim of the retaliation—collateral damage, so to speak, of the employer's unlawful act. To the contrary, injuring him was the employer's intended means of harming Regalado. Hurting him was the unlawful act by which the employer punished her.

RESULT   The judgment of the Sixth Circuit was reversed. Thompson could sue for retaliation.

Special Applications of Title VII

Civil rights legislation was founded on the fundamental premise that individuals should not be denied a job or an opportunity on the job because of their race, color, religion, national origin, or sex. The law has expanded beyond that basic premise to reach more subtle forms of discrimination.

Sexual Stereotyping

In *Price Waterhouse v. Hopkins*,[61] Ann Hopkins was denied a partnership in the accounting firm PricewaterhouseCoopers after being told by the policy board that, to improve her

---

61. 490 U.S. 228 (1989).

chances for partnership, she should "walk more femininely, talk more femininely, dress more femininely, wear make-up, have her hair styled, and wear jewelry." The U.S. Supreme Court concluded that the evidence produced by Hopkins was sufficient to establish that sexual stereotyping played a part in the firm's decision not to promote her and held that it constituted discrimination based on sex. With respect to sexual stereotyping, the Court stated: "An employer who objects to aggressiveness in women but whose positions require this trait places women in an intolerable and impermissible Catch-22: out of a job if they behave aggressively and out of a job if they don't. Title VII lifts women out of this bind."[62] In addition, although the case dealt with gender discrimination, the Court expressly stated that all references to gender and all principles announced in the opinion "apply with equal force to discrimination based on race, religion, or national origin."

Pregnancy Discrimination

The Pregnancy Discrimination Act provides that discrimination on the basis of pregnancy is, on its face, a form of sex discrimination under Title VII.[63] For example, the U.S. Court of Appeals for the Sixth Circuit held that a female employee who was promised a promotion to supervisor, but was offered a lesser promotion after her employer learned she was pregnant, made out a prima facie case of discrimination.[64]

These protections are not absolute, however. In *Reeves v. Swift Transportation Co.*,[65] a former employee who was pregnant sued Swift claiming that she was wrongfully terminated when she became pregnant. Swift terminated the employee pursuant to a policy that denied light-duty work to employees who could not perform heavy lifting and also had not been injured on the job. The U.S. Court of Appeals for the Sixth Circuit affirmed the district court's grant of summary judgment in favor of Swift. The court stated: "Swift's light-duty policy is indisputably pregnancy-blind. It simply does not grant or deny light work on the basis of pregnancy, childbirth, or related medical conditions. It makes this determination on the nonpregnancy-related basis of whether there has been a work-related injury or condition."

Fetal-Protection Policies

Certain substances used in manufacturing are harmful to the fetus being carried by a pregnant woman. In an effort to avoid such harm, and related lawsuits for unsafe working environments, some companies adopted so-called *fetal-protection policies*, which barred a woman from certain

jobs unless her inability to bear children was medically documented. In *International Union, United Automobile, Aerospace & Agriculture Implement Workers of America, UAW, v. Johnson Controls, Inc.*,[66] the U.S. Supreme Court held that Johnson Controls' policy, which precluded women with childbearing capacity from working at jobs in which lead levels were defined as excessive, was a facially discriminatory policy forbidden under Title VII and ruled that women cannot be excluded from certain jobs because of their childbearing capacity. The Court stated that "[d]ecisions about the welfare of future children must be left to the parents who conceive, bear, support, and raise them rather than to the employers who hire those parents."

In the wake of *Johnson Controls*, employers have been forced to walk a fine line between avoiding discrimination related to pregnancy and limiting or reducing potential workplace hazards. For example, in *Asad v. Continental Airlines, Inc.*,[67] Asad sued Continental under state tort laws claiming that Continental was responsible for her newborn son's cerebral palsy. Asad had requested a job transfer for the duration of her pregnancy to escape exposure to carbon monoxide fumes. Continental refused the transfer, citing *Johnson Controls* and other cases holding that the Pregnancy Discrimination Act (PDA) does not require employers to "accommodate" pregnant women.[68] The U.S. District Court for the Northern District of Ohio deviated from prior court rulings when it held that although *Johnson Controls* demonstrated that employers could not prevent women who are or who may become pregnant from working in an environment that may be hazardous to a fetus, "the PDA and Title VII should not prevent an employer from temporarily transferring a pregnant woman, at her request, for the protection of her fetus."

Family Responsibilities

As of 2009, the Center for Work-Life Law and the Hastings College of the Law at the University of California had identified more than 2,000 cases of *family responsibility discrimination (FRD)*, also referred to as maternal wall discrimination, based on sexual stereotyping.[69] Although the traditional way to prove disparate treatment under Title VII is by use of comparative evidence (that is, evidence of how nonprotected class members are treated), the U.S. Court of Appeals for the Second Circuit ruled in *Back v. Hastings on*

---

62. *Id.*

63. 42 U.S.C. § 2000e(k).

64. Lulaj v. Wackenhut Corp., 512 F.3d 760 (6th Cir. 2008).

65. 446 F.3d 637 (6th Cir. 2006).

66. 499 U.S. 187 (1991).

67. 328 F. Supp. 2d 772 (N.D. Ohio 2004).

68. *See* Int'l Union, United Auto., Aerospace & Agric. Implement Workers of Am., UAW v. Johnson Controls, Inc., 499 U.S. 187 (1991); Spivey v. Beverly Enters., Inc., 196 F.3d 1309 (11th Cir. 1999); Armstrong v. Flowers Hosp., Inc., 33 F.3d 1308 (11th Cir. 1994); Duncan v. Children's Nat'l Med. Ctr., 702 A.2d 207 (D.C. App. 1997).

69. Stephanie Bornstein & Robert J. Rathmell, *Caregivers as a Protected Class?: The Growth of State and Local Laws Prohibiting Family Responsibilities Discrimination*, CTR. FOR WORK-LIFE LAW (Dec. 2009), *available at* http://www.worklifelaw.org/pubs/LocalFRDLawsReport.pdf.

Hudson Union Free School District[70] that disparate treatment can also be proved by evidence of gender stereotyping:

> The defendants argue that stereotypes about women or mothers are not based upon gender, but rather, "gender plus parenthood," thereby implying that such stereotypes cannot, without comparative evidence of what was said about fathers, be presumed to be "on the basis of sex.". . . [It is particularly] clear, however, that, at least where stereotypes are considered, the notions that mothers are insufficiently devoted to work, and that work and motherhood are incompatible, are properly considered to be, themselves, gender-based.

The *Back* case involved a school psychologist who was denied tenure because her employer assumed that, because she had children, she would not continue to work hard if she was granted tenure. In another case, an outstanding lawyer was not offered a promotion because her employer assumed she would not be willing to travel because she was a mother.[71]

FRD can also affect fathers. One study found that fathers who took parental leave were recommended for fewer rewards and had lower performance ratings than mothers.[72] FRD affects blue-collar workers as well as professionals. In addition to disparate treatment and disparate impact cases, plaintiffs have also brought FRD cases based on hostile environment. For example, a jury found that a woman had been subjected to a hostile work environment based on evidence that her supervisor complained about absences caused by her son's ear infections, attached signs ("Out—Sick Child") to her cubicle when she had to care for him, informed her that she had to make up "every minute" she was away from the office for doctor's appointments, warned her not to get pregnant again, and threw a phone book on her desk and told her to find a pediatrician whose office was open after hours.[73]

Interracial Association

In *Holcomb v. Iona College*,[74] a white assistant coach of the Iona College basketball team alleged that he was fired because he was married to an African American woman. The U.S. Court of Appeals for the Second Circuit joined the Fifth, Sixth, and Eleventh Circuits in ruling that Title VII protects employees from discrimination based on their association with a person of a different race. The court reasoned that "where an employee is subjected to adverse action because an employer disapproves of interracial association, the employee suffers discrimination because of the employee's own race."

English-Only Laws

The national origin provisions of Title VII have been used to challenge workplace rules that prohibit employees from speaking any language other than English at work. The EEOC has taken the position that language is closely linked with national origin, so English-only policies can have a disparate impact on Hispanic employees and others whose native language may not be English.[75] Federal courts have agreed with the EEOC.

For example, the U.S. Court of Appeals for the Tenth Circuit reversed a grant of summary judgment to a Title VII defendant after finding that the plaintiffs had made out a prima facie case that the defendant's English-only rule created a hostile environment for Hispanic employees. The court noted that an English-only policy itself, not just its effect, may create or contribute to the hostility of the work environment:

> Here, the very fact that the [defendant] City would forbid Hispanics from using their preferred language could reasonably be construed as an expression of hostility to Hispanics. At least that could be a reasonable inference if there was no apparent legitimate purpose for the restrictions. It would be unreasonable to take offense at a requirement that all pilots flying into an airport speak English in communications with the tower or between planes; but hostility would be a reasonable inference to draw from a requirement that an employee calling home during a work break speak only in English. The less the apparent justification for mandating English, the more reasonable it is to infer hostility toward employees whose ethnic group or nationality favors another language.[76]

Dress Codes

Although employers have the right to enact and enforce dress codes, these codes can result in legal claims involving religious and sexual discrimination and harassment. The trend of employers allowing employees to wear casual clothing has the potential to further complicate this matter.

Employees have based claims of religious discrimination on their employer's refusal to let them wear turbans rather than protective headgear. In response, the Occupational Safety and Health Administration amended its regulations to exempt persons wearing turbans from its hard-hat requirements.

In the following case, the court considered whether a clothing retailer violated Title VII when it refused to hire a Muslim woman because she wore a head scarf.

---

70. 365 F.3d 107 (2d Cir. 2004).

71. Trezza v. Hartford, Inc., 1998 U.S. Dist. LEXIS 20206 (S.D.N.Y. 1998).

72. Lori Jablczynski, *Striking a Balance Between the "Parental" Wall and Workplace Equality: The Male Caregiver Perspective*, 31 WOMEN'S RTS. L. REP. 309, 317 (2010).

73. Walsh v. Nat'l Computer Sys., Inc., 332 F.3d 1150 (8th Cir. 2003).

74. 521 F.3d 130 (2d Cir. 2008).

75. Barbara Yuill, *Employment Discrimination—Language: At Panel Discussion on National Origin Bias EEOC Says English-Only Challenges Are Rising*, 66 U.S.L.W. 2375 (1997).

76. Maldonado v. City of Altus, 433 F.3d 1294 (10th Cir. 2006).

EEOC v. Abercrombie & Fitch Stores, Inc.

United States District Court for the Northern District of Oklahoma 798 F. Supp. 2d 1272 (N.D. Okla. 2011).

FACTS   Samantha Elauf, a Muslim since birth, has worn a traditional head scarf in public since reaching the age of puberty. She considers it a "representation and reminder of her faith, a religious symbol, a symbol of Islam and of modesty." In June 2008, she applied for a job at the Abercrombie Kids store in Woodland Hills Mall in Tulsa, Oklahoma. Abercrombie requires its employees to comply with a strict "Look Policy," which requires employees to dress in clothing and merchandise consistent with those sold at the store. It also prohibits facial hair, necklaces, bracelets, and hats.

Heather Cooke, the assistant store manager, interviewed Elauf. At the interview, Elauf wore clothes consistent with those sold at the store, as well as her head scarf. Cooke did not inquire about Elauf's scarf at the interview and did not tell her about the Look Policy, although she did tell Elauf to wear clothing consistent with that sold by Abercrombie and not to wear heavy makeup or nail polish. Although Cooke was under the impression that Elauf wore the scarf for religious reasons, she was unsure whether it would conflict with the store's Look Policy against head gear. She contacted her store manager about the issue and recommended that Elauf be hired for the position.

Cooke's store manager was also unsure how to handle the situation so he forwarded the matter to the district manager, Randall Johnson. Johnson told Cooke not to hire Elauf because she wore the head scarf, which was the equivalent of wearing a hat. Johnson said that if Elauf was allowed to wear one, other employees would think they could as well. At Johnson's prompting, Cooke threw away her initial assessment of Elauf, including the scores that would allow her to be recommended for the position, and lowered the scores on her appearance because of the scarf so that she would receive a subpar assessment. Elauf was not hired as a result.

The EEOC sued on behalf of Elauf pursuant to Title VII, alleging that Abercrombie discriminated against her on the basis of her religion by failing to reasonably accommodate her religious beliefs. Both parties moved for summary judgment.

ISSUE PRESENTED   Is a clothing retailer, whose image is based on the look of its sales personnel, required to make an exception for a potential employee whose religious beliefs require her to wear a head scarf inconsistent with the company's dress code?

SUMMARY OF OPINION   The U.S. District Court for the Northern District of Oklahoma began by stating that Title VII requires an employer to offer reasonable accommodations for an employee's religious beliefs unless doing so would cause "undue hardship on the conduct of the employer's business." The court found that Elauf established a prima facie case that she was discriminated against for her religious beliefs: her belief requires her to wear a head scarf; the donning of that scarf is in violation of Abercrombie's Look Policy; Abercrombie was on notice that Elauf wore a head scarf due to her religious beliefs; and she was subsequently not hired as a result.

Abercrombie attempted to rebut Elauf's showing of a prima facie case by alleging that wearing the head scarf was not a "bona fide religious belief," because those beliefs were not "sincerely held" and because it was a cultural rather than religious belief. The court rejected Abercrombie's assertion that because Muslim women are not required by the Quran to wear a head scarf, wearing a scarf is not a religious belief. Elauf "testified that she considers the head scarf to be a representation and reminder of her faith, a religious symbol, a symbol of Islam and of modesty." Additionally, the court explained, the "broad definition of 'religion' does not require that a belief have a textual basis." It was enough that Elauf believed that *she* should wear a head scarf because of her religion.

Further, just because Elauf did not pray five times a day, or even every day as devout, practicing Muslims do, did not mean that her belief was not sincerely held. The court found the record devoid of *any* evidence that Elauf's belief was animated by motives of deception and fraud. The record showed that she had consistently worn the scarf in the presence of unfamiliar males and in public since age thirteen, and "[t]here is no evidence Elauf has sought or received financial gain by wearing the head scarf."

CONTINUED

Abercrombie then argued that allowing Elauf to wear a head scarf would result in an "undue hardship" for the company. The court explained that an "accommodation which results in 'more than a de *minimus* cost' is an undue hardship to the employer and the employer need not provide the accommodation." However, the court explained, "[a]ny proffered hardship . . . must be actual; [a]n employer cannot rely merely on speculation. A claim of undue hardship cannot be supported by merely conceivable or hypothetical hardship. . . . The *magnitude* as well as the *fact* of hardship must be determined by examination of the facts of each case."

Although several Abercrombie executives testified that they believed that granting Elauf an exception to the Look Policy would have a negative impact on the brand, sales, and compliance, none had conducted any studies. Nor could they cite specific examples to support their opinion. Instead, Abercrombie relied on an expert who testified extensively about the importance of the in-store experience to Abercrombie's marketing strategy and opined that the granting of even one exception to the Look Policy would negatively affect the brand. The court concluded that his opinion was too speculative to establish actual hardship because he failed to take account of the fact that Abercrombie had granted numerous exceptions to the Look Policy since 2001, including eight or nine recent head scarf exceptions.

The court ruled that Abercrombie had failed to meet its burden of establishing that granting Elauf an exception to the Look Policy would have caused undue hardship. As a result, Abercrombie violated Title VII when it did not hire Elauf.

RESULT   The EEOC's motion for partial summary judgment as to liability was granted. The employer failed to reasonably accommodate Elauf's religious beliefs.

Defenses Under Title VII

Title VII sets forth several statutory defenses to claims of discriminatory treatment. Of these, the defense of bona fide occupational qualification is most frequently cited.

Bona Fide Occupational Qualification

Title VII provides that an employer may lawfully hire an individual on the basis of religion, sex, or national origin if religion, sex, or national origin is a *bona fide occupational qualification (BFOQ)* reasonably necessary to the normal operation of that particular business. This is known as the *BFOQ defense.* The BFOQ defense is not available when discriminatory treatment is based on a person's race or color. Because BFOQ is an affirmative defense, the employer has the burden of showing a reasonable basis for believing that the category of persons (for example, women) excluded from a particular job was unable to perform that job.

The BFOQ defense has been narrowly construed. EEOC regulations provide that gender will not qualify as a BFOQ when a gender-based restriction is based on (1) assumptions of the comparative employment characteristics of women in general (such as the assumption that women have a higher turnover rate than men); (2) stereotyped characterizations of the sexes (for example, that men are less capable of assembling intricate equipment than women); or (3) the preferences of coworkers, employers, or customers for one gender or the other.[77] Gender will be considered a BFOQ when physical attributes are important for authenticity (as with actors) or when a gender-based restriction is necessary to protect the rights of others to privacy (as with restroom attendants).

Seniority and Merit Systems

Title VII states that it is not unlawful for employers to apply different standards of compensation, or different terms, conditions, or privileges of employment pursuant to a bona fide seniority or merit system, provided that such differences are not the result of an intention to discriminate because of race, color, religion, sex, or national origin. This is considered an exemption from Title VII rather than an affirmative defense. Consequently, the plaintiff has the burden of proving the employer had a discriminatory intent or illegal purpose in implementing the seniority or merit system. Moreover, although a disproportionate impact may be used as evidence of discriminatory intent, such an impact is not, in itself, sufficient to establish discriminatory intent.

After-Acquired Evidence

When an employee initiates a suit under Title VII, the employer will sometimes learn during the course of discovery that the individual violated company rules. Under these circumstances, employers have argued that the plaintiff's

---

77. 29 C.F.R. pts. 1604.2(a)(1)(i)–1604.2(a)(1)(iii).

discrimination claim should fail because, had the employer known of the employee misconduct, the employee would have been discharged anyway.

In *McKennon v. Nashville Banner Publishing Co.*,[78] the U.S. Supreme Court held that after-acquired evidence of misconduct does not bar a discrimination claim. But the employee misconduct is not ignored: remedies available to plaintiffs in cases involving misconduct should be limited to back pay and should not include reinstatement or front pay.

Remedies Under Title VII

In addition to back pay, front pay, and other compensatory damages, as well as reinstatement and other injunctive relief, a prevailing plaintiff may be able to recover punitive damages in certain cases of intentional discrimination.

Punitive Damages

Punitive damages may be awarded under Title VII only in cases of "intentional discrimination," that is, cases that do not rely on the disparate impact theory of discrimination.[79] To recover punitive damages, the complaining party must demonstrate that the employer engaged in a discriminatory practice or practices "with malice or with reckless indifference to the federally protected rights of an aggrieved individual." The employee is not required to show that the employer engaged in egregious misconduct, however. Rather, the employee must show that the employer had the requisite discriminatory mental state. Punitive damages are available and can be awarded even if the jury awarded no compensatory damages.[80] (Punitive damages are not available in suits against a government, governmental agency, or political subdivision.)

Even if the employee can show the requisite malice or indifference, the employer still may not be liable for punitive damages. If the employer has engaged in "good-faith efforts" to comply with Title VII, then it is not vicariously liable for punitive damages based on discriminatory employment decisions by managerial agents when those decisions were contrary to the company's good faith efforts. To hold otherwise, the Supreme Court reasoned, would reduce the incentive for employers to implement anti-discrimination programs.

The U.S. Court of Appeals for the Fourth Circuit affirmed a compensatory damages award of $600,000, based on evidence that the defendant's managers had created a racially hostile environment through their constant use of racial slurs and insults and the defendant's failure to respond to repeated complaints by the plaintiffs' shop steward, but the court overturned the punitive damages

award of $1.2 million.[81] The court held that even though the employer's antiharassment policy and training had been ineffective to stop the hostile environment, they operated as a total bar to a punitive damages award:

> While the ineffectiveness of an antiharassment policy defeats an employer's affirmative defense . . . , a policy's ineffectiveness alone cannot demonstrate the lack of good faith required for justifying an award of punitive damages. If it could, employers with antiharassment policies who failed on their affirmative defenses would automatically be exposed to punitive damages . . . .

Caps on Liability

In federal cases, compensatory and punitive damages available for discrimination based on sex or religion are capped by the Civil Rights Act of 1991 at $50,000 for employers of 100 or fewer employees, $100,000 for employers with 101 to 200 employees, $200,000 for employers with 201 to 500 employees, and $300,000 for employers with more than 500 employees.[82] These compensatory caps do not apply to intentional racial or ethnic discrimination, however. In addition, front pay is not considered compensatory damages, so it is not subject to the cap on compensatory awards.[83] Employees claiming discrimination frequently sue under state employment-discrimination laws, which often do not include caps on damages.

Courts may also decide to limit the amount of compensatory damages awarded a plaintiff. For example, the Supreme Court of Michigan threw out a $21 million jury award to a sexual harassment plaintiff on the basis that it was excessive.[84]

AGE DISCRIMINATION

As the baby boomers, who comprise a substantial percentage of the American workforce, grow older, the issue of age discrimination in employment has become more visible. By 2018, workers over the age of fifty-five will constitute nearly 25% of the workforce.[85]

The Age Discrimination in Employment Act (ADEA) prohibits age discrimination in employment with respect to individuals aged forty years or older. To establish a prima facie case of age discrimination under the ADEA,

---

78. 513 U.S. 352 (1995).

79. Kolstad v. Am. Dental Ass'n, 527 U.S. 526 (1999).

80. *See id.*; Timm v. Progressive Steel Treating, Inc., 137 F.3d 1008 (7th Cir. 1998); Cush-Crawford v. Adchem Corp., 271 F.3d 352 (2d Cir. 2001); Corti v. Storage Tech. Corp., 304 F.3d 336 (4th Cir. 2002).

81. White v. BFI Waste Servs., LLC, 198 F. App'x 283 (4th Cir. 2006).

82. Civil Rights Act of 1991, Pub. L. No. 102-106, § 1977(a)(b)(3), 105 Stat. 1071 (1991).

83. Pollard v. E.I. du Pont de Nemours & Co., 532 U.S. 843 (2001). *But see* Peyton v. DiMario, 287 F.3d 1121 (D.C. Cir. 2002) (stating that awards of front pay may be considered too speculative, and thus reduced, if the length of time for which the front pay was awarded is considered too great).

84. Gilbert v. DaimlerChrysler Corp., 685 N.W.2d 391 (Mich. 2004).

85. *See* U.S. Dep't of Labor, Bureau of Labor Statistics, *Employment Projections: 2008–18* (Dec. 10, 2009), *available at* http://www.bls.gov/news.release/ecopro.nr0.htm.

the employee must prove that he or she (1) was within the protected age group, (2) was qualified for the position at issue, (3) suffered an adverse employment action, and (4) was replaced by a sufficiently younger person.[86] Individuals under age forty have no protection from discrimination based on age. Courts have held that the employer, not the individual making the discriminatory decision, is liable for age discrimination.[87]

The substantive provisions of the ADEA are similar in many respects to those of Title VII. The ADEA generally prohibits age discrimination with respect to employee hiring, firing, and compensation, as well as with respect to the terms, conditions, and privileges of employment.

Unlike Title VII, which authorizes claims in any case where an improper consideration was "a motivating factor" for an adverse employment action, the ADEA does not authorize mixed-motive age discrimination claims.[88] Thus, in an ADEA case, "[a] plaintiff must prove by a preponderance of the evidence (which may be direct or circumstantial), that age was the 'but-for' cause of the challenged employer decision."[89]

As with Title VII, creation of a hostile environment because of age is a form of age discrimination.[90] The ADEA also prohibits retaliation against an individual aged forty or older because of the individual's opposition to unlawful age discrimination, or because he or she has made a charge or testified or assisted in an investigation, proceeding, or litigation under the ADEA.

Although the ADEA protects individuals over the age of forty, age discrimination cannot be inferred simply because the replacement employee is outside the protected class.[91] In other words, replacing a forty-year-old employee with a thirty-nine-year-old employee does not give rise to a stronger inference of discrimination than replacing a fifty-two-year-old employee with a forty-year-old employee. Rather, "the fact that a replacement is substantially younger than the plaintiff is a far more reliable indicator of age discrimination."

Even so, the ADEA prohibits unlawful age discrimination among persons within the protected age group. Thus, for example, if two individuals aged forty-one and fifty-three apply for the same position, the employer may not lawfully reject either applicant on the basis of age. On the other hand, an employer may still have engaged in age discrimination by rejecting someone over forty in favor of another person over forty if the chosen candidate is substantially younger than the

rejected candidate.[92] The ADEA does not protect younger workers over forty against older workers, however.[93]

A finding of liability for intentional discrimination under the ADEA can be based solely on the plaintiff's prima facie case of discrimination together with sufficient evidence for a reasonable fact finder to reject the employer's nondiscriminatory explanation for its decision.[94] In order to create a genuine issue of material fact as to whether the employer's nondiscriminatory explanation is pretextual, the plaintiff must "point to some evidence, direct or circumstantial, from which a fact finder could reasonably either (1) disbelieve the employer's articulated legitimate reasons; or (2) believe that an invidious discriminatory reason was more likely than not a motivating or determinative cause of the employer's action."[95]

The ADEA does not guarantee workplaces "free from the ordinary ebb and flow of power relations and inter-office politics." In *Suarez v. Pueblo International, Inc.*,[96] the U.S. Court of Appeals for the First Circuit held that Ramon Suarez, the fifty-nine-year-old president of CaribAd (a subsidiary of Pueblo International), was not constructively discharged based on age when Pueblo was restructured and most of CaribAd's employees were relocated to corporate headquarters, leaving Suarez alone in an office with a receptionist. Although Suarez was told that the in-house advertising for which he had been responsible was being transferred to someone else and that he would be responsible for bringing in new clients, he maintained his position as president and continued to be paid his salary of $190,000 a year. The court stated that "[i]n that rarified [sic] financial atmosphere . . . an increase in work requirements that does not surpass reasonable expectations" cannot sustain a constructive discharge claim. Even if Pueblo was attempting to marginalize Suarez, the "unpleasantness, hurt feelings, and wounded pride" that resulted did not create working conditions that were "so onerous, abusive or unpleasant that a reasonable person in the employee's position would have felt compelled to resign."

Disparate Impact and the Defense of a Reasonable Factor Other Than Age

Employer actions that on their face do not discriminate based on age may still violate the ADEA if they have a statistically significant impact on workers over forty.[97]

---

86. Anderson v. Consol. Rail Corp., 297 F.3d 242 (3d Cir. 2002).

87. Stults v. Conoco, Inc., 76 F.3d 651 (5th Cir. 1996).

88. Gross v. FBL Fin. Servs., Inc., 557 U.S. 167 (2009).

89. *Id.*

90. Crawford v. Medina Gen. Hosp., 96 F.3d 830 (6th Cir. 1996) (finding the hostile work environment claim a "relatively uncontroversial proposition").

91. O'Connor v. Consol. Coin Caterers Corp., 517 U.S. 308 (1996).

92. *Id. See also* D'Cunha v. Genovese/Eckerd Corp., 479 F.3d 193, 195 (2d Cir. 2007).

93. Gen. Dynamics Land Sys., Inc. v. Cline, 540 U.S. 581 (2004). *See* Rules & Regulations, 72 Fed. Reg. 36,873, which was amended to conform with the U.S. Supreme Court's holding in *General Dynamics Land Systems, Inc. v. Cline.*

94. Reeves v. Sanderson Plumbing Prods., Inc., 530 U.S. 133 (2000).

95. Tomasso v. Boeing Co., 445 F.3d 702, 706 (3d Cir. 2006) (citing Fuentes v. Perskie, 32 F.3d 759, 764 (3d Cir. 1994)).

96. 229 F.3d 49 (1st Cir. 2000).

97. Smith v. City of Jackson, Miss., 544 U.S. 228 (2005).

Nevertheless, the scope of disparate impact liability is narrower under the ADEA than under Title VII. Recognizing that "age, unlike race or other classifications protected by Title VII, not uncommonly has relevance to an individual's capacity to engage in certain types of employment," the Supreme Court ruled that employees must identify the specific test, requirement, or practice that is responsible for any observed statistical disparities. It is not enough to point to a generalized policy that leads to such an impact.[98] Moreover, even if the employee identifies the relevant practice, the employer has a defense if the employer bases its decision on a *"reasonable factor other than age"* (the *RFOA defense*).[99] The employer in a disparate impact case has the burden of proving that its decision was made based on such reasonable factors. The employer is not required to show business necessity, however.

Older Workers' Benefit Protection Act

The Older Workers' Benefit Protection Act[100] (OWBPA) prohibits age discrimination in providing employee benefits. It also establishes minimum standards for employees who waive their rights under the ADEA.

To meet the minimum standards, the employee waiver must be "knowing and voluntary." The employee must be given at least twenty-one days to consider whether to enter into an agreement waiving rights under the ADEA. This period is extended to forty-five days when the waiver is in connection with an early retirement or exit-incentive plan offered to a group or class of employees. The agreement must also give the employee a period of at least seven days following execution of the agreement during which the employee may revoke it. An employee who has accepted a severance payment in exchange for waiving his or her rights under the ADEA can still sue the employer for violation of the ADEA without having to return the payment if the waiver was not made in accordance with the OWBPA.[101]

Employers may revoke a proposed early retirement agreement during the time frame that the OWBPA gives employees to act on it. For example, the U.S. Court of Appeals for the Eighth Circuit held that an employer could revoke a separation agreement containing a waiver of claims under the ADEA and provide a new, less valuable agreement, after the employer learned that the employee had made defamatory statements about the company.[102]

Defenses

An employer faced with an age discrimination claim may assert in its defense that (1) age is a BFOQ reasonably necessary to the normal operation of the business (extremely difficult to prove); (2) the differential treatment is based on reasonable factors other than age (the RFOA defense discussed earlier in the chapter); (3) the employer's action is based on a bona fide seniority system or employee benefit plan—such as a retirement, pension, or insurance plan—that is not invoked as a subterfuge to evade the purposes of the ADEA; or (4) the discharge or discipline of a protected individual was for good cause.[103] Although these defenses are set forth in the ADEA itself, employers should proceed with caution because the courts construe them strictly.

Remedies Under the ADEA

Employees who bring successful claims under the ADEA or the OWBPA are entitled to both equitable relief, which includes hiring, wage adjustments, promotion, or reinstatement, and monetary relief.[104] Monetary remedies include back pay, front pay, and liquidated damages. Liquidated damages equal to the amounts owing to a person as a result of the violation are provided only in the event of willful violations by the employer. Compensatory damages and punitive damages are also available under the ADEA.

DISABILITY DISCRIMINATION

Title I of the Americans with Disabilities Act (ADA) prohibits employers from discriminating against a qualified individual because of a disability in regard to job application procedures, hiring, advancement, discharge, compensation, job training, and other terms, conditions, and privileges of employment. Such discrimination includes the use of selection criteria to screen out individuals with disabilities unless the criteria are job related and consistent with business necessity. The ADA requires employers to make "reasonable accommodations" as requested by employees who have a "physical or mental impairment that substantially limits a major life activity."

Impermissible Discrimination

Under the ADA, employers are prohibited from (1) intentionally discriminating against disabled persons and (2) engaging in employment practices that are not intentionally discriminatory, but have the effect of discriminating against disabled persons or perpetuating the past effects of such

---

98. This is the standard of proof the U.S. Supreme Court imposed in *Wards Cove Packing Co. v. Atonio*, 490 U.S. 642 (1986), for disparate impact cases under Title VII before Congress expanded the coverage of Title VII in the Civil Rights Act of 1991 (§ 2, 105 Stat. 1071 (1991)).

99. Meacham v. Knolls Atomic Power Lab., 554 U.S. 84 (2008).

100. 29 U.S.C. § 623(f).

101. Oubre v. Entergy Operations, Inc., 522 U.S. 422 (1998).

102. Ellison v. Premier Salons Int'l, Inc., 164 F.3d 1111 (8th Cir. 1999).

103. 29 U.S.C. § 623(f).

104. Equal Emp't Opportunity Comm'n, *When a Charge Is Filed Against My Company, available at* http://archive.eeoc.gov/employers/charges-filed.html (last modified Dec. 17, 2001).

discrimination. The term "discriminate" as construed by the ADA includes the following prohibited practices:

1. Limiting, segregating, or classifying an applicant or employee because of his or her disability so as to adversely affect his or her opportunities or status.

2. Entering into a contractual relationship with an employment or referral agency, union, or other organization that has the effect of subjecting applicants or employees with a disability to prohibited discrimination.

3. Using standards, criteria, or methods of administration that have the effect of discriminating or perpetuating the effects of discrimination because of disability.

4. Not making reasonable accommodations to the known physical or mental limitations of an otherwise qualified applicant or employee with a disability, unless to do so would impose undue hardship on the employer.

5. Denying job opportunities to an otherwise qualified applicant or employee with a disability in order to avoid having to make reasonable accommodations for that disability.

6. Using qualification standards or employment tests that tend to screen out individuals with disabilities, unless the standards or tests are shown to be job related and consistent with business necessity.

7. Failing to select and conduct job testing in such a way as to ensure that when the test is administered to an applicant or employee with a disability that impairs his or her sensory, manual, or speaking skills, the results of the test accurately reflect the skills or aptitude that test is designed to measure, rather than reflecting the sensory, manual, or speaking impairment.

The employee must be able to attend work to be considered a "qualified individual" within the meaning of the ADA. Thus, an employee diagnosed with depression who was unable to attend work did not qualify for protection under the ADA.[105]

Both disparate treatment and disparate impact cases can be brought under the ADA.[106] In addition, the U.S. Courts of Appeals for the Fourth, Fifth, Eighth, and Tenth Circuits have determined that employees can also bring a claim for a hostile work environment under the ADA.[107]

The ADA prohibits employers from discriminating against employees who have an "association" with someone with a disability.[108] A plaintiff can establish an *association claim* by showing that (1) the plaintiff was qualified for the position, (2) the plaintiff was subject to an adverse employment action, (3) the plaintiff was known to have a relative with a disability, and (4) the adverse employment action occurred under a circumstance that raised a reasonable inference that the relative's disability was a determining factor in the decision.[109] For example, the U.S. Court of Appeals for the Seventh Circuit held that an employee could raise a claim of "association discrimination" when the employer fired her because her husband's medical bills, which were paid by the employer's health plan, were too costly.[110]

Seven federal circuits have held that the ADA does not bar employers from providing less coverage for mental and emotional disabilities than for physical disabilities.[111] However, the Paul Wellstone and Pete Domenici Mental Health Parity and Addiction Equity Act[112] requires employers with fifty or more employees that provide group health insurance with mental health coverage to pay mental illness and addiction expenses on terms (such as deductibles, copayments, and covered hospital days and out-patient visits) that are on a par with the coverage offered for physical illnesses. Employers can obtain an exemption if providing parity would increase the total costs of health coverage by more than a specified percentage.

Definition of Disability

The ADA defines a "person with a disability" as (1) a person with a physical or mental impairment that substantially limits one or more of that person's major life activities, (2) a person with a record of a physical or mental impairment that substantially limits one or more of that person's major life activities, or (3) a person who is regarded as having such an impairment. The ADA Amendments Act of 2008 (ADAAA)[113] provides that "disability" is to be broadly construed and rejected cases, such as *Sutton v. United Airlines, Inc.*,[114] in which the Supreme Court narrowed the protection provided by the ADA. Congress instructed courts to focus primarily on whether the employer met its responsibility under the ADA, not on whether the plaintiff meets the definition of disability.[115]

Physical or Mental Impairment

The first and second prongs of the ADA's definition of disability focus on whether the individual has, or has a record of, a physical or mental impairment. The *Code of Federal Regulations* defines a physical or mental impairment as:

---

105. Leslie v. Cumulus Media, Inc., 814 F. Supp. 2d 1326 (S.D. Ala. 2011).

106. Raytheon Co. v. Hernandez, 540 U.S. 44 (2003).

107. Fox v. Gen. Motors Corp., 247 F.3d 169 (4th Cir. 2001); Flowers v. S. Reg'l Physician Servs., Inc., 247 F.3d 229 (5th Cir. 2001); Shaver v. Indep. Stave Co., 350 F.3d 716 (8th Cir. 2003); Lanman v. Johnson County, Kansas, 393 F.3d 1151 (10th Cir. 2004).

108. 42 U.S.C. § 12112(b)(4).

109. Larimer v. IBM Corp., 370 F.3d 698 (7th Cir. 2004).

110. De Witt v. Proctor Hosp., 517 F.3d 944 (7th Cir. 2008).

111. Moilanen v. Educ. Minn., 2009 WL 397863 (D. Minn. Feb. 17, 2009). Similarly, the U.S. Court of Appeals for the Second Circuit held that an employer did not violate the ADA when it offered different long-term disability benefits for physical and mental disabilities as long as every employee was offered the same plan. EEOC v. Staten Island Sav. Bank, 207 F.3d 144 (2d Cir. 2000).

112. Pub. L. No. 110-343, 122 Stat. 3765 (2008). *See* Appendix C.

113. Pub.L. No. 110-325, 122 Stat. 3553 (2008).

114. 527 U.S. 471 (1999).

115. ADAAA § 2(b)(5).

1. Any physiological disorder, or condition, cosmetic disfigurement, or anatomical loss affecting one or more body systems, such as neurological, musculoskeletal, special sense organs, respiratory (including speech organs), cardiovascular, reproductive, digestive, genitourinary, immune, circulatory, hemic, lymphatic, skin, and endocrine; or

2. Any mental or psychological disorder, such as intellectual disability (formerly termed "mental retardation"), organic brain syndrome, emotional or mental illness, and specific learning disabilities.[116]

Neither the ADA nor the *Code of Federal Regulations* lists all of the diseases or conditions that qualify as a "physical or mental" impairment, but the ADAAA expressly extended protection to workers with diabetes, epilepsy, and cancer.[117] The ADAAA prohibits employers from discriminating against disabled employees who have an impairment that is episodic or in remission; however, the ADAAA requires that workers prove that they have a disability that "would substantially limit a major life activity when active."[118]

Physical characteristics, such as skin color, weight, or height within the normal range, are not physical impairments, nor are personality traits, such as rudeness, irresponsible behavior, or a short temper. In addition, environmental, cultural, or economic disadvantages, such as lack of education or a prison record, are not impairments. For example, a person who cannot read due to dyslexia, which is a learning disability, has an impairment and is thus disabled. In contrast, a person who cannot read because he or she did not go to school does not have a disability because failure to attend school is not an impairment.

Substantially Limits a Major Life Activity
An impairment is a disability under the ADA only if it substantially limits an individual's abilities to perform a major life activity as compared with most people in the general population. *Major life activity* includes walking, seeing, hearing, speaking, working, performing manual tasks, reproducing, eating, communicating, learning, concentrating, and the operation of major bodily functions such as the liver.[119] Courts will consider the impairment's nature and severity, how long it will last or is expected to last, and its expected impact.[120] According to the

ADAAA, "substantially limits" is not "meant to be a demanding standard." Therefore, the determination of whether an impairment substantially limits a major life activity "should not demand extensive analysis."

The determination of whether an impairment substantially limits a major life activity is "made without regard to the ameliorative effects of mitigating measures [other than ordinary eyeglasses or contact lenses] such as . . . medication, medical supplies, equipment, or appliances . . . ; use of assistive technology; reasonable accommodations or auxiliary aids or services, or learned behavioral or adaptive neurological modifications."[121] For example, diabetes is "assessed in terms of its limitations on major life activities when the diabetic does *not* take insulin injections or medicine and does not require behavioral adaptations such as a strict diet."[122]

Regarded as Disabled
An individual is also protected under the ADA if he or she is subject to an action prohibited by the ADA, such as termination or failure to hire, based on an impairment that is not transitory and minor. This provision recognizes that societal stereotypes and prejudices may constrain individuals more than their actual limitations. The individual need not show that the perceived impairment limits the ability to perform a major life activity. In other words, an individual might be "regarded as" disabled even if he or she does not actually have a disability, if the employer treats him or her as if the condition constituted a disability. Individuals who are only regarded as disabled are not entitled to reasonable accommodations.

Exclusions
Although the definition of a disability under the ADA is relatively vague, the statute clearly excludes certain things. For example, the ADA specifically excludes homosexuality, bisexuality, sexual-behavior disorders, compulsive gambling, kleptomania, and pyromania from the definition of a disability.

Psychoactive-substance-use disorders resulting from current illegal use of drugs, including the use of alcohol in the workplace against the employer's policies, are also excluded from the ADA's definition of a disability. Although "current use" is not specifically defined in the statute, it has been interpreted to mean "the drug use was sufficiently recent to justify the employer's reasonable belief that the drug abuse remained an ongoing problem" and "recently enough to indicate that the individual is actively engaged in such conduct."[123] In contrast, an employee or applicant who no longer actively uses drugs or alcohol on

116. 29 C.F.R. pt. 1630.2.

117. Equal Emp't Opportunity Comm'n, *Fact Sheet on EEOC's Final Regulations Implementing the ADAAA, available at* http://www1.eeoc.gov//laws/regulations/adaaa_fact_sheet.cfm?renderforprint=1.

118. EEOC Interpretive Guidance on Title I of the Americans with Disabilities Act, 29 C.F.R. pt. 1630, app. (May 24, 2011).

119. EQUAL EMPLOYMENT OPPORTUNITY COMMISSION COMPLIANCE MANUAL, Notice Concerning the Americans with Disabilities Act (ADA) Amendments Act of 2008, 2009 WL 4782013 (E.E.O.C.C.M) (Aug. 2009).

120. *Id.*

121. Rohr v. Salt River Project Agric. Improvement & Power Dist., 555 F.3d 850 (9th Cir. 2009).

122. *Id.*

123. Mauerhan v. Wagner Corp., 649 F.3d 1180 (10th Cir. 2011).

the work site, but who is involved in or has completed a supervised rehabilitation program, may be regarded as a disabled person.[124] Also, although an individual may not be fired on the basis of his or her alcoholism, an employer may discharge the person based on behavior related to the alcoholism.[125]

Reasonable Accommodation

The ADA requires employers to make reasonable accommodations to an employee's disability as long as doing so does not cause the employer "undue hardship." Thus, even if a disability precludes an individual from performing the essential functions of the position or presents a safety risk, the employer is required to assess whether there is a reasonable accommodation that will permit the individual to be employed despite the disability. There is, however, no duty to make a reasonable accommodation for an individual who is deemed disabled solely because he or she is "regarded as" disabled.

To establish liability under the ADA, the employee generally must have requested an accommodation from the employer; it is the employee's initial request for an accommodation that triggers the employer's obligation to provide one.[126] An employee who fails to provide the employer with necessary medical information is precluded from claiming that the employer failed to provide reasonable accommodation.[127] Employers must train supervisors to recognize when a reasonable request for accommodation has been made.[128]

Title I sets forth a nonexhaustive list of what might constitute *reasonable accommodation*, including the following: (1) making work facilities accessible; (2) restructuring jobs or modifying work schedules; (3) reassigning the individual to another job; (4) acquiring or modifying equipment or devices; (5) modifying examinations, training materials, or policies; and (6) providing qualified readers or interpreters or other similar accommodations for individuals with disabilities. An employer is not required to provide special training for an employee with a disability or to hire another employee to assist the disabled employee.[129]

At least nine circuit courts have found that once a request for accommodation is made, an employer must be proactive and make a reasonable effort to determine the

appropriate accommodation.[130] A minimum requirement seems to be that the employer should discuss potential accommodations with the disabled employee and not make unilateral decisions regarding the adequacy of potential accommodations.[131] Courts have not been receptive to claims that an employer should be required to transfer the plaintiff to a new supervisor.[132]

In some cases, however, reassignment may be deemed a necessary reasonable accommodation. In *Smith v. Midland Brake, Inc., Division of Echlin, Inc.*,[133] the U.S. Court of Appeals for the Tenth Circuit found that the employer could have reassigned the employee to another job within the company after he became unable to perform his job because of a chronic skin condition. The court said that the ADA's reasonable accommodation requirement would be transformed into a "hollow promise" if it merely extended the right "to compete equally with the rest of the world for a vacant position" to disabled workers.

In contrast, in *Huber v. Wal-Mart Stores, Inc.*,[134] the U.S. Court of Appeals for the Eighth Circuit held that the employer did not violate the ADA by refusing to reassign a dry grocery order filler at a Wal-Mart store to a vacant router position after she suffered a permanent injury to her right arm that prevented her from performing the essential functions of her order filler job. Instead of automatically reassigning her to the router position, Wal-Mart required her to compete for the job with other applicants pursuant to its policy of hiring the most qualified applicant for the job. The court stated: "[T]he ADA is not an affirmative action statute and does not require an employer to reassign a qualified disabled employee to a vacant position when such a reassignment would violate a legitimate, nondiscriminatory policy of the employer to hire the most qualified candidate."

An employer does not have to accommodate a disabled employee if doing so would conflict with seniority rules under the employer's collective bargaining agreement.[135] In *U.S. Airways, Inc. v. Barnett*,[136] however, the Supreme Court held that an employer's unilaterally imposed seniority system (not embodied in a collective bargaining

---

124. *See* Brown v. Lucky Stores, Inc., 246 F.3d 1182 (9th Cir. 2001).

125. James Podgers, *Disability and DUIs: ADA Claims by Fired or Demoted Alcoholic Employees Fail*, A.B.A. J., Feb. 1996, at 46.

126. Hayes v. Wal-Mart Stores, Inc., 781 F. Supp. 2d 1080 (D. Ore. 2011).

127. *Id.*

128. *Employment Discrimination-Disability: Employers Should Train Supervisors in ADA Accommodation Duty, EEOC Official Advises*, 69 U.S.L.W. 2254–55 (2000).

129. Hammel v. Eau Galle Cheese Factory, 407 F.3d 852, 867 (7th Cir. 2005).

130. *See, e.g.*, Griffin v. United Parcel Serv., 661 F.3d 216 (5th Cir. 2011) ("[W]hen an employer's unwillingness to engage in a good faith interactive process leads to a failure to reasonably accommodate an employee, the employer violates the ADA."); Colwell v. Rite Aid Corp., 602 F.3d 495 (3d Cir. 2010) ("[O]nce proper notice has been provided . . . both parties have a duty to assist in the search for an appropriate reasonable accommodation and to act in good faith.").

131. Bultemeyer v. Fort Wayne Cmty. Schs., 100 F.3d 1281 (7th Cir. 1996).

132. *See* Mark C. Weber, *Unreasonable Accommodation and Undue Hardship*, 62 FLA. L. REV. 1119, 1158 n.180 (2010).

133. 180 F.3d 1154 (10th Cir. 1999).

134. 486 F.3d 480 (8th Cir. 2007).

135. *See, e.g.*, EEOC v. Sharp Mfg. Co. of Am., Div. of Sharp Elecs. Corp., 534 F. Supp. 2d 797 (W.D. Tenn. 2008).

136. 535 U.S. 391 (2002).

agreement) that conflicts with a reassignment that is a reasonable accommodation under the ADA will not necessarily serve to bar the reassignment. In this case, an employee who suffered a serious back injury while working asked his employer to reassign him to another job in the company's mail room. Two employees with greater seniority planned to exercise their seniority right to transfer to jobs in the mail room, thereby preventing the disabled employee from working there. Although a seniority system is ordinarily sufficient to show that accommodation is not reasonable under the ADA, the Supreme Court ruled that an employee may present evidence of special circumstances that make an exception to the seniority rule reasonable under particular facts: "[T]he plaintiff might show, for example, that the employer, having retained the right to change the system unilaterally, exercises the right fairly frequently, reducing employee expectations that the system will be followed—to the point where the requested accommodation will not likely make a difference."

Defenses Under the ADA

Defenses available to an employer under the ADA include undue hardship, business necessity, and permissible exclusion.

Undue Hardship

A reasonable accommodation is not required if it would impose an undue hardship on the employer. The ADA defines *undue hardship* to mean an activity requiring significant difficulty or expense when considered in light of (1) the nature and cost of the accommodation needed; (2) the overall financial resources of the facility, the number of persons employed at the facility, the effect on expenses and resources, or any other impact of the accommodation on the facility; (3) the overall financial resources of the employer and the overall size of the business with respect to the number of employees and the type, number, and location of its facilities; and (4) the type of operation of the employer, including the composition, structure, and functions of the workforce, and the geographic separateness and administrative or fiscal relationship of the facility in question to the employer.

One accommodation that was deemed unreasonable involved an employee with depression and various anxiety-related disorders who sued when the employer did not honor his request for a less stressful work environment. The U.S. Court of Appeals for the Third Circuit ruled that transferring the employee away from the stressful work environment was not a reasonable accommodation because it would impose extraordinary administrative costs on the employer.[137]

Business Necessity

Employers may also defend their actions by showing that they had to discriminate against an applicant or employee with a disability due to a business necessity. In *Belk v. Southwestern Bell Telephone Co.*,[138] the U.S. Court of Appeals for the Eighth Circuit ruled that employment tests, qualification standards, and other selection criteria are acceptable under the ADA if they are related to the job and consistent with business necessity. Southwestern Bell had argued that it had job-related reasons for not accommodating a worker who wore a leg brace during a physical performance test for a technician job.

In *EEOC v. Exxon Corp.*,[139] the U.S. Court of Appeals for the Fifth Circuit analyzed Exxon's policy, adopted in response to the 1989 *Exxon Valdez* oil spill disaster, of permanently removing any employee who had undergone treatment for substance abuse from certain safety-sensitive positions. The EEOC sued, arguing that Exxon had to prove that the class of individuals posed a "direct threat" to the health or safety of others. The court rejected this argument, stating that Exxon could justify its policy as a business necessity. Whereas the "direct threat" test focuses on the individual employee and the specific risk posed by the employee's disability, the "business necessity" defense concerns whether a safety policy constitutes a business necessity; therefore, both the magnitude of possible harm and the probability of harm must be evaluated.

In *Tice v. Centre Area Transportation Authority*,[140] the U.S. Court of Appeals for the Third Circuit held that a transportation authority did not violate the ADA by ordering a post-hiring physical examination of a bus driver who had repeatedly taken medical leave due to a back injury. The examination was job related and consistent with the business necessity of determining whether the employee was physically fit to perform his job.

Permissible Exclusion

An applicant or employee who is disabled may be excluded from the employment opportunity only if, by reason of the disability, he or she (with or without reasonable accommodation) cannot perform the essential functions of the job or if the individual's employment poses a significant risk to the health or safety of the employee or others.

Inability to Perform Essential Functions   In determining whether a job function is essential, the ADA requires that consideration be given to the employer's judgment as to which functions are essential, but it also looks to any written job description prepared *before* advertising or interviewing for the job commenced. The applicant or

---

137. Gaul v. Lucent Techs., Inc., 134 F.3d 576 (3d Cir. 1998).

138. 194 F.3d 946 (8th Cir. 1999).
139. 203 F.3d 871 (5th Cir. 2000).
140. 247 F.3d 506 (3d Cir. 2001).

employee has to prove only that he or she is able to perform the essential functions of the job, not all of the functions.[141]

Direct Threat   An employer cannot deny a job due to risk of future injury to the employee or others, unless, given the person's current condition, there is a probability of substantial harm. For example, the U.S. Court of Appeals for the Eleventh Circuit ruled that a dental office acted lawfully when it laid off a hygienist who tested positive for the human immunodeficiency virus (HIV). The court concluded that the hygienist posed a direct threat to the health and safety of others, because his job included engaging in invasive, exposure-prone activities, such as cleaning teeth, on a frequent basis.[142] The presence of sharp instruments on which the hygienist could prick his hand increased the risk of HIV transmission. Employers cannot rely on their own physician's opinion, however; risk of injury must be based on generally accepted medical opinion.

In *Chevron USA, Inc. v. Echazabal*,[143] the U.S. Supreme Court held that the "direct threat" defense under the ADA applies to employees who pose a direct threat to their own health or safety even if they pose no threat to other persons. Although Echazabal worked for various maintenance contractors at Chevron's El Segundo, California oil refinery, Chevron refused to hire him because he had a liver disease that might be aggravated by exposure to solvents and chemicals in the refinery. Chevron also asked the maintenance contractor that employed Echazabal to remove him from the refinery or assign him to a position where he would not be exposed to solvents or chemicals. Echazabal sued Chevron, alleging that it had violated the ADA. The Supreme Court found that Chevron's reasons for denying employment to Echazabal were reasonable: Chevron wished to avoid time lost to sickness, excessive turnover from medical retirement or death, litigation under state law, and the risk of violating the Occupational Safety and Health Act. The Court concluded that if an employer hires an individual who knowingly consents to the particular dangers the job would pose to him, "there is no denying that the employer would be asking for trouble." The employer's decision to hire "would put Congress's policy in the ADA, [and] a disabled individual's right to operate on equal terms within the workplace, at loggerheads with the competing policy of OSHA, to ensure the safety of 'each' and 'every' worker."

HIV Discrimination

Due to advances in drug treatments, more individuals are living healthy, productive lives while infected with HIV. This is called asymptomatic HIV disease. When an individual's immune system is compromised and the person becomes ill due to HIV-related complications, the individual is considered symptomatic. Acquired immune deficiency syndrome (AIDS) refers to the most serious stage of symptomatic HIV disease. Both asymptomatic and symptomatic HIV-positive individuals are disabled within the meaning of the ADA.[144]

In the context of HIV disease, courts have narrowly construed the direct threat defense in accordance with medical evidence that HIV cannot be transmitted through casual contact. Thus, only those professions that could lead to the transmission of bodily fluids, such as healthcare, are given closer analysis under the direct threat exception.

Dealing with HIV Disease in the Workplace

An employer cannot justify discrimination against a person who is HIV positive on the basis of coworker or customer preference. Similarly, the fact that the employment of someone with HIV disease will increase group health insurance costs or cause absenteeism does not make discrimination permissible.

In *Leonel v. American Airlines, Inc.*,[145] the U.S. Court of Appeals for the Ninth Circuit held that American Airlines may have violated the ADA by refusing to hire HIV-positive flight attendant candidates who did not reveal their medical status as part of a medical examination that was conducted before the company had completed its background checks. The court stated:

> Both the ADA and [the equivalent state law] deliberately allow job applicants to shield their private medical information until they know that, absent an inability to meet the medical requirements, they will be hired, and that if they are not hired, the true reason for the employer's decision will be transparent. American's attempt to focus on the evaluation rather than the collection of medical information squares with neither the text nor the purposes of the statutes. Whether or not it looked at the medical information it obtained from the appellants, American was not entitled to get the information at all until it had completed the background checks, unless it can demonstrate it could not reasonably have done so before initiating the medical examination process.

The court also held that American may have violated the plaintiffs' rights to privacy under the California Constitution by conducting complete blood count tests on their blood samples without notifying them or obtaining their consent.

Many states recognize either a common law or a constitutional right to privacy that protects individuals from improper communication of their HIV status, even when the information is true and was properly obtained for a

---

141. Fisher v. Vizioncore, Inc., 2011 WL 2883292 (7th Cir. July 20, 2011).

142. Waddell v. Valley Forge Dental Assocs., Inc., 276 F.3d 1275 (11th Cir. 2001).

143. 536 U.S. 73 (2002).

144. Bragdon v. Abbott, 524 U.S. 624 (1998).

145. 400 F.3d 702 (9th Cir. 2005).

specific purpose. Statutes prohibiting disclosure of medical information, specifically HIV-related information, may also be a source of employer liability. Thus, HIV-related information should be kept in confidence among individuals who need to know.

The employer also runs the risk of being sued for libel or slander if careless statements are made about employees. For example, falsely accusing an employee of having AIDS could be grounds for a defamation suit. Truth, however, is a complete defense.

Genetic Discrimination

Even before passage of the Genetic Information Nondiscrimination Act of 2008 (GINA),[146] the EEOC took the position that the ADA prohibits discrimination on the basis of a diagnosed genetic predisposition toward an asymptomatic condition or illness.[147] GINA prohibits employers with at least fifteen employees from using genetic information to make decisions about hiring, firing, or compensation.[148] GINA also prohibits health insurance companies from using genetic information to deny benefits or raise premiums for individual policies (it was already illegal to exclude individuals from a group plan because of their genetic profile).

Remedies Under the ADA and GINA

The ADA and GINA are enforced in the same manner as Title VII, and the same remedies are available. Compensatory and punitive damages for discrimination based on disability or genetic information are subject to the same caps as those applicable to discrimination based on sex or religion. Employers who violate either act can be fined as much as $300,000 for each violation.

The ADA also prohibits retaliation against an individual for exercising his or her rights under the statute. The federal courts are split over the availability of compensatory and punitive damages for retaliation claims, however. The U.S. Court of Appeals for the Seventh Circuit held that damages are not recoverable,[149] but district courts in other circuits have held that both compensatory and punitive damages are available.[150] Based on the Supreme Court's reasoning in *Gomez-Perez v. Potter*[151] that a private action for retaliation could be inferred from a ban on age discrimination, the better argument seems to be that under the ADA damages are recoverable for retaliation.

FAMILY AND MEDICAL LEAVE ACT

Under the Family and Medical Leave Act of 1993 (FMLA),[152] eligible employees are entitled to twelve weeks of unpaid job-protected leave per year. An employee may use leave under the Act in four situations: (1) the birth of a child; (2) the placement of an adopted or foster-care child with the employee; (3) care of a child, a parent, or a spouse; or (4) a serious health condition that renders the employee unable to do his or her job. As discussed below, two types of leave related to military service are also available. Whereas the focus of the ADA is to demonstrate that an employee can work despite a disability, the objective of the FMLA is to provide time off to an employee who cannot work because of family responsibility or a serious health condition. To be eligible for a family leave, the employee must have worked at the place of employment for at least twelve months and have completed at least 1,250 hours of service to the employer during that twelve-month period.

The National Defense Authorization Act of 2008[153] amended the FMLA by adding two categories of unpaid, job-protected leave for military families. Coverage was expanded by the National Defense Authorization Act for Fiscal Year 2010. Eligible employees may take up to twelve weeks of FMLA *qualifying exigency leave* to handle exigencies related to a family member's active duty military service or call to active duty. "Qualifying exigencies" include (1) short notice deployment and deployment to a foreign country; (2) military events and related activities; (3) child-care and school activities; (4) financial and legal arrangements; (5) counseling; (6) rest and recuperations; (7) post-deployment activities; and (8) additional activities to address other events that arise out of the covered service member's active duty or call to active duty status, provided that the employer and employee agree that such leave shall qualify as an exigency and agree to both the timing and duration of the leave.[154]

Eligible employees can also take up to twenty-six weeks of FMLA *covered service member family leave* to care for a spouse, son, daughter, parent, or next of kin who has a serious injury or illness incurred or aggravated by service in the line of active duty. Leave is also available to care for certain veterans. The Department of Labor has defined "next of kin" of a covered service member as the nearest blood relative other than the covered service member's spouse, parent, son, or daughter in the following order

146. Pub.L. No. 110-233, 122 Stat. 881 (2008). For the EEOC regulations, see 29 C.F.R. § 1635.1.

147. *EEOC Commissioner Says ADA Bans Genetic Discrimination*, CORP. COUNS. WKLY. (BNA), Apr. 12, 2000, at 7.

148. 42 U.S.C.A. § 2000e(b).

149. Kramer v. Banc of Am. Sec. LLC, 355 F.3d 961 (7th Cir. 2004).

150. *See, e.g.,* Baker v. Windsor Republic Doors, 635 F. Supp. 2d 765 (W.D. Tenn. 2009); Edwards v. Brookhaven Sci. Assocs. LLC, 390 F. Supp. 2d 225, 234 (E.D.N.Y. 2005).

151. 128 S. Ct. 1931 (2008)

152. Pub. L. No. 103-3, 107 Stat. 6 (codified at 5 U.S.C. § 6381 *et seq.* and 29 U.S.C. § 2601 *et seq.*).

153. Pub. L. No. 110-181, 122 Stat. 3 (2008).

154. Jonathan D. Rosenfeld & Julie Murphy Clinton, *New FLMA Regulations Effective January 2009*, WILMERHALE, Dec. 24, 2008, *available at* http://www.wilmerhale.com/new_fmla_regulations_effective_january_2009_12-24-2008/.

of priority: blood relatives who have been granted legal custody of the covered service member by court decree or statutory provisions, brothers and sisters, grandparents, aunts and uncles, and first cousins, unless the covered service member has specifically designated in writing another blood relative as his or her nearest blood relative for purposes of covered service member leave. EEOC regulations provide that eligible employees can take more than one twenty-six-week leave if the leave is to care for a different covered service member or if the same covered service member has a subsequent injury or illness. However, an eligible employee cannot take more than twenty-six weeks of leave in any single twelve-month period.[155]

The FMLA's requirements are a floor, not a ceiling, for what employers can provide their employees in terms of leave. If employers provide for more generous leave, however, they must give employees notice regarding the consequences of taking the extra leave.[156]

An employee cannot waive his or her right to leave time under the FMLA. But the employer may require, or an employee may choose, to substitute any or all accrued paid leave for the leave time that is provided for under the Act. Employers have no obligation to give employees advance notice that their paid leave will be counted toward the unpaid leave provided by the FMLA.[157]

Reinstatement

In general, the employer is required to restore the employee to the same position, or one with equivalent benefits, pay, and other terms and conditions of employment, following the expiration of FMLA leave. However, an employer may still terminate an employee during the family medical leave if the employer would have made the same decision had the employee not taken the leave. For example, the U.S. Court of Appeals for the Eighth Circuit held that an employer did not violate the FMLA by firing an employee on FMLA pregnancy leave because the employer produced nondiscriminatory, legitimate reasons for terminating the employee unrelated to her FMLA leave.[158]

Similarly, the U.S. Court of Appeals for the Eleventh Circuit held that an employee taking leave under the FMLA does not have an absolute right to reinstatement if his or her employment is terminated during the leave as part of a general reduction in force (RIF) by the employer.[159] The court explained: "An employee has no greater right to reinstatement or to other benefits and conditions of employment than if the employee had been continuously employed during the FMLA leave period." The burden of proof is on the employer denying reinstatement to show that it would have discharged the employee even if he or she had not been on FMLA leave.

An employer is also not required to reinstate key employees to their previous positions if the employer determines that "such denial is necessary to prevent substantial and grievous economic injury to the operations of the employer." "Key employee" is defined as a salaried employee who is among the highest-paid 10% of the employees located within seventy-five miles of the facility at which the subject employee is employed. EEOC regulations require the employer to notify an employee, at the time the leave is requested, of his or her status as a key employee and of the consequence of taking a leave.[160]

Remedies

To vindicate rights under the FMLA, a plaintiff may sue both the employer and his or her supervisor individually.[161] This interpretation is distinctive because a supervisor generally cannot be sued in his or her individual capacity under Title VII, the ADEA, or the ADA. In addition, despite states' general immunity from private actions under the Eleventh Amendment, the U.S. Supreme Court has held that employees can sue state employers for FMLA violations.[162]

VETERANS' REEMPLOYMENT RIGHTS

The Uniformed Services Employment and Reemployment Rights Act of 1994 (USERRA)[163] protects the civilian jobs of members of the uniformed services of the United States. The deployment of U.S. troops, including large numbers of reservists, to Afghanistan and Iraq has increased the interest in USERRA protections.

Service in the uniformed services is defined as follows:

[T]he performance of duty on a voluntary or involuntary basis in a uniformed service under competent authority and includes active duty, active duty for training, initial active duty for training, inactive duty training, full-time National Guard duty, a period for which a person is absent from a position of employment for the purpose of an examination to determine the fitness of the person to perform any such duty, and a period for which a person is absent from employment for the purpose of performing funeral honors duty.[164]

---

155. *Id.*

156. *See* Kosakow v. New Rochelle Radiology Assocs., P.C., 274 F.3d 706 (2d Cir. 2001).

157. *See* Ragsdale v. Wolverine World Wide, Inc., 535 U.S. 81 (2002).

158. Wierman v. Casey's Gen. Stores, 638 F.3d 984 (8th Cir. 2011).

159. O'Connor v. PCA Family Health Plan, Inc., 200 F.3d 1349 (11th Cir. 2000).

160. Neel v. Mid-Atlantic of Fairfield, LLC, 778 F. Supp. 2d 593 (D. Md. 2011).

161. Rynders v. Williams, 650 F.3d 1188 (8th Cir. 2011). *But see* Mitchell v. Chapman, 343 F.3d 811 (6th Cir. 2003) (holding that the FMLA does not impose individual liability on public agency employees).

162. Nev. Dep't of Human Res. v. Hibbs, 538 U.S. 721 (2003).

163. 38 U.S.C. §§ 4301–4335.

164. 38 U.S.C. § 4303(13).

Covered employers include "any person, installation, organization, or other entity that pays salary or wages for work performed or that has control over employment opportunities," including federal and state government employers.[165]

Section 4312 of USERRA requires an employer to rehire covered employees, and section 4311 prohibits employers from treating those employees differently after they are rehired. Section 4316 prevents employers from dismissing the employees without cause for a limited period of time (the length of the protected period depends on the length of military service). USERRA also protects an employee from adverse employment decisions when the employee's membership in the uniformed services is a motivating factor in the employer's decision.[166] USERRA also prohibits other forms of discrimination because of an employee's military status or service. For example, a district court granted summary judgment to an active duty serviceman who was denied employment as a police officer, because his active duty prevented him from beginning service until two months after the police department's start date. The employer argued that it had refused to employ the serviceman because of his unavailability to report to work, not his status, but the court disagreed: "This contention can be dispatched quickly: it ignores the plain language of section 4311(a), which prohibits discrimination based not only on a person's status as a member of the uniformed services, but also on the service member's 'obligation to perform service.'"[167] In addition, reemployment must be to a position comparable "to the position he would have held had he remained continuously in his civilian employment."[168]

Remedies

A person claiming violation of USERRA may file a complaint with the U.S. Secretary of Labor, request that the U.S. Attorney General file a lawsuit on his or her behalf, or file a civil lawsuit in state or federal court. A court may (1) order an employer to comply with the act, (2) award back pay and front pay, and (3) award an additional amount equal to the pay award as liquidated damages if it finds that the employer willfully failed to comply with the Act. The court may also exercise full equity powers. USERRA allows a successful plaintiff to recover his or her attorneys' fees, expert witness fees, and other litigation expenses.[169]

AFFIRMATIVE ACTION

Affirmative-action programs are generally viewed as a means of remedying past acts of discrimination. Such programs are usually established pursuant to court orders, court-approved consent decrees, or federal and state laws that impose affirmative-action obligations on government contractors.

Executive Order 11246 requires federal government contractors to include certain provisions in every government contract not exempted by the order. In these provisions, the contractor agrees (1) not to discriminate in employment on the basis of race, color, religion, sex, or national origin; (2) to take affirmative steps to prevent discrimination; and (3) to file equal opportunity surveys every other year.[170] In some cases, a contractor's affirmative-action plan must be put in writing. Although individuals have no private right of action based on an alleged violation of the order, the Department of Labor, through its Office of Federal Contract Compliance Programs, can impose a wide range of sanctions, including terminating a government contract and disqualifying the contractor from entering into any future government contracts.[171] Government contractors are subject to affirmative-action obligations under certain federal laws as well, including the Vocational Rehabilitation Act of 1973 and the Vietnam Era Veterans' Readjustment Assistance Act of 1972.

The Civil Rights Act of 1991[172] limited the ability of persons to challenge affirmative-action litigated judgments and consent decrees. A person cannot challenge a judgment or consent decree if any of the following three conditions is applicable: (1) he person had actual notice of the proposed judgment or order sufficient to let that person know that the judgment or decree might adversely affect the interests and legal rights of that person and had an opportunity to present objections (2) the person had a reasonable opportunity to present objections to the judgment or order or (3) the person's interests were adequately represented by another person who had previously challenged the judgment or order on the same legal grounds and with a similar factual situation.

As explained in Chapter 4, the U.S. Supreme Court has held that both state and federal government-mandated affirmative-action plans are subject to strict scrutiny under the Equal Protection Clause.[173] In reinstating a reverse-discrimination claim by a white-owned construction company that had lost a contract to a minority-owned business, the Court held that benign and invidious racial classifications should be subject to the same standards. This ruling was significant because it required the government to show a specific history of discrimination in order to justify preferential treatment of minority-owned businesses in government contracts.

165. 38 U.S.C. § 4303(4)(A).

166. Newport v. Ford Motor Co., 91 F.3d 1164, 1167 (8th Cir. 1996).

167. McLain v. City of Somerville, 424 F. Supp. 2d 329 (D. Mass. 2006).

168. Rogers v. City of San Antonio, 392 F.3d 758, 763 (5th Cir. 2004).

169. 38 U.S.C. § 4323(h)(2).

170. Exec. Order No. 11246, 3 C.F.R. 339 (1964–1965), *reprinted in* 42 U.S.C. § 2000e (1994).

171. The Office of Federal Contract Compliance Programs' regulations overhauling the thirty-year-old requirements for affirmative action under Executive Order 11246 were published in the November 13, 2000 issue of the *Federal Register*, 65 Fed. Reg. 68,022, and took effect on December 13, 2000.

172. Pub. L. No. 102-166, 105 Stat. 1071 (1991).

173. Adarand Constructors, Inc. v. Peña, 515 U.S. 200 (1995).

In 1998, in *Lutheran Church–Missouri Synod v. FCC*,[174] the U.S. Court of Appeals for the District of Columbia Circuit struck down the Federal Communications Commission's affirmative-action requirements for radio and television broadcast licenses. The court held that *Adarand*'s requirement of strict scrutiny applied not just to racial preferences in hiring, but to any race-conscious decision making that affects employment opportunities, even if it does not establish preferences, quotas, or set-asides. The court explained:

> [W]e do not think it matters whether a government hiring program imposes hard quotas, soft quotas, or goals. Any one of these techniques induces an employer to hire with an eye toward meeting the numerical target. As such, they can and surely will result in individuals being granted a preference because of their race.

The court also held that even if the FCC's interest in fostering diverse programming could be deemed a compelling state interest, the FCC's equal employment opportunity rules were not narrowly tailored to foster diverse programming. In response to *Lutheran Church*, the FCC adopted new rules that require broadcast licensees to disseminate information about job openings to all members of the community to ensure that all potential applicants have the opportunity to compete for jobs.[175]

As discussed in Chapter 4, in *Grutter v. Bollinger*,[176] the U.S. Supreme Court upheld the University of Michigan Law School's admissions policy, which took race and ethnicity into account in an effort to achieve student body diversity but did not use numerical quotas. In a companion case,[177] the Supreme Court invalidated the University of Michigan's undergraduate admissions policy, which used mechanistic numerical formulas to admit more applicants of color. Unlike the Law School—which included race and ethnicity as just two of many factors used to make admissions decisions—the undergraduate programs specified one set of required grade point averages and board scores for whites granted automatic admission and another, lower set of grades and board scores for nonwhites granted automatic admission. Similarly, the Court held that a Seattle public school district that had not operated legally segregated schools could not voluntarily adopt a student assignment plan that relied on race to determine which public high schools children would attend.[178] Nor could a school district

in Jefferson County, Kentucky, whose court-ordered desegregation decree had been dissolved, use racial guidelines to assign elementary school students to particular schools.[179]

As explained in Chapter 4, the Equal Protection Clause applies only to state actors. Affirmative-action programs by private employers have primarily been challenged under Title VII. In *United Steelworkers of America v. Weber*,[180] the U.S. Supreme Court upheld a collective bargaining agreement containing an affirmative-action plan giving preference to African American employees entering skilled-craft training positions. Concluding that Title VII did not preclude all private, voluntary, race-conscious affirmative-action programs, the Court noted that the plan (1) like Title VII, was designed to break down patterns of racial segregation and hierarchy, (2) "does not unnecessarily trammel the interests of white employees," and (3) was a temporary measure intended to eliminate rather than maintain racial balance. The EEOC has promulgated regulations regarding voluntary affirmative-action plans.[181]

In *Taxman v. Board of Education*,[182] the U.S. Court of Appeals for the Third Circuit struck down a school board's affirmative-action plan as a violation of Title VII. The plan gave preference to minority teachers over nonminority teachers in layoff decisions when teachers were equally qualified. The court read the Supreme Court's ruling in *United Steelworkers* as permitting race-based employment decisions only when they are necessary to remedy past discrimination. A mere desire to promote diversity in education was not sufficient to warrant a discriminatory policy. In *Ricci v. DeStefano*,[183] the Supreme Court held that invalidating exam scores that would result in promoting no African Americans violated Title VII because it was intentional discrimination based on race.

APPLICABILITY OF CIVIL RIGHTS LAWS TO TEMPORARY WORKERS

The EEOC has responded to the growth in the number of temporary or contingent workers by extending potential liability for discrimination against such workers to both

---

174. 141 F.3d 344 (D.C. Cir. 1998).

175. 47 C.F.R. pt. 73.2080 (2000).

176. 539 U.S. 306 (2003).

177. Gratz v. Bollinger, 539 U.S. 244 (2003). Voters in Michigan subsequently amended the Michigan Constitution to limit affirmative action. In *Fisher v. University of Texas at Austin*, 631 F.3d 213 (5th Cir. 2011), *cert. granted*, 2012 WL 538328 (2012), the U.S. Court of Appeals for the Fifth Circuit upheld a policy that included race as one of many factors considered for undergraduate admission based on the compelling state interest in ensuring a "critical mass" of minority students at the university.

178. Parents Involved in Cmty. Schs. v. Seattle Sch. Dist. No. 1, 551 U.S. 701 (2007).

179. Meredith. v. Jefferson County Bd. of Ed., 551 U.S. 701 (2007). This case was decided in the same opinion as *Parents Involved in Community Schools v. Seattle School District No. 1*.

180. 443 U.S. 193 (1979).

181. *See* 29 C.F.R. § 1608.1–12.

182. 91 F.3d 1547 (3d Cir. 1996).

183. 129 S. Ct. 2658 (2009) (Case 13.1).

the employment agencies or temporary staffing firms and their client-employers.[184] If both the staffing firm and its client have the right to control the worker, they are treated as joint employers, and both are subject to liability for both back and front pay, as well as compensatory and punitive damages.

If the staffing firm learns that one of its clients has discriminated against a temporary employee, the firm should not assign other workers to that work site unless the client has taken the necessary corrective and preventive measures to ensure that the discrimination will not recur. Otherwise, the staffing firm will be liable, along with the client, if a worker later assigned to that client is subjected to similar misconduct.

THE EXTRATERRITORIAL REACH OF U.S. EMPLOYMENT DISCRIMINATION LAW

In 1991, Congress amended Title VII to protect U.S. citizens employed in a foreign country by a U.S. employer or a U.S.-controlled employer. The ADEA and the ADA also apply extraterritorially to the same extent as Title VII.

The EEOC has provided guidance on how to determine whether an entity is a U.S. employer.[185] The nationality of an entity is determined on a case-by-case basis, taking into consideration the following factors: (1) the entity's place of incorporation, (2) the principal place of business, (3) contacts within the United States, (4) the nationality of dominant shareholders and/or those holding voting control, and (5) the nationality and location of management. An entity that is incorporated in the United States will generally be deemed a U.S. entity.

Even if a foreign entity is not deemed to be a U.S. entity, it will still be covered if it is "controlled by" a U.S. entity. The determination of whether a U.S. employer controls an entity is based on the interrelation of the companies' operations, common management, centralized control of labor relations, and common ownership or financial control of the U.S. employer and the foreign entity.[186]

Section 109 of Title VII makes it clear, however, that "it shall not be unlawful," under either Title VII or the ADA, for an employer to act in violation of either statute if compliance would cause the employer to violate the law of the foreign country in which the employee's workplace is located. For example, an employer may be permitted to deny employment to women in a country that prohibits women from working, even though this practice violates Title VII.

---

184. The text of the EEOC's guidance on the application of employment-discrimination laws to contingent workers (Contingent Worker Guidance) is available at http://www.eeoc.gov/policy/docs/conting.html (last modified July 6, 2000). The text of the EEOC's guidance on the application of the ADA to contingent workers, which supplements the Contingent Worker Guidance, is available at http://www.eeoc.gov/policy/docs/guidance-contingent.html (last modified Jan. 23, 2001).

185. Equal Emp't Opportunity Comm'n, *Enforcement Guidance on Application of Title VII and the Americans with Disabilities Act*, available at http://www.eeoc.gov/policy/docs/extraterritorial-vii-ada.html (last modified Apr. 24, 2003).

186. 42 U.S.C. § 2000e-1(c)(3).

GLOBAL VIEW

Globalization, Cultural Norms, and Workplace Discrimination

When engaging in business overseas, managers should familiarize themselves with the employment-discrimination laws of the countries in which they are doing business. "Today, geographic barriers are disappearing, and the way we do business is changing," said Nandan Nilekani, Infosys's chief executive.[187] "Multicultural interaction is becoming a very important part of our work environment."[188] Legally astute managers attend to both changing legal requirements and cultural differences.

European Union

The member states of the European Union (EU) have (1) banned workplace discrimination and harassment on the basis of sex, religion, age, race, ethnic origin, disability, and

sexual orientation;[189] (2) banned retaliation or other adverse treatment in reaction to a complaint or other action aimed at enforcing compliance with the principle of equal treatment; (3) established judicial or administrative bodies to enforce equal treatment in the workplace; and (4) removed any caps on awards for discrimination cases (although each member state is permitted to establish its own system of remedies). The relevant EU directives left it up to the member states to implement appropriate sanctions to avoid discrimination and harassment. Any EU citizen claiming to be the victim of discrimination can also file a claim in the European Court of

CONTINUED

---

187. Saritha Rai, *Harassment Suit in U.S. Shifts India's Work Culture*, N.Y. Times, Sept. 5, 2002.

188. *Id.*

189. Equal Treatment Directive, European Parliament and Council Directive 2002/73/EC, 2002 O.J. (L 269) (Oct. 5); Equal Treatment Framework Directive, Council Directive 2000/78/EC, 2000 O.J. (L 308) (Nov. 27); Race Equality Directive, Council Directive 2000/43/EC, 2000 O.J. (L 180) 22 (June 29).

Norebbo/Shutterstock

Justice in Luxembourg. Even though the European Commission mandated that all member states have uniform laws regarding employment discrimination, each member state implements and utilizes these directives in different ways.

In trying discrimination cases, EU member states are required to utilize a burden of proof mechanism similar to the U.S. concepts of disparate treatment and disparate impact. "Disparate treatment" is called "direct discrimination," and "disparate impact" is called "indirect discrimination" in the EU. Direct discrimination analysis ensures that the burden of proof shifts if the complainant establishes "facts [from] which it may be presumed that there has been direct or indirect evidence of discrimination." Indirect discrimination occurs "where a provision, criterion, or practice would put persons of a racial or ethnic origin at a particular disadvantage compared with other persons, unless that provision, criterion, or practice is objectively justified by a particular aim." Like U.S. courts, European courts look at percentages to determine whether a protected class has been disadvantaged by a particular employment practice.

In the case of race and sex discrimination claims, once the employee presents credible evidence that would allow a presumption that discrimination has occurred, the employer must prove that there has been no violation of the principle of equal treatment. This makes it easier for employees to prove direct discrimination in a European court than in the United States.

India

Indian anti-discrimination law has developed slowly since the implementation of the Indian Constitution in 1950. The constitution prohibits discrimination in employment on the basis of religion, race, color, caste, sex, disability, descent, place of birth, or residence.[190]

Perhaps the greatest struggle for equal rights has involved members of the Dalit caste (formerly called "untouchables"). These people occupy India's lowest caste and are viewed as unclean by higher-caste Hindus. In an effort to end the caste system, India passed the Protection of Civil Rights Act in 1955[191] and implemented an affirmative-action program for government workers. One purpose of this Act was to enable Dalits to obtain jobs other than the low-paying and undesirable occupations to which they were traditionally relegated. Attempts by the Indian government to extend the affirmative-action program to the private sector have been strongly opposed by Indian industry. However, most of India's major information technology companies have adopted the United Nations Global Compact's principles regarding the elimination of discrimination with respect to employment and occupation.[192]

India has ratified the UN Convention on the Rights of Persons with Disabilities. The Persons with Disabilities Act of 1995 mandates that 3% of government jobs be reserved for persons with disabilities.[193]

The Indian government passed its first law concerning rights for women in the workplace in 1948. The law prohibited women from cleaning certain machinery in factories and granted female factory workers maternity leave for up to twelve weeks.[194] Since then, other laws mandating equal pay, maternity benefits, and equal opportunity in hiring have been passed. Sexual harassment is perhaps the most recent area of gender anti-discrimination law to be developed. In 1997, the Indian Supreme Court recognized sexual harassment in the workplace as not only a personal injury to the affected woman, but also a violation of her fundamental human rights. In its ruling, the Supreme Court issued guidelines making employers responsible for both preventive and remedial measures to make the workplace safe for women.[195]

India has no specific provisions governing age discrimination. Employers are generally free to establish age limits for any job according to their requirements.

Japan

Article 14 of the Japanese Constitution provides that "all of the people are equal under the law and there shall be no discrimination in political, economic or social relations because of race, creed, sex, social status, or family origin."[196] Despite this provision, Japanese anti-discrimination law is not very developed. Japan has no statutes prohibiting discrimination on the basis of race or national origin (most likely because Japan is generally a racially homogeneous society). Some Japanese courts, however, have permitted ethnic minorities to invoke international human rights law to challenge discrimination.[197] For example, in 1998 a Brazilian reporter was awarded 1.5 million yen ($12,500) after being ejected from a jewelry store because the store refused to serve foreigners. Although the judge noted that there was no statute banning discrimination against foreigners, the store owner's actions constituted an illegal tort under Japanese law because the reporter's basic human rights "to dignity and honor" were violated. As a result, the owner was liable for the mental anguish he caused.[198]

190. UNESCO, *India—Constitution*, *available at* http://www.unesco.org/most/rr3indi.htm.

191. Hillary Mayel, *India's "Untouchables" Face Violence, Discrimination*, Nat'l Geographic News, July 2, 2003, *available at* http://news.nationalgeographic.com/news/2003/06/0602_030602_untouchables.html.

192. Karine Schomer, *Culture Matters: Workforce Diversity in India and the U.S.*, Sourcingmag.com, http://www.sourcingmag.com/content/c070212a.asp?action=print.

193. Office of the Chief Commissioner for Persons with Disabilities (Govt. of India), Office Memorandum, *Consolidated Instructions of DOP&T on 3% Reservation*, Dec. 29, 2005, *available at* http://www.ccdisabilities.nic.in/page.php?s=reg&t=yb&p=dop_t.

194. Mines Act of 1952. *See* Ajmal Edappagath, *Gender Sensitive Legislative Legislation and Policies in India* (2001), *available at* http://www.unescap.org/esid/GAD/Events/EGMICT2001/edappagath.pdf.

195. Laxmi Murthy, *The Cost of Harassment*, IndiaNest.com, Aug. 11, 2002, http://www.boloji.com/wfs/wfs066.htm.

196. International Labor and Employment Laws 32-50–32-52 (Timothy J. Darby & William L. Keller eds., 2007).

197. Holning Lau, *Introduction to the Symposium Issue: Pluralism in Asia*, 36 N.C. J. Int'l L. & Com. Reg. 499 (2011).

198. Timothy Webster, *Reconstituting Japanese Law: International Norms and Domestic Litigation*, 30 Mich. J. Int'l L. 211 (2008).

Japan signed the UN Convention on the Rights of Persons with Disabilities in 2007 but, as of January 2012, Japan had not yet ratified it. Japan has been preparing for ratification by conducting studies and research projects on accommodation for people with disabilities.[199]

Laws regarding sex discrimination are the most highly developed discrimination laws in Japan. The Equal Employment Opportunity Law of 1985 (EEOL) prohibits discrimination against women in employment recruitment, hiring, assignment, promotion, training, education, fringe benefits, and termination. Amendments enacted in 1997 imposed a duty on employers to prevent sexual harassment and added sanctions, which were not present in the original law, to enforce these new provisions. In addition, when an employer violates the EEOL, the Labor Minister can publicize that fact.

Although twelve women were successful in procuring a court order upholding a $1.6 million award against a company for systematically discriminating against them in pay and promotions, many Japanese job seekers, labor lawyers, economists, and women's rights advocates interviewed by the *New York Times* said that the law had "had little real impact, and the old patterns of consignment of women to non-career positions [had] continued unabated."[200] The World Economic Forum ranked Japan ninety-eighth in its 2011 Gender Gap study,[201] and the Minister of Labor came under attack after he called women "child-bearing machines."[202]

Japan's Employment Promotion Law, which became effective in 2007, addresses employment discrimination based on age in recruiting and hiring. It applies to old and young, as well as domestic and foreign, employees.

---

199. Jin Nakagawa, *Future of Disability Law in Japan: Employment and Accommodation*, 33 Loy. L.A. Int'l & Comp. L. Rev. 173 (2010).

200. Howard W. French, *Diploma at Hand, Japanese Women Find Glass Ceiling Reinforced with Iron*, N.Y. Times, Jan. 1, 2001, at A4. *See also* Martin Flacker, *Career Women in Japan Find a Blocked Path*, N.Y. Times, Aug. 6, 2007.

201. World Economic Forum, *The Global Gender Gap*, available at http://reports.weforum.org/global-gender-gap-2011/.

202. Kyodo News, *Yanagisawa Apologizes Anew, Adds Gaffe*, Japan Times, Feb. 8, 2007, *available at* http://search.japantimes.co.jp/cgi-bin/nn20070208a2.html.

Mike Price/Shutterstock

THE RESPONSIBLE MANAGER

HONORING EMPLOYEES' CIVIL RIGHTS

Managers must be diligent in preventing and correcting any unlawful discrimination either in the preemployment process or during employment. Legally astute managers recognize the value of a diverse workforce that reflects the company's range of customers, suppliers, and other stakeholders.

Management should develop a written policy that (1) clearly outlines discriminatory acts prohibited by federal, state, and local statutes, and (2) prohibits retaliation against employees who complain about discrimination. Employees should be advised that any form of discrimination is inappropriate. The policy should have an enforcement mechanism and should clearly state that violations of the policy will result in poor performance reviews or termination. Such a policy will not only curb discriminatory acts but, in the event that litigation should arise, will also demonstrate that management diligently attempted to prevent such behavior.

The firm should also create an environment in which employees feel comfortable bringing complaints against fellow workers and supervisors. There should be at least two individuals in the company, a male and a female, to whom such complaints may be brought. Because supervisors are often the discriminators, an employee should not be required to first complain to his or her supervisor. Managers should not keep reports of harassment confidential, even if requested to do so by the employee. Each complaint should be thoroughly investigated, and, if necessary, the violator should be punished.

Although the establishment of a comprehensive policy is one way to prevent unlawful discriminatory practices, it is not sufficient in itself. Managers must also abide by the policy and comply with all federal, state, and local statutes prohibiting unlawful discrimination; supervisors should undergo training regarding such laws.[203] If management participates in discriminatory acts, the firm's employees will have little incentive to abide by its policy against discrimination and will hesitate to bring a claim for discriminatory treatment.

It is crucial that employers make sure that they do not retaliate against employees who have filed discrimination claims. Although employers often perceive discrimination claims by an employee as an act of disloyalty, retaliation for these claims will make it more likely that the employer will be found liable by a jury or judge, even if the initial claim would not have supported liability.

Employers should also create nondiscriminatory policies and procedures for hiring new employees. The employer

---

203. California codified this recommendation in 2004 by requiring that all supervisors employed in companies of more than fifty employees undergo harassment training every two years. Cal. Gov't Code § 12950.1 (West 2007).

CONTINUED

should avoid relying on word-of-mouth recruitment practices, which tend to reach a disproportionate number of persons of the same race or ethnicity as the employer's current employees, and should use media designed to reach people in both minority and nonminority communities. When advertising vacant positions, employers should use a job posting system that allows for an open and fair application process. The job advertisements themselves should not express a preference or limitation based on race, color, religion, gender, national origin, or age unless such specifications are based on bona fide occupational qualifications.

Employers should also train employees in interviewing to ensure that interviewers ask proper questions and use objective hiring criteria. Although federal laws do not expressly prohibit preemployment inquiries concerning an applicant's race, color, national origin, sex, marital status, religion, or age, such inquiries are disfavored because they create an inference that these factors will be used as selection criteria. Such inquiries may also be expressly prohibited under state law. As a general rule, recruitment personnel should ask themselves, "What information do I really need to decide whether an applicant is qualified to perform this job?"

With respect to the ADA, employers should be proactive and engage in an interactive process with employees requesting accommodation. If an employer explores every option but still cannot find a way to provide an accommodation, the employer should inform the individual and ask if he or she has any suggestions.[204] Employers should create a paper trail to document the actions they took to find an accommodation.

Employers may also want to consider employment practice liability insurance (EPLI) to protect against discrimination

claims. Interest in EPLI has been growing.[205] Areas of coverage include wage and hour, punitive damages, sexual harassment, discrimination, wrongful termination, breach of contract, invasion of privacy, emotional distress, libel or slander, benefits mismanagement, negligent compensation, promotion or hiring decisions, and third-party liability.[206]

Dating and romantic relationships between employees at a company can lead to discrimination and sexual harassment claims, particularly when there is a significant power and age gap between partners. Such relationships are very perilous. If the parties have a falling-out, the subordinate may claim that the relationship was not consensual and say that he or she feared adverse employment consequences for rebuffing the manager's advances. To address this problem, IBM instituted a policy that allows a manager to become involved with a subordinate as long as the manager transfers to another job within or outside the company, so that he or she is not supervising or evaluating the performance of the subordinate involved. Yale University prohibits sexual relationships between teachers and students and established a website entitled "Sexual Misconduct Response at Yale"[207] to address violations of its policies against all types of sexual misconduct.

---

204. *Interactive Process Helps Employers Prevail, but Isn't Required*, Corp. Couns. Wkly. (BNA), Jan. 10, 2001, at 12.

205. By 2005, approximately half the companies with 250 employees or more had some type of EPL insurance, and 19% of companies with 25 to 49 employees had such coverage. Richard S. Betterley, *The Betterley Report: Employment Practices Liability Insurance Market Survey 2010*, Dec. 2010, *available at* http://betterley.com/samples/EPLI10_nt.pdf; V. John Ella, *Employment Practices Liability Insurance Comes of Age*, Hennepin Law., Aug. 24, 2010, *available at* http://hennepin.timberlakepublishing.com/article.asp?article=1453&paper=1&cat=147.

206. Betterley, *supra* note 205; *What Is Employment Practices Liability Insurance, or EPLI?*, Business Insurance Now, http://www.businessinsurancenow.com/employment-practices-liability/ (last visited Nov. 22, 2011).

207. http://www.smr.yale.edu.

A MANAGER'S DILEMMA

Putting It into Practice

Can Jokes Create a Hostile Environment?

Catherine Van Order is a manager at American Eagle's hangar at the Miami International Airport. The hangar's workforce consists of eighty mechanics, including a small number of African Americans, Latinos, and white ex-strikers from Eastern Air Lines who are earning half as much as they did at their old employer. American Eagle is struggling to regain the public's confidence after two of its planes suffered fatal crashes. Although the airline is downsizing in two other southern cities, it wants to increase its business to

Latin America and the Caribbean, so it has hired more staff at the Miami airport. Workers are assigned heavy workloads at low pay and have to work with aging equipment in run-down facilities, leading to a great deal of tension at the Miami airport hangar.

Employees have tried to ease the tension by playing practical jokes on each other and making wisecracks. These jokes have included sexual and ethnic jokes along with comments about people's appearance, including weight, and their

CONTINUED

religion. Employees posted cartoons depicting black mechanics as gorillas or starving Somalis on the bulletin board. When Van Order suggested to one of the mechanics that the joking was getting out of control, he told her that people were just making fun of stereotypes and that nobody was trying to be personally offensive to their coworkers.

Although no employees complained to her about the joking, Van Order issued a memo setting forth the company's policy on discrimination and harassment. Several employees then told her that the memo had affected morale;

without the joking, workers seemed tense and anxious, and were less productive. Within several weeks, the joking commenced again and escalated when a poster of a black basketball player with a mop on his head and a watermelon in his hand was posted in the locker room. After this incident, Van Order spoke to several African American workers about it, but they seemed reluctant to talk. She sensed that they were quiet for fear of either losing their jobs or becoming the victim of hostile treatment by their coworkers. What should Van Order do?

INSIDE STORY

The Social Network of Employment Discrimination

Job seekers everywhere are using the Internet to pursue career opportunities, and employers are responding in kind by researching blogs and social networking websites like MySpace, Facebook, Twitter, and LinkedIn to find out more about job applicants and employees.[208] A 2009 Careerbuilder.com survey of more than 2,600 managers found that 45% of them were using Internet search engines and social media networks to research applicants, more than double the percentage (22%) in the previous year.[209] The study found that 35% of the employers decided not to extend offers of employment to applicants based on content found on the social media networks.

This increased use of the Internet by employers has raised new concerns that employers may misuse information available on the Web in making employment decisions. Although an employment application submitted over the Internet may not reveal protected characteristics, such as religion, political views, national origin, race, or sexual preference, an employer may be able to discover this information by searching profiles available on social networking websites. An employer may also discover photos or writings related to an applicant's religion, political views, national origin, race, or sexual history. It may also be difficult for an employer to determine whether information obtained through the Internet is credible; yet the employer may use this information to make an adverse employment decision regarding that applicant.

Another concern is that an employer may violate discrimination laws by searching the Internet for information only about specific applicants, such as women or minorities. Even if an employer conducts Internet searches for all applicants, it may show discriminatory bias toward some. For example, an employer may view a photo of an African American male holding a beer at a bar with a hip-hop DJ more negatively than a photo of a Caucasian male holding a beer at a rock 'n' roll bar with other white males wearing fraternity shirts.[210]

Employers may also use information obtained from the Internet to make adverse employment decisions about existing employees. There are numerous stories about employees who have been fired for content posted on their blogs or profiles on social networking sites. For example, a teacher at a Catholic school in Las Vegas was fired after posting on his MySpace page that he was gay; a Florida sheriff's deputy was fired after posting on his MySpace page that he was a heavy drinker and was fascinated with female breasts. Programmer Mark Pilgrim was fired after his manager followed a link from an online manual to Pilgrim's blog and discovered an essay about his past addictions to nicotine, alcohol, and marijuana.[211] Ellen Simonetti, a Delta Air Lines flight attendant, posted provocative pictures of herself in uniform on her blog. Delta terminated her because the company believed the photographs were inappropriate and a misuse of her uniform. Simonetti then filed a sex discrimination lawsuit because Delta had allowed male employees to post

CONTINUED

208. Lydia Dishman, *Monster.com's SeeMore Helps Recruiters Scout the Talent in the Resume Haystack*, FAST COMPANY, July 21, 2011, *available at* http://www.fastcompany.com/1768437/recruiters-start-your-search-engines-monstercoms-seemore-uses-semantics-to-find-talent.

209. Jenna Wortham, *More Employers Use Social Networks to Check Out Applicants*, N.Y. TIMES, AUG. 20, 2009; *Monster*, BUS. INSIDER, *available at* http://www.businessinsider.com/blackboard/monster (last modified Apr. 19, 2011).

210. George Lenard, *Employers Using Facebook for Background Checking, Part I*, GEORGE'S EMP. BLAWG (Dec. 5, 2006), *available at* http://www.employmentblawg.com/2006/employers-using-facebook-for-background-checking-part-i/.

211. Paul S. Gutman, *Say What? Blogging and Employment Law in Conflict*, 27 COLUM. J.L. & ARTS 145 (Fall 2003).

pictures of themselves in their uniforms on other websites.[212] In 2008, New England Patriots cheerleader Caitlin Davis was fired when a photo surfaced on Facebook showed her holding a sharpie next to a passed-out partygoer who had been covered in phallic symbols, swastikas, and the phrase "I'm a Jew."[213] In November 2011, a judge ruled that a first-grade teacher in New Jersey should be fired for a Facebook comment she made about her students: "I'm not a teacher—I'm a warden for future criminals!" The judge stated that this comment "demonstrated a complete lack of sensitivity to the world in which her students live."[214]

In response to employers' increased use of the Internet, the Office of Federal Contract Compliance Programs (OFCCP) instituted a rule in 2006 to ensure that federal contractors do not discriminate against minorities and women who apply for jobs on the Internet. The rule requires all federal contractors to maintain records of Internet résumés viewed, the race and gender of applicants, and which applicants were hired. If an employer uses a search function to find qualified applicants, it must save information about the search, including when it was conducted, the criteria used, and the names of the applicants identified through the search.[215]

As discussed in Chapter 12, certain Internet posts by workers about the terms and conditions of employment are protected collective action under the National Labor Relations Act. For example, an employee working at the nonprofit organization Hispanics United of Buffalo vented on Facebook, on a nonworking Saturday, about a coworker's accusation that she did not do enough for the organization's clients. The coworker reported the posting to a supervisor, who fired the employee who had posted comment, citing the company's social media policy banning cyber harassment of coworkers. After the employee reported the incident to the National Labor Relations Board, a judge ruled that employees were within their rights to converse about their working conditions and ordered reinstatement.[216]

In light of the trend toward researching employees and job applicants online, employees and applicants should assume that employers will read everything posted about them on the Internet. Indeed, certain employers have gone so far as to ask applicants to open their Facebook page during an interview or to provide their password, sparking new concerns about privacy and the legality of such requests. Employers trying to protect themselves should develop policies and procedures regarding the use of Internet searches to ensure that they will not be used in a discriminatory manner. The Internet is dramatically changing the availability of information related to employees and job applicants, but it remains to be seen how employment-discrimination laws will be applied to many of the new search techniques.

212. David W. Garland & Linda B. Katz, *Employers: Don't Get Bogged in Blogs*, 5–6 BENDER'S LAB. & EMP. BULL. 3 (June 1, 2005).

213. Dylan Love, *17 People Who Were Fired for Using Facebook*, BUSINESS INSIDER, May 11, 2011, *available at* http://www.businessinsider.com/facebook-fired-2011-5.

214. Emil Protalinski, *Teacher Should Be Fired for Facebook Comment, Judge Rules*, ZDNET, Nov. 15, 2011, *available at* http://www.zdnet.com/blog/facebook/teacher-should-be-fired-for-facebook-comment-judge-rules/5375.

215. Tresa Baldas, *Web Hiring Rule May Trigger New Suits*, NAT'L L.J., Dec. 7, 2005; Ida Bergstrom, *Facebook Can Ruin Your Life. And So Can MySpace, Bebo*, Feb. 10, 2008, *available at* http://www.independent.co.uk/life-style/gadgets-and-tech/news/facebook-can-ruin-your-life-and-so-can-myspace-bebo-780521.html.

216. *Employees Can't Be Fired for Facebook Complaints, Judge Says*, FORBES, Sept. 8, 2011.

KEY WORDS AND PHRASES

adverse employment action   394

back pay   394

bona fide occupational qualification (BFOQ)   409

covered service member family leave   418

disparate impact   395

disparate treatment   395

family responsibility discrimination (FRD)   406

fetal-protection policies   406

front pay   394

hostile environment harassment   398

major life activity   414

qualifying exigency leave   418

quid pro quo harassment   398

reasonable accommodation (disability)   415

reasonable factor other than age (RFOA) defense   412

sexual stereotyping   399

undue hardship   416

QUESTIONS AND CASE PROBLEMS

1. Beginning in 1996, Tanisha Matthews, an Apostolic Christian, worked as an overnight stocker at Wal-Mart's store in Joliet, Illinois. In September 2005, during a break in the overnight shift, Matthews took part in a conversation about God and homosexuality. The next day an employee informed a manager that Matthews had made inappropriate comments about gays to a gay employee named Amy. Over the next three months, Wal-Mart investigated the incident by interviewing and obtaining statements from employees who were present during the conversation. In her statement, Amy reported that Matthews was "screaming over her" that God does not accept gays, they should not "be on earth," and they will "go to hell" because they are not "right in the head." Five other employees confirmed that Matthews had said that gays are sinners and are going to hell.

   Wal-Mart fired Matthews after concluding that she had engaged in serious harassment in violation of Wal-Mart's Discrimination and Harassment Prevention Policy. This policy, which Matthews was aware of at the time of the incident, prohibits employees from engaging in conduct that could reasonably be interpreted as harassment based on an individual's status, including sexual orientation, and provides that employees who violate the policy will receive "coaching and/or other discipline, up to and including termination." Wal-Mart has a "zero tolerance" policy for harassment "regardless of whether such conduct rises to the level of unlawful discrimination or harassment" and treats serious harassment as gross misconduct and grounds for immediate termination.

   Matthews filed suit, alleging that terminating her for stating that gays will go to hell—a belief that she maintains is an aspect of her Apostolic Christian faith—constitutes unlawful discrimination under Title VII. Is she correct? [*Matthews v. Wal-Mart Stores, Inc.*, 417 F. App'x 552 (7th Cir. 2011).]

2. In May 2003, Jennifer Willis, senior account manager at Coca Cola Enterprises, called her supervisor and said she was sick and unable to come to work. She also told him she was pregnant, but did not specify that she was sick because of the pregnancy. When she called in the next day, a Tuesday, to find out where she should report to work, she was told that she needed a medical release. She told her supervisor that she had a doctor's appointment on "Wednesday," which the supervisor assumed was the next day, but the appointment was actually scheduled for the following Wednesday. Willis had no further contact with her employer until Thursday of the next week, when company officials arrived at her home to recover her company car. At that point, she contacted her employer and was eventually brought in for a meeting where she was informed that she had been terminated for violating the company's "No Call/No Show" policy. Under this policy, "an employee absent from work for three consecutive days without notifying the supervisor during that period will be considered to have voluntarily resigned." Willis filed a lawsuit in which she claimed that her termination was discriminatory. Does Willis have a valid claim? How should Coca Cola Enterprises respond? [*Willis v. Coca Cola Enterprises, Inc.*, 445 F.3d 413 (5th Cir. 2006).]

3. In September 1998, Christie Helm was hired as an administrative assistant for both Judge Frederick Stewart and Judge Robert Bednar in the First Judicial District of Kansas. Judge Stewart began sexually harassing Helm shortly after she was hired. For several years, the harassment primarily involved touching Helm's rear end, thighs, and legs. Additionally, in 1999, Judge Stewart forced a kiss on Helm in front of the courthouse.

   Helm took a medical leave of absence during the spring and early summer of 2006. After Helm returned to work, Judge Stewart started touching her inappropriately again. During the spring of 2007, the harassment began to escalate. Throughout March and April, Judge Stewart would regularly close the door of his office and kiss Helm. In addition, he once put his hands up Helm's skirt. In late May or early June 2007, Judge Stewart put his hands up Helm's skirt and penetrated her vagina with his finger. He also told her that he wanted to have sex with her on the couch in his chambers and make her have an orgasm. In June 2007, Judge Stewart unbuttoned Helm's blouse on two different occasions and fondled her breasts.

   Between 2003 and 2007, Helm complained to her coworker Karen Connor about Judge Stewart on approximately ten different occasions. She never mentioned specifics, stating only that Judge Stewart made her uncomfortable. In late June or early July 2007, Helm approached David King, the chief judge of the First Judicial District, and told him that Judge Stewart had done something inappropriate and made her feel uncomfortable. She did not disclose any details, however. Chief Judge King advised her of the procedure for making a complaint. He also told her that if she wished to make a complaint, the First Judicial District "would stand beside and support her fully and that there would be no consequence to her as a result of making the complaint." Helm said that she wanted to think about whether to make a complaint, and Chief Judge King responded, "Well, don't take too long, because if you don't do anything, I'm going to have to do something since you've conveyed this to me."

   Helm came back to Chief Judge King the same day and said that she had resolved the matter with Judge Stewart and did not wish to pursue it further. Chief Judge King relayed his conversation with Helm to Steven Crossland, the court administrator, but neither King nor Crossland made a report to the Office of Judicial Administration (OJA). In July 2007, Helm requested medical leave so that she could seek treatment for alcohol and drug abuse. She was given permission to take unpaid leave under the Family and Medical Leave Act after she exhausted her sick leave and vacation.

   On August 8, 2007, before Helm was scheduled to return to work, she reported to Judge Bednar that Judge Stewart had sexually harassed her. Helm told Judge Bednar that the harassment was "basically verbal, but it had gotten to touching or had involved touching." She also informed Judge Bednar about her previous conversations with Chief Judge King.

Judge Bednar immediately reported Helm's complaint to Chief Judge King and Steven Crossland. Crossland notified the OJA of the complaint later that same day. Crossland planned to talk to Helm and Chief Judge King when she returned to work on August 13, 2007, about changing her duties so that she would not have to work for Judge Stewart anymore. Helm did not return to work on August 13.

On September 18, 2007, Helm was arrested following an altercation with her husband. She was charged with aggravated battery (a felony) and domestic battery and disorderly conduct (both misdemeanors). Helm ultimately entered into a diversion agreement that included her stipulation to facts that satisfied the elements of the three charged offenses. On December 3, 2007, Chief Judge King sent Helm a letter informing her that the conduct to which she admitted violated three provisions of the Kansas Court Personnel Rules. He further explained that her decision to enter into a diversion on a felony charge disqualified her from accessing defendants' criminal histories under the rules established for the Kansas Criminal Justice Information System. This precluded her from carrying out her duties as an administrative assistant.

Helm responded in a letter dated December 7, 2007. She provided a number of reasons why she should be allowed to continue working for the First Judicial District, including the fact that Ron Chance, the court administrator who preceded Crossland, had entered into a diversion on a DUI charge and had not been fired. Helm suggested that her criminal prosecution and the proposed termination represented retaliation for her complaining about Judge Stewart's sexual harassment. One week later, Chief Judge King wrote to Helm again and informed her that she was terminated effective immediately. He rejected Helm's attempt to compare her situation to Chance's, explaining that Helm was the only employee that he knew who had admitted to facts constituting a felony offense against another person.

Helm filed a charge of discrimination against the State of Kansas with the EEOC, in which she alleged sexual harassment and retaliatory discharge in violation of Title VII. What result? [*Helm v. Kansas*, 656 F.3d 1277 (10th Cir. 2011).]

4. Benjamin Endres was an officer in the Indiana State Police. Soon after Indiana began licensing casinos, Endres was assigned by lottery to a full-time position as a Gaming Commission agent at the Blue Chip Casino in Michigan City, Indiana. Gaming Commission agents certify gambling revenue, investigate complaints from the public about the gaming system, and conduct licensing investigations for the casinos and their employees. Endres, a Baptist, believed that he must neither gamble nor help others do so, because games of chance are sinful.

Endres told the State Police that he was willing to enforce general vice laws at casinos, but that providing the specialized services required of Gaming Commission agents would violate his religious beliefs because it would facilitate gambling. When the State Police refused his request for a different assignment, Endres refused to report for duty and was fired for insubordination.

Endres sues under Title VII, contending that the State of Indiana discriminated against him on account of his religion by failing to reasonably accommodate his religious beliefs. The State of Indiana moves to dismiss the claim. How should the court rule? [*Endres v. Indiana State Police*, 349 F.3d 922 (7th Cir. 2003).]

5. Amaani Lyle applied for the position of writers' assistant for a television show about the lives of young, sexually active adults. During her interview, she was told that one of the most important aspects of the job was taking very copious and detailed notes for the writers' meetings, where story lines, jokes, and dialogue were discussed. She was also told that she must type incredibly fast. Four months after she was hired, the producers fired Lyle because she consistently missed very important story lines and jokes during the writers' meetings and typed too slowly.

Lyle subsequently filed a claim for sexual harassment. She claimed that during the writers' meetings, the writers constantly engaged in discussions about anal and oral sex, discussed their sexual exploits both real and fantasized, commented on the sexual nature of the female actors on the show, made and displayed crude drawings of women's breasts and vaginas, pretended to masturbate, and altered the words on the scripts and other documents to create new words such as "tits" and "penis."

Warner Brothers defended on the basis that the writers' job was to create jokes, dialogue, and story lines for an adult-oriented situation comedy:

> [B]ecause "Friends" deals with sexual matters, intimate body parts and risqué humor, the writers of the show are required to have frank sexual discussions and tell colorful jokes and stories (and even make expressive gestures) as part of the creative process of developing story lines, dialogue, gags, and jokes for each episode. Lyle, as a writers' assistant, would reasonably be exposed to such discussions, jokes, and gestures.

Who should prevail on Lyle's sexual harassment claim? [*Lyle v. Warner Brothers Television Productions*, 132 P.3d 211 (Cal. 2006).]

6. Kenneth Horgan was diagnosed as HIV positive in 1990 but kept his illness confidential. In February 2001, he began working as a sales manager for Morgan, a linen and uniform rental services company. In January 2008, he was promoted to general manager of the Chicago facility. In July 2009, the company's president and Horgan's supervisor, Timothy Simmons, asked to meet with Horgan for what Simmons called a "social visit." During that meeting, he told Horgan that he was "really worried about him" and demanded to know what was going on with him, telling Horgan that "if there was something medical going on, [he] needed to know."

Although Horgan insisted that nothing was going on that would interfere with his work, Simmons "continued to insist that there was something physical or mental" that was affecting Horgan. At that point, Horgan felt compelled to tell Simmons that he was HIV positive, but he assured Simmons that his condition had no effect on his ability to perform his job duties. Simmons then asked about his prognosis, and Horgan replied that he had been HIV positive for a long time, that his condition was under control, and that he had not yet progressed to AIDS. Simmons then asked "how he could ever perform his job with his HIV positive condition and how he could continue to work with a terminal illness." Simmons also said that "a General Manager needs to be respected by the employees and have the ability to lead" and then added that he "did not know how [Horgan] could lead if employees knew about his condition."

Simmons ended the meeting by telling Horgan that he needed to "recover" and that he should "go on vacation" and "leave the plant immediately." Simmons then discussed the issue with Morgan's owner. The next day Horgan received a copy of an e-mail sent to all general managers and corporate staff indicating that "effective immediately" Horgan was "no longer a member of Morgan []."

Horgan brought suit, claiming that he was terminated because of his disability in violation of the ADA and that Simmons's questioning was an impermissible medical inquiry in violation of the ADA. Who will prevail? [*Horgan v. Simmons*, 704 F. Supp. 2d 814 (N.D. Ill. 2010).]

7. Burnett was a janitor for Habitat, a property management business. His job required him to lift heavy objects. In October 2003, Burnett told Polo, his supervisor, that he had a medical problem. Polo offered to transfer Burnett to a different location, but Burnett declined because of his "weak bladder" and the reduced access to a restroom at the other location. After he missed work for a week in December, Burnett presented Polo with a copy of a doctor's examination that showed he had a serious prostate problem. When he met with Polo to discuss his absence, Burnett said he was feeling sick and compared his symptoms to his brother-in-law's symptoms before he was diagnosed with prostate cancer. In January 2004, Burnett told another supervisor that he was going to have a prostate biopsy at the end of the month. A short time later, Polo reprimanded Burnett for wasting time, and Burnett filed a union grievance.

After the biopsy, Burnett returned to work with a doctor's treatment plan that restricted him from heavy lifting or strenuous activity. Burnett claimed that his supervisors ignored these restrictions, and he submitted two vacation requests. Polo denied the second request and told Burnett that the treatment plan was not important. Burnett said he was going home because he felt sick, and Polo terminated

him the next day for insubordination. A week after he was terminated, Burnett was diagnosed with prostate cancer. Burnett claimed Habitat violated the FMLA by denying him leave and violated the ADA. Did Habitat violate the FMLA? The ADA? What defense will Habitat assert? Did Burnett's supervisors exercise good business judgment? Act ethically? [*Burnett v. LFW Inc.*, 472 F.3d 471 (7th Cir. 2006).]

8. Mo-Tech manufactures molds for the consumer products, automotive, medical, and computer industries. In 2007, it laid off its three oldest and most skilled mold-makers—Richard Rahlf, Frank Stelter, and Scott Johnson—in a reduction in force (RIF). When these three employees began working in the 1980s, molds were made manually. In the early 1990s, Mo-Tech began using a Computer Numerical Control machine (CNC) to help make the molds. A CNC machine is programmed by a mold-maker to the product specifications and directs the production of the mold. Clients often design parts for CNC-generated models, and the CNC technology makes the process easier and faster. Consequently, there is greater need for mold-makers proficient in this technology than for those trained in traditional manual mold-making. Despite the growing popularity of the CNC machine, Mo-Tech did not require or provide its employees with formal training on it. Instead, employees were trained on the job when CNC machines were available. Rahlf practiced on the CNC machines at work; Stelter and Johnson each attended CNC training in the 1990s.

Mo-Tech claimed that its RIF was necessary to meet changing client needs and address anticipated reductions in workload and profitability. The company's stated goal "was to shift the work that remained to the more efficient and less labor intensive CNC mold making process while reducing the total number of Class A manual mold makers employed to reflect the anticipated decrease in its workload." To determine which mold-makers to let go, three Mo-Tech managers ranked the mold-makers based on several factors, including CNC proficiency, general mold-making efficiency, and their own observations of each employee's work. Within one year after firing the plaintiffs, Mo-Tech hired new (and younger) mold-makers, and its sales increased.

Rahlf, Stelter, and Johnson claimed that Mo-Tech's stated reason for terminating them was pretextual on five grounds: (1) there was no need for a RIF, (2) Mo-Tech failed to review their performance evaluations, (3) Mo-Tech did not follow its own termination criteria, (4) Mo-Tech destroyed the evidence it relied on to make the decision, and (5) Mo-Tech changed its reasons for the termination. What must the plaintiffs show to establish a prima facie case of age discrimination? Does the employer have a valid defense? How might it have avoided this lawsuit? [*Rahlf v. Mo-Tech Corp.*, 642 F.3d 633 (8th Cir. 2011).]

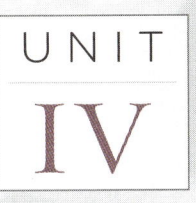

UNIT

IV

THE REGULATORY ENVIRONMENT

CHAPTER 14

CRIMINAL LAW

INTRODUCTION

IMPACT ON CORPORATE BEHAVIOR

Criminal law is a powerful tool for controlling corporate behavior and ensuring ethical conduct. Primary areas of concern for many managers include bribery, compliance with environmental laws, worker safety, government contracts, securities fraud, antitrust law compliance, and securities trading by officers and directors.

White-collar crime in the United States costs more than $300 billion annually.[1] By comparison, personal and household crimes account for the relatively paltry sum of $15.7 billion.[2] According to one survey, one-third of the companies in the world have engaged in criminal misconduct.[3]

Criminal liability may be imposed in several ways. Individuals are always responsible for their own criminal acts, even if they were following orders from top management. In certain limited circumstances, supervisors may be vicariously liable for the acts of their subordinates. Corporations (and other business entities) may also be found guilty of crimes based on the illegal conduct of their employees.

CHAPTER OVERVIEW

This chapter defines the elements necessary to create criminal liability. It discusses the statutory sources of criminal law and then describes criminal procedure—the mechanics of a criminal action, the plea options, and the trial. The chapter then explains

a number of constitutional issues, including search warrant requirements and the privilege against self-incrimination. The chapter continues with a discussion of the Federal Sentencing Guidelines. Then it summarizes a variety of white-collar crimes, including violations of the Racketeer Influenced and Corrupt Organizations Act, wire and mail fraud, money laundering, computer crime, and obstruction of justice. The chapter also provides a list of penalties and concludes with a brief description of federal amnesty and leniency programs.

DEFINITION OF A CRIME

A *crime* is an offense against the public at large. It may be defined as any act that violates the duties owed to the community, for which the offender must make satisfaction to the public. Conviction of a crime can lead to a substantial fine, a prison sentence, or even the death penalty. Because the results of a criminal conviction can be so serious, an act is criminal only if it is defined as such in a federal or state statute or a local ordinance enacted by a city or county. In contrast, much of civil law was developed by the courts without applicable statutes or ordinances. A criminal charge and prosecution are brought by either the state or the federal government. Under most federal and state laws, crimes are divided into two categories. A *felony* is a crime punishable by death or by imprisonment for more than one year. A *misdemeanor* is a less serious crime, punishable by a fine or a jail sentence of one year or less.

SOURCES OF CRIMINAL LAW

By some estimates, the *United States Code* contains more than 4,500 federal criminal offenses.[4] If one includes the *Code of Federal Regulations*, that number increases to almost 15,000.[5]

1. Federal Bureau of Investigation, *Seattle Division: What We Investigate* (2011), *available at* http://www.fbi.gov/seattle/about-us/what-we-investigate/priorities.
2. Federal Bureau of Investigation, *Crime in the United States 2010* (2011), *available at* http://www.fbi.gov/about-us/cjis/ucr/crime-in-the-u.s/2010/crime-in-the-u.s.-2010 (last visited Dec. 12, 2011).
3. *Financial Misrepresentation Leads Concerns in New Corporate Economic Crime Survey*, Corp. Couns. Wkly. (BNA), July 23, 2003, at 227.
4. Gary Fields & John R. Emshwiller, *As Criminal Laws Proliferate, More Are Ensnared*, Wall St. J., July 23, 2011.
5. John Baker, *Revisiting the Explosive Growth of Federal Crimes*, Heritage Found., June 16, 2008.

The criminal statutes of the individual states are similar to their federal counterparts, but they are not exactly the same. This is because most states have adopted the Model Penal Code but have modified it to meet their own needs. The *Model Penal Code* is a set of criminal law statutes that were proposed by the National Conference of Commissioners on Uniform State Laws for adoption by the states.

ELEMENTS OF A CRIME

Two elements are necessary to create criminal liability: (1) an act that violates an existing criminal statute and (2) the requisite state of mind.

The Criminal Act

The term *actus reus* (guilty act or wrongful deed) is often used to describe the act in question. A crime is not committed unless some overt act has occurred. Merely thinking about a criminal activity is not criminal.

The State of Mind

The statute that defines the criminal act also defines the requisite state of mind. Generally, a crime is not committed unless the criminal act named in the statute is performed with the requisite state of mind, known as *mens rea* (guilty mind). The U.S. Supreme Court has characterized the requirement of "a relation between some mental element and punishment for a harmful act [as] almost as instinctive as the child's familiar exculpatory 'But I didn't mean to.'"[6] When statutory language is ambiguous, the traditional assumption is that some *mens rea* is required.[7]

Mens Rea: *Negligence, Recklessness, and Intent*

The three forms of *mens rea* are negligence, recklessness, and intention to do wrong. Negligence is the least culpable state of mind, and intention to do wrong is the most culpable. Generally speaking, crimes associated with a higher degree of culpability are punished more severely. Convictions for intentional homicide, for instance, bring penalties far more harsh than those for negligent homicide.

Negligence is the failure to see the possible negative consequences of one's actions that a reasonable person would have seen. Individuals may be negligent even if they did not know that their conduct could cause harm. All that is necessary is a showing that a reasonable person would have known of the possible harm. A reasonable person is often thought of as a rational person using ordinary care under the circumstances.

Recklessness is the conscious disregard of a substantial risk that one's actions will result in the harm prohibited by the statute. Recklessness is found when the individual knew of the possible harm of his or her act but ignored the risk. A person has an *intention to do wrong* when he or she consciously intends to cause the harm prohibited by the statute, or when he or she knows such harm is substantially certain to result from his or her conduct.

The commonly invoked platitude "ignorance of the law is no excuse" is true as a general principle. Nevertheless, this is an imprecise rule that, taken alone, does not tell courts how to apply the *mens rea* requirements of particular criminal statutes. There is often substantial room for interpretation and debate when construing the *mens rea* requirement.

For example, criminal statutes often require willful or knowing misconduct or both. Although "willful" is a "word of many meanings whose construction is often dependent on the context in which it appears,"[8] in general, a *willful* act is "one undertaken with a 'bad purpose.' In other words, in order to establish a 'willful' violation of a statute, 'the Government must prove that the defendant acted with knowledge that his conduct was unlawful.'"[9] The defendant does not need to have known which particular law he or she was breaking, however; it is sufficient that the defendant knew that he or she was violating some law.

In contrast, the term *knowingly* requires proof of knowledge of the facts that constitute the offense, not knowledge of unlawfulness, unless the text of the statute dictates a different result. For example, a person cannot be convicted of knowingly acquiring food stamps in a manner not authorized by the statute or regulations unless he knew that he was acquiring food stamps in an unauthorized or illegal manner.[10] Similarly, to convict a defendant for "knowingly transfer[ing], possess[ing], or us[ing], without lawful authority, a means of identification of another person,"[11] the government must prove that the defendant knew that the "means of identification" that he or she unlawfully transferred, possessed, or used did in fact belong to another person, as opposed to being a counterfeit. It is not enough to show that the defendant knew that he or she was transferring, possessing, or using a means of identification without lawful authority, unless the government also shows that the defendant knew that this means of identification belonged to another person.[12]

---

6. Morissette v. United States, 342 U.S. 246, 250–51 (1952).

7. Liparota v. United States, 471 U.S. 419 (1985).

8. Bryan v. United States, 524 U.S. 184, 191 (1998).

9. *Id.*; *see also* Safeco Ins. Co. of Am. v. Burr, 551 U.S. 47 (2007) (differentiating between the meaning of "willful" in criminal and civil contexts and holding that mere recklessness is sufficient in a civil case).

10. *Liparota*, 471 U.S. 419.

11. 18 U.S.C.A. § 1028A(a)(1).

12. Flores-Figueroa v. United States, 556 U.S. 646 (2009).

In contrast, consider the intention-to-do-wrong requirement in the context of the federal false-statement statute.[13] The statute makes it a crime to "knowingly and willfully" make any false statement or representation "in any manner within the jurisdiction of any department or agency of the United States." Suppose that a woman made a statement to a federal agent knowing that the statement was false but without knowing that the person to whom she directed the statement was a federal agent. Would this defendant be convicted? The U.S. Supreme Court ruled that she would be.[14] The Court applied the "intention-to-do-wrong" requirement only to the "false-statement" portion of the statute. In other words, it required only that the defendant knowingly lied to a person who was in fact a federal agent, rather than that she knowingly lied to a person she knew was a federal agent.

Strict Liability

Under certain statutes, a person can be guilty regardless of his or her state of mind or degree of fault. This is known as *strict liability*. Typically, strict liability statutes address issues of public health and safety[15] or involve "dangerous or deleterious devices or products or obnoxious waste materials,"[16] such as grenades[17] and opium.[18] Strict liability statutes are generally disfavored, and most courts will require clear legislative intent to impose strict liability before they will dispense with *mens rea* as an element of a crime.[19] As a result, a court may require knowledge of wrongdoing even when the statute is silent on the mental state required. (Vicarious criminal liability for regulatory offenses is discussed later in the chapter.)

CRIMINAL VERSUS CIVIL LIABILITY

Civil law, particularly tort law (discussed in Chapter 9), compensates the victim for legal wrongs committed against a person or his or her property. Criminal law protects society by punishing the criminal. It does not compensate the victim. The victim of a crime may bring a civil suit for damages against the perpetrator, however.

---

13. 18 U.S.C. § 1001.

14. United States v. Yermian, 468 U.S. 63 (1984).

15. *See, e.g.*, United States v. Park, 421 U.S. 658 (1975) (Food, Drug and Cosmetic Act).

16. United States v. Int'l Minerals & Chem. Corp., 402 U.S. 558, 564–65 (1971).

17. United States v. Freed, 401 U.S. 601 (1971).

18. United States v. Balint, 258 U.S. 250 (1922) (holding that a person could be guilty of undocumented sales of certain narcotics even if he did not know that the drugs he was selling were "narcotics" within the ambit of the Narcotic Act of 1914).

19. *See, e.g.*, Staples v. United States, 511 U.S. 600 (1994).

Many regulatory statutes provide for both criminal and civil sanctions. An individual or a firm may therefore be sued under both criminal and civil law for a single act. Violation of a criminal statute is *negligence per se*; this means that in a subsequent civil suit, the court will accept the criminal conviction as sufficient proof that the defendant was negligent, that is, that he or she did not act with the care a reasonably prudent person would have used under the same circumstances. Consequently, defendants must carefully review their criminal defense strategy in light of possible future civil litigation.

Burden of Proof

Criminal trials impose a much heavier *burden of proof* than civil cases. In a criminal case, the accused is presumed innocent until proved guilty beyond a reasonable doubt. In most civil cases, the plaintiff only needs to establish the facts by a preponderance of the evidence.

This difference in the degree of proof required is typical of the procedural and constitutional safeguards protecting defendants' rights throughout criminal proceedings. In a criminal case, the formidable resources of the state are focused on an individual. In this contest of unequal strength, it seems only fair to require the state to meet a higher standard of proof.

CRIMINAL PROCEDURE

A criminal action begins with the arrest of the person suspected of a crime and proceeds through a preliminary hearing to plea bargaining and trial.

Arrest

After a person is *arrested* (taken into custody against his or her will for criminal prosecution or interrogation), he or she is taken to a police station and *booked*; that is, the charges against him or her are written in a register. The arresting police officer must then file a report with the prosecutor. Based on this report, the prosecutor decides whether to press charges against the arrested person. If charges are to be pressed, many states require that the accused be taken before a public judicial official, usually a justice of the peace or magistrate, to be informed of the charges. *Bail*, the amount of money a defendant must post as a bond to guarantee his or her appearance at trial, is often determined during this initial appearance before the public official. Sometimes a defendant will be released from custody pending trial on his or her own recognizance without having to post bail.

Plea

If the charge is only a misdemeanor, the accused will be asked at this initial appearance whether he or she pleads guilty or not guilty. In the case of a felony, the next step in many states is a *preliminary hearing*, at which the prosecutor must present evidence demonstrating probable cause that the defendant committed the felony. Following this hearing, formal charges are usually filed either by the prosecutor through an *information*, a document filed with the court, or by a grand jury through an *indictment*. The accused is then arraigned before a trial court judge. At the arraignment, the accused is informed of the charges against him or her and asked to enter a *plea* of guilty or not guilty. If the defendant enters a plea of not guilty, the case is set for trial.

The accused can also plead *nolo contendere*, which means that he or she does not contest the charges. For the purpose of the criminal proceedings, a plea of *nolo contendere* is equivalent to a guilty plea. Unlike a guilty plea, however, a plea of *nolo contendere* cannot be introduced at a subsequent civil trial. Therefore, a *nolo contendere* plea may be used by corporate defendants who anticipate civil suits based on the same activity for which they face criminal charges.

Plea Bargaining, Immunity, and Consent Decrees

Very few cases ever reach trial. Most are resolved through plea bargaining between the accused and the prosecutor. *Plea bargaining* is the process whereby the prosecutor agrees to reduce the charges in exchange for a guilty plea from the accused.

Frequently, a lower-ranking member of a criminal conspiracy will "cop a plea," that is, provide the prosecutor with testimony incriminating his or her criminal superiors, in exchange for a reduced sentence or immunity from prosecution. The immunity granted may be either use immunity or transactional immunity. *Use immunity* prohibits the testimony of the witness from being used against that witness in any way. *Transactional immunity*, which is broader, prohibits any criminal prosecution of the witness that relates to any matter discussed in his or her testimony.

Some courts have challenged the offer of leniency in exchange for testimony as a violation of the federal statute forbidding the exchange of "anything of value" for testimony.[20] The twelve federal courts of appeals that have considered the issue, however, have all rejected that challenge and allow the government to offer leniency.[21] As one circuit court judge put it:

> To pay a witness, other than an expert witness, for his testimony is irregular and in fact is unlawful in federal trials. . . . The practice of paying witnesses for their testimony

apparently is forbidden in trials in the state courts of Wisconsin as well. To pay in money, that is; immunity from prosecution, a lighter sentence, placement in a witness-protection program, and other breaks are lawful coin in this realm.[22]

Consent decrees are common in the corporate context. A *consent decree* is a court order based on an agreement by the defendant corporation to take measures to remedy the problem that led to the criminal charges. Like a plea of *nolo contendere*, a consent decree cannot be introduced as evidence of guilt in a subsequent civil trial.

Trial

A criminal trial proceeds in much the same way as the civil trials discussed in Chapter 3. There are opening statements, direct examination and cross-examination of witnesses, and closing arguments. The jury then deliberates to reach a verdict of guilty or not guilty.

Sentencing

If the defendant is convicted, the court will proceed with sentencing. State and federal criminal statutes normally specify penalties that include both jail or prison time and monetary fines. The length of the sentence and the amount of the fine usually fall within a specified range. In a state court, if the defendant is found guilty, the judge generally has sentencing discretion within that range. Under the Federal Sentencing Guidelines, as interpreted by the U.S. Supreme Court, a sentencing court is required to consider the criteria and ranges specified by the guidelines but has discretion to depart from them as the judge sees fit.[23]

CONSTITUTIONAL PROTECTIONS

The U.S. Constitution affords criminal defendants a number of important rights and protections.

Ex Post Facto Clause

Under the *Ex Post Facto Clause* of the U.S. Constitution,[24] a person can be convicted of a crime only if his or her actions constituted a crime at the time they occurred. As the U.S. Supreme Court explained: "To fall within the ex post facto prohibition, a law must be retrospective—that is, it must apply to events occurring before its enactment—and

20. 18 U.S.C. § 201(c)(2).

21. United States v. Souffront, 338 F.3d 809 (7th Cir. 2003). The Federal Circuit, which hears primarily patent claim appeals, has not yet considered the issue.

22. Mataya v. Kingston, 371 F.3d 353, 359 (7th Cir. 2004).

23. United States v. Booker, 543 U.S. 220 (2005).

24. U.S. Const. art. I, § 10.

it must disadvantage the offender affected by it, by altering the definition of criminal conduct or increasing the punishment for the crime."[25]

The Ex Post Facto Clause also prevents a person from having to bear legal consequences for an act when such legal consequences did not exist at the time the act was committed. For example, it is unconstitutional to apply less strict proof requirements to establish a conviction than were imposed when the criminal act was committed.[26] Similarly, the Supreme Court struck down a California statute that permitted the resurrection of otherwise time-bound prosecutions for sex-related child abuse.[27] The clause does not, however, preclude courts from retroactively applying judicially created modifications to federal statutes and regulations as long as the prior law put the defendant on notice that his or her conduct was wrongful.[28]

There is a split in the circuits over the applicability of the clause to administrative regulations. The U.S. Court of Appeals for the Tenth Circuit applied the Ex Post Facto Clause to an agency regulation that was legislative in nature,[29] but the First Circuit declined to do so.[30] The U.S. Court of Appeals for the Third Circuit ruled in a civil case that the Ex Post Facto Clause bars application of a new agency regulation that alters substantive rights or obligations, but does not bar application of a new regulation that merely clarifies what those existing rights and obligations have always been.[31] Accordingly, there was no impermissible retroactive effect when a new Securities and Exchange Commission rule clarifying what constitutes short-swing trading under section 16(b) was applied to securities trades made before the new rule took effect.

Fourth Amendment Protections

The Fourth Amendment to the U.S. Constitution provides:

> The right of the people to be secure in their persons, houses, papers, and effects, against unreasonable searches and seizures, shall not be violated, and no Warrants shall issue, but upon probable cause, supported by Oath or affirmation, and particularly describing the place to be searched, and the persons or things to be seized.

This provision was intended to prevent the arbitrary and intrusive searches that had characterized British rule during the American colonial period, and it applies only to actions by government officials, unless a private person is acting on behalf of the government. As discussed in detail below, courts have struggled to strike the appropriate balance between the individual's reasonable expectation of privacy and the government's legitimate need to secure evidence of wrongdoing to prevent criminal acts and apprehend criminals.

The Arrest Warrant Requirement

An arrest is a Fourth Amendment seizure. A valid arrest requires *probable cause*, that is, a reasonable belief that the suspect has committed a crime or is about to commit a crime. Certain stops and searches may be justified without a showing of probable cause, however, such as brief questioning when police observe unusual conduct that leads to a reasonable suspicion of criminal activity.

In general, an arrest warrant is required only for arrests in the suspect's own home or in another person's home. The Fourth Amendment does not require that a warrant be obtained prior to an arrest in a public place when the officer has reasonable suspicion to believe a felony has been committed by the individual or when a misdemeanor has been committed in the officer's presence. In determining what is "reasonable suspicion," the Supreme Court has deemed nervous, evasive behavior on the part of the suspect to be relevant. For example, the Court held that an arrest made by police officers patrolling a high-crime area was reasonable when the suspect fled after spotting the officers.[32] Stating that headlong flight is a "consummate act of evasion," the Court reasoned that "determination of reasonable suspicion must be based on common sense judgments and inferences about human behavior."

The Search Warrant Requirement

The Fourth Amendment prohibits only "unreasonable searches and seizures" without a search warrant. The courts have wrestled with defining what is "unreasonable" and what constitutes a "search."

Reasonable and Unreasonable Expectations of Privacy: The *Katz* Test A touchstone of the Supreme Court's analysis in Fourth Amendment cases is whether the individual has a reasonable expectation of privacy under the circumstances. In the Court's landmark Fourth Amendment case *United States v. Katz*,[33] Justice John Marshall Harlan's concurring opinion framed the issue as follows: Has government action intruded on an individual's subjective expectation of privacy? If so, is that expectation one that society deems reasonable? If an individual has a subjective privacy expectation that society deems reasonable, then the

25. Lynce v. Mathis, 519 U.S. 433, 441 (1997).

26. Carmell v. Texas, 529 U.S. 513 (2000) (overturning the conviction of a man for sexually assaulting his stepdaughter based on her testimony alone because, at the time the offenses occurred, Texas law required corroborating evidence).

27. Stogner v. California, 539 U.S. 607 (2003).

28. Rogers v. Tennessee, 532 U.S. 451 (2001).

29. Smith v. Scott, 223 F.3d 1191 (10th Cir. 2000). *Accord* United States v. Bell, 991 F.2d 1445 (8th Cir. 1993) (subjecting Federal Sentencing Guidelines to ex post facto analysis).

30. Dominique v. Weld, 73 F.3d 1156 (1st Cir. 1996).

31. Levy v. Sterling Holding Co., 544 F.3d 493 (3d Cir. 2008).

32. Illinois v. Wardlow, 528 U.S. 119 (2000).

33. 389 U.S. 347 (1967).

police are not entitled to conduct a search or seizure without first obtaining a warrant. Conducting a warrantless search or seizure under those circumstances would be deemed "unreasonable" and a violation of the Fourth Amendment under the *Katz* test. In contrast, if the person being searched does not have a subjective expectation of privacy or has an expectation that society would not consider objectively reasonable, then no warrant is required. In such a case, a warrantless search would not be considered "unreasonable."

In applying this framework, courts have held that a citizen's interest in freedom from governmental intrusions is particularly strong in his or her private home—a person clearly has a reasonable expectation of privacy there. In places open to the public, law enforcement has been given broader scope. Thus, the Supreme Court permitted a warrantless search of garbage cans placed at curbside for collection, where the garbage was readily accessible to animals and strangers, including the trash haulers who could have sorted through it before commingling it with garbage collected from other dwellings.[34] Similarly, the Court permitted warrantless searches of business offices when the government agent entered during business hours and observed whatever was visible to customers or the public from the public areas of the premises.[35] No search warrant is required for government officials to search an individual's bank deposit records either.[36] An individual

lowers the expectation of privacy by revealing his or her affairs to the bank and assumes the risk that the information will be revealed to the government.

Other well-established exceptions to the search warrant requirement include (1) a search incident to a lawful arrest, (2) a search of an automobile if there is probable cause to believe evidence of a crime will be found, (3) a search and seizure of anything discovered by police in plain view if the officers are legitimately on the premises, (4) a stop and frisk of a suspect if the officer reasonably believes the suspect is dangerous, (5) a search when the owner or a person who appears to have authority voluntarily and intelligently consents to the search, and (6) any instance when the police are in "hot pursuit" or when the evidence may disappear before a warrant can be obtained (e.g., blood samples containing alcohol). If a person is validly arrested, the officer has the authority to search the arrestee and the area immediately within the arrestee's control to protect the officer's safety.

The Supreme Court has drawn a line between visual inspection and tactile examination, however. A border patrol officer cannot touch or squeeze a bus passenger's carry-on bag placed in the overhead rack, even though other passengers might also be expected to touch the bag.[37]

In the following case, the court considered whether an employer may consent to a search of a company-owned computer used by an employee, despite the employee's expectation of privacy in his office.

34. *See* California v. Greenwood, 486 U.S. 35 (1988).
35. *See* Marshall v. Barlow's, Inc., 436 U.S. 307 (1978).
36. *See* United States v. Miller, 425 U.S. 435 (1976).

37. Bond v. United States, 529 U.S. 334 (2000).

| A CASE IN POINT | *Summary* | Case 14.1 |

United States v. Ziegler

United States Court of Appeals for the Ninth Circuit
474 F.3d 1184 (9th Cir. 2007).

FACTS Frontline Processing's Internet service provider tipped off the FBI that a Frontline employee had accessed child pornography from a work computer. The FBI immediately contacted Frontline's information technology (IT) department, which determined that Jeffrey Ziegler, Frontline's director of operations, had searched for and accessed child pornography from his work computer. Frontline started monitoring Ziegler's Internet activity through his browser's cache files, where it found evidence of child pornography. Frontline routinely monitored workplace computers, and its employees were aware of its monitoring capabilities.

Members of the Frontline IT department obtained a key to Ziegler's office from the chief financial officer, entered the office, and made two copies of Ziegler's computer hard drive (there was some dispute over whether the FBI directed the Frontline employees to act, or whether they did so on their own or at the direction of the CFO). Frontline's corporate counsel turned over all the materials to the FBI and indicated that the company would comply fully with the investigation.

In his pretrial motions, Ziegler argued that the FBI obtained the materials without a warrant and, thus, conducted an illegal search that violated the Fourth Amendment. Even though the district court found that the FBI had directed the company to enter Ziegler's office and make the copies, it denied his motions, explaining that Ziegler had no expectation of privacy in "the files he accessed on the Internet."

Ziegler entered into a plea agreement, but reserved his right to appeal the district court's denial of his pretrial motions.

CONTINUED

ISSUES PRESENTED   Does an employee have an expectation of privacy in his workplace computer sufficient to suppress images of child pornography sought to be admitted into evidence in a criminal prosecution? If so, could the employer provide valid consent to a search of the employee's computer?

SUMMARY OF OPINION   On appeal, Ziegler argued that the district court had erred in finding that he did not have a legitimate expectation of privacy in his office and computer. He compared the workplace computer to the desk drawer or file cabinet given Fourth Amendment protection in prior cases. The Government argued that Ziegler did not have an objectively reasonable expectation of privacy.

The U.S. Court of Appeals for the Ninth Circuit began its analysis by noting that the Fourth Amendment protects people, not places. A criminal defendant may invoke the protections of the Fourth Amendment only if he can show that he had a legitimate expectation of privacy in the place searched or the item seized. A legitimate expectation of privacy is established where there is "(1) a subjective expectation of privacy; and (2) an objectively reasonable expectation of privacy." The first element was established in this case because Ziegler locked his office door and used a password on his computer. The court concluded that the second element was also established, because employees of private-sector employers have some expectation of privacy in their offices.

Because Ziegler had an expectation of privacy in his office, the remaining question was whether the search of his office and the copying of his hard drive were "unreasonable" within the meaning of the Fourth Amendment. This search was conducted without a warrant, so it was "unreasonable" unless it fell within one of the narrow exceptions to the warrant requirement. Although a search of private property without a warrant is generally unreasonable, if a third party with "common authority over or other sufficient relationship to the premises or effects sought to be inspected" provides consent, a warrant may not be necessary.

In this case, the court found that even when an employee believes that his private office will not be subject to a search without his consent, the employer may provide the necessary consent to search the employee's office. Furthermore, the court found that the computer was not personal property, despite Ziegler's password, because company administrators retained "complete administrative access," regularly monitored Internet traffic from company computers, and informed employees of the company's monitoring efforts. Thus, Frontline could consent to a search of Ziegler's office and work computer, and the search did not violate the Fourth Amendment.

RESULT   The U.S. Court of Appeals for the Ninth Circuit affirmed the lower court's decision denying Ziegler's pretrial suppression motion. The computer files were admissible.

Suspicionless Drug Testing and Administrative Searches   In general, a search or seizure is unreasonable "in the absence of individualized suspicion of wrongdoing."[38] Nonetheless, the Supreme Court has upheld "certain regimes of suspicionless searches where the program was designed to serve 'special needs, beyond the normal need for law enforcement.' "[39] These include the random drug testing of student-athletes,[40] U.S. Customs Service employees seeking transfer or promotion to certain positions,[41] and railway employees involved in train accidents or found to be in violation of particular safety regulations.[42] Conversely, the Supreme Court struck down the mandatory drug testing of candidates for high state office in Georgia after noting that these officials typically did not perform high-risk, safety-sensitive tasks and that the statute was not enacted in response to any fear or suspicion of drug use by state officials.[43] The Court also invalidated a program that tested pregnant women for drugs without their consent and then turned over positive results to the police, because it primarily served law enforcement aims.[44]

---

38. City of Indianapolis v. Edmond, 531 U.S. 32 (2000).

39. *Id.*

40. Vernonia Sch. Dist. 47J v. Acton, 515 U.S. 646 (1995).

41. Treasury Emps. v. Von Raab, 489 U.S. 656 (1989).

42. Skinner v. Ry. Labor Executives' Ass'n, 489 U.S. 602 (1989).

43. Chandler v. Miller, 520 U.S. 305 (1997) ("However well meant, the candidate drug test Georgia has devised [impermissibly] diminishes personal privacy for a symbol's sake.").

44. Ferguson v. Charleston, 532 U.S. 67 (2001).

The Court has permitted suspicionless searches for certain administrative purposes, including inspections of fire-damaged structures to determine the cause of a blaze,[45] buildings to ensure compliance with a city housing code,[46] and the premises of a "closely regulated" business.[47] A warrantless inspection of a closely regulated business will be reasonable only if (1) there is a "substantial" government interest that informs the regulatory scheme pursuant to which the inspection is made; (2) the warrantless inspections are necessary to further the regulatory scheme; and (3) the inspection program, in terms of the certainty and regularity of its application, provides a constitutionally adequate substitute for a warrant.[48]

Searches Employing New Technology The framers of the Fourth Amendment protections could not have conceived of the technological tools at the disposal of today's law enforcement agencies. In the seminal *Katz* decision, the Supreme Court ruled that the government could not use an electronic bug on the outside of a pay-phone booth without a warrant. More than thirty years later, in *Kyllo v. United States*,[49] the Court ruled that police may not use infrared thermal-image scanners to scan homes without a warrant. The scanners reveal artificial heat sources, such as heat being released from grow lights for hidden marijuana crops. The Court characterized "the right of a man to retreat into his own home and there be free from unreasonable governmental intrusion" as being at "the very core" of the Fourth Amendment. Thus, "[i]n the home . . . all details are intimate details, because the entire area is held safe from prying government eyes." Recognizing that future technology may make it possible to literally see through the walls of a dwelling and stressing the importance of drawing not only a firm but also a "bright" line at the entrance to the house, the Court ruled, "Where, as here, the Government uses a device that is not in general public use, to explore details of the home that would previously have been unknowable without physical intrusion, the surveillance is a 'search' and is presumptively unreasonable without a warrant."

"It's a boy!"

Michael Shaw/The New Yorker Collection/www.cartoonbank.com

The dissent argued that there is "a distinction of constitutional magnitude" between through-the-wall surveillance that gives the observer or listener direct access to information in a private area, on the one hand, and the thought processes used to draw inferences from information in the public domain obtained from off-the-wall surveillance on the other hand. The thermal-imaging device detected only the heat emitted from the exterior of the house, which could have been observed by a neighbor or passerby. As such, the dissent argued, use of the device did not amount to a search and was "perfectly reasonable."[50]

A more contested issue is whether police may obtain the names and electronic addresses of the persons to whom a defendant has sent e-mail without first securing a warrant. Law enforcement personnel argue that this is equivalent to obtaining pen registers listing telephone calls, which are available without a warrant. Defense lawyers and privacy advocates claim that an e-mail list is far more intrusive and revealing because the names and addresses convey much more information than a series of telephone numbers.

The U.S. Court of Appeals for the Ninth Circuit addressed this issue in the following case.

---

45. Michigan v. Tyler, 436 U.S. 499 (1978).

46. Camara v. Mun. Court of San Francisco, 387 U.S. 523 (1967).

47. New York v. Burger, 482 U.S. 691 (1987).

48. United States v. Argent Chem. Labs., Inc., 93 F.3d 572 (9th Cir. 1996).

49. 533 U.S. 27 (2001).

50. *Id.* at 46. The Canadian Supreme Court accepted this argument when it upheld warrantless infrared surveillance in *R. v. Tessling*, [2004] 3 S.C.R. 432 (Can.).

A CASE IN POINT	*Summary*	Case 14.2

United States v. Forrester

United States Court of Appeals for the Ninth Circuit
512 F.3d 500 (9th Cir. 2008).

FACTS Following a lengthy government investigation, Forrester and Alba were indicted and charged with conspiracy to manufacture and distribute the illegal drug Ecstasy. During its investigation of Forrester and Alba's Ecstasy-manufacturing operation, the government employed various computer surveillance techniques to monitor Alba's e-mail and Internet activity. The surveillance began in May 2001, after the government applied for and received court permission to install a pen register analogue, known as a "mirror port," on Alba's account with

CONTINUED

PacBell Internet. The mirror port was installed at PacBell's connection facility in San Diego, and it enabled the government to learn the to/from addresses of Alba's e-mail messages, the Internet protocol (IP) addresses of the websites that Alba visited, and the total volume of information sent to or from his account.

At trial, the jury convicted Forrester and Alba. On appeal, Alba contended that the government's surveillance of his e-mail and Internet activity violated the Fourth Amendment and fell outside the scope of the then-applicable federal pen register statute.

ISSUE PRESENTED   Do searches of e-mail and Internet activity constitute an unreasonable search in violation of the Fourth Amendment, or do they fall within the scope of the federal pen register statute?

SUMMARY OF OPINION   The U.S. Court of Appeals for the Ninth Circuit first outlined the reasoning allowing the use of pen registers as discussed in the seminal case *Smith v. Maryland*.[51] According to the Supreme Court, people do not have a subjective expectation of privacy in telephone numbers that they dial because they "realize that they must 'convey' phone numbers to the telephone company, since it is through telephone company switching equipment that their calls are completed." Therefore, the use of a pen register is not a Fourth Amendment search. Importantly, the Court distinguished pen registers from more intrusive surveillance techniques on the ground that "pen registers do not acquire the *contents* of communications" but rather obtain only the addressing information associated with phone calls.

The court began its discussion of the present case by pointing out that neither it nor any other circuit had spoken to the constitutionality of the computer surveillance techniques in question. The court concluded that the surveillance techniques employed by the government in this case are constitutionally indistinguishable from the use of a pen register. First, e-mail and Internet users, like the telephone users in *Smith*, rely on third-party equipment in order to engage in communication. Therefore, just like telephone users dialing phone numbers, e-mail and Internet users have no expectation of privacy in the to/from addresses of their messages or the IP addresses of the websites they visit, because they should know that this information will be used by Internet service providers to direct the routing information. Second, e-mail to/from addresses and IP addresses constitute addressing information and do not necessarily reveal any more about the underlying contents of communication than do phone numbers. Finally, the pen register in *Smith* was able to disclose not only the phone numbers dialed but also the number of calls made. According to the court, there is no constitutional difference between this aspect of the pen register and the government's monitoring of the total volume of data transmitted to or from Alba's account.

RESULT   The conviction was upheld. The e-mail to/from addresses, IP addresses, and the amount of Internet data transmitted were permissibly obtained without a warrant.

---

51. 442 U.S. 735 (1979).

Traffic Stops and Checkpoints   The Supreme Court has given police broad scope to stop motorists suspected of traffic violations. If a police officer makes a traffic stop based on an objective belief that there is probable cause to believe a traffic violation has occurred, then it is irrelevant that the police officer might have used the violation only as a pretext to stop the car.[52] Police officers need not inform detained drivers that they are "legally free to go" before asking for consent to search their vehicles.[53] A police officer may order passengers out of a vehicle during the course of a traffic stop,[54] but the police cannot conduct a full car search after issuing a routine traffic citation unless the driver consents.[55] If the vehicle's occupants are arrested, however, then officers may lawfully search the arrestees as well as the area within their immediate reach during the arrest to ensure both the

---

52. *Whren v. United States*, 517 U.S. 806 (1996).

53. *Ohio v. Robinette*, 519 U.S. 33 (1996).
54. *Maryland v. Wilson*, 519 U.S. 408 (1997).
55. *Knowles v. United States*, 525 U.S. 113 (1998).

officers' safety and the preservation of evidence.[56] Once the scene is secure and the arrested individuals pose no threat to the officers or evidence, however, a warrant may be required before a broader search, including a search of the interior of the car, may be conducted.[57]

Recognizing the government's interest in policing the nation's borders and intercepting illegal aliens, the Supreme Court upheld brief, suspicionless seizures of motorists at two fixed Border Control checkpoints located on major U.S. highways less than one hundred miles from the Mexican border.[58] The Supreme Court also upheld highway sobriety checkpoints designed to detect signs of intoxication and to remove impaired drivers from the road.[59] Checkpoints tailored to find witnesses to a particular criminal incident are permissible as well.[60]

But the Court struck down highway checkpoints aimed at the discovery and interdiction of illegal narcotics: "When law enforcement authorities pursue primarily general crime control purposes at checkpoints . . . , stops can only be justified by some quantum of individualized suspicion."[61] The Court distinguished between sobriety checkpoints to protect the public from an "immediate, vehicle-bound threat of life and limb" and narcotics stops "justified only by the generalized and ever-present possibility that interrogation and inspection may reveal that any given motorist has committed a crime." The Court made it clear that sobriety checkpoints, border searches, searches at airports and government buildings, and "roadblocks set up to thwart imminent terrorist attack or to catch a dangerous criminal who is likely to flee by way of a particular route" are permitted. The Court left open the legality of a checkpoint program with the primary purpose of checking driver's licenses and a secondary purpose of interdicting narcotics.

In a subsequent case, the Supreme Court upheld a suspicionless search outside a car by a drug-detection dog during a lawful traffic stop for speeding, which revealed the presence of marijuana.[62] Unlike the thermal-imaging device at issue in *Kyllo*, which could have detected lawful activity within the home—including "at what hour each night the lady of the house takes her daily sauna and bath"—a well-trained narcotics-detection dog's sniff and alert reveal "no information other than the location of a substance that no individual has any right to possess."

Obtaining a Search Warrant

When a search warrant is required, a law enforcement agent must persuade a "neutral and detached" magistrate that a search is justified. The rights of private citizens are protected by the requirement that a magistrate, rather than a law enforcement agent, determine whether probable cause exists for the search.

A valid search warrant must (1) be based on probable cause, (2) be supported by an oath or affirmation, and (3) describe in specific detail (with particularity) what is to be searched or seized. Probable cause is determined by the totality of the circumstances, balancing the privacy rights of the individual against the government's law enforcement needs.

When government authorities obtain a warrant to conduct a physical search of a business, the scope of the search typically must have some limits. To obtain a broad warrant to conduct a sweeping raid of a company, the government must show that the company is "pervaded by fraud." The "pervaded by fraud" exception applies only to companies that are little more than "boiler room" sales operations engaged only negligibly in legitimate business activities.[63]

The Exclusionary Rule

The *exclusionary rule* is virtually unique to the U.S. legal system. It generally prohibits the introduction in a criminal trial of evidence that was obtained by an illegal search or seizure in violation of the Fourth Amendment (or in violation of the Fifth Amendment's ban on self-incrimination, discussed below). Illegal evidence includes evidence found when the search went beyond the scope of the warrant, evidence gathered without a warrant when a warrant was required, and evidence acquired directly or indirectly as a result of an illegal search, arrest, or interrogation (called *fruit of the poisonous tree*).

The exclusionary rule is often criticized in the media as simply a device to set guilty criminals free on a technicality. Supporters of the rule argue that it is necessary to protect personal freedom.

Exceptions to the Exclusionary Rule

The two most important exceptions to the exclusionary rule are the good faith exception and the inevitable discovery exception.

The *good faith exception* provides that evidence obtained by police in good faith will not be excluded from trial even if it was obtained in violation of the Fourth Amendment.[64] Because the exclusionary rule was designed to deter police misconduct, the Supreme Court reasoned that no deterrent purpose would be served by excluding evidence that the police acquired while acting in good faith. The good faith exception also covers errors made by court personnel. As a result, if police conduct an unconstitutional search relying on erroneous information from a court employee, the exclusionary rule will not apply.

56. Chimel v. California, 395 U.S. 752 (1969).

57. Arizona v. Gant, 162 P.3d 640 (Ariz. 2007).

58. United States v. Martinez-Fuerte, 428 U.S. 543 (1976).

59. Mich. Dep't of State Police v. Sitz, 496 U.S. 444 (1990).

60. Illinois v. Lidser, 540 U.S. 419 (2004).

61. City of Indianapolis v. Edmond, 531 U.S. 32 (2000).

62. Illinois v. Caballes, 543 U.S. 405 (2005).

63. *In re* Grand Jury Investigation Concerning Solid State Devices, Inc., 130 F.3d 853 (9th Cir. 1997).

64. United States v. Leon, 468 U.S. 897 (1984).

The *inevitable discovery exception* provides that illegally obtained evidence can lawfully be introduced at trial if it can be shown that the evidence would inevitably have been found by other legal means.[65] For example, *United States v. Pimentel*[66] involved Duroyd Manufacturing Company, a defense contractor that falsified documents and charges to the Defense Department. Evidence of this fraud was contained in a letter to Duroyd from one of its subcontractors, which the government obtained in an illegal search. The court denied Duroyd's request to exclude the letter from evidence. Because the contract gave the Defense Department's auditors the right to examine all "books, records, documents and other evidence . . . sufficient to reflect properly all direct and indirect costs . . . incurred for the performance of this contract," the court concluded that this letter would inevitably have been discovered.

Fifth Amendment Protections

The Fifth Amendment prohibits forced self-incrimination, double jeopardy, and criminal conviction without due process of law.

Protection Against Self-Incrimination

The Fifth Amendment provides that no person "shall be compelled in any criminal case to be a witness against himself." This protection against self-incrimination extends to the preliminary stages in the criminal process as well as the trial itself.

In the landmark self-incrimination case *Miranda v. Arizona*,[67] the Supreme Court ruled that a statement made by a defendant in custody is admissible only if the defendant was informed prior to police interrogation of his or her constitutional right to remain silent and to have counsel present. These warnings are referred to as the *Miranda warnings*.

More than three decades later, the Supreme Court invalidated a federal statute[68] that purported to overturn the *Miranda* rule, reasoning that "Miranda's constitutional character prevailed against a federal statute that sought to restore the old regime of giving no warnings and litigating most statements' voluntariness."[69] The Court also held that the police may not purposefully question first and warn later, that is, question a suspect in custody, obtain a confession, and then provide the *Miranda* warnings and obtain another confession.[70] If, however, the police mistakenly forget to read an accused his or her *Miranda* rights during the first stage of an interrogation, the post-*Miranda* confession may be admissible.[71]

The Fifth Amendment privilege against self-incrimination applies only to compelled testimonial evidence. Requiring defendants to provide tangible evidence such as fingerprints, body fluids (urine and blood), or voice or handwriting samples does not violate the Fifth Amendment prohibition against self-incrimination. Requiring a person to appear in a lineup also does not violate the privilege.

The privilege does not extend to investigations by certain self-regulatory organizations, such as the Financial Industry Regulatory Authority (FINRA), which is the private body authorized by the Securities and Exchange Commission (SEC) to regulate securities broker-dealers and registered representatives.[72] As a condition of membership, securities firms and professionals must agree to give on-the-record testimony whenever requested by FINRA. FINRA can bar individuals and firms from the securities business if they refuse to appear and testify. But if a FINRA investigation becomes too intertwined with an investigation by the SEC, creating such a "close nexus" that seemingly private behavior may be treated as that of the state,[73] then the privilege against self-incrimination may apply.[74]

Business Records and Papers and the Collective Entity Doctrine   The Fifth Amendment protection for business records and papers is very limited. Corporations (and other business entities) enjoy no protection. Under the *collective entity doctrine*, the Supreme Court has held that the custodian of records for a collective entity (such as a corporation) may not resist a subpoena for such records on the ground that the act of production will incriminate him or her.[75] Nonetheless, the custodian cannot be compelled to testify as to the contents of the documents if that testimony would incriminate him or her personally.

The Fifth Amendment privilege may not be invoked to resist compliance with a regulatory regime as long as that regime is designed with a public purpose unrelated to the enforcement of criminal laws.[76] Thus, when government regulations require a business to keep certain records, those records can be used against the reporting individual in a criminal prosecution.

The business records compiled by a sole proprietor may have some protection if the government cannot authenticate

65. Nix v. Williams, 467 U.S. 431 (1984).

66. 810 F.2d 366 (2d Cir. 1987).

67. 384 U.S. 436 (1966).

68. 18 U.S.C. § 3501.

69. Dickerson v. United States, 530 U.S. 428 (2000).

70. Missouri v. Seibert, 542 U.S. 600 (2004).

71. Oregon v. Elstad, 470 U.S. 298 (1985).

72. *See* D.L. Cromwell Invs., Inc v. NASD Regulation, Inc., 279 F.3d 155 (2d Cir. 2002) (holding that the National Association of Securities Dealers (NASD), predecessor to FINRA, did not engage in state action when requiring testimony even though the respondent faced a parallel criminal investigation).

73. Brentwood Acad. v. Tennessee Secondary Sch. Athletic Ass'n, 531 U.S. 288, 295 (2001).

74. *See, e.g., In re* Frank P. Quattrone, Securities Exchange Act Release No. 53,547 (Mar. 24, 2006) (holding that summary disposition was improper when registered principal alleged facts suggesting the NASD might have been acting jointly with the SEC and therefore was a state actor subject to the Fifth Amendment).

75. *See* Braswell v. United States, 487 U.S. 99 (1988).

76. *See* Shapiro v. United States, 335 U.S. 1 (1948).

the documents without the proprietor. In that case, the act of furnishing the documents may have the qualities of self-incriminating testimony.[77] In short, although a person can be required to hand over specified documents, he or she cannot be required to assist in identifying sources of information.[78]

Foreign Prosecutions A witness in a U.S. proceeding who is not facing prosecution in the United States may not invoke the privilege to avoid having to give testimony that might incriminate the witness in another country, unless the other sovereign is itself bound by the privilege.[79] The Supreme Court has left open the question of whether the privilege against self-incrimination may be asserted if the cooperation between the United States and another country has reached a point at which prosecution in the other country could not fairly be characterized as "foreign."

No Double Jeopardy

The *Double Jeopardy Clause* of the Fifth Amendment protects criminal defendants from multiple prosecutions for the same offense. If the defendant is found not guilty, then the prosecutor may not appeal the verdict. If the defendant is found guilty, however, the defendant can appeal. Double jeopardy does not bar a second prosecution if the first proceeding ended in a hung jury or if a guilty verdict was reversed on appeal.

There are important limitations on the protection against double jeopardy. A single criminal act may result in several statutory violations for which the defendant may be prosecuted even if each prosecution is based on the same set of facts. For example, if the defendant operated a securities scam, a prosecutor could bring criminal charges for securities law violations, wire and mail fraud, false statements, and tax evasion. The Double Jeopardy Clause also does not protect against prosecutions by different governments (such as state and federal) based on the same underlying facts. Thus, after the two police officers who beat Rodney King in 1991 were acquitted on California state criminal charges, spawning the 1992 Los Angeles riots, they could still be tried and convicted one year later on federal charges for violating King's civil rights.

Finally, the prohibition against double jeopardy does not preclude a civil suit against a criminal defendant by the victim. Thus, although O.J. Simpson was acquitted on criminal murder charges in 1996, the families of his alleged victims were still able to secure multimillion-dollar judgments against Simpson in a 1997 civil trial.

Civil and Criminal Prosecutions by the Government

The government often seeks both civil sanctions (such as fines) and criminal punishment for the same illegal conduct. The Double Jeopardy Clause protects only against the imposition of multiple *criminal* punishments for the same offense. Legislative intent is the guiding factor in determining whether a particular penalty is "civil" or "criminal." When the legislature has indicated an intention to establish a civil sanction, courts should rarely transform it into a criminal penalty for double jeopardy purposes.[80]

Bar on Use of Involuntary Confessions

When the conduct of law enforcement officials in obtaining a confession is outrageous or shocking, the *Due Process Clauses* of the Fifth and Fourteenth Amendments bar the government from using the involuntary confession, even if the *Miranda* warnings were given. For example, physical coercion or brutality invalidates a confession. In contrast, the courts have usually held that misleading or false verbal statements that induce the suspect to confess are not grounds for invalidating the confession unless the statements rise to the level of unduly coercive threats.

A Florida appeals court invalidated a confession elicited through the use of fabricated (and false) laboratory reports linking the defendant to the crime.[81] Other courts, however, have indicated that there is no "bright line" that dictates that all uses of false documents are unconstitutional. These courts have held that confessions similarly obtained were in fact "voluntary," after considering the "totality of the circumstances."[82]

Before a confession of guilt will be admitted into evidence, the trial judge must determine whether the confession was voluntarily made, as required by the Due Process Clauses. Nonetheless, the erroneous admission at trial of a coerced confession will not always automatically require that the conviction be overturned.[83]

Sixth Amendment Protections

The Sixth Amendment grants criminal defendants a number of procedural protections, including a right to counsel and to a trial by jury.

Assistance of Counsel

The defendant in most criminal prosecutions has the right "to have the Assistance of Counsel." This means, first, that the accused has the right to his or her own attorney.

---

77. *See* Fisher v. United States, 425 U.S. 391 (1976). *See also Braswell*, 487 U.S. 99.

78. United States v. Hubbell, 530 U.S. 27 (2000) (holding that "the constitutional privilege against self-incrimination protects the target of a grand jury investigation from being compelled to answer questions designed to elicit information about the existence of sources of potentially incriminating evidence").

79. United States v. Balsys, 524 U.S. 666 (1998).

80. Hudson v. United States, 522 U.S. 93 (1997).

81. Florida v. Cayward, 552 So. 2d 971 (Fla. App. 1989).

82. *See, e.g.,* Sheriff, Washoe County v. Bessey, 914 P.2d 681 (Nev. 1996); Arthur v. Virginia, 480 S.E.2d 749 (Va. App. 1997); Lincoln v. Maryland, 882 A.2d 944 (Md. Ct. Spec. App. 2005).

83. *See* Arizona v. Fulminante, 499 U.S. 279 (1991) (holding that the harmless error test applies to determine whether conviction must be overturned).

If the defendant cannot afford an attorney, he or she is entitled to a court-appointed attorney. Second, once taken into custody, the accused must be informed of his or her right to counsel as part of the *Miranda* warnings. Third, the assistance of counsel must be effective, that is, within the range of competence required of attorneys in criminal cases. In practice, counsel is presumed to be effective; only in outrageous cases is counsel considered ineffective.

Fourth, an attorney must be appointed for an appeal of a verdict.

In the following case, the court considered whether the federal government violated managers' Sixth Amendment rights when it pressured their employer to refrain from advancing their legal expenses as a condition to not prosecuting the employer for allegedly creating and marketing fraudulent tax shelters.

| A CASE IN POINT | *In the Language of the Court* | Case 14.3 |

United States v. Stein

United States Court of Appeals for the Second Circuit
541 F.3d 130 (2d Cir. 2008).

Facts   In January 2003, U.S. Deputy Attorney General Larry D. Thompson promulgated a policy statement articulating "principles" to govern the U.S. Justice Department's discretion in bringing prosecutions against business organizations. This "Thompson Memorandum" explained that prosecutors should inquire "whether the corporation appears to be protecting its culpable employees and agents . . . *through the advancing of attorneys fees . . . .*"

After evidence surfaced that partners at the accounting firm KPMG might have been involved in the creation and marketing of fraudulent tax shelters, KPMG retained Robert S. Bennett of the law firm Skadden Arps to formulate a "cooperative approach" for KPMG to use in dealing with federal authorities. Part of Bennett's strategy included a decision to "clean house": KPMG partners, including Jeffrey Stein, would leave their positions, and KPMG would agree to pay for their representation in any actions brought against them for their activities in the firm. Prior to the issuance of the Thompson Memorandum, KPMG's long-standing policy was to pay legal fees and expenses of its personnel in all cases without condition or cap. Under the new "Fees Policy," however, fee advancement would continue as long as the employees cooperated with the government, but would terminate once an employee was indicted. Assistant U.S. Attorneys continuously emphasized the need for KPMG to consider the Thompson Memorandum, and they even demanded that KPMG circulate a memorandum advising employees that they could "meet with investigators without the assistance of counsel." The government also implied that an agreement not to prosecute was unlikely given KPMG's level of cooperation and its assistance to its executives.

On August 29, 2005, KPMG entered into a deferred prosecution agreement under which KPMG admitted extensive wrongdoing, paid a $456 million fine, and committed to cooperate in any future government investigation or prosecution. On the same day, the government indicted six defendants, including Stein. Pursuant to the new Fees Policy, KPMG promptly stopped advancing legal fees to the indicted employees.

In January 2006, thirteen defendants moved to dismiss the indictment based on the government's interference with KPMG's advancement of fees. The district court concluded that but for the Thompson Memorandum and the prosecutors' conduct, KPMG would have paid the defendants' legal fees and expenses without consideration of cost. The court ruled that the government's conduct violated the defendants' rights to fairness in the criminal process and counsel under the Fifth and Sixth Amendments, and it dismissed the indictment against the thirteen defendants. The government appealed.

Issues Presented   Did the promulgation and enforcement of KPMG's Fees Policy amount to state action under the Constitution? If so, did the government thereby deprive the defendants of their Sixth Amendment right to counsel?

Opinion   JACOBS, J., writing for the U.S. Court of Appeals for the Second Circuit:

"A nexus of state action exists between a private entity and the state when the state exercises coercive power, is entwined in the management or control of the private actor, or provides the private actor with *significant encouragement*, either overt or covert, or when the private

CONTINUED

actor operates as a *willful participant in joint activity* with the State or its agents, is controlled by an agency of the State, has been delegated a public function by the state, or is *entwined with governmental policies.*"

.   .   .   .

KPMG's adoption and enforcement of the Fees Policy amounted to "state action" because KPMG "operate[d] as a willful participant in joint activity" with the government, and because the [U.S. Attorney's Office] "significant[ly] encourage[d]" KPMG to withhold legal fees from defendants upon indictment.

.   .   .   .

It is true, of course, that the Sixth Amendment right to counsel typically attaches at the initiation of adversarial proceedings . . . . But the analysis can not end there. . . . The fact that *events were set in motion prior to indictment with the object of having, or with knowledge that they were likely to have, an unconstitutional effect upon indictment* cannot save the government. This conduct, unless justified, violated the Sixth Amendment.

.   .   .   .

[T]hese defendants can easily demonstrate interference in their relationships with counsel and impairment of their ability to mount a defense based on [the Trial Judge]'s non-erroneous findings that the post-indictment termination of fees "caused them to restrict the activities of their counsel," and thus to limit the scope of their pre-trial investigation and preparation. . . . As [the Trial Judge] found, these defendants "have been forced to limit their defenses . . . for economic reasons and . . . they would not have been so constrained if KPMG paid their expenses." We therefore hold that these defendants were also deprived of their right to counsel under the Sixth Amendment.

RESULT   The U.S. Court of Appeals for the Second Circuit affirmed the judgment of the district court dismissing the defendants' indictment.

CRITICAL THINKING QUESTIONS

1. To what extent, if any, could the prosecutors in this case have encouraged the adoption of the principles of the Thompson Memorandum without crossing constitutional boundaries?

2. Could a private company's legal fee policy, based in reliance on the Thompson Memorandum, be a constitutionally sound policy *absent* any outside government coercion?

Jury Trial

Defendants in most criminal cases have the right to a jury trial. Jury trials are not required, however, in cases in which the authorized punishment for the charged offense is six months or less. A jury is also not required in juvenile proceedings. State court juries consist of six to twelve individuals, with a minimum of six jurors. Federal courts have twelve jurors. To render a verdict in a federal criminal trial, the jury must reach a unanimous decision. Juries of six in state courts must also be unanimous to render a verdict in a criminal case, but the U.S. Supreme Court has not ruled on juries of seven or more.

Other Procedural Rights

The Sixth Amendment also guarantees the right to a speedy trial and the right to confront and cross-examine witnesses.

The latter, which is embodied in the *Confrontation Clause*, can limit the prosecution's ability to introduce prior statements by witnesses not subject to cross-examination at trial.[84]

Eighth Amendment Protections

The Eighth Amendment prohibits cruel and unusual punishment. Although the U.S. Supreme Court has repeatedly upheld the death penalty in cases involving murder, it ruled in a five-to-four decision in 2008 that a defendant convicted of raping his eight-year-old stepdaughter could not be executed.[85] The Court stated that the death penalty was available only in cases involving murder and crimes

84. Crawford v. Washington, 541 U.S. 36 (2004).
85. Kennedy v. Louisiana, 554 U.S. 407 (2008).

INTERNATIONAL SNAPSHOT

In China, more than sixty different crimes carry the death penalty, including tax fraud, bribery, and certain other economic crimes. In 2007, the Chinese government executed Wang Zhendong, chair of a company that took $385 million from the public through a Ponzi scheme, as well as two mid-level professionals at the China Construction Bank who were convicted of a $52 million fraud.

In 2011, Ji Wenhua, president of Yintai Real Estate and Investment Group, was sentenced to death for cheating investors out of more than $1.1 billion. In the same year, Zhang Chunjiang, an executive at China Mobile, was sentenced to death for accepting more than $1.15 million in bribes while working at a series of state-run telecom companies.

Even regulators are not exempt from the harshest of punishments. Zheng Xiaoyu, a former food and drug official, was executed in 2007 after being convicted of accepting bribes from pharmaceutical companies. In 2011, the Chinese government executed Xu Maiyong and Jiang Renjie, former mayors of booming eastern cities, who took bribes worth more than $15.4 million in connection with real estate projects.

Xiao Yang, President of the Supreme People's Court, defended his country's liberal use of the death penalty: "It is necessary to use the death penalty in China to punish criminals who commit extremely serious crimes in order to safeguard state security, public interests, and smooth operation of economic construction."

SOURCES: Al Lewis, *In China, Execution Is Critical*, DEN. POST, July 17, 2007, at C1; Ariana Eunjung Cha, *Art Fraud Yields Death Sentence*, WASH. POST, Mar. 20, 2007, at D1; Keith Bradsher, *A Chinese Banker Is Convicted, and a Message Is Sent*, N.Y. TIMES, Aug. 13, 2005, at 2; David Barboza, *Former China Mobile Official Sentenced in Bribery Case*, N.Y. TIMES, July 23, 2011, at B7; D. Collins, *Chinese Fund Managers Sentenced to Death After Cheating Investors Out of 1 Billion USD*, CHINA MONEY REP., Nov. 10, 2011.

against the state, such as treason, espionage, and terrorism. In an opinion by Justice Kennedy, joined by Justices Stevens, Souter, Ginsburg, and Breyer, the Court recognized the "hurt and horror" suffered by child rape victims but cautioned, "When the law punishes by death, it risks its own sudden descent into brutality, transgressing the constitutional commitment to decency and restraint."

NONCONSTITUTIONAL PROTECTIONS

In a criminal prosecution, the prosecutor is obligated to share certain evidence with the defendant, including all evidence that the defendant specifically requests and any exculpatory evidence regardless of whether the defendant has requested it. To neutralize the natural advantage of the state against the individual defendant, more requirements to reveal evidence are imposed on the prosecutor than on the defendant. Nonetheless, the defendant may be required to reveal certain information to the prosecutor, such as statements made by witnesses who have testified in a sworn statement.

Attorney–Client Privilege

The communications between a criminal defendant and his or her attorney are protected from disclosure by the attorney–client privilege, which was discussed in detail in Chapter 3. When criminal charges are brought against a corporate employee who is represented by a lawyer paid by the corporation, it may be unclear to whom the attorney–client privilege belongs. Is the client the employee charged with the offense, the corporation that is paying the lawyer, or both? In general, a client must establish a relationship with the attorney for the attorney–client privilege to apply. Thus, if the employee wants to be treated as the client, the employee should obtain an engagement letter from the attorney that expressly states that the employee is the client even though the employer is paying the attorney's fees. In-house counsel investigating possible violations of law usually represent the corporation, not the individual employees who might be questioned by counsel. As discussed further below, a willingness to waive the attorney–client privilege has become an important bargaining chip for firms facing a possible indictment or sentencing.

FEDERAL SENTENCING GUIDELINES

Congress created the U.S. Sentencing Commission, an independent agency in the judicial branch, to provide an honest, fair, and effective federal sentencing system that would impose reasonably uniform sentences for similar criminal offenses committed by similar offenders. The Sentencing Commission established the Federal Sentencing Guidelines, which created categories of "offense behavior" and "offender characteristics."

Although the Guidelines initially required the sentencing court to select a sentence (up to the maximum authorized by statute for each federal crime) from within the Guidelines ranges specified by the combined categories, the U.S. Supreme Court ruled that judges may depart from the Guidelines in the unusual case that presents an aggravating or mitigating circumstance not adequately taken into consideration by the Sentencing Commission.[86] The Court pointed out, however, that

---

86. United States v. Booker, 543 U.S. 220 (2005) (holding that the mandatory nature of the Guidelines violated the Sixth Amendment right to be found guilty by a jury only upon proof beyond a reasonable doubt of all elements of the crime charged). *See also* Apprendi v. New Jersey, 530 U.S. 466 (2000) (holding that any fact—other than the existence of a prior conviction—that increases the penalty for a crime beyond the prescribed statutory minimum must be submitted to a jury and proved beyond a reasonable doubt). The *Booker* Court recognized "the authority of a judge to exercise broad discretion in imposing a sentence within a statutory range" and stated that "the defendant has no right to a jury determination of the facts that a judge deems relevant."

"[i]n most cases, as a matter of law, the Commission will have adequately taken all relevant factors into account, and no departure will be legally permissible. In those instances, the judge is bound to impose a sentence within the Guidelines range."[87] If the sentence comes up for review on appeal, the Supreme Court instructed the court of appeals to determine whether the sentence is unreasonable in light of a variety of mitigating and aggravating circumstances. Sentences will be upheld on appeal if they are procedurally and substantively reasonable. A sentence is procedurally reasonable if it is free from procedural defects, such as a failure to accurately calculate the Guidelines recommendations. A sentence is substantively reasonable if it is reasonable in light of the circumstances that a case presents.[88]

Individuals

Congress abolished federal parole in 1984. Rather than permit a parole commission to decide how much of a sentence an offender will actually serve, an offender serves the full sentence imposed by the court, less approximately 15% for good behavior.

Under the Guidelines, individuals are sentenced to prison using offense levels, their criminal history, and other factors deemed relevant by the sentencing judge. For example, when sentencing a defendant convicted of garden-variety mail and wire fraud, the court would first consider the individual's criminal history. For a perpetrator with no history, the base offense level is 6. The offense level is then increased depending on the amount of the loss. If the loss is more than $400 million, then an increase of 30 levels is applied to arrive at a recommended base offense level of 36. An offense level of 36 would correspond to somewhere between 188 and 405 months in prison; for perpetrators with an extensive criminal history, the Guidelines would recommend sentences at the high end of the range. The recommended fine for individuals convicted of this offense level would be between a minimum of $20,000 and a maximum of $200,000.

Organizations

The Federal Sentencing Guidelines for Organizations, originally enacted in 1991, specify stiff fines for companies convicted of fraud, antitrust violations, and most types of corporate wrongdoing. According to the Sentencing Commission, the Guidelines for Organizations were "designed so that the sanctions imposed upon organizations and their agents . . . will provide just punishment, adequate deterrence, and

incentives for organizations to maintain internal mechanisms for preventing, detecting and reporting criminal conduct."[89]

The Guidelines take a carrot-and-stick approach. The "stick" is that organizations are held liable for the criminal actions of all their employees and agents. The "carrot" is that a company's maintenance of a meaningful voluntary compliance program is deemed a mitigating factor that will reduce otherwise applicable fines.[90] A company can also achieve significant mitigation of fines by cooperating with or self-reporting misconduct to authorities. Corporate directors risk violating their fiduciary duty of care if they fail to take advantage of all mitigation measures available under the Guidelines.[91]

The Guidelines apply to all companies with two or more members but recognize that smaller organizations may have more informal compliance programs. They suggest that "[a]s appropriate, a large organization should encourage small organizations (especially those that have, or seek to have, a business relationship with the large organization) to implement effective compliance and ethics programs."[92]

Determining the Sentence

Exhibit 14.1 shows the steps involved in calculating the recommended fine for an organization convicted of a crime, and Exhibit 14.2 shows the tables used in the calculation. The first step in calculating the sentence for a particular crime is to determine the recommended base fine, which depends on the severity of the crime. For instance, money laundering is considered a more serious offense than price-fixing; thus, the base fine for price-fixing is $20,000 (offense level 10 in Exhibit 14.2), whereas the base fine for laundering money instruments (such as checks) is $1.6 million (offense level 23). If this base fine is exceeded by either the organization's gain or the victim's (or society's) loss from the crime, then that amount will supplant the base fine.

The second step is to adjust the base fine to reflect the culpability of the organization. The culpability score is used to determine minimum and maximum multipliers,

87. *Booker*, 543 U.S. 220.

88. Charles Doyle, Congressional Research Service, Mail and Wire Fraud: A Brief Overview of Federal Criminal Law 8–9 (2011).

89. Itamar Sittenfeld, *Federal Sentencing Guidelines*, Internal Auditor, Apr. 1996, at 58.

90. Kathryn Keneally, *White Collar Crime: Corporate Compliance Programs: From the Sentencing Guidelines to the Thompson Memorandum—and Back Again*, Champion, June 2004.

91. David Hess, *A Business Ethics Perspective on Sarbanes–Oxley and the Organizational Sentencing Guidelines*, 105 Mich. L. Rev. 1781, 1790 n.54 (2007).

92. U.S. Sentencing Guidelines Manual, Effective Compliance and Ethics Programs, ch. 8, § 8B2.1 (2011), *available at* http://www.ussc.gov/Guidelines/2011_guidelines/Manual_PDF/Chapter_8.pdf.

EXHIBIT 14.1   Determining the Fine for Non-Criminal-Purpose Organizations Under the Federal Sentencing Guidelines

Step 1	Step 2	Step 3	Step 4

Base Fine
The greatest of:
1. Offense level amount
2. Pecuniary gain to offender
3. Pecuniary loss to victim or society

×

Minimum & Maximum Multipliers

=

Guideline Fine Range

→

Determining the Fine Within the Range

or

Departing from the Range

Culpability Score
1. Involvement in or tolerance of criminal activity
2. Prior history
3. Violation of an order
4. Obstruction of justice
5. Effective program to prevent and detect violations of law

SOURCES: Jennifer Moore, *Corporate Culpability Under the Federal Sentencing Guidelines*, 34 ARIZ. L. REV. 743, 783 (1992); U.S. SENTENCING GUIDELINES MANUAL ch. 8 & apps. (2011).

as shown in the lower part of Exhibit 14.2. The base fine is then multiplied by the minimum and maximum multipliers to determine the recommended fine range. A culpability score starts at a baseline of five points out of ten. Points are then added or subtracted based on various criteria, including whether (1) management condoned or willfully ignored the criminal misconduct, (2) management assisted authorities in their investigation, and (3) the organization had an effective compliance and ethics program in place at the time of the misconduct to not only prevent and detect criminal conduct but also facilitate compliance with all applicable laws. For example, the culpability score can be reduced by five points for timely and full cooperation and acceptance of responsibility.[93]

Cooperation and Mitigation   Although the 2004 version of the Guidelines required firms to waive the attorney–client privilege and work-product protection to receive full credit for cooperation, the Sentencing Commission removed the waiver requirement language from the amended Guidelines issued in 2006.[94] The *United States v. Stein*[95] decision put additional pressure on prosecutors not to require waivers.

As mentioned earlier, the possibility of fine mitigation serves as a strong incentive for organizations to adopt and maintain effective compliance and ethics programs. Exhibit 14.3 sets forth the seven requirements that must be satisfied under the Guidelines (as amended as of

November 1, 2011) for mitigation due to the existence of an effective compliance and ethics program.[96]

Letting Employees Take the Rap

When facing a criminal probe, corporations have increasingly responded to the Guidelines' encouragement to cooperate with authorities by winning leniency for themselves at the expense of their employees. Because the Guidelines call on corporations to apply "adequate discipline" to employees deemed responsible for criminal violations, a company has an incentive to isolate a small group of "fall guys," fire them, and cooperate with the federal government in their prosecution. This pattern frequently occurs even though it can often be difficult to determine who is really responsible for corporate crimes.[97]

Although it may be appropriate to let a true "rogue" employee take the rap, under certain circumstances, scapegoating raises fundamental questions of fairness. William S. Laufer warns that scapegoating is most likely to result in "self-deception, denial of responsibility, and lack of repentance" when top management is complicit or middle management tacitly encourages employees to engage in wrongdoing in spite of a comprehensive compliance program, when senior executives and managers condoned the commission of the offense or consciously disregarded knowledge of the illegality, when the person being blamed is far subordinate to those cooperating with the government, and when the firm "purchases" the trappings of compliance to impress regulators.[98]

---

93. Keneally, *supra* note 90.

94. U.S. SENTENCING GUIDELINES MANUAL app. C, amend. 695 (2011), at 183, *available at* http://www.ussc.gov/Guidelines/2011_Guidelines/Manual_PDF/Appendix_C_Vol_III.pdf.

95. 541 F.3d 130 (2d Cir. 2008) (Case 14.3).

96. U.S. SENTENCING GUIDELINES MANUAL ch. 8, § 8B2.1 (2011).

97. *See, e.g.*, Dean Starkman, *More Firms Let Employees Take the Rap*, WALL ST. J., Oct. 9, 1997, at B3.

98. William S. Laufer, *Corporate Prosecution, Cooperation, and the Trading of Favors*, 87 IOWA L. REV. 653, 659–60 (2002).

EXHIBIT 14.2	Determining Penalties for Organizations

Offense Level Fine Table for Organizations

Offense Level	Amount of Fine
6 or less	$ 5,000
7	7,500
8	10,000
9	15,000
10	20,000
11	30,000
12	40,000
13	60,000
14	85,000
15	125,000
16	175,000
17	250,000
18	350,000
19	500,000
20	650,000
21	910,000
22	1,200,000
23	1,600,000
24	2,100,000
25	2,800,000
26	3,700,000
27	4,800,000
28	6,300,000
29	8,100,000
30	10,500,000
31	13,500,000
32	17,500,000
33	22,000,000
34	28,500,000
35	36,000,000
36	45,500,000
37	57,500,000
38 or more	72,500,000

Table of Minimum and Maximum Multipliers for Organizations

Culpability Score	Minimum Multiplier	Maximum Multiplier
10 or more	2.00	4.00
9	1.80	3.60
8	1.60	3.20
7	1.40	2.80
6	1.20	2.40
5	1.00	2.00
4	0.80	1.60
3	0.60	1.20
2	0.40	0.80
1	0.20	0.40
0 or less	0.05	0.20

SOURCE: U.S. SENTENCING GUIDELINES MANUAL ch. 8, pt. C, §§ 8C2.4 & 8C2.6 (2011).

INDIVIDUAL LIABILITY FOR CRIMINAL ACTS

Liability may be imposed on the person who actually committed the crime, on that person's supervisors, and on the corporation (or other entity) that employed the violator. Individuals face direct liability for their own acts and, under certain circumstances, vicarious liability for the acts of others.

Direct Liability

If an officer, director, or employee commits a crime against the employer (such as theft, embezzlement, or forgery), that person will be prosecuted as an individual. Even when individuals commit crimes with the intent of trying to benefit the firm, they will still be prosecuted as individuals and held responsible for their acts. As discussed below, that person's supervisor may also be held responsible.

If a supervisor asks an employee to commit an act that the employee suspects is criminal, the employee should bear two things in mind. First, if there is a criminal prosecution, it is not a valid defense for the employee to state that he or she was just following the orders of upper-level officers or directors of the corporation. Second, as discussed in Chapter 12, in the vast majority of jurisdictions, an employee cannot be terminated for refusing to commit a criminal act.

Vicarious Liability

Vicarious liability (also called *imputed liability*) is the imposition of liability on one party for wrongs committed by another. Under the theory of vicarious liability, officers, directors, and managers may, under certain limited circumstances, be found guilty of a crime committed by employees under their supervision. Although the criminal statutes imposing vicarious liability on corporate officers usually require that the officer commit some wrongful act, failure to provide adequate supervision or to satisfy a duty imposed by the statute is typically sufficient to fulfill this requirement.

The more delicate issue is what kind of *mens rea*, or mental state, is required to find a corporate officer vicariously liable for a crime. In cases involving criminal vicarious liability, the crucial questions are most often, "How much did the manager know?" and "How much does the statute require that the manager know before he or she can be held criminally liable?"

Responsible Corporate Officer Doctrine

Under the *responsible corporate officer doctrine*, a corporate officer may be found guilty of a crime if he or she bore a "responsible relation" to a violation of a statute dealing

---

EXHIBIT 14.3   Key Components of an Effective Corporate Compliance and Ethics Program

To take advantage of the provisions in the Federal Sentencing Guidelines that reduce culpability for a company with an effective compliance and ethics program, a company must:

1. Establish compliance standards and procedures reasonably capable of reducing the prospect of criminal activity and otherwise promote an organizational culture that encourages ethical conduct and commitment to compliance with the law. A viable code of conduct is a good starting point.

2. Assign the board of directors the responsibility for overseeing the compliance effort. The company should assign a high-ranking person with adequate authority to be in charge of the program, to take "day-to-day operational responsibility," and to report on the program's effectiveness periodically to high-level personnel and, as appropriate, the governing authority.

3. Use due care in delegating authority. The company must not delegate substantial discretionary authority to individuals who have previously engaged in any criminal or unethical misconduct. The fox can't guard the hen house.

4. Periodically, provide mandatory training to effectively communicate the standards to all employees and other agents. Training should include a discussion of the laws applicable to the business and focus on helping employees identify risk areas. A well-designed video can help ensure ongoing training about the standards. Good online training tools are available as well.

5. Adopt mechanisms for monitoring compliance with the standards and reporting criminal misconduct without fear of retribution. The company should have and publicize a system for reporting that ensures anonymity or confidentiality to encourage reporting of misconduct.

6. Consistently enforce the standards through investigation and adequate discipline. The company must be willing to discipline violators through salary reduction, poor performance ratings, and termination of employment. When employees report misconduct, the company must take steps to respond. The company should also provide incentives to ensure compliance with the program.

7. Adopt procedures for feedback and correction. After an offense has been detected, the organization must take all reasonable steps to respond adequately to the offense and to prevent further offenses—including making any necessary modifications to its compliance program. Some sort of auditing or monitoring system should be in place to ensure the program is working.

---

with "products which may affect the health of customers,"[99] that is, if the officer had the power to prevent the violation and failed to do so. In applying this doctrine, it is important to remember that two different but interwoven issues are involved. The first is a vicarious liability issue: whether an officer bears responsibility for the actions of his or her subordinates. The second is a *mens rea* issue: whether the officer must have known about or intended the violation before he or she can be held personally criminally liable.

The Supreme Court applied the responsible corporate officer doctrine in *United States v. Park*.[100] John Park was the CEO of Acme Markets, a national retail food chain that employed 36,000 people and operated 874 retail outlets. On two separate occasions, the Food and Drug Administration (FDA) had advised Park that the company was storing food in rodent-infested warehouses. Although Park had been told by a vice president that the problem had been taken care of after the first FDA visit, he failed to personally investigate even after the FDA visited a second time and again complained of rats in the warehouses.

Despite Acme's size and the multiple layers of authority between Park and the employees who had been instructed to eliminate the rodents in the warehouses, Park was found guilty as an individual of distributing "adulterated" food in violation of the Food, Drug and Cosmetic Act (FDCA), a misdemeanor punishable by a minimum fine of $10,000 and imprisonment for up to one year. The Court noted that "Congress has seen fit to enforce the accountability of responsible corporate agents dealing with products which may affect the health of customers" by enacting "rigorous" penal sanctions. Corporate officers have a "duty to implement measures that will insure that violations will not occur"; in other words, the FDCA imposed "requirements of foresight and vigilance."

The responsible corporate officer doctrine is applied most frequently to strict liability offenses. When a statute requires that a defendant "knowingly" commit a wrongful act, courts have ruled that the responsible corporate officer doctrine cannot be used to convict officers unless there is direct or circumstantial

---

99. United States v. Park, 421 U.S. 658 (1975). *See also* United States v. Dotterweich, 320 U.S. 277 (1943) (holding that criminal sanctions can be imposed on the corporate officers who have a "responsible relation" to the offending acts of the corporation even in the absence of proof that the officers were conscious of the wrongdoing).

100. 421 U.S. 658 (1975).

proof of knowledge.[101] For example, the Federal Meat Inspection Act and certain environmental statutes, such as the Comprehensive Environmental Response, Compensation, and Liability Act (CERCLA) and the Resource Conservation and Recovery Act (RCRA) (discussed in Chapter 15), require that defendants knowingly commit wrongful acts before being found guilty. Even though these statutes clearly concern public health and safety, the appellate courts required a showing of knowledge.[102]

In many circumstances, courts take a broad view of what constitutes knowledge, however, and do not require the government to prove that a defendant knew the specific legal details related to a violation.[103] The principle applies in the responsible corporate officer context as well. For example, the U.S. Court of Appeals for the Seventh Circuit ruled that to establish an RCRA violation, the government need not show that the defendant knew the offending material was hazardous waste as defined by Environmental Protection Agency regulations. It was sufficient that the defendant understood that the material "had the potential to be harmful to others or the environment, . . . the waste was not an innocuous substance."[104] Appellate courts have also held that knowledge may be inferred in appropriate circumstances.[105] For example, in *United States v. Self*,[106] the U.S. Court of Appeals for the Fifth Circuit stated: "[W]hile knowledge of prior illegal activity is not conclusive as to whether a defendant possessed the requisite knowledge of later illegal activity, it most certainly provides circumstantial evidence of the defendant's later knowledge from which the jury may draw the necessary inference."

Appellate courts have used the responsible corporate officer doctrine to impose fines under the Occupational Safety and Health Act[107] and the Radiation Control for Health and Safety Act.[108] Initially, the federal courts did not apply the doctrine to felony charges, and judges refused to impose lengthy sentences based on the doctrine. This changed in 2001 when the U.S. Court of Appeals for the Eleventh Circuit sentenced two defendants to stiff prison terms for violations of the Clean Water Act and RCRA by employees under their supervision.[109]

The threat of a prison term can be a strong incentive for corporate actors to accept a plea bargain. In 2007, three Purdue Frederick executives charged pursuant to the responsible corporate officer doctrine with violating FDA regulations avoided jail time by pleading guilty to misdemeanor misbranding charges related to marketing of the company's OxyContin pain relief drug.[110] The defendants agreed to pay a combined $34.5 million in fines.

In the following case, the court considered whether the trustee could be held criminally liable for violations of National Forest regulations by the trust.

101. *See, e.g.*, United States v. MacDonald & Watson Waste Oil Co., 933 F.2d 35 (1st Cir. 1991) ("[I]n a crime having knowledge as an express element, a mere showing of official responsibility . . . is not an adequate substitute for direct or circumstantial proof of knowledge."). Similarly, the U.S. District Court for the Western District of Missouri held that "something more than a mere status should be required before civil penalties are assessed against corporate officers for knowing violations of the [Federal Hazardous Substances Act]." United States v. Shelton Wholesale, Inc., 1999 U.S. Dist. LEXIS 15980 (W.D. Mo. Sept. 21, 1999). *But see* United States v. Int'l Minerals & Chem. Corp., 402 U.S. 558 (1971) (holding that officers of a chemical company were "under a species of absolute liability for violation of the regulations [proscribing knowing failure to record shipment of chemicals] despite the 'knowingly' requirement").

102. *See, e.g.*, United States v. Agnew, 931 F.2d 1397 (10th Cir. 1991).

103. *See e.g.*, United States v. Kung-Shou Ho, 311 F.3d 589 (5th Cir. 2002).

104. United States v. Kelly, 167 F.3d 1176, 1179 (7th Cir. 1999).

105. *See, e.g.*, United States v. Johnson & Towers, Inc., 741 F.2d 662, 669–70 (3d Cir. 1984) (holding that "knowledge" in an RCRA criminal prosecution "may be inferred by the jury as to those individuals who hold the requisite responsible positions with the corporate defendant").

106. 2 F.3d 1071, 1087–88 (5th Cir. 1993).

107. *See, e.g.*, United States v. Doig, 950 F.2d 411 (7th Cir. 1991).

108. *See, e.g.*, United States v. Hodges X-Ray, Inc., 759 F.2d 557 (6th Cir. 1985).

109. *See, e.g.*, Hansen v. United States, 262 F.3d 1217 (11th Cir. 2001) (Case 15.4).

110. *General Counsel to Pay $8 M in OxyContin Flap*, Conn. L. Trib., July 2, 2007, at 3.

A CASE IN POINT	*Summary*	Case 14.4

United States v. Freed

United States Court of Appeals for the Eleventh Circuit
189 F. App'x 888 (11th Cir. 2006).

FACTS Susan Freed is the trustee of Enota Mission Trust, which owns the Enota campground. In 1999, a Forest Service Ranger discovered blaze marks and vegetation damage on trails in the National Forest leading to Enota, as well as cut-down trees and improvements made to a dam on a nearby creek, which flowed onto the Enota property. In response to these findings, the Ranger notified Freed that these changes and improvements were in violation of National Forest regulations and illegal. The notifications called for the improvements to be removed and for no further modifications to be made to the land. Freed did not comply with these orders, as subsequent visits by the Rangers revealed. Freed was found guilty of various

CONTINUED

violations before a magistrate judge, who found her guilty as a responsible corporate agent of Enota Mission Trust. The district court affirmed the convictions, and Freed appealed.

ISSUE PRESENTED   Is the responsible corporate officer doctrine limited to cases involving health and safety?

SUMMARY OF OPINION   The U.S. Court of Appeals for the Eleventh Circuit was quick to reject Freed's assertion that the district court mistakenly applied vicarious liability principles to find her guilty of these offenses. Freed contended that the responsible corporate officer doctrine applies only to public health and safety regulations concerning "dangerous or deleterious devices or products or obnoxious waste materials." The court rejected this argument, reasoning that the doctrine applies when a corporation is liable for an offense because "the only way in which a corporation can act is through the individuals who act on its behalf." To impose liability, the government must produce "evidence sufficient to warrant a finding by the trier of facts that the defendant had, by reason of his position in the corporation, responsibility and authority either to prevent in the first instance, or promptly to correct, the violation complained of, and that he failed to do so."

RESULT   The conviction was upheld. The defendant was in a position of responsibility with regard to Enota and thus was criminally liable under the responsible corporate officer doctrine.

Impossibility Defense

A corporate officer may escape liability if he or she did everything possible to ensure legal compliance, but the company was still unable to comply with the applicable standards. In these circumstances, the officer can argue the defense of impossibility. According to the U.S. Court of Appeals for the Second Circuit: "To establish the *impossibility defense*, the corporate officer must introduce evidence that he exercised extraordinary care and still could not prevent violations of the Act."[111]

CORPORATE LIABILITY FOR CRIMINAL ACTS

Under the doctrine of *respondeat superior*, which means "let the superior give answer," a corporation (or other business entity) can be held liable for criminal offenses committed by its employees if the acts were committed within the scope of their employment (whether actual or apparent). (The application of *respondeat superior* in civil cases was discussed in Chapters 5 and 9.) Although a small minority of state courts have held that a corporation cannot be guilty of a non-strict liability crime—that is, a crime requiring a guilty mental state such as "knowledge" or "intent"—it is now the generally accepted rule that a corporation may be convicted of a crime (such as negligent homicide) for which a specific guilty mental state is essential. In such cases, the knowledge or intent of the corporation's employees and agents is imputed to

the corporation.[112] For example, the Pennsylvania Superior Court held a bus company criminally liable for homicide by vehicle when a low-level employee, the driver of a school bus owned by the corporation, ran over and killed a six-year-old who was crossing in front of the bus.[113] The bus driver could not see the child because mirrors that were required by state statute were missing. In many cases, the legislature has clearly indicated (either in the language of the statute or in legislative history) a desire to impose criminal liability on corporations; courts consistently enforce such legislative intent.[114] Judicial imputation is limited by the practical reality of a corporation's nature. For instance, because a corporation's intent is by definition that of its employees, it cannot engage in a conspiracy with only one employee.[115]

In cases involving misdemeanor offenses or regulatory crimes, the well-established rule is that a corporation is criminally liable for all violations committed by any of its agents or employees.[116] Even in the case of felonies, the corporation will almost always be vicariously liable if upper management or the board of directors adopted a policy or issued instructions that caused an employee to violate the law. Even if an agent acted contrary to a corporate policy or express instructions, the corporation may still be

---

111. United States v. Gel Spice Co., 773 F.2d 427 (2d Cir. 1985) (quoting United States v. New England Grocers Co., 488 F. Supp. 230 (D. Mass. 1980)) (emphasis added).

112. *See, e.g.,* Boise Dodge v. United States, 51 F.3d 1390 (9th Cir. 1969); Vaughn & Sons, Inc. v. State, 737 S.W.2d 805 (Tex. Crim. App. 1987); 18 AM. JUR. 2D *Corporations* § 2137 (1985).

113. Commonwealth v. McIlwain Sch. Bus Lines, 423 A.2d 413 (Pa. Super. 1980).

114. *See, e.g.,* Hanlester Network v. Shalala, 51 F.3d 1390 (9th Cir. 1995); People v. Mattiace, 568 N.E.2d 1189 (N.Y. 1990).

115. United States v. Sain, 141 F.3d 463 (3d Cir. 1998).

116. *See* 18 AM. JUR. 2D *Corporations* § 2136 (1985).

EXHIBIT 14.4 Factors Used by the Department of Justice to Decide Whether to Indict a Corporation

The factors federal prosecutors should consider in determining whether to charge a corporation are:

1. The nature and seriousness of the offense.

2. The pervasiveness of the wrongdoing within the corporation, including complicity or condonation by corporate management.

3. History of similar misconduct.

4. Timely and voluntary disclosure of the wrongdoing and willingness to cooperate.

5. The existence and adequacy of the corporation's preexisting compliance program.

6. Remedial actions, including efforts to implement or improve a compliance program, replace responsible management, discipline or terminate wrongdoers, pay restitution, and cooperate with relevant government agencies.

7. Collateral consequences of criminal liability, including disproportionate harm to nonculpable persons.

8. The adequacy of the prosecution of individuals responsible for the corporation's malfeasance.

9. The adequacy of civil or regulatory remedies.

SOURCE: *Principles of Federal Prosecution of Business Organizations*, UNITED STATES ATTORNEYS MANUAL § 9-28.300, *available at* http://www.justice.gov/usao/eousa/foia_reading_room/usam/title9/28mcrm.htm#9-28.300 (last visited Nov. 27, 2011).

criminally liable if the agent was acting within his or her apparent authority (and, in some states, at least in part for the benefit of the corporation). For example, a company was convicted of bribery after the manager of a gambling facility and dog track offered bribes to a state representative's law partner to influence the legislator's stance on proposed laws affecting the company.[117] The U.S. Court of Appeals for the First Circuit upheld the company's conviction even though an executive had clearly prohibited the payment of bribes. The fact that the bribe had been offered for the benefit of the corporation by the manager responsible for maintaining relationships with local political figures was sufficient to sustain the company's conviction.

As a practical matter, courts have been willing to impose liability on the corporation if the agent's actions involved or were at least "tolerated" by management.[118] Typically, courts make this determination based on the totality of the circumstances surrounding the agent's actions. For example, if the illegal conduct is performed or tolerated by a high managerial agent acting on behalf of the corporation within the scope of his or her office or employment, then the corporation can be held criminally liable even if the corporation's board of directors did not condone the action. Thus, a court upheld the conviction of Penn Valley Resorts for criminal involuntary manslaughter, reckless endangerment, and furnishing liquor to minors and visibly intoxicated persons after its president agreed to provide dinner and an open bar for sixty undergraduate students.[119] A twenty-year-old minor became noticeably intoxicated at the dinner and caused an automobile accident in which he was killed en route back to the university.

Deciding Whether to Prosecute a Business Organization

Prosecutors have discretion when deciding whether to prosecute a corporation or other business entity. The nine factors the U.S. Attorney General uses to make this determination are set forth in Exhibit 14.4.

Earlier versions of the guidelines for determining whether to prosecute a company had indicated that it was appropriate to consider whether a company had waived its right to attorney–client privilege and work-product protection when determining whether it had cooperated with prosecutors.[120] In addition, companies often refused to support employees or officers who were believed to be the architects of the underlying improper conduct.[121]

In response to pressure from business interests, the defense bar, the courts, and legislators, Deputy Attorney general Mark R. Filip announced in 2008 that credit for cooperation will not depend on the corporation's waiver of attorney–client or work-product privileges but on voluntary and timely disclosure of all relevant facts.[122] Although corporations are free to waive privilege, the revised principles direct prosecutors not to request waivers of nonfactual or "core" attorney–client communications or work product. They also instruct prosecutors not to consider a corporation's advancement of employees' legal fees or its participation in a joint defense agreement when evaluating cooperativeness.[123]

---

117. United States v. Potter, 463 F.3d 9 (1st Cir. 2006). *See also* United States v. Automated Med. Lab., Inc., 770 F. 2d 399 (4th Cir. 1985).

118. *See* Minnesota v. Christy Pontiac–GMC, Inc., 354 N.W.2d 17 (Minn. 1984).

119. Commonwealth v. Penn Valley Resorts, Inc., 494 A.2d 1139 (Pa. Super. 1985).

120. E. Lawrence Barcella Jr. et al., *Cooperation with Government Is a Growing Trend*, NAT'L L.J., July 19, 2004, at S2.

121. *Id.*

122. Press Release, U.S. Dep't of Justice, Justice Department Revises Charging Guidelines for Prosecuting Corporate Fraud (Aug. 29, 2008), *available at* http://www.usdoj.gov/oda/dc/2008/August/08-odag-757, html (last visited Sept. 18, 2008).

123. *See generally* Harry First, *Branch Office of the Prosecutor: The New Role of the Corporation in Business Crime Prosecution*, 89 N.C. L. Rev. 23 (2010). The decision in *United States v. Stein*, 541 F.3d 130 (2d Cir. 2008) (Case 14.3), helped spark these changes in policy.

IN BRIEF

Liability for Criminal Actions

Type of Defendant	Standard for Liability
Individual	An individual can perpetrate a crime against the corporate employer (e.g., embezzlement) or for the benefit of the corporation (e.g., price-fixing). The individual must have performed *actus reus* (criminal act) with *mens rea* (guilty mind).
Corporate officers	Officers can be directly liable for failing to supervise their subordinates. In addition to individual liability for their own acts, officers may, under certain limited circumstances, be vicariously liable for crimes committed by employees under their supervision. Under the responsible corporate officer doctrine, officers can be liable for criminal actions of their subordinates if the officer bore a "responsible relation" to the violation of law. Traditionally, the doctrine was limited to violations of strict liability statutes involving public health or safety where the officer is charged with a misdemeanor or the prosecution proves, through direct or circumstantial evidence, that the officer knew of the violation. Increasingly, courts are applying the doctrine to felonies requiring knowledge or intent.
Corporations (and other business entities)	*Respondeat superior* liability. A corporation is criminally liable for (1) all misdemeanor offenses and regulatory crimes committed by any of its agents or employees; (2) all crimes committed pursuant to top management's corporate policy or express instructions; and (3) all crimes committed by employees if the acts were committed (a) within the scope of their employment (whether actual or apparent and, in some states, also in furtherance of the corporation's business interests) or (b) were tolerated by top management.

 WHITE-COLLAR CRIME

White-collar crime is violation of the law by a corporation (or other business entity) or one of its managers. White-collar employees—that is, managers or professionals—may be either the victims or the perpetrators of crime. Most white-collar crime is nonviolent.

Many white-collar criminal statutes do not have a *mens rea* requirement. It is, therefore, possible to commit a crime in the corporate setting without having the intention of breaking the law.

Crime Against the Employer

Examples of crimes committed by an employee against his or her employer include theft, embezzlement, fraud, acceptance of a bribe, and certain computer-related crimes.

Theft, technically known as *larceny*, is simply the taking of property without the owner's consent. White-collar theft ranges from taking home pens and paper from the office to stealing money through the company's computer system.

Embezzlement is the taking of money or property that is lawfully in the employee's possession by reason of his or her employment. For example, a company's treasurer who takes money that belongs to the company by writing checks to dummy accounts is guilty of embezzlement.

Fraud is any deception intended to induce someone to part with property or money. Fraud may involve a false representation of fact, whether by words or by conduct, or concealment of something that should have been

disclosed. Examples of fraud include padding an expense account, submitting falsely inflated insurance reimbursement bills, and doctoring financial statements to influence the company's stock price.

Acceptance of a bribe may also be a crime against the employer. For example, a sales representative cannot legally accept a kickback from a purchaser of his or her employer's products. Similarly, a purchasing agent for a corporation must not accept a bribe from an outside salesperson.

Employees and outsiders may also commit a variety of computer crimes, including computer fraud, hacking, and transmitting viruses. These are discussed later in this chapter.

Crimes Perpetrated by the Corporation and Its Agents

Examples of crimes perpetrated by corporations (and other business entities) and employees or agents acting on their behalf include consumer fraud, securities fraud, tax evasion, and environmental pollution. Corporations can also commit crimes against other corporations. Examples include price-fixing (discussed in Chapter 16) and misappropriation of trade secrets or violations of copyright or trade secret laws (discussed in Chapter 11).

The balance of this section is devoted to a description of the most common types of white-collar crimes. The maximum penalties for many of the most common types of white-collar crimes are listed in Exhibit 14.5. They are grouped by the public policies they further, as set out in Chapter 1.

EXHIBIT 14.5 Penalties for White-Collar Crime

Offense	Maximum Fine or Penalty	Maximum Sentence	Comments
Public Policy Objective: Promote Economic Growth by Facilitating Capital Markets			
Failure to register nonexempt security offering (*Securities Act of 1933, 15 U.S.C. § 77x*)	$10,000	5 years	Purchasers can recover damages equal to the difference between purchase price and fair market value at time of suit or, if securities have been sold, difference between purchase price and sale price.
Unlawfully engaging in a swap transaction (*Dodd–Frank Wall Street Reform and Consumer Protection Act, § 723; 7 U.S.C. § 13(a)(5)*)	$1 million	10 years	Swaps include derivatives, such as equity swaps.
Insider trading of securities (*Securities Exchange Act of 1934, 15 U.S.C. § 78ff; Dodd–Frank Wall Street Reform and Consumer Protection Act, 15 U.S.C. § 78u-6*)	$5 million for individuals and $25 million for corporations for willful violations. SEC can also recover a civil fine of up to three times profit gained or loss avoided. Brokerage firms can be fined up to $2.5 million if they "knew or recklessly disregarded" information that would indicate insider trading by employees.	20 years	Contemporaneous traders can recover damages equal to the amount of profit gained or loss avoided. Tippers and all direct and remote tippees are jointly and severally liable. Whistleblowers whose tips lead to convictions can recover bounty payments as high as 30% of fines and penalties paid by the defendant.
Securities fraud (*Securities Exchange Act of 1934, 15 U.S.C. § 78ff; Rule 10b-5; Dodd–Frank Wall Street Reform and Consumer Protection Act, 15 U.S.C. § 78u-6*)	$5 million for individuals and $25 million for corporations for willful violations	20 years	Private plaintiffs can recover damages equal to the difference between price paid to purchase or sell security and what would have been paid absent the fraud. Whistleblowers whose tips lead to convictions can recover bounty payments as high as 30%.
Public company securities fraud (*Sarbanes–Oxley Act of 2002, 18 U.S.C. § 1348*)	$5 million for individuals and $25 million for corporations for willful violations	25 years	
False certification of SEC periodic reports or financial statements by CEO or CFO (*Sarbanes–Oxley Act of 2002, 18 U.S.C. § 1350*)	$1 million or $5 million if executive acted willfully	10 years or 20 years if executive acted willfully	
Failure of accountants to keep audit documents and work papers for at least five years (*Sarbanes–Oxley Act of 2002, 18 U.S.C. § 1520*)	Greater of $250,000 fine per violation for individuals ($500,000 for organizations) and twice gain to violators or loss to victims for knowing and willful violations	10 years for knowing and willful violations	

© Cengage Learning 2013

CONTINUED

EXHIBIT 14.5   Penalties for White-Collar Crime (Continued)

Offense	Maximum Fine or Penalty	Maximum Sentence	Comments
Public Policy Objective: Promote Economic Growth by Giving Incentives to Innovate			
Copyright infringement *(Copyright Act, 18 U.S.C. § 2319)*	Greater of $250,000 fine per violation for individuals ($500,000 for organizations) and twice gain to violators or loss to victims	5 years for first offense; 10 years for subsequent convictions	
Patent infringement *(Patent Act, 35 U.S.C. §§ 281, 283–285)*	No criminal penalties	No criminal penalties	Civil remedies include injunctions to protect against infringement and damages to compensate for infringement. A court may triple the amount of damages and in exceptional cases award attorneys' fees to prevailing party.
Misappropriation of trade secrets *(Economic Espionage Act, 18 U.S.C. § 1831)*	$500,000 for an individual and $10 million for corporation for intentional and knowing violations	15 years	
Public Policy Objective: Protect Workers			
Willful violation of workplace safety laws resulting in death of an employee *(Occupational Safety and Health Act (OSH Act), 29 U.S.C. § 666)*	$10,000 for first offender; $20,000 for subsequent convictions	6 months for first offender; 12 months for subsequent convictions	
Willful violations of Employee Retirement Income Security Act (ERISA) *(Sarbanes–Oxley Act of 2002, 29 U.S.C. § 1131)*	$100,000 for individuals; $500,000 for organizations	10 years	
Retaliation against whistleblowers who report securities law violations to government agencies *(Sarbanes–Oxley Act of 2002, 18 U.S.C. § 1513)*	Greater of $250,000 fine per violation for individuals ($500,000 for organizations) and twice gain to violators or loss to victims	10 years	Whistleblower can also sue to recover damages resulting from retaliatory acts.
Public Policy Objective: Promote Consumer Welfare by Ensuring Safe Products and Services			
Sale of adulterated or misbranded food or drug *(Food, Drug and Cosmetic Act, 21 U.S.C. § 333)*	$1,000 for first offenses without intent to defraud or mislead; $10,000 for subsequent convictions or first offenses with intent to defraud or mislead	1 year for first offenses without intent to defraud or mislead; 3 years for subsequent convictions or first offenses with intent to defraud or mislead	

CONTINUED

EXHIBIT 14.5   Penalties for White-Collar Crime (Continued)

Offense	Maximum Fine or Penalty	Maximum Sentence	Comments
Sale of drug without required FDA approval *(Food, Drug and Cosmetic Act, 21 U.S.C. § 333)*	$250,000 per violation for knowing violations	10 years for knowing violations	
Public Policy Objective: Promote Consumer Welfare by Facilitating Low-Cost Goods and Services			
Price-fixing and other antitrust violations *(Sherman Act, 15 U.S.C. §§ 1–3)*	$1 million per violation for individuals; $100 million for corporations	10 years	
Payment of bribes or failure to have adequate internal accounting controls *(Foreign Corrupt Practices Act, 15 U.S.C. § 78dd-2)*	$100,000 for individuals and $2 million for corporations; under the Alternative Fines Act, fines can be twice gross gain of corrupt bribe.	5 years	
Public Policy Objective: Promote Consumer Welfare by Facilitating Innovative Products and Services			
See "Promote Economic Growth by Giving Incentives to Innovate" above.			
Public Policy Objective: Promote Consumer Welfare by Preventing Deceptive Practices			
Mail or wire fraud *(Mail Fraud Act, 18 U.S.C. § 1341, or Wire Fraud Act, 18 U.S.C. § 1343)*	Greater of $250,000 fine per violation for individuals ($500,000 for organizations) and twice gain to violators or loss to victims; $1 million for violations that affect financial institutions	20 years; 30 years for violations that affect financial institutions	Violation of these acts can trigger civil and criminal liability under the Racketeer Influenced and Corrupt Organizations Act (RICO).
Money laundering *(18 U.S.C. § 1956)*	Greater of $250,000 for individuals ($500,000 for organizations) and twice the value of the property involved in the transaction	20 years	
Computer fraud *(Computer Fraud and Abuse Act, 18 U.S.C. § 1030)*	Greater of $250,000 fine per violation for individuals ($500,000 for organizations) and twice gain to violators or loss to victims	10 years for first-time offenders; 20 years for subsequent offenders	
Racketeering *(Racketeer Influenced and Corrupt Organizations Act (RICO), 18 U.S.C. § 1963)*	Greater of $250,000 fine per violation for individuals ($500,000 for organizations) and two times the defendant's gain or the victim's loss; forfeiture of all property wrongfully acquired or maintained	Life	Any injured person may also sue to recover threefold the damages sustained and the cost of the suit, except no private right of action based solely on securities fraud (18 U.S.C. § 1964).
Bribery *(18 U.S.C. § 201)*	Greater of $250,000 fine per violation for individuals ($500,000 for organizations) and twice gain to violators or loss to victims and three times the value of the bribe	15 years	

CONTINUED

EXHIBIT 14.5   Penalties for White-Collar Crime (Continued)

Offense	Maximum Fine or Penalty	Maximum Sentence	Comments
Public Policy Objective: Promote Public Welfare by Promoting Effective Administration of Justice			
Obstruction of justice (18 U.S.C. §§ 1501–20)	Greater of $250,000 fine per violation for individuals ($500,000 for organizations) and twice gain to violators or loss to victims		Includes altering or destroying documents with intent to impair their use in an official proceeding; offering or promoting false testimony; and threatening or intimidating witnesses, jurors, or court officials.
Perjury (18 U.S.C. § 1621)	Greater of $250,000 fine per violation for individuals ($500,000 for organizations) and twice gain to violators or loss to victims	5 years	Falsehood must be relevant to inquiry.
Tampering with a record or otherwise impeding an official proceeding (Sarbanes–Oxley Act of 2002, 18 U.S.C. § 1512)	Greater of $250,000 fine per violation for individuals ($500,000 for organizations) and twice gain to violators or loss to victims	20 years	
Public Policy Objective: Promote Public Welfare by Collecting Taxes and Spending Money			
False statements to U.S. Government (False Statements Act, 18 U.S.C. § 1001)	Greater of $250,000 fine per violation for individuals ($500,000 for organizations) and twice gain to violators or loss to victims for knowing and willful violations	5 years for knowing and willful violations; 8 years if offense involves terrorism	
Tax fraud or evasion (Internal Revenue Code, 26 U.S.C. § 7201)	$100,000 for individuals ($500,000 for corporations) plus costs of prosecution	5 years	Violations include willful attempts to evade any tax imposed under the Code, including employee withholding requirements, willful delivery of a fraudulent return to the Secretary of the Treasury, and any false statements in a tax return.
False claims for reimbursement to U.S. Government (False Claims Act, 18 U.S.C. § 287)	Greater of $250,000 fine per violation for individuals ($500,000 for organizations) and twice gain to violators or loss to victims for knowing and willful violations	5 years	U.S. Government includes any individual or any agency in civil, military, or naval service.
Public Policy Objective: Promote Public Welfare by Protecting the Environment			
Unlawful transport or disposal of hazardous waste (Resource Conservation and Recovery Act (RCRA), 42 U.S.C. § 6928)	$50,000 per day for first-time offenders and $100,000 per day for subsequent violations; $250,000 for knowingly endangering others and $1 million for organizations that knowingly endanger others	2 years for first-time offenders and 4 years for subsequent violations; 15 years for knowingly endangering others	Imposes "cradle to the grave" responsibility for generators of hazardous waste and requires disposal in a licensed facility.
Unlawful disposal of hazardous materials in water (Clean Water Act, 33 U.S.C. § 1319)	Not less than $2,500 nor more than $25,000 per day for negligent first-time violations; $50,000 per day for subsequent violations; $250,000 for first-time knowing endangerment and $500,000 for subsequent knowing endangerment violations; $1 million for organizations that knowingly endanger others for the first time and $2 million for subsequent violations	1 year for negligent first-time violations and 2 years for subsequent violations; 15 years for first-time knowing endangerment and 30 years for subsequent violations	

Racketeering Under the Racketeer Influenced and Corrupt Organizations Act (RICO)

The Racketeer Influenced and Corrupt Organizations Act (RICO)[124] was originally designed to combat organized crime and to provide an enforcement mechanism against syndicate bosses and masterminds who might otherwise escape liability. Today, the criminal provisions of RICO are one of a prosecutor's most powerful weapons for fighting classic white-collar crimes. RICO has proved particularly effective against groups of traders, brokers, and others who have developed a continuous relationship of passing and trading on inside information.

RICO prohibits (1) the investment in any enterprise of income derived from racketeering, (2) the acquisition of an interest in an enterprise through a pattern of racketeering activity, (3) participation in an enterprise through a pattern of racketeering activity involving at least two related predicate acts in a ten-year period, and (4) conspiring to engage in any of these activities.

RICO Requirements

RICO broadly defines an *enterprise* as "any individual, partnership, corporation, association, or other legal entity, and any union or group of individuals associated in fact although not a legal entity." The enterprise need not be engaged in business or have profit as an aim.[125] Groups recognized by the courts as enterprises for RICO purposes include members of an anti-abortion group,[126] People for the Ethical Treatment of Animals (PETA),[127] and a street gang called the Nasty Boys.[128] *Racketeering activity* is defined to include various state and federal offenses, specifically including mail and wire fraud and fraud in the sale of securities. Consequently, almost any business fraud can serve as the basis for a criminal RICO violation.

To demonstrate a *pattern* of racketeering activity, a plaintiff must show that at least two related predicate acts have occurred within a ten-year period. Two isolated acts are not considered sufficient.

Private Civil Actions

In addition to criminal penalties, the statute grants a civil private right of action that permits individuals to recover treble damages (that is, three times their actual damages) and also their costs and attorneys' fees. The private right of action was apparently intended as a tool against businesses fueled by funds generated through organized crime. The statute contains no explicit requirement that organized crime be involved, however, and RICO has been used in numerous civil suits against legitimate businesses.

To prevail in a civil case under RICO, the plaintiff must demonstrate that the defendant committed an "overt act . . . in furtherance of a RICO conspiracy."[129] Thus, a president fired for reporting activity that violated RICO did not have a private cause of action against his former employer because the termination of his employment was not a racketeering activity. In the Private Securities Litigation Reform Act of 1995,[130] Congress foreclosed the use of the RICO civil private right of action against alleged perpetrators of securities fraud. Denying the potential for RICO-based shareholder lawsuits was one of many measures in this statute that were designed to curb abusive shareholder litigation. Criminal RICO charges can still be based on securities fraud, however.

Limits on the Use of RICO

Although RICO is generally given a liberal construction to ensure that Congress's intent is not frustrated by an overly narrow reading of the statute, its reach is not unlimited. In *Reves v. Ernst & Young*,[131] purchasers of demand notes from a farmers' cooperative brought a securities fraud and RICO action against the cooperative's auditors. The U.S. Supreme Court held that the accountants hired to perform an audit of the cooperative's records did not exert control over the company or "participate in the operation or management" of the cooperative's affairs. Such a finding of participation would have been necessary to find the accountants liable under RICO for failing to inform the cooperative's board of directors that the cooperative was insolvent. As clarified by the U.S. Court of Appeals for the Seventh Circuit, "participation" requires that one "knowingly agree to perform the services of a kind which facilitate the activities of those who are operating the enterprise in an illegal manner."[132]

Reves is an important case for accountants, underwriters, attorneys, and others who work with a company issuing securities. Such persons can no longer be found liable under RICO just because they were involved in the offering process. Instead, some involvement in the management of the issuer of the securities is required.

Mail and Wire Fraud

Next to RICO, the Mail and Wire Fraud Acts[133] may be the prosecutor's most powerful weapon against white-collar crime. Chief Justice Warren Burger characterized the Mail Fraud Act as a "stopgap" provision that criminalizes conduct that a court finds morally reprehensible but that is not mentioned in any other criminal statute.

124. 18 U.S.C.A. §§ 1961–68.

125. United States v. Muyet, 994 F. Supp. 501, 511 (S.D.N.Y. 1998) (the RICO statute does not require the government to prove that the enterprise operated with a financial purpose).

126. Tompkins v. Cyr, 202 F.3d 770 (5th Cir. 2000).

127. Huntingdon Life Scis. v. Rokke, 986 F. Supp. 982 (E.D. Va. 1997).

128. *Muyet*, 994 F. Supp. at 511.

129. Beck v. Prupis, 529 U.S. 494 (2000).

130. Pub. L. No. 104-67, § 107, 109 Stat. 737, 758 (1995) (codified at 18 U.S.C.A. § 1964(c)).

131. 507 U.S. 170 (1993).

132. Brouwer v. Raffensperger, 199 F.3d 961 (7th Cir. 2000).

133. 18 U.S.C. §§ 1343, 1341.

To establish *mail fraud or wire fraud* under the Acts, the prosecutor must demonstrate (1) the existence of a scheme intended to defraud or to obtain money or property by fraudulent means and (2) the use of the mails or of interstate telephone lines in furtherance of the fraudulent scheme. The U.S. Supreme Court has broadly construed "fraud" to encompass "everything designed to defraud by representations as to the past or present, or suggestions and promises as to the future."[134]

Federal prosecutions under these Acts have involved such diverse activities as defense procurement fraud, insurance fraud, false financial statements fraud, medical advertising fraud, tax fraud, divorce mill fraud, and securities fraud. In *Schmuck v. United States*,[135] the U.S.

Supreme Court upheld an indictment for mail fraud even though the use of the mail was merely incidental to the scheme to defraud. Wayne T. Schmuck, a used-car distributor, had purchased used cars, rolled back their odometers, and sold them to Wisconsin retail dealers at prices artificially inflated by the low-mileage readings. The unwitting dealers relied on the altered readings and resold the cars to customers at inflated prices. The dealers consummated these transactions by mailing title-application forms to the state authorities on behalf of the buyers. The Supreme Court held that the mailings at issue satisfied the mailing element of the crime of mail fraud.

In the following case, the Supreme Court considered whether an executive's alleged failure to provide "honest services" to his employer constituted fraud under the Acts.

---

134. Durland v. United States, 161 U.S. 306, 313 (1896).
135. 489 U.S. 705 (1989).

| A CASE IN POINT | *Summary* | Case 14.5 |

Skilling v. United States

Supreme Court of the United States
130 S. Ct. 2896 (2010).

FACTS   Founded in 1985, Enron Corporation grew from its headquarters in Houston, Texas, into one of the world's leading energy companies.[136] Jeffrey Skilling steadily rose through the corporation's ranks, serving as president and chief operating officer and, then, beginning in February 2001, as chief executive officer. Six months later, on August 14, 2001, Skilling resigned from Enron.

Less than four months after Skilling's departure, Enron spiraled into bankruptcy. An investigation conducted by the U.S. Department of Justice uncovered an elaborate conspiracy to prop up Enron's short-run stock price by overstating the company's financial well-being. On July 7, 2004, a grand jury indicted Skilling; Kenneth Lay, Enron's former chair; and Richard Causey, Enron's former chief accounting officer. Count 1 of the indictment charged Skilling with conspiracy to commit "honest-services" mail and wire fraud by depriving Enron and its shareholders of the intangible right to his honest services as well as conspiracy to commit securities fraud. After a four-month trial, the jury found Skilling guilty of nineteen counts, including conspiracy.

ISSUE PRESENTED   Does conduct that results in a deprivation of an employer's intangible right to honest services constitute mail and wire fraud?

SUMMARY OF OPINION   The U.S. Supreme Court began by reviewing the origin and subsequent application of the honest-services doctrine. The Mail and Wire Fraud Acts prohibit "any scheme or artifice to defraud, *or for obtaining money or property by means of false or fraudulent pretenses, representations, or promises.*" Emphasizing Congress's use of the disjunctive "or," the courts of appeals initially "interpreted the term 'scheme or artifice to defraud' to include deprivations not only of money or property, but also of intangible rights," such as the right to honest services from employees. Honest-services claims centered on the harm to the employer, not the gain to the defendant. In 1987, in *McNally v. United States*,[137] the U.S. Supreme Court rejected the doctrine. The next year, Congress enacted a new statute, codified in section 1346, "specifically to cover one of the 'intangible rights' that lower courts had protected . . . prior to *McNally*: 'the intangible right of honest services.'"

CONTINUED

---

136. Enron is discussed further in the "Inside Story" in Chapter 2.
137. 483 U.S. 350 (1987).

The Court surveyed the cases decided before *McNally* and found that the "'vast majority' of the honest-services cases involved offenders who, in violation of a fiduciary duty, participated in bribery or kickback schemes." Thus, the Court had "no doubt that Congress intended § 1346 to reach *at least* bribes and kickbacks." Reading the statute to proscribe a wider range of offensive conduct would, the Court concluded, raise due process concerns because the statute would be overly vague: "To preserve the statute without transgressing constitutional limitations, we now hold that § 1346 criminalizes *only* the bribe-and-kickback core of the pre-*McNally* case law."

RESULT The Supreme Court ruled that Skilling did not commit honest-services fraud because he did not engage in bribes or kickbacks. The case was remanded to the appeals court for a determination of whether the honest-services fraud instruction was harmless error. Skilling's conviction on the other counts was not affected by this decision.

COMMENT On remand, the U.S. Court of Appeals for the Fifth Circuit ruled that the invalid jury instruction permitting conviction for conspiracy to commit honest-services fraud was harmless because there was overwhelming evidence that the jury would still have convicted Skilling of conspiracy to commit securities fraud even if there had been no instruction regarding honest-services fraud.[138]

138. 638 F.3d 480 (5th Cir. 2011).

A prosecution for wire and mail fraud can be brought in addition to other prosecutions based on the same events. Thus, the defendant may be charged with violation of the securities laws, the tax laws, or the Truth in Lending Act, as well as with wire or mail fraud. Indeed, it is rare for a white-collar criminal prosecution to be brought without alleging a violation of the Wire and Mail Fraud Acts. Violation of the Wire and Mail Fraud Acts can also trigger RICO liability. As a result, wire and mail fraud and RICO prosecutions often proceed in tandem.

This prosecutorial ability to bring charges under various statutes increases the plea-bargaining power of the government. By presenting multiple statutory violations to the jury, the prosecutor also increases the chances of conviction and the likelihood of a stiffer sentence.

Money Laundering

Especially in the wake of the terrorist attacks on September 11, 2001, which may have been financed at least in part by funds improperly held and transferred abroad by U.S. financial institutions, the federal government has stepped up its investigation and prosecution of cases involving *money laundering*, that is, the transfer of funds derived from unlawful activities with the intent of concealing or disguising the location, source, ownership, or control of said funds.[139] Although the statute does not require the prosecution to prove that the defendant

intended to create an appearance of legitimate wealth, it does require the prosecution to prove that the defendant's secrecy in hiding the money was part of a larger "design" to disguise the source or nature of the money.

False Statements to the U.S. Government

The False Statements Act provides:

Whoever, in any manner within the jurisdiction of any department or agency of the United States knowingly and willfully

1. falsifies, conceals or covers up by any trick, scheme, or device a material fact;

2. makes any false, fictitious or fraudulent statements or representations; or

3. makes or uses any false writing or document knowing the same to contain any false, fictitious or fraudulent statement or entry, shall be fined or imprisoned . . . or both.[140]

Although not used as frequently as the Wire and Mail Fraud Acts, the False Statements Act has become an effective tool for criminal prosecutions of businesses and employees who deal dishonestly with governmental administrative agencies. For example, in *United States v. Yermian*,[141] an employee of Gulton Industries, a defense contractor, was convicted of making false statements to the Department of Defense in connection with his application for a security clearance.

139. 18 U.S.C. § 1956. Cuellar v. United States, 553 U.S. 550 (2008).

140. 18 U.S.C. § 1001.

141. 581 F.2d 595 (7th Cir. 1978).

"Let's just say someone has slipped out of the top one per cent."

Charles Barsotti/The New Yorker Collection/www.cartoonbank.com

False Claims to the U.S. Government and *Qui Tam* *Plaintiffs*

Since the late 1980s, the U.S. government has used a civil statute, the False Claims Act (FCA),[142] to attack defense-contract, health-care fraud, and mortgage fraud. Often these civil suits lead to criminal prosecution under other federal statutes, such as the Mail and Wire Fraud Acts. A number of states and municipalities have enacted their own false claim acts.[143]

Both the government and private parties (usually whistleblowers), acting on the government's behalf as

---

142. 31 U.S.C. § 3729 *et seq.*

143. *State False Claim Acts*, TAXPAYERS AGAINST FRAUD EDUC. FUND, *available at* http://www.taf.org/statefca.htm.

HISTORICAL PERSPECTIVE

White-Collar Crime

The term "white-collar crime" was first used in 1939 when Edwin Sutherland coined it in a speech about "crime in relation to business" that he was presenting to the American Sociological Society.[a] Sutherland defined white-collar crime as a "crime committed by a person of respectability and high social status in the course of his occupation."[b] Sutherland promoted the idea—revolutionary for his time—that wealthy or high-status individuals commit crimes, too. Prior to Sutherland's work, crime was viewed primarily as a reaction to poverty and thus endemic to the lower classes.

Sutherland asserted that "crime is not so highly concentrated in the lower class as the usual statistics indicate."[c] He further pointed out that the cost of white-collar crime was much higher than that of street crime.[d] Sutherland went on to argue: "The financial loss from white-collar crime, great as it is, is less important than the damage to social relations. White-collar crimes violate trust and therefore create distrust, which lowers social morale and produces social disorganization on a large scale."[e] Nonetheless, white-collar criminals were not "regarded as real criminals."[f]

According to Sutherland, the "robber barons" of the late nineteenth and early twentieth centuries (including J.P. Morgan and John D. Rockefeller) were notorious examples of white-collar criminals.[g] These corporate titans openly exploited labor for their own gain and created monopolies violating the Sherman Antitrust Act of 1890, but they did not go to prison.[h]

After the stock market crash of 1929 and the ensuing Great Depression crippled the financial markets, Congress enacted the Securities Act of 1933 and the Securities Exchange Act of 1934 "to set limits on what people can do in the name of profit."[i] Yet it was not until 1961, seventy years after the passage of the Sherman Antitrust Act, that the first white-collar criminals were sent to jail.[j] Seven executives at major companies implicated in a price-fixing conspiracy, including General Electric and Westinghouse, were sentenced to thirty days, less time for good behavior.[k] During the first seventy years of the Sherman Act, the government brought 1,580 antitrust cases against corporations, but all of them resulted in civil penalties.[l]

Prosecution of white-collar crime did not become commonplace until the mid-1970s. It was only after the Watergate break-in and a series of scandals involving bribery of foreign governments that the federal government began targeting white-collar crime as a high-priority area.[m]

By the mid-1980s and early 1990s, a number of high-profile corporate crime cases were making headlines. These included a series of insider trading cases involving Ivan Boesky, Michael Milken, and Drexel Burnham Lambert (discussed in the "Inside Story" in Chapter 22). Of the fourteen Wall Street crooks convicted in the 1980s, former junk-bond king Milken received the longest sentence—ten years.[n] He ended up serving only twenty-two months, however.

Even before the Milken scandal was over, the government had a new target: the savings and loan industry. The most high-profile case involved Lincoln Savings & Loan, headed by

CONTINUED

Charles Keating. Its collapse—dubbed "the largest public-finance scandal of the century"[o]—cost the U.S. taxpayers $2.5 billion. Keating was convicted in 1992 of fraud, racketeering, and securities violations and sentenced to ten years in prison. He served four and one-half years before his sentence was overturned. In 1999, he pleaded guilty to defrauding investors and was sentenced to the time he had already served.

One expert commented that the "criminal sanction is generally reserved for the losers, the scamsters, the low-rent crime."[p] He compared the fate of "starched-collar criminals" who loot companies of millions or billions of dollars with that of petty thieves:

The starched-collar S&L crooks got an average of 36.4 months in the slammer. Those who committed burglary—generally swiping $300 or less—got 55.6 months; car thieves got 38 months; and first-time drug offenders, 64.9 months. Now compare the costs of the two kinds of crime: The losses from all bank robberies in the U.S. in 1992 $35 million. That's about 1% of the estimated cost of Charles Keating's fraud at Lincoln Savings & Loan.[q]

After the spate of accounting scandals at the turn of the millennium, the U.S. government took a tougher stance on corporate crime. As seen in Exhibit 14.6, multiple executives charged over the ensuing years were sentenced to upwards of two decades in prison. As a U.S. attorney commented in 2003 after the former chief executive of Rite Aid, Martin Grass, was sentenced to eight years in prison for accounting fraud, "This conviction . . . should serve as a warning for corporate executives: if you lie to the investing public, to grand juries, to investigators, regulators and prosecutors, you will be vigorously investigated and prosecuted."[r]

After WorldCom was forced to file for bankruptcy in 2002 as a result of $11 billion in accounting fraud, the former CFO Scott D. Sullivan pleaded guilty and was the key witness against his former boss CEO Bernie Ebbers. Ebbers was convicted in March 2005 of securities fraud, conspiracy to commit securities fraud, and filing false reports with the Securities and Exchange Commission.[s] He had borrowed $400 million from WorldCom, secured by his WorldCom stock, and prosecutors claimed that he perpetrated the fraud to reverse the slide in WorldCom's stock price. Ebbers took the stand in his own defense and played down his expertise, testifying, "I don't know about technology and I don't know about finance and accounting."[t] Ebbers also testified that he was unaware of what the WorldCom CFO was doing. The jury didn't buy it. According to a posting by the father of juror Sarah Nulty, the jury "concluded that with his personal fortune evaporating and the company he built sinking, it was inconceivable that Ebbers was not paying attention" to WorldCom's finances.[u]

One source pointed out that without convictions of the top guys, little else matters: when it comes to restoring the public confidence in the courts and Wall Street, all the guilty pleas on earth won't amount to much if their purpose is to gain evidence against CEOs who nonetheless wind up tap-dancing their way to freedom on a smile and a handshake and the assurance that they're really, really stupid.[v] Ebbers's conviction, coupled with the CEO and CFO certification requirements imposed by the Sarbanes–Oxley Act of 2002, appeared to spell the demise of the "aw shucks" or "it wasn't me" defense.[w]

EXHIBIT 14.6	A Sampling of Executives on Trial		
The CEO	**The Crime**	**Plea/Trial Outcome**	**Punishment/Status**
Diana D. Brooks *Sotheby's Holdings*	Price-fixing conspiracy with rival Christie's.	Pleaded guilty (2000)	Sentenced to 6 months under house arrest and 3 years on probation; also paid a $350,000 fine and performed 1,000 hours of community service.
Sam Waksal *ImClone*	Securities fraud, conspiracy, insider trading, obstruction of justice, perjury, bank fraud, and tax evasion.	Pleaded guilty (2002)	Sentenced to 7¼ years in federal prison and fined $4.3 million.
Martha Stewart *Martha Stewart Living Omnimedia*	Making false statements, obstruction, and conspiracy.	Convicted (2004)	Served 5 months followed by 5 months of home confinement; also paid a fine of $30,000.
Oral Suer *United Way*	Transporting stolen money across state lines, making false statements, and concealing facts about an employee retirement plan.	Pleaded guilty (2004)	Served 27 months and ordered to pay $497,000 in restitution.
John Rigas *Adelphia Communications*	Conspiracy, bank fraud, and securities fraud, but acquitted of wire fraud charges.	Convicted (2004)	Sentenced to 15 years.

CONTINUED

| EXHIBIT 14.6 | A Sampling of Executives on Trial (Continued) | | |

The CEO	The Crime	Plea/Trial Outcome	Punishment/Status
Bernie Ebbers *WorldCom*	Securities fraud, conspiracy to commit fraud, and filing false reports with the SEC.	Convicted (2005)	Sentenced to 25 years.
Dennis Kozlowski *Tyco International*	Conspiracy, grand larceny, and securities fraud.	Convicted (2005)	Sentenced to between 8⅓ and 25 years.
Sanjay Kumar *Computer Associates International*	Securities fraud, conspiracy, and obstruction of justice.	Pleaded guilty (2006)	Sentenced to 12 years and fined $8 million.
Jeffrey Skilling *Enron*	Insider trading, securities fraud, wire fraud, making false statements, and conspiracy to commit wire and securities fraud.	Convicted (2006)	Originally sentenced to more than 24 years in prison and fined $45 million; then resentencing ordered.
Kenneth Lay *Enron*	Bank fraud, making false statements to banks, conspiracy, wire fraud, and securities fraud.	Conviction vacated (2006)	Convicted in May 2006 but died of heart failure in Colorado less than two months later. Because Lay's appeal was pending at his death, his convictions were voided.
Walter Forbes *Cendant*	Wire, mail, and securities fraud; insider trading; making false statements to the SEC; and conspiracy.	Convicted (2006)	Sentenced to 12 years and 7 months; also ordered to pay a $3.3 billion fine.
Gregory Reyes *Brocade Communications Systems*	Securities fraud based on stock option backdating scheme.	Convicted (2007)	Sentenced to 21 months and fined $15 million.
Bernard L. Madoff *Bernard L. Madoff Investment Securities*	Securities fraud, money laundering, perjury, and theft.	Pleaded guilty (2009)	Sentenced to 150 years.
Raj Rajaratnam *Galleon Group*	Insider trading and conspiracy.	Convicted (2011)	Sentenced to 11 years and ordered to pay $63.8 million in fines and forfeitures.
Lee Farkas *Taylor Bean & Whitaker*	Bank, wire, and securities fraud.	Convicted (2011)	Sentenced to 30 years and ordered to pay $38.5 million in gains.
Denis M. Field *BDO Seidman*	Running an illegal tax shelter scheme.	Convicted (2011)	Was awaiting sentencing as of 2011.

© Cengage Learning 2013

Just as the dust appeared to be settling on the spate of corporate scandals that sent a record number of former CEOs and CFOs to prison, the financial community was shocked by the collapse of the subprime mortgage market in 2008. As discussed more fully in the "Inside Story" in Chapter 23, both federal and state criminal cases were ongoing as of 2011.

a. This speech was later published as Edwin H. Sutherland, *White-Collar Criminality*, 1 Am. Soc. Rev. 1 (1940).

b. Edwin H. Sutherland, White Collar Crime: The Uncut Version (1983).

c. Sutherland, *supra* note a, at 4.

d. *Id.* at 4–5.

e. *Id.* at 8.

f. *Id.*

g. *Id.* at 2.

h. Leland Hazard, *Are Big Businessmen Crooks?*, Atlantic Monthly, Nov. 1961.

i. Cynthia Crossen, *A Thirties Revelation: Rich People Who Steal Are Criminals, Too*, Wall St. J., Oct. 15, 2003, at B1.

j. *Id.*

k. Hazard, *supra* note h.

l. *Id.*

m. Peter J. Henning, *Testing the Limits of Investigating and Prosecuting White Collar Crime: How Far Will the Courts Allow Prosecutors to Go?*, 54 U. Pitt. L. Rev. 405 (1993).

n. *Michael Milken: Junked*, Economist, Nov. 24, 1990, at 90.

o. *The S&L Mess*, U.S. News & World Rep., Nov. 26, 1990, at 13.

p. Clifton Leaf, *White-Collar Criminals*, Fortune, Mar. 18, 2002, at 68.

q. *Id.* at 76.

r. Adrian Michaels, *Former Rite Aid Chief Jailed*, Fin. Times, May 28, 2004, at 32.

s. Jonathan D. Glater & Ken Belson, *Ebbers, on Witness Stand, May Have Lost His Case*, N.Y. Times, Mar. 16, 2005, at C1.

t. *Id.* at C8.

u. *Id.* at C9.

v. Christopher Byron, *The CEO Dunce Card*, N.Y. Post, July 26, 2004, at 37.

w. Joann S. Lublin & Christopher Rhoads, *It Better Not Be Lonely at the Top in the New World of Today's CEO*, Wall St. J., Mar. 16, 2005, at A10.

qui tam plaintiffs, can bring civil suits to recover treble damages and penalties from persons who submit false claims for government funds knowingly or with recklessness or deliberate ignorance of their truth or falsity. In 2000, the U.S. Supreme Court rebuffed a challenge to the *qui tam* provisions when it held that whistleblowers have standing under Article III of the U.S. Constitution to sue on the government's behalf.[144]

The *qui tam* plaintiffs receive "bounties" of up to 25% of the recovery. Since 1986, the United States had recovered more than $21 billion through FCA *qui tam* cases, of which more than $2 billion was paid to the whistleblowers who brought the cases.[145] Congress created similar incentives for whistleblowers in cases involving violations of securities law, commodities law, and the Foreign Corrupt Practices Act (FCPA) in the Dodd–Frank Wall Street Reform and Consumer Protection Act, with bounties up to 30% of recoveries in excess of $1 million.

Fighting Health-Care Fraud Health-care fraud and abuse in the United States costs between $100 and $170 billion each year.[146] The presence of third-party payors, such as private insurance companies and government programs, increases the opportunities and incentives to cheat rather than compete on price.

The Department of Justice focused first on the clinical laboratory industry, then on the major hospital chains, and most recently on pharmaceutical companies.[147] The Health Insurance and Portability Account Act of 1996 (HIPAA)[148] created several new criminal offenses, including health-care fraud,[149] theft or embezzlement in connection with a health-care offense,[150] false statements relating to a health-care offense,[151] and obstruction of a criminal investigation of a health-care offense.[152] Although firms convicted of felony health-care fraud are ineligible to participate in federal health-care programs, the government has been reluctant to use its power to bar major drug companies from doing business with federal programs, such as Medicare or Medicaid, for fear of harming the elderly and poor clients who rely on the drugs these companies provide.[153] Instead,

the government is increasingly going after the individual executives involved.[154]

In 2010 alone, the U.S. Attorney's Office brought criminal health-care fraud charges against 931 defendants, the most ever in a single fiscal year.[155] Criminal convictions in health-care fraud cases increased from 59 in 1992 to 263 in 1999, to 726 in 2010.[156] In 2010, the government secured a record $4 billion in health-care fraud judgments and settlements.[157]

Exhibit 14.7 presents a sampling of health-care fraud settlements of $100 million or more in the period from 2001 to 2011. Since 1999, the government has recouped more than $12 billion from health-care fraud cases.[158]

Computer Crime

White-collar crime often involves computers. Computers may be used not only to commit the offense but also to hide or destroy the evidence. Even if computer crime is detected, it often goes unreported. Most businesses, especially financial institutions, do not want it publicly known that an employee or an outsider used the company's computer system to steal from the company or access confidential files.

Despite ongoing efforts to thwart it, computer crime continues to flourish.[159] Computer crime can take several forms. *Computer fraud* is the use of a computer to steal company or government funds. This type of theft generally involves improper or unauthorized access to the computer system and the creation of false data or computer instructions. The computer system then generates fraudulent transfers of funds or bogus checks that are cashed by the wrongdoer.

More than forty different sections of the federal criminal code may apply to thefts by computer, ranging from embezzlement to wire fraud. Most computer-aided thefts can also be prosecuted under traditional state larceny laws. Other computer crimes can be prosecuted under a multitude of other laws that normally apply to non-computer-related crime.[160] The Economic Espionage Act and child pornography statutes, as well as bootlegging, identity theft, and stalking laws, are all applicable to crimes committed with the use of computers.

144. Vt. Agency of Natural Res. v. United States *ex rel.* Stevens, 529 U.S. 765 (2000).

145. *Department of Justice Fraud Statistics Overview 1987–2007*, Taxpayers Against Fraud Educ. Fund, *available at* http://www.taf.org/STATS-FY-2007.pdf.

146. *A Review of Healthcare Fraud and Abuse in America*, AAOMS Committee on Healthcare & Advocacy, Mar. 1, 2011, at 2.

147. Terry Carter, *Drug Wars*, A.B.A. J., Dec. 1, 2002, at 40; Bruce Japsen, *Targets Change in Drug Probes*, Chi. Trib., Dec. 27, 2001, at 1.

148. Pub. L. No. 104-191, 110 Stat. 1936 (1996).

149. 18 U.S.C. § 1347.

150. 18 U.S.C. § 669.

151. 18 U.S.C. § 1035.

152. 18 U.S.C. § 1518.

153. Julie Schmit, *Drug Companies Dodge Ban from Medicare, Medicaid*, USA Today, Aug. 16, 2004, at 3B.

154. For example, the CEO of Forest Labs faced an individual ban from Medicaid & Medicare. *See* http://www.pharmalot.com/2011/04/forest-ceo-faces-ban-from-medicaid-medicare/.

155. Press Release, U.S. Dep't of Justice, Assistant Attorney General Lanny A. Breuer Speaks at the American Health Lawyers Association and Health Care Compliance Association's 2011 Fraud and Compliance Forum, Sep. 26, 2011, *available at* http://www.justice.gov/criminal/pr/speeches/2011/crm-speech-110926.html.

156. *Id.*

157. *Id.*

158. *Id.*

159. Federal Bureau of Investigation, *2005 FBI Computer Crime Survey*, at 6, *available at* http://www.digitalriver.com/v2.0-img/operations/naievigi/site/media/pdf/FBIccs2005.pdf.

160. For a list of laws relevant to computer crime, see U.S. Dep't of Justice, Computer Crime & Intellectual Prop. Section, *Computer Crime Legal Resources, available at* http://www.cybercrime.gov/cclaws.html.

EXHIBIT 14.7   Sampling of Health-Care Fraud Cases Resulting in Payments of More Than $100 Million

Company (Date of Plea, Conviction, or Settlement)	Crime	Settlement/Penalty
Vencor, Inc. (2001)	Settled claims alleging that the company submitted false claims to government insurance programs, including Medicare and Medicaid.	$244.5 million, including $104.5 million in civil fines under the False Claims Act, $25 million in fines for claims that were not fraudulent, $90 million to Medicare, and $25 million to the states. The company neither admitted nor denied wrongdoing.
TAP Pharmaceuticals (2001)	Pleaded guilty to criminal conspiracy to violate the Prescription Drug Marketing Act. The company used illegal kickbacks to doctors to induce them to prescribe its prostate cancer drug, Lupron, which was more expensive than other available drugs. Kickbacks included money as "educational grants" as well as expensive dinners, parties, golf and ski trips, and TVs/VCRs. The company gave doctors free samples with the understanding that they would bill Medicare and Medicaid for the drugs. The company also ensured that doctors received profits by charging them substantially less than the federal government paid for the drug. Losses totaled an estimated $145 million.	$875 million, including a $290 million criminal fine under the Prescription Drug Marketing Act, a $559 million civil fine under the False Claims Act, and $25.5 million in civil fines to the states. TAP agreed to employ a corporate integrity agreement as part of its settlement.
Bristol–Myers Squibb (2003)	Settled charges that the company paid $72.5 million to competitors and illegally prolonged patents on its antidepressant, BuSpar, and cancer drugs, Taxol and Platinol, to prevent generic entry for these three drugs, which contributed $2 billion in annual revenues.	$670 million, with $155 million going to state governments and the rest to affected private groups. The company agreed to a 10-year ban on its practice of filing patents to gain an automatic 30-month delay on the entry of generic versions of its off-patent drugs.
HCA, Inc. (2003)	After pleading guilty in 2000 to 14 criminal counts of defrauding government health insurance programs by an estimated $650 million, HCA settled additional claims in 2003. HCA defrauded Medicare and other federal programs by overcharging for services and provided kickbacks to doctors to induce them to refer patients to HCA hospitals.	In period from 2000 to 2003, $1.7 billion, including $631 million in civil fines, $250 million to Medicare, and $17.6 million for state Medicaid programs. HCA agreed to increase the strength and scope of its compliance program.
Abbott Laboratories (2003)	Pleaded guilty to one count of obstructing a federal inquiry into allegations that the company sold or gave away its nutritional pumps to nursing homes and hospitals at discounted prices and charged Medicare and Medicaid higher prices.	$600 million, including $200 million in criminal fines and $400 million in civil fines. The company agreed to institute a corporate integrity agreement to monitor its marketing practices.
Pfizer/Warner–Lambert (2004)	Two criminal counts for violating the Federal Food, Drug and Cosmetic Act by marketing its epilepsy drug, Neurontin, for unapproved uses. The company also promoted its drug by giving kickbacks to physicians.	$430 million, including a $240 million criminal fine, $152 million in civil fines under the False Claims Act, and $38 million to consumer protection agencies. The company agreed to improve its corporate compliance program.
Serono Group (2005)	Pleaded guilty to improperly marketing an AIDS drug, Serostim, by supplying doctors with testing software that would register "body cell mass" loss in AIDS patients even if they had not lost weight. The company also admitted bribing doctors to prescribe its drug.	$704 million in total penalties, including criminal fines of $136.9 million. $305 million of the civil damages went to the federal government, with the remainder split among state Medicaid programs.

CONTINUED

EXHIBIT 14.7   Sampling of Health-Care Fraud Cases Resulting in Payments of More Than $100 Million (Continued)

Company (Date of Plea, Conviction, or Settlement)	Crime	Settlement/Penalty
St. Barnabas Hospitals (2006)	Falsely increased the costs of treating patients in order to obtain $500 million in supplemental payments from Medicare.	$265 million to the federal government. The company also agreed to have its Medicare billing practices monitored by an outside party for 6 years.
Tenet Healthcare (2006)	Settled claims that the hospital chain improperly billed Medicare for supplemental payments, bribed physicians to refer patients to Tenet hospitals, and "upcoded" patient records to reflect more costly care than had been provided.	In a settlement valued at $900 million, Tenet agreed to pay $725 million and to discontinue its pursuit of another $175 million in outstanding Medicare bills. Tenet made an initial payment of $450 million and agreed to a schedule of quarterly payments. Tenet also agreed to hire an outside firm to review its compliance programs.
Amerigroup Corp. (2006 and 2007)	Found guilty of Medicaid fraud for illegally discriminating against patients, such as pregnant women, with potentially costly medical conditions. In 2007, a federal judge ruled that the company had filed more than 18,000 false Medicare claims.	$344 million in total. The jury awarded treble damages of $144 million in the first trial. The court imposed a $190 million penalty in the second case.
Purdue Frederick Co. (2007)	Three executives pleaded guilty to misdemeanor criminal charges that the drugmaker "misbranded" the company's OxyContin as a less addictive alternative to other painkillers. The complaint alleged that sales officials used misleading data to convince doctors to accept the claim.	$600 million in total, with $470 million to state and federal agencies and $130 million to settle civil suits brought by patients who became addicted. The three executives agreed to pay a combined $34.5 million in fines and were sentenced to 3 years' probation and 400 hours of community service.
Bristol–Myers Squibb (2007)	Paid bribes to physicians in return for prescribing the company's drugs and marketed an antipsychotic for off-label uses.	$515 million and a 5-year corporate integrity agreement with the Department of Health and Human Services.
Merck & Co. (2008)	Sold several drugs to hospitals and physicians at discounted prices, up to 90% off, that were not offered to Medicare.	$650 million settlement, with $431 million split among 49 states and the remainder allocated to the federal government.
Pfizer (2009)	Illegally marketing the painkiller Bextra.	$2.3 billion settlement and agreed to plead guilty to criminal charges.
GlaxoSmithKline (2011)	Marketed drugs for unapproved uses.	$3 billion settlement to resolve U.S. criminal and civil investigations.
Merck & Co. (2011)	Making false claims about the safety of painkiller Vioxx and marketing it for unapproved uses.	$950 million settlement total, with $361.6 million to pay fine for illegal promotion and $630 million to settle civil charges that it made false statements about the drug's safety.

The ability of computer hackers to access protected governmental and financial records is a particular concern. The total number of reported such incidents reached 107,439 in 2010, a 39% increase from 2009.[161]

The private sector has been equally afflicted. Hackers have stolen credit card numbers, transmitted highly destructive viruses, and shut down popular online sites.[162] Online fraud alone accounted for $550 million in consumer losses in 2009, more than

---

161. OFFICE OF MGMT. & BUDGET, FISCAL YEAR 2010 REPORT TO CONGRESS ON THE IMPLEMENTATION OF THE FEDERAL INFORMATION SECURITY MANAGEMENT ACT OF 2002 (2010), *available at* http://www.whitehouse.gov/sites/default/files/omb/assets/egov_docs/FY10_FISMA.pdf.

162. For a discussion of the computer crime laws applicable to different types of cybercrime, see Xiaomin Huang, Peter Radowski III & Peter Roman, *Computer Crimes*, 44 AM. CRIM. L. REV. 285 (2007).

twice that reported in 2008.[163] In 2011, the Securities and Exchange Commission clarified public companies' obligation to disclose vulnerability to cyber attacks in their periodic reports.[164] The "Inside Story" in this chapter discusses the efforts to combat cybercrime in more detail.

The Computer Fraud and Abuse Act   The Computer Fraud and Abuse Act (CFAA)[165] is the mainstay of federal computer fraud legislation. It prohibits (1) accessing a "protected computer" without authorization or exceeding authorized access; (2) knowingly transmitting a program, information, code, or command that results in intentionally causing "damage" without authorization to a protected computer; (3) knowingly and with intent to defraud trafficking in any password or similar information through which a protected computer may be accessed without authorization; and (4) threatening to cause damage to a protected computer. *Protected computer* is defined to include any computer used in "interstate or foreign commerce or communication." As a result, computers used in a crime need not be located in different jurisdictions as long as they are connected to the Internet.[166] Thus, the explosive growth in the use of the Internet has greatly expanded the types of activities covered by the Act. "Damage" is defined as "any impairment to the integrity or availability of data, a program, a system, or information." Collecting and disseminating confidential information impairs the integrity of that data and therefore causes damage, even when no data are physically damaged or erased.[167]

The CFAA also makes illegal the knowing transmission of computer viruses. A *computer virus* is a computer program that can replicate itself into other programs without any subsequent instruction, human or mechanical. A computer virus may destroy data, programs, or files, or it may prevent user access to a computer (*denial-of-service attacks*). The proliferation of networks of personal computers has created millions of entry points for viruses. A virus can be concealed in any software and then passed on to other computers through attachments to e-mail, information services, disks, or other means.

The following case addressed the split among the federal circuits as to whether a breach of the duty of loyalty automatically terminates an agent's authority to access a protected computer, thereby making the agent's access to the computer unauthorized within the meaning of the CFAA.

---

163. Stuart Pfeifer, *Internet Fraud's U.S. Price Tag Put at $550 Million*, L.A. TIMES, Mar. 15, 2010.

164. U.S. Securities & Exchange Comm'n, CF Disclosure Guidance: Topic No. 2 (Oct. 13, 2011), *available at* http://www.sec.gov/divisions/corpfin/guidance/cfguidance-topic2.htm.

165. 18 U.S.C. § 1030.

166. *See* Shurgard Storage Ctrs., Inc. v. Safeguard Self Storage, Inc., 119 F. Supp. 2d. 1121, 1127 (W.D. Wash. 2000). *See also* James R. Eiszner, *Drew Case Raises Specter of Criminal Exposure for Online Intelligence Gathering*, CORP. COUNS. WKLY. (BNA) Aug. 20, 2008, at 264 (cautioning that obtaining information from a public website may be a criminal violation if person knows that the terms and conditions of the site deny authorization for that use).

167. *Shurgard Storage Ctrs.*, 119 F. Supp. 2d 1121.

A CASE IN POINT	***In the Language of the Court***	**Case 14.6**

United States v. Nosal

United States Court of Appeals for the Ninth Circuit
642 F.3d 781 (9th Cir. 2011), rehearing en banc granted, 661 F.3d 1180 (9th Cir. 2011).

FACTS   From April 1996 to October 2004, defendant David Nosal worked as an executive for the executive search firm Korn/Ferry International. When Nosal left Korn/Ferry in October 2004, he signed an agreement not to compete with Korn/Ferry for one year. Shortly after leaving his employment, Nosal engaged three Korn/Ferry employees to help him start a competing business. These employees obtained trade secrets and other proprietary information by using their user accounts to access the Korn/Ferry computer system, including its highly confidential Searcher database. Korn/Ferry required all its employees to enter into agreements that restricted the use and disclosure of all such information, except for legitimate Korn/Ferry business.

The government indicted Nosal and the Korn/Ferry employees and charged them with violating the Computer Fraud and Abuse Act (CFAA) by exceeding the employer's authorized access. Nosal filed a motion to dismiss the indictment, arguing that Korn/Ferry employees could not have acted "without authorization," nor could they have "exceed[ed] authorized access," because they had permission to access the computer and its information under certain circumstances. The district court ruled for the defendants, reasoning that a criminal violation for accessing a protected computer "without authorization" or in "excess of authorized access" occurs only when initial access or the access of certain information is not permitted in the first instance. Because the conspirators had authority to obtain protected information for legitimate Korn/Ferry *business purposes*, they did not exceed their authorized access by doing so, even if they acted with a fraudulent intent. The Government appealed.

CONTINUED

ISSUE PRESENTED Does a breach of an employer's computer use policy automatically terminate an agent's authority to access protected computer data?

OPINION TROTT, J., writing for the U.S. Court of Appeals for the Ninth Circuit:

We are not faced in this appeal with an argument that Nosal's accomplices accessed the Searcher database "without authorization." The question we must answer here is whether those accomplices could have *exceeded* their authorized access by accessing information that they were entitled to access only under limited circumstances. We hold that an employee "exceeds authorized access" under § 1030 when he or she violates the employer's computer access restrictions—including use restrictions.

We held in [*LVRC Holdings, LLC v.*] *Brekka*[168] that it is the *employer's* actions that determine whether an employee acts without authorization to access a computer in violation of [the CFAA]. Brekka was an employee at an addiction treatment center who was negotiating with his employer, LVRC Holdings, for the purchase of an ownership interest in the business. During the course of those negotiations, Brekka emailed several business documents to his and his wife's personal email accounts. The negotiations broke down, and Brekka left his employment with LVRC. LVRC later discovered the emails Brekka had sent to himself and sued him under § 1030(g), which provides for a private right of action under the CFAA.

Relying primarily on *International Airport Centers, LLC v. Citrin*,[169] LVRC argued that Brekka had acted "without authorization" because by accessing and emailing the documents he acted contrary to his employer's interest. In *Citrin*, the Seventh Circuit held that an employee loses authorization to use a computer when the employee violates a state law duty of loyalty because, based on common law agency principles, the employee's actions terminated the employer-employee relationship "and with it his authority to access the [computer]." In the Seventh Circuit, therefore, an employee accesses a computer "without authorization" the moment the employee uses a computer or information on a computer in a manner adverse to the employer's interest.

We rejected the *Citrin* approach as inconsistent with our conclusion that, for purposes of [the CFAA], it is the action of the *employer* that determines whether an employee is authorized to access the computer:

> If the employer has not rescinded the defendant's right to use the computer, the defendant would have no reason to know that making personal use of the company computer in breach of a state law fiduciary duty to an employer would constitute a criminal violation of the CFAA. It would be improper to interpret a criminal statute in such an unexpected manner.

. . . .

Our decision today that an employer's use restrictions define whether an employee "exceeds authorized access" is simply an application of *Brekka's* reasoning. As we held in that case, "[i]t is the employer's decision to allow or to terminate an employee's authorization to access a computer that determines whether the employee is with or 'without authorization.'". . . Therefore, the only logical interpretation of "exceeds authorized *access*" is that the employer *has placed* limitations on the employee's "permission to use" the computer and the employee has violated—or "exceeded"—those limitations.

We do face a substantial factual distinction in this case: the existence of access restrictions instituted by the employer. The employee in *Brekka* had unfettered access to the company computer—"LVRC and Brekka did not have a written employment agreement, nor did LVRC promulgate employee guidelines that would prohibit employees from emailing LVRC documents to personal computers." Therefore, Brekka did not exceed his authorized access any more than he acted without

CONTINUED

168. 581 F.3d 1127 (9th Cir. 2009).
169. 440 F.3d 418 (7th Cir. 2006).

authorization: he was entitled to obtain the information because he had not acted in a way that violated any access restrictions.

By contrast, Korn/Ferry employees were subject to a computer use policy that placed clear and conspicuous restrictions on the employees'access both to the system in general and to the Searcher database in particular. By using their authorized access to defraud Korn/Ferry in violation of Korn/Ferry's access restrictions, Nosal's accomplices certainly had fair warning that they were subjecting themselves to criminal liability. . . . Nosal's argument that the government's "Orwellian" interpretation would improperly criminalize certain actions depending only on the vagaries and whims of the employer is foreclosed by *Brekka*, which held unequivocally that under § 1030 the employer determines whether an employee is authorized. . . .Therefore, as long as the employee has knowledge of the employer's limitations on that authorization, the employee "exceeds authorized access" when the employee violates those limitations. It is as simple as that.

. . . .

The other circuits that have addressed the meaning of "exceeds authorized access" in the context of employers' access restrictions have also determined that the phrase encompasses such restrictions. . . .[170] [W]e now join our sister circuits.

. . . .

Today, we clarify that under the CFAA, an employee accesses a computer in excess of his or her authorization when that access violates the employer's access restrictions, which may include restrictions on the employee's use of the computer or of the information contained in that computer. We reaffirm our previous conclusion that "an individual who is authorized to use a computer for certain purposes but goes beyond those limitations is considered by the CFAA as someone who has 'exceed[ed] authorized access.'"

RESULT   Because the conspirators violated Korn/Ferry's use restriction by accessing protected information for illegitimate purposes, the appeals court reversed the district court's decision granting the defendant's motion for summary judgment. Thereafter, the U.S. Court of Appeals for the Ninth Circuit agreed to hear the case en banc.

CRITICAL THINKING QUESTIONS

1. Is a computer or its information "damaged" within the meaning of the CFAA if intruders alter existing log-on programs to copy user passwords to a file that the hackers can retrieve later if, after retrieving the newly created password file, the intruders restore the altered log-in file to its original condition?

2. Would an employee be criminally liable for computer fraud if she used her work computer to check the latest football scores in violation of a no-personal-use policy?

---

170. The Ninth Circuit cited cases from the First, Fifth, and Eleventh Circuits on this point.

Computer Piracy   *Computer piracy* is the theft or misuse of computer software. (With the increasing value and decreasing size of computer equipment, the theft of computer hardware is increasing. This is larceny, not computer piracy, however.)

Concerned about the increasing amount of computer software theft, Congress amended the Copyright Act in 1980 to cover computer software. (Copyright law is discussed further in Chapter 11.) Most states have also made the theft of computer software a crime.

Crimes Involving Intellectual Property

Chapter 11 discussed criminal liability under the Copyright Act, the No Electronic Theft Act, the Digital Millennium Copyright Act, and the Economic Espionage Act.

The Foreign Corrupt Practices Act

The Foreign Corrupt Practices Act,[171] discussed further in Chapter 24, makes it a crime for any U.S. firm or any firm controlled by a U.S. firm to make payments to an official of a foreign government in an attempt to influence the actions of the official. The Act also requires detailed record keeping and internal control measures by all public companies, whether international or purely domestic.

Antitrust Laws

Criminal prosecutions under the antitrust laws are discussed in Chapter 16.

---

171. 15 U.S.C. § 78dd-2.

Securities Law Violations

As explained further in Chapter 21, the offer and sale of securities are governed by a complex set of federal and state laws and regulations, which are enforced with criminal penalties.

Federal Securities and Commodities Laws Both the Securities Act of 1933[172] and the Securities Exchange Act of 1934[173] provide criminal penalties in addition to civil sanctions for offering and selling securities without an exemption, securities fraud, insider trading, and other violations. The Dodd–Frank Wall Street Reform and Consumer Protection Act[174] added a prohibition to the Commodity Exchange Act for engaging in an unauthorized swap transaction. As discussed in the "Inside Story" in Chapter 6, the SEC regulates security swaps, and the Commodity Futures Trading Commission regulates all other swaps, such as credit default swaps and other non-securities-based derivatives.

State Blue Sky Laws The states also impose criminal sanctions for violations of their *blue sky laws.* For example, the Wisconsin Court of Appeals upheld the securities fraud conviction of a man who borrowed $140,000 from his girlfriend in 2001 to start a new business without disclosing that he had filed for bankruptcy three years earlier and was sentenced to jail in 1990 for larceny. Although the definition of "security" was similar under state and federal law, the court noted that Wisconsin securities law "at least impliedly casts a wider net."[175] Ignorance of these laws is no excuse. As Judge Easterbrook of the U.S. Court of Appeals for the Seventh Circuit remarked, "No one with half a brain can offer 'an opportunity to invest in our company' without knowing that there is a regulatory jungle out there."[176]

Obstruction of Justice, Perjury, and Related Offenses

The Sarbanes–Oxley Act increased the penalties for existing obstruction-of-justice offenses, such as jury and witness tampering and destroying evidence while a government investigation or lawsuit is pending or imminent.[177] It also created several new crimes, including (1) destroying corporate audit working papers, records, or analyses within five years after the completion of the audit;[178] (2) destroying, altering, or falsifying records relevant to potential future federal investigations or bankruptcy;[179] and (3) retaliating against an individual who provided a law enforcement officer with any truthful information relating to the commission or possible commission of a federal offense.[180] (See Appendix K.)

If government prosecutors are uncertain whether they can get a conviction on a substantive crime, they are increasingly turning to related cover-up crimes, such as obstruction of justice and perjury. A person commits *perjury* when he or she takes an oath to tell the truth and willfully and contrary to such an oath states a material matter that he or she does not believe to be true.[181]

The conviction of Martha Stewart, chief executive of Martha Stewart Living Omnimedia, in 2004 is a prime example of this phenomenon. She was initially suspected of insider trading when she sold her ImClone stock after Samuel Waksal, ImClone's CEO, learned that the Food and Drug Administration had denied approval for ImClone's new cancer drug. Stewart truthfully told investigators that Waksal had not tipped her to sell her shares, but she claimed that she had a preexisting agreement with her broker at Merrill Lynch to sell her shares if the price dropped below $60. She also told investigators that her broker had not told her that Waksal was selling ImClone stock. When her broker's assistant admitted that there was no prior sell agreement and testified that he had informed Stewart that Waksal was selling, Stewart was prosecuted for obstruction of justice. She was never indicted for insider trading, however, because it was not clear that knowing Waksal was selling was, by itself, material nonpublic information obtained in breach of a duty of trust or confidence. In short, Stewart was convicted of lying about a crime for which she was never charged.[182]

One of the first cases testing the revised obstruction-of-justice statutes under Sarbanes–Oxley involved Thomas Trauger, a former partner at the accounting firm Ernst & Young. Trauger was charged in September 2003 with obstruction of justice under 18 U.S.C. § 1519 for altering and destroying documents related to one of his audit clients, NextCard. After Trauger was notified that banking regulators had requested the accounting work papers relating to the audit of NextCard's 2000 fiscal year, Trauger allegedly told a fellow employee to "beef up" the work papers to make it appear as though the auditing team had been "right on the mark" all along. The men went into a computerized archive for the work papers and revised them, then deleted the original work papers from the system.[183] Trauger then proceeded to hand over the revised

---

172. 15 U.S.C.A. § 77a *et seq.*

173. 15 U.S.C.A. § 78a *et seq.*

174. Pub. L. No. 111-203, 124 Stat. 1376 (2010).

175. Wisconsin v. McGuire, 735 N.W. 2d 555 (Wisc. Ct. App. 2007).

176. Mueller v. Sullivan, 141 F.3d 1232 (7th Cir. 1998).

177. *See generally* Note, *The Obstruction of Justice Nexus Requirement After Arthur Andersen and Sarbanes–Oxley*, 93 CORNELL L. REV. 401 (2008).

178. 18 U.S.C. § 1520.

179. 18 U.S.C. § 1519.

180. 18 U.S.C. § 1513.

181. 18 U.S.C. § 1621.

182. *The Trial of Martha*, WALL ST. J., Feb. 13, 2004, at A12.

183. Kurt Eichenwald, *U.S. Charges Ernst & Young Ex-Partner in Audit Case*, N.Y. TIMES, Sept. 26, 2003, at C1.

work papers to investigators. In October 2004, Trauger pleaded guilty to obstruction of justice and was sentenced to five years in prison. His plea was viewed as a triumph of the new Sarbanes–Oxley provision. As one U.S. attorney explained, "This is one of the first cases in which an auditor has pled guilty to destroying key documents in an effort to obstruct a federal investigation."[184]

OTHER FEDERAL REGULATORY AND TAX OFFENSES

A large number of federal regulatory laws provide for criminal as well as civil penalties for their violation. Several of the more important are discussed in this section.

Environmental Laws

As explained in Chapter 15, the federal environmental laws provide for criminal sanctions against both corporate and individual violators. For example, any person who knowingly falsifies any records required to be maintained under the Clean Water Act may be fined and imprisoned. Prison terms and fines are doubled for subsequent violations. The Resource Conservation and Recovery Act (RCRA)[185] imposes criminal penalties on both the corporation and individual employees who dispose of hazardous waste without the appropriate RCRA permit.

Worker Safety Laws

Both federal and state laws provide sanctions for failure to provide a safe working environment. For example, in 2011, the U.S. Attorney reached a $209 million settlement with Alpha Natural Resources, successor to Massey Energy Company, to settle criminal and civil charges against the company arising out of the deadliest mining disaster in forty years. Twenty-nine miners were killed in a mine explosion in 2010 caused by inadequate ventilation and excessive coal dust. The Mine Safety and Health Administration, which attributed the accident to "a culture that valued production over safety," cited the company for 369 violations, including twelve "flagrant" ones, and levied a $10.8 million civil fine.[186]

The Occupational Safety and Health Act

As discussed in Chapter 12, the Occupational Safety and Health Act (OSH Act),[187] which applies to all employers engaged in a business affecting interstate commerce, imposes both civil and criminal penalties.

State Law Prosecutions of Workplace Safety Hazards

As noted in Chapter 12, state prosecutors have taken an aggressive approach toward workplace safety hazards that result in injuries. Employers have tried to defend against such charges by claiming that the OSH Act preempts state prosecutions based on failure to maintain workplace safety. The U.S. Courts of Appeals for the First and Third Circuits rejected this argument,[188] and several other courts have adopted the First Circuit's reasoning.[189]

Tax Laws

Certain violations of the Internal Revenue Code are subject to criminal penalties. The strictest penalties are found in section 7201,[190] which prohibits willful attempts to evade any tax imposed under the Code, including failure to comply with employee withholding requirements. Section 7206 forbids any false statements in a tax return, and section 7207 criminalizes the willful delivery of a fraudulent return to the Secretary of the Treasury.

Tax evasion is an illegal practice whereby a person intentionally does not pay his or her tax liability, often by hiding funds in offshore tax havens—countries that impose little or no tax liability. Most countries allow individuals and firms to invest their money wherever they please but obligate them to report all of their income to the tax authorities in their home country. It is estimated that the U.S. Treasury loses as much as $100 billion a year due to illegal international tax maneuvering.[191]

Experts recognize that ending tax evasion will require global cooperation:

> Without vigorous and coordinated action by governments to ensure that the right legislative framework is in place, that tax administrations have the necessary information, tools and resources to address the problem, and without greater bilateral and multilateral cooperation, offshore tax evasion will continue to grow and undermine the integrity of national tax systems. No one country by itself can meet this challenge.[192]

A tax fraud prosecution must allege willful misconduct on the part of the accused. Consequently, prosecutors in

---

184. Stephen Taub, *Auditor Pleads on Document Cover-Up*, CFO.com, Nov. 2, 2004.

185. 42 U.S.C. § 6901 *et seq.*

186. Kris Maher, *Feds Blame Owner of Mine*, WALL ST. J., Dec. 7, 2011, at A3.

187. 29 U.S.C. § 651 *et seq.* & 29 U.S.C.A. § 651 *et seq.*

188. *See* Pedraza v. Shell Oil Co., 942 F.2d 48 (1st Cir. 1991); Lindsey v. Caterpillar, Inc., 480 F.3d 202 (3d Cir. 2007).

189. *See, e.g.*, Wickham v. Am. Tokyo Kasei, Inc., 927 F. Supp. 293 (N.D. Ill. 1996); Donovan v. Beloit Co., 655 N.E.2d 313 (Ill. App. Ct. 1995).

190. 26 U.S.C. § 7201.

191. Tom Herman, *Tax Evasion: Crackdown on Overseas Accounts*, FISCAL TIMES, June 16, 2010.

192. *Hearings on Offshore Tax Evasion Before the S. Fin. Comm.*, 110th Cong. (May 3, 2007) (statement of Jeffrey Ownes, Director of OECD Center for Tax Policy and Administration), *available at* http://www.senate.gov/-finance/hearings/testimony/2007test/050307testjo.pdf.

tax fraud cases often add a mail fraud charge, which can result in a conviction even if willful misconduct is not proved. Moreover, mail fraud, unlike tax fraud, can be the basis for a RICO claim.

Section 6672 imposes civil liability for a penalty equal to the amount of a corporation's unpaid federal employment taxes on "those with the power and responsibility within the corporate structure for seeing that the taxes withheld from various sources are remitted to the Government."[193] Thus, if an entrepreneur responsible for writing the check to the U.S. Treasury for employee withholding used that money to fund operations instead, he or she would be liable for this penalty. The U.S. Court of Appeals for the Ninth Circuit has ruled that a person cannot be held liable for failure to pay over taxes unless the party (1) was the person required to collect, truthfully account for, and pay over the tax; and (2) willfully refused to pay the tax.[194]

---

193. Monday v. United States, 421 F.2d 1210, 1214 (7th Cir. 1970).
194. Teel v. United States, 529 F.2d 903 (9th Cir. 1976).

AMNESTY AND LENIENCY PROGRAMS

In an effort to promote self-policing and self-reporting, the federal government will provide amnesty or leniency to offenders who proactively report and remedy violations. Examples include the Department of Justice's amnesty for price-fixing cartels (discussed in Chapter 16) and the Environmental Protection Agency's leniency for violations detected by voluntary self-audits (discussed in Chapter 15). These policies work primarily by "making companies an offer they shouldn't refuse."[195]

---

195. This phrase was the title of a speech given by Deputy Assistant Attorney General Gary Spratling in 1999 about the Department of Justice's amnesty policy. Gary R. Spratling, Making Companies an Offer They Shouldn't Refuse: The Antitrust Division's Corporate Leniency Policy—An Update, Address at the Bar Association of the District of Columbia's 35th Annual Symposium on Associations and Antitrust, Washington D.C. (Feb. 16, 1999).

THE RESPONSIBLE MANAGER

ENSURING CRIMINAL LAW COMPLIANCE

Managers can take various actions to create a culture that values both organizational integrity and compliance with the spirit and the letter of the law. First, the company should develop a code of ethics, as discussed in Chapter 2. All criminal acts should be outlawed by the code. The code of ethics should have an enforcement mechanism, and it should clearly state that violations of the code will result in sanctions, such as salary reductions, poor performance ratings, and, in extreme cases, termination of employment.

The company should develop and implement a comprehensive program to ensure compliance with laws and regulations. The audit committee of the board of directors should oversee the program. The corporation should also have educational programs to teach employees about the laws applicable to their areas of responsibility and to remind them about the provisions of the compliance program. Outside firms can be hired to review the corporation's compliance program and suggest areas for improvement.

A good reporting structure is crucial. Corporate in-house counsel should be independent and report suspected criminal activity directly to the board of directors. They should not succumb to pressure from division managers to give the go-ahead to an action that they believe may violate a criminal statute. Firms should also self-report violations. Prosecutors and courts are more inclined to mitigate the punishment of a corporation if it consistently reports the criminal misconduct of its employees.

It should be clear throughout the company that ethical behavior is expected. What top management does when it sees criminal law–related problems will influence all employees. It is much harder for employees to justify committing criminal acts against the corporation when they cannot claim that top management is also guilty of violating the law. Criminal misconduct is often a function of goal-setting and performance measures that induce people to do what they should not do. Managers should be careful to avoid sending mixed signals that reward (or demand) performance at all costs regardless of compliance with the law.

If the company is faced with a possible criminal investigation, prompt action is important. Prior to contacting the authorities, the company should seek the immediate advice of outside counsel. If employees are interviewed in connection with an internal investigation, both internal and outside counsel should make it clear that they are representing the company, and not the employee. Managers should be careful when turning over information about internal investigations

CONTINUED

to prosecutors because they may inadvertently waive the attorney–client privilege applicable to notes prepared by outside counsel.

Managers disregard rumors of unlawful behavior at their peril. According to Harry Brandon, a business intelligence specialist with Smith Brandon International, 75% of investigations uncover proof of a violation.[196] If the rumors are true, not only is the company in trouble, but managers with knowledge, or a reasonable suspicion, of the offending activities may face civil claims and perhaps criminal charges.

Documents will be a primary source of information in any investigation.[197] Whenever an investigation appears likely, managers should remind all employees to retain physical and electronic documents, including e-mails. As discussed in Chapter 3, disposing of documents in anticipation of a government investigation can result in significant penalties, including charges of obstruction of justice, and future juries may draw negative inferences about the purpose behind the document destruction.

Although companies may be reluctant to investigate and self-report violations, it is better to know about a problem and deal with it than to let it persist and get out of control. No corporate compliance program is foolproof, but an effective program can "prevent and detect most violations; reduce financial litigation, regulatory,

and reputational harm; get mitigation credit under the Sentencing Guidelines; and help set a tone in investigations that shows the company cares about doing business the right way."[198] It can also help shield officers and directors from vicarious liability.

Corporate compliance may even be a source of competitive advantage.[199] According to the consulting firm Deloitte & Touche, "companies that follow both the letter and the spirit of the law by taking a 'values-based' approach to ethics and compliance will have a distinct advantage in the marketplace. Benefits of this approach can include improvements to a company's market performance, brand equity, and shareholder value."[200] In addition to the direct costs of sanctions (such as fines and punitive damages) and the legal costs associated with litigation and appeals, illegality can divert funds from strategic investments, tarnish a firm's image with customers and other stakeholders, raise capital costs and reduce sale volume,[201] and sap employee morale.

196. Joseph Finder, *The CEO's Private Investigation*, Harv. Bus. Rev., Oct. 2007, at 54.

197. Michael N. Levy, Michael L. Spafford & Lothlorien S. Redmond, *The Changing Nature of Internal Probes*, Fin. Executive, Jan. 1, 2007, at 51.

198. Karen L. Shapiro, *10 Steps to a Better Day*, Bus. L. Today, Sept.–Oct. 2003, at 43.

199. K. Schatterly, *Increasing Firm Value Through Detection and Prevention of White-Collar Crime*, 24 Strategic Mgmt. J. 587 (2003). *See also* Constance E. Bagley, Winning Legally: How to Use the Law to Create Value, Marshal Resources, and Manage Risk 47–86 (2005) (outlining a nine-step program for strategic compliance management).

200. Deloitte & Touche, *Ethics and Corporate Compliance: The Advantages of a Value-Based Approach, available at* http://www.deloitte.com/dtt/cda/doc/content/Ethics_Compliance%20final%20E.pdf.

201. David A. Baucus & Melissa S. Baucus, *Paying the Piper: An Empirical Examination of Longer-Term Financial Consequences of Illegal Corporate Behavior*, 40 Acad. Mgmt. J. 129 (1997).

A MANAGER'S DILEMMA

Putting It into Practice

From Cookie-Jar Reserves to Booking Sales of "Buggy" Software

You are the chief financial officer of X-Ray Corporation, the largest subsidiary of Medtech, a publicly traded medical-imaging firm. When you report to Medtech's CEO that X-Ray had better-than-expected earnings for the quarter ended June 30, 2011, the CEO asks you to "hold some of them back" as a cushion in case other subsidiaries report lower-than-expected earnings in future quarters. How would you respond? Suppose that you tell the CEO that you can't do that because this "cookie-jar reserve" would violate Generally Accepted Accounting Principles, but the CEO warns that failure to create the reserve would be a career-limiting move. What would you do?

What if, instead of an earnings surplus over analysts' projections, X-Ray Corporation had lower-than-expected earnings due to unforeseen bugs in the software for its new suite of imaging equipment? How would you respond to a request from the CEO to book sales in the quarter ending June 30, 2011, that would not actually be finalized until July 2011, which is when X-Ray's engineers predict that the bugs will be worked out?[202]

202. This feature is based, in part, on a scenario described in Carol J. Loomis, *Lies, Damned Lies, and Managed Earnings*, Fortune, Aug. 2, 1999, at 92.

Norebbo/Shutterstock

INSIDE STORY

Fighting Cybercrime

From a criminal's viewpoint, cybercrime is appealing for a number of reasons. It is a nonviolent and often easy way to make money; it does not involve personal interaction with the victims; and it has only recently come to be regarded as a serious crime. The Department of Justice, the FBI, the Federal Trade Commission (FTC), the U.S. Postal Service, and state, local, and foreign governments are working together to catch cybercrooks.[203]

According to the FBI's Internet Crime Complaint Center (IC3), the FTC received more than 300,000 Internet-related fraud reports in 2010.[204] Losses in the United States from cybercrime in 2009 alone were estimated to be $560 million: 16% from scams where crooks pretended to represent the FBI, 11.9% from nondelivery of merchandise or payment, and 9.8% from advanced fee fraud scams.[205] In 2007, U.S. consumers were taken for $3.2 billion in "phishing" scams.[206] (In phishing schemes, criminals use fake e-mail messages to induce consumers to divulge personal information.) In early 2008, Yahoo discovered that 7.8 billion links established through searches on its website led to sites that were either designed or altered to help criminals steal information.[207] Criminals have become more businesslike and brazen, even advertising credit card numbers for sale online.[208] The burgeoning industry now has specialists—such as "bot herders" who control a network of computers by infecting them with disguised software—available for hire by groups that need their services to engage in criminal computing activities.[209]

Defendants have been sent to prison for violating both the Federal CAN-SPAM Act and state analogues. For example, in 2004 Jeremy Jaynes was sentenced to nine years in prison for violating Virginia's antispam statute after he e-mailed 10,000 messages to America Online customers. The severity of the sentence reflected the fact that "juries are now familiar with spam and are willing to impose tough sentences for the non-violent but annoying crime."[210]

That same year, federal officials announced fifty-three convictions as part of "Operation Web Snare," which had targeted identity theft, fraud, counterfeit software, computer intrusions, and other online crimes. The crimes affected more than 150,000 victims and caused estimated losses of more than $215 million.[211] Dan Larkin, head of the IC3, characterized Operation Web Snare as "not the end but rather the start of such investigations."[212]

Also in 2004, the Department of Justice announced the first successful conviction in "Operation Fastlink."[213] Jathan Desir pleaded guilty to three counts of copyright infringement and conspiracy to commit copyright infringement for pirating software, movies, videogames, and music. Investigators conducted more than 120 searches in twenty-seven states and eleven foreign countries and identified almost 100 individuals worldwide as leaders or high-level members of various international piracy organizations.

203. Brian C. Lewis, *Prevention of Computer Crime Amidst International Anarchy*, 41 Am. Crim. L. Rev. 1353 (2004).

204. Internet Crime Complaint Center, 2010 Internet Crime Report 6 (2010), *available at* http://www.ic3.gov/media/annualreport/2010_IC3Report.pdf.

205. *Id.*

206. Brian Krebs, *Cyber Crime 2.0: In 2007, Online Fraud Got More Targeted and Sophisticated*, Wash. Post Online, Dec. 20, 2007, http://www.washingtonpost.com.

207. Deborah Gage, *Web Peril Where You Least Expect It*, Seattle Post-Intelligencer, May 7, 2008, at A1.

208. Mark Helm, *135 Arrested in Cybercrime Cases*, Milwaukee J. Sentinel, May 17, 2003, at 3A; Carlos Campos, *Internet Fraud Crackdown Leads to 130 Arrests in the U.S.*, Atlanta J. Const., May 17, 2003, at 3F.

209. *Id.*

210. Wendy Leibowitz, *Nine-Year Sentence for Felony Spam Shows Jury Viewed E-mail Torrent as Serious Crime*, U.S.L.W., Nov. 10, 2004, at 912.

211. Jon Swartz, *Hackers Hijack Federal Computers*, USA Today, Aug. 31, 2004, at 1B; Thomas Claburn, *Feds Target Scofflaws and Spammers*, Info. Wk., Aug. 30, 2004, at 22.

212. *Id.*

213. Press Release, U.S. Dep't of Justice, First "Operation Fastlink" Defendant Pleads Guilty to Online Software Piracy (Dec. 22, 2004), *available at* http://www.usdoj.gov/opa/pr/2004/December/04_crm_801.htm.

KEY WORDS AND PHRASES

QUESTIONS AND CASE PROBLEMS

1. Antoine Jones and several others were the subjects of an FBI–Metropolitan Police Department task force investigation of narcotics violations. As part of the investigation, authorities conducted telephone wiretaps and installed a Global Positioning System (GPS) in Jones's Jeep without a valid warrant. Police used the GPS to track Jones's movements twenty-four hours a day for four weeks. The district court admitted all evidence obtained during the police investigation, and the jury found Jones guilty of conspiracy to distribute and to possess with intent to distribute cocaine.

On appeal, Jones argued that his conviction should be overturned because the police violated his constitutional rights by tracking his movements with the warrantless use of a GPS device. Is GPS tracking a "search" requiring a warrant? Is obtaining GPS data from cell towers? [*United States v. Jones,* 132 S. Ct. 945 (2012).]

2. Acting on a tip, two inspectors from the Environmental Protection Agency took samples of the wastewater discharged from a paper mill by accessing sewer pipes through a manhole located on the edge of company property 300 feet from where the water dumped into the public sewer system. The mill and its owner were indicted on criminal environmental law charges based, in part, on the test results from those samples. Are the test results admissible at trial? [*Riverdale Mills Corp. v. Pimpare,* 392 F.3d 55 (1st Cir. 2004).]

3. Bert's Sporting Goods, Inc., with stores located throughout the state of Lys, sells a wide variety of sporting goods, including guns. Section 123.45 of the Lys Penal Code requires sellers of guns to verify that the purchaser has not committed a felony within the last five years. If the purchaser has committed a felony within the last five years, the seller is not allowed to make the sale. Selling a gun to a recent felon is considered a misdemeanor and is punishable by up to one year in jail and/or a maximum $10,000 fine.

Jim Dandy, who was convicted of a felony under Lys's penal code four years ago, went to purchase a gun at one of the Bert's Sporting Goods stores. Joe Mountain, a salesman at Bert's, sold Dandy the gun without asking for identification or checking to see whether Dandy was a convicted felon.

As a matter of fact, Mountain never checked whether any of the customers to whom he sold guns were felons. Mountain did not know of the Lys law requiring him to check on the customer's prior criminal history. However, Jay Lake, Mountain's supervisor, knew of the law and also knew that Mountain never checked whether a customer was a felon. Bert, the sole shareholder and director of Bert's Sporting Goods, Inc., knew about the law but did not know that Mountain did not check on his customers' prior criminal history.

Dandy used the gun in a robbery and shot two police officers during his getaway. He was never captured. Can Mountain be punished under section 123.45 of the Lys Penal Code? What about Lake? Bert? Bert's Sporting Goods, Inc.? What penalties should be assessed? [See, e.g., *Staples v. United States,* 511 U.S. 600 (1994).]

4. Barry Engel was president of Gel Spice Company, which imported, processed, and packaged spices. As president, he was responsible for the purchasing and storing of spices in the company's warehouse in Brooklyn, New York. In June 1972, the Food and Drug Administration (FDA) inspected the Gel Spice warehouse and found widespread rodent infestation. On reinspection in August 1972, the FDA found evidence of continuing infestation. Following the two 1972 inspections, the FDA considered a criminal prosecution against Gel Spice. Before referring the case to the Department of Justice, however, the FDA conducted an additional inspection. At that July 1973 inspection, no evidence of rodent infestation was found, and the criminal prosecution was dropped. Three years later, in July 1976, the FDA inspected Gel Spice and again found active rodent infestation. Four additional inspections were performed from 1977 to 1979, each of which revealed continuing infestation. Thereafter, the government instituted criminal proceedings against Gel Spice and its president, Barry Engel. Under what theory of criminal liability could Engel be held liable for violating the Food, Drug and Cosmetic Act? Can Engel successfully assert any defense? [*United States v. Gel Spice Co.*, 773 F.2d 427 (2d Cir. 1985).]

5. An American Wrecking Corporation (AWC) employee was killed when bricks fell on him as he prepared a section of building for demolition. AWC was cited for willfully violating the Occupational Safety and Health Act (OSH Act) governing the removal of loose material during the demolition process. Willful violations of the Act can serve as the basis of criminal complaints. AWC filed a review petition. At hearing, the Occupational Safety and Health Administration Review Committee's experts testified that the bricks were unstable and should have been taken down, while company employees stated that they believed that the bricks had been supported by iron in the structure. The administrative law judge ruled that the company had willfully violated the statute by not removing the bricks because the hazardous condition should have been obvious to the demolition supervisor. On appeal, should this ruling be upheld? If so, what would be the appropriate sentence? [*American Wrecking Corp. v. Secretary of Labor*, 351 F.3d 1254 (D.C. Cir. 2003).]

6. Bermel Enterprises, Inc. is a supplier of computer programming consulting services to the federal government. In completing their time reports, Alex and Margot Frankel, two Bermel systems analysts, have consistently overstated the time they spent working on the government projects. These time reports determine how much money the government pays the company. Additionally, Michelle Laff, a manager at Bermel, has falsified the results of systems tests conducted on the computer systems installed for the government. As a result, the systems appear to be bug-free when, in fact, they contain many errors.

What criminal charges may the government bring against the employees? Against Larry Bermel, owner of Bermel Enterprises, Inc.? Against Bermel Enterprises, Inc. itself?

7. Joseph Russo and Everett James Garner entered into an agreement to establish a building materials manufacturing business, Panel Building Systems, Inc. (PBS). To obtain capital to fund the development of the new company, Russo applied for a $630,000 loan from the U.S. Small Business Administration (SBA). On the loan application, Russo stated that he was the president and 100% owner of PBS. PBS subsequently defaulted on the loan, and the SBA suffered losses of about $474,000. During the SBA's investigation of the default, it was revealed that the actual president of PBS was Garner, not Russo, and that Garner had a poor financial record. Russo later admitted that he knew the information supplied on the loan application was false and that the false information was supplied in order to secure a loan from the SBA. Russo was sued for knowingly and willfully making a false statement to the federal government under 18 U.S.C. § 1001, which requires willful intent to deceive.

Russo claimed that although he knew the information supplied on the loan application was false, he lacked willful intent to deceive the federal government because he always intended to be president and CEO of PBS. Russo also argued that he thought Garner was a wealthy man and that he did not know Garner had a poor financial record. Did Russo have willful intent to deceive the federal government? [*United States v. Russo*, 202 F.3d 283 (10th Cir. 2000).]

8. Shurgard Storage Centers, the industry leader in full- and self-service storage facilities in both the United States and Europe, sued its competitor Safeguard Self Storage for allegedly embarking on a "systematic" scheme to hire away key employees for the purpose of obtaining trade secrets. Shurgard claimed that Eric Leland, a Shurgard employee subsequently hired by Safeguard, used Shurgard's computers to access various trade secrets and proprietary information belonging to Shurgard and to send e-mails containing the information to Safeguard. Leland was still employed by Shurgard at the time he sent the e-mails.

Shurgard alleged violations of the Computer Fraud and Abuse Act as well as misappropriation of trade secrets, conversion, unfair competition, and tortious interference with a business expectancy. Safeguard moved to dismiss the CFAA claims. [*Shurgard Storage Centers, Inc. v. Safeguard Self Storage, Inc.*, 119 F. Supp. 2d 1121 (W.D. Wash. 2000).]

CHAPTER 15

ENVIRONMENTAL LAW

INTRODUCTION

ROLE IN BUSINESS MANAGEMENT

Environmental law consists of numerous federal, state, and local laws with the common objective of protecting human health and the environment. These laws are of great concern to a variety of firms, many of which may not have considered environmental liability when they first went into business.

Some industries (such as petroleum, mining, and chemical manufacturing) are well accustomed to intense government regulation of the environmental effects of their operations. In the last forty years, however, the scope and impact of environmental laws have grown steadily. Today, real estate owners and investors, developers, insurance companies, and financial institutions find that their operations, too, are often affected by laws and regulations intended to protect the environment. In addition, concerns about climate change have prompted virtually every company to consider ways to reduce its *carbon footprint*, the amount of carbon dioxide and other greenhouse gases it releases into the air.

Failure to comply with environmental laws can result in large judgments and punitive fines for companies, as well as criminal penalties (including imprisonment) for the corporate executives responsible for these violations. In 2004, an executive at an asbestos removal company was sentenced to twenty-five years in prison, the longest sentence ever issued under federal environmental laws, after being convicted of a decade's worth of Clean Air Act violations. The executive had repeatedly ordered workers to remove asbestos without wetting it first and had falsified at least 1,500 air quality reports.[1] Dissatisfaction with a company's environmental record can lead to adverse publicity, activist protests, consumer boycotts, and more stringent regulation.

Conversely, as General Electric discovered after it launched its ecomagination business initiative in 2005, "green is green."[2] As discussed in Chapter 2, GE not only reduced its own emissions and water consumption but also enhanced its revenues by selling more energy-efficient jet engines, locomotives, and power plants. In the period from 2004 to 2006 alone, GE saved more than $100 million a year in energy costs by utilizing solar panels, switching to natural gas, cutting emissions in the manufacture of locomotive engines, and adopting other conservation techniques.[3]

CHAPTER OVERVIEW

This chapter examines four federal environmental laws that illustrate the importance of environmental regulation for an expanding scope of business activities. The Clean Air Act, the Clean Water Act, and the Resource Conservation and Recovery Act are discussed as examples of environmental statutes that control the release of pollutants into the air, water, and land. The Comprehensive Environmental Response, Compensation, and Liability Act is discussed as an example of a remedial statute with broad application to all kinds of businesses and individuals. In addition, the chapter addresses the potential liability under the environmental laws of shareholders, directors, officers, and managers, as well as affiliated companies and lenders. The chapter also outlines the key elements of effective compliance programs and concludes with a discussion of international efforts to stop global warming.

---

1. Michelle York, *Father and Son Get Long Terms in Defective Asbestos Removal*, N.Y. TIMES, Dec. 24, 2004, at A5.

2. Amanda Griscom Little, *G.E.'s Green Gamble*, VANITY FAIR, July 2006.

3. Martin LaMonica, *Newsmaker: Stirring GE's Ecomagination*, CNET NEWS.COM, Oct. 26, 2007.

OVERVIEW OF ENVIRONMENTAL LAWS

In recent decades, growing awareness of the environmental problems posed by an industrial society has led to an increase in the number and reach of environmental laws and regulations at both the federal and state levels.

Common Law Nuisance

Prior to the 1950s, the federal government left environmental concerns largely up to the states.[4] State law often required the abatement or segregation of public nuisances to control industrial and agricultural activities that interfered with the health or comfort of the community. A public nuisance is "an unreasonable interference with a right common to the general public."[5] Thus, industrial odors, noise, smoke, and pollutants of all kinds were the subjects of numerous lawsuits that attempted to balance the legitimate business interests of the polluter with the private interests of the surrounding community. The public nuisance doctrine was mostly used to prosecute out-of-state polluters, however,[6] because states feared causing economic harm by prosecuting local companies.[7]

A federal general common law of public nuisance emerged to deal "with air and water in their ambient or interstate aspects."[8] For example, one state was permitted to bring a federal common law suit to abate pollution emanating from another state.[9]

The need to file a lawsuit in each case and the complexity of the common law made nuisance a cumbersome way to control environmental pollution in an industrial society, however. Moreover, a lawsuit could not prevent pollution; it could only provide a remedy after the fact.

Today, state and federal regulatory programs have largely replaced common law nuisance as a means of pollution control. As seen in *American Electric Power Co. v. Connecticut*,[10] discussed later in this chapter, states and other parties have continued to bring nuisance claims in an attempt to force reductions in the emission of greenhouse gases.

Environmental Statutes and Regulations

Environmental law consists of federal and state statutes, administrative regulations, and the administrative and judicial interpretations of their meaning. Environmental statutes establish policy, set goals, and authorize the executive branch or one of its administrative agencies to adopt regulations specifying how the law will be implemented. The statutes and regulations are interpreted and applied in administrative and judicial proceedings. In addition, administrative agencies, such as the Environmental Protection Agency (EPA), often issue policy statements and technical guidance, which do not have the force of law but guide enforcement efforts and provide assistance to the regulated community.

Three Categories

There are three broad categories of environmental law. The largest category consists of laws that regulate the release of pollutants into the air, water, or ground. These laws usually authorize the government to issue and enforce permits for release of pollutants. They may also authorize emergency responses and remedial action if, for example, improper waste disposal or accidental chemical spills threaten human health or the environment. Statutes in this category include the Clean Air Act; the Federal Water Pollution Control Act, as amended by the Clean Water Act; the Solid Waste Disposal Act, as amended by the Resource Conservation and Recovery Act (RCRA); the Comprehensive Environmental Response, Compensation, and Liability Act (CERCLA or Superfund);[11] and similar state laws. These four federal pollution-control laws are discussed in this chapter.

A second category governs the manufacture, sale, distribution, and use of chemical substances as commercial products. This category includes (1) the Federal Insecticide, Fungicide and Rodenticide Act, which applies to pesticide products; and (2) the Toxic Substances Control Act, which applies to all chemical substances either manufactured in or imported into the United States, excluding certain substances that are regulated under other federal laws. The Safe Drinking Water Act, which governs the quality of drinking water served by public drinking-water systems, can also be included in this category.

A third category includes laws that require government decision makers to take into account the effects of their decisions on the quality of the environment. These include the National Environmental Policy Act of 1969 (NEPA),[12] which is discussed in Chapter 18, and similar laws adopted by most states. NEPA affects

---

4. ROBERT V. PERCIVAL ET AL., ENVIRONMENTAL REGULATION: LAW, SCIENCE, AND POLICY 89 (6th ed. 2009).

5. RESTATEMENT (SECOND) OF TORTS § 821B (1979).

6. *See, e.g.*, Georgia v. Tenn. Copper Co., 206 U.S. 230 (1907) (enjoining a Tennessee copper smelting company from discharging noxious gas from its operation, which carried over into Georgia).

7. PERCIVAL ET AL., *supra* note 4.

8. Illinois v. Milwaukee, 406 U.S. 91, 103 (1972).

9. *See, e.g.*, *Tenn. Copper Co.*, 206 U.S. 230; Missouri v. Illinois, 180 U.S. 208 (1901).

10. 131 St. Ct. 2527 (2011) (Case 15.2).

---

11. As amended by the Superfund Amendments and Reauthorization Act of 1986, the Superfund Recycling Equity Act of 1999, and the Small Business Liability Relief and Brownfields Revitalization Act of 2002. *See* the Superfund section on laws, policy, and guidance on the EPA's website, http://www.epa.gov/superfund/policy/index.htm.

12. Codified, as amended, at 42 U.S.C. §§ 4321–4370f. *See also* Monsanto Co. v. Geerston Seed Farms, 130 S. Ct. 2743 (2010) (Case 17.1).

Under the treaty between members of the European Union, "environmental protection is to be integrated into the definition and implementation of all Community activities and policies" and not just segregated to legislation enacted specifically to address broad environmental concerns. Central to environmental policy acts is the requirement that the government expressly consider environmental values in its decision making and that it document this consideration in written environmental impact reports that can be reviewed by the public. These requirements are especially important when the government itself is responsible for major development projects.

all business activities that require governmental authorizations, permits, or licenses.[13]

Natural Resources Laws

Although environmental law contributes to the protection of natural resources, it generally does not include wilderness preservation, wildlife protection,[14] coastal zone management, energy conservation, national park designation, and the like. Those laws are commonly referred to as *natural resources laws*. Nor does environmental law cover land-use regulation and zoning. Such laws, which are generally administered by local governments, are commonly referred to as land-use laws and are discussed in Chapter 18.

⊘ ADMINISTRATION OF ENVIRONMENTAL LAWS

Both federal and state agencies administer the environmental laws.

---

13. The U.S. Supreme Court upheld the Federal Motor Carrier Safety Administration's proposed rules concerning Mexican motor carriers even though the agency did not consider the environmental impact of having more Mexican trucks after an executive order was issued allowing a larger number to cross the U.S. border. Dep't of Transp. v. Pub. Citizens, 541 U.S. 752 (2004). The Court reasoned that because the agency lacked discretion to prevent these cross-border operations, neither NEPA nor the Clear Air Act required an evaluation of their environmental effects.

14. The Ninth Circuit ruled that dolphins, whales, and other cetaceans did not have standing under the Endangered Species Act (ESA) to sue to challenge the Navy's use of active sonar. Cetacean Cmty. v. Bush, 386 F.3d 1169 (9th Cir. 2004). The court dismissed as dicta its statement in *Palila v. Hawaii Department of Land & Natural Resources,* 852 F.2d 1106, 1107 (9th Cir. 1988), that the Hawaiian Palila bird "has legal status and wings its way into federal court as a plaintiff in its own right" to enforce the ESA. In *Loggerhead Turtle v. County Council of Volusia County, Florida,* 148 F.3d 1231 (11th Cir. 1998), however, the Eleventh Circuit held that certain endangered species of turtles had Article III standing to sue under the ESA.

Environmental Protection Agency

The *Environmental Protection Agency (EPA)* administers all the federal laws that set national goals and policies for environmental protection, except the National Environmental Policy Act, which is administered by the Council on Environmental Quality. The EPA was created in 1970 by an executive order and operates under the supervision of the President. The EPA administrator and assistant administrators are appointed by the President with the advice and consent of the Senate. The EPA is, however, neither an independent agency nor a cabinet-level department.

Several of the assistant administrators are responsible for administering the agency's regulatory programs; others have internal administrative functions. These national program managers share responsibility with the ten regional administrators who head the ten EPA regional offices. The national managers at headquarters develop policy and set goals for the regional offices. The regional administrators take responsibility for day-to-day program operation.

State Programs

State agencies administer state laws and, with the authorization of the EPA, federal laws as well. State environmental laws and programs often predate the comparable federal programs. Moreover, many states have laws that are more stringent and more comprehensive than the federal laws. For example, California's hazardous-waste-management laws, water-quality-control laws, underground-tank regulations, and ban on the land disposal of certain hazardous wastes all predate and, in some cases, provided the model for subsequent federal legislation.

In light of these preexisting state environmental programs and the need to reduce the EPA's administrative burden, Congress gave the EPA the authority to authorize or approve a state program in lieu of the federal program in that state. The EPA does not delegate its federal authority; it merely approves a state program as "equivalent to or more stringent than" the federal program and then refrains from implementing the federal program in that state. The EPA generally provides oversight, however. It retains its enforcement authority and may revoke its authorization if the state program fails to meet federal requirements. In addition, as discussed further below, in some instances the EPA invokes federal preemption (discussed in Chapter 4) to prevent the states from imposing stricter standards than the ones mandated by the EPA.

Industry Participation

Environmental laws and regulations are constantly changing as new threats to human health and the environment become apparent and new ways are discovered to manage such threats safely and economically. Congressional or administrative agency staff may be unaware of how a proposed law or regulation may affect a particular industry and usually welcome constructive industry participation in the law- and rule-making process, especially when a company can propose alternative ways to accomplish the same legislative goals.

THE CLEAN AIR ACT

The Clean Air Act[15] sets four types of air quality goals. First, it requires the EPA to establish *national ambient air quality standards (NAAQS)*, which are the maximum levels of pollutants in the outdoor air that, with adequate margins of safety, are compatible with public health.[16] Standards must be set without regard for cost considerations.[17] The EPA has set standards for six pollutants: (1) particulate matter, (2) sulfur dioxide, (3) ozone, (4) nitrogen dioxide, (5) carbon monoxide, and (6) lead. (EPA regulation of carbon dioxide and other greenhouse gases is discussed below.) Every state and locality must seek to achieve and maintain these national air quality

standards, which are revised periodically. Section 112 of the Act mandates technology-based standards to reduce listed hazardous air emissions from major sources in designated industrial categories; additional regulation is possible if needed to protect public health with an "ample margin of safety." If a nonattainment area fails to develop an adequate plan to attain the national standard, the federal government is required to impose penalties, such as bans on construction of new sources of pollution, limits on drinking-water hookups, withholding of federal funds for combating air pollution, and limits on the use of federal highway funds. By affecting decisions concerning land use and transportation, as well as imposing emission controls, the law helps determine which areas of the country and which industrial sectors will be able to grow.

Second, the Clean Air Act requires that air quality in those areas that already meet the NAAQS not be allowed to deteriorate. Third, the Act requires the preservation of natural visibility within the major national parks and wilderness areas. Fourth, it requires the EPA to establish emission standards that protect public health, with an ample margin of safety, from hazardous air pollutants.[18]

The law also requires reductions in vehicle tail-pipe emissions of certain pollutants and the use of reformulated gasoline. It mandates that fleets use clean, low-emission fuels in some nonattainment areas. Major sources of some 200 hazardous air pollutants are required to meet emission limits based on best available control technology. Electric power plants must reduce emissions that lead to the formation of acid rain. Finally, the law phased out methylchloroform and chlorofluorocarbons and placed limitations on the production of certain substitute chemicals.

In the following case, the U.S. Court of Appeals for the District of Columbia Circuit invalidated a rule that would have relieved electric power plants from an obligation to use best available technology to reduce mercury emissions.

---

15. 42 U.S.C. § 7401 *et seq.* The Fifth Circuit held that the Clean Air Act was a valid exercise of Congress's power under the Commerce Clause in *United States v. Ho*, 311 F.3d 589 (5th Cir. 2002).

16. The U.S. Supreme Court rejected claims that the Act constituted an unconstitutional delegation of legislative power because it arguably left the EPA free to set the NAAQS at any point between zero and concentrations that would yield a "killer fog." *Whitman v. Am. Trucking Ass'ns*, 531 U.S. 457 (2001).

17. *Id.*

18. *See also* Massachusetts v. EPA, 549 U.S. 497 (2007) (rejecting the EPA's contention that the agency was not authorized to regulate new vehicle emissions as a means of combating global warming and pointing out that the Clean Air Act granted the agency the power to regulate emissions and that policy considerations were irrelevant to that mandate).

| **A CASE IN POINT** | *Summary* | **Case 15.1** |

New Jersey v. EPA

United States Court of Appeals for the District of Columbia
517 F.3d 574 (D.C. Cir. 2008).

FACTS   In 2000, the EPA concluded that it was "appropriate and necessary" to regulate mercury emissions from coal- and oil-fired electric utility steam generating units (EGUs) because mercury emissions from EGUs "present significant hazards to public health and the environment." When mercury drops out of the air, it accumulates in rivers and streams and is stored in the tissues of fish. If pregnant women or children eat the fish, the mercury can cause the child to suffer serious developmental problems. In 2005, the EPA issued a rule purporting to remove coal- and oil-fired EGUs from the section 112 list (the Delisting Rule). A second rule adopted that same year (1) set performance standards pursuant to section 111 for new coal-fired EGUs; (2) established a national mercury emissions cap for new and existing EGUs, allocating each state and certain tribal areas a mercury emissions budget; and (3) created a voluntary

CONTINUED

market-based cap-and-trade program for new and existing coal-fired EGUs. In a *cap-and-trade system*, plants' allowable emissions would be capped, and plants that emitted more than their allotments could buy credits from plants with emissions below the specified levels. New Jersey and fourteen other states, the City of Baltimore, and various environmental organizations sued to invalidate both rules on the grounds that the EPA violated section 112's plain text when it delisted the EGUs and acted in an arbitrary and capricious manner when it reversed its determination that regulation of the EGUs' release of mercury was appropriate and necessary.

ISSUE PRESENTED   Did the EPA violate the Clean Air Act when it removed EGUs from the list of sources of mercury pollution listed in the Clean Air Act after having previously determined that the release of mercury from the plants was hazardous to human health?

SUMMARY OF OPINION   The U.S. Court of Appeals for the District of Columbia Circuit began by noting that Congress's concern about the EPA's slow pace in regulating sources of hazardous air pollution resulted in amendments to the Clean Air Act in 1990 that eliminated much of the EPA's discretion to regulate sources of hazardous air pollution. In the eighteen years following the passage of section 112 in 1970, the EPA had listed only eight pollutants and established standards for only seven of these, which addressed only a limited selection of possible pollution sources. The court explained that the 1990 amendments required the EPA to regulate more than 100 specific pollutants, including mercury. Congress gave the EPA the power, pursuant to section 112(c)(9), to remove sources of pollutants from the section 112 list, but only after determining that "emissions from no source in the category or subcategory concerned . . . exceed a level which is adequate to protect public health with an ample margin of safety and no adverse environmental effect will result from emissions from any source." Because the EPA failed to make the requisite finding before adopting the Delisting Rule, the court invalidated that rule and the rule purporting to regulate EGUs under section 111.

The court rejected the EPA's argument that it had the authority to remove coal- and oil-fired plants from the section 112(c) list at any time that it made a negative "appropriate and necessary" finding. The court also rejected, as contrary to the EPA's 2000 determination, the agency's assertion that the EGUs were not a source meeting the statutory criteria for listing under section 112. Citing *Chevron, U.S.A., Inc. v. Natural Resources Defense Council, Inc.,*[19] the court ruled that Congress had directly spoken to the issue of delisting and that "the court, as well as the agency, must give effect to the unambiguously expressed intent of Congress."[20] The court characterized the EPA's reasoning as "the logic of the Queen of Hearts, substituting EPA's desires for the plain text of section 112(c)(9)." (In Lewis Carroll's *Alice in Wonderland,* the Queen of Hearts declares, "Sentence first—verdict afterwards.") Because the EPA failed to make the findings required by section 112(c)(9) to delist the EGUs from the section 112(c)(1) list, both EPA rules were invalid.

RESULT   Both the Delisting Rule and the cap-and-trade rules were invalidated.

COMMENTS   Environmentalists cautioned that the invalidated cap-and-trade system could result in "hot spot[s]" of pollution if local plants could buy their way out of the obligation to use the best available technology to cut mercury emissions.[21] Commenting on the EPA's attempt to delist mercury, Professor Robert Percival of the University of Maryland remarked, "It's fairly clear that even judges that are, you know, not that fond of environmental regulation are kind of appalled at how willing the [George W. Bush administration] has been to try to bend the law."[22] EPA spokesperson Jonathan Shrader criticized the court's ruling, saying, "We have now no control over existing power plants, which should be of concern to the American people."[23] He asserted that the court's ruling invalidated a program that would have reduced mercury emissions by 70%.

---

19. 467 U.S. 837 (1984).

20. Quoting *id.* at 842–44.

21. David A. Fahrenthold & Steven Mufson, *Court Rejects Emission "Trades,"* WASH. POST, Feb. 9, 2008.

22. *Id.*

23. *Id.*

Federal and State Regulation of Greenhouse Gases

As a result of the increase in the buildup of carbon dioxide, methane, nitrous oxides, and other so-called greenhouses gases in the atmosphere, the earth is in the midst of unprecedented global climate change.[24] Increased greenhouse gas levels trap more heat radiated from the earth, causing a net warming effect.[25]

Although some greenhouse effect occurs naturally, the rapid increase in the atmospheric concentration of greenhouse gases in the past several decades is directly correlated with human activity.[26] Carbon dioxide and other gases are released into the atmosphere by the combustion of fossil fuels and other human activities; the destruction of rainforests reduces the amount of carbon dioxide being removed by the trees. Climate change could severely damage the world's ecosystem. Predicted consequences include severe flooding in coastal communities, water shortages and subsequent crop failures in poor countries, more powerful hurricanes and tropical cyclones, and other damaging changes. Such changes could disrupt, if not destroy, the livelihoods of hundreds of millions of people.[27]

According to a report released in 2007 by the United Nations Intergovernmental Panel on Climate Change (IPCC), global warming is "unequivocal" and "very likely" accelerated by human activity.[28] Global average air and ocean temperatures have increased, widespread melting of snow and ice has occurred, and global average sea levels have risen. An IPCC report released in 2011 predicted that severe heat waves and other extreme weather will intensify,[29] causing increased mortality and disease.[30]

Although most scientists agree that human beings are contributing significantly to climate change, public skepticism about climate change and its causes persists. A 2011 Gallup poll found that 51% of Americans view global warming as a personal threat, down from 66% in 2008.[31]

Section 108(a) of the Clean Air Act requires the EPA to publish air quality for any "pollutant" that contributes to air pollution that may endanger public health or welfare if its presence "in the ambient air results from numerous or diverse mobile or stationary sources."[32] The General Counsel of the EPA initially took the position that carbon dioxide satisfied the definition of "air pollutant" under the Act, but was not considered "reasonably . . . anticipated to endanger public health or welfare," the endangerment finding necessary for the pollutant's regulation.[33] In 1999, nineteen organizations filed a petition with the EPA asserting that in light of this legal opinion and the mounting evidence of climate change, the EPA was required to issue an endangerment finding and to regulate the emission of greenhouse gases from new motor vehicles.[34]

In 2007, in *Massachusetts v. EPA*,[35] the U.S. Supreme Court confirmed the EPA's authority under the Act to regulate carbon dioxide and other greenhouse gases emitted by motor vehicles and directed the EPA to make a finding regarding its obligation to regulate such emissions. The Court also ordered the EPA to consider whether it should provide a waiver under the Clean Air Act to permit California to impose the tough fuel economy standards embodied in section 43018.5(b)(1) of the California Health and Safety Code. California's standards were stricter than those imposed under federal law. Stressing the need for a uniform set of national standards, the EPA denied California's waiver request on December 19, 2007.[36] A federal court refused to lift an injunction prohibiting California from enforcing its fuel economy standards until a waiver of federal preemption is granted or federal legislation permitting their enforcement is enacted.[37]

In 2012, the EPA imposed limits of less than 1,000 pounds of carbon dioxide per megawatt-hour on new coal-fired power plants. Emissions from existing coal-fired plants and natural gas powered plants are not subject to these limits.

Before the Supreme Court handed down its decision in *Massachusetts v. EPA*[38] and the EPA began regulating greenhouse gases, parties frustrated with the EPA's choice not to regulate greenhouse gases brought suit not under the Clean Air Act, but under federal and state public nuisance law. The plaintiffs argued that the Clean Air Act did not displace federal common law in the area of regulating emissions of carbon dioxide. The U.S. Supreme Court addressed the issue in the following case.

---

24. PERCIVAL ET AL., *supra* note 4, at 1136.

25. *Id.*

26. *Id.* at 1137; CONTRIBUTION OF WORKING GROUP I TO THE FOURTH ASSESSMENT REPORT OF THE INTERGOVERNMENTAL PANEL ON CLIMATE CHANGE 2007 (S. Solomon et al. eds., 2007).

27. CONTRIBUTION OF WORKING GROUP I, *supra* note 26.

28. *Id.*

29. FIRST JOINT SESSION OF WORKING GROUPS I AND II: IPCC SREX SUMMARY FOR POLICYMAKERS 6 (Nov. 18, 2011), *available at* http://ipcc-wg2.gov/SREX/images/uploads/SREX-SPM_Approved-HiRes_opt.pdf.

30. Environmental Protection Agency, Proposed Endangerment and Cause or Contribute Findings for Greenhouse Gases Under Section 202(a) of the Clean Air Act, 74 Fed. Reg. 18,886 (2009).

31. Jeffrey M. Jones, *In U.S., Concerns About Global Warming Stable at Lower Levels*, GALLUP, Mar. 14, 2011.

32. 42 U.S.C. § 7408(a)(1).

33. PERCIVAL ET AL., *supra* note 4, at 509.

34. *Id.*

35. 549 U.S. 497 (2007).

36. *EPA Begins Rule on Greenhouse Gas Registry; Will Avoid Duplicative Reporting, Official Says*, 76 U.S.L.W. 2471 (2008).

37. Cent. Valley Chrysler-Jeep, Inc. v. Goldstene, 563 F. Supp. 2d 1158 (E.D. Cal. 2008).

38. 549 U.S. 497 (2007).

A CASE IN POINT

American Electric Power Co. v. Connecticut.

Supreme Court of the United States
131 S. Ct. 2527 (2011).

In the Language of the Court

Case 15.2

FACTS In 2004, eight states, New York City, and three land trusts brought an action against American Electric Power Company and four other electric power corporations that together owned and operated fossil-fuel-fired power plants in twenty states. The plaintiffs alleged that the defendants were the largest emitters of carbon dioxide in the country. By contributing to global warming, the plaintiffs argued, the defendants' emissions "substantially and unreasonably interfered with public rights," in violation of the federal common law of interstate nuisance, or, in the alternative, of state tort law. The states and New York City argued that public lands, infrastructure, and health were at risk from climate change. The land trusts alleged that climate change would destroy habitats for animals and rare species of trees and plants on land owned by the trusts. The plaintiffs sought injunctive relief requiring the defendants to cap their carbon dioxide emissions and to further reduce them by a specified amount each year.

The district court dismissed both suits as presenting nonjusticiable political questions. The U.S. Court of Appeals for the Second Circuit reversed, deeming it "error to equate a political question with a political case." The defendants appealed.

ISSUE PRESENTED Does the Clean Air Act preempt federal or state public nuisance claims against emitters of greenhouse gases?

OPINION GINSBURG, J., writing for the U.S. Supreme Court:

The petitioners [the power companies] contend that the federal courts lack authority to adjudicate this case. Four members of the Court would hold that at least some plaintiffs have Article III standing under *Massachusetts*,[39] which permitted a State to challenge EPA's refusal to regulate greenhouse gas emissions, and, further, that no other threshold obstacle bars review. Four members of the Court, adhering to a dissenting opinion in *Massachusetts*, or regarding that decision as distinguishable, would hold that none of the plaintiffs have Article III standing. We therefore affirm, by an equally divided Court, the Second Circuit's exercise of jurisdiction and proceed to the merits. [*Editor's note:* Justice Sotomayor took no part in the consideration or decision of the case.]

. . . .

"There is no federal general common law," *Erie R. Co. v. Tompkins*[40] famously recognized. In the wake of *Erie,* however, a keener understanding developed. . . . *Erie* [] sparked "the emergence of a federal decisional law in areas of national concern." The "new" federal common law addresses "subjects within national legislative power where Congress has so directed" or where the basic scheme of the Constitution so demands. Environmental protection is undoubtedly an area "within national legislative power," one in which federal courts may fill in "statutory interstices," and, if necessary, even "fashion federal law." As the Court stated in [*Illinois v. Milwaukee*[41]]: "When we deal with air and water in their ambient or interstate aspects, there is a federal common law."

. . . .

Recognition that a subject is meet for federal law governance, however, does not necessarily mean that federal courts should create the controlling law. . . . And where, as here, borrowing the law of a particular State would be inappropriate, the Court remains mindful that it does not have creative power akin to that vested in Congress.

. . . .

CONTINUED

39. *Id.*
40. 304 U.S. 64 (1938).
41. 406 U.S. 91 (1972).

The defendants argue that considerations of scale and complexity distinguish global warming from the more bounded pollution giving rise to past federal nuisance suits. . . . The plaintiffs, on the other hand, contend that an equitable remedy against the largest emitters of carbon dioxide in the United States is in order and not beyond judicial competence.

. . . .

We need not address the parties' dispute in this regard. For it is an academic question whether, in the absence of the Clean Air Act and the EPA actions the Act authorizes, the plaintiffs could state a federal common law claim for curtailment of greenhouse gas emissions because of their contribution to global warming. Any such claim would be displaced by the federal legislation authorizing EPA to regulate carbon-dioxide emissions.

. . . .

The test for whether congressional legislation excludes the declaration of federal common law is simply whether the statute "speak[s] directly to [the] question" at issue.

. . . .

We hold that the Clean Air Act and the EPA actions it authorizes displace any federal common law right to seek abatement of carbon-dioxide emissions from fossil-fuel fired power plants. *Massachusetts* made plain that emissions of carbon dioxide qualify as air pollution subject to regulation under the Act. And we think it equally plain that the Act "speaks directly" to emissions of carbon dioxide from the defendants' plants.

. . . .

The plaintiffs argue, as the Second Circuit held, that federal common law is not displaced until EPA actually exercises its regulatory authority, *i.e.*, until it sets standards governing emissions from the defendants' plants. We disagree.

. . . .

The critical point is that Congress delegated to EPA the decision whether and how to regulate carbon-dioxide emissions from power plants; the delegation is what displaces federal common law.

. . . .

The plaintiffs also sought relief under state law, in particular, the law of each State where the defendants operate power plants. . . . In light of our holding that the Clean Air Act displaces federal common law, the availability *vel non* [or not] of a state lawsuit depends, *inter alia*, on the preemptive effect of the federal Act. . . . None of the parties have briefed preemption or otherwise addressed the availability of a claim under state nuisance law. We therefore leave the matter open for consideration on remand.

RESULT   The Clean Air Act displaces any federal common law right to seek abatement of carbon dioxide emissions from fossil-fuel-fired power plants. The case was remanded for a determination of whether a claim was available under state nuisance law.

COMMENTS   Commentators split on the efficacy of the Court's decision. Libertarians and others disagree with the holding, arguing that using the common law to address environmental pollution concerns is in fact better than relying on centralized administrative agencies. Any degree of climate change could produce the sorts of harms, such as flooding of a neighbor's land due to rising sea temperatures, that common law nuisance has long addressed. Others, however, commended the decision for avoiding the "torrent of litigation" that could ensue if the door were opened to climate-based nuisance suits.[42]

---

42. Jonathan H. Adler, *The Supreme Court Disposes of a Nuisance Suit*: American Electric Power v. Connecticut, 2011 CATO SUP. CT. REV. 295, 317 (2011).

A rider to the 2008 Consolidated Appropriations Act signed by President Bush on December 26, 2007, directed the EPA "to require mandatory reporting of greenhouse gases above appropriate thresholds." Many saw this as a necessary first step in creating a national cap-and-trade program.

In 2008, the EPA sent the Office of Management and Budget a draft proposal for regulating greenhouse gas emissions from vehicles under the Clean Air Act. In response, the Departments of Agriculture, Commerce, Energy, and Transportation declared that "the Clean Air Act is fundamentally ill-suited to the effective regulation of greenhouse gas emissions."[43] Edward Lazear, chair of the Council of Economic Advisers, and John H. Marburger, director of the Office of Science and Technology Policy, asserted that "acting in a globally uncoordinated fashion will put the United States at a competitive disadvantage. . . . If businesses in other countries do not suffer the penalty for emitting greenhouse gases, production has an incentive to move abroad."[44] As discussed in the "Global View" in this chapter, the United States did not ratify the global limits on greenhouse gases in the Kyoto Protocol. Others expressed skepticism that EPA regulations are burdensome on the economy, finding "little evidence" that environmental regulations cause significant job loss.[45] Indeed, some argue, limiting greenhouses gases would create a job boom in "green" industries.

On December 7, 2009, EPA Administrator Lisa Jackson, appointed by the Obama administration, issued a finding that the current and projected concentrations of the six key greenhouse gases in the atmosphere—carbon dioxide, methane, nitrous oxide, hydrofluorocarbons, perfluorocarbons, and sulfur hexafluoride—"threaten the public health and welfare of current and future generations."[46] The Administrator also determined that the combined emissions of these greenhouse gases from new motor vehicles contribute to the greenhouse gas pollution that threatens public health and welfare.[47] These findings were a legal predicate to setting standards for greenhouse gas emissions from mobile sources under the statute. In May 2010, the EPA issued a final rule to address greenhouse gas emissions from both stationary and nonstationary sources. The rule required passenger cars, light-duty trucks, and medium-duty passenger vehicles for model years 2012 through 2016 to meet a 35.5 miles per gallon (MPG) standard.[48] The final rule also set thresholds for stationary sources of greenhouse gas emissions that define when permits are required for new and existing industrial facilities; however, all but the largest commercial facilities are excluded under the 2010 rule. The EPA committed to undertake another rulemaking and issue a final rule no later than July 1, 2012, to address phasing in smaller stationary source emitters.[49]

THE CLEAN WATER ACT

The Federal Water Pollution Control Act was adopted in 1972 and was substantially amended by the Clean Water Act of 1977 and by the Water Quality Act of 1987. The Act, as amended, is commonly referred to as the Clean Water Act.[50] The principal goal of the Clean Water Act is to eliminate the discharge of pollutants into the navigable waters of the United States.

Navigable waters are all "waters of the United States which are used in interstate commerce," including "all freshwater wetlands that are adjacent to all other covered waterways." In *Solid Waste Agency of Northern Cook County v. Army Corps of Engineers*,[51] the U.S. Supreme Court ruled that an abandoned sand and gravel pit in northern Illinois that provided habitat for migratory birds did not constitute "navigable waters" within the meaning of the Clean Water Act. The Court held that the Act does not apply to ponds that are not adjacent to open water, reasoning that the term "navigable" in the statute reflected Congress's intention to limit application of the Clean Water Act to waters that are or have been navigable in fact or that could reasonably be made so. Permitting federal jurisdiction over ponds and mudflats would impinge on the states' traditional power over land and water use. In *Rapanos v. United States*,[52] the Court further refined its interpretation of "waters of the United States" to include "those relatively permanent, standing or continuously flowing bodies of water 'forming geographic features'" such as streams, oceans, rivers, and lakes, but excluding "channels through which water flows intermittently or ephemerally, or channels that periodically provide drainage for rainfall."[53]

43. *EPA Proposal Lacks Agency Support, Is Not Administrative Policy, OMB Says*, 77 U.S.L.W. 2058 (2008).

44. *Id.*

45. Jia Lynn Yang, *Do Federal Regulations Really Kill Jobs? Economists Say Overall Impact on Employment Is Minimal*, Wash. Post.Com (Nov. 13, 2011).

46. Environmental Protection Agency, *Endangerment and the Cause or Contribute Findings for Greenhouse Gases Under Section 202(a) of the Clean Air Act* (Nov. 2011), *available at* http://epa.gov/climatechange/endangerment.html.

47. *Id.*

48. *See* the Regulations and Standards section on Transportation and Climate on the EPA's website, http://epa.gov/otaq/climate/regulations.htm#finalR.

49. Environmental Protection Agency, *Final Rule: Prevention of Significant Deterioration and Title V Greenhouse Gas Tailoring Rule* (2011), *available at* http://www.epa.gov/nsr/documents/20100413fs.pdf.

50. 33 U.S.C. § 1251 *et seq.*

51. 531 U.S. 159 (2001).

52. 547 U.S. 715 (2006).

53. *Id.* at 739.

National Pollutant Discharge Elimination System

The principal regulatory program established by the Clean Water Act is the *National Pollutant Discharge Elimination System (NPDES)*, which requires permits for the discharge of pollutants from any point source to navigable waters. EPA regulations establish *national effluent limitations*, which impose increasingly stringent restrictions on pollutant discharges, based on the availability of economically achievable treatment and recycling technologies. More stringent restrictions are imposed on new sources through the setting of national standards of performance. General and specific industry pretreatment standards are set for discharges to *publicly owned sewage treatment works (POTWs)*. The pretreatment standards are designed to ensure the effective operation of the POTW and to avoid the pass-through of pollutants. The POTW, in turn, must comply with its own NPDES permit for the discharge of treated waters. The NPDES program is administered largely through approved state programs, although the EPA maintains NPDES authority in areas not within the jurisdictions of states having EPA-approved programs.

Individual Liability of Corporate Officers

A corporate officer can be held civilly liable under the Clean Water Act if he or she had the authority to exercise control over the activity that caused the unlawful discharge. A corporate officer can also be held criminally responsible if he or she knowingly violated the Act.

In *United States v. Iverson*,[54] the U.S. Court of Appeals for the Ninth Circuit upheld a one-year prison sentence for the president and chair of the board of CH20, Inc., a manufacturer of acid cleaners and alkaline compounds, after finding that he had actual authority to prevent the company's dumping of industrial waste into a sewer. The executive was also fined $75,000 and received an additional sentence of three years of supervised release.

Similarly, the owner of a steel drum recycling company was found to have directed employees to dispose of hazardous waste water in various clandestine ways, from dumping it directly into sewers to bribing a city worker to put drums of waste in the city incinerator. He even ordered the construction of a fake evaporation tank that deceived enforcement officials into believing that contaminated water was being properly handled. Calling the owner's actions "environmental homicide," the district court judge sentenced to him to thirteen years in prison and ordered him to pay $14,000 in restitution.[55]

THE RESOURCE CONSERVATION AND RECOVERY ACT

The Solid Waste Disposal Act, as amended by the Resource Conservation and Recovery Act of 1976 and the Hazardous and Solid Waste Amendments of 1984 (RCRA),[56] governs the management of hazardous wastes. The Act authorizes the EPA to identify and list hazardous wastes, to develop standards for the management of hazardous wastes by generators and transporters of wastes, and to set standards for the construction and operation of hazardous waste treatment, storage, and disposal facilities. RCRA covers current and future hazardous waste treatment facilities. Abandoned or historically polluted sites are governed by the Comprehensive Environmental Response, Compensation, and Liability Act (CERCLA), discussed later in this chapter. The Federal Facility Compliance Act of 1992 and the Land Disposal Program Flexibility Act of 1996 strengthened enforcement of RCRA at federal facilities and eased RCRA-based restrictions on the disposal of certain types of waste, respectively.[57]

Cradle-to-Grave Responsibility

RCRA imposes "cradle-to-grave" responsibility on generators of hazardous waste. Each generator must obtain an EPA identification number and use a transportation manifest when transporting wastes for treatment or disposal. This allows the EPA to track the transportation, treatment, and disposal of hazardous wastes from the generator's facility to the final disposal site. A manifest is also required to transport hazardous wastes to an authorized storage facility.

RCRA bans the disposal of hazardous wastes on land without treatment to render them less hazardous. To comply with the EPA's requirements for disposal on land, companies that generate hazardous waste may have to make substantial capital investments in treatment systems or incur increased costs for having wastes treated elsewhere prior to disposal.

Generators of hazardous waste must certify that they have a program in place to reduce the quantity and toxicity of their wastes. They must also certify that they are disposing of their wastes in a manner that, to the extent practicable, minimizes future threats to human health and the environment.

Owners and operators of hazardous waste facilities must obtain permits and comply with stringent standards for the construction and operation of their facilities. These standards include maintaining certain liability insurance

---

54. 162 F.3d 1015 (9th Cir. 1998).

55. Richard Danielson, *Lutz Man Gets 13 Years for Toxic Waste Dumping*, ST. PETERSBURG TIMES, Aug. 17, 1999, at 1B.

56. 42 U.S.C. § 6901 *et seq.*

57. *See* the Wastes section on laws and regulations on the EPA's website, http://www.epa.gov/epawaste/laws-regs/index.htm.

ECONOMIC PERSPECTIVE

Externalities and the Tragedy of the Commons

A key concept in environmental economics is the idea of externalities. An externality is an effect of a purchase or use decision by one set of parties on others who did not have a choice and whose interest was not taken into account. For example, if a company can release its waste into a nearby river without having to pay for the harm it causes to those downstream, that is a negative externality. The result is a loss of allocative efficiency because all of the costs associated with the firm's activities are not reflected in its prices.

Another type of externality arises out of the exploitation of commonly owned natural resources, such as public grazing land or the sea or the air. Commonly owned resources are especially susceptible to overexploitation because the marginal cost to the private entity exploiting the resources is close to zero and the benefits are limitless. This problem is known as the "tragedy of the commons."

The tragedy of the commons arises when individuals, who are assumed to be rational, self-maximizing beings, exploit a limited shared resource and ultimately contribute to its depletion, even though each individual is aware at the time that there will be a detrimental impact in the long term. A commons has been defined as a resource where the prevention of overexploitation through physical or institutional means is costly and a single user's exploitation of the resource limits the availability of the resource to others. For example, consider a hypothetical plot of pastureland, open to all nearby shepherds. As a rational being, each shepherd seeks to maximize his or her personal gain. Given the opportunity, a shepherd will bring one more animal onto the land to graze. Since he or she receives all of the proceeds from herding and selling the animal, the incremental benefit to the shepherd is +1. The negative component is a function of the additional overgrazing created by one more animal. This negative value, however, will be only a fraction of –1, because it will be spread out among all the shepherds. Behaving rationally, a shepherd will maximize his or her overall benefit by continuing to increase his or her flock. Every other shepherd, however, will do the same thing. Therein lies the tragedy: eventually, the pastureland will be depleted, and no one will be able to graze sheep there.[a]

Since its inception, this well-settled concept has been important in the environmental context, including pollution and climate change. The "commons" at issue is the atmosphere, which is freely accessible to the entire global population. Like the herders in the hypothetical pasture, companies and individuals emit greenhouse gases and other pollutants to gain an individual, incremental benefit. Collectively, these emissions contribute to the degradation of the atmospheric commons. Like the herders, no single nation has an incentive to reduce its emissions, because such reductions will drastically reduce the nation's own realized benefits while only slightly diminishing the collective harm to the atmosphere.[b]

The most plausible economic solutions to the tragedy of the commons range from privatizing the commons to subjecting the commons to a central governing authority. In the context of climate change, policy proposals have addressed both ends of the spectrum: privatizing the disposal of carbon emissions into the atmosphere via tradable permits, and establishing globally allocated emissions limits enforced by regulatory oversight. Critics of unilateral regulations imposed by subglobal governments say such measures are irrational under the tragedy of the commons theory. On this logic, certain policymakers have attempted to justify the United States' failure to ratify the Kyoto Protocol. They argue that developing nations, such as China, will soon emit even more greenhouse gases than the developed nations. Because the Protocol does not limit developing nations' emissions to the same degree that it limits those of the developed nations, there will be a "free-rider" effect: the developing countries will gain an unfair competitive advantage because they will be able to sell their products at a lower price because they do not have to internalize the cost of their emissions.[c] The success of the post-Kyoto efforts to deal with climate change will depend in substantial part on the ability of all emitters to address these issues.

---

a. Garrett Hardin, *The Tragedy of the Commons*, Sci., Dec. 18, 1968, at 1243, 1243–44.
b. Kirsten H. Engel & Scott R. Saleska, *Subglobal Regulations of the Global Commons: The Case of Climate Change*, 32 Ecology L.Q. 183, 190–91 (2005).
c. *Id.*

---

coverage and providing financial assurances that show the owner/operator has the financial wherewithal to close the facility at the appropriate time and to maintain it properly after closure.

Even though hazardous waste transporters and treatment and storage facilities are closely regulated, companies that generate hazardous wastes must carefully select treatment, transportation, and disposal facilities. Liability may be imposed not only on the persons who "own or operate" the facility but also on those who have used the facility for the storage, treatment, or disposal of wastes. Persons who "contributed" to the improper waste disposal are also potentially liable. This includes individuals, such as officers who had no direct involvement in the disposal but had the authority to control the corporation's actions and failed to do so.

Criminal Liability

Although RCRA imposes strict civil liability, a criminal violation requires some sort of knowledge. In particular, RCRA provides criminal sanctions for any person who "knowingly transports any hazardous waste identified or listed under this subchapter to a facility which does not have a permit."[58] As explained in Chapter 14, it is not always clear how far down the sentence the word "knowingly" travels.

In *United States v. Hayes International Corp.*,[59] the U.S. Court of Appeals for the Eleventh Circuit held that knowledge of the regulation banning transport of hazardous waste to an unlicensed facility is not an element of the offense. Furthermore, the defendants could be found guilty even if they did not know that the substance being disposed of was a hazardous waste within the meaning of the regulations. It was enough that they knew that they were disposing of a mixture of paint and solvents. The court distinguished *Liparota v. United States*,[60] which required knowledge that the purchase of food stamps was illegal, on the grounds that (1) the food stamp law required "knowing violation of a regulation" and (2) RCRA, unlike the food stamp law, was a public welfare statute involving a heavily regulated area with great ramifications for the public health and safety. The court concluded that it was fair to charge those who chose to operate in such an area with knowledge of the regulatory provisions.

The court held, however, that the government did have to prove that the defendants knew that the facility to which the waste was sent did not have a permit. Thus, even if the transporters did not know a permit was required, as long as they knew the facility did not have one or knew that they had not inquired, that would be sufficient knowledge for a conviction. Such knowledge could be shown circumstantially. For example, given that it is common knowledge that properly disposing of wastes is an expensive task, if someone is willing to take away wastes at an unusually low price or under unusual circumstances, then a juror could infer that the transporter knew that the wastes were not being taken to a licensed facility.

The court did acknowledge that mistake of fact would be a defense if the defendants had had a good faith belief that the materials were being recycled. The regulations applicable at the time provided an exemption from the permit requirement for waste that was recycled. The court distinguished a case in which the U.S. Supreme Court had held that a person who believed in good faith that he was shipping distilled water, when in fact he was shipping dangerous acid, did not "knowingly" ship dangerous chemicals in violation of applicable regulations.[61] Unlike the defendant in that case, the defendants in *Hayes* knew what was being shipped—a combination of waste and solvents—and they did not have a good faith belief that the materials were being recycled. Therefore, the convictions were upheld.

In *United States v. Wasserson*,[62] the U.S. Court of Appeals for the Third Circuit held that generators of hazardous waste, who do not themselves carry out the disposal of such waste, could face liability under both the transportation *and* disposal offenses under RCRA. Under section 6928(d)(5), it is a violation to "knowingly transport[] without a manifest, or cause[] to be transported without a manifest, any hazardous waste . . . ." Under section 6928(d)(2)(A), it is a violation to "knowingly . . . dispose[] of any hazardous waste . . . without a permit . . . ." The court rejected the defendant's contention that only the actual disposer of hazardous waste was intended to be penalized under section 6928(d)(2)(A). According to the court, one who causes, aids, or abets any permitless disposal of hazardous waste is subject to liability under that section as well.

In applying its new standard, the court reversed the trial court's decision granting the defendant generator's motion for summary judgment as to the disposal charge. The court noted that the defendant had extensive knowledge of proper hazardous waste disposal procedures, yet delegated disposal work to an employee inexperienced in proper methods. Due to the defendant's failure to make a proper inquiry and to provide a manifest to accompany the waste, the evidence was sufficient to show that the defendant was "willfully blind" to the ultimate destination of his hazardous waste. As such, the defendant had effectively "aided and abetted" in the permitless disposal of hazardous waste in violation of section 6928(d)(2)(A).

THE FEDERAL SUPERFUND LAW (CERCLA)

More than any other environmental law, the Comprehensive Environmental Response, Compensation, and Liability Act (CERCLA) of 1980, as amended,[63] has affected individuals and businesses that do not themselves produce environmental pollutants. CERCLA

---

58. 42 U.S.C. § 6928(d)(1).

59. 786 F.2d 1499 (11th Cir. 1986).

60. 471 U.S. 419 (1985).

61. United States v. Int'l Minerals & Chem. Corp., 402 U.S. 558 (1971).

62. 418 F.3d 225 (3d Cir. 2005).

63. 42 U.S.C. § 9601 *et seq.*

authorizes the federal government to investigate and take remedial action in response to a release or threatened release of hazardous substances into the environment. CERCLA established the *Hazardous Substance Superfund* to finance federal response activity. Through 2007, the Superfund had been replenished with tax revenue numerous times, for a total of more than $32 billion in appropriations.[64]

How federal Superfund money is spent is determined in part by the EPA's National Priorities List, which identifies sites that may require remedial action. The EPA lists the sites in a rulemaking proceeding based on a *hazard ranking score*, which represents the degree of risk that the site presents to the environment and public health.

Strict Liability

The courts have interpreted the liability provisions of CERCLA broadly in order to effectuate the statute's remedial policies. With few exceptions, CERCLA imposes strict liability, meaning that any of the potentially responsible parties are liable regardless of fault. It is now well established, for example, that the present owner of the land is liable for the cleanup of hazardous substances disposed of on the land by another person (usually a previous owner or tenant), unless it can establish the third-party defense (also called the innocent landowner defense), discussed later in this chapter.

Potentially Responsible Parties

The EPA may undertake remedial action itself or require the potentially responsible parties to do so. The *potentially responsible parties (PRPs)* include (1) the present owner or operator of the facility, (2) the owner or operator at the time of disposal of the hazardous substance, (3) any person who arranged for treatment or disposal of hazardous substances at the facility, and (4) any person who transported hazardous substances to or selected the facility.[65] If the EPA performs the remedial work, it can recover its cleanup costs from the responsible parties. CERCLA does not permit punitive damages absent a showing of recklessness.

Lessee as Owner

Certain courts have held lessees of contaminated property liable as "owners" under CERCLA, reasoning that site control is a sufficient indicator of ownership to impose owner liability on lessees or sublessors. The U.S. Court of Appeals for the Second Circuit rejected this approach, reasoning that site control confuses the two statutorily distinct

---

> ### INTERNATIONAL SNAPSHOT
>
> A fundamental element of the U.S. environmental scheme is that the polluter pays. The European Union (EU) has also adopted this policy: "The cost of preventing and eliminating nuisances must, as a matter of principle, be borne by the polluter."[a] The EU's policy on the environment is designed to (1) preserve, protect, and improve the quality of the environment; (2) protect human health; (3) ensure prudent and rational utilization of natural resources; and (4) promote measures at the international level to deal with regional or worldwide environmental problems.
>
> This concept has also been introduced in Asia. Taiwan, for example, enacted an environmental law modeled, in part, on CERCLA, with modifications to address the local culture, issues, and concerns. On a smaller scale, the government of Delhi, India, has begun enforcing local litter and recycling ordinances more stringently under the "polluter pays" principle.
>
> When the laws of other nations are closely patterned on U.S. laws, compliance may be easier for U.S. companies operating in those countries; nonetheless, close attention should be paid to the differences between the U.S. laws and the laws of other countries. As other governments embrace U.S. pollution remediation principles, the United States may find itself in an awkward position. For example, Suresh Prabhu, India's former environment minister, remarked: "The polluters pay principle is internationally accepted today. So if the US and other rich countries are responsible for 70% of all the [greenhouse gases] in the atmosphere today, it's their responsibility to ensure the world doesn't hurtle towards an environmental crisis."[b]
>
> ---
>
> **a.** Objective 17, Restatement of the Objectives and Principles of a Community Environment Policy, 1977 O.J. (C 139).
>
> **b.** Nitin Sethi, *UN Report Tells India to Clean Up*, TIMES OF INDIA, Oct. 31, 2007.

---

categories of owner and operator under CERCLA.[66] Instead, the Second Circuit ruled, the critical question is whether the lessee's status is that of a de facto owner. In determining whether a lessee is an owner, important factors to consider are (1) the length of the lease and whether it allows the owner/lessor to determine how the property is used; (2) whether the owner has the power to terminate the lease before it expires; (3) whether the lessee can sublet the property without notifying the owner; (4) whether the lessee must pay taxes, insurance, assessments, and operation and maintenance costs; and (5) whether the lessee is responsible for making structural repairs.

Joint and Several Liability

The law permits the imposition of joint and several liability on owners, operators, and other responsible parties, which means that any one responsible party can be held liable for the total amount of response (cleanup)

---

64. U.S. Gov't Accountability Office, *Superfund: Funding and Reported Costs of Enforcement and Administration Activities* (July 18, 2008), at 2.

65. 42 U.S.C. § 9607.

66. Commander Oil Corp. v. Barlo Equip. Corp., 215 F.3d 321 (2d Cir. 2000), *cert. denied*, 531 U.S. 979 (2000).

costs and natural resource damage even though others may also be responsible for the release. A responsible party who incurs costs cleaning up a toxic-waste site can seek cost recovery, or *contribution*, from other responsible parties. In resolving contribution claims, the court may allocate response costs among liable parties using such equitable factors as the court determines are appropriate.[67] Of course, the right of contribution is of value only if the other parties are still in existence and able to pay. Many times, they are not. Thus, joint and several liability allows the government to select financially sound parties from whom to collect response costs and puts the burden of recovering these costs from other responsible parties on the selected defendants.

A party may escape joint and several liability if it can prove that it contributed to only a divisible portion of the harm or that it was the source of waste that, when mixed with other hazardous waste, did not contribute to the release and cleanup costs that followed. The party bears the burden of establishing a reasonable basis for apportioning liability.[68]

Liability of Affiliated Companies and Piercing the Corporate Veil

Corporate relatives also face potential CERCLA liability under certain circumstances. In *United States v. Bestfoods*,[69] the U.S. Supreme Court outlined the responsibility a parent corporation has for the hazardous waste disposal activities of a subsidiary. There are two bases for imposing liability on parent corporations for facilities ostensibly operated by their subsidiaries: (1) as an owner of a subsidiary whose corporate veil has been pierced and (2) as an operator of the facility.

Derivative Liability as an Owner

A parent corporation will have derivative CERCLA liability as an owner for its subsidiary's actions when (but only when) there are grounds for piercing the subsidiary's corporate veil. As explained more fully in Chapter 19, such a collapsing of the legal distinction between parent and subsidiary is appropriate only if the corporation is just a sham or if the distinction is a fiction meant simply to protect shareholders from illegal activity.

In its initial ruling in *Bestfoods*, the U.S. Court of Appeals for the Sixth Circuit had turned to Michigan corporate law to decide whether to pierce the Michigan firm's corporate veil. Other courts have turned to federal common law, that is, the principles found in cases that the courts have developed for interpreting federal statutes like CERCLA. Under federal common law, courts may give less respect to the corporate form than under the common law of many states.

Direct Liability as an Operator of the Subsidiary's Facility

A parent corporation will have direct liability for its own actions if it operates a facility owned by its subsidiary. To be deemed an operator, the parent corporation "must manage, direct, or conduct operations specifically related to pollution, that is, operations having to do with the leakage or disposal of hazardous waste, or decisions about compliance with environmental regulations."[70] Thus, the question is not whether the parent operates the subsidiary, but rather whether it operates the facility.

The Supreme Court acknowledged in *Bestfoods* that it is common for directors of a parent corporation to serve as directors of its subsidiary. Directors and officers holding positions with both the parent and its subsidiary can and do legitimately "change hats" to represent the two corporations separately. Courts generally presume that the directors are wearing their "subsidiary hats," and not their "parent hats," when managing the subsidiary. As a result, the parent is not liable just because dual officers and directors made policy decisions and supervised activities at the subsidiary's facility. But if an agent of the parent who wears only the parent's hat manages or directs activities at the subsidiary's facility, then the parent company may be held directly liable as an operator.

The parent company may also be directly liable if (1) the parent operates the facility in the stead of its subsidiary or alongside the subsidiary in some sort of joint venture, or (2) a dual officer or director departs so far from the norms of parental influence exercised through dual officeholding as to serve the parent in operating the facility, even when ostensibly acting on behalf of the subsidiary. Activities involving the facility that are consistent with the parent's investor status (such as monitoring the subsidiary's performance, supervising the subsidiary's finance and capital budget decisions, and articulating general policies and procedures) should not give rise to direct operator liability for the parent.

Successor Liability

Another important issue is *successor liability*, that is, the responsibility an acquirer of corporate assets has for the liabilities of the seller. Ordinarily, a purchaser of corporate assets—as opposed to a purchaser of all the stock of a corporation or a merger partner—does not automatically assume any of the seller's liabilities. The doctrine of

---

67. In *Browning-Ferris Industries of Illinois v. TerMaat*, 195 F.3d 953 (7th Cir. 1999), the U.S. Court of Appeals for the Seventh Circuit held that if one party has been required to pay the entire cost of cleaning up a site to which several other parties also contributed hazardous waste, the other parties can be held jointly and severally liable for contribution.

68. United States v. Alcan Aluminum Corp., 990 F.2d 711 (2d Cir. 1993).

69. 524 U.S. 51 (1998).

70. *Id.*

successor liability arose out of attempts by companies to evade liability by selling the bulk of their business or assets to another firm and then distributing the proceeds to their shareholders, thereby leaving creditors with no assets to collect against. Although this aspect of corporate law is normally a province of state common law, several federal courts refer to a federal common law of successor liability for environmental cleanup under CERCLA.

The U.S. Courts of Appeals for the Third,[71] Fourth,[72] Fifth,[73] Seventh, and Eighth[74] Circuits have taken the position that the doctrine of successor liability under CERCLA should be fashioned by reliance on federal common law. For example, the Seventh Circuit reasoned that resort to federal common law was warranted to achieve national uniformity in interpreting CERCLA and to prevent parties from frustrating the statute's aims by incorporating under the laws of states that restrict successor liability.[75]

In contrast, the First,[76] Second,[77] Sixth,[78] Ninth,[79] and Eleventh[80] Circuits relied on state common law to determine successor liability. For example, in *New York v. National Services Industries*,[81] the Second Circuit read *Bestfoods*[82] to require reference to state corporate law to determine when there should be successor liability.

It abandoned the substantial continuity test it had embraced in an earlier case.[83] The *substantial continuity test* (sometimes referred to as the *continuity of enterprise approach*) imposes successor liability when the purchaser of assets "maintains the same business, with the same employees doing the same jobs, under the same supervisors, working conditions, and production process, and produces the same products for the same customers" as the seller corporation.[84] Although several states employ this test, the majority of states impose successor liability only when there is a single corporation after the transfer of assets with the same shareholders and directors before and after the acquisition.[85] Because most states apply this more stringent *mere continuation (identity) test*, the Second Circuit applied the traditional common law rule, which states that a corporation acquiring the assets of another takes on its liabilities only when (1) the acquirer has expressly or implicitly agreed to assume them, (2) the transaction may be viewed as a de facto merger or consolidation, (3) the successor is the mere continuation of the predecessor, or (4) the transaction is fraudulent. In a subsequent case,[86] the Second Circuit ruled that a de facto merger requires continuity of ownership.

Liability of Lenders and Fiduciaries

Lenders face potential liability under CERCLA because foreclosure of a contaminated property potentially makes them an owner. The Asset Conservation, Lender Liability, and Deposit Insurance Protection Act of 1996[87] excluded from the definition of "owner or operator" a lender that did not participate in the management of a facility prior to foreclosure. Participation in management means "actually participating in the management or operational affairs" of the facility. Mere capacity to influence management is not a sufficient basis for imposing operator liability on a lender. Thus, a lender may hold "indicia of ownership," such as a deed of trust, to protect its security interest without facing liability as long as it does not actually manage or operate the facility.

Although a lender may take steps to sell the property (or re-lease rental property) if the debtor defaults and may even buy it at the foreclosure sale, without automatically becoming a potentially responsible party, the lender must attempt to sell or re-lease the property as soon as practicable for a commercially reasonable price. Failure to do so will make the lender potentially liable as an owner.

71. United States. v. Gen. Battery Corp., 423 F.3d 294 (3d Cir. 2005); Smith Land & Improvement Corp. v. Celotex Corp., 851 F.2d 86 (3d Cir. 1988) (holding that in resolving the issue of successor liability, the district court must consider national uniformity. "[O]therwise, CERCLA aims may be evaded easily by a responsible party's choice to arrange a merger or consolidation under the laws of particular states which unduly restrict successor liability").

72. United States v. Carolina Transformer Co., 978 F.2d 832 (4th Cir. 1992); United States v. Monsanto Co., 858 F.2d 160 (4th Cir. 1988).

73. Matter of Bell Petroleum Servs., Inc., 3 F.3d 889 (5th Cir. 1993) ("[a]ccordingly, Congress has suggested, and we agree, that common-law principles of tort liability set forth in the *Restatement* provide sound guidance" when determining successor liability under CERCLA).

74. K.C. 1986 Ltd. P'ship v. Read Mfg., 472 F.3d 1009 (8th Cir. 2007).

75. North Shore Gas Co. v. Salomon, Inc., 152 F.3d 642 (7th Cir. 1998).

76. Cyr v. B. Offen & Co., 501 F.2d 1145 (1st Cir. 1974); United States v. Davis, 261 F.3d 1, 54 (1st Cir. 2001) (noting that *Bestfoods* "left little room" for the creation of a special federal rule of liability under CERCLA).

77. New York v. Nat'l Servs. Indus., 352 F.3d 682 (2d Cir. 2003). *Accord* Ne. Conn. Econ. Alliance, Inc. v. ATC P'ship, 861 A.2d 473 (Conn. 2004).

78. Anspec Co. v. Johnson Controls, Inc. 922 F.2d 1240 (6th Cir. 1991); City Mgmt. Corp. v. U.S. Chem. Co., 43 F.3d 244 (6th Cir. 1994).

79. Atchison, Topeka & Santa Re Ry. Co. v. Brown & Bryant, Inc., 159 F.3d 358 (9th Cir. 1998) (noting that expansion of CERCLA successor liability under federal common law was not permissible, due to recent Supreme Court decision undermining the notion that federal common law governed).

80. Redwing Carriers, Inc. v. Saraland Apartments, 94 F.3d 1489 (11th Cir. 1996) (holding that state law determines liability of limited partners under CERCLA).

81. 353 F.3d 682 (2d Cir. 2003).

82. 524 U.S. 51 (1998).

83. B.F. Goodrich v. Betkoski, 99 F.3d 505 (2d Cir. 1996).

84. United States v. Carolina Transformer Co., 978 F.2d 832 (4th Cir. 1992).

85. *Id.*

86. New York v. Nat'l Servs. Indus., 460 F.3d 201 (2d Cir. 2006).

87. 42 U.S.C. § 9601(20).

The liability of a fiduciary, such as a trustee, is limited to the assets held in trust. There is also a safe harbor for fiduciaries that undertake lawful response actions, but the safe harbor does not protect against negligence that causes or contributes to the release or threatened release of hazardous substances.[88]

Defenses

There are five defenses to liability under CERCLA. The defendant can avoid liability by showing that the release of hazardous substances was caused solely by (1) an act of God (that is, an unavoidable natural disaster, such as an earthquake); (2) an act of war; or (3) the act or omission of a third party, provided that certain other requirements are met. A fourth defense for purchasers of *brownfields*, contaminated sites that are eligible for cleaning and reclaiming with assistance from the Superfund, was added by the Brownfields Revitalization Act. A fifth defense is available for recyclers against claims brought by private parties but not against claims by the federal or state government.

Third-Party or Innocent Landowner Defense

To assert the *third-party defense* (also referred to as the *innocent landowner defense*), a defendant must show that the third party responsible for the release was not an employee and had no contractual relationship with the person asserting the defense. If the facility was acquired from the third party, the written instrument of transfer (usually a deed) is deemed to create a contractual relationship unless the purchaser acquired the facility after the hazardous substances were disposed of and without any knowledge or reason to know that hazardous substances had previously been disposed of at the facility. To establish that the purchaser had no reason to know that hazardous substances were disposed of at the facility, the purchaser must show that, prior to the sale, it undertook "all appropriate inquiry into the previous ownership and uses of the property consistent with good commercial or customary practice in an effort to minimize liability."[89]

The EPA initially declined to define what constituted "all appropriate inquiry," but was instructed to do so by the 2002 Small Business Liability Relief and Brownfields Revitalization Act. After forming a negotiated rulemaking committee comprising environmental engineers, representatives of industry, state and local government officials, and community activists, the EPA promulgated a final rule in 2007 that gave prospective purchasers definitive guidance on what is necessary to prove the appropriate inquiry required for the third-party defense.[90] The requirements are summarized in Exhibit 15.1.

Brownfields and Ready-for-Reuse Certificates

The Brownfields Revitalization Act[91] makes it possible for acquirers of certain contaminated sites to avoid liability for legacy (that is, preexisting) contamination on the site. Landowners must comply with all institutional controls and guidelines issued by the EPA. For example, a landowner must take "reasonable steps" to prevent future or continuing releases of hazardous materials onto the land. Failure to comply with the guidelines exposes landowners to liability for the entire cleanup costs.[92] A full review of federal and state EPA guidelines is recommended to determine what constitutes "reasonable steps."

To offer more certainty to acquirers of contaminated sites, the EPA will, under certain circumstances, issue certificates of reuse under RCRA. The EPA issued its first certificate of reuse to a steel plant in Oklahoma in 2002. This certificate "verifies that environmental conditions on this property are protective of its current use and anticipated future uses."[93] These reuse certificates are incentives to clean up formerly contaminated land.

Recyclers

The Superfund Recycling Equity Act of 1999 exempts recyclers from liability in private-party actions under CERCLA. They remain liable in suits brought by the state or federal government, however. Under the statute, a person "who arranged for recycling of a recyclable material shall not be liable under [CERCLA's cost recovery and contribution sections] with respect to such material." The term "recyclable material" includes lead-acid and nickel-cadmium used in batteries.[94]

Retroactive Application

In *United States v. Olin Corp.*,[95] the U.S. Court of Appeals for the Eleventh Circuit ruled that owners can be held liable for hazardous waste disposed of before CERCLA became law. The court reasoned that "Congress's twin goals of cleaning up pollution that occurred prior to December 11, 1980, and of assigning responsibility to culpable parties

---

88. 42 U.S.C. § 9607(n).

89. 42 U.S.C. § 9601(35)(B).

90. 70 Fed. Reg. 66,070 (Nov. 1, 2005); *see also* the section on Brownfields and Land Revitalization on the EPA's website, http://www.epa.gov/brownfields/aai/aaifs.pdf.

91. Small Business Liability Relief and Brownfields Revitalization Act, Pub. L. No. 107-118, 115 Stat. 2356 (2002); *see also* Robert Dahlquist & Tiffany Barzal, *Ah: Relief from CERCLA. But Where's the Relief?*, 12 BUS. LAW. 39 (2003), for an excellent discussion of the relief from Superfund liability granted to some small businesses. The Economic Development Administration Reauthorization Act of 2003, Pub. L. No. 108-373, 118 Stat. 1756 (2004), provided for a demonstration program to encourage the use of solar energy technologies at brownfields sites. Up to $5 million for each fiscal year from 2004 through 2008 was authorized to develop "brightfield" sites.

92. These guidelines are available at http://www.epa.gov/compliance/resources/policies/cleanup/superfund/common-elem-guide.pdf. *See also EPA Guidance Issued on Avoiding Liability for Properties Tainted by Contiguous Sites*, 72 U.S.L.W. 2448 (2003).

93. *First-Ever Certificate of Reuse Awarded Under RCRA to Oklahoma Steelmaking Plant*, 71 U.S.L.W. 2061 (2002).

94. Gould Inc. v. A&M Battery & Tire Serv., 232 F.3d 162 (3d Cir. 2000).

95. 107 F.3d 1506 (11th Cir. 1997).

EXHIBIT 15.1   What Constitutes "All Appropriate Inquiry" Under CERCLA?

To avail itself of the third-party defense, the landowner or prospective purchaser must hire an environmental professional, as defined in the final rule, to conduct a site assessment. That assessment must include:

- Interviews with past and present owners, operators, and occupants.
- Reviews of historical sources of information.
- Reviews of federal, state, tribal, and local government records.
- Visual inspections of the facility and adjoining properties.
- Commonly known or reasonably ascertainable information.
- An assessment of the degree of obviousness of the presence or likely presence of contamination at the property and the ability to detect the contamination.

Additional inquiries that must be conducted by or for the prospective landowner include:

- Searches for environmental cleanup liens.
- Assessments of any specialized knowledge or experience of the prospective landowner.
- An assessment of the relationship of the purchase price to the fair market value of the property, if the property was not contaminated.
- Commonly known or reasonably ascertainable information.

The rule specifies that any assessment conducted in accordance with ASTM standard E1527-05 (Standard Practice for Environmental Site Assessments: Phase I Environmental Site Assessment Process) will comply with the rule and thereby satisfy the requirement of "all appropriate inquiry."

SOURCE: Section on Brownfields and Land Revitalization at the EPA's website, http://www.epa.gov/brownfields/aai/aaifs.pdf.

---

can be achieved only through retroactive application of CERCLA's response cost liability provisions."

Subsequent to the Eleventh Circuit's decision in this case, the U.S. Supreme Court held in *Eastern Enterprises v. Apfel*[96] that retroactive application of the Coal Industry Retiree Health Benefit Act of 1992 to a company that had abandoned its coal business in 1965 violated the Takings Clause of the Fifth Amendment to the U.S. Constitution. Although defendant firms have argued in several cases that *Eastern Enterprises* overrules all previous decisions holding that CERCLA could be constitutionally applied retroactively, four federal circuit courts (the U.S. Courts of Appeals for the First,[97] Second, Sixth, and Eighth

Circuits), as well as several federal district courts (including the Eastern District of Virginia, the Northern District of New York, the Western District of Arkansas, and the District of New Jersey),[98] have rejected this argument and upheld the retroactive application of CERCLA.

Extraterritorial Application

In what appears to be the first application of CERCLA to activity outside the United States, the court in the following case permitted an action to proceed against a Canadian smelter that dumped hazardous waste into a river that ran into Washington State.

---

96. 524 U.S. 498 (1998).
97. O'Neil v. Picillo, 883 F.2d 176 (1st Cir. 1989) (finding that CERCLA may be applied to both pre-enactment conduct and pre-enactment costs incurred by the government).

98. United States v. Alcan Aluminum Corp., 315 F.3d 179, 189–90 (2d Cir. 2003) (listing post–*Eastern Enterprises* decisions finding retroactive application of CERCLA constitutional). *But see* Gen. Elec. Co. v. EPA, 360 F.3d 188 (D.C. Cir. 2004) (ordering district court to consider General Electric's pre-enforcement constitutional challenge).

A CASE IN POINT   *In the Language of the Court*   **Case 15.3**

Pakootas v. Teck Cominco Metals, Ltd.

United States District Court for the Eastern District of Washington
2004 U.S. Dist. LEXIS 23041 (E.D. Wash. Nov. 8, 2004).

FACTS   Plaintiffs Joseph A. Pakootas and Donald R. Michel, enrolled members of the Confederated Tribes of the Colville Reservation, sued to enforce a unilateral administration order (UAO) by the U.S. EPA requiring the defendant, Teck Cominco Metals, Ltd. (TCM), to investigate and determine the full nature of the contamination at the "Upper Columbia River Site" due to materials disposed of into the Columbia River from the defendant's smelter. TCM is a Canadian corporation that owned and operated a smelter in Trail, British Columbia, located approximately ten Columbia River miles north of the United States–Canada border. The State of Washington was also a plaintiff, having intervened in the litigation as a matter of right under CERCLA.

CONTINUED

TCM moved to dismiss the action, contending that the U.S. court did not have subject matter or personal jurisdiction and that the plaintiffs' complaints failed to state claims on which relief could be granted.

ISSUE PRESENTED   Does a U.S. court have the power to enforce the provisions of CERCLA against a Canadian corporation for actions taken by that corporation in Canada?

OPINION   MCDONALD, J., writing for the U.S. District Court for the Eastern District of Washington:

A. Subject Matter Jurisdiction

This case arises under CERCLA and, therefore, there is a federal question which confers subject matter jurisdiction on this court.

. . . .

B. Personal Jurisdiction

. . . .

Absent one of the traditional bases for personal jurisdiction—presence, domicile, or consent—due process requires a defendant have "certain minimum contracts with [the forum state] such that the maintenance of the suit does not offend traditional notions of fair play and substantial justice." *International Shoe Co. v. Washington.*[99] The forum state must have a sufficient relationship with the defendants and the litigation to make it reasonable to require them to defend the action in a federal court located in that state. . . .

The extent to which a federal court can exercise personal jurisdiction, absent the traditional bases of consent, domicile or physical presence, depends on the nature and quality of defendant's "contacts" with the forum state. . . .

If a non-resident, acting entirely outside of the forum state, intentionally causes injuries within the forum state, local jurisdiction is presumptively reasonable. Under such circumstances, the defendant must "reasonably anticipate" being haled into court in the forum state. Personal jurisdiction can be established based on: (1) intentional actions; (2) expressly aimed at the forum state; (3) causing harm, the brunt of which is suffered, and which defendant knows is likely to be suffered, in the forum state. . . .

The facts alleged in the individual plaintiffs' complaint and the State of Washington's complaint-in-intervention satisfy this three-part test. The complaints allege that from approximately 1906 to mid-1995, defendant generated and disposed of hazardous substances directly into the Columbia River and that these substances were carried downstream into the waters of the United States where they have eventually accumulated and cause continuing impacts to the surface water and ground water, sediments, and biological resources which comprise the Upper Columbia River and Franklin D. Roosevelt Lake. . . . This disposal causes harm which defendant knows is likely to be suffered downstream by the State of Washington and those individuals, such as Pakootas and Michel, who fish and recreate in the Upper Columbia River and Lake Roosevelt.

The burden is on the defendant to prove the forum's exercise of jurisdiction would not comport with "fair play and substantial justice.". . .

. . . .

The exercise of jurisdiction over defendant TCM does not offend traditional notions of fair play and substantial justice. The burden on defendant in defending in this forum is not great. Trail, B.C. is located approximately 10 miles from the Eastern District of Washington. For reasons discussed below, the court finds the exercise of personal jurisdiction over defendant does not

CONTINUED

---

99. 326 U.S. 310 (1945).

create any conflicts with Canadian sovereignty. It is obvious the State of Washington has a significant interest in adjudicating this dispute, as evidenced by its intervention as a plaintiff, and venue is proper here under CERCLA.

. . . .

C. Failure to State a Claim

A Rule 12(b)(6) dismissal is proper only where there is either a "lack of a cognizable legal theory" or "the absence of sufficient facts alleged under a cognizable legal theory.". . .

Defendant contends the UAO cannot be enforced against a Canadian corporation based on conduct which occurred in Canada. . . .

. . . CERCLA's definition of "environment" is limited to waters, land, and air under the management and authority of the United States, within the United States, or under the jurisdiction of the United States.

. . . The court . . . will assume this case involves an extraterritorial application of CERCLA to conduct occurring outside U.S. borders. In doing so, however, the court does not find that said application is an attempt to regulate the discharges at the Trail smelter, but rather simply to deal with the effects thereof in the United States.

Congress has the authority to enforce its laws beyond the territorial boundaries of the United States. It is, however, a longstanding principle of American law "that legislation of Congress, unless a contrary intent appears, is meant to apply only within the territorial jurisdiction of the United States.". . .

. . . .

"[I]f Congressional intent concerning extraterritorial application cannot be divined, then courts will examine additional factors to determine whether the traditional presumption against extraterritorial application should be disregarded in a particular case." First, "the presumption is generally not applied where the failure to extend the scope of the statute to a foreign setting will result in adverse effects within the United States."

. . . .

Here, defendant TCM contends the presumption against extraterritorial application is not defeated because CERCLA is "bare of any language affirmatively evidencing any intent to reach foreign sources." There is no dispute that CERCLA, its provisions and its "sparse" legislative history, do not clearly mention the liability of individuals and corporations located in foreign sovereign nations for contamination they cause within the U.S. At the same time, however, there is no doubt that CERCLA affirmatively expresses a clear intent by Congress to remedy "domestic conditions" within the territorial jurisdiction of the U.S. That clear intent, combined with the well established principle that the presumption is not applied where failure to extend the scope of the statute to a foreign setting will result in adverse effects within the United States, leads this court to conclude that extraterritorial application of CERCLA is appropriate in this case.

. . . .

There is no direct evidence that Congress intended extraterritorial application of CERCLA to conduct occurring outside the United States. There is also no direct evidence that Congress did not intend such application. There is, however, no doubt that Congress intended CERCLA to clean up hazardous substances at sites within the jurisdiction of the United States. That fact, combined with the well-established principle that the presumption against extraterritorial application generally does not apply where conduct in a foreign country produces adverse effects within the United States, leads the court to conclude that extraterritorial application of CERCLA is not precluded in this case. The Upper Columbia River Site is a "domestic condition" over which the United States has sovereignty and legislative control.

CONTINUED

Extraterritorial application of CERCLA in this case does not create a conflict between U.S. laws and Canadian laws.

. . . .

Because the fundamental purpose of CERCLA is to ensure the integrity of the domestic environment, we expect that Congress intended to proscribe conduct associated with the degradation of the environment, regardless of the location of the agents responsible for said conduct.

RESULT   The motion to dismiss was denied so that the case could proceed.

CRITICAL THINKING QUESTIONS

1. Would the Canadian government be able to cite this case as precedent for holding U.S. companies liable under Canadian law for acid rain in Canada?[100]

2. What public policy considerations are involved when deciding whether to apply U.S. environmental laws to conduct occurring outside the United States? Are they the same as those implicated when deciding whether to apply U.S. antitrust,[101] employment-discrimination,[102] securities,[103] or copyright and trademark law[104] to conduct occurring outside the United States?

100. *See* Shi-Ling Hsu & Austen L. Parrish, *Litigating Canada–U.S. Transboundary Harm: Intentional Environmental Lawmaking and the Threat of Territorial Reciprocity*, 48 VA. J. INT'L L. 1 (2007).

101. Envtl. Def. Fund v. Massey, 986 F.2d 528 (D.C. Cir. 1993).

102. Carnero v. Boston Scientific Corp., 433 F.3d 1 (1st Cir. 2006).

103. Tamari v. Bache & Co., 730 F.2d 1103 (7th Cir. 1984).

104. Suba Films v. MGM–Pathe Commc'ns Co., 24 F.3d 1088 (9th Cir. 1994).

ENVIRONMENTAL JUSTICE

In 1992, the EPA created the Office of Environmental Justice and began integrating environmental justice into the agency's policies, programs, and activities. *Environmental justice* refers to the belief that decisions with environmental consequences (such as where to locate incinerators, dumps, factories, and other sources of pollution) should not discriminate against poor and minority communities. Because such decisions usually require state or municipal permits, environmental justice concerns are often enforced by the federal government against states, cities, and counties.

ENFORCEMENT ACTIVITIES AND SANCTIONS FOR NONCOMPLIANCE

Enforcement of environmental laws includes the monitoring of regulated companies' compliance with the laws, remediation of problems, and the punishment of violators.

Agency Inspections

The environmental laws give broad authority to the administering agencies to conduct on-site inspections of plant facilities and their records. Many laws authorize the collection of samples for analysis. Inspections may be conducted routinely or in response to reports or complaints from neighbors or employees. If criminal violations are suspected, the agency may be required to obtain a search warrant before conducting a nonroutine inspection. Violations observed during the inspection may result in civil or criminal enforcement actions.

Administrative and Civil Enforcement Actions

Because the environmental laws are intended to accomplish such important societal goals and violations of the laws may cause serious harm or injury, environmental regulatory agencies generally are given strong enforcement powers. For a first violation, the agency might issue a warning and impose a schedule for compliance. If the schedule is not met or the violations are repeated, more aggressive enforcement action will likely follow. Such action may take the form of an administrative order to take specified steps to achieve compliance or a formal administrative complaint containing an assessment of administrative penalties. The penalties vary. Because they can be assessed for each day of each violation, they can be substantial for repeated, multiple, or long-standing violations.

Criminal Prosecution

In more egregious cases, the enforcing agency may refer the case to the U.S. Attorney's office or its state counterpart for criminal prosecution. In most instances, courts are authorized to impose penalties of $2,500 to $100,000 per day for negligent or knowing violations of the federal environmental statutes and to sentence individuals to prison terms of one year or more.[105] Any person who knowingly violates the law and who knows at that time that he or she thereby places another person in imminent danger of death or serious bodily injury can be fined up to $250,000 and imprisoned for up to fifteen years. Fines and terms of imprisonment are doubled for subsequent offenses.[106] In some cases, the agency may have authority to close down the violator's operations.

The EPA often recommends against criminal prosecution by the Department of Justice if the company self-reports and cooperates with the EPA. Any protection against criminal prosecution gained by voluntary disclosures under the audit policy applies only to the company, however. Officers and employees may still be subject to criminal liability based on information disclosed by the company.

The following case has been described as the most expansive application to date of the responsible corporate officer doctrine in a criminal case. It makes it clear that even self-reporting may not prevent a prison sentence.

---

105. *See, e.g.*, 33 U.S.C. § 1319 & 42 U.S.C. § 6928.
106. 33 U.S.C. § 1319(c).

INTERNATIONAL SNAPSHOT

Although historically pollution laws were often not enforced in India, in November 1999, the Supreme Court of India ordered New Delhi authorities to comply with its 1996 order to close approximately 90,000 small factories that were polluting residential areas in the capital city or to relocate them to areas outside the city. The businesses included leather, fertilizer, chemical, food processing, and paint plants that polluted the city's air and water sources. After the India Supreme Court issued the order, thousands of workers violently protested the closure of the factories by torching buses, blocking major roads, and throwing stones.[a] These protests essentially shut down the capital for a week. Opponents of the closures argued that shutting down the small factories, which provided employment to approximately one million people and generated business worth more than $1 billion annually, would cripple the city's economy.[b] The India Supreme Court argued that the closures were necessary to protect public health and stated that it would not be influenced by the protests: "The court will not withdraw its orders just because hooligans have taken to the streets."[c] The governments of the rapidly industrializing states of Haryana and Uttar Pradesh, which are just north of New Delhi, ran advertisements encouraging factories to relocate there.[d]

---

a. Celia W. Dugger, *A Cruel Choice in New Delhi: Jobs vs. a Safer Environment*, N.Y. TIMES, Nov. 24, 2000.

b. Ranjit Devrai, *Development—India: Thousands of Jobless Question Green Concerns*, INTER PRESS SERVICE, Dec. 29, 2000.

c. Dugger, *supra* note a.

d. Kartik Goyal, *India: Neighbouring States Gain As Delhi Shuts Polluting Units*, REUTERS ENG. NEWS SERVICE, Dec. 29, 2000.

A CASE IN POINT	*In the Language of the Court*	Case 15.4

United States v. Hansen

United States Court of Appeals for the Eleventh Circuit
262 F.3d 1217 (11th Cir. 2001).

FACTS Christian Hansen founded the Hanlin Group in 1972 and served as its CEO until April 1993. The Hanlin Group operated a chemical plant in Brunswick, Georgia, through its subsidiary LCP Chemicals–Georgia (LCP). The plant employed about 150 workers. Before Hanlin acquired the Brunswick facility in 1979, the site had been occupied by other companies that had produced and dumped hazardous materials on the land and the surrounding area. LCP constructed a wastewater treatment system and obtained a permit in 1990 to dump "treated" water into Purvis Creek, a nearby waterway. Although LCP had represented that its treatment facilities could process seventy gallons of water per minute, in fact, the facility could process only thirty-five gallons per minute. In August 1992, the Occupational Safety and Health Administration cited the plant for safety hazards associated with contaminated water on the cell room floors.

Hanlin filed for bankruptcy in 1991. Soon thereafter, Christian asked his son Randall to join LCP as an executive vice president to help turn the facility around.

In February 1992, James Johns, the Brunswick plant manager, informed Randall that, without "extensive work" on the wastewater treatment system, the plant could not operate for more than a few days without willfully violating environmental regulations. Randall attempted to raise additional funds by selling excess equipment and reducing the payroll, but the funds available for maintenance, repair, and environmental compliance remained limited. All major projects and all capital and extraordinary expenditures required the approval of the Hanlin board, the Hanlin bankruptcy creditors' committee, and the bankruptcy court. Although

CONTINUED

Randall requested funds to address the wastewater problems, the funds were usually not released.

Later that year, Randall visited the plant again after meeting with representatives from the EPA and was told by Alfred Taylor, the new plant manager, that the water treatment problem was growing even more serious. Taylor testified at trial that Randall was "just as concerned as they were" about the problems and authorized him to hire a task force to help solve the problem.

After a year and a half of more violations, which were duly reported to the state and federal EPA by Randall and LCP, Randall and his managers considered shutting down the facility either permanently or temporarily. But Randall told his managers, "They won't let me do that." In April 1993, the board removed Christian as CEO and elected Randall in his place. Randall also served as plant manager of the Brunswick facility from July through September 1993.

Randall searched for a suitable buyer with the resources and capital to fix the plant's problems. During this time, he received reports of the continuing violations at the plant.

In June 1993, the Georgia Environmental Protection Division (EPD) proposed a revocation of LCP's license to dump wastewater into Purvis Creek. In July and August 1993, Christian told employees to pump wastewater into drums containing oil, even though he knew that wastewater mixed with oil could not be run through the wastewater treatment system. He also advised employees not to dump any more water into Purvis Creek. Employees repeatedly told Randall, Christian, and Taylor that water was running out of the treatment facility's doors due to breaks in the beams. These employees were told that conditions would change as soon as the plant had a cash infusion from a buyer, but that nothing more could be done at that time.

During this period, Randall found a buyer that was willing to advance funds to help alleviate the releases of hazardous waste. Although conditions briefly improved, the deal fell through, and the Georgia EPD revoked LCP's license in September 1993, forcing LCP to close the plant entirely. Randall requested $1.5 million from the bankruptcy court to deal with the environmental impacts of a full plant closure, but his request was denied.

Following the closure, the facility was turned over to the U.S. EPA for cleanup, which cost approximately $50 million. Shortly thereafter, the U.S. Attorney's office indicted Christian and Randall Hansen and Taylor for violating numerous environmental laws from 1984 through the plant's final shutdown in 1994. The government also indicted Douglas Hanson, LCP's environmental and health and safety manager. Hanson pleaded guilty to violating CERCLA and the Endangered Species Act and testified against Christian, Randall, and Taylor.

Christian Hansen was convicted of violating the Clean Water Act (CWA), the Resource Conservation and Recovery Act (RCRA), and CERCLA, and he was sentenced to 108 months in prison. Randall was convicted of violating the CWA and RCRA and was sentenced to 46 months in prison. Taylor was convicted of violating the CWA, RCRA, and CERCLA and was sentenced to 78 months in prison. All three appealed their convictions.

ISSUE PRESENTED When may corporate officers and plant managers be held individually guilty as operators of a hazardous waste facility under the CWA, RCRA, and CERCLA?

OPINION PER CURIAM, by the U.S. Court of Appeals for the Eleventh Circuit:

The indictment alleged that the defendants, "after learning that the Brunswick facility was disposing of hazardous wastes . . . without a RCRA permit, continued to operate the Brunswick facility in such a manner as to continue the disposal of these hazardous wastes without expending adequate funds . . . to prevent the disposal of such hazardous wastes into the environment." The jury was instructed that the defendants were responsible for the acts of others that they "willfully directed," "authorized," or aided and abetted by "willfully joining together with [another] person in the commission of a crime." . . .

CONTINUED

a. Hansen

. . . .

The testimony at trial indicated that Christian Hansen was aware that wastewater was permitted to flow out the cell room back door in June 1993, and directed the use of the old Bunker C storage tanks for storage of wastewater, including the inadequately treated wastewater from the treatment system, from July through September 1993. Although the acts continued after Hansen left his decision-making position, the acts occurred at his direction. This evidence was sufficient for the jury to reasonably conclude beyond a reasonable doubt that his acts were in furtherance of the violations. . . .

b. Randall

Randall claims that the government presented no evidence that he personally treated, stored, or disposed of a hazardous waste, personally effected a CWA violation, or instructed an agent to do so. He maintains that, under the laws of bankruptcy and corporate governance, he lacked the authority to close the plant or to allocate the funds for the needed capital improvements. He contends that LCP needed the bankruptcy court's approval to use the bankruptcy estate's assets, or to obtain a new debt, to perform the needed repairs at the Brunswick plant.

In February 1994, LCP applied to the bankruptcy court for the funds "to shutdown" the plant and for new equipment, but the motion was denied. . . . LCP Board of Directors member James Mathis testified that Randall was responsible for "running the day-to-day operations of the company" once he became the interim CEO and COO. . . .

LCP, as a debtor in possession, could use the property of the estate in the ordinary course of business, but needed court approval to use, sell, or lease, other than in the ordinary course of business, property of the estate. It could obtain secured credit . . . in the ordinary course of business, but needed court approval to obtain unsecured credit or to incur unsecured debt other than in the ordinary course of business. Bankruptcy does not insulate a debtor from environmental regulatory statutes. In reviewing an injunction to clean up a hazardous waste site, the U.S. Supreme Court commented:

> We do not suggest that [the debtor's] discharge [in bankruptcy] will shield him from prosecution for having violated the environmental laws . . . or for criminal contempt for not performing his obligations under the injunction prior to bankruptcy. . . . We do not hold that the injunction . . . against any conduct that will contribute to the pollution of the site or the State's wasters is dischargeable in bankruptcy. . . . Finally, we do not question that anyone in possession of the site . . . must comply with the environmental laws. . . . Plainly, that person or firm may not maintain a nuisance, pollute the waters of the State, or refuse to remove the source of such conditions.[107]

Although Randall claims that his role as Executive Vice-President and acting CEO was limited to financial matters, he also received daily reports about the plant's operations and environmental problems, wrote and received memos regarding specific plant operational problems, received monthly written environmental reports, and oral environmental reports. He admitted that Hanlin's bankruptcy was not an excuse for violating environmental laws. There is no indication that he asked the Hanlin Board or the bankruptcy court to close the plant. The evidence indicates that he apparently misled them into believing that environmental compliance was not a problem. After the Georgia EPD attempted to revoke the plant's [dumping] permit in June 1993, Randall contested the revocation, explaining that the plant's CWA violations were due to a lightning strike and equipment failures, and asserted that "LCP has already taken steps to improve the situation." This evidence was sufficient for the jury to conclude that Randall's actions were in furtherance of the violations.

CONTINUED

107. Ohio v. Kovacs, 469 U.S. 274, 284–85 (1985).

c. Taylor

Taylor argues that he should not be held responsible for the environmental violations that occurred after he resigned as plant manager. Taylor resigned as plant manager on 16 July 1993, but returned shortly thereafter as a project engineer and continued in that position until the plant closed. . . .

Although Taylor left his managerial position, he continued to work in a position in which he directed or authorized acts of the employees on environmental and safety problems. . . . This evidence was sufficient for the jury to conclude beyond a reasonable doubt that these acts were in furtherance of the violations.

RESULT   The defendants' convictions were supported by the evidence and were, accordingly, upheld.

COMMENTS   The Justice Department has responded to criticism that environmental crime prosecutors are "overreaching by criminalizing what should be handled through the civil or regulatory process" with a resolute stance of continuing to criminally pursue those it considers violators.

CRITICAL THINKING QUESTIONS

1. Is it fair to hold an officer criminally liable for environmental problems when the officer lacks the funds to fix the problems or to shut the plant down properly to prevent further violations?

2. Is it fair to attribute corporate actions to the corporation's officers when they never instructed or encouraged their employees to violate the environmental laws?

Self-Reporting Requirements

Many statutes and regulations require regulated companies to report certain facts to the EPA, such as the concentrations or the amounts of pollutants discharged from a facility, or both. These reports may indicate a violation and may therefore prompt an enforcement action by the agency. There are severe penalties for filing false reports, including criminal sanctions for knowingly providing false information to a government agency.

EPA INCENTIVES FOR SELF-POLICING

The EPA's audit policy statement on self-policing is designed "to enhance protection of human health and the environment by encouraging regulated entities to voluntarily discover, promptly disclose and expeditiously correct violations of Federal environmental requirements."[108] If a company meets all nine conditions for leniency set forth in Exhibit 15.2 or all except the first one (that the discovery is made through systematic monitoring), then the EPA will generally opt not to pursue criminal proceedings.[109]

Parties that meet these nine conditions for leniency are also eligible for a substantial reduction in civil penalties or the elimination of the gravity component of civil penalties.[110] Companies that fulfill all the conditions except the first can receive 75% mitigation of gravity-based civil penalties.[111] As an additional incentive, the EPA may "refrain from routine audits."[112]

A company may also qualify under the policy if, after having been found liable for violations at one facility, it discloses similar violations at others. The voluntary disclosure policy has been widely used. To date, more than 670 companies have made voluntary disclosures, resulting in the resolution of claims at more than 1,300 facilities.[113]

---

108. Environmental Protection Agency, *Incentives for Self-Policing: Discovery, Disclosure, Correction and Prevention of Violations, Final Policy Statement* (May 11, 2000), at 16–28.

109. *Id.*

110. The gravity component is that portion of the penalty over and above the violator's economic gain from noncompliance.

111. Environmental Protection Agency, *supra* note 108.

112. *Id.*

113. Peyton Sturges, *Revisions to EPA Audit Policy Dovetail with Enforcement Initiatives, Official Says,* 68 U.S.L.W. 2576 (2000). In the spring of 2003, the EPA announced that it had waived $1.5 million in fines payable by East Coast–based companies after they self-reported violations occurring as far back as 1994 and as recently as 2001. The violations ranged from failing to file appropriate waste authorization forms to misreporting the qualities of dangerous chemicals being dumped by the companies. *EPA Waives $1.5 Million in Potential Fines Against Companies Reporting Own Violations,* 71 U.S.L.W. 2551 (2003).

EXHIBIT 15.2   Conditions for Leniency Under the EPA's Audit Policy Statement

1. *Systematic discovery of the violation through an environmental audit or a compliance management system:* The violation must have been discovered through either (a) an environmental audit or (b) a compliance management system that reflects due diligence in preventing, detecting, and correcting violations.

2. *Discovery and disclosure independent of government or third-party plaintiff*: The entity must discover the violation independently. That is, the violation must be discovered and identified before the EPA or another government agency likely would have identified the problem either through its own investigative work or from information received through a third party.

3. *Correction and remediation:* The entity must remedy any harm caused by the violation and expeditiously certify in writing to appropriate federal, state, and local authorities that it has corrected the violation.

4. *Preventing recurrence:* The regulated entity must agree to take steps to prevent a recurrence of the violation after it has been disclosed. Preventive steps may include, but are not limited to, improvements to the entity's environmental auditing efforts or compliance management system.

5. *No repeat violations:* Repeat offenders are not eligible to receive audit policy credit. Under the repeat violations exclusion, the same or a closely related violation must not have occurred at the same facility within the past three years.

6. *Other violations excluded:* Policy benefits are not available for violations that result in serious actual harm to the environment or that may have presented an imminent and substantial endangerment to public health or the environment. When events of such a consequential nature occur, violators are ineligible for penalty relief and other incentives under the audit policy.

7. *Cooperation:* The regulated entity must cooperate as required by the EPA and provide the EPA with the information it needs to determine policy applicability. The entity must not hide, destroy, or tamper with possible evidence following discovery of potential environmental violations.

8. *Voluntary disclosure:* The violation must have been identified voluntarily, and not through a monitoring, sampling, or auditing procedure that is required by statute, regulation, permit, judicial or administrative order, or consent agreement.

9. *Prompt disclosure:* The entity must disclose the violation in writing to the EPA within twenty-one calendar days after discovery.

SOURCE: Environmental Protection Agency, *Incentives For Self-Policing: Discovery, Disclosure, Correction and Prevention of Violations, Final Policy Statement* (May 11, 2000), at 16–28.

MANAGEMENT OF ENVIRONMENTAL COMPLIANCE

Legally astute managers recognize the need to adopt corporate policies and create management systems to ensure that company operations are protective of human health and the environment and meet market and societal expectations. These programs generally include several key elements.

Corporate Policy

A strong corporate policy of environmental protection, adopted and supported at the highest levels of management, is usually the keystone of an effective program. Mere compliance with environmental laws may not be enough. A practice that is lawful today could nevertheless lead to environmental harm and future liability. For example, underground storage of flammable materials was once considered a sound practice and was actually required by many local fire codes. Little thought was given to the possibility of leaks or spillage around the tanks, with resulting harm to underground water supplies. If the risks had been perceived properly, double containment could have been provided when the tanks were first installed. This lack of foresight caused many companies to incur substantial costs for groundwater restoration.

The corporate policy should require every employee to comply with environmental laws. It should encourage management to consider more stringent measures than those required by law if such measures are necessary to protect human health and the environment. Finally, the policy should encourage a cooperative and constructive relationship with government agency personnel and should support active participation in legislative and administrative rulemaking proceedings.[114]

Well-Defined Organizational Structure and Crisis-Management Plan

Management of environmental compliance requires a well-defined organizational structure with clearly delineated responsibilities and reporting relationships. The complex and technical nature of environmental laws and regulations requires a highly trained professional staff with legal and technical expertise.

---

114. *EPA May Recommend Not Prosecuting Companies That Uncover, Report Crimes*, 66 U.S.L.W. 2520 (1998). The official EPA statement of its policy is available at http://www.epa.gov/compliance/resources/policies/index.html.

A company should have policies and procedures for reporting environmental law violations to corporate management and for managing the company's reporting obligations to government agencies. Top management also needs to ensure that whistleblowers are not subject to retaliation.

Environmental problems are what Max Bazerman and Michael Watkins call "predictable surprises."[115] Therefore, every company should have a crisis-management plan in place that designates someone other than the CEO to coordinate the response. That response, in turn, should include immediate stabilization of the situation, objective inquiry into it, and some immediate action to assure the company's constituencies that things are being put under control. For that reason, constituencies must receive information as the response continues. To the extent that crises are at least foreseeable, more detailed plans should be developed ahead of time.[116] (The "Inside Story" in this chapter discusses BP's failure to adequately manage its massive oil spill in the Gulf of Mexico.)

Education and Training

A corporation can be held liable for the malfeasance of its employees acting within the scope of employment, even if they acted contrary to company policies. At the same time, an employee involved in illegal conduct can be held personally criminally liable, even if he or she was just following orders from a supervisor. In addition, as explained in this chapter and in Chapter 14, under certain circumstances, the corporate executive officers responsible for operating or overseeing the operation of facilities or activities involving hazardous waste can be civilly and criminally liable for illegal conduct by the employees under their supervision.

The most essential component of good environmental management is comprehensive education and training. Every employee must know about and understand the company's environmental policy and recognize his or her responsibilities in carrying it out.

Record Keeping, Accounting, and Disclosure

Good record-keeping and cost-accounting systems are also essential. Many environmental laws require certain records to be developed and maintained for specified periods of time. These laws should be consulted when a company develops a record-retention policy. The company should also develop cost-accounting procedures that will allow it to forecast and report the costs of environmental compliance.

Publicly traded companies must carefully evaluate the costs of complying with environmental law and potential environmental liabilities in order to meet the disclosure and reporting requirements of the Securities and Exchange Commission (SEC). The SEC requires disclosure of environmental enforcement proceedings and litigation, as well as estimated costs of environmental compliance, including capital expenditures and any effects of compliance on earnings and competitive position that may be material. The SEC uses information provided by the EPA in enforcing these reporting requirements. In particular, FIN 47 requires companies to include any future environmental liabilities, particularly those related to closing a facility, in their financial statements. According to American Bar Association estimates, FIN 47 reduced the 2005 after-tax earnings of Eli Lilly & Co. by $22 million, Commonwealth Edison by $42 million, Ford Motor Company by $251 million, and Citigroup by $49 million.[117]

The SEC also requires public companies to make certain disclosures concerning climate change. Specifically, companies are required to disclose risks they face as a result of existing or pending legislation or regulations that concern climate change. Furthermore, they must consider and disclose, when material, the impact on their business of treaties or "international accords" relating to climate change. They must also assess and disclose any indirect consequences of regulation or business trends, as well as the significant physical effects that climate change will have on their operations and results.[118]

Periodic Environmental Audits

An important step in comprehensively managing environmental liability and reducing penalties for noncompliance is to conduct periodic environmental audits. Such candid, internal self-assessments document and measure (1) compliance with occupational health and safety requirements; (2) compliance with federal, state, and local emissions limits and other requirements of a company's licensing, if any; (3) current practices for the generation, storage, and disposal of hazardous wastes; and (4) potential liability for past disposal of hazardous substances. Audits should also test the effectiveness of the management system and ensure that all instances of noncompliance are corrected.

Although such programs can generate valuable information for management, they may also be self-incriminating. A thorough audit that reveals contaminated properties, shoddy disposal practices, and lax compliance with regulations will certainly aid a company seeking to improve its environmental compliance. If the results of such an audit were publicly available, however, plaintiffs in the discovery

---

115. MAX H. BAZERMAN & MICHAEL D. WATKINS, PREDICTABLE SURPRISES (2004).

116. Stanley Sporkin, A Plan for Crisis Management and Avoidance, Address at the Nonprofit Risk Management Institute (Nov. 12, 1997).

117. Kaija Wilkinson, *SOX Offshoot: Poison the Land, Prepare to Pay*, BIRMINGHAM BUS. J., Feb. 17, 2006.

118. *See* SECURITIES AND EXCHANGE COMMISSION, COMMON GUIDANCE REGARDING DISCLOSURE RELATED TO CLIMATE CHANGE (2010).

IN BRIEF

Developing an Environmental Compliance Program

In evaluating or developing an environmental program, a manager should consider the following areas and ask the following questions:

1. *Achieving and maintaining compliance:*
   - What laws and regulations affect the company's facilities?
   - What procedures effectively balance compliance costs with liability?
   - How can those procedures be communicated to those responsible for their implementation?
   - How can employees be persuaded that they have a stake in the program's success?

2. *Obtaining timely notice of new requirements:*
   - What is being done to keep abreast of new requirements?
   - Will management receive notice early enough to make necessary changes cost-effectively?

3. *Influencing future requirements:*
   - What environmental laws and regulations are on the horizon?
   - How are they being tracked?
   - What is being done to influence their wording and enactment?

4. *Monitoring compliance accurately:*
   - What kind of monitoring is required?
   - Who will perform that monitoring?
   - How will the results be assessed?

5. *Timely and accurate reporting:*
   - When must a manager report information to regulators?
   - What procedures ensure that reportable incidents are brought to management's attention?
   - Does the company have databases for tracking chemical use and other technical information?

6. *Responding to emergencies:*
   - What systems are in place to respond to emergencies?
   - Are responsible employees trained to respond appropriately?

7. *Maintaining community relations:*
   - How strong is the company's relationship with the surrounding community?
   - What kind of programs are in place to maintain and expand that relationship?
   - How would management expect the community to respond to emergencies?

SOURCE: Based on Steven J. Koorse, *When Less Is More—Trouble*, BUS. L. TODAY, Sept.–Oct. 1997, at 24.

stage of litigation could use the audit results to further their case. For that reason, several states have enacted laws making such information privileged in order to encourage companies to produce and use it. At least one court has established a qualified privilege for certain self-critical analyses.[119]

The more stringent governmental financial reporting required by the Sarbanes–Oxley Act of 2002 has prompted auditors to take a closer look at the actual procedures used by in-house environmental managers. The requirement that the CEO and CFO of public companies certify the accuracy of their financial statements provides yet another reason for companies to perform in-house environmental evaluations with diligence and foresight.[120]

Many businesses are complying with standards established by nongovernmental certification programs.[121] Environmental certification programs verify that the activities of certified firms are environmentally appropriate. The International Organization for Standardization (ISO) environmental management program and the chemical

119. Reichhold Chems., Inc. v. Textron, Inc., 157 F.R.D. 522 (N.D. Fla. 1994).

120. Goodwin Procter, *LLP, Environmental Law Advisory*, June 2004.

121. Errol E. Meidinger, *Environmental Certification and U.S. Environmental Law: Closer Than You May Think*, 31 ENVTL. L. REP. 10162 (2001).

industry's Responsible Care program are two of the most widely used programs. Complying with these standards offers a number of benefits. The EPA has enacted a number of policies that promote certification, including the "Performance Track" program that gives special treatment to businesses meeting certification-like requirements. Among the prerequisites for qualifying for both ISO and Performance Track are (1) the adoption of an in-house environmental management system, (2) a commitment to improve environmental performance and open reporting to the public, and (3) a record of compliance with environmental requirements. Companies that meet the requirements enjoy streamlined monitoring, record keeping, and reporting under the Clean Air Act and Clean Water Act and greater flexibility in installing "best available control technology" under the Clean Air Act.[122] Furthermore, a number of major international banks have agreed to finance environmentally sensitive projects, such as power plants, dams, and pipelines, only if the projects also qualify under international environmental and social-impact standards.[123]

Preparing for Agency Inspections

Government agencies may undertake inspections with little or no advance notice. The company should be prepared in advance for such an event by having a protocol for handling the inspection. Individuals trained in the company protocol should accompany the inspector to ensure that the inspection is conducted properly and within the inspector's authority. The person who accompanies the inspector should prepare a report to management and make sure that any instances of noncompliance identified during the inspection are corrected.

Public and Community Relations

The manner in which a company handles an environmental problem can also have an important impact on its public image, its relationship with the community where it is located, and the economic damages it will suffer. A company can gain credibility and respect by handling an environmental accident in a proactive and fair manner.

For example, Eastman Kodak's response to an environmental problem increased its standing in the city of Rochester, New York, where it is headquartered. When the local newspaper reported that toxic chemicals from Kodak had seeped into the bedrock beneath the soil and were moving underground toward homes, panic erupted and the prices of the homes plummeted. The company instituted a series of homeowner relief programs to assure homeowners that they would lose no money as a result of the decline in value of their homes. Kodak offered discounted refinanced mortgages and home improvement grants to encourage people

to stay in their homes rather than sell them. For those who wanted to sell, the company agreed to pay the difference between the selling price and the home's market value before the environmental problem was discovered. If a house took longer than three months to sell, Kodak supplied interest-free bridge loans so that owners could move into their new homes before their old homes were sold. The president of the neighborhood association that represented 5,000 Rochester households commented, "The program was a perfect example of a company being proactive in their interactions with the community. Everyone I know [from the polluted area] felt they were given a good deal. I've not heard any objections."[124]

Long-Term Strategies and the Importance of Being Proactive

The company should develop strategies for reducing the costs of compliance and the risk of liability over the long term. These might include minimizing the amounts and kinds of pollutants produced, developing ways to recycle waste products, and investing in new technologies to render wastes nonhazardous. If hazardous wastes are produced, the company should have procedures for evaluating and selecting well-managed and well-constructed treatment and disposal facilities.

It is critical for managers to understand that "[e]nvironmental regulation is a constantly evolving part of the normal business landscape."[125] For example, California had a regulation that provided that if the EPA waived federal preemption or if Congress passed legislation permitting California to impose its stricter fuel economy standards, then automobile and truck manufacturers had only forty-five days to conform to the tougher California standards. When asked to insulate manufacturers from this California rule, the U.S. District Court for the Eastern District of California refused, reasoning:

> Plaintiffs' arguments suggest, without actually so stating, that at least some of the Plaintiff auto manufacturers made a conscious decision to proceed on the assumption that a waiver of federal preemption would never be granted by the EPA. If it turns out that the manufacturers that made that assumption are wrong, those Plaintiff auto manufacturers may well be at a significant disadvantage relative to auto manufacturers that are currently positioned more favorably with respect to compliance. But, so far as this court can discern, the choice to proceed as though California would never be granted waiver of federal preemption is fundamentally just a business decision that, like any other, may have negative consequences if wrongly made. It is not up to the courts to deflect the burden of such business decisions.[126]

122. *Id.*

123. Michael Phillips & Mitchell Pacelle, *Banks Accept Environmental Rules*, WALL ST. J., June 4, 2003, at A2.

124. *Uncivil Action*, 9 TREASURY & RISK MGMT. 25 (Jan.–Feb. 1999).

125. Cent. Valley Chrysler-Jeep, Inc. v. Goldstene, 563 F. Supp. 2d 1158 (E.D. Cal. 2008).

126. *Id.*

GLOBAL VIEW

Global Warming: Kyoto and Beyond

As the 2012 Kyoto Protocol deadline approached, world leaders were left to wonder whether the first global effort to combat greenhouse gas emissions had had any substantial positive impact on this key world issue. The Kyoto Protocol is an amendment to the United Nations Framework Convention on Climate Change, which was ratified by thirty-seven industrialized countries (excluding the United States) that pledged to reduce harmful greenhouse gas emissions to an average of 5% below the levels emitted in 1990. Each country was assigned a level of emissions of carbon dioxide gases that it was allowed to emit, but it was also allowed to trade or purchase emissions credits from other (often developing) countries in order to meet the assigned goals.[127]

Even though the United States produces nearly a quarter of the world's greenhouse gases each year, President George W. Bush opposed the ratification of Kyoto.[128] He cited the cost of reductions and the fact that Kyoto exempted developing countries, such as Indonesia and China—currently, the world's top carbon polluter[129]—from the emissions caps applicable to industrialized nations.[130] In 2006 alone, China built 114,000 megawatts of fossil-fuel-based generating capacity, almost all of it coal fired.[131] Critics of Kyoto argued that dramatic, and very costly, reductions in U.S. emissions would not reduce global levels of greenhouse gases if these other countries were not subject to the same limits.[132]

The European Union (EU) adopted a cap-and-trade system in 2005 as a way to meet the requirements set forth in Kyoto. A cap-and-trade system is a market-based system that caps the amount of carbon dioxide that companies, such as power generators, are allowed to emit.[133] If a company emits more than the amount allotted, it must then cut its emissions levels, buy allowances from more efficient companies, or buy extra allowances at government auctions. Even with cap and trade, emissions in the EU still rose about 1% a year from 2005 to 2008.[134] The failure of the system to reduce emissions was blamed on too many carbon permits handed out by the

national governments. When officials designed the system, they based the emissions caps on estimates provided by the EU member states. Each country received its data from the companies emitting the harmful gases, and by providing high estimates, the companies received more permits and therefore had no incentive to overhaul their factories or to install emissions-reducing technology.[135]

The United Nations administers a pollution-trading program whereby poorer countries can sell pollution credits to polluters in rich countries, which can use the credits to help satisfy Kyoto or EU limits. The program was designed to spur investment in pollution-control technology in poorer countries to enable them to cut emissions without curtailing economic growth.[136]

In theory, the United States would be able to cut emissions to 71% below their 2005 levels by 2050 if it adopted a nationwide cap-and-trade system.[137] For example, a bill proposed by U.S. Senators John Warner of Virginia and Joe Lieberman of Connecticut would have reduced U.S. emissions of greenhouse gases by 18% by 2020.[138] Critics asserted that a national cap-and-trade law would stifle the economy and result in the loss of up to 4 million U.S. jobs by 2030 as well as cost $660 billion per year to enforce.[139] President Obama endorsed the plan, arguing that it would create green jobs and protect the environment, but the cap-and-trade bill quickly died when it reached the Senate floor.[140]

In October 2011, California unveiled the first statewide cap-and-trade program to reduce greenhouse gases in the United States. Set to begin in 2013, the program established a continuously decreasing cap on greenhouse emissions from the state's 600 largest producers of carbon emissions. It also set up a trading system utilizing emissions allowances and offsets designed to reward the most efficient companies.[141]

In November 2011, the Australian Parliament approved an emissions trading plan that is second in size only to the EU's. Under the new regulations, a carbon tax will be imposed on the country's 500 largest emitters, and a market-based trading program will be implemented in 2015.[142]

CONTINUED

127. United Nations Framework Convention on Climate Change, *Fact Sheet: The Kyoto Protocol, available at* http://unfccc.int/files/press/backgrounders/application/pdf/fact_sheet_the_kyoto_protocol.pdf.

128. Bryan Walsh, *How to Win the War on Global Warming*, TIME, Apr. 16, 2008.

129. Roger Harrabin, *China "Now Top Carbon Polluter,"* BBC NEWS, Apr. 14, 2008.

130. Steven Lee Myers, *Bush to Skip U.N. Talks on Global Warming*, N.Y. TIMES, Sept. 24, 2007.

131. Keith Bradsher, *China's Green Energy Gap*, N.Y. TIMES, Oct. 24, 2007.

132. Walsh, *supra* note 128.

133. Leila Abboud & Stephen Power, *U.S. Aims to Skirt Flaws in Europe's Carbon Limits; Cap-and-Trade Bill to Stress Auctions, Balance for Permits*, WALL ST. J., May 30, 2008, at A4.

134. *Id.*

135. *Id.*

136. Charles Forelle, *French Firm Cashes in Under U.N. Warming Program*, WALL ST. J., July 23, 2008.

137. Steve Mufson, *Is This Green Enough? We Can Clean Up Our Act, but It'll Cost Us*, WASH. POST, Apr. 20, 2008, at B1.

138. H. Josef Hebert, *Senate Votes to Begin Global Warming Debate*, ASSOC. PRESS, June 2, 2008.

139. Walsh, *supra* note 128.

140. Eric Pooley, *Why the Climate Bill Failed*, TIME, June 9, 2008.

141. Editorial, *California's Persistence*, N.Y. TIMES, Oct. 24, 2011, at A22.

142. Matt Siegel, *Australian Senate Approves Emissions Trading Plan*, N.Y. TIMES, Nov. 7, 2011.

In high-profile meetings in Copenhagen in 2009 and Cancún in 2010, leaders from across to world failed to extend legally binding commitments under the Kyoto framework. Many developed nations were unwilling to make significant binding commitments without obligatory targets for emerging nations. As a result, countries only made nonbinding reduction "pledges," which might result in no reductions at all. The Cancún Agreement did establish a Green Climate Fund, under which rich countries pledged $100 billion to support emissions reduction and climate change adaptation programs in poor countries.

A December 2011 meeting in Durban, South Africa, produced similarly modest results. After extended negotiations, the representatives from 200 countries (including the United States, the EU members, China, and India) were unable to come to a legally binding agreement. They did, however, undertake to reach "an agreed outcome with legal force" by 2015 that would commit all countries, both developed and developing (including Brazil, China, and India), to start reducing carbon emissions by 2020 at the earliest. Critics questioned whether major developing countries would actually follow through on even this vague promise, however, given their historic opposition to any binding agreements.[143] The Durban participants also reiterated their commitment to the Green Climate Fund and clarified that the funds may be used for private as well as public initiatives.

The so-called Durban platform anticipates that the Kyoto Protocol will be extended to 2017 or 2020 (with the date to be set in future sessions), but Canada announced its withdrawal from the Kyoto Protocol the next day. Noting that Kyoto did not bind the world's two largest polluters (the United States and China) and that Canada's failure to meet its Kyoto targets could cost the nation $14 billion (in Canadian dollars) for carbon emission permits to offset its increased emissions, the Canadian environmental minister declared: "It's now clear that Kyoto is not the path forward to a global solution to climate change. If anything, it's an impediment."[144] While Russia supported Canada's decision, Japan called it "disappointing" and China condemned it as "preposterous."[145]

143. *See* John M. Broder, *Climate Talks in Durban Yield Limited Agreement*, N.Y. TIMES, Dec. 12, 2011, at A9.

144. *Canada Pulls Out of Kyoto Protocol*, GUARDIAN.CO.UK, Dec. 12, 2011.

145. Damian Carrington & Adam Vaughan, *Canada Condemned at Home and Abroad for Pulling Out of Kyoto Treaty*, GUARDIAN.CO.UK, Dec. 13, 2011.

Mike Price/Shutterstock

THE RESPONSIBLE MANAGER

MANAGING ENVIRONMENTAL RISKS

Several sources of potential environmental liability present risks to the parties in business transactions. In evaluating a company for purposes of acquisition, investment, or financing, a manager must consider that the company's earnings may be affected by the costs of compliance with environmental laws. The value of its equipment assets may be affected by regulatory limitations that make the equipment obsolete. Its ability to expand in existing locations may be impaired as a result of limitations on new sources of air emissions or the lack of nearby waste treatment or disposal facilities. A company's cash flow may be affected by additional capital investments or by increased operating costs necessitated by environmental regulations. Failure to comply with existing regulations may lead to the imposition of substantial penalties, also affecting cash flow. Small companies or companies that are highly leveraged may not be able to meet these additional demands for cash.

Similarly, a small company may not be able to survive the imposition of liability for response costs under CERCLA or similar state laws. Potential liabilities may not be properly reflected in the company's financial statements. Finally, a company's operations or the condition of its properties may present risks of injury to other persons and their property, giving rise to possible tort claims.

The most important element in managing the risk of these potential liabilities is *due diligence*, that is, a systematic and ongoing process for determining whether property contains or emits hazardous substances and whether the company is in compliance with environmental laws. The object of environmental due diligence investigations is to identify and characterize the risks associated with the properties and operations involved in the business transaction. Such investigations have become highly sophisticated undertakings, often requiring the use of technical consultants and legal counsel with special expertise. Although much of the effort focuses on the review of company documents and available public records, it may also involve physical inspections of the properties, including soil and groundwater sampling and analysis. Care should be taken to avoid negligent soil investigations, which can create liability for disposal of hazardous waste. Environmental due diligence may represent a significant cost of the transaction and may take much longer to complete than traditional due diligence efforts.

The scope of the due diligence effort will depend on the nature of the assets and the structure of the transaction. For example, if the transaction is a simple purchase and sale of real estate, then the due diligence can be limited

CONTINUED

to the property to be acquired and its surroundings. If the transaction involves the acquisition of a business with a long history of operations in many locations, however, then the due diligence investigation must cover not only the current operating locations but also prior operating locations and the sites used for off-site disposal of wastes. This is particularly true when a company is acquired by merger because the surviving company takes over all of the liabilities of the disappearing company.

Allocation of the risk of liability under CERCLA and other environmental laws has become a significant issue in the negotiation of business transactions. The parties can, by contract, allocate the identified risks of environmental liability by undertaking specified obligations, assuming and retaining contingent liabilities, adjusting the purchase price, making representations and warranties, giving indemnities, and the like. But care must be exercised when the identified risks are not yet quantifiable. For example, if liability for response costs is accepted in return for a reduction in the purchase price, it should be borne in mind that response costs often exceed by a wide margin the initial estimate provided by a consultant or government agency.

It is also important to remember that contractual arrangements to shift environmental liability are not binding on federal or state governments. Thus, even if the seller of a piece of property agrees to indemnify the purchaser for any environmental claims arising out of the seller's activities, the EPA can still recover response costs from the present owner. The present owner could sue the seller for indemnification and contribution, but the present owner will bear the entire cleanup cost if the previous owner is insolvent or has insufficient assets.

Under CERCLA, secured lenders, and in some cases equity investors, may be deemed liable for response costs as present operators if they participate in the day-to-day management of the borrower's facilities. If a lender takes title at foreclosure, it may also be deemed liable for response costs as a present owner unless it attempts to dispose of the property reasonably quickly. Thus, the risk of hazardous substance releases on the subject property should be carefully evaluated in connection with the loan application. The operations of the borrower should also be carefully reviewed to evaluate the risks they present during the life of the loan. If a release of hazardous substances occurs on the property, its value as collateral is impaired. If the borrower defaults, the lender may not be able to recover the outstanding amount of the debt.

In trying to protect against diminishment of the value of collateral, a lender must be careful not to participate in management, however. Overly strict loan covenants that involve the lender in making operational decisions (such as approval of major capital expenditures) may create operator liability for the lender.

In addition, some states have adopted *superlien* provisions, which secure recovery of response costs incurred by state agencies. Where a superlien exists, it may take priority over existing security interests.

When an owner leases property, it must take care to evaluate the environmental risks of the tenant's operations. Use of the property should be carefully limited to prevent any unauthorized activities. If the tenant's activities present significant risks, financial assurances in the form of parent corporation guarantees, letters of credit, or performance bonds might be obtained to ensure that any damage caused by the tenant will be remedied. Tenants also should be cautious in taking possession of property formerly occupied by others. Many tenants perform *baseline assessments* to establish the environmental condition of the property at both the commencement and the termination of the lease. These assessments may provide some protection from liability for conditions caused by prior or succeeding tenants.

Although the use of laws, regulations, and standards, referred to as "command and control" policy, is still an important tool for ensuring that companies' operations do not pollute the environment, many corporations have gone beyond simply complying with the laws.[146]

Responsible corporations have broadened their focus to include the materials they use in production, as well as the pollutants they generate. After scrutinizing both their inputs and their outputs, companies are implementing principles of "eco-efficiency" in their operations by using less energy, fewer new materials, and more reused and recycled materials. Indeed, some companies are working not just to reduce waste but to eliminate it altogether. This process involves looking at whole systems, rather than the individual parts, to create designs that take advantage of feedback loops within the company's operations. Companies are also working with other firms for both economic and environmental benefit. For example, *industrial ecology* is an approach that advocates a systems approach to eco-efficiency and applies it to groups of corporations working together.

Michael E. Porter and Claas van der Linde maintain that firms can not only remain competitive but even gain competitive advantage through *innovation offsets*, technological advantages gained by companies that meet the challenge of environmental regulations and discover lower costs and better-quality products as a result.[147] Some corporations have implemented the concept of *strategic environmental management*, which advocates placing environmental

CONTINUED

146. *See* Carl Frankel, In Earth's Company: Business, Environment, and the Challenge of Sustainability (1998).

147. Michael E. Porter & Claas van der Linde, *Green and Competitive: Ending the Stalemate*, in Michael E. Porter, On Competition 351–75 (1980).

management on the profit side of the corporation rather than the cost side. This represents a profound shift in how companies view their relationship with the environment.

Finally, certain corporations have successfully exploited the opportunities created by environmental problems.[148] Auto companies have introduced hybrid cars and SUVs with reduced emissions and increased gas mileage and are racing to develop vehicles powered by fuel cells. Energy companies are also investing in developing alternative sources of energy.

Forest Reinhardt has identified five approaches that companies can use to incorporate environmental issues into their business model: (1) differentiate their products by making them environmentally friendly and, as a result, command high prices; (2) "manage" competitors by imposing a set of private regulations or helping government write rules; (3) cut costs by implementing environmental practices; (4) manage risk and reduce lawsuits and accidents; and (5) make systemic changes concerning environmental issues that will redefine competition in their markets.[149]

148. *See* C. Nehrt, *Maintainability of First Mover Advantages When Environmental Regulations Differ Between Countries*, 23 ACAD. MGMT. REV. 77 (1998); J. Alberto Aragon-Correa & Sanjay Sharma, *A Contingent Resource-Based View of Proactive Corporate Environmental Strategy*, 28 ACAD. MGMT. REV. 71 (2003).

149. FOREST REINHARDT, DOWN TO EARTH: APPLYING BUSINESS PRINCIPLES TO ENVIRONMENTAL MANAGEMENT (2000).

A MANAGER'S DILEMMA

Putting It into Practice

Exporting Environmental Compliance

American Widgets is a manufacturing company that has gained a large share of the international widget market, largely because of its high quality and competitive pricing. The disposal of the company's wastes has become increasingly expensive, however. A new ban on land disposal will require the company to incinerate one of its largest waste streams. Plants of competitors located in Southeast Asia and South America are subject to increasing environmental regulation modeled after the laws in the United States, but they are not subject to a land-disposal ban and will have a significant competitive advantage over plants located in the United States. Jimmy Tsai, an American Widgets manager, is considering the possibility of locating a new plant in Southeast Asia. What factors should he take into account? What alternatives are there besides relocation?

INSIDE STORY

BP Oil Spill

On April 20, 2010, an explosion aboard the *Deepwater Horizon*, an oil rig drilling one mile below the Gulf of Mexico for BP, led to the largest accidental oil spill in history. For eighty-six days, the well gushed a total of 185 million gallons of oil into the Gulf.[150] As of July 2011, the oil had contaminated more than 1,000 miles of coastline in Alabama, Florida, Louisiana, and Mississippi,[151] potentially affecting more than 8,000 species of animals.[152]

At the outset, the response effort was plagued by a lack of preparation, organization, and sense of urgency by federal, state, and local governments, as well as BP. The federal government repeatedly underestimated the extent of the spill, and BP was unwilling to support any estimation efforts. Initially, BP claimed that estimating oil flow was very difficult and resisted requests by scientists to use sophisticated instruments to get a more accurate estimate.[153] Interior Secretary Ken Salazar, frustrated by BP's response, at one point threatened to push the company out of the effort entirely.

CONTINUED

150. *Gulf of Mexico Oil Spill* (2010), N.Y. TIMES, Oct. 17, 2011.

151. Jim Polson, *BP Oil Still Ashore One Year After End of Gulf Spill*, BLOOMBERG.COM, July 15, 2011.

152. David Biello, *The BP Spill's Growing Toll on the Sea Life of the Gulf*, YALE ENV'T, June 9, 2010, at 360.

153. Justin Gillis, *Giant Plumes of Oil Forming Under the Gulf*, N.Y. TIMES, May 16, 2010, at A1.

Alabama, Louisiana, and Mississippi incurred significant economic damage to their fishing and tourism industries after the National Oceanic and Atmospheric Administration (NOAA) closed commercial and recreational fishing in approximately 36% of federal waters in the Gulf of Mexico.[154] The affected waters remained closed until November 15, 2010. Estimates of the damage sustained by Louisiana's fishing industry alone reached $2.5 billion. Tourism is one of the top drivers of the Gulf economy, and the U.S. Travel Association estimated that the spill could cost coastal economies $23 billion.[155] In an attempt to alleviate the impact, BP gave $25 million to the state of Florida to promote the uncontaminated portions of its beaches and $78 million to the state of Louisiana to help tourism and test and advertise seafood.[156] Other coastal states affected by the spill received similar awards.

A joint report released in September 2011 by the Interior Department and the Coast Guard concluded that BP, which was running behind schedule and over budget in completing drilling of the well, took numerous shortcuts that contributed to the spill.[157] The report concluded that BP, as well as Transocean, the well's owner, and Halliburton, which was in charge of cementing operations on the well, all ultimately contributed to the spill. According to the report, the companies failed to operate the drilling rig in a safe and responsible manner, recklessly endangered their workers, did not follow proper well control procedures, and failed to properly maintain safety equipment, including the blowout preventer. A presidential panel concluded that the spill was preventable and that the companies involved took a series of hazardous, time-saving steps without sufficient consideration of the risks.[158]

BP CEO Tony Hayward ultimately lost his job after displaying a seemingly insensitive attitude toward the disaster. At one point he remarked, "I'd like my life back."[159] While testifying before the House Energy and Commerce Committee, he attempted to avoid any responsibility by insisting that he "wasn't involved" with the decisions leading up to the explosion and thus could not pass judgment on them.[160] As criticism of his operational performance intensified, Hayward stepped down as the head of BP's response effort in June 2010. His position was filled by American BP executive Bob Dudley, in an effort to "isolate the 'toxic' side of the company and dilute some of the anti-British feeling aimed at [Hayward]," according to the company.[161] Dudley replaced Hayward as CEO of BP after Hayward resigned in July 2010.

The Oil Pollution Act of 1990 limited BP's liability for non-cleanup costs to $75 million, but after meeting with President Obama soon after the explosion, BP agreed to set up a $20 billion compensation fund for victims of the oil spill and to pay all cleanup and remediation costs regardless of the liability cap.[162] BP assured the public that the fund would be used for natural resource damage, individual compensation, and reimbursement of state and local response costs, but would not cover fines and penalties.[163] Since the explosion, about 475,000 claims have been filed by individuals and businesses seeking emergency damage awards from the fund. The emergency program, which ended in November 2010, paid out a total of $2.2 billion; the next phase of payouts focused on lump-sum final settlements for those affected by the spill.[164] As of October 2011, BP had paid roughly $7 billion out of the fund.[165] Altogether, the cost of the spill to BP was estimated at $40 billion.[166]

In October 2011, a part owner of the well, Anadarko Petroleum, agreed to pay $4 billion to settle claims relating to the oil spill. Under the terms of the settlement, Anadarko, which had a 25% stake in the well, dropped its allegations of gross negligence against BP, received indemnification against certain claims, and transferred its stake in the well back to BP.[167] Together with two previous settlements, the $4 billion from Anadarko allowed BP to end its payments into its $20 billion compensation fund by early 2012, a year ahead of schedule.[168] BP applauded the settlement, saying it should be an example for the contractors Transocean and Halliburton, which have consistently denied any liability in the spill. The extent of these companies' liability, as well as BP's, will ultimately be determined by a federal court in New Orleans hearing a civil lawsuit filed by the Department of Justice against BP and eight other companies. The amount of damages sought by the suit was not specified, but analysts predicted that it could reach into the tens of billions of dollars.[169]

---

154. *BP Oil Spill: NOAA Modifies Commercial and Recreational Fishing Closure in the Oil-Affected Portions of the Gulf of Mexico*, Southeast Fishery Bull., June 21, 2010.

155. U.S. Travel Association, *Potential Impact of the Gulf Oil Spill on Tourism* (July 21, 2010).

156. Brian Skoloff & Jane Wardell, *BP's Oil Spill Costs Grow, Gulf Residents React*, Assoc. Press, Nov. 2, 2010.

157. John M. Broder, *U.S. Acts to Fine BP and Top Contractors for Gulf Oil Spill*, N.Y. Times, Oct. 13, 2011, at A18.

158. *Gulf of Mexico Oil Spill (2010)*, *supra* note 150

159. Jad Mouawad & Clifford Krauss, *Another Torrent BP Works to Stem: Its C.E.O.*, N.Y. Times, June 4, 2010, at A1.

160. Sam Gustin, *BP CEO Tony Hayward Steps Down from Gulf Oil Spill Oversight*, Daily Fin., June 18, 2010.

161. Terry Macalister, *BP Hives Off "Toxic" Gulf Spill Operation to Dilute Anti-British Feeling in US*, Guardian, June 4, 2010.

162. Erica Werner, *Federal Law May Limit BP Liability in Oil Spill*, Assoc. Press, May 3, 2010.

163. Noah Brenner, *Hayward Says Spill "Never Should Have Happened,"* Upstream, June 17, 2010.

164. *Gulf of Mexico Oil Spill (2010)*, *supra* note 150.

165. Julia Werdigier, *Ending Dispute, Well Partner Settles with BP for $4 Billion*, N.Y. Times, Oct. 18, 2011, at B7.

166. Skoloff & Wardell, *supra* note 156.

167. *Id.*

168. Sylvia Pfeifer, *Anadarko Relief Puts Focus on Dudley's Review*, Fin. Times, Oct. 18, 2011.

169. *Gulf of Mexico Oil Spill (2010)*, *supra* note 150.

KEY WORDS AND PHRASES

baseline assessments   509

brownfields   494

cap-and-trade system   483

carbon footprint   479

continuity of enterprise approach   493

contribution   492

due diligence   508

environmental justice   498

environmental law   479

Environmental Protection Agency
(EPA)   481

Hazardous Substance Superfund   491

industrial ecology   509

innocent landowner defense   494

mere continuation (identity) test   493

national ambient air quality standards
(NAAQS)   482

national effluent limitations   488

National Pollutant Discharge Elimination
System (NPDES)   488

natural resources laws   481

navigable waters   487

potentially responsible parties
(PRPs)   491

publicly owned sewage treatment works
(POTWs)   488

strategic environmental
management   509

substantial continuity test   493

successor liability   492

superlien   509

third-party defense   494

QUESTIONS AND CASE PROBLEMS

1. Northeastern Pharmaceutical and Chemical Company (NEPACCO) had a manufacturing plant in Verona, Missouri, that produced various hazardous and toxic by-products. The company pumped the byproducts into a holding tank, which a waste hauler periodically emptied. Michaels founded the company, was a major shareholder, and served as its president. In 1971, a waste hauler named Mills approached Ray, a chemical-plant manager employed by NEPACCO, and proposed disposing of some of the firm's wastes at a nearby farm. Ray visited the farm and, with the approval of Lee, the vice president and a shareholder of NEPACCO, arranged for disposal of wastes at the farm.

   Approximately eighty-five 55-gallon drums were dumped into a large trench on the farm. In 1976, NEPACCO was liquidated, and the assets remaining after payment to creditors were distributed to its shareholders. Three years later the EPA investigated the area and discovered dozens of badly deteriorated drums containing hazardous waste buried at the farm. The EPA took remedial action and then sought to recover its costs under RCRA and other statutes. From whom and on what basis can the government recover its costs? [*United States v. Northeastern Pharmaceutical & Chemical Co.*, 810 F.2d 726 (8th Cir. 1986).]

2. George Lu was named the executive director of the Cornell University Foundation, a nonprofit association organized to support the university. As part of its efforts, the foundation has begun a program to preserve open-space land and ecologically sensitive environments near the university's campus in upstate New York. The foundation plans to buy or receive gifts of land, especially from alumni, and then sell the land to public entities for permanent preservation. The difference between the purchase price and the sale price will be used to finance the association's efforts and to support Cornell generally. One of Lu's first tasks is to develop a protocol and prepare model agreements for making acquisitions.

   a. As a nonprofit, educational organization, does the association have potential liability under the environmental laws?

   b. What procedures should Lu establish to protect the association from potential environmental law liabilities in connection with its acquisitions?

   c. What kinds of contractual arrangements should be considered to protect the association from environmental law liabilities? [*See, e.g., United States v. Alcan Aluminum Corp.*, 34 E.R.C. 1744 (N.D.N.Y. 1991).]

3. In 1960, Brown & Bryant, Inc. (B&B) began operating an agricultural chemical distributions business, purchasing pesticides and other chemical products from suppliers, including Shell Oil Company. When a certain chemical bought from Shell would arrive at B&B's warehouse in tanker trucks, it was transferred from the trucks to a bulk storage tank located on B&B's primary parcel. From there, the chemical was transferred to other trucks, tanks, and rigs. During each of these transfers, leaks and spills could—and often did—occur. Aware that spills of the chemical were occurring frequently among its distributors, in the late 1970s Shell took several steps to encourage the safe handling of its products. Despite these improvements, B&B remained a "sloppy operator." In 1983, a state agency began investigating B&B's violation of hazardous waste laws, and the EPA soon followed suit. To recoup cleanup costs, the EPA filed suit against several parties, including Shell. The EPA argued that Shell was an "arranger" subject to liability under CERCLA because it had arranged for the disposal of hazardous substances through its sale and delivery, even though it did not "intend" to dispose of a hazardous substance. Does the EPA have a valid argument? Is mere knowledge that spills and leaks occurred sufficient grounds for concluding that Shell "arranged for" the disposal of the chemical under CERCLA? [*Burlington Northern & Sante Fe Railway Co. v. United States*, 129 S. Ct. 1870 (2009).]

4. The City of Florence, a municipal corporation organized under the laws of Alabama, purchased property for the purpose of encouraging industrial development within the county where the city is located. Florence leased the property to Stylon, a corporation that planned to construct and operate a ceramic tile manufacturing factory on the property. Florence issued bonds to finance the purchase of the property and mortgaged the property to First National Bank of Florence, pledging that Stylon's rent payments for the property would be used to secure the repayment on the bonds held by the bank.

Stylon operated a tile manufacturing facility on the property for approximately twenty years until it went bankrupt. During that time, it discharged hazardous substances, which contaminated the property. After Stylon went bankrupt, Monarch Tile, Inc. leased the property for fifteen years from the City of Florence, with the city retaining title. Subsequently, Monarch purchased the property from the city.

After Monarch discovered the contamination, it notified the EPA and was directed to remediate pursuant to CERCLA. Monarch brought suit against the City of Florence for contribution under CERCLA. The City of Florence argued that it was not liable because it held ownership of the property primarily to protect its security interest. How should the court rule? Should the National Bank of Florence or the former Stylon shareholders be forced to contribute to the cost of remediation? [*Monarch Tile Inc. v. City of Florence*, 212 F.3d 1219 (11th Cir. 2000).]

5. Gregg Entrepreneur is organizing a small company to manufacture a new biotechnology product. Entrepreneur will be a principal shareholder and president of the company. What measures should Entrepreneur take to ensure that his company operates in compliance with environmental laws?

Despite all the measures Entrepreneur has taken to ensure environmental law compliance, his vice president of operations reports that the production manager has been disposing of wastes into the sewer in violation of national pretreatment standards and that she has been submitting false reports to the publicly owned sewage treatment works (POTWs) to cover up the violations. All of the reports have been signed by the vice president of operations, who had no knowledge that they contained false statements. What steps should Entrepreneur take? Should he report the violations to the POTWs even if doing so could result in personal civil or criminal liability? What about the vice president? The production manager? What is Entrepreneur's ethical responsibility? [*See, e.g., United States v. Alley*, 755 F. Supp. 771 (N.D. Ill. 1990).]

6. A Colorado silver mine was owned by a company that went bankrupt. The three main creditors of the bankrupt firm formed the Raytheon Mine Company (RMI) as part of the plan of reorganization. RMI ran and operated the mine and gave each creditor a percentage of its stock commensurate with the original bankrupt company. Biller Company was one such minor creditor and never owned more than 20% of RMI. Years after the money owed Biller Company was repaid and Biller had sold its interest in the mine, the government assessed serious environmental cleanup costs under CERCLA. Biller's former partners in RMI brought a claim for contribution against Biller as a successor in interest to the tainted land to recover part of the cleanup costs. Will their claim be successful? [*Raytheon Construction Inc. v. Asarco Inc.*, 368 F.3d 1214 (10th Cir. 2003).]

7. After paying to clean the portion of the Mohawk River around its oil refinery and storage operation, Niagara Mohawk Power Corporation (NMPC) filed claims for contribution against several other companies that had maintained facilities in the area. One of the companies, Mohawk Valley Oil (MVO), had used a parcel to store oil as part of its own petroleum business. On one side of that parcel was the river and on the opposite side was land used by a tar manufacturing company, Tar Asphalt Services (TAS). Among other activities, TAS washed tar from its trucks with kerosene. TAS allowed the contaminated runoff to flow across MVO's property into the river. MVO became aware of this practice after it purchased the land and took steps to prevent the runoff from reaching its property as it developed the location. NMPC argued that although MVO had prevented additional kerosene-tainted water from flowing across its property, it had done nothing to remediate the prior disposals and therefore remained liable under CERCLA. Does failing to prevent contaminated water from crossing one's property qualify as a "disposal" of hazardous waste under CERCLA? What liability would MVO have faced if it had failed to take steps to prevent the runoff from TAS's activities once it became aware of it? [*Niagara Mohawk Power Corp. v. Jones Chemical Inc.*, 315 F.3d 171 (2d Cir. 2003).]

8. Geronimo Villegas, co-owner and vice president of Plaza Health Laboratories, Inc., a blood-testing laboratory in New York, was convicted of knowingly discharging pollutants into the Hudson River in violation of the Clean Water Act. On at least two occasions, Villegas loaded containers of numerous vials of human blood (some infected with the hepatitis-B virus) generated from his business into his personal car and drove to his residence in New Jersey. Once at his condominium complex, Villegas removed the containers from his car and carried them to the edge of the Hudson River. On one occasion, he carried two containers of the vials to the bulkhead that separated his condominium complex from the river; at low tide, he placed the containers in a crevice in the bulkhead that was below the high-water line. One day, a group of eighth graders on a field trip discovered numerous glass vials containing human blood along the shore. All of the vials were traced back to Plaza Health Laboratories. Villegas appealed his conviction, arguing that his crime cannot be prosecuted under the Clean Water Act because his conduct failed to meet the elements necessary to bring a claim under the Act. What result? [*United States v. Plaza Health Laboratories, Inc.*, 3 F.3d 643 (2d Cir. 1993).]

CHAPTER 16

ANTITRUST

INTRODUCTION

ANTITRUST VIOLATORS DO THE TIME AND PAY THE FINE

The first U.S. antitrust law, the Sherman Act, was passed by Congress in 1890 as fear of corporate power grew during the Progressive Era. The Sherman Act was part of a populist movement to combat the rise of trusts in such basic industries as oil and steel. The *trusts* were powerful associations of companies with the intention and power to create a monopoly or otherwise interfere with the free course of trade. "You must heed [the voters'] appeal or be ready for the socialist, the communist, and the nihilist," Senator John Sherman declared during the debate over his bill. The Sherman Act's general prohibitions have evolved over the past hundred years through judicial decisions, which reflect changing political sentiment and economic theory.

The basic principle of the *antitrust laws* is that the economy functions best when firms are free to compete vigorously with one another. In a competitive economy, the consumer enjoys better goods at lower prices, or, as economists say, consumer welfare is maximized. If, however, competition is decreased or eliminated by firms seeking jointly or independently to wield monopoly power, consumers suffer and the performance of the economy declines.

Antitrust statutes contain very general prohibitions on business conduct. These general prohibitions often have little content until courts apply them to the particular facts of a case. Thus, bright lines that clearly separate lawful from unlawful conduct are rare in this field. A business practice that harms competition in one market setting might not harm competition in another. The courts and agencies that enforce the antitrust laws must distinguish between the pernicious and the benign.

One of the few bright lines is the ban on horizontal price-fixing. In one of the world's largest price-fixing scams, representatives of Roche Holding A.G., BASF A.G., and Rhone-Poulenc SA met regularly in the Black Forest to fix prices for vitamins and vitamin additives. In 1999, Roche and BASF paid more than $725 million in U.S. criminal fines. Rhone-Poulenc escaped U.S. criminal charges because it was the first member of the *cartel* to cooperate with the U.S. Justice Department. The European Union (EU) levied fines of 855.2 million euros against all three firms plus several others involved in the scheme. Four high-ranking officials at Roche and BASF were sent to prison and fined $650,000.[1]

As trade barriers continue to be broken down and the global market becomes more integrated, the antitrust laws of the major commercial countries will need to be better harmonized or at least made more transparent to provide greater predictability as to which country's law applies. The EU's competition law is quickly replacing U.S. antitrust law as the model for other countries as they develop their own competition laws.

CHAPTER OVERVIEW

This chapter offers a general overview of the federal antitrust laws. It begins with a discussion of sections 1 and 2 of the Sherman Act and then addresses the Clayton Act provisions relating to mergers and combinations. The chapter outlines the Robinson–Patman Act's prohibitions on price discrimination and briefly discusses the Federal Trade Commission Act. It concludes with a discussion of the extraterritorial application of the U.S. antitrust laws, the EU competition laws, and the extraterritorial effect of the EU laws.

---

1. Harry First, *Antitrust at the Millennium (Part II): The Vitamins Cases and the Coming of International Competition Law*, 68 ANTITRUST L.J. 711 (2001).

JURISDICTIONAL REACH: INTERSTATE OR FOREIGN TRADE AND COMMERCE

The Sherman Act applies only to "trade or commerce" among states or with foreign nations. The phrase "commerce among the several States" extends the reach of the Act as far as constitutionally allowed under the Commerce Clause.[2] The resulting scope of antitrust jurisdiction therefore encompasses more than restraints on trade that are motivated by a desire to limit interstate commerce or that have their sole impact on interstate commerce. The commerce requirement is satisfied when the defendant's conduct (1) directly interferes with the flow of goods in the stream of commerce or (2) has a substantial effect on interstate commerce.

AGREEMENTS IN RESTRAINT OF TRADE: SECTION 1 OF THE SHERMAN ACT

Section 1 of the Sherman Act provides that "[e]very contract, combination in the form of trust or otherwise, or conspiracy, in restraint of trade or commerce among the several States, or with foreign nations, is declared to be illegal."[3] On its face, section 1 appears to prohibit all concerted activity that restrains trade. Yet almost every business transaction restrains trade to a certain extent. A contract, for example, restrains the parties from doing things that would constitute a breach, such as selling goods to someone else. Read literally, section 1 would outlaw every type of business transaction involving more than one party. In order to avoid an unworkable construction of the Sherman Act, the courts have construed section 1 to prohibit only those restraints of trade that *unreasonably* restrict competition.

For liability to attach under section 1, a plaintiff must demonstrate that (1) there is a contract, combination, or conspiracy among separate entities; (2) it unreasonably restrains trade; (3) it affects interstate or foreign commerce; and (4) it causes an antitrust injury (the concept of antitrust injury is addressed later in this chapter).

What Constitutes a Contract, Combination, or Conspiracy?

Section 1 does not prohibit unilateral activity in restraint of trade. Acting by itself, an individual or firm may take any action, no matter how anticompetitive, and not violate section 1. Similarly, a parent corporation and its wholly owned subsidiary cannot "agree" within the concerted-action requirement of section 1.[4] (In contrast, section 2 of the Sherman Act, discussed later in this chapter, does prohibit some forms of unilateral conduct.)

A joint venture comprising two competitors may also be treated as a single entity. For example, Texaco and Shell Oil formed a joint venture called Equilon to consolidate their operations in the western United States. They pooled their resources and shared the risks of and profits from Equilon's activities but marketed their gasoline under two brands rather than one. Because Texaco and Shell participated in the market jointly through their investments in Equilon, the Supreme Court ruled that the pricing decision made by Equilon did not constitute illegal price-fixing between competitors.[5]

Because conspiracies are inherently secretive, requiring direct proof of a conspiracy would likely permit many companies engaging in unlawful activities to escape liability. On the other hand, because unilateral behavior is not a violation, courts must be careful not to unduly relax the requirement that conspiracy be proved.

In general, courts are more willing to base liability solely on *circumstantial*, or indirect, *evidence* in cases involving horizontal arrangements than they are when vertical restraints are involved. *Horizontal agreements* are those between firms that compete directly with each other at the same level of production or distribution, such as retailers selling the same range of products. *Vertical agreements* are those between firms at different levels of production or distribution, such as an automaker and its dealers or a clothing retailer and its supplier.

Horizontal restrictions are generally considered more inherently anticompetitive than vertical restraints because they reduce *interbrand competition*, that is, competition between companies producing the same type of product or service. As a result, horizontal restraints are more likely to result in higher prices or lower quality for a class of goods or services. In contrast, vertical restraints reduce *intrabrand competition*, that is, competition among firms producing or distributing the same brand; the restraints may or may not reduce interbrand competition. Courts look more favorably on reductions in intrabrand competition when there is vigorous interbrand competition that can prevent the reduction in intrabrand competition from harming consumers.

Proving a Horizontal Conspiracy

Sometimes, there is direct evidence that competitors expressly agreed to fix prices or divide markets. The courts will not require evidence of an explicit agreement to violate the law, however. As the U.S. Court of Appeals for the Ninth Circuit recognized, a "knowing wink can mean

---

2. Summit Health, Ltd. v. Pinhas, 500 U.S. 322, 329 n.10 (1991).
3. 15 U.S.C. § 1.
4. Copperweld Corp. v. Independence Tube Corp., 467 U.S. 752 (1984).
5. Texaco, Inc. v. Dagher, 547 U.S. 1 (2006).

more than words."[6] But merely showing that ostensibly independent firms consistently set prices at the same levels and change prices at the same time (*conscious parallelism*) is insufficient to prove a horizontal conspiracy to fix prices. Particularly when a homogeneous product or service is involved, common pricing can result either from illegal price-fixing or from vigorous competition.

Accordingly, the courts will not infer an agreement or conspiracy from parallel behavior unless the plaintiff shows additional facts or "*plus factors*." Thus, a complaint that alleges only parallelism without any plus factors should be dismissed.[7] In contrast, parallel behavior that

would appear to be contrary to the economic interests of the defendants, were they acting independently, can support an inference of conspiracy.[8] Even in such a case, a court will not infer a conspiracy if the defendants can produce reasonable business explanations for the behavior. Other circumstantial evidence of an agreement, such as a meeting between two defendants, may be a plus factor. Increasing prices and persistent profits despite a decline in demand for the good or service may also be plus factors.

In the following case, the court considered whether tobacco companies had conspired to fix prices.

6. Esco Corp. v. United States, 340 F.2d 1000, 1007 (9th Cir. 1965).

7. Bell Atl. Corp. v. Twombly, 550 U.S. 544 (2007).

8. Theatre Enters., Inc. v. Paramount Film Distrib. Corp., 346 U.S. 537 (1954).

| A CASE IN POINT | *In the Language of the Court* | Case 16.1 |

Williamson Oil Co. v. Philip Morris USA

United States Court of Appeals for the Eleventh Circuit
346 F.3d 1287 (11th Cir. 2003).

FACTS Between 1993 and 2000, Philip Morris (PM), R.J. Reynolds (RJR), Brown & Williamson (B&W), and Lorillard (collectively, the manufacturers) produced more than 97% of the cigarettes sold in the United States. During the early 1990s, as the price gap widened between premium brands, such as Marlboro and Camel, and discount brands, such as Basic and Doral, some "premium smokers" began to shift to nonpremium brands. By 1993, nonpremium brands had captured more than 40% of the U.S. market. Although this trend benefited RJR and B&W, it was undesirable for premium-intensive manufacturers, such as PM and Lorillard. This prompted PM to look for ways to reverse the trend toward discount cigarettes. In 1993, PM announced that it was cutting the retail price of Marlboro cigarettes, the best-selling brand in America, by $.40 per pack and forgoing price increases on other premium brands "for the forseeable future." This price cut was followed by price cuts to PM's other premium brands. PM's price cuts set off a price war, as RJR, B&W, and Lorillard matched PM's retail price reductions, which cut into the market share held by the discount brands.

Later, however, RJR announced that it would no longer sacrifice profitability for market share and increased the price of its premium and discount brands. The other manufacturers matched the increase within a couple of weeks. Eleven more parallel increases occurred between May 1995 and January 2000.

A class of several hundred cigarette wholesalers sued the manufacturers, alleging that they had conspired to fix cigarette prices at unnaturally high levels, which resulted in wholesale list price overcharges of nearly $12 billion. The district court entered summary judgment in favor of the manufacturers after concluding that the wholesalers had failed to demonstrate the existence of a "plus factor." The wholesalers appealed.

ISSUE PRESENTED What types of conduct may constitute "plus factors" necessary to create an inference of a price-fixing conspiracy?

OPINION MARCUS, J., writing for the U.S. Court of Appeals for the Eleventh Circuit:

"[T]he distinctive characteristic of oligopoly is recognized interdependence among the leading firms: the profit-maximizing choice of price and output for one depends on the choices made by others."

When they are the product of a rational, independent calculus by each member of the oligopoly, as opposed to collusion, these types of synchronous actions have become known as "conscious parallelism." The Court has defined this phenomenon as "the process, not in itself

CONTINUED

unlawful, by which firms in a concentrated market might in effect share monopoly power, setting their prices at a profit-maximizing, supracompetitive level by recognizing their shared economic interests and their interdependence with respect to price and output decisions." . . .

As numerous courts have recognized, it often is difficult to determine which of these situations—illegal price fixing or conscious parallelism—is present in a given case. . . .

. . . .

. . . [P]rice fixing plaintiffs are relegated to relying on indirect means of proof. The problem with this reliance on circumstantial evidence, however, is that such evidence is by its nature ambiguous, and necessarily requires the drawing of one or more inferences in order to substantiate claims of illegal conspiracy. . . .

. . . .

. . . "[T]o survive a motion for summary judgment . . . a plaintiff seeking damages for [collusive price fixing] . . . must present evidence that 'tends to exclude the possibility' that the alleged conspirators acted independently." Evidence that does not support the existence of a price fixing conspiracy any more strongly than it supports conscious parallelism is insufficient to survive a defendant's summary judgment motion. . . .

In applying these principles, we have fashioned a test under which price fixing plaintiffs must demonstrate the existence of "plus factors" that remove their evidence from the realm of equipoise and render that evidence more probative of conspiracy than of conscious parallelism. . . .

. . . .

. . . [T]he district court delineated . . . distinct factors that appellants had denominated "plus factors." These are: "(1) signaling of intentions; (2) permanent allocations programs; (3) monitoring of sales; (4) actions taken contrary to economic self-interest." . . .

. . . .

. . . [W]e are satisfied that none of the actions on which appellants' arguments are based rise to the level of plus factors. . . . Indeed, when all of appellees' actions are considered together, the class has established nothing more than that the tobacco industry is a classic oligopoly, replete with consciously parallel pricing behavior, and that its members act as such.

RESULT   The appeals court affirmed the district court's grant of summary judgment for the defendants. The suit was dismissed.

COMMENTS   This case supports the strategy of "price leadership," whereby a firm with significant market share publicly announces its pricing policy, which other competitors elect to follow. As long as there is no explicit or implied agreement to act in concert, price leadership has withstood judicial scrutiny.

CRITICAL THINKING QUESTIONS

1. The court stated that the plaintiffs in this case simply proved that the defendants acted as rational oligopolists. What sort of evidence would establish that the defendants actually were engaging in an illegal price-fixing scheme?

2. The court recognized that there are economic costs associated with using circumstantial evidence to distinguish between lawful conscious parallel decision making within an oligopoly and illegal collusive price-fixing. What are some of these economic costs?

Proving a Vertical Conspiracy

Since the mid-1980s, the courts have generally been unwilling to allow proof of vertical conspiracies by circumstantial evidence alone. Unlike competitors, firms in a vertical arrangement have many legitimate reasons to communicate with each other. Therefore, a plaintiff seeking to prove an unlawful conspiracy must introduce evidence that tends to exclude the possibility that the firms acted independently when setting prices.[9] Evidence of action that could be either concerted or independent is insufficient to prove a section 1 violation under this test.

What Constitutes an Unreasonable Restraint of Trade?

Even if firms agreed to act in concert, their behavior is illegal only if it results in an *unreasonable* restraint of trade. There are two approaches to analyzing the reasonableness of a restraint: the *per se* rule and the rule of reason.

Per se Violations

Per se analysis condemns practices that are considered completely void of redeeming competitive rationales. This is appropriate when the practice always or almost always tends to restrict competition and decrease output. Once identified as *illegal per se*, a practice will not be examined further for its procompetitive justifications. *Horizontal price-fixing*, such as an agreement between retailers to set a common price for a product, is the classic example of a *per se* violation of section 1.

A school of economic thought, known as the Chicago School, maintains that market forces defeat most anticompetitive practices. Its proponents question the efficacy of the government's regulation of commerce and markets, arguing that attempts at regulation often actually decrease the competitiveness of markets. As the U.S. Supreme Court has embraced this scholarship, the number of truly *per se* violations of the antitrust laws has declined.

The Rule of Reason

If the plaintiff has not proved a *per se* violation, the activity will be evaluated under the *rule of reason*. The objective of this rule is to determine whether, on balance, the activity promotes or restrains competition, or to put it differently, helps or harms consumers. In short, the U.S. antitrust laws are designed to protect consumers not to protect competitors. (As discussed in the "Global View" in this chapter, European competition law is more protective of competitors.) When analyzing particular behavior, the court will consider the structure of the market as well as the defendant's actions to ascertain the anticompetitive and procompetitive effects of the challenged practice. Activity that has a substantial net anticompetitive effect is deemed an unreasonable, and therefore, illegal, restraint of trade.

Types of Horizontal Restraints

Restraints between direct competitors, such as price-fixing, market division, and some kinds of group boycotts, have traditionally been treated as *per se* violations of section 1 of the Sherman Act. Trade associations may also be found to be acting unlawfully under the rule of reason in some circumstances.

Horizontal Price-Fixing

Horizontal price-fixing agreements include (1) setting prices (including maximum prices); (2) setting the terms of sale, such as customer credit terms; (3) setting the quantity or quality of goods to be manufactured or made available for sale; or (4) rigging bids (agreements between or among competitors to fix contract bids). For example, it is illegal *per se* for Competitor 1 and Competitor 2 to agree that Competitor 1 will submit an artificially high bid on Contract A to enhance the likelihood that Competitor 2 will win that contract in exchange for Competitor 2's agreement to submit an artificially high bid on Contract B. This is illegal even if there is a much larger Competitor 3 that is likely to win both bids if Competitors 1 and 2 bid against each other.

Horizontal Market Division and Nonprice Horizontal Restraints

The U.S. Supreme Court considers horizontal market divisions so inherently anticompetitive as to constitute *per se* violations of section 1. *Horizontal market division* can take various forms: competitors might divide up a market by class of customer, by brand of product, by geographic territory, or by restricting product output. Market division is prohibited even if it is intended to enable small competitors to compete with larger companies and to thereby foster interbrand competition.[10] The *per se* ban on horizontal market division extends to potential as well as actual competitors.[11]

Group Boycotts

Although a firm generally may choose to do business with whomever it wants, an agreement among competitors to refuse to deal with another competitor—a *group boycott*—was initially treated as a *per se* violation of section 1. For example, the U.S. Supreme Court held that manufacturers of appliances could not agree with a distributor's competitors to refrain from selling to the distributor or to do so only at higher prices. Such an agreement was treated as a *per se* violation of section 1 even though there was no agreement on the exact price, quantity, or quality of the appliances to be sold.[12]

More recently, the Supreme Court has evaluated certain forms of group boycotts under the rule of reason. For example, the Court refused to apply the *per se* rule when a wholesale purchasing cooperative of office-supply retailers

9. Monsanto Co. v. Spray-Rite Serv. Corp., 465 U.S. 752 (1984).

10. United States v. Topco Assocs., Inc., 405 U.S. 596 (1972).
11. Palmer v. BRG of Ga., Inc., 498 U.S. 46 (1990).
12. Klor's, Inc. v. Broadway–Hale Stores, Inc., 359 U.S. 207 (1959).

expelled a member for violating a cooperative bylaw requiring notification of changes in ownership. The Court noted that there was no showing that the cooperative possessed market power or unique access to a business element necessary for effective competition.[13] (The concept of market power is addressed later in this chapter.) Applying the rule of reason analysis instead, the Court concluded that the members' decision to expel the plaintiff was not an unreasonable restraint because cooperatives need to establish and enforce reasonable rules to function effectively. Furthermore, the expulsion did not completely exclude the plaintiff from access to the cooperative's wholesale operations.

Trade Associations: Group Boycotts, Exchanges of Information, and Standards Setting

Courts often do not look favorably on attempts at self-regulation by trade and professional associations, particularly when such attempts result in group boycotts. For example, the U.S. Supreme Court struck down as a violation of the Sherman Act a minimum fee schedule for lawyers published by a county bar association, which was enforced through the prospect of professional discipline from the Virginia State Bar Association.[14]

Other types of self-regulation, however, will be upheld under the rule of reason if the presumptive economic benefits outweigh any potential economic harm. For example, the California Dental Association (CDA) adopted a code of ethics that included a section prohibiting dentists from soliciting patients with any false or misleading communication. The guidelines forbade advertising that referred to "low" or "reasonable" prices, offered volume discounts, or made any claims about quality of service, ostensibly because such statements could mislead consumers by implying unverifiable superiority over other dentists' services.

The U.S. Court of Appeals for the Ninth Circuit initially held that the CDA had violated section 5 of the Federal Trade Commission Act because it prevented its members from engaging in truthful, nonmisleading advertising offering discounts or claims about service quality. The U.S. Supreme Court reversed, holding that the Ninth Circuit had erred by engaging in a *"quick look,"* or abbreviated, *rule of reason analysis* that failed to consider a number of theories under which the CDA restrictions on advertising might prove procompetitive. On remand, the Ninth Circuit found no antitrust violation, pointing out several ways in which the CDA's guidelines would have a net procompetitive effect: (1) the guidelines required dentists to disclose their regular and discounted rates, thereby allowing a price-conscious consumer to determine from the ads which dentist actually offered a lower fee;

(2) restricting advertising in the dental market, where there is strong customer loyalty, was less detrimental than restricting advertising in markets where consumers are much more likely to switch brands; and (3) the restrictions did not amount to a complete ban on advertising.[15]

Trade and professional associations often disseminate information among their members. Association agreements rarely state goals that violate the Sherman Act, so courts will consider the structure of the market, and the type and timeliness of the information exchanged, to determine whether the exchange of information facilitates anticompetitive behavior, such as price-fixing or market division.

When a market has few competitors, they are more likely than a large group to be able to reach and enforce an agreement. Therefore, the more concentrated the industry, the more closely courts will scrutinize the exchange of information.

The type of information exchanged also plays a critical role in the analysis. Information that does not involve prices or terms of sale receives less scrutiny by the courts. For example, cooperative industrial research, market surveys, and joint advertising concerning the industry are permissible. Similarly, the exchange of information concerning contractors whose payments were two months in arrears was deemed a reasonable way to help members avoid contractor fraud.[16] In contrast, a hardwood manufacturers' trade association violated section 1 when it disseminated (1) a weekly report listing the names of companies that sold lumber and the prices at which they sold it and (2) monthly reports discussing future price trends and future estimates of production.[17] Members could use the information to police secret agreements setting uniform prices or terms. In another case, the Supreme Court found no violation when a manufacturers' association disseminated information on average costs and the terms of past transactions but did not identify individual sellers or buyers and did not discuss future pricing.[18]

Standards-making activities by trade associations are generally procompetitive and are often permissible.[19] Standards permit the sale of compatible products from different manufacturers, thereby increasing competition and making it easier for buyers to compare products. For example, DVD manufacturers compete only on price and features because all players will play all DVDs. Standards also make it easier to introduce complementary new technologies by reducing buyers' concern that they will be left with incompatible products. Industry standards may give

---

13. Nw. Wholesale Stationers, Inc. v. Pac. Stationery & Printing Co., 472 U.S. 284 (1985).

14. Goldfarb v. Va. State Bar, 421 U.S. 773 (1975).

15. Cal. Dental Ass'n v. FTC, 224 F.3d 942 (9th Cir. 2000).

16. Cement Mfrs. Protective Ass'n v. United States, 268 U.S. 588 (1925).

17. Am. Column & Lumber Co. v. United States, 257 U.S. 377 (1921).

18. Maple Flooring Mfrs. Ass'n v. United States, 268 U.S. 563 (1925).

19. Radiant Burners v. Peoples Gas Co., 364 U.S. 656 (1961).

rise to antitrust claims if they are structured to favor a specific company or technology, however.[20]

Companies with existing technologies can, however, impermissibly use standards to stifle competition. For example, the U.S. Supreme Court found that the vice president of the dominant manufacturer of a safety device for heating boilers, who was also vice chairman of a trade association subcommittee that promulgated the standards for this device, violated section 1 when he conspired with other members of the subcommittee to misrepresent the standards in order to discourage customers from buying a new manufacturer's products.[21]

League Rules

Some products, such as sporting events, may require horizontal restraints in order to exist at all. The Supreme Court recognized in 1996 that "clubs that make up a professional sports league are not completely independent economic competitors, as they depend upon a degree of cooperation for economic survival."[22] Nonetheless, in a case decided in 2010, *American Needle, Inc. v. National Football League*,[23] the Court rejected the argument that the thirty-two teams in the National Football League (NFL) and their owners should be viewed as a single entity not capable of concerted conduct. The Court noted: "The NFL teams do not possess either the unitary decisionmaking quality or the single aggregation of economic power characteristic of independent action. Each of the teams is a substantial, independently owned, and independently managed business."[24] The NFL had created National Football League Properties (NFLP) to develop, license, and market the thirty-two teams' intellectual property. After the NFLP granted a ten-year exclusive license to Reebok for NFL-team-branded hats and other gear, a firm

---

20. *See, e.g.,* Addamax Corp. v. Open Software Found., Inc., 888 F. Supp. 274 (D. Mass. 1995).

21. Am. Soc'y of Mech. Eng'rs v. Hydrolevel Corp., 456 U.S. 556 (1982).

22. Brown v. Pro Football, Inc., 518 U.S. 231, 248–50 (1996). *See also* Nat'l Collegiate Athletic Ass'n v. Bd. of Regents of Univ. of Okla., 468 U.S. 85, 101 (1984).

23. 130 S. Ct. 2201 (2010).

24. *Id.* at 2212.

that was previously licensed to use NFL trademarks on its hats sued, alleging a violation of section 1. The Court concluded that the grant of the exclusive license was concerted action subject to section 1 but explained, "Football teams that need to cooperate are not trapped by antitrust law." Because "restraints on competition are essential if the product is to be available at all," league restraints are not *per se* illegal but are instead judged according to the "flexible Rule of Reason."

Types of Vertical Restraints

Unlawful *vertical restraints*, that is, restraints between firms at different levels in the chain of distribution, include price-fixing, market division, tying arrangements, and some franchise agreements.

Vertical Price-Fixing

Agreements on price between firms at different levels of production or distribution can be as anticompetitive as agreements between direct competitors at the same level of production or distribution. Although for decades the U.S. Supreme Court took the position that both maximum and minimum vertical price-fixing (also referred to as *resale price maintenance* or *RPM*) are *per se* illegal, it now evaluates both under the rule of reason.

The Supreme Court eliminated the ban on *maximum* vertical price restrictions, which prohibit a retailer from selling at a price higher than that set by the manufacturer, in 1997.[25] The Court reasoned that setting maximum prices does not necessarily prevent price competition. Suppliers may sell their product at whatever price they choose, subject to a price cap. The cap is arguably pro-competitive, because it may be lower than what might otherwise have been charged, especially when supplies are limited.

The Supreme Court's shift from *per se* to rule of reason treatment of *minimum* resale price maintenance in the following case proved particularly contentious, both on and off the Court.

---

25. State Oil Co. v. Khan, 522 U.S. 3 (1997).

A CASE IN POINT	*Summary*	Case 16.2

Leegin Creative Leather Products, Inc. v. PSKS, Inc.

Supreme Court of the United States
551 U.S. 877 (2007).

FACTS Leegin Creative Leather Products sells a variety of women's fashion accessories under the brand name "Brighton," in more than 5,000 retail stores, mostly small, independent boutiques and specialty stores. PSKS operates Kay's Kloset, a women's apparel store that started purchasing Brighton goods from Leegin in 1995. In 1997, Leegin instituted the "Brighton Retail Pricing and Promotion Policy," pursuant to which it refused to sell to retailers that discounted Brighton goods below Leegin's suggested retail prices. In its letter to retailers regarding the policy, Leegin stated that it was adopting the policy to give its retailers

CONTINUED

sufficient margins to provide customers with the service central to its distribution strategy and expressed concern that discounting harmed Brighton's reputation and brand image.

A year after instituting this policy, Leegin introduced the "Heart Store Program," which offered retailers incentives to become Heart Stores; in exchange, retailers pledged, among other things, to sell at Leegin's suggested prices. Although Kay's became a Heart Store, the parties appear to have agreed subsequently that it would not be a Heart Store after 1998. Despite losing this status, Kay's continued to increase its Brighton sales. In December 2002, Leegin discovered that Kay's had been marking down Brighton's entire line by 20%. Although Kay's contended it did so to compete with nearby retailers who were also discounting the line, Leegin requested that Kay's stop discounting. When Kay's refused, Leegin stopped selling to the store.

PSKS sued Leegin, alleging that Leegin had violated the antitrust laws by "enter[ing] into agreements with retailers to charge only those prices fixed by Leegin." At trial Leegin argued that it had established a lawful unilateral pricing policy, but the jury agreed with PSKS and awarded it $1.2 million. The court trebled the damages and added reimbursement for PSKS's attorneys' fees and costs, increasing the judgment to almost $4 million. On appeal, Leegin did not dispute that it had entered into vertical price-fixing agreements with its retailers. Instead, it argued that the court should have applied the rule of reason when evaluating its conduct. The U.S. Court of Appeals for the Fifth Circuit rejected this argument, explaining that it was bound by the Supreme Court's 1911 decision in *Dr. Miles Medical Co. v. John D. Park & Sons Co.*,[26] in which the Court established the rule that it is *per se* illegal for a manufacturer to agree with its distributor to set the minimum price that the distributor can charge for the manufacturer's goods. Leegin appealed.

ISSUE PRESENTED   Should vertical minimum resale price maintenance agreements continue to be treated as *per se* unlawful?

SUMMARY OF OPINION   The U.S. Supreme Court overruled *Dr. Miles* after finding that it was based on "formalistic" legal doctrine rather than "demonstrable economic effect." The Court reasoned that the doctrine of *stare decisis* did not compel its continued adherence to the *per se* rule against vertical price restraints because "respected authorities in the economic literature suggest the *per se* rule is inappropriate, and there is now widespread agreement that resale price maintenance can have procompetitive effects."

In particular, minimum resale price maintenance can stimulate interbrand competition by enticing retailers selling the same brand to invest in services or promotions that improve the manufacturer's position against rivals. Even though the minimum vertical price restraints eliminate intrabrand price competition, they prevent a discounter from free-riding on the marketing efforts or customer service provided by a rival selling the same brand. For example, a retailer selling high-end home theater systems would have no incentive to build an expensive showroom staffed by well-trained sales representatives if a customer could spend hours choosing the best system in the showroom, then walk across the street and buy the same product from a discounter operating out of a warehouse. Minimum prices can also protect the high-status image of a premium brand. Given these potentially procompetitive effects of RPM, the Court concluded that the *per se* rule was no longer appropriate.

RESULT   The Supreme Court held that vertical price restraints are to be judged by the rule of reason and remanded the case for a determination of whether the restraints had a net procompetitive effect.

COMMENTS   In a dissent joined by Justices Stevens, Souter, and Ginsburg, Justice Breyer sharply criticized the majority for overturning almost 100 years of precedent without meeting the factors that *stare decisis* requires before the Court overrules an earlier case. According to Justice Breyer, (1) the Court applies *stare decisis* more rigidly in statutory than

CONTINUED

26. 220 U.S. 373 (1911).

in constitutional cases, (2) the Court sometimes overrules cases that it decided wrongly only a reasonably short time earlier, (3) the fact that a decision creates an unworkable legal regime argues in favor of overruling, (4) the fact that a decision unsettles the law may argue in favor of overruling it, (5) the fact that a case involves property rights or contract rights where reliance interests are involved argues against overruling it, and (6) the fact that a rule of law has become embedded in the national culture argues strongly against overruling it. Applying these factors to the instant case, Justice Breyer concluded that *Dr. Miles* should not have been overruled.

As for the economic arguments, Justice Breyer pointed out the difference between the theoretical world of economics and the real world of business:

> [E]conomics can, and should, inform antitrust law. But antitrust law cannot, and should not, precisely replicate economists' (sometimes conflicting) views. That is because law, unlike economics, is an administrative system the effects of which depend upon the content of rules and precedents only as they are applied by judges and juries in courts and by lawyers advising their clients. And that fact means that courts will often bring their own administrative judgment to bear, sometimes applying rules of per se unlawfulness to business practices even when those practices sometimes produce benefits.

The dissent also predicted that the majority's decision could add $300 billion annually to consumers' costs. One year after the *Leegin* decision, the *Wall Street Journal* reported that manufacturers of consumer electronics, pet food, baby goods, and home furnishings were cutting off supplies to discounters who sold their products for less than the minimum price.[27] Manufacturers claimed that minimum prices were necessary to prevent "discount stigma," to "prevent customers from feeling 'cheated' for having paid more," and to keep discounters from "free-riding" on rival retailers' advertising and other expenses.[28]

---

27. Joseph Pereira, *Price-Fixing Makes Comeback After Supreme Court Ruling*, WALL ST. J., Aug. 18, 2008, at A1 & A12.
28. *Id.* at A12.

Nonprice Vertical Restraints and Vertical Market Division

Vertical market division is an arrangement imposed by a manufacturer on its distributors or dealers that limits the freedom of the dealer to market the manufacturer's product. Such an agreement may establish exclusive distributorships, territorial or customer restrictions, location clauses, areas of primary responsibility, and the like. Nonprice vertical restrictions are judged under the rule of reason.

As with price restraints, the central inquiry in cases involving nonprice vertical restraints is whether the reduction in intrabrand competition is justified by interbrand competition. The higher the market share of a particular manufacturer's product, the greater the likelihood that a decline in intrabrand competition will violate the rule of reason. For example, suppose Pixel Unlimited controls 80% of the market for high-definition television (HDTVs) in Atlanta, Georgia, and sells its products through five independent retail outlets. Pixel agrees with three of its dealers to terminate the other two. The reduction in competition among Pixel dealers might arguably increase interbrand HDTV competition, but given Pixel's high market share, that increase may not offset the anticompetitive effect of the decrease in Pixel

intrabrand competition. Accordingly, the reduction in the number of Pixel dealers might violate section 1.

Exclusive Distributorships   In an *exclusive distributorship*, a manufacturer may limit itself to a single distributor in a given territory or line of business, refusing to sell to other potential distributors in that territory or line of business. Exclusive distributorships have been upheld under the rule of reason when there is some competitive pressure that limits the market power of the retailers holding them. Exclusive automobile dealerships for particular geographic regions are the classic example. This restriction on intrabrand competition is permissible because of the intense interbrand competition among U.S. and foreign automobile manufacturers.

Territorial and Customer Restrictions   *Territorial* and *customer restrictions* prevent a dealer or distributor from selling outside a certain territory or to a certain class of customers. For example, a Dow representative selling industrial chemicals might be permitted to sell only to hardware stores, and only in a specified area. Vertical territorial or customer restrictions are not *per se* violations of section 1 but are instead judged under the rule of reason. Because nonprice restrictions often increase interbrand competition, an accompanying reduction of intrabrand competition may be permissible.

Dual Distributors   A manufacturer that sells its goods both wholesale and at retail is called a *dual distributor*. Early decisions held that restraints imposed by dual distributors were illegal *per se* on the basis that such arrangements were unlikely to create the efficiencies and increased competition created by permissible forms of vertical nonprice agreements. The trend in recent decisions, however, is to analyze such restraints under the rule of reason.

Product Bundling and Other Tying Arrangements

Tying arrangements can be challenged under section 1 of the Sherman Act or section 3 of the Clayton Act. In a *tying arrangement*, the seller will sell product A (the *tying*, or desired, product) to the customer only if the customer agrees to purchase product B (the *tied* product) from the seller. A tying arrangement is a way of forcing a buyer to purchase a product or service it would not buy on the product's or service's own merits.

For example, suppose Metro Cable expands its cable television service into a new town. The public utilities commission grants Metro the exclusive right to provide cable service in the town. Metro is a subsidiary of Moviemax, a company that provides a cable television movie channel for subscribers. To improve Moviemax's profit margin, the marketing vice president decides to require all of Metro's customers to subscribe to Moviemax. In this example, the tying product is the basic cable service. The tied product is the Moviemax television channel.

Tying arrangements may unreasonably restrain trade by making it difficult for competitors to sell their goods to customers who are obliged to buy the tied product. In the Moviemax example, the tying arrangement would make it more difficult for other movie channels, such as HBO, to sell their product to cable customers in the new town. Tying arrangements also restrict the freedom of choice of purchasers who are forced to buy the tied product.

A firm's ability to translate power in one market into power in another is often a function of product complementarity. If one needs product B (for example, bicycle helmets) to use product A (bicycles), then the firm controlling the market for product A (bicycles) will have a good shot at forcing consumers to buy the complementary product (bicycle helmets) from it. Unfortunately, the courts have not fashioned any precise formula that firms can use to determine ahead of time whether a bundle or integration of products is an antitrust violation or just shrewd business.

To establish a tying arrangement, a plaintiff must show that (1) the tying and tied products are separate products, (2) the availability of the tying product is conditioned on the purchase of the tied product, (3) the party imposing the tie has enough market power in the tying product market to force the purchase of the tied product, and (4) a "not insubstantial" amount of commerce in the tied product is affected.

Separate Products   It is sometimes difficult to determine whether separate products are involved. Firms often label or market a combination of goods and services as a single product, but the courts focus on whether a separate demand exists for each product. For example, in one case the U.S. Supreme Court found that below-market financing that was provided to buyers of prefabricated metal homes was a separate product from the homes themselves. In contrast, the Supreme Court ruled that the provision of anesthesia and surgery were not separate products because consumers did not use anesthesia alone.[29]

Condition of Sale   If the tying product can be purchased on nondiscriminatory terms, without the tied product, there is no tie. It has been suggested that a manufacturer should not make a second product so technologically interdependent with the purchased product that technology, rather than contract terms, forces customers to buy both. To date, however, these technological ties have been found lawful as long as there is no separate demand for the products involved, or the interdependent products provide consumers with functionalities not available if the products are purchased separately.[30]

Market Power   The nature and extent of the market power required for a tying arrangement are frequently litigated. As the U.S. Supreme Court defines it, market power is "the power to force a purchaser to do something that he would not do in a competitive market."[31] Ordinarily, market power is inferred from a firm's predominant share of the market, but patented or copyrighted products may confer market power in tying cases when there are high switching costs. For example, the Supreme Court ruled that Kodak's refusal to sell patented parts to independent service organizations could constitute an illegal tie because it forced the owners of expensive Kodak copiers with a long life to purchase service from Kodak. For this purpose, the relevant market was defined as Kodak copiers.[32] The Court remanded the case to the U.S. Court of Appeals for the Ninth Circuit for a determination of whether Kodak's refusal to sell the patented parts was unreasonable under the rule of reason.

In the following case, the Supreme Court eliminated the presumption that a tie between a patented product and a nonpatented product is illegal *per se*.

---

29. Jefferson Parish Hosp. Dist. No. 2 v. Hyde, 466 U.S. 2 (1984).
30. *See, e.g.*, Microsoft Corp. v. United States, 147 F.3d 935 (D.C. Cir. 1998).
31. Eastman Kodak Co. v. Image Technical Servs., Inc., 504 U.S. 451 (1992).
32. *Id.*

| *Summary* | Case 16.3

Illinois Tool Works, Inc. v. Independent Ink, Inc.

Supreme Court of the United States
547 U.S. 28 (2006).

FACTS   Trident, Inc. and its parent Illinois Tool Works, Inc. (collectively, Trident) manufacture industrial printing systems that include a patented ink jet printhead and ink container and unpatented ink. Trident sells its systems to original equipment manufacturers (OEMs) that are licensed by Trident to incorporate the printheads and ink containers into printers that they sell to customers for use in printing bar codes on cartons and packages. The license agreement requires the OEM to purchase ink exclusively from Trident and further provides that neither the OEM nor its customers will refill the containers with ink of any kind.

Independent Ink developed an ink similar to the ink sold by Trident. Independent Ink sued Trident and sought to invalidate its patents on the grounds that Trident illegally tied the sale of its patented printhead and ink container to the purchase of the unpatented ink in violation of section 1 of the Sherman Act. After the U.S. Court of Appeals for the Federal Circuit held that a patented tying product necessarily conferred market power on Trident, Trident appealed.

ISSUE PRESENTED   Does the fact that a product in a tying arrangement is patented create a presumption of market power in that product?

SUMMARY OF OPINION   In a unanimous decision, the U.S. Supreme Court traced the history of tying arrangements, noting that they have been condemned (1) as "improper extensions of the patent monopoly" under the doctrine of patent misuse, (2) as "contracts in restraint of trade under § 1 of the Sherman Act," (3) as "unfair methods of competition under § 5 of the Federal Trade Commission Act," and (4) as "contracts tending to create a monopoly under § 3 of the Clayton Act." Early decisions assumed that "[t]ying arrangements serve hardly any purpose beyond the suppression of competition."

In *International Salt Co. v. United States*,[33] the Court held that leases of patented machines that required lessees to use the defendant's unpatented salt products violated section 1 of the Sherman Act and section 3 of the Clayton Act as a matter of law. This presumption that a patented tying product is always anticompetitive originated in the doctrine of *patent misuse*, which creates a defense to infringement when a patentee uses its patent "as the effective means of restraining competition with its sale of an unpatented article."

The Court reevaluated the *International Salt* rule in light of a subsequent change in patent misuse law. Congress had excluded certain conduct from triggering the patent misuse defense when it first codified the patent laws. In 1988, Congress amended the patent statute to eliminate the presumption of market power in patent misuse cases altogether.[34] Although this amendment pertained only to patent misuse and did not refer to the antitrust laws, the Court reasoned that this change in the patent law "invites a reappraisal of the *per se* rule announced in *International Salt*." The Court concluded that it "would be absurd to assume that Congress intended to provide that the use of a patent that merited punishment as a felony [under the antitrust laws] would not constitute 'misuse'" under the patent law. Given that the presumption of market power in antitrust law originated in patent law, "it would be anomalous to preserve the presumption in antitrust after Congress has eliminated its foundation."

The Court further explained that the "vast majority of the academic literature" disapproved of a presumption of market power. In addition, both the Department of Justice and the Federal Trade Commission have adopted guidelines that do "not presume that a patent, copyright, or trade secret necessarily confers market power upon its owner." Accordingly, the Court concluded that tying arrangements involving patented products should be evaluated under the rule of reason rather than under the *per se* rule articulated in *International Salt*.

CONTINUED

---

33. 332 U.S. 392 (1947).

34. 35 U.S.C. § 271(d).

RESULT The Court overruled *International Salt* and vacated the judgment of the Federal Circuit. The case was remanded to the district court to give International Ink a fair opportunity to introduce evidence defining the relevant market and proving that Trident possessed power within it.

COMMENTS This opinion highlights the links between intellectual property law and antitrust, demonstrating how legislative developments in one area of the law may influence the judiciary's interpretation of another. It is also yet another example of the Supreme Court's shift from *per se* to rule of reason analysis for most antitrust claims.

Effect on Commerce Plaintiffs can meet the requirement that a "not insubstantial" amount of commerce be affected by showing that more than a trifling dollar amount is involved.

Business Justification Courts apply the rule of reason when evaluating most tying arrangements and thus will consider the business justifications proffered by the tying firm. For example, the U.S. Court of Appeals for the Ninth Circuit upheld Mercedes–Benz's policy of requiring its dealers to sell only factory-made parts.[35] The court found that this tying arrangement was justified by the assurance it provided to Mercedes that service on its automobiles, important in preserving its high-quality image, would not be performed with substandard parts.

Some lower courts have also allowed tying arrangements in fledgling industries. For example, one court upheld a tying arrangement whereby purchasers of cable television satellite antennas were required to purchase service contracts to ensure proper functioning of the antennas.[36] The U.S. Court of Appeals for the D.C. Circuit held that the rule of reason should be used to decide whether Microsoft had illegally tied its Internet Explorer browser to the Windows operating system.[37]

Franchise Agreements

A *franchise* is a business relationship in which one party (the franchisor) grants to another party (the franchisee) the right to use the franchisor's name and logo and to distribute the franchisor's products from a specified locale. (Franchises are discussed further in Chapter 19.) Vertical market division between a franchisor and a franchisee may be lawful when interbrand competition is enhanced by the limitation on intrabrand competition.[38] Such division may take the form of limits on the number of franchisees in a geographic region and restrictions on the sale of franchisor products to specifically franchised locations.

Antitrust issues are also raised when a franchisor, in an effort to promote uniformity and name recognition, imposes certain limitations on the franchisee. For example, McDonald's franchisees might be required to decorate their restaurants in an approved fashion and have all their employees wear approved uniforms.

Requirements for the franchisee to purchase goods or equipment from the franchisor have been challenged as illegal tying arrangements. In *Queen City Pizza, Inc. v. Domino's Pizza, Inc.*,[39] Domino's Pizza franchisees claimed that Domino's illegally tied the right to use its name and registered trademarks to a requirement that its franchisees purchase ingredients, materials, and supplies for use in their restaurants from Domino's or Domino's approved suppliers, thus forcing plaintiffs to pay above-market prices for their ingredients, materials, and supplies. Although the plaintiffs argued that the relevant market should be narrowly limited to pizza and ingredients approved by Domino's for sale to its franchisees, the U.S. Court of Appeals for the Third Circuit held that "ingredients, supplies, materials, and distribution services used by and in the operation of Domino's pizza stores" could not, as a matter of law, constitute a relevant market for antitrust purposes. The court appeared to be influenced by the fact that the alleged illegal tie of fresh dough to the purchase of other ingredients from Domino's was disclosed to the franchisees in the franchise agreement, so the franchisees had the opportunity to evaluate these potential costs against Domino's competitors' costs before they purchased the franchise. This opinion has significantly reduced the ability of franchisees to use antitrust laws to attack restrictive terms in their franchise agreements. Unless the franchisor (1) has a high share of the relevant franchisor product or opportunity or, perhaps, (2) keeps the purchase requirement a secret from the would-be franchisee and makes it difficult for the franchisee to recoup its investment in the franchise, franchisee tying claims are likely to fail.

---

35. Mozart Co. v. Mercedes–Benz of N. Am., Inc., 833 F.2d 1342 (9th Cir. 1987).

36. United States v. Jerrold Elecs. Corp., 187 F. Supp. 545 (E.D. Pa. 1960), *aff'd*, 365 U.S. 567 (1961).

37. United States v. Microsoft Corp., 253 F.3d 34 (D.C. Cir. 2001).

38. Cont'l T.V., Inc. v. GTE Sylvania, Inc., 433 U.S. 36 (1977).

39. 124 F.3d 430 (3d Cir. 1997).

MONOPOLIES: SECTION 2 OF THE SHERMAN ACT

Section 2 of the Sherman Act provides that "[e]very person who shall monopolize, or attempt to monopolize, or combine or conspire with any other person or persons, to monopolize any part of the trade or commerce among the several States, or with foreign nations, shall be deemed guilty of a felony."[40]

A firm that possesses monopoly power is able to set prices at noncompetitive levels, harming both consumers and competitors. Consequently, section 2 condemns actual or attempted monopolization of any market. Unlike section 1, section 2 does not require an agreement or any other collective action; unilateral conduct may violate section 2.

Section 2 does not, however, prohibit the mere possession of monopoly power. The offense of monopolization has two elements: a status element and a conduct element. The plaintiff must show first that the defendant has monopoly power in a relevant market (the status element) and then that the defendant willfully acquired or maintained that power through anticompetitive acts (the conduct element). As one court explained, "to be condemned as exclusionary, a monopolist's act must have 'anticompetitive effect.' That is, it must harm the competitive *process* and thereby harm consumers. In contrast, harm to one or more *competitors* will not suffice."[41] A firm that has monopoly power thrust upon it by circumstances or attains it by superior performance does not violate section 2. As Judge Learned Hand explained more than sixty-five years ago:

> A single producer may be the survivor out of a group of active competitors, merely by virtue of his superior skill, foresight and industry. In such cases a strong argument can be made that, although the result may expose the public to the evils of monopoly, the Act does not mean to condemn the resultant of those very forces which it is its prime object to foster: finis opus coronat ["the end crowns the work"].[42]

Market Power

Courts define *market power* (also called *monopoly power*) as the power to control prices or exclude competition in a relevant market. Market power is marked by supracompetitive prices (that is, prices that are higher than they would be in a competitive market) over an extended period of time and the unavailability of substitute goods or services. The determination of whether a particular corporation has market power usually requires complex economic analysis. Presumptions based on market share and other structural characteristics of markets are used to simplify the analysis; in practice, however, each case turns on its unique (and usually disputed) facts.

Defining the Relevant Market

Competition takes place in discrete markets. Therefore, the existence of market power can be determined only after the relevant market for the product is determined. Markets have two components: a product component and a geographic component.

Multiple-Brand Product Market The *multiple-brand product market* is made up of product or service offerings by different manufacturers or sellers that are economically interchangeable and may therefore be said to compete. Sometimes it is easy to identify substitutes. No one would deny that Coca-Cola competes against Pepsi. Frequently, the question is more complex. Does Coca-Cola compete against Dr Pepper? Probably. Against powdered iced tea? That is harder to say.

These questions are important because the power of a seller to set prices above competitive levels is limited by the ability of purchasers to substitute other products. If purchasers are unable to substitute other goods in the face of a price increase, the seller can set prices at monopoly levels. Thus, the product market is that collection of goods or services that customers deem to be practically substitutable.

Single-Brand Product Market In some cases, a single brand of a product or service may constitute a separate market in a section 2 analysis. For example, the U.S. Supreme Court held in *Eastman Kodak Co. v. Image Technical Services, Inc.* that "[b]ecause service and parts for Kodak equipment are not interchangeable with other manufacturers' service and parts, the relevant market from the Kodak-equipment owner's perspective is composed of only those companies that service Kodak machines."[43] The Court rejected Kodak's motion for summary judgment on the basis that the relevant market was all copy machines and that Kodak could not have market power as to Kodak parts and service for copy machines, because it did not have market power in copy machines. Evidence in the case showed that Kodak controlled nearly 100% of the Kodak parts market and 80% to 95% of the Kodak service market, so Kodak-equipment owners had no readily available substitutes. Because of the high costs of switching to another brand, consumers could not readily change copy-machine manufacturers if Kodak unilaterally raised its service fees.

Geographic Market Competition is also affected by geographic restraints on product movement. If a firm in Michigan is the only maker of widgets in the Midwest, it

---

40. 15 U.S.C. § 2.

41. *See* Rambus Inc. v. FTC, 522 F.3d 456 (D.C. Cir. 2008).

42. United States v. Aluminum Co. of Am., 148 F.3d 416, 430 (2d Cir. 1945).

43. 504 U.S. 451 (1992).

has the potential to exercise market power unless widget makers from other parts of the country can profitably ship their products to that area. Some markets are national or even international in scope, for example, the markets for long-distance telephone service, supercomputer sales, and nuclear power plant designs. Other markets are localized, for example, markets for products that are expensive to transport, such as wet cement. The contours of geographic markets may also be affected by government regulations that confine firms to certain regions.

By defining the geographic market, antitrust courts try to separate firms that affect competition in a given region from those that do not. The geographic market encompasses all firms that compete for sales in a given area at current prices or would compete in that area if prices rose by a modest amount.

Determining Market Share

Once the relevant market is determined, the plaintiff must show that, within this market, the defendant possessed market, or monopoly, power. The Supreme Court has held that monopoly power may be inferred from a firm's predominant share of the market, because a dominant share of the market often carries with it the power to control output across the market and thereby control prices. How a relevant market is defined often determines whether a particular firm has a dominant share of the market. For example, if the relevant market is the market for imported mineral water, Perrier's competitors would include other imported mineral-water sellers like Pellegrino, and Perrier would hold a major share of that market. On the other hand, if the market is defined as all mineral water (including, for example, Calistoga and Poland Springs), then Perrier's market share would be considerably smaller.

In one case, the Supreme Court found that 87% of the market was a predominant share sufficient to create a presumption of market power. As a general proposition, firms with market shares in excess of 60% are especially vulnerable to section 2 litigation. When a single brand of a product or service constitutes the relevant market, market share may be 100%.

Barriers to Entry

Market shares alone do not conclusively establish market power. The plaintiff must also show that new competitors face high market barriers to entry and that current competitors lack the ability to expand their output to challenge a monopolist's high prices. Common entry barriers include patents, governmental licenses or approvals, control of essential or superior resources, entrenched buyer preferences, economies of scale, and, according to some authorities, high initial capital requirements. Courts will also look at profit levels, market trends, pricing patterns, product differentiation, and government regulation. Essentially, the court is trying to determine the likelihood that another company will become a viable competitor in the relevant market if there is a small but significant nontransitory increase in price levels.

ECONOMIC PERSPECTIVE

The Regulation of Natural Monopolies

In the imagined world of perfect competition, *productive efficiency* (an equilibrium in which only the lowest-cost producers of goods and services survive) and *allocative efficiency* (an equilibrium in which scarce societal resources are allocated to the production of various goods and services up to the point where the cost of the resources equals the benefit society reaps from their use) would go hand in hand. In the real world, however, this is not always so. For example, the most cost-efficient way to provide landline telephone connections to homes is to link all of the homes to one central station, using one set of lines. Competition would require duplication of this expensive "last-mile" infrastructure; productive efficiency is best served by a monopoly. But the pricing policy of a monopolist is not controlled by competition. Consequently, the unregulated price of local telephone service would rise above the socially efficient level, and allocative efficiency would be impaired (see Exhibit 16.1). This can be remedied only by regulation of such industries, which are known as *natural monopolies*.

For many years, the American Telephone and Telegraph Company (AT&T) enjoyed a regulated monopoly in both local and long-distance telecommunications. The provision of long-distance service is not a natural monopoly because more than one network of intercity telephone lines can be profitably operated. Nonetheless, there was no competition in long-distance service because AT&T controlled access to the lines to individual homes.

In 1974, the U.S. government brought an antitrust suit against AT&T, charging monopolization of the

CONTINUED

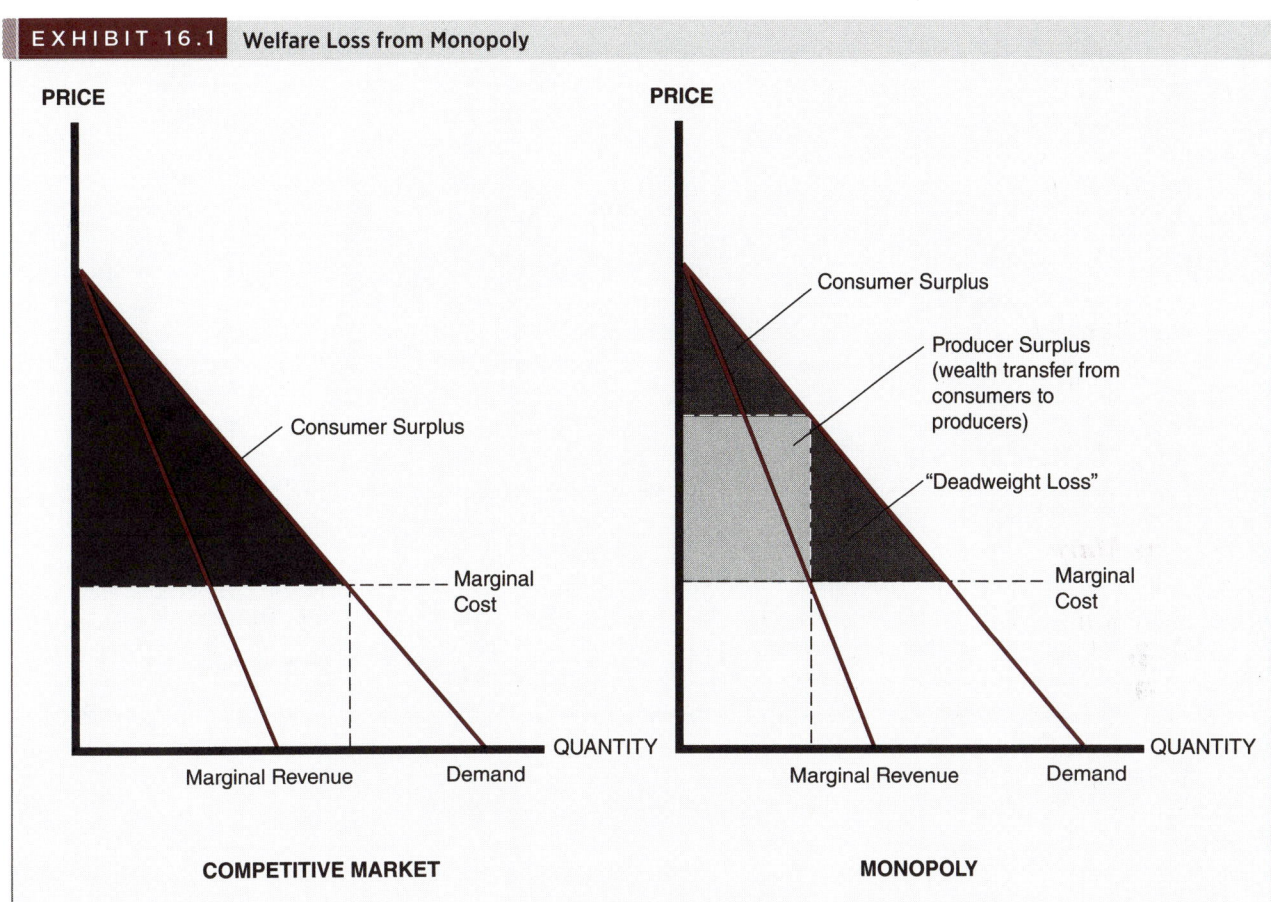

EXHIBIT 16.1 Welfare Loss from Monopoly

COMPETITIVE MARKET

MONOPOLY

DEFINITION OF TERMS

Consumer surplus The difference between the value of a good to consumers (measured by the price they would be willing to pay for the good) and the price they actually must pay to obtain the good.

Producer surplus The difference between the cost to producers of producing a good (measured by the minimum price at which they would sell a given quantity of the good) and the price they actually receive in the market.

Total surplus The sum of producer and consumer surplus. Total surplus represents the difference between the cost to society of the inputs used to make a good, including raw materials and labor, and the value of the finished good to society. Total surplus measures the overall increase in societal wealth attributable to production of a good.

Deadweight loss The difference between total surplus in a competitive market and total surplus in a monopolized market.

SOURCE: @Ingram Pinn/Financial Times, Apr. 5, 2000.

telecommunications industry in violation of section 2 of the Sherman Act. The case was decided in 1983.[a] In 1984, AT&T signed a consent decree to enable competition to flourish in the long-distance market. The decree provided for (1) the breakup of AT&T's monopoly over local service by creating seven regional telecommunications companies, known as the Baby Bells, and (2) a complex set of rules to ensure that both AT&T and other companies providing long-distance service, such

as MCI and Sprint, would have equal access to the local networks. The Baby Bells continued to be subject to regulation because each of them still enjoyed a monopoly in the provision of local telephone service until new technologies, such as cellphones and cable- and Internet-based phone service, obviated the need for mandated access to the Baby Bells' local phone landlines.

Similar issues arose in connection with high-speed Internet digital subscriber line (DSL) service when

independent service providers sought to compete with the Baby Bells. Because competing providers of DSL service still had to access the lines that connected homes and businesses to the Baby Bells' telephone network, the Federal Communications Commission (FCC) initially required the incumbent phone companies to sell transmission service to independent DSL providers. After 2005,[b] robust competition from cable companies and satellite and wireless services prompted the FCC

CONTINUED

to abandon this forced sharing requirement.[c] The FCC did, however, require AT&T to provide wholesale "DSL transport service" to independent firms at a price no greater than the retail price of AT&T's DSL service as a condition to approving the merger of former Baby Bell BellSouth Corporation with AT&T.[d]

Nonetheless, the Supreme Court rejected a "price-squeezing" claim under section 2 of the Sherman Act by independent DSL service providers (ISPs), which alleged that AT&T was monopolizing the DSL market in California by setting a high wholesale price for DSL transport and a low retail price for its DSL Internet service, and thereby squeezing the ISPs' profit margins.[e] The Court ruled that a price-squeezing claim may not be brought under section 2 when (1) the defendant has no *antitrust* obligation to sell imports to the competitors and (2) the retail price does not constitute predatory pricing, which requires both (a) below-cost retail pricing

and (b) a "dangerous probability" that the defendant will realize lost profits by raising prices later. Although the FCC required AT&T to provide access at "just and reasonable rates," this did not create an antitrust duty to deal.

The Court had previously held in *Verizon Communications Inc. v. Law Offices of Curtis V. Trinko,*[f] "that a firm with no antitrust duty to deal with its rivals at all is under no obligation to provide those rivals with a 'sufficient' level of service."[g] The Court considered it anomalous to permit "AT&T [to] bankrupt the plaintiffs by refusing to deal altogether," yet require it to price both its wholesale and retail products "in a manner that preserves its rivals' profit margins."[h] Imposing such a duty would require courts to police both wholesale and retail prices, and thereby assume "day-to-day controls characteristic of a regulatory agency," a task for which courts are ill-suited.

In a concurring opinion in which Justices Stevens, Souter, and Ginsburg

joined, Justice Breyer similarly reasoned that a competitor of "a regulated firm (which, if a natural monopolist, is lawfully such) cannot win an antitrust case simply by showing that it is 'squeezed' between the regulated firm's wholesale price (to the plaintiff) and its retail price (to customers for whose business both firms compete)." The concurrence encouraged the ISPs to seek regulatory relief from the FCC, not antitrust relief from the courts.

a. United States v. Am. Tel. & Tel. Co., 552 F. Supp. 131 (D.D.C. 1982), *aff'd sub nom.* Maryland v. United States, 460 U.S. 1001 (1983).
b. *In re* Appropriate Framework for Broadband Access to Internet Over Wireless Facilities, 20 FCC Rcd. 14853, 14853 (2005).
c. Pac. Bell Tel. Co. v. Linkline Commc'ns, Inc., 555 U.S. 438 (2009).
d. *Id.*
e. *Id.*
f. 540 U.S. 398 (2004).
g. *Pac. Bell Tel. Co.,* 555 U.S. 438.
h. *Id.*

Monopolistic Intent

Once the presence of market power is established, the defendant's intent is relevant. Some cases hold that the plaintiff must prove that the defendant's conduct lacks a legitimate business purpose. Other cases hold that the initial burden is on the defendant to prove a legitimate business purpose; if it does so, the plaintiff must then prove a monopolistic intent. It is possible to prove intent through evidence of statements by the monopolist's executive expressing a desire to eliminate competition. Hostility between competitors is commonplace, however, and may even be beneficial to vigorous competition. Therefore, the courts often require that monopolistic intent be proved by evidence of conduct (not merely statements) that is inherently anticompetitive.

A defendant may rebut allegations of monopolistic intent by showing that its success in the marketplace is the result of "superior skill, foresight and industry."[44] A monopoly earned by superior performance is not unlawful. Indeed, the law recognizes that the possibility of attaining such a monopoly may be a powerful incentive to vigorous competition, which benefits consumers. Therefore, a key issue in section 2 litigation is whether the defendant acquired or maintained its monopoly by procompetitive acts or by anticompetitive acts. Anticompetitive acts include predatory pricing and, under limited circumstances, refusals to deal.

44. United States v. Aluminum Co. of Am., 148 F.2d 416, 430 (2d Cir. 1945).

Predatory Pricing

Predatory pricing is the attempt to eliminate rivals by undercutting their prices to the point where they lose money and go out of business, leaving the monopolist unrestrained by competition and thus able to raise its prices. The courts have struggled to develop principles that distinguish between such anticompetitive pricing and the procompetitive pricing that occurs when a more efficient firm competes vigorously yet fairly against its rivals. In the latter case, the more efficient firm could undercut its rivals, forcing them out of business, and a lawful monopoly would result.

Courts will usually find pricing legal when the prices are above average variable cost but below average total cost and the company has excess capacity. (*Variable cost* is the cost of producing the next incremental unit; *total cost* includes variable cost and fixed costs, such as rent and overhead.) If a company does not have excess capacity, the legality of the pricing depends on the company's intent and the nature of the market. If, for example, costs will fall dramatically as the company progresses along the learning curve, then it is legal to price below average variable cost. At some point, though, pricing below cost becomes economically irrational unless the predator is anticipating the long-term gains that would result from destroying its rivals.

The Supreme Court has recognized that predatory pricing is self-defeating in all but a few market scenarios: "predatory pricing schemes are rarely tried, and even more rarely successful."[45] Having eliminated its rivals, the predator needs to keep both its old rivals and new entrants out of the market when it raises its prices to recoup its losses. That will be difficult as the high prices—and high profits—can be expected to attract new entrants. Unless barriers to entry or other factors make a market structurally conducive to monopolization, pricing below cost is not a Sherman Act violation, regardless of whether the defendant had monopolistic intent.[46] This has been referred to as the *rule of impossibility*.[47] Accordingly, the Supreme Court requires a plaintiff claiming predatory pricing to prove both (1) that the prices and other direct revenues for the practice complained of are below an appropriate measure of the defendant's costs, and (2) that the defendant has a dangerous probability of recouping its investment "losses" by later raising prices above competitive levels.

In *Weyerhaeuser Co. v. Ross-Simmons Hardwood Lumber Co.*,[48] the Supreme Court held that the same test also applies to predatory buying claims. Ross-Simmons accused Weyerhaeuser of paying too much for alder logs and not using what it bought, with the goal of driving out competing sawmills that used wood in furniture and other products. The Court found that the risk of chilling procompetitive behavior was as serious in this case as in predatory pricing cases. Therefore, only higher bidding that leads to predatory pricing in the relevant output market should constitute a basis for predatory bidding liability.

Refusal to Deal and the Essential Facilities Doctrine

As a general proposition, the antitrust laws do not prevent a firm from deciding with whom it will or will not deal. Yet the courts have long recognized that there are limited circumstances in which a unilateral refusal to deal may allow a firm to acquire or maintain monopoly power.

A monopolist has a duty to deal with its rivals when it controls an *essential facility*, that is, some resource necessary to its rivals' survival that they cannot feasibly duplicate. A court considers four elements in an essential-facility case: (1) whether the defendant prevents would-be competitors from using the facility, (2) whether it is feasible for the defendant to permit access to the facility by its would-be competitors, (3) whether the defendant has monopoly power and control of the facility, and (4) whether the competitors are able to duplicate the essential facility.[49] The essential-facility doctrine does not require a firm to share resources that are merely useful, that would allow competitors to compete more

effectively, or that the competitors could duplicate on their own. Recent Supreme Court cases have sharply curtailed plaintiffs' ability to force a monopolist to deal with rivals.[50]

In 1995, the Federal Trade Commission and the Department of Justice issued *Antitrust Guidelines for the Licensing Intellectual Property*.[51] These guidelines set forth three core principles: (1) the standard antitrust analysis applies to intellectual property, (2) intellectual property rights do not necessarily confer market power, and (3) licensing is generally procompetitive and subject to rule of reason analysis.

The U.S. Court of Appeals for the Federal Circuit upheld Xerox's policy of not selling or licensing its patented products and copyrighted software to independent service organizations.[52] The Federal Circuit declined to inquire into the subjective motivation behind Xerox's refusal to sell or license its patented and copyrighted works, finding that the antitrust defendant's subjective motivation is immaterial. The court held that in the absence of illegal tying, fraud on the Patent and Trademark Office or the Copyright Registrar, or sham litigation, Xerox's enforcement of its statutory intellectual property rights did not violate the antitrust laws.

Other Anticompetitive Acts

In *Cascade Health Solutions v. PeaceHealth*,[53] the U.S. Court of Appeals for the Ninth Circuit held that selling a bundle of products at a price that was less than what the products would cost individually was insufficient to establish a section 2 violation unless the discounted bundle was sold at a price less than an appropriate measure of the seller's cost. Above-cost pricing by a monopolist, coupled with exclusionary conduct, can give rise to a violation of section 2,[54] at least when the monopolist has unconstrained market power. For example, a court concluded that 3M's practice of offering bundled rebates across multiple product lines was tantamount to an illegal tying arrangement because (1) 3M had a 90% market share in the transparent tape market, and (2) the practice "forclose[d] portions of the market to a potential competitor who does not manufacture an equally diverse group of products and who therefore cannot make a comparable offer."[55] Other

---

45. Brooke Grp. Ltd. v. Brown & Williamson Tobacco Corp., 509 U.S. 209, 226 (1993).

46. Matsushita Elec. Indus. Co. v. Zenith Radio Corp., 475 U.S. 574 (1986).

47. *See, e.g., Brooke Grp.*, 509 U.S. 209.

48. 549 U.S. 312 (2007).

49. *See* Aspen Skiing Co. v. Aspen Highlands Skiing Corp., 472 U.S. 585 (1984).

50. *See, e.g.,* Pac. Bell Tel. Co. v. Linkline Commc'ns, Inc., 555 U.S 438 (2009).

51. The guidelines are available at http://www.ftc.gov/bc/0558.pdf.

52. CSU, LLC v. Xerox Corp., 203 F.3d 1322 (Fed. Cir. 2000). *But see* Image Technical Servs., Inc. v. Eastman Kodak Co., 125 F.3d 1195 (9th Cir. 1997) (in a tying case, holding that Kodak's refusal to sell replacement copier parts to independent service organizations was not justified by a desire to exploit its patents or copyrights). *See* Constance E. Bagley & Gavin Clarkson, *Adverse Possession for Intellectual Property: Adopting an Ancient Concept to Resolve Conflicts Between Antitrust and Intellectual Property Laws in the Information Age*, 16 Harv. J.L. & Tech. 327 (2003), for a proposed standard to reconsider these approaches.

53. 515 F.3d 883 (9th Cir. 2008).

54. *See, e.g.,* LePage's, Inc. v. 3M, 324 F.3d 141 (3d Cir. 2001) (holding that bundled all-or-nothing rebate tied to multiple product lines was illegal).

55. *Id.*

practices that can indicate the presence of monopolistic intent include the allocation of markets and territories, price-fixing, fraudulently obtaining a patent, or engaging in sham litigation against a competitor. Firms can also incur section 2 liability by acquiring or maintaining monopoly power through corporate mergers or acquisitions.

INTERNATIONAL SNAPSHOT

After ten years of drafting, China's Anti-Monopoly Law became effective on August 1, 2008. Loosely based on European and U.S. antitrust laws, the law includes four substantive sections that (1) prohibit certain types of agreements unless they fall within exemptions set forth in the law, (2) prohibit behavior classified as abuse of dominant market position, (3) establish a broad scheme for reviewing mergers (as well as a procedure for national security review of transactions),[a] and (4) prohibit abuse of government administrative powers for compliance. The law also contains certain miscellaneous provisions, including a provision that prohibits undefined "abuses" of intellectual property rights.

Although the law is largely neutral on its face, it includes some unique Chinese considerations, in particular those that reflect China's socialist heritage. For example, the declared purpose of the law is to protect the public interest and to promote the socialist market economy. The law recognizes that many key industries are controlled by large state-owned enterprises and prohibits these enterprises from abusing their dominant positions or legal monopolies to the detriment of consumers. The law also refers to trade associations, which often control the behavior of Chinese industries, by prohibiting such associations from organizing business operations to engage in monopolistic conduct. At the same time, however, the law provides that trade associations "shall strengthen self-discipline of the industries, provide guidance for enterprises in their industries to compete lawfully, and protect the order of market competition."[b]

In 2009, the Chinese Commerce Ministry used the law to condition Japan-based Mitsubishi Rayon Company's $1 billion acquisition of Lucite International Group Ltd., based in the United Kingdom, on Lucite's agreement to spin off half of its Chinese production capacity within five years and to sell the compound methylmethacrylate (MMA), which is used in the production of plastics, to a third party in China at cost.[c] The Ministry also prohibited Mitsubishi from acquiring any Chinese producer of MMA for five years or from building new Chinese factories to make MMA. Without these conditions, the combined company would have controlled 64% of the Chinese market for MMA. Also in 2009, the Ministry blocked Coca-Cola's proposed purchase of Huiyuan Juice Group Ltd.

---

a. The Chinese State Council published the Regulation on Notification Thresholds for Concentration of Undertakings in August 2008. These regulations supplement the merger control rules under the Anti-Monopoly Law. Peter J. Wang, H. Stephen Harris Jr. & Yizhe Zhang, *New Merger Notification Thresholds Under the AML Published*, JONES DAY (Aug. 2008), *available at* http://www.jonesday.com/pubs/pubs_detail.aspx?pubID=S5384.

b. Peter J. Wang, H. Stephen Harris Jr. & Yizhe Zhang, *New Chinese Anti-Monopoly Law*, JONES DAY (Oct. 2007), *available at* http://www.jones-day.com/pubs/pubs_detail.aspx?pubID=S4662.

c. Aaron Back & J.R. Wu, *China Flexes Global Merger Clout, Imposes Conditions on Lucite Deal*, WALL ST. J., Apr. 28, 2009, at B6.

To be actionable, the exclusionary conduct "must harm the competitive *process* and thereby harm consumers."[56] The courts have made it clear that "harm to one or more *competitors* will not suffice."[57]

For example, the Federal Trade Commission (FTC) unsuccessfully sued Rambus, Inc., a computer memory developer that had created a proprietary form of DRAM (dynamic random access memory), for illegal monopolization after its design became the industry standard. The FTC claimed that Rambus violated section 2 of the Sherman Act when it failed to disclose its intellectual property interests in four technologies being considered by the Electronic Industries Alliance, a standard-setting organization (SSO), of which Rambus was a member. The SSO's patent policy required its members to disclose patents and patent applications "related to" its standardization work. After Rambus formally withdrew from the SSO, the SSO incorporated four of Rambus's inventions into what became the dominant standard for computer memory products. When Rambus attempted to enforce its patents, the FTC ordered Rambus to charge a limited royalty for three years and then no royalty thereafter. The U.S. Court of Appeals for the District of Columbia Circuit overturned the FTC's order after concluding that the FTC had failed to prove that Rambus's failure to disclose its patent applications had allowed the company to monopolize the relevant markets.[58] The court explained:

> Deceptive conduct—like any other kind—must have an anti-competitive effect in order to form the basis of a monopolization claim. "Even an act of pure malice by one business competitor against another does not, without more, state a claim under the federal antitrust laws," without proof of "a dangerous probability that [the defendant] would monopolize a particular market."[59] . . . Cases that recognize deception as exclusionary hinge, therefore, on whether the conduct impaired rivals in a manner tending to bring about or protect a defendant's monopoly power.

Because the FTC expressly left open the likelihood that the SSO "would have standardized Rambus's technologies *even if Rambus had disclosed* its intellectual property," there was insufficient proof that the nondisclosure had caused the resultant monopoly.

Derivative Markets and Monopoly Leveraging

Ordinarily, section 2 liability is restricted to monopolistic behavior within the specific market in which the firm has market power. Through leveraging, however, a firm with monopoly power in one market can use that power to gain an advantage in a separate market. It is clear that

---

56. *See, e.g.*, Rambus Inc. v. FTC, 522 F.3d 456 (D.C. Cir. 2008).

57. *Id.*

58. *Id.*

59. Brooke Grp. Ltd. v. Brown & Williamson Tobacco Corp., 509 U.S. 209, 225 (1993).

when such an advantage amounts to monopoly power in the second market, the firm has violated section 2. Leveraging that confers only a "competitive advantage" in a market does not violate section 2 unless the plaintiff can prove that there is a dangerous probability of successfully monopolizing a second market.[60]

Thus, the two largest proprietary computerized airline reservation systems did not violate section 2 merely because the systems gave them a competitive advantage in the air-transportation market by listing their flights first.[61] The court held that unless the monopolist uses its power in the first market to acquire and maintain a monopoly in the second market, or to attempt to do so, there is no section 2 violation. The plaintiffs had conceded that the two airlines did not have a monopoly in the leveraged, downstream air-transportation market and that there was no dangerous probability that either defendant would acquire such a monopoly. Therefore, their section 2 claims were rejected.

In the following case, the court considered whether Abbott Laboratories' pricing of its HIV drugs constituted illegal monopoly leveraging.

60. Spectrum Sports, Inc. v. McQuillan, 506 U.S. 447 (1993); Verizon Commc'ns Inc. v. Law Offices of Curtis v. Trinko, 540 U.S. 398 (2004).

61. Alaska Airlines, Inc. v. United Airlines, Inc., 948 F.2d 536 (9th Cir. 1991).

A CASE IN POINT	*Summary*	Case 16.4

John Doe 1 v. Abbott Laboratories

United States Court of Appeals for the Ninth Circuit
571 F.3d 930 (9th Cir. 2009).

FACTS John Does 1 and 2 represented HIV patients and their medical plans, which purchase Norvir, a drug made by Abbott Laboratories. Norvir is used to boost the effectiveness of the protease inhibitors used to fight HIV disease. These inhibitors are manufactured by Abbott and other pharmaceutical firms. Although Abbott first marketed Norvir as a protease inhibitor, it proved more useful as a booster. Once the boosting effect of Norvir became known, Abbott's competitors started promoting Norvir as a booster to be taken with their own inhibitors. Subsequently, Abbott increased the price of Norvir from $1.71 to $8.57 per 100 milligrams but did not increase the price of its own "boosted" protease inhibitor Kaletra, which contains the boosting drug found in Norvir. The plaintiffs alleged that Abbott was unlawfully leveraging its monopoly in the booster market in an attempt to monopolize the boosted protease inhibitor market, but they did not allege that Abbott was selling Kaletra below its cost.

The district court denied Abbott's motion for summary judgment, and Abbott appealed.

ISSUE PRESENTED Do allegations of monopoly leveraging through pricing conduct in two markets state a claim under section 2 of the Sherman Act, absent an antitrust refusal to deal in the monopoly market or below-cost pricing in the second market?

SUMMARY OF OPINION The U.S. Court of Appeals for the Ninth Circuit applied the *Linkline*[62] holding to the facts of this case and found no section 2 violation. In *Linkline*, independent Internet service providers (ISPs) unsuccessfully sued AT&T for price-squeezing. AT&T sold DSL access to the ISPs at purportedly high wholesale prices and charged lower retail prices for its own DSL service than the ISPs could afford to charge. The Supreme Court held that section 2 did not ban the mere possession of monopoly power or the practice of charging monopoly prices when AT&T was under no antitrust duty to sell the inputs to its rivals.

The court found that Abbott's conduct was the functional equivalent of the price squeeze that occurred in *Linkline*:

> Either way, the alleged vice is that Abbott is using its monopoly position in the booster market to raise the price of Norvir while selling its own boosted inhibitor at too low a price. And either way, this puts the squeeze on competing producers of protease inhibitors that depend on Norvir for their boosted effectiveness and consumer acceptance.

Because there was no refusal to deal in the booster market and no allegation that Abbott was selling below cost, the plaintiffs failed to state a valid claim under section 2.

RESULT The district court's decision was reversed, and the claims against Abbott were dismissed.

62. Pac. Bell Tel. Co. v. Linkline Commc'ns, Inc., 555 U.S. 438 (2009). This case is discussed in the "Economic Perspective" in this chapter.

PRICE DISCRIMINATION: THE ROBINSON–PATMAN ACT

Section 2 of the Clayton Act, as amended by the Robinson–Patman Act, prohibits *price discrimination*, that is, selling the same tangible product to different purchasers at the same level of distribution at different prices. By outlawing price discrimination, Congress believed that it could protect independent businesses by preventing the formation of monopolies. The legislators assumed that price discrimination was the means by which trusts were built and that discriminatory price concessions were the means by which large retail chains expanded at the expense of smaller independent retailers.

Elements of a Robinson–Patman Case

Most Robinson–Patman claims involve either "primary line" or "secondary line" price discrimination. Robinson–Patman claims for *primary line* (or predatory pricing) *violations* are virtually identical to predatory pricing claims under the Sherman Act. Few primary line claims meet the current standard, which makes attempts to monopolize illegal only if they present a "dangerous probability of success." *Secondary line violations* typically involve a "disfavored" purchaser that brings a suit against a seller, or the seller's "favored" purchaser, for giving the favored purchaser better pricing.

Six elements must be proved to establish secondary line discrimination under the Robinson–Patman Act: (1) there must be discrimination in price, that is, a difference in the price at which goods are sold, in the terms and conditions of sale, or in such items as freight allowances or rebates; (2) some part of the discrimination must involve sales in interstate commerce, that is, at least one sale must be across state lines; (3) the discrimination must involve sales for use, consumption, or resale within the United States; (4) there must be discrimination between different purchasers; (5) the discrimination must involve sales of tangible commodities of like grade and quality; and (6) there must be a probable injury to competition. The probable injury to competition is assessed at three levels: (1) the seller level, (2) the buyer level, and (3) the customer level. The Supreme Court has stated that a "hallmark of the requisite competitive injury... is the diversion of sales or profits from a disfavored purchaser to a favored purchaser."[63]

Defenses

Even if a plaintiff has shown the elements of a Robinson–Patman violation, the following defenses are available.

Not Actual Competitors for Same Customer

A manufacturer is not liable for secondary line price discrimination in the absence of a showing that the manufacturer discriminated between dealers competing to sell the manufacturer's product to the same retail customer.[64] Because interbrand competition is the "primary concern of antitrust law," a manufacturer may offer a greater discount to a particular dealer to compete against another brand. As long as the plaintiff is not competing for that same customer's business, it cannot establish a Robinson–Patman violation by showing that the manufacturer offered it a less favorable discount on an order from a different customer.

Not Taking Advantage of Available Discounts

The Robinson–Patman Act permits discrimination that arises from discounts and allowances that a company affirmatively offers to all competing customers. A customer who fails to take advantage of such an offer cannot claim an actionable injury.

Meeting the Competition

Discriminatory prices are not prohibited if the seller acted in "good faith to meet an equally low price of a competitor."[65] As defined by the Federal Trade Commission, good faith is "a flexible and pragmatic, not a technical or doctrinaire, concept. The standard of good faith is simply the standard of the prudent businessman responding fairly to what he reasonably believes is a situation of competitive necessity."[66]

Cost Justification

Price differentials that would otherwise be prohibited by the Robinson–Patman Act are not prohibited if the differentials "make only due allowance for differences in the cost of manufacture, sale or delivery resulting from the differing methods or quantities" in which the goods are sold and delivered (such as costs of billing; credit losses; costs of advertising, promotion, and selling; and freight and delivery charges).[67] To establish this defense and justify the price reduction, the defendant must show actual cost savings, not merely generalized assertions of cost savings. The FTC interprets this defense restrictively. In addition, compiling the necessary paper trail is expensive.

Changing Conditions

The Robinson–Patman Act does not prohibit price changes from time to time in response to changing conditions affecting the market for or the marketability of the goods concerned. Such conditions include, but are not limited to, actual or imminent deterioration of perishable goods, obsolescence of seasonal goods, distress sales under court

63. Volvo Trucks N. Am., Inc. v. Reeder-Simco GMC, Inc., 546 U.S. 164 (2006).

64. *Id.*

65. 15 U.S.C. § 13(b).

66. *In re* Cont'l Baking Co., 63 F.T.C. 2071, 2163 (1963).

67. 15 U.S.C. § 13(a).

process, or sales in good faith when the seller discontinues its business in the goods concerned.

The changing-conditions defense has generally been confined to situations caused by the physical characteristics of the product, such as the perishable nature of fruit. For example, a court permitted price differentials on bananas from a single shipload because they reflected the perishable nature of bananas.

MERGERS: SECTION 7 OF THE CLAYTON ACT

If a merger or acquisition unreasonably restrains trade, it violates section 1 of the Sherman Act. If it results in monopolization, it violates section 2. These statutes, however, are rarely invoked to challenge mergers. Dissatisfied with the ability of the government to attack mergers under the Sherman Act, Congress amended the Clayton Act in 1950 to prohibit mergers that threatened to harm competition. Section 7 of the Clayton Act provides:

> No person engaged in commerce or in any activity affecting commerce shall acquire, directly or indirectly, the whole or any part of the stock or other share capital and no person subject to the jurisdiction of the Federal Trade Commission shall acquire the whole or any part of the assets of another person engaged also in commerce or in any activity affecting commerce, where in any line of commerce or in any activity affecting commerce in any section of the country, the effect of such acquisition may be substantially to lessen competition, or to tend to create a monopoly.[68]

Hart–Scott–Rodino Antitrust Improvements Act: Premerger Notifications

The U.S. Department of Justice and the Federal Trade Commission act as enforcement agents for the federal antitrust laws. As part of this mandate, they are responsible for determining whether potential business combinations or significant acquisitions of assets (including those involving exclusive licenses) are likely to lessen competition in any given market. Although the Justice Department and the FTC evaluate all transactions that they believe may raise competitive concerns, certain acquisitions and other transactions require companies to comply with the federal notification and preclosing waiting period requirements set forth in the Hart–Scott–Rodino Antitrust Improvements Act of 1976, as amended (the HSR Act). The resulting waiting period provides these antitrust regulators with an important preclosing window to investigate (and challenge) transactions that they believe may be anticompetitive.

Jurisdictional Thresholds

Transactions that do not exceed the $50 million (as adjusted) size-of-transaction threshold are not subject to the HSR Act notification and waiting period requirements. If the transaction exceeds the $200 million (as adjusted) size-of-transaction threshold, then HSR Act jurisdiction is satisfied without needing to consider the size-of-person test (although even then various technical exemptions can come into play that can result in no filing being required). If the transaction is valued between $50 million (as adjusted) and $200 million (as adjusted), then no HSR Act filing or waiting period is required unless the parties satisfy a separate $100 million/$10 million (as adjusted) size-of-person test.

The size-of-transaction and other HSR Act jurisdictional thresholds are adjusted annually based on the prior year's percentage growth (or decrease) in the gross national product. The FTC typically publishes the adjusted thresholds in late January, and they take effect in late February. As of December 2011, the adjusted $50 million and $200 million size-of-transaction thresholds were $66 million and $263 million, respectively; the adjusted $100 million and $10 million size-of-person thresholds were $131.9 million and $13.2 million, respectively.[69]

In calculating the size of the transaction, parties must follow the HSR Act's valuation rules, which focus not just on the purchase price or merger consideration but, when different, on the total value of the voting securities and/or assets to be held as a result of the transaction. For example, a minority shareholder who is acquiring the remaining outstanding shares of an issuer has to value its entire post-transaction stake. For these reasons, parties to transactions that initially might appear to be valued at less than $50 million (as adjusted) must ensure that they calculate the value of the transaction properly.

The size-of-person test focuses on the annual net sales and total assets of both the specific buyer and the target and the companies or individuals in the chain of control (the "control group"). As a result, a very small target can still end up satisfying part of the size-of-person test, even the $100 million (as adjusted) part of the test, if it happens to be controlled by a large company or a very wealthy individual.

To satisfy the $100 million/$10 million (as adjusted) size-of-person test, one party (most commonly, the acquirer) must, together with its control group, have either annual net sales or total assets of at least $100 million (as adjusted). In addition, the other party (typically, the target) must, together with its control group, have either annual net sales or total assets of at least $10 million (as adjusted). An exception to this "either–or" approach applies when a target, together with its control group, is not engaged in manufacturing. In such cases, a company satisfies the

---

68. 15 U.S.C. § 18.

69. Federal Trade Comm'n, Revised Jurisdictional Thresholds for Section 7a of the Clayton Act, 76 Fed. Reg. 4349–50 (Jan. 25, 2011).

$10 million (as adjusted) part of the test only if it, together with its control group, has total assets of at least $10 million (as adjusted).

Filings and Waiting Period

If an HSR filing is required, both sides must submit filings. The acquiring party must pay a filing fee based on a three-tiered filing fee structure. Filings are required even when the target company actively opposes the transaction, as in the case of a hostile tender offer. The parties must disclose certain information and produce various documents regarding the parties themselves and the proposed transaction. For example, the HSR filing must include offering memoranda (whether prepared by investment advisers or in-house), board books, slide presentations, memos to senior managers or board members, and other documents relating to the proposed acquisition. In 1999, the FTC filed an enforcement action against Blackstone Capital Partners, and one of Blackstone's partners who signed the Hart–Scott–Rodino filing on behalf of Blackstone, for failing to file a copy of a board document showing competitive problems that should have been attached as an exhibit to the HSR filing. Blackstone paid $2.785 million in civil penalties to settle the FTC suit, and the individual partner paid $50,000. This was the first time in the history of the HSR premerger reporting program that the FTC named an individual in a civil penalty action for violation of the HSR rules.

After making any required filings under the HSR Act, the parties will face a waiting period that lasts for a set number of days depending on the type of transaction (typically thirty calendar days for most transactions, including mergers, and fifteen calendar days for cash tender offers), unless the reviewing agency (1) approves a request for early termination and cuts the waiting period short or (2) launches a formal investigation by issuing a Second Request, demanding more information and materials about the parties, competition in the affected market(s), or the proposed transaction.

If the reviewing agency issues a Second Request, the waiting period does not start to run again until the parties have complied with the (typically very burdensome) request. As a practical matter, receipt of a Second Request often delays the transaction for at least three months, even if the transaction is ultimately approved. In particularly antitrust-sensitive transactions, the delay can be even longer. For example, the Justice Department did not publicly clear the XM/Sirius transaction until March 24, 2008, more than a year after the parties each received a Second Request.

Merger Guidelines

In connection with their enforcement obligations, the FTC and the Justice Department have together developed a series of guidelines as to the kinds of transactions that are likely to be challenged as violations of the Clayton Act.

Under the 2010 Horizontal Merger Guidelines,[70] the FTC and the Justice Department seek to determine whether a proposed corporate combination will more likely than not reduce competition. Although the Guidelines state that "evaluation of competitive alternatives available to customers is always necessary at some point in the analysis," they recognize that the competitive analysis need "not start with market definition." Instead, the 2010 Guidelines permit the FTC and Justice Department to use another "tool" if it would "more directly predict the competitive effects of a merger."[71]

As an aid to the interpretation of market data, the Justice Department uses the *Herfindahl–Hirschman Index (HHI)* of market concentration. The HHI is calculated by summing the squares of the individual market shares of all the firms in the market. For example, in a market with four competitors having market shares of 35%, 25%, 25%, and 15%, the HHI is 2,700 ($35^2 + 25^2 + 25^2 + 15^2 = 1,225 + 625 + 625 + 225 = 2,700$). Proposed mergers ordinarily require no further analysis if (1) the postmerger HHI is under 1,000; (2) the postmerger HHI falls between 1,000 and 1,800, and the change in the HHI is less than 100; or (3) the postmerger HHI is above 1,800, and the change in the HHI is less than 50. Historically, the reviewing agency has often not challenged mergers that involve market shares and concentrations that fall outside the above zones.

Litigation Under Section 7

Although the Department of Justice's merger guidelines are of considerable persuasive value, the standards applied by the courts differ in several significant respects. A court's

---

---

70. The guidelines are available at http://www.ftc.gov/os/2010/08/100819hmg.pdf (last revised Aug. 19, 2010).

71. See James A. Keyle & Kenneth B. Schwartz, *"Tally-Ho!": UPP and the 2010 Horizontal Merger Guidelines*, 77 ANTITRUST L.J. 587 (2011).

analysis may also vary depending on the type of merger or corporate combination that has been challenged.

Horizontal Mergers

A *horizontal merger* is the combining of two or more competing companies at the same level in the chain of production and distribution. The first step in determining the lawfulness of such a merger is to identify the relevant product and geographic markets. Courts use the same standards used under section 2 of the Sherman Act. Once the market is defined, the court will look primarily at three factors: (1) the market shares of the firms involved in the transaction, (2) the level of concentration in the market, and (3) whether the market is structurally conducive to anticompetitive behavior.

The classic case of *United States v. Philadelphia National Bank*[72] illustrates this method of analysis. In the early 1960s, Philadelphia National Bank (PNB) was the second largest bank in the Philadelphia market, which consisted of forty-two commercial banks in the metropolitan area of Philadelphia, Pennsylvania, and its three contiguous counties. After PNB signed a merger agreement with Girard Bank, the third largest bank in the same market, the United States sued to enjoin the merger on the grounds that it would violate section 7 of the Clayton Act.

The merger would have resulted in PNB's controlling at least 30% of the commercial banking business in the four-county Philadelphia metropolitan area, a market share that the U.S. Supreme Court viewed as an unacceptable threat to competition. After the merger, the two largest banks would control 59% of the market, whereas before the merger the two largest banks controlled only 44%. This increase in concentration also worried the Court. Neither the high level of government regulation of the banking business nor the banks' provision of services and intangible credit, rather than tangible products, made the banking industry immune from the anticompetitive effects of undue concentration. Because of these three elements, the Court directed the district court to enter judgment enjoining the merger. The Court explained:

> [A] merger which produces a firm controlling an undue percentage share of the relevant market, and results in a significant increase in the concentration of firms in that market is so inherently likely to lessen competition substantially that it must be enjoined in the absence of evidence clearly showing the merger is not likely to have such anticompetitive effects.

The 30% market share that the Court held to be excessive has been taken by many lower courts to create a presumption of illegality. The Supreme Court has insisted, however, that no single numerical standard can be applied to all markets. In the absence of a highly concentrated market, most courts today will not find a section 7 violation unless the merging firms have a combined market share of at least 30%.

In 2008, the Justice Department approved a merger between satellite radio's two principal carriers, XM Satellite Radio Holdings, Inc. and Sirius Satellite Radio, Inc. Although critics argued that the relevant market was satellite radio and that the proposed merger would create a vertical monopoly for the 17 million satellite radio customers, the Justice Department concluded that satellite radio was a small slice of a larger market that included radio and other music delivery services, such as Apple iPods and online entertainment.[73] In contrast, the FTC effectively blocked AT&T's proposed merger with T-Mobile in 2011.

Even if a merger or combination is determined to be presumptively illegal on the basis of market shares, the defendants may still show that the transaction is not likely to decrease competition. For example, if there are no barriers to entry in the relevant market, any transitory increase in concentration will be quickly eroded by the entry of new competitors into the market. If one of the combined firms is failing, the proposed transaction may be the only alternative to that failure. In either of these cases, section 7 liability can be avoided.

Vertical Mergers

A *vertical merger* is the acquisition by one company of another company at a higher or lower level in the chain of production and distribution. For example, the merger of an airplane manufacturer and an airplane-engine manufacturer would be a vertical merger. In vertical merger cases, courts tend to focus on whether the merger has excluded competitors from a significant sector of the market. For example, section 7 was held to be violated when competing suppliers were denied access to approximately 25% of the highly concentrated automobile market. When the market is less concentrated, however, the courts will analyze the market more thoroughly to determine whether the transaction has any anticompetitive effects.

Conglomerate Mergers

In the 1960s and 1970s, many academics and government prosecutors favored expanding section 7 prohibitions to cover mergers that were neither horizontal nor vertical in the traditional sense. This effort to prohibit *conglomerate mergers*—that is, the acquisition of a company by another company in a different line of business—has largely been abandoned. Because the merging companies are in different markets, there is no threat to competition.

---

72. 374 U.S. 321 (1963).

73. Miriam Marcus, *XM and Sirius Pay to Play*, FORBES.com (July 24, 2008), http://www.forbes.com/2008/07/24/xm-sirius-merger-closer-markets-cx_mlm_0724markets40.html.

IN BRIEF

Major Areas of Antitrust Concern

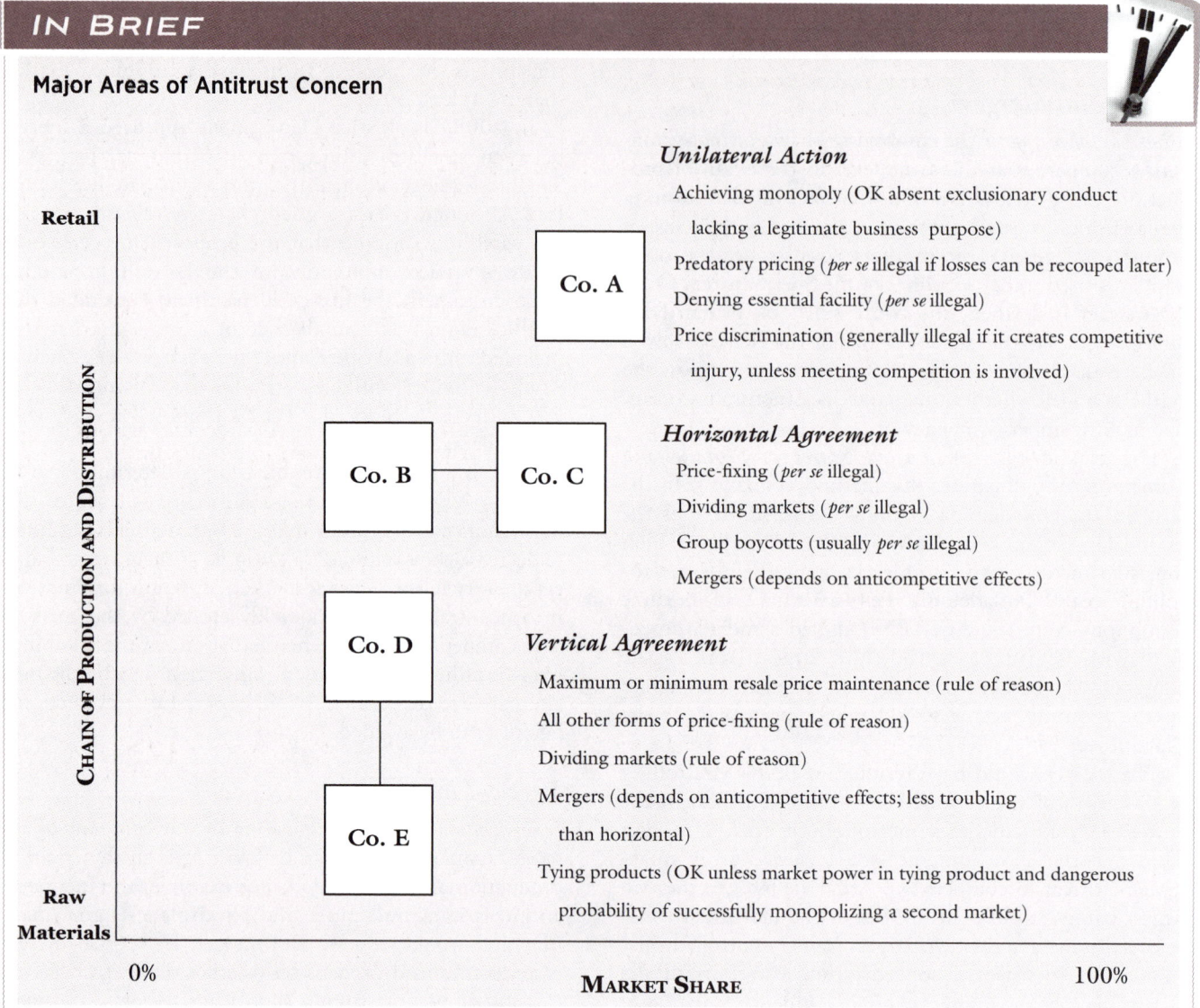

Unilateral Action

Achieving monopoly (OK absent exclusionary conduct
lacking a legitimate business purpose)

Predatory pricing (*per se* illegal if losses can be recouped later)

Denying essential facility (*per se* illegal)

Price discrimination (generally illegal if it creates competitive
injury, unless meeting competition is involved)

Horizontal Agreement

Price-fixing (*per se* illegal)

Dividing markets (*per se* illegal)

Group boycotts (usually *per se* illegal)

Mergers (depends on anticompetitive effects)

Vertical Agreement

Maximum or minimum resale price maintenance (rule of reason)

All other forms of price-fixing (rule of reason)

Dividing markets (rule of reason)

Mergers (depends on anticompetitive effects; less troubling
than horizontal)

Tying products (OK unless market power in tying product and dangerous
probability of successfully monopolizing a second market)

Retail ... **Raw Materials**

CHAIN OF PRODUCTION AND DISTRIBUTION

Co. A, Co. B — Co. C, Co. D, Co. E

0% **MARKET SHARE** 100%

One theory advanced during this period has endured, although it has rarely been applied. A merger between firms that are not competitors at the time of the acquisition but that might, without the merger, have become competitors may be held to violate section 7. This is because potential competition is useful in keeping prices at competitive levels. When prices rise above competitive levels, potential competitors will have an incentive to enter the market and charge competitive prices. When there is no such potential entrant into the market, there is no pressure to keep prices at competitive levels. Monopoly pricing may result.

Consequently, it can be argued that a merger violates section 7 if a plaintiff proves that (1) the market is highly concentrated; (2) one of the merging firms is an actual, substantial competitor in the market and the other is one of a small number of firms that might have entered the market; (3) entry of the latter firm would be reasonably likely to have procompetitive effects; and (4) without the

merger, entry by the latter firm was likely. Some attorneys argue that a merger does not have to eliminate an actual potential entrant in order to violate section 7. Under this theory (which the Justice Department embraced in the 2010 Guidelines), it is sufficient if the merger eliminates a perceived potential entrant.

UNFAIR METHODS OF COMPETITION: SECTION 5 OF THE FEDERAL TRADE COMMISSION ACT

Section 5 of the Federal Trade Commission Act (FTC Act) is broader than the other antitrust laws. It provides that "unfair methods of competition in or affecting commerce and unfair or deceptive acts or practices in or affecting

commerce, are hereby declared unlawful." Congress did
not define these terms; instead, it empowered the Federal
Trade Commission, an independent administrative agency,
to determine what practices violate section 5 so that it can
be adapted to changing business practices. For example, the
FTC relied on section 5 when it sued Rambus for alleged
illegal monopolization resulting from its deception about
its patent position. Chapters 9 and 17 provide examples of
unfair or deceptive practices affecting consumers.

The FTC has the exclusive power to enforce the FTC
Act. It can conduct investigations of suspected antitrust
violations and issue interpretive rulings, general statements
of policy, trade regulation rules, and guidelines defining
unfair or deceptive practices. It can also issue cease-and-
desist orders against violators, which can be appealed to a
federal court.

STATE-ACTION EXEMPTION

More than sixty-five years ago, the Supreme Court declared that the antitrust laws apply to anticompetitive
actions by private parties, not to anticompetitive actions
by state legislatures or administrative bodies. Thus, state
action is exempt as long as (1) there is a clear state purpose to displace competition, and (2) the state provides
adequate public supervision. For example, the California
legislature passed a law designed to limit the production
of raisins and consequently to raise their price. Given that
California produced nearly one-half of the world's raisins,
the effect of this statute on interstate commerce was substantial. Nevertheless, the Supreme Court enunciated and
applied the state-action exemption in this case.[74]

The courts have refused to extend the exemption to
local municipalities except in certain limited circumstances.[75] The Local Government Antitrust Act of 1984,[76]
enacted to allay municipalities' fears of treble damages,

expressly eliminated local governments' liability for antitrust damages but preserved equitable remedies, such as
injunctions. The Act extended immunity from damages
to all officials or employees acting in an official capacity.

ANTITRUST ENFORCEMENT

Federal antitrust laws provide for both government and
private lawsuits. The two federal agencies responsible for
enforcing U.S. antitrust laws are the Justice Department,
through its Antitrust Division, and the FTC.

Criminal Violations of the Sherman Act

Violations of the Sherman Act may be prosecuted by
the Justice Department as felonies.[77] Corporations can
be fined up to $100 million for each violation, and the
fines can be increased under other statutes to the greater
of twice the gain to the competitors or twice the loss to
the victims. Individuals can be fined up to $1 million for
each violation and imprisoned for up to ten years. The
Justice Department views horizontal price-fixing as "hard
crime," to be punished by prison sentences whenever possible. Indeed, under the Federal Sentencing Guidelines,
some term of confinement is recommended for individuals convicted of horizontal price-fixing, bid rigging, or
market-allocation agreements; in most cases, first-time offenders serve a minimum sentence of six to twelve months.

Amnesty

In an effort to promote self-policing and self-reporting, the
Justice Department will provide amnesty to offenders who
believe they may have been involved in criminal antitrust
violations and who cooperate with the Antitrust Division.
The necessity of providing incentives to cooperate is particularly compelling in price-fixing cases given the nature
of cartels: "Because cartel activities are hatched and carried out in secret, obtaining the cooperation of insiders is
the best, and often the only way to crack a cartel."[78] The
Justice Department imposes six conditions for so-called
Type A amnesty from criminal prosecution:

1. The Antitrust Division of the U.S. Department of Justice has
not yet received information from any other source about the
conspiracy.

2. The applicant takes prompt and effective action to terminate
its involvement in the illegal activity upon its discovery of the
conspiracy.

74. Parker v. Brown, 317 U.S. 341 (1943).

75. See, e.g., City of Columbia v. Omni Outdoor Adver., Inc., 499 U.S. 365
(1991).

76. 15 U.S.C. §§ 34–36.

77. See Federal Trade Comm'n, *FTC Guide to the Antitrust Laws, available
at* http://www.ftc.gov/bc/antitrust/antitrust_laws.shtm (last updated
July 8, 2008).

78. R. Hewitt Pate, International Anti-Cartel Enforcement, Address at the
2004 ICN Cartels Workshop, Sydney, Australia (Nov. 21, 2004), at 5–6,
available at http://www.usdoj.gov/atr/public/speeches/206428.pdf.

3. The applicant reports the wrongdoing with candor and completeness and provides full, continuing, and complete cooperation throughout the investigation.

4. The applicant's confession is truly a corporate act as opposed to isolated confessions of individual executives or officials.

5. The applicant makes restitution to the injured parties.

6. The applicant did not coerce another party to participate in the illegal activity and was not the leader or originator of the illegal activity.[79]

Type B amnesty may be available, at the discretion of the Department of Justice, even after the investigation is under way if (1) the applicant is the first to qualify for amnesty with respect to the illegal activity; (2) the Antitrust Division does not yet have evidence against the applicant that is likely to result in a sustainable conviction; (3) the applicant took prompt and effective action to terminate its part in the activity upon the discovery of the illegal activity; (4) the applicant reports the illegal activity with candor and completeness and provides full, continuing, and complete cooperation that advances the Division's investigations; (5) the confession embodies a corporate act, not just isolated confessions of individuals; (6) the applicant makes restitution where possible; and (7) granting amnesty would not be unfair to others, considering the nature of the illegal activity, the applicant's role in it, and the time when the applicant came forward.[80]

Under either type, the Justice Department may bring criminal charges if the company or its agents fail to fulfill the conditions.[81] In such a proceeding, the defendants may use the amnesty agreement as a defense and show that they did not violate its terms.

Civil Suits by Federal or State Governments

The U.S. government may also (1) bring civil actions to enforce the antitrust laws and (2) sue for treble damages to recover for injury to its business or property resulting from an antitrust violation. The Justice Department enforces the Sherman and Clayton Acts through civil suits in the federal courts. The FTC enforces the Clayton Act and the FTC Act provisions on "unfair methods of competition" (but not the Sherman Act), primarily through administrative proceedings. Pursuant to a liaison agreement, the Justice Department refers all civil Robinson–Patman Act matters to the FTC for action. Although enforcement of the Robinson–Patman Act is a

low priority of the FTC,[82] private enforcement through civil litigation continues.

Finally, state attorneys general may bring civil actions under the Sherman Act for injuries sustained by residents in their respective states. In these *parens patriae actions*, treble damages may also be recovered. For example, in 2004, New York attorney general Eliot Spitzer filed a civil complaint accusing insurance broker Marsh & McLennan of arranging bidding procedures that steered business to insurers based on kickbacks to Marsh, rather than following procedures in the best interest of the clients purchasing insurance. Marsh settled the lawsuit in 2005 by agreeing to pay $850 million in restitution to the injured clients. The stock prices of insurers mentioned in the complaint dropped sharply, and at least six insurance company executives pleaded guilty to criminal charges.[83]

Injunctive Relief and Damages for Violations of Section 7 of the Clayton Act and the Hart–Scott–Rodino Antitrust Improvements Act

In the event of a violation of section 7 of the Clayton Act, the Justice Department, through the courts, and the FTC, through its own administrative proceedings, may seek (1) divestiture of acquired stock or assets; (2) sale of particular subsidiaries, divisions, or lines of business; (3) compulsory sale of needed materials to a divested firm; (4) compulsory sharing of technology; or (5) temporary restrictions on the defendant's own output or conduct. Justice Department or FTC action can delay, and perhaps unwind, a corporate merger or acquisition. State attorneys general may also sue to enforce section 7, and they have begun to do so with increasing frequency.

In April 2007, a district court judge dismissed the FTC's request to temporarily block Whole Foods Market's $565 million purchase of rival Wild Oats Market. The FTC had argued that the proposed transaction would reduce competition in the market for "premium, natural, and organic supermarkets," but the district court concluded that the relevant market was the wider supermarket industry. After the transaction closed in August 2007, Whole Foods began the process of integrating the companies, including closing a number of former Wild Oats stores, rebranding several other Wild Oats stores as Whole

---

79. U.S. Dep't of Justice, *Frequently Asked Questions Regarding the Antitrust Division's Leniency Program and Model Leniency Letters*, Nov. 19, 2008, *available at* http://www.justice.gov/atr/public/criminal/239583.htm (last visited Nov. 22, 2011).

80. *Id.*

81. Stolt-Nielsen, S.A. v. United States, 442 F.3d 177 (3d Cir. 2006).

82. In 1984, the FTC declared that the Robinson–Patman Act was protectionist legislation that has been costly to the consumer because its underlying goal is to protect individual competitors rather than competition in general. Since then the FTC has initiated only two Robinson–Patman enforcement actions. Irving Scher, *Corporations Should Keep in Mind the Threat of Private Litigation When Ensuring Robinson–Patman Act Compliance*, CORP. COUNS. WKLY. (BNA), Jan. 16, 2002, at 24.

83. Michael Bobelian, *Marsh Settles, Agrees to Pay $850 Million*, N.Y. L.J., Feb. 1, 2005, *available at* http://www.law.com/jsp/article.jsp?id=1107178525241.

Foods stores, and disposing of some of the other Wild Oats assets. Although the FTC typically does not appeal when it fails to secure a preliminary injunction, in this case it appealed the district court's decision. In July 2008, the U.S. Court of Appeals for the District of Columbia Circuit concluded that the district court had applied the wrong test in defining the relevant market and had underestimated the FTC's likelihood of success. As a result, the appellate court reversed the district court's denial of the preliminary injunction and remanded the case to the district court.[84] Ultimately, Whole Foods reached a settlement agreement with the FTC, whereby Whole Foods divested thirty-one Wild Oats stores and relinquished rights to the Wild Oats brand.[85]

Private Suits

The civil actions brought by private parties in the wake of criminal prosecutions can have drastic financial consequences. Private plaintiffs (sometimes called private attorneys general) are entitled to recover three times the damages they have sustained as a result of violations of the Sherman Act or the Clayton Act. (Enforcement of the FTC Act is reserved to the FTC.) Liability for antitrust damages is joint and several among all of the conspirators, so each conspirator is potentially liable for treble damages for the losses caused by all of the defendants. Participants in the massive international conspiracy to raise the price of vitamins and vitamin additives paid more than $1.4 billion to settle the civil lawsuits.[86] Microsoft paid about $4.6 billion to resolve antitrust lawsuits brought by seven companies, including Sun Microsystems, Time Warner, Inc. (on behalf of America Online), IBM, Novell, Gateway, and Burst.com.[87] (The "Inside Story" discusses the Justice Department's and European Commission's antitrust cases against Microsoft.)

Competitors of merging firms may also bring actions for injunctive relief. Recently, however, some courts have come to look with disfavor on such actions, fearing that they might halt mergers that would actually intensify competition.

Antitrust Injury

To recover damages, a plaintiff must establish that it sustained an *antitrust injury,* that is, a loss due to a competition-reducing aspect or effect of the defendant's violation of the antitrust laws. A plaintiff may not recover under the antitrust laws for losses that resulted from competition as such.

The Supreme Court ruled in *Atlantic Richfield Co. v. USA Petroleum,*[88] that maximum resale price maintenance (RPM) does not rise to an antitrust injury in the absence of predatory pricing. The Court reasoned that when the prices under an RPM program are set at nonpredatory levels, there is generally no anticompetitive effect, even though such pricing may reduce the market share of competitors or the price that they may charge consumers. As a result, the competitor may not recover damages under the antitrust laws. (The *ARCO* case was decided seven years before the Court's decision in *State Oil Co. v. Khan,*[89] which eliminated *per se* treatment of maximum RPM, and in many ways it laid the groundwork for that decision.)

Standing

To prevent private parties from jumping on the treble-damages bandwagon, the U.S. Supreme Court requires that a private plaintiff have *standing* to sue; that is, the plaintiff must have suffered an injury from the defendant's violation of the antitrust law. For example, a consumer buying goods from an innocent middleman does not have standing to recover from a manufacturer who was a member of a price-fixing cartel.[90]

THE EXTRATERRITORIAL REACH OF U.S. ANTITRUST LAW

Sections 1 and 2 of the Sherman Act expressly apply to "trade or commerce . . . with foreign nations," so they clearly have extraterritorial reach. Because sections 2 and 3 of the Clayton Act apply to price discrimination, tying arrangements, and exclusive-dealing contracts for commodities sold "for use, consumption, or resale within the United States," they have no extraterritorial reach.

Enforcement of Sherman Act

International Guidelines promulgated by the Antitrust Division of the Justice Department and the FTC provide that, in enforcing the antitrust laws, the agencies will take account of "international comity," defined as "respect among co-equal sovereign nations [that] plays a role in determining the recognition which one nation allows within its territory to the legislative, executive, or judicial acts of another nation."[91] (The comity doctrine is discussed further in Chapter 24.) Section 3 of the guidelines lists the following factors that the agencies will consider: (1) the significance to the violation of conduct within the

84. FTC v. Whole Foods Mkt., 533 F. 3d 869 (D.C. Cir. 2008).

85. Ashby Jones, *Making Sense of the Whole Foods/FTC Antitrust Settlement,* WALL ST. J., Mar. 6, 2009.

86. David Barboza, *$1.1 Billion to Settle Suit on Vitamins,* N.Y. TIMES, Nov. 4, 1999.

87. Jonathan Kim, *RealNetworks, Microsoft Settle Suit,* WASH. POST, Oct. 12, 2005.

88. 495 U.S. 328 (1990).

89. 522 U.S. 3 (1997).

90. California v. ARC Am. Corp., 490 U.S. 93 (1989).

91. FTC & U.S. Dep't of Justice, *Antitrust Enforcement Guidelines for International Operations,* Apr. 1995, *available at* http://www.justice.gov/atr/public/guidelines/internat.htm.

United States versus conduct outside the United States; (2) the nationality of the parties involved; (3) the presence or absence of an intent to affect U.S. consumers, markets, or exporters; (4) the significance and foreseeability of the effects on the United States versus the effects abroad; (5) the existence of reasonable expectations that would be furthered or defeated by the action; (6) the degree of conflict with foreign law and economic policies; (7) the extent to which the enforcement actions of another country may be affected; and (8) the effectiveness of foreign enforcement versus U.S. enforcement.

To avoid disputes with foreign governments, the U.S. courts apply the *sovereign immunity* doctrine. As discussed in Chapter 24, if a foreign firm's anticompetitive activity was directed by the government, then U.S. antitrust laws will not be enforced. If, however, the foreign government tolerates but does not require the anticompetitive acts, then the U.S. antitrust laws apply.

The basic U.S. rule for evaluating extraterritorial conduct affecting U.S. *imports* (where the anticompetitive conduct occurs offshore, but the adverse impact is felt by purchasers in the United States) is the purpose and effects test. The Sherman Act will apply to conduct by foreign partners in a foreign nation when (1) the intent of the parties is to affect commerce within the United States and (2) their conduct actually affects commerce in the United States. Defendants cannot defend such conduct by arguing that applicable foreign law conflicts with U.S. law unless their compliance with the laws of both countries is impossible.[92] In *United States v. Nippon Paper Industries Co.*,[93] the U.S. Court of Appeals for the First Circuit held that conduct by a non-U.S. company outside the United States that has an effect on commerce in the United States could form the basis for a criminal antitrust case.

Under the Foreign Trade Antitrust Improvement Act of 1982 (the FTAIA),[94] antitrust conduct (whether by U.S. or foreign firms and whether occurring in the United States or elsewhere) that affects U.S. *exports* can be regulated under the Sherman or FTC Act if it has a "direct, substantial and reasonably foreseeable effect of restraining U.S. exports." Section 4 of the Export Trading Act (also known as the Webb–Pomerene Export Act)[95] exempts conduct affecting the export of goods by an association of U.S.-based firms that would otherwise violate the Sherman Act if the conduct does not (1) have an anticompetitive effect in the United States, (2) injure domestic competitors of the association members, or (3) "artificially or intentionally enhance or depress prices within" the United States. To gain and maintain this exemption, the association must file its articles of agreement and annual reports with the FTC.

The U.S. antitrust authorities are less aggressive in dealing with conduct affecting U.S. exports when anticompetitive U.S. domestic conduct affects foreign markets. As the U.S. Supreme Court explained in *F. Hoffman–La Roche Ltd. v. Empagran S.A.*,[96] the FTAIA seeks to make clear that section 1 of the Sherman Act does not prevent American exporters and firms doing business abroad from entering into business arrangements, however anticompetitive, as long as those arrangements adversely affect only foreign markets. It does so by removing export activities and other commercial activities that take place abroad from the Sherman Act's reach, unless those activities adversely affect (1) domestic commerce, (2) imports to the United States, or (3) exporting activities of one engaged in such activities within the United States. The Court also ruled that it was unreasonable to apply the Sherman Act to conduct that is significantly foreign "insofar as that conduct causes independent foreign harm and that foreign harm alone gives rise to the plaintiff's claim."

Many countries do not accept treble damages as a remedy. For example, the United Kingdom does not allow any recovery in excess of single damages. Suppose a U.S. court awards a U.S. corporation (USCO) $15 million in damages, after trebling, in a suit against a U.K. corporation (UKCO). When USCO attempts to collect $15 million of UKCO's assets, the U.K. court will treat two-thirds of the $15 million award, or $10 million, as an illegal treble-damages award. Thus, USCO will be able to recover only $5 million in the U.K. court. Even when a U.S. court finds a foreign corporation in violation of the antitrust laws, any award of damages is meaningless without foreign enforcement of the award, unless the foreign corporation has assets in the United States that can be attached to satisfy the judgment.

U.S. Control over Offshore Mergers and Other Consolidations

The Justice Department and the FTC have generally required HSR reports for (1) U.S. acquisitions of foreign-based assets or securities and (2) foreign acquisitions of U.S.-based assets or securities that meet the HSR jurisdictional requirements. For example, the FTC fined German auto-parts maker Mahle GmbH $5.1 million in 1997 for failing to alert the agencies to its $40 million purchase of 40.1% of a Brazilian rival's voting stock. The FTC found that it had authority to intervene because both companies had U.S. subsidiaries.

No HSR notification is required (1) if a U.S. or foreign person acquires foreign assets unless those assets generated sales in or into the United States in excess of $50 million during the most recent fiscal year; (2) if a U.S. person acquires voting securities of a foreign issuer unless the issuer either (a) holds assets in the United States with an aggregate

---

92. Hartford Fire Ins. Co. v. California, 509 U.S. 764 (1993).

93. 109 F.3d 1 (1st Cir. 1997).

94. 15 U.S.C. §§ 1, 6a, 45.

95. 18 U.S.C. §§ 61–65.

96. 542 U.S. 155 (2004).

value in excess of $50 million or (b) made aggregate sales in or into the United States in excess of $50 million during the most recent fiscal year; or (3) if a foreign person acquires voting securities of a foreign issuer unless (a) the sale confers control of the issuer to the buyer and (b) the issuer either (i) holds assets in the United States with an aggregate value in excess of $50 million or (ii) made aggregate sales in or into the United States in excess of $50 million during the most recent fiscal year. Foreign acquisitions of foreign assets are exempt if the size of the transaction is less than $200 million and (1) the aggregate sales of the acquirer and acquired person in or into the United States are less than $110 million, (2) the aggregate assets of the acquirer and acquired person located in the United States are less than $110 million, and (3) the size-of-person test is not exceeded. This exemption protects small acquisitions by foreign buyers of foreign persons doing business with the United States.[97] (Like the other HSR jurisdictional requirements, these thresholds are adjusted annually. For example, the $50 million threshold was adjusted to $66 million in 2011.)

---

97. 16 C.F.R. pts. 802.51, 802.52.

GLOBAL VIEW

Antitrust Laws in the European Union

In the European Union, the principal rules of competition law are set forth in Articles 81 and 82 of the Treaty of Amsterdam and the Merger Control Regulation.[98] Firms doing business in the EU must also comply with the various antitrust laws of member nations. However, to the extent that EU law applies and conflicts with the laws of a member nation, EU law will prevail.

Article 81 addresses conduct similar to that addressed in section 1 of the Sherman Act, namely, "concerted practices which have the object or effect of preventing, restraining or distorting competition with the Common Market." It includes a nonexclusive list of prohibited activities, including price-fixing, output restrictions, market allocations, discriminatory practices, and tying arrangements. However, the European Commission has issued a number of "block" or group exemptions, which exempt whole categories of agreements. Even if a block exemption is not available, individual exemptions can be granted for specific agreements; the process for obtaining them is long and complex, however. Exemptions are binding on the EU and on the member nations' national authorities and courts.

One of the major differences between U.S. and EU competition laws is the EU's approach to vertical territorial restraints. Although the EU generally prohibits horizontal agreements between competitors in the same way as U.S. antitrust laws, the EU takes a stricter view of vertical arrangements because of their tendency to impede continent-wide market integration. As a result, although U.S. manufacturers are free to appoint exclusive distributors in each state, similar exclusive arrangements are suspect in the EU unless made pursuant to applicable block exemptions.

Article 82 prohibits abuse of an entity's dominant position. It is in some ways stricter than section 2 of the Sherman Act, because the definition of the relevant market is narrower and the degree of market power that makes a company dominant is less. The question of what constitutes a dominant position is complex and depends on a number of factors, such as the firm's market share in the relevant market, the competitive pressures it faces, its ability to control price, and barriers to entry to its market. The concept of what constitutes "abuse" is also broader than the U.S. concept of "monopolization." In contrast to the broad language in section 2 of the Sherman Act, Article 86 lists four types of conduct that constitute abuse of dominant position: imposing unfair pricing, limiting production, employing discriminatory trade practices, and imposing a tying arrangement.[99]

Although EU competition law shares the U.S. antitrust goal of preventing abuse of market power, there are substantive differences between the two laws. EU law is concerned with the effects of anticompetitive actions on competitors as well as consumers, whereas U.S. law focuses primarily on consumers. There are also material differences in enforcement. The European Commission has the primary responsibility for enforcing EU competition laws. Unlike U.S. law, EU law does not include a private right of action, there is no criminal enforcement authority, and treble damages are not available. Many member states have a private right of action for violation of their local competition laws, however.[100]

Extraterritorial Reach of EU Antitrust Law

EU competition law has an international component similar to the U.S. law announced in *Hartford Fire Insurance Co. v. California*.[101] On the import side, if foreign or domestic firms

CONTINUED

---

98. *See Rules of Application and Procedure for Articles 81 and 82 of the EC Treaty*, updated July 7, 2005, *available at* http://europa.eu/legislation_summaries/other/l26042_en.htm.

99. Mark R. Sandstrom & David N. Goldsweig, Negotiating and Structuring International Commercial Transactions 421 (2003).

100. Elizabeth Morony & Ingrid Cope, *Private Antitrust Remedies: Latest Developments*, Global Couns., Mar. 2003, at 32.

101. 509 U.S. 764 (1993).

engage in conduct outside the EU that, had it occurred within the EU, would have violated the EU antitrust laws, and that conduct has the purpose and effect of distorting competition within the EU, then violators can be prosecuted in the EU. On the export side (that is, can EU antitrust laws be used to protect U.S. markets?), there is no EU legislation that is equivalent to the Webb–Pomerene Export Act. Nonetheless, the language of the Treaty of Amsterdam does not appear to put EU export cartels in jeopardy unless they have impacts within the EU.

The EU and its predecessors have enforced its laws against U.S. companies doing business in Europe for many years. For example, in 1980, the European Commission sued IBM, the world's largest computer manufacturer, claiming that IBM had abused its dominant position in the supply of two key products—the central processing unit (CPU) and the operating system—for its most powerful range of computers, System/370, in an effort to control the markets for the supply of all products compatible with System/370. The alleged abuses included (1) failing to supply other manufacturers in sufficient time with the technical interface information needed to permit competitive products to be used with System/370, (2) not offering System/370 CPUs without main memory included in the price, (3) not offering System/370 CPUs without the basic software included in the price, and (4) refusing to supply certain software installation services to users of non-IBM CPUs. In 1984, IBM agreed to offer its System/370 CPUs either without main memory or with only such capacity as was strictly required for testing and to disclose, in a timely manner, sufficient interface information to enable competitors to attach both their hardware and their software products to System/370. IBM had previously advised the European Commission that it had taken steps to make installation services available to all users of its software and was in the course of unbundling all software.[102]

In 2007, the EU issued a "statement of objections" alleging that Intel had violated EU law "with the aim of excluding its main rival, AMD," from the market for the widely used x86 computer chip. The charges alleged three types of antitrust violations: (1) offering substantial rebates to computer makers if they agreed to obtain most of their CPU chips from Intel, (2) making payments to induce computer makers to delay or cancel the launch of products that used AMD chips, and (3) providing strategic customers with below-cost CPU chips in an attempt to outbid AMD.[103] The European Commission fined Intel a record 1.06 billion euros (the equivalent of $1.45 billion) in 2009 for its abuse of the computer chip market.[104]

The EU case is only one of a series of global investigations into Intel's business practices. In March 2005, Japan's Fair Trade Commission found that Intel had violated Japan's antimonopoly laws by illegally forcing full or partial exclusivity with five Japanese computer companies; instead of imposing a fine, the Commission called on Intel to change some of its practices. In July 2008, South Korea's antitrust regulator announced that it would order Intel to pay $25.4 million for violating its fair trade rules by offering rebates to South Korea computer manufacturers and undercutting AMD.[105] AMD also sued Intel in Japan and the United States for antitrust violations, and a U.S. class action filed by Dell stockholders claimed Intel illegally paid Dell more than $1 billion per year to not purchase microprocessors from its competitors.[106] In 2009, AMD agreed to drop all pending antitrust litigation against Intel pursuant to an agreement whereby Intel agreed to pay AMD $1.25 billion and share chip technology through a five-year cross-licensing agreement.[107]

EU Control over Offshore Mergers and Other Consolidations

The EC Merger Control Regulation[108] requires a more stringent merger analysis than is required by U.S. law because of both the EU's greater willingness to consider theories of competitive harm and its greater reliance on input from competitors. In addition, the fact that the EU can prohibit a merger without going to court gives the EU's Merger Task Force power and discretion that exceed that of its U.S. counterparts.

The Merger Control Regulation provides that in determining whether to challenge a merger within its jurisdiction, the EU must decide whether the merger is "compatible with the common market." The substantive test applied is whether a concentration will "create or strengthen a dominant position as a result of which effective competition would be significantly impeded in the common market or a substantial part of it." Although the analysis is similar to U.S. law, the outcome can be different. For example, as discussed in the "Global View" in Chapter 1, even though the U.S. government had approved General Electric's $49 billion bid for Honeywell International, the European Commission vetoed the deal in January 2001, on the basis that GE might have been able to drive competitors out of the aerospace market by offering customers a complete package of GE engines, Honeywell avionics, and financing from GE Capital Aviation Services. The EU's decision was criticized in the United States, where regulators are inclined to allow businesses to pursue such synergies.[109]

102. Commission of the European Communities, Fourteenth Report on Competition Policy (1984).

103. Jennifer L. Schenker, *Europe's Tough Case Against Intel*, BUS. WK., July 27, 2007.

104. James Kanter, *Europe Fines Intel a Record $1.45 Billion in Antitrust Case*, N.Y. TIMES, May 13, 2009.

105. Kelly Olsen, *S. Korea to Hit Intel with $25.4M Antitrust Fine*, USA TODAY, June 5, 2008.

106. Schenker, *supra* note 103.

107. Arik Hesseldahl & Cliff Edwards, *Intel and AMD Reach a Landmark Settlement*, BLOOMBERGBUSINESSWEEK, Nov. 12, 2009.

108. The text is available at http://eurlex.europa.eu/LexUriServ/LexUriServ.do?uri=CELEX:32004R0139:EN:HTML (last amended Jan. 20, 2004).

109. *Q&A: GE's Failed Merger*, BBC NEWS, July 4, 2001, *available at* http://news.bbc.co.uk/2/hi/business/1421879.stm.

THE RESPONSIBLE MANAGER

AVOIDING ANTITRUST VIOLATIONS

Although a manager can never eliminate all possible antitrust violations, implementing a number of steps can help to avoid them. The underlying purpose of the antitrust statutes is to benefit consumers by promoting competition. The economy functions best when firms compete vigorously, but fairly, with one another. In antitrust, however, the line between legal and illegal conduct is often blurry. Consequently, there are few bright-line rules that a manager can give to his or her employees. Rather, the manager must identify the activities or conditions that most often trigger antitrust liability, such as discussions with competitors and activities that may increase concentration in any market that is already highly concentrated.

Discussions among competitors receive the highest degree of antitrust scrutiny. Trade and professional associations are particularly vulnerable. If they disseminate information that identifies parties to individual transactions and the prices of even past or current individual transactions, the antitrust laws may be violated. Equally hazardous is the dissemination of information that may result in market division or output restriction. As a general rule, any trade association information concerning prices should be immediately forwarded to in-house or outside counsel to address potential antitrust concerns.

Antitrust scrutiny is also heightened whenever price is discussed, even between manufacturers and retailers. An agreement between a manufacturer and a distributor that sets the minimum price the distributor may charge end consumers will be analyzed under the rule of reason. It may also violate applicable state laws even if it does not violate federal law.

Finally, antitrust scrutiny is heightened where markets are highly concentrated. The fewer the entities that compete in a particular market, the more likely that illegal agreements in restraint of trade among them can be effectuated and that mergers can lead to unlawful monopolies. Consequently, corporations operating in concentrated markets should be particularly cautious. A manager can obtain rough approximations of market concentration from company counsel.

Employees should be encouraged, through an appropriate award system, to inform the manager whenever any of the above "red flags" appear. A manager should not hesitate to seek assistance from counsel in analyzing any activity that might violate the antitrust laws. The manager should also be careful to avoid any situation that could be interpreted as evidence of illegal activity. If a manager attending a trade show, for example, hears competitors discussing price or other terms of sale, the manager should leave the room, preferably in a manner that calls attention to his or her departure, such as by spilling a drink while leaving a group of competitors having drinks at a bar. In the event that a manager learns that his or her company has violated U.S. antitrust laws, the manager should consider the possibility of reporting the violation to the government in exchange for amnesty.

Common sense and education are the keys. Actions that do not seem fair usually are not. Continuing education programs will keep corporate employees aware of potential antitrust problems. A manager should always stress that short-term gains through unethical or illegal behavior are always outweighed by longer-term losses, particularly in the area of antitrust with its treble-damages awards. At the same time, it is important for employees to understand that winning market share through the sale of superior or cheaper products or services is not illegal. As Judge Learned Hand cautioned more than sixty-five years ago, "The successful competitor, having been urged to compete, must not be turned upon when he wins."[110] For a firm with market power, the difference between an exhortation to "kill the competition" and "make a product everyone will want to buy" can be determinative.

---

110. United States v. Aluminum Co. of Am., 148 F.2d 416, 430 (2d Cir. 1945).

A MANAGER'S DILEMMA

Putting It into Practice

Illegal Price-Fixing or Just Good Customer Service?

You are the vice president for marketing at Explorer Technology (ET), a manufacturer of plasma screens. During a meeting with your staff, several pricing proposals are made with strong arguments to support each proposal.

a. ET should set a minimum price per set that the wholesalers can charge.

b. ET should set a maximum price per set that the wholesalers can charge.

c. The wholesalers can charge any price they want within a certain range; if they charge a higher price, they must give the customer a rebate coupon for the differential.

CONTINUED

d. The wholesalers can charge any price they want, but if they advertise a price that is less than ET's specified minimum advertised price, the wholesalers are not entitled to receive the marketing funds that ET provides to wholesalers that do not advertise prices that are less than the specified minimum advertised price.

After the meeting, you are considering the pros and cons of each plan so that you can make a recommendation to the president. Although each plan has different marketing advantages, your staff estimates that each will result in approximately the same level of sales. What other factors should you consider before making your recommendation? What are the legal pros and cons of each proposal? What else do you need to know before calculating the legal trade-offs among the proposals?

INSIDE STORY

Google Replaces Microsoft as Antitrust Poster Child

A cartoonist once quipped that you know you've really arrived when the Justice Department's Antitrust Division is knocking at your door. By this measure, Google has definitely arrived. Google controls more than 65% of the U.S. search market, and commentators are drawing parallels between its ever-growing reach and the Microsoft practices that the FTC formally began investigating in 1991.

According to *The Huffington Post*:

There are many similarities between modern day Google and Microsoft circa 1991. Both companies are enormous, highly profitable and indispensable for consumers—and both have been accused of using their massive reach to choke off their competitors. . . . [Both] have used similar strategies to grow their empires. Both seek to be at the core of consumers' digital interactions, whether powering their PCs or their web browsing, and strive to stay dominant by aggressively expanding their offerings so that users never have to exit the Google or Microsoft ecosystem. Just as Microsoft wanted to provide both the software used on computers, in the form of its Windows operating system, and the gateway to the web, via the Internet Explorer browser, Google aims to extend its reach to serve consumers not only when they search, but when they send emails, place calls, look for directions and buy a smartphone. Google has essentially made it possible to do everything online without ever leaving its network of properties, a move that recalls Microsoft's own efforts to manage the user experience on desktops and laptops.[111]

The rise of Google and the resurgence of Apple, Inc. at the expense of Microsoft show how dynamic markets are. Former IBM CEO Louis Gerstner blamed IBM's loss of market share to firms like Microsoft on the decade-long antitrust battle waged by the Justice Department.[112] Will Microsoft suffer the same fate? Will Google?

In 1994, the U.S. Department of Justice's Antitrust Division charged Microsoft with unlawful monopoly and restraint of trade under sections 1 and 2 of the Sherman Act. These practices included charging per-processor royalties, whereby personal computer (PC) manufacturers were offered a discount if they agreed to pay a royalty to Microsoft for each computer processor sold, regardless of whether the unit was shipped with the Microsoft operating system or a competitor's operating system.

The government based its case on the notion of "network economics," a condition in which the value of owning a product rises as other consumers own the same product. Because most PC owners used Microsoft's operating system, the regulators argued, Microsoft could coerce them into buying other products simply by tying the two together.

Microsoft argued, however, that operating systems are dynamic and must respond to consumer demand and technological advances. Microsoft reasoned that although operating systems initially did not include modules for data compression, memory management, file backup, or device driving, these functions were integrated into the operating system over time as consumers began to expect them as standard rather than options.

In 1995, Microsoft abandoned its per-processor pricing arrangements and signed a consent decree with the Department of Justice that prohibited it from conditioning the license of its operating system to original equipment manufacturers (OEMs) on their agreement to license other Microsoft products. Microsoft, however, retained the right to develop integrated products.

CONTINUED

111. Bianca Bosker, *Google Antitrust Inquiry: Microsoft's History Looms Large*, HUFFINGTON POST (June 23, 2011), http://www.huffington-post.com/2011/06/23/google-antitrust-inquiry-_n_883389.html.

112. LOUIS V. GERSTNER, JR., WHO SAYS ELEPHANTS CAN'T DANCE? INSIDE IBM'S HISTORIC TURNAROUND (2002).

Thereafter, Microsoft bundled a version of Windows 95 with its Internet Explorer (IE) web browser at no additional cost and prohibited OEMs from disassembling the package. PC operating systems had always served to coordinate a user's access to various sources of information, including internal hard drives, floppy disk drives, random access memory, and CD-ROM drives. With the birth of the Internet, Microsoft reasoned that it was time for operating systems to also provide access to the World Wide Web. By this logic, integration of web browsers was the natural next step in operating system evolution.

Within two years, Internet Explorer had garnered more than 40% of the web browser market, largely at the expense of Netscape Communications Corporation, which had developed the wildly popular Navigator browser. No doubt, IE's rapid success was due in part to Microsoft's bundling of IE with Windows at no additional cost. Its functionality, however, made it a worthy rival to Navigator.

In October 1997, the Justice Department petitioned the U.S. District Court for the District of Columbia to find Microsoft in contempt of court for violating the 1995 consent decree and to fine the company $1 million per day until it complied by unbundling Windows and IE. Although the trial court did not find Microsoft in contempt, it issued a preliminary injunction prohibiting Microsoft from further conditioning its licensing of PC operating system software (including Windows 95 or any successor version) on the licensing of any Microsoft browser, pending development of the record.

In May 1998, the U.S. Court of Appeals for the District of Columbia stayed the injunction insofar as it applied to Windows 98 (which further integrated IE into the operating system).[113] The court held that the United States had presented no evidence suggesting Windows 98 was not an integrated product and thus exempt from the prohibitions of the consent decree. The court ruled that, at least for purposes of deciding whether products were integrated within the meaning of the consent decree, the test was whether the integrated product provided functionalities and advantages that consumers could not themselves achieve by buying both products and using them together. The court also questioned the competency of judges to dictate what features should be included in an operating system.

The Justice Department filed a wide-ranging complaint against Microsoft in May 1998. The attorneys general of twenty states filed similar suits the same day. The Justice Department alleged that Microsoft's restrictive agreements with Internet and online service providers (such as America Online) and Internet content providers, whereby those companies agreed not to license, distribute, or promote non-Microsoft products (or to do so only on terms that materially disadvantaged such products), and Microsoft's agreements with OEMs restricting

modification or customization of the PC boot-up sequence and screen, unreasonably restricted competition in violation of section 1. The complaint also alleged that Microsoft had engaged in a series of anticompetitive practices (including tying and unreasonably exclusionary agreements) with the purpose and effect of maintaining its PC operating system monopoly and extending that monopoly to the Internet browser market in violation of section 2.

In 2000, the district court held that Microsoft had violated section 1 by tying Internet Explorer to Windows and had attempted to monopolize the browser market in violation of section 2, but it rejected the Justice Department's exclusive dealing claim under section 1 on the basis that Microsoft's agreements for IE did not foreclose enough of the relevant market to constitute a violation.[114] Evidence of monopolistic intent included statements by a Microsoft executive that Microsoft should "cut off Netscape's air supply"[115] and "knife the baby."[116]

The district court ordered that Microsoft be split into two companies, with one selling the Window's operating system and the other selling Microsoft's Office suite of word-processing, spreadsheet generation, and other applications. Microsoft immediately appealed.

In 2001, the U.S. Court of Appeals for the District of Columbia affirmed the district court's judgment that Microsoft had violated section 2 of the Sherman Act by employing anticompetitive means to maintain a monopoly in the operating system market but reversed the finding that Microsoft had violated section 2 of the Sherman Act by illegally attempting to monopolize the Internet browser market.[117] The Ninth Circuit also reversed the finding that Microsoft had committed a *per se* violation of section 1 by unlawfully tying its browser to its operating system and remanded this issue to the trial court for reconsideration under the rule of reason. The Justice Department subsequently elected not to pursue the tying issue.

Later that year, Microsoft, the Justice Department, and nine of the eighteen states that had joined in the litigation agreed to a settlement. The remaining nine states rejected the settlement and pressed for stiffer penalties in the penalty phase of the litigation, but Judge Colleen Kollar-Kotelly rejected most of the tougher penalties proposed by the states as overbroad

CONTINUED

---

113. Microsoft Corp. v. United States, 147 F.3d 935 (D.C. Cir. 1998).

114. United States v. Microsoft Corp., 84 F. Supp. 2d 9 (D.D.C. 1999).

115. Andrew Orlowski, *Microsoft "Killed Dell Linux"—States*, THE REGISTER, Mar. 19, 2002, *available at* http://www.theregister. co.uk/2002/03/19/microsoft_killed_dell_linux_states/.

116. *Id.*

117. United States v. Microsoft Corp., 253 F.3d 34 (D.C. Cir. 2001). The court of appeals also reversed the finding that Microsoft had committed a *per se* violation of section 1 by unlawfully tying its browser to its operating system and remanded this issue to the trial court for consideration under the rule of reason (the Justice Department subsequently elected not to pursue the tying issue).

and instead relied heavily on the earlier settlement proposal. Key elements of the remedy included the following:

- Microsoft must allow PC makers to add or substitute competitive products to handle popular tasks like web browsing. Microsoft programs will remain on the machine, however.

- Microsoft cannot enter into agreements with PC makers, independent service providers, and others to sell only Microsoft products, although Microsoft is allowed to provide financial incentives to them for promoting Microsoft products, such as offering PC makers discounts if they agree to use all-Microsoft products on their desktop computers.

- There is no restriction on Microsoft's ability to develop and bundle new features into its operating system.

- Microsoft is required to disclose application program interfaces, along with related technical information, which Microsoft Middleware utilizes to interoperate with the Windows platform. In a small concession to the states, Judge Kollar-Kotelly expanded the definition of "Microsoft Middleware" to include server/network computing and interactive television software, although she refused to include handheld devices or web services.

- The plaintiffs are required to appoint a committee to coordinate enforcement of the remedial decree. Plaintiffs may also select a compliance officer who will serve as a high-level Microsoft employee, but retain a significant amount of autonomy and independence from the company.

Judge Kollar-Kotelly retained jurisdiction over the implementation of the consent decree and asked Microsoft to designate a member of its board of directors to oversee its implementation.

Although the settlement with the U.S. regulators permitted Microsoft to continue to freely bundle new technologies into the operating system in the United States, in 2004 the European Commission ordered Microsoft to offer a version of its Windows operating system with its MediaPlayer software stripped out. The Commission also required Microsoft to license certain of its proprietary tools to its competitors so that their software could communicate more effectively with the Windows operating system. When negotiations broke down with Microsoft, the European Commission sued. In 2007, the European Court of First Instance (CFI) upheld the Commission's findings, its imposition of a then-record 497 million euro ($666 million) fine, and its order.[118] Microsoft ultimately paid more than $2.7 billion in fines, penalties, and costs.

In 2008, the EU opened new investigations into Microsoft's practices after receiving complaints that it was competing unfairly in the market for web browsers by using the Internet Explorer software. The EU also investigated whether Microsoft was making it too hard for its rivals to work with its Office suite applications.[119] As a result of these investigations, Microsoft announced that it would not bundle Internet Explorer with the version of Windows to be sold in Europe. In 2009, the EU agreed that Microsoft could offer to include a "ballot box" screen option to let Internet users choose their browser from twelve options, including Internet Explorer.

Microsoft's obligations under the agreement with the U.S. Justice Department expired in May 2011. Now, the focus of antitrust concern has transferred over to Google, whose practices are currently being investigated by both the FTC and EU. Critics of the company claim that its dominant share of the search market gives it unparalleled influence over what users are exposed to when searching on the Internet. As Google has expanded its products' reach to include other areas, such as mapping, shopping, and travel, other companies are accusing Google of giving its own products better placement in search results. If true, this could be hurting smaller companies and consumers, who are denied the benefits of the best search results.

According to the *Washington Post*, Google takes the position that its users are free to use other search engines and that "when [Google] places its own results higher than others, it's merely trying to give users the information they want faster."[120] As one Google spokesperson put it: "Our goal in making changes to the way we present search results is to get people the information they're looking for as quickly and effortlessly as possible."[121]

Despite the looming antitrust investigations in the United States and Europe, Google continues to expand its empire and offer more services. Its search results now include photos and other information about local businesses, which puts the company in direct competition with other websites like Yelp and Citysearch.[122]

Meanwhile, Apple has also faced scrutiny over its newfound dominance. One class-action lawsuit claimed that Apple maintained an illegal music store monopoly through iTunes by preventing music files sold by competitors from playing on Apple's iPods. Apple faced a similar situation in 2005, when it was sued by consumer groups in France for its iTunes–iPod tie-in.

The IBM, Microsoft, Google, and Apple cases raise the question of whether technology markets are too inherently fluid to be effectively regulated by nation-states. Given the U.S. Supreme Court's acceptance of the Chicago School's approach to market economics, such an argument is likely to have more sway in the United States than in the EU.

---

118. For a summary of the CFI decision, *see generally* Constance E. Bagley, *Commission of the European Communities v. Microsoft Corporation* (Yale Sch. of Mgmt. Case No. 07-054, 2007).

119. James Kanter, *Harsh Words for Microsoft Technology*, N.Y. TIMES, June 11, 2008, at C8.

120. Jia Lynn Yang, *Google Faces Antitrust Glare on Capitol Hill*, WASH. POST, Sept. 20, 2011.

121. Bianca Bosker, *Google Adds More of Its Own Goodies to Search Results, Despite Antitrust Concerns*, HUFFINGTON POST (Nov. 2, 2011), http://www.huffingtonpost.com/2011/11/02/google-adds-search-features_n_1071323.html.

122. *Id.*

KEY WORDS AND PHRASES

QUESTIONS AND CASE PROBLEMS

1. You work in sales and are friendly with a sales representative from one of your employer's competitors. Your children are in the same class at school, so you see each other frequently. While watching a Saturday soccer game, you talked about a new sales promotion that your company plans to offer. Is it ethical to have such a conversation? Is it legal? Should it matter whether the promotion is the subject of an advertisement in the trade magazines?

2. The two largest newspapers in Chicago are the *Chicago Tribune* and the *Sun Times*, and the two largest supplemental news providers are the New York Times News Service and the Los Angeles Times/Washington News Service. In addition to printing the work of its own staff, the *Tribune* has a contract with the New York Times News Service pursuant to which the Service provides news and other material of interest to the *Tribune* on an exclusive basis in the Chicago area. The *Sun Times* has a similar exclusive arrangement with the Los Angeles Times/Washington News Service. As a result of these exclusive contracts, Chicago's third largest newspaper, the *Daily Herald*, could not obtain newsfeed from either service. It was also unable to obtain newsfeed from the third most popular provider because it was owned by the *Tribune*, which refused to license its stories to a competitor in its home market. The *Daily Herald* challenged this pattern of exclusive distributorships as a violation of section 1 of the Sherman Act, claiming that it effectively denied the *Herald* the opportunity to subscribe to the best supplemental news services. Does a pattern of exclusive distributorships in a market violate the Sherman Act? In what way could the news services'

practices harm consumers? What if the *Herald* could show that it had tried to outbid the *Tribune* or the *Sun Times* for their supplemental news service subscriptions? Would the *Herald's* argument be stronger if the exclusive agreements were long-term agreements? [*Paddock Publications, Inc. v. Chicago Tribune Co.*, 103 F.3d 42 (7th Cir. 1996).]

3. Research in Motion (RIM), manufacturer of the BlackBerry smartphone, sued its direct competitor Motorola, alleging that Motorola violated section 2 of the Sherman Act when it broke a commitment to standard-setting organizations to license patents that covered wireless communications technology included in international standards on "fair, reasonable, and nondiscriminatory" (FRAND) terms. What would RIM have to prove to establish this claim? [*Research in Motion Ltd. v. Motorola, Inc.*, 644 F. Supp. 2d 788 (N.D. Tex. 2008).]

4. Gerber, Heinz, and Beech-Nut, manufacturers of baby food, account for essentially the entire market in the United States. A number of retail stores filed an antitrust class action against the companies alleging that they had violated section 1 of the Sherman Act by engaging in an unlawful conspiracy to fix prices. The class presented evidence that sales representatives employed by the three companies exchanged price information about their products, including, on occasion, sending each other advance notice of price increases. The class of store owners also introduced evidence of e-mails indicating that the companies were aware of anticipated price increases before they were announced in the market. One memo stated that Heinz would not try to secure a majority base of distribution in a sales

area because it had agreed to a "truce" with Gerber. Did the companies violate the antitrust laws? Would you need any additional evidence to make this determination? [*In re Baby Food Antitrust Litigation*, 166 F.3d 112 (3d Cir. 1999).]

5. Will a dealer who sells a manufacturer's products in an exclusive territory be able to successfully sue the manufacturer under the Robinson–Patman Act if the manufacturer is offering lower prices to dealers in other exclusive territories? [*Volvo Trucks N. Am., Inc. v. Reeder-Simco GMC, Inc.*, 546 U.S. 164 (2006).]

6. U.S. manufacturers want to bring a suit against Japanese manufacturers, alleging a conspiracy to take over the U.S. automobile industry by exporting low-priced products to the United States while keeping the prices artificially high in Japan. The U.S. manufacturers tell you, their attorney, that the Japanese manufacturers have formed an association in which they discuss market conditions in the United States, potential or actual import restrictions, surcharges, and simplification of export procedures, as well as other topics.

    a. In light of these facts, what are the chances of successfully bringing an antitrust suit against these manufacturers? Assume that there are no conflict-of-law or other procedural problems created by the manufacturers being in another country.

    b. What if instead of discussing the topics listed above, the manufacturers discussed the details of individual sales, production, inventories, current price lists, and future price trends?

    c. What if they discussed average costs, freight rates, and terms of past transactions without identifying buyers or sellers? [*Matsushita Electric Industrial Co. v. Zenith Radio Corp.*, 475 U.S. 574 (1986).]

7. Leegin Creative Leather Products, Inc. is a manufacturer of leather apparel. In order to focus its brand on quality, Leegin refused to sell its products to retailers who intended to sell the products below Leegin's suggested retail prices. Five years after establishing this policy, Leegin discovered that Kay's Kloset was selling its products below the recommended prices. When Kay's refused to comply with Leegin's request to raise prices, Leegin stopped shipping its products to Kay's. PSKS, Inc., Kay's parent company, sued Leegin, claiming violation of antitrust laws. What facts would each party have to marshal to prove its case? What result? [*PSKS, Inc. v. Leegin Creative Leather Products, Inc.*, 615 F.3d 412 (5th Cir. 2010).]

8. Locked-out professional basketball players Carmelo Anthony, Chauncey Billups, Kevin Durant, Leon Powe, and Kawhi Leonard file a class-action lawsuit against the National Basketball Association (NBA). The plaintiffs allege that by refusing to allow players to work, the NBA created an illegal group boycott, price-fixing agreement, and price restraint in violation of the Sherman Act. The only offers the owners made to settle the dispute would drastically reduce player salaries and effectively wipe out the competitive market for most NBA players. What result? Was filing this suit an effective tactic by the players? How would you respond if you were the lead negotiator for the owners? [*Brown v. Pro Football, Inc.*, 518 U.S. 231 (1996); *American Needle, Inc. v. National Football League*, 130 S. Ct. 2201 (2010).]

CHAPTER 17

CONSUMER PROTECTION

INTRODUCTION

ROLE OF CONSUMER PROTECTION LAW IN BUSINESS

Historically, consumers had little recourse in the event of a dispute with a vendor, manufacturer, producer, service provider, or creditor. Consumer transactions were commonly governed by the concept of *caveat emptor* ("let the buyer beware"). Today, the standard has shifted closer to *caveat venditor* ("let the seller beware"). Federal and state laws protect consumers from unsafe or harmful consumer products, unfair and deceptive trade practices, fraud, and misleading or discriminatory credit requirements. Managers must, of course, comply with the law. In addition, by being proactive, working with administrative agencies, and promoting industry self-regulation, managers may be able to both protect brand equity and forestall burdensome new regulatory restrictions. Conversely, failure to meet societal expectations leads to more government regulation.

Consumer protection law should not be confused with product liability law, discussed in Chapter 10. Product liability law provides a common law remedy enforced by private action, whereas consumer protection law provides a statutory remedy enforced by the government (and, in some cases, also by private parties).

CHAPTER OVERVIEW

This chapter examines three primary areas of consumer protection law and the agencies, departments, and commissions that administer and enforce them: (1) consumer health and safety (including the regulation of food, drugs, medical devices, automobiles, broadcasting, and the Internet); (2) unfairness, deception, and fraud (including the regulation of advertising, packaging and labeling, pricing, warranties, and certain sales practices); and (3) consumer credit. The discussion focuses primarily on federal legislation, although numerous state-law topics are also discussed. In general, consumer protection law at the state level is more stringent than federal law, and, as discussed in the "Global View," product safety and environmental standards in the European Union are higher than those in the United States. Privacy protection is discussed in Chapter 9, and consumer bankruptcy is described in Chapter 23.

COMMISSIONS AND AGENCIES

Federal regulatory agencies involved in consumer protection are either independent commissions or executive branch agencies. Independent commissions include the Federal Trade Commission, the Federal Communications Commission, the Securities and Exchange Commission, the Federal Reserve Board, and the Consumer Product Safety Commission.

The Federal Trade Commission, for example, has five commissioners appointed by the president and confirmed by the Senate for seven-year terms. No more than three of them can be from the same political party. The commissioners make decisions by majority vote and issue rules.

Executive branch regulatory agencies are located in cabinet departments. For example, the Food and Drug Administration is located within the U.S. Department of Health and Human Services, the Consumer Financial Protection Bureau is part of the Federal Reserve Board, and the National Highway Traffic Safety Administration is located in the U.S. Department of Transportation.

A number of federal, state, and local regulatory agencies protect consumers' health and safety, including the Food and Drug Administration (FDA), the Department of Agriculture, the Department of Transportation's National Highway Traffic Safety Administration, and the Consumer Product Safety Commission. For example, pursuant to the Food, Drug and Cosmetic Act,[1] the FDA monitors the production and sale of more than $1 trillion

---

1. 21 U.S.C. § 321 *et seq.*

of food and medical products each year. In addition to specifying the proper labeling of food, drugs, medical devices, and cosmetics, the FDA also regulates the new-drug approval process. The Federal Trade Commission also regulates the packaging and labeling of certain products.

Numerous state laws cover such items as food, drugs, medical devices, cosmetics, clothing, tobacco, smoking, alcohol, and gambling. State and local laws also require restaurant inspections and regulate the competency of professional workers through the granting of various occupational licenses.

The "In Brief" identifies the key federal commissions and agencies charged with administering major consumer protection laws.

IN BRIEF

Consumer Protection Laws and Their Administration

Agency, Department, or Commission	Consumer Credit	Unfairness, Deception, and Fraud	Consumer Health and Safety
Federal Trade Commission Established: 1914 Commissioners: 5	Credit advertising; Fair Credit Reporting Act; Fair Debt Collection Practices Act; Equal Credit Opportunity Act.	Advertising; unfair or deceptive sales practices; identity theft.	Privacy.
Consumer Financial Protection Bureau (Federal Reserve Board) Established: 2010 Director: 1	Credit advertising.	Consumer credit terms, including home mortgages; education.	
Food and Drug Administration (U.S. Department of Health and Human Services) Established: 1930 Commissioner: 1			Labeling of food (except meat, poultry, and eggs), drugs, and cosmetics; adulterated food and cosmetics; approval of drugs and medical devices; tobacco; domestic and international product quality and safety.
U.S. Department of Agriculture Established: 1862			Labeling of meat, poultry, and eggs; inspection of meat, poultry, and egg processing facilities.
National Highway Traffic Safety Administration (NHTSA) (U.S. Department of Transportation) Established: 1970 Administrator: 1			Automobile safety standards; driver and highway safety.
Consumer Product Safety Commission Established: 1972 Commissioners: 3			Consumer Product Safety Act (CPSA) protect consumers from risk of injury or death from products such as toys, cribs, power tools, cigarette lighters, and household chemicals.
Federal Communications Commission Established: 1934 Commissioners: 5		Telemarketing.	Broadcast and Internet standards.
U.S. Postal Service Established: 1775 Reorganized: 1970		Sales practices.	
Securities and Exchange Commission Established: 1934 Commissioners: 5		Securities fraud, insider trading, disclosure requirements, regulation of broker-dealers and exchanges.	

CONTINUED

Agency, Department, or Commission	Consumer Credit	Unfairness, Deception, and Fraud	Consumer Health and Safety
Federal Reserve Board Established: 1913 Governors: 7	Truth in Lending Act (Regulation Z); Consumer Leasing Act (Regulation M); Equal Credit Opportunity Act (Regulation B); Electronic Fund Transfer Act (Regulation E).		
U.S. Department of Labor Established: 1913	Garnishment of wages.		
Bankruptcy courts	Chapter 13 consumer bankruptcy.		

© Cengage Learning 2013

FOOD SAFETY AND LABELING

The Food and Drug Administration and the Department of Agriculture have the primary responsibility for food safety and labeling. The Environmental Protection Agency regulates pesticides and genetically modified crops and organisms.

Product Definition: Food or Drug?

Because the distinction between drugs and food is important in the application of both the mislabeling and the adulteration provisions of the Food, Drug and Cosmetic Act, as well as in the drug-approval process, the FDA must categorize each product. *Drugs* include (1) articles intended for use in the diagnosis, cure, mitigation, treatment, or prevention of disease; and (2) articles (other than food) intended to affect the structure or any function of the body. Thus, many things that are, in fact, food may fit this definition. For example, orange juice might be used to prevent disease. Under the Act, *food* is defined as (1) articles used for food or drink, (2) chewing gum, and (3) articles used for components of either.

In general, the FDA looks at the intended use of a product in determining how to categorize it. Intent may be apparent from the manufacturer's purpose or from consumers' reasons for using the product, or it may be inferred from labels, promotional material, or advertisements.

FDA Standards for Food Condemnation

The FDA protects consumer health and safety through the confiscation of contaminated or adulterated foods. Tainted food causes more than 3,000 deaths annually in the United States and an estimated 128,000 hospitalizations.[2]

The standards for condemnation differ depending on whether the product is a natural food or contains additives. A natural food is *adulterated* if it "consist[s] in whole or in part of any filthy, putrid or decomposed substance,

or if it is otherwise unfit for food." All foods contain some level of unavoidable natural defects, so the FDA sets minimum tolerance standards for defects that will be tolerated. Articles that exceed those minimum levels are deemed adulterated and seized by the FDA. An *additive* is anything not inherent in the food product, including pesticide residue, unintended environmental contaminants, and substances unavoidably added from packaging. If an additive (in the quantity present in the food product) is injurious to any group in the general population, then the product will be deemed adulterated.

As discussed in Chapter 14, the chief executive officer of a food company was held vicariously and strictly criminally liable for introducing adulterated articles into interstate commerce.[3] Managers should develop and implement adequate policies and checks to ensure the proper handling and storage of food. If a problem is brought to a manager's attention, he or she should immediately report it to a supervisor and personally ensure that it is remedied.

In January 2011, President Obama signed into law the Food Safety Modernization Act (FSMA),[4] the first major overhaul of the FDA since 1932. The Act emphasizes the FDA's role in preventing foodborne disease and focuses on several main areas: increasing inspections of food manufacturing and processing facilities, requiring these facilities to take preemptive measures to prevent contamination, identifying foods at high risk for foodborne illness outbreaks, and developing an electronic tracking system that will follow food from "farm to fork." Importers must now verify the safety of food from their suppliers, and the FDA is working more closely with foreign governments and increasing its inspection of foreign food facilities. The FDA now has the authority to block foods from facilities or countries that refuse U.S. inspection. The FSMA also calls for increased collaboration among all food safety agencies whether they be federal, state, local, territorial, tribal, or foreign.[5]

---

2.   Food & Drug Admin., *What You Need to Know About Foodborne Illness-Causing Organisms in the U.S.*, available at http://www.fda.gov/food/resourcesforyou/consumers/ucm103263.htm (last updated Apr. 11, 2011).

3.   United States v. Park, 421 U.S. 658 (1975).

4.   Pub. L. No. 111-353, 124 Stat. 3885 (2011).

5.   Margaret A. Hamburg, *Food Safety Modernization Act: Putting the Focus on Prevention*, WHITE HOUSE BLOG, Jan. 3, 2011, http://www.whitehouse.gov/blog/2011/01/03/food-safety-modernization-act-putting-focus-prevention.

Role of the U.S. Department of Agriculture

The primary consumer protection activities of the U.S. Department of Agriculture (USDA) all involve food. The USDA inspects facilities engaged in the slaughtering or processing of meat, poultry, and egg products; prevents the sale of mislabeled meat or poultry products; and offers producers a voluntary grading program for various agricultural products. In August 2010, the FDA ordered the recall of more than half a billion eggs after laboratory testing confirmed the presence of salmonella. The tainted eggs had been distributed to fourteen states throughout the country and caused 2,000 illnesses.[6]

Pesticides and Human-Made Bugs

Under the Food, Drug and Cosmetic Act, the FDA shares with the Environmental Protection Agency (EPA) the responsibility for regulating pesticide residues on food. The EPA regulates pesticides and establishes tolerances under the Act. The FDA enforces the tolerance levels and deems a food to be adulterated if its residues exceed those levels.

Scientists have created genetically engineered (GE) insects and microbes to fight pests, such as the glassy-winged sharpshooter, which has destroyed more than $14 billion worth of grapes and other crops in California. The EPA issues permits for the use of bioengineered insects and pathogens.

Genetically Modified Food and Other Crops

The FDA authorized the sale of genetically modified food in 1992 but did not require that it be labeled as such. In 2000, the National Academy of Science recommended that the federal government increase its regulation of genetically modified foods. Although the report did not find that genetically modified food was unsafe, it urged scientists to develop better methods for identifying potential allergens and called on regulatory agencies to monitor the

environmental impact of genetically modified organisms (GMOs).[7] The "Genetically Engineered Food Right to Know Act" was first introduced in Congress in 2003[8] and has been reintroduced multiple times since then,[9] but it has always failed to pass.

At the state level, Vermont requires the labeling of genetically modified seeds, and Alaska requires the labeling of transgenic fish.[10] As of 2011, fourteen states were debating whether to mandate labeling for genetically modified foods.[11]

The Animal and Plant Health Inspection Service (APHIS), a division of the USDA, has the authority to regulate certain GE crops pursuant to the USDA's power to prevent the introduction and dissemination of plant pests under the Plant Protection Act (PPA).[12] APHIS's regulations provide that certain engineered organisms and products are presumed to be "plant pests" and therefore "regulated articles" under the PPA until APHIS determines otherwise. In the following case, the Supreme Court considered whether the USDA had properly deregulated the sale of the Roundup Ready Alfalfa plant, a genetically engineered strain of alfalfa that is resistant to the weed killer Roundup.

6.   Associated Press, *Recall Expands to More Than Half a Billion Eggs*, MSNBC, Aug. 20, 2011, *available at* http://www.msnbc.msn.com/id/38741401/ns/health-food_safety/t/recall-expands-more-half-billion-eggs/#.TtWYunrWNmg.

7.   GMOs are discussed further in Chapter 24.

8.   *See, e.g.*, H.R. 2916, 108th Cong. (2003).

9.   H.R. 5269, 109th Cong. (2005); H.R. 6636, 110th Cong. (2008); H.R. 5577, 111th Cong. (2010).

10. Pallavi Gogoi, *States Move to Label Cloned Food*, Bus. Wk., Mar. 4, 2008.

11. Lyndsey Layton, *States Lead Debate over Modified Food Labeling*, WASH. POST, May 19, 2011.

12. 7 U.S.C. § 7701 *et seq.*

A CASE IN POINT	*In the Language of the Court*	Case 17.1

Monsanto Co. v. Geertson Seed Farms

Supreme Court of the United States
130 S. Ct. 2743 (2010).

FACTS   Monsanto Company developed Roundup Ready Alfalfa (RRA), an alfalfa plant that has been genetically engineered to be tolerant of glyphosate, the active ingredient in the herbicide Roundup. Monsanto licensed its intellectual property rights to Forage Genetics International (FGI), the exclusive developer of RRA seed.

APHIS initially classified RRA as a regulated article under the Plant Protection Act and limited its use to 300 field trials over an eight-year period. In 2004, Monsanto and FGI sought nonregulated

CONTINUED

status for two strains of RRA. In response, APHIS prepared a draft environmental assessment (EA) analyzing the likely environmental impact of the requested deregulation. It then published a notice in the *Federal Register* advising the public of the deregulation petition and soliciting public comments on its draft EA. Notwithstanding substantial evidence that RRA genes could transfer to other plants, APHIS issued a Finding of No Significant Impact and decided to deregulate RRA unconditionally without preparing an environmental impact statement (EIS).

Approximately eight months after APHIS deregulated RRA, two conventional alfalfa seed farms and environmental groups concerned about food safety (the respondents) sued the Secretary of Agriculture and certain other officials, claiming that APHIS violated the National Environmental Policy Act of 1969 (NEPA)[13] by deregulating RRA without first completing an EIS. The district court accepted APHIS's finding that RRA does not have any harmful health effects on humans or livestock but concluded that APHIS violated NEPA by deregulating RRA without first preparing an EIS. In particular, the court found that APHIS's EA failed to answer substantial questions concerning the extent to which (1) complete deregulation would lead to the transmission of the gene conferring glyphosate tolerance from RRA to organic and conventional alfalfa or (2) the introduction of RRA would contribute to the development of Roundup-resistant weeds. The court (1) vacated APHIS's deregulation decision; (2) ordered APHIS to prepare an EIS before it made any decision on Monsanto's deregulation petition; (3) enjoined the planting of any RRA in the United States after March 30, 2007, pending APHIS's completion of the required EIS; and (4) imposed certain conditions suggested by APHIS on the handling and identification of already-planted RRA. They included mandatory isolation distances between RRA and non-genetically-engineered alfalfa fields in order to mitigate the risk of gene flow; a requirement that planting and harvesting equipment that had been in contact with RRA be cleaned prior to any use with conventional or organic alfalfa; and identification and handling requirements for RRA seed. After the U.S. Court of Appeals for the Ninth Circuit affirmed the trial court's decision, Monsanto and FGI (the petitioners) appealed. They challenged the scope of the relief granted but did not dispute the existence of a NEPA violation.

ISSUE PRESENTED   Did the district court abuse its discretion when it enjoined APHIS from partially deregulating RRA pending completion of the EIS and issued a nationwide injunction against the planting of RRA?

OPINION   ALITO, J., writing on behalf of the U.S. Supreme Court:

I
A

In deciding whether to grant nonregulated status to a genetically engineered plant variety, APHIS must comply with NEPA , which requires federal agencies "to the fullest extent possible" to prepare an environmental impact statement (EIS) for "every recommendation or report on proposals for legislation and other major Federal actio[n] significantly affecting the quality of the human environment.". . .

An agency need not complete an EIS for a particular proposal if it finds, on the basis of a shorter "environmental assessment" (EA), that the proposed action will not have a significant impact on the environment. Even if a particular agency proposal requires an EIS, applicable regulations allow the agency to take at least some action while the EIS is being prepared.

. . . .

II
A

At the threshold, respondents contend that petitioners lack standing to seek our review of the lower court rulings at issue here. We disagree.

Standing under Article III of the Constitution requires that an injury be concrete, particularized, and actual or imminent; fairly traceable to the challenged action; and redressable by a favorable

CONTINUED

---

13.   42 U.S.C. § 4321 *et seq.* NEPA is discussed further in Chapter 15.

ruling.[14] Petitioners here satisfy all three criteria. Petitioners are injured by their inability to sell or license RRA to prospective customers until such time as APHIS completes the required EIS. Because that injury is caused by the very remedial order that petitioners challenge on appeal, it would be redressed by a favorable ruling from this Court.

. . . .

B

. . . Petitioners argue that respondents have failed to show that any of the named respondents is likely to suffer a constitutionally cognizable injury absent injunctive relief. We disagree.

Respondents include conventional alfalfa farmers. Emphasizing "the undisputed concentration of alfalfa seed farms," the District Court found that those farmers had "established a 'reasonable probability' that their organic and conventional alfalfa crops will be infected with the engineered gene" if RRA is completely deregulated. A substantial risk of gene flow injures respondents in several ways. For example, respondents represent that, in order to continue marketing their product to consumers who wish to buy non-genetically-engineered alfalfa, respondents would have to conduct testing to find out whether and to what extent their crops have been contaminated. Respondents also allege that the risk of gene flow will cause them to take certain measures to minimize the likelihood of potential contamination and to ensure an adequate supply of non-genetically-engineered alfalfa.

Such harms, which respondents will suffer even if their crops are not actually infected with the Roundup-ready gene, are sufficiently concrete to satisfy the injury-in-fact prong of the constitutional standing analysis. Those harms are readily attributable to APHIS's deregulation decision, which, as the District Court found, gives rise to a significant risk of gene flow to non-genetically-engineered varieties of alfalfa. Finally, a judicial order prohibiting the growth and sale of all or some genetically engineered alfalfa would remedy respondents' injuries by eliminating or minimizing the risk of gene flow to conventional and organic alfalfa crops. We therefore conclude that respondents have constitutional standing to seek injunctive relief from the complete deregulation order at issue here.

. . . .

III

A

The District Court sought to remedy APHIS's NEPA violation in three ways. First, it vacated the agency's decision completely deregulating RRA; second, it enjoined APHIS from deregulating RRA, in whole or in part, pending completion of the mandated EIS; and third, it entered a nationwide injunction prohibiting almost all future planting of RRA. Because petitioners and the Government do not argue otherwise, we assume without deciding that the District Court acted lawfully in vacating the deregulation decision. . . .

B

"[A] plaintiff seeking a permanent injunction must satisfy a four-factor test before a court may grant such relief. A plaintiff must demonstrate: (1) that it has suffered an irreparable injury; (2) that remedies available at law, such as monetary damages, are inadequate to compensate for that injury; (3) that, considering the balance of hardships between the plaintiff and defendant, a remedy in equity is warranted; and (4) that the public interest would not be disserved by a permanent injunction." The traditional four-factor test applies when a plaintiff seeks a permanent injunction to remedy a NEPA violation.

. . . .

In our view, none of the traditional four factors governing the entry of permanent injunctive relief supports the District Court's injunction prohibiting partial deregulation. . . .

CONTINUED

---

14.   Horne v. Flores, 129 S. Ct. 2579 (2009).

Respondents in this case brought suit under the APA [Administrative Procedure Act] to challenge a particular agency order: APHIS's decision to *completely* deregulate RRA. The District Court held that the order in question was procedurally defective, and APHIS decided not to appeal that determination. At that point, it was for the agency to decide whether and to what extent it would pursue a *partial* deregulation. If the agency found, on the basis of a new EA, that a limited and temporary deregulation satisfied applicable statutory and regulatory requirements, it could proceed with such a deregulation even if it had not yet finished the onerous EIS required for complete deregulation. If and when the agency were to issue a partial deregulation order, any party aggrieved by that order could bring a separate suit under the Administrative Procedure Act to challenge the particular deregulation attempted.

In this case, APHIS apparently sought to "streamline" the proceedings by asking the District Court to craft a remedy that, in effect, would have partially deregulated RRA until such time as the agency had finalized the EIS needed for a complete deregulation. To justify that disposition, APHIS and petitioners submitted voluminous documentary submissions in which they purported to show that the risk of gene flow would be insignificant if the District Court allowed limited planting and harvesting subject to APHIS's proposed conditions. Respondents, in turn, submitted considerable evidence of their own that seemed to cut the other way. This put the District Court in an unenviable position. "The parties' experts disagreed over virtually every factual issue relating to possible environmental harm, including the likelihood of genetic contamination and why some contamination had already occurred."

The District Court may well have acted within its discretion in refusing to craft a judicial remedy that would have *authorized* the continued planting and harvesting of RRA while the EIS is being prepared. It does not follow, however, that the District Court was within its rights in *enjoining* APHIS from allowing such planting and harvesting pursuant to the authority vested in the agency by law. When the District Court entered its permanent injunction, APHIS had not yet exercised its authority to partially deregulate RRA. Until APHIS actually seeks to effect a partial deregulation, any judicial review of such a decision is premature.

Nor can the District Court's injunction be justified as a prophylactic measure needed to guard against the possibility that the agency would seek to effect on its own the particular partial deregulation scheme embodied in the terms of APHIS's proposed judgment. Even if the District Court was not required to adopt that judgment, there was no need to stop the agency from effecting a partial deregulation in accordance with the procedures established by law. Moreover, the terms of the District Court's injunction do not just enjoin the *particular* partial deregulation embodied in APHIS's proposed judgment. Instead, the District Court barred the agency from pursuing *any* deregulation—no matter how limited the geographic area in which planting of RRA would be allowed, how great the isolation distances mandated between RRA fields and fields for growing non-genetically-engineered alfalfa, how stringent the regulations governing harvesting and distribution, how robust the enforcement mechanisms available at the time of the decision, and—consequently—no matter how small the risk that the planting authorized under such conditions would adversely affect the environment in general and respondents in particular.

. . . .

Based on the analysis set forth above, it is clear that the order enjoining any deregulation whatsoever does not satisfy the traditional four-factor test for granting permanent injunctive relief. Most importantly, respondents cannot show that they will suffer irreparable injury if APHIS is allowed to proceed with any partial deregulation, for at least two independent reasons.

First, if and when APHIS pursues a partial deregulation that arguably runs afoul of NEPA, respondents may file a new suit challenging such action and seeking appropriate preliminary relief. Accordingly, a permanent injunction is not now needed to guard against any present or imminent risk of likely irreparable harm.

CONTINUED

Second, a partial deregulation need not cause respondents any injury at all, much less irreparable injury; if the scope of the partial deregulation is sufficiently limited, the risk of gene flow to their crops could be virtually nonexistent. . . .

Of course, APHIS might ultimately choose not to partially deregulate RRA during the pendency of the EIS, or else to pursue the kind of partial deregulation embodied in its proposed judgment . . . . Until such time as the agency decides whether and how to exercise its regulatory authority, however, the courts have no cause to intervene. Indeed, the broad injunction entered here essentially pre-empts the very procedure by which the agency could determine, independently of the pending EIS process for assessing the effects of a *complete* deregulation, that a *limited* deregulation would not pose any appreciable risk of environmental harm.

. . . .

We now turn to petitioners' claim that the District Court erred in entering a nationwide injunction against planting RRA. . . . We agree that the District Court's injunction against planting went too far, but we come to that conclusion for two independent reasons.

First, the impropriety of the District Court's broad injunction against planting flows from the impropriety of its injunction against partial deregulation. If APHIS may partially deregulate RRA before preparing a full-blown EIS—a question that we need not and do not decide here—farmers should be able to grow and sell RRA in accordance with that agency determination. Because it was inappropriate for the District Court to foreclose even the possibility of a partial and temporary deregulation, it necessarily follows that it was likewise inappropriate to enjoin any and all parties from acting in accordance with the terms of such a deregulation decision.

Second, respondents have represented to this Court that the District Court's injunction against planting does not have any meaningful practical effect independent of its vacatur [that is, the order vacating the permanent deregulation of RRA]. An injunction is a drastic and extraordinary remedy, which should not be granted as a matter of course. If a less drastic remedy (such as partial or complete vacatur of APHIS's deregulation decision) was sufficient to redress respondents' injury, no recourse to the additional and extraordinary relief of an injunction was warranted.

RESULT   The district court order invalidating APHIS's total deregulation of RRA was upheld, but the Supreme Court struck down both the injunction banning APHIS from partially deregulating RRA pending completion of the required EIS and the injunction banning the planting of RRA pending APHIS's preparation of an EIS. APHIS has the authority to decide whether to partially deregulate RRA based on a new EA or, if APHIS deems it necessary, an EIS.

CRITICAL THINKING QUESTIONS

1. During the two years RRA was unregulated, more than 3,000 farmers in forty-eight states planted approximately 220,000 acres of RRA. Does the Court's suggestion that the conventional alfalfa farmers and environmental groups can bring another suit if they are not satisfied with APHIS's new EA provide adequate redress for an uncontested NEPA violation?

2. Given the reasoning in this case, what facts would a plaintiff have to prove to justify an injunction against the deregulation of a genetically engineered crop?

The USDA, FDA, and EPA have stepped up periodic inspections to address unauthorized releases of genetically engineered crops. The USDA inspects crops engineered to produce pharmaceutical or industrial compounds seven times a year, both during and after the growing season. The USDA inspects other types of GE crops at least once a year in each state in which a field trial is done.

In 2007, the USDA's Investigative and Enforcement Services (IES) fined Scott Company $500,000, the maximum allowable, for multiple violations, including allowing GE grasses to form pollen that might have pollinated plants outside the field trial site, exceeding the allowable acreage in a field trial, missing records for particular field trial sites, allowing unauthorized movement of regulated

GE grass to locations outside the field trial site, and lacking adequate borders around field trial sites.[15]

Although coordination and enforcement by the USDA, FDA, and EPA have significantly improved since 2000, the Government Accountability Office (GAO) has recommended that the three agencies can enhance their coordination by articulating a common desired outcome; agreeing on roles and responsibilities; establishing joint strategies; identifying and addressing needs by leveraging resources; establishing compatible policies, procedures, and other means; reinforcing agency accountability for joint efforts through reports and plans; and developing mechanisms to monitor, report, and analyze results.[16]

Cloned Meat and Milk

In 2008, the FDA authorized the sale of food from cloned animals and decided not to require labels for cloned food after concluding that meat and milk from cloned animals were "as safe to eat as food from conventionally bred animals."[17] In response, state legislators introduced mandatory labeling bills in thirteen states, including California, New Jersey, and Kentucky.[18] The California House and Senate passed a mandatory labeling and tracking bill in 2007, but it was vetoed by Governor Arnold Schwarzenegger on the grounds that it was "unworkable, costly, and unenforceable."[19] The Cloned Food Labeling Act, which Senator Barbara Mikulski (D.-Md.) first introduced in 2007, would require that food from cloned animals bear the label: "This product is from a cloned animal or its progeny." Senator Mikulski explained the bill's rationale: "Labeling does two things. It gives consumers the right to know and allows scientists to monitor."[20] The bill never became law.

Irradiated Foods

In December 1997, the FDA authorized the irradiation of fresh and frozen red meat as a means of killing foodborne bacteria (including *E. coli*) and lengthening shelf life. During irradiation, food is passed through a sealed chamber, where it is exposed to gamma ray radiation from cobalt 60 or cesium 137 or to an electron beam. FDA regulations require irradiated foods to be prominently and conspicuously labeled with the radura symbol (a stylized green flower) and the words "Treated with Radiation" or "Treated by Irradiation."

For many consumers, irradiation conjures up images of mushroom clouds and the nuclear reactor meltdown in 1986 at Chernobyl in Ukraine or the near meltdown at the Fukushima Dai-ichi reactor in Japan in 2011.[21] Nonetheless, experts have predicted that consumers will eventually be won over by irradiation's safety and effectiveness in protecting against bacteria and other microbes. Former FDA commissioner Dr. David Kessler drew parallels to the public's shunning of pasteurized milk in the early twentieth century and the initial distrust of microwave ovens in the 1970s.[22] Although the amount of irradiated beef Americans eat has increased each year, irradiated beef currently accounts for only one-tenth of 1% of the beef marketed in the United States. Labeling it costs more than labeling regular beef, and if the irradiation is not done with great precision, the meat does not taste very good.[23]

Organic Foods

Sales of organic products in the United States amounted to approximately $28.6 billion in 2010.[24] Uniform standards promulgated by the USDA for organic food ban the use of pesticides, genetic engineering, growth hormones, and irradiation. They also require dairy cattle to have access to pasture. Foods grown and processed according to the standards may bear the seal "USDA Organic."[25]

Other Food Labeling Requirements

The FDA has primary responsibility for regulating the packaging and labeling of food (except meat, poultry, and eggs, which are under the jurisdiction of the USDA), drugs, medical devices, and cosmetics. The Fair Packaging and Labeling Act[26] requires prepackaged foods to bear labels containing the name and address of the manufacturer, packer, or distributor; the net quantity, placed in a uniform location on the front panel; the quantity in servings, with the net quantity of each serving stated; and the quantity listed in certain other ways, depending on how the product is classified. This last provision requires dual declarations of sizes (for example, one quart and thirty-two ounces) and forbids the use of potentially misleading terms such as "jumbo

15. U.S. Gov't Accountability Office, GAO -09-60, Genetically Engineered Crops: Agencies Are Proposing Changes to Improve Oversight but Could Take Additional Steps to Enhance Coordination and Monitoring (Nov. 2008), *available at* http://www.gao.gov/new.items/d0960.pdf.

16. *Id.* at 25.

17. Gogoi, *supra* note 10.

18. *Id.*

19. *Id.*

20. *Id.*

21. Martha Groves, *Less-Than-Glowing Image Hampers Food Irradiation*, L.A. Times, Mar. 15, 1998, at A1.

22. Joanna Ramey, *Food Industry Groups Near Start of Irradiation Campaign*, SupermarketNews, Apr. 17, 1998, at 23.

23. James Andrews, *Is It Time to Accept Food Irradiation?*, Food Safety News, Sept. 30, 2011, *available at* http://www.foodsafetynews.com/2011/09/is-it-time-to-accept-food-irradiation/.

24. *2011 Organic Industry Survey*, Organic Trade Ass'n, Apr. 2011.

25. Frederic J. Frommer, *What's Organic? Some Worry New USDA Label Will Change Organic Farming*, Assoc. Press, Jan. 16, 2001.

26. 15 U.S.C. § 1451 *et seq.*

Free trade treaties have made the U.S. food market one of the most open in the world. Yet problems with imported food, such as the salmonella outbreak in the summer of 2008 caused by jalapeño and serrano peppers grown in Mexico, present challenges for regulators. Effective September 30, 2008, the U.S. Department of Agriculture requires all stores to label unprocessed beef, pork, lamb, veal, chicken, and nuts with the country of origin. Restaurants, other food service providers, and retail grocery stores that buy less than $230,000 per year in fresh fruits and vegetables are exempt. As a result, only about 30% of the U.S. beef supply, 11% of all pork, 39% of chicken, and 40% of all fruit and vegetable supplies may be covered by the requirement at the retail level.[a]

The USDA estimated that labeling would cost $2.6 billion in the first year and $500 million annually thereafter. Many retailers and meat producers see little benefit for the consumer, particularly because the law does not cover processed foods. Mark Dopp, a senior vice president for the American Meat Institute, asked, "What can they learn from seeing the country? This tells nothing about safety."[b] Ultimately, the burden of ensuring safe food may fall on the globalized food industry.

a. REMY JURENAS, CONG. RES. SERV., COUNTRY-OF-ORIGIN LABELING FOR FOODS (Jul. 15, 2010), *available at* http://www.fas.org/sgp/crs/misc/RS22955.pdf.

b. Bob LaMendola, *Do You Know Where Your Beef Comes From? New Labels Soon Will Tell You Nations of Origin of More Foods*, SUN-SENTINEL (Fla.), Sept. 23, 2008.

quart" and "super ounce." Many supermarkets provide unit-pricing information so that consumers can more easily compare the prices of competing products. Manufacturers of goods that are to be exported also need to consider foreign labeling requirements, such as language translations, country of origin disclosures, and weight conversions.

Nutrition Facts

The Nutrition Labeling and Education Act of 1990[27] (1) requires nutrition labeling of almost all foods through a nutrition panel entitled "Nutrition Facts," (2) requires expanded ingredient labeling, and (3) restricts nutrient content claims and health claims. FDA regulations govern the use of nutrient claims, such as "light," "fat free," and "low calorie," and provide uniform definitions so that these terms mean the same for any product on which they appear.

More than 90% of processed food must carry nutrition information. Exceptions include plain coffee and tea, delicatessen items, and bulk food. The Nutrition Facts panel must include the amount per serving of saturated fat, trans fat, cholesterol, dietary fiber, sodium, and other nutrients. These panels also provide information on how the food fits into an overall daily diet. Point-of-purchase nutrition information is voluntary under the Act for many raw foods, including meat, poultry, raw fish, and fresh produce. The information may be shown in a poster or chart at a butcher's counter or a produce stand.

PepsiCo's Frito-Lay division was the first major food company to eliminate trans fats from its potato chips and other products. "Trans fat" is a form of partially hydrogenated oil that improves the shelf life and taste of products but contributes to fatal and nonfatal coronary heart disease.[28] PepsiCo prominently labeled its products "0 trans fats" before the FDA labeling requirement went into effect in 2006, thereby gaining a marketing edge.

As discussed in the "Inside Story" in Chapter 1, public health officials have increasingly put pressure on chain restaurants to display the number of calories their offerings contain next to each item on the menu. New York City was among the first cities to require chain restaurants to post calorie information on their menus. As of 2011, eighteen state and local governments had passed a similar requirement.

In 2011, the FDA proposed a rule that would require any restaurant with twenty or more locations, including chain restaurants, coffee shops, bakeries, and vending machines, to "clearly and prominently" display on menus the calorie content of food.[29] This proposed regulation was issued pursuant to a requirement imposed by the Patient Protection and Affordable Care Act. Although certain sectors of the food service industry have lobbied against the labeling requirement, the National Restaurant Association supports it, deeming a uniform federal requirement preferable to a patchwork of state and federal regulations. The movie theater industry, which earns up to a third of its income from selling popcorn and other foods and drinks, has lobbied the FDA to exempt theater concession stands from the labeling requirement on the theory that people go to the theater to see movies, not to eat meals.

Health Claims

The Nutrition Labeling and Education Act of 1990 permits manufacturers to make health claims for foods on labels without FDA approval as a new drug, or the risk of sanctions for issuing a *misbranded* product, as long as the claim has been certified by the FDA as being supported by significant scientific agreement. The FDA has approved several health claims for foods, including the relationship between calcium and osteoporosis, fiber-containing products and cancer, fruits and vegetables and cancer, folate and neural tube defects, and soluble fiber and coronary heart disease.

DRUGS AND MEDICAL DEVICES

Drugs and medical devices, as well as drug advertising, are regulated by the FDA.

27. 21 U.S.C. §§ 301, 321, 337, 343, 371.

28. 64 Fed. Reg. 62,772 (Nov. 17, 1999).

29. Lyndsey Layton, *FDA Proposal Would Require Chain Restaurants to Display Calorie Information*, WASH. POST, Apr. 1, 2011.

FDA Standards for Drug Approval

The FDA has the authority to require that certain drugs be available only by prescription. If a drug authorized only for prescription use is sold over-the-counter, then it is misbranded, and the FDA will halt its sale. In general, the FDA will require prescription use only when a drug is toxic, requires a physician's supervision for safe use, or is addictive.

The first step in the approval process for new drugs is their classification by the Drug Enforcement Administration (DEA) into one of five schedules based on potential for abuse and currently accepted medical use. Only Schedule I drugs, those with the highest potential for abuse and no currently accepted medical use, cannot be approved by the FDA.

The drug-approval process for non-Schedule I drugs begins with preclinical research (which includes animal testing) aimed at the discovery and identification of drugs that are sufficiently promising to study in humans. The drug maker then submits this preclinical research, along with a document called "Claimed Exemption for Investigational New Drug," to the FDA. The FDA can then permit or deny continued research. If approved for investigational purposes, a drug will be tested in humans in three separate phases, with FDA review at the end of each phase. This framework is designed to protect the safety of the human subjects used in the study, to develop necessary data on the drug, and to ensure that all studies are done properly. Once all of the testing data are assembled, they are submitted to the FDA, which may approve or deny the application. Approval is based on a drug's safety and effectiveness. The approval may require marketing restrictions, and it can be contested by anyone. The FDA must also approve the description of a drug (for example, labels and package inserts).

Drugs with a high potential for therapeutic gain and no satisfactory alternative may be given priority (expedited) review by the FDA. In addition, through open protocols, such drugs may be available during the investigational stage to people not within the clinical test group. For example, people with AIDS may have access to new drugs under investigation if studies yield preliminary evidence of effectiveness.

As discussed in Chapter 10, generic drugs can be approved on a showing that they are identical to approved brand-name drugs. The Biologics Price Competition and Innovation Act of 2009 authorized the FDA to approve certain biologic drugs, which are derived from living cells and dispensed by injection, based on biosimilarity. By 2015, biologic drugs worth more than $51 billion will lose patent protection. Even with this legislation, analysts anticipate that it will take three to five years and $100 million to $150 million to develop a biosimilar drug. Even so, the cost savings over the brand-name versions are likely to be substantial.

ethical consideration

Drug companies provide financial support to academic researchers in the form of employment or consulting fees, research funds, money to attend symposiums, and speaking honoraria. Should scientists disclose their ties to drug companies when publishing articles about their research? Should drug companies disclose these financial ties? Should investigators limit how much money a researcher can receive from drug companies? Should the FDA require disclosure?

The Food and Drug Administration Modernization Act of 1997[30] speeded up the approval of new drugs and medical devices and made it easier for seriously ill patients to obtain experimental drugs. The Act permits the FDA to use outside reviewers to evaluate certain drugs and medical devices. It also includes a safe harbor for the distribution by drug manufacturers of certain third-party materials concerning "off-label" uses of their drugs.[31] "Off-label" uses are uses of a drug other than those for which it was approved. A physician can prescribe a drug to serve any purpose that he or she thinks is appropriate regardless of whether the drug was initially approved for that use, but the FDA restricts companies' ability to promote off-label uses.[32] In 2009, Pfizer paid $2.3 billion in fines to resolve civil and criminal charges resulting from violations of this ban.[33]

The U.S. Supreme Court struck down the provisions of the Food and Drug Administration Modernization Act that exempted compounded drugs from the FDA's approval requirements only if the compounding pharmacy refrained from advertising particular compounded drugs.[34] Compounding is a process whereby a pharmacist, pursuant to a physician's prescription, mixes ingredients to create a medication for a particular patient, usually because the patient is allergic to an ingredient in a mass-produced product. The Court held that the ban violated the Free Speech Clause of the First Amendment. The Court recognized the importance of the government's interests in preserving the effectiveness and integrity of the FDA's new-drug approval process while also permitting compounding to create drugs produced on such a small scale that it would be prohibitively expensive to require them to undergo safety and efficiency testing. Nonetheless, the Court concluded that the speech restrictions were more extensive than necessary to serve these interests. The Court identified several non-speech-related means of drawing a line between compounding

---

30. 21 U.S.C. § 301 *et seq.*
31. 21 U.S.C. § 360aaa *et seq.*
32. *See* 65 Fed. Reg. 14,286 (Mar. 16, 2000).
33. Rita Rubin, *Pfizer Fined $2.3 Billion for Illegal Marketing in Off-Label Drug Case,* USA TODAY, Sept. 3, 2009.
34. Thompson v. W. States Med. Ctr., 535 U.S. 357 (2002).

and large-scale manufacturing that the government never even considered. The Court admonished Congress that "[i]f the First Amendment means anything, it means that regulating speech must be a last—not first—resort."

As discussed in Chapter 10, FDA approval of the label on a brand-name prescription drug does not preempt state failure-to-warn claims arising out of injuries caused by that drug even though the drug bears the FDA-mandated label.[35] In contrast, because generic drugs must bear the same label as their brand-name counterpart, federal law preempts state failure-to-warn claims related to approved generic drugs as long as they bear the FDA-mandated label.[36]

In 2004, Merck & Co. issued a voluntary recall of the popular anti-inflammatory drug Vioxx after finding that the drug increased the risk of heart attacks and strokes. The FDA had approved Vioxx in 1999 to treat pain and inflammation caused by osteoarthritis and rheumatoid arthritis. In 2000, Merck submitted a safety study to the FDA that found an increased risk of heart attacks and strokes in patients taking the drug. Although the FDA implemented labeling changes to reflect the study's findings two years later, it did not issue a public health advisory until the fall of 2004, *after* Merck had voluntarily withdrawn Vioxx from the market.

The FDA's failure to respond to evidence that Vioxx was a potentially dangerous substance sparked renewed criticism of the agency, including allegations that the FDA is too closely aligned with the commercial interests of the pharmaceutical producers that it is tasked to regulate.[37] Hardly the agency's only misstep in recent years, the Vioxx scandal was one in a string of drug-safety controversies that spurred renewed calls for FDA regulatory reform. Reformers assert that the FDA should be restructured to give the agency the authority to recall drugs and to impose significant fines on drug companies for safety violations.[38] Having an independent and effective FDA is particularly important in light of the U.S. Supreme Court's decisions holding that FDA approval of a medical device preempts state-law product liability claims[39] and that FDA approval of a generic drug preempts state-law failure-to-warn claims.[40] Although Congress voted to overhaul the FDA's regulation of the food industry with the Food Safety Modernization Act,[41] it has yet to overhaul the FDA's regulation of the drug industry.

FDA Approval of Medical Devices

The FDA must also approve *medical devices*. A medical device is defined as follows:

> an instrument, apparatus, implement, machine, contrivance, implant, in vitro reagent, or other similar or related article, including a component part, or accessory which is: recognized in the official National Formulary, or the United States Pharmacopoeia, or any supplement to them; intended for use in the diagnosis of disease or other conditions, or in the cure, mitigation, treatment, or prevention of disease, in man or other animals; or intended to affect the structure or any function of the body of man or other animals, and which does not achieve any of its primary intended purposes through chemical action within or on the body of man or other animals and which is not dependent upon being metabolized for the achievement of any of its primary intended purposes.[42]

Certain devices require extensive premarket review; others are subject to less rigorous review. As with drugs, the FDA may mandate certain warnings. As discussed in Chapter 10, if a medical device has undergone full premarket FDA review and the manufacturer provides the FDA-mandated warnings, then state-law failure-to-warn-claims are preempted. If, however, the device was exempt from full review, then the manufacturer could still be found liable under state product liability law for failure to warn.[43]

Drug Advertising

The FDA permits drug companies to advertise prescription drugs on television and radio. Drug companies can tout a drug's benefits without listing all of the side effects and explaining how to properly use the drug. Television ads must warn of major risks, however, and provide a quick way (such as a toll-free telephone number, Web address, or magazine advertisement) for consumers to obtain full information about the drug.

Health Claims and the Labeling of Dietary Supplements

Dietary supplements include products such as vitamins, minerals, herbs, and amino acids. The sale of dietary supplements is regulated only when the supplement contains a new dietary ingredient or poses a safety risk.[44] As with foods, however, health claims on dietary supplements can cause

35. Wyeth v. Levine, 555 U.S. 555 (2009).

36. Pliva, Inc. v. Mensing, 131 S. Ct. 2567 (2011) (Case 10.4).

37. Alicia Mundy, *Congress Moves to Beef Up FDA as Crisis Mounts*, WALL ST. J., July 30, 2008, at A4.

38. *Id.*

39. Riegel v. Medtronic, Inc., 552 U.S. 312 (2008).

40. *Pliva*, 131 S. Ct. 2567 (Case 10.4).

41. Pub. L. No. 111-353, 124 Stat. 3885 (2011).

42. Food & Drug Admin., *Is the Product a Medical Device?*, *available at* http://www.fda.gov/medicaldevices/deviceregulationandguidance/overview/classifyyourdevice/ucm051512.htm (last updated Mar. 3, 2010).

43. *See, e.g.*, Degelmann v. Advanced Med. Optics, Inc., 659 F.3d 835 (9th Cir. 2011).

44. Dietary Supplement Health and Education Act of 1994, 21 U.S.C. §§ 350b, 342(f).

them to be characterized as drugs. The Nutrition Labeling and Education Act created a safe harbor for health claims on dietary supplements akin to that provided for food but delegated to the FDA the task of establishing a procedure and standard governing the validity of health claims.

FDA regulations authorize a health claim only if there is substantial scientific agreement among experts that the claim is supported by the totality of publicly available scientific evidence.[45] The FDA specifies the types of claims that manufacturers of dietary supplements may make without prior review by the FDA and those that require prior authorization.[46]

In addition, manufacturers need to register with the FDA pursuant to the Public Health Security and Bioterrorism Preparedness and Response Act of 2002[47] before producing or selling supplements. In 2007, the FDA published comprehensive regulations for Current Good Manufacturing Practices for those who manufacture, package, or hold dietary supplement products. These regulations focus on practices that ensure the identity, purity, quality, strength, and composition of dietary supplements.

The FDA came under heavy fire in 2003 when Steve Bechler, a twenty-three-year-old pitcher for the Baltimore Orioles baseball team, died suddenly during spring training workouts in Florida after taking Xenadrine, a legal over-the-counter drug containing a weight-loss supplement known as ephedra. Shortly thereafter, a young football player's sudden death was also linked to ephedra. Critics blasted the FDA for allowing the drug to be marketed over-the-counter without significant warnings. In response, the FDA banned the use of ephedra in any dietary supplements and advised consumers to stop using any products containing ephedra.[48]

More recently, the FDA highlighted the harmful effects of caffeinated alcoholic beverages. Consuming alcohol, a depressant, and caffeine, a stimulant, can result in heart attacks.[49] Caffeine can mask the sensory cues on which drinkers may rely to determine how intoxicated they are. Thus, individuals drinking caffeinated alcoholic beverages may consume more alcohol—and become more intoxicated—than they realize. In November 2010, the FDA sent warning letters to four manufacturers making malt versions of these drinks cautioning that caffeine is an "unsafe food additive" because the manufacturers have failed to show that the direct addition of caffeine to their malt beverages is "generally recognized as safe" by qualified experts. Rather, there is evidence that the combinations of caffeine and alcohol in these products pose a public health concern.[50] Seven states have announced bans on the drinks until the FDA announces a nationwide ban.[51]

LABELING OF OTHER PRODUCTS

The Federal Trade Commission (FTC) has the primary responsibility for regulating the packaging and labeling of commodities other than food, drugs, medical devices, and cosmetics.

Clothing

Numerous federal laws regulate the labeling of clothing. Among these are the Wool Products Labeling Act,[52] the Fur Products Labeling Act,[53] the Flammable Fabrics Act,[54] and the Textile Fiber Products Identification Act.[55] Each of these acts is intended to protect distributors and consumers against misbranding and false advertising.

Alcohol

The Bureau of Alcohol and Tobacco Tax and Trade, a branch of the Treasury Department, regulates everything that appears on packages of alcoholic beverages and bottles of wine. The Bureau's regulations attach legal meanings to various statements made on wine labels, including the vintage year, grape variety, producer, and alcohol content. Warnings are also required to alert those who are allergic to sulfites that wine contains trace amounts of the substances, which may be used as a preservative and are also produced naturally during fermentation. Bottles, cans, and packages of wine, beer, and spirits are required to carry a congressionally mandated warning label, which states that alcohol consumption increases the risks of birth defects, warns that consuming alcoholic beverages can impair one's ability to drive a car, and cautions against the use of alcohol when operating machinery.[56]

45. 21 C.F.R. pt. 101.14(c).

46. *FDA Regulates Statements Made on Effects of Dietary Supplements*, 68 U.S.L.W. 2392–93 (Jan. 11, 2000).

47. Pub. L. No. 107–188, 116 Stat. 594 (2002).

48. Jennifer Warner, *FDA Issues Final Ban on Ephedra*, WebMD, Feb. 6, 2004, *available at* http://my.webmd.com/content/article/81/97056.htm.

49. Clayton Sandell, *Doctors: Alcohol–Caffeine Drinks Pose Health Risk to College-Age Fans*, ABC News, Oct. 20, 2010, *available at* http://abcnews.go.com/Health/MindMoodNews/high-alcohol-high-caffeine-drinks-pose-health-danger/story?id=11928034#.TuopO3rWNmg.

50. Food & Drug Admin., *Consumer Updates: Serious Concerns over Alcoholic Beverages with Added Caffeine*, available at http://www.fda.gov/ForConsumers/ConsumerUpdates/ucm233987.htm (last updated Dec. 8, 2011).

51. *Caffeinated Alcoholic Beverages: A Growing Public Health Concern?*, Sci. Daily, Nov. 29, 2010, *available at* http://www.sciencedaily.com/releases/2010/11/101129203338.htm.

52. 15 U.S.C. § 68 *et seq.*

53. 15 U.S.C. § 69 *et seq.*

54. 15 U.S.C. § 1191 *et seq.*

55. 15 U.S.C. § 70 *et seq.*

56. Dan Berger, *Modern Wine Industry Still Fears the "Feds" but for Labeling Reasons*, L.A. Times, Nov. 24, 1989, at H2; *see generally* 27 C.F.R. pts. 4, 5 & 7 (Alcohol & Tobacco Tax & Trade Bureau, Department of the Treasury).

"Made in USA"

The FTC specifies when manufacturers and marketers can label their products "Made in USA." Under the FTC's Made in USA policy, "all or virtually all" of the product must be made in the fifty states, the District of Columbia, or the U.S. territories and possessions. "All or virtually all" means that all significant parts and processing that go into the product must be of U.S. origin. A manufacturer or marketer must have a reasonable basis, based on competent and reliable evidence, to support its claim that the product was made in the USA.[57] Apple can legally tout that its latest iPhone was created in California, but it must also state that it was "Made in China."

State Labeling Laws

Many states have enacted labeling laws aimed at protecting consumers from dangerous products. Historically, these laws have sought to protect consumers from risks that involved the danger of imminent bodily harm. Of particular note is California's Safe Drinking Water and Toxic Enforcement Act of 1986, better known as Proposition 65. Proposition 65 provides that "no person . . . shall knowingly and intentionally expose any individual to a chemical known to the state to cause cancer or reproductive toxicity without first giving clear and reasonable warning to such individual."[58] The law requires the governor to compile a list of the chemicals requiring warnings and to update the list annually. The current list includes ingredients such as alcohol, certain color dyes, aspirin, and marijuana smoke, as well as potential contaminants such as lead and mercury.[59] The labeling requirements apply to manufacturers, producers, packagers, and retail sellers; the warnings may be in the form of product labels, signs at retail outlets, or public advertising. An example of a Proposition 65 warning is: "Warning: This product contains a chemical known to the State of California to cause birth defects or other reproductive harm."

The FDA has the authority to issue regulations that preempt state labeling requirements, such as Proposition 65, and it has done so when the state labeling requirements serve to frustrate the FDA's labeling scheme or make unsubstantiated warnings that serve to diminish the impact of valid warnings. For example, the FDA did this in 2008 when Proposition 65 required that nicotine replacement therapy bear a warning label for pregnant women. The FDA believed that the warning label required by Proposition 65 did not properly communicate the benefits of the product and might deter women from using the product in lieu of smoking, an activity that would be far less healthy than using the product. The California Supreme Court ultimately agreed with FDA that the state requirement was preempted in regard to this product.[60]

BROADCASTING AND THE INTERNET

The Federal Communications Commission (FCC) has the authority to regulate broadcasting and aspects of the Internet.

Broadcasting

The FCC is charged with ensuring that broadcast media are competitive and operate for the public's benefit and use. Licenses cannot be transferred or assigned without the permission of the FCC and a finding that such a transfer will serve the public interest. Enforcement of many of the FCC's policies is achieved primarily through its ability to withhold license renewals. The FCC can also levy fines.

In 2003, Congress invalidated FCC regulations that would have relaxed the limits on concentrated media ownership in the United States.[61] In 2007, the FCC again attempted to relax restrictions to permit the same company to own a newspaper and broadcast station in the same market. In 2011, the U.S. Court of Appeals for the Third Circuit struck down those regulations, finding that the concentration rules are necessary to preserve competition and promote diverse sources of news.[62] As of 2011, the FCC was considering whether its current media ownership rules are effective in achieving its main goals of competition, localism, and diversity.[63] Congressional Democrats have urged the agency to preserve the rules limiting media ownership;[64] many Republicans support relaxing the restrictions.

The Indecency Ban

The Public Communications Act of 1992 and applicable regulations provide that "[w]hoever utters any obscene, indecent, or profane language by means of radio communication [between the hours of 6 a.m. and 10 p.m.] shall be fined under this title or imprisoned not more than two years, or both."[65] In the following case, the U.S. Supreme Court considered whether the FCC has the authority to ban broadcasts with "fleeting expletives."

57. FTC Bureau of Consumer Protection, "Made in USA" and Other U.S. Origin Claims: Notice, 62 Fed. Reg. 63,756 (Dec. 7, 1997).

58. CAL. HEALTH & SAFETY CODE § 25,249.6.

59. EPA (California), Office of Environmental Health Hazard Assessment, *Chemicals Known to the State to Cause Cancer or Reproductive Toxicity*, Nov. 18, 2011, *available at* http://oehha.ca.gov/prop65/prop65_list/files/P65single111811.pdf.

60. Dowhal v. SmithKline Beecham Consumer Healthcare, 32 Cal. 4th 910 (2004).

61. S.J. Res. 17, 108th Cong. (2003).

62. Prometheus Radio Project v. FCC, 373 F.3d 372 (3dCir. 2011).

63. Edward Wyatt, *F.C.C. Begins Review of Regulations on Media Ownership*, N.Y. TIMES, May 25, 2010.

64. Gautham Nagesh, *Lawmakers Tell FCC to Preserve Local Media Ownership Rules*, THE HILL, Dec. 6, 2011, http://thehill.com/blogs/hillicon-valley/technology/197589-lawmakers-tell-fcc-to-preserve-local-media-ownership-rules.

65. 18 U.S.C. § 1464; 106 Stat. 954, note following 47 U.S.C. § 303.

A CASE IN POINT	*Summary*	Case 17.2

Federal Communications Commission v. Fox Television Stations, Inc.

Supreme Court of the United States
556 U.S. 502 (2009).

FACTS   The Federal Communications Commission levied an indecency fine against Fox Television Stations, Inc. for the single use of expletives in two of its 2002 and 2003 Billboard Music Awards. During the 2002 awards, Cher stated in her acceptance speech: "People have been telling me I'm on the way out every year, right? So fuck 'em." In 2003, a presenter stated: "Have you ever tried to get cow shit out of a Prada purse? It's not so fucking simple."

Fox protested the fine and filed a petition for review of the FCC's order.[66] The U.S. Court of Appeals for the Second Circuit overturned the agency's order, finding that the Commission's reasoning was inadequate under the Administrative Procedure Act (APA), and the FCC appealed.

ISSUES PRESENTED   Did the FCC correctly determine that the broadcast of vulgar expletives violates federal restrictions on the broadcast of "any obscene, indecent, or profane language" when the expletives are used only once in a single broadcast? Is the FCC ban constitutional?

SUMMARY OF OPINION   The U.S. Supreme Court explained that an FCC indecency finding requires two determinations. First, the material falls within the "subject matter scope of [the] indecency definition—that is, the material must describe or depict sexual or excretory organs or activities." Second, the broadcast is *patently offensive* as measured by contemporary community standards for the broadcast medium."

The FCC considers three factors when deciding whether material is patently offensive:

> (1) *the explicitness or graphic nature* of the description or depiction of sexual or excretory organs or activities; (2) whether the material *dwells on or repeats at length* descriptions of sexual or excretory organs or activities; (3) *whether the material appears to pander or is used to titillate, or whether the material appears to have been presented for its shock value.*

Prior to its *Golden Globes* ruling,[67] issued in response to Bono's use of the "F-Word" in his acceptance speech at the 2003 Golden Globes Awards, the FCC took the position that "isolated or fleeting broadcasts of the 'F-Word' . . . are not indecent or would not be acted upon." In *Golden Globes*, it explicitly ruled that "any such interpretation is no longer good law. . . ." The Commission explained that the "strict dichotomy between 'expletives' and 'descriptions or depictions of sexual or excretory functions' is artificial and does not make sense in light of the fact that an 'expletive's' power to offend derives from its sexual or excretory meaning."

The U.S. Court of Appeals for the Second Circuit reasoned that the Administrative Procedure Act and the Supreme Court decision in *State Farm*[68] require agencies to make clear "'why the original reasons for adopting the [displaced] rule or policy are no longer dispositive'" as well as "'why the new rule effectuates the statute as well as or better than the old rule.'" The Supreme Court rejected this standard of review, finding "no basis in the Administrative Procedure Act or in our opinions for a requirement that all agency change be subjected to more searching review." *State Farm* only requires "a reasoned analysis for the change beyond that which may be required when an agency *does not act* in the first instance." Although an agency "may not . . . depart from a prior policy *sub silentio* or simply disregard rules that are still on the books," and it must present good reasons for the new policy,

> it need not demonstrate to a court's satisfaction that the reasons for the new policy are *better* than the reasons for the old one; it suffices that the new policy is permissible under the statute, that there are good reasons for it, and that the agency *believes* it to be better, which the conscious change of course adequately indicates.

CONTINUED

---

66. FCC 06-166 (Nov. 6, 2006).

67. *Complaints Against Various Broadcast Licenses Regarding the Airing of the "Golden Globes Awards" Program* (Memorandum Opinion & Order), 19 FCC Rcd. 4985 (Mar. 18, 2004).

68. Motor Vehicle Mfrs. Ass'n of United States, Inc. v. State Farm Mut. Auto. Ins. Co., 463 U.S. 29 (1983).

The Court rejected the suggestion that agency actions that implicate constitutional liberties should be subjected to stricter review, reasoning: "If the Commission's action here was not arbitrary or capricious in the ordinary sense, it satisfies the Administrative Procedure Act's 'arbitrary [or] capricious' standard; its lawfulness under the Constitution is a separate question to be addressed in a constitutional challenge."

On the merits, the Court concluded that the FCC's new enforcement policy and its order finding that the broadcasts were indecent were neither arbitrary nor capricious. The FCC acknowledged that it had changed its position, and the Court found it "certainly reasonable to determine that it made no sense to distinguish between literal and nonliteral uses of offensive words, requiring repetitive use to render only the latter indecent." Technological advances that have made it easier to bleep out offending words further supported the FCC's new enforcement policy.

The Court acknowledged that there is "scant empirical evidence" demonstrating the harmful effect of broadcast profanity on children but explained:

> One cannot demand a multiyear controlled study, in which some children are intentionally exposed to indecent broadcasts (and insulated from all other indecency), and others are shielded from all indecency. It is one thing to set aside agency action under the Administrative Procedure Act because of failure to adduce empirical data that can readily be obtained. It is something else to insist upon obtaining the unobtainable. Here it suffices to know that children mimic the behavior they observe—or at least the behavior that is presented to them as normal and appropriate. . . . If enforcement had to be supported by empirical data, the ban would effectively be a nullity.

The Court concluded that it was not arbitrary or capricious for the FCC to consider the patent offensiveness of isolated expletives on a case-by-case basis. It also found reasonable the FCC's prediction that a *per se* exemption for fleeting expletives would lead to increased use of such expletives.

Noting that the Second Circuit did not definitively rule on the constitutionality of the FCC's indecency policies and that the Supreme Court is the court of final review, "not of first view," the Court declined to reach the broadcasters' First Amendment challenges even though "[i]t is conceivable that the Commission's orders may cause some broadcasters to avoid certain language that is beyond the Commission's reach under the Constitution."

RESULT   The Supreme Court reversed the Second Circuit's finding that the FCC's indecency policy violated the APA and remanded the case to the Second Circuit for a determination of whether the FCC's policy on "fleeting expletives" was constitutional.

COMMENTS   On remand, the U.S. Court of Appeals for the Second Circuit struck down the FCC's indecency policy as unconstitutionally vague in violation of the First Amendment.[69] The court reasoned that "[i]t is well-established that indecent speech is fully protected by the First Amendment."[70] Nonetheless, "restrictions on expletives in broadcast radio and television are subject to a lower level of scrutiny than the strict scrutiny which is applied in most contexts involving content-based restrictions of this kind because of its pervasiveness and its accessibility to children."[71] As a result, the court subjected the FCC order to intermediate scrutiny.[72]

The court explained that the vagueness doctrine serves several important objectives in the First Amendment context. First, it provides fair notice, which is particularly important with respect to content-based speech restrictions "because of [their] obvious chilling effect on

CONTINUED

---

69. Fox Television Stations, Inc. v. FCC, 613 F.3d 317 (2d Cir. 2010), *cert. granted*, 131 S. Ct. 3065 (2011).

70. Reno v. Am. Civil Liberties Union, 521 U.S. 844, 874–75 (1997).

71. FCC v. Pacifica Found., 438 U.S. 726, 748-49 (1978).

72. *See* FCC v. League of Women Voters, 468 U.S. 364 (1984).

free speech." Vague regulations "inevitably lead citizens to steer far wider of the unlawful zone than if the boundaries of the forbidden areas were clearly marked." Second, the vagueness doctrine is based "on the need to eliminate the impermissible risk of discriminatory enforcement."

The Commission argued that its three-factor "patently offensive" test gave broadcasters fair notice of what it will find indecent. However, the court characterized the Commission's reasoning as "repetition of one or more of the factors without any discussion of how it applied them." For example, the court questioned the FCC's conclusion that the use of "bullshit" in an *NYPD Blue* episode was patently offensive but that "dickhead," "pissed off," "up yours," and "kiss my ass" were not. The FCC found that the word "bullshit" is indecent because it is "vulgar, graphic and explicit" but concluded that the word "dickhead" was not indecent because it was "not sufficiently vulgar, explicit, or graphic." The court concluded that the FCC policy "hardly gives broadcasters notice of how the Commission will apply the factors in the future." Such notice is especially important because "[t]he English language is rife with creative ways of depicting sexual or excretory organs or activities, and even if the FCC were able to provide a complete list of all such expressions, new offensive and indecent words are invented every day."[73] The Supreme Court granted certiorari in 2011.

CRITICAL THINKING QUESTIONS

1. Is a court qualified to make inferences about how public attitudes toward indecent language have changed since the FCC began levying sanctions in the 1970s?

2. Is this decision consistent with the Supreme Court's invalidation of the California statute banning the sale of violent video games to minors?[74]

---

73. *Fox Television Stations*, 613 F.3d at 330.
74. Brown v. Entm't Merchs. Ass'n, 131 S. Ct. 2729 (2011) (Case 4.3).

During the 2004 Super Bowl halftime performance, a "wardrobe malfunction" caused Janet Jackson's breast to be exposed on national television for nine-sixteenths of a second. Many viewers were outraged, and the National Football League and MTV (the group that sponsored and prepared the show) were embarrassed. The FCC assessed $550,000 in fines against twenty CBS affiliates for violating its indecency requirements. The U.S. Court of Appeals for the Third Circuit initially overturned the FCC's fine, reasoning that it was arbitrary and capricious and in violation of the Administrative Procedure Act.[75] That decision was subsequently vacated by the Supreme Court with orders to reconsider the decision in light of the Court's ruling in Fox.[76] On remand, the Third Circuit invalidated the fine a second time, after concluding that its original decision had actually been strengthened by the Supreme Court's ruling in *Fox*. In *Fox*, the Court acknowledged that the FCC's *Golden Globes Order* had "broken new ground" from previous policy. The policy in place prior to the *Golden Globes Order* did not make a distinction between fleeting expletives and fleeting images, and prior policy exempted all fleeting material, whether words or images. Thus, the Third Circuit reasoned, holding CBS liable under that order would raise due process concerns because the 2004 halftime show at issue was broadcast before the FCC altered its policy. As a result, the imposition of a penalty against CBS constituted an arbitrary and capricious punishment in violation of the APA.[77]

Internet

The Internet also raises free speech issues, as discussed in Chapter 4. As explained in Chapters 9 and 14, the Internet has spawned new types of fraudulent schemes, such as online auction fraud, pyramid schemes, and securities fraud. The

ethical consideration

On average, an American child sees about 8,000 murders on television before reaching high school. How should programming managers respond to scientific evidence that television violence leads to more violent behavior by children? What additional precautions (such as time, place, and manner restrictions), if any, should they take to protect children?

---

75. CBS Corp. v. FCC, 535 F.3d.167 (3d Cir. 2008).

76. FCC v. CBS Corp., 129 S. Ct. 2176 (2009).
77. CBS Corp. v. FCC, 663 F. 3d 122 (3d Cir. 2011).

FTC, the U.S. Department of Justice, and the Securities and Exchange Commission actively prosecute offenders.

As discussed in Chapter 6, the FCC took action against Comcast, the country's second-largest Internet provider, in 2008 after concluding that Comcast had violated the federal *net neutrality policy* by hindering transfers of large data files by customers who use peer-to-peer file-sharing programs, such as BitTorrent, to share music and video.[78]

After the U.S. Court of Appeals for the D.C. Circuit invalidated the FCC's net neutrality policy,[79] the FCC promulgated a new—but very similar—policy, but this time it based its authority on a different statute. Verizon has filed suit against the FCC to challenge the new net neutrality rules.[80]

THE CONSUMER PRODUCT SAFETY COMMISSION

Congress created the Consumer Product Safety Commission (CPSC), an independent regulatory agency, in 1972 and substantially increased its budget and powers in 2008. The Consumer Product Safety Act[81] and related legislation[82] gave the CPSC the authority to set consumer product safety standards, such as performance or product-labeling specifications. The CPSC is charged with protecting the public against unreasonable risks of injury associated with consumer products and assisting consumers in evaluating the comparative safety of such products. The CPSC has no jurisdiction over tobacco products, firearms, pesticides, motor vehicles, food, drugs, medical devices, or cosmetics. These matters are regulated by other entities, such as the FDA.

Before implementing a mandatory safety standard, the CPSC must find that voluntary standards are inadequate. CPSC standards must also be reasonably necessary to eliminate an unreasonable risk of injury that the regulated product presents. When making this determination, the Commission weighs the standard's effectiveness in preventing injury against its effect on the cost of the product. The CPSC maintains an Injury Information Clearinghouse to collect and analyze information relating to the causes and prevention of death, injury, and illness associated with consumer products.

Any interested person may petition the CPSC to adopt a standard and may resort to judicial remedies if the CPSC denies the petition. One obvious concern for the Commission is that producers motivated solely by short-term profits may not be willing or able to self-regulate. The

CPSC itself can begin a proceeding to develop a standard by publishing a notice in the *Federal Register* inviting any person to submit an offer to do the development. Within a specified time limit, the CPSC can then accept such an offer, evaluate the suggestions submitted, and publish a proposed rule. The issuance of the final standard is subject to notice and comment by interested persons.

It is unlawful to manufacture for sale, offer for sale, distribute in commerce, or import into the United States a consumer product that does not conform to an applicable standard. Violators are subject to civil penalties, criminal penalties, injunctive enforcement and seizure, private suits for damages, and private suits for injunctive relief. This means that if a product cannot be made free of unreasonable risk of personal injury, the CPSC may ban its manufacture, sale, or importation altogether. The supplier of any already-distributed products that pose a substantial risk of injury may be compelled by the CPSC to repair, modify, or replace the products, or refund the purchase price.

Consumer Product Safety Improvement Act of 2008

On August 14, 2008, President George W. Bush signed the Consumer Product Safety Improvement Act of 2008 (the 2008 Act).[83] Characterized by *The Wall Street Journal* as "the biggest overhaul of U.S. product-safety rules in a generation,"[84] this Act sought to strengthen consumer product safety standards and modernize and re-energize the CPSC in the wake of a media onslaught that dubbed 2007 "The Year of the Recall."

There were 472 voluntary recalls involving nearly 110 million products in 2007. As discussed in this chapter's "Inside Story," most of the recalls involved lead-tainted paint and other hazards in imported children's toys. The scandals damaged the reputations and performance of major U.S. importers and retailers, including Mattel, Inc. and Wal-Mart Stores, Inc. Worldwide, Mattel alone recalled about 2.8 million toys due to lead-contaminated paint and 18.2 million toys due to a design flaw.[85] The recalls spurred public outrage and weakened consumer confidence in manufacturers and retailers.

Although passage of the law was largely motivated by widespread concern over children's toys, the 2008 Act affects virtually all manufacturers, importers, distributors, and retailers of consumer products. Some of the most significant provisions of the Act include (1) widespread bans on lead and phthalates (a material used in some plastics), (2) new safety standards and test procedures, (3) mandatory third-party testing and certification for imported children's

78. John Dunbar, *FCC Rules Against Comcast: Firm Ordered to End Delays on File-Sharing Traffic*, Assoc. Press, Aug. 2, 2008.

79. Comcast Corp. v. FCC, 600 F.3d 42 (D.C. Cir. 2010) (Case 6.2).

80. Cecilia Kang, *Verizon Sues over Net Neutrality Rules*, Wash. Post, Sept. 30, 2011.

81. 15 U.S.C. § 2051 *et seq.*

82. *See, e.g.*, the Hazardous Substances Labeling Act, the Child Protection Act, and the Child Protection and Toy Safety Act. 15 U.S.C. § 2052.

83. Pub. L. No. 110–314, 122 Stat. 3016 (2008).

84. Melanie Trottman, *Lawmakers Clinch Deal to Overhaul Product Safety*, Wall St. J., July 29, 2008, at A1.

85. Nicholas Casey, *Mattel Issues Third Major Recall: Top Toy Brands Barbie, Fisher-Price Are Latest Facing Lead-Paint Issues*, Wall St. J., Sept. 5, 2007, at A3.

products, (4) mandatory product tracking labels and product registration, and (5) new warnings in advertising and on websites for toys and games. It also banned most shipments of faulty products to other nations, from which they had historically found their way back onto U.S. store shelves.

The 2008 Act placed more inspectors at U.S. ports to examine imported products. Before this law was passed, CPSC officials relied mostly on agents from Customs and Border Protection to investigate products at the borders. Hardly optimal partners, these agencies tended to look for counterfeit products, rather than goods that might not comply with safety standards.

Perhaps the most significant aspect of the 2008 Act was its effort to institutionally strengthen the CPSC, which was overwhelmed, underfunded, and ill-equipped to manage the recall crisis. The agency's budget in 2007 was only $62 million, one-seventh the size of the FDA's budget for food safety alone.[86] The CPSC, which once boasted 1,000 federal employees, had shrunk to a low of 420 employees under President George W. Bush and had the capability to investigate only 10% to 15% of the reported injuries or deaths linked to consumer goods. The 2008 Act increased the CPSC staff to 500 and called for an increase in its budget of more than 50% by 2013. The CPSC requested a budget of $122 million for 2012 to support 610 full-time employees.[87]

The 2008 Act increased civil fines from $5,000 to $100,000 per offense, with each day of violation of the Act constituting a separate offense. The maximum civil penalty for a related series of violations was increased more than tenfold, from $1.25 million to $15 million. Additionally, the 2008 Act provided protection from retaliation for employees who blow the whistle on manufacturers, private labelers, retailers, or distributors to expose violations of any CPSC-enforced product safety requirements.

Although many manufacturers criticized the 2008 Act and warned that it would threaten their international competitiveness, for some the Act may offer a potential competitive advantage. For example, the Act sets tougher standards for makers of all-terrain vehicles, which could work to the advantage of U.S. producers hit hard by cheaper vehicles produced in China. Although imports currently account for 44% of consumer products sold in the United States, they account for more than 75% of CPSC product recalls, suggesting that the Act will affect foreign producers more than domestic manufacturers.[88]

The CPSC's SaferProducts Website and Database

The 2008 Act also required the CPSC to establish a database of consumer complaints and accident reports. To implement this mandate, the CPSC created a new consumer-friendly website, SaferProducts.gov. The website went live in March 2011. As of July 7, 2011, it had attracted 5,464 consumer complaints.[89] The CPSC notifies the manufacturer within five days of any complaint filed against it. The manufacturer then has fifteen days to respond to the complaint by (1) submitting a response, (2) challenging the complaint as false, or (3) asserting that the complaint will disclose a trade secret. If a response is filed, it appears alongside the complaint in the database. If a manufacturer claims that a complaint is false or that it would disclose a trade secret, the CPSC can use its discretion to decide whether to withhold the complaint or to publish it in the database.

Critics argue that because the alleged hazards reported on the database have not been verified, the site threatens manufacturers' profits and misleads consumers. CPSC spokesperson Scott Wolfson acknowledged that 204 complaints misidentified the products' manufacturers. Of the 5,464 complaints submitted, only 38% were deemed to have sufficient information to merit publication.[90] The CPSC displays a disclaimer on the website, noting that complaints may not have been verified.

In October 2011, the database faced its first legal challenge when a manufacturer that wished to remain anonymous filed suit in federal district court as "Company Doe" to prevent the CPSC from publishing a report alleging that a product caused injury to a child, which the company described as "baseless."[91] The company requested that all documents pertaining to the lawsuit be sealed; otherwise the harm it would suffer could not be redressed.

Notwithstanding the tougher regulation, sales of unsafe products continue. In 2010, the CPSC initiated 427 recalls of unsafe products, affecting a total of 124.7 million products.[92] That year, Fisher-Price, a unit of Mattel, issued the largest recall, involving more than 10 million children's toys and other products sold in the United States.[93]

---

86. Tom Lowry & Lorraine Woellert, *More Paper Tiger Than Watchdog? The Consumer Product Safety Agency Is Overwhelmed and Underfunded*, Bus. Wk., Sept. 3, 2007, at 45.

87. Consumer Product Safety Comm'n, *2012 Performance Budget Request to Congress*, Feb. 2011, *available at* http://www.cpsc.gov/cpscpub/pubs/reports/2012plan.pdf.

88. Christie L. Grymes, Kelley Drye & Warren LLP, *"The Year of the Recall": CPSC Lessons to Learn*, Metropolitan Corp. Couns., July 22, 2008, *available at* http://www.metrocorpcounsel.com/current.php?artType=view&artMonth=June&artYear=2008&EntryNo=8363.

89. U.S. Gov't Accountability Office, GAO-12-30, Report to Congress: Consumer Product Safety Commission: Action Needed to Strengthen Identification of Potentially Unsafe Products (Oct. 2011), *available at* http://www.gao.gov/new.items/d1230.pdf.

90. *Id.*

91. Ann Carrins, *Company Anonymously Challenges Consumer Website*, N.Y. Times, Nov. 2, 2011.

92. Consumer Product Safety Comm'n, 2010 Annual Report to the President and Congress (2010), *available at* http://www.cpsc.gov/cpscpub/pubs/reports/2010rpt.pdf; *Only One-Fifth of Americans Are Aware They Purchased a Recalled Product*, Consumer Rep., Jan. 4, 2011, *available at* http://pressroom.consumerreports.org/pressroom/2011/01/only-one-fifth-of-americans-are-aware-they-purchased-a-recalled-product.html.

93. Consumer Product Safety Comm'n, *The Fisher-Price Recall: More Than 10 Million Products*, Sept. 30, 2010, http://www.cpsc.gov/onsafety/2010/09/the-fisher-price-recall-more-than-10-million-products/.

State Product Safety Laws

More than fifteen states have adopted their own product safety laws. For example, two University of Chicago professors, whose son died when his Playskool Travel-Lite portable crib collapsed while he was napping, initiated Illinois's Children's Product Safety Act, which was signed into law in August 1999. Michigan followed suit and enacted the same law in June 2000.[94]

The 2008 Act explicitly prohibits the CPSC from preempting any cause of action under state or local common law or state statutory law regarding damage claims, and it grants authority to state attorneys general to enforce CPSC regulations. The 2008 Act allows the CPSC to exempt state statutes from federal preemption if the state's standards or regulations provide more protection and do not unduly burden interstate commerce. Therefore, states can continue to enforce many of the safety requirements that were in effect before enactment of the 2008 Act.

AUTOMOBILES

Automobile safety has seen enormous gains since Ralph Nader first brought the issue to the nation's attention in the 1960s.[95] The National Highway Traffic Safety Administration (NHTSA), an agency of the U.S. Department of Transportation, has the power to establish motor vehicle safety standards,[96] establish a National Motor Vehicle Safety Advisory Council, engage in testing and development of motor vehicle safety, prohibit the manufacture or importation of substandard vehicles, and develop tire safety.[97] In addition, the NHTSA is charged with developing national standards for driver safety performance, accident reporting, and vehicle registration and inspection. States refusing to comply with established federal standards are denied federal highway funds.[98] As discussed in the "Inside Story" in Chapter 10, the NHTSA fined Toyota Motor Company for mishandling claims of unintended acceleration.

PRIVACY PROTECTIONS

As discussed in Chapter 9, technological developments, especially the Internet, have made it possible to amass large amounts of detailed personal information, causing

Scott McNealy, CEO of Sun Microsystems, to quip, "You have zero privacy. . . . Get over it."[99] The 2012 amendments to Google's privacy policies, which permit Google to aggregate information from Google searches, YouTube viewing, Android smartphone location, and other data, sparked new concerns both because Google does not permit users to opt out of this aggregation and because some courts take the view that data shared with third parties is not entitled to Fourth Amendment protection.

In response to public concerns about identity theft and other violations of privacy, state and federal governments have enacted and proposed a variety of laws dealing with the collection and transmission of private data and the transmission of unsolicited e-mail (*spam*). Many of these laws are discussed in Chapter 9.

In 2010, approximately 262 billion spam e-mail messages were sent worldwide every twenty-four hours.[100] Using a spam virus, spammers are able to infect computers and turn them into "zombie computers" that can send thousands of e-mails daily without the user's knowledge.[101]

The Controlling the Assault of Non-Solicited Pornography and Marketing Act of 2003 (the CAN-SPAM Act)[102] preempted earlier state laws regulating spam. The CAN-SPAM Act has four main provisions: (1) it bans false and misleading header information and subject lines; (2) it requires the sender to include a response mechanism whereby the receiver can opt out of any future commercial messages from the sender; (3) the sender must clearly identify the message as an advertisement and include a valid physical mail address; and (4) any messages that contain sexually explicit material must include the warning "SEXUALLY-EXPLICIT" in the subject line. The CAN-SPAM Act is enforced by the Federal Trade Commission (and state attorneys general),[103] with criminal cases being brought by the Department of Justice. Violation of CAN-SPAM can subject the sender to fines of up to $11,000 and imprisonment. In 2009, Alan Ralsky, known as the "Godfather of Spam," and four co-conspirators pleaded guilty to violations under the CAN-SPAM Act, as well as conspiracy to commit wire fraud and money laundering. They admitted to hijacking tens of thousands of computers to send up to 70 million spam e-mails *per day* to pump up prices of Chinese penny stocks and then selling the stocks at inflated prices. The government alleged that Ralsky made profits of as much as $3 million from the operation, which began in 2004. Ralsky was sentenced by a federal judge to fifty-one months in prison, ordered to forfeit $250,000 seized by the government in 2007, and faced up to five years of probation.[104]

Internet service providers (ISPs) can also sue violators under the CAN-SPAM Act. In 2011, Yahoo! won a $610 million judgment against Nigerian and Thai scammers that sent more than 11.6 million hoax e-mails through its e-mail system, telling people that they had won the lottery and all they needed to do to get their prize was to wire money to cover fees.[105] In *Gordon v. Does 1-10*,[106] the U.S. Court of Appeals for the Ninth Circuit held that a private plaintiff must be a bona fide ISP to sue under the CAN-SPAM Act.

Consumers have also banded together to file class-action suits for failure to safeguard their personal information from scammers. For example, TD Ameritrade entered into a settlement agreement after being sued in a class action for allowing account holders' e-mail addresses to be leaked to scammers. The settlement called for a judgment between $2.5 million and $6.5 million.[107]

The onslaught of spam text messages sent to cellphones has resulted in regulatory action as well as litigation by the wireless carriers and by consumers hit with charges for unwanted text messages. Unlike junk e-mail, a spam text message costs the recipient between ten and twenty cents for those who do not have unlimited text messaging plans.[108] Even customers with unlimited plans may encounter unwanted charges.[109] Consumers have sued text spammers for violating the Telephone Consumer Protection Act,[110] which prohibits marketers from using automatic telephone dialing systems to make calls to cellphones unless the owners have consented.[111] Most major carriers voluntarily comply with the Mobile Marketing Association's Best Consumer Practices[112] and will often remove unwanted charges and block texts at the customer's request.

The FCC has instituted a ban on spam messages sent to wireless devices if they are sent to or from an Internet domain name; however, this ban does not cover "short" messages sent from one mobile device to another through a phone number.[113] In 2011, the FTC settled its first text spam lawsuit. The FTC had sued Philip Flora for violations of the Federal Trade Commission Act's ban on "unfair or deceptive" practices and for violations of the CAN-SPAM Act, including deceiving consumers by representing a government affiliation and sending commercial e-mails without the required return address and opt-out provisions. Flora allegedly sent 5.5 million unsolicited commercial texts, 85 messages per minute per day, to wireless handhelds to promote his debt relief and loan modification programs.[114] In his settlement with the FTC, Flora was banned from sending or aiding anyone in the delivery of unwanted text messages that promote a commercial product and was ordered to pay $32,000.[115]

UNFAIRNESS, DECEPTION, AND FRAUD

A number of regulatory agencies, both federal and state, are involved in the area of unfair and deceptive trade practices and consumer fraud. They include the Federal Trade Commission, the Food and Drug Administration, the Federal Communications Commission, the U.S. Postal Service, the U.S. Department of Housing and Urban Development, and the Securities and Exchange Commission. (Securities fraud is discussed in Chapter 22.) These federal agencies regulate advertising, packaging and labeling, pricing, warranties, and numerous sales practices. State attorneys general and state departments of consumer affairs are also involved on the state level in protecting

---

104. Hibah Yousef, *"Godfather of Spam" Going to Prison*, CNN Money, Nov. 30, 2009, *available at* http://money.cnn.com/2009/11/24/technology/King_of_spam_lawsuit_fraud_Ralsky/.

105. Julianne Pepitone, *Yahoo Wins $610 Million from Lottery Scammers*, CNN Money, Dec. 7, 2011, *available at* http://money.cnn.com/2011/12/07/technology/yahoo_spam/?source=cnn_bin.

106. 2011 WL 5909156 (9th Cir. Nov. 28, 2011).

107. *TD Ameritrade Data Breach Class Action Settlement of Alleged Identity Theft & Email Spam Class Action Lawsuit*, Class Action Lawsuits in the News, Jan. 15, 2011, *available at* http://classactionlawsuitsinthenews.com/class-action-notices/td-ameritrade-data-breach-class-action-settlement-of-alleged-identity-theft-email-spam-class-action-lawsuit/.

108. Ken Hart, *Advertising Sent to Cellphones Opens New Front in War on Spam*, Washingtonpost.com, Mar. 10, 2008, http://www.washingtonpost.com/wp-dyn/content/article/2008/03/09/AR2008030902213.html?hpid+topnews.

109. *See* Laura Northrop, *Watch Out: Spam Texts Could Be Text Scams*, Consumerist, Dec. 31, 2010, *available at* http://consumerist.com/2010/12/watch-out-spam-texts-could-be-text-scams.html.

110. 47 U.S.C. § 227 (1991).

111. Wendy Davis, *FTC Brings First SMS Spam Case*, MediaPost News, Feb. 23, 2011, *available at* http://www.mediapost.com/publications/article/145547/ftc-brings-first-sms-spam-case.html.

112. Mobile Marketing Ass'n, *U.S. Consumer Best Practices Version 6.0*, Mar. 1, 2011, *available at* http://mmaglobal.com/bestpractices.pdf.

113. Federal Communications Comm'n, *Spam: Unwanted Text Messages and E-Mail*, *available at* http://www.fcc.gov/guides/spam-unwanted-text-messages-and-email.

114. Davis, *supra* note 111.

115. Dan Kaplan, *FTC Settles with SMS Marketer over Spam Allegations*, SC Mag., Sept. 29, 2011, *available at* http://www.scmagazine.com/ftc-settles-with-sms-marketer-over-spam-allegations/article/213163/.

consumers through their administration of various state labeling laws, state warranty provisions (such as "lemon laws"), state deceptive sales practices statutes, and state privacy laws.

Deceptive Advertising and Warranties

Consumers are bombarded daily with the competing claims of various advertisers trying to generate new sales. From billboards to television to banner ads on websites and even the back of grocery receipts, advertisers vie for the consumer's attention. In this competitive environment, companies sometimes make claims that are deceptive or false. Legal solutions to this problem have historically involved three separate approaches: the common law, statutory law, and regulatory law. Regulatory law, enacted and enforced through the Federal Trade Commission, has proved to be the most effective vehicle for combating false advertisements.

Common Law

A traditional common law approach provides two remedies for a consumer who has been misled by false advertising. First, a consumer can sue for breach of contract. Such a claim may be difficult to prove because the courts usually consider an advertisement to be only an offer to deal, not a contract. A consumer might also sue for the tort of deceit (also called fraudulent misrepresentation). As discussed in Chapter 9, *deceit* requires the proof of several elements, including knowledge by the seller that the misrepresentation is false. In addition, the misrepresentation must be one of fact and not opinion, which can be a difficult distinction to make in the context of advertising.

Statutory Law

The Uniform Commercial Code (UCC) and the Lanham Trademark Act protect consumers from certain types of false advertising. As discussed in Chapter 8, section 2-313 of the UCC provides that any statement, sample, or model may constitute an *express warranty* if it is part of the basis of the bargain. Thus, an advertising term may be construed as an express warranty for a product. If the product does not conform to the representation made, the warranty is breached.

The Lanham Trademark Act[116] forbids the use of any false "description or representation" in connection with any goods or services and provides a private cause of action for any competitor injured by any other competitor's false claims. The purpose of the Act is to ensure truthfulness in advertising and to eliminate misrepresentations of quality regarding one's own product or the product of a competitor. Neither consumers nor retailers have

standing to sue for violations of the Lanham Act—only direct commercial competitors or surrogates for direct commercial competitors have standing to pursue claims under the Act.[117]

For example, in 2011 Procter & Gamble, producer of the CoverGirl makeup line, was forced to pull an advertisement containing a photograph of music artist Taylor Swift. The ad showed Swift with full, voluptuous lashes with a disclaimer at the bottom of the image stating that Swift's lashes were digitally enhanced postproduction. The National Advertising Division of the Council of Business and Bureau Claims remarked, "You can't use a photograph to demonstrate how a cosmetic will look after it is applied to a woman's face and then—in the mice type—have a disclosure that says 'okay, not really.'"[118]

FTC Regulatory Law

The Federal Trade Commission is charged with preventing unfair and deceptive trade practices, including false advertising. Among the areas that the FTC has addressed under section 5 of the Federal Trade Commission Act are deceptive price and quality claims and false testimonials and mock-ups.[119] If the FTC believes a violation of section 5 exists, it will attempt to negotiate a consent order with the alleged violator. A *consent order* is an agreement to stop the activity that the FTC has found illegal. If an agreement cannot be reached, the matter will be heard by an administrative law judge. The judge's decision can be appealed to the full Commission, and its decision can be appealed to a U.S. court of appeals. Exhibit 17.1 lists the top twenty consumer fraud complaints that the FTC received in 2010.

> **ethical**consideration
>
> Procter & Gamble Company recruited 600,000 moms for Vocalpoint, a word-of-mouth marketing program it developed to pitch its own and other companies' products. P&G gives these moms talking points, samples, and coupons in an attempt to enhance its customer base through personal endorsements.[a] Is this an acceptable form of marketing or a dangerous commercialization of human relations? Should the person spreading the product message be required to disclose her affiliation with P&G?
>
> **a.** *I Sold It Through the Grapevine*, Bus. Wk., May 29, 2006.

---

116. 15 U.S.C. §§ 1114–27.

117. Conte Bros. Auto., Inc. v. Quaker State-Slick 50, Inc., 165 F.3d 221 (3d Cir. 1998).

118. Joyce Eng, *Taylor Swift CoverGirl Ad Banned for Excessive Photoshopping*, TV Guide, Dec. 21, 2011, *available at* http://www.tvguide.com/News/Taylor-Swift-Ad-Banned-1041042.aspx.

119. Other applications of section 5 are discussed in Chapter 16. (*See* Appendix F on page A-16.)

EXHIBIT 17.1	FTC Top Consumer Fraud Complaints in 2010		
Rank	Category	Complaints	Percent
1	Identity theft	250,854	19
2	Debt collection	144,159	11
3	Internet services	65,565	5
4	Prizes, sweepstakes, lotteries	64,085	5
5	Shop-at-home catalog sales	60,205	4
6	Imposter scams	60,158	4
7	Internet auctions	56,107	4
8	Foreign money/counterfeit check scams	43,866	3
9	Telephone and mobile services	37,388	3
10	Credit cards	33,258	2
11	Advance fee loans and credit protection/repair	31,726	2
12	Banks and lenders	29,967	2
13	Credit bureaus, information furnishers, and report users	28,724	2
14	Mortgage foreclosure relief and debt management	28,584	2
15	Television and electronic media	28,245	2
16	Business opportunities, employment agencies, and work-at-home plans	24,123	2
17	Health care	21,710	2
18	Computer equipment and software	20,833	2
19	Travel, vacations, and timeshare plans	18,836	1
20	Auto-related complaints	15,787	1

SOURCE: Federal Trade Comm'n, *Consumer Sentinel Data Book for January–December 2010*, Mar. 2011, *available at* http://www.ftc.gov/sentinel/reports/sentinel-annual-reports/sentinel-cy2010.pdf.

FTC remedies include civil damages, affirmative advertising (which means the advertiser must include specific information), counter or corrective advertising, and cease and desist orders. A *cease and desist order* instructs the advertiser to stop using the methods deemed unfair

ethical consideration

A newspaper's publication of an article entitled "A Car Buyer's Guide to Sanity," which taught consumers how to negotiate lower prices, so angered car dealers that they pulled at least $1 million worth of advertising from the newspaper. The FTC challenged the dealers' actions under the antitrust laws, claiming that they had deprived consumers of essential price information in the form of newspaper advertising and had chilled the newspaper from publishing similar stories in the future.[a] Should the government become embroiled in an advertiser's decision to pull advertising from a news publication? Was the advertisers' conduct ethical?

or deceptive. In one case, the FTC required the maker of Listerine to cease and desist from making the claim that Listerine prevented colds and sore throats or lessened their severity. Tests performed by the FTC revealed that this claim, which the company had made for more than fifty years, was false. To counteract years of false claims, the FTC required the company to disclose in any future advertisements for Listerine that, contrary to prior advertising, Listerine did not help prevent colds or sore throats or lessen their severity. The order applied to the next $10 million of Listerine advertising.[120]

Deceptive Price   One example of deceptive pricing practices involves the sale of advertised items at higher prices to customers unaware of the advertised price. In one case, a person purchased a blue 1986 Chevrolet Celebrity with 29,000 miles from an automobile dealer for $8,524.[121] The buyer did not know that the dealership was currently advertising a blue 1986 Celebrity with 29,000 miles for

a. Anthony Ramirez, *Car Dealers to Stop Ad Threat*, S.F. CHRON., Aug. 2, 1995, at B3.

120. Warner–Lambert Co. v. FTC, 562 F.2d 749 (D.C. Cir. 1977).

121. Affrunti v. Vill. Ford Sales, Inc., 597 N.E.2d 1242 (Ill. App. Ct. 1992).

$6,995 in a local newspaper. When he returned home, the buyer saw the ad and telephoned the dealership to demand that the deal be renegotiated. The salesman refused, claiming that the advertised car had been sent to auction. The customer sued under the Illinois Consumer Fraud Act, which forbids false misrepresentations as well as omission of material facts. The trial court held that the dealership had a duty to inform the customer of the advertised price and awarded him the difference in the prices, plus costs.

Deceptive pricing practices also include offers of free merchandise with a purchase and two-for-one deals when the advertiser recovers the cost of the free merchandise by charging more than the regular price for the merchandise bought. Another example of deceptive pricing is bait and switch advertising. An advertiser violates the FTC *bait and switch advertising* rules if it refuses to show an advertised item, fails to have a reasonable quantity of the item in stock, fails to promise to deliver the item within a reasonable time, or discourages employees from selling the advertised item.

Quality Claims   Advertisements often include quality claims. To determine whether an advertiser has made a deceptive quality claim, the FTC must first identify the claim and then determine whether the claim is substantiated. Quality claims made without any substantiation are considered deceptive. For example, the FTC concluded that the marketers of Doan's pills had disseminated false and deceptive statements when they claimed the pills were

---

ethicalconsideration

Should free-market, competitive forces determine the price of "essential" goods such as pharmaceuticals, or should their prices be regulated? What constitutes "reasonable" profits on a product such as AZT and the cocktail of protease inhibitors recommended for people with HIV or AIDS?[a] Is the answer the same for drugs sold in Africa as for drugs sold in the United States?

---

a. For a complete discussion of the AZT controversy, see *Ethics, Pricing and the Pharmaceutical Industry,* J. Bus. Ethics, Aug. 1992, at 617. See also Brian O'Reilly, *The Inside Story of the AIDS Drug,* Fortune, Nov. 5, 1990, at 112.

---

more effective at relieving back pain than other over-the-counter pain relievers without any reasonable basis for substantiating the representations.[122] In contrast, obvious exaggerations and vague generalities are considered *puffing* and are not deemed deceptive because they are unlikely to mislead consumers. (Puffing is also discussed in Chapter 8.)

In the following case, a purchaser of the over-the-counter painkiller Aleve sued its distributor for false advertising in violation of California's Unfair Competition Law (UCL), which has been interpreted in accordance with the FTC Act.

---

122. Novartis Corp. v. FTC, 223 F.3d 783 (D.C. Cir. 2000).

| A CASE IN POINT | *In the Language of the Court* | Case 17.3 |

Lavie v. Procter & Gamble Co.

California Court of Appeal
129 Cal. Rptr. 2d 486 (Cal. App. 2003).

FACTS   Zion Lavie developed a stomach ulcer after using Aleve, an over-the-counter drug distributed by Procter & Gamble Company. He sued P&G, alleging that the company had engaged in false advertising. Aleve's advertising campaign explicitly claimed that Aleve was gentler on the stomach than aspirin. The plaintiff claimed that this implied that Aleve would not cause any stomach upset. The trial court granted summary judgment for P&G and dismissed all claims. Lavie appealed.

ISSUE PRESENTED   Should false advertising claims be based on what a reasonable consumer would understand, or should they be based on what the "least sophisticated consumer" would think about a product and its corresponding advertising?

OPINION   KLINE, J., writing on behalf of the California Court of Appeal:

The Attorney General and district attorneys have an independent role in the enforcement of this state's false advertising laws. They are authorized to prosecute violations of the UCL criminally and may also seek redress through the bringing of civil law enforcement cases seeking equitable relief and civil penalties beyond those available to private parties. . . .

Asserting that an advertisement violates the law if it is false or if it has the capacity to mislead unwary, unsophisticated or the most gullible consumers, the Attorney General maintains, the "trial court's failure to apply the 'least sophisticated consumer' standard as the measure of deception and the court's imposition of responsibility on consumers to investigate the merits of advertising claims were error."

CONTINUED

We disagree. California and federal courts applying the UCL have never applied a "least so-phisticated consumer standard," absent evidence that the ad targeted particularly vulnerable customers. Rather, they have consistently applied a standard closer to an ordinary or "rea-sonable consumer" standard to evaluate unfair advertising claims. Nor do we view the court's application of the "reasonable consumer" standard as requiring consumers to investigate the merits of advertising claims.

. . . .

As *Haskell* observed, "[T]he reasonable person standard is well ensconced in the law in a variety of legal contexts in which a claim of deception is brought. It is the standard for false advertising and unfair competition under the Lanham Act; for securities fraud, for deceit and misrepresentation and for common law unfair competition."[123]

. . . .

Haskell also relied upon the FTC's interpretation of the Federal Trade Commission Act because of the relationship between the UCL and the federal act. "[T]he Unfair Business Practices Act is one 'of the so-called "little FTC Acts" of the 1930's, enacted by many states in the wake of amendments to the Federal Trade Commission Act enlarging the commission's regulatory jurisdiction to include unfair business practices that harmed, not merely the interests of busi-ness competitors, but of the general public as well.' Because of this relationship between the [UCL] and the Federal Trade Commission Act, judicial interpretations of the federal act have persuasive force. Since 1982 the FTC has interpreted 'deception' in Section 5 of the Federal Trade Commission Act to require a showing of 'potential deception of "consumers acting rea-sonably in the circumstances," not just any consumers.'"

. . . .

Unless the advertisement targets a particular disadvantaged or vulnerable group, it is judged by the effect it would have on a reasonable consumer. As noted by the FTC many years ago: "Perhaps a few misguided souls believe, for example, that all 'Danish pastry' is made in Denmark. Is it, therefore, an actionable deception to advertise 'Danish pastry' when it is made in this country? Of course not. A representation does not become 'false and deceptive' merely because it will be unreasonably misunderstood by an insignificant and unrepresentative seg-ment of the class of persons to whom the representation is addressed."

RESULT   The appeals court affirmed the dismissal of the complaint. P&G's ads were not misleading.

CRITICAL THINKING QUESTIONS

1. Would you interpret the statement that Aleve is gentler on the stomach than aspirin to mean that it will not cause an ulcer?

2. Why shouldn't advertisers be required to ensure that their ads do not mislead the most gullible consumers?

---

123. Haskell v. Time, Inc., 857 F. Supp. 1392 (E.D. Cal. 1994).

Testimonials and Mock-ups   Testimonials and endorse-ments in which the person endorsing a product does not, in fact, use or prefer it are considered to be deceptive and therefore in violation of the FTC Act. It is also deceptive for the endorser to imply falsely that he or she has superior knowledge or experience.

It is also illegal to show an advertisement purporting to be a product demonstration that is, in fact, a mock-up or simulation. For example, the FTC successfully challenged

a series of three television commercials for Colgate–Palmolive Company's Rapid Shave shaving cream. Each commercial featured a sandpaper test, in which Rapid Shave was applied to a substance that appeared to be sandpaper, and immediately thereafter a razor was shown shaving the substance clean. Meanwhile, an announcer informed the audience that "[t]o prove Rapid Shave's super-moisturizing power, we put it right from the can onto this tough, dry sandpaper. It was apply . . . soak . . . and off in a stroke."

The FTC charged that the commercials were false and deceptive. Evidence disclosed that sandpaper of the type depicted in the commercials could not be shaved immediately following the application of Rapid Shave but required a soaking period of approximately eighty minutes. The evidence also showed that the substance resembling sandpaper was in fact a simulated prop, or "mock-up," made of plexiglass to which sand had been applied. Ultimately, the U.S. Supreme Court agreed with the FTC and decided that the commercials were unlawfully deceptive.[124]

Infomercials

Infomercials, also known as long-form marketing programs or direct response television, are advertisements generally presented in the format of half-hour television talk shows or news programs. Their very format, however, may present problems by blurring the line between advertising and regular television programming.[125]

In response to numerous complaints alleging deceptive advertising in infomercials, the infomercial industry established an internal watchdog agency, the National Infomercial Merchandising Association, in 1990, thereby forestalling greater government regulation. The association offers guidelines to combat deceptive practices, endorses legitimate infomercial producers, and reports violations to the FTC.

Magnuson–Moss Warranty Act

In addition to the statutory protections provided by the UCC for express and implied warranties, the federal government has passed a law that is designed to inform consumers about the products they buy: the Magnuson–Moss Warranty Act.[126] As explained in Chapter 8, the Act does not require any seller to provide a written warranty. If, however, a seller offers a written warranty, then the Act requires certain disclosures. In addition, it restricts disclaimers for implied warranties and permits consumers to sue violators of the Act and to recover damages plus costs, including reasonable attorneys' fees.

A manufacturer or seller offering a written warranty on consumer goods costing more than $15 must "fully and conspicuously disclose in simple and understandable language the terms and conditions of the warranty." The FTC has issued various rules relating to this provision, including one that requires consumer notification that some states do not allow certain manufacturer exclusions or limitations. A manufacturer or seller that offers a written warranty on consumer goods costing more than $10 must also state whether the warranty is full or limited.[127]

The Act prohibits sellers offering a written warranty from disclaiming *implied warranties*, such as the implied warranty of merchantability. These implied warranties may be limited to the duration of the written warranty, however. In such a case, the written warranty must be designated as "limited." A seller is permitted to disclaim all implied warranties but only if it does not offer any written warranty or service contract at all and sells a product "as is."

FTC rules allow a seller to establish an informal dispute resolution procedure and to require consumers to use this procedure before filing a lawsuit under the Act. Magnuson–Moss also requires that the warrantor be given an opportunity to remedy its noncompliance before a lawsuit is filed. Courts in six states have held that the Magnuson–Moss Warranty Act does not invalidate arbitration provisions in a written warranty.[128] However, courts in four other states reached the opposite conclusion.[129]

State Lemon Laws

A majority of states have laws dealing with warranties on new cars and new mobile homes. These *lemon laws* are designed to protect consumers from defective products that cannot be adequately fixed. The statutes vary considerably from state to state, but there are several common features. In general, a new vehicle must conform to the warranty given by the manufacturer. This means that if, after a reasonable number of attempts (usually four), the manufacturer or dealer is unable to remedy a defect that substantially impairs the value of the vehicle, the vehicle must be replaced or the purchase price refunded. Lemon laws also typically require replacement or refund if a new vehicle has been out of service ("in the shop") for thirty days during the statutory warranty period.

In addition to permitting the revocation of a sales contract, state lemon laws are designed to encourage informal resolution of disputes concerning defective new vehicles. They do this by requiring that a consumer use a manufacturer's arbitration program before litigating, as long as the manufacturer has established an informal dispute resolution program that complies with FTC regulations. Some states, including New York, have adopted their own standards for these dispute resolution programs.

Sales Practices

A number of state and federal agencies currently regulate sales practices, including the FTC, the FCC, the

---

124. FTC v. Colgate–Palmolive Co., 380 U.S. 374 (1965).

125. Karen Zagor & Gary Mead, *Illumination from the Stars: A Look at the New-Found Respectability of So-Called "Infomercials,"* FIN. TIMES, Nov. 5, 1992, at 18.

126. 15 U.S.C. § 2301 *et seq.*

127. For further discussion of the Magnuson–Moss Act, *see* Chapter 8.

128. *See* Davis v. S. Energy Homes, Inc., 305 F.3d 1268 (11th Cir. 2002); Jones v. Gen. Motors Corp., 640 F. Supp. 2d 1124 (D. Ariz. 2009); Hemphill v. Ford Motor Co., 206 P.3d 1 (Kan. App. 2009); Borowiec v. Gateway 2000, Inc., 808 N.E.2d 957 (Ill. 2004); Walker v. DaimlerChrysler Corp., 856 N.E.2d 90 (Ind. App. 2006); Pack v. Damon Corp., 320 F. Supp. 2d 545 (E.D. Mich. 2004).

129. *See* Koon's Ford of Baltimore, Inc. v. Lobach, 919 A.2d 722 (Md. App. 2007); Parkerson v. Smith, 817 So. 2d 529 (Miss. 2002); Rickard v. Teynor's Homes, Inc., 279 F. Supp. 2d 910 (N.D. Ohio 2003); Browne v. Kline Tysons Imps., Inc., 190 F. Supp. 2d 827 (E.D. Va. 2002).

Postal Service, and the Department of Housing and Urban Development. Their regulations may apply to all industries or be industry specific, such as the FTC's rules for sellers of used cars or state insurance regulations. For example, Prudential Insurance Company of America paid more than $2.7 billion to settle claims that its agents had engaged in illegal sales tactics, including tricking policyholders into cashing in old policies with accrued cash-surrender value to purchase new expensive ones with no surrender value, making false promises that dividends would build up quickly enough to pay for premiums, and disguising insurance policies as retirement programs.

Sometimes laws of general application can be invoked to protect consumers. For example, a lawyer in Washington, D.C., won two state court judgments totaling $11.6 million against affiliates of Tele-Communications, Inc. for charging excessive late fees on monthly cable television bills.[130] He successfully argued that the fees violated the general principle of contract law that damages assessed for breach of contract cannot be disproportionate to the actual harm caused by the breach.

State Deceptive Practices Statutes

Most state consumer protection laws are directed at deceptive trade practices and prohibit sellers from providing false or misleading information to consumers. Although there is considerable variation among state laws, they often provide more stringent protections than federal laws.

UCC Unconscionability Principle

Also on the state level, the Uniform Commercial Code protects consumers from unfair sales practices through the unconscionability principle contained in section 2-302 of the UCC, as discussed in Chapter 8. This section prohibits the enforcement of any contracts, or contract provisions, for the sale of goods that are so unfair and one-sided that they shock the conscience of the court.

Door-to-Door Sales

Door-to-door sales are initiated and concluded at a buyer's home. They pose special risks because individuals may feel more pressure to buy something from someone standing at their door, or they may make a purchase just to get rid of a persistent salesperson. As a result, the FTC has mandated a three-day cooling-off period during which a consumer may rescind a door-to-door purchase. Under FTC rules, the seller must also notify a buyer of the right to cancel. Laws in some states provide longer periods during which consumers can cancel a sale.

Referral Sales and Pyramid Sales

A number of states have enacted legislation restricting referral and pyramid sales. In a *referral sale*, the seller offers the buyer a commission, rebate, or discount for furnishing the seller with a list of additional prospective customers. The discount, however, is usually contingent on the seller actually making later sales to the prospects provided by the original customer. In a *pyramid selling* scheme, a consumer is recruited as a product "distributor" and receives commissions based on the products he or she sells and on the recruitment of additional sellers (and may even receive commissions on the sales of the recruits). The problem with both referral and pyramid sales is that unless the buyer or "distributor" becomes involved early in the chain, the supply of prospective recruits is quickly exhausted.

Telemarketing

The Telemarketing and Consumer Fraud and Abuse Prevention Act[131] enhanced the FTC's power to combat abusive or deceptive telemarketing practices, including credit card laundering. The FTC adopted limits on when telemarketers can make unsolicited calls and, together with the FCC, created a national Do-Not-Call Registry. Consumers who put their phone numbers on the list can limit unsolicited commercial telemarketing calls. In addition, state securities commissioners and the FTC continue to fight investment-related telemarketing fraud ranging from ostrich ranching in Idaho to digital fingerprint identification in Indiana and worthless oil and gas programs in Kentucky.

Mail-Order Sales

Unscrupulous mail-order sales practices have led to a high incidence of consumer complaints with resultant state and federal regulation. Sellers must respond to consumer mail orders by shipping merchandise or offering refunds within a reasonable time. Unsolicited or unordered merchandise sent by U.S. mail may be kept or disposed of by the recipient without incurring any obligation to the sender. Book and record clubs are generally legal as long as they comply with state-law provisions requiring sellers to provide consumers with forms or announcement cards that the consumer may use to instruct the seller not to send the offered merchandise. The U.S. Postal Service has authority to assess criminal and civil penalties for fraudulent mail schemes that injure consumers.

In 2010, Congress passed the Restore Online Shoppers' Confidence Act,[132] which is designed to protect consumers from *data passing*, the practice whereby a merchant transfers a customer's payment information to another merchant for a separate online sale without requiring the

---

130. Eben Shapiro, *Attorney Finds a Way to Battle Bills' Late Fees*, Wall St. J., Oct. 6, 1997, at B1.

131. Pub. L. No. 103-297, 108 Stat. 1545 (1994).
132. Pub. L. No. 111-345, 124 Stat. 3618 (2010).

customer to reenter the payment information or give consent to the transfer of that information. Third-party merchants involved in data passing then charge consumers for memberships, products, and services they did not want or authorize.

For example, after a consumer submitted credit or debit card information to make a purchase on a retailer's website but before the purchaser clicked to confirm the purchase, an ad from an outside marketer would pop up offering a free trial for magazines, a club membership, or other services. The initial purchase could not be completed until the consumer agreed to the free trial or clicked on a less-noticeable link to decline. If the consumer accepted the free trial, he or she would have to cancel the product or service once the trial ended to avoid being charged. Many consumers did not realize this and were surprised when they were automatically billed by the third-party marketer that obtained the billing information from the retailer.[133]

The Act contains two primary prohibitions. First, it prohibits and prevents Internet-based post-transaction third-party sales of the sort described above. Second, it imposes specific requirements on negative option offers, in which the seller interprets the consumer's silence, or failure to take an affirmative action to reject goods or services or cancel an agreement, as acceptance of the offer.[134]

Industry-Specific Sales Practices

Since the early 1980s, the FTC has become more involved in regulating the sales practices of specific industries. For example, the FTC requires used-car sellers to affix a Buyer's Guide label to the cars that they sell.[135] The label provides information about the car's warranty and any service contract provided by the dealer. If the car is sold without a warranty, the label must state that the car is being sold "as is."

A related and well-developed area of state and federal consumer law prohibits tampering with car odometers. Consumers purchasing a motor vehicle rely heavily on odometer readings as an indication of a car's safety and reliability. It is a federal crime to tamper with car odometers.[136]

On the state level, industry-specific regulation covers the insurance industry. State insurance commissioners both establish regulations regarding the disclosure of information to prospective policyholders and set maximum rates within a state.

Real Estate Sales

A number of state and federal laws, including the Federal Real Estate Settlement Procedures Act[137] and the Interstate Land Sales Full Disclosure Act,[138] protect consumers in real estate transactions. For example, the costs of title insurance, taxes, and fees for attorneys, appraisers, and brokers must be disclosed, and lenders must give home buyers an estimate of settlement costs and provide a statement showing the annual percentage rate for the mortgage. Certain disclosure requirements of the Truth in Lending Act apply to real estate credit transactions as well. In some transactions, real estate buyers have the right to cancel the purchase contract if certain information is not disclosed to them or if other procedures are not properly followed.

In response to fraudulent practices used in the sale of subdivided land for investment purposes or for second or retirement homes, Congress passed the Interstate Land Sales Full Disclosure Act in 1968, which is administered by the Secretary of the Department of Housing and Urban Development (HUD). Under the Act, the Secretary created the Office of Interstate Land Sales Registration and imposed federal disclosure requirements on the sale of 100 or more lots of undeveloped subdivided land akin to those required for the offer of securities under the Securities Act of 1933. The Act gives the Secretary of HUD the power to bring suit in federal district court to enjoin sales by developers who have not registered in accordance with the Act. Purchasers affected by a promoter's wrongdoing have a private cause of action and may cancel the purchase contract.

As discussed in Chapter 18 and the "Inside Story" in Chapter 23, the Dodd–Frank Wall Street Reform and Consumer Protection Act imposed new requirements for loans secured by home mortgages.

STATE OCCUPATIONAL LICENSING

State departments of consumer affairs protect the public by examining and licensing firms and individuals who possess the necessary education and demonstrated skills to perform their services competently. Among the occupations generally regulated are accountants, architects, barbers, contractors, cosmetologists, dentists, dry cleaners, marriage counselors, nurses, pharmacists, physical therapists, physicians, and social workers. Attorneys are regulated by state bar associations and the courts. As noted in Chapter 7, any person required to be licensed who is in fact not licensed cannot enforce a promise to pay for unlicensed work. State departments of consumer affairs

133. Eileen Ambrose, *Law Aims to Protect Online Shoppers from Shady Marketers*, BALTIMORE SUN, Feb. 8, 2011.

134. Dean W. Harvey, *"Data Pass" and Online Negative Option Marketing Now Deceptive Trade Practices*, ANDREWS KURTH LLP, Apr. 19, 2011, *available at* http://www.andrewskurth.com/pressroom-publications-780.html.

135. 16 C.F.R. pt. 455 (Used Motor Vehicle Trade Regulation Rule).

136. 49 U.S.C. § 32703.

137. 12 U.S.C. § 2601 *et seq.*

138. 15 U.S.C. § 1701 *et seq.*

also investigate and resolve consumer complaints and hold public hearings involving consumer matters.

CONSUMER CREDIT

Because credit plays an important role in many consumer transactions, a number of consumer protection laws address this area. Federal consumer credit law can be confusing because many of the acts have similar names. These complex acts and regulations are all part of the lengthy Consumer Credit Protection Act (CCPA),[139] which was initially passed by Congress in 1968. Since 1968, several additional acts (or titles) have been added to the original legislation.

The Consumer Financial Protection Act, promulgated as part of the Dodd–Frank Wall Street Reform and Consumer Protection Act of 2010 (Dodd–Frank), also added significant protections for borrowers, including limits on prepayment penalties. Perhaps most importantly, the Consumer Financial Protection Act imposed a duty on consumer lenders (including mortgage lenders) to make a good faith determination that the consumer has a reasonable ability to repay the loan and all applicable taxes, insurance, and assessments at the time of its consummation.

The Consumer Financial Protection Bureau

As discussed in Chapter 6, Dodd–Frank established the Consumer Financial Protection Bureau (CFPB) to protect consumers from unfair, deceptive, and abusive credit practices. The Bureau has conducted three "Know Before You Owe" campaigns designed to better inform consumers about credit cards, mortgages, and student loans. The CFPB has also drafted and field-tested new mortgage disclosure forms, pursuant to the Truth in Lending Act (discussed below) and the Real Estate Settlement Procedures Act.

In one of the its first moves, the CFPB created a joint task force to combat scams targeted at homeowners seeking modifications of their mortgages to avoid foreclosure. It has also published an interim report analyzing the 5,074 consumer credit card complaints received since it commenced operations in July 2010.[140]

Although it had a productive first year, the CFPB's progress was hindered by the absence of a named director. Without a director, the CFPB could only commence investigations and bring cases pursuant to the powers transferred to it from the Federal Trade Commission, the Federal Deposit Insurance Corporation, and other federal regulators under Dodd–Frank. Even though the CFPB could, from the outset, enforce existing laws against financial institutions,[141] only the director has the power to issue new final rules.

As noted in Chapter 6, President Obama nominated former Ohio Attorney General Richard Cordray to the post in July 2011. Five months later, Senate Republicans blocked a floor vote on his nomination, stating that they would not accept any nominee for director unless Dodd–Frank was amended to replace the position of director with a five-member outside board to provide more oversight.[142] In what the *Washington Post* dubbed "a bold act of political defiance,"[143] President Obama announced on January 4, 2012, that he had appointed Cordray as director during a three-day congressional recess. The Constitution gives the President the power to make appointments to fill vacancies during periods when Congress is in recess, to ensure that the government can continue to function.[144] Interim appointees can remain in their posts for one year, until the end of the next Senate session, during which time they must either win confirmation from the Senate or step down.

Republican President George W. Bush made 171 recess appointments during his first six years in office. In 2007, Democrat Senate leader Harry Reid moved to block recess appointments by holding regular pro forma sessions even when members were not present because of a congressional break. These "sessions" would be held only a minute or two every third day, but they permitted the Senate to deny that the President had the power to make a recess appointment.[145] The text of the Constitution does not state how long Congress must be in recess, but when the Constitution was originally enacted, Congress was expected to meet only a few months each year.[146]

Overview of Consumer Credit Protection Act (CCPA)

Exhibit 17.2 provides an overview of the CCPA and indicates the provisions that are omitted from the discussion in this chapter.

139. 15 U.S.C. § 1601 *et seq.*

140. CONSUMER FINANCIAL PROTECTION BUREAU, REPORT TO CONGRESS: BUILDING THE CFPB: A PROGRESS REPORT (July 18, 2011), *available at* http://www.consumerfinance.gov/wp-content/uploads/2011/07/Report_BuildingTheCfpb1.pdf.

141. Josh Boak, *Consumer Financial Protection Bureau Can Open Without Chief*, POLITICO, June 16, 2011, *available at* http://www.politico.com/news/stories/0611/57142.html.

142. Stephen Koff, *Richard Cordray's Nomination Fails in U.S. Senate Because of Dispute over Consumer Financial Protection Bureau*, CLEVELAND PLAIN DEALER, Dec. 8, 2011, *available at* http://www.cleveland.com/open/index.ssf/2011/12/richard_cordrays_nomination_fa.html.

143. David Nakamura & Felicia Sonmez, *Obama Appoints Richard Cordray to Head Consumer Watchdog Bureau*, WASH. POST, Jan. 5, 2012.

144. U.S. CONST. art. II, § 2, cl. 3.

145. Bruce Ackerman, *Washington Standoff: Obama Should Fight the Senate on Recess Appointments, but Not This Way*, L.A. TIMES, Jan. 6, 2012.

146. Peter M. Shane, *Recess Appointments and President Obama's Surprising Restraint*, HUFFINGTON POST POLITICS, Jan. 6, 2012, http://www.huffingtonpost.com/peter-m-shane/recess-appointments-and-p_b_1190404.html.

EXHIBIT 17.2   Consumer Credit Protection Act (CCPA)

Title	Consumer Credit Protection Act
I.	Truth in Lending Act (TILA)
	Chapter 1: General Provisions [omitted]
	Chapter 2: Credit Transactions
	Chapter 3: Credit Advertising
	Chapter 4: Fair Credit Billing Act
	Chapter 5: Consumer Leasing Act [omitted]
II.	Extortionate Credit Transactions
III.	Restriction on Garnishment
IV.	National Commission on Consumer Finance [omitted]
V.	General Provisions [omitted]
VI.	Fair Credit Reporting Act
VII.	Equal Credit Opportunity Act
VIII.	Fair Debt Collection Practices Act
IX.	Electronic Fund Transfer Act

© Cengage Learning 2013

"Which carries more favorable interest rates, an auto loan or a home improvement loan? My mobile home needs a new transmission."

Aaron Bacall/The New Yorker Collection/www.cartoonbank.com

Truth in Lending Act

The Truth in Lending Act (TILA), Title I of the Consumer Credit Protection Act, is intended "to assure a meaningful disclosure of credit terms so that the consumer will be able to compare more readily the various credit terms available and avoid the uninformed use of credit, and to protect the consumer against inaccurate and unfair credit billing and credit card practices."[147] In particular, the Act makes uniform the actuarial method for determining the rate of charge for consumer credit and requires certain disclosures. It is not a *usury statute*, however, and does not set maximum interest rates. TILA applies only to credit transactions between creditors and individual consumers, not to credit transactions between two consumers. Typical transactions covered by TILA include car loans, student loans, and home improvement loans; credit cards (such as Visa and MasterCard), which permit deferred payment over a period of time; charge cards (such as American Express), which require payment of the full balance on receipt of the bill; and certain real estate loans in which the amount financed is less than $25,000.

Congress directed the Federal Reserve Board to issue regulations for the enforcement and interpretation of TILA. To that end, the Federal Reserve has produced model disclosure forms for use with credit sales and loans. The two most important terms in a TILA disclosure statement are the *finance charge* (interest over the life of the loan expressed as a dollar amount) and the annual percentage rate (interest expressed as a percentage), which are both defined in the Federal Reserve Board's

Regulation Z.[148] Regulation Z also contains provisions dealing with disclosure of the terms of any credit or mortgage insurance offered in connection with a loan.

Regulation Z requires marketing materials for credit cards to prominently display a table that clearly states the annual percentage rate and other critical information (including the annual fee). The annual percentage rate for purchases and the variable rate information, grace period, minimum finance charge, method of computing the balance, cash advance fees, and overlimit fees, as well as any other fees that vary by state, must be printed in a box in at least eighteen-point type to prevent information from being hidden in the "fine print." In addition, the overall disclosure statement must be printed in at least twelve-point type and be "readily noticeable" and in a "reasonably understandable form."[149] Consumers can be required to arbitrate their claims in individual arbitrations if they agreed to do so when applying for or procuring credit and are not forced to relinquish statutorily protected rights.[150]

TILA draws a distinction between open-end credit and closed-end credit. *Open-end credit* occurs when the parties intend the creditor to make repeated extensions of credit (for example, Visa or MasterCard); *closed-end credit* involves only one transaction (for example, a car or house loan). Open-end consumer credit plans must make certain

147. 15 U.S.C. § 1601.

148. 12 C.F.R. pt. 226.

149. *Consumer Credit—Truth in Lending: Fed Issues Final Regulation Under TILA Requiring New Clarity for Card Disclosures,* 69 U.S.L.W. 2200 (2000).

150. Thompson v. Ill. Title Loans, Inc., 2000 U.S. Dist. LEXIS 232 (N.D. Ill. Jan. 6, 2000).

disclosures at three separate times: (1) in an initial disclosure statement when the account is opened, (2) in subsequent periodic billing statements, and (3) annually when a consumer must be notified of his or her rights under the Fair Credit Billing Act. In general, the required information includes finance and other charges, security interests (collateral), previous balance and credits, identification of transactions, closing date and new balance, and annual percentage rates and period rates.

New disclosure rules, which went into effect in February 2010, require credit card companies to indicate on monthly billing statements how long it will take to pay off the balance by making only the minimum monthly payment and how much that will cost at the applicable interest rate. For example, if a cardholder owing $3,000 at an interest rate of 14.4% makes the minimum monthly payment of $90, then it will take eleven years and payments of $4,745 to pay off the balance.[151] Credit card companies are required to disclose monthly and year-to-date totals for fees paid and interest charges and also must notify the cardholder at least forty-five days before raising interest rates, changing certain fees (such as annual fees or late fees), or making any other significant changes to the terms of the credit card.

Closed-end credit plans require disclosure of at least the following for each transaction: identity of creditor, amount financed, finance charge, annual percentage rate, variable rate, payment schedule, total of payments, total sale price, prepayment provisions, late payment fee, security interest, credit insurance, loan assumption policy, and required deposit. Special rules apply for certain residential mortgages and adjustable-rate transactions.

TILA limits the liability of credit cardholders to $50 per card for unauthorized charges made before a card issuer is notified that the card has been lost or stolen. Once a card issuer has been notified, a cardholder incurs no liability from unauthorized use. In addition, a credit or charge card company cannot bill a consumer for unauthorized charges if the card was improperly issued by the card company.

Home Equity Lending Plans, Subprime Mortgages, and Predatory Lending

TILA provides specific protections for consumers who use their home as collateral for a second mortgage or an open-end line of credit. Because losing one's home has such significant consequences, Congress felt special disclosure requirements were in order. TILA provides consumers with a *right of rescission* (that is, a right to cancel the contract) whenever their home is used as collateral except for original construction or acquisition. These cancellation

rights are generally available for three days if all procedures are properly followed by the lender, three years if they are not. TILA also mandates disclosure of up-front costs, repayment schedules, and the annual percentage rate and its method of calculation.

Notwithstanding these disclosures, millions of Americans were duped into toxic subprime mortgages.[152] Communities of color were particularly hard hit by *predatory lending*, mortgage loans secured by the borrower's house made at subprime interest rates to borrowers who often lacked the ability to repay the loans. These loans tended to be concentrated in low-income communities and used to repay consumer debt rather than for housing purposes. Because the loans were often based solely on the homeowner's equity in the home, without regard to the borrower's income and thus his or her ability to repay the loan, foreclosures were common. Although subprime lending enabled many Americans with modest incomes and poor credit histories to buy homes, these loans have cost millions of borrowers their homes and brought others near the brink of financial ruin. In 2004, the Federal Reserve Board fined Citigroup a record $75 million for violating regulations against predatory lending practices.

A 2007 study by researchers at New York University found that home buyers in predominantly black and Hispanic neighborhoods in New York City were more likely to get their mortgages from a subprime lender than were home buyers in white neighborhoods. According to NYU's Furman Center for Real Estate and Urban Policy, this disparity held true even when median income levels were comparable.[153] This study confirmed the suspicion that certain mortgage brokers offering subprime mortgages worked only in certain neighborhoods or tended to offer white borrowers better rates than equally qualified African American or Hispanic customers.

Effective on October 2009, the Federal Reserve Board revised Regulation Z to add rules designed to protect mortgage customers from predatory lending practices and "higher-priced" mortgages and to discourage prepayment penalties. As discussed in Chapter 18, the Dodd–Frank Act prohibits prepayment penalties for adjustable-rate and "not-qualified mortgages." Other protections added by Dodd–Frank are discussed in the "Inside Story" in Chapter 23.

Credit Advertising

TILA includes specific provisions that regulate credit advertising. The idea behind these provisions is that consumers equipped with complete and accurate credit information will be able to find the best terms. Regulation Z requires that any advertised specific credit terms actually

---

151. Board of Governors of the Federal Reserve, *What You Need to Know: New Credit Card Rules Effective Feb. 22, available at* http://www.federalreserve.gov/consumerinfo/wyntk_creditcardrules.htm (last updated Mar. 11, 2010).

152. Arkadi Kuhlmann, *Putting the "Own" Back in Homeowners*, WALL ST. J., Apr. 11, 2011, at A15.

153. Manny Fernandez, *Study Finds Disparities in Mortgages by Race*, N.Y. TIMES, Oct. 15, 2007.

be available and that any credit terms (for example, the finance charge or annual percentage rate) mentioned in the advertisement be explained fully. The FTC enforces the advertising provisions of Regulation Z. For example, all credit card advertising must have a "Schumer Box" (named after the New York Senator who championed the regulation) that contains all basic credit card information. Unlike the other sections of TILA, this provision does not give consumers a private cause of action to sue credit advertisers directly.

In 2009, Congress passed the Credit Card Accountability Responsibility and Disclosure Act (Credit CARD Act),[154] which, among other things, bans retroactive rate increases on existing balances due to "any time, any reason" and severely limits increases due to default. In general, credit card companies may not retroactively increase rates on existing balances unless a promotional rate has expired, the variable indexed rate has increased, or payments are more than sixty days late. If the cardholder does trigger the default rate because of a sixty-day delinquency, the bank must restore the lower rate once the cardholder demonstrates six months of consecutive on-time payments.

The Credit CARD Act also requires that contract terms be clearly spelled out and remain stable for the entire first year. It requires that institutions give cardholders a reasonable time to pay the monthly bill, at least twenty-one calendar days from the time of mailing, and it prohibits late-fee traps such as weekend deadlines, due dates that change each month, and deadlines that fall in the middle of the day. The Act requires the institution to obtain the consumer's permission to process transactions that would put the account balance over the limit, and it restricts fees on subprime, low-limit credit cards. The Act also requires credit card companies to apply excess payments to the highest interest balance first and ends the confusing and unfair practice of "double-cycle billing," in which the issuer uses the balance in a previous month to calculate interest charges on the current month.[155]

---

154. Pub. L. No. 111-24, 123 Stat. 1734 (2009).

155. Press Release, Office of the Press Secretary, Fact Sheet: Reforms to Protect American Credit Card Holders (May 22, 2009), *available at* http://www.whitehouse.gov/the_press_office/Fact-Sheet-Reforms-to-Protect-American-Credit-Card-Holders.

Credit Billing

The Fair Credit Billing Act requires creditors, such as credit card companies, to respond to consumer complaints with an acknowledgment of the complaint, followed by a reasonable investigation to determine whether the complaint is justified. Companies cannot evade this requirement by canceling a cardholder's account.

For example, in 1982, American Express Company canceled a cardholder's account during a dispute about incorrect billings. American Express argued that its contract with the cardholder allowed it to revoke a credit card at any time for any reason, but the U.S. Court of Appeals for the District of Columbia ruled that the Fair Credit Billing Act's protections could not be waived.[156] As the court explained:

> The rationale of consumer protection legislation is to even out the inequalities that consumers normally bring to the bargain. To allow such protection to be waived by boiler plate language of the contract puts the legislative process to a foolish and unproductive task. A court ought not impute such nonsense to a Congress intent on correcting abuses in the market place.

Hence, the Fair Credit Billing Act protected the cardholder from the revocation of his account despite the provisions of the Cardmember Agreement purporting to permit American Express to cancel the account at any time.

Extortionate Credit Transactions

The CCPA prohibits any *extortionate extension of credit*, that is, the extension of credit where the parties expect nonpayment to result in bodily harm.

Restrictions on Garnishment

Garnishment is the legal procedure by which a creditor may collect a debt by attaching a portion of the debtor's weekly wages. The CCPA restricts the amount of a debtor's wages that is available for garnishment to the lesser of (1) 25% of the "disposable earnings" for that week (defined by the Act as the amount remaining after deductions required by law) or (2) the amount by which "disposable earnings" for that week exceed thirty times the current federal minimum hourly wage. The Secretary of Labor enforces the provisions of this title. Some states prohibit garnishment of wages altogether.

Fair Credit Reporting Act

Almost everyone over the age of eighteen has a credit report on file somewhere. Lenders look to these various reporting agencies for information on an individual's creditworthiness. Because negative information in a credit

---

156. Gray v. Am. Express Co., 743 F.2d 10 (D.C. Cir. 1984).

report can make obtaining credit considerably more difficult, it is important for consumers to be able to access these credit reports and to correct any false information before it is reported to lenders or shared with another reporting agency's computer.

Under the Fair Credit Reporting Act of 1970 (FCRA),[157] as amended by the Fair and Accurate Credit Transactions Act of 2003 (FACT Act), consumers can request all information (except medical information) on themselves, the source of the information, and any recent recipients of a report. The FCRA also gives consumers a right to have corrected copies of their credit reports sent to creditors. The FTC has the primary responsibility for the enforcement of the FCRA.

Credit bureaus must investigate disputed information in credit reports and resolve consumer complaints within thirty days. They must give the consumer written notice of the results of the investigation within five days after it is completed. The credit-reporting agency must go beyond the original source of information to determine whether it is accurate. Thus, when a consumer notified the agency that she had never held the credit cards her report showed as being delinquent, the agency could not just rely on the credit card companies' statements that the applications for the cards had the correct information. Instead, the agency should have checked the handwriting on the credit applications and determined whether the applications were obtained by fraud.[158]

When a consumer tells a credit-reporting agency that he or she disputes a charge, the agency is required to notify the furnisher of the information that the information provided is in dispute. The creditor must then conduct a "reasonable" investigation and review all relevant information to determine whether it is accurate.[159] Any finding that information is inaccurate or incomplete must be reported to all national credit bureaus. Under certain circumstances, consumers can require the firm that furnished disputed information to the credit bureau to reinvestigate the accuracy of the information it passed on to the bureau. A furnisher is liable for providing inaccurate information if it "knows or has reasonable cause to believe that the information is inaccurate."[160]

As noted in Chapter 9, the FACT Act gave consumers new tools to fight identity theft and to correct erroneous information resulting from the fraudulent use of credit cards and accounts. The FACT Act does not, however, contain an express private cause of action for consumers harmed by erroneous credit reports.

The FCRA also contains restrictions on *investigative consumer reporting*, that is, reports that contain information on character and reputation, not just credit history. In most cases, a consumer must be notified in writing that such a report may be made. This requirement applies to potential or current employers as well.

Before asking a credit bureau or private investigator for a report on a credit applicant or employee, the lender or employer must notify the individual in writing that a report may be used and obtain the individual's consent. Neither a lender nor an employer may rely on a credit or investigative consumer report to take adverse action (including denying credit or denying a job applicant a position, reassigning or terminating an employee, or denying a promotion), unless it first provides the individual with a "pre-adverse action disclosure," which includes a copy of the report and the FTC's "A Summary of Your Rights Under the Fair Credit Reporting Act." Lenders and employers who fail to obtain permission before requesting a credit or investigative report or to provide the pre-adverse action disclosures are subject to suits for damages (including punitive damages for deliberate violations) by individuals and civil penalties by the FTC.

After a lender or an employer has taken adverse action, it must give the individual notice—orally, in writing, or electronically—that the action has been taken. The notice must include (1) the name, address, and phone number of the credit bureau or private investigator that supplied the report; (2) a statement that the credit bureau or investigator did not make the decision to take adverse action and cannot give specific reasons for it; and (3) a notice of the individual's right to dispute the accuracy or completeness of any information the bureau or investigator furnished and the individual's right upon request to an additional free report from the credit bureau or investigator within sixty days.

Lenders that use risk-based pricing must provide notices to consumers who receive loans on "material terms that are materially less favorable than the most favorable terms available to a substantial portion of consumers . . . based in whole or in part on a consumer report."[161]

Equal Credit Opportunity Act

The Equal Credit Opportunity Act was originally intended to address the difficulty many women faced in obtaining credit, but it has since been expanded to prohibit discrimination against credit applicants on many other grounds. The current list of protected categories includes gender, marital status, race, color, religion, national origin, and age (except that older applicants may be given favorable treatment). The Act also prohibits discrimination against applicants who derive their income from public assistance or have exercised in good faith any right under the CCPA. The FACT Act generally prohibits lenders from using medical information about a consumer as a factor in decisions about credit eligibility.

---

157. 15 U.S.C. § 1681.

158. Cushman v. Trans Union Corp., 115 F.3d 220 (3d Cir. 1997).

159. Johnson v. MBNA Am. Bank, NA, 357 F.3d 426 (4th Cir. 2004).

160. FACT Act § 312(b).

161. FACT Act § 311.

Unlike most of the other lending acts discussed in this chapter, the Equal Credit Opportunity Act applies to business credit as well as consumer credit. In general, the rejection of an application for credit triggers the Act and various compliance steps, which include written notification of the reasons for denial. The regulations also establish methods for evaluating the creditworthiness of an applicant.

Fair Debt Collection Practices Act

The Fair Debt Collection Practices Act (FDCPA), which is enforced by the FTC, regulates debt collectors and debt collection practices and provides a civil remedy for anyone injured by a violation of the statute. In general, FTC guidelines require collectors to tell the truth and not to use any deceptive means to collect a debt or locate a debtor. For example, a collector sending a dunning letter must state very clearly and explicitly the amount owed.

The Act covers only third-party debt collectors (for example, collection agencies) or someone pretending to be a third-party collector. First-party debt collectors (for example, retail store collection departments) are not covered, although the FTC can reach these collectors under its duty to address "unfair and deceptive trade practices" under section 5 of the Federal Trade Commission Act. The U.S. Court of Appeals for the Second Circuit held that a letter from an attorney for a landlord demanding that a tenant pay back rent within three days or face eviction was subject to the FDCPA.[162] The court held that past due rent is a debt and that the lawyer's letter was a debt collection "communication" within the meaning of the statute.

People who write bad checks for goods and services are also protected from abusive debt collection practices by the FDCPA. The U.S. Courts of Appeals for the Seventh,[163] Eighth,[164] Ninth,[165] and Tenth[166] Circuits have each held that the payment obligation that arises from a bounced check is a "debt" within the meaning of the Act even though the transaction did not involve an offer or extension of credit.

Electronic Fund Transfer Act: Debit Cards and Preauthorized Fund Transfers

The Electronic Fund Transfer Act, passed by Congress in 1978, covers online debit cards issued by banks for use with automatic teller machines (ATMs) and point-of-sale transactions, as well as preauthorized electronic fund transfers or automatic payments from a consumer's account. As with credit cards, banks are prohibited from sending out debit cards except in response to a consumer's request.

The Federal Reserve Board has issued regulations and model forms for banks to use to satisfy disclosure requirements under the Act. In general, the Federal Reserve forms ensure disclosure of contract terms, potential customer liability for unauthorized use (as with credit cards, customer liability is usually limited to no more than $50), and consumer complaint procedures. Banks are also required to issue receipts with every ATM transaction and to mail periodic statements showing electronic fund transfer activity on a consumer's account during the period. For preauthorized transfers or automatic payments, banks are required to provide either (1) written or oral notice within two days of the scheduled transaction date that the transaction did or did not occur or (2) a telephone line for consumers to call and ascertain whether the transfer occurred. Most financial institutions have adopted the latter approach.

Online debit cards are usually PIN–protected; that is, cash cannot be withdrawn from an ATM and a deduction cannot be made at a point-of-sale terminal unless the holder uses a personal identification number (PIN). In contrast, off-line debit cards (which may bear the Visa or MasterCard logo) have the characteristics of both an ATM card and a credit card, and they can be used without a PIN. For example, the holder of an off-line debit card can authorize a deduction from his or her bank account by signing a charge slip at a restaurant. Visa and MasterCard voluntarily agreed to impose a $50 cap on liability for their off-line debit cards.

162. Romea v. Heiberger & Assocs., 163 F.3d 111 (2d Cir. 1998).

163. Bass v. Stolper, Koritzinsky, Brewster & Neider, S.C., 111 F.3d 1322 (7th Cir. 1997).

164. Duffy v. Landberg, 133 F.3d 1120 (8th Cir. 1998).

165. Charles v. Lundgren & Assocs., P.C., 119 F.3d 739 (9th Cir. 1997).

166. Johnson v. Riddle, 305 F.3d 1107 (10th Cir. 2002).

EXHIBIT 17.3 State Credit Laws

Area Law Covers	Examples	Primary Goals
Installment sales	Legal interest rates, late charges, deferral charges, and other permissible charges	Place caps on late charges and limit remedies, attorney's fees, and rights to assign sales contract.
Consumer loans	Mortgages and private loans	Set maximum permissible interest rate, with exceptions available for special license holders
Credit cards	Credit card repayment rates, credit card fees	Stop exploitation by credit card companies.

© Cengage Learning 2013

State Laws Regulating Consumer Credit

All states have statutes regulating consumer credit. Two types of consumer credit transactions are addressed primarily at the state level: installment sales and loans to consumers. State statutes vary widely, and an attempt to create uniform state laws on consumer credit through adoption of the Uniform Consumer Credit Code (UCCC, called the U–Triple C) has been largely unsuccessful. The UCCC is intended to replace a state's consumer credit laws, including those that regulate usury, installment sales, consumer loans, truth in lending, and garnishment. The UCCC has been adopted by only a handful of states, however, and in each of those it has been so significantly altered that little

uniformity remains. Exhibit 17.3 summarizes common provisions in state credit laws.

Credit card companies have found a way around particularly stringent state credit card fee limits and usury laws by moving their operations to states with more lax laws. The Supreme Court ruled that the usury laws of the state in which the card company is located apply.[167] Thus, a bank with credit card operations in a state that permits high rates, such as South Dakota or Delaware, can charge a resident of Massachusetts the high rates of interest and fees permitted in the state of operation even though they are in excess of the Massachusetts limits.

---

167. Marquette Nat'l Bank of Minneapolis v. First of Omaha Serv. Corp., 439 U.S. 299 (1978).

GLOBAL VIEW

Norebbo/Shutterstock

International Recycling and Chemical Safety Standards

Although the United States initially set the standard for consumer and environmental protection, the European Union (EU) is increasingly replacing America as the leader in environmental and chemical policy development.[168] Three significant environmental policies, including two directives and one regulation, are being implemented in the twenty-seven member states that comprise the European Union.

The first directive, WEEE,[169] is intended to increase the recovery and recycling of electrical and electronic equipment. The second, RoHS,[170] outlines restrictions on the use of certain hazardous substances in the production of such equipment. These measures, adopted in 2003, require manufacturers

to dispose of consumers' used electronic equipment free of charge and prohibit the export of hazardous waste to developing countries outside the EU for disposal.

Unlike American policy, these measures demand significant producer accountability, placing the burden of environmental responsibility entirely on the manufacturer. European producers are now required to finance the recycling, reprocessing, and safe disposal of regulated equipment and its components. Advocates of the policies hope that these requirements will provide substantial incentives for producers to design environmentally friendly electrical and electronic equipment and to consider waste management when designing new products. In the past, public authorities, not private manufacturers, were responsible for both waste management and the risk assessment of chemicals.

The WEEE directive regulates the production of products in ten different categories, including large household appliances, small household appliances, information technology and telecommunications equipment, consumer equipment, lighting equipment, electrical and electronic tools, toys and leisure and sports equipment, medical devices, monitoring and control instruments, and automatic dispensers. The RoHS

---

168. Henrik Selin & Stacy D. VanDeveer, *Raising Global Standards: Hazardous Substances and E-Waste Management in the European Union*, 48 ENV'T 6–17 (Dec. 2006).

169. Council directive 2002/96/EC on waste electrical and electronic equipment (WEEE); Council directive 2003/108/EC amending Council directive 2002/96/EC on waste electrical and electronic equipment (WEEE).

170. Council directive 2002/95/EC on the restriction of the use of certain hazardous substances (RoHS) in electrical and electronic equipment.

directive overlaps and supplements the WEEE directive, limiting the use of six toxic substances in eight of the ten product categories addressed by WEEE. These substances include four heavy metals (lead, mercury, cadmium, and hexavalent chromium) and two chemicals (PBB and PBDE), all of which are common in electrical and electronic goods produced in Europe and around the world. Each EU state is expected to design its own implementation system to enforce these directives.

In 2007, the European Union adopted a third chemical regulation, REACH (registration, evaluation, and authorization of chemicals). Perhaps the world's most stringent and rigorous policy on potentially hazardous chemical substances, this initiative requires registration and evaluation of more than 30,000 existing chemical substances and of any new ones that may be developed. At present, there is little information available on most of the tens of thousands of chemicals used in existing products. REACH is designed to yield data on these chemicals, particularly in the areas of emissions, toxicity, the ecosystem, and effect on human health. For the first time, producers are required to present risk assessment data for every new substance before introducing it to the market. The technical, scientific, and administrative aspects of REACH are managed by the European Chemicals Agency located in Helsinki, Finland.[171]

Extensive negotiations among the European Commission, the European Council, and the European Parliament led to the development of these three policy initiatives. These governmental entities developed these policies with input from concerned lobbyists representing private-sector and civil society groups, and the EU adopted the three initiatives notwithstanding significant resistance from organized industry in Europe and abroad.

Since the adoption of these regulations, the member states of the EU have attempted to translate the broad directives into concrete national legislation. A number of EU countries had adopted domestic electronics waste legislation before 2003 and needed only to make limited additions. Germany, the Netherlands, Denmark, and Sweden pioneered much of the EU's policy on substantial producer responsibility; officials in these countries labored to "trade up" their strict regulations to the EU level. For many other countries, however, the implementation of these directives required a massive overhaul of domestic legislation.

Opponents of the new legislation expressed concerns about the economic costs to individual firms and consumers as well as potentially adverse implications for international trade and jobs. The European Commission estimated that REACH alone would cost the chemical industry between 2.8 and 5.2 billion euros over eleven years.[172]

Major chemical companies, including Bayer and Shell Chemicals, argued that the economic burden of enforcement would threaten their competitiveness. According to the Environmental Data Services (ENDS), REACH "attracted more hostility from industry than any other item of EU environmental legislation in 30 years."[173]

Roughly one in fourteen people in the world lives in the European Union, which has an economy of almost $15 trillion and a population of more than 500 million.[174] Given that almost all multinational companies operate or sell their products in the EU, these regulatory standards will almost certainly have significant implications for international trade. Firms operating in the United States and in Asia must comply with EU product rules and standards in order to sell their products in Europe.

In recent years, Asian countries have responded favorably to the European policies. South Korea and China passed WEEE- and RoHS-inspired legislation in 2007 and 2009, respectively. Although Japan does not have any direct WEEE or RoHS regulations, a 2006 ministerial ordinance directs that some electronic products exceeding a specified amount of the nominated toxic substances must carry a warning label.[175]

Substantial opposition to these regulations continues to come from the United States, however. Many American companies criticized the EU's invocation of the precautionary principle to justify its identification and assessment of risks. The *precautionary principle* provides guidance for protecting public health and the environment in the face of uncertain risks and stipulates that the absence of full scientific certainty shall not be used as a reason to postpone measures where there is a risk of serious or irreversible harm to public health or the environment.[176] Critics argue that the EU has stifled scientific and industrial innovation and ignored the basic reality that a certain amount of risk is unavoidable in industry and in everyday life. Many in the U.S. government and industry have also expressed concern about the potential costs (estimated to be in the billions of dollars) and jobs lost as a result of compliance with these strict regulations.

---

171. European Chemicals Agency, *ECHA Mission*, *available at* http://echa. europa.eu/about/mission_en.asp.

172. *Q&A: Reach Chemicals Legislation*, BBC News, Nov. 28, 2005, *available at* http://news.bbc.co.uk/2/hi/europe/4437304.stm.

173. Environmental Data Services, *REACH Caught Up in EU's Competitiveness Agenda*, ENDS REPORT 346, Nov. 2003, at 51–53.

174. Central Intelligence Agency, *The World Factbook* (2010), *available at* https://www.cia.gov/library/publications/the-world-factbook/geos/ ee.html (last updated Nov. 15, 2011); Matej Hruska, *EU Population Tops 500 Million*, Bus. Wk., July 29, 2010, *available at* http://www. businessweek.com/globalbiz/content/jul2010/gb20100729_623637. htm.

175. Ministry of Economy, Trade and Industry, *Law for the Promotion of Effective Utilization of Resources*, *available at* http://www.meti. go.jp/policy/recycle/main/english/law/promotion.html (last updated Jan. 25, 2007).

176. *See generally* PROTECTING PUBLIC HEALTH AND THE ENVIRONMENT: IMPLEMENTING THE PRECAUTIONARY PRINCIPLE (Carolyn Raffensberger & Joel Tickner eds., 1999).

THE RESPONSIBLE MANAGER

COMPLYING WITH CONSUMER PROTECTION LAWS

Managers have a responsibility to make sure that current and potential customers are treated fairly and in a manner that will not subject them to economic or physical injury. Supervisors must take steps to ensure that employees are aware of, and in compliance with, various federal and state consumer protection regulations. Because both managers and employees can be held legally accountable for their actions (and criminally liable in some cases), companies should educate employees about important consumer law topics.

In a competitive marketplace, managers often feel the need to be aggressive in advertising products or services. Nonetheless, managers must refrain from making claims that may be deceptive or false. The FTC and state attorneys general aggressively pursue companies that make false advertising claims. Remedies can include civil damages and corrective advertising campaigns, which can cost millions of dollars.

Consider Volvo's ill-fated "Bear Foot" advertising campaign in 1990, which almost destroyed thirty years of consistent brand messaging that equated Volvo with safety. The ad showed a Volvo suffering no damage after being driven over by a monster truck. The ad failed to disclose, however, that the internal structure of the Volvo had been reinforced and that the pillars in competing cars had been weakened for the commercial. According to five-time Clio award winner Mike Moser, "When people found out that the demonstration was rigged, the credibility of the brand was suddenly on shaky ground. People had bought into safety's being a core value of Volvo. . . . These same people didn't want to hear that Volvo didn't believe its own demonstration."[177]

The attorney general of Texas called the Volvo ads "a hoax and a sham"[178] and fined Volvo and its ad agency, Scali, McCabe, Sloves, $150,000 each for deceptive advertising. Volvo withdrew the spots and ran corrective ads in nineteen Texas newspapers, *USA Today*, and *The Wall Street Journal*. One month later, Scali, McCabe, Sloves resigned from the Volvo account. The incident cost the agency $40 million in annual revenues and the jobs of thirty-five to fifty staffers.[179]

Business leaders should not be satisfied merely to meet minimum government standards. Mere compliance may not be sufficient to release a manager or his or her company from liability when the manager has superior product information and should have taken additional precautions. Managers whose companies extend credit to customers need to be aware that many discriminatory practices in the extension of credit are illegal under the Equal Credit Opportunity Act. Some states also prohibit discrimination in credit based on sexual orientation.

Legally astute managers embrace the opportunity to self-regulate or, at least, work closely with a regulatory agency to establish industry standards that meet the concerns of both the agency and the company. A good example of a self-regulating industry is the infomercial industry. Faced with possible government regulation, the industry established its own watchdog agency. In doing so, it was able to avert government involvement and the possibility of more restrictive regulation. The Consumer Product Safety Improvement Act of 2008 and the Credit Card Accountability Responsibility and Disclosure Act of 2009 are just two examples of the tougher regulation that results when firms fail to meet society's expectations of appropriate behavior.

---

177. Mike Moser, United We Brand 16 (2001).

178. Bruce Horovitz, *Volvo, Agency Fined $150,000 Each for TV Ad Commercials*, L.A. Times, Aug. 22, 1991.

179. Joshua Levine, *Image Maker, Heal Thyself*, Forbes, May 27, 1991.

A MANAGER'S DILEMMA

Putting It into Practice

Downplaying Hazards and Keeping Product Liability Settlements Confidential

Frequently, companies are reluctant to generate negative publicity about their product, so they try to negotiate with the CPSC to issue a press release that uses language that minimizes the hazards. For example, the company may issue a press release announcing a "recall for repair" rather than a straight recall. Is this ethical? Good business practice?

Suppose that you are the product manager for your company's portable infant playpen. Two infants suffocate after their caregivers fail to properly latch the sides open, permitting the unit to collapse. The CPSC orders a recall of the playpens but requires only minimal publicity about the recall. Should you do more than the CPSC requires to publicize the recall? What would you do if you knew that another three infants would die the same way if you did not publicize the recall? Suppose the parents of the third infant to die sue your company. Is it ethical to settle the case on the condition that the settlement be kept confidential?[180] Is it good business practice?

---

180. Felcher, *supra* note 94.

INSIDE STORY

Toxic Toys

In 2007, tests of a child's backpack made in China revealed lead levels as high as 4,600 parts per million, almost eight times the 600 parts per million standard for lead paint set by the CPSC.[181] Of the 40 million children's toys and accessories recalled for safety reasons in the United States in 2007, 30 million were manufactured in China. They included backpacks, vinyl baby bibs, pencil cases, an infant wrist rattle, and a toy bear.[182]

Mattel alone executed three major recalls in the summer of 2007 for products including the Barbie Living Room Play Set, Fisher-Price Bongo Band Toys, and "Sarge" toy cars from the Walt Disney movie *Cars*, all of which were believed to contain lead-contaminated paint. Items from the Barbie, Batman, Doggie Day Care, and Polly Pocket toy lines were also recalled when it was discovered that they included tiny magnets that could injure children if swallowed. In total, Mattel recalled about 2.8 million toys due to lead paint and 18.2 million toys due to a design flaw. All of the recalled toys were made in China. In light of the summer recalls, Mattel's stock fell more than 27% from its fifty-two-week high in April 2007.[183] These recalls spurred public outrage and weakened consumer confidence in manufacturers and retailers selling products made outside the United States.

Exposure to lead, by children chewing on lead toys or repeatedly playing with toys containing lead, has been proved to cause severe neurological and behavioral problems.[184] Toys and other products made for children containing lead paint were banned in the United States in the 1970s, but items made in China were not subject to the same regulations that applied to toys manufactured in the United States.

Children's products also often contain phthalates, a family of chemicals that make plastics softer. A study conducted by the Center for Reproductive Epidemiology at the University of Rochester Medical School found that infants exposed to phthalate levels were more likely to have liver and kidney cancer later in life.[185]

As the recalls mounted, the CPSC acknowledged that more needed to be done to protect U.S. consumers, but it lacked the resources to act.[186] For example, the CPSC stated in a 2007 budget report that "because of resource limitations," it would be curtailing efforts aimed at preventing children from drowning in swimming pools and bathtubs.[187]

In an attempt to cut the problem off at the source, Nancy A. Nord, the acting head of the CPSC, traveled to China in September 2007 to ask Chinese officials to stop using lead paint on export toys.[188] As a result of these talks, China agreed to stop the use of lead paint on toys exported to the United States, to hold regular product safety talks with American regulators, to help the United States trace products to their source when problems arise, and to cooperate on improving the overall safety of toy exports.

Although Chinese toys accounted for many of the toys recalled, Chinese manufacturing methods were not always at fault. In September 2007, after the largest single recall, involving 18 million toys, Mattel, Inc. issued a public apology to China for causing damage to the country's reputation.[189] According to Mattel, the recall had nothing to do with Chinese manufacturing problems and actually resulted from Mattel's own "design flaw," namely, using tiny magnets that could fall off the toys and become deadly if swallowed.

In July 2008, Congress passed the Consumer Product Safety Improvement Act, which, among other things, banned lead and phthalates in children's products and ordered the creation of a new database of complaints and accident reports for goods. Notwithstanding the enhanced regulation, there is still trouble in Toyland. A 2011 CPSC report indicated that toy-related deaths of kids younger than fifteen had increased from 2010 levels with toy-related injuries remaining "alarmingly high."[190] In one of the largest toy recalls in recent years, Fisher-Price, a unit of Mattel, recalled more than 10 million tricycles, high chairs, and other children's products in 2010, following a variety of injuries, mishaps, and safety concerns.

181. Jad Mouawad, *550,000 More Chinese Toys Recalled for Lead*, N.Y. TIMES, Sept. 27, 2007.

182. Kevin Diaz & H.J. Cummins, *House Bans Lead from Children's Toys; A Local Boy's Death from Lead Poisoning Sparked the Move for Product Safety*, STAR TRIB., July 31, 2008, *available at* http://www.startribune.com/politics/national/congress/26122814.html?page=1&c=y.

183. Casey, *supra* note 85.

184. Mouawad, *supra* note 181.

185. Lyndsey Layton, *Lawmakers Agree to Ban Toxins in Children's Items*, WASH. POST, July 29, 2008, at A1.

186. Eric S. Lipton & David Barboza, *As More Toys Are Recalled, Trail Ends in China*, N.Y. TIMES, June 19, 2007.

187. *Id.*

188. Associated Press, *China Signs Pact to Ban Lead Paint in Export Toys*, N.Y. TIMES, Sept. 12, 2007.

189. Nicholas Casey, *Mattel Seeks to Placate China with Apology*, WALL ST. J., Sept. 22, 2007, at A1.

190. Jayne O'Donnell, *Toys Are Getting Safer, but Injuries Still Alarming*, USA TODAY, Nov. 16, 2011.

KEY WORDS AND PHRASES

additive   553

adulterated   553

bait and switch advertising   574

caveat emptor   551

caveat venditor   551

cease and desist orders   573

closed-end credit   580

consent order   572

deceit   572

dietary supplements   562

drug   553

express warranty   572

extortionate extension of credit   582

finance charge   580

food   553

garnishment   582

implied warranties   576

lemon laws   576

medical devices   562

misbranded   560

net neutrality policy   568

open-end credit   580

precautionary principle   586

predatory lending   581

puffing   574

pyramid selling   577

referral sale   577

Regulation Z   580

right of rescission   581

spam   570

usury statute   580

QUESTIONS AND CASE PROBLEMS

1. Ravlona, a cosmetic company, has developed an innovative makeup that holds fast on the skin for thirty-six hours. The makeup uses a new chemical dye recently developed by the in-house research team at Ravlona. The dye is manufactured from commonly used dyes that are converted to different forms with a platinum catalyst. The catalyst must be present in order to retard the natural fading of the dye, but when the makeup is applied, some of the catalyst leaches into the skin. Preliminary research has shown that this leaching may cause long-term damage, but the effects would not be noticeable for ten to twenty years. Assume that there are no federal rules regulating the presence of platinum in cosmetics. If you were the marketing director at Ravlona, would you feel comfortable introducing this product to the market even though problems may emerge ten or twenty years down the line? Is Ravlona obligated to disclose the findings of its study to the FDA?

2. Virginia passed a statute that made it a crime to falsify the transmission information in any unsolicited e-mail message. The only way to send an anonymous e-mail message is to employ false routing information, such as the sender's domain name or Internet service provider address. Virginia construed the law as a prohibition on lying to commit trespass, that is, the unauthorized use of e-mail servers. Is the Virginia statute a valid exercise of state power? [*Jaynes v. Virginia*, 666 S.E.2d 303 (Va. 2008).]

3. In 1989, John M. Stevenson began receiving phone calls from bill collectors regarding overdue accounts that were not his. After Stevenson obtained a copy of his credit report from TRW, Inc., a credit-reporting agency, he discovered numerous errors in the report. The report included information on accounts that belonged to another John Stevenson; it also included accounts belonging to his estranged son, John Stevenson, Jr., who had fraudulently obtained some of the disputed accounts by using the senior Stevenson's Social Security number. In all, Stevenson disputed sixteen accounts, seven inquiries, and much of the identifying information.

   TRW investigated the complaint. On February 9, 1990, it told Stevenson that all disputed accounts containing negative credit information had been removed. Inaccurate information, however, either continued to appear on Stevenson's reports or was reentered after TRW had deleted it. Stevenson then filed suit, alleging both common law libel and violations of the Fair Credit Reporting Act. Did TRW violate the Fair Credit Reporting Act in its handling of Stevenson's dispute? [*Stevenson v. TRW, Inc.*, 987 F.2d 288 (5th Cir. 1993).]

4. McCoy was the holder of a credit card issued by Chase Bank. The cardholder agreement provided that McCoy was eligible for "preferred rates" as long as he met certain conditions. If any of those conditions were not met, Chase reserved the right to raise the rate, up to a pre-set maximum, and to apply the change to both existing and new balances. Chase increased his interest rate due to his delinquency or default and applied that increase retroactively. McCoy filed suit pursuant to TILA. Does the Federal Reserve Board's Regulation Z require subsequent disclosure because the rate increase constitutes a "change in terms"? [*Chase Bank U.S.A., N.A. v. McCoy*, 131 S. Ct. 871 (2011).]

5. In a 1991 attempt to persuade soft drink bottlers to switch from 7UP to Sprite, Coca-Cola Company, the distributor of Sprite, developed a promotional campaign entitled "The Future Belongs to Sprite." In its presentation, Coca-Cola used charts and graphs to compare the two drinks' relative sales and market share during the previous decade. The campaign was especially targeted at seventy-four "cross-franchise" bottlers, which distribute 7UP along with Coca-Cola products other than Sprite. After Coca-Cola made the presentation to eleven of these cross-franchise bottlers, five decided to switch from 7UP to Sprite. In response,

Seven-Up Company filed suit against Coca-Cola, alleging that the presentation violated the Lanham Act's prohibition on misrepresentations "in commercial advertising or promotion." Coca-Cola argued that its presentation was not sufficiently disseminated to the public to constitute advertising under the statute. Was Coca-Cola's presentation "advertising" and therefore subject to the Lanham Act? [*Seven-Up Co. v. Coca-Cola Co.*, 86 F.3d 1379 (5th Cir. 1996).]

6. Facebook users must register with the website and agree to Facebook's Statement of Rights and Responsibilities (SRR). On registration, users are given unique usernames and passwords to access their own user profiles as well as the profiles of their "friends." Only registered users have the ability to send messages to each other through the Facebook website. The SRR prohibits any activity that would impair the operation of Facebook's website, including the use of data mining "bots" to gain access to users' login information, the posting of unsolicited advertising on the website, or the circulation of such advertising via e-mail, or any commercial use of the Facebook website without Facebook's prior authorization. Facebook alleges that Philip Porembski is a registered Facebook user who is bound by the SRR. Since October 2008, Porembski and others (the defendants) allegedly have obtained login credentials for at least 116,000 Facebook accounts without authorization, and they have sent more than 7.2 million spam messages to Facebook users. According to Facebook, the messages ask recipients to click on a link to a "phishing" site designed to trick users into divulging their Facebook login information. Once users divulge the information, the defendants use it to send spam messages to the users' friends, repeating the cycle. In addition, certain spam messages allegedly redirect users to websites that pay the defendants for each user visit. Facebook filed suit asserting that the defendants' phishing and spamming activities are in violation of the Controlling the Assault of Non-Solicited Pornography and Marketing Act (CAN-SPAM Act). Is there a violation? If so, how will the court calculate damages? [*Facebook, Inc. v. Fisher*, 2011 WL 250395 (N.D. Cal. Jan. 26, 2011).]

7. Debra Dugan was a customer at TGI Friday's Mt. Laurel restaurant. The TGIF menu listed prices for all food items and wine, but it did not list prices for beer, mixed drinks, or soft drinks. Dugan was charged an undisclosed amount for beverages while dining at a TGIF restaurant. On one occasion, Dugan purchased Coors Lite beer at the bar and was charged $2.00 per serving. She then sat at a nearby table, made a second order for the same beer, and was charged $3.59 per serving. Dugan filed suit, alleging that TGIF's activities constitute unconscionable commercial practices—calling them (1) a "bait and switch" and (2) an unlawful practice under New Jersey's Consumer Fraud Act (CFA). TGIF filed a motion to dismiss the complaint for failure to state a claim. What result? [*Dugan v. TGI Friday's, Inc.*, 2011 WL 5041391 (N.J. Super. App. Div. Oct. 25, 2011).]

8. In April 2006, the law firm Carlisle, McNellie, Rini, Kramer & Ulrich filed a complaint in Ohio state court on behalf of its client, Countrywide Home Loans, Inc., seeking foreclosure of a mortgage held by Countrywide on real property owned by Karen L. Jerman. The complaint included a "Notice," later served on Jerman, stating that the mortgage debt would be assumed to be valid unless Jerman disputed it in writing. Jerman's lawyer sent a letter disputing the debt, and Carlisle sought verification from Countrywide. When Countrywide acknowledged that Jerman had, in fact, already paid the debt in full, Carlisle withdrew the foreclosure lawsuit. Jerman then filed a lawsuit seeking class certification and damages under the Fair Debt Collection Practices Act (FDCPA), because Carlisle stated that her debt would be assumed valid unless she disputed it in writing. Is there a violation? If so, is ignorance of the law's requirements an affirmative defense? [*Jerman v. Carlisle, McNellie, Rini, Kramer & Ulrich LPA*, 130 S. Ct. 1605 (2010).]

CHAPTER 18

REAL PROPERTY AND LAND USE

INTRODUCTION

IMPORTANCE

It is difficult to imagine any business enterprise that does not involve real property in some way. From the global company with factories and retail outlets on several continents to a mail-order business operated out of a rented apartment, real estate is important to the successful functioning of most businesses. In the past several decades, there has been an explosion in the real estate field due to the securitization of mortgages and the public marketing of interests in commercial real estate and home mortgages through real estate investment trusts and other vehicles. The subprime mortgage crisis of 2008 (which is the subject of the "Inside Story" in this chapter) underscores the impact a decline in the real estate sector can have on the global economy.

Real estate law has its roots in both English common law and Spanish civil law. Many of the laws are determined by municipalities, others by the state. In recent years, the federal government has played an increasingly active role through tax policy and environmental regulations (discussed in Chapter 15). The federal government is also interested in the safety of real estate (through the Occupational Safety and Health Administration), physical access to commercial facilities (under the Americans with Disabilities Act), foreign investment in U.S. real estate, and the preservation of parklands.

CHAPTER OVERVIEW

This chapter discusses the forms of real estate ownership and the transfer of ownership, including the different types of deeds and the effect of recording statutes. It explains the role of brokers and the effect of express and implied warranties concerning the condition of real property. The chapter outlines the alternatives to acquiring real property for cash, including tax-deferred exchanges, sales and leasebacks, and real estate investment trusts. It then describes certain types of preliminary agreements, including option contracts, rights of first refusal, and letters of intent. Methods of financing are also addressed, as are leasing and lease terms. Finally, the chapter discusses obligations under the Americans with Disabilities Act and governmental regulation of the use of real property by the exercise of police and condemnation powers, including the circumstances in which government restrictions on land use are deemed "takings" requiring compensation of the owner under the U.S. Constitution.

FORMS OF OWNERSHIP

Real property can be held in a variety of ways. A business will normally own real estate in the name of the firm. Whether the firm is organized as a partnership (general or limited), a corporation, or a limited liability company will depend on tax, financial, securities, and liability factors. The choice of the proper entity for owning real estate is particularly important at the beginning of an investment or development. It may be difficult to make a change at a later date without adverse tax consequences. The issue of choice of entity is discussed further in Chapter 19.

Individual

In the simplest type of ownership, property is owned by a single individual. From a business perspective, individual ownership is often undesirable because the individual owner may be liable in tort for any accidents occurring on the property. The risk of unlimited personal liability can, however, be reduced by obtaining liability insurance.

Ownership rights can also be shared by two or more individuals. Forms of co-ownership include tenancy in common, joint tenancy, tenancy by the entirety, and community property. Though not a form of co-ownership, a trust also involves more than one person.

Tenancy in Common

Tenants in common each own an undivided fractional interest in a parcel of real property. Two or more persons can hold property as tenants in common. For example, one tenant in common may have a two-thirds interest and another a one-third interest. Regardless of the percentage ownership interest, each tenant in common has an equal right to possession of the property, and no co-tenant has the right of exclusive possession of the property against any other co-tenant. Each co-tenant does, however, have the right to exclude any third party. Co-tenants share the income and burdens of ownership. The interest of a tenant in common is assignable and inheritable without the consent of any other co-tenant.

Joint Tenancy

In a *joint tenancy*, property is owned in equal shares by two or more individuals. The key characteristic of a joint tenancy is the right of survivorship. If a joint tenant dies, his or her interest passes automatically to the remaining joint tenant or tenants. If a single joint tenant attempts to convey his or her interest in the property separately, however, the joint tenancy is destroyed and converted into a tenancy in common. Use of joint tenancy property in a business may also terminate the joint tenancy.[1]

Tenancy by the Entirety

Historically, English common law recognized a special type of co-ownership of real property between husband and wife called *tenancy by the entirety.* Like joint tenancy, tenancy by the entirety includes a right of survivorship. Unlike a joint tenancy, however, neither spouse can convey an individual interest to a third party and thereby terminate the right of survivorship. Additionally, unlike joint tenancy, where joint tenants have equal rights to possession of the property, tenancy by the entirety entitled only the husband to the possession, use, and enjoyment of the property. In effect, he acted as a guardian over the wife's interest.

About one-half of the states recognize tenancy by the entirety. Most states have retained the indestructible right of survivorship, but they give the husband and wife equal rights to the possession, use, and revenues of the property. Additionally, the modern view is that divorce converts a tenancy by the entirety to a tenancy in common.[2]

Community Property

In Arizona, California, Idaho, Louisiana, Nevada, New Mexico, Texas, Washington, and Wisconsin, property acquired by either spouse during marriage (other than separate property, as defined below) is considered to be *community property*; that is, each spouse owns an undivided one-half interest in the property. Property acquired prior to the marriage or by gift or inheritance or with separate property during the marriage is *separate property*, belonging solely to the spouse who acquired it before marriage or used separate property to buy it or received it by gift or inheritance, unless the spouse owning the property has converted it to community property. Separate property is converted into community property when (1) one spouse gifts the separate property to the other spouse, (2) the parties treat the separate property in such a manner that a presumption of a gift arises, or (3) the separate and common property have been commingled, or mixed together.

Conveyance   Community property cannot be conveyed unless both spouses execute the instrument by which the conveyance is effected. However, even if one spouse does not sign the instrument, if both spouses were present during negotiations and were fully aware of the terms and conditions, then the nonsigning spouse may not claim that the transaction is void due to the absence of his or her signature.[3]

The community-property interest of a spouse may be separately willed upon death. In the absence of a will, community property passes to the other spouse.

Effect of Divorce   Most of the cases interpreting what is or is not community property arise in the divorce context. Community-property laws vary from state to state. Complicated issues can arise, for example, when one spouse inherits land from his or her family (which is separate property at the date of inheritance), but subsequently one or both spouses improve or develop the property. In this case, some or all of the inherited property may turn into community property. Similarly, if one spouse uses separate property as seed capital for a business that he or she operates during the marriage, then part of the value of the business will be separate property and part will be community property.

Trust

Property may be held in a *trust*, whereby the property is owned and controlled by one person, the *trustee*, for the benefit of another, the *beneficiary*. The duration of the trust, the powers of the trustee and the trustor (the person creating the trust), and the express rights of the beneficiary are set forth in a trust agreement.

Real Estate Investment Trusts (REITs)

Real estate investment trusts, commonly referred to as *REITs*, can provide a good tax vehicle for investors seeking to invest in a portfolio of real property. REITs sell beneficial shares that are traded in the stock markets, and they

---

1. Williams v. Dovell, 96 A.2d 484 (Md. 1953).
2. *See, e.g.,* Markland v. Markland, 21 So. 2d 145 (Fla. 1945).
3. Calvin v. Salmon River Sheep Ranch, 658 P.2d 972 (Idaho 1983).

permit small investors to invest in a diversified portfolio of real estate, similar to an investment in common stocks through a mutual fund.

As long as at least 90% of a REIT's net income is distributed to shareholder–beneficiaries, the REIT itself pays no income tax; taxes are paid at the shareholder–beneficiary level only.[4] REITs are limited in the types of operations they may conduct. For instance, 95% of the income derived from the REIT must meet certain income source tests.[5] These tests ensure that REITs are used principally for passive investment and for investments in real estate or real estate–related assets. Ownership concentration is also limited: no five persons may own more than 50% of the REIT's beneficial interests; often the percentage of shares a shareholder may own is limited to 9.9% or less.[6]

General Partnership

When property is held in a general partnership, the partners have rights similar to those of co-tenants, and each partner is liable for any debts of the partnership remaining after the partnership assets are exhausted. A general partner has no right to possess partnership property for other than partnership purposes. In addition, a general partner may not assign his or her individual interest in specific partnership property. On the other hand, a general partner can effectively convey the entire partnership property to a bona fide purchaser who has no knowledge of any restriction that might exist on the general partner's authority to convey partnership property.

Limited Partnership

Real property may be held in a limited partnership, consisting of one or more general partners, who manage the property, and one or more limited partners. The liability of a limited partner is usually restricted to the amount of capital the limited partner has contributed or agreed to contribute to the partnership. Typically, limited partners will indemnify the general partners with the indemnity secured by the value of the real estate assets. The authority of the general partner to convey the property is determined by the limited partnership agreement and the jurisdiction's limited partnership law.

Corporation

A corporation may own real property. Corporate authority to convey the property is governed by the corporation's certificate of incorporation and bylaws, as well as the jurisdiction's corporate law. The board of directors must authorize most transfers of real property.

---

4. RALPH L. BLOCK, INVESTING IN REITS: REAL ESTATE INVESTMENT TRUSTS 11 (4th ed. 2012).

5. *See* 26 U.S.C.A. § 856(c)(2).

6. THEODORE S. LYNN ET AL., REAL ESTATE INVESTMENT TRUSTS § 11:50 (2011).

Limited Liability Company

Generally, the preferred form of ownership for real property is now the limited liability company or LLC. Authority to convey property is governed by the operating agreement as well as the jurisdiction's LLC law. The board of managers must authorize most transfers of real property.

TRANSFER OF OWNERSHIP

Ownership of land is normally transferred by a document known as a *deed*, which is recorded at a public office, typically the office of the county recorder in the county where the real property is located. (As discussed later in the chapter, a group of companies sought to supplant this system with a private system for recording deeds of trust and mortgages, called the Mortgage Electronic Registration System, often with disastrous consequences for both borrowers and lenders.) Any document transferring an interest in real estate, such as a deed or a lease, is called a *conveyance*. The person conveying the property is the *grantor*, and the person to whom the property is conveyed is the *grantee*. Occasionally, though seldom in business, ownership is obtained through an installment sales contract, with the deed to follow when payment for the real estate has been completed. Ownership of property subject to probate is transferred by a court order from the probate court.

In most purchases of real estate, the interest conveyed is a *fee simple* interest, that is, absolute ownership of the property. However, many other transactions, such as a lease, convey less than an absolute ownership interest in the property.

Title

A seller of real estate is generally required to convey *marketable title*, that is, an interest in the property free from defects. Defects that make a title unmarketable include any cloud on the title that would cause the buyer to receive less than a fee simple interest. For example, the existence of a lien on the property would constitute a defect of title sufficient to make the title unmarketable. In contrast, a fifty-year-old easement allowing neighbors to use a five-inch strip of the property for a fence probably is not sufficiently burdensome to render a title defective. If the title is found to be unmarketable prior to closing, the buyer may agree to purchase the property anyway or can elect to cancel the deal entirely.

The type of interest (usually fee simple) and the quality of title (that is, whether it is marketable) are set forth in a deed executed by the party conveying the property. The type of deed determines the scope of the warranties granted.

Types of Deeds

An interest in real property can be conveyed only by a signed deed that specifically describes that interest and is delivered to and accepted by a named grantee. There are three basic types of deeds: quitclaim deeds, grant deeds, and warranty deeds. These differ in the specific express warranties they contain.

Quitclaim Deed

A *quitclaim deed* contains no warranties, and the grantor conveys only whatever right, title, and interest, if any, the grantor holds at the time of execution. A quitclaim deed does not convey *after-acquired title*, that is, title acquired by the grantor after the deed is executed.

Grant Deed

A *grant deed* contains implied warranties that (1) the grantor has not previously conveyed the same property or any interest in it to another person, and (2) the title is marketable. A grant deed also conveys after-acquired title. This means that if at the date the deed is executed the grantor does not have title to the real property referred to in the grant deed, but subsequently acquires it, the title will be automatically transferred to the grantee.

Warranty Deed

A *warranty deed* contains the implied warranties of a grant deed; in addition, the grantor expressly warrants the title to and the quiet possession of the property. Warranty deeds may also contain other express warranties as well.

Adverse Possession

In unusual circumstances, a person can acquire legal ownership of a piece of property by adverse possession (also known as *squatter's rights*). To acquire a parcel of land by *adverse possession*, (1) a person must possess the land for the period of time specified by the state statute (usually between fifteen and twenty-two years); (2) the current owner of the land must have actual constructive notice of the adverse possession; (3) the possession must continue uninterrupted for the specified period; (4) the person possessing the property must not have a legal right to be there (thus, the possession must be "adverse" to the current owner's rights); and (5) the possession must not be shared with another, such as the current owner or the general public. At first blush, adverse possession appears to reward illegal possession, but the doctrine is designed to ensure that land is used in the most efficient, publicly beneficial manner. Landowners who have no use for their land are forced to give it to those who will put it to a more economic use. The grace period of fifteen-plus years offers ample time for a conscientious landowner to commence eviction proceedings, which would destroy the adverse possession.

Representations, Warranties, and the Duty to Disclose

In the past, real estate transactions were governed by the traditional rule of *caveat emptor* ("let the buyer beware"). Under this rule, the seller of a house or other property made no warranties to the buyer other than those expressly included in the deed or written contract of sale. Current law is more protective of the buyer, especially when a person is buying a house.

Implied Warranty of Habitability

A majority of the states impose an implied warranty of habitability on commercial builders of houses. As with the Uniform Commercial Code's implied warranty of merchantability for sales of goods (discussed in Chapter 8), under the *implied warranty of habitability* builders warrant that the house is in reasonable working order and is of reasonably sound construction. Because builders have a major hand in determining the overall fitness of a building, courts have deemed it appropriate to hold them responsible for its initial condition. This warranty applies only to the original builders, *not* to subsequent sellers. Thus, secondary sellers are not burdened by an implied warranty of habitability. A number of courts have extended the warranty of habitability to protect individual lessees of residential property.

Implied Warranty of Suitability

A small minority of jurisdictions recognize an implied warranty of suitability for purpose in leases of real property for commercial use, such as office space.[7] A warranty of suitability means that at the inception of the lease there are no latent defects in the premises that will prevent them from being used for their intended purpose and that the premises will remain in a suitable condition.

Seller's Duty to Disclose

The traditional rule of *caveat emptor* is also giving way to a duty on sellers to disclose defects in real property. In most states, sellers have an obligation to disclose any known defect that (1) materially affects the value of the property and (2) could not reasonably be discovered by the buyer. As the following case illustrates, sellers—and their brokers[8]—can be held liable for the nondisclosure of certain off-site conditions that materially affect the value of the property.

---

7. *See, e.g.*, Reste Realty Corp. v. Cooper, 53 N.J. 444 (1969) (recognizing an implied warranty of suitability in commercial leases); Gym-N-I Playgrounds, Inc. v. Snider, 220 S.W.3d 905 (Tex. 2007). *Contra* Serv. Oil Co. v. White, 218 Kan. 87 (1975) (refusing to recognize implied warranty of suitability); Golub v. Colby, 120 N.H. 535 (1980) ("[W]e decline to extend, to commercial leases, the implied warranty of habitability found to exist in residential leases.").

8. Real estate brokers must fully disclose all material facts within their knowledge concerning the property being sold. RULES OF THE VERMONT REAL ESTATE COMMISSION r. 31(b) (1987). The Vermont Supreme Court extended this to off-site conditions in *Carter v. Gugliuzzi*, 168 Vt. 48 (1998).

Strawn v. Canuso

Supreme Court of New Jersey
657 A.2d 420 (N.J. 1995).

FACTS The plaintiffs comprised more than 150 families who purchased new homes in Voorhees Township. The homes were developed and marketed by companies controlled by the Canuso family. The home buyers sought damages against the Canusos and their companies because—unbeknownst to the buyers—the new homes they purchased had been constructed near the Buzby Landfill. Between 1966 and 1978, large amounts of hazardous materials and chemicals were dumped at the Buzby Landfill. Toxic materials escaped, contaminating the groundwater and air. The federal Environmental Protection Agency recommended that the site be considered for a Superfund cleanup.

The home buyers alleged that the developers and brokers knew of the Buzby Landfill and its environmental hazards before they considered the site for residential development but failed to disclose those facts to the families when they purchased their homes. The representatives of the Canuso brokerage and development companies were instructed never to disclose the existence of the Buzby Landfill, even when asked about such conditions. The lower court found in favor of the home buyers.

ISSUE PRESENTED Do the developers of new homes and the real estate brokers marketing those homes have a duty to disclose to prospective buyers that the homes were constructed near an abandoned hazardous waste dump?

OPINION O'HERN, J., writing for the New Jersey Supreme Court:

[A] seller of real estate or a broker representing the seller would be liable for nondisclosure of on-site defective conditions if those conditions were known to them and unknown and not readily observable by the buyer. Such conditions, for example, would include radon contamination and a polluted water supply. . . .

. . . [T]he principal factors shaping the duty to disclose have been the difference in bargaining power between the professional seller of residential real estate and the purchaser of such housing, and the difference in access to information between the seller and the buyer. Those principles guide our decision in this case.

The first factor causes us to limit our holding to professional sellers of residential housing (persons engaged in the business of building or developing residential housing) and the brokers representing them. . . . Hence, we believe that it is reasonable to extend to such professionals a similar duty to disclose off-site conditions that materially affect the value or desirability of the property.

. . . Defendants used sales-promotion brochures, newspaper advertisements, and a fact sheet to sell the homes in the development. That material portrayed the development as located in a peaceful, bucolic setting with an abundance of fresh air and clean lake waters. Although the literature mentioned how far the property was from malls, country clubs, and train stations, "neither the brochures, the newspaper advertisements nor any sales personnel mentioned that a landfill [was] located within half a mile of some of the homes."

. . . .

We hold that a builder-developer of residential real estate or a broker representing it is not only liable to a purchaser for affirmative and intentional misrepresentation, but is also liable for nondisclosure of off-site physical conditions known to it and unknown and not readily observable by the buyer if the existence of those conditions is of sufficient materiality to affect the habitability, use, or enjoyment of the property and, therefore, render the property substantially less desirable or valuable to the objectively reasonable buyer.

RESULT The verdict in favor of the home buyers was affirmed. The defendants had violated their duty to disclose the existence of the landfill.

CONTINUED

COMMENTS   The New Jersey legislature subsequently limited sellers' obligations in the New Residential Construction Off-Site Conditions Disclosure Act.[9]

In *Urman v. South Boston Savings Bank*,[10] the Massachusetts Supreme Judicial Court followed *Strawn* and held that a seller is required to disclose known off-site physical conditions in appropriate circumstances but concluded that a lender with limited knowledge of an off-site toxic contamination that had previously been cleaned up and that posed no demonstrable future danger to the condominium in question had no duty to disclose it to the buyer. In contrast, the District Court of Appeal in Florida ruled that *Strawn* is "not consistent with the law of this State."[11]

CRITICAL THINKING QUESTIONS

1. Would the court have reached a different result if the sellers had not touted the development's bucolic setting, fresh air, and clean lake waters?

2. Why should a seller of commercial property have less obligation to disclose adverse off-site conditions than a seller of houses?

---

9. N.J. STAT. ANN. § 43: 3C-1 *et seq.*
10. 424 Mass. 165 (1997).
11. Ribak v. Centex Real Estate Corp., 702 So. 2d 1316 (Fla. Dist. Ct. App. 1997).

Contractual Protections and Due Diligence

A skillful buyer will request express contractual representations and warranties from the seller as to the condition of the property. This is particularly important in commercial transactions, because courts are less willing to impose implied warranties and a duty to disclose when the buyer is a commercial entity, rather than an individual. From the seller's perspective, the representations and warranties are a potential source of liability. From the buyer's perspective, the representations and warranties provide some assurance that the buyer is getting what it expected. If nothing else, the negotiation of representations and warranties frequently leads to additional disclosures regarding the physical condition of the property.

The buyer should not rely on representations and warranties as an alternative to its own careful investigation of the condition of the property, however. Although the seller is generally required to indemnify the buyer against liability arising from the inaccuracy of any of its representations and warranties, the right to indemnification is not worth much if the seller does not have the resources to back it up. Perhaps more important, defects in the property can seriously disrupt the buyer's operations and business.

RECORDING STATUTES AND TITLE INSURANCE

Deeds and other instruments of conveyance, including mortgages, must be recorded with a government official in a public office, where copies will be available to anyone.

The documents must be in *recordable form*. The requirements vary from state to state, but they typically include legibility and some type of notarization by a notary public. The record in the public office is the principal basis for determining the state of title of real estate.

The Uniform Real Property Electronic Recording Act, enacted by twenty-five states as of 2011, standardizes the execution and recording of electronic real estate documents.[12] The Act makes it possible to "sign," deliver, and record documents electronically over the Internet, making the expensive, time-consuming "sit-down" closing and trip to the recording office a thing of the past. There are still some practical barriers to overcome, however, including the inability of many town recording offices to accept electronically signed documents and the lack of standardized regulations and procedures.[13]

Recording statutes establish an orderly process by which claims to interests in real property can be resolved. There are three types of recording statutes: (1) race statutes, (2) pure notice statutes, and (3) race–notice statutes. The law of the state where the real property is located should always be checked before closing a transaction.

Under *race statutes*, recording is a race—the rule is "first in time is first in right." The first to record a deed

---

12. The final version of the Act is available at http://www.law.upenn.edu/bll/archives/ulc/urpera/URPERA_Final_apr05-1.pdf.
13. Scott Brede, *An Idea Before Its Time*, CONN. L. TRIB., Feb. 26, 2002. *See also* NORTH CAROLINA: UNIFORM REAL PROPERTY ELECTRONIC RECORDING ACT: REPORT FROM THE NORTH CAROLINA RECORDING COUNCIL (2011), *available at* http://www.secretary.state.nc.us/ecomm/pdf/ERC%20Standards%20Final%203-7-2011.pdf.

has superior rights, even if he or she knew that someone else had already bought the property but had failed to record the deed.

Under *pure notice statutes*, a person who has notice that someone else has already bought the property cannot validate his or her deed by recording it first. Notice may be actual or constructive. Courts may find *constructive notice* if a reasonable inquiry (for instance, inspection of the property) would have disclosed the prior interest. A pure notice statute protects good faith subsequent purchasers. A *good faith subsequent purchaser* is one who purchases for value, in good faith, without knowledge of a prior outstanding interest. Thus, if a subsequent purchaser acquires a deed and has no notice (actual or constructive) of a prior deed at that time, then he or she will have superior rights. *Race–notice statutes* protect only those good faith subsequent purchasers who record their deed before the prior purchaser records its deed.

As of 2011, only Louisiana and North Carolina have race statutes that apply to all conveyances, including deeds. Other states, including Delaware and Maryland, have race statutes applicable to mortgages but notice or race–notice statutes for deeds. The other states are split about evenly between pure notice statutes and race–notice statutes.[14]

Title Searches, Insurance, and Escrows

Despite the existence of recording statutes, the condition of the title to a specific property and the priority of any claims against the property are often difficult to ascertain. In some states, title is searched by attorneys, in others by title abstract companies on which attorneys rely, and in still others by title insurance companies. Title insurance companies may also insure the condition of title or the priority of one's interest. In some states, lawyers' opinions are still used rather than title insurance. It is important to review a title report or insurance policy carefully before acquiring title to property. The exceptions listed in the report or policy may be defects in title.

Blindly relying on any attorney's or title company's title abstract can be dangerous. The New Hampshire Supreme Court ruled that attorneys are not vicariously liable for relying on a faulty title report, unless they were negligent in choosing or supervising the title abstractor.[15] Thus, the buyer should make sure that the title company or the attorney issuing a title report is reputable and competent.

Extent of Coverage

A title insurance policy insures against loss as a result of (1) undisclosed liens or defects in the title to the property or (2) errors in the title abstract, that is, the summary of the relevant recorded deeds and liens. Generally, the policy limit is the purchase price of the property or the amount of the *encumbrance*, that is, the claim against the property.

Escrow

In addition to issuing title insurance policies, title companies often hold the purchase money in *escrow*, that is, in a special account, until the conditions for the sale have all been met. The money is then paid to the seller. If the sale does not go through, the money is returned to the would-be purchaser. Banks also perform this service, and in some jurisdictions there are separate escrow companies.

The *escrow agent* acts as a neutral stakeholder, allowing the parties to close the transaction without the physical difficulties of passing instruments and funds between the parties. Additionally, it is the duty of the escrow agent to coordinate the closing with the recording of documents, the issuance of title insurance, and other activities that take place concurrently with the closing.

Neutral Party   As a neutral party, the escrow agent is an agent of all parties to the transaction and must follow their specific instructions. Because an escrow agent has a fiduciary duty to all of the parties, it cannot act when the parties have submitted conflicting instructions. Generally, if the parties fail to resolve conflicts between instructions, the escrow agent will go to court for a resolution of the conflict.

BROKERS

The market for real estate is imperfect, and brokers facilitate its operation by bringing buyers and sellers together.

Compensation

A broker is customarily retained by the seller through a listing agreement, which must be in writing to be enforceable. Generally, the broker receives a percentage of the gross selling price (or aggregate rental income) as compensation. To the extent that the buyer's or lessee's broker is compensated, it is usually by sharing the commission paid by the seller.

Listing Agreements

There are several types of listing agreements: open, exclusive, and net.

Open Listing

In an *open listing*, the listing broker will receive a commission only if he or she procures a ready, willing, and able buyer. It is understood that the seller will be contracting with more than one broker, so the first broker to procure a buyer will receive the commission. Because of

---

14. *See* Jesse Dukeminier et al., Property 667–69 (7th ed. 2010).
15. Lawyers Title Ins. Corp. v. Groff, 808 A.2d 44 (N.H. 2002).

the uncertainty of earning a commission even if a buyer is found, it is hard to get a broker to work diligently to sell a commercial property with an open listing.

Exclusive Listing

An *exclusive listing* grants the broker the right to sell the property for a specified period of time; any sale of the property during the term of the listing will entitle the broker to a commission. If a seller has dealt with particular potential buyers before signing an exclusive listing agreement, the seller may wish to exclude them from the agreement.

Net Listing

A *net listing* involves a completely different compensation scheme: the broker will receive any sales proceeds in excess of the net listing amount specified by the seller. Net listings are uncommon.

Regulation of Brokers

In most states, real estate brokers are heavily regulated. As noted earlier, they have broad duties to disclose information about the property being sold or leased and, under certain circumstances, about off-site conditions.

Licensing

Real estate brokers are generally required to have a license to perform brokerage activities. Anyone who engages in brokerage activities without a license will not be able to sue successfully to recover his or her fee. Brokerage activities are broadly defined to include effecting or negotiating (1) any sale or offer to sell, or purchase or offer to purchase, real property or a business opportunity and (2) any leases, loans secured by real property, or real property sales contracts. A mere finder, who does nothing more than introduce two parties for a fee, does not need a broker's license.

In many states, real estate brokers must report and keep records of their transactions. Brokers may also be required to meet continuing education requirements and maintain up-to-date knowledge regarding the particulars of real estate loans.

Agency Relationship

Brokers are fiduciaries. Brokers may also be subject to regulations concerning the disclosure of the agency relationship between the broker and the parties to the transaction. As a general rule, a broker may not act for more than one person in a transaction without the knowledge and consent of all parties to the transaction. When a broker acts for both the buyer and the seller, the relationship is characterized as a *dual agency*. In most instances, a dual agent is prohibited from disclosing to the buyer, without the consent of the seller, that the seller is willing to sell the property for less than the listing price. Similarly, a dual agent may not disclose to the seller that the buyer is willing to pay a price higher than the listing price. Agency issues are discussed further in Chapter 5.

ACQUISITIONS AND DISPOSITIONS

Acquisitions and dispositions of real estate interests are contracted for in the same manner as most commercial transactions. Although standardized contracts are often used in relatively simple transactions (such as the conveyance of a single-family residence or a small commercial property), most large transactions require custom-drafted contracts.

Sales

Generally, contracts for the sale of an interest in real property are the result of protracted negotiations between the parties. In addition to essential terms such as price, time of closing, and method of payment, common areas of negotiation include types of acceptable financing, the condition of title, the allocation of closing costs and taxes, and compliance with zoning laws, building codes, and environmental regulations. In many purchase and sale agreements, the most heavily negotiated provisions are the seller's representations and warranties concerning the condition of the property.

Tax-Deferred Exchanges

An alternative to acquiring real property for cash is a *tax-deferred exchange*, whereby the seller exchanges its property for another piece of property. Such transactions can have favorable tax consequences. In particular, the capital gains tax owed by the seller may be deferred if the seller (1) is disposing of a property held for investment or for productive use in a trade or business and (2) is acquiring a property that qualifies under the Internal Revenue Code. Tax-deferred exchanges take many forms. The most common is the three-party exchange, in which the buyer purchases a piece of property designated by the seller and exchanges it for the seller's property. Because these exchanges can be complex, it is prudent to consult an attorney specializing in tax and real estate issues when acquiring real property through a tax-deferred exchange.

Sales and Leasebacks

A *sale and leaseback* arrangement involves a simultaneous two-step transaction. In the first step, an institutional lender with funds to invest, such as a life insurance company or a pension fund, purchases real property from a company. In the second step, or often simultaneously, the property is leased back to the company for its use. The term of the lease is long, often ranging from twenty to forty years. The length of the term influences how the lease will be accounted for on the balance sheet. A longer-term lease may be capitalized as an asset on the balance sheet, whereas an *operating lease* (typically with a shorter term) will not appear on the balance sheet at all. The tenant may have the option of repurchasing the property on or before the termination date of the lease.

The amount of rent payable is structured so that during the term of the lease, the lessor will recoup the purchase price of the property and realize an acceptable return on its investment. The lessee pays all taxes and maintenance and operating costs.

Synthetic Leases

Synthetic leases were commonly used in the 1990s to take advantage of the differences between the tax and accounting rules governing leases. In a *synthetic lease*, the transaction is treated as a conventional operating lease for accounting purposes, so it does not appear on the balance sheet. Payments under the lease are treated merely as rent. At the same time, for tax purposes, the lessee of the property treats the transaction as though it had purchased the property and obtained a loan from the seller. Thus, payments under the lease are treated as debt service on the loan, and the lessee may take favorable interest payment deductions as well as depreciation write-offs.[16]

Following the collapse of Enron in the early 2000s, various off-balance sheet financing transactions, such as synthetic leases, were heavily scrutinized. The Financial Accounting Standards Board (FASB) subsequently issued statements restricting the risk that a lessee could assume under a synthetic lease. Stricter regulations and a tarnished public image of synthetic lease financing contributed to the decline in their popularity. As a result, many companies reverted to "sales and leasebacks" as an alternative financing mechanism. Given the current market conditions and the difficulty in financing real estate transactions, however, companies with good credit capable of supporting a secured financing have begun to revisit synthetic leases.[17]

Transactions with Foreigners

Sales of real property interests in the United States to non-resident aliens are regulated by the federal government. Under the Foreign Investment in Real Property Tax Act (FIRPTA), the purchaser of a U.S. real property interest from a foreign person is required to withhold 10% of the purchase price to ensure that U.S. capital gains tax is paid on the sale. Additionally, the Agricultural Foreign Investment Disclosure Act requires foreign acquirers of U.S. agricultural land to file an informational report with the U.S. Secretary of Agriculture.

ENVIRONMENTAL DUE DILIGENCE

Because liability under federal and state environmental laws and regulations can be so large as to overshadow any other economic aspect of the property, the buyer or lessee should diligently investigate whether there are toxic or hazardous substances on or under the property. As explained in Chapter 15, under the Comprehensive Environmental Response, Compensation, and Liability Act (CERCLA), the current owner or operator of a contaminated facility is potentially jointly and severally liable with the prior owner or the operator of the facility at the time of waste disposal for the costs associated with cleaning up the facility. If the prior owner is insolvent or nonexistent, the current owner may be responsible for the entire cleanup. This liability attaches even if the current owner purchased the property with no knowledge of the prior contamination, unless it can show that it made all due inquiry and still had no reason to know about the contamination.

In addition, office workers and other tenants have successfully sued building owners and construction contractors for injury or fear of future injury due to asbestos on the premises.[18] Litigation related to potentially toxic mold is also increasing, causing some to call toxic mold "the new asbestos."[19]

PRELIMINARY AGREEMENTS

Often the parties to a real estate transaction are able to reach a general agreement on terms and conditions but need more time to negotiate specific representations and warranties or to investigate the property further. A number of alternatives to the traditional contract for the sale of real property have been developed. These include option contracts, rights of first refusal, and letters of intent.

Option Contract

In an *option contract*, the potential buyer pays the seller for the right, but not the obligation, to purchase the property during a given time period. The option gives the buyer time to conduct investigations, determine whether the purchase of the property is economically feasible, and obtain financing. The seller receives payment for taking the property off the market for a specified period of time.

16. Gerard R. Boyce, *Synthetic Leases: The Hard Facts*, N.Y. L.J., Jan. 13, 2000.

17. Timothy J. Oxley, *Synthetic Lease Financing Revisited*, 26(1) REAL EST. FIN. 31–33 (June 2009).

18. Susan Warren, *Asbestos Quagmire*, WALL ST. J., Jan. 27, 2003, at B1.

19. John M. Simon & Thomas J. Trautner Jr., *Mold: Should Your Client Be Worried?*, 13 BUS. L. TODAY 36–39 (2004).

To be enforceable, an option contract must be in writing, and consideration must be paid to the seller. Additionally, the option contract must state the major terms of the proposed purchase agreement and must specify the manner in which the option may be exercised. It is also advisable to record the option to provide constructive notice to third parties and thereby prevent the sale of the property to a third party before the option has expired.

Right of First Refusal

A *right of first refusal* is the right, conferred by a written contract, to purchase the property on the same terms offered by or to a third party. Perhaps its most frequent use is with a tenant of a leasehold interest. The holder of the right of first refusal should require that it be recorded.

A right of first refusal can chill the owner's ability to sell the property. Few buyers will want to start investigations and negotiations knowing that they could lose the deal if the party with the right of first refusal exercises its right. Consequently, the owner will often want to modify the right of first refusal to give the holder only the right to negotiate the purchase of the property before the seller enters negotiations with another party. This is sometimes called a *right of first negotiation*. Another method of accommodating the needs of the seller is to provide for a very short time, such as seventy-two hours, for the holder to exercise its right of first refusal.

Letter of Intent

A letter of intent may create the right to acquire an interest in a specific property. A *letter of intent* sets forth the general terms and conditions of a proposed purchase until a formal acquisition agreement can be signed. Although the parties often view letters of intent as unenforceable, courts have increasingly treated them as enforceable contracts. In one case, the court focused on the conduct of the parties to determine whether an enforceable agreement was intended despite express written statements to the contrary in the letter of intent.[20] Consequently, if the parties do not wish to be bound by their letters of intent, they must ensure that the terms and conditions are not set forth so specifically that a binding legal obligation is created; they must also conduct themselves consistently with the absence of a binding contract.

When properly utilized, letters of intent allow the parties to investigate the proposed transaction to determine whether it is worth pursuing. Although letters of intent are generally not as effective as options or rights of first refusal in removing property from the market, they can create an ethical commitment to consummate the transaction. In some states, the execution of a letter of intent creates an implied covenant of good faith and fair dealing between the parties, requiring good faith negotiation of a formal acquisition agreement.

FINANCING

Financing the purchase of real estate may involve borrowing funds for a long or short term. The loan is usually secured by a lien on the property, known as a *mortgage* or a *deed of trust*. Although these two documents are virtually the same, the name varies from state to state. Generally, in the northeastern and southern states, the document conferring a security interest in real property is called a mortgage, whereas in the Midwest and on the West Coast, it is known as a deed of trust. Conceptually, a mortgage and a deed of trust secure a lien in different ways, but they operate to create the same end result. The party granting the mortgage is the *mortgagor*; the recipient of the mortgage, usually the lender, is called the *mortgagee*.

Most large lenders use standard documents for loan agreements, although changes are sometimes made. In substantial transactions, it is essential that all documents be reviewed and negotiated by all parties to the transaction and their counsel.

The availability of financing depends on the intrinsic value of the property or on both its value and its potential for the production of income. The types of financing available are almost unlimited. Some of the more common forms are discussed in this section.

Permanent Loans

The most common type of real estate loan is the *permanent loan*. This is usually a long-term loan, repaid over five, ten, or sometimes up to twenty years.

Fixed-Rate Loans

Traditionally, permanent loans have had a fixed interest rate, that is, the rate of interest does not change over the term of the loan. The lender assumes the risk of losing the benefit of any increase in interest rates, and the borrower assumes the risk of losing the benefit of any decrease.

In order to benefit from any increases in market interest rates, many lenders reserve the right to *call* (that is, demand repayment of) fixed-rate loans after a specified period, often after five, ten, or fifteen years. Conversely, to prevent borrowers from refinancing their obligation when market interest rates fall below the fixed interest rate of the loan, some lenders insert a lock-in clause to prohibit prepayments of principal or impose a penalty, called a *prepayment penalty*, if the loan is paid off early. Usually, the penalty declines with time.

The Dodd–Frank Wall Street Reform and Consumer Protection Act prohibits a lender from imposing prepayment penalties for adjustable-rate residential mortgages

---

20. Computer Sys. of Am. v. Int'l Bus. Machs. Corp., 795 F.2d 1086 (1st Cir. 1986).

and nonqualified mortgages, such as subprime mortgages (discussed below). For qualified home mortgages, prepayment penalties are capped at 3% for the first year, 2% for the second year, and 1% for the third year, with no penalty permissible after year three. Dodd–Frank also prohibits lenders from offering a loan with a prepayment penalty without also offering a loan that does not have a prepayment penalty.

Adjustable-Rate Loans

Adjustable-rate loans allow lenders to avoid the risk of fluctuating interest rates. In an *adjustable-rate loan*, the rate of interest is often set at a fixed number of percentage points over a specified standard or benchmark rate (often the six-month London Interbank Offered Rate, known as LIBOR, or the *prime rate*, which is the rate at which major financial institutions offer to lend to their most creditworthy customers). Over the term of the loan, the interest rate fluctuates with changes in the benchmark rate or index. The interest rate is usually adjusted annually or semiannually. The total amount of the change over the term of the loan is generally subject to some cap or maximum top rate. A floor may also be established to ensure that the interest rate does not fall below a specified percentage.

Subprime Mortgages   As discussed more fully in the "Inside Story" in this chapter, there was a surge in the number of subprime *adjustable-rate mortgages (ARMs)* in the period from 2002 to 2007.[21] The Department of Housing and Urban Development (HUD) characterizes a lender as *subprime* if (1) most of its business involves refinancing rather than purchasing loans and (2) the lender does not sell a significant portion of its portfolio to the two government-sponsored housing agencies, the Federal National Mortgage Association (Fannie Mae) and the Federal Home Loan Mortgage Corporation (Freddie Mac).

Points

In addition to interest, real estate lenders often charge a loan fee, called *points*. The fee is the amount funded, multiplied by a fixed percentage. Each 1% is a point. For example, a 2½-point fee on a $100,000 loan would be $2,500. Points are usually paid up front at the time the loan is made.

Construction Loans

Construction loans generally have a term slightly longer than the estimated construction period. On completion of construction, the developer obtains either permanent (take-out) financing or interim (gap) financing and repays the construction lender. If the construction loan comes due before the permanent financing is available, the developer obtains *interim* or *gap financing* to pay off the loan. This financing is provided by someone other than the construction lender and is for a longer term. A *take-out commitment* is an agreement by a lender to replace the construction loan with a permanent loan, usually after certain conditions, such as the timely completion of the project, have been met.

Development Loans

Developers use construction loans for the acquisition and improvement of commercial properties and *development loans* for the acquisition, subdivision, improvement, and sale of residential properties. Funds are advanced by the lender as development progresses. The lender normally requires that the developer obtain performance bonds and personal guaranties by its principals. From the lender's perspective, development loans are riskier than construction loans because repayment of a development loan depends on the developer's ability to sell parcels of the development.

Equity Participation by Lender

Many lenders attempt to increase their yield from real estate projects by participating in the *equity*, or ownership, of the property. The developers can benefit from the higher loan-to-value ratio, lower interest rates, and slower repayment terms that a participating lender will accept.

Equity participation by lenders is a relatively recent phenomenon. Historically, federal and state statutes prohibited banks and other lenders from owning real estate. In recent years, however, these statutory restraints have been substantially relaxed. Lenders need to ensure that their equity participation does not result in an effective interest rate in excess of state usury limits.

Wraparound Financing

Occasionally, an owner will require financing in addition to an existing loan secured by a deed of trust or mortgage on the property. Unless the second lender is willing to take a position subordinate to the holder of the first loan with respect to rights to the property, the owner will need to obtain a second loan sufficient to satisfy (pay off) the first loan and still provide sufficient funds to meet its financing requirements.

Paying off the first loan may not be economically attractive, however, because of prepayment penalties or because the interest rate on the first loan may be lower than the rate available on a new loan. In such instances, wraparound financing can provide additional funds without requiring the owner to first pay off the original loan.

---

21. Christopher L. Foote, Kristopher Gerardi, Lorenz Goette & Paul S. Willen, *Subprime Facts: What (We Think) We Know About the Subprime Mortgage Crisis and What We Don't* (Fed. Reserve Bank of Boston, Working Paper No. 08-2, May 30, 2008).

In a *wraparound financing* transaction, the second lender lends the owner the additional funds and agrees to take over the servicing of the first loan. In exchange, the owner executes a deed of trust or mortgage and an all-inclusive note, covering the combined amount of the first and second loans. The new lender benefits because the rate charged on the all-inclusive note is higher than the weighted-average interest rates of the first and second loans. The owner benefits because the interest rate on the all-inclusive note is lower than the rate it would have to pay if it paid off the first loan and took out a new loan to cover the entire amount.

Foreclosure and Rights of Redemption

If the mortgagor fails to repay the loan, then the mortgagee may resort to foreclosure. *Foreclosure* is the legal process by which a mortgagee puts a piece of property up for sale to the public to raise cash in order to pay off a debt owed by the mortgagor to the mortgagee. The property is sold to the highest bidder; the proceeds are then first used to satisfy the debt obligation (plus interest) of the unpaid first mortgage and court costs. The proceeds are then used to pay any other secured creditors holding a mortgage or deed of trust on the property. The remainder, if any, is distributed to the mortgagor. The exact details of the foreclosure process differ from state to state. Generally,

creditors receive payment in the order in which they secured their debts. However, secondary creditors may condition a second mortgage or loan on the mortgagor getting prior creditors to waive their rights to first payment in the event of a foreclosure. The mortgagor receives nothing until all creditors with a security interest in the property are paid in full.

In some states, the lender can bid the amount of the outstanding indebtedness in the foreclosure sale. If the lender is the highest bidder, it acquires the property, and the debt is extinguished. Some states provide *rights of redemption*, which give the mortgagor and certain other categories of interested persons the right to redeem (reacquire) the property within a statutory limited period, ranging from two months to two years after the sale. If the foreclosure amount plus interest is not paid by the expiration of the redemption period, the purchaser at the foreclosure sale receives the deed and clear ownership of the land. A *short sale* occurs when a lender accepts a discounted payment on a mortgage to enable the mortgagor to avoid bankruptcy or foreclosure. Not all lenders will accept a short sale. Even if a lender does agree to a short sale, there is no guarantee that the lender will not legally pursue the mortgagor for the deficiency unless the lender so agrees.

Before foreclosing on property, the lender needs to ensure that it holds a valid security interest. This was a key issue in the following case.

A CASE IN POINT	*Summary*	Case 18.2

U.S. Bank National Association v. Ibanez

Supreme Judicial Court of Massachusetts
941 N.E.2d 40 (Mass. 2011).

FACTS   In 2005, Antonio Ibanez took out a loan for the purchase of residential property, secured by a mortgage to the lender Rose Mortgage. Several days later, Rose Mortgage executed an assignment of the mortgage in blank (meaning the assignment did not specify the name of the assignee). The blank space was at some point stamped with the name of Option One Mortgage Corporation as the assignee. Later, Option One executed an assignment of the Ibanez mortgage in blank, which was later assigned to Lehman Brothers. Ultimately, the Ibanez mortgage was pooled with other mortgage loans and assigned to U.S. Bank, which converted them into mortgage-backed securities.

U.S. Bank claimed that the assignment to it occurred through a private placement memorandum (PPM), an unsigned offer of mortgage-backed securities that indicated that each loan would be identified in a future trust agreement. U.S. Bank relied solely on the PPM, as it was unable to produce the purported trust agreement naming it as assignee.

In 2007, U.S. Bank filed a complaint to foreclose on the Ibanez mortgage. In the complaint, it represented that it was the "owner (or assignee) and holder" of the Ibanez mortgage. At the foreclosure sale, U.S. Bank purchased the Ibanez property. More than a year after the sale, a "successor-in-interest" to Option One, which was until then the record holder of the Ibanez mortgage, executed an assignment of that mortgage to U.S. Bank.

U.S. Bank brought an action seeking a declaration that the mortgagor's title had been extinguished and that it was the fee simple owner of the foreclosed property. The Land Court Department held that the foreclosure sale was invalid because U.S. Bank, which was not the original mortgagee, had failed to make the required showing that it was the holder of the mortgage at the time of foreclosure. U.S. Bank appealed.

CONTINUED

ISSUE PRESENTED   Based on the documentation provided to the court by U.S. Bank, was it a valid assignee of the mortgage in question with authority to foreclose on the mortgaged property?

SUMMARY OF OPINION   The Supreme Judicial Court of Massachusetts began by noting that one of the terms of the power of sale that must be strictly adhered to is the restriction on who is entitled to foreclose. Any effort to foreclose by a party lacking "jurisdiction and authority" to carry out the foreclosure is void. Because U.S. Bank was not the original mortgagee, it had to prove its authority to foreclose as the eventual assignee of the original mortgagee.

Like a sale of land itself, the assignment of a mortgage is a conveyance of an interest in land that requires a writing signed by the grantor. In Massachusetts, a "title theory state," a mortgage is a transfer of legal title in a property to secure a debt. Therefore, when a person borrows money to purchase a home and gives the lender a mortgage, the homeowner retains only equitable title in the home; the legal title is held by the mortgagee. When mortgage loans are pooled together and converted to mortgage-backed securities, the mortgagees still retain legal title to property and should be treated as such.

After describing the legal requirements of an assignment, the court reviewed the documentation provided by U.S. Bank to determine whether a valid assignment existed. U.S. Bank argued that it was assigned the mortgage under the PPM, which included an offer for mortgage loans to be identified in a trust agreement. The court concluded that this document did not qualify as a valid assignment for several reasons. First, the PPM only furnished evidence of a future intent to assign mortgages to U.S. Bank; it did not constitute proof of their actual assignment. Second, even if there was language of present assignment, U.S. Bank did not produce a schedule of the specifically identified loans that was an exhibit of that agreement, so it failed to show that the Ibanez mortgage was included among them. Finally, U.S. Bank failed to furnish any evidence that the entity assigning the mortgage ever held the mortgage to be assigned. The last assignment of the mortgage on record was from Rose Mortgage to Option One. There was no evidence that Option One ever assigned the mortgage to anyone else before the foreclosure sale. Accordingly, U.S. Bank's claim that it acquired fee simple title to the property by purchasing it at the foreclosure sale was rejected.

RESULT   Based on the documentation submitted to the court, Option One, not U.S. Bank, was the mortgage holder at the time of the foreclosure. Because U.S. Bank did not have the authority to foreclose on the property, the foreclosure sale was set aside.

COMMENTS   The court's decision in *Ibanez* has been hailed by some as an indictment of securitized lending (the practice of bundling mortgages and selling them as mortgage-backed securities to investors) that largely adhered to prior Massachusetts case law.[22] Others see the decision as a departure from the common practice of relying on post-foreclosure assignments of mortgages as providing sufficient authority to foreclose.[23]

---

22. Christopher J. DeCosta, U.S. Bank v. Ibanez: *The Mortgage Industry's Documentation Practices in Focus*, 55 B.B.J. 23 (Spring 2011).

23. *Id.*

Frustrated with the costs of complying with state laws regarding the recording of mortgage assignments, Fannie Mae, Freddie Mac, and other lenders created the Mortgage Electronic Registration System (MERS), a private, parallel recording system, in 1993.[24] Under this streamlined process, MERS is the mortgagee of record for all the mortgages registered with the company. When loan servicing is transferred from one MERS member to another MERS member via a purchase and sale agreement, no assignment of record is needed because MERS remains the mortgage lien holder. MERS was thus established in part to facilitate the bundling of debt and securitization of loans. Its lack of transparency has been blamed

---

24. Tanya Marsh, Sidebar, *Foreclosures and the Failure of the American Land Title Recording System*, 111 COLUM. L. REV. 19 (2011).

"Remember, not one word about his foreclosure."

Tom Cheney/The New Yorker Collection/www.cartoonbank.com

for hiding shoddy record keeping by lenders prior to and during the residential foreclosure crisis.[25] R.K. Arnold resigned as CEO of MERS in 2011. Although under scrutiny, the company had not, as of early 2012, officially been accused of any wrongdoing.[26]

Shoddy mortgage paperwork, involving several shortcuts known collectively as "robo-signing," led many of the nation's largest banks to temporarily halt foreclosures in the fall of 2010. Overwhelmed with paperwork, processors had signed thousands of documents without verifying the information they contained. Both bankers and the lawyers who submitted robo-signed documents to courts have been criticized for essentially lying under oath. A nationwide investigation by various county registers of deeds revealed that illegal or questionable mortgage paperwork has tainted the deeds of tens of thousands of homes since the late 1990s.[27]

In early 2012, Bank of America, Wells Fargo, JPMorgan Chase, Citigroup, and Ally Financial agreed to pay $26 billion to settle federal and state claims arising out of robo-signing and other questionable foreclosure and servicing practices. The deal also eliminated "dual-tracking," whereby a lender negotiates a loan modification while simultaneously proceeding to foreclose on the home. The settlement does not preclude federal or state governments from bringing criminal cases for fraud during the loan origination process or suits for securities law violations when the mortgages were bundled and sold to investors as securities.

APPRAISAL METHODS

The value of an income-producing property may be appraised by (1) the cost approach, which adds the cost of constructing a given improvement on the property to the value of the unimproved land; (2) the market approach, which looks at the selling prices in recent sales of properties with similar income-producing characteristics; or (3) the income approach, which establishes the present value of the estimated annual cash flow over the anticipated holding period. The income approach is generally favored because it provides a basis for comparison; the cost approach is rarely used.

The appraisal of property is an inexact science and is relatively unregulated by state governments. Because the funds available to a developer, and the financial institution's loan fees, are based on the property's appraised value, the appraiser may be pressured to inflate the appraisal. Although increased loan fees and increased funds for development may provide short-term benefits, inflated appraisals can have disastrous long-term effects. For example, the savings and loan crisis in the 1980s (which cost taxpayers in excess of $300 billion) was in part caused by inflated appraisals that induced savings and loan associations to make reckless loans.

Inflated appraisals also contributed to the subprime crisis of 2008.[28] Dodd–Frank requires that appraisals be done by an appraiser independent of the lender and made it unlawful to coerce, extort, collude with, instruct, bribe, or intimidate an appraiser in an attempt to influence the independent judgment of the appraiser. The Act also established a hotline for complaints and authorized the Consumer Financial Protection Bureau to investigate those complaints.

PROTECTIVE LAWS FOR BORROWERS

Every jurisdiction has laws that regulate the conduct of lenders and protect borrowers, especially the interest rate that can be charged (*usury laws*) and the remedies available if a borrower fails to pay on time or is otherwise in default. Both sets of laws are designed primarily to protect individuals, not businesses. Many of the default laws originated during the Great Depression to protect farmers. Such laws include the rights of redemption discussed earlier.

In recent years, usury laws have tended to disappear because an out-of-date usury law (e.g., limiting the interest rate to 8% when the prevailing market rate is 12%) will simply cause loan money to go to a more liberal jurisdiction. In some states, however, the usury laws still apply unless a corporation holds the title to the property. In other states, equity participation by a lender may result in an illegally high interest rate. The penalties for violating the usury laws can be severe, and treble damages are sometimes available. A borrower cannot effectively agree to waive the benefits of a usury law; such a waiver is considered contrary to public policy.

25. *Id.*

26. Michael Powell & Gretchen Morgenson, *MERS? It May Have Swallowed Your Loan*, N.Y. TIMES, Mar. 6, 2011, at BU1.

27. Pallavi Gogoi, *Robo-Signing Practices Older, More Pervasive Than First Thought*, ASSOC. PRESS, Sep. 1, 2011, *available at* http://www.huffingtonpost.com/2011/09/01/robo-signing-practices-1990s_n_945867.html.

28. Mitch Weiss, *Following AP Report, Appraisers Call for Reform*, WASH. POST, Aug. 20, 2008.

Fair lending laws prohibit racial discrimination in lending practices. The Department of Housing and Urban Development (HUD) is responsible for enforcing these laws.

COMMERCIAL LEASING

A *commercial lease* is both (1) a conveyance of an interest in real property from the landlord (also called the *lessor*) to the tenant (also called the *lessee*) and (2) a contract that governs the respective rights and obligations of the parties during the lease term. Because most firms do not own the premises in which their business operations are conducted, the availability and the terms and conditions of commercial leasing can be crucial to the success or failure of the business.

Types of Leases

There are four types of commercial leases: office leases, retail leases, industrial leases, and ground leases.

Office Leases

Most tenants occupy only a portion of an office building. Unless the tenant is to occupy a substantial portion of the building, the lessor will ordinarily present a standard lease form used for all of the tenants of the building. Because the lessor is more interested in having occupants than in obtaining any particular tenant as an occupant, it is often unwilling to negotiate each lease provision separately or to permit the tenant to prepare the lease. In a tight market for tenants, however, there is more room for negotiation.

Retail Leases

In the negotiation of retail leases, the focus is on the operation of the tenant's business. Retail leases frequently contain a *percentage rent clause* that requires the tenant to pay the lessor a percentage of its gross sales, in addition to a base monthly rent.

Environmental issues can be a significant concern in retail leases. Having a paint store or a dry cleaner as a tenant can impose liability on the landlord under federal and state environmental laws and regulations.

Industrial Leases

Industrial leases tend to have a five-year term with renewal options. They usually contemplate substantial capital improvements by the tenant in the form of plant and equipment. Industrial leases are almost always *triple net*, which means that the tenant pays all taxes, insurance, and operating maintenance expenses. Additionally, because the industrial use tends to be very site-specific, assignments of industrial leases are usually allowed only on the sale of the tenant's business; subleasing is usually strictly prohibited.

Ground Leases

A *ground lease* is a very long-term lease, sometimes as long as ninety-nine years. Ground leases are used when a landowner desires to obtain a steady return of income from undeveloped commercial property without the expense of improving or managing the property. Alternatively, a ground lease may be proposed by a tenant that does not wish to invest its own funds in the land but is willing to erect improvements for its own use and at its own risk.

Assignments and Subleases

If the premises fail to meet the tenant's needs, or if the tenant can no longer afford the lease, it may wish to assign or sublease the property. An *assignment* of a lease is a permanent transfer of the lease to a third party. The third party acquires the tenant's rights under the lease; however, the tenant remains liable for the rent if the third party defaults unless the lessor has agreed to look only to the third party. A *sublease* is a temporary transfer of the lease to a third party.

Landlords may be hesitant to grant the tenant the right to assign or sublease to a stranger, however. Moreover, landlords are often concerned about the financial wherewithal of any assignees or sublessees. Therefore, most leases require the landlord's written consent for an assignment or a sublease. Most landlords are willing to provide in the lease that they will not withhold consent unreasonably, and some leases allow for assignment without the landlord's consent if the assignee has the same credit rating as the assignor. In an escalating market, a lease may develop a substantial bonus value if market rents exceed the rent due under the lease. Therefore, the landlord may condition the assignment or sublease on the tenant's paying over any bonus value or splitting it with the landlord.

Hidden Issues

Leases, especially commercial and retail leases, invariably contain a dizzying number of provisions and terms. Most of these terms are straightforward, but they should *always* be reviewed carefully to find any possible out clauses, also known as *early termination clauses*. Any provision that would allow the lessor or lessee to cancel the lease without completing the full term or paying the complete value of the lease is considered an *out clause*. Most leases contain a few standard out clauses involving complete destruction of the property, and all leases are subject to implied out clauses such as frustration of purpose.[29] Some leases, however, contain terms that

---

29. If a lessee enters into a lease with a lessor for a very specific purpose that is frustrated by events over which the party wishing to terminate the lease had no control (for example, a reporter rents a room in London to see a coronation procession that is postponed because the would-be king gets appendicitis), then a court may void the lease and release the lessee from the obligation to pay any further rent because the purpose of the lease (to see the procession) has been frustrated. *See* Krell v. Henry, [1903] 2 K.B. 740 (C.A.).

ordinarily would not be grounds for invalidating the entire lease. For example, an owner of a mall may guarantee that it will maintain a certain percentage of occupancy. If occupancy drops below that percentage, the tenant may have the right to opt out of the lease. These clauses can easily be overlooked in a lease of twenty-five pages or more but can become very important if such circumstances ever come to pass.

ENVIRONMENTAL ISSUES

As discussed in Chapter 15, no one should ever lease or buy real property or take a security interest in real property without first considering the impact of federal and state environmental laws.

National Environmental Policy Act and State Analogues

The National Environmental Policy Act (NEPA)[30] requires all federal agencies to preserve and enhance the environment so that "man and nature can exist in productive harmony, and fulfill the social, economic, and other requirements of present and future generations of Americans." To implement this goal, NEPA requires all agencies of the federal government to consider the environmental consequences of their actions. Most states have adopted environmental quality laws similar to NEPA, which require state and local agencies to consider the environmental impact of their decisions.

Environmental Impact Statement

As part of any proposal for legislation or other major governmental action that may significantly affect the quality of the environment, the government must generally include an *environmental impact statement (EIS)*. The EIS considers (1) the environmental impact of the proposed action, (2) any adverse environmental effects that the proposed action would unavoidably have, (3) alternatives to the proposed action, (4) the relationship between the short-term uses of the environment and the maintenance and enhancement of long-term productivity, and (5) any irretrievable commitments of resources that the proposed action would involve.

Some actions are categorically exempt from the EIS requirement because they do not have any environmental impact. If an action is not categorically exempt, the agency involved prepares an *environmental assessment (EA)*, which identifies any significant impact on the environment. If the EA indicates that the action will not have a significant impact on the environment, no EIS is prepared. If there may be a significant impact, an EIS is required. In some cases, courts have determined that an EIS may not be required when the agency proposing the action performs an environmental review substantially equivalent to an EIS.

Enforcement

NEPA and its state-law counterparts are enforced mainly through litigation by persons who wish to challenge a governmental agency's decision. For example, alfalfa farmers and environmental groups sued the U.S. Department of Agriculture for failing to prepare an EIS before deregulating the sale of Roundup Ready Alfalfa, a genetically modified strain resistant to the herbicide Roundup.[31] NEPA and state-law complaints have been used extensively by groups opposing real estate developments and federal leases of public lands for private use. Such litigation can delay projects for many years.

Planning

Planning for compliance with NEPA or its state-law counterparts is an important part of planning for any business project that requires state or federal decisions, approvals, or permits. This means not only preparing an EIS, if required, but also planning the project to minimize adverse effects on the environment.

Environmental Assessment

Certain states require a detailed evaluation of the effects of a proposed development project on the environment before they will approve it. The state may also require the developer to discuss alternatives to the proposed project and to identify measures that would mitigate adverse environmental effects.

CERCLA and the Development of Brownfields

As discussed in Chapter 15, the Comprehensive Environmental Response, Compensation, and Liability Act (CERCLA) generally holds current owners, as well as the owners at the time of disposal, jointly and severally liable for the costs of remediating any hazardous waste. Thus, if developers buy a piece of property that requires cleanup, they stand a good chance of having to pay the entire cleanup cost even if it is so prohibitive as to make their original investment a loss.

For decades, so-called *brownfields*—such as dumps, landfills, and abandoned factory lots with actual or suspected hazardous contamination—have gone unused even though they are often in exceptional locations. Many of

---

30. 42 U.S.C. § 4321 *et seq.*

31. Monsanto Co. v. Geertson Seed Farms, 130 S. Ct. 2743 (2010) (Case 17.1).

these long neglected eyesores are now being reclaimed and are once again thriving.[32]

The Small Business Liability Relief and Brownfields Revitalization Act of 2002[33] and related state legislation encourage private groups to attempt to clean up brownfields by letting them off the hook for the entire cleanup cost. If the buyer is a "bona fide prospective purchaser," as defined in the Act, then it can avoid liability for so-called legacy contamination, that is, waste disposed of on the site prior to the acquisition. To qualify as a *bona fide prospective purchaser (BFPP)*, the buyer cannot have contributed to the contamination of the brownfield in the first place. In addition, the buyer must (1) conduct a diligent investigation of the property and report any contamination to the appropriate governmental authorities; (2) exercise appropriate care concerning the contamination to stop future or continuing release of contaminants; (3) cooperate with any authorized group, including the federal government, to conduct a cleanup of the property; and (4) obey any land-use restrictions on the property.[34]

GOVERNMENT REGULATION OF LAND USE

Land use is most heavily regulated at the local level, although several states regulate at least some aspects of land use on a regional or statewide level. For example, the state of Florida has preempted the authority of local jurisdictions to regulate land use. "City" is used here to refer to both cities and counties unless otherwise noted. The specific laws and regulations applicable in each state and local jurisdiction must be consulted to understand how land use in that jurisdiction is regulated. Federal and state laws concerning environmental matters, such as air and water quality and the protection of wetlands and endangered species, can also affect the permitted uses of property. Aspects are discussed in Chapter 15.

The legal basis for land-use planning and regulation is the *police power*, that is, the inherent authority of a city or county to protect the health, safety, and welfare of its residents. The courts have been interpreting the police power to give it a wider and wider scope. Its exercise is no longer limited to addressing immediate threats to the public health and safety, such as fires or unsanitary conditions. The U.S. Supreme Court explained:

> The concept of the public welfare is broad and inclusive. . . . The values it represents are spiritual as well as physical, aesthetic as well as monetary. It is within the power of the

Legislature to determine that the community should be beautiful as well as healthy, spacious as well as clean, well-balanced as well as carefully patrolled.[35]

Under this broad reading of public welfare, regulations as varied as architectural review, rent control, limitations on condominium conversions, and restrictions on off-site advertising signs have all been upheld as being appropriate uses of a city's police power.

Rent Control

In 1999, the California Supreme Court upheld the City of Santa Monica's rent control law, which, among other things, established maximum allowable rents, provided for adjustments of allowable rents, and prohibited evictions except in specified circumstances.[36] The law's stated purpose was to prevent owners from exploiting a growing shortage of affordable housing units by charging unreasonably high rents. A landlord challenged the rent control law, arguing that it did not accomplish its stated purpose but rather caused "gentrification" in Santa Monica.

The California Supreme Court "recogniz[ed] the well-established case law of the United States Supreme Court and of this court holding that ordinary rent control statutes are generally constitutionally permissible exercises of governmental authority," but the court also noted that particular decisions of public agencies charged with administering rent control may be deemed to be unconstitutional if they deprive landlords of a fair rate of return. In addition, rent control laws must possess certain structural features that safeguard against confiscatory results. The Fifth Amendment is violated when a land-use regulation "does not substantially advance legitimate state interests." In this instance, the court concluded that Santa Monica's interest in preventing "excessive and unreasonable rent increases" was a legitimate government interest, regardless of whether the primary beneficiaries of this protection were tenants with low income or merely moderate income. The court noted that "with rent control, as with most other such social and economic legislation, we leave to legislative bodies rather than the courts to evaluate whether the legislation has fallen so far short of its goals as to warrant repeal or amendment."

Eminent Domain

Federal, state, and local governments have the power to acquire private property needed for a public purpose through *eminent domain*. The government is required by

---

32. This discussion is based in part on John Holusha, *Town Dump #146's Buried Treasure: Location*, N.Y. TIMES, Apr. 4, 2004, at 1.

33. Pub. L. No. 107-118, 115 Stat. 2356 (2001).

34. David Farer, *Brownfields Redevelopment Initiatives: Federal and Selected State Developments*, in A.L.I.—A.B.A., THE IMPACT OF ENVIRONMENTAL LAW ON REAL ESTATE TRANSACTIONS 501–90 (2003).

35. Berman v. Parker, 348 U.S. 26 (1954).

36. SMB, Ltd. v. Superior Court of Los Angeles County, 968 P.2d 993 (Cal. 1999).

the Fifth Amendment to the U.S. Constitution (made applicable to the states by the Fourteenth Amendment) to pay just compensation for property acquired by eminent domain. As the U.S. Supreme Court explained, the "paradigmatic taking requiring just compensation is a direct government appropriation or physical invasion of private property," however minor.[37] In the following case, the U.S. Supreme Court considered whether a town could use eminent domain to require private landowners to sell their houses and other property to a private developer.

---

37. Lingle v. Chevron U.S.A., 544 U.S. 528 (2005).

| A CASE IN POINT | *Summary* | Case 18.3 |

Kelo v. City of New London

Supreme Court of the United States
545 U.S. 469 (2005).

FACTS   The City of New London, Connecticut, wanted to develop a nonblighted residential area in order to revitalize its ailing economy. In particular, the city had approved a development plan that called for construction of a waterfront hotel, restaurants, retail stores, residences, office space, and marinas. Instead of developing the property itself, the city proposed to have it developed by a private developer. Nine landowners refused to sell to the private development agent, so the city initiated condemnation proceedings.

ISSUE PRESENTED   Does a redevelopment plan designed to spur economic growth by transferring nonblighted private residential property to a private developer constitute a public use?

SUMMARY OF OPINION   The U.S. Supreme Court began by explaining:

Two polar propositions are perfectly clear. On the one hand, it has long been accepted that the sovereign may not take the property of A for the sole purpose of transferring it to another private property owner B, even though A is paid just compensation. On the other hand, it is equally clear that a State may transfer property from one private party to another if future "use by the public" is the purpose of the taking.

The Court propounded a broad definition of public use: "For more than a century, our public use jurisprudence has wisely eschewed rigid formulas and intrusive scrutiny in favor of affording legislatures broad latitude in determining what public needs justify the use of the takings power." The takings in this case advanced a public purpose, namely, economic development: "Promoting economic development is a traditional and long accepted function of government." The Court refused to adopt a rule requiring that the city establish to a "reasonable certainty" that the expected public benefits, such as new jobs and increased tax revenues, would actually accrue from the development plan. It also declined to second-guess the city's determinations as to what lands it needed to acquire in order to effectuate the project.

RESULT   The city could use its power of eminent domain to force private owners to sell their houses and other property to the private development agent.

COMMENTS   In a sharply worded dissent joined by Chief Justice Rehnquist and Justices Scalia and Thomas, Justice O'Connor accused the majority of washing out any distinction between private and public use of property and cautioned:

Under the banner of economic development, all private property is now vulnerable to being taken and transferred to another private owner, so long as it might be upgraded—i.e., given to an owner who will use it in a way that the legislature deems more beneficial to the public—in the process.

She predicted:

The beneficiaries of this decision] are likely to be those citizens with the disproportionate influence and power in the judicial process, including large corporations and development firms. As for the victims, the government now has license to transfer

CONTINUED

property from those with fewer resources to those with more. The Framers cannot have intended this perverse result.

In response to this decision, a number of states adopted laws prohibiting the taking of private property for purposes of private redevelopment. Instead, eminent domain was limited to traditional public purposes, such as building schools, roads, or public parks.

Regulatory Takings

Although the range of activities a city can engage in is broad, there are limitations on the police power. A city may not act arbitrarily or capriciously in enacting or applying land-use regulations. In addition, land-use regulations are sometimes challenged on the ground that they amount to an unconstitutional taking of the property without just compensation.

Regulation that completely deprives an owner of all economically beneficial use of his or her property (a *regulatory taking* or *inverse condemnation*) constitutes a taking requiring just compensation. But a regulation may not require compensation if it merely limits the owner's ability to realize the highest economic value for the property. For example, in *Penn Central Transportation Co. v. City of New York*,[38] the U.S. Supreme Court held that the City of New York did not effect a taking requiring just compensation when it denied Penn Central permission to build a fifty-story office building over Grand Central Terminal. New York City had designated Grand Central a landmark under the Landmarks Preservation Law, which restricted the owner's right to substantially alter the building. Although the application for the construction of the building met all local zoning requirements, Penn Central was denied permission under the landmarks law. Rejecting Penn Central's claim that the application of the landmarks law had deprived it of its property without just compensation, the Supreme Court emphasized that application of the law did not interfere with "Penn Central's primary expectation concerning the use of the parcel" or prevent Penn Central from earning a "reasonable return" on its investment.

In *Lucas v. South Carolina Coastal Council*,[39] the U.S. Supreme Court considered whether South Carolina's desire to prevent harmful or noxious uses justified its Beachfront Management Act, which effectively barred Lucas, the owner of two residential lots purchased in 1986 for $975,000, from erecting any permanent structure on his parcels. The Supreme Court held that if the Act did no more than duplicate the result under the state's common law nuisance law, then no compensation would be required. But, if the Act prohibited an activity not prohibited by common law nuisance and denied the owner all economically viable use of his land, then compensation may be required. The Court put the burden of proof on the state to show that its regulation was not a taking.

In *Palazzolo v. Rhode Island*,[40] the U.S. Supreme Court ruled that landowners may challenge regulations they consider to be takings requiring compensation even if the regulations were already in place at the time the person challenging the regulations purchased the property. In the past, it was assumed that anyone purchasing property with regulatory restrictions on it was paying a lower price and purchasing the property with the understanding that its use was restricted. *Palazzolo* represented a major extension of the rights that theretofore were generally reserved for owners whose property was later burdened by new regulations.

In *Tahoe-Sierra Preservation Council Inc. v. Tahoe Regional Planning Agency*,[41] the U.S. Supreme Court ruled that a five-year moratorium on development in the Lake Tahoe Basin imposed by the Tahoe Regional Planning Agency did not constitute a taking requiring compensation. Unlike a physical taking of property for public use, which requires compensation, a regulatory taking limiting the private use of land automatically entitles the owner to compensation only when the regulation removes all the economic value of a piece of property. In all other cases, courts must look to see whether the "regulatory taking went too far," based on "essentially ad hoc, factual inquiries." In this case, the temporary nature of the regulations weighed against a finding of a taking. In addition, the Court reasoned, imposing strict compensation rules on future decision-making bodies might cause them to be less likely to make fair and just decisions out of fear that the costs might be prohibitive. The need to keep these bodies objective and focused on making the most socially beneficial decisions, despite the costs, was a major factor in the Court's decision.

The Court initially held in *Agins v. Tiburon*[42] that a regulatory taking occurs if the regulation does not substantially advance legitimate state interests. Twenty-five years later, the Court changed course in *Lingle v. Chevron U.S.A.*[43] and ruled that "the 'substantially advances'

38. 438 U.S. 104 (1978).
39. 505 U.S. 1003 (1992).
40. 533 U.S. 606 (2001).
41. 535 U.S. 302 (2002).
42. 447 U.S. 255 (1980).
43. 544 U.S. 528 (2005).

formula is not a valid method of identifying compensable regulatory takings" and accordingly "has no proper place in our takings jurisprudence." The Court explained that the "substantially advances" inquiry reveals nothing about the magnitude or character of the burden a particular regulation imposes on private property rights. Nor does it provide any information about how any regulatory burden is distributed among property owners. As a result, "this test does not help to identify those regulations whose effects are functionally comparable to government appropriation or invasion of private property." While acknowledging that its language in *Agins* was "regrettably imprecise," the Court pointed out that the decision in *Lingle v. Chevron* "does not require us to disturb any of our prior holdings," because "in no case have we found a compensable taking based on such an inquiry."

In *Stop the Beach Renourishment, Inc. v. Florida Department of Environmental Protection*,[44] the U.S. Supreme Court once again revisited the regulatory takings doctrine. In that case, beachfront property owners challenged Florida legislation allowing the State to restore eroded beach and take title to the newly added land. Under Florida common law, a beachfront property owner takes title to accretions (gradual additions of sand and sediment) to his or her property, and the State owns the submerged land as well as avulsions (rapid additions of sand and sediment). Under the Florida statute, any accretions to land formed by avulsions belong to the State. The challengers argued that the legislation, which treated the filling of submerged land for beach restoration as an avulsion, effectively restricted their common law right to take title to any subsequent accretions. The Florida Supreme Court held that the legislation did not unconstitutionally deprive beachfront property owners of their right to future accretions. On appeal, the property owners argued that the Florida Supreme Court's decision effected a taking by transforming private property rights into public property rights. The U.S. Supreme Court affirmed the Florida Supreme Court's decision, finding that the right to accretions is a future contingent interest and not a vested property right. A plurality of the Court agreed that the Takings Clause applies to the judiciary, reasoning that "[i]t would be absurd to allow a State to do by judicial decree what the Takings Clause forbids it to do by legislative fiat." In so holding, the Court denied Florida's contention that no judicial taking occurs unless the court's decision has no "fair and substantial basis." The Court stated that precedent "provide[s] no support for the proposition that takings effected by the judicial branch are entitled to special treatment, and in fact suggest[s] the contrary." Instead, the landowners must prove the elimination of an established property right, which they failed to do here.

Takings questions also arise when a regulatory agency imposes a condition that must be satisfied before a building permit or other land-use approval is granted. This issue is addressed as part of the discussion of regulatory schemes that follows.

Regulatory Schemes

The fundamental components of most land-use regulatory schemes are a general plan, a zoning ordinance, and a subdivision ordinance. Some jurisdictions also employ more specialized planning documents, often called specific plans or community plans, that function somewhere between the general plan and the zoning ordinances.

The General Plan and Other Planning Documents

Many cities have a general development plan, known variously as the general plan, *city plan, master plan,* or *comprehensive plan.* (All such plans are referred to in this chapter as the general plan.) A *general plan* is a long-range planning document that addresses the physical development and redevelopment of a city. It is comprehensive in that it addresses the entire city and a wide range of concerns, such as housing, natural resources, public facilities, transportation, and the permitted locations for various land uses. It includes goals, objectives, policies, and programs related to these concerns.

The practical effect of the general plan varies from state to state. In some states, a general plan is not required at all. In certain states, the general plan is strictly an advisory document that need not be adhered to when planning decisions are made. In other states, the plan functions as the "constitution" for development, and by law, planning decisions (such as zoning, subdivision approval, and road and sewer construction) must be consistent with it. When the general plan has this significance, anyone contemplating development of a specific piece of property should determine what the general plan says about the allowed uses for that property. The general plan may also provide important information about the city's policies regarding growth, where and when public services and facilities will be provided, and whether developers will be expected to provide or pay for needed infrastructure.

If development of the type contemplated is not authorized by the general plan, a general plan amendment will be required. The general plan may also be amended to preclude a contemplated development. Authorization of a type of development in the general plan is not, however, a guarantee that a specific development will be permitted. The development must also be authorized by the zoning ordinance, and other land-use approvals could be required.

Some jurisdictions employ other planning documents in addition to the general plan. Called *specific plans,*

---

44. 130 S. Ct. 2592 (2010).

POLITICAL | PERSPECTIVE

The Oregon Land-Use Referendum: A State Divided

Certain states, including Florida, Louisiana, Mississippi, and Texas, require compensation for property owners if newly enacted land-use regulations reduce the property's value by at least 25%. In 2004, voters in Oregon passed Measure 37, which required cities and counties either (1) to pay fair market compensation for *any* diminution in value due to land-use regulations enacted after the purchase of the property or (2) to exempt the property owner from the regulation. Rules enacted to meet federal requirements or to protect the community from public nuisances and safety hazards did not trigger a right to compensation.[a]

In support of Measure 37, farmers argued that Oregon's thirty-one-year-old land-use regulations left them with insufficient funds for retirement and unfairly forced property owners, rather than taxpayers, to pay the cost of socially imposed goals.[b] Property owners in rural areas were particularly critical of "urban policy makers and the urban elite," who established urban growth boundaries around cities and tried to keep development within them.[c]

After landowners took advantage of the new development freedom provided by Measure 37 and proposed the construction of 100,000-plus homes, subdivisions, and office buildings on their open land, opinion polls and newspaper pundits revealed that many Oregonians were suffering from "voter's remorse." On November 6, 2007, the voters passed Measure 49 by 62% of the vote.[d] It rescinded Measure 37 and significantly scaled back the property rights the first measure had granted. Measure 49 permits landowners to build up to three houses on their property if such construction was allowed when they acquired the property. That number is increased to ten if (1) ten houses were permitted when the owners acquired their property and (2) the owners have suffered reductions in property values that justify additional home sites. Measure 49 protects farmlands, forestlands, and lands with groundwater shortages by prohibiting subdivisions on these lands and prevents property owners from using Measure 49 to override current zoning laws prohibiting commercial and industrial developments on restricted lands. With the enactment of Measure 49, the state projected that only about 13,000 new houses would be built in the countryside, a fraction of the new construction expected after Measure 37 was passed.

a. Timothy B. Wheeler, *Md. Edgy as Ore. Eases Sprawl Curbs*, BALTIMORE SUN, Dec. 2, 2004, at 1B.
b. Felicity Barringer, *Property Rights Law May Alter Oregon Landscape*, N.Y. TIMES, Nov. 26, 2004, at A3.
c. *Oregon Voters Deal Blow to Good Planning*, NEWS TRIB. (Tacoma, Wash.), Nov. 8, 2004, at B10.
d. Blaine Harden, *Oregon Rethinks Easing Land-Use Limits: Trying to Untie Poperty Owners' Hands, Voters Also Ended Some Checks on Sprawl*, WASH. POST, Mar. 11, 2007, at A8.

special plans, community plans, area plans, and a number of other names, these plans usually encompass just a portion of the city's geographic area. They may focus on areas in particular need of planning, such as a downtown area slated for redevelopment, an environmentally sensitive area, a transportation corridor, or an area facing unusual development pressure. Typically, these plans are more detailed than the general plan.

Zoning Regulations

Zoning is the division of a city into districts and the application of specific land-use regulations in each district. Zoning regulations are divided into two classes: (1) regulations regarding the structural and architectural design of buildings (such as height or bulk limitations), and (2) regulations regarding the uses, such as commercial or residential, to which buildings within a particular district may be put. These types of regulations are employed both in traditional zoning systems and in more recently developed approaches to zoning.

Traditional Zoning Traditional zoning separates different land uses. For example, residential areas are separate from commercial and industrial areas, and residential areas of varying densities are separate. This approach to zoning finds its roots in the earliest land-use regulations, which promoted health and safety by separating residences from certain types of manufacturing and service industries. Early zoning also protected property values by preventing apartments from being built near more desirable single-family dwellings.

Planned Unit Development Although many cities still employ some form of traditional zoning, others have adopted different approaches. For example, under *planned unit development (PUD)* zoning, the land-use regulations for a given piece of property reflect the proposed development plans for that property. These plans may include a mixture of uses, such as residential, office, and retail commercial, which could not be accommodated under the separation of uses required by traditional zoning. Residential development may be clustered on a portion of the property, creating densities higher than those permitted under traditional zoning but also providing larger areas of open space. Planned offices or industrial parks may be subject to covenants and restrictions such as regulated setbacks or signage. Many feel that this more flexible approach to zoning allows more creativity and shows greater sensitivity to environmental and aesthetic concerns.

Zoning Relief   Variances and conditional-use permits may create exceptions to a zoning ordinance. A *variance* allows a landowner to construct a structure or to carry on an activity not otherwise permitted under the zoning regulations. It allows the property owner to use the property in a manner basically consistent with the established regulations, with such minor variations as are necessary to avoid inflicting a unique hardship on that property owner. In some states, variances may be granted to allow uses not authorized by the zoning regulations. In other states, variances are limited to sanctioning deviations from regulations governing physical standards, such as minimum lot size, the maximum number of square feet that may be developed, and off-street parking requirements.

A *conditional-use permit* allows uses that are not permitted as a matter of right under the zoning ordinance. The permit imposes conditions to ensure that the use will be appropriate for the particular situation.

Nonconforming Uses   A *nonconforming* use is an existing use that was originally lawful but does not comply with a later-enacted zoning ordinance. A zoning ordinance may not compel immediate discontinuance of a nonconforming use (unless it constitutes a public nuisance). A city can, however, require that nonconforming uses be eliminated within a reasonable time or on application for a building permit to modify the premises.

Subdivision Process

Frequently, development requires the division of land into separate parcels. This process is known as *subdivision*. It is a necessary step in residential development and often in industrial or commercial development.

The subdivision process allows the city to regulate new development and to limit harm, deterioration of water quality, soil erosion, and building in areas subject to earth movement. The subdivider may also be required to address, for example, the impact of the subdivision on views and other aesthetic concerns or on traffic circulation.

Conditions and Unconstitutional Takings

Frequently, to win approval for a subdivision (or other land-use permit), the subdivider or landowner must provide streets, utilities, sewers, drainage facilities, and other infrastructure to serve the subdivision or other development. It may also be required to dedicate land for parks, schools, libraries, and fire stations and to pay impact fees to offset the increased burden on public facilities and services resulting from the development. The conditions may include constructing on-site or off-site facilities or paying fees for purposes as varied as acquiring parkland or providing day-care centers, public art, or low-income housing.

Conditions to a land-use approval will be upheld if they are reasonably related to the burdens on the community created by the development being approved. Thus, if the development will result in an influx of residents or employees, a fee to fund traffic improvements made necessary by that influx will be upheld. In the absence of the legally required relationship between a condition to an approval and the impacts of the development being approved (the *nexus*), however, the condition may be struck down as an unconstitutional taking.

For example, in the case of *Nollan v. California Coastal Commission*,[45] James and Marilyn Nollan sought a permit from the California Coastal Commission to demolish their existing single-story beachfront house and replace it with a two-story, three-bedroom house approximately three times larger than the existing structure. Public beaches were located within one-half mile to the north and south of the Nollans' property. Finding that the new house would further obstruct the ocean view, increase private use of the beach, and establish a "psychological barrier" to access to the nearby public beaches, the commission approved the construction subject to the condition that the Nollans dedicate an easement for public access across the portion of their property lying between the high-water mark and a seawall approximately ten feet inland. The Nollans successfully challenged this condition. The U.S. Supreme Court held that the dedication condition amounted to an unconstitutional taking because there was no nexus between the requirement of an easement for public access and the stated interest of reducing obstacles to the ocean view as well as "psychological barriers" to using the beach. The Court concluded by saying that if the government wanted an easement across the Nollans' property, "it must pay for it."

In *Dolan v. City of Tigard*,[46] the Supreme Court held that there has to be a showing of "rough proportionality" between the conditions imposed on a permit and the nature and extent of the proposed development's impact. The Court ruled that a city could not require Dolan to dedicate a portion of her property to a pedestrian/bicycle pathway as a condition to permitting the expansion of her retail sales facility. The Court acknowledged that the enlarged retail sales facility would increase traffic on the streets of the

---

45. 483 U.S. 825 (1987).
46. 512 U.S. 374 (1994).

IN BRIEF

Limits on Land-Use Regulation

1. Any direct government appropriation or physical invasion of private property, however minor, requires just compensation.

2. Government takings and regulations must be reasonably related to the public welfare.

3. Regulations cannot deny the owner all economically beneficial use of its land.

4. Conditions to a land-use approval must be reasonably related to the burdens on the community created by the development being approved (nexus).

5. There must be rough proportionality between the conditions imposed and the nature and extent of the proposed development's impact.

central business district by roughly 435 additional trips per day. The Court also noted that dedications for streets, sidewalks, and other public ways are generally reasonable exactions to avoid excessive congestion for a proposed property use. The Court concluded, however, that the city had not met its burden of demonstrating that the additional number of vehicle and bicycle trips generated by Dolan's development was reasonably related to the city's requirement for dedication of the pedestrian/bicycle easement. Thus, the exaction amounted to an unconstitutional taking.

In *Monterey v. Del Monte Dunes at Monterey, Ltd.*,[47] the U.S. Supreme Court held that *Dolan's* rough proportionality test applies only to exactions and not to outright denials of permission to develop. The Court explained:

> Although in a general sense concerns for proportionality animate the Takings Clause, we have not extended the rough proportionality test of *Dolan* beyond the special context of exactions—land-use decisions conditioning approval of development on the dedication of property to public use. The rule applied in *Dolan* considers whether dedications demanded as conditions of development are proportional to the development's anticipated impacts. It was not designed to address, and is not readily applicable to, the much different questions arising where, as here, the landowner's challenge is based not on excessive exactions but on denial of development. We believe, accordingly, that the rough proportionality test of *Dolan* is inapposite to a case such as this one.

A city's imposition of a condition on the grant of a permit can also be challenged under the Equal Protection Clause. For example, the U.S. Supreme Court recognized that a valid claim for relief existed when a village "intentionally demanded a 33-foot easement as a condition to connecting [one property owner's] property to the municipal water supply where the village required only a 15-foot easement from similarly situated property owners."[48]

Vested Development Rights

Until a developer obtains a *vested right*—that is, a fully guaranteed right—to develop a property, the regulations governing that property may be changed. In other words, a developer has no claim to the land-use regulations in effect when the property was acquired, when preliminary steps to development were taken, or at any other time prior to the vesting of the right to develop. A change in the land-use regulations prior to vesting may, therefore, preclude a development that would have been permissible under the regulations in force at the time the property was acquired.

In some states, the right to develop vests when substantial work is done and substantial liabilities are incurred in reliance on a building permit. In other states, vesting is tied to obtaining the "last discretionary approval" required for development. States differ on what constitutes the last discretionary approval.

Early Vesting

Mechanisms to allow early vesting are available in certain states. One such mechanism is a development agreement, which is authorized in Arizona, California, Colorado, Florida, Hawaii, and Nevada. In those states, the development project is governed by the land-use regulations in effect at the time the development agreement is entered into, and the project is immune from subsequent changes in the regulations.

PHYSICAL ACCESSIBILITY TO COMMERCIAL FACILITIES AND PLACES OF PUBLIC ACCOMMODATION

Under the Americans with Disabilities Act (ADA),[49] any new renovations or alterations to commercial facilities must be accessible to persons with disabilities, including those in wheelchairs. The Act defines *commercial facilities* as all structures except those intended for residential use. This accessibility rule applies only to the areas being renovated, and it requires compliance only to the extent feasible.

New construction is subject to more complex accessibility rules. In building new structures, architects and builders must comply with regulations established by the U.S. Attorney General regarding accessibility. In general, new structures must be designed and constructed so that

---

47. 526 U.S. 687 (1999).

48. Vill. of Willowbrook v. Olech, 528 U.S. 562 (2000).

49. 42 U.S.C. § 12101 *et seq.*

they are "readily accessible to and usable by individuals with disabilities," unless it is structurally impossible to do so.

Violation of the physical-accessibility rules for renovations and new construction can result in a private lawsuit or action by the U.S. Attorney General. Violators may be required to pay damages as well as civil penalties of up to $50,000 for a first violation and $100,000 for subsequent violations.

The ADA also requires minor physical changes to existing workplaces to accommodate workers with disabilities. For example, the ADA mandates removal of architectural barriers in existing stores, offices, and firms where the removal is "readily achievable." Modifications are readily achievable if they are easy to accomplish and can be done without significant expense. Readily achievable changes might include ramping a few steps or lowering a public telephone for wheelchair users, installing grab bars in restrooms, putting raised Braille symbols on elevator controls, and rearranging office furniture to provide increased accessibility.

In addition, the ADA requires that individuals with disabilities have access to "the full and equal enjoyment of the goods, services, facilities, privileges, advantages, or accommodations of any place of public accommodation." *Public accommodation* is defined to include, among other things, a restaurant, place of lodging, place of entertainment, place of public gathering, and place of exercise or recreation.

In *Stevens v. Premier Cruises*,[50] a plaintiff confined to a wheelchair successfully sued Premier Cruises for failing to make all areas of its cruise ship wheelchair accessible. The U.S. Court of Appeals for the Eleventh Circuit ruled that "those portions of the cruise ship that come within the statutory definition of 'public accommodation' are subject to the public accommodation provisions" of the ADA. The Third Circuit ruled that arenas subject to the ADA do not have to provide spectators in wheelchairs sight lines over standing spectators, however.[51]

In contrast, Oregon Paralyzed Veterans of America and three of its members successfully sued two movie theater companies that did not provide wheelchair-bound patrons with "lines of sight" comparable to those provided to members of the general public who did not use wheelchairs.[52] The theaters located all of the wheelchair-accessible seating in the first few rows, forcing wheelchair-bound patrons to "sit in seats that are objectively uncomfortable, requiring them to crane their necks and twist their bodies in order to see the screen, while non-disabled patrons have a wide range of comfortable viewing locations from which to choose." The court found it "simply inconceivable that

this arrangement could constitute 'full and equal enjoyment' of movie theater services by disabled patrons."

Under certain circumstances, screening or eligibility requirements imposed from a central location that the disabled person may never actually visit may also be covered under the ADA.[53] Courts are split on when discrimination not occurring at a physical location constitutes discrimination in a "public accommodation." Some courts require a nexus between the nonphysical service and the actual, physical premises of the public accommodation. In *Rendon v. Valleycrest Productions, Ltd.*,[54] the court found that the plaintiffs demonstrated a nexus between the challenged service (an automated telephone selection process for a TV game show) and the premises of the public accommodation, namely, the physical television studio. In contrast, the court in *Access Now, Inc. v. Southwest Airlines Co.*,[55] found that no nexus existed between Southwest Airlines' online "virtual ticket counter" and a physical, concrete place of public accommodation.

Other courts take a more expansive view of what constitutes "public accommodation." For example, the First and Seventh Circuits have suggested that the term encompasses more than just physical structures and reaches facilities open to the public through electronic space, including websites.[56]

Thus, some experts believe that the ADA will be applied to require certain websites to adopt special coding or features to provide access to individuals with disabilities.[57] In *National Federation of the Blind v. Target Corp.*,[58] the court found that a group of blind persons stated a valid claim under the ADA where Target's website did not contain certain features that would allow them full access to the site. In 2010, the U.S. Department of Justice issued an advance notice of proposed rulemaking that would require that public offerings of goods and services via the Internet be made accessible to individuals with disabilities.

The ADA also prohibits discrimination on the basis of disability by public entities unless the discrimination is necessary to avoid substantial risk to the disabled person or others.[59] One case involved the city of

---

50. 215 F.3d 1237 (11th Cir. 2000).

51. Caruse v. Blockbuster–Sony Music Entm't Ctr. at the Waterfront, 193 F.3d 730 (3d Cir. 1999).

52. Or. Paralyzed Veterans of Am. v. Regal Cinemas Inc., 339 F.3d 1126 (9th Cir. 2003).

---

53. 42 U.S.C. § 12101 *et seq.*

54. 294 F.3d 1279 (11th Cir. 2002).

55. 227 F. Supp. 2d 1312 (S..D. Fla. 2002).

56. *See* Carparts Distribution Ctr., Inc. v. Auto. Wholesaler's Ass'n of New England, Inc., 37 F.3d 12, 19–20 (1st Cir. 1994) (holding that "public accommodation" encompasses more than actual physical structures and includes the defendant insurance company); Doe v. Mut. of Omaha Ins. Co., 179 F.3d 557, 559 (7th Cir. 1999) (noting, in dicta, that a "place of public accommodation" encompasses facilities open to the public in both physical and electronic space, including websites).

57. *See Disabled Access Laws and Internet Web Sites—An Unsettled Area,* 72 U.S.L.W. 2371–73 (2004).

58. 452 F. Supp. 2d 946 (N.D. Cal. 2006).

59. MX Group Inc. v. Covington, Kentucky, 293 F.3d 326 (6th Cir. 2002).

Covington, Kentucky, which had refused to grant a permit to a group that sought to establish a methadone clinic for recovering drug addicts. The city expressed concerns about a possible increase in crime and drug use if the clinic were located in the area. MX Group, Inc. successfully brought an action on behalf of heroin addicts under the ADA and the Vocational Rehabilitation Act to require the city to grant the permit. The U.S. Court of Appeals for the Sixth Circuit first held that the ADA's prohibitions against discrimination on the basis of disability apply to zoning and permits. It then explained that the goal of the ADA is to protect disabled individuals from deprivations based on prejudice, stereotypes, or unfounded fears. Accordingly, the determination of whether a development would pose a significant risk turns on an individualized assessment of the nature, duration, and severity of the risk and the probability that the potential injury will actually occur. If a significant risk is present, then the challenging party must show that the risk can be ameliorated by reasonable modifications. If it cannot be ameliorated, ADA protections are unavailable. Because Covington's denial of the permit was based on stereotypes, prejudice, and unfounded fears, it violated the ADA.

Mike Price/Shutterstock

THE RESPONSIBLE MANAGER

BUYING AND USING REAL ESTATE

The typical manager who does not deal with real estate full-time will probably find that there are more laws, administrative regulations, and governmental practices associated with real estate than with many other management activities. The manager will not always be able to rely on common sense in managing real estate because the laws and administrative practices related to real property can have surprising effects.

Before acquiring real estate, legally astute managers (1) determine whether the property is properly located for the company's operations; (2) ascertain whether the improvements, if already built, comply with applicable building codes and are suitable for the company; (3) determine whether the facility complies with physical-accessibility regulations under the Americans with Disabilities Act; (4) determine whether previous owners have fully complied with federal, state, and local environmental and hazardous waste laws and confirm that the company will not be liable under any of those laws; (5) decide whether the company should lease or buy the property; (6) decide, if the property is rental property, for how long and under what terms it should be leased; (7) decide, if the property is for sale, how best to negotiate the purchase contract and finance the purchase; and (8) keep senior executives and/or the board of directors informed about the manager's actions and decisions throughout the process.

The magnitude of the investment and the permanence of the acquisition render these decisions some of the most important that a manager will make. Although large corporations generally have a department for facilities management, smaller organizations often do not. The manager will need to have access to responsible professionals, including knowledgeable commercial/industrial real estate brokers, attorneys who specialize in real estate and environmental law, and environmental consultants. If the company is acquiring bare land and building its own improvements, the manager will also need to have available expertise in planning and land use. With the heavy use of outside consultants comes the responsibility of managing the consultants and controlling the costs.

Similar responsibilities accompany the occupancy of real estate. If a company occupies premises under a *full-service lease*, which requires the lessor to maintain the property, the tenant's responsibilities may be limited to seeing that the services provided by the lessor are adequate. Most manufacturing companies do not occupy leased premises on a full-service basis, however. Thus, the managers may be responsible for continuing maintenance, repairs, and compliance with laws, including environmental laws. In any type of occupancy, management must always plan ahead to ensure that the facilities will continue to be adequate for present and future operations. It is often difficult to anticipate future needs, and it is easy to overspend or, conversely, to fail to anticipate a new demand.

Finally, managers are likely to find that they have less control than desired over real estate decisions. For example, building or other occupancy permits may need to be obtained from several agencies, such as building departments and fire departments. Those agencies may not be responsive to a company's urgent demands, and the officials involved may have a great deal of discretion in both the timing of the approval and the interpretation of the applicable laws. Delays beyond the company's control frequently try managers' patience and cause inconvenience and downtime. In both the acquisition or the disposition phase, legally astute managers allow considerable extra time for delay.

A MANAGER'S DILEMMA

Putting It into Practice

A Multiplicity of Interests

In 1986, Triple Five of Minnesota, Inc. secured the development rights for the land on which the Mall of America in Bloomington, Minnesota, was built. Teachers Insurance and Annuity Association provided $650 million in construction financing, which was converted into an equity interest in Mall of America Company LP (MOAC LP). MOAC LP was the managing partner and owner of 99% of the Mall of America Company (MOAC), which owned the Mall. MOAC LP was a partnership between Teachers, which owned 55% of MOAC LP, and Mall of America Associates (MOAA), which owned 45%. MOAA was a 50/50 partnership between Triple Five and a limited partnership controlled by the Melvin and Herbert Simon family (Si-Minn LP). Si-Minn LP became the managing partner of MOAA in 1987.

Teachers had always received the entire income generated by the Mall, but MOAA was paid a management fee of 5% of the Mall's gross income per year. Si-Minn LP, the actual manager of the Mall, received 80% of this fee, and Triple Five, which had no day-to-day responsibility for managing the Mall, received 20%. In March of 1998, both Triple Five and Si-Minn LP became aware that Teachers was considering selling all or part of its interests in the Mall, which it had the right to do.

A company controlled by the Simon family is considering acquiring 50% of Teachers' interests in the Mall. Are there any legal or ethical constraints on the company's ability to acquire Teachers' interests?[60]

---

60. *See* Triple Five of Minn., Inc. v. Simon, 404 F.3d 1088 (8th Cir. 2005).

INSIDE STORY

Countrywide Financial: Subprime Mortgages and Shattered Dreams

In 2004, Countrywide Financial Corporation became the largest U.S. mortgage lender, in part by using aggressive sales techniques and lowering lending standards. Along with other lenders, Countrywide introduced exotic mortgages that allowed borrowers to qualify for larger mortgages. The most common type of subprime mortgage originated in the 2002–2007 period was a "2/28" hybrid ARM, with the interest rate fixed for the loan's first two years and then adjustable every six months for the remaining twenty-eight years (or until the loan was paid off).[61] Countrywide also sold "pay option ARMs," an adjustable-rate mortgage loan that gives the borrower a choice of payment methods, including making a minimum payment that is less than the interest owed. If the borrower elects this payment option, the difference between the interest owed and the interest actually paid is added to his or her outstanding loan balance each month in a process known as "negative amortization." A borrower who elected this method of payment also faced steeply elevated interest rates.[62]

As competition for these risky loans grew, Countrywide joined other lenders in relaxing its standards for borrowing. Although many borrowers with "good" credit (that is, a FICO® score above 620, the number generally considered the cutoff

for prime borrowers) were steered toward subprime mortgages, many subprime borrowers had FICO scores below 620. In addition, regardless of their credit scores, most subprime borrowers (1) had high loan-to-value ratios (the ratio of the loan to the value of the house ranged from an average of 85% for the lowest-score borrowers to 95% for the highest-score borrowers in 2005–2006); (2) high debt-to-income ratios (often in excess of 40%); and (3) were unwilling (or unable) to fully document their income and assets. By the end of the housing boom in 2004, the fraction of fully documented loans had dropped below 70% for borrowers with FICO scores less than 620 and below 40% for borrowers with FICO scores above 660. Only about 10% of the borrowers with outstanding subprime loans in the mid-2000s would have qualified for prime loans.[63]

When housing prices fell, many subprime borrowers had *negative equity*, that is, an outstanding mortgage balance in excess of the value of the house. Researchers calculated that a borrower whose property's value had fallen by more than 20% since the initial purchase was more than fifteen times more likely to lose his or her house to foreclosure than a homeowner whose property had appreciated by 20%.[64]

CONTINUED

---

61. Foote, Gerardi, Goette & Willen, *supra* note 21.

62. Bob Tedeschi, *New Rules for "Exotic" Loans*, N.Y. TIMES, Oct. 15, 2006, § 11, at 13.

63. *Id.*

64. *Id.*

During the second half of 2007, Countrywide suffered $1.6 billion in mortgage-related losses. By the end of 2007, more than 5% of Countrywide's $28.42 billion in pay option ARMs were at least ninety days overdue, and 71% of its pay option ARM borrowers had opted to make only the minimum payments. Deteriorating credit market conditions forced Countrywide into a merger with Bank of America in 2008 in exchange for $2.8 billion of Bank of America stock,[65] a fraction of Countrywide's 2007 market value of $25 billion.[66]

Dubbed a "deal from hell,"[67] the acquisition of Countrywide is expected to cost Bank of America tens of billions of dollars in inherited litigation settlements. The bank has also seen a substantial decline in profits, with losses of $20.6 billion in earnings in the second quarter of 2011 alone.[68] In 2010, Bank of America agreed to pay $600 million to settle shareholder lawsuits claiming that Countrywide concealed mounting risks as it loosened standards for loans.[69] Many investors opted out of the initial agreement in hopes of bringing future lawsuits against the bank. In late 2011, American International Group (AIG) sued Bank of America in an effort to recover more than $10 billion in losses it claims it suffered when Countrywide misrepresented the quality of the mortgages placed in securities and sold to investors.[70]

In June 2008, California, Illinois, and Florida filed lawsuits against Countrywide and its founder and CEO Angelo Mozilo for deceptive mortgage practices. By early 2009, eight more states had joined the suit. Under the terms of the settlement, Countrywide agreed to modify tens of thousands of loans and establish a mortgage aid program to prevent struggling borrowers from losing their homes.[71] Some states, including New York and Delaware, chose to opt out of any settlement agreement in order to preserve the right to bring future lawsuits against the company. In August 2011, Nevada sought to end its participation in the settlement agreement, alleging that Bank of America raised the interest rates on struggling borrowers and failed to provide loan modifications to qualified homeowners as required under the deal.[72]

In October 2010, Mozilo paid $67.5 million to settle a civil securities fraud lawsuit brought by the Securities and Exchange Commission (SEC).[73] In February 2011, the Department of Justice ended a two-year criminal investigation into Mozilo's actions without taking any action against him.[74]

In December 2011, Bank of America agreed to pay $335 million to resolve claims that its Countrywide unit had engaged in pervasive discrimination against minority borrowers across forty-one states. The plaintiffs alleged that between 2004 and 2008 Countrywide charged more than 200,000 minority borrowers higher fees and interest rates than it charged white borrowers with similar credit profiles.[75]

Also in December 2011, the SEC brought civil actions against six former executives at Fannie Mae and Freddie Mac, which were created by Congress to buy mortgages from lending institutions, such as Countrywide, and then either hold them in investment portfolios or resell them as mortgage-backed securities to investors. After it became apparent that Fannie Mae and Freddie Mac had insufficient capital to withstand the housing crisis, the federal government took control of them in September 2008 and infused $200 billion of taxpayers' money in an effort to keep them afloat. The SEC alleged that Fannie and Freddie did not adequately disclose the firms' exposure to risky mortgages prior to the financial crisis. According to the SEC complaint, from 2007 to 2008 Freddie Mac executives indicated that the company's exposure was from $2 billion to $6 billion when it was actually as high as $244 billion. Similarly, although Fannie Mae's executives stated that its exposure was about $4.8 billion, the amount was in fact almost ten times greater.[76]

The role of Fannie and Freddie in the 2008 financial crisis has been fiercely debated. The Financial Crisis Inquiry Commission, created by Congress in 2009, concluded that the two firms "contributed to the crisis but were not a primary cause."[77]

As discussed in the "Inside Story" in Chapter 23, the Dodd–Frank Wall Street Reform and Consumer Protection Act of 2010 placed certain restrictions on lending practices. The Act also created the Consumer Financial Protection Bureau, which is discussed in the "Inside Story" in Chapter 6 and in Chapter 17.

65. *Bank of America Becomes Nation's Largest Mortgage Lender*, Buff. L.J., July 7, 2007, *available at* http://www.lawjournalbuffalo.com/news/article/current/2008/07/07/101176/bank-of-america-becomes-nations-largest-mortgage-lender.

66. E. Scott Reckard, *His Star Tarnished, Mozilo Exits Stage*, L.A. Times, July 1, 2008, § C, at 1.

67. Steven M. Davidoff, *For Bank of America, Countrywide Bankruptcy Is Still an Option*, N.Y. Times, Aug. 11, 2011.

68. *Id.*

69. David Benoit, *BlackRock, Calpers Reach New Settlement on Countrywide Claims*, Dow Jones Newswires, Nov. 22, 2011, *available at* http://online.wsj.com/article/BT-CO-20111122-713923.html.

70. Louise Story & Gretchen Morgenson, *A.I.G. Sues Bank of America over Mortgage Bonds*, N.Y. Times, Aug. 8, 2011, at A1.

71. *Bank Settles Countrywide Mortgage Lawsuit*, Assoc. Press, Feb. 11, 2009, *available at* http://www.cbsnews.com/8301-500395_162-4503045.html.

72. Gretchen Morgenson, *Nevada Sees Violations of Mortgage Agreement*, N.Y. Times, Aug. 30, 2011, at B1.

73. Peter Lattman, *Criminal Investigation of Countrywide Chief Has Ended*, NYTimes.com, Feb. 19, 2011, http://dealbook.nytimes.com/2011/02/19/criminal-investigation-of-countrywide-chief-ends/.

74. *Id.*

75. Charlie Savage, *Countrywide Will Settle a Bias Suit*, N.Y. Times, Dec. 22, 2011, at B1.

76. David Glovin & Joshua Gallu, *Freddie Mac, Fannie Mae Ex-CEOs Sued for Understating Loans*, Bloomberg.Com, Dec. 16, 2011, http://www.bloomberg.com/news/2011-12-16/sec-sues-former-freddie-mac-chief-executive-richard-syron-in-new-york.html.

77. *Federal National Mortgage Association Fannie Mae*, Times Topics, *available at* http://topics.nytimes.com/top/news/business/companies/fannie_mae/index.html.

KEY WORDS AND PHRASES

QUESTIONS AND CASE PROBLEMS

1. In 1973, William Arnholt and his then wife, Marie Arnholt, purchased a parcel of land abutting a stream. They remained there until 1993, when they were divorced. Pursuant to their divorce decree, Marie continued to reside in the home until 1995, at which time William took possession of the home. Since the purchase of the land in 1973, William treated a barbed-wire fence on the other side of the stream as his property's boundary line. Over the years, he planted as many as 150 trees on the sides of the stream and buttressed the stream banks with bricks and tiles. He also began mowing the area on the opposite side of the stream and storing materials and automobiles not far from the stream. Carlisle is the owner of an adjoining parcel on which sits the disputed area. After disputes between

Carlisle and Arnholt arose, Arnholt filed a complaint seeking title to the disputed property on the grounds of adverse possession. Did Arnholt meet all of the requirements of adverse possession? [*Arnholt v. Carlisle*, 2011 WL 2436590 (Ohio Ct. App. 2011).]

2. Ace owns Blueacre, a forty-acre parcel of unimproved real estate on the outskirts of a burgeoning city in the state of Calvada. In June 1999, the legislature of Calvada approved the construction of a freeway adjacent to Blueacre. Shortly after the completion of the freeway in 2006, Ace was approached by Greenhorn, who desired to construct an apartment building on Blueacre. Greenhorn is a licensed general contractor previously employed by several large apartment building developers. Although Greenhorn could not arrange financing to purchase Blueacre outright, he was able to negotiate a sixty-year ground lease from Ace on the express condition that Greenhorn complete construction of the apartment building before July 1, 2011. The lease was duly executed by both Ace and Greenhorn, and a memorandum of the lease was legally recorded.

Greenhorn obtained a $10 million loan at 9% interest that was due and payable on or before July 1, 2011, from Construction Lender. To secure repayment of the construction loan, Greenhorn executed a leasehold mortgage in favor of Construction Lender and legally recorded it.

Concurrently with the funding of the construction loan, Greenhorn obtained a standby commitment from Permanent Lender to advance $10 million at 7% interest contingent on (1) the issuance of certificates of occupancy for 80% of the apartment building and (2) the leasing of 60% of the total rentable space of the apartment building to tenants acceptable to Permanent Lender. Greenhorn contracted with various subcontractors for the construction of the apartment building. Certificates of occupancy for 80% of the apartment building were issued on or before May 31, 2011. Certificates of occupancy for the remaining units were not obtained until July 3, 2011. The leasing of units was hampered by the availability of apartments at a lower cost in competing complexes. As of May 31, 2011, Permanent Lender had approved leases for only 45% of the rentable space.

Fearful of defaulting on the construction loan, Greenhorn approached both Construction Lender and Permanent Lender and was successful in negotiating a letter of intent involving Greenhorn, Construction Lender, and Permanent Lender, whereby it was agreed in principle that the term of the construction note would be extended to December 31, 2011, subject to approval by counsel for both Construction Lender and Permanent Lender. On execution of the letter of intent, the officer of Construction Lender negotiating it exclaimed that he was glad that an agreement had been reached to extend the construction loan. The officer representing Permanent Lender replied that he should receive a memento to mark the importance of the occasion.

Subsequently, Permanent Lender suffered record defaults in its mortgage business, its lending policies were scrutinized by the federal regulatory authorities, and its reserve requirements were substantially increased. Unbeknownst to Greenhorn and Construction Lender, Permanent Lender was no longer in a position to fund the permanent loan because of its increased reserve requirements.

Prior to December 31, 2011, Greenhorn submitted executed leases to Permanent Lender sufficient to meet the 60% lease contingency. The financial condition of the tenants who signed these leases was equal to or greater than that of the tenants previously approved by Permanent Lender. Recognizing the tight position that Permanent Lender was in, its attorneys uncovered an ancient deed restriction that precluded the sale or lease of Blueacre or any portion thereof to any person of Chinese descent. Based on this restriction, Permanent Lender refused to approve several leases to individuals with Chinese surnames. As a result, Greenhorn was unable to fulfill the 60% lease contingency prior to December 31, 2011, and Permanent Lender refused to fund the permanent loan.

On January 5, 2012, Construction Lender sent a notice of default to Greenhorn and announced its intent to foreclose the leasehold mortgage. What are the legal rights and obligations of Ace, Greenhorn, Construction Lender, and Permanent Lender? Has each of the parties acted ethically?

3. Patricia and Bobby Star were married in New Mexico in July 2003. They had been living together since 2000. In July 2010, they separated. They had purchased a residence as joint tenants in April 2002. Bobby made the down payment from his separate funds. The mortgage payments were made out of commingled funds before and after marriage.

In August 2004, Patricia founded BioGene Corporation, a biotechnology firm, with $20,000 that she received as an inheritance from her grandmother. All of the stock of BioGene was issued in Patricia's name, and Patricia worked full-time for BioGene. Bobby retained his job with another employer and was not involved in the operations of BioGene. Due to limited financial resources, Patricia did not draw a salary from BioGene until August 2010. In September 2010, BioGene's first product was approved by the Food and Drug Administration. Shortly thereafter, Patricia sold all of her BioGene stock to a large pharmaceutical concern for $30 million. Two days after the sale of the stock, Patricia filed for dissolution of the marriage.

Is the residence that Patricia and Bobby acquired community property or property held in joint tenancy? Would it matter if after marriage they had written a document stating that they wanted to hold the property as community property? In joint tenancy? Does Bobby have any interest in the proceeds from the sale of the BioGene stock?

4. The Blixseths entered into a purchase agreement with American Capital Corporation (ACC) for three parcels of real estate in Newport, Rhode Island. One was vacant, the second parcel had a mansion on it, and the third had a carriage house. Although ACC knew that all three parcels were located within the Newport Historic District and subject to the rules and regulations of the Newport Historic District Commission, it did not disclose that fact to the Blixseths. A Rhode Island statute provides that a buyer may

terminate a sale if an undisclosed condition is a "materially deficient condition." Will the Blixseths be able to void the purchase and sale agreement? [*American Capital Corp. v. Blixseth*, 563 F. Supp. 2d 316 (D.R.I. 2008).]

5. Lucy Dunworth, developer of a shopping mall, entered into an easement and operating agreement with three major department stores. One of the covenants in the agreement was that each occupant promised to operate its store area as a first-class department store under its trade name for a twenty-year period. The occupants each purchased their commercial space in fee (that is, they actually purchased the land) from the developer. Kaufman—Straus Company, one of the tenants, sold its place to a discount store two years later. The other two first-class department stores brought an action against the discount store because it was not a first-class operation. What is the result? [*Net Realty Holding Trust v. Franconia Properties, Inc.*, 544 F. Supp. 759 (E.D. Va. 1982).]

6. Hermanson Family Limited owns several commercial buildings in a historic block of shops and restaurants called Larimer Square. Kevin Williams, who suffers from paraplegia and is confined to a wheelchair, visited Larimer Square frequently and noticed that architectural barriers prevented him from accessing many of the stores. Specifically, a 5.5-inch iron stoop at the entrance of one of the buildings owned by Hermanson blocked wheelchair access. In addition, the door to the store was recessed from the storefront and added another barrier to wheelchair access.

    Williams brought suit against Hermanson under the Americans with Disabilities Act. At trial, Williams introduced a conceptual sketch drawn by an architectural consultant of a ramp design that would provide wheelchair accessibility. The designer was able to offer a rough construction cost estimate of $10,000. On cross-examination, it became clear that the designer had not worked all the design features of the architectural barriers into his drawing. Williams also introduced testimony by an accountant who testified that installing the ramps would have immaterial financial impacts and would be easily accomplished. The lower court found for the building owner after concluding that Williams did not meet the burden of showing the suggested method of barrier removal was "readily achievable." On appeal, what result? [*Colorado Cross Disability Coalition v. Hermanson Family Limited Partnership*, 264 F.3d 999 (10th Cir. 2001).]

7. In an effort to minimize the adverse effects on the supply of housing for low-income, elderly, and disabled persons caused by the conversion or demolition of hotel rooms, San Francisco passed the Residential Hotel Unit Conversion and Demolition Ordinance, which made it unlawful to eliminate a residential hotel without first obtaining a conversion permit.

    To obtain a permit, applicants were required to (1) construct new residential units comparable to the converted ones; (2) construct or rehabilitate housing for low-income, disabled, or elderly persons; or (3) pay an "in lieu fee" equal to the replacement site acquisition and construction costs.

    Owners of the San Remo Hotel sought to convert the hotel from mixed residential-tourist use to all tourist use. They paid an in lieu fee of $567,000 in return for the permit, then sued to recover the fee. They argued that the ordinance violated the California Constitution, which provides: "Private property may be taken or damaged for public use only when just compensation, ascertained by a jury unless waived, has first been paid to, or into court for, the owner." Was the conversion fee a compensable taking? [*San Remo Hotel LP v. San Francisco*, 41 P.3d 87 (Cal. 2002).]

8. Vinton Watson, an avid race car driver, owned and kept several figure eight racing cars in an unenclosed parking lot. The City of Indianola subsequently adopted a land-use ordinance requiring the enclosure of "figure eight cars," among other racing vehicles, when two or more such cars are present. Watson sued the City, arguing that the ordinance created an uncompensated regulatory taking by requiring him to install a fence and thereby reducing the overall value of the property. The district court applied the takings standard from *Penn Central* and found for the City. The court determined that the erection of a fence did not cause a "physical invasion" and that the City had passed the ordinance for a legitimate public purpose, namely, the promotion of "community aesthetics." On appeal, Watson argued that the court should have applied the alternative regulatory taking test that courts apply to physical invasions of private property, as in *Nollan* and *Dolan*. Who is right? What public policies are implicated? [*Iowa Assurance Corp. v. City of Indianola, Iowa*, 650 F.3d 1094 (8th Cir. 2011).]

CORPORATE GOVERNANCE, OWNERSHIP, AND CONTROL

CHAPTER 19

FORMS OF BUSINESS ORGANIZATIONS

INTRODUCTION

CHOOSING THE PROPER FORM OF BUSINESS ENTITY

One of the first questions facing any entrepreneur starting a business is which form of business organization will best suit the enterprise. In weighing the advantages and disadvantages associated with the various forms, four considerations take on primary importance. First, to what extent will the personal assets of the founders and investors be exposed to the liabilities of the business? Second, which format will make the business most attractive to potential investors, lenders, and employees? Third, what costs are associated with creating and maintaining the organization? Finally, how can taxes be minimized?

Founders enjoy a broad range of options. The decision on the entity form comes in the earliest stages in the life of a business, but it is nonetheless a crucial one. Changing the form of organization can be very costly. Not only will administrative and legal fees be incurred, but a change may also give rise to tax liability or cause a business opportunity to be lost. Thus, at the outset of their venture, entrepreneurs should carefully consider its expected evolution and choose the form of organization accordingly. In addition, once the form of entity is chosen, its managers must be diligent to comply with all statutory requirements.

CHAPTER OVERVIEW

This chapter begins with an examination of the advantages and disadvantages of the most frequently used forms of business organizations: sole proprietorships, general and limited partnerships, limited liability partnerships, corporations (including S corporations), and limited liability companies, as well as a new vehicle for socially motivated firms, the benefit corporation. Next, the chapter summarizes the basic tax treatment of these different entities. The remainder of the chapter offers a more detailed discussion of how partnerships and corporations are structured and operated. Chapter 20 discusses the fiduciary duties of corporate officers, directors, and controlling shareholders and how power is allocated between the shareholders and the directors of a corporation in contested contests for corporate control.

SOLE PROPRIETORSHIPS

The sole proprietorship is the simplest and most prevalent form of business enterprise in the United States. In a *sole proprietorship*, one individual owns all of the assets of the business and is solely and personally liable for all of its debts, contract obligations, and tort liabilities. In other words, the sole proprietor is the business. Any individual who conducts business without creating a separate organization is operating as a sole proprietorship.

There are no formal requirements for forming a sole proprietorship. If, however, the business operates under a *fictitious business name*—that is, a name other than the name of the owner—then that name must be registered with the state. A sole proprietorship ends on the discontinuation of the business or the death of the proprietor, whichever is earlier.

Advantages of a sole proprietorship include the flexibility afforded by having one person in complete control of the business. Also, because a sole proprietorship can be created without formal agreements or state filings, it is the easiest and least costly form of business organization to set up. Sole proprietorships pay only one level of income tax—the proprietor reports income and losses from the business on his or her personal tax returns. Finally, the proprietor receives all of the profits generated by the business.

If the business loses money, however, the proprietor alone bears liability for the losses, and all of his or her assets are therefore at risk. This element of risk is the major disadvantage of the sole proprietorship. In addition, it is more difficult for sole proprietorships to raise capital. A sole proprietor can only tap personal funds and borrow money.

GENERAL PARTNERSHIPS

A *general partnership* is created when two or more persons agree to place their money, efforts, labor, or skills in a business and to share the profits and losses.[1] Their agreement can be express or implied, but they must share in real profits, not just receive wages or compensation.

Absent an express agreement to the contrary, each partner has some control over the business, and each may have the authority to bind the partnership with respect to third parties. In some respects, a partnership is like a marriage or a family. Its members share not only the benefits of the relationship but the burdens as well.

A partnership is treated as an entity separate from its partners and can acquire property in its own name. Property that is not acquired in the name of the partnership is nonetheless partnership property if the instrument transferring title refers to (1) the person taking title as a partner or (2) the existence of the partnership.

One of the key advantages of a partnership is that it allows for a wide variety of operational and profit-sharing arrangements. In essence, partners may agree to any terms in forming a partnership as long as they are not illegal or contrary to public policy. An example of this flexibility is that partners may contribute either capital or services to the partnership. Suppose Abigail and Caroline decide to form a partnership, called Rad Waves, to manufacture windsurfing equipment. Caroline contributes the start-up and operating capital, and Abigail contributes only her management services. Even though Abigail has not contributed capital to the partnership, she is (unless agreed otherwise) an equal partner with Caroline in Rad Waves.

Like a sole proprietorship, a partnership has the advantage of being subject to only one level of tax. Though it must file an informational return with the Internal Revenue Service (IRS), a partnership does not pay income taxes as a separate entity. Instead, the profit earned (or loss incurred) by the partnership (whether distributed or not) "passes through" to the individual partners, who report it as income (or loss) on their individual returns. Thus, a partnership is a *pass-through entity*.

Unlike a sole proprietorship, which terminates on the death of the owner, a partnership is not automatically dissolved on a partner's death, bankruptcy, or withdrawal. Instead, the partners holding a majority of the partnership interests may elect to continue the general partnership within ninety days after the occurrence of such an event.

General partnerships face a disadvantage similar to sole proprietorships in that individual partners are subject to personal liability for the obligations of the partnership. Thus, if the partnership is unable to pay its debts, honor its contracts, or satisfy its tort liabilities, the creditors of the partnership have claims against the assets of individual partners.

JOINT VENTURES

A *joint venture* is a one-time partnership of two or more persons for a specific purpose, such as the construction of a hydroelectric dam or a cogeneration plant. Like a general partnership, a joint venture requires that the parties (1) share a community of interest; (2) have the mutual right to direct and govern; (3) share the partnership's profits and losses; and (4) combine their property, money, effort, skill, or knowledge in the undertaking. Unlike a general partnership, a joint venture is not a continuing relationship; it terminates when the project is completed.

In a joint venture, the authority of one member to bind the partnership is more limited than in a general partnership. To avoid inadvertently conferring apparent authority to bind the other members, a joint venture should make it clear in its dealings with third parties that it is a joint venture and not a partnership. This distinction should be reflected in the entity's name and in the recitation of its legal status in its contracts.

LIMITED LIABILITY PARTNERSHIPS

The *limited liability partnership (LLP)* is designed primarily for groups of professionals, such as law firms and accounting firms. LLPs are created by filing the appropriate forms with a central state agency. A major advantage of the LLP form for existing partnerships, such as law firms and accounting firms, is that they can attain LLP status without significant modification of the business's partnership agreement. Like other forms of partnerships, LLPs retain pass-through taxation treatment.

The main function of an LLP is to insulate its partners from *vicarious liability* for certain partnership obligations, such as liability arising from the *malpractice*, or negligent or wrongful conduct, of another partner. Partners in an LLP usually have unlimited liability for their own malpractice.

State LLP statutes are not uniform, however. Most statutes provide that liability will be limited at least for debts and obligations arising from the malpractice of other partners. However, a few states, such as Minnesota and New York, protect partners from commercial liabilities (such as trade debt) as well.[2] This expanded protection further narrows the distinction between an LLP and a limited liability company.

---

1. Section 101(6) of the Revised Uniform Partnership Act (RUPA) of 1997 defines a partnership as "an association of two or more persons to carry on as co-owners a business for profit." This discussion is based on the RUPA, which has been adopted by a majority of the states.

2. Elizabeth G. Hester, *Keeping Liability at Bay*, Bus. L. Today, Jan.–Feb. 1996, at 60.

LIMITED PARTNERSHIPS

A *limited partnership* is a special type of partnership consisting of general partners and limited partners. *General partners* of a limited partnership remain jointly and severally liable for partnership obligations (just like partners in a general partnership), and they are responsible for the management of the partnership. In contrast, *limited partners* assume no liability for partnership debts beyond the amount of capital they have contributed, and they have no right to participate in the management of the partnership.

Limited partnerships are often used to raise capital—the limited liability for limited partners makes them attractive to investors. Returning to the Rad Waves example, suppose the general partners desire to raise capital to finance a sportswear line to promote their other products. To do so, they restructure their partnership as a limited partnership with Abigail and Caroline remaining as general partners. They can now offer an investor a limited partnership interest in the business, renamed Rad Waves, L.P. If Olivia contributes $1,000 to the partnership, she becomes a limited partner in Rad Waves (assuming compliance with the relevant state statute), and her personal liability for Rad Waves' obligations is limited to her $1,000 investment.

This ability to attract investors with the assurance of limited liability is the main advantage of a limited partnership. A limited partnership is more difficult to create than a general partnership. Unlike a general partnership, a limited partnership does not come into existence until a certificate of limited partnership has been filed with the appropriate state agency. Moreover, courts generally take a strict approach to the formal requirements of limited partnership status. If a partnership runs afoul of those requirements, courts will treat it as a general partnership instead.

CORPORATIONS

A *corporation* is an organization authorized by state law to act as a legal entity distinct from its owners. As a separate legal entity, the corporation has its own name and operates with specified powers to achieve the specific purposes set out in its *corporate charter* (also called its *articles of incorporation* or *certificate of incorporation*). Most charters give corporations the broad power to engage in any lawful business. Corporations are owned by *shareholders* (also called *stockholders*), who have purchased an ownership stake in the business. The *board of directors*, which is elected by the shareholders, has central decision-making authority. The board of directors typically employs officers to manage the day-to-day operations of the business.

One of the most attractive features of the corporation is that the liability of its shareholders is limited to their investments. Only the corporation itself is responsible for its liabilities. (An important exception to this general rule, the piercing the corporate veil theory, is discussed later in this chapter.) This cap on liability permits entrepreneurs and investors to undertake risky ventures without the worry that they will lose personal assets if things go badly.

Another benefit of a corporation is its ability to raise significant capital by selling transferable ownership shares of corporate stock (also known as equity) to investors. Finally, corporations have the advantage of perpetual life. Thus, if a key investor dies or decides to sell his or her interest in the business, the corporation as an entity continues to exist and to conduct business.

C Corporations

The main disadvantage of the corporate form of organization is that it is usually subject to two levels of taxation: both corporate and shareholder unless it is eligible for and elects S corporation status (discussed below). Any corporation not meeting the requirements for an S corporation is automatically a *C corporation* (so-named because it is taxed in accordance with the rules set forth in Subchapter C of the Internal Revenue Code). A C corporation pays tax on the income generated by the business, and the shareholders pay tax on that same income when it is distributed as dividends.

S Corporations

Some closely held corporations can avoid this double taxation by electing to be treated as S corporations under Subchapter S of the Internal Revenue Code. An *S corporation* is taxed as a pass-through entity. In other words, the corporation itself is not taxed on its income; rather, the shareholders pay tax on their pro rata shares of the corporation's income. An election to be taxed under Subchapter S does not affect the status of the organization as a corporation for state corporate law purposes. Any corporation that has not elected to be an S corporation or that fails to continue to meet the requirements for an S corporation is automatically a C corporation.

To qualify for S corporation status, a corporation must satisfy the following requirements:

1. The corporation must have no more than 100 shareholders, all of whom must be individuals who are citizens of the United States or U.S. resident aliens, or certain types of tax-exempt organizations, trusts, or estates.

2. The corporation must have only one class of stock.

3. The corporation must be domestic.

4. The corporation must file a timely election signed by all the shareholders to be treated as an S corporation.

5. The corporation must not be an ineligible corporation, which includes certain financial institutions, insurance companies, and domestic international sales corporations.[3]

---

3. Internal Revenue Service, *S Corporations, available at* http://www.irs.gov/businesses/small/article/0,,id=98263,00.html (last updated Jan. 18, 2012).

Close Corporations

Some states have enacted laws that give close corporations extra operating flexibility. A *close corporation* is a corporation that (1) has elected in its charter to be treated as a close corporation and (2) has a "small" number of shareholders, typically no more than thirty. A corporation must elect to become a close corporation by stating in its certificate of incorporation that it is a close corporation; otherwise, regardless of the number of shareholders, the corporation will not be treated as a close corporation.

State close corporation laws permit significant departures from the formalities required of traditional corporations.[4] Under some state statutes, if a close corporation's shareholders agree not to observe corporate formalities relating to meetings of directors or shareholders in connection with the management of its affairs, then the bypassing of these formalities may not be considered a factor in deciding whether to pierce the corporate veil and hold the shareholders personally liable. In addition, many statutes permit the shareholders of a close corporation to manage the corporation directly—instead of delegating that responsibility to the directors or officers—as long as a certain percentage of the shareholders agree to this in writing.

Closely Held Corporations

It is important to distinguish between a close corporation—one that conforms to the rules set forth by the state of incorporation to legally qualify as such—and a closely held corporation. A *closely held corporation* may have any number of shareholders, but it is characterized by the absence of a market for its stock.[5] If a court characterizes a corporation as closely held, it will often impose a greater duty of loyalty and care on the corporation's directors and majority shareholders. These impositions are *not* codified, however, and exist only in common law and traditional business practices.[6]

LIMITED LIABILITY COMPANIES

A *limited liability company (LLC)* combines the tax advantages of a pass-through entity with the limited liability advantages of a corporation. Like corporations and limited partnerships, the LLC is a creature of state law. However, as discussed below, many LLC statutes give the founders and investors flexibility to shape their duties and responsibilities by contract. To form an LLC, a charter document must be filed with the appropriate state agency (usually the office of the secretary of state). This LLC charter document is typically called the *articles of organization* (as in California) or the *certificate of formation* (as in Delaware). The name of the business must include the initials L.L.C. or the words Limited Liability Company.

The owners of an LLC are called *members*. The rights, obligations, and powers of the members, managers, and officers are set forth in an *operating agreement*. The members elect the *managers* who, like a board of directors, are responsible for managing the business, property, and affairs of the company. The managers appoint the officers of the company.

Unless a business is organized as a corporation under state law or is publicly held, the IRS's "check the box" regulations permit the founders to decide whether the entity is to be taxed as a corporation or a pass-through entity. State-law corporations and publicly traded entities are always taxed as corporations. Accordingly, LLCs are not taxed at the firm level unless they elect to be taxed as corporations.

The LLC form of business organization offers the advantages of both the limited partnership and the S corporation without their respective drawbacks. Properly formed LLCs are taxed as partnerships, but unlike the general partners in limited partnerships, even the controlling persons in LLCs can limit their liability to the amount invested. Moreover, all owners of an LLC can participate fully in the management of the business. Like a partnership, an LLC can have flexible allocations of profits and losses. The main advantage of the LLC form over the S corporation is the lack of restrictions on shareholders and the ability to have more than one class of securities. Specifically, in contrast to an S corporation, there is no limit on the number of members an LLC can have, and its investors can be corporations, partnerships, and foreigners.

One disadvantage of the LLC form of business organization is the cost of preparing a customized operating agreement. Although standardized forms[7] provide a good starting point for drafting, they must be tailored to the individual company and the needs of its members. The courts have made it clear that the operating agreement "defines the scope, structure, and personality of limited liability companies."[8]

For example, the Delaware Limited Liability Company Act provides, "It is the policy of this chapter to give the maximum effect to the principle of freedom of contract and to the enforceability of limited liability company

---

4. *See, e.g.*, CAL. CORP. CODE § 300(e).

5. Donahue v. Rodd Electrotype Co. of New England, 328 N.E.2d 505 (Mass. 1975).

6. For more on closely held corporations and how they are operated, see American Bar Association Committee on Corporate Laws, *Managing Closely Held Corporations: A Legal Guidebook*, 58 BUS. LAW. 1077–126 (2003).

7. *See, e.g.*, GUIDE TO ORGANIZING AND OPERATING A LIMITED LIABILITY COMPANY IN CALIFORNIA (Allan B. Dubott ed., 2001), published by the Partnerships and Unincorporated Business Organizations Committee of the Business Law Section of the State Bar of California. This guide includes annotated sample short-form and long-form operating agreements and other useful exemplars.

8. R&R Capital, LLC v. Buck & Doe Run Valley Farms, LLC, 2008 Del. Ch. LEXIS 115, at *1 (Aug. 19, 2008).

agreements."[9] Section 18-1101(c) further provides that "[t]o the extent that a member or manager has duties (including fiduciary duties) to a limited liability company or to another member or manager . . . the member's or manager's . . . duties may be expanded or restricted or eliminated by provisions in the limited liability company agreement . . . ."[10]

The members may not enter into an agreement that contravenes any mandatory provisions of the Delaware LLC Act, but the mandatory provisions are generally intended to protect third parties, not necessarily the contracting members. As Delaware Chancellor Chandler explained, "The allure of the limited liability company . . . would be eviscerated if the parties could simply petition this court to renegotiate their agreements when relationships sour."[11] Although the LLC Act explicitly bars members from "eliminat[ing] the implied contractual covenant of good faith and fair dealing,"[12] courts are loathe to interject duties not required by the Act or to invalidate waivers of obligation set forth in the operating agreement, especially when the members are all sophisticated parties. Although the implied covenant of good faith and fair dealing "requires a 'party in a contractual relationship to refrain from arbitrary or unreasonable conduct which has the effect of preventing the other party to the contract from receiving the fruits' of the bargain,"[13] the mere exercise of contractual rights, without more, cannot constitute a breach of the implied covenant of good faith and fair dealing. Thus, the implied covenant "is not a panacea for the disgruntled litigant" and should not be used to fill a gap in a contract with an implied term unless it was clear from the contract that the "parties would have agreed to proscribe the act later complained of . . . had they thought to negotiate with respect to the matter."[14] So, for example, the Delaware Court of Chancery upheld provisions in an operating agreement whereby the members waived their right to seek dissolution of the LLC or to appoint a receiver.[15]

In the following case, the court considered the contours of the covenant of good faith and fair dealing.

---

9. 6 DEL. CODE § 18-1101 (b).

10. 6 DEL. CODE § 18-1101 (c).

11. *R&R Capital*, 2008 Del. Ch. LEXIS 115, at *8.

12. 6 DEL. CODE § 18-1101 (c).

13. Dunlap v. State Farm Fire & Cas. Co., 878 A.2d. 434, 442 (Del. 2005).

14. Fisk Ventures, LLC v. Segal, 2008 WL 1961156 at *10 (Del. Ch. May 7, 2008) (Case 19.1).

15. *R&R Capital*, 2008 Del. Ch. LEXIS 115.

| A CASE IN POINT | *Summary* | Case 19.1 |

Fisk Ventures, LLC v. Segal

Delaware Court of Chancery
2008 WL 1961156 (Del. Ch. May 7, 2008).

FACTS Dr. Andrew Segal founded Genitrix, LLC, a Delaware limited liability company, in 1996 to develop and market biomedical technology. Equity in Genitrix was divided into three classes of membership. In exchange for the patent rights Segal transferred to the LLC, Segal's capital account was credited with $500,000, and he retained approximately 55% of the Class A membership interest. The remainder of the Class A interest was granted to other individuals not involved in this suit. Segal originally served as both president and chief executive officer of Genitrix.

In the initial round of financing, H. Fisk Johnson contributed $843,000 in return for a sizable portion of the Class B membership interest. The remainder of the Class B interest was owned by Fisk Ventures, LLC and Stephen Rose. The Class B investors were granted a put right whereby they could require the company to purchase any or all of their Class B membership interest at any time at a price determined by an independent appraisal. Various other investors contributed more than $1 million for the Class C membership. The Class C investors were mostly passive, leaving the power in the LLC essentially divided between the Class A and Class B members.

The agreement provided that the board of member representatives was responsible for managing the business and affairs of the company and required a 75% vote of the board for most decisions. The board initially consisted of four members, two appointed by Johnson and two appointed by Segal.

From its inception, Genitrix was strapped for cash. After Segal told the board that the company would require $2.6 million for human trials, Johnson stated that he was unwilling to be the sole financier of the company. Johnson and Fisk Ventures offered to contribute another $2 million in convertible debt if the company agreed to try to raise an additional $5 million

CONTINUED

from other investors over the following two years. During the course of negotiating the terms of the Fisk Ventures note, Segal proposed that the Class B put right be suspended. The Class B members refused to suspend or relinquish this right, although they did indicate that they had no immediate or foreseeable intention of exercising it. Segal's efforts to raise the additional $5 million ultimately failed. The balance of power then shifted, and the board was expanded to five seats. The Class B members were given the right to appoint a representative to the newly created seat, and Segal was replaced as CEO by Chris Pugh, another employee of Genitrix. In August 2006, Pugh left Genitrix to work for another firm, leaving just Segal and another employee. The other employee left in May 2007, leaving the company with no office, no capital funds, no grant funds, and no revenue. Although the Class B members invited Segal to propose terms under which they might purchase his interest in the company, the Class B members rejected those terms in June 2007. Fisk Ventures subsequently sued to dissolve Genitrix. Segal counterclaimed against Fisk Ventures and Johnson, arguing that they had breached the LLC agreement, the implied covenant of good faith and fair dealing implicit in the agreement, and their fiduciary duty to the company. The case against Johnson was dismissed on procedural grounds.

ISSUE PRESENTED Under what circumstances will a member's exercise of its negotiated veto and put rights constitute a breach of the operating agreement, the implied covenant of good faith and fair dealing, or the member's fiduciary duty to the founder?

SUMMARY OF OPINION The Delaware Court of Chancery dismissed the breach-of-contract claims because Segal had failed to allege breaches of any duties set forth in the operating agreement. The court noted that the agreement gave both the Class A and Class B members specified rights and protections and in no way did it

> obligate one class to acquiesce to the wishes of the other simply because the other believes its approach is superior or in the interest of the Company. To find otherwise—that is to find that the court must decide whose business judgment was more in keeping with the LLC's best interest—would cripple the policy underlying the LLC Act promoting freedom of contract.

The court found no evidence that any of the Class B board representatives had acted with gross negligence or willful misconduct, in bad faith, or in knowing violation of the law. The court recognized that perhaps Genitrix would have been able to obtain financing if the Class B members had been willing to relinquish their put right, but it stated that their refusal to do so was not in bad faith.

The court also rejected Segal's claim that Fisk had violated fiduciary duties to him. The operating agreement eliminated fiduciary duties to the maximum extent permitted by law when it flatly stated that members had no duties other than those expressly articulated in the agreement. Section 18-1101(c) of the Delaware Limited Liability Company Act specifically provides that "to the extent that a member or manager has duties, including fiduciary duties, to a limited liability company or to another member or manager, the members' or managers' duties may be expanded or restricted or eliminated by provisions in the limited liability company agreement. . . ." Thus, a member's exercise of its negotiated veto and put rights did not violate the implied covenant of good faith and fair dealing or the member's fiduciary duty to the founder.

RESULT Segal's claims for breach of contract, breach of the implied covenant of good faith and fair dealing, and breach of fiduciary duty against Fisk were dismissed.

COMMENTS The court observed:

> [A]nyone in Dr. Segal's position would be understandably frustrated by the demise of Genitrix, a company in which he has invested monetary, temporal, intellectual, and emotional resources. Nevertheless, such frustration cannot justify the *post hoc* refashioning of the bargain he struck with Johnson and the Class B investors in the Class B agreement.

Section 409(a) of the New York Limited Liability Company Law provides that "[a] manager shall perform his or her duties as a manager . . . in good faith and with that degree of care that an ordinarily prudent person in a like position would use under similar circumstances." New York courts have held that managers of an LLC have a fiduciary duty to the limited liability company (breaches of which can be addressed in a derivative action brought on behalf of the company)[16] and may also owe a fiduciary duty directly to the other members of the LLC.[17] For example, one court held that the managing member of a New York LLC had a fiduciary duty to a co-member to make full disclosure of all material facts.[18] Thus, the extent of managers' duties to other members and the ability of members to eliminate those duties by contract vary by state.[19]

BENEFIT CORPORATIONS

Another new and developing form of business corporation is the *benefit corporation (B corporation)*. A B corporation is a for-profit corporation that uses the power of business to solve social and environmental problems.[20] B corporations are required to "have a purpose of creating general public benefit" in addition to their other corporate purposes.[21] (A somewhat similar new type of entity with both business and charitable purposes is the *low-profit limited liability company*, also called an "*L3C.*") Benefit corporations must distribute to shareholders an annual benefit report providing information about their social and environmental performance benchmarked against a third-party standard.

Importantly, directors of B corporations have no duty to maximize shareholder value even when there is a change of control. Instead, they are required to consider the effects of any action on (1) the ability of the corporation to accomplish its benefit purpose; (2) the corporation's shareholders; (3) the employees and workforce of the corporation and its suppliers; (4) customers; (5) the community; (6) the environment; and (7) "the short-term and long-term interests of the benefit corporation, including benefits that may accrue to the benefit corporation from its long-term plans and the possibility that these interests may be best served by the continued independence of the benefit corporation."[22] The directors may also take other

factors into account, such as the intent and conduct of any potential acquirer. Importantly, directors of a B corporation have no duty to give priority to the interests of any one group over the interests of another unless the certificate of incorporation so provides.

As of January 31, 2012, seven states (including California, New York, and Virginia) have enacted benefit corporation legislation, and the legislation is pending in three states: Michigan, Pennsylvania, and North Carolina.[23] There are more than 450 certified B corporations in over sixty industries.

INCOME TAX CONSIDERATIONS

The analysis that follows is concerned solely with federal income tax consequences under the Internal Revenue Code of 1986, as amended and in force as of January 1, 2012. Many state income tax provisions follow the federal rules, but there can be substantial differences. Because provisions in the tax laws change often, it is more important to understand the general issues than to strive for a detailed knowledge of the tax laws for any given year.

Comparing Taxable Entities with Pass-Through Entities

The tax treatment of C corporations is different from that of pass-through entities (such as partnerships, S corporations, and LLCs) in several respects. Each may have favorable or unfavorable tax consequences, depending on the circumstances.

Property Transfers

Because a C corporation is a separate taxable entity, a transfer of cash or any other kind of property between the corporation and its owners is a taxable transaction unless it comes within one of the statutory exceptions in Subchapter C. It is easier to transfer property to and from a partnership or an LLC on a tax-free basis than it is with either a C corporation or an S corporation. For example, a transfer of property to either type of corporation in exchange for stock is tax-free only if the persons transferring the property own, immediately after the transaction, 80% or more of the stock of the corporation to which the property is transferred. In contrast, an exchange of property for a share in a partnership is tax-free regardless of the transferor's percentage share in the partnership.

Similarly, property that has appreciated in value may be more easily distributed tax-free from a partnership or an LLC than from a corporation. Neither the partnership nor the LLC is subject to tax on the appreciated property, and the partner receiving the property is not taxed until

16. Tzolis v. Wolf, 884 N.E.2d 1005 (N.Y. 2008).

17. DeFazio v. Wallis, 2009 WL 2207556 (N.Y. Sup. Dec. 7, 2009).

18. Salm v. Feldstein, 20 A.D.3d 469, 799 N.Y.S.2d 104 (2d Dept. 2005).

19. *See generally* Thomas M. Madden, *Do Fiduciary Duties of Managers and Members of Limited Liability Companies Exist as with Majority Shareholders of Closely Held Corporations?*, 12 DUQ. BUS. L.J. 211 (2010).

20. *What Is a B Corp?*, B LAB, *available at* http://bcorporation.net/about.

21. *See, e.g.*, N.Y. BUS .CORP. LAW § 1706.

22. *See, e.g.*, CAL. CORP. CODE § 14620; N.Y. BUS. CORP. LAW § 1707.

23. *Benefit Corp Information Center: State by State Status*, B LAB, *available at* http://www.benefitcorp.net/.

he or she subsequently sells it. This can be particularly important for venture capital funds, which often make distributions of illiquid stock in the portfolio companies in which the fund has invested. If the fund is organized as a partnership or LLC, these securities can be distributed to the partners or members tax-free, with no tax due until the partner or member sells the securities. In contrast, a corporation will be taxed on the appreciation in value at the time of the transfer just as if it had sold the property for cash, and the shareholders will be taxed on the fair market value of the property they have received. Thus, with a C corporation, there will be both a corporate-level tax and a shareholder-level tax on the distribution. For an S corporation, the taxable income is passed through and will be taxed only at the shareholder level.

Cash Distributions

The income of a C corporation is taxed at the corporate level when earned, and it is taxed again at the individual level when it is distributed. This double taxation does not occur with the other forms of business organizations. This difference alone may make a pass-through entity preferable to a C corporation as the chosen form of business organization.

Double taxation can be reduced in two ways. First, the tax liability of the corporation can be reduced to the extent that corporate income can be offset by tax-deductible payments to shareholders. For example, if personal services are a major source of the corporation's income, payment of employee compensation to shareholders active in the business will reduce the corporation's taxable income. If capital investment is a major source of income, payment of interest or rent to shareholders may provide similar relief. Second, the tax liability of the shareholders can be reduced to the extent that the business income is retained by the corporation and not distributed to shareholders. However, the accumulated earnings of a corporation may be taxed if they are not being retained for a legitimate corporate business purpose.

Cash distributions from partnerships and S corporations are tax-free to the recipients up to the amount of their previous capital contributions less any income previously passed through to them. Distributions from C corporations, on the other hand, generally result in taxable dividend income to the shareholders.

Operating Losses

If the business operations of a C corporation produce a loss, as is frequently the case with start-up companies and real estate investments in their early years, the operating loss will be recognized at the corporate level. This means that the shareholders receive no tax benefits from the operating loss, and the corporation receives no benefit until it has operating income against which its prior losses can be deducted.

In contrast, if the same business is operated by a partnership, LLC, or S corporation, then the operating loss each year will be passed through to the individual partners or shareholders. They may, if certain tax law requirements are satisfied, deduct the operating loss from their other income. Under the limits on passive losses, only owners who materially participate in the business may deduct its losses from their other ordinary income (such as wages or interest). Passive investors may not deduct such losses from ordinary income, but they can use passive losses to offset passive gains (such as capital gains on the sale of stock).

Capitalization

The tax laws impose no restrictions on a C corporation's capitalization. As business needs require, the corporation may issue common stock, preferred stock, bonds, notes, warrants, options, and other instruments. These instruments may confer the right to varying degrees of control and varying shares of earnings and may be convertible, redeemable, or callable. The tax treatment of each type of capital instrument may differ from its classification by the corporation, however. For example, shareholder debt may be treated as stock if the corporation has too little *equity capital*, that is, capital received in exchange for shares in the ownership of the corporation. As a consequence, tax-deductible "interest" payments may be recast as nondeductible "dividends" that are taxable to the shareholders.

Allocation of Losses

Items of partnership (or LLC) income or loss generally can be allocated to specific partners (or members) at specific times as long as these allocations have a substantial economic effect apart from tax considerations. Thus, an LLC can allocate a disproportionate amount of losses or depreciation to a particular member in the early years and allocate a disproportionate amount of later income to the same member until the loss is recovered. This form of allocation may generate a valuable tax deferral for that member.

No comparable allocation can be made by a C corporation, except to a limited extent by capitalizing the corporation with different classes of stock and debt. An S corporation is even more limited in this respect. It may have only one class of stock, and all income and losses must be allocated strictly in proportion to stock ownership.

Ability to Raise Venture Capital

Although pass-through entities (such as partnerships, LLCs, and S corporations) offer many tax advantages, they are rarely used for a business that intends to raise money from venture capitalists. Instead, the C corporation is usually used for two reasons. First, most venture capital firms raise money from large institutional investors, such as pension funds, university endowments, and the like. Nonprofit entities such as these can invest in

IN BRIEF

Choice of Business Entity: Pros and Cons

The following chart lists the principal considerations in selecting the form of business entity and applies them to the C corporation, S corporation, general partnership, limited partnership, limited liability company, and limited liability partnership. The considerations are listed in no particular order, in part because their importance will vary depending on the nature of the business, its sources of financing, and the plan for providing financial returns to the owners (for example, distributions of operating income, a public offering, or a sale of the business). Other factors that are not listed will also influence the choice of entity. In addition, the "yes" or "no" format oversimplifies the applicability of certain attributes.

	C Corporation	S Corporation	General Partnership	Limited Partnership	Limited Liability Company	Limited Liability Partnership
Limited liability	Yes	Yes	No	Yes[a]	Yes	Yes[b]
Flow-through taxation	No	Yes	Yes	Yes	Yes	Yes
Simplicity/low cost	Yes	Yes	No	No	No	No
Limitations on eligibility	No	Yes	No	No	No	No
Limitations on capital structure	No	Yes	No	No	No	No
Ability to take public	Yes	Yes[c]	No[d]	No[d]	No[d]	No[d]
Flexible charter documents	No	No	Yes	Yes	Yes	Yes
Ability to change structure without tax	No	No	Yes	Yes	Yes	Yes
Favorable employee incentives (including incentive stock options)	Yes	Yes/No[e]	No[f]	No[f]	No[f]	No[f]
Qualified small business stock exclusion for gains	Yes[g]	No	No	No	No	No
Special allocations	No	No	Yes	Yes	Yes	Yes
Tax-free in-kind distributions	No	No	Yes	Yes	Yes	Yes

a. Limited liability for limited partners only; a limited partnership must have at least one general partner with unlimited liability.

b. Partners in LLPs generally are protected from liability for malpractice and other wrongful conduct of fellow partners; states are split on whether LLP partners can be held individually liable for other partnership liabilities, such as commercial debt.

c. An S corporation would convert to a C corporation upon a public offering because of the number of shareholders.

d. Although the public markets are generally not available for partnership offerings, partnerships (including LLPs) and LLCs can be incorporated without tax and then taken public.

e. Although an S corporation can issue incentive stock options, the inability to have two classes of stock limits favorable pricing of the common stock offered to employees.

f. Although partnership and LLC interests can be provided to employees, they are poorly understood by most employees. Moreover, tax-favored incentive stock options are not available.

g. A special low capital gains rate is available for stock of U.S. C corporations with not more than $50 million in gross assets at the time the stock is issued if the corporation is engaged in an active business and the taxpayer holds the stock for at least five years.

securities and receive their income and capital gains tax-free only if the issuer of the securities is not a pass-through entity. Otherwise, the nonprofits will be deemed to have received unrelated business income, which is fully taxable. Second, most start-ups want the ability to sell securities to outside investors at a significantly higher price than was paid by the founders at the outset. To justify the price differential, and avoid having some of the value of the founders' shares treated as employee compensation, companies issue two classes of stock: common stock to the founders and preferred stock to the outside investors. Because an S corporation cannot have more than one class of stock, the C corporation is usually the easiest vehicle to use.

AGENCY LAW AND LIMITED LIABILITY

It is critical for individuals acting on behalf of any business entity to make it clear whether they are acting on their own or as agents of a separate legal entity. Failure to do this can result in personal liability for the manager involved. For example, if a person signs a contract in his or her own name, without indicating the name of the business entity on behalf of which he or she is acting, then the person is personally liable if the undisclosed principal fails to perform its obligations.

In addition, owners of a limited liability entity who are active in the operation of the business can be held directly liable for their own tortious acts, as happened in the following case.

| A CASE IN POINT | *In the Language of the Court* | Case 19.2 |

Estate of Countryman v. Farmers Cooperative Association

Supreme Court of Iowa
679 N.W.2d 598 (Iowa 2004).

FACTS On Labor Day in 1999, an explosion caused by stray propane gas destroyed the home of Jerry Usovsky, killing seven people and seriously injuring several others. The survivors and the estates of the deceased filed a lawsuit based on several tort theories. Among those named in the complaint were Double Circle and Farmers Cooperative Association of Keota (Keota).

Double Circle, which delivered the propane prior to the accident, was a limited liability company, and Keota was its 95% owner. Keota's executive board also served as Double Circle's executive board. An agreement between Double Circle and Keota stated that Keota was responsible for Double Circle's "human resource and management safety" activities.

The complaint alleged that Keota was personally liable for the accident. Keota moved for summary judgment, arguing that the structure of Double Circle as an LLC protected Keota from personal liability as long as Keota operated within its prescribed duties as a limited liability manager of Double Circle. The trial court granted summary judgment, and the plaintiffs appealed.

ISSUE PRESENTED Can a member of an LLC be held personally liable in tort for its actions as a manager of the LLC?

OPINION CADY, J., writing on behalf of the Iowa Supreme Court:

The limited liability company, "LLC" as it is now known, is a hybrid business entity that is considered to have the attributes of a partnership for federal income tax purposes and the limited liability protections of a corporation. As such, it provides for the operational advantages of a partnership by allowing the owners, called members, to participate in the management of the business. Yet, the members and managers are protected from liability in the same manner shareholders, officers, and directors of a corporation are protected.

. . . .

Sections 490A.601 and 490A.603 of the [Iowa Limited Liability Company] Act generally provide that a member or manager of a limited liability company is not personally liable for acts or debts of the company solely by reason of being a member or manager, except in the following situations: (1) the ILLCA expressly provides for the person's liability; (2) the articles of organization provide for the person's liability; (3) the person has agreed in writing to be personally liable; (4) the person participates in tortious conduct; or (5) a shareholder of a corporation would be personally liable in the same situation, except that the failure to hold meetings and related formalities shall not be considered.

While liability of members and managers is limited, the statute clearly imposes liability when they participate in tortious conduct. This approach is compatible with the longstanding approach to liability in corporate settings, where, under general agency principles, corporate officers and directors can be liable for their torts even when committed in their capacity as an officer. This approach has been explained as follows: Agency law generally, and Iowa law in particular, has long recognized that if a person commits a tort while acting for another person, the tortfeasor is personally liable for the tort, even if the person for whom he is acting is also vicariously liable for the same wrong. In other words, a person's status as an agent confers no immunity with respect to the person's own tort liability. Thus, if a member of a limited liability company injures another person while working in the course of the firm's business, the member is personally liable for that harm along with the company, just as the member would be if he worked for a firm organized as a corporation, a partnership, or any other business form.

CONTINUED

Keota suggests that liability of an LLC member or manager for tortious conduct is limited to conduct committed outside the member or manager role. Yet, this approach is contrary to the corporate model and agency principles upon which the liability of LLC members and managers is based, and cannot be found in the language of the statute. We acknowledge that the "participation in tortious conduct" standard would not impose tort liability on a manager for merely performing a general administrative duty.

. . . .

It is also important to recognize that this case is not about holding an officer, director, or shareholder of Keota personally liable for participating in tortious conduct. Plaintiffs have not sued individual members of Keota. Instead, the lawsuit filed by the plaintiffs seeks to hold Keota liable for participating in certain torts as the designated manager of an LLC. . . . While members and managers of an LLC are generally not personally liable for the acts of an LLC, Keota must also be viewed as a separate "legal" person.

. . . .

We conclude that Keota is not protected from liability if it participated in tortious conduct in performing its duties as manager of Double Circle.

RESULT   The court found that Keota could potentially be liable and remanded the case back to the trial court.

CRITICAL THINKING QUESTIONS

1. If Keota were owned in part by another LLC, Company X, could the plaintiffs also hold Company X liable for the accident?

2. Under what circumstances would the members of the Keota executive board who also sat on the Double Circle executive board be personally liable to the members of Double Circle? To third parties injured by the tortious conduct of Double Circle?

PARTNERSHIP MECHANICS

This section describes in more detail how partnerships are formed, operated, and terminated.

Formation of a General Partnership

A general partnership can be created with nothing more than a handshake and a general understanding between the partners. For example, students agree to work together on a business plan; a baker and a chef agree to open a restaurant together; an engineer and a mechanic agree to design bicycles together—in each case, a partnership is formed. The intention of one party alone, however, cannot create a partnership. There must be a meeting of the minds. Hence, in the Rad Waves example, if Caroline viewed her agreement with Abigail as forming a partnership, but Abigail contemplated a mere employee–employer relationship, then there is no partnership.

A partnership does not require a minimum amount of capital in order to be formed. Partners usually contribute cash or property, or agree to provide personal services, to the partnership. In some instances, a partnership interest may be received as a gift. The partnership need not be given a name. There may or may not be a written partnership agreement.

Without a Written Agreement

If there is no written partnership agreement, the laws of the state where the parties are doing business will determine whether the relationship will be treated as a partnership or some other relationship, such as an agency. If the relationship is recognized as a partnership, state partnership laws will govern the partnership and prescribe the rights of the partners if there is no written agreement. Some provisions of those laws could lead to undesirable business results.

In the Rad Waves example, Abigail and Caroline could form a partnership with a simple oral agreement. Under state partnership law, however, Abigail and Caroline will be required to share the profits and losses equally. Furthermore, until the partnership is terminated, neither partner may withdraw capital without the consent of the other. If they admit a third partner, his or her death could terminate the partnership even if Abigail and Caroline prefer to continue it. These are just a few examples of the dangers of forming a partnership without a written partnership agreement.

In the following case, the Court of Appeal of California considered whether a partnership existed between two women who had discussed a business idea but never drafted documents expressly creating a partnership.

Holmes v. Lerner

Court of Appeal of California
88 Cal. Rptr. 2d 130 (Cal.
App. 1999).

In the Language of the Court — Case 19.3

FACTS Sandra Lerner was a successful entrepreneur and an experienced businessperson. She and her husband were the original founders of Cisco Systems. When Lerner sold her interest in Cisco, she received a substantial amount of money, which she invested, in part, in a venture capital limited partnership called "& Capital Partners."

Patricia Holmes met Lerner in late 1993, when Lerner visited Holmes's horse training facility to arrange for the training and boarding of two horses that Lerner was importing from England. In 1995, Lerner and Holmes traveled to England to attend a horse show and to make arrangements to ship the horses to the United States. On this trip, Lerner decided that she wanted to celebrate her fortieth birthday by going pub crawling in Dublin. Lerner was wearing what Holmes termed "alternative clothes" and black nail polish, and she encouraged Holmes to do the same. Holmes did not like black nail polish, however, and was unable to find a suitable color in the English stores. At Lerner's mansion outside London, Lerner gave Holmes a manicure kit, telling her to see if she could find a color she would like to wear. Holmes looked through the kit, tried different colors, and eventually developed her own purple color by layering a raspberry color over black nail polish. Lerner also found the color attractive.

On July 31, 1995, the two women returned from England and stayed at Lerner's West Hollywood condominium while they waited for the horses to clear quarantine. While sitting at the kitchen table, they discussed nail polish colors. Len Bosack, Lerner's husband, was in and out of the room during the conversations. For approximately an hour and a half, Lerner and Holmes worked with the colors in a nail kit to try to re-create the purple color Holmes had made in England so that they could have the color in a liquid form, rather than having to layer two colors.

Lerner said to Holmes: "This seems like a good [thing], it's something that we both like, and isn't out there. Do you think we should start a company?" Holmes responded: "Yes, I think it's a great idea." Lerner told Holmes that they would have to do market research and determine how to have the polishes produced, and that there were many things they would have to do. Lerner said: "We will hire people to work for us. We will do everything we can to get the company going, and then we'll be creative, and other people will do the work, so we'll have time to continue riding the horses." Holmes agreed that they would do those things. They did not separate out which tasks each of them would do, but planned to do it all together.

Lerner then called David Soward, the general partner of & Capital and her personal business consultant. Holmes heard her say, "Please check Urban, for the name, Urban Decay, to see if it's available and if it is, get it for us." Holmes knew that Lerner did not joke about business and was certain, from the tone of her voice, that Lerner was serious about the new business. The telephone call to secure the trademark for Urban Decay confirmed in Holmes's mind that they were forming a business based on the concepts they had originated in England and at the kitchen table that day.

Holmes knew that she would be taking the risk of sharing in losses as well as potential success, but the two friends did not discuss the details at that time. Lerner's housekeeper heard Lerner tell Holmes: "It's going to be our baby, and we're going to work on it together." After Holmes left, the housekeeper asked Lerner what gave her the idea to go into the cosmetics business, given that her background was in computers. Lerner replied: "It was all Pat's idea over in England, but I've got the money to make it work." Lerner told her housekeeper that she hoped to sell Urban Decay to Estée Lauder for $50 million.

Although neither Lerner nor Holmes had any experience in the cosmetics business, they began work on their idea immediately. They met frequently in August and September at Lerner's home and experimented with nail colors.

Prior to the first scheduled August meeting, Holmes told Lerner she was concerned about financing the venture. Lerner told her not to worry because Lerner thought they could convince Soward that the nail polish business would be a good investment. Holmes and Lerner

CONTINUED

discussed their plans for the company and agreed that they would attempt to build it up and then sell it. Lerner and Holmes discussed the need to visit chemical companies and hire people to handle the daily operations of the company. However, the creative aspect, ideas, inspiration, and impetus for the company came from Holmes and Lerner.

The participants in these meetings referred to them as "board meetings," even though there was no formal organizational structure and, technically, no board. They discussed financing, and Soward reluctantly agreed to commit $500,000 toward the project. Urban Decay was financed entirely by & Capital, the venture capital partnership composed of Soward as general partner and Lerner and her husband as the only limited partners. Neither Lerner nor Holmes invested any of their individual funds.

Lerner and Soward went to Kirker Chemical Company later in August 1995 and learned about mixing and manufacturing nail polish colors. Lerner discouraged Holmes from accompanying them. At the second board meeting, in late August, Soward introduced Wendy Zomnir, a friend of his former fiancée, as an advertising and marketing specialist. Holmes was enthusiastic about Zomnir, and they decided to hire her. At the conclusion of the September board meeting, after Holmes had left, Lerner and Soward secretly made Zomnir an offer of employment, which included a percentage ownership interest in Urban Decay. Holmes did not learn of the terms of the offer until a couple of meetings later, when Lerner or Soward referred to Zomnir as the "chief operating officer" of Urban Decay.

In early October, after Holmes learned of the secret offer to Zomnir, she asked Lerner to define her role at Urban Decay. Lerner responded, "Your role is anything you want it to be." When Holmes asked to discuss the issue in more detail, Lerner turned and walked away.

In December 1995, Urban Decay Cosmetics LLC was organized. Holmes asked for a copy of the articles of incorporation but was given only two pages showing the name and address of the company. On December 31, Holmes sent a fax to Lerner stating that it had been difficult to discuss her position in Urban Decay with Lerner. Holmes asked Lerner: "What are my responsibilities and obligations, and what are my rights or entitlements?" and "What are my current and potential liabilities and assets?" She requested that Lerner provide the information in writing. Soward intercepted the fax and called Holmes, asking: "What's going on?" Holmes explained that she wanted a written agreement, and Soward apologized, telling her that Lerner had asked him to get "something . . . in writing" to Holmes. Soward told Holmes that *no one* in the company had a written statement of their percentage interest in the company yet. Soward asked: "What do you want, 1 percent, 2 percent?" When Holmes did not respond, he told her that 5% was high for an idea. Holmes told him: "I'm not selling an idea. I'm a founder of this company." Soward exclaimed: "Surely you don't think you have fifty percent of this company?" Holmes told him that it was a matter between her and Lerner and that Soward should speak to Lerner. Soward agreed to talk to Lerner.

During January and February, an early press release stated: "The idea for Urban Decay was born after Lerner and her horse trainer, Pat Holmes, were sitting around in the English countryside." Lerner approved the press release. In February 1996, an article was printed in the *San Francisco Examiner* containing the following quote from Lerner: "Since we couldn't find good nail polish, in cool colors there must be a business opportunity here. Pat had the original idea. Urban Decay was my spin."

In March 1996, Holmes received a document from Soward offering her a 1% ownership interest in Urban Decay. Soward explained that Urban Decay had been formed as a limited liability company, which was owned by its members. For the first time, Holmes realized that she was now being asked to become a minor partner.

Holmes filed a complaint against Lerner and others claiming the existence of an oral contract making them partners. The trial court found in favor of Holmes, and Lerner appealed.

ISSUE PRESENTED   Can a general partnership be created through actions and words without any formal documentation?

CONTINUED

OPINION   MARCHIANO, J., writing for the Court of Appeal of California:

Holmes testified that she and Lerner did not discuss sharing profits of the business during the July 31 "kitchen table" conversation. Throughout the case, Lerner and Soward have contended that without an agreement to share profits, there can be no partnership. . . .

[The] statutory predecessor of the Uniform Partnership Act (UPA) defined a partnership as: "the association of two or more persons, for the purpose of carrying on business together, and dividing its profits between them."[24]

The applicable version of the UPA omitted the language regarding division of profits and defined a partnership as: "an association of two or more persons to carry on as co-owners a business for profit." When the legislature enacts a new statute, replacing an existing one, and omits express language, it indicates an intent to change the original act. We can only conclude that the omission of the language regarding dividing profits from the definition of a partnership was an intentional change in the law.

. . . .

Lerner and Soward argue that the agreement between Lerner and Holmes was too indefinite to be enforced. The cases they rely on do not support the argument. . . . The parties' outward manifestations must show that the parties all agreed "upon the same thing in the same sense." If there is no evidence establishing a manifestation of assent to the "same thing" by both parties, then there is no mutual consent to contract and no contract formation. The terms of a contract are reasonably certain if they provide a basis for determining the existence of a breach and for giving an appropriate remedy. There is no requirement, the intention to form a joint venture being otherwise present, that the parties must agree upon the post-acquisition management and operation of the property. In addition, there is nothing unusual about a partnership in which one party supplies an idea which the other party brings into a substantive form. Many businesses and great industrial organizations have sprouted from the germ of an idea in the mind of some man. When the idea is reduced to concrete form and put into action in the form of a business enterprise, an invention, a book, an opera or a theatrical production, the results of the idea are subject to private ownership. . . . The agreement between Holmes and Lerner was to take Holmes' idea and reduce it to concrete form. They decided to do it together, to form a company, to hire employees, and to engage in the entire process together.

. . . .

[T]he evidence is flatly and irreconcilably conflicting. A finding that no partnership had been formed, had one been made, would have had considerable evidentiary support. As the finding which was made of the formation and the existence of the partnership has ample support in evidence which was accepted by the trial judge as substantial and which was taken as true by him, we cannot disturb the judgment here.

RESULT   The Court of Appeal of California affirmed the trial court's decision that an express agreement to divide profits is not a prerequisite to proving the existence of a partnership.

CRITICAL THINKING QUESTIONS

1. How could Lerner and Holmes have avoided this dispute?
2. Did Lerner behave ethically?

24. CAL. CORP. CODE § 16001.

With a Written Agreement

A written partnership agreement can override many of the provisions of partnership statutes that could turn out to be undesirable to the partners. It can prevent future misunderstandings and also provide for a dispute resolution mechanism, such as arbitration.

A partnership agreement usually includes (1) the term of the partnership's existence, (2) the capital characteristics of the partnership, (3) the division of profits and losses between the partners, (4) partnership salaries or withdrawals, (5) the duties of the partners, and (6) the consequences to the partnership if a partner decides to sell his or her interest in the partnership or becomes incapacitated or dies. Also included are the name of the partnership, the names and addresses of the partners, the type of business to be conducted, and the location of the business.

Drafting a partnership agreement focuses the partners' attention on matters that they might not consider if they made less formal arrangements.[25] For example, will all partners have an equal voice in management? What limits will be placed on the managing partners? How will disputes be settled? May a partner be expelled? May new partners be admitted? If so, by what process?

Operation of a General Partnership

Unlike a corporation, which has a centralized board of directors and a staff of hired executives for decision making, a general partnership is characterized by direct owner management and control of the business. Each partner's assets are vulnerable to the poor business decisions of the fellow partners. It is therefore important that each partner have a voice in the business decisions of the partnership.

A partnership may choose to cede managerial control of the business to one or more of its partners. Unless the partners expressly agree otherwise, partnership law requires unanimous agreement of all partners on all but the most ordinary matters. If the partners in an informal partnership cannot agree on a decision, they may disband the partnership, distribute its assets, and terminate it.

Each partner is an agent of the partnership for the purpose of its business unless the partnership has filed with the secretary of state a statement specifying which partners have authority for entering into certain transactions on behalf of the partnership, as specified in sections 105 and 303 of the Revised Uniform Partnership Act (RUPA) (1997). Each partner in a general partnership is liable for the debts incurred by another partner acting in the name of the partnership if that partner had express authority to incur the debt or was carrying on the business of the partnership in the usual way.

For example, if Abigail and Caroline form Rad Waves as a general partnership, they will each be responsible for the full amount of any liabilities incurred by the partnership or by either partner acting within the scope of her authority as a partner. Hence, Caroline's personal assets can be seized if Rad Waves' partnership assets are insufficient to satisfy a judgment against Rad Waves. Caroline's personal assets might also be seized if Rad Waves breaches a contract entered into by Abigail on behalf of the partnership.

Fiduciary Duty

Partners owe one another certain fiduciary duties, in particular, a duty of loyalty and a duty of care. Partners must also discharge their duties to the partnership and to one another in accordance with the obligation of good faith and fair dealing.

Among the duty of loyalty obligations listed in the RUPA are (1) accounting to the partnership and holding as trustee for it any property, profit, or benefit; (2) refraining from dealing with the partnership as or on behalf of a party having an interest adverse to the partnership; and (3) refraining from engaging in grossly negligent or reckless conduct, intentional misconduct, or a knowing violation of the law.

Be aware, however, that although some states, such as Delaware, have adopted the RUPA in its entirety, many states have chosen to tailor their own version, creating subtle differences that can be significant. For example, the California Uniform Partnership Act implies a higher fiduciary duty than the RUPA by analogizing partnership law with trust law rather than with corporate law.[26]

Dissolution, Winding Up, and Termination of a General Partnership

Dissolution of a general partnership occurs when the partners no longer carry on the business together. A partnership may be dissolved for many reasons. The agreed term for the partnership may expire, or the partners may decide to dissolve the partnership prior to the expiration of the agreed term. A particular undertaking specified in the partnership agreement may be completed. One or more partners may desire to dissolve the partnership. (Unless there is an agreement to the contrary, withdrawal or death of a general partner results in the dissolution of the partnership.) A partner may be expelled, and the remaining partners may thereafter agree to terminate the partnership. A partner may die or go bankrupt, and the agreement may not provide for the partnership's continuation.

A partnership will also be dissolved if the business for which the partnership was formed becomes unlawful—for example, if there is a war between the countries of two or more of the partners. In such a case, the partnership will be dissolved regardless of the wishes of the partners. In other situations, a court may issue a decree of dissolution if a partner becomes disabled, insane, or otherwise unable to perform as a partner. Courts also have the power to dissolve a partnership when a partner willfully breaches the agreement or performs in such a manner as to make it impractical to carry on the partnership. Because the purpose of partnerships is to make a profit, a partnership may be dissolved by court decree if it becomes apparent that

---

25. *See* Eleena de Lisser, *Partnership Prenuptials*, WALL ST. J., Sept. 25, 1999, at 12.

26. Al Li, *Taking Care of Your Partners: A Brief Reminder of Fiduciary Duties in the Venture Firm*, GRAY CARY VENTURE SERVICES E-ALERT, July 2003.

the partnership is unprofitable and lacks any real prospect of success. If the partnership has reasonable prospects of earning money in the future, however, it may not be dissolved by court decree despite recent losses.

On dissolution, all of the partners' authority ceases except their authority to complete transactions begun but not yet finished and to wind up the partnership. *Winding up* involves settling the accounts and liquidating the assets of the partnership for the purpose of making distributions and terminating the concern. The liabilities and obligations of the partners do not end at dissolution; the partnership continues throughout the winding-up period.

During the winding-up process, the partners' fiduciary duties to one another continue. The winding-up partners may not run the business for their own benefit but must account as trustees to the withdrawing partners or to the estate of a deceased partner.

Termination occurs when all the partnership affairs are wound up and the partners' authority to act for the partnership is completely extinguished. A dissolved partnership may terminate or may be continued by a new partnership formed by the remaining partners (including perhaps the estate or heirs of a deceased partner).

LIMITED PARTNERSHIP REQUIREMENTS

The basic rules that govern formation, operation, and termination of general partnerships apply to limited partnerships as well. Some additional requirements are placed on limited partnerships, however.

Formal Requirements

In addition to the requirement that a certificate of limited partnership be filed with the appropriate state authority, most state statutes require that the partnership agreement clearly designate the limited partners as such. Any partnership that does not substantially meet this and other statutory requirements will be treated as a general partnership, with mutual liability and apparent authority attaching to each partner. A person who intended to be only a limited partner may face unlimited personal liability for all of the partnership's debts if there has not been substantial compliance in good faith with the formal requirements.

The Uniform Limited Partnership Act provides that persons who contributed capital to a business erroneously believing that they were becoming limited partners in a limited partnership will not be liable as general partners if, upon ascertaining the mistake, they promptly renounce their interest in the profits of the business.[27] A person who believed in good faith that he or she had become a limited

partner is liable only to third parties that both transacted business with the purported limited partnership before the certificate of limited partnership was filed and reasonably believed that the person was a general partner at the time of the transaction.[28]

Limited Participation

A limited partner's liability is limited unless he or she takes part in the control of the business. Thus, if limited partners have a voice in the business decisions of the partnership, they are opening themselves up to the possibility of liability beyond their original capital investment. Furthermore, limited partners may contribute money or property to the partnership, but generally not services. Hence, in the Rad Waves example, if Olivia assists with the design of the sportswear line, in most states her liability could exceed her original $1,000 capital contribution. Therefore, limited partners should not take part in any partnership activity beyond monitoring the progress of their investment and exercising such statutory rights as the right to vote on the removal of a general partner. Moreover, the limited partner's name cannot appear in the name of the partnership without incurring unlimited liability.

INCORPORATION

Incorporation is the process by which a corporation is formed. The corporate statutes of each state set forth the steps that must be taken to establish a corporation in that state. Many state statutes are based in whole or in part on the Model Business Corporation Act, an annotated uniform statute prepared by academics and practitioners. The state under whose laws a corporation is formed is called the corporation's *corporate domicile*. A corporation is not limited to doing business in its corporate domicile. It can conduct business as a *foreign corporation* in other states. Typically, to do so, it must file a statement of foreign corporation with the appropriate secretary of state and state taxing authority.

Where to Incorporate

Corporations may incorporate in any state; it need not be the state in which most of their business is located. Two important factors affect the decision of where to incorporate: (1) the costs of incorporation in a given state, and (2) the relative advantages and disadvantages of that state's corporation laws. If the corporation is privately held and its business will be conducted largely within one state, incorporation in that state is probably the best choice. If the corporation will be large from the outset or will be engaged in substantial interstate business, however, then

---

27. If such a renunciation is not effectuated, the putative limited partners face liability in an individual capacity for debts of the partnership. Reiman v. Int'l Hospitality Group, Ltd., 614 A.2d 925 (D.C. 1992).

28. *See, e.g.,* CAL. REVISED UNIF. LTD. P'SHIP ACT § 15633.

incorporation in a jurisdiction with the most advantageous corporate statutes and case law should be considered.

Corporation laws may be favorable either to management or to the shareholders. Some states, such as Delaware, are considered to be pro-management because their statutes and court decisions tend to give control on a wide range of issues to the officers and directors. Other states, such as California, make it difficult for corporate managers to do certain things without the approval and participation of the shareholders. These states are regarded as pro-shareholder.

Since the mid-1930s, Delaware has been considered the preeminent state for incorporation. Fifty percent of the companies on the New York and Nasdaq Stock Exchanges are incorporated in Delaware, and more than 65% of *Fortune* 500 companies are Delaware companies. Consequently, Delaware corporate law is considered the standard in America and much of the world.[29]

The Delaware General Corporation Law is a dynamic statute designed to give corporations maximum flexibility in ordering their affairs. The Delaware Court of Chancery, established in 1792, hears (without juries) all cases involving corporate law issues and has rendered thousands of written opinions interpreting virtually every provision of the Delaware General Corporation Law.[30]

An examination of the Delaware statute helps highlight some of the key corporate governance choices. The power to elect the board of directors is the primary way in which shareholders exercise control, and all jurisdictions provide for it. Delaware permits, but does not require, cumulative voting (discussed further below), which allows a minority shareholder greater opportunity to elect someone to the board. Delaware also permits a *staggered* (or *classified*) *board*, whereby directors serve for specified terms, usually three years, with only a fraction of them up for reelection at any one time. Delaware prohibits the removal of directors on a classified board without cause, unless the certificate of incorporation provides otherwise. Thus, a classified board makes it more difficult to replace the entire board at once, which can be important in a change-of-control contest. Although classified boards used to be the norm in Delaware, institutional investors have successfully pressured many large Delaware corporations to declassify their boards.

All corporations incorporated in California, except publicly traded companies, must have cumulative voting and cannot have a staggered board. In addition, as explained further in Chapter 20, Delaware permits broader

---

INTERNATIONAL SNAPSHOT

Before a business incorporates abroad, its management should consult a lawyer in the country in which the incorporation is to take place to be advised of the country's laws governing tax, labor, and corporate issues. Parties contemplating a partnership or joint venture should note that civil law jurisdictions usually do not recognize common law–style partnerships. Instead, they look through the partnership to the partners and view the partners as the legal owners.

---

limitations on directors' personal monetary liability than California.

The primary reason a company would choose to incorporate in California, or any other state rather than Delaware, is cost.[31] When deciding whether to incorporate in the local state or Delaware, entrepreneurs must weigh the advantages Delaware provides for managers against the expense of paying Delaware corporate franchise taxes, the expense of hiring lawyers familiar with Delaware law, and the possibility of having to defend a lawsuit in Delaware. Businesses incorporated in their local state often reincorporate in Delaware once they have grown large enough to justify the effort and expense of reincorporation.

How to Incorporate

To create a corporation, one or more incorporators must prepare the certificate or articles of incorporation (or the corporate charter). This document must be filed with the appropriate state governmental agency, usually the secretary of state for the jurisdiction that will become the corporate domicile.

The certificate of incorporation is generally quite short. For example, the Pennsylvania Business Corporation Law specifies that the certificate need only set forth the name of the corporation, the location and mailing address of the corporation's registered office in Pennsylvania, a brief statement of the purpose of the corporation, the term for which the corporation is to exist (which may be perpetual), the total number of shares that the corporation is authorized to issue, the name and mailing address of each of the incorporators, and a statement of the number of shares to be purchased by each.

Section 204 of the Pennsylvania Business Corporation Law, like most modern corporation statutes, goes on to provide that the purpose clause "may consist of or include a statement that the corporation shall have unlimited power to engage in and to do any lawful act concerning any or all lawful business for which corporations may be incorporated under this act." Pennsylvania's corporate law goes on to specify corporate powers, so there is no need to have a long purpose clause in the certificate of incorporation. Indeed, to do so invites trouble because one might inadvertently exclude an activity in which the corporation may later want to engage.

After the certificate of incorporation is filed, the incorporators adopt the *bylaws*, that is, the rules governing the corporation (including the number of authorized directors), and elect the initial board of directors. This can be done either at an organizational meeting or by unanimous written consent. The incorporators are exclusively empowered to place the directors in office. After electing the board of directors, the incorporators sign a written resignation. The directors then have an organizational meeting at which they (1) ratify the adoption of the bylaws by the incorporators or adopt new bylaws, (2) appoint officers, (3) designate a bank as depository for corporate funds, (4) authorize the sale of stock to the initial shareholders, and (5) determine the consideration to be received in exchange for such shares—cash, other property, or past services rendered to the corporation. Exhibit 19.1 outlines the steps required to form a corporation.

Defective Incorporation

Because a corporation exists only by statute, not by common law, any defect in the incorporation process can have the effect of denying corporate status. A business organization that was intended to function as a corporation but has failed to comply with the statutory requirements is in fact a partnership or, if there is only one shareholder, a sole proprietorship. The owners will not enjoy the protection of limited liability and can be held personally responsible for all debts of the enterprise. The courts have, however, developed several doctrines to avoid this result if it would be unfair.

De Jure Corporation

When incorporation has been done correctly, a *de jure corporation* is formed. This means that the entity is a corporation by right and cannot be challenged. Most jurisdictions will find de jure corporate status as long as the incorporators have substantially complied with the incorporation requirements. For example, substantial compliance will be found even if the incorporators failed to obtain a required signature or submitted an improper notarization.

De Facto Corporation

If the incorporators cannot show substantial compliance, a court may treat the entity as a *de facto corporation*, that is, as a corporation in fact even though it is not technically a corporation by law. For the court to find a de facto corporation, the incorporators must demonstrate that they were unaware of the defect and that they made a good faith effort to incorporate correctly. For example, if a clerk for the secretary of state delayed filing the certificate, the business would not be a corporation de jure, but it would probably be a corporation de facto.

Corporation by Estoppel

An entity that is neither a de jure nor a de facto corporation may be a *corporation by estoppel*. If a third party, in all of its transactions with the enterprise, acts as if it were doing business with a corporation, the third party is prevented or *estopped* from claiming that the enterprise is not a corporation.[32] It is considered unfair to permit the third party to reach shareholders' personal assets when all along it believed it was dealing with a corporation whose shareholders had limited liability.

---

32. *See, e.g.,* Cranson v. Int'l Bus. Machs. Corp., 200 A.2d 33 (Md. 1964).

EXHIBIT 19.1 Steps Required to Form a Corporation

1. Select a corporate name and agent for service of process.

2. File the certificate of incorporation (also known as articles of incorporation or charter in some jurisdictions) signed by the incorporator(s).

3. Sign action by the incorporator(s) that:
   - Adopts bylaws.
   - Specifies initial directors.

4. Obtain written resignation of the incorporator(s).

5. Hold first directors' meeting or take action by unanimous written consent of the directors to:
   - Ratify the adoption of the bylaws by the incorporator(s) or the adoption of new bylaws.
   - Elect officers.
   - Authorize issuance of stock.
   - Authorize corporate bank account.

PIERCING THE VEIL OF A CORPORATION OR LIMITED LIABILITY COMPANY

The corporation is built around the central premise of limited liability. Under certain circumstances, however, courts will deny this central premise and hold the shareholders liable for claims against the corporation. A court will *pierce the corporate veil* in this way if necessary to prevent the evasion of statutes, the perpetration of fraud, or other activities against public policy. The need to pierce arises only if the corporation is unable to pay its own debts.

There are two legal approaches to piercing the corporate veil. The *alter ego theory* applies when the owners of a corporation have so mingled their own affairs with those of the corporation that the corporation does not exist as a distinct entity—instead, it is an alter ego of its owners. The *undercapitalization theory* applies when the corporation is a separate entity, but its deliberate lack of adequate capital allows it to skirt potential liabilities. Such undercapitalization constitutes a fraud upon the public.

Courts usually apply some combination of these theories. A court is more inclined to pierce the corporate veil when it suspects wrongdoing or bad faith on the part of shareholders. Because a publicly traded corporation generally does not have one controlling shareholder, attempts to pierce the veil of such corporations are rare. Usually, the cases involve small, closely held corporations or subsidiaries of larger corporations.

Courts have used the same approach to decide whether to pierce the veil of a limited liability company (LLC) and hold its members personally liable. For example, the Court of Appeal of Louisiana held that Insulation Sales and Service, Inc. (ISS), the majority owner of AAI Ventures, L.L.C., was liable for monies owed under a contract between AAI and Patrick Hamilton, an individual hired to provide general management services to AAI in connection with its subcontract to remove asbestos from a casino.[33] AAI, which was formed to do the asbestos removal work at the casino, was undercapitalized; the separate corporate existence of AAI and its affiliated companies was disregarded; individuals associated with the casino project were unsure of coworkers' job titles or the employers of record; employees of one organization were housed at the offices of other organizations; and AAI had no employees—its accounting was handled by employees of ISS. The discussion that follows applies to both corporations and LLCs.

Alter Ego Theory

A court will consider several factors when deciding whether a corporation is merely the alter ego of a shareholder.

Domination by Controlling Shareholder

If an individual or another corporation owning most of the stock of the corporation exerts so much control that the standard corporate decision-making mechanisms are not in operation, the court may find that the corporation has no separate mind, will, or existence of its own.

For example, following its acquisition of Atlanta-based HBO & Co. (HBOC), McKesson, a California-based health-care company, allowed HBOC to survive as its wholly owned subsidiary. Later that year McKesson announced that for several years prior to the merger HBOC had improperly recorded more than $50 million in revenue. The announcement caused the value of McKesson's stock to plummet. Following the precipitous drop in value, McKesson brought a suit of unjust enrichment against former HBOC shareholders who had traded in their overvalued stock for equivalently valued McKesson stock. The judge denied the claim, finding it would be an unwarranted piercing of the corporate veil. Although the companies had not become completely merged, McKesson exercised such control over HBOC that its shareholders, after giving final approval of the merger agreement, were, in effect, merely McKesson shareholders. McKesson argued that it had to sue the shareholders directly because suing its own subsidiary would harm itself, but the judge found that if suing HBOC would amount to suing itself, then the HBOC shareholders, as McKesson shareholders, were protected against such an attack.[34]

Commingling of Assets

The courts will also examine whether the books and funds of the corporation and of the controlling shareholder have been commingled; for example, whether the shareholder uses company checks to make personal purchases or payments.

Bypassing Formalities

If an action that requires approval by the board proceeds without a board meeting being held, or if other procedural rules (such as the requirement of an annual shareholders' meeting) are consistently broken, the courts will be inclined to view the corporation as the instrument of the controlling shareholder unless the corporation qualifies as a statutory close corporation under the law of the state of incorporation. As noted earlier, the bypassing of these formalities is not a factor in deciding whether to pierce the veil of a close corporation.

Undercapitalization Theory

When deciding whether a corporation is undercapitalized, a court will consider whether the founders should

---

33. *Hamilton v. AAI Ventures, L.L.C.,* 768 So. 2d 298 (La. Ct. App. 2000).

34. *McKesson HBOC, Inc. v. N.Y. State Common Ret. Fund,* 339 F.3d 1087 (9th Cir. 2003).

have reasonably anticipated that the corporation would be unable to pay the debts or liabilities it would incur. (Of course, the amount of capital invested does not have to guarantee business success—if it did, all failed businesses would be deemed undercapitalized.)

For example, assume a new corporation is formed to build airplanes, an activity that requires large expenditures and entails substantial risks of liability for third-party injury. The corporation has raised only $1,000 in capital. It is obvious that the corporation will run out of funds quickly and be unable to pay its bills. It will not have money to buy adequate product liability insurance or to self-insure against claims for injuries caused by defective airplanes. Because of the undercapitalization, a court may ignore the corporate form and hold the owners of the corporation personally liable for its debts and liabilities.

The above example is an exaggerated case. In reality, it is often difficult for a court to decide how much capital is enough. Two judges examining the same facts may come to different conclusions as to whether the owner should have reasonably anticipated that the corporation would need more capital. Judges may also disagree as to whether undercapitalization alone is sufficient grounds to pierce the corporate veil. In the following classic case, the majority opinion and the minority dissent reflect two sides of this issue.

A CASE IN POINT	*In the Language of the Court*	Case 19.4

Walkovszky v. Carlton

Court of Appeals of New York
223 N.E.2d 6 (N.Y. 1966).

FACTS The plaintiff was severely injured in New York City when he was run down by a taxicab owned by the defendant, Seon Cab Corporation. The individual defendant, Carlton, was a shareholder of ten corporations, including Seon, each of which had two cabs registered in its name. Each cab was covered by only the minimum $10,000 per cab automobile liability insurance required by New York law.

Although seemingly independent of one another, these corporations were, according to the plaintiff, "operated . . . as a single entity, unit and enterprise" with regard to financing, supplies, repairs, employees, and garaging, and all were named as defendants. The plaintiff also asserted that the multiple corporate structure constituted an unlawful attempt "to defraud members of the general public" who might be injured by the cabs. He therefore sought to hold their sole shareholder personally liable for his injury.

ISSUE PRESENTED May the corporate veil be pierced solely because the corporation is undercapitalized?

OPINION FULD, J., writing for the New York Court of Appeals:

The law permits the incorporation of a business for the very purpose of enabling its proprietors to escape personal liability but, manifestly, the privilege is not without its limits. Broadly speaking, the courts will disregard the corporate form, or, to use accepted terminology, "pierce the corporate veil," whenever necessary "to prevent fraud or to achieve equity."

. . . .

The individual defendant is charged with having "organized, managed, dominated and controlled" a fragmented corporate entity but there are no allegations that he was conducting business in his individual capacity. . . . The corporate form may not be disregarded merely because the assets of the corporation, together with the mandatory insurance coverage of the vehicle which struck the plaintiff, are insufficient to assure him the recovery sought. . . . [I]f the insurance coverage required by statute "is inadequate for the protection of the public, the remedy lies not with the courts but with the Legislature." It may very well be sound policy to require that certain corporations must take out liability insurance which will afford adequate compensation to their potential tort victims. However, the responsibility for imposing conditions on the privilege of incorporation has been committed by the Constitution to the Legislature and it may not be fairly implied, from any statute, that the Legislature intended, without the slightest discussion or debate, to require of taxi corporations that they carry automobile liability insurance over and above that mandated by the Vehicle and Traffic Law.

RESULT Plaintiff Walkovszky cannot sue Carlton in his individual capacity unless the complaint is amended to allege alter ego.

CONTINUED

DISSENT   KEATING, J., dissenting from the majority opinion:

From their inception these corporations were intentionally undercapitalized for the purpose of avoiding responsibility for acts which were bound to arise as a result of the operation of a large taxi fleet having cars out on the street 24 hours a day and engaged in public transportation. And during the course of the corporations' existence all income was continually drained out of the corporations for the same purpose.

The issue presented by this action is whether the policy of this State, which affords those desiring to engage in a business enterprise the privilege of limited liability through the use of the corporate device, is so strong that it will permit that privilege to continue no matter how much it is abused, no matter how irresponsibly the corporation is operated, no matter what the cost to the public. I do not believe that it is.

[*Editor's Note*: Judge Keating then cited with approval a California Supreme Court case[35] holding that the corporate veil could be pierced based on undercapitalization alone.]

. . . .

What I would merely hold is that a participating shareholder of a corporation vested with a public interest, organized with capital insufficient to meet liabilities which are certain to arise in the ordinary course of the corporation's business, may be held personally responsible for such liabilities. Where corporate income is not sufficient to cover the cost of insurance premiums above the statutory minimum or where initially adequate finances dwindle under the pressure of competition, bad times or extraordinary and unexpected liability, obviously the shareholder will not be held liable.

COMMENTS   In *Walkovszky*, the court rejected the argument that undercapitalization alone constituted fraud. The court suggested, however, that the plaintiff amend the complaint to allege that the individual defendants were "shuttling . . . personal funds in and out of the corporation 'without regard to formality and to suit their immediate convenience,'" thus stating a valid cause of action under the alter ego theory. In *Browning-Ferris Industries of Illinois, Inc. v. TerMaat*,[36] the U.S. Court of Appeals for the Seventh Circuit held that undercapitalization alone did not justify piercing the corporate veil of an Illinois corporation operating a garbage dump.

CRITICAL THINKING QUESTIONS

1. From a public policy standpoint, with which opinion do you agree, the majority or the dissent?

2. Would the result have been different if defendant Carlton's name had been conspicuously displayed on the sides of all of the taxis owned by the various corporations of which Carlton was the sole shareholder and if Carlton actually serviced, inspected, repaired, and dispatched the taxis?

---

35. Minton v. Cavaney, 364 P.2d 473 (Cal. 1961).

36. 195 F.3d 953 (7th Cir. 1999).

Tort Versus Contract

A tort plaintiff's contact with the corporation (for example, being hit by a taxi) may be completely involuntary. Many courts are therefore more sympathetic to the tort victim who faces an undercapitalized corporate defendant than to a plaintiff seeking to pierce the corporate veil in a breach-of-contract case. Why should someone who voluntarily contracted to provide credit to a weakly capitalized corporation, perhaps charging a premium interest rate in so doing, later be entitled to reach the owner's personal assets? After all, the creditor had, or could have negotiated, access to the corporation's financial statements. The voluntary decision to do business with the undercapitalized company contrasts quite sharply with the plight of a party who is a victim of a tort committed by an officer or employee of the corporation. If, however, a shareholder misrepresents the financial condition of the corporation when negotiating a contract, then courts will pierce the corporate veil.

Reverse Piercing

Under certain circumstances, some jurisdictions will permit *reverse piercing*, whereby a corporation may be held liable for the debts of a shareholder. For example, in what the California Court of Appeal called "[p]erhaps, the oldest reverse piercing case,"[37] *Kingston Dry Dock Co. v. Lake Champlain Transportation Co.*,[38] the U.S. Court of Appeals for the Second Circuit held, as a matter of federal law, that a parent corporation may be liable for the acts of its subsidiary when the parent directly intervened in the transaction "ignoring the subsidiary'[s] paraphernalia of incorporation, directors and officers."[39]

MANAGEMENT OF THE CORPORATION

Corporate control is apportioned among the directors, officers, and shareholders. The directors are the overall managers and guardians of the corporation. The officers are the day-to-day managers. The shareholders, as the residual owners of the corporation, do not participate directly in management, but they elect the directors. The shareholders also must approve certain major transactions.

Directors

Most state statutes provide that the business and the affairs of the corporation shall be managed, and all corporate powers shall be exercised by, or under the direction of, the board of directors. The board typically delegates the management of the day-to-day operations of the business of the corporation to the officers or, less often, to a management company. A member of the board may also serve as an officer. Such a person is called an *inside director*. A director who is not also an officer is called an *outside director*. An understanding of the dynamics between the board and the officers is essential to comprehend the workings of a corporation.

Officers

The officers appointed by the board of directors are agents of the corporation and have the power to act on its behalf. A corporation will normally have a chief executive officer (often called president), a secretary, a chief financial officer, and other officers as designated in the bylaws or determined by the board.

Any number of offices may be held by the same person unless the articles or bylaws provide otherwise. Officers are chosen by the board and serve at the pleasure of the board. If an officer is terminated in violation of an employment contract, the officer cannot sue to get his or her job back but can sue for damages. An officer may resign at any time on written notice to the corporation. The corporation can sue for damages if an officer's resignation breaches his or her employment contract.

Shareholders

Shareholders are virtually never involved in the day-to-day operations of a corporation. As discussed more fully in Chapter 20, shareholders' main "power" in the corporation is their right to elect directors who will run the company in their stead.

Voting Rights

The shareholders elect the directors. In some states, directors can be removed by the shareholders with or without cause at any time. In other states, such as Delaware, a director who is elected to a staggered or classified board (where directors serve for designated multiyear terms, usually not to exceed three years) may not be removed without cause, unless the certificate of incorporation provides otherwise. The shareholders might be able to accomplish the same result by first eliminating the charter or bylaw provision requiring the staggered board and then voting to remove the directors, however. In addition, certain transactions, such as a merger or the sale of substantially all of the corporation's assets, can be approved only by a vote of the shareholders.

Shareholders can act by voting at a meeting or by written consent. A shareholder who cannot be present at a meeting can vote by *proxy*, that is, by a written authorization for another person to vote on his or her behalf. Only *shareholders of record*, that is, persons whose names appear on the corporation's shareholder list on a specified date, are entitled to vote.

No action can be taken at a shareholders' meeting unless there is a *quorum*; the quorum requirements are set forth in each state's corporate statute. In most jurisdictions, there is no quorum unless the holders of at least 50% of the outstanding shares are present in person or by proxy.

Cumulative Voting Versus Straight Voting in the Election of Directors Some states permit, and some require, *cumulative voting*, whereby each shareholder may cast all of his or her votes for one nominee or allocate them among the nominees as the shareholder sees fit. A shareholder's total number of votes is thus equal to the number of directors to be elected multiplied by the number of shares owned by the shareholder. Cumulative voting gives minority shareholders a greater likelihood of electing at least one director.

37. Postal Instant Press, Inc. v. Kaswa Corp., 77 Cal. Rptr. 3d 96 (Cal. App. 2008).

38. 31 F.2d 265 (2d Cir. 1929).

39. *Id.* at 267.

In an election permitting cumulative voting, the number of shares, x, required to elect a given number of directors, y, may be calculated by the following formula:

$$x = \frac{y \times z}{1 + d} + 1$$

where z is the total number of shares voting, and d is the total number of directors to be elected.[40]

To illustrate, assume a shareholder wants to elect three directors ($y = 3$) to a board with five members up for election ($d = 5$). The corporation has 100 shares outstanding, and they are all voted ($z = 100$). Then

$$x = \frac{3 \times 100}{1 + 5} + 1$$
$$x = 51$$

With cumulative voting, a shareholder would need 51 shares to elect three directors.

In contrast, with *straight voting*, a shareholder can cast one vote for each share the shareholder owns for each nominee. Thus, a shareholder who owns 51 shares can cast 51 votes for each vacant director position. Consequently, a shareholder who controls more than half the voting stock of a corporation can effectively elect the entire board of directors.

Class Voting   Class voting occurs when the charter or applicable corporate law requires one class of stock, usually preferred, to approve a given proposal while other classes of stock are excluded from the vote. For example, a charter might require all mergers and sales of substantially all of the assets to be approved by both a majority of the common shares voting as a class and a majority of the preferred shares voting as a class. Class voting is often sought by investors attempting to protect their control of certain key decisions even if they lose majority control of the corporation's voting equity.

Courts generally will enforce class-voting provisions but tend to construe them quite literally. In *Benchmark Capital Partners IV, L.P. v. Vague*,[41] the Delaware Court of Chancery reaffirmed its position that a class-voting provision should be narrowly construed even if it appears that a majority shareholder crafted a transaction to avoid triggering the provision. Thus, a group of shareholders who were guaranteed the right to vote as a class on any change in the corporate charter that would dilute their rights or holdings in the corporation were held to have no right to a class vote on a merger that might dilute their equity interest.

Including Shareholder Proposals in the Company's Proxy Statement

The Securities and Exchange Commission (SEC) requires publicly traded companies to include certain shareholder proposals in the proxy statement the board sends to shareholders to solicit proxies for the election of directors. Shareholder activists have used shareholder proposals extensively to raise social, political, and corporate governance issues. Early examples included proposals for companies to stop doing business in South Africa to protest the policy of apartheid (mandated segregation of blacks and whites). More recently, shareholder proposals have focused more on corporate governance issues, such as eliminating classified boards and giving shareholders a right to vote on executive compensation (so-called Say on Pay.)[42] As discussed in Chapter 20, the Dodd–Frank Wall Street Reform and Consumer Protection Act gave shareholders of public companies the right to vote on advisory (that is, nonbinding) resolutions regarding executive compensation and severance agreements (so-called golden parachutes). In the wake of the Supreme Court's decision in *Citizens United*[43] expanding corporations' ability to directly fund political advertising and indirectly support individual candidates, shareholders in a number of companies have proposed enhanced disclosure of the board's policies and procedures for spending corporate funds on electioneering.

Shareholders have also focused on nanotechnology, energy sustainability, and the economic and environmental effects of global warming.[44] For example, the SEC ruled that (1) ExxonMobil could not omit a request that the board establish a committee to study and report to shareholders on how the company can become a leader in developing environmentally sustainable technology to make the United States energy independent and (2) General Electric could not omit a request that the board prepare a global warming report.[45]

SEC Rule 14a–8 under the Securities Exchange Act of 1934 allows companies to exclude proposals that relate to the "ordinary business" of the company. The SEC staff has advised corporations that they may not omit any of the following types of shareholder proposals from proxy materials: (1) requests that the board seek shareholder approval prior to adopting a "poison pill" antitakeover device (discussed in Chapter 20), (2) limits on the compensation of nonemployee directors, (3) compensation for senior officers, (4) a reduction in pension benefits, (5) requests that the company dissociate itself from any "offensive" advertising, (6) increased retirement benefits, and (7) a dividend

40. Constance E. Bagley & David J. Berger, Proxy Contests: Strategic Considerations (1998).

41. 2002 WL 1732423 (Del. Ch. 2002).

42. Lisa M. Fairfax, *Shareholder Democracy on Trial: International Perspective on the Effectiveness of Increased Shareholder Power*, 3 Va. L. & Bus. Rev. 1 (2008).

43. Citizens United v. Fed. Election Comm'n, 130 S. Ct. 876 (2010) (discussed in Chapter 4).

44. *Climate and Energy Resolutions 2011*, Investor Network on Climate Risk, *available at* http://www.ceres.org/incr/engagement/corporate-dialogues/shareholder-resolutions/resolutions-2011 (reporting that 111 climate change–related shareholder proposals were filed in 2011 alone).

45. *"Ordinary Business" Is Still Unclear in 2008 Proxy Season*, Corp. Couns. Wkly. (BNA), July 30, 2008, at 237.

ethical consideration

Edward Hall and Harry Hall were 50% owners of Hall Contractors and the corporation's only directors. Edward died, leaving all of his assets to his widow. Harry (the only surviving director at that point) appointed his own wife to fill the vacancy on the board. Initially, Harry and his wife refused to call a shareholder meeting. Even when one was called, Harry simply did not show up to vote. As a result, Edward's widow could never generate a quorum for a shareholder vote to replace Harry's wife with an impartial director. The corporation never paid dividends to Edward or his widow and did not intend to pay dividends in the future. As a result, Edward's widow's stock in the corporation became worthless. Did Harry and his wife have a legal right to do what they did?[a] Were they acting ethically? Would the answer be different if the case involved a corporation like IBM or Google?

a. Hall v. Hall, 506 S.W.2d 42 (Mo. Ct. App. 1974).

---

increase.[46] Corporations also may not exclude proposals relating to board structure, voting procedures, nominating procedures, or qualifications of directors.[47] In addition, corporations may not exclude "shareholder proposals that seek to establish a procedure in the company's governing documents for the inclusion of one or more shareholder director nominees in the company's proxy materials."[48]

Shareholder Nomination of Directors

As discussed earlier, corporate law proceeds on the assumption that the shareholders will elect the directors who in turn are responsible for overseeing management.

46. Michael Bologna, *Shareholder Proposals*, Corp. Couns. Wkly. (BNA), Feb. 20, 2003, at 60.

47. Shareholder Proposal Relating to the Election of Directors, 72 Fed. Reg. 70,450 (Dec. 6, 2007), *available at* http://www.sec.gov/rules/final/2007/34-56914.pdf.

48. 17 C.F.R 240.14a-8(i)(8).

In practice, the CEO is often also the chair of the board and significantly influences both the selection of directors and the board's agenda.[49] As a result, the board may fail to exercise the necessary oversight.

The corporate excesses of recent years have led to renewed calls for greater director independence. In public companies, a separate, independent committee of directors is charged with nominating directors for election. In 2003, the SEC adopted rules that require companies to disclose more information about the nomination process, including whether the company pays a third party to help find suitable directors and the company's minimum requirements for its director nominees.[50]

In 2010, the SEC adopted Rule 14a–11, the so-called *proxy access rule*, which made it possible for shareholders who have held at least 3% of a public company's stock for at least three years to nominate candidates for the board and solicit proxies without having to go through the considerable expense of commencing a proxy contest.[51] The rule required management to include certain shareholder nominations in management's proxy statement and on its proxy voting card. In the following case, the court considered whether Rule 14a–11 was a valid exercise of the SEC's authority under the Securities Exchange Act of 1934 to regulate the solicitation of proxies.

49. *See* Constance E. Bagley & Richard H. Koppes, *Leader of the Pack: A Proposal for Disclosure of Board Leadership Structure*, 34 San Diego L. Rev. 149 (1997).

50. Disclosure Regarding Nominating Committee Functions and Communications Between Security Holders and Boards of Directors, Release No. 34-48825, 68 Fed. Reg. 69,204 (Dec. 11, 2003). For a more detailed discussion, see Task Force on Shareholder Proposals of the Committee on Federal Regulation of Securities of the Section of Business Law of the American Bar Association, *Report on Proposed Changes in Proxy Rules and Regulations Regarding Procedures for the Election of Corporate Directors*, 59 Bus. Law. 109–25 (2003).

51. Securities & Exchange Comm'n, Facilitating Shareholder Director Nominations, 74 Fed. Reg. 29,024, 29,025–26 (June 18, 2009).

A CASE IN POINT	*Summary*	Case 19.5

Business Roundtable v. SEC

United States Court of Appeals for the District of Columbia Circuit 647 F.3d 1144 (D.C. Cir. 2011).

FACTS The Business Roundtable and U.S. Chamber of Commerce, both of which have members that issue publicly traded securities, challenged the validity of Exchange Act Rule 14a-11. When adopting Rule 14a-11, the SEC had concluded that the rule could create "potential benefits of improved board and company performance and shareholder value" sufficient to "justify [its] potential costs." The Business Roundtable and Chamber of Commerce claimed that the rule violated the Administrative Procedure Act (APA) because the SEC had failed to adequately consider the rule's effect on "efficiency, competition, and capital formation" as required by section 3(f) of the Exchange Act.[52]

CONTINUED

52. 15 U.S.C. § 78c(f).

ISSUE PRESENTED   Did the SEC violate the Administrative Procedure Act when it promulgated the proxy access rule?

SUMMARY OF OPINION   The U.S. Court of Appeals for the District of Columbia Circuit began by explaining that any agency action that is "arbitrary, capricious, and an abuse of discretion, or otherwise not in accordance with law" violates the APA and is, therefore, invalid. The Exchange Act requires the SEC to ensure that its decisions are made on a rational factual basis and take into account potential economic implications. The court concluded that the SEC failed to meet this standard.

The court determined that the SEC had "inconsistently and opportunistically framed the costs and benefits of the rule; failed adequately to quantify the certain costs or to explain why those costs could not be quantified; neglected to support its predictive judgments; contradicted itself; and failed to respond to substantial problems raised by commenters." For example, the SEC failed to consider the consequences of nominations by union and state pension funds under the rule, which might be designed to extract employee concessions unrelated to shareholder value, and to evaluate how often shareholders would initiate election contests. In addition, because the SEC did not address the extent to which Rule 14a-11 will take the place of traditional proxy contests, it had no way of knowing whether the rule would facilitate enough election contests to be of net benefit.

The court faulted the SEC for relying exclusively on "two relatively unpersuasive" studies to conclude that the proxy access rule would improve board performance and increase shareholder value by facilitating the election of dissident shareholder nominees. The court pointed out that there were numerous studies that tended to show that enhanced proxy access would not achieve these objectives.

The court ruled that the SEC had neglected its statutory obligation to assess the economic consequences of the rule by failing to make "tough choices" about which of competing estimates regarding proxy contests was most plausible or to hazard a guess as to which was correct. Accordingly, the rule was arbitrary and capricious on its face and therefore invalid.

RESULT   The court vacated Rule 14a-11. Public companies are not required to include shareholder nominations in management's proxy materials.

COMMENTS   The SEC elected not to appeal the decision invalidating Rule 14a-11. Proxy solicitor Georgeson, Inc. predicted that activists will seek access to management's proxy statement for their nominees by submitting shareholder proposals on a company-by-company basis pursuant to Rule 14a-8.[53]

53. GEORGESON, INC., 2011 ANNUAL CORPORATE GOVERNANCE REVIEW (2011), *available at* http://www.georgeson.com/usa/acgr.php.

Majority Voting

Management proxy statements typically give shareholders two choices when voting for directors: "For" and "Withhold Authority." Until recently, the vast majority of corporations used a *plurality standard*, whereby a director could be elected as long as he or she received a plurality of the votes cast for any nominee, without regard to the number of votes withheld. In 2006, the most common shareholder proposals were those to require *majority voting*, whereby a director must receive a majority of the shares voted to be elected. By 2007, more than 50% of the S&P 500 companies had adopted some type of majority voting.[54] One popular variation—"plurality-plus"—provides that directors who fail to receive a majority of the votes cast must tender their resignations, which the company must then decide whether to accept.[55] In a true majority voting system, a director must receive a majority of the votes cast to be elected.

Shareholder Inspection Rights and Access to the Shareholder List

Shareholders have a common law right to inspect the corporate books and records, including the stock register and/or shareholder list, the minutes of board meetings and

54. Fairfax, *supra* note 42.

55. *Id.*

shareholder meetings, the bylaws, and books of account. In making the examination, shareholders are permitted the assistance of an accountant, lawyer, or other expert.

In most states, the right of inspection is limited by the requirement that the inspection be conducted for a "proper purpose." States vary in their interpretation of this limit. Some jurisdictions construe "proper purpose" liberally, leaving shareholder inspection rights virtually unfettered. These states reason that inspection rights should be broad because everything that affects a corporation eventually has an effect on its shareholders. Other states, more concerned with the potential for the inspection right to be an abusive tool, protect against "fishing expeditions" by requiring more than a vague allegation of mismanagement to establish a proper purpose.

In one of the most famous cases in American corporate history, the Minnesota Supreme Court ruled that a shareholder of Honeywell, Inc., who opposed the Vietnam War and sought to persuade Honeywell to cease producing antipersonnel fragmentation bombs for use in the war, did not have a right to Honeywell's shareholder list or the corporate records dealing with weapons and munitions manufacture.[56] The court explained: "Considering the huge size of many modern corporations and the necessarily complicated nature of their bookkeeping, it is plain that to permit thousands of stockholders to roam at will through their records would render impossible . . . the proper carrying on of their business." Because "the power to inspect may be the power to destroy," the court ruled that Delaware law (which governed the case because Honeywell was incorporated in Delaware) requires the shareholder to assert some concern with investment return. In this case, the shareholder's avowed purpose in buying Honeywell stock was to place himself in a position to try to impress his social and political opinions upon Honeywell's management and its other shareholders. Such an interest, the court concluded, could hardly be deemed a proper purpose germane to his economic interest as a shareholder.

Many of the most intense shareholder inspection battles involve access to the list of shareholders. Shareholders seeking to change a corporate policy or gain control of the board of directors want to identify and target their message to the holders of large blocks of stock. To do this, the insurgents need a copy of the shareholder list. Precisely because the list is so valuable to management's shareholder critics, incumbent managers are likely to resist efforts to obtain it.

Acknowledging that access to the shareholder list can be vital to a successful corporate power struggle, some jurisdictions allow such access without requiring a proper purpose, provided that the shareholder owns a substantial block of shares. For example, section 1600(a) of the

ethical consideration

In 2003, Hewlett-Packard (HP) and Compaq were involved in the largest high-tech merger in history. Walter Hewlett, son of the company's founder and an HP director, commenced a proxy contest to oppose the merger. On the day the stockholders were to vote, Deutsche Asset Management, a division of Deutsche Bank, suddenly changed most of its votes from against the merger to approval. The investment giant's sudden turnaround accounted for 17 million HP shares, nearly 1% of the company's stock. What Walter Hewlett did not know at the time was that HP's directors, who were in favor of the merger, had secretly hired Deutsche Bank and agreed to pay it $1 million to advise HP concerning the merger. Deutsche Bank was to receive another $1 million on the successful completion of the merger.[a] The merger was approved by a margin of roughly 2% of the company's stock. Was Deutsche Bank's conduct legal? Ethical?

a. *In re* Deutsche Asset Mgmt., Inc., SEC Admin. Proc. File No. 11226 (Aug. 19, 2003); also see Susan Beck, *Proxy Wars*, AM. LAW. NEWS GROUP, May 2002.

California Corporations Code provides that any 5% shareholder can inspect and copy the record of shareholders' names and addresses and shareholdings during usual business hours upon five business days' written notice.

Proxy contests, whereby insurgents propose their own slate of directors or rally to oppose a board proposal by sending out their own proxy statement and soliciting proxies for their candidates or position, continue to be an important technique for obtaining control of a publicly traded company or opposing a particular transaction proposed by the incumbent board of directors.[57] Under the SEC's regulation for the solicitation of proxies, publicly traded companies must either mail the proxy materials for the insurgents seeking to elect their own directors or provide a shareholder list. Most companies elect to mail the materials, so insurgents often rely on state inspection statutes to gain access to shareholder lists.[58]

Shareholder Suits

Shareholders generally have a right to sue individually and directly for specific harm done to them. However, shareholders alleging corporate mismanagement leading to harm to the corporation as a whole must usually sue derivatively in the name of the corporation in a shareholder derivative action. In such a case, the recovery is paid to the corporation, not any individual shareholder.

---

56. State *ex rel.* Pillsbury v. Honeywell, Inc., 191 N.W.2d 406 (Minn. 1971).

57. CONSTANCE E. BAGLEY & DAVID BERGER, PROXY CONTESTS: PREPARING FOR THE CAMPAIGN (1998).

58. *See generally* CONSTANCE E. BAGLEY & DAVID BERGER, PROXY CONTESTS: CONDUCTING THE CAMPAIGN (1998).

To determine whether a claim is direct or derivative, Delaware courts focus on "(1) who suffered the alleged harm (the corporation or the suing stockholders, individually); and (2) who would receive the benefit of any recovery or other remedy (the corporation or the stockholders, individually)."[59] Also relevant is whether the plaintiffs have demonstrated that they can prevail without showing an injury to the corporation, which depends in part on the identity of the person or entity to whom a duty was owed. When a group of former shareholders sued the former chair of Syncor International Corporation for alleged misconduct that caused them to receive a lower price for their shares when the company was sold, the Delaware Court of Chancery applied this standard and concluded that the plaintiffs had stated a derivative claim that belonged to the corporation.[60] Because the plaintiffs were no longer Syncor shareholders, they had no standing to pursue the claim on Syncor's behalf. Their case was dismissed.

As discussed further in Chapter 20, before bringing a shareholder derivative action, the plaintiff shareholder must first demand that the directors bring suit on behalf of the corporation or prove that such a demand would be futile. Often companies will set up a special litigation committee to decide whether a suit is warranted. Because the would-be defendants are often fellow directors, a court may not honor the committee's decision not to sue unless the committee was truly independent.[61]

STRUCTURAL CHANGES IN A CORPORATION

State laws establish mechanisms by which the fundamental structure of the corporation can be changed. These changes can range from a reorganization of the enterprise to the end of the corporation as a separate entity. Because structural changes have far-reaching consequences, they cannot be made easily.

State corporation law prohibits certain changes, such as a merger or the sale of substantially all of the corporation's assets, unless they are approved by both the board of directors *and* the shareholders. Approval by the shareholders usually means approval by a simple majority of the outstanding shares, but the certificate of incorporation may require approval by a larger majority, such as two-thirds of the shareholders. Such a requirement for supermajority approval reflects the importance of structural changes.

As discussed in Chapter 16, companies contemplating acquisitions and mergers meeting the size requirements set forth in the Hart–Scott–Rodino Antitrust Improvements Act must file a premerger notification with the Federal Trade Commission and the Department of Justice. This notification enables the federal agencies to review the anticompetitive effects of the proposed merger before the combination occurs.

Merger

A *merger* is the combination of two or more corporations into one. The *disappearing corporation* no longer maintains its separate corporate existence but becomes part of the *surviving corporation*. The surviving corporation assumes, that is, becomes responsible for, all of the liabilities and debts of the disappearing corporation and automatically acquires all of its assets by operation of law. The new corporation may take on the name of one of the parties to the merger, or a new corporate name may be chosen.

An agreement of merger, negotiated between the two companies, will specify such crucial matters as who will comprise the management team of the new enterprise. A merger generally cannot occur unless the boards and the shareholders of both companies approve the transaction. Once the requisite approval is given, the agreement of merger is filed with the secretary of state.

In a noncash merger, the shares in the disappearing corporation are automatically converted into shares in the surviving corporation. Shareholders are required to surrender their old stock certificates for new certificates representing the stock of the surviving corporation. If a shareholder does not surrender the old certificate, it is deemed by operation of law to represent shares of the surviving corporation.

In a cash merger, some shareholders (usually the public shareholders) are required to surrender their shares in the disappearing corporation for cash. They retain no interest in the surviving corporation. Hence, such a merger is also called a *freeze-out merger*.

Sale of Assets

A company may want to acquire the assets of another company, but not its liabilities. To achieve this goal, it can purchase all or most of the other company's assets without merging with the other company. The proceeds of the asset sale can be distributed to the selling company's shareholders as part of a dissolution of the corporation. Alternatively, the selling company may choose to continue its corporate existence and invest the proceeds of the asset sale in a new business.

A sale of all or substantially all of the assets of a corporation must be approved by both the board and the shareholders of the selling company. Most states consider a sale of 50% or more of the assets of a company to be a sale of substantially all of the assets. On the theory that the acquisition of assets is a routine management decision, in which the shareholders should not be involved, some

---

59. Tooley v. Donaldson, Lufkin & Jenrette, Inc., 845 A.2d 1031 (Del. 2004).

60. *In re* Syncor Int'l Corp. S'holders Litig., 857 A.2d 994 (Del. Ch. 2004).

61. *See, e.g., In re* Oracle Corp. Derivative Litig., 824 A.2d 917 (Del. Ch. 2003).

states do not require that the transaction be approved by the shareholders of the acquiring company.

Appraisal Rights

In a merger or a sale of assets, *dissenting shareholders*—those who voted against the transaction—are frequently granted *appraisal rights*, that is, the right to receive in cash the fair value of the shares they were forced to give up as a result of the transaction. This right is available only if the transaction was subject to shareholder approval and if the dissenting shareholder complies with certain statutory procedures.

In *M.P.M. Enterprises, Inc. v. Gilbert*,[62] the Delaware Supreme Court held that for purposes of calculating the amount due shareholders exercising appraisal rights, "fair value" is "the value of the company to the stockholder as a going concern, rather than its value to a third party as an acquisition." Using projected revenue growth, terminal value in five years, and an appropriate discount rate, the court determined that the equity value of M.P.M. Enterprises was $156.33 million, even though Cookson Group PLC had agreed to buy M.P.M. for $65 million plus up to $73.6 million in subsequent payments, contingent on earnings.

TENDER OFFERS AND STOCK REPURCHASES

One company may gain control of another by buying a majority of its voting shares, rather than by merging with it or purchasing its assets.

Tender Offers

A *tender offer* is a public offer to all the shareholders of a corporation to buy their shares at a stated price, usually higher than the market price. The party making the offer is called a *bidder* or sometimes a *raider* because of the hostile nature of the bid. The bidder may offer either cash or other securities in exchange for the stock it seeks to acquire. The bidder is often a new corporation formed for the purpose of making the offer.

The shareholders are free to reject or accept the tender offer without the approval of the board of the target. If shareholders sell sufficient stock to the bidder, it will acquire control of the *target corporation*. Hence, this transaction is commonly described as a *takeover*. Because a takeover is almost certain to result in substantial changes in the corporate structure of the target, tender offers are the subject of much regulation by federal statutes, as well as by the laws of the individual states. In addition, as discussed more fully in Chapter 20, the boards of many public companies have enacted defensive tactics designed to thwart hostile tender offers.

An example of a takeover that results in a major change in corporate structure is the *second-step back-end merger*. The bidder first acquires more than 50% of the shares of a company through a tender offer and replaces the target company's board of directors with its own people. The new board then approves the merger of the target company into a company owned by the bidder, with the shareholders of the target company receiving cash or securities for their stock. As the majority shareholder of the target company, the bidder can outvote any dissenters and provide the required shareholder approval. The remaining shareholders are thus frozen out of the new company, and the bidder ends up with all the equity.

Section 203 of the Delaware General Corporation Law prohibits publicly held corporations from engaging in certain business combinations, including mergers, with an interested stockholder (defined as the owner of 15% or more of the outstanding voting stock of the corporation) for a period of three years following the time the stockholder became interested unless (1) the board of directors approved the transaction that resulted in the stockholder becoming an interested stockholder; (2) the interested stockholder owns at least 85% of the corporation; or (3) the business combination is approved by the board of directors and authorized at an annual or special meeting of stockholders, and not by written consent, by the affirmative vote of at least $66\,{}^{2}/_{3}\%$ of the outstanding voting stock that is not owned by the interested stockholder.[63] A Delaware corporation can opt out of this rule by including a provision in its charter expressly electing not to be governed by this section.

Leveraged Buyouts

Any tender offer or other stock purchase can be structured as a *leveraged buyout (LBO)*, that is, a stock purchase financed by debt. In many LBOs, the group of investors seeking to gain control of a corporation includes members of corporate management. The debt financing an LBO is typically secured by the assets of the target company (such as real estate or plant and equipment), and it may take the form of an issuance of bonds, a commercial bank loan, or a loan from an investment bank. An LBO often results in a high debt load, which requires the company to make a series of substantial interest payments. As discussed in Chapter 23, LBOs can raise fraudulent conveyance issues.

Self-Tender Offers and Going-Private Transactions

A corporation can offer to repurchase its own shares, either in a privately negotiated transaction or through a

---

62. 731 A.2d 790 (Del. 1999).

63. 8 DEL. CODE § 203.

tender offer available to the public shareholders. A large-scale repurchase can result in the corporation's *going private*, that is, having fewer than 300 shareholders and ceasing to be required to file public periodic reports under the Securities Exchange Act of 1934 (discussed further in Chapter 21). A host of SEC rules regulates share repurchases and going-private transactions.[64] A number of small public companies have elected to go private (also known as "going dark") to avoid the expense of complying with the record-keeping and certification requirements imposed by the Sarbanes–Oxley Act of 2002. A report by the Government Accountability Office found that "public companies with $75 million or less in market capitalization paid a median of $1.14 in audit fees for every $100 in revenue under the act, compared to just 13 cents for every $100 by companies with over $1 billion in market capitalization."[65]

---

64. For a more detailed discussion of stock repurchases, see Matthew Haftner, *Stock Repurchases Can Provide Important Benefits to Corporations/Stockholders, but Care Needed to Avoid Pitfalls*, 29 U.S.L.W. 232 (2001).

65. Angus Loten, *Sarbanes-Oxley Takes Toll on Smaller Firms*, INC. (May 8, 2006), *available at* http://www.inc.com/news/articles/200605/sarbox.html.

THE RESPONSIBLE MANAGER

CHOOSING THE APPROPRIATE BUSINESS ORGANIZATION

The individuals who participate in the creation of a business organization will often go on to become its managers. These managers have a strong incentive to maximize the new enterprise's potential for success. To do this, several concerns must be addressed during the entity-selection process.

First, a founder should define and clarify the business goals of the enterprise in a business plan. For example, if the enterprise will need capital from a large number of individuals, it will be necessary to ensure limited liability for some or all of these investors. A general partnership would not be suitable, as there would be no limited liability for passive investors.

If several persons work together on an informal basis with a common business objective, and then one leaves, the *forgotten founder* problem can arise. The person who left may have ownership rights in the enterprise. Such rights can be based on the laws of intellectual property if the person leaving created a protectable piece of property, such as a patentable invention or computer software that is protected by copyright law. (Intellectual property is discussed in Chapter 11.) Even if a founder created no protectable intellectual property before leaving, he or she may have been a partner in an informal oral general partnership if the parties were sharing profits and losses. As such, that founder would be entitled to a share of the partnership assets.

One way to mitigate the forgotten founder problem is to incorporate early and issue shares that are subject to vesting over time. A common vesting schedule provides that if a person leaves in the first year, he or she forfeits all rights to any stock. Under this approach, called *cliff vesting*, one-quarter of the stock is often vested at the end of the first year. The remainder is vested monthly over the next three to four years.

If early incorporation is not feasible or is otherwise undesirable, it is important to spell out in writing at the beginning of a joint project what will happen if someone leaves. Otherwise, those who remain could find themselves sued years down the road for a share of the company that finally is formed, a partnership interest, or royalties for use of intellectual property.

If a general partnership is chosen, there are additional concerns. For example, it is important to put the partnership agreement in writing. As we have seen, a written partnership agreement is not always absolutely necessary to form a partnership, but creating one forces people to think through their business objectives and relationships before they begin working together.

Once an entity has been established, the founders will oversee the process of capitalization. To decide what percentages of debt and equity are to be used in financing the operation, managers should have a realistic idea of the existing demand and the distinct markets for both types of financing. In addition, managers must be aware of the rates at which the corporation can borrow money and the terms that debt and equity holders will require. Tax considerations are crucial to this process.

The final capital structure can take a variety of forms, and much creativity can be employed in this area. Entrepreneurs and investors will often seek assistance from attorneys specializing in finance and tax law, as well as from accountants and investment bankers. The more a manager understands about capitalization, however, the better the manager can utilize the information provided by lawyers, bankers, and accountants to achieve a suitable capital structure.

Mike Price/Shutterstock

A MANAGER'S DILEMMA
Putting It into Practice

When Is a Partner Not a Partner?

In February 1990, Collette Bohatch was named a partner in the Washington, D.C. office of Butler & Binion, a Houston-based law firm. John McDonald was then the managing partner of the firm's D.C. office, which worked almost exclusively for Pennzoil. Bohatch soon became privy to internal firm reports showing the number of hours each attorney worked, billed, and collected. After reviewing such reports, she became concerned that McDonald was overbilling Pennzoil.

On July 15, 1990, Bohatch met with Louis Paine, Butler & Binion's managing partner, to report her concerns about McDonald's billing practices. Paine told Bohatch he would investigate. The following day, McDonald met with Bohatch and told her that Pennzoil was not satisfied with her work and wanted her work to be supervised. Bohatch later testified that this was the first time she had ever heard criticism of her work for Pennzoil.

After looking into Bohatch's complaint and discussing the allegations with Pennzoil's in-house counsel, who said

that Pennzoil believed the firm's bills were reasonable, Paine informed Bohatch in August that he found no basis for her contentions. Paine also told her that she should begin to look for other employment. In June 1991, she was informed that that month's partnership distribution would be her last. She was asked to leave by November.

Bohatch filed suit for breach of fiduciary duty and other claims in October 1991. The firm voted to expel her three days later. At trial, a jury found that the firm had breached its fiduciary duty to Bohatch. The court of appeals reversed, holding that the firm's only duty to Bohatch was not to expel her in bad faith. Bohatch appealed. Did Butler & Binion fulfill its legal obligations to Bohatch? Did it act ethically? Should it matter whether Bohatch was correct about the overbilling?[66]

---

66. *See* Bohatch v. Butler, 977 S.W.2d 543 (Tex. 1998).

INSIDE STORY

Focus on Franchises

Although franchises are not a separate form of business entity in the traditional sense, they are a common business arrangement that is subject to regulation by both the Federal Trade Commission (FTC) and a number of states. Approximately 900,000 franchises were operating in the United States in 2010 with more than a trillion dollars in annual retail sales.[67] Well-known franchisors include McDonald's, Century 21, Avis Rent-a-Car, Realty World America, and Dunkin' Donuts.

A *franchise* is commonly understood to refer to a business arrangement whereby the franchisor receives cash up front, followed by monthly payments based on a reseller's gross receipts, in exchange for granting the franchisee the right to use the franchisor's trademarks, marketing plan, and other proprietary information. Certain state statutes define the term far more broadly, however, and may bring within their ambit product distribution arrangements between manufacturers and dealers that many managers would not have considered to be franchises.[68] Because franchise laws can override the parties'

contractual arrangements (for example, by prohibiting termination of the relationship without good cause), manufacturers may find themselves constrained in their ability to alter their supply chains to take advantage of new distribution channels, such as the Internet. Absent a contrary statutory provision, however, franchise arrangements are generally governed by the contract between the franchisor and franchisee.[69]

Advantages and Disadvantages of Franchising

A franchise offers individuals the opportunity to own their own business without having to start from scratch. Furthermore, a new franchisee can capitalize on the enormous capital inherent in large, established franchises. For example, a company like Best Buy can sell electronics at a considerably lower price

CONTINUED

---

67. Robert W. Emerson, *Franchise Encroachment*, 47 Am. Bus. L.J. 191 (2010).

68. *See* Thomas J. Collin, *State Franchise Laws and the Small Business Franchise Act of 1999: Barriers to Efficient Distribution*, 55 Bus. Law. 1699 (2000).

69. *See, e.g.*, Carvel Corp. v. Noonan, 818 N.E.2d 1100, 1105 (N.Y. 2004) ("the relationship between franchisors and franchisees is a complex one; while cooperative, it does not preclude all competition; and the extent to which competition is allowed should be determined by the contracts between the parties, not by courts or juries seeking after the fact to devise [such] a code of conduct.").

because of the company's ability, in the aggregate, to stock expensive items that tend to become outdated quickly.[70]

On the other hand, the quality of customer service and the level of individual attention sometimes deteriorate as a result of the less flexible business plan imposed by the franchisor. Although there is a trend toward larger franchises, some franchisees are finding niches by encouraging their employees to spend more time with customers, responding more promptly to problems, and empowering sales representatives to make decisions on the spot.[71]

Definition of "Franchise"

State franchise statutes tend to use either a marketing plan or a community of interest definition, with the marketing plan definition being more prevalent. The definition of "franchise" used by the FTC is broad enough to encompass relationships that would be included under either state definition.

Marketing Plan Definition   The California Business and Professions Code, which is representative, defines a franchise as a contract or agreement, either expressed or implied, whether oral or written, between two or more persons by which:

(a) A franchisee is granted the right to engage in the business of offering, selling, or distributing goods or services under a marketing plan or system prescribed in substantial part by a franchisor; and

(b) The operation of the franchisee's business pursuant to that plan or system is substantially associated with the franchisor's trademark, service mark, trade name, logotype, advertising, or other commercial symbol designating the franchisor or its affiliate; and

(c) The franchisee is required to pay, directly or indirectly, a franchise fee.[72]

The courts have construed the requirement for a marketing plan very liberally. It can be as little as a quota of copiers to sell in a specific territory, coupled with a requirement that the distributor's personnel participate in mandatory product training,[73] or an agreement with a boat manufacturer specifying that the dealer was to advertise intensively, conduct a variety of promotions, and carry the boat manufacturer's array of accessory sales devices.[74]

Similarly, it takes very little to satisfy the requirement for a franchise fee. Although many states exclude payments for goods at a bona fide wholesale price, payments for

videocassettes, posters, and brochures to promote the manufacturer's product have been viewed as franchise fees when they were required by the manufacturer or recommended as essential for the successful operation of the business.

Community of Interest Definition   The New Jersey definition of "franchise" is representative of state statutes using the community of interest definition:

> "Franchise" means a written arrangement for a definite or indefinite period, in which a person grants to another person a license to use a trade name, trade mark, service mark, or related characteristics, and in which there is a community of interest in the marketing of goods or services at wholesale, retail, by lease, agreement, or otherwise.[75]

Some states, including Hawaii and Minnesota, also require payment of a franchise fee.

The supplier is deemed to have given the requisite license if the distributor has the right to identify itself as an authorized dealer even if the distributor does not have the right to use the supplier's name as part of its own business name. A community of interest in the marketing of goods is also easily shown, and it is present in most supplier–dealer arrangements. For example, courts have found that a community of interest existed when (1) a "consultant" was required to pay an information services firm 1% of the proceeds received from each loan placed by the consultant using the information, and (2) a dealer made significant investments that were specific to the supplier's goods or services and therefore were not fully recoverable upon termination of the relationship.[76]

Venue for Resolving Disagreements

One major difficulty inherent to franchises is determining where they actually are located and therefore where disputes should be resolved. Should a single Wendy's restaurant in Jersey City be considered to be located in New Jersey for purposes of lawsuits against the Wendy's Corporation? To decide where a franchise is located, the Wisconsin Supreme Court has developed a nine-point, nonexclusive test that concentrates on the "substance" rather than the physical "location" of the franchise, in this case, a dealership.[77] State public policy leans toward forcing franchisors to settle disputes that arise in the state's territory under the state's laws. In 2000, California invalidated all clauses in franchise agreements that mandated non-California venues for dispute resolution.[78] If states did not force franchises to obey their laws, franchisors could simply pick and choose which states to be "from" so as to take advantage of franchisor-friendly legislation.

CONTINUED

70. *See* Anne Field, *Your Ticket to a New Career?*, BUS. WK. INVESTOR, May 12, 2003, at 100.

71. Michael Selz, *Caring for Profits*, WALL ST. J., Sept. 25, 2000, at 8.

72. CAL. BUS. & PROF. CODE §§ 20001(a)–(c).

73. Wright-Moore Corp. v. Ricoh Corp., 908 F.2d 128 (7th Cir. 1990).

74. Boat & Motor Mart v. Sea Ray Boats, Inc., 825 F.2d 1285 (9th Cir. 1987).

75. N.J. STAT. ANN. § 56:10-3(a).

76. Collin, *supra* note 68, at 1722.

77. Baldewein Co. v. Tri-Clover, Inc., 606 N.W.2d 145 (Wis. 2000).

78. Jones v. GNC Franchising, Inc., 211 F.3d 495 (9th Cir. 2000).

State Registration and Disclosure Requirements

Thirteen states (including California, Illinois, Indiana, New York, Virginia, and Wisconsin) require franchisors to register before they can sell franchises in that state and to provide presale disclosure to prospective franchisees in the form of a Uniform Franchise Offering Circular (UFOC). Two additional states (Michigan and Oregon) do not require registration or the filing of offering circulars but do require franchisors to provide presale disclosures.[79] All fifteen states also have broad antifraud provisions, prohibiting any person from making any untrue statement of material fact, or a material omission, in connection with the offer or sale of a franchise in the state.

State Franchise Laws: No Termination Without Good

Cause   In the 1960s and early 1970s, a number of state legislatures adopted laws to protect local businesses investing in franchises from the superior bargaining power of large franchisors. These statutes typically prohibit termination or nonrenewal except where there is good cause, such as (1) failure by the franchisee to comply with any material and reasonable obligation under the franchise agreement or (2) conduct by the franchisee that substantially impairs the franchisor's trademark or trade name.

Although manufacturers may feel justified in terminating a distribution arrangement if the franchisee's performance is "sub-par," according to Thomas J. Collin of Thompson Hine LLP, "[c]ases finding that sub-par performance constitutes good cause for termination are scarcer than hen's teeth . . . ."[80] As a result, a franchisor who seeks to terminate a dealer for lack of market penetration or performance "faces a steep uphill climb."[81] In some states, such as New Jersey and Indiana, the franchisor cannot terminate the franchise even if it has bona fide business reasons for doing so, such as a desire to eliminate distributors' exclusive territories or to terminate distributors in order to sell directly to end users.

FTC's Franchise Rule

The Federal Trade Commission's Franchise Rule, as amended effective July 1, 2008, requires franchisors to provide a prospective franchisee with a UFOC at least fourteen calendar days before the franchisee signs the contract with the franchisor or pays any money to the franchisor.[82] The amended Franchise Rule adopted, for the most part, the UFOC guidelines developed and administered by the North American Securities Administrators Association, thereby harmonizing to a large extent the federal rule with state franchise disclosure laws. Unlike the state rules, however, the Franchise Rule does not require disclosure of risk factors.

The Franchise Rule requires a franchisor to make material disclosures in five general categories: (1) the nature of the franchisor and the franchise system, (2) the franchisor's financial viability, (3) the costs involved in purchasing and operating a franchised outlet, (4) the terms and conditions that govern the franchise relationship, and (5) the names and addresses of current franchisees who can share their experiences within the franchise system and thus help the prospective franchisee to verify independently the franchisor's claims. In addition, franchisors must have a reasonable basis and substantiation for any earnings claims made to prospective franchisees and must disclose the basis and assumptions underlying any such earnings claims.

Presale disclosure is intended to enable prospective franchisees to conduct their own due diligence investigations and to ensure that franchisees understand the relationships they are entering into, including any product source restrictions and any right to protected territories. The FTC enforces the Franchise Rule, and there is no implied private right of action for its violation.

Franchise Relationship Issues   Many franchisees have criticized the FTC for not addressing what they consider to be the greatest problem in franchising today: postsale "abusive franchise relationships." They have urged the FTC to use its power under section 5 of the Federal Trade Commission Act to ban as unfair practices postcontract covenants not to compete, obligations to purchase supplies or inventory from specified providers when comparable items are available at cheaper prices from alternative suppliers, and encroachment on a franchisee's market territory. Encroachment occurs "when a franchisor sells a franchisee an outlet in a certain location, and then a few months later, sells another outlet a few blocks away to someone else."[83] The new establishment diverts customers and revenues away from the original franchisee, but the franchisor is often still better off because it is receiving its percentage royalty from two stores. According to Susan Kezios, president and founder of the American Franchisee Association, "McDonald's wants to have a Big Mac five minutes away from every man, woman, and child. . . . They don't give a rat's ass if they devalue your asset [in the process]."[84] Although the Iowa Franchise Act protects against encroachment, regardless of the terms of the franchise agreement, other states do not.[85]

The FTC has argued that it has no authority to address these so-called abuses because (1) there is insufficient evidence to show that the various alleged franchisor abuses are prevalent or result in substantial injury when viewed from the standpoint of the franchising industry as a whole; (2) the benefits to consumers

CONTINUED

---

79. Federal Trade Comm'n, *State Offices Administering Franchise Disclosure Laws, available at* http://www.ftc.gov/bcp/franchise/netdiscl.shtm (last visited Jan. 21, 2012).

80. Collin, *supra* note 68, at 1732.

81. *Id.*

82. Disclosure Requirements and Prohibitions Concerning Franchising and Business Opportunities, 72 Fed. Reg. 15,443 (Mar. 30, 2007), 16 C.F.R. pts. 436 & 437 (2007) [hereinafter "Franchise Rule"].

83. Deidre Shesgreen, *Franchisees Seek Protection on the Hill*, LEGAL TIMES, Jan. 4, 1999, at 1. *See also* Emerson, *supra* note 67.

84. Shesgreen, *supra* note 83.

85. Emerson, *supra* note 67.

and existing franchisees flowing from the franchisor's contractual terms outweigh complaints or allegations of "oppression" by individual franchisees; and (3) the contractual provisions that prospective franchisees voluntarily read, agree to, and sign are "reasonably avoidable."[86] The 2007 amendments do, however, require (1) disclosure in the UFOC of whether the franchisor or an affiliate (a) has the right to make sales within the franchisee's territory or (b) has used, or has the right to use, other channels of distribution, such as the Internet, catalog sales, or telemarketing; (2) a breakdown in the UFOC of how many company-owned outlets were acquired from franchisees or sold to franchisors during the preceding three years; (3) a warning in the UFOC when the franchisee is not granted an exclusive territory; (4) disclosure in the UFOC of all material lawsuits involving the franchise relationship in the last fiscal year filed by or against a franchisor; and (5) disclosure of a franchisor's use of confidentiality clauses that prohibit or restrict existing or former franchisees from discussing their experiences with prospective franchisees.

Matthew Shay, vice president and chief counsel of the International Franchise Association (which counts McDonald's and KFC among its members), sharply criticized proposed federal legislation—the Small Business Franchise Act of 1999—that would have required good cause for termination, given franchisees more freedom in choosing where they buy their supplies, and prohibited encroachment.[87] Shay claimed that the bill would "rewrite every condition and every term in a franchise agreement" and "impose such extreme restrictions on franchising that it would basically kill the business."[88] David J. Kaufman, a senior partner at Kaufman, Feiner, Yamin, Gilden & Robbins LLP, which represents some of the nation's largest franchise systems, has called for federal preemption of all state franchise relationship laws, which he called "pernicious in their impact upon the logistical and profitable operation of franchise networks, both the franchisor in question and all of its franchisees."[89] As of 2012, it appeared unlikely that Congress would take such a dramatic step.

---

86. *Subcomm. on Commerce, Trade and Consumer Prot. of the House Comm. on Energy and Commerce*, 107th Cong. (June 25, 2002) (testimony of J. Howard Beales III, Director of the Federal Trade Commission's Bureau of Consumer Protection), *available at* http://ftc.gov; Franchise Rule, *supra* note 82.

87. H.R. 3308, 106th Cong. (1999), reproduced as Appendix I to the *Report of the American Bar Association Section of Antitrust Law on Proposed Small Business Franchise Act, available at* http://www.ftc.gov/bcp/rulemaking/franchise/comments/comment025.htm.

88. *Id.*

89. Eryn Gable, *The Future of Franchise Laws: A Look Ahead at Franchise Legislation That Could Be Considered by the New Congress,* ENTREPRENEUR (2001), *available at* http://www.entrepreneur.com/franchises/franchisezone/viewpoint/article37332.html.

KEY WORDS AND PHRASES

QUESTIONS AND CASE PROBLEMS

1. Amy Rockwell was a brilliant but penniless electrical engineer. She had designed a new type of cogeneration plant that she believed had great commercial potential. On January 15, she approached Benjamin Furst, a successful and experienced manager in the energy field, with the idea of starting Cogen, Inc., a corporation devoted to building a plant based on this new design. Furst was enthusiastic. On January 28, he enlisted the support of Clyde Pfeffer, a well-known venture capitalist who had retired from venture capital work but was looking to invest the proceeds of his past endeavors. On February 16, Pfeffer gave the green light to establish the new enterprise.

   Furst retained the law firm of Wilson Scott Associates to handle the details of incorporation. Andrea Scott, one of the partners, drafted the articles of incorporation, signed them as the incorporator, and filed them with the secretary of state on February 28. She then advised her clients that the articles had been filed. Because of a typographical error, the articles of incorporation filed with the secretary of state referred to the company as Cogene, not Cogen.

   Rockwell, Furst, and Pfeffer decided that they would save further expense by completing the incorporation process without any more assistance from Wilson Scott. On March 3, they held what they called the meeting of incorporators to elect the directors and proceeded to elect themselves to the board. As board members, they appointed themselves as the company's officers. They typed up the minutes of this meeting.

   On March 4, the daily operations of Cogen, Inc. commenced. In all of their transactions with third parties, the officers represented themselves as doing business for the corporation. One of these transactions was with Firstloan Bank, which lent the company $5 million. The representations in the loan agreement stated that the corporation had been duly formed, that it existed as a valid corporation under Texas law, and that the shares of stock owned by the various shareholders had been duly authorized and were fully paid.

   On May 5, the corporation began building its cogeneration plant. Three months later, energy prices dropped drastically, and there was no longer a need for a cogeneration facility in that location. The corporation was forced to default on the bank loan. The lawyers for the bank, on being informed that it would not receive any more loan payments, reviewed the original loan documents, the articles of incorporation, and the minutes of the first meeting of the incorporators. On reviewing these documents, they initiated an action directly against the three founders in their individual capacity for liability on the bank loan.
   a. Should the founders have done anything differently?
   b. Are the founders personally liable for the bank loan?

2. Roberto Martinez was the sole force behind In Over Our Heads, Inc., a corporation designed to run a year-round community swimming pool. The enterprise was incorporated in the correct manner in January, with Martinez as the sole director and shareholder. Martinez contributed $100,000 of starting capital, which was just enough to purchase the pool, finance initial advertising, and leave a reserve of $10,000. The corporation had no liability insurance.

   On March 10, the pool opened for business. The corporation operated with a profit over the next few months. In June, Martinez took a two-week vacation in Europe and used a check from the company bank account to purchase his airline ticket. In November, he decided to have the pool repainted. Because business had slowed and the corporation's bank account did not have sufficient funds, Martinez wrote a personal check for this job.

   Martinez feared he would not make enough money through the winter to turn a profit, so he decided to take a part-time job as a telephone salesperson for a real estate company. He used the swimming pool's office phone to make his calls and made a substantial profit.

   On February 11, a child drowned in the pool. The parents brought a suit for wrongful death against the corporation and against Martinez in his individual capacity as owner. At the time of the suit, the corporation had the $10,000 reserve and less than $1,000 in its bank account. Because of these limited funds, the child's parents hoped to recover most of their damages directly from Martinez.

   What arguments can be made to hold Martinez liable for any debt of the corporation arising from this death? Should they prevail? How could Martinez have protected himself against such potential liability? Can an owner–manager of a small corporation guarantee that he or she will not be held liable for the corporation's debts? [See, e.g., Zoran Corp. v. Chen, 185 Cal. App. 4th 799 (2010).]

3. Vince Lutriario claims that the defendant, A World of Pets and Supplies (A World of Pets), sold him a dog infected with giardia, which put Lutriario's children at risk of catching the parasite. When Lutriario sought to recover the price of the dog and the costs he incurred in curing the dog, the marshal who went to A World of Pets was told the store no longer existed and was now A World of Pups. Lutriario had previously talked to the owner of A World of Pets (also the owner of A World of Pups) and arranged a payment plan to be reimbursed. Now, however, the defendant sought an order vacating the judgment that led to that plan and claimed that A World of Pups was distinct and separate from the original defendant, A World of Pets. Despite the name change, there still appeared to be

continuity not only of management and owner, but also of physical location, assets, and the general business operation. Was there a de facto merger between the two "Worlds"? [*Lutriario v. A World of Pets & Supplies, Ltd.*, 26 Misc. 3d 1219(A) (Civ. Court, Richmond County, 2010 Levine, J.).]

4. Francis McQuade was the manager of the New York Giants baseball team. Charles Stoneham (father of Horace Stoneham, who acquired the baseball franchise in 1936 and moved it from New York to San Francisco in 1958) owned a majority of the stock of the company that owned the Giants and sold shares in that company to McQuade and John McGraw. As part of this transaction, these three shareholders each agreed to use his best efforts to continue to keep each of the others as directors and officers of the company at their present salaries. Stoneham and McGraw subsequently failed to use their best efforts to continue to keep McQuade as a director and treasurer of the company. McQuade sued for specific performance of the agreement. What result? [*McQuade v. Stoneham*, 189 N.E. 234 (N.Y. 1934).]

5. Water, Waste & Land, Inc. was a land development and engineering company doing business under the name "Westec." Donald Lanham and Larry Clark were managers and also members of Preferred Income Investors, L.L.C. (P.I.I.), a limited liability company organized under the Colorado Limited Liability Company Act (the LLC Act).

   In March 1995, Clark contacted Westec about the possibility of hiring Westec to perform engineering work in connection with the construction of a fast-food restaurant known as Taco Cabana. In the course of preliminary discussions, Clark gave his business card to representatives of Westec. The business card included Lanham's address, which was also the address listed as P.I.I.'s principal office and place of business in its articles of organization filed with the secretary of state. Section 7-80-208 of the LLC Act provides that the filing of the articles of organization serves as constructive notice of a company's status as an LLC.

   Although the name Preferred Income Investors, L.L.C. was not on the business card, the letters "P.I.I." appeared above the address on the card. There was, however, no indication as to what the acronym meant or that P.I.I. was an LLC.

   Although Westec never received a signed contract from Lanham, in mid-August it did receive verbal authorization from Clark to begin work. Westec completed the engineering work and sent a bill for $9,183.40 to Lanham. No payments were made on the bill. Westec filed a claim in county court against Clark and Lanham individually as well as against P.I.I. Are Clark and Lanham personally liable to Westec? How might Clark, Lanham, and Westec have avoided this dispute? [*Water, Waste & Land, Inc. v. Lantham*, 955 P.2d 997 (Colo. 1998) (en banc).]

6. Ernie Jameson is a design engineer with a proven track record in the field of electronic musical instruments. He recently designed a new VLSI (very large scale integrated) chip. This chip is meant to be the heart and soul of a digital sampling keyboard to be called Echo. Jameson believes the Echo will set a new industry standard. He wishes to organize a business enterprise to build and market it. He has a meeting with his lawyer and conveys to her the following bits of information:

   a. It will take approximately two years to turn the VLSI chip into a marketable product.

   b. Jameson has more than $200,000 in savings from previous ventures. He does not want any of that money at risk in this new venture. However, he wants a part of the ownership; he is unsure what percentage he wants.

   c. Currently, five private investors are willing to put money into this venture. Only two of the five want to play an active role in the enterprise. Jameson is willing to give these two some limited control.

   d. Jameson knows that he is not qualified to manage the new endeavor. Nonetheless, he wants a significant say in how it proceeds.

   e. Five more investors could be attracted to this project, but only if they could be guaranteed some fixed return on their money or could realize immediate tax benefits from investing.

   f. Jameson would like Bernie Lord, a manager much in demand in the electronics field, to be his CEO. It would take significant incentives to attract him to the enterprise.

   Jameson is not committed to using any particular type of business organization; he is interested in weighing the alternatives. What possible types of business organizations could accommodate the needs of the various players? What are the advantages and disadvantages of each alternative? Which one should Jameson choose?

7. Tyson Foods, a chicken distributor, and IBP, a beef and pork distributor, signed a merger agreement after an active auction for IBP. Before signing the agreement, Tyson conducted extensive due diligence and learned that IBP was facing business and financial problems, including a downturn in the beef industry, evidence of accounting fraud in an IBP subsidiary, and recently reduced cash flow. The agreement contained a material adverse change (MAC) clause, which relieved Tyson of its obligation to consummate the merger if there were "any event, occurrence, or development of a state of circumstances or facts which had or reasonably could be expected to have a Material Adverse Effect." After the merger agreement was signed, both Tyson and IBP reported disappointing earnings for two quarters. Tyson then purported to terminate the merger agreement, and IBP sued for specific performance. Does IBP's poor performance in subsequent quarters constitute a Material Adverse Effect giving Tyson the right to terminate the merger agreement? [*IBP v. Tyson*, 789 A.2d 14 (Del. Ch. 2001).]

8. Plaintiffs Monica Allen and Shantese Thomas were injured by lead paint while living at a property owned by Hard Assets, LLC. The plaintiffs sued Jay Dackman, a member of the LLC at the time it owned the property, alleging he was liable for their injuries. Dackman has had limited involvement with the property. He has never visited the property, and neither he nor the LLC was aware that the plaintiffs were occupying the property until after the LLC had acquired it. Once they realized this fact, they took legal action to have the plaintiffs removed. The applicable housing code imposes liability on any individual who "owns, holds, or controls" the title to the property. Is Dackman liable for the plaintiffs' injuries? What are the policy arguments in favor of both parties? [*Allen v. Dackman*, 991 A.2d 1216 (Md. 2010).]

CHAPTER 20

DIRECTORS, OFFICERS, AND CONTROLLING SHAREHOLDERS

INTRODUCTION

FIDUCIARY DUTIES

Directors and officers are agents of the corporation and owe a fiduciary duty to the corporation they serve.[1] Under certain circumstances, a controlling shareholder owes a fiduciary duty to other shareholders as well.

These duties take two basic forms: a duty of care and a duty of loyalty. Generally, the *duty of care* requires fiduciaries to make informed and reasonable decisions and to exercise reasonable supervision of the business. The *duty of loyalty* mandates that fiduciaries act in good faith and in what they believe to be the best interest of the corporation, subordinating their personal interests to the welfare of the corporation. As then Judge Benjamin Cardozo stated, many forms of conduct permissible in the business world for those acting at arm's length are forbidden to those bound by fiduciary ties. A trustee, he said, is held to something stricter than the morals of the marketplace. Not mere honesty, but a "punctilio of an honor the most sensitive" is the standard of behavior with which fiduciaries must comply.[2] As discussed further below, directors' duties of care and loyalty include a duty to act in good faith.[3]

CHAPTER OVERVIEW

This chapter outlines the duties of directors, officers, and controlling shareholders. First, it analyzes the duty of care in terms of the most applicable judicial doctrine, the business judgment rule. Next, the chapter analyzes the duty of good faith and addresses issues arising under the duty of loyalty, including corporate opportunities. It then discusses the fiduciary duties of directors that arise when the directors must decide whether to sell the company or resist a corporate takeover bid. Legislative responses to these issues are also described. Executive compensation is discussed, as are the duties of controlling shareholders in connection with sales of corporate control and squeeze-out mergers. Finally, the chapter outlines the takeover rules in the European Union.

THE BUSINESS JUDGMENT RULE AND THE DUTY OF CARE

In cases challenging board decisions for breach of the duty of care, the courts generally defer to the business judgment of the directors, acknowledging that courts are ill equipped to second-guess directors' decisions at a later date. Thus, under the *business judgment rule*, as long as certain standards are met, a court will presume that the directors have acted in good faith and in the honest belief that the action taken was in the best interest of the company. The court will not question whether the action was wise or whether the directors made an error of judgment or a business mistake.

To take advantage of the rule, the directors must have made an informed decision with no conflict between their personal interests and the interests of the corporation and its shareholders. Courts will not respect directors' business judgment if the directors (1) were interested in the transaction, (2) did not act in good faith, (3) acted in a manner that cannot be attributed to a rational purpose, or (4) reached their decision by a grossly negligent process.[4]

---

1. Gantler v. Stephens, 965 A.2d 695 (Del. 2009) (holding that "the fiduciary duties of officers are the same as those of directors").
2. Meinhard v. Salmon, 164 N.E. 545, 546 (N.Y. 1928) (Case 5.1).
3. For a discussion of the fiduciary duties of directors of a corporation near insolvency or in bankruptcy, see Myron M. Sheinfeld & Judy Harris Pippitt, *Fiduciary Duties of Directors of a Corporation in the Vicinity of Insolvency and After Initiation of a Bankruptcy Case*, 60 BUS. LAW. 79 (2004).

4. Brehm v. Eisner, 746 A.2d 244 (Del. 2000).

If the business judgment rule does not apply to a transaction, courts generally shift to directors the burden of proving that their acts were not grossly negligent (or in cases involving transactions in which the directors are interested, that the transaction was fair and reasonable).

Informed Decision

The business judgment rule is applicable only if the directors make an informed decision. The general corporation law of most jurisdictions authorizes directors to rely on the reports of officers and certain outside experts. However, passive reliance on such reports may result in an insufficiently informed decision, as in the following landmark case.

| A CASE IN POINT | *Summary* | Case 20.1 |

Smith v. Van Gorkom

Supreme Court of Delaware
488 A.2d 858 (Del. 1985).

FACTS Trans Union Corporation was a publicly traded, diversified holding company engaged in the railcar-leasing business. Its stock was undervalued, largely due to accumulated investment tax credits. Jerome W. Van Gorkom, the chair of the board of Trans Union, was reaching retirement age. He asked the chief financial officer, Donald Romans, to work out the per-share price at which a leveraged buyout could be done, given current cash flow. Romans came up with $55, based on debt-servicing requirements. He did not attempt to determine the intrinsic value of the company. Van Gorkom later met with Jay Pritzker and worked out a merger at $55 per share. Trans Union stock was then trading at about $37 per share.

Van Gorkom called a board meeting for September 20, 1980, on one day's notice, to approve the merger. All of the directors were familiar with the company's operations as a going concern, but they were not apprised of the merger negotiations before the board meeting on September 20. They were also familiar with the company's current financial status; a month earlier they had discussed a Boston Consulting Group strategy study. The ten-member board included five outside directors who were CEOs or board members of publicly held companies, as well as a former dean of the University of Chicago Business School.

Copies of the merger agreement were delivered to the directors, but too late for study before or during the meeting. The meeting began with a twenty-minute oral presentation by chairman Van Gorkom. The chief financial officer then described how he had arrived at the $55 figure. He stated that it was only a workable number, not an indication of a fair price. Trans Union's president stated that he thought the proposed merger was a good deal.

The board approved the merger after a two-hour meeting. Board members later testified that they had insisted that the merger agreement be amended to ensure that the company was free to consider other bids before the closing; however, neither the board minutes nor the merger documents clearly reflected this.

Plaintiff Smith sued to challenge the board's action, arguing that the merger price was too low. The Delaware Court of Chancery held that, given the premium over the market value of Trans Union stock, the business acumen of the board members, and the effect on the merger price of the prospect of other bids, the board was adequately informed and did not act recklessly in approving the Pritzker deal. In making its findings, the court relied in part on actions taken by the board after the meeting on September 20, 1980, that were intended to cure defects in the directors' initial level of knowledge. Smith appealed.

ISSUE PRESENTED Were directors who accepted and submitted to the shareholders a proposed cash merger at a premium over market without determining the intrinsic value of the company grossly negligent in failing to inform themselves adequately before making their decision?

SUMMARY OF OPINION The Delaware Supreme Court reversed the lower court and held that the directors were grossly negligent in failing to reach a properly informed decision. They were not protected by the business judgment rule even though there were no allegations

CONTINUED

of bad faith, fraud, or conflict of interest. The court found that the directors could not reasonably base their decision on the inadequate information presented to the board. They should have independently valued the company.

The court found that the directors had inadequate information as to (1) the role of Van Gorkom, Trans Union's chair and chief executive officer, in initiating the transaction; (2) the basis for the proposed purchase price of $55 per share; and, most important, (3) the intrinsic value of Trans Union, as opposed to its current and historical stock price. The court held that in the absence of any apparent crisis or emergency, it was grossly negligent for the directors to approve the merger after a two-hour meeting, with eight of the ten directors having received no prior notice of the proposed merger.

The court stated:

> None of the directors, management or outside, were investment bankers or financial analysts. Yet the board did not consider recessing the meeting until a later hour that day (or requesting an extension of Pritzker's Sunday evening deadline) to give it time to elicit more information as to the sufficiency of the offer, either from inside management (in particular Romans) or from Trans Union's own investment banker, Salomon Brothers, whose Chicago specialist in mergers and acquisitions was known to the Board and familiar with Trans Union's affairs. Thus, the record compels the conclusion that on September 20 the Board lacked valuation information adequate to reach an informed business judgment as to the fairness of $55 per share for sale of the Company.

The court additionally held that the directors' subsequent efforts to find a bidder willing to pay more than Pritzker were inadequate to cure the infirmities of their uninformed exercise of judgment.

The court rejected the directors' argument that they properly relied on the officers' reports presented at the board meeting. A pertinent report may be relied on in good faith, but not blindly. The directors were duty bound to make reasonable inquiry of Van Gorkom (the chief executive officer) and Romans (the chief financial officer). If they had done so, the inadequacy of those officers' reports would have been apparent. Van Gorkom's summary of the terms of the deal was inadequate because he had not reviewed the merger documents and was basically uninformed as to the essential terms. (Indeed, he had signed the merger agreement without reading it while at the opening of the Chicago Lyric Opera.) Romans's report on price was inadequate because it was just a cash flow feasibility study, not a valuation study.

The court also held that the mere fact that a substantial premium over the market price was being offered did not justify board approval of the merger. A premium may be one reason to approve a merger, but sound information as to the company's intrinsic value is required to assess the fairness of an offer. In this case, there was no attempt to determine the company's intrinsic value.

RESULT   The Delaware Supreme Court held that the Trans Union directors were grossly negligent in making an uninformed decision regarding the proposed merger agreement. Their decision was not protected by the business judgment rule. The case was remanded to the Delaware Court of Chancery for an evidentiary hearing to determine the fair value of the shares based on Trans Union's intrinsic value on September 20, 1980, the day when the board met to consider Pritzker's offer. If the chancellor found that value to be higher than $55 per share, the directors would be liable for the difference.

COMMENTS   The case was settled for $23.5 million—$13.5 million in excess of the directors' liability insurance coverage. Although the purchasers, the Pritzker family, ultimately paid the amount by which the settlement exceeded the directors' coverage, they were not legally obligated to do so.

CONTINUED

Smith v. Van Gorkom is one of the most debated corporate law cases ever decided. Three years after the decision, one of the key defendants—Trans Union's CEO, Jerome W. Van Gorkom—wrote an article giving the defendants' side of the story. The article makes it clear that the defendants and the Delaware Supreme Court had very different views about what the directors actually did and what their options really were.

In his article, Van Gorkom stated that at the September 20 meeting:

> The directors, all broadly experienced executives, realized that an all-cash offer with a premium of almost 50% represented an unusual opportunity for the shareholders. They also knew, however, that $55 might not be the highest price obtainable. At the meeting, therefore, there was considerable discussion about seeking an outside "fairness opinion" that might shed further light on the ultimate value of the company.[5]

Furthermore, Van Gorkom explained:

> Acceptance of the offer was not a decision by the directors that the company should be sold for $55 a share. The acceptance was the only mechanism by which the offer could be preserved for the shareholders. *They* would make the ultimate decision as to the fairness of the price and they would do so only after the free market had had ample time in which to determine if $55 was the top value obtainable. The market's opinion would be definitive and worth infinitely more to the shareholders than any theoretical evaluation opinion that the directors could obtain in 39 hours or even longer. On this reasoning the offer was accepted.[6]

Following the meeting, the Trans Union directors hired Salomon Brothers to conduct an intensive search for a higher bidder. In addition, Van Gorkom stated that once the $55 offer became a matter of public knowledge, an auction occurred in the market with Trans Union's stock sometimes selling above $56 on the New York Stock Exchange. After three months of the intensive search and the public auction, no higher bid was ever received. "[T]he market had proven beyond a shadow of a doubt that $55 was the highest price obtainable."[7]

Van Gorkom believed that he and the other Trans Union directors wholeheartedly fulfilled their fiduciary obligations. He concluded that their actions clearly should have been protected under the business judgment rule.

---

5. J.W. Van Gorkom, *Van Gorkom's Response: The Defendant's Side of the Trans Union Case*, MERGERS & ACQUISITIONS, Jan.–Feb. 1988.

6. *Id.*

7. *Id.*

Reliability of Officers' Reports

As *Van Gorkom* underscores, not every statement of an officer can be relied on in good faith, and no statement is entitled to blind reliance. The passivity of the Trans Union directors in *Van Gorkom* unquestionably influenced the court's finding of gross negligence:

> Here, the record establishes that the Board did not request its Chief Financial Officer, Romans, to make any valuation study or review of the proposal to determine the adequacy of $55 per share for sale of the Company. On the record before us: The Board rested on Romans' elicited response that the $55 figure was within a fair price range within the context of a leveraged buy-out. No director sought any further information from Romans. No director asked him why he put $55 at the bottom of his range. No director asked Romans for any details as to his study, the reason why it had been undertaken or its depth. No director asked to see the study; and no director asked Romans whether Trans Union's finance department could do a fairness study within the remaining 36-hour period available under the Pritzker offer. . . . [If he had been asked,] Romans . . . presumably would have . . . informed the Board of his view, and the widespread view of Senior Management, that the timing of the offer was wrong and the offer inadequate.[8]

---

8. Smith v. Van Gorkom, 488 A.2d 858, 876–77 (Del. 1985).

When the CEO, Van Gorkom, told the board that $55 per share was fair, no questions were asked:

> The Board thereby failed to discover that Van Gorkom had suggested the $55 price to [the bidder] Pritzker and, most crucially, that Van Gorkom had arrived at the $55 figure based on calculations designed solely to determine the feasibility of a leveraged buy-out. No questions were raised either as to the tax implications of a cash-out merger or how the price for the one million share option granted Pritzker was calculated.[9]

Reliability of Experts' Reports

Two principles regarding the use of experts' reports emerge from the cases. First, a board should engage a reputable investment banking firm, aided if necessary by an outside appraiser, (1) to prepare a valuation study and (2) to give a written opinion as to the financial fairness of the transaction and of any related purchase of assets or options.

Second, directors have a duty to pursue reasonable inquiry and to exercise reasonable oversight in connection with their engagement of investment bankers and other advisers. A conclusory fairness opinion (that is, an opinion that merely states a conclusion without giving the factual grounds for that conclusion) of an investment banker, however expert, is not a sufficient basis for a board decision, particularly if the investment banker's conclusion is questionable in light of other information known to the directors. As the directors of SCM Corporation learned in *Hanson Trust PLC v. ML SCM Acquisition, Inc.*,[10] an expert's opinion must be in writing and be reasoned.

SCM was the target of a hostile tender offer by a British conglomerate, Hanson Trust PLC. SCM's board negotiated a friendly management leveraged buyout led by "white knight" Merrill Lynch. As part of this agreement, SCM granted Merrill Lynch an *asset lock-up option* to purchase two of SCM's divisions, considered to be SCM's key assets or *crown jewels*. The option was exercisable if Merrill Lynch was not successful in acquiring control of SCM. A lock-up option is a kind of consolation prize for the loser in a bidding war; depending on how it is priced, a lock-up option can have the effect of deterring other bids. Merrill Lynch represented in negotiations that it would not proceed with its leveraged buyout offer without the lock-up.

SCM's investment banker, Goldman Sachs, issued a written fairness opinion on the overall deal, stating that the sale of SCM to Merrill Lynch was fair to the shareholders of SCM from a financial point of view. A partner at Goldman Sachs also orally advised SCM's

directors that the option prices were "within the range of fair value." However, the directors did not inquire what the range of fair value was or how it was calculated. Unfortunately for the directors, the banker had not in fact calculated the fair value of the two divisions. Although the directors knew that the two divisions generated more than two-thirds of SCM's earnings, they never asked the investment banker why the divisions were being sold for less than half the total purchase price. The U.S. Court of Appeals for the Second Circuit held that the SCM directors' "paucity of information" and "their swiftness of decision-making" strongly suggested a breach of the duty of care. The asset lock-up was struck down. As in the case of officers' reports, blind reliance on the reports of experts creates a risk that the directors will not receive the protection of the business judgment rule.

Reasonable Supervision

As fiduciaries, directors have a responsibility to exercise reasonable supervision over corporate operations. In the leading case, *In re Caremark International Inc. Derivative Litigation*,[11] the Delaware Court of Chancery held that directors cannot satisfy their obligation to be reasonably informed concerning the corporation's compliance with the law and its business performance unless they assure themselves that the organization has in place reasonably designed information and reporting systems to provide senior management and the board itself with timely and accurate information as a matter of ordinary operations. The level of detail required is a question of business judgment. Although even a rationally designed information and reporting system will not eliminate the possibility that the corporation will violate laws or regulations, the board is required to exercise a good faith judgment that the corporation's information and reporting system is, in concept and design, adequate to assure the board that appropriate information will come to its attention in a timely manner. Failure to exercise adequate supervision may, in theory at least, render a director liable for losses caused by noncompliance with applicable legal standards.[12]

In the following case, the court considered whether the board of Citigroup could be held personally liable in a shareholder derivative suit for the bank's massive losses on its subprime mortgage portfolio. (A *shareholder derivative suit* is a suit brought by a shareholder on behalf of the corporation.)

---

9. *Id.* at 877.
10. 781 F.2d 264 (2d Cir. 1986).
11. 698 A.2d 959 (Del. Ch. 1996).
12. The Court of Chancery noted that the federal Organizational Sentencing Guidelines offer powerful incentives for corporations to have in place compliance programs to detect violations of law, promptly report violations to appropriate public officials when discovered, and take prompt, voluntary remedial efforts.

A CASE IN POINT

In re Citigroup Inc. Shareholder
Derivative Litigation

Court of Chancery of Delaware
946 A.2d 106 (Del. Ch. 2009).

Summary   Case 20.2

FACTS   In late 2005, housing prices, artificially inflated by speculation and easily available credit, began to plateau and then to deflate. Adjustable-rate mortgages began to reset, leaving homeowners with higher monthly payments, which led to an increase in defaults and foreclosures.

During this period, Citigroup, a global financial services company, was exposed to the subprime lending market through its involvement in collateralized debt obligations (CDOs), which are repackaged pools of lower-rated securities created by obtaining asset-backed securities like residential mortgage backed securities (RMBSs) and then selling rights to the cash flows from those securities in classes with different levels of risk and return. Citigroup was also exposed to the subprime mortgage market through its use of structured investment vehicles (SIVs), which are created by selling short-term debt and buying longer-term debt to yield higher returns.

A group of plaintiffs, including Montgomery County Employees' Retirement Fund and City of New Orleans Employees' Retirement System, sued a number of Citigroup directors who were members of the Audit and Risk Management Committee and considered audit committee experts. The plaintiffs alleged that from as early as 2006, the defendant directors and officers caused and allowed Citigroup to engage in subprime lending that ultimately left the bank exposed to massive losses by late 2007. In particular, the plaintiffs alleged that the defendants breached their fiduciary duty by (1) failing to adequately oversee and manage Citigroup's exposure to the problems in the subprime mortgage market, even when there were obvious "red flags," and (2) failing to ensure that Citigroup's financial reporting and other disclosures were thorough and accurate. They also alleged a waste of Citigroup's corporate assets.

ISSUE PRESENTED   What do shareholders have to allege to demonstrate that it would be futile to demand that the board sue the directors for failure to adequately protect the corporation from exposure to the subprime lending market?

SUMMARY OF OPINION   The Delaware Court of Chancery began by explaining the procedure whereby shareholders can bring a shareholder derivative action to recover damages to the corporation caused by a breach of fiduciary duty by the directors. Because the board of directors is usually responsible for deciding when the corporation should bring a lawsuit, shareholders must either make a pre-suit demand that the board authorize the lawsuit or show that such a demand would be futile. To show futility, the allegations must raise a reasonable doubt that "(1) the directors are disinterested and independent [or] (2) the challenged transaction was otherwise the product of a valid exercise of business judgment."

In this case, the plaintiffs did not question the independence of the directors. Nor did they attack a specific business decision of the board. Because they did not make a pre-suit demand, the plaintiffs had to allege particularized facts that create a reasonable doubt that the board would properly exercise its independent and disinterested business judgment when responding to a demand.

The court rejected the plaintiffs' assertion that a demand would have been futile because the directors' failure to oversee Citigroup's business subjected them to the risk of personal liability. The court explained that demand is excused based on a possibility of personal director liability only when a plaintiff can show director conduct that is so egregious on its face that substantial director liability exists.

The court then applied the *Caremark* standard to determine whether the Citigroup directors were liable for failure to oversee the business. Under *Caremark*, plaintiffs must show that the directors knew they were not discharging their fiduciary obligations or that the directors displayed a conscious disregard for their responsibilities, that is, something close to bad faith.

The burden is on the plaintiffs to rebut the presumption of good faith. A plaintiff can plead bad faith by alleging with particular facts that a director knowingly violated a fiduciary duty

CONTINUED

or failed to act in accord with a known duty to act, which demonstrates a conscious disregard for his or her duties. The court recognized that corporate directors have a duty to implement and monitor a system of oversight, but it explained that this obligation does not eviscerate the protections of the business judgment rule. Those protections are designed to allow corporate directors and managers to pursue risky transactions without the risk of being held personally liable if their decisions turn out poorly. The court noted that it is almost impossible, in hindsight, to determine whether directors properly evaluated risk and thus made the "right" business decision.

After analyzing the complaint, the court concluded that the allegations were insufficient to reasonably conclude that the defendants faced a substantial likelihood of personal liability that would prevent them from considering a demand impartially. The court further found that the allegations of the futility of a demand regarding the waste claims were also insufficient.

RESULT   The court dismissed the shareholder derivative suit. The allegations in the complaint were insufficient to show that a demand on the directors would have been futile.

COMMENTS   Although shareholders have the right to bring derivative suits for breach of fiduciary duty by the directors, "[i]n practice, however, many corporate lawyers will tell you that 'these rights are so limited as to be almost nonexistent,'" given the internal authority wielded by boards and managers and the expansive protections afforded by the business judgment rule."[13] Thus, the dissenters in *Citizens United* found little comfort in the majority's assertion that shareholders could use their corporate democracy rights to prevent a board from using corporate funds against their wishes in political campaigns.

---

13. Citizens United v. Fed. Election Comm'n, 130 S. Ct. 876, 978 (2010) (Stevens, J., concurring in part and dissenting in part) (citing Margaret Blair & Lynn Stout, *A Team Production Theory of Corporate Law*, 85 VA. L. REV. 247, 320 (1999)).

The U.S. District Court for the Central District of California refused to dismiss failure-to-supervise claims against inside and outside directors who served on the Finance, Credit, Audit & Ethics, and Operations & Public Policy Committees at Countrywide Financial Corporation.[14] The plaintiffs alleged that the defendant directors ignored red flags related to the deteriorating quality of the mortgages underwritten by Countrywide, including increasing delinquency rates, exponentially rising negative amortizations, and other signs of loan nonperformance. The plaintiffs alleged that "a pervasive 'culture' encouraged underwriters to grant risky loans to unqualified borrowers." Because "ongoing access to the secondary mortgage market requires the consistent production of quality mortgages and servicing of those mortgages at levels that meet or exceed secondary mortgage market standards," the defendant directors allegedly "either knew, or proceeded with deliberate recklessness with respect to, the fact that originating loans to borrowers who could not pay back their mortgages would ultimately be counterproductive, lucrative as it was in the short term."

Responsibility for SEC Filings

The Securities and Exchange Commission (SEC) has emphasized the affirmative responsibility of officers and directors under the federal securities laws to ensure the accuracy and completeness of public company filings with the SEC, such as annual and quarterly reports and proxy statements.[15] In addition, as discussed further in Chapter 21, the Sarbanes–Oxley Act of 2002 requires the chief executive officer and the chief financial officer to certify the accuracy of public companies' SEC filings and the adequacy of internal controls.

Officers and directors are required to conduct a full and informed review of the information contained in the final draft of the filings. If an officer or director knows or should have known about an inaccuracy in a proposed filing, he or she has an obligation to correct it. An officer or director may rely on the company's procedures for determining what disclosure is required only if he or she has a reasonable basis for believing that those procedures are effective and have resulted in full consideration of those issues.

---

14. *In re* Countrywide Fin. Corp. Derivative Litig., 554 F. Supp. 2d 1044 (C.D. Cal. 2008).

15. Report of Investigation Pursuant to Section 21(a) of the Securities Exchange Act of 1934 Concerning the Conduct of Certain Former Officers and Directors of W.R. Grace & Co., Exchange Act Release No. 39, 157 (Sept. 30, 1997).

If a director or officer is aware of facts that might have to be disclosed, he or she must go beyond the established procedures to inquire into the reasons for nondisclosure. Officers and directors cannot blindly rely on legal counsel's conclusions about the need for disclosure if they are aware of facts that seem to suggest that disclosure is required. They must raise the issue specifically with disclosure counsel, telling counsel exactly what they know and asking specifically whether disclosure is required. If they are not satisfied with the answers provided, they should insist that the documents be revised before they are filed with the SEC.

Disinterested Decision

Even when the board makes an informed decision, the business judgment rule is not applicable if the directors have a financial or other personal interest in the transaction at issue.[16] For example, if a board dominated by *inside directors* (that is, directors who are also officers of the corporation) sets executive compensation, they can be required to prove to a court that the transaction was fair and reasonable. To be disinterested in the transaction normally means that the directors can neither have an interest on either side of the transaction nor expect to derive any personal financial benefit from the transaction (other than benefits that accrue to all shareholders of the corporation, which are not considered self-dealing).

Even if one or more individual directors have an interest in the transaction, the board's decision may still be entitled to the protection of the business judgment rule if the transaction is approved by a majority of the

disinterested directors. If the board delegates too much of its authority or is too much influenced by an interested party, however, then the entire board may be tainted with that individual's personal motivations and lose the protection of the business judgment rule.

In some jurisdictions, a relevant factor in determining whether a board is disinterested is whether the majority of the board consists of outside directors. The fact that outside directors receive directors' fees but not salaries is viewed as heightening the likelihood that the directors were not motivated by personal interest. Application of these rules in the context of takeovers, mergers, and acquisitions is discussed later in this chapter.

Statutory Limitations on Directors' Liability for Breach of Duty of Care

Cases such as *Van Gorkom* had a devastating impact on the market for directors' and officers' liability insurance and on the availability of qualified outside directors. In response, Delaware adopted legislation in 1986 to allow shareholders to limit the monetary liability of directors for breaches of the duty of care (but not the duty of loyalty or good faith) in any suit brought by the corporation or in a shareholder derivative suit. Most other states followed suit. Delaware and most other states require that the limitation be contained in the original certificate of incorporation or in an amendment approved by a majority of the shareholders. The statutes do not affect directors' liability for suits brought by third parties; they merely allow the shareholders to agree that, under certain circumstances, they will not seek monetary recovery against the directors. The directors' liability for breach of the duty of loyalty may not be limited. Also, most states do not allow officers (as compared with directors) to be exonerated from liability for breach of the duty of care or the duty of loyalty.

Delaware's Statute

Section 102(b)(7) of the Delaware Corporation Code permits the certificate of incorporation to include a provision limiting or eliminating the personal liability of directors to the corporation or to its shareholders for monetary damages for breach of fiduciary duty. Such a provision cannot, however, eliminate or limit the liability of a director for (1) any breach of the director's duty of loyalty to the corporation or its shareholders, (2) acts or omissions that are not in good faith or that involve intentional misconduct or knowing violation of law, (3) unlawful payments of dividends or stock purchases, or (4) any transaction from which the director derived an improper personal benefit.

California's Statute

Section 204(a)(10) of the California Corporation Code, which applies to corporations organized under California law, is more restrictive. In addition to the

---

16. *See, e.g.*, Gantler v. Stephens, 965 A.2d 695 (Del. 2009).

four exceptions contained in the Delaware statute, California prohibits the elimination or limitation of director liability for (1) acts or omissions that show a reckless disregard for the director's duty to the corporation or its shareholders in circumstances in which the director was aware, or should have been aware, of a risk of serious injury to the corporation or its shareholders; and (2) an unexcused pattern of inattention that amounts to an abdication of the director's duties to the corporation or its shareholders.

Although other states apply their corporate governance rules only to corporations incorporated there, California imposes its pro-shareholder provisions on so-called privately held *quasi-foreign corporations*. Such corporations are incorporated elsewhere but (1) have more than 50% of their stock owned by California residents and (2) derive more than 50% of their sales, payroll, and property tax from activities in California. As a result, a privately held quasi-foreign corporation will be subject to California's more restrictive limits on monetary liability even though the state of incorporation (e.g., Delaware) is more permissive.

DUTY OF GOOD FAITH

Allegations of failure to act in good faith take on special significance in cases involving corporations that have eliminated directors' personal liability for breaches of the duty of care. Because the statutes authorizing such limitations list failures to act in good faith separately from breaches of the duty of loyalty, courts have started to focus more directly on good faith, especially when the directors had no personal interest in the transaction at hand.

In certain cases, the duty of good faith may be subsumed within the duty of loyalty. As the Delaware Supreme Court explained, "'[a] director cannot act loyally towards the corporation unless she acts in the good faith belief that her actions are in the corporation's best interest.'"[17]

But, as Chancellor Chandler explained in litigation arising out of Walt Disney Company's termination payments to Michael Ovitz, in certain instances:

> The fiduciary duties of care and loyalty, as traditionally defined, may not be aggressive enough to protect shareholder interests when the board is well advised, is not legally beholden to the management or a controlling shareholder and when the board does not suffer from other disabling conflicts of interest, such as a patently self-dealing transaction. Good faith may serve to fill this gap and ensure that the persons entrusted *by shareholders* to

govern Delaware corporations do so with an honesty of purpose and with an understanding of whose interests they are there to protect.[18]

On appeal, the Delaware Supreme Court stated:

> "[I]ssues of good faith are (to a certain degree) inseparably and necessarily intertwined with the duties of care and loyalty. . . ." But, in the pragmatic, conduct-regulating legal realm which calls for more precise conceptual line drawing, the answer is that grossly negligent conduct, without more, does not and cannot constitute a breach of the fiduciary duty to act in good faith. The conduct that is the subject of due care may overlap with the conduct that comes within the rubric of good faith in a psychological sense, but from a legal standpoint those duties are and must remain quite distinct. Both our legislative history and our common law jurisprudence distinguish sharply between the duties to exercise due care and to act in good faith, and highly significant consequences flow from that distinction.[19]

As a result, mere gross negligence was not enough to constitute the lack of good faith that would have subjected the disinterested directors to personal monetary liability. To invoke an exception to a section 102(b)(7) exculpatory provision, the plaintiff must make "a strong showing of misconduct,"[20] such as "intentionally acting 'with a purpose other than that of advancing the best interests of the corporation,' acting 'with the intent to violate applicable positive law,' or 'intentionally fail[ing] to act in the face of a known duty to act.'"[21]

In *Stone v. Ritter*,[22] the Delaware Supreme Court recognized that "good faith may be described colloquially as part of a 'triad' of fiduciary duties," but ruled that the obligation to act in good faith does not establish an independent fiduciary duty that stands on the same footing as the duties of care and loyalty. Only the latter two duties, where violated, "may directly result in liability, whereas a failure to act in good faith may do so, but indirectly."[23] As a result, in Delaware, a failure to act in good faith, taken alone, does not appear to give rise to liability.

Nonetheless, as seen in the following case, directors who consciously ignore known risks of noncompliance risk losing the protection of both the business judgment rule and any exculpatory provisions in their corporate charter.

---

17. Stone v. Ritter, 911 A.2d 362, 370 (Del. 2006) (quoting Guttman v. Huang, 823 A.2d 492, 506 n.34 (Del. Ch. 2003)).

18. *In re* Walt Disney Co. Derivative Litig., 907 A.2d 693, 760 n.487 (Del. Ch. 2005).

19. *In re* Walt Disney Co. Derivative Litig., 906 A.2d 27, 65 (Del. 2006).

20. *Id.*

21. *In re* Lear Corp. S'holder Litig., 967 A.2d 640, 653–54 (Del. Ch. 2008).

22. 911 A.2d 362 (Del. 2006).

23. *Id.*

| A CASE IN POINT | *In the Language of the Court* | Case 20.3 |

In re Abbott Laboratories
Derivative Shareholders Litigation

*United States Court of Appeals for
the Seventh Circuit*
325 F.3d 795 (7th Cir. 2003).

FACTS   In 1999, Abbott Laboratories, an Illinois corporation, entered into a consent decree that required it to pay a $100 million fine, at the time the largest penalty ever imposed for a civil violation of Food and Drug Administration (FDA) regulations. The FDA also required Abbott to withdraw 125 types of medical diagnostic test kits, destroy certain inventory, and make a number of corrective changes in its manufacturing procedures after six years of quality control violations. Abbott shareholders brought a shareholder derivative suit alleging that the directors breached their fiduciary duties when they failed to take necessary action to correct repeated noncompliance problems brought to Abbott's attention by the FDA in the period from 1993 until 1999.

Not only had the FDA sent Abbott a Form 483 noting deviations from the requirements set forth in the FDA's "Current Good Manufacturing Practice" after each of its thirteen inspections of Abbott's Abbott Park and North Chicago facilities, but the FDA had also sent four formal certified Warning Letters to Abbott. The first was sent to David Thompson, president of Abbott's Diagnostics Division (ADD), on October 20, 1993. The letter stated that the FDA had found adulterated in vitro diagnostic products and warned: "Failure to correct these deviations may result in regulatory action being initiated by the Food and Drug Administration without further notice. These actions include, but are not limited to, seizure, injunction, and/or civil penalties." A second Warning Letter was sent to Thompson on March 28, 1994, with a copy to Duane Burnham, Abbott's CEO and board chair.

On January 11, 1995, the *Wall Street Journal* reported that the FDA had uncovered a wide range of flaws in Abbott's quality assurance procedures used in assembling its diagnostic products. In July 1995, the FDA and Abbott entered into a Voluntary Compliance Plan to work together to correct Abbott's deficiencies. In February 1998, after finding continued deviations from the regulations, the FDA sent Abbott the equivalent of a Warning Letter closing out the plan. In 1999, the FDA sent the fourth and final Warning Letter to Miles White, a member of Abbott's board and the current CEO. White had replaced Burnham as CEO in April 1999.

The plaintiffs did not demand that the members of Abbott's board institute an action against themselves for breach of their fiduciary duties, arguing that such a demand would be futile. Under applicable law, such a demand is not required if the plaintiffs plead facts showing that the directors faced a substantial likelihood of liability for their actions. In particular, "demand can only be excused where facts are alleged with particularity which create a reasonable doubt that the directors' action was entitled to the protections of the business judgment rule."[24] The district court dismissed the complaint, and the plaintiffs appealed.

ISSUE PRESENTED   Is it a breach of directors' duty of good faith for them to fail to follow up on repeated notices of regulatory noncompliance?

OPINION   WOOD, J., writing on behalf of the U.S. Court of Appeals for the Seventh Circuit:

Plaintiffs in *Abbott* allege facts that the directors were aware of known violations, providing evidence that there was direct knowledge through the Warning Letters and as members of the Audit Committee. Under proper corporate governance procedures—the existence of which is not contested by either party in *Abbott*—information of the violations would have been shared at the board meetings. In addition, plaintiffs have alleged that, as fiduciaries, the directors all signed the annual SEC forms which specifically addressed government regulation of Abbott's products. The *Abbott* case is clearly distinguished from the "unconsidered" inaction in *In re Caremark*.[25]

. . . .

CONTINUED

---

24. Aronson v. Lewis, 473 A.2d 805, 808 (Del. 1984), *overruled on other grounds by* Brehm v. Eisner, 746 A.2d 244 (Del. 2000).

25. 698 A.2d 959, 967 (Del. Ch. 1996).

The district court noted, correctly, that the plaintiffs did not allege that Abbott's reporting system was inadequate. . . . Where there is a corporate governance structure in place, we must then assume the corporate governance procedures were followed and that the board knew of the problems and decided no action was required. . . .

. . . .

Delaware law states that director liability may arise from the breach of the duty to exercise appropriate attention to potentially illegal corporate activities or from "an *unconsidered failure of the board to act* in circumstances in which due attention would, arguably, have prevented the loss." *In re Caremark.* The court held that "a sustained or systematic failure of the board to exercise oversight . . . will establish the lack of good faith that is a necessary condition to [director] liability." . . .

Given the extensive paper trail in *Abbott* concerning the violations and the inferred awareness of the problems, the facts support a reasonable assumption that there was a "sustained and systematic failure of the board to exercise oversight," in this case intentional in that the directors knew of the violations of law, took no steps in an effort to prevent or remedy the situation, and that failure to take any action for such an inordinate amount of time resulted in substantial corporate losses, establishing a lack of good faith. We find that six years of noncompliance, inspections, 483s, Warning Letters, and notice in the press, all of which then resulted in the largest civil fine ever imposed by the FDA and the destruction and suspension of products which accounted for approximately $250 million in corporate assets, indicate that the directors' decision to not act was not made in good faith and was contrary to the best interests of the company. With respect to demand futility based on the directors' conscious inaction, we find that the plaintiffs have sufficiently pleaded allegations, if true, of a breach of the duty of good faith to reasonably conclude that the directors' actions fell outside the protection of the business judgment rule. . . .

The directors contend that they are not liable under Abbott's certificate of incorporation provision which exempts the directors from liability [for breach of the duty of care]. Directors are not protected by that provision when a complaint alleges facts that infer a breach of loyalty or good faith. [*Editor's note:* The court stated that the burden of establishing good faith rests with the director seeking protection under the exculpatory provision.]

Plaintiffs in *Abbott* accused the directors not only of gross negligence, but of intentional conduct in failing to address the federal violation problems, alleging "a conscious disregard of known risks, which conduct, if proven, cannot have been undertaken in good faith."

RESULT   The plaintiffs pleaded sufficient facts to prove that the directors were not entitled to the protection of the business judgment rule. The plaintiffs' claims were also not precluded by Abbott's charter provision. The trial court's dismissal of the complaint was reversed. The plaintiffs could proceed with the derivative action.

COMMENTS   The directors were potentially liable even though a majority of the board was independent and there were no allegations of self-dealing.

CRITICAL THINKING QUESTIONS

1. Would the independent directors have been liable if the CEO and board chair had not given them copies of the FDA Warning Letters?
2. If you had been an independent director on Abbott's board, how would you have responded upon receiving notice of the second FDA Warning Letter?

DUTY OF LOYALTY

To comply with their duty of loyalty, directors and managers must act in good faith and subordinate their own interests to those of the corporation and its shareholders. As a result, when a shareholder attacks a transaction in which managers or directors are engaged in self-dealing or have a self-interest other than that of a corporate fiduciary, the courts will closely review the merits of the deal. Traditionally, such a transaction has been voidable unless its proponents could show that it was fair and reasonable to the corporation.

Corporate Opportunities

One central corollary of the fiduciary duty of loyalty is that officers and directors may not take personal advantage of a business opportunity that rightfully belongs to the corporation. This is known as the *corporate opportunity doctrine.* For example, suppose that a copper-mining corporation is actively looking for mining sites. If an officer of the corporation learns of an attractive site in the course of his business for the corporation, the officer may not buy it for himself. If the officer attempts to do so, a shareholder can block the sale or impose a *constructive trust* on any profits the officer makes from the acquisition, that is, force the officer to hold the profits for the benefit of the corporation and pay them over to the corporation on request.

The courts have devised several tests for determining whether an opportunity belongs to a corporation. Perhaps the most widely used is the *line-of-business test.* Under this test, if an officer, director, or controlling shareholder learns of an opportunity in the course of her business for the corporation and the opportunity is in the corporation's line of business, a court will not permit the officer, director, or controlling shareholder to keep the opportunity for herself.

For example, the Delaware Supreme Court ruled in a classic case that the president and director of Loft, Inc., a company engaged in manufacturing candies, syrups, beverages, and foodstuffs, could not set up a new corporation to acquire the secret formula and trademarks of Pepsi Cola.[26] He had unsuccessfully sought a volume discount for Loft's purchases of syrup from the Coca-Cola Company and was contemplating substituting Pepsi for Coke.

If an officer or director develops an idea on company time using company resources, a court will be more likely to find a breach of fiduciary duty if the officer or director then leaves to pursue the idea. If the officer or director has signed an assignment of inventions, then the idea will usually belong to the company under the terms of that agreement. Even without such an agreement, use of company time or resources may restrict the ability of the officer or director to define the line of business narrowly.

Other courts have considered whether (1) it would be fair for the fiduciary to keep the opportunity, (2) the corporation has an expectancy or interest growing out of an existing right in the opportunity, or (3) the interference by the fiduciary will hinder the corporation's purposes. Because different states apply different tests, a corporate fiduciary should always consult local counsel if there is any question of the fiduciary's usurpation of a corporate opportunity.

An officer or director presented with a corporate opportunity is required to disclose it to the disinterested directors, who may then accept or reject the opportunity. Disclosure is required even when the officers or directors taking advantage of the opportunity, acting in their capacity as controlling shareholders, could have prevented the corporation from pursuing it. For example, *Thorpe v. CERBCO Inc.*[27] involved two brothers who were officers, directors, and controlling shareholders of CERBCO. When a potential acquirer brought up the possibility of buying one of CERBCO's subsidiaries, the brothers instead proposed to sell their own shares to the acquirer. Because the brothers (in their capacity as shareholders) could have blocked every viable sale of the subsidiary, CERBCO was not in fact able to take advantage of the opportunity. Thus, CERBCO suffered no damages as a result of this lost opportunity because there was zero probability of the sale occurring (due to the brothers' lawful right to vote against it). Nevertheless, the brothers were fiduciaries of CERBCO and, as such, had the duty to present the sale opportunity to CERBCO. The court held that the brothers were not entitled to the profit gained by their breach of this duty. As a result, they were not entitled to keep the profit they had made on the sale of their stock to the potential acquirer of CERBCO's subsidiary and had to disgorge all of their gains to the corporation.

DUTY OF CANDOR

When requesting shareholder action, directors have a duty to disclose "fully and fairly" all material facts.[28] The directors of First Niles Financial violated this duty when they stated in a proxy statement that "[a]fter careful deliberations, the board determined in its business judgment [that a merger] proposal was not in the best interests of the Company or our shareholders," when in fact the board had not objectively considered the merits of the merger proposal.[29] In *Malone v. Brincat,*[30] the Delaware Supreme Court went a step further and held that whenever directors disseminate information to shareholders, the fiduciary duties of care, loyalty, and good faith apply, even if no shareholder action is sought. As a result, the court held that "directors who knowingly disseminate false information that results in corporate injury or damage to an individual stockholder violate their fiduciary duty, and may be held accountable in a manner appropriate to the circumstances."[31]

---

26. Guth v. Loft, Inc., 5 A.2d 503 (Del. 1939).

27. 703 A.2d 645 (Del. 1997).

28. Stroud v. Grace, 606 A.2d 75, 84 (Del. 1992).

29. Gantler v. Stephens, 965 A.2d 695 (Del. 2009).

30. 722 A.2d 5 (Del. 1998).

31. *Id.* at 9.

DUTIES IN THE CONTEXT OF MERGERS, ACQUISITIONS, AND TAKEOVERS

The decision whether to merge or sell a corporation is generally protected by the business judgment rule.[32] In deciding whether to sell a company and on what terms, directors should consider seven key factors: (1) the company's intrinsic value, (2) the appropriateness of delegating negotiating authority to management, (3) nonprice considerations, (4) the reliability of officers' reports to the board, (5) the reliability of experts' reports, (6) the investment banker's fee structure, and (7) the reasonableness of any defensive tactics. As explained earlier, the directors must act in good faith and be adequately informed.

The Company's Intrinsic Value

The ability to make an informed decision as to the acceptability of a proposed buyout price requires knowledge of the company's intrinsic value. Determining intrinsic value entails more than an assessment of the premium of the offering price over the market price per share of the company's stock. When, as in *Van Gorkom*, it is believed that the market has consistently undervalued the company's stock, evaluating the offered price by comparing it with the market price is, according to the Delaware Supreme Court, "faulty, indeed fallacious."[33]

Thus, the directors must do more than assess the adequacy of the premium and compare it with the premiums paid in other takeovers in the same or similar industries. They must also assess the intrinsic or fair value of the company (or division) as a going concern and on a liquidation basis.

Practitioners have read *Van Gorkom* as virtually mandating participation by an investment banker if directors are to avoid personal liability. Although the *Van Gorkom* court expressly disclaimed such an intention, for all practical purposes, directors should look to both internal and external sources for guidance. The most reliable valuation information will consist of financial data supplied by management and evaluated by investment bankers knowledgeable about the industry and recent merger and acquisition activity.

The *Hanson Trust*[34] decision makes it clear, however, that the mere presence of investment bankers in the target's boardroom will not shield its directors from personal liability. In that case, the Goldman Sachs partner's oral opinion that the option prices were "within the range of fair value" did not withstand the scrutiny of the Second Circuit on appeal.

Delegation of Negotiating Authority

If members of management are financial participants in the proposed transaction, the delegation of negotiation responsibilities to management or inside directors will expose the board to greater risks of liability. The Second Circuit observed in *Hanson Trust*:

> SCM's board delegated to management broad authority to work directly with Merrill to structure an LBO proposal, and then appears to have swiftly approved management's proposals. Such broad delegations of authority are not uncommon and generally are quite proper as conforming to the way that a Board acts in generating proposals for its own consideration. However, when management has a self-interest in consummating an LBO, standard post hoc review procedures may be insufficient. . . . SCM's management and the Board's advisers presented the various agreements to the SCM directors more or less as *faits accompli*, which the Board quite hastily approved. . . . In short, the Board appears to have failed to ensure that alternative bids were negotiated or scrutinized by those whose only loyalty was to the shareholders.[35]

Nonprice Considerations

In evaluating a buyout proposal, directors have a fiduciary duty to familiarize themselves with any material nonprice provisions of the proposed agreement. Directors are duty bound to consider separately whether such provisions are in the best interest of the company and its shareholders or, if not, whether the proposal as a whole, notwithstanding such provisions, is in the best interest of their constituencies.

In *Van Gorkom*, for example, several outside directors maintained that Pritzker's merger proposal was approved with the understanding that "if we got a better deal, we had a right to take it."[36] The directors also asserted that they had "insisted" on an amendment reserving to Trans Union the right to disclose proprietary information to competing bidders. However, the court found that the merger agreement reserved neither of these rights to Trans Union. In the court's view, the directors had "no rational basis" for asserting that their acceptance of Pritzker's offer was conditioned on a market test of the offer or that Trans Union had a right to withdraw from the agreement in order to accept a higher bid.

Directors should therefore ensure not only that they correctly understand the nonprice provisions of a proposed merger agreement but also that the provisions find their way into the definitive agreement. They should verify this by reading the documents prior to execution.

---

32. *Gantler*, 965 A.2d 695.

33. Smith v. Van Gorkom, 488 A.2d 858, 876 (Del. 1985) (Case 20.1).

34. Hanson Trust PLC v. ML SCM Acquisition, Inc., 781 F.2d 264 (2d Cir. 1986).

35. *Id.* at 277.

36. *Van Gorkom*, 488 A.2d at 879.

Takeover Defenses

The business judgment rule creates a powerful presumption of validity in favor of the directors of a corporation. As noted earlier, the business judgment rule does not apply if the directors have an interest in the transaction being acted on. If a hostile raider is successful, it is probably going to replace the company's management and board of directors as its first step after assuming control. Thus, the directors arguably have a personal interest whenever a board takes defensive action to oppose a hostile takeover.

Unocal *Proportionality Test*

Unocal Corp. v. Mesa Petroleum Co.[37] established the principle that the business judgment rule applies to takeover defenses, provided that the directors can show that they had reasonable grounds for believing that the unwelcome suitor posed a threat to corporate policy and effectiveness and that the defense was a reasonable response to that threat. This enhanced judicial scrutiny is designed to guard against "the omnipresent specter that a board may be acting primarily in its own interests, rather than those of the corporation and its shareholders."[38]

The Delaware Supreme Court further explained:

> If a defensive measure is to come within the ambit of the business judgment rule, it must be reasonable in relation to the threat posed. This entails an analysis by the directors of the nature of the takeover bid and its effect on the corporate enterprise. Examples of such concerns may include: inadequacy of the price offered, nature and timing of the offer, questions of illegality, the impact on "constituencies" other than shareholders (i.e., creditors, customers, employees, and perhaps even the community generally), the risk of nonconsummation, and the quality of securities being offered in the exchange. While not a controlling factor, it also seems to us that a board may reasonably consider the basic stockholder interests at stake, including those of short term speculators, whose actions may have fueled the coercive aspect of the offer at the expense of the long term investor.[39]

If the directors succeed in making this initial showing, then they are entitled to the protection of the business judgment rule. Under those circumstances, the Delaware Supreme Court stated:

> [U]nless it is shown by a preponderance of the evidence that the directors' decisions were primarily based on perpetuating themselves in office, or some other breach of fiduciary duty such as fraud, overreaching, lack of good faith, or being uninformed, a court will not substitute its judgment for that of the board.[40]

Two-tier offers, in which a hostile bidder offers cash consideration in the first stage to gain control and then offers securities in a second-step merger, are deemed particularly coercive, especially when coupled with the threat of greenmail. (*Greenmail* occurs when a raider acquires stock in a target company and then threatens to commence a hostile takeover unless its stock is repurchased by the target at a premium over the market price.) Even if shareholders consider the price inadequate, they might well feel coerced into tendering in the first stage for fear of receiving securities of even less value in the second stage. As discussed below, defensive tactics, including shareholder rights plans (also called poison pills), can protect shareholders from coercive tender offers.

Duty to Maximize Shareholder Value Under *Revlon*

Once the judgment is made that a sale or breakup of the corporation is in the best interests of the shareholders or is inevitable, directors have a fiduciary duty to obtain the best available price for the shareholders. This rule was first articulated in a case involving a hostile takeover bid for Revlon, Inc. by Pantry Pride.[41]

After initially resisting the takeover attempt, the Revlon board elected to go forward with a friendly buyout from another company at a lower price than that offered by the hostile bidder. The Revlon board sought to justify the lower price by pointing out the benefits of the friendly buyout for other corporate constituencies, such as the Revlon noteholders. The hostile bidder sued to enjoin the friendly buyout.

The Delaware Supreme Court required the Revlon board to seek the highest price for the shareholders. The court defined the duty of the directors as follows:

> The Revlon board's authorization permitting management to negotiate a merger or buyout with a third party was a recognition that the company was for sale. The duty of the board had thus changed from the preservation of Revlon as a corporate entity to the maximization of the company's value at a sale for the stockholders' benefit. . . . The directors' role changed from defenders of the corporate bastion to auctioneers charged with getting the best price for the stockholders at a sale of the company.[42]

Not every change of corporate control necessitates an auction, however.[43] If fairness to shareholders and the minimizing of conflicts of interest can be demonstrated, the added burden of having an auction may not be necessary. The Delaware Supreme Court declined to make a specific rule for determining when a market test

---

37. 493 A.2d 946 (Del. 1985).

38. *Id.* at 954.

39. *Id.* at 954–55.

40. *Id.* at 958.

41. Revlon, Inc. v. MacAndrews & Forbes Holdings, Inc., 506 A.2d 173 (Del. 1986).

42. *Id.* at 182.

43. Barkan v. Amsted Industries, Inc., 567 A.2d 1279 (Del. 1989).

(or "market check") is required. The court simply stated: "[I]t must be clear that the board had sufficient knowledge of relevant markets to form the basis for its belief that it acted in the best interests of the shareholders."[44]

It is doubtful that the directors' failure to consider every conceivable alternative would in itself amount to a breach of fiduciary duty. Such a rule would be unduly harsh. In hindsight, a complaining shareholder could almost always conjure up at least one alternative that the directors failed to consider. As the Delaware Supreme Court stated, "No court can tell directors exactly how to accomplish" the goal of maximizing shareholder value.[45] Thus, a board might reasonably conclude that delaying the signing of a merger agreement to do a premarket check was not worth the risk of losing an attractive offer.[46] On the other hand, the failure of a board to consider any alternatives at all, or the unwillingness of a board to negotiate with anyone other than its chosen white knight (or with the initial offeror), would be a breach of fiduciary duty unless there were special circumstances.

When Is a Company in Revlon Mode?

The case of *Paramount Communications, Inc. v. Time Inc.*[47] examined the question of what constitutes an event triggering the *Revlon* duty to maximize shareholder value. (A company with such an obligation is deemed to be in *Revlon mode*.) Time had entered into a friendly stock-for-stock merger agreement with Warner Communications. Under that agreement, roughly 60% of the stock of the new combined entity Time–Warner would be held by former public shareholders of Warner. The merger agreement was subject to the approval of Time's shareholders.

Shortly before the Time shareholder vote was to take place, Paramount Communications made a hostile, unsolicited cash tender offer for all Time shares. In response, Time proceeded with its own highly leveraged cash tender offer to acquire 51% of Warner, to be followed by a back-end, second-step merger of the two companies. This tender offer, which would preclude acceptance of the Paramount tender offer, did not require approval by the Time shareholders. Paramount challenged the actions of Time's directors in opposing its offer, arguing that the Time board had put Time in the *Revlon* mode when it agreed to the stock merger with Warner.

The Delaware Supreme Court held that this transaction did not trigger *Revlon* duties because there was no change in control. Majority control shifted from one "fluid aggregation of unaffiliated shareholders" to another and remained in the hands of the public. As a result, the

Time board could properly take into account such intangibles as the desire to preserve the Time culture and journalistic integrity in deciding to reject Paramount's hostile tender offer, which was arguably worth more to shareholders than the Time–Warner combination. The court considered this to be a strategic alliance, not a sale of Time to Warner, which would have triggered the *Revlon* duty to maximize shareholder value.

Relying heavily on the precedent established by the *Paramount v. Time* case, Paramount entered into a friendly merger agreement with Viacom, Inc. in September 1993. At the time Paramount agreed to merge with Viacom, control of Paramount was vested in the "fluid aggregation of unaffiliated stockholders," and not in a single person, entity, or group. Sumner Redstone was the CEO, chair, and majority shareholder of Viacom. After the proposed merger, he would be the controlling shareholder of the combined Paramount–Viacom entity. When QVC Network, Inc. made a hostile unsolicited offer for Paramount that was worth $1.3 billion more than Viacom's offer, the Paramount board refused to negotiate with QVC and instead stood by its merger agreement with Viacom.

QVC then sued the Paramount directors, arguing that the Paramount board had put Paramount in the *Revlon* mode when it committed to a transaction that would shift control of Paramount from the public shareholders to Redstone. The Paramount board argued that it had no duty to maximize shareholder value because it was pursuing a strategic alliance with Viacom, not a breakup of the company. The Delaware Supreme Court rejected this argument and ruled that the Paramount directors had an obligation to continue their search for the best value reasonably available to the stockholders.[48]

The court ruled:

> [W]hen a corporation undertakes a transaction which will cause: (a) a change in corporate control; or (b) a break-up of the corporate entity, the directors' obligation is to seek the best value reasonably available to the stockholders. This obligation arises because the effect of the Viacom-Paramount transaction, if consummated, is to shift control of Paramount from the public stockholders to a controlling stockholder, Viacom.[49]

Regardless of the present Paramount board's vision of a long-term strategic alliance with Viacom, once the Paramount–Viacom deal was consummated, Redstone would have the power to alter that vision. Furthermore, once control shifted, the current Paramount stockholders would have no leverage to demand another control premium in the future.

---

44. *Id.* at 1288.

45. Lyondell Chem. Co. v. Ryan, 970 A.2d 235 (Del. 2009).

46. *In re* Smurfit-Stone Container Corp. S'holder Litig., 2011 WL 2028076 (Del. Ch. May 20, 2011).

47. 571 A.2d 1140 (Del. 1990).

48. Paramount Commc'ns, Inc., v. QVC Network, Inc., 637 A.2d 34 (Del. 1994).

49. *Id.* at 48.

IN BRIEF

Application of the Business Judgment Rule

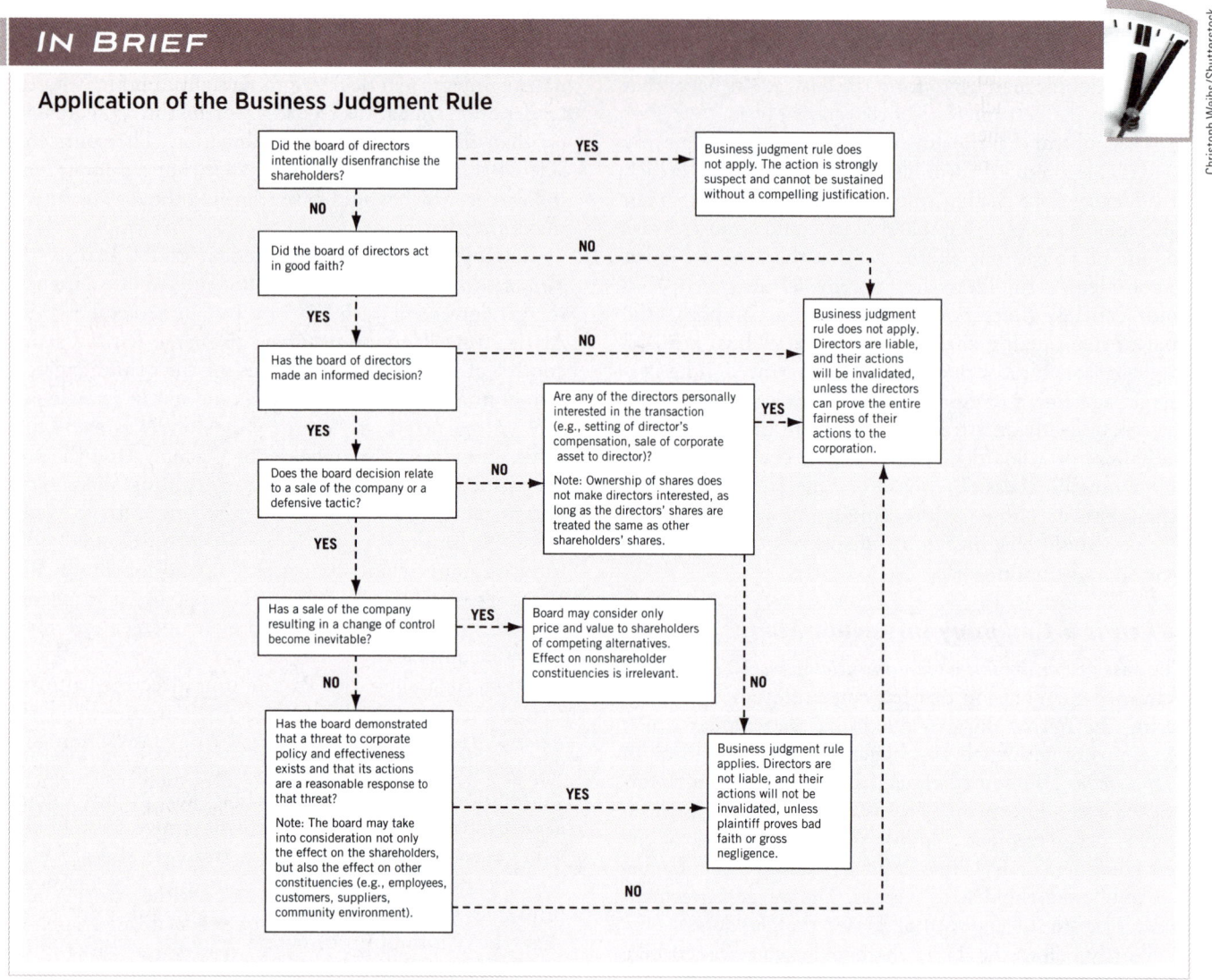

The Delaware Supreme Court was highly critical of the process the Paramount board followed:

> The directors' initial hope and expectation for a strategic alliance with Viacom was allowed to dominate their decision-making process to the point where the arsenal of defensive measures established at the outset was perpetuated (not modified or eliminated) when the situation was dramatically altered. QVC's unsolicited bid presented the opportunity for significantly greater value for the stockholders and enhanced negotiating leverage for the directors. Rather than seizing those opportunities, the Paramount directors chose to wall themselves off from material information which was reasonably available and to hide behind the defensive measures as a rationalization for refusing to negotiate with QVC or seeking other alternatives.[50]

In *In re Lukens Inc. Shareholders Litigation*,[51] the Delaware Court of Chancery concluded that a merger

of Lukens with Bethlehem Steel triggered *Revlon* duties even though more than 30% of the merger consideration consisted of shares of common stock of Bethlehem, a widely held company with no controlling stockholder. Because 62% of the consideration was cash, the court concluded that "for a substantial majority of the then-current shareholders, 'there is no long run.'"[52] The Delaware Court of Chancery also applied Revlon to a merger in which public shareholders received half their merger consideration in stock of the acquirer and half in cash.[53]

The fact that a shareholder has filed a Schedule 13D disclosing its right to acquire 8% of the target's stock and its interest in possibly acquiring the target does not put the target in *Revlon* mode.[54] Therefore, the target board did violate its fiduciary duties when it adopted a "wait and see" approach.

The "In Brief" provides a decision tree for analyzing when the business judgment rule will apply to board decisions.

50. *Id.* at 51.

51. 757 A.2d 720 (Del. Ch. 1999), *aff'd*, 757 A.2d 1278 (Del. 2000).

52. *Id.* at 732 n.25.

53. *In re* Smurfit-Stone Container Corp. S'holder Litig., 2011 WL 2028076 (Del. Ch. May 20, 2011).

54. Lyondell Chem. Co. v. Ryan, 970 A.2d 235 (Del. 2009).

Deal Protection Devices

Often the parties to a friendly merger will use *deal protection devices*, such as no-talk provisions, to dissuade other bidders and thereby protect the consummation of the friendly merger transaction. Defensive devices can be economic, structural, or both.

No-Talk Provisions

Delaware courts are highly skeptical of agreements that purport to limit directors' ability to fulfill what they in good faith perceive their fiduciary duties to be. For example, the Court of Chancery refused to enforce a no-talk clause in a stock-for-stock merger agreement between Capital Re Corporation and ACE Limited. The *no-talk clause* permitted Capital Re to engage in discussions with and provide information to other bidders only if the board concluded, based on the written opinion of outside legal counsel, that engaging in discussions or providing information was required to prevent the board from breaching its fiduciary duties to its stockholders.[55] Although Capital Re's counsel opined that negotiating with other bidders was consistent with the board's fiduciary duties, counsel did not state that the board was *required* to discuss an offer by another bidder. The court indicated that a provision that purports to prevent a board from talking with other bidders, even if the directors determine that they have a fiduciary duty to do so, is "particularly suspect when a failure to consider other offers guarantees the consummation of the original transaction, however more valuable an alternate transaction may be and however less valuable the original transaction might have become since the merger agreement was signed."[56]

The court did suggest that a no-talk clause with no *fiduciary out* (a clause allowing the board of directors to negotiate with other bidders or to terminate a merger agreement) might be permissible if (1) the stockholders could freely vote for or against the existing merger agreement and choose among the present merger, a subsequent merger, or no merger at all; or (2) the board agreed to the provision as a way to end an auction for sale of a company after a thorough canvass of the market. While acknowledging the tension between a vested contract right and the board's duty to determine what its own fiduciary duties require, the court concluded that a contract right must give way when (1) "the acquirer knew, or should have known, of the target board's breach of fiduciary duty"; (2) the "transaction remains pending"; and (3) "the board's violation of fiduciary duty relates to policy concerns that are especially significant."[57]

On the other hand, courts are more likely to permit *no-shop agreements*, whereby the target agrees not to actively solicit other bidders but retains the right to negotiate with parties that submit unsolicited bids to the target. Once again, such devices are more likely to withstand attack when they are put into place after a canvass of the market and as a condition to a bidder's willingness to make a favorable bid.

Breakup Fees

In exchange for providing a fiduciary out, a bidder will usually demand that some predetermined amount of money be paid to it if the deal fails to close because the target terminates the agreement. *Termination* or *breakup fees* are sometimes characterized as liquidated damages provisions, and they are often 2% to 3% of the value of the deal. They are usually intended to help make the bidder whole for its out-of-pocket expenses (for attorneys, investment bankers, and the like) and lost opportunity costs.

For example, in December 2011, AT&T agreed to pay Deutsche Telecom, T-Mobile's parent, a breakup fee of $4 billion—$3 billion in cash and $1 billion in other assets—after AT&T abandoned the deal due to antitrust concerns.[58] In mergers of equals, where there is no clear buyer or seller, there are often reciprocal termination fee provisions. For example, the 2009 merger agreement between Black & Decker and Stanley Works contained a $125 million termination fee for either party.[59] Although courts in Delaware and elsewhere have upheld termination fees in the 1% to 3% range under either the business judgment rule or the standard of reasonableness applied to liquidated damages provisions, fees that are so large as to constitute "showstoppers" are much more likely to be struck down.[60]

Options

The Delaware Supreme Court struck down a put option Paramount had granted to Viacom, which would have given Viacom an additional $1 billion if its deal with Paramount fell through.[61] The court upheld the 1.5% breakup fee as a valid liquidated damages provision, however.

---

55. ACE Ltd. v. Capital Re Corp., 747 A.2d 95 (Del. Ch. 1999).

56. *Id.* at 106.

57. *Id.* at 105–06.

58. Trevis Team, *AT&T Deal Demise Gives T-Mobile Big Dowry for New Marriage*, FORBES, Dec. 22, 2011, *available at* http://www.forbes.com/sites/greatspeculations/2011/12/22/att-deal-demise-gives-t-mobile-big-dowry-for-new-marriage/.

59. *See* Steven M. Davidoff, *The Deal Professor's 2009 in Review: Part II: The Deals*, N.Y. TIMES, Dec. 30, 2009, *available at* http://dealbook.nytimes.com/2009/12/30/the-deal-professors-2009-in-review-part-ii-the-deals/.

60. For an interesting empirical analysis of deals involving breakup fees and other forms of lock-ups, see John C. Coates IV & Guhan Subramanian, *A Buy-Side Model of M&A Lockups: Theory and Evidence*, 53 STAN. L. REV. 307 (2000).

61. Paramount Commc'ns, Inc. v. QVC Network, Inc., 637 A.2d 34 (Del. 1994).

Other Devices

In the following case, the Delaware Supreme Court considered whether the directors of an insolvent publicly traded corporation breached their fiduciary duty when they agreed to submit a merger agreement to a stockholder vote, knowing that the stockholders with a majority of the voting power had agreed unconditionally to vote all of their shares in favor of the inferior offer.

A CASE IN POINT	*Summary*	Case 20.4

Omnicare, Inc. v. NCS Healthcare, Inc.

Supreme Court of Delaware
818 A.2d 914 (Del. 2003).

FACTS NCS Healthcare, Inc., a leading independent provider of pharmacy services to skilled nursing facilities and other long-term care institutions, became insolvent after changes in the timing and level of reimbursements by government and third-party payors adversely affected market conditions in the health-care industry. The price of its common stock dropped from about $20 in January 1999 to a range of $0.09 to $0.50 per share by early 2002 when Omnicare, Inc. offered to pay $313,750,000 for NCS's assets in a proposed asset sale in bankruptcy. Omnicare's offer was less than the amount of NCS's outstanding debt and would have resulted in no recovery for NCS's stockholders.

NCS's operating performance was improving by early 2002, when NCS contacted Genesis Health Ventures, Inc. in hopes of negotiating a transaction that would provide some recovery for NCS's stockholders. An independent committee of NCS board members, who were neither NCS employees nor major NCS stockholders, negotiated a transaction whereby Genesis agreed to repay the NCS senior debt in full, assume the trade debt, purchase the NCS notes or exchange them for cash and stock, and provide $24 million in value for the NCS common stock.

Genesis had previously lost a bidding war for another company when Omnicare made a last-minute overbid. Genesis told NCS that it was unwilling to be a stalking horse for a higher Omnicare bid and insisted on an exclusivity agreement that prevented NCS from negotiating with other bidders for a short period of time.

After NCS entered into the agreement, Omnicare concluded that NCS was negotiating a transaction with a competitor that would potentially present a competitive threat. In light of a run-up in the price of the NCS common stock, Omnicare also came to believe that whatever transaction NCS was negotiating probably included a payment for its stock. Omnicare then proposed a transaction that included $3 cash for the common shares but was conditioned on negotiating a merger agreement, obtaining certain third-party consents, and completing its due diligence. Although Omnicare's economic terms were attractive, the due diligence condition weakened its offer.

Genesis agreed to improve its offer by, among other things, increasing the payment to the stockholders by 80% but stipulated that the transaction had to be approved by midnight the next day or else it would terminate the discussions and withdraw its offer. After "balancing the potential loss of the Genesis deal against the uncertainty of Omnicare's letter," the NCS special committee and full board concluded that the only reasonable alternative was to approve the Genesis transaction. The NCS board authorized the voting agreements with the two majority stockholders, whereby they agreed to vote for the Genesis deal, and agreed to submit the merger agreement to the NCS stockholders regardless of whether the board continued to recommend the merger under section 251(c) of the Delaware General Corporation Law.

Shortly thereafter, Omnicare made an irrevocable offer to acquire the NCS stock for $3.50 per share in cash. The NCS board then withdrew its recommendation that the stockholders vote in favor of the NCS–Genesis merger agreement, and NCS's financial adviser withdrew its fairness opinion. Nonetheless, the stockholder agreement ensured NCS stockholder approval of the Genesis merger. Omnicare then sued to prevent the consummation of the inferior Genesis transaction.

ISSUE PRESENTED Did the directors of an insolvent publicly traded company violate their fiduciary duty when they entered into an agreement for a "bullet-proof" sale of the company to the "only game in town"?

CONTINUED

SUMMARY OF OPINION The Delaware Supreme Court began by explaining that a board's management decision to enter into and recommend a merger transaction can become final only when ownership action is taken by a vote of the stockholders. As a result, "a board of directors' decision to adopt defensive devices to protect a merger agreement may implicate the stockholders' right to effectively vote contrary to the initial recommendation of the board in favor of the transaction."

The court then reasoned that there is an "omnipresent specter" of conflicts of interest when a board of directors acts to prevent stockholders from effectively exercising their right to vote contrary to the will of the board. To be protected under the business judgment rule, defensive devices adopted by the board to protect the original merger transaction must withstand enhanced judicial scrutiny under the *Unocal* standard applied to antitakeover devices. The court explained that the board "does not have unbridled discretion to defeat perceived threats by any draconian means available." Defensive measures that are either preclusive or coercive are, by definition, considered draconian and invalid.

Enhanced judicial scrutiny requires (1) a "judicial determination regarding the adequacy of the decisionmaking process employed by the directors, including the information on which the directors based their decision," and (2) "a judicial examination of the reasonableness of the directors' action in light of the circumstances then existing." The directors have the burden of proving that they were adequately informed and acted reasonably. As long as the deal protection devices are not draconian and are within a range of reasonableness, a court will not substitute its judgment for that of the board.

The court first considered whether the NCS directors had demonstrated that they had reasonable grounds for believing that a danger to corporate policy and effectiveness existed. The threat identified by the NCS board was the possibility of losing the Genesis offer and being left with no comparable alternative transaction.

The court then applied the second stage of the *Unocal* test, which required the NCS directors to demonstrate that their defensive response was reasonable in relation to the threat posed. The court explained that this inquiry involves a two-step analysis. First, the NCS directors were required to establish that the merger deal protection devices adopted in response to the threat were not "coercive" or "preclusive." Second, they had to demonstrate that their response was within a "range of reasonable responses" to the threat perceived.

In this case, the court concluded that the deal protection devices the NCS board agreed to were *both* preclusive and coercive. The tripartite defensive measures—the section 251(c) provision, the voting agreements, and the absence of an effective fiduciary out clause—made it "mathematically impossible" and "realistically unattainable" for the Omnicare transaction or any other proposal to succeed, no matter how superior the proposal. Although the minority stockholders were not forced to vote for the Genesis merger, they were required to accept it because it was a *fait accompli*. The court concluded that the NCS directors' defensive devices were not within a reasonable range of responses to the perceived threat of losing the Genesis offer because they were preclusive and coercive. As a result, the devices were unenforceable.

The court went on to hold that the deal protection devices were unenforceable for a second independent reason. Taken together, they completely prevented the board from discharging its fiduciary responsibilities to the minority stockholders.

Although the NCS board was seeking to ensure that the NCS creditors were paid in full and that the NCS stockholders received the highest value available for their stock, the NCS board did not have authority to accede to the Genesis demand for an absolute "lock-up." Because the directors of a Delaware corporation have a continuing obligation to discharge their fiduciary responsibilities, as future circumstances develop, after approving the merger with Genesis, the NCS board was required to negotiate a fiduciary out clause to protect the NCS stockholders if the Genesis transaction became an inferior offer. "By acceding to Genesis' ultimatum for complete protection in futuro, the NCS board disabled itself from exercising

CONTINUED

its own fiduciary obligations at a time when the board's own judgment is most important, i.e., receipt of a subsequent superior offer." Although the stockholders with majority voting power "had an absolute right to sell or exchange their shares with a third party at any price," the NCS directors had a supervening responsibility to discharge their fiduciary duties on a continuing basis.

The court explained:

> Any board has authority to give the proponent of a recommended merger agreement reasonable structural and economic defenses, incentives, and fair compensation if the transaction is not completed. To the extent that defensive measures are economic and reasonable, they may have become an increased cost to the proponent of any subsequent transaction. Just as defensive measures cannot be draconian, however, they cannot limit or circumscribe the directors' fiduciary duties.

RESULT   The provisions in the merger agreement requiring a stockholder vote on the Genesis deal were invalid, so the NCS board was not required to put the Genesis deal to a stockholder vote.

COMMENTS   This case resulted in a rare three–two split decision of the Delaware Supreme Court. The dissenting opinion by Chief Justice Veasey, with whom Justice Steele joined, pointed out that the merger agreement and the voting commitments of the majority stockholders concluded a lengthy search and intense negotiation process in the context of insolvency and creditor pressure where no other viable bid had emerged:

> Going into negotiations with Genesis, the NCS directors knew that, up until that time, NCS had found only one potential bidder, Omnicare. Omnicare had refused to buy NCS except at a fire sale price through an asset sale in bankruptcy. Omnicare's best proposal at that stage would not have paid off all creditors and would have provided nothing for stockholders. Genesis expressed interest that became increasingly attractive. Negotiations with Genesis led to an offer paying creditors off and conferring on NCS stockholders $24 million—an amount infinitely superior to the prior Omnicare proposals.

> But there was, understandably, a sine qua non. In exchange for offering the NCS stockholders a return on their equity and creditor payment, Genesis demanded certainty that the merger would close. If the NCS board would not have acceded to the Section 251(c) provision, if [the majority shareholders] had not agreed to voting agreements and if NCS had insisted on a fiduciary out, there would have been no Genesis deal! Thus, the only value-enhancing transaction available would have disappeared.

> The Majority invalidates the NCS board's action by announcing a new rule that represents an extension of our jurisprudence. That new rule can be narrowly stated as follows: A merger agreement entered into after a market search, before any prospect of a topping bid has emerged, which locks up stockholder approval and does not contain a "fiduciary out" provision, is per se invalid when a later significant topping bid emerges. As we have noted, this bright-line, per se rule would apply regardless of (1) the circumstances leading up to the agreement and (2) the fact that stockholders who control voting power had irrevocably committed themselves, *as stockholders,* to vote for the merger. Narrowly stated, this new rule is a judicially-created "third rail" that now becomes one of the given "rules of the game," to be taken into account by the negotiators and drafters of merger agreements. In our view, this new rule is an unwise extension of existing precedent.

> The NCS board's actions—as the Vice Chancellor correctly held—were reasonable in relation to the threat because the Genesis deal was the "only game in town," the NCS directors got the best deal they could from Genesis and—but for the emergence of Genesis on the scene—there would have been no viable deal.

CONTINUED

Because the deal protection measures were not adopted unilaterally by the board to fend off an existing hostile offer, the dissent argued that the majority's reliance on the discussion in an earlier case of "draconian" antitakeover measures was misplaced.

In a second dissenting opinion, Justice Steele chided the majority:

> In effect, the majority has adopted the "duck" theory of contract interpretation. In my view, just as all ducks have their season and the wary hunter carefully scans the air to determine which duck may and which may not be shot at a given time on a certain day, the same holds true for distinguishing between contract provisions that could in another context be deemed truly defensive measures demanding enhanced scrutiny by a court. When certain, or when in doubt that the "duck" is not in season, courts, like prudent waterfowls, should defer.

ALLOCATION OF POWER BETWEEN THE DIRECTORS AND THE SHAREHOLDERS

A key issue that emerges from cases involving hostile takeovers and defensive tactics is who gets to decide whether the corporation should be sold—the board of directors or the shareholders. Theoretically, the board of directors is the guardian of the shareholders' interests, but the interests and obligations of the two groups sometimes conflict.

Frequently, a hostile takeover attempt presents such a conflict. Sometimes the proposed terms are attractive to the shareholders because the acquiring corporation offers to pay a substantial premium for their stock. The board of directors, however, may believe that the acquiring company's plans for the corporation are ultimately destructive, as in the case of a *bust-up takeover*, in which the acquired corporation is taken apart and its assets sold piecemeal. The directors may have legitimate concerns about the effect of such a takeover on the company's employees or on the community where the corporation is located. Or the directors might believe that the long-term value of the company is greater than the price being offered. Of course, directors might oppose a transaction just so they can remain on the corporation's board, in violation of their legal obligation to put the corporation's interests before their own.

Poison Pills

One of the first cases addressing the allocation of power between the directors and the shareholders in deciding whether the corporation should be sold involved a *poison pill* or *shareholder rights plan*, a plan that would make any takeover not approved by the directors prohibitively expensive.[62] In 1984, the directors of Household International, fearing that Household might be taken over and busted up, adopted a poison pill in the form

of a Preferred Share Purchase Rights Plan without first securing shareholder approval. This plan provided that, under certain triggering circumstances, common shareholders would receive a "right" for every common share of Household. In the event of a merger in which Household was not the surviving corporation, the holder of each common share of Household would have the right to purchase $200 of the common stock of the acquiring company for only $100. If these rights were triggered and exercised, they would dilute the value of the stock of the acquiring company, making a takeover prohibitively expensive for the acquirer.

The Delaware Supreme Court upheld the board's power to adopt the plan. The court found that the plan did not usurp the shareholders' ability to receive tender offers and to sell their shares to a bidder without board approval of the sale. Household's poison pill left "numerous methods to successfully launch a takeover." For example, a bidder could make a tender offer on the condition that the board redeem the rights, that is, buy them back for a nominal sum before they were triggered. A bidder could set a high minimum of shares and rights to be tendered; it could solicit consents to remove the board and replace it with one that would redeem the rights; or it could acquire 50% of the shares and cause Household to self-tender for the rights. In a *self-tender*, the company would agree to buy back the shareholders' rights for a fair price.

The court also found that the plan did not fundamentally restrict the shareholders' right to conduct a proxy contest. In a *proxy contest*, someone wishing to replace the board with his or her own candidates must acquire a sufficient number of shareholder votes to do so. Such votes are usually represented by *proxies*, or limited written powers of attorney entitling the proxy holder to vote the shares owned by the person giving the proxy. The court found that a proxy contest could be won with an insurgent ownership of less than 20% (the threshold for triggering distribution of the rights) and that the key to success in a proxy contest is the merit of the insurgent's arguments, not the size of his or her holdings.

---

62. Moran v. Household Int'l, Inc., 500 A.2d 1346 (Del. 1985).

The court concluded that the decision to adopt the poison-pill plan was within the board's authority. Moreover, because the directors "reasonably believed Household was vulnerable to coercive acquisition techniques and adopted a reasonable defensive mechanism to protect itself," the court held that the board had discharged its fiduciary duty appropriately under the business judgment rule.

Although the Delaware Supreme Court upheld the adoption of a poison-pill plan in *Moran*, it reserved judgment on how such a plan would operate in practice. In particular, it left open the question of when directors must redeem the poison-pill rights to permit shareholders to tender their shares to a bidder.

The question of whether a board must redeem a pill is fact-specific—a court will look at all of the circumstances in making its decision. Certain factors will favor keeping the pill in place. These include (1) a tender offer that is only slightly above the market price of the stock; (2) a tender offer for less than all of the shares; (3) an active attempt by the board to solicit other offers; (4) a conscious effort by the board to allow its outside directors, deemed more disinterested, to make the decisions in this area; and (5) the fact that the tender offer is only in its early stages.

In the following case, the court considered whether a corporation could keep a poison pill in place to rebuff an any-or-all fully financed cash offer at a premium over the trading price of the target's stock.

| A CASE IN POINT | *Summary* | Case 20.5 |

Air Products & Chemicals, Inc. v. Airgas, Inc.

Court of Chancery of Delaware
16 A.3d 48 (Del. Ch. 2011).

FACTS   Air Products is the world's largest supplier of hydrogen and helium to technology, energy, industrial, and health-care customers globally. Airgas is a domestic supplier and distributor of industrial, medical, and specialty gases. Its staggered board had adopted a poison pill with a 15% threshold in 2007. Airgas has not opted out of section 203 of the Delaware General Corporation Law, which prohibits business combinations with any interested shareholder for a period of three years after the time the person became an interested shareholder, unless certain conditions are met. The Airgas certificate of incorporation requires supermajority approval of certain business combinations.

The Airgas stock had been trading in the $40s and $50s through most of 2007–2008, but it dropped as low as $27 in March 2009 and then rebounded to $41.64 in the fall of 2009. In October 2009, John McGlade, CEO of Air Products, approached the CEO of Airgas, Peter McCausland, and proposed that Air Products acquire Airgas at a price of $60 in Air Products stock per share of Airgas stock. After McCausland rejected McGlade's advances, Air Products launched a fully financed hostile public tender offer for any and all Airgas shares at a price of $60 cash in February 2010. During the ensuing year, Air Products raised its offer to a "best and final" offer of $70 cash per share. After Airgas's two investment banks, Goldman Sachs and Bank of America Merrill Lynch, opined that Airgas was worth at least $78 per share, the Airgas board rejected the offer as "clearly inadequate." All of the Airgas directors, including three nominated by Air Products and elected in a proxy contest, voted not to redeem the poison pill. Thus, Airgas blocked the bid, foreclosing its shareholders' opportunity to tender their shares to Air Products. Air Products and certain Airgas shareholders then filed suit to require Airgas to redeem its poison pill.

ISSUE PRESENTED   In the context of an any-or-all cash hostile tender offer, under what circumstances must the board of directors of the target redeem a poison pill?

SUMMARY OF OPINION   Chancellor Chandler began his opinion on behalf of the Delaware Court of Chancery by stating:

> In essence, this case brings to the fore one of the most basic questions animating all of corporate law, which relates to the allocation of power between directors and stockholders. That is, "when, if ever, will a board's duty to 'the corporation and its shareholders' require [the board] to abandon concerns for 'long term' values (and other constituencies) and enter a current share value maximizing mode?" More to the point, in the context of a hostile tender offer, who gets to decide when and if the corporation is for sale?

CONTINUED

The court applied the *Unocal* standard of enhanced judicial scrutiny to evaluate the Airgas board's decision not to redeem its poison pill. Under the two prongs of *Unocal,* the board must show (1) that it had reasonable grounds to believe that a threat to corporate policy and effectiveness existed and (2) that any board action taken to rebut that threat was reasonable.

The court found that the Airgas board satisfied the first *Unocal* prong. The board comprised a majority of independent directors who relied on several outside independent financial advisers to reach its conclusion that Air Products' $70 offer was "clearly inadequate." Therefore, the board reasonably believed that the offer was inadequate and that it posed a legitimate threat if Airgas stockholders were to accept it.

The court next determined that Airgas's defensive measures were reasonable responses to the legally cognizable threat of an inadequately priced offer from Air Products. Even though there was evidence that the Airgas shareholders were fully informed about the board's view concerning the value of Airgas and the Air Products offer, the court found a risk of *substantive coercion* because a majority of the Airgas shareholders would likely have tendered into an offer that the board deemed inadequate. As the court explained:

> Inadequate price has become a form of "substantive coercion" as that concept has been developed by the Delaware Supreme Court in its takeover jurisprudence. That is, the idea that Airgas's stockholders will disbelieve the board's views on value (or in the case of merger arbitrageurs who may have short-term profit goals in mind, they may simply ignore the board's recommendations), and so they may mistakenly tender into an inadequately priced offer. Substantive coercion has been clearly recognized by our Supreme Court as a valid threat.

The poison pill was not impermissibly preclusive because it did not make a successful contest for Airgas impossible. It only delayed a successful proxy contest for control of the Airgas board, so it did not unduly interfere with the franchise rights of the Airgas stockholders. Chancellor Chandler expressed his own personal view that the Airgas poison pill had "served its legitimate" purpose but acknowledged that, under existing Delaware law, the power to defeat an inadequate hostile tender offer ultimately lies with the board of directors.

RESULT   The board of directors did not breach its fiduciary duties to the Airgas stockholders when it refused to redeem the poison pill. The court dismissed the plaintiffs' claims with prejudice.

COMMENTS   Unlike the Trans Union board, the Airgas board was advised by top investment banks and relied on both internal and external valuations before deciding that Air Products' offer was inadequate. Its bankers analyzed management's financial projections, research analysts' estimates for Airgas, discounted cash flow valuations of Airgas using various EBITDA multiples and discount rates, and historical stock prices, and they considered the fact that Airgas generally emerges later from economic recessions than Air Products. The directors relied not only on their bankers' inadequacy opinions but also on management's five-year strategic plan to support their conclusion that Airgas was worth at least $78 per share.

Significantly, the court answered "no" to the question, "[Can] a board 'just say never' to a hostile tender offer?" Chancellor Chandler explained:

> Only a board of directors found to be acting in good faith, after reasonable investigation and reliance on the advice of outside advisors, which articulates and convinces the Court that a hostile tender offer poses a legitimate threat to the corporate enterprise, may address that perceived threat by blocking the tender offer and forcing the bidder to elect a board majority that supports its bid.

It is important to note the reference to "corporate enterprise," which suggests that the board may take into account factors other than shareholder return when deciding whether to rebuff a hostile offer. It remains to be seen whether a board could keep a pill in place if its own advisers conclude that the offered price exceeds their estimated value of the target's shares.

The Delaware Court of Chancery struck down a so-called *dead-hand pill*, which could be redeemed only by the directors in office before the hostile bidder gained control or their designated successors.[63] The court held that the dead-hand provision violated the requirement under section 141 of the Delaware General Corporation Law that the directors manage the business and affairs of the corporation because it gave one category of directors distinctive voting rights that were not shared by the other directors. Although the Delaware statute permits different directors to be given distinctive voting rights, those rights must be set forth in the certificate of incorporation, which was not the case here.

The court also held that the dead-hand feature violated the directors' duty of loyalty for two reasons. First, the provision failed to meet the more exacting *Blasius*[64] standard (after the case of the same name in which the Delaware Court of Chancery first articulated this standard) applicable to defensive tactics touching upon issues of control because it purposefully disenfranchised the company's shareholders without any compelling justification. In particular, "even in an election contest fought over the issue of the hostile bid, the shareholders will be powerless to elect a board that is both willing and able to accept the bid." Instead, the shareholders "may be forced to vote for [incumbent] directors whose policies they reject because only those directors have the power to change them." Second, the dead-hand provision failed to satisfy *Unocal's* requirement that the defense be proportionate to the threat because it was preclusive: it eliminated the use of a proxy contest as a possible means to gain control.

The Delaware Supreme Court also struck down a so-called *no-hand pill*, which could not be redeemed for six months even if the insurgent's slate of directors was elected and wanted to redeem it.[65] The delayed redemption provision in the plan would have prevented a new board of directors from redeeming the plan in order to facilitate a transaction that would serve the stockholders' best interests, even under circumstances where the board would be required to do so because of its fiduciary duty to the stockholders. Because the delayed redemption provision impermissibly circumscribed the board's statutory power under section 141(a) to manage the business and affairs of the company and the directors' ability to fulfill their concomitant fiduciary duties, the delayed redemption provision was invalid.

Protecting the Shareholder Franchise and the *Blasius* Standard of Review

A number of takeover cases have drawn a distinction between the exercise of two types of corporate power: (1) the power over the assets of the corporation, and (2) the power relationship between the board and the shareholders.[66] As explained earlier, directors have broad power over the assets of the corporation. Such decisions are generally protected by the business judgment rule or subjected to *Unocal's* proportionality analysis if they relate to defensive tactics. As Delaware Chancellor William Allen explained in *Paramount Communications, Inc. v. Time Inc.*, "[t]he corporation law does not operate on the theory that directors, in exercising their powers to manage the firm, are obligated to follow the wishes of a majority of shares."[67] Thus, the Time directors had the power to acquire Warner Communications even though the holders of a majority of Time's stock would have preferred to take Paramount's offer. Or, as the Delaware Court of Chancery put it, "[d]irectors are not thermometers, existing to register the ever-changing sentiments of stockholders."[68]

If a board's unilateral decision to adopt a defensive measure touches on issues of voting control, however, then further judicial scrutiny is required to protect the shareholder franchise essential for corporate democracy. In particular, the court must decide whether the board purposefully disenfranchised its shareholders (that is, interfered with their right to elect the directors). If so, then under the *Blasius* standard, the action is strongly suspect and cannot be sustained without a compelling justification.[69]

Protecting the shareholder franchise is critical because the business judgment rule provides the directors and officers with great latitude in managing the day-to-day affairs of the corporation. As a result, shareholders who are displeased with the business performance generally have only two options: sell their shares or vote to replace the incumbent board members. The corporate governance system loses a key control if unhappy shareholders cannot vote the directors out of office.

For example, in *Chesapeake Corp. v. Shore*,[70] the Delaware Court of Chancery held that a supermajority bylaw provision adopted by the board of Shorewood Packing Corporation to thwart a hostile bid by Chesapeake Corporation was "a preclusive, unjustified impairment of the Shorewood stockholders' right to influence their company's policies through the ballot box." The provision increased the number of Shorewood shares needed to amend the bylaws from a simple majority to 60%. Because Shorewood's management controlled almost 24% of its stock, the supermajority provision made it virtually impossible for Chesapeake to garner enough votes to amend the bylaws to eliminate the

---

63. Carmody v. Toll Bros., Inc., 723 A.2d 1180 (Del. Ch. 1998).

64. Blasius Indus., Inc. v. Atlas Corp., 564 A.2d 651 (Del. Ch. 1988).

65. Quickturn Design Sys., Inc. v. Shapiro, 721 A.2d 1281 (Del. 1998).

---

66. *See* Hilton Hotels Corp. v. ITT Corp., 978 F. Supp. 1342 (D. Nev. 1997).

67. Fed. Sec. L. Rep. (CCH) 94,514 (Del. Ch. July 14, 1989), *aff'd*, 571 A.2d 1140 (Del. 1990).

68. *In re* Lear Corp. S'holder Litig., 967 A.2d 640 (Del. Ch. 2008).

69. *See* Stroud v. Grace, 606 A.2d 75 (Del. 1992); Unitrin, Inc. v. Am. Gen. Corp., 651 A.2d 1361 (Del. 1995); Blasius Indus., Inc. v. Atlas Corp., 564 A.2d 651 (Del. Ch. 1988).

70. 771 A.2d 293, 297 (Del. Ch. 2000).

classified board so that it could unseat the current directors and install a new board amenable to its offer.

The Shorewood board claimed that Chesapeake's offer posed two threats: (1) the price was grossly inadequate, so Shorewood stockholders faced great harm if they sold their stock at that price; and (2) "there was a danger that Shorewood stockholders would be confused about the intrinsic value of the company, fail to understand management's explanation as to why the market was undervaluing their stock, and mistakenly tender consents to Chesapeake to facilitate its unfair offer."[71] The court found the threat of confusion "at best quite a weak one" in light of (1) the fact that more than 80% of Shorewood's shares were held by management and institutional holders, (2) the ability of the board to engage in a more vigorous communication campaign, and (3) the fact that reputable analysts were already tracking the stock. Although the court acknowledged that the price offered might be inadequate, it held that the supermajority bylaw was "an extremely aggressive and overreaching response to a very mild threat."[72] Instead, if the board truly believed that price inadequacy was the problem, it could have taken Chesapeake up on its offer to negotiate price and structure.

71. *Id.* at 306.

72. *Id.* at 343.

DUTY OF DIRECTORS TO DISCLOSE PRELIMINARY MERGER NEGOTIATIONS

Directors can face a difficult decision when deciding whether they must disclose an offer to buy the company or the company's participation in merger negotiations. As is discussed more fully in Chapter 22, disclosure can be required even if the parties have not reached an agreement in principle on the price and structure of the transaction. The U.S. Supreme Court held in *Basic, Inc. v. Levinson*[73] that such "soft information" can be material.

Managers planning a management buyout (MBO) of a company face a real conflict of interest in deciding whether to disclose their offer to the public because disclosure will often bring forth competing bidders. Prudent directors, like the independent directors of RJR Nabisco when faced with CEO Ross Johnson's bid, will often require public announcement of the bid even if it puts the company "in play."

73. 485 U.S. 224 (1988).

POLITICAL | PERSPECTIVE

The Pennsylvania Antitakeover Statute

One of the nation's toughest state antitakeover statutes, Pennsylvania Senate bill 1310, also known as Act 36, was signed into law by Governor Bob Casey (a Democrat) on April 27, 1990.[a] An examination of the events surrounding the enactment of this controversial statute highlights the ever-changing battle over defining, shaping, and reshaping the law in this area, as well as the role that politics can play in that process.

Background

The impetus for drafting the statute came from the Belzberg family's hostile takeover bid for Armstrong World Industries, Inc., a *Fortune* 500 company specializing in flooring and furnishings, headquartered in Lancaster, Pennsylvania. After Armstrong's board

rejected the Belzbergs' offer to buy the company, the Belzbergs' holding company, First City Financial Corporation, initiated a proxy fight for control of four directors' seats on the board. The shareholders' meeting, at which the results of the proxy fight were to be announced, was scheduled for April 30, 1990.

Noah W. Wenger (a Republican), the state senator from the Lancaster district, introduced a comprehensive antitakeover bill while the Belzbergs and Armstrong were in the midst of their conflict. The bill, drafted in part by the Pennsylvania Chamber of Business and Industry, was designed not only to throw a wrench into the plans of corporate raiders in general but perhaps also to impede the Belzberg bid in particular.

The Statute

Pennsylvania's antitakeover statute attacks hostile bids for corporate control on three major fronts. First, it requires controlling persons (defined as those who own, or control proxies for, 20% of a company's stock) to disgorge—that is, give back to the company—any profits they make by selling stock of the company within eighteen months after becoming a controlling person. Such disgorgement is required if stock acquired within twenty-four months before or within eighteen months after becoming a controlling person is sold by the controlling person within eighteen months after becoming a controlling person.

This provision is aimed at those who, after failed takeover attempts, try to reap short-term profits by

CONTINUED

selling acquired stock at a premium. Institutional investors and other shareholders who launch proxy fights for purposes other than gaining control of a majority of the board are exempted from the disgorgement provision.

Second, the statute expands the directors' ability to consider other constituencies when making change-of-control decisions. Subsection (d) of section 511 provides an expansive list of constituencies that a director may consider when exercising his or her duty to the corporation:

In discharging the duties of their respective positions . . . directors may, in considering the best interests of the corporation, consider to the extent they deem appropriate:

(1) The effects of any action upon *any or all groups affected by such action,* including shareholders, employees, suppliers, customers and creditors of the corporation, and upon communities in which offices or other establishments of the corporation are located.

(2) The short-term and long-term interests of the corporation, including benefits which may accrue to the corporation from its long-term plans and the *possibility that these interests may be best served by the continued independence of the corporation.*

(3) The resources, intent and conduct (past, stated and potential) of the person seeking to acquire control of the corporation.

(4) *All other pertinent factors.* (Emphasis added.)

In addition, the directors are not required to regard any particular corporate interest or the interest of any group as "a dominant or controlling interest or factor." The implication is clear. A director's duty when considering a proposal for a change of control is not simply to maximize shareholder value.

Third, like some other states' antitakeover statutes, the Pennsylvania law deprives a shareholder of its voting rights when it crosses certain ownership lines, placed at 20%, 33%, and 50% of the company's stock. The voting rights can be regained only if the holders of a majority of the shares—excluding holders of shares acquired in the previous twelve months—give their approval at a special shareholders' meeting.

The statute also protects the employees of a company that is taken over. Existing labor contracts must be honored, and a successful bidder must pay severance benefits to employees who lose their jobs within two years of the takeover.

Corporations are allowed to opt out of various provisions of the antitakeover statute. In the first two years after it was enacted, more than 66 corporations

(including Westinghouse Electric) of the estimated 200 corporations affected by the statute opted out of at least one of its subchapters.[b]

In 1998, the Pennsylvania statute proved important in the successful effort by Mellon Bank (a Pennsylvania corporation) to thwart a hostile bid by the Bank of New York.[c] In rejecting Bank of New York's $23.6 billion offer (which represented a premium of 28% over Mellon's closing stock price the day before the offer was announced and a premium of 34% over Mellon's average closing stock price over the last thirty trading days), the chair of Mellon's board seemed to be invoking the Pennsylvania statute when he criticized the proposed merger as not benefiting "our shareholders, employees, customers and—in particular—the communities we serve."[d]

---

a. The independent sections are codified as 15 PA. CONS. STAT. ANN. §§ 511, 512, 1721, 2502 (1990); 15 PA. CONS. STAT. ANN. §§ 2561–67, 2571–74, 2581–83, 2585–88 (1990).

b. Jeffrey L. Silberman, *How Do Pennsylvania Directors Spell Relief?* Act 36, 17 DEL. J. CORP. L. 115 (1992).

c. *See* Bloomberg News, *In Pennsylvania, Watch Out What You Try to Take Over: Thanks to Tough Rules, Mellon Bank Is Able to Flatly Reject an Offer from Bank of New York,* L.A. TIMES, Apr. 23, 1998, at D7.

d. Associated Press, *Mellon Bank Sues Bank of New York to Avoid Takeover; $23 Billion Bid Was Rejected,* STAR TRIB. (Minneapolis), Apr. 24, 1998, at D1.

EXECUTIVE COMPENSATION

Since 2002, a number of actions have been taken in reaction to the compensation excesses of the late 1990s and the early 2000s. The Sarbanes–Oxley Act (SOX) of 2002[74] required more timely disclosure of executive pay deals, prohibited loans to officers and directors, and required CEOs and CFOs to return performance-based pay or profits from stock sales following restatements of financial results that involve misconduct *(clawbacks).*

The Dodd–Frank Wall Street Reform and Consumer Protection Act's "Say on Pay" provision gives shareholders of public companies an advisory vote on company payment practices for top executives.[75] These votes must occur at least once every three years. Companies must also hold a "frequency" vote at least once every six years during which shareholders can decide whether they want annual, biannual, or triennial advisory voters on executive pay. Public companies must also hold a shareholder advisory vote on executive change-of-control benefits (so-called *golden parachutes).*

Equity Compensation Arrangements

It has been the prevailing wisdom for decades that an executive will be more motivated to perform to the best of his or her ability if the executive is a shareholder of the

---

74. Sarbanes–Oxley Act of 2002, Pub. L. No. 107-204, 116 Stat. 745 (2002) (codified as amended in scattered sections of 11, 15, 18, 28, 29 U.S.C.A.).

75. Dodd–Frank Wall Street Reform and Consumer Protection Act, Pub. L. No. 111-201, § 951, 124 Stat. 1376, 1899–1900 (2010).

company. Equity compensation plans are seen as a flexible way to share ownership with employees, reward them for performance, and attract and retain a motivated staff. There is not, however, a consensus as to the most appropriate way to achieve such a result, nor is there a consensus as to what is the best balance between equity ownership and nonequity forms of compensation.

Stock Options

A *stock option* gives the person to whom it is granted (the *optionee*) the right to buy a certain number of shares at a fixed price for a fixed number of years, but usually no more than ten years (the *exercise period*). The price at which the optionee can exercise the options by purchasing the stock is called the *exercise price*. Stock option plans provide benefits to the executive only if the stock price rises above the stock option exercise price. In 2004, the Financial Accounting Standards Board (FASB) issued rules that require companies to expense stock option awards. The Internal Revenue Code assesses a steep penalty on stock options granted with an exercise price less than the fair market value of the stock on the date of grant.[76]

Although stock options gained popularity as a means of aligning the interests of executives with those of the shareholders of their companies, critics believe that options have backfired. They argue that at best, options have promoted a short-term focus, and at worst, they have created an incentive for executives to inflate company earnings and make irresponsible forecasts. In some cases, executives have even fraudulently manipulated earnings in an attempt to keep stock prices high, while they exercised their options and sold their stock at inflated prices. Gary Winnick of Global Crossing, Ltd. and Dennis Kozlowski of Tyco International were among the many executives who apparently used this *pump and dump* strategy to their personal advantage as the Internet bubble began to burst.

Studies have also found an inverse relationship between the number of options that key executives hold and the success of their corporations. Interestingly, however, studies have also shown that broad-based employee stock ownership appears to increase sales, employment, and productivity.[77]

Restricted Stock Plans

In the context of executive compensation, *restricted stock* usually means stock subject to vesting restrictions. Restricted stock plans are frequently used in the private company context where the stock is sufficiently inexpensive that the executive can afford to purchase a substantial

portion of it. In the publicly traded company context, however, generally the company's stock is "too expensive" for the executive to purchase and hold a substantial portion. Accordingly, a publicly traded company will more often give restricted stock to the executive without payment by the executive other than the requirement for continued service for the employer.

For example, an employee might be given stock, or be allowed to purchase stock (sometimes at a discount from fair market value), but be required to forfeit the stock if his or her employment ends before the restrictions have been removed (e.g., when the stock vests either by the employee working for the company for a certain period of time or after certain performance goals have been met). Some plans allow the restrictions to lapse gradually (e.g., 25% of the shares vest at the end of the first year of employment and monthly thereafter for the next thirty-six months). Other plans provide that the restrictions do not lapse until the end of the period (e.g., all of the shares of stock vest after the employee has worked for the company for four years).

SEC Disclosure Requirements

The SEC requires public companies to provide comprehensive disclosure about executive compensation and requires the board of directors to approve and be legally responsible for their company's report on pay practices. According to former SEC Chairman Richard C. Breeden, "the best protection against abuses in executive compensation is a simple weapon—the cleansing power of sunlight and the power of an informed shareholder base."[78]

Each public company must provide in the proxy statement for its annual meeting of stockholders (or in its Annual Report on Form 10–K, if not incorporated by reference from the proxy statement) detailed tabular and narrative disclosure relating to total compensation, holdings of equity-related interests, pension plans, and other retirement and postemployment compensation. The principal disclosure vehicle for executive compensation is the Summary Compensation Table,[79] which presents compensation data for the company's principal executive officer, the principal financial officer, and the three most highly compensated other executive officers for each of the company's last three completed fiscal years. If a company provides severance, retirement, or other change-of-control benefits to a named executive officer (golden parachutes), the company must include a narrative disclosure of the material terms of the arrangements and quantify the estimated payments for each separate triggering event. Golden parachutes and other material executive compensation events must also be promptly disclosed on Form 8–K.

---

76. For a discussion of the tax treatment of stock options and other equal compensation, see Constance E. Bagley & Craig E. Dauchy, The Entrepreneur's Guide to Business Law 91–109 (4th ed. 2012).

77. Nat'l Ctr. for Employee Ownership, *Largest Study Yet Shows ESOPs Improve Performance and Employee Benefits*, available at http://nceo.org/library/esop_perf.html (last visited Dec. 27, 2011).

78. Marilyn F. Johnson et al., *An Empirical Analysis of the SEC's 1992 Proxy Reforms on Executive Compensation* 4 (Research Paper No. 1679, Feb. 2001), *available at* http://gsbapps.stanford.edu/researchpapers/library/RP1679.pdf.

79. *See id.* at 11.

The compensation disclosure in the proxy statement (or annual report) must include a section called "Compensation Discussion and Analysis" (CD&A). The CD&A is a narrative overview that explains the material elements of compensation for the company's named executive officers and is intended to provide the public with insight into the company's compensation policies and decision-making process. It must describe the objectives of the company's compensation program, what the compensation program is designed to reward, each element of compensation and why the company chooses to pay each element, how the company determines the amount (and, if applicable, the formula) for each element of pay, and how each compensation element and the company's decisions regarding that element fit into the company's overall compensation objectives and affect decisions regarding other elements. The rules also require the compensation committee report to state that the committee has reviewed and discussed the CD&A with management, and based on its review and discussions, the committee has recommended to the board that the CD&A be included in the company's proxy statement.[80]

Stock Exchange Requirements

Companies listed on the New York Stock Exchange must have compensation committees composed entirely of independent directors, and the Nasdaq requires listed companies to have compensation determined either by an independent compensation committee or by a majority of independent directors. Although the NYSE and Nasdaq requirements for compensation committees do not bind directors of nonlisted companies, they signal the standards to which courts may hold directors of all companies.[81]

Shareholder Proposals and Votes

The 2011 annual meeting season generated forty shareholder proposals related to executive compensation, representing 16.7% of the total number of shareholder proposals on corporate governance issues.[82] The vast majority of pay packages submitted to the nonbinding advisory vote required by Dodd–Frank passed.[83]

Key Principles Related to Compensation

Reports issued by the Conference Board Commission on Public Trust and Private Enterprise, the Business Roundtable, and the National Association of Corporate Directors' Blue Ribbon Commission on Executive Compensation and the Role of the Compensation Committee highlight the following key principles relating to compensation.

First, a strong and independent compensation committee should oversee and understand the entire executive compensation package and engage its own advisers and consultants. (As noted earlier, both the NYSE and the Nasdaq listing standards require independent compensation committees.) There should be no family relationships, personal friendships, or prior business or philanthropic relationships between the committee members and the executives for whom the committee is determining compensation. At a minimum, the CEO should not participate in compensation committee meetings or compensation issues considered by the board of directors.[84]

Second, executive compensation should have a significant performance-based component (some part of which can be equity incentives). Many institutional investors are also calling for a clearer link between pay and performance. For example, Institutional Shareholder Services, Inc. (ISS) supports shareholder proposals advocating the use of performance-based equity awards, unless the proposal is overly restrictive or the company demonstrates that at least 50% of the shares awarded to the top five officers are already performance based.[85] Now that FAS 123R requires that all options be expensed, the pay-for-performance mandate is likely to spill over into stock option vesting.

Third, benchmarking should be discouraged because it facilitates what some refer to as the "Lake Woebegon Effect," whereby all executives (and as a result, their compensation) are deemed by their board to be above average.[86] This leads to escalating executive compensation packages as companies seek to stay ahead of at least half of their peers. A report by former SEC Chairman Richard Breeden, the court-appointed monitor for MCI/WorldCom, suggests that a logical starting point for executive compensation might be the 25th percentile, rather

80. McGuireWoods, *A Comprehensive Analysis of the SEC's Executive Compensation Disclosure Rules* (Jan. 2007), *available at* http://www.mcguirewoods.com/news-resources/publications/taxation/analysis_SEC_executive_compensation.pdf.

81. Joseph M. Poerio, *New Bearings for Compensation Committees: Five Steps for Getting Executive Compensation Right*, J. Rep.: L. & Pol'y (Bureau of Nat'l Affairs, Benefits Practice Ctr., Executive Compensation Library, Compensation, Feb. 2004).

82. GEORGESON, INC., 2011 ANNUAL CORPORATE GOVERNANCE REVIEW 16 (2011), *available at* http://www.georgeson.com/usa/download/acgr/acgr2011.pdf.

83. James R. Copland, *Proxy Monitor 2011: A Report on Corporate Governance and Shareholder Activism*, PROXY MONITOR (Sept. 2011), at 2.

84. Martin Mack, Corporate Ethics and CEO Compensation 39–40 (May 2008) (unpublished Senior Honors Thesis, University of Rhode Island), *available at* http://digitalcommons.uri.edu/ (search for "Martin Mack"; then follow the hyperlink) (last visited Dec. 27, 2011).

85. *ISS 2004 Policy Changes*, FREDERIC W. COOK & CO., INC., Jan. 16, 2004, http://www.fwcook.com/alert_letters/1-16-04%20ISS%202004%20Policy%20Changes.pdf.

86. Scott Schaefer & Rachel M. Hayes, *CEO Pay and the Lake Wobegon Effect*, SOCIAL SCIENCE RESEARCH NETWORK, Dec. 11, 2008, *available at* http://papers.ssrn.com/sol3/papers.cfm?abstract_id=966332.

than the 75th percentile.[87] Benchmark data can be useful, but compensation committees need to examine competitive pay packages more carefully and sprinkle those packages with performance incentives.

Fourth, executives should be subject to acquire-and-hold policies that force them to retain a significant equity stake in their employers. Ownership guidelines have two purposes: (1) to align the long-term interests of executives and shareholders, and (2) to prevent executives from focusing on short-term increases in stock price at the expense of long-term performance. Presumably, these goals could be accomplished by option terms that prohibit option exercise for a substantial period of time; the leveraged nature of options would have a bigger financial impact on executives.

Fifth, executive compensation should be transparent and conspicuously disclosed. Disclosure of executive and director compensation is very important to institutional shareholders. Companies should clearly spell out, in terms that will be understood by investors, the company's compensation programs and philosophy, including the performance criteria on which certain compensation will be paid and the rationale for the salary levels, incentive payments, and stock option grants of top executive officers.

Thoughtful companies will respond with well-constructed, well-communicated compensation programs that place greater emphasis on performance than has been the case in the past.[88] (The "Inside Story" discusses some of the recent excesses in executive compensation.)

DUTIES OF CONTROLLING SHAREHOLDERS

A shareholder who owns sufficient shares to outvote the other shareholders, or to otherwise set corporate policy, and thus to control the corporation is known as a *controlling shareholder*. A person owning a majority of the outstanding shares is almost always a controlling shareholder, but persons owning a lower percentage (30%, for example) may still be deemed controlling if the shares are widely dispersed and there are no other large holders. In certain situations, controlling shareholders owe a fiduciary duty to the corporation and to its other shareholders. Generally, controlling shareholders have a responsibility to minority shareholders to control the corporation in a fair, just, and equitable manner (the standard of *entire fairness*). They may not engage in a bad faith scheme to drain off the corporation's earnings, thereby ensuring that minority shareholders are frozen out of all financial benefits.[89]

In 2011, the Delaware Court of Chancery held Grupo Mexico, the controlling shareholder of Southern Peru Copper Corporation (a public company traded on the New York Stock Exchange), liable for $1.3 billion in damages after a purportedly independent special board committee agreed to merge Southern Peru Copper with Minera Mexico, a private company owned by Grupo Mexico, at an inflated price.[90] Investment bank Goldman Sachs had opined that the transaction was fair from a financial perspective to the stockholders of Southern Peru and had provided a written fairness opinion, but the special committee did not ask Goldman to update its fairness analysis at the time of the stockholder vote on the transaction—nearly five months after the special committee had voted to recommend it—despite rising Southern Peru share prices and better-than-expected performance. The court explained: "Where, as here, a controlling stockholder stands on both sides of a transaction, the interested defendants are 'required to demonstrate their utmost good faith and the most scrupulous inherent fairness of the bargain.'" The court faulted both the special committee and Goldman for focusing "on finding a way to get the terms of the Merger structure proposed by Grupo Mexico to make sense, rather than aggressively testing the assumption that the Merger was a good idea in the first place." In concluding that Grupo Mexico had breached its duty of loyalty, the court explained that a reasonable special committee would not have taken the results of Goldman's discounted cash flow analyses "and blithely moved on to relative valuation, without any continuing and relentless focus on the actual give-get involved in real cash terms." Thus, the special committee "turn[ed] the gold that it held (market-tested Southern Peru stock worth in cash its trading price) into silver (equating itself on a relative basis to a financially-strapped, non-market tested selling company), and thereby devalue[d] its own acquisition currency."

Sale of Control

The obligation not to exercise control in a manner that intentionally harms the corporation and minority shareholders spills over into a sale of control. For instance, if a controlling shareholder knows or has reason to believe that the purchaser of its shares intends to use controlling power to the detriment of the corporation, the controlling shareholder has a duty not to transfer the power of management to such a purchaser.

---

87. Richard C. Breeden, *Restoring Trust, Report to The Hon. Jed S. Rakoff, The United States District Court for the Southern District of New York on Corporate Governance of the Future of MCI, Inc.* (Aug. 2003), at 97, *available at* http://law.du.edu/images/uploads/restoring-trust.pdf.

88. This discussion has drawn on Cooley Godward LLP, *Compensation Issues in the 2004 Proxy Season: Stormy Weather Ahead?*, Feb. 17, 2004, *available at* http://www.cooley.com/news/alerts.aspx?id=38514520.

89. Sugarman v. Sugarman, 797 F.2d 3 (1st Cir. 1986).

90. *In re* S. Peru Copper Corp. S'holder Derivative Litig., 2011 WL 6440761 (Del. Ch. Dec. 20, 2011).

A controlling interest in a corporation usually commands a higher price per share than a minority interest. Does this control premium belong to the corporation or to the majority shareholder? The widely accepted rule is that controlling shareholders normally have a right to derive a premium from the sale of a controlling block of stock.[91] For instance, in *Zetlin v. Hanson Holdings, Inc.*,[92] the New York Court of Appeals commented:

> In this action plaintiff Zetlin contends that minority stockholders are entitled to an opportunity to share equally in any premium paid for a controlling interest in the corporation. This rule would profoundly affect the manner in which controlling stock interests are now transferred. It would require, essentially, that a controlling interest be transferred only by means of an offer to all stockholders, that is, a tender offer. This would be contrary to existing law and if so radical a change is to be effected it would be best done by the Legislature.

In extreme circumstances, however, courts may be willing to characterize the control premium as a corporate asset, thus entitling minority shareholders to a portion. The U.S. Court of Appeals for the Second Circuit took such an approach in *Perlman v. Feldmann*.[93] *Perlman* involved Newport Steel Corporation, whose mills produced steel sheets for sale to manufacturers of steel products. C. Russell Feldmann was the chair of the board of directors and president of the corporation; he was also the controlling shareholder. In August 1950, when the supply of steel was tight due to the Korean War, Feldmann and some other shareholders sold their stock to a syndicate of end users of steel who were interested in securing a source of supply.

Minority shareholders brought a shareholder derivative suit to compel the controlling shareholders to account for, and make restitution of, their gains from the sale. The court held that the consideration received by the defendants included compensation for the sale of a corporate asset, namely, the ability of the board to control the allocation of the corporation's product in a time of short supply.

Note that the court did not seek to prohibit majority shareholders from ever selling their shares at a premium; it was careful to circumscribe its holding with an emphasis on the extreme market conditions:

> We do not mean to suggest that a majority stockholder cannot dispose of his controlling block of stock to outsiders without having to account to his corporation for profits or even never do this with impunity when the buyer is an interested customer, actual or potential, for the corporation's product. But when the sale necessarily results in a sacrifice of this element of corporate good will and consequent unusual profit to the fiduciary who has caused the sacrifice, he should account for his gains. So when in a time of market shortage, where a call on a corporation's product commands an unusually large premium, in one form or another, we think it sound law that a fiduciary may not appropriate to himself the value of this premium.[94]

The following classic case involved elements of abuse of control and sale of control. The dominant shareholders took a series of steps to ensure that they would participate in the financial benefits of the company without letting the minority shareholders also participate.

---

91. *See, e.g.,* Essex Universal Corp. v. Yates, 305 F.2d 572 (2d Cir. 1962).
92. 397 N.E.2d 387, 389 (N.Y. 1979).
93. 219 F.2d 173 (2d Cir. 1955).

94. *Id.* at 178.

A CASE IN POINT	*Summary*	Case 20.6

Jones v. H.F. Ahmanson & Co.

Supreme Court of California
460 P.2d 464 (Cal. 1969).

FACTS   The shares of the United Savings and Loan Association were not actively traded due to their high book value, the closely held nature of the association, and the failure of its management to provide information to shareholders, brokers, or the public.

In 1958, investor interest in shares of savings and loan associations and holding companies increased. Savings and loan stocks that were publicly marketed enjoyed a steady increase in market price. The controlling shareholders of the United Savings and Loan Association decided to create a mechanism by which the association, too, could attract investor interest. They did not, however, attempt to render the association's shares more readily marketable.

Instead, a holding company, the United Financial Corporation of California, was incorporated in Delaware on May 8, 1959. On May 14, pursuant to a prior agreement, certain association shareholders owning a majority of the association's stock exchanged their shares for those of United Financial.

After the exchange, United Financial held 85% of the association's outstanding stock. The former majority shareholders of the association had become the majority shareholders of United Financial and continued to control the association through the holding company. They did not offer the minority shareholders of the association an opportunity to exchange their shares.

CONTINUED

The first public offering of United Financial stock was made in June 1960. An additional public offering in February 1961 included a secondary offering (that is, an offering by selling share-holders) of 600,000 shares. There was active trading in the United Financial shares. Sales of the association shares, however, decreased from 170 shares per year before the formation of United Financial to half that number by 1961. United Financial acquired 90% of the associa-tion's shares that were sold.

A shareholder of the association brought suit, on behalf of herself and all other similarly situ-ated minority shareholders, against United Financial and the individuals and corporations that had set up the holding company. The plaintiff contended that the defendants' course of con-duct constituted a breach of fiduciary duty owed by the majority shareholders to the minority. She alleged that they had used their control of the association for their own advantage and to the detriment of the minority when they created United Financial, made a public market for its shares that rendered the association's stock unmarketable except to United Financial, and then refused either to purchase the minority's association stock at a fair price or to exchange the stock on the same terms afforded to the majority. She further alleged that they had created a conflict of interest that might have been avoided had they offered all association shareholders the opportunity to participate in the initial exchange of shares.

ISSUE PRESENTED   Did the majority shareholders who transferred their shares to a holding corporation, then took it public without allowing the minority to exchange their shares, breach their fiduciary duty to the minority shareholders?

SUMMARY OF OPINION   The California Supreme Court began its analysis by stating that the majority shareholders, acting either singly or in concert, have a fiduciary responsibil-ity to the minority and to the corporation. They must use their ability to control the corpora-tion fairly. They may not use it to benefit themselves alone or in a manner detrimental to the minority. Any use to which they put their power to control the corporation must benefit all shareholders proportionately and must not conflict with the proper conduct of the corpora-tion's business. The court summarized the rule as one of "inherent fairness from the viewpoint of the corporation or those interested therein."

The court noted that the controlling shareholders of the association could have taken advantage of the bull market in savings and loan stock in two other ways. They could have caused the association to effect a stock split, thereby increasing the number of outstand-ing shares, or they could have created a holding company and permitted all shareholders to exchange their shares before offering the holding company's shares to the public. Either course would have benefited all of the shareholders alike, although the majority shareholders would have had to relinquish some of their control shares. Instead, the defendants chose to set up a holding company that they controlled and did not allow the minority shareholders to exchange their association shares for shares of the holding company. Moreover, the market created by the defendants for United Financial shares would have been available for associa-tion shares had the defendants chosen a stock split of the association's shares.

The court stated that when a controlling shareholder sells or exchanges its shares, the transaction is subject to close scrutiny, particularly if the majority receives a premium over market value for its shares. If the premium constitutes payment for what is properly a corporate asset, all shareholders are entitled to a proportionate share of the premium (citing *Perlman v. Feldmann*). The defen-dants' exchange of association stock for United Financial stock was an integral part of a scheme that the defendants could have reasonably foreseen would destroy the potential public market for association stock. The remaining association shareholders would thus be deprived of the opportu-nity to realize a profit from those intangible characteristics that attach to publicly marketed stock.

RESULT   The majority shareholders who transferred their shares to a holding corporation, then took it public without allowing the minority to exchange their shares, breached their fiduciary duty to the minority shareholders. The minority shareholders were awarded dam-ages that would place them in a position at least as favorable as the majority shareholders had created for themselves.

Freeze-outs

The Delaware Supreme Court has held that a majority shareholder may *freeze out* the minority, that is, force the minority shareholders to convert their shares into cash, as long as the transaction is fair.[95] Sometimes a freeze-out is effected by merging a subsidiary into its parent, as in *Rosenblatt v. Getty Oil Co.*[96] In this case, Skelly Oil Company and Mission Corporation merged into Getty Oil Company, which was indirectly the majority shareholder of both Skelly and Mission. All three corporations were in the oil business. At issue was the fairness of the exchange ratio in the merger, that is, the ratio that would be used to convert the minority shareholders' stock into cash.

The Delaware Supreme Court stated that the concept of fairness in parent–subsidiary mergers has two aspects: fair dealing and fair price. Both must be examined together in resolving the ultimate question of entire fairness.

As to fair dealing, a court will look at the timing of the transaction; how it was initiated, structured, negotiated, and disclosed to the board; and how director and shareholder approval was obtained. The court cited a number of factors leading to a conclusion of fair dealing by Getty, including the adversarial nature of the negotiations between the parties to the merger.

Regarding fair price, a court will look at such economic factors as asset value, market value, earnings, and future prospects, and at any other elements that affect the intrinsic value of a company's stock. Both Getty and Skelly believed that the real worth of an oil company is centered in its reserves. Therefore, the court was especially impressed with the fact that they had employed D & M, a petroleum consulting engineering firm with a worldwide reputation and with nearly thirty-seven years of experience, to estimate Getty's and Skelly's respective oil and natural gas reserves. The court concluded that Getty had dealt fairly with the Skelly minority shareholders in the merger.

Although the controlling shareholder may be permitted to negotiate a deal for the sale of the entire company, the board of directors of the target must still determine the intrinsic value of the company and the maximum shareholder value reasonably attainable so that it has an informed basis for recommending the proposed deal to the minority stockholders or for suggesting that the minority stockholders vote against the deal and exercise their appraisal rights.[97] The representatives of the controlling shareholder on the target board owe the target's minority shareholders "an uncompromising duty of loyalty."[98] This includes an obligation to provide the minority full and accurate information about the company even if the minority has no right to vote on the deal.

Greenmail

Delaware courts analyze the payment of greenmail in the same way they analyze other defensive tactics under *Unocal.* Greenmail is a purchase of a dissident shareholder's stock by the issuer at a premium over market, often in exchange for a *standstill agreement*, whereby the shareholder agrees not to commence a tender offer or proxy contest or to buy additional shares of the issuer for a period of time, often ten years. If the board demonstrates that the shareholder to be bought out poses a threat to corporate policy and effectiveness and the repurchase of shares at a premium is a reasonable response to that threat, then the payment will be protected by the business judgment rule.[99]

95. Weinberger v. UOP, Inc., 457 A.2d 701 (Del. 1983).

96. 493 A.2d 929 (Del. 1985).

97. McMullin v. Beran, 765 A.2d 910 (Del. 2000).

98. *Id.* at 923.

99. *See also* Grobow v. Perot, 539 A.2d 180 (Del. 1988) (upholding repurchase by General Motors of GM stock and notes from H. Ross Perot at a "giant premium").

GLOBAL VIEW

Hostile Takeovers in the European Union

Takeovers in the European Union (EU) are governed by the European Union Directive on Takeover Bids (DTB), one of the most ambitious and highly contested pieces of legislation to pass the European Parliament. Adopted in April 2004, after thirty years of political wrangling among the EU member states, its aim was to open up European markets; harmonize the conflicting laws that regulate the economies of individual member states; and create clarity, transparency, and legal certainty through a set of common, universal rules governing shareholders' rights and defensive mechanisms in the event of takeover bids. Originally intended as a major step toward an integrated European capital market, the legislation foundered over sharp differences between the competitive, liberal, "Anglo-Saxon" version of shareholder rights and the coordinated, protectionist, "Rhenish" model.[100]

The United Kingdom and Ireland supported provisions that would ease takeover restrictions across Europe, arguing that takeovers would facilitate restructuring and

CONTINUED

100. SIMON HIX, ABDOUL G. NOURY & GERARD ROLAND, DEMOCRATIC POLITICS IN THE EUROPEAN PARLIAMENT 200 (2007).

Norebbo/Shutterstock

prepare companies for tougher competition in the global market. Germany, Sweden, and Norway, however, pressed for the protection of their national antitakeover defenses. In an effort to reach a consensus, the European Parliament ultimately left adoption of the two key articles that would have sharply limited the ability of target firms to adopt takeover defenses (Articles 9 and 11) to the discretion of individual member states. The result was a gutted and largely symbolic bill that left national antitakeover statutes mostly intact.[101]

As passed, the DTB consists of twenty-three articles, which together stipulate greater transparency, a mandatory bid rule, and an optional British-style "neutrality rule." The Directive applies to takeover bids for securities of an EU company whose securities are admitted to trading on a regulated market in at least one member state, but it specifically excludes takeover bids for securities issued by member states' central banks.[102]

Article 9, the contentious *neutrality rule*, generally requires the target's board of directors to remain neutral when faced with a hostile takeover bid and stipulates that once a takeover bid has been launched, the target's board cannot adopt any antitakeover devices, such as poison pills, without first obtaining the specific approval of shareholders.[103] The *mandatory bid provision* prohibits coercive two-tier offers by requiring any person who acquires 30% or more of a target company's stock to offer to buy all remaining shares at the highest price paid to acquire the 30% block.[104]

The *breakthrough rule* in Article 11 was designed to weaken the differential voting structures common in German and Nordic companies. It enables the hostile bidder to break through prebid defenses, such as multiple voting rights and other measures that distribute control rights in a manner that is disproportionate to the cash flow rights, thereby ensuring that a bidder that acquires a majority of the equity can successfully mount a takeover. Germany, France, and the Scandinavian countries bitterly resisted the rule's adoption.[105]

To break the deadlock, the drafters added Article 12, which allows the member states to opt out of the neutrality rule and breakthrough rule altogether. As a result, firms in each member state can retain the antitakeover defenses legal under existing national laws. Fritz Bolkestein, the EU Commissioner responsible for the Directive, was so angry at the extent of the compromise that he threatened to withdraw the Directive entirely, but he could not gain sufficient support from the other Commissioners.[106] According to an EU Commission report, only 1% of listed companies in the EU will apply the breakthrough rule on a mandatory basis.[107]

101. Luca Enriques, *EC Company Law Directives and Regulations: How Trivial Are They?*, 27 U. PA. J. INT'L ECON. L. 1 (2006).

102. Directive 2004/25/EC of the European Parliament and of the Council of 21 April 2004 on Takeover Bids, O.J. (L 142), 12 (Sept. 18, 2008), *available at* http://eur-lex.europa.eu/LexUriServ/LexUriServ.do?uri=CELEX:32004L0025:EN:HTML.

103. Matteo Gatti, *Optionality Arrangements and Reciprocity in the European Takeover Directive*, 5 EUR. BUS. ORG. L. REV. 553 (2005).

104. Harald Baum, *Takeover Law in the EU and Germany: Comparative Analysis of a Regulatory Model*, 3 U. TOKYO J. L. & POL. 60 (2006).

105. HIX, NOURY & ROLAND, *supra* note 100, at 204.

106. *EU Approves New Takeover Rules*, BBC NEWS, Nov. 28, 2003, *available at* http://news.bbc.co.uk/2/hi/business/3243074.stm.

107. Aoife White, *EU: Many European Governments Reluctant to Lift Takeover Barriers*, ASSOC. PRESS, Feb. 27, 2007, *available at* http://www.sddt.com/news/article.cfm?SourceCode=20070227faa.

Mike Price/Shutterstock

THE RESPONSIBLE MANAGER

CARRYING OUT FIDUCIARY DUTIES

Officers, directors, and controlling shareholders are fiduciaries. They owe their principal (the corporation and its shareholders) undivided loyalty. They must act in good faith. They may not put their own interests before those of the corporation and its shareholders. They cannot, for example, fight off a hostile takeover just to keep their jobs. They cannot use the company's confidential information for their personal gain.

Officers and directors also owe the corporation and its shareholders a duty of care. They should act with the care reasonable persons would use in the management of their own property. They have a duty to make only informed decisions. They cannot rely blindly on the advice of other people, even experts.

The duty to make informed decisions, which is a part of the duty of care, takes various forms. In the context of takeovers, board members cannot reject an offer without taking sufficient time to analyze its merit. Managers must be able to demonstrate that they made their decisions only after sufficient deliberation and after review of all relevant

CONTINUED

information. They should consider the possible effects of both the monetary and the nonmonetary aspects of the transaction.

A manager should never sign a document without reading it first. Ideally, each director should read the document the board is asked to approve. If that is not practical, the directors should demand and read a written summary prepared by counsel. They should also make sure that the officers who are authorized to sign the agreement have read it before signing it.

A manager should be informed as to the rules regarding the duty of care in the company's state of incorporation. Some jurisdictions permit the shareholders to amend the articles of incorporation to relieve directors of any financial liability for violations of the duty of care. But even with such provisions in place, directors must still act in good faith and in what they honestly believe is the best interest of the corporation. Otherwise, they will breach their duty of loyalty. Such a breach can not only result in monetary liability but can also demoralize the shareholders and employees of the corporation, making it difficult to maintain a high level of ethical behavior among them.

In a situation involving a potential conflict of interest, a manager should excuse himself or herself and leave the decision to others who do not have a conflict. It is common, for example, to establish special independent committees of the board of directors, either to examine the fairness of a management offer to acquire the company or to review the merits of shareholder litigation against the directors or officers.

A repurchase of stock at a premium from a dissident (or unhappy) shareholder may violate both the directors' duty to the corporation and the shareholder's duty to the other shareholders. Different courts view such repurchases differently, and local counsel should always be consulted. It is often appropriate for the board not only to obtain a written opinion from counsel that such a repurchase is permissible but also to convene a special independent committee of directors to decide whether the consideration that will be paid for the stock is fair.

Any controlling shareholder engaging in a transaction such as a merger with the company it controls must be able to prove that the transaction is fair both procedurally and substantively. The use of independent committees, advised by independent financial consultants and counsel, helps show procedural fairness, as does a willingness to negotiate the proposed transaction with such a committee on an arm's length basis. Paying a fair price for corporate assets or for shares of a corporation shows substantive fairness. The fairness of a price can be demonstrated by evidence of competing offers or independent appraisals or evaluations. The form of compensation of the appraiser or investment banker should not give that person an interest in the outcome of the appraisal or of the transaction. It is often preferable to pay the appraiser or investment banker a flat fee regardless of whether the deal goes through, rather than an incentive fee based on the value of the deal struck.

Certain acts of directors, officers, and controlling shareholders are both illegal and unethical, such as the seizing of a corporate opportunity by an officer. Other conduct may be legal yet ethically questionable, such as the payment of greenmail.

Some situations present conflicting ethical concerns. The Delaware Supreme Court has held that the directors must maximize shareholder value, that is, get the best price available, if they decide to sell control of the corporation. Yet a sale to a bust-up artist who will sell the company's assets, or to a union buster, might adversely affect the corporation's other constituencies, such as employees, suppliers, and the community in which the corporation does business.[108] A manager should try to select a course of action that protects the corporation's constituencies without sacrificing the shareholders' right to the best price. If the management team itself bids for the company, the board may find itself forced to become an auctioneer whose sole goal is to get the best price for the shareholders.

A board of directors can use various defensive measures to prevent a hostile takeover, provided that the measures are reasonable in relation to the threat posed and that the board considers it in the best interests of the company and its constituencies for the company to remain independent. Any measures designed to interfere with the shareholder franchise require proof by the directors of a compelling justification.

Similarly, if the board adopts a strategy resulting in a change of control of a corporation, it cannot use defensive tactics such as no-shop provisions (whereby the board agrees not to consider other offers) or large asset or stock lock-ups to deter competing bidders. In short, if the board agrees to a change of control, it breaches its fiduciary duties if it makes competing offers impossible by adopting a scorched-earth policy that leaves the successful bidder with a depleted target. Although legal counsel will advise managers and directors in this area, knowledge of the rules of the game is essential to good management.

---

108. See Constance E. Bagley & Karen L. Page, *The Devil Made Me Do It: Replacing Corporate Directors' Veil of Secrecy with the Mantle of Stewardship*, 36 SAN DIEGO L. REV. 897 (1999), for a discussion of the legal, economic, and organizational behavioral aspects of directors' consideration of factors other than simply shareholder return when acting on behalf of the corporation.

Norebbo/Shutterstock

A MANAGER'S DILEMMA

Putting It into Practice

Should Mickey Pay Greenmail?

In March 1984, a group headed by Saul Steinberg purchased more than 2 million shares of stock of Walt Disney Productions, the owner of Disneyland. Disney responded by announcing that it would acquire the Arvida Corporation for $200 million in newly issued Disney stock and would assume Arvida's $190 million debt. The Steinberg group countered with a shareholder derivative suit in federal court, seeking to block the Arvida transaction. All of the proceeds of such a suit (less expenses) go to the corporation for the benefit of all of its shareholders.

While the shareholder derivative suit was pending, the Steinberg group proceeded to acquire 2 million additional shares of Disney stock, increasing its ownership position to approximately 12% of the outstanding Disney shares. On June 8, 1984, the Steinberg group advised Disney's

directors of its intention to make a tender offer for 49% of the outstanding shares at $67.50 a share and its intention to later tender for the balance at $72.50 a share.

Should the Disney directors offer to repurchase all the Disney stock held by the Steinberg group at a premium and to reimburse the estimated cost incurred in preparing the tender offer in return for the Steinberg group's agreement not to purchase any more Disney stock and to drop the Arvida litigation? Is it legal or ethical for the Steinberg group to agree not to oppose a motion to dismiss the Arvida litigation? To sell its shares at a premium not offered to other Disney shareholders?[109]

---

109. *See* Heckman v. Ahmanson, 214 Cal. Rptr. 177 (Cal. Ct. App. 1985).

INSIDE STORY

Occupy Wall Street and the Long Twilight of Imperial CEOs

One of the rallying cries of the leaderless resistance movement Occupy Wall Street is, "We are the 99 percent."[110] In 2008, the top 1% of earners took in more than 20% of the earnings (including capital gains).[111] The top 0.1% garnered more than 10% of all personal income for an average of $1.7 million or more, including capital gains.[112] By September 17, 2011, when the Occupy Wall Street protesters flooded into lower Manhattan, income disparity in the United States had reached the highest levels since the Great Depression.[113] Income gaps translate into larger gaps in standardized test scores between rich and poor children and gaps in completion of college as well as economic segregation "with the rich flocking together in new exurbs and gentrifying pockets where lower- and middle-income families cannot afford to live."[114]

Initiated by the Canadian activist group Adbusters, the Occupy movement seeks to encourage greater social and economic equality through measures such as eliminating corporate influence in politics, reforming the tax structure, and creating jobs. The movement rapidly spread to 100 cities in the United States and more than 1,500 cities globally.[115]

Although hedge fund operator John Paulson became a poster child for compensation excess (he was paid $4.9 billion in 2010 after successfully betting against the subprime home mortgage market), 41% of the top 0.1% were executives, managers, and supervisors at nonfinancial companies.[116] (Sports figures and media stars comprised only about 3%.) While pay for 90% of working Americans has remained flat since the 1970s, executive compensation at the largest firms has quadrupled. Market systems are designed to increase economic efficiency by rewarding those who are most productive to society, but this can result in a regime that "allow[s] the big winners to feed their pets better than the losers can feed their children."[117]

CONTINUED

---

110. *About Occupy Wall Street*, http://occupywallst.org/about/ (last visited Dec. 29, 2011).

111. Sabrina Tavernise, *Middle-Class Areas Shrink as Income Gap Grows*, *New Report Finds*, N.Y. TIMES, Nov. 15, 2011.

112. *Id.*

113. Peter Whoriskey, *With Executive Pay, Rich Pull Away from Rest of America*, WASH. POST, June 18, 2011.

114. Tavernise, *supra* note 111.

115. *About Occupy Wall Street*, *supra* note 110.

116. Whoriskey, *supra* note 113.

117. ARTHUR M. OKUN, EQUALITY AND EFFICIENCY: THE BIG TRADEOFF 1 (1975).

hxdbzxy/Shutterstock

Some attribute high executive compensation not to good economics but to overly cozy relationships between CEOs and their boards. Consider corporate governance at WorldCom before massive fraud destroyed roughly $200 billion in shareholder value, put tens of thousands of employees out of work, and wiped out the entire value of stock held in employee retirement accounts as well as the value of accumulated equity-based compensation.[118]

According to Richard C. Breeden, corporate monitor of WorldCom during its 2003 bankruptcy proceedings, WorldCom's CEO Bernard J. Ebbers "was allowed nearly imperial reign over the affairs of the Company, without the board of directors exercising any apparent restraint on his actions, even though he did not appear to possess the experience or training to be remotely qualified for his position."[119] The WorldCom board had allowed "lavish compensation," including more than $400 million in "loans" to Ebbers, which were unlikely ever to be repaid. It also approved a $238 million "compensation slush fund," which Ebbers could allocate to favored executives or employees, with no standards or supervision. Citing Lord Acton's remark in 1887 that "power tends to corrupt and absolute power corrupts absolutely," Breeden stated that "'backbone' and 'fortitude' may be the most important qualities needed by a director of a public company."

As a condition to emerging from bankruptcy, WorldCom, which is now known as MCI, Inc., was required to convert its articles of incorporation into a governance constitution, which could be changed only with prior shareholder consent. MCI was required to:

- Give a group of shareholders the power to nominate their own candidates for inclusion in the management proxy statement if the group did not agree with the board's proposed candidates.

- Create the position of nonexecutive chair of the board.

- Ban the issuance of stock options without prior shareholder approval.

- Expense both stock options and restricted stock grants on its financial statements.

- Ban a staggered board, set ten-year term limits for directors, and restrict independent directors to a maximum of three boards, including the MCI board.

- Prohibit related-party transactions involving board members.

- Compensate directors solely with cash and require them to utilize not less than 25% of those fees to purchase MCI stock, which had to be held until they left the board.

- Have the board of directors meet at least eight times a year, hold an annual strategic review, and attend annual refresher training on topics relating to board responsibilities.

- Limit change-in-control devices, such as poison pills.

In the fall of 2004, in the wake of a corporate scandal involving Marsh & McLennan Companies, the largest insurance brokerage firm in the United States, the *Wall Street Journal* commented: "The long twilight of imperial CEOs—who run opaque giants that are granted unquestioning trust from shareholders—finally is coming to an end. True, the imperial CEO is harder to get rid of than Rasputin. But this seems to be it."[120]

Reports of the demise of the imperial CEO proved premature. The subprime mortgage crisis set off renewed scrutiny of executive pay and perks. The collapse of the mortgage industry and the ensuing credit crisis could cost the U.S. economy $1 trillion. At a time when working families struggled with ballooning mortgage payments, falling real estate prices, mortgage foreclosure, and job losses, the executives of companies at the center of the crisis have collected hundreds of millions of dollars in compensation. As Representative Henry Waxman, chair of the U.S. House Committee on Oversight and Government Reform, put it: "The obvious question is this: How can a few executives do so well when their companies do so poorly?"[121]

The former CEO of the failing subprime mortgage firm Countrywide Financial, Angelo Mozilo, received millions in executive compensation before the firm crashed and burned. Although Citigroup CEO Charles Prince technically received no severance package, he left the firm with $29.5 million in stock options, grants, and other perks after Citibank's bets on the subprime mortgage market drove the bank to near insolvency. AIG CEO Martin Sullivan, who was later named one of the "Worst CEOs of All Time" by *Time*, collected $47 million from the company after he was fired. CEO Ken Lewis left Bank of America in 2009 with $53 million in pension benefits. Meanwhile, Merrill Lynch CEO Stanley O'Neal collected a $160 million severance package, even after leaving the bank with an $8 billion write-down.[122]

The Bush administration's $700 billion bailout of the banks weakened by the collapse of the mortgage-backed securities market capped executive compensation at banks receiving federal money, but those limits lapsed when the banks repaid the federal funds. (The bailout and associated regulatory reforms are discussed in more detail in the "Inside Story" in Chapter 23.)

---

118. Breeden, *supra* note 87.

119. *Id.*

120. *See* Jesse Eisinger, *AIG's Chief Shows Signs of Humility as Spitzer Probe Rattles the Industry*, WALL ST. J., Oct. 20, 2004, at C1.

121. Mike Hall, *CEOs Pocket Big Pay While Their Companies Tank*, AFL–CIO NOW BLOG NEWS, Mar. 7, 2008, *available at* http://blog.aflcio.org/2008/03/07/ceos-pocket-big-pay-while-their-companies-tank/.

122. Ben Walsh, *7 of the Most Outrageous Severance Packages in Recent Wall Street History*, BUS. INSIDER, Dec. 15, 2011, *available at* http://www.businessinsider.com/7-outrageous-severance-packages-2011-12?op=1.

KEY WORDS AND PHRASES

asset lock-up option   661

breakthrough rule   689

breakup fee   673

business judgment rule   657

bust-up takeover   677

clawbacks   682

constructive trust   668

controlling shareholder   685

corporate opportunity doctrine   668

deal protection devices   673

duty of care   657

duty of loyalty   657

entire fairness   685

exercise price   683

fiduciary out   673

freeze out   688

golden parachutes   682

greenmail   670

inside directors   664

line-of-business test   668

mandatory bid provision   689

neutrality rule   689

no-shop agreement   673

no-talk clause   673

poison pill   677

proxy   677

proxy contest   677

quasi-foreign corporation   665

restricted stock   683

Revlon mode   671

self-tender   677

shareholder derivative suit   661

shareholder rights plan   677

stock option   683

standstill agreement   688

substantive coercion   679

termination fee   673

QUESTIONS AND CASE PROBLEMS

1. In 2007, eBay started an online classifieds business called Kijiji. eBay designedKijiji to compete with Craigslist, the most widely used online classifieds website in the United States. At the time that it startedKijiji, eBay owned 28.4% of Craigslist and was one of only three stockholders. As a result of choosing to compete with Craigslist and pursuant to the Craigslist stockholders' agreement, eBay lost certain contractual consent rights and the right of first refusal over the shares it owned. The other two stockholders asked eBay to sells its shares back to the company or to a third party, but eBay refused. The two stockholders responded, in their capacity as directors, by (1) adopting a plan that restricted eBay from purchasing additional Craigslist shares and hampered eBay's ability to sell its shares to third parties, (2) implementing a staggered board to make it impossible for eBay to unilaterally elect a director to the Craigslist board, and (3) seeking to obtain a right of first refusal in Craigslist's favor over the shares eBay owned through a scheme that reduced eBay's ownership in Craigslist from 28.4% to 24.9%. eBay sued, asserting that the other two stockholders had breached the fiduciary duties they owed eBay as a minority stockholder. What result? [*eBay Domestic Holdings, Inc. v. Newmark*, 16 A.3d 1 (Del. Ch. 2010).]

2. Lee Gray was a director, president, and treasurer of HMG/ Courtland Properties, Inc. (HMG), a publicly held real estate investment trust, and of its investment adviser Courtland Group, Inc. As such, he negotiated the terms of a joint venture with Norman Fieber, another HMG director, for the development of a portfolio of properties located in the northeastern United States. During the course of the negotiations, Gray told Fieber that Martine Avenue Associates, a general partnership controlled by Gray and his sister, would be interested in co-investing with Fieber as a buyer of an interest in the properties. Neither Gray nor Fieber disclosed that possibility to HMG, but all parties agreed that the negotiated price was fair and reasonable. Martine did ultimately join a group of investors on Fieber's side of the transaction in May 1986, but HMG did not learn of Gray's economic interest in Martine until October 1996. Did either Gray or Fieber violate their fiduciary duties to HMG? [*HMG/Courtland Properties, Inc. v. Gray*, 749 A.2d 94 (Del. Ch. 1999).]

3. Missouri Fidelity Union Trust Life Insurance Company stock was trading at $2.63 per share. Eight directors sold their shares for $7.00 per share, conditioned on the resignation of eleven of the fifteen directors of the corporation and the provision that five nominees of the buyer be elected as a majority of the executive and investment committees. Did the directors violate their fiduciary duty? Would the answer be different if the directors had controlled a majority of the voting stock? [*Snyder v. Epstein*, 290 F. Supp. 652 (E.D. Wis. 1968).]

4. The After-School Care Corporation owned more than forty day-care centers specializing in providing care to elementary-school-aged children in the afternoons. The president of the company, Clark Holmes, received a phone call at work one day from Marney Stein, the owner and sole proprietor of Pro Providers, a firm that owned six nursery schools for children aged two to four. Stein indicated that she wanted to sell Pro Providers for $1 million and asked if After-School were interested. Holmes proposed the sale to the After-School board of directors. The directors were divided on the issue because they were not certain whether branching out into nursery care would be a smart move. As funds were not available, however, they saw no need to vote on the issue at that time.

Holmes decided that he would try to purchase Pro Providers on his own. After securing a loan, Holmes entered into negotiations with Stein. They agreed on a price of $900,000, and the sale went through. Holmes did not inform the board of his activity until after the sale was completed.

A shareholder is considering suing Holmes for breach of fiduciary duty. Does she have a valid claim? Should it matter that Holmes plans to expand one of the Pro Provider nursery schools into a nursery/after-school center?

5. The Engulf Corporation is a large media and entertainment conglomerate with its stock trading on the New York Stock Exchange. Engulf is a major producer of films and videos and also publishes several magazines. The company has a shareholder rights plan (that is, a poison pill), which would make any hostile takeover financially prohibitive unless the pill is redeemed by Engulf's board of directors. On January 10, the Megaclout Corporation, in a move designed to gain control of Engulf, announced a tender offer for 51% of Engulf's shares at $140, an $11 premium over the market price.

On January 14, in a meeting that lasted more than thirteen hours, the Engulf board of directors met to consider Megaclout's offer. Engulf's lawyers and investment bankers attended and made detailed presentations on the adequacy of the offer. The next day, the directors officially announced that they believed the Megaclout offer was unacceptable for two reasons: (1) the long-term value of the Engulf stock ranged from $160 to $170, so $140 was financially inadequate; and (2) Engulf had a distinct corporate culture that included special ways of doing business, an outstanding record of management–employee relations, and strong support of community projects in the towns in which Engulf businesses were located. Acceptance of Megaclout's tender offer would pose a direct threat to this corporate culture. For these reasons, the board refused to redeem the poison pill.

Megaclout brought suit as an Engulf shareholder against the Engulf board of directors, demanding that the board redeem the poison pill, which would allow all the shareholders to decide whether they wanted to accept the offer by tendering their shares.
   a. Must the Engulf board of directors redeem the poison pill at this time?
   b. The board argues that the offer, which is $11 over the market price of the stock, is financially inadequate. Is the argument convincing? Why or why not?
   c. Should managers be concerned about corporate constituencies other than shareholders, such as employees or communities in which businesses are located? What if these different concerns conflict?

6. Shlensky was a minority shareholder of Chicago National League Ball Club, Inc., which owned and operated the Chicago Cubs baseball team. The defendants were directors of the club. Shlensky alleged that since 1935 when night baseball was introduced, every major league team except the Cubs has scheduled most of its home games at night. This has allegedly been done for the specific purpose of maximizing attendance, thereby maximizing revenue and income.

The Cubs have sustained losses from their direct baseball operations. Shlensky attributed the losses to inadequate attendance at the Cubs' home games, which are played at Wrigley Field. He feels that if the directors continue to refuse to install lights at Wrigley Field and schedule night baseball games, the Cubs will continue to sustain similar losses.

Shlensky further alleged that Philip Wrigley, the president of the corporation, refused to install lights not, as Wrigley claims, for the welfare of the corporation, but because of his personal opinion that "baseball is a daytime sport." Shlensky charged the other directors with acquiescing in Wrigley's policy.

In his complaint, Shlensky claimed that the directors were acting for reasons contrary to the business interests of the corporation and wasting corporate assets. Have the directors failed to exercise reasonable care in the management of the corporation's affairs? Does the directors' decision fall within the scope of their business judgment? [*Shlensky v. Wrigley,* 237 N.E.2d 776 (Ill. App. Ct. 1968).]

7. McDonald, a potential buyer of financial institutions, visited Halbert at the Tulane Savings and Loan Association. Halbert was president, manager, and chair of the board, and, along with his wife, the owner of 53% of the stock of the association. McDonald asked if the association was for sale. Halbert replied that it was not for sale but that he and his wife would sell their controlling stock for $1,548 per share. Halbert did not tell the association's board of directors or its shareholders about McDonald's interest in acquiring the association.

In addition to agreeing to sell his stock, Halbert also agreed to cause the association to withhold the payment of dividends. After Halbert's shares were purchased, Halbert, who had not yet relinquished his corporate offices, helped McDonald solicit the minority shareholders' shares and even advised them that, because McDonald was going to withhold dividends for ten to twenty years, they ought to take his offer of $300 per share. McDonald bought some of the minority shares at $300 and others for between $611 and $650.

Did Halbert owe the minority shareholders a fiduciary duty? If so, what was his duty in selling his majority stock position? Was his conduct ethical? [*Brown v. Halbert,* 76 Cal. Rptr. 781 (Cal. App. Ct. 1969).]

8. In 1995, Walt Disney Company hired Michael Ovitz, a longtime friend of Disney's CEO Michael Eisner, as president. Ovitz lacked experience managing a diversified public company, although he was being considered for high-level executive positions in other companies. Ovitz's five-year employment agreement, which was negotiated solely by Eisner and the board of directors, gave Ovitz a base salary of $1 million a year, a discretionary bonus, and two sets of stock options. The agreement included a provision stating that termination without cause would entitle Ovitz to his remaining salary through September 30, 2000, a $10 million severance payment, an additional $7.5 million for each fiscal year remaining under the agreement, and the immediate vesting of the first 3 million stock options. Soon after Ovitz took office, problems arose. In 1996, Eisner and Ovitz arranged for Ovitz to leave Disney on a no-fault basis with $130 million in termination compensation pursuant to the employment agreement. Did the board of directors breach its fiduciary duty when it agreed to the no-fault termination provisions in Ovitz's employment agreement? Did Ovitz violate his fiduciary duty as an officer when he accepted the no-fault termination payment? [*In re Walt Disney Co. Derivative Litigation,* 906 A.2d 27 (Del. 2006).]

UNIT

VI

SECURITIES AND FINANCIAL TRANSACTIONS

CHAPTER 21

PUBLIC AND PRIVATE OFFERINGS OF SECURITIES

INTRODUCTION

RAISING CAPITAL THROUGH SECURITIES OFFERINGS

Most businesses reach a certain point at which the founders' initial capital investment and ongoing bank loans are insufficient for continued growth. At this juncture, the directors and managers of the company must decide whether to rein in the company's growth consistent with its existing capital asset base or to sell an interest in the company to raise capital for continued expansion. Although entrepreneurs often turn first to family, friends, and wealthy individual investors (*angels*), and then to venture capitalists, many companies will eventually seek to raise capital through an initial public offering of the company's shares. Even those companies that can internally generate the cash flow for growth may decide to sell securities to spread the concentration of risk in the business venture and to give the founders, early investors, and venture capitalists liquidity and an exit vehicle.

Because registered public offerings are very expensive (usually costing more than $1 million in out-of-pocket expenses alone), sales of securities to private investors or venture capitalists are almost always structured to be exempt from the federal registration requirements. Whether the directors and managers of a company seek an exemption or go through the public offering process, they must understand and comply with federal and state securities laws. Ignorance of these laws is no excuse. As Judge Frank Easterbrook put it, "No one with half a brain can offer an opportunity to invest in our company without knowing that there is a regulatory jungle out there."[1]

CHAPTER OVERVIEW

This chapter first provides an overview of the federal and state statutory schemes that regulate the offer and sale of securities. It then defines the key terms "security," "offer," and "sale" under the Securities Act of 1933 (the *1933 Act*). Next, the chapter describes the public offering process, including the registration of securities. It then discusses several exemptions from registration for offerings by the issuer, including the exemptions under SEC Regulation D and the *crowdfunding* exemption added in 2012.

The chapter goes on to outline the exemptions for secondary offerings by shareholders, the restrictions on the resale of registered and unregistered securities, offerings outside the United States under Regulation S, and sales to qualified institutional buyers under Rule 144A. The chapter then briefly describes the regulation of the derivatives markets under the Dodd–Frank Wall Street Reform and Consumer Protection Act. The periodic reporting and certain other requirements under the Securities Exchange Act of 1934 (the *1934 Act*) are also identified. The chapter looks at liability for failure to meet the registration and prospectus-delivery requirements under section 12(a)(1) of the 1933 Act and then discusses liability for misstatements or omissions in the registration statement. The discussion focuses first on section 11 of the 1933 Act, under which issuers are strictly liable for misstatements or omissions in a registration statement and certain officers, all directors, accountants, and underwriters are liable if they fail to act with due diligence. It then turns to section 12(a)(2) of the 1933 Act, which provides a remedy for any person who purchases a security in a registered or unregistered public offering by means of a misleading prospectus or oral communication. The broader antifraud

---

1. Mueller v. Sullivan, 141 F.3d 1232 (7th Cir. 1998).

CONTINUED

provisions contained in section 10(b) of the 1934 Act and Rule 10b-5 (which apply to both registered and exempt offerings of securities) and the prohibitions against selective disclosure in Regulation FD are discussed in Chapter 22.

THE FEDERAL STATUTORY SCHEME

The two principal federal acts that regulate securities transactions and issuers, the Securities Act of 1933 (the 1933 Act)[2] and the Securities Exchange Act of 1934 (the 1934 Act),[3] were adopted during the depths of the Great Depression. Both acts have been amended numerous times since their adoption. The federal securities laws embody three beliefs: (1) investors should be provided with full information prior to investing, (2) corporate insiders should not be allowed to use nonpublic information concerning their companies to their own financial advantage, and (3) misled investors should receive adequate relief even in the absence of common law fraud. As discussed in Chapter 6, the market turmoil in 2008 that led to the most extensive federal intervention in the financial markets

---

2.   15 U.S.C. § 77a.
3.   15 U.S.C. § 78a.

since the Great Depression resulted in further strengthening of the federal regulations governing the securities, banking, and insurance industries and new regulation of over-the-counter derivative contracts.

The 1933 Act

In adopting the 1933 Act, the U.S. Congress sought to ensure that investors would receive adequate disclosure of material information about the issuer and its business and the offering. The Act requires that promoters of securities offerings register them with the Securities and Exchange Commission (SEC), an agency of the U.S. government, and provide prospective purchasers with a prospectus containing material information about the issuer and the offering, unless the security or the type of transaction is exempt from registration.

Congress rejected suggestions that it also regulate the terms or quality of securities offerings. As a result, investors are not protected from making highly speculative or foolish investments. The 1933 Act requires only that they be advised of all material facts before they invest their money.

In addition to requiring registration, the 1933 Act expressly creates private rights of action for certain violations of its provisions. This means that in addition to public enforcement by the SEC or criminal proceedings by the U.S. Attorney's Office, any investor can bring a private suit for damages.

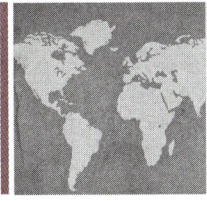

winnond/Shutterstock

HISTORICALPERSPECTIVE

From the Securities Act of 1933 to TARP to the Dodd–Frank Wall Street Reform and Consumer Protection Act of 2010 to the JOBS Act of 2012

After the stock market crash of 1929, distrust of the nation's financial markets was widespread. Regulations governing securities offerings in the United States stem from the public and governmental outrage at the markets' excesses. According to Representative (later Speaker of the House) Sam Rayburn:

> Millions of citizens have been swindled into exchanging their savings for worthless stocks. The fraudulent promoter has taken an incredible toll from confiding people. . . .

These hired officials of our great corporations who permitted, who promoted, who achieved the extravagant expansion of the financial structure of their respective companies today present a pitiable spectacle. Five years ago they arrogated to themselves the greatest privileges. They scorned the interference of the Government. They dealt with their stockholders in the most arbitrary fashion. They called upon the people to bow down to them as the

real rulers of the country. Safe from the pitiless publicity of Government supervision, unrestrained by Federal statute, free from any formal control, these few men, proud, arrogant, and blind, drove the country to financial ruin. Some of them are fugitives from justice in foreign lands; some of them have committed suicide; some of them are under indictment; some of them are in prison; all of them are in terror of the consequences of their own deeds.[a]

CONTINUED

Seventy-five years after Rayburn's observations, excesses in the financial markets would once again lead to governmental intervention and regulation.

After nearly eight years of favoring the deregulation of the financial industry, the George W. Bush administration aggressively interceded in the private markets in the fall of 2008 to quell panic and stabilize the nation's leading financial institutions. This dramatic change in regulatory policy began in earnest when the venerable investment bank Bear Stearns, badly damaged by the subprime mortgage crisis, sold itself to JPMorgan Chase in a fire sale in March 2008. (The subprime mortgage crisis of 2007–2008 is discussed further in the "Inside Story" in Chapters 18 and 23.) The U.S. government paid more than $150 billion to bail out and recapitalize Fannie Mae and Freddie Mac, the government-sponsored home mortgage giants devastated by the subprime mortgage crisis; it paid another $150 billion to keep insurance behemoth American International Group (AIG) from collapsing. AIG had issued $440 billion in credit-default swaps insuring the repayment of mortgage-backed securities and other debt. Originally procured by investors to guarantee the repayment of bonds in case the issuer defaulted, *credit-default swaps* became a popular vehicle for hedge funds and other traders betting on how close a firm was to insolvency.[b] In a controversial decision, the U.S. Treasury Department paid AIG's counterparties 100 cents on the dollar.

The value of a swap or other financial derivative contract depends in part on the counterparty's solvency and its ability to honor its obligations. Brooksley Born, then chair of the Commodity Futures Trading Commission (CFTC), had warned in 1998 that the explosion of the financial derivatives market allowed traders "to take positions that may threaten our regulatory markets or, indeed, our economy, without the knowledge of any federal regulatory authority."[c] Her colleagues on the Working Group on Financial Markets—Alan Greenspan, chair of the Federal Reserve; SEC chair Arthur Levitt Jr.; and U.S. Treasury Secretary Robert Rubin—voiced "grave concerns" about her proposal to regulate the financial derivatives market. Deputy Treasury Secretary Lawrence Summers criticized her for "casting a shadow of regulatory uncertainty over an otherwise thriving market,"[d] and Congress passed a law in 2000 that exempted swaps from oversight by the CFTC and the SEC. The massive but unregulated swaps markets only aggravated the downward pressure on financial institutions already burdened by subprime mortgage-backed securities. On September 26, 2008, SEC Chair Christopher Cox admitted that "the last six months have made it abundantly clear that voluntary regulation does not work."[e]

Investment bank Lehman Brothers declared bankruptcy on September 15, 2008. Thereafter, the Federal Reserve, at the urging of U.S. Treasury Secretary (and former chair and CEO of Goldman Sachs) Henry Paulson and with Wall Street's cooperation, waived the normal review process and opportunity for public comment and approved in a matter of days a major overhaul of the structure of the last two major independent investment banks in the United States, Goldman Sachs and Morgan Stanley.[f] Both firms announced on September 21 that they would become commercial bank-holding companies subject to permanent on-site regulation by the Federal Reserve. Their decision to become regulated commercial banks marked the end of an era and instantly altered the landscape of modern Wall Street.

The Federal Reserve immediately extended credit to the firms' broker-dealer subsidiaries and sent the message that it would not allow these powerhouses to go under. Becoming bank-holding companies enabled Goldman and Morgan Stanley to tap the Fed's so-called discount window and to extend Federal Deposit Insurance Corporation (FDIC) coverage to more of their client accounts. In exchange, the firms subjected themselves to greater government scrutiny that could limit their ability to engage in potentially risky but lucrative strategies, such as borrowing heavily to make securities and financial derivative trades.

The Senate passed what became the Emergency Economic Stabilization Act[g] on October 1, 2008, by a vote of 74 to 25. On Friday, October 3, the House passed the bill by a vote of 263 to 171. President George W. Bush signed it into law a few hours later.

The statute authorized the Secretary of the Treasury to "immediately provide authority and facilities that the Secretary of the Treasury can use to restore liquidity and stability to the financial system of the United States" and granted the Secretary the power to "purchase . . . troubled assets from any financial institution, on such terms and conditions as determined by the Secretary."[h] Congress initially appropriated $700 billion for this Troubled Asset Relief Program (TARP).

In his testimony before the U.S. Senate, Treasury Secretary Paulson claimed that the bill would stabilize the economy, improve liquidity in the credit market, and stimulate investor confidence.[i] In fact, the Act failed to spark the hoped-for rebound in the stock market; on Monday, October 6, the Dow Jones Average dropped more than 700 points and fell below 10,000 for the first time in four years.

In early October 2008, the Federal Reserve announced its intention to start lending directly to nonfinancial firms by buying up short-term corporate debt (commercial paper) for the first time since the Great Depression. On October 14, President Bush announced that the Treasury Department would spend up to $250 billion of the $700 billion authorized by the bailout law to buy non-voting senior preferred shares in the nation's commercial banks. Secretary Paulson had summoned the CEOs of the nine largest U.S. banks to the Treasury Department on October 13 and told them in no uncertain terms that they had no choice but to accept $125 billion in government funds in exchange for preferred stock "for their own good and that of the country."[j] As part of the deal, the banks were required to limit executive compensation and to agree not to increase dividends to their common shareholders. President Bush promised that "government's role will

CONTINUED

"Now we just have to sit back and wait for the Fed to bail us out."

Christopher Weyant/The New Yorker Collection/www.cartoonbank.com

be limited and temporary" and that the partial nationalization of the nation's banks, which was patterned after Britain's purchase of equity stakes in its major banks, was a short-term move. The FDIC also temporarily guaranteed most new debt issued by insured banks and expanded government insurance to cover all non-interest-bearing accounts in an effort to staunch cash withdrawals by small businesses.

By early 2012, roughly $413 billion of the TARP funds had been disbursed; of this amount, around $278 billion was subsequently repaid. In addition, the government earned roughly $40 billion in interest, dividends, and other income. The total net cost of TARP to the U.S. taxpayers is estimated to exceed $50 billion.[k]

A number of members of Congress reported significant resistance to the bailouts from their constituents, who were outraged that the measure appeared to unfairly enrich the same executives who may have caused

the financial crisis in the first place. Bloomberg News reported that the top five Wall Street investment banks paid their senior executives more than $5 billion in the five years before Lehman Brothers filed for bankruptcy.[l]

Public indignation sparked again in 2009 when a number of banks that had received TARP funds, AIG, and other Wall Street firms announced that they were paying almost $20 billion in bonuses to their traders and executives. AIG alone awarded $165 million in bonuses for the year ended December 31, 2008.[m] The TARP limits of executive compensation were strengthened in February 2009 after President Obama called the bonuses "shameful."[n]

In June and July of 2010, the House (by a vote of 237-192) and the Senate (by a vote of 60-39) passed the Dodd-Frank Wall Street Reform and Consumer Protection Act[o]—the most sweeping reform of the U.S. financial markets since the Great Depression. As discussed in

the "Inside Story" in Chapter 6, the Act created the Consumer Financial Protection Bureau and imposed new regulations on the $55 trillion credit-default swap market and other derivatives trading. Efforts to create electronic swaps trading platforms were predicated on the premise that greater transparency around the pricing of derivatives would bring structure and stability to this heretofore "dark market."[p]

When President Obama signed the bill, he stated that the reforms in the Dodd-Frank Act "represent the strongest consumer financial protections in history."[q] U.S. Treasury Secretary Timothy Geithner explained: "It was designed to lay a stronger foundation for innovation, economic growth and job creation with robust protections for consumers and investors and tough constraints on risk-taking."[r]

Many Republicans voiced disapproval of Dodd-Frank, however, and only six Republican senators voted in favor of the bill. Former Speaker of the House and 2012 Republican presidential candidate Newt Gingrich charged that Dodd-Frank was a negative influence on the economy, which is "making it harder to make loans for housing, and it is crippling small business borrowing," partly by "crushing independent banks." In one presidential debate, he stated: "If they would repeal [Dodd-Frank] tomorrow morning, you would have a better housing market the next day."[s]

The need to create more jobs in the wake of the Great Recession trumped concerns expressed by SEC Chair Mary Shapiro and others about unduly deregulating offerings by so-called emerging growth companies. By a vote of 380-41 in the House and 73-26 in the Senate, Congress passed the Jumpstart Our Business Startups Act (the *JOBS Act*) in March 2012 and President Obama signed it in April 2012.[t]

CONTINUED

a. House Consideration, Amendment and Passage of H.R. 5480, May 5, 1932, 77 Cong. Rec. 2910, 2918 (1933), *reprinted in* 1 Federal Securities Laws: Legislative History, 1933–1982, at 2948 (1983).

b. David Cho & Zachary A. Goldfarb, *3 Agencies Vie for Oversight of Swaps Market*, Wash. Post, Aug. 21, 2008, at D1.

c. Anthony Faiola, Ellen Nakashima & Jill Drew, *What Went Wrong*, WASH. POST, Oct. 15, 2008, at A1.

d. *Id.*

e. Damian Paletta & Deborah Solomon, *U.S. Rewrites Financial Playbook*, WALL ST. J., Oct. 8, 2008, at A2.

f. Aaron Lucchetti & Kate Kelly, *Goldman, Morgan Rewrite Playbooks*, WALL ST. J., Oct. 2, 2008, at C1.

g. Pub. L. No. 110-343, 122 Stat. 3765 (2008).

h. Amendment to the Senate Amendment to H.R. 3997 (Emergency Economic Stabilization Act of 2008), *available at* http://financialservices.house.gov/essa/ayo08c04_xml.pdf.

i. Press Release, U.S. Dep't of the Treasury, Testimony by Secretary Henry M. Paulson, Jr. before the Senate Banking Committee on Turmoil in U.S. Credit Markets (Sept. 23, 2008), *available at* http://www.treas.gov/press/releases/hp1153.htm.

j. *Bush Outlines $250B Bank Share Buy-Up: U.S. Will Invest Funds Allocated by $700 Billion Bailout Package in Big Banks*, CBS NEWS, Oct. 14, 2008, *available at* http://www.cbsnews.com/stories/2008/10/13/national/main4516862.shtml; Damian Paletta, Jon Hilsenrath & Deborah Solomon, *At Moment of Truth, U.S. Forced Big Bankers to Blink*, WALL ST. J., Oct. 15, 2008, at A1.

k. *Quarterly Report to Congress*, OFFICE OF THE SPECIAL INSPECTOR GENERAL FOR THE TROUBLED ASSET RELIEF PROGRAM, Jan. 26, 2012, *available at* http://www.sigtarp.gov/reports/congress/2012/January_26_2012_Report_to_Congress.pdf.

l. Susan Sward, *Many Pitfalls in CEO Compensation*, S.F. CHRON., Sept. 27, 2008, at C1, C2.

m. Helene Cooper, *Obama Orders Treasury Chief to Try to Block A.I.G. Bonuses*, N.Y. TIMES, Mar. 16, 2009.

n. Sheryl Gay Stolberg & Stephen Labaton, *Obama Calls Wall Street Bonuses "Shameful,"* N.Y. TIMES, Jan. 29, 2009.

o. Pub. L. No. 111-203, 124 Stat 1376 (2010).

p. David Bogoslaw, *Short Sellers: Unfairly Targeted in the Market Crisis?*, BUS. WK., Oct. 14, 2008, *available at* http://www.msnbc.msn.com/id/27162814/.

q. *Obama's Remarks at Signing of Dodd–Frank Wall Street Reform and Consumer Protection Act*, COUNCIL ON FOREIGN RELATIONS, July 21, 2010, *available at* http://www.cfr.org/united-states/obamas-remarks-signing-dodd-frank-wall-street-reform-consumer-protection-act/p22682.

r. Timothy Geithner, *A Dodd–Frank Retreat Deserves a Veto*, WALL ST. J., July 20, 2011.

s. *Republican Debate Transcript, Tampa, Florida, January 2012*, COUNCIL ON FOREIGN RELATIONS, Jan. 23, 2012, *available at* http://www.cfr.org/us-election-2012/republican-debate-transcript-tampa-florida-january-2012/p27180.

t. Pub. L. No. 112-106, 126 Stat. 306 (2012).

The 1934 Act

The 1934 Act sought to build on the 1933 Act by implementing a policy of continuous disclosure. Companies of a certain size and with a certain number of shareholders or whose stock is traded on a national securities exchange are required to file periodic reports with the SEC. The 1934 Act also contains stringent antifraud provisions and implements filing requirements for insiders dealing in their own company's stock. In addition, the 1934 Act established a framework for the self-regulation of the securities industry under the ultimate supervision of the SEC.

Exhibit 21.1 briefly describes the main sections of the 1933 and 1934 Acts. More detailed excerpts from both acts and the SEC regulations adopted thereunder can be found in Appendices G and H of this book.

Private Securities Litigation Reform Act of 1995

As discussed in more detail in Chapter 22, the Private Securities Litigation Reform Act of 1995 (the Litigation Reform Act)[4] amended the 1933 and 1934 Acts to add a variety of procedural provisions designed to correct perceived abuses in private securities litigation that increased

---

4. Pub.L. No. 104-67, 109 Stat. 737 (1995) (codified in scattered sections of 15 U.S.C.).

EXHIBIT 21.1	Selected Sections of the 1933 and 1934 Acts

1933 Act

- *Section 2*—defines terms, including security, offer, sale, and underwriter.

- *Sections 3 and 4*—list exempt securities and describe exempt transactions.

- *Section 5*—requires the registration of all securities offered and sold in the United States (unless an exemption from registration is available) and the delivery of a prospectus.

- *Sections 6–8 and 10*—outline the general procedures of the registration process and detail the guidelines for the registration statement and the accompanying prospectus.

- *Sections 11 and 12*—describe the penalties, elements of liability, damages, and parties held liable for violation of the 1933 Act.

1934 Act

- *Section 10*—prohibits the use of manipulative and deceptive devices in connection with the purchase or sale of registered or unregistered securities.

- *Section 12*—lists the reporting requirements for registered public companies.

- *Section 16*—provides the reporting requirements for insiders (including directors, officers, and principal shareholders) and limits certain insider transactions.

the cost of raising capital and chilled corporate disclosure to investors.

Securities Litigation Uniform Standards Act of 1998

The Securities Litigation Uniform Standards Act of 1998[5] requires the removal of securities fraud cases from state to federal court in many circumstances. Only state securities cases that are not class actions and do not involve more than fifty plaintiffs can be tried in state court. Congress's goal was to create national standards for fraud cases brought against companies traded on the national securities exchanges (such as the New York Stock Exchange and the Nasdaq Global Market). The so-called *Delaware carve-out* permits shareholders to bring a state-law class-action suit against a corporation and its directors for breach of preexisting common law fiduciary disclosure obligations.

Sarbanes–Oxley Act of 2002

In the wake of Enron's collapse, Congress hastily, and by an impressive margin (99–0 in the Senate and 423–3 in the House), passed the most sweeping securities legislation since the 1934 Act. The Sarbanes–Oxley Act of 2002[6] (SOX) contains eleven titles, which attempt to eradicate specific problems that Congress believed caused numerous corporate debacles around the turn of the millennium.

SOX created the Public Company Accounting Oversight Board (PCAOB) to regulate and inspect the public accounting firms that provide audit reports for publicly traded companies that are (1) registered under section 12 of the 1934 Act, (2) required to file reports under section 15(d) of that act, or (3) have filed a registration statement under the 1933 Act. The PCAOB also has the authority to set auditing standards for public company audits and to adjudicate issues related thereto.

In an attempt to mitigate the conflicts of interest present when accounting firms provide auditing services to corporate clients for whom they also do consulting, tax planning, or other accounting work, SOX prohibits the provision of nonaudit services to audit clients in all but very limited circumstances (see Appendix K). It also makes it illegal for any person to attempt to improperly influence the auditors.

In the most sweeping federal regulation of corporate governance to date, SOX and the regulations adopted by the SEC thereunder:

- Mandated the composition and authority of audit committees at public companies.

- Required corporations to disclose whether they have a financial expert on their audit committee.

- Prohibited personal loans to executives and members of the board of directors.

- Gave the SEC the authority to order CEOs and CFOs to forfeit certain bonuses and profits if their employer is required to restate its financial statements due to material noncompliance with securities laws.

- Generally prohibited insiders from trading during pension fund blackout periods.

- Required corporations to disclose whether they have a code of ethics applicable to senior financial officers and, if not, to disclose why not.

- Empowers the SEC to indefinitely restrict "unfit" persons from serving as officers or directors of a public company.

- Required management to maintain internal controls to facilitate accurate financial reporting and disclosure and to have the adequacy of those controls certified by the auditors. The Dodd–Frank Act exempted public companies with a market capitalization of less than $75 million from SOX's internal controls audit requirement.

Sarbanes–Oxley also:

- Mandated enhanced financial disclosures in periodic reports.

- Provided for enhanced SEC review of periodic reports.

- Mandated additional disclosures of transactions involving directors, officers, and principal stockholders.

- Required more rapid disclosure of material changes in a reporting company's financial conditions or operations on Form 8-K.

- Required CEOs and CFOs to certify the accuracy and completeness of SEC periodic reports, including the financial statements contained therein.

In an effort to reduce securities analysts' conflicts of interest, SOX created new, severe criminal penalties for those who defraud shareholders of publicly held corporations. It extended the statute of limitations on certain actions brought by defrauded investors, and it provided that debts incurred from judgments or settlements relating to securities fraud are nondischargeable in bankruptcy. SOX also required that auditors retain records relevant to financial audits for seven years after the completion of the audit.

SOX increased maximum fines for securities and mail and wire fraud by tens of millions of dollars and increased the maximum duration of imprisonment by as much as tenfold. SOX created stiff criminal penalties (as much as twenty years' imprisonment and a $5 million fine) for officers who certify noncompliant financial reports, with similarly severe penalties for tampering with records relevant

---

5. 15 U.S.C. § 77p(d).
6. Pub. L. No. 107-204, 116 Stat. 745 (codified in scattered sections of 15, 18, 28 & 29 U.S.C.).

to an official proceeding or otherwise impeding such a proceeding. The Act strongly urged CEOs to sign federal income tax returns.

As noted in Chapter 12, two sections of SOX protect whistleblowers and informants. Discriminating against or discharging an informant was made a criminal offense punishable by a substantial fine or imprisonment for as long as ten years, or both.

Dodd–Frank Wall Street Reform Act and Consumer Protection Act of 2010

As discussed in the "Inside Story" in Chapter 6 and in the "Historical Perspective" in this chapter, the Dodd–Frank Wall Street Reform and Consumer Protection Act overhauled regulation of the U.S. financial sector. This included greater regulation of hedge funds, which are private investment partnerships that historically accept only high-wealth investors and use a wide range of high-risk investment strategies, including leverage and the trading of equity default swaps, puts, calls, and other financial derivatives, to boost their return.

SEC RULES AND REGULATIONS

Since Congress enacted the 1934 Act, the SEC has used its power as an administrative agency to adopt a number of rules and regulations. The SEC uses these rules and regulations to address some of the ambiguity of the securities acts, make case-specific exemptions, carry out informal discretionary actions, and conduct investigations regarding compliance with the securities acts.

For instance, in 1972, the SEC adopted Rule 144 to clarify when investors can sell stock not acquired in a registered offering (*restricted stock*) without being deemed an "underwriter." In 1982, the SEC adopted Regulation D with rules that outlined the requirements and limitations for exempt private offerings and offerings by small businesses. Subsequently, it adopted Rule 701 to exempt offers and sales of securities pursuant to employee benefit plans. Regulation A was revised to make it easier for small businesses to raise capital without going through a registered offering. As discussed in Chapter 19, the SEC adopted Rule 14a–11 to give major shareholders the right to have their nominees for directors included in management's proxy statement, but the U.S. Court of Appeals for the District of Columbia invalidated the rule.[7]

STATE BLUE SKY LAWS

In addition to the federal securities laws, state statutes called *blue sky laws* also regulate offerings and sales of securities. These laws were the precursors to federal securities

---

INTERNATIONAL SNAPSHOT

On most U.S. stock exchanges, foreign securities are traded in the form of American Depository Receipts (ADRs). The securities themselves are held by a financial institution called a depository, which issues the ADRs traded by foreign investors and handles any foreign-exchange transactions. This structure allows the foreign securities to trade at a per-share price level customary in the U.S. market. In addition, it allows investors to trade interests in foreign securities in compliance with U.S. clearance and settlement requirements.

regulation and were "aimed at promoters who 'would sell building lots in the blue sky in fee simple.'"[8] An issuer selling securities must comply not only with the federal securities laws but also with the securities laws of all of the states in which the securities are offered or sold. This usually includes the state where the issuer is headquartered, the state from which any offering materials are dispatched or where any oral offers are made, the state where the offerees have their domicile, and the state to which offering materials are sent.[9]

Fortunately, many states, the District of Columbia, and Puerto Rico have adopted the Uniform Securities Act, so there is some consistency among state laws. Other states, including New York and California, have retained their own versions of securities regulatory schemes. In some respects, the state laws are stricter than their federal counterparts. For example, New York's Martin Act[10] prohibits a broader range of fraud than the 1934 Act.

Like the federal statutes, the Uniform Securities Act emphasizes disclosure as the primary means of protecting investors. Some states, however, authorize the securities administrator to deny a securities selling permit unless he or she finds that the issuer's plan of business and the proposed issuance of securities are fair, just, and equitable. Even if the state statute does not specifically include this provision, a state securities commissioner can usually deny registration or qualification to sell in that state until he or she is satisfied that the offering is fair. This process is referred to as *merit review*.

Congress passed the Capital Markets Efficiency Act of 1996[11] in part to provide more uniformity between federal and state securities regulation. The Act precludes states from requiring pre-offer and pre-sale notice filings and from imposing merit review requirements in connection with offerings pursuant to Rule 506 under Regulation D. States may require only the type of filing required by the

---

7. Bus. Roundtable v. SEC, 647 F.3d 1144 (D.C. Cir. 2011) (Case 19.5).

8. SEC v. Edwards, 540 U.S. 389 (2004) (Case 21.1).

9. For a summary of the private-offering exemptions in certain states, see CONSTANCE E. BAGLEY & CRAIG E. DAUCHY, THE ENTREPRENEUR'S GUIDE TO BUSINESS LAW 186–93 (4th ed. 2011).

10. N.Y. GEN. BUS. LAW §§ 352–53.

11. Pub. L. No. 104-290, 110 Stat. 3416 (1996).

SEC (including any amendments), a consent to service of process, and a filing fee. The law similarly preempted state registration requirements and merit review in connection with most initial public offerings registered with the SEC. It also provided federal preemption for the issuance of securities to "qualified purchasers." The SEC has proposed that the definition of "qualified purchasers" be the same as the one for "accredited investors" under Regulation D.

DEFINITION OF TERMS

It is necessary to define three basic terms used in the 1933 Act—security, offer, and sale. Their meanings in a securities law context may be different from their everyday meanings.

Security

The term *security* for purposes of the 1933 Act—and most other securities statutes—is much broader than the common conception of the term. Section 2(1) of the 1933 Act defines a security as:

> any note, stock, treasury stock, bond, debenture, evidence of indebtedness, certificate of interest or participation in any profit-sharing agreement, collateral-trust certificate, pre-organization certificate or subscription, transferable share, investment contract, voting-trust certificate, certificate of deposit for a security, fractional undivided interest in oil, gas, or other mineral rights, any put, call, straddle, option, or privilege on any security, certificate of deposit, or group or index of securities (including any interest therein or based on the value thereof), or any put, call, straddle, option, or privilege entered into on a national securities exchange relating to foreign currency, or, in general, any interest or instrument commonly known as a "security," or any certificate of interest or participation in, temporary or interim certificate for, receipt for, guarantee of, or warrant or right to subscribe to or purchase, any of the foregoing.

Because "security" is defined so broadly, the circumstances of a particular transaction must be analyzed to determine whether it does, in fact, involve a security and is subject to regulation. Certain investments that are commonly agreed to be securities include the stock and bonds of public and private companies. In *Landreth Timber Co. v. Landreth*,[12] the U.S. Supreme Court held that the sale of a business through a sale of 100% of its stock is a securities transaction if the stock sold possesses all of the characteristics traditionally associated with common stock. This is the case even though the success of the venture going forward depends on the efforts of the buyer, not the seller.

Yet some investments, which by their name fall into the definition of securities, are not necessarily considered securities. An example is the stock in a cooperative association owning an apartment building; an occupant of the building owns shares of stock that are inextricably linked to the lease of a particular unit of the building. In *United Housing Foundation v. Forman*,[13] the U.S. Supreme Court held that because the dwelling was used as a place of habitation, the inducement to purchase was solely to acquire living space and not to invest for profit. Consequently, the Court ruled that the shares of stock were not securities under the 1933 Act.

Investment Contract

An investment may be characterized as a security even if it involves the transfer of an interest in real property or another physical asset. Any transaction that involves an investment of money in a common enterprise with profits to come solely from the efforts of others is deemed to be an *investment contract* and thus a security. This test was first enunciated in *SEC v. W.J. Howey Co.*[14] The U.S. Supreme Court held that the offer and sale of parcels of land bearing citrus trees, coupled with optional management contracts pursuant to which the promoter cared for the trees, constituted an investment contract and hence a security under section 2(1) of the 1933 Act. The following case further elaborated on this test.

---

12. 471 U.S. 681 (1985).
13. 421 U.S. 837 (1975).
14. 328 U.S. 293 (1946).

A CASE IN POINT	*In the Language of the Court*	Case 21.1

SEC v. Edwards

Supreme Court of the United States
540 U.S. 389 (2004).

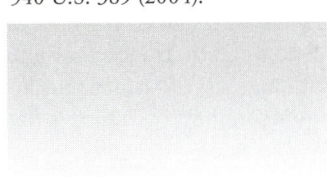

FACTS Charles Edwards was the chair, CEO, and sole shareholder of ETS Payphones, Inc. Acting partly through a subsidiary also controlled by Edwards, ETS sold payphones to the public. The payphones were offered in a variety of packages, but virtually all purchasers chose a package that included a site lease, a five-year leaseback and management agreement, and a buyback agreement, at a total cost of around $7,000. ETS guaranteed $82 per month (a 14% annual return) to purchasers under the leaseback and management agreement. ETS also promised to refund the full purchase price of the package at the end of the lease or within 180 days of the purchaser's request.

CONTINUED

ETS boasted in its brochure that "[v]ery few business opportunities can offer the potential for ongoing revenue generation that is available in today's pay telephone industry." Unfortunately, the payphones did not generate enough revenue for ETS to make its payments to purchasers under the leaseback agreements. ETS was forced to rely on funds from new investors to meet its obligations, and in 2000, the company filed for bankruptcy.

The SEC brought an action alleging that Edwards and ETS had sold securities in violation of various provisions of the 1933 and 1934 Acts. Edwards argued that schemes offering a fixed rate of return are not investment contracts because (1) they do not give the purchasers capital appreciation or the earnings of the enterprise and (2) the return is not "derived solely from the efforts of others," because the purchasers have a contractual entitlement to the return.

ISSUE PRESENTED   For purposes of the federal securities laws, does a moneymaking scheme fall outside the definition of an investment contract simply because the promised rate of return is fixed rather than variable?

OPINION   O'CONNOR, J., writing on behalf of a unanimous U.S. Supreme Court:

"Congress' purpose in enacting the securities laws was to regulate investments, in whatever form they are made and by whatever name they are called." To that end, it enacted a broad definition of "security," sufficient "to encompass virtually any instrument that might be sold as an investment."

. . . .

The test for whether a particular scheme is an investment contract was established in our decision in *SEC v. W.J. Howey Co.* We look to "whether the scheme involves an investment of money in a common enterprise with profits to come solely from the efforts of others." This definition "embodies a flexible rather than a static principle, one that is capable of adaptation to meet the countless and variable schemes devised by those who seek the use of the money of others on the promise of profits."

In reaching that result, we first observed that when Congress included "investment contract" in the definition of security, it "was using a term the meaning of which had been crystallized" by state courts' interpretation of their "blue sky" laws. . . . Thus, when we held that "profits" must "come solely from the efforts of others," we were speaking of the profits that investors seek on their investment, not the profits of the scheme in which they invest. We used "profits" in the sense of income or return, to include, for example, dividends, other periodic payments, or the increased value of the investment.

There is no reason to distinguish between promises of fixed returns and promises of variable returns for purposes of the test, so understood. In both cases, the investing public is attracted by representations of investment income, as purchasers were in this case by ETS' invitation to "watch the profits add up." Moreover, investments pitched as low-risk (such as those offering a "guaranteed" fixed return) are particularly attractive to individuals more vulnerable to investment fraud, including older and less sophisticated investors. Under the reading respondent advances, unscrupulous investments could evade the securities laws by picking a rate of return to promise. We will not read into the securities laws a limitation not compelled by the language that would so undermine the laws' purposes.

. . . .

The Eleventh Circuit's perfunctory alternative holding, that respondent's scheme falls outside the definition because purchasers had a contractual entitlement to a return, is incorrect and inconsistent with our precedent. We are considering investment contracts. The fact that investors have bargained for a return on their investment does not mean that the return is not also expected to come solely from the efforts of others.

CONTINUED

RESULT   Edwards and ETS had offered and sold securities.

CRITICAL THINKING QUESTIONS

1. Why was the Supreme Court unwilling to exclude contracts guaranteeing a fixed rate of return from the definition of security?

2. Are mortgage notes, sold with a package of management services and a promise to repurchase the notes in the event of default, securities?

There is a split in the circuits as to whether the "common enterprise" element of the *Howey* test can be met simply by showing "vertical commonality" between the promoter and the investor or whether there must be "horizontal commonality," that is, multiple investors who pool their funds and receive a pro rata share of the profits or buy very similar assets that are managed jointly.[15] The majority of circuits use horizontal commonality to identify a common enterprise. A number of states, for purposes of their blue sky laws, define the term "investment contract" more broadly than the federal definition[16] and do not require commonality or sole reliance on the efforts of others.

Federal courts have also relaxed the sole reliance requirement. Although the *Howey* test required that the investor rely solely on the efforts of others for the expectation of profits, subsequent federal decisions have established that, under certain circumstances, there can be an investment contract, and thus a security, even if the investor participates in the generation of profits.[17] For example, an interest in a general partnership is generally held not to be a security because each partner by law has the right to exercise control in the operation of the partnership. But the courts have found a general partnership interest to be a security if it meets any of the following three tests:

1. The partnership agreement leaves so little power to the partners that the arrangement is tantamount to a limited partnership.

2. The investor is so inexperienced in business affairs that he or she is incapable of intelligently exercising his or her partnership powers.

3. The investor is so dependent on the unique management ability of the promoter or manager that he or she cannot replace the manager or exercise meaningful partnership powers.[18]

A limited partnership interest is almost always held to constitute a security because the limited partners, to protect their limited liability, are prohibited by law from taking part in the control of the partnership business. An interest in real estate is not in itself considered a security, though it may be a security if it is combined with a management contract, as in *Howey*.

The SEC and at least thirty-five state securities regulators have taken the position that interests in a limited liability company (LLC) are securities. Regulators base their conclusion on either of two theories: LLC interests constitute an investment contract under *Howey*, or they have all the characteristics of stock. Nonetheless, the U.S. Court of Appeals for the Fourth Circuit ruled that an equity interest in an LLC was not a security.[19] The court reasoned that the interest held by Robinson, a member of the LLC, was not an investment contract because he held 33,333 of the company's 133,333 shares, was treasurer of the company, took a seat on the board of managers, had the right to appoint two of the seven members of the board of managers, and was a member of the company's executive committee. As a result, Robinson was able to exercise control over his investment. The Fourth Circuit also rejected Robinson's argument that the membership certificates had all the characteristics of stock. The LLC members did not have a right to receive dividends based on their equity percentage as common shareholders typically do. Instead, Robinson received 100% of the LLC's net profits up to a certain amount, after which the funds were distributed pro rata to all equity holders. Common stock is typically negotiable, but Robinson's interest was not. Apparently, there was also some dispute as to whether Robinson's interest retained any voting rights if transferred. Because it was not an investment contract and did not have all the characteristics of stock, Robinson's LLC interest did not qualify as a security. As of 2011, the U.S. Supreme Court had not ruled on this issue.

Family Resemblance Test

Promissory notes and other evidences of indebtedness may or may not constitute a security, depending on the factual context. In *Reves v. Ernst & Young*,[20] the U.S. Supreme

---

15. *See, e.g.*, SEC v. ETS Payphones, Inc., 408 F.3d 727 (11th Cir. 2009) (holding vertical commonality is the test for determining whether investors operated under a common enterprise); *In re* J.P. Jeanneret Assocs., Inc., 769 F. Supp. 2d 340 (S.D.N.Y. 2011) (holding horizontal commonality is the test for determining a common enterprise).

16. *See, e.g.*, King v. Pope, 91 S.W.3d 314, 321 (Tenn. 2002).

17. SEC v. Glenn W. Turner Enters., Inc., 474 F.2d 476 (9th Cir. 1973).

18. The test to determine whether a general partnership constitutes a security was set forth in *Williamson v. Tucker*, 645 F.2d 404 (5th Cir. 1981), and later applied in *Holden v. Hagopian*, 978 F.2d 1115 (9th Cir. 1992).

19. Robinson v. Glynn, 349 F.3d 166 (4th Cir. 2003).

20. 494 U.S. 56 (1990).

Court set forth the *family resemblance test* for determining which types of notes are securities. Under this test, a promissory note is initially presumed to be a security based on the literal language of the securities acts ("The term 'security' means any note . . ."). This presumption may be rebutted, however, by a showing that the note bears a "strong resemblance" (in terms of four specific factors) to an enumerated category of instruments commonly held not to constitute securities, such as notes delivered in connection with consumer financing, notes secured by a home mortgage, and short-term notes secured by accounts receivable. The four specific factors used in evaluating an instrument are:

1. The motivations that would prompt a reasonable seller and buyer to enter into the transaction.

2. The plan of distribution of the instrument.

3. The reasonable expectations of the investing public.

4. Whether some factor, such as the existence of another regulatory scheme, significantly reduces the risk of the instrument, thereby rendering application of the federal securities laws unnecessary.

The "In Brief" on page 711 provides a decision tree for determining whether an instrument is a security and for analyzing the securities registration requirements.

Offer

Section 2(3) of the 1933 Act defines an *offer* as "every attempt or offer to dispose of, or solicitation of an offer to buy, a security or interest in a security, for value." This definition is much broader than that in contract law. An offer that is unacceptably vague for contract law purposes may still constitute an offer for federal securities law purposes. Section 2(3) expressly provides, however, that preliminary negotiations or agreements between an issuer and an underwriter or among underwriters do not constitute an offer to sell.

Sale

A *sale* is defined by section 2(3) to include "every contract of sale or disposition of a security or interest in a security, for value." The crucial term in this definition is *value.* The courts have defined "value" very broadly—more broadly, for example, than in state corporation statutes, which require that stock can be issued only for "value" in the form of cash, property, or compensation for past services.

⟨⟩ REGISTRATION OF SECURITIES OFFERINGS

Once it is determined that an investment offering does, in fact, involve a security, the issue of registration must be addressed. Section 5 of the 1933 Act requires the registration

of all offers and sales of securities in the United States, unless an exemption from registration is available. Section 5 can be summarized as follows.

1. Section 5(a) prohibits the sale of a nonexempt security before a registration statement has been filed with the SEC except pursuant to an applicable exemption. The *registration statement* consists of filing forms, the *prospectus*—the disclosure document that an issuer of securities provides to prospective purchasers—and certain exhibits. Except in the case of certain seasoned public companies (as defined below), section 5(c) prohibits any offer to sell or buy a nonexempt security before the registration statement is filed.

2. During the waiting period between the filing of the registration statement and the date the registration statement becomes effective with the SEC, written and oral offers to sell the security may be made, but all written offers (except those made by certain large publicly traded companies, as discussed below) must either be made pursuant to a prospectus meeting the requirements of section 10 (a *statutory prospectus*) or be accompanied or preceded by a statutory prospectus.

3. Once the registration statement becomes effective with the SEC (referred to as *going effective*), sales of securities may be consummated, but (again, except in the case of certain large issuers) any written offer or sale of a security made within forty days after the registration statement is declared effective must be preceded or accompanied by a statutory prospectus.

In general, every public offering of nonexempt securities must be registered with the SEC. The registration requirement is designed to ensure that certain information is filed with the SEC and distributed to potential investors by means of a prospectus. Unlike certain state securities authorities, the SEC does not have the statutory authority to approve or disapprove an offering on its merits. Instead, the registration process is designed to ensure that the information provided to investors is accurate and complete. The general procedures to be followed in the registration process are found in sections 6 and 8 of the 1933 Act.

An initial public offering (IPO) is an expensive and time-consuming effort that typically takes at least twelve to sixteen weeks from start to finish.[21] Securities lawyers, independent accountants, investment bankers, and a printer all become involved in the process.

A principal advantage of registering a securities offering with the SEC is that the registered securities are nonrestricted and may be traded relatively freely in a *secondary offering*, that is, a subsequent offering by a person other than the issuer. Like primary offerings by the issuer, secondary offerings must either be registered with the SEC or be exempt from registration. As discussed further below, section 4(1) is the most frequently used exemption for

---

21. The process of doing an initial public offering is discussed in detail in Bagley & Dauchy, *supra* note 9, at 717–44.

secondary offerings. It permits nonaffiliates to sell non-restricted securities without registration, regardless of the size of the offering or the number of offerees. (*Affiliates* include officers, directors, and controlling shareholders. The SEC has a rebuttable presumption that any shareholder owning 10% or more of the issuer's stock is an affiliate.)

The Role of the Underwriters

A public offering of securities is typically, though not necessarily, underwritten by one or more investment banking firms.

Firm Commitment Underwriting

In a *firm commitment underwriting*, the underwriters agree to purchase the entire offering, thus effectively shifting the risk of the offering from the issuer to the underwriters. The managing investment banks in an IPO are referred to as the *book-running managers*. The other underwriters are typically known as *co-managers*. The book-running managers negotiate the terms of the offering (most importantly, the offering price and number of shares offered) and the underwriter discount with the issuer and put together an underwriting group (the *syndicate*). In an IPO, the underwriters typically buy stock from the issuer at a discount from the public offering price (usually 6% to 7% of the public offering price) and then sell the stock to the public at the full price. Each member of the underwriting group agrees to purchase a certain number of securities once the offering is declared effective by the SEC.

In theory, such a commitment places the underwriters in a risky position. In practice, the book-running managers will not go forward with the offering unless they have tentative offers from buyers for as many as two to five times the number of shares being offered. Accordingly, the underwriting agreement between the issuer and the book-running managers (as the representative of the underwriting group) and the agreements among the members of the underwriting group are typically not signed until immediately before the offering is declared effective by the SEC. The price at which the securities will be offered and the underwriters' commission are usually not formally determined until the evening before the offering goes effective.

Once the offering becomes effective, the underwriters attempt to sell the securities that they are obligated to purchase. Most firm underwriting agreements are of short duration. Usually, the sale closes within two business days after the agreement is signed. As of the closing date, the underwriters are obligated to purchase any securities that remain unsold.

Because a firm commitment underwriting will provide the issuer with a predetermined amount of money within a specified period, it is attractive to issuers. A firm commitment underwriting is also attractive to investors because it implies that the underwriters themselves are willing to take a risk on the offering. Because it places the members of the underwriting group at risk for the amount of the offering, broker–dealers and investment bankers will usually agree to a firm underwriting only if they are certain that they will be able to sell the offered securities quickly. Such certainty will depend on a variety of factors, including the amount of money being sought, the performance and prospects of the company, whether the company is seasoned or relatively new, and the condition of the public securities market.

Best-Efforts Underwriting

In a *best-efforts underwriting*, the underwriters do not agree to purchase the securities being offered. Instead, they agree to use their best efforts to find buyers at an agreed-on price. Best-efforts underwritings are often used for IPOs or for companies that are unseasoned.

A best-efforts offering leaves the risks of the offering entirely with the issuer. Nevertheless, some established, successful companies may prefer a best-efforts offering because the cost of distribution is lower than for a firm commitment underwriting.

The Registration Statement

Sections 7 and 10 of the 1933 Act, and the rules promulgated by the SEC under the Act, contain detailed guidelines as to what must be included in the registration statement and the accompanying prospectus. Regulations C and S–K, adopted by the SEC pursuant to the 1933 Act, list the general information required in connection with most public registrations.[22] In addition, the SEC has issued a variety of forms that list the information required in connection with particular types of transactions.

Companies planning to list their securities on a national exchange, such as the Nasdaq Global Market or the New York Stock Exchange, must satisfy that exchange's listing requirements and register the company under the 1934 Act. Registration under the 1934 Act subjects the company and its officers and directors to additional securities law requirements (discussed later in this chapter) and typically takes effect simultaneously with the effectiveness of the registration statement filed under the 1933 Act.

Forms

Securities offered in an IPO are registered in a registration statement meeting the requirements of *Form S–1*. The registration statement must include a complete description of the securities being offered, the business of the issuer, the risk factors, the management, and the major shareholders. It must also include audited financial statements.

Form S–3 is a "short form" used by a category of companies that have timely filed periodic reports under the 1934 Act for at least twelve months and have a widespread

---

22. 17 C.F.R. pt. 230.400 *et seq.*; 17 C.F.R. pt. 229.

following in the marketplace. An issuer can use Form S–3 for an offering of common stock only if the aggregate market value of the voting and nonvoting stock held by nonaffiliates is $75 million or more.

For companies filing on Form S–3, information about the registrant that has been reported in annual and quarterly reports filed under the 1934 Act need not be provided to investors in the prospectus, unless there has been a material change in the registrant's affairs or financial statements. Such reports are incorporated by reference and are deemed a part of the prospectus for liability purposes.

Prospectus

The tone of a prospectus frequently strikes nonlawyers as dry, bleak, and confusing. Such a perception arises out of the conflicting purposes of the prospectus. On the one hand, it is a selling document, designed to present the best possible view of the investment and the issuing company. On the other hand, it is a disclosure document, an insurance policy against claims of securities fraud. This second function usually predominates. The prospectus usually contains only provable statements of fact, with numerous disclaimers regarding the future success of the issuer. Businesspeople, accustomed to presenting their company in the best possible light, frequently have difficulty adjusting to the somber tone of the prospectus.

Companies are required to use plain English in the design and language of the cover page, summary, and risk factors sections of the prospectus.[23] In these sections, companies must (1) use short sentences with everyday words, (2) avoid legal jargon and highly technical business terms, (3) use the active voice, (4) not use multiple negatives, and (5) use bulleted lists for complex information, if possible. Companies are encouraged, but not required, to use plain English throughout the prospectus.

Due Diligence

A key step in preparing the registration statement is the process of *due diligence*, whereby the company, the underwriters, and their respective counsel assemble and review the information about the company in the registration statement. The company must be prepared to back up every claim it makes in the prospectus. Even if the claim is stated as an opinion (such as "The company believes that it is the industry leader"), the company must be able to demonstrate the reasonableness of its belief. Underwriters cannot simply rely on the representations of the issuer or the issuer's officers but must perform their own independent due diligence investigation. They should go beyond the corporate documents provided by the issuer and examine information in press releases and news

reports concerning key competitors and others important to the issuer's business.[24] Underwriters should also monitor relevant websites and public agency filings.

Registration Procedure

The registration statement must be filed with the SEC. Section 8 of the 1933 Act provides that the registration statement automatically becomes effective on the twentieth day after filing, unless the SEC fixes an earlier date. Virtually all registrants file their registration statement with language stating that it will not become effective until declared effective by the SEC; this ensures that the SEC staff will have the necessary time (which usually exceeds the statutory twenty-day period) to review the filing. Each amendment to the registration statement filed prior to the effective date starts the twenty-day period running again. If the SEC has consented to the amendment, the waiting period may be accelerated. If, however, the SEC finds that the registration statement is materially defective in some respect, it may, after notice and a hearing, issue a stop order suspending the effectiveness of the offering.

Review

Registration statements received by the SEC are subject to review by the SEC staff, which typically takes about thirty days from the date of filing. The extent of the review is usually affected by the nature of the offering and the number of filings that the SEC must review. In general, all first-time registrants will receive a complete review. Most repeat registrants will receive a more limited review, and some will receive no review.

Comments of the SEC staff are conveyed through a letter of comment, which is generally mailed to the issuer's counsel. Members of the SEC staff are usually available to discuss these letters of comment either by telephone or in person. Although the comment letters contain only suggestions without force of law, they generally result in the filing of an amendment to the registration statement. Acceding to the staff's reasonable suggestions is less expensive and less time-consuming than fighting an issue in an administrative hearing and in court. The amended registration statement is usually filed with a letter from counsel answering, item by item, the issues raised by the staff.

SEC review includes staff analysis of the text of the prospectus, the financial statements, and the exhibits to the registration statement. For example, in 2000, the SEC staff required several companies seeking to go public to reduce their revenues by the value of warrants or cheap stock issued to customers that had placed large orders for the start-up's products. Dubbed a "unique marriage of

---

23. On January 24, 2000, as part of Regulation M–A, the SEC extended the plain English requirements to the summary sheet for tender offers, mergers, and going-private transactions.

24. *See* Robert Alan Spanner, *Limiting Exposure in the Offering Process*, REV. SEC. & COMMODITIES REG. 64–66 (Apr. 8, 1987), for a long but useful list of tasks that should be undertaken by officers, directors, underwriters, and counsel engaged in the public offering of securities.

convenience" by the *Wall Street Journal*,[25] the practice was particularly prevalent in the highly competitive telecommunications industry, where new companies sought an edge when battling industry giants such as Cisco Systems. In turn, the network operators had an incentive to buy the products because their firms could make far more on their investments in the start-up after it went public than they spent on the equipment. The practice of issuing cheap stock or warrants in exchange for orders also raised the specter of a pyramid-type scheme. Purchasers were buying new equipment not because of their faith in the product but as a way to inflate the value of the start-up so that it could go public at an unrealistically high valuation. Public investors stood to get hurt when sales to nonaffiliated purchasers (i.e., purchasers that received neither the cheap stock nor warrants) failed to materialize.

Waiting Period

The time between the filing of the registration statement and its becoming effective is called the *waiting period* or the *quiet period* because the law severely limits what the issuer and underwriters may say or publish during this time. No sale of securities can occur prior to the effectiveness of the registration statement; however, the underwriters may assemble selling groups, distribute copies of the preliminary prospectus, and even solicit (but not accept) offers to buy the securities.

The preliminary prospectus—sometimes referred to as a *red-herring prospectus* because a notice on the cover states in red ink that it is not final and is subject to revision—is an incomplete version of the final prospectus. It sets forth the proposed range for the selling price and omits the names of the underwriters except for the lead underwriters, whose names appear on the cover page. The preliminary prospectus usually is not distributed until all changes needed to respond to SEC staff comments are incorporated.

Selling efforts during the waiting period must be done in strict compliance with the securities laws. They usually include distribution of the preliminary prospectus and *roadshows*, that is, oral presentations to large institutional investors in key cities in the United States, Europe, and Asia. The roadshow often includes an Internet component as well. The material presented in the roadshow must be consistent with, and cannot go beyond, the information contained in the preliminary prospectus. In the case of IPOs at least, no written materials other than the preliminary prospectus are typically distributed to the potential investors.

The SEC calls sales literature and other written communications that offer securities but do not meet the statutory requirements for a prospectus a *free writing prospectus*. All methods of communication, other than oral communications, are deemed written communications.[26] Thus,

any communication that is written, printed, broadcast, or embodied in any form of electronic media (such as audiotapes, videotapes, facsimiles, CD-ROMs, electronic mail, Internet websites, computer networks, and other forms of computer data compilation) is treated as a written communication. A live telephone call is not deemed a written communication even if it is carried over the Internet, but "blast" voice-mail messages are.

In an IPO, the issuer cannot use written sales literature or other free writing prospectuses unless they are accompanied or preceded by the preliminary prospectus filed with the SEC. A prospectus is deemed to accompany an electronic free writing prospectus if the free writing prospectus contains a hyperlink to the statutory prospectus. Live roadshows are deemed oral communications, but an electronic roadshow is considered a free writing prospectus. As such, it must be filed with the SEC and made available electronically to unrestricted audiences. The SEC reasoned that this treatment of electronic roadshows strikes "the appropriate balance between the need to market an issuer's securities to institutional investors and the desires of retail and other investors to have access to issuer information, such as management presentations, that are normally available only at roadshows that often have not been open to retail investors generally."[27]

Issuers are required to file all free writing prospectuses with the SEC when they are first used. They are not deemed part of the registration statement, however, and therefore do not subject the issuer or underwriters to potential section 11 liability, unless the issuer elects to include them in the registration statement. Both oral communications and free writing prospectuses do, however, subject the issuer and underwriters to potential liability under section 12(a)(2). (Liability under sections 11 and 12(a)(2) is discussed later in this chapter.)

The issuing company and its underwriters must be careful about the information they release to the public during the waiting period. Conditioning the market with a news article or press release about the company and its upcoming offering is referred to as *gun-jumping*. Gun-jumping may violate the 1933 Act, and the SEC may require the issuer to postpone the offering. For example, the SEC required Web Van, the Internet grocer, to postpone its IPO after it released significant information not contained in its prospectus during a conference call as part of its roadshow.

The SEC has established a bright-line period ending thirty days prior to the filing of a registration statement, during which issuers may communicate (orally or in writing) without risk of violating the gun-jumping provisions as long as (1) the communication does not reference a securities offering, (2) the communication is made "by or on behalf of the issuer," and (3) the issuer takes reasonable steps within its control to prevent further distribution or publication of the information during the thirty-day period immediately before the issuer files the registration

25. Scott Thurm, *SEC Questions Start-Ups' Cheap Stock Sales to Customers*, WALL ST. J., Sept. 26, 2000, at C1.
26. Securities Offering Reform, 69 Fed. Reg. 67,392 (Nov. 17, 2004).
27. *Id.*

statement. The safe harbor is not available to offerings by a blank check company, a shell company, an issuer offering penny stock, a registered investment company, or a business development company. (A *blank check company* is a development-stage company that has no specific business plan or has a business plan to acquire a currently unknown business.) Offerings in connection with business combinations and exchange offers are also excluded.

Special Rules for Well-Known Seasoned Issuers and Emerging Growth Companies

So-called *well-known seasoned issuers*, defined generally as firms eligible to use Form S–3 that have at least a $700 million public common equity float, are permitted to make unrestricted oral and written offers before the registration statement is filed, without violating the gun-jumping provisions. As a result, well-known seasoned issuers may use a free writing prospectus at any time.

Eligible seasoned issuers and eligible well-known seasoned issuers are also not required to deliver a copy of the preliminary prospectus before using a free writing prospectus. Instead, they are required only to notify the recipient of the free writing prospectus, through a required legend, of where the recipient can access or hyperlink to the preliminary or base prospectus by using the URL provided for the prospectus.

The JOBS Act permits so-called *emerging growth companies,* defined generally as companies with gross annual revenue of less than $1 billion, to do an initial public offering without meeting all the onerous requirements otherwise applicable. Such companies may go public with only two years of audited financial statements; they can "test the waters" prior to or during a public offering by meeting with institutional accredited investors and qualified institutional buyers; and their investment banks may publish

research reports about such companies even if the banks are participating in the offering.

Going Effective and Delivery of the Final Prospectus

Once a registration statement has been informally cleared by the SEC staff or the registrant has received notice that the registration statement will not be reviewed, the company files a pre-effective amendment with the SEC. This is typically accompanied by a request that the waiting period be accelerated so that the registration statement will become effective at a particular date and time. Without the request for acceleration, the registration statement would not become effective until the expiration of an additional twenty-day period.

Offers to buy can be accepted only after the registration statement is declared effective by the SEC. Information concerning the price of the securities and underwriting arrangements is filed with the SEC as part of the final prospectus. Before consummating sales of registered securities, the issuer must give each purchaser a copy of the final prospectus. Supplemental sales literature, which in most cases need not be reviewed by the SEC, may be provided to prospective purchasers. Any sales literature distributed within forty days after the date of effectiveness must be preceded or accompanied by the final prospectus. Often the underwriters will run a *tombstone ad* to publicize their involvement in the offering.

USE OF SOCIAL MEDIA AND CROWDFUNDING

Issuers, underwriters, and investment advisers need to ensure that employees do not use social media in ways that violate the securities laws.[28] The SEC suggests that firms create compliance procedures specific to social media, including usage guidelines, content standards, and systems of monitoring.[29] To discourage misleading information from being posted on social media sites, the SEC recommends that firms that allow third parties to post on their social media sites implement safeguards to avoid violations of the securities laws. In particular, the SEC warns of the possibility that the "like" feature might be considered a testimonial or a statement of a client's experience with, or endorsement of, an investment adviser or broker–dealer.

On January 4, 2012, the SEC brought an action against investment adviser Anthony Fields for making fraudulent offers of more than $500 billion in securities using various social media sites and issued an alert regarding the use

---

ethical consideration

During the dot.com boom of the 1990s, shares of IPOs—*hot issues*—were in incredibly high demand and were often allocated by underwriters to corporate executives in hopes of securing more investment banking business from the executives' firms. Asked about this practice of *spinning*, Cristina Morgan, former managing director of investment banking at Hambrecht & Quist, remarked, "Is it appropriate? Well, yeah." She reasoned: "If you sell doughnuts, you do everything you can to enhance the image and service of your doughnut shop to customers. You're just doing your job. That's what we all are doing."[a] Morgan asserted that the amounts involved, often 500 to 1,000 shares, were so small compared to the net worth of her clients that the IPO allocations could not have influenced the corporate decisions made by the executives who received them. Is spinning legal? Ethical?

---

a. Morgan is quoted in Michael Siconolfi, *Hambrecht & Quist Goes on Offensive on "Spinning,"* WALL ST. J., Nov. 26, 1997, at C1, C20. *See also* Michael Siconolfi, *SEC, NASD Begin Probes of IPO "Spin" Accounts,* WALL ST. J., Nov. 13, 1997, at A3; New York v. McLeod, 45 A.D.3d 282 (N.Y. App. Div. Nov. 1, 2007).

---

28. *Regulatory Notice 10-06: Social Media Web Sites,* FIN. INDUS. REGULATORY AUTH. (Jan. 2010), *available at* http://www.finra.org/web/groups/industry/@ip/@reg/@notice/documents/notices/p120779.pdf.

29. Securities & Exchange Comm'n, Office of Compliance Inspections & Examinations, *Investment Adviser Use of Social Media,* 2 NAT'L EXAMINATION RISK ALERT 1 (Jan. 4, 2012), *available at* http://www.sec.gov/about/offices/ocie/riskalert-socialmedia.pdf.

of social media by investment advisers.[30] The SEC alert addressed failure to maintain required books and records, failure to implement adequate compliance policies, and publication of false and materially misleading information on social media websites.

The JOBS Act permits private issuers to use online platforms, such as Kickstarter and Profunder, to raise up to $1 million within any twelve-month period without having to register the securities under the 1933 Act. All such transactions must be effected through an SEC-approved broker or funding portal. Purchasers with annual income or net worth of less than $100,000 may not invest more than $2,000 or 5% of the investor's annual income or net worth; other purchasers may not invest more than 10% of their annual income or net worth in any given year.

SHELF REGISTRATION

Rule 415 under the 1933 Act provides for the *shelf registration* of securities, that is, the registration of a number of securities at one time for issuance later. The securities can then be issued over a period of time, for example, in connection with continuous acquisition programs or employee stock-benefit plans, or they can be issued at a later date, for example, when interest rates or market conditions are more favorable. Shelf registration can result in reduced legal, accounting, and printing expenses and increased competition among potential underwriters. Moreover, the issuer can respond more flexibly to rapidly changing market conditions by varying the structure and terms of the securities on short notice.

---

30. Anthony Fields, Exchange Act Release No. 66,091, 2012 WL 12719 (Jan. 4, 2012), *available at* http://www.sec.gov/litigation/admin/2012/33-9291.pdf.

IN BRIEF

Decision Tree Analysis of Securities Registration Requirements

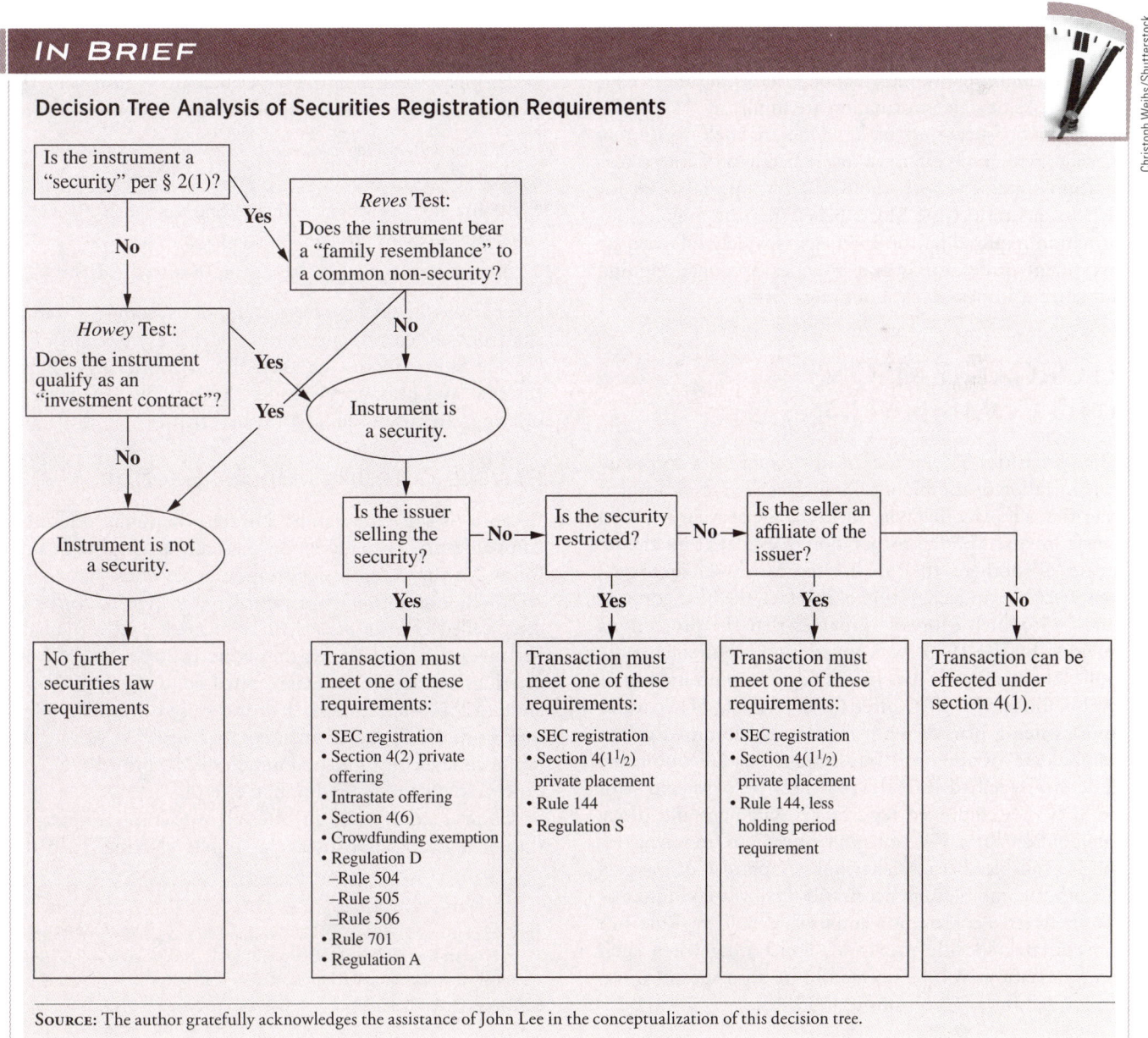

SOURCE: The author gratefully acknowledges the assistance of John Lee in the conceptualization of this decision tree.

Christoph Weihs/Shutterstock

Registration is intended to ensure that current information is available to prospective underwriters and purchasers of securities. Accordingly, shelf registration is restricted to offerings in which the information contained in the registration statement will not become stale or inaccurate after some months or years.

Rule 415 limits the availability of shelf registration to eleven types of offerings, which can be broken down into two basic categories: (1) traditional shelf offerings, and (2) offerings of securities of certain large, publicly traded companies that are eligible to use short-form registration procedures such as Form S–3.

Traditional shelf offerings include (1) securities offered pursuant to employee benefit plans; (2) securities offered or sold pursuant to dividend or interest reinvestment plans; (3) warrants, rights, or securities to be issued upon conversion of other outstanding securities; (4) mortgage-related securities; and (5) securities issued in connection with business combination transactions. With respect to offerings by certain large, publicly traded companies, the SEC has decided that because the market receives a steady stream of high-quality information concerning these issuers, the risks of stale information are minimal.

Seasoned issuers may make *automatic shelf registration offerings*, which are effective immediately on filing a registration statement with the SEC. The special rules for such issuers reflect the SEC's belief that the ongoing information required by the 1934 Act is widely followed by investment professionals and provides adequate ongoing and current information about these firms.

REORGANIZATIONS AND COMBINATIONS

When securities holders are asked to approve a corporate reorganization or combination—such as a reclassification of securities, a merger involving an exchange of securities, or a transfer of assets of one corporation in exchange for the securities of another—they are in effect faced with an investment decision. In recognition of this fact, the SEC adopted Rule 145, which expressly provides that the protections provided by the 1933 Act's registration requirements are applicable to certain types of business reorganizations and combinations. An offer, offer to sell, or sale of securities occurs when a plan of reorganization is submitted to the shareholders for approval. Transactions that fall within the guidelines specified in Rule 145 must be registered with the SEC in a combined registration statement and proxy statement on *Form S–4*, unless an exemption from registration is available. Because shareholder approval of mergers and other combinations necessarily involves communications between a corporation and its shareholders, Rule 145 also contains specific provisions concerning when such communications will be deemed to be a prospectus or an offer to sell for purposes of the 1933 Act.

EXEMPTIONS FOR OFFERINGS BY THE ISSUER

In adopting the 1933 Act registration provisions, Congress provided exemptions from registration when there is no practical need for it or the costs would outweigh the public benefits. Exemptions from registration fall into two categories: exempt securities and exempt transactions.

Exempt securities, listed in section 3 of the 1933 Act, include the following:

1. Any security issued or guaranteed by the United States or any state of the United States.

2. Any security issued or guaranteed by any national bank.

3. Any security issued by a charitable organization.

4. Any security that is part of an issue offered and sold only to persons residing within a single state or territory, if the issuer is a resident of the same state or territory. (Note: Even though the intrastate offering exemption is listed under section 3, the SEC treats it as a transactional exemption under section 4.)

Exempt transactions are described in section 4 of the 1933 Act. They include the following:

1. "Transactions by any person other than an issuer, underwriter or dealer" (section 4(1)).

2. "Transactions by an issuer not involving any public offering" (section 4(2), the private-offering exemption).

3. Offers and sales solely to "accredited investors" (section 4(5)).

Most state blue sky laws have exemptions from registration that roughly correspond to the federal exemptions. The "Inside Story" in this chapter discusses offerings on the Internet and on issuer websites. Exemptions for offshore offerings are discussed later in this chapter.

Private Offerings Under Section 4(2)

Because of the expense and burdens of public offerings, companies trying to raise money usually attempt to qualify for an exemption from registration. They most frequently rely on the exemption for private offerings. A *private offering*, often called a *private placement*, is directed to selected qualified investors, rather than to the public. In 2010 alone, private offerings in the United States raised about $1.4 trillion—about $250 million more than was raised in public offerings in the U.S. capital markets that year.[31] A private offering can be consummated more quickly and with far less expense than a registered public offering.

Under section 4(2), an offering is exempt from registration if it does not involve a "public offering."[32] In the

---

31. Craig M. Lewis, *Unregistered Offerings and the Regulation D Exemption*, SECURITIES & EXCHANGE COMM'N (2011), http://www.sec.gov/info/smallbus/acsec/acsec103111presentation-regd.pdf.

32. Securities Act Release No. 285, Fed. Sec. L. Rep. (CCH) ¶ 2740 (1935).

landmark case *SEC v. Ralston Purina Co.*,[33] the Supreme Court rejected a simple numeric test to decide what constitutes a public offering and held that the determination of whether a transaction is a public or private offering depends primarily on the sophistication of the offerees. Absent a showing of special circumstances, employees are indistinguishable from other members of the investing public as far as the securities laws are concerned. If an offering is made to those who are not able "to fend for themselves," the transaction is a public offering. An important factor affecting this determination is whether the offerees have access to the same kind of information that the 1933 Act would make available through a registration statement. Courts also considered whether the offerees could both understand and bear the risk of the investment. Because issuers had to demonstrate that each offeree (not just each purchaser) was sophisticated, reliance on section 4(2) was an uncertain and somewhat risky proposition.

Regulation D: Safe-Harbor Exemptions

To provide greater certainty and promote capital creation for small businesses, the SEC adopted Regulation D.[34] *Regulation D* offers a safe harbor for those seeking exemption from registration. An issuer that does not comply with all of the requirements of the applicable rule will not necessarily fail to have an exemption because the transaction may still meet the more general conditions of section 4(2).

Rules 501–503 define terms and concepts applicable to one or more of the exemptions.

Accredited Investors

The concept of an accredited investor, derived from earlier federal regulations and state securities laws, is based on the idea that certain investors are so financially sophisticated that they do not need all the protections afforded by the securities laws. Rule 501 defines an *accredited investor* as any one of the following:

1. Any national bank.
2. Any corporation, business trust, or charitable organization with total assets in excess of $5 million.
3. Any director, executive officer, or general partner of the issuer.
4. Any natural person who had individual income in excess of $200,000 in each of the two most recent years, or joint income with that person's spouse in excess of $300,000 in each of those years, with a reasonable expectation of reaching the same income level in the current year.

5. Any natural person whose individual net worth, or joint net worth with that person's spouse, excluding the primary residence, exceeds $1 million at the time of the purchase.
6. Any trust with assets greater than $5 million with the purchase directed by a sophisticated investor.
7. Any private development company.
8. Any entity in which all of the equity owners are accredited investors.

Three Types of Exemptions

Regulation D contains three separate exemptions from registration, defined by Rules 504, 505, and 506.

Rule 504   Rule 504 exempts offerings of up to $1 million within a twelve-month period. There may be an unlimited number of purchasers under Rule 504. Rule 504 is not available to issuers registered under the 1934 Act—known as public companies—or to investment companies such as mutual funds. It is also not available to blank check companies. The issuer must file a notice on Form D with the SEC within fifteen days after the first sale of securities.

Rule 504 generally prohibits public solicitation and general advertising unless (1) the securities are offered exclusively in one or more states that (a) provide for the registration of the securities and (b) require the public filing and delivery to investors of a substantive disclosure document before sale, and the offering is made in accordance with those state provisions; or (2) securities are offered exclusively pursuant to state-law exemptions from registration that permit general solicitation and general advertising, and all purchasers are accredited investors.

Rule 505   Rule 505 exempts offerings of up to $5 million (up to $50 million after the JOBS Act is fully implemented) within a twelve-month period as long as the issuer reasonably believes that there are not more than thirty-five unaccredited investors. General solicitations and advertising are not permitted unless all purchasers are accredited investors or qualified institutions. Rule 505 is not available to investment companies. Rule 505 requires that certain specified information be provided to purchasers (unless all are accredited investors). This information is generally compiled in a private-placement memorandum (described later) or offering circular. Rule 505 also requires that purchasers have the opportunity to ask questions and receive answers concerning the terms of the offering. A notice on Form D must be filed with the SEC within fifteen days of the first sale of securities.

Rule 506   Rule 506, adopted by the SEC under section 4(2), exempts offerings that in the issuer's reasonable belief are limited to no more than thirty-five unaccredited investors, provided that the issuer reasonably believes immediately prior to making any sale that each unaccredited investor, either alone or with his or her purchaser representative, has enough business and financial experience to evaluate the

---

33. 346 U.S. 119 (1953).
34. Proposed Revision of Certain Exemptions from the Registration Provisions of the Securities Act of 1933 for Transactions Involving Limited Offers and Sales, 46 Fed. Reg. 41,791-01 (proposed Aug. 18, 1981) (to be codified at 17 C.F.R. pts. 230, 239).

merits and risks of the prospective investment. There can be an unlimited number of accredited investors, and there is no limit on the amount that can be raised. General solicitations and advertising are not permitted, however.

Like Rule 505, Rule 506 requires that certain specified information be provided to purchasers (unless all purchasers are accredited investors) and that purchasers have the opportunity to ask questions and receive answers concerning the terms of the offering. A notice on Form D must be filed with the SEC within fifteen days of the first sale of securities.

Integration of Offerings

If an issuer makes successive offerings within a limited period of time, the SEC may *integrate* the offerings; that is, it may deem them to be part of a single offering. Integrating two or more offerings may increase the number of unaccredited investors beyond acceptable limits, resulting in the loss of a private-offering exemption. To determine whether offerings should be integrated, the SEC and the courts consider whether the offerings (1) are part of a single plan of financing, (2) involve the issuance of the same class of securities, (3) are made at or about the same time, (4) involve the same type of consideration, and (5) are made for the same general purpose.

Rule 502(a) provides an integration safe harbor for Regulation D offerings. Under Rule 502(a), offers and sales made more than six months before the start of a Regulation D offering or more than six months after its completion will almost never be considered part of the Regulation D offering, provided that the same issuer makes no offers or sales of a similar class of securities during those six-month periods.

If a company decides to abandon a proposed public offering due, for example, to a lack of investor interest, Rule 155(c) provides a way to shift to a private offering without having to wait the six months normally required to avoid integration of the two offerings. To qualify, issuers (1) may not sell any securities in the abandoned offering, (2) must wait thirty calendar days after withdrawal of the registration statement, and (3) must disclose to each offeree in the subsequent offering specific information related to the abandoned offering. There is also a private-to-registered safe harbor that permits a similar shift from a private offering to a registered public offering.

Section 4(5) Exemption

Section 4(5) of the 1933 Act exempts offers and sales by any issuer to an unlimited number of accredited investors, provided that no offers or sales are made to any nonaccredited investors, the aggregate offering price does not exceed $5 million, and there is no public solicitation or advertising in connection with the offering. The section 4(5) definition of "accredited investor" includes banks, insurance companies, and employee benefit plans for which the investment decision is made by a bank, insurance company, or registered adviser.

Regulation A

Under *Regulation A*, U.S. and Canadian companies that are not required to report under the 1934 Act may offer and sell up to $5 million of securities in a twelve-month period, of which up to $1.5 million may be sold by the selling security holders. Regulation A is not available to investment companies, companies issuing oil and gas rights, or blank check companies.

Under Rule 262, the "bad boy" provision, Regulation A is unavailable if the issuer or its officers, directors, principal shareholders, or affiliates have been subject to specified proceedings, convictions, injunctions, or disciplinary orders from the SEC or other regulatory agencies arising from the securities business or postal fraud. To disqualify the company from using Regulation A, the misconduct must have occurred within five years preceding the filing, or within ten years for officers, directors, and principal shareholders.

Testing the Waters

Regulation A issuers can determine interest in a proposed offering prior to filing an offering statement with the SEC. The issuer need only file a solicitation-of-interest document with the SEC, along with copies of any written or broadcast media ads. There is no prohibition on general solicitation or advertising. Radio and television broadcasts and newspaper ads are permitted to determine investor interest in the offering.

No sales may be made or payment received during the testing-the-waters period. To move forward, the company must file Form 1–A with the SEC, and the Regulation A offering statement must be qualified by the SEC. Once the offering statement is filed, testing-the-waters activity ceases. Sales can be made only after the passage of a required waiting period, usually twenty days from the time of the last solicitation of interest.

Offerings to Employees, Directors, Consultants, and Advisers

Securities offered pursuant to equity compensation plans must be either registered or exempt from registration.

Registration—Publicly Traded Companies

In general, federal registration of shares to be issued pursuant to a compensatory stock plan of a company that is publicly traded in the United States can be done relatively simply by registering the shares to be issued pursuant to the plan on SEC Form S–8.

Exemption from Registration—Privately Held Companies

Nonpublic companies that are not registered pursuant to the 1934 Act often faced a problem when instituting employee stock plans. If the company relies on Rule 504 of Regulation D issued pursuant to the 1933 Act, it can issue only $1 million in stock in one twelve-month period. Because employee offerings are usually continuous, the issuer may face serious offering integration problems. It is seldom practical to shut down a stock plan for six months to take advantage of Regulation D's integration safe harbor.

In response to these problems, the SEC adopted Rule 701, which, subject to certain conditions and limitations, exempts offers and sales of securities made pursuant to either (1) a written compensatory benefit plan for employees, directors, general partners, trustees (if the issuer is a business trust), officers, consultants, or advisers; or (2) a written contract relating to the compensation of such persons. If the benefit plan is for consultants or advisers, they must render bona fide services not connected with (1) the offer and sale of securities in a capital-raising transaction or (2) promoting a market for the issuer's securities. Exempt compensatory benefit plans include purchase, savings, option, bonus, stock appreciation, profit-sharing, thrift-incentive, and pension plans.

Under Rule 701, if total sales (not offerings) of stock[35] during a twelve-month period do not exceed the greater of

(1) $1 million, (2) 15% of the total assets of the issuer, or (3) 15% of the outstanding securities of the class being offered and sold, the offerings are exempt from registration. Other than providing a copy of the benefit plan or contract under which the options or securities are awarded, there are no specific disclosure requirements under Rule 701 for sales up to $5 million in a twelve-month period. If, during a twelve-month period, total sales to the specified class of persons above are more than $5 million, the issuer must disclose certain additional information, such as risk factors, a summary of the material terms of the plan, and certain financial information. Rule 701 provides additional integration relief for issuers who sell both under Rule 701 and under Rules 504, 505, or 506 of Regulation D or section 4(2) of the 1933 Act. Offerings under Rule 701 are not integrated with those under Regulation D or section 4(2), and vice versa.

Exhibit 21.2 summarizes the key elements of certain exemptions from registration for offerings by the issuer.

THE PRIVATE-PLACEMENT MEMORANDUM

The *private-placement memorandum* (also called an *offering circular*) is the private-offering counterpart to the prospectus. Like the prospectus, the private-placement memorandum is both a selling document and a disclosure document. The disclosure function is usually primary, so the memorandum may not be as upbeat as the issuer might like.

---

35. In measuring sales, all options granted during the period are considered part of the aggregate sales, with the sales price defined as the option exercise price as of the date of grant. Repriced options are treated as new grants; however, credit is given so that double-counting does not occur. Shares issued pursuant to restricted stock or compensatory stock purchases are calculated as of the date of sale. For deferred compensation equity plans, measurements are based on the date of an irrevocable election to defer compensation. In calculating securities for the 15% rules, currently exercisable or convertible options, warrants, rights, and other securities are treated as outstanding. Nat'l Ctr. for Employee Ownership, *Exemption from Securities Registration Under Rule 701* (2002), *available at* http://www.nceo.org/library/rule701.html.

EXHIBIT 21.2   **Key Elements of Certain Federal Exemptions from Registration**

Type of Exemption	Dollar Limit of the Offering	Limits on the Purchasers	Purchaser Qualifications	Issuer Qualifications
Section 4(2)	No limit	Generally limited to a small number of offerees able to understand and bear risk	Offerees and purchasers must have access to information and be sophisticated investors.	No limitations
Regulation D[a]				
Rule 504[b]	Up to $1 million in 12 months	No limit	No requirements	Not a 1934 Act public reporting company, an investment company, or a blank check company
Rule 505[c]	$5 million in 12 months (increases to $50 million after the JOBS Act is fully implemented)	No limit on the number of accredited investors but limited to 35 unaccredited investors	No requirements for unaccredited investors	Not an investment company
Rule 506[c]	No limit	No limit on the number of accredited investors but limited to 35 unaccredited investors	Unaccredited investors must be sophisticated, that is, have sufficient knowledge and experience in financial matters to evaluate the investment.	No limitations

CONTINUED

EXHIBIT 21.2   Key Elements of Certain Federal Exemptions from Registration (Continued)

Type of Exemption	Dollar Limit of the Offering	Limits on the Purchasers	Purchaser Qualifications	Issuer Qualifications
Regulation A[d]	$5 million in 12 months, with a maximum $1.5 million sold by selling security holders	No limit	No requirements	A U.S. or Canadian company, but not a 1934 Act public reporting company, an investment company, a blank check company, a company issuing oil/gas/mineral rights, or a company disqualified under "bad boy" provisions of Rule 262
Rule 701[e,f]	The greater of $1 million or 15% of the total assets of the issuer or 15% of the outstanding securities of the same class	No limit on the number of employees, directors, general partners, officers, advisers, and consultants	Advisory and consulting services must not be connected with the offer and sale of securities in a capital-raising transaction.	Not a 1934 Act public reporting company or an investment company

a. All issuers relying on these exemptions are required to file a notice on Form D with the SEC within fifteen days after the first sale of securities.

b. This exemption does not depend on the use of any type of disclosure document.

c. A disclosure document meeting the specified SEC requirements is mandatory if there are any unaccredited investors.

d. The issuer must file a disclosure document with the SEC and have it qualified before securities are sold. Testing the waters is permitted after a solicitation-of-interest document is filed with the SEC.

e. Disclosure is required if sales exceed $5 million in a twelve-month period.

f. Must be pursuant to written compensatory benefit plans or written contracts relating to compensation.

The content of the private-placement memorandum is determined by the exemption on which the issuer relies. For example, Rule 502(b) under Regulation D provides that if an issuer is selling securities under Rule 505 or 506 to any purchaser that is not an accredited investor, certain specified information must be provided to the purchaser, including audited financial statements. On the other hand, if the issuer is offering securities under Rule 504 or only to accredited investors, or in reliance on the general section 4(2) exemption, then the issuer is not required to provide any specific information. State blue sky laws may also influence the content and format of a private-placement memorandum.

In many circumstances, no private-placement memorandum is technically required. Nonetheless, an issuer is usually well advised to create such a document in order to clearly demonstrate the disclosure made to prospective investors. Such disclosure is important to rebut claims of securities fraud, a topic discussed in Chapter 22.

EXEMPTIONS FOR SECONDARY OFFERINGS

A principal advantage of registering a securities offering with the SEC and the appropriate state securities authorities is that the securities may be traded relatively freely following the IPO. In contrast, securities issued in a private placement cannot be sold in a secondary offering, that is, a subsequent offering by a person other than the issuer, unless they are either registered or exempt from registration. Securities issued in a private placement are thus called *restricted securities.*

Because securities offered in private offerings are unregistered, their subsequent transfer is restricted, and their price will be discounted accordingly. In addition, purchasers of privately offered securities may demand a greater voice in the operation of the business or sweeteners such as dividend preferences or mandatory redemption privileges, which force the company to repurchase the stock on the occurrence of certain events.

Exhibit 21.3 summarizes certain key definitions and terms related to the resale of equity securities.

ethicalconsideration

Because federal law requires only disclosure of all material information, who bears the responsibility for ensuring the quality and fairness of an offering? The managers and directors of the issuing company? The investment bankers? The securities lawyers?

> **EXHIBIT 21.3** Key Definitions and Terms Related to the Resale of Equity Securities
>
> - **Restricted securities** "Securities issued in a transaction not involving a public offering." [Rule 144]
>
> - **Issuer** "Every person who issues or proposes to issue any security." [Section 2(4)]
>
> - **Affiliate** Any officer, director, or major shareholder (generally presumed to include a person owning at least 10% of the issuer's stock). Someone who controls, or is controlled by, or co-controls the issuer. [Rule 144]
>
> - **Underwriter** "Any person who has purchased from an issuer with a view to, or offers or sells for an issuer in connection with, the distribution of any security." For purposes of this definition, "issuer" includes "any person directly or indirectly controlling or controlled by the issuer, or any person under direct or indirect common control with the issuer." [Section 2(11)]
>
> - **"Not an underwriter"** A person who meets the safe-harbor requirements of Rule 144:
>
>   1. Adequate public information available.
>
>   2. Six-month holding period for reporting issuers and one year for nonreporting issuers (unless affiliate sells unrestricted securities).
>
>   3. Sales limitations for any three-month period: the greater of 1% of the outstanding securities of the class and the average weekly trading volume for the preceding four weeks.
>
>   4. Must sell through a broker or directly to a market maker.
>
>   5. Form 144 filing if more than 5,000 shares or greater than $50,000 aggregate price in three months.
>
>   6. Must have bona fide intention to sell within a reasonable amount of time after filing Form 144.
>
> - **Rule 144A** A nonaffiliate may resell without restriction to a "qualified institutional buyer."

Section 4(1) Exemption

Section 4(1) of the 1933 Act provides that "transactions by any person other than an issuer, underwriter, or dealer" are exempt from registration. Section 2 of the 1933 Act defines an *issuer* as any person "who issues or proposes to issue any security." A *dealer* is defined as "any person who engages either for all or part of his time, directly or indirectly, as agent, broker, or principal, in the business of offering, buying, selling, or otherwise dealing or trading in securities issued by another person."

An *underwriter* is defined as "any person who has purchased from an issuer with a view to, or offers or sells for an issuer in connection with, the distribution of any security." As used in the definition of an underwriter, the term "issuer" includes "any person directly or indirectly controlling or controlled by the issuer, or any person under direct or indirect common control with the issuer." For example, the sale of securities to the public by a controlling shareholder or other affiliate of the issuer (so called *control securities*) is a transaction involving an underwriter. Affiliates include officers, directors, and major shareholders. The SEC has a rebuttable presumption that anyone owning at least 10% of the issuer's stock is an affiliate. Thus, the section 4(1) exemption is generally unavailable, for resales by affiliates.

If the person desiring to sell unrestricted securities is not an issuer, underwriter, or dealer, he or she may sell the securities without registration under section 4(1). There is no limit on the size of the offering or the number of offerees. Section 4(1) is the exemption most often relied on by persons who sell securities in the secondary market in an ordinary transaction involving a broker.

Rule 144

The SEC adopted *Rule 144* in 1972 to reduce the uncertainty associated with the definition of the term "underwriter." If the requirements of Rule 144 are met, then restricted and control securities may be sold publicly without registration. Rule 144 is intended merely to provide objective criteria for deciding whether a person is an underwriter; it is not meant to be the exclusive means through which restricted or control securities may be sold. Exhibit 21.4 depicts the alternatives available for resales of equity securities pursuant to Rule 144 by affiliates and nonaffiliates.

Equity Securities

Under Rule 144, a person selling equity securities is *not an underwriter* if the following conditions are met:

1. Adequate current public information must be available concerning the issuer. This requirement effectively means that the issuer must be a publicly traded company that has complied with the periodic reporting requirements imposed by the 1934 Act (discussed later in this chapter).

2. Securities issued by a *reporting issuer* (that is an issuer that has been subject to the reporting requirements of section 13 or 15(d) of the 1934 Act for at least ninety days before the Rule 144 sale) must have been beneficially owned—with all economic rights belonging to the owner—and fully paid for at least six months prior to the date of sale. The holding period is one year in the case of securities issued by a nonreporting issuer.

EXHIBIT 21.4   Resales of Equity Securities Under Rule 144

	Affiliate or Person Selling on Behalf of an Affiliate	Nonaffiliate (and Has Not Been an Affiliate During the Prior Three Months)
Restricted Securities of Reporting Issuers	*During six-month holding period*—no resales under Rule 144 permitted. *After six-month holding period*—may resell in accordance with all Rule 144 requirements including: • Current public information • Volume limitations • Manner-of-sale requirements for equity securities • Filing of Form 144	*During six-month holding period*—no resales under Rule 144 permitted. *After six-month holding period but before one year*—unlimited public resales under Rule 144 except that the current public information requirement still applies. *After one-year holding period*—unlimited public resales under Rule 144; need not comply with any other Rule 144 requirements.
Restricted Securities of Nonreporting Issuers	*During one-year holding period*—no resales under Rule 144 permitted. *After one-year holding period*—may resell in accordance with all Rule 144 requirements including: • Current public information • Volume limitations • Manner-of-sale requirements for equity securities • Filing of Form 144	*During one-year holding period*—no resales under Rule 144 permitted. *After one year holding period*—unlimited public resales under Rule 144; need not comply with any other Rule 144 requirements.

SOURCE: SEC Release No. 33–8869, Revisions to Rule 144 and Rule 145, 72 Fed. Reg. 71,545, 71,551 (Dec. 17, 2007).

3. In any three-month period, the seller must not sell more than the greater of (a) 1% of the outstanding securities of the class and (b) the average weekly trading volume in the securities during the four calendar weeks preceding the filing of the notice of sale on Form 144.

4. The securities must be sold in "broker's transactions" or "riskless principal transactions," as defined in the 1933 Act, or directly to a "market maker," as defined in the 1934 Act. Solicitation of offers to buy is not permitted, and no commissions for the sale may be paid to any person other than the broker who executes the order of sale.

5. If the amount of the securities sold during any three-month period will exceed 5,000 shares or have an aggregate sale price in excess of $50,000, a notice on Form 144 must be filed with the SEC and with the principal stock exchange (if any) on which the securities are traded.

6. The person filing the Form 144 must have a bona fide intention to sell the securities within a reasonable time after the filing of the notice.

A person who is not an affiliate of the issuer and has not been an affiliate for three months preceding the sale (1) may sell restricted securities issued by a reporting or a nonreporting issuer without regard to items 1, 3, 4, and 5 above if he or she has owned the securities for at least one year prior to their sale; and (2) may sell restricted securities issued by a reporting issuer without regard to items 1, 3, 4, and 5 if he or she has owned the securities for at least six months prior to their sale. This is of particular importance for shareholders of privately held companies that do not file 1934 Act reports.

Usually, restricted securities are identified as such by legends appearing on the face or back of their stock certificates. Accordingly, an opinion from the issuer's attorney may be required before a broker–dealer or transfer agent is willing to consummate a transaction involving restricted securities. Certificates issued following a sale pursuant to Rule 144 may be issued without restrictive legends.

If an affiliate of the issuer wants to sell control securities, then he or she must sell in accordance with Rule 144 (except for the six-month holding period requirement, which is inapplicable if the securities being sold were acquired in a registered offering) or use another available exemption. One alternative is the *section 4(1½) exemption* for private offerings by an affiliate. These offerings would qualify as private placements under section 4(2) if made by the issuer. Thus, the securities can be offered only to persons who are capable of bearing and understanding the risk of the investment and who acquire the securities for investment purposes only and not with a view to distribution.

Debt Securities

The manner-of-sale restrictions set forth in item 4 above do not apply to resales of debt securities (including nonparticipatory preferred stock and certain asset-backed securities). The volume limitations (item 3) for the resale of debt securities are the greatest of (1) 1% of the shares or other units of the class of debt securities outstanding, (2) the average trading volume in such securities, and (3) 10% of the tranche or class of nonparticipatory preferred stock being sold. After an IPO, stock issued pursuant to equity compensation plans is generally registered with the SEC on Form S-8, which makes shares issued pursuant to such plans unrestricted and freely tradable.

Rule 701

Employee shares issued to nonaffiliates prior to an IPO under written compensatory plans may generally be sold pursuant to Rule 701 ninety days after the IPO. Employee shares held by affiliates may also be sold ninety days after the IPO, subject to the Rule 144 volume limitations.

Rule 144A

Rule 144A permits the resale of unregistered securities to *qualified institutional buyers*—that is, institutional investors holding and managing $100 million or more of securities—if the securities are not of the same class as any securities of the issuer listed on a U.S. securities exchange or quoted on an automated interdealer quotation system (such as the Nasdaq Global Market). The rule creates a safe harbor for trading unregistered securities that are often issued to institutional investors in private placements and are generally subject to Rule 144's holding periods. The creation of a secondary market for eligible unregistered securities has increased their liquidity and value and reduced the private-offering discount for them.

If a transaction meets the terms of Rule 144A, it is deemed not to be a distribution. Therefore, the seller is not an underwriter as defined in the 1933 Act. If the seller is also not an issuer or dealer, it may rely on the section 4(1)

exemption for transactions by persons who are not issuers, underwriters, or dealers, as long as it resells only to other qualified institutional buyers.

Dealers may also take advantage of Rule 144A. Under section 4(3) of the 1933 Act, dealers are entitled to an exemption from registration, unless they are participants in a distribution or in a transaction taking place within a specified period after securities have been offered to the public. If a transaction complies with Rule 144A, the dealer will be deemed not to be a participant in a distribution, and the securities will be deemed not to have been offered to the public. Accordingly, the transaction will be exempt from registration.

Rule 144A is a nonexclusive exemption. If the requirements of Rule 144A cannot be met, the parties to the transaction may still rely on the facts-and-circumstances analysis commonly associated with non-public transfers of unregistered stock. For example, the so-called section 4(1½) exemption for private resales of restricted securities may apply. In general, a section 4(1½) offering is an offering by a person other than the issuer (usually either a control person or the holder of restricted unregistered stocks) that would, if it had been done by the issuer, be eligible for the section 4(2) private-offering exemption.

Offerings Offshore and Regulation S

Regulation S clarified the general rule that any offer or sale outside the United States is not subject to the federal registration requirements. The SEC had long taken the position that the section 5 registration requirements do not apply to offers and sales effected in a manner that would result in the securities coming to rest abroad. Transactions meeting the requirements of certain safe harbors for the issuance and resale of securities set forth in Regulation S are deemed to occur outside the United States.

All offers and sales of any security under Regulation S must be made in *offshore transactions*, defined as transactions in which no offer is made to a person in the United States and either (1) the buyer is outside the United States at the time the buy order is originated; or (2) the transaction is one executed in, on, or through the facilities of a designated offshore securities market. No directed selling efforts may be made in the United States.

Regulation S has enabled U.S. companies to offer securities abroad with greater certainty that such securities are exempt from registration. Additionally, the combination of Rule 144A and Regulation S has expanded the private-placement market by increasing the liquidity of privately placed securities.

Exhibit 21.5 provides a flow chart of the registration and exemption requirements applicable to primary and secondary offerings of securities.

EXHIBIT 21.5 An Outline of Registration and Exemption Requirements

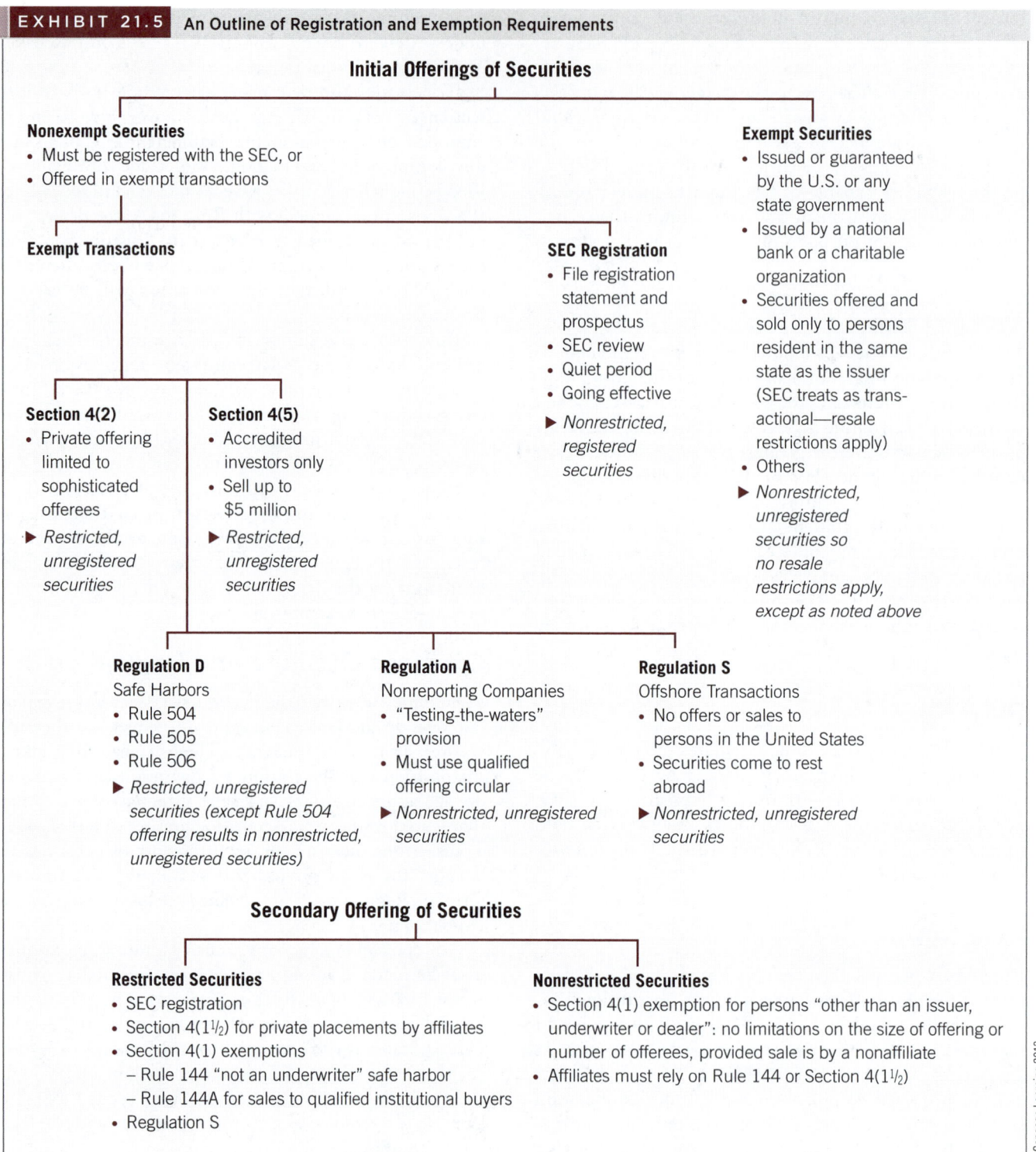

REPORTING REQUIREMENTS OF PUBLIC COMPANIES

The completion of a public offering does not terminate the issuer's relationship with the SEC. Under section 15(d) of the 1934 Act, a company with registered securities in a public offering must file periodic reports. Usually, the company must also register the class of equity securities offered to the public with the SEC under section 12 of the 1934 Act. Whereas the 1933 Act requires the registration of specific offerings of securities, the 1934 Act requires the registration of specific *classes* of securities.

Section 12 Reports

Under section 12 of the 1934 Act, an issuer engaged in interstate commerce and having total assets exceeding $10 million must register with the SEC each nonexempt class of security that (1) is listed on a national stock exchange or (2) is an equity security held of record by at least 500 persons (that number increases to 2,000 if no more than 500 of the holders of record are unaccredited; individuals holding securities pursuant to employee compensation plans are not included in either threshold). One reason why Facebook filed a registration statement for an IPO in 2012 was that it was approaching the pre-JOBS Act threshold of 500 persons. Registration under the 1934 Act subjects the issuer to various reporting requirements and to certain rules and regulations concerning proxies, tender offers, insider trading, and the like. A company registered under section 12 is commonly referred to as a public or *reporting company*. Registration under the 1934 Act is intended to supplement the 1933 Act registration and to ensure that current information concerning the issuer is available to the public, enabling investors to make informed decisions about securities purchases and sales.

The following are some of the significant requirements associated with becoming a registered company under section 12 of the 1934 Act:

- *Quarterly report on Form 10-Q* An unaudited quarterly statement of operations and financial condition must be filed with the SEC on Form 10-Q within forty days after the end of each fiscal quarter.

- *Annual report on Form 10-K* An annual audited report must be filed with the SEC on Form 10-K within sixty, seventy-five, or ninety days (depending on the type of issuer) after the end of the issuer's fiscal year.

- *Special report on Form 8-K* A special report on Form 8-K must be filed with the SEC within four business days after certain events, including changes in control; acquisitions or dispositions of key assets; resignation of directors or auditors; entry into or termination of material agreements that are not made in the ordinary course of business; material impairments; specific issues affecting listing; determinations that past financial statements can no longer be relied on; temporary suspension of trading under employee pension plans; waiver of a provision of the company's code of ethics; creation of, or triggering events that accelerate or increase, obligations under off-balance-sheet arrangements; and costs associated with exit or disposal activities.

The periodic reports must include in narrative form Management's Discussion & Analysis of Financial Condition and Results of Operations (MD&A). The SEC has identified three principal objectives of the MD&A:

- To provide a narrative explanation of a company's financial statements that enables investors to see the company through the eyes of management.

- To enhance the overall financial disclosure and provide the context within which financial information should be analyzed.

- To provide information about the quality of, and potential variability of, a company's earnings and cash flow so that investors can ascertain the likelihood that past performance is indicative of future performance.[36]

Among the topics requiring disclosure within the MD&A are certain off-balance-sheet arrangements of the sort created by Enron, discussed further in Chapter 2.

Other Sections of the 1934 Act

Other sections of the 1934 Act regulate such activities as proxy solicitations, insider trading, and tender offers.

Proxy Solicitations

The proxy regulation provisions of section 14 of the 1934 Act apply to all public companies. They govern the solicitation of written powers of attorney, or *proxies*, that give the proxy holder the right to vote the shares owned by the person who signs the proxy card. As explained in Chapter 19, proxy solicitations relate to management and shareholder proposals as well as to the election of the board of directors.

Insider Trading Reports

Section 16 of the 1934 Act requires executive officers, directors, and persons holding more than 10% of the equity securities of a public company (which includes certain security-based swaps) to file ownership reports on Forms 4 and 5 with the SEC initially, when they acquire or dispose of securities, and on an annual basis. (These reports are described more fully in Chapter 22.) Purchases and sales of the public issuer's equity securities (including sales back to the issuer) must be reported within two business days. Insiders of companies not registered under the 1934 Act are not required to file regular reports with the SEC. Trading by insiders is also subject to section 16(b)'s short-swing trading restrictions and section 10(b)'s antifraud provisions, which are discussed in Chapter 22.

Tender Offers

Any person making a *tender offer* to shareholders, whereby shareholders are asked to sell their shares to that person for a stated price, must comply with the tender offer rules found in section 14 of the 1934 Act. Some rules, such as the requirement that a tender offer be left open for at least twenty business days, apply if the company has a significant number of shareholders even if it is not registered under the 1934 Act. Other rules, such as the rule giving shareholders the right to withdraw their shares once they are tendered and

---

36. Interpretation: Commission Guidance Regarding MD&A, SEC Release Nos. 33-8350, 34-48960, 17 C.F.R. pts. 211, 231, 241 (Dec. 29, 2003).

the rule requiring proration if the offer is oversubscribed, apply only if the company is registered under the 1934 Act.

Schedule 13D

Under section 13, any person acquiring beneficial ownership of more than 5% of the equity shares of a reporting company (including certain security-based swaps) must file a Schedule 13D within ten days after crossing the 5% mark. The Schedule 13D must disclose the number of shares acquired and the intentions of the person acquiring them. Often the person acquiring the shares will state that it is buying the shares for investment purposes only. Sometimes, however, the company suspects an ulterior motive, such as preparation for a hostile takeover attempt.

Although it is clear that a person who buys voting equity securities has beneficial ownership of them, questions may arise when a person engages in derivative transactions, such as equity swaps, as seen in the following hotly contested case.

| **A CASE IN POINT** | *Summary* | **Case 21.2** |

CSX Corp. v. The Children's Investment Fund Management (UK) LLP

United States District Court for the Southern District of New York
562 F. Supp. 2d 511 (S.D.N.Y. 2008).

FACTS   The Children's Investment Fund Management (TCI) and 3G Fund, the two defendant hedge funds, acquired large economic positions in CSX Corporation, one of the largest railroads in the United States, through the use of total return equity swaps (TRSs). TCI was widely regarded as an "activist" hedge fund, and it made its initial investment in TRSs referenced with CSX stock in October 2006. When TCI's efforts to force CSX to go private in a leveraged buyout or change its operations were largely rebuffed, TCI began contacting other hedge funds, including 3G, and encouraged them to acquire CSX shares or swaps referenced to those shares. 3G bought its first shares of CSX common stock in February 2007. By November 2007, 3G owned shares and swaps that gave it an aggregate economic exposure of 4.9% of the company. TCI and 3G did not disclose their interest in CSX until December 2007 on the theory that prior to that date they did not beneficially own the shares referenced by the swaps.

In mid-December 2007, TCI and 3G filed a Schedule 13D disclosing that at that time they collectively owned 8.3% of CSX shares outstanding. The Schedule 13D also disclosed that TCI had cash-settled equity swap arrangements with eight counterparties that gave it economic exposure to approximately 11% of CSX's shares outstanding, but TCI disclaimed beneficial ownership of the underlying shares referenced by the TRSs.

TCI and 3G commenced a proxy fight in which they sought to elect their nominees to five of the twelve seats on the CSX board of directors at the annual meeting scheduled to take place on June 25, 2008. CSX sued, alleging that the defendants had failed to file a Schedule 13D on a timely basis and that the Schedule 13D and the proxy statement they eventually filed were false and misleading. CSX sought, among other things, an order precluding the defendants from voting their shares (that is, *share sterilization*).

A *total return equity swap* is a type of derivative security whereby two counterparties agree to exchange cash flows on two financial instruments over a specific period of time. Counterparty A (the "short" party) agrees to pay Counterparty B (the "long" party) cash flows equal to the sum of (1) any cash distributions, such as interest or dividends, that Counterparty A would have received had it held the referenced security and (2) either (a) an amount equal to the market appreciation of the value of the referenced security over the term of the swap (if the TRS is cash-settled) or, what is economically the same thing, (b) the security in exchange for its value on the last refixing date prior to the winding up of the transaction (if the TRS is settled in kind). In turn, Counterparty A is entitled to receive (1) an amount equal to the interest at the negotiated rate that would have been payable had Counterparty B actually loaned Counterparty A the purchase price of the referenced security, plus (2) any decrease in the market value of the referenced security.

In this case, the short counterparties, which included Deutsche Bank, Citigroup Global Markets, and Morgan Stanley, hedged their short exposures by purchasing a number of CSX shares roughly equal to the shares referenced in the swaps. Although the hedging institutions had no economic interest in the CSX stock, they were the beneficial owners of the CSX shares because they had the right to vote them.

CONTINUED

ISSUE PRESENTED   Does an investor who has entered into total return swaps for more than 5% of a public company's common stock have an obligation to file a Schedule 13D?

SUMMARY OF OPINION   The U.S. District Court for the Southern District of New York began by stating:

> Some people deliberately go close to the line dividing legal from illegal if they see a sufficient opportunity for profit in doing so. A few cross that line and, if caught, seek to justify their actions on the basis of formalistic arguments, even when it is apparent that they have defeated the purpose of the law.
>
> This is such a case.

The court explained the economic effect of swaps:

> In practical economic terms, a TRS referenced to stock places the long party in substantially the same economic position that it would occupy if it owned the referenced stock or security. There are two notable exceptions. First, since it does not have record ownership of the referenced shares, it does not have the right to vote them. Second, the long party looks to the short party, rather than to the issuer of the referenced security, for distributions and the marketplace for any appreciation in value.

From the point of view of the short party, it is entitled to have the long party place it in the same economic position it would have been in had it advanced the long party an amount equal to the market value of the referenced security (the notional amount).

Although some institutions will not vote shares held to hedge TRS risk, others will tend to vote as the counterparty desires. Others claim to vote as they determine in their sole discretion. Skeptical of this claim, the court noted that "one may suppose that banks seeking to attract swap business will understand that activist investors will consider them to be more attractive counterparties if they vote in favor of the positions that their client indicates."

The court explained that by using swaps to conceal its activities, the long party can avoid having other investors bid up the referenced stock in anticipation of a tender offer or other change-of-control contest, thereby maximizing the long party's potential profit. The use of swaps also permits a long party that is interested in persuading an issuer to alter its policies, but is not willing to commence an all-out battle for control, to wait to announce its emergence as a powerful player until a moment of its choosing. In other words, the court stated, "it permits a long party to ambush an issuer with a holding far greater than five percent."

The court further noted that TRS transactions are privately negotiated and their terms may be varied at any time, as long as the counterparties agree. As a result, a TRS that at its inception required cash settlement may be settled in kind—that is, by delivery of the referenced shares of the long party—as long as the parties consent. This makes it possible for the long party either to unwind the swaps by acquiring the referenced shares in swiftly consummated private transactions or to prompt the short counterparty to dispose of the shares to raise the cash necessary to unwind the swaps, thereby releasing a ready supply of shares to the market at times and in circumstances effectively chosen and known principally by the long party.

Quoting the U.S. Court of Appeals for the Second Circuit in *GAF Corp. v. Millstein*,[37] the court stated that the Schedule 13D filing requirements were adopted "to alert the marketplace to every large, rapid accumulation of securities, regardless of technique employed, which might represent a potential shift in corporate control." Under Rule 13d–3(a), a person is deemed to have beneficial ownership of a security if that person has the power to vote, or to direct the voting of, the security or has the power to dispose of, or to direct the disposition of, the security. Rule 13d–3(b) goes on to provide that any person who, directly or indirectly, uses any arrangement with the purpose or effect of divesting that person of beneficial ownership as

CONTINUED

---

37. 453 F.2d 709, 717 (2d Cir. 1971), *cert. denied*, 406 U.S. 910 (1972).

part of a plan or scheme to evade the reporting requirements is deemed to be the beneficial owner of that security.

The court acknowledged that the TCI swap agreements did not give TCI any legal rights with respect to the voting or disposition of the CSX shares referenced therein. Nor did they require the short counterparties to acquire CSX shares to hedge their positions. There was also no evidence that TCI and any of its counterparties had explicit agreements that the banks would vote their hedge shares in a certain way. Nonetheless, the court found the evidence overwhelming that the counterparties did in fact hedge their short positions by purchasing shares of CSX common stock on virtually a share-for-share basis either on the day of or the day following the commencement of the swap. The court characterized this as "precisely what TCI contemplated and, indeed, intended." Similarly, with minor exceptions, whenever TCI terminated a swap, the counterparty sold the same number of physical shares that were referenced in the unwound swap and did so on the same date that the swap was terminated to avoid the risk that holding the physical shares would have entailed once the downside protection of the swap had been removed. Although the court found no evidence that TCI had explicitly directed the banks to purchase the hedge shares upon entering into the swaps or to sell them upon termination, the court stated:

> On this record, it is quite clear that TCI significantly influenced the banks to purchase the CSX shares that constituted their hedges because the banks, as a practical matter and as TCI both knew and desired, were compelled to do so. It significantly influenced the banks to sell the hedge shares when the swaps were unwound for the same reasons.

In summary, the court concluded that there were substantial reasons for finding that TCI was the beneficial owner under Rule 13d–3(a) of the CSX shares held as hedges by its short counterparties. First, "TCI manifestly had the economic ability to cause its short counterparties to buy and sell the CSX shares." Second, although the court found the voting situation "a bit murkier," it concluded that TCI was in a position to influence the counterparties, especially Deutsche Bank, with respect to the exercise of their voting rights. The court reasoned that focusing just on TCI's legal rights based on its swap contracts elevated form over substance, noting: "The securities markets operate in the real world, not in a law school contracts classroom. Any determination of beneficial ownership that failed to take account of the practical realities of that world would be open to the gravest abuse."

Interestingly, having gone through this detailed analysis under Rule 13d–3(a), the court ultimately punted on the legal question of whether TCI was the beneficial owner of the referenced CSX shares under that section. Instead, the court based its holding on Rule 13d–3(b) and ruled that "the evidence that TCI created and used TRSs, at least in major part, for the purpose of preventing the vesting of beneficial ownership of CSX shares in TCI and as part of a plan or scheme to evade the reporting requirements of Section 13(d) is overwhelming." The court also upheld the trier of facts's conclusion that TCI had formed a group that beneficially owned more than 5% of CSX's stock no later than February 13, 2007, and granted CSX's motion for a permanent injunction restraining the defendants from further violations of section 13(d) of the 1934 Act. The court, however, rejected CSX's assertion that the Schedule 13D and the proxy statements issued by TCI and 3G were materially misleading.

The court also rejected CSX's request for share sterilization after concluding that it was constrained by precedent from ordering sterilization. Although the defendants' actions altered the corporate electorate, they did not give the defendants effective control. The court added, however, that "were the Court free as a matter of law . . . to grant such an injunction, whether on the basis that such relief was warranted to afford deterrence or on another basis, it would do so."

RESULT The court ruled that TCI and 3G had violated the requirement to file the Schedule 13D within ten days following formation of their group on February 13, 2007, and enjoined

CONTINUED

them from further violations of section 13(d). It denied CSX's request for an injunction that would have enjoined the defendants from voting the 6.4% of CSX shares they had acquired between February 23, 2007, and the date of the trial.

COMMENTS   In an amici curiae brief filed with the U.S. Court of Appeals for the Second Circuit on July 18, 2008, five former SEC commissioners, including Arthur Levitt, Joseph A. Grundfest, and Roberta S. Karmel, urged the appeals court to affirm the lower court's decision. The securities industry, various financial markets associations, and the International Swaps and Derivatives Association called for a reversal.[38]

On appeal, the Second Circuit vacated the injunction against voting the shares because sufficient information was available to the shareholders before the vote and remanded the case for a determination by the trial court of "whether the Defendants formed a group for the purpose of 'acquiring, holding, voting or disposing,' of CSX shares owned outright, and, if so, a date by which at the latest such a group was formed."[39] Dodd–Frank required the SEC to make a finding of whether security-based swaps should be counted for purposes of calculating beneficial ownership. On June 8, 2011, the SEC readopted Rule 13d–3 without change, thereby preserving the status quo (and uncertainty) regarding when security-based swaps confer beneficial ownership.[40]

---

38. *Former SEC Commissioners Filed a Brief Urging the Second Circuit to Affirm "CSX" Decision*, CORP. COUNS. WKLY. (BNA), July 30, 2008, at 233.

39. CSX Corp. v. The Children's Inv. Fund Mgmt. (UK) LLP, 654 F.3d 276 (2d Cir. 2011).

40. Beneficial Ownership Reporting Requirements and Security-Based Swaps, SEC Release No. 34-64628, 2011 WL 2246370 (July 11, 2011).

VIOLATION OF THE REGISTRATION AND PROSPECTUS-DELIVERY REQUIREMENTS: SECTION 12(A)(1) OF THE 1933 ACT

As explained above, section 5 of the 1933 Act provides that, absent an exemption, all securities must be registered and may be sold only after delivery of a prospectus meeting the requirements of the 1933 Act. The penalty for violation of section 5 is simple and severe. Section 12(a)(1) provides that, absent an exemption, anyone who offers or sells a security without an effective registration statement or by means of a noncomplying prospectus is liable to the purchaser for rescission or damages. In effect, the purchaser is given a put: if the investment proves successful, the investor can keep the shares, but if, within one year from the date of purchase, the investment proves unprofitable, the investor can get his or her money back.

Elements of Liability

To establish a section 12(a)(1) claim, the plaintiff must show that the defendant sold or offered securities without an effective registration statement, or by means of a noncomplying prospectus, through the use of interstate transportation or communication. A plaintiff typically satisfies the interstate transportation or communication requirement by proving that the mails, telephone, or other interstate means were used in the offer or sale to that particular plaintiff. The plaintiff must file suit within one year from the date the securities were offered or sold. Section 12(a)(1) imposes a standard of strict liability. The plaintiff need not show that the defendant acted willfully or negligently, but only that the defendant committed the act of selling unregistered and nonexempt securities.

Damages

If the plaintiff still owns the securities, he or she is entitled to rescind the purchase. To rescind, the plaintiff returns the securities, together with any income (such as dividends) he or she received from them, in exchange for the price paid for the securities, plus interest. If the plaintiff has sold the securities, he or she is entitled to recover damages—usually the difference between what was paid and what was received for the securities at sale.

Who May Be Sued

The severity of the remedy under section 12(a)(1) has led to questions about who may be considered to have offered or sold securities within the meaning of the statute. It clearly includes the issuer. But what about others involved in an unregistered securities transaction, such as attorneys, accountants, underwriters, and investment bankers?

Section 12(a)(1) provides that "any person who . . . offers or sells a security," in violation of the registration requirement, "shall be liable to the person purchasing such security from him." To be considered a seller, a nonowner must successfully solicit the purchase and be motivated at least in part by a desire to serve his or her own financial interests or those of the securities owner.[41] Thus, mere promotion of a security does not necessarily make a person a seller under section 12(a)(1), even if that promotion is a substantial factor in inducing the purchase of the security.

Who May Sue

Anyone who purchases shares issued in violation of the registration requirements may bring suit. If the securities were sold to a number of persons, then a plaintiff may bring a class-action suit, which will be filed on behalf of all persons who purchased the illegally issued securities.

SECTION 11 OF THE 1933 ACT

Section 11 provides a remedy for a person who purchases a security pursuant to a misleading registration statement. Section 11 applies only to registered securities. The section is the longest and most detailed civil liability provision in the 1933 Act. It spells out who may sue, who may be sued, the elements of the offense, the permitted defenses, and the damages that may be awarded. Under section 11, an issuer of securities is liable for its false statements or misleading omissions even if the issuer had no intent to defraud and was not even negligent in ascertaining the truth.

Who May Sue

Any person who has purchased a registered security may sue under section 11, but this is subject to a tracing requirement.

Tracing Requirement

The purchaser must prove that the security at issue was actually one of those sold pursuant to the misleading registration statement.[42] Although this requirement does not present a problem for direct purchasers of an IPO, open-market purchasers may find it difficult to trace their

securities back to a sale made under the defective registration statement.

Class Actions

Plaintiffs in a section 11 case typically bring a class action, in which the named plaintiffs act on behalf of themselves and "all others similarly situated." The advantage to the plaintiffs (and their attorneys) of proceeding in this manner is that the individual plaintiffs' claims, worth only a few hundred or a few thousand dollars, together often amount to millions of dollars.

Who May Be Sued

Section 11 lists, and thereby limits, the entities and persons who may be sued: (1) the issuer offering the security; (2) the underwriters; (3) any member of the board of directors at the time of the offering; (4) persons who gave their consent to be named in the registration statement as future directors; (5) every person who signed the registration statement (under section 6(a) of the 1933 Act, it must be signed by the issuer, its principal executive officer, its principal financing officer, and its principal accounting officer); and (6) experts who consented to give authority to the "expertized" portion of the registration statement, such as accountants who audited the financial statements contained in it. No person can be named in the registration statement as an expert unless that person has consented in writing to being named.

All defendants in a section 11 case generally have joint and several liability for violations, meaning that one defendant can be held responsible for all the damages awarded to the plaintiff, even if that defendant was only partially responsible for the violation. The one exception is that outside directors who did not commit knowing violations are generally liable only for the portion of the damages attributable to their percentage of responsibility.

Plaintiffs often allege that persons or entities other than those specified in section 11 are liable under a theory of secondary liability, such as aiding and abetting or conspiracy. Most (but not all) courts have rejected such attempts to expand liability under section 11. The U.S. Supreme Court ruled in 1994 that a private plaintiff may not maintain an aiding and abetting suit under section 10(b),[43] and it seems unlikely that the Court would extend section 11 to include aiders and abettors.[44]

In the following case, the court considered whether a credit rating agency was an underwriter of securities based on collateralized debt obligations.

---

41. Pinter v. Dahl, 486 U.S. 622 (1988).

42. *See, e.g.,* Lee v. Ernst & Young LLP, 294 F.3d 969, 976–77 (8th Cir. 2002); DeMaria v. Andersen, 318 F.3d 170 (2d Cir. 2003) (holding that after-market purchasers who can trace their shares to an allegedly misleading registration statement have standing to sue under section 11).

43. Cent. Bank of Denver, N.A. v. First Interstate Bank of Denver, N.A., 511 U.S. 164 (1994).

44. *See also* Stoneridge Inv. Partners v. Scientific-Atlanta, Inc., 552 U.S. 148 (2008) (rejecting "scheme liability" in fraud cases under section 10(b) of the 1934 Act) (Case 22.6).

| A CASE IN POINT | *Summary* | Case 21.3 |

In re **Lehman Bros. Mortgage-Backed Securities Litigation**

United States Court of Appeals for the Second Circuit
650 F.3d 167 (2d Cir. 2011).

FACTS Mortgage pass-through certificates are a type of mortgage-backed security. These certificates are based on a pool of mortgages acquired by a "sponsor" and pooled by a "depositor" into a securitized trust, which in turn sells the certificates to underwriters to offer to investors. The trusts pay out distributions to holders of the certificates from principal and interest payments made by the individual mortgage borrowers. Rating agencies assign the certificates different risk levels, or "tranches" of risk, ranging from the least risky (AAA rating) to the most risky or likely to default. The tranches are created using credit enhancement techniques, such as subordinating lower tranches to absorb losses first, overcollateralizing the loan pools in excess of the bond amount, or creating an excess spread fund to cover the difference between the interest collected from borrowers and the amounts owed to investors.

Between 2005 and 2007, plaintiffs in this class-action suit purchased about $155 billion in mortgage pass-through certificates registered with the SEC that had been rated by the defendants—Standard & Poor's (a subsidiary of McGraw Hill), Moody's Investors Service, Inc., and/or Fitch, Inc. (collectively, "Rating Agencies"). The plaintiffs alleged that the Rating Agencies provided preliminary ratings when the issuing banks were "shopping" for ratings and that they also negotiated the amount of credit enhancements and percentage of AAA certificates for each mortgage pool once chosen. Moreover, the plaintiffs alleged that the Rating Agencies helped determine the composition of loan pools, the certificates' structures, and the amount and kinds of credit enhancement for particular tranches, partly by providing their modeling tools to the banks' traders to help them achieve specific ratings.

During the 2008 mortgage crisis, after the values of the plaintiffs' certificates declined due to a downgrading by the Rating Agencies, the plaintiffs sued various entities involved in their offerings. The plaintiffs claimed that the Rating Agencies were liable as underwriters or control persons for misstatements or omissions in securities offering documents in violation of sections 11 and 15 of the 1933 Act. The Rating Agencies moved to dismiss all claims against them. The district court granted this motion, ruling that the Rating Agencies were not "underwriters" under the meaning of the 1933 Act when they participated in creating the securities because they did not purchase them for resale. Nor did the Rating Agencies' power to influence or persuade the primary violators constitute the requisite "practical ability to direct the actions of people who issue or sell securities" necessary for controlling-person liability under section 15.

ISSUES PRESENTED Are rating agencies that helped select a pool of mortgages for a mortgage-backed security "underwriters" under the 1933 Act? Are they controlling persons under section 15?

SUMMARY OF OPINION The U.S. Court of Appeals for the Second Circuit defined "underwriter" based on statutory text, judicial precedent, and legislative intent, concluding that, to qualify as an "underwriter" under section 11 of the 1933 Act, "a person must have participated, directly or indirectly, in the purchase of securities with a view toward distribution, or in the sale or offer of securities in connection with a distribution." The court further ruled that the Rating Agencies' conduct did not make them underwriters, as their efforts in structuring or creating securities occurred during the initial stages of securitization, not during efforts to sell the certificates to investors. Because the Rating Agencies did not participate in the distribution of the securities, they were not underwriters.

Although the court recognized that the plaintiffs had adequately pleaded primary section 11 violations by the certificates' issuers and the depositors, it concluded that the Rating Agencies did not control the primary violators as required for liability under section 15 of the 1933 Act. The court adopted the definition it had previously articulated for "control" under section 20(a), namely, "the power to direct or cause the direction of the management and policies of the

CONTINUED

primary violators, whether through the ownership of voting securities, by contract, or otherwise." The court then concluded that the plaintiffs had failed to adequately plead control. At most, their allegations suggested that the Rating Agencies provided advice and "strategic direction" on how to structure transactions to achieve particular ratings. According to the court, this involvement in transaction-level decisions is inadequate to establish a power to direct the primary violators' "management and policies."

RESULT   The Second Circuit affirmed the dismissal of the plaintiffs' claims.

CRITICAL THINKING QUESTIONS

1. If underwriter status did apply to any party who provided nondistribution services to an offeror, rather than being restricted to distribution-related participation, what additional actors in the securitization process might be considered "underwriters"?

2. What ethical obligations do rating agencies have when participating in the securitization process?

Elements of Liability

The elements of a section 11 offense are straightforward. The plaintiff must show that, at the time the registration statement became effective, it (1) contained a false or misleading statement of a material fact or (2) omitted to state a material fact required to be stated in the registration statement or necessary to make the statements contained in the registration statement not misleading.

The Supreme Court has defined a *material fact* as one that a reasonable investor would most likely have considered important in deciding whether to buy or sell—that is,

what a reasonable hypothetical investor would have considered important, not necessarily what the actual investor considered important. The Supreme Court has held that an omitted fact is material if there is "a substantial likelihood that the disclosure of the omitted fact would have been viewed by the reasonable investor as having significantly altered the 'total mix' of information made available."[45] The following case further explored the definition of materiality.

---

45. TSC Indus. v. Northway, Inc., 426 U.S. 438, 449 (1976).

A CASE IN POINT	*Summary*	Case 21.4

Rosenzweig v. Azurix Corp.

United States Court of Appeals for the Fifth Circuit
332 F.3d 854 (5th Cir. 2003).

FACTS   In 1999, Enron Corporation formed Azurix, a global water and wastewater company. Azurix planned to take advantage of what appeared to be a trend toward privatization by acquiring and operating government-owned facilities. Azurix did an initial public offering in 1998 after securing a thirty-year concession from the province of Buenos Aires, Argentina. The offering price was around $20 per share. Enron took Azurix private in 2000 by buying all the public's shares at $8 per share.

Shareholders who had purchased Azurix stock in the secondary market brought this action, alleging, among other things, that the defendants had violated the federal securities laws by making misrepresentations and omissions in press releases and public filings. In particular, the plaintiffs alleged that the defendants knew that Azurix's business plan was fundamentally flawed and that the Buenos Aires concession was plagued with problems, but they nevertheless fraudulently inflated Azurix's stock price by making misleading optimistic representations and concealing the truth. The defendants challenged the materiality of the alleged misrepresentations and omissions.

ISSUE PRESENTED   What constitutes materiality for purposes of a section 11 claim?

SUMMARY OF OPINION   The U.S. Court of Appeals for the Fifth Circuit declared that "[t]he generalized, positive statements about the company's competitive strengths, experienced management, and future prospects" were not material, noting that "Azurix was under no duty to cast its business in a pejorative, rather than a positive light." More specific remarks

CONTINUED

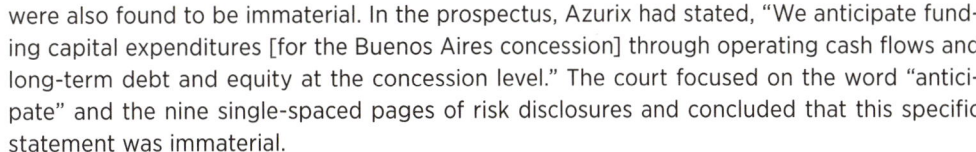

were also found to be immaterial. In the prospectus, Azurix had stated, "We anticipate funding capital expenditures [for the Buenos Aires concession] through operating cash flows and long-term debt and equity at the concession level." The court focused on the word "anticipate" and the nine single-spaced pages of risk disclosures and concluded that this specific statement was immaterial.

The plaintiffs also claimed that the investing public was led to believe that the defendants had performed due diligence on the Buenos Aires concession, as well as others, which was either a material misrepresentation or an omission. The court agreed with the trial court that "a rational investor would not have relied on the due diligence statements contained in the prospectus," in light of the risk disclosures. The court described other, allegedly misleading, specific statements as "obviously immaterial puffery."

RESULT The Fifth Circuit affirmed the dismissal of the plaintiffs' claims.

COMMENTS The plaintiffs also brought claims under section 12, but those claims were dismissed because the plaintiffs lacked standing. Additionally, the court pointed out that the claims were insufficiently particular and that the inferences of intent to deceive were weak.

The plaintiff does not have to establish that he or she read the prospectus or relied on the misstatement or omission except in the following instance: A plaintiff who purchases a security on the open market after the issuing company has released its income statements for the year following the registration statement must show that the misrepresentation in the prospectus influenced his or her decision to buy.

Defenses

Section 11 sets forth several defenses. The defenses of no reliance and no causation focus on the effects of the misstatements on the behavior of investors and the market, while the defense of due diligence looks to the culpability of the defendants.

No Reliance

The defense of no reliance relates to the investor's knowledge. Investors who know that there was a misstatement or omission cannot claim to have relied on it; they are presumed to have acted despite the misstatement or omission. Thus, if the defendant can establish that the plaintiff actually knew that a statement was false or that there was an omission, there is no liability under section 11. Again, note that investors need not prove that they actually relied on the misstatement or omission or even read the prospectus.

No Causation

The defense of no causation focuses on the link between the misstatement and the investor's loss. Even if there was a misstatement or omission of a material fact, a defendant will not be liable if it can show that the misstatement or omission did not actually cause the plaintiff to suffer any loss. In other words, the plaintiff may have lost money on a trade, but that loss may not have been due to the defendant's conduct. This showing typically consists of an expert analysis of the various factors that influenced the price movements of the securities in question. Developments in this area are discussed in Chapter 22.

Due Diligence

The defense of due diligence focuses on the behavior of the defendants. It is available to all defendants except the issuing company. A defendant is not liable for a misrepresentation or omission if it acted with due diligence, meaning that it (1) conducted a reasonable investigation and (2) reasonably believed (a) that the statements made were true and (b) that there were no omissions that made those statements misleading. A reasonable investigation is what a prudent person managing his or her own property would conduct.

The primary wrinkle in the due diligence defense arises in connection with the expertized portions of the registration statement, such as audit reports on the company's financial statements, appraisal reports, or engineering reports. The experts are, of course, responsible for their own reports, provided that the reports are identified as having been prepared by them and that the experts have given their consent to the use of their reports in the registration statement. The experts are generally not responsible under section 11 for portions of the registration statement other than their reports.

Nonexpert defendants are generally entitled to rely on the experts. They can establish due diligence by showing that they had no reasonable basis to believe that the experts' reports were misleading and, in fact, did not believe them to be misleading. But, as the U.S. District Court for the Southern District of Texas explained in the Enron securities litigation:

[T]here are no rigid or clear standards or rules for measuring what is reasonable, since that determination varies with the circumstances of each case, but an underwriter's reliance on audited financial statements may not be automatic. What constitutes a "red flag" or "storm warning" in the context of § 11 claims that would demonstrate that a defendant had "no reasonable ground to believe and did not believe" that the expertized portions of a registration statement are true "depends upon the facts and context of a particular case." . . . Where red flags appear, the underwriter must

"look deeper and question more" in its due diligence investigation." The existence of red flags can create a duty to investigate even audited financial statements."[46]

The case that follows was the first to articulate the due diligence standards applicable to the various participants in the offering process and remains an accurate statement of the law.

---

46. *In re* Enron Corp. Sec., Derivative & MDL-1446 "ERISA" Litig., 2005 U.S. Dist. LEXIS 39927 (S.D. Tex. 2005). A group of investment banks, accountants, lawyers, and others agreed to pay $7.2 billion, the largest recovery in a class action, to settle securities claims by investors who bought Enron securities before the firm imploded in 2001. *Court Clears $688 M Fee Award to Lead Counsel in Enron Litigation*, CORP. COUNS. WKLY. (BNA), Sept. 17, 2008, at 285.

| A CASE IN POINT | *Summary* | Case 21.5 |

Escott v. BarChris Construction Corp.

United States District Court for the Southern District of New York
283 F. Supp. 643 (S.D.N.Y. 1968).

FACTS   BarChris was in the business of building bowling alleys. It obtained capital through a public offering in May 1961. Due to financial problems, the company filed for protection under the Bankruptcy Act in October 1962. A class action followed, alleging section 11 claims against the company, its officers and directors, and its underwriters.

ISSUES PRESENTED   When is the due diligence defense available to the principal officers or the inside directors of the issuer? May a chief financial officer rely on the audited financial statements if he had reason to believe those statements were incorrect? Have outside directors and underwriters, who relied on management's statements and made no independent investigation, acted with due diligence?

SUMMARY OF OPINION   The U.S. District Court for the Southern District of New York first found that both the expertized and the nonexpertized portions of the registration statement were misleading. Every defendant raised the defense of due diligence except the issuer, to whom the defense was not available.

The court applied the most stringent standards to the company's principal officers and inside directors (that is, the directors who were also officers of the corporation). It first noted that principal officers and inside directors who sign a registration statement have a significant burden. Because of their extensive knowledge of the company's affairs, it is rare that they can successfully establish a due diligence defense. The court held that the chief financial officer was not entitled to rely on the outside auditors as to the accuracy of the financial statements because he had reason to believe that those statements were incorrect. The court concluded that the liability of principal officers and inside directors approaches that of the company itself. They cannot escape liability for the nonexpertized portions of the statement even if they did not read the statement, did not understand it, and relied on assistants and lawyers to make adequate disclosures.

The court then considered the liability of two outside directors who had become directors a month before the offering. Neither had read the registration statement in final form, and both had relied on assurances from the officers that everything was in order. The court ruled that section 11 imposes liability on directors, no matter how new they are. Individuals are presumed to know their responsibility when they become directors. A director can escape liability only by using that degree of reasonable care to investigate the facts that a prudent person would employ in the management of his or her own property. The court concluded that a prudent person would not act in an important matter without any knowledge of the relevant facts, in sole reliance on representations of persons who were comparative strangers, and on general information that did not purport to cover the particular case.

CONTINUED

The court then considered whether the underwriters had established the due diligence defense. The court concluded that the underwriters had made no effectual attempt at verification. The court ruled that it was not sufficient to ask management questions, obtain answers that, if true, would be thought satisfactory, and let the matter go at that without seeking to ascertain from the records whether the answers were, in fact, true and complete. The court explained:

> [I]n a sense, the positions of the underwriter and the company's officers are adverse. It is not unlikely that statements made by company officers to an underwriter to induce him to underwrite may be self-serving. They may be unduly enthusiastic. As in this case, they may, on occasion, be deliberately false.

The underwriters argued that the prospectus is the company's prospectus, not theirs. But the court ruled that the 1933 Act makes no such distinction. Prospective investors rely on the reputation of the underwriters when deciding whether to purchase the securities. The court explained:

> The purpose of Section 11 is to protect investors. To that end the underwriters are made responsible for the truth of the prospectus. If they may escape that responsibility by taking at face value representations made to them by the company's management, then the inclusion of underwriters among those liable under Section 11 affords the investors no additional protection. To effectuate the statute's purpose, the phrase "reasonable investigation" must be construed to require more effort on the part of the underwriters than the mere accurate reporting in the prospectus of "data presented" to them by the company. It should make no difference that this data is elicited by questions addressed to the company officers by the underwriters, or that the underwriters at the time believe that the company's officers are truthful and reliable. In order to make the underwriters' participation in this enterprise of any value to the investors, the underwriters must make some reasonable attempt to verify the data submitted to them. They may not rely solely on the company's officers or on the company's counsel. A prudent man in the management of his own property would not rely on them.

RESULT   None of the defendants could rely on the due diligence defense, except the outside directors, who were permitted to rely on the opinion of the auditors as to the audited financial statements.

COMMENTS   The degree of reliance a participating underwriter may place on a principal underwriter remains unclear. The court in *BarChris* summarily noted that the participating underwriters who relied solely on the primary underwriters did not establish due diligence. An SEC release has since suggested that a participating underwriter has met its due diligence requirements if it satisfies itself that the managing underwriter has made the kind of investigation the participant would have performed were it the manager.

The incorporation of an issuer's 1934 Act periodic and special reports in short-form registration statements filed on Form S–3 has truncated the time spent by the issuer and underwriters preparing and reviewing the prospectus. Nevertheless, the SEC and the courts have rejected the argument that integrated disclosure relieves an underwriter or directors of the duty they otherwise would have to conduct an adequate due diligence investigation.[47] The SEC has called on underwriters to use "anticipatory and continuous due diligence programs," such as designating one law firm to act as underwriters' counsel, holding 1934 Act report drafting sessions, and conducting meetings of management, prospective underwriters, and underwriters' counsel shortly after the release of quarterly

CONTINUED

---

47. *See, e.g., In re* WorldCom Sec. Litig., 346 F. Supp. 2d 628, 669 (S.D.N.Y. 2004) (citing the SEC's recommendation that "underwriters concerned about the time pressure created by integrated disclosure . . . 'arrange [their] due diligence procedures over time for the purpose of avoiding last minute delays in an offering environment characterized by rapid market changes.'").

earnings.[48] Although underwriters "are not being asked to duplicate the work of auditors,"[49] they must conduct a reasonable investigation. Moreover:

> If their initial investigation leads them to question the accuracy of financial reporting, then the existence of an audit or a *comfort letter* [in which the accountant describes the review it has conducted of unaudited interim financial statements and of certain numbers in the prospectus] will not excuse the failure to follow through with a subsequent investigation of the matter. If red flags arise from a reasonable investigation, underwriters will have to make sufficient inquiry to satisfy themselves as to the accuracy of the financial statements, and if unsatisfied, they must demand disclosure, withdraw from the underwriting process, or bear the risk of liability.[50]

Directors should also carefully review the 1934 Act reports and conduct a reasonable investigation.[51]

---

48. SEC Release No. 6499, 1983 WL 408321, at 6.

49. *WorldCom*, 346 F. Supp. 2d at 684.

50. *Id.*

51. *See, e.g., In re* Enron Corp. Sec., Derivative & "ERISA" Litig., 258 F. Supp. 2d 576 (S.D. Tex. 2003) (refusing to dismiss claims, as invalid as a matter of law, that the Enron directors were liable under section 11 for misstatements in audited quarterly and annual financial statements incorporated in Enron's registration statement because the reasonableness of the directors' investigation and the reasonable ground for their belief in and reliance on the expertized financial statement or expert opinion were questions of fact that had to be determined by a jury).

Bespeaks Caution Doctrine

According to another defense, the judicially created *bespeaks caution doctrine*, a court may determine that the inclusion of sufficient cautionary statements in a prospectus renders immaterial any misrepresentations and omissions contained therein. The doctrine is based on the proposition that a statement or omission must be considered in context, so accompanying statements may render it immaterial as a matter of law. Cautionary language will render an alleged omission or misrepresentation immaterial only if the cautionary statements are substantive and tailored to specific future projections, estimates, or opinions in the prospectus.

Not all courts have adopted the bespeaks caution doctrine. In 1994, the Fifth Circuit stated:

> [C]autionary language is not necessarily sufficient, in and of itself, to render predictive statements immaterial as a matter of law. . . . The appropriate inquiry is whether, under all the circumstances, the omitted fact or the prediction without a reasonable basis "is one [that] a reasonable investor would consider significant in [making] the decision to invest, such that it alters the total mix of information available about the proposed investment." Inclusion of cautionary language . . . is, of course, relevant to the materiality inquiry. . . . Nevertheless, cautionary language as such is not dispositive of this inquiry.[52]

---

52. Rubinstein v. Collins, 20 F.3d 160 (5th Cir. 1994).

Litigation Reform Act Safe Harbor for Forward-Looking Statements

The Litigation Reform Act provides a statutory safe harbor for certain forward-looking statements by issuers subject to the 1934 Act's reporting requirements and persons acting on their behalf. It is not available for IPOs or offerings by a blank check company, a partnership, a limited liability company, or a direct participation investment program, however. The safe harbor also does not apply to any forward-looking statement included in a financial statement prepared in accordance with generally accepted accounting principles.

The safe harbor provides two independent and alternative grounds for precluding liability. Under the first prong, liability for a written or oral forward-looking statement is precluded if it was identified by the speaker as a forward-looking statement and accompanied by meaningful cautionary statements that identify important factors that could cause actual results to differ materially from those in the statement. Even if the statement does not satisfy these criteria, a second prong precludes liability for a forward-looking statement unless the person who made the statement did so with actual knowledge that the statement was false or misleading. A company is not liable for a forward-looking statement it issues unless the plaintiff proves that the statement was made by, or with the approval of, an executive officer who had actual knowledge that the statement was false or misleading. This safe harbor is discussed further in Chapter 22.

Damages

Section 11 sets forth the damages recoverable for violation of its provisions. If the plaintiff has not sold the securities in question, the recoverable damages are the amount paid for each security minus its value at the time the plaintiff brings the claim. The value at the time the plaintiff brings the claim is usually the market price, unless the market price has been affected by the misrepresentation or omission. If the securities have been sold before the plaintiff brings the claim, the recoverable damages are the amount paid for the securities minus the amount received at sale.

SECTION 12(A)(2) OF THE 1933 ACT

Section 12(a)(2) provides a remedy for any person who purchases a security by means of a misleading prospectus (free writing, preliminary, or final) or oral communication. To establish a section 12(a)(2) claim, the plaintiff must prove that (1) through the mails or other means of interstate commerce, (2) the defendant offered or sold a security, (3) by means of a prospectus or oral communication, (4) that included a material misrepresentation or omission. Materiality under section 12(a)(2) is the same as materiality under section 11. The plaintiff must bring the section 12(a)(2) action within one year from when he or she discovered or should have discovered the fraud, or three years after the sale, whichever is the shorter.

The purchaser may rescind the purchase unless the defendant proves that the depreciation in the value of the security resulted from factors unrelated to the alleged misstatement or omission. If the purchaser has sold the security, he or she generally may recover damages equal to the difference between what was paid and what was received for the security. If the defendant demonstrates that part or all of the decline in the value of the security was caused by factors other than the misstatement or omission alleged in the complaint, then the plaintiff may not recover damages based on that portion of the decline.

Section 12(a)(2) does not require the plaintiff to prove that he or she relied on the misrepresentation or that the defendant acted with *scienter*, that is, an intent to deceive. On the other hand, section 12(a)(2) applies only to those who offer or sell a security.

In *Gustafson v. Alloyd Co.*,[53] the Supreme Court limited section 12(a)(2) to public offerings but did not define the term. The Court held that section 12(a)(2) did not apply to a private placement exempt under section 4(2). The Court reasoned that a stock purchase agreement was not a prospectus under section 10 and thus was not a prospectus for purposes of section 12(a)(2) either.

Gustafson makes it clear that section 12(a)(2) liability extends to fraudulent statements or omissions in statutory prospectuses used in a registered public offering, as well as in documents used to sell securities exempt under section 3. It is not yet clear whether the term "public offering" applies to (1) all offerings not exempted under section 4(2) or (2) only offerings that must be registered under section 5 and offerings of securities exempted under section 3. The latter reading would exclude offerings under Regulation D, Rule 144A, and Regulation S from section 12(a)(2)'s reach. Several courts have held that Rule 144A or Regulation S offerings could be "public" for purposes of section 12(a)(2).[54] Others have reached the opposite result.[55]

Resales by affiliates under Rule 144 should not fall within the scope of section 12(a)(2). However, resales by affiliates that would constitute a distribution under traditional section 2(11) analysis are probably public offerings subject to section 12(a)(2).[56]

Section 12(a)(2) clearly applies to oral communications made in connection with a registered public offering. It would also appear to extend to selling documents, such as a brochure sent to investors along with the statutory prospectus, used in connection with registered offerings.

Who May Be Sued

Section 12(a)(2)'s language relating to who may be liable is identical to that of section 12(a)(1): anyone who "offers or sells" a security by means of a misleading prospectus or oral communication. Accordingly, most courts treat sections 12(a)(1) and 12(a)(2) as the same for the purposes of identifying potential defendants and limit the potential defendants to those in privity with the plaintiff or those who solicited the securities sale for financial gain. Those in privity would include the issuer in direct offerings to the public and underwriters, brokers, and dealers having a direct contractual relationship with the plaintiff in underwritten offerings.

Reasonable Care Defense

Section 12(a)(2) provides a defense of reasonable care. A defendant (including the issuer) will not be liable for a section 12(a)(2) violation if it can prove that it did not know, and in the exercise of reasonable care

---

53. 513 U.S. 561 (1995).

54. *See, e.g.*, Newby v. Enron Corp., 310 F. Supp. 2d 819 (S.D. Tex. 2004); Sloane Overseas Fund v. Sapiens Int'l Corp., 941 F. Supp. 1369 (S.D.N.Y. 1996).

55. *See, e.g., In re* Hayes Lemmerz Int'l, Inc. Equity Sec. Litig., 271 F. Supp. 2d 1007 (E.D. Mich. 2003).

56. *See* Stephen M. Bainbridge, *Securities Act Section 12(2) After the Gustafson Debacle*, 50 Bus. Law. 1231, 1258 (1995).

could not have known, about the misrepresentations or omissions. In contrast to the due diligence defense of section 11, the defense of reasonable care is not spelled out in detail.

Commentators have suggested that reasonable care may require a defendant to undertake an investigation. In *Sanders v. John Nuveen & Co.*,[57] the U.S. Court of Appeals for the Seventh Circuit held that there is no difference between the duties imposed on an underwriter by section 11, which requires a reasonable investigation, and section 12(a)(2). An underwriter, the Seventh Circuit held, must look beyond published data and undertake some investigation of that part of the data that is verifiable. Because the underwriter in *Sanders* did not examine the issuing company's records, contracts, or tax returns, the underwriter did not act with reasonable care.

Liability of Controlling Persons

Section 15 of the 1933 Act imposes liability on anyone who "controls any person liable under Section 11 or 12." Section 15 of the 1933 Act deals only with civil liability for false registration statements and information contained in prospectuses and communications. Section 20(a) of the 1934 Act provides for broader *controlling-person liability*, although it does allow for a "good faith defense." Congress did not define the term "control" in either act but left it for the courts to decide:

> It was thought undesirable to attempt to define the term. It would be difficult if not impossible to enumerate or to anticipate the many ways in which actual control may be exerted. A few examples of these methods used are stock ownership, lease, contract, and agency. It is well known that actual control sometimes may be exerted through ownership of much less than a majority of the stock of a corporation either by the ownership of such stock alone or through such ownership in combination with other factors.[58]

Unfortunately, the courts do not agree as to when there is controlling-person liability. Some courts will find control if the defendant simply had the power to directly or indirectly control or influence corporate policy or the power to control the general affairs of an entity.[59] Others require that the defendant actually participated in the securities violation.[60] The majority of courts will find liability if a person merely possessed the power to control the specific activity that is the basis for the securities violation, regardless of whether that power was exercised,

provided that the person did actually exercise some degree of general control or influence over the entity primarily liable.

A controlling person is usually an officer, director, or major shareholder of the company. The U.S. Court of Appeals for the Eleventh Circuit adopted a variation of the majority rule for establishing controlling-person liability in *Brown v. Enstar Group, Inc.*[61] In that case, Kinder-Care, Inc. (KCI) planned to spin off its wholly owned subsidiary, Kinder-Care Learning Centers, Inc. (KCLC). KCI's chair, Perry Mendel, was also the chair of KCLC. KCLC conducted a public offering, reducing KCI's holdings of KCLC to 87%. In preparation for a further restructuring plan that would completely separate the two entities, Mendel resigned as chair of KCI but stayed on as chair of KCLC. Instead of spinning off the subsidiary, KCI decided to offer KCI shareholders rights to purchase the KCI-owned shares of KCLC stock. KCI prepared and issued a prospectus to its shareholders to that end. After the restructuring was complete, KCI changed its name to The Enstar Group, Inc.

The issue in *Brown* was whether Mendel could be held liable as a controlling person of KCI for alleged omissions and fraud in the prospectus. The Eleventh Circuit held that the trial court correctly dismissed the complaints against Mendel because he "neither possessed nor exercised power over the entity primarily liable."[62] Mendel failed the first half of the following test:

> [A] defendant is liable as a controlling person if he or she had the power to control the general affairs of the entity primarily liable at the time the entity violated the securities laws . . . [and] had the requisite power to directly or indirectly control or influence the specific corporate policy which resulted in the primary liability.[63]

Although the majority rule requires actual participation in the operations of the corporation in general, *Brown* requires only that the defendant have power over the corporation in general, whether or not that power is exercised. If Mendel had still been the chair of KCI's board, he probably would have been liable under the *Brown* rule, but perhaps not under the majority rule, depending on his level of participation in the operations of KCI in general. Notably, in the overwhelming majority of jurisdictions, a high-ranking official who simply signs a fraudulent document will be subject to controlling-person liability.

Neither section 15 of the 1933 Act nor section 20(a) of the 1934 Act imposes strict liability on controlling persons. Controlling persons are not liable under section 15 if they had no knowledge of the facts giving

---

57. 619 F.2d 1222 (7th Cir. 1980), *cert. denied*, 450 U.S. 1005 (1981).

58. H.R. REP. No. 73-1383, § 19 at 26 (1934).

59. *See, e.g.*, Abbott v. Equity Group, Inc., 2 F.3d 613 (5th Cir. 1993).

60. *See, e.g.*, Sharp v. Coopers & Lybrand, 649 F.2d 175 (3d Cir. 1981) (interpreting identical language in section 20(a) of the 1934 Act to require culpable participation in the securities violation).

61. 84 F.3d 393 (11th Cir. 1996).

62. *Id.* at 397 n.6.

63. *Id.* at 396 (internal quotation marks omitted).

rise to the controlled person's alleged liability and had no reasonable ground to believe in the existence of such facts. Controlling persons under section 20(a) have a defense if they acted in good faith and did not directly or indirectly induce the violation. The majority view is that the defendant bears the burden of establishing the defenses of "no knowledge" and no "reasonable ground to believe," or "good faith" and lack of inducement. Generally, these defenses are established by proving that the defendant acted in good faith and took reasonable measures, in light of the situation, to prevent the securities violation.[64]

---

64. SEC v. W.J. Howey Co., 328 U.S. 293 (1946).

CRIMINAL PENALTIES

In addition to having to buy back the securities or pay damages, violators of state or federal securities laws also face criminal penalties, including fines and imprisonment. Under section 24 of the 1933 Act, any person who willfully violates the provisions of the Act shall upon conviction be fined not more than $10,000 or imprisoned for up to five years, or both. A violation can be willful even if the defendant did not know that the transaction at issue involved securities or that the law was being violated. In cases claiming false statements or omissions of material facts, the government need show only that the defendant knew what investors were and were not being told, accompanied by proof that the statement or omissions were objectively material. Penalties under the 1934 Act are set forth in Chapter 14.

THE RESPONSIBLE MANAGER

COMPLYING WITH REGISTRATION REQUIREMENTS

Promoters, entrepreneurs, and managers should be familiar with the *Howey* test. Certain arrangements that normally are not thought of as securities may run afoul of the requirements set forth in the 1933 and 1934 Acts.

Any person offering securities must comply with the registration requirements of the 1933 Act as well as any applicable blue sky laws. This includes start-up companies, as well as large, publicly traded companies. Failure to comply gives the purchaser of the security the right to keep the proceeds if the investment is successful or to return the security to the seller if the investment does not turn out as hoped. Moreover, as explained in Chapter 14, a willful failure to comply is a criminal offense. Even if a security is exempt from registration, it is not exempt from the antifraud provisions of the 1934 Act, as discussed in Chapter 22.

The preparation of a private-placement memorandum is an involved process that requires an intimate knowledge of the statutory requirements. Managers face considerable liability for incorrect or misleading statements, so they should consult experienced counsel when preparing these documents.

Any person involved in a public offering of securities has a legal and ethical duty to ensure that the prospectus contains no misleading statements or omissions. Experts, such as accountants, have a particularly heavy responsibility. The underwriters and outside directors cannot rely passively on the representations of management.

Violations of these rules give rise to both civil and criminal liability.

Managers should work closely with counsel during the waiting period to ensure that there are no gun-jumping problems due to eagerness of the underwriter or the company's public relations department. It is very important that the company not issue an abnormal number of press releases or increase the amount of its advertising prior to the registration going effective. In other words, the manager should make sure that the company remains quiet and does not depart from its ordinary routine.

Securities held by officers, directors, and other affiliates cannot be freely resold even if they were initially issued in a registered offering. They must be sold under Rule 144, subject to its volume and public information requirements, or in a private offering to sophisticated, eligible buyers. Companies must put legends on affiliates' share certificates, issue stop-transfer orders to the transfer agent, or take other such steps as may be reasonable to ensure compliance with these rules.

In addition, managers should ensure that there are no material misstatements or omissions in any other public disclosures (for example, reports on Form 10–K or Form 10–Q or oral statements to the public). Even if there is no legal obligation to disclose a particular fact, once a disclosure is made, the statements contained in it must be truthful and complete.

A MANAGER'S DILEMMA

Putting It into Practice

To IPO or Not to IPO?

Interchange Corporation of Laguna Hills, California, operates a targeted search advertising network. Its primary competitors are Google and Yahoo. Last year, Interchange reported a $60,000 profit on sales of $8.7 million. The company's founders want to take Interchange public.

The IPO market is beginning to heat up again, and many companies in competitive industries need both the capital and the perception of credibility offered by being publicly held. A few relatively recent, high-profile offerings may provide ample coattails on which Interchange's stock could ride. On the other hand, the risks of taking a young company, particularly a technology company, public remain high. The demand for technology companies has not fully rebounded, and the prices of the sixty technology companies that offered stock last year suffered an average decline

of 5% over the same period. Also, it is particularly difficult for investors to predict the success of young companies with inexperienced management teams.

If there is a market for the offering, should Interchange go ahead with the IPO? Should it matter whether Interchange is operating at a loss? Should companies offer their stock publicly simply because the public is willing to purchase it? What other factors should be taken into consideration? Given that Interchange is short on cash, should it offer its outside counsel a 5% equity share in lieu of traditional hourly fees?[65]

---

65. *See* Robert C. Kahrl & Anthony T. Jacono, *"Rush to Riches": The Rules of Ethics and Greed Control in the Dot.Com World*, 2 MINN. INTELL. PROP. REV. 51 (2001), *available at* http://mipr.umn.edu/archive/v2n1/jacono.pdf.

INSIDE STORY

Offerings on the Internet, Crowdfunding, and Issuer Websites

In 1995, Spring Street Brewing Company became the first company to conduct an initial public offering over the Internet.[66] Spring Street raised $1.6 million in an offering exempt under Regulation A. The securities were qualified under the blue sky laws of eighteen states, on the assumption that the majority of potential purchasers resided in those states.

Other small companies have done offerings of up to $1 million under Rule 504 of Regulation D, which does not prohibit general solicitation for offerings of up to $1 million. The JOBS Act requires the SEC to promulgate rules permitting crowdfunding and to eliminate the ban on general solicitation and general advertising in certain Rule 506 offerings sold only to accredited investors and qualified purchasers. Prior to the JOBS Act, the SEC generally required issuers relying on Rules 505 or 506 to make the sites offering the securities accessible only by password and only by investors shown by questionnaire to be accredited.[67]

Companies doing registered offerings can post the registration statement on their website. In addition, NETRoadshow and other firms make audiovisual transmissions of live investor

roadshows available via the Internet. The transmission is not edited for content and contains the oral presentations by management, questions and answers, and charts and graphics presented at the roadshow.[68] As noted earlier, electronic roadshows must be made available to unrestricted audiences.

In 2000, the SEC issued an interpretive release providing guidance on the electronic delivery of documents, website content, and online offerings.[69] The release made it clear that a hyperlink embedded within a prospectus causes the hyperlinked information to be treated as part of the prospectus. In 2008, the SEC provided additional guidance, which made it clear that a company is liable for hyperlinks to third-party information that the issuer was involved in preparing (entanglement) or explicitly or implicitly endorsed or approved (*adoption*).[70] To determine whether the issuer has adopted the hyperlinked information, the key consideration is whether the context of the hyperlink creates a reasonable inference

CONTINUED

---

66. *See* Constance E. Bagley & John Arledge, *SEC Could Ease Offerings of Securities via the Web*, NAT'L L.J., Jan. 13, 1997, at B9.

67. *See* Constance E. Bagley & Robert J. Tomkinson, *Internet Is Seeing Its Share of Securities Offerings*, NAT'L L.J., Feb. 2, 1998, at C3.

68. *Id.* at C4.

69. Use of Electronic Media, SEC Release No. 34-42728 (Apr. 28, 2000), *available at* http://www.sec.gov/rules/interp/interparchive/interparch2000.shtml.

70. Commission Guidance on the Use of Company Web Sites, SEC Release No. 34–58288, 73 Fed. Reg. 45862–01 (Aug. 7, 2008).

that the issuer has approved or enclosed it. "Exit notices" and "intermediate screens" can help clarify the source of the information. Although not determinative, a prominently displayed statement that the issuer is not responsible for third-party information and does not endorse it can help avoid confusion. A disclaimer will not protect an issuer from liability, however, if the issuer knew or was reckless in not knowing that the hyperlinked information was materially false or misleading.

A company is not required to update archived information available on its site as long as it makes it clear that the information is historical and speaks only as of the date of initial publication. To avoid confusion, experts recommend that the issuer prominently indicate the release date on all posted materials and put archived materials in a separate part of the website.[71]

But the fact that information on a website is close to the prospectus does not, by itself, make the information an offer within the meaning of the securities laws. For issuers in the process of registering, however, website contents qualify as written communications subject to section 5 of the 1933 Act and so can constitute gun-jumping if they condition the market.

All companies and individuals offering to sell or selling securities online must be registered brokers in accordance with section 15(b) of the 1934 Act. As long as a broker solicits investors, the broker must be registered, even if the broker merely owns the required software and equipment and leases it to the issuer for purposes of an IPO.[72]

Sometimes graphics, images, or audio material in a document cannot be easily reproduced in electronic form. According to Rule 304, electronic versions of the documents must include a fair and accurate narrative description, tabular representation, or transcript of the omitted material. Any graphic, image, or audio material in the version delivered to investors is deemed part of the electronic version delivered to the SEC. Thus, plaintiffs cannot seek rescissionary damages under section 12(a) on the theory that they purchased securities relying on the printed prospectus and only the securities described in the electronic version (the one delivered to the SEC) were registered.[73] Plaintiffs can, however, seek relief under section 11, alleging either that one version of the prospectus was misleading or that the different versions of the prospectus, taken together, were misleading.[74]

The SEC provides an Internet-based system called Electronic Data Gathering, Analysis, and Retrieval (EDGAR). EDGAR provides companies that are required to file documents with the SEC an efficient and fair way to publicly present those documents. Collection, validation, indexing, acceptance, and forwarding are automated on the site.

---

71. Mark Hoffman & Barbara Nepf, *SEC Issues Guidance Regarding Corporate Websites*, DLA PIPER CORP. GOVERNANCE (Aug. 20, 2008), *available at* http://www.dlapiper.com/sec_guidance_corporate_websites/(last accessed Oct. 1, 2008).

72. *See* In the Matter of Salvani and MainStreetIPO.com, Inc. (July 26, 2001), *available at* http://www.sec.gov/litigation/admin/34-44590.htm.

73. *See* DeMaria v. Andersen, 318 F.3d 170, 175 (2d Cir. 2003).

74. *See id.* at 179.

KEY WORDS AND PHRASES

QUESTIONS AND CASE PROBLEMS

1. Life Partners, Inc. is the leading promoter of interests in viatical settlements, whereby investors purchase at a discount interests in a pool consisting of life insurance benefits of terminal AIDS patients. Is Life Partners engaged in the sale of securities? [*SEC v. Life Partners, Inc.*, 102 F.3d 587 (D.C. Cir. 1996).]

2. Rock Corporation proposes to merge with Quarry, Inc. Quarry will first obtain the approval of its shareholders; then, by operation of law, the Quarry shares will become shares of the survivor corporation, Rock Quarry, Inc. Is it necessary to register the Rock Quarry shares?

   Suppose that prior to the merger Felda Flintstone owned 30% of Quarry's stock that she had acquired three years before in a private placement. She will own only 2% of the Rock Quarry shares and will not be an officer or director of Rock Quarry. May she freely resell her Rock Quarry shares? Would it matter whether they were registered in connection with the merger?

3. Susan Newton, age thirty-eight, founded her own software firm at age fifteen and acquired her stock in an offering under Rule 505 of Regulation D. Newton grew her firm to $20 million in revenues before EBM Corporation purchased it in exchange for EBM common stock in a private placement under section 4(2). Newton is no longer an officer of EBM or active in the day-to-day management, but she sits on the board of directors of EBM and owns 15% of its outstanding common stock. She proposes to sell all of her EBM stock to the public. The stock is actively traded on the Nasdaq Global Market. Are there any restrictions on her ability to sell her EBM shares?

4. In January, Arbor Corporation, a paper company with annual sales of more than $2 billion and assets of more than $5 billion, issued 4 million registered common shares at an average price of $50 per share. In preparing the registration statement, Charles Controller relied on a report by Acme Appraisers, which stated that the company's woodlands were worth $900 million. Acme's report was not included in the registration statement, and Acme was not mentioned in the prospectus. Ollie Olson, the company's newly elected outside director (and Controller's brother-in-law) questioned whether the woodland estimate might be too high. Controller reassured him that "if the numbers are good enough for our CPAs, they're good enough for me."

   In February, the company discovered that the woodland appraisal was overstated by $150 million. Management and the directors were livid about the error. To add to Arbor's problems, a major competitor shocked the industry by announcing that it will double its paper production capacity. Arbor's stock price is now $20 per share.

   Do the shareholders have a basis for a suit? Who can they sue? What problems or defenses will they likely encounter? Assuming that the suit is otherwise successful, how will damages be determined?

5. Duke Distribution, Inc. recently had a public offering of its shares. The company's attorneys, its CPAs, and the underwriter's attorneys worked diligently to meet a tight deadline that management had imposed. Unfortunately, in its haste to meet the deadline, Duke's team failed to include several items in the registration statement. The prospectus failed to mention that while Duke's inventory-to-sales ratio was constant over the past few years, most competitors' ratios had declined significantly over the same period. It also failed to mention that the company leases warehouses from a partnership consisting of three of its directors. The leases require rent that is about 8% higher than the market rate for equivalent facilities. After the IPO, the company engaged in additional transactions with insiders.

   Now the economy has softened and competition has increased. The price of Duke stock has fallen from $15 to $10. Is there a cause of action? Against whom? What are the defenses?

6. SG Ltd., a Dominican corporation, operates a website called StockGeneration. The website's "virtual stock exchange" offers "players" the opportunity to invest real money in eleven "virtual companies," one of which is called the "privileged company." The privileged company, the website proclaims, is "supported by the owners of SG, this is why its value constantly rises; on average at a rate of 10% monthly (this is approximately 215% annually)." Is SG selling securities? [*SEC v. SG Ltd.*, 265 F.3d 42 (1st Cir. 2001).]

7. The price of an IPO is set jointly by the company and the lead underwriters. For at least five decades, studies have

shown that IPOs generally trade on the open market at a price significantly higher than the offering price.

Until the late 1990s, IPOs were underpriced by 5% to 20%, but in the "hot issues" market of 1998 to 2000, IPOs frequently surged to 100% to 200% of the offering price on the first day of trading. In the period from October 1982 to June 1998, the number of shares traded in the first five days after the IPO was on average equal to 85% of the shares offered. In the period from July 1998 to 2000, the number of shares traded in the first five days after IPOs increased to more than 350% of the shares issued.

Would an issuer or investors have any basis for suing the lead underwriters if post-IPO they learned that the underwriter had signaled to potential purchasers that they would be allocated shares in high-demand IPOs only if they were willing to buy additional shares in the aftermarket at prices above the IPO price or to purchase less attractive IPO shares or to pay excessive commissions? If so, how would the issuer or investors prove that they had been damaged by such an undisclosed arrangement? If the arrangement had been disclosed to the issuer, would purchasers in the aftermarket have any claims against the issuer and its officers and directors or against the lead underwriters and their officers and directors? [*Credit Suisse Securities (USA) LLC v. Billing*, 551 U.S. 264 (2007); *In re Initial Public Offering Securities Litigation*, 241 F. Supp. 2d 281 (S.D.N.Y. 2003); *Xpedior Creditor Trust v. Credit Suisse First Boston (USA), Inc.*, 309 F. Supp. 2d 459 (S.D.N.Y. 2003).]

8. The SEC brought a civil enforcement action against Platforms Wireless International Corporation and William Martin, Platforms's former chair and CEO, for selling 17.45 million unregistered securities to the public in violation of the registration provisions of section 5 of the 1933 Act. Platforms had transferred the 17.45 million unregistered shares to Intermedia Video Marketing Company as compensation for consulting services. Intermedia then transferred those shares to François Draper and Benefit Consultants. At the time of the transfers, Martin was an officer of Intermedia and represented himself to be its president and CEO. Soon after receiving the stock from Intermedia, Draper and Benefit Consultants sold the shares to the public for more than $1.7 million.

The defendants claimed that the issuance of shares by Platforms to Intermedia qualified for an exemption under section 4(2) because they took reasonable care to ensure that Intermedia was not an underwriter. They further claimed the sale of the Platforms stock by Draper and Benefit Consultants was exempt under section 4(1) and Rule 144(k).

Under section 4(2) of the 1933 Act, "transactions by an issuer not involving any public offering" are exempted from registration. The parties agreed that the transactions would not qualify for the section 4(2) exemption unless Platforms and Martin complied with Rule 502(d) and took reasonable care to assure that Platforms was not issuing securities to an underwriter within the meaning of section 2(11) of the Act. Under Rule 502(d), "reasonable care" can be demonstrated by:

> (1) Reasonable inquiry to determine if the purchaser is acquiring the securities for himself or herself or for other persons;
>
> (2) Written disclosure to each purchaser prior to sale that the securities have not been registered under the Act and, therefore, cannot be resold unless they are registered under the Act or unless an exemption from registration is available; and
>
> (3) Placement of a legend on the certificate or other document that evidences the securities stating that the securities have not been registered under the Act and setting forth or referring to the restrictions on transferability and sale of the securities.

Platforms and Martin conceded that they did not take any of these three actions but noted that Rule 502(d) does not list these actions as the exclusive method to demonstrate reasonable care. Rather, it creates a safe harbor. Platforms and Martin claimed that their "reasonable care" could be demonstrated by their reliance on opinion letters written by Platforms's general counsel stating that the transfers complied with a safe harbor from 1933 Act registration requirements. The opinion letters stated that counsel had "relied on" the representation Platforms made to the effect that Intermedia was not an affiliate of Platforms.

Are either the section 4(2) or section 4(1) exemptions available to Platforms and Martin? What could they have done differently to have avoided this lawsuit? [*SEC. v. Platforms Wireless International Corp.*, 617 F.3d 1072 (9th Cir. 2010).]

CHAPTER 22

SECURITIES FRAUD AND INSIDER TRADING

INTRODUCTION

MAINTAINING THE INTEGRITY OF THE SECURITIES MARKETS

Many attribute the size and success of the U.S. capital markets to the transparency and perceived fairness of the securities markets, which is a direct result of the registration requirements imposed by the Securities Act of 1933 (the 1933 Act), the periodic reporting requirements imposed by the Securities Exchange Act of 1934 (the 1934 Act), and the antifraud provisions in both acts. Each company that takes advantage of the capital markets has a legal and ethical duty to ensure the integrity of those markets. Securities fraud, in any form, erodes investor confidence and makes it more difficult and expensive for honest businesses to raise capital. As the market turbulence in 2008 demonstrated, investors will abandon the capital markets if they lose confidence in their fairness or integrity.[1] As the U.S. Supreme Court so aptly put it in *Basic, Inc. v. Levinson*, no one "would knowingly roll the dice in a crooked crap game."[2]

The meltdown in the subprime mortgage market in 2007 and 2008 (the subject of the "Inside Story" in Chapter 23) spawned numerous investigations by the Securities and Exchange Commission (SEC) and the Financial Industry Regulatory Authority to determine "who knew what when and what did they disclose to the marketplace along the way."[3] Linda Chatman Thomsen, head of the SEC's enforcement division, indicated that "'tone at the top,' ethical culture, call it whatever you want" would be an important factor in the ultimate outcome of the investigations, including the decision whether to seek criminal sanctions.[4] Areas of investigation include misrepresentations and omissions in offering circulars, prospectuses, SEC reports, and press releases; possible manipulative rumormongering and short selling; insider trading; and conflicts of interest and breaches of fiduciary duty.

For example, the SEC sued the former CEOs of Freddie Mac and Fannie Mae, Richard Syron and Daniel Mudd, respectively, and four other executives for securities fraud after the U.S. Treasury had to pay more than $151 billion to bail out the two government-sponsored mortgage firms. Together, they guarantee more than $5 trillion in home mortgages.[5] The SEC alleged that Fannie Mae had understated its exposure to subprime loans by $40 billion and that Freddie Mac had reported that its single-family guarantee business had exposure of $2 billion to $6 billion related to subprime loans when, in fact, it had exposure of roughly $141 billion.[6] Both Fannie Mae and Freddie Mac agreed to cooperate with the SEC in its litigation against the former executives. They also agreed to the statement of facts presented in the SEC's complaint against the executives, while neither admitting nor denying their own liability.[7]

Public company shareholders, including retirement funds and other institutional investors, have filed a raft of subprime-related private suits alleging (1) securities fraud by issuers and their executives for allegedly misleading investors about the health of their firms; (2) misrepresentations

---

1. Joe Nocera, *A Day (Gasp) Like Any Other*, N.Y. TIMES, Oct. 6, 2008.
2. 485 U.S. 224, 246–47 (1988).
3. Quoting Cheryl Scarboro, associate director of the SEC's division of enforcement. *SEC Pursuing Dozens of Investigations Regarding Subprime Mortgage Industry*, 76 U.S.L.W. 2484, 2485 (2008); *New FINRA Task Force Is Investigating Nine Regulated Firms for Subprime Misdeeds*, 76 U.S.L.W. 2727 (2008).
4. *SEC Pursuing Dozens of Investigations, supra* note 3.
5. Nick Timiraos, *Homing in on Fannie, Freddie*, WALL ST. J., Dec.12, 2011, at A3.
6. SEC v. Syron, 2011 WL 6268191 (S.D.N.Y. Dec. 16, 2011); SEC v. Mudd, 2011 WL 6268192 (S.D.N.Y. Dec. 16, 2011).
7. Press Release, Securities & Exchange Comm'n, Commission Charges Former Fannie Mae And Freddie Mac Executives with Securities Fraud: Companies Agree to Cooperate in SEC Actions (Dec. 16, 2011), *available at* http://www.sec.gov/news/digest/2011/dig121611.htm.

by underwriters, including Deutsche Bank Securities and Bear Stearns, in offering documents; and (3) securities fraud and breach of fiduciary duty by credit rating agencies, including Standard & Poor's and Moody's, that allegedly failed to disclose that they had "assigned excessively high ratings to bonds backed by risky subprime mortgages—including bonds packaged as collateralized debt obligations—which was materially misleading to investors concerning the quality and relative risk of these investments."[8]

CHAPTER OVERVIEW

This chapter focuses on section 10(b) of the 1934 Act and Rule 10b-5, which prohibit the use of any fraudulent, manipulative, or deceptive device in connection with the purchase or sale of a security. It sets forth the seven elements necessary in a Rule 10b-5 securities fraud case and the fraud-on-the-market theory of liability. The chapter discuss the safe harbor for certain forward-looking statements as well as section 17(a) of the 1933 Act, under which the U.S. government can bring fraud claims, and the securities fraud offense added by the Sarbanes-Oxley Act of 2002. It then identifies the legal elements of an insider trading case and discusses SEC Regulation FD's ban on selective disclosure. Finally, it explains the rules for calculating the recoverable profits from short-swing trading and outlines the requirements for reporting by insiders.

OVERVIEW OF ANTIFRAUD PROVISIONS

The principal antifraud provisions of the federal securities laws are sections 11 and 12(a)(2) of the 1933 Act and section 10(b) of the 1934 Act. As explained in Chapter 21, section 11 applies only to registered offerings, and section 12(a)(2) applies only to public offerings not exempt from the 1933 Act's registration requirements. In contrast, section 10(b) of the 1934 Act, which makes it unlawful for any person to use a fraudulent, manipulative, or deceptive device in connection with the purchase or sale of a security, applies to all purchases and sales of securities, regardless of whether they are registered or exempt from registration.

Section 10(b) gives the SEC power to prohibit individuals and companies from engaging in securities fraud by authorizing the SEC to prescribe specific rules for the

protection of investors. The SEC promulgated Rule 10b–5 to encourage disclosure of information relevant to the investing public, to protect investors, and to deter fraud in the securities industry.

Rule 10b–5 also prohibits *insider trading*, that is, trading securities based on material nonpublic information in violation of a duty to the corporation or its shareholders or the source of the information. SEC Rules 10b5–1 and 10b5–2, which are excerpted in Appendix I, clarify certain aspects of insider trading.

Section 16(b) of the 1934 Act regulates "short-swing" trading by insiders of publicly traded companies. In particular, it allows a public corporation to recover the profits earned by any officer or director of the corporation or any person who owns more than 10% of the corporation's securities as a result of purchases and sales, or sales and purchases, of the corporation's securities within a six-month period.

RULE 10B–5

Rule 10b–5 states:

It shall be unlawful for any person, directly or indirectly, by the use of any means or instrumentality of interstate commerce, or of the mails, or of any facility of any national securities exchange,

(1) to employ any device, scheme, or artifice to defraud,

(2) to make any untrue statement of a material fact or to omit to state a material fact necessary in order to make the statements made, in the light of the circumstances under which they were made, not misleading, or

(3) to engage in any act, practice, or course of business which operates or would operate as a fraud or deceit upon any person, in connection with the purchase or sale of any security.

More suits are brought under Rule 10b–5 than under any other provision of securities law, including those, such as sections 11 and 12(a)(2) of the 1933 Act, that explicitly create private rights of action. Although there is some overlap, Rule 10b–5 extends to misconduct not covered by other securities laws. Under Rule 10b–5, managers could be liable for misleading statements contained in any document—such as a press release or a letter to shareholders or a posting on a website—or even a speech to a trade association, as long as the statements were made in a manner reasonably calculated to influence the investing public. In addition, Rule 10b–5 applies to both registered and nonregistered securities.

Since 1946, courts have held that Rule 10b–5 creates an implicit private right of action, giving individual investors the right to sue a violator for damages. Although the Supreme Court in recent decisions has shown increasing hostility toward implied rights of action under other

---

8. *Subprime Mortgage Crisis Generating New Areas of Litigation*, CORP. COUNS. WKLY. (BNA), Nov. 28, 2007, at 368.

provisions of the securities laws, Congress "ratified" the implied private right of action for violations of section 10(b) and Rule 10b–5 in the Private Securities Litigation Reform Act.[9] The Supreme Court has been reluctant to expand the class of persons liable under these provisions, however.[10]

Elements of a Rule 10b-5 Cause of Action

To recover damages from a defendant under Rule 10b–5, a plaintiff must show each of the following elements:

1. The defendant used either an instrumentality of interstate commerce or the mails or a facility of a national securities exchange.

2. The defendant made a statement that either misrepresented or omitted a fact.

3. The fact was of material importance.

4. The misrepresentation or omission was made with *scienter* (culpable state of mind).

5. The statement or omission was made in connection with the purchase or sale of securities.

6. The plaintiff acted in reliance either on the defendant's misrepresentation or on the assumption that the market price of the stock accurately reflected its value.

7. The defendant's misrepresentation or omission caused the plaintiff to suffer losses.

Each element is discussed in a separate section below.

---

9. Stoneridge Inv. Partners, LLC v. Scientific-Atlanta, Inc., 552 U.S. 148 (2008) (citing the reference in 15 U.S.C. § 78u-4(b) to "any private action" arising under the 1934 Act) (Case 22.6).

10. Janus Capital Group, Inc. v. First Derivative Traders, 131 S. Ct. 2296 (2011).

INTERSTATE COMMERCE

Both section 10(b) and Rule 10b–5 apply only to activities involving interstate commerce. The requirement that the defendant used interstate commerce, the mails, or a national securities exchange gives Congress the power to regulate the defendant's conduct under the Commerce Clause of the U.S. Constitution. The requirement is usually easy to satisfy. Use of interstate commerce includes use of a radio broadcast heard in more than one state; use of a newspaper advertisement in a newspaper delivered to more than one state; or use of a telephone wired for interstate calls, even if no interstate calls were actually made. Use of the mails includes sending a letter within a state because the mail is an instrumentality of interstate commerce. Use of a national securities exchange includes use of any facility of such an exchange.

MISSTATEMENT OR OMISSION

A *misstatement* is a misrepresentation of a fact; in other words, a lie. An *omission* is a fact left out of a statement, such that the statement becomes misleading. For purposes of private actions under Rule 10b–5, "the maker of a statement is the person or entity with ultimate authority over the statement, including its content and whether and how to communicate it."[11]

Misstatement

In the following landmark case, a company's attempts to dispel rumors were found to misrepresent the facts.

---

11. *Id.* at 2302.

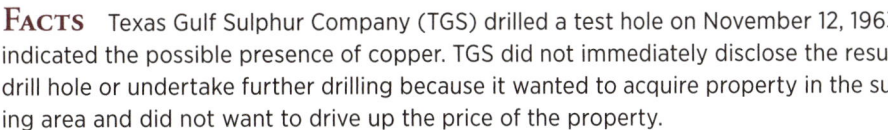

| A CASE IN POINT | *Summary* | Case 22.1 |

SEC v. Texas Gulf Sulphur Co.

United States District Court for the Southern District of New York
312 F. Supp. 77 (S.D.N.Y. 1970),
aff'd, 446 F.2d 1301 (2d Cir. 1971).

FACTS Texas Gulf Sulphur Company (TGS) drilled a test hole on November 12, 1963, which indicated the possible presence of copper. TGS did not immediately disclose the results of its drill hole or undertake further drilling because it wanted to acquire property in the surrounding area and did not want to drive up the price of the property.

On April 12, 1964, in response to rumors about the copper discovery, TGS issued a press release. By this time, the company had confirmed the presence of copper. Preliminary tests indicated that the amount was significant. The press release, however, minimized the importance of the discovery. It said (in part):

> For Immediate Release
>
> TEXAS GULF SULPHUR COMMENT ON TIMMINS, ONTARIO, EXPLORATION NEW YORK, April 12—The following statement was made today by Dr. Charles F. Fogarty, executive vice president of Texas Gulf Sulphur Company, in regard to the company's drilling operations near Timmins, Ontario, Canada. Dr. Fogarty said:
>
> During the past few days, the exploration activities of Texas Gulf Sulphur in the area of Timmins, Ontario, have been widely reported in the press, coupled with rumors

CONTINUED

of a substantial copper discovery there. These reports exaggerate the scale of operations, and mention plans and statistics of size and grade of ore that are without factual basis and have evidently originated by speculation of people not connected with TGS.

The facts are as follows. TGS has been exploring in the Timmins area for six years as part of its overall search in Canada and elsewhere for various minerals—lead, copper, zinc, etc. During the course of this work, in Timmins as well as in Eastern Canada, TGS has conducted exploration entirely on its own, without the participation by others. Numerous prospects have been investigated by geophysical means and a large number of selected ones have been core-drilled. These cores are sent to the United States for assay and detailed examination as a matter of routine and on advice of expert Canadian legal counsel. No inferences as to grade can be drawn from this procedure.

Most of the areas drilled in Eastern Canada have revealed either barren pyrite or graphite without value; a few have resulted in discoveries of small or marginal sulfide ore bodies. Recent drilling on one property near Timmins has led to preliminary indications that more drilling would be required for proper evaluation of this prospect. The drilling done to date has not been conclusive, but the statements made by many outside quarters are unreliable and include information and figures that are not available to TGS.

The work done to date has not been sufficient to reach definite conclusions and any statement as to size and grade of ore would be premature and possibly misleading. When we have progressed to the point where reasonable and logical conclusions can be made, TGS will issue a definite statement to its stockholders and to the public in order to clarify the Timmins project.

The SEC contended that TGS's April 12 release was a misstatement because it left investors with an impression that was contrary to the known facts at the time.

ISSUE PRESENTED   Does a press release giving a misleading impression about the results of a drilling operation violate Rule 10b-5?

SUMMARY OF OPINION   The U.S. District Court for the Southern District of New York acknowledged that the timing of disclosure is a matter for the business judgment of the corporate officers. When a company chooses to issue a press release to respond to spreading rumors regarding its activities, it must, however, describe the true picture at the time of the press release. This should include the basic facts known, or which reasonably should be known, to the drafters of the press release. Such facts are necessary to enable the investing public to make a reasonable appraisal of the existing situation.

Because the press release misled reasonable investors to believe either that there was no ore discovery or that any discovery was not a significant one, TGS violated section 10(b) and Rule 10b-5.

RESULT   TGS violated section 10(b) and Rule 10b-5.

COMMENTS   A company may have excellent reasons to attempt to dispel rumors. TGS, for example, had an interest in keeping the find quiet in order to keep down the acquisition costs of land. Or consider a company involved in merger negotiations that is asked by the press whether there is any reason for unusual trading in its stock. The company may well want to keep the negotiations under wraps for a variety of legitimate reasons. Yet, if it states that it is unaware of any corporate developments, when in fact material negotiations are under way, it runs the risk of Rule 10b-5 liability.[12]

---

12. *See, e.g.*, Basic, Inc. v. Levinson, 485 U.S. 224 (1988) (discussed further below).

A prediction about the future can be a misstatement, but only if the person making the prediction does not believe it at the time. A prediction is not a guarantee, and it does not become a misstatement simply because the facts do not develop as predicted. If there is no reasonable basis for a prediction, however, then it is a misstatement because the person who made it could not honestly have believed it.[13] As discussed later in this chapter, the Private Securities Litigation Reform Act of 1995 (the Litigation Reform Act) contains a safe harbor for certain forward-looking statements.

Omission

It is clear that a company must be careful if it chooses to speak. What if it chooses not to speak?

The general rule is that a company has no general duty under Rule 10b–5 to reveal corporate developments unless the company or its insiders (1) trade in its securities, (2) recommend trading to someone else, or (3) disclose the information as a *tip*—that is, a disclosure made to an individual and withheld from the general public. The fact that information is material does not, in itself, give rise to a duty to disclose.[14] Thus, when a plaintiff alleges fraud under section 10(b) based on nondisclosure, there can be no fraud absent a duty to speak.

The securities laws require that certain information be disclosed in registration statements; annual, quarterly, and special reports; and proxy solicitations. In particular, Management's Discussion and Analysis of Financial Condition and Results of Operations must disclose any known material event or uncertainty that would cause reported financial information not to be necessarily indicative of future operating results or financial condition.[15] Stock exchange rules require that issuers promptly reveal material developments unless there is a business reason not to do so.

Silence or a "no comment" statement in response to rumors will not lead to liability if the company has not previously spoken on the subject and insiders are not trading or tipping. There is a caveat, however: a policy of not commenting on rumors must be adhered to in the face of both true and untrue rumors. If the company always says "no comment" when the rumor is true but provides facts to dispel untrue rumors, then the "no comment" acts as an admission that the rumor is true.

Although keeping silent may be safer under Rule 10b–5, in many cases that will be hard to do. If a corporation's

INTERNATIONAL SNAPSHOT

Under the London Stock Exchange rules, if a listed company's share price moves significantly on the basis of rumor and the rumor is true, the company must disclose the existence of the rumored event. For example, in January 1998, drug powerhouse SmithKline Beecham PLC was required to disclose that it was engaged in merger negotiations with American Home Products after rumors of a deal sent shares of both companies rising.[a] Although there is no numerical threshold for disclosure, a rule of thumb is that a 10% move in the stock triggers the duty to disclose the accuracy of truthful rumors. On the other hand, if the rumors are not true, then the company can continue to say "no comment."

a. Steven Lipin & Sara Calian, *Did U.K.'s Strict Rules Spur Deal?*, WALL ST. J., Feb. 2, 1998, at C1.

stock is traded on rumors of some major development, silence may contribute to disorderly market activity, distrust of company management, and possible abuse by those with access to inside information. Moreover, a blanket "no comment" policy makes it impossible to dispel false but damaging rumors.

Once the company has said something about a particular topic, it has a duty to disclose enough relevant facts so that the statement is not inaccurate, incomplete, or misleading.[16] The statement may be an obligatory one. Or the statement may be voluntary; for example, a company may choose to publicize information about favorable new developments or to respond to unfavorable rumors. Whether the statement is obligatory or voluntary, the company's officials must tell the whole truth with respect to that topic or risk being sued later for a misleading omission.

An omission can occur when a company makes a statement that was true at the time it was made but becomes misleading in light of later events. There is a duty to correct when "a company makes a historical statement [of a material fact] that at the time made, the company believed to be true, but as revealed by subsequently discovered information actually was not."[17] In contrast, the duty to update—which may arise when a statement, reasonable at the time it is made, becomes misleading due to a subsequent event—is more limited.[18] There is no duty to update if the original statement was not material,[19] or "when the original statement was not forward looking and does not contain some factual representation that remains 'alive' in

---

13. *See* Va. Bankshares v. Sandberg, 501 U.S. 1083 (1991) (holding that a statement as to beliefs or opinions may be actionable if the opinion is known by the speaker at the time it is expressed to be untrue or to have no reasonable basis in fact).

14. Backman v. Polaroid Corp., 910 F.2d 10 (1st Cir. 1990).

15. *See* Item 303 of SEC Regulation S–K, Management's Discussion and Analysis of Financial Condition and Results of Operations, 17 C.F.R. § 229.303(a)(3)(ii).

16. *See* Dale E. Barnes, Jr. & Constance E. Bagley, *Great Expectations: Risk Management Through Risk Disclosure*, 1 STAN. J.L. BUS. & FIN. 155 (1994).

17. Stransby v. Cummins Engine Co., 51 F.3d 1329 (7th Cir. 1995). Corrective disclosures do not need to be fact-for-fact corrections as long as they disclose the truth obscured by the fraudulent statements. Alaska Elec. Pension Fund v. Flowserve Corp., 572 F.3d 221 (5th Cir. 2009).

18. *See, e.g., In re* Time Warner, Inc. Sec. Litig., 9 F.3d 259 (2d Cir. 1993).

19. Hillson Partners Ltd. P'ship v. Adage, Inc., 42 F.3d 204 (4th Cir. 1994).

the minds of investors as a continuing representation."[20] In contrast, if investors are reasonably relying on the previous statements, the company can be liable for failing to disclose the new information. For example, a company incurs a duty to update its financial projections when a projection changes or the company discovers that the projection was incorrect from the outset. A "pattern of disclosure" does not bind a corporation to continue disclosure in that manner, however.[21] Thus, even though MEMC Electronic Materials had a history of providing timely updates about production disruptions, the U.S. Court of Appeals for the Eighth Circuit held that the company was not liable for failing to disclose production problems at two of its plants for over a month.

The following case addressed the issue of whether a company has a duty to update or correct statements that have become misleading in light of subsequent events.

20. *In re* Int'l Bus. Machs. Corp. Sec. Litig., 163 F.3d 102 (2d Cir. 1998). *See also In re* Burlington Coat Factory Sec. Litig., 114 F.3d 1410 (3d Cir. 1997).

21. Minneapolis Firefighters' Relief Ass'n v. MEMC Elec. Materials, Inc., 641 F.3d 1023 (8th Cir. 2011).

| A CASE IN POINT | *Summary* | Case 22.2 |

Weiner v. Quaker Oats Co.

United States Court of Appeals for the Third Circuit
129 F.3d 310 (3d Cir. 1997).

Facts   On November 2, 1994, the Quaker Oats Company and Snapple Beverage Corporation announced that Quaker would acquire Snapple in a tender offer and merger transaction for $1.7 billion in cash. The market disapproved of the deal. Subsequent to the announcement, Quaker's stock price fell $7.375 per share—approximately 10% of the stock's value.

To finance the acquisition, Quaker had obtained $2.4 billion of credit from a banking group led by NationsBank Corporation. The Snapple acquisition nearly tripled Quaker's debt, from approximately $1 billion to approximately $2.7 billion. The acquisition also increased Quaker's total debt-to-total capitalization ratio to approximately 80%.

Over the course of the year prior to its acquisition of Snapple, Quaker had announced in several public documents the company's guideline for debt-to-equity ratio and its expectations for earnings growth. The announcements formed the basis for the plaintiffs' action.

In its 1993 Annual Report (dated October 4, 1993), Quaker stated that "our debt-to-total capitalization ratio at June 30, 1993 was 59 percent, up from 49 percent in fiscal 1992. For the future, our guideline will be in the upper-60 percent range." Quaker's president reiterated this "guideline" in a letter contained in the same Annual Report. Quaker's Form 10–Q for the quarter ended September 30, 1993 (filed with the SEC in November 1993) repeated the total debt-to-total capitalization ratio guideline.

In its 1994 Annual Report (dated September 23, 1994), Quaker stated that "we are committed to achieving real earnings growth of at least 7 percent over time." In addition, the report noted that Quaker's total debt-to-total capitalization ratio was 68.8%, "in line with our guideline in the upper-60 percent range."

Negotiations between Quaker and Snapple apparently began in the spring of 1994. By early August 1994, Quaker had advised Snapple that it was interested in pursuing a merger of the two companies and had commenced a due diligence investigation. As noted, the merger was completed in November of that year.

The gist of the plaintiffs' complaint was that, even if Quaker's announcements about its total debt-to-total capitalization ratio and projected earnings growth were true at the time they were made, Quaker still had a duty to update or correct those statements if it knew they had become materially misleading in light of subsequent events. The plaintiffs alleged that (1) Quaker knew those statements were materially misleading as soon as it was reasonably certain the Snapple merger would be finalized, and (2) Quaker had such certainty at least sometime prior to its formal announcement of the merger on November 2, 1994.

The district court dismissed both portions of the plaintiffs' claim, on the basis that neither Quaker's statements relating to its total debt-to-total capitalization ratio nor its statements relating to its projected earnings growth were material. The plaintiffs appealed.

CONTINUED

ISSUE PRESENTED Under what circumstances do a corporation and its officers have a duty to update, or at least not to repeat, particular projections regarding the corporation's financial condition (for example, total debt-to-total capitalization ratio or earnings growth projections)?

SUMMARY OF OPINION The U.S. Court of Appeals for the Third Circuit began by explaining that the plaintiffs' claims related to the debt–equity ratio were claims of nondisclosure. In general, section 10(b) and Rule 10b–5 do not impose a duty on defendants to correct prior statements—particularly statements of intent—as long as those statements were true when made. However, "[t]here can be no doubt that a duty exists to correct prior statements, if the prior statements were true when made but misleading if left unrevised." To avoid liability in such circumstances, the company must disseminate notice of its change of intent in a "timely fashion."

The court first addressed the plaintiffs' claim that the defendants' statements in the months leading up to the merger improperly omitted mention of the planned increase in the total debt-to-total capitalization ratio guideline. Specifically, the court looked to the defendants' repeated claim of an "upper 60-percent range" total debt-to-total capitalization ratio guideline even after the merger with Snapple became a probability. Ultimately, the court found that a reasonable fact finder could determine that Quaker's statements would have been "material" to a reasonable investor and, hence, that Quaker had a duty to update such statements when they became unreliable.

In performing its analysis, the court of appeals invoked the standard of materiality of an omitted statement as set forth in *Basic, Inc. v. Levinson*: "An omitted fact is material if there is a substantial likelihood that a reasonable shareholder would consider it important in deciding how to [proceed]."[22] By including the total debt-to-total capitalization ratio guideline in three separate reports, Quaker may well have created the reasonable understanding among investors that the ratio guideline was a number to which Quaker attached "considerable significance." Furthermore, it would have been "entirely reasonable" for an investor to assume that the company would make another prediction if it expected the ratio to change significantly in the ensuing year. Because the alleged omissions were not "so obviously unimportant to an investor that reasonable minds cannot differ on the question of materiality," the district court erred when it ruled them inactionable as a matter of law.

The Third Circuit rejected the district court's reasoning that requiring Quaker to disclose the possibility that it might seek loans to finance an acquisition (and thus experience a higher total debt-to-total capitalization ratio) would essentially require disclosure of the acquisition negotiations. The court explained that Quaker had the ability to communicate a projected increase in its debt ratio without alerting investors to the impending merger. Quaker had previously demonstrated this ability when it announced plans to increase the ratio substantially in its 1993 Annual Report for a variety of reasons unrelated to acquiring other companies.

The court then turned to plaintiffs' claim based on defendants' projections of earnings growth. The court first examined the statement of Quaker's CEO at the August 1994 public meeting that Quaker was "confident of achieving at least 7% real earnings growth" in fiscal 1995. This statement, explained the court, was not a vague expression of optimism but instead a specific figure representing a defined period. Furthermore, the statement contained no explicit "cautionary language," which would have rendered the statement immaterial as a matter of law.

However, for the statement to have a deleterious effect, it would have had to remain "alive" in the market, unmodified, until the merger was announced. The court focused on a second statement made in Quaker's 1994 Annual Report, more than five weeks prior to the merger announcement, that "we are committed to achieving a real earnings growth of at least 7 percent *over time*." According to the court, no reasonable investor would find material a prediction of

CONTINUED

---

22. 485 U.S. 224 (1988).

7% growth followed by the qualifier "over time." Because no reasonable finder of fact could conclude that the projection influenced prudent investors, that claim was properly dismissed.

RESULT   The claim relating to Quaker's total debt-to-total capitalization ratio guideline was reinstated and remanded to the district court for trial; the dismissal of the claim relating to Quaker's earnings growth projections was affirmed.

CRITICAL THINKING QUESTIONS

1. Given that a wealth of data compiled by market analysts demonstrates that, over the long run, stock prices follow corporate earnings, which piece of information would you find more important when deciding whether to buy or sell Quaker stock: (a) forecasts relating to the company's total debt-to-total capitalization ratio or (b) forecasts relating to the company's real earnings growth?

2. Would an announcement by Quaker that it was contemplating increasing its total debt-to-total capitalization ratio have "tipped the market" to a pending acquisition?

There is a duty to disclose the results of product safety tests if they make previously disclosed test results false. For example, A.H. Robins Company, a pharmaceutical manufacturer, reported in 1970 that its Dalkon Shield intrauterine contraceptive device was safe and effective. In 1972, internal studies indicated that the Dalkon Shield was not as safe or effective as originally reported.[23] The U.S. Court of Appeals for the Second Circuit held that Robins's omission of the new information rendered its earlier statements misleading. Because investors were still relying on the statement that the Dalkon Shield was safe, the company had a duty to correct that statement once it learned that it was inaccurate.

Statements by Third Parties and Entanglement

Even if the company itself did not publish the misleading projection, make the statement, or start the rumor, it may nevertheless have a duty to reveal all of the facts regarding the issue. This is the case when the company is so entangled with the third party's statement that the statement can be attributed to the company. The company is then responsible for making sure that the statement is accurate. For example, if a company makes it a practice to review and correct drafts of analysts' forecasts, then the company implicitly represents that the corrected forecast is in accord with the company's view, and it has a duty to reveal all facts necessary to ensure that the analyst's report is not misleading.[24] Similarly, a company's distribution of copies of an analyst's report to investors or other members of the public or the posting of an analyst's report on the company's website may be construed as an implied representation that the information in the report is accurate or reflects the company's views.

MATERIAL FACT

A buyer or seller of stock cannot recover damages just because an executive misrepresented or omitted a fact about the company. The fact must be material. As explained in Chapter 21, a fact is material if a reasonable investor would consider it important in deciding how to act. Materiality is judged at the time of the misstatement or omission. Materiality is not affected by the intent of the party making the statement. There can be liability even if the manager did not know that the omitted or misrepresented fact came within the legal definition of a material fact.

In the following case, the Supreme Court gave further guidance on what constitutes a material fact.

---

23. Ross v. A.H. Robins Co., 607 F.2d 545 (2d Cir. 1979).

24. *See, e.g.*, Stack v. Lobo, 903 F. Supp. 1361 (N.D. Cal. 1995).

A CASE IN POINT	*Summary*	Case 22.3

Matrixx Initiatives v. Siracusano

Supreme Court of the United States
131 S. Ct. 1309 (2011).

FACTS   Matrixx Initiatives is an over-the-counter pharmaceutical company that sells an over-the-counter cold remedy through its wholly owned subsidiary Zicam LLC. Between 1999 and 2003, Matrixx received several complaints from physicians and Zicam consumers alleging a connection between the use of Matrixx's leading product, Zicam Cold Remedy, and loss of smell (anosmia). Even after being notified of a presentation at the American Rhinologic Society describing eleven Zicam users who lost their sense of smell after using the product,

CONTINUED

Matrixx made announcements that Zicam was "poised for growth in the upcoming cough and cold season" and expected that revenues would "be up in excess of 50% and that earnings, per share for the full year [would] be in the 25 to 30 cent range." In an SEC report, Zicam reported the potential "material adverse effect" that could result from consumer complaints of anosmia but did not disclose that two consumers had already sued.

In early 2004, Matrixx's stock price fell by about 22% when Dow Jones Newswires reported that, in light of at least three lawsuits, the Food and Drug Administration (FDA) was investigating the complaints that Zicam may have caused some users to lose their sense of smell. Matrixx revived its stock price with a press release stating that there had been no reports of loss of smell in clinical trials of Zicam and that anosmia can result from the common cold. The stock price fell again when a *Good Morning America* special reported that more than a dozen Zicam users had lost their sense of smell. Matrixx reported to the SEC that, after meeting with "physicians and scientists to review current information on smell disorders," it determined that "there is insufficient scientific evidence at this time to determine if [Zicam], when used as recommended, affects a person's ability to smell." A few weeks later, Matrixx stated to the press that it would begin "animal and human studies to further characterize these post-marketing complaints."

Shareholders brought a class action against Matrixx alleging that the firm violated Rule 10b–5 and section 10(b) when it made misleading statements that failed to disclose reports of the possible link between Zicam and anosmia in an effort to maintain artificially high prices for Matrixx securities. Matrixx argued that the adverse event reports were not material information as no statistical significance was shown between these reports of anosmia and use of the Zicam product. Plaintiffs countered that materiality should be determined by the "total mix of information" test.

ISSUE PRESENTED   If an issuer knows that information about possible side effects of a drug could affect its stock price, does it have an obligation to disclose the information even if there is no statistical link between use of the drug and the adverse effect?

SUMMARY OF OPINION   The U.S. Supreme Court began by rejecting Matrixx's argument that a bright-line rule should be used when assessing the materiality of adverse events associated with Zicam's products. A categorical rule, reasoned the Court, would "artificially exclud[e]" information that "would otherwise be considered significant to the trading decision of a reasonable investor." The Court further rejected Matrixx's assumption that statistical evidence was the only valid measure of causation. Statistically significant data are not always available, and ethical considerations may arise from performing clinical trials in order to obtain statistically significant evidence.

In support of its reasoning, the Court pointed to the fact that the FDA often relies on evidence other than statistically significant data in assessing causation. For instance, the FDA considers the "strength of the association," "temporal relationship of product use and the event," "consistency of findings across available data sources," and "degree of benefit the product provides, including availability of other therapies," among other factors. Moreover, the FDA may make regulatory decisions against drugs on evidence giving rise to only a suspicion of causation.

Just as the FDA and other regulators act on the basis of evidence that is not statistically significant, the Court concluded, in certain cases reasonable investors would as well. In line with this reasoning, the Court adopted the "total mix of information" test as advocated by the plaintiffs. Under this test, the question is whether a *reasonable* investor would have viewed undisclosed information "as having *significantly* altered the 'total mix' of information made available." The mere existence of adverse reports will not satisfy this standard; instead, the court can look to the "source, content, and context of the reports."

Applying the "total mix" standard, the Court concluded that the plaintiffs had adequately pleaded materiality. Matrixx had received reports from three medical professionals and

CONTINUED

researchers about eleven different cases of consumers losing their sense of smell after using Zicam. In addition, several product liability suits had been brought against the company suggesting a causal link between Zicam use and anosmia. The company was also aware of the presentation given to the American Rhinologic Society, which suggested a temporal relationship between Zicam use and the onset of anosmia. Despite being aware of this evidence, Matrixx did not perform studies of its own and thus had no basis to reject the adverse findings in its subsequent press releases.

The Court further found that consumers likely would have viewed the risk associated with Zicam use as substantially outweighing the benefit of using the product, particularly in light of the existence of many alternative products on the market. Considering that Zicam Cold Remedy accounted for 70% of Matrixx's sales, the Court concluded that the plaintiffs had alleged facts suggesting a significant risk to the commercial viability of Zicam.

The Court next rejected Matrixx's argument that it did not act with the requisite level of scienter (knowledge) in failing to disclose its knowledge of adverse events to investors. According to the Court, a plaintiff must prove that the defendant acted with "deliberate recklessness" in order to satisfy the scienter requirement. In this case, the inference that Matrixx acted recklessly was "as compelling, if not more compelling, than the inference that it simply thought the reports did not indicate anything meaningful about adverse reactions." The allegations raised by the plaintiffs, when taken collectively, gave rise to a "cogent and compelling" inference that Matrixx chose not to disclose the adverse reports not because it believed they were meaningless, but because it understood their likely effect on the market.

RESULT   Matrixx's motion to dismiss the complaint was denied. The plaintiffs had stated a valid claim under Rule 10b–5 and section 10(b), so their case could proceed to trial.

Although it is not always possible to predict which facts a court will consider material, certain matters are almost always considered material. For example, any statements about the earnings, distributions, or assets of a company (unless the misrepresentation is inadvertent and concerns a minor amount) are material. In 1999, the SEC accounting staff cautioned companies and their auditors against using "rules of thumb" to determine whether errors in the financial statements are material.[25] Even if two errors net out to zero, they can still be material. For example, an overstatement of revenues can be material even if it is accompanied by an overstatement of cost of goods sold. The SEC staff also stated that any intentional misstatement of a number in the financial statements is, by definition, material.

Significant facts about a parent or a subsidiary are usually material. These include the discovery of embezzlement or falsification of financial statements, an impending tender offer, or the loss of a manufacturer's major customer. Other facts that are probably material include inability to obtain supplies, increased costs of supplies, a decision to close a plant, information regarding the outlook in the industry, an intention to market a new product or cease marketing an old one, potential liability for damages in a lawsuit, a major discovery or product development, cost overruns, a change in management or compensation of corporate officers, and an increase in real estate taxes. As

this list illustrates, a material fact is any fact that is likely to affect the market value of the company's stock.

The Supreme Court has recognized that for contingent or speculative events, such as negotiations regarding a potential merger, it can be difficult to tell whether a reasonable investor would consider the omitted fact material at the time. The Court has declined to adopt a bright-line rule, however; materiality is a fact-specific determination.[26] If a misstatement or omission concerns a future event, such as a potential merger, its materiality will depend on a balancing of the probability that the event will occur and the anticipated magnitude of the event in light of the totality of the company's activity.

Thus, the materiality of preliminary merger discussions in any particular case depends on the facts. Generally, to assess the probability that the event will occur, a fact finder will look to indicia of interest in the transaction at the highest corporate levels. Without attempting to catalog all such possible factors, the Court has noted by way of example that board resolutions, instructions to investment bankers, and actual negotiations between principals or other intermediaries may serve as indicia of interest.[27] To assess the magnitude of the transaction to the issuer of the securities allegedly manipulated, a fact finder will consider such facts as the size of the two corporate entities and of the potential premiums over market value. No particular event

---

25. Staff Accounting Bulletin No. 99, 1999 WL 1123073 (SEC Aug. 12, 1999).

26. Basic, Inc. v. Levinson, 485 U.S. 224 (1988).
27. *Id.*

or factor short of closing the transaction is either necessary or sufficient by itself to render merger discussions material.

Vague statements of corporate optimism that are not capable of objective verification and mere puffing are immaterial as a matter of law because reasonable investors would not rely on them in making investment decisions.[28] For example, the U.S. Court of Appeals for the Second Circuit characterized a statement made on October 15, 1992, by Jim Clippard, the director of investor relations of International Business Machines Corporation (IBM), that "we're not—despite your anxiety—concerned about being able to cover the dividend for quite a foreseeable time" as an immaterial expression of optimism, not a guarantee, because he qualified it by noting that "this is a relatively short-term period of economic difficulty we're going through. And we think that we can ride through this with no problem [whatsoever] as far as [the] dividend is concerned."[29] The court held that there was no duty to *correct* the statement when the CFO concluded in late November 1992 that the dividend was likely to be cut because, at the time the statement was made (October 15, 1992), IBM did not have a plan or need to alter the dividend. The court also held that "there is no duty to *update* vague statements of optimism or expressions of opinion." (Emphasis added.) In another case, however, a prediction that the company "expects . . . a net income of approximately $1.00 a share" for the fiscal year that would close in two months was held to be a material statement.[30]

Bespeaks Caution Doctrine

As explained in Chapter 21, under the judicially developed *bespeaks caution doctrine*, a court may determine that the inclusion of sufficient cautionary statements in a document renders immaterial any misrepresentation and omission contained therein. The doctrine applies only to projections, estimates, and other forward-looking statements that are

---

ethical consideration

Managers of companies frequently act as promoters, describing the company's products to the press and the public in an aggressive, upbeat manner. It is reasonable to expect them to engage in a certain amount of puffing and exaggeration. Are these exaggerations ethically justifiable as long as they do not violate the securities laws?

accompanied by precise cautionary language that adequately discloses the risks involved. The cautionary language must relate to the specific information that the plaintiffs allege is misleading[31] and reflect what the speaker knows or strongly suspects. As one judge commented, "The doctrine of bespeaks caution provides no protection to someone who warns his hiking companion to walk slowly because there might be a ditch ahead when he knows with near certainty that the Grand Canyon lies one foot away."[32]

Unlike the safe harbor provided in the Litigation Reform Act, the bespeaks caution doctrine applies to forward-looking statements in any context, including initial public offerings. The legislative history of the Litigation Reform Act (which is discussed further below) makes it clear that Congress did not intend its statutory safe-harbor provisions to replace the judicial bespeaks caution doctrine or to foreclose further development of that doctrine by the courts.

SCIENTER

Rule 10b–5 does not impose liability for innocent misstatements or omissions. The misstatements or omissions must be made with scienter, that is, a mental state embracing the intent to deceive, manipulate, or defraud. Intent to deceive means that the defendant says something he or she believes is untrue with the expectation that others will rely on the statement, or that the defendant omits a fact in the hope that the omission will cause others to misunderstand what he or she does say. Scienter is more than mere negligence or lack of care.

The Litigation Reform Act requires the plaintiff to plead with particularity specific facts giving rise to a "strong inference" that the defendant acted with scienter. The Supreme Court clarified this pleading requirement in the following case.

---

28. *See, e.g.,* Raab v. Gen. Physics Corp., 4 F.3d 286 (4th Cir. 1993) (holding that statements in annual report that company expected 10% to 30% growth rate over the next several years and was "poised to carry the growth and success of 1991 well into the future" were immaterial puffing); San Leandro Emergency Med. Group Profit Sharing Plan v. Philip Morris Cos., 75 F.3d 801 (2d Cir. 1996) (holding that statement that company was "optimistic" about its earnings in 1993 and that it should deliver income growth consistent with its historically superior performance was mere puffery and lacked the sort of definite positive projections that might require later correction).

29. *In re* Int'l Bus. Machs. Corp. Sec. Litig., 163 F.3d 102 (2d Cir. 1998).

30. Marx v. Computer Scis.Corp., 507 F.2d 485 (9th Cir. 1974).

31. *See, e.g.,* Grossman v. Novell, Inc., 120 F.3d 1112 (10th Cir. 1997).

32. *In re* Prudential Sec., Inc. P'ships Litig., 930 F. Supp. 68, 72 (S.D.N.Y. 1996).

A CASE IN POINT	*Summary*	Case 22.4

Tellabs, Inc. v. Makor Issues & Rights

Supreme Court of the United States
549 U.S. 1276 (2007).

FACTS After Tellabs, Inc., a fiber optics equipment manufacturer, announced that demand for its TITAN 5500 and TITAN 6500 switching systems had declined and lowered its revenue forecasts, its stock price dropped sharply. The plaintiffs sued, alleging that Tellabs's CEO had misled investors when he misrepresented that demand for its products was strong. The CEO

CONTINUED

did not sell any Tellabs's securities during the period in question. The district court dismissed the complaint, which contained allegations from twenty-seven anonymous sources. The U.S. Court of Appeals for the Seventh Circuit reversed after concluding that the complaint was sufficient to create a strong inference of scienter because a reasonable person could infer scienter from the facts alleged. Tellabs appealed.

ISSUES PRESENTED   What must a plaintiff allege to meet the heightened pleading standards for scienter under the Litigation Reform Act? Can fraud be pleaded with sufficient particularity if the plaintiff relies on unnamed confidential sources?

SUMMARY OF OPINION   The U.S. Supreme Court acknowledged that Congress did not clearly define what was required to create a "strong inference" of scienter, but reasoned that the phrase should be interpreted in a workable manner that would promote the Reform Act's goal of deterring "frivolous, lawyer-driven litigation, while preserving investors' ability to recover on meritorious claims." After analyzing the ordinary meaning of the word "strong," the Court concluded that a strong inference must be more than merely "reasonable" or "permissible." It has to be "powerful," "cogent and compelling." Thus, a complaint will survive a motion to dismiss "only if a reasonable person would deem the inference of scienter cogent and at least as compelling as any opposing inference one could draw from the facts alleged." The Court made it clear that no single factor is determinative and rejected the defendant CEO's assertion that he could not have had scienter because he sold no stock during the period of alleged fraud. Instead, the significance to be ascribed to the lack of sales, or any other single fact, "depends on the entirety of the complaint."

RESULT   The Seventh Circuit's ruling was vacated, and the case was remanded to the appeals court to determine whether the complaint satisfied the stricter pleading standards set forth by the Supreme Court. If it did not, then the case would be dismissed.

COMMENTS   On remand, the Seventh Circuit adhered to its earlier finding that the plaintiffs had adequately pleaded a strong inference of scienter.[33] In an opinion by Judge Richard Posner, the court concluded that it is "conceivable, yes, but it is exceedingly unlikely" that the false statements "were the result of merely careless mistakes at the management level based on false information fed it from below, rather than of an intent to deceive or a reckless indifference to whether the statements were misleading." The court noted that the TITAN 5500 and 6500 were the company's key products and that they "were to Tellabs as Windows XP and Vista are to Microsoft." Moreover, almost all the false statements quoted in the complaint were made by the CEO, who sat at the "top of the corporate pyramid." The court found it "very hard to credit" the defendants' claim that no member of senior management involved in authorizing "the public statements knew they were false" and stated that the defendants had failed to tell a "plausible story" that might "dispel our incredulity."

---

33. Makor Issues & Rights Ltd. v. Tellabs Inc., 513 F.3d 702 (7th Cir. 2008).

In *Higginbotham v. Baxter International Inc.*,[34] the U.S. Court of Appeals for the Seventh Circuit ruled that information from anonymous sources must be discounted when considering whether there are plausible competing inferences: "Perhaps these confidential sources have axes to grind. Perhaps they are lying. Perhaps they don't even exist." Although such statements are not to be ignored, usually the discount will be "steep."[35] In *South Ferry LP #2 v. Killinger*,[36] the U.S. Court of Appeals for the Ninth

Circuit held that an allegation that key officials know facts critical to the company's "core operations" is "usually," but not always, insufficient in and of itself to create a strong inference of scienter.

Recklessness

The U.S. Supreme Court acknowledged in *Tellabs* that there is a split in the circuits on whether recklessness is sufficient for a finding of scienter, but it declined to resolve the issue. On remand, the Seventh Circuit equated scienter with intent to deceive or recklessness.

In a case involving Silicon Graphics, the U.S. Court of Appeals for the Ninth Circuit held that the Litigation

---

34. 495 F.3d 753 (7th Cir. 2007).
35. *Id.*
36. 542 F.3d 776 (9th Cir. 2008).

Reform Act precludes liability under section 10(b) for mere recklessness.[37] Instead, a "heightened form of recklessness, i.e., deliberate or conscious recklessness, at a minimum, is required to establish a strong inference of intent." In *Matrixx Initiatives v. Siracusano*,[38] the Supreme Court assumed, without deciding, that deliberate recklessness is sufficient to establish scienter because the defendant did not challenge that aspect of the decision by the U.S. Court of Appeals for the Ninth Circuit on appeal.

The U.S. Court of Appeals for the Second Circuit held that recklessness is sufficient for a showing of scienter in *Kasaks v. Novak*.[39] It defined reckless conduct as "conduct which is 'highly unreasonable' and which represents 'an extreme departure from the standards of ordinary care . . . to the extent that the danger was either known to the defendant or so obvious that the defendant must have been aware of it.'" Under certain circumstances, a finding of recklessness can be based on "facts demonstrating that defendants failed to review or check information that they had a duty to monitor, or ignored obvious signs of fraud," but "[c]orporate officials need not be clairvoyant; they are only responsible for revealing those material facts reasonably available to them." Thus, plaintiffs cannot just allege "fraud by hindsight." In addition, "as long as the public statements are consistent with reasonably available data, corporate officials need not present an overly gloomy or cautious picture of current performance and future prospects."

To avoid liability, officers should investigate what the facts are before making any statement. Managers should make no statement unless they in good faith believe it to be true. The investigation must be fairly thorough. At least in the Second Circuit, an officer may be liable for misrepresenting facts that he or she should have been aware of, even if the officer was not in fact aware of them. For example, directors may be deemed to have knowledge of facts in the corporate books regardless of whether they have actually examined the books.

These tough pleading requirements make it more important than ever for insiders to avoid trading while in possession of material nonpublic information. Plaintiffs can be expected to claim that insiders who sold before the announcement of bad news knew of the impending negative developments and sold their stock while the market price was artificially high, thereby "cashing in" on their alleged misrepresentations and omissions.[40] This arguably creates an inference of fraud.

For example, the U.S. Court of Appeals for the Ninth Circuit characterized Oracle CEO Larry Ellison's sale of $900,000 of Oracle stock approximately one month prior to the announcement of lower-than-expected sales as "suspicious" and ruled that the unusual stock sales supported a strong inference of scienter.[41] Ellison had not sold any Oracle stock in the previous five years. Although Ellison sold only 2.1% of his Oracle stock, the court reasoned that "where, as here, stock sales result in a truly astronomical figure, less weight should be given to the fact that they may represent a small portion of the defendant's holdings." Although the sales, taken alone, may not have created a strong inference of scienter, when they were coupled with (1) evidence that Oracle maintained an internal database of sales that was monitored by top executives, (2) Oracle customers' billing and payment histories that were corroborated by a former Oracle senior manager and showed improper revenue accounting, and (3) the Oracle executives' detail-oriented management style, the plaintiffs had made allegations that in their totality created a strong inference that Oracle and its top three executives acted with scienter. Characterizing this as "far from a cookie-cutter complaint," the court concluded by stating: "The PSLRA [Litigation Reform Act] was designed to eliminate frivolous or sham actions, but not actions of substance."

It is not yet clear how the U.S. Supreme Court will rule on this issue. Until there is a definitive ruling, managers and companies are well advised to assume that insider trading shortly before the announcement of bad news can create an inference of fraud sufficient to satisfy the Litigation Reform Act's pleading requirements.

IN CONNECTION WITH THE PURCHASE OR SALE OF ANY SECURITY

Rule 10b–5 requires that the conduct occur "in connection with the purchase or sale of any security." This requirement defines both those who can sue and those who can be sued under Rule 10b–5.

The U.S. Supreme Court has made it clear that only persons who actually purchase or sell securities can sue under Rule 10b–5. Persons who have not purchased (or sold) cannot sue on the theory that they would have purchased (or sold) had they known the true facts. Thus, liability under Rule 10b–5 does not extend to the whole world of potential investors but only to those who actually buy or sell stock after a misstatement or omission.

---

37. *In re* Silicon Graphics, Inc. Sec. Litig., 183 F.3d 970 (9th Cir. 1999).

38. 131 S. Ct. 1309 (2011) (Case 22.3).

39. 216 F.3d 300 (2d Cir. 2000). *Accord* Greebel v. FTP Software, Inc., 194 F.3d 185 (1st Cir. 1999) (holding that the Litigation Reform Act did not alter preexisting scienter requirements for securities fraud cases). *Cf. In re* Comshare, Inc. Sec. Litig., 183 F.3d 542 (6th Cir. 1999) (holding that allegations giving rise to a strong inference of recklessness are sufficient to pass muster but that facts showing a mere motive and opportunity to commit fraud are not).

40. *See* Dale E. Barnes, Jr. & Karen Kennard, *Greater Expectations: Risk Disclosure Under the Private Securities Litigation Reform Act of 1995—An Update*, 2 Stan. J.L. Bus. & Fin. 331, 347–48 (1996).

41. Nursing Home Pension Fund v. Oracle Corp., 380 F.3d 1226 (9th Cir. 2004).

Certain states permit suits under their blue sky laws by investors who allege that they did not sell their securities because of the defendants' fraud (*holder claims*). The Supreme Court, however, ruled that the Securities Litigation Uniform Standards Act of 1998 bars all state securities fraud class actions, including holder claims.[42] As a result, plaintiffs cannot bring holder claims as a class action in state court. They cannot be brought in federal court either because the plaintiffs did not purchase or sell securities based on the fraud.

Parties that can be sued under Rule 10b–5 are those that make or are responsible for misstatements or omissions in connection with the purchase or sale of securities. Statements are made "in connection with" the purchase or sale of securities if they were made in a manner reasonably calculated to influence the investing public or if they were of the sort on which the investing public might reasonably rely.

For example, the U.S. Court of Appeals for the Third Circuit held that fraudulent financial statements issued by Cendant during the course of its tender offer for American Bankers Insurance Group (ABI) were misrepresentations made "in connection with" the plaintiffs' purchase of ABI shares during Cendant's tender offer even though the plaintiffs had neither purchased any Cendant shares nor tendered shares of ABI stock to Cendant.[43] The plaintiffs had alleged that Cendant's misrepresentations artificially inflated the price at which they purchased their ABI shares, and that they suffered a loss when those misrepresentations were disclosed to the public and the merger agreement between Cendant and ABI was terminated.

---

42. Merrill Lynch, Pierce, Fenner & Smith Inc. v. Dabit, 547 U.S. 71 (2006).

43. Semerenko v. Cendant Corp., 223 F.3d 165 (3d Cir. 2000).

In summary, a company must be careful to monitor its public statements, such as those made in periodic reports, press releases, proxy solicitations, and annual reports, and on the company's website. Even when addressing noninvestors, such as creditors or labor union representatives, a manager should exercise caution if the statements can reasonably be expected to reach investors.

RELIANCE

To establish liability under Rule 10b–5, investors must show that they relied either directly or indirectly on the misrepresentation or omission. If the investors did not rely on the misstatement or omission in deciding to buy or sell stock, then any loss they incurred cannot be blamed on the person that made the misrepresentation or omission.

Direct Reliance

A plaintiff may show reliance by showing that he or she was aware of the misstatement by the defendant and traded based on that misrepresentation. For example, if a plaintiff read a press release that overstated the issuer's earnings and traded on the basis of that misrepresentation, then that constitutes direct reliance. In the case of an omission, the U.S. Supreme Court has ruled that the plaintiff will be presumed to have relied on the omission if it was material. That presumption of reliance can be rebutted—that is, shown to be not true—by a showing that the plaintiff would have bought (or sold) the stock even if the omitted fact had been included.

In the following case, the seller of stock in a private placement sought to avoid liability for allegedly deceptive oral statements and omissions based on a nonreliance clause in the stock purchase contract.

A CASE IN POINT	*Summary*	Case 22.5

Emergent Capital Investment Management, LLC v. Stonepath Group, Inc.

United States Court of Appeals for the Second Circuit
43 F.3d 189 (2d Cir. 2003).

FACTS   Emergent Capital Investment Management, LLC invested $2 million in Net Value Holdings, Inc. (NETV), now Stonepath Group, Inc. The investment arose out of a meeting set up by Lee Hansen, director and president of NETV and the former roommate and personal friend of Mark Waldron. Mark Waldron and Daniel Yun, the managing members of Emergent, owned 90% of Emergent's stock. Andrew Panzo, the chair and CEO of NETV, had a long history of collaborating with Howard Appel, who had been barred for life by the National Association of Securities Dealers from associating with any member of that organization in any capacity. In the negotiations leading up to the purchase, NETV executives represented, orally and in a brochure, that NETV's largest investment was a $14 million purchase of a 12% equity interest in Brightstreet.com. In fact, the Brightstreet.com investment amounted to only $4 million. NETV never mentioned any connection to Appel, who allegedly played a significant role in NETV's founding, financing, and control.

Emergent and NETV executed a stock purchase agreement, in which NETV made extensive warranties and representations regarding its capital structure, indebtedness, involvement in litigation, ownership and leases of real and personal property, and other matters connected with its business. Further, the agreement contained a passage stating that the agreement and accompanying documents "contained the entire understanding and agreement among

CONTINUED

the parties . . . and superseded any prior understandings or agreements" between or among any of them.

Appel and Panzo apparently engaged in a number of investment schemes whereby Appel would acquire control of a public shell corporation and subsequently install Panzo as a director or senior officer. The company would transfer substantial quantities of stock to affiliates of Appel and Panzo, and the two men would, "through extraordinarily complex corporate legal maneuvers," end up with large amounts of stock. They would then sell the stock at a high price, leaving behind a virtually worthless company.

Between January and March 2000, the price of NETV's stock hovered between $10 and $30 per share. The stock subsequently fell to less than $1 per share. As the stock fell, Emergent demanded rescission of the agreement. NETV refused, prompting Emergent to sue for securities fraud under Rule 10b–5. Emergent alleged that NETV had misrepresented the size of the Brightstreet.com investment and had failed to disclose the company's connection to Appel.

ISSUE PRESENTED   Does a nonreliance clause in a stock purchase agreement preclude liability in cases of misrepresentations or omissions?

SUMMARY OF OPINION   The U.S. Court of Appeals for the Second Circuit first explained that the plaintiff had to establish reasonable reliance on the alleged misrepresentations or omissions. The reasonableness of the reliance is judged in light of the entire context of the transaction, including factors such as its complexity and magnitude, the sophistication of the parties, and the content of any agreements between them.

As for the misrepresentation concerning the Brightstreet.com investment, the court noted that the plaintiff had secured from the defendants extensive contractual representations concerning NETV's financial condition and operations. Because Emergent was a sophisticated investor, it should have protected itself by insisting that the representation regarding the Brightstreet.com investment be included in the stock purchase agreement. The court ruled that Emergent's failure to require such a representation in the agreement precluded a finding of reasonable reliance on the misrepresentation.

Unlike the affirmative misrepresentation, the omissions of Panzo's investment history and of NETV's ties to Appel were not known by Emergent. As a result, Emergent could not have protected itself against them in the agreement. The court held that the plaintiff had sufficiently alleged that, but for the omissions, the purchase would not have taken place. Further, the court found that the plaintiff had sufficiently asserted that Emergent's loss was a foreseeable consequence of the defendants' omissions, particularly in light of the drastic price declines that occurred in the shares of the other companies controlled by Panzo and Appel.

RESULT   The dismissal of Emergent's claim regarding the misstatement of the value of the Brightstreet.com investment was affirmed, but the dismissal of Emergent's claim regarding Panzo's investment history and NETV's connection to Appel was vacated. Emergent could pursue the latter claim.

COMMENTS   Given the "sophistication of the parties," the Second Circuit expected the buyer to include every material fact in the purchase agreement. In effect, the court reasoned that if a statement was important enough to be relied on by a sophisticated investor, then it should have been included in the agreement.

The Seventh Circuit reached a similar result in *Rissman v. Rissman*.[44] As Judge Easterbrook noted, "Prudent people protect themselves against the limitations of memory (and the temptation to shade the truth) by limiting their dealings to those memorialized in writing, and promoting the primacy of the written word is a principal function of the federal securities laws." The court also rejected the argument that the no-reliance clause should be ignored as mere "boilerplate." Judge Easterbrook explained that "the fact that language has been used before does not make it less binding when used again. Phrases become boilerplate when many parties find that the language serves their ends. That's a reason to enforce the promises, not to disregard them."

---

44. 213 F.3d 381 (7th Cir. 2000).

Fraud on the Market

In the securities market, direct reliance is rare because transactions usually are not conducted on a face-to-face basis. The market is interposed between the parties, providing important information to them in the form of the market price. As one court put it: "The market is acting as the unpaid agent of the investor, informing him that, given all the information available to it, the value of the stock is worth the market price."[45]

The theory underlying this view is known to economists as the *efficient-market theory*. It holds that in an open and developed securities market, the price of a company's stock equals its true value. The market is said to evaluate information efficiently and to incorporate it into the price of a company's securities.

Against this background, the courts have approved the *fraud-on-the-market theory*: If the information available to the market is incorrect, then the market price will not reflect the true value of the stock. Under this theory, an investor who purchases or sells a security is presumed to have relied on the market, which in turn relied on the misstatement or omission when it set the price of the security.

The Supreme Court first embraced this theory in *Basic, Inc. v. Levinson*[46] and then reiterated it in *Erica P. John Fund, Inc. v. Halliburton Co.*: "Because the market 'transmits information to the investor in the processed form of a market price,' we can assume . . . that an investor relies on public misstatements whenever he 'buys or sells stock at the price set by the market.'"[47]

Thus, plaintiffs do not have to show that they read or heard a defendant's misstatement in order to recover damages from that defendant. Instead, reliance is presumed if the investor shows that (1) the defendant made a public material misrepresentation that would have caused reasonable investors to misjudge the value of the defendant's stock and (2) the investor traded shares of the defendant's stock in an open securities market after the misrepresentations were made and before the truth was revealed.

A defendant can rebut the fraud-on-the-market presumption by showing that the plaintiff traded or would have traded despite knowing the statement was false. For example, an insider who is aware of nonpublic information that results in the stock being undervalued, but who sells for other reasons, cannot be said to have relied on the integrity of the market price.

Lower courts have declined to apply the fraud-on-the-market presumption in cases that do not involve an efficient, open, and developed market. The courts have identified at least five factors to consider in identifying an efficient market: (1) sufficient weekly trading volume, (2) sufficient reports and analyses by investment professionals, (3) the presence of market makers and arbitrageurs, (4) the existence of issuers eligible to file Form S–3 short-form registration statements, and (5) a historical showing of immediate price response to unexpected events or financial releases. In short, for a market to be open and developed, it must have a large number of buyers and sellers and a relatively high level of trading activity and frequency. It also must be a market where prices rapidly reflect new information.

Truth on the Market

Defendants have also used the efficient-market theory to their advantage. For example, even if the defendant makes overly optimistic sales projections for a product, there is no fraud on the market if the market makers were privy to the truth. In such a case, an investor who did not directly rely on the misrepresentation (for example, by actually reading a misleading press release) cannot successfully assert a securities fraud claim based on fraud on the market.

As the U.S. Court of Appeals for the Ninth Circuit explained, in a fraud-on-the-market case, a defendant's failure to disclose material information may be excused if that information has been made credibly available to the market by other sources: "[I]ndividuals who hear [only good news or only bad news] may receive a distorted impression . . . , and thus may have an actionable claim. But the market, and any individual who relies only on the price established by the market, will not be misled."[48]

A defendant is not relieved of its duty to disclose material information unless that information has been transmitted to the public with a degree of intensity and credibility sufficient to counterbalance any misleading impression created by the defendant. A brief mention of the omitted fact in a few poorly circulated or lightly regarded publications would be insufficient.

CAUSATION

To prevail, a plaintiff must prove that the defendant's misstatement, omission, or other deceptive conduct caused him or her to suffer economic loss (so-called *loss causation*). In *Dura Pharmaceuticals, Inc. v. Broudo*,[49] the U.S. Supreme Court ruled that allegedly false and misleading statements about Dura Pharmaceuticals' Albuterol Spiros asthma medication delivery device could not have caused the plaintiff investor's loss because the market price of the stock did not decline after the corrective disclosure was made. As a result, the plaintiff failed to prove loss causation. The Court rejected the Ninth Circuit's assertion that loss causation "merely requires pleading that the price at the time of purchase was overstated and sufficient identification of the cause."

---

45. *In re* LTV Sec. Litig., 88 F.R.D. 134, 143 (N.D. Tex. 1980).

46. 485 U.S. 224 (1988).

47. 131 S. Ct. 2179, 2185 (2011) (quoting Basic, Inc. v. Levinson, 485 U.S.224, 244, 247 (1988)).

48. *In re* Apple Computer Sec. Litig., 886 F.2d 1109 (9th Cir. 1989).

49. 544 U.S. 336 (2005).

Loss causation is primarily an economic question—what factors influenced the price of the security? Suppose, for example, that investors in an oil company claim that a misrepresentation by the company of the value of its oil reserves caused them to suffer losses. The claim is based on the contention that the stock price was maintained at an artificially high level as a result of the misrepresentation. The investors attribute the subsequent drop in the stock price to the revelation of the true facts. At trial, the defendants present the testimony of an economist that the drop in the stock price was caused by a drop in the price of oil and was not attributable to any misrepresentation of the value of the oil reserves. If the jury believes this expert, then the plaintiffs will have failed to prove their claim. Thus, proponents of the efficient-market theory may be right when they predict that an entire Rule 10b–5 case may boil down to one question: Did the misleading statement artificially affect the market price?

In early 2005, the U.S. Court of Appeals for the Second Circuit dismissed securities fraud claims against Merrill Lynch & Co., its star analyst Henry M. Blodget, and other research analysts for allegedly issuing false and misleading analyst reports on two Internet companies—24/7 Media and Interliant.[50] Merrill Lynch had acted as lead underwriter for two public offerings by 24/7 Media and as co-lead underwriter of Interliant's initial public offering. The plaintiffs alleged that Blodget and other research analysts issued knowingly or recklessly false bullish research reports to generate investment banking business for Merrill.

The plaintiffs suing Merrill did not claim to have read Merrill's reports or to have bought 24/7 Media or Interliant shares through the firm. Instead, they asserted fraud on the market. To prevail, the plaintiffs had to show loss causation, that is, that "the misstatement or omission concealed something from the market that, when disclosed, negatively affected the value of the security." The plaintiffs did not allege that Merrill "doctored" the facts or hid the risks, the price volatility of the stocks, the negative earnings-per-share ratios, or the consistent quarterly losses. There was also no allegation that the market reacted negatively to a corrective disclosure regarding the falsity of Merrill's positive recommendations. The Second Circuit declared this "fatal" to the plaintiffs' case. The court also rejected the plaintiffs' efforts to characterize Merrill's actions as market manipulation in violation of Rule 10b–5(a) and (c).

An earlier investigation of analyst conflicts of interest by New York Attorney General Eliot Spitzer had led to Merrill's agreement in 2002 to pay $100 million to settle New York's civil complaint and spawned more than 100 class-action complaints. Ultimately, ten investment banking firms paid more than $1 billion in a global settlement reached in 2003 to settle government investigations of the incestuous relationships between the firms' research groups—which purported to provide objective research reports—and their investment banking arms, which used favorable analyst coverage to garner more investment banking business.

The scandal resulted in a new SEC regulation—*Regulation Analyst Certification (Regulation AC)*[51]—which prohibits analysts from issuing reports that they do not personally believe to be true and requires the disclosure of any analyst compensation arrangements related to the specific recommendation or views contained in the research report.[52] The SEC has suggested that violation of Regulation AC may give rise to a private right of action under section 10(b) and Rule 10b–5.[53] Moreover, the SEC stated, "even without Regulation AC, analysts may be found to have violated the anti-fraud provisions of the federal securities laws if they make baseless recommendations that they disbelieve."[54]

The Sarbanes–Oxley Act of 2002 created a new crime, *securities fraud involving a publicly traded company.*[55] The Act made it a felony to knowingly execute or attempt to execute a scheme or artifice (1) to defraud any person in connection with any security of a publicly traded company or (2) to obtain, by means of false or fraudulent pretenses, representations, or promises, any money or property in connection with the purchase or sale of any security of a publicly traded company. The provision applies to any security of an issuer that has a class of securities registered under section 12 of the 1934 Act or that is required to file reports under section 15(d) of the 1934 Act. Congress thereby made it clear that any fake or misleading statements reasonably calculated to affect the public securities markets—such as those made by Henry Blodget of Merrill Lynch, Jack Grubman of Citigroup, and other securities analysts who touted stocks they privately called "junk" or worse—constitute securities fraud.

CALCULATION OF DAMAGES

The measure of damages in a Rule 10b–5 case is typically the out-of-pocket loss, that is, the difference between what the investor paid (or received) and the fair value of the stock on the date of the transaction. Alternatively, investors can elect to rescind the transaction, returning what they received and getting back what they gave. In the court's discretion, *prejudgment interest*—that is, interest on the amount of the award between the date the

---

50. Lentell v. Merrill Lynch & Co., 396 F.3d 161 (2d Cir. 2005).

51. Regulation Analyst Certification, 17 C.F.R. §§ 242.500–242.505.

52. *See* Securities Exchange Act Release No. 47,384 (Feb. 20, 2003), 68 Fed. Reg. 9482 (Feb. 27, 2003).

53. *Id. See also* Robert F. Serio & Matthew S. Kahn, *Private Rights of Action May Emerge from Sarbanes–Oxley Act,* Corp. Couns. Wkly. (BNA), Apr. 19, 2006, at 127.

54. Regulation Analyst Certification, *supra* note 51.

55. 18 U.S.C. § 1348.

securities were purchased and the date of the judgment—may also be awarded. Punitive damages are not available.

In theory, damages must be proved with reasonable certainty. In practice, however, damages are awarded on the basis of expert testimony, which can be highly conjectural. For example, a claim that a company's failure to reveal negative information about its new product artificially inflated the price of its stock is quite difficult to evaluate with any scientific certainty because even the experts often do not agree to what extent any particular piece of information affects the price of a company's securities.

In addition, the number of traders who can claim damage can only be estimated. For example, in-and-out traders' trades are included in the total volume of trading; but such traders who buy, then quickly sell, suffer no damage if they sell the securities before the price drop.

Evidence of damages is therefore often presented by comparing the stock's performance with the industry or market performance, on the assumption that the industry or the market was not subject to the same artificial inflation. This clearly remains a fertile field for argument and future litigation.

STATUTE OF LIMITATIONS

Suits under section 10(b) must be brought within two years after the date the plaintiff discovered the facts constituting the violation (including the defendant's state of mind)[56] or within five years after the violation occurred, whichever is earlier.[57] The five-year limit has been construed as a statute of repose that "may expire before a plaintiff discovers he has been wronged or even before damages have been suffered at all."[58]

LITIGATION REFORM ACT SAFE HARBOR FOR FORWARD-LOOKING STATEMENTS

The Private Securities Litigation Reform Act provides issuers subject to the 1934 Act's reporting requirements and persons acting on their behalf a two-prong safe harbor for certain forward-looking statements.[59] *Forward-looking statements* include (1) a statement containing a projection of revenues, income, earnings per share, capital expenditures, dividends, capital structure, or other financial items; (2) a statement of the plans and objectives of management for future operations, including plans relating to the issuer's products and services; (3) a statement of future economic performance, including any such statement

in Management's Discussion and Analysis of Financial Condition and Results of Operations (MD&A) required to be included by the SEC; and (4) any statement of the assumptions underlying or relating to any such statement.

The safe harbor does not apply to forward-looking statements in connection with (1) an initial public offering; (2) an offering of securities by a blank check company; (3) a rollup or going-private transaction; (4) a tender offer; or (5) an offering by a partnership, limited liability company, or direct participation investment program. The safe harbor also does not apply to any forward-looking statement included in (1) a financial statement prepared in accordance with generally accepted accounting principles or (2) a report of beneficial ownership on Schedule 13D.

As explained in Chapter 21, the statutory safe harbor for forward-looking statements was designed to promote market efficiency by encouraging companies to disclose projections and other information about their future prospects. Anecdotal evidence indicated that corporate counsel were advising their clients to say as little as possible due to fear that if the company failed to satisfy its announced earning projections—perhaps due to an industry downturn or the timing of a large order or release of a new product—the company would automatically be sued.

Under the first prong of the safe harbor, a person is protected from liability for a misrepresentation or omission based on a written forward-looking statement as long as the statement (1) is identified as forward-looking and (2) is accompanied by meaningful cautionary statements identifying important factors that could cause actual results to differ materially from those projected in the statement. The safe harbor also protects oral forward-looking statements if the person making the statement (1) identifies the statement as forward-looking, (2) states that results may differ materially from those projected in the statement, and (3) identifies a readily available written document (such as a document filed with the SEC) that contains factors that could cause results to differ materially.

The stated factors must be relevant to the projection and of a nature that could actually affect whether the forward-looking statement is realized. Boilerplate warnings will not suffice. Failure to include the particular factor that ultimately causes the forward-looking statement not to come true will not mean that the statement automatically is not protected by the safe harbor. The company must disclose all important factors, not all factors. In this respect, the safe harbor provides greater protection than the bespeaks caution doctrine.

For example, in *Harris v. Ivax Corp.*,[60] the U.S. Court of Appeals for the Eleventh Circuit held that a generic drug manufacturer was not liable for securities fraud despite its failure to disclose the possibility of a $104 million reduction in the carrying value of goodwill for several of its businesses. The company's cautionary language was

---

56. Merck & Co. v. Reynolds, 130 S. Ct. 1784 (2010).

57. 28 U.S.C. § 1658(b).

58. *In re* Exxon Mobil Corp. Sec. Litig., 500 F.3d 189 (3d Cir. 2007).

59. 15 U.S.C.S. § 77z-2.

60. 182 F.3d 799 (11th Cir. 1999).

adequate even though it did not explicitly mention the factor that ultimately belied the forward-looking statement. The court explained: "When an investor has been warned of risks of a significance similar to that actually realized, she is sufficiently on notice of the danger of the investment to make an intelligent decision about it according to her own preferences for risk and reward."

When a court is ruling on a motion to dismiss based on this prong of the safe harbor, the state of mind of the person making the statement is not relevant. The court looks only at the cautionary language accompanying the forward-looking statement.

Even if a person cannot rely on this first prong, there is an independent prong based on the state of mind of the person making the statement. A person or business entity will not be liable in a private lawsuit involving a forward-looking statement unless the plaintiff proves that the person or business entity made a false or misleading forward-looking statement with actual knowledge that it was false or misleading. A statement by a business entity will come within the safe harbor unless it was made by or with the approval of an executive officer of the entity with actual knowledge by that officer that the statement was false or misleading.

LIABILITY OF SECONDARY ACTORS

In addition to suing the person trading and the person who made the misleading statement or omission, private plaintiffs and the SEC often sue other parties, such as accountants, lawyers, or banks, for section 10(b) violations under a variety of theories.

Primary Liability

Secondary actors can be liable in private suits if their conduct satisfies the requirements for primary liability.[61] For example, the U.S. Court of Appeals for the Ninth Circuit ruled in *McGann v. Ernst & Young*[62] that an auditor that produced a fraudulent audit report knowing that its client would include the audit opinion in its annual report on Form 10–K filed with the SEC committed fraudulent acts "in connection with" the trading of securities and thus was subject to primary liability under section 10(b) of the 1934 Act. The court cited *SEC v. Texas Gulf Sulphur Co.*,[63] which stands for the proposition that any false and misleading assertions made "in a manner reasonably calculated to influence the investing public" are made "in connection with" the purchase or sale of securities within

the meaning of section 10(b). Section 10(b) does not limit liability to those who actually trade securities. One who "introduces fraudulent information into the securities market does no less damage to the public because that party did not trade stocks."[64] Therefore, Ernst & Young could be liable for a primary violation of section 10(b) if the plaintiff could prove that Ernst & Young made a misleading statement in the audit opinion, knowing that the opinion would be included in its client's Form 10–K.

McGann involved an alleged failure to disclose that caused the audit opinion to be false and misleading. Accountants are generally not responsible for misrepresentations or omissions in other parts of a document that they did not certify.[65]

Similarly, the Second Circuit held that a securities broker could be held primarily liable for market manipulation in violation of section 10(b) and Rule 10b–5 when he followed a stock promoter's directions to execute stock trades designed to create the appearance of an actual market for a company's shares and thereby artificially raise the stock price.[66] The court stated that the broker would be liable if he knew, or was reckless in not knowing, that the trades were manipulative, even if he did not share the promoter's specific overall purpose of manipulating the market for the stock.

Aiding and Abetting

In *Central Bank of Denver, N.A. v. First Interstate Bank of Denver, N.A.*,[67] the Supreme Court ruled that a private plaintiff may not maintain an aiding and abetting suit under section 10(b). In that case, the plaintiff had attempted to hold the bank that was the indenture trustee for a municipal bond issue secondarily liable as an *aider and abettor* of the fraud perpetrated by the issuers of the bonds. In reaching its decision, the Supreme Court noted the vexatious nature of Rule 10b–5 suits and the fact that such suits require secondary actors to expend large sums for pretrial defense and the negotiation of settlements. The Court went on to state:

> This uncertainty and excessive litigation can have ripple effects. For example, newer and smaller companies may find it difficult to obtain advice from professionals. A professional may fear that a newer or smaller company may not survive and that business failure would generate securities litigation against the professional, among others. In addition, the increased costs incurred by professionals because of the litigation and settlement costs under 10b–5 may be passed on to their client companies, and in turn incurred by the company's investors, the intended beneficiaries of the statute.[68]

61. Stoneridge Inv. Partners, LLC v. Scientific-Atlanta, Inc., 552 U.S. 148 (2008) (Case 22.6).
62. 102 F.3d 390 (9th Cir. 1996).
63. 401 F.2d 833 (2d Cir. 1968) (Case 22.1).
64. *Id.*
65. *See* Shapiro v. Cantor, 123 F.3d 717 (2d Cir. 1997).
66. SEC v. U.S. Envtl., Inc., 155 F.3d 107 (2d Cir. 1998).
67. 511 U.S. 164 (1994).
68. *Id.* at 189.

The SEC can still bring aider-and-abettor cases seeking damages or injunctive relief under section 10(b). To prove that a person is an *aider and abettor*, it is necessary to show (1) the existence of a primary violation of section 10(b) or Rule 10b–5, (2) the defendant's knowledge of (or recklessness as to) that primary violation, and (3) substantial assistance of the violation by the defendant.

Conspiracy

In *Dinsmore v. Squadron, Ellenoff, Plesent, Sheinfeld & Sorkin*,[69] the U.S. Court of Appeals for the Second Circuit

---

69. 135 F.3d 837 (2d Cir. 1998).

applied *Central Bank's* reasoning to a claim of conspiracy to fraudulently buy or sell securities and held that there is no implied private cause of action for conspiracy under section 10(b).

Scheme Liability

In the following case, the U.S. Supreme Court extended *Central Bank* to bar claims against third parties that engaged in fraudulent business transactions designed to enable the issuer to artificially inflate its earnings (so-called *scheme liability*).

| A CASE IN POINT | *In the Language of the Court* | Case 22.6 |

Stoneridge Investment Partners, LLC v. Scientific-Atlanta, Inc.

Supreme Court of the United States
552 U.S. 148 (2008).

FACTS   Charter Communications, Inc., a cable operator, allegedly engaged in a variety of fraudulent practices so that its quarterly reports would meet Wall Street expectations for cable subscriber growth and operating cash flow. The fraud included misclassification of its customer base, delayed reporting of terminated customers, improper capitalization of costs that should have been shown as expenses, and manipulation of the company's billing cutoff dates to inflate reported revenues. In late 2000, Charter executives realized that, despite these efforts, the company would miss projected operating cash-flow numbers by $15 to $20 million.

To help meet the shortfall, Charter decided to alter its existing arrangements with Scientific-Atlanta and Motorola, which supplied Charter with the digital cable converter (set top) boxes that Charter furnished to its customers. Charter arranged to overpay the two suppliers $20 for each set top box it purchased until the end of the year, with the understanding that they would return the overpayment by purchasing advertising time from Charter at inflated prices. Charter recorded the advertising purchases as revenue and capitalized its purchases of the set top boxes, thereby inflating revenue and operating cash flow by approximately $17 million. The transactions had no economic substance, and Charter's accounting treatment violated generally accepted accounting principles.

To keep Arthur Andersen, Charter's auditor, from discovering the link between Charter's increased payments for the boxes and the advertising purchases, the companies drafted documents to make it appear that the transactions were unrelated and were conducted in the ordinary course of business. In particular, following a request from Charter, Scientific-Atlanta sent documents to Charter stating—falsely—that it faced increased production costs and was increasing the price for set top boxes, by $20 per box, for the rest of 2000. As for Motorola, Charter entered into a written contract whereby it agreed to purchase from Motorola a specific number of set top boxes and to pay liquidated damages of $20 for each unit it did not take. The contract was made with the expectation that Charter would fail to purchase all the units and would pay Motorola the liquidated damages.

To return the additional money from the set top box sales, Scientific-Atlanta and Motorola signed contracts with Charter to purchase advertising time for a premium. The new set top box agreements were backdated to make it appear that they were negotiated a month before the advertising agreements. The backdating was important to convey the impression that the negotiations were unconnected, a point Arthur Andersen considered necessary for separate treatment of the transactions. The inflated number was shown on financial statements filed with the SEC and reported to the public.

Scientific-Atlanta and Motorola had no role in preparing or disseminating Charter's financial statements. They booked the transactions as a wash in their own financial statements,

CONTINUED

in accordance with generally accepted accounting principles. The plaintiff purchasers of Charter stock filed a securities fraud class action under section 10(b) of the 1934 Act and SEC Rule 10b–5, alleging that the two suppliers knew or were in reckless disregard of Charter's intention to use the transactions to inflate its revenues and knew that the resulting financial statements issued by Charter would be relied on by research analysts and investors.

The district court dismissed the complaint for failure to state a claim on which relief could be granted, and the U.S. Court of Appeals for the Eighth Circuit affirmed.

ISSUE PRESENTED   Are customer/supplier companies that agreed to arrangements that allowed an issuer to mislead its auditor liable in a private action under section 10(b) of the 1934 Act?

OPINION   KENNEDY, J., writing on behalf of the U.S. Supreme Court:

In this suit investors sought to impose liability on entities who, acting both as customers and suppliers, agreed to arrangements that allowed the investors' company to mislead its auditor and issue a misleading financial statement affecting the stock price. We conclude the implied right of action does not reach the customer/supplier companies because the investors did not rely upon their statements or representations. We affirm the judgment of the Court of Appeals.

I

In *Central Bank*, the Court determined that § 10(b) liability did not extend to aiders and abettors. The Court found the scope of § 10(b) to be delimited by the text, which makes no mention of aiding and abetting liability.

. . . .

The decision in *Central Bank* led to calls for Congress to create an express cause of action for aiding and abetting within the Securities Exchange Act. . . . Congress did not follow this course. Instead, in § 104 of the Private Securities Litigation Reform Act of 1995 (PSLRA)[70] it directed prosecution of aiders and abettors by the SEC.[71]

. . . .

II

. . . .

A

Reliance by the plaintiff upon the defendant's deceptive acts is an essential element of the § 10(b) private cause of action. It ensures that, for liability to arise, the "requisite causal connection between a defendant's misrepresentation and a plaintiff's injury" exists as a predicate for liability. We have found a rebuttable presumption of reliance in two different circumstances. First, if there is an omission of a material fact by one with a duty to disclose, the investor to whom the duty was owed need not provide specific proof of reliance. Second, under the fraud-on-the-market doctrine, reliance is presumed when the statements at issue become public. The public information is reflected in the market price of the security. Then it can be assumed that an investor who buys or sells stock at the market price relies upon the statement.

Neither presumption applies here. Respondents [Scientific-Atlanta and Motorola] had no duty to disclose; and their deceptive acts were not communicated to the public. No member of the investing public had knowledge, either actual or presumed, of respondents' deceptive acts during the relevant times. Petitioner [the plaintiff investors], as a result, cannot show reliance upon any of respondents' actions except in an indirect chain that we find too remote for liability.

CONTINUED

---

70. 109 Stat. 757.

71. 15 U.S.C. § 78t(e).

Invoking what some courts call "scheme liability," petitioner nonetheless seeks to impose liability on respondents even absent a public statement. In our view this approach does not answer the objection that petitioner did not in fact rely upon respondents' own deceptive conduct. Liability is appropriate, petitioner contends, because respondents engaged in conduct with the purpose and effect of creating a false appearance of material fact to further a scheme to misrepresent Charter's revenue. The argument is that the financial statement Charter released to the public was a natural and expected consequence of respondents' deceptive acts; had respondents not assisted Charter, Charter's auditor would not have been fooled, and the financial statement would have been a more accurate reflection of Charter's financial condition. That causal link is sufficient, petitioner argues, to apply *Basic*'s presumption of reliance to respondents' acts. In effect petitioner contends that in an efficient market investors rely not only upon the public statements relating to a security but also upon the transactions those statements reflect. Were this concept of reliance to be adopted, the implied cause of action would reach the whole marketplace in which the issuing company does business; and there is no authority for this rule.

. . . .

[W]e conclude respondents' deceptive acts, which were not disclosed to the investing public, are too remote to satisfy the requirement of reliance. It was Charter, not respondents, that misled its auditor and filed fraudulent financial statements; nothing respondents did made it necessary or inevitable for Charter to record the transactions as it did.

The petitioner invokes the private cause of action under § 10(b) and seeks to apply it beyond the securities markets—the realm of financing business—to purchase and supply contracts—the realm of ordinary business operations. The latter realm is governed, for the most part, by state law. It is true that if business operations were used, as alleged here, to affect securities markets, the SEC enforcement power may reach the culpable actors. It is true as well that a dynamic, free economy presupposes a high degree of integrity in all of its parts, an integrity that must be underwritten by rules enforceable in fair, independent, accessible courts. Were the implied cause of action to be extended to the practices described here, however, there would be a risk that the federal power would be used to invite litigation beyond the immediate sphere of securities litigation and in areas already governed by functioning and effective state-law guarantees. Our precedents counsel against the extension.

. . . .

Petitioner's theory, moreover, would put an unsupportable interpretation on Congress' specific response to *Central Bank* in § 104 of the PSLRA. Congress amended the securities laws to provide for limited coverage of aiders and abettors. Aiding and abetting liability is authorized in actions brought by the SEC but not by private parties. See 15 U.S.C. § 78t(e). Petitioner's view of primary liability makes any aider and abettor liable under § 10(b) if he or she committed a deceptive act in the process of providing assistance. Were we to adopt this construction of § 10(b), it would revive in substance the implied cause of action against aiders and abettors except those who committed no deceptive act in the process of facilitating the fraud; and we would undermine Congress' determination that this class of defendants should be pursued by the SEC and not by private litigants.

. . . .

III

Secondary actors are subject to criminal penalties, and civil enforcement by the SEC. The enforcement power is not toothless. Since September 20, 2002, SEC enforcement actions have collected over $10 billion in disgorgement and penalties, much of it for distribution to injured investors. In addition, some state securities laws permit state authorities to seek fines and restitution from aiders and abettors.[72] All secondary actors, furthermore, are not necessarily

CONTINUED

---

72. *See, e.g.*, Del. Code Ann. tit. 6, § 7325 (2005).

immune from private suit. The securities statutes provide an express private right of action against accountants and underwriters in certain circumstances, and the implied right of action in § 10(b) continues to cover secondary actors who commit primary violations.

RESULT The judgment of the court of appeals was affirmed. The section 10(b) and Rule 10b–5 claims against Scientific-Atlanta and Motorola were subsequently dismissed.[73]

DISSENT STEVENS, J., with whom Souter and Ginsburg, JJ., joined:[74]

The Court's conclusion that no violation of § 10(b) giving rise to a private right of action has been alleged in this case rests on two faulty premises: (1) the Court's overly broad reading of *Central Bank,* and (2) the view that reliance requires a kind of super-causation—a view contrary to both the Securities and Exchange Commission's (SEC) position . . . and our holding in *Basic Inc. v. Levinson.*

I

. . . The Court correctly explains why the statute covers nonverbal as well as verbal deceptive conduct. The allegations in this case—that respondents produced documents falsely claiming costs had risen and signed contracts they knew to be backdated in order to disguise the connection between the increase in costs and the purchase of advertising—plainly describe "deceptive devices" under any standard reading of the phrase.

What the Court fails to recognize is that this case is critically different from *Central Bank* because the bank in that case did not engage in any deceptive act and, therefore, did not itself violate § 10(b). . . . The facts of this case would parallel those of *Central Bank* if respondents had, for example, merely delayed sending invoices for set-top boxes to Charter. Conversely, the facts in *Central Bank* would mirror those in the case before us today if the bank had knowingly purchased real estate in wash transactions at above-market prices in order to facilitate the appraiser's overvaluation of the security. *Central Bank,* thus, poses no obstacle to petitioner's argument that it has alleged a cause of action under § 10(b).

II

The Court's next faulty premise is that petitioner is required to allege that Scientific-Atlanta and Motorola made it "necessary or inevitable for Charter to record the transactions in the way it did" in order to demonstrate reliance. . . . In *Basic Inc.,* we stated that "[r]eliance provides the requisite causal connection between a defendant's misrepresentation and a plaintiff's injury." The Court's view of the causation required to demonstrate reliance is unwarranted and without precedent.

. . . The holding in *Basic* is surely a sufficient response to the argument that a complaint alleging that deceptive acts which had a material effect on the price of a listed stock should be dismissed because the plaintiffs were not subjectively aware of the deception at the time of the securities' purchase or sale.

. . . Reliance is often equated with "transaction causation." Transaction causation, in turn, is often defined as requiring an allegation that but for the deceptive act, the plaintiff would not have entered into the securities transaction. Even if but-for causation, standing alone, is too weak to establish reliance, petitioner has also alleged that respondents proximately caused Charter's misstatement of income; petitioner has alleged that respondents knew their deceptive acts would be the basis for statements that would influence the market price of Charter stock on which shareholders would rely. Thus, respondents' acts had the foreseeable effect of causing petitioner to engage in the relevant securities transactions. . . .

The Court's view of reliance is unduly stringent and unmoored from authority. The Court first says that if the petitioner's concept of reliance is adopted, the implied cause of action "would

CONTINUED

73. Stoneridge Inv. Partners, LLC v. Scientific-Atlanta, Inc., 519 F.3d 730 (8th Cir. 2008).

74. Justice Breyer took no part in the consideration or decision of this case.

reach the whole marketplace in which the issuing company does business." The answer to that objection is, of course, that liability only attaches when the company doing business with the issuing company has *itself* violated § 10(b). The Court next relies on what it views as a strict division between the "realm of financing business" and the "ordinary business operations." But petitioner's position does not merge the two: A corporation engaging in a business transaction with a partner who transmits false information to the market is only liable where the corporation *itself* violates § 10(b). Such a rule does not invade the province of "ordinary" business transactions.

. . . .

Finally, the Court relies on the course of action Congress adopted after our decision in *Central Bank* to argue that siding with petitioner on reliance would run contrary to congressional intent. . . . Congress stopped short of undoing *Central Bank* entirely, instead adopting a compromise which restored the authority of the SEC to enforce aiding and abetting liability. . . . That Congress chose not to restore the aiding and abetting liability removed by *Central Bank* does not mean that Congress wanted to exempt from liability the broader range of conduct that today's opinion excludes.

The Court is concerned that such liability would deter overseas firms from doing business in the United States or "shift securities offerings away from domestic capital markets." But liability for those who violate § 10(b) "will not harm American competitiveness; in fact investor faith in the safety and integrity of our markets *is* their strength. The fact that our markets are the safest in the world has helped make them the strongest in the world."

CRITICAL THINKING QUESTIONS

1. Are there any circumstances under which secondary actors who did not themselves make an actionable omission or representation could still be liable under section 10(b)?[75]

2. Do strict securities antifraud rules make the U.S. capital markets more or less attractive to foreign investors?

---

75. *See* James Stengel, Steven Fink & Kristen Fournier, Stoneridge Investment v. Scientific Atlanta, Inc., LEXIS NEXIS EXPERT COMMENT. (Feb. 2008).

---

ethicalconsideration

Accountants must sign a written consent before their audited report can be included in a registration statement. Before doing so, they generally conduct an *S–1 review*, which is a review of events subsequent to the date of the certified balance sheet in the registration statement to ascertain whether any material change has occurred in the company's financial position that should be disclosed to prevent the financial statements from being misleading. This review includes comparing recent financial statements to earlier ones, reading minutes of the shareholders' and directors' meetings, and investigating changes in material contracts, bad debts, and newly discovered liabilities.

Suppose that, in the course of the S–1 review, the accountants learn that the company's earnings have dropped dramatically from earnings for the comparable periods included in the registration statement. Should the accountants refuse to sign the consent for inclusion of their opinion on the financial statements for the previous period unless the adverse results are disclosed in the prospectus?

Controlling Persons

Section 20(a) imposes joint and several liability on every person who, directly or indirectly, controls another person who is liable under the 1934 Act,[76] unless the controlling person acted in good faith and did not directly or indirectly induce the acts constituting the violation. This provision is generally interpreted in the same way as section 15 of the 1933 Act, which was discussed in Chapter 21. Thus, to be liable as a controlling person, the defendant must "in some meaningful sense [be] a culpable participant in the primary violation."[77]

SECTION 17(A)

Section 17(a) of the 1933 Act prohibits fraud in connection with the sale of securities. It is similar in scope to section 10(b) of the 1934 Act, but section 17(a) does not

---

76. Morrison v. Nat'l Australia Bank Ltd., 130 S. Ct. 2869 (2010).

77. Boguslavsky v. Kaplan, 159 F.3d 715, 720 (2d Cir. 1998); STMicroelectronics v. Credit Suisse Group, 775 F. Supp. 2d 525 (E.D.N.Y. 2011).

require proof of scienter. The SEC and the U.S. Attorney's Office can use section 17(a) to prosecute securities fraud, but private parties cannot sue based on it.

SEC ACTIONS

The SEC has broad power to investigate apparent violations of section 10(b), Rule 10b–5, and section 17(a); to order the violator to stop its wrongful conduct; and to recommend criminal prosecution for willful violations. As noted above, although private plaintiffs may not sue for aiding and abetting a section 10(b) violation or for conspiring, the SEC can sue aiders and abettors for injunctive relief and damages under section 10(b).

Since 1972, the SEC has permitted defendants to settle civil enforcement cases without admitting or denying liability. Although the policy was adopted, at least in part, to prevent defendants from settling and then claiming publicly that they were not at fault,[78] no-fault settlements made it possible for firms to settle SEC cases without making an admission of fault, which could be used against the firm in a private action.[79] In the following case, the court surprised many when it rejected a no-fault settlement between the SEC and Citigroup.

---

78. Bob Van Voris, *SEC Policy Challenged in Judge's Rejection of $285 Million Citigroup Deal*, Bloomberg.com (Nov. 29, 2011), http://www.bloomberg.com/news/2011-11-29/sec-policy-challenged-in-judge-s-rejection-of-citigroup-deal.html.

79. Elizabeth G. Olson, *Will the SEC–Citi Settlement Rejection Make a Difference?*, CNN Money (Dec. 1, 2011), http://management.fortune.cnn.com/2011/12/01/will-the-sec-citi-settlement-rejection-make-a-difference/?section=magazines_fortune.

| A CASE IN POINT | *Summary* | Case 22.7 |

SEC v. Citigroup Global Markets, Inc.

United States District Court for the Southern District of New York
2011 WL 5903733 (S.D.N.Y. Nov. 28, 2011).

FACTS The SEC alleged that Citigroup created a billion-dollar fund in 2007 that was primarily made up of subprime residential-mortgage-backed securities that were projected to lose money. It sold these "dubious assets" to investors even after it realized that "the market for mortgage-backed securities was beginning to weaken." Citigroup ostensibly knew that investors would be unlikely to invest in the fund if it disclosed "its intention to use the vehicle to short a hand-picked set of [poorly rated assets]." Correspondingly, Citigroup misrepresented the assets as "attractive investments rigorously selected by an independent investment adviser" without disclosing that Citigroup as a firm took a short position in those same assets. Investors in the fund lost more than $700 million while Citigroup made about $160 million in profits.

Even though the SEC's claims seemed to suggest an allegation of scienter of fraudulent activities, the SEC only charged Citigroup with negligence in violation of sections 17(a)(2) and (3) of the 1933 Act. The SEC presented the court with a proposed "Consent Judgment" under which Citigroup agreed to pay the SEC $285 million, including the forfeiture of its $160 million in profits. The proposed Consent Judgment enjoined Citigroup from committing securities fraud and required the bank to implement measures to prevent future securities fraud.

ISSUE PRESENTED Under what circumstances will a court reject a no-fault Consent Judgment agreed to by the SEC and the defendant firm?

SUMMARY OF OPINION Refusing to be a "mere handmaiden" to a privately negotiated settlement on the basis of unknown facts, the U.S. District Court for the Southern District of New York did not approve the Consent Judgment because it lacked "any proven or admitted facts upon which to exercise even a modest degree of independent judgment." The court applied the same standard of review it had used when it rejected a proposed settlement between the SEC and Bank of America about two years earlier, namely "whether the proposed Consent Judgment . . . is fair, reasonable, adequate, and in the public interest."[80] Disagreeing with the SEC, the court reasoned that it had to consider the public interest because part of the relief requested was an injunction, which always requires consideration of the public interest.[81] The court refused to let the SEC be the "sole determiner of what is

CONTINUED

---

80. SEC v. Bank of Am. Corp., 653 F. Supp. 2d 507 (S.D.N.Y. 2009) (characterizing the proposed Consent Judgment as "a contrivance designed to provide the S.E.C. with the facade of enforcement and the management of the Bank with a quick resolution of an embarrassing inquiry—all at the expense of the sole alleged victims, the shareholders.").

81. eBay, Inc. v. MercExchange, 547 U.S. 388, 391 (2006).

in the public interest," reasoning that to satisfy the constitutional doctrine of separation of powers, the court "must still exercise a modicum of independent judgment in determining whether the requested deployment of its injunctive powers will serve, or disserve, the public interest."

The court noted that if it had approved the Consent Judgment, the public would be "deprived of ever knowing the truth in a matter of obvious public importance." As the court explained:

> [I]n any case like this that touches on the transparency of financial markets whose gyrations have so depressed our economy and debilitated our lives, there is an overriding public interest in knowing the truth. In much of the world, propaganda reigns, and truth is confined to secretive, fearful whispers. Even in our nation, apologists for suppressing or obscuring the truth may always be found. But the S.E.C., of all agencies, has a duty, inherent in its statutory mission, to see that the truth emerges; and if it fails to do so, this Court must not, in the name of deference or convenience, grant judicial enforcement to the agency's contrivances.

The court criticized the "SEC's long-standing policy . . . of allowing defendants to enter into Consent Judgments without admitting or denying the underlying allegations" because it "deprives the Court of even the most minimal assurance that the substantial injunctive relief it is being asked to impose has any basis in fact." The court was concerned that Citigroup did not contest the allegations yet would not admit to them. As a result, Citigroup would be able to (and most likely would) dispute the facts in any parallel litigation. Furthermore, the court stressed, the practice of allowing Consent Judgments without an admission of fault encourages businesses to view such consent agreements with the SEC as a cost of doing business rather than a settlement over the facts.

The court concluded that it had inadequate information over how the Consent Judgment would affect the public interest and ruled that the Consent Judgment was "neither fair, nor reasonable, nor adequate, nor in the public interest." Although the court acknowledged that the interests of the parties might have be satisfied by the agreement, it stated that their interests "cannot be automatically equated with the public interest, especially in the absence of a factual base" on which to assess the resolution.

RESULT   The proposed settlement was rejected, and the court ordered the parties to be ready to try the case in July 2012.

COMMENTS   The SEC announced its intention to appeal Judge Jed. S. Rakoff's decision in a statement issued by its director of enforcement Robert Khuzami: "We believe the district court committed legal error by announcing a new and unprecedented standard that inadvertently harms investors by depriving them of substantial, certain and immediate benefits."[82] After its settlement with Citigroup was rejected, the SEC changed its policy to prohibit no-fault settlements in civil cases when a defendant admits guilt in a companion criminal case or is convicted or enters into a no-prosecution agreement with the U.S. Department of Justice.[83]

CRITICAL THINKING QUESTIONS

1. How might litigating the case, rather than settling with the SEC, affect Citigroup in potential private actions? Will other corporate defendants be willing to settle if they have to admit fault?

2. Would the result have been the same if the SEC had agreed to settle the case for only damages? If so, how will this case affect future cases?

82. Edward Wyatt, *Citing "Legal Error," S.E.C. Says It Will Appeal Rejection of Citigroup Settlement*, N.Y. TIMES, Dec. 16, 2011.

83. Edward Wyatt, *S.E.C. Changes Policy on Firms' Admissions of Guilt*, N.Y. TIMES, Jan. 7, 2012.

RESPONSIBILITY OF AUDITORS TO DETECT AND REPORT ILLEGALITIES

The Litigation Reform Act added a new section 10A to the 1934 Act to promote disclosure by independent public accountants of illegal acts committed by their publicly traded audit clients. Each audit must include, in accordance with generally accepted auditing standards, (1) procedures designed to provide reasonable assurance of detecting illegal acts that would have a direct and material effect on the determination of financial statement amounts, (2) procedures designed to identify material related-party transactions (such as those involving officers, directors, and controlling shareholders of the company being audited), and (3) an evaluation of whether there is substantial doubt about the ability of the company to continue as a going concern during the ensuing fiscal year. The Sarbanes–Oxley Act of 2002 also requires auditors to report on the adequacy of the company's internal controls (see Appendix N).

If, in the course of the audit, the independent public accountant detects or otherwise becomes aware of information indicating that an illegal act has or may have occurred (regardless of whether it is perceived to have a material effect on the financial statements), then the accountant must (1) determine whether it is likely that an illegal act has occurred and, if so, determine and consider the possible effect on the financial statements; and (2) inform the appropriate level of the management of the company. The accountant must ensure that the audit committee, or the board of directors in the absence of such a committee, is adequately informed with respect to the illegal acts, unless the illegal act is clearly inconsequential. If after informing the audit committee (or board in the absence of an audit committee), the accountant concludes that (1) the illegal act has a material effect on the financial statements of the company, (2) senior management has not taken timely and appropriate remedial actions with respect to the illegal act, and (3) the failure to take remedial action is reasonably expected to warrant departure from a standard audit report or resignation, then the accountant must, as soon as practicable, directly report its conclusions to the full board of directors. The board is then required to notify the SEC within one business day after its receipt of the report. If the board fails to do so, the accountant must furnish the SEC a copy of its report (or the documentation of any oral report given).

DEFINITION OF INSIDER TRADING

"Insider trading" refers in general terms to trading by persons (often insiders, such as officers and directors) based on material nonpublic information. Section 10(b) does not expressly ban insider trading, and the law in this area has developed on a piecemeal basis. Because there is no statutory definition of insider trading, the safest course is never to trade while in possession of material nonpublic information; however, such a premise is unduly restrictive. The nature of insider trading can best be understood by examining the purposes underlying the laws that prohibit it.

Two fundamental goals of the securities laws are to protect the investing public and to maintain fair and efficient securities markets. Allowing a party who knows that the market is incorrectly pricing a security to exploit another party's ignorance of that fact is fundamentally unfair. Yet, if an efficient market is to be maintained, market professionals, such as securities analysts, must be given an incentive to ferret out the truth about companies and their prospects. There would be no incentive if the persons who expended the time and effort to piece together the truth were precluded from either trading on that information or selling it to others in the form of a tip or analyst report. Moreover, section 10(b) bans only fraudulent, manipulative, and deceptive practices.

In light of this need to promote an efficient market and the language of section 10(b), the Supreme Court has held that a trade based on material nonpublic information is illegal only if (1) there is a breach of duty by the person trading to the issuer of the securities being traded; (2) the person trading is the recipient of a tip—a piece of inside information—from a person who breached a duty to the issuer by giving a tip;[84] or (3) the person trading or the tipper violated a duty of trust or confidence owed the source of the nonpublic information.[85] (The person giving the tip is known as the *tipper*; the person receiving it is known as the *tippee*.) The first two types are covered by the *classical theory of insider trading*, which prohibits insiders of a firm from trading that firm's securities based on material nonpublic information. The third is based on the *misappropriation theory*, which prohibits anyone from trading or tipping based on material nonpublic information in violation of a duty of trust or confidence owed the source of that information.

Classical Theory of Insider Trading

An *insider* is a person with access to confidential information about a company and an obligation of disclosure of nonpublic material information to other traders before trading in that company's securities. Thus, an insider must either disclose material nonpublic information in his or her possession before trading or refrain from trading. The fundamental question in a classical insider trading case is whether this disclosure obligation should be imposed on a particular trader.

---

84. Dirks v. SEC, 463 U.S. 646 (1983).

85. United States v. O'Hagan, 521 U.S. 642 (1997).

Traditional Insiders

Traditional insiders include (1) officers and directors, (2) employees, (3) controlling shareholders, and (4) the corporation itself. As discussed in Chapter 20, corporate officers and directors have a fiduciary obligation of loyalty and care to the corporation and its shareholders. They also have the greatest access to sensitive information regarding corporate events. Because they are required to subordinate their self-interests to the interests of the shareholders, it is illegal for them to trade in the stock of the corporation they serve based on nonpublic information. Similarly, employees have a duty of loyalty and may not personally profit from the confidential information that they receive in the course of their employment. Even if an insider resigns before trading, he or she will still be liable for trading on the basis of material inside information learned while on the job. Controlling shareholders often have access to confidential information and have a fiduciary duty not to exploit that information at the expense of minority shareholders.

Often a corporation (or other issuer) will engage in the purchase or sale of its own securities. Under these circumstances, the corporation and those acting on its behalf are deemed insiders and therefore must not trade while in possession of material nonpublic information.

Temporary Insiders

Outside attorneys, accountants, consultants, investment bankers, and rating agencies who are not directly employed by the corporation, but who acquire confidential information through the performance of professional services, are also considered insiders. The U.S. Supreme Court extended liability under section 10(b) to such *temporary insiders* in footnote 14 in *Dirks v. SEC*.[86]

Tippees of Insiders

In most cases, a tippee of an insider will have no independent duty to the shareholders of the company in whose securities the tippee is trading. Tippees are subject to liability under Rule 10b–5 only if they can be considered derivative insiders (or under the misappropriation theory, discussed below). A tippee will not be held liable as a *derivative insider* unless the insider's duty of disclosure can somehow be imposed on the tippee.

Thus, under the classical theory of insider trading, a tippee is not liable unless the tippee and the tipper join in a co-venture to exploit the information. Only in such a case will the fiduciary duty of the tipper be derivatively imposed on the tippee. For the tippee to be liable, therefore, the tipper must have a duty to the company not to disclose the information that the tipper breached by seeking to benefit personally from the disclosure of the

information to the tippee. The benefit sought by the tipper can be either tangible or intangible. Intangible benefits might include an enhanced reputation as "someone in the know" or the intangible benefit received through the giving of gifts.

The requirement that the tipper be seeking some benefit implies that the tipper must desire that the tippee trade on the information, but it is unclear whether such a showing is necessary. For example, the tipper could derive a benefit merely from impressing the tippee with his or her access to confidential information. Such a desire could stem from social or career aspirations of the tipper and could have nothing to do with the stock-trading ramifications of the information.

In a classic case of illegal tipping, the former CEO of ImClone, Samuel D. Waksal, was convicted in 2003 of telling his daughter and father to sell their ImClone stock based on his nonpublic knowledge that the Food and Drug Administration (FDA) was denying approval of ImClone's anticancer drug Erbitex. In the course of sentencing Waksal to more than seven years in prison and ordering him to pay a $3 million fine, Judge William H. Pauley III stated:

> The harm that you wrought is truly incalculable. You abused your position of trust as chief executive officer of a major corporation and undermined the public's confidence in the integrity of the financial markets. Then you tried to lie your way out of it, showing a complete disregard for the firm administration of justice.[87]

Judge Pauley further rebuked Waksal, saying, "Your spectacular success in building ImClone into a company worthy of inclusion in the Nasdaq 100 led you to disconnect from reality and, most importantly, from the rule of law."[88]

The SEC sued Samuel Waksal's father in 2003 to recover the $7 million in profits he earned when he sold his ImClone shares before the public announcement of the FDA's rejection of the drug application. The complaint alleged that Samuel Waksal intended to bestow a gift of illegal profits or illegal loss avoidance on his father by telling him about the impending announcement of bad news and that his father knew that he should not have traded on that information.[89]

The tippee is liable only if he or she knew or should have known that the tipper's disclosure of the confidential information constituted a fiduciary breach. If the tippee has reason to know that the insider's disclosure was wrong or against the interest of the corporation,

---

86. 463 U.S. 646 (1983).

87. Constance L. Hays, *Former Chief of ImClone Is Given 7-Year Term,* N.Y. TIMES, June 11, 2003, at C1.

88. *Id.*

89. Constance L. Hays, *Waksal's Father Named in S.E.C. Suit,* N.Y. TIMES, Oct. 11, 2003, at C3.

the tippee's actual knowledge will be irrelevant. For example, the U.S. Court of Appeals for the Sixth Circuit upheld the conviction of Kelly Hughes and her husband Kevin Stacy after they purchased thousands of shares of Worthington Foods, just days before its acquisition by Kellogg Company. Hughes received material nonpublic information about the acquisition from Roger Blackwell, a director of Worthington, and Blackwell's wife then shared that information with Stacy.[90] They earned profits of $104,955. The court concluded that Hughes was a knowledgeable investor who would have known that Blackwell was breaching his duty to Worthington when he shared information about the acquisition. Hughes and Stacy were each sentenced to prison (thirty-three months for Hughes, twenty-seven for Stacy) and three years of supervised release, and each was fined $53,443. These fines were in addition to the $104,955 Hughes and Stacy were ordered to disgorge as a result of a civil case brought by the SEC.[91]

Remote Tippees

Remote tippees—that is, the tippees of tippees—may be found to have violated section 10(b) and Rule 10b–5 even if they are completely unacquainted with and removed from the original insider tipper. However, remote tippees are not liable unless they knew or should have known that the first-tier tipper was breaching a fiduciary duty in passing on the nonpublic information.[92] The phrase "should have known" is key to this formulation. It means that tippees cannot insulate themselves from liability merely by failing to inquire as to the source of the information. If a tippee has reason to suspect that the information was wrongfully acquired, such conscious avoidance of knowledge will not prevent a finding of scienter.

Misappropriation Theory of Insider Trading

The Supreme Court expanded the class of possible defendants to include so-called outsiders when it embraced the misappropriation theory in *United States v. O'Hagan*.[93] Under the misappropriation theory, a Rule 10b–5 violation occurs when a person breaches a fiduciary duty to the source of the nonpublic information by trading on that information after secretly misappropriating it for his or her own use. The trader can be held liable even if he or she is not an insider of the company whose securities are traded and has no independent duty of disclosure to the person

from whom the securities were bought or sold. Thus, the Court explained:

> Under this theory, a fiduciary's undisclosed, self-serving use of a principal's information to purchase or sell securities, in breach of a duty of loyalty and confidentiality, defrauds the principal of the exclusive use of that information. In lieu of premising liability on a fiduciary relationship between company insider and purchaser or seller of the company's stock, the misappropriation theory premises liability on a fiduciary-turned-trader's deception of those who entrusted him with access to confidential information.[94]

The case involved James Herman O'Hagan, a partner of the law firm Dorsey & Whitney, who had purchased stock and options for stock in Pillsbury Company prior to the public announcement of a tender offer for Pillsbury's stock by Grand Met PLC. O'Hagan possessed material nonpublic information about Grand Met's intentions, which he had obtained as a partner of the law firm representing Grand Met in connection with its acquisition of Pillsbury. O'Hagan realized a profit in excess of $4 million on his Pillsbury-related transactions. The U.S. Supreme Court upheld O'Hagan's criminal conviction of securities fraud under section 10(b) and Rule 10b–5, reasoning that "it makes scant sense to hold a lawyer like O'Hagan a § 10(b) violator if he works for a law firm representing the target of a tender offer, but not if he works for a law firm representing the bidder. The text of the statute requires no such result."

The Court also upheld O'Hagan's conviction for violating Rule 14e–3(a), which prohibits a person with nonpublic information about a pending tender offer that he or she knows or has reason to know has been acquired directly or indirectly from the offeror or the target or someone working on their behalf from trading on that information. (See Appendix J for the full text of Rule 14e–3.) The Supreme Court ruled that the SEC had not exceeded its powers under section 14(e) when it adopted Rule 14e–3, which does not require proof that the trader breached any fiduciary duty.

Liability under the misappropriation theory requires deception, that is, "feigning fidelity to the source of the information."[95] As a result, if the trader discloses to the source of the nonpublic information that he plans to trade on the basis of that information, then "there is no 'deceptive device' and thus no § 10(b) violation."[96]

In the following case, the U.S. Court of Appeals for the Ninth Circuit applied *O'Hagan* to a director of a major shareholder of an acquisition target who traded the target's stock based on nonpublic information about the potential acquisition.

---

90. United States v. Hughes, 505 F.3d 578 (6th Cir. 2007).

91. SEC v. Blackwell, 2007 WL 1169362 (S.D. Ohio Apr. 18, 2007).

92. SEC v. Musella, 678 F. Supp. 1060 (S.D.N.Y. 1988).

93. 521 U.S. 642 (1997).

94. *Id.* at 652.

95. *Id.* at 655.

96. *Id.*

SEC v. Talbot

*United States Court of Appeals for
the Ninth Circuit*
530 F.3d 1085 (9th Cir. 2008).

FACTS   On April 18 or 19, 2003, LendingTree's CEO Doug Lebda told Fidelity Financial's Vice President Brent Bickett that LendingTree was negotiating a sale of the firm to a third party on terms that were favored by a majority of the LendingTree board. Fidelity owned approximately 10% of LendingTree's common stock. Lebda did not disclose the name of the potential acquirer, but he did tell Bickett that he "would need to keep this information confidential." Bickett then relayed that information to Fidelity's CEO William Foley.

On April 22, 2003, Fidelity held its quarterly board meeting, which J. Thomas Talbot, an attorney and Fidelity board member, attended. Foley told the board that negotiations were proceeding for a third party to acquire LendingTree. Foley informed the board that the name of the acquirer was unkown, but he indicated that Fidelity "would make about $50 million on the transaction." According to Terry Christensen, another board member, Foley informed the board that Fidelity's stock in LendingTree "would be acquired at a very attractive price," between $16 and $18, which represented a 23% to 29% increase over LendingTree's closing price of $12.97 per share on April 22, 2003. Talbot remembered the meeting differently, declaring that, although he could "not recall the exact words spoken . . . some person or company might be interested in acquiring LendingTree, Inc. . . . and [Fidelity] would benefit if the transaction occurred."

Although Foley did not tell the board that the information was confidential, one board member, Cary Thompson, said "something to the effect that this is inside information, no one trade in the stock. Make sure you don't do anything with the stock." All board members present at the meeting, except for Talbot, considered the LendingTree information to be confidential.

Various directors testified as to their understanding of how far along the negotiations had proceeded between LendingTree and the unnamed acquirer, as conveyed by Foley: "far along, and it would be announced as a deal shortly thereafter" (Thompson); "advanced discussions" (Bickett); and that "it looked like there was going to be a transaction" (Christensen). Talbot interpreted Foley's words as far less definite, understanding the information about LendingTree to be a "rumor," not a "factual statement."

On April 24, 2003, two days after the meeting, Talbot purchased 5,000 shares of LendingTree on margin at approximately $13.50 per share for a total of $67,000. Talbot testified that Foley's comments at the April 22, 2003 board meeting regarding LendingTree "triggered [his] conduct on April 23rd to look into [LendingTree] more carefully." Talbot continued to monitor LendingTree's stock closely. After being satisfied that "the price was moving up . . . [a]nd the volume was solid," he purchased on margin an additional 5,000 shares at $14.50 per share for $72,500 on April 30, 2003.

On May 5, 2003, three major events occurred. First, Fidelity executed an agreement with the acquiring company, USA Interactive Corporation, and LendingTree to vote its shares in favor of the acquisition. Second, LendingTree and USA Interactive issued a press release announcing the acquisition. Third, LendingTree's stock rose roughly 41% on the news, immediately after which Talbot sold all of his LendingTree shares for a profit of $67,881.20. LendingTree stock closed on Monday, May 5, at $20.72, up $6.03 from its previous closing price of $14.69 on Friday, May 2. Talbot resigned from the Fidelity board on September 19, 2003.

On June 23, 2004, the SEC brought a civil action against Talbot alleging that he had traded on material, nonpublic information in violation of section 10(b) of the 1934 Act and Rule 10b–5. The district court held that Talbot could not be liable under the misappropriation theory because there was no continuous chain of fiduciary relationship from LendingTree to Fidelity to Talbot. With respect to whether the information Talbot received at the Fidelity board meeting was material, the district court held that it could not make that determination one way or the other as a matter of law. There were genuine issues of material fact that a jury would have to consider to decide whether the information was material or not. The SEC appealed.

ISSUE PRESENTED   Did a director of a major shareholder of an acquisition target violate Rule 10b–5 and section 10(b)of the 1934 Act when he traded in the stock of the target while in possession of nonpublic information concerning a possible acquisition of the target?

CONTINUED

SUMMARY OF OPINION The U.S. Court of Appeals for the Ninth Circuit characterized this as a "textbook" case of misappropriation. Talbot, as a member of Fidelity's board, owed a duty of trust and confidence to Fidelity, the "source" of the information on which he traded. That information was "entrusted" to him by Fidelity in his capacity as a Fidelity director. Thus, Talbot violated his fiduciary duty to Fidelity when he secretly traded LendingTree securities on the basis of that information. The appeals court rejected the trial court's reasoning that the trader and the "originating source" must be linked through a continuous chain of fiduciary relationships for liability to attach under the misappropriation theory. It was sufficient that Talbot breached a duty to Fidelity.

The court also rejected Talbot's assertion that he was not obligated to keep the information in question confidential given his belief that the acquisition was merely a "rumor." Nor was the fact that Foley had not expressly stated that the information was confidential a defense: "Corporate officers and directors are not permitted to use their position of trust and confidence to further their private interests. While technically not trustees, they stand in a fiduciary relation to the corporation and its stockholders." Thus, as a matter of law, Talbot's conduct contravened the purposes of the Exchange Act as articulated in *O'Hagan*:

> An animating purpose of the Exchange Act . . . [is] to insure honest securities markets and thereby promote investor confidence. Although informational disparity is inevitable in the securities markets, investors likely would hesitate to venture their capital in a market where trading based on misappropriated nonpublic information is unchecked by law. An investor's informational disadvantage vis-à-vis a misappropriator with material, nonpublic information stems from contrivance, not luck; it is a disadvantage that cannot be overcome with research or skill.[97]

The court next considered whether the information at issue was material as a matter of law. An omitted fact is material "if there is a substantial likelihood that a reasonable investor would consider it important in deciding whether to buy or sell securities." In determining materiality, a court will consider several factors, including an increase in the stock price after public announcement of a merger, whether the information comes from an insider, and whether information concerning a potential acquisition is accompanied by "implied certainty" or other measures of quantification.

The Ninth Circuit agreed with the district court's finding that a genuine issue of material fact existed regarding materiality. Evidence supporting a finding of materiality included Foley's indication to the board that Fidelity stood to make a $50 million profit on the acquisition, the common perception among other directors that the acquisition was in advanced stages, the fact that Talbot purchased LendingTree stock just two days after learning this information, and the stock price increase of 41% on announcement of the acquisition. Evidence supporting a finding of immateriality included the fact that Talbot understood the transaction to be a mere "rumor" and his recollection that no one discussed when exactly the acquisition would occur. Due to the conflicting evidence, a question of material fact existed as to the materiality of the information on which Talbot traded, which would have to be resolved at trial.

RESULT The district court's summary judgment in favor of Talbot was reversed. Talbot could be held liable under the misappropriation theory if the jury concluded at trial that the information Talbot knew about the possible acquisition of LendingTree was material.

CRITICAL THINKING QUESTIONS

1. Would the misappropriation theory apply to a case in which a person defrauded a bank into giving him a loan, or embezzled cash from another, and then used the proceeds of the misdeed to purchase securities?

2. If a fiduciary disclosed to the source of nonpublic information that she planned to trade on that information, would trading on that information constitute a section 10(b) violation? Would it violate any other laws? Would it be ethical?

97. *Id.* at 658–59.

The misappropriation theory widens the class of persons who can be found liable for insider trading, but the requirement that there must be a duty of trust or confidence remains a limiting factor. For instance, an outsider who infers from the movements of corporate executives that an event will likely take place owes no duty to the corporation or its employees.

Rules 10b5–1 and 10b5–2

In 2000, the SEC sought to clarify several aspects of insider trading by promulgating Rules 10b5–1 and 10b5–2 (which are set forth in Appendix I).

Trading Based on Nonpublic Information

Rule 10b5–1 provides that any person who purchases or sells securities of any issuer on the basis of material nonpublic information about the security or issuer violates section 10(b) if the purchase or sale was in breach of a duty of trust or confidence owed directly, indirectly, or derivatively to (1) the issuer or its security holders or (2) any other person who is the source of the material nonpublic information. A trade is "on the basis of" material nonpublic information if the person trading was aware of the information at the time of the trade, unless the person can demonstrate that:

1. Before becoming aware of the information, he or she (a) entered into a binding contract to purchase or sell, (b) gave instructions for the trade, or (c) adopted a written plan to trade; and

2. The contract, instruction, or plan either (a) specified the amount of securities to be traded and the price, or (b) included a written formula or algorithm for determining the amount and price, or (c) did not permit the person to exercise any subsequent influence over how, when, and whether to trade; and

3. The trade was pursuant to the contract, instruction, or plan.

Thus, Rule 10b5–1 creates a presumption that persons who trade while in possession of material nonpublic information trade on the basis of that information unless the trade is pursuant to a preexisting *10b5–1 plan.* The rule was adopted in response to several cases in which the court held that a person who trades while in possession of inside information violates Rule 10b–5 only if he or she decided to trade based on that information.

The affirmative defense is designed to cover situations in which the person trading can demonstrate that the material nonpublic information was not a factor in the trading decision. It permits those who would like to plan securities transactions in advance, at a time when they are not aware of material nonpublic information, to carry out those preplanned transactions at a later time, even if they later become aware of material, nonpublic information.

ethicalconsideration

Members of Congress and their staff often meet with lobbyists and constituents to discuss proposed and pending litigation. If a lobbyist trades on the basis of that information, is either the lobbyist or the member of Congress or the staffer liable for insider trading? Would it violate section 10(b) for a member of Congress or staffer to trade based on nonpublic information learned about a key bill under consideration? Are any such trades ethical? Would it be legal for a hedge fund to pay a political intelligence firm to provide nonpublic information about congressional deliberations?[a] Would it be ethical? Should Congress restrict the transfer of such information or trading based on it?[b] What public policies and ethical considerations are implicated?

a. Matt Levine, *What Congressman Would You Buddy Up with to Help with Your Insider Trading?*, DEALBREAKER, Oct. 4, 2011, *available at* http://dealbreaker.com/2011/10/what-congressman-would-you-buddy-up-with-to-help-with-your-insider-trading/#more-54623.

b. *See* Stop Trading on Congressional Knowledge Act of 2012 (STOCK Act), Pub. L. No. 112-105, 126 Stat. 291 (2012).

Duty of Trust or Confidence SEC Rule 10b5–2 sets forth a nonexclusive list of three situations in which a person is deemed to have a duty of trust or confidence for purposes of the misappropriation theory of insider trading. A duty of trust or confidence exists (1) whenever a person agrees to maintain information in confidence; (2) when two people have a history, pattern, or practice of sharing confidences such that the recipient of the information knows or reasonably should know that the person communicating the material nonpublic information expects that the recipient will maintain its confidentiality; and (3) when a person receives or obtains material nonpublic information from a spouse, parent, child, or sibling unless the recipient of the information can demonstrate that, under the facts and circumstances of that family relationship, no duty of trust or confidence existed.

MAIL AND WIRE FRAUD

An employee who trades or tips using confidential information belonging to his or her employer can be liable under the Mail and Wire Fraud Acts. For example, the U.S. Supreme Court upheld the mail and wire fraud conviction of R. Foster Winans, a Dow Jones employee who wrote the *Wall Street Journal* column "Heard on the Street," after he gave two stockbrokers information about his soon-to-be-published columns.[98] They used the information to make trades based on the anticipated positive market response to the column's publication. The Court held that if

---

98. Carpenter v. United States, 484 U.S. 19 (1987).

IN BRIEF

Decision Tree Analysis of Insider Trading Laws

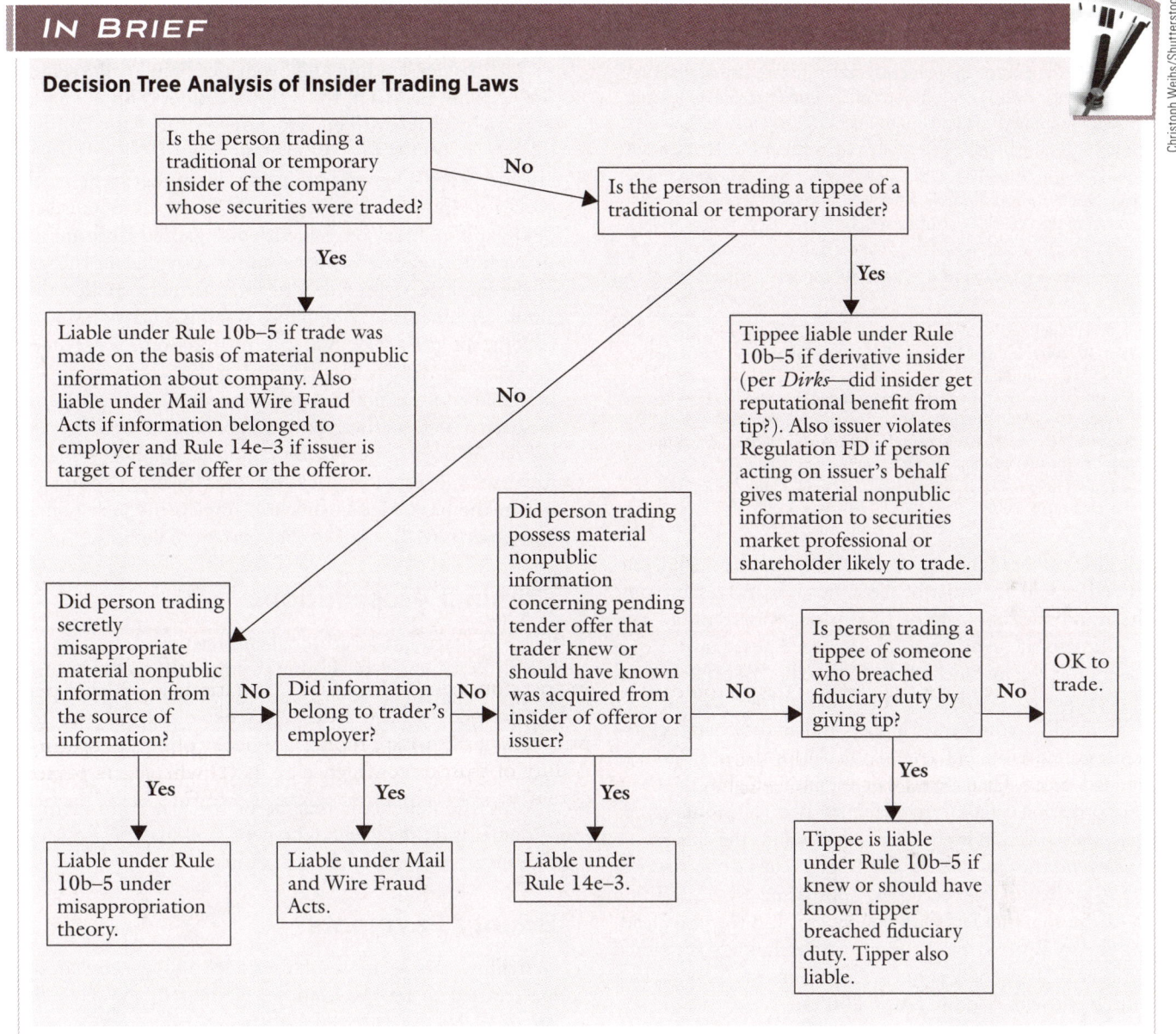

© Cengage Learning 2013

a business generates confidential information and has the right to control the use of that information prior to public disclosure, then use of that information to trade can be prohibited under the wire and mail fraud statutes. Thus, even though neither Winans nor the stockbrokers traded in Dow Jones stock, Winans was liable for mail and wire fraud because he wrongfully gave his employer's confidential information to the traders.

RICO

A securities fraud claim cannot be used as a predicate act in a civil case under the Racketeer Influenced and Corrupt Organizations Act (RICO) (discussed in Chapter 14) unless the defendant has been criminally convicted in connection with the fraud. However, a criminal conviction under the Wire and Mail Fraud Acts for misappropriation of an employer's confidential information may, assuming other requirements are met, be the basis for a civil RICO case.

ENFORCEMENT OF ANTIFRAUD PROHIBITIONS

Persons who violate the antifraud provisions of the federal securities laws are subject to private suits for damages, civil enforcement actions by the SEC, and criminal prosecution.

Private Actions

In private actions, the plaintiff must be an actual purchaser or seller of securities, and the plaintiff's loss must have been proximately caused by the acts of the defendant.

INTERNATIONAL SNAPSHOT

In 2008, the European Union responded to large auditor settlements and awards by authorizing member states to permit auditors to limit their liability to their audit clients by contract.[a] Auditors in the United States have renewed calls for limits, arguing that the growth of their clients' market capitalization and the concentration of public company audits by the Big Four accounting firms (PricewaterhouseCoopers, Ernst & Young, KPMG, and Deloitte) could leave the markets in chaos if one of the Big Four failed as a result of a massive judgment against it.[b]

a. Jennifer Hughes, *FRC Gives Liability Reform Guidance*, FIN. TIMES, June 30, 2008. In May 2008, the European Commission stated that unlimited auditor liability was "no longer tenable," and the internal market and services commissioner recommended that the EU member states introduce legislation to limit auditor liability. *Id.* The U.K. Financial Reporting Council has authorized contractual limits on liability but requires them to be approved each year by the shareholders. *Id.*

b. Jennifer Hughes, *US Auditors Renew Calls for Liability Limits,* FIN. TIMES, Sept. 1, 2008.

All contemporaneous traders, that is, persons who purchased or sold securities of the same class at the same time the fraud was ongoing or the insider was trading, have standing to sue. Any amounts disgorged pursuant to court order or at the instance of the SEC will offset the amount of damages recoverable by contemporaneous traders.

In insider trading cases, tippers and all direct and remote tippees are jointly and severally liable for the illicit gain or avoided losses. That means that any individual in the chain of information can be found liable for all of the profits gained or losses avoided in every transaction within the chain.

Defendants in one of the largest class-action settlements in history agreed to pay approximately $7.2 billion to Enron shareholders who bought stock in the years leading up to Enron's bankruptcy.[99] Shareholders recovered another high payout, about $6.2 billion, in a class-action settlement with WorldCom in 2005.[100]

SEC Enforcement Actions

In an SEC civil enforcement action, violators may be liable for damages and disgorgement of profits and may be subject to other penalties and injunctions prohibiting future violations. Both in deciding whether to seek corporate penalties and in determining the magnitude of the penalty, the SEC focuses principally on two considerations: (1) Did the corporation obtain a direct benefit as a result of the violation? (2) Will the penalty recompense or further harm the injured shareholders?[101] The SEC assessed a record $750 million fine against WorldCom, prompting

complaints that large fines further injure shareholders already hurt by management's wrongdoing.

The Insider Trading and Securities Fraud Enforcement Act of 1988, passed in the wake of insider trading charges against Michael Milken and Drexel Burnham Lambert in the late 1980s (discussed more fully in this chapter's "Inside Story"), provided strong encouragement to the brokerage industry to police itself. A brokerage house can be fined if it "knew or recklessly disregarded" information that would indicate insider trading activities on the part of its employees. Intended to force firms to police their employees, institute compliance systems, and monitor suspicious activities, the Act specifically requires registered brokers and dealers to maintain and enforce reasonably designed written policies and procedures to prevent the misuse of material nonpublic information. Although this legislation does not explicitly require it, many commentators have suggested that it is prudent for other companies not in the brokerage business to implement such policies and procedures in light of their potential liability.

Criminal Prosecutions

The SEC itself has no criminal enforcement power. As discussed in Chapter 14, criminal prosecutions are brought by the Department of Justice through the U.S. Attorney's Office, often on referral from the SEC. If criminally convicted of a willful violation, a defendant faces fines and/or imprisonment. Willfulness has been interpreted as awareness by the defendant that he or she was committing a wrongful act; the defendant need not specifically know that he or she was violating a statute.

Bounty Payments

Individuals whose tips result in insider trading prosecutions are entitled to receive bounties, similar to the payments provided by the Internal Revenue Service in tax cases. These bounties can be as high as 10% of any revenues recovered from a defendant through penalties or settlement. In May 2011, the SEC adopted rules, pursuant to section 922 of the Dodd–Frank Act, creating a whistleblower program that rewards individuals for successful enforcement actions by the SEC.[102] The rules also provide incentives for whistleblowers to report the violations internally first.

SELECTIVE DISCLOSURE AND REGULATION FD

Regulation FD (Fair Disclosure) prohibits the practice of *selective disclosure,* whereby issuers of publicly traded securities would disclose material nonpublic information, such

99. *In re* Enron Corp. Sec., Derivative, and ERISA Litig., 586 F. Supp. 2d 732, 740 (S.D. Tex. 2008).

100. *In re* WorldCom Inc. Sec. Litig., 388 F. Supp. 2d 319 (S.D.N.Y. 2005).

101. *SEC Unveils Statement of Penalty Principles with Announcement of McAfee Settlement*, CORP. COUNS. WKLY. (BNA), Jan. 11, 2006, at 9.

102. Press Release, Securities & Exchange Comm'n, SEC Adopts Rules to Establish Whistleblower Program (May 25, 2011), *available at* http://www.sec.gov/news/press/2011/2011-116.htm.

as advance warnings of earning results, to securities analysts or selected institutional investors before making full disclosure of the same information to the general public. Those privy to the information were able to make a profit or avoid a loss at the expense of those kept in the dark. According to the SEC, this led "to a loss of investor confidence in the integrity of our capital markets. Investors who see a security's price change dramatically and only later are given access to the information responsible for that move rightly question whether they are on a level playing field with market insiders."[103]

Selective disclosure also threatened the integrity of the securities markets by creating "the potential for corporate management to treat material information as a commodity to be used to gain or maintain favor with particular analysts or investors."[104] Analysts might feel pressure to report favorably about a company for fear of being excluded from calls and meetings to which other analysts were invited. Finally, the SEC reasoned, "Whereas issuers may once have had to rely on analysts to serve as information intermediaries, issuers now can use a variety of methods to communicate directly with the market." These include Internet webcasting and teleconferencing. Accordingly, the SEC concluded: "Technological limitations no longer provide an excuse for abiding the threats to market integrity that selective disclosure represents."[105]

Regulation FD provides that whenever an issuer, or a person acting on its behalf, discloses material nonpublic information to securities market professionals or holders of the issuer's securities who may well trade on the basis of the information, the issuer must publicly disclose that same information simultaneously (for intentional disclosures) or promptly (for nonintentional disclosures). Market professionals include broker–dealers, investment advisers and investment managers, investment companies and hedge funds, and official persons thereof. A disclosure is considered intentional only if the person knows, or is reckless in not knowing, that the information he or she is communicating is both material and nonpublic. In cases of nonintentional disclosure, the issuer must disclose the information to the public as soon as practical (but no later than twenty-four hours) after a senior official learns of the disclosure and knows (or is reckless in not knowing) that the information disclosed was both material and nonpublic. No public disclosure is required for communications (1) made to a person who owes the issuer a duty of trust or confidence (such as an investment banker, accountant, or attorney); (2) made to any person who expressly agrees to maintain the information in confidence; (3) with a credit rating agency; or (4) made in connection with most offerings of securities registered under the 1933 Act.

Information is material if there is a substantial likelihood that a reasonable shareholder would consider it important in making an investment decision. Types of information or events likely to be considered material include (1) earnings information; (2) mergers, acquisitions, tender offers, or changes in assets; (3) new products or developments involving customers or suppliers; (4) changes in control or management; (5) changes in auditors; (6) defaults on senior securities, repurchase plans, or stock splits; and (7) bankruptcies. The SEC cautioned that an official who engages in a private discussion with an analyst seeking guidance about earnings estimates "takes on a high degree of risk under Regulation FD."[106] On the other hand, an issuer is not prohibited from disclosing nonmaterial information to an analyst even if, unbeknown to the issuer, that piece of information helps the analyst complete a "mosaic" of information that, taken together, is material.

To avoid creating a chilling effect on issuers' willingness to communicate with outsiders, the SEC expressly provided that private parties cannot sue issuers for violations of Regulation FD. It is not an antifraud rule, and failure to make a public disclosure required solely by Regulation FD is not in and of itself a violation of Rule 10b–5. If an issuer fails to comply with Regulation FD, the SEC is empowered to bring an enforcement action and can seek an injunction and/or civil monetary penalties.

OTHER REQUIREMENTS APPLICABLE TO OFFICERS, DIRECTORS, AND GREATER-THAN-10% SHAREHOLDERS

In addition to the prohibition against trading based on material nonpublic information, section 16 of the 1934 Act and section 306 of the Sarbanes–Oxley Act impose several additional requirements on officers, directors, and greater-than-10% shareholders of publicly traded firms.

Short-Swing Trading

Section 16(b) of the 1934 Act governs *short-swing trading*—the purchase and sale, or the sale and purchase, by officers, directors, and greater-than-10% shareholders of equity securities of a public company registered under the 1934 Act within a six-month period. Unlike section 10(b), which requires scienter (that is, a showing of bad intent), liability is imposed under section 16(b) regardless of the insider's state of mind.

Although the purpose of section 16(b) is to prevent insiders of publicly held companies from exploiting information not generally available to the public in order to secure quick profits, it need not be proved that the insider

---

103. Selective Disclosures and Insider Trading, SEC Release Nos. 33-7881, 34-43154, IC-24599, 17 C.F.R. pts. 240, 243, 249 (Aug. 15, 2000).

104. *Id.*

105. *Id.*

106. *Id.*

actually possessed any material nonpublic information at the time the insider traded in the securities. To establish liability under section 16(b), it is sufficient to prove that an insider purchased and then sold, or sold and then purchased, equity securities within a period of six months.

Definition of an Equity Security

An *equity security* includes (1) any stock or similar security; (2) any security that is convertible, with or without consideration, into such a security; (3) any security carrying any warrant or right to subscribe to or purchase such a security; (4) any such warrant or right; and (5) any other security that the SEC deems to be of a similar nature and that, for the protection of investors or in the public interest, the SEC considers appropriate to treat as an equity security. Thus, equity securities may include hybrids that ordinarily are not considered equity securities, such as convertible debt securities that have not been registered under the 1934 Act.

Special problems can arise in connection with the grant and exercise of stock options and other derivative securities. A set of complicated rules embodied largely in Rule 16b–3, adopted by the SEC under section 16(b) of the 1934 Act, governs this area. Before becoming an officer or director, a person should consult counsel to avoid inadvertent section 16(b) liability.

Persons Covered

Section 16(b) applies to officers, directors, and greater-than-10% shareholders.

Officer or Director   A person may be liable under section 16(b) if he or she was an officer or director at the time of either the purchase or the sale. It is not necessary that both transactions occur during the person's tenure.

For example, if an officer purchased 100 shares of XYZ Corporation common stock at $10 per share on January 1, resigned as an officer on February 1, then sold 100 shares of XYZ common stock at $20 per share on March 1, she would be liable for $1,000 of short-swing profits because she was an officer when she made the January 1 purchase. Similarly, if a person purchased 100 shares of XYZ Corporation at $10 per share on January 1, became an officer of XYZ Corporation on February 1, and sold the shares at $20 on March 1, that person would be liable for $1,000 of short-swing profits because he was an officer at the time of the sale. On the other hand, if an officer who had not traded for more than six months before March 1 resigned on March 1, bought 100 shares of XYZ Corporation at $10 on April 1, then sold them at $20 on April 2, she would not have recoverable profits because she was not an officer or director at the time of either the purchase or the sale.

Greater-than-10% Shareholder   The rule is different for persons who are not officers or directors but are beneficial owners of more than 10% of the issuer's equity securities. Such persons are liable under section 16(b) only if they hold more than 10% of the securities both at the time of the purchase and at the time of the sale. The transaction whereby the person becomes a 10% shareholder does not count.

For example, if a person who previously owned less than 10% of the shares of XYZ Corporation's stock purchased 10.5% of XYZ Corporation's common stock at $10 on January 1, then sold those shares at $20 on March 1, he would have no recoverable short-swing profits. However, if the same person had purchased another 2% of XYZ common stock in February, then the February purchase could be matched against the March sale because he owned more than 10% of the stock at the time of the February purchase and also at the time of the March sale.

Beneficial Ownership of Shares

Officers, directors, and greater-than-10% shareholders can be liable for purchases and sales of shares they do not own of record but are deemed to own beneficially. Under section 16(b), a person will be considered the *beneficial owner* of any securities held by his or her immediate family—his or her spouse, any minor children, or any other relative living in his or her household. There is a rebuttable presumption that a person is the beneficial owner of any securities over which he or she has the practical power to vest title in himself or herself, or from which he or she receives economic benefits (such as sales proceeds) substantially equal to those of ownership.

Purchases and sales of securities held beneficially by an officer, director, or greater-than-10% shareholder will be attributed to that person in determining his or her liability for short-swing trading. For example, the purchase of securities by an officer's husband could be matched under section 16(b) with the sale of other securities by the officer herself within six months of her husband's purchase, thereby resulting in liability for short-swing profits. Thus, any officer, director, or greater-than-10% shareholder planning a purchase or sale must consider not only his or her own trading record but also the record of those persons whose securities he or she is deemed to own beneficially.

Purchase and Sale Within Six Months

To result in recoverable short-swing profits, the purchase and sale, or sale and purchase, must have occurred "within any period of less than six months." That period commences on the day on which the first purchase or sale occurred and ends at midnight two days before the corresponding date in the sixth succeeding month. For example, for a transaction on January 1, the six-month period ends at midnight on June 29, two days before July 1.

Profit Calculation

To calculate the profits recoverable under section 16(b), the sale price is compared with the purchase price. If several purchases and sales occur within a six-month period, the lowest purchase price will be matched with the highest sale price; then the next lowest purchase price with the next highest sale price; and so on, regardless of the order in which the purchases and sales actually occurred. Matching purchases and sales in this manner maximizes the recoverable profit.

The shares that are sold need not be the same shares that were purchased. Any purchase and any sale will incur liability if they occur less than six months apart, regardless of whether the transactions involve the same shares. For example, if on January 1, an officer of XYZ Corporation sold 100 shares of XYZ common stock that he had held for ten years, then on February 1 purchased 200 shares of XYZ common stock at a lower price, he would be liable for the short-swing profits on 100 of the shares. The January 1 sale would be matched with the February 1 purchase, even though the officer had held the securities for ten years before he sold them.

Short-swing profits cannot be offset by trading losses that were incurred in the same period. Thus, there may be recoverable profits under section 16(b) even though the officer or director suffered a net loss on the trading transactions.

The following example illustrates the "lowest-in, highest-out" matching principle just described. Assume that an officer made purchases and sales, each of 100 shares, as follows:

Date	Transaction	Price
Jan. 1	Purchase	$ 9
Jan. 30	Sale	10
Feb. 15	Sale	15
Feb. 28	Purchase	12
Mar. 15	Purchase	6
Mar. 30	Sale	4

These transactions will result in a recoverable short-swing profit of $1,000, calculated as follows. The February 15 sale is matched with the March 15 purchase, for a profit of $15 − $6 = $9 per share, or $900. Then the January 30 sale is matched with the January 1 purchase, for a profit of $10 − $9 = $1 per share, or $100. Even though the March 15 purchase at $6 per share and the subsequent sale at $4 per share resulted in a loss of $2 per share, or $200, that loss will not be taken into account. The officer will have to surrender $900 + $100 = $1,000, even though she actually realized only $200 of net profit in the trading transactions (total sales of $2,900 less purchases of $2,700).

Unorthodox Transactions

If a purchase or sale by an officer, director, or greater-than-10% shareholder that would otherwise result in recoverable short-swing profits was involuntary and did not involve the payment of cash, and if there was no possibility of speculative abuse of inside information, then a court may hold that it was an *unorthodox transaction* to which no liability will attach. These situations generally arise in the context of exchanges in mergers and other corporate reorganizations, stock conversions, stock reclassifications, and tender offers in which securities are sold or exchanged for consideration other than cash.[107] Embracing the judicial doctrine, the SEC exempts certain noncash mergers, reclassifications, and consolidations under amendments to Rule 16b–7 adopted in 2005. In contrast, an exchange of securities by an officer, director, or greater-than-10% shareholder for cash in a tender offer or acquisition would almost certainly be deemed a sale for which the person receiving the cash could be liable under section 16(b).

Filing of Beneficial Ownership Reports

Section 16(a) of the 1934 Act requires officers, directors, and greater-than-10% shareholders of companies that have registered any class of equity securities under the 1934 Act to file beneficial-ownership reports with the SEC and with any national securities exchange on which their company's equity securities are listed. Within ten days after becoming an officer or director, a person must file an initial ownership report on Form 3, even if the person does not beneficially own any securities of the company at that time. In the case of greater-than-10% shareholders, a Form 3 must be filed within ten days of the date they acquire a greater-than-10% interest. (In addition, as noted in Chapter 21, any person who acquires more than 5% of the voting securities of a public company must file a Schedule 13D within ten days after the date he or she acquired the more-than-5% stake. An amendment to the Schedule 13D must be filed promptly after any material change in beneficial ownership or investment purpose.)

Subsequently, an officer, director, or greater-than-10% shareholder must file a Form 4 within two business days after any transaction resulting in any change in beneficial ownership. For example, a transaction executed on Tuesday, September 3, would have to be reported to the SEC by the close of business (5:30 P.M. Eastern time) on Thursday, September 5. In the initial Form 4, an officer or director must report all purchases or sales that occurred within the previous six months, even if those transactions were effected before the person became an officer or director. A Form 5 showing changes in beneficial ownership

---

107. *See, e.g.,* At Home Corp. v. Cox Commc'ns Inc., 446 F.3d 403 (2d Cir. 2006) (finding no section 16(b) "purchase" when insider acquired stock in At Home by acquisition of three third-party intermediaries that held warrants for At Home stock because the acquisition of the three cable systems holding At Home's stock "entail[ed] appreciable risks and opportunities independent of the risks and opportunities that inhere in the stock of the issuer," likening it to "speculating in tractors by buying a farm").

during the preceding year must be filed annually within forty-five days after the issuer's fiscal year-end.

Acquisitions and dispositions of shares acquired by officers or directors pursuant to employee benefit plans must also be reported within two business days on Form 4 even if the transactions are exempt from short-swing recovery under Rule 16b-3. A person who ceases to be an officer or director must continue to report any changes in beneficial ownership that occur within six months of the last reportable transaction while he or she was an officer or director.

The SEC has brought enforcement actions to force executives to file these ownership reports within the required time frame. Publicly traded companies must disclose in their proxy statements and in their annual reports on Form 10–K whether their officers and directors have complied with their section 16(a) reporting obligations.

Prohibition on Selling Short

Section 16(c) of the 1934 Act prohibits officers or directors from *selling* any of their company's equity *securities short*, that is, from selling a security that the seller does not own. If the officer or director owns the security being sold, he or she must deliver it within twenty days after the sale or deposit it in the mails or other usual channels of delivery within five days. If the officer or director fails to do this, he or she will be liable under section 16(c) unless (1) he or she acted in good faith and was unable to make the delivery

or deposit within the specified time, or (2) he or she acted in good faith and satisfying the time requirements would have caused undue inconvenience or expense.

SOX Ban on Trading During Blackout Periods and Mandated Disgorgement After Financial Restatements

Section 306[108] of the Sarbanes–Oxley Act (SOX)[109] prohibits officers and directors from trading equity securities acquired in connection with their services as officers or directors during any retirement plan blackout period. A *blackout period* is any period longer than three business days during which 50% or more of the participants in a retirement plan are prevented from trading. Private actions to recover any profit realized by the offender may be brought by the issuer or derivatively on its behalf by a shareholder.

Section 304 provides that the chief executive and chief financial officers of an issuer required to restate its financial statements "as a result of misconduct" must disgorge all bonuses and incentive- and equity-based compensation received in the twelve months following the filing of the faulty document as well as all profits realized from the sale of the issuer's securities during that period.[110]

---

108. 15 U.S.C. § 7244.

109. Pub. L. No. 107-204, 116 Stat. 745 (2002).

110. 15 U.S.C. § 7243.

GLOBAL VIEW

Insider Trading in the European Union and China

The European Union (EU) Market Abuse Directive[111] requires member states to enact national legislation punishing primary and secondary insiders who trade publicly held securities on the basis of "inside information," which is defined as nonpublic information "a reasonable investor would be likely to use as part of the basis of his investment decisions."[112] Primary insiders include officers, directors, employees, and shareholders of the issuer as well as persons who have access to inside information by virtue of their professional duties. Secondary insiders are those who obtain inside information from primary insiders, that is, tippees.

Issuers are required to maintain lists of persons working for them with access to inside information, and senior managers must report changes in beneficial ownership to the appropriate national authority within five business days.[113] In addition,

the principle of "equal treatment" prohibits the selective disclosure of inside information.

Although the EU Directive does not on its face embrace the misappropriation theory, persons who obtain information as a result of their professional duties are deemed primary insiders even if they have no fiduciary duty to the issuer. Thus, trading by a person like O'Hagan[114] would violate European law.

The legislation in China banning insider trading is based in substantial part on the U.S. regulatory approach[115] and is enforced by the China Securities Regulatory Commission (CSRC). Although there are very few reported cases, research suggests that insider trading in the Chinese markets is "widespread," "everyday," "extensive," and "ingrained."[116] One interviewee remarked: "Many people do not trade shares unless they have inside information. We simply have no choice in such an environment."[117]

---

111. European Parliament and Council Directive 2003/6/EC on Insider Dealing and Market Manipulation (Market Abuse), 2003 O.J. (L 96). This supersedes Commission Directive 89/592: Coordinating Regulations on Insider Dealing.

112. Commission Directive 2003/124/EC, 2003 O.J. (L 339).

113. Commission Directive 2004/72/EC, 2004 O.J. (L 162).

114. United States v. O'Hagan, 521 U.S. 642 (1997).

115. HUI HUANG, INTERNATIONAL SECURITIES MARKETS: INSIDER TRADING LAW IN CHINA 25–26 (2006).

116. *Id.* at 38.

117. Quoted in *id.*

THE RESPONSIBLE MANAGER

PREVENTING SECURITIES FRAUD AND INSIDER TRADING

Managers have an obligation not to mislead investors in company public announcements, periodic reports, or speeches. Although a company may remain silent about material developments if neither the company nor insiders are trading, early disclosure is often the better course. This gives all investors equal access to current information about the company. There is a trade-off here, however. Sometimes the company's business or transactions may be in a state of flux. For example, a party with no visible source of financing may have made an offer to buy the company's assets. In this case, it may be worse to disclose the offer and get the market's hopes up than to wait and see if the offer is real. Managers, together with their lawyers, must make these judgment calls.

Another reason for early disclosure is to avoid illegal insider trading. A company must make disclosure if it knows its insiders, such as officers or directors, are trading in the company's securities.

Any forward-looking statements should be identified as such and be accompanied by meaningful cautionary language identifying important factors that could cause actual results to differ materially from those in the forward-looking statement. It is often helpful to (1) prioritize the order of risk factors, (2) state the risk in the first sentence, (3) be specific, (4) convey the magnitude of the risk, and (5) focus risk factors on the negatives without softening them by including positives.

Trading by a manager based on material nonpublic information is illegal. It violates the manager's fiduciary duty to subordinate his or her personal interests to the interests of the corporation and shareholders he or she serves. A manager is given access to nonpublic information not for the manager's own personal gain but to better enable the manager to serve his or her principal—the corporation and its shareholders. Violation of those rules erodes both shareholder confidence and the confidence of investors generally in the capital markets. It is also unethical.

A manager cannot give tips to others in exchange for money or even just to enhance his or her reputation as "someone in the know." A manager should carefully guard the information given in confidence by his or her employer or client. Managers must also instill these values in their subordinates. Everyone, from the person who empties the trash or runs the copy machine to the person who occupies the largest office in the executive suite, must be told to follow these rules or risk dismissal. This edict should be made clear in the corporation's code of ethics and in its personnel manual. All corporations, and especially brokerage firms, without adequate procedures in place to prevent illegal

insider trading face potential liability for their insiders' illegal trades.

Inquiries into insider trading tend to focus on high-volume trading that occurs before major corporate announcements. Enforcement agencies generally watch organized trading rings and well-known public figures because of their high profiles, but ordinary investors and isolated violations are also detected and prosecuted. Surveillance groups monitor daily trading and investigate any suspicious activity. Social media make it easier for regulators to find potential tippers and tippees.

A company cannot disclose material information only to certain favored analysts. This is unfair to the public investors and can result in liability for the company and for the manager who tips an analyst whose clients then trade based on the tip. It also violates Regulation FD.

A company's policy on insider trading[118] should prohibit any person associated with the company from trading in any security, regardless of whether it was issued by the company, based on material nonpublic information. The policy should also ban passing on material nonpublic information to outsiders who may trade (tipping). It should require persons who are likely to obtain material nonpublic information on a regular basis to pre-clear all purchases and sales of the company's securities. The policy should also (1) describe the legal penalties for insider trading and the company's potential liability for the insider trading violations of its employees and (2) provide that any employee who violates the policy may be terminated.

An officer or director of a public company who buys and sells securities within a six-month period has a legal and ethical responsibility to come forward and pay all profits over to the corporation. This is true even if the short-swing trade was inadvertent, as might happen if an officer sold securities not realizing that his or her spouse had bought securities less than six months before. A corporation that discovers a short-swing trade must try to persuade the insider to voluntarily turn the profits over to the corporation. If the insider refuses to do so, the corporation has an obligation to bring suit to recover the profits from the short-swing trading. If a corporation fails to bring suit, any shareholder has the right to sue on behalf of the corporation.

Officers and directors of public companies must report their security holdings and their trades in a timely manner.

CONTINUED

---

118. Aspects of this discussion are drawn from *Effective Company Policy May Avoid Violations, ABA Told,* Corp. Couns. Wkly. (BNA), Aug. 11, 1999, at 2.

Disregard of these filing requirements breeds contempt for the law and encourages illegal or unethical behavior by others in the organization.

Each manager has a role to play in preventing securities fraud and insider trading. As with preventing the other types of criminal behavior described in Chapter 14, legally astute managers lead by example. If a manager permits his or her company to engage in unlawful or unethical conduct, the manager exposes himself or herself and the company to considerable risk of civil and criminal liability. Such a manager is also likely to encourage illegal behavior by subordinates. Although many executives complained mightily about the costs of Sarbanes–Oxley, especially the requirements in section 404[119] that (1) management maintain a sound internal-control structure for financial reporting and assess its effectiveness and (2) the auditors attest to the soundness of management's assessment and report on the state of the overall financial control system, a number of firms ranging from PepsiCo and Iron Mountain (a $1.8 billion records and information company) to Yankee Candle and RSA Security "approached the new law with something like gratitude."[120]

Section 906 of SOX made "willful failure" to portray the true state of the company's operations and financial condition a crime, and sections 302 and 404 require the CEO and CFO to attest personally to the effectiveness of the firm's internal control over financial reporting.[121] Compliance with these requirements led to (1) improved job-description documentation, training, oversight, and performance evaluation at BlackRock, an investment firm with more than $450 billion in assets under management, which survived the subprime mortgage crisis unscathed; (2) fewer unenforceable contracts and miscalculated rent escalations at a Fortune 1000 real estate company; (3) significant gains in efficiency at Iron Mountain; and (4) standardized software at Manpower.[122] While acknowledging that "[f]ear can be a powerful generator of upstanding conduct," Deloitte & Touche partner Stephen Wagner and Deloitte Consulting partner Lee Dittmar point out that "business runs on discovering and creating value."[123] They go on to assert: "The procrastinators need to start viewing the Sarbanes–Oxley Act of 2002 as an ally in that effort."[124]

---

119. *See* Appendix K.

120. Stephen Wagner & Lee Dittmar, *The Unexpected Benefits of Sarbanes–Oxley*, Harv. Bus. Rev., Apr. 2006, at 133.

---

121. False certifications may give rise to private actions under section 10(b) and Rule 10b–5. Certification of Disclosure in Companies' Quarterly and Annual Reports, SEC Release No. 8124 (Aug. 28, 2002).

122. Wagner & Dittmar, *supra* note 120.

123. *Id.* at 140.

124. *Id.*

Norebbo/Shutterstock

A Manager's Dilemma

Putting It into Practice

When May an Accountant Look the Other Way?

In 1984, several individuals (including David Greenberg) formed seven limited partnerships to develop and operate a chain of 100 "Video USA" video rental stores. One hundred and sixteen limited partners, who had invested $13 million in three private placements, sued accounting firm Touche Ross, among others, for securities fraud. They alleged that Touche Ross (1) had failed to disclose that David Greenberg was a convicted felon; that his twelve-year-old son was the sole officer, director, and shareholder of one of the corporations that served as a general partner; and that the principals used fraudulent invoices and made fraudulent claims against insurance companies; and (2) had prepared the materially misleading financial projections attached as exhibits to the offering memoranda. Touche Ross did not issue an opinion or certification as to any part of the offering documents. Attached to each of the projections that Touche Ross issued was a letter stating that the projection was based on management's "knowledge and belief" and cautioning that the projection "does not include an evaluation of the support for the assumptions underlying the projections." If you were the account manager at Touche Ross and learned about Greenberg's felony conviction and the existence of fraudulent invoices, what would you have done? Is Touche Ross liable under section 10(b) to the limited partners?[125]

---

125. Shapiro v. Cantor, 123 F.3d 717 (2d Cir. 1997).

INSIDE STORY

From Michael Milken to Raj Rajaratnam: Insider Trading Spreads from Junk Bonds to Hedge Funds

The philosopher George Santayana once said, "Those who cannot remember the past are condemned to repeat it."[126] In 2007, Linda Thomson, the SEC enforcement director, reported that insider trading among Wall Street professionals "appears to be rampant again."[127] She and others attributed the spike in cases to the fact that the younger professionals working in hedge funds and brokerage firms "were very young or not even born during the era of the high profile Dennis Levine prosecution in the 1980s."[128] Although U.S. Attorney General Richard Thornburgh warned back in 1990 that "white-collar criminals are never so powerful or clever that they cannot be caught by diligent and persistent law enforcement efforts,"[129] the subsequent insider trading convictions of Samuel Waksal (former CEO of ImClone), Raj Rajaratnam (former manager of the Galleon Group hedge fund), and others suggest that many still have not taken this message to heart.

Dennis Levine and Ivan Boesky

In addition to information gained from monitoring trading, prosecutors and enforcement agencies investigating suspicious activity rely heavily on information gathered from informers and persons already under indictment. For example, the arrest and prosecution of Dennis Levine and Ivan Boesky in 1986 set off the most comprehensive investigation of securities trading practices in the history of federal regulation.

Levine, a former managing director of investment bank Drexel Burnham Lambert, was charged with illegal trading in approximately fifty-four stocks. As a result of cooperation by Levine, the SEC was able to bring insider trading charges against one of Wall Street's richest and most active speculators, Ivan Boesky.

Boesky made his career and fortune as a risk arbitrageur who concentrated on the purchase and sale of stock in target corporations that were the subject of tender offers. Generally, the acquiring corporation pays a premium for the stock of the target corporation; thus, people who invest prior to the announcement of the acquisition are in a position to make swift and substantial profits. The SEC alleged that Levine, who worked on mergers and acquisitions, passed on information to Boesky, who was able to purchase shares in the target

prior to public announcement of the impending takeover. It is further believed that Boesky offered Levine a 5% commission for any information leading to an initial stock purchase and a 1% commission for information pertaining to stocks already owned by Boesky.

In all, Boesky was alleged to have made approximately $50 million through these insider trading activities. Both Levine and Boesky pleaded guilty to criminal charges. Boesky settled the SEC's civil charges by agreeing to pay $100 million and to cooperate with the government in future prosecutions of others. Boesky was sentenced to three years in prison and ultimately served two years.

Drexel Burnham Lambert

Approximately two years later, with the cooperation of Ivan Boesky, the SEC charged Drexel Burnham Lambert and four of its prominent employees, including the head of its junk-bond department, Michael Milken. According to the SEC, Drexel had entered into a secret agreement with Boesky to defraud its clients and drive up the price of target-company stocks. The complaint alleged that Drexel utilized Boesky to engage in *stock parking*—the temporary sale of shares to another entity or individual so as to hide the true ownership of the shares in order to avoid tax-reporting requirements or the net-margin requirements of the securities laws applicable to brokerage firms. Drexel, which assisted companies interested in acquisitions, was also accused of advising Boesky to purchase massive amounts of shares in certain companies in order to give the appearance of active trading in them and to drive up the takeover price.

In December 1988, Drexel agreed to plead guilty to six felony counts and to pay $650 million in fines and restitution—at the time, "by far the largest penalty ever paid in a securities case."[130] It agreed to pay an additional $30 million to settle civil charges in April 1989. As a condition to the settlement, Drexel was required to cooperate in the investigation of Milken and to fire him. The firm collapsed soon thereafter.

Michael Milken

In 1990, Milken pleaded guilty to six felony counts, ranging from securities and mail fraud to tax evasion and conspiracy.[131] He agreed to pay a fine of $200 million and to put

CONTINUED

126. E.D. Hirsch, Jr., Joseph F. Kett & James Trefil, The New Dictionary of Cultural Literacy, § Proverbs (3d ed. 2005).

127. *Insider Trading Appears to Be Rampant Again, Says Thomson*, Corp. Couns. Wkly. (BNA), Oct. 31, 2007, at 332.

128. *Id.*

129. *Id.* For an excellent detailed account of the insider trading scandals of the 1980s, see James B. Stewart, Den of Thieves (1991).

130. Larry Reibstein & Carolyn Friday, *Nailing the Junk Kings*, Newsweek, Jan. 2, 1989, at 44.

131. Laurie P. Cohen, *Public Confession: Milken Pleads Guilty to Six Felony Counts and Issues an Apology*, Wall St. J., Apr. 25, 1990, at A1.

$400 million into a fund for restitution to defrauded investors. Milken was sentenced to ten years in prison but was released after serving only twenty-two months. He was also banned for life from acting as a securities broker or dealer. U.S. Attorney General Richard Thornburgh characterized Milken's crimes as "some of the most serious efforts undertaken to manipulate and subvert Wall Street's securities markets."[132]

Raj Rajaratnam and Rajat Gupta

In October 2011, Sri Lankan–born billionaire Raj Rajaratnam was sentenced to eleven years in federal prison—the longest sentence ever given for insider trading—after being found guilty on all fourteen counts of securities fraud and conspiracy to commit securities fraud. Rajaratnam was also fined $10 million and ordered to forfeit $53.8 million in profits gained from the scheme. He was ordered to pay an additional $92.8 million in a civil case brought by the SEC. Other participants in scheme also received lengthy sentences: Zvi Goffer, ten years; Craig Drimal, five-and-a half years; and Jason Goldfarb, three years.

Unlike the majority of the other twenty-six defendants, Rajaratnam pleaded not guilty and refused to cooperate in the convictions of his circle of informants. Some of the key evidence presented against Rajaratnam came from wiretaps, which historically have been used only in criminal cases involving drug trafficking and organized crime.

Rajat Gupta, former CEO of McKinsey & Co. and a board member of Goldman Sachs and Procter & Gamble, was both sued by the SEC and criminally indicted for assisting in Rajaratnam's insider trading scheme. Gupta allegedly gave inside information to Rajaratnam concerning the earnings, financial performance, and business transactions of Goldman Sachs and Procter & Gamble.[133] For example, Gupta allegedly notified Rajaratnam of Goldman Sachs's decision to accept a $5 billion investment by Berkshire Hathaway, a multinational holding company. Gupta called Rajaratnam approximately sixteen seconds after the end of the telephone board meeting in which this decision was made, and Rajaratnam caused Galleon funds to purchase about $27 million of Goldman Sachs stock about four minutes later, two minutes before the close of the market. Galleon Group sold these stocks the following day, for an illegal profit of about $840,000.

Under the standard set forth in the *Dirks* case, Gupta faces liability for insider trading as a tipper only if he personally benefited, in either a tangible or an intangible way, from the disclosure of this nonpublic material information. The indictment against Gupta states that he "provided the inside information to Rajaratnam because of Gupta's friendship and business relationships with Rajaratnam. Gupta benefitted and hoped to benefit from his friendship and business relationships with Rajaratnam in various ways, some of which were financial." Although the financial relationships listed in the indictment mostly occurred before the alleged insider trading activities, at least one of the financial relationships existed during the pertinent time: Gupta and Rajaratnam were partners in a private equity fund. In Gupta's defense, his lawyer pointed out that Gupta did not share in any of the profits Rajaratnam earned while trading on inside information, and Gupta lost his entire $10 million investment in a fund managed by Rajaratnam. As of early 2012, both the criminal and SEC cases against Gupta were ongoing.

Operation Perfect Hedge

The Federal Bureau of Investigation (FBI) also used wiretaps in the criminal and civil cases brought in January 2012 against traders who allegedly netted $78 million in illegal profits after a Dell employee leaked quarterly financial information in violation of Dell's policies. Three of the seven individual criminal defendants, who include executives at top hedge funds snared in the FBI's "Operation Perfect Hedge," have already pleaded guilty. The SEC also filed civil charges against Diamondback Capital Management, Level Global Investors, and the seven individual traders. According to U.S. Attorney Preet Bharara, insider trading has become "rampant and routine."[134] Janice K. Fedarcyk, assistant director in charge of the FBI's New York office, cautioned: "If you are engaged in insider trading, what distinguishes you from the dozens who have been charged is not that you haven't been caught, it's that you haven't been caught yet."[135]

---

132. *Id.*
133. SEC v. Gupta, No. 11 Civ. 7566(JSR), 2011 WL 5977579 (S.D.N.Y. Nov. 30, 2011).

134. David S. Hilzenrath, *Two Major Hedge Funds Charged in Insider Trading Case*, WASH. POST, Jan. 18, 2012.
135. *Id.*

KEY WORDS AND PHRASES

QUESTIONS AND CASE PROBLEMS

1. During a session with her psychiatrist, Dr. Robert Willis, Joan Weill mentioned in confidence the imminent merger of the company headed by her husband, Sanford Weill, with another company. Willis, on hearing of the merger, communicated the information to Martin Sloate, who traded in the company's securities for his own account and for his customers' accounts.

   Did Weill, Willis, or Sloate engage in illegal insider trading? Was the conduct of the parties ethical? [*SEC v. Willis*, 777 F. Supp. 1165 (S.D.N.Y. 1991).]

2. Ernst & Young (EY) accountancy firm audited the financial statements of semiconductor company Broadcom Corporation. In 2005, EY issued an unqualified opinion that Broadcom's financial statements from 2003 to 2005 accurately portrayed Broadcom's finances. Broadcom offered stock options as part of its compensation package for officers, directors, and key employees and secretly backdated certain option grants so that option recipients received the largest possible gain. For example, if the market price increased from $10 on January 1 to $12 on January 15, then options granted on January 15 might be dated January 1 and have an exercise price of $10. Because issuers are required to take a charge against earnings for the value of the option, including the difference between the strike price and the fair market value on the date of grant, backdating has the effect of understating the compensation expense and thereby overstating the company's reported net income in each of the years in which the options vest. In 2007, Broadcom issued a restatement for 1998 to 2005 in which it acknowledged that it had improperly accounted for $2.2 billion in income, mostly due to improper option backdating. As a result, every financial statement issued during this time period was false and misleading. After Broadcom agreed to pay $12 million to settle civil charges brought by the SEC, the New Mexico State Investment Council led a civil suit against EY for knowing, or being deliberately reckless in not knowing, that its 2005 opinion was materially false and misleading due to Broadcom's stock option backdating scheme. The plaintiffs alleged that:

   • EY knew the material consequences of a May 2000 backdated option grant that would have resulted in a $700 million charge to Broadcom's financial results but, in violation of generally accepted auditing standards (GAAS), signed off on the grant without obtaining documentation.

   • EY knew that several significant option grants were approved on dates when Broadcom's compensation committee was not legally constituted due to the death of one of the two committee members.

   • EY presided over corrective reforms in 2003 to prevent and detect any future instances of improper stock option awards without questioning the integrity of Broadcom's accounting for options granted prior to the corrective reforms.

   • EY was deliberately reckless in ignoring a number of "red flags" that should have alerted it to the potential for material misstatements related to stock-based compensation.

   Did EY violate section 10(b) or Rule 10b–5? Would it matter if the EY employees who participated in the 2005 audit were unaware of the earlier alleged backdating, given that EY continuously served as Broadcom's auditor during that time period? [*New Mexico State Investment Council v. Ernst & Young LLP*, 641 F.3d 1089 (9th Cir. 2011).]

3. Gallop, Inc. is a toy manufacturer specializing in games for boys and girls aged eight to twelve. On March 30, Gallop had predicted first-quarter earnings of $.20 per share. On April 15, Gallop received a fax from its key distributor reporting a $10 million claim for personal injury of a nine-year-old child who was allegedly injured by a design defect in Gallop's most popular product line, the Spartan Warriors. Gallop's outside counsel was instructed to prepare a press release describing the claim. Before the press release was sent to the copy center at Gallop's executive office, the vice president of marketing, one director, and the outside counsel sold all of their Gallop shares at the prevailing market price of $25.25 per share.

   Collin Copier, who ran the photocopying machine at Gallop's executive office, saw the draft press release; called his broker, Barbara Broker; told her about the press release; and ordered her to sell the 500 shares of Gallop that Copier had acquired in Gallop's initial public offering. Broker then called her best client, Charleen Client, and suggested that she sell her 100,000 shares of Gallop stock but did not tell her why. Client agreed, and Broker sold Copier's and Client's stock at $25.25 a share right before the market closed on April 17.

   The press release was publicly announced and was reported on the Business Wire after the market closed on April 17.

The next day, Gallop's stock dropped to $20.75 per share. A class-action suit has been brought, and the SEC has commenced enforcement proceedings. Criminal prosecution is threatened by the U.S. Attorney's Office.

What are the bases on which each proceeding could be brought? Who is potentially liable? For how much?

4. Cameron Winklevoss, Tyler Winklevoss, and Divya Narendra (the Winklevosses) claim that Mark Zuckerberg stole the idea for Facebook from them. In the course of mediation, the Winklevosses signed a settlement agreement with Zuckerberg, stipulating that the Winklevosses would surrender ConnectU, their competing social networking site, in return for cash and Facebook stock.

   Facebook later sued to enforce this settlement agreement. ConnectU argued that the agreement was unenforceable, in part because Facebook allegedly violated Rule 10b–5 by misleading the Winklevosses to believe that Facebook's stock was worth four times more than its later stated value. If Facebook did violate Rule 10b–5, the Winklevosses would be entitled to cancel the settlement agreement under section 29(b) of the 1934 Act, which renders voidable "[e]very contract made in violation of any provision of [the securities laws, rules, or regulations], and every contract . . . the performance of which involves [such a] violation." The Winklevosses assert that a settlement proviso that barred them from "further claims against Facebook" does not preclude their Rule 10b–5 claim because section 29(a) of the 1934 Act provides that "any condition, stipulation or provision binding any person to waive compliance with [the securities laws, rules, or regulations] shall be void."

   Do the Winklevosses have a valid claim under Rule 10b–5? Should it matter that the alleged misrepresentations occurred during negotiations in a dispute rather than in the course of normal business? Would a confidentiality agreement concerning statements made during mediation, which would prevent the Winklevosses from presenting evidence for their Rule 10b–5 claim, be void under section 29(a)? Is Facebook required to disclose this dispute in the prospectus for its initial public offering? [*Facebook, Inc. v. Pacific Northwest Software, Inc.,* 640 F.3d 1034 (9th Cir. 2011).]

5. In a May 2001 quarterly report, American Express disclosed that although it had lost $182 million from its high-yield debt investments in the first quarter of 2001, "[t]otal losses on these investments for the remainder of 2001 [were] expected to be substantially lower than in the first quarter." Several pages after this statement, there was a cautionary statement that the report "contain[ed] forward-looking statements, which are subject to risks and uncertainties" and that "[f]actors that could cause actual results to differ materially from these forward-looking statements include . . . potential deterioration in the high-yield sector, which could result in further losses."

   After an evaluation of the investments, American Express issued a press release in July 2001 announcing that it would be taking an $826 million loss due to "additional write-downs in [its] high-yield debt portfolio . . . and

losses associated with rebalancing the portfolio towards lower-risk securities." Plaintiff purchasers of American Express stock sued the company and a number of executives for securities fraud under sections 10(b) and 20(a), alleging that American Express knew the statement in its May quarterly report predicting a significantly smaller loss was misleading at the time it was made. What factors are important in determining whether safe-harbor protection applies? [*Slayton v. American Express Co.*, 604 F.3d 758 (2d Cir. 2010).]

6. Texas International Speedway, Inc. (TIS) filed a registration statement for $4,398,900 in securities with the proceeds to be used to construct an automobile racetrack called the Texas International Speedway. The entire issue was sold on the offering date, October 30, 1969. On November 30, 1970, TIS filed for bankruptcy.

   The prospectus stated that the speedway was under construction. It also included a pro forma balance sheet showing that, on completion of the public offering and application of the proceeds to the construction costs of the speedway, TIS would have $93,870 in cash on hand on the speedway's opening date.

   The TIS prospectus warned that "THESE SECURITIES INVOLVE A HIGH DEGREE OF RISK" and that the construction costs might be underestimated. If the plaintiff investors present evidence from which a jury could infer that, on the effective date of the registration statement, the two officers and directors of TIS and its accountant knew that the cost of construction was understated and that consequently TIS's working capital position would not be as favorable as the prospectus reflected, will the plaintiffs win a suit under section 10(b) and Rule 10b–5? What would be the result if the Litigation Reform Act applied? [*Huddleston v. Herman & MacLean*, 640 F.2d 534 (5th Cir. 1981), *rev'd in part and aff'd in part*, 456 U.S. 914 (1982).]

7. In 1998, after working at two banks for about ten years, Bryan J. Mitchell helped found MCG Capital Corporation, a venture capital firm that invested in the media, communications, and technology sectors. MCG went public in 2001, and Mitchell served as its CEO and chair of the board. Various documents filed with the SEC stated that Mitchell "earned a B.A. in economics from Syracuse University." In fact, he attended Syracuse for only three years and did not graduate. After being pressured by a journalist, Mitchell disclosed the misrepresentation to the MCG board. The same day, the company issued a press release correcting the statement. The board subsequently stripped Mitchell of his title as chair of the board and made him repay certain bonuses and loans.

   The press responded negatively to "another CEO that lied about his résumé" and speculated about "what else might not be right." On the day the press release was issued, MCG's stock price dropped from $11.85 per share to $8.40 but fully recovered within a month.

   Shareholders sued, alleging that the misrepresentation violated section 11 of the 1933 Act, section 10(b) of the 1934 Act, and Rule 10b–5.

Was Mitchell's lie about having a college degree material? Would your answer be the same if a CEO lied about (1) having experience with an initial public offering and subsequent acquisition and (2) leading a company from conception to human clinical trials? If you had been a member of the MCG board, would you have been comfortable keeping Mitchell as CEO? [*Greenhouse v. MCG Capital Corp.*, 392 F.3d 650 (4th Cir. 2004); *SEC v. Reys*, 712 F. Supp. 2d 1170 (W.D. Wash. 2010).]

8. Janus Capital Group, Inc. (JCG) is a publicly traded company that created the Janus Investment Fund, a family of mutual funds. Janus Investment Fund is a separate legal entity owned entirely by its mutual fund investors. The Janus Investment Fund retained JCG's wholly owned subsidiary, JCM, to be its investment adviser and administrator. JCM provides Janus Investment Fund with investment advisory services, which include the day-to-day management and administrative services necessary for the operation of the Janus Fund. All of the officers of Janus Fund are also officers of JCM, but only one member of Janus Investment Fund's board of trustees is associated with JCM.

As required by the securities laws, Janus Investment Fund issued prospectuses describing the investment strategy and operations of its mutual funds to investors. The prospectuses for several funds represented that the funds were not suitable for market timing, the strategy of making buy or sell decisions based on predicted future market movements, and suggested that JCM would implement policies to curb the practice.

After New York's attorney general brought a suit against JCM for using market timing strategies, investors pulled out of Janus Investment Fund, causing JCG's stock price to fall about 25%. JCG stockholders brought a class action against JCG and JCM for violations of Rule 10b–5 and section 10(b). They alleged that the prospectuses "created the misleading impression that [JCG and JCM] would implement measures to curb market timing in the Janus [mutual funds]."

Rule 10b–5 prohibits "mak[ing] any untrue statement of a material fact" in connection with the purchase or sale of securities. Did JCM "make" the false statements by preparing the prospectuses the Janus Investment Fund filed with the SEC? Would it matter if JCM was aware of market timing in the Janus Fund before the prospectuses were filed but never shared this information with the Janus Fund board? Is JCM liable for violating any other provisions in the 1934 Act? [*Janus Capital Group, Inc. v. First Derivative Traders*, 131 S. Ct. 2296 (2011).]

CHAPTER 23

DEBTOR–CREDITOR RELATIONS AND BANKRUPTCY

INTRODUCTION

SALVAGING A BUSINESS IN FINANCIAL TROUBLE

A business generally decides to borrow when it needs funds and believes it is in a position to repay a loan with interest. Although lenders sometimes take equity positions in a borrower, whereby they receive returns based on the profits or losses of the borrower, lenders in a loan transaction are entitled only to interest at a stated rate on the amount borrowed (generally called the *principal*) and the return of the principal at the end of the term.

When a business is in trouble, it will inevitably run short of cash and fall behind in its payments. Creditors may be temporarily appeased, but those with collateral will ultimately pursue foreclosure; others will file lawsuits in a race for the remaining assets. Defending against these actions can absorb resources and hamper management's ability to cure the company's underlying ills. Successful collection can cripple or kill the business. Even if all debts can be paid, the equity holders in the company will suffer. The collapse of a large enterprise could leave many unemployed and send disruptive waves through related industries.

The legal tools used to stem this potentially destructive tide are found mainly in the Bankruptcy Code.[1] The U.S. Constitution gives Congress the power to enact bankruptcy laws. A successful reorganization under Chapter 11 of the Bankruptcy Code results in the restructuring of financial relationships among the owners and creditors of a business and, ideally, the preservation of a viable going concern. Even when reorganization is not possible, the bankruptcy system is designed to realize the maximum value from the available assets, provide equitable distribution among claimants, and foster fair and efficient administration through a collective or multiparty process.

The Bankruptcy Abuse Prevention and Consumer Protection Act of 2005 (BAPCPA) was the first major revision to the Bankruptcy Code since 1978. It was intended to prevent abuse by making it more difficult for many individuals

to receive a complete discharge in bankruptcy. To do this, the BAPCPA imposed an income-based test to determine whether individuals who file for bankruptcy should be required to repay some or all of their debts.

In fiscal year 2011, nonbusiness bankruptcies totaled just over 1.4 million, an 8% decrease from 2010.[2] Business bankruptcy filings during fiscal year 2011 were down 14% from the same period in 2010, an indication of the slow yet promising economic growth following the recession.[3] The vast majority of these bankruptcy filings involved businesses with fewer than one hundred employees. In 2010, 106 public companies sought bankruptcy protection, a decrease of 49% from 2009. The size of the public company bankruptcies also decreased from $594 billion in combined assets in 2009 to $89 billion in 2010.[4] The bankruptcy filing by Lehman Brothers Holdings, Inc. in September 2008, which listed more than $613 billion of debt, was the largest bankruptcy filing in history.[5]

CHAPTER OVERVIEW

This chapter summarizes the typical terms of a loan agreement. It then categorizes commercial loans according to the type of lender, the purposes to

CONTINUED

---

2. Press Release, Admin. Office of U.S. Courts, Bankruptcy Filings Down in Fiscal Year 2011 (Nov. 7, 2011), *available at* http://www.uscourts.gov/News/NewsView/11-11-07/Bankruptcy_Filings_Down_in_Fiscal_Year_2011.aspx.

3. *See* Kate Rogers, *Bankruptcy Filings Down in 2011, Economy Not As "Starkly Dysfunctional,"* FoxBusiness.Com, Jul. 13, 2011, http://www.foxbusiness.com/personal-finance/2011/07/12/fewer-people-filing-for-bankruptcy/.

4. *Report: Corporate Bankruptcies Fell in 2010*, Am. L. Daily, Jan. 11, 2011, *available at* http://www.law.com/jsp/tal/PubArticleTAL.jsp?id=1202477803060&slreturn=1.

5. Yalman Onaran & Christopher Scinta, *Lehman Makes Largest Bankruptcy Filing in History*, Fin. Post, Sept. 15, 2008, *available at* http://www.financialpost.com/story.html?id=790965.

---

1. Codified in scattered sections of 11 U.S.C.

which the loan proceeds will be applied, and whether the loan is secured or unsecured. The terms of a typical security agreement, together with methods for perfecting a security interest under Article 9 of the Uniform Commercial Code, are discussed. Equipment leasing, guaranties, subordination, and lender liability are addressed. This is followed by a discussion of business bankruptcies under Chapters 11 and 7 of the Bankruptcy Code, consumer bankruptcies under Chapters 7 and 13, and international bankruptcies under Chapter 15. The chapter also includes a discussion of workouts.

LOAN AGREEMENTS

The basic structure of loan agreements is surprisingly standard. Lenders are concerned about the administration of the loan, their ongoing relationship with the borrowers, and the rights they have if the borrowers breach their promises. At times, these concerns must be addressed in specially tailored documentation; generally, however, banks use a collection of standard forms, which are distributed to loan officers along with instructions for their use. This section discusses the basic features common to all loan agreements.

Parties to the Agreement

The parties to a loan agreement are the lender and the borrower. There may be more than one lender and more than one borrower.

Lenders

When two or more lenders, usually banks, make a loan to a borrower together, it is called a syndicated loan. In a *syndicated loan*, the lenders enter into concurrent direct obligations with the borrower to make a loan, typically on a pro rata basis. The loan is coordinated by a lead lender that serves as agent for all of the lenders in disbursing the funds, collecting payments of interest and principal, and administering and enforcing the loan.

In a *participation loan*, the original lender sells shares to other parties, called participants. Each participant acquires an undivided interest in the loan. The sale may be made without the borrower's involvement. The purpose of either a syndicated or a participation loan is to spread the risk of the borrower's default among lenders, particularly when the transaction involves a sizable loan.

Borrowers

Multiple borrowers are usually related entities, such as a parent corporation and its subsidiaries. Corporate law recognizes each corporation as a separate entity, but from the lender's perspective, the parent and its subsidiaries are one economic entity. If each subsidiary is jointly and severally liable for the entire debt, a subsidiary's obligation may outweigh the economic benefit it receives from the loan. (To the extent the loan is used by the parent rather than the subsidiary, the transaction may be invalidated as to the subsidiary as a fraudulent transfer under state law and the Federal Bankruptcy Code, as discussed below, but that is more of a concern for the lender than the borrower.)

Additional Parties

In more complicated transactions, additional parties may become involved in the negotiations for a loan, even though they are not parties to the loan agreement. For example, in a leveraged buyout, the acquisition of a company is financed largely by debt secured by its assets. The lender will want assurances from the seller that the assets being sold to the borrower are free and clear of all liens, and this may affect the structure of the buyout; or, if the seller is taking a note from the buyer for part of the purchase price, the lender will want to negotiate an agreement with the seller setting forth their relative rights to repayment. In a construction loan, the construction lender will advance sufficient funds to complete the construction project with the expectation of being repaid when a permanent, long-term lender steps in. In such a situation, the construction lender will negotiate with the permanent lender as well as the borrower.

In certain types of project financings, a limited partnership may be formed for the sole purpose of constructing, say, a power plant. Normally, the general partner's liability is unlimited, but for tax and other reasons, a lender may agree that it will look only to the partnership's assets for repayment of a loan. In such a case, the lender will need to assure itself that the limited partnership has sufficient resources to repay the loan.

In all of these examples, the lender has a legitimate interest in seeing that the borrower's relationships with third parties will not adversely affect the loan.

Commitment to Make a Loan

A loan agreement may be preceded by a *term sheet*, which is a letter outlining the terms and conditions on which the lender will lend. A commitment to make a loan generally need not be in writing to be enforceable, but an oral promise may be difficult to enforce because reasonable people may honestly have different recollections of what was said. Nevertheless, a jury may award damages for breach of an oral loan commitment.[6]

A number of states have enacted legislation providing that loan commitments must be in writing to be enforceable.[7] Even in the absence of such legislation, a prudent

---

6. *See, e.g.*, Landes Constr. Co. v. Royal Bank of Canada, 833 F.2d 1365 (9th Cir. 1987).

7. *See, e.g.*, GA. CODE ANN. § 13-5-30(7); NEB. REV. STAT. §§ 45-1, 112 to 45-1, 113.

lender will use a written term sheet or commitment letter to specify the terms of a proposed loan (including the amount, the interest rate, fees, and repayment provisions) and to disclaim any obligation to lend until additional investigation is completed, additional terms and conditions are negotiated, and formal documentation is signed.

Description of the Loan

A loan agreement contains the lender's promise to lend a specified amount of money. Frequently, this will be the only promise that the lender will make in the loan agreement. The loan agreement also describes the mechanics by which funds will be disbursed, the rate of interest to be charged, the manner of computing such interest, and the repayment terms.

Mechanics of Funding

The funds are usually credited to the borrower's account if the lender is a bank, or sent by wire transfer to an account specified by the borrower if the lender is another type of entity. If timing is important, the borrower will want to discuss the logistical details of the loan agreement, such as the lender's deadline for sending wire transfers. Logistics may be critical if the lender and the borrower are in different time zones or if there are multiple lenders, as in a syndicated loan.

Interest Rates

Interest rates may be fixed or *floating*, that is, fluctuating throughout the life of the loan according to the interest rate the lender would pay if it borrowed the funds in order to relend them. Fixed-rate term loans are common from insurance companies; banks generally prefer a floating rate. The floating rate may be pegged to the bank's *prime rate*, that is, the lowest published rate of interest at which the bank lends to its best and most creditworthy commercial customers. Because a bank may lend money at a rate below its so-called prime rate, banks often use the term *base rate* or *reference rate* instead. Some banks include an explicit statement that the prime (or base or reference) rate

is not the bank's best or lowest rate. The floating rate may be expressed either as a percentage of the prime rate (such as 110% of the prime rate) or, more commonly, as the sum of the prime rate and a specified number of percentage points (such as the prime rate plus 20 percentage points).

Alternatively, the floating rate may be pegged to the London Interbank Offered Rate (LIBOR) or to the certificate of deposit (CD) rate. These rates are based on the theoretical cost that a bank incurs to obtain, for a given period of time, the funds it will lend. A *spread* (or margin) is added to this cost to arrive at the actual interest rate. Frequently, a loan agreement will offer prime-rate, LIBOR, and CD-rate options for the borrower to select during the life of the loan.

The *London Interbank Offered Rate (LIBOR)* interest rate is based on the cost of borrowing offshore U.S. dollars in the global interbank market, which today is centered in several locations in addition to London; LIBOR is published in the business sections of all major daily newspapers (or on their websites). Deposits made through the interbank offering market are generally for periods of one, two, three, six, nine, or twelve months; LIBOR loans are made for corresponding periods. At the end of an interest period, the borrower may elect to (1) roll over the LIBOR loan, that is, to continue it for another interest period; (2) repay the loan; or (3) convert it to a loan based on a different interest rate.

The *certificate of deposit (CD) rate* is based on the average of the bid rates quoted to the bank by dealers in the secondary market for the purchase at face value of the bank's CDs in a given amount and for a given term. CD-rate loans are commonly available for interest periods of 30, 60, 90, or 180 days.

Computation of Interest

Interest is generally computed on a daily basis according to one of several methods. Under the *365/360 method*, the nominal annual interest rate is divided by 360, and the resulting daily rate is then multiplied by the outstanding principal amount and the actual number of days in the payment period. Thus, for a year of 365 or 366 days, the actual rate of interest will be greater than the nominal annual rate.

Under the *365/365 method*, the daily rate is determined by dividing the nominal annual interest rate by 365 (or 366, in leap years); then this daily rate is multiplied by the outstanding principal amount and the actual number of days in the payment period. Under the *360/360 method*, it is assumed that all months have thirty days; thus, the monthly interest amounts are always the same.

The method used to compute interest is significant when large principal amounts are involved. It may also be significant if the lender or the loan is subject to state *usury* laws, which limit the maximum rate of interest that may be charged. National banks and other specified classes of lenders are subject to federal legislation that preempts state usury laws, and many states permit higher interest rates for exempt commercial transactions over a given dollar amount. Unless a state or federal exemption applies, lenders and borrowers should analyze whether a loan is usurious by virtue of its terms and conditions. For example, compensation paid for a loan, such as commitment fees, expenses, and prepayment penalties, may be treated as interest.

Repayment Terms

A *revolving loan* is a line of credit that may be advanced and repaid from time to time at the borrower's discretion, subject to a final maturity date when all sums outstanding become due and payable. In a *term loan*, any advanced amounts may not be reborrowed; the lender may require the entire loan to be repaid in one lump sum on maturity, in which case the borrower only pays interest on the loan prior to maturity, or in equal or unequal installments of principal and interest. Often a loan agreement will incorporate both a term and a revolving facility. The term loan might finance an acquisition or the buildout of a plant, and the revolving line will provide day-to-day working capital.

Agreements for term or revolving loans may also call for mandatory prepayment when certain events occur. For example, in a receivables and inventory line of credit, a prepayment will be required if the level of receivables and/or inventory supporting the outstanding borrowings drops. A sale of assets outside the ordinary course of business or financial earnings below a specified level may also mandate a prepayment.

Asset-Based Loans

In structuring a loan agreement, the fact that a loan is secured or unsecured is not particularly significant, except in certain types of asset-based financing in which the amount lent is determined according to the levels of assets available from time to time. One example of an asset-based loan is a revolving line of credit based on receivables, inventory, or both. Subject to certain criteria as to what inventory or receivables are acceptable to the lender, the borrower borrows against such assets and repays the loans on a revolving basis out of collections of the receivables generated from the sale of inventory. Sometimes payments may be made directly to the lender through such mechanisms as a locked-box or blocked account, which allows the lender to take the outstanding loan repayments out of the collected proceeds before they are distributed to the borrower.

Representations and Warranties

Before committing to make a loan, a lender will investigate the potential borrower's financial condition and creditworthiness. It will also require the borrower to make certain representations and warranties, including representations about the borrower's legal status and good standing; that all necessary actions have been taken to authorize the proposed borrowing; that regulatory and other approvals that might be required for the borrowing have been obtained; that the borrower has good and marketable title to all of its assets, including any assets that constitute collateral for the loan; that the loan agreement is legal, valid, and binding; and that no default has occurred or would result from entering into the loan agreement.

The purpose of these representations and warranties is to specify the assumptions on which the lender is willing to lend. The representations and warranties serve as a checklist of major areas of investigation by the lender. They also provide a framework for the borrower to examine its legal and financial position.

Qualifications

Often a borrower will state that a representation is true to the best of its knowledge. The borrower will want to be held accountable only for what it knows, but the lender will want the borrower to take steps to ascertain the accuracy of its representations. The risk that a representation will prove to be untrue is usually placed on the borrower rather than the lender. Any qualification based on the borrower's knowledge is therefore likely to be phrased in terms of what the borrower either knows or should know after diligent inquiry. It may include a definition of the appropriate standard of diligence.

In the loan agreement, the borrower states that the representations and warranties are true and complete as of the date of the loan agreement. Although they do not apply prospectively, the loan agreement may provide that if advances are to be made, the representations and warranties will be updated as of the time of the advances.

Truthfulness of Representations

Before a disbursement is made under the loan agreement, the lender may require an opinion of counsel and a certification by an independent public accountant, confirming the representations made by the borrower. The lender's obligation to continue to lend will likewise be conditioned on the continuing truthfulness of the representations in the loan agreement.

Conditions to Closing

If the basic assumptions and facts on which the lender has relied change materially after a commitment to lend has been made, the lender will reevaluate the loan. It may (1) refuse to advance the funds committed, (2) refuse to advance additional funds if some disbursements have already been made, or (3) accelerate the maturity of the loan. The loan agreement will specify the conditions that must be met before the lender's obligations arise under the agreement. These are known as *conditions precedent*.

Authority to Approve the Loan

The lender will require evidence that the borrower's internal requirements for approving the loan have been met. Thus, the lender may ask for copies of the relevant corporate resolutions, with a certification by the corporate secretary, and certification of the incumbency of the officers authorized to execute the loan agreement.

Completion of Documents

In addition to the loan agreement, the lender will typically require a promissory note and, if the loan is secured, a security agreement and financing statements.

Payment of Fees

Some fees, such as commitment fees, must be paid before any funds are disbursed, although lenders often allow fees to be paid out of loan advances. In such instances, the lender deducts the fees from any advance and disburses the net advance.

Other Conditions

Other conditions may apply in certain circumstances. For example, in the case of a term loan to finance a merger or acquisition, the lender will condition any disbursement on the consummation of the merger or acquisition.

Regulatory approval may be required because of the nature of the borrower's business. In such cases, the particular permits and approvals that must be obtained or issued before the lender is willing to disburse funds will be listed.

As explained in Chapter 15, lenders have become increasingly concerned about the liability they may face when real property held by them, either as security or outright after a foreclosure, is required to comply with environmental cleanup laws. The lender may, therefore, require an opinion of environmental counsel, an environmental audit by qualified consultants and engineers, and indemnity agreements with the borrower and with any third parties that may be responsible for the environmental condition of the property.

Covenants

Covenants are the borrower's promises that it will or will not take specific actions as long as either a commitment or a loan is outstanding. If a covenant is breached, the lender can terminate the loan agreement and require the borrower to repay the loan. The list of covenants imposed on the borrower can be quite lengthy.

The borrower's obligations may also affect nonparties to the loan agreement. For example, the lender may require that the borrower and its subsidiaries maintain a specified net worth, computed on a consolidated basis. The loan agreement cannot directly impose such an obligation on the subsidiaries because they are not parties to it, but the agreement can require the borrower to cause its subsidiaries to comply with the covenant. Such a covenant assumes that the borrower is in a position to influence the nonparties' actions.

Affirmative Covenants

Affirmative covenants state the actions that the borrower will take, for example, maintain its corporate existence, pay taxes, maintain insurance, and comply with applicable laws. The borrower is usually required to keep the lender informed of its financial condition and to submit unaudited financial reports monthly or quarterly and audited financial reports annually. Financial tests relating to income statement and balance sheet items may be imposed. A catchall covenant will require the borrower to inform the lender of any material adverse change in its operations or financial condition.

Negative Covenants

Negative covenants state the actions that the borrower cannot take; for example, the borrower cannot incur additional debt beyond a specified amount and cannot grant liens other than those specifically enumerated or arising in the ordinary course of business. (A *lien* is a claim on property that secures a debt owed by the owner of the property.)

Scope

Covenants are generally heavily negotiated. Because financial covenants are based on projections of future financial results, flexibility is required in long-term loans. The lender will generally base the covenants on financial projections that the borrower provides to it. A borrower will resist any covenants that appear to interfere with the control and operation of its business. A lender sensitive to borrowers' fears of lender control will draft its covenants carefully to impose the minimum control needed to protect its right to be repaid. For example, a provision that effectively gives the lender the right to select the borrower's management is difficult to justify. Lawsuits, some resulting in multimillion-dollar punitive judgments against unduly interfering lenders, have alerted lenders to the need for caution in drafting and enforcing such provisions.

Events of Default

A loan agreement lists the events that will trigger the lender's right to terminate (or "call") the loan, accelerate the repayment obligations, and, if the loan is secured, take possession of the property securing the loan. These events, known as the *events of default*, usually include (1) failure to pay on time the amounts due under the loan agreement, (2) making false or misleading representations or warranties in connection with the loan, (3) failure to live up to any covenant in the loan agreement, (4) insolvency, and (5) a material adverse change in the borrower's financial or other condition. A borrower is often reluctant to sign onto a loan agreement with a material adverse change clause (commonly referred to as a "MAC" clause) because it gives the lender some discretion with respect to what constitutes default, unlike the other events of default that have bright-line rules. The lender, on the other hand, wants that provision as a safeguard against the occurrence of an event that the lender did not consider at the time the loan was made.

Some events of default may be outside the borrower's control. For example, if a loan is made to a corporation on the strength of the lender's confidence in a particular individual's management ability, the death of that individual may be included as an event of default. Similarly, involuntary liens or legal judgments against the borrower, although more or less outside the borrower's control, change the fundamental bases on which a loan was originally made.

Cross-Default

A *cross-default* provision provides that any breach by the borrower under any other loan agreement constitutes an event of default. A borrower will want the provision to apply only to a serious breach of a loan agreement covering a loan larger than a specified minimum. The borrower may also want the lender to agree that the borrower's breach of another agreement will not constitute an event of default under the loan agreement unless the other lender terminates its loan on account of the breach. The lender, on the other hand, will want a broad definition of the events of default. It will want the right to join with other creditors to negotiate some form of protection for its position as soon as the borrower's financial condition deteriorates.

If the borrower does breach another agreement, the lender and borrower may renegotiate the terms and conditions on which the loan will remain outstanding. For example, the lender may agree to continue the loan in exchange for new or additional collateral, new guaranties, or a higher rate of interest. Such negotiations are a practical alternative to the more drastic measure of terminating the loan. Note, however, that if the borrower seeks bankruptcy, any efforts to restructure the loan will be subject to the jurisdiction of the bankruptcy court.

Remedies for Default

The default section sets forth the lender's remedies for default. A lender may waive a default or forbear from enforcing its rights because the cost of modification or forbearance may be less than the cost of calling the loan. If the lender *waives* a default (that is, relinquishes its right to call the loan based on such default) or *forbears* a default (that is, decides not to exercise any of its remedies for the forbearance period), it may exact additional consideration from the borrower in the form of an increase in the interest rate or additional security or charge the borrower a modification or forbearance fee.

Any waiver should be in writing to avoid any misunderstanding as to its scope or the terms and conditions on which it is being granted, including any additional obligations that the borrower will now be expected to satisfy. In lender liability lawsuits, express terms in a loan agreement have been found to be superseded by oral or written communications between the lender and the borrower or by the actions of the borrower or lender. Reducing understandings to writing and avoiding actions that may be inconsistent with the written documents will avoid surprises and failed expectations on both sides.

COMMERCIAL LOAN CATEGORIES

Commercial loans can be categorized by lender or by purpose.

Loans Categorized by Lender

Commercial loans are most commonly made by banks, insurance companies, venture debt funds, and purchasers of *commercial paper*, that is, short-term corporate indebtedness. Both banks and insurance companies are highly regulated. Extensive federal and state legislation prescribes the types of entities that may call themselves banks, who may own them, and what they may or may not do once they open for business. Similarly, insurance companies are restricted by state legislation in connection with their business of insuring against risk. The regulatory framework within which banks, insurance companies, and other types of lenders operate affects their sources and availability of funds; these factors in turn affect the terms on which they offer to lend money. Banks generally are more flexible in the length of the terms of their loans, their interest rate formulas, and the mechanics of their loan administration. Insurance companies typically offer medium- to long-term loans at fixed interest rates. Whether a lender is a bank or an insurance company, it may have particular expertise in the industry in which the borrower does business or in making loans for particular purposes. Venture debt funds are subject to fewer regulations and often can make loans that bank or insurance company lenders would not consider.

Loans Categorized by Purpose

A borrower may require funds to meet everyday working capital needs, to finance an acquisition of assets or a business, or to finance a real estate construction project or an engineering project. Under regulations promulgated by the Board of Governors of the Federal Reserve System, lenders and borrowers may not enter into transactions whereby secured credit will be used to acquire stock, unless certain requirements are met. As discussed in the "Inside Story" in this chapter, the Dodd–Frank Wall Street Reform and Consumer Protection Act imposed new limits on the use of leverage in connection with futures contracts, options, swaps, and other derivative contracts.

Apart from these basic restrictions and additional restrictions that apply to borrowers in regulated industries, borrowers may borrow money for a wide variety of reasons. These reasons dictate whether the loan will be a term loan or a revolving loan.

Term Loans

Funds required for a specific purpose, such as an acquisition or a construction project, are generally borrowed in the form of a term loan. A specified amount is borrowed, either in a lump sum or in installments, to be repaid on a specified date (known as the *maturity date*) or *amortized* (paid off over a period of time). For example, in an acquisition the buyer may be required to pay the purchase price up front and thus will require a lump-sum loan. By contrast, the owner of a construction project will require a loan to be disbursed in installments as scheduled progress payments become due. Amounts repaid under a term loan cannot be reborrowed.

Revolving Loans

A borrower may project its working capital needs for a given period but desire flexibility as to the exact amount of money borrowed at any given time. A revolving loan or *revolving line of credit* allows the borrower to borrow the amount it requires, up to a specified maximum. The borrower may also reborrow amounts it has repaid (hence the term "revolving"). The lender requires a *commitment fee* as consideration for its promise to keep the commitment available, as it receives no interest on amounts not borrowed.

SECURED TRANSACTIONS UNDER THE UCC

In making a loan, the lender relies on the borrower's cash flow, the borrower's assets, or the proceeds of another loan as sources of repayment. If the lender relies solely on the borrower's promise to repay the loan, the lender's recourse for nonpayment is limited to suing the borrower. Even if the lender sues the borrower, it stands in no better position than other general creditors of the borrower and has no special claim to any of the borrower's specific assets as a source of repayment. Because of this risk, lenders often refuse to make loans without *collateral*, that is, property belonging to the borrower that becomes the lender's if the loan is not repaid. A loan backed by collateral is known as a *secured loan*. Unsecured loans, if they are available, are priced at a higher rate to reflect the greater risk to the lender.

If the borrower fails to repay a secured loan, the lender, in addition to suing, may *foreclose* on—that is, take constructive or actual possession of—the collateral and either

sell it to repay the debt or keep it in satisfaction of the debt. (Chapter 18 discusses issues surrounding home foreclosures.) Under some *antideficiency laws* and *one-form-of-action laws*, however, lenders seeking remedies against real property security may be restricted from suing the borrower personally. Where a lender has recourse to the borrower or to other property of the borrower and exercises such rights, the lender may be precluded from foreclosing on real estate mortgaged by the borrower. These laws, which date back to the Great Depression, are designed to protect borrowers from forfeiting their properties to overzealous lenders.

The mechanics of taking a security interest in personal property and fixtures, and the consequences of taking such a security interest, are governed by Article 9 of the Uniform Commercial Code (UCC), which provides a unified, comprehensive scheme for all types of *secured transactions*, that is, loans or other transactions secured by the borrower's collateral.[8] Article 9, however, does not apply to liens on real property, and various state and federal laws preempt the UCC in the areas of ship mortgages, mechanic's liens, and aircraft liens. Notices of security interests in copyrights are commonly filed in the U.S. Copyright Office, in addition to being perfected as general intangibles under the UCC. Article 9 also does not apply to security interests subject to a landlord's lien, to a lien given by statute or other rule of law for services or materials, or to a right of setoff. A *right of setoff* permits one party to automatically deduct amounts owed to it by the other party from the payments the first party makes to the second party. Security interests in securities are governed by Article 8 of the UCC.

Terminology

Part 1 of Article 9 defines terms. In place of the various common law security devices, the UCC uses the single term *security interest* for any interest in personal property or fixtures used as collateral to secure payment or the performance of an obligation. The parties to a secured transaction are (1) the *debtor*, that is, the person who owes payment or other performance of the obligation secured, whether or not that person owns or has rights in the collateral; and (2) the *secured party*, that is, the lender, seller, or other person in whose favor there is a security interest. A *security agreement* is an agreement that creates or provides for a security interest.

Formal Requirements

Part 2 of Article 9 sets forth the formal requirements to create an enforceable security interest and describes the rights of the parties to a security agreement. If the secured party takes possession of the collateral, an oral agreement

---

8. A full-text version of UCC Article 9 is available at http://www.law.cornell.edu/ucc/9/.

is sufficient to create a security interest; otherwise, a signed security agreement containing a description of the collateral is required. For a security interest to be enforceable, value must have been given for it, and the debtor must have rights in the collateral. These requirements do not have to be fulfilled in any particular order. When all of the requirements have been met, a security interest is said to have *attached*.

Rights and Remedies

The remainder of Article 9 sets forth the rights of the secured party against other creditors of the debtor; the rules for *perfecting* a security interest, that is, making it valid as against other creditors of the debtor; and the remedies available to a secured party when a debtor defaults.

Security Agreements

A security agreement identifies the parties and the property to be used as collateral. It may also specify the debtor's obligations and the lender's remedies in case of default.

Parties to the Agreement

Security agreements typically use the UCC terminology to identify the parties. In a loan transaction, the secured party is the lender. The debtor is the borrower, if it owns the collateral or if a third-party property owner has authorized it to use its property for collateral. If the third-party property owner acts as a guarantor of the borrower's obligation, it may also be referred to as the debtor. (Guaranties are discussed later in this chapter.)

Granting Clause

Unless the security interest is a possessory interest (traditionally called a *pledge*), the security agreement must be signed by the debtor and expressly grant a security interest in some specified property. The standard operative words are: "The debtor hereby grants to the secured party a security interest in . . . ." The UCC does not require a precise form, but the collateral must be described.

Description of the Collateral

The description of the collateral does not have to be specific, as long as it reasonably identifies what is described. For example, a working capital loan may be secured by receivables and inventory, with the inventory described simply as "inventory" or, in longer documents, as "inventory and any goods held for sale or lease." A secured party will frequently take a security interest in all of the debtor's assets—not only fixed assets, inventory, and receivables, but also intellectual property, including patents, trademarks, and copyrights. Loans to finance the purchase of specific property, such as an equipment loan, will typically be secured by the property purchased, and the security agreement will contain a description of that property.

After-Acquired Property

After-acquired property is property acquired by the debtor after it signs the security agreement. After-acquired assets may be included in the security agreement either in addition to, or as replacements of, currently owned assets. A security interest in after-acquired collateral will attach when the debtor acquires rights in the collateral, assuming that the other prerequisites for attachment have been met. Lenders will typically require the collateral to include after-acquired property.

Proceeds

The UCC provides that, unless otherwise agreed, a security agreement gives the secured party a security interest in the proceeds if the collateral is sold, exchanged, collected, or otherwise disposed of. The security interest is equally effective against cash, accounts, or whatever else is received from the transaction. This feature makes a security interest created under Article 9 a *floating lien*.

Debtor's Obligations

The debtor is obligated to repay the debt and to pay interest and related fees, charges, and expenses. In addition, the debtor will have nonmonetary obligations, such as obligations to maintain prescribed standards of financial well-being, measured by net worth, cash flow, and debt coverage (the ratio of debt to equity). These obligations are typically set forth in detail in a loan agreement or a promissory note, although occasionally they may be found in a security agreement.

Cross-Collateralization

The collateral for one loan may be used to secure obligations under another loan. This is done by means of a *cross-collateralization* provision—sometimes called a *dragnet clause*—in the security agreement. For example, an inventory and receivables line of credit may be secured not only by inventory and receivables but also by equipment owned by the borrower and already held by the lender as collateral for an equipment loan. Thus, if the lender forecloses on the equipment, any proceeds in excess of the amounts owed under the equipment loan will be available to pay down the inventory and receivables line of credit. Similarly, if the equipment loan is cross-collateralized with collateral for the inventory and receivables line of credit, any proceeds realized from foreclosure of the inventory and receivables will be available to pay down the equipment loan.

Remedies for Default of a Security Agreement

The remedies described in a security agreement track the rights and procedures set forth in Article 9. After default, the secured party has the right to take possession of the collateral without judicial process if this can be done without breach of the peace. The secured party may then dispose of the collateral at a public or private sale. If there is a surplus from the sale of the collateral, the secured party is required to return it to the debtor. If there is a deficiency, the debtor remains liable for that amount. The proceeds from the sale must be applied in this order: (1) to the reasonable expenses of foreclosure and, if provided for in the agreement, reasonable attorneys' fees and legal expenses; (2) to the satisfaction of the obligations secured; and (3) to the satisfaction of indebtedness secured by a subordinate security interest, if a written demand for such satisfaction is timely received. The secured party also has the option to retain the collateral (with the debtor's consent and after notice to, and with the consent of, any junior lienholders or other third parties claiming an interest in the collateral) in partial, as well as in full, satisfaction of the debt.

Although the UCC establishes a framework within which the lender may exercise its remedies, some details must be provided by contract. For example, the parties may agree to apply the proceeds of a foreclosure sale to attorneys' fees and legal expenses, or they may agree that the debtor will assemble the collateral and make it available to the secured party at a designated place. Such provisions are subject to the requirement that the secured party's disposition of the collateral must be commercially reasonable. This term is not defined in the UCC, but it is generally interpreted to require conformity with prevailing standards and to prevent one party from taking undue advantage of another. The secured party and the debtor are free to fashion a mutually acceptable standard of commercial reasonableness, however, and security agreements often contain a description of such standards.

Perfecting a Security Interest

To protect its rights in the collateral, a lender must ensure that its security interest is perfected, that is, valid against the debtor's other creditors and against the debtor's trustee in bankruptcy. The UCC does not define perfection; instead, it describes the situations in which an unperfected security interest will be subordinated to the rights of third parties. For example, a security interest is subordinated to the rights of a person who becomes a lien creditor before the security interest is perfected. *Subordination* to lien creditors means in effect that the security interest is not valid against the debtor's trustee in bankruptcy.

Methods of Perfection

Security interests can be perfected by (1) taking possession of the collateral, (2) taking control of the collateral, (3) filing a financing statement, (4) automatically, or (5) recording with the appropriate federal office.

By Possession   A security interest in goods, instruments (other than certificated securities, which are covered by Article 8 of the UCC—see below), negotiable instruments, or chattel paper may be perfected by the secured party's taking possession of the collateral. A security interest in money may be perfected only by possession. Although filing a financing statement perfects a security interest in negotiable instruments and chattel paper, possession is the preferred means of perfection, as a bona fide purchaser of a negotiable instrument or chattel paper will be senior to a secured party that perfects by filing.

By Control   A security interest in a deposit account or a letter-of-credit right may be perfected only by taking control of the collateral. In the case of a deposit account, the lender and borrower enter into an account control agreement with the borrower's bank, whereby the borrower relinquishes control of its deposit account and the bank agrees to disburse amounts in the account directly to the lender for repayment of the loan if the lender demands payment.

By Filing   For all types of personal property, including negotiable instruments such as promissory notes (but excluding money, deposit accounts, and letter-of-credit rights), perfection may be accomplished by filing a financing statement. Standard printed forms, known as *UCC–1 forms*, are widely available for this purpose.

Automatic Perfection   Some security interests require neither possession nor filing for perfection. For example, a *purchase-money security interest* in consumer goods (created when the seller of consumer goods lends the buyer the money with which to buy them) is automatically perfected. Under certain circumstances, a security interest in a certificated security or an instrument is temporarily perfected without filing or possession. Automatic perfection is of limited duration, however, and must be followed by possession or filing if perfection is to survive for a longer period.

Federal Recording   Registered copyrights can be perfected only by federal recording with the U.S. Copyright Office. Although a security interest in patents or trademarks is perfected by a UCC filing, a prudent lender will also file its security agreement with the Patent and Trademark Office to protect its security interest against bona fide purchasers for value.

Security Interests in Uncertificated Securities

The once fundamental distinction between possessory and nonpossessory security interests became blurred with the introduction of uncertificated, or book-entry, securities. Article 8 of the UCC, which governs investment securities, was revised in 1977 to provide for the creation and perfection of security interests in certificated and uncertificated securities. These topics were then removed from Article 9, except for cross-references to the applicable sections of Article 8.

Filing Procedure

The purpose of perfection by filing is to provide notice "to the world" that assets of one person are subject to the security interest of another. If a security interest is not perfected by possession, the collateral remains in the debtor's possession and control. This occurs, for example, when the collateral is intangible (such as accounts), or when possession by the secured party is impractical (as in the case of inventory). A centralized system gives effective public notice that property in the possession and under the apparent control of the debtor is actually subject to the rights of another. The filing system enables a prospective creditor to determine whether, in claiming its rights to such assets, it will be competing with other creditors or with a trustee in bankruptcy. It also enables a purchaser of goods to determine whether the seller's creditors have any claims against the goods. (Under certain circumstances, a purchaser of goods is protected from liens on the goods created by the seller; for example, buyers in the ordinary course of business, e.g., consumers, are protected from inventory liens on a seller's goods.)

What to File

To perfect a nonpossessory security interest in personal property, a financing statement must be filed. The financing statement is a one-page form that tells the world that a secured party may have a security interest in a debtor's property. It needs to contain only the correct name and address of the debtor and the secured party and an indication of the collateral in which a security interest has been or may be granted. If a financing statement covers crops grown or to be grown or goods that are or will become fixtures, the UCC also requires a legal description of the land concerned.

Where to File

For most debtors and in most cases, the proper place to file is in the office of the secretary of state in the state where the debtor is located. If the debtor moves, then a financing statement must be filed in the new jurisdiction. Location is determined by the jurisdiction of organization for corporate-type debtors, including corporations, limited liability companies, and limited liability partnerships. A nonregistered organization is located at its place of business if it has only one place of business, and at its chief executive's office if it has more than one place of business. Most foreign debtors are deemed to be located in the District of Columbia. A security interest in collateral closely associated with real property, such as fixtures, growing crops, timber, or minerals, must be filed in the state where the real property is located in the office in which a mortgage on real estate would be recorded; this is usually the county recorder's office in the county where the real property is located.

When to File

A financing statement may be filed in advance of the transaction or the execution of the security agreement. This is important because, under the UCC, a security interest is perfected when the statement is filed. Thus, the first secured party to file has priority over other parties with security interests in the same debtor's property, unless special priority rules apply, as in the case of purchase-money security interests.

EQUIPMENT LEASING

To conserve its working capital, a company may decide to lease needed equipment rather than purchase it. Leasing sometimes offers an attractive alternative to borrowing funds to purchase equipment because a leasing company may be willing to provide more lenient terms than a bank or other lender. A leasing company may also be willing to accept a greater credit risk than banks, but it will probably charge higher interest rates than a bank to accommodate the greater credit risk involved. A newer enterprise may sometimes be asked for a security deposit or personal guaranty in connection with an equipment lease.

When equipment is leased, three parties are involved: the seller of the equipment, the leasing company, and the user of the equipment. The user determines its needs and negotiates a purchase price for the equipment; then the user engages a leasing company to purchase the equipment and lease it to the user. The manufacturer or seller of the equipment may lease it to the user, either directly or through a leasing subsidiary, but third-party leasing companies are more frequently used.

Differences Between Finance and True Leases

An equipment lease that serves the purpose of financing is known as a *finance lease*. A finance-lease agreement differs from a true lease in several ways: (1) it gives the lessor some degree of control over the use, alteration, and location of the equipment; (2) it prohibits major changes in the user's business operations without the lessor's consent, unless the lessee first repays the lessor in full; (3) the lessee is required to keep the equipment in good repair and to insure it against loss or damage; (4) the lessor is given a security interest in the equipment and may foreclose and sell the equipment in the event of the user's default; and (5) the rights and remedies of the lessor and lessee are governed by Article 9 of the UCC in addition to the terms of the lease agreement.

For accounting purposes, a finance lease is treated as a long-term debt of the lessee, who is deemed to own the leased equipment; the lessee may therefore enjoy tax benefits such as depreciation deductions. If the lessee has the right to purchase the equipment at the end of the lease term, the lease will often provide that the purchase price will be the fair market value of the equipment at that time.

GUARANTIES

A *guaranty* is an undertaking by one person, the *guarantor*, to become liable for the obligation of another person, the *primary debtor*. A guaranty allows the party that is to receive payment to look to the guarantor in the event that the primary debtor fails to pay. The guarantor can be an individual, a corporation, a partnership, a limited liability company, or any other type of entity willing to lend its credit support to another's obligation. The most common form of guaranty is that indebtedness or other payment obligations of another will be paid when due. A *guaranty of performance*, a less common form, assures that specified nonpayment obligations will be performed. The type of guaranty and the duties of the guarantor are determined by the language of the guaranty instrument. The statute of frauds requires that a guaranty be in writing to be enforceable.

Lenders often require a guaranty when a credit analysis indicates that the borrower's credit is not sufficient to support the requested loan. The lender will evaluate the credit of each guarantor and decide whether to make the loan based on the combined credit of the borrower and the guarantors. A lender may also require guaranties from officers, directors, or shareholders of a borrower, especially when the borrower is a closely held corporation. To protect its position under a guaranty, a lender may require that the guarantor refrain from incurring additional debt or granting liens on its assets.

Payment Versus Collection

Under a *guaranty of payment*, the guarantor's obligation to pay the lender is triggered, immediately and automatically, when the primary debtor fails to make a payment when due. In contrast, under a *guaranty of collection*, the guarantor becomes obliged to pay only after the lender has attempted unsuccessfully to collect the amount due from the primary debtor. With a collection guaranty, the lender generally has to file a lawsuit and take other steps to collect the debt before calling on the guarantor to pay (unless the primary debtor is insolvent or otherwise clearly unable to pay). This condition makes enforcement of collection guaranties so cumbersome and expensive that lenders almost always require payment guaranties.

Limited Versus Unlimited

A guarantor's liability under a guaranty may be either limited or unlimited. With a *limited guaranty*, the maximum amount of the guarantor's liability is expressly stated in the guaranty instrument. This maximum liability is usually a specific dollar amount, although it can be based on other criteria, such as a percentage of the primary debtor's total indebtedness to the lender.

Restricted Versus Continuing

A *restricted guaranty* is enforceable only with respect to a specified transaction or series of transactions. A guaranty that covers all future obligations of the primary debtor to the lender is referred to as a *continuing guaranty*. The objective of the continuing guaranty is to make the guarantor liable for any debt incurred at any time by the primary debtor, regardless of whether the debt was contemplated at the time the guaranty was entered into. Lenders naturally favor continuing guaranties over restricted guaranties.

In many jurisdictions, a continuing guaranty may be revoked by the guarantor during his or her lifetime. Such a revocation prevents the guarantor from becoming liable for debts incurred by the primary debtor in connection with transactions entered into after the revocation date. The death of the guarantor also revokes a guaranty, but the guarantor's estate remains liable for debts incurred by the primary debtor prior to the guarantor's death.

Discharging the Guarantor

A lender that makes a guaranteed loan must avoid any actions that would have the effect of discharging the guarantor, such as altering the terms of the agreement between the lender and the primary debtor (for example, increasing the interest rate on the loan or increasing the amount of the scheduled payments), extending the time for payment of the loan or renewing the indebtedness, or releasing or impairing the lender's rights with respect to collateral pledged by the primary debtor. A well-drafted guaranty can alleviate some of these potential pitfalls through an express waiver of the guarantor's legal, equitable, and statutory rights in connection with any such modifications. The best approach, however, is for the lender to obtain the written consent of the guarantor in the form of an affirmation of the guaranty before making any material change to the arrangement between the lender and the primary debtor.

Guaranties Versus Letters of Credit

As explained in Chapter 24, a standby letter of credit can often be used in place of a guaranty. Uniform standards for standby letters of credit can be incorporated into the letter of credit by reference to the International Chamber of Commerce's International Standby Practices (ISP98).[9]

Fraudulent Conveyances

A guaranty may be attacked as a fraudulent conveyance under the Federal Bankruptcy Code or state fraudulent transfer statutes. Under many fraudulent transfer statutes, assets may be recovered and transfers avoided under

---

9. ICC Pub. No. 590 (1998). Note that the UCP (Uniform Customs and Practice for Documentary Credits Pub. No. 600 (1993, rev. 2007)) is more often used for standby letters of credit than ISP98.

circumstances that constitute "actual fraud" or "constructive fraud." Fraud is actual when the assets are transferred with intent to hinder, delay, or defraud creditors by putting the assets out of the creditors' reach. Fraud is constructive when an asset is transferred for less than reasonably equivalent value and other factors, such as the insolvency of the debtor, are present.

A guaranty may be a fraudulent conveyance, if without conferring a benefit on the guarantor, it makes the guarantor's assets unavailable to creditors other than the party receiving the guaranty. For example, if the guarantor did not receive fair value in exchange for giving its guaranty and was insolvent at the time it gave its guaranty, or if the guarantor was rendered insolvent or left with unreasonably small capital as a result of giving its guaranty, the party receiving the guaranty may have an unfair advantage over other creditors of the guarantor. In such a case, the other creditors would be able to invalidate the guaranty. A lender must carefully examine these issues before accepting a guaranty.

Upstream Guaranty

With an *upstream guaranty*, subsidiaries guarantee, or pledge their assets as security for, the parent's debt. An upstream guaranty may be found fraudulent if the guarantor received none of the loan proceeds or received an inadequate amount compared to the liability it incurred. Other creditors of the subsidiary (and the subsidiary's minority shareholders, if the subsidiary is less than wholly owned by the parent) may claim that the lender, as the beneficiary of the guaranty, received an unfair advantage at the other creditors' (or minority shareholders') expense.

Leveraged Buyouts

Leveraged buyouts, in which the acquisition of a company is financed largely through debt, may be subject to attack as fraudulent conveyances. For example, if a leveraged buyout is structured so that a newly formed corporation will acquire the stock of the target company using proceeds from a loan, the lender's source of repayment will be dividends paid from the target company to the borrower. To ensure that such a source of repayment will be available, the lender may require the target company to give a guaranty, which may or may not be secured by the target's assets. Alternatively, the lender may require a merger between the target company and the borrower. Such guaranties or mergers will be invalidated if the target company both (1) failed to receive a reasonably equivalent value and (2) was left insolvent, with assets that were unreasonably small in relation to its business, or with insufficient working capital.

Voidable Preferences

A transfer from a debtor to a creditor that results in a reduction in the guaranty liability of an insider may be a voidable preference if it occurs within one year of the date the debtor files for bankruptcy.[10] For example, suppose that on February 1, 2010, ABC Corporation borrows $1 million from Friendly Bank and that Henri-Claude, a major shareholder of ABC Corporation, guarantees the loan. ABC Corporation makes a $100,000 payment to Friendly Bank on March 1, 2011. On October 1, 2011, ABC Corporation files bankruptcy. ABC Corporation's creditors will be able to set aside the $100,000 payment because it reduced Henri-Claude's guarantor liability dollar for dollar and thereby preferred an insider of ABC Corporation.

SUBORDINATION

A *debt subordination* is an agreement whereby one or more creditors of a common debtor agree to defer payment of their claims until another creditor of the same debtor is fully paid. The indebtedness that is subordinated under the agreement is referred to as the subordinated or *junior debt*. The indebtedness that benefits from the subordination is called the *senior debt*.

The primary purpose of a debt subordination is to protect the senior creditor in the event of the debtor's insolvency. As long as the debtor is solvent, both the junior debt holder and the senior debt holder can expect to be paid. If the debtor becomes insolvent, there will be insufficient assets to satisfy all of its creditors. In such circumstances, creditors can expect to receive only a partial payment on their claims. In subordinating its claim, the holder of the junior debt agrees to yield its right of payment to the senior creditor until the senior creditor has been paid in full.

Corporations frequently use subordinated debt as a means of raising capital. The use of subordinated notes or subordinated debentures (long-term secured bonds) may have certain advantages over equity financing. For example, the interest payable on subordinated debt will be tax-deductible. In addition, the interest rate payable on subordinated debt is often less than the dividend rate that would have to be offered on comparable preferred stock.

Indebtedness to Insiders

When a borrower seeks a short-term loan from a bank or other commercial lender, the lender will often require that the borrower's indebtedness to insiders, such as officers, directors, and shareholders, be subordinated. This is especially true when the borrower is a closely held corporation and the insider debt is significant in relation to the amount of the lender's loans.

---

10. *See, e.g.,* Levit v. Ingersoll Rand Fin. Corp. (*In re* V.N. Deprizio Constr. Co.), 874 F.2d 1186 (7th Cir. 1989).

Lien Subordination

A *lien subordination* is an agreement between two secured creditors whose respective security interests, liens, or mortgages attach to the same property. The subordinating party agrees that the lien of the other creditor will have priority notwithstanding the relative priorities that the parties' liens would otherwise have under applicable law. Unlike debt subordination, a lien subordination does not limit the right of the subordinating party to accept payment from the debtor. Instead, the lien subordination has the effect of limiting the subordinating party's recourse to the collateral until the prior secured party's claim has been satisfied.

Equitable Subordination

A creditor's claim may be involuntarily postponed through application of the doctrine of *equitable subordination*, a doctrine developed in bankruptcy law to prevent one creditor, through fraud or other wrongful conduct, from increasing its recovery at the expense of other creditors of the same debtor. The court will order that the creditor that acted wrongfully shall receive no payment from the debtor until the claims of all other creditors have been fully paid.

⊕ LENDER LIABILITY

Lenders may be liable to borrowers based on several theories of lender liability.

Breach of Contract

A breach of contract results from a lender's failure to act or to refrain from acting as required by the terms of a loan document or other agreement. For example, a lender's unexcused failure to honor a promise to make a loan will give rise to a breach-of-contract claim. Compensatory damages may be awarded to place the borrower in the same position it would have been in if the lender had properly performed the agreement.

Breach of Duty of Good Faith

Some cases have imposed an implied obligation of good faith and fair dealing on lenders. This duty requires the lender to act reasonably and fairly in dealing with the borrower and in exercising its rights and remedies under the loan documents and under applicable law. In the following case, the court considered whether the bank violated its duty of good faith.

A CASE IN POINT	*Summary*	Case 23.1

Tufankjian v. Rockland Trust Co.

Appeals Court of Massachusetts
57 Mass. App. Ct. 173 (2003).

FACTS In the fall of 1993, Charles Tufankjian sought to acquire a Toyota dealership. He signed an agreement to purchase for approximately $1.4 million and subsequently applied to Rockland Trust Company for loans to finance the acquisition. While he was awaiting a response, a representative of Rockland Trust approached him and indicated that the bank would finance the entire purchase of the dealership. The representative encouraged Tufankjian to consider floor-plan financing as well (meaning the financing of the dealership's inventory), which Tufankjian refused. A week later, Rockland approved his loan, offering to lend Tufankjian $700,000 at a fixed 7.5% interest rate for five years and at a floating rate for the remaining five years. Additional financing would be provided by a Small Business Administration (SBA) loan at a separate interest rate. Tufankjian was unfamiliar with SBA loans, so Rockland put him in contact with Kristen Teixeira, a vice president of Rockland in charge of SBA loans. Teixeira "guaranteed" Tufankjian that the interest rate applicable to the SBA portion of the loan would not exceed 6.5%. Tufankjian agreed to proceed with the loan on these terms. Pursuant to Rockland's request, Tufankjian filled out certain paperwork and sought an appraisal of the dealership.

Rockland and Tufankjian signed a commitment letter in which the only interest rate quoted referred to the $700,000 bank loan. SBA financing, in the amount of $560,000, was referred to in the commitment letter only as a condition of the bank's loan. After Tufankjian questioned Teixeira as to the omitted "guarantee" in the commitment letter, she again assured him the rate would be 6.5%. Prior to the closing, Tufankjian was informed that despite Teixeira's assurances, the interest rate on the SBA loan would in fact exceed 6.5%. Tufankjian subsequently met with the president and vice president of Rockland, neither of whom could honor Teixeira's guarantee.

Ultimately, conflict between the parties resulted in the loan not being consummated. Tufankjian was forced to refinance his loan from other sources with terms less favorable than those originally guaranteed by Teixeira. Following the purchase of his dealership, Tufankjian brought suit

CONTINUED

against Rockland, alleging breach of contract and breach of the duty of good faith and fair dealing. A jury returned a verdict for Tufankjian and awarded him $232,116 in damages. The trial court granted the bank's motion for judgment notwithstanding the verdict on Tufankjian's breach-of-contract claim, but it adopted the jury's finding on the breach of good faith and fair dealing charge. The bank appealed, arguing that the trial judge entered an inconsistent judgment by separating the two charges.

ISSUE PRESENTED   Did the lender's conduct amount to a breach of the duty of good faith and fair dealing?

SUMMARY OF OPINION   The Appeals Court of Massachusetts began by noting that in Massachusetts, every contract implies good faith and fair dealing by the parties in its performance. This duty translates to an "implied term" or condition of the contractual agreement. The parties to a contract, then, have an understanding that "neither party shall do anything that will have the effect of destroying or injuring the right of the other party to receive the fruits of the contract."

The court concluded that Rockland Trust took a number of positions and actions that were designed to force financial concessions from Tufankjian and injured his right to receive the fruits of the contract. The bank played an essential role in financing the proposed dealership, both in terms of financing directly and in providing assistance to Tufankjian. The bank knew Tufankjian was relying on its advice and expertise and used that reliance to try to "sweeten the deal."

The court pointed to several instances to illustrate its conclusion. The bank had continuously attempted to improve on the deal by including floor-plan financing and a higher interest rate, despite Tufankjian's repeated refusals. The bank officer also portrayed Tufankjian in a negative light at a meeting with an SBA loan screener, suggesting he would be unable to repay the loan. Further, the appraisal, which the bank was responsible for obtaining, was not completed on time. In addition, the bank required Tufankjian to hire a more expensive, out-of-state appraiser rather than a less expensive in-state one. Once the bank refused to guarantee the 6.5% interest rate on the SBA loan, the bank indicated it would lend all of the money for the dealership, but only at a rate of 7.5% with floor-plan financing or at a 9.5% rate without the floor-plan financing.

The bank, according to the court, was thus seeking to "'recapture opportunities forgone on contracting' as determined by [Tufankjian's] reasonable expectations" and to secure a better deal for itself.

RESULT   The appellate court held that the trial jury was warranted in finding that the lender breached the duty of good faith and fair dealing and, therefore, breached the contract with the borrower. Judgment for Tufankjian was affirmed.

When there is a fiduciary relationship between the lender and the borrower or when the parties are of unequal bargaining strength, punitive damages may be recoverable for breach of the implied duty of good faith and fair dealing. For example, the U.S. Court of Appeals for the Sixth Circuit affirmed a judgment of $1.5 million compensatory damages and punitive damages against the Irving Trust Company. The company was found to have breached an implied covenant of good faith and fair dealing when it failed to give notice to the borrower before refusing to make further advances under a discretionary line of credit.[11] However, other courts have held that principles of good faith could not be used to override express contract terms.[12]

Fraudulent Misrepresentation

A lender may be liable for making false statements to a borrower if, for example, it represents that it will make a loan facility available when, in fact, it has decided not to extend any credit to the borrower. If a fiduciary relationship exists between the lender and the borrower, the lender may have an additional duty to disclose information if nondisclosure would result in an injury to the borrower. Both compensatory and punitive damages may be recovered for fraudulent misrepresentation.

Economic Duress

If the lender pressures the borrower into doing something that the borrower is not required to do under the loan documents, a court may find the lender's action constitutes *economic duress*. For example, a threat by the lender

---

11. K.M.C. Co. v. Irving Trust Co., 757 F.2d 752 (6th Cir. 1985).

12. Khan & Nate's Shoes No. 2, Inc. v. First Bank, 908 F.2d 1351 (7th Cir. 1990); Taggart & Taggart Seed Inc. v. First Tenn. Bank Nat'l Ass'n, 684 F. Supp. 230 (E.D. Ark. 1988), *aff'd*, 881 F.2d 1080 (8th Cir. 1989).

to accelerate a loan, unless the borrower provides additional collateral, may constitute economic duress if there is no default under the loan documents. Compensatory and punitive damages may be recovered for economic duress.

Tortious Interference

The lender was found liable for tortious interference with the borrower's corporate governance in *State National Bank of El Paso v. Farah Manufacturing Co.*,[13] which set a precedent for claims of this kind. In this case, the loan agreement between the bank lenders and the borrower prohibited any change in the borrower's management "which any two Banks shall consider, for any reason whatsoever, to be adverse to the interests of the Banks." The lenders disapproved of a certain individual and threatened to accelerate the loan if the borrower reappointed him as chief executive officer. In response to this threat, the borrower appointed a series of CEOs proposed by the lenders. After its financial position seriously deteriorated during the tenure of these chief executives, the borrower sued the banks for tortious interference.

The Texas Court of Appeals held that the banks had wrongfully interfered with the borrower's right to have its affairs managed by competent directors and officers who would maintain a high degree of undivided loyalty to the company. The interference compelled the election of directors and officers whose particular business judgment, inexperience, and divided loyalty proximately resulted in injury to the borrower. The banks were liable for the losses suffered by the borrower while under the bank-imposed management, resulting in a judgment in excess of $18 million against the banks. However, most other courts have not recognized a lender's interference with a borrower's corporate governance as an independent basis of liability.[14]

Intentional Infliction of Emotional Distress

A bank was found liable for intentional infliction of emotional distress when, after deciding not to make any additional advances to the borrower, bank officials publicly ridiculed him, pointing at him, using profanities, and laughing about his financial difficulties. To recover for intentional infliction of emotional distress, the lender's conduct must be extreme and outrageous and must intentionally or recklessly cause emotional distress to the borrower. Compensatory and punitive damages are recoverable.

Negligence and General Tort Liability

Claims that do not fall into one of the other established categories may be characterized as negligence or general tort liability. As explained in Chapter 9, negligence is the failure to exercise reasonable care, resulting in injury to the borrower. General tort liability arises from conduct that intentionally causes injury to a borrower.

Statutory Bases of Liability

A lender may be liable to the borrower if it violates a statutory standard of conduct. For example, the federal Racketeer Influenced and Corrupt Organizations Act (RICO) has been used by private litigants to recover for fraud or misrepresentation by banks or other lenders. The treble damages available under RICO provide an incentive for borrowers to claim RICO violations in their lender liability suits.

Federal antitying statutes prohibit banks and thrifts from conditioning a loan or other financial service on the borrower's purchase of an unrelated property or service from the lender, or on the borrower's providing to the lender a product or service unrelated to the original loan. A lender may be subject to penalties in cases brought by the Securities and Exchange Commission (SEC) for aiding or abetting a borrower in violating federal securities laws if it knew, or should have known, that a violation was taking place or if it is found to be a controlling person with respect to the borrower. Under the federal Comprehensive Environmental Response, Compensation, and Liability Act (CERCLA, discussed in Chapter 15) and state-law counterparts, if the lender falls within the statutory definition of an owner or operator of a site contaminated by hazardous wastes and does not come within the statutory safe harbor for lenders, it may find itself liable for all the costs of cleanup even if they exceed the amount of the loan.

To protect itself from contract or tort liability in connection with a loan, the lender will include an indemnification clause in the loan agreement, whereby the borrower agrees to defend, indemnify, and hold harmless the lender and its agents from any claims and liabilities arising from the loan transaction. A separate environmental indemnity is often used in real estate transactions to insulate the lender from liability under environmental laws.

SPECIAL DEFENSES AVAILABLE TO THE FEDERAL INSURERS OF FAILED BANKS AND SAVINGS AND LOANS

When a bank has failed, the Federal Deposit Insurance Corporation (FDIC) takes control. During the savings and loan debacle of the 1980s, the Resolution Trust

---

13. 678 S.W.2d 661 (Tex. App. 1984), *overruled in part by* Wal-Mart Stores v. Sturges, 52 S.W.3d 711 (Tex. 2001).

14. Benjamin Mintz, *Revisiting Lender Liability Claims Under New Theory*, Nat'l L.J., July 11, 2005, at 15–16.

Corporation (RTC) took control of the failed savings and loan associations (S&Ls). In the past, both the FDIC and the RTC employed a common law principle known as the *D'Oench, Duhme doctrine*[15] to increase the value of the failed institution by making it easier for federal agencies to collect on outstanding loans.

D'Oench, Duhme bars many claims and defenses a borrower might otherwise have against conservators and receivers that might have been valid against the failed bank itself. In particular, the doctrine bars enforcement of any agreements (including secret agreements) unless those agreements are in writing and have been approved contemporaneously by the bank's board or loan committee and recorded in the bank's written records. This permits federal and state bank examiners to rely exclusively on the bank's written records when evaluating the worth of the bank's assets.[16] It has also been used as a defense to breach-of-contract and tort claims based on oral promises or arrangements.[17] Congress effectively codified the holding of *D'Oench, Duhme* in the Dodd–Frank Wall Street Reform and Consumer Protection Act.[18]

The defense is available only to banking transactions engaged in by federally insured institutions. It does not apply to nonbanking transactions or to transactions engaged in by a bank's nonbank subsidiaries.

✦ MANAGEMENT DUTIES MAY SHIFT WHEN A COMPANY ENTERS INSOLVENCY ZONE

Generally, directors of a corporation owe their fiduciary duties to the corporation and its shareholders (see Chapter 20). Creditors are expected to protect their interests by contract. When a corporation is insolvent, however:

> [T]he value of creditors' contract claims may be affected by management's business decisions in a way it was not before insolvency. At the same time, as long as insolvency persists, shareholder value is essentially worthless and shareholders no longer occupy the position of residual claimants. Because insolvency shifts the residual risk of management decisions from shareholders to creditors, at least some of the duties formerly owed by directors only to shareholders are owed also to creditors upon that circumstance, or so the theory goes.[19]

Thus, directors of a corporation that is insolvent or "in the zone of insolvency" may owe fiduciary duties to the corporation's creditors.[20] Directors, as well as officers and, in most jurisdictions, those who aid, abet, or conspire with the directors or officers, may be personally liable to the bankrupt estate for breach of fiduciary duty.[21]

It is often not clear when a corporation becomes insolvent. Under fraudulent transfer law, insolvency is generally defined as an excess of liabilities over the value of assets. Under the principles of fiduciary obligations, however, insolvency is usually defined as an inability to pay debts as they mature. Even though not insolvent in the bankruptcy sense, a business is insolvent in the equity sense if its assets lack liquidity.

It is even less clear when a company enters the *zone of insolvency*. There is no test or definition for the "zone of insolvency," although case law suggests that a company may enter the zone when there is a substantial risk that the company will be unable to pay its debts when they come due or the company is operating with unreasonably small capital that "connotes a condition of financial debility short of insolvency (in either the bankruptcy or equity sense) but which makes insolvency reasonably foreseeable."[22]

The scope of the duty owed to creditors of a firm in the zone of insolvency varies by jurisdiction. Minnesota courts have adopted a narrow view that management owes no duty of care to the creditors of an insolvent corporation and that management's fiduciary obligation consists solely of a prohibition against self-dealing and insider preferences.[23] California applies a form of the "trust fund doctrine," whereby once a corporation becomes insolvent, its assets "become a trust fund for the benefit of all creditors in order to satisfy their claims,"[24] but it limits the directors' "extra-contractual" duties to creditors "to the avoidance of actions that divert, dissipate, or unduly risk corporate assets that might otherwise be used to pay creditors claims."[25] This includes self-dealing and preferential treatment of creditors. The California Court of Appeal declined to extend even this limited duty to directors of firms operating in the "zone" or "vicinity" of insolvency.

The Delaware Supreme Court held that (1) creditors may not bring a direct action for breach of fiduciary duty

---

15. From the U.S. Supreme Court case of the same name, *D'Oench, Duhme & Co. v. FDIC*, 315 U.S. 447 (1942).

16. *Alexandria Assocs. v. Mitchell Co.*, 2 F.3d 598 (5th Cir. 1993).

17. *See, e.g.*, *Murphy v. FDIC*, 208 F.3d 959 (11th Cir. 2000), *cert. dismissed*, 531 U.S. 1107 (2001).

18. 12 U.S.C.A. § 5390(a)(6).

19. *Berg & Berg Enters., LLC v. Boyle*, 178 Cal. App. 4th 1020, 1039 (2009) (explaining the rationale behind cases holding that directors have a fiduciary duty to creditors of an insolvent corporation).

20. *Geyer v. Ingersoll Publ'ns Co.*, 621 A.2d 784, 787 (Del. Ch. 1992).

21. *See In re* Healthco Int'l, Inc., 208 B.R. 288, 309–10 (Bankr. D. Mass. 1997); *Crowthers McCall Pattern, Inc. v. Lewis*, 129 B.R. 992, 999 (S.D.N.Y. 1991); *Amerifirst Bank v. Bomar*, 757 F. Supp. 1365, 1380 (S.D. Fla. 1991).

22. *In re Healthco Int'l*, 208 B.R. at 301–02.

23. *St. James Capital Corp. v. Pallet Recycling Ass'n of N. Am., Inc.*, 589 N.W.2d 511 (Minn. Ct. App. 1999). *See also Bank of Am. v. Musselmann*, 222 F. Supp. 2d 792, 800 (E.D. Va. 2002).

24. *CarrAmerica Realty Corp. v. NVIDIA Corp.*, 2006 WL 2868979, *5 (N.D. Cal. Sept. 29, 2006).

25. *Berg & Berg Enters., LLC v. Boyle*, 178 Cal. App. 4th 1020, 1042 (2009).

ethical consideration

In many foreign countries, directors are personally liable if they allow a company to continue to conduct any business while it is insolvent. What are the reasons for imposing personal liability on the directors of an insolvent company? Although directors are not personally liable for all business conducted by an insolvent company in the United States, is it ethical for the directors of an insolvent company to allow the company to continue to transact business?

against the directors of a corporation while the corporation is in the zone of insolvency; (2) creditors have standing to maintain derivative claims on behalf of the corporation for breach of fiduciary duty against the directors of the corporation when the corporation is in fact insolvent; but (3) creditors have no right to assert direct claims for breach of fiduciary duty against directors even when the corporation is insolvent.[26] In contrast, courts in New York,[27] Illinois,[28] and Florida[29] have held that directors and officers of both insolvent corporations and corporations operating in the zone of insolvency owe a fiduciary duty to creditors to minimize losses upon insolvency.

Deepening Insolvency

A number of bankruptcy and other federal courts have held that plaintiffs, often bankruptcy trustees or other bankruptcy estate representatives, could pursue a cause of action against a corporation's directors and others for deepening insolvency. Courts define *deepening insolvency* as the "fraudulent prolongation of a corporation's life beyond insolvency,"[30] resulting in "damage . . . inflicted by the diminution of its assets and income,"[31] and similarly as the "fraudulent expansion of corporate debt and prolongation of corporate life."[32]

The Delaware Supreme Court rejected this cause of action when it affirmed the Delaware Court of Chancery's decision in *Trenwick America Litigation Trust v. Ernst & Young, L.L.P.*[33] As Chancellor Strine explained:

Delaware law imposes no absolute obligation on the board of a company that is unable to pay its bills to cease operations and to liquidate. Even when the company is insolvent, the board may pursue, in good faith, strategies to maximize the value of the firm. . . .

If the board of an insolvent corporation, acting with due diligence and good faith, pursues a business strategy that it believes will increase the corporation's value, but that also involves the incurrence of additional debt, it does not become a guarantor of that strategy's success. That the strategy results in continued insolvency and an even more insolvent entity does not in itself give rise to a cause of action. Rather, in such a scenario, the directors are protected by the business judgment rule. To conclude otherwise would fundamentally transform Delaware law.[34]

OVERVIEW OF BANKRUPTCY LAW

Modern bankruptcy law in the United States began with the Bankruptcy Act of 1898. It has been amended multiple times since.

The Bankruptcy Code[35] is divided into chapters. Chapters 1, 3, and 5 include definitions and provisions for the administration of bankruptcy proceedings that apply to all forms of bankruptcy. The most common forms of bankruptcy are liquidation under Chapter 7, reorganization under Chapter 11, and consumer debt readjustment under Chapter 13. Chapters 7 and 11 are available to individuals and most business organizations, but Chapter 13 is available only to individuals.[36] Chapter 15 governs ancillary and other cross-border bankruptcy cases. The remaining chapters govern bankruptcies of municipalities, stockbrokers, railroads, and farmers.

Bankruptcy Courts

The bankruptcy courts are part of the federal district court system; a bankruptcy court is attached to each federal district court. Bankruptcy judges, who are appointed by the President and serve for fourteen-year terms, hear and enter final judgments in *core proceedings* regarding bankruptcy cases (e.g., allowing creditor claims, deciding preferences, confirming plans of reorganization). In *noncore proceedings* (e.g., decisions on personal-injury torts and wrongful death proceedings),[37] the bankruptcy courts

26. N. Am. Catholic Educ. Programming, Inc., v. Gheewalla, 930 A.2d 92 (Del. 2007).

27. N.Y. Credit Men's Adjustment Bureau v. Weiss, 110 N.E.2d 397 (N.Y. 1953); Pereira v. Cogan, 2001 WL 243537, at 9–10 (S.D.N.Y. Mar. 8, 2001).

28. *In re* Ben Franklin Retail Stores, Inc., 225 B.R. 646, at 653 (Bankr. N.D. Ill. 1998), *aff'd in relevant part*, 2000 WL 28266 (N.D. Ill. 2000).

29. *In re* Toy King Distribs., Inc., 256 B.R. 1 (Bankr. M.D. Fla. 2000).

30. Schacht v. Brown, 711 F.2d 1343, 1350 (7th Cir. 1983).

31. *Id.* at 1348.

32. Official Comm. of Unsecured Creditors v. R.F. Lafferty & Co., 267 F.3d 340 (3d Cir. 2001).

33. Trenwick Am. Litig. Trust v. Billett, 931 A.2d 438 (Del. 2007).

34. 906 A.2d 168, 174 (Del. Ch. 2006).

35. Title 11 of the *United States Code*.

36. The Bankruptcy Code specifically authorizes the court to convert a case under Chapter 11 or 13 to a case under Chapter 7 or to dismiss a case for cause.

37. N. Pipeline Constr. Co. v. Marathon Pipe Line Co., 458 U.S. 50 (1982).

submit proposed conclusions of law and findings of fact to the federal district court, which reviews them and issues the final judgment. Although district courts review the judgments of bankruptcy courts in core proceedings, they apply the usual limited appellate standards and thus will not set aside findings of facts unless they are clearly erroneous.[38]

In the following case, the Supreme Court limited the power of bankruptcy courts to decide certain core issues.

---

38. Stern v. Marshall, 131 S. Ct. 2594 (2011) (Case 23.2).

| A CASE IN POINT | *Summary* | Case 23.2 |

Stern v. Marshall

Supreme Court of the United States
131 S. Ct. 2594 (2011).

Facts   Vickie Lynn Marshall, a former model known publicly as Anna Nicole Smith, married billionaire J. Howard Marshall II in 1994. At the time of their marriage, Vickie was twenty-six and J. Howard was eighty-nine.[39] J. Howard died about eighteen months later. Although he had showered Vickie with gifts during their courtship and marriage, she was left nothing under his will. Before J. Howard died, she filed a suit in Texas probate court, asserting that her stepson Pierce Marshall, J. Marshall's younger son, had fraudulently induced J. Howard to sign a living trust that did not include her, even though J. Howard meant to give her half of his property. Pierce denied any fraudulent activity.

After J. Howard's death, Vickie filed a petition for bankruptcy in the Central District of California. Pierce filed a complaint in that proceeding, in which he contended that Vickie had defamed him by inducing her lawyers to tell members of the press that he had fraudulently gained control over his father's assets. The complaint sought a declaration that Pierce's defamation claim was not dischargeable in the bankruptcy proceeding. Thereafter, Pierce filed a proof of claim for the defamation action in the bankruptcy court. Vickie responded by asserting truth as a defense to the alleged defamation and by filing a counterclaim for tortious interference with the gift she had expected from J. Howard. The bankruptcy court granted Vickie's motion for summary judgment on the defamation claim in 1999 and, after a bench trial, awarded her more than $400 million in compensatory damages and $25 million in punitive damages after finding "overwhelming" evidence of fraud. Vickie then voluntarily dismissed her claims before the Texas probate court, and the trust and will were given full effect by that court.[40]

Pierce challenged the bankruptcy court's award, claiming that the court had no authority to render judgment on the counterclaim because (1) it was not a core claim, within the meaning of 28 U.S.C. § 157(b), and (2) even if it were a core claim, the statute conferring authority on the bankruptcy court to hear such a claim was unconstitutional. The district court concluded that the counterclaim was not a core claim, so it engaged in an independent review of the case. Even though the Texas probate court had entered a judgment in Pierce's favor, the district court found that Pierce had tortiously interfered with Vickie's expectancy, and it awarded her $44 million in compensatory damages and $44 million in punitive damages. The U.S. Court of Appeals for the Ninth Circuit reversed, ruling that the counterclaim was not a core proceeding. Because the Texas probate court was "the earliest final judgment entered on matters relevant to this proceeding," the Ninth Circuit ruled that the district court should have given it preclusive effect. Vickie died of an overdose of prescription drugs in 2007. Her estate appealed.

Issues Presented   Is a counterclaim for tortious interference with an expected gift, filed in response to a bankruptcy claim for defamation, a core matter subject to the jurisdiction of the bankruptcy court under the Bankruptcy Code? If so, is conferring that authority on the bankruptcy court a violation of Article III of the U.S. Constitution?

Summary of Opinion   The U.S. Supreme Court first concluded that the tortious interference counterclaim was a core proceeding within the meaning of section 157 of Title 11 because it arose "in a bankruptcy case or under Title 11." It rejected the argument that some core proceedings will arise in a Title 11 case or under Title 11 and some will not. The Court also rejected Pierce's assertion that the bankruptcy court had no jurisdiction because the

CONTINUED

---

39. David G. Savage, *Oilman Wanted Inheritance for Wife, Lawyer Says*, L.A. Times, Oct. 29, 1999.
40. Marshall v. Marshall, 547 U.S. 293 (2006).

defamation claim was a personal-injury tort. Without determining what constitutes a "personal injury tort," within the meaning of the statute, the Court concluded that Pierce consented to the bankruptcy court's adjudication of his defamation claim (and forfeited any argument to the contrary) when he failed to seek withdrawal of the claim until he had litigated it before the bankruptcy court for twenty-seven months: "Pierce repeatedly stated to the Bankruptcy Court that he was happy to litigate there. We will not consider his claim to the contrary, now that he is sad." Accordingly, the Supreme Court held that the bankruptcy court did have the statutory authority to enter a final judgment on Vickie's counterclaim.

The Court then considered whether this congressional grant of authority was consistent with Article III's mandate that "[t]he judicial Power of the United States, shall be vested in one supreme Court, and in such inferior Courts as the Congress may from time to time ordain and establish." Because "the Framers sought to ensure that each judicial decision would be rendered, not with an eye toward currying favor with Congress or the Executive, but rather with the '[c]lear heads . . . and honest hearts' deemed 'essential to good judges,'" Article III judges have lifetime tenure. In contrast, bankruptcy judges serve for fourteen-year terms.

The Court rejected Vickie's assertion that the entry of final judgment on her claim was constitutional because the defendant in her counterclaim was himself a creditor who had filed a claim in her bankruptcy proceeding. It also rejected her argument that her counterclaim was a matter of "public right" that can be decided outside the judicial branch. The Court first recognized that the executive branch could adjudicate certain public rights, such as title to property belonging to a customs collector who had failed to transfer payments to the federal government that he had collected on its behalf, in *Murray's Lessee v. Hoboken Land & Improvement Co.*[41] Subsequent cases extended the doctrine to cases involving the government as a party in its sovereign capacity under a statute conferring statutory public rights, claims based on a federal regulatory scheme, and cases "in which resolution of the claim by an expert government agency is deemed essential to a limited regulatory objective within the agency's authority." For example, the Commodities Futures Trading Commission had the authority to adjudicate a customer's claim against a broker for violations of the federal commodities law.[42] In *Granfinanciera, S.A. v. Nordberg*,[43] the Court ruled that the private rights exception did not apply to a fraudulent conveyance claim filed on behalf of a bankruptcy estate against a noncreditor in the bankruptcy proceeding. The Court ruled that Vickie's counterclaim was a private right that did not come within the private rights exception. Even though Pierce had previously stated that he was "happy" to litigate his claim in bankruptcy court, the Supreme Court concluded that "Pierce did not truly consent to resolution of Vickie's claim in the bankruptcy court proceedings. He had nowhere else to go if he wished to recover from Vickie's estate." Because the "Bankruptcy Court below lacked the constitutional authority to enter final judgment on a state law counterclaim that is not resolved in the process of ruling on a creditor's proof of claim," its final judgment was vacated.

RESULT The Court affirmed the decision of the court of appeals in favor of Pierce. Vickie's estate was not entitled to any relief.

COMMENTS The Court predicted that its decision would "not change all that much," stating that "the question presented here is a 'narrow' one." In a dissent joined by Justices Ginsburg, Sotomayor, and Kagan, Justice Breyer disagreed:

> Consider a typical case. A tenant files for bankruptcy. The landlord files a claim for unpaid rent. The tenant asserts a counterclaim for damages suffered by the landlord's (1) failing to fulfill his obligations as lessor, and (2) improperly recovering possession of the premises by misrepresenting the facts in housing court. This state-law counterclaim does not "ste[m]" from the bankruptcy itself, it would not "necessarily

CONTINUED

---

41. 59 U.S. 272 (1856).

42. Commodity Futures Trading Comm'n v. Schor, 478 U.S. 833 (1986).

43. 492 U.S. 33 (1989).

be resolved in the claims allowance process," and it would require the debtor to prove damages suffered by the lessor's failures, the extent to which the landlord's representations to the housing court were untrue, and damages suffered by improper recovery of possession of the premises. Thus, under the majority's holding, the federal district judge, not the bankruptcy judge, would have to hear and resolve the counterclaim.

Why is that a problem? Because these types of disputes arise in bankruptcy court with some frequency. Because the volume of bankruptcy cases is staggering, involving almost 1.6 million filings last year, compared to a federal district court docket of around 280,000 civil cases and 78,000 criminal cases. . . . Because under these circumstances, a constitutionally required game of jurisdictional ping-pong between courts would lead to inefficiency, increased cost, delay, and needless additional suffering among those faced with bankruptcy.

Initiation of a Bankruptcy Proceeding

A bankruptcy case begins when a petition is filed with the bankruptcy court by the debtor or by one or more of its creditors. In a *voluntary proceeding*, the debtor files the petition and initiates the case, whereas one or more creditors initiate an *involuntary proceeding*.

A voluntary petition must be signed and sworn under oath and must state that the debtor has debts; the debtor does not have to declare insolvency. The petition must include (1) a list of secured and unsecured creditors (including addresses and amount of debt); (2) a list of all property owned by the debtor, including any property claimed to be exempt; (3) a statement of the financial affairs of the debtor; and (4) a list of the debtor's current income and expenses.

An involuntary petition must allege that the debtor is not paying its debts as they come due. If the debtor has more than twelve creditors, the petition must be signed by at least three creditors. If there are twelve or fewer creditors, any creditor can sign. The signing creditor(s) must have valid unsecured claims of at least $10,000 in the aggregate, and the debtor must file the same schedules filed by voluntary debtors.

The filing of the petition constitutes an *order for relief.* If the debtor challenges an involuntary petition for bankruptcy, a trial is held to determine whether an order for relief should be granted. If the order is granted, the case is accepted for further proceedings.

Bankruptcy Estate

On the filing of a bankruptcy petition, a new entity, called the bankruptcy estate, is created. The *bankruptcy estate* comprises "all legal or equitable interests of the debtor in property as of the commencement of the case."[44]

Exempt Property

Exempt property is excluded from the bankruptcy estate. Intended to provide for the debtor's future needs, it generally includes, among other things, an interest up to a specified amount in equity in property used as a residence and burial plots (the homestead exemption); one motor vehicle; certain household goods and personal items; some special deposits or cash; tools or books used in the debtor's trade; any unmatured life insurance policy; professionally prescribed health aids; a number of government benefits, including Social Security, veteran's, disability, unemployment compensation, and public assistance benefits; alimony or support payments; and personal-injury awards.

Subject to a cap on homestead exemptions in limited circumstances, (discussed later in this chapter), the Bankruptcy Code also allows states to enact their own exemptions. Some states give debtors the option of choosing between federal and state exemptions, while others require debtors to follow state law. State exemptions are frequently higher than under the federal exemption scheme. For example, Florida, Iowa, Kansas, Oklahoma, South Dakota, Texas, and the District of Columbia have unlimited homestead exemptions.[45]

The Bankruptcy Code permits debtors to nullify involuntary liens that impair their allowable exemptions. They can even invalidate consensual liens on most household items, tools of the trade, or health aids, unless the secured creditor financed the debtor's purchase of the property or was given possession of it. To take full advantage of the exemptions, debtors often convert assets from nonexempt to exempt forms before filing their bankruptcy cases. They must be careful not to take steps that could be considered fraudulent, however, because fraudulent conduct could jeopardize their right to discharge existing debts.

---

44. 11 U.S.C. § 541(a)(1).

45. Carol A. Pettit & Vastine D. Platte, Cong. Research Serv., R40891, Homestead Exemptions in Bankruptcy After the Bankruptcy Abuse Prevention and Consumer Protection Act of 2005 (BAPCPA) 2 (Aug. 25, 2011).

Meeting of Creditors

A meeting of creditors must be held within a reasonable period of time after the order for relief, but in no event earlier than twenty or later than forty days after entry. The bankruptcy judge cannot attend the meeting, but the debtor must appear and answer questions.

Appointment of Trustee or Debtor-in-Possession

In Chapter 7 cases, an interim trustee is appointed by the court when an order for relief is entered. A permanent trustee is elected at the first meeting of the creditors. Once appointed, the *trustee* becomes the legal representative of the debtor's estate.

In most Chapter 11 cases, the debtor is left in place to operate the business and is referred to as the *debtor-in-possession (DIP)*. The DIP has the same powers as the trustee but also has the power to operate the business during the bankruptcy proceeding. The court may appoint a trustee in a Chapter 11 proceeding only on a showing of cause (fraud, dishonesty, or gross mismanagement by the debtor or its managers). Even if a trustee is not appointed, however, the court may appoint an examiner to investigate the Chapter 11 debtor's financial affairs.

Administration of Claims

Unsecured creditors must file a *proof of claim* stating the amount of their claim in a form provided by the court within time periods established by the jurisdiction in which the case is filed. The proof of claim requirement in a Chapter 11 bankruptcy is deemed satisfied for claims listed in the debtor's schedules as uncontingent and undisputed (unless the creditor wishes to claim more than the debtor acknowledges is due).

A creditor's claim must be allowed by the court before a creditor is permitted to participate in the bankruptcy estate. Except for personal-injury or wrongful-death claims, which are triable to a jury in the district court, disputed claims are normally resolved through a hearing before the bankruptcy judge. If a resolution would unduly delay administration of the bankruptcy case (such as when a claim is contingent upon a future event), the bankruptcy court will estimate the allowable amount of certain claims.

Some claims are limited in bankruptcy. For example, a terminated employee's damages claim may not exceed one year's compensation. Unless the estate can pay all claims in a liquidation, postpetition interest is allowed only to secured creditors that can recover it from their collateral. Perhaps most significantly, section 502(b)(6) of the Bankruptcy Code limits the amount of damages a landlord may collect from a bankrupt tenant (who rejects the lease) to the amount of unpaid back rent equal to the greater of (1) one year's rent or (2) 15% of the rent for the remaining term, not to exceed three years' rent. Many debtors holding a large number of unfavorable long-term leases have filed for bankruptcy to take advantage of this provision.

In *In re El Toro Materials Co.*,[46] the U.S. Court of Appeals for the Ninth Circuit held that tort damages claimed by a landlord are not subject to the section 502(b)(6) cap. El Toro leased property from Saddleback Community Church, paying $28,000 per month in rent. When El Toro filed for bankruptcy and rejected the lease, Saddleback brought an adversary proceeding against El Toro for $23 million in damages, alleging that El Toro left a million tons of wet clay "goo," mining equipment, and other materials on the property. The court analyzed the key issues as follows:

> The structure of the cap—measured as a fraction of the remaining term—suggests that damages other than those based on a loss of future rental income are not subject to the cap. It makes sense to cap damages for lost rental income based on the amount of expected rent. Landlords may have the ability to mitigate these damages by re-leasing or selling the premises, but will suffer injury in proportion to the value of their lost rent in the meantime. In contrast, collateral damages are likely to bear only a weak correlation to the amount of rent: A tenant may cause a lot of damage to a premises leased cheaply, or cause a little damage to premises underlying an expensive leasehold.[47]

Distribution of Property

A secured creditor's claim to the debtor's estate has priority over unsecured creditors' claims to the extent that the property of the estate consists of the creditor's collateral. The statutory priority of unsecured claims is as follows:

1. Alimony and child support.

2. Fees and expenses of administering the estate, including court costs, trustee fees, attorneys' fees, appraisal fees, and other administrative costs.

3. Claims arising in the ordinary course of business after the date of the filing of the petition but before the earlier of (a) the appointment of the trustee or (b) the issuance of the order for relief.

4. Unsecured claims for $10,950[48] per employee in wages, salary, or commissions earned by each employee of the debtor within the 180 days immediately preceding the filing of the petition (all other salary claims are treated as a claim of a general unsecured creditor).

5. Unsecured claims for up to $10,950 per employee for contributions to employee benefit plans based on services performed within 180 days immediately preceding the filing of the petition.

6. Claims up to $5,400 for each farmer or fisher against debtors who operate or own facilities for storing grain or processing fish.

---

46. Saddleback Valley Cmty. Church v. El Toro Materials Co. (*In re El Toro Materials Co.*), 504 F.3d 978 (9th Cir. 2007).

47. *Id.* at 980.

48. The amounts specified in this list are adjusted every three years.

7. Consumer claims up to $2,425 per claim for deposits with or prepayments to the debtor for undelivered property or the purchase of services that were not delivered or provided by the debtor.

8. Certain tax obligations owed by the debtor.

9. Wrongful-death or personal-injury claims resulting from the operation of a motor vehicle if such operation was unlawful because the debtor was intoxicated.

10. Claims of general unsecured creditors.

Each class must be paid in full before any lower class is paid. If a class cannot be paid in full, the claims of that class are paid proportionately. If anything is left after all of the creditors listed above are paid in full, the balance is returned to the debtor.

PROVISIONS APPLICABLE TO ALL BANKRUPTCIES

Certain provisions apply in all bankruptcy cases. They include the good faith requirement; the automatic stay; the debtor's ability to assume, assign, or reject most executory contracts and leases; and the bankruptcy court's ability to void certain transactions.

Good Faith Requirement

A debtor does not have to show it is insolvent to file for bankruptcy. Some debtors may face a liquidity crisis that cannot be untangled without judicial intervention. A notable example of this is the bankruptcy filing by Texaco after a jury in Texas awarded Pennzoil more than $10 billion (see the "Inside Story" in Chapter 7).

On the other hand, courts have resisted the use of bankruptcy when they perceive that it is being used in bad faith. For example, in *In re Integrated Telecom Express, Inc.*,[49] the board of directors of Integrated Telecom authorized commencement of a Chapter 11 proceeding if the company's negotiations with its landlord to reduce its long-term lease obligations proved unsuccessful. The board then instructed management to send the landlord a letter threatening that the company would file a Chapter 11 bankruptcy case and avail itself of the landlord cap if the landlord refused to settle. When the landlord refused to settle, Integrated Telecom filed a Chapter 11 petition and moved to reject the lease. According to its schedules, Integrated Telecom had $105.4 million in cash, $20 million of insurance to cover any liability associated with a pending class-action securities lawsuit, and other assets valued at $1.5 million. On the liability side, the landlord filed a proof of claim asserting that the present value of the company's remaining lease obligations (without applying the landlord cap) was approximately $26 million; Integrated Telecom's bankruptcy schedule listed other liabilities totaling approximately $430,000 (the class-action plaintiffs in the securities litigation sought a total of $93.24 million in damages, but Integrated Telecom disputed those claims and amounts).

Both the bankruptcy court and the district court had concluded that Integrated Telecom faced financial distress, but the U.S. Court of Appeals for the Third Circuit did not see how bankruptcy offered Integrated Telecom any relief from this distress. Although Integrated Telecom's assets were threatened by the collapse of the company's business model, there was no evidence that the value of its assets could be preserved or maximized in an orderly liquidation under Chapter 11. Although Integrated Telecom's desire to take advantage of the cap on landlord claims provided by section 502(b)(6) did not establish bad faith, it also did not, in and of itself, establish good faith. As a result, the court reversed the district court's denial of the landlord's motion to dismiss and remanded the case to the bankruptcy court with instructions to dismiss Integrated Telecom's Chapter 11 petition.

Automatic Stay

The most immediate and dramatic advantage of any bankruptcy filing is the *automatic stay*, which instantly suspends most litigation and collection activities against the debtor, its property, or that of the bankruptcy estate as well as setoffs of any debt owing to the debtor against any claim against the debtor. Many debtors file for bankruptcy on the eve of foreclosure to forestall the loss of crucial assets; others file primarily to stave off litigation or collection activities. The latter group includes such notable bankruptcy refugees as Dow Corning (facing 19,000 lawsuits involving 400,000 women claiming immune-system illness caused by silicon breast implants), Johns–Manville (sued for thousands of asbestos-related injuries), and Texaco (unable to post a bond while appealing the multibillion-dollar judgment against it for interfering with Pennzoil's efforts to acquire Getty Oil). By stopping creditors in their tracks, the automatic stay provides a breathing spell that can enable a Chapter 11 debtor to focus on operating the business and reorganizing its financial affairs.

There are only a few exceptions to the automatic stay. Three of these are the most notable. First, several types of securities and similar financial transactions are not stayed. Second, the automatic stay does not stay the commencement or continuation of a criminal action against the debtor. Third, it does not stay any action to enforce a government's police or regulatory power. These exceptions are narrowly interpreted.

The U.S. Supreme Court has ruled that a bank could, without violating the automatic stay, put a temporary administrative hold on the portion of the bankrupt debtor's checking account that the bank claimed was subject to setoff.[50] The Court reasoned that a bank account is not money belonging to the depositor but rather represents a

---

49. 384 F.3d 108 (3d Cir. 2004).

50. Citizens Bank of Md. v. Strumpf, 516 U.S. 16 (1995).

ethicalconsideration

Would it be ethical for the manager of a company about to file bankruptcy to withdraw all company funds from accounts at banks to which the company owes money to avoid having an administrative hold imposed on the accounts?

"The check is in the cloud."

Barbara Smaller/The New Yorker Collection/www.cartoonbank.com

promise by a bank to pay the depositor an amount equal to the money in the account. Therefore, by imposing an administrative hold, the bank does not exercise dominion over the bankrupt's property. Rather, the hold represents a temporary refusal of a creditor to pay a debt that is subject to setoff against a debt owed by the bankrupt entity. The Court ruled that there is no setoff unless the creditor intends to permanently settle accounts.

The automatic stay prevents creditors from enforcing a clause in their agreements, referred to as an *ipso facto clause*, that expressly permits termination in the event of a bankruptcy filing. For example, in *In re Computer Communications, Inc.*,[51] Codex Corporation had entered into a joint marketing and development agreement with Computer Communications, Inc. (CCI), pursuant to which Codex agreed to make minimum quarterly purchases of equipment and software from CCI. After CCI filed a Chapter 11 petition, Codex notified CCI that it was terminating the agreement pursuant to an ipso facto clause in the agreement. CCI sued in bankruptcy court, alleging that Codex's termination of the agreement violated the Bankruptcy Code's automatic stay provision. The bankruptcy court held that Codex had willfully violated the

ethicalconsideration

Computer Communications, Inc. (CCI) extended its agreement with Codex only two days before filing for bankruptcy. It seems clear that Codex would not have renewed the agreement if it had known that CCI was going to declare bankruptcy. The managers of CCI locked in a favorable contract by concealing their intentions from Codex. Was the CCI managers' conduct unethical or just good business?

51. 824 F.2d 725 (9th Cir. 1987).

automatic stay and awarded general damages of $4,750,000 (apparently based on loss of projected profits), plus $250,000 in punitive damages, and the U.S. Court of Appeals for the Ninth Circuit affirmed.

The stay is not a permanent shield, however. The court may authorize creditors to resume collection efforts, most often foreclosure on collateral, for cause—that is, if there is inadequate protection of the creditors' property interests, such as when the value of the collateral declines with use and no replacement security is provided. Relief from the stay will also be granted if the debtor has no equity in property and a stay is not necessary for effective reorganization. Such relief from the automatic stay becomes more likely as time passes without progress toward reorganization. The automatic stay is rarely lifted to permit garden-variety litigation against the debtor, however.

When economic conditions worsen, workouts in the shadow of foreclosure become more common. A *workout* is an out-of-court settlement that restructures the debtor's financial affairs in much the same way that a confirmed plan would, but it binds only those who expressly consent. Sometimes, a creditor will require a debtor to agree to waive its right to an automatic stay in the event of bankruptcy as a condition to agreeing to a workout. Bankruptcy courts are generally wary of enforcing prepetition waivers of the automatic stay for the benefit of one secured creditor on the basis that the debtor's other creditors have a right to be heard and to object to a grant of such relief. As seen in the following case, however, courts will under certain circumstances enforce a prebankruptcy waiver of the automatic stay.

A CASE IN POINT	*Summary*	Case 23.3

In re **Bryan Road**

United States Bankruptcy Court for the Southern District of Florida 389 B.R. 297 (Bankr. S.D. Fla. 2008).

FACTS The lender, which had commenced a judicial foreclosure proceeding against its borrower, the owner of a 210 "dray stack" boat storage facility, was awarded final judgment setting a date for the foreclosure sale. On the morning of the foreclosure sale, however, the lender agreed to continue the foreclosure sale for two months in order to give the owner time to refinance and save the project. In exchange, the lender required the owner to include a provision in the forbearance agreement whereby the lender would be relieved from the automatic stay in the event of bankruptcy. When the hoped-for financing fell through, the owner filed a

Chapter 11 bankruptcy just before the rescheduled foreclosure sale. The lender filed a motion for relief from the stay, asking the bankruptcy court to enforce the prebankruptcy relief from stay waiver in the forbearance agreement. The motion was appealed by the owner as well as the official committee of unsecured creditors and junior lienholders.

ISSUE PRESENTED   Is a prebankruptcy waiver of the automatic stay in a prepetition workout enforceable?

SUMMARY OF OPINION   In its decision on the lender's relief of stay motion, the U.S. Bankruptcy Court for the Southern District of Florida noted that prepetition waivers of the automatic stay will be given "no particular effect" when included as part of initial loan documents, but will be given "the greatest effect if entered into during the course of prior (and subsequently aborted) Chapter 11 proceedings." In considering whether stay relief should be granted based on a prepetition waiver, the court looked at four nonexclusive factors: (1) the sophistication of the party making the waiver; (2) the consideration for the waiver, including the creditor's risk and the length of time the waiver covers; (3) whether other parties are affected, including unsecured creditors and junior lienholders; and (4) the feasibility of the debtor's plan. The court found that the first two factors had been met. It also noted the existence of junior lienholders and approximately $1 million of disputed unsecured claims. However, because the court also found that the debtor's plan was not feasible, it concluded that there was likely no value for the unsecured creditors in the boat storage project and that the junior lienholders could protect their interests under state law. Putting these factors together, the bankruptcy court concluded that the forbearance agreement, including the prebankruptcy waiver of the automatic stay, should be enforced.

RESULT   The bankruptcy court lifted the automatic stay.

Ability to Assume, Assign, or Reject Executory Contracts and Leases

Sections 365(a) and 365(f) of the Bankruptcy Code give the trustee (or debtor-in-possession in the case of a Chapter 11 reorganization) the option of assuming, assigning, or rejecting most prebankruptcy *executory contracts*—that is, contracts that have not yet been fully performed—or unexpired leases. Assumption preserves the debtor's rights and duties under the existing relationship, whereas rejection terminates them. Even if a contract or lease contains contractual restrictions barring assignment, any assumed contract or lease can be sold and assigned intact if the prospective assignee's future performance is adequately assured.

In general, debtors will reject unfavorable contracts and assume favorable ones. For example, if an executory contract or unexpired lease is a valuable asset, the DIP will want to assume it so that it can be preserved for the reorganizing business or sold at a profit. Assumption is advantageous when it allows the debtor to sell or buy goods at a favorable price or to lease space or equipment at better-than-market rents. Even if a contract or lease is in default, the debtor can still assume it, provided that the debtor cures the default, compensates for the breach, and gives adequate assurance of future performance. Once assumed, the contract or lease obligations are allowable as administrative expenses, as with other authorized postpetition transactions.

On the other hand, by rejecting a disadvantageous contract or lease, the debtor can escape burdensome performance obligations. The nondebtor party to the contract or lease will be deemed to have a prepetition damages claim for breach and thus will be treated like others whose claims arose from prebankruptcy transactions. If a DIP does not include an executory contract in its reorganization plan, the contract is deemed to have been rejected.

Collective Bargaining Agreements

The rules for avoiding collective bargaining agreements (CBAs) changed after Frank Lorenzo, then CEO of Continental Airlines, used Chapter 11 to avoid the company's CBAs in the early 1980s. After the labor unions rejected his demands for sizable wage concessions, Lorenzo took Continental into a Chapter 11 proceeding and repudiated its CBAs. Continental emerged from bankruptcy as a nonunion carrier with a reduced wage structure.

Organized labor protested the use of the Bankruptcy Code by Lorenzo (and, increasingly, others) to break unions. In 1984, Congress responded by enacting section 1113 of the Bankruptcy Code, which sets forth the following procedural prerequisites to a debtor's rejection of a CBA: (1) the debtor must make a proposal to the union to modify the CBA that incorporates changes necessary to permit reorganization; (2) the proposal must be based on the most complete and reliable information available at the time; (3) the debtor must provide the union with such relevant information as is necessary to evaluate the proposal; (4) the debtor must meet at reasonable times with the union between the time of making the proposal and the time of the hearing on rejection; and (5) at the meetings, the debtor must confer in good faith in attempting to reach mutually satisfactory modifications of the CBA.

Steps 1 through 3 must be completed prior to filing a motion to reject the CBA, but steps 4 and 5 can take place after the motion is filed. If the procedural steps are satisfied, the bankruptcy court will consider the following substantive elements in deciding whether to reject the CBA: (1) the proposed modifications must be necessary to allow the debtor to reorganize and must be submitted in good faith; (2) the proposed modifications must assure that all creditors, the debtor, and all affected parties are treated fairly and equitably; (3) the union must have refused to accept the proposal without good cause; and (4) the balance of the equities must favor rejection.

The section 1113 requirements have been applied differently by different courts. For example, the U.S. Court of Appeals for the Third Circuit has held that the standard to measure "necessary modifications" to the CBA encompasses only the modifications necessary for the debtor's short-term survival or to prevent liquidation.[52] The U.S. Court of Appeals for the Second Circuit, however, has held that satisfaction of the necessity requirement requires proof that the modifications sought are "necessary, but not absolutely minimal, changes that will enable the debtor to complete its reorganization successfully."[53]

Notwithstanding the procedural protections provided by section 1113, major airlines continue to use bankruptcy as a tool to reduce their labor costs. In 2006, the bankruptcy court for the Southern District of New York found that Northwest Airlines had satisfied all of the procedural requirements of section 1113 for rejection of its CBA. Turning to the substantive elements, the court found the CBA could be rejected because (1) the necessity for change was evidenced by the undisputed fact that Northwest could not reorganize if its labor costs remained unchanged, (2) the union lacked good cause because the union had voted down the debtor's proposal despite its acceptance by union leadership, and (3) the balance of the equities favored rejection of the CBA.[54] That same year, in a case involving Delta Air Lines, another bankruptcy court in the Second Circuit also approved the rejection of a CBA.[55] In 2011, American Airlines followed its rivals United Airlines, U.S. Airways, Northwest, and Delta into bankruptcy. The airline had been involved in fruitless negotiations with the union for several years. According to American's incoming CEO Tom Horton, "The world changed around us, [and] [i]t became increasingly clear that the cost gap between us and our competitors was untenable."[56]

Limitations

Section 365(c) provides an exception to the debtor's usual right to assume, assign, or reject executory contracts and unexpired leases. It provides that the debtor may not assume or assign an executory contract or unexpired lease if "applicable laws excuse a party . . . to such contract or lease from accepting performance from or rendering performance to an entity other than the debtor" unless the other party consents to the assignment or assumption.[57]

Intellectual Property Licenses

In the early cases, courts tended to permit the assumption and assignment of both exclusive and nonexclusive intellectual property (IP) licenses, including copyright, patent, and trademark licenses, even if the IP license expressly prohibited assignment without the licensor's consent. In more recent decisions, however, certain courts have invoked section 365(c) to limit the ability of debtors to assign or even assume IP licenses without the licensor's consent. Certain, but not all, courts treat a debtor's election to assume a license and perform it itself differently from an election to assume a license and then assign it to a third party.

Assumption of Licenses The U.S. Courts of Appeals for the First and Fifth Circuits allow a debtor to assume an IP license that is subject to section 365(c), even over the objection of a nondebtor licensor, as long as the debtor licensee does not actually intend to assign the license to a third party. This approach is called the "actual test."[58] On the other hand, the U.S. Courts of Appeals for the Third, Fourth, and Ninth Circuits have held that a debtor may not assume an IP license subject to section 365(c) when applicable nonbankruptcy law prohibits assignment without consent, even if the debtor has no actual intention to assign its license. Once the license is assumed, these courts create a "hypothetical" third party to whom the license will be assigned. For this reason, the analysis is referred to as the "hypothetical test."

52. Wheeling–Pittsburgh Steel v. United Steelworkers, 791 F.2d 1074 (3d Cir. 1986).

53. Truck Drivers Local 807 v. Carey Transp., Inc., 816 F.2d 82 (2d Cir. 1987).

54. *In re* Northwest Airlines Corp., 2006 Bankr. LEXIS 1159 (Bankr. S.D.N.Y. June 29, 2006).

55. *In re* Delta Air Lines, Case No. 05-17923 (Bankr. S.D.N.Y. July 21, 2006). *See generally* Jeremy R. Johnson, *The Rejec-tion of Collective Bargaining Agreements—New Cases and Developments*, DLA Piper News & Insights, *available at* http://www.dlapiper.com/rejection_of_collective_bargaining/.

56. Kyle Peterson & Matt Daily, *American Airlines Files for Bankruptcy*, Reuters, Nov. 29, 2011.

57. *See, e.g., In re* Footstar, Inc., 323 B.R. 566 (Bankr. S.D.N.Y. 2005) (debtors sought to assume certain agreements with Kmart granting the debtors the exclusive right to operate footwear departments in certain Kmart stores).

58. Institut Pasteur v. Cambridge Biotech Corp., 104 F.3d 489 (1st Cir. 1997), *cert. denied*, 521 U.S. 1120 (1997), *abrogated by* Hardemon v. City of Boston, 1998 WL 148382 (1st Cir. 1998), *overruling recognized by* Beal Bank, S.S.B. v. Waters Edge Ltd. P'ship, 248 B.R. 668 (D. Mass. 2000); Bonneville Power Admin. v. Mirant Corp., 440 F.3d 238 (5th Cir. 2006).

Despite this predominantly licensor-favorable backdrop, the courts in several more recent decisions have sided with Chapter 11 debtors. This emerging trend is particularly noteworthy because two of the decisions came from the Southern District of New York, where many of the largest Chapter 11 bankruptcy cases (including Enron, WorldCom, Delphi, Dana, Northwest Airlines, and Delta Air Lines) have been filed. In *In re Footstar, Inc.*,[59] a 2005 case that did not involve IP licenses, the bankruptcy court for the Southern District of New York adopted a new "literal" reading of section 365(c). Noting that the section's use of the word "trustee" does not include the debtor or the DIP, the court held that the right of the nondebtor party to object to assignment does not by itself affect the right of the DIP (as opposed to a trustee) to assume an executory contract. In 2007, the bankruptcy court, faced with the same issue, expressly rejected the "hypothetical test" and embraced the *Footstar* decision as "consistent in outcome with the decisions of" those courts following the "actual" theory.[60]

Assignment of Copyright Licenses   At least one bankruptcy court has held that a nonexclusive copyright license is nonassignable in a bankruptcy proceeding in the absence of consent by the licensor or express contractual provisions to the contrary.[61] Authorities differ on the assignability of exclusive copyright licenses. One school of thought holds that exclusive copyright licenses are freely assignable; this would suggest that assignment is generally appropriate even if the copyright license expressly prohibits assignment.[62] In contrast, the highly regarded treatise *Nimmer on Copyright* concludes that a copyright licensor may restrict assignment of even an exclusive copyright license by express contractual restrictions; this approach would suggest that assignment is appropriate unless there is an express contractual restriction to the contrary.[63] A third school of thought holds that Congress did not grant exclusive licensees the right to freely transfer their licenses. This approach would suggest that assignment should be prohibited unless consent is first obtained.

Assignment of Patent Licenses   At least one bankruptcy court has held that nonexclusive patent licenses are not assignable under section 365(c) without the consent of the licensor.[64]

Assignment of Trademark Licenses   Case law appears to support the proposition that trademark licenses are assignable without consent.[65] In 2005, however, Billy Blanks

of the Billy Blanks® Tae Bo® fitness program successfully moved the U.S. District Court for the District of Nevada to compel rejection of its trademark license on the basis that contracts that cannot be assigned by the debtor without the nondebtor party's consent under the hypothetical test cannot be assumed by the debtor either.[66] Although the decision was appealed to the U.S. Court of Appeals for the Ninth Circuit, the debtor, N.C.P. Marketing, reached a settlement of the case prior to the oral argument. However, N.C.P. Marketing and certain other parties filed an objection to the trustee's motion for approval of the settlement, and in February 2008, the bankruptcy court denied the motion for approval and instead approved a sale of the appeal rights and certain other assets to the objecting parties.

Sale of Property

Bankruptcy can facilitate favorable sales of assets other than contracts or leases. For example, if partition or division of property jointly owned by the debtor and another is impractical and a separate sale of the debtor's undivided interest would yield significantly less for the estate, the debtor can sell both interests and disburse the net proceeds proportionately, as long as the resulting benefit would outweigh the detriment to the other owner. Similarly, the debtor may sell property free and clear of liens or other interests (which normally will be shifted to the proceeds) if the price will exceed all encumbrances or if the nondebtor's interest is in bona fide dispute. Thus, although the debtor's sale before bankruptcy might be stymied, a bankruptcy proceeding can sometimes break the logjam and allow the debtor to pass clear title.

This cleansing power of bankruptcy extends beyond specific property. It can be the key to successful reorganization through the sale of the entire business or through new capital infusions. When a business is troubled and its future is in doubt, potential investors may shy away, despite the venture's intrinsic worth. Similarly, the price a prospective going-concern purchaser will pay may be seriously depressed by the fear that acquiring all of the assets will subject the buyer to the debtor's obligations under doctrines of successor liability (discussed in Chapter 10). The same investors or buyers are more willing to recognize the true value of the debtor's business if the transaction proceeds under a confirmed plan or other court order that quantifies or cuts off preexisting claims. Subject to possible constitutional due process protections for unknown future claimants, bankruptcy can dispel uncertainties that would otherwise prevent the debtor from realizing the equity in its business.

Avoiding Powers

The Bankruptcy Code provides trustees with certain *avoiding powers* that they can use to invalidate or reverse

---

59. 323 B.R. 566 (Bankr. S.D.N.Y. 2005).

60. *In re* Adelphia Commc'ns, 359 B.R. 65 (Bankr. S.D.N.Y. 2007).

61. *In re* Patient Educ. Media, 210 B.R. 237 (S.D.N.Y. 1997).

62. *Id.*

63. *See* NIMMER ON COPYRIGHT § 10.01[C][4] (2008).

64. Everex Sys. v. Cadtrak, 89 F.3d 673 (9th Cir. 1996).

65. *In re* Rooster, Inc., 100 B.R. 228 (Bankr. E.D. Pa. 1989).

66. *In re* N.C.P. Mktg. Group, Inc., 337 B.R. 230 (D. Nev. 2005).

certain prebankruptcy transactions that would unfairly benefit the debtor or certain creditors.

Fraudulent Conveyances

Section 548 of the Bankruptcy Code gives the court the power to avoid *fraudulent conveyances*. In general, these arise from transactions that occurred within a year before bankruptcy that (1) are actually intended to hinder, delay, or defraud creditors or (2) provide less than reasonably equivalent value in exchange and leave the debtor insolvent or without sufficient capital to engage in business or to pay expected debts. Thus, a leveraged buyout that leaves a company with insufficient capital and high debt leverage after the payouts to equity holders may be voidable as a fraudulent conveyance.[67] Most states have roughly parallel fraudulent transfer laws, but the Bankruptcy Code's version may be broader. For example, the state laws may be inapplicable to distressed foreclosure sales that are noncollusive and procedurally proper; bankruptcy law has been applied to invalidate such sales if the proceeds are less than 70% of the collateral's fair market value. Thus, although a good faith buyer should have a lien for the value given (which is usually the amount of the secured debt), the bankruptcy trustee may be able to reverse the foreclosure and recapture equity. However, in *BFP v. Resolution Trust Corp.*,[68] the U.S. Supreme Court affirmed the dismissal of a fraudulent transfer proceeding by a Chapter 11 debtor, holding that the price received at a mortgage foreclosure sale conclusively established the "reasonably equivalent value" of the mortgage property as long as the requirements of the state's foreclosure law were met.

Preferences

Preferences are transfers to (or for the benefit of) creditors on account of antecedent (that is, preexisting) debts that are made from an insolvent debtor's property within ninety days before bankruptcy and that enable the creditors to receive more than they would through a Chapter 7 liquidation. (The preference window is enlarged to a year before bankruptcy if the benefited creditor is an *insider*—that is, someone in a position to control the debtor's conduct, such as a relative, partner, director, officer, or substantial shareholder.) Preferences are avoidable in bankruptcy to discourage creditors from dismembering a troubled business in their race for its assets and to foster equal distribution among similarly situated claimants. Subject to limited exceptions, the bankruptcy court can recover voluntary or involuntary preferential payments and strip away preferential security interests or collection liens, all for the benefit of the bankruptcy estate.

A payment is a preference only if it is for an antecedent debt. To avoid penalizing creditors that continue to deal in a customary fashion with the debtor during its slide into bankruptcy, current payments in the ordinary course of business cannot be recovered as preferences.[69] In *Union Bank v. Wolas*,[70] the U.S. Supreme Court held that payments on long-term debt, as well as payments on short-term debt, may qualify for the ordinary course of business exception to the trustee's power to avoid preferential transfers if (1) the loan was incurred in the ordinary course of the debtor's business and of the bank's business, (2) the payments were made in the ordinary course of business, and (3) the payments were made according to ordinary business terms.

In a 2007 decision, the U.S. Court of Appeals for the Ninth Circuit held that even a first-time transaction can qualify for the ordinary course of business defense to preferences. The Ninth Circuit set forth the following special rule when a first-time debt is involved:

> [W]hen we have no past debt between the parties with which to compare the challenged one, the instant debt should be compared to the debt agreements into which we would expect the debtor and creditor to enter as a part of their ordinary business operations. . . . [A] first-time debt must be ordinary in relation to this debtor's and this creditor's past practices when dealing with other, similarly situated parties. Only if a party has never engaged in similar transactions would we consider more generally whether the debt is similar to what we would expect of similarly situated parties, where the debtor is not sliding into bankruptcy.

Having established the new test, the court reversed the grant of summary judgment to the defendant in this case because it found the proof presented was inadequate.[71]

The *earmarking doctrine*, whereby a payment to a preexisting creditor may not be recoverable as a preference if the funds for the repayment were provided by some other creditor and not by the debtor, can sometimes be asserted as a defense to preference claims. For example, the U.S. Court of Appeals for the Ninth Circuit has held that the earmarking defense applies when a lender agrees to pay a specific creditor, even when the lender does not pay the creditor directly, but instead advances the funds to the debtor for payment to the selected creditor.[72]

Setoff Rights

A creditor exercising a setoff right automatically deducts what the debtor owes the creditor from what the creditor owes the debtor. By analogy to the preference provision, creditors who exercise setoff rights within ninety days before bankruptcy can be required to disgorge such offsets to the extent that they decreased their obligations to the debtor within the ninety-day period.

---

67. *See, e.g.*, United States v. Tabor Court Realty Corp., 803 F.2d 1288 (3d Cir. 1987), *cert. denied*, 483 U.S. 1005 (1987).

68. 511 U.S. 531 (1994).

69. 11 U.S.C. § 547(c)(2).

70. 502 U.S. 151 (1991).

71. *In re* Ahaza Sys., Inc., 482 F.3d 1118 (9th Cir. 2007).

72. *In re* Superior Stamp & Coin Co., 223 F.3d 1004 (9th Cir. 2000).

Statutory Liens

The bankruptcy court can avoid certain statutory liens, including those that first arise upon insolvency or that would not have been enforceable against a bona fide purchaser of the encumbered property when the bankruptcy was filed. This prevents state law from creating hidden priorities that would distort the federal bankruptcy distribution scheme.

CHAPTER 11 REORGANIZATIONS

Chapter 11 is designed for reorganizing troubled businesses, from single-asset limited partnerships and joint ventures, such as Dow Corning, the manufacturer of silicon breast implants, to huge publicly held corporations, such as the oil giant Texaco, the pharmaceutical manufacturer A.H. Robins, the retailer Kmart, and the investment bank Lehman Brothers. Chapter 11 has two primary objectives: (1) to rehabilitate a troubled debtor and (2) to maximize the return to creditors. It has the added benefit of maintaining jobs and preserving other economic benefits to the community. The goal of Chapter 11 is to reorganize the debtor with a new capital structure so that it can emerge from bankruptcy as a viable concern. Chapter 11 is available to individuals, partnerships, corporations, unincorporated associations, and railroads. It is not available to banks, savings and loan associations, credit unions, insurance companies, stockbrokers, or commodity brokers. The majority of Chapter 11 proceedings are filed by corporations.

The treatment of a Chapter 11 debtor's creditors and owners and the future of its business are set forth in a plan developed by one or more of the parties. If the plan meets the statutory requirements and is confirmed by the court, it becomes a master contract that redefines the legal relationships among all who have claims against (or interests in) the debtor; it binds even those who do not consent to its terms.

Obtaining Credit

Often the DIP's first priority is to stay in business and continue (or resume) providing goods and services to customers at a profit. Yet, as observed at the outset, poor cash flow often paves the way to Chapter 11. Although the bankruptcy system does not manufacture money, it may enhance or create some funding possibilities.

Customers' Payments

The debtor's liquidity crisis sometimes stems from a secured lender's insistence that all encumbered customer payments be applied to the loan, leaving little or no cash for operations. If a bankruptcy petition is filed, customer payments on prebankruptcy accounts will remain the lender's cash collateral, but the court may authorize the DIP to use the funds if the lender's position is adequately protected. Such protection might be found in surplus collateral that gives the lender an ample equity cushion or by granting the lender a substitute lien on postpetition inventory and receivables. Of course, the court may underestimate the need for protection, and this risk may prod an otherwise recalcitrant lender to negotiate terms for use of its cash collateral.

Extension of Unsecured Credit

Filing for reorganization may encourage suppliers (and perhaps other lenders) to extend unsecured credit. During the debtor's prebankruptcy decline, conventional trade terms (such as payment due thirty days after invoice) often become unavailable as the debtor falls behind on accounts payable and word of its shaky condition spreads. Fearful that they may recover only pennies on the dollar from credit sales if the debtor collapses, vendors begin requiring cash on delivery or even in advance, which aggravates the debtor's problems. The same suppliers, particularly those that are sophisticated and value the debtor's patronage most, may be willing to resume regular credit transactions with the DIP.

Flexibility returns because postpetition debts incurred in the ordinary course of doing business are allowable as administrative expenses, which are accorded priority over virtually all other unsecured claims. Thus, vendors that extend postpetition credit expect full payment on those transactions. In so doing, they may strengthen the debtor's business and promote a greater recovery on their prepetition claims.

Secured Borrowings

The debtor's ability to borrow on a secured basis can be similarly enhanced in a Chapter 11 reorganization, mainly because collateral may be more available. For example, assets acquired after the bankruptcy petition is filed (other than those derived directly from prebankruptcy collateral) will not be subject to prepetition security agreements designed to cover such after-acquired property. Therefore, a debtor that can produce inventory or generate accounts receivable after the bankruptcy filing may have enough unencumbered property to support new secured loans. Moreover, if credit is not otherwise available, the court can authorize borrowing that is secured by a *priming lien*—a lien that is senior to a previously granted security interest—provided that the preexisting lienholder is adequately protected. Thus, for example, a first mortgage on raw land might be involuntarily subordinated to a new lien that will secure a DIP-developer's construction financing.

Court Oversight

On occasion, the bankruptcy court's oversight alone may help the debtor arrange new secured loans. By obtaining court approval after giving appropriate notice to other creditors, lenders can virtually immunize their repayment rights and security interests from the attacks by other creditors that sometimes undermine prebankruptcy loans.

Turnover of Debtor's Property

Although usually less expeditious than borrowing, other bankruptcy tools can also help the DIP obtain funds for operations and enhance the value of the estate. Almost anyone can be compelled to turn over property of the estate that could be used by the DIP. Thus, if adequate protection is provided, a lender that has frozen the debtor's deposit accounts at the banking institution or a taxing authority that has seized them may be required to relinquish these funds.

The Plan of Reorganization

The debtor has the exclusive right to file a plan of reorganization with the bankruptcy court within the first 120 days after the date of the order for relief. The debtor also has the right to obtain creditor approval of the plan within the first 180 days after the date of the order. The court has discretion to extend these time periods in complex cases. After that, any party may propose a plan.

All plans divide claims and equity interests into separate classes according to their legal attributes. For example, lienholders' claims are classified by collateral and rank (often resulting in one claim per class, because each lien confers distinct rights and usually secures only one claim). Relevant priority claims (such as wages or consumer deposits) are put into discrete classes, separate from general unsecured claims. Holders of preferred shares are grouped separately from common shareholders.

A plan must also prescribe treatment for the claims and interests in each class. Some plans simply extend the time for repaying debts; others reduce the amounts payable. A reduction in the amount payable is known as a *composition*. In many cases, creditors exchange all or part of their claims for preferred or common stock or other ownership interests in the business, thereby diluting or extinguishing the rights of the prebankruptcy shareholders. Sometimes the entire business will be sold free of claims, with creditors dividing the sale proceeds. A plan can even call for liquidation and distribution comparable to the Chapter 7 process (to be discussed later in this chapter). Unless they agree otherwise, priority claimants usually are entitled to full payment when the plan becomes effective, except that prepetition unsecured taxes may be paid in installments over six years from the assessment date, with interest at the market rate.

In addition, the plan must explain the intended means for its execution. Plans often provide for payments from cash on hand, future earnings, asset sales, new capital contributions, or some combination of sources.

Confirmation

To be confirmed, a plan must meet numerous statutory requirements. If these requirements are met and all impaired classes accept the plan, the plan should be confirmed. Under certain circumstances, a plan can be confirmed over the objection of creditors.

General Requirements

Some of the less technical requirements are discussed below.

Feasibility   The plan must be feasible. There is no point in replacing the debtor's existing obligations with a new set of obligations that the debtor cannot meet.

Best Interests of Creditors   Unless accepted unanimously, the plan must pass the *best interests of creditors test*. Dissenters must be given a bundle of rights with a current value at least as great as the distribution they would receive through a Chapter 7 liquidation.

Disclosure Statement   Before deciding whether to accept the plan, creditors and shareholders are entitled to receive a disclosure statement that the court has found contains adequate information to enable them to make an informed judgment. This disclosure process largely displaces otherwise applicable laws and regulations governing the issuance and sale of securities, including the requirements of the Securities Act of 1933, described in Chapter 21.

Impaired Claims   If a plan impairs any class of claims, it cannot be confirmed unless at least one impaired class accepts it (excluding favorable votes cast by insiders). Claims are considered *impaired* if the plan does not provide for full cash payment on its effective date and if it alters the creditors' legal, equitable, or contractual rights in any way (except by curing defaults and reinstating the maturity of the claim).

Acceptance   A creditor class accepts the plan if the affirmative ballots constitute a simple majority and represent two-thirds of the total claim amounts of those voting. An equity class accepts if the favorable ballots represent two-thirds of the voted interests.

Cramdown Confirmation

Even when a class rejects a plan, the plan can still be confirmed by a *cramdown*, that is, confirmed over the objections of creditors. A cramdown can occur only if the court finds that the plan does not discriminate unfairly and that it is fair and equitable, and if at least one noninsider, impaired class has voted to accept the plan. Although the phrases "does not discriminate unfairly" and "fair and equitable" both have technical meanings that are open to interpretation, the phrase "fair and equitable" is more frequently the subject of debate. If the rejecting class consists of secured claims, the plan ordinarily can be found fair and equitable only if creditors will retain their liens until they receive full payment in cash of the secured claims. The cash payments must have a present value at least as great as the present value of the collateral. If the debtor elects to retain and use the creditor's collateral, the value of the collateral (and thus the secured claim) is the replacement value, that is, what the debtor would have to pay for comparable property.[73] For other creditors and equity holders, the plan will be considered fair and equitable only if no class junior to the naysayers will receive anything under the plan or if the rejecting class is to receive value equivalent to immediate payment in full.

Thus, to cramdown a plan that would distribute stock in satisfaction of claims, the proponent must show that the stock will neither overpay nor underpay those who receive it. The value of the stock turns on the going-concern value of the business, which is often a controversial issue. When classes have not accepted a debt-for-stock plan, the confirmation hearing can easily become a battle among expert witnesses arguing over whether higher or lower multiples or multipliers should be used to capitalize the reorganized debtor's expected earnings, which are themselves subject to competing projections.

Plan Negotiations

Because confirmation by cramdown is both difficult and uncertain, plan proponents frequently try to draft terms that will encourage broad acceptance. For the first 120 days (or for a longer or shorter time that the court may fix), only the debtor can propose a plan. After this exclusivity period expires, any party may propose a plan. Thus, a debtor that does not bargain reasonably may be faced with a competing plan that might be threatened or proposed by a major secured creditor or by the official committee that is appointed in Chapter 11 cases to represent the interests of unsecured creditors. Even if the debtor is the only party proposing a plan, an endorsement from the creditors' committee can be essential to obtain the creditor support necessary to achieve confirmation without a cramdown. Taken together, these dynamics promote negotiation and accommodation among the interested parties. Most successful plans in large Chapter 11 cases reflect such compromises.

Discharge

Confirmation under Chapter 11 can give reorganized debtors a new financial beginning under the plan through a *discharge* of (that is, relief from) their debts. Because entities such as corporations or partnerships are not eligible for a discharge under Chapter 7, they will similarly not be discharged under Chapter 11 in the event of a liquidation. If the business is rehabilitated, however, then the debtor

entity is liable for preconfirmation claims only insofar as they are expressly preserved by the plan.

No bankruptcy discharge, whether under Chapter 11 or otherwise, protects the debtor's co-obligors, such as guarantors or joint tortfeasors. Increasingly, however, to facilitate the debtor's reorganization, courts are enjoining collecting actions by third parties against nondebtor parties (such as sureties or guarantors of the debtor) under the court's general equitable powers pursuant to section 105(a) of the Bankruptcy Code. The use of these section 105(a) injunctions is the subject of much controversy. The U.S. Courts of Appeals for the Second[74] and Seventh Circuits[75] have upheld the power of bankruptcy courts under section 105(a) to issue temporary and permanent injunctions against third parties, as well as third-party releases under certain factual circumstances. In contrast, the U.S. Court of Appeals for the Ninth Circuit[76] does not permit permanent third-party releases under a plan pursuant to section 105(a). In addition, section 524(g) affords the bankruptcy court the power to issue a channeling injunction in asbestos bankruptcies to provide similar injunctive relief to certain third parties, including insurance carriers, whose liability is derivative from the debtor's liability.

WORKOUTS AND PREPACKAGED AND PRENEGOTIATED CHAPTER 11 CASES

The high transaction costs, adverse publicity, and uncertainty of a Chapter 11 bankruptcy can be disadvantageous for debtors and creditors alike, so the parties often seek alternatives.

Workouts

To avoid a Chapter 11 filing, the parties often try to negotiate a workout. Workouts are forged in the shadow of bankruptcy, and the parties measure their concessions against the obvious alternative. The debtor and major creditors may be willing to accept something less than unanimity (for example, to preclude dissenters from extorting preferred treatment), but the deal will unravel if there are too many holdouts. When this risk is apparent from the outset, the workout agreement can be drafted in the form of a Chapter 11 plan. If necessary, and provided the information disclosed in soliciting assent to the agreement was adequate, the debtor can then file for reorganization and use the prepetition votes to transform the workout into a prepackaged Chapter 11 bankruptcy (discussed below).

---

73. Assocs. Commercial Corp. v. Rash, 520 U.S. 953 (1997).

74. SEC v. Drexel Burnham Lambert Group, Inc. (*In re* Drexel Burnham Lambert Group, Inc.), 960 F.2d 285, 293 (2d Cir. 1992); *see also In re* Lyondell Chem. Co., 402 B.R. 571 (Bankr. S.D.N.Y. 2009).

75. *In re* Airadigm Commc'ns, Inc., 519 F.3d 640 (7th Cir. 2008).

76. *In re* Am. Hardwoods, Inc., 885 F.2d 621 (9th Cir. 1989).

The foundation of any successful workout is trust. Creditors will not sign an agreement that leaves the business in the hands of managers they consider to be dishonest or incompetent. If the debtor has lost credibility by misleading creditors or evading their reasonable inquiries (a common problem), its management may need to recruit and defer to a turnaround specialist in order to restore confidence. Full disclosure and candor are especially important when creditors are agreeing to accept partial payment in full satisfaction of undisputed debts. The debtor's misrepresentation or concealment of material facts probably would invalidate an otherwise binding release.

Regardless of its terms, a workout agreement cannot stop the debtor from taking refuge in Chapter 11 if the restructured obligations prove too great. The right to file bankruptcy cannot be waived. Sometimes, however, creditors have strategic reasons to defer the debtor's filing, perhaps to buttress their positions with new guaranties or to season transfers against the avoiding powers. In any event, if the debtor has broken faith with the workout pact, the court may consider previous creditor concessions in deciding whether to lift the stay, allow creditors to propose a plan at the outset, appoint a trustee, or convert the case to a Chapter 7 liquidation.

Prepackaged Chapter 11 Cases

A prepackaged Chapter 11 case is a popular method for restructuring a troubled company. In a *prepackaged bankruptcy*, the company solicits votes on its plan of reorganization before filing for bankruptcy. It files for Chapter 11 protection only after obtaining the required votes in favor of the plan. If the debtor is a publicly held company, the vote solicitation and the SEC filing are made promptly after the company and its creditors have agreed on the terms.

Although companies use prepackaged bankruptcies to implement many strategies, a company most commonly files a prepackaged Chapter 11 bankruptcy when it believes that the sale of its assets will exceed the costs of the bankruptcy, because the Chapter 11 filing will allow it to sell the assets free and clear of liens. One of the reasons that buyers like these bankruptcy sales is that after competitive bidding and notice to all creditors, the sales are approved by the bankruptcy court. As a result, it is unlikely that the buyer of the assets of a company that has filed a prepackaged Chapter 11 case will be sued later for fraudulent conveyance.

Prenegotiated Chapter 11 Cases

A prenegotiated Chapter 11 case combines the advantages of a prebankruptcy negotiation with creditors with the benefits of a postbankruptcy solicitation of votes on the plan of reorganization. In a *prenegotiated bankruptcy*, the debtor files its Chapter 11 petition as soon as it can after reaching agreement on the terms of the restructuring with its key creditors. Votes on the plan are not solicited until after the bankruptcy case is filed, however.

Companies and creditors may prefer a prenegotiated Chapter 11 to a prepackaged Chapter 11 for several reasons. First, complying with federal securities laws is easier in a prenegotiated Chapter 11 due to various provisions in the Bankruptcy Code and the federal securities laws. Second, a company filing a prenegotiated Chapter 11 does not have to publicly disclose its financial condition prior to the filing, which allows the company to run its operations as smoothly as possible during the prefiling period.

A prenegotiated Chapter 11 has one major disadvantage, however. If the debtor is a public company, the earliest the vote solicitation can begin is usually a month after the debtor files for bankruptcy. This means that creditors with nonpublic knowledge of the debtor's financial condition are unable to trade in the debtor's stock during this gap period.[77]

Another possible disadvantage of a prenegotiated Chapter 11 is that the debtor may not be able to obtain a binding postpetition commitment by the participating creditors to support a plan with certain specified terms. This commitment most often takes the form of a lockup.

CHAPTER 7 LIQUIDATIONS

In a Chapter 7 bankruptcy, sometimes called a *straight bankruptcy*, the trustee liquidates the estate and distributes the proceeds, first to secured creditors (to the extent of their collateral) and then in the prescribed order discussed earlier in the chapter and pro rata within each level. Any persons, including individuals, partnerships, and corporations, may be debtors in a Chapter 7 proceeding, although certain types of businesses (including banks, savings and loan associations, credit unions, insurance companies, and railroads) cannot file a Chapter 7 proceeding.

Individual Debtors

Individual debtors normally are discharged (that is, relieved) from bankruptcy (that is, prepetition) obligations, except for certain nondischargeable debts such as (1) taxes, (2) educational loans (unless repayment would constitute an undue hardship), (3) spousal or child support, (4) fines or penalties, (5) drunk-driving liabilities, and (6) claims arising from "willful and malicious injury by the debtor" under section 523(a)(6) of the Bankruptcy Code. Punitive damages awarded on account of the debtor's fraudulent acquisition of money, property, services, or credit are also nondischargeable.[78]

In *Kawaauhau v. Geiger*,[79] the U.S. Supreme Court found that a medical malpractice claim was discharged because there was no proof that the debtor's tortious conduct was intended to cause psychological or economic

---

77. Neil Cummings, *Smoothing the Way*, DAILY DEAL, Mar. 7, 2003.

78. Cohen v. de la Cruz, 523 U.S. 213 (1998).

79. 523 U.S. 57 (1998).

harm. Several bankruptcy courts subsequently have applied *Geiger* to Title VII discrimination cases, finding that sexual harassment claims were also dischargeable.[80] More recently, however, the U.S. Bankruptcy Appellate Panel for the Eighth Circuit ruled that a Title VII judgment for retaliation in a sexual harassment case was not dischargeable. The panel held that the issues in the Title VII case were essentially the same—whether the defendant had acted willfully and maliciously—and that the jury's finding of retaliation foreclosed the defendant from relitigating the issues of willfulness and malice in bankruptcy court.[81] This ruling is particularly significant since it comes from the same panel that decided *Kawaauhau v. Geiger*.

In assessing whether a student loan is dischargeable on the basis that repayment would constitute an undue hardship, the most widely used criteria are whether the debtor, for most of the loan repayment period, can maintain a minimal standard of living on current income and expenses; whether the debtor has made good faith repayment efforts; the amount of the debt; the accumulation of interest; and the debtor's claimed expenses and current standard of living. A bankruptcy court may partially discharge student loans when full repayment would impose undue hardship on a debtor.

A Chapter 7 discharge is not available to debtors who have received a discharge in a Chapter 7 bankruptcy filed in the preceding eight years or in a Chapter 13 case filed in the preceding six years. It will also be denied if the debtor has mistreated his or her creditors or abused the system, such as by fraudulently transferring or concealing property, destroying or falsifying financial information, or disobeying lawful court orders. (Unlike in Chapter 7, a debtor's prior misconduct or discharge within the past six years will not bar a Chapter 13 discharge.) The same debts that are nondischargeable under Chapter 7 are also excluded from a Chapter 11 discharge. Also, a Chapter 11 plan that calls for the liquidation and cessation of a business will only afford a discharge to individuals who would have been eligible for one in Chapter 7.

An individual who has filed under Chapter 7 can enter into a contract with a creditor (a *reaffirmation agreement*) whereby the debtor agrees to repay a debt even though the debt would otherwise be discharged in the debtor's bankruptcy case. The creditor must file the reaffirmation agreement with the bankruptcy court, which has the power to disapprove the agreement if the court finds that it is not in the debtor's best interests.

From 1985 to 1997, Sears, Roebuck & Co. unlawfully dunned more than 200,000 consumers who had outstanding debt on Sears credit cards and had filed for bankruptcy protection. Sears persuaded them to sign reaffirmation agreements but failed to file the agreements with the bankruptcy courts. In June 1997, Sears entered into a settlement with the Federal Trade Commission whereby it agreed to refund $100 million to consumers for its improper credit card collection practices.[82] Sears also agreed to write off the unpaid portion of the balances on the invalid reaffirmation agreements.[83]

An individual Chapter 7 debtor cannot retain possession of personal property in which a creditor has a purchase-money security interest unless the debtor, no later than forty-five days after the first meeting of creditors, either enters into a reaffirmation agreement or redeems the property. If the debtor fails to take action within forty-five days, the automatic stay is terminated with respect to such property, and the property is no longer estate property, thereby allowing the creditor to exercise its nonbankruptcy law remedies.[84]

Bankruptcy Abuse Prevention and Consumer Protection Act of 2005

In an effort to "help ensure that debtors who *can* pay creditors *do* pay them,"[85] the Bankruptcy Abuse Prevention and Consumer Protection Act of 2005 established an objective income test that bankruptcy judges must use to determine whether an individual can file for the relatively prompt total discharge offered by Chapter 7 or must agree to a three- to five-year repayment plan pursuant to Chapter 13. (Chapter 13 bankruptcies are discussed below.) If an individual's monthly income (minus monthly expenses) is above his or her state's median income and the debtor can pay at least $6,000 over five years ($100 per month), then he or she will usually not qualify for Chapter 7 bankruptcy. Instead, the debtor is required to file under Chapter 13. The BAPCPA also requires individuals who file for bankruptcy to pay for credit counseling; gives top priority to a spouse's claims for child support among creditors' claims against a debtor; provides special accommodations in the application of the income test for active-duty members of the armed services, low-income veterans, and debtors with serious medical conditions; and restricts the homestead exemption to $125,000 if the debtor bought his or her residence within three years and four months before filing for bankruptcy. Thus, wealthy individuals in states with unlimited homestead exemptions who file for bankruptcy may still keep their mansions and ranches if they bought them at least three years and four months

---

80. Sanger v. Busch, 311 B.R. 657 (Bankr. N.D.N.Y. 2004).

81. Sells v. Porter, 375 B.R. 822 (B.A.P. 8th Cir. 2007).

82. Robert Berner & Bruce Ingersoll, *Sears to Repay Card Holders $100 Million*, WALL ST. J., June 5, 1997, at A3.

83. The U.S. Court of Appeals for the Seventh Circuit has held that there is no private right of action for damages for a creditor's failure to file debt discharge agreements with the bankruptcy court. Cox v. Zale Del., Inc., 239 F.3d 910 (7th Cir. 2001).

84. Philip R. Principe, *Did BAPCPA Eliminate the "Fourth Option" for Individual Debtors' Secured Property?*, AM. BANKRUPTCY INST. (Oct. 1, 2005), *available at* http://www.abiworld.org/AM/Template.cfm?Section=Home&TEMPLATE=/CM/ContentDisplay.cfm&CONTENTID=52516.

85. Ransom v. FIA Card Servs., N.A., 131 S. Ct. 716, 721 (2011).

Winding-up proceedings in Australia are essentially *ex parte*: only the creditors appear before the court. As a result, debtors do not have the same recourse as under U.S. bankruptcy rules. Other countries, such as Germany, do not provide for the complete discharge of debts in bankruptcy; instead, they only arrange for the debts to be paid over time.

before filing, but many workers saddled with uninsured medical expenses can no longer receive a prompt discharge under Chapter 7.

Nonindividual Debtors

Chapter 7 does not provide a discharge for corporations, partnerships, or similar business entities. Once their assets are sold, these debtors essentially become defunct shells whose unpaid obligations have no significance. Thus, from the vantage point of the debtor firm's management, the only virtue of a liquidation may be that the task of selling property and paying creditors falls to a trustee. The principals of closely held companies are often better advised to avoid bankruptcy and to handle these chores themselves. Rather than adhering to the pro rata distribution model, they may wish to prefer some creditors by channeling funds first to those who are most likely to pursue them personally (such as holders of guaranties). Also, they may not want to expose earlier transactions (such as preferential payments) to scrutiny by a trustee, who can become a more troublesome foe than any of the company's creditors by invoking the avoiding powers discussed above.

CONSUMER BANKRUPTCY UNDER CHAPTER 13

Chapter 13 (consumer bankruptcy) of the Bankruptcy Code deals with adjustments to the debt of an individual or a married couple with regular income. Although an individual with income below the BAPCPA threshold may be the subject of a Chapter 7 liquidation or file for a Chapter 11 reorganization, only individuals and small proprietorships are eligible undrer Chapter 13.

Chapter 13 Requirements

Individuals with regular income, including wage earners and individuals engaged in business, may qualify for Chapter 13 status if their unsecured debts do not exceed $360,475 and their secured debts do not exceed $1,081,400.[86] Chapter 13 is similar to a reorganization in that it provides for a court-appointed plan for repaying creditors. If the debtor makes all the payments required by the plan, then the debts listed in the plan will be discharged.

Chapter 13 plans can be proposed only by debtors and usually are quite simple. The plan ordinarily allows the debtor to retain all of his or her assets, not just those that would be exempt. However, the debtor must agree to pay all future "projected disposable income," which would be the debtor's to keep in a Chapter 7 or

---

86. These are the dollar limits as of January 1, 2012; the limits are adjusted every three years. Debtors with debts in excess of these limits who wish to reorganize rather than liquidate must consider Chapter 11.

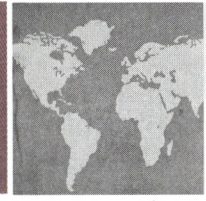

HISTORICAL PERSPECTIVE

From Mosaic Law to Vulture Capitalists

The principle that debtors should be permitted to discharge certain debts has ancient roots. As early as 1400 B.C., Mosaic law required unconditional forgiveness of debts every seven years to encourage a proper focus on social relationships. The word "bankruptcy" is believed to have evolved from the Latin words "banca" and "rupta," referring to the broken bench or moneychangers' table left behind by failed merchants fleeing from their creditors. In A.D. 1542, during the reign of King Henry VIII, English lawmakers

passed a Bankruptcy Act to regulate failing English merchants. Under this law, debtors were considered quasi criminals. Over the centuries, strong sanctions for insolvency, including imprisonment, generally made bankruptcy a remedy for creditors rather than a relief for debtors. For example, a 1604 amendment to the Bankruptcy Act permitted the debtor's ear to be cut off.

The roots of the American bankruptcy system can be traced to the experiences of colonists who were

refugees from debtors' prisons in Europe. The drafters of the U.S. Constitution, recognizing the importance of debtor relief, gave Congress the exclusive right to establish national bankruptcy laws and thereby override the states' treatment of debtors and creditors.

During the nineteenth century, debtors' prisons fell out of favor for humanitarian reasons—and for the more practical reason that imprisoned debtors could not repay their debts. Starting around 1800, Congress would

CONTINUED

enact bankruptcy protection laws to ease the pain of an economic crisis and then repeal them when the financial situation improved. In 1898, when a severe depression forced many railroads into receivership, Congress used its bankruptcy power to enact the laws that became the foundation for the current U.S. bankruptcy system. The Bankruptcy Act of 1898 enabled failing railroads and other businesses to continue operating while reorganizing, generally stripping shareholders of their interests. In 1915, the U.S. Supreme Court declared that one of the law's purposes was to protect honest debtors. In 1934, the Supreme Court held that a man who had pledged his future wages to repay a $300 loan could not be forced to turn over his wages after he declared bankruptcy.[a]

The Bankruptcy Act of 1898 was overhauled in 1938, when Congress created the Chapter 13 consumer debt adjustment process. In 1978, Congress enacted the Bankruptcy Reform Act, which created the Bankruptcy Code that exists today. That legislation, the result of nearly a decade of intensive study and debate about problems in the bankruptcy system and proposed reforms, made sweeping changes in the law, most of them favorable to debtors.

In light of the massive defaults on junk bonds in 1989 and the early 1990s, some began to question whether Congress had given debtors too much relief under the Bankruptcy Code. The lead-in to a 1990 *Forbes* article on the subject expressed this concern: "In the old days, a debt was an obligation and bankruptcy was a disgrace. Nowadays bond issuers concoct ever more ways to stiff investors."[b]

In an effort to curb the ease of filing for bankruptcy, Congress passed the Bankruptcy Abuse Prevention and Consumer Protection Act in 2005. Credit card companies, hospitals, and other corporate lobbyists pushed hard for the BAPCPA over the objections of consumer advocates, legal scholars, retired bankruptcy judges, and others who claimed that it was too favorable to creditors.[c]

In the wake of the subprime mortgage crisis, a number of scholars and consumer advocates have called on Congress to give bankruptcy courts the power to reduce the principal owing on home mortgages.[d] Although the Bankruptcy Code enables judges to modify loans on vacation homes, farms, and commercial properties, Congress carved out an exception for primary residences in 1978 to promote the flow of capital to the housing market. This "anti-modification rule" precludes a homeowner who files for bankruptcy from modifying the terms of his or her primary mortgage. This rule has thus made bankruptcy an ineffective means of stemming the tide of foreclosures.

Proponents of changing the anti-modification rule argue that lenders are foreclosing on homeowners with negative equity—a mortgage balance in excess of the home's current value—who could have stayed in their homes and made their monthly payments if they could have renegotiated the loan and had the principal reduced. Often homes are sold at foreclosure sales for far less than the principal amount outstanding, which hurts not only the homeowner but also the investors who own the mortgage-backed securities. As a result, investment groups have pushed for bankruptcy reform and advocated broader use of voluntary principal reductions by servicers to combat foreclosures.

Banks and loan servicers have opposed any measures to do away with the anti-modification rule, arguing that it would unfairly reward borrowers who do not pay their mortgages and increase the cost of credit. The Federal Reserve Bank of Cleveland found, however, that the use of bankruptcy courts to address the farm foreclosure crisis in the 1980s did not negatively affect the cost or availability of credit.[e]

---

a. Local Loan Co. v. Hunt, 292 U.S. 234 (1934).

b. Matthew Schifrin, *Enough Already!*, FORBES, May 28, 1990, at 126.

c. Mark Neis, *History of BAPCPA: Special Interest Legislation at Its Worst*, KANSAS BANKRUPTCY LAW INFORMATION, *available at* http://www. bankruptcykansas.info/2008/06/04/bapcpa-special-interest-legislation-at-its-worst/ (last accessed Sept. 17, 2008).

d. *See, e.g., Opportunity Funding Corporation Economic Stabilization White Paper* (Yale Sch. of Management, Nov. 30, 2010), *available at* mba.yale.edu.

e. Thomas J. Fitzpatrick IV & James B. Thomson, *Stripdowns and Bankruptcy: Lessons from Agricultural Bankruptcy Reform*, FED. RESERVE BANK OF CLEVELAND (2010), *available at* http://www.clevelandfed.org/research/commentary/2010/2010-9.cfm)

Chapter 11 bankruptcy, to a disbursing trustee for the duration of the plan.[87] Creditors holding claims secured by a mortgage, deed of trust, or security interest are entitled to the equivalent of the present value of their lien rights, except that Chapter 13 plans cannot modify home mortgage loans unless they provide for payments to cure default. Unlike under Chapter 11, creditors do not vote on Chapter 13 plans. They can, however, object to confirmation if the plan is proposed in bad faith, is not feasible, does not pay all disposable income to the disbursing trustee, or offers them less than they would get in a Chapter 7 liquidation.

A Chapter 13 plan may be either a composition plan or an extension plan. In a *composition plan*, creditors receive a percentage of the indebtedness, and the debtor is discharged of the remaining obligation. In an *extension plan*, creditors receive the entire indebtedness, but the period for payment is extended beyond the original due date.

---

87. Hamilton v. Lanning, 130 S. Ct. 2464 (2010).

IN BRIEF

Advantages and Disadvantages of Bankruptcy

CATEGORY	ADVANTAGES	DISADVANTAGES
Debtors	*Automatic Stay* • Instantly suspends most litigation and collection activities against the debtor, its property, or the bankruptcy estate.	*Administrative Costs* • Legal and accounting expenses. • Official creditors' committee fees.
	Control • Debtor retains possession of the bankruptcy estate (unless a trustee is appointed). • Chapter 11 permits the debtor to operate in the ordinary course of business.	*Reduction in Autonomy* • Creditor oversight. • Management's ability to make and implement decisions rapidly and autonomously is curtailed.
	Contracts, Leases, and Property • Debtor-in-possession (DIP) has option of assuming or rejecting prebankruptcy executory contracts or unexpired leases. • DIP may (in certain circumstances) sell property free and clear of liens or other interests.	*Stigma of Bankruptcy* • Morale or confidence problems among staff, vendors, or customers. • Customer anxiety regarding future warranty claims or product support.
Creditors	*Enhanced Value and Participation* • Preserves going-concern value of an insolvent business. • DIP more accountable due to bankruptcy reporting and notice requirements.	*Suspension of Individual Remedies* • Automatic stay stalls foreclosure. • Nondebtor parties to executory contracts and unexpired leases are left in limbo.
	Equitable Distribution • When inequitable conduct by any creditor (typically an insider) has prejudiced others, bankruptcy court has authority to subordinate all or part of transgressor's claim to payment of other creditors.	*Unequal Effects* • Some bankruptcy procedures affect various creditors unequally (e.g., avoiding actions, claim caps, equitable subordination).
	Involuntary Petitions • Creditors may file an involuntary petition for relief under Chapter 7 or (more rarely) Chapter 11 and force the debtor into bankruptcy.	*Reduced Distribution* • Only a small fraction of Chapter 11 cases filed result in a successful reorganization. Continued operation results in less funds to distribute at liquidation.

After completing all plan payments, the debtor obtains a Chapter 13 discharge. An earlier discharge may be granted in hardship cases if the creditors have received at least as much as they would have under Chapter 7. Apart from the hardship situation, this fresh start (sometimes called *super discharge*) will extinguish otherwise nondischargeable debts (such as claims for fraud, theft, willful and malicious injury, or drunk driving), but not spousal or child support.

Advantages and Disadvantages of Chapter 13

Chapter 13 has many advantages for overextended consumers. For example, the filing of a bankruptcy petition stops all creditor collection activity other than the filing of a claim in the bankruptcy proceeding. As a result, it is often used by homeowners who fall behind on mortgage payments to stop foreclosure proceedings, allowing the cure of mortgage arrears over time—typically five years. In addition, unlike what happens in a Chapter 7 liquidation, a Chapter 13 debtor does not surrender any assets. A good faith effort to pay creditors can preserve goodwill and future credit prospects.

Unfortunately, two out of three Chapter 13 debtors are unable to make the payments outlined in their plan,[88] leaving them with no discharge of their unpaid debts unless they convert from Chapter 13 to Chapter 7.[89] After conversion, the debtor's nonexempt property is liquidated, and the debtor receives a Chapter 7 discharge.

A study found that blacks were roughly twice as likely as whites to be steered by their lawyers into the more costly Chapter 13 instead of filing for straight bankruptcy under Chapter 7.[90] This was true even when the researchers controlled for assets, income, education, and home ownership.

---

88. Tara Siegel Bernard, *Blacks Face Bias in Bankruptcies, Study Suggests*, N.Y. TIMES, Jan. 20, 2012.

89. It is not clear whether a debtor who converts from Chapter 13 to Chapter 7 must complete the "means test." The U.S. Bankruptcy Court for the District of Rhode Island concluded that a converting debtor must complete the means test (*In re* Perfetto, 361 B.R. 27 (Bankr. D.R.I. 2007)), but the U.S. Bankruptcy Court for the District of New Jersey held that a converting debtor is not subject to the means test (*In re* Fox, 2007 Bankr. LEXIS 1865 (Bankr. D.N.J. June 1, 2007)).

90. Bernard, *supra* note 88.

CHAPTER 15

Chapter 15 deals with cross-border insolvencies. It incorporates the Model Law on Cross-Border Insolvencies promulgated by the United Nations Commission on International Trade Law (UNCITRAL) and approved by the UN General Assembly in 1997.[91] Chapter 15's

---

91. Model Law on Cross-Border Insolvencies, May 30, 1997, 36 I.L.M. 1386 (1997).

basic procedure is straightforward: a case is commenced when a foreign representative files a petition for recognition of a foreign proceeding. As long as recognition would not be manifestly contrary to U.S. public policy, the court must enter an order recognizing the foreign proceeding. If recognition is granted as a foreign main proceeding, the debtor receives protection and rights similar to those of U.S.-based debtors, including the automatic stay.

THE RESPONSIBLE MANAGER

MANAGING DEBTOR–CREDITOR RELATIONS

It has become fashionable in some circles to view Chapter 11 as a strategic option for creative business planning. Apart from the fresh start granted to individual debtors, however, the bankruptcy system generally respects a debtor's obligations existing under state or other federal law; it merely provides a forum for dealing fairly, efficiently, and flexibly with the rights of all the creditors and equity holders. Thus, although insolvency is not a prerequisite for relief, a bankruptcy filing is generally not appropriate unless the business is in serious financial difficulties.

If those difficulties are present, the bankruptcy system can be an effective mechanism for overcoming them while preserving a productive enterprise. Yet for each celebrated success, there are countless failed Chapter 11 cases, in which no plan is confirmed and creditors are left with less than they would have received through prompt liquidation. This is partly the price of giving depressed businesses the chance to rebound, but it also reflects fundamental problems.

Many debtors, most of them single-asset or other small businesses, file Chapter 11 cases without any realistic prospect for reorganization. In some instances, the principals refuse to recognize and deal with financial ills until the business is too weak to survive. Continuing their ostrichlike pattern, they then file a Chapter 11 petition, awash in a sort of terminal euphoria and not recognizing that liquidation is inevitable. Other debtors see the writing on the wall but file to buy time, hoping for a miracle cure. Still others file merely to postpone management's impending unemployment.

Congress gave creditors the means to protect their interests, however. If management acts improperly, a trustee can be appointed; if reorganization is improbable, the case can be dismissed or converted to a Chapter 7 liquidation. Unfortunately, these remedies are rarely invoked before the creditors' interests are seriously prejudiced. Not surprisingly, individual unsecured creditors tend to be reluctant to throw good money after bad by policing the debtor's conduct. For the same reason (though with less justification), they frequently decline to serve or participate actively on the official

creditors' committee, so this watchdog may be somnolent or nonexistent in smaller cases. Thus, unless a secured creditor is motivated to overcome this inertia, a Chapter 11 case may have a bleak outcome.

Unless prompted by an interested party, the bankruptcy judge ordinarily will not intervene until the situation becomes egregious, as when the DIP does not comply with the rules, such as those requiring regular financial and tax reporting. Because the court is not well equipped to investigate the progress of each Chapter 11 debtor, an abusive case can languish for a considerable time before the court itself initiates corrective action.

The effectiveness of the bankruptcy system depends largely on knowledgeable and responsible conduct by the interested parties. In general, both debtors and creditors benefit by addressing financial problems early and pursuing a constructive workout. Because the charged emotional climate often makes this difficult, it is important to obtain objective and practical advice from counsel. If a workout is not possible, the debtor's management should consider whether a reorganization is plausible before filing for relief under Chapter 11. If the case is filed, creditors must recognize that meaningful participation, ideally through the official creditors' committee, is usually necessary to protect their interests.

Directors of a corporation in financial trouble assume new responsibilities to protect not only shareholders but the entire community of interests represented by creditors, employees, and other parties with a stake in the continued viability of the corporation. Once a corporation enters the zone of insolvency, the directors owe a fiduciary duty to creditors as well as shareholders.

A responsible manager must understand lender liability risks. The following steps will help lenders minimize those risks.

In negotiating loan terms, the lender should indicate clearly that any commitment must be in writing and approved by the loan committee or other appropriate officials of the

CONTINUED

lender. The lender's written communications to the borrower should disclaim any commitment if none is intended.

The lender should avoid provisions in loan documents giving it a broad right to control the borrower's management decisions or day-to-day business activities. The lender should refrain from using its financial leverage to influence such activities as the selection of management, the hiring or firing of employees, or the payment of other creditors.

The loan documents should contain a merger clause stating that the written loan documents supersede any prior oral understandings and that the borrower is not relying on any prior oral promise or representation by the lender. The loan documents should provide that any amendment, modification, or waiver of the terms of the documents or of the rights of the parties must be in writing and signed by both the lender and the borrower.

The lender may ask the borrower to insert in the loan documents a waiver of its right to a jury trial. Juries are often perceived as sympathetic to borrowers; a judge may be less likely to award large compensatory or punitive damages to the borrower.[92] The lender may want to specify in the loan documents that any legal action by the borrower must be brought in a court in a specific state or city to avoid the possible disadvantage the lender may have as a defendant in a court in the borrower's home territory. The lender may want to add an arbitration clause to the loan documents, stating that any

disputes arising under the loan documents will be resolved through binding arbitration instead of litigation in a court.

The lender should maintain accurate and complete credit files supporting all the actions it takes. Virtually all of the documents in the lender's files may be subject to legal discovery; it is wise to assume that any entry in the credit files may someday be read to a judge or jury in a lender liability case.

The lender should not threaten to take actions that are not yet authorized or that it does not actually intend to take. The lender should give reasonable warning and, if possible, written notice to the borrower before terminating a line of credit, changing an established course of conduct, accelerating a loan, or exercising any remedies. In a workout situation, when the borrower is trying to renegotiate a loan it cannot pay, or when it becomes apparent that the borrower may be preparing a lender liability suit, the lender should consult with legal counsel.

Except when acting as a trustee or other fiduciary, the lender should refrain from giving any legal, financial, or investment advice to the borrower that might create a fiduciary relationship between the lender and the borrower. The lender should be cautious about giving other creditors the borrower's financial history or opinions as to the borrower's creditworthiness.

At all times the lender's loan officers should behave professionally, regardless of their level of frustration with the borrower. Any personality conflicts with the borrower should be avoided. If a personality conflict does develop, the matter should be transferred to other loan officers.

---

92. Note, however, that the California Supreme Court has held that a waiver of a jury trial is unenforceable. Grafton Partners LP v. Superior Court, 116 P.3d 479 (Cal. 2005).

A MANAGER'S DILEMMA

Putting It into Practice

When Is a Dividend an Unlawful Preference?

MNVA was a Minnesota corporation engaged in operating a short-line freight railroad. Larry and Diane Wood were officers and directors and major shareholders of MNVA, and DMVW was a wholly owned subsidiary of MNVA. In August 1994, MNVA agreed in principle to the terms of a letter of intent with Pioneer Railcorp under which Pioneer agreed to acquire MNVA's operating assets by purchasing MNVA's stock. MNVA decided to spin off DMVW to MNVA shareholders as part of the reorganization of MNVA in connection with the sale to Pioneer. In October 1994, the deal between MNVA and Pioneer was restructured as a sale of assets. On November 21, 1994, the MNVA board of directors determined that it would be able to pay its debts in the ordinary course of business after the proposed distribution of DMVW stock to MNVA shareholders and approved the distribution of DMVW stock to the existing MNVA shareholders in

proportion to the percentage of stock they owned in MNVA. No consideration was paid to MNVA for the distribution of DMVW stock. DMVW became an independently operated entity after the distribution. In December 1994, MNVA sold its assets to Pioneer in exchange for $1 and the assumption of certain secured debts; it thereafter ceased operations.

In May 1996, Helm Financial obtained a state court judgment against MNVA for railcar leasing fees in the amount of $96,028, plus interest and attorneys' fees and costs, but MNVA had insufficient assets to pay them. According to MNVA, during the course of winding up its affairs, it was unable to pay all of its creditors in full because it experienced an "unexpected shortfall" after losing several substantial claims, including one against the Minnesota Department of Transportation for reimbursement of track rehabilitation expenses.

CONTINUED

In June 1997, Helm sued MNVA, DMVW, and the individual officers and directors of MNVA, alleging that the distribution of DMVW stock to the MNVA shareholders defrauded MNVA's creditors in violation of the Minnesota Uniform Fraudulent Transfer Act and constituted an unlawful preference of the defendant officers, directors, and shareholders over MNVA's creditors in breach of their fiduciary duty to the creditors. Helm alleged that the spinoff left MNVA insolvent because DMVW was MNVA's most valuable asset.

Was the distribution of the DMVW stock a fraudulent transfer? Did the Woods violate their fiduciary duty to creditors, such as Helm? Under the Minnesota corporation law, a distribution to shareholders is permitted only when "the corporation will be able to pay its debts in the ordinary course of business after making the distribution and the board does not know before the distribution is made that the determination was or has become erroneous." Did the Woods and their fellow officers and directors act ethically? Would your answer be different if instead of distributing shares of a subsidiary as a dividend, the board had voted to repay preexisting loans from the Woods to MNVA?[93]

---

93. Helm Fin. Corp. v. MNVA R.R., Inc., 212 F.3d 1076 (8th Cir. 2000).

INSIDE STORY

Laissez-Faire Lending, Securitization, and Derivatives Trading Wreak Havoc on the Global Economy

In 2001, the U.S. economy was reeling from a recession induced by the Internet bubble of the late 1990s and the attacks on the World Trade Center and the Pentagon. In response, the Federal Reserve began cutting interest rates dramatically in order to expand the money supply and encourage borrowing. The idea was that spending was patriotic, and everyone, from President George W. Bush on down, encouraged Americans to go shopping and buy, buy, buy.

Lenders responded by approving *subprime mortgage loans*, which carried above-market interest rates to compensate for the added risk of default, often to borrowers with poor credit. Lenders and mortgage brokers also created risky, new nontraditional mortgages, such as *2-28 loans*, which offered a low initial teaser interest rate that stayed fixed for two years, after which the loan reset to a higher adjustable rate for the remaining twenty-eight years of the loan, and *negative amortization loans*, under which the debtor pays only the interest every month but owes a huge balloon payment at the end of the term. Record low interest rates, combined with loosening lending standards, pushed real estate prices to record highs during 2005.

Lenders were able to sell off their mortgages in the secondary market and collect origination fees, which freed them up for more lending. The investors that bought these mortgages securitized them into bonds that they sold to investors through *collateralized debt obligations*, or *CDOs*. The global CDO market rose from $125 billion in 2004 to $475 billion in 2006. Credit rating agencies, such as Moody's and Standard & Poor's, were willing to put their "AAA" or "A+" credit rating on many of these securities, signaling their relative safety as an investment, even though some argued (at least in retrospect) that the agencies should have foreseen the high default rates for subprime borrowers and given the CDOs much lower ratings. Nevertheless, as a result of the favorable ratings, investors were willing to purchase the CDOs, which in turn led to a huge demand for subprime loans.[94] Many investors bought credit-default swaps from companies like insurance giant American International Group (AIG), at relatively low premiums, to insure against defaults in the underlying debt. Because the Commodity Futures Modernization Act of 2000 exempted credit-default swaps and other derivatives from regulation as either futures contracts under the Commodity Exchange Act or securities under the federal securities laws and exempted them from state regulation as insurance products, AIG was not required to reserve against future claims.

When interest rates began to rise in the middle of 2006, new home sales stalled, and median prices halted their climb. Homeowners were not able to refinance their subprime mortgages and were unable to pay the higher rates when their loans were adjusted upward. This led to increased mortgage foreclosures. As increasing numbers of consumers filed for bankruptcy protection, lenders lost money on defaulted mortgages and were left with property that was worth less than the amount originally owed. In many cases, the losses were large enough to result in lender bankruptcies.

Despite mounting evidence, the federal government resisted calls for the government to get involved. In March 2007, Treasury Secretary Henry Paulson stated that economic growth was healthy and that the housing market was nearing a turnaround. In June 2007, Ben Bernanke, Chair of the Board of

CONTINUED

---

94. Eric Petroff, *Who Is to Blame for the Subprime Crisis?*, INVESTOPEDIA. COM, http://investopedia.com/printable.asp?a=/articles/07/subprime-blame.asp (last visited Sept. 15, 2008).

Governors of the Federal Reserve, declared that "fundamental factors—including solid growth in incomes and relatively low mortgage rates—should ultimately support the demand for housing, and at this point, the troubles in the sub-prime sector seem unlikely to seriously spill over to the broader economy or the financial system." He also stated, "It is not the responsibility of the Federal Reserve . . . to protect lenders and investors from the consequences of their financial decisions."[95] Paulson cautioned against a "rush" to regulation, and two Treasury undersecretaries, writing in *The Financial Times* in September 2007, criticized calls for "immediate regulation."[96]

By December 2007, however, the Federal Reserve acknowledged that a number of home mortgage lenders had aggressively sold deceptive loans to borrowers who had little chance of repaying them and proposed a broad set of restrictions on exotic mortgages and high-cost loans for people with weak credit.[97]

In July 2008, Congress passed the Housing and Economic Recovery Act to provide some relief for families struggling to make their mortgage payments and to bolster the Federal National Mortgage Association (Fannie Mae) and the Federal Home Loan Mortgage Corporation (Freddie Mac). Fannie Mae is the leading market-maker in the U.S. secondary mortgage market, and Freddie Mac buys mortgages on the secondary market, pools them, and sells them as mortgage-backed securities to investors on the open market. Together, they own or guarantee about half of the United States' $12 trillion mortgage market. Although the Act allowed the Federal Housing Administration (FHA) to insure up to $300 billion in new thirty-year fixed-rate mortgages for at-risk borrowers in owner-occupied homes if their lenders agreed to write down loan balances to 90% of the homes' current appraised value, many lenders refused to write down their loans. The Act also gave the U.S. Treasury temporary authority to lend a financial hand to Fannie Mae and Freddie Mac if the Treasury deemed it necessary to help stabilize markets.[98] Finally, the Act included a number of tax relief provisions aimed at shoring up the ailing housing market.

In September 2008, the government seized control of Fannie Mae and Freddie Mac to try to stabilize the troubled housing and financial market. Under the Treasury Department plan, both companies were placed into a government conservatorship to be run by the Federal Housing Finance Agency. The Treasury Department was issued $1 billion in senior preferred stock paying 10% interest, from each company, as well as warrants representing ownership stakes of 79.9% in each company, but could be required to put up as much as $100 billion for each, if funds were required to keep the companies afloat as losses mounted. "This is a shareholder bailout financed by the U.S. taxpayers," declared Armando Falcon, Jr., formerly the chief regulator of Fannie Mae and Freddie Mac.[99]

A week later, Lehman Brothers, the fourth largest investment bank in the United States, saddled with $60 billion of bad real estate debt, was forced to file for Chapter 11. Merrill Lynch, the nation's largest brokerage and one of the country's top issuers of mortgage-backed securities, sold itself to Bank of America to avoid bankruptcy after it reported it lost more than $45 billion on its mortgage-backed investments.[100] Meanwhile, AIG, staggered by losses stemming from the credit crisis, sought $40 billion from the Federal Reserve. Although the government initially announced that it would not bail out the company or provide any guarantees, it quickly agreed to provide up to $85 billion in loans in a move that gave the Federal Reserve an 80% stake in AIG.[101] By 2012, the U.S. Treasury had funded a $185 billion bailout of AIG.[102] In a controversial move, AIG subsequently paid its counterparties, including Goldman Sachs and Deutsche Bank, 100 cents on the dollar for the credit-default swaps it had underwritten.

After the U.S. Treasury spent almost $800 billion bailing out the troubled banks, calls for financial reform reached a crescendo. The Dodd–Frank Wall Street Reform and Consumer Protection Act of 2010 requires securitizers selling mortgage-backed securities and other debt-collateralized securities to retain an economic interest of at least 5% of the credit risk in the assets they pool and then sell as securities (so-called *skin in the game*). The Act also increased government oversight of the previously unregulated swaps markets. First, it brought transparency by requiring real-time reporting and mandating that standardized swaps be traded on transparent exchanges. Second, the Act required over-the-counter swaps to be cleared by regulated clearinghouses, which would manage the risks associated with them.[103] Third, it established a comprehensive system of regulation for swaps dealers and exchanges. Finally, the Act required the Commodity Futures Trading Commission

CONTINUED

---

95. James Quinn, *What Banks and the Government Are Not Telling Us About 2009—The Next Shoes You Hear Drop May Be Very Loud Ones*, CUTTING EDGE NEWS, Aug. 4, 2008, *available at* http://www.thecuttingedgenews.com/index.php?article=685.

96. Editorial, *Things Go Better with Rules*, N.Y. TIMES, Sept. 30, 2007, at § 4, 11.

97. Edmund L. Andrews, *In Reversal, Fed Approves Plan to Curb Risky Lending*, N.Y. TIMES, Dec. 19, 2007, at A1.

98. Jeanne Sahadi, *Bush Signs Housing Rescue Law*, CNNMONEY.COM, July 30, 2008, http://money.cnn.com/2008/07/30/news/economy/housing_bill_Bush/index.htm.

99. Neil Irwin & Zachary A. Goldfarb, *Feds Take Over Mortgage Giants*, SAN JOSE MERCURY NEWS, Sept. 8, 2008, at A1.

100. Dina Temple-Raston, *Foundering Wall Street Giants Seek Help, Cash*, NPR, Sept. 15, 2008, *available at* http://www.npr.org/templates/story/story.php?storyId=94624580.

101. Jack Reerink & Douwe Miedema, *Morgan Stanley and Goldman Slide as HBOS in Takeover Talks*, REUTERS, Sept. 17, 2008.

102. Barry Ritholtz, *Credit Default Swaps Are Insurance Products, It's Time We Regulated Them as Such*, WASH. POST, Mar. 10, 2012.

103. For a criticism of this requirement, see Zachary J. Gubler, *The Financial Innovation Process: Theory and Application*, 36 DEL. J. CORP. L. 55 (2011).

(CFTC) to set position limits "'as appropriate' and 'to the maximum extent practicable, in its discretion' in order to protect against excessive speculation and manipulation while ensuring that the markets retain sufficient liquidity for bona fide hedgers and that their price discovery functions are not disrupted."[104] The Dodd–Frank Act did not, however, subject credit-default swaps to regulation by the states as insurance products or require the setting aside of reserves.[105]

In 2011, the CFTC issued final rules limiting the net long and short positions a trader can take in twenty-eight physical commodities (such as metals, oil, and agricultural commodities) traded on a designated contract market and futures, options, and other swaps based on those commodities.[106] So-called *bona fide hedging* transactions are exempt from these limits. Because this exemption applies only to swaps based on physical commodities, it does not apply to financial hedging transactions.

As discussed in Chapters 6 and 17, the Act also created the Consumer Financial Protection Bureau. In addition, it imposed limits on the terms and conditions of residential mortgages, which are discussed in Chapter 18.

---

104. Commodity Futures Trading Comm'n, Position Limits for Futures and Swaps, 76 Fed. Reg. 71626-01 (Nov. 18, 2011).

105. Ritholtz, *supra* note 102.

106. Commodity Futures Trading Comm'n, Position Limits for Futures and Swaps, 17 C.F.R. pt. 151.

KEY WORDS AND PHRASES

QUESTIONS AND CASE PROBLEMS

1. Pluris, Inc. had $50 million in net operating losses (NOLs) when its directors voted to assign all its assets to an assignee for the benefit of creditors. Its largest creditor, Berg & Berg Enterprises, had tried unsuccessfully to persuade the board to file for bankruptcy instead so that it could reorganize Pluris and take advantage of its NOLs. Under certain circumstances, a debtor with NOLs can merge with a firm with taxable income and thereby transfer the tax value of the NOLs to the other firm. Berg sued the directors of Pluris, in their individual capacity, claiming that they had breached their fiduciary duty to creditors by failing to make any reasonable inquiry into other possible approaches, such as a reorganization, which might or would have yielded greater value for creditors. Berg alleged that once the directors realized that their own equity investment in Pluris was worthless, they "took the easiest path for themselves" by assigning the assets and then "'washed their hands' of the matter." Who should prevail? Does it matter whether Pluris was insolvent or in the zone of insolvency at the time of the assignment? Does it matter where Pluris is incorporated? What, if any, defenses might be available to the directors? [*Berg & Berg Enterprises, LLC v. Boyle*, 178 Cal. App. 4th 1020 (2009).]

2. ABC Food Corporation, a food company with annual sales of more than $1 billion, operated a paper division that supplied ABC with packaging for its food products. ABC's management determined that the company should concentrate on its core business of manufacturing food products and recommended to the board of directors that the assets of the paper division be sold.

   Newcorp, Inc. is a newly formed corporation with two shareholders who have experience in the timber industry. Those two shareholders also jointly own Lumber Corporation, which operates two lumber mills in the state of Washington. Newcorp was formed specifically to acquire the assets of ABC's paper division.

   On February 1, 2011, ABC and Newcorp signed a letter of intent specifying a closing no later than July 1, 2011, subject to Newcorp obtaining satisfactory financing. The letter of intent provided that ABC and Newcorp would enter into a long-term contract whereby Newcorp would supply specified quantities of paper packaging to ABC.

   On February 15, 2011, Newcorp approached the Bank of Hope to request a term loan to acquire the assets of ABC's paper division and a revolving line of credit to meet its day-to-day working capital requirements. On March 31, 2011, the Bank of Hope delivered to Newcorp a letter stating that it would agree to extend a credit facility to Newcorp on the terms and conditions described in a term sheet attached to the letter.

   Bank of Hope required, as a condition to its credit facility, that the credit be secured by all fixed and current assets of Newcorp. Carlos Banker, the account officer for the bank, took all steps necessary to give the bank a valid first-priority lien on all collateral.

   A major source of revenue for Newcorp will be the long-term supply contract with ABC. The Bank of Hope is requiring an assignment of the supply contract that prohibits ABC and Newcorp from making any amendments to the contract without the bank's consent. One of the terms of the Bank of Hope's loan is a guaranty from each shareholder and from Lumber Corporation.

   a. You are a manager of Newcorp. What objections would you have to such an assignment?
   b. You are a manager of ABC. Any objections?
   c. You are the president of Newcorp. As president, you will be involved in the day-to-day operations of Newcorp. What arguments might you make against giving such a guaranty?
   d. You own 51% of the stock of Newcorp, and you made loans to Newcorp during the initial stages of its existence. You have since left the running of Newcorp to the president and other managers. What arguments could you make against giving such a guaranty?
   e. You are the Bank of Hope's attorney. What advice would you give the bank about taking a guaranty from Lumber Corporation?

3. Assume the facts in Question 2. On June 1, 2011, Revolving Credit Bank took over the revolving line of credit from Bank of Hope and acquired Bank of Hope's security interest in Newcorp's accounts receivable and inventory. Beginning in early 2012, due to a combination of internal and external conditions, Newcorp's business failed to generate sufficient revenue to meet its debt obligations.

The loan agreement between Newcorp and Revolving Credit Bank contains an advance clause, which states that Revolving Credit Bank may, at its discretion, advance up to $2 million based on eligible accounts receivable and inventory. Revolving Credit Bank informed Newcorp that Newcorp has failed to maintain certain financial covenants contained in their credit agreement. Without declaring a default, Revolving Credit Bank then required Newcorp to establish a locked-box arrangement with the bank so that all payments made to Newcorp could be used first to repay any advances outstanding. On March 1, 2012, Newcorp's treasurer called Revolving Credit Bank's account officer and asked for a $350,000 advance to cover checks that would be presented to the bank that day. Revolving Credit Bank refused to lend the full amount requested but did advance $200,000 to pay certain suppliers.

a. You are the manager of one of Newcorp's trade creditors that has not been paid. Do you have any rights against Revolving Credit Bank?

In April 2012, Newcorp began to have difficulty meeting its monthly repayment obligations on the term loan from the Bank of Hope. Although Newcorp never missed a payment, the payments were all a few days late. In May 2012, Carlos Banker called the treasurer at Newcorp, assuring him that the Bank of Hope "would stand by the company" and that Newcorp should do whatever it could to keep the payments current. In September 2012, Revolving Credit Bank, concerned about continuing deteriorating conditions, decided to initiate foreclosure proceedings. The Bank of Hope followed suit only after Revolving Credit Bank began foreclosure proceedings.

b. You are a manager of Newcorp. What defenses would you raise against Revolving Credit Bank's foreclosure? Against the Bank of Hope's foreclosure?

c. You are a manager of Revolving Credit Bank. How would you respond to Newcorp's arguments?

d. You are a manager of the Bank of Hope. How would you respond to Newcorp's arguments? Should the Bank of Hope proceed to foreclose against the plant? What recourse does the Bank of Hope have against Newcorp if it does not foreclose? Does it have any recourse against any other party?

e. You are a manager of ABC and hold a junior deed of trust on the property. How would you react to the Bank of Hope's latest action?

4. Venito, Inc. has just filed a voluntary petition under Chapter 11. Its primary asset was an unexpired lease for 9,000 square feet of office space in New York City at a rent of $27.50 per square foot (market rate in 2011). The lease was signed on January 31, 2007, and expires on January 31, 2015. Concurrent with execution of the lease, Venito paid a $1 million security deposit ($500,000 in cash and $500,000 in the form of a letter of credit). The lease includes a provision stating that it terminates upon the lessee's insolvency or on the filing of either a voluntary or an involuntary petition in bankruptcy by the lessee. The lease also prohibits assignment or subletting without the landlord's consent. Venito had not paid rent for three months prior to the petition date, and it is currently in default on the lease. Prior to the petition date, the landlord had started eviction proceedings by serving a three-day notice to quit, but it had not yet retaken physical possession of the building.

Venito has a license from Langhorn, Inc. to make, use, and sell a patented product. The license provides that it terminates upon the licensee's insolvency or on the filing of a voluntary or involuntary bankruptcy proceeding by the licensee. It also provides that the license cannot be assigned without Langhorn's consent. At the time that Venito filed its petition, it had not paid license fees for three months, but Langhorn had not yet sent a notice of default as required by the license. Subsequent to filing the petition, Venito filed a motion to assume the license and assign it to Radical Media.

a. Assume that rental rates have increased to $50 per square foot. Venito has filed a motion with the bankruptcy court to approve assumption of the lease and assignment of it to Radical Media. Venito proposes to keep the $350,000 profit it will make on assignment of the lease. Is the lease an executory contract? Can Venito assume and assign the lease without the landlord's consent? Can the landlord file a motion to dismiss Venito's case for bad faith? Who will keep the profit on the lease assignment?

b. Assume that rental rates have fallen to $10 per square foot, Venito does not pay the rent for two months after the petition date, and Venito files a motion to reject the lease. What rights/claims does the landlord have regarding the unpaid rent? Can Venito reject the lease? What are the landlord's rights to the cash and letter-of-credit security deposits?

c. Does the license from Langhorn terminate upon the filing of the bankruptcy petition? Can it be assumed and/or assigned without Langhorn's consent? Can Langhorn terminate the license after the bankruptcy filing? What must Venito do to assume and assign the license?

5. Filene's Basement, Inc. hired Kathleen Mason as president of Filene's Basement Division and chief merchandising officer in May 1999. Mason left a high-paying position as president of Home Goods, Inc. to join Filene's at a time when it was already experiencing financial difficulty. The parties signed an employment agreement that provided, among other things, that Mason would receive three years' salary and other fringe benefits in the event she was terminated without cause. Filene's filed for relief under Chapter 11 in August 1999. After the filing, Mason continued to provide services pursuant to the prepetition employment agreement and received the salary and benefits specified in the agreement. According to Mason, she was induced to remain with the company by the DIP's postpetition promise that her employment agreement was in effect and would be honored. She also spoke with her attorney about the status of the agreement, and he recommended that the DIP seek formal bankruptcy approval of the agreement.

Meanwhile, Filene's operations were quickly downsized: thirty-five of its fifty-five stores were closed shortly after the petition date, and on November 9, 1999, Mason was notified that she was being put on "administrative leave," with pay, pending a motion by the DIP to reject her employment agreement. In February 2000, the bankruptcy court granted the motion to reject the employment agreement; Mason was terminated four days later. Mason then filed a "Request for Payment of Chapter 11 Expenses," in which she claimed that her termination benefits specified in the employment agreement were entitled to first priority as administrative expenses because she was terminated after rendering postpetition services. The Official Committee of Unsecured Creditors opposed the request. What will Mason argue in support of her claim for termination benefits? What will the committee argue in opposition? Who wins and on what basis? What, if anything, could have been done to avoid this dispute? [*In re FBI Distribution Corp. v. Mason*, 330 F.3d 36 (1st Cir. 2003).]

6. After Marvel Entertainment Group filed for bankruptcy protection under Chapter 11, tensions arose between several of the creditors. Eventually, one creditor acquired control of Marvel, thereby assuming the roles of DIP and creditor. The new DIP and the other creditors attempted to settle their claims against the estate, but negotiations broke down. The new DIP then commenced adverse litigation against the other creditors. The other creditors petitioned for the appointment of a trustee, arguing that the new DIP was incapable of neutrality. The district court appointed a trustee, and the new DIP appealed. Is acrimony between the DIP and certain creditors sufficient cause to justify appointment of a trustee? [*In re Marvel Entertainment Group, Inc.*, 140 F.3d 463 (3d Cir. 1998).]

7. Southmark, a Texas corporation, sold the Double Diamond Ranch in Nevada to the Double Diamond Ranch Limited Partnership (Double Diamond), retaining an option to buy back part of the ranch. Southmark later filed for bankruptcy in Texas. As part of its Chapter 11 reorganization plan, it assumed various executory contracts by filing a notice of assumption. The plan provided that all executory contracts not listed were deemed rejected. The notice did not list the option to buy back the ranch.

Double Diamond itself then filed for bankruptcy in Nevada. The committee administering the Double Diamond bankruptcy decided to sell the ranch to South Meadows Properties Limited Partnership. The committee asked the bankruptcy court to allow sale of the ranch free and clear of Southmark's option. A free-and-clear sale was appropriate only if the option was no longer valid because it had been stripped away in the Texas bankruptcy proceeding. The Nevada bankruptcy court held that the option was an executory contract that had been rejected in Southmark's bankruptcy. Therefore, it allowed Double Diamond to sell the ranch to South Meadows free and clear of Southmark's option. Southmark appealed.

If Southmark had given written notice of its intent to exercise the option, but had not yet paid the purchase price before filing for bankruptcy, would the option have been an executory contract? The option agreement expressly provided that the option was for a period of fifteen years "provided, however, that the option granted herein shall terminate in the event Southmark files for protection under Chapter 11 for the Bankruptcy Code." Is an option to buy property an executory contract? Why wasn't the option automatically terminated when Southmark filed under Chapter 11? [*Unsecured Creditors Committee of Robert L. Helms Construction & Development Co. v. Southmark Corp.*, 139 F.3d 702 (9th Cir. 1998).]

8. Bank of America National Trust and Savings Association was the major creditor of the debtor, 203 North LaSalle Street Partnership, an Illinois real estate limited partnership. The value of the partnership property mortgaged to the bank was less than the balance due, leaving the bank with an unsecured deficiency of $38.5 million. The partnership sought to cramdown over the bank's objection a plan whereby (1) the bank's $38.5 million unsecured deficiency claim would be discharged for an estimated 16% of its present value, and (2) certain former partners of the partnership would contribute $6.125 million in new capital over the course of five years, in exchange for the partnership's entire ownership of the reorganized debtor. The old equity holders were the only ones given the right to contribute new capital in exchange for equity. A senior class of impaired creditors objected. What arguments will the impaired creditors make in opposition to the plan? What arguments will the equity holders make in support of the plan? Should the plan be approved? [*Bank of America National Trust & Savings Ass'n v. 2003 North La Salle Street Partnership*, 526 U.S. 434 (1999).]

INTERNATIONAL BUSINESS

CHAPTER 24

INTERNATIONAL LAW AND TRANSACTIONS

INTRODUCTION

MANAGING IN A GLOBAL ECONOMY

Total U.S. trade in goods and services reached $4.76 trillion in 2011, representing $2.1 trillion in exports and $2.66 trillion in imports.[1] Firms of all sizes are taking advantage of the global markets. In 2010, General Motors sold more cars and trucks in China than it did in the United States.[2] Eighty percent of Facebook's users live outside the United States.[3] In addition, there is a growing internationalization of production and service delivery, with both manufacturing and services being outsourced. The effects of the U.S. subprime mortgage crisis on the global credit markets[4] and the European sovereign debt crisis on U.S. exports and securities markets show how interconnected the world has become.

International treaties and trade regimes, ranging from bilateral friendship, navigation, and commerce agreements to the regional North American Free Trade Agreement (NAFTA) and the multilateral World Trade Organization, form a major part of the legal and economic environment in which businesses operate. The most comprehensive effort to achieve regional integration is the European Union, which has an ultimate objective of complete economic, monetary, and political integration of its expanding number of member states.

Managers in today's global economy can expect to engage in many types of international business transactions, including the sale and leasing of goods and services, transfers and licensing of technology, equity investments, and international lending. These transactions create a wealth of issues and risks, but they also provide opportunities that may not be seen in many domestic transactions. Because of the many overlapping laws and regimes, companies engaging in cross-border transactions rely heavily on contractual arrangements to address issues such as choice of law and the mechanism for dispute resolution.

CHAPTER OVERVIEW

This chapter begins with a discussion of the most common legal systems used by the world's countries. It discusses the various sources of international law, including treaties, customary practices, and decisions of international, national, and regional courts. The chapter explains how national laws of both home and host countries are used to regulate the activities of multinational companies. It then outlines the U.S. trade regime and certain international trade regimes such as NAFTA and the World Trade Organization. It outlines the various types of regional trading alliances, focusing on the European Union, which is the most visible example of an economic union. It then shifts to a review of some of the legal issues involved in international business transactions, as well as the laws that govern doing business with and litigating against foreign governments. The chapter concludes with a discussion of international joint ventures.

TYPES OF LEGAL SYSTEMS

The legal systems used by the world's countries vary dramatically. A domestic company must follow the laws of its home country. A multinational company must also follow the laws of all of the host countries in which it operates, as well as a variety of international treaties, customs, and trade practices. Unfortunately, these laws sometimes are in conflict with each other.

The laws of a multinational company's home country govern activities that occur within that country's borders.

1. *See Annual Trade Highlights: 2011*, U.S. CENSUS BUREAU, *available at* http://www.census.gov/foreign-trade/statistics/highlights/annual.html.
2. Tom Krisher & Yuri Kageyama, *GM Sells More Vehicles in China Than in U.S.*, USA TODAY, Jan. 23, 2010.
3. *Statistics*, FACEBOOK, http://www.facebook.com/press/info.php?statistics (last visited Jan. 26, 2012).
4. Carolyn Said, *Home Values Hold in Few Places in Bay Area*, SFGATE.COM, Aug. 12, 2008, http://www.sfgate.com/cgi-bin/article.cgi?f=/c/a/2008/08/11/BULK1293VV.DTL.

The home country may also have laws that attempt to regulate business activities of the company that are conducted outside the home country's borders. For example, U.S. antitrust, foreign corrupt practices, and product safety laws purport to regulate certain offshore business activities of companies. Other laws and measures, including export law, sanctions, and embargoes, are designed to regulate the international trade activities of these companies.

The laws of the host countries in which a multinational company operates affect the company in a variety of ways. Some of the laws, such as labor, securities, banking, consumer protection, environmental, and intellectual property laws, are primarily designed to regulate the company's conduct within the host country; many of these have been addressed in other chapters of this book.

A host country may also enact laws that are intended to regulate foreign-owned firms that are operating within the jurisdiction of the host country. On occasion, host countries have nationalized certain foreign-owned businesses. Some countries also regulate the percentage of foreign ownership of businesses that are incorporated within their borders. Many countries impose restraints on the ability of a multinational business to *repatriate*, or return to its home country, profits earned in the host country.

Understanding and applying these laws becomes more difficult if the countries involved use different legal systems. The United Kingdom and most of its former colonies, including the United States, use a common law system, which is based primarily on a collection of decisions rendered by judges in individual cases. Most other countries have adopted civil law systems, which are primarily based on comprehensive legal codes, often developed from a single drafting event. A few countries have adopted other legal systems such as religious law systems or combinations or derivatives of the common law and civil law systems.

Common Law

Common law legal systems are used in countries that are or were British territories or colonies (with the exception of a few British colonies that had adopted civil law systems before they were taken over by the British). *Common law legal systems* primarily rely on case law and precedents. As a result, common law judges use accumulated past judicial decisions to form general rules (*precedents*) to serve as guidelines for similar cases in the future. A judge can depart from precedent and establish a new rule, however, if the case presents different or new considerations and facts. This new rule itself becomes precedent if it is accepted and subsequently used in other cases by different judges or if it is adopted by the highest court in a jurisdiction, in which case the new rule is binding on lower courts. (The doctrine of *stare decisis*, which embodies this reliance on precedent, is discussed further in Chapter 3).

An important, but not a distinguishing, aspect of common law systems is the existence of different levels of courts to define and further refine the law, starting with the trial courts that normally consist of a single judge and a jury. To reach a judgment or verdict, the jury in a jury trial or the judge in a bench trial determines the facts in accordance with the law set forth by the judge. Appellate courts, forming the next level in the judicial common law system, consist of judges and only review whether the judge of the trial court applied the correct principles of law.

Statutes and codes exist in common law systems. They are created either through *codification*, a process in which existing common law positions are restated and laid down in a statute, or by enacting new *statutory law* that is not based on existing common law rules. As discussed in Chapter 4, courts can declare statutory law unconstitutional in common law systems.

The principle of equity is unique to common law legal systems. The very formal character of the traditional English common law system, especially with regard to remedies, made exceptions necessary. As a result, the English common law system incorporated the royal prerogative to grant these exceptions, referred to as *equity*, in individual cases in the interest of justice. Initially, common law and equity were separate systems, each with its own courts. Later, these two systems were merged, but, even today, the distinction between common law and equity remains important. For example, the Seventh Amendment to the U.S. Constitution guarantees the right to a jury trial "in suits at common law," but no similar right is guaranteed in equity proceedings. As a result, it is necessary to ascertain whether a claim is legal or equitable in order to determine whether a jury trial is constitutionally guaranteed.

Although the U.S. legal system is undeniably rooted in the English common law legal system,[5] there are a number of differences between the current British and U.S. common law systems. Unlike the U.S. system, the British common law system does not use juries in civil cases, and it allows for only limited *discovery* (the phase in a civil lawsuit before the trial, when each party can request documents and other evidence from the other party). The British system has no procedures for *class-action lawsuits,* but it does permit *representative suits* in which a claim is made on behalf of a potentially affected group.[6] Britain prohibits the payment of lawyers on a *contingency fee* basis (in which the attorney receives a percentage of the judgment awarded to his or her client), and it requires the losing party in a lawsuit to pay both its own attorneys' fees and those of the prevailing party. The British system has two types of lawyers: solicitors and barristers. A *solicitor* is allowed to perform legal services outside the court, but only *barristers* may argue in court.

---

5. The state of Louisiana, which was once a French, and later a Spanish, colony, is the only U.S. state that has a civil law system for matters that are not criminal in nature.

6. The British common law also includes the concept of a group legal order (GLO), which is a procedure whereby a judge hears related cases together.

Civil Law

Civil law legal systems are based on Roman law as consolidated between A.D. 529 and 534 in the Corpus Juris Civilis (also called Justinian's Code after Justinian, the Roman emperor who initiated the consolidation). In the eighteenth century, strong national systems were established all over Europe, and this led to the creation of separate national codes. The most prominent example was the French Napoleonic Code (Code Napoléon), which influenced the development of other national civil codes, especially in countries that were once under French control.

Today, civil law systems are found in other areas besides Europe. For example, Japan, South Korea, and Taiwan used the German Civil Code as the basis of their respective civil law regimes.

Civil law relies primarily on statutory laws that are embodied in a unified code. Lower courts usually cannot declare these statutes unconstitutional. Civil law systems generally draw a strong distinction between *private law* (the area of the law in which the sole function of government is the recognition and enforcement of private rights, e.g., civil and commercial codes) and *public law* (the area of the law that focuses on the effectuation of the public interest by state action, e.g., constitutional law, administrative law, and criminal law). Some civil law countries have different courts for private and public law, and some also separate criminal courts from administrative courts within their court system.

Traditionally, civil law statutes and codes tend to be more abstract than codified common law to cover a wider range of facts. Civil law judges use analogies to apply the existing statutes and codes to new cases and discuss the underlying general principles at length. Judges also often use the work of legal scholars in reasoning and deciding the case at hand. Far less frequently, civil law judges use decisions in prior cases to further refine their decisions.

Judges play a different role in civil law systems than in common law systems. Common law judges are expected to be more creative when applying the law than civil law judges are. In addition to applying the law, common law judges also create law to balance the power of the legislature and executive branch. In contrast, a civil law judge is bound by the existing statutes and codes as they were created by the legislature. In common law systems, the judge is a neutral party in the proceedings, whereas a civil law judge assumes many of the roles of a lawyer in a common law system, such as deciding what evidence needs to be developed or produced.

This discussion has focused on how common law and civil law systems differ, but increasingly there are also similarities. As case law has become more important in civil law systems and statutory law has become more important in common law systems, the differences between the two legal systems have become less distinct.

Other Families of Law

Although common law and civil law systems predominate, some countries have adopted other forms of legal systems, many of which are rooted in or based on religious principles and orders.

Islamic

The traditional Islamic rules and laws that regulate Muslim life are called *Sharia* (also Shari'a or Shariah). Civil law in Islamic countries is interpreted in harmony with the Sharia. The duty to honor agreements and observe good faith in commercial dealings is a central premise of Islamic law. Islamic trade and commerce is governed by the concepts of Zakat, Riba (or Ribaa), and Gharar. *Zakat* is the allocation of certain taxes to deprived and poor people as a welfare contribution. *Riba* prohibits unearned or unjustified (illicit) profits and can therefore lead to problems when interest is charged on loans. Islamic law forbids excessive *Gharar*, or an event whose outcomes are unknown, if it will lead to exploitation and injustice. Gambling contracts have excessive Gharar, which usually renders them void. An open-ended contract or a contract under which one party does not know what it will receive or has to provide may also be problematic.

In the following case, the court considered whether an amendment to the Oklahoma Constitution that prohibited Oklahoma courts from applying Sharia and other international law was constitutional.

A CASE IN POINT	*Summary*	Case 24.1

Awad v. Ziriax

United States Court of Appeals for the Tenth Circuit
2012 WL 50636 (10th Cir. Jan. 10, 2012).

FACTS   On November 2, 2010, just over 70% of the Oklahoma voters approved an amendment to the Oklahoma Constitution called the "Save Our State Amendment," which provided that in making judicial decisions, Oklahoma "courts shall not look to the legal precepts of other nations or cultures. Specifically, the courts shall not consider international law or Sharia law." Without intervention, the proposed amendment would likely have been certified by the Oklahoma Election Board on November 9, 2010, and thereby have become part of the Oklahoma state constitution.

On November 4, Muneer Awad sued the members of the Election Board, seeking to prevent the certification of the election results. Awad, an American citizen residing in Oklahoma, was

CONTINUED

the executive director of the Oklahoma Chapter of the Council on American-Islamic Relations. As a Muslim, he adhered to the religious principles from the Koran and the teachings of Mohammed.

In his suit, Awad alleged that the Save Our State Amendment violated his rights under both the Establishment and Free Exercise Clauses of the First Amendment to the U.S. Constitution. Specifically, he objected to the amendment's singling out his religion for negative treatment. He claimed that implementation of the amendment would cause multiple adverse consequences, such as stigmatizing him and others who practice the Muslim faith, inhibiting the practice of Islam, disabling a court from probating his last will and testament (which contained references to Sharia law), limiting the relief Muslims can obtain from Oklahoma state courts, and fostering excessive entanglement between the government and his religion. After the district court granted Awad's motion for a preliminary injunction preventing the certification of the proposed amendment, the members of the Oklahoma Election Board appealed.

ISSUE PRESENTED Does a state constitutional amendment prohibiting state courts from considering Sharia law violate the Establishment or the Free Exercise Clause of the U.S. Constitution?

SUMMARY OF OPINION The U.S. Court of Appeals for the Tenth Circuit first determined that the plaintiff had Article III standing to bring his suit. The court next considered whether the district court had abused its discretion in granting the preliminary injunction. To obtain a preliminary injunction, a plaintiff must show that four factors weigh in his or her favor: (1) the plaintiff is substantially likely to succeed on the merits; (2) the plaintiff will suffer irreparable injury if the injunction is denied; (3) the plaintiff's threatened injury outweighs the injury the opposing party will suffer under the injunction; and (4) the injunction would not be adverse to the public interest.

To weigh the first factor, the court first had to decide which legal test governed the Establishment Clause claim. Because the proposed amendment provided "explicit and deliberate distinctions" among religions, the court concluded that the strict scrutiny test set forth in *Larson v. Valente*[7] applied. Under this heightened standard, a law that discriminates among religions can survive scrutiny only if it is "closely fitted" to the furtherance of a compelling government interest.

To show a compelling government interest, the government must demonstrate that the recited harms are real, not merely conjectural, and that the regulation will in fact alleviate these harms in a direct way. The court rejected the assertion that "Oklahoma certainly has a compelling interest in determining what law was applied in Oklahoma courts." This may be a valid state interest, the court reasoned, but this general statement alone is not sufficient to establish a *compelling* interest. Moreover, the members of the Election Board provided no evidence of a concrete real problem. Thus, any harm they sought to remedy with the proposed amendment was speculative. Even if the proposed amendment satisfied the compelling interest factor, the court ruled that its complete ban of Sharia law is "hardly an exercise of narrow tailoring."

The court agreed that the plaintiff was likely to face irreparable injury absent an injunction. A plaintiff suffers irreparable injury when the court would be "unable to grant an effective monetary remedy after a full trial . . . ." Because damages would be difficult to ascertain for a claim of government condemnation of one's religion, the court held that the plaintiff was likely to face irreparable injury absent an injunction.

The court then looked to the third factor, the balance of harms. Under the heightened standard of review, the plaintiff had to show that his threatened injury outweighed any injury to the members of the Election Board caused by granting the injunction. While recognizing that the voters of Oklahoma have a strong interest in having their political will expressed, the

CONTINUED

7. 456 U.S. 228 (1982).

court emphasized that when a publicly supported law is likely unconstitutional, their interests do not outweigh the plaintiff's interest in having his constitutional rights protected. The appellants were not able to point to a specific instance where an Oklahoma court had applied Sharia law or the law of any foreign nation. The court reasoned that delayed implementation of a measure that does not appear to address any immediate problem generally will not cause material harm. Accordingly, the court agreed that the plaintiff had made a strong showing that his threatened injury outweighed any potential harm to the appellants in granting the injunction.

Finally, the court considered whether the preliminary injunction would be adverse to the public interest. Although federal courts should be wary of interfering with the voting process, the court indicated that "it is always in the public interest to prevent the violation of a party's constitutional rights."

Having found that the district court did not abuse its discretion when it preliminarily enjoined the certification of the proposed amendment based on the Establishment Clause, the appeals court did not reach the plaintiff's Free Exercise claim.

RESULT   The district court did not abuse its discretion when it enjoined the certification of the Save Our State Amendment.

COMMENTS   The U.S. Supreme Court has on occasion considered international law when addressing the constitutionality of domestic laws. For example, in *Roper v. Simmons*,[8] the Supreme Court considered international views when considering whether it was constitutional to execute convicts for crimes committed when they were juveniles. The Court emphasized that it has historically looked to the laws of other countries as instructive for its interpretation of the Eight Amendment's prohibition of "cruel and unusual punishments." The Court acknowledged the overwhelming weight of international opinion against the juvenile death penalty before making its own determination banning the practice.

Similarly, the Supreme Court looked to laws in other countries when deciding whether a Texas statute that barred two individuals of the same sex from engaging in certain intimate sexual acts violated the U.S. Constitution. In *Lawrence v. Texas*,[9] the Court cited the British Parliament's ban on such laws several decades earlier as well as a European Court of Human Rights' decision that laws proscribing homosexual conduct were invalid under the European Convention on Human Rights. The Court also cited authority in all member countries of the Council of Europe that were at odds with such laws. The Court ultimately sided with the growing trend in the international community to invalidate laws against consensual homosexual conduct and struck down the Texas statute.

CRITICAL THINKING QUESTIONS

1. Can a U.S. court enforce a clause in a contract specifying that Sharia law will apply?

2. When, if ever, should a national court look to decisions of courts in other nations when interpreting its constitution?

8.   543 U.S. 551 (2005).
9.   539 U.S. 558 (2003).

Hindu

Classical Hindu law contained a set of rules, customs, and usages to guide the life and beliefs of Hindus. In today's India, Hindu law is applied only to very personal matters, namely, marriage, divorce, and inheritance/succession questions, and is therefore referred to as "personal law." Most other legal issues in India are governed by codified Indian law, which is a secular law based on English common law but tailored to the needs of Indian society.

Socialist

The term "socialist law" is used for the legal systems in socialist and communist states. Socialist law systems are based on civil law systems with changes and additions

IN BRIEF

Comparison of Common Law and Civil Law

Common Law	Civil Law
Developed in England during 12th and 13th centuries	Origins in Roman Republic
Adversarial	Inquisitional
Case-based	Code-based
Inductive (specific to general)	Deductive (general to specific)
Relies on precedent	Little reliance on precedent
Little distinction between public and private law	Distinguishes between public and private law
Equity courts/theories	Equitable doctrines, if any, must be written into the code
Judicial system usually drawn as a pyramid with the "highest" court at the top	Judicial system divided between private law courts and public law courts
Jury system (at least in criminal cases)	No or limited jury system
Strict rules of evidence	Looser rules of evidence
Pretrial discovery	Limited pretrial discovery
Integrated court system with courts of general jurisdiction to adjudicate criminal and most types of civil cases	Specialty court systems and specialty courts to deal with different areas of law (constitutional, criminal, administrative, commercial, and civil or private law)
Single event trial	Trials involve an extended process with a series of successive hearings and consultations
Judges act as managers or referees of the lawyers, who play adversarial roles, and judges are secondary to the lawyers.	Judges use inquisitorial process with judge as principal interrogator of witnesses.
Judges search creatively for an answer to a question or issue among many potentially applicable judicial precedents.	Judges are appliers of the law.
Judges are selected as part of the political process for a specific judicial post that they hold for life or for a specified term, with no automatic system of advancement to higher courts as a reward for services.	Judges are usually part of the civil service of the country.

© Cengage Learning 2013

from the respective ideological background (mostly Marxist-Leninist). One of the most important aspects of a socialist system is public ownership of property and the means of production. Today, only a very small number of states still have socialist law systems. Some of them, such as China, have adapted their legal systems to account for the market-oriented changes in their economic system and do grant certain property rights.

SOURCES OF INTERNATIONAL LAW

The term "international law" does not stand for a specific body of law or a set of rules or regulations. Instead, it refers to different legal principles that together comprise the laws of the international community. International law is often divided between public international law and private international law. *Public international law* governs the relationships among nation-states, whereas *private*

international law governs the relationships between private parties engaged in transactions across national borders. *Supranational law* is another legal principle of international law, under which nations submit their decision-making authority to a common organization or institution.

National law is normally enacted by the legislative body of a country, but there is no similar legislative body that creates international law. Therefore, in most cases,[10] at least two nations are involved in creating the legal rules that will be applied as international law.

Treaties

Most international rules of law are set forth in written agreements between or among two or more countries, called *treaties*. Such agreements may also be referred to

---

10. In some instances, unilateral actions, such as declarations of a state, can also be regarded as creating binding legal effects.

as conventions, pacts, protocols, or accords.[11] The Vienna Convention on the Law of Treaties defines a "treaty" as "an international agreement concluded between States in written form and governed by international law . . . ."[12] This Convention, which was signed but not ratified by the United States, sets the rules for all phases of a treaty, including negotiation, signature, ratification, entry into force, and termination.

There are now more than 158,000 treaties in existence. Each country must determine who is authorized to enter into a treaty on its behalf; in most countries, the authorization is granted in the constitution. For example, the U.S. Constitution grants the President the power to enter into treaties "by and with the Advice and Consent of the Senate, [. . .] provided two-thirds of the Senators present concur."[13] Often the President delegates this constitutional power to negotiate treaties to other parts of the executive branch.

The U.S. Constitution prohibits states from entering "into any Treaty, Alliance or Confederation,"[14] but the U.S. Supreme Court has allowed the states to enter into treaties that do not "encroach upon or impair the supremacy of the United States."[15] In *Crosby v. National Foreign Trade Council,*[16] the Supreme Court made it clear that the authority of states and localities in this area is very limited. The Commonwealth of Massachusetts had passed a law that barred governmental entities in Massachusetts from buying goods or services from companies doing business with Burma (Myanmar) at a time when federal legislation imposed mandatory and conditional sanctions on Burma. The U.S. Supreme Court ruled that the Massachusetts law unconstitutionally infringed on federal foreign affairs power in violation of the Foreign Commerce Clause of the U.S. Constitution and was, therefore, preempted by federal law. The Court found that "[i]n this case, the state Act is an obstacle to the federal Act's delegation of discretion to the President of the United States to control economic sanctions against Burma."

The consent of a nation to enter into a treaty is expressed not by signing the treaty, but through the process of ratification or accession.[17] *Ratification* is a twofold process that occurs both on the national level, where it is governed by the laws of the nation that has to ratify the treaty, and on the international level, where it is often governed by the treaty itself. Only a nation that is an original party to the treaty can ratify it, but, through the process of *accession*, a nation that was not an original party can elect to participate in the treaty at a later time.

Treaties can be breached by one or more countries, and disputes can arise from these breaches or alleged breaches. These disputes can lead to adjudication in international courts, but more often these disputes are decided by national courts.

The Supremacy Clause of the U.S. Constitution states that "all treaties . . . which shall be made . . . under the Authority of the United States shall be the supreme Law of the land; and the Judges in every State shall be bound thereby."[18] In the following case, the U.S. Supreme Court considered whether a decision by the International Court of Justice (ICJ) that flowed from treaties in which the United States submitted to ICJ jurisdiction is directly enforceable as domestic law in U.S. state courts.

---

11. Treaties can bind two states bilaterally or more than two states multilaterally.

12. Vienna Convention on the Law of Treaties, art. 2(1)(a), May 23, 1969, 1155 U.N.T.S. 331.

13. U.S. Const., art. II, § 2, cl. 2.

14. U.S. Const., art. I, § 10.

15. Virginia v. Tennessee, 148 U.S. 503, 518 (1893).

16. 530 U.S. 363 (2000).

17. Vienna Convention on the Law of Treaties, art.11, *supra* note 12.

18. U.S. Const. art.VI, cl. 2.

| A CASE IN POINT | *In the Language of the Court* | Case 24.2 |

Medellín v. Texas

Supreme Court of the United States
552 U.S. 491 (2008).

FACTS   The International Court of Justice, located in The Hague, is a tribunal established pursuant to the United Nations Charter to adjudicate disputes between member states. The ICJ Statute, which is annexed to the Charter, provides the organizational framework and governing procedures for cases brought before the ICJ.[19] In 1969, the United States ratified the Vienna Convention on Consular Relations of April 24, 1963, and the Optional Protocol Concerning the Compulsory Settlement of Disputes to the Vienna Convention. Article 36 of the Vienna Convention requires that foreign nationals who are arrested or detained must be given notice "without delay" of their right to have their embassy or consulate notified of their arrest. The Optional Protocol provides that disputes arising out of the interpretation or application of the Vienna Convention "shall lie within the compulsory jurisdiction of the

CONTINUED

---

19. The ICJ Statute sets forth two ways for a nation to consent to ICJ jurisdiction: (1) it may consent generally to jurisdiction on any question arising under a treaty or general international law, or (2) it may consent specifically to jurisdiction over a particular category of cases or disputes pursuant to a separate treaty.

International Court of Justice." The United States originally consented to the general jurisdiction of the ICJ when it filed a declaration recognizing compulsory jurisdiction under the ICJ Statute. By ratifying the Optional Protocol, the United States consented to the specific jurisdiction of the ICJ with respect to claims arising out of the Vienna Convention.[20]

In 1997, José Ernest Medellín, a Mexican national, was convicted of capital murder and sentenced to death in Texas for the gang rape and brutal murders of two Houston teenagers on June 24, 1993. When Medellín was arrested, he was given *Miranda*[21] warnings, and a few hours later he gave a detailed written confession. Local law enforcement officers did not inform him of his Vienna Convention right to notify the Mexican consulate of his detention. He first raised his Vienna Convention claim in his first application for state postconviction relief, but both the trial court and the Texas Court of Criminal Appeals rejected the claim, finding that he had failed to show that the nonnotification had affected the validity of his conviction or punishment.

In 2004, in the *Case Concerning Avena and Other Mexican Nationals*[22] brought by Mexico against the United States, the ICJ held that, because of violations of the Vienna Convention, fifty-one named Mexican nationals (including Medellín) were entitled to review and reconsideration of their state court convictions and sentences in the United States. When Medellín's appeal found its way to the U.S. Court of Appeals for the Fifth Circuit, he raised the ICJ's ruling in *Avena*, but the Fifth Circuit denied relief.[23] Medellín appealed to the U.S. Supreme Court, which granted certiorari. Before the Supreme Court heard the case, President Bush issued a Memorandum to the United States Attorney General in which he asserted that the United States would "discharge its international obligations" under *Avena* "by having State courts give effect to the decision." While Medellín's second appeal was under consideration in Texas, the Supreme Court decided *Sanchez-Llamas v. Oregon*,[24] a case that did not involve the individuals named in the *Avena* judgment; the Court held that, contrary to the ICJ's determination, the Vienna Convention did not preclude the application of state default rules. The Texas Court of Criminal Appeals subsequently dismissed Medellín's second appeal, holding that neither the *Avena* decision nor the Memorandum was "binding federal law" that could displace the State's limitations on the filing of successive habeas applications. The U.S. Supreme Court granted certiorari for a second time.

ISSUES PRESENTED Are the procedural protections afforded by a treaty duly ratified by the United States automatically binding on the States? If not, can the President require a state court to review and reconsider a conviction without regard to state procedural default rules?

OPINION ROBERTS, C.J., writing on behalf of the U.S. Supreme Court:

No one disputes that the *Avena* decision . . . constitutes an *international* law obligation on the part of the United States. But not all international law obligations automatically constitute binding federal law enforceable in United States courts. The question we confront here is whether the *Avena* judgment has automatic *domestic* legal effect such that the judgment of its own force applies in state and federal courts.

This Court has long recognized the distinction between treaties that automatically have effect as domestic law, and those that—while they constitute international law commitments—do not by themselves function as binding federal law. . . . [W]hile treaties "may comprise international commitments . . . they are not domestic law unless Congress has either enacted

CONTINUED

---

20. The United States withdrew from general ICJ jurisdiction in October 1985. In 2005, the United States withdrew from the Optional Protocol.

21. *Miranda* warnings are derived from the Supreme Court's decision in *Miranda v. Arizona*, 384 U.S. 436 (1966).

22. 2004 I.C.J. 12.

23. Medellín v. Dretke, 371 F.3d 270 (5th Cir. 2004).

24. 548 U.S. 331 (2006).

implementing statutes or the treaty itself conveys an intention that it be 'self-executing' and is ratified on these terms."

A treaty is, of course, "primarily a compact between independent nations." . . . Only "if the treaty contains stipulations which are self-executing, that is, require no legislation to make them operative, [will] they have the force and effect of a legislative enactment."

Medellín . . . contend[s] that the Optional Protocol, United Nations Charter, and ICJ Statute supply the "relevant obligation" to give the *Avena* judgment binding effect in the domestic courts of the United States. Because none of these treaty sources creates binding federal law in the absence of implementing legislation, and because it is uncontested that no such legislation exists, we conclude that the *Avena* judgment is not automatically binding domestic law.

. . . .

The most natural reading of the Optional Protocol is a bare grant of jurisdiction. . . . The Protocol says nothing about the effect of an ICJ decision and does not itself commit signatories to comply with an ICJ judgment. The Protocol is similarly silent as to any enforcement mechanism.

The obligation on the part of signatory nations to comply with ICJ judgments derives . . . from Article 94 of the United Nations Charter. . . .

. . . The Article is not a directive to domestic courts. It does not provide that the United States "shall" or "must" comply with an ICJ decision, nor indicate that the Senate that ratified the U.N. Charter intended to vest ICJ decisions with immediate legal effect in domestic courts. . . .

. . . .

The pertinent international agreements, therefore, do not provide for implementation of ICJ judgments through direct enforcement in domestic courts, and "where a treaty does not provide a particular remedy, either expressly or implicitly, it is not for the federal courts to impose one on the States through lawmaking of their own.". . .

Our conclusion that *Avena* does not by itself constitute binding federal law is confirmed by the "postratification understanding" of signatory nations. There are currently 47 nations that are parties to the Optional Protocol and 171 nations that are parties to the Vienna Convention. Yet neither Medellín nor his *amici* have identified a single nation that treats ICJ judgments as binding in domestic courts.

. . . .

[*Editor's Note:* The Court then rejected Medellín's argument that the ICJ judgment is binding on state courts by virtue of the President's Memorandum:

> The President has an array of political and diplomatic means available to enforce international obligations, but unilaterally converting a non-self-executing treaty into a self-executing one is not among them. . . . [T]he terms of a non-self-executing treaty can become domestic law only in the same way as any other law—through passage of legislation by both Houses of Congress, combined with either the President's signature or a congressional override of a Presidential veto.]

RESULT   The Court affirmed the judgment of the Texas Court of Criminal Appeals that the ICJ judgment was not directly enforceable as domestic law in a state court in the United States. Medellín's appeal was dismissed, and he was executed in Texas in 2008.

COMMENTS   In a dissent joined by Justices Ginsburg and Souter, Justice Breyer argued that the ICJ treaty was "self-executing" based on a reading of other treaties that had gone into effect without additional congressional action. He observed that the decision could have the effect of "diminishing our nation's reputation abroad as a result of our failure to follow the 'rule of law' principles that we preach."

CONTINUED

CRITICAL THINKING QUESTIONS

1. Justice Breyer appended a list of seventy treaties that the United States has ratified with ICJ dispute resolution provisions similar to those contained in the Optional Protocol, many of which relate to property rights, contract and commercial rights, trademarks, civil liability for personal injury, rights of foreign diplomats, taxation, domestic-court jurisdiction, and similar matters. Will uncertainty about the enforceability of ICJ judgments rendered under these treaties in the United States undermine efforts by the signatories of these treaties to create effective international dispute resolution procedures in a world where commerce, trade, and travel have become more international? Will this decision make it more difficult for the United States to convince other countries to come to the table to negotiate treaties related to business, the environment, intellectual property protection, and other important international issues?

2. To provide consistency in the interpretation of contracts for the sales of goods involving companies located in different countries, the Convention on the International Sale of Goods (CISG) sets forth a set of contract principles that purport to bind all companies located in countries that are signatories to the CISG (the CISG is discussed in more detail in Chapter 8). The United States is a signatory to the CISG. Given the *Medellín* decision, will the CISG still be binding on U.S. businesses that enter into contracts with companies located in other signatory countries?

Customary International Law

Another form of international law, *customary international law,* is created by *customary practice.* Whereas treaties between nations are comparable to contracts between private parties in national legal systems, customary international law is analogous to "established practice" and "commercial usage" as they are known in the commercial laws of many nations. Customary practice arises from continuous practice, not from a legislative action. Thus, a state must give its express consent to be bound by a treaty, but it implicitly consents to customary practice through continuous observation of the practice.

Treaties and customary practice often complement each other. Customary practices are sometimes used to interpret treaties, and treaties often codify, clarify, or modify existing customary practices.

The Alien Tort Statute (ATS)[25] grants U.S. federal district courts jurisdiction over claims "by an alien for a tort only, committed in violation of the law of nations or a treaty of the United States." In the following case, the court considered whether corporations can be liable for human rights abuses under the ATS as a matter of customary international law.

25. 28 U.S.C. § 1350.

A CASE IN POINT	*Summary*	Case 24.3

Kiobel v. Royal Dutch Petroleum Co.

United States Court of Appeals for the Second Circuit
621 F.3d 111 (2d Cir. 2010), *cert. granted,* 132 S. Ct. 472 (2011).

FACTS Defendants Royal Dutch Petroleum Company (Royal Dutch) and Shell Petroleum Development Company of Nigeria, Ltd. (SPDC), a subsidiary of Shell Transport and Trading Company PLC (Shell), engaged in oil exploration and production in the Ogoni region of Nigeria for several decades. In response to SPDC and Royal Dutch's activities, residents of the Ogoni region organized a group named the "Movement for Survival of Ogoni People" to protest the environmental effects of oil exploitation in the region. According to the plaintiffs, who are residents of Nigeria, the defendants responded in 1993 by enlisting the aid of the Nigerian government to suppress the Ogoni resistance. Throughout 1993 and 1994, Nigerian military forces allegedly shot and killed Ogoni residents and attacked Ogoni villages—beating, raping, and arresting residents and destroying or looting property—with the assistance of the defendants.

The plaintiffs brought claims against the defendants under the Alien Tort Statute for aiding and abetting the Nigerian government in alleged violations of the law of nations. Specifically, the plaintiffs brought claims of aiding and abetting (1) extrajudicial killing; (2) crimes against humanity; (3) torture or cruel, inhuman, and degrading treatment; (4) arbitrary arrest and

CONTINUED

detention; (5) violation of the rights to life, liberty, security, and association; (6) forced exile; and (7) property destruction.

In 2006, the district court dismissed the plaintiffs' claims for aiding and abetting property destruction; forced exile; extrajudicial killing; and violations of the rights to life, liberty, security, and association. The district court reasoned that customary international law did not define those violations with sufficient particularity. The district court denied the defendants' motion to dismiss with respect to the remaining claims of aiding and abetting arbitrary arrest and detention; crimes against humanity; and torture or cruel, inhuman, and degrading treatment. Recognizing the importance of the issues presented and the substantial grounds for difference of opinion, the district court certified its entire order for immediate review by the U.S. Court of Appeals for the Second Circuit.

ISSUE PRESENTED   Does liability under the Alien Tort Statute extend to corporations that aid and abet human rights violations as a matter of customary international law?

SUMMARY OF OPINION   The U.S. Court of Appeals for the Second Circuit began by noting that although it had never directly addressed whether its jurisdiction under the ATS extended to civil actions against corporations, the issue had been "lurking" in its ATS jurisprudence for quite some time. To resolve this question, the court proceeded in two steps. First, it determined which body of law, international or domestic, governs the question of "who is liable for what." After concluding that international law governed, the court then considered whether corporations can be subject to liability for violations of customary international law.

The Second Circuit concluded that the Supreme Court's decision in *Sosa v. Alvarez-Machain*,[26] its own precedents, and international law required it to apply international law, not domestic law, to determine the scope of liability for violations of customary international law under the ATS. In *Sosa*, the Supreme Court instructed the lower federal courts to consider "whether *international law* extends the scope of liability for a violation of a given norm to the perpetrator being sued, if the defendant is a private actor such as a corporation or individual." The Second Circuit has consistently adhered to the method prescribed in *Sosa*. For example, in *Presbyterian Church of Sudan v. Talisman Energy, Inc.*,[27] the Second Circuit looked to international law to determine the circumstances in which aiders and abettors could be liable for violations of the customary international law of human rights. In other cases, the court also looked to international law to determine whether state officials and private individuals could be held liable under the ATS. The court acknowledged that the "idea that corporations are 'persons' with duties, liabilities, and rights has a long history in American domestic law," but held that "the ATS requires federal courts to look beyond rules of domestic law—however well-established they may be—to examine the specific and universally accepted rules that the nations of the world treat as binding *in their dealings with one another*."

International law is not silent on the question of the *subjects* of international law, nor does international law leave to the individual states the responsibility of defining those subjects. Rather, observed the court, "[t]he concept of international person is . . . derived from international law." The court looked to decisions of the International Military Tribunal at Nuremberg after World War II to support its stance. The Tribunal's decisions explicitly recognized *individual liability* for the violation of specific, universal, and obligatory norms of the customary international law of human rights. The Tribunal rejected the defendants' arguments that "international law is concerned with the actions of sovereign states, and provides no punishment for individuals." Instead, the Tribunal declared that "*international law* imposes duties and liabilities upon individuals as well as upon states" and that "individuals can be punished for violations of international law." More recently, although there was a proposal to grant the International Criminal Court (ICC) jurisdiction over corporations and other "juridical" persons,

CONTINUED

---

26. 542 U.S. 692 (2004).

27. 582 F.3d 244 (2d Cir. 2009).

"that proposal was soundly rejected, and the Rome Statute,[28] the ICC's constitutive document, hews to the tenet set forth in Nuremberg that international norms should be enforced by the punishment of the individual men and women who violate them."

After concluding that international law governs the scope of liability under the ATS, the court next considered whether corporations are subject to liability under international customary law. To attain the status of a rule of customary law, a norm must be "specific, universal, and obligatory." The court ultimately consulted authority derived from international tribunals and international treaties to determine whether corporate liability has satisfied this threshold.

The court found it particularly significant that no international tribunal of which it was aware has *ever* held a corporation liable for a violation of the law of nations. The court looked again to the trials at Nuremberg, which it called the "single most important source of modern customary international law concerning liability for violations of fundamental human rights." The London Charter, which established the Tribunal at Nuremberg, granted the Tribunal jurisdiction over *natural persons only*. The Charter granted the Tribunal the authority to declare organizations "criminal," but ultimately the purpose of this authority was to facilitate the prosecution of *individuals* who were members of the organizations. Thus, surmised the court, at the time of the Nuremberg trials, corporate liability was not recognized as a "specific, universal, and obligatory" norm of customary international law. Subsequent international tribunals have continued to limit jurisdiction to "natural persons." Thus, according to the court, the concept of corporate liability for violations of customary international law has not even begun to "ripen[ ]" into a universally accepted norm of international law.

Although all treaties ratified by more than one state provide *some* evidence of the custom and practice of nations, "a treaty will only constitute *sufficient proof* of a norm of *customary international law* if an overwhelming majority of States have ratified the treaty, *and* those States uniformly and consistently act in accordance with its principles." That a provision appears in one treaty (or more), therefore, is not proof of a well-established norm of *customary* international law. Although a small number of recent international treaties that imposed liability on corporations have been ratified by an "overwhelming majority" of states, these treaties do not address the subject matter of human rights. To find that these treaties create rules of customary international law that reach beyond their subject matter would mean that the rule applies to nations that have not yet ratified it. To do this, warned the court, would be "wholly inappropriate and without precedent" and would contravene the international comity the ATS was enacted to promote. Finally, the few specialized treaties imposing liability on corporations have not had such influence that a general rule of corporate liability has become a norm of customary international law. Having found "no historical evidence of an existing or even nascent norm of customary international law imposing liability on corporations for violations of human rights," the court held that corporate liability for human rights violations is not a "specific, universal, and obligatory" norm of customary international law. Accordingly, the defendants were not subject to suit under the ATS.

RESULT   The order of the district court was affirmed insofar as it dismissed some of the plaintiffs' claims against the defendants and reversed insofar as it declined to dismiss the plaintiffs' remaining claims. The plaintiffs' suit was dismissed in its entirety due to lack of subject matter jurisdiction.

CRITICAL THINKING QUESTIONS

1. Is this decision consistent with the U.S. Supreme Court's reasoning in *Citizens United v. Federal Election Commission*[29]?

2. How does the court draw the line between customary norms that have been universally accepted and those that have not?

---

28. The Rome Statute of the International Criminal Court, art. 25(1), *opened for signature* July 17, 1998, 37 I.L.M. 1002, 1016 (limiting the ICC's jurisdiction to "natural persons").

29. 130 S. Ct. 876 (2010). See Chapter 4.

Decisions of International, National, and Regional Courts

Although there are a number of international courts, these courts do not have exclusive jurisdiction over international disputes. For example, Article 34 of the statute creating the International Court of Justice states that "[o]nly States may be parties in cases before the Court."[30] The European Court of Justice at Luxembourg deals with cases brought by member states of the European Union (EU), cases brought by EU institutions, and cases brought by individuals or corporations against EU institutions and member states. Similarly, the European Court of Human Rights is authorized to hear complaints filed by states or by individuals about violations of the human rights protected by the Human Rights Convention. Because of the limited authority of these international courts to hear disputes involving private parties, many international disputes must be resolved by national courts. As a result, courts on a national as well as an international level are also a source of international law.

National Laws

National laws can affect both foreign-owned businesses and international business activities. Certain laws have extraterritorial application.

National Laws Directed at Foreign-Owned Businesses

Certain national laws are designed to limit foreign-owned businesses.

Constraints on Foreign Ownership Some governments try to protect what they regard as their country's key industries, such as the energy and media industries, by limiting the allowed percentage of foreign ownership. Another constraint on foreign ownership is to restrict the profits that can be returned by a multinational company to its home country through limits on repatriation.

Nationalization, Expropriation, Confiscation, and Privatization Host countries sometimes pass laws that directly affect foreign-owned business operations in their country. If a host country decides to assert ownership over some or all of a company's assets, *nationalization* takes place. If the host country compensates the company for its lost assets, this process of nationalization is referred to as *expropriation*; if no compensation is provided, it is called *confiscation*. (The "Global View" in this chapter discusses the nationalization of certain oil fields in Venezuela.) The reverse situation in which property ownership is transferred from a nation to a private entity is called *privatization*.

The Overseas Private Investment Corporation (OPIC), a U.S. governmental agency, specializes in providing insurance for eligible U.S. investors against certain defined risks, including political risks such as expropriation. To be eligible for OPIC insurance, an investor must be (1) a U.S. citizen, (2) a U.S. partnership or corporation substantially owned by U.S. citizens, or (3) a foreign business at least 95% owned by a U.S. citizen or by a U.S. partnership or corporation. OPIC insures U.S. investors' interests only in "friendly" countries—that is, those that have investment-protection agreements (bilateral treaties of friendship, and navigation and commerce, or FNCs, or bilateral investment treaties, or BITs) with the United States. Coverage is also available for inconvertibility of foreign-currency remittances and losses due to hostile action during civil unrest.[31]

National Laws Directed at International Business Activities

Other national laws are designed to regulate international business activities.

Sanctions *Sanctions* may be imposed by one country (or a group of countries) against another country in an effort to influence that country's behavior. *Economic sanctions* can include boycotts of goods, refusal to maintain commercial relationships, tariffs, quotas, and other penalties. Sanctions may lead to so-called trade wars, when a country retaliates by imposing tariffs on the goods of the country that imposed sanctions on it.[32]

Embargoes An *embargo* is a special kind of sanction that is declared by a country or, more frequently, a group of countries against all commerce of another country. As with other sanctions, the goal is to force the embargoed country to change its behavior or policies. An embargo often isolates the affected country and is intended to create economic suffering. Well-known examples of international embargoes are the embargo against goods coming out of or going into South Africa, which was imposed during the 1980s because of the country's apartheid politics, the United Nations embargo imposed on Iraq after the invasion of Kuwait in 1990 that lasted until the invasion of Iraq in 2003 by the United States and its allies, and the European Union's oil embargo against Iran in response to the development of its nuclear program in January 2012.

---

30. Statute of the International Court of Justice, as annexed to the Charter of the United Nations, June 26, 1945, 59 Stat. 1031, T.S. No. 993, 3 Bevans 1153 (entered into force Oct. 24, 1945).

31. OPIC publishes a number of handbooks that describe its programs and services. They are available from the Information Officer, Overseas Private Investment Corporation, Office of External Affairs, 1100 New York Avenue NW, Washington, D.C. 20527.

32. Other forms of sanctions are *diplomatic sanctions* (removal or reduction of a diplomatic relationship) or *military sanctions* (military blockades or interventions).

Export Laws   Export laws are another important form of sanction. Almost every country has its own export laws.[33] Forty-one countries, among them the United States and most western European countries, participate in the Wassenaar Arrangement.[34] The Arrangement was created to promote greater transparency and responsibility regarding the transfer of armaments and sensitive *dual-use* goods and technologies that have both military and nonmilitary applications. It facilitates the voluntary exchange of information among member states and creates a forum to assess the scope of coordination of national export control policies. In December 2001, the Arrangement was extended in an effort to prevent terrorists and terrorist groups and organizations from acquiring armaments and sensitive dual-use items.

Extraterritorial Application of National Laws

Increasingly, countries are asserting the right to regulate activities that occur beyond their borders, a practice known as *extraterritoriality.* For example, both the United States and the European Union have asserted the right to apply their antitrust laws to the activities of U.S. firms, on the basis that the company's activities have adversely affected competition within their respective markets. See the "Inside Story" in Chapter 1 for a discussion of the EU's decision to block General Electric's acquisition of Honeywell International and the "Inside Story" in Chapter 16 for a summary of the U.S. and EU antitrust actions against Microsoft.

Certain product safety standards also have extraterritorial application. For example, pharmaceutical products exported to the United States must be produced in facilities that adhere to the manufacturing practices established by the U.S. Food and Drug Administration (FDA). Similarly, airplanes built overseas for use in U.S. airspace must be built according to Federal Aviation Administration (FAA) standards in FAA-certified facilities. Investment contracts for such export projects need to reflect the production standards required by U.S. law.

INTERNATIONAL PRIVACY LAWS

As discussed in Chapter 9, a number of countries regulate the exchange and transfer of identifiable personal information and data. The type and extent of the regulations, as well as the degree to which they are implemented and enforced, vary from country to country. Several countries have addressed the issue of the cross-border transfer of personal information and have taken steps to prevent the circumvention of existing national laws governing the storage, processing, and disclosure of such information through "off-shoring" of such activities.

It is not always easy for multinational companies to determine which privacy laws and regulations apply to their activities, or might apply, if they do business outside their home country, especially when they are offering products or services on the Internet. Although the answer to this question will always depend on the specific privacy-related practices of the company, a multinational company that collects personal information from residents of a foreign country is likely to fall under the privacy laws and regulations in that country because most national privacy laws and regulations are intended to protect the citizens and/or residents of the country in which the law or regulation was enacted.

FOREIGN CORRUPT PRACTICES ACT

Another key example of a national law with extraterritorial application is the U.S. Foreign Corrupt Practices Act. Following the discovery that more than 400 American corporations had paid bribes or made questionable payments abroad, the U.S. Congress enacted the Foreign Corrupt Practices Act (FCPA)[35] in 1977 as an amendment to the Securities Exchange Act of 1934 (the 1934 Act).

The FCPA prohibits any payment by a company, its employees, or its agents directly or indirectly to a foreign government official or a foreign political party for the purpose of improperly influencing government decisions in order to obtain business abroad. The statute is violated even if the bribe is only offered but never paid.

An exception is made for payments to low-ranking officials who merely expedite the nondiscretionary granting of a permit or license (*facilitating payments*). A second exception is made for payments to foreign businesses, as long as they are not acting as conduits for the money to pass to the foreign government.

As discussed in the "Inside Story" in this chapter, companies sometimes attempt carry out illegal practices through the use of agents or intermediaries. Intermediaries, who may include shipping and customs agents, vendors, and contractors, are under less direct control and supervision by the company making the payment. Accordingly, a company may find it easier to escape scrutiny for questionable activities procured through intermediaries than through its own employees. The FCPA attempts to stem this practice by establishing two sources of intermediary liability. First, the Act's anti-bribery provision makes it unlawful to make a payment to an intermediary knowing that all or part of such payment is going to be made to a foreign official for the purpose of influencing that official

---

33. Sometimes the participation of a country in different international conventions may lead to various layers of export controls in the country.

34. The Wassenaar Arrangement on Export Controls for Conventional Arms and Dual-Use Goods and Technologies was adopted in 1996 and updated in 2007.

35. 15 U.S.C. § 78dd-1 *et seq.*

in order to obtain business. Second, under the books and records provisions, companies are required to exercise due diligence and implement internal controls to ensure that payments to intermediaries are properly classified and are not disguised bribes.

Liability under the FCPA intermediary provisions is not reserved solely for companies engaging in willful misconduct. Companies seeking to avoid liability under the Act due to third-party conduct should establish an effective FCPA compliance program. This should include performing adequate due diligence before an intermediary relationship is created and having the intermediary certify that (1) it is not owned by a public official, (2) it understands and will comply with the FCPA, (3) it has not made improper payments in the past, and (4) it will not make improper payments in the future. Another precaution is to require that requests for use of agents, particularly in suspect countries, be reviewed by the legal or compliance department. Additionally, it may be wise to document any arrangements in writing and clearly identify the terms of any payments to be made. Such an agreement should also limit the intermediary's use of subcontractors. Once an intermediary relationship is established, managers should periodically investigate the intermediaries to confirm that no misconduct is occurring. Managers should also require detailed documentation for expense reimbursement, require annual FCPA certifications, and review requests for payments.[36]

Directors, officers, employees, or agents of a corporation who willfully violate the prohibited payments portion of the FCPA are subject to a $100,000 fine and up to five years in prison; the corporation can be fined up to $2 million or, if greater, twice its profits from the illegal activity.

The FCPA also imposes record-keeping requirements on all public companies that file periodic reports with the Securities and Exchange Commission (SEC) under the 1934 Act. This portion of the FCPA was designed to prevent companies from developing a slush fund and then accounting for questionable payments as legitimate business expenses. Even if a U.S. public company does not engage in international trade, it still must comply with the FCPA's record-keeping requirements.

Under these requirements, each corporation must keep records that accurately reflect the dispositions of its assets and must implement internal controls to ensure that its transactions are completed as authorized by management. Periodic reports must be filed. Failure to maintain the appropriate records and procedures is a violation, whether or not there is payment of a bribe. The record-keeping provisions of the FCPA do not contain any specific penalties, but record-keeping violations may give rise to civil and criminal liability under the Securities Act of 1933

and the Securities Exchange Act of 1934 (discussed in Chapters 21 and 22).

Since 1977, when the United States became the first major industrial country to ban bribes, it has encouraged other countries to adopt similar prohibitions. The United States scored a major victory when it helped persuade the Organization for Economic Co-operation and Development (OECD) and its members to adopt the international convention on bribery (discussed further in Chapter 2).

Britain's Bribery Act of 2011 gave the Serious Fraud Office (SFO) the authority to prosecute not only individuals who pay or receive bribes but also their employer if the firm failed to adopt "adequate procedures" to prevent bribery. A whistleblower identified only as a "BP employee" triggered both internal BP and SFO investigations by sending a letter in March 2012 to BP CEO Robert Dudley and the SFO, alleging that a senior BP employee in the tanker chartering division had been receiving cash bribes from a supplier for more than five years.

INTERNATIONAL BANKING REGIME

In an effort to encourage common banking standards and formulate broad supervisory guidelines and oversight practices at foreign banks, the Basel Committee was established in 1974. The Committee's members include Argentina, Australia, Belgium, Brazil, Canada, China, France, Germany, Hong Kong SAR, India, Indonesia, Italy, Japan, Korea, Luxembourg, Mexico, the Netherlands, Russia, Saudi Arabia, Singapore, South Africa, Spain, Sweden, Switzerland, Turkey, the United Kingdom, and the United States. The Committee does not possess any formal supranational supervisory authority, and its conclusions do not have legal force. Rather, it formulates broad supervisory standards and guidelines and recommends statements of best practice in the expectation that individual member states will take steps to implement them.

In response to the financial crisis of 2008, the Committee and its oversight body (the Group of Governors and Heads of Supervision) moved aggressively to develop sound supervisory standards worldwide. In January 2012, the Committee adopted new global standards (called "Basel III") to address both firm-specific risks and broader, system-wide risks that can build up across the banking sector over time.[37] These measures are designed to improve the banking sector's ability to absorb shocks arising from financial and economic stress, improve risk management and governance, and strengthen banks' transparency and disclosures.

---

36. David Isaak, *FCPA Compliance—Navigating the Minefield of Intermediaries*, CURRENTS: INT'L TRADE L.J. 26 (Winter 2008).

37. Basel Committee on Banking Supervision, *History of the Basel Committee and Its Membership*, BANK FOR INT'L SETTLEMENTS, *available at* http://www.bis.org/bcbs/history.htm (last visited Feb. 10, 2012).

U.S. TRADE REGIME

U.S. trade laws are generally designed to restrict or to facilitate imports and exports. Imports are restricted primarily by means of *tariffs* (government fees an importer must pay when importing merchandise from another country) and quantitative limitations such as *quotas*. Conversely, imports may be facilitated through exemption from U.S. tariffs. Exports are controlled by means of *export licenses*. Exports may be facilitated by federal subsidies, tax breaks, and other legislation, including section 301 of the Trade Act of 1974 (Trade Act) (discussed later in this chapter).

The Role of Government Branches and Agencies in Trade Relations

Trade laws are enacted by Congress pursuant to the Commerce Clause of the U.S. Constitution, and they are administered by the federal government and its administrative agencies. Congress has the power to regulate all aspects of foreign commerce, including imports and exports, foreign investment, licensing of technology, and other commercial activities.

The Role of the President

As chief executive, the President has broad power to administer U.S. trade laws and negotiate trade agreements, but the President cannot regulate trade without congressional delegation or approval.

The President's Power to Restrict Trade

Over the years, Congress has authorized the President to regulate or restrict trade and other economic activity when necessary to protect the U.S. national security, foreign policy, or economy. The International Emergency Economic Powers Act of 1977[38] limited the President's authority to restrict trade and other commercial transactions to instances when a national emergency has been declared in response to an "unusual and extraordinary threat, which has its source in whole or substantial part outside the United States, to the national security, foreign policy or economy of the United States."

The economic sanctions imposed under these laws are administered by the Office of Foreign Assets Control in the Department of the Treasury, which issues appropriate regulations. To varying degrees, the regulations apply not only to transactions in the United States, but also to transactions by foreign affiliates of U.S. companies and to transactions abroad involving U.S. property. The application of the regulations to foreign subsidiaries or operations of U.S. companies has caused considerable

"What about business—which branch is that?"

difficulty, particularly for companies subjected to conflicting requirements imposed by foreign governments on their foreign affiliates.[39]

Trade Promotion Authority   Another way for the President to influence U.S. international trade is the so-called Trade Promotion Authority or *fast-track negotiating authority. Trade Promotion Authority* allows the President to negotiate trade agreements and then submit them for an up or down vote by Congress with no amendments permitted. This authority includes mechanisms for the negotiation, consideration, and implementation of trade agreements. Although Congress gave the President fast-track authority in the U.S. Trade Promotion Authority Act of 2002,[40] it expired in July 2007. The Senate refused to extend this authority to President Obama in September 2011.[41]

Administrative Agencies

The agencies primarily responsible for administration of the trade laws are the U.S. Trade Representative (USTR), the Department of Commerce, the Department of State, the Department of the Treasury, the U.S. International Trade

38. 50 U.S.C. §§ 1701–06.

39. *See, e.g.,* Dresser Indus., Inc. v. Baldrige, 549 F. Supp. 108 (D.D.C. 1982) (French subsidiary of U.S. company unsuccessful in enjoining application of sanctions by U.S. Department of Commerce for failure to honor U.S. prohibition on exports of certain types of equipment to the Soviet Union even though French subsidiaries had been ordered by the French government to honor prior contractual commitments to ship the equipment).

40. 19 U.S.C. §§ 3803–05.

41. Doug Palmer, *Senate Rejects Trade Promotion Authority for Obama,* REUTERS, Sept. 20, 2011, *available at* http://www.reuters.com/article/2011/09/20/us-usa-trade-congress-idUSTRE78J6FU20110920.

Commission, and U.S. Customs and Border Protection (which is part of the Department of Homeland Security).

The USTR, with the assistance of the other agencies, is responsible for the development of U.S. trade policy and the negotiation of trade agreements with other countries. The USTR makes all policy decisions concerning the operation of these agreements. The Department of Commerce is generally responsible for implementing U.S. trade policy, enforcing certain import relief laws and export controls, and promoting U.S. exports. The Department of State administers controls on munitions exports and defends U.S. economic interests through U.S. embassies abroad.

The Department of the Treasury administers embargoes imposed on U.S. trade with countries such as Iran, Cuba, and North Korea. The International Trade Commission is an independent agency with a variety of responsibilities, including investigating the effect of imports on U.S. industries. U.S. Customs and Border Protection enforces all U.S. customs laws and import restrictions and collects U.S. tariffs. Other agencies, such as the U.S. Department of Agriculture, administer restrictions on U.S. trade falling in their particular areas of responsibility; in this, they are assisted by U.S. Customs and Border Protection.

The Interagency Committee   The President makes trade policy decisions based on the recommendations of an interagency committee, headed by the USTR. In addition to the agencies listed above, the committee includes members from the Department of Labor, the Council of Economic Advisers, and other agencies interested in trade policy. Private interests are typically given the opportunity to express their views to any of these agencies or to the interagency committee directly. For example, tariffs on a particular product are rarely changed without first consulting the affected industry. Government officials at all the agencies are generally receptive to requests and comments from U.S. companies. In many cases, public hearings are held before decisions are made.

Export-Import Bank   The Export-Import Bank of the United States (Ex-Im Bank) was created to provide financing for the purchase of U.S. exports. The Ex-Im Bank is the U.S. government's response to foreign governments' export subsidies. By offering financing at below-market interest rates, the Ex-Im Bank allows U.S. exporters to compete with foreign companies. For example, in 2011 the Ex-Im Bank approved an $805 million loan to South Africa's state-owned electric company to build massive newer coal-fired power plants.[42]

Laws Affecting Exports

Several U.S. laws serve to facilitate or, in some cases, control exports.

Export Administration Act

The Export Administration Act of 1979[43] (EAA) was the primary restriction on U.S. exports until it expired for the last time in August 2001.[44] A new version of the EAA was passed by the Senate in 2001, but the House blocked it because of concern that the new version weakened controls on potentially dangerous technologies.[45] It authorized the Secretary of Commerce to prohibit exports when necessary to protect national security, carry out U.S. foreign policy, enforce U.S. nuclear nonproliferation policy, or prevent the export of goods that are in short supply. However, the export licensing system created under the authority of the EAA has been continued under the International Emergency Economics Powers Act (IEEPA), pursuant to a presidential executive order.

Export restrictions apply to exports of technology (referred to as technical data) as well as goods. The export restrictions that have had the most serious adverse consequences for U.S. exporters competing for business abroad are those that control high technology and its products. The Omnibus Trade and Competitiveness Act of 1988,[46] reflecting the importance attached to the trade deficit and the need to promote U.S. exports, removed many controls on exports, particularly to friendly countries.

U.S. export controls are enforced by a system of export licenses. Certain categories of commodities and technical data may not be exported without an export license from the Commerce Department's Bureau of Export Administration. The Bureau decides whether to grant an export license based on a number of factors, including the nature of the item to be exported, the country to which it is to be shipped, the foreign consignee, and the use to which the item will be put.

U.S. export restrictions apply not only to exports from the United States but also to many reexports of U.S.-origin goods and technology to third countries by other countries and to exports from other countries of certain foreign-made articles that are direct products of U.S. technology. In addition, the transfer of technical data to a foreign citizen in the United States is generally considered to be an export, which means that an export license is required. Such transfers include verbal exchanges of technology on U.S. soil and visits by foreign nationals to U.S. plants.

---

42. Constance E. Bagley, Haris Aqeel & Eva T. Zlotnicka, *South Africa's Energy Crisis Reconciling Economic Growth with Environmental Protection* (Yale Sch. of Mgmt. Case No. 11-015, 2011).

43. 50 U.S.C.A. app. § 2401 *et seq.*

44. IAN F. FERGUSSON, CONG. RESEARCH SERV., RL31832, EXPORT ADMINISTRATION ACT: EVOLUTION, PROVISION, AND DEBATE (last updated July 15, 2009), *available at* http://fas.org/sgp/crs/secrecy/RL31832.pdf.

45. *Id.*

46. 19 U.S.C. § 2905(a).

Export Administration Regulations (EARs)

The Bureau of Industry and Security (BIS) in the Department of Commerce issues Export Administration Regulations (EARs) that apply to shipments of nonmilitary and dual-use goods and technology.[47]

The Arms Export Control Act

The Arms Export Control Act,[48] which authorizes the U.S. Secretary of State to prohibit exports of munitions and munitions technology from the United States, is administered by the Office of Munitions Control of the State Department, which issues the International Traffic in Arms Regulations (ITARs) and operates a licensing system similar to that of the Commerce Department, based on the United States Munitions List.[49] The Commerce and State Departments both issue advisory opinions to exporters concerning the applicability of export controls to specific transactions.

Penalties for Violations of Export Regulations

There are substantial criminal and civil penalties for violations of U.S. export regulations. For munitions export control violations, the statute authorizes a maximum criminal penalty of $1 million per violation and, for an individual person, up to ten years in prison. In addition, munitions violations can result in the imposition of a maximum fine of $500,000 per violation of the ITARs. Currently, for dual-use export control violations, criminal penalties can reach a maximum of $500,000 per violation and, for an individual person, up to ten years in prison. Dual-use violations can also be subject to civil fines up to $12,000 per violation.[50]

In 2007, ITT Corporation was fined $100 million for violating the Arms Export Control Act in connection with the transfer of classified materials (including information about night vision goggles) without proper authority to engineers in China, Singapore, and the United Kingdom as part of ITT's outsourcing program. ITT was given the option of spending half of the fine on the development of advanced night vision technology, in which case the U.S. government would receive the rights to all technology that ITT developed and even be allowed to share this technology with ITT's competitors.[51]

In 2009, seventy-two-year-old John Reece Roth, a former University of Tennessee professor, was convicted of violating the Arms Export Control Act for exporting technical information relating to a U.S. Air Force contract to research and develop specialized plasma technology for use in Unmanned Air Vehicles (UAVs) to a citizen in China. He was sentenced to four years in prison.[52]

Section 301

Section 301 of the Trade Act of 1974 (section 301)[53] is the principal U.S. statute addressing unfair foreign practices affecting U.S. exports of goods or services. It may be used to enforce U.S. rights under international trade agreements and to respond to unreasonable, unjustifiable, or discriminatory foreign government practices that burden or restrict U.S. commerce. Specifically, section 301 authorizes the USTR to investigate alleged unfair practices of foreign governments that impede U.S. exports of goods and services. Subject to certain exceptions, the USTR has discretionary authority to take action in response to foreign government practices if it determines that an act or policy (1) violates trade agreements with the United States or (2) is unjustifiable (that is, in violation of the international legal rights of the United States) and burdens or restricts U.S. commerce.

The Omnibus Trade and Competitiveness Act of 1988 created a program known as *Super 301*, which required the USTR to draw up a list of the foreign governments whose practices pose the most significant barriers to U.S. exports and to immediately commence section 301 investigations with respect to these practices. Similarly, under the *Special 301 provisions* in U.S. trade law, the USTR identifies those countries that deny adequate and effective protection for intellectual property rights or deny fair and equitable market access for persons that rely on intellectual property protection. Countries that have the most onerous or egregious practices and whose practices have the greatest adverse impact on the relevant U.S. products are designated as "priority foreign countries" and are subject to section 301 investigations. Other countries with less severe problems protecting intellectual property rights are placed on a "watch list" or "priority watch list" and are monitored closely.[54]

For example, China has been on the priority watch list as a result of concerns about its respect for intellectual property rights. In March 2011, China's Sinovel, the world's second-largest wind turbine manufacturer, abruptly refused

47. See the EAR section of the website of the Bureau of Industry and Security at http://www.bis.doc.gov/policiesandregulations/index.htm#ear for more information.

48. 22 U.S.C. §§ 2751–96.

49. 22 C.F.R. pt. 121.

50. *An Overview of U.S. Export Controls*, EXPORT CONTROL, *available at* http://www.exportcontrol.org/links/1373c.aspx (last visited Jan. 14, 2012).

51. *ITT Fined $100 Million for Illegal Exports*, CNNMONEY.COM, Mar. 27, 2007, http://money.cnn.com/2007/03/27/news/international/itt_export/index.htm.

52. Press Release, FBI, Former University of Tennessee Professor John Reece Roth Sentenced to 48 Months in Prison for Illegally Exporting Military Research Technical Data (July 1, 2009), *available at* http://www.fbi.gov/knoxville/press-releases/2009/kx070109.html.

53. 19 U.S.C. § 2411.

54. U.S. INTERNATIONAL TRADE COMMISSION, THE YEAR IN TRADE: OPERATION OF THE TRADE AGREEMENTS PROGRAM DURING 1998, 50TH REPORT 87, 91 (1998).

shipments of wind turbine electrical systems and control software from American Superconductor, resulting in a 70% reduction of the firm's revenues and a loss of more than $700 million in undelivered components on existing contracts.[55] Subsequently, evidence emerged that Sinovel had promised $1.5 million to Dejan Karabasevic, a Serbian employee of American Superconductor in Austria, in exchange for American Superconductor's trade secrets. Karabasevic confessed to the crime and is now serving time in an Austrian prison. American Superconductor has filed multiple lawsuits against Sinovel, seeking more than $1.2 billion in damages, cease and desist orders, and copyright remedies.

In his 2012 State of the Union address, President Obama announced the creation of the Fair Trade Enforcement Unit to end unfair trade practices that hinder U.S. growth.[56] To enforce fair global trade, the Unit will organize a global team of investigators and resources, conduct more import inspections to prevent counterfeit/unsafe goods from coming to the United States, and ensure that no foreign company has a financing advantage over American manufacturers. The likely focus of the Unit will be on China's trade practices and the trade deficit with China, which has cost the United States 2.8 million jobs over the last decade.

Laws Affecting Imports

The United States has various laws limiting or otherwise regulating imports.

Tariffs

Tariffs are the basic tool for limiting imports to protect domestic industries. Today, most tariffs are *ad valorem tariffs*, meaning that the importer must pay a percentage of the value of the imported merchandise. For instance, a 10% tariff on a shipment of imports valued at $10,000 will result in a *duty*, that is, a required payment, of $1,000.

U.S. tariffs are established by federal law and can be changed only by statute or by administrative action authorized by statute. Congress frequently changes U.S. tariffs. In addition, Congress has periodically delegated to the President the authority to reduce U.S. tariffs in exchange for tariff concessions by other nations. Congress has also delegated to the President the power to increase tariffs temporarily in order to protect domestic industries in certain specified situations.

The Harmonized Tariff Schedule   The United States has accepted an internationally harmonized tariff system.

Current tariffs are found in a document entitled the *Harmonized Tariff Schedule of the United States (HTS).*[57] The HTS lists the tariffs on goods imposed by Congress and by the President, based on their country of origin.

For each product category, there are two basic rates of duty. One column applies to most countries (column 1), and the second applies to several less favored countries, such as Cuba and North Korea (column 2). These columns reflect tariffs imposed by Congress or negotiated by the President. U.S. tariffs vary not only by the country of origin but also by the article's *tariff classification*, that is, where it is best described in the HTS.

The duty paid on an imported article depends on the value assigned to it by U.S. Customs and Border Protection, that is, on the *customs valuation* of the article. The lower the valuation, the lower the duty. The general rule of customs valuation in the United States is that the value of an article for customs purposes is the *transaction value*, which is the price indicated on the sales invoice.

U.S. customs laws are administered by U.S. Customs and Border Protection. Its headquarters are in Washington, D.C., but the agency has a district office at every U.S. port of entry. Tariff rulings by the district offices can be appealed to headquarters and then to the U.S. Court of International Trade. Appeals from this court are to the U.S. Court of Appeals for the Federal Circuit and then to the U.S. Supreme Court.

Tariff Preferences   Pursuant to authority delegated by Congress, the President has established preferential tariffs for imports from certain developing countries. The most important are embodied in the *Generalized System of Preferences (GSP).*

The GSP, which was agreed to multilaterally, is a program developed by the industrialized countries to assist developing nations by improving their ability to export. The GSP has been used to integrate developing countries into the international trade system and to encourage beneficiary countries to eliminate or reduce barriers to trade and to enforce intellectual property rights. Under the GSP, the President has designated certain products as eligible for duty-free treatment if they are produced in developing countries designated as eligible beneficiaries of the program.[58]

An eligible product receives duty-free treatment only if 35% or more of the value of the product was added in an eligible country. There are also limitations on the volume of eligible articles that may be imported from a single country. If the volume limitation is exceeded, the product is automatically removed from the category of eligible imports from that country.

If a country is found to be sufficiently competitive, the President can remove it from the program, either entirely

55. Jonathan Weisman, *U.S. to Share Cautionary Tale of Trade Secret Theft to Chinese Official*, N.Y. TIMES, Feb. 14, 2012.

56. Kerri Shannon, *Obama's Trade Enforcement Unit and the Looming Trade War with China*, MONEY MORNING, Jan. 25, 2012, *available at* http://moneymorning.com/2012/01/25/obamas-trade-enforcement-unit-and-the-looming-trade-war-with-china/.

57. Published by the U.S. International Trade Commission.

58. 19 U.S.C. §§ 2461–66.

or with respect to individual products. This process is referred to as "graduation." For example, the Republic of Trinidad and Tobago was graduated from the program effective 2010 because, as of 2007, the World Bank classified it as a "high income" country. Countries can also be removed from the GSP program for policy reasons, such as failure to protect intellectual property rights. The program is reviewed annually to determine which countries and products should be removed from or added to the program. The program is administered for the President by the USTR.

Import Relief Laws

In a series of laws, known collectively as the *import relief laws*, Congress has authorized the President to raise U.S. tariffs on specified products and to provide other forms of import protection to U.S. industries. These laws vary as to the nature of the unfair practice (if any) to which they are directed, the degree of injury required in order to obtain relief, the nature of the relief authorized, the agencies authorized to provide the relief, and the amount of discretion given to the President in determining whether to grant relief.

Section 201 Section 201 of the Trade Act of 1974 (*section 201*)[59] provides for temporary relief to domestic industries seriously injured by increasing imports, regardless of whether unfair practices are involved. It is sometimes called the *fair trade law*. The relief is designed to give the U.S. industry a few years (normally no more than five) to adjust to import competition.

The U.S. International Trade Commission (ITC) investigates petitions filed by U.S. industries. If the ITC makes an affirmative finding of injury from imports, it recommends specific import relief, such as higher duties or quantitative limits on imports. The President must provide the recommended relief unless he or she finds that it would not be in the national economic interest, as defined in the law. Because import relief always has economic costs, such as inflationary effects, the President may decide not to provide relief.

The Omnibus Trade and Competitiveness Act of 1988[60] encourages petitioning industries to submit plans illustrating how they would use section 201 relief to adjust to import competition. It further provides that the ITC should recommend relief that not only addresses the injury caused by imports but also facilitates the domestic industry's adjustment to import competition. As a complement to that, the law provides that the President can grant either import relief or other appropriate relief within his or her legal authority. Thus, the law encourages making relief conditional on the ability of the

domestic industry to meet the competition or to transfer its resources elsewhere.

Relationship Between WTO Dispute Settlement Process and U.S. Trade Laws

Whether U.S. trade laws like sections 201 and 301 of the Trade Act of 1974 give the President (acting through the U.S. Trade Representative) the ability to take unilateral action to penalize countries with trade practices that threaten American interests, without going through the dispute settlement process established by the World Trade Organization (WTO), is a matter of some debate. (The WTO, which will be discussed in detail later in the chapter, is an international institution that regulates global trade.) On their face, the U.S. laws seem to allow for this result, and the legislative history of the U.S. statute implementing the Uruguay Round and creating the WTO suggests that Congress did not intend for the WTO dispute resolution process to displace the powers vested in the USTR. The implementing legislation includes the following language:

> Sec. 102(a) RELATIONSHIP OF AGREEMENTS TO UNITED STATES LAW—(1) UNITED STATES LAW TO PREVAIL IN CONFLICT—No provision of any of the Uruguay Round Agreements, nor the application of any such provision to any person or circumstance, that is inconsistent with any law of the United States shall have effect. (2) CONSTRUCTION.— Nothing in this Act shall be construed—(A) to amend or modify any law of the United States . . . (B) to limit any authority conferred under any law of the United States.

On the other hand, the United States has generally attempted to use Trade Act powers after the WTO has authorized such actions. For example, the President's Statement of Administrative Action, issued by President Clinton, provided that the United States will use section 301 only in a WTO "compliant manner."

Nonetheless, the United States has not always awaited WTO authorization before taking action under the Trade Act. For example, the United States and Canada imposed sanctions on the European Union in response to its rules on hormone-treated meat imports since 1999. Previously, the European Union had outright banned meat that had been treated with hormones. In 1998, the WTO found that these rules were inconsistent with WTO rules and authorized the United States and Canada to impose sanctions comprising a 100% duty on EU imports to a value of $116.8 million. In 2003, the EU adopted new rules that ban the use of one of six hormones used in raising cattle—oestradiol 17—after scientific studies showed that it promotes cancer and harms genes and substantial evidence showed that it is harmful to human health. In response, the United States and Canada unilaterally imposed sanctions against the EU without first testing the legality of the new rules at the WTO. In 2008, the WTO condemned these actions as a clear violation of WTO

---

59. 19 U.S.C. § 2251.

60. 15 U.S.C. §§ 78dd-1, 78dd-2, 78ff.

rules.[61] Over the years, the EU has commissioned studies to address the scientific basis of its ban on hormone-treated meat and has reaffirmed its position. In January 2009, the USTR announced higher tariffs on some EU products, which the EU claimed constituted an "escalation" of the dispute and "more punitive" than the existing sanctions. Following a series of negotiations, in May 2009 the EU and the United States finally agreed on a settlement to resolve the long-standing trade dispute.[62] In March 2011, the EU and Canada reached a temporary solution to the beef dispute: Canada agreed to suspend trade sanctions, and the EU agreed to increase market access and opportunities for beef imports.[63]

The Antidumping Law   The antidumping law, codified in the Tariff Act of 1930, as amended,[64] is the most frequently used import relief law. If a U.S. industry is materially injured by imports of a product being *dumped* in the United States (that is, sold below the current selling price in the exporter's home market or below the exporter's cost of production), then the law imposes an antidumping duty on the dumped product. The amount of the duty is equal to the amount of the *dumping margin*, that is, the difference between the U.S. price and the price in the exporting country. If the International Trade Commission determines that dumping has occurred and caused material injury, the Commerce Department is required to impose duties on the imports sold at less than fair value.

Section 337   Section 337 of the Tariff Act of 1930 (*section 337*)[65] provides that if a U.S. industry is injured (or there is a restraint or monopolization of trade in the United States) by reason of unfair acts in the importation of articles into the United States, an order must be issued requiring the exporters and importers to cease the unfair acts or, if necessary, excluding imports of the offending articles from all sources. This law applies to unfair competition of all kinds not covered in other import relief laws, but it is most commonly used in cases involving patent or trademark infringement. Relief is mandatory unless the President disapproves the ITC's decision, which seldom happens.

The Omnibus Trade and Competitiveness Act of 1988 eliminated the requirement to show economic injury in cases involving intellectual property rights (infringement of patents, trademarks, and copyrights). The Act affected most section 337 cases and made it significantly easier for U.S. companies to obtain relief under this statute.

The Buy American Act   Under the Buy American Act,[66] federal agencies, when procuring supplies and equipment, must give a preference to products made in the United States unless their price is a certain percentage higher than the price of the equivalent foreign product. Products are deemed to be American made, and therefore eligible for the preference, if they are manufactured in the United States and at least 50% of the components are American made.

As explained later in this chapter, preferences to domestic industry in government procurement are a common form of nontariff barrier to imports that was addressed in one of the GATT codes. Pursuant to the code (the Agreement on Government Procurement),[67] many U.S. agencies have joined foreign agencies in eliminating this preference. Defense-related articles are not subject to the agreement, however, and still receive the Buy American Act preference.

INTERNATIONAL TRADE REGIMES

In order to achieve its trade goals, both with respect to the regulation of imports and the facilitation of exports, the United States engages its trade partners in a wide array of bilateral, regional, and multilateral trade agreements. Bilateral agreements tend to be limited in subject matter, covering matters such as tariffs, taxes, and intellectual property rights. Several of the regional and multilateral agreements, such as the North American Free Trade Agreement and the World Trade Organization, have their own dispute settlement mechanisms, which were negotiated as part of each agreement.

North American Free Trade Agreement

The trilateral North American Free Trade Agreement (NAFTA)[68] provides for the gradual elimination of all barriers to trade among the United States, Canada, and Mexico and for the free cross-border movement of goods and services among the territories of the three signatories. Designed to improve all three countries' economies and to benefit 390 million consumers with lower-priced goods and increased investment opportunities, NAFTA established the world's largest free trade zone by covered area. Congress approved the agreement on November 17, 1993, and it went into effect on January 1,

61. Press Release, World Trade Org., WTO Condemns US and Canada Sanctions on EU Goods in Hormone-Treated Meat Dispute (Mar. 31, 2008), *available at* http://trade.ec.europa.eu/doclib/docs/2008/april/tradoc_138477.pdf.

62. RENÉE JOHNSON & CHARLES E. HANRAHAN, CONG. RESEARCH SERV., RL40449, THE U.S.-EU BEEF HORMONE DISPUTE (Dec. 6, 2010), *available at* http://www.nationalaglawcenter.org/assets/crs/R40449.pdf.

63. Press Release, European Comm'n on Trade, EU Commission and Canada Reach Provisional Solution in Beef Dispute (Mar. 17, 2011), *available at* http://trade.ec.europa.eu/doclib/press/index.cfm?id=685.

64. 19 U.S.C. §§ 1673–77.

65. 19 U.S.C. § 1337.

66. 41 U.S.C. §§ 10a–d.

67. 18 I.L.M. 1052 (1979).

68. North American Free Trade Agreement, U.S.-Can.-Mex., Dec. 17, 1992, 32 I.L.M. 605 (1993).

1994, at which time the United States eliminated the majority of its tariffs on Mexican goods. Mexico had eliminated all tariffs on U.S. capital goods by 2003.

In addition to eliminating its custom duties, each country is required to accord national treatment to the goods of the other nations in accordance with Article III of GATT (discussed below). The agreement also substantially reduced the barriers to government procurement and has effectively resulted in totally open procurement.

NAFTA prohibits new restrictions on investment and on trade in services among the three countries. It includes major provisions relating to specific industries, such as agriculture, telecommunications, and energy. In addition, it established special rules of origin to ensure that only products originating in the United States, Canada, or Mexico enjoy duty-free treatment. Certificates of origin are required on all goods being exported among the three countries to certify that the good qualifies as an "originating" good.

The pact also provides for the adequate protection and enforcement of intellectual property rights and attempts to ensure that these rights do not become barriers to trade. Each country was required to implement several international agreements regarding intellectual property rights, such as the Berne Convention for the Protection of Literary and Artistic Works (dealing with copyrights) and the Paris Convention for the Protection of Industrial Property Rights (dealing with patents).

NAFTA explicitly protects the continued enforceability of U.S. environmental regulations and includes a mechanism for sanctions if Mexico fails to enforce its own environmental laws. In addition, a NAFTA side agreement set up a three-nation mechanism, the Commission for Environmental Cooperation, to address environmental disputes. Any country or private interest group that believes that a nation is not enforcing its environmental laws may complain. If the Commission determines that a violation has occurred, it can impose a fine of up to $20 million or impose trade sanctions on the offending country. Through June 2011, seventy-six citizen submissions had been filed.[69] Since 1992, Mexico has enacted a number of major environmental statutes and numerous regulations (often modeled on U.S. environmental laws) and has dramatically improved its environmental enforcement regime.[70] Even so, some environmentalists have faulted the Commission for not demanding more, especially in the area of transboundary cleanup and remediation.[71]

The North American Agreement on Labor Cooperation, a side agreement that established National Administrative Offices (NAOs) in the United States, Mexico, and Canada to hear complaints about worker abuse, has had little impact.[72] Although NAOs are restricted to reviewing and issuing a report on the complaint,[73] they can request the establishment of an Evaluation Committee of Experts (ECE) to further analyze the matter. If a matter is not resolved by the ECE, the disputing parties can request consultations and the formation of arbitration panels.[74] Human rights organizations and U.S. unions have argued that violations relating to freedom of association, collective bargaining, and strikes should also give rise to fines and trade sanctions, not just the high-level ministerial consultations called for in the side agreement.[75]

When one of the parties to NAFTA violates the treaty, an impartial arbiter may approve punitive sanctions against the offending country. An example was the sanctions levied by Mexico against the United States in response to U.S. limits on the use of Mexican trucks and drivers to transport goods from Mexico into the interior of the United States. Even though a successful pilot program between 2007 and 2009 showed that U.S. concerns about lower safety standards on Mexican rigs were overblown because Mexican and U.S. trucks had similar safety records, Congress killed the program in 2009 in response to strong objections from the Teamsters Union.

An impartial arbiter found that the United States had violated NAFTA and granted Mexico permission to levy punitive tariffs on $2.4 billion in U.S. exports. In July 2011, the United States and Mexico reached an agreement to end the eighteen-year dispute. Mexican trucks are now permitted to travel throughout the United States, subject to strict monitoring to ensure that they do not operate dangerously when inside the United States, and Mexico is phasing out its tariffs. The deal enables more efficient and cheaper cross-border shipping and is expected to create jobs and increase exports.[76]

Efforts to build on NAFTA by creating a Free Trade Area of the Americas (FTAA) have been stalled since 2005.

The World Trade Organization (WTO) and the GATT

Besides negotiating bilateral and regional preferential agreements, the United States participates in the World Trade Organization (WTO), the successor to the General

---

69. *Article 14: Submissions on Enforcement Matters*, COMM'N FOR ENVTL. COOPERATION, June 13, 2011.

70. *NAFTA at 10: Environmentalists Have Mixed Feelings*, CHARLES STEWART MOTT FOUND., Sept. 1, 2004, *available at* http://www.mott.org/recentnews/news/2004/nafta.aspx.

71. Joel Millman, *Nafta's Do-Gooder Side Deals Disappoint*, WALL ST. J., Oct. 15, 1997, at A19.

72. ROBERT G. FINBOW, LIMITS OF REGIONALISM: NAFTA'S LABOUR ACCORD 253 (2006).

73. Brianna Busch, *Free Trade Agreements and Labor Considerations After the NAALC: How the U.S.–Chile Free Trade Agreement Created a Faulty Template*, 4 INT'L BUS. L. REV. 59, 65f (2004).

74. Gary Clyde Hufbauer & Jeffrey J. Schott, NAFTA REVISITED: ACHIEVEMENTS AND CHALLENGES 125 (2005).

75. *Labor Rights and Trade: Guidance for the United States in Trade Accord Negotiations* (Human Rights Watch Briefing Paper), HUMAN RIGHTS WATCH, Oct. 30. 2002, *available at* http://www.hrw.org/press/2002/10/laborrights-bck.htm (last visited Sept. 22, 2008).

76. Editorial, *Lessons from a Trade Spat with Mexico*, WASH. POST, July 9, 2011.

Agreement on Tariffs and Trade (GATT), entered into in 1994. The WTO came into existence on January 1, 1995,[77] after the conclusion of the Uruguay Round of GATT multilateral trade negotiations.

The WTO oversees all of the agreements reached in the Uruguay Round,[78] and it is the principal multilateral mechanism devoted to the regulation of international trade. As of 2011, the WTO had 157 members, with more than twenty-five other countries waiting to join.[79]

The GATT has had a profound effect on world trade.[80] Tariffs today are, on average, a small fraction of what they were when the GATT was formed in 1947. The Uruguay Round, the eighth in the history of the GATT, was the most ambitious GATT round ever held. The 117 nations represented at the Uruguay Round agreed to reduce their tariffs by an average of one-third over six years. In addition, agricultural tariffs were reduced by 36% in industrial nations and by 24% in developing nations. For the first time, agriculture, services, textiles, and investment services were covered by international rules of fair trade, as was the protection of intellectual property rights. The agreement, also for the first time, protected the right of service-sector companies to operate on foreign soil free of discriminatory laws.

The WTO agreement requires member states to participate in the Multilateral Trade Agreements, including (1) fourteen Agreements on Trade in Goods (including GATT 1994), (2) the General Agreement on Trade in Services (GATS), (3) the Agreement on Trade-Related Aspects of Intellectual Property Rights (TRIPS), (4) the Understanding on Rules and Procedures Governing the Settlement of Disputes (DSU), and (5) the Trade Policy Review Mechanism (TPRM). These agreements are binding on all members of the WTO. In 2001, the WTO initiated the Doha Development Round to further lower trade barriers around the world. Key issues included cutting rich countries' farm subsidies and providing a special safeguard mechanism (SSM) to protect poor farmers by allowing a country to protect its farmers by imposing special tariffs on agricultural imports in the event of a surge of these imports. While the United States claimed that the SSM levels had been set too low, India and China refused to agree to a higher threshold.[81] Other unresolved issues included

provisions giving special and differential treatment to developing countries and problems that developing countries are having in implementing current trade obligations.[82]

One Doha success involved balancing the interests of pharmaceutical companies in developed countries that hold patents on medicines and the public health needs of developing countries. In 2003, WTO members approved a decision that offered an interim waiver under the TRIPS Agreement to allow a member country to export pharmaceuticals made under compulsory licenses to the least developed countries and certain other members.

After Russia, Montenegro, and Samoa joined the WTO as full members in 2011, Robert Sturdy of the European Parliament's Trade Delegation commented: "Although it is now clear that a deal surrounding the Doha Development Round is dead, it is encouraging to see that the WTO is still making progress on multilateral level."[83]

Basic Principles of the WTO

Six basic principles undergird the GATT and its successor, the WTO: (1) most favored nation treatment, (2) bound tariffs, (3) national treatment, (4) gradual freer trade through negotiation, (5) fair competition, and (6) encouragement of development and economic reform.[84]

Most Favored Nation Treatment

The *most favored nation (MFN)* principle is the foundation of the current world trading system. Each WTO member must accord to all other member countries tariff treatment no less favorable than it provides to any other country. In other words, if the United States agrees to lower its tariff on imports of a product from a certain country, it must grant the same treatment to all other WTO members. (The Generalized System of Preferences and other preferential agreements discussed above are exceptions to the MFN principle and are authorized by the GATT.) The theory behind the MFN principle is that world trade will be enhanced if countries avoid discriminating among themselves and creating trading blocs that expand trade within the blocs but restrict trade among them.

The GATT encourages regional economic integration and participation in free trade areas and customs unions, however. A *free trade area* is created when a group of states reduce or eliminate tariffs among themselves but maintain their own individual tariffs as to other states.

77. Agreement Establishing the World Trade Organization, Apr. 15, 1994, 33 I.L.M. 1132 (1994).

78. Final Act Embodying the Results of the Uruguay Round of Multilateral Trade Negotiations, Apr. 15, 1994, 33 I.L.M. 1140 (1994).

79. Editorial, *Russia as a WTO Member*, JAPAN TIMES, Jan. 16, 2012, *available at* http://www.japantimes.co.jp/text/ed20120116a1.html.

80. General Agreement on Tariffs and Trade, *opened for signature* Oct. 30, 1947, T.I.A.S. No. 1700, 55 U.N.T.S. 187.

81. Thomas W. Hertel, Will Martin & Amanda M. Leister, *Potential Implications of a Special Safeguard Mechanism in the WTO: The Case of Wheat* (World Bank Development Research Group Agriculture & Rural Development Team Policy Research Working Paper No. 5334, June 2010), *available at* http://www-wds.worldbank.org/servlet/WDSContentServer/WDSP/IB/2010/06/06/000158349_20100606235900/Rendered/PDF/WPS5334.pdf.

82. IAN F. FERGUSSON, CONG. RESEARCH SERV., RL32060, WORLD TRADE ORGANIZATION NEGOTIATIONS: THE DOHA DEVELOPMENT AGENDA 16 (updated Jan. 18, 2008).

83. Robert Sturdy, *Robert Sturdy in Geneva for World Trade Organization Ministerial Conference*, Dec. 17, 2011, http://robertsturdymep.com/2011/12/17/robert-sturdy-in-geneva-for-world-trade-organization-ministerial-conference/.

84. *Understanding the WTO, Basics: Principles of the Trading System*, WORLD TRADE ORG., *available at* http://www.wto.org/english/thewto_e/whatis_e/tif_e/fact2_e.htm (last visited Jan. 18, 2012).

A *customs union* is similar but involves the establishment of a common tariff for all other states.

Once a free trade area or customs union is established, GATT rules apply to the area or union as a whole and not to the constituent states. Members of the WTO may participate in free trade areas or customs unions only if the area or union does not establish higher duties or more restrictive commercial regulations for other WTO countries.

Bound Tariffs

A second basic principle of the GATT is the concept of *bound tariffs.* Each time tariffs are reduced, they become bound; that is, they may not be raised again. If any country raises its bound tariffs, it must compensate the other WTO members, normally through other tariff concessions.

National Treatment

A third basic principle is *national treatment.* WTO members may not discriminate against imported products in favor of domestically produced "like products." Thus, for example, special taxes on imported goods are illegal if not applied equally to domestic products. The determination of what is a "like product" is done on a case-by-case basis by examining such factors as (1) the product's end uses in a given market; (2) consumers' tastes and habits, which vary from country to country; and (3) the product's properties, nature, and quality.[85]

Gradual Freer Trade Through Negotiation

The WTO lists lowering trade barriers as one of the most obvious means of encouraging trade, but recognizes that adjustments are required. Countries are allowed to introduce changes gradually through "progressive liberalization," and developing countries are allowed more time to fulfill their obligations.

Fair Competition

The WTO recognizes that "free trade" cannot be free of all regulations and allows tariffs and other forms of protection, but within a system of rules dedicated to open, fair, and undistorted competition.

Encouragement of Development and Economic Reform

The WTO aims at encouraging members that are developing countries to implement trade liberalization programs and to take on obligations that are required of developed countries.

85. *See, e.g.,* World Trade Org., Appellate Body Report, *Japan—Taxes on Alcoholic Beverages,* WT/DS8/AB/R, WT/DS10/AB/R & WT/DS11/AB/4, 1997 BDIEL AD LEXIS 27 (Oct. 4, 1996) (shochu and vodka are like products, so Japan could not tax imported vodka at a higher rate than domestic shochu).

ethical consideration

France and other European countries have typically required a majority of television programming to be of European origin, thereby limiting American-made programs to less than 50% of the total television broadcasts. France imposes a tax on tickets for American movies and uses the money generated from the taxes to underwrite French films.[a]

For years, Canada has been concerned that the U.S. media would turn the country into a mini–United States. In April 1998, federal regulators in Ottawa adopted a requirement that at least 35% of music played by commercial radio stations on weekdays between 6 a.m. and 6 p.m. must be Canadian selections played in their entirety.[b] In June 1999, similar restrictions were imposed on the distribution of movies in Canada by U.S. movie companies, as well as on ads in publications in order to bolster local Canadian magazines.[c] Liza Frulla, the Minister of Canadian Heritage, claimed that these measures were necessary because "Canadians must be able to find their own reflection in the music, films, television programs and literature created by our artists and distributed in our country."[d] Cultural policies were exempted in part from NAFTA.

An earlier attempt by Canada to impose an 80% excise tax on advertisements in split-run editions of periodicals was struck down by the WTO as a violation of Article III's requirement of national treatment.[e] A split-run edition of a magazine is one in which the publisher who is located in a foreign country inserts some domestic content as well as domestic advertising in the magazine that is originally targeted at the readership of the foreign country.

To what extent should media companies worry about protecting local culture? Should popular tastes prevail, or is it acceptable for governments to protect expressions of local culture by minimizing foreign competition through quotas?

a. Alan Riding, *Filmmakers Seek Protection from US Dominance,* N.Y. Times, Feb. 4, 2003, at E3.
b. Canadian Radio-Television & Telecommunications Comm'n, *Canadian Content Requirements for Music on Canadian Radio* (last modified Mar. 14, 2002), *available at* http://www.crtc.gc.ca/Eng/cancon/r_cdn.htm.
c. Department of Canadian Heritage, *Backgrounder: Canada-U.S. Agreement on Magazines, available at* http://www.pch.gc.ca/pc-ch/org/sectr/ac-ca/pol/magazines/fact-info/magbk1-eng.cfm (last updated Jun. 4, 2000).
d. News Release Communiqué, Department of Canadian Heritage, The Government of Canada Submits Its Comments Concerning the Preliminary Draft of the Convention on the Protection of the Diversity of Cultural Contents and Artistic Expressions (Nov. 19, 2004), *available at* http://www.mondialisations.org/php/public/art.php?id=15608&lan=EN.
e. World Trade Org., Appellate Body Report, *Canada—Certain Measures Concerning Periodicals,* WT/DS31/AB/R, 1997 BDIEL AD LEXIS 12 (June 30, 1997).

Other GATT and WTO Principles

Tariffs are not the only barrier to trade.

Nontariff Barriers

In some cases, countries have replaced tariffs with *nontariff barriers (NTBs)* as a means of protecting domestic industries threatened by import competition. For example, the preference often given to domestic products in government procurement can reduce the volume of imports. International codes designed to reduce nontariff barriers were negotiated during the Tokyo Round of the GATT (which occurred from 1973 to 1979). Further efforts to reduce NTBs, specifically those arising from regulatory measures that explicitly or effectively protect domestic industries, are reflected in the Agreement on Technical Barriers to Trade and the Agreement on the Application of Sanitary and Phytosanitary Measures.

Environmental and Health Exceptions and the SPS Agreement

The GATT gives member states the right to adopt and enforce measures "relating to the conservation of exhaustible natural resources" as well as measures "necessary to protect human, animal or plant life or health." Such measures cannot be applied in an arbitrary or unjustifiably discriminatory manner, however; nor may they be used as a disguised restriction on trade.

This exception to national treatment has been construed very narrowly.[86] A WTO appellate body upheld a ruling of a dispute settlement panel that France's ban on white asbestos was justified to protect the health of French workers under Article XX(b) of GATT; this was the first case in which the WTO upheld national public-health protections.[87] In contrast, the U.S. reformulated

gasoline standards (adopted as part of the Clean Air Act Amendments in 1990), which imposed tougher baselines for foreign producers and refiners, were successfully challenged by Venezuela and Brazil.[88] The Committee on Trade and Environment, established under the auspices of the WTO to make recommendations on the need for rules to enhance the positive interaction between trade and environmental measures for the promotion of sustainable development, has done little to date.

The Agreement on the Application of Sanitary and Phytosanitary Measures (SPS Agreement), adopted as part of the Uruguay Round, deals with additives, contaminants, toxins, and disease-carrying organisms in food. The SPS Agreement gives WTO member states the right to take sanitary and phytosanitary measures that are "necessary" for the protection of human, animal, or plant life and health. In addition to not being discriminatory or used as disguised restrictions on trade, the measures cannot be "more trade restrictive than required" to achieve their appropriate level of protection. A measure is more trade restrictive than required if there is a reasonably available and feasible alternative that would accomplish the same result.

In the following case, the United States, Canada, and Argentina successfully challenged what they regarded as an EU moratorium on the approval of biotech products based on insufficient scientific evidence. The case highlights the different approaches of the EU and the United States with respect to the regulation of biotech products and genetically modified organisms (GMOs). Until 2004, when this case was initiated, the EU had followed a "precautionary approach" under which precaution is seen as a temporary measure until further risk assessment is possible ("harmful until proven safe"). The U.S. approach is diametrically different ("safe until proven otherwise") and had been criticized as deregulatory and "laissez-faire" by the EU. As a result of the United States' successful challenge of the EU approach, the EU was required to adopt changes to its regulatory regime to make it more similar to the U.S. regime.

---

86. *See* Thomas J. Schoenbaum, *International Trade and Protection of the Environment: The Continuing Search for Reconciliation*, 91 Am. J. Int'l L. 268 (1997).

87. World Trade Org., Appellate Body Report, *European Communities—Measures Affecting Asbestos and Asbestos-Containing Products*, WT/DS135/AB/R (Mar. 12 2001).

88. United States—Standards for Reformulated and Conventional Gasoline, 35 I.L.M. 274 (1996).

| **A CASE IN POINT** | *Summary* | **Case 24.4** |

EC—Measures Affecting the Approval and Marketing of Biotech Products

World Trade Organization Dispute Settlement Body
WT/DS291, WT/DS292, & WT/DS293 (adopted Nov. 21, 2006).

FACTS In June 1999, five European Community (EC) member states declared that they would not approve biotech products for commercialization until new EC legislation (Directive 2001/18) concerning the labeling and traceability (the ability to document each step in food and animal feed production from the farm to the consumer) of genetically modified organisms (GMOs) had been adopted by member states. This declaration triggered U.S. charges that the EC was engaging in a de facto moratorium of agricultural biotechnology products.

In May 2003, the United States informed the EC that it would seek WTO consultations to end the alleged moratorium on the basis, among others, that it violated the WTO Agreement on the Application of Sanitary and Phytosanitary Measures (the SPS Agreement). The United States

CONTINUED

appended to its complaint a list of biotech product applications for commercialization that had been submitted to EC member states from April 1999 through July 2001, all of which were either pending approval or had been withdrawn. As of 2003, the U.S. State Department claimed at least $300 million in lost sales of genetically modified corn and soy products.

The EC argued that the filing of the complaint was "legally unwarranted, economically un-founded and politically unhelpful." Several weeks later, President George W. Bush asserted that the alleged moratorium was hindering efforts to reduce hunger in Africa. Because the EC consultation did not result in the ending of the alleged moratorium, in August 2003 the WTO Dispute Settlement Body (DSB) announced the formation of a single panel to rule on the case.

The EC argued that Article 5.7 of the SPS Agreement allowed WTO members to establish a provisional SPS measure without a risk assessment because of the insufficiency of scientific evidence and uncertainty about risks that make it impossible to carry out a full risk assess-ment. Regulatory review delays resulting from requests by regulators to obtain sufficient rele-vant scientific evidence to perform a risk assessment, design risk management measures, and formulate risk communication measures should not, therefore, be characterized as "undue delay" in violation of the SPS Agreement. As an example of the delay required for thorough regulatory review, the EC noted the three-year delay before Canada approved Monsanto's application to commercialize genetically engineered wheat.

The United States, on the other hand, argued that the EC could not defend its moratorium as provisional measures resulting from insufficient evidence. The earlier rendering of a positive scientific assessment by an EC scientific committee was sufficient to require final approval of the biotech products.

The United States cited the following passage in the appellate body's ruling in the Japan-apples case as support for its argument:

> [T]he application of Article 5.7 [of the SPS Agreement] is triggered not by the exis-tence of scientific uncertainty, but rather by the insufficiency of scientific evidence. The text of Article 5.7 is clear: it refers to "cases where relevant scientific evidence is insufficient," not to "scientific uncertainty." The two concepts are not interchange-able. Therefore, we are unable to endorse Japan's approach of interpreting Article 5.7 through the prism of "scientific uncertainty."[89]

(The Japan-apples case dealt with a complaint by the United States brought before the WTO concerning certain requirements and prohibitions imposed by Japan with respect to the im-portation of apple fruit from the United States.)

ISSUE PRESENTED   What level of scientific evidence is sufficient to allow WTO member states to take precautionary measures in connection with biotech products and GMOs?

SUMMARY OF OPINION   The final ruling of the panel was issued in May 2006 after the panel sought expert advice, and the DSB adopted the panel reports in November 2006. The panel found that a de facto moratorium on approvals of biotech products was in effect when the panel was established. The panel further found that the EC had violated its obliga-tions under the SPS Agreement by applying this moratorium because the moratorium had led to "undue delays" in approval processes for biotech products. The panel concluded that the EC had prevented approvals through its acts and omissions and that these procedural decisions to delay final substantive approval decisions violated Articles 5.1 and 2.2 of the SPS Agreement. The approval procedures therefore led to "undue delay," which is inconsistent with the SPS Agreement.

With regard to EC member states' safeguard measures, the panel found that the EC also violated the SPS Agreement because these safeguard measures were not based on risk

CONTINUED

89. WT/DS245/AB/R, ¶ 179.

assessments that satisfied the SPS Agreement and were maintained without sufficient scientific evidence in violation of Articles 5.1 and 2.2 of the SPS Agreement.

The panel rejected the EC's argument that its measures in connection with biotech products were measures to preserve biodiversity under the competence of the Cartagena Protocol on Biosafety and outside the WTO's competence. (The panel explained that the WTO is not bound by the standards in the Cartagena Protocol.)

RESULT   The DSB found that the EC's de facto moratorium, the EC's approval measures, and the EC member states' safeguard measures violated the requirements of the SPS Agreement. No damages were awarded to the plaintiff.

COMMENTS   The EU ended its de facto moratorium and introduced more permissive rules for the approval of biotech products. This WTO ruling will likely become a precedent for future WTO panels that deal with food safety, the environmental impact of food production, and related topics.

WTO Dispute Settlement Procedures

The WTO Understanding on Rules and Procedures Governing the Settlement of Disputes sets forth the procedures for resolving disputes. A panel of experts is established at the request of a complaining party. Panel reports are adopted virtually automatically unless they are rejected by consensus of the WTO members (including the member–complainant that filed the case in question).

The nature of the WTO as an international institution raises issues that do not arise in the context of implementing domestic judicial decisions. In the domestic setting, a court order has the force of law, and compliance with such orders is ultimately backed by the physical power of governmental authorities. By contrast, a WTO member can respond to losing a case before a panel or appellate body of the WTO by (1) implementing the recommendations and rulings, (2) providing compensation, or (3) accepting suspension of concessions by the winning party or parties.

To date, the express preference of the United States has been for members to comply with WTO rulings and implement such changes to national law and policy as are necessary to achieve compliance with the applicable WTO agreement. This strong preference—and the United States' willingness to act on it—helps explain why the United States moved expeditiously to change the U.S. tax law to implement a 2000 WTO decision involving foreign sales corporations (FSCs). These offshore corporations had been permitted to exempt from U.S. income taxation a portion of the revenue earned on sales of U.S.-origin goods outside the United States.[90] In response to the WTO ruling, the United States eliminated this tax preference.

The United States has used the WTO dispute settlement process both as a means of vindicating rights in particular cases and as a way of communicating to its trading partners that the United States expects them to take seriously compliance with the WTO rules. The United States has been an active user of the WTO dispute settlement process, having used it in ninety-five cases from January 1995 to December 2011.[91] Since its establishment in 1994, the WTO has received a total of 426 complaints from one member country against another. The United States has been a party to 210 or 49.3% of those disputes, the highest percentage of any member.[92]

Although the United States has for the most part been successful in pursuing these matters, the United States has also lost its share of cases. After winning or obtaining concessions in its first fourteen cases, the United States lost for the first time in December 1997, when the WTO rejected Eastman Kodak Company's claims that Fuji Photo Film and the Japanese government had erected internal barriers to trade in Japan. The *Kodak* ruling sparked criticism of the WTO. In the words of then Senator John Ashcroft (R-Mo.), the ruling raised "serious questions about the credibility of this international body and of the U.S. trade representative's capacity to secure and defend free-trade agreements."[93]

By September 2011, the United States had lost forty-four of the fifty-eight proceedings initiated by other WTO member countries.[94] In addition to the *Kodak* ruling, the

90. *See* Press Release, U.S. Trade Representative (Sept. 30, 2000) (announcing that the United States and the European Union had reached an agreement regarding procedures for reviewing whether replacement legislation for the then-current FSC regime was WTO consistent and urging Congress to complete this action as expeditiously as possible). For further discussion of this matter, *see infra* note 96.

91. *Snapshot of WTO Cases Involving the United States*, OFFICE OF U.S. TRADE REPRESENTATIVE (last updated Dec. 21, 2011), *available at* http://www.ustr.gov/webfm_send/3216. http://www.ustr.gov/ assets/ Trade_Agreements/Monitoring_Enforcement/Dispute_Settlement/ WTO/asset_upload_file562_5696.pdf.

92. *Summary and Analysis of World Trade Organization Cases Lost by the United States*, ECONOMYINCRISIS.ORG, *available at* http://www.economyincrisis.net/sites/all/pdf/WTOstudyEIC.pdf.

93. Robert S. Greenberger et al., *WTO's Kodak Ruling Heightens Trade Tensions*, WALL ST. J., Dec. 8, 1997, at A3.

94. *Summary and Analysis of World Trade Organization Cases Lost by the United States*, *supra* note 92.

losses included WTO decisions concerning reformulated gasoline,[95] provisions of the U.S. tax code giving preferred treatment to U.S. foreign sales corporations,[96] and the U.S.

___

95. Venezuela and Brazil had complained that the United States was discriminating against gasoline imports and violating national treatment principles when it applied stricter rules on the chemical characteristics of imported gasoline than it did for domestically refined gasoline. The dispute panel agreed with Venezuela and Brazil and found that the United States was in violation of WTO rules. The Appellate Body upheld the panel's conclusions. The parties agreed to implement the decision within fifteen months from the decision of the Appellate Body. Appellate Body Report, *United States—Standards for Reformulated and Conventional Gasoline*, WT/DS2/R (Jan. 29, 1996).

96. The WTO ruled in February 2000 that the exemption provisions for FSCs constituted an illegal export subsidy under WTO rules. Appellate Body Report, *United States—Tax Treatment for "Foreign Sales Corporations,"* WT/DS108/AB/R (Feb. 24, 2000). The WTO Appellate Body affirmed this decision in 2002 and approved the EU's request for more than $4 billion in retaliatory tariffs.

final affirmative determinations of sales at less than fair value (dumping) with respect to shrimp from Ecuador.[97]

Timetable

The timetable for resolving disputes is flexible, but normally a case should not take more than one year (fifteen months if the case is appealed) to run the full course from consultation among the countries involved in the dispute (with mediation by the WTO director–general if the parties cannot resolve the dispute themselves) to a ruling by the Dispute Settlement Body. Exhibit 24.1 presents the timetable for resolution of the reformulated gasoline cases brought by Venezuela and Brazil against the United States.

___

97. *United States—Anti-Dumping Measure on Shrimp from Ecuador*, DS335 (2005).

___

EXHIBIT 24.1   Timetable for WTO Dispute Settlement Process in Practice: Reformulated Gasoline Decision

On January 23, 1995, Venezuela complained to the WTO Dispute Settlement Body that, pursuant to amendments to the U.S. Clean Air Act adopted in 1990, the United States applied stricter rules on the chemical characteristics of imported gasoline than it did for domestically refined gasoline. Brazil joined the case in April 1996. The following chart shows the actual timetable for resolution of the dispute.[a]

Time (0 = start of case)	Target/Actual Period	Date	Action
−5 years		1990	U.S. Clean Air Act amended.
−4 months		September 1994	U.S. restricts gasoline imports under Clean Air Act.
0	*"60 days"*	23 January 1995	Venezuela complains to Dispute Settlement Body, asks for consultation with U.S.
+1 month		24 February 1995	Consultations take place but no accord reached.
+2 months		25 March 1995	Venezuela asks Dispute Settlement Body for a panel.
+2½ months	*"30 days"*	10 April 1995	Dispute Settlement Body agrees to appoint panel, and U.S. does not block. (Brazil starts complaint, requests consultation with U.S.)
+3 months		28 April 1995	Panel appointed. (On 31 May, panel assigned to Brazilian complaint as well.)
+6 months	*9 months (target is 6–9)*	10–12 July and 13–15 July 1995	Panel meets.
+11 months		11 December 1995	Panel gives interim report to U.S., Venezuela, and Brazil for comment.
+1 year		29 January 1996	Panel circulates final report to Dispute Settlement Body.
+1 year, 1 month		21 February 1996	U.S. appeals.
+1 year, 3 months	*"60 days"*	29 April 1996	Appellate body submits report.
+1 year, 4 months	*"30 days"*	20 May 1996	Dispute Settlement Body adopts panel and appeal reports.

CONTINUED

EXHIBIT 24.1   Timetable for WTO Dispute Settlement Process in Practice: Reformulated Gasoline Decision (Continued)

Time (0 = start of case)	Target/Actual Period	Date	Action
+1 year, 10½ months		3 December 1996	U.S. and Venezuela agree on what U.S. should do (implementation period is 15 months from 20 May).
+1 year, 11½ months		9 January 1997	U.S. makes first of monthly reports to Dispute Settlement Body on status of implementation.
+2 years, 7 months		19–20 August 1997	U.S. signs new regulation (19 August). End of agreed implementation period (20 August).

a. *Settling Disputes; Case Study: The Timetable in Practice*, WORLD TRADE ORG., *available at* http://www.wto.org/english/thewto_e/whatis_e/tif_e/disp3_e.htm (last visited Jan. 5, 2012).

© Cengage Learning 2013

REGIONAL ECONOMIC INTEGRATION

Regional alliances play an important role in the promotion of international trade. More than one hundred regional alliance agreements are in existence. These regional trading alliances vary significantly, but they all achieve some amount of economic integration among the members. Regional alliances can be divided into five groups: free trade areas, customs unions, common markets, economic unions, and political unions. As explained earlier, a free trade area encourages trade among its members by eliminating trade barriers. NAFTA, which reduces tariffs and nontariff barriers among Canada, Mexico, and the United States, is an example of a free trade area.

A customs union not only eliminates internal trade barriers among its members but also adopts common external trade policies toward countries that are not members. The Mercosur (or Mercosul) Accord, an agreement among Argentina, Brazil, Paraguay, and Uruguay, is an example of a customs union.

A *common market* has the features of a customs union, but goes a step further by eliminating barriers that restrict the movement of labor, capital, and technology among the member nations. The European Economic Area, an agreement by EU members and several other European countries to promote the free movement of factors of production among them, is an example of a common market.

A *political union* represents the complete political and economic integration of the member states. The integration of the thirteen separate colonies under the Articles of Confederation for the United States is an example of a political union.

In an *economic union*, internal trade barriers are abolished, restrictions on mobility of factors of production among members are eliminated, and the economic policies of the member states (monetary, fiscal, taxation, and social welfare programs) are fully integrated so as to blend the member states' economies into a single entity. The European Union, discussed below, is the most visible example of an economic union.

The European Union

The European Union, formerly known as and still often referred to as the European Community, is an intergovernmental organization of twenty-seven European states. The EC/EU was established through the following treaties: the European Coal and Steel Community (established in 1951); the European Atomic Energy Commission (Euratom, established in 1957); the Treaty of Rome, which established the European Economic Community (EEC) in 1957;[98] the Single European Act (1987); and the Treaty on European Union[99] (also known as the Maastricht Treaty), which established the European Union in 1993. The Treaty of Lisbon (also known as the Reform Treaty) was signed in December 2007 in Lisbon, Portugal, and all twenty-seven member states have ratified it, the last being the Czech Republic on November 3, 2009. The Lisbon Treaty included the Constitution for Europe as well as a number of changes to the structure of the EU.[100]

From the beginning, the intention of the European Community was to create a common market, which was formally established in 1993. The EU is now well down the path to economic, monetary, and political union. As of 2012, the EU member states are Austria, Belgium, Bulgaria, Cyprus, the Czech Republic, Denmark, Estonia, Finland, France, Germany, Greece, Hungary, Ireland, Italy, Latvia, Lithuania, Luxembourg, Malta, the Netherlands, Poland, Portugal, Romania, Slovakia, Slovenia, Spain, Sweden, and the United Kingdom. Croatia, Iceland, the Republic of Macedonia, Montenegro, and Turkey are official membership candidates; Albania, Bosnia and Herzegovina, Kosovo, and Serbia are potential membership candidates.

Goods, services, people, and capital can move almost as freely within the EU as within a single country. There

---

98. Treaty Establishing the European Economic Community, Mar. 25, 1957, 298 U.N.T.S. 11.

99. Treaty on European Union, Feb. 7, 1992, 1992 O.J. (C 224) 1, 31 I.L.M. 247 (1992).

100. *See infra* under "Principal EU Institutions" for more information on the institutional changes of the Treaty of Lisbon.

are no tariff barriers among the states, and all states apply a single set of tariffs (called the *common customs tariff*) on goods imported from outside the EU.

The creation of the single EU market has had profound effects on U.S. businesses. It has facilitated the formation of larger European companies with a bigger home market and has increased large-scale research and development in Europe. At the same time, the single market has created a larger market for American goods and has made the EU a more attractive place in which to invest.

The EU negotiates international trade agreements on behalf of the member states, but all agreements (including negotiations with the WTO) must be approved by the individual states. The EU has the exclusive power to take action against dumping in the EU by companies in non-member countries. Agriculture is centrally coordinated through the Common Agricultural Policy, which supports prices of agricultural products and promotes the modernization of agriculture throughout the EU.

As discussed in Chapter 16, EU competition law has been used to prevent companies from engaging in private restraints of trade affecting the member states. For example, in 2004, the European Commission found that the bundling of the Windows operating system with the Microsoft Windows Media Player abused Microsoft's dominant position in the market; Microsoft was required to offer a version of the operating system without the Media Player installed. In 2006, the European Court of First Instance annulled the Commission's decision to allow the merger of Bertelsman Music Group and Sony Music Entertainment to form Sony BMG.

Principal EU Institutions

Seven institutions are primarily responsible for governing the EU: (1) the European Commission, (2) the Council of Ministers, (3) the European Parliament, (4) the European Court of Justice, (5) the European Court of Auditors, (6) the European Council, and (7) the European Central Bank.

The European Commission   The European Commission is the executive branch of the EU and comprises twenty-seven individuals appointed by the governments of the member states (with each member state appointing one member). Commissioners are expected to act independently of their national governments. With a staff of almost 33,000 civil servants, the Commission is at the heart of the EU's policy-making process.

The Commission formulates recommendations, addresses opinions to members, and may bring member states before the European Court of Justice for failure to carry out their obligations under the Maastricht and Rome Treaties.

The Council of Ministers   The Council of Ministers, officially known as the Council of the European Union, is the legislative body of the EU and enacts legislation based on proposals referred to it by the European Commission. Members of the Council are appointed by the governments of the member states, but unlike the Commission members, they represent the interests of their respective states.

EU legislation may be in the form of *regulations*, which are directly applicable in the member states without the need for national measures to implement them. Legislation may also take two other forms. One is the *directive*, which is a law directing member states to enact certain laws or regulations. Directives are binding with respect to the objective to be achieved but allow national authorities to choose the form and means of implementation. The other form of legislation is the *decision*, which is an order directed at a specific person or member state.

The European Parliament   The 785 members of the European Parliament (EP) are the only EU policymakers elected directly by the citizens of the member states, generally in proportion to the population of each state. The Parliament must be consulted twice on each legislative proposal. First, it considers the proposed law at the committee level; then it expresses its opinion by a vote in plenary session. If the EP rejects a proposal, the law can be enacted only by a unanimous vote of the Council of Ministers. The EP can also amend European Commission proposals. If the Commission supports the EP amendment, the amended proposal can be defeated only by a unanimous vote of the Council of Ministers. Finally, the Parliament has the power to dismiss the Commission with a two-thirds vote and to reject the Commission's annual budget.

The European Court of Justice   The European Court of Justice (ECJ) is the judicial branch of the EU. Its role is to interpret the treaties establishing the EU and to determine whether national laws, as applied by the national courts, are consistent with those obligations. The ECJ has been a major force in affirming the powers of community institutions and the development of a single market.

The ECJ comprises up to fifteen judges and nine advocates general appointed by the national governments. In 2010, a total of 1,406 new cases were brought before the ECJ— 631 new cases and 385 references for preliminary ruling. Of these, the ECJ decided 574.[101] There are five primary avenues to the ECJ:[102]

1. *Failure to comply.* The Commission advises a company or a country that it has failed to comply with a directive or regulation. If the company or country contests the Commission's ruling, then the matter is brought before the ECJ.

---

101. Press Release No. 13/11, European Court of Justice, Statistics Concerning Judicial Activity in 2010: References for a Preliminary Ruling Have Never Been Dealt with So Quickly (Mar. 2, 2011), *available at* http://curia.europa.eu/jcms/upload/docs/application/pdf/2011-03/cp110013en.pdf.

102. The author gratefully acknowledges the assistance of Professor Claude Mosseri-Marlio in the preparation of this discussion of the ECJ.

2. *Annulment.* Any member state or EU institution (that is, Commission, Council, or Parliament) may ask the ECJ to annul an EU decision as contrary to the Rome Treaty.

3. *Failure to act.* Member states or EU institutions may ask the ECJ to declare that a country, the Council of Ministers, or the Commission has failed to take a required action. Individuals who are personally and directly concerned may intercede in the proceeding.

4. *Civil liabilities.* National courts and individuals may ask the ECJ for a ruling that the EU or a national government is liable for damages for an act or failure to act.

5. *Preliminary rulings.* National courts can ask for an opinion as to whether a national law conflicts with one or more articles of the Rome or Maastricht Treaties and request guidance as to how EU law should be interpreted and applied to the matter at hand. Most of the ECJ's cases fall into this category.

In an effort to reduce a backlog, a junior court—the Court of First Instance—was created in 1989. It hears administrative cases, competition cases, dumping suits involving countries outside the EU, and intellectual property cases. Appeals from the Court of First Instance to the ECJ can be made only on matters of law, not matters of fact.

The European Court of Auditors The European Court of Auditors is composed of one member from each European member state. The Court has no judicial functions, but it acts as an external independent investigatory audit agency, monitoring and inspecting the EU budget to determine whether it has been correctly implemented. The European Court of Auditors reports any problems it finds and prepares annual reports for the European Parliament.

European Council Under the Treaty of Lisbon, the European Council became an EU institution. It comprises the heads of the member states of the EU and the President of the European Commission and constitutes the highest political body of the EU.

The European Central Bank Under the Treaty of Lisbon, the status of the European Central Bank (ECB) also changed to that of an EU institution. The ECB is based in Frankfurt, Germany, and came onstream on July 1, 1998. Its primary duty is to maintain price stability, usually by lowering or raising interest rates. The Maastricht Treaty required all member states to converge their economic and monetary policies with the goal of creating a single European currency, the *euro.* The convergence criteria called for the member states to harmonize their budget deficits, inflation levels, public-sector debt, and long-term interest rates at specific target levels and to achieve exchange rate stability. These efforts culminated in the creation of the European Monetary Union (EMU) on January 1, 1999.

Eleven EU members qualified for initial participation in the euro: Austria, Belgium, Finland, France, Germany, Ireland, Italy, Luxembourg, the Netherlands, Portugal, and Spain. Greece was permitted to adopt the euro in 2001 after lowering its budget deficits and inflation; Slovenia adopted it in 2007, Cyprus and Malta in 2008, Slovakia in 2009, and Estonia in 2011. The United Kingdom and Denmark are eligible to adopt the euro, but they have taken a wait-and-see approach. Latvia is scheduled to adopt the euro in 2014, and Romania is scheduled to adopt it in 2015. Bulgaria, the Czech Republic, Hungary, Lithuania, and Sweden do not yet have target dates to adopt the euro. By giving up their national currencies, members of the EMU have relinquished control of their exchange rates and monetary policies to the ECB.

On January 1, 1999, all currencies of participating member states were irrevocably locked together at a specified conversion rate, and the euro became the official currency for the participating member states. Beginning in 2009, the economic instability of a few member states, including Greece, Ireland, and Portugal, resulted in instability for the union as a whole. After the extent of Greek debt was revealed, markets reacted by increasing interest rates not only for Greek debt, but also for borrowing by Spain, Portugal, and Ireland. In early 2010, the EU and the International Monetary Fund put together a series of bailout packages for Greece that totaled 110 billion euros ($163 billion). In May, leaders approved a contingency fund of 500 billion euro (about $680 billion) for the EU at large. In November, European officials arranged a bailout of 85 billion euros (roughly $112 billion) for Ireland. The hope was that this show of financial force would reassure markets about the solvency of euro countries.

The crisis posed great risks to many of the Continent's banks, which had invested heavily in government bonds, and forced deep cuts in government spending, which drove up unemployment and put several countries back into deep recessions. The economic crisis gradually became a political one as well, leading to the ouster of governments in Ireland, Portugal, Greece, and Italy.

After the leaders of France and Germany told Greece in early 2012 to move forward with promised economic changes or risk losing the next installment of bailout funds, Greece's newly installed prime minister, Lucas Papademos, agreed to deeper spending cuts. The EU agreed in February 2012 to give Greece an additional $170 billion in bailout loans in exchange for Greece's agreement to bring its sovereign debt down to 120.5% of gross domestic product by 2020. After holders of the Greek sovereign debt were forced in March 2012 to accept a reduction in principal to secure the bailout by the European Central Bank, the International Swaps and Derivatives Association declared that Greece had officially defaulted, thereby triggering payments of $2.5 billion to the holders of $3.2 billion of credit-default swaps on the Greek debt. This amounted to 78.5 cents on the dollar. (In contrast, when the U.S. Treasury bailed out insurance giant AIG, it paid 100 cents on the dollar to the holders of AIG's credit-default swaps.)

The contagion spread from Greece to other parts of Europe. In January 2012, Standard & Poor's downgraded France's credit rating from AAA rating to AA+ due to France's sovereign debt exposure and concerns about deficit spending. The ratings agency also cut Portugal's credit to junk status and downgraded Italy's,[103] putting further stress on the euro.

Emissions Trading Scheme

As of January 1, 2012, the European Union implemented the Emissions Trading Scheme (ETS), a tax on international airlines, in an effort to reduce the presence of climate-changing gases in European airspace. Under the system, airlines flying to or from Europe must obtain certificates for carbon dioxide emissions. They will get free credits to cover most flights in 2012 but must buy or trade for credits thereafter. The EU unilaterally implemented the tax, which is opposed by industry leaders and governments, including China, India, Russia, and the United States. EU Transport Commissioner Siim Kallas acknowledged the growing opposition to the scheme but stated that the EU would not bow to pressure to suspend it. China has barred its carriers from paying the tax, arguing that Asian carriers are unfairly penalized in favor of Middle Eastern carriers because the tax is based on distance in flight. China estimates the tax would cost Chinese airlines an additional $124 million per year.[104] One Malaysian carrier, AirAsia X, says it will eliminate flights to Europe because the increase in jet fuel prices combined with the new tax has made those flights less profitable.[105] There is concern that the implementation of this scheme could start a trade war between Europe and the rest of the world.

Challenges

Notwithstanding the tremendous progress toward European integration, challenges remain. There is no European citizenship—a nonnational can vote in local but not national elections. There is no European company law or Europe-wide insurance. Rules for pension plans are not coordinated, and plans cannot hold nonnational shares of stock. There is still no tax harmonization; national varieties include value-added, income, company, capital gains, wealth, and inheritance taxes. Critics of the EU's continuous enlargement think several of the new members and candidates for membership are too different from the existing (or core) EU countries in social, cultural, and economic terms. In addition, as noted above, the sovereign debt crisis has put addition strain on the monetary union.

---

103. *European Debt Crisis*, N.Y. TIMES, Jan. 30, 2012.

104. *EU "Risks Trade War" over Carbon Trading Scheme*, BBC NEWS, Feb. 13, 2012, *available at* http://www.bbc.co.uk/news/business-17008172.

105. Associated Press, *EU Open to Negotiations but Won't Scrap Airline Carbon Emissions Tax*, WASH. POST, Feb. 13, 2012.

STRUCTURING INTERNATIONAL OPERATIONS

A U.S. business can structure its international operations in a variety of ways. A business can establish a presence in a foreign country to supervise or manage sales with little or no investment by setting up a liaison, representative, or branch office in the host country. The scope of permissible activities, capital requirements, and tax liabilities of each of these forms of representation vary with the legal scheme of the host jurisdiction.

Typically, the greater the scope of permissible activities, the more stringent the capitalization and taxation rules. Thus, representative and liaison offices are generally limited to providing services on behalf of a home office. They cannot engage in manufacturing operations, and typically they can conduct only limited sales support and marketing activities. In countries with very limited or no provision for such operations, companies may be forced to choose between use of an agent or distributor on the one hand and a branch or subsidiary on the other.

A branch office can perform certain kinds of services, such as import and export, provided it is formally capitalized, registers with local government authorities, and pays income and other required taxes. Legally, the lack of local limited liability protection is one reason not to use a branch office. Many companies have subsidiaries that are entirely separate legal entities, with their own capital structure, boards of directors, and officers. Different tax treatment is a second reason to favor a subsidiary rather than a foreign office when establishing an overseas presence. Another issue that should not be overlooked is the burden of disclosing and possibly restating company financials under local regulations.

CONTRACTING ACROSS NATIONAL BORDERS

An international contract, like a domestic one, may reallocate rights, obligations, and risks differently from what they would be in the absence of the contract under applicable law. In an international context, however, the practices common to the parties may be fewer, their assumptions and expectations more divergent, and the risks greater. There is, in short, more ground to be covered to ensure a true meeting of the minds—and more risk and uncertainty in proceeding without one.

Payment and Letters of Credit

Because the parties to an international transaction may not be well known to each other, a very common payment mechanism for international transactions is the opening (that is, the establishment) of a documentary credit, commonly known as a *letter of credit*. The buyer or borrower (the *applicant*) enters into a contract with the issuing bank, which is usually in the buyer's or borrower's jurisdiction. The issuing bank issues a letter of credit in favor of the seller or lender (the *beneficiary*). The *documentary letter of credit (L/C)* provides for payment by the issuing bank to the beneficiary upon tender by the beneficiary (or its agent or assignee) of specified documents. The nature of these specified documents is based on the terms of the contract between the applicant and the beneficiary.

Two sets of rules can apply to L/Cs in international transactions. The first is Article 5 of the U.S. Uniform Commercial Code (UCC), which varies slightly from state to state. The second set of rules is set forth in the International Chamber of Commerce's Uniform Customs and Practice for Documentary Credits (UCP), the most recent version of which is contained in a document often cited in bank L/C forms as Uniform Customs and Practice for Documentary Credits.[106]

There are significant differences between UCC Article 5 and the UCP. For example, UCC Article 5, as interpreted by most U.S. courts, provides that, once established, an L/C is irrevocable unless otherwise agreed. The UCP, by its terms, establishes the opposite presumption: an L/C is revocable at the issuing bank's option and without prior notice to or agreement of the beneficiary, unless the contract and the L/C expressly state that the L/C is irrevocable. These rules, as much as the terms of the underlying sales contract, can determine the outcome of a payment dispute.

The parties can elect to have their L/C governed by UCC Article 5 or by the UCP, and they should be specific about their choice.[107] It is also prudent to expressly specify in the L/C whether it is revocable or irrevocable.

Guaranties and Standby Letters of Credit in Financing Transactions

Guaranties and standby letters of credit are also often used to provide security for those providing financing for a major construction project in another country. If the political or credit risks of a country are perceived to be especially great, an entity in the host country, often an instrumentality of the host country government, may be called on to act as the guarantor. Under a *guaranty* arrangement, a local financial institution guarantees, for the benefit of the project owners, that the lender will be repaid if the project principals are unable to pay, as long as the parties to the project have adhered to the contracts.

U.S. law prohibits U.S. banks from issuing guaranties, so a standby letter of credit is sometimes used to provide payment or repayment comfort. Under a *standby letter of credit*, payment is usually conditioned upon a brief statement, in language previously agreed on by the applicant and the beneficiary, that the applicant is in default or has failed to perform an obligation to the beneficiary under the construction or similar project and the beneficiary is therefore entitled to payment from the issuing bank. Unlike the common form of guaranty, the creditor only has to tender the specified document and is not required to establish that the debtor breached its obligations in the underlying contract. This means that a guarantor can raise any defenses that the primary debtor could have raised, whereas a bank that issued a standby letter of credit cannot inquire into the underlying transaction or assert the defenses that the applicant has.

Although letters of credit are therefore more secure, they cost money, and, in an ongoing relationship, the buyer usually presses for more favorable payment terms. In the multinational-corporation context, having a well-known parent company guarantee a local affiliate's obligations is a fairly common cost-saving alternative to an L/C.

INVESTMENT ABROAD

Before investing outside the United States, U.S. firms should (1) assess their investment goals and competitive position; (2) consider the economic, political, geographic, legal, and labor conditions in the host country; and (3) address any financial issues, such as currency considerations, project capitalization, and taxation.

Investment Goals and Competitive Position

A business plan for investing abroad must begin with an assessment of the investor's goals and the firm's competitive position. The attractiveness of a prospective investment in a given host country can vary greatly depending on these factors.

Local Market Penetration

For legal or business reasons, some markets are almost inaccessible to U.S. manufacturers wishing to sell their products. Developing countries may lack hard currency—that is, convertible foreign exchange—and these shortages may limit their purchase of imports. Applicable laws may restrict imports of certain products but grant benefits to foreign investors wishing to manufacture those products locally. To penetrate these types of markets, the only practical approach may be to invest in a local manufacturing facility. Certain Asian countries permit only local companies to establish retail businesses—another example of how foreign companies may be prevented from competing in certain markets.

---

106. ICC Publication No. 600, Revision 2007, which formally commenced on July 1, 2007.

107. Certain provisions in revised UCC Article 5 cannot be varied by agreement; as a practical matter, however, the nonvariable rules are unlikely to conflict with any UCP rule.

Regional Base

U.S. businesses that wish to compete in Europe or Asia may need to establish manufacturing, marketing, and/or service centers in the relevant region to gain credibility with local customers. U.S. businesses may also need to be on-site to sustain their local sources of supplies for operations elsewhere. Regional bases can reduce transportation costs, enhance time-to-market responses, help avoid cultural difficulties, and generally help the home office monitor the business pulse of the region. They also avoid potential problems with distributors or agents not wholly committed to the products or not aligned with the foreign parent. The challenge of integrating an expatriate with the local business environment is the corollary of this issue of aligning locally hired managers with the overall corporate mission and goals.

Cheaper Production Costs

Developing countries typically offer cheaper labor and raw materials than more industrialized countries. These lower costs are often the primary reason for U.S. business investment in foreign manufacturing operations. As discussed below, however, the assessment of true production costs is not limited to a line item comparison of the costs of each element of production. Intangible issues such as labor efficiency, reliability of supplies, local labor law requirements, and political stability can affect the true costs of production.

Host Country Conditions

Prospective investors need to consider the economic, political, geographic, legal, and labor conditions in the host country.

Economic Conditions

The host country's economic condition is usually a high-profile issue in the investment evaluation process. Per capita income, for example, may determine whether a particular country is a realistic market for a particular product or whether it is a likely source of inexpensive labor. Economic growth trends can suggest both a growing consumer market and increasing labor costs. The monetary system is also important because the existence of a readily convertible currency and the nature of the currency-exchange laws will determine whether profits can be easily repatriated (that is, transferred abroad). In a country with a high inflation rate, local suppliers may be reluctant to perform on long-term contracts, and capital and working loans may be more expensive.

The U.S. Department of Commerce, the U.S. Foreign Commercial Service, and the U.S. Department of State regularly publish reports on the economic conditions of various countries collected from a network of commercial officers stationed at U.S. embassies and consulates throughout the world. They collect and analyze economic data and are available on-site to assist U.S. businesses in interpreting how the data may be relevant to an investment project.

Political Conditions

Political instability inevitably leads to some degree of legal and economic instability. Generally, investors are mainly concerned with the reliability and stability of the local legal institutions that enforce contracts and protect property rights. Changes of government in Western democracies can lead to changes in the legal and policy environment that dramatically affect the economic results of foreign investments but do not undermine the rule of law. Other political systems may have a stable regime, but with a corrupt judicial and legislative system that does not offer effective legal recourse for investors. At the outer extreme, violent political or civil divisions can lead to the complete collapse of the rule of law. Business can still be done in such an environment, but written contractual terms become insignificant next to practical considerations of power, possession, and protection.

A prospective foreign investor must, therefore, look beyond the reasonableness of the contract, the competence of its foreign business counterpart, and the desirability of the site to determine whether (1) the existing government and its policies are aligned with the needs of the project and (2) that government or its policies are likely to change in adverse ways. Managers should analyze both (1) political risks, such as expropriation, partial nationalization, and serious operational restrictions, which often stem from a change in the overall political orientation; and (2) legal risks, such as changes in tax, customs, employment, and other laws that do not represent an inherent shift against private ownership or foreign investment.

Geographic Conditions

Climatic and geographic conditions can directly affect the production and transportation of products. Severe weather in certain seasons can affect delivery schedules. Consequently, it is important to ascertain the breadth and reliability of the transportation system and other infrastructure available.

The nature, cost, and development status of a prospective site are major considerations. In some countries (such as Vietnam or the Philippines where foreign nationals can only purchase condominiums or townhouses), foreign investors are not permitted to own land but can, often with the assistance of a local partner, obtain long-term land-use rights. If the capital investment will be large relative to the parent company's assets, a foreign investor may want to consider investing only in countries that offer guaranties concerning expropriation or in friendly developing countries where U.S. investors are eligible for OPIC insurance (discussed earlier in the chapter). Sometimes a country may seek to attract investment to certain areas by offering attractive land-use terms and new infrastructure.

Mistaken assumptions about issues such as land rights and use, flood control, power supply, fire protection, utility service, legal and informal employee protections, and the like can present the most significant hidden operational hazard in foreign direct investment. It is critical for the investor and its legal and business advisers to probe these areas aggressively in their due diligence.

Legal Conditions

Managers should ask whether local laws and courts offer predictability, uniformity, and evenhanded enforcement. Also, is the judicial system speedy, efficient, and inexpensive? Beyond the letter of the laws, their effectiveness depends on political conditions and the nature of the legal and administrative organs that interpret and enforce them. A reliable court system or comparable dispute resolution forum (such as an established arbitration system) is essential; without it, the investor will have little leverage to enforce contracts or invoke commercial laws.

Sources of necessary supplies should be secure, and their transportation and storage not subject to rampant theft. The existence of a reasonably diligent and fair law enforcement network is a factor to be considered in this regard.

Foreign investors must develop a working knowledge of the applicable host country laws and acceptable forums for dispute resolution, and they should obtain professional advice from local attorneys. These professionals can also assist in providing accurate contract translations where required. It is not uncommon for a country to require that the definitive text of a contract be in the local language (for example, consumer contracts in the Canadian province of Quebec must be drawn up in French, unless the parties expressly agree otherwise), but an accurate English version is critical.

Many countries offer a variety of vehicles for foreign investment. A foreign investor can select the investment format most appropriate to its project in a foreign country, just as a U.S. business can choose to operate domestically as a sole proprietorship; a general, limited, or limited liability partnership; a limited liability company; or a corporation. Each form is subject to its own set of laws, which affect management structure, equity investment requirements, limitation of investor liabilities, and taxation.

Often, though, businesses have less structural flexibility in foreign jurisdictions. In contrast to the United States, in some countries more prestige is attached to specific forms (for example, in some European countries, the private limited company form may be perceived as a less serious commitment than the public limited company form). Country handbooks published by international accounting firms, local law firms, and the U.S. government contain useful information on such issues.

The licensing or contribution of technology by the U.S. business to the foreign business is often a component of an equity investment project. For example, some countries' investment laws or policies may limit the portion of the foreign party's equity investment that can be attributable to intellectual property, as compared with cash or equipment. Certain restrictions on technology use also may be invalid under local technology licensing laws.

A would-be investor should check for bilateral tax or investment treaties that grant reciprocal rights to businesses from the host and investor countries. These treaties may offer significant benefits, such as avoidance of double taxation (that is, taxation by both the host and investor countries) and guaranties against uncompensated expropriation by the host government. The U.S. State Department compiles records of ratified treaties and their signatories. A quick review of this information can provide a sense of the relative involvement of various nations in international conventions that affect foreign investment.

Labor Conditions

A leading reason for investing abroad is to take advantage of relatively low labor costs in a foreign country. The true cost of labor, however, is more than the hourly or daily wage. It includes labor efficiency, trainability, reliability, and adherence to quality control standards. In addition, the labor and foreign investment laws of some countries, particularly those with socialist economies, require employers to fund a wide range of employee benefits that are not expected by U.S. investors. These benefits include housing, travel, education, and food subsidies, as well as the more common retirement, health insurance, and maternity benefits. Many nations do not permit employers to terminate an employee without just cause, which can make it difficult to terminate inefficient or redundant workers. Local labor laws may limit the degree to which employees may be treated differently, thus restricting flexibility in incentive compensation.

Financial Issues

Several common financial concerns for an equity investor in a foreign project include currency considerations, project funding and capitalization, and taxation.

Currency Considerations

The currency in which the foreign entity does business and in which its assets and obligations are denominated can be a major concern for a U.S. investor in many developing countries. The ideal is an open economy (1) without currency and other monetary restrictions and (2) with a currency tied directly to the dollar or at least to another stable major currency such as the euro. This minimizes the fluctuations in investment results due solely to currency issues relative to those inherent in the fundamental

IN BRIEF

Going Global

Market Conditions and Competition
- Product/service market fundamentals
- Distribution/operational realities
- Personnel and management
- Location
- Currency
- Competitors
- Achieving "local touch"

Legal Mores of Foreign Country
- Rule of law
- Corruption
- Judicial integrity

Substantive Foreign Law
- Exchange controls
- Import/export costs and controls
- Employment law
- Taxes, both foreign and domestic
- Securities
- Antitrust
- Formation, governance, and dissolution of a foreign entity

Sociopolitical and Economic Climate of Host Country
- Long-term economic stability
- Stable pro-market consensus
- Attitude toward foreign investors

© Cengage Learning 2013

economics of the business. In the second-best case, the prices of inputs and outputs are primarily denominated in hard currency, even though the local currency is the unit of account (a common requirement). This is most typical in export and processing operations. Often, however, the investor will find that local currency controls and financing restrictions are a significant issue. In that case, hedging contract commitments and planning capital allocation across currencies and in view of governmental restrictions will be an integral part of establishing and implementing a successful financial plan.

Local financial institutions are often restricted in offering foreign-currency loans. At the same time, foreign banks outside the host country may be reluctant to offer capital loans if local currency profits may not be freely convertible for loan repayment. Project proceeds, or even host country project properties, may not offer sufficient security for a loan from a foreign financial institution. Consequently, the foreign investor may be required to obtain and provide security entirely outside the host jurisdiction for any loans it desires.

The availability and cost of hard currency can be a major issue when the host country currency is not freely convertible. It may be of less concern to a foreign investor that expects to earn hard currency through exports of either the project's products or other local products purchased with its local currency profits. This latter arrangement is known as *countertrade.*

Cash-flow hedging methods are increasingly common in countries that maintain restrictive controls on foreign exchange. For example, a company with both import and export activities might structure import payments to match hard-currency inflows in order to reduce potential exchange rate losses. If the local currency is depreciating rapidly, inflows of hard-currency earnings may lag behind offsetting import payments. As a currency is devalued, import costs rise. Potential exchange rate losses can be avoided by delaying the conversion of export receivables into local currency until imported goods are paid for.

The currency denomination also affects the capitalization of an investment project. For example, a foreign partner in a joint venture may agree to contribute a specified amount of U.S. dollars over time, with the host country partner making an equal contribution in the local currency. If the local currency depreciates against the U.S. dollar, the foreign partner will end up making a greater than 50% contribution to the joint venture in local currency terms. Some reconciliation of paid-in capital and share pricing may be needed under local law. Unequal contributions may also arise where local law requires foreign-currency capital contributions to be valued at an official exchange rate that fails to reflect the local currency's true value. These currency risks can be addressed by careful contract drafting and, where possible, through currency swaps and hedging.

Project Capitalization

Foreign businesses typically require fixed capital (often for construction costs) and working capital for daily operations. Local laws and practices may not permit the flexibility in capital structure available in the United States. The reliability and attractiveness of a host nation in this regard may be affected by factors such as political risk, currency-convertibility laws, profit-repatriation restrictions, local banking laws and practices, and the enforceability of guaranties or security agreements. As noted earlier, the lenders will usually require the borrower to secure its repayment obligations by providing a standby letter of credit or guaranty.

Taxation

Careful tax planning can minimize the risk of withholding taxes and double income taxation and can enable the investor to take advantage of local tax benefits. One simple way of addressing tax risks is a *gross-up clause*, whereby the local party is obligated to pay all taxes other than those specifically allocated to the foreign party. In this way, the foreign party avoids the risk of tax increases or unknown taxes. Some countries prohibit such reallocation of responsibility for the payment of certain taxes, however, and will not recognize gross-ups. As a result, a gross-up, though simple in concept, often is not the most efficient way of addressing certain tax issues.

The United States has bilateral tax treaties with more than fifty countries. The treaties seek to avoid double taxation of U.S.-based businesses and individuals. Some treaties also impose tax ceilings on certain types of income; for example, one treaty imposes a 10% tax ceiling on passive income such as royalties from technology licenses or rental income. Bilateral tax treaties may not affect all the taxes applicable to a foreign investment project or to an individual expatriate employee's income; when a tax treaty provision is applicable, however, and offers more favorable tax treatment than the comparable domestic tax rule, the treaty rule will generally apply.

Tax credits may be available to U.S. businesses engaged in foreign projects that are taxed by the host country. Such credits are available for the amount of foreign taxes paid up to a certain limit, which is derived by dividing the foreign-source taxable income by the total taxable income (which includes all foreign- and domestic-source income) and multiplying that fraction by the U.S. tax liability on the total taxable income. (Thus, if foreign tax rates exceed U.S. rates, no credit is available for the excess in the current year.) Foreign tax credits for any one year cannot exceed the amount of foreign income taxes that have been paid or accrued, but taxes in excess of the limitation can be carried back two years and forward five years, subject to each year's tax credit limit.

Noncommercial Issues

Many noncommercial issues can affect the desirability of operating a business abroad. Knowledge of the language and customs of the host country, or the use of proficient interpreters, is essential to the success of a business venture abroad. Stories abound concerning the gaffes of U.S. investors who, because of language difficulties or cultural misunderstandings, offended their foreign partners, misinterpreted contract negotiations, miscalculated the effect of their business operations, or simply could not maintain effective working relationships with their foreign counterparts. Contract terms, both legal and technical, require accurate translation to ensure effective implementation.

The business customs of a host country can have a substantial impact on local business operations on very basic levels. A frank, direct management style may be welcomed in some countries, but in others, it may be viewed as arrogant and gauche. Gift giving may be appropriate, even expected, behavior in certain circumstances; in other situations, it may be regarded as unethical and possibly illegal.

International direct-dial land phones, cellular phones, fax machines, and Internet access are common business tools in some regions but may not be available in some developing countries. Even postal or courier services may be unreliable. Such infrastructural deficiencies need to be reflected in contract provisions requiring timely notice or delivery of documents.

Developing countries may also lack reliable transportation infrastructure, which can affect the delivery of raw materials within a host country. Inadequate port facilities can lead to delayed shipments abroad and lost sales. Inefficient or corrupt customs officials can have similar effects in delaying business transactions and increasing their cost.

In many developing countries, an expatriate manager and staff may be essential to provide needed skills and to proselytize the corporate culture and goals to local staff. To attract qualified personnel to hardship posts, a company usually must offer a compensation package that includes income premiums and benefits. If expatriate staff must pay considerable income tax to the host country, further additional compensation may have to be paid to counteract this disadvantage. Local managers may resent the higher compensation of their expatriate counterparts, however, and local laws may require that local managers receive comparable compensation.

Personal safety may be an issue in some countries, effectively precluding the assignment of personnel with families. It may also be difficult to extend comparable company health and life insurance benefits to expatriate employees.

DISPUTE RESOLUTION IN INTERNATIONAL TRANSACTIONS

As in domestic trade and transactions, disputes may arise in international trade and transactions. When parties to a contract are from different nations, a dispute between the parties can lead to a collision between at least one party's expectations and a foreign legal regime. Managers engaged in resolving disputes outside the United States need to be mindful of important differences between U.S. practices and those elsewhere. Key differences include (1) greater willingness in some countries, such as Japan, to submit important business cases to arbitration and mediation; (2) limited or no opportunity for discovery; and (3) a requirement in the United Kingdom and many other countries that the loser pay the winner's attorneys' fees.

Dispute Resolution Mechanisms

International law provides several possible methods for the resolution of disputes: negotiation, good offices, mediation, inquiry, conciliation, arbitration, and litigation.

Negotiation is a very informal process in which the goal is to reach a compromise. Often the parties try negotiation before resorting to other means of dispute resolution.

Good offices is a process used mainly in the area of public international law. A third party (often a disinterested government) brings the parties together by establishing communication and providing a site where the parties can meet, often in secret. Increasingly, international organizations are taking the role of the disinterested third party.

Mediation is very similar to good offices and often is used in private international law disputes. In mediation, the third (disinterested) party is called the mediator and plays a more active role than the third party in good offices. The mediator facilitates the communications of the parties and may also intervene in a constructive way (for example, to propose a settlement). A mediator works to reconcile the opposing claims and to appease the feelings of resentment that may have arisen between the parties. Like good offices, mediation is generally nonbinding.

Inquiry is done by a commission of inquiry that is established ad hoc, often after a violation of international law. Two contending governments review the finding of the commission, with the goal of achieving an acceptable solution to the dispute at hand.

Conciliation is a more formal method of dispute resolution. It is similar to inquiry but adds a "cooling-off" period. In addition, the parties agree in advance to accept the finding of the commission.

In *arbitration*, a legal process is carried out by a tribunal that is often very similar to a court. The parties must decide in advance whether the arbitration decision will be final and binding and not subject to review by any courts. Unless such a stipulation is made, the dispute may be reviewed by a court without reference to the arbitration (*de novo review*), rendering the arbitration decision unenforceable.

Litigation, which is a legal proceeding conducted in the court system of a state or nation, is the most structured method of dispute resolution. Few managers appreciate being hauled into a foreign-language court 5,000 miles from their home office and being held to unfamiliar legal standards. Many European and Asian business leaders, for example, are uncomfortable with the U.S. legal system's discovery procedures for obtaining evidence prior to trial through depositions, written interrogatories, and document production. Often the parties can draft an arbitration clause to their mutual satisfaction, but once litigation has begun, the parties cannot "negotiate around" many rules of a legal system, even if both are willing to do so.

Arbitration can be preferable to litigation for several reasons. First, arbitration is potentially more flexible and allows the structure, formalities, and proceedings to be tailored to the specific case at hand. Second, international arbitral bodies often have more experience in dealing with international commercial disputes than their judicial counterparts. Another benefit is that arbitral bodies, unlike courts, can keep the nature and the outcome of the dispute confidential, and they may provide a more level playing field than some judicial systems. Finally, as discussed below, arbitral awards in many cases are enforceable in countries where a foreign court's judgment would not be.

In 1985, IBM Corporation set a precedent when it turned to international arbitration to resolve a major dispute with Fujitsu, Ltd., a Japanese electronics firm that was trying to gain access to IBM's mainframe programming materials. IBM claimed that Fujitsu had violated IBM copyrights by copying IBM software to develop its own operating system software. The arbitrators ultimately ruled that Fujitsu was entitled to obtain access to IBM's programs to develop and market imitations of IBM's mainframe software products in exchange for license fees of approximately $800 million.

In 2000, Toshiba America Information Systems, Inc. used mediation to settle a class action involving allegations that the company had manufactured and distributed faulty floppy-diskette controllers.[108] Toshiba agreed to pay approximately $2.1 billion in cash and to provide hardware replacement and coupons to repair the allegedly defective equipment.

Many multinational ventures stipulate by contract that certain disputes will be decided by binding arbitration. Bilateral Investment Treaties (BITs) may also require countries to arbitrate disputes with foreign investors.

The Complexity of Arbitration and Litigation: The Cases Brought Against Chevron by the Government of Ecuador and the Residents of the Lago Agrio Region

The multiyear dispute between Chevron (and its predecessor Texaco) and the government of Ecuador and the residents of the Lago Agrio region of the Ecuadorian Amazon graphically demonstrates how complex the interplay of arbitration and multicountry litigation involving both nation-states and individuals can be. In 1993, residents of Ecuador's oil-rich Oriente region (the Lago Agrio plaintiffs or LAPs) sued Chevron in the U.S. District Court for the Southern District of New York alleging that its subsidiary TexPet "improperly dumped . . . toxic by-products of the drilling process into the local rivers" and constructed a pipeline that "leaked large quantities of petroleum into the environment," causing both personal injuries and catastrophic environmental damage.[109] At the time, both Chevron and the Ecuadorian government vigorously opposed having the plaintiffs' claims litigated in the United States. Ecuador refused to waive its sovereign immunity in the New York district court and was not a party to the

---

108. *Shaw v. Toshiba Am. Info. Sys., Inc.*, 91 F. Supp. 2d 942 (E.D. Tex. 2000).

109. *Republic of Ecuador v. Chevron Corp.*, 638 F.3d 384 (2d Cir. 2011).

LAPs' original action against Chevron. Chevron moved to dismiss the LAPs' suit based on *forum non conveniens* (discussed in Chapter 3 and further below) and international *comity*, the principle under which a court will enforce another country's judgments under certain conditions.

In 1994, while the litigation was ongoing in the Southern District of New York, Chevron entered into a settlement with the Ecuadorian government and its government-owned oil company, Petroecuador. Under the settlement, Texaco "funded certain environmental remediation projects in exchange for . . . a release from liability for environmental impact falling outside the scope of that settlement." The settlement was finalized in 1998, after Chevron spent roughly $40 million on the remediation.

After Chevron agreed in writing to be sued in Ecuador, to accept service of process in Ecuador, and to waive any defenses based on the statute of limitations that might have matured since the filing of the complaint, the district court in New York dismissed the LAPs' complaint. The LAPs responded by refiling their claims in court in Lago Agrio, Ecuador, in 2004.

In September 2009, Chevron initiated BIT arbitration against Ecuador seeking (1) a declaration that Chevron and TexPet "have no liability or responsibility for environmental impact . . . or for performing further environmental remediation"; (2) a declaration that Ecuador has breached both the BIT and the terms of its release agreement with TexPet; (3) an order requiring Ecuador to inform the Lago Agrio court that Chevron has "been released from all environmental impact . . . and that Ecuador and Petroecuador are responsible for any remaining and future remediation work"; (4) a declaration that Ecuador or Petroecuador is exclusively liable for any judgment that may be issued in the Lago Agrio litigation; (5) an order requiring Ecuador to indemnify, protect, and defend Chevron in connection with the Lago Agrio litigation, including payment of all damages that may be awarded against Chevron; and (6) attorneys' fees, litigation costs, arbitration costs, moral damages, and interest.

In December 2009, Ecuador petitioned the district court in New York to stay the BIT arbitration, arguing that Chevron's initiation of arbitration and pursuit of such broad relief violated the promises that Chevron had previously made in order to secure the dismissal of the LAPs' case in the New York court based on *forum non conveniens*. Shortly thereafter, the LAPs also sued in New York to stay the arbitration "to the extent it would seek dismissal, nullification or avoidance of any judgment" in the Lago Agrio litigation. The district court in New York refused to stay the arbitration and granted Chevron's motion to dismiss the suits by both the Ecuadorian government and the LAPs. Ecuador and the LAPs appealed.

While the appeal was still pending, the BIT arbitral panel issued an interim order directing Ecuador to take all measures at its disposal to suspend or cause to be suspended the enforcement of any judgment against Chevron

in the Lago Agrio litigation. A few days later, the Lago Agrio court entered an $8.6 billion judgment against Chevron.

In *Republic of Ecuador v. Chevron Corp.*,[110] the U.S. Court of Appeals for the Second Circuit upheld the New York district court's refusal to stay Chevron's initiation of BIT arbitration against Ecuador. The court explained that arbitration under the Bilateral Investment Treaty signed by both the United States and Ecuador falls under the United Nations Convention on the Recognition and Enforcement of Foreign Arbitral Awards (the New York Convention), which governs agreements that are "commercial and . . . not entirely between citizens of the United States." The New York Convention "promote[s] the enforcement of arbitral agreements in contracts involving international commerce so as to facilitate international business transactions." The Federal Arbitration Act (FAA) implements the New York Convention, and it brings with it "a national policy favoring arbitration of claims that parties contract to settle in that manner."

Ecuador moved to stay the BIT arbitration under the FAA, arguing that Chevron, having previously agreed to litigate against the LAPs in Lago Agrio, was "estopped from accepting, ha[s] waived [its] right to accept, or ha[s] otherwise rejected [its] right" to arbitration under the BIT. The Second Circuit disagreed, finding that the dispute between Ecuador and Chevron was properly brought to BIT arbitration. By signing the BIT, Ecuador agreed to resolve investment disputes through arbitration under the rules of the United Nations Commission on International Trade Law (UNCITRAL). Article 21 of those rules states that the arbitrator "shall have the power to rule on objections that it has no jurisdiction, including any objections with respect to the existence or validity of the . . . arbitration agreement." Having consented to sending challenges to the "validity" of the arbitration agreement to the arbitral panel, Ecuador cannot now "disown its agreed-to obligation to arbitrate . . . the question[s] of arbitrability." Because Ecuador's waiver and estoppel claims went to the validity of the arbitration agreement, Article 21 required that they be decided by the arbitral panel, not by the courts.

Similarly, the Second Circuit rejected Ecuador's argument that Chevron was estopped from pursuing the BIT arbitration because it had agreed to litigate the LAPs' case in Ecuador in order to secure a dismissal of the case brought by the LAPs in New York. The court explained that BIT arbitration is designed to settle investment disputes between foreign investors and host governments. The individual plaintiffs in the Lago Agrio litigation were not parties to the BIT, so that treaty has no application to their claims. As a result, their claims cannot be resolved by BIT arbitration. Because Chevron's agreement to litigate in

---

110. *Id.*

Ecuador was made with different plaintiffs—the LAPs, not the Ecuadorian government—the court found no inherent conflict between the BIT arbitration between Ecuador and Chevron and the Lago Agrio litigation. The court concluded that the existence of those parallel proceedings—one in which Chevron asserts wrongdoing on the part of Ecuador and another in which the plaintiffs assert wrongdoing on the part of Chevron—made it clear that the Lago Agrio litigation could coexist with BIT arbitration.

In the following case, Chevron sought an injunction prohibiting the enforcement of the judgment rendered by the Lago Agrio court, based on alleged corruption in the Ecuadorian judiciary.

A CASE IN POINT	*Summary*	Case 24.5

Chevron Corp. v. Naranjo

United States Court of Appeals for the Second Circuit
667 F.3d 232 (2d Cir. 2012).

FACTS From 1964 through 1992, Chevron and various partners, including the Ecuadorian government, engaged in oil extraction in the Lago Agrio region of the Ecuadorian Amazon. In 1993, the Lagro Agrio plaintiffs (LAPs) brought suit in the Southern District of New York, alleging a variety of environmental, health, and other tort claims related to the extraction activities. The district court dismissed the plaintiffs' claims due to *forum non conveniens* after Chevron agreed to litigate the LAPs' claims in Ecuador.

In 2004, the LAPs initiated a lawsuit against Chevron in Ecuador. In 2005, the LAPs' lawyer Steven R. Donziger solicited Joseph Berlinger, a prominent New York documentary filmmaker, to make a film "to tell his clients' story." A version of the film, entitled *Crude*, included footage suggesting that Richard Cabrera Vega, the purportedly independent expert appointed by the Ecuadorian court, had worked hand-in-glove with the LAPs in his investigations. After discovering the footage, Chevron launched dozens of discovery proceedings, which allowed the company to gain access to a significant amount of previously unexposed information, including Donziger's litigation files and several hundred hours of outtakes from Berlinger's film.

The outtakes contained Donziger's unedited characterizations of his negative view of the Ecuadorian judiciary; the LAPs' litigation, legislative, and political strategies; and a discussion of how the LAPs planned to use any resulting Ecuadorian judgment to force a quick settlement with Chevron. Chevron also discovered a memo in Donziger's litigation files detailing his strategy of using the judgment enforcement for settlement leverage.

On the basis of this evidence, Chevron alleged that the Ecuadorian judgment was fundamentally tainted by fraud. In particular, Chevron accused Donziger of covert illicit participation in the selection of Cabrera as an "independent" expert and of ghost-writing Cabrera's entire report. Chevron also alleged that "Donziger engaged in other threats against the Ecuadorian judiciary, by mobilizing protesters to intimidate the court by surrounding it on the dates of key hearings, and by enlisting political pressure from elected officials, including the President of Ecuador."

Chevron presented its allegations of fraud to the Ecuadorian trial court. Nevertheless, in February 2011, the Ecuadorian trial court found Chevron liable for $8.6 billion of damages, with a $8.6 billion punitive damages award to be added unless Chevron apologized within fourteen days of the opinion's issuance. Chevron did not apologize, resulting in a judgment of $17.2 billion against the company.

Chevron then filed suit in the Southern District of New York. In addition to money damages related to several civil claims, Chevron sought a permanent injunction under the Declaratory Judgment Act and the Recognition Act barring the enforcement, anywhere in the world outside Ecuador, of any judgment rendered against it by the Ecuadorian courts. The district court, persuaded by Chevron's portrayal of a politically and judicially corrupt nation, granted the injunction. Specifically, the court concluded that Chevron was likely to show at a subsequent trial that the Ecuadorian court system is incapable of producing a judgment that New York courts can respect under the Recognition Act, because "the Ecuadorian judicial system 'no longer acts impartially, with integrity and firmness in applying the law and administering justice . . . .'"

Donziger and the LAPs appealed the district court's decision granting the preliminary injunction.

CONTINUED

ISSUE PRESENTED   May a U.S. district court preliminarily enjoin the enforcement in any jurisdiction outside Ecuador of an allegedly corrupt judgment by an Ecuadorian court?

SUMMARY OF OPINION   The U.S. Court of Appeals for the Second Circuit began its analysis by observing that the Uniform Foreign Money-Judgments Recognition Act supports the enforcement of foreign judgments that are "final, conclusive and enforceable where rendered even though an appeal therefrom is pending or it is subject to appeal." There are ten exceptions to that presumption of enforceability: two mandate nonrecognition, and the remaining eight leave the question of nonrecognition to the court's discretion. One of the mandatory exceptions requires that a court not enforce a judgment if "the judgment was rendered under a system which does not provide impartial tribunals or procedures compatible with the requirements of due process of law." The court may also exercise its discretion and decline recognition if "the judgment was obtained by fraud."

The court quickly dismissed Chevron's complaints under these provisions of the Recognition Act on a procedural basis. The sections on which Chevron relied merely provided *exceptions* from the circumstances in which a holder of a foreign judgment can obtain enforcement of that judgment in New York; they do not create an affirmative cause of action to declare foreign judgments void and to enjoin their enforcement. The court reasoned that the Recognition Act and the common law principles it encapsulates are motivated by an interest to *provide* for the enforcement of foreign judgments, not to prevent them. Thus, the Recognition Act (as well as its exceptions) has the underlying purpose of facilitating trust among nations and their judicial systems.

In addition to the procedural pitfalls of Chevron's reliance on the Recognition Act, the court also raised international comity concerns. In enacting the Recognition Act, New York undertook to act as a responsible participant in an international system of justice—not to set up its courts as a "transnational arbiter to dictate to the entire world which judgments are entitled to respect and which countries' courts are to be treated as international pariahs." Even though this was only an anti-*enforcement* injunction as opposed to a more significant anti-*suit* injunction, the court concluded that a decision by a court in one jurisdiction to decline to enforce a judgment rendered in a foreign jurisdiction plainly touches on international comity concerns. Those concerns become even "graver" when a court in one country attempts to preclude the courts of every other nation from even *considering* the effect of that foreign judgment. Because Chevron's claims under the Recognition Act failed on procedural grounds, the court did not further address these international comity concerns.

The court next rejected Chevron's characterization of its claims as a simple declaratory action under the federal Declaratory Judgment Act (DJA). The DJA gives a district court the discretion to "declare the legal rights and other legal relations of any interested party seeking such declaration." Simply put, the court stated, that discretion does not extend to the declaration of rights that do not exist under law. Like a preliminary injunction, a declaratory judgment relies on a valid legal predicate. Because the Recognition Act did not provide that legal predicate, Chevron could not use the DJA to obtain relief.

The court noted that the LAPs hold a judgment from an Ecuadorian court, which they may seek to enforce in any country in the world where Chevron has assets. At the present time, there is no indication that they will select New York as one of the jurisdictions where they will seek enforcement efforts. Therefore, the court concluded, nothing will be gained by rendering a decision now about the effect in New York of a foreign judgment that may never be presented in New York. Instead, a better remedy is available: Chevron can present its defense to the recognition and enforcement of the Ecuadorian judgment in New York if, as, and when the LAPs seek to enforce their judgment in New York.

RESULT   The judgment of the district court was reversed, and the preliminary injunction was vacated. The case was remanded to the district court with the instruction to dismiss Chevron's claim for injunctive and declaratory relief under the Recognition Act.

Limited Discovery

Discovery rules in foreign countries are not as liberal as U.S. rules and frequently allow the parties to obtain relatively little information or none at all. As a result, if litigation in an American court concerns either an American corporation's foreign subsidiary or one of its offices located in a foreign country, obtaining documents or taking depositions of the employees located in the foreign country may prove difficult. Although litigants can obtain an order from a U.S. court that permits them to petition the court of the foreign country to obtain discovery to be used in the United States, the process is lengthy, and many countries will allow only very limited discovery or none at all. Even the United Kingdom, which has a legal system similar to the U.S. system, permits only limited discovery.

In addition, the process for taking discovery in foreign countries is frequently different from the U.S. practice. For example, countries often require a judge to be present at depositions, making the procedure more formal and controlled than it is in the United States, where only lawyers and witnesses are present.

Recovery of Attorneys' Fees

Virtually every western European country uses the "British rule"—also known as the "loser pays" rule—which requires the losing party at trial to pay the legal costs, including attorneys' fees, of the winner. The American system, by contrast, requires each litigant to bear its own attorneys' fees regardless of the trial's outcome, unless there is a contract providing that the loser must pay the winner's attorneys' fees. Efforts by the Republican majority in Congress in the mid-1990s to adopt the British rule as part of the "Contract With America" failed.[111]

The British rule is intended to compel potential litigants to evaluate the merits of their case carefully before involving the justice system. It can deter plaintiffs from filing frivolous claims to extort a settlement and defendants from adopting outlandish positions.[112] At the same time, the threat of being saddled with their opponents' costs can discourage potential litigants, particularly the poor, from asserting justifiable claims.[113] The fee-shifting rule can also inhibit the development of the law, as the financial risk of asserting novel or untested legal theories becomes too great.

Choice of Law and Choice of Forum

Since most international transactions are conducted on a contract basis, most disputes involving international transactions relate to an alleged past or future contractual relationship. Crucial considerations in any dispute will be which law applies to the contract and which country's courts have jurisdiction over the dispute.

The substantive terms of a contract are typically subject to the laws of a single jurisdiction, which will clarify, modify, or even void the provisions of the contract. If a contract leaves an issue open, the applicable law may fill the gap, disregarding the parties' unwritten intentions. Certain provisions may be included to address requirements of laws of other jurisdictions (for example, U.S. export controls may affect non-U.S. contracts). Even if the written contract addresses an issue, that provision may be affected by what is allowed or required under the relevant local law. It is important, therefore, to understand not only what the parties wish to do but also what they are permitted to do. Achieving this understanding can be difficult. Familiar legal terms in one jurisdiction may have a different meaning and effect in another. Hence, it is often of utmost importance to have advisers in each jurisdiction who understand the relevant differences between that jurisdiction and others and can fully address the intricacies of cross-border transactions.

International contracts should generally include explicit choice-of-law and choice-of-forum provisions to avoid later disputes over which law applies and which country's courts (or other dispute resolution tribunals) have jurisdiction. It is important to remember, however, that under certain circumstances a court will not honor the parties' choice-of law provision. As explained further in Chapter 3, this is most likely to occur when application of the chosen law would violate the public policy of the jurisdiction in which the lawsuit is brought. For example, an Indian court will not enforce a postemployment covenant not to compete against an Indian employee living in India, even if the employer is based in Massachusetts and the employment contract specifies that the law of the Commonwealth of Massachusetts (which will enforce reasonable covenants not to compete) will govern the employment relationship. To enforce the covenant would violate India's strong public policy in favor of employees' right to ply their trade.

When jurisdiction and choice of law are not specified in the contract and are disputed, the court in which the suit is filed will apply *conflict-of-laws rules*, which usually focus on the significance of each country's relationship to the contract. These principles (sometimes referred to as principles of private international law) vary in some respects from country to country, and the process of litigating them can be extended and expensive. Consequently, it is prudent to address these issues in advance.

As explained in Chapter 8, if both parties to an international contract are nationals of countries that are signatories to the United Nations Convention on Contracts for the International Sale of Goods (CISG), the rules of that convention may apply, unless the parties opt out of the CISG rules. CISG rules also apply if the country whose law applies (as determined by the contract or by conflict-of-laws principles) is a signatory to CISG.

---

111. This part of the "Contract With America" was proposed by Jim Ramstad (R-Minn.) in the 104th Congress in a bill entitled "The Common Sense Legal Reforms Act" (H.R. 956). It failed to pass the House of Representatives.

112. *Less Litigation, More Justice*, WALL ST. J., Aug. 14, 1991.

113. AGENDA FOR CIVIL JUSTICE REFORM IN AMERICA 24 (1991).

A contract party may be willing to accept the substantive law of the other party's country but prefer that any disputes be submitted to a neutral forum. In such a case, an international arbitral organization is commonly specified.

Commonly selected international arbitral forums include the International Chamber of Commerce (ICC) in Paris, the International Center for the Settlement of Investment Disputes (ICSID), the London Court of International Arbitration (LCIA), the Arbitration Institute of the Stockholm Chamber of Commerce, and the Arbitration Institute of the Zurich Chamber of Commerce. Each international arbitral body has its own procedural rules. Internationally accepted arbitration rules, such as those adopted by the United Nations Commission on International Trade Law (UNCITRAL), may also be used in conjunction with the parties' own methods of selecting an arbitral panel. This latter type of arrangement is referred to as ad hoc arbitration. If there is no mutually convenient venue for the arbitration, the parties will often designate a place that is comparably distant and inconvenient for both parties.

Enforcement of Awards

After a dispute has ended, the awards must be enforced, but enforcement across national borders can present additional problems. Under the principle of comity, a court will generally enforce another country's judgments when three conditions are met: (1) reciprocity is extended between the countries (that is, the countries must have agreed to mutually honor each other's court decisions, usually by way of a treaty), (2) proper notice is given to the defendant, and (3) the foreign court's judgment does not violate domestic statutes or treaty obligations. U.S. courts, however, generally do not require reciprocity in order to honor foreign judgments.[114]

Since 1979, seventy-two countries, including the United States, have become members of the Convention on Jurisdiction and Foreign Judgments in Civil and Commercial Matters[115] under the auspices of the Hague Conference on Private International Law. As of January 2012, 146 countries, including the United States and most of the major trading nations, are parties to the 1958 United Nations Convention on the Recognition and Enforcement of Foreign Arbitral Awards (often referred to as the New York Convention).[116] Its purpose is "to unify standards by which agreements to arbitrate are observed and arbitral awards are enforced in signatory countries." The New York Convention requires signatory countries to recognize and enforce foreign arbitration awards except in

very limited circumstances. As a result, arbitration awards of another country can often be enforced more readily in a foreign court than foreign judgments.

Forum Non Conveniens

Defendants in international disputes often invoke the doctrine of *forum non conveniens*, claiming that the forum chosen by the plaintiff is not convenient. To prevail on a motion to dismiss a case under this doctrine, the defendant must first show that an adequate alternative forum exists. "However, it is only 'in rare circumstances . . . where the remedy provided by the alternative forum . . . is so clearly inadequate or unsatisfactory, that there is no remedy at all,' that this requirement is not met."[117] As the U.S. Court of Appeals for the Second Circuit explained: "'The availability of an adequate alternative forum does not depend on the existence of the identical cause of action in the other forum,' nor on identical remedies."[118]

Thus, for example, England was deemed an adequate forum even though the Sherman Act and certain common law claims were not available and English courts had never awarded money damages in an antitrust case.[119] Trinidad was deemed adequate even though the plaintiff, who potentially could recover $8 million in the United States, was likely limited to $570,000 in Trinidad.[120]

After showing the adequacy of the alternative forum, the defendant must demonstrate that the ordinarily strong presumption favoring the plaintiff's chosen forum is countered by the public and private interest factors identified by the U.S. Supreme Court in *Gulf Oil Corp. v. Gilbert*.[121] In *Gilbert*, the Supreme Court outlined four public interest factors for courts to weigh: (1) administrative difficulties associated with court congestion, (2) the unfairness of imposing jury duty on a community with no relation to the litigation, (3) the "local interest in having localized controversies decided at home," and (4) the interest in avoiding difficult problems in resolving conflict-of-law issues and applying foreign law. The private interest factors enumerated in *Gilbert* include (1) ease of access to evidence; (2) the availability of compulsory process to compel the attendance of unwilling witnesses; (3) the cost of willing witnesses' attendance; (4) if relevant, the possibility of a view of the premises; and (5) all other factors that might make a trial quicker or less expensive.

In the following case, the court applied the doctrine of *forum non conveniens* to determine whether a case should be transferred from a U.S. court to Peru.

---

114. *See* Restatement (Second) of Conflict of Laws § 6 cmt. k, § 98 cmt. e (1971).

115. The Convention is available at http://www.hcch.net/index_en.php?act=conventions.text&cid=78.

116. The current status of the New York Convention can be found at http://www.uncitral.org/uncitral/en/uncitral_texts/arbitration/NYConvention_status.html.

117. Lueck v. Sundstrand Corp, 236 F.3d 1137, 1143 (9th Cir. 2001).

118. Norex Petroleum Ltd. v. Access Indus., Inc., 416 F.3d 146, 158 (2d Cir. 2005).

119. Capital Currency Exch., N.V. v. Nat'l Westminster Bank PLC, 155 F.3d 603 (2d Cir. 1998).

120. Alcoa S.S. Co. v. M/V Nordic Regent, 654 F.2d 147 (2d Cir. 1980) (en banc).

121. 330 U.S. 501 (1947).

Carijano v. Occidental
Petroleum Corp.

*United States Court of Appeals for
the Ninth Circuit*
643 F.3d. 1216 (9th Cir. 2011).

FACTS Twenty-five members of the Achuar indigenous group (the Achuar plaintiffs) and Amazon Watch, a nonprofit Montana corporation headquartered in California, sued Occidental Petroleum, one of the largest oil and gas companies in the United States, in Los Angeles County Superior Court for environmental contamination and release of hazardous waste as a result of Occidental's petroleum and oil exploration in Peru. The Achuar are dependent for their existence upon the rain forest lands and waterways along the Corrientes and Macusari Rivers in the northern region of Peru. Occidental built dozens of wells, a 530-kilometer network of pipelines, refineries, and separation batteries for processing crude oil, as well as roads, heliports, and camps to support its operations near the Corrientes and Macusari Rivers. Occidental sold its stake in the Peruvian oil fields to the Argentine oil company Pluspetrol in 2000.

The complaint alleged that Occidental knowingly utilized out-of-date methods for separating crude oil that contravened U.S. and Peruvian law, resulting in the discharge of millions of gallons of toxic oil by-products into the area's waterways. Achuar children and adults came into frequent contact with the contaminants by using polluted rivers and tributaries for drinking, washing, and fishing. Tests have shown potentially dangerous levels of lead and cadmium in the blood of a significant number of affected individuals. The Achuar plaintiffs have reported gastrointestinal problems, kidney trouble, and skin rashes that they attribute to the pollution. Environmental damage as a result of the pollution includes decreasing yields of edible fish, the death or disease of animals hunted by the Achuar after drinking river water, and a reduction in agricultural productivity and land values. The plaintiffs assert claims for common law negligence, strict liability, battery, medical monitoring, wrongful death, fraud and misrepresentation, public and private nuisance, trespass, and intentional infliction of emotional distress, as well as a violation of California's Unfair Competition Law. They seek damages, injunctive and declaratory relief, restitution, and disgorgement of profits on behalf of the individual plaintiffs and two proposed classes.

Amazon Watch began working with the Achuar communities in 2001. Representatives of Amazon Watch traveled to the region several times in the ensuing years and helped produce a documentary film about the contamination. Amazon Watch officials also communicated with Occidental representatives in Los Angeles throughout 2005 and 2006, both at public shareholder events and in private meetings. Amazon Watch organized public relations campaigns in both Peru and Los Angeles designed to respond to statements by Occidental about its Peruvian operations.

Although Occidental has its headquarters in Los Angeles County, Occidental removed the suit to federal district court where it successfully moved for dismissal on the ground that Peru is a more convenient forum. Occidental also moved to dismiss Amazon Watch as a plaintiff without standing. The district court found that Peru was an adequate alternative forum but did not decide whether the Amazon Watch plaintiff lacked standing because that was moot in light of the dismissal of the suit on *forum non conveniens* grounds. The Achuar plaintiffs appealed.

ISSUE PRESENTED Did the district court abuse its discretion when it dismissed the Achuar plaintiffs' lawsuit on *forum non conveniens* grounds?

SUMMARY OF OPINION The U.S. Court of Appeals for the Ninth Circuit began by noting that *forum non conveniens* is "an exceptional tool to be employed sparingly," and not a "doctrine that compels plaintiffs to choose the optimal forum for their claim."

To prevail on a motion to dismiss based on *forum non conveniens*, a defendant bears the burden of demonstrating that an adequate alternative forum exists and that the balance of private and public interest factors favors dismissal. In determining whether the district court abused its discretion in concluding that Occidental satisfied its burden, the court examined (1) the adequacy of the alternative forum, (2) the private and public factors and the deference

CONTINUED

owed a plaintiff's chosen forum, and (3) the district court's decision to dismiss the plaintiffs' case without imposing any conditions on the dismissal.

The district court properly determined that Peru provides an adequate alternative forum for the plaintiffs to pursue their claims against Occidental. An alternative forum is deemed adequate if (1) the defendant is amenable to process there and (2) the other jurisdiction offers a satisfactory remedy. Occidental is amenable to process in Peru because of its previous business activities in the country as well as its stipulation to service of process and jurisdiction there.

The district court also correctly concluded that Occidental met its burden of proving that Peru could offer the plaintiffs a satisfactory remedy. The district court was presented with expert affidavits by both parties and did not abuse its discretion in disregarding the plaintiffs' experts, who stated that damages fulfill a purely compensatory, not punitive, function in Peru and that it may be difficult for an "indeterminate group of persons (or class) such as the 'Achuar communities'" to recover, in favor of Occidental's expert, who stated that "Peruvian law has analogies for all the substantive legal theories on which the lawsuit filed in the Los Angeles jurisdiction is based."

The district court also did not abuse its discretion in determining that Peru is not disqualified as an adequate forum due to fraud or corruption. The plaintiffs produced experts who described the Achuar plaintiffs as a group as being victims of discrimination in Peru due to their ethnicity, poverty, and isolation and stated that Peru's judicial system has refused to intervene. The district court was within its discretion to credit Occidental's expert, who provided detailed examples of the availability of filing fee waivers for the indigent and outreach programs for indigenous groups. The district court properly concluded that the evidence contained in the plaintiffs' expert affidavits was too generalized and anecdotal "to pass value judgments on the adequacy of Peru's judicial system."

Nonetheless, there is a strong presumption in favor of the plaintiffs' choice of forum, which may be overcome only when private and public interest factors point to trial in the alternative forum. Although plaintiffs may be entitled to less deference when the court makes an express finding that they are forum shopping, those concerns were "muted" here. Amazon Watch had been engaged in the subject matter of the dispute for six years before the filing of this claim. Moreover, the plaintiffs did not strategically choose a random or only tangentially relevant forum. Los Angeles is the home forum of both Occidental and Amazon Watch, as well as a forum that has strong connection to the subject matter of this case. And while the case concerns past operations and injury in Peru, the complaint includes claims based on decisions made in and policies emerging from Occidental's corporate headquarters in Los Angeles.

The district court erred in neglecting to analyze each individual private factor and instead looked only generally to witnesses and evidence located in California as compared to witnesses and evidence located in Peru. For example, the parties' residences did not weigh in favor of dismissal. Occidental maintains its headquarters in California; Amazon Watch's principal place of business is in San Francisco, California, and it has an office in Malibu, California. Although the Achuar plaintiffs do not live in California, they indicated willingness to travel to the United States in the event of trial.

The district court also erred in finding that the California forum was inconvenient for the litigants. The district court cited the substantial cost of airfare to transport the Achuar plaintiffs to the United States for trial. It did not, however, consider the flip side of transporting the Occidental defendants and witnesses as well as the Amazon Watch plaintiff and witnesses to Peru for trial. When this cost is considered, this factor is neutral because there is hardship either way.

The district court also erred in finding that access to evidence weighed in favor of dismissal. Rather than evaluating the materiality and importance of anticipated witnesses' testimony,

CONTINUED

the district court relied on the number of witnesses located in Peru versus the number located in California. However, the proper consideration is whether the witnesses in Peru are unwilling to testify. Occidental did not satisfy its burden of showing that the Peruvian witnesses were unwilling to testify in California.

In addition, the physical site in Peru was less important now because Occidental withdrew from the site in 2000. The district court also failed to consider that Amazon Watch's principal place of business is in California and that key employees and relevant documentary evidence within its control are in California. Moreover, many of the events involving the group that form the basis for its claims occurred in the state. After taking into account all of the relevant considerations, the court concluded that the evidentiary factor was neutral.

Most critically, the district court failed to give any consideration to whether a judgment against Occidental could be enforced in Peru. California generally enforces foreign judgments, as long as they are issued by impartial tribunals that have afforded the litigants due process. In contrast, compelling evidence of disorder in the Peruvian judiciary leads to reasonable doubts as to the enforceability of a judgment in Peru. Because the district court did not require Occidental to agree, as a condition for dismissal, that any Peruvian judgment could be enforced against it in the United States or anywhere else it held assets, Occidental remains free to attack any Peruvian judgment on due process grounds under California's foreign judgments statute. The private factor of the enforceability of judgments thus weighs against dismissal.

In weighing the public factors related to the interests of the forums, the district court weighed Peru's stake in a case involving its own "lands and citizens" against California's "interest in ensuring that businesses incorporated or operating within its borders abide by the law," and concluded that the local interests factor favored dismissal. However, the district court did not adequately consider California's substantial interest in providing a forum for those harmed by the actions of its citizen corporations. In addition, the basis of Amazon Watch's Unfair Competition Law claim against Occidental is for actions taking place in California—a California plaintiff suing a California defendant for actions that occurred within California. Therefore, although both sides have significant interests in the outcome of the litigation, the local interest factor favors neither side entirely.

The district court did not abuse its discretion in finding that the factor of court congestion and burden was neutral, as both forums have similarly crowded dockets. The district court also did not err in finding the choice-of-law factor neutral because there are reasonable arguments on both sides as to which law, Peruvian or Californian, applies.

In weighing the factors, the private factors based on convenience and evidentiary concerns favored neither side, while the residence of the parties and enforceability of the judgment factors weighed against dismissal. All of the public interest factors were neutral. Thus, the court concluded that the private and public factors, taken together, failed to "establish . . . oppressiveness and vexation to a defendant . . . out of all proportion to plaintiff's convenience" and also failed to outweigh the deference owed to the plaintiff Amazon Watch's chosen forum.

In addition, the district court abused its discretion when it did not condition its dismissal of the Los Angeles action on Occidental's agreement to litigate in Peru because "there is a justifiable reason to doubt that a party [namely, Occidental] will cooperate with the foreign forum." Here, there was reason to suspect that Occidental will move to dismiss the Peruvian claims when they are refiled pursuant to the Peruvian statute of limitations. The district court could have cured this by imposing the proper conditions on the dismissal.

RESULT   The district court erred in granting Occidental's motion to dismiss on *forum non conveniens* grounds without requiring that Occidental waive any statute of limitations defenses that would not have been available in California. The dismissal of the case was reversed so that the plaintiffs could maintain their suit in the Los Angeles courts.

Suing Foreign Governments

Sovereign immunity and the act-of-state doctrine are international legal principles that affect the rights of private commercial parties when a government becomes involved in or interferes with an international commercial transaction.

Sovereign Immunity

The doctrine of *sovereign immunity* prevents the courts of one country from hearing suits against the governments of other countries. The rationale underlying this rule is that all sovereign states are equal and none may subject others to their laws.

The needs of commerce have gradually tempered this rule. Because private entities often enter into commercial transactions with foreign governments, it became apparent that allowing a government to have complete immunity from all suits was not desirable. Thus, the concept of absolute immunity has yielded to the restrictive theory of sovereign immunity, which allows immunity for a government's public activities but not for its commercial activities.

The Foreign Sovereign Immunities Act of 1976 (FSIA)[122] is the U.S. codification of the restrictive theory of immunity. FSIA was designed to eliminate the inconsistencies associated with politically initiated decisions to grant or withhold sovereign immunity in particular cases. It empowered the courts to determine when sovereign immunity applies "by reference to the nature of the course of conduct or particular transaction or act." The U.S. Supreme Court held in *Republic of Austria v. Altmann*[123] that FSIA even applies retroactively.

FSIA is the sole basis for obtaining jurisdiction over a foreign government in U.S. courts. FSIA grants a blanket immunity to foreign states except in cases in which (1) the foreign state expressly or impliedly waives its immunity; (2) the foreign state engages in commercial activities; (3) the foreign state expropriates property in violation of international law (that is, seizes it without proper compensation); (4) property in the United States that is immovable or was acquired by gift or succession is at issue; (5) the foreign state commits certain noncommercial torts; (6) suit is brought to enforce a maritime lien under admiralty (maritime) law; or (7) the defendant wishes to file a counterclaim in a suit initiated by the foreign state.

The *commercial activity exception* to sovereign immunity provides that a foreign sovereign or its agencies and instrumentalities shall not be immune from the jurisdiction of the courts of the United States or of the states in any case in which the action is based on an act (1) that takes place outside the territory of the United States in connection with a commercial activity of the foreign sovereign elsewhere and (2) that causes a direct effect in the United States. As the U.S. Court of Appeals for the Second Circuit explained: "If the sovereign's activity is commercial in nature and has a direct effect in the United States, then the jurisdictional nexus is met, no immunity attaches, and a district court has the authority to adjudicate disputes based on that activity."[124] For example, in *Republic of Argentina v. Weltover, Inc.,*[125] the U.S. Supreme Court held that Argentina's unilateral rescheduling of bond payments had a "direct effect" in the United States because New York was the place of payment.

FSIA is particularly relevant to U.S. companies that do or intend to do business with state-owned or state-managed enterprises, such as those in China and Vietnam. The exception from immunity for the commercial activities of these entities may not always be clear, however. In addition, if the contract is between a foreign, wholly owned subsidiary of a U.S. company and a foreign, state-owned enterprise, the fact that the U.S. parent is affected by a breach of the contract may not give rise to any remedial rights under U.S. law. If the nature of the foreign party to a contract or the subject matter of a contract is not clearly commercial, it may be advisable to require the foreign government to waive sovereign immunity in the contract.

Act-of-State Doctrine

The *act-of-state doctrine* applies to the noncommercial acts of a government that affect foreign business interests within that government's territory. The doctrine was most clearly expressed by the U.S. Supreme Court in *Underhill v. Hernandez,*[126] when it stated that "the courts of one country will not sit in judgment on the acts of the government of another, done within its own territory." Pursuant to this doctrine, U.S. courts are extremely reluctant to provide a legal remedy under U.S. law for the public acts of a foreign government. As a result, U.S. businesses generally cannot look to the U.S. courts for protection from or compensation for acts such as expropriation, unless there is a bilateral treaty between the United States and the foreign country that specifies the procedural and substantive rights of a U.S. investor in that country. As mentioned earlier, however, OPIC (the Overseas Private Investment Corporation) will insure U.S. businesses against certain host government acts, such as expropriation or restrictions on the conversion of local currency earnings.

---

122. 28 U.S.C. § 1330.
123. 541 U.S. 677 (2004).
124. Commercial Bank of Kuwait v. Rafidain Bank, 15 F.3d 238, 241 (2d Cir. 1994).
125. 504 U.S. 607 (1992).
126. 168 U.S. 250, 252 (1897).

GLOBAL VIEW

Venezuela and the Hazards of International Joint Ventures

In theory, international joint ventures allow each partner to benefit from the comparative advantages of the other, generating a healthy profit for both. Even when the parties clearly specify management and ownership rights in the joint venture agreement, however, the risk of nationalization and expropriation is a constant hazard, particularly in developing or politically unstable countries. As evidenced by Big Oil's experience in the early twenty-first century in Venezuela, rules on foreign investment may change at any time—often without warning—putting a joint venturer's capital, resources, technologies, and profits at risk.

In the early 1990s, Venezuela reopened its oil fields to foreign investors after the unsuccessful nationalizations of the 1970s. Lured by generous tax concessions and eager to profit from what would become the fifth-largest oil export market in the world,[127] foreign firms invested more than $20 billion in so-called strategic associations to develop Venezuela's oil fields. Then, in 1998, after seven years of soaring profits for oil companies, the political climate changed dramatically. Hugo Chávez was elected President of Venezuela on a platform that called for the creation of a National Constituent Assembly to write a new Venezuelan constitution. Chávez had strong support from the poorest classes, who had seen their living standards decline significantly over the previous decade.

As part of his "Bolívarian Revolution," Chávez moved Venezuela abruptly toward socialism and promised to redistribute the oil wealth to the country's poor. Venezuela began insisting on strict compliance with OPEC's production quotas in order to raise oil prices. Severe political turmoil and instability ensued. In 2001, Chávez bypassed the Venezuelan Congress and promulgated a new Hydrocarbons Law, which went into effect in 2002. The new law provided that all oil production and distribution were the domain of the Venezuelan state and required that the state-owned oil company, Petróleos de Venezuela SA (PdVSA), be given at least 51% of the capital stock in all future joint ventures.[128] The law also raised royalty rates (with the exception of high-risk joint ventures targeting extra-heavy crude oil production) from 16.7% to 30%—making them the highest in the world.[129]

Shortly after the passage of the Hydrocarbons Law, business leaders led a two-month national strike and shut down economic activity. Chávez responded by declaring that Venezuela's oil reserves were of "strategic importance" to

Venezuela and must be kept under state control. Petroleum production and refining by PdVSA ceased almost entirely during this period. Chávez used this as an opportunity to fire 19,000 of the company's experienced employees—more than half of the workforce—and to replace them with workers loyal to him.

In 2004, the oil industry was again hit hard when Chávez unilaterally increased the royalty rate on oil production from the Orinoco heavy crude strategic associations from 1% to 16.6%. The world's largest oil companies, including Chevron, ExxonMobil, ConocoPhillips, and British Petroleum (BP), felt the brunt of the change.[130] Less than a year later, Chávez targeted foreign oil investors directly and announced that all international strategic associations must comply with the Hydrocarbons Law, convert to joint ventures, and relinquish majority control of their investments to the state. The firms faced a sharp deadline to sign the new joint venture agreements, which mandated up to 80% ownership by PdVSA. Chávez threatened that if the oil companies refused to comply, he would seize their oil fields for the state. Before the joint ventures could be formed, the foreign companies were required to pay $3 billion in back tax claims.[131]

Chevron, Statoil, Total, and BP signed the agreements, giving PdVSA an average of 78% equity participation in the former strategic associations. After ExxonMobil and ConocoPhillips refused to hand over their 60% to 80% ownership interests to PdVSA,[132] the Venezuelan government seized their lucrative oil fields in 2007 and refused to pay cash compensation.[133] ExxonMobil moved straight to international arbitration at the International Center for Settlement of Investment Disputes (ICSID) in 2007 in accordance with a Bilateral Investment Treaty with Venezuela that requires arbitration. The ICSID is an autonomous international institution established under the Convention on the Settlement of Investment Disputes Between States and Nationals of Other States that operates under the auspices of the World Bank. More than 140 countries, including Venezuela, are signatories.

Chávez responded by banning ExxonMobil from ever doing business in Venezuela and proclaiming in his weekly radio and TV broadcast that "they will never steal from us again, the ExxonMobil bandits, imperialist white-collar thieves who

CONTINUED

---

127. *US Energy Security Plans Threatened by Militant Venezuela*, OIL & ENERGY TRENDS, Sept. 16, 2005, at 3.

128. Fabiola Sanchez, *New Law Tightens State Control over Venezuela's Oil Industry*, ASSOC. PRESS WORLDSTREAM, Nov.27, 2001.

129. *Id.*

130. Brian Ellsworth, *Venezuela Defends Tax Increase on Four Oil Projects*, N.Y. TIMES, Oct. 12, 2004, at C6.

131. Natalie Obiko Pearson, *South America Goes Nationalist with Its Oil and Gas amid High World Prices*, ASSOC. PRESS, Oct. 13, 2005.

132. *ConocoPhillips, ExxonMobil Pull Out of Venezuela Oil Sector*, AGENCE FRANCE PRESSE—ENGLISH, June 26, 2007.

133. Natalie Obiko Pearson, *Venezuela: No Cash Compensation for Takeover of Oil Companies in Orinoco*, ASSOC. PRESS FIN. WIRE, May 3, 2007.

corrupt and oust governments and supported the invasion of Iraq . . . ."[134] ConocoPhillips also petitioned the ICSID for damages from Venezuela.[135]

In December 2011, ExxonMobil was granted $907 million by the International Chamber of Commerce for the 2007 seizure of the Cerro Negro heavy crude project; the ICSID was expected to confirm

the award in 2012.[136] ExxonMobil has a pending arbitration proceeding against the government of Venezuela in which it is demanding $12 billion. Some predicted that the ICSID would award something closer to $1 billion. In January 2012, President Chávez announced that Venezuela would refuse to obey future ICSID decisions and formally began the process of withdrawing from the Convention on the Settlement of Investment Disputes Between States and Nationals of Other States, which it had signed in 1996.

134. *Id.*

135. *Venezuela to Exit World Bank Investment Dispute Tribunal*, Wall St. J., Jan. 15, 2012.

136. *Id.*

THE RESPONSIBLE MANAGER

EXPANDING INTO INTERNATIONAL MARKETS

Before expanding into international markets, legally astute managers take into consideration not only market conditions but also the laws and mores of the foreign country. Examples of substantive laws that may affect a foreign business are import/export regulations, employment law, tax law, securities law, and antitrust law. A company that follows the correct form of doing business but fails to recognize or understand local law may reduce its profitability. A company considering foreign investments should therefore carefully analyze the sociopolitical and economic climate of the prospective host country, in addition to obtaining a clear understanding of the legal, regulatory, and administrative regimes and the foreseeable future changes to these.

One way in which companies typically expand into the international marketplace is through direct sales to customers. Direct sales may pose several problems for the company, however, including export regulations, international contract law, letters of credit, import regulations, and the use of local representatives.

If costs do not justify opening a local office, a firm will often retain a local representative to oversee the sale of its products. If the transaction is not correctly structured, however, the company may find that it has a dependent agent in the foreign country—that it has, under local law, opened an office in the foreign country. Transactions thought to be tax-free will, in fact, be subject to corporate tax, and the local agent may have acquired additional rights and protections under local employment law.

A company can also conduct business in a foreign country by acquiring an existing company. Such transactions are governed by the laws regulating foreign investment in the country. Tax issues will play a predominant role in determining the form of the acquisition and the method of future operation.

A firm may also choose to create a new entity distinct from the parent corporation. This entity could be a corporation with 100% foreign ownership or a joint venture in the form of a corporation or partnership. Local law will define the regulations and restrictions to be imposed on the firm.

Common restrictions include requiring majority local ownership or that a majority of the board be resident directors. In many countries, investors may specify whether the entity is to be treated as a partnership or a corporation for U.S. tax purposes. Every jurisdiction seems to have some unique wrinkles in the areas of formation and administration; matters taken for granted by locals may surprise and create delays for foreign investors.

Local advisers experienced in dealing with foreign investors can help smooth the process and minimize surprises on both practical issues and matters of substantive and procedural law. Special attention should be paid to coordinating tax/accounting and legal advice within the context of the investor's business goals. The investor must recognize, though, that sometimes foreign lawyers and accountants take a compartmentalized rather than interdisciplinary approach—they may be accustomed to performing only a technical role and may not wish to act as general business advisers. It is important that the investor's point person, the transaction manager, actively set expectations and coordinate the advisory process.

This is perhaps nowhere more important than in the tax area. Even similar tax systems will differ in significant respects, and only rarely can one find a single individual who is thoroughly versed in the laws of two jurisdictions and their interrelations. It is important to coordinate carefully and start early in the planning stage to uncover potential problem areas. Obtaining tax credits is a relatively obvious issue. More subtle issues can appear in many contexts. An agreement, exchange of assets, or other transaction that creates no tax liability or is not deemed a tax event in one country may create income tax liability in another. For example, stock dividends and splits are not taxable in the United States and other major economies because there is no change of economic substance. Thus, it might not occur to a U.S. manager, tax lawyer, or accountant to inquire and discover that they may be taxable in other countries.

CONTINUED

Corporate laws also vary by jurisdiction. The U.S. system of corporate law and procedure is relatively flexible. Most other jurisdictions have less permissive rules regarding capital structure, dissolution, corporate formalities, and officers and directors, as well as different penalties for noncompliance. An investor may not be able to form, operate, and close down the entity how and when it wants, and achieving the desired management structure may prove impossible or impractical.

If the company employs workers in the host country, it is subject to a system of employment laws, regulations, and customs that is more restrictive and more protective of workers than U.S. law. Restricted use of foreign personnel, required proportions of local workers, prescribed terms of employment, and difficulty in terminating unsatisfactory employees are all common issues. The foreign investor may have to compromise its employment policies to satisfy local requirements.

In some areas, such as environmental law, many developing countries are far less regulated than the United States, but the investor should expect to see these countries' legal regimes eventually catch up. Legal advantages, like business advantages, are often transitory. The investor needs to evaluate and understand both areas to develop the knowledge of and sensitivity to local conditions needed to make the right investment decision.

A MANAGER'S DILEMMA

Putting It into Practice

Should U.S. Companies Sell Products Banned in the United States in Other Countries?

Domingo Castro Alfaro, a Costa Rican resident and employee of Standard Fruit Company, and eighty-one other Costa Rican employees and their wives brought suit against Dow Chemical Company and Shell Oil Company. The employees claimed that while they were working on a banana plantation in Costa Rica for Standard Fruit Company, they suffered personal injuries as a result of exposure to Dibromochloropropane (DBCP). DBCP is a pesticide manufactured by Dow and Shell, which allegedly was furnished to Standard Fruit, an American subsidiary of Dole Fresh Fruit Company, headquartered in Boca Raton, Florida. The employees exposed to DBCP allegedly suffered several medical problems, including sterility.

After the U.S. Environmental Protection Agency (EPA) banned DBCP in the United States, Shell and Dow apparently shipped several hundred thousand gallons of the pesticide to Costa Rica for use by Standard Fruit. Alfaro sued Dow and Shell in Texas in April 1984, alleging that handling DBCP caused the employees serious personal injuries for which Shell and Dow were liable under the theories of product liability, strict liability, and breach of warranty. Under the doctrine of *forum non conveniens*, the defendants argued that Texas was not a convenient forum in which to litigate this case. Should the court grant the defendants' motion to dismiss? Was the conduct of Dow Chemical and Shell Oil ethical? Was Standard Fruit's use of the U.S.-banned pesticide ethical? Were the defendants arguing inconvenient forum to avoid a jury trial and Texas laws regarding personal injury and wrongful death? If so, is that ethical? If goods are not consistent with some sets of standards but are basically okay, is it ethical to sell them? If they are dangerous, how dangerous is too dangerous? Should it matter whether consumers in a developing country cannot afford products meeting higher but more expensive Western standards?[137]

137. Dow Chem. Co. v. Alfaro, 786 S.W.2d 674 (Tex. 1990).

INSIDE STORY

Siemens and Halliburton Caught in FCPA Web After Their Intermediaries Pay Bribes to Government Officials

Both Siemens AG, the Germany-based manufacturer of industrial and consumer products, and U.S. defense contractor Halliburton agreed to pay hundreds of millions of dollars in fines after their so-called intermediaries paid bribes to government officials in violation of the Foreign Corrupt Practices Act (FCPA). In 2008, Siemens reached an unprecedented settlement to resolve SEC charges that the company had violated the FCPA's antibribing and books and records provisions. The SEC complaint alleged that Siemens paid bribes on various projects, including the design and construction of metro transit lines in Venezuela, power plants in Israel, and refineries in Mexico. The company also allegedly used bribes to obtain business such as developing mobile

CONTINUED

telephone networks in Bangladesh, national identity cards in Argentina, and medical devices in Vietnam, Canada, and Russia. Siemens also paid kickbacks to Iraqi ministries in connection with sales of power stations and equipment to Iraq under the United Nations Oil for Food Program. In all, Siemens earned more than $1.1 billion in profits from these and other transactions.[138]

The SEC complaint alleged that between 2001 and 2007, the company engaged in elaborate payment schemes that concealed their corrupt nature and that lax internal controls allowed these schemes to occur. Siemens made thousands of payments to third-party intermediaries in an effort to obscure the purpose for, and recipients of, the money. Authorizations were sometimes made on Post-it notes, which were subsequently destroyed so that no permanent record was kept. Siemens also maintained slush funds and off-books accounts and utilized a vast system of intermediaries to facilitate the illicit payments. In all, Siemens made payments totaling at least $1.4 billion to bribe government officials in return for business and payments to third-party intermediaries totaling $391 for illicit purposes, such as commercial bribery and embezzlement.[139]

Under the terms of the settlement, Siemens agreed to pay $350 million in disgorgement to settle the SEC's charges and a $450 million criminal fine to settle a parallel suit brought by the U.S. Department of Justice. Siemens also paid a criminal fine of $569 million to the Office of the Prosecutor General in Munich, Germany.[140]

The misconduct at Siemens involved all levels of management, and the SEC complaint alleged that top executives hampered an effective FCPA compliance program and at times rewarded bribery. In December 2011, the SEC charged seven former Siemens executives with violating the FCPA for their role in a decade-long bribery scheme involving a $1 billion contract to produce national identity cards for Argentine citizens. The SEC complaint alleged that one of the executives left Siemens in order to act as an intermediary in the scheme. Siemens paid bribes totaling more than $100 million to high-ranking officials including two former Argentine presidents and former cabinet members. The executives allegedly falsified documents and created sham contracts to facilitate the illegal payments.[141]

In another notable case, KBR, Inc. and its former parent company Halliburton Company agreed in 2009 to a settlement with the SEC following alleged violations of the FCPA's intermediary liability provisions. The settlement of $579 million was the largest combined settlement paid by U.S. companies in the FCPA's history. The SEC charged that KBR subsidiary Kellogg Brown & Root, LLC had bribed Nigerian officials over a ten-year period in order to obtain construction contracts. The SEC also claimed that KBR and Halliburton both engaged in books and records violations and internal controls violations related to the bribery.[142]

Kellogg Brown & Root, LLC's predecessor entities (Kellogg, Brown & Root, Inc. and The M.W. Kellogg Company) were members of a four-company joint venture that won construction contracts worth more than $6 billion. As early as 1994, members of the joint venture engaged in a scheme to bribe Nigerian officials in order to obtain the construction contracts. Albert Stanley, the former CEO of the predecessor entities, along with others involved in the joint venture, met with Nigerian government officials and their representatives on numerous occasions to arrange for bribe payments. To conceal the illicit payments, the joint venture entered into sham contracts with agents in Japan and the United Kingdom, who funneled the money to Nigerian officials.

The SEC complaint also alleged that members of the joint venture formed a "cultural committee" to implement the bribery scheme. As the joint venture was compensated for construction projects, it would in turn make payments to bank accounts held by the agents in Japan and the United Kingdom. The committee determined that the agent from the United Kingdom would be used to pay high-ranking Nigerian officials, while the agent from Japan would be used to pay lower-ranking Nigerian officials. Payments to the two agents exceeded $180 million. After receiving the money, the agents would make substantial payments into accounts controlled by Nigerian officials.[143]

In 1998, Halliburton acquired Dresser Industries, Inc., the parent company of The M.W. Kellogg Company. The SEC complaint alleged that following the Dresser acquisition, Halliburton failed to implement adequate internal control measures to oversee its foreign sales agents and failed to enforce its existing internal controls. Halliburton's due diligence investigation into the United Kingdom agent failed to detect evidence of the bribery scheme, and Halliburton made no such due diligence investigation into the Japanese agent. As a result, many Halliburton records contained false information concerning the payments made to the foreign agents.[144]

As part of the SEC settlement, KBR and Halliburton agreed to disgorge $177 million in ill-gotten profits derived from the scheme. In a parallel criminal proceeding brought by the U.S. Department of Justice, Kellogg Brown & Root, LLC was charged with four counts of violating the antibribery provisions of the FCPA. Kellogg Brown & Root, LLC pleaded guilty to the charges, agreeing to pay a criminal fine of $402 million and to retain a monitor to review and evaluate KBR's policies as they relate to compliance with the FCPA.[145]

138. Press Release, Securities & Exchange Comm'n, SEC Charges Siemens AG for Engaging in Worldwide Bribery (Dec. 15, 2008).

139. *Id.*

140. *Id.*

141. Press Release, Securities & Exchange Comm'n, SEC Charges Seven Former Siemens Executives with Bribing Leaders in Argentina (Dec. 13, 2011).

142. Press Release, Securities & Exchange Comm'n, SEC Charges KBR and Halliburton for FCPA Violations (Feb. 11, 2009).

143. *Id.*

144. *Id.*

145. *Id.*

KEY WORDS AND PHRASES

accession 838

act-of-state doctrine 878

ad valorem tariffs 850

applicant 864

beneficiary 864

bound tariffs 855

civil law legal system 834

class-action lawsuits 833

codification 833

comity 870

commercial activity exception 878

common customs tariff 861

common law legal system 833

common market 860

conciliation 869

confiscation 844

conflict-of-laws rules 873

countertrade 867

customary international law 841

customary practice 841

customs union 855

customs valuation 850

directive 861

documentary letter of credit (L/C) 864

dual-use 845

dumped 852

dumping margin 852

duty 850

economic union 860

embargo 844

equity 833

euro 862

export license 847

expropriation 844

extraterritoriality 845

facilitating payments 845

fair trade law 851

fast-track negotiating authority 847

forum non conveniens 870

free trade area 854

Generalized System of Preferences (GSP) 850

good offices 869

gross-up clause 868

guaranty 864

Harmonized Tariff Schedule of the United States (HTS) 850

import relief laws 851

inquiry 869

letter of credit 864

mediation 869

most favored nation (MFN) 854

national treatment 855

nationalization 844

nontariff barriers (NTBs) 856

political union 860

private international law 837

private law 834

privatization 844

public international law 837

public law 834

quotas 847

ratification 838

regulations 861

repatriate 833

sanctions 844

section 201 851

section 301 849

section 337 852

Sharia 834

sovereign immunity 878

Special 301 provisions 849

standby letter of credit 864

statutory law 833

Super 301 849

supranational law 837

tariff classification 850

tariffs 847

Trade Promotion Authority 847

transaction value 850

treaty 837

QUESTIONS AND CASE PROBLEMS

1. A fast-growing U.S. beverage company wishes to import mineral water and has asked you, its vice president for purchasing, to recommend foreign sources. You know that sources exist in France, Canada, and Australia. What U.S. trade laws should you consider in choosing among these sources?

   Suppose that you determine that the best source of mineral water for your purposes is France, but a tariff makes imports from that country noncompetitive. How could you seek a reduction in this tariff?

2. IMOD and Wye Oak Technology entered into a contract on August 16, 2004, for the refurbishment and disposal of Iraqi military equipment. The contract required Wye Oak to "use all reasonable commercial efforts . . . in the development of markets and sales prospects for Military equipment." IMOD agreed to provide offices in Iraq for Wye Oak to facilitate the broker activities, but Wye Oak was "responsible for its own administrative costs." As for compensation, the contract

called for IMOD to pay Wye Oak a commission equal to 10% of any sale of equipment and a commission equal to 10% of any refurbishment costs. The contract required IMOD to make "full payment" of these commissions "immediately upon presentation" to it of invoices by Wye Oak. The contract was signed by Dr. Bruska Noori Shaways, secretary general of IMOD, and Dale C. Stoffel, president of Wye Oak. On the same day the contract was executed, Shaways signed a letter addressed to Stoffel, which stated:

   Wye Oak . . . is commissioned as the sole and exclusive agent for the recovery and sale of all Iraqi Ministry of Defense material described as scrap military equipment in the territory of Iraq. Related thereto, Wye Oak is also commissioned to inventory, assess and recover any such equipment it determines as recoverable for the use or sale on behalf of the Ministry of Defense of the Republic of Iraq.

Less than five months later, Stoffel attended a meeting in Baghdad to discuss contract performance. Three days after the meeting, while still in Iraq, he was shot and killed by unidentified assailants. On July 20, 2009, Wye Oak filed suit against Iraq, but not IMOD, in the U.S. District Court for the Eastern District of Virginia, seeking damages for breach of contract. Iraq moved to dismiss the suit for lack of subject matter jurisdiction, arguing that it was immune from suit under the Foreign Sovereign Immunities Act (FSIA). Wye Oak claimed that there was no immunity because the breach of contract occurred outside the territory of the United States in connection with commercial activity that caused a direct effect on the United States. Who will prevail? What public policies are implicated? [*Wye Oak Technology, Inc. v. Republic of Iraq*, 666 F.3d 205 (4th Cir. 2011).]

3. Optomagic, Inc. is a U.S. corporation that produces optomagic gizmos. Production of optomagic gizmos involves a confidential gizmo-processing technique (which is described in printed confidential Optomagic manuals), labor-intensive processing, and inclusion of an optomagic component for which Optomagic was granted a U.S. patent six months ago. The optomagic component has widespread uses in the space, aviation, and medical industries.

Eight months ago, in the African country of Varoom, a relatively peaceful popular uprising resulted in the removal of the "old guard" leaders, who had favored a strong, centrally planned economy. The new provisional government called for free elections in one year, began taking immediate steps to reform the economy, and promised to liberalize foreign investment laws to attract foreign investors.

Because the government bureaucracy is still in some disarray, it is extremely helpful, as a practical matter, to have close contacts with a government official who can speed the review and approval process for applications for foreign investment. During a recent official tour of the United States, Dr. Segun Ayantuga, the minister of health and welfare of Varoom, visited Optomagic's manufacturing facility in Boston, Massachusetts. Ayantuga is an eminent surgeon and a strong proponent of bringing advanced medical technology to his developing country so that the best medical care can be made available to the public. In addition, to earn badly needed foreign exchange for Varoom, he is interested in finding labor-intensive U.S. industries that may be able to produce products in Varoom for export to more developed countries. Optomagic is very interested in the newly emerging markets of Africa, and in Varoom in particular. Optomagic would also like to obtain gizmonium, a raw material necessary for the production of optomagic gizmos, which is found in great abundance in the mountains of Varoom, but which, under Varoomian law, is available only to Varoomian enterprises.

Two weeks after his visit to Optomagic, Ayantuga wrote to the CEO of Optomagic to make the following proposal. Ayantuga and a state-owned medical clinic, Varoom Medical, are interested in establishing a joint venture in Varoom with Optomagic. Current Varoomian law limits foreign investment interests in Varoomian enterprises to 50% of the total investment. Ayantuga states that, although under local law the Varoomian partners share equal responsibility for the management of the venture, they will in fact defer to Optomagic in all material matters related to the operation of the manufacturing facility. In addition, Ayantuga assures Optomagic that the foreign investment law is likely to be liberalized within the year. As his investment in the venture, Ayantuga offers to contribute his lease interest in certain property in Varoom and to ensure that all the necessary government permits for the construction and licensing of the facility are obtained. Ayantuga expresses his confidence in being able to obtain all the government approvals for the proposed project because "our government has recently issued a decree emphasizing the national importance of upgrading our health-care industries."

The father of Optomagic's CEO emigrated from Varoom sixty years ago. He is excited about the developments in Varoom and finds Ayantuga to be a delightful, dynamic man. He is convinced that Optomagic should move into Varoom now, before its competitors do.

Your assignment is to put together a business plan for the proposed joint venture, assuming that it's going to cost something up front but will be worth the expense in the long run. The CEO wants a preliminary report in two weeks to take to the board of directors, which will be considering establishing a wholly owned subsidiary in Cairo, Egypt, to operate prospective sales and manufacturing facilities in Africa. He also wants a comprehensive report to follow in another four weeks.

a. You have full access to your expert in-house legal counsel, who has experience in international projects. How can you best use her to assist in putting your plan together? What issues of particular importance should be addressed by counsel for inclusion in the preliminary report?

b. Given the uncertainty in the development of Varoom's foreign investment laws (and its government), what types of terms or conditions do you think should be included in the contract for the proposed joint venture to protect against unexpected changes in the laws or government policies? What is your evaluation of the desirability of other forms of protection?

c. Are there any legal problems with including Ayantuga as an investor in the project? As a paid consultant?

4. Upon further general inquiry on behalf of Optomagic, you learn the following facts in addition to those set forth in Question 3. First, Varoom has a patent law and a trademark-registration law and is a signatory of the Paris and Madrid Conventions, but it has no copyright law. Second, Varoomian law provides that licenses of foreign technology cannot (1) unreasonably restrict the geographic market for such exports, (2) require that the Varoomian party purchase components or raw materials from the foreign party, or (3) restrict use of the technology by the Varoomian licensee beyond a term of ten years without approval from the supervising ministry (which in this case is the Ministry of Health).

What other information do you need to determine how best to protect Optomagic's intellectual property rights in the proposed venture? Based on what you do know, what steps should be taken to maximize the protection of Optomagic's intellectual property rights? What U.S. laws will apply to the contribution, licensing, or other transfer of optomagic gizmo components by Optomagic to the joint venture? What license and joint venture contract terms are important to obtain?

Varoom Medical is prepared to invest 950 million baninis (U.S. $1 = 1,000 baninis) over the first five years of the project. Its commitment will be backed by a standby letter of credit to be issued by the National People's Bank of Varoom, a state-owned bank. What more do you need to know about the proposed capital contribution to be made by Varoom Medical and the standby letter of credit from the bank? Would you impose any additional conditions or requirements on the proposed contribution and the letter of credit? What do you suggest that Optomagic contribute as its share of capital to the proposed joint venture? What factors do you need to consider to make that decision?

5. Assume the facts in Question 3. You begin to consider the labor force that the joint venture will need. Ayantuga suggests that the venture technicians should make regular technical training visits to Optomagic's facility in Boston, Massachusetts. Ayantuga also suggests that he can arrange to select the Varoomian technicians for the joint venture. Monthly salaries in Varoom for the relevant types of workers are 70% lower than in the United States. However, Varoom's labor laws require that all enterprises (1) provide employees with housing and health insurance subsidies equal to 50% of their salaries; (2) engage in mandatory arbitration with the local labor bureau prior to termination of any employee for any reason; and (3) in the case of foreign-invested enterprises, pay local managers salaries and benefits that are comparable to those of the expatriate management personnel of the foreign-invested enterprise.
    a. How would you assess the legal and economic advantages and disadvantages of the employees that Ayantuga has proposed be hired?
    b. Is there another way to structure the workforce?
    c. What U.S. laws may apply to the training of joint venture technicians at Optomagic's U.S. facilities?
    d. Would you recommend that resident expatriate management personnel, or just visiting technicians, be assigned to the prospective project? Why? What qualities do you think an expatriate employee in Varoom should have?

6. In addition to the facts covered in Questions 3 through 5, you learn that the banini is not freely convertible into dollars. The Varoom foreign-exchange and tax laws provide that a foreign-invested joint venture can repatriate up to 50% of its foreign-exchange earnings, subject to a repatriation tax of 15% (in addition to the tax imposed on the joint venture's income). Banini profits can be exchanged only upon prior approval by the supervising ministry (each ministry is allocated a quota of baninis for which it can approve an exchange into foreign currencies). In addition, Varoom's foreign investment law requires that

foreign-invested enterprises export a minimum of 50% of their products.
    a. What alternatives exist to repatriating foreign-currency earnings in the prospective venture?
    b. What U.S. laws, if any, might apply to exports of optomagic gizmos to the United States from Varoom?

7. Adidas Promotional Retail Operations, Inc., Sports Chalet, and Offside Soccer (Adidas) are California retailers that sell athletic shoes made from the hides of the red kangaroo, the eastern grey kangaroo, and the western grey kangaroo. Viva! International Voice for Animals, an international nonprofit organization devoted to protecting animals, sued Adidas for violating section 653o of the California Penal Code, which was enacted to prevent the extinction of species that the California legislature deemed threatened. It provides in relevant part: "It is unlawful to import into this state for commercial purposes, to possess with intent to sell, or to sell within the state, the dead body, or any part thereof, of any . . . kangaroo."

The Federal Endangered Species Act of 1973 (ESA) was enacted to halt and reverse the trend toward species extinction. Section 6(f) of the Act states:

> Any state law . . . which applies with respect to the importation or exportation of, or interstate or foreign commerce in, endangered species or threatened species is void to the extent that it may . . . effectively (1) permit what is prohibited by this Act or by any regulation which implements this chapter, or (2) prohibit what is authorized pursuant to an exemption or permit provided for in this Act or in any regulation which implements this Act.

The ESA also includes a saving provision that states that the Act should not be construed to void any more restrictive state law.

During the twentieth century, a commercial market developed in Australia for kangaroo hides and meat. By the early 1970s, the kangaroo population had dropped to the point that the Australian state and federal governments instituted protective measures, including a ban on exports and species-specific quotas on the killing of kangaroos for commercial use.

In 1974, the U.S. Fish and Wildlife Service listed the red, eastern grey, and western grey kangaroos as threatened species under the ESA, which carries a prohibition on importation subject to exemptions and permits issued under the ESA. The Fish and Wildlife Service subsequently banned commercial import of these species until the Australian states harvesting them could assure the United States that their taking would not be detrimental to their survival. In 1981, the Service issued a special final rule lifting the ban on commercial import of these species. In 1995, the Service removed the three kangaroo species from the ESA's list of endangered or threatened species on the basis of their successful recovery. Once the three species had been deleted under the ESA, their import into the United States was not prohibited by federal law.

In its defense, Adidas argued that section 653o of the California Penal Code was preempted by the Endangered Species Act because the California law undermined federal actions taken under the ESA to influence the Australian state and federal governments to preserve threatened kangaroo species. How will Adidas support this argument? What arguments will Viva! make in support of section 653o of the Penal Code? Which party will prevail? [*Viva! International Voice for Animals v. Adidas Promotional Retail Operations, Inc.*, 162 P.3d 569 (Cal. 2007).]

8. The Drug Enforcement Administration (DEA) approved using Mexican nationals to abduct Alvarez-Machain, also a Mexican national, from Mexico to stand trial in the United States for a DEA agent's torture and murder. After his acquittal, Alvarez sued the United States for false arrest under the Federal Tort Claims Act (FTCA), which waives the sovereign immunity of the United States in suits "for . . . personal injury . . . caused by the negligent or wrongful act or omission of any [government] employees while acting within the scope of his office or employment." However, the Act limits its waiver of sovereign immunity in a number of ways, including an exception for "[a]ny claim arising in a foreign country." The U.S. district court dismissed the FTCA claim against the DEA, but the U.S. Court of Appeals for the Ninth Circuit reversed the district court's dismissal. What arguments can Alvarez-Machain make to support his FTCA claim against the U.S. government? What arguments can the United States make to support the dismissal of Alvarez-Machain's suit? Which party will prevail? [*Sosa v. Alvarez-Machain*, 542 U.S. 692 (2004).]

APPENDICES

APPENDIX A: The Constitution of the United States of America

PREAMBLE

We the People of the United States, in Order to form a more perfect Union, establish Justice, insure domestic Tranquility, provide for the common defence, promote the general Welfare, and secure the Blessings of Liberty to ourselves and our Posterity, do ordain and establish this Constitution for the United States of America.

ARTICLE I

Section 1. All legislative Powers herein granted shall be vested in a Congress of the United States, which shall consist of a Senate and House of Representatives.

Section 2. The House of Representatives shall be composed of Members chosen every second Year by the People of the several States, and the Electors in each State shall have the Qualifications requisite for Electors of the most numerous Branch of the State Legislature.

No Person shall be a Representative who shall not have attained to the Age of twenty five Years, and been seven Years a Citizen of the United States, and who shall not, when elected, be an Inhabitant of that State in which he shall be chosen.

Representatives and direct Taxes shall be apportioned among the several States which may be included within this Union, according to their respective Numbers, which shall be determined by adding to the whole Number of free Persons, including those bound to Service for a Term of Years, and excluding Indians not taxed, three fifths of all other Persons. The actual Enumeration shall be made within three Years after the first Meeting of the Congress of the United States, and within every subsequent Term of ten Years, in such Manner as they shall by Law direct. The Number of Representatives shall not exceed one for every thirty Thousand, but each State shall have at Least one Representative; and until such enumeration shall be made, the State of New Hampshire shall be entitled to chuse three, Massachusetts eight, Rhode Island and Providence Plantations one, Connecticut five, New York six, New Jersey four, Pennsylvania eight, Delaware one, Maryland six, Virginia ten, North Carolina five, South Carolina five, and Georgia three.

When vacancies happen in the Representation from any State, the Executive Authority thereof shall issue Writs of Election to fill such Vacancies.

The House of Representatives shall chuse their Speaker and other Officers; and shall have the sole Power of Impeachment.

Section 3. The Senate of the United States shall be composed of two Senators from each State, chosen by the Legislature thereof, for six Years; and each Senator shall have one Vote.

Immediately after they shall be assembled in Consequence of the first Election, they shall be divided as equally as may be into three Classes. The Seats of the Senators of the first Class shall be vacated at the Expiration of the second Year, of the second Class at the Expiration of the fourth Year, and of the third Class at the Expiration of the sixth Year, so that one third may be chosen every second Year; and if Vacancies happen by Resignation, or otherwise, during the Recess of the Legislature of any State, the Executive thereof may make temporary Appointments until the next Meeting of the Legislature, which shall then fill such Vacancies.

No Person shall be a Senator who shall not have attained to the Age of thirty Years, and been nine Years a Citizen of the United States, and who shall not, when elected, be an Inhabitant of that State for which he shall be chosen.

The Vice President of the United States shall be President of the Senate, but shall have no Vote, unless they be equally divided.

The Senate shall chuse their other Officers, and also a President pro tempore, in the Absence of the Vice President, or when he shall exercise the Office of President of the United States.

The Senate shall have the sole Power to try all Impeachments. When sitting for that Purpose, they shall be on Oath or Affirmation. When the President of the United States is tried, the Chief Justice shall preside: And no Person shall be convicted without the Concurrence of two thirds of the Members present.

Judgment in Cases of Impeachment shall not extend further than to removal from Office, and disqualification to hold and enjoy any Office of honor, Trust, or Profit under the United States: but the Party convicted shall nevertheless be liable and subject to Indictment, Trial, Judgment, and Punishment, according to Law.

Section 4. The Times, Places and Manner of holding Elections for Senators and Representatives, shall be prescribed in each State by the Legislature thereof; but the Congress may at any time by Law make or alter such Regulations, except as to the Places of chusing Senators.

The Congress shall assemble at least once in every Year, and such Meeting shall be on the first Monday in December, unless they shall by Law appoint a different Day.

Section 5. Each House shall be the Judge of the Elections, Returns, and Qualifications of its own Members, and a Majority of each shall constitute a Quorum to do Business; but a smaller Number may adjourn from day to day, and may be authorized to compel the Attendance of absent Members, in such Manner, and under such Penalties as each House may provide.

Each House may determine the Rules of its Proceedings, punish its Members for disorderly Behavior, and, with the Concurrence of two thirds, expel a Member.

Each House shall keep a Journal of its Proceedings, and from time to time publish the same, excepting such Parts as may in their Judgment require Secrecy; and the Yeas and Nays of the Members of either House on any question shall, at the Desire of one fifth of those Present, be entered on the Journal.

Neither House, during the Session of Congress, shall, without the Consent of the other, adjourn for more than three days, nor to any other Place than that in which the two Houses shall be sitting.

Section 6. The Senators and Representatives shall receive a Compensation for their Services, to be ascertained by Law, and paid out of the Treasury of the United States. They shall in all Cases, except Treason, Felony and Breach of the Peace, be privileged from Arrest during their Attendance at the Session of their respective Houses, and in going to and returning from the same; and for any Speech or Debate in either House, they shall not be questioned in any other Place.

No Senator or Representative shall, during the Time for which he was elected, be appointed to any civil Office under the Authority of the United States, which shall have been created, or the Emoluments whereof shall have been increased during such time; and no Person holding any Office under the United States, shall be a Member of either House during his Continuance in Office.

Section 7. All Bills for raising Revenue shall originate in the House of Representatives; but the Senate may propose or concur with Amendments as on other Bills.

Every Bill which shall have passed the House of Representatives and the Senate, shall, before it become a Law, be presented to the President of the United States; If he approve he shall sign it, but if not he shall return it, with his Objections to the House in which it shall have originated, who shall enter the Objections at large on their Journal, and proceed to reconsider it. If after such Reconsideration two thirds of that House shall agree to pass the Bill, it shall be sent together with the Objections, to the other House, by which it shall likewise be reconsidered, and if approved by two thirds of that House, it shall become a Law. But in all such Cases the Votes of both Houses shall be determined by Yeas and Nays, and the Names of the Persons voting for and against the Bill shall be entered on the Journal of each House respectively. If any Bill shall not be returned by the President within ten Days (Sundays excepted) after it shall have been presented to him, the Same shall be a Law, in like Manner as if he had signed it, unless the Congress by their Adjournment prevent its Return in which Case it shall not be a Law.

Every Order, Resolution, or Vote to which the Concurrence of the Senate and House of Representatives may be necessary (except on a question of Adjournment) shall be presented to the President of the United States; and before the Same shall take Effect, shall be approved by him, or being disapproved by him, shall be repassed by two thirds of the Senate and House of Representatives, according to the Rules and Limitations prescribed in the Case of a Bill.

Section 8. The Congress shall have Power To lay and collect Taxes, Duties, Imposts and Excises, to pay the Debts and provide for the common Defence and general Welfare of the United States; but all Duties, Imposts and Excises shall be uniform throughout the United States;

To borrow Money on the credit of the United States;

To regulate Commerce with foreign Nations, and among the several States, and with the Indian Tribes;

To establish an uniform Rule of Naturalization, and uniform Laws on the subject of Bankruptcies throughout the United States;

To coin Money, regulate the Value thereof, and of foreign Coin, and fix the Standard of Weights and Measures;

To provide for the Punishment of counterfeiting the Securities and current Coin of the United States;

To establish Post Offices and post Roads;

To promote the Progress of Science and useful Arts, by securing for limited Times to Authors and Inventors the exclusive Right to their respective Writings and Discoveries;

To constitute Tribunals inferior to the supreme Court;

To define and punish Piracies and Felonies committed on the high Seas, and Offenses against the Law of Nations;

To declare War, grant Letters of Marque and Reprisal, and make Rules concerning Captures on Land and Water;

To raise and support Armies, but no Appropriation of Money to that Use shall be for a longer Term than two Years;

To provide and maintain a Navy;

To make Rules for the Government and Regulation of the land and naval Forces;

To provide for calling forth the Militia to execute the Laws of the Union, suppress Insurrections and repel Invasions;

To provide for organizing, arming, and disciplining, the Militia, and for governing such Part of them as may be employed in the Service of the United States, reserving to the States respectively, the Appointment of the Officers, and the Authority of training the Militia according to the discipline prescribed by Congress;

To exercise exclusive Legislation in all Cases whatsoever, over such District (not exceeding ten Miles square) as may, by Cession of particular States, and the Acceptance of Congress, become the Seat of the Government of the United States, and to exercise like Authority over all Places purchased by the Consent of the Legislature of the State in which the Same shall be, for the Erection of Forts, Magazines, Arsenals, dock-Yards, and other needful Buildings;—And

To make all Laws which shall be necessary and proper for carrying into Execution the foregoing Powers, and all other Powers vested by this Constitution in the Government of the United States, or in any Department or Officer thereof.

Section 9. The Migration or Importation of such Persons as any of the States now existing shall think proper to admit, shall not be prohibited by the Congress prior to the Year one thousand eight hundred and eight, but a Tax or duty may be imposed on such Importation, not exceeding ten dollars for each Person.

The privilege of the Writ of Habeas Corpus shall not be suspended, unless when in Cases of Rebellion or Invasion the public Safety may require it.

No Bill of Attainder or ex post facto Law shall be passed.

No Capitation, or other direct, Tax shall be laid, unless in Proportion to the Census or Enumeration herein before directed to be taken.

No Tax or Duty shall be laid on Articles exported from any State.

No Preference shall be given by any Regulation of Commerce or Revenue to the Ports of one State over those of another: nor shall Vessels bound to, or from, one State be obliged to enter, clear, or pay Duties in another.

No Money shall be drawn from the Treasury, but in Consequence of Appropriations made by Law; and a regular Statement and Account of the Receipts and Expenditures of all public Money shall be published from time to time.

No Title of Nobility shall be granted by the United States: And no Person holding any Office of Profit or Trust under them, shall, without the Consent of the Congress, accept of any present, Emolument, Office, or Title, of any kind whatever, from any King, Prince, or foreign State.

Section 10. No State shall enter into any Treaty, Alliance, or Confederation; grant Letters of Marque and Reprisal; coin Money; emit Bills of Credit; make any Thing but gold and silver Coin a Tender in Payment of Debts; pass any Bill of Attainder, ex post facto Law, or Law impairing the Obligation of Contracts, or grant any Title of Nobility.

No State shall, without the Consent of the Congress, lay any Imposts or Duties on Imports or Exports, except what may be absolutely necessary for executing its inspection Laws: and the net Produce of all Duties and Imposts, laid by any State on Imports or Exports, shall be for the Use of the Treasury of the United States; and all such Laws shall be subject to the Revision and Controul of the Congress.

No State shall, without the Consent of Congress, lay any Duty of Tonnage, keep Troops, or Ships of War in time of Peace, enter into any Agreement or Compact with another State, or with a foreign Power, or engage in War, unless actually invaded, or in such imminent Danger as will not admit of delay.

ARTICLE II

Section 1. The executive Power shall be vested in a President of the United States of America. He shall hold his Office during the Term of four Years, and, together with the Vice President, chosen for the same Term, be elected, as follows:

Each State shall appoint, in such Manner as the Legislature thereof may direct, a Number of Electors, equal to the whole Number of Senators and Representatives to which the State may be entitled in the Congress; but no Senator or Representative, or Person holding an Office of Trust or Profit under the United States, shall be appointed an Elector.

The Electors shall meet in their respective States, and vote by Ballot for two Persons, of whom one at least shall not be an Inhabitant of the same State with themselves. And they shall make a List of all the Persons voted for, and of the Number of Votes for each; which List they shall sign and certify, and transmit sealed to the Seat of the Government of the United States, directed to the President of the Senate. The President of the Senate shall, in the Presence of the Senate and House of Representatives, open all the Certificates, and the Votes shall then be counted. The Person having the greatest Number of Votes shall be the President, if such Number be a Majority of the whole Number of Electors appointed; and if there be more than one who have such Majority, and have an equal Number of Votes, then the House of Representatives shall immediately chuse by Ballot one of them for President; and if no Person have a Majority, then from the five highest on the List the said House shall in like Manner chuse the President. But in chusing the President, the Votes shall be taken by States, the Representation from each State having one Vote; A quorum for this Purpose shall consist of a Member or Members from two thirds of the States, and a Majority of all the States shall be necessary to a Choice. In every

Case, after the Choice of the President, the Person having the greater Number of Votes of the Electors shall be the Vice President. But if there should remain two or more who have equal Votes, the Senate shall chuse from them by Ballot the Vice President.

The Congress may determine the Time of chusing the Electors, and the Day on which they shall give their Votes; which Day shall be the same throughout the United States.

No person except a natural born Citizen, or a Citizen of the United States, at the time of the Adoption of this Constitution, shall be eligible to the Office of President; neither shall any Person be eligible to that Office who shall not have attained to the Age of thirty five Years, and been fourteen Years a Resident within the United States.

In Case of the Removal of the President from Office, or of his Death, Resignation or Inability to discharge the Powers and Duties of the said Office, the same shall devolve on the Vice President, and the Congress may by Law provide for the Case of Removal, Death, Resignation or Inability, both of the President and Vice President, declaring what Officer shall then act as President, and such Officer shall act accordingly, until the Disability be removed, or a President shall be elected.

The President shall, at stated Times, receive for his Services, a Compensation, which shall neither be increased nor diminished during the Period for which he shall have been elected, and he shall not receive within that Period any other Emolument from the United States, or any of them.

Before he enter on the Execution of his Office, he shall take the following Oath or Affirmation: "I do solemnly swear (or affirm) that I will faithfully execute the Office of President of the United States, and will to the best of my Ability, preserve, protect and defend the Constitution of the United States."

Section 2. The President shall be Commander in Chief of the Army and Navy of the United States, and of the Militia of the several States, when called into the actual Service of the United States; he may require the Opinion, in writing, of the principal Officer in each of the executive Departments, upon any Subject relating to the Duties of their respective Offices, and he shall have Power to grant Reprieves and Pardons for Offenses against the United States, except in Cases of Impeachment.

He shall have Power, by and with the Advice and Consent of the Senate to make Treaties, provided two thirds of the Senators present concur; and he shall nominate, and by and with the Advice and Consent of the Senate, shall appoint Ambassadors, other public Ministers and Consuls, Judges of the supreme Court, and all other Officers of the United States, whose Appointments are not herein otherwise provided for, and which shall be established by Law; but the Congress may by Law vest the Appointment of such inferior Officers, as they think proper, in the President alone, in the Courts of Law, or in the Heads of Departments.

The President shall have Power to fill up all Vacancies that may happen during the Recess of the Senate, by granting Commissions which shall expire at the End of their next Session.

Section 3. He shall from time to time give to the Congress Information of the State of the Union, and recommend to their Consideration such Measures as he shall judge necessary and expedient; he may, on extraordinary Occasions, convene both Houses, or either of them, and in Case of Disagreement between them, with Respect to the Time of Adjournment, he may adjourn them to such Time as he shall think proper; he shall receive Ambassadors and other public Ministers; he shall take Care that the Laws be faithfully executed, and shall Commission all the Officers of the United States.

Section 4. The President, Vice President and all civil Officers of the United States, shall be removed from Office on Impeachment for, and Conviction of, Treason, Bribery, or other high Crimes and Misdemeanors.

ARTICLE III

Section 1. The judicial Power of the United States, shall be vested in one supreme Court, and in such inferior Courts as the Congress may from time to time ordain and establish. The Judges, both of the supreme and inferior Courts, shall hold their Offices during good Behaviour, and shall, at stated Times, receive for their Services a Compensation, which shall not be diminished during their Continuance in Office.

Section 2. The judicial Power shall extend to all Cases, in Law and Equity, arising under this Constitution, the Laws of the United States, and Treaties made, or which shall be made, under their Authority;—to all Cases affecting Ambassadors, other public Ministers and Consuls;—to all Cases of admiralty and maritime Jurisdiction;—to Controversies to which the United States shall be a Party;—to Controversies between two or more States;—between a State and Citizens of another State;—between Citizens of different States;—between Citizens of the same State claiming Lands under Grants of different States, and between a State, or the Citizens thereof, and foreign States, Citizens or Subjects.

In all Cases affecting Ambassadors, other public Ministers and Consuls, and those in which a State shall be a Party, the supreme Court shall have original Jurisdiction. In all the other Cases before mentioned, the supreme Court shall have appellate Jurisdiction, both as to Law and Fact, with such Exceptions, and under such Regulations as the Congress shall make.

The Trial of all Crimes, except in Cases of Impeachment, shall be by Jury; and such Trial shall be held in the State where the said Crimes shall have been committed; but when not committed within any State, the Trial shall be at such Place or Places as the Congress may by Law have directed.

Section 3. Treason against the United States, shall consist only in levying War against them, or, in adhering to their Enemies, giving them Aid and Comfort. No Person shall be convicted of Treason unless on the Testimony of two Witnesses to the same overt Act, or on Confession in open Court.

The Congress shall have Power to declare the Punishment of Treason, but no Attainder of Treason shall work Corruption of Blood, or Forfeiture except during the Life of the Person attainted.

ARTICLE IV

Section 1. Full Faith and Credit shall be given in each State to the public Acts, Records, and judicial Proceedings of every other State. And the Congress may by general Laws prescribe the Manner in which such Acts, Records and Proceedings shall be proved, and the Effect thereof.

Section 2. The Citizens of each State shall be entitled to all Privileges and Immunities of Citizens in the several States.

A Person charged in any State with Treason, Felony, or other Crime, who shall flee from Justice, and be found in another State, shall on Demand of the executive Authority of the State from which he fled, be delivered up, to be removed to the State having Jurisdiction of the Crime.

No Person held to Service or Labour in one State, under the Laws thereof, escaping into another, shall, in Consequence of any Law or Regulation therein, be discharged from such Service or Labour, but shall be delivered up on Claim of the Party to whom such Service or Labour may be due.

Section 3. New States may be admitted by the Congress into this Union; but no new State shall be formed or erected within the Jurisdiction of any other State; nor any State be formed by the Junction of two or more States, or Parts of States, without the Consent of the Legislatures of the States concerned as well as of the Congress.

The Congress shall have Power to dispose of and make all needful Rules and Regulations respecting the Territory or other Property belonging to the United States; and nothing in this Constitution shall be so construed as to Prejudice any Claims of the United States, or of any particular State.

Section 4. The United States shall guarantee to every State in this Union a Republican Form of Government, and shall protect each of them against Invasion; and on Application of the Legislature, or of the Executive (when the Legislature cannot be convened) against domestic Violence.

ARTICLE V

The Congress, whenever two thirds of both Houses shall deem it necessary, shall propose Amendments to this Constitution, or, on the Application of the Legislatures of two thirds of the several States, shall call a Convention for proposing Amendments, which, in either Case, shall be valid to all Intents and Purposes, as part of this Constitution, when ratified by the Legislatures of three fourths of the several States, or by Conventions in three fourths thereof, as the one or the other Mode of Ratification may be proposed by the Congress; Provided that no Amendment which may be made prior to the Year One thousand eight hundred and eight shall in any Manner affect the first and fourth Clauses in the Ninth Section of the first Article; and that no State, without its Consent, shall be deprived of its equal Suffrage in the Senate.

ARTICLE VI

All Debts contracted and Engagements entered into, before the Adoption of this Constitution shall be as valid against the United States under this Constitution, as under the Confederation.

This Constitution, and the Laws of the United States which shall be made in Pursuance thereof; and all Treaties made, or which shall be made, under the Authority of the United States, shall be the supreme Law of the Land; and the Judges in every State shall be bound thereby, any Thing in the Constitution or Laws of any State to the Contrary notwithstanding.

The Senators and Representatives before mentioned, and the Members of the several State Legislatures, and all executive and judicial Officers, both of the United States and of the several States, shall be bound by Oath or Affirmation, to support this Constitution; but no religious Test shall ever be required as a Qualification to any Office or public Trust under the United States.

ARTICLE VII

The Ratification of the Conventions of nine States shall be sufficient for the Establishment of this Constitution between the States so ratifying the Same.

AMENDMENT I [1791]

Congress shall make no law respecting an establishment of religion, or prohibiting the free exercise thereof; or abridging the freedom of speech, or of the press; or the right of the people peaceably to assembly, and to petition the Government for a redress of grievances.

AMENDMENT II [1791]

A well regulated Militia, being necessary to the security of a free State, the right of the people to keep and bear Arms, shall not be infringed.

AMENDMENT III [1791]

No Soldier shall, in time of peace be quartered in any house, without the consent of the Owner, nor in time of war, but in a manner to be prescribed by law.

Amendment IV [1791]

The right of the people to be secure in their persons, houses, papers, and effects, against unreasonable searches and seizures, shall not be violated, and no Warrants shall issue, but upon probable cause, supported by Oath or affirmation, and particularly describing the place to be searched, and the persons or things to be seized.

Amendment V [1791]

No person shall be held to answer for a capital, or otherwise infamous crime, unless on a presentment or indictment of a Grand Jury, except in cases arising in the land or naval forces, or in the Militia, when in actual service in time of War or public danger; nor shall any person be subject for the same offence to be twice put in jeopardy of life or limb; nor shall be compelled in any criminal case to be a witness against himself, nor be deprived of life, liberty, or property, without due process of law; nor shall private property be taken for public use, without just compensation.

Amendment VI [1791]

In all criminal prosecutions, the accused shall enjoy the right to a speedy and public trial, by an impartial jury of the State and district wherein the crime shall have been committed, which district shall have been previously ascertained by law, and to be informed of the nature and cause of the accusation; to be confronted with the witnesses against him; to have compulsory process for obtaining witnesses in his favor, and to have the Assistance of Counsel for his defence.

Amendment VII [1791]

In Suits at common law, where the value in controversy shall exceed twenty dollars, the right of trial by jury shall be preserved, and no fact tried by jury, shall be otherwise re-examined in any Court of the United States, than according to the rules of the common law.

Amendment VIII [1791]

Excessive bail shall not be required, nor excessive fines imposed, nor cruel and unusual punishments inflicted.

Amendment IX [1791]

The enumeration in the Constitution, of certain rights, shall not be construed to deny or disparage others retained by the people.

Amendment X [1791]

The powers not delegated to the United States by the Constitution, nor prohibited by it to the States, are reserved to the States respectively, or to the people.

Amendment XI [1798]

The Judicial power of the United States shall not be construed to extend to any suit in law or equity, commenced or prosecuted against one of the United States by Citizens of another State, or by Citizens or Subjects of any Foreign State.

Amendment XII [1804]

The Electors shall meet in their respective states, and vote by ballot for President and Vice-President, one of whom, at least, shall not be an inhabitant of the same state with themselves; they shall name in their ballots the person voted for as President, and in distinct ballots the person voted for as Vice-President, and they shall make distinct lists of all persons voted for as President, and of all persons voted for as Vice-President, and of the number of votes for each, which lists they shall sign and certify, and transmit sealed to the seat of the government of the United States, directed to the President of the Senate;—The President of the Senate shall, in the presence of the Senate and House of Representatives, open all the certificates and the votes shall then be counted;— The person having the greatest number of votes for President, shall be the President, if such number be a majority of the whole number of Electors appointed; and if no person have such majority, then from the persons having the highest numbers not exceeding three on the list of those voted for as President, the House of Representatives shall choose immediately, by ballot, the President. But in choosing the President, the votes shall be taken by states, the representation from each state having one vote; a quorum for this purpose shall consist of a member or members from two-thirds of the states, and a majority of all states shall be necessary to a choice. And if the House of Representatives shall not choose a President whenever the right of choice shall devolve upon them, before the fourth day of March next following, then the Vice-President shall act as President, as in the case of the death or other constitutional disability of the President.—The person having the greatest number of votes as Vice-President, shall be the Vice-President, if such number be a majority of the whole number of Electors appointed, and if no person have a majority, then from the two highest numbers on the list, the Senate shall choose the Vice-President; a quorum for the purpose shall consist of two-thirds of the whole number of Senators, and a majority of the whole number shall be necessary to a choice. But no person constitutionally ineligible to the office of President shall be eligible to that of Vice-President of the United States.

Amendment XIII [1865]

Section 1. Neither slavery nor involuntary servitude, except as a punishment for crime whereof the party shall have been duly convicted, shall exist within the United States, or any place subject to their jurisdiction.

Section 2. Congress shall have power to enforce this article by appropriate legislation.

AMENDMENT XIV [1868]

Section 1. All persons born or naturalized in the United States, and subject to the jurisdiction thereof, are citizens of the United States and of the State wherein they reside. No State shall make or enforce any law which shall abridge the privileges or immunities of citizens of the United States; nor shall any State deprive any person of life, liberty, or property, without due process of law; nor deny to any person within its jurisdiction the equal protection of the laws.

Section 2. Representatives shall be apportioned among the several States according to their respective numbers, counting the whole number of persons in each State, excluding Indians not taxed. But when the right to vote at any election for the choice of electors for President and Vice President of the United States, Representatives in Congress, the Executive and Judicial officers of a State, or the members of the Legislature thereof, is denied to any of the male inhabitants of such State, being twenty-one years of age, and citizens of the United States, or in any way abridged, except for participation in rebellion, or other crime, the basis of representation therein shall be reduced in the proportion which the number of such male citizens shall bear to the whole number of male citizens twenty-one years of age in such State.

Section 3. No person shall be a Senator or Representative in Congress, or elector of President and Vice President, or hold any office, civil or military, under the United States, or under any State, who having previously taken an oath, as a member of Congress, or as an officer of the United States, or as a member of any State legislature, or as an executive or judicial officer of any State, to support the Constitution of the United States, shall have engaged in insurrection or rebellion against the same, or given aid or comfort to the enemies thereof. But Congress may by a vote of two-thirds of each House, remove such disability.

Section 4. The validity of the public debt of the United States, authorized by law, including debts incurred for payment of pensions and bounties for services in suppressing insurrection or rebellion, shall not be questioned. But neither the United States nor any State shall assume or pay any debt or obligation incurred in aid of insurrection or rebellion against the United States, or any claim for the loss or emancipation of any slave; but all such debts, obligations and claims shall be held illegal and void.

Section 5. The Congress shall have power to enforce, by appropriate legislation, the provisions of this article.

AMENDMENT XV [1870]

Section 1. The right of citizens of the United States to vote shall not be denied or abridged by the United States or by any State on account of race, color, or previous condition of servitude.

Section 2. The Congress shall have power to enforce this article by appropriate legislation.

AMENDMENT XVI [1913]

The Congress shall have power to lay and collect taxes on incomes, from whatever source derived, without apportionment among the several States, and without regard to any census or enumeration.

AMENDMENT XVII [1913]

Section 1. The Senate of the United States shall be composed of two Senators from each State, elected by the people thereof, for six years; and each Senator shall have one vote. The electors in each State shall have the qualifications requisite for electors of the most numerous branch of the State legislatures.

Section 2. When vacancies happen in the representation of any State in the Senate, the executive authority of such State shall issue writs of election to fill such vacancies: Provided, That the legislature of any State may empower the executive thereof to make temporary appointments until the people fill the vacancies by election as the legislature may direct.

Section 3. This amendment shall not be so construed as to affect the election or term of any Senator chosen before it becomes valid as part of the Constitution.

AMENDMENT XVIII [1919]

Section 1. After one year from the ratification of this article the manufacture, sale, or transportation of intoxicating liquors within, the importation thereof into, or the exportation thereof from the United States and all territory subject to the jurisdiction thereof for beverage purposes is hereby prohibited.

Section 2. The Congress and the several States shall have concurrent power to enforce this article by appropriate legislation.

Section 3. This article shall be inoperative unless it shall have been ratified as an amendment to the Constitution by the legislatures of the several States, as provided in the Constitution, within seven years from the date of the submission hereof to the States by the Congress.

AMENDMENT XIX [1920]

Section 1. The right of citizens of the United States to vote shall not be denied or abridged by the United States or by any State on account of sex.

Section 2. Congress shall have power to enforce this article by appropriate legislation.

AMENDMENT XX [1933]

Section 1. The terms of the President and Vice President shall end at noon on the 20th day of January, and the terms of Senators and Representatives at noon on the 3d day of January, of the years in which such terms would have ended if this article had not been ratified; and the terms of their successors shall then begin.

Section 2. The Congress shall assemble at least once in every year, and such meeting shall begin at noon on the 3d day of January, unless they shall by law appoint a different day.

Section 3. If, at the time fixed for the beginning of the term of the President, the President elect shall have died, the Vice President elect shall become President. If the President shall not have been chosen before the time fixed for the beginning of his term, or if the President elect shall have failed to qualify, then the Vice President elect shall act as President until a President shall have qualified; and the Congress may by law provide for the case wherein neither a President elect nor a Vice President elect shall have qualified, declaring who shall then act as President, or the manner in which one who is to act shall be selected, and such person shall act accordingly until a President or Vice President shall have qualified.

Section 4. The Congress may by law provide for the case of the death of any of the persons from whom the House of Representatives may choose a President whenever the right of choice shall have devolved upon them, and for the case of the death of any of the persons from whom the Senate may choose a Vice President whenever the right of choice shall have devolved upon them.

Section 5. Sections 1 and 2 shall take effect on the 15th day of October following the ratification of this article.

Section 6. This article shall be inoperative unless it shall have been ratified as an amendment to the Constitution by the legislatures of three-fourths of the several States within seven years from the date of its submission.

AMENDMENT XXI [1933]

Section 1. The eighteenth article of amendment to the Constitution of the United States is hereby repealed.

Section 2. The transportation or importation into any State, Territory, or possession of the United States for delivery or use therein of intoxicating liquors, in violation of the laws thereof, is hereby prohibited.

Section 3. This article shall be inoperative unless it shall have been ratified as an amendment to the Constitution by conventions in the several States, as provided in the Constitution, within seven years from the date of the submission hereof to the States by the Congress.

AMENDMENT XXII [1951]

Section 1. No person shall be elected to the office of the President more than twice, and no person who has held the office of President, or acted as President, for more than two years of a term to which some other person was elected President shall be elected to the office of President more than once. But this Article shall not apply to any person holding the office of President when this Article was proposed by the Congress, and shall not prevent any person who may be holding the office of President, or acting as President, during the term within which this Article

becomes operative from holding the office of President or acting as President during the remainder of such term.

Section 2. This article shall be inoperative unless it shall have been ratified as an amendment to the Constitution by the legislatures of three-fourths of the several States within seven years from the date of its submission to the States by the Congress.

AMENDMENT XXIII [1961]

Section 1. The District constituting the seat of Government of the United States shall appoint in such manner as the Congress may direct:

A number of electors of President and Vice President equal to the whole number of Senators and Representatives in Congress to which the District would be entitled if it were a State, but in no event more than the least populous state; they shall be in addition to those appointed by the states, but they shall be considered, for the purposes of the election of President and Vice President, to be electors appointed by a state; and they shall meet in the District and perform such duties as provided by the twelfth article of amendment.

Section 2. The Congress shall have power to enforce this article by appropriate legislation.

AMENDMENT XXIV [1964]

Section 1. The right of citizens of the United States to vote in any primary or other election for President or Vice President, for electors for President or Vice President, or for Senator or Representative in Congress, shall not be denied or abridged by the United States, or any State by reason of failure to pay any poll tax or other tax.

Section 2. The Congress shall have power to enforce this article by appropriate legislation.

AMENDMENT XXV [1967]

Section 1. In case of the removal of the President from office or of his death or resignation, the Vice President shall become President.

Section 2. Whenever there is a vacancy in the office of the Vice President, the President shall nominate a Vice President who shall take office upon confirmation by a majority vote of both Houses of Congress.

Section 3. Whenever the President transmits to the President pro tempore of the Senate and the Speaker of the House of Representatives his written declaration that he is unable to discharge the powers and duties of his office, and until he transmits to them a written declaration to the contrary, such powers and duties shall be discharged by the Vice President as Acting President.

Section 4. Whenever the Vice President and a majority of either the principal officers of the executive departments or of such other body as Congress may by law provide, transmit to the President pro tempore of the Senate and the Speaker of the House of Representatives their written declaration that the President is unable to discharge the powers and duties of his office, the Vice President shall immediately assume the powers and duties of the office as Acting President.

Thereafter, when the President transmits to the President pro tempore of the Senate and the Speaker of the House of Representatives his written declaration that no inability exists, he shall resume the powers and duties of his office unless the Vice President and a majority of either the principal officers of the executive department or of such other body as Congress may by law provide, transmit within four days to the President pro tempore of the Senate and the Speaker of the House of Representatives their written declaration and the President is unable to discharge the powers and duties of his office. Thereupon Congress shall decide the issue, assembling within forty-eight hours for that purpose if not in session. If the Congress, within twenty-one days after receipt of the latter written declaration, or, if Congress is not in session, within twenty-one days after Congress is required to assemble, determines by two-thirds vote of both Houses that the President is unable to discharge the powers and duties of his office, the Vice President shall continue to discharge the same as Acting President; otherwise, the President shall resume the powers and duties of his office.

AMENDMENT XXVI [1971]

Section 1. The right of citizens of the United States, who are eighteen years of age or older, to vote shall not be denied or abridged by the United States or by any State on account of age.
Section 2. The Congress shall have power to enforce this article by appropriate legislation.

AMENDMENT XXVII [1992]

No law, varying the compensation for the services of the Senators and Representatives, shall take effect, until an election of Representatives shall have intervened.

APPENDIX B: Title VII of the Civil Rights Act of 1964 [Excerpts]

TITLE VII OF THE CIVIL RIGHTS ACT OF 1964—THE EMPLOYMENT DISCRIMINATION SECTION

Section 703. Unlawful Employment Practices. (a) It shall be an unlawful employment practice for an employer—

(1) to fail or refuse to hire or to discharge any individual, or otherwise to discriminate against any individual with respect to his compensation, terms, conditions, or privileges of employment, because of such individual's race, color, religion, sex, or national origin; or

(2) to limit, segregate, or classify his employees or applicants for employment in any way which would deprive or tend to deprive any individual of employment opportunities or otherwise adversely affect his status as an employee, because of such individual's race, color, religion, sex, or national origin.

(b) It shall be an unlawful employment practice for an employment agency to fail or refuse to refer for employment, or otherwise to discriminate against, any individual because of his race, color, religion, sex, or national origin, or to classify or refer for employment any individual on the basis or his race, color, religion, sex, or national origin.

(c) It shall be an unlawful employment practice for a labor organization—

(1) to exclude or to expel from its membership, or otherwise to discriminate against, any individual because of his race, color, religion, sex, or national origin;

(2) to limit, segregate, or classify its membership or applicants for membership, or to classify or fail or refuse to refer for employment any individual, in any way which would deprive or tend to deprive any individual of employment opportunities, or would limit such employment opportunities or otherwise adversely affect his status as an employee or as an applicant for employment, because of such individual's race, color, religion, sex, or national origin; or

(3) to cause or attempt to cause an employer to discriminate against an individual in violation of this section.

(d) It shall be an unlawful employment practice for any employer, labor organization, or joint labor-management committee controlling apprenticeship or other training or retraining, including on-the-job training programs to discriminate against any individual because of his race, color, religion, sex, or national origin in admission to, or employment in, any program established to provide apprenticeship or other training.

(e) Notwithstanding any other provision of this subchapter—

(1) it shall not be an unlawful employment practice for an employer to hire and employ employees, for an employment agency to classify, or refer for employment any individual, for a labor organization to classify its membership or to classify or refer for employment any individual, or for an employer, labor organization, or joint labor-management committee controlling apprenticeship

or other training or retraining programs to admit or employ any individual in any such program, on the basis of his religion, sex, or national origin in those certain instances where religion, sex, or national origin is a bona fide occupational qualification reasonably necessary to the normal operation of that particular business or enterprise, and

(2) it shall not be an unlawful employment practice for a school, college, university, or other educational institution or institution of learning to hire and employ employees of a particular religion if such school, college, university, or other educational institution or institution of learning is, in whole or in substantial part, owned, supported, controlled, or managed by a particular religion or by a particular religious corporation, association, or society, or if the curriculum of such school, college, university, or other educational institution or institution of learning is directed toward the propagation of a particular religion.

(f) As used in this subchapter, the phrase "unlawful employment practice" shall not be deemed to include any action or measure taken by an employer, labor organization, joint labor-management committee, or employment agency with respect to an individual who is a member of the Communist Party of the United States or of any other organization required to register as a Communist-action or Communist-front organization. . . .

(g) Notwithstanding any other provision of this subchapter, it shall not be an unlawful employment practice for an employer to fail or refuse to hire and employ any individual for any position, for an employer to discharge any individual from any position, or for an employment agency to fail or refuse to refer any individual for employment in any position, or for a labor organization to fail or refuse to refer any individual for employment in any position, if—

(1) the occupancy of such position, or access to the premises in or upon which any part of the duties of such position is performed or is to be performed, is subject to any requirement imposed in the interest of the national security of the United States . . . and

(2) such individual has not fulfilled or has ceased to fulfill that requirement.

(h) Notwithstanding any other provision of this subchapter, it shall not be an unlawful employment practice for an employer to apply different standards of compensation, or different terms, conditions, or privileges of employment pursuant to a bona fide seniority or merit system, or a system which measures earnings by quantity or quality of production or to employees who work in different locations, provided that such differences are not the result of an intention to discriminate because of race, color, religion, sex, or national origin, nor shall it be an unlawful employment practice for an employer to give and act upon the results of any professionally developed ability test provided that such test, its administration or action upon the results is not designed, intended or used to discriminate because of race, color, religion, sex, or national origin. . . .

(j) Nothing contained in this subchapter shall be interpreted to require any employer, employment agency, labor organization, or joint labor-management committee subject to this subchapter to grant preferential treatment to any individual or to any group because of the race, color, religion, sex, or national origin of such individual or group on account of an imbalance which may exist with respect to the total number or percentage of persons of any race, color, religion, sex, or national origin employed by any employer, referred or classified for employment by any employment agency or labor organization, or admitted to, or employed in, any apprenticeship or other training program, in comparison with the total number or percentage of persons of such race, color, religion, sex, or national origin in any community, State, section, or other area, or in the available work force in any community, State, section, or other area.

Section 704. Other Unlawful Employment Practices. (a) It shall be an unlawful employment practice for an employer to discriminate against any of his employees or applicants for employment, for an employment agency, or joint labor-management committee controlling apprenticeship or other training or retraining, including on-the-job training programs, to discriminate against any individual, or for a labor organization to discriminate against any member thereof or applicant for membership, because he has opposed any practice made an unlawful employment practice by this subchapter, or because he has made a charge, testified, assisted, or participated in any manner in an investigation, proceeding, or hearing under this subchapter.

(b) It shall be an unlawful employment practice for an employer, labor organization, employment agency, or joint labor-management committee controlling apprenticeship or other training or retraining, including on-the-job training programs, to print or publish or cause to be printed or published any notice or advertisement relating to employment by such an employer or membership or any classification or referral for employment by such a labor organization, or relating to any classification or referral for employment by such an employment agency, or relating to admission to, or employment in, any program established to provide apprenticeship or other training by such a joint-labor-management committee, indicating any preference, limitation, specification, or discrimination, based on race, color, religion, sex, or national origin, except that such a notice or advertisement may indicate a preference, limitation, specification, or discrimination based on religion, sex or national origin when religion, sex, or national origin is a bona fide occupational qualification for employment.

APPENDIX C: Americans with Disabilities Act of 1990 [Excerpts] and ADA Amendments Act of 2008 [Excerpts]

AMERICANS WITH DISABILITIES ACT OF 1990 [EXCERPTS]

Title I– Employment

Sec. 101. Definitions

As used in this title: . . .

(8) Qualified individual with a disability. The term "qualified individual with a disability" means an individual with a disability who, with or without reasonable accommodation, can perform the essential functions of the employment position that such individual holds or desires. For the purposes of this title, consideration shall be given to the employer's judgment as to what functions of a job are essential, and if an employer has prepared a written description before advertising or interviewing applicants for the job, this description shall be considered evidence of the essential functions of the job.

(9) Reasonable accommodation. The term "reasonable accommodation" may include

(A) making existing facilities used by employees readily accessible to and usable by individuals with disabilities; and (B) job restructuring, part-time or modified work schedules, reassignment to a vacant position, acquisition or modification of equipment or devices, appropriate adjustment or modifications of examinations, training materials or policies, the provision of qualified readers or interpreters, and other similar accommodations for individuals with disabilities.

(10) Undue Hardship.

(A) *In general.* The term "undue hardship" means an action requiring significant difficulty or expense, when considered in light of the factors set forth in subparagraph(B).

(B) *Factors to be considered.* In determining whether an accommodation would impose an undue hardship on a covered entity, factors to be considered include

(i) the nature and cost of accommodation needed under this Act;

(ii) the overall financial resources of the facility or facilities involved in the provision of the reasonable accommodation; the number of persons employed at such facility; the effect on expenses and resources, or the impact otherwise of such accommodation upon the operation of the facility;

(iii) the overall financial resources of the covered entity; the overall size of the business of a covered entity with respect to the number of its employees; the number, type, and location of its facilities; and

(iv) the type of operation or operations of the covered entity, including the composition, structure, and functions of the workforce of such entity; the geographic separateness, administrative, or fiscal relationship of the facility or facilities in question to the covered entity.

Sec. 102. Discrimination

(a) General Rule. No covered entity shall discriminate against a qualified individual with a disability because of the disability of such individual in regard to job application procedures, the hiring, advancement, or discharge of employees, employee compensation, job training, and other terms, conditions, and privileges of employment.

(b) Construction. As used in subsection (a), the term "discriminate" includes

(1) limiting, segregating, or classifying a job applicant or employee in a way that adversely affects the opportunities or status of such applicant or employee because of the disability of such applicant or employee;

(2) participating in a contractual or other arrangement or relationship that has the effect of subjecting a covered entity's qualified applicant or employee with a disability to the discrimination prohibited by this title (such relationship includes a relationship with an employment or referral agency, labor union, an organization providing fringe benefits to an employee of the covered entity, or an organization providing training and apprenticeship programs);

(3) utilizing standards, criteria, or methods of administration

(A) that have the effect of discrimination on the basis of disability; or

(B) that perpetuate the discrimination of others who are subject to common administrative control;

(4) excluding or otherwise denying equal jobs or benefits to a qualified individual because of the known disability of an individual with whom the qualified individual is known to have a relationship or association;

(5)(A) not making reasonable accommodations to the known physical or mental limitations of an otherwise qualified individual with a disability who is an applicant or employee, unless such covered entity can demonstrate that the accommodation would impose an undue hardship on the operation of the business of such covered entity; or

(B) denying employment opportunities to a job applicant or employee who is an otherwise qualified individual with a disability, if such denial is based on the need of such covered entity to make reasonable accommodation to the physical or mental impairments of the employee or applicant;

(6) using qualification standards, employment tests or other selection criteria that screen out or tend to screen out an individual with a disability or a class of individuals with disabilities unless the standard, test or other selection criteria, as used by the covered entity, is shown to be job-related for the position in question and is consistent with business necessity; and

(7) failing to select and administer tests concerning employment in the most effective manner to ensure that, when such test is administered to a job applicant or employee who has a disability that impairs sensory, manual, or speaking skills, such test results accurately reflect the skills, aptitude, or whatever other factor of such applicant or employee that such test purports to measure, rather than reflecting the impaired sensory, manual, or speaking skills of such employee or applicant (except where such skills are the factors that the test purports to measure). . . .

Sec. 104. Illegal Use of Drugs and Alcohol

(b) Rules of Construction. Nothing in subsection (a) shall be construed to exclude as a qualified individual with a disability an individual who

(1) has successfully completed a supervised drug rehabilitation program and is no longer engaging in the illegal use of drugs, or has otherwise been rehabilitated successfully and is no longer engaging in such use;

(2) is participating in a supervised rehabilitation program and is no longer engaging in such use; or

(3) is erroneously regarded as engaging in such use, but is not engaging in such use; except that it shall not be a violation of this Act for a covered entity to adopt or administer reasonable policies or procedures, including but not limited to drug testing, designed to ensure that an individual described in paragraph (1) or (2) is no longer engaging in the illegal use of drugs. . . .

Sec. 107. Enforcement.

(a) Powers, Remedies, and Procedures. The powers, remedies, and procedures set forth in sections 705, 706, 707, 709, and 710 of the Civil Rights Act of 1964 (42 U.S.C. 2000e-4, 2000e-5, 2000e-6, 2000e-8, and 2000e-9) shall be the powers, remedies, and procedures this title provides to the Commission, to the Attorney General, or to any person alleging discrimination on the basis of disability in violation of any provision of this Act, or regulations promulgated under section 106, concerning employment.
(b) Coordination. The agencies with enforcement authority for actions which allege employment discrimination under this title and under the Rehabilitation Act of 1973 shall develop procedures to ensure that administrative complaints filed under this title and under the Rehabilitation Act of 1973 are dealt with in a manner that avoids duplication of effort and prevents imposition of inconsistent or conflicting standards for the same requirements under this title and the Rehabilitation Act of 1973. The Commission, the Attorney General, and the Office of Federal Contract Compliance Programs shall establish such coordinating mechanisms (similar to provisions contained in the joint regulations promulgated by the Commission and the Attorney General at part 42 of title 28 and part 1691 of title 29, Code of Federal Regulations, and the Memorandum of Understanding between the Commission and the Office of Federal Contract Compliance Programs dated January 16, 1981 (46 Fed. Reg. 7435, January 23, 1981)) in regulations implementing this title and Rehabilitation Act of 1973 not later than 18 months after the date of enactment of this Act.

Sec. 108. Effective Date.

This title shall become effective 24 months after the date of enactment.

ADA Amendments Act of 2008 [Excerpts]

Sec. 2. Findings and Purposes

(a) Findings. Congress finds that

(1) in enacting the Americans with Disabilities Act of 1990 (ADA), Congress intended that the Act "provide a clear and comprehensive national mandate for the elimination of discrimination against individuals with disabilities" and provide broad coverage;

(2) in enacting the ADA, Congress recognized that physical and mental disabilities in no way diminish a person's right to fully participate in all aspects of society, but that people with physical or mental disabilities are frequently precluded from doing so because of prejudice, antiquated attitudes, or the failure to remove societal and institutional barriers;

(3) while Congress expected that the definition of disability under the ADA would be interpreted consistently with how courts had applied the definition of a handicapped individual under the Rehabilitation Act of 1973, that expectation has not been fulfilled;

(4) the holdings of the Supreme Court in Sutton v. United Air Lines, Inc., 527 U.S. 471 (1999) and its companion cases have narrowed the broad scope of protection intended to be afforded by the ADA, thus eliminating protection for many individuals whom Congress intended to protect;

(5) the holding of the Supreme Court in Toyota Motor Manufacturing, Kentucky, Inc., v. Williams, 534 U.S. 184 (2002) further narrowed the broad scope of protection intended to be afforded by the ADA;

(6) as a result of these Supreme Court cases, lower courts have incorrectly found in individual cases that people with a range of substantially limiting impairments are not people with disabilities;

(7) in particular, the Supreme Court, in the case of Toyota Motor Manufacturing, Kentucky, Inc., v. Williams, 534 U.S. 184 (2002), interpreted the term "substantially limits" to require a greater degree of limitation than was intended by Congress; and

(8) Congress finds that the current Equal Employment Opportunity Commission ADA regulations defining the term "substantially limits" as "significantly restricted" are inconsistent with congressional intent, by expressing too high a standard. . . .

Sec. 4 Disability Defined and Rules of Construction

(a) Definition of Disability. Section 3 of the Americans with Disabilities Act of 1990 (42 U.S.C. 12102) is amended to read as follows:

"Sec. 3. Definition of Disability.

"As used in this Act:

"Disability. The term 'disability' means, with respect to an individual

"(A) A physical or mental impairment that substantially limits one or more major life activities of an individual;

"(B) a record of such an impairment; or

"(C) being regarded as having such an impairment (as described in paragraph (3)).

"(2) Major Life Activities.

"(A) In *General.* For purposes of paragraph (1), major life activities include, but are not limited to, caring for oneself, performing manual tasks, seeing, hearing, eating, sleeping, walking, standing, lifting, bending, speaking, breathing, learning, reading, concentrating, thinking, communicating, and working.

"(B) *Major Bodily Functions.* For purposes of paragraph (1), a major life activity also includes the operation of a major bodily function, including but not limited to, functions of the immune system, normal cell growth, digestive, bowel, bladder, neurological, brain, respiratory, circulatory, endocrine, and reproductive functions.

"(3) Regarded As Having Such An Impairment. For purposes of paragraph (1)(C):

"(A) An individual meets the requirement of 'being regarded as having such an impairment' if the individual establishes that he or she has been subjected to an action prohibited under this Act because of an actual or perceived physical or mental impairment whether or not the impairment limits or is perceived to limit a major life activity.

"(B) Paragraph (1)(C) shall not apply to impairments that are transitory and minor. A transitory impairment is an impairment with an actual or expected duration of 6 months or less.

"(4) Rules Of Construction Regarding The Definition Of Disability. The definition of 'disability' in paragraph (1) shall be construed in accordance with the following:

"(A) The definition of disability in this Act shall be construed in favor of broad coverage of individuals under this Act, to the maximum extent permitted by the terms of this Act.

"(B) The term 'substantially limits' shall be interpreted consistently with the findings and purposes of the ADA Amendments Act of 2008.

"(C) An impairment that substantially limits one major life activity need not limit other major life activities in order to be considered a disability.

"(D) An impairment that is episodic or in remission is a disability if it would substantially limit a major life activity when active.

"(E) (i) The determination of whether an impairment substantially limits a major life activity shall be made without regard to the ameliorative effects of mitigating measures such as—

"(I) medication, medical supplies, equipment, or appliances, low-vision devices (which do not include ordinary eyeglasses or contact lenses), prosthetics including limbs and devices, hearing aids and cochlear implants or other implantable hearing devices, mobility devices, or oxygen therapy equipment and supplies;

"(II) use of assistive technology;

"(III) reasonable accommodations or auxiliary aids or services; or

"(IV) learned behavioral or adaptive neurological modifications.

"(ii) The ameliorative effects of the mitigating measures of ordinary eyeglasses or contact lenses shall be considered in determining whether an impairment substantially limits a major life activity.

"(iii) As used in this subparagraph

"(I) the term 'ordinary eyeglasses or contact lenses' means lenses that are intended to fully correct visual acuity or eliminate refractive error; and

"(II) the term 'low-vision devices' means devices that magnify, enhance, or otherwise augment a visual image. . . . "

APPENDIX D: Sherman Antitrust Act [Excerpts]

Section 1. Every contract, combination in the form of trust or otherwise, or conspiracy, in restraint of trade or commerce among the several States, or with foreign nations, is hereby declared to be illegal. Every person who shall make any contract or engage in any such combination or conspiracy shall be deemed guilty of a felony, and, on conviction thereof, shall be punished by fine not exceeding $10,000,000 if a corporation, or, if any other person, $350,000 or by imprisonment not exceeding three years, or by both said punishments in the discretion of the court.

Section 2. Every person who shall monopolize, or attempt to monopolize, or conspire with any other person or persons, to monopolize any part of the trade or commerce among the several States, or with foreign nations, shall be deemed guilty of a felony, and, on conviction thereof, shall be punished by fine not exceeding $10,000,000 if a corporation, or, if any other person, $350,000 or by imprisonment not exceeding three years, or by both said punishments, in the discretion of the court.

APPENDIX E: Clayton Act of 1914 [Excerpts]

Section 3. That it shall be unlawful for any person engaged in commerce, in the course of such commerce, to lease or make a sale or contract for sale of goods, wares, merchandise, machinery, supplies, or other commodities, whether patented or unpatented, for use, consumption, or resale within the United States or . . . other place under the jurisdiction of the United States, or fix a price charged therefor, or discount from, or rebate upon, such price, on the condition, agreement, or understanding that the lessee or purchaser thereof shall not use or deal in the goods, wares, merchandise, machinery, supplies, or other commodities of a competitor or competitors of the lessor or seller, where the effect of such lease, sale, or contract for sale or such condition, agreement, or understanding may be to substantially lessen competition to tend to create a monopoly in any line of commerce.

Section 4. That any person who shall be injured in his business or property by reason of anything forbidden in the antitrust laws may sue therefor in any district court of the United States in the district in which the defendant resides or is found, or has an agent, without respect to the amount in controversy, and shall recover threefold the damages by him sustained, and the cost of suit, including a reasonable attorney's fee.

Section 4A. Whenever the United States is hereafter injured in its business or property by reason of anything forbidden in the antitrust laws it may sue therefor in the United States district court for the district in which the defendant resides or is found or has an agent, without respect to the amount in controversy, and shall recover actual damages by it sustained and the cost of suit.

Section 4B. Any action to enforce any cause of action under sections 4 or 4A shall be forever barred unless commenced within four years after the cause of action accrued. No cause of action barred under existing law on the effective date of this act shall be revived by this Act.

Section 6. That the labor of a human being is not a commodity or article of commerce. Nothing contained in the antitrust laws shall be construed to forbid the existence and operation of labor, agricultural or horticultural organizations, instituted for the purposes of mutual help, and not having capital stock or conducted for profit, or to forbid or restrain individual members of such organizations from lawfully carrying out the legitimate objects thereof; nor shall such organizations or the members thereof, be held or construed to be illegal combinations or conspiracies in restraint of trade, under the antitrust laws.

Section 7. That no person engaged in commerce shall acquire, directly or indirectly, the whole or any part of the stock or other share capital and no corporation subject to the jurisdiction of the Federal Trade Commission shall acquire the whole or any part of the assets of another corporation engaged also in commerce, where in any line of commerce in any section of the country, the effect of such acquisition may be substantially to lessen competition, or to tend to create a monopoly.

No person shall acquire, directly or indirectly, the whole or any part of the stock or other share capital and no corporation subject to the jurisdiction of the Federal Trade Commission shall acquire the whole or any part of the assets of one or more corporations engaged in commerce, where in any line of commerce in any section of the country, the effect of such acquisition, of such stocks or assets, or of the use of such stock by the voting or granting of proxies or otherwise, may be substantially to lessen competition, or to tend to create a monopoly.

This section shall not apply to persons purchasing such stock solely for investment and not using the same by voting or otherwise to bring about, or in attempting to bring about, the substantial lessening of competition . . . .

Section 8. . . . No person shall, at the same time, serve as a director or officer in any two or more corporations (other than banks, banking associations, and trust companies) that are—

(A) engaged in whole or in part in commerce; and

(B) by virtue of their business and location of operation, competitors, so that the elimination of competition by agreement between them would constitute a violation of any of the antitrust laws; if each of the corporations has capital, surplus, and undivided profits aggregating more than $10,000,000 as adjusted pursuant to paragraph (5) of this subsection.

APPENDIX F: Federal Trade Commission Act of 1914 [Excerpts]

UNFAIR METHODS OF COMPETITION PROHIBITED

Section 5. Unfair methods of competition unlawful; prevention by Commission—declaration. Declaration of unlawfulness; power to prohibit unfair practices.

(a) (1) Unfair methods of competition in or affecting commerce, and unfair or deceptive acts or practices in or affecting commerce, are declared unlawful.

. . .

(b) Any person, partnership, or corporation who violates an order of the Commission to cease and desist after it has become final, and while such order is in effect, shall forfeit and pay to the United States a civil penalty of not more than $10,000 for each violation, which shall accrue to the United States and may be recovered in a civil action brought by the Attorney General of the United States. Each separate violation of such an order shall be a separate offense, except that in the case of a violation through continuing failure or neglect to obey a final order of the Commission, each day of continuance of such failure or neglect shall be deemed a separate offense.

APPENDIX G: Securities Act of 1933 [Excerpts]

Prohibitions Relating to Interstate Commerce and the Mails

Sec. 5. (a) Unless a registration statement is in effect as to a security, it shall be unlawful for any person, directly or indirectly—

(1) to make use of any means or instruments of transportation or communication in interstate commerce or of the mails to sell such security through the use or medium of any prospectus or otherwise; or

(2) to carry or cause to be carried through the mails or in interstate commerce, by any means or instruments of transportation, any such security for the purpose of sale or for delivery after sale.

[PROSPECTUS REQUIREMENTS]

(b) It shall be unlawful for any person, directly or indirectly—

(1) to make use of any means or instruments of transportation or communication in interstate commerce or of the mails to carry or transmit any prospectus relating to any security with respect to which a registration statement has been filed under this title, unless such prospectus meets the requirements of section 10, or

(2) to carry or to cause to be carried through the mails or in interstate commerce any such security for the purpose of sale or for delivery after sale, unless accompanied or preceded by a prospectus that meets the requirements of subsection (a) of section 10.

[PROHIBITION AGAINST OFFERS PRIOR TO REGISTRATION]

(c) It shall be unlawful for any person, directly or indirectly, to make use of any means or instruments of transportation or communication in interstate commerce or of the mails to offer to sell or offer to buy through the use or medium of any prospectus or otherwise any security, unless a registration statement has been filed as to such security, or while the registration statement is the subject of a refusal order or stop order or (prior to the effective date of the registration statement) any public proceeding or examination under section 8.

CIVIL LIABILITIES ON ACCOUNT OF FALSE REGISTRATION STATEMENT

Sec. 11. (a) In case any part of the registration statement, when such part became effective, contained an untrue statement of a material fact or omitted to state a material fact required to be stated therein or necessary to make the statements therein not misleading, any person acquiring such security (unless it is proved that at the time of such acquisition he knew of such untruth or omission) may, either at law or in equity, in any court of competent jurisdiction, sue—

[SIGNERS OF REGISTRATION STATEMENT]

(1) every person who signed the registration statement;

[DIRECTORS AND PARTNERS]

(2) every person who was a director of (or person performing similar functions), or partner in, the issuer at the time of the filing of the part of the registration statement with respect to which his liability is asserted;

[PERSONS NAMED AS BEING, OR ABOUT TO BECOME, DIRECTORS OR PARTNERS]

(3) every person who, with his consent, is named in the registration statement as being or about to become a director, person performing similar functions, or partner;

[Accountants, Engineers, Appraisers, and Other Professional Persons]

(4) every accountant engineer, or appraiser, or any person whose profession gives authority to a statement made by him, who has with his consent been named as having prepared or certified any part of the registration statement, or as having prepared or certified any report or valuation which is used in connection with the registration statement, with respect to the statement in such registration statement, report, or valuation, which purports to have been prepared or certified by him;

[Underwriters]

(5) every underwriter with respect to such security.

[Purchase After Publication of Earning Statement]

If such person acquired the security after the issuer has made generally available to its security holders an earning statement covering a period of at least twelve months beginning after the effective date of the registration statement, then the right of recovery under this subsection shall be conditioned on proof that such person acquired the securities relying on such untrue statement in the registration statement or relying upon the registration statement and not knowing of such omission, but such reliance may be established without proof of the reading of the registration statement by such person.

[Defenses of Persons Other Than Issuer]

(b) Notwithstanding the provisions of subsection (a) no person, other than the issuer, shall be liable as provided therein who shall sustain the burden of proof—

[Resignation Before Effective Date]

(1) that before the effective date of the part of the registration statement with respect to which his liability is asserted (A) he had resigned from or had taken such steps as are permitted by law to resign from, or ceased or refused to act in, every office, capacity or relationship in which he was described in the registration statement as acting or agreeing to act, and (B) he had advised the Commission and the issuer in writing, that he had taken such action and that he would not be responsible for such part of the registration statement; or

[Statements Becoming Effective Without Defendants Knowledge]

(2) that if such part of the registration statement became effective without his knowledge, upon becoming aware of such fact he forthwith acted and advised the Commission, in accordance with paragraph (1), and, in addition, gave reasonable public notice that such part of the registration statement had become effective without his knowledge; or

[Belief on Reasonable Grounds That Statements Were True]

(3) that (A) as regards any part of the registration statement not purporting to be made on the authority of an expert, and not purporting to be a copy of or extract from a report or valuation of an expert and not purporting to be made on the authority of a public official document or statement, he had, after reasonable investigation, reasonable ground to believe and did believe, at the time such part of the registration statement became effective, that the statements therein were true and that there was no omission to state a material fact required to be stated therein or necessary to make the statements therein not misleading; and

[Statement Made on Authority of Defendant as Expert]

(B) as regards any part of the registration statement purporting to be made upon his authority as an expert or purporting to be a copy of or extract from a report or valuation of himself as an expert, (i) he had, after reasonable investigation, reasonable ground to believe and did believe, at the time such part of the registration statement became effective, that the statements therein were true and that there was no omission to state a material fact required to be stated therein or necessary to make the statements therein not misleading, or (ii) such part of the registration statement did not fairly represent his statement as an expert or was not a fair copy of or extract from his report or valuation as an expert; and

[Statement Made on Authority of Expert Other Than Defendant]

(C) as regards any part of the registration statement purporting to be made on the authority of an expert (other than himself) or purporting to be a copy of or extract from a report or valuation of an expert (other than himself), he had no reasonable ground to believe and did not believe, at the time such part of the registration statement became effective, that the statements therein were untrue or that there was an omission to state a material fact required to be stated therein or necessary to make the statements therein not misleading, or that such part of the registration statement did not fairly represent the statement of the expert or was not a fair copy of or extract from the report or valuation of the expert; and

[Statement Made by Official Person; Copy of Public Official Document]

(D) as regards any part of the registration statement purporting to be a statement made by an official person or purporting to be a copy of or extract from a public official document, he had no reasonable ground to believe and did not believe, at the time such part of the registration statement became effective, that the statements therein were untrue, or that there was an omission to state a material fact required to be stated therein or necessary to make the statements therein not misleading, or that such part of the registration statement did not fairly represent the statement made by the official person or was not a fair copy of or extract from the public official document.

["REASONABLE" INVESTIGATION AND "REASONABLE" GROUNDS FOR BELIEF]

(c) In determining, for the purpose of paragraph (3) of subsection (b) of this section, what constitutes reasonable investigation and reasonable ground for belief, the standard of reasonableness shall be that required of a prudent man in the management of his own property.

[PERSON BECOMING UNDERWRITER AFTER EFFECTIVENESS OF REGISTRATION STATEMENT]

(d) If any person becomes an underwriter with respect to the security after the part of the registration statement with respect to which his liability is asserted has become effective, then for the purposes of paragraph (3) of subsection (b) of this section such part of the registration statement shall be considered as having become effective with respect to such person as of the time when he became an underwriter.

[AMOUNT OF DAMAGES; BOND FOR COSTS OF SUIT]

(e) The suit authorized under subsection (a) may be to recover such damages as shall represent the difference between the amount paid for the security (not exceeding the price at which the security was offered to the public) and (1) the value thereof as of the time such suit was brought, or (2) the price at which such security shall have been disposed of in the market before suit, or (3) the price at which such security shall have been disposed of after suit but before judgment if such damages shall be less than the damages representing the difference between the amount paid for the security (not exceeding the price at which the security was offered to the public) and the value thereof as of the time such suit was brought: Provided, that if the defendant proves that any portion or all of such damages represents other than the depreciation in value of such security resulting from such part of the registration statement, with respect to which his liability is asserted, not being true or omitting to state a material fact required to be stated therein or necessary to make the statements therein not misleading, such portion of or all such damages shall not be recoverable. In no event shall any underwriter (unless such underwriter shall have knowingly received from the issuer for acting as an underwriter some benefit, directly or indirectly in which

all other underwriters similarly situated did not share in proportion to their respective interests in the underwriting) be liable in any suit or as a consequence of suits authorized under subsection (a) of this section for damages in excess of the total price at which the securities underwritten by him and distributed to the public were offered to the public. In any suit under this or any other section of this title the court may, in its discretion, require an undertaking for the payment of the costs of such suit, including reasonable attorney's fees, and if judgment shall be rendered against a party litigant, upon the motion of the other party litigant, such costs may be assessed in favor of such party litigant (whether or not such undertaking has been required) if the court believes the suit or the defense to have been without merit, in an amount sufficient to reimburse him for the reasonable expenses incurred by him, in connection with such suit, such costs to be taxed in the manner usually provided for taxing of costs in the court in which the suit was heard.

[JOINT AND SEVERAL LIABILITY]

(f) (1) Except as provided in paragraph (2), All or any one or more of the persons specified in subsection (a) shall be jointly and severally liable, and every person who becomes liable to make any payment under this section may recover contribution as in cases of contract from any person who, if sued separately, would have been liable to make the same payment, unless the person who had become liable was, and the other was not, guilty of fraudulent misrepresentation.

(2)(A) The liability of an outside director under subsection (e) shall be determined in accordance with Section 21D(f) of the Securities Exchange Act of 1934.

[*Ed.*: Section 21D(f) provides that any person found liable shall be jointly and severally liable for all damages awarded the plaintiff only if the trier of fact specifically determines that the person knowingly committed a violation of the securities laws. Otherwise (except for uncollectible amounts, as described below), a person is liable solely for the portion of the judgment that corresponds to that person's percentage of responsibility (such percentage to be determined by considering both the nature of the person's conduct and the nature and extent of the causal relationship between the person's conduct and the damages incurred by the plaintiff). If part of the judgment owed by all defendants remains uncollectible, then each defendant has joint and several liability for the uncollectible share if the plaintiff is an individual with a net worth less than $200,000 and the recoverable damages represent more than 10 percent of that net worth. Otherwise, each defendant is liable for the uncollectible share in proportion to his or her percentage of responsibility up to a maximum of 50 percent of that person's proportionate share of liability.]

(B) For purpose of this paragraph, the term "outside director" shall have the meaning given such term by rule or regulation of the commission.

[LIMITATION ON AMOUNT OF DAMAGES]

(g) In no case shall the amount recoverable under this section exceed the price at which the security was offered to the public.

Civil Liabilities Arising in Connection with Prospectuses and Communications

Sec. 12. (a) *In General*—Any person who—

(1) offers or sells a security in violation of section 5, or

OFFERS OR SELLS BY USE OF INTERSTATE COMMUNICATIONS OR TRANSPORTATION

(2) offers or sells a security (whether or not exempted by the provisions of section 3, other than paragraph (2) of subsection (a) thereof), by the use of any means or instruments of transportation or communication in interstate commerce or of the mails, by means of a prospectus or oral communication, which includes an untrue statement of a material fact or omits to state a material fact necessary in order to make the statements, in the light of the circumstances under which they were made, not misleading (the purchaser not knowing of such untruth or omission), and who shall not sustain the burden of proof that he did not know, and in the exercise of reasonable care could not have known, of such untruth or omission, shall be liable, subject to subsection (b), to the person purchasing such security from him, who may sue either at law or in equity in any court of competent jurisdiction, to recover the consideration paid for such security with interest thereon, less the amount of any income received thereon, upon the tender of such security, or for damages if he no longer owns the security.

(b) *Loss Causation.*—In an action described in subsection (a)(2), if the person who offered or sold such security proves that any portion or all of the amount recoverable under subsection (a)(2) represents other than the depreciation in value of the subject security resulting from such part of the prospectus or oral communication, with respect to which the liability of that person is asserted, not being true or omitting to state a material fact required to be stated therein or necessary to make the statement not misleading, then such portion or amount, as the case may be, shall not be recoverable.

APPENDIX H: Securities Exchange Act of 1934 [Excerpts]

REGULATION OF THE USE OF MANIPULATIVE AND DECEPTIVE DEVICES

Sec. 10. It shall be unlawful for any person, directly or indirectly, by the use of any means or instrumentality of interstate commerce or of the mails, or of any facility of any national securities exchange—

   . . .

[USE OR EMPLOYMENT OF MANIPULATIVE OR DECEPTIVE DEVICES]

(b) To use or employ, in connection with the purchase or sale of any security registered on a national securities exchange or any security not so registered, any manipulative or deceptive device or contrivance in contravention of such rules and regulations as the commission may prescribe as necessary or appropriate in the public interest or for the protection of investors.

   . . .

[DIRECTORS, OFFICERS, AND PRINCIPAL STOCKHOLDERS]

Sec. 16. (a) Every person who is directly or indirectly the beneficial owner of more than 10 per centum of any class of any equity security (other than exempted security) which is registered pursuant to section 12 of this title, or who is a director or an officer of the issuer of such security, shall file, at the time of the registration of such security on a national securities exchange or by the effective date of a registration statement filed pursuant to section 12(g) of this title, or within ten days after he becomes such beneficial owner, director, or officer, a statement with the Commission (and, if such security is registered on a national securities exchange, also with the exchange) of the amount of all equity securities of such issuer of which he is the beneficial owner, and within ten days after the close of each calendar month thereafter, if there has been a change in such ownership during such month, shall file with the Commission (and if such security is registered on a national securities exchange, shall also file with the exchange), a statement indicating his ownership at the close of the calendar month and such changes in his ownership as have occurred during such calendar month.

[PROFITS REALIZED FROM PURCHASE AND SALES WITHIN PERIOD OF LESS THAN SIX MONTHS]

(b) For the purpose of preventing the unfair use of information which may have been obtained by such beneficial owner, director, or officer by reason of his relationship to the issuer, any profit realized by him from any purchase and sale, or any sale and purchase, of any equity security of such issuer (other than an exempted security) within any period of less than six months, unless such security was acquired in good faith in connection with a debt previously contracted, shall inure to and be recoverable by the issuer, irrespective of any intention on the part of such beneficial owner, director, or officer in entering into such transaction of holding the security purchased or of not repurchasing the security sold for a period exceeding six months. Suit to recover such profit may be instituted at law or in equity in any court of competent jurisdiction by the issuer, or by the owner of any security of the issuer in the name and in behalf of the issuer if the issuer shall fail or refuse to bring such suit within sixty days after request or shall fail diligently to prosecute the same thereafter; but no such suit shall be brought more than two years after the date such profit was realized. This subsection shall not be construed to cover any transaction where such beneficial owner was not such both at the time of the purchase and sale, or the sale and purchase, of the security involved, or any transaction or transactions which the Commission by rules and regulations may exempt as not comprehended within the purpose of this subsection.

APPENDIX I: Rules 10b-5, 10b5-1, and 10b5-2 from Code of Federal Regulations

REGULATIONS ADOPTED BY THE SECURITIES AND EXCHANGE COMMISSION PURSUANT TO SECTION 10(B) OF THE SECURITIES EXCHANGE ACT OF 1934

§ 240.10b-5 Employment of manipulative and deceptive devices.

It shall be unlawful for any person, directly or indirectly, by the use of any means or instrumentality of interstate commerce, or of the mails or of any facility of any national securities exchange,

(1) to employ any device, scheme, or artifice to defraud,

(2) to make any untrue statement of a material fact or to omit to state a material fact necessary in order to make the statements made, in light of the circumstances under which they were made, not misleading, or

(3) to engage in any act, practice, or course of business which operates or would operate as a fraud or deceit upon any person, in connection with the purchase or sale of any security.

[13 Fed. Reg. 8, 183 (Dec. 22, 1948), as amended at 16 Fed. Reg. 7,928 (Aug. 11, 1951)]

§ 240.10b5–1 TRADING "ON THE BASIS OF" MATERIAL NONPUBLIC INFORMATION IN INSIDER TRADING CASES.

Preliminary Note to § 240.10b5–1: This provision defines when a purchase or sale constitutes trading "on the basis of" material nonpublic information in insider trading cases brought under Section 10(b) of the Act and Rule 10b–5 thereunder. The law of insider trading is otherwise defined by judicial opinions construing Rule 10b–5, and Rule 10b5–1 does not modify the scope of insider trading law in any other respect.

(a) General. The "manipulative and deceptive devices" prohibited by Section 10(b) of the Act (15 U.S.C. 78j) and § 240.10b–5 thereunder include, among other things, the purchase or sale of a security of any issuer, on the basis of material nonpublic information about that security or issuer, in breach of a duty of trust or confidence that is owed directly, indirectly, or derivatively, to the issuer of that security or the shareholders of that issuer, or to any other person who is the source of the material nonpublic information.

(b) Definition of "on the basis of." Subject to the affirmative defenses in paragraph (c) of this section, a purchase or sale of a security of an issuer is "on the basis of" material nonpublic information about that security or issuer if the person making the purchase or sale was aware of the material nonpublic information when the person made the purchase or sale.

(c) Affirmative defenses. (1)(i) Subject to paragraph (c) (1) (ii) of this section, a person's purchase or sale is not "on the basis of" material nonpublic information if the person making the purchase or sale demonstrates that:

(A) Before becoming aware of the information, the person had:

(1) Entered into a binding contract to purchase or sell the security,

(2) Instructed another person to purchase or sell the security for the instructing person's account, or

(3) Adopted a written plan for trading securities;

(B) The contract, instruction, or plan described in paragraph (c) (1) (i) (A) of this Section:

(1) Specified the amount of securities to be purchased or sold and the price at which and the date on which the securities were to be purchased or sold;

(2) Included a written formula or algorithm, or computer program, for determining the amount of securities to be purchased or sold and the price at which and the date on which the securities were to be purchased or sold; or

(3) Did not permit the person to exercise any subsequent influence over how, when, or whether to effect purchases or sales; provided, in addition, that any other person who, pursuant to the contract, instruction, or plan, did exercise

such influence must not have been aware of the material nonpublic information when doing so; and

(C) The purchase or sale that occurred was pursuant to the contract, instruction, or plan. A purchase or sale is not "pursuant to a contract, instruction, or plan" if, among other things, the person who entered into the contract, instruction, or plan altered or deviated from the contract, instruction, or plan to purchase or sell securities (whether by changing the amount, price, or timing of the purchase or sale), or entered into or altered a corresponding or hedging transaction or position with respect to those securities.

(ii) Paragraph (c) (1) (i) of this section is applicable only when the contract, instruction, or plan to purchase or sell securities was given or entered into in good faith and not as part of a plan or scheme to evade the prohibitions of this section.

(iii) This paragraph (c) (1) (iii) defines certain terms as used in paragraph (c) of this Section.

(A) Amount. "Amount" means either a specified number of shares or other securities or a specified dollar value of securities.

(B) Price. "Price" means the market price on a particular date or a limit price, or a particular dollar price.

(C) Date. "Date" means, in the case of a market order, the specific day of the year on which the order is to be executed (or as soon thereafter as is practicable under ordinary principles of best execution). "Date" means, in the case of a limit order, a day of the year on which the limit order is in force.

(2) A person other than a natural person also may demonstrate that a purchase or sale of securities is not "on the basis of" material nonpublic information if the person demonstrates that:

(i) The individual making the investment decision on behalf of the person to purchase or sell the securities was not aware of the information; and

(ii) The person had implemented reasonable policies and procedures, taking into consideration the nature of the person's business, to ensure that individuals making investment decisions would not violate the laws prohibiting trading on the basis of material nonpublic information. These policies and procedures may include those that restrict any purchase, sale, and causing any purchase or sale of any security as to which the person has material nonpublic information, or those that prevent such individuals from becoming aware of such information.

[65 Fed. Reg. 51,716, 51,737 (Aug. 24, 2000)]

§ 240.10b5–2 Duties of trust or confidence in misappropriation insider trading cases.

Preliminary Note to § 240.10b5–2: This section provides a non-exclusive definition of circumstances in which a person has a duty of trust or confidence for purposes of the "misappropriation" theory of insider trading under Section 10(b) of the Act and Rule 10b–5. The law of insider trading is otherwise defined by judicial opinions construing Rule 10b–5, and Rule 10b5–2 does not modify the scope of insider trading law in any other respect.

(a) Scope of Rule. This section shall apply to any violation of Section 10(b) of the Act (15 U.S.C. 78j(b)) and § 240.10b–5 thereunder that is based on the purchase or sale of securities on the basis of, or the communication of, material nonpublic information misappropriated in breach of a duty of trust or confidence.

(b) Enumerated "duties of trust or confidence." For purposes of this section, a "duty of trust or confidence" exists in the following circumstances, among others:

(1) Whenever a person agrees to maintain information in confidence;

(2) Whenever the person communicating the material nonpublic information and the person to whom it is communicated have a history, pattern, or practice of sharing confidences, such that the recipient of the information knows or reasonably should know that the person communicating the material nonpublic information expects that the recipient will maintain its confidentiality; or

(3) Whenever a person receives or obtains material nonpublic information from his or her spouse, parent, child, or sibling; provided, however, that the person receiving or obtaining the information may demonstrate that no duty of trust or confidence existed with respect to the information, by establishing that he or she neither knew nor reasonably should have known that the person who was the source of the information expected that the person would keep the information confidential, because of the parties' history, pattern, or practice of sharing and maintaining confidences, and because there was no agreement or understanding to maintain the confidentiality of the information.

[65 Fed. Reg. 51,716, 51,738 (Aug. 24, 2000)]

APPENDIX J: Rule 14e–3 from Code of Federal Regulations

§ 240.14e-3 Transactions in securities on the basis of material, nonpublic information in the context of tender offers. (a) If any person has taken a substantial step or steps to commence, or has commenced, a tender offer (the "offering person"), it shall constitute a fraudulent, deceptive or manipulative act or practice within the meaning of section 14(e) of the Act for any other person who is in possession of material information relating to such tender offer which information he knows or has reason to know is nonpublic and which he knows or has reason to know has been acquired directly or indirectly from:

(1) The offering person,

(2) The issuer of the securities sought or to be sought by such tender offer, or

(3) Any officer, director, partner or employee or any other person acting on behalf of the offering person or such issuer, to purchase or sell or cause to be purchased or sold any of such securities or any securities convertible into or exchangeable for any such securities or any option or right to obtain or dispose of any of the foregoing securities, unless within a reasonable time prior to any purchase or sale such information and its source are publicly disclosed by press release or otherwise.

(b) A person other than a natural person shall not violate paragraph (a) of this section if such person shows that:

(1) The individual(s) making the investment decision on behalf of such person to purchase or sell any security described in paragraph (a) of this section or to cause any such security to be purchased or sold by or on behalf of others did not know the material, nonpublic information; and

(2) Such person had implemented one or a combination of policies and procedures, reasonable under the circumstances, taking into consideration the nature of the person's business, to ensure that individual(s) making investment decision(s) would not violate paragraph (a) of this section, which policies and procedures may include, but are not limited to, (i) those which restrict any purchase, sale and causing any purchase and sale of any such security or (ii) those which prevent such individual(s) from knowing such information.

(c) Notwithstanding anything in paragraph (a) of this section to contrary, the following transactions shall not be violations of paragraph (a) of this section:

(1) Purchase(s) of any security described in paragraph (a) of this section by a broker or by another agent on behalf of an offering person; or

(2) Sale(s) by any person of any security described in paragraph (a) of this section to the offering person.

(d)(1) As a means reasonably designed to prevent fraudulent, deceptive or manipulative acts or practices within the meaning of section 14(e) of the Act, it shall be unlawful for any person described in paragraph (d)(2) of this section to communicate material, nonpublic information relating to a tender offer to any other person under circumstances in which it is reasonably foreseeable that such communication is likely to result in a violation of this section except that this paragraph shall not apply to a communication made in good faith:

(i) To the officers, directors, partners or employees of the offering person, to its advisors or to other persons, involved in the planning, financing, preparation or execution of such tender offer;

(ii) To the issuer whose securities are sought or to be sought by such tender offer, to its officers, directors, partners, employees or advisors or to other persons, involved in the planning, financing, preparation or execution of the activities of the issuer with respect to such tender offer; or

(iii) To any person pursuant to a requirement of any statute or rule or regulation promulgated thereunder.

(2) The persons referred to in paragraph (d)(1) of this section are:

(i) The offering person or its officers, directors, partners, employees or advisors;

(ii) The issuer of the securities sought or to be sought by such tender offer or its officers, directors, partners, employees or advisors;

(iii) Anyone acting on behalf of the persons in paragraph (d)(2)(i) of this section or the issuer or persons in paragraph (d)(2)(ii) of this section; and

(iv) Any person in possession of material information relating to a tender offer which information he knows or has reason to know is nonpublic and which he knows or has reason to know has been acquired directly or indirectly from any of the above.

[46 FR 60418 (SEPT. 12, 1980)]

APPENDIX K: Sarbanes–Oxley Act of 2002 [Excerpts]

Sec. 201. Services Outside the Scope of Practice of Auditors.

(g) *Prohibited Activities.* Except as provided in subsection (h), it shall be unlawful for a registered public accounting firm (and any associated person of that firm, to the extent determined appropriate by the [Securities and Exchange] Commission) that performs for any issuer any audit required by this title or the rules of the Commission under this title or . . . Board, the rules of the Public Company Accounting Oversight Board, to provide to that issuer, contemporaneously with the audit, any non-audit service, including—

(1) bookkeeping or other services related to the accounting records or financial statements of the audit client;

(2) financial information systems design and implementation;

(3) appraisal or valuation services, fairness opinions, or contribution-in-kind reports;

(4) actuarial services;

(5) internal audit outsourcing services;

(6) management functions or human resources;

(7) broker or dealer, investment adviser, or investment banking services;

(8) legal services and expert services unrelated to the audit; and

(9) any other service that the Board determines, by regulation, is impermissible.

(h) *Preapproval Required for Non-Audit Services.* A registered public accounting firm may engage in any non-audit service, including tax services, that is not described in any of paragraphs (1) through (9) of subsection (g) for an audit client, only if the activity is approved in advance by the audit committee of the issuer, in accordance with subsection (i). [Codified at 15 U.S.C. § 78j-1.]

Sec. 302. Corporate Responsibility for Financial Reports.

(a) *Regulations Required.* The Commission shall, by rule, require, for each company filing periodic reports under section 13(a) or 15(d) of the Securities Exchange Act of 1934, that the principal executive officer or officers and the principal financial officer or officers, or persons performing similar functions, certify in each annual or quarterly report filed or submitted under either such section of such Act that—

(1) the signing officer has reviewed the report;

(2) based on the officer's knowledge, the report does not contain any untrue statement of a material fact or omit to state a material fact necessary in order to make the statements made, in light of the circumstances under which such statements were made, not misleading;

(3) based on such officer's knowledge, the financial statements, and other financial information included in the report, fairly present in all material respects the financial condition and results of operations of the issuer as of, and for, the periods presented in the report;

(4) the signing officers—

(A) are responsible for establishing and maintaining internal controls;

(B) have designed such internal controls to ensure that material information relating to the issuer and its consolidated subsidiaries is made known to such officers by others within those entities, particularly during the period in which the periodic reports are being prepared;

(C) have evaluated the effectiveness of the issuer's internal controls as of a date within 90 days prior to the report; and

(D) have presented in the report their conclusions about the effectiveness of their internal controls based on their evaluation as of that date;

(5) the signing officers have disclosed to the issuer's auditors and the audit committee of the board of directors (or persons fulfilling the equivalent function)—

(A) all significant deficiencies in the design or operation of internal controls which could adversely affect the issuer's ability to record, process, summarize, and report financial data and have identified for the issuer's auditors any material weaknesses in internal controls; and

(B) any fraud, whether or not material, that involves management or other employees who have a significant role in the issuer's internal controls; and

(6) the signing officers have indicated in the report whether or not there were significant changes in internal controls or in other factors that could significantly affect internal controls subsequent to the date of their evaluation, including any corrective actions with regard to significant deficiencies and material weaknesses.

[Codified at 15 U.S.C. § 7241.]

Sec. 404. Management Assessment of Internal Controls.

(a) *Rules Required.* The Commission shall prescribe rules requiring each annual report required by section 13(a) or 15(d) of the Securities Exchange Act of 1934 to contain an internal control report, which shall—

(1) state the responsibility of management for establishing and maintaining an adequate internal control structure and procedures for financial reporting; and

(2) contain an assessment, as of the end of the most recent fiscal year of the issuer, of the effectiveness of the internal control structure and procedures of the issuer for financial reporting.

(b) *Internal Control Evaluation and Reporting.* With respect to the internal control assessment required by subsection (a), each registered public accounting firm that prepares or issues the audit report for the issuer shall attest to, and report on, the assessment made by the management of the issuer. An attestation made under this subsection shall be made in accordance with standards for attestation engagements issued or adopted by the Board. Any such attestation shall not be the subject of a separate engagement.

[Codified at 15 U.S.C. § 7262.]

Sec. 802. Criminal Penalties for Altering Documents.
Whoever knowingly alters, destroys, mutilates, conceals, covers up, falsifies, or makes a false entry in any record, document, or tangible object with the intent to impede, obstruct, or influence the investigation or proper administration of any matter within the jurisdiction of any department or agency of the United States or any [bankruptcy] case filed under title 11, or in relation to or contemplation of any such matter or case, shall be fined under this title, imprisoned not more than 20 years, or both.

[Codified at U.S.C. § 1519.]

GLOSSARY

A

abandonment (of a trademark) The failure to use a mark after acquiring legal protection may result in the loss of rights, and such loss is known as abandonment.

abrogate To annul the states' Eleventh Amendment immunity.

absolute privilege In defamation cases, the right of the defendant to publish with impunity a statement known by the defendant to be false.

acceptance An agreement to the amount offered for certain services or products. Acceptance may be verbal, written, or implied by action.

accession A process whereby a nation that was not an original party to a treaty can elect to participate in the treaty at a later time.

accord *See* Accord and Satisfaction.

accord and satisfaction An agreement to accept performance that is different from what is called for in the contract.

accredited investor Under Rule 501 of SEC Regulation D, an "accredited investor" is any one of the following: (1) a national bank; (2) a corporation, business trust, or charitable organization with total assets in excess of $5 million; (3) a director, executive officer or general partner of the issuer; (4) a natural person who had individual income in excess of $200,000 in each of the two most recent years, or joint income with that person's spouse in excess of $300,000 in each of the two most recent years, with a reasonable expectation of reaching the same income level in the current year; (5) any natural person whose individual net worth, or joint net worth with that person's spouse, excluding the primary residence, exceeds $1 million at the time of purchase; (6) a trust with assets greater than $5 million with the purchase directed by a sophisticated investor; (7) a private developing company; or (8) an entity in which all the equity owners are accredited investors.

act-of-state doctrine The doctrine that states that the courts of one country will not sit in judgment on the acts of the government of another done within its own territory.

actual authority The express or implied power of an agent to act for and bind a principal to agreements entered into by an agent.

actual cause Proof that but for the defendant's negligent conduct the plaintiff would not have been harmed.

actual damages The amount required to repair or to replace an item or the decrease in market value caused by tortious conduct. Actual damages restore the injured party to the position it was in prior to the injury. Also called *compensatory damages*.

actual intent The subjective desire to cause the consequences of an act, or the belief that the consequences are substantially certain to result from it.

actual malice A statement made with the knowledge that it is false or with a reckless disregard for the truth.

actus reus (guilty deed) A crime; a criminal act.

ad valorem tariffs Tariffs for which the importer must pay a percentage of the value of the imported merchandise.

additive Anything not inherent in a food product—including pesticide residues, unintended environmental contaminants, and unavoidably added substances from packaging.

adhesion contracts An unfair type of contract by which sellers offer goods or services on a take-it-or-leave-it basis, with no chance for consumers to negotiate for goods except by agreeing to the terms of said contract.

adjustable-rate loan Loans that allow lenders to avoid the risk of fluctuating interest rates. The rate of interest is often set at a fixed number of percentage points over a specified standard.

adjustable-rate mortgages (ARMs) Mortgages that start out with a low fixed rate and usually adjust upward within two to five years as the rate resets.

administrative law judge (ALJ) The presiding official at an administrative proceeding who has the power to issue an order resolving the legal dispute.

adoption Process by which a securities issuer explicitly or implicitly endorses or approves third-party information.

adulterated Consisting in whole or in part of any filthy, putrid, or decomposed substance, or otherwise unfit for food.

adverse employment action Action by an employer that materially affects the terms and conditions of employment, such as employee compensation or job responsibilities.

adverse possession Ownership of property that is not occupied by its owner for a certain period of time may be transferred to those who have been unlawfully occupying it and openly exercising rights of ownership. Such a transfer is usually not reflected in the official land records. Also called *squatter's rights*.

affidavit A written or printed declaration or statement of facts, made voluntarily, and confirmed by the oath or affirmation of the party making it, taken before a person having authority to administer such oath or affirmation.

affiliate Any person who controls an issuer of securities, or is controlled by the issuer, or is under common control. Includes officers, directors, and major shareholders of a corporation.

affirmative covenants The borrower's promise to do certain things under the loan agreement.

affirmative defense The admission in an answer to a complaint that defendant has acted as plaintiff alleges, but denies that defendant's conduct was the real or legal cause of harm to plaintiff.

after-acquired property The property a debtor acquires after the execution of a security agreement.

after-acquired title If, at the date of execution of a grant deed, the grantor does not have title to the real property referred to in the grant deed but subsequently acquires it, such after-acquired title is deemed automatically transferred to the grantee.

agency A relationship in which one person (the agent) acts for or represents another person (the principal).

agency by estoppel When the principal leads a third party to believe that a person is his or her agent, the principal is estopped (prevented) from denying that the person is his or her agent.

agency by ratification An agency formed when a principal approves or accepts the benefits of the actions of an otherwise unauthorized agent.

agent A person who manages a task delegated by another (the principal) and exercises whatever discretion is given to the agent by the principal.

aided-in-the-agency doctrine *See* Aided-in-the-Agency-Relation Doctrine.

aided-in-the-agency-relation doctrine An agency principle whereby the principal may be held vicariously liable for the wrongful acts of an agent acting outside of the scope of authority because the principal provided the instrumentality or created the circumstances that made it possible for the agent to commit the wrongful act.

aided-in the agency relation theory An employee is aided in accomplishing a tort by the existence of the agency relationship.

aider and abettor A person with knowledge of (or recklessness as to) a primary criminal violation who provides substantial assistance to the primary violation.

allocative efficiency An equilibrium in which scarce societal resources are allocated to the production of various goods and services up to the point where the cost of the resources equals the benefit society reaps from their use.

alter ego theory When owners have so mingled their own affairs with those of a corporation that the corporation does not exist as a distinct entity, it is an alter ego (second self) of its owners, permitting the piercing of the corporate veil.

alternative dispute resolution (ADR) Alternative techniques, such as negotiation, mediation, arbitration, med-arb, arb-med, minitrials, and summary jury trials, to resolve disputes without litigation.

alternative minimum tax (AMT) A tax law that was passed to prevent higher income taxpayers from paying too little tax because they were able to take advantage of a variety of tax deductions or exclusions, including the spread on exercise of an incentive stock option. Taxpayers who may be subject to AMT must calculate their taxable income in two ways and pay whichever formula yields the higher tax.

***amici curiae* brief** An appellate brief filed by interested parties (literally, "friends of the court") who are not themselves parties to the case on appeal.

amortize To pay the principal of a loan over a period of time.

angels Wealthy individual investors to whom entrepreneurs often turn for equity capital after exhausting the funds available from family and friends.

answer The instrument by which defendant admits or denies the various allegations stated in the complaint against the defendant.

anticipatory repudiation If a party indicates before performance is due that it will breach the contract, there is an anticipatory repudiation of the contract.

antideficiency laws Statutes that restrict lenders seeking remedies against real property security from suing the borrower personally. If a lender has recourse to the borrower or to other property of the borrower, and exercises such rights, the lender may be precluded from foreclosing on real estate mortgaged by the borrower. Alternatively, if the holder of a mortgage or deed of trust secured by real property forecloses on the property, the lender may be precluded from suing the borrower personally to recover whatever is still owing after a foreclosure sale. Also called *one-form-of-action laws.*

antitrust injury The damages sustained by a plaintiff in an antitrust suit as a result of the defendant's anticompetitive conduct.

antitrust laws The laws that seek to identify and forbid business practices that are anticompetitive. Also called *competition laws.*

apartheid Prior to its abolition in the 1980s, an official policy of racial segregation in South Africa that relegated its black citizens to a second-class status in employment, housing, and opportunity.

apparent authority A principal, by words or actions, causes a third party to reasonably believe that an agent has authority to act for or bind the principal.

appellant The person who is appealing a judgment or seeking a writ of certiorari. Also called a *petitioner.*

appellate jurisdiction The power of the Supreme Court and other courts of appeal to decide cases that have been tried in a lower court and appealed.

appellee The party in a case against whom an appeal is taken; that is, the party who has an interest adverse to setting aside or reversing the judgment. Also called *respondent.*

applicant Person (the buyer in a sales transaction) requesting an issuing bank to provide a letter of credit in favor of another party called the beneficiary (the seller in a sales transaction).

appraisal rights In a merger or sale of assets, shareholders who voted against the transaction have appraisal rights, that is, the right to receive the fair cash value of the shares they were forced to give up as a result of the transaction.

appropriate collective bargaining unit A collective bargaining unit in which the employees share a community of interest; that is, they have similar compensation, working conditions, and supervision, and they work under the same general employer policies.

appropriation of a person's name or likeness Unauthorized use of a person's name or likeness for financial gain.

arbitrary and capricious standard If an agency has a choice between several courses of action, the court will presume that the chosen course is valid unless the person challenging it shows that it lacks any rational basis.

arbitrary marks A real word whose ordinary meaning has nothing to do with the trademarked product.

arbitration The resolution of a dispute by a neutral third party.

arbitration clause A clause that specifies that in the event of a dispute arising out of a contract, the parties will arbitrate specific issues in a stated manner.

arbitrator The neutral third party who conducts an arbitration to resolve a dispute.

arb-med A shortened form of arbitration/mediation, a procedure whereby parties present their case to an arbitrator who makes an award but keeps it secret while the parties try to resolve the dispute through mediation. If the mediation fails, then the arbitrator's award is unsealed and becomes binding on the parties.

area plan A planning document that usually encompasses just a portion of the city's geographic area.

arrest To deprive a person of his or her liberty by legal authority. Taking, under real or assumed authority, custody of another for the purpose of holding or detaining him or her to answer a criminal charge or civil demand.

articles of incorporation The basic document filed with the appropriate governmental agency upon the incorporation of a business. The contents are prescribed in the general corporation statutes but generally include the name, purpose, agent for service of process, authorized number of shares, and classes of stock of a corporation. It is executed by the incorporator(s). Also called the *charter* or the *certificate of incorporation.*

articles of organization The charter document for a limited liability company. Also called *certificate of formation.*

assault An intent to create a well-grounded apprehension of an immediate harmful or offensive contact. Generally, assault also requires some act (such as a threatening gesture) and the ability to follow through immediately with the battery.

asset lock-up option A lock-up option relating to assets of the target company.

assignment The transfer by a tenant of all or a portion of rented premises.

assumption of risk The expressed or implied consent by plaintiff to defendant to take the chance of injury from a known and appreciated risk.

at-will contract An employment relationship of indefinite duration.

attached If the three basic prerequisites of a security interest exist (agreement, value, and collateral), the security interest becomes enforceable between the parties and is said to attach. Also called *attachment*.

attorney-client privilege The common law rule that a court cannot force the disclosure of confidential communications between client and client's attorney.

attractive nuisance Artificial conditions on land for which an owner is liable for physical injury to child trespassers if (1) the owner knew or should have known that children were likely to trespass; (2) the condition is one the owner would reasonably know involved an unreasonable risk of injury to such children; (3) the children, because of their youth, did not discover the condition or realize the risk involved; (4) the utility to the owner of maintaining the condition is not great; (5) the burden of eliminating the risk is slight compared with the magnitude of the risk to the children; and (6) the owner fails to exercise reasonable care to protect the children.

automatic stay Feature of bankruptcy filing that instantly suspends most litigation and collection activities against the debtor, its property, or property of the bankruptcy estate.

avoiding powers The powers bankruptcy trustees can use to invalidate or reverse certain prebankruptcy transactions.

B

back pay A damage remedy in an employment discrimination case to compensate the plaintiff for lost salary and benefits.

bad faith A breach of the duty to act in good faith.

bad faith exception An exception to the at-will employment relationship for breach of the implied covenant of good faith and fair dealing.

bail The amount of money a defendant must post as a bond to guarantee his or her appearance at trial.

bait and switch advertising An area of deceptive pricing in which an advertiser refuses to show an advertised item, fails to have a reasonable quantity of the item in stock, fails to promise to deliver the item within a reasonable time, or discourages employees from selling the item.

bankruptcy estate Virtually all of a debtor's existing assets, less exempt property.

baseline assessments In order to mitigate liability under CERCLA and other environmental statutes, many tenants perform baseline assessments to establish the environmental condition of the property at both the commencement and the termination of the lease.

base rate The lowest rate of interest publicly offered by major lending institutions to their most creditworthy customers. Also called *reference rate* or *prime rate*.

battle of the forms A conflict between an offer and acceptance for the purchase of goods. Occurs when the parties negotiate the essential terms of the contract (for example, quantity, quality, and delivery date) but exchange standard preprinted forms that contain conflicting terms instead of executing a single, fully integrated contract.

baseline assessments The appraisal performed by a tenant that establishes the environmental condition of leased property at the commencement and termination of the lease.

battery The intentional, non-consensual harmful or offensive contact with an individual's body or with those things in contact with or closely connected with it.

bench trial A trial in which a judge, not a jury, decides all issues.

beneficial owner A person is considered to be a beneficial owner of any securities held by his or her immediate family, spouse, any minor children, and any other relative living in his or her household.

beneficiary An individual who is benefited by a trust or a will.

benefit corporation (B corporation) A form of for-profit corporation, which is authorized only in certain states, that is not required to maximize shareholder value even when a change in control or break-up is inevitable. A B corporation is required to distribute to shareholders an annual benefit report providing information about their social and environmental performance, using third parties as a benchmark.

bespeaks caution doctrine A doctrine whereby a court may determine that the inclusion of sufficient cautionary statements in a prospectus or other document renders immaterial any misrepresentations and omissions contained therein.

best-efforts underwriting A situation wherein the underwriters do not agree to purchase the securities being offered but instead agree to use their best efforts to find buyers at an agreed-on price. These underwritings are often used for initial public offerings or for companies that are unseasoned.

best interests of creditors test In a Chapter 11 bankruptcy case, dissenters must be given a bundle of rights the current value of which is at least as great as the distribution they would receive through a Chapter 7 liquidation.

best mode The best way the inventor knows of making an invention at the time of filing the patent application.

bicameralism The state of being composed of two legislative chambers; in the case of the United States, the Congress consists of the House of Representatives and the Senate.

bidder The party who makes a tender offer.

bilateral contract A promise given in exchange for another promise.

bills of attainder A law enacted to punish individuals or an easily ascertainable member of a group and prohibited by Article I, Section 9, of the U.S. Constitution.

Bill of Rights The first ten amendments to the Constitution.

binding arbitration When arbitration parties agree on a resolution and are bound by the arbitrator's decision.

blackout period Any period longer than three business days during which 50 percent or more of the participants in a retirement plan are prevented from trading the employer's securities.

blank check company A development-stage company that has no specific business plan or whose business plan is to acquire a presently unknown business.

blue sky laws A popular name for the state statutes that regulate and supervise offerings and sales of securities to persons in that state.

blurring Dilution of a famous trademark that occurs when a non-famous mark reduces the strong association between the owner of the famous mark and its products.

board of directors The individuals elected by the shareholders of a corporation who by law are responsible for the overall management of a corporation.

bona fide occupational qualification (BFOQ) A requirement that an employer places on certain jobs that actually requires that the person in that job has a certain gender, religion, or national origin.

book-running managers The managing investment banks in a public offering of securities; they negotiate the terms of the offering (most importantly the offering price and the number of shares offered) and the underwriter discount with the issuer (and any selling stockholders); and they assemble the underwriting group.

booked Having criminal charges against someone who has been arrested written in a register at a police station.

bound tariffs The WTO principle that holds that each time tariffs are reduced, they may not be raised again.

breakthrough rule A provision in Article 11 of the European Union Directive on Takeover Bids that permits a hostile bidder to weaken a target company's prebid differential voting structures to ensure that a bidder that acquires a majority of the target's equity can successfully mount a takeover.

breakup fee An amount agreed to in a merger agreement to be paid to a friendly suitor company if the agreement with the target company is not consummated through no fault of the friendly suitor company.

brownfields Property contaminated with hazardous waste that can be acquired and used without assumption of liability for the cleanup of all the legacy contamination.

browse-wrap agreement An online agreement that appears on a website but does not require the user to take any action to express his or her assent to the terms of use. To be enforceable, a user is deemed to have assented to the terms of use by the continued use of the website, as long as the terms of use are conspicuous.

burden of proof The requirement of a prosecutor in a criminal case to establish a defendant's guilt beyond a reasonable doubt.

business judgment rule In a case challenging a board decision, this rule holds that as long as directors have made an informed decision and are not interested in the transaction being considered, a court will not question whether the directors' action was wise or whether they made an error of judgment or a business mistake.

bust-up takeover An acquisition in which the acquired corporation is taken apart and its assets are sold piecemeal.

bylaws The internal rules governing a corporation.

C

C corporation A business organization that is taxed at both the entity level and the owner level.

call To demand repayment of fixed-rate loans or securities after a specified period, often after five, ten, or fifteen years.

capacity The ability (requisite presence of mind) to enter into a binding contract.

cap-and-trade system A system whereby allowable emissions are capped by law, and facilities that emit more than their allotments are required to buy credits from plants with emissions below the specified levels.

carbon footprint The amount of carbon dioxide and other greenhouse gases released into the air by a person or facility.

cartel A group of competi`tors that agrees to set prices.

caveat emptor (let the buyer beware) This maxim summarizes the rule that a purchaser must examine, judge, and test for himself or herself. It does not apply where strict liability, warranty, or other consumer protection laws protect consumer-buyers.

caveat venditor "Let the seller beware."

cease and desist orders An order of an administrative agency or court prohibiting a person or business firm from continuing a particular course of conduct.

cert. denied Indicates that a writ of certiorari was sought but denied by the Supreme Court.

certificate of deposit (CD) rate The CD rate is based on the average of the bid rates quoted to the bank by dealers in the secondary market for the purchase at face value of certificates of deposit of the bank in a given amount and for a given term.

certificate of formation The charter document for a limited liability company. Also called *articles of organization*.

certificate of incorporation *See* Articles of Incorporation.

certification mark A mark placed on a product or used in connection with a service that indicates that the product or service in question has met the standards of safety or quality that have been created and advertised by the certifier.

choice-of-forum clause or provision The clause in a contract wherein the parties agree in advance to the jurisdiction in which a dispute arising out of their agreement must be litigated.

circumstantial evidence The indirect (not based on personal knowledge or observation) evidence of certain facts that, taken alone, do not prove a particular conclusion but, if taken as a whole, give a trier of fact a reasonable basis for asserting a certain conclusion is true.

cite The citation of the court's decision in a case.

civil law legal system Legal system based on the Roman law as consolidated by the Corpus Juris Civilis in A.D. 533 and 534.

civil procedure The methods, procedures, and practices that govern the processing of a civil lawsuit from start to finish.

claims (under patent law) The description of those elements of an invention that will be protected by the patent.

class action If the conduct of the defendant affected numerous persons in a common way, litigation or arbitration may be brought as a class action by a representative of the class of persons affected.

classical theory of insider trading Prohibits insiders of a firm from trading that firm's securities based on material nonpublic information.

classified board A board on which directors serve for specified terms, usually three years, with only a fraction of them up for reelection at any one time. Also called *staggered board*.

clawback provisions Contract provisions that give an employer the right to recoup some or all of an employee's stock option gain if he or she goes to work for a competitor within a certain period of time following exercise of the option.

click-wrap license An online license agreement that presents the user with a notice on his or her computer screen that requires the user to agree to the terms of the license by clicking on an icon.

cliff vesting A common vesting schedule that provides that if a person granted stock options leaves within a certain period of time after employment (usually six months or a year), he or she forfeits all rights to any stock.

close corporation A corporation owned by a limited number of shareholders, usually thirty, most of whom are actively involved in the management of the corporation, that elects close corporation status in its charter.

closed-end credit Credit that involves only one transaction, such as a car or house loan.

closely held corporation A corporation characterized by the absence of a market for its stock, though it may have any number of shareholders.

Code of Federal Regulations (CFR) A multi-volume codification of federal regulations and rules.

codification The process by which existing common law principles are restated and laid down in a statute.

codified To collect and arrange items, such as statutes or regulations, systematically.

collateral The property belonging to a borrower that will become the lender's if the loan is not repaid.

collateralized debt obligations (CDOs) Mortgages packaged together and securitized into bonds and other debt securities. Often sold in tranches.

collective entity doctrine Under this doctrine, the custodian of records for a collective entity (such as a corporation) may not resist a subpoena for such records on the ground that the act of production will incriminate him or her.

co-managers Underwriters in a public offering of securities selected by the book-running managers.

comfort letter Letter that describes the review the accountant has conducted of unaudited interim financial statements and of certain numbers in the prospectus.

comity A situation whereby a court will enforce another country's judgments under certain conditions.

Commerce Clause The constitutional clause that gives Congress the power to regulate commerce with other nations, with Indian tribes, and between states.

commercial activity exception An exception to the blanket immunity from suits provided by the Foreign Sovereign Immunity Act for cases in which the foreign state was engaged in commercial activities.

commercial facilities (under Americans with Disabilities Act) All structures and facilities except those intended for residential use.

commercial impracticability Provision in Section 2-615 of the Uniform Commercial Code that excuses a failure to perform if performance is made impractical by an event unforeseen by the contract.

commercial lease A contract that conveys an interest in real property from the landlord to the tenant and governs the respective rights and obligations of the parties during the lease term.

commercial paper Short-term corporate indebtedness.

commitment fee The fee payable to a lender in connection with a revolving loan as consideration for its promise to keep the commitment available.

common customs tariff A single set of tariffs applied by all European Union (EU) member states on goods imported from outside the EU.

common law Also known as *case law,* or the legal rules made by judges when they decide a case where no constitution, statute, or regulation exists to resolve the dispute.

common law legal system A legal system that primarily relies on case law and precedents and is used in most countries that are or were British territories or colonies.

common market The customs union in which there are no tariffs on trade among its members, and a single set of tariffs applies to goods imported from outside the union.

community plan *See* Specific Plan.

community property The property acquired during marriage with assets earned by either spouse during the marriage.

comp (compensatory) time Extra paid vacation time granted instead of extra pay for overtime work.

comparative fault Reduced recovery for an injured party because of misuse or abuse of manufacturer's product.

comparative negligence The doctrine by which courts decide amount of award to be given a plaintiff based on the amount (percentage) of negligence plaintiff demonstrated when injured by defendant.

compensatory damages In an action for breach of contract, the amount necessary to make up for the economic loss caused by the breach.

compensatory justice Aims at compensating people for the harm done by another.

complaint The statement of plaintiff's grievance that makes allegations of the particular facts giving rise to dispute and states the legal reason why plaintiff is entitled to a remedy, the request for relief, the explanation why the court applied to has jurisdiction over the dispute, and whether plaintiff requests a jury trial.

composition A reduction in the amount payable to creditors pursuant to a composition plan.

composition plan A composition plan in a Chapter 13 proceeding is a plan in which creditors receive a percentage of the indebtedness, and the debtor is discharged of the remaining obligation.

computer fraud The unauthorized access of a computer used by the federal government, by various types of financial institutions, or in interstate commerce with the intent to alter, damage, or destroy information or to prevent authorized use of the such computers.

concerted activity Under the National Labor Relations Act, the exercise by employees of their rights to band together for mutual aid and protection that is engaged in with or on the authority of other employees and not solely by and on behalf of one employee.

conciliation A more formalized method of dispute resolution that is similar to inquiry but adds the element of acceptance in advance of the result of the commission by the parties and a "cooling-off" period.

condition An event or state of facts.

condition precedent A condition that must be met before a party's obligations to perform arise under a contract.

conditional-use permit A method of relief from the strict terms of a zoning ordinance that provides for other uses of real property that are not permitted as a matter of right, but for which a use permit must be obtained.

confidentiality agreement A way to avoid future claims by settling a case where the parties agree not to disclose the terms of the settlement.

confiscation The process of nationalization when the host country does not compensate the company for its lost assets.

conflict-of-laws rules When choice of law is disputed, the court in which the suit is filed will apply conflict of laws principles to determine which state's or country's laws should govern the dispute. They usually focus on the significance of each state's or country's relationship to the parties and the contract.

Confrontation Clause Clause in the U.S. Constitution that limits the prosecution's ability to introduce prior statements by witnesses not subject to cross-examination at trial.

conglomerate merger A combination of firms that were not competitors at the time of the acquisition, but that may, absent the merger, have become competitors.

conscious parallelism In business, the act of consistently setting prices at the same levels and changing prices at the same time as competitors.

consent decree A judgment entered by the consent of the parties whereby the defendant agrees to stop the alleged illegal activity without admitting guilt or wrongdoing. Also called *consent order*.

consent order An agreement to stop the activity that a regulatory agency has found unlawful.

consequential damages Compensation for losses that occur as a foreseeable result of a breach of contract. Actual damages represent the damage, loss, or injury that flows directly and immediately from the act of the other party; in contrast, consequential damages refer to damage, loss, or injury flowing from some of the consequences or results of such act.

consideration A thing of value (money, services, an object, a promise, forbearance, or giving up the right to do something) exchanged in a contract.

construction (of a statute) Interpretation of a statute within that agency's area of expertise.

constructive notice Notice attributed by the existence of a properly recorded deed.

constructive trust A trust imposed on profits derived from an agent's breach of fiduciary duty.

continuing guaranty A guaranty that covers all future obligations of the primary debtor to the lender.

continuity of enterprise approach *See* Substantial Continuity Test.

contract A legally enforceable promise or set of promises.

contribution The doctrine that provides for the distribution of loss among several defendants by requiring each to pay its proportionate share to one who has discharged the joint liability of the group.

contributory copyright infringement Inducing, causing, or materially contributing to the infringing conduct of another with knowledge of the infringing activity.

contributory patent infringement One party knowingly sells an item that has one specific use that will result in the infringement of another's patent.

contributory negligence Plaintiff was negligent in some manner when injured by defendant.

control securities The sale of securities to the public by a controlling shareholder or other affiliate of the issuer is a transaction involving an underwriter.

controlling-person liability A person (or other entity), usually an officer or director of a company, responsible and liable for a securities violation.

controlling shareholder A shareholder who owns sufficient shares to outvote the other shareholders, and thus to control the corporation.

conversion The exercise of dominion and control over the personal property, rather than the real property (land), of another. Term includes any unauthorized act that deprives an owner of his or her personal property permanently or for an indefinite time.

conveyance An instrument transferring an interest in real estate, such as a deed or lease.

copyright The legal right to prevent others from copying the expression embodied in a protected work.

core proceedings Proceedings of bankruptcy cases such as allowing creditor claims, deciding preferences, and confirming plans of reorganization.

corporate charter The document issued by a state agency or authority granting a corporation legal existence and the right to function as a corporation. Also called the *articles or certificate of incorporation*.

corporate domicile The state under whose laws a corporation is formed.

corporate opportunity doctrine The doctrine that holds that a business opportunity cannot legally be taken advantage of by an officer, director, or controlling shareholder if it is in the corporation's line of business.

corporation An organization authorized by state law to act as a legal entity distinct from its owners.

corporation by estoppel When a third party, in all its transactions with an enterprise, acts as if it were doing business with a corporation, the third party is prevented or estopped from claiming that the enterprise is not a corporation.

counterclaim A legal claim by defendant in opposition to or as a deduction from claim of plaintiff.

counterfeit mark A spurious trademark (1) that is used in combination with trafficking in goods or services, (2) that is identical to, or substantially indistinguishable from, a registered trademark, and (3) the use of which is likely to cause confusion or mistake or to deceive; or a spurious designation that is identical with, or substantially indistinguishable from, the holder of the right to use the designation.

counteroffer A new offer by the initial offeree that rejects and modifies the terms originally proposed by the offeror.

countertrade A foreign investor uses its local currency profits to purchase local products for sale abroad.

covenant The borrower's promise to the lender that it will or will not take specific actions as long as either a commitment or a loan is outstanding.

covenant not to compete An agreement, generally part of a contract of employment or a contract to sell a business, in which the covenantor agrees for a specific period of time and within a particular area to refrain from competition with the covenantee. Also called a *noncompete agreement*.

cover A buyer's obligation to buy substitute goods elsewhere after the seller has defaulted.

covered service member family leave The Family and Medical Leave Act of 1993, as amended by the National Defense Authorization Act of 2008, entitles eligible employees to up to twenty-six weeks of unpaid, job-protected time off from work to care for a spouse, son, daughter, parent, or next of kin who has a serious injury or illness incurred or aggravated by service in the military.

cramdown A bankruptcy relief plan confirmed over the objections of creditors.

credit default swaps A financial derivative contract used by lenders to hedge against a default by the borrower. Also used by hedge funds and other traders betting on how close a firm is to insolvency.

creditor beneficiary Third party to a contract that the promisee enters into in order to discharge a duty to said third party.

crime An offense against the public at large; an act that violates the duties owed to the community, for which the offender must make satisfaction to the public.

criminal An individual or entity that has been convicted of a crime.

cross-collateralization A provision in a loan agreement whereby the collateral for one loan may be used to secure obligations under another loan.

cross-default Any breach by the borrower under any other loan agreement will constitute an event of default under the subject loan agreement.

crowdfunding An offering of securities of up to $1 million per year exempt from SEC registration pursuant to the JOBS Act of 2012.

cumulative voting The process by which a shareholder can cast all its votes for one director nominee or allocate them among nominees as it sees fit.

customary international law A form of international law analogous to established practice and commercial usage as they are known in the commercial laws of many nations.

customary practice A form of international law whereby treaties between nations can be compared to "established practice" or "commercial usage" as they are known in the commercial laws of many nations.

customer restrictions Restrictions that prevent a dealer or distributor from selling to a certain class of customer.

customs union A group of countries that reduce or eliminate tariffs between themselves, but establish a common tariff for trading with all other states.

customs valuation The value assigned to an imported article by the U.S. Customs Service.

cybersquatting The registration of a domain name that is confusingly similar or identical to a protected trademark, where the person registering the domain name has no legitimate interest in that particular domain name and registers and uses it in bad faith.

D

***D'Oench, Duhme* doctrine** A doctrine that bars many claims and defenses against conservators and receivers that might have been valid against the failed bank or savings and loan itself. It bars enforcement of agreements unless those agreements are in writing and have been approved contemporaneously by the bank's board or loan committee and recorded in the bank's written records.

deceit Requires the proof of several elements, including knowledge by the seller that the misrepresentation is false.

***de facto* (in fact) corporation** When incorporators cannot show substantial compliance with incorporation requirements, a court may find a corporation is a *de facto* corporation (corporation in fact), even though it is not technically a corporation by law, if the incorporators demonstrate that they were unaware of the defect and that they made a good faith effort to incorporate correctly.

***de jure* (by law) corporation** When incorporators have substantially complied with incorporation requirements, the entity is a *de jure* corporation (a corporation by right).

de novo Anew; a *de novo* proceeding takes place when a case has been successfully appealed and will be litigated again from the beginning.

deal protection devices These devices dissuade other bidders and thereby protect the consummation of the friendly merger transaction favored by the target.

dealer Under the Securities Act of 1933, any person who engages either for all or part of his or her time, directly or indirectly, as agent, broker, or principal, in the business of offering, buying, selling, or otherwise dealing or trading in securities issued by another person.

debt subordination An agreement whereby one or more creditors of a common debtor agree to defer payment of their claims until another creditor of the same debtor is fully paid.

debtor Under the Uniform Commercial Code, the person who owes payment or other performance of the obligation secured, whether or not that person owns or has rights in the collateral.

debtor-in-possession (DIP) In most Chapter 11 bankruptcy cases the debtor is left in place to operate the business and is referred to as the debtor-in- possession (DIP). The DIP has the same powers as a trustee in bankruptcy, but also has the power to operate the debtor's business during the bankruptcy proceeding.

deceit *See* Fraudulent Misrepresentation.

deed A written document transferring an interest in real estate that is recorded at a public office where title documents are filed.

deed of trust A document evidencing a loan to buy real property secured by a lien on the real property. Also called a *mortgage*.

defamation The intentional communication to a third party of an untrue statement of fact that injures the plaintiff's reputation or good name by exposing the plaintiff to hatred, ridicule, or contempt.

default judgment A judgment that may be entered in favor of the plaintiff if the defendant does not file an answer within the time required.

defendant The person defending or denying; the party against whom relief or recovery is sought in an action or suit. The accused in a criminal case.

defined benefit pension plan A plan in which an employee's retirement benefit is expressed as a monthly annuity, the exact amount of which is calculated based on variables such as (1) number of years of service, (2) average compensation, (3) marital status, and (4) age at which benefits begin.

defined contribution pension plan A plan in which an employer agrees only to make specific contributions, usually a percentage of salary, so the payout is dependent on both the total contributions and the plan's investment performance.

Delaware carve-out Permits shareholders to bring a state law class-action suit against a corporation and its directors for breach of preexisting common law fiduciary disclosure obligations.

denial-of-service attacks Computer viruses that prevent user access to an Internet site.

deontological theory of ethics An ethical theory that focuses on the motivation behind an action rather than the consequences of an action.

depeçage A choice-of-law doctrine under which the court is permitted to apply the laws of different states to different issues when more than one state has an interest in the outcome of a case.

deposition The oral questioning of any person who may have helpful information about the facts of a case.

derivative insider A person, such as a tippee, upon whom the insider's duty of disclosure is imposed.

derivative works Works based upon a copyrighted work.

descriptive mark The identifying marks that directly describe (size, color, use of) the goods sold under the mark.

design defect A type of product defect that occurs when the product is manufactured according to specifications, but its inadequate design or poor choice of materials causes it to be defective.

design patent A patent that protects any novel, original, and ornamental design for an article of manufacture.

detrimental reliance Occurs when an offeree has changed his or her position because of justifiable reliance on an offer.

development loans Loans used for the acquisition, subdivision, improvement, and sale of residential properties.

dietary supplements Products such as vitamins, minerals, herbs, and amino acids.

diplomatic sanctions The removal or reduction of a diplomatic relationship.

direct copyright infringement Occurs when one party is alleged to have violated at least one of the five exclusive rights of the copyright holder by its own actions.

direct damages The difference between the market price at the time the buyer or seller learned of the other party's breach and the contract price for goods.

direct patent infringement The making, use, or sale of any patented invention in the jurisdiction where it is patented during the term of the patent.

direct representation Rules that apply for an agent acting in the name of a principal pursuant to express, implied, or apparent authority, whether or not the principal's identity is revealed at the time the agent acts or is to be revealed later.

directed verdict After the presentation of evidence in a trial before jury, either party may assert that other side has not produced enough evidence to support the legal claim or defense alleged. The moving party then requests that the judge take the case away from the jury and direct that a verdict be entered in favor of the moving party.

directive A form of European Union legislation that is a law directing member states to enact certain laws or regulations.

disappearing corporation In a merger of two corporations, the corporation that no longer maintains its separate corporate existence is the disappearing corporation.

discharge Relieve.

discovery The process through which parties to a lawsuit collect evidence to support their claims.

discovery-of-injury statutes Statutes that provide that the statute of limitations does not begin to run until the person discovers the injury.

discretionary review The Supreme Court can decide which cases within its jurisdiction it will adjudicate.

dismissed with prejudice The plaintiff is precluded from asserting the same claims in another case.

dismissed without prejudice The plaintiff is permitted to refile the complaint (or an amended version thereof) and recommence litigation of the same claims.

disparagement Untrue statements derogatory to the quality or ownership of a plaintiff's goods or services, that the defendant knows are false, or to the truth of which the defendant is consciously indifferent.

disparate impact The systematic exclusion of women, ethnic groups, or others in a protected class from employment through testing and other selection procedures.

disparate treatment Intentional discrimination against a person by employer by denying the person employment or a benefit or privilege of employment because of race, religion, sex, national origin, age, or disability.

Disposal Rule This regulation applies to individuals and organizations of any size that obtain information from consumer reporting agencies. These recipients are required to take reasonable measures to protect against unauthorized access to or use of sensitive consumer information (such as names, addresses, and Social Security numbers) in connection with its disposal.

dispute negotiation Backward-looking negotiation that addresses past events that have caused disagreement.

disqualified disposition A sale of stock originally acquired pursuant to an incentive stock option that causes the recipient of the option to lose tax-favored treatment.

dissenting shareholder A shareholder who voted against a merger, sale of assets, or other reorganization.

dissolution The designation of the point in time when partners no longer carry on their business together.

distributive justice A theory of justice that looks to how the burden and benefits of a particular situation of a system are distributed.

distributive negotiations Negotiations in which the only issue is the distribution of the fixed pie. Also called *zero-sum negotiations*.

diversity jurisdiction The power of U.S. district courts to decide lawsuits between citizens of two different states when amount in controversy, exclusive of interest and all costs, exceeds $75,000.

doctrine of equivalents The doctrine that holds that a direct infringement of a patent has occurred when a patent is not literally copied, but is replicated to the extent that the infringer has created a product or process that works in substantially the same way and accomplishes substantially the same result as the patented invention.

doctrine of first sale *See* First Sale Doctrine.

doctrine of self-publication A doctrine that provides that a defamatory communication by an employer to an employee may constitute publication if the employer could foresee that the employee would be required to repeat the communication, for instance, to a prospective employer.

documentary letter of credit (L/C) A letter of credit issued by a bank that provides for payment by the bank to the beneficiary upon tender by the beneficiary (or its agent or assignee) of specified documents; frequently used to secure payment for goods and repayment of loans in international transactions.

domain name The unique name that identifies an Internet site. Domain names always have two or more parts, separated by dots. The part on the left is the most specific, and the part on the right is the most general.

donee beneficiary Third party to a contract to whom promisee does not owe an obligation, but rather wishes to confer a gift or a right of performance.

dormant commerce clause An implied constitutional limitation on state action affecting interstate commerce even in the absence of preempting federal legislation.

double jeopardy A law that forbids being tried twice for the same crime.

Double Jeopardy Clause A clause of the Fifth Amendment of the U.S. Constitution that protects criminal defendants from multiple prosecutions for the same offense.

dragnet clause In a security agreement, a provision giving the secured party a security interest in all the debtor's property and in the proceeds from the sale of such property.

drug Defined by the Food, Drug and Cosmetic Act to include (1) articles intended for use in the diagnosis, cure, mitigation, treatment, or prevention of disease; and (2) articles (other than food) intended to affect the structure or any function of the body.

dual distributor A manufacturer that sells its goods both at wholesale and at retail.

dual use The state of goods and technologies that have both military and nonmilitary applications.

due diligence The identification and characterization of risks associated with property and operations involved in various business transactions. A defense available to a defendant (other than the issuer) in a securities violation case concerning a registration statement who (1) conducted a reasonable investigation, and (2) reasonably believed that (a) the statements made were true, and (b) that there were no omissions that made those statements misleading.

Due Process Clauses (Fifth and Fourteenth Amendments) A clause in the Fifth and Fourteenth Amendments of the U.S. Constitution that provides that the government (federal or state) shall not "deprive any person of life, liberty, or property without due process of law." Among other things, it prohibits the government from using involuntary confessions, even if the *Miranda* warnings were given, when the conduct of the law enforcement officials in obtaining a confession is deemed outrageous or shocking, among other things.

dumping Sale of imported products in the United States below the current selling price in the exporter's home market or below the exporter's cost of production.

dumping margin The difference between the U.S. price for foreign goods and the price of those goods in their country of origin.

duress Coercion.

duty (1) The obligation to act as a reasonably prudent person would act under the circumstances to prevent an unreasonable risk of harm to others. (2) The required payment on imports.

duty of care The fiduciary duty of agents, officers, and directors to act with the same care that a reasonably prudent person would exercise under similar circumstances. Sometimes expressed as the duty to use the same level of care a reasonably prudent person would use in the conduct of his or her own affairs.

duty of loyalty The fiduciary duty of agents, officers, and directors to act in good faith and in what they believe to be the best interest of the principal or the corporation.

duty of obedience The fiduciary duty of agents, officers, and directors to obey all reasonable orders of his or her principal.

E

early termination clause An out clause or provision that would allow the lessor or lessee to cancel the lease without completing the full term or paying the complete value of the lease.

earmarking doctrine A bankruptcy doctrine whereby a payment to a preexisting creditor may not be recoverable as a preference if the funds for the repayment were provided by some other creditor and not by the debtor.

economic duress The coercion of the borrower, threatening to do an unlawful act that might injure the borrower's business or property.

economic loss rule A common law doctrine that bars a plaintiff who is in privity of contract with the defendant or who has entered into a commercial transaction involving the defendant from bringing a lawsuit for negligence based solely on economic losses.

economic sanction A sanction imposed by one country (or a group of countries) against the commerce of another country in an effort to influence that country's behavior.

economic strike A union strikes employers when they are unable to extract acceptable terms and conditions of employment through collective bargaining.

economic union A union within which internal trade barriers are abolished, restrictions on mobility of factors of production among members are eliminated, and the economic policies of the member states (monetary, fiscal, taxation, and social welfare programs) are fully integrated in order to blend the member state economics into a single entity.

electronic agents Autonomous computer programs that can be dispatched by the user to execute certain tasks.

embargo A special kind of sanction against all commerce of one country that is declared by a country, or more frequently, a group of countries.

embezzlement The acquisition by an employee of money or property by reason of some office or position, which money or property the employee takes for personal use.

emerging growth companies Defined in the JOBS Act of 2012 as companies with gross annual revenue of less than $1 billion.

eminent domain The power of state and federal governments to take private property for government uses for which property owners are entitled to just compensation.

***en banc* hearing** A hearing at which all the judges of a court of appeals sit together to hear and decide a particularly important or close case.

encumbrance A claim against real property.

enterprise Any individual, partnership, corporation, association, or other legal entity, and any union or group of individuals associated in fact although not a legal entity.

entire fairness A corporate law requirement of fair dealing and fair price applicable to parent-subsidiary mergers and certain other transactions with a controlling shareholder. When evaluating fair dealing, a court will look at the timing of the transaction; how it was initiated, structured, negotiated, and disclosed to the board; and how director and shareholder approval was obtained. When ascertaining whether a price is fair, a court will look at such economic factors as asset value, market value, earnings, and future prospects, and at any other elements that affect the intrinsic value of a company's stock.

environmental assessment (EA) A document that identifies any significant impact of a development on the environment.

environmental impact statement (EIS) A required document for any proposal for legislation or other major governmental action that may significantly affect the quality of the environment.

environmental justice The notion that decisions with environmental consequences (such as where to locate incinerators, dumps, factories, and other sources of pollution) should not discriminate against poor and minority communities.

environmental laws The numerous federal, state, and local laws with the common objective of protecting human health and the environment.

Environmental Protection Agency (EPA) Federal agency that administers all of the federal laws that set national goals and policies for environmental protection, except for the National Environmental Policy Act, which is administered by the Council on Environmental Quality.

equal dignities rule Under this rule if an agent acts on behalf of another (its principal) in signing an agreement of the type that must under the statute of frauds be in writing, the authority of the agent to act on behalf of the principal must also be in writing.

equitable relief An injunction issued by the court to prohibit a defendant from continuing in a certain course of activity or to require a defendant to perform a certain activity.

equitable subordination The doctrine that prevents one creditor, through fraud or other wrongful conduct, from increasing its recovery at the expense of other creditors of the same debtor.

equity The value of real property that exceeds the liens against it.

equity capital The cash or property contributed to an enterprise in exchange for an ownership interest.

equity security An equity security includes (1) any stock or similar security; (2) any security that is convertible, with or without consideration, into such a security; (3) any security carrying any warrant or right to purchase such a security; (4) any such warrant or right; and (5) any other security that the Securities and Exchange Commission (SEC) deems to be of a similar nature and that, for the protection of investors or in the public interest, the SEC considers appropriate to treat as an equity security.

***Erie* doctrine** In a diversity action in federal court, except as to matters governed by the U.S. Constitution and acts of Congress, the law to be applied in any case is the law of the state in which the federal court is situated.

escrow The system by which a neutral stakeholder (escrow agent) allows parties to a real property transaction to fulfill the various conditions of the closing of the transaction without the physical difficulties of passing instruments and funds between the parties.

escrow agent A neutral stakeholder who facilitates the transfer of real property between interested parties.

essential facility Under antitrust law, a resource necessary to a company's rivals' survival that they cannot economically or feasibly duplicate.

Establishment Clause A clause in the First Amendment that prohibits the establishment of a religion by the federal government.

Ethical Business Leader's Decision Tree A guide for managers to use when deciding how to act.

euro The common currency used in those members of the European Union that have agreed to accept it in lieu of their former national currency. For example, France has abandoned use of the French franc in favor of the euro.

events of default The events contained in a loan agreement that will trigger the lender's right to terminate the loan, accelerate the repayment obligations, and, if the loan is secured, take possession of the property securing the loan.

***ex post facto* clause (after the fact)** Clause in the U.S. Constitution prohibiting laws that punish actions that were not illegal when performed.

***ex post facto* laws** Laws that punish actions that were not illegal when performed; prohibited by Article I, Section 9, and Article I, Section 10.

exclusionary rule The evidence obtained in an unlawful search or interrogation cannot be introduced into evidence at trial against a defendant.

exclusive distributorship An agreement in which a manufacturer limits itself to a single dealer or distributor in a given territory.

exclusive listing A listing that grants the real estate broker the right to sell the property; any sale of the property during the term of the listing will entitle the broker to a commission.

executive privilege The type of immunity granted the president against the forced disclosure of presidential communications made in the exercise of executive power.

executory contract Contracts that have not yet been performed and involve an exchange of promises.

exemplary damages Damages awarded to a plaintiff over and above what will fairly compensate it for its loss. They are intended to punish the defendant and deter others from engaging in similar conduct. Also called *punitive damages.*

exempt employee An employee who is exempt from the minimum-wage and overtime requirements of the Federal Labor Standards Act; such an employee is generally paid a salary instead of an hourly wage.

exempt securities Securities listed in Section 3 of the Securities Act of 1933, including any security (1) issued or guaranteed by the United States or any state of the United States, (2) issued or guaranteed by any national bank, (3) issued by a charitable organization, and (4) that is part of an issue offered and sold only to persons residing within a single state or territory, if the issuer is a resident of the same state or territory.

exempt transactions Transactions described in Section 4 of the 1933 Act that include those (1) by any person other than an issuer, underwriter or dealer and (2) by an issuer not involving any public offering.

exercise price The price at which the recipient of an option (the optionee) can exercise the option by purchasing the underlying stock. It is usually the market price of the stock at the time the option was granted. Also called *strike price.*

exhaustion of administrative remedies A court will not entertain an appeal from the administrative process until an agency has had a chance to act and all possible avenues of relief before the agency have been fully pursued.

expectation damages In the case of breach of contract, refers to remuneration that puts a plaintiff into the cash position the plaintiff would have been in if the contract had been fulfilled.

export license The control of exports.

express authority The power of an agent to act for a principal based on that agent's justifiable belief that the principal has authorized him or her to do so; may be given by the principal's actual words or by an action that indicates the principal's consent.

express warranty An explicit guarantee by the seller that the goods purchased by a buyer will have certain qualities.

expropriation The process of nationalization when the host country compensates the company for its lost assets.

extension plan A plan in a Chapter 13 bankruptcy proceeding in which creditors receive the entire indebtedness, but the period for payment is extended beyond the original due date.

extortionate extension of credit Making a loan for which violence is understood by the parties as likely to occur in the event of nonpayment.

extraterritoriality A practice whereby countries assert the right to regulate activities that occur beyond their borders.

F

facilitating payments Under the Foreign Corrupt Payments Act, payments to low-ranking officials who merely expedite the nondiscretionary granting of a permit or license or performance of an administrative act.

failure to warn Failure of a product to carry adequate warnings of the risks involved in the normal use of the product.

fair lending laws Laws that prohibit discrimination in lending practices.

fair trade law A federal law providing for temporary relief to domestic industries seriously injured by increasing imports, regardless of whether unfair practices are involved.

fair use doctrine The doctrine that protects from liability a defendant who has infringed a copyright owner's exclusive rights when countervailing public policies predominate. Activities such as literary criticism, social comment, news reporting, educational activities, scholarship, or research are traditional fair use domains.

false imprisonment The confinement of an individual without that individual's consent and without lawful authority.

family resemblance test A test for determining whether an instrument is a security by asking whether it bears a family resemblance to any nonsecurity.

family responsibility discrimination (FRD) Employment discrimination based on stereotypes of parental roles and responsibilities. Also referred to as *maternal wall discrimination*.

fanciful mark A coined term having no prior meaning until used as a trademark in connection with a particular product.

fast-track negotiating authority Congressional legislation allowing the president to negotiate trade agreements and then submit them for an up or down vote by Congress with no amendments permitted.

Federal Arbitration Act (FAA) The federal law requiring courts to honor agreements to arbitrate and arbitration awards.

federalism System of government created by the U.S. Constitution that gives certain powers to the federal government, while reserving other powers to the states.

federal question When a dispute concerns federal law, namely, a legal right arising under the U.S. Constitution, a federal statute, an administrative regulation issued by a federal government agency, federal common law, or a treaty of the United States, it is said to raise a federal question.

Federal Rules of Civil Procedure (FRCP) The procedural rules that govern civil litigation.

Federal Rules of Evidence (FRE) Federal rules governing the admissibility of evidence in litigation in federal court.

fee simple Title to property that grants owner full right of disposition during his or her lifetime that may be passed on to owner's heirs and assigns forever.

felony An offense punishable by death or prison term exceeding one year.

fetal-protection policy A company policy that bars a woman from certain jobs unless her inability to bear children is medically documented.

fictitious business name The name of a business that is other than that of the owner.

fiduciary duty The obligation of a trustee or other fiduciary to act for the benefit of the other party.

fiduciary out A clause allowing the board of directors to negotiate with other bidders or to terminate a merger agreement.

file-wrapper estoppel The doctrine that prevents a patent owner involved in infringement from introducing any evidence at odds with the information contained in the owner's application on file with the U.S. Patent and Trademark Office.

final-offer arbitration A form of arbitration used most notably in baseball salary disputes; each side submits its "best and final" offer to the arbitrator, who must choose one of the two proposals.

finance charge Interest over the life of a loan, expressed as a dollar amount.

financing lease Under a financing lease (commonly used to finance the acquisition of expensive capital equipment and vehicles such as airplanes, locomotives, and ships), the parties expect the lessee to purchase the leased equipment at the end of the lease term at an agreed-upon residual value.

firm commitment underwriting The underwriters agree to purchase the entire offering, thus effectively shifting the risk of the offering from the issuer to the underwriters.

firm offer Under the Uniform Commercial Code, an offer signed by a merchant that indicates that the offer will be kept open and is not revocable, for lack of consideration, during the time stated, or for a reasonable period of time if none is stated, but in no event longer than three months.

first sale doctrine (copyrights) Codified in Section 109(a) of the Copyright Act, a copyright owner has exhausted its statutory right to control distribution of a copyrighted item once the owner sells the item and thereby puts it in the stream of commerce. As a result, once the copyright owner sells a copyrighted product, it cannot prevent its resale or transfer to others.

first sale doctrine (patents) An authorized sale of patented articles exhausts the patent holder's exclusive rights as to that article, to the extent that the article embodies the invention. The patent holder is then precluded from obtaining any further royalties or imposing any further restrictions on the article or its subsequent sale or transfer.

fixtures The items of personal property that are attached to real property and that cannot be removed without substantial damage to the item.

floating Interest rates that fluctuate throughout the life of the loan according to the interest rate that the lender would pay if it borrowed the funds in order to relend them.

floating lien In a security interest, if the collateral is sold, exchanged, collected, or otherwise disposed of, the security interest is equally effective against cash, account, or whatever else is received from the transaction.

food Defined by the Food, Drug and Cosmetic Act as (1) articles used for food or drink; (2) chewing gum; and (3) articles used for components of either.

forbears A lender does not exercise any of its remedies for the forbearance period.

foreclose To take constructive or actual possession of collateral or real property subject to a mortgage or deed of trust.

foreclosure The legal process by which a mortgagee may put up a piece of property for sale in the public arena to raise cash in order to pay off a debt owed by the mortgagor to the mortgagee.

foreign corporation A corporation doing business in one state though chartered or incorporated in another state is a foreign corporation as to the first state.

forgotten founder A problem that can arise when several persons work together on an informal basis with a common business objective, and then one leaves. The person who left (the forgotten founder) may have ownership rights in the enterprise.

Form S–1 The registration statement used in an initial public offering of securities.

Form S–3 An abbreviated form of registration statement that is available to companies that have filed periodic reports under the Securities Exchange Act of 1934 for at least three years and have a widespread following in the marketplace.

Form S–4 A combined securities registration statement and proxy statement.

forum non conveniens A doctrine whereby a suit is dismissed because an alternate, more convenient forum is available.

forum shopping A party to a lawsuit attempts to have a case tried in a particular court or jurisdiction where the party believes the most favorable judgment or verdict will be received.

forward-looking statement A statement by a publicly traded company (1) containing a projection of revenues, income, earnings per share, capital expenditures, dividends, capital structure, or other financial items; (2) of management's plans and objectives for future operations, including plans relating to the issuer's products and services; (3) of future economic performance, including any such statement in management's discussion and analysis of financial condition or in the results of operations required to be included by the SEC; and (4) of the assumptions underlying or relating to any such statement.

401(k) plan A defined contribution pension plan funded with contributions by the participants or a combination of participant and employer contributions.

franchise A business relationship in which one party (the franchisor) grants to another party (the franchisee) the right to use the franchisor's name and logo and to distribute the franchisor's products from a specified locale.

fraud Any intentional deception that has the purpose of inducing another in reliance upon the deception to part with some property or money. Fraud may involve false representations of fact, whether by words or conduct; false allegations; omission (especially by fiduciary); or concealment of something that should have been disclosed.

fraud in the factum A type of fraud that occurs when a party is persuaded to sign one document thinking that it is another.

fraud in the inducement A type of fraud that occurs when a party makes a false statement to persuade the other party to enter into an agreement.

fraud-on-the-market theory The theory that holds that if the information about a company available to the market is incorrect, then the market price will not reflect the true value of the stock.

fraudulent conveyance The direct or indirect transfer of assets to a third party with actual intent to defraud or have inadequate consideration in circumstances when the transferor is insolvent.

fraudulent misrepresentation Deceit; intentionally misleading by making material misrepresentations of fact that the plaintiff relied on that cause injury to the plaintiff.

Free Exercise Clause A clause in the First Amendment that prohibits certain, but not all, restrictions on the practice of religion.

free writing prospectus Any written offer under Section 2(a)(10) of the 1933 Act and subject to liability under Section 12(a)(2).

freeze out The majority forces the minority shareholders to convert their shares into cash, as long as the transaction is fair.

freeze-out merger In a merger with a controlling shareholder, some shareholders (usually the public shareholders) are required to surrender their shares in the disappearing corporation for cash.

front pay A damage remedy in an employment discrimination case that is generally equal to the compensation the employee would have received had he or she not been unlawfully discharged.

fruit of the poisonous tree Evidence acquired directly or indirectly as a result of an illegal search or arrest is generally inadmissible.

frustration of purpose Frustration of purpose occurs when performance is possible, but changed circumstances have made the contract useless to one or both of the parties.

full-service lease A lease that requires the lessor to maintain the property that a company is occupying, which means, in turn, that the tenant's responsibilities may be limited to seeing that the services provided are adequate.

full warranty The warranty that gives the consumer the right to free repair or replacement of a defective product.

G

gap financing Financing that a developer obtains to pay off a construction loan when it becomes due before the permanent financing is available. Also called *interim financing*.

garnishment The legal procedure by which a creditor may collect a debt by attaching a portion of a debtor's weekly wages.

general partners Partners of a general or limited partnership responsible for managing the partnership. They are jointly and severally liable for partnership obligations.

general partnership A form of business organization between two or more persons in which the partners share in the profits or losses of a common business enterprise.

general plan A long-range planning document that addresses the physical development and redevelopment of a city.

general release An agreement by person engaging in a dangerous activity to assume all risks and hold the party offering access to said dangerous activity free of all liability.

Generalized System of Preferences (GSP) A tariff program developed by industrialized countries to assist developing nations by improving their ability to export.

genericism The use of a trademark as a generic name for the product, for example, "a Kleenex" for "tissue."

Gharar A tenet of Islamic trade and commerce that refers to an event where the outcomes are unknown.

going effective A term used to describe the process whereby the SEC permits a registered offer or sale to proceed.

going private Also known as "going dark," small public companies "go private" when they have fewer than 300 shareholders and are no longer required to file public periodic reports under the Securities Exchange Act of 1934.

golden parachutes Executive compensation and severance agreements typically provided when there is a change of control of a company, such as a merger or sale of assets.

good faith exception An exception to the exclusionary rule that provides that evidence obtained by police in good faith will not be excluded from trial, even if it was obtained in violation of the Fourth Amendment.

good faith subsequent purchaser A person who acquires real property for fair value without being aware of a disputed claim to the property.

good offices A process mainly used in the area of public international law, by which a third party (often a disinterested government) brings the parties together through establishing communication and providing a site where the parties can meet, often in secrecy.

goods As defined in Article 2 of the Uniform Commercial Code, all things (including specially manufactured goods) that are movable at the time of identification to the contract for sale.

government-contractor defense The limited immunity available for manufacturers that produce products to the specifications of government contracts.

grant deed A deed that contains implied warranties that the grantor has not previously conveyed the same property or any interest in it to another person and that the title is marketable.

grantee A person to whom real property is conveyed.

grantor A person conveying real property.

gray market A market where products are sold outside the normal channel of distribution, often at a discounted price.

greenmail Payment by a target company to buy back shares owned by a potential acquiror at a premium over market. The acquiror in exchange agrees not to pursue its hostile takeover bid.

gross-up clause The clause in foreign investment contracts by which local partner or licensee is obligated to pay all taxes other than those specifically allocated to the foreign partner.

ground lease A lease for land on which a building will be built.

group boycott An agreement among competitors to refuse to deal with another competitor.

guarantor The person who agrees to be liable for the obligation of another person.

guaranty An undertaking by one person to become liable for the obligation of another person.

guaranty of collection Under a guaranty of collection, the guarantor becomes obliged to pay only after the lender has attempted unsuccessfully to collect the amount due from the primary debtor.

guaranty of payment A provision that holds guarantor's obligation to pay the lender is triggered, immediately and automatically, if the primary debtor fails to make a payment when due.

guaranty of performance A guaranty that specified nonpayment obligations will be performed.

gun-jumping A violation of the securities laws that occurs when an issuer or underwriter conditions the market with a news article, press release, or speech about a company engaged in the registration of its securities.

H

H-1B visa A work authorization issued by the U.S. Citizenship and Immigration Services that is available only for foreign workers in professional and specialty occupations (generally those involving a bachelor's degree or its equivalent), such as computer programmers, engineers, doctors, or fashion models, where the employer can show an inability to recruit qualified workers in the United States.

Harmonized Tariff Schedule of the United States (HTS) A U.S. government document that lists the tariffs on goods imposed by Congress and by the president pursuant to the Trade Agreements Program, based on the country of origin.

Hazardous Substance Superfund Finances federal activity to investigate and take remedial action in response to a release or threatened release of hazardous substances to the environment.

hearing The phase of arbitration that is similar to a trial.

Herfindahl-Hirschman Index (HHI) An aid to the interpretation of market data when determining the anticompetitive effect of a merger; the HHI of market concentration is calculated by summing the squares of the individual market shares of all the firms in the market.

holder claims Lawsuits pursuant to certain state blue sky laws by investors who allege that they did not sell their securities because of the defendants' fraud. Not available in federal court.

horizontal agreement A conspiracy agreement between firms that compete with each other on the same level of production or distribution.

horizontal market division An agreement among competitors to divide a market according to class of customer or geographic territory; it violates antitrust law.

horizontal merger A corporate combination of actual or prospective competitors.

horizontal price-fixing An agreement between competitors at the same level of distribution to set a common price for a product; it violates antitrust law.

hostile environment harassment The creation of a hostile working environment, such as continually subjecting an employee to ridicule and racial slurs, or unwanted sexual advances.

hot issues Shares of high-demand initial public offerings.

I

I-9 The Employment Eligibility and Verification Form that the U.S. government requires all employers to complete and keep on file to identify the identity and employment eligibility of all persons they hire.

identification to the contract Setting aside or otherwise designating the particular goods for sale under a contract.

identity theft Taking an individual's information (such as Social Security number and mother's maiden name) and using that information to fraudulently obtain credit or commit other financial crimes.

illegal contract A contract is illegal if its formation or performance is expressly forbidden by a civil or criminal statute, or if a penalty is imposed for doing the act agreed upon.

illegal *per se* A practice that is illegal regardless of its impact on the market or its procompetitive justifications.

illusory promise A promise that either does not in fact confer any benefit on the promisee or subject the promisor to any detriment.

impaired A characteristic of a claim when the plan does not provide for full cash payment on its effective date and if it alters the creditors' legal, equitable, or contractual rights in any way.

implied authority The power of an agent to do whatever is reasonable to complete the task he or she has been instructed to undertake.

implied contract An employment agreement—implied from such facts as long-term employment; receipt of raises, bonuses and promotions; and assurance from management that the employee was doing a good job—that the employee would not be terminated except for good cause.

implied covenant of good faith and fair dealing An implied covenant in every contract that imposes on each party a duty not to do anything that will deprive the other party of the benefits of the agreement.

implied ratification Implied ratification occurs when the principal, by his or her silence or failure to repudiate the agent's act, acquiesces in it.

implied warranties Representations about the quality or suitability of a product that are implied, not explicitly stated. *See also* Implied Warranty of Fitness for a Particular Purpose and Implied Warranty of Merchantability.

implied warranty of fitness for a particular purpose The warranty whereby goods involving the following elements are judged satisfactory for the buyer's purpose: (1) the buyer must have a particular purpose for the goods; (2) the seller must have known or have had reason to know of that purpose; (3) the seller must have known or had reason to know that the buyer was relying on the seller's expertise; and (4) the buyer must have relied upon the seller.

implied warranty of habitability A warranty made by a commercial seller of houses in which the seller warrants that the house is in reasonable working order and is of reasonably sound construction.

implied warranty of merchantability The warranty by which all goods sold by merchants in the normal course of business must meet following criteria: (l) pass without objection in the trade under the contract description; (2) be fit for the ordinary purposes for which such goods are used; (3) be within the variations permitted by the agreement, of even kind, quality and quantity within each unit and among all units involved; (4) be adequately contained, packaged, and labeled as the agreement may require; and (5) conform to the promises or affirmations of fact made on the container or label, if any.

import relief laws A series of laws through which Congress has authorized the president to raise U.S. tariffs on specified products and to provide other forms of import protection to U.S. industries.

impossibility An excuse for nonperformance based on the destruction of something vital to the performance of the contract or another unforeseen event that makes performance of the contract impossible.

impossibility defense A defense to strict liability in which a corporate officer might not be held strictly (and vicariously) liable if he or she did everything possible to ensure legal compliance to applicable standards, even though the company was still unable to comply.

impracticability A situation in which performance of a contract is possible but commercially impractical.

improper means Deceitful actions through which party obtains trade secrets of another.

imputed liability The imposition of civil or criminal liability on one party for the wrongful acts of another. Also called *vicarious liability*.

in loco parentis (in place of the parent) Refers to actions of a custodian, guardian, or other person acting in the parent's place.

***in personam* jurisdiction** Personal jurisdiction based upon the residence or activities of the person being sued. It is the power that a court has over the defendant itself, in contrast to the court's power over the defendant's interest in property (*quasi in rem* jurisdiction) or power over the property itself (*in rem* jurisdiction).

***in rem* jurisdiction** Jurisdiction over property based upon the location of the property at issue in the lawsuit.

incentive stock option (ISO) A stock option that qualifies for favorable tax treatment Internal Revenue Code Section 422, granted to an employee of a corporation to buy stock at a specified price (at least 100% of fair market value on the date of grant) for a specified period of time (no more than ten years).

incidental damages In an action for breach of contract, the lesser and relatively minor damages that a nonbreaching party incurs in mitigating damages resulting from the breach, such as the charges, expenses, and commissions incurred in stopping delivery; the cost of the transportation, care, and custody of goods after a breach; and the expenses incurred in connection with the return or subsequent disposition of goods that are the subject of the contract.

incorporation The process by which a corporation is formed.

indemnification The doctrine that allows a defendant to recover its individual loss from a co-defendant whose relative blame is greater or who has contractually agreed to assume liability.

indemnity A right to reimbursement for loss.

independent contractor A person is deemed to be an independent contractor only if the employer neither exercises control over the means of performing the work nor the end result of that work.

indictment Formal charges filed by a grand jury.

indirect patent infringement One party's active inducement of another party to infringe a patent.

indirect representation Rules that apply when an intermediary acts on instructions and on behalf of, but not in the name of, a principal, or when the third party does not know or have reason to know that the intermediary is acting as an agent.

inducement to infringe A party's active encouragement of another party to infringe a patent or copyright. Applies to those who supply a product or service that has substantial non-infringing uses if the supplier also encourages that product or service to be used in an infringing fashion.

industrial ecology A concept that advocates a systems approach to ecoefficiency and applies it to groups of corporations working together.

inevitable disclosure doctrine A doctrine that permits a former employer to prevent an employee from working for a competitor when the new position will require the employee to disclose or use the trade secrets of the former employer.

inevitable discovery exception An exception to the exclusionary rule that provides that illegally obtained evidence can lawfully be introduced at trial if it can be shown that the evidence would inevitably have been found by other legal means.

infomercial An advertisement generally presented in the format of half-hour television talk shows or news programs.

informal discretionary action The administrative agencies' decision-making process for repetitive actions that are inappropriate to litigate in courts.

information The formal charges filed with the court in a criminal case.

injunction A remedy granted by the court that requires defendant to perform or cease from performing some activity.

injurious falsehood False statements knowingly made that lead to economic loss for a plaintiff.

in loco parentis (*in place of the parents*) Obligations to ensure the safety of children and to serve as role models.

innocent landowner defense In a case under the Comprehensive Environmental Responsibility, Contribution, and Liability Act, a potentially responsible current owner can assert this defense if the release or disposal of hazardous materials was by a third party who was not an employee and with whom the current owner had no contractual relationship. Also called the *third-party defense*.

innovation offsets Technological advantages gained by companies that met the challenge of environmental regulations and discovered lower costs and better quality products as a result.

inquiry Done by a commission of inquiry that is established ad hoc, often after a violation of international law, it consists of two contending governments reviewing the finding of the commission with the goal to come to an acceptable solution for the dispute at hand.

inside director A member of a board who is also an officer.

insider A person with access to confidential information and an obligation of disclosure to other traders in the marketplace.

insider trading Trading securities based on material nonpublic information, in violation of a duty to the corporation or its shareholders or others.

integrate When an issuer makes successive sales of securities within a limited period of time, the Securities and Exchange Commission may integrate the successive sales; that is, it may deem them to be part of a single sale for purposes of deciding whether there was an exemption from registration.

intellectual property Any product or result of a mental process that is given legal protection against unauthorized use.

intent The actual, subjective desire to cause the consequences of an act, or the belief that the consequences are substantially certain to result from it.

intent to be bound An oral or written statement or an action signaling that a party intended to enter into a contract.

intention to do wrong Subjective intent or desire to do wrong or intent to take action substantially certain to cause a wrong to occur.

intentional infliction of emotional distress Outrageous conduct by the individual inflicting the distress; intention to cause, or reckless disregard of the probability of causing, emotional distress; severe emotional suffering; and actual and proximate (or legal) causation of the emotional distress.

interbrand competition The price competition between a company and its competitors that sell a different brand of the same product.

interference with contractual relations A defendant intentionally induces another to breach a contract with a plaintiff.

interference with prospective business advantage Intentional interference by the defendant with a business relationship the plaintiff seeks to develop, which interference causes loss to the plaintiff.

interim financing Financing that a developer obtains to pay off a construction loan when it becomes due before the permanent financing is available. Also called *gap financing*.

interrogatory Written question to a party to a lawsuit and its attorney.

intrabrand competition The price competition among the different dealers selling products produced by the same company.

intrusion Objectionable prying, such as eavesdropping or unauthorized rifling through files. It includes the act of wrongfully entering upon or taking possession of property of another.

invasion of privacy Prying or intrusion that would be objectionable or offensive to a reasonable person, including eavesdropping, rifling through files one has no authorization to see, public disclosure of private facts, or unauthorized use of an individual's picture in an advertisement or article with which that person has no connection.

inverse condemnation The taking of private real property for a public use; requires payment of just compensation.

investigative consumer reporting Report that contains information on character and reputation, not just credit history.

investment contract A type of security created by an investment of money in a common enterprise with profits to come solely from the efforts of others.

investors Persons putting up cash or property in exchange for an equity interest in an enterprise.

invitee A business visitor who enters premises for the purposes of the possessor's business.

involuntary proceeding An involuntary proceeding in bankruptcy that is initiated when one or more of the debtor's creditors files a bankruptcy petition with the bankruptcy court.

ipso facto **clause** A clause in a contract that expressly permits termination of the contract in the event of a bankruptcy filing by one or both parties to the contract.

irrevocable letter of credit A letter of credit that cannot be amended or canceled without the consent of the beneficiary and the issuing bank.

irrevocable offer An offer that cannot be revoked. Arises (1) when an option contract has been entered into or (2) when an offeree has relied on an offer to its detriment.

issuer A company that offers or sells any security.

J

JOBS Act Jumpstart Our Business Startups Act of 2012 makes funding more accessible for startups, small businesses, and entrepreneurs.

joint and several liability In a case in which the court determines that multiple defendants are at fault; the doctrine whereby a plaintiff may collect the entire judgment from any single defendant, regardless of the degree of that defendant's fault.

joint tenancy A specialized form of co-ownership involving real property owned in equal shares by two or more persons who have a right of survivorship if one joint tenant dies.

joint venture A one-time group of two or more persons in a single specific business enterprise or transaction.

judgment n.o.v. (*j.n.o.v.* **)** The attorney can make a motion to reverse the jury verdict on the grounds that the evidence of the prevailing party was so weak that no reasonable jury could have resolved the dispute in that party's favor.

judgment notwithstanding the verdict (judgment n.o.v.) Reverses the jury verdict on the grounds that the evidence of the prevailing party was so weak that no reasonable jury could have resolved the dispute in that party's favor. Also called *judgment n.o.v. (non obstante veredicto, notwithstanding the verdict)*.

judicial review The power of federal courts to review acts of the legislative and executive branches of government to determine whether they violate the Constitution.

junior debt Indebtedness that is subordinated under a debt subordination agreement.

K

Kantian theory An ethical theory that looks to the form of an action, rather than the intended result, in examining the ethical worth.

know-how Detailed information on how to make or do something.

knowingly Knowledge by a defendant of the facts that constitute an offense. Defendant is generally deemed to knowingly violate a statute even if he or she was not aware that the conduct at issue was unlawful, unless the text of the statute dictates a different result. Contrast with *willful*.

L

larceny Theft. The taking of property without the owner's consent.

legal astuteness The ability of a manager to communicate effectively with counsel and to work together to solve complex problems.

legal duty The requirement to act reasonably under the circumstances to avoid harming another person.

lemon laws Laws designed to protect consumers from defective products that cannot be adequately fixed, such as new cars and new mobile homes.

lessee A tenant or one to whom an interest in real property is conveyed.

lessor A landlord or one who conveys an interest in real property.

letter of credit (L/C) A payment mechanism for international sales transactions involving a bank in the buyer's jurisdiction that commits to pay the seller. Also called a *documentary credit*.

letter of intent An instrument entered into by the parties to a real estate or other transaction for the purpose of setting forth the general terms and conditions of a purchase and sale agreement until a formal legal commitment can be made through the execution of a formal acquisition agreement.

leveraged buyout (LBO) A takeover financed with loans secured by the acquired company's assets, in which groups of investors, often including management, use borrowed money along with some of their own money to buy back the company's stock from its current shareholders.

libel A written communication to a third party by a defendant of an untrue statement of fact that injures a plaintiff's reputation.

licensee Anyone who is privileged to enter upon land of another because the possessor has given expressed or implied consent.

lien A claim on a property that secures a debt owed by the owner of the property.

lien subordination An agreement between two secured creditors whose respective security interest, liens, or mortgages attach to the same property. The subordinating party agrees that the lien of the other creditor shall have priority notwithstanding the relative priorities that the parties' liens would otherwise have under applicable law.

limited fund class action A class action in which the total of the aggregated liquidated claims exceeds the fund available to satisfy them.

limited guaranty A guaranty in which the maximum amount of the guarantor's liability is expressly stated in the guaranty instrument.

limited liability company (LLC) A form of business entity authorized by state law that is taxed like a limited partnership and provides its members with limited liability, but like a corporation gives its members the right to participate in management without incurring unlimited liability.

limited liability partnership (LLP) A form of limited partnership designed primarily for professionals who typically do business as a partnership that insulates its partners from vicarious liability for certain partnership obligations.

limited partners The participants in a limited partnership whose liability for partnership business is limited to their capital contribution.

limited partnership A form of business organization in which limited partners must refrain from actively participating in the management of the partnership but are liable for the debts of the partnership only up to the amount they personally contributed to the partnership.

limited warranty The warranty that limits the remedies available to the consumer for a defective product.

line-item veto Allowed the president to sign a bill into law and then cancel any dollar amounts that he or she believed to be fiscally irresponsible. Declared unconstitutional by the U.S. Supreme Court.

line-of-business test If an officer, director, or controlling shareholder learns of an opportunity in the course of business for the corporation, and if the opportunity is in the corporation's line of business, a court will not permit that person to keep the opportunity for personal gain.

liquidated damages The amount of money stipulated in a contract to be paid to non-breaching party should one of the parties breach the agreement.

living wage ordinances Local ordinances that require employers to pay wages approximating the real cost of living in the locality, which is often significantly higher than the applicable federal or state minimum wage.

London Interbank Offered Rate (LIBOR) An interest rate based on the cost of borrowing offshore U.S. dollars in the global interbank market, centered in several locations in addition to London.

long-arm statute A state statute that subjects an out-of-state defendant to jurisdiction when the defendant is doing business or commits a civil wrong in the state.

loss causation The misstatement or omission concealed something from the market that, when disclosed, negatively affected the value of the security.

M

mail fraud A scheme intended to defraud or to obtain money or property by fraudulent means through use of the mails.

major life activity Under the Americans with Disabilities Act, an activity that an average person can perform with little or no difficulty, such as walking, seeing, hearing, and speaking.

majority voting A requirement that a nominee for the board of directors of a corporation must receive a majority of the shares voted to be elected. Contrast with *plurality voting*.

malicious defense A tort committed when a defendant creates false material evidence and gives false testimony advancing the evidence.

malicious prosecution A plaintiff can successfully sue for the tort of malicious prosecution if he or she shows that a prior proceeding was instituted against him or her maliciously and without probable cause or factual basis.

malpractice A claim of professional negligence.

managers Persons elected by the members (owners) of a limited liability company who, like a board of directors in a corporation, are responsible for managing the business, property, and affairs of the company.

mandatory arbitration One party will not do business with the other unless it agrees to arbitrate any future claims.

mandatory bid provision Prohibits coercive two-tier hostile tender offers and market purchases by requiring any person who acquires 30 percent or more of a target company's stock to offer to buy all remaining shares at the highest price paid to acquire the 30 percent block.

manufacturing defect A flaw in a product that occurs during production, such as a failure to meet the design specifications.

market power The power to control market prices or exclude competition in the relevant market. Also called *monopoly power*.

market-share liability The liability for damages caused by a manufacturer's products assessed based on a manufacturer's national market share.

marketable title Title to property that is fee simple and is free of liens or encumbrances.

material fact A fact that a reasonable investor would most likely have considered important in deciding whether to buy or sell his or her stock.

maturity date The date a term loan becomes due and payable.

med-arb A form of dispute resolution whereby the parties to a dispute enter mediation with the commitment to submit the dispute to binding arbitration if mediation fails to resolve the conflict.

mediation A form of dispute resolution whereby the parties agree to try to reach a solution themselves with the assistance of a neutral third party who helps them find a mutually satisfactory solution.

medical device Defined by the Food and Drug Administration as an instrument, apparatus, implement, machine, contrivance, implant, in vitro reagent, or other similar or related article, including a component part, or accessory that is recognized in the official National Formulary, or the United States Pharmacopoeia, or any supplement to them; intended for use in the diagnosis of disease or other conditions, or in the cure, mitigation, treatment, or prevention of disease, in man or other animals; or intended to affect the structure or any function of the body of man or other animals, and that does not achieve any of its primary intended purposes through chemical action within or on the body of man or other animals and that is not dependent upon being metabolized for the achievement of any of its primary intended purposes.

mediator The third party who helps the parties in mediation find a mutually satisfactory solution.

members The owners of a limited liability company.

mens rea **(guilty state of mind)** Criminal intent.

merchant As defined in Article 2 of the Uniform Commercial Code, a person who deals in goods of the kind or otherwise by its occupation holds itself out as having knowledge or skill peculiar to the practices or goods involved in the transaction.

mere continuation (identity) A doctrine of successor liability whereby a firm that acquires the assets of a target firm is liable for the debts of the target firm when, after the asset purchase, there is a single corporation with the same shareholders and directors as the target firm prior to the asset purchase.

merger The combination of two or more corporations into one.

merger agreement An agreement between two companies to combine those companies into one.

merit review A review by a state securities commissioner to determine whether the issuer's plan of business and the proposed issuance of securities are fair, just, and equitable.

minitrial A cross between arbitration and negotiation, truncated presentation of evidence conducted by lawyers, usually with business persons present.

Miranda **warnings** Once a person is placed in custody, he or she cannot be questioned by the police unless first advised of his or her constitutional rights to remain silent and to have counsel present.

mirror image rule A common law contract rule that requires acceptance to contain the exact same terms as the offer.

misappropriation theory A basis for an insider trading claim under SEC Rule 10b-5 when a person breaches a fiduciary duty to the source of the nonpublic information by trading on that information after misappropriating it for his or her own use.

misbranding False or misleading labeling prohibited by federal and state statutes. Includes claiming unsubstantiated medicinal benefits for a food, inadequate labeling for a drug, or selling over-the-counter a drug for which a prescription is required.

misdemeanor An offense lower than a felony, punishable by fine or imprisonment for less than one year (not in a penitentiary).

misrepresentation A misleading or false representation of the facts intended to deceive another party.

misstatement (Rule 10b–5) A misrepresentation of a fact; a lie.

mistake of fact A mistake about an underlying fact that may make a contract voidable.

mistake of judgment A mistake of judgment occurs when the parties make an erroneous assessment about the value of what is bargained for.

mitigate Lessen.

Model Panel Code A set of criminal law statutes that were proposed by the National Conference of Commissioners on Uniform State Laws for adoption by the states.

money laundering The transfer of funds derived from unlawful activities with the intent of concealing or disguising the location, source, ownership, or control of said funds.

monopoly power The power to control market prices or exclude competition in the relevant market. Also called *market power*.

mortgage A loan to buy real property secured by a lien on the real property. Also called *deed of trust*.

mortgagee The recipient of a mortgage, usually the lender.

mortgagor The party granting a mortgage, usually the owner of the real property securing a loan.

most favored nation (MFN) The principle that holds that each member country of the World Trade Organization (WTO) must accord to all other WTO members tariff treatment no less favorable than it provides to any other country.

motion Formally requests the court to take some action.

motion for judgment on the pleadings A motion filed immediately after the complaint and answer have been filed. One party, usually the defendant, argues that the pleadings alone demonstrate that the action is futile.

motion for summary judgment A motion requesting the trial judge to decide a case as a matter of law, without a trial, when there are no material facts in dispute.

motion to dismiss The formal request that the court terminate lawsuit on the ground that plaintiff's claim is technically inadequate.

multiple-brand product market A market made up of product or service offerings by different manufacturers or sellers that are economically interchangeable and may therefore be said to compete.

mutual rescission An agreement by both parties to a contract to terminate the contract. A mutual rescission is itself a type of contract.

mutuality of obligation Both parties in a bilateral contract are obligated to perform their side of the bargain.

N

national ambient air quality standards (NAAQS) The permissible levels of pollutants in the ambient or outdoor air that, with adequate margins of safety, are required to protect public health; set forth in the Clean Air Act.

national effluent limitations EPA regulations that impose increasingly stringent restrictions on pollutant discharges, based on the availability of economically achievable treatment and recycling technologies.

National Pollutant Discharge Elimination System (NPDES) The principal regulatory program established by the Clean Water Act; requires permits for the discharge of pollutants from any point source to navigable waters.

national treatment The World Trade Organization principle that holds that WTO members must not discriminate against imported products in favor of domestically produced products.

nationalization When a host country decides to assert ownership over some or all of a company's assets.

natural monopolies An absence of market competition that results from structural or other impediments to economically efficient competition among firms.

natural resource law The laws that govern wilderness protection, wildlife protection, coastal zone management, energy conservation, and national park designation.

navigable waters The waters of the United States and the territorial seas, as well as lakes and streams that are capable of being used for purposes of navigation.

negative amortization loans Under which the debtor pays only the interest every month but owes a huge balloon payment at the end of the term.

negative Commerce Clause *See* Dormant Commerce Clause.

negative convenant The borrower's promise of what it undertakes not to do under the loan agreement.

negative equity An outstanding mortgage balance in excess of the value of the house or other property securing the loan.

negligence A breach of the requirement that a person act with the care a reasonable person would use in the same circumstances.

negligence *per se* Violation of a statute that shifts the burden to the defendant to prove the defendant was not negligent once the plaintiff shows that the defendant violated a statute and the violation caused an injury.

negligent-hiring theory An employer is negligent if the employer hires an employee who endangers the health and safety of other employees.

negligent infliction of emotional distress A tort committed when the defendant negligently inflicts emotional distress that causes the plaintiff some form of physical injury.

negotiation The give and take people engage in when coming to terms with each other.

net listing A real estate listing in which the broker receives any sales proceeds in excess of the net listing amount specified by the seller.

net neutrality policy A policy adopted by the FCC in 2011 that prohibits wired broadband providers from blocking lawful content, applications, services, and non-harmful devices. Under this policy wireless providers are also barred from blocking lawful websites or applications that compete with voice or video services. The policy further forbids wired broadband providers from discriminating in the transmission of lawful network traffic.

neutrality rule Requires the target's board of directors to remain neutral when faced with a hostile takeover bid and stipulates that once a takeover bid has been launched, the target's board cannot adopt any antitakeover devices, such as poison pills, without first obtaining the specific approval of shareholders. Applicable in certain member states of the European Union.

nexus The legally required relationship between a condition to a land-use approval and the impacts of the development being approved.

1933 Act (Securities Act of 1933) Principal federal act that regulates offerings and sales of securities by generally requiring the registration of securities with the SEC and the delivery of a prospectus.

1934 Act (Securities Exchange Act of 1934) Principal federal act that prohibits securities fraud and requires companies of a certain size and with a certain number of shareholders or whose stock is traded on a national securities exchange to file periodic reports with the SEC.

nolo contendere (I will not contest it) A plea that means the accused does not contest the charges.

non-core proceedings (bankruptcy) Proceedings deemed not core to a bankruptcy case (e.g., decision on personal-injury torts and wrongful death proceedings). Bankruptcy courts submit proposed conclusions of law and findings of fact to a federal district court, which reviews them and issues the final judgment.

nominative use A fair-use defense to a trademark infringement action that permits use of a trademark when necessary for purposes of identifying another producer's product, not the user's own product.

non obstante veredicto Latin for "notwithstanding the verdict."

nonbinding arbitration Arbitration in which the parties are not bound by the arbitrator's decision.

nonconforming use An existing land use that was lawful but that does not comply with a later-enacted zoning ordinance.

nonexempt employee An employee that is n ot exempt from the minimum wage and overtime requirements of the Federal Labor Standards Act; such an employee is often paid an hourly wage.

noninfringement In a patent dispute, the defense of noninfringement asserts that the allegedly infringing matter does not fall within the claims of the issued patent.

nontariff barriers (NTBs) Barriers to trade other than tariffs that have in some cases replaced tariffs as a means of protecting domestic industries threatened by import competition.

no-shop agreement An agreement whereby the target agrees not to actively solicit other bidders but retains the right to negotiate with parties who submit unsolicited bids to the target.

no-talk clause A clause permitting a corporation to engage in discussions with and provide information to other bidders only if the board has concluded, based on the written opinion of outside legal counsel, that engaging in discussions or providing information was required to prevent the board from breaching its fiduciary duties to its stockholders.

not an underwriter Under Rule 144, an affiliate or a person selling restricted securities is not an underwriter if certain conditions (e.g., holding period, volume limitations, manner of sale, filing of Form 144, and available public information) are met.

novation The method of contract modification by which the original contract is canceled and a new one is written with perhaps only one change, such as substitution of a new party.

novel (patents) An invention is novel if it was not anticipated; i.e., if it was not previously known or used by others in the United States and was not previously patented or described in a printed publication in any country.

nuisance A thing or activity that unreasonably and substantially interferes with an owner's use and enjoyment of owner's property.

O

obvious risk If the use of a product carries an obvious risk, the manufacturer will not be held liable for injuries that result from ignoring the risk.

offer (contracts) A proposal to enter into a contract. Proposal may be verbal, written, or implied by action.

offer (securities) Every attempt or offer to dispose of, or solicitation of an offer to buy, a security or interest in a security, for value.

offeree A person to whom an offer is made.

offering circular Also known as a private placement memorandum, this circular is the private offering counterpart to the prospectus and is both a selling document and a disclosure document.

offeror A person making an offer.

offshore transaction A security transaction in which no offer is made to a person in the United States and either (1) at the time the buy order is originated, the buyer is outside the United States; or (2) the transaction is one executed in, on, or through the facilities of a designated offshore securities market.

ombudsperson A person who hears complaints, engages in fact finding, and generally promotes dispute resolution through information methods such as counseling or mediation.

omission (Rule 10b–5) A company or its managers fail to tell the whole truth about a material fact, causing reasonable investors to take away an impression contrary to the true facts.

one-form-of-action laws *See* Antideficiency Laws.

open-end credit Credit in which the creditor makes repeated extensions of credit (for example, Visa or MasterCard).

open listing A real estate listing in which the broker receives a commission only if he or she procures a ready, willing, and able buyer.

operating agreement A contract that sets forth the rights, obligations, and powers of the owners, managers, and officers of a limited liability company.

operating lease Typically a short-term lease that does not appear on the balance sheet.

oppression An inequality of bargaining power that results in no real negotiation and an absence of meaningful choice for one party to the contract.

option contract A contract in which the offeror promises to hold an offer open for a certain amount of time.

order for relief The filing of a bankruptcy petition constitutes an order for relief. If the debtor challenges an involuntary petition for bankruptcy, a trial is held to determine whether an order for relief should be granted.

original jurisdiction The power of the U.S. Supreme Court to take cognizance of a case at its inception, try it, and pass judgment upon the law and facts. Distinguished from appellate jurisdiction.

out clause A provision that would allow the lessor or lessee to cancel the lease without completing the full term or paying the complete value of the lease.

output contract A contract under which a buyer promises to buy all the products that the seller produces.

outside director A member of a board who is not also an officer.

outside sales employee An employee that has the primary duty of either making sales or obtaining orders or contracts for services or for the use of facilities and who is customarily and regularly engaged away from the employer's place of business in performing such duty.

override (of a president's veto) The ability of Congress to annul a president's veto by a two-thirds vote of both the House of Representatives and the Senate.

P

parens patriae **(parent of the country) action** Antitrust suits brought by state attorneys general for injuries sustained by residents of their respective states.

parol evidence rule If there is a written contract that the parties intended would encompass their entire agreement, oral evidence of prior or contemporaneous statements will not be permitted to vary or alter the terms of the contract.

partial summary judgment A summary judgment granted on some issues of a case while other issues proceed to trial.

participation in a breach of fiduciary duty A tort committed when the defendant induces another party to breach its fiduciary duty to the plaintiff.

participation loan A loan in which the original lender sells shares to other parties, called participants.

pass-through entity A business organization that is not a separate taxpayer; all its income and losses are passed through and taxed to its owner. S Corporations, partnerships, and limited liability companies are pass-through entities.

patent A government-granted right to exclude others for a stated period of time (usually 20 years) from making, using, or selling within the government's jurisdiction an invention that is the subject of the patent.

patent misuse In a patent dispute, a defense asserting that although the defendant has infringed a valid patent, the patent holder has abused its patent rights and therefore has lost, at least temporarily, its right to enforce them.

pattern An involvement in racketeering activity demonstrated by at least two predicate acts occurring within a ten-year period.

penumbra The peripheral rights that are implied by the specifically enumerated rights in the Bill of Rights.

pension plan An employee retirement benefit plan established, and usually funded at least in part, by an employer.

per se **analysis** A form of antitrust analysis that condemns practices that are completely void of redeeming competitive rationales.

percentage rent clause A clause frequently contained in retail leases that requires the tenant to pay, in addition to a base monthly rent, a percentage of its gross sales to the landlord.

perfect tender rule A Uniform Commercial Code rule that gives the buyer an absolute right to reject any goods not meeting all the contract requirements, including time of delivery.

perfecting (under the UCC) In connection with security interests, perfection refers to making the security interest valid as against other creditors of the debtor.

perjury An act by a person who takes an oath to tell the truth yet willingly and contrary to such oath states a material matter that he or she does not believe to be true.

permanent loan Usually a long-term loan used to acquire property that is repaid over five, ten, or sometimes up to twenty years.

personal jurisdiction The power of state court to hear (decide) a civil case based upon residence or location of activities of the person being sued.

petitioner The person who is appealing a judgment or seeking a writ of certiorari. Also called *appellant*.

pierce the corporate veil When a court denies limited liability to a corporation and holds shareholders personally responsible for claims against the corporation, the court has pierced the corporate veil.

plaintiff A person who brings an action; the party who complains or sues in a civil action and is so named on the record. The prosecution in a criminal case (i.e., the state or the United States in a federal case).

planned unit development (PUD) The land use regulations for a given piece of property that reflect the proposed development plans for that property. PUD allows for mixture of uses for property not possible under traditional zoning regulations.

plant patent A patent issued for new strains of asexually reproducing plants.

plea The response by a defendant in criminal case of guilty, not guilty, or *nolo contendere*.

plea bargaining The process by which the prosecutor agrees to reduce the charges in exchange for a guilty plea from the accused.

pleadings The formal allegations by the parties to a lawsuit of their respective claims and defenses.

pledge A type of security interest whereby the creditor or secured party takes possession of the collateral owned by the debtor.

plenary Complete, sufficient, unqualified.

plurality standard A process whereby a nominee for the board of directors can be elected as long as he or she receives a plurality of the votes cast for any nominee, without regard to the number of votes withheld. Contrast with *majority voting*.

plus factors (antitrust) Parallel behavior that would appear to be contrary to the economic interests of the defendants, were they acting independently; supports an inference of conspiracy.

points A one-time charge to a borrower buying real property (in addition to interest) computed by a lender by multiplying the amount funded by a fixed percentage.

poison pill A plan that would make any takeover of a corporation prohibitively expensive. Also called *shareholder rights plan*.

police power The general power granted state and city governments to protect the health, safety, welfare, or morals of its residents.

political union A union that represents the complete political and economic integration of the member states.

posthearing The final phase of arbitration in which the arbitrator renders his or her award after considering all the evidence presented in the prehearing and the hearing.

potentially responsible parties (PRPs) Parties potentially responsible for damages that include the present owner or operator of a facility, the owner or operator at the time of disposal of a hazardous substance, any person who arranged for treatment or disposal of hazardous substances at a facility, and any person who transported hazardous substances to or selected the facility.

power of attorney A written instrument that authorizes a person, called an attorney-in-fact (who need not be a lawyer), to sign documents or perform certain specific acts on behalf of another person.

prayer The request for relief in a complaint.

precautionary principle Provides guidance for protecting public health and the environment in the face of uncertain risks and stipulates that the absence of full scientific certainty shall not be used as a reason to postpone measures where there is a risk of serious or irreversible harm to public health or the environment.

precedents General rules that are to be used as guidelines for similar cases in the future.

precontractual liability The claims by the disappointed party if contract negotiations fail before a contract has been finalized.

predatory lending Involves mortgage loans secured by the borrower's house that are made at subprime interest rates to borrowers who often lack the ability to repay them. Also includes certain payday loans at exorbitant but legal interest rates.

predatory pricing The act of pricing below the producer's actual cost with the intent of driving other competitors out of the market, thus enabling the person engaging in predatory pricing to raise prices later.

preempt A federal law takes precedence when state law conflicts with federal law.

preemption defense (product liability) The immunity granted manufacturers if they meet minimum standards of conduct under certain regulatory schemes.

preferences Transfers to (or for the benefit of) creditors on account of antecedent debts that are made from an insolvent debtor's property within ninety days before bankruptcy (one year if creditor is insider) and that enable the creditors to receive more than they would through a Chapter 7 liquidation.

prehearing The first stage in arbitration in which parties may submit trial-like briefs, supporting documents, and other written statements making their case.

prejudgment interest The interest on the amount of an award from the date of the injury to the date of judgment.

preliminary hearing A hearing in which the prosecutor presents evidence demonstrating probable cause that the defendant committed the crime.

premises liability A theory under which a building owner may be found liable for violating its general duty to manage the premises and warn of dangers, such as asbestos.

prenegotiated bankruptcy In a prenegotiated bankruptcy, the debtor files its Chapter 11 bankruptcy petition as soon as it can after it has reached agreement on the terms of the restructuring with its key creditors, but votes on the plan are not solicited until after the bankruptcy case is filed.

prenuptial agreement An agreement entered into before marriage that sets forth the manner in which the parties' assets will be distributed and the support to which each party will be entitled, in the event the parties get divorced.

prepackaged bankruptcy A workout plan approved by key creditors and the debtor before the debtor files bankruptcy; it becomes the plan of reorganization in a Chapter 11 bankruptcy.

prepayment penalty A clause whereby a lender imposes a penalty if the loan is paid off early.

preponderance of the evidence The evidence offered in a civil trial that is more convincing than the evidence presented in opposition to it.

price discrimination Sellers charge different prices to purchasers in interstate sales for commodities of like grade and quality.

primary debtor The person with an obligation for which the guarantor becomes liable.

primary line violation Under the Robinson-Patman Act, a primary line violation occurs where the discriminating seller's price impacts competition with the seller's competitors.

prime rate The lowest rate of interest publicly offered by major lending institutions to their most creditworthy customers. Better practice dictates using the terms "base rate" or "reference rate" because sometimes lenders offer a loan below prime.

priming lien A lien that is senior to a previously granted security interest.

principal A person who delegates a portion of his or her tasks to another person who represents the principal as an agent.

prior art Developments or pre-existing art that relates to a claimed invention.

prior restraints Prohibitions barring speech before it occurs.

private international law Law that governs the relationships between private parties engaged in transactions across national borders.

private law The area of the law in which the sole function of government is recognition and enforcement of private rights, e.g., civil and commercial codes.

private nuisance Interference with a person's use and enjoyment of his or her land and water.

private offering An offering to selected individuals or entities who have the ability to evaluate and bear the risk of the investment; that is, they have the ability to fend for themselves. Also called *private placement*.

private placement *See* Private Offering.

private-placement memorandum A booklet offered by entrepreneurs seeking financing from private individual investors that furnishes information about themselves and their enterprise.

privatization The transfer of property ownership from a nation to a private entity.

Privileges and Immunities Clause (Fourteen Amendment) Provides that no state "shall make or enforce any law which shall abridge the privileges or immunities of citizens of the United States."

privity of contract The relationship that exists between the parties to a contract.

probable cause As applied to an arrest or a search warrant, a reasonable belief that the suspect has committed a crime or is about to commit a crime. Mere suspicion or belief, unsupported by facts or circumstances, is insufficient.

procedural due process The parties whose rights are to be affected are entitled to be heard and, in order that they may enjoy that right, they must be notified before adverse action is taken.

product A tangible item, as opposed to a service.

product liability The liability of a manufacturer or seller of a product that because of a defect, causes injury to a purchaser, user, or bystander.

product line theory A theory of successor liability whereby a corporation purchasing the assets of another is liable for the target company's debts where the purchaser continues to manufacture the same product line as the target company, under the same name and with no outward indication of any change of ownership, even if the particular item was manufactured and sold by the target company prior to the acquisition. Usually applied only in product-liability cases.

promisee In contract law, the promisee is the person to whom the promise (contract) was made.

promisor In contract law, the promisor is the person who made the promise.

promissory estoppel A promise that the promisor should reasonably expect to induce action or forbearance on the part of the promisee or a third person and that does induce such action or forbearance can create liability for reliance damages if injustice can be avoided only by providing some relief when promise is broken.

promissory fraud A type of fraud that occurs when one party induces another to enter into a contract by promising to do something without having the intention to carry out the promise.

proof of claim A claim filed by creditors on uncontingent and undisputed debt.

prospectus Any document that is designed to produce orders for a security, whether or not the document purports on its face to offer the security for sale or otherwise to dispose of it for value. The descriptive document that an issuer of securities provides to prospective purchasers.

protected computer A computer used in interstate or foreign commerce.

protected expression The part of a work that is subject to copyright protection.

proximate cause A reasonably foreseeable consequence of the defendant's negligence, without which no injury would have occurred.

proxy A written authorization by a shareholder to another person to vote on the shareholder's behalf.

proxy access rule A rule adopted by the SEC in 2010 that would have given shareholders that have held at least 3% of a public company's stock for at least three years to nominate candidates for the board and solicit proxies without having to go through the considerable expense of commencing a proxy contest. Although the SEC rule was invalidated by the U.S. Court of Appeals for the Federal Circuit, shareholder activists have proposed shareholder resolutions to amend the corporate charter to give certain large shareholders similar access to management's proxy materials.

proxy contest A battle for corporate control whereby someone wishing to replace the board with its own candidates seeks to acquire a sufficient number of shareholder votes to do so.

public accommodation Under Americans with Disabilities Act, includes any place of public accommodation, such as a restaurant, place of lodging, place of entertainment, place of public gathering, and place of exercise or recreation.

public disclosure of private facts The publication of a private fact that is not newsworthy. The matter must be private, such that a reasonable person would find publication objectionable. Unlike in a defamation case, truth is not a defense.

public figures Individuals, who, by reason of their achievements or the vigor and success with which they seek the public's attention, are injected into the public eye.

public international law Law that governs the relationships between and the interactions of nations.

public law The area of the law that focuses on effectuation of the public interest by state action, e.g., constitutional law, administrative law, and criminal law.

public officials Include legislators, judges, and police officers.

public nuisance Unreasonable and substantial interference with the public health, safety, peace, comfort, convenience, or utilization of land.

public policy exception An exception to the general employment at will doctrine that prohibits an employer from discharging an employee for a reason that violates public policy.

publication Communication to a third party.

publicly owned sewage treatment works (POTWs) General and specific industry pretreatment standards are set for discharges to publicly owned sewage treatment works (POTWs).

puffing The expression of opinion by a seller regarding goods; not a warranty.

punitive damages Damages awarded to a plaintiff over and above what will fairly compensate it for its loss. They are intended to punish the defendant and deter others from engaging in similar conduct. Also called *exemplary damages*.

purchase-money security interest A security interest created when a seller lends the buyer the money to buy the seller's goods.

pure notice statutes Under these statutes, a person who has notice that someone else has already bought the real property cannot validate his or her deed by recording it first.

pyramid selling A scheme whereby a consumer is recruited as a product "distributor" and receives commissions based on the products he or she sells and on the recruitment of additional sellers.

 Q

qualified institutional buyer Institutional investors holding and managing $100 million or more of securities.

qualified privilege When defending a claim of defamation, a party has a qualified privilege (1) to make statements to protect one's own personal interests, including statements to a peer review committee; (2) to make statements to protect legitimate business interests, such as statements to a prospective employer; and (3) to provide information for the public interest, such as credit reports. Unlike an absolute privilege, a qualified privilege may be lost if the person making the statement abuses the privilege.

qualifying exigency leave Unpaid, job-protected leave for military families to handle exigencies related to a family member's active–duty military service or call to active duty.

quantum meruit A basis for equitable relief by a court when there was no contract between the parties, but one party has received a benefit for which it has not paid.

quasi-foreign corporation A corporation incorporated outside of California, for example, but with more than 50 percent of its stock owned by California residents and with more than 50 percent of its sales, payroll, and property tax derived from activities in California.

qui tam plaintiff A plaintiff suing on the government's behalf, often entitled to a share of the amount recovered.

"quick look" rule of reason The "quick look" rule of reason is used whenever the practice has obvious anticompetitive effects but is not illegal per se; it allows for immediate inquiry into procompetitive justifications.

quid-pro-quo (this for that) harassment The specific, job-related adverse action, such as denial of a promotion, in retaliation for a worker's refusal to respond to a supervisor's sexual advances.

quiet period The time between filing of securities registration statement and the date the registration statement becomes effective. Also called the *waiting period*.

quitclaim deed A deed that contains no warranties; the grantor conveys only any right, title, and interest held by the grantor, if any, at the time of execution.

quorum The holders of more than 50 percent of the outstanding shares of a corporation.

quotas Tariffs and quantitative limitations that place restrictions on imports.

R

race statutes Under these statutes, recording is a race—the rule is "first in time is first in right." The first to record a deed has superior rights, regardless of whether he or she knew that someone else had already bought or claimed an interest in the real property.

race–notice statutes These statutes protect only a good faith subsequent purchaser who recorded its deed before the prior purchaser recorded its deed.

racketeering activity The state and federal offenses involving a pattern of illegal acts, including mail and wire fraud.

raider In a hostile takeover, a third party who seeks to obtain control of a corporation, called the target, over the objections of its management.

ratification A principal affirms through words or actions a prior act of an agent that did not bind the principal.

ratify An agreement by an individual, after the individual becomes competent or reaches the age of majority, to be bound by contracts entered into while the person was incompetent or a minor; a principal's agreement to be bound by the acts of an agent.

rational basis test A test under which a discriminatory classification will be held valid if there is any conceivable basis upon which the classification might relate to a legitimate governmental interest; applies to all classifications that relate to matters of economics or social welfare.

Rawlsian moral theory A deontological line of thought that aims to maximize the utility of the worst off person in society.

reaffirmation agreement A contract with a creditor whereby an individual who has filed bankruptcy under Chapter 7 agrees to repay a debt even though the debt would otherwise be discharged in the debtor's bankruptcy case.

real estate investment trust (REIT) A tax-advantaged pool of real property.

reasonable accommodation (of a disability) Even if a disability precludes an applicant or employee from performing the essential functions of a position or presents a safety risk, an employer is required to assess whether there is a reasonable accommodation that will permit the individual to be employed despite the disability if the employee requests an accommodation and provides the employer with the necessary medical information. Reasonable accommodations include (1) making work facilities accessible; (2) restructuring jobs or modifying work schedules; (3) reassigning the individual to another job; (4) acquiring or modifying equipment or devices; (5) modifying examinations, training materials, or policies; and (6) providing qualified readers or interpreters or other similar accommodations for individuals with disabilities.

reasonable–alternative-design-requirement A requirement in a product liability case that the plaintiff prove that defendant acted wrongly or negligently in choosing an unsafe design.

reasonable care under the circumstances A standard requiring landowners to act in a reasonable manner with respect to entrants on their land, with liability hinging on the foreseeability of harm.

reasonable factor other than age (RFOA) defense In an age discrimination case, an employer's affirmative defense that its actions were based on reasonable factors other than age. Contrast with *business necessity*.

recklessness In the criminal context, conscious disregard of a substantial risk that an individual's actions would result in the harm prohibited by a statute.

recognitional picketing Picketing that strives to force the employer to recognize a labor union as a collective bargaining agent for its employees.

recognized hazard Under the Occupational Safety and Health Act, a workplace condition that is obviously dangerous or is regarded by an employer or other employers in the industry as dangerous.

record The oral and written evidence presented at an administrative hearing.

recordable form The requirements established by the state regarding how title to real estate is filed and recorded. Requirements generally include legibility and notarization.

recording statutes Statutes that establish an orderly process by which claims to interests in real property can be recorded as part of the public record and resolved.

red-herring prospectus Preliminary prospectus; incomplete version of the final prospectus.

reference rate The lowest rate of interest publicly offered by major lending institutions to their most creditworthy customers.

referendum A vote by the electorate to approve or reject a treaty or other governmental action.

referral sale The seller offers the buyer a commission, rebate, or discount for furnishing the seller with a list of additional prospective customers.

registered mask work Highly detailed transparencies that represent the topological layout of semiconductor chips.

registration statement The registration statement consists of filing forms and the prospectus, the disclosure document that an issuer of securities provides to prospective purchasers.

Regulation A A regulation whereby $5 million of securities can be offered and sold in a twelve-month period, of which up to $1.5 million may be sold by the selling security holders.

Regulation Analyst Certification (Regulation AC) An SEC regulation that prohibits analysts from issuing reports that they do not personally believe to be true and requires the disclosure of any analyst compensation arrangements related to the specific recommendation or views contained in the research report.

Regulation D An SEC regulation that offers a safe harbor for those seeking exemption from securities registration under the Securities Act of 1933. An issuer that fails to comply with all of the requirements of the applicable rule may still be able to rely on the private-offering exemption in Section 4(2).

Regulation FD (Fair Disclosure) An SEC regulation that provides that whenever an issuer, or a person acting on its behalf, discloses material nonpublic information to securities market professionals or holders of the issuer's securities who may well trade on the basis of the information, the issuer must publicly disclose that same information simultaneously or promptly.

Regulation S An SEC regulation that has clarified the general rule that any offer or sale outside the United States is not subject to the federal registration requirements.

Regulation Z Regulations issued by the Federal Reserve Board to interpret and enforce the federal Truth-in-Lending Act.

regulations The rules of order prescribed by superior or competent authority relating to action of those under its control.

regulatory negotiations (reg-neg) A style of administrative rulemaking in which representatives of major groups convene with an administrative agency and work out a compromise through negotiation on the substance of new regulations.

regulatory taking The taking by the government of private real property for a public use; requires payment of just compensation.

reliance damages The awards made to a plaintiff for any expenditures made in reliance on a contract that was subsequently breached.

remand The power of a court of appeal to send a case back to a lower court for reconsideration.

remote tippee Recipient of a tip from another tippee other than the original tippee.

repatriate The act of a multinational business returning profits earned in a host country to its home country.

repatriation A constraint on foreign ownership to restrict the profits that can be returned by a multinational company to its home country.

reporter The published volumes of case decisions by a particular court or group of courts.

reporting company A company registered under Section 12 of the Securities Exchange Act of 1934 that subjects issuers to various reporting requirements and to certain rules and regulations concerning proxies, tender offers, and insider trading.

reporting issuer An issuer that has been subject to the reporting requirements of Section 13 or 15(d) of the 1934 Act for at least ninety days before a Rule 144 sale.

representation and warranties Highly negotiated provisions in a purchase-and-sale contract concerning the parties and the stock, goods, or other assets being sold.

representation election An election among employees to decide whether they want a union to represent them for collective bargaining.

requests for production of documents Requests for documents such as medical records and personal files to be produced as part of the discovery process before a trial.

requirements contract A contract under which the buyer agrees to buy all of a specified commodity the buyer needs from the seller and the seller agrees to provide that amount.

***res ipsa loquitur* (the thing speaks for itself)** The doctrine that allows a plaintiff to prove breach and causation indirectly.

resale price maintenance An agreement on minimum price between firms at different levels of production or distribution that violates antitrust law.

resource-based view (RBV) A firm's resources can be a source of sustained competitive advantage if they are valuable, rare, and imperfectly imitable by competitors and have no strategically equivalent substitutes.

***respondeat superior* (let the master answer)** The doctrine under which an employer may be held vicariously or secondarily liable for the negligent or intentional conduct of the employee that is committed in the scope of the employee's employment.

respondent The party in a case against whom an appeal is taken; the party who has an interest adverse to setting aside or reversing the judgment.

responsible corporate officer doctrine A criminal law doctrine that, under certain circumstances, imposes vicarious liability on an officer responsible for compliance based on the actions of subordinates.

restatement Former common law rules in a particular subject area (e.g., contracts, torts) integrated into formal collections that a judge or legislature is free to adopt.

restitution An award made to a plaintiff of a benefit improperly obtained by the defendant.

restricted guaranty A guaranty in which the guarantor's liability is enforceable only with respect to a specified transaction or series of transactions.

restricted securities Securities issued in a private placement; they cannot be resold or transferred unless they are either registered or exempt from registration. The most common exemption is pursuant to Securities and Exchange Commission Rule 144.

restricted stock A conditional grant of shares of a company's stock, with vesting contingent upon continued employment for a specified period of time.

restricted stock unit (RSU) A promise to pay a bonus in the future in the form of shares of a company's stock. An RSU is usually subject to vesting conditions so that it is not paid unless the vesting conditions are satisfied.

retributive justice A theory that states that every crime demands payment in the form of punishment.

reverse piercing A doctrine whereby a corporation (including a subsidiary) may be held liable for the debts of a shareholder (including a parent corporation).

reversibility An ethical theory that looks to whether one would want a rule applied to one's self.

revival statutes State and federal statutes that allow plaintiffs to file lawsuits that have been barred by the running of the statute of limitations.

***Revlon* mode** A company is said to be in *Revlon* mode when a change of control or breakup of the company has become inevitable.

revoke To annul an offer by rescission.

revolving line of credit A line of credit that allows a borrower to borrow whatever sums it requires up to a specified maximum amount and reborrow amounts it has repaid.

revolving loan A loan that allows a borrower to borrow whatever sums it requires up to a specified maximum amount and to reborrow amounts it has repaid.

Riba A tenet of Islamic trade and commerce that prohibits unearned or unjustified (illicit) profits and can therefore lead to problems in the area of interest on loans.

right of first negotiation Gives the holder the right to negotiate the purchase of the property before the seller enters negotiations with another party.

right of first refusal A contract that provides the holder with the right to purchase property on the same terms and conditions offered by or to a third party.

right of redemption Gives the mortgagor and certain other categories of interested persons the right to redeem or get back foreclosed property within a statutorily limited period.

right of rescission A right to cancel a contract.

right of setoff Permits Party A to deduct automatically from payments due Party B amounts that are due from Party B to Party A.

ripeness A court will not hear agency cases if they are not ripe for decision, for example, after a rule is adopted but before the agency seeks to apply it to a particular case.

roadshow Oral presentations to large institutional investors in key cities in the United States, Europe, and Asia.

rule of impossibility The rule under which claims of predation are rejected because the marketplace in question cannot be successfully monopolized.

rule of reason The rule that takes into account a defendant's actions as well as the structure of the market to determine whether an activity promotes or restrains competition.

Rule 10b-5 An SEC regulation adopted pursuant to Section 10(b) of the Securities Exchange Act of 1934 that prohibits individuals and companies from engaging in fraudulent, manipulative, or deceptive practices in connection with the offer or sale of securities.

Rule 144 A safe harbor designed to reduce the uncertainty associated with the definition of the term "underwriter," this SEC rule permits nonissuers to sell restricted and control securities publicly without registration as long as the Rule's requirements are met.

S

S–1 review A review by the auditor of events subsequent to the date of the certified financial statements included in the securities registration statement to ascertain whether any material change has occurred in the company's financial position that should be disclosed in the final prospectus to prevent the financial statements from being materially misleading.

S Corporation A corporation meeting certain requirements that is taxed only at the owner level.

Safeguard Rule Requires financial services firms to protect consumer privacy by (1) promulgating a written information security plan, (2) designating at least one employee to coordinate the plan, (3) identifying and assessing the risks to customer financial information, and (4) evaluating the safeguards for controlling these risks.

sale (securities) Includes "every contract of sale or disposition of a security or interest in a security, for value."

sale and leaseback A simultaneous two-step transaction, whereby an institutional lender purchases real property from a company, and the property is leased back to the company for its use.

sanctions Laws imposed by one country (or a group of countries) against the commerce of another country as an effort to influence that country's behavior, for example with regard to international law.

satisfaction *See* Accord and Satisfaction.

Say on Pay proposal Annual shareholder advisory votes on a company's executive pay policies and practices.

scheme liability Fraudulent business transactions designed to enable the issuer to artificially inflate its earnings.

scienter An intent to deceive.

second-step back-end merger The second step in a corporate takeover whereby the shareholders who did not tender their shares receive cash or securities in a subsequent merger.

secondary boycott A strike against an employer with whom a union has no quarrel in order to encourage it to stop doing business with an employer with whom it does have a dispute.

secondary line violation Typically involves a "disfavored" purchaser that brings a suit against a seller, or the seller's "favored" purchaser, for giving the favored purchaser better pricing.

secondary meaning A descriptive trademark becomes protectable by acquiring secondary meaning, or sufficient consumer recognition through sufficient use and/or advertising of the goods under the mark.

secondary offering A securities offering by a person other than the issuer.

Section 4(1 ½) exemption An exemption for a private offering of securities by an affiliate that would qualify as a private placement under Section 4(2) of the Securities Act of 1933 if made by the issuer.

Section 83(b) election When filed, the employee elects to pay tax at the time restricted stock is purchased in an amount equal to what would be due if the stock were not subject to vesting.

Section 201 Provides for temporary relief to U.S. industries seriously injured by increasing imports, regardless of whether unfair practices are involved. It is sometimes called the fair trade law.

Section 301 Authorizes the U.S. Trade Representative to investigate alleged unfair practices of foreign governments that impede U.S. exports of both goods and services.

Section 337 Provides that if a U.S. industry is injured (or there is a restraint or monopolization of trade in the United States) by reason of unfair acts in the importation of articles into the United States, an order must be issued requiring the exporters and importers to cease the unfair acts or, if necessary, excluding imports of the offending articles from all sources.

Section 423 plan An employee stock purchase plan (ESPP) satisfying Internal Revenue Code Section 423, which permits an employee to defer paying tax on the discount from the fair market value of stock purchased via the plan until the employee sells the stock.

secured loan A loan backed up by collateral.

secured party The lender, seller, or other person in whose favor there is a security interest.

secured transaction A loan or other transaction secured by collateral put up by the borrower.

securities fraud involving a publicly traded company A crime created by the Sarbanes-Oxley Act of 2002, it is a felony to knowingly execute or attempt to execute a scheme or artifice (1) to defraud any person in connection with any security of a publicly traded company or (2) to obtain, by means of false or fraudulent pretenses, representations, or promises, any money or property in connection with the purchase or sale of any security of a publicly traded company.

security Any note, stock, treasury stock, bond, debenture, evidence of indebtedness, certificate of interest or participation in any profit-sharing agreement, collateral trust certificate, pre-organization certificate or subscription, transferable share, investment contract, voting-trust certificate, certificate of deposit for a security, fractional undivided interest in oil, gas, or other mineral rights; any put, call, straddle, option, or privilege on any security, certificate of deposit, or group or index of securities (including any interest therein or based on the value thereof); or any put, call, straddle, option, or privilege entered into on a national securities exchange relating to foreign currency; or, in general, any interest or instrument commonly known as a "security," or any certificate of interest or participation in temporary or interim certificate for, receipt for, guarantee of, or warrant or right to subscribe to or purchase, any of the foregoing.

security agreement An agreement that creates or provides for a security interest.

security interest Any interest in personal property, fixtures or letters of credit and accounts that is used as collateral to secure payment or the performance of an obligation.

selective disclosure A practice whereby issuers of publicly traded securities disclose material nonpublic information, such as advance warnings of earnings results, to securities analysts or selected institutional investors before making full disclosure of the same information to the general public.

self-publication A doctrine giving an employee a claim for defamation when the employer makes a false assertion in firing an employee, which the employer could reasonably expect the employee to repeat to a prospective employer.

self-tender An offer by a corporation to buy back its stock or shareholder rights for a fair price.

selling securities short The sale of securities the seller does not own.

senior debt Indebtedness that benefits from a debt subordination agreement.

separate property Property that belongs solely to the spouse who acquired it before marriage or received it by gift or inheritance.

separation of powers The distinct authority of governance granted the three branches of U.S. government (executive, legislative, and judicial) by the U.S. Constitution.

sequestration order A governmental order that requires spending levels to be reduced below the levels provided in the budget.

service mark A legally protected identifying mark connected with services.

service of process Notifying a defendant of a claim.

settlement conference A conference a judge may hold to give each side a candid assessment of the strengths and weaknesses of its case and the likely outcome if the case goes to trial.

sexual stereotyping Discrimination against employees because they are not "manly" enough men or "womanly" enough women. Illegal under Title VII of Civil Rights Act.

share sterilization An order precluding the defendants from voting their shares.

shareholder A holder of equity securities of a corporation. Also called *stockholder*.

shareholder derivative suit A lawsuit brought against directors or officers of a corporation by a shareholder on behalf of the corporation.

shareholder of record The persons whose names appear on a corporation's shareholder list on a specified date who are entitled to vote.

shareholder primacy Maximization of shareholder wealth, not legally mandated.

shareholder rights plan *See* Poison Pill.

Sharia The traditional Islamic rules and body of laws that regulate Muslim life.

shelf registration The registration of a number of securities at one time for issuance later.

short-swing trading The purchase and sale or sale and purchase by an officer, director, or greater-than-10 percent shareholders of securities of a public company within a six-month period.

show-how Nonsecret information used to teach someone how to make or do something; generally not legally protectable.

shrink-wrap license A license that customers cannot read when they purchase software but are deemed to have accepted when they open the wrapping around the envelope containing the discs.

signing statement A document attached to a bill at its execution describing the president's interpretation of that law.

SIMPLE Plan Retirement plans for employers with fewer than one hundred employees that are similar to 401(k) plans, but have stricter rules and simpler administration, that allow employees to defer a portion of their salaries on a pretax basis into an investment fund set up by the employer.

slander A spoken communication to a third party by a defendant of an untrue statement of fact that injures a plaintiff's reputation.

slander *per se* Words that are slanderous in and of themselves. Only statements that a person has committed a serious crime, has a loathsome disease, is guilty of sexual misconduct, or is not fit to conduct business are slanderous *per se*.

sole proprietorship One person owns all the assets of the business, has complete control of the business, and is solely liable for all the debts of the business.

solicitor A type of lawyer in the British system who is allowed to perform legal services outside the court.

sophisticated user defense An affirmative defense in a product liability case based on failure to warn whereby a manufacturer is not liable to a sophisticated user of its product for failure to warn of a risk, harm, or danger, if the sophisticated user knew or should have known of that risk, harm, or danger.

sovereign acts doctrine The government cannot be held liable for breach of contract due to legislative or executive acts of general application.

sovereign immunity The doctrine that prevents the courts of one country from hearing a suit against the government of another country.

spam Unsolicited e-mails.

Special 301 Provisions Provisions in U.S. trade law under which the U.S. Trade Representative identifies countries that deny adequate and effective protection for intellectual property rights or deny fair and equitable market access for persons who rely on intellectual property protection.

special plan *See* Specific Plan.

specific performance A court order to a breaching party to complete the contract as promised.

specific plan A planning document in addition to a general plan that usually encompasses just a portion of a city's geographic area; typically more detailed than the general plan.

specifications The description of an invention in a patent application in its best mode and the manner and process of making and using the invention so that a person skilled in the relevant field may make and use the invention.

spinning The practice whereby underwriters would distribute IPO shares to a corporate executive in exchange for the investment banking business of the executive's corporation.

split in the circuits When different courts of appeals disagree on a legal issue.

spoliation inference Inference, as instructed to a jury, that missing or altered evidence should be presumed to have been unfavorable to the party causing its destruction or loss.

spread (1) A margin that is added to the cost that a bank incurs to obtain, for a given period of time, the funds it will lend, in order to arrive at the actual interest rate for a loan. (2) The difference between the strike price of a stock option and the fair market value of the stock at the time the optionee exercises the option.

squatter's rights *See* Adverse Possession.

staggered board A board on which directors serve for specified terms, usually three years, with only a fraction of them up for reelection at any one time. Also called *classified board*.

standby letter of credit A method of securing a party's performance, whereby an issuing bank undertakes to pay a sum of money to the person (the beneficiary) to which performance is due on presentation of certain documents specified in the letter of credit, usually a brief statement (in language agreed on by the two parties) that the other party is in default and the beneficiary is entitled to payment from the issuing bank.

standing A party to a lawsuit has standing if the person seeking relief is the proper party to advance the litigation, has a personal interest in the outcome of the suit, and will benefit from a favorable ruling.

standstill agreement An agreement whereby the shareholder agrees not to commence a tender offer or proxy contest or to buy additional shares of the issuer for a period of time, often ten years.

stare decisis (to abide by) The doctrine that holds that once a court resolves a particular issue, other courts addressing a similar legal problem generally follow the initial court's decision.

state-of-the-art defense A defense against claims based on a manufacturer's compliance with the best available technology (that may or may not be synonymous with the custom and practice of the industry).

state secrets doctrine A doctrine that bars the discovery or admission of evidence that would expose confidential matters that, in the interest of national security, should not be divulged.

statute of frauds A statute that requires that certain contracts, such as contracts conveying an interest in real property, must be in a signed writing to be enforceable in a court.

statute of limitations A time limit, defined by the statute, within which a lawsuit must be brought.

statute of repose A time limit that cuts off the right to assert a cause of action after a specified period of time from the date the product is sold.

statutory bar An inventor is denied patent protection in the event that prior to one year before the inventor's filing, the invention was (1) patented; (2) publicly used or sold in the United States; or (3) described in a printed publication in the United States or a foreign country.

statutory law Law that is based on statutes, not on existing common law rules.

statutory prospectus A prospectus for a registered offering of securities meeting the requirements of Section 10 of the Securities Act of 1933.

stock option A contract that allows an individual to buy a certain number of shares of a company's stock at a certain price (typically the fair market value of the stock at the time the option is granted) within a certain timeframe (typically five to ten years), but ending upon termination of employment.

stock parking The temporary sale of shares to another entity or individual to avoid tax reporting requirements or the net margin requirements of the securities laws applicable to brokerage firms.

straight bankruptcy A Chapter 7 bankruptcy in which the trustee liquidates the estate and distributes the proceeds first to secured creditors (to the extent of their collateral) and then in a prescribed order, pro rata within each level.

straight voting A voting process whereby a shareholder can cast one vote for each share the shareholder owns for each nominee.

strategic compliance management Term coined by **Professor** Constance E. Bagley to describe a legally astute top management team's ability to go beyond mere compliance with law to seek opportunities to increase a firm's realizable value. Includes ability to frame the cost of complying with government regulations as an investment, not an expense.

strategic environmental management A concept that advocates placing environmental management on the profit side of the corporation rather than on the cost side. An example of strategic compliance management.

strict liability Liability without fault. The concept that sellers are liable for all defective products. Also imposed for abnormally dangerous (or ultrahazardous) activities and toxic torts.

strict scrutiny test Under this test, a discriminatory classification will be held valid only if it is necessary to promote a compelling state interest and narrowly tailored; applies to classifications based on race or religion.

strike price The price (which is generally the market price of the stock at the time the stock option is granted) at which an optionee can exercise his or her stock option by purchasing the stock. Also referred to as the *grant price*.

subdivision A division of land into separate parcels for development purposes.

subject matter jurisdiction The specific types of cases enumerated under Article III of the U.S. Constitution to be decided by the Supreme Court and lower courts established by Congress.

subject matter test The privilege that protects the communications or discussions of any company employee with counsel as long as the subject matter of the communication relates to that employee's duties and the communication is made at the direction of a corporate superior.

sublease An act by a tenant of renting out all or a portion of property the tenant has rented from a landlord.

subordination Relegation to a lesser position, usually in respect to a right or security.

subprime Debt issued by a lender that (1) predominantly refinances rather than makes or purchases loans and (2) does not sell a significant portion of its portfolio to the two government sponsored housing financing agencies.

subprime mortgage loans Loans that carry above-market interest rates to compensate for the added risk of default, to borrowers with poor credit.

subsequent remedial measures A manufacturer's later fix of a dangerous condition or improvement of a design in a product that has been found to be inherently defective.

substantial continuity test A test that imposes successor liability when the purchaser of assets maintains the same business, with the same employees doing the same jobs, under the same supervisors, working conditions, and production process, and produces the same products for the same customers as the seller corporation. Also known as the *continuity of enterprise approach*.

substantial evidence standard Under this standard, the courts defer to an administrative agency's factual determinations in formal adjudications even if the record would support other factual conclusions.

substantial factor test An actual-cause test whereby the plaintiff or prosecutor seeks to hold liable multiple defendants, including any person who played a substantial role in causing the harm or violation.

substantially related test A test under which a discriminatory classification will be held valid if it furthers a governmental interest that is "important" or "substantial" and it prevents real, not conjectural, harm "in a direct and material way"; applies to classifications such as gender and legitimacy of birth.

substantive coercion A threat that shareholders may agree to sell their shares in an otherwise noncoercive tender offer out of ignorance about the target company's true value. Also occurs when management structures a deal in such a way that deprives shareholders of a meaningful choice.

substantive due process The constitutional guarantee that no person shall be arbitrarily deprived of life, liberty, or property; the essence of substantive due process is protection from arbitrary and unreasonable action.

successor liability Individuals or entities who acquire an interest in a business or in real property may be held liable for personal injury and property or environmental damage resulting from acts (including sale of products) of the predecessor entity or previous owner.

suggestive mark A trademark that suggests something about a product without directly describing it.

summary judgment A procedural device available for disposition of a controversy without trial. A judge will grant summary judgment only if all of the written evidence before the court clearly establishes that there are no disputed issues of material fact and the party who requested the summary judgment is entitled to prevail as a matter of law.

summary jury trial (SJT) Parties to a dispute put their cases before a real jury, which renders a nonbinding decision.

summons The official notice to a defendant that a lawsuit is pending against the defendant in a particular court.

Super 301 A provision of the Omnibus Trade Act of 1988 that required the U.S. Trade Representative to draw up a list of the foreign governments whose practices pose the most significant barriers to U.S. exports, and to immediately commence Section 301 investigations with respect to these practices.

super discharge After completing all payments in accordance with a Chapter 13 bankruptcy plan, the debtor obtains a Chapter 13 discharge (sometimes called a super discharge), which extinguishes otherwise nondischargeable debts (such as claims for fraud, theft, willful and malicious injury, or drunk driving), but not spousal or child support.

superlien An instrument that secures recovery of environmental cleanup response costs incurred by state agencies.

supervisor Anyone possessing specified personnel functions if the exercise of that authority is not of a merely routine or clerical nature, but requires the use of independent judgment.

supranational law A principle of international law, under which nations submit their decision-making authority to a common organization or institution.

surprise The extent to which the supposedly agreed on terms of the bargain are hidden in a densely printed form drafted by the party seeking to enforce the disputed terms.

surviving corporation In a merger of two corporations, the corporation that maintains its corporate existence is the surviving corporation.

syndicate An underwriting group in a public offering; each member agrees to purchase a certain number of the securities of the issuer once the offering is declared effective by the Securities and Exchange Commission.

syndicated loan In a syndicated loan, the lenders enter into concurrent direct obligations with the borrower to make a loan, typically on a pro rata basis. The loan is coordinated by a lead lender that serves as agent for all the lenders in disbursing the funds, collecting payments of interest and principal, and administering and enforcing the loan.

synthetic lease A lease that is treated as a conventional operating lease for accounting purposes (so does not appear on the lessee's balance sheet) but is treated as if the lessee had purchased the property and obtained a loan from the seller for tax purposes.

systems approach to business and society The descriptive framework that integrates legal and societal considerations with mainstream theories of competitive advantage and social responsibility.

T

take-out commitment An agreement by a lender to replace the construction loan with a permanent loan, usually after certain conditions, such as the timely completion of the project, have been met.

takeover A bidder acquires sufficient stock from a corporation's shareholders to obtain control of the corporation.

target The subject of a tender offer or hostile corporate takeover attempt. Also a company that another firm controls after acquiring it via merger, a sale of stock by the target's shareholders, or a sale of substantially all the assets of the target.

target corporation A corporation that a friendly or hostile bidder is seeking to acquire, often in a merger or sale of assets or through a tender offer.

tariff classification The tariff on articles imported to the United States is determined by their description on the Harmonized Tariff Schedule.

tariffs The basic tool for limiting imports to protect domestic industries.

tarnishment Dilution of a famous trademark that occurs when use of the famous mark in connection with a particular category of goods or goods of an inferior quality reduces the positive image associated with the products bearing the famous mark.

tax-deferred exchange A transfer of real property for an alternative piece of real property meeting certain requirements.

tax evasion The illegal practice whereby a person intentionally does not pay his or her tax liability.

teleological theory of ethics An ethical theory concerned with the consequences of something. The good of an action is to be judged by the effect of the action on others.

temporary insiders For purposes of bans on insider trading, outside attorneys, accountants, consultants, and investment bankers who are not directly employed by the corporation, but who acquire confidential information through the performance of professional services.

10b5-1 plan A securities trading plan meeting the requirements of SEC Rule 10b5-1. There is a presumption that persons who trade while in possession of material nonpublic information trade on the basis of that information unless the trade is pursuant to a preexisting 10b5–1 plan.

tenancy by the entirety A special type of co-ownership of real property between husband and wife; like joint tenancy, it includes a right of survivorship.

tenants in common The individuals who own undivided interests in a parcel of real property.

tender of delivery Under Article 2 of the Uniform Commercial Code, when the seller notifies the buyer that it has the goods ready for delivery.

tender offer A public offer to all the shareholders of a corporation to buy their shares at a stated price, usually higher than the market price.

term loan A loan for a specified amount funded in a lump sum or in installments to be repaid on a specified maturity date or paid off over a period of time.

term sheet A letter that outlines the terms and conditions on which a lender will lend.

termination The point after the dissolution of a partnership when all the partnership affairs are wound up and partners' authority to act for the partnership is completely extinguished.

termination fee *See* Breakup Fee.

territorial restrictions Restrictions that prevent a dealer or distributor from selling outside a certain territory.

third-party beneficiary One who does not give consideration for a promise yet has legal rights to enforce the contract. A person is a third-party beneficiary with legal rights when the contracting parties intended to benefit that person.

third-party defense In a case under the Comprehensive Environmental Responsibility, Contribution, and Liability Act, a potentially responsible current owner can assert this defense if the release or disposal of hazardous materials was by a third party who was not an employee and with whom the current owner had no contractual relationship. Also called the *innocent landowner defense*.

360/360 method A method for calculating interest whereby it is assumed that all months have 30 days; thus the monthly interest amounts are always the same.

365/360 method A method for calculating interest whereby the nominal annual interest rate is divided by 360, and the resulting daily rate is then multiplied by the outstanding principal amount and the actual number of days in the payment period.

365/365 method A method for calculating interest whereby the daily rate is determined by dividing the nominal annual interest rate by 365 (or 366, in leap years), then this daily rate is multiplied by the outstanding principal amount and the actual number of days in the payment period.

tip Disclosure of a fact made to an individual and withheld from the general public.

tippee A person who receives inside information.

tipper A person who gives inside information.

tombstone ad A newspaper advertisement surrounded by bold black lines identifying the existence of a public offering and indicating where a prospectus may be obtained.

tort A civil wrong causing injury to a person, his or her property, or certain economic relationships.

total-activity test A combination of tests used to determine where a company engaged in multistate operations is domiciled; considers all aspects of the corporate entity, including the nature and scope of the company's activities.

total cost Variable cost plus fixed costs, such as rent and overhead.

total return equity swap A type of derivative security whereby two counterparties agree to exchange cash flows on two financial instruments over a specific period of time. One counterparty generally buys the equity securities underlying the swap.

trade dress A manifestation of trademark law, the concept of trade dress is to protect the overall look of a product as opposed to just a particular design.

trade name A trade name or a corporate name identifies and symbolizes a business as a whole, as opposed to a trademark, which is used to identify and distinguish the various products and services sold by the business.

Trade Promotion Authority A law that allows the president to negotiate trade agreements and then submit them for an up or down vote by Congress with no amendments permitted.

trade secret Information that derives independent economic value from not being generally known and that is subject to reasonable efforts to maintain its secrecy.

trademark A word or symbol used on goods or with services that indicates their origin.

traditional insiders For purposes of bans on insider trading, persons employed by an issuer who acquire confidential information by performing duties within or on behalf of their employer. Traditional insiders include (1) officers and directors, (2) employees, (3) controlling shareholders, and (4) the corporation itself.

traditional shelf offerings The registration of (1) securities offered pursuant to employee benefit plans; (2) securities offered or sold pursuant to dividend or interest reinvestment plans; (3) warrants, rights, or securities to be issued upon conversion of other outstanding securities; (4) mortgage-related securities; and (5) securities issued in connection with business combination transactions.

transaction value The price of an imported article indicated on a sales invoice.

transactional immunity The prohibition from prosecution granted a witness that relates to any matter discussed in that person's testimony.

treaty An international agreement concluded between states in written form and governed by international law.

trespass to chattels When personal property is interfered with but not taken, destroyed, or substantially altered (i.e., not converted), there is a trespass to chattels. Also called *trespass to personal property*.

trespass to land The intentional invasion of real property (below the surface or in the airspace above) without consent of the owner.

trespass to personal property When personal property is interfered with but not taken, destroyed, or substantially altered (i.e., not converted), there is said to be a trespass to personal property. Also called *trespass to chattels*.

triple net lease A type of industrial lease that requires the tenant to pay all taxes, insurance, and maintenance expenses.

trust (1) A combination of competitors who act together to fix prices, thereby stifling competition. (2) A manner of holding property that is controlled by a trustee for the benefit of a beneficiary.

trustee The legal representative of a bankrupt debtor's estate.

tying arrangement A business arrangement whereby a seller will sell product A (the tying or desired product) to the customer only if the customer purchases product B (the tied product) from the seller.

U

UCC-1 Form In most states, this is the form a secured creditor uses for a financing statement under the Uniform Commercial Code.

ultrahazardous Under tort law, an activity of a defendant is deemed ultrahazardous when it (1) necessarily involves a risk of serious harm to persons or property that cannot be eliminated by the exercise of utmost care and (2) is not a matter of common usage. Also called *abnormally dangerous*.

unavoidably unsafe product A product, such as a vaccine, that is generally beneficial but is known to have harmful side effects in some cases.

unconscionable A contract term that is oppressive or fundamentally unfair.

unconscionability As under common law, unconscionability can be either procedural (relating to the bargaining process) or substantive (relating to the provisions of the contract).

undercapitalization theory A corporation is a separate entity, but its lack of adequate capital may constitute a fraud on the public. May be a basis for piercing corporate veil.

underwriter Any person who has purchased any security from an issuer with a view to, or offers or sells for an issuer in connection with, the distribution of any security.

undisclosed principal Use of an agent so that the third party to an agreement does not know or have reason to know of a principal's identity or existence.

undue hardship An affirmative defense under the Americans with Disabilities Act that relieves an employer of the obligation to make reasonable accommodations for an employee's disability because doing so would constitute an undue hardship for the employer.

undue influence Sufficient influence and power over another as to make genuine assent impossible.

unfair labor practice strike A union strikes an employer for the employer's failure to bargain in good faith.

unfair labor practices Unlawful misconduct by an employer to employees exercising union rights.

unilateral contract A promise given in exchange for an act. Offer can be accepted only by performing the act.

universalizability An ethical theory that asks whether one would want everyone to perform in this manner.

unjust enrichment The unfair appropriation of the benefits of negotiation of contracts for the party's own use.

unorthodox transaction The purchase or sale by an officer, director, or greater-than-10 percent shareholder that would otherwise result in recoverable short-swing profits but is involuntary and does not involve the payment of cash, and there is no possibility of speculative abuse of insider information.

upstream guaranty A guaranty whereby subsidiaries guarantee the parent corporation's debt, or pledge their assets as security for the parent corporation's debt.

use immunity The prohibition on the use of the testimony of a witness against that witness in connection with the case in which that person is testifying or another case.

useful article doctrine The doctrine that holds that copyrightable pictorial, graphic, and sculptural works include works of artistic craftsmanship insofar as their form but not their mechanical or utilitarian aspects are concerned.

useful life statutes Statutes that provide manufacturers and sellers protection from product liability claims after a specified period of time has elapsed since the product was sold.

usury Charging an amount of interest on a loan that is in excess of the maximum specified by applicable law.

usury laws State statutes that set legal caps on what interest rates lenders may charge.

usury statutes Laws that limit the interest rate on loans and usually provide that any loan agreement in violation of the statute is unenforceable.

utilitarianism A major teleological system of ethics that stands for the proposition that the ideal is to maximize the total benefit for everyone involved.

utility patent A patent that protects any novel, useful, and nonobvious process, machine, manufacture, or composition of matter; or any novel, useful, and nonobvious improvement of such process, machine, manufacture, or composition of matter.

V

vacate The power of a court of appeal to nullify a previous court's ruling.

value Cash, property, or compensation for past services.

variable cost The cost of producing the next incremental unit.

variance A method of relief from the strict terms of a zoning ordinance that allows a landowner to construct a structure or carry on an activity not otherwise permitted under zoning regulations.

venue The particular county or geographical area in which a court with jurisdiction may hear and determine a case.

vertical agreement An agreement between firms that operate at different levels of production or distribution.

vertical market division An agreement between a company and a dealer or distributor that prevents the dealer or the distributor from selling outside a certain territory or to a certain class of customer.

vertical merger A combination between firms at different points along the chain of distribution.

vertical restraint Unlawful restraint between firms at different levels in the chain of distribution, including price-fixing, market division, tying arrangements, and some franchise agreements.

vested right The right of a developer to develop property sometimes, but not always, obtained when a building permit is issued, substantial work is done, and substantial liabilities are incurred in reliance of that permit.

veto power The power of the president to prevent permanently or temporarily the enactment of a law created by Congress that does not meet his or her approval.

vicarious copyright infringement A doctrine that imposes liability on a third party for a direct copyright infringer's actions if the third party (a) has the right and ability to control the infringer's acts and (b) receives a direct financial benefit from the infringement.

vicarious liability The imposition of civil or criminal liability on one party (e.g., an employer) for the wrongful acts of another (e.g., an employee). Also called *imputed liability*.

voidable Unenforceable at the option of one party.

voir dire Questioning of potential jurors to determine possible bias.

voluntary proceeding A voluntary proceeding in bankruptcy filing begins when the debtor files a petition with the bankruptcy court.

W

waiting period The period between the filing of the registration statement and the date the registration statement becomes effective with the SEC. Also called the *quiet period*.

waive To refrain from exercising certain rights.

warranty deed A warranty deed is similar to a grant deed. In addition to the implied warranties contained in a grant deed, the grantor of a warranty deed also expressly warrants the title to and the quiet possession of the property to grantee.

welfare benefit plans Employee medical, dental, and disability plans that are subject to ERISA's rules on reporting, disclosure, and fiduciary responsibility.

well-known seasoned issuers Firms eligible to use Form S-3 with $700 million of public common equity float and permitted to make unrestricted oral and written offers before the registration statement is filed without violating the gun-jumping provisions.

whistleblowing When an employee reports an employer's unlawful or wrongful conduct to a supervisor, inside counsel or ombudsperson, the board of directors, the government, or the public.

white-collar crime Nonviolent violations of the law by companies or their managers.

willful A defendant acting with knowledge that his conduct is unlawful. Contrast with *knowingly*.

winding up The process of settling partnership affairs after dissolution.

wire fraud A scheme intended to defraud or to obtain money or property by fraudulent means through use of telephone systems.

work made for hire A copyrightable work created by an employee within the scope of his or her employment, or a work in one of nine listed categories that is specially commissioned through a signed writing that states that the work is a "work made for hire."

work-product doctrine Protects information, including the private memoranda and personal thoughts of the attorney, created by the attorney while preparing a case for trial.

workout An out-of-court settlement between debtors and creditors that restructures the debtor's financial affairs in much the same way that a confirmed bankruptcy plan would, but it only binds those who expressly consent.

wraparound financing The transaction in which a new lender lends the owner of mortgaged real property additional funds and agrees to take over the servicing of the first loan. In exchange, the owner executes a deed of trust or mortgage and an all-inclusive note, covering the combined amount of the first and new loans.

writ of certiorari An order written by the U.S. Supreme Court when it decides to hear a case, ordering the lower court to certify the record of proceedings below and send it up to the U.S. Supreme Court.

wrongful discharge An employee termination without good cause that (1) violates public policy; (2) breaches an implied contract; or (3) violates the implied covenant of good faith and fair dealing.

Z

zone of danger The area in which an individual is physically close enough to a victim of an accident as to also be in personal danger.

zone of insolvency There is no test or definition. The law suggests that a company may enter the zone when there is a substantial risk that the company will be unable to pay its debts.

zoning The division of a city into districts and the application of specific land use regulations in each district.

INDEX

Q